Department of Economic and Social Affairs, Statistics Division
Département des affaires économiques et sociales, Division de statistique

1999
Industrial Commodity Statistics
Yearbook
Production Statistics (1990-1999)

Annuaire
de statistiques industrielles par produit
Statistiques de production (1990-1999)

United Nations • Nations Unies
New York, 2001

CENTRAL MISSOURI
STATE UNIVERSITY
Warrensburg
Missouri

NOTE

Symbols of United Nations documents are composed of capital letters combined with figures.

General disclaimer

The designations employed and the presentation of material in this publication do not imply the expression of any opinion whatsoever on the part of the Secretariat of the United Nations concerning the legal status of any country, territory, city or area, or of its authorities, or concerning the delimitation of its frontiers or boundaries.

Where the designation "country or area" appears in the headings of tables, it covers countries, territories, cities or areas. In prior issues of this publication, where the designation "country" appears in the headings of tables, it should be interpreted to cover countries, territories, cities or areas.

NOTE

Les cotes des documents de l'Organisation des Nations Unies se composent de lettres majuscules et de chiffres.

Déni de responsabilité

Les appellations employées dans cette publication et la présentation des données qui y figurent n'impliquent de la part du Secrétariat de l'Organisation des Nations Unies aucune prise de position quant au statut juridique des pays, territoires, villes ou zones, ou de leurs autorités, ni quant au tracé de leurs frontières ou limites.

L'appellation "pays ou zone" figurant dans les titres des rubriques des tableaux désigne des pays, des territoires, des villes ou des zones. L'appellation "pays" figurant dans certaines rubriques des tableaux de numéros antérieurs de cette publication doit être interprétée comme désignant des pays, des territoires, des villes ou des zones.

ST/ESA/STAT/SER.P/39

UNITED NATIONS PUBLICATION

Sales No. E/F.02.XVII.2

PUBLICATION DES NATIONS UNIES

Numéro de vente : E/F.02.XVII.2

ISBN 92-1-061195-0
ISSN 0257-7208

Inquiries should be directed to:
SALES SECTION
UNITED NATIONS
NEW YORK, NY 10017

Adresser toutes demandes de renseignements à la :
SECTION DES VENTES
NATIONS UNIES
NEW YORK, NY 10017

CONTENTS - TABLE DES MATIERES

CONTENTS (continued) - TABLE DE MATIERES (suite)

INTRODUCTION

This is the thirty-third in a series of annual compilations of statistics on world industry designed to meet both the general demand for information of this kind and the special requirements of the United Nations and related international bodies. Beginning with the 1992 edition, the title of the publication was changed to *Industrial Commodity Statistics Yearbook* as the result of a decision made by the United Nations Statistical Commission at its twenty-seventh session to discontinue, effective 1994, publication of the *Industrial Statistics Yearbook, volume I, General Industrial Statistics* by the Statistics Division of the United Nations. The United Nations Industrial Development Organization (UNIDO) has become responsible for the collection and dissemination of general industrial statistics while the Statistics Division of the United Nations continues to be responsible for industrial commodity production statistics. The previous title, *Industrial Statistics Yearbook*, volume II, *Commodity Production Statistics*, was introduced in the 1982 edition. The first seven editions in this series were published under the title *The Growth of World Industry* and the next eight editions under the title *Yearbook of Industrial Statistics*.

This edition of the Yearbook contains annual quantity data on production of industrial commodities by country, geographical region, economic grouping and for the world. A standard list of about 530 commodities (about 590 statistical series) has been adopted for the publication. Most of the statistics refer to the ten-year period 1990-1999 for about 200 countries and areas.

Ce recueil annuel de statistiques industrielles mondiales est le trente-troisième d'une série qui a pour vocation de répondre à la fois à la demande générale d'informations dans ce domaine et aux besoins particuliers de l'Organisation des Nations Unies et des organismes internationaux qui lui sont apparentés. La Commission de statistique ayant décidé, à sa vingt-septième session, que la Division de statistique de l'Organisation des Nations Unies interromprait à partir de 1994 la publication du volume I intitulé *Industrial Statistics Yearbook, Volume I, General Industrial Statistics*, le titre de cet ouvrage est devenu, à partir de 1992, *Annuaire de statistiques industrielles (par produit) (Industrial Commodity Statistics Yearbook)*. En effet, l'Organisation des Nations Unies pour le développement industriel (ONUDI) a été chargée de recueillir et de diffuser les statistiques industrielles générales, tandis que la Division de statistique de l'ONU continue d'être responsable de statistiques de production par produit. Depuis 1982, cet ouvrage s'intitulait *Annuaire des statistiques industrielles, Volume II : Statistiques de production (par produit)*; les sept premières éditions avaient été publiées sous le titre *La croissance de l'industrie mondiale*, et les huit suivantes, sous le titre *Annuaire de statistiques industrielles*.

Cette édition de l'Annuaire présente des statistiques de production annuelle de produits industriels par pays, par zone géographique et par groupement économique et des données mondiales. Une liste de base d'environ 530 produits (environ 590 séries statistiques) a été retenue. La plupart des statistiques portent sur la période de 10 ans allant de 1990 à 1999 et concernent quelque 200 pays ou zones.

Presentation of statistics

In principle, the production data refer to the total industrial production of each commodity during the years indicated and within the national boundaries of each country. The data should thus include: (a) the production of industrial establishments for which the commodity is a primary product; (b) the production of industrial establishments for which it is a secondary product; (c) the production of industrial establishments for which it is an intermediate product. Unless otherwise stated in the footnotes, production by non-industrial establishments, such as farm production of dairy products, is excluded.

Selection, ordering and coding of commodities

The selection of industrial commodities is based on a list of products and materials[1] prepared by the Statistics Division for the 1973 World Programme of Industrial Statistics. Definitions of commodities are provided at the end of each relevant table. These definitions are based largely on the description of related items of the Brussels Tariff Nomenclature (BTN)[2].

The coding of the commodities has been based on the codes of the *International Standard Industrial Classification of All Economic Activities (ISIC)*[3] *Rev.2*. The first four digits of the six-digit code number relate to the pertinent ISIC industry group of which the commodity is a principal product.

---

[1] Recommendations for the 1973 World Programme of Industrial Statistics, part II, *List of Selected Products and Materials*, Statistical Papers, Series M, No. 54 (part II) (United Nations publication, Sales No. E.71.XVII.16).

[2] Customs Co-operation Council, Explanatory Notes to the Brussels Nomenclature (Brussels, 1955).

[3] Statistical Papers, Series M, No. 4, Rev. 2 (United Nations publication, Sales No. E.68.XVII.8).

Présentation des statistiques

En principe, les données relatives à la production portent sur la production industrielle totale de chaque produit pendant les années indiquées et à l'intérieur des frontières nationales de chaque pays. Elles devraient donc indiquer, pour chacun de ces produits : a) la production des établissements industriels pour lesquels il s'agit d'un produit primaire; b) la production des établissements industriels pour lesquels il s'agit d'un produit secondaire; c) la production des établissements industriels pour lesquels il s'agit d'un produit intermédiaire. Sauf indication contraire figurant en note, les données s'entendent à l'exclusion de la production des établissements non industriels (production agricole de produits laitiers, par exemple).

Choix, classement et codage des produits

Le choix des produits industriels repose sur une liste de produits et matières[1] établie par la Division de statistique en vue du Programme mondial de statistiques de l'industrie de 1973. Les définitions des produits sont indiquées à la fin des tableaux correspondants. Elles s'inspirent en grande partie de la description des éléments correspondants de la Nomenclature douanière de Bruxelles (NDB)[2].

Le codage des produits a été établi d'après celui de la *Classification internationale type, par industrie, de toutes les branches d'activité économique (CITI)*[3] *Rev.2*. Les quatre premiers des six chiffres que comprend l'indicatif correspondent au groupe de la CITI dont le produit considéré est un produit principal.

---

[1] Recommandations pour le Programme mondial de statistiques industrielles de 1973, deuxième partie, *Liste partielle de produits et matières*, Études statistiques, Série M, No 54 (deuxième partie) (publication des Nations Unies, numéro de vente F.71.XVII.16).

[2] Conseil de coopération douanière, notes explicatives de la Nomenclature douanière de Bruxelles (Bruxelles, 1955).

[3] Études statistiques, Série M, No 4, Rév.2 (publication des Nations Unies, numéro de vente: F.68.XVII.8).

The remaining two digits indicate the position of the item within the set of commodities pertaining to this industry group. In a few cases, however, a seventh digit has been introduced to provide more detail for a given commodity than the aforementioned list of selected products and materials would allow. As a result, the data previously shown under "Copper, refined", for example, have now been broken down to supply additional information on the production of primary and secondary refined copper separately. As a rule, where two or more units of measurement are recommended, the series are differentiated by the use of capital letters "A", "B" etc. following the basic code. In a few cases, however, these letters also relate to the components of a given item. Where the code for a commodity contains letter "M", the data are shown in terms of metal content of metal-bearing ores and concentrates.

The corresponding code for the commodity based on the *Standard International Trade Classification (SITC, Rev.3)*[4] is shown at the end of the definition. In this case, also, a six-digit code number is used, the first five digits being the code number of the most closely related SITC item and the sixth digit indicating whether the item is the equivalent of the SITC item (use of zero in the sixth place) or only part of it (use of 1, 2 etc. in the sixth place).

At the end of the publication are two annexes. Annex I is an index of commodities in alphabetical order. Annex II is a preliminary table of correspondence between the ISIC-based commodity codes and the SITC, Revised,[5] SITC, Rev. 2[6], SITC, Rev.3[4] and Harmonized System (HS) codes[7].

Les deux autres chiffres correspondent à la position du produit considéré à l'intérieur du cet groupe. Dans certains cas, on a ajouté un septième chiffre pour fournir sur un produit donné des indications plus détaillées que la Liste partielle de produits et matières susmentionnée. C'est ainsi que l'on a dissocié les données antérieurement fournies sous la rubrique "Cuivre affiné" pour présenter des informations complémentaires sur la production primaire et la production secondaire de cuivre affiné. En règle générale, lorsque plusieurs unités de mesures sont recommandées, les séries sont différenciées par l'utilisation de lettres majuscules "A", "B", etc., à la suite de l'indicatif principal. Dans un petit nombre de cas, toutefois, ces lettres correspondent aussi aux éléments d'une position donnée. Lorsque l'indicatif d'un produit contient la lettre "M", les données sont fournies en poids de métal contenu dans les minerais métalliques et les concentrés.

La position du produit dans la *Classification type pour le commerce international (CTCI, Rev. 3)*[4] est indiquée au bout de la définition. Dans ce cas, on utilise aussi un indicatif à six chiffres : les cinq premiers correspondent à la position de la CTCI la plus proche et le sixième précise s'il y a identité (auquel cas ce chiffre est un zéro) ou correspondance partielle seulement (ce chiffre étant alors 1, 2 et ainsi de suite).

On trouvera à la fin de la publication deux annexes. L'annexe I est l'index alphabétique des produits. L'annex II est une table de correspondance provisoire entre les indicatifs d'après la CITI et les indicatifs de la CTCI Révisée [5], CTCI, Rev.2[6], CTCI, Rev.3[4] et du Système harmonisé (SH)[7].

[4]   Standard International Trade Classification, Revision 3, Statistical Papers, Series M, No. 34/Rev.3 (United Nations publication, Sales No. E.86.XVII.12).
[5]   Statistical Papers, Series M, No. 34 (United Nations publication, Sales No. E.61.XVII.6).
[6]   Standard International Trade Classification, Revision 2, Statistical Papers, Series M, No. 34/Rev.2 (United Nations publication, Sales No. E.75.XVII.6).
[7]   Customs Co-operation Council, The Harmonized Commodity Description and Coding System (Brussels, 1985).

[4]   Classification type pour le commerce international (troisième version révisée), Études statistiques, Série M, No 34/Rev.3 (publication des Nations Unies, numéro de vente : F.86.XVII.12).
[5]   Études statistiques, Série M, No 34 (publication des Nations Unies, numéro de vente : F.61.XVII.6).
[6]   Classification type pour le commerce international (deuxième version révisée), Études statistiques, Série M, No 34/Rév.2 (publication des Nations Unies, numéro de vente : F.75.XVII.6).
[7]   Conseil de coopération douanière, "Système harmonisé de désignation et de codification des marchandises", Bruxelles,1985.

Comparability of the data

The metric system of weights and measures has been used throughout the volume. While efforts have been made to ensure the comparability of the series published for each commodity through the use of standard definitions and units of measurement, the compilation of the data in standard form has occasionally presented difficulties. In some cases, for example, units of measurement other than the recommended units have been used in reporting and, in these cases, the data have been converted into the recommended units either by the use of standard conversion factors or by ad hoc conversion factors. The latter have been utilized in the compilation of certain tables in the publication; some of these factors are only of an approximate character and have been employed solely to obtain a reasonable measure of international comparability on the tables. A list of conversion factors is given following the introduction. In other cases, however, the data could not be converted into the recommended units for lack of appropriate conversion factors.

Aggregates and estimation of missing data

Most of the tables in the publication contain aggregate figures for various country groupings. The aggregates are shown for commodities for which it is believed a satisfactory degree of comparability exists in the series for different countries. They represent the summation of the country data shown in the tables and include estimates for missing data. However, the data for the former Czechoslovakia, former USSR and former Yugoslavia are shown in the tables and included in the aggregate figures only prior to 1991 or 1992 (see paragraphs about country order and nomenclature below). After that, the data for the individual republics of the former countries are shown and included in the respective regional and world totals. It should be noted that the former USSR republics are listed under the appropriate continental regions (Asia and Europe). Therefore, from 1991 the regional and subregional (East Europe, EEC) totals are not always comparable with those for the previous years.

Comparabilité des données

Le système métrique a partout été utilisé. Malgré les efforts faits pour assurer la comparabilité des séries publiées pour chaque produit, en appliquant des définitions et des unités de mesure normalisées, la collecte des données sous une forme normalisée n'est pas toujours allée sans mal. Dans les cas, par exemple, où elles ont été fournies dans des unités de mesure autres que les unités recommandées, elles ont été converties dans les unités recommandées à l'aide soit de facteurs de conversion normalisés, soit, pour l'établissement de certains tableaux, de facteurs de conversion spéciaux dont quelques-uns ne sont qu'approximatifs et n'ont été employés que pour assurer des possibilités raisonnables de comparaison des tableaux entre les divers pays. On trouvera à la suite de l'introduction une liste des facteurs de conversion utilisés. Il y a cependant des cas où les données n'ont pu être converties dans les unités recommandées, faute de facteurs de conversion appropriés.

Agrégats et estimation des données manquantes

La plupart des tableaux présentés font apparaître des agrégats pour des groupes de pays. Ces agrégats sont fournis dans le cas des produits pour lesquels les séries nationales disponibles sont aisément comparables. Ils représentent la somme des données nationales figurant dans les tableaux, complétée, le cas échéant, par des estimations des données manquantes. Les données relatives à la Tchécoslovaquie, à l'ex-URSS et à l'ex-Yougoslavie ne sont présentées et incluses dans les totaux que jusqu'à 1990 ou 1991 (voir le paragraphe sur le Classement par pays et nomenclature ci-dessous). A partir de 1991 ou 1992 les données relatives à chacune des républiques des pays précités sont présentées et incluses dans les totaux respectifs mondial et régional. On notera que les républiques de l'ex-URSS ont été classées avec les régions appropriées (l'Asie et l'Europe). Par conséquent, à partir de 1991, les totaux régionaux et sous-régionaux (Europe de l'Est, CEE) ne sont pas toujours comparables à ceux des années antérieures.

In providing the estimates of the missing data for a given country and commodity, the following methods have been utilized:

(a)   When data are available for less than five years of the period shown, the average of the years is used for the missing data;

(b)   When data are available for five or more years of the period shown, estimates for the missing data are derived from a linear regression, using the least squares method, applied to the reported data.

When some data in a given table are shown in units of measurement other than the unit indicated for that table and conversion of such data to the standard unit is not possible, aggregate figures are not published.

Sources

Like the previous issues, the *Industrial Commodity Statistics Yearbook* has been prepared by the Statistics Division of the United Nations with the generous cooperation of the national statistical authorities.

Acknowledgement is also due to the following specialized agencies and intergovernmental bodies whose publications have been utilized in updating our statistics: Commonwealth Secretariat (London), Food and Agriculture Organization of the United Nations (Rome), International Atomic Energy Agency (Vienna), International Coffee Organization (London), International Monetary Fund (Washington, D.C.), International Rubber Study Group (London), International Sugar Organization (London), International Wheat Council (London), International Energy Agency of the Organisation for Economic Co-operation and Development (Paris), Organisation

Les estimations correspondant aux données manquantes pour un pays et un produit donnés sont établies de la façon suivante :

a)   Lorsque les données disponibles portent sur moins de cinq années de la période considérée, on utilise, pour les données manquantes, la moyenne des années disponibles;

b)   Lorsque les données disponibles pour la période considérée portent sur cinq ans ou davantage, les estimations correspondant aux données manquantes sont obtenues par régression linéaire, suivant la méthode des moindres carrés appliquée aux données existantes.

Lorsque, dans un tableau, certaines données sont fournies dans des unités de mesure autres que l'unité indiquée pour ce tableau et qu'elles ne peuvent pas être converties dans l'unité normalisée, aucun agrégat n'est donné.

Sources

Comme les éditions précédentes, l'*Annuaire de statistiques industrielles (par produit)* a été établi par la Division de statistique de l'Organisation des Nations Unies, auquel les services statistiques nationaux ont largement prêté leur concours.

La Division de statistique se doit aussi de remercier les institutions spécialisées et les organes intergouvernementaux dont elle a utilisé les publications pour mettre à jour les statistiques, à savoir le Secrétariat du Commonwealth (Londres), l'Organisation des Nations Unies pour l'alimentation et l'agriculture (Rome), l'Agence internationale de l'énergie atomique (Vienne), l'Organisation internationale du café (Londres), le Fonds monétaire international (Washington), le Groupe international d'étude du caoutchouc (Londres), l'Organisation internationale du sucre (Londres), le Conseil international du blé (Londres), l'Agence

for Economic Co-operation and Development (Paris), Organisation of American States (Washington, D.C.), Organization of Petroleum Exporting Countries (Vienna), Statistical Office of the European Communities (Luxembourg) and United Nations Conference on Trade and Development (Geneva).

Governmental agencies, private institutes and associations and others to whom credit is also due for the valuable information used in this publication are as follows: Lloyd's Register of Shipping (London), Metallgesellschaft Aktiengesellschaft (Frankfurt), United States Bureau of Mines (Washington, D.C.), United States Department of Agriculture (Washington, D.C.) and World Bureau of Metal Statistics (London).

Country order and nomenclature

In the tables, the countries are arranged in continental and regional order irrespective of their political status. The order followed for the continental division is as follows: Africa; America, North; America, South; Asia, excluding the former USSR (beginning 1991, including former USSR Asian Republics); Europe, excluding the former USSR (beginning 1991, including former USSR European Republics); former USSR; and Oceania.

For reasons of space or geographical clarity, some country names in the tables have been abbreviated. These abbreviated country names are, of course, intended to be of purely geographical significance to the reader and to convey no political implications whatsoever.

internationale de l'énergie de l'Organisation de coopération et de développement économiques (Paris), l'Organisation de coopération et de développement économique (Paris), l'Organisation des États américains (Washington), l'Organisation des pays exportateurs de pétrole (Vienne), l'Office de statistique des Communautés européennes (Luxembourg) et la Conférence des Nations Unies sur le commerce et le développement (Genève).

Pour la présente publication, la Division de statistique est en outre redevable d'informations utiles aux services nationaux, instituts et associations privées et autres organismes suivants: Registre des transports maritimes de la Lloyd's (Londres), Metallgesellschaft Aktiengesellschaft (Francfort), Office des mines des États-Unis (Washington), Ministère américain de l'agriculture (Washington) et World Bureau of Metal Statistics (Londres).

Classement par pays et nomenclature

Dans les tableaux, les pays sont classés par continent et par région, indépendamment de leur statut politique. Le classement adopté pour la répartition par continent est le suivant : Afrique; Amérique du Nord; Amérique du Sud; Asie, sans l'ex-URSS (à partir de 1991, y compris les républiques asiatiques de l'ex-URSS); Europe, sans l'ex-URSS (à partir de 1991, y compris les républiques européennes de l'ex-URSS); ex-URSS; Océanie

Pour des raisons de place ou de clarté, certains noms de pays ont été abrégés dans les tableaux. Il est bien entendu que ces abréviations n'ont pas de signification politique.

For the period covered in this edition the following changes and deviations should be noted:

Cambodia was formerly listed as Democratic Kampuchea;

China: The data published under the heading "China" exclude those for Taiwan Province.

Hong Kong: Pursuant to a Joint Declaration signed on 19 December 1984, the United Kingdom restored Hong Kong to the People's Republic of China with effect from 1 July 1997; the People's Republic of China resumed the exercise of sovereignty over the territory with effect from that date.

Czech Republic, Slovakia: Data for the Czech Republic and Slovakia, where available, are shown separately under the appropriate country name. For periods prior to 1992, data for the former Czechoslovakia are shown under the country name 'Czechoslovakia (former)'.

Germany: Through accession of the German Democratic Republic to the Federal Republic of Germany with effect from 3 October 1990, the two German states have united to form one sovereign State. As from the date of unification, the Federal Republic of Germany acts in the United Nations under the designation of Germany. Data prior to 1991 pertain to the territorial boundaries of the Federal Republic of Germany and the former German Democratic Republic prior to 3 October 1990.

Il convient de noter les changements et déviations suivantes pour la période décrite dans cette édition:

Le *Cambodge* apparaissait antérieurement sous le nom de Kampuchea démocratique;

Chine: Les données qui sont présentées sous le terme "Chine" ne comprennent pas celles relatives à la province de Taiwan.

Hong Kong: Conformément á une Déclaration commune signée le 19 décembre 1984, le Royaume-Uni a rétrocédé Hong Kong á la République populaire de Chine, avec effet au 1er juillet 1997; la souveraineté de la République populaire de Chine s'exerce à nouveau sur le territoire à compter de cette date.

République tchèque, Slovaquie: Les données relatives à la République tchèque et à la Slovaquie, lorsqu'elles sont disponibles, sont présentées séparément sous le nom de chacun des pays. Pour la période précédant 1992, les données relatives à l'ancienne Tchécoslovaquie sont, sauf indication contraire, présentées sous le titre 'Tchécoslovaquie (anc.)'.

Allemagne: En vertu de l'adhésion de la République démocratique allemande à la République fédérale d'Allemagne, prenant effet le 3 octobre 1990, les deux États allemands se sont unis pour former un seul État souverain. À compter de la date de l'unification, la République fédérale d'Allemagne est désignée à l'ONU sous le nom d'Allemagne. Les données relatives à la période antérieure à 1991 correspondent aux limites territoriales de la République fédérale d'Allemagne et l'ancienne République démocratique allemande avant le 3 octobre 1990.

Myanmar was formerly listed as Burma.

Palau was formerly listed as Pacific Islands.

Former USSR: In 1991, the Union of Soviet Socialist Republics formally dissolved into fifteen independent republics (Armenia, Azerbaijan, Belarus, Estonia, Georgia, Kazakhstan, Kyrgyzstan, Latvia, Lithuania, Republic of Moldova, Russian Federation, Tajikistan, Turkmenistan, Ukraine and Uzbekistan). Beginning 1991 (resp. 1992 for commodities related to energy and some agricultural products), data are shown for the individual republics. Prior to 1991 (resp. 1992), data are shown for the former USSR.

Yemen: On 22 May 1990 Democratic Yemen and Yemen merged to form a single State. Since that date they have been listed as *Yemen*.

Yugoslavia, SFR: Data provided for Yugoslavia prior to 1991 (prior to 1992 for commodities related to energy and some agriucltural products) refer to the Socialist Federal Republic of Yugoslavia which was composed of six republics, whereas data provided for Yugoslavia after that year refer to the Federal Republic of Yugoslavia which is composed of two republics (Serbia and Montenegro).

Le *Myanmar* apparaissait antérieurement sous le nom de Birmanie.

Palaos apparaissa⊂t antérieurement sous le nom d'Iles du Pacifique.

L'ex-*URSS*: En 1991, l'Union des Républiques socialistes soviétiques s'est séparée en 15 républiques indépendantes (Arménie, Azerbaïdjan, Bélarus, Estonie, Fédération de Russie, Géorgie, Kazakhstan, Kirghizistan, Lettonie, Lituanie, Ouzbékistan, République de Moldova, Tadjikistan, Turkménistan, Ukraine. A partir de 1991 (ou 1992 pour les produits relatives au secteur de l'énergie et certains produits agricoles), les données sont présentées pour l'ex- URSS.

Yémen: Le Yémen et le Yémen démocratique ont fusionné le 22 mai 1990 pour ne plus former qu'un seul État, qui depuis lors apparaît sous le nom *Yémen*.

Yougoslavie (RSF): Les données fournies pour la Yougoslavie avant 1991 (avant 1992 pour les produits relatives au secteur de l'énergie et certains produits agricoles) se rapportent à la République socialiste fédérative de Yougoslavie, qui était composée de six républiques, alors que les données fournies pour la Yougoslavie après cet année se rapportent à la République fédérale de Yougoslavie, qui est composée de deux républiques (Serbie et Monténégro).

Explanation of symbols

The following symbols have been employed in making entries in the tables:

...	Data not available
..	Not applicable
0	Magnitude nil or less than half of the unit of measurement employed
*	Provisional or estimated figure
#	A marked break in the series; data prior to the sign not comparable

Decimal figures are always preceded by a period (.).

Explication des symboles

Les symboles employés dans les tableaux sont les suivants :

...	Données non disponibles
..	Sans Objet
0	Grandeur nulle ou inférieure à la moitié de l'unité de mesure utilisée
*	Chiffre provisoire ou estimatif
#	Marque une interruption dans la série et la non-comparabilité des données précédant le symbole

Les décimales sont toujours précédées d'un point (.).

Note. The metric system of weights and measures has been employed in the Industrial Statistics Yearbook. In this system, the relationship between units of volume and capacity is: 1 litre = 1 cubic decimeter exactly (as decided by the 12th International Conference of Weights and Measures. New Delhi, November 1964).

Section A shows the equivalent of the basic metric, British imperial and United States units of measurement. According to an agreement between the national standard institutions of English speaking nations, the British and United States units of length, area and volume are now identical, and based on the yard = 0.9144 metre exactly. The weight measures in both systems are based on the pound = 0.45359237 kilogram exactly. (Reference: Weights and Measures Act 1963 (London), and Federal Register announcement of 1 July 1959: Refinement of Values for the Yard and Pound (Washington D.C.).)

Section B shows various derived or conventional conversion coefficients and equivalents.

Section C shows other conversion coefficients or factors which have been utilized in the compilation of certain tables in the Industrial Commodity Statistics Yearbook. Some of these are only of an approximate character and have been employed solely to obtain a reasonable measure of international comparability on the tables.

For a comprehensive surveys of international and national systems of weights and measures and of units weights for a large number of commodities in different countries, see World Weights and Measures, Statistical Papers, Series M. No. 21, Rev. 1 (United Nations publication Sales No. 66.XVII.3).

Remarque. L'Annuaire de statistiques industrielles utilise le système mètrique pour les poids et mesures. La relation entre unités métriques de volume et de capacité est: 1 litre = 1 décimètre cube (dm^3) exactement (comme ce fut décidé à la Conférence internationale de poids et mesures, New Delhi, novembre 1964).

La section A fournit les équivalents principaux des systèmes de mesure métrique, britannique et américain. Suivant un accord entre les institutions de normalisation nationales des pays de langue anglaise, les mesures britanniques et américaines de longueur, superficie et volume sont désormais identiques, et sont basées sur le yard = 0.9144 mètre exactemet. Les mesures de poids se rapportent, dans les deux systèmes, à la pound (livre) = 0.45359237 kilogramme exactement. (Référence: Weights and Measures Act 1963 (Londres), et Federal Register Announcement of 1 July 1959: Refinement of Values for the Yard and Pound (Washington D.C.).)

La section B fournit divers coefficients et facteurs de conversion convertionnels ou dérivés.

La section C fournit d'autres coefficients ou facteurs de conversion utilisés dans l'élaboration de certains tableaux de l'Annuaire de statitiques industrielles par produit e sont que des approximations et n'ont été utilisés que pour obtenir un degré raisonnable de comparabilité sur le plan international.

Pour une étude d'ensemble des systèmes internationaux et nationaux de poids et mesures, et d'unités de poids pour un grand nomibre de proudits dans différents pays, voir World Weights and Measure, Etudes statistiques, Série M., No. 21, Rev. 1 (publication des Nations Unies, numéro de vente: 66.XVII.3)

A. Equivalents of metric, British imperial and United States units of measure
Equivalents des unités métriques, britanniques et américaines

Metric units Unités métriques	British imperial and U.S. Equivalents Equivalent en mesures britanniques et des Etats-Unis	British imperial and U.S. units Unités britanniques et des Etats-Unis	Metric equivalents Equivalents en Mesures métriques	
Length-Longeur:				
1 centimetre-centimètre (cm)..	0.3937008 inch	1 inch...........................	2.540	cm
1 metre-mètre (m).................	3.280840 feet	1 foot...........................	30.480	cm
1 kilometre – kilomètre (km)....	1.093613 yard	1 yard...........................	0.9144	m
	0.6213712 mile	1 mile...........................	1609.344	m
	0.5399568 int. naut. mile	1 international nautical ml.	1852.000	m
Area - Superficie:				
1 square centimetre - cm^2.....	0.1550003 square inch	1 square inch.................	6.45160	cm^2
1 square metre - m^2............	10.763910 square feet	1 square foot.................	9.290304	dm^2
	1.195990 square yards	1 square yard.................	0.83612736	m^2
1 hectare –ha....................	2.471054 acres	1 acre.........................	0.4046856	ha^2
1 square kilometre - km^2......	0.3861022 square mile	1 square mile.................	2.589988	km^2
Volume:				
1 cubic centimetre - cm^3........	0.06102374 cubic inch	1 cubic inch....................	16.38706	cm^3
1 cubic metre - m^3.................	35.31467 cubic feet	1 cubic foot....................	28.316847	dm^3
	1.307951 cubic yards	1 cubic yard....................	0.76455486	m^3
Capacity - Capacité:				
1 litre (l)............................	0.8798766 imp. Quart	1 British imperial quart......	1.136523	l
	1.056688 U.S. liq. Quart	1 U.S. liquid quart............	0.9463529	l
	0.908083 U.S. dry quart	1 U.S. dry quart...............	1.1012208	l
1 hectolitre (hl)....................	21.99692 imp. Gallons	1 imperial gallon..............	4.546092	l
	26.417200 U.S. gallons	1 U.S. gallon..................	3.785412	l
	2.749614 imp. Bushels	1 imperial bushel.............	36.368735	l
	2.837760 U.S. bushels	1 U.S. bushel..................	35.239067	l
Weight or mass – Poids				
1 kilogram (kg)....................	35.27396 av. Ounces	1 av. ounce...................	28.349523	G
	32.15075 troy ounces	1 troy ounce..................	31.10348	g
	2.204623 av. Pounds	1 av. pound..................	453.59237	g
		1 central (100 lb.)...........	45.359237	kg
	1.1023113 short tons	1 hundredweight (112 lb.).	50.802345	kg
1 ton - tonne (t)....................	0.9842065 long tons	1 short ton (2000 lb.).......	0.9071847	t
		1 long ton (2240 lb.)........	1.0160469	t

British Imperial and U.S. units Unités britanniques et des Etats-Unis	Metric equivalents Equivalents en mesures métriques	Metric units Unités métriques	British imperial and US Equivalent Equivalents en mesures Britanniques et des Etats-Unis
Ship tonnage - Tonnage de navire:			
1 register ton - tonne de jauge (GRT)..	2.83 m³ 100 cu.ft.	1 cubic metre..........	0.353 GRT 0.841 British shipping tons 0.885 U.S. shipping tons
1 British shipping ton.......................	1.19 m³ 42 cu.ft.		
1 U.S. shipping ton...........................	1.13 m³ 40 cu. ft.		
1 deadweight ton (dwt ton).............	1.016047 t 1 long ton	1 metric ton...........	0.984 dwt ton
Energy - Energie:			
1 British horsepower (hp)................	0.7457 KW	1 kilowatt (KW).......	1.34102 hp
1 horsepower - cheval vapeur (cv)....	0.735499 kW		1.35962 cv
Alcohol - Alcool:			
1 imperial proof gallon...................	0.57 imp. gallons of pure alcohol at 511F 2.59 litres of pure alcohol at 10.6°C	1 litre of pure alcohol at 10.61C.......... 1 litre of pure alcohol at 15.6°C............	0.386 imp.proof gallons 0.528 US proof gallons
1 U.S. proof gallon........................	0.5 U.S. gallon of pure alcohol at 60°F 1.893 litre d'alcool pur à 15.61C		

B. Various conventional or derived coefficients employed in Industrial Commodity Statistics Yearbook tables
Divers coefficients conventionnels ou dérivés utilisés dans les tableaux de l=Annuaire de statistiques industrielles

FOREST PRODUCTS - PRODUITS FORESTIERS

Wood (general) - Bois (general)

10³ board feet	=	2,3597 cubic metres	1 cubic metre =	423.8 board feet
10³ square metres (1 mm thickness)	=	1 cubic metre	=	1000 square metres (1mm thickness)
10³ square feet (1/8 inch thickness)	=	0.295 cubic metres	=	3390 square feet (1/8 inch thickness)

Sawnwood, coniferous -   Sciages, conifères

1 standard (Petrograd)	=	4.6723 cubic metres	1 cubic metre =	0.214 standard (Petersburg)
1 metric ton	=	1.82 cubic metres	=	0.55 metric tons

Sawnwood, broadleaved - Sciages, non-conifères

1 standard (Petrograd)	=	4.6723 cubic metres	1 cubic metre =	0.214 standard (Petersburg)
1 metric ton	=	1.43 mètres cubes	=	0.7 metric tonnes

Railway sleepers - Traverses pour voles ferrées

1 metric ton	=	1.28 cubic metres	1 cubic metre =	0.78 metric tonnes

Plywood - Contre-plaqués

1 metric ton	=	1.54 cubic metres	1 cubic metre =	0.65 metric tonnes

Veneer sheets - Feuilles de placages

1 metric ton	=	1.33 cubic metres	1 cubic metre =	0.75 metric tonnes

Particle board - Panneaux de particules

1 metric ton	=	1.54 cubic metres	1 cubic metre =	0.65 metric tonnes

Fibreboard, compressed - Panneaux de fibres, durs

1 metric ton	=	1.053 cubic metres	1 cubic metre =	0.95 metric tonnes

Fibreboard, non-compressed - Panneaux de fibres, isolants

1 metric ton	=	4 cubic metres	1 cubic metre =	0.25 metric tonnes

MINERALS - PRODUITS MINERAUX

Molybdenum - Minerais de molybdène

1 ton molybdenite (MoS_2) = 0.5995 tons molybdenum (Mo) | 1 ton molybdenum = 1.668 tons molybdenite

Vanadium - Minerais de vanadium

1 ton vanadium pentoxide (V_2O_5) = 0.5602 tons vanadium (V) | 1 ton vanadium = 1.7861 tons vanadium pentoxide

Tungsten - Minerais de tungstène

1 ton tungsten trioxide (WO_3) = 0.79303 tons tungsten (W) | 1 ton tungsten = 1.26098 tons tungsten trioxide

Chromium - Mineraiss de chrome

1 ton of chromic oxide (Cr_2O_3) = 0.68425 ton chromium (Cr) | 1 ton chromium = 1.46145 tons chromium Oxide

---

TEXTILES - TEXTILES

Cotton fabrics - Tissus de cotton

1 metric ton	=	7194 square metres	10^3 sq. metres	=	0.1264 metric tons
10^3 metres	=	1195 square metres		=	837 metres

Linen fabrics - Tissus de lin

1 metric ton	=	2721 square metres	10^3 sq. metres	=	0.367 metric tons
10^3 metres	=	928 square metres		=	1078 metres

Woollen fabrics -- Tissus de laine

1 metric ton	=	2807 square metres	10^3 sq. metres	=	0.3563 metric tons
10^3 metres	=	1650 square metres		=	606 metres

Silk and synthetic fabrics - Tissus de soie et de fibres synthétiques

1 metric ton	=	9017 square metres	10^3 sq. metres	=	0.1109 metric tons
10^3 metres	=	1370 square metres		=	703 metres

Jute fabrics - Tissus de jute

1 metric ton	=	2108 square metres	10^3 sq. metres	=	0.4744 metric tons

---

CHEMICALS- PRODUITS CHIMIQUES

Acetylene - Acétylène

1 cubic metre = 1.105 kilograms | 1 kilogram = 0.905 cubic metres

Ethyl alcohol - Alcool éthylique

1 litre = 0.789 kilograms | 1 kilogram = 1.2674 litres

1 cubic metre = 0.789 metric tons | 1 metric ton = 1.2674 cubic metres

SELECTED ENERGY CONVERSION FACTORS - FACTEURS DE CONVERSION POUR CERTAINS PRODUITS EN MATIERE D'ENERGIE

Crude petroleum

1 barrel	= 42 U.S. gallons
	= 34.97 imperial gallons
	= 158.99 litres
	= 0.15899 cubic metres.

1 cubic metre = 6.2898 barrels.

The equivalent of barrels in metric tons depends on the specific gravity of the petroleum which varies from country to country. The average specific gravity for each producing country is indicated in the table on the production of crude petroleum in the Energy Statistics Yearbook.

Natural Gas and Manufactured Gas (Gasworks Gas and Coke-oven Gas)
Data for all gases are presented in terajoules. For comparison with earlier years, multiply teracalories with a factor of 4.1868 to obtain terajoules.

Petroleum products.
The following approximate coefficients have been used to convert original data, expressed in capacity of volume, into metric tons:

Pétrole brut

1 baril	= 42 gallons E.U.
	= 34.97 gallons britanniques
	= 158.99 litres
	= 0.15899 m³

1m³ = 6.2898 barils.

L'équivalent du baril en tonnes métriques dépend du poids spécifique du pétrole qui varie d'un pays à l'autre. Le poids spécifique moyen utilisé pour chaque pays producteur se trouve dans l'Annuaire des statistiques de l'énergie dans le tableau relatif à la production de pétrole brut.

Gaz naturel et gaz manufacturé (Gaz d'usines et de cokeries)
Les données pour tous les gaz sont présentées en terajoules. Pour permettre la comparaison avec les editions antérieures, il faut multiplier les téracalories par un facteur de 4.1868 afin d'obtenir des terajoules.

Dérivés du pétrole
Les coefficients approximatifs suivants ont été utilisés pour convertir en tonnes métriques les données de base, exprimées en capacité ou en volume:

Product	Kilolitres = m³	000 gallons imperial britannique	000 gallons U.S. - E.U.	U.S. barrels Barils E.U.	Produits
Liquefied petroleum gas........	0.54	2.4549	2.0441	0.08585	Gaz de pétrole liquéfié
Naphtha............................	0.72	3.2731	2.7255	0.1145	Naphta
Motor spirit.......................	0.74	3.3641	2.8012	0.1177	Essence
Aviation spirit....................	0.73	3.3186	2.7633	0.1161	Essence avion
Kerosene, white spirit and jet Fuel.................................	0.81	3.6823	3.0662	0.1288	Pétrole lampant, white-spirit carburéacteur
Distillate fuel oils.................	0.87	3.9551	3.2933	0.1383	Huiles légères
Residual fuel oils.................	0.95	4.3188	3.5961	0.1510	Huiles lourdes
Lubricating oils...................	0.90	4.0915	3.4069	0.1431	Huiles de graissage
Bitumen (asphalt)...............	1.04	4.7279	3.9368	0.1653	Bitume (asphalte)
Paraffin wax......................	0.80	3.6369	3.0283	0.1272	Paraffine
Petroleum coke..................	1.14	5.1825	4.3154	0.1812	Coke de pétrole
Natural gasolene................	0.63	2.8640	2.3848	0.1002	Gazoline naturelle
Plant condensates..............	0.70	3.1822	2.6498	0.1113	Le condensat de raffinerie
Fuel oils n.o.s.	0.91	4.1369	3.4447	0.1447	Huiles légères et lourdes non spécifiées

Coal equivalent [1](metric tones unless otherwise indicated):

Coal,anthracite and bituminous...	1.0
Coal riquettes...	1.0
Cokesof coal...	0.9
Brown coal and lignite..	0.385
Cokes of brown coal or lignite..	0.67
Briquettes of brown coal and lignite...	0.67
Peat for fuel..	0.325
Peat briquettes..	0.5
Crude petroleum...	1.454
Natural gas liquids (weighted average)...	1.542
Liquefied petroleum gases...	1.554
Natural gasoline...	1.532
Condensate and other..	1.512
Motor spirit..	1.5
Kerosene and jet fuel..	1.474
Gas-diesel oils...	1.45
Residual fuel oils..	1.416
Natural gas (terajoules[2])..	34.131
Manufactured gas (terajoules[2])	34.131

Equivalent en houille [1](tonnes métriques sauf indication contraire):

Charbon, anthracite et la houille bitumineuse..............................	1.0
Briquettes de charbon..	1.0
Cokes de charbon...	0.9
Charbon brun et lignite...	0.385
Cokes de charbon brun ou de lignite...	0.67
Briquettes de charbon brun ou de lignite.....................................	0.67
Tourbe pour combustible...	0.325
Briquettes de tourbe..	0.5
Pétrole brut..	1.454
Condensats provenant du gaz naturel (moyenne pondéré).............	1.542
Gaz de pétrole liquéfié...	1.554
Gazoline naturelle...	1.532
Condensat et autres..	1.512
Essence...	1.5
Pétrole lampant et carburéacteur...	.474
Gaz oil fuel oil fluides..	1.45
Huile lourde..	1.416
Gaz naturel (terajoules[2])...	34.131
Gaz d'usine (terajoules[2])..	34.131

Coal equivalent (metric tons) of hydro, nuclear and geothermal electricity:
1000 kWh = 0.123

Equivalent en houille (tonnes mètriques) d'électricitè, hydraulique, nucleare et géothermique:
1000 kWh = 0.123

---

[1] It should be noted that the base used for coal equivalency comprises 7000 calories/gramme.
[2] Under standard conditions of 151C. 1013.25 mbar. dry.

[1] Veuillez noter que l'équivalence en houille est faite sur la base de 7000 calories/gramme.
[2] En volume standard (à 151C, 1013.25 mbar, gaz sec).

Hard Coal
Houille
ISIC-BASED CODE - CODE BASE CITI

2100-01

Unit : Thousand metric tons | Unité : Milliers de tonnes métriques

Country or area	1990	1991	1992	1993	1994	1995	1996	1997	1998	1999	Pays ou zone
Africa	**182526**	**186102**	**182312**	**189873**	**203790**	**214313**	**213682**	**227211**	**231798**	**251065**	**Afrique**
Algeria*	10	15	15	20	20	22	22	23	23	...	Algérie*
Botswana	794	784	901	890	901	910	728	776	924	...	Botswana
Cameroon*	1	1	1	1	1	1	1	1	1	...	Cameroun*
Dem. Rep. of Congo	78	*80	*83	*90	*92	*93	*95	*95	*96	...	Rép. dém. du Congo
Morocco	526	551	576	604	650	650	506	376	*269	...	Maroc
Mozambique*	40	42	40	40	40	38	20	18	18	...	Mozambique*
Niger	172	172	170	*172	*172	*173	*173	*174	*174	...	Niger
Nigeria	76	138	87	41	*130	*140	*140	*140	*59	...	Nigéria
South Africa	174784	178196	174392	182276	195749	206211	206362	219869	*224827	...	Afrique du Sud
Swaziland	160	123	100	50	*182	171	129	*150	*150	...	Swaziland
United Rep.Tanzania*	4	4	4	4	4	5	5	5	5	...	Rép. Unie de Tanzanie*
Zambia	377	380	395	*400	*380	*360	*325	*280	205	...	Zambie
Zimbabwe	5504	5616	5548	5285	5469	5539	5176	5304	*5047	...	Zimbabwe
America, North	**894282**	**867289**	**857176**	**813448**	**896422**	**898863**	**926974**	**953991**	**975224**	**992555**	**Amérique du Nord**
Canada	37672	39911	32315	35310	36645	38590	40031	41252	*38293	...	Canada
Mexico	2963	2321	1605	1701	2103	1645	1712	1897	*2141	...	Mexique
United States	853647	825057	823256	776437	857674	858628	885231	910842	*934790	...	Etats-Unis
America, South	**29820**	**30304**	**31639**	**31329**	**34144**	**36618**	**39412**	**44701**	**47893**	**52110**	**Amérique du Sud**
Argentina	270	292	215	167	348	305	311	250	*289	...	Argentine
Brazil	4595	5188	4731	4595	5134	5199	4805	5647	5516	...	Brésil
Chile	2183	2208	1626	1355	1182	1038	1004	1044	940	...	Chili
Colombia	20468	19992	21905	21223	22665	25869	29595	32592	*33671	...	Colombie
Peru	115	67	90	98	74	143	58	22	*21	...	Pérou
Venezuela	2189	2557	3072	3891	4741	4064	3639	5146	*7456	...	Venezuela
Asia	**1396218**	**1555606**	**1601754**	**1636459**	**1729346**	**1848616**	**1905189**	**1887209**	**1767680**	**2049827**	**Asie**
Afghanistan[1]	105	94	8	*7	*6	*5	3	*2	*2	...	Afghanistan[1]
Bhutan	2	*2	56	46	64	68	64	54	*50	...	Bhoutan
China[2]	1079883	1087406	1116369	1149745	1239902	1360730	1397000	1372820	*1250000	...	Chine[2]
Georgia	..	...	200	82	44	43	23	5	*14	...	Géorgie
India[3]	201829	226857	233883	246041	254658	265574	285522	296255	*297866	...	Inde[3]
Indonesia	7330	13715	21147	27584	31238	41517	47339	52074	*60321	...	Indonésie
Iran(Islamic Rep. of)[1]	*1100	986	971	970	1293	1138	1211	*1024	*1169	...	Iran(Rép. islamique)[1]
Japan	8262	8053	7598	7218	6933	6261	6480	4275	*3665	...	Japon
Kazakhstan	..	...	122391	107204	99811	79615	73240	70174	*68058	...	Kazakhstan
Korea,Dem.Ppl's.Rep.*	68000	70000	71000	72000	71500	71000	70400	65613	62332	...	Corée,Rép.pop.dém.de*
Korea, Republic of	17217	15058	11970	9443	7438	5720	4951	4512	4361	...	Corée, République de
Kyrgyzstan	..	1517	1040	736	746	463	370	500	*400	...	Kirghizistan
Lao People's Dem. Rep.*	1	1	1	1	1	1	1	1	1	...	Rép. dém. pop. lao*
Malaysia	105	180	80	397	134	112	83	100	*351	...	Malaisie
Mongolia	595	2200	1957	1569	1355	1290	*1380	1171	*989	...	Mongolie
Myanmar[3]	31	36	37	33	31	35	31	*29	*31	...	Myanmar[3]
Nepal	...	...	2	2	2	6	6	8	*16	...	Népal
Pakistan[4]	3143	3054	3099	3267	3534	3043	3638	3553	*3159	...	Pakistan[4]
Philippines	1243	1262	1661	1582	1449	1318	1106	1079	*999	...	Philippines
Thailand	0	0	22	16	12	5	3	0	*0	...	Thaïlande
Turkey	2745	2762	2830	2789	2838	2248	2441	2513	*2156	...	Turquie
Uzbekistan	..	...	200	152	200	74	74	59	*68	...	Ouzbékistan
Viet Nam	4627	5204	5232	5575	6157	8350	9823	11388	*11672	...	Viet Nam
Europe	**375097**	**680450**	**677054**	**611606**	**550557**	**551744**	**521452**	**511098**	**466823**	**393267**	**Europe**
Belgium	2357	2108	1197	971	753	637	560	427	*312	...	Belgique
Bulgaria	143	128	248	263	173	194	138	102	*92	...	Bulgarie
Croatia	...	...	120	105	96	75	64	49	*51	...	Croatie
Denmark	...	...	0	0	10	22	64	23	*0	...	Danemark
Czechoslovakia(former)	[5]22371	19522	..	..	..	..	..	..	..	...	Tchécoslovaquie(anc.)
Czech Republic[5]	..	..	18481	18297	17376	17169	16531	16069	*16112	...	République tchèque[5]
France incl. Monaco	11199	10910	10248	8990	8109	8495	7755	6286	*5375	...	France y compris Monaco
Germany	..	*72744	*72153	64175	57623	58858	53157	51212	*45339	...	Allemagne
Germany(Fed.Rep.)	76553	..	..	..	..	..	..	..	..	...	Allemagne(Rép.féd.)
Hungary[5]	169	85	83	0	0	0	0	0	*0	...	Hongrie[5]

For general note and footnotes, see end of table. | Voir la fin du tableau pour la remarque générale et les notes.

Hard Coal (continued)
Houille (suite)

ISIC-BASED CODE - CODE BASE CITI

2100-01

Unit : Thousand metric tons   Unité : Milliers de tonnes métriques

Country or area	1990	1991	1992	1993	1994	1995	1996	1997	1998	1999	Pays ou zone
Ireland	35	1	1	1	1	1	0	0	*0	...	Irlande
Italy and San Marino	58	21	111	10	0	0	0	0	*0	...	Italie y comp. St. Marin
Norway,Svlbd.J.Myn. l	303	330	391	268	301	292	230	386	*328	...	Norvège,Svalbd,J.May
Poland	147736	140376	131620	130047	133127	136190	137094	137129	*115145	...	Pologne
Portugal	281	270	221	197	147	0	*0	*0	*0	...	Portugal
Romania	4446	3828	4098	1224	1365	1148	1323	1752	*1406	...	Roumanie
Russian Federation	..	...	210432	193136	176754	176918	166516	159807	*153084	...	Fédération de Russie
Spain[5]	14743	13916	14718	14046	14056	13590	13613	13754	*12287	...	Espagne[5]
Sweden	11	28	37	4	0	0	0	0	*0	...	Suède
Ukraine	..	...	127900	111600	91300	83528	74132	75514	*75767	...	Ukraine
United Kingdom[5]	94397	94921	84893	68199	49284	54556	50197	48495	*41420	...	Royaume-Uni[5]
Yugoslavia	..	...	102	73	82	71	78	93	*105	...	Yougoslavie
Yugoslavia, SFR	292	..	..	..	..	..	..	..	..	..	Yougoslavie, RSF
USSR (former)	473931	..	..	..	..	..	..	..	..	..	URSS (anc.)
Oceania	**161040**	**167139**	**177899**	**179880**	**179396**	**194309**	**196771**	**209954**	**221994**	**237115**	**Océanie**
Australia[4]	158834	164644	175130	176955	176650	191055	193437	206816	*218959	...	Australie[4]
New Zealand[3]	2206	2495	2769	2925	2746	3254	3334	3138	*3035	...	Nouvelle-Zélande[3]
Total	**3512914**	**3486890**	**3527834**	**3462595**	**3593655**	**3744463**	**3803480**	**3834164**	**3711412**	**3975939**	**Total**

General Note.

Coal with a high degree of coalification, and with a gross calorific value above 24 MJ/kg (5700 kcal/kg) on an ash-free but moist basis, and with a reflectance index of vitrinite of 0.5 and above. Slurries, middlings and other low grade coal products, which cannot be classified according to the type of coal from which they are obtained, are included under hard coal. (SITC, Rev.3: 32110-0, 32120-0).

[1] Twelve months beginning 21 March of year stated.
[2] Including lignite.
[3] Twelve months beginning 1 April of year stated.
[4] Twelve months ending 30 June of year stated.
[5] Including recovered slurries.

Remarque générale.

Charbon à haut degré de houillification et de pouvoir calorifique brut supérieur à 24 MJ/kg (5700 kcal/kg) mesuré sans cendre, mais sur base humide, pour lequel l'indice de réflectance du vitrain est égal ou supérieur à 0,5. Les schlamms, les mixtes et autres produits du charbon de faible qualité qui ne peuvent être classés en fonction du type de charbon dont ils sont derivés, sont inclus dans cette rubrique. (CTCI, Rev.3: 32110-0, 32120-0).

[1] Période de douze mois commençant le 21 mars de l'année indiquée.
[2] Y compris la lignite.
[3] Période de douze mois commençant le 1er avril de l'année indiquée.
[4] Période de douze mois finissant le 30 juin de l'année indiquée.
[5] Y compris les schlamms récupérés.

Lignite
Lignite

ISIC-BASED CODE - CODE BASE CITI

2100-04

Unit : Thousand metric tons　　　　　　　　　　　　　　　　　　　　　　　　Unité : Milliers de tonnes métriques

Country or area	1990	1991	1992	1993	1994	1995	1996	1997	1998	1999	Pays ou zone
America, North	**113651**	**112882**	**119249**	**119849**	**122880**	**122482**	**124428**	**124334**	**124759**	**131209**	**Amérique du Nord**
Canada	30659	31224	33047	33706	36179	36336	35840	37434	*37075	...	Canada
Mexico	3078	3174	4499	4905	6795	7675	8593	8499	*9091	...	Mexique
United States	79914	78484	81703	81238	79906	78471	79995	78401	*78593	...	Etats-Unis
America, South	**40**	**40**	**60**	**42**	**40**	**40**	**38**	**36**	**35**	**32**	**Amérique du Sud**
Chile*	40	40	60	42	40	40	38	36	35	...	Chili*
Asia	**100742**	**112410**	**118436**	**118652**	**127081**	**129999**	**133596**	**137067**	**140253**	**153432**	**Asie**
India[1]	15020	15263	16207	17157	19201	22108	22281	23031	*23300	...	Inde[1]
Japan	15	15	17	16	*16	*16	*16	*16	*16	...	Japon
Kazakhstan	..	...	4152	4669	4815	3740	3591	2473	*1715	...	Kazakhstan
Korea,Dem.Ppl's.Rep.*	22000	23000	24000	27000	26500	26000	25500	23766	22578	...	Corée,Rép.pop.dém.de*
Kyrgyzstan	..	1956	1111	985	550	280	273	280	*280	...	Kirghizistan
Mongolia	6562	4837	4290	4040	3655	3581	*3731	3753	*4068	...	Mongolie
Myanmar[1]	*38	*39	*39	*25	*22	*23	*22	28	*28	...	Myanmar[1]
Philippines*	3	3	3	3	3	3	3	3	3	...	Philippines*
Tajikistan	..	...	200	200	103	27	20	20	*20	...	Tadjikistan
Thailand	12421	14689	15335	15530	17083	18416	21474	23393	*20163	...	Thaïlande
Turkey	44683	43346	48601	45372	51533	52825	53922	57416	*65227	...	Turquie
Uzbekistan	..	...	4481	3655	3600	2980	2763	2888	*2855	...	Ouzbékistan
Europe	**777669**	**771671**	**751129**	**709060**	**699516**	**634779**	**633242**	**605452**	**581986**	**554330**	**Europe**
Albania	*2070	1087	800	600	169	163	101	70	*49	...	Albanie
Austria	2448	2081	1771	1691	1391	1297	1108	1130	*1140	...	Autriche
Belgium	...	1473	979	971	753	637	560	427		...	Belgique
Bosnia and Herzegovina	..	..	*2000	*1500	1400	1640	*1690	*1741	*1794	...	Bosnie-Herzégovine
Bulgaria	31544	28323	30087	28769	28584	30636	28104	26929	*30019	...	Bulgarie
Croatia	..	...	0	11	7	7	2	0	*0	...	Croatie
Czechoslovakia(former)	83749	80812	..	..	..	..	..	..	..	..	Tchécoslovaquie(anc.)
Czech Republic	..	..	73855	73984	66058	57947	59692	57446	*51417	...	République tchèque
Estonia	..	..	18849	14915	14530	13310	14735	14383	*12464	...	Estonie
France incl. Monaco	2333	1966	1578	1672	1501	1401	799	1030	*737	...	France y compris Monaco
Germany	..	*279578	241812	221801	241812	192757	187239	177159	*166035	...	Allemagne
Germany(Fed.Rep.)	107589	..	..	..	..	..	..	..	..	..	Allemagne(Rép.féd.)
German D.R.(former)*	280000	..	..	..	..	..	..	..	..	..	R.D.A. (anc.)*
Greece	51896	52695	55051	54817	56741	57662	59781	58844	*60884	...	Grèce
Hungary	15842	15050	15748	14616	14111	14588	15190	15589	*14650	...	Hongrie
Italy and San Marino	956	940	714	995	267	380	296	102	*189	...	Italie y comp. St. Marin
Poland	67584	69406	66852	68105	66770	63547	63845	63169	*62820	...	Pologne
Romania	33737	28578	33662	38527	39182	39973	40546	32055	*24825	...	Roumanie
Russian Federation[2][3]	..	...	126832	112778	95292	85894	90179	85224	*78835	...	Fédération de Russie[2][3]
Slovakia	..	..	3522	2301	2363	3759	3829	3915	*3951	...	Slovaquie
Slovenia	..	...	5573	5121	4854	4884	4768	4953	4891	...	Slovénie
Spain	21070	19646	18681	17458	15500	14813	13679	12587	*13675	...	Espagne
Ukraine	..	...	5779	4148	3100	2296	1587	1436	*1409	...	Ukraine
United Kingdom[4]	5	3	3	3	2	0	0	0	0	...	Royaume-Uni[4]
Yugoslavia	..	...	40003	37360	38269	39939	38367	40563	*43967	...	Yougoslavie
T.F.Yug.Rep. Macedonia	..	...	6978	6917	6860	7249	7145	6700	*8176	...	L'ex-RY Macédoine
Yugoslavia, SFR	75556	..	..	..	..	..	..	..	..	..	Yougoslavie, RSF
USSR (former)[2]	**156588**	**..**	**..**	**..**	**..**	**..**	**..**	**..**	**..**	**..**	**URSS (anc.)[2]**
Oceania	**46203**	**49559**	**50902**	**47824**	**49004**	**50944**	**53926**	**58388**	**65882**	**65858**	**Océanie**
Australia[5]	45990	49386	50723	47648	48752	50751	53712	58156	*65600	...	Australie[5]
New Zealand[1]	213	173	179	176	252	193	214	232	*282	...	Nouvelle-Zélande[1]
Total	**1194893**	**1046563**	**1039776**	**995427**	**998521**	**938244**	**945230**	**925277**	**912915**	**904861**	**Total**

General Note.
Coal with a low degree of coalification which has retained the anatomical structure of the vegetable matter from which it was formed. Its gross calorific value is less than 24 MJ/kg (5700 kcal/kg) on an ash-free but moist basis, and its reflectance index of vitrinite is less than 0.5. (SITC, Rev.3: 32221-0).

Remarque générale.
Charbon d'un faible degré de houillification qui a gardé la structure anatomique des végétaux dont il est issu. Son pouvoir calorifique brut est inférieur à 24 MJ/kg (5700 kcal/kg) mesuré sans cendre mais sur base humide et son indice de réflectance du vitrain est inférieur à 0,5. (CTCI, Rev.3: 32221-0).

For footnotes, see end of table.　　　　　　　　　　　3　　　　　　　　　　Voir la fin du tableau pour les notes.

Lignite (continued)
Lignite (suite)

Footnotes

[1] Twelve months beginning 1 April of year stated.

[2] Including oil shale.

[3] Including lignite briquettes.

[4] Great Britain only.

[5] Twelve months ending 30 June of year stated.

Notes.

[1] Période de douze mois commençant le 1er avril de l'année indiquée.

[2] Y compris le schiste bitumineux.

[3] Y compris les briquettes de lignite.

[4] Grande Bretagne seulement.

[5] Période de douze mois finissant le 30 juin de l'année indiquée.

Crude petroleum
Pétrole brut
ISIC-BASED CODE - CODE BASE CITI
2200-01A

Unit : Thousand metric tons   Unité : Milliers de tonnes métriques

Country or area	1990	1991	1992	1993	1994	1995	1996	1997	1998	1999	Pays ou zone
Africa	**300602**	**318811**	**327827**	**312484**	**309925**	**318658**	**324647**	**330400**	**334888**	**340106**	**Afrique**
Algeria	37021	37698	36333	35184	35455	35907	38009	38194	*39103	...	Algérie
Angola	23553	24731	26544	25346	27193	32132	34777	*35149	*36382	...	Angola
Benin	193	185	128	213	178	131	112	90	*62	...	Bénin
Cameroon	7835	7235	6790	6610	5809	5398	*5215	*5510	*5905	...	Cameroun
Congo	8028	8054	8637	9537	9562	9268	10370	11598	*12710	...	Congo
Côte d'Ivoire	*955	*1010	9590	872	*348	314	1263	1272	*1282	...	Côte d'Ivoire
Dem. Rep. of Congo	1459	1325	1122	1135	1124	*1146	*1148	*1151	*1155	...	Rép. dém. du Congo
Egypt	44032	45581	46080	45464	44356	44436	42837	41650	*40286	...	Egypte
Equatorial Guinea	...	...	125	234	242	339	857	2997	*4099	...	Guinée équatoriale
Gabon	13494	14710	14660	15584	17214	18246	18277	18597	*18195	...	Gabon
Libyan Arab Jamah.	67162	72180	69117	65536	66210	67655	67413	69347	*67461	...	Jamah. arabe libyenne
Morocco	15	12	11	10	8	5	5	12	*12	...	Maroc
Nigeria	86335	94655	97850	95260	91045	92157	92805	93640	*96960	...	Nigéria
South Africa	...	...	5652	6849	6817	7273	7389	*7400	*7300	...	Afrique du Sud
Tunisia	4511	5190	5188	4650	4364	4251	4170	3793	*3976	...	Tunisie
America, North	**588593**	**603961**	**587246**	**583685**	**579180**	**572891**	**569028**	**581462**	**564172**	**556354**	**Amérique du Nord**
Barbados	62	62	65	63	62	63	50	45	*80	...	Barbade
Canada	76226	75939	78855	84761	89566	91828	91745	96569	*85966	...	Canada
Cuba	726	748	936	975	1258	1638	1644	1628	*1869	...	Cuba
Guatemala	215	202	306	352	365	467	729	975	*1272	...	Guatemala
Mexico	132469	145650	145395	145815	145188	141319	148454	157846	*160266	...	Mexique
Trinidad and Tobago	7863	7442	7009	6396	6769	6746	6673	6179	*6352	...	Trinité-et-Tobago
United States	371032	373918	354680	345323	335972	330830	319733	318220	*308367	...	Etats-Unis
America, South	**213687**	**225861**	**232394**	**244528**	**260965**	**276739**	**307150**	**324898**	**330047**	**378637**	**Amérique du Sud**
Argentina	24784	25329	28617	30485	34278	35888	40311	42837	*42275	...	Argentine
Bolivia[1]	971	1029	1029	969	1134	1314	1456	1495	*1738	...	Bolivie[1]
Brazil	31614	31229	31569	32252	33804	34907	39401	42777	49570	...	Brésil
Chile	842	755	619	584	594	417	363	270	242	...	Chili
Colombia	22155	21978	22759	23498	23560	30253	32431	33760	*37267	...	Colombie
Ecuador	14566	14945	17949	19797	17391	20100	19243	20123	*20681	...	Equateur
Peru	6528	5725	5798	6566	6348	6071	5999	5956	*5662	...	Pérou
Suriname	218	266	*269	*271	272	275	245	246	*248	...	Suriname
Venezuela[1]	112009	124605	123785	130106	143584	147514	167701	177434	*172364	...	Venezuela[1]
Asia	**1118298**	**1137851**	**1203085**	**1254676**	**1266436**	**1279174**	**1298562**	**1350734**	**1418575**	**1480470**	**Asie**
Azerbaijan	..	...	10696	9971	9308	8946	8890	8822	*11247	...	Azerbaïdjan
Bahrain	2101	2133	2063	2029	2011	1975	1930	1934	*1869	...	Bahreïn
Bangladesh	*[2]19	[2]16	[2]30	*[2]30	[2]6	10	7	1	*1	...	Bangladesh
Brunei Darussalam	6695	7245	8689	8306	8911	8470	8242	8135	*8050	...	Brunéi Darussalam
China	138306	140992	142097	145237	146082	150044	157334	160741	*161000	...	Chine
Georgia	..	...	100	100	74	47	128	134	*119	...	Géorgie
India[3]	33311	31007	28035	26508	30896	32200	33189	33830	*32972	...	Inde[3]
Indonesia	70199	78323	74169	73480	73941	73421	73969	74059	*65487	...	Indonésie
Iran(Islamic Rep. of)[4]	158814	171285	171708	181210	179123	181358	182152	178726	*180265	...	Iran(Rép. islamique)[4]
Iraq	100638	13776	21100	23482	25840	27019	28374	56502	*104038	...	Iraq
Israel	13	11	9	8	4	7	4	0	*0	...	Israël
Japan	540	751	625	570	543	531	518	498	*450	...	Japon
Jordan	16	7	3	0	2	2	2	2	*2	...	Jordanie
Kazakhstan	..	...	21934	19572	18544	17932	21050	23409	*23819	...	Kazakhstan
Kuwait,part Ntl.Zone	59550	9061	53783	95291	101664	101666	101891	101687	*103939	...	Koweït et prt.Zne.N.
Kyrgyzstan	..	143	113	88	88	89	100	85	*77	...	Kirghizistan
Malaysia	30028	30769	31631	31586	32155	33327	33737	33104	*33980	...	Malaisie
Myanmar[3]	647	707	722	674	680	473	401	395	*382	...	Myanmar[3]
Oman	34018	35128	36807	38571	40150	42324	44019	44925	*44573	...	Oman
Pakistan[2]	2619	3151	3014	2937	2774	2664	2826	2854	*2756	...	Pakistan[2]
Philippines	245	165	463	471	237	135	47	42	*41	...	Philippines
Qatar	19062	18831	20462	18995	18273	18450	18606	26168	*29009	...	Qatar
S.Arabia,pt.Ntrl.Zn	319622	404620	416420	412280	403382	406171	407280	417326	*431312	...	Arab.saoud,p.Zn.neut
Syrian Arab Republic	22941	24600	27100	29400	29900	30500	30070	28150	*27650	...	Rép. arabe syrienne
Tajikistan	..	...	57	49	32	24	20	25	*19	...	Tadjikistan
Thailand	1280	1308	1408	1247	1326	1190	1322	1374	*1513	...	Thaïlande

For general note and footnotes, see end of table.   Voir la fin du tableau pour la remarque générale et les notes.

Crude petroleum (continued)
Pétrole brut (suite)

ISIC-BASED CODE - CODE BASE CITI

2200-01A

Unit : Thousand metric tons   Unité : Milliers de tonnes métriques

Country or area	1990	1991	1992	1993	1994	1995	1996	1997	1998	1999	Pays ou zone
Turkey	3712	4364	4276	3892	3696	3516	3500	3449	*3223	...	Turquie
Turkmenistan	..	..	4653	3900	3360	3500	4025	5149	*6375	...	Turkménistan
United Arab Emirates	101959	109444	103962	103720	104066	103215	103816	105892	*108010	...	Emirats arabes unis
Uzbekistan	..	...	3293	3944	5500	5171	4977	5102	*5335	...	Ouzbékistan
Viet Nam	2695	4000	5520	6312	7000	7620	8803	10090	*12500	...	Viet Nam
Dem. Yemen (former)*	800	..	..	..	..	..	..	..	..	..	Yémen dém. (anc.)*
Yemen (former)*	8468	..	..	..	..	..	..	..	..	..	Yémen (anc.)*
Yemen	..	9431	8143	10816	16868	17177	17333	18124	*18562	...	Yémen
Europe	206099	590299	636125	599951	603702	604319	616672	619866	614032	630275	Europe
Albania	1067	845	585	568	535	521	488	366	*368	...	Albanie
Austria	1149	1280	1180	1155	1100	1036	965	972	*959	...	Autriche
Belarus	..	...	2000	2005	2000	1932	1860	1822	*1830	...	Bélarus
Bulgaria	60	58	53	43	36	43	32	28	*33	...	Bulgarie
Croatia	..	...	1917	1895	1577	1500	1469	1533	*1589	...	Croatie
Denmark	5994	7092	7756	8265	9118	9169	10121	11360	*11432	...	Danemark
Czechoslovakia(former)	123	140	..	..	..	..	..	..	..	..	Tchécoslovaquie(anc.)
Czech Republic	..	..	82	61	128	146	152	163	*179	...	République tchèque
France incl. Monaco	3024	2952	2866	2752	2769	2503	2107	1780	*1698	...	France y compris Monaco
Germany	..	3405	*3279	3064	2938	2926	2874	2804	*2934	...	Allemagne
Germany(Fed.Rep.)	3594	..	..	..	..	..	..	..	..	..	Allemagne(Rép.féd.)
German D.R. (former)*	39	..	..	..	..	..	..	..	..	..	R.D.A. (anc.)*
Greece	773	789	653	537	500	435	483	436	*293	...	Grèce
Hungary	1974	1841	1769	1654	1575	1668	1476	1360	*1260	...	Hongrie
Italy and San Marino	4641	4307	4479	4620	4877	5208	5430	5926	*5600	...	Italie y comp. St. Marin
Lithuania	..	...	64	73	93	128	155	212	*277	...	Lituanie
Netherlands	3533	3258	2845	2672	3437	2721	2221	2069	*1714	...	Pays-Bas
Norway,Svlbd.J.Myn. I	79663	91383	104481	111854	125043	134617	152752	152491	*146166	...	Norvège,Svalbd,J.May
Poland	160	157	200	235	284	292	317	289	*360	...	Pologne
Romania	7929	6791	6615	6713	6737	6717	6626	6517	*6309	...	Roumanie
Russian Federation	..	...	399337	351496	315764	305107	299498	303868	*301406	...	Fédération de Russie
Slovakia	..	..	*70	67	*67	*74	71	64	*60	...	Slovaquie
Slovenia	..	...	2	2	2	2	1	1	1	...	Slovénie
Spain	795	1067	1073	874	807	652	512	371	*529	...	Espagne
Sweden	3	3	1	0	5	4	*4	0	*0	...	Suède
Ukraine	..	...	4474	4248	4200	4058	4098	4134	*3900	...	Ukraine
United Kingdom	88010	86833	89179	93950	119032	121794	121930	120321	*124222	...	Royaume-Uni
Yugoslavia	..	...	1165	1148	1078	1066	1030	979	*913	...	Yougoslavie
Yugoslavia, SFR	3568	..	..	..	..	..	..	..	..	..	Yougoslavie, RSF
USSR (former)	552559	..	..	..	..	..	..	..	..	..	URSS (anc.)
Oceania	31732	32281	29350	29078	27534	28090	25501	26055	26903	23057	Océanie
Australia [2]	25465	25432	22311	21836	20262	21615	19551	19508	*20949	...	Australie [2]
New Zealand [3]	1767	1849	1739	1842	1772	1475	1950	2587	*2054	...	Nouvelle-Zélande [3]
Papua New Guinea*	4500	5000	5300	5400	5500	5000	4000	3960	3900	...	Papouasie-Nvl-Guinée*
Total	3011570	2909064	3016027	3024402	3047742	3079871	3141560	3233415	3288617	3408899	Total

General Note.

Mineral oil consisting of a mixture of hydrocarbons of natural origin, yellow to black in colour, of variable specific gravity and viscosity,including crude mineral oils extracted from bituminous minerals (shale, bituminous sand, etc.). (SITC, Rev.3: 33300-0A).

Remarque générale.

Huile minérale constituée d'un mélange d'hydrocarbures d'origine naturelle, de couleur variant du jaune au noir, d'une densité et d'une viscosité variables. Figurent également dans cette rubrique les huiles minérales brutes extraites de minéraux bitumineux (schiste, sable, etc.). (CTCI, Rev.3: 33300-0A).

[1] Including condensate production.
[2] Twelve months ending 30 June of year stated.
[3] Twelve months beginning 1 April of year stated.
[4] Twelve months beginning 21 March of year stated.

[1] Y compris la production des condensats d'usine.
[2] Période de douze mois finissant le 30 juin de l'année indiquée.
[3] Période de douze mois commençant le 1er avril de l'année indiquée.
[4] Période de douze mois commençant le 21 mars de l'année indiquée.

Natural gasolene
Gazoline naturelle

ISIC-BASED CODE - CODE BASE CITI

2200-07A

Unit : Thousand metric tons   Unité : Milliers de tonnes métriques

Country or area	1990	1991	1992	1993	1994	1995	1996	1997	1998	1999	Pays ou zone
Africa	**34**	**30**	**34**	**33**	**32**	**31**	**31**	**35**	**36**	**35**	**Afrique**
Tunisia	34	30	34	33	32	31	31	35	*36	...	Tunisie
America, North	**18598**	**19015**	**20359**	**21211**	**21532**	**21715**	**20951**	**21656**	**21671**	**23301**	**Amérique du Nord**
Canada	4147	4339	4807	5330	5880	5645	5378	*5540	*5548	...	Canada
Mexico*	3165	2854	3401	3688	3704	3825	3310	3811	3815	...	Mexique*
Trinidad and Tobago	7	*7	*7	*7	36	*35	*35	*30	*30	...	Trinité-et-Tobago
United States[1]	11279	11815	12144	12186	11912	12210	12228	12275	*12278	...	Etats-Unis[1]
America, South	**1322**	**1385**	**1354**	**1564**	**1669**	**1701**	**1738**	**1792**	**1766**	**2043**	**Amérique du Sud**
Argentina	270	260	*260	*250	*250	*250	*250	*200	*200	...	Argentine
Bolivia	81	91	*102	98	101	*104	103	46	*46	...	Bolivie
Chile	104	87	83	87	85	74	69	59	64	...	Chili
Colombia*	76	97	61	60	60	60	60	70	57	...	Colombie*
Ecuador	29	36	40	48	43	*42	*42	*42	*42	...	Equateur
Peru	*3	*20	*13	*6	*7	*7	*7	7	*7	...	Pérou
Venezuela	759	794	*795	1015	1123	1164	1207	1368	*1350	...	Venezuela
Asia	**7687**	**6920**	**7037**	**6241**	**6304**	**7022**	**7199**	**7401**	**7504**	**7614**	**Asie**
Brunei Darussalam	*65	78	95	99	100	100	98	*98	*98	...	Brunéi Darussalam
India[2]	184	291	320	0	0	0	0	0	*0	...	Inde[2]
Iran(Islamic Rep. of)[3]	*1700	*1800	1916	*1422	*1500	*1400	*1550	*1675	*1750	...	Iran(Rép. islamique)[3]
Iraq*	510	0	0	0	0	0	0	0	0	...	Iraq*
Kuwait,part Ntl.Zone	*600	*80	*0	*0	*0	824	*850	*865	*880	...	Koweït et prt.Zne.N.
S.Arabia,pt.Ntrl.Zn	4517	...	...	...	...	...	...	...	...	...	Arab.saoud,p.Zn.neut
Syrian Arab Republic	*16	*16	*20	*0	*0	*0	*0	0	*0	...	Rép. arabe syrienne
Thailand	95	138	169	203	187	181	184	246	*259	...	Thaïlande
Europe	**391**	**372**	**173**	**176**	**162**	**396**	**441**	**443**	**443**	**471**	**Europe**
Hungary	384	370	173	173	159	393	438	*440	*440	...	Hongrie
Poland	7	2	0	...	...	...	...	...	...	...	Pologne
Total	**28032**	**27722**	**28957**	**29225**	**29699**	**30865**	**30360**	**31327**	**31420**	**33464**	**Total**

General Note.

Light spirit extracted from wet natural gas, often in association with crude petroleum. It is used as petroleum refinery and petrochemical plant input and is also used directly for blending with motor spirit without further processing. (SITC, Rev.3: 34420-1A).

Remarque générale.

Essence légère extraite du gaz naturel humide, souvent en association avec le pétrole brut. Elle est utilisée comme charge dans les raffineries de pétrole et les usines pétrochimiques et aussi employée directement en mélange avec le carburant auto sans traitement supplémentaire. (CTCI, Rev.3: 34420-1A).

[1] Including condensate production.
[2] Twelve months beginning 1 April of year stated.
[3] Twelve months beginning 21 March of year stated.

[1] Y compris la production des condensats d'usine.
[2] Période de douze mois commençant le 1er avril de l'année indiquée.
[3] Période de douze mois commençant le 21 mars de l'année indiquée.

Natural gas
Gaz naturel
ISIC-BASED CODE - CODE BASE CITI
2200-10B

Unit : Petajoules   Unité : Petajoules

Country or area	1990	1991	1992	1993	1994	1995	1996	1997	1998	1999	Pays ou zone
Africa	**2786**	**2972**	**2939**	**3058**	**2964**	**3526**	**3803**	**4205**	**4296**	**4786**	**Afrique**
Algeria	2013	2104	2038	2102	1996	2431	2619	2955	*3156	...	Algérie
Angola*	21	22	22	21	20	21	21	22	22	...	Angola*
Egypt	*265	*303	*328	376	411	530	563	581	*482	...	Egypte
Gabon	4	31	32	33	30	32	30	29	*26	...	Gabon
Libyan Arab Jamah.	242	255	264	248	249	247	251	256	*248	...	Jamah. arabe libyenne
Morocco	2	*2	1	1	1	1	1	1	*1	...	Maroc
Nigeria	156	172	172	197	178	186	213	228	*230	...	Nigéria
South Africa	*70	*71	*72	72	72	72	72	*64	*54	...	Afrique du Sud
Tunisia	13	*13	*11	*8	*7	*6	*33	68	*77	...	Tunisie
America, North	**24137**	**25796**	**26405**	**26689**	**28302**	**28248**	**29105**	**29480**	**28967**	**31814**	**Amérique du Nord**
Barbados	1	1	1	1	1	1	1	1	*1	...	Barbade
Canada	4197	4434	4874	5346	5885	6207	6414	6530	*6713	...	Canada
Cuba	1	1	1	1	1	1	1	1	1	...	Cuba
Mexico*	1481	1548	1565	1113	1143	1122	1275	1315	1420	...	Mexique*
Trinidad and Tobago	202	234	232	202	256	263	298	317	*331	...	Trinité-et-Tobago
United States	18255	19578	19733	20027	21016	20654	21117	21317	*20502	...	Etats-Unis
America, South	**2260**	**2389**	**2520**	**2909**	**3204**	**3332**	**3261**	**3559**	**3600**	**4261**	**Amérique du Sud**
Argentina	793	886	*899	925	996	1062	1032	1215	*1248	...	Argentine
Bolivia	101	100	108	107	128	*147	150	134	*128	...	Bolivie
Brazil	151	147	159	173	180	193	216	240	252	...	Brésil
Chile	69	61	70	67	73	70	69	75	68	...	Chili
Colombia	*153	*162	*152	166	*172	190	208	253	*265	...	Colombie
Ecuador	10	12	12	13	15	15	26	*24	*15	...	Equateur
Peru	27	24	26	27	28	28	28	30	*25	...	Pérou
Venezuela	956	997	1095	1431	1612	1626	1533	1587	*1599	...	Venezuela
Asia	**9149**	**13609**	**13756**	**14819**	**15324**	**16493**	**17873**	**18293**	**18675**	**21099**	**Asie**
Afghanistan[1]	*8	*8	7	*7	*7	*7	*6	*6	*5	...	Afghanistan[1]
Azerbaijan	..	...	297	257	240	250	238	225	*211	...	Azerbaïdjan
Bahrain	213	202	*202	254	249	*264	273	*288	*311	...	Bahreïn
Bangladesh[2]	154	184	195	211	233	265	274	270	*293	...	Bangladesh[2]
Brunei Darussalam	*408	353	361	374	383	415	417	*417	*404	...	Brunéi Darussalam
China	596	626	615	726	761	777	871	983	*1008	...	Chine
Georgia	..	...	1	2	0	0	0	0	*0	...	Géorgie
India[3]	389	438	456	*460	664	*718	1021	732	*996	...	Inde[3]
Indonesia	2345	1899	1989	2062	2289	2444	*2983	*2983	*2937	...	Indonésie
Iran(Islamic Rep. of)[1]	943	1005	975	727	1576	1506	1576	1934	*1951	...	Iran(Rép. islamique)[1]
Iraq	110	72	89	99	124	124	126	119	*115	...	Iraq
Israel	1	1	1	1	1	1	0	1	*0	...	Israël
Japan	84	88	89	90	93	91	91	93	*94	...	Japon
Jordan	...	...	5	6	10	10	10	10	*11	...	Jordanie
Kazakhstan	..	...	304	253	169	223	246	306	*300	...	Kazakhstan
Kuwait,part Ntl.Zone	204	75	102	243	233	362	363	362	*370	...	Koweït et prt.Zne.N.
Kyrgyzstan	..	...	2	1	2	1	1	2	*1	...	Kirghizistan
Malaysia	*502	*617	*671	862	902	*1368	*1376	*1557	*1497	...	Malaisie
Myanmar[3]	35	33	33	41	51	57	61	66	*64	...	Myanmar[3]
Oman	103	106	131	158	175	169	177	209	*235	...	Oman
Pakistan[2]	467	488	519	548	580	586	623	652	*652	...	Pakistan[2]
Qatar	*218	292	448	527	527	527	535	679	*764	...	Qatar
S.Arabia,pt.Ntrl.Zn	1195	1293	1343	1401	1471	1484	1613	1769	*1827	...	Arab.saoud,p.Zn.neut
Syrian Arab Republic	*64	*74	*77	76	*80	*90	*102	*140	*200	...	Rép. arabe syrienne
Tajikistan	..	...	2	2	1	1	2	1	*1	...	Tadjikistan
Thailand	226	281	301	339	382	396	449	561	*581	...	Thaïlande
Turkey	8	8	8	8	8	7	8	10	*22	...	Turquie
Turkmenistan	..	...	2040	2478	1361	1353	1326	653	*500	...	Turkménistan
United Arab Emirates	872	1007	865	895	1007	1222	1319	1417	*1446	...	Emirats arabes unis
Uzbekistan	..	...	1627	1711	1746	1774	1783	1848	*1877	...	Ouzbékistan
Viet Nam	0	*0	*0	*0	*0	*0	*0	*0	*1	...	Viet Nam
Europe	**8693**	**33418**	**33951**	**33403**	**32777**	**33008**	**34771**	**33443**	**34069**	**34272**	**Europe**
Albania	9	6	4	4	2	1	1	1	*1	...	Albanie

For general note and footnotes, see end of table.   Voir la fin du tableau pour la remarque générale et les notes.

Natural gas (continued)
Gaz naturel (suite)

ISIC-BASED CODE - CODE BASE CITI

2200-10B

Unit : Petajoules   Unité : Petajoules

Country or area	1990	1991	1992	1993	1994	1995	1996	1997	1998	1999	Pays ou zone
Austria	45	51	55	57	52	57	57	55	*60	...	Autriche
Belarus	..	...	10	10	11	10	10	10	*11	...	Bélarus
Bulgaria	0	0	1	2	2	2	2	1	*1	...	Bulgarie
Croatia	..	...	61	69	61	75	68	65	*60	...	Croatie
Denmark	122	151	157	173	189	205	358	342	*277	...	Danemark
Czechoslovakia(former)	23	19	..	..	..	..	..	..	..	..	Tchécoslovaquie(anc.)
Czech Republic	..	..	6	8	9	9	8	8	*8	...	République tchèque
France incl. Monaco	112	166	163	134	137	130	112	99	*85	...	France y compris Monaco
Germany	..	630	616	612	641	668	726	718	*706	...	Allemagne
Germany(Fed.Rep.)	546	..	..	..	..	..	..	..	..		Allemagne(Rép.féd.)
German D.R.(former)*	55	..	..	..	..	..	..	..	..		R.D.A. (anc.)*
Greece	6	6	6	4	2	2	2	2	*2	...	Grèce
Hungary	160	161	151	163	175	176	167	156	*138	...	Hongrie
Ireland	88	89	88	100	102	105	101	89	*65	...	Irlande
Italy and San Marino	653	696	685	730	769	760	761	734	*724	...	Italie y comp. St. Marin
Netherlands	2541	2872	2881	2930	2779	2805	3171	2814	*2676	...	Pays-Bas
Norway,Svlbd.J.Myn. I	1101	1189	1229	1246	1374	1480	1955	2010	*1997	...	Norvège,Svalbd,J.May
Poland	100	111	108	138	143	146	151	149	*151	...	Pologne
Romania	959	828	737	702	621	605	576	499	*467	...	Roumanie
Russian Federation	..	...	23850	22940	22193	21952	22139	21240	*21997	...	Fédération de Russie
Slovakia	..	..	*12	9	11	12	11	10	*9	...	Slovaquie
Slovenia	..	...	1	0	0	1	0	0	0	...	Slovénie
Spain	59	55	48	27	8	17	20	7	*5	...	Espagne
Ukraine	..	...	754	724	690	709	718	707	*701	...	Ukraine
United Kingdom	2028	2248	2294	2586	2775	3049	3630	3700	*3901	...	Royaume-Uni
Yugoslavia	..	...	32	33	31	33	25	26	*28	...	Yougoslavie
Yugoslavia, SFR*	86	..	..	..	..	..	..	..	..	..	Yougoslavie, RSF*
USSR (former)	27530	..	..	..	..	..	..	..	..	..	URSS (anc.)
Oceania	980	943	1112	1174	1236	1343	1399	1408	1431	1685	Océanie
Australia[2]	797	746	903	971	1046	1163	1194	1189	*1238	...	Australie[2]
New Zealand[3]	180	193	206	201	187	177	202	216	*190	...	Nouvelle-Zélande[3]
Papua New Guinea*	3	3	3	3	3	3	3	3	3	...	Papouasie-Nvl-Guinée*
Total	75537	79127	80683	82053	83808	85951	90213	90386	91038	97917	Total

General Note.
A mixture of hydrocarbon compounds and small quantities of non-hydrocarbons existing in the gaseous phase, or in solution with oil in natural underground reservoirs at reservoir conditions. It may be subclassified into associated (i.e., that originating from fields producing both liquid and gaseous hydrocarbons), dissolved, or non-associated gas (i.e., that originating from fields producing only hydrocarbons in gaseous form). Methane recovered from coal mines and sewage gas are also included as well as natural gas liquified for transportatioon. Excluded is natural gas used for repressuring and reinjection, as well as gas flared, vented or otherwise wasted, and shrinkage accruing to processing for the extraction of natural gas liquids. (SITC, Rev.3: 34320-0B).

Remarque générale.
Mélange de composés d'hydrocarbures et de petites quantités de composants autres que des hydrocarbures existant en phase gazeuse ou en solution huileuse dans des réservoirs souterrains naturels, dans les conditions du réservoir. Ils peuvent être subdivisés en trois catégories: gaz associé (c'est-à-dire provenant de gisements qui produisent à la fois des hydrocarbures liquides et gazeux), gaz dissous, ou gaz non-associé (c'est-à-dire provenant de gisements qui produisent seulement des hyrocarbures gazeux). Sont également inclus dans cette rubrique le méthane récupéré dans les mines de charbon et le gaz de gadoues, ainsi que le gaz naturel liquéfié en vue du transport. Sont exclus en revanche le gaz utilisé aux fins de repressurisation ou de réinjection, le gaz brûlé aux torches, éventé ou autrement perdu, ainsi que la freinte résultant du traitement du gaz naturel en vue de l'extraction des liquides. (CTCI, Rev.3: 34320-0B).

[1] Twelve months beginning 21 March of year stated.
[2] Twelve months ending 30 June of year stated.
[3] Twelve months beginning 1 April of year stated.

[1] Période de douze mois commençant le 21 mars de l'année indiquée.
[2] Période de douze mois finissant le 30 juin de l'année indiquée.
[3] Période de douze mois commençant le 1er avril de l'année indiquée.

Iron-bearing ores
Minerais ferrifères

ISIC-BASED CODE - CODE BASE CITI

2301-01M

Unit : Thousand metric tons

Unité : Milliers de tonnes métriques

Country or area	1990	1991	1992	1993	1994	1995	1996	1997	1998	1999	Pays ou zone
Africa	**32045**	**28873**	**28841**	**30076**	**29065**	**29451**	**29741**	**30916**	**30621**	**28642**	**Afrique**
Algeria	1589	1277	1364	1250	1089	1208	1212	872	963	[1]900	Algérie
Egypt	1202	1072	1196	1095	1352	* [1]1100	* [1]1700	* [1]1400	* [1]1500	* [1]1500	Egypte
Liberia	2490	804	1142	[1]0	[1]0	[1]0	[1]0	...	...	...	Libéria
Mauritania	[1]6800	6660	5743	6890	7526	* [1]7000	* [1]7384	* [1]7605	* [1]7410	* [1]7475	Mauritanie
Morocco	88	58	48	34	38	28	7	7	5	4	Maroc
South Africa	18962	18119	18460	18367	[1]18903	[1]19806	* [1]19115	* [1]20600	* [1]20400	* [1]18442	Afrique du Sud
Tunisia	154	203	178	190	155	122	129	145	120	121	Tunisie
Zimbabwe	760	680	710	2250	2	187	194	287	*223	[1]200	Zimbabwe
America, North	**61775**	**61854**	**59344**	**60724**	**63346**	**66512**	**64135**	**66711**	**67453**	**61381**	**Amérique du Nord**
Canada[2]	22178	22152	19973	21223	23084	22343	20984	22743	23734	20262	Canada[2]
Mexico	3902	3901	4120	4256	3500	4592	3908	3946	3995	4589	Mexique
United States[3]	35695	35801	35251	35245	36762	39577	39243	40022	39724	36530	Etats-Unis[3]
America, South	**124262**	**124276**	**117172**	**119392**	**125103**	**134849**	**132387**	**143182**	**144085**	**133525**	**Amérique du Sud**
Argentina	444	89	3	1	[1]28	[1]0	[1]0	[1]0	[1]0	* [1]0	Argentine
Bolivia	79	102	35	32	0	0	[1]0	[1]0	[1]0	...	Bolivie
Brazil	[4]103200	[4]103000	[4]98309	[4]100344	[1]103227	[1]112793	[1]112000	[1]122184	* [1]124210	* [1]114207	Brésil
Chile	5035	5164	4450	4517	5167	5233	5621	5437	5681	5215	Chili
Colombia	289	274	310	226	[1]317	* [1]300	* [1]330	* [1]350	* [1]295	* [1]320	Colombie
Peru	2181	2460	1977	3474	4637	3948	2916	2966	[1]2885	[1]2583	Pérou
Venezuela	13034	13187	12088	10798	11727	* [1]12575	* [1]11520	* [1]12245	* [1]11014	* [1]11200	Venezuela
Asia	**131149**	**136825**	**144624**	**166928**	**173810**	**191354**	**179044**	**203034**	**188725**	**179446**	**Asie**
Azerbaijan	..	462	360	374	...	2	4	2	7	0	Azerbaïdjan
China	86080	88490	96420	117366	119514	133475	118920	139701	125739	119073	Chine
India	35633	37492	36802	38237	41249	43114	43601	48474	46123	46973	Inde
Indonesia[5]	84	85	164	215	197	198	242	278	320	321	Indonésie[5]
Iran(Islamic Rep. of)	1800	2700	2350	2137	* [1]4300	6463	7427	6218	*8175	* [1]6000	Iran(Rép. islamique)
Japan[6]	21	19	25	6	1	1	2	2	1	1	Japon[6]
Korea,Dem.Ppl's.Rep.[1]	*4400	*4700	*4900	*4900	*4900	*5100	*5100	4700	*4700	*3900	Corée,Rép.pop.dém.de[1]
Korea, Republic of	169	124	124	123	107	103	124	166	133	228	Corée, République de
Malaysia	192	215	175	128	134	[1]123	[1]208	[1]172	* [1]243	* [1]216	Malaisie
Philippines	6	...	...	0	0	0	0	12	...	...	Philippines
Thailand	75	139	248	118	90	21	25	26	53	71	Thaïlande
Turkey	2689	2396	3053	3324	3167	2754	3391	3283	3227	2658	Turquie
Europe	**22163**	**120392**	**123602**	**97219**	**89041**	**91628**	**85783**	**87616**	**86207**	**86975**	**Europe**
Albania	...	...	...	...	4	...	...	...	...	...	Albanie
Austria	762	703	541	448	510	* [1]660	[1]504	* [1]490	* [1]500	* [1]500	Autriche
Bulgaria	321	182	239	266	268	270	282	264	*83	*75	Bulgarie
Czechoslovakia(former)	490	478	..	..	..	..	..	..	..	..	Tchécoslovaquie(anc.)
Finland	78	33	23	11	7	...	...	...	...	...	Finlande
France[7]	2655	2256	1697	798	708	432	429	145	0	3	France[7]
Greece	800	* [1]815	* [1]610	* [1]575	* [1]810	* [1]800	* [1]810	...	...	* [1]600	Grèce
Norway	1453	1593	1522	1537	1672	1453	1130	360	381	...	Norvège
Poland	2	2	2	0	0	0	...	...	...	...	Pologne
Portugal	5	4	5	6	5	[1]5	[1]7	* [1]7	* [1]7	* [1]7	Portugal
Romania	326	290	247	207	216	203	198	173	110	94	Roumanie
Russian Federation	..	51280	45536	42677	41589	44264	41047	40875	41572	46297	Fédération de Russie
Slovakia	..	..	*370	545	442	498	[1]190	[1]200	[1]215	[1]200	Slovaquie
Spain	1439	1763	1334	1140	[1]992	[1]1073	[1]588	[1]0	* [1]53	* [1]0	Espagne
Sweden*	12382	12641	28470	11840	12720	13270	13600	13990	13380	11580	Suède*
Ukraine	..	48347	43000	37164	29097	28695	26993	30379	29173	27414	Ukraine
United Kingdom[8]	2	...	2	1	1	1	1	1	1	1	Royaume-Uni[8]
Yugoslavia, SFR	1444	..	..	..	..	..	..	..	..	..	Yougoslavie, RSF
USSR (former)	133578	..	..	..	..	..	..	..	..	..	URSS (anc.)
Oceania	**83281**	**71344**	**73797**	**74563**	**79556**	**84876**	**91819**	**95829**	**98925**	**94546**	**Océanie**
Australia[9]	83281	71344	73797	74563	79556	84876	91819	95829	98925	94546	Australie[9]
Total	**588253**	**543564**	**547380**	**548902**	**559921**	**598670**	**582909**	**627288**	**616016**	**584515**	**Total**

For general note and footnotes, see end of table.

Voir la fin du tableau pour la remarque générale et les notes.

Iron-bearing ores (continued)
Minerais ferrifères (suite)

General Note.

Fe content of iron ores and concentrates and all other iron-bearing ores and concentrates intended for treatment for iron recovery. (SITC, Rev.3: 28150-1M, 28160-1M).

[1] Source: U. S. Geological Survey, (Washington, D. C.).
[2] Shipments.
[3] Including metal content of by-product ore.
[4] Content of ores.
[5] Content of iron sand concentrate.
[6] Including iron content of iron sand and pyrites.
[7] Beginning 1998, production was reduced up to 95% due to the closing of Arbed mines.
[8] Great Britain only.
[9] Twelve months ending 30 June of year stated.

Remarque générale.

Contenu en Fe des minerais de fer et concentrés et tous autres minerais ferrifères et concentrés, destinés à être traités en vue de l'extraction du fer. (CTCI, Rev.3: 28150-1M, 28160-1M).

[1] Source: U.S. Geological Survey, (Washington, D.C.).
[2] Expéditions.
[3] Y compris la teneur en métal des minerais de récupération.
[4] Teneur des minerais.
[5] La teneur en fer des concentrés de sables ferrugineux.
[6] Y compris la teneur en fer des sables ferrugineux et des pyrites.
[7] A partir de 1998, la fermeture des mines d'Arbed a causé une réduction de 95% de la production.
[8] Grande Bretagne seulement.
[9] Période de douze mois finissant le 30 juin de l'année indiquée.

Copper-bearing ores
Minerais cuprifères

ISIC-BASED CODE - CODE BASE CITI

2302-01M

Unit : Thousand metric tons / Unité : Milliers de tonnes métriques

Country or area	1990	1991	1992	1993	1994	1995	1996	1997	1998	1999	Pays ou zone
Africa	**1235**	**923**	**815**	**681**	**656**	**607**	**584**	**600**	**564**	**471**	**Afrique**
Botswana	20.6	20.6	20.4	20.1	22.8	20.5	23.3	19.8	22.1	21.0	Botswana
Dem. Rep. of Congo	[1]355.5	[1]250.0	[1]144.0	[1]46.0	[1][2]30.0	[1][2]30.0	[1][2]40.2	[1][2]37.7	[1][2]41.0	[3]35.0	Rép. dém. du Congo
Morocco	[4]11.1	[4]10.9	[4]9.6	[4]11.5	[4]10.0	[4]10.1	[4]10.5	[4]10.5	8.9	7.1	Maroc
Namibia[1][2]	32.5	35.0	34.4	33.1	26.6	22.5	14.8	20.3	5.0	...	Namibie[1][2]
South Africa[1]	178.7	192.9	167.0	166.0	183.9	199.6	[3]152.6	[3]153.1	[3]166.0	[3]144.3	Afrique du Sud[1]
Zambia	621.6	400.0	[3]429.5	[3]396.2	[3]373.2	[3]316.0	[3]334.0	[3]352.9	[3]315.0	[3]260.0	Zambie
Zimbabwe[1]	14.8	13.8	9.6	8.2	9.3	8.1	8.9	6.0	6.0	...	Zimbabwe[1]
America, North	**2653**	**2738**	**2802**	**2836**	**2775**	**2909**	**2951**	**2989**	**2951**	**2577**	**Amérique du Nord**
Canada	[1]771.5	[1]809.6	[1]761.6	[1]733.6	[1]616.8	[1]723.7	[1]688.4	658.0	705.0	614.2	Canada
Cuba	2.0	[3]2.0	[3]1.5	[3]1.5	[3]2.9	[3]2.0	[3]2.0	[3]1.0	[3]1.0	[3]1.0	Cuba
Mexico[1]	291.3	296.1	[3]279.0	301.1	305.5	[3]333.6	[3]340.7	[3]390.5	[3]384.6	[3]361.8	Mexique[1]
United States[5]	1587.7	1630.0	1760.0	1800.0	1850.0	1850.0	1920.0	1940.0	1860.0	1600.0	Etats-Unis[5]
America, South	**1977**	**2278**	**2389**	**2502**	**2642**	**2971**	**3678**	**4087**	**4448**	**5200**	**Amérique du Sud**
Argentina	0.4	0.4	0.3	0.0	[3]0.0	[3]0.0	[3]0.0	[3]30.4	[3]170.3	* [3]210.0	Argentine
Bolivia	[1]0.2	[1]0.0	[1]0.1	[1]0.1	[1]0.1	[1]0.1	[1]0.1	[1]0.2	[1]0.0	[3]0.1	Bolivie
Brazil	36.4	37.0	39.8	42.2	[3]39.7	[3]48.9	[3]46.2	[3]40.0	* [3]34.5	* [3]31.2	Brésil
Chile[1]	1616.3	1855.1	1966.9	2078.5	2233.9	2509.6	3144.2	3511.5	3757.8	4421.6	Chili[1]
Colombia	0.3	3.3	2.2	0.0	[2]2.6	[2]2.8	[2]2.2	[2]1.8	[2]2.0	[3]1.0	Colombie
Ecuador* [3]	0.1	0.1	0.1	0.1	0.1	0.1	0.1	0.1	0.1	0.1	Equateur* [3]
Peru	323.4	382.3	379.1	381.3	365.7	409.7	485.6	503.0	483.3	536.3	Pérou
Asia	**840**	**900**	**1003**	**1062**	**1106**	**1265**	**1302**	**1390**	**1643**	**1760**	**Asie**
China	[3]295.9	[3]304.0	[3]332.6	347.0	395.6	441.9	436.4	494.0	480.0	509.3	Chine
Cyprus[1][6]	0.4	0.2	0.2	0.1	[2]0.0	[2]0.0	0.0	0.0	0.0	0.0	Chypre[1][6]
India	59.7	58.2	56.0	55.5	52.8	48.8	40.1	46.0	41.7	35.5	Inde
Indonesia	139.5	203.5	289.2	296.1	339.9	481.8	561.1	579.9	842.2	926.3	Indonésie
Iran(Islamic Rep. of)[3]	65.8	84.3	105.0	86.6	117.9	102.2	107.6	118.7	128.0	134.0	Iran(Rép. islamique)[3]
Japan[4]	12.9	15.0	12.1	10.3	6.0	2.4	1.1	0.9	1.1	1.0	Japon[4]
Korea,Dem.Ppl's.Rep.* [3]	15.0	15.0	16.0	16.0	16.0	16.0	16.0	16.0	14.0	14.0	Corée,Rép.pop.dém.de* [3]
Malaysia[3]	24.3	25.6	28.6	25.2	25.3	20.8	20.2	18.8	13.9	5.0	Malaisie[3]
Myanmar[3]	4.6	4.6	3.7	3.6	5.0	5.3	4.8	2.9	6.7	26.7	Myanmar[3]
Philippines	182.0	148.0	126.1	136.2	112.1	102.6	62.3	48.6	[3]46.5	[3]35.2	Philippines
Turkey	39.8	41.8	33.4	84.9	34.9	[2]43.4	[2]52.2	64.5	68.9	73.2	Turquie
Europe	**890**	**917**	**860**	**904**	**893**	**933**	**958**	**944**	**949**	**935**	**Europe**
Albania	[3]11.5	[3]3.7	[3]0.9	14.0	8.7	16.7	10.8	0.9	2.3	0.9	Albanie
Bulgaria[2]	32.9	47.2	47.4	60.4	75.5	75.5	84.8	75.5	75.5	...	Bulgarie[2]
Czechoslovakia(former)	6.4	4.2	..	..	..	..	..	..	..	..	Tchécoslovaquie(anc.)
Finland	17.5	16.2	15.4	13.7	13.2	9.8	9.3	[3]9.0	[3]9.0	[3]10.0	Finlande
France	0.3	0.2	[3]0.1	[3]0.1	[3]0.2	[3]0.0	[3]0.0	[3]0.0	[3]0.0	...	France
German D.R.(former)	3.4	..	..	..	..	..	..	..	..	..	R.D.A. (anc.)
Norway[4]	23.0	19.9	12.7	8.7	7.4	6.8	7.4	6.7	2.8	[3]0.0	Norvège[4]
Poland	369.6	381.7	372.6	430.8	423.6	431.1	472.6	464.6	490.9	523.1	Pologne
Portugal	167.4	166.1	150.5	150.4	130.3	[3]134.2	[3]109.9	[3]106.5	[3]114.6	[3]99.5	Portugal
Romania	32.0	26.4	24.7	25.3	26.0	24.5	24.4	22.6	19.1	16.5	Roumanie
Spain	14.2	8.9	9.4	3.2	[3]4.9	[3]23.0	[3]37.5	[3]37.8	[3]37.0	[3]2.0	Espagne
Sweden[2][4]	73.5	81.7	89.1	88.9	79.4	83.6	71.7	86.6	73.7	...	Suède[2][4]
United Kingdom	1.0	0.3	[2]0.0	[2]0.0	[2]0.0	[2]0.0	[2]0.0	[2]0.0	[2]0.0	...	Royaume-Uni
Yugoslavia	..	119.4	97.8	68.0	84.8	87.6	82.5	87.4	84.6	62.8	Yougoslavie
T.F.Yug.Rep. Macedonia	..	40.7	39.1	40.1	38.7	40.7	47.2	46.8	39.1	38.2	L'ex-RY Macédoine
Yugoslavia, SFR	137.0	..	..	..	..	..	..	..	..	..	Yougoslavie, RSF
USSR (former)[7]	900.0	..	..	..	..	..	..	..	..	..	URSS (anc.)[7]
Oceania	**459**	**526**	**558**	**629**	**639**	**605**	**654**	**647**	**755**	**872**	**Océanie**
Australia[8]	*306.0	*328.0	371.0	427.0	432.0	376.0	484.0	560.0	590.0	689.0	Australie[8]
Papua New Guinea	153.2	198.3	187.0	202.2	206.6	229.4	170.2	86.8	165.4	182.6	Papouasie-Nvl-Guinée
Total	**8953**	**8282**	**8426**	**8614**	**8710**	**9291**	**10128**	**10658**	**11310**	**11815**	**Total**

For general note and footnotes, see end of table.   Voir la fin du tableau pour la remarque générale et les notes.

Copper-bearing ores (continued)
Minerais cuprifères (suite)

ISIC-BASED CODE - CODE BASE CITI
2302-01M

General Note.
Cu content of copper ores and concentrates and all other copper-bearing ores and concentrates intended for treatment for copper recovery. (SITC, Rev.3: 28310-1M+).

[1] Content of all copper-bearing materials in the form they are to be used or exported.
[2] Source: World Metal Statistics, (London).
[3] Source: U. S. Geological Survey, (Washington, D. C.).
[4] Content of concentrates.
[5] Copper content calculated as recoverable.
[6] Excluding copper content of iron pyrites.
[7] Source: Metallgesellschaft Aktiengesellschaft, (Frankfurt).
[8] Twelve months ending 30 June of year stated.

Remarque générale.
Contenu en Cu des minerais de cuivre et concentrés et tous autres minerais cuprifères et concentrés, destinés à être traités en vue de l'extraction du cuivre. (CTCI, Rev.3: 28310-1M+).

[1] Teneur en cuivre de tous les matériaux prêts à être utilisés ou exportés.
[2] Source: World Metal Statistics,(Londres).
[3] Source: U.S. Geological Survey, (Washington, D.C.).
[4] Teneur des concentrés.
[5] Teneur considérée récupérable au niveau de fonte.
[6] Non compris la teneur en cuivre des pyrites de fer.
[7] Source: "Metallgesellschaft Aktiengesellschaft", (Francfort).
[8] Période de douze mois finissant le 30 juin de l'année indiquée.

Nickel-bearing ores
Minerais nickelifères

ISIC-BASED CODE - CODE BASE CITI

2302-04M

Unit : Metric tons   Unité : Tonnes métriques

Country or area	1990	1991	1992	1993	1994	1995	1996	1997	1998	1999	Pays ou zone
Africa	**60464**	**60606**	**57388**	**63378**	**63310**	**58754**	**65651**	**65778**	**72423**	**70262**	**Afrique**
Botswana	19022	19294	18873	21621	19041	18088	22095	20157	22851	22898	Botswana
South Africa[2]	[1]30000	[1]30000	[1]28400	[1]29868	[1]30751	[1]29803	[1]33861	[1]34830	36700	36200	Afrique du Sud[2]
Zimbabwe	11442	11312	10115	11889	13518	10863	9695	10791	[1]12872	[1]11164	Zimbabwe
America, North	**262434**	**273679**	**267885**	**256935**	**228069**	**270748**	**290436**	**298722**	**291557**	**290143**	**Amérique du Nord**
Canada[2]	195004	188098	186384	188080	152136	181820	192649	190529	186177	186236	Canada[2]
Cuba	*38400	35400	[1]32190	[1]28972	[1]25787	[1]40845	[1]51289	[1]59041	[1]65080	[1]64407	Cuba
Dominican Republic[1]	28700	44661	42641	37423	50146	46523	45168	49152	40300	39500	Rép. dominicaine[1]
United States[3]	330	5520	6670	2460	0	1560	1330	0	0	0	Etats-Unis[3]
America, South	**24100**	**26376**	**29372**	**32154**	**27706**	**29124**	**25245**	**31936**	**36764**	**43784**	**Amérique du Sud**
Brazil[1]	24100	26376	29372	32154	27706	29124	25245	31936	36764	43784	Brésil[1]
Asia	**117464**	**115819**	**124241**	**104740**	**128051**	**145126**	**146764**	**140060**	**135628**	**147700**	**Asie**
China	[1]33204	[1]30379	[1]32806	30772	36908	41786	43800	46600	[1]48700	[1]50100	Chine
Indonesia	[1]68300	[1]71681	[1]77600	[1]65757	[1]81175	[1]88183	[1]87911	75300	[1]74063	[1]89100	Indonésie
Myanmar	[4]160	[4]59	[4]35	[4]259	[4]73	[4]82	[4]50	[4]27	[4]25	* [1]50	Myanmar
Philippines	15800	13700	13800	7952	9895	15075	15003	18133	[1]12840	[1]8450	Philippines
Europe	**42112**	**39090**	**30859**	**25264**	**29801**	**26772**	**26871**	**24125**	**22482**	**19512**	**Europe**
Albania	[1]8800	[1]7500	[1]150	0	0	0	0	0	0	0	Albanie
Finland	10812	10332	10311	8862	7652	3439	2136	[1]3252	[1]1967	[1]730	Finlande
German D.R.(former)[5]	900	..	..	..	..	..	..	..	..	..	R.D.A. (anc.)[5]
Greece[1]	18500	19300	17000	12940	18821	19947	21600	18419	16985	16050	Grèce[1]
Norway	[1]3100	[1]1958	[1]3398	[1]3462	[1]3328	[1]3386	[1]3135	[1]2454	3530	[1]2732	Norvège
USSR (former)[5]	212000	..	..	..	..	..	..	..	..	..	URSS (anc.)[5]
Oceania	**151227**	**168591**	**156624**	**165092**	**163323**	**218712**	**229779**	**252043**	**258319**	**231062**	**Océanie**
Australia[6]	66180	68768	[7]57000	68000	66000	98000	105000	115000	133000	121000	Australie[6]
New Caledonia	85047	99823	99624	97092	97323	120712	124779	137043	[1]125319	[1]110062	Nouvelle-Calédonie
Total	**869801**	**684161**	**666369**	**647563**	**640260**	**749236**	**784746**	**812664**	**817173**	**802463**	**Total**

General Note.
Ni content of nickel ores and concentrates and all other nickel-bearing ores and concentrates intended for treatment for nickel recovery. (SITC, Rev.3: 28410-1M+).

Remarque générale.
Contenu en Ni des minerais de nickel et concentrés et tous autres minerais nickelifères et concentrés, destinés à être traités en vue de l'extraction du nickel. (CTCI, Rev.3: 28410-1M+).

[1] Source: U. S. Geological Survey, (Washington, D. C.).
[2] Content of concentrates.
[3] Shipments.
[4] Government production only.
[5] Source: Metallgesellschaft Aktiengesellschaft, (Frankfurt).
[6] Twelve months ending 30 June of year stated.
[7] Source: World Metal Statistics, (London).

[1] Source: U.S. Geological Survey, (Washington, D.C.).
[2] Teneur des concentrés.
[3] Expéditions.
[4] Production de l'Etat seulement.
[5] Source: "Metallgesellschaft Aktiengesellschaft", (Francfort).
[6] Période de douze mois finissant le 30 juin de l'année indiquée.
[7] Source: World Metal Statistics,(Londres).

Bauxite
Bauxite

ISIC-BASED CODE - CODE BASE CITI

2302-07

Unité : Milliers de tonnes métriques

Unit : Thousand metric tons Country or area	1990	1991	1992	1993	1994	1995	1996	1997	1998	1999	Pays ou zone
Africa	**17174**	**16558**	**15222**	**16437**	**14471**	**16324**	**16084**	**16927**	**15449**	**15361**	**Afrique**
Ghana	381	400	[1]338	482	426	513	473	[1]519	[1]443	[1]353	Ghana
Guinea	15341	14862	13625	14784	[1]13300	[1]15800	[1]15600	[1]16400	[1]15000	[1]15000	Guinée
Mozambique	7	8	9	6	10	11	11	8	6	8	Mozambique
Sierra Leone	1445	1288	* [1]1250	[1]1165	[1]735	[1]0	[1]0	[1]0	[1]0	...	Sierra Leone
America, North	**11545**	**11667**	**11412**	**11239**	**11887**	**10971**	**11857**	**12088**	**12774**	**11699**	**Amérique du Nord**
Dominican Republic[2]	85	7	0	0	0	0	[3]0	[3]0	...	...	Rép. dominicaine[2]
Jamaica[2]	10965	11610	11367	11184	11787	10871	11757	11988	12674	11699	Jamaïque[2]
United States[3]	495	50	45	55	100	100	100	100	100	...	Etats-Unis[3]
America, South	**15433**	**17092**	**18837**	**21018**	**23340**	**25591**	**22229**	**23015**	**23387**	**24346**	**Amérique du Sud**
Brazil	9876	10414	13573	14435	13033	15039	[1]10998	[1]11671	[1]11961	[1]12880	Brésil
Guyana	1424	1346	895	897	[1]1732	[1]2028	[1]2475	[1]2467	[1]2600	[1]3300	Guyana
Suriname	3267	3136	3252	3156	3803	3502	3647	[1]3877	[1]4000	[1]4000	Suriname
Venezuela	866	2196	1117	2530	4772	[1]5022	[1]5109	[1]5000	4826	4166	Venezuela
Asia	**11018**	**16252**	**16838**	**16846**	**16000**	**11786**	**12786**	**13187**	**19927**	**20519**	**Asie**
China	3655	5926	6661	6468	6621	1585	1755	2201	* [1]8200	* [1]8500	Chine
India	4984	5013	5145	5535	4913	5565	6076	6108	6610	6854	Inde
Indonesia[2]	1206	1406	804	1320	1342	899	842	809	1056	*[1]1116	Indonésie[2]
Kazakhstan	..	...	3036	2911	2584	3318	3346	3416	3437	3607	Kazakhstan
Malaysia	[4]398	[4]377	331	69	162	184	219	279	161	[1]223	Malaisie
Pakistan[5]	2	3	[1]3	[1]5	[1]5	[1]3	[1]4	[1]5	[1]5	[1]11	Pakistan[5]
Turkey	773	484	859	538	373	232	544	369	458	208	Turquie
Europe	**8764**	**5595**	**4986**	**4324**	**3375**	**3559**	**3433**	**3336**	**3081**	**3318**	**Europe**
Albania	...	...	* [1]4	2	2	1	1	4	4	0	Albanie
Croatia	..	122	7	1	1	1	0	[1]0	[1]0	[1]0	Croatie
France	490	[3]183	[3]104	[3]151	[3]128	[3]131	[3]165	[3]164	[3]80	...	France
Greece	2511	2165	2085	2231	2201	2165	1713	1828	1700	[1]1883	Grèce
Hungary	2559	2013	1721	1561	836	1015	1056	743	909	935	Hongrie
Italy	0	9	[1]98	[1]90	[1]23	[1]11	[1]0	[1]0	[1]0	[1]0	Italie
Romania	247	200	175	186	184	175	175	127	162	[1]0	Roumanie
Spain	1	1	0	0	0	0	0	0	...	...	Espagne
Yugoslavia	..	900	792	102	0	60	323	470	226	500	Yougoslavie
Yugoslavia, SFR	2953	..	..	..	..	..	..	..	..	..	Yougoslavie, RSF
USSR (former)* [1]	4200	..	..	..	..	..	..	..	..	..	URSS (anc.)* [1]
Oceania	**39983**	**41831**	**34788**	**41180**	**41286**	**42308**	**43308**	**42990**	**44878**	**46444**	**Océanie**
Australia[5]	39983	41831	34788	41180	41286	42308	43308	42990	44878	46444	Australie[5]
Total	**108117**	**108995**	**102082**	**111044**	**110360**	**110540**	**109697**	**111543**	**119496**	**121687**	**Total**

General Note.
Gross weight of crude ore mined. (SITC, Rev.3: 28510-0).

[1] Source: U. S. Geological Survey, (Washington, D. C.).
[2] Dried equivalent of crude ore.
[3] Source: World Metal Statistics, (London).
[4] Data refer to Peninsular Malaysia only.
[5] Twelve months ending 30 June of year stated.

Remarque générale.
Poids brut du minerai brut naturel. (CTCI, Rev.3: 28510-0).

[1] Source: U.S. Geological Survey, (Washington, D.C.).
[2] Equivalent desséché de minerai brut.
[3] Source: World Metal Statistics,(Londres).
[4] Données se rapportant à la Malaisie péninsulaire seulement.
[5] Période de douze mois finissant le 30 juin de l'année indiquée.

Lead-bearing ores
Minerais plombifères

ISIC-BASED CODE - CODE BASE CITI

2302-10M

Unit : Thousand metric tons

Unité : Milliers de tonnes métriques

Country or area	1990	1991	1992	1993	1994	1995	1996	1997	1998	1999	Pays ou zone
Africa	**162**	**174**	**171**	**201**	**186**	**183**	**184**	**174**	**182**	**177**	**Afrique**
Algeria[1]	1.9	1.9	1.5	1.5	1.1	1.4	1.0	1.3	1.2	1.2	Algérie[1]
Morocco[1]	66.1	70.6	72.4	79.1	72.1	70.1	74.2	74.3	79.4	78.8	Maroc[1]
Namibia[1][2]	18.0	15.0	15.0	11.6	13.9	16.1	15.3	13.6	13.3	10.0	Namibie[1][2]
Nigeria	0.1	0.2	0.2	0.2	[2]0.0	[2]0.0	[2]0.0	[2]0.0	...	...	Nigéria
South Africa[1]	70.2	76.3	[3]75.4	[3]100.2	[3]95.8	[3]88.0	[3]89.0	[3]83.0	[3]84.1	80.2	Afrique du Sud[1]
Tunisia[1][4]	1.8	0.8	0.8	0.5	2.0	7.0	4.7	1.4	4.3	6.3	Tunisie[1][4]
Zambia	4.1	9.0	[3]6.1	[3]7.6	[3]0.6	[3]0.0	[3]0.0	[3]0.0	[3]0.0	...	Zambie
America, North	**928**	**892**	**927**	**730**	**715**	**772**	**872**	**826**	**825**	**807**	**Amérique du Nord**
Canada	233.4	248.1	339.6	183.1	166.4	210.8	257.3	186.2	161.2	162.2	Canada
Greenland	18.0	[2]0.0	[2]0.0	[2]0.0	[2]0.0	...	...	...	...	...	Groënland
Honduras[2]	5.8	8.7	10.8	3.6	2.8	2.6	4.7	5.9	4.3	5.2	Honduras[2]
Mexico	174.1	157.9	[2]169.6	181.0	175.3	164.3	[2]173.8	[2]174.7	[2]166.1	[2]120.0	Mexique
United States	497.0	477.0	407.0	362.0	370.0	394.0	436.0	459.0	493.0	[2]520.0	Etats-Unis
America, South	**271**	**273**	**256**	**259**	**268**	**282**	**292**	**307**	**302**	**311**	**Amérique du Sud**
Argentina[1]	23.4	23.7	18.0	11.8	10.0	10.5	[2]11.3	[2]13.8	[2]15.0	[2]15.6	Argentine[1]
Bolivia	19.9	20.8	20.0	21.2	19.7	20.4	16.5	18.6	13.8	[2]10.1	Bolivie
Brazil[5]	16.0	9.2	[2]2.5	[2]0.1	[2]1.3	[2]11.6	[2]13.2	[2]14.3	[2]14.3	[2]14.3	Brésil[5]
Chile	1.1	1.1	[6]0.3	[6]0.3	[6]1.0	[6]0.9	[6]1.4	[6]1.3	[6]0.3	[6]0.4	Chili
Colombia[2]	0.3	0.6	0.6	0.4	0.3	0.3	0.3	0.3	0.3	0.3	Colombie[2]
Ecuador*[2]	0.2	0.2	0.2	0.2	0.2	0.2	0.2	0.2	0.2	0.2	Equateur*[2]
Peru	209.7	217.9	214.0	224.7	235.0	237.6	248.9	258.2	257.7	270.5	Pérou
Asia	**567**	**552**	**526**	**529**	**639**	**693**	**833**	**889**	**651**	**742**	**Asie**
China	363.9	352.2	329.9	346.3	461.9	514.2	643.4	711.9	469.8	561.5	Chine
India	35.6	45.5	50.5	44.5	45.4	47.2	48.4	51.6	57.8	56.8	Inde
Iran(Islamic Rep. of)	*12.0	12.6	*12.4	[2]14.7	[2]18.3	[2]15.9	[2]15.7	[2]18.2	[2]13.4	[2]14.0	Iran(Rép. islamique)
Japan[1]	18.7	18.3	18.8	16.5	9.9	9.7	7.8	5.2	6.2	6.1	Japon[1]
Korea,Dem.Ppl's.Rep.[2]	80.0	80.0	75.0	80.0	80.0	80.0	80.0	75.0	70.0	70.0	Corée,Rép.pop.dém.de[2]
Korea, Republic of[1]	14.9	12.6	13.6	7.4	2.2	4.1	[2]5.1	[2]3.6	[2]7.1	[2]3.6	Corée, République de[1]
Myanmar*[2]	2.7	2.8	2.8	2.2	2.3	2.4	2.2	1.9	2.2	2.0	Myanmar*[2]
Thailand[1]	20.9	15.7	11.2	5.6	7.7	9.1	19.7	5.0	6.1	9.5	Thaïlande[1]
Turkey	18.4	12.1	11.6	11.4	11.2	10.4	11.0	16.7	18.6	18.2	Turquie
Europe	**480**	**409**	**386**	**355**	**363**	**355**	**340**	**358**	**340**	**322**	**Europe**
Austria	2.2	3.3	1.8	2.0	0.0	[3]0.0	[3]0.0	[3]0.0	[3]0.0	...	Autriche
Bulgaria[2]	57.0	43.6	39.0	34.0	32.0	33.0	28.5	32.0	25.0	18.0	Bulgarie[2]
Czechoslovakia(former)[1]	3.0	3.4	..	..	..	..	..	..	..	..	Tchécoslovaquie(anc.)[1]
Finland	2.4	2.5	0.9	[3]0.0	[3]0.0	[3]0.0	[3]1.2	[3]2.0	[3]2.0	...	Finlande
France[1]	0.8	1.0	0.0	0.0	0.0	[3]0.0	[3]0.0	[3]0.0	[3]0.0	...	France[1]
Germany(Fed.Rep.)[7]	8.6	..	..	..	..	..	..	..	..	...	Allemagne(Rép.féd.)[7]
Greece[1][2]	26.2	31.7	28.3	28.8	28.4	20.4	8.4	19.3	18.0	16.0	Grèce[1][2]
Ireland[1]	35.2	39.9	43.0	44.5	46.1	46.1	45.4	43.1	36.5	[2]45.0	Irlande[1]
Italy[1]	14.5	12.4	17.0	5.0	12.7	14.0	12.6	10.9	6.3	[2]6.0	Italie[1]
Norway[1]	3.0	3.9	4.2	2.2	3.6	1.5	2.1	2.2	[2]1.0	[2]0.0	Norvège[1]
Poland	[3]45.4	[3]47.3	[3]51.0	[3]49.0	[3]51.6	[3]58.1	[3]58.7	[3]54.8	[3]59.6	68.0	Pologne
Romania	24.7	16.2	16.8	16.9	23.8	23.2	21.4	19.4	15.1	17.5	Roumanie
Slovenia	..	2.8	1.5	1.0	0.8	[2]0.0	[2]0.0	0.0	0.0	...	Slovénie
Spain	58.5	44.4	30.3	25.4	[2]23.8	[2]30.1	[2]23.8	[2]23.9	[2]18.8	[2]18.0	Espagne
Sweden[1][2]	98.3	91.1	105.3	111.7	112.8	100.1	98.8	108.6	114.4	115.0	Suède[1][2]
United Kingdom[1][8]	[3]1.4	[3]1.0	[3]1.0	[3]1.0	[3]1.0	[3]1.6	[3]1.8	[3]1.6	[3]1.6	[2]1.0	Royaume-Uni[1][8]
Yugoslavia	..	33.9	22.6	9.3	6.7	11.7	20.6	20.6	24.8	4.6	Yougoslavie
T.F.Yug.Rep. Macedonia	..	30.4	23.6	23.7	19.3	15.7	16.9	*19.5	16.8	12.3	L'ex-RY Macédoine
Yugoslavia, SFR	99.1	..	..	..	..	..	..	..	..	..	Yougoslavie, RSF
USSR (former)[2]	450.0	..	..	..	..	..	..	..	..	...	URSS (anc.)[2]
Oceania	**511**	**542**	**569**	**554**	**540**	**460**	**516**	**516**	**571**	**662**	**Océanie**
Australia[9]	*511.0	*542.0	569.0	554.0	540.0	460.0	516.0	516.0	571.0	662.0	Australie[9]
Total	**3370**	**2842**	**2835**	**2627**	**2709**	**2744**	**3037**	**3069**	**2871**	**3021**	**Total**

For general note and footnotes, see end of table.

Voir la fin du tableau pour la remarque générale et les notes.

General Note.
Pb content of lead ores and concentrates and all other lead-bearing ores and concentrates intended for treatment for lead recovery. (SITC, Rev.3: 28740-1M+).

[1] Content of concentrates.
[2] Source: U. S. Geological Survey, (Washington, D. C.).
[3] Source: World Metal Statistics, (London).
[4] Excluding content of mixed ores or concentrates.
[5] Content of ores.
[6] Including lead content in zinc concentrates.
[7] Excluding lead content in pyrites.
[8] Including zinc content.
[9] Twelve months ending 30 June of year stated.

Remarque générale.
Contenu en Pb des minerais de plomb et concentrés et tous autres minerais plombifères et concentrés, destinés à être traités en vue de l'extraction du plomb. (CTCI, Rev.3: 28740-1M+).

[1] Teneur des concentrés.
[2] Source: U.S. Geological Survey, (Washington, D.C.).
[3] Source: World Metal Statistics,(Londres).
[4] Non compris la teneur des minerais mixtes ou concentrés.
[5] Teneur des minerais.
[6] Y compris la teneur en plomb contenu dans les concentrés de zinc.
[7] Non compris la teneur en plomb contenu dans les pyrites.
[8] Y compris la teneur en zinc.
[9] Période de douze mois finissant le 30 juin de l'année indiquée.

Zinc -bearing ores
Minerais zincifères

ISIC-BASED CODE - CODE BASE CITI

2302-13M

Unit : Thousand metric tons

Unité : Milliers de tonnes métriques

Country or area	1990	1991	1992	1993	1994	1995	1996	1997	1998	1999	Pays ou zone
Africa	**221**	**207**	**193**	**210**	**208**	**236**	**231**	**212**	**265**	**278**	**Afrique**
Algeria[1]	8.0	7.9	7.5	6.8	5.6	7.0	5.9	6.8	8.6	9.8	Algérie[1]
Dem. Rep. of Congo[1][2]	61.8	42.4	36.0	10.0	0.6	0.8	1.2	1.2	1.2	...	Rép. dém. du Congo[1][2]
Morocco[1]	20.8	26.8	22.0	65.4	78.1	79.6	79.3	89.3	112.3	112.4	Maroc[1]
Namibia[3]	37.7	33.2	36.1	28.4	33.4	30.2	35.9	39.7	42.1	37.0	Namibie[3]
Nigeria	0.1	0.1	0.1	0.1	* [3]0.1	* [3]0.1	...	...	...	...	Nigéria
South Africa	74.8	66.6	[2]69.8	[2]78.2	[2]76.4	[2]74.0	[2]77.0	[2]72.1	[2]69.6	[1]69.7	Afrique du Sud
Tunisia[1]	7.3	5.2	2.3	1.3	12.9	44.2	31.9	2.9	31.2	48.9	Tunisie[1]
Zambia	10.9	[2]24.8	[2]19.2	[2]19.7	[2]1.0	[2]0.0	[2]0.0	[2]0.0	[2]0.0	...	Zambie
America, North	**2123**	**2035**	**2246**	**1898**	**1963**	**2148**	**2265**	**2120**	**2196**	**2265**	**Amérique du Nord**
Canada	1203.1	1148.2	1324.7	1007.3	984.0	1113.4	1222.4	1069.0	1008.9	1021.0	Canada
Greenland[3]	47.9	0.0	0.0	0.0	0.0	...	...	...	...	...	Groënland[3]
Honduras[3]	29.6	38.3	29.0	18.3	23.6	27.1	37.0	39.5	36.6	41.0	Honduras[3]
Mexico	[4]299.0	[4]301.1	[4]340.7	[4]359.8	[4]357.1	[3]363.7	[3]377.6	[3]379.3	[3]395.4	[3]360.0	Mexique
United States	543.0	547.0	552.0	513.0	598.0	644.0	628.0	632.0	755.0	843.0	Etats-Unis
America, South	**904**	**974**	**990**	**1024**	**1026**	**1095**	**1092**	**1240**	**1154**	**1209**	**Amérique du Sud**
Argentina[1]	38.7	39.3	41.0	31.4	26.9	32.1	[3]31.1	[3]33.4	[3]35.6	[3]35.8	Argentine[1]
Bolivia	[1]103.8	[1]129.8	[1]143.9	[1]122.6	[1]100.7	[1]146.1	[1]147.1	[1]154.5	[1]152.1	145.2	Bolivie
Brazil[5]	138.0	135.0	[3]149.0	[3]171.8	[3]177.6	[3]188.5	[3]117.3	[3]152.6	[3]87.5	[3]96.5	Brésil[5]
Chile[1]	25.1	31.0	29.7	29.4	31.0	35.4	36.0	34.4	10.1	32.3	Chili[1]
Colombia[3]	0.4	0.4	0.3	0.3	0.0	0.0	0.0	0.0	0.0	...	Colombie[3]
Ecuador[3]	0.1	0.1	0.1	0.0	0.1	*0.1	*0.1	0.1	*0.1	*0.1	Equateur[3]
Peru	598.2	638.1	626.2	668.1	690.0	692.3	760.4	865.3	868.8	899.5	Pérou
Asia	**1338**	**1417**	**1434**	**1408**	**1615**	**1665**	**1733**	**1783**	**1731**	**1885**	**Asie**
China	763.1	749.8	753.3	729.3	990.3	1000.6	1161.0	1209.7	1121.8	1278.8	Chine
India	[1]90.2	[1]158.4	[1]184.3	177.9	169.9	180.1	171.2	185.7	212.7	224.0	Inde
Iran(Islamic Rep. of)	26.0	50.0	[3]66.0	[3]77.0	[3]72.9	[3]145.1	[3]76.3	[3]76.5	[3]82.0	[3]80.0	Iran(Rép. islamique)
Japan[1]	127.3	133.0	134.5	118.6	100.7	95.7	79.7	71.6	67.7	64.3	Japon[1]
Korea,Dem.Ppl's.Rep.[3]	230.0	200.0	200.0	210.0	210.0	210.0	210.0	210.0	200.0	190.0	Corée,Rép.pop.dém.de[3]
Korea, Republic of[1]	27.8	22.0	21.9	13.8	7.1	7.7	[3]8.4	[3]9.0	[3]21.0	[3]19.7	Corée, République de[1]
Myanmar[1][6]	2.2	1.5	[3]1.1	[3]0.9	[3]1.3	[3]0.7	[3]0.6	[3]0.5	[3]0.5	[3]0.3	Myanmar[1][6]
Philippines[1]	0.1	0.1	[2]0.0	0.0	0.0	0.0	0.0	0.0	...	...	Philippines[1]
Thailand[3]	61.5	87.0	62.0	70.0	55.0	16.2	11.4	8.9	19.6	27.0	Thaïlande[3]
Turkey	10.0	14.9	10.7	10.2	7.5	9.1	14.9	11.0	6.3	0.6	Turquie
Europe	**1147**	**1059**	**966**	**874**	**822**	**833**	**768**	**795**	**769**	**778**	**Europe**
Austria	17.9	15.9	16.4	20.0	0.0	0.0	[2]0.0	[2]0.0	[2]0.0	...	Autriche
Bulgaria[3]	34.7	29.1	29.0	30.0	29.0	26.0	19.8	20.0	17.0	12.0	Bulgarie[3]
Finland	53.9	57.3	32.8	22.5	3.7	16.4	26.3	[3]30.8	[3]30.0	[3]30.0	Finlande
France[1]	23.8	26.9	16.5	13.8	0.0	[2]0.0	[2]0.0	[2]0.0	[2]0.0	...	France[1]
Germany(Fed.Rep.)[7]	58.1	..	..	..	..	..	..	..	..	...	Allemagne(Rép.féd.)[7]
Greece[1][3]	26.7	30.0	27.5	24.9	17.2	14.5	13.6	17.8	29.1	18.9	Grèce[1][3]
Ireland[1]	166.5	187.5	194.1	193.7	194.5	184.1	164.2	160.4	181.0	[3]226.0	Irlande[1]
Italy[1]	43.2	36.4	32.5	3.8	21.3	22.7	10.5	8.0	2.7	[3]0.0	Italie[1]
Norway[1]	17.5	19.6	21.5	15.1	15.9	9.9	9.0	6.7	0.9	[3]12.0	Norvège[1]
Poland[3]	153.0	144.7	151.7	150.9	151.0	154.5	159.0	158.3	155.0	153.0	Pologne[3]
Romania	36.0	26.3	25.8	28.0	35.4	36.7	32.1	31.7	25.7	26.5	Roumanie
Slovenia	..	8.9	6.9	3.8	2.1	[2]0.0	[2]0.0	0.0	0.0	[3]0.0	Slovénie
Spain	260.9	261.9	204.7	171.2	170.1	[3]172.5	[3]140.1	[3]171.8	[3]128.1	[3]110.0	Espagne
Sweden[1][3]	164.0	161.2	171.5	168.6	159.9	167.1	160.3	155.4	164.7	175.0	Suède[1][3]
United Kingdom	6.7	1.1	[2]0.0	[2]0.0	[2]0.0	[2]0.0	[2]0.0	[2]0.0	[2]0.0	...	Royaume-Uni
Yugoslavia	..	31.4	19.6	9.8	6.8	11.5	18.0	18.9	20.3	4.3	Yougoslavie
T.F.Yug.Rep. Macedonia	..	20.8	15.5	18.0	15.4	16.8	15.0	*15.5	14.3	10.2	L'ex-RY Macédoine
Yugoslavia, SFR	83.8	..	..	..	..	..	..	..	..	..	Yougoslavie, RSF
USSR (former)* [3]	750.0	..	..	..	..	..	..	..	..	..	URSS (anc.)* [3]
Oceania	**863**	**1001**	**1022**	**1053**	**1025**	**915**	**1039**	**1060**	**1038**	**1142**	**Océanie**
Australia[1][8]	863.4	1001.0	1022.0	1053.0	1025.0	915.0	1039.0	1060.0	1038.0	1142.0	Australie[1][8]
Total	**7347**	**6692**	**6852**	**6467**	**6659**	**6892**	**7129**	**7210**	**7153**	**7557**	**Total**

For general note and footnotes, see end of table.

Voir la fin du tableau pour la remarque générale et les notes.

Zinc -bearing ores (continued)
Minerais zincifères (suite)

ISIC-BASED CODE - CODE BASE CITI

2302-13M

General Note.
Zn content of zinc ores and concentrates and all other zinc-bearing ores and concentrates intended for treatment for zinc recovery. (SITC, Rev.3: 28750-1M+).

Remarque générale.
Contenu en Zn des minerais de zinc et concentrés et tous autres minerais zincifères et concentrés, destinés à être traités en vue de l'extraction du zinc. (CTCI, Rev.3: 28750-1M+).

[1] Content of concentrates.
[2] Source: World Metal Statistics, (London).
[3] Source: U. S. Geological Survey, (Washington, D. C.).
[4] Content of all zinc-bearing materials in the form they are to be used or exported.
[5] Content of ores.
[6] Government production only.
[7] Source: Metallgesellschaft Aktiengesellschaft, (Frankfurt).
[8] Twelve months ending 30 June of year stated.

[1] Teneur des concentrés.
[2] Source: World Metal Statistics,(Londres).
[3] Source: U.S. Geological Survey, (Washington, D.C.).
[4] Teneur en zinc de tous les matériaux prêts à être utilisés ou exportés.
[5] Teneur des minerais.
[6] Production de l'Etat seulement.
[7] Source: "Metallgesellschaft Aktiengesellschaft", (Francfort).
[8] Période de douze mois finissant le 30 juin de l'année indiquée.

Tin-bearing ores
Minerais stannifères

ISIC-BASED CODE - CODE BASE CITI

2302-16M

Unit : Metric tons

Unité : Tonnes métriques

Country or area	1990	1991	1992	1993	1994	1995	1996	1997	1998	1999	Pays ou zone
Africa	**6161**	**4451**	**3457**	**1748**	**387**	**697**	**396**	**171**	**235**	**232**	**Afrique**
Burundi[1]	*54	*74	*110	*10	0	15	25	0	23	10	Burundi[1]
Cameroon*[1]	3	3	3	3	2	2	1	1	1	1	Cameroun*[1]
Dem. Rep. of Congo[1]	2220	1520	1020	0	0	0	0	0	...	...	Rép. dém. du Congo[1]
Namibia[1]	900	#11	11	4	4	2	0	0	0	0	Namibie[1]
Niger	38	*[1]20	60	18	*[1]20	*[1]20	*[1]10	*[1]10	*[1]10	*[1]20	Niger
Nigeria	[1]192	[1]217	[1]415	178	208	357	150	[1]150	[1]200	[1]200	Nigéria
Rwanda[1]	*734	*730	*500	*400	*50	*242	200	*0	0	0	Rwanda[1]
South Africa	1140	1042	[1]582	*[1]450	[1]0	[1]0	[1]0	[1]0	[1]0	0	Afrique du Sud
Uganda*[1]	25	25	30	3	3	43	0	0	0	0	Ouganda*[1]
United Rep.Tanzania*[1]	15	6	8	12	9	3	0	0	0	0	Rép. Unie de Tanzanie*[1]
Zambia[1]	1	6	2	12	9	3	0	0	0	0	Zambie[1]
Zimbabwe	839	797	716	658	82	[1]10	[1]10	[1]10	[1]1	[1]1	Zimbabwe
America, North	**3950**	**4500**	**155**	**99**	**3**	**1**	**2**	**5**	**5**	**5**	**Amérique du Nord**
Canada	3844	4392	58	0	0	[1]0	...	...	...	...	Canada
Mexico	6	[1]12	[1]1	[1]3	*[1]3	[1]1	[1]2	[1]5	[1]5	[1]5	Mexique
United States	*[2]100	*[2]96	*[2]96	96	0	0	0	0	0	...	Etats-Unis
America, South	**61279**	**52697**	**53560**	**59444**	**52921**	**54067**	**61423**	**59915**	**51662**	**56120**	**Amérique du Sud**
Argentina	123	0	0	0	0	0	...	...	...	...	Argentine
Bolivia[3]	17248	16829	16516	18634	16027	14419	14802	12898	11308	12516	Bolivie[3]
Brazil	39096	29300	[1]27000	[1]26500	[1]16619	*[1]17317	[1]19617	[1]19065	[1]14607	[1]13200	Brésil
Peru	4812	6568	10044	14310	20275	[1]22331	27004	[1]27952	25747	30404	Pérou
Asia	**117011**	**108582**	**100740**	**92617**	**96084**	**109847**	**128720**	**129867**	**133052**	**120368**	**Asie**
China	42055	42104	43947	46554	54076	61913	69700	67500	[1]70100	[1]61700	Chine
Indonesia	31284	30348	30384	28584	30612	38378	51024	55176	53952	[1]47754	Indonésie
Lao People's Dem. Rep.[1]	300	300	300	300	200	200	906	*1030	*895	*703	Rép. dém. pop. lao[1]
Malaysia	28480	20712	14328	10380	6456	6408	5174	5070	5760	[1]7340	Malaisie
Myanmar[4][5]	292	181	297	436	[1]814	[1]747	[1]459	[1]335	[1]221	[1]149	Myanmar[4][5]
Thailand[1]	14600	14937	11484	6363	3926	2201	1457	756	2124	2722	Thaïlande[1]
Europe	**8881**	**8155**	**5018**	**7536**	**6234**	**6728**	**7018**	**3069**	**6802**	**4849**	**Europe**
Czechoslovakia(former)	336	10	..	..	..	..	..	..	..	..	Tchécoslovaquie(anc.)
German D.R.(former)[6]	1800	..	..	..	..	..	..	..	..	..	R.D.A. (anc.)[6]
Portugal	3318	5833	3011	5334	4330	4626	4716	[1]2667	[1]3000	[1]3000	Portugal
Spain	27	12	7	2	[1]4	*[1]2	*[1]2	*[1]2	*[1]2	*[1]2	Espagne
United Kingdom	3400	2300	2000	2200	1900	2100	2300	400	3800	...	Royaume-Uni
USSR (former)*[6]	13000	..	..	..	..	..	..	..	..	..	URSS (anc.)*[6]
Oceania	**8256**	**5664**	**6204**	**7048**	**7972**	**7999**	**9172**	**9284**	**10100**	**9822**	**Océanie**
Australia[7]	*8256	5664	6204	7048	7972	7999	9172	9284	10100	9822	Australie[7]
Total	**218538**	**184049**	**169134**	**168492**	**163601**	**179339**	**206731**	**202311**	**201856**	**191396**	**Total**

General Note.
Sn content of tin concentrates and all other tin-bearing ores and concentrates intended for treatment for tin recovery. (SITC, Rev.3: 28760-1M+).

Remarque générale.
Contenu en Sn des minerais d'étain et concentrés et tous autres minerais stannifères et concentrés, destinés à être traités en vue de l'extraction de l'étain. (CTCI, Rev.3: 28760-1M+).

[1] Source: U. S. Geological Survey, (Washington, D. C.).
[2] Source: World Metal Statistics, (London).
[3] Content of ores plus metal exported.
[4] Government production only.
[5] Content of concentrates.
[6] Source: Metallgesellschaft Aktiengesellschaft, (Frankfurt).
[7] Twelve months ending 30 June of year stated.

[1] Source: U.S. Geological Survey, (Washington, D.C.).
[2] Source: World Metal Statistics,(Londres).
[3] Teneur des minerais plus métal exporté.
[4] Production de l'Etat seulement.
[5] Teneur des concentrés.
[6] Source: "Metallgesellschaft Aktiengesellschaft", (Francfort).
[7] Période de douze mois finissant le 30 juin de l'année indiquée.

Manganese-bearing ores
Minerais manganifères

ISIC-BASED CODE - CODE BASE CITI

2302-19M

Unit : Thousand metric tons — Unité : Milliers de tonnes métriques

Country or area	1990	1991	1992	1993	1994	1995	1996	1997	1998	1999	Pays ou zone
Africa	**3153**	**2252**	**1929**	**1870**	**2018**	**2355**	**2525**	**2364**	**2453**	**2494**	**Afrique**
Gabon[1]	*1118.5	*748.0	*718.0	*595.0	*663.0	891.0	915.0	879.0	*966.0	*966.0	Gabon[1]
Ghana	98.0	104.3	*[1]106.0	173.6	129.2	98.5	215.0	[1]149.0	[1]172.0	173.0	Ghana
Morocco	25.3	30.4	25.2	21.8	[2]15.7	[2]15.9	[2]15.1	[2]15.8	[2]14.5	14.9	Maroc
South Africa[1]	1911.0	*1369.0	*1080.0	*1080.0	*1210.0	*1350.0	*1380.0	*1320.0	*1300.0	*1340.0	Afrique du Sud[1]
America, North	**166**	**93**	**153**	**135**	**112**	**174**	**173**	**193**	**187**	**169**	**Amérique du Nord**
Mexico*[1]	166.0	93.0	153.0	135.0	112.3	174.2	173.4	192.8	187.0	169.0	Mexique*[1]
America, South	**963**	**840**	**679**	**735**	**877**	**956**	**996**	**846**	**853**	**654**	**Amérique du Sud**
Argentina	0.7	1.0	0.2	...	...	0.0	...	...	...	...	Argentine
Bolivia	[1]0.0	0.2	0.0	0.0	0.0	0.0	...	...	...	...	Bolivie
Brazil	[3]950.0	[3]826.0	[1][3]664.0	[1][3]716.0	[1]858.0	[1]935.0	[1]977.0	[1]828.0	[1]838.0	[1]641.0	Brésil
Chile	12.5	13.2	14.9	18.8	18.2	20.2	18.3	17.3	14.3	11.9	Chili
Asia	**4735**	**5146**	**5521**	**4619**	**4529**	**5744**	**5638**	**4795**	**4923**	**3988**	**Asie**
China	...	...	4279.7	3749.2	3517.3	4707.0	4417.3	3706.2	3654.2	2404.0	Chine
Georgia*[1]	..	...	148.0	89.0	44.0	30.0	29.0	...	...	...	Géorgie*[1]
India	574.2	617.7	723.4	647.9	637.9	683.3	695.9	626.5	587.3	600.9	Inde
Indonesia[1]	5.0	...	...	...	...	...	...	...	...	...	Indonésie[1]
Iran(Islamic Rep. of)	*11.5	15.8	12.8	18.7	[1]13.0	...	...	...	...	...	Iran(Rép. islamique)
Kazakhstan	..	...	334.2	89.3	295.0	284.3	468.9	426.1	634.1	944.0	Kazakhstan
Philippines	15.0	4.1	13.8	1.2	0.0	0.0	0.0	0.0	...	...	Philippines
Thailand*	8.0	5.0	3.8	...	...	...	...	...	...	...	Thaïlande*
Turkey	0.0	0.0	0.7	12.8	11.5	12.7	0.0	7.9	19.2	10.4	Turquie
Europe	**96**	**2128**	**1848**	**1381**	**1088**	**1021**	**979**	**975**	**688**	**673**	**Europe**
Bulgaria	11.0	8.7	6.9	4.0	...	5.6	13.1	14.2	...	...	Bulgarie
Greece[1][2]	2.0	...	...	...	...	...	...	...	...	...	Grèce[1][2]
Hungary*[1]	18.0	9.0	5.0	18.0	17.0	...	...	...	...	...	Hongrie*[1]
Italy	1.7	2.2	2.1	2.1	1.9	1.7	1.7	0.6	0.3	...	Italie
Romania	45.6	28.4	21.1	27.0	33.6	28.1	26.0	19.1	[4]19.0	[4]11.0	Roumanie
Ukraine	..	2078.1	1810.6	1328.2	1024.3	968.6	920.0	922.2	638.7	630.5	Ukraine
Yugoslavia, SFR	18.1	..	..	..	..	..	..	..	..	..	Yougoslavie, RSF
USSR (former)	2561.0	..	..	..	..	..	..	..	..	..	URSS (anc.)
Oceania	**915**	**701**	**596**	**1043**	**944**	**1005**	**1056**	**1105**	**794**	**790**	**Océanie**
Australia	*[5]915.0	*[5]701.2	[1]596.0	[1]1043.0	*[1]944.0	[5]1005.0	[5]1056.0	[5]1105.0	[5]794.0	[5]790.0	Australie
Total	**12590**	**11161**	**10726**	**9784**	**9568**	**11256**	**11368**	**10277**	**9898**	**8767**	**Total**

General Note.

Mn content of manganese ores and concentrates and all other manganese-bearing ores and concentrates intended for treatment for manganese recovery. (SITC, Rev.3: 28770-1M+).

Remarque générale.

Contenu en Mn des minerais de manganèse et concentrés et tous autres minerais manganifères et concentrés, destinés à être traités en vue de l'extraction du manganèse. (CTCI, Rev.3: 28770-1M+).

[1] Source: U. S. Geological Survey, (Washington, D. C.).
[2] Content of concentrates.
[3] Content of ores.
[4] Source: Annual Bulletin of Steel Statistics for Europe, America and Asia, United Nations Economic Commission of Europe (Geneva).
[5] Twelve months ending 30 June of year stated.

[1] Source: U. S. Geological Survey, (Washington, D.C.).
[2] Teneur des concentrés.
[3] Teneur des minerais.
[4] Source: Bulletin annuel de statistiques de l'acier pour l'Europe, l'Amérique et l'Asie. Commission économique des Nations Unies pour l'Europe (Genève).
[5] Période de douze mois finissant le 30 juin de l'année indiquée.

Chromium-bearing ores, Cr content
Minerais chromifères, Cr contenu

ISIC-BASED CODE - CODE BASE CITI

2302-22M1

Unit : Thousand metric tons

Unité : Milliers de tonnes métriques

Country or area	1990	1991	1992	1993	1994	1995	1996	1997	1998	1999	Pays ou zone
Africa	**1639**	**1678**	**1226**	**981**	**1297**	**1956**	**1945**	**2289**	**2376**	**2502**	**Afrique**
Madagascar	35	41	43	[1]43	[1]27	[1]35	[1]45	* [1]46	* [1]34	* [1]35	Madagascar
South Africa* [1]	1416	1448	1009	851	1093	1678	1676	2033	2138	2250	Afrique du Sud* [1]
Sudan* [1]	4	3	3	3	8	13	4	10	6	3	Soudan* [1]
Zimbabwe	185	186	171	83	170	[1]230	[1]220	[1]200	[1]198	[1]214	Zimbabwe
America, North	**11**	**14**	**15**	**5**	**6**	**9**	**11**	**13**	**16**	**12**	**Amérique du Nord**
Cuba	11	* [1]14	* [1]15	[1]5	[1]6	[1]9	[1]11	* [1]13	* [1]16	* [1]12	Cuba
America, South	**124**	**97**	**135**	**92**	**108**	**148**	**135**	**99**	**119**	**115**	**Amérique du Sud**
Brazil	124	[1]97	* [1]135	[1]92	[1]108	[1]148	[1]135	* [1]99	* [1]119	* [1]115	Brésil
Asia	**621**	**1525**	**1705**	**1528**	**1533**	**2222**	**1415**	**1930**	**1557**	**1692**	**Asie**
China	* [1]8	* [1]7	* [1]7	* [1]16	* [1]19	201	130	200	[1]50	[1]53	Chine
India	285	328	319	323	343	509	435	452	422	506	Inde
Indonesia [1]	*2	*1	*1	*1	*1	*3	*4	*1	2	2	Indonésie [1]
Iran(Islamic Rep. of)	*28	61	65	48	[1]106	[1]111	[1]43	[1]56	[1]69	[1]84	Iran(Rép. islamique)
Japan [2]	2	* [2]	* [2]	* [2]	* [0]	* [0]	* [0]	* [0]	* [0]	...	Japon [2]
Kazakhstan [1]	..	...	*1050	*870	*631	*725	*357	*593	*480	721	Kazakhstan [1]
Myanmar [1]	*0	*0	*2	*0	*0	1	1	1	1	1	Myanmar [1]
Oman [1]	*0	*0	*1	*3	*2	*2	*5	6	9	9	Oman [1]
Pakistan	*6	* [1]9	* [1]7	* [1]7	* [1]2	* [1]5	* [1]8	* [1]9	* [1]9	18	Pakistan
Philippines	[3]26	* [1]57	* [1]20	10	11	23	19	17	9	[1]6	Philippines
Turkey [1]	*250	*282	228	230	381	624	384	562	463	254	Turquie [1]
United Arab Emirates [1]	...	...	*0	*6	*17	*11	*17	*18	25	20	Emirats arabes unis [1]
Viet Nam	5	6	4	...	[1]21	[1]8	[1]12	[1]15	[1]18	[1]17	Viet Nam
Europe	**239**	**227**	**240**	**222**	**217**	**257**	**230**	**278**	**270**	**250**	**Europe**
Albania	91	35	16	33	11	31	30	29	20	[1]28	Albanie
Finland	121	131	180	145	160	171	164	[1]194	[1]202	[1]183	Finlande
Greece*	25	[1]11	[1]1	[1]3	[1]2	[1]2	[1]4	[1]4	[1]4	[1]4	Grèce*
Russian Federation [1]	..	...	36	36	43	50	32	50	43	33	Fédération de Russie [1]
T.F.Yug.Rep. Macedonia	..	9	7	4	*2	*4	*0	2	* [1]2	* [1]2	L'ex-RY Macédoine
Yugoslavia, SFR*	2	..	..	..	..	..	..	..	..	..	Yougoslavie, RSF*
USSR (former)* [1]	1100	..	..	..	..	..	..	..	..	..	URSS (anc.)* [1]
Oceania	**2**	**0**	**2**	**0**	**0**	**0**	**0**	**0**	**0**	**0**	**Océanie**
New Caledonia	*2	* [1]0	* [1]2	0	0	0	0	0	...	...	Nouvelle-Calédonie
Total	**3735**	**3541**	**3323**	**2828**	**3161**	**4592**	**3736**	**4610**	**4339**	**4570**	**Total**

General Note.
Cr content of chromium ores and concentrates and all other chromium-bearing ores and concentrates intended for treatment for Cr recovery. (SITC, Rev.3: 28791-1M).

Remarque générale.
Contenu en Cr des minerais de chrome et concentrés et tous autres minerais chromifères et concentrés destinés à être traités en vue de l'extraction du chrome. (CTCI, Rev.3: 28791-1M).

[1] Source: U. S. Geological Survey, (Washington, D. C.).
[2] Content of concentrates.
[3] Twelve months ending 30 June of year stated.

[1] Source: U.S. Geological Survey, (Washington, D.C.).
[2] Teneur des concentrés.
[3] Période de douze mois finissant le 30 juin de l'année indiquée.

Tungsten-bearing ores, W content
Minerais tungstifères, W contenu

ISIC-BASED CODE - CODE BASE CITI

2302-25M1

Unit : Metric tons — Unité : Tonnes métriques

Country or area	1990	1991	1992	1993	1994	1995	1996	1997	1998	1999	Pays ou zone
Africa	254	330	174	173	66	58	78	58	198	94	**Afrique**
Burundi* [1]	...	...	...	...	...	22	16	16	10	10	Burundi* [1]
Dem. Rep. of Congo* [1]	17	15	0	0	0	0	...	...	...	...	Rép. dém. du Congo* [1]
Rwanda	196	277	128	141	*[1]30	19	62	42	188	84	Rwanda
Uganda	*4	4	[1]16	[1]5	[1]12	[1]17	[1]0	...	...	...	Ouganda
Zimbabwe [2]	1	1	[1]0	[1]0	[1]0	[1]0	...	...	...	...	Zimbabwe [2]
America, North	633	640	612	610	600	737	638	629	580	493	**Amérique du Nord**
Mexico	183	190	[1]162	160	150	[1]287	[1]188	[1]179	[1]130	[1]43	Mexique
United States*	450	...	...	...	...	...	...	...	...	...	Etats-Unis*
America, South	3140	3095	1821	995	1038	1652	1163	972	703	...	**Amérique du Sud**
Argentina	*30	15	[1]0	[1]0	[1]0	*[1]0	...	...	...	...	Argentine
Bolivia	1278	1343	1073	362	583	826	733	647	627	[1]334	Bolivie
Brazil	422	500	[1]205	[1]245	[1]196	[1]98	[1]99	[1]40	[1]0	[1]0	Brésil
Peru	1410	1237	543	388	259	728	331	285	76	[1]0	Pérou
Asia	35495	35270	28131	24261	29156	29594	28270	26688	25948	25032	**Asie**
China* [1]	32000	31800	25000	21600	27000	27400	26500	25000	24700	24000	Chine* [1]
India	11	4	2	2	3	3	2	0	0	[1]0	Inde
Japan	254	279	[1]347	[1]66	[1]0	0	[1]0	[1]0	...	0	Japon
Kazakhstan* [1]	..	...	200	350	122	249	0	0	0	0	Kazakhstan* [1]
Korea, Dem. Ppl's. Rep.* [1]	1000	1000	1000	1000	900	900	900	900	800	700	Corée, Rép. pop. dém. de* [1]
Korea, Republic of	1266	780	247	[1]0	[1]0	[1]0	[1]0	[1]0	0	...	Corée, République de
Malaysia	0	[1]2	[1]3	[1]2	...	...	...	...	...	...	Malaisie
Mongolia* [1]	...	...	...	...	0	34	17	26	35	16	Mongolie* [1]
Myanmar [1]	443	356	531	524	544	531	334	272	178	87	Myanmar [1]
Tajikistan* [1]	..	...	200	150	100	75	50	0	0	0	Tadjikistan* [1]
Thailand	269	227	92	[1]80	[1]40	*[1]52	*[1]37	*[1]30	*[1]35	*[1]29	Thaïlande
Uzbekistan* [1]	..	...	300	300	300	300	300	250	200	200	Ouzbékistan* [1]
Viet Nam [1]	...	...	...	...	...	50	130	210	0	0	Viet Nam [1]
Europe	2955	8773	12655	8873	4059	7013	5189	5436	5254	5560	**Europe**
Austria	1500	1400	[1]1489	[1]105	[1]0	[1]738	[1]1413	[1]1400	*[1]1423	*[1]1610	Autriche
Portugal	1405	971	1121	[1]768	[1]59	[1]875	[1]776	[1]1036	*[1]831	*[1]450	Portugal
Russian Federation* [1]	..	...	10000	8000	4000	5400	3000	3000	3000	3500	Fédération de Russie* [1]
Spain	8	50	*45	0	0	0	0	0	...	...	Espagne
United Kingdom [1]	42	9	0	0	0	...	...	...	...	...	Royaume-Uni [1]
USSR (former) [1]	8800	...	..	..	..	..	..	..	..	..	URSS (anc.) [1]
Oceania	691	237	159	23	11	0	0	0	0	0	**Océanie**
Australia	[3]691	[3]237	[1]159	[1]23	[1]11	[3]0	[3]0	[3]0	[3]0	[3]0	Australie
Total	51968	48345	43552	34935	34930	39054	35338	33783	32683	31513	**Total**

General Note.
W content of tungsten concentrates and all other tungsten-bearing ores and concentrates intended for treatment for W recovery. (SITC, Rev.3: 28792-1M).

Remarque générale.
Contenu en W des minerais concentrés de tungstène et tous autres minerais tungstifères ou concentrés contenant du tungstène, destinés à être traités en vue de l'extraction du tungstène. (CTCI, Rev.3: 28792-1M).

[1] Source: U. S. Geological Survey, (Washington, D. C.).
[2] Limited coverage. Twelve months ending 30 September of the year.
[3] Twelve months ending 30 June of year stated.

[1] Source: U. S. Geological Survey, (Washington, D.C.).
[2] Couverture limitée. Période de douze mois finissant au 30 septembre de l'année indiquée.
[3] Période de douze mois finissant le 30 juin de l'année indiquée.

Ilmenite
Ilménite
ISIC-BASED CODE - CODE BASE CITI
2302-271

Unit : Thousand metric tons

Unité : Milliers de tonnes métriques

Country or area	1990	1991	1992	1993	1994	1995	1996	1997	1998	1999	Pays ou zone
Africa	**46**	**60**	**60**	**63**	**47**	**0**	**0**	**0**	**0**	**0**	**Afrique**
Sierra Leone [1]	...	60.4	60.3	62.9	47.4	0.0	0.0	0.0	0.0	...	Sierra Leone [1]
America, North	**601**	**601**	**601**	**601**	**601**	**601**	**601**	**601**	**601**	**601**	**Amérique du Nord**
United States [2]	...	...	...	...	...	...	...	...	601.0	...	Etats-Unis [2]
America, South	**114**	**69**	**77**	**91**	**97**	**102**	**98**	**97**	**103**	**105**	**Amérique du Sud**
Brazil [1]	114.1	69.1	76.6	90.6	97.4	102.1	98.0	97.2	103.0	...	Brésil [1]
Asia	**1061**	**828**	**775**	**800**	**631**	**660**	**701**	**665**	**685**	**696**	**Asie**
China [1]	*150.0	*150.0	*150.0	155.0	155.0	160.0	...	...	...	...	Chine [1]
India	300.5	258.8	245.3	264.2	297.4	298.4	231.5	315.0	363.9	379.5	Inde
Malaysia [1]	530.2	336.4	338.0	279.0	116.7	151.7	244.6	167.5	124.7	128.5	Malaisie [1]
Sri Lanka	69.9	66.2	38.3	81.1	[1]60.4	50.3	67.6	23.7	*37.1	...	Sri Lanka
Thailand	[1]10.7	[1]17.1	2.9	20.7	1.6	0.0	0.0	0.0	0.0	0.0	Thaïlande
Europe	**789**	**615**	**708**	**713**	**826**	**812**	**734**	**750**	**589**	**698**	**Europe**
Norway	788.5	615.4	708.1	713.1	826.4	812.4	734.3	[1]750.0	588.9	...	Norvège
USSR (former) [1]	430.0	..	..	..	..	..	..	..	..	..	URSS (anc.) [1]
Oceania	**1605**	**1328**	**1790**	**1804**	**1782**	**1980**	**2071**	**2100**	**2352**	**2163**	**Océanie**
Australia [3]	1605.0	1328.0	[1]1790.0	[1]1804.0	[1]1782.0	[1]1980.0	2071.0	2100.0	2352.0	2163.0	Australie [3]
Total	**4646**	**3502**	**4011**	**4072**	**3985**	**4156**	**4205**	**4213**	**4330**	**4264**	**Total**

General Note.

Gross weight of ilmenite concentrates. (SITC, Rev.3: 28783-1).

[1] Source: U. S. Geological Survey, (Washington, D. C.).
[2] Including rutile.
[3] Twelve months ending 30 June of year stated.

Remarque générale.

Poids brut de concentrés d'ilménite. (CTCI, Rev.3: 28783-1).

[1] Source: U.S. Geological Survey, (Washington, D.C.).
[2] Y compris le rutile.
[3] Période de douze mois finissant le 30 juin de l'année indiquée.

Molybdenum-bearing ores
Minerais molybdénifères

ISIC-BASED CODE - CODE BASE CITI

2302-28M

Unit : Metric tons

Unité : Tonnes métriques

Country or area	1990	1991	1992	1993	1994	1995	1996	1997	1998	1999	Pays ou zone
America, North	**76999**	**67387**	**60028**	**49450**	**59123**	**73896**	**67899**	**73354**	**65489**	**55250**	**Amérique du Nord**
Canada[2]	[1]12188	[1]11437	8870	10250	9723	9113	8789	7612	6240	6250	Canada[2]
Mexico	3200	2550	[3]1458	2400	2600	[3]3883	[4]4210	[4]4842	[3]5949	* [3]6000	Mexique
United States[1]	61611	53400	49700	36800	46800	60900	54900	60900	53300	43000	Etats-Unis[1]
America, South	**18009**	**17528**	**20469**	**19676**	**20580**	**21310**	**21082**	**25599**	**29641**	**32740**	**Amérique du Sud**
Chile[1]	13830	14434	14840	14899	15949	17899	17415	21337	25297	27269	Chili[1]
Peru	4179	3094	5629	4777	4631	3411	3667	4262	4344	5471	Pérou
Asia	**19353**	**21475**	**42720**	**43977**	**25889**	**38046**	**35397**	**38990**	**36332**	**34149**	**Asie**
Armenia*[3]	..	...	1000	500	500	1500	1800	1800	2500	2500	Arménie*[3]
China	[3]15700	[3]16000	37318	39208	[3]21400	[3]33000	[3]29600	[3]33300	* [3]30000	* [3]27900	Chine
Iran(Islamic Rep. of)*[3]	...	...	1320	700	670	560	600	600	600	600	Iran(Rép. islamique)*[3]
Japan*[1]	...	661	564	619	651	689	596	698	632	585	Japon*[1]
Kazakhstan*[3]	..	...	100	100	100	75	100	100	100	110	Kazakhstan*[3]
Korea, Republic of	171	239	#8	[3]0	[3]2	[3]0	[3]0	[3]0	[3]0	...	Corée, République de
Mongolia[3]	...	...	1610	2050	2066	1822	2201	1992	2000	1954	Mongolie[3]
Turkey[4]	100	100	100	100	0	0	0	0	0	...	Turquie[4]
Uzbekistan*[3]	..	...	700	700	500	400	500	500	500	500	Ouzbékistan*[3]
Europe	**150**	**6639**	**11000**	**10500**	**4200**	**3400**	**2400**	**2400**	**2400**	**2800**	**Europe**
Bulgaria	[3]150	[3]160	[4]200	[4]200	[4]200	[4]400	[4]400	[4]400	[4]400	*400	Bulgarie
Russian Federation*[3]	..	...	10800	10300	4000	3000	2000	2000	2000	2400	Fédération de Russie*[3]
USSR (former)*[3]	11000	..	..	..	..	..	..	..	..	..	URSS (anc.)*[3]
Oceania	**11**	**3**	**0**	**0**	**0**	**0**	**0**	**0**	**0**	**0**	**Océanie**
Australia[1][5]	11	3	[4]0	[4]0	[4]0	[4]0	[4]0	[4]0	[4]0	...	Australie[1][5]
Total	**125522**	**113032**	**134217**	**123603**	**109792**	**136652**	**126778**	**140343**	**133862**	**124939**	**Total**

General Note.
Mo content of molybdenum ores and concentrates and all other molybdenum-bearing ores and concentrates intended for treatment for molybdenum recovery. (SITC, Rev.3: 28781-0M, 28782-0M).

Remarque générale.
Contenu en Mo des minerais de molybdène et concentrés et tous autres minerais molybdénifères et concentrés, destinés à être traités en vue de l'extraction du molybdène. (CTCI, Rev.3: 28781-0M, 28782-0M).

[1] Content of concentrates.
[2] Shipments.
[3] Source: U. S. Geological Survey, (Washington, D. C.).
[4] Source: World Metal Statistics, (London).
[5] Twelve months ending 30 June of year stated.

[1] Teneur des concentrés.
[2] Expéditions.
[3] Source: U.S. Geological Survey, (Washington, D.C.).
[4] Source: World Metal Statistics,(Londres).
[5] Période de douze mois finissant le 30 juin de l'année indiquée.

Tantalum and Niobium (Columbium) concentrates
Concentrés de tantale et de niobium (colombium)

ISIC-BASED CODE - CODE BASE CITI

2302-29

Unit : Metric tons

Unité : Tonnes métriques

Country or area	1990	1991	1992	1993	1994	1995	1996	1997	1998	1999	Pays ou zone
Africa	**196**	**389**	**333**	**279**	**97**	**124**	**154**	**284**	**294**	**192**	**Afrique**
Dem. Rep. of Congo[1][2]	36	57	29	20	4	4	0	0	0	0	Rép. dém. du Congo[1][2]
Nigeria[1][2]	44	44	40	40	30	65	57	60	70	70	Nigéria[1][2]
Rwanda	81	177	170	171	56	54	97	224	224	122	Rwanda
Zimbabwe[1][2]	35	111	94	48	7	1	0	0	0	0	Zimbabwe[1][2]
America, North	**5620**	**5610**	**5300**	**5420**	**5274**	**5360**	**5380**	**5286**	**5338**	**5448**	**Amérique du Nord**
Canada[1][2][3]	5620	5610	5300	5420	5274	5360	5380	5286	5338	5448	Canada[1][2][3]
America, South	**29710**	**30790**	**29800**	**22875**	**31575**	**31375**	**32790**	**43090**	**56530**	**50330**	**Amérique du Sud**
Brazil[1][2][3]	29710	30790	29800	22875	31575	31375	32790	43090	56530	50330	Brésil[1][2][3]
Asia	**13**	**7**	**10**	**10**	**10**	**10**	**10**	**10**	**10**	**10**	**Asie**
Malaysia[1][2]	4	...	...	...	...	...	...	...	...	10	Malaisie[1][2]
Thailand[1][2]	9	3	...	...	...	...	...	...	...	...	Thaïlande[1][2]
Europe	**10**	**10**	**8**	**6**	**6**	**0**	**0**	**0**	**0**	**0**	**Europe**
Spain[1][2]	10	10	8	6	6	0	0	0	0	...	Espagne[1][2]
Oceania	**529**	**703**	**656**	**495**	**700**	**900**	**920**	**1010**	**1150**	**1230**	**Océanie**
Australia[1][2]	529	703	656	495	700	900	920	1010	1150	1230	Australie[1][2]
Total	**36078**	**37509**	**36107**	**29085**	**37662**	**37769**	**39254**	**49680**	**63322**	**57210**	**Total**

General Note.
Gross weight of tantalum and niobium (columbium) concentrates. (SITC, Rev.3: 28785-1).

Remarque générale.
Poids brut de concentrés de tantale et de niobium (colombium). (CTCI, Rev: 28785-1).

[1] Excluding columbium and tantalum-bearing tin concentrates and slags.

[2] Source: U. S. Geological Survey, (Washington, D. C.).

[3] Concentrates of columbite, tantalite, pyrochlore and microlite.

[1] Non compris les concentrés d'étain et scories stannifères comprenant colombium et tantale.

[2] Source: U.S. Geological Survey, (Washington, D.C.).

[3] Concentrés de colombium, de tantale, de pyrochlore et de microlite.

Niobium (Columbium) concentrates
Concentrés de niobium (colombium)

ISIC-BASED CODE - CODE BASE CITI

2302-291M

Unit : Metric tons — Unité : Tonnes métriques

Country or area	1990	1991	1992	1993	1994	1995	1996	1997	1998	1999	Pays ou zone
Africa	**65**	**77**	**69**	**59**	**18**	**27**	**23**	**23**	**30**	**30**	**Afrique**
Dem. Rep. of Congo[1]	9	15	8	5	1	1	0	0	0	0	Rép. dém. du Congo[1]
Nigeria[1]	18	15	17	17	13	26	23	23	30	30	Nigéria[1]
Rwanda[1]	33	30	30	30	#3	0	0	0	0	...	Rwanda[1]
Zimbabwe[1]	5	17	14	7	1	0	0	0	0	0	Zimbabwe[1]
America, North	**3394**	**3366**	**3284**	**3424**	**3300**	**2357**	**2331**	**2300**	**2311**	**2370**	**Amérique du Nord**
Canada[2]	3394	3366	3284	3424	3300	[1]2357	[1]2331	[1]2300	[1]2311	[1]2370	Canada[2]
America, South	**12371**	**12866**	**12545**	**9580**	**13200**	**13100**	**13700**	**18000**	**23600**	**21000**	**Amérique du Sud**
Brazil[1][2]	12371	12866	12545	9580	13200	13100	13700	18000	23600	21000	Brésil[1][2]
Asia	**3**	**2**	**3**	**3**	**3**	**3**	**3**	**3**	**3**	**3**	**Asie**
Malaysia[1]	1	...	...	...	...	...	...	...	...	...	Malaisie[1]
Thailand[1]	2	1	...	...	...	...	...	...	...	...	Thaïlande[1]
Oceania	**69**	**94**	**69**	**50**	**81**	**109**	**112**	**125**	**140**	**140**	**Océanie**
Australia[1]	69	94	69	50	81	109	112	125	140	140	Australie[1]
Total	**15902**	**16405**	**15970**	**13116**	**16602**	**15596**	**16169**	**20451**	**26084**	**23543**	**Total**

General Note.
Nb content of niobium (columbium) ores and concentrates. (SITC, Rev.3: 28785-11M).

Remarque générale.
Contenu en Nb des minerais de niobium (colombium) et concentrés. (CTCI, Rev: 28785-11M).

[1] Source: U. S. Geological Survey, (Washington, D. C.).
[2] Including Nb content of pyrochlore.

[1] Source: U.S. Geological Survey, (Washington, D.C.).
[2] Y compris le contenu en Nb des minerais de pyrochlore.

Tantalum concentrates
Concentrés de tantale

ISIC-BASED CODE - CODE BASE CITI

2302-292M

Unit : Metric tons

Unité : Tonnes métriques

Country or area	1990	1991	1992	1993	1994	1995	1996	1997	1998	1999	Pays ou zone
Africa	**90**	**121**	**107**	**87**	**49**	**46**	**45**	**45**	**45**	**45**	**Afrique**
Dem. Rep. of Congo[1]	10	16	8	6	1	1	0	0	0	0	Rép. dém. du Congo[1]
Mozambique[1]	42	...	...	...	...	...	...	...	...	...	Mozambique[1]
Nigeria[1]	2	2	2	2	2	3	3	3	3	3	Nigéria[1]
Rwanda[1]	24	22	22	22	#2	0	0	0	0	...	Rwanda[1]
Zimbabwe[1]	12	39	33	15	2	0	0	0	0	0	Zimbabwe[1]
America, North	**100**	**114**	**54**	**14**	**36**	**33**	**55**	**49**	**57**	**52**	**Amérique du Nord**
Canada	100	114	54	14	36	[1]33	[1]55	[1]49	[1]57	52	Canada
America, South	**90**	**84**	**60**	**50**	**50**	**50**	**55**	**55**	**90**	**90**	**Amérique du Sud**
Brazil[1]	90	84	60	50	50	50	55	55	90	90	Brésil[1]
Asia	**12**	**21**	**31**	**25**	**34**	**70**	**59**	**70**	**56**	**98**	**Asie**
Thailand	...	...	...	25	34	70	59	70	56	98	Thaïlande
Europe	**3**	**2**	**2**	**2**	**2**	**0**	**0**	**0**	**0**	**0**	**Europe**
Spain[1]	3	2	2	2	2	0	0	0	0	...	Espagne[1]
Oceania	**165**	**218**	**224**	**170**	**238**	**274**	**276**	**302**	**330**	**350**	**Océanie**
Australia[1]	165	218	224	170	238	274	276	302	330	350	Australie[1]
Total	**460**	**560**	**478**	**348**	**409**	**473**	**490**	**521**	**578**	**635**	**Total**

General Note.
Ta content of tantalum bearing ores and concentrates. (SITC, Rev.3: 28785-12M).

Remarque générale.
Contenu en Ta des minerais de tantale et concentrés. (CTCI, Rev.3: 28785-12M).

[1] Source: U. S. Geological Survey, (Washington, D. C.).

[1] Source: U.S. Geological Survey, (Washington, D.C.).

Vanadium-bearing ores
Minerais vanadifères

ISIC-BASED CODE - CODE BASE CITI

2302-31M

Unit : Metric tons

Unité : Tonnes métriques

Country or area	1990	1991	1992	1993	1994	1995	1996	1997	1998	1999	Pays ou zone
Africa	**17106**	**14962**	**14285**	**15051**	**16350**	**16297**	**14770**	**15590**	**18868**	**16000**	**Afrique**
South Africa [1] [2]	17106	14962	14285	15051	16350	16297	14770	15590	18868	16000	Afrique du Sud [1] [2]
Asia	**4761**	**5789**	**6348**	**6053**	**6543**	**14882**	**15158**	**16158**	**16758**	**17258**	**Asie**
China* [1]	4500	4500	4700	5000	5400	13700	14000	15000	15500	16000	Chine* [1]
Japan* [1]	...	...	245	252	252	245	245	245	245	245	Japon* [1]
Kazakhstan* [1]	..	...	1400	800	878	924	900	900	1000	1000	Kazakhstan* [1]
Korea, Republic of	...	35	3	1	...	...	...	...	...	...	Corée, République de
Europe	**222**	**11532**	**11200**	**13000**	**12100**	**11200**	**11200**	**9200**	**9100**	**9000**	**Europe**
Hungary* [1]	...	200	200	200	200	200	200	200	100	0	Hongrie* [1]
Russian Federation* [1]	..	...	11000	12800	11900	11000	11000	9000	9000	9000	Fédération de Russie* [1]
USSR (former) [1] [3]	9500	..	..	..	..	..	..	..	..	..	URSS (anc.) [1] [3]
Total	**31589**	**32284**	**31833**	**34104**	**34993**	**42379**	**41128**	**40948**	**44726**	**42258**	**Total**

General Note.

V content of vanadium ores and concentrates and all other vanadium-bearing ores and concentrates intended for treatment for vanadium recovery. (SITC, Rev. 3: 28785-2M).

[1] Source: U. S. Geological Survey, (Washington, D. C.).
[2] Including vanadium content of slag.
[3] Vanadium contained in exported slags. Excluding production for domestic consumption or for export in any form except slag.

Remarque générale.

Contenu en V des minerais de vanadium et concentrés et tous autres minerais vanadifères ou concentrés, destinés à être traités en vue de l'extraction du vanadium. (CTCI, Rev.3: 28785-2M).

[1] Source: U.S. Geological Survey, (Washington, D.C.).
[2] Y compris la teneur en vanadium des scories.
[3] Vanadium contenu dans les scories exportées. Non compris la production destinée à la consommation intérieure ou à l'exportation sous toute forme forme autre que de scories.

Zirconium ores and concentrates
Minerais de zirconium et concentrés

ISIC-BASED CODE - CODE BASE CITI
2302-32

Unit : Metric tons

Unité : Tonnes métriques

Country or area	1990	1991	1992	1993	1994	1995	1996	1997	1998	1999	Pays ou zone
Africa	**151536**	**230000**	**243000**	**243000**	**243000**	**260000**	**260000**	**265300**	**300000**	**400000**	**Afrique**
South Africa* [1]	151536	230000	243000	243000	243000	260000	260000	265300	300000	400000	Afrique du Sud* [1]
America, North	**102942**	**104009**	**109025**	**105325**	**105325**	**105030**	**105836**	**105108**	**105325**	**105325**	**Amérique du Nord**
Canada	...	...	...	...	...	574	1380	*652	...	...	Canada
United States [2]	102073	103140	108156	...	...	...	...	...	...	...	Etats-Unis [2]
America, South	**16907**	**18600**	**16874**	**13252**	**17064**	**16343**	**15560**	**19252**	**19300**	**19500**	**Amérique du Sud**
Brazil	16907	[1]18600	[1]16874	[1]13252	[1]17064	[1]16343	[1]15560	[1]19252	[1]19300	[1]19500	Brésil
Asia	**60172**	**69952**	**53199**	**51792**	**59792**	**60761**	**56379**	**54018**	**47045**	**49750**	**Asie**
China* [1]	15000	15000	15000	15000	15000	15000	15000	15000	15000	15000	Chine* [1]
India* [1]	18000	18200	18000	17000	18000	18000	19000	19000	19000	19000	Inde* [1]
Indonesia* [1]	...	2500	2500	2500	2500	2000	2000	105	231	250	Indonésie* [1]
Malaysia [1]	4279	5579	2608	2184	1656	3790	4511	4050	*4000	*2500	Malaisie [1]
Sri Lanka	[1]19727	[1]26100	13368	[1]14401	[1]22310	21971	15863	15863	*8814	[1]13000	Sri Lanka
Thailand	490	2573	1723	707	326	[1]0	5	[1]0	[1]0	0	Thaïlande
Europe	**..**	**48499**	**42162**	**42500**	**43000**	**62652**	**60080**	**70745**	**71293**	**71800**	**Europe**
Russian Federation* [1]	..	...	...	2500	3000	2652	5080	5745	6293	6800	Fédération de Russie* [1]
Ukraine* [1]	..	...	40000	40000	40000	60000	55000	65000	65000	65000	Ukraine* [1]
Oceania	**425000**	**317000**	**355000**	**414000**	**511000**	**527000**	**496000**	**411000**	**427000**	**354000**	**Océanie**
Australia	425000	317000	[1]355000	[1]414000	[1]511000	527000	496000	411000	427000	354000	Australie
Total	**756556**	**788059**	**819260**	**869869**	**979181**	**1031786**	**993855**	**925423**	**969963**	**1000375**	**Total**

General Note.
Gross weight of zirconium concentrates. (SITC, Rev.3: 28784-0).

Remarque générale.
Poids brut de concentrés de zirconium. (CTCI, Rev.3: 28784-0).

[1] Source: U. S. Geological Survey, (Washington, D. C.).
[2] Beginning 1993, data are confidential.

[1] Source: U.S. Geological Survey, (Washington, D.C.).
[2] A partir de 1993, les données sont confidentielles.

Antimony-bearing ores
Minerais stibifères

ISIC-BASED CODE - CODE BASÉ CITI

2302-34M

Unit : Metric tons Unité : Tonnes métriques

Country or area	1990	1991	1992	1993	1994	1995	1996	1997	1998	1999	Pays ou zone
Africa	**5104**	**4835**	**4230**	**4386**	**4774**	**5772**	**5294**	**3575**	**4403**	**5428**	**Afrique**
Morocco	188	190	[1]197	[1]180	[1]175	[1]198	[1]152	[1]160	[1]160	[1]150	Maroc
South Africa[2]	[1]4815	[1]4485	[1]3779	[1]4111	[1]4534	[1]5537	[1]5137	[1]3415	4243	5278	Afrique du Sud[2]
Zimbabwe[2]	101	160	254	[1]95	[1]65	[1]37	[1]5	[1]0	[1]0	[1]0	Zimbabwe[2]
America, North	**3758**	**4422**	**2495**	**2416**	**2899**	**3375**	**3821**	**3674**	**2667**	**2955**	**Amérique du Nord**
Canada	[3][4]565	[3][4]429	[3][4]796	566	630	665	[1]1716	[1]529	[1]428	[1]566	Canada
Guatemala	[4]868	[4]590	[4]275	[4]90	[4]296	[4]665	[1]880	[1]880	[1]440	[1]440	Guatemala
Honduras	* [1]25	...	[4]0	[4]0	[4]0	[4]0	[4]0	[4]0	[4]0	...	Honduras
Mexico[5]	*1800	2900	1064	1494	[1]1758	[1]1783	[1]983	[1]1909	[1]1301	[1]1500	Mexique[5]
United States	[6]500	[6]500	360	266	215	262	242	356	498	449	Etats-Unis
America, South	**8761**	**7564**	**6333**	**5775**	**7435**	**6656**	**6792**	**6459**	**5195**	**5260**	**Amérique du Sud**
Bolivia[5]	8454	7287	6022	5556	7050	6426	6487	5999	4735	[1]4800	Bolivie[5]
Peru[5]	307	277	311	219	385	230	305	[1]460	* [1]460	* [1]460	Pérou[5]
Asia	**55695**	**61944**	**59575**	**64431**	**94575**	**128152**	**131555**	**133577**	**99367**	**102120**	**Asie**
China*[1]	54800	58300	52000	60000	91000	125000	129000	131000	97400	100000	Chine*[1]
Kyrgyzstan*[1]	..	...	3000	2500	2000	1500	1200	1200	150	100	Kirghizistan*[1]
Myanmar	[1]0	9	[4]0	[4]0	[4]0	[4]0	[4]0	[4]0	[4]0	...	Myanmar
Pakistan[7]	6	8	* [1]12	* [1]0	* [1]0	* [1]6	[1]0	[1]0	[1]0	[1]0	Pakistan[7]
Tajikistan*[1]	..	...	1500	1200	1000	1000	1000	1200	1500	1800	Tadjikistan*[1]
Thailand[5]	337	62	278	[1]620	[1]500	[1]230	[1]70	[1]60	[1]200	[1]190	Thaïlande[5]
Turkey	552	288	2785	111	75	416	285	117	117	[1]30	Turquie
Europe	**2035**	**7721**	**10000**	**7120**	**7000**	**6000**	**6000**	**6000**	**4000**	**4000**	**Europe**
Austria	469	0	0	0	0	[4]0	[4]0	[4]0	[4]0	...	Autriche
Czechoslovakia(former)	917	297	..	..	..	..	..	..	..	..	Tchécoslovaquie(anc.)
Italy	240	77	0	0	0	0	[4]0	[4]0	[4]0	...	Italie
Russian Federation*[1]	..	...	10000	7120	7000	6000	6000	6000	4000	4000	Fédération de Russie*[1]
Yugoslavia, SFR	409	..	..	..	..	..	..	..	..	..	Yougoslavie, RSF
USSR (former)*[1]	9000	..	..	..	..	..	..	..	..	..	URSS (anc.)*[1]
Oceania	**1297**	**1496**	**1701**	**2300**	**1300**	**900**	**1800**	**1900**	**1800**	**1800**	**Océanie**
Australia	1297	1496	[1]1701	[1]2300	[1]1300	[1]900	[1]1800	[1]1900	[1]1800	[1]1800	Australie
Total	**85650**	**87982**	**84334**	**86428**	**117983**	**150855**	**155262**	**155185**	**117432**	**121563**	**Total**

General Note.
Sb content of antimony ores and concentrates and all other antimony-bearing ores and concentrates intended for treatment for antimony recovery. (SITC, Rev.3: 28799-1M).

Remarque générale.
Contenu en Sb des minerais d'antimoine et concentrés, ainsi que tous autres minerais stibifères et concentrés destinés à être traités en vue de l'extraction de l'antimoine. (CTCI, Rev.3: 28799-1M).

[1] Source: U. S. Geological Survey, (Washington, D. C.).
[2] Content of concentrates.
[3] Including antimonial lead; prior to 1986, shipments of antimony concentrates.
[4] Source: World Metal Statistics, (London).
[5] Content of all antimony-bearing materials in the form they are to be used or exported.
[6] Source: Metallgesellschaft Aktiengesellschaft, (Frankfurt).
[7] Twelve months ending 30 June of year stated.

[1] Source: U.S. Geological Survey, (Washington, D.C.).
[2] Teneur des concentrés.
[3] Y compris les plomb antimonieux; avant 1986, expéditions de concentrés d'antimoine.
[4] Source: World Metal Statistics,(Londres).
[5] Teneur en antimoine de tous les matériaux prêts à être utilisés ou exportés.
[6] Source: "Metallgesellschaft Aktiengesellschaft", (Francfort).
[7] Période de douze mois finissant le 30 juin de l'année indiquée.

Cobalt-bearing ores
Minerais cobaltifères

ISIC-BASED CODE - CODE BASE CITI

2302-37M

Unit : Metric tons   Unité : Tonnes métriques

Country or area	1990	1991	1992	1993	1994	1995	1996	1997	1998	1999	Pays ou zone
Africa	**26869**	**17891**	**13730**	**8256**	**5558**	**8785**	**10374**	**11148**	**19058**	**13595**	**Afrique**
Botswana	205	208	208	205	225	271	406	334	335	332	Botswana
Dem. Rep. of Congo[1][2]	19000	9900	5700	2459	826	1670	2000	3500	6000	7000	Rép. dém. du Congo[1][2]
Morocco	[1][2]194	[1][2]325	[1][2]461	[1][2]397	[2]419	[2]537	[2]553	[2]785	[2]316	1043	Maroc
South Africa*[1]	350	350	350	265	358	288	350	400	370	380	Afrique du Sud*[1]
Zambia[1][3]	6999	6990	6910	4840	3600	5908	6959	6037	11900	4700	Zambie[1][3]
Zimbabwe	121	118	101	[1]90	130	111	106	92	[1]137	[1]140	Zimbabwe
America, North	**3784**	**3271**	**3373**	**3211**	**2888**	**3739**	**7725**	**7791**	**8061**	**7484**	**Amérique du Nord**
Canada	2184	2171	2223	2150	1916	2148	[1]5714	[1]5709	[1]5861	[1]5324	Canada
Cuba[1]	1600	*1100	*1150	1061	972	1591	2011	2082	2200	2160	Cuba[1]
America, South	**400**	**400**	**400**	**400**	**400**	**400**	**400**	**400**	**400**	**700**	**Amérique du Sud**
Brazil*[1]	400	400	400	400	400	400	400	400	400	700	Brésil*[1]
Asia	**359**	**880**	**1260**	**840**	**570**	**1280**	**490**	**500**	**340**	**400**	**Asie**
China*[1]	...	...	260	240	270	980	190	200	40	100	Chine*[1]
Kazakhstan*[1]	..	...	1000	600	300	300	300	300	300	300	Kazakhstan*[1]
Europe	**873**	**4323**	**4236**	**3677**	**3131**	**3591**	**3354**	**3317**	**3200**	**3300**	**Europe**
Albania	*[1]600	*[1]600	*[1]20	10	10	0	0	0	0	0	Albanie
Finland[4]	273	234	216	167	121	...	...	...	...	...	Finlande[4]
Russian Federation*[1]	..	...	4000	3500	3000	3500	3300	3300	3200	3300	Fédération de Russie*[1]
USSR (former)*[1]	2400	..	..	..	..	..	..	..	..	..	URSS (anc.)*[1]
Oceania	**2664**	**2205**	**2400**	**2700**	**3300**	**3600**	**3900**	**4000**	**4300**	**5200**	**Océanie**
Australia	[5][6]1864	[5][6]1405	[1]1600	[1]1900	[1]2300	[1]2500	[1]2800	[1]3000	[1]3300	[1]4100	Australie
New Caledonia[1]	*800	*800	*800	*800	1000	1100	1100	1000	*1000	*1100	Nouvelle-Calédonie[1]
Total	**37349**	**28970**	**25399**	**19084**	**15847**	**21395**	**26243**	**27156**	**35359**	**30679**	**Total**

General Note.
Co content of cobalt ores and concentrates and all other cobalt-bearing ores and concentrates intended for treatment for cobalt recovery. (SITC, Rev.3: 28793-0M).

Remarque générale.
Contenu en Co des minerais de cobalt et concentrés et tous autres minerais cobaltifères et concentrés destinés à être traités en vue de l'extraction du cobalt. (CTCI, Rev.3: 28793-0M).

[1] Source: U. S. Geological Survey, (Washington, D. C.).
[2] Content of concentrates.
[3] Metal recovered.
[4] Content of cupriferous pyrites.
[5] Twelve months ending 30 June of year stated.
[6] Content of nickel concentrates.

[1] Source: U.S. Geological Survey, (Washington, D.C.).
[2] Teneur des concentrés.
[3] Métal récupéré.
[4] Teneur des pyrites cuprifères.
[5] Période de douze mois finissant le 30 juin de l'année indiquée.
[6] Teneur des concentrés de nickel.

Mercury
Mercure

ISIC-BASED CODE - CODE BASE CITI

2302-40M

Unit : Metric tons   Unité : Tonnes métriques

Country or area	1990	1991	1992	1993	1994	1995	1996	1997	1998	1999	Pays ou zone
Africa	**646**	**438**	**489**	**458**	**414**	**292**	**368**	**447**	**169**	**181**	**Afrique**
Algeria	637	430	469	458	[1]414	[1]292	[1]368	* [1]447	169	181	Algérie
Morocco[1]	...	...	*20	0	0	0	0	0	...	...	Maroc[1]
America, North	**1297**	**398**	**85**	**240**	**240**	**243**	**243**	**243**	**243**	**243**	**Amérique du Nord**
Mexico[1]	735	340	#21	12	*12	*15	*15	*15	*15	*15	Mexique[1]
United States[2]	562	[3]58	[3]64	...	...	...	...	...	...	...	Etats-Unis[2]
Asia	**1060**	**1409**	**1421**	**1177**	**915**	**1190**	**1139**	**1491**	**903**	**881**	**Asie**
China* [1]	1000	760	580	520	470	780	510	830	230	200	Chine* [1]
Kyrgyzstan	..	...	736	577	379	360	584	[1]610	638	646	Kirghizistan
Tajikistan* [1]	..	...	100	80	55	50	45	40	35	35	Tadjikistan* [1]
Turkey	[1]60	[1]25	[1]5	[1]0	...	0	0	...	0	0	Turquie
Europe	**1299**	**965**	**333**	**357**	**632**	**1682**	**1035**	**1033**	**845**	**730**	**Europe**
Czechoslovakia(former)	126	75	..	..	..	..	..	..	..	..	Tchécoslovaquie(anc.)
Finland[1]	141	74	75	98	83	90	88	90	*80	*80	Finlande[1]
Russian Federation* [1]	..	..	70	60	50	50	50	50	50	50	Fédération de Russie* [1]
Slovakia[1]	..	..	...	50	50	*0	*0	*0	*20	*0	Slovaquie[1]
Slovenia	..	9	12	...	6	5	[1]5	[1]5	0	[1]0	Slovénie
Spain	962	...	[1]36	[1]64	[1]393	[1]1497	[1]862	* [1]863	* [1]675	* [1]600	Espagne
Ukraine* [1]	..	...	100	80	50	40	30	25	20	...	Ukraine* [1]
Yugoslavia, SFR*	70	..	..	..	..	..	..	..	..	..	Yougoslavie, RSF*
USSR (former)* [1]	2100	..	..	..	..	..	..	..	..	..	URSS (anc.)* [1]
Total	**6402**	**3210**	**2328**	**2232**	**2201**	**3407**	**2785**	**3214**	**2160**	**2035**	**Total**

General Note.
Total Hg recovered from mercury-bearing ores and concentrates. (SITC, Rev.3: 28799-2M).

Remarque générale.
Poids total du mercure extrait des minerais ou concentrés contenant du mercure. (CTCI, Rev.3: 28799-2M).

[1] Source: U. S. Geological Survey, (Washington, D. C.).
[2] Beginning 1993, data are confidential.
[3] Limited coverage.

[1] Source: U.S. Geological Survey, (Washington, D.C.).
[2] A partir de 1993, les données sont confidentielles.
[3] Couverture limitée.

Silver-bearing ores
Minerais argentifères

ISIC-BASED CODE - CODE BASE CITI

2302-46M

Unit : Metric tons   Unité : Tonnes métriques

Country or area	1990	1991	1992	1993	1994	1995	1996	1997	1998	1999	Pays ou zone
Africa	**579**	**613**	**493**	**627**	**631**	**481**	**439**	**484**	**507**	**475**	**Afrique**
Algeria* [1]	3	3	4	2	2	2	2	2	2	2	Algérie* [1]
Dem. Rep. of Congo* [1]	84	80	18	18	12	1	1	1	1	1	Rép. dém. du Congo* [1]
Ghana* [1]	1	1	2	2	2	3	2	3	4	4	Ghana* [1]
Morocco	190	230	168	[1]309	[1]328	[1]204	[1]200	[1]261	* [1]306	* [1]300	Maroc
Namibia	92	91	89	[2]72	[2]64	[2]69	[2]42	[2]34	[2]17	...	Namibie
South Africa	161	171	176	[2]193	[2]196	[2]174	169	155	161	152	Afrique du Sud
Tunisia* [1]	2	1	1	1	3	4	3	1	1	1	Tunisie* [1]
Zambia	[3]25	[3]17	[3]18	[2 3]18	[2 3]12	[1]9	[1]9	[1]7	[1]8	[1]8	Zambie
Zimbabwe	21	19	17	12	12	15	11	20	[1]7	[1]7	Zimbabwe
America, North	**5902**	**5477**	**5314**	**4971**	**4484**	**5221**	**5462**	**6136**	**5996**	**5581**	**Amérique du Nord**
Canada	1381	1261	1147	888	740	1285	1309	1222	[1]1196	* [1]1246	Canada
Dominican Republic	[1]22	[1]22	13	1	9	21	17	12	[1]7	[1]4	Rép. dominicaine
Honduras [2]	31	43	35	24	28	30	36	40	43	...	Honduras [2]
Mexico	2346	2290	2317	[2]2416	[2]2215	[2]2324	[2]2528	[2]2679	[2]2686	[2]2338	Mexique
Nicaragua [1]	1	1	2	2	2	1	2	3	4	*3	Nicaragua [1]
United States	2121	1860	1800	1640	1490	1560	1570	2180	2060	1950	Etats-Unis
America, South	**2840**	**2910**	**2980**	**3082**	**3096**	**3499**	**3589**	**3560**	**3845**	**4097**	**Amérique du Sud**
Argentina	83	70	45	43	38	48	50	* [1]53	* [1]36	* [1]39	Argentine
Bolivia	310	337	282	333	352	425	386	387	404	[1]422	Bolivie
Brazil	60	50	50	[1]108	[1]50	[1]50	[1]30	* [1]27	* [1]34	* [1]34	Brésil
Chile	655	676	1025	970	983	1041	1147	1091	1341	1380	Chili
Colombia	7	8	8	[2]7	[2]6	[1]6	[1]6	[1]4	[1]5	[1]5	Colombie
Peru	1725	1769	1570	[2]1621	[2]1667	[1]1929	[1]1970	[1]1998	[1]2025	[1]2217	Pérou
Asia	**662**	**1260**	**2091**	**2071**	**2130**	**3451**	**2512**	**2685**	**3081**	**3186**	**Asie**
China* [1]	130	150	800	840	810	910	1140	1300	1400	1400	Chine* [1]
India	35	36	47	56	46	36	40	54	55	54	Inde
Indonesia	[4]67	[4]80	[4]90	[2 4]90	[2]107	[1]276	[1]255	[1]219	[1]349	[1]292	Indonésie
Japan	150	171	178	[1]137	[1]134	[1]100	[1]85	* [1]87	* [1]94	[1]94	Japon
Kazakhstan* [1]	..	...	500	500	506	489	468	465	470	575	Kazakhstan* [1]
Korea,Dem.Ppl's.Rep.* [1]	50	50	50	50	50	50	50	50	50	50	Corée,Rép.pop.dém.de* [1]
Korea, Republic of	148	113	184	215	257	343	[1]254	[1]268	400	* [1]489	Corée, République de
Malaysia	[5]13	[5]13	[5]15	[5]14	[5]13	[1]11	[1]10	[1]10	[1]7	[1]5	Malaisie
Myanmar	[6]7	[6]5	[6]5	[1]2	[1]6	[1]4	[1]4	[1]2	* [1]3	* [1]4	Myanmar
Philippines	47	39	33	32	30	28	24	21	18	18	Philippines
Turkey	15	48	134	75	106	1139	112	139	165	130	Turquie
Uzbekistan* [1]	..	...	55	60	65	65	70	70	70	75	Ouzbékistan* [1]
Europe	**1794**	**2504**	**2530**	**2313**	**2465**	**2207**	**1951**	**2061**	**2058**	**2007**	**Europe**
Bulgaria	[5]54	[5]37	* [1]35	* [1]35	* [1]30	* [1]35	* [1]49	* [1]32	* [1]24	* [1]25	Bulgarie
Czechoslovakia(former) [5]	15	28	..	..	..	..	..	..	..	..	Tchécoslovaquie(anc.) [5]
Finland [7]	29	27	6	1	...	...	...	...	...	...	Finlande [7]
France	8	8	13	[1]1	[1]1	[1]1	[1]2	[1]2	* [1]2	* [1]2	France
Germany(Fed.Rep.) [5]	8	..	..	..	..	..	..	..	..	..	Allemagne(Rép.féd.) [5]
German D.R.(former) [1]	20	..	..	..	..	..	..	..	..	..	R.D.A. (anc.) [1]
Greece	[2]63	[2]70	[2]61	[2]59	[2]45	[1]33	[1]17	[1]45	[1]45	[1]44	Grèce
Ireland	7	10	13	[1]13	[1]17	[1]14	[1]15	[1]13	* [1]13	* [1]12	Irlande
Italy	104	176	127	93	121	[1]14	[1]9	[1]10	[1]10	[1]10	Italie
Poland	832	899	798	767	1064	1001	935	1038	1108	1100	Pologne
Portugal	1	1	#38	36	32	37	[1]36	[1]34	[1]32	[1]30	Portugal
Romania* [1]	80	80	73	70	70	60	60	60	60	60	Roumanie* [1]
Russian Federation* [1]	..	...	800	800	600	600	400	400	350	375	Fédération de Russie* [1]
Spain	246	197	206	158	[2]175	[1]102	[1]66	[1]66	[1]65	[1]25	Espagne
Sweden	220	253	281	[1]255	[1]276	[1]268	[1]272	[1]304	* [1]299	* [1]300	Suède
United Kingdom	2	2	...	[2]0	[2]0	[2]0	[2]0	[2]0	[2]0	...	Royaume-Uni
Yugoslavia	..	68	78	25	18	26	74	41	34	8	Yougoslavie
Yugoslavia, SFR [7]	105	..	..	..	..	..	..	..	..	..	Yougoslavie, RSF [7]
USSR (former) [1]	1400	..	..	..	..	..	..	..	..	..	URSS (anc.) [1]
Oceania	**1282**	**1296**	**1342**	**1249**	**1123**	**1011**	**1083**	**1057**	**1388**	**1662**	**Océanie**

For general note and footnotes, see end of table.   Voir la fin du tableau pour la remarque générale et les notes.

Silver-bearing ores (continued)
Minerais argentifères (suite)

ISIC-BASED CODE - CODE BASE CITI

2302-46M

Unit : Metric tons — Unité : Tonnes métriques

Country or area	1990	1991	1992	1993	1994	1995	1996	1997	1998	1999	Pays ou zone
Australia	[2]1173	[2]1180	[2]1248	[2]1152	[2]1045	941	1024	1009	1332	1594	Australie
Fiji[1]	1	0	1	1	1	2	2	*3	*2	*3	Fidji[1]
Papua New Guinea	108	116	93	96	77	68	57	45	54	65	Papouasie-Nvl-Guinée
Total	**14459**	**14060**	**14750**	**14313**	**13929**	**15870**	**15036**	**15983**	**16875**	**17008**	**Total**

General Note.

Ag content of silver ores and concentrates and all other silver-bearing ores and concentrates intended for treatment for silver recovery. (SITC, Rev.3: 28911-1M).

Remarque générale.

Contenu en Ag des minerais d'argent et concentrés et tous autres minerais argentifères et concentrés, destinés à être traités en vue de l'extraction de l'argent. (CTCI, Rev.3: 28911-1M).

[1] Source: U. S. Geological Survey, (Washington, D. C.).
[2] Source: World Metal Statistics, (London).
[3] Silver recovered.
[4] Silver content of concentrates only.
[5] Source: Metallgesellschaft Aktiengesellschaft, (Frankfurt).
[6] Government production only.
[7] Silver refined from copper, lead and zinc ore.

[1] Source: U.S. Geological Survey, (Washington, D.C.).
[2] Source: World Metal Statistics,(Londres).
[3] Argent récupéré.
[4] Teneur en argent des concentrés seulement.
[5] Source: "Metallgesellschaft Aktiengesellschaft", (Francfort).
[6] Production de l'Etat seulement.
[7] Argent affiné provenant de minerais de cuivre, plomb et zinc.

Uranium-bearing ores
Minerais uranifères

ISIC-BASED CODE - CODE BASE CITI

2302-52M

Unit : Metric tons   Unité : Tonnes métriques

Country or area	1990	1991	1992	1993	1994	1995	1996	1997	1998	1999	Pays ou zone
Africa	**9219**	**7803**	**6883**	**6818**	**7191**	**7063**	**7780**	**7984**	**8213**	**7493**	**Afrique**
Gabon	709	678	589	556	650	652	568	470	725	...	Gabon
Namibia	3211	2450	1660	1679	1895	2016	2447	2905	2780	...	Namibie
Niger	2839	2963	2965	2914	2975	2974	3329	3499	3714	...	Niger
South Africa	2460	1712	1669	1669	1671	1421	1436	1110	994		Afrique du Sud
America, North	**12149**	**11220**	**11467**	**.10335**	**10936**	**12797**	**14138**	**14201**	**12732**	**14445**	**Amérique du Nord**
Canada	8729	8160	9297	9155	9647	10473	11706	12031	10922	...	Canada
United States	3420	3060	2170	1180	1289	2324	2432	2170	1810	...	Etats-Unis
America, South	**14**	**18**	**123**	**150**	**185**	**171**	**16**	**30**	**7**	**58**	**Amérique du Sud**
Argentina	9	18	123	126	79	65	16	30	7	...	Argentine
Brazil	5	0	0	24	106	106	0	0	0	...	Brésil
Asia	**1149**	**6421**	**6715**	**6305**	**4985**	**3972**	**3459**	**3654**	**4016**	**2056**	**Asie**
China	800	800	955	780	480	500	560	570	590	...	Chine
India	[1]230	[1]200	[1]150	[1]148	[1]155	[1]155	[1]207	[1]207	207	...	Inde
Kazakhstan	..		2802	2700	2240	1630	1210	1090	1270	...	Kazakhstan
Mongolia	89	101	105	54	72	20	0	0	0	...	Mongolie
Pakistan	[2]30	[2]30	[2]23	[2]23	[2]23	[2]23	[2]23	[2]23	23	...	Pakistan
Uzbekistan	..	...	2680	2600	2015	1644	1459	1764	1926	...	Ouzbékistan
Europe	**7334**	**8354**	**7690**	**7343**	**6105**	**5439**	**5781**	**5389**	**5298**	**4434**	**Europe**
Belgium	39	38	36	34	40	25	28	27	15	...	Belgique
Bulgaria	405	240	150	100	70	0	0	0	0	...	Bulgarie
Czech Republic	..	..	...	950	541	600	604	603	610	...	République tchèque
France incl. Monaco	2841	2477	2149	1730	1053	1016	930	572	507	...	France y compris Monaco
Germany	..	1207	232	116	47	35	39	28	30	...	Allemagne
Germany(Fed.Rep.)	2972		..	..	..	..	..	..	..	..	Allemagne(Rép.féd.)
Hungary	490	417	430	380	413	210	200	200	*200	...	Hongrie
Portugal	111	28	28	32	24	18	15	17	19	...	Portugal
Romania	210	160	120	120	120	120	105	107	132	...	Roumanie
Russian Federation	..	...	2640	2697	2541	2160	2605	2580	2530	...	Fédération de Russie
Slovenia	..	...	2	0	0	0	0	0	0	...	Slovénie
Spain	213	196	187	184	256	255	255	255	255	...	Espagne
Ukraine	..	...	1000	1000	1000	1000	1000	1000	1000	...	Ukraine
Yugoslavia, SFR	53	..	..	..	..	..	..	..	..	..	Yougoslavie, RSF
Oceania	**3530**	**3776**	**2334**	**2256**	**2208**	**3712**	**4975**	**5488**	**4910**	**5717**	**Océanie**
Australia	[2]3530	[2]3776	[2]2334	[2]2256	[2]2208	[2]3712	[2]4975	[2]5488	4910	...	Australie
Total	**33395**	**37592**	**35212**	**33207**	**31610**	**33154**	**36149**	**36746**	**35176**	**34204**	**Total**

General Note.
U content of uranium ores and concentrates and all other uranium-bearing ores and concentrates intended for treatment for uranium recovery. (SITC, Rev. 3: 28610-0M)

Remarque générale.
Contenu en U des minerais d'uranium et concentrés et tous autres minerais uranifères et concentrés, destinés à être traités en vue de l'extraction de l'uranium (CTCI, Rev. 3: 28610-0M).

[1] Twelve months beginning 1 April of year stated.
[2] Twelve months ending 30 June of year stated.

[1] Période de douze mois commençant le 1er avril de l'année indiquée.
[2] Période de douze mois finissant le 30 juin de l'année indiquée.

Gold-bearing ores
Minerais aurifères

ISIC-BASED CODE - CODE BASE CITI

2302-55M

Unit : Kilograms Unité : Kilogrammes

Country or area	1990	1991	1992	1993	1994	1995	1996	1997	1998	1999	Pays ou zone
Africa	**657741**	**670732**	**692415**	**706729**	**677060**	**633415**	**602415**	**612963**	**605265**	**612800**	**Afrique**
Botswana	46	20	165	192	234	86	5	28	1	8	Botswana
Burundi[1]	*9	*25	*32	*20	#1000	2000	2200	*1500	*1500	*1500	Burundi[1]
Cameroon*[1]	10	10	10	#1000	800	800	1000	1000	1000	1000	Cameroun*[1]
Central African Rep.	300	240	[1]155	*[1]153	*[1]138	*[1]97	*[1]90	*[1]90	*[1]100	*[1]100	Rép. centrafricaine
Congo	3	12	0	2	0	0	37	31	54	12	Congo
Dem. Rep. of Congo*[1]	9300	8800	9000	8700	11100	10000	8200	9600	4800	4000	Rép. dém. du Congo*[1]
Ethiopia	848	*2000	2652	[1]3387	*[1]2370	*[1]4500	*[1]2500	*[1]3000	*[1]2500	*[1]2000	Ethiopie
Gabon[1]	80	50	70	120	*72	*70	*70	*70	*70	*70	Gabon[1]
Ghana[1]	16840	26310	31000	38911	43478	53087	49211	*54662	*72540	*81000	Ghana[1]
Kenya	*[1]25	17	2	*[1]20	10	151	72	*[1]440	*[1]388	*[1]400	Kenya
Liberia*[1]	600	600	700	700	700	800	700	500	800	1000	Libéria*[1]
Madagascar[1]	216	*500	*500	*500	*500	38	*50	*50	*50	*50	Madagascar[1]
Mali	4317	5352	6099	5939	5677	6291	7340	*[1]18400	*[1]22800	*[1]25700	Mali
Mauritania	...	...	826	1266	[1]1738	[1]1196	*[1]189	*[1]0	[1]0	[1]0	Mauritanie
Namibia	[2]1605	[2]1850	[1][2]2030	[1]1954	[1]2445	[1]2394	[1]2145	[1]2417	[1]1882	[1]2100	Namibie
Rwanda	700	*[1]1000	*[1]1000	*[1]1000	*#[1]100	*[1]26	*[1]25	*[1]25	*[1]20	*[1]20	Rwanda
South Africa	602997	601110	614100	[1]619201	[1]580201	[1]523809	498300	490600	465100	451300	Afrique du Sud
Sudan*[1]	100	50	#1000	1600	3000	3700	4500	5000	5000	6000	Soudan*[1]
United Rep.Tanzania	[1]1628	3851	4525	[1]3264	[1]2861	[1]320	[1]318	*[1]300	*[1]720	*[1]6100	Rép. Unie de Tanzanie
Zambia[1]	129	136	271	235	124	91	*119	*290	*765	*740	Zambie[1]
Zimbabwe	16900	17820	18278	18565	20512	[1]23959	25344	24960	[1]25175	[1]29700	Zimbabwe
America, North	**476069**	**482726**	**504659**	**495834**	**489287**	**494438**	**522666**	**565043**	**563407**	**528545**	**Amérique du Nord**
Canada	167373	175282	160351	153129	145156	152032	166378	171479	166089	...	Canada
Costa Rica*[1]	460	550	550	260	358	400	510	502	483	300	Costa Rica*[1]
Dominican Republic	4353	3160	2375	354	1538	3288	3659	2349	[1]1424	651	Rép. dominicaine
Honduras[1]	156	180	163	111	106	110	*142	*150	*150	*150	Honduras[1]
Mexico	8338	8400	9900	[1]9792	[1]13888	[1]20292	[1]24477	[1]26001	[1]25427	[1]22477	Mexique
Nicaragua[1]	*1200	1154	1320	1188	1241	1316	*1500	*2562	*3834	*2700	Nicaragua[1]
United States	294189	294000	330000	331000	327000	317000	326000	362000	366000	341000	Etats-Unis
America, South	**206111**	**201334**	**210172**	**208444**	**230846**	**229955**	**247657**	**262518**	**269977**	**315758**	**Amérique du Sud**
Argentina	1399	1725	1106	937	937	837	723	[1]2289	[1]20400	[1]38515	Argentine
Bolivia	5198	9239	9821	11988	12791	14405	12634	13291	14445	11787	Bolivie
Brazil[1]	[3]102000	[3]89600	85862	69894	72397	64424	60011	*58488	*49567	*40900	Brésil[1]
Chile	27503	28879	34473	33637	38786	44585	53098	49486	44990	46668	Chili
Colombia	29352	30000	29900	[1]27471	[1]20762	*[1]21136	*[1]22073	*[1]18811	*[1]18813	*[1]19000	Colombie
Ecuador[1]	10700	12200	12300	12500	13000	7410	7208	*3070	*3500	*4000	Equateur[1]
French Guiana	550	1000	[1]2140	[1]2800	[1]2270	[1]3000	*[1]3000	*[1]3000	*[1]3000	*[1]3000	Guyane française
Guyana[1]	1500	1840	2475	9614	11710	9005	12006	*13521	13500	13500	Guyana[1]
Peru	20179	22606	24242	30318	47799	57743	64885	77940	94214	128088	Pérou
Suriname*[1]	30	30	300	300	300	300	300	300	300	300	Suriname*[1]
Venezuela	7700	[1]4215	[1]7553	[1]8985	[1]10094	[1]7110	[1]11719	*[1]22322	*[1]7248	*[1]10000	Venezuela
Asia	**156376**	**184951**	**214152**	**227920**	**237306**	**263959**	**292284**	**330262**	**367965**	**377148**	**Asie**
China*	[1]100000	[1]120000	125000	130000	132000	140000	[1]145000	[1]175000	[1]178000	[1]170000	Chine*
India	2207	2041	1850	2075	2373	2036	2892	2846	2683	2442	Inde
Indonesia	9355	13889	37986	41576	44843	[1]64031	[1]83564	[1]86927	[1]124018	[1]130000	Indonésie
Japan	7303	8299	8893	9352	9551	9185	8627	8384	8601	9405	Japon
Korea,Dem.Ppl's.Rep.*[1]	5000	5000	5000	5000	5000	5000	5000	5000	5000	5000	Corée,Rép.pop.dém.de*[1]
Korea, Republic of	5225	6911	6220	10443	12332	[1]13418	[1]14096	[1]14852	...	[1]25730	Corée, République de
Malaysia	[4]2600	[4]2800	[4]3500	[1]4462	[1]4085	[1]3162	[1]2830	[1]4487	[1]3394	[1]3449	Malaisie
Philippines	24591	25916	25608	24917	27037	27023	30180	32671	34038	31027	Philippines
Thailand	...	...	...	...	85	104	...	...	...	...	Thaïlande
Europe	**22847**	**26418**	**26239**	**19953**	**21208**	**19260**	**20779**	**17895**	**21248**	**18471**	**Europe**
Finland	1503	1818	1663	304	963	1459	1336	[1]3000	[1]3000	[1]3000	Finlande
France	4236	3085	[1][2]2910	[1]3034	[1]5078	[1]4615	[1]5651	*[1]4350	*[1]4500	*[1]5000	France
Germany(Fed.Rep.)[5][6]	18	..	..	..	..	..	..	..	..	...	Allemagne(Rép.féd.)[5][6]
Hungary[4]	500	600	600	500	200	500	500	500	500	...	Hongrie[4]
Portugal	276	264	149	...	...	...	...	...	...	...	Portugal
Spain	6814	7431	6572	6060	[4]5900	[1]4131	[1]2763	[1]1824	[1]3295	[1]3600	Espagne
Sweden	5000	6300	[4]5800	[4]6500	[4]6400	[1]6528	[1]6145	[1]6777	[1]5944	[1]4400	Suède

For general note and footnotes, see end of table. Voir la fin du tableau pour la remarque générale et les notes.

Gold-bearing ores (continued)
Minerais aurifères (suite)

ISIC-BASED CODE - CODE BASE CITI

2302-55M

Unit : Kilograms   Unité : Kilogrammes

Country or area	1990	1991	1992	1993	1994	1995	1996	1997	1998	1999	Pays ou zone
Yugoslavia	..	6920	8545	3325	2437	1797	4154	1214	3779	1811	Yougoslavie
Yugoslavia, SFR[7]	4500	..	..	..	..	..	..	..	..	..	Yougoslavie, RSF[7]
USSR (former)[1]	302000	..	..	..	..	..	..	..	..	..	URSS (anc.)[1]
Oceania	272183	300857	326326	322196	329028	318084	340405	360904	390921	379375	Océanie
Australia	* [1]244000	* [1]234000	* [1]243000	[1]247196	[1]256188	248570	272930	299440	316150	302760	Australie
Fiji	4116	2743	3701	[1]3713	[1]3535	[1]3496	[1]4452	* [1]4671	* [1]3690	* [1]4500	Fidji
New Zealand[1]	4630	6760	10531	11161	10118	12132	*11879	*11350	*7700	*7100	Nouvelle-Zélande[1]
Papua New Guinea	19402	57324	69057	60096	59156	53861	51119	45418	62346	62015	Papouasie-Nvl-Guinée
Solomon Islands	35	30	37	[1]30	[1]31	[1]25	[1]25	[1]25	[1]1035	[1]3000	Iles Salomon
Total	2093327	1867018	1973963	1981075	1984735	1959111	2026205	2149584	2218783	2232097	Total

General Note.
Au content of gold ores and concentrates and all other gold-bearing ores and concentrates intended for treatment for gold recovery. (SITC, Rev.3: 28919-2M).

Remarque générale.
Contenu en Au des minerais d'or et concentrés et tous autres minerais aurifères et concentrés, destinés à être traités en vue de l'extraction de l'or. (CTCI, Rev.3: 28919-2M).

[1] Source: U. S. Geological Survey, (Washington, D. C.).
[2] Smelter production only.
[3] Gold refined from domestic ores only.
[4] Source: World Metal Statistics, (London).
[5] Gold refined, including gold recovered as a by-product.
[6] Beginning 1981, official data are confidential. Data shown are U. S. Bureau of Mines (Washington, D.C.) estimates.
[7] Gold refined from copper, lead and zinc ores only.

[1] Source: U.S. Geological Survey, (Washington, D.C.).
[2] Production des fonderies seulement.
[3] Or affiné provenant de minerais indigène seulement.
[4] Source: World Metal Statistics,(Londres).
[5] Or affiné, y compris l'or récupéré comme sous produit.
[6] A partir de 1981, les chiffres sont confidentiels. Les données officielles publiées se rapportent aux estimations du 'U. S. Bureau of Mines' (Washington, D.C.).
[7] Or affiné provenant de minerais de cuivre, plomb et zinc seulement.

Slate
Ardoise

ISIC-BASED CODE - CODE BASE CITI
2901-01

Unit : Thousand metric tons   Unité : Milliers de tonnes métriques

Country or area	1990	1991	1992	1993	1994	1995	1996	1997	1998	1999	Pays ou zone
Africa	**29**	**26**	**26**	**22**	**22**	**24**	**38**	**11**	**24**	**20**	**Afrique**
South Africa	29	[1]26	[1]26	[1]22	[1]22	[1]24	[1]38	[1]11	[1]24	...	Afrique du Sud
America, North	**33**	**30**	**26**	**33**	**35**	**36**	**25**	**25**	**30**	**29**	**Amérique du Nord**
United States[2]	33	30	26	33	35	36	25	25	30	29	Etats-Unis[2]
America, South	**68**	**68**	**68**	**68**	**68**	**73**	**81**	**83**	**85**	**85**	**Amérique du Sud**
Brazil[1]	50	...	*50	50	50	50	50	50	50	50	Brésil[1]
Peru[1]	*18	*18	*18	18	18	23	31	33	35	35	Pérou[1]
Asia	**152**	**148**	**141**	**137**	**133**	**137**	**135**	**138**	**137**	**137**	**Asie**
India	25	21	14	10	6	10	8	11	10	10	Inde
Syrian Arab Republic	127	...	...	...	...	...	...	...	...	...	Rép. arabe syrienne
Europe	**2965**	**7404**	**6840**	**6320**	**6603**	**6110**	**5237**	**5551**	**5306**	**5572**	**Europe**
Croatia	..	158	154	135	171	131	145	0	...	...	Croatie
France	43	43	42	29	24	* [1]27	* [1]26	[1]31	[1]30	...	France
Germany[1]	..	...	55	67	89	90	90	70	70	..	Allemagne[1]
Germany(Fed.Rep.)[1]	12	..	..	..	..	..	..	..	..	..	Allemagne(Rép.féd.)[1]
Greece	...	...	...	528	509	668	653	...	...	...	Grèce
Italy[1]	120	*120	*120	*120	*120	120	107	100	100	...	Italie[1]
Norway	38	...	...	...	...	...	...	...	...	...	Norvège
Poland	68	54	57	50	41	37	36	37	25	27	Pologne
Portugal	23	24	35	57	66	[1]30	[1]20	[1]30	46	46	Portugal
Russian Federation	..	4204	3799	3301	3317	2351	1544	2073	1715	1951	Fédération de Russie
Spain	1686	1720	1610	1519	1814	2326	2151	2216	2212	2323	Espagne
Sweden	26	23	14	14	12	17	19	20	16	17	Suède
United Kingdom[3][4]	359	360	326	462	402	275	408	347	425	361	Royaume-Uni[3][4]
USSR (former)	27042	..	..	..	..	..	..	..	..	..	URSS (anc.)
Total	**30289**	**7676**	**7101**	**6580**	**6862**	**6379**	**5516**	**5809**	**5581**	**5843**	**Total**

General Note.
Slate including slate not further worked than roughly split, roughly squared or squared by sawing. Roofing slate and mosaic cubes are excluded. (SITC, Rev.3: 27311-0).

Remarque générale.
Ardoise, y compris l'ardoise brute, refendue, dégrossie ou simplement débitée par sciage, à l'exclusion de l'ardoise de couverture et des cubes pour mosaïques. (CTCI, Rev.3: 27311-0).

[1] Source: U. S. Geological Survey, (Washington, D. C.).
[2] Sold or used by producers.
[3] Including waste used for constructional fill and powder and granules used in manufacturing.
[4] Great Britain only.

[1] Source: U.S. Geological Survey, (Washington, D.C.).
[2] Vendu ou utilisé par les producteurs.
[3] Y compris les déchets utilisés pour le remblayage ainsi que les poudres et granules employées en manufacture.
[4] Grande Bretagne seulement.

Marble, travertines etc.
Marbre, travertins etc.

ISIC-BASED CODE - CODE BASE CITI

2901-04

Unit : Thousand cubic metres

Unité : Milliers de mètres cubes

Country or area	1990	1991	1992	1993	1994	1995	1996	1997	1998	1999	Pays ou zone
Africa											**Afrique**
Algeria[1]	27	31	...	...	...	...	...	...	...	...	Algérie[1]
Cameroon[1]	...	...	...	...	550	550	560	560	580	...	Cameroun[1]
Egypt	40	58	62	16	30	25	58	128	[2][3]27	148	Egypte
Ethiopia[2]	...	...	...	...	[4]184	85	84	93	152		Ethiopie[2]
Madagascar[1][3]	3	3	3	1	1	1	1	1	...	...	Madagascar[1][3]
Mozambique	0	0	1	1	2	1	1	0	0	1	Mozambique
Namibia[1][2][3]	13	10	0	13	12	17	13	14	9	...	Namibie[1][2][3]
Nigeria[3]	2	11	11	[1]3	8	[1]67	[1]29	[1]30	[1]30	...	Nigéria[3]
South Africa[2]	4	[1][3]12	[1][3]17	[1][3]21	[1][3]5	[1][3]1	[1][3]3	...	...	...	Afrique du Sud[2]
America, North											**Amérique du Nord**
Canada[3]	771	641	650	705	728	...	...	...	...	...	Canada[3]
Guatemala[1][2]	15	11	11	7	3	3	1	*3	*3	...	Guatemala[1][2]
Honduras[1][2][4]	84	96	100	95	90	93	94	95	95	...	Honduras[1][2][4]
Mexico[1][3]	681	750	860	[2]987	[2]1086	[2]899	[2]659	[2]517	[2]664	...	Mexique[1][3]
United States[3][5]	26	39	30	36	36	40	28	41	41	40	Etats-Unis[3][5]
America, South											**Amérique du Sud**
Argentina[3]	33	46	31	43	[1]25	[1]25	[1]34	[1]45	[1]45	...	Argentine[3]
Brazil[1][2]	[3]180	[3]200	[3]200	200	200	200	200	200	200	...	Brésil[1][2]
Chile[2][3]	1	1	[1]1	[1]1	[1]2	[1]6	[1]0	[1]1	1	1	Chili[2][3]
Colombia[1][2][3]	32	33	35	35	75	130	170	191	190	...	Colombie[1][2][3]
Ecuador[2][3]	[1]2	[1]2	2	[1]9	[1]10	[1]11	[1]17	[1]1	[1]1	...	Equateur[2][3]
Peru[1]	[3]25	35	15	[2][3]13	[2][3]12	[2][3]15	[2][3]13	[2][3]10	[2][3]10	[2]8	Pérou[1]
Uruguay[1][2][3]	4	4	4	4	5		0	0	...	0	Uruguay[1][2][3]
Venezuela[2][3]	61	129	134	...	...	...	...	...	...	...	Venezuela[2][3]
Asia											**Asie**
Armenia[4]	..	529	120	57	40	51	57	42	43	38	Arménie[4]
Cyprus[3]	82	73	58	75	42	30	21	25	7	2	Chypre[3]
India[2]	1711	1972	2178	2176	2666	3122	3576	*3576	...	...	Inde[2]
Indonesia[1][2]	[4]1	[4]0	[4]2	[4]3	[4]15	10	8	3	142	1	Indonésie[1][2]
Iran(Islamic Rep. of)	[1][3]5470	[1][3]5500	[1][3]5230	[1][3]4010	[1][3]5590	[1][3]5590	*[1][3]5590	*[1][3]5590	*7420	...	Iran(Rép. islamique)
Jordan[1][2]	[3]484	[3]180	[3]200	[3]112	112	112	100	58	135	...	Jordanie[1][2]
Nepal[1]	[2][3]161	[2][3]25	[2][3]20	[2][3]28	[2][3]28	[6]28	[6]692	[6]775	[6]659	[6]653	Népal[1]
Oman[1][2][3]	35	35	54	76	70	145	117	169	170	...	Oman[1][2][3]
Pakistan[3][7]	267	282	...	...	...	...	...	...	...	...	Pakistan[3][7]
Philippines[2][3]	23	65	66	33	13	6	4	3	0	0	Philippines[2][3]
Syrian Arab Republic	43	42	41	53	...	...	...	...	...	...	Rép. arabe syrienne
Thailand[2]	[3]55	[3]75	[3]87	[3]88	[3]87	[3]97	145	51	18	14	Thaïlande[2]
Turkey	26	#116	199	215	204	281	476	413	633	747	Turquie
Yemen[4]	..	44	39	21	11	12	82	83	...	...	Yémen[4]
Europe											**Europe**
Austria[3]	[8]27	[8]28	[8]22	[8]22	[8]22	#433	308	361	400	381	Autriche[3]
Belgium	...	...	...	...	1289	[3]1372	[3]1144	[3]1151	[3]1325	[3]1503	Belgique
Croatia	..	47	41	36	36	35	39	38	35	...	Croatie
France	[2]4	[2]3	[2]2	[2]2	3	...	...	...	...	...	France
Germany(Fed.Rep.)	45	..	..	..	..	..	...	...	..	..	Allemagne(Rép.féd.)
Greece	266	242	220	639	890	585	654	...	...	...	Grèce
Italy	4820	[1]4650	[1]5720	[1][3]4010	[1][3]4110	[1][3]5100	[1][3]5713	[1][3]5600	[1][3]5600	...	Italie
Portugal	[2]316	[2]338	962	896	[3]896	[3]941	[3]945	[3]1084	[3]1323	[3]1338	Portugal
Slovenia[3]	..	17	15	12	11	10	33	28	31	32	Slovénie[3]
Spain[3]	2020	2068	1178	#119641	126677	137199	137556	141637	163482	171752	Espagne[3]
Sweden[3]	6	6	4	2	6	2	...	...	...	...	Suède[3]
Switzerland[3]	8	7	9	5	5	4	...	...	...	...	Suisse[3]
Yugoslavia	..	[4]234	[4]67	[4]72	[4]45	[4]73	[4]63	[4]68	66	40	Yougoslavie
T.F.Yug.Rep. Macedonia	..	18	16	15	13	12	10	8	8	7	L'ex-RY Macédoine

For general note and footnotes, see end of table.

Voir la fin du tableau pour la remarque générale et les notes.

Marble, travertines etc. (continued)
Marbre, travertins etc. (suite)

ISIC-BASED CODE - CODE BASE CITI

2901-04

General Note.

Marble, travertines, ecaussine and other similar hard calcareous monumental and building stone and alabaster, provided that their apparent specific gravity is 2.5 or more (that is, effective weight in kg/1000 cubic cm), presented in the mass or in form of blocks, slabs or sheets. Stones identifiable as mosaic cubes or as paving flagstones are excluded. (SITC, Rev.3: 27312-0).

[1] Source: U. S. Geological Survey, (Washington, D. C.).
[2] Marble only.
[3] In thousand metric tons.
[4] In thousand square metres.
[5] Sold or used by producers.
[6] Incomplete coverage.
[7] Twelve months ending 30 June of year stated.
[8] Including granite, porphyry, sandstone etc.

Remarque générale.

Marbre, travertin, écaussine et autres pierres calcaires dures analogues de taille ou de construction, d'une densité moyenne apparente égale ou supérieure à 2,5 (poids en kg/dm cube), à l'état brut ou sous forme de blocs, moëllons ou plaques, à l'exclusion des cubes pour mosaïques et des dalles de pavage. (CTCI, Rev.3: 27312-0).

[1] Source: U.S. Geological Survey, (Washington, D.C.).
[2] Marbre seulement.
[3] En milliers de tonnes métriques.
[4] En milliers de mètres carrés.
[5] Vendu ou utilisé par les producteurs.
[6] Couverture incomplète.
[7] Période de douze mois finissant le 30 juin de l'année indiquée.
[8] Y compris le granite, le porphyre, le grès, etc.

Granite, porphyry, sandstone etc.
Granite, porphyre, grès etc.

ISIC-BASED CODE - CODE BASE CITI
2901-07

Unit : Thousand metric tons — Unité : Milliers de tonnes métriques

Country or area	1990	1991	1992	1993	1994	1995	1996	1997	1998	1999	Pays ou zone
Africa											**Afrique**
Egypt[1]	242	182	113	128	102	126	108	66	...	...	Egypte[1]
Namibia[2][3]	5	8	7	3	12	5	5	7	7	...	Namibie[2][3]
South Africa[4]	[3]387	[2][3]673	[2][5]575	[2][5]528	[2][5]619	[2][5]718	[2][5]709	[2][5]804	[2][5]669	...	Afrique du Sud[4]
Zimbabwe[2][3]	70	80	91	40	107	122	109	110	126	...	Zimbabwe[2][3]
America, North											**Amérique du Nord**
Canada	19524	16297	19096	17909	16279	...	...	...	...	...	Canada
United States[6]	691	708	665	738	671	640	652	630	605	634	Etats-Unis[6]
America, South											**Amérique du Sud**
Argentina	[7]46	[7]54	[7]54	[7]99	[2]5320	[2]7156	[2]7922	[2]12069	[2]12095	...	Argentine
Brazil[1][2][3]	60000	50300	60000	60000	60000	60000	60000	60000	60000	...	Brésil[1][2][3]
Peru[2][3]	2	2	2	2	2	2	2	2	2	2	Pérou[2][3]
Venezuela	158	270	208	*195	[2][3]264	[2][3]236	[2][3]286	[2][3]400	[2][3]314	...	Venezuela
Asia											**Asie**
Cyprus[8]	208	120	71	472	1320	769	77	28	40	63	Chypre[8]
India[9]	4066	4289	3046	4887	8129	7071	7758	*7758	...	...	Inde[9]
Indonesia[2][3]	*1200	*1200	2907	2767	5129	5386	4827	6138	4801	4107	Indonésie[2][3]
Iran(Islamic Rep. of)	...	15	525	212	[2][3]20	[2][3]20	[2][3]20	[2][3]20	[2][3]40	...	Iran(Rép. islamique)
Korea, Republic of	983	1017	1017	1034	1033	1079	954	859	843	1344	Corée, République de
Pakistan	1436	2520	...	...	...	...	...	...	...	...	Pakistan
Philippines[9]	67	105	106	118	108	119	35	18	18	101	Philippines[9]
Singapore[3]	6371	...	...	...	...	...	...	...	...	...	Singapour[3]
Turkey	...	...	...	...	...	...	251	164	160	189	Turquie
Europe											**Europe**
Austria	...	...	...	...	...	650	599	443	516	594	Autriche
Belgium[3]	3020	2649	3655	3512	[1][2]2105	[1][2]2115	[1][2]2115	[1][2]2115	[1][2]1915	...	Belgique[3]
Denmark[10]	[1]226	...	...	...	26	29	31	20	24	50	Danemark[10]
Czech Republic	..	..	...	...	379	328	340	403	351	188	République tchèque
Finland	161	193	231	236	245	239	194	239	282	296	Finlande
France	352	263	...	...	...	...	...	...	...	...	France
Germany	..	...	...	...	...	85	66	87	246	...	Allemagne
Germany(Fed.Rep.)[1]	25	...	...	..	..	..	..	..	..	...	Allemagne(Rép.féd.)[1]
Greece	...	...	...	1474	1127	1493	1931	...	...	...	Grèce
Hungary	51	34	30	22	25	21	...	#675	531	1282	Hongrie
Italy[2]	4300	4300	3300	2800	2800	2800	1867	1900	1900	...	Italie[2]
Latvia	..	[1]15	[1]20	[1]1	[1]1	[1]6	[1]7	[1]11	[1]6	3	Lettonie
Poland	3775	1748	...	...	...	...	...	...	...	...	Pologne
Portugal	11705	12856	14438	17772	17335	18729	18749	...	555	562	Portugal
Slovakia							12861	14107	...	...	Slovaquie
Slovenia	..	4	4	2	5	5	60	51	58	74	Slovénie
Spain	22322	22314	29015	25072	24776	27053	26014	26795	28740	30176	Espagne
Sweden	106	[2][3]91	86	76	80	67	107	99	102	93	Suède
United Kingdom	...	...	...	595	608	[2][9]19694	[2][9]17522	[2][9]18774	[2][9]18975	...	Royaume-Uni
Yugoslavia	..	...	36	28	24	23	9	16	22	26	Yougoslavie
T.F.Yug.Rep. Macedonia[1]	..	1	1	...	...	...	...	...	...	...	L'ex-RY Macédoine[1]

General Note.

Monumental and building stones, including such stone not further worked than roughly split, roughly squared or squared by sawing, such as granite, porphyry, basalt, sandstone and other hard indigenous rocks. (SITC, Rev.3: 27313-0).

[1] In thousand cubic metres.
[2] Source: U. S. Geological Survey, (Washington, D. C.).
[3] Granite only.
[4] Domestic sales plus exports.
[5] Granite and norite only.
[6] Sold or used by producers.
[7] Granite in blocks only.
[8] Building stone only.
[9] Sandstone only.
[10] Sales.

Remarque générale.

Pierres de taille et de construction, telles que le granit, le porphyre, le basalte, le grès et autres roches dures naturelles, brutes, dégrossies ou simplement débitées par sciage. (CTCI, Rev.3: 27313-0).

[1] En milliers de mètres cubes.
[2] Source: U.S. Geological Survey, (Washington, D.C.).
[3] Granite seulement.
[4] Ventes nationales plus exportations.
[5] Granite et norite seulement.
[6] Vendu ou utilisé par les producteurs.
[7] Granite en blocs seulement.
[8] Pierre de construction seulement.
[9] Grès seulement.
[10] Ventes.

Limestone flux and calcareous stone
Castine et pierres à chaux et à ciment
ISIC-BASED CODE - CODE BASE CITI
2901-10

Unit : Thousand metric tons   Unité : Milliers de tonnes métriques

Country or area	1990	1991	1992	1993	1994	1995	1996	1997	1998	1999	Pays ou zone
Africa											**Afrique**
Cameroon* [1]	57	57	57	[2]57	[2]57	[2]57	[2]50	[2]50	[2]50	...	Cameroun* [1]
Egypt[3]	16000	18000	17000	18000	18000	18000	18000	23000	25000	27000	Egypte[3]
Ethiopia[1][2]	100	90	100	100	700	3215	3300	3300	3400	...	Ethiopie[1][2]
Kenya[1][2]	18	...	...	425	330	331	632	732	732	...	Kenya[1][2]
Malawi[1][2]	113	175	175	126	174	176	134	258	260	...	Malawi[1][2]
Namibia[1][4]	10	...	...	...	...	...	...	...	...	...	Namibie[1][4]
Nigeria	1136	1379	1753	1935	2908	3128	[1]2095	[1]2000	[1]2000	...	Nigéria
South Africa	19944	[1][5]21494	[1][5]19782	[1][5]18215	[1][5]19548	[1][5]19738	[1][5]22038	[1][5]22214	[1][5]19754	...	Afrique du Sud
Zambia[1]	772	739	[2]680	[2]632	[2]668	[2]700	[2]700	[2]700	[2]700	...	Zambie[1]
Zimbabwe[2]	[1]1252	[1]1428	1365	[1]1036	[1]1658	[1]1499	[1]1425	[1]1027	[1]1473	...	Zimbabwe[2]
America, North											**Amérique du Nord**
Belize[1][2]	237	300	300	250	300	310	310	310	315	...	Belize[1][2]
Canada	86519	66471	65522	66437	69769	...	...	...	...	...	Canada
Costa Rica[1]	1600	1300	1300	1500	1500	1500	1500	1500	1600	...	Costa Rica[1]
Dominican Republic[2]	[3]491	[1][3]449	[1][3]589	[1]0	[1]0	[1]0	[1]0	[1]0	[1]0	...	Rép. dominicaine[2]
El Salvador[1][2]	1700	1900	2200	2600	2600	2800	3000	3000	3000	...	El Salvador[1][2]
Guatemala[1][2]	1415	...	...	*1500	1146	1407	1280	*1500	*1500	...	Guatemala[1][2]
Honduras[1][2]	460	500	450	400	400	450	450	450	450	...	Honduras[1][2]
Jamaica	[1][2]6050	[1][2]5480	[1][2]4300	3319	3319	3385	3351	3350	3200	...	Jamaïque
Mexico[1][2]	27400	29500	31800	33985	36020	32873	37641	*43706	44372	...	Mexique[1][2]
Panama[1]	393	338	716	725	757	762	613	326	333	...	Panama[1]
Trinidad and Tobago[1][2]	600	1030	1400	1580	1600	1600	1600	1219	1100	...	Trinité-et-Tobago[1][2]
United States[6]	...	333	375	366	366	363	350	346	373	446	Etats-Unis[6]
America, South											**Amérique du Sud**
Argentina	8299	9012	10573	10740	*11970	*11491	[1][2]12315	[1][2]13439	[1][2]13500	...	Argentine
Brazil[1][2]	60000	60000	60000	60000	60000	60000	60000	60000	60000	...	Brésil[1][2]
Chile	3776	3998	4890	5650	6305	5912	6009	5678	5998	5618	Chili
Colombia[1][2]	17000	15700	16000	15701	14000	19248	14151	13392	15000	...	Colombie[1][2]
Ecuador[1][2]	3890	3660	3160	3707	6229	4089	3491	4261	4200	...	Equateur[1][2]
Paraguay[2]	811	840	850	1020	1060	1133	1145	1107	917	1016	Paraguay[2]
Peru[1][2]	3000	3200	1480	1610	1600	4315	4363	4097	5508	4307	Pérou[1][2]
Uruguay[1][2]	750	750	750	750	750	750	789	1240	1516	...	Uruguay[1][2]
Venezuela[1][2]	12600	11400	14300	14900	11649	12189	15873	14177	13670	...	Venezuela[1][2]
Asia											**Asie**
Bangladesh[7]	38	42	43	23	24	28	21	28	[1]26	[1]27	Bangladesh[7]
Bhutan[1]	220	220	167	[2]190	[2]232	[2]267	[2]275	* [2]270	[2]272	...	Bhoutan[1]
Cyprus	7	7	6	6	7	6	6	6	5	7	Chypre
India	70512	77558	80453	83602	93747	97558	103241	110934	113571	128189	Inde
Indonesia[1][2]	9510	2573	3796	*4000	20814	13143	*15000	6329	6575	15540	Indonésie[1][2]
Iran(Islamic Rep. of)[2]	*18300	13792	15216	20684	*28000	*30131	*31961	*33025	*31015	...	Iran(Rép. islamique)[2]
Japan	198224	206839	203854	200455	202481	201096	202894	201399	183955	180193	Japon
Jordan[1][2]	4	136	115	[3]5336	[3]5340	[3]6000	[3]8000	[3]12388	[3]8031	...	Jordanie[1][2]
Korea, Republic of	50846	59329	60918	66673	76191	74013	88091	92206	71735	...	Corée, République de
Myanmar[2]	41	42	45	53	54	55	[1]54	49	...	...	Myanmar[2]
Nepal[1]	180	222	368	296	350	370	489	369	484	500	Népal[1]
Pakistan	[7]7736	[7]8409	* [1]8760	[1]9074	[1]9096	[1]9769	9740	9492	11167	9467	Pakistan
Philippines[2]	3818	5384	10225	5356	19945	6681	6710	10216	27714	13379	Philippines[2]
Qatar[1][2]	810	...	...	*900	*900	*900	*900	*900	...	...	Qatar[1][2]
Sri Lanka[1][2]	642	621	600	*650	*670	746	813	901	...	...	Sri Lanka[1][2]
Thailand	19697	19782	25609	33040	43882	48248	53085	61401	37494	49358	Thaïlande
Turkey	4221	6784	9201	10852	15608	31174	40458	49686	52047	46251	Turquie
Viet Nam[2]	...	...	...	...	...	1041	992	1069	939	971	Viet Nam[2]
Europe											**Europe**
Austria	...	...	...	...	...	3733	3328	3399	3312	3750	Autriche
Belgium	31893	34256	33394	30941	*33400	[1][2]33000	[1][2]33000	* [1][2]30000	[1][2]30000	...	Belgique
Bulgaria	6185	3922	2887	2894	3556	5258	5354	4970	3537	3382	Bulgarie
Croatia	..	200	405	315	508	728	968	1081	1202	...	Croatie
Denmark[8]	1587	1353	1024	803	955	1092	993	827	697	...	Danemark[8]
Czechoslovakia(former)	12146	7442	...	...	...	...	...	...	...	...	Tchécoslovaquie(anc.)

For general note and footnotes, see end of table.   Voir la fin du tableau pour la remarque générale et les notes.

Limestone flux and calcareous stone (continued)
Castine et pierres à chaux et à ciment (suite)

ISIC-BASED CODE - CODE BASE CITI

2901-10

Unit : Thousand metric tons   Unité : Milliers de tonnes métriques

Country or area	1990	1991	1992	1993	1994	1995	1996	1997	1998	1999	Pays ou zone
Czech Republic	..	..	7232	5515	5272	4959	5233	7170	6886	6610	République tchèque
Estonia	..	6904	3470	1996	2240	2594	2674	2702	3713	3210	Estonie
Finland	4278	3354	2901	2669	2963	3295	3304	2665	2776	2798	Finlande
France	8486	8192	7402	2010	6410	[1]9780	[1]9200	[1]11433	[1]11000	...	France
Germany	..	...	63966	60706	...	24239	24393	22872	21594	...	Allemagne
Germany(Fed.Rep.)	49650	..	..	..	..	..	..	..	..	..	Allemagne(Rép.féd.)
German D.R.(former)	15761	..	..	..	..	..	..	..	..	..	R.D.A. (anc.)
Greece	...	...	...	13038	13195	13262	13499	...	...	...	Grèce
Hungary	8877	5948	4825	5148	5693	5761	4796	4779	4802	5010	Hongrie
Ireland	[2]9258	[1][2]8500	[1][2]9000	[1][2]8500	[1][2]9000	1851	2411	2509	2393	6968	Irlande
Italy[1]	120000	120000	125000	[2]120000	[2]120000	[2]120000	[2]120000	* [2]120000	* [2]120000	...	Italie[1]
Latvia	..	...	...	...	...	...	...	...	363	437	Lettonie
Lithuania	..	...	...	...	...	1162	1035	1003	1462	1078	Lituanie
Malta[1][2]	2400	2350	2300	2200	2200	2000	2000	2000	...	...	Malte[1][2]
Norway	4071	[1][2]4000	[1][2]3500	[1][2]3500	[1][2]4357	...	1094	1593	4131	4290	Norvège
Poland	20581	18455	18769	19692	23361	24292	22607	24455	23219	25109	Pologne
Portugal	21425	21309	21848	22610	24629	[1]15000	[1]35370	[1]15000	[1]15000	...	Portugal
Slovakia	..	..	3045	3723	3729	3833	2327	3078	3291	3159	Slovaquie
Slovenia	..	1055	1041	820	...	...	1325	1187	997	1271	Slovénie
Spain	123626	134946	133895	#0	0	0	0	0	...	0	Espagne
Sweden	3809	*3809	3712	3668	3976	4174	4329	4175	4014	3519	Suède
United Kingdom[2]	12641	94860	89398	93305	102844	94636	86564	87752	89274	91485	Royaume-Uni[2]
Yugoslavia	..	1363	742	574	965	1238	1392	1259	1741	1040	Yougoslavie
T.F.Yug.Rep. Macedonia	..	10	6	3	2	2	1	...	...	...	L'ex-RY Macédoine
Yugoslavia, SFR[1][2]	8500	..	..	..	..	..	..	..	..	..	Yougoslavie, RSF[1][2]
Oceania											**Océanie**
Australia	[7]13283	* [1]12000	* [1]12000	* [1]12000	* [1]12000	* [1]12000	[1]12000	[1]12000	[1]12000	[1]12000	Australie
New Zealand	[1]3000	...	[1]1459	[1]1577	1542	1543	1520	[1]1623	[1]1500	[1]1500	Nouvelle-Zélande

General Note.

Limestone flux and limestone and calcareous rocks commonly used for the manufacture of lime or cement, excluding building or monumental stone. Those materials in powdered form for soil improvement are included. Dolomite and chalk are excluded. (SITC, Rev.3: 27322-0).

Remarque générale.

Castine et pierres à chaux et à ciment proprement dites, à l'exclusion des pierres de taille et de construction. Cette position comprend la pierre utilisée sous forme de poudre pour l'amendement des terres. Elle ne comprend pas la dolomie et la craie. (CTCI, Rev.3: 27322-0).

[1] Source: U. S. Geological Survey, (Washington, D. C.).
[2] Limestone only.
[3] In thousand cubic metres.
[4] Including marble.
[5] Including dolomite.
[6] Sold or used by producers.
[7] Twelve months ending 30 June of year stated.
[8] Sales.

[1] Source: U.S. Geological Survey, (Washington, D.C.).
[2] Calcaire seulement.
[3] En milliers de mètres cubes.
[4] Y compris le marbre.
[5] Y compris la dolomie.
[6] Vendu ou utilisé par les producteurs.
[7] Période de douze mois finissant le 30 juin de l'année indiquée.
[8] Ventes.

Sand, silica and quartz
Sables, siliceux et quartzeux

ISIC-BASED CODE - CODE BASE CITI

2901-13

Unit : Thousand metric tons   Unité : Milliers de tonnes métriques

Country or area	1990	1991	1992	1993	1994	1995	1996	1997	1998	1999	Pays ou zone
Africa											**Afrique**
Egypt[1][2]	13000	16000	14000	14000	30000	14000	17000	21000	20000	21000	Egypte[1][2]
Ethiopia[3]	[1]1250	[1]1000	[1]700	[1]1000	[4]6040	[1]1600	[1]1600	[1]1600	...	...	Ethiopie[3]
Nigeria	1	1	1	1	1	...	...	...	...	...	Nigéria
South Africa[3]	[5]1986	[5]2068	[5]1750	1738	1920	2180	2167	[6]2479	[6]3000	...	Afrique du Sud[3]
Zambia[3][4]	1000	...	...	...	...	...	...	...	...	...	Zambie[3][4]
America, North											**Amérique du Nord**
Belize	206	...	...	...	...	...	...	...	...	...	Belize
Canada[3]	[7]2081	[7]1495	[7]1754	[7]1600	[6]1600	[6]1689	[6]1558	[6]1690	[6]1700	...	Canada[3]
Costa Rica[3][4]	1020	...	...	1200	1400	1500	1400	1400	...	...	Costa Rica[3][4]
Cuba[3]	* [8]500	* [8]500	* [8]450	* [8]400	[6]300	[6]300	[6]300	[6]300	[6]300	...	Cuba[3]
Dominica	...	...	...	51	59	51	...	...	...	...	Dominique
Guatemala	[3][9]30	[3][9]17	[3][9]34	[3][9]27	17	107	67	81	[3]50	...	Guatemala
Jamaica	...	...	[3]20	[3]21	[3]18	20	16	12	[3][6]12	...	Jamaïque
Mexico[10]	*1000	...	[3]1129	[3]1310	[3]1361	[3]1292	[3]1425	[3]1564	[3]1600	...	Mexique[10]
Nicaragua[3][4]	1064	...	...	...	...	...	...	...	...	...	Nicaragua[3][4]
Panama[3][9]	15	18	23	23	23	23	23	23	23	...	Panama[3][9]
United States[11][12]	851852	731200	859200	895200	918300	935200	941800	980500	1098200	1138900	Etats-Unis[11][12]
America, South											**Amérique du Sud**
Argentina	10226	11378	11931	16858	[1][3]14615	[1][3]16012	[1][3]16872	[1][3]16850	...	...	Argentine
Chile[13]	542	486	484	459	543	597	583	554	641	577	Chili[13]
Colombia[3]	703	...	...	850	850	900	900	900	...	...	Colombie[3]
Ecuador[3]	52	[5]33	[5]36	[5]49	[5]34	[5]26	[5]24	[5]43	[5]40	...	Equateur[3]
Peru[3][8]	...	...	152	115	100	92	76	80	...	...	Pérou[3][8]
Suriname[1][3]	160	...	...	...	...	...	...	...	...	...	Suriname[1][3]
Uruguay[3][4]	2000	...	...	...	...	...	...	...	...	...	Uruguay[3][4]
Venezuela	254	176	61	483	102	[3]679	[3]763	[3]885	[3]900	...	Venezuela
Asia											**Asie**
Armenia[2]	..	1478	322	126	199	38	40	186	83	61	Arménie[2]
Brunei Darussalam	743	724	653	844	1007	1285	1789	1872	...	...	Brunéi Darussalam
Georgia[2]	..	...	509	127	26	43	55	117	167	90	Géorgie[2]
India[14]	3458	3516	3613	3619	3220	3125	3473	3779	4607	5539	Inde[14]
Indonesia[3]	...	...	[8]400	240	588	279	300	320	300	...	Indonésie[3]
Iran(Islamic Rep. of)	...	61359	70400	69764	...	...	...	...	...	...	Iran(Rép. islamique)
Israel[15][16]	94	...	...	...	...	...	...	...	...	...	Israël[15][16]
Korea, Republic of[1][2]	30970	48670	34588	39730	49179	55864	61984	65423	47607	52169	Corée, République de[1][2]
Kyrgyzstan[2]	...	2463	969	606	182	214	160	194	246	283	Kirghizistan[2]
Pakistan	[17]136	[17]143	[3][8]135	[3][8]168	[3][8]170	[3][8]170	[3][8]165	[3][8]165	...	158	Pakistan
Philippines	[5]256	275	745	103	130	118	31	21	16	[5]64	Philippines
Sri Lanka[13]	1	...	...	...	...	...	...	...	...	...	Sri Lanka[13]
Syrian Arab Republic[2][4]	13210	12374	11242	20178	23636	20636	21558	16277	18549	28040	Rép. arabe syrienne[2][4]
Tajikistan[2]	..	1627	991	744	474	286	78	94	81	214	Tadjikistan[2]
Thailand	444	678	612	477	481	337	457	521	328	535	Thaïlande
Turkey	1792	2144	1916	1713	2113	2103	4026	2837	3408	3725	Turquie
Turkmenistan	..	2304	1908	2055	1856	1788	1506	1252	1424	...	Turkménistan
Viet Nam[2][18]	...	...	...	...	...	14363	17147	22395	25431	28988	Viet Nam[2][18]
Europe											**Europe**
Austria	16337	18027	17474	16927	19104	# [13]1516	[13]1380	[13]1432	[13]1278	[13]1552	Autriche
Belgium[19]	14693	14922	14725	14063	...	...	...	...	...	...	Belgique[19]
Bulgaria[2][20]	32224	9466	8406	8069	8701	9759	9069	7522	...	...	Bulgarie[2][20]
Croatia	..	177	40	23	31	32	44	164	152	...	Croatie
Denmark[21]	[2]2616	[2]2170	[2]1923	[2]1741	1887	1671	2070	3600	3868	4661	Danemark[21]
Czech Republic	..	...	...	...	...	...	1619	1869	1758		République tchèque
Estonia	..	5073	2140	404	1380	585	962	1819	1793	1423	Estonie
Finland	711	351	255	330	328	321	705	...	...	73	Finlande
France[22]	89071	87750	80804	88915	75699	187229	169784	170955	173739	...	France[22]
Germany	..	181336	...	206672	235904	* #[9]113	9455	8953	8795	...	Allemagne
Germany(Fed.Rep.)	153871		...	..	..	...	...	...	...	...	Allemagne(Rép.féd.)
Greece	[3][5]94	...	...	402	343	...	...	...	...	...	Grèce
Hungary	1750	1621	847	...	875	1723	1615	1815	1634	2831	Hongrie

For general note and footnotes, see end of table.   Voir la fin du tableau pour la remarque générale et les notes.

Sand, silica and quartz (continued)
Sables, siliceux et quartzeux (suite)

ISIC-BASED CODE - CODE BASE CITI

2901-13

Unit : Thousand metric tons / Unité : Milliers de tonnes métriques

Country or area	1990	1991	1992	1993	1994	1995	1996	1997	1998	1999	Pays ou zone
Iceland	4200	...		[2,3,4]3600	[2,3,4]3600	[2,3,4]3600	[2,3,4]3600	[2,3,4]3600	...	...	Islande
Italy[3,5]	*4300	*4200	*4000	3100	2700	3000	2950	3000	3000	...	Italie[3,5]
Latvia	..	[2,23]2572	[2,23]859	[2,23]439	[2]176	[2]137	[2]183	[2]168	[2]229	5	Lettonie
Luxembourg[1]	760	...	...	...	...	...	...	...	...	...	Luxembourg[1]
Netherlands[24]	25137	24480	23237	#[25]1163	[25]3695	[25]6958	[25]8717	[25]11868	[25]14843	[25]13555	Pays-Bas[24]
Norway	...	...	...	...	...	...	...	1327	1188	862	Norvège
Poland	[13]33	[13]29	[13]31	56	40	14	55	78	27	9	Pologne
Portugal	2060	2663	3170	4508	4334						Portugal
Republic of Moldova[2]	..	2583	1217	[26]331	[26]256	[26]229	[26]218	[26]265	[26]263	[26]261	Rép. de Moldova[2]
Romania	2081	1607	978	864	831	909	907	713	1049	763	Roumanie
Russian Federation	..	653518	463108	343087	266426	[2]68571	[2]48556	[2]44243	[2]40624	[2]40286	Fédération de Russie
Slovenia	..	328	324	229	281	303	286	282	295	318	Slovénie
Spain	[3,4]3843	[3,4]2945	3169	2506	2577	1918	2808	2892	3492	3631	Espagne
Sweden	...	...	...	...	388	428	366	374	395	388	Suède
Ukraine		[1,2]50550	[1,2]31725	[1,2]23382	[1,2]20775	[1,2]8520	[1,2]4027	[1,2]3709	[1,2]3498	[1]3570	Ukraine
United Kingdom	[18,27]11617	[18,27]97918	...	3587	...	4343	4861	[3]4800	[3]4800	...	Royaume-Uni
Yugoslavia	..	2002	1013	218	271	273	1169	351	524	322	Yougoslavie
T.F.Yug.Rep. Macedonia	..	123	111	69	99	94	77	48	39	8	L'ex-RY Macédoine
Oceania											**Océanie**
Australia	[17]33856	...	...	[3]32000	[3]32500	[3]32500	[3]32500	*[3]32500	...	...	Australie
New Caledonia[28]	96	127	181	76	102	...	...	...	...	...	Nouvelle-Calédonie[28]
New Zealand	415	...	500	720	361	659	533	...	...	...	Nouvelle-Zélande

General Note.
Commercially-extracted sand used in building, in glass industry, for cleaning metals etc. (SITC, Rev.3: 27331-0).

Remarque générale.
Sables provenant d'exploitations commerciales, utilisés dans la construction, la verrerie, le décapage des métaux, etc. (CTCI, Rev.3: 27331-0).

[1] Sand only.
[2] In thousand cubic metres.
[3] Source: U. S. Geological Survey, (Washington, D. C.).
[4] Sand and gravel.
[5] Silica only.
[6] Industrial sand and gravel.
[7] Silica and quartz only.
[8] Including gravel.
[9] Silica and sand only.
[10] Quartz and glass sand only.
[11] Industrial sand and construction sand and gravel.
[12] Sold or used by producers.
[13] Quartz only.
[14] Twelve months beginning 1 April of year stated.
[15] Excluding silica.
[16] Marketed local production.
[17] Twelve months ending 30 June of year stated.
[18] Including gravel, excluding quartz and silica.
[19] Sand and quartz only.
[20] Including gravel and crushed stone.
[21] Sales.
[22] Industrial sand from quarries and alluvial sand. Excluding crushed sand.
[23] Sand only, excluding sand used in glass industry.
[24] Industrial sand only.
[25] Production by establishments employing 20 or more persons.
[26] Excluding Transnistria region.
[27] Great Britain only.
[28] Calcareous sand of coral origin.

[1] Sable seulement.
[2] En milliers de mètres cubes.
[3] Source: U.S. Geological Survey, (Washington, D.C.).
[4] Sable et gravier.
[5] Silice seulement.
[6] Sable et gravier industriels.
[7] Silice et quartz seulement.
[8] Y compris les graviers.
[9] Silice et sable seulement.
[10] Quartz et sable utilisé dans la verrerie seulement.
[11] Sable industriel et de construction, et gravier.
[12] Vendu ou utilisé par les producteurs.
[13] Quartz seulement.
[14] Période de douze mois commençant le 1er avril de l'année indiquée.
[15] Non compris la silice.
[16] Production locale commercialisée.
[17] Période de douze mois finissant le 30 juin de l'année indiquée.
[18] Y compris les graviers. Non compris le quartz et la silice.
[19] Sables et quartz seulement.
[20] Y compris les graviers et les pierres concassées.
[21] Ventes.
[22] Sables industriels de carrières et sables d'alluvions. Les sables de concassage sont exclus.
[23] Sable seulement, non compris le sable utilisé pour l'industrie du verre.
[24] Sables industriels seulement.
[25] Production des établissements occupant 20 personnes ou plus.
[26] Non compris la région de Transnistrie.
[27] Grande Bretagne seulement.
[28] Sable calcaire d'origine corallienne.

Gravel and crushed stone
Graviers et pierres concassées

ISIC-BASED CODE - CODE BASE CITI

2901-16

Unit : Thousand metric tons

Unité : Milliers de tonnes métriques

Country or area	1990	1991	1992	1993	1994	1995	1996	1997	1998	1999	Pays ou zone
Africa											**Afrique**
Algeria[1][2]	4974	4691	5353	5106	5419	5531	4805	4220	3881	3709	Algérie[1][2]
Botswana[1][2]	755	1124	994	*910	*712	973	845	1092	997	1466	Botswana[1][2]
Dem. Rep. of Congo[3][4]	450	360	280	200	200	200	200	200	200	...	Rép. dém. du Congo[3][4]
Egypt[2][5]	14000	8000	7000	7000	31000	9000	10000	12000	12000	13000	Egypte[2][5]
Ethiopia[2]	...	...	...	...	...	...	...	...	56	50	Ethiopie[2]
Madagascar[2]	...	...	...	...	17	21	14	15	13	...	Madagascar[2]
Swaziland[2]	*155	*129	*233	254	185	[3]114	[3]221	[3]456	[3]453	...	Swaziland[2]
Zambia[3][6]	500	500	500	500	117	200	200	200	200	...	Zambie[3][6]
America, North											**Amérique du Nord**
Antigua and Barbuda	...	...	...	...	...	...	119	90	...	...	Antigua-et-Barbuda
Canada	[3][6]244316	[3][6]214410	[3][6]238134	[3][6]237000	[3][6]247148	[3][6]228163	[6]213831	*225495	217650	...	Canada
Costa Rica[3][6]	1020	1050	1100	1200	1400	1500	1400	1400	...	...	Costa Rica[3][6]
Guatemala	[3][6]2388	521	533	1238	1019	1207	1387	1045	1197	...	Guatemala
Jamaica	[3][6]2380	[3][6]1210	[3][6]1350	[3][6]1549	700	1800	836	1928	[7]1840	...	Jamaïque
Mexico[2][3][6]	82400	83700	88900	91311	95881	83056	95523	103740	98650	...	Mexique[2][3][6]
Panama[3]	470	1940	2450	[6]2500	[6]2700	[6]3000	[6]3000	[6]3000	[6]3000	...	Panama[3]
Trinidad and Tobago[2][6]	548	...	...	...	...	...	...	...	...	...	Trinité-et-Tobago[2][6]
United States[8][9]	1108580	997000	1050000	1120000	1230000	1260000	1330000	1410000	1510000	1540000	Etats-Unis[8][9]
America, South											**Amérique du Sud**
Argentina	*3700	[3][5]7150	[3][5]6810	[3][5]7800	[3][5]8391	[3][5]5819	[3][5]5550	[3][5]6062	[3][5]6000	...	Argentine
French Guiana[3][6]	2800	3000	2400	2400	3000	...	...	...	...	...	Guyane française[3][6]
Guyana[3][4]	42	55	73	75	136	136	136	136	136	...	Guyana[3][4]
Suriname[3]	85	85	85	85	85	85	85	85	85	...	Suriname[3]
Uruguay[3][5]	500	500	500	500	500	500	#17700	40109	40192	...	Uruguay[3][5]
Venezuela[6]	3735	3688	4096	2071	1398	[3]4629	[3]3660	[3]4218	[3]3681	...	Venezuela[6]
Asia											**Asie**
Armenia[2]	..	3198	775	221	174	52	72	150	90	94	Arménie[2]
Brunei Darussalam	335	347	291	631	1708	1812	1757	1326	...	...	Brunéi Darussalam
Cyprus[1]	5250	5450	6120	6300	6000	6200	7290	6990	8400	9150	Chypre[1]
Georgia[2]	..	...	48	4	2	21	19	11	...	1	Géorgie[2]
India	...	...	...	1284	3116	2590	2608	*2608	...	...	Inde
Israel	[6]14554	[3][4]17100	[3][4]17100	[3][6]31515	[3][6]31500	[3][6]31500	[3][6]31500	[3][6]31500	[3][6]31500	...	Israël
Korea, Republic of[2][5]	22124	30958	22989	17599	13575	7348	8356	3798	1828	1541	Corée, République de[2][5]
Kyrgyzstan[2]	..	4091	1610	562	266	209	134	229	229	272	Kirghizistan[2]
Oman[3][6]	...	5900	6540	*7000	*8000	9395	9629	9800	9800	...	Oman[3][6]
Pakistan	...	[5][10]8	...	...	[3]170	[3]170	[3]165	[3]165	[3]170	17	Pakistan
Philippines[6]	31345	31353	31573	33385	32956	56310	74893	80060	71254	64841	Philippines[6]
Syrian Arab Republic[2][11]	799	1276	1051	1075	982	1358	1156	279	151	153	Rép. arabe syrienne[2][11]
Tajikistan[2]	..	3233	1524	877	566	435	132	87	116	...	Tadjikistan[2]
Turkmenistan	..	7273	7187	5473	4452	3738	3355	3061	2866	...	Turkménistan
Europe											**Europe**
Austria	14772	17066	17148	18187	14344	#41324	47977	47797	44960	47241	Autriche
Belgium	10171	10828	12203	10762	28631	29616	26889	25431	25939	29959	Belgique
Croatia	..	5286	4216	4066	4212	4392	5347	12317	13470	...	Croatie
Denmark	[2][12]8659	...	[2][12]9511	...	[12]12311	[2][3]25000	[2][3]23000	[2][3]23000	[2][3]23000	...	Danemark
Czechoslovakia(former)	46681	25175	..	..	..	..	..	..	..	..	Tchécoslovaquie(anc.)
Czech Republic	..	..	15693	20755	16637	19399	24553	25244	23313	23219	République tchèque
Estonia	..	5014	1396	658	599	711	584	671	1363	955	Estonie
Finland	*40505	33824	29606	29960	27232	28208	28475	40993	42084	34212	Finlande
France	156556	163845	149790	159768	154890	[3][6]181000	[3][6]165200	[3][6]170560	[3][6]171500	...	France
Germany	...	...	...	...	321452	...	...	...	...	...	Allemagne
German D.R.(former)[7]	69452	...	...	...	...	...	...	...	...	...	R.D.A. (anc.)[7]
Greece	...	...	...	41149	39613	36495	38922	...	123	...	Grèce
Hungary	9582	6317	9702	9100	11155	14996	13635	14688	14064	16843	Hongrie
Iceland	24	23	18	19	19	17	[2][3][6]3600	[2][3][6]3600	[2][3][6]3600	...	Islande
Ireland	[7]7762	[3][6]7000	[3][6]7000	[3][6]7500	[3][6]7800	[6]13823	[6]19281	[6]22205	[6]25173	30782	Irlande
Latvia	..	[2]4834	[2]1438	[2]476	582	758	894	832	1060	1660	Lettonie
Luxembourg[13]	345	...	...	...	...	...	...	...	...	...	Luxembourg[13]
Netherlands	8805	7212	6543	[14]4903	[14]5380	[14]5020	[14]6025	[14]6855	[14]6345	[14]6943	Pays-Bas

For general note and footnotes, see end of table.

Voir la fin du tableau pour la remarque générale et les notes.

Gravel and crushed stone (continued)
Graviers et pierres concassées (suite)

ISIC-BASED CODE - CODE BASE CITI

2901-16

Unit : Thousand metric tons / Unité : Milliers de tonnes métriques

Country or area	1990	1991	1992	1993	1994	1995	1996	1997	1998	1999	Pays ou zone
Norway[1]	4525	...	...	...	...	...	...	...	...	...	Norvège[1]
Poland	13560	12414	13617	11284	12808	13388	15230	17018	15847	18205	Pologne
Republic of Moldova[2]	..	788	312	[15]62	[15]103	[15]110	[15]84	[15]57	[15]38	[15]24	Rép. de Moldova[2]
Romania[2]	12699	12567	6202	5197	5871	6798	6422	5340	3500	3104	Roumanie[2]
Russian Federation[2]	..	300815	282158	166181	130101	121195	101726	91235	88448	94394	Fédération de Russie[2]
Slovakia	..	..	...	4423	3969	4720	10360	8817	9818	6870	Slovaquie
Slovenia	..	[2]2837	[2]917	[2]2928	[2]3182	[2]3786	9577	9702	9996	12168	Slovénie
Sweden	33255	37481	25850	27479	22411	32173	26804	30817	35721	40609	Suède
Switzerland	155	...	...	...	...	23705	21756	21138	14875	18100	Suisse
Ukraine	..	[2]135425	[2]114271	[2]63077	[2]42952	[2]35404	23232	[2]21593	24784	20738	Ukraine
United Kingdom	...	...	...	221906	239566	202054	179600	[3][4]197900	...	...	Royaume-Uni
Yugoslavia[2]	..	1868	1427	594	687	692	818	1161	1334	789	Yougoslavie[2]
T.F.Yug.Rep. Macedonia[2]	..	107	88	69	83	86	95	86	71	82	L'ex-RY Macédoine[2]
Yugoslavia, SFR	10735	...	...	..	..	..	..	..	..	..	Yougoslavie, RSF
Oceania											**Océanie**
Australia	[10]89257	[3]80000	[3]80000	[3]80000	[3]80000	[3]80000	[3]80000	[3]80000	[3]80000	[3]80000	Australie
Fiji[2][3][6]	839	800	73	427	148	...	...	...	...	...	Fidji[2][3][6]
New Caledonia[2]	224	240	189	408	454	...	...	...	...	...	Nouvelle-Calédonie[2]
New Zealand	[3]18000	...	[3]17872	[3]20124	19147	22553	23342	...	...	...	Nouvelle-Zélande

General Note.

Pebbles and crushed or broken stone, gravel, macadam and tarred macadam of a kind commonly used for concrete aggregates, for road metalling or for railway or other ballast. Flint and shingle are included. (SITC, Rev.3: 27340-0).

Remarque générale.

Cailloux et pierres broyées ou concassées, graviers, macadam avec ou sans enrobement, du type communément utilisé comme granulats pour le béton, comme matériel d'empierrement des routes et comme ballast pour les voies de chemin de fer ou autres, y compris les silex et les galets. (CTCI, Rev.3: 27340-0).

[1] Including sand.
[2] In thousand cubic metres.
[3] Source: U. S. Geological Survey, (Washington, D. C.).
[4] Crushed stone.
[5] Gravel only.
[6] Sand and gravel.
[7] Including sand, silica and quartz.
[8] Crushed stone and industrial gravel.
[9] Sold or used by producers.
[10] Twelve months ending 30 June of year stated.
[11] Stone only.
[12] Sales.
[13] Excluding crushed stone.
[14] Production by establishments employing 20 or more persons.
[15] Excluding Transnistria region.

[1] Y compris le sable.
[2] En milliers de mètres cubes.
[3] Source: U.S. Geological Survey, (Washington, D.C.).
[4] Pierres concassées.
[5] Graviers seulement.
[6] Sable et gravier.
[7] Y compris sable, silice et quartz.
[8] Pierres concassées et graviers industriels.
[9] Vendu ou utilisé par les producteurs.
[10] Période de douze mois finissant le 30 juin de l'année indiquée.
[11] Pierres seulement.
[12] Ventes.
[13] Non compris les pierres concassées.
[14] Production des établissements occupant 20 personnes ou plus.
[15] Non compris la région de Transnistria.

Clay (total production)
Argile (production totale)

ISIC-BASED CODE - CODE BASE CITI

2901-19

Unit : Thousand metric tons   Unité : Milliers de tonnes métriques

Country or area	1990	1991	1992	1993	1994	1995	1996	1997	1998	1999	Pays ou zone
Africa	**8770**	**11975**	**11181**	**11886**	**11980**	**11809**	**12716**	**16846**	**10955**	**11802**	**Afrique**
Algeria	71	57	*60	37	*47	*49	[1]47	[1]40	[1]33	39	Algérie
Burundi	[1]5	7	[1]10	* [1]5	* [1]5	*1	* [1]1	* [1]1	* [1]1	1	Burundi
Egypt	7534	10775	10041	10638	10706	10509	11358	15482	9715	10687	Egypte
Ethiopia[1][2]	*1	*0	*0	*1	*0	*0	*0	*0	0	...	Ethiopie[1][2]
Kenya	0	0	1	2	...	1	1	[1]1	[1]1	...	Kenya
Madagascar	* [1]0	* [1]0	* [1]1	* [1]1	* [1]1	* [1]1	* [1]2	* [1]2	* [1]2	2	Madagascar
Morocco	[1]56	[1]47	[1]46	[1]49	[1]48	[1]44	[1]57	*74	*61	*65	Maroc
Mozambique	9	34	0	100	1	8	12	13	14	11	Mozambique
Nigeria	31	51	53	62	105	97	[1]102	[1]100	110	110	Nigéria
Senegal	* [1]115	* [1]129	* [1]112	* [1]119	* [1]119	* [1]120	* [1]120	* [1]100	* [1]100	80	Sénégal
South Africa	[1]490	[1]414	[1]415	[1]393	[1]421	452	474	491	422	310	Afrique du Sud
Tunisia[1]	350	...	...	...	...	...	...	...	...	...	Tunisie[1]
United Rep.Tanzania* [1]	2	2	1	0	0	0	0	...	...	...	Rép. Unie de Tanzanie* [1]
Zambia[1]	6	...	...	...	...	...	...	...	...	...	Zambie[1]
Zimbabwe	100	103	[1]85	123	[1]170	[1]171	[1]186	[1]186	[1]140	140	Zimbabwe
America, North	**43806**	**41934**	**41103**	**41628**	**43164**	**44033**	**44004**	**42862**	**42944**	**43912**	**Amérique du Nord**
Costa Rica[1]	*200	...	...	...	401	410	410	412	415	...	Costa Rica[1]
Guatemala	* [1]11	* [1]15	* [1]16	* [1]15	* [1]4	* [1]5	* [1]5	* [1]5	* [1]4	4	Guatemala
Mexico	[1]331	[1]353	[1]321	[1]347	[1]352	[1]311	[1]366	[1]398	[1]573	747	Mexique
Panama[1]	212	...	...	...	407	307	123	47	52	...	Panama[1]
United States[3]	43052	41000	40200	40700	42000	43000	43100	42000	41900	42200	Etats-Unis[3]
America, South	**6589**	**6539**	**7088**	**8961**	**12636**	**13127**	**6666**	**11051**	**11036**	**13551**	**Amérique du Sud**
Argentina	2606	2703	3134	4535	3797	3470	[1]390	[1]352	[1]262	...	Argentine
Brazil	* [1]1151	* [1]1061	* [1]943	* [1]1030	* [1]1184	* [1]1218	* [1]1245	* [1]1505	1592	1592	Brésil
Chile	34	65	60	68	74	12	14	15	13	...	Chili
Colombia* [1]	1920	1984	2050	2100	6700	7300	3957	8040	8000	...	Colombie* [1]
Ecuador[1]	8	12	6	12	7	45	87	*50	*50	...	Equateur[1]
Paraguay* [1]	74	74	74	74	74	66	17	67	67	...	Paraguay* [1]
Peru* [1]	53	22	15	15	36	35	33	30	27	...	Pérou* [1]
Uruguay[1]	150	...	...	150	150	150	41	59	41	...	Uruguay[1]
Venezuela	593	512	700	977	614	...	...	...	...	...	Venezuela
Asia	**6552**	**6792**	**7065**	**8138**	**7429**	**10532**	**13012**	**12915**	**10235**	**10760**	**Asie**
Armenia* [1]	..	...	...	...	...	...	3	3	3	...	Arménie* [1]
Azerbaijan	..	104	101	84	79	40	46	39	39	0	Azerbaïdjan
Bangladesh[4]	[1]7	7	2	2	3	7	7	9	[1]8	[1]8	Bangladesh[4]
Hong Kong SAR	17	...	...	...	...	...	...	...	...	...	Hong-Kong RAS
Cyprus	428	441	463	458	403	407	390	372	344	394	Chypre
India	871	874	767	1819	911	1036	968	[1]843	[1]992	[1]977	Inde
Indonesia[1]	166	162	249	56	67	40	41	[5]656	[5]9	[5]27	Indonésie[1]
Iran(Islamic Rep. of)	[1]115	[1]124	[1]330	[1]398	[1]300	[1]321	450	[1]615	[1]605	715	Iran(Rép. islamique)
Israel[1]	*46	*57	...	*40	40	40	40	40	40	40	Israël[1]
Japan	977	893	* [1]809	765	783	765	*610	*561	*578	*558	Japon
Jordan[1]	39	...	...	...	...	...	...	...	...	...	Jordanie[1]
Korea, Republic of	115	111	116	106	138	117	160	154	113	...	Corée, République de
Malaysia[1]	153	187	245	250	253	211	*210	187	*181	209	Malaisie[1]
Myanmar[6]	5	2	2	3	2	2	6	5	2	1	Myanmar[6]
Pakistan[4]	1895	2111	...	...	...	...	...	...	...	...	Pakistan[4]
Philippines	...	...	[1]795	[1]710	[1]807	[1]817	[1]814	[1]815	13	10	Philippines
Sri Lanka	28	21	18	22	[1]8	[1]16	[1]8	[1]20	[1]24	25	Sri Lanka
Thailand	348	382	487	614	534	610	711	521	417	371	Thaïlande
Turkey	456	400	500	666	956	3958	6406	5933	4725	5129	Turquie
Viet Nam	75	99	76	...	...	...	...	...	...	...	Viet Nam
Europe	**62359**	**57478**	**52086**	**51921**	**40068**	**51954**	**52102**	**56938**	**56741**	**62179**	**Europe**
Austria	473	351	460	415	527	454	205	304	275	239	Autriche
Belgium	[2]161	[2]188	[2]171	[2]139	* [1]300	* [1]300	* [1]300	* [1]300	* [1]300	* [1]300	Belgique
Bulgaria	315	346	195	196	241	360	375	352	418	559	Bulgarie
Croatia	..	32	11	9	10	7	10	13	14	...	Croatie
Denmark[7]	[1][2]17	[2]17	...	...	*10	*12	*11	*3	*3	10	Danemark[7]
Czechoslovakia(former)	872	705	..	...	...	...	...	...	...	..	Tchécoslovaquie(anc.)

For general note and footnotes, see end of table.   Voir la fin du tableau pour la remarque générale et les notes.

Clay (total production) (continued)
Argile (production totale) (suite)

ISIC-BASED CODE - CODE BASE CITI

2901-19

Unit : Thousand metric tons / Unité : Milliers de tonnes métriques

Country or area	1990	1991	1992	1993	1994	1995	1996	1997	1998	1999	Pays ou zone
Czech Republic	..	..	598	702	1327	1519	1465	1636	1791	1404	République tchèque
Estonia	..	534	292	169	200	108	109	210	298	335	Estonie
Finland	20	18	8	11	11	18	19	...	...	...	Finlande
France	450	382	339	272	312	[1]390	[1]371	[1]377	[1]375	[1]390	France
Germany	..	8127	...	8330	8751	6221	6031	6405	5988	..	Allemagne
Germany(Fed.Rep.)	8538	..	...	..	..	..	..	..	..	..	Allemagne(Rép.féd.)
Greece	[5]234	[5]190	[5]174	1915	1590	2385	2861	...	...	...	Grèce
Hungary	[5]74	[5]71	[5]21	[5]19	[5]21	[5]23	[5]22	#1442	926	1127	Hongrie
Italy	982	934	622	851	1082	1428	1451	1477	1680	1821	Italie
Latvia	..	...	...	..	..	..	..	...	...	266	Lettonie
Poland	523	443	362	316	319	275	248	199	175	140	Pologne
Portugal	1053	1074	1267	1534	1328	1628	2074	3637	3787	3806	Portugal
Romania	7799	6276	4313	4244	4199	203	158	116	100	78	Roumanie
Russian Federation	..	430	347	478	401	486	398	468	459	905	Fédération de Russie
Slovakia	..	..	...	...	...	...	...	158	74	63	Slovaquie
Slovenia	..	23	29	29	13	10	#297	385	347	357	Slovénie
Spain	19840	17807	18657	14929	13866	16187	18180	18657	20617	21608	Espagne
Sweden	0	0	..	...	..	...	...	36	71	64	Suède
Ukraine	..	1402	1022	678	534	580	587	866	435	648	Ukraine
United Kingdom	[8]20798	[8]17649	...	16230	4545	18893	16447	[1]15749	[1]13955	...	Royaume-Uni
Yugoslavia	..	153	103	38	70	57	68	64	75	40	Yougoslavie
T.F.Yug.Rep. Macedonia	..	60	31	8	12	11	16	23	28	20	L'ex-RY Macédoine
Yugoslavia, SFR	210	..	..	..	..	..	..	..	..	..	Yougoslavie, RSF
USSR (former)* [1][5]	4500	..	..	..	..	..	..	..	..	..	URSS (anc.)* [1][5]
Oceania	**7968**	**9556**	**9559**	**9912**	**9895**	**9648**	**9649**	**9632**	**9835**	**9869**	**Océanie**
Australia	[4]7866	...	...	[1]9755	[1]9775	[1]9596	[1]9596	[1]9597	[1]9795	[1]9825	Australie
New Zealand	[1]102	...	[1]83	[1]157	120	52	53	[1]35	[1]40	...	Nouvelle-Zélande
Total	**140544**	**134273**	**128081**	**132446**	**125172**	**141103**	**138148**	**150243**	**141746**	**152072**	**Total**

General Note.

All natural crude clayey substances consisting of earth or rocks of sedimentation origin with basis of aluminium silicates such as kaolin, bentonite, andalusite etc. Expanded clays are excluded. (SITC, Rev.3: 27826-0, 27827-0, 27829-0).

[1] Source: U. S. Geological Survey, (Washington, D. C.).
[2] Kaolin only.
[3] Sold or used by producers.
[4] Twelve months ending 30 June of year stated.
[5] Kaolin and bentonite only.
[6] Government production only.
[7] Sales.
[8] Great Britain only.

Remarque générale.

Toutes substances argileuses naturelles à l'état brut, constituées de roches ou terres sédimentaires à base silico-alumineuse telles que le kaolin, la bentonite, l'andalousite etc., à l'exclusion des argiles expansées. (CTCI, Rev.3: 27826-0,27827-0,27829-0).

[1] Source: U.S. Geological Survey, (Washington, D.C.).
[2] Kaolin seulement.
[3] Vendu ou utilisé par les producteurs.
[4] Période de douze mois finissant le 30 juin de l'année indiquée.
[5] Kaolin et bentonite seulement.
[6] Production de l'Etat seulement.
[7] Ventes.
[8] Grande Bretagne seulement.

Bentonite
Bentonite

ISIC-BASED CODE - CODE BASE CITI

2901-191

Unit : Thousand metric tons · Unité : Milliers de tonnes métriques

Country or area	1990	1991	1992	1993	1994	1995	1996	1997	1998	1999	Pays ou zone
Africa	**233**	**244**	**174**	**273**	**294**	**302**	**307**	**348**	**250**	**258**	**Afrique**
Algeria	42	30	35	24	25	20	20	22	20	18	Algérie
Egypt	5	6	4	6	2	4	[1]1	[1]1	[1]2	[1]2	Egypte
Morocco	11	9	8	10	25	29	[1]40	50	33	37	Maroc
Mozambique	9	34	0	100	1	8	12	13	11	11	Mozambique
South Africa	[1]66	[1]65	[1]44	[1]50	[1]72	[1]71	* [1]48	76	48	51	Afrique du Sud
Zimbabwe[1]	100	100	83	*83	169	170	*186	*186	*136	*140	Zimbabwe[1]
America, North	**3628**	**3587**	**3099**	**2977**	**3394**	**3898**	**3814**	**4135**	**4010**	**4282**	**Amérique du Nord**
Guatemala[1]	*9	*12	*13	*12	4	*6	*4	*4	*4	*4	Guatemala[1]
Mexico	[1]145	[1]145	[1]136	[1]95	100	[1]73	* [1]70	112	[1]186	* [1]209	Mexique
United States[2]	3474	3430	2950	2870	3290	3820	3740	4020	3820	4070	Etats-Unis[2]
America, South	**328**	**284**	**244**	**221**	**287**	**289**	**341**	**361**	**365**	**363**	**Amérique du Sud**
Argentina	107	108	98	97	113	[1]111	[1]135	[1]114	[1]131	* [1]130	Argentine
Brazil	175	160	[1]131	[1]113	[1]145	[1]150	[1]186	[1]224	[1]210	* [1]210	Brésil
Chile	1	1	1	1	1	1	1	1	1	1	Chili
Peru	* [1]45	[1]15	[1]14	10	28	27	19	22	[1]22	[1]22	Pérou
Asia	**1038**	**1177**	**1558**	**1410**	**1536**	**1723**	**1656**	**2395**	**1747**	**2096**	**Asie**
Armenia	..	...	...	...	...	[1]0	[1]3	3	* [1]3	* [1]3	Arménie
Cyprus	82	58	59	[1]52	[1]47	51	66	99	122	139	Chypre
Georgia[1]	..	...	...	...	*13	13	13	12	11	*12	Géorgie[1]
India	242	291	328	230	323	427	433	*433	...	...	Inde
Indonesia[1]	6	22	18	14	14	*26	*26	654	1	*5	Indonésie[1]
Iran(Islamic Rep. of)	35	64	66	54	[1]72	[1]55	* [1]85	109	*118	* [1]115	Iran(Rép. islamique)
Israel[1][3]	4	4	...	...	...	...	...	...	...	...	Israël[1][3]
Japan	549	554	534	517	484	478	469	496	444	428	Japon
Myanmar[4]	0	1	1	0	1	2	[1]5	5	2	1	Myanmar[4]
Pakistan	[1]3	[1]5	[1]6	[1]8	[1]11	[1]6	* [1]15	[1]16	[1]14	17	Pakistan
Philippines	[1]15	42	32	6	4	8	3	0	4	2	Philippines
Thailand	...	3	8	3	5	8	11	3	6	5	Thaïlande
Turkey	97	68	439	457	516	605	482	521	566	900	Turquie
Turkmenistan	..	...	* [1]50	52	42	40	41	40	27	...	Turkménistan
Europe	**1126**	**1356**	**937**	**2200**	**2408**	**3047**	**3058**	**2503**	**2631**	**2824**	**Europe**
Bulgaria	129	67	33	26	20	96	118	112	200	367	Bulgarie
Croatia	..	17	10	8	10	7	10	7	8	[1]8	Croatie
Denmark[5]	...	...	0	0	6	8	8	...	...	10	Danemark[5]
Czech Republic[1]	..	..	...	...	65	54	59	110	125	*160	République tchèque[1]
Finland	4	3	1	2	2	5	5	...	...	...	Finlande
France[1]	10	10	6	6	*7	*0	*0	*0	*0	...	France[1]
Germany	..	...	257	245	227	323	283	[1]511	[1]478	* [1]500	Allemagne
Germany(Fed.Rep.)	223	..	..	..	..	..	..	..			Allemagne(Rép.féd.)
Greece	88	110	85	506	654	840	[1]974	[1]943	[1]950	* [1]950	Grèce
Hungary	55	32	16	17	21	[1]23	[1]15	[1]15	[1]17	* [1]16	Hongrie
Italy	228	391	151	327	374	591	472	510	580	563	Italie
Poland	69	35	18	9	1	2	2	...	0	0	Pologne
Romania	165	91	57	46	41	42	44	27	25	21	Roumanie
Slovakia	..	..	...	...	..	...	...	79	70	62	Slovaquie
Spain	151	259	157	[6]869	[6]903	[6]982	[6]990	* [1]150	* [1]150	* [1]150	Espagne
T.F.Yug.Rep. Macedonia	..	50	22	5	7	4	8	14	18	11	L'ex-RY Macédoine
USSR (former)[1]	2700	..	..	..	..	..	..	..	..	..	URSS (anc.)[1]
Oceania	**37**	**43**	**43**	**37**	**36**	**39**	**49**	**48**	**49**	**50**	**Océanie**
Australia*[1]	35	35	35	35	35	35	35	35	35	35	Australie*[1]
New Zealand[1]	2	...	...	2	1	4	*14	13	14	*15	Nouvelle-Zélande[1]
Total	**9090**	**6691**	**6055**	**7118**	**7955**	**9298**	**9224**	**9790**	**9051**	**9873**	**Total**

For general note and footnotes, see end of table. · Voir la fin du tableau pour la remarque générale et les notes.

Bentonite (continued)
Bentonite (suite)

ISIC-BASED CODE - CODE BASE CITI
2901-191

General Note.

Bentonite is a clay derived from volcanic ash, largely used as an ingredient of moulding sand, as a filtering and de-colourizing agent in oil refining, and for de-greasing of textiles. (SITC, Rev.3: 27827-0).

[1] Source: U. S. Geological Survey, (Washington, D. C.).
[2] Sold or used by producers.
[3] Metabentonite only.
[4] Government production only.
[5] Sales.
[6] Including fuller's earth.

Remarque générale.

La bentonite, matière argileuse provenant de cendres d'origine volcanique, principalement utilisée dans la préparation du sable de moulage, comme élément filtrant et décolorant dans le raffinage des huiles et pour le dégraissage des textiles. (CTCI, Rev.3: 27827-0).

[1] Source: U.S. Geological Survey, (Washington, D.C.).
[2] Vendu ou utilisé par les producteurs.
[3] Metabentonite seulement.
[4] Production de l'Etat seulement.
[5] Ventes.
[6] Y compris terre à foulon.

Fuller's earth
Terre à foulon

ISIC-BASED CODE - CODE BASE CITI

2901-192

Unit : Thousand metric tons   Unité : Milliers de tonnes métriques

Country or area	1990	1991	1992	1993	1994	1995	1996	1997	1998	1999	Pays ou zone
Africa	**176**	**180**	**162**	**168**	**157**	**140**	**122**	**109**	**112**	**112**	**Afrique**
Algeria[1]	[2]8	[2]5	[2]4	[2]3	[2]5	* [2]5	*5	*5	*5	*4	Algérie[1]
Morocco[1][3]	45	38	38	39	23	15	17	24	*28	*28	Maroc[1][3]
Senegal* [1][2]	115	129	112	119	119	120	100	80	80	80	Sénégal* [1][2]
South Africa	[1][2]8	[1][2]8	[1][2]8	[1][2]7	[1][2]10	0	0	0	0	0	Afrique du Sud
America, North	**2337**	**2781**	**2451**	**2486**	**2676**	**2656**	**2642**	**2421**	**2468**	**2608**	**Amérique du Nord**
Mexico	[1]30	[1]41	[1]41	[1]36	36	[1]16	[1]42	[1]51	* [1]48	* [1]48	Mexique
United States[4]	2307	2740	2410	2450	2640	2640	2600	2370	2420	2560	Etats-Unis[4]
America, South	**2**	**2**	**2**	**2**	**2**	**2**	**2**	**2**	**2**	**2**	**Amérique du Sud**
Argentina* [1]	[2]2	2	2	2	2	2	2	2	2	2	Argentine* [1]
Asia	**142**	**146**	**137**	**109**	**207**	**72**	**59**	**58**	**70**	**73**	**Asie**
India	20	31	38	88	38	59	46	*46	...	...	Inde
Pakistan	14	23	[1]22	[1]21	[1]15	[1]13	* [1]13	* [1]12	* [1]15	16	Pakistan
Philippines	...	...	...	0	154	0	0	0	...	...	Philippines
Europe	**8263**	**6955**	**5221**	**5019**	**4842**	**5125**	**4796**	**4621**	**4026**	**2711**	**Europe**
Germany	..	708	673	[1]670	[1]498	[1]529	[1]491	[1]511	* [1]500	* [1]500	Allemagne
Germany(Fed.Rep.)	653	..	..	..	..	..	..	..	..	..	Allemagne(Rép.féd.)
Italy	46	23	30	12	20	34	26	22	29	60	Italie
Portugal	327	301	...	...	...	...	...	...	...	...	Portugal
Romania	6955	5648	3909	3785	3732	4004	3688	3522	2982	1664	Roumanie
Spain* [1][2]	54	73	92	85	85	94	94	90	90	90	Espagne* [1][2]
United Kingdom[5]	228	202	203	153	193	150	183	162	111	83	Royaume-Uni[5]
Oceania	**20**	**15**	**15**	**15**	**15**	**15**	**15**	**15**	**15**	**15**	**Océanie**
Australia* [1][2]	20	15	15	15	15	15	15	15	15	15	Australie* [1][2]
Total	**10940**	**10079**	**7988**	**7799**	**7898**	**8009**	**7635**	**7226**	**6693**	**5520**	**Total**

General Note.

Fuller's earth is a natural earthy material extensively used to decolourize and deodorize vegetable and mineral oils, fat sand waxes. (SITC, Rev.3: 27829-1).

Remarque générale.

La terre à foulon, une matière terreuse naturelle très employée pour décolorer et désodoriser les huiles, graisses et cires végétales et minérales. (CTCI, Rev.3: 27829-1).

[1] Source: U. S. Geological Survey, (Washington, D. C.).
[2] Attapulgite.
[3] Smectite only.
[4] Sold or used by producers.
[5] Great Britain only.

[1] Source: U.S. Geological Survey, (Washington, D.C.).
[2] Attapulgite.
[3] Smectite seulement.
[4] Vendu ou utilisé par les producteurs.
[5] Grande Bretagne seulement.

Kaolin
Kaolin
ISIC-BASED CODE - CODE BASE CITI
2901-193

Unit : Thousand metric tons

Unité : Milliers de tonnes métriques

Country or area	1990	1991	1992	1993	1994	1995	1996	1997	1998	1999	Pays ou zone
Africa	**310**	**352**	**370**	**327**	**351**	**448**	**615**	**546**	**552**	**567**	**Afrique**
Algeria	[1]20	[1]22	[1]21	[1]13	17	24	24	19	14	17	Algérie
Burundi[1]	5	7	10	*5	*5	*1	*1	*1	*1	*1	Burundi[1]
Egypt	149	186	203	157	195	233	293	259	286	314	Egypte
Ethiopia* [1]	1	0	0	1	0	0	0	0	0	0	Ethiopie* [1]
Kenya	0	0	1	2	...	1	1	...	...	...	Kenya
Madagascar[1]	0	0	1	*1	*1	*2	*2	*2	*2	*2	Madagascar[1]
Nigeria	1	1	1	2	0	12	# [1]102	[1]100	[1]110	* [1]110	Nigéria
South Africa	[1]132	[1]134	[1]132	[1]147	[1]132	175	192	164	138	122	Afrique du Sud
United Rep.Tanzania* [1]	2	2	1	0	0	...	...	...	...	...	Rép. Unie de Tanzanie* [1]
America, North	**9920**	**9740**	**8887**	**9049**	**8986**	**9702**	**9374**	**9515**	**9979**	**9650**	**Amérique du Nord**
Guatemala[1]	2	3	3	*3	0	0	0	0	*0	*0	Guatemala[1]
Mexico	[1]156	[1]167	[1]144	[1]216	216	[1]222	[1]254	[1]235	[1]339	* [1]490	Mexique
United States	[2]9762	[3]9570	[3]8740	[3]8830	[3]8770	[3]9480	[3]9120	[3]9280	[3]9640	[3]9160	Etats-Unis
America, South	**3067**	**3112**	**3086**	**3251**	**7960**	**8540**	**5267**	**9468**	**9539**	**9520**	**Amérique du Sud**
Argentina	[1]34	[1]47	[1]44	[1]42	50	[1]40	[1]64	[1]47	[1]47	* [1]45	Argentine
Brazil	975	900	[1]811	[1]916	[1]1038	[1]1067	[1]1058	[1]1280	[1]1381	* [1]1381	Brésil
Chile	33	64	59	67	73	11	13	14	12	4	Chili
Colombia* [1]	1920	1984	2050	2100	6700	7300	3957	8040	8000	8000	Colombie* [1]
Ecuador	[1]8	[1]12	6	[1]12	[1]7	[1]45	[1]87	* [1]7	* [1]7	* [1]7	Equateur
Paraguay* [1]	74	74	74	74	74	66	67	67	67	67	Paraguay* [1]
Peru	* [1]8	* [1]7	1	5	8	8	14	8	[1]8	* [1]8	Pérou
Venezuela	15	24	41	35	[1]10	[1]3	[1]8	[1]5	[1]17	[1]8	Venezuela
Asia	**2191**	**2259**	**2498**	**2405**	**2447**	**2901**	**3023**	**3570**	**3284**	**3491**	**Asie**
Bangladesh[1] [4]	7	7	2	2	3	7	7	7	8	8	Bangladesh[1] [4]
India	724	815	668	645	732	831	775	791	741	752	Inde
Indonesia[1]	160	140	231	42	53	14	*15	*2	*9	*21	Indonésie[1]
Iran(Islamic Rep. of)	80	60	[1]264	[1]254	[1]228	[1]266	365	485	452	* [1]600	Iran(Rép. islamique)
Israel* [1]	42	53	53	40	40	40	40	40	40	40	Israël* [1]
Japan	165	130	123	110	138	182	141	111	105	73	Japon
Korea, Republic of	115	111	116	106	138	117	160	154	113	...	Corée, République de
Malaysia[1]	153	187	245	250	253	211	210	187	*177	*209	Malaisie[1]
Pakistan	62	45	37	37	[1]48	[1]31	[1]55	* [1]66	[1]71	* [1]65	Pakistan
Philippines	...	...	...	...	...	...	...	...	1	...	Philippines
Sri Lanka	8	8	7	*7	* [1]8	[1]16	[1]8	[1]20	[1]24	* [1]25	Sri Lanka
Thailand	348	382	487	614	534	610	711	521	417	371	Thaïlande
Turkey	251	219	186	211	186	490	450	1099	1042	1089	Turquie
Turkmenistan	..	...	...	...	...	...	...	2	2	...	Turkménistan
Viet Nam	75	99	76	...	...	...	...	...	...	...	Viet Nam
Europe	**10348**	**8866**	**9714**	**8024**	**8619**	**8125**	**8666**	**8097**	**7990**	**8077**	**Europe**
Austria[5]	473	351	460	415	527	...	...	...	...	...	Autriche[5]
Belgium	161	188	171	139	* [1]300	* [1]300	* [1]300	* [1]300	* [1]300	* [1]300	Belgique
Bulgaria	186	106	104	111	*145	168	189	173	155	144	Bulgarie
Denmark[6]	17	17	0	0	[1]4	[1]4	[1]3	[1]3	0	0	Danemark[6]
Czechoslovakia(former)	533	425			..	..	..	..	..	..	Tchécoslovaquie(anc.)
Czech Republic	..	..	428	390	652	758	742	822	1101	1049	République tchèque
Finland	7	7	7	8	8	12	14	...	...	...	Finlande
France	[7]370	[7]370	[7]387	[7]295	[7]294	[1]345	[1]326	[1]332	[1]330	* [1]325	France
Germany	..	...	2930	...	...	1199	1063	980	953	...	Allemagne
Germany(Fed.Rep.)	3207	..	..	..	..	..	..	..	..	..	Allemagne(Rép.féd.)
German D.R.(former)	464	..	..	..	..	..	..	..	..	..	R.D.A. (anc.)
Greece	146	80	89	...	77	95	[1]60	[1]60	[1]60	[1]60	Grèce
Hungary	19	14	2	...	...	...	...	#1044	549	696	Hongrie
Italy	67	58	33	55	58	86	130	181	248	296	Italie
Poland	48	44	42	48	53	53	72	84	82	89	Pologne
Portugal[1]	108	*150	*194	*178	182	*180	177	*180	*180	*180	Portugal[1]
Romania	117	84	58	48	48	49	45	29	25	25	Roumanie
Russian Federation	..	...	...	...	...	...	39	48	41	65	Fédération de Russie
Slovenia		21	23	20	3	...	...	...	...	...	Slovénie
Spain	[1]468	[1]538	[1]379	386	474	519	632	610	705	740	Espagne

For general note and footnotes, see end of table.

Voir la fin du tableau pour la remarque générale et les notes.

Kaolin (continued)
Kaolin (suite)

ISIC-BASED CODE - CODE BASE CITI
2901-193

Unit : Thousand metric tons

Unité : Milliers de tonnes métriques

Country or area	1990	1991	1992	1993	1994	1995	1996	1997	1998	1999	Pays ou zone
Sweden	0	0	...	...	...	...	...	36	71	64	Suède
Ukraine	..	999	840	621	282	287	249	238	202	222	Ukraine
United Kingdom	...	...	...	...	3605	3075	3658	[1][6]2400	[1][6]2392	[1][6]2304	Royaume-Uni
Yugoslavia	..	12	9	5	7	5	6	5	5	4	Yougoslavie
T.F.Yug.Rep. Macedonia	..	10	9	3	5	7	8	9	10	9	L'ex-RY Macédoine
Yugoslavia, SFR	210	..	..	..	..	..	..	..	..	..	Yougoslavie, RSF
USSR (former)[1]	1800	..	..	..	..	..	..	..	..	..	URSS (anc.)[1]
Oceania	225	211	208	207	241	224	236	242	246	275	Océanie
Australia*[1]	200	190	180	180	200	210	210	220	220	250	Australie*[1]
New Zealand[1]	25	21	28	27	41	14	26	22	*26	*25	Nouvelle-Zélande[1]
Total	27861	24540	24764	23262	28604	29940	27181	31439	31590	31579	Total

General Note.
Kaolin, a high grade, white or nearly white plastic clay used in the porcelain and paper making industries. Kaolin-bearing sands are excluded. (SITC, Rev.3: 27826-0).

Remarque générale.
Le kaolin est une argile plastique blanche, ou presque blanche, de première qualité, servant de matière première dans l'industrie de la porcelaine et de matière de charge dans la fabrication du papier. Les sables kaoliniques ne sont pas compris. (CTCI, Rev.3: 27826-0).

[1] Source: U. S. Geological Survey, (Washington, D. C.).
[2] Kaolin sold or used by producers.
[3] Sold or used by producers.
[4] Twelve months ending 30 June of year stated.
[5] Including bleaching earths.
[6] Sales.
[7] Including kaolinitic clay.

[1] Source: U. S. Geological Survey, (Washington, D. C.).
[2] Argiles kaoliniques vendues ou utilitisées par les producteurs.
[3] Vendu ou utilisé par les producteurs.
[4] Période de douze mois finissant le 30 juin de l'année indiquée.
[5] Y compris les terres décolorantes.
[6] Ventes.
[7] Y compris les argiles kaoliniques.

Andalusite, kyanite and sillimanite
Andalousite, cyanite et sillimanite

ISIC-BASED CODE - CODE BASE CITI

2901-194

Unit : Thousand metric tons   Unité : Milliers de tonnes métriques

Country or area	1990	1991	1992	1993	1994	1995	1996	1997	1998	1999	Pays ou zone
Africa	**284**	**213**	**233**	**189**	**208**	**207**	**234**	**252**	**240**	**141**	**Afrique**
South Africa	[1][2]284.3	[1][2]210.4	[1][2]230.6	[2]188.3	[1][2]206.8	206.4	233.7	251.2	236.2	136.9	Afrique du Sud
Zimbabwe[2]	[3]0.2	[3]2.5	[3]2.0	[3]0.9	[3]1.0	0.9	0.1	1.1	3.8	4.0	Zimbabwe[2]
America, North	**90**	**90**	**90**	**90**	**90**	**90**	**90**	**90**	**90**	**90**	**Amérique du Nord**
United States[1]	...	...	...	...	...	...	...	...	90.0	90.0	Etats-Unis[1]
America, South	**1**	**1**	**1**	**1**	**1**	**1**	**1**	**1**	**1**	**1**	**Amérique du Sud**
Brazil[3]	1.0	[2]1.0	[2]0.6	[2]0.6	[2]0.6	[2]0.6	[2]0.6	[2]0.6	[2]0.6	[2]0.6	Brésil[3]
Asia	**59**	**44**	**33**	**26**	**17**	**21**	**18**	**22**	**21**	**24**	**Asie**
China[2]	...	...	...	...	2.5	2.5	2.5	3.0	3.0	3.0	Chine[2]
India[5]	[2]57.1	[2]41.6	30.1	23.0	14.5	18.0	15.5	18.5	18.3	21.4	Inde[5]
Europe	**54**	**54**	**54**	**53**	**54**	**64**	**74**	**71**	**69**	**65**	**Europe**
France[2][6]	50.0	50.0	50.0	50.0	50.0	60.0	70.0	67.0	65.0	65.0	France[2][6]
Spain	[2][6]3.6	[2][6]3.6	[2][6]3.6	[2][6]3.0	[2][6]3.5	[2][6]3.5	[2][6]3.5	[2][6]3.5	[2][6]3.5	0.0	Espagne
Oceania	**1**	**1**	**1**	**1**	**1**	**1**	**1**	**1**	**1**	**1**	**Océanie**
Australia[2][5]	0.9	0.9	0.9	0.9	0.9	0.9	0.9	0.9	0.9	1.1	Australie[2][5]
Total	**489**	**402**	**410**	**359**	**370**	**383**	**417**	**436**	**421**	**322**	**Total**

General Note.
Andalusite, Kyanite (or disthene) and sillimanite are natural anhydrous aluminium silicates used as refractories. (SITC, Rev.3: 27829-2).

Remarque générale.
L'andalousite, la cyanite (ou disthène) et la sillimanite sont des silicates d'aluminium anhydres naturels, utilisés comme produits réfractaires. (CTCI, Rev.3: 27829-2).

[1] Andalusite and sillimanite.
[2] Source: U. S. Geological Survey, (Washington, D. C.).
[3] Kyanite.
[4] Until1 1998 the data are confidential.
[5] Kyanite and sillimanite.
[6] Andalusite.

[1] Andalousite et sillimanite.
[2] Source: U.S. Geological Survey, (Washington, D.C.).
[3] Cyanite.
[4] Jusqu'à l'année 1998 les donnés sont confidentiélles.
[5] Cyanite et sillimanite.
[6] Andalousite.

Magnesite
Magnésite

ISIC-BASED CODE - CODE BASE CITI

2901-22

Unit : Thousand metric tons

Unité : Milliers de tonnes métriques

Country or area	1990	1991	1992	1993	1994	1995	1996	1997	1998	1999	Pays ou zone
Africa	**156**	**121**	**77**	**82**	**83**	**101**	**89**	**99**	**88**	**84**	**Afrique**
Egypt	9.4	5.0	7.5	9.0	9.8	11.3	6.5	...	...	...	Egypte
South Africa	114.2	[1]92.6	[1]60.1	[1]67.4	[1]71.7	[1]84.6	[1]71.4	76.7	74.3	74.0	Afrique du Sud
Zimbabwe	32.6	23.3	9.0	6.0	* [1]1.6	5.6	[1]10.7	[1]13.1	[1]4.3	...	Zimbabwe
America, North	**1**	**1**	**1**	**2**	**1**	**0**	**0**	**0**	**0**	**0**	**Amérique du Nord**
Mexico[1]	0.6	0.6	...	1.5	1.1	0.3	0.2	0.2	0.3	...	Mexique[1]
America, South	**686**	**616**	**1020**	**241**	**290**	**333**	**318**	**305**	**319**	**54**	**Amérique du Sud**
Brazil[1]	...	...	[2]1001.0	232.7	279.5	316.0	305.7	294.6	308.3	...	Brésil[1]
Colombia[1]	19.3	18.8	18.8	8.8	10.7	17.5	12.6	10.5	10.5	...	Colombie[1]
Asia	**5081**	**5177**	**4862**	**3809**	**5421**	**6099**	**6871**	**6573**	**7155**	**5955**	**Asie**
China[1]	*2170.0	*1650.0	*1510.0	*1230.0	2050.0	2100.0	2400.0	2400.0	2450.0	...	Chine[1]
India	528.7	530.6	540.9	374.6	334.5	345.1	377.5	373.5	349.9	329.8	Inde
Iran(Islamic Rep. of)	[1][3]1.4	[1][3]29.3	[1][3]36.2	[1]49.4	[1][3]40.0	83.6	110.8	116.3	121.8	...	Iran(Rép. islamique)
Korea,Dem.Ppl's.Rep.[1]	1500.0	1600.0	1600.0	1600.0	1600.0	1600.0	1600.0	1600.0	1500.0	1000.0	Corée,Rép.pop.dém.de[1]
Nepal[1]	25.0	...	...	...	...	...	...	...	...	...	Népal[1]
Pakistan	7.3	4.2	[1]6.5	[1]4.2	[1]4.5	[1]16.9	15.0	6.7	3.4	3.5	Pakistan
Philippines	3.7	13.6	18.8	0.3	1.0	0.4	0.3	0.7	0.7	0.7	Philippines
Thailand	0.2	0.0	...	...	...	...	...	...	...	...	Thaïlande
Turkey	845.1	1324.2	1124.5	525.6	1365.5	1928.1	2341.9	2050.8	2703.7	1724.7	Turquie
Europe	**6363**	**5857**	**4628**	**4493**	**3933**	**3841**	**3945**	**4122**	**4050**	**3733**	**Europe**
Austria	1179.2	909.1	999.2	627.0	654.1	[1]784.0	[1]624.0	[1]700.0	[1]650.0	...	Autriche
Czechoslovakia(former)	2703.7	1552.7	..	..							Tchécoslovaquie(anc.)
Greece	[1]697.0	[1]590.0	[1]250.0	434.4	512.4	556.8	532.5	[1]623.1	[1]650.0	...	Grèce
Poland	23.3	8.1	12.9	13.0	16.4	21.5	19.3	6.4	5.7	...	Pologne
Slovakia	..	..	..	953.3	634.5	380.3	...	...	...	...	Slovaquie
Slovenia	..	...	...	1.0	2.9	1.0	...	...	0.0	...	Slovénie
Spain	444.4	558.2	418.2	663.0	[1]400.0	[1]491.4	[1]483.7	[1]500.0	[1]500.0	...	Espagne
Ukraine	..	710.2	788.6	490.0	259.4	213.1	227.3	221.6	192.1	215.7	Ukraine
United Kingdom	...	...	...	1251.2	1378.9	...	...	...	...	...	Royaume-Uni
Yugoslavia	..	212.6	186.8	60.2	74.2	77.4	85.7	98.4	80.9	30.6	Yougoslavie
USSR (former)[1]	1700.0	..	..	..	..	..	..	..	..	..	URSS (anc.)[1]
Oceania	**51**	**242**	**242**	**261**	**286**	**234**	**312**	**180**	**337**	**279**	**Océanie**
Australia	[4]50.8	...	...	[1]260.6	[1]285.6	233.8	312.0	180.1	336.6	278.9	Australie
Total	**14037**	**12014**	**10829**	**8888**	**10014**	**10609**	**11534**	**11279**	**11948**	**10105**	**Total**

General Note.
Natural magnesium carbonate, whether or not calcined, other than purified magnesium oxide. (SITC, Rev3.: 27824-0).

Remarque générale.
Carbonate de magnésium naturel, calciné ou non, à l'exclusion de l'oxyde de magnésium purifié. (CTCI, Rev.3: 27824-0).

[1] Source: U. S. Geological Survey, (Washington, D. C.).
[2] Gross weight.
[3] Twelve months beginning 21 March of year stated.
[4] Twelve months ending 30 June of year stated.

[1] Source: U. S. Geological Survey, (Washington, D.C.).
[2] Poids brut.
[3] Période de douze mois commençant le 21 mars de l'année indiquée.
[4] Période de douze mois finissant le 30 juin de l'année indiquée.

Chalk
Craie

ISIC-BASED CODE - CODE BASE CITI

2901-25

Unit : Thousand metric tons   Unité : Milliers de tonnes métriques

Country or area	1990	1991	1992	1993	1994	1995	1996	1997	1998	1999	Pays ou zone
America, South	**470**	**163**	**163**	**163**	**163**	**101**	**101**	**101**	**101**	**101**	**Amérique du Sud**
Peru* [1]	470	...	...	...	...	101	101	101	101	101	Pérou* [1]
Asia	**136**	**222**	**152**	**130**	**161**	**157**	**131**	**121**	**123**	**146**	**Asie**
India	132	137	109	109	154	147	123	115	119	140	Inde
Kazakhstan	..	81	38	16	2	3	1	1	0	0	Kazakhstan
Pakistan	[2]4	[2]4	...	...	...	[1]7	[1]7	[1]5	[1]4	[1]6	Pakistan
Europe	**15422**	**15775**	**19877**	**18204**	**16973**	**19621**	**17596**	**17948**	**18259**	**18697**	**Europe**
Belarus	..	120	103	86	68	97	64	75	79	78	Bélarus
Belgium	337	378	#6159	5409	...	...	...	...	...	...	Belgique
Bulgaria	35	40	27	22	23	26	18	20	...	...	Bulgarie
Croatia	..	33	26	31	42	31	33	33	26	...	Croatie
Denmark[3]	341	363	355	386	414	366	359	422	344	344	Danemark[3]
Germany	..	...	...	440	445	924	1010	1093	1022	..	Allemagne
Germany(Fed.Rep.)	412	..	..	..	..	..	..	..	..	..	Allemagne(Rép.féd.)
German D.R.(former)	112	..	..	..	..	..	..	..	..	..	R.D.A. (anc.)
Poland	139	159	175	156	176	...	...	...	...	...	Pologne
Romania	228	221	149	168	162	151	168	141	124	91	Roumanie
Russian Federation	..	1665	1267	786	675	3576	2350	2255	2440	3038	Fédération de Russie
Slovenia	..	3	2	1	2	2	2	1	1	1	Slovénie
Spain	609	599	659	598	791	788	785	802	814	822	Espagne
Sweden	29	40	28	86	121	108	65	79	62	...	Suède
Ukraine	..	1296	1144	958	746	349	242	209	119	111	Ukraine
United Kingdom[4]	13129	10317	9171	9076	10236	9949	9239	9550	9934	9667	Royaume-Uni[4]
T.F.Yug.Rep. Macedonia	..	1	1	...	...	...	...	...	...	...	L'ex-RY Macédoine
Yugoslavia, SFR	51	..	..	..	..	..	..	..	..	..	Yougoslavie, RSF
Total	**16028**	**16160**	**20191**	**18496**	**17297**	**19879**	**17828**	**18171**	**18483**	**18944**	**Total**

General Note.
Natural calcium carbonate. Phosphatic chalk, steatite and powder chalk prepared are excluded. (SITC, Rev.3: 27891-0).

Remarque générale.
Carbonate de calcium naturel, à l'exclusion de la craie phosphatée, de la stéatite et de la poudre de craie préparée. (CTCI, Rev.3: 27891-0).

[1] Source: U. S. Geological Survey, (Washington, D. C.).
[2] Twelve months ending 30 June of year stated.
[3] Sales.
[4] Great Britain only.

[1] Source: U.S. Geological Survey, (Washington, D.C.).
[2] Période de douze mois finissant le 30 juin de l'année indiquée.
[3] Ventes.
[4] Grande Bretagne seulement.

Natural phosphates, gross weight
Phosphates naturels, poids brut
ISIC-BASED CODE - CODE BASE CITI
2902-04

Unit : Thousand metric tons
Unité : Milliers de tonnes métriques

Country or area	1990	1991	1992	1993	1994	1995	1996	1997	1998	1999	Pays ou zone
Africa	**38110**	**35255**	**36394**	**32383**	**34126**	**35557**	**37413**	**39984**	**39607**	**38839**	**Afrique**
Algeria	1128	1090	1173	717	763	757	[1]1051	[1]1068	1155	1097	Algérie
Burkina Faso* [1]	15	15	18	15	15	...	...	...	...	...	Burkina Faso* [1]
Egypt	1505	1865	2089	1585	864	1044	1238	1428	1059	1165	Egypte
Mali	8	8	7	5	4	3	3	...	...	...	Mali
Morocco	21396	17900	19145	18305	20335	20186	20792	23084	22644	22163	Maroc
Senegal	2147	1741	2300	1863	1718	1682	1625	1706	1700	1700	Sénégal
South Africa [1]	3165	3180	3080	2466	2545	2822	2655	2732	2739	2900	Afrique du Sud [1]
Togo	2314	2965	2083	[1]1794	[1]2145	[1]2570	[1]2731	[1]2631	[1]2250	[1]1700	Togo
Tunisia	6259	6352	6335	5476	5565	6302	7151	7222	7951	8006	Tunisie
United Rep.Tanzania [1]	25	22	22	4	22	21	28	3	2	2	Rép. Unie de Tanzanie [1]
Zimbabwe	148	117	142	153	150	154	[1]123	[1]94	[1]91	[1]90	Zimbabwe
America, North	**46962**	**48711**	**47530**	**35747**	**41662**	**44137**	**46096**	**46628**	**44970**	**41614**	**Amérique du Nord**
Mexico	604	[1]596	[1]515	[1]237	[1]547	[1]622	[1]682	[1]714	[1]756	[1]1000	Mexique
Neth.Antil. and Aruba* [1]	15	15	15	10	15	15	...	...	...	...	Antill.néer.et Aruba* [1]
United States	46343	48100	47000	35500	41100	43500	45400	45900	44200	40600	Etats-Unis
America, South	**3231**	**3506**	**3397**	**3698**	**4131**	**4066**	**4131**	**4723**	**4912**	**4619**	**Amérique du Sud**
Brazil	2968	3280	3300	[1]3420	[1]3937	[1]3888	[1]3823	[1]4270	[1]4421	[1]4100	Brésil
Chile	14	14	18	15	10	[1]12	[1]17	[1]13	[1]15	[1]15	Chili
Colombia [1]	37	32	32	45	48	50	40	45	50	50	Colombie [1]
Peru [1]	47	18	37	37	37	30	103	104	104	104	Pérou [1]
Venezuela [1]	165	162	10	...	99	86	148	291	322	350	Venezuela [1]
Asia	**34423**	**35675**	**41390**	**35926**	**37221**	**33815**	**36253**	**41229**	**40960**	**40486**	**Asie**
China	21552	21396	23198	[1]21200	[1]24100	[1]19300	[1]21000	[1]24500	[1]25000	[1]25100	Chine
India	[2]675	[2]684	[2]690	[2]1036	[2]1097	[2]1309	[2]1341	1142	[2]1262	[2]1136	Inde
Indonesia [1]	*2	*6	*8	*7	*7	*8	*8	1	1	2	Indonésie [1]
Iraq* [1]	900	400	600	800	1000	1000	1000	1000	1000	1000	Iraq* [1]
Israel	2428	2267	2372	2662	2779	2642	2450	[1]4047	[1]4050	[1]4100	Israël
Jordan	6080	4850	5227	4215	4216	4983	5355	5895	5925	[1]6000	Jordanie
Kazakhstan	..	...	7000	[1]4000	[1]1700	* [1]1700	* [1]1700	* [1]1000	* [1]100	* [1]0	Kazakhstan
Korea,Dem.Ppl's.Rep.* [1]	500	500	500	510	510	520	520	520	450	350	Corée,Rép.pop.dém.de* [1]
Pakistan	333	321	...	[1]14	[1]15	[1]10	[1]10	[1]8	[1]9	4	Pakistan
Philippines	* [1]3	22	61	45	5	* [1]32	* [1]30	* [1]30	* [1]30	* [1]30	Philippines
Sri Lanka	[1]33	[1]20	[1]26	[1]36	[1]32	[1]32	34	30	*37	30	Sri Lanka
Syrian Arab Republic	1633	1469	1265	930	1202	1598	2188	2471	2494	2127	Rép. arabe syrienne
Thailand	[1]10	[1]6	[1]8	[1]11	8	9	4	4	3	4	Thaïlande
Turkey	0	4	65	97	* [1]80	* [1]80	0	0	0	0	Turquie
Viet Nam	* [1]274	319	* [1]290	* [1]363	* [1]470	592	613	581	599	*603	Viet Nam
Europe	**548**	**492**	**571**	**629**	**658**	**686**	**656**	**695**	**721**	**705**	**Europe**
Denmark	[3]2	[3]0	0	[3]1	[3]1	[3]1	[3]0	[3]0	[3]0	[3]0	Danemark
Estonia	..	20	0	0	0	...	...	...	...	...	Estonie
Finland	546	472	571	628	657	680	651	[1]690	[1]716	[1]700	Finlande
USSR (former) [1]	33500	..	..	..	..	..	..	..	..	..	URSS (anc.) [1]
Oceania	**933**	**534**	**749**	**636**	**634**	**501**	**511**	**492**	**488**	**602**	**Océanie**
Australia	[4]7	4	[1]2	[1]2	[1]21	[1]5	[1]1	[1]1	[1]1	[1]2	Australie
Nauru [1]	926	530	747	634	613	496	510	491	487	600	Nauru [1]
Total	**157707**	**124173**	**130031**	**109020**	**118432**	**118762**	**125059**	**133751**	**131657**	**126864**	**Total**

General Note.
Natural calcium phosphates, natural aluminium calcium phosphates, apatite and phosphatic chalk. Guano is excluded. (SITC, Rev.3: 27230-0).

Remarque générale.
Phosphates de calcium naturels, les phosphates alumino-calciques naturels, l'apatite et les craies phosphatées, à l'exclusion du guano. (CTCI, Rev3: 27230-0).

[1] Source: U. S. Geological Survey, (Washington, D. C.).
[2] Acid and metallurgical grade.
[3] Sales.
[4] Twelve months ending 30 June of year stated.

[1] Source: U.S. Geological Survey, (Washington, D.C.).
[2] Grade de métallurgique et d'acide.
[3] Ventes.
[4] Période de douze mois finissant le 30 juin de l'année indiquée.

Natural phosphates, P2O5 content
Phosphates naturels, P2O5 contenu

ISIC-BASED CODE - CODE BASE CITI

2902-04M

Unit : Thousand metric tons   Unité : Milliers de tonnes métriques

Country or area	1990	1991	1992	1993	1994	1995	1996	1997	1998	1999	Pays ou zone
Africa	**12210**	**11244**	**11669**	**10139**	**10691**	**11565**	**11713**	**13142**	**13287**	**12885**	**Afrique**
Algeria[1]	333	322	340	220	226	500	320	330	358	0	Algérie[1]
Burkina Faso	1	1	1	...	...	...	...	...	...	...	Burkina Faso
Egypt[1]	286	413	500	390	178	207	222	240	*320	*320	Egypte[1]
Mali	2	2	2	...	...	...	...	...	...	...	Mali
Morocco[1][2]	6906	5700	6180	5778	6274	6399	6552	*7848	*7850	*7850	Maroc[1][2]
Senegal[1]	777	630	830	606	*576	*545	*478	*575	*540	*650	Sénégal[1]
South Africa[1]	1190	1210	1170	962	995	1101	1036	1066	*1068	*1100	Afrique du Sud[1]
Togo[1]	840	1076	760	540	780	930	980	*955	*812	*610	Togo[1]
Tunisia[3]	1815	1842	1837	1588	1614	1828	2074	2094	2306	2322	Tunisie[3]
United Rep.Tanzania	8	[1]7	[1]7	[1]7	[1]0	[1]7	[1]9	[1]1	* [1]1	* [1]1	Rép. Unie de Tanzanie
Zimbabwe[1]	52	41	42	*45	*45	*45	*39	*30	*29	*29	Zimbabwe[1]
America, North	**14346**	**14680**	**14260**	**10772**	**12264**	**12980**	**13505**	**13514**	**13127**	**12100**	**Amérique du Nord**
Mexico[1]	174	180	160	72	164	180	205	214	*227	*300	Mexique[1]
United States	14172	14500	14100	10700	12100	12800	13300	13300	12900	11800	Etats-Unis
America, South	**1102**	**1250**	**1415**	**1433**	**1439**	**1410**	**1438**	**1623**	**1699**	**1597**	**Amérique du Sud**
Brazil	1051	1200	...	...	[1]1387	[1]1364	[1]1353	[1]1500	[1]1560	[1]1450	Brésil
Chile[1]	...	...	...	3	3	5	3	4	4	Chili[1]
Colombia	8	* [1]7	* [1]7	* [1]9	* [1]10	* [1]11	[1]8	[1]9	* [1]11	* [1]11	Colombie
Peru[1]	6	6	12	12	12	9	32	32	*37	*37	Pérou[1]
Venezuela	34	34	35	...	[1]27	[1]23	[1]40	[1]79	[1]87	[1]95	Venezuela
Asia	**9079**	**10594**	**12378**	**10221**	**11452**	**10352**	**11037**	**12586**	**12644**	**12496**	**Asie**
China	4700	6500	6959	[1]6350	[1]7430	[1]5790	[1]6300	[1]7530	* [1]7500	* [1]7530	Chine
India	190	188	197	264	278	329	338	308	384	342	Inde
Indonesia*[1]	1	2	2	2	2	2	2	0	0	0	Indonésie*[1]
Iraq*[1]	270	120	180	240	300	300	300	300	300	300	Iraq*[1]
Israel[1]	1104	1070	1130	1148	1232	1264	1201	1250	*1288	*1300	Israël[1]
Jordan[1]	2007	1458	1410	1367	1399	1655	1765	1940	*1968	*1980	Jordanie[1]
Kazakhstan	..	...	1800	209	86	140	120	91	16	26	Kazakhstan
Korea,Dem.Ppl's.Rep.[1]	160	*160	*160	*163	*163	*164	164	164	*142	*105	Corée,Rép.pop.dém.de[1]
Pakistan*[1]	...	...	...	...	3	2	2	2	2	2	Pakistan*[1]
Philippines*[1]	1	7	2	31	7	11	10	10	10	10	Philippines*[1]
Sri Lanka	33	20	26	25	* [1]11	* [1]10	* [1]12	* [1]10	* [1]10	* [1]10	Sri Lanka
Syrian Arab Republic[1]	511	425	395	286	371	477	670	*730	*765	*635	Rép. arabe syrienne[1]
Thailand[1]	3	*2	*2	*3	*2	*3	1	1	*1	*1	Thaïlande[1]
Turkey	0	[1]1	[1]20	15	[1]24	[1]24	...	0	0	0	Turquie
Viet Nam	96	* [1]88	* [1]93	* [1]116	* [1]144	* [1]181	* [1]143	* [1]250	* [1]258	* [1]255	Viet Nam
Europe	**199**	**7567**	**4940**	**4048**	**3315**	**3706**	**3569**	**4081**	**4085**	**4567**	**Europe**
Estonia	..	2	0	0	0	...	...	...	...	...	Estonie
Finland	199	174	211	232	242	251	240	240	235	[1]260	Finlande
Russian Federation	..	7391	4729	3816	3073	3454	3328	3840	3849	4306	Fédération de Russie
USSR (former)[1]	10200	..	..	..	..	..	..	..	..	..	URSS (anc.)[1]
Oceania	**358**	**205**	**288**	**244**	**238**	**191**	**194**	**187**	**185**	**230**	**Océanie**
Australia[1]	3	1	0	0	5	1	0	0	*0	*0	Australie[1]
Nauru[1]	355	204	288	244	233	190	194	*187	*185	*230	Nauru[1]
Total	**47494**	**45540**	**44951**	**36857**	**39399**	**40204**	**41456**	**45133**	**45027**	**43875**	**Total**

General Note.
P$_2$O$_5$ content of natural calcium phosphate, natural aluminium calcium phosphate, apatite and phosphatic chalk. Guano is excluded. (SITC, Rev.3: 27230-0).

Remarque générale.
Poids de P$_2$O$_5$ contenu dans les phosphates de calcium naturels, les phosphates alumino-calciques naturels, l'apatite et les craies phosphatées, à l'exclusion du guano. (CTCI, Rev.3: 27230-0).

[1] Source: U. S. Geological Survey, (Washington, D. C.).
[2] Including production for Western Sahara.
[3] Content of concentrates.

[1] Source: U.S. Geological Survey, (Washington, D.C.).
[2] Y compris les données relatives au Sahara Occidental.
[3] Teneur des concentrés.

Potash salts, crude
Sels de potasse bruts

ISIC-BASED CODE - CODE BASE CITI

2902-07

Unit : Thousand metric tons — Unité : Milliers de tonnes métriques

Country or area	1990	1991	1992	1993	1994	1995	1996	1997	1998	1999	Pays ou zone
America, North	**9425**	**9156**	**8750**	**8344**	**9437**	**10546**	**9510**	**10389**	**10501**	**9529**	**Amérique du Nord**
Canada	7372	7406	7040	6834	8037	[1]9066	[1]8120	[1]8989	[1]9201	[1]8329	Canada
United States	2053	1750	1710	1510	1400	1480	1390	1400	1300	1200	Etats-Unis
America, South	**91**	**121**	**105**	**228**	**255**	**238**	**264**	**302**	**348**	**372**	**Amérique du Sud**
Brazil[1]	66	101	85	173	234	215	243	280	326	350	Brésil[1]
Chile[1]	25	20	20	55	21	23	21	22	*22	*22	Chili[1]
Asia	**2769**	**3354**	**3453**	**3534**	**3697**	**4074**	**3375**	**3019**	**3147**	**2975**	**Asie**
China[1]	*29	*32	*21	*25	*74	*80	*110	115	*120	*125	Chine[1]
Israel	[1][2]1310	1958	2086	2139	2073	2214	[1]1500	[1]1488	[1]1500	[1]1750	Israël
Jordan	1430	1364	1346	1370	1550	1780	1765	1416	1527	[1]1100	Jordanie
Europe	**7562**	**13072**	**13501**	**10621**	**10674**	**11698**	**11572**	**13091**	**13231**	**13818**	**Europe**
Belarus	..	...	3600	2679	3021	3211	3305	4202	4481	4553	Bélarus
Denmark[3]	0	...	3	...	0	0	0	0	0	0	Danemark[3]
France[4]	1404	1224	1236	960	936	869	812	725	454	346	France[4]
Germany	..	3902	* [1]3461	2711	2793	[1]3278	[1]3332	[1]3423	[1]3581	[1]3600	Allemagne
Germany(Fed.Rep.)	2723	..	..	..	..	..	..	..	..	..	Allemagne(Rép.féd.)
German D.R.(former)	2100	..	..	..	..	..	..	..	..	..	R.D.A. (anc.)
Italy	66	43	162	0	0	0	...	...	...	...	Italie
Russian Federation	..	...	[1]3470	[1]2628	[1]2498	2831	2685	3487	* [1]3500	* [1]4200	Fédération de Russie
Spain	781	683	700	800	[1]684	[1]760	[1]717	[1]640	[1]585	[1]550	Espagne
Ukraine	..	495	340	288	162	167	93	48	22	69	Ukraine
United Kingdom[1]	488	495	529	555	580	582	618	565	608	500	Royaume-Uni[1]
USSR (former)[1]	9000	..	..	..	..	..	..	..	..	..	URSS (anc.)[1]
Total	**28847**	**25703**	**25809**	**22727**	**24063**	**26556**	**24721**	**26801**	**27227**	**26694**	**Total**

General Note.
K₂O content or equivalent of various mined potash salts. Manufactured fertilizers are not included. (SITC, Rev.3: 27240-0).

Remarque générale.
Equivalent en K₂O des divers sels de potasse d'extraction. Cette rubrique ne comprend pas les engrais artificiels. (CTCI, Rev.3: 27240-0).

[1] Source: U. S. Geological Survey, (Washington, D. C.).
[2] Twelve months beginning 1 April of year stated.
[3] Sales.
[4] Recovered quantities of K₂O.

[1] Source: U.S. Geological Survey, (Washington, D.C.).
[2] Période de douze mois commençant le 1er avril de l'année indiquée.
[3] Ventes.
[4] Quantités de K₂O récupérées.

Sulphur, native
Soufre natif

ISIC-BASED CODE - CODE BASE CITI

2902-10

Unit : Thousand metric tons

Unité : Milliers de tonnes métriques

Country or area	1990	1991	1992	1993	1994	1995	1996	1997	1998	1999	Pays ou zone
America, North	**5166**	**3910**	**3030**	**2002**	**3783**	**3973**	**3723**	**3643**	**2623**	**2603**	**Amérique du Nord**
Mexico[1]	1440	1040	710	102	...	...	...	...	...	...	Mexique[1]
United States	3726	2870	2320	1900	*2960	*3150	*2900	*2820	*1800	*1780	Etats-Unis
America, South	**73**	**70**	**85**	**78**	**79**	**86**	**79**	**83**	**88**	**91**	**Amérique du Sud**
Bolivia	[2]2	3	0	0	0	0	...	...	...	...	Bolivie
Brazil[2]	*6	*6	*18	22	21	22	25	*25	...	...	Brésil[2]
Chile[2]	29	19	24	1	1	...	...	...	...	...	Chili[2]
Colombia[2]	32	38	39	51	53	60	49	54	...	...	Colombie[2]
Ecuador[2]	*4	*4	*4	4	4	4	4	*4	...	...	Equateur[2]
Asia	**1198**	**993**	**894**	**833**	**684**	**464**	**468**	**499**	**512**	**344**	**Asie**
China*[2]	320	320	320	330	330	160	170	200	210	250	Chine*[2]
Indonesia[2]	4	*4	*4	4	4	4	4	4	...	...	Indonésie[2]
Iran(Islamic Rep. of)[2][3]	30	...	...	...	...	...	...	...	...	...	Iran(Rép. islamique)[2][3]
Iraq*[2]	800	250	250	250	250	250	250	250	250	...	Iraq*[2]
Philippines	7	...	...	...	...	...	...	...	...	...	Philippines
Turkey	37	39	39	27	17	0	0	0	0	0	Turquie
Turkmenistan	..	343	244	186	47	14	8	9	12	...	Turkménistan
Europe	**4790**	**33149**	**14319**	**13216**	**23775**	**13925**	**11662**	**11378**	**10728**	**7624**	**Europe**
Bulgaria	16	14	14	17	15	25	26	25	...	...	Bulgarie
Denmark[4]	12	6	7	10	7	8	7	4	3	4	Danemark[4]
Czechoslovakia(former)	56	55	..	..	..	..	..	..	..	..	Tchécoslovaquie(anc.)
Czech Republic	..	..	40	...	...	...	...	...	...	...	République tchèque
Finland	46	40	38	34	43	39	51	...	...	...	Finlande
Lithuania	..	26	9	11	10	15	23	35	41	27	Lituanie
Poland	4660	3935	2917	1893	2163	2427	1783	1719	1404	1248	Pologne
Russian Federation	..	27597	10006	10849	21178	11133	9564	9410	9073	6154	Fédération de Russie
Ukraine	..	1476	1288	362	319	238	168	100	97	80	Ukraine
Total	**11227**	**38122**	**18327**	**16130**	**28321**	**18448**	**15932**	**15603**	**13951**	**10663**	**Total**

General Note.

Unrefined sulphur extracted by melting or otherwise from mineral sulphur occurring in the free state. Sulphur obtained from Frasch-process mines is included. Sublimed sulphur, precipitated sulphur and colloidal sulphur are excluded. (SITC, Rev.3: 27411-1).

[1] Frasch only.
[2] Source: U. S. Geological Survey, (Washington, D. C.).
[3] Twelve months beginning 21 March of year stated.
[4] Sales.

Remarque générale.

Soufre non raffiné obtenu, par fusion ou autrement, du soufre minéral brut à l'état naturel (soufre natif). Cette position comprend le soufre extrait par le procédé Frasch mais non le soufre sublimé, le soufre précipité, ou le soufre colloïdal. (CTCI, Rev.3: 27411-1).

[1] Frasch seulement.
[2] Source: U.S. Geological Survey, (Washington, D.C.).
[3] Période de douze mois commençant le 21 mars de l'année indiquée.
[4] Ventes.

Iron pyrites, unroasted
Pyrites de fer non grillées

ISIC-BASED CODE - CODE BASE CITI

2902-13

Unit : Thousand metric tons   Unité : Milliers de tonnes métriques

Country or area	1990	1991	1992	1993	1994	1995	1996	1997	1998	1999	Pays ou zone
Africa	**294**	**288**	**276**	**273**	**323**	**230**	**255**	**240**	**224**	**213**	**Afrique**
South Africa	...	...	...	...	[1]252	[1]159	[1]184	168	[1]152	141	Afrique du Sud
Zimbabwe	67	70	66	72	71	71	...	...	...	...	Zimbabwe
Asia	**7222**	**7199**	**6982**	**6620**	**6509**	**6463**	**6526**	**6487**	**4947**	**4241**	**Asie**
China[1]	...	...	...	...	*5870	*5930	*5990	*6040	*4490	3860	Chine[1]
India	94	106	130	115	118	141	144	125	89	10	Inde
Japan	[2]108	[2]63	[2]64	1	1	1	1	2	* [2]2	...	Japon
Kazakhstan* [1]	...	...	...	...	200	71	71	0	0	...	Kazakhstan* [1]
Philippines	[2]429	...	[1][2]350	* [1]317	* [1]320	* [1]320	* [1]320	* [1]320	...	...	Philippines
Europe	**9676**	**9222**	**8920**	**7536**	**7567**	**6829**	**6622**	**6740**	**6758**	**6207**	**Europe**
Bulgaria[1]	180	180	170	150	150	150	150	150	...	...	Bulgarie[1]
Czechoslovakia(former)[1]	140	...	..	..	..	..	..	..	..	..	Tchécoslovaquie(anc.)[1]
Finland	659	568	667	665	840	875	813	...	...	...	Finlande
Germany(Fed.Rep.)[1]	340	..	..	..	..	..	..	..	..	...	Allemagne(Rép.féd.)[1]
Greece	[1]100	[1]60	[1]55	[1]50	[1]50	...	19	...	...	...	Grèce
Italy	806	550	441	377	258	0	0	...	...	...	Italie
Norway	296	307	374	88	1	...	...	...	...	...	Norvège
Portugal	98	12	...	...	...	...	...	...	...	...	Portugal
Romania	567	449	451	163	227	145	52	67	...	...	Roumanie
Russian Federation* [1]	..	...	...	...	700	450	400	400	400	...	Fédération de Russie* [1]
Spain	1638	1327	884	721	[1]342	[1]404	[1]438	[1]424	[1]430	...	Espagne
Sweden	252	89	37	0	...	...	...	...	...	...	Suède
United Kingdom	4600	...	...	...	...	...	...	...	...	...	Royaume-Uni
Yugoslavia	..	145	456	2	249	0	0	0	0	...	Yougoslavie
Total	**17192**	**16709**	**16178**	**14429**	**14399**	**13522**	**13403**	**13467**	**11929**	**10661**	**Total**

General Note.
All unroasted iron pyrites and unroasted cupreous pyrites. Chalco-pyrite and gem marcasite are excluded. (SITC, Rev.3: 27420-0).

Remarque générale.
Toutes les pyrites de fer non grillées, y compris les pyrites cuivreuses non grillées, mais à l'exclusion de la chalcopyrite et de la marcassite utilisée en bijouterie. (CTCI, Rev.3: 27420-0).

[1] Source: U. S. Geological Survey, (Washington, D. C.).
[2] Concentrates only.

[1] Source: U.S. Geological Survey, (Washington, D.C.).
[2] Concentrés seulement.

Fluorspar, excluding precious stones
Spath fluor, non compris les pierres precieuses

ISIC-BASED CODE - CODE BASE CITI

2902-16

Unit : Thousand metric tons · Unité : Milliers de tonnes métriques

Country or area	1990	1991	1992	1993	1994	1995	1996	1997	1998	1999	Pays ou zone
Africa	**545**	**496**	**480**	**412**	**402**	**421**	**415**	**405**	**437**	**457**	**Afrique**
Egypt[2]	[1]1.3	[1]1.8	[1]1.7	[1]0.8	[1]0.5	[1]0.6	* [1]0.7	*0.7	*0.7	*0.7	Egypte[2]
Kenya	[3]78.5	[3]77.4	[3]80.6	[3]78.7	[3]89.2	[3]80.2	[2 4]83.0	[2 4]68.7	[2 4]60.9	[2 4]98.0	Kenya
Morocco	[2 4]86.5	[2 4]74.6	[2 4]85.5	[2 4]70.0	[2 4]85.0	105.8	95.9	103.8	105.0	83.1	Maroc
Namibia	27.1	34.6	40.4	[2]43.5	[2 4]52.2	[2 4]36.9	[2 4]32.3	[2 4]23.2	* [2 4]40.7	[2 4]57.6	Namibie
South Africa[5]	311.0	*270.3	258.1	[2]218.0	[2]174.3	[2]195.9	201.9	* [2]207.0	228.6	217.5	Afrique du Sud[5]
Tunisia[4]	41.0	37.6	13.8	1.4	0.4	1.9	1.3	1.8	0.8	0.6	Tunisie[4]
America, North	**723**	**428**	**415**	**343**	**284**	**573**	**532**	**553**	**598**	**564**	**Amérique du Nord**
Canada[2 4]	25.0	0.0	0.0	0.0	0.0	...	...	...	...	...	Canada[2 4]
Mexico	634.0	370.0	364.0	[2 3]283.0	[2 3]235.0	[2 3]522.0	[2 3]524.0	[2 3]552.8	* [2 3]598.0	* [2 3]564.0	Mexique
United States[6]	63.5	58.0	51.0	60.0	49.0	51.0	8.2	0.0	0.0	0.0	Etats-Unis[6]
America, South	**90**	**101**	**100**	**98**	**94**	**94**	**65**	**85**	**79**	**79**	**Amérique du Sud**
Argentina	[3]20.0	[3]20.0	[3]19.0	[2 3]4.6	[2]3.6	[2]5.1	[2]5.7	[2]7.2	[2]7.2	[2]7.0	Argentine
Brazil	70.3	81.3	81.0	[2 3]92.9	[2 3]89.9	[2 3]89.3	[2 3]59.0	[2 3]78.0	[2 3]72.1	[2 3]72.0	Brésil
Asia	**2740**	**2939**	**3000**	**3104**	**2855**	**2985**	**3156**	**3288**	**3357**	**3434**	**Asie**
China[2 3]	1700.0	1700.0	1900.0	2100.0	*2000.0	*2000.0	*2150.0	*2300.0	*2350.0	*2400.0	Chine[2 3]
India[3]	31.7	22.0	22.8	27.2	29.4	27.0	25.1	16.9	4.1	48.1	Inde[3]
Iran(Islamic Rep. of)	4.8	12.3	12.0	* [2]10.0	[2]22.2	[2]20.2	19.0	*17.0	[2]26.0	[2]20.0	Iran(Rép. islamique)
Japan* [2]	...	...	...	236.3	...	...	...	...	...	...	Japon* [2]
Korea,Dem.Ppl's.Rep.* [2 7]	40.0	41.0	41.0	41.0	40.0	40.0	39.0	39.0	30.0	25.0	Corée,Rép.pop.dém.de* [2 7]
Korea, Republic of	0.6	0.3	0.1	0.3	0.1	0.0	0.0	0.0	0.0	...	Corée, République de
Mongolia	[7]614.0	755.2	622.1	536.8	383.2	526.9	565.1	567.1	612.0	597.1	Mongolie
Pakistan	[1]8.4	[1]1.4	[2 3]5.0	[2]5.1	[2]13.4	[2]2.8	[2]0.4	[2]1.1	[2]1.0	[2]0.2	Pakistan
Tajikistan* [2]	..	...	...	8.0	10.0	9.0	9.0	9.0	9.0	9.0	Tadjikistan* [2]
Thailand[3]	94.8	62.1	56.5	48.4	23.7	24.1	17.2	7.8	3.7	13.0	Thaïlande[3]
Turkey	[2]10.0	[2]5.0	[2]3.1	0.9	6.7	8.9	4.8	3.9	5.0	4.8	Turquie
Uzbekistan* [2]	..	...	...	90.0	90.0	90.0	90.0	90.0	80.0	80.0	Ouzbékistan* [2]
Europe	**856**	**842**	**693**	**654**	**788**	**732**	**717**	**709**	**662**	**685**	**Europe**
Czechoslovakia(former)[2 3]	46.9	40.0	..	..	..	..	..	..	..	..	Tchécoslovaquie(anc.)[2 3]
France[5]	257.9	200.0	130.9	132.8	254.1	[2]130.0	[2]111.0	[2]110.0	[2]110.0	[2]107.0	France[5]
Germany[2]	..	...	...	40.0	35.6	39.1	32.4	*24.0	*25.0	*28.0	Allemagne[2]
Germany(Fed.Rep.)	74.6		..	..	..	..	..	..	..	..	Allemagne(Rép.féd.)
German D.R.(former)[3]	66.7		..	..	..	..	..	..	..	..	R.D.A. (anc.)[3]
Greece[1 2]	0.2	0.2	0.2	...	...	...	...	...	...	...	Grèce[1 2]
Italy[2]	[5]122.5	[5]98.5	[5]80.0	[5]60.0	[3]67.9	[3]124.7	[3]126.5	[3]126.0	[3]107.0	[3]110.0	Italie[2]
Romania* [2 7]	15.0	14.0	15.0	15.0	15.0	15.0	15.0	15.0	15.0	15.0	Roumanie* [2 7]
Russian Federation* [2]	..	...	..	250.0	250.0	250.0	250.0	250.0	220.0	250.0	Fédération de Russie* [2]
Spain[3]	153.7	117.6	101.1	[2]87.0	* [2]107.0	[2]118.4	[2]116.5	* [2]120.0	* [2]120.0	* [2]133.0	Espagne[3]
Sweden[1 3]	0.2	0.2	...	0.0	...	...	...	...	...	...	Suède[1 3]
United Kingdom[2]	[3]118.5	[3]77.9	[3]76.1	[3]70.3	[3]58.0	[3]55.0	65.0	*64.0	*65.0	*42.0	Royaume-Uni[2]
USSR (former)[2 3]	380.0	..	..	..	..	..	..	..	..	..	URSS (anc.)[2 3]
Total	**5335**	**4806**	**4689**	**4611**	**4422**	**4806**	**4885**	**5041**	**5133**	**5219**	**Total**

General Note.

Fluorspar (or fluorite) is natural calcium floride occurring as solid masses streaked with varied colours, or in agglomerated crystals of various colours. Fluorspar in the form of precious stones is excluded. (SITC, Rev.3: 27854-0).

Remarque générale.

Le spath fluor (ou fluorine) est un fluorure de calcium qui se présente, dans la nature, soit en masses compactes comportant des zones diversement colorées, soit en cristaux agglomérés de couleur variable. Le spath fluor ayant le caractère de pierres gemmes n'est pas compris. (CTCI, Rev.3: 27854-0).

[1] Grade unspecified.
[2] Source: U. S. Geological Survey, (Washington, D. C.).
[3] Acid and metallurgical grade.
[4] Acid grade.
[5] Acid, metallurgical and ceramic grade.
[6] Shipments.
[7] Metallurgical grade.

[1] Teneur du minerai non spécifiée.
[2] Source: U.S. Geological Survey, (Washington, D.C.).
[3] Grade de métallurgique et d'acide.
[4] Grade d'acide.
[5] Grade de céramique, de métallurgique et d'acide.
[6] Expéditions.
[7] Grade metallurgique.

Barytes, whether or not calcined
Barytine même calciné

ISIC-BASED CODE - CODE BASE CITI

2902-19

Unit : Thousand metric tons
Unité : Milliers de tonnes métriques

Country or area	1990	1991	1992	1993	1994	1995	1996	1997	1998	1999	Pays ou zone
Africa	**455**	**531**	**509**	**430**	**291**	**364**	**371**	**439**	**443**	**438**	**Afrique**
Algeria	[1]53	[1]44	[1]51	[1]47	[1]22	[1]30	[1]31	[1]40	36	51	Algérie
Egypt	3	2	2	1	1	2	...	...	...	...	Egypte
Kenya	[2]0	[2]0	20	14	20	...	...	...	...	...	Kenya
Morocco	364	435	401	350	230	290	283	343	353	329	Maroc
South Africa	[2]2	[2]5	[2]4	[2]2	[2]2	6	[2]7	[2]2	1	3	Afrique du Sud
Tunisia	30	44	29	15	15	8	15	13	8	4	Tunisie
Zimbabwe	3	1	2	1	*1	*1	*1	*2	...	...	Zimbabwe
America, North	**806**	**706**	**563**	**607**	**726**	**854**	**1191**	**1007**	**729**	**698**	**Amérique du Nord**
Canada	44	47	35	[2]59	[2]55	[2]61	[2]58	[2]77	[2]90	[2]126	Canada
Guatemala[2]	0	0	2	*2	*1	*1	1	*1	*1	*1	Guatemala[2]
Mexico	332	211	200	...	[2]87	[2]248	[2]470	[2]237	[2]162	[2]137	Mexique
United States[3]	430	448	326	315	583	543	662	692	476	434	Etats-Unis[3]
America, South	**234**	**111**	**89**	**78**	**126**	**132**	**106**	**134**	**128**	**131**	**Amérique du Sud**
Argentina	40	24	10	[2]15	[2]28	[2]29	[2]14	[2]10	[2]2	[2]1	Argentine
Bolivia	[2]0	1	0	0	3	[2]11	[2]5	4	2	[2]6	Bolivie
Brazil	56	65	50	[2]32	[2]31	[2]31	[2]40	[2]52	[2]47	[2]47	Brésil
Chile	3	3	3	2	4	3	[2]3	[2]3	1	1	Chili
Colombia[2]	5	9	9	5	*7	21	7	*1	*1	*1	Colombie[2]
Peru	*[2]130	[2]9	[2]17	24	53	37	37	64	[2]75	[2]75	Pérou
Asia	**3160**	**3072**	**2536**	**2650**	**2812**	**2818**	**3705**	**4541**	**4568**	**3547**	**Asie**
Afghanistan[2,4]	2	2	2	2	2	2	2	2	*2	*2	Afghanistan[2,4]
China*[2]	1750	1600	1500	1500	1800	1800	2800	3500	3300	2800	Chine*[2]
Georgia[5]	..	...	15	5	3	12	2	3	0	0	Géorgie[5]
India	633	650	481	526	531	443	382	453	661	205	Inde
Iran(Islamic Rep. of)	[2,4]77	[2,4]191	[2,4]181	[2,4]226	[2,4]139	[4]161	[4]159	[4]150	[4]178	[2]170	Iran(Rép. islamique)
Kazakhstan[2,5]	..	...	...	...	90	83	50	38	9	13	Kazakhstan[2,5]
Korea,Dem.Ppl's.Rep.[2]	...	...	...	110	*110	*120	*110	*120	*100	*70	Corée,Rép.pop.dém.de[2]
Korea, Republic of	[2]3	[2]1	[2]0	[2]0	[2]0	[2]0	[2]0	*[2]0	0	*[2]0	Corée, République de
Lao People's Dem. Rep.	...	...	...	...	2	2	*[2]6	*[2]8	*[2]9	*[2]7	Rép. dém. pop. lao
Malaysia	47	[2]16	[2]11	[2]12	[2]17	[2]17	[2]17	[2]3	[2]2	[2]12	Malaisie
Myanmar[6]	10	11	14	16	22	35	25	17	22	25	Myanmar[6]
Pakistan	25	26	29	[2]26	[2]20	[2]15	[2]19	[2]23	[2]21	18	Pakistan
Philippines	0	0	*[2]1	*[2]1	*[2]0	*[2]0	[2]0	[2]0	[2]0	...	Philippines
Saudi Arabia[2]	...	...	...	...	5	6	8	8	8	7	Arabie saoudite[2]
Thailand	108	93	27	24	14	21	20	37	96	68	Thaïlande
Turkey	367	249	63	118	57	101	105	179	160	150	Turquie
Europe	**853**	**923**	**829**	**725**	**930**	**684**	**680**	**622**	**555**	**505**	**Europe**
Belgium*[2]	35	35	30	30	30	30	30	30	40	30	Belgique*[2]
Bosnia and Herzegovina	..	..	10	...	...	...	...	...	...	...	Bosnie-Herzégovine
Bulgaria	...	...	...	...	*[2]120	*[2]150	*[2]120	*[2]120	100	[7]100	Bulgarie
Czechoslovakia(former)	70	46	..	..							Tchécoslovaquie(anc.)
France	91	152	96	74	351	[2]75	*[2]75	*[2]75	*[2]75	*[2]60	France
Germany	..	..	155	[2]131	[2]127	[2]122	[2]121	[2]119	*[2]120	*[2]120	Allemagne
Germany(Fed.Rep.)	148									..	Allemagne(Rép.féd.)
German D.R. (former)[2]	27	..	..	..	..	..	..	..	..	..	R.D.A. (anc.)[2]
Greece[2,5]	1	1	*1	*1	*1	1	1	1	1	1	Grèce[2,5]
Ireland[2]	101	94	71	*53	0	0	0	0	*0	...	Irlande[2]
Italy	44	87	81	53	58	44	43	27	32	25	Italie
Poland[2]	25	18	16	20	27	25	22	3	0	0	Pologne[2]
Portugal[2]	1	1	0	0	*0	*0	*0	*0	*0	...	Portugal[2]
Romania	74	57	48	48	29	18	13	13	10	5	Roumanie
Russian Federation*[2]	..	...	...	...	70	70	70	60	60	60	Fédération de Russie*[2]
Slovakia	..	..	...	...	*[2]25	*[2]25	[2]45	[2]62	[2]15	13	Slovaquie
Spain	7	6	6	[2]18	[2]28	[2]29	*[2]28	*[2]28	*[2]28	*[2]26	Espagne
United Kingdom[2]	68	86	77	55	*54	*85	102	74	64	55	Royaume-Uni[2]
Yugoslavia, SFR	21	..	..	..	..	..	..	..	..	..	Yougoslavie, RSF
USSR (former)[2]	500	..	..	..	..	..	..	..	..	..	URSS (anc.)[2]

For general note and footnotes, see end of table.
Voir la fin du tableau pour la remarque générale et les notes.

Barytes, whether or not calcined (continued)
Barytine même calciné (suite)

ISIC-BASED CODE - CODE BASE CITI

2902-19

Unit : Thousand metric tons   Unité : Milliers de tonnes métriques

Country or area	1990	1991	1992	1993	1994	1995	1996	1997	1998	1999	Pays ou zone
Oceania	11	11	11	11	11	12	12	15	13	12	Océanie
Australia* [2]	11	11	11	11	11	12	12	15	13	12	Australie* [2]
Total	6019	5354	4537	4501	4897	4864	6065	6758	6435	5329	Total

General Note.

Naturally occurring barium sulphate (barytes - sometimes known as heavy spar) and barium carbonate (witherite). Refined or chemically produced barium sulphate and barium carbonate are excluded. Including calcined witherite, which consists largely of impure barium oxide. (SITC, Rev.3: 27892-0).

Remarque générale.

Le sulfate de baryum naturel, également nommé barytine et, dans certains pays, spath pesant, et le carbonate de baryum naturel ou withérite. Le sulfate de baryum et le carbonate de baryum, raffinés ou obtenus par voie chimique, sont exclus. Y compris la withérite calcinée, qui est essentiellement constituée par de l'oxyde de baryum impur. (CTCI, Rev.3: 27892-0).

[1] Ground baryte only.
[2] Source: U. S. Geological Survey, (Washington, D. C.).
[3] Sold or used by producers.
[4] Twelve months beginning 21 March of year stated.
[5] Baryte concentrates.
[6] Government production only.
[7] Source: The Chemical Industry, Organisation for Economic Co-operation and Development (OECD), (Paris).

[1] Barytine moulue seulement.
[2] Source: U.S. Geological Survey, (Washington, D.C.).
[3] Vendu ou utilisé par les producteurs.
[4] Période de douze mois commençant le 21 mars de l'année indiquée.
[5] Concentrés de barytine.
[6] Production de l'Etat seulement.
[7] Source: l'Industrie chimique, Organisation de coopération et de développement économiques (OCDE), (Paris).

Borate minerals, crude
Minéraux boratés bruts

ISIC-BASED CODE - CODE BASE CITI

2902-22

Unit : Thousand metric tons

Unité : Milliers de tonnes métriques

Country or area	1990	1991	1992	1993	1994	1995	1996	1997	1998	1999	Pays ou zone
America, North	**1090**	**1240**	**1010**	**1060**	**1110**	**1190**	**1150**	**1190**	**1170**	**1220**	**Amérique du Nord**
United States[1]	1090.0	1240.0	1010.0	1060.0	1110.0	1190.0	1150.0	1190.0	1170.0	1220.0	Etats-Unis[1]
America, South	**312**	**253**	**378**	**312**	**341**	**607**	**537**	**489**	**639**	**700**	**Amérique du Sud**
Argentina	144.0	115.6	125.0	146.3	215.0	[2]345.0	[2]342.0	[2]270.0	...	...	Argentine
Bolivia[2]	...	14.0	23.0	12.0	10.0	10.0	7.0	...	...	...	Bolivie[2]
Chile	131.8	97.1	202.7	117.1	85.9	211.3	149.0	170.6	280.1	324.7	Chili
Peru[2]	20.0	26.0	27.0	36.5	30.0	40.6	39.0	40.0	...	...	Pérou[2]
Asia	**2138**	**1917**	**1933**	**2056**	**2283**	**2072**	**2563**	**2748**	**2959**	**2627**	**Asie**
China[2]	*75.0	*93.0	*127.0	[3]155.4	[3]188.2	[3]294.6	[3]157.0	[3]140.0	...	...	Chine[2]
Kazakhstan[2]	..	...	10.0	8.0	7.0	8.4	5.7	...	...	...	Kazakhstan[2]
Turkey	2062.8	1814.2	1796.1	1892.4	2087.6	1768.9	2400.6	2602.4	2754.1	2414.8	Turquie
Europe	**130**	**126**	**147**	**137**	**137**	**139**	**140**	**137**	**136**	**136**	**Europe**
Finland	11.8	3.0	3.2	3.6	3.5	5.3	6.1	...	...	...	Finlande
Germany	..	123.2	143.7	...	...	...	...	...	...	...	Allemagne
Germany(Fed.Rep.)	117.8	..	..	..	..	..	..	..	..	..	Allemagne(Rép.féd.)
USSR (former)[2]	175.0	..	..	..	..	..	..	..	..	..	URSS (anc.)[2]
Total	**3844**	**3536**	**3468**	**3565**	**3871**	**4008**	**4390**	**4563**	**4904**	**4683**	**Total**

General Note.

Crude natural borate minerals as extracted, concentrates (whether or not calcined) of such materials, and crude natural boric acid as obtained by evaporation of the water left after the condensation of the natural vapours escaping from the earth in certain regions, or by evaporating water drawn from underground sources in those regions. Excluding boric acid containing more than 85 percent H_3BO_3 calculated on the dry weight. (SITC, Rev.3: 27894-0).

Remarque générale.

Les minéraux boratés naturels impurs, dans l'état où ils sont extraits ou obtenus sous forme de concentrés (calcinés ou non), ainsi que l'acide borique naturel brut, tel qu'il provient de l'évaporation des eaux de condensation des vapeurs naturelles issues du sol de certaines régions, ou des eaux captées des nappes sousterraines de ces régions. Non compris l'acide borique contenant plus de 85 pour cent de BO_3H_3 sur produit sec. (CTCI, Rev.3: 27894-0).

[1] Sold or used by producers.
[2] Source: U. S. Geological Survey, (Washington, D. C.).
[3] B_2O_3 equivalent.

[1] Vendu ou utilisé par les producteurs.
[2] Source: U.S. Geological Survey, (Washington, D.C.).
[3] B_2O_3 équivalent.

Arsenic (Arsenic trioxide)
Arsenic (Trioxyde d'arsenic)

ISIC-BASED CODE - CODE BASE CITI

2902-25

Unit : Metric tons   Unité : Tonnes métriques

Country or area	1990	1991	1992	1993	1994	1995	1996	1997	1998	1999	Pays ou zone
Africa	**2976**	**2300**	**2960**	**3192**	**6944**	**6070**	**7002**	**5874**	**5175**	**5000**	**Afrique**
Ghana[1]	...	*500	*500	902	#3897	4409	5443	4577	*5000	*5000	Ghana[1]
Namibia[1][2]	1637	1800	2460	2290	3047	1661	1559	1297	175	0	Namibie[1][2]
America, North	**5295**	**5156**	**4540**	**4700**	**4650**	**3870**	**3192**	**3249**	**2823**	**2750**	**Amérique du Nord**
Canada[1]	485	236	236	250	250	*250	*250	*250	*250	*250	Canada[1]
Mexico[1]	[2]4810	[2]4920	[2]4290	[2]4450	[2]4400	[2]3620	[2]2942	2999	2573	2500	Mexique[1]
America, South	**6630**	**7944**	**7297**	**7275**	**4677**	**4626**	**9867**	**9593**	**9487**	**10014**	**Amérique du Sud**
Bolivia	[1]300	463	633	663	341	362	255	282	284	*280	Bolivie
Chile[1]	5830	6820	6020	6200	4050	4076	8000	8350	*8400	*8000	Chili[1]
Peru	[1][2]500	[1][2]661	[2]644	[2]412	[2]286	188	1612	961	803	1734	Pérou
Asia	**14972**	**17784**	**21542**	**16540**	**20040**	**23040**	**17040**	**17040**	**17540**	**18040**	**Asie**
China[1]	9000	10000	14000	14000	*18000	*21000	*15000	*15000	*15500	*16000	Chine[1]
Iran(Islamic Rep. of)[1]	382	552	492	500	*500	500	500	500	500	500	Iran(Rép. islamique)[1]
Japan[1]	[2]500	[2]500	50	40	*40	*40	*40	*40	*40	*40	Japon[1]
Kazakhstan*[1]	..	...	2000	2000	1500	1500	1500	1500	1500	1500	Kazakhstan*[1]
Philippines[1]	5090	5000	5000	0	0	0	0	0	0	...	Philippines[1]
Europe	**20040**	**9338**	**13200**	**13700**	**16200**	**15100**	**13100**	**12550**	**11500**	**10500**	**Europe**
Belgium[1]	3000	2500	2000	2000	*2000	*2000	*2000	*2000	*1500	*1500	Belgique[1]
France[1]	[2]6480	[2]2000	[2]2000	[2]3000	* [2]6000	* [2]5000	*3000	*2500	*2000	*1000	France[1]
Germany[1]	..	...	300	300	*300	*250	*250	*250	*200	*200	Allemagne[1]
Germany(Fed.Rep.)[1][2]	360	..	..	..	..	..	..	..	..	..	Allemagne(Rép.féd.)[1][2]
Portugal[1]	[2]200	[2]200	[2]150	[2]150	* [2]150	* [2]100	*100	*50	*50	*50	Portugal[1]
Russian Federation*[1]	..	...	2500	2000	1500	1500	1500	1500	1500	1500	Fédération de Russie*[1]
Sweden[1][2]	10000	2500	...	...	...	...	...	...	...	...	Suède[1][2]
USSR (former)[1][2]	7800	..	..	..	..	..	..	..	..	..	URSS (anc.)[1][2]
Total	**57713**	**42522**	**49539**	**45407**	**52511**	**52706**	**50201**	**48306**	**46525**	**46304**	**Total**

General Note.
Arsenic trioxide (As$_2$O$_3$) (arsenous oxide, white arsenic), obtained by roasting arseniferous ores of nickel and silver or arsenical pyrites. It may sometimes contain impurities (arsenic sulphide, sulphur, antimonous oxide etc.). (SITC, Rev.3: 52222-1).

[1] Source: U. S. Geological Survey, (Washington, D. C.).
[2] Including calculated arsenic trioxide equivalent of output of elemental arsenic and arsenic compounds other than trioxide.

Remarque générale.
Anhydride arsénieux (As$_2$O$_3$) (trioxyde d'arsenic, oxyde arsénieux, arsenic blanc). On l'obtient par grillage de minerais arsénifères de nickel et d'argent ou de pyrites arsenicales. Il peut contenir des impuretés: sulfure d'arsenic, soufre,oxyde antimonieux, etc. (CTCI, Rev.3: 52222-1).

[1] Source: U.S. Geological Survey, (Washington, D.C.).
[2] Y compris l'équivalent en arsenique trioxide dans la production d'arsenique élémentaire et composés d'arsenique autre que l'arsenique trioxide.

Salt, unrefined
Sel, non raffiné

ISIC-BASED CODE - CODE BASE CITI

2903-01

Unit : Thousand metric tons

Unité : Milliers de tonnes métriques

Country or area	1990	1991	1992	1993	1994	1995	1996	1997	1998	1999	Pays ou zone
Africa	**3052**	**2836**	**2897**	**2742**	**2885**	**2657**	**3333**	**3659**	**4101**	**4261**	**Afrique**
Algeria	117	103	103	59	75	[1]178	[1]178	[1]137	[1]172	[1]175	Algérie
Angola* [1]	30	40	20	30	30	30	30	30	30	30	Angola* [1]
Cape Verde[1]	*4	*4	*4	*4	*4	*4	5	6	*7	*7	Cap-Vert[1]
Egypt	1125	891	936	972	1116	1193	1632	2024	2488	2588	Egypte
Ethiopia[1]	110	93	110	53	*[2]5	*[2]5	*[2]5	*[2]1	*[2]1	*[2]1	Ethiopie[1]
Ghana* [1]	50	50	50	50	50	50	50	50	50	50	Ghana* [1]
Kenya	32	110	*[1]102	*[1]75	[1]71	71	41	*[1]6	*[1]22	*[1]25	Kenya
Madagascar	[1]49	*[1]30	*[1]30	*[1]30	76	52	42	37	27	*[1]50	Madagascar
Mali* [1]	5	5	5	5	5	5	6	5	6	6	Mali* [1]
Mauritius	6	6	7	7	7	7	7	6	6	7	Maurice
Morocco	158	144	164	151	176	173	165	257	127	156	Maroc
Mozambique	47	45	23	...	...	[1]40	[1]60	[1]60	[1]60	[1]60	Mozambique
Niger	*[1]3	*[1]3	*[1]3	*[1]3	3	*[1]3	*[1]3	*[1]3	[1]2	[1]2	Niger
Senegal	91	61	20	37	106	25	113	122	138	145	Sénégal
Somalia* [1]	2	1	1	1	1	1	2	1	1	1	Somalie* [1]
South Africa	[1]728	[1]665	[1]702	[1]613	[1]414	311	290	327	358	358	Afrique du Sud
Sudan* [1]	68	75	75	75	75	75	50	50	45	50	Soudan* [1]
Tunisia	402	441	460	435	528	319	557	437	466	455	Tunisie
Uganda[1]	*5	*5	*5	10	*10	*10	*10	*10	*5	*5	Ouganda[1]
United Rep.Tanzania	[1]20	64	77	83	[1]84	[1]105	[1]87	*[1]90	*[1]90	*[1]90	Rép. Unie de Tanzanie
America, North	**56643**	**56817**	**56099**	**59186**	**61579**	**62407**	**64667**	**64326**	**64949**	**67939**	**Amérique du Nord**
Bahamas[1]	751	1096	809	850	*900	*900	*900	*900	*900	*900	Bahamas[1]
Canada	11191	11000	11088	10895	12267	10875	12248	*13192	13497	12678	Canada
Cuba	200	[1]200	[1]185	[1]185	*[1]175	*[1]180	*[1]180	*[1]180	*[1]180	*[1]180	Cuba
Dominican Republic	30	...	...	[1]62	[1]58	[1]53	[1]61	23	12	12	Rép. dominicaine
El Salvador[1]	3	7	...	*30	*30	*30	*31	95	89	90	El Salvador[1]
Guatemala	60	*[1]100	*[1]46	*[1]47	*[1]48	*[1]48	*[1]48	*[1]48	*[1]48	*[1]50	Guatemala
Honduras* [1]	32	32	30	30	25	25	25	25	25	25	Honduras* [1]
Jamaica	...	17	21	18	18	20	18	17	16	19	Jamaïque
Mexico	7135	7594	[1]7395	[1]7490	[1]7458	[1]7670	*[1]8508	[1]7933	[1]8412	[1]8500	Mexique
Netherlands Antilles[1]	*350	*350	*350	*300	420	424	*366	432	487	500	Antilles néerlandaises[1]
Nicaragua[1]	15	*15	*15	*15	*15	*15	*15	14	*15	*15	Nicaragua[1]
Panama	22	26	31	19	*[1]20	*[1]22	*[1]22	*[1]22	*[1]23	*[1]23	Panama
Puerto Rico* [1]	41	41	45	45	45	45	45	45	45	...	Porto Rico* [1]
United States	36794	36300	36000	39200	40100	42100	42200	41400	41200	44900	Etats-Unis
America, South	**7627**	**7720**	**8988**	**9551**	**11170**	**11014**	**11747**	**13647**	**14819**	**14744**	**Amérique du Sud**
Argentina	833	943	952	1033	834	*1009	*1100	[1]841	[1]850	[1]850	Argentine
Brazil	3883	3795	[1]5261	[1]6180	[1]6043	[1]5800	[1]5384	[1]6516	[1]6837	[1]6900	Brésil
Chile	1835	1676	1672	1443	3178	3494	4043	5488	6207	6074	Chili
Colombia	676	676	[1]547	[1]400	[1]565	[1]235	[1]577	[1]373	[1]495	[1]490	Colombie
Peru	*[1]200	*[1]200	*[1]238	125	150	126	293	79	[1]80	[1]80	Pérou
Venezuela	200	[1]430	[1]318	[1]370	*[1]400	*[1]350	*[1]350	*[1]350	*[1]350	*[1]350	Venezuela
Asia	**29873**	**34964**	**39972**	**40550**	**41364**	**41045**	**41251**	**43439**	**35254**	**41491**	**Asie**
Afghanistan	[3]35	[1][3]12	[1][3]12	[1][3]13	[1][3]13	[1][3]13	*[1]13	[1]13	*[1]13	*[1]13	Afghanistan
Armenia	..	103	61	45	47	33	26	23	25	27	Arménie
Azerbaijan	..	85	22	4	7	7	7	5	4	3	Azerbaïdjan
Bangladesh[2]	408	516	719	331	694	952	...	...	...	...	Bangladesh[2]
Cambodia[1]	*40	*40	*40	*40	*40	*40	*40	40	*40	*40	Cambodge[1]
China	20226	24100	*[1]28100	*[1]29500	[1]29746	[1]29780	[1]29035	[1]30830	22425	28124	Chine
Indonesia* [1]	600	610	630	650	650	670	670	680	650	680	Indonésie* [1]
Iran(Islamic Rep. of)	[1][3]848	[1][3]901	[1][3]1018	[1][3]720	[1][3]1050	[3]721	[1]1411	*[1]1383	*[1]1502	[1]1500	Iran(Rép. islamique)
Iraq	249	118	*[1]250	[1]300	*[1]250	*[1]250	*[1]250	*[1]250	*[1]250	*[1]300	Iraq
Israel	[4]402	[4]399	...	...	*[1]1120	*[1]900	*[1]800	*[1]800	*[1]800	*[1]900	Israël
Japan	[5][6]1378	[5][6]1379	[1][5][6]1405	[1]1378	[1]1387	[1]1351	[1]1390	[1]1400	[1]1400	[1]1400	Japon
Jordan	18	18	15	*[1]26	*[1]26	*[1]25	50	24	20	*[1]200	Jordanie
Kazakhstan	..	995	964	763	527	313	230	36	180	16	Kazakhstan
Korea,Dem.Ppl's.Rep.* [1]	580	580	590	590	600	600	590	590	550	500	Corée,Rép.pop.dém.de* [1]
Korea, Republic of	669	599	[1]772	[1]750	*[1]760	520	*339	334	252	502	Corée, République de
Kuwait	...	...	32	41	37	34	34	43	41	39	Koweït
Lao People's Dem. Rep.	...	...	...	...	10	11	*[1]14	*[1]18	[1]39	[1]40	Rép. dém. pop. lao

For general note and footnotes, see end of table.

Voir la fin du tableau pour la remarque générale et les notes.

ISIC-BASED CODE - CODE BASE CITI

2903-01

Unit : Thousand metric tons   Unité : Milliers de tonnes métriques

Country or area	1990	1991	1992	1993	1994	1995	1996	1997	1998	1999	Pays ou zone
Lebanon* [1]	3	3	3	3	3	3	4	4	4	4	Liban* [1]
Mongolia	16	0	0	0	1	1	1	[1]1	[1]1	[1]1	Mongolie
Myanmar[7]	27	47	47	59	59	...	...	...	...	...	Myanmar[7]
Pakistan	[2]735	[2]712	[1]863	[1]909	[1]860	[1]952	* [1]958	[1]1061	[1]1053	1190	Pakistan
Philippines	490	493	496	535	531	613	618	687	728	704	Philippines
Sri Lanka	63	53	116	[1]43	44	71	82	88	*67	79	Sri Lanka
Syrian Arab Republic	127	74	84	113	100	111	72	119	178	104	Rép. arabe syrienne
Tajikistan	..	73	45	63	73	65	48	60	59	51	Tadjikistan
Thailand[1]	219	225	313	362	*388	*481	*630	655	646	650	Thaïlande[1]
Turkey	1889	1438	1417	1527	1354	1444	1979	2308	2171	2146	Turquie
Turkmenistan	..	650	483	173	107	254	271	215	220	*240	Turkménistan
Viet Nam	593	583	594	...	...	689	709	743	867	918	Viet Nam
Yemen (former)	220	..	..	..	..	..	..	..	..	..	Yémen (anc.)
Yemen	..	116	107	123	118	71	135	136	...	...	Yémen
Europe	45177	49267	47167	42608	42684	45864	47146	45105	43788	43778	Europe
Austria	715	765	702	716	785	1361	1295	1238	1206	1433	Autriche
Croatia	..	18	29	30	22	22	19	17	24	[1]18	Croatie
Denmark[8]	522	550	528	591	307	603	599	531	485	571	Danemark[8]
Finland	5	2	6	4	5	5	2	...	...	...	Finlande
France	7168	6924	5866	5470	4764	4122	3654	4063	3330	* [1]3000	France
Germany	..	...	7738	7131	7087	8639	10072	8788	8062	...	Allemagne
Germany(Fed.Rep.)	6351	..	..	..	..	..	..	..	..	..	Allemagne(Rép.féd.)
German D.R.(former)	4082	..	..	..	..	..	..	..	..	..	R.D.A. (anc.)
Greece	182	129	143	[1]175	[1]206	[1]143	140	[1]150	* [1]150	* [1]150	Grèce
Italy	[9]3752	[9]3504	[9]3366	[9]3021	[9]3396	[9]3430	[1][9]3541	[1][9]3510	[1][9]3600	3338	Italie
Netherlands	3653	3417	[1]3628	* [1]3500	* [1]3500	[1]4976	[1]5530	* [1]5000	* [1]5500	* [1]5000	Pays-Bas
Poland	4055	3840	3887	3817	4074	4214	4163	3979	4005	4212	Pologne
Portugal	726	653	563	525	* [1]644	587	[1]610	* [1]600	597	559	Portugal
Romania[10]	4262	3255	2556	2190	2201	2489	2689	2612	2220	2197	Roumanie[10]
Russian Federation[11]	..	...	...	..	...	..	...	...	..	1611	Fédération de Russie[11]
Slovenia	..	8	7	12	11	3	4	7	20	48	Slovénie
Spain	3377	3172	2705	2842	3497	3685	3437	3445	3700	3774	Espagne
Switzerland	254	348	276	267	305	443	* [1]300	* [1]300	* [1]300	* [1]300	Suisse
Ukraine	..	8394	7409	3877	3237	2867	2848	2623	2297	2185	Ukraine
United Kingdom	5697	5200	[1]6100	[1]6790	* [1]7000	* [1]6650	* [1]6610	* [1]6600	[1]6600	* [1]5800	Royaume-Uni
Yugoslavia	..	39	47	39	32	14	22	28	78	64	Yougoslavie
Yugoslavia, SFR[12]	376	..	..	..	..	..	..	..	..	..	Yougoslavie, RSF[12]
USSR (former)	14747	..	..	..	..	..	..	..	..	..	URSS (anc.)
Oceania	7268	7872	7773	7817	7765	8260	8335	8382	9024	9268	Océanie
Australia	[2]7188	[2]7792	[1]7693	[1]7737	[1]7685	8210	8255	8315	8959	9203	Australie
New Zealand	[1]80	[1]80	[1]80	[1]80	* [1]80	* [1]50	80	[1]67	* [1]65	* [1]65	Nouvelle-Zélande
Total	164387	159475	162896	162454	167447	171247	176479	178559	171935	181482	Total

General Note.

Sodium chloride or common salt (NaCl), irrespective of the source from which it is obtained and the degree of purity or concentration. Refined salt, salt liquors and sea water are excluded. (SITC, Rev.3: 27830-1).

Remarque générale.

Chlorure de sodium ou sel ordinaire (NaCl), sans distinction de provenance ni de degré de pureté ou de concentration, à l'exclusion du sel rafinné, des saumures et de l'eau de mer. (CTCI, Rev.3: 27830-1).

For footnotes, see end of table.   Voir la fin du tableau pour les notes.

Salt, unrefined (continued)
Sel, non raffiné (suite)

ISIC-BASED CODE - CODE BASE CITI

2903-01

Footnotes

[1] Source: U. S. Geological Survey, (Washington, D. C.).
[2] Twelve months ending 30 June of year stated.
[3] Twelve months beginning 21 March of year stated.
[4] Marketed quantities.
[5] Production in licensed plants only.
[6] Twelve months beginning 1 April of year stated.
[7] Government production only.
[8] Sales.
[9] Including brine.
[10] Including refined salt.
[11] Refined salt.
[12] Excluding rock salt.

Notes.

[1] Source: U.S. Geological Survey, (Washington, D.C.).
[2] Période de douze mois finissant le 30 juin de l'année indiquée.
[3] Période de douze mois commençant le 21 mars de l'année indiquée.
[4] Quantités commercialisées.
[5] Production des usines agréées seulement.
[6] Période de douze mois commençant le 1er avril de l'année indiquée.
[7] Production de l'Etat seulement.
[8] Ventes.
[9] Y compris la saumure.
[10] Y compris le sel raffiné.
[11] Sel raffiné.
[12] Non compris le sel gemme.

Diamonds, industrial
Diamants industriels

ISIC-BASED CODE - CODE BASE CITI

2909-01

Unit : Thousand carats

Unité : Milliers de carats

Country or area	1990	1991	1992	1993	1994	1995	1996	1997	1998	1999	Pays ou zone
Africa	**27404**	**36530**	**27319**	**35142**	**35428**	**37108**	**41730**	**44258**	**46516**	**43247**	**Afrique**
Angola[1]	73	62	80	15	30	#300	250	124	364	120	Angola[1]
Botswana	5206	#16506	15946	14730	15550	16802	17707	20111	19772	21348	Botswana
Central African Rep.[1]	78	82	107	125	131	130	120	100	200	150	Rép. centrafricaine[1]
Côte d'Ivoire[1]	3	4	4	...	...	22	100	100	100	100	Côte d'Ivoire[1]
Dem. Rep. of Congo[1]	16500	14814	4570	13620	13000	13000	17000	17600	18900	14500	Rép. dém. du Congo[1]
Gabon*[1]	100	100	100	100	100	100	100	...	...	...	Gabon*[1]
Ghana[1]	487	140	590	484	473	505	573	166	160	160	Ghana[1]
Guinea[1]	8	6	5	#33	75	91	40	40	100	100	Guinée[1]
Liberia	60	60	90	[1]90	[1]60	[1]90	[1]90	[1]120	[1]150	[1]400	Libéria
Namibia[1]	15	20	30	20	0	0	0	71	73	105	Namibie[1]
Sierra Leone[1]	12	83	116	68	100	101	108	100	50	75	Sierra Leone[1]
South Africa[1]	4800	4600	5600	5700	5800	5880	5550	5540	6460	6000	Afrique du Sud[1]
Swaziland	17	23	51	62	...	...	...	...	...	...	Swaziland
United Rep.Tanzania	[1]45	30	30	41	17	49	54	...	...	...	Rép. Unie de Tanzanie
America, North	**87200**	**90000**	**90000**	**103000**	**104000**	**115000**	**114000**	**125000**	**140000**	**208000**	**Amérique du Nord**
United States*	...	90000	90000	103000	104000	115000	114000	125000	140000	208000	Etats-Unis*
America, South	**1243**	**1266**	**1188**	**1461**	**1198**	**701**	**708**	**725**	**785**	**785**	**Amérique du Sud**
Brazil[1]	900	900	665	1000	600	600	600	600	600	600	Brésil[1]
Guyana	15	29	46	51	...	...	...	...	...	...	Guyana
Venezuela	328	337	477	410	563	[1]66	[1]73	[1]90	[1]150	[1]150	Venezuela
Asia	**826**	**836**	**824**	**883**	**888**	**942**	**942**	**943**	**945**	**971**	**Asie**
China[1]	*800	*800	*800	*850	*850	*900	*900	900	900	920	Chine[1]
India	3	12	3	#13	16	20	20	20	23	29	Inde
Indonesia[1]	*23	24	21	20	22	22	22	23	...	...	Indonésie[1]
Europe	..	**8429**	**8911**	**8000**	**10000**	**10500**	**10500**	**10500**	**11500**	**11500**	**Europe**
Russian Federation[1]	..	...	...	8000	10000	10500	10500	10500	11500	11500	Fédération de Russie[1]
USSR (former)*[1]	6804	..	..	..	..	..	..	..	..	..	URSS (anc.)*[1]
Oceania	**17300**	**18000**	**22100**	**23000**	**23800**	**22381**	**23096**	**22100**	**22500**	**16381**	**Océanie**
Australia	17300	18000	22100	23000	23800	22381	[1]23096	[1]22100	[1]22500	[1]16381	Australie
Total	**140777**	**155061**	**150342**	**171486**	**175315**	**186633**	**190977**	**203526**	**222247**	**280884**	**Total**

General Note.
Mine and alluvial production of rough, uncut and unpolished diamonds for industrial uses. Industrial diamonds comprise all stones the colour, size and texture of which do not permit their use as jewellery, for example, boart, carbonado etc. Diamonds in the form of grit or powder are included. (SITC, Rev.3: 27710-0).

Remarque générale.
Production de diamants bruts, non taillés et non polis, en provenance de mines ou d'alluvions, destinés à des usages industriels. Cette rubrique comprend toutes les pierres dont la couleur, la dimension ou la structure interdisent leur emploi en joaillerie, par exemple les borts, les carbonados etc., ainsi que les diamants sous forme d'égrisés et de poudres. (CTCI, Rev.3: 27710-0).

[1] Source: U. S. Geological Survey, (Washington, D. C.).

[1] Source: U.S. Geological Survey, (Washington, D.C.).

Gypsum, crude
Gypse brut

ISIC-BASED CODE - CODE BASE CITI

2909-02

Unit : Thousand metric tons   Unité : Milliers de tonnes métriques

Country or area	1990	1991	1992	1993	1994	1995	1996	1997	1998	1999	Pays ou zone
Africa	2419	2930	3018	2946	3142	3596	3381	3203	3858	4111	**Afrique**
Algeria	49	49	48	...	...	*[1]250	*[1]250	*[1]275	*[1]275	*[1]275	Algérie
Angola[1]	57	57	57	50	0	0	*0	*0	*0	...	Angola[1]
Egypt	1279	1239	1425	1199	1481	2361	2092	1839	2423	2666	Egypte
Ethiopia[1]	2	2	3	3	*[2]31	[2]124	*[2]124	*[2]120	*[2]100	*[2]100	Ethiopie[1]
Kenya	[1][2]36	[1][2]36	1	2	...	1	1	[1]1	[1]1	[1]1	Kenya
Libyan Arab Jamah.	4	...	...	...	3	1	0	0	0	0	Jamah. arabe libyenne
Mali	1	1	1	[1]1	*[1]1	*[1]0	*[1]1	*[1]0	*[1]1	*[1]1	Mali
Mauritania	[1]8	3	3	4	4	...	...	...	...	...	Mauritanie
Morocco[1]	450	450	450	450	*450	*450	*450	*450	*450	*450	Maroc[1]
Niger	[1]1	[1]1	[1]2	[1]2	2	*[1]2	*[1]2	*[1]2	*[1]2	*[1]2	Niger
Sierra Leone	4	4	4	...	...	...	...	...	...	...	Sierra Leone
Somalia[1]	3	1	2	...	...	*2	*1	*1	*2	*2	Somalie[1]
South Africa	384	420	334	...	[1]304	[1]288	[1]341	397	486	505	Afrique du Sud
Sudan[1][2]	5	7	10	10	*10	*10	*5	*5	*5	*5	Soudan[1][2]
Tunisia[1]	100	*650	*650	*650	*650	*100	*100	*100	*100	*100	Tunisie[1]
United Rep.Tanzania[1][2]	36	9	27	1	8	1	9	*9	*9	...	Rép. Unie de Tanzanie[1][2]
America, North	28788	25983	27678	29144	30868	30056	32306	33552	34589	39223	**Amérique du Nord**
Canada	[2][3]7978	[2][3]6727	[2][3]7295	[3]7563	[3]8110	8055	8202	*8628	8095	9345	Canada
Cuba	132	132	127	...	...	*[1]130	*[1]130	*[1]130	*[1]130	*[1]130	Cuba
Dominican Republic	150	[1]118	[1]83	[1]85	[1]93	[1]95	[1]86	113	76	27	Rép. dominicaine
El Salvador[1]	5	5	5	5	*5	*5	*5	*6	*6	*6	El Salvador[1]
Guatemala[1]	66	52	73	75	89	*90	28	*30	*30	*30	Guatemala[1]
Honduras[1]	27	27	26	26	*26	*26	*26	*28	*30	*30	Honduras[1]
Jamaica	88	136	100	109	164	188	251	132	154	232	Jamaïque
Mexico[1]	5430	4770	5160	5340	[2]5040	[2]4854	[2]6065	[2]5869	[2]7045	[2]7000	Mexique[1]
Nicaragua[2]	12	[1]16	[1]9	[1]11	*[1]11	*[1]13	*[1]13	*[1]16	*[1]23	*[1]23	Nicaragua[2]
United States[4]	14900	14000	14800	15800	17200	16600	17500	18600	19000	22400	Etats-Unis[4]
America, South	2337	2549	2840	2638	2782	2734	3060	4101	4866	4847	**Amérique du Sud**
Argentina[1]	362	383	514	519	550	590	633	697	*650	*650	Argentine[1]
Brazil	653	750	[1]888	[1][2]747	[1][2]834	[1][2]953	[1][2]1126	[1][2]1396	[1][2]1630	[1][2]1630	Brésil
Chile	254	336	424	511	552	464	520	398	781	886	Chili
Colombia	499	499	598	[1]439	[1]450	*[1]450	*[1]522	*[1]565	*[1]560	*[1]560	Colombie
Ecuador[1]	32	24	24	24	108	2	2	2	2	2	Equateur[1]
Paraguay[1]	5	5	5	5	*5	*5	*5	5	*5	*4	Paraguay[1]
Peru	[1]150	*[1]160	*[1]35	38	15	25	65	65	*[1]35	*[1]35	Pérou
Uruguay[1]	145	145	145	145	145	145	130	943	1123	1000	Uruguay[1]
Venezuela	237	247	207	210	123	[1]100	[1]57	[1]30	[1]80	[1]80	Venezuela
Asia	34098	34233	36438	35165	31770	34442	35856	37009	33233	34957	**Asie**
Afghanistan[1]	3	3	3	3	*3	*3	*3	*3	*3	*3	Afghanistan[1]
Armenia	..	172	69	50	35	34	17	18	15	12	Arménie
Azerbaijan	..	81	52	21	20	6	2	2	3	2	Azerbaïdjan
China	10424	10618	11970	*[1]10600	*[1]6820	*[1]7340	*[1]7780	[1]9100	*[1]9000	*[1]9000	Chine
Cyprus	37	18	35	69	89	153	94	234	297	182	Chypre
Georgia	..	...	7	2	1	1	1	4	6	6	Géorgie
India	1662	1560	1802	1686	1646	2195	2210	2195	2267	3288	Inde
Iran(Islamic Rep. of)	[1]7720	[1]8050	[1]8720	[1]8600	[1]8430	8285	8570	8900	[1]9750	*[1]9750	Iran(Rép. islamique)
Iraq[1]	380	190	380	450	*300	*250	*200	*200	*250	*250	Iraq[1]
Israel[1]	38	26	48	48	*48	*50	*50	*60	*60	*60	Israël[1]
Japan[1]	[5]6350	4508	4322	3953	3873	5334	5432	5371	5305	5500	Japon[1]
Jordan[1]	93	55	83	195	193	*190	*190	194	176	180	Jordanie[1]
Kyrgyzstan	..	15	6	0	0	0	0	0	0	0	Kirghizistan
Lao People's Dem. Rep.	[1]53	[1]77	[1]80	[1]80	130	124	[1]113	[1]114	[1]130	[1]135	Rép. dém. pop. lao
Lebanon[1]	2	2	2	2	*2	*2	*3	*3	*3	*3	Liban[1]
Mongolia[1]	32	25	25	25	*25	*25	*25	*25	*25	*10	Mongolie[1]
Myanmar[6]	34	33	31	28	38	35	39	39	37	46	Myanmar[6]
Pakistan	491	468	[1]462	[1]535	[1]607	[1]314	*[1]504	*[1]550	[1]249	242	Pakistan
Philippines	[7]118	[1][2]28	[1][2]25	[1][2]0	[1][2]0	[1][2]0	[1]0	[1]0	...	...	Philippines
Saudi Arabia[1]	375	375	269	327	*375	370	363	*365	330	*330	Arabie saoudite[1]
Syrian Arab Republic	179	183	235	303	304	336	358	330	325	395	Rép. arabe syrienne
Tajikistan	..	33	49	4	4	1	22	26	32	32	Tadjikistan

For general note and footnotes, see end of table.   Voir la fin du tableau pour la remarque générale et les notes.

Gypsum, crude (continued)
Gypse brut (suite)

ISIC-BASED CODE - CODE BASE CITI

2909-02

Unit : Thousand metric tons / Unité : Milliers de tonnes métriques

Country or area	1990	1991	1992	1993	1994	1995	1996	1997	1998	1999	Pays ou zone
Thailand	5753	7196	7111	7455	8140	8533	8934	8558	4334	5005	Thaïlande
Turkey	172	324	432	493	487	670	754	525	463	354	Turquie
Turkmenistan	..	15	17	9	6	5	5	4	3	...	Turkménistan
United Arab Emirates	89	*[1]95	*[1]95	*[1]95	*[1]95	*[1]90	*[1]90	*[1]90	*[1]90	*[1]90	Emirats arabes unis
Viet Nam[1]	27	*30	*30	*30	*0	*0	*0	*0	*0	...	Viet Nam[1]
Yemen (former)[1]	66	..	..	..	..	..	..	..	..	..	Yémen (anc.)[1]
Yemen	..	50	78	102	99	96	97	99	[1]80	[1]80	Yémen
Europe	**27125**	**27773**	**22781**	**22313**	**22776**	**23409**	**22307**	**21713**	**23099**	**23851**	Europe
Austria	753	653	764	874	1012	586	374	349	311	...	Autriche
Belarus	..	134	85	37	20	16	21	23	17	27	Bélarus
Bosnia and Herzegovina	..	..	150	...	...	...	...	...	...		Bosnie-Herzégovine
Bulgaria	494	#63	125	143	161	163	169	156	[1][2]183	[1][2]180	Bulgarie
Czechoslovakia(former)	744	624		...	...	...	...	...	...		Tchécoslovaquie(anc.)
France	5800	5708	[5]5160	[5]5000	*[1][2]5200	*[1][2]4800	[1][2]4550	*[1][2]4500	*[1][2]4500	*[1][2]4500	France
Germany	..	...	...	...	...	1175	1021	1240	1094	...	Allemagne
Germany(Fed.Rep.)	2172										Allemagne(Rép.féd.)
German D.R.(former)	300	..	..	..	..	..	..	..	..	..	R.D.A. (anc.)
Greece	630	665	658	630	630	692	732	[1]663	[1]600	[1]600	Grèce
Hungary[1]	[2]112	[2]110	*120	125	*[2]150	*[2]198	*[2]190	*[2]190	*[2]180	*[2]180	Hongrie[1]
Ireland[1]	394	342	343	318	367	406	422	*477	*450	*450	Irlande[1]
Italy[1]	1260	1290	1300	1200	1361	2362	*1275	*1300	*1300	*1300	Italie[1]
Latvia	..	337	...	60	61	79	64	117	119	97	Lettonie
Poland	916	788	843	832	1055	1023	1028	1035	1029	1163	Pologne
Portugal	309	359	[1]417	[1]459	521	538	*[1][2]521	*[1][2]500	*[1][2]500	*[1][2]500	Portugal
Republic of Moldova	..	531	535	[8]260	[8]280	[8]269	[8]197	[8]158	[8]100	[8]180	Rép. de Moldova
Romania	798	599	499	#83	124	111	91	215	297	308	Roumanie
Russian Federation	..	2281	1416	1104	789	697	1534	559	609	867	Fédération de Russie
Slovenia	..	..	151	...	...	...	...	...	...		Slovénie
Spain	7673	7212	4990	6467	6497	7495	7259	7477	9058	9511	Espagne
Switzerland[1]	230	230	200	299	*298	*300	*300	*300	*300	...	Suisse[1]
Ukraine	..	959	697	434	243	130	175	70	68	97	Ukraine
United Kingdom	*[9]3990	*[9]3501	*[9]2994	[1]2500	*[1]2500	*[1]2000	*[1]2000	*[1]2000	*[1]2000	*[1]1800	Royaume-Uni
Yugoslavia	..	43	48	18	40	40	44	32	28	34	Yougoslavie
T.F.Yug.Rep. Macedonia	..	60	37	36	33	28	39	51	55	76	L'ex-RY Macédoine
Yugoslavia, SFR	550	..	..	..	..	..	..	..	..	..	Yougoslavie, RSF
USSR (former)[1]	4720	..	..	..	..	..	..	..	..	..	URSS (anc.)[1]
Oceania	**1885**	**2000**	**2000**	**2000**	**2000**	**2000**	**2000**	**2100**	**2100**	**2100**	Océanie
Australia	1885	[1]2000	[1]2000	[1]2000	*[1]2000	*[1]2000	*[1]2000	*[1]2100	*[1]2100	*[1]2100	Australie
Total	**101372**	**95468**	**94756**	**94206**	**93337**	**96237**	**98910**	**101678**	**101745**	**109089**	Total

General Note.
Gypsum is a natural hydrated calcium sulphate generally white and friable. Anhydrite is a natural anhydrous form of calcium sulphate used in the manufacture of sulphuric acid and of certain types of plaster. (SITC, Rev.3: 27323-0).

Remarque générale.
Le gypse est un sulfate de calcium naturel hydraté, généralement friable et de couleur blanche. L'anhydrite est une forme anhydre du sulfate de calcium naturel, utilisée dans la fabrication de l'acide sulfurique et de certains genres de plâtres. (CTCI, Rev.3: 27323-0).

[1] Source: U. S. Geological Survey, (Washington, D. C.).
[2] Including anhydrite.
[3] Shipments.
[4] Excluding byproduct gypsum.
[5] Gypsum consumed.
[6] Government production only.
[7] Including byproduct gypsum.
[8] Excluding Transnistria region.
[9] Great Britain only.

[1] Source: U.S. Geological Survey, (Washington, D.C.).
[2] Y compris l'anhydrite.
[3] Expéditions.
[4] Non compris le gypse obtenu comme sous-produit.
[5] Le gypse consommé.
[6] Production de l'Etat seulement.
[7] Y compris le gypse obtenu comme sous-produit.
[8] Non compris la région de Transnistria.
[9] Grande Bretagne seulement.

Abrasives, natural (pozzolan, pumice etc.)
Abrasifs naturels (pouzzolane, pierre ponce etc.)

ISIC-BASED CODE - CODE BASE CITI

2909-04

Unit : Thousand metric tons
Unité : Milliers de tonnes métriques

Country or area	1990	1991	1992	1993	1994	1995	1996	1997	1998	1999	Pays ou zone
Africa	**218**	**232**	**244**	**207**	**245**	**466**	**452**	**436**	**450**	**445**	**Afrique**
Burkina Faso[1]	...	...	...	...	11.0	11.0	11.0	10.0	10.0	...	Burkina Faso[1]
Cameroon[1][2]	130.0	130.0	130.0	130.0	101.9	90.0	80.0	100.0	105.0	...	Cameroun[1][2]
Cape Verde[1][2]	53.0	53.0	53.0	25.0	5.0	5.0	1.0	1.0	...	...	Cap-Vert[1][2]
Ethiopia[1]	23.0	37.0	49.0	40.0	#127.0	360.0	360.0	325.0	...	...	Ethiopie[1]
America, North	**951**	**921**	**981**	**948**	**969**	**991**	**1076**	**1040**	**1041**	**1074**	**Amérique du Nord**
Costa Rica[1]	4.9	8.0	8.0	8.0	8.0	8.0	8.0	8.0	8.0	...	Costa Rica[1]
Dominica	[1][3]100.0	[1][3]100.0	[1][3]100.0	[1][3]100.0	[1][3]100.0	[1][3]100.0	[1]100.0	[1]100.0	92.6	...	Dominique
Guadeloupe[1]	[2]220.0	[2]230.0	[2]220.0	[2]210.0	[2]210.0	[2]210.0	210.0	210.0	210.0	...	Guadeloupe[1]
Guatemala	15.0	[1][3]6.1	[1][3]6.6	[1][3]6.3	[1][3]6.0	[1][3]6.2	[1]6.3	[1]6.3	...	...	Guatemala
Martinique[1]	[3]140.0	[3]150.0	[3]140.0	[3]130.0	[3]130.0	130.0	130.0	130.0	130.0	...	Martinique[1]
Mexico[1]	...	...	25.0	25.0	*25.0	8.2	9.9	8.3	12.2	...	Mexique[1]
United States[5]	[4]442.8	[4]401.4	[4]481.0	[4]469.0	[4]490.0	[6]529.0	[6]612.0	[6]577.0	[6]583.0	[6]643.0	Etats-Unis[5]
America, South	**464**	**424**	**494**	**549**	**679**	**638**	**901**	**1091**	**1452**	**1654**	**Amérique du Sud**
Argentina	125.0	[1]69.7	[1]89.1	[1]89.0	[1]131.7	[1]74.9	[1]81.3	[1]147.2	[1]140.0	...	Argentine
Chile	[2]305.1	[2]320.9	[2]384.7	[2]448.2	[2]451.6	[2]465.8	[1]500.0	[2]490.8	[2]911.9	[2]957.5	Chili
Ecuador[1]	34.0	33.5	20.6	12.2	95.2	97.0	319.9	453.3	400.0	...	Equateur[1]
Asia	**244**	**880**	**991**	**871**	**1213**	**1360**	**1296**	**1173**	**1156**	**2177**	**Asie**
India	5.3	27.4	23.0	48.4	66.1	62.3	42.3	76.9	133.1	190.8	Inde
Iran(Islamic Rep. of)	[1]238.0	[1]215.0	[1]330.0	[1]185.0	[1]200.0	452.9	480.0	415.0	444.0	...	Iran(Rép. islamique)
Turkey	[3]0.6	...	...	...	[1]947.2	[1]845.0	[1]774.0	[1]681.0	[1]579.0	...	Turquie
Europe	**8120**	**8357**	**8269**	**7893**	**8260**	**7093**	**6954**	**7049**	**6965**	**6548**	**Europe**
Austria	21.5	20.7	18.9	17.4	19.2	21.7	...	...	...	...	Autriche
France	[2]373.7	[2]435.1	[2]403.9	[2]127.3	[1]490.0	[1]427.0	[1]400.0	[1]477.0	[1]460.0	...	France
Germany	...	...	[1]591.0	[1]647.0	[1]504.0	312.3	299.2	338.0	214.0	...	Allemagne
Germany(Fed.Rep.)[1][7]	105.0	...									Allemagne(Rép.féd.)[1][7]
Greece	[1]1460.0	[1]981.0	[1]1300.0	[1]1200.0	[1]1285.0	860.0	864.4	...	...	...	Grèce
Iceland	[3]29.5	[3]34.7	[3]37.9	[1]45.0	[1]23.0	[1]30.0	...	103.2	96.8	100.3	Islande
Italy[1]	5225.0	5200.0	5000.0	5200.0	5200.0	4650.0	4600.0	4600.0	4600.0	...	Italie[1]
Slovenia[1]	...	...	*50.0	*40.0	*40.0	*40.0	40.0	40.0	40.0	...	Slovénie[1]
Spain	905.7	969.0	812.1	554.1	623.9	677.4	[1]600.0	[1]600.0	737.1	845.3	Espagne
T.F.Yug.Rep. Macedonia[1]	...	...	...	...	75.0	75.0	75.0	100.0	100.0	...	L'ex-RY Macédoine[1]
USSR (former)	6.8	..								..	URSS (anc.)
Oceania	**25**	**53**	**112**	**69**	**117**	**77**	**91**	**197**	**190**	**190**	**Océanie**
New Zealand	25.0	[1]52.6	112.5	69.2	116.8	[1]77.1	[1]90.6	[1]196.7	[1]190.0	[1]190.0	Nouvelle-Zélande
Total	**10030**	**10867**	**11091**	**10538**	**11483**	**10626**	**10770**	**10985**	**11254**	**12088**	**Total**

General Note.
Data in this table refer to the production of natural abrasives such as pozzolan, pumice and volcanic cinder. Unless otherwise stated, production of other abrasives including emery, natural corundum, tripoli and garnet is not included. Precious or semi-precious stone dust or powder are also excluded. (SITC, Rev.3: 27722-1, 27729-1).

Remarque générale.
Les données se rapportent à la production des abrasifs naturels (pouzzolane, pierre ponce, lapilli et cendre volcanique). Sauf avis contraire, cette rubrique ne comprend ni les autres abrasifs, i.e. émeri, corindon naturel, "tripoli" et grenat, ni les égrisés et les poudres de pierres précieuses et semi-précieuses. (CTCI, Rev.3: 27722-1,27729-1).

[1] Source: U. S. Geological Survey, (Washington, D. C.).
[2] Pozzolan.
[3] Pumice.
[4] Including pumice for use other than as an abrasive. Also including volcanic cinders used principally for ballast.
[5] Excluding volcanic cinder.
[6] Sold or used by producers.
[7] Including pumice and pumicite for construction purposes.

[1] Source: U.S. Geological Survey, (Washington, D.C.).
[2] Pouzzolane.
[3] Pierre ponce.
[4] Y compris la pierre ponce utilisée autrement que comme abrasif. Y compris également les cendres volcaniques utilisées essentiellement comme ballast.
[5] Non compris les cendres volcaniques.
[6] Vendu ou utilisé par les producteurs.
[7] Y compris la pierre ponce et le lapilli utilisés dans la construction.

Graphite, natural
Graphite naturel

ISIC-BASED CODE - CODE BASE CITI

2909-07

Unit : Metric tons   Unité : Tonnes métriques

Country or area	1990	1991	1992	1993	1994	1995	1996	1997	1998	1999	Pays ou zone
Africa	**44489**	**34200**	**30836**	**29296**	**28788**	**30898**	**32354**	**44301**	**33443**	**31742**	**Afrique**
Madagascar	18036	11372	8910	13118	14593	16119	11295	15397	13748	...	Madagascar
Mozambique	...	...	...	...	[1]430	[1]3019	[1]3283	5125	5889	4007	Mozambique
Namibia[1]	0	200	200	0	0	...	...	...	...	...	Namibie[1]
United Rep.Tanzania[1]	...	...	...	...	...	359	#6776	*11000	0	*0	Rép. Unie de Tanzanie[1]
Zimbabwe	16384	[1]12903	[1]12346	[1]7142	[1]7890	11381	11000	[1]12779	[1]13806	[1]13800	Zimbabwe
America, North	**24918**	**37258**	**32400**	**48500**	**30863**	**34388**	**40412**	**47982**	**43461**	**44000**	**Amérique du Nord**
Mexico	24918	37258	32400	[1]48500	[1]30863	[1]34388	[1]40412	[1]47982	[1]43461	* [1]44000	Mexique
America, South	**29208**	**27050**	**29434**	**34820**	**33372**	**28053**	**31254**	**40587**	**61369**	**61400**	**Amérique du Sud**
Argentina	318	[1]85	[1]20	[1]20	[1]25	[1]25	...	...	...	...	Argentine
Brazil	28890	26965	[1]29414	[1]34800	[1]33347	[1]28028	[1]31254	[1]40587	[1]61369	* [1]61400	Brésil
Asia	**894970**	**799815**	**657200**	**463047**	**335217**	**406544**	**371085**	**484706**	**348554**	**181402**	**Asie**
China	678900	589300	508300	[1]310000	[1]183000	[1]204000	[1]185000	[1]310000	158270	* [1]28000	Chine
India	59140	68265	78185	83956	103053	136263	117761	112786	135668	108821	Inde
Korea,Dem.Ppl's.Rep.[1]	35000	35000	38000	*38000	*38000	*40000	*40000	40000	35000	*25000	Corée,Rép.pop.dém.de[1]
Korea, Republic of	99600	76791	8412	5910	4300	1938	1820	992	0	0	Corée, République de
Myanmar[2]	45	40	0	0	0	0	...	...	...	...	Myanmar[2]
Pakistan	18	...	...	...	...	...	...	...	...	...	Pakistan
Sri Lanka	3555	3831	3307	[1]5163	[1]2946	4325	6486	5910	4598	4563	Sri Lanka
Turkey	18712	26570	[1]20978	[1]20000	3900	[1]20000	[1]20000	* [1]15000	[1]15000	* [1]15000	Turquie
Europe	**54136**	**137000**	**108318**	**51731**	**53176**	**55463**	**84302**	**58152**	**46315**	**51316**	**Europe**
Austria	[3]22705	[3]27003	[3]19596	[3]4146	[3]12211	[1][3]11877	[1][3]12000	[1]12000	[1]12000	* [1]12000	Autriche
Czechoslovakia(former)	5557	4269	..	..	...	...	...	...	..	..	Tchécoslovaquie(anc.)
Czech Republic	..	..	7764	6515	...	...	...	...	...	...	République tchèque
Germany	..	...	[1]11963	[1]4473	[1]4369	[1]5214	36357	...	[1]1000	* [1]1000	Allemagne
Germany(Fed.Rep.)[1][4]	8000										Allemagne(Rép.féd.)[1][4]
Norway	5000	[1]6930	[1]7000	[1]6500	[1]5566	[1]2588	[1]2500	* [1]2600	[1]2500	* [1]2500	Norvège
Romania	8795	5296	2303	2494	2335	2179	2931	2573	1951	1041	Roumanie
Russian Federation	..	37791	33569	17103	11721	13629	13928	14275	12966	15670	Fédération de Russie
Sweden	...	...	...	...	...	...	...	...	3654	4504	Suède
Ukraine	..	41077	22044	6421	5755	8757	5367	6289	5104	7461	Ukraine
USSR (former)[1]	80000	..	..	..	..	..	..	..	..	..	URSS (anc.)[1]
Total	**1127721**	**1035323**	**858188**	**627394**	**481416**	**555346**	**559407**	**675728**	**533142**	**369860**	**Total**

General Note.
Natural graphite (plumbago or black lead) regardless of carbon content. (SITC, Rev.3: 27822-0).

Remarque générale.
Graphite naturel (plombagine ou mine de plomb), quelle qu'en soit la teneur en carbone. (CTCI, Rev.3: 27822-0).

[1] Source: U. S. Geological Survey, (Washington, D. C.).
[2] Twelve months ending 31 March of year stated.
[3] Crude production.
[4] Marketable production.

[1] Source: U.S. Geological Survey, (Washington, D.C.).
[2] Période de douze mois finissant le 31 mars de l'année indiquée.
[3] Production brute.
[4] Production commercialisable.

Asbestos
Amiante

ISIC-BASED CODE - CODE BASE CITI

2909-10

Unit : Thousand metric tons   Unité : Milliers de tonnes métriques

Country or area	1990	1991	1992	1993	1994	1995	1996	1997	1998	1999	Pays ou zone
Africa	**503**	**477**	**459**	**430**	**401**	**422**	**327**	**337**	**249**	**259**	**Afrique**
Algeria	169	158	157	141	129	133	77	99	69	75	Algérie
Egypt	0	1	1	1	1	1	1	2	[1]2	* [1]2	Egypte
South Africa	146	149	124	[1]104	[1]92	[1]89	[1]57	[1]50	27	19	Afrique du Sud
Swaziland[1]	...	...	...	...	27	29	26	26	28	*28	Swaziland[1]
Zimbabwe	161	142	150	157	152	170	166	160	[1]123	* [1]135	Zimbabwe
America, North	**702**	**707**	**603**	**537**	**535**	**525**	**516**	**462**	**315**	**344**	**Amérique du Nord**
Canada	686	687	587	523	525	[1]516	506	[1]455	[1]309	* [1]337	Canada
United States	...	[2]20	[2]16	[2]14	[2]10	[2]9	[2]10	[2]7	[2]6	[1]7	Etats-Unis
America, South	**218**	**218**	**191**	**193**	**200**	**178**	**178**	**178**	**178**	**178**	**Amérique du Sud**
Brazil	[3]210	[3]210	...	[1]185	[1]192	[1]170	[1]170	[1]170	[1]170	* [1]170	Brésil
Colombia[1]	8	8	...	...	...	...	...	...	...	...	Colombie[1]
Asia	**285**	**918**	**807**	**688**	**602**	**580**	**584**	**583**	**603**	**579**	**Asie**
China	192	213	230	[1]240	* [1]303	* [1]263	* [1]293	* [1]245	298	292	Chine
India	26	28	42	42	28	24	27	26	20	18	Inde
Iran(Islamic Rep. of)	3	3	3	3	* [1]5	* [1]5	* [1]5	* [1]5	* [1]5	* [1]5	Iran(Rép. islamique)
Japan[1]	4	5	*30	*25	*21	*20	*18	*18	*18	*18	Japon[1]
Kazakhstan	..	517	387	272	140	161	134	182	155	139	Kazakhstan
Korea, Republic of	2	0	2	0	0	0	...	...	...	...	Corée, République de
Pakistan	46	136	...	...	...	...	...	...	...	...	Pakistan
Syrian Arab Republic	12	16	22	15	14	16	...	...	...	...	Rép. arabe syrienne
Europe	**85**	**1665**	**1452**	**925**	**699**	**781**	**706**	**805**	**673**	**743**	**Europe**
Bulgaria[3]	1	0	1	1	0	0	0	0	...	...	Bulgarie[3]
Greece	[1]73	[1]60	* [1]30	[1]57	[1]56	75	75	* [1]80	* [1]70	* [1]60	Grèce
Italy	4	4	0	0	0	0	...	...	...	...	Italie
Russian Federation	..	1599	1420	867	643	706	630	724	602	683	Fédération de Russie
Yugoslavia	..	2	1	0	0	0	1	0	1	0	Yougoslavie
Yugoslavia, SFR[4]	7	..	..	..	..	..	..	..	..	..	Yougoslavie, RSF[4]
USSR (former)[1]	2400	..	..	..	..	..	..	..	..	..	URSS (anc.)[1]
Total	**4192**	**3986**	**3512**	**2773**	**2436**	**2486**	**2311**	**2364**	**2018**	**2103**	**Total**

General Note.
Crude, washed or ground asbestos. (SITC, Rev.3: 27840-0).

Remarque générale.
Amiante brut, lavé ou broyé. (CTCI, Rev.3: 27840-0).

[1] Source: U. S. Geological Survey, (Washington, D. C.).
[2] Sales.
[3] Asbestos fibres only.
[4] Excluding asbestos powder.

[1] Source: U. S. Geological Survey, (Washington, D.C.).
[2] Ventes.
[3] Fibres d'amiante seulement.
[4] Non compris l'amiante en poudre.

Mica in book form (sheet and splittings)
Mica sous forme feuilletée (en feuilles et en lamelles)

ISIC-BASED CODE - CODE BASE CITI

2909-131

Unit : Metric tons   Unité : Tonnes métriques

Country or area	1990	1991	1992	1993	1994	1995	1996	1997	1998	1999	Pays ou zone
Africa	**2680**	**2617**	**2661**	**2890**	**2069**	**2036**	**2550**	**1233**	**2509**	**2110**	**Afrique**
Madagascar[1][2]	...	680	798	880	356	432	450	603	600	*600	Madagascar[1][2]
Morocco	...	...	...	* [2]1500	* [2]1500	[2]564	* [2]600	* [2]600	* [2]600	210	Maroc
Zimbabwe[2]	...	...	...	510	213	1040	*1500	30	1309	*1300	Zimbabwe[2]
America, North	**20853**	**24778**	**24203**	**23937**	**23253**	**22528**	**21773**	**18475**	**18390**	**18500**	**Amérique du Nord**
Canada[1][2]	12000	17000	17500	*17500	*17500	*17500	*17500	*17500	*17500	*17500	Canada[1][2]
Mexico[1][2]	...	...	...	6437	5753	5028	4273	975	890	1000	Mexique[1][2]
America, South	**5900**	**5790**	**7473**	**7820**	**7520**	**6000**	**7397**	**4400**	**2563**	**2400**	**Amérique du Sud**
Argentina	[3]400	[2]610	[2]373	* [2]720	* [2]720	* [2]700	* [2]297	* [2]300	* [2]300	* [2]300	Argentine
Brazil[2]	5000	*5080	*7000	*7000	*6700	*5200	*7000	*4000	*2163	*2000	Brésil[2]
Peru	[2]500	* [2]100	* [2]100	* [2]100	* [2]100	* [2]100	*100	[2]100	[2]100	* [2]100	Pérou
Asia	**15855**	**15861**	**18110**	**15465**	**47518**	**55179**	**48762**	**43077**	**44790**	**46695**	**Asie**
India[2]	...	...	...	2082	2055	1728	1894	1794	1489	*1500	Inde[2]
Iran(Islamic Rep. of)	...	...	...	[2]1224	* [3]3000	*3894	*5444	*1086	1200	...	Iran(Rép. islamique)
Korea, Republic of	4765	[2]5127	[2]7732	* [2]7500	[2]37470	[2]43709	[2]35923	[2]34489	38459	* [2]39000	Corée, République de
Malaysia[1][2]	...	...	...	4659	4993	5848	5501	5708	3642	3800	Malaisie[1][2]
Europe	**10099**	**128339**	**160795**	**138840**	**112058**	**112628**	**110507**	**110500**	**112500**	**112500**	**Europe**
France* [2]	...	...	...	8000	10000	10000	8000	8000	10000	10000	France* [2]
Romania	7	1	0	0	0	0	...	...	...	...	Roumanie
Russian Federation[2]	..	...	*150000	129000	100000	100000	100000	100000	100000	*100000	Fédération de Russie[2]
Spain	913	1052	2081	1840	...	[1][2]2628	[1][2]2507	* [1][2]2500	* [1][2]2500	* [1][2]2500	Espagne
Yugoslavia, SFR	750	..	..	..	..	..	..	..	..	..	Yougoslavie, RSF
Total	**55386**	**177385**	**213243**	**188952**	**192418**	**198371**	**190989**	**177685**	**180752**	**182205**	**Total**

General Note.
Data refer to crude mica, which consists of mica crystals, of irregular shape, size and thickness, covered with earth (books); mica sheets, obtained by rifting cobbed and trimmed books and mica splittings, obtained by rifting sheet mica. (SITC, Rev.3: 27852-1).

Remarque générale.
Les données se rapportent au mica brut sous forme de cristaux de forme, de surface et d'épaisseur irregulières, encore enrobés de matières terreuses (books); au mica en feuilles, obtenu par clivage de 'books' préalablement dégrossis puis ébarbés et au mica en lamelles, obtenu par simple clivage de feuilles de mica. (CTCI, Rev.3: 27852-1).

[1] Including scrap.
[2] Source: U. S. Geological Survey, (Washington, D. C.).
[3] Mica sheets only.

[1] Y compris les déchets.
[2] Source: U.S. Geological Survey, (Washington, D.C.).
[3] Mica en feuilles seulement.

Mica waste and powder
Déchets et poudre de mica

ISIC-BASED CODE - CODE BASE CITI

2909-132

Unit : Metric tons   Unité : Tonnes métriques

Country or area	1990	1991	1992	1993	1994	1995	1996	1997	1998	1999	Pays ou zone
Africa	**1765**	**1883**	**2079**	**1991**	**1973**	**2137**	**1515**	**1432**	**1556**	**1010**	**Afrique**
South Africa	[1]1765	[2]1883	[2]2079	[2]1991	[2]1973	[2]2137	[2]1515	1432	1556	1010	Afrique du Sud
America, North	**97000**	**75000**	**84000**	**92000**	**95000**	**98000**	**103000**	**110000**	**104000**	**111000**	**Amérique du Nord**
United States	97000	75000	84000	92000	95000	98000	103000	110000	104000	111000	Etats-Unis
America, South	**500**	**1038**	**635**	**1226**	**1104**	**2643**	**1840**	**3228**	**3200**	**3000**	**Amérique du Sud**
Argentina[2]	500	1038	635	1226	1104	2643	1840	3228	3200	*3000	Argentine[2]
Asia	**3371**	**2134**	**1958**	**1113**	**1665**	**7590**	**3509**	**4409**	**5567**	**5039**	**Asie**
India	2822	1934	1758	913	1465	1240	1109	909	1067	1039	Inde
Sri Lanka[2]	...	200	200	*200	*200	#6350	2400	3500	4500	*4000	Sri Lanka[2]
Europe	**3122**	**2456**	**1399**	**1161**	**1306**	**1557**	**1068**	**1319**	**1404**	**883**	**Europe**
Denmark	...	...	0	[3]1	[3]0	[3]0	[3]0	[3]0	[3]0	[3]0	Danemark
Romania	2736	2070	1013	774	920	1171	682	933	1018	497	Roumanie
Sweden	...	...	...	...	...	386	...	...	...	...	Suède
Total	**105759**	**82511**	**90071**	**97491**	**101048**	**111927**	**110932**	**120388**	**115727**	**120932**	**Total**

General Note.
Data refer to mica waste (scrap) and powder. (SITC, Rev.3: 27852-2).

Remarque générale.
Les données se rapportent aux déchets et à la poudre de mica.
(CTCI, Rev.3: 27852-2)

[1] Scrap only.
[2] Source: U. S. Geological Survey, (Washington, D. C.).
[3] Sales.

[1] Déchets seulement.
[2] Source: U.S. Geological Survey, (Washington, D.C.).
[3] Ventes.

Talc, powdered steatite and pyrophyllite
Talc ou stéatite pulverisée et la pyrophyllite

ISIC-BASED CODE - CODE BASE CITI

2909-14

Unit : Thousand metric tons | Unité : Milliers de tonnes métriques

Country or area	1990	1991	1992	1993	1994	1995	1996	1997	1998	1999	Pays ou zone
Africa	**24**	**25**	**30**	**22**	**23**	**35**	**52**	**66**	**55**	**52**	**Afrique**
Egypt	6	8	8	5	4	15	30	35	*27	*27	Egypte
Morocco	...	...	...	...	...	...	2	3	3	3	Maroc
South Africa[1]	14	13	17	[2]13	[2]14	[2]15	[2]19	[2]27	[2]24	[2]21	Afrique du Sud[1]
Zimbabwe	1	2	2	1	[1][3]2	[1][3]2	[1][3]1	[1][3]1	[1][3]1	*[1][3]1	Zimbabwe
America, North	**1422**	**1167**	**1139**	**1090**	**1080**	**1187**	**1081**	**1137**	**1068**	**1024**	**Amérique du Nord**
Canada	[4]137	[4]115	[4]122	[1]108	[1]130	[1]116	[1]77	[1]73	[1]78	*[1]79	Canada
Mexico[1]	13	12	20	[3]14	[3]15	[3]11	[3]10	[3]14	[3]19	[3]20	Mexique[1]
United States[5]	1272	1040	997	968	935	1060	994	1050	971	925	Etats-Unis[5]
America, South	**510**	**524**	**476**	**534**	**719**	**514**	**507**	**509**	**511**	**510**	**Amérique du Sud**
Argentina	18	23	22	[1]19	[1]19	[1]17	[1]14	[1]16	[1]18	*[1]17	Argentine
Brazil	[3]470	[1]478	[1]430	[1]480	[1]666	[1]451	[1]452	[1]452	[1]452	*[1]452	Brésil
Chile	1	1	1	5	5	4	4	4	4	*4	Chili
Colombia	10	10	11	[1]20	[1]18	[1]19	[1]15	[1]15	[1]15	[1]15	Colombie
Peru[1]	9	10	10	[2]9	[2]9	[2]22	[2]21	[2]21	[2]21	[2]21	Pérou[1]
Uruguay[1]	2	2	2	*2	*2	*1	1	1	1	*1	Uruguay[1]
Asia	**5152**	**4111**	**4124**	**3793**	**3916**	**4138**	**5689**	**6199**	**5455**	**5570**	**Asie**
China[1]	2545	2600	2650	2300	2400	2400	4000	4100	3800	*3900	Chine[1]
India	406	480	414	421	409	541	513	475	482	528	Inde
Iran(Islamic Rep. of)	31	15	32	31	*[1][3]27	*[1][3]20	[3]26	[3]29	[3]30	[1][3]20	Iran(Rép. islamique)
Japan	[1]1272	#[3]66	[3]61	[3]57	[3]50	[3]57	[1][3]56	[3]27	[3]22	[3]21	Japon
Korea,Dem.Ppl's.Rep.[1]	170	170	170	180	180	180	180	180	150	*120	Corée,Rép.pop.dém.de[1]
Korea, Republic of[1]	...	...	...	699	743	819	799	1020	868	*875	Corée, République de[1]
Nepal[1][6]	2	3	4	[3]1	[3]2	[3]2	[3]5	[3]7	[3]7	[3]7	Népal[1][6]
Pakistan[1]	30	34	24	47	37	35	34	45	49	*50	Pakistan[1]
Thailand[1]	34	49	39	[2]50	[2]64	[2]80	[2]72	[2]312	[2]42	*[2]44	Thaïlande[1]
Turkey	6	3	3	6	*[1]4	*[1]4	*[1]4	*[1]4	*[1]5	*[1]5	Turquie
Europe	**1161**	**1516**	**1483**	**1230**	**1231**	**1311**	**1243**	**1305**	**1331**	**1446**	**Europe**
Austria	134	161	160	[1][7]137	[1][7]131	[1][7]132	[1][7]130	162	178	175	Autriche
Bulgaria	17	2	0	1	1	1	1	0	0	...	Bulgarie
Finland	343	313	323	348	395	405	345	[1][8]350	[1][3]350	460	Finlande
France	285	310	319	282	278	297	321	335	363	377	France
Germany[1]	..	...	24	[3]11	[3]12	[3]14	[3]10	[3]9	[3]15	[3]15	Allemagne[1]
Greece	[1]14	[1]1	[1]1	*[1][7]1	*[1][7]0	1	3	*[1][7]0	1	*[1][7]0	Grèce
Hungary[1]	10	10	[3]2	[3]2	[3]2	[3]1	*[3]1	*[3]1	*[3]1	*[3]1	Hongrie[1]
Italy	152	162	184	141	138	159	133	141	134	124	Italie
Norway	100	80	80	*[1][3]50	*[1][3]28	*[1][3]30	*[1][3]30	*[1][3]30	*[1][3]28	*[1][3]28	Norvège
Portugal	8	[1]8	[1]9	[1][3]9	[1][3]8	8	[1][3]8	[1][3]8	10	10	Portugal
Romania[3]	24	15	6	9	9	10	10	8	8	8	Roumanie[3]
Russian Federation	..	338	260	132	109	102	80	98	79	108	Fédération de Russie
Spain	44	34	65	58	[1][7]65	[1][7]112	[1][7]110	[1][7]110	[1][7]110	*[1][7]110	Espagne
Sweden	*[1][3]15	*[1][3]19	*[1][3]10	*[1][3]20	*[1][3]20	*[1][3]25	*[1][3]30	*[1][3]25	*[1][3]25	0	Suède
United Kingdom	[9]15	[9]11	[9]10	0	0	[1]4	[1]5	[1]6	[1]5	*[1]5	Royaume-Uni
T.F.Yug.Rep. Macedonia	..	38	30	30	36	10	25	21	23	25	L'ex-RY Macédoine
USSR (former)[1]	500	..								..	URSS (anc.)[1]
Oceania	**234**	**216**	**215**	**215**	**215**	**215**	**215**	**215**	**215**	**215**	**Océanie**
Australia	234	216	215	*[1]215	*[1]215	*[1]215	*[1]215	*[1]215	*[1]215	*[1]215	Australie
Total	**9004**	**7559**	**7466**	**6884**	**7183**	**7399**	**8787**	**9430**	**8635**	**8817**	**Total**

General Note.
Earth materials used chiefly as a source for industrial talcs. The mineral talc is commonly but not necessarily a major constituent. Steatite, i.e. soapstone, French chalk etc. and pyrophyllite are included under this heading. Material that has been ground to size is included. (SITC, Rev.3: 27893-0).

Remarque générale.
Terres utilisées surtout comme source de talcs industriels. Le talc minéral en est généralement, mais non pas nécessairement, un constituant important. Sont incluses la stéatite (improprement appelée craie de Briançon ou craie d'Espagne) et la pyrophyllite. La matière moulue à la finesse désirée est incluse. (CTCI, Rev.3: 27893-0).

For footnotes, see end of table.

Voir la fin du tableau pour les notes.

Talc, powdered steatite and pyrophyllite (continued)
Talc ou stéatite pulverisée et la pyrophyllite (suite)

ISIC-BASED CODE - CODE BASE CITI

2909-14

Footnotes
[1] Source: U. S. Geological Survey, (Washington, D. C.).
[2] Talc and pyrophyllite only.
[3] Talc only.
[4] Shipments.
[5] Data refer to talc only; data on pyrophyllite are confidential.

[6] Twelve months beginning 16 July of year stated.
[7] Steatite only.
[8] Source: United Nations Economic Commission for Europe (ECE), (Geneva).

[9] Great Britain only.

Notes.
[1] Source: U.S. Geological Survey, (Washington, D.C.).
[2] Talc et prophyllite seulement.
[3] Talc seulement.
[4] Expéditions.
[5] Les données se rapportent aux talc seulement; les données sur la pyrophyllite sont confidentielles.
[6] Période de douze mois commençant le 16 juillet de l'année indiquée.
[7] Steatite seulement.
[8] Source: Commission économique des Nations Unies pour l'Europe (CEE), (Genève).
[9] Grande Bretagne seulement.

Peat for fuel
Tourbe comme combustible

ISIC-BASED CODE - CODE BASE CITI

2909-17

Unit : Thousand metric tons

Unité : Milliers de tonnes métriques

Country or area	1990	1991	1992	1993	1994	1995	1996	1997	1998	1999	Pays ou zone
Africa	**11**	**10**	**12**	**10**	**10**	**10**	**10**	**5**	**5**	**5**	**Afrique**
Burundi	11	[1]10	[1]12	[1]10	[1]10	[1]10	[1]10	* [1]5	* [1]5	* [1]5	Burundi
America, South	**7**	**1**	**1**	**3**	**3**	**4**	**3**	**3**	**3**	**2**	**Amérique du Sud**
Argentina	7	1	1	3	3	4	...	...	...	...	Argentine
Europe	**14537**	**24416**	**29730**	**21037**	**23185**	**25380**	**27699**	**20359**	**15520**	**21318**	**Europe**
Belarus	..	3888	4181	2922	3482	3145	2847	2768	2035	3090	Bélarus
Estonia	..	574	657	467	645	583	652	497	163	558	Estonie
Finland	5993	6414	7568	7972	8270	9967	11372	* [1]7000	* [1]6000	* [1]7000	Finlande
Germany[1]	..	...	...	180	180	180	180	180	*180	*180	Allemagne[1]
Germany(Fed.Rep.)	230	..	..	..	..	..	..	..	..	..	Allemagne(Rép.féd.)
Ireland[1]	6430	4770	5414	3975	4696	4788	6578	4351	*4500	*5300	Irlande[1]
Latvia	..	298	408	334	435	299	356	362	46	315	Lettonie
Lithuania	..	70	107	52	90	67	73	74	60	85	Lituanie
Netherlands[1]	300	*300	*300	*300	*300	*0	*0	*0	*0	*0	Pays-Bas[1]
Norway[1]	1	*1	*1	*1	*1	*0	*0	*0	*0	*0	Norvège[1]
Romania	153	75	17	26	19	6	2	...	...	...	Roumanie
Russian Federation	..	4725	7779	2530	2928	4401	4103	3363	1767	3462	Fédération de Russie
Spain	69	68	56	48	42	48	* [1]60	* [1]60	* [1]60	0	Espagne
Sweden[1]	1361	*1400	*1400	*1400	*800	*800	700	1000	*120	*800	Suède[1]
Ukraine	..	1653	1662	830	1297	1096	776	704	589	528	Ukraine
USSR (former)	**11189**	..	..	..	..	..	..	..	..	..	**URSS (anc.)**
Oceania	**12**	**11**	**11**	**11**	**15**	**15**	**15**	**15**	**15**	**15**	**Océanie**
Australia[1]	12	*11	*11	*11	*15	*15	*15	*15	*15	*15	Australie[1]
Total	**25756**	**24438**	**29754**	**21061**	**23213**	**25409**	**27727**	**20382**	**15543**	**21340**	**Total**

General Note.

The data refer to peat used as fuel. Peat is the first stage in the metamorphosis of vegetable matter to coal. It has a high percentage of moisture and a gross calorific value of 3700 to 4000 calories/ gramme. Unless otherwise stated, peat briquettes are excluded. (SITC, Rev.3: 32230-1).

Remarque générale.

Les données se rapportent à la tourbe utilisée comme combustible. La tourbe représente la première étape de la transformation de la matière végétale en houille. Elle a une teneur élevée en eau et un pouvoir calorifique brut de 3700 à 4000 cal/g. Sauf indication contraire, les agglomérés de tourbe ne sont pas compris. (CTCI, Rev3: 32230-1).

[1] Source: U. S. Geological Survey, (Washington, D. C.).

[1] Source: U.S. Geological Survey, (Washington, D.C.).

Peat for agricultural use
Tourbe à usage agricole

ISIC-BASED CODE - CODE BASE CITI

2909-18

Unit : Thousand metric tons · Unité : Milliers de tonnes métriques

Country or area	1990	1991	1992	1993	1994	1995	1996	1997	1998	1999	Pays ou zone
America, North	**1467**	**1465**	**1427**	**1518**	**1526**	**1658**	**1450**	**1715**	**1812**	**2037**	**Amérique du Nord**
Canada	[1]775	[1]833	[1]828	[1]902	[1]952	* [1]1010	901	*1054	1127	* [2]1306	Canada
United States	692	632	599	616	574	648	549	661	685	731	Etats-Unis
America, South	**3**	**3**	**1**	**3**	**3**	**0**	**0**	**0**	**0**	**0**	**Amérique du Sud**
Argentina	3	3	[2]1	[2]3	[2]3	[2]0	[2]0	[2]0	[2]0	[2]0	Argentine
Asia	**20**	**20**	**20**	**20**	**20**	**20**	**20**	**20**	**20**	**20**	**Asie**
Israel[2]	20	20	...	...	...	...	...	...	...	...	Israël[2]
Europe	**3096**	**83659**	**66242**	**40118**	**24886**	**16563**	**11483**	**8717**	**9127**	**9568**	**Europe**
Belarus	..	12021	17849	4430	2190	961	533	253	107	308	Bélarus
Denmark[2]	50	[3]184	[3]195	[3]189	[3]190	* [3]205	[3]204	* [3]205	* [3]205	* [3]200	Danemark[2]
Estonia	..	136	214	193	629	469	448	505	202	741	Estonie
Finland	569	647	944	862	*1017	*881	*1285	358	* [2]400	* [2]400	Finlande
France[2]	200	*200	*200	*200	*200	*200	*200	*200	*200	*200	France[2]
Germany[2]	..	...	...	2739	*2800	*2800	*2800	*2800	*2800	*2800	Allemagne[2]
Germany(Fed.Rep.)[2]	1500	..	..	..	..	..	..	..	..	..	Allemagne(Rép.féd.)[2]
Hungary[2]	64	*65	*65	*65	*65	48	*45	*45	*45	*45	Hongrie[2]
Ireland[2]	229	249	300	300	250	*300	*300	*300	*300	*300	Irlande[2]
Latvia	..	1365	377	94	203	198	163	164	111	567	Lettonie
Lithuania	..	594	255	135	321	163	182	221	142	305	Lituanie
Norway[2]	30	*30	*30	*30	*30	*30	*30	*30	*30	*30	Norvège[2]
Poland[2][4]	200	167	134	410	109	199	198	*206	*200	*200	Pologne[2][4]
Russian Federation	..	53295	36657	27809	15581	9076	4293	2762	3834	2855	Fédération de Russie
Slovakia	..	...	...	...	...	...	...	252	...	...	Slovaquie
Sweden[2]	254	*263	*260	*250	*250	*300	*300	*350	*200	*250	Suède[2]
Ukraine	..	11678	5738	2160	799	481	250	66	99	115	Ukraine
USSR (former)[2]	150000	..	..	..	..	..	..	..	..	..	URSS (anc.)[2]
Total	**154586**	**85147**	**67690**	**41659**	**26435**	**18241**	**12953**	**10452**	**10959**	**11625**	**Total**

General Note.
The data refer to peat for agricultural or domestic use. This series includes crushed peat, peat litter etc. used in stables, for soil improvement or for other purposes. It does not include fibres of peat prepared for textile use and flower pots and other articles of peat, including insulating sheets for buildings obtained by cutting or moulding. (SITC, Rev.3: 32230-2).

Remarque générale.
Les données se rapportent à la tourbe à usage domestique ou agricole. Cette série comprend la tourbe écrasée et celles qui sont employées pour la litière des animaux, l'amendement du sol ou tous autres usages. La série ne comprend pas toutefois les fibres de tourbe ligneuse traitées en vue de leur utilisation comme textiles et les pots à fleurs et autres articles en tourbe taillée ou moulée, ainsi que les plaques de tourbe comprimée, employées comme isolants dans la construction. (CTCI, Rev.3: 32230-2).

[1] Shipments.
[2] Source: U. S. Geological Survey, (Washington, D. C.).
[3] Sales.
[4] Including peat for fuel.

[1] Expéditions.
[2] Source: U.S. Geological Survey, (Washington, D.C.).
[3] Ventes.
[4] Y compris tourbe comme combustible.

Diamonds, gem
Diamants de joaillerie

ISIC-BASED CODE - CODE BASE CITI

2909-19

Unit : Thousand carats

Unité : Milliers de carats

Country or area	1990	1991	1992	1993	1994	1995	1996	1997	1998	1999	Pays ou zone
Africa	**22021**	**23220**	**28739**	**19558**	**22918**	**26190**	**25931**	**27690**	**28541**	**28457**	**Afrique**
Angola[1]	1060	899	1100	130	270	2600	2250	1110	2400	1080	Angola[1]
Botswana[1]	12150	...	11200	10300	10550	11500	12400	15100	14800	15000	Botswana[1]
Central African Rep.[1]	303	296	307	370	401	400	350	. 400	330	400	Rép. centrafricaine[1]
Côte d'Ivoire[1]	9	11	11	...	...	53	202	207	210	210	Côte d'Ivoire[1]
Dem. Rep. of Congo[1]	2914	3000	8930	2010	4000	4000	3600	3000	3300	3500	Rép. dém. du Congo[1]
Gabon*[1]	400	400	400	400	400	400	400	...	...	...	Gabon*[1]
Ghana[1]	163	560	104	106	118	126	142	664	649	649	Ghana[1]
Guinea[1]	119	91	90	134	306	274	165	165	300	300	Guinée[1]
Liberia[1]	40	40	60	60	40	60	60	80	150	600	Libéria[1]
Namibia[1]	750	1170	1520	1120	1312	1382	1402	1345	1394	1995	Namibie[1]
Sierra Leone[1]	66	160	180	90	155	113	162	300	200	225	Sierra Leone[1]
South Africa[1]	3826	3800	4600	4600	5050	5070	4400	4500	4300	4000	Afrique du Sud[1]
Swaziland	25	34	36	...	...	...	...	...	...	...	Swaziland
United Rep.Tanzania[1]	60	70	70	...	...	...	...	...	...	...	Rép. Unie de Tanzanie[1]
Zimbabwe[1]	...	...	...	26	104	114	300	321	10	0	Zimbabwe[1]
America, South	**685**	**709**	**963**	**1274**	**687**	**808**	**306**	**465**	**407**	**407**	**Amérique du Sud**
Brazil[1]	600	600	653	1000	300	676	200	300	300	300	Brésil[1]
Guyana[1]	5	7	8	...	...	...	...	...	...	...	Guyana[1]
Venezuela	80	[1]102	[1]302	[1]267	[1]380	[1]125	[1]99	[1]158	[1]100	[1]100	Venezuela
Asia	**210**	**211**	**214**	**244**	**246**	**247**	**249**	**248**	**249**	**249**	**Asie**
China[1]	*200	*200	*200	*230	*230	*230	*230	230	230	230	Chine[1]
India	3	3	8	7	9	10	12	11	12	12	Inde
Indonesia[1]	7	8	6	...	...	...	...	...	...	...	Indonésie[1]
Europe	..	**8429**	**8911**	**8000**	**10000**	**10500**	**10500**	**10500**	**11500**	**11500**	**Europe**
Russian Federation[1]	..	...	...	8000	10000	10500	10500	10500	11500	11500	Fédération de Russie[1]
USSR (former)[1]	7500	..	..	...	..	..	..	..	..	..	URSS (anc.)[1]
Oceania	**17300**	**18000**	**18100**	**18800**	**19500**	**18300**	**18897**	**18100**	**18400**	**13403**	**Océanie**
Australia[1]	17300	18000	18100	18800	19500	18300	18897	18100	18400	13403	Australie[1]
Total	**47716**	**50569**	**56927**	**47876**	**53351**	**56045**	**55883**	**57003**	**59097**	**54016**	**Total**

General Note.
Mine and alluvial production of rough, uncut and unpolished diamonds intended for gem stones. (SITC, Rev.3: 66721-0).

Remarque générale.
Production de diamants bruts, non taillés et non polis, destinés à la joaillerie, en provenance de mines et d'alluvions. (CTCI, Rev.3: 66721-0).

[1] Source: U. S. Geological Survey, (Washington, D. C.).

[1] Source: U.S. Geological Survey, (Washington, D.C.).

Beef and veal, fresh (Total production)
Viande de boeuf ou de veau, non préparée (Production totale)

ISIC-BASED CODE - CODE BASE CITI

3111-01

Unit : Thousand metric tons

Unité : Milliers de tonnes métriques

Country or area	1990	1991	1992	1993	1994	1995	1996	1997	1998	1999	Pays ou zone
Africa	**3726**	**3861**	**3949**	**3908**	**3794**	**3842**	**3946**	**4132**	**4225**	**4343**	**Afrique**
Algeria	89.5	94.3	96.5	98.2	100.6	100.6	99.0	102.0	103.0	117.0	Algérie
Angola	59.0	60.0	66.0	66.0	65.0	65.0	71.0	77.0	85.0	85.0	Angola
Benin	15.4	15.6	16.4	16.3	17.5	18.5	19.5	20.4	19.8	21.1	Bénin
Botswana	41.9	44.2	47.4	48.7	38.2	45.9	44.1	38.2	37.3	37.1	Botswana
Burkina Faso	37.3	38.5	38.5	39.6	39.6	40.2	47.3	49.5	50.6	51.7	Burkina Faso
Burundi	12.4	12.4	13.7	13.7	12.4	12.4	13.0	10.4	11.1	9.2	Burundi
Cameroon	72.4	74.3	76.6	78.7	80.8	83.2	85.4	87.8	89.5	89.5	Cameroun
Cape Verde	0.4	0.3	0.3	0.4	0.4	0.3	0.7	0.5	0.6	0.4	Cap-Vert
Central African Rep.	40.6	42.0	44.0	45.0	45.0	48.0	61.4	50.0	51.0	51.0	Rép. centrafricaine
Chad	73.2	74.9	79.1	70.0	56.9	68.0	73.5	72.8	82.5	81.1	Tchad
Comoros	0.9	1.0	1.0	1.0	1.0	1.0	1.0	0.9	1.0	1.0	Comores
Congo	2.0	1.6	1.6	1.6	1.7	1.7	1.7	1.8	1.8	1.7	Congo
Côte d'Ivoire	31.0	32.7	34.2	34.2	34.4	36.3	37.0	37.7	38.4	39.0	Côte d'Ivoire
Dem. Rep. of Congo	21.8	19.3	19.6	20.2	18.5	17.0	15.0	15.6	14.5	14.0	Rép. dém. du Congo
Djibouti	2.2	3.0	3.0	3.2	3.5	3.3	3.5	3.5	3.6	3.6	Djibouti
Egypt	304.0	335.0	342.7	361.0	382.2	393.9	452.8	548.4	559.9	571.5	Egypte
Eritrea	...	...	...	9.2	9.8	10.0	12.2	14.3	15.8	18.3	Erythrée
Ethiopia,incl.Eritrea	245.0	245.0	244.0	...	...	...	...	...	...	...	Ethiopie,incl.Erythrée
Ethiopia	...	...	...	230.0	230.0	235.0	267.0	270.0	274.0	290.0	Ethiopie
Gabon	0.9	1.0	1.1	1.1	1.1	1.2	1.1	1.1	1.1	1.1	Gabon
Gambia	3.1	3.2	2.8	2.9	2.9	3.0	3.0	3.1	3.2	3.3	Gambie
Ghana	19.7	20.6	20.0	20.1	20.5	20.7	20.9	12.3	13.7	13.8	Ghana
Guinea	9.8	10.4	11.0	11.7	12.5	14.5	14.9	15.3	15.5	15.8	Guinée
Guinea-Bissau	3.3	3.4	3.6	3.9	3.9	4.0	4.0	4.1	4.1	4.2	Guinée-Bissau
Kenya	250.0	247.0	230.0	225.0	230.0	240.0	260.0	270.0	243.0	252.0	Kenya
Lesotho	12.9	12.8	14.1	15.0	12.8	13.5	12.0	15.0	12.0	10.5	Lesotho
Liberia	1.0	1.0	1.0	1.0	1.0	1.0	1.0	1.0	1.0	1.0	Libéria
Libyan Arab Jamah.	24.0	30.6	26.6	25.6	22.1	21.6	14.5	39.4	43.1	14.9	Jamah. arabe libyenne
Madagascar	142.8	143.4	144.1	144.7	145.4	146.0	146.6	147.3	147.9	147.9	Madagascar
Malawi	16.9	17.1	16.8	17.6	14.0	14.0	16.4	18.2	17.2	17.0	Malawi
Mali	71.5	74.1	78.0	80.6	83.2	84.5	85.8	88.4	91.1	93.6	Mali
Mauritania	17.0	19.7	18.2	9.2	9.4	9.6	10.2	10.2	10.2	10.3	Mauritanie
Mauritius	2.1	2.3	2.5	2.6	2.8	2.4	2.4	2.4	2.6	3.0	Maurice
Morocco	144.9	149.0	145.0	150.0	125.0	122.1	103.0	125.0	120.0	130.0	Maroc
Mozambique	40.5	39.0	36.0	37.8	36.0	36.8	36.9	37.5	37.8	38.1	Mozambique
Namibia	38.9	45.7	48.8	49.0	49.5	47.7	45.8	29.8	38.3	38.5	Namibie
Niger	28.0	24.5	31.5	32.5	34.0	35.0	36.0	38.0	39.0	40.0	Niger
Nigeria	204.3	205.0	210.0	244.4	264.3	266.9	280.0	294.0	297.0	298.0	Nigéria
Réunion	1.3	1.1	1.1	1.2	1.1	1.2	1.1	1.2	1.3	1.3	Réunion
Rwanda	14.1	14.4	13.1	12.0	10.4	10.4	11.4	13.5	15.6	17.7	Rwanda
Sao Tome and Principe	0.1	0.1	0.1	0.1	0.1	0.1	0.1	0.1	0.1	0.1	Sao Tomé-et-Principe
Senegal	42.6	43.7	44.0	44.8	45.6	46.0	46.3	47.5	48.0	48.0	Sénégal
Seychelles	0.1	0.1	0.1	0.1	0.1	0.0	0.0	0.0	0.0	0.0	Seychelles
Sierra Leone	5.2	5.2	5.5	5.7	5.9	5.9	6.0	6.2	6.4	6.6	Sierra Leone
Somalia	46.2	40.7	36.3	41.8	44.0	49.5	53.9	60.5	61.6	58.3	Somalie
South Africa	661.0	700.0	745.0	651.0	554.0	521.0	481.0	484.0	518.0	553.0	Afrique du Sud
Sudan	218.2	231.4	226.0	215.0	212.3	224.8	226.4	250.0	265.0	276.0	Soudan
Swaziland	10.8	12.9	13.8	15.3	13.5	14.0	13.3	13.6	14.4	13.8	Swaziland
Togo	5.2	5.1	5.3	5.3	5.3	6.5	6.8	6.5	6.9	6.8	Togo
Tunisia	39.0	41.0	43.5	47.9	49.2	50.4	52.2	50.4	53.4	57.5	Tunisie
Uganda	81.2	84.0	86.0	91.5	84.3	86.4	87.5	88.5	93.0	96.0	Ouganda
United Rep.Tanzania	195.2	196.6	199.1	203.0	205.0	206.0	209.0	211.0	218.0	223.0	Rép. Unie de Tanzanie
Zambia	36.0	37.3	38.1	41.9	43.2	37.5	39.5	27.9	27.5	29.5	Zambie
Zimbabwe	81.7	83.8	94.1	75.4	67.4	73.2	67.4	73.6	73.7	95.4	Zimbabwe
America, North	**13119**	**13156**	**13290**	**13238**	**13999**	**14445**	**14632**	**14661**	**14861**	**15276**	**Amérique du Nord**
Antigua and Barbuda	0.5	0.6	0.6	0.6	0.6	0.5	0.5	0.5	0.5	0.5	Antigua-et-Barbuda
Barbados	1.0	0.9	1.0	0.9	0.9	0.9	0.9	0.6	0.6	0.6	Barbade
Belize	1.5	1.4	1.5	1.4	1.4	1.4	1.3	1.5	1.2	1.2	Belize
British Virgin Islands	0.1	0.1	0.1	0.1	0.1	0.1	0.1	0.1	0.1	0.1	Iles Vierges britanniques
Canada	900.1	866.0	898.8	859.6	899.5	928.2	1016.3	1076.3	1148.1	1238.0	Canada
Costa Rica	87.5	94.0	80.9	81.9	91.5	92.2	96.4	86.1	82.0	75.4	Costa Rica
Cuba	136.2	90.4	76.8	65.5	60.3	64.4	68.4	67.6	69.4	72.7	Cuba

For general note and footnotes, see end of table.

Voir la fin du tableau pour la remarque générale et les notes.

Beef and veal, fresh (Total production) (continued)
Viande de boeuf ou de veau, non préparée (Production totale) (suite)

ISIC-BASED CODE - CODE BASE CITI
3111-01

Unit : Thousand metric tons

Unité : Milliers de tonnes métriques

Country or area	1990	1991	1992	1993	1994	1995	1996	1997	1998	1999	Pays ou zone
Dominica	0.5	0.5	0.5	0.5	0.5	0.5	0.5	0.5	0.5	0.5	Dominique
Dominican Republic	82.5	84.3	83.0	85.5	80.7	79.8	80.3	79.2	80.0	82.7	Rép. dominicaine
El Salvador	27.2	23.5	22.1	24.7	26.9	27.3	26.7	34.7	34.0	33.7	El Salvador
Grenada	0.1	0.1	0.1	0.1	0.1	0.1	0.1	0.1	0.1	0.1	Grenade
Guadeloupe	3.0	2.8	2.9	3.1	3.2	3.4	3.2	3.4	3.4	3.4	Guadeloupe
Guatemala	66.6	51.7	40.5	48.1	51.8	53.8	54.1	54.4	54.5	47.0	Guatemala
Haiti	24.0	25.0	27.0	28.8	27.8	23.9	28.0	28.0	30.8	31.0	Haïti
Honduras	46.0	45.1	44.4	44.5	45.0	22.8	25.4	25.8	28.3	21.0	Honduras
Jamaica	15.0	16.1	18.2	15.6	15.8	16.7	15.6	14.5	14.3	14.7	Jamaïque
Martinique	2.6	2.5	2.5	2.3	2.3	2.3	2.6	2.6	2.6	2.6	Martinique
Mexico	1113.9	1188.7	1247.2	1256.5	1364.7	1412.3	1329.9	1340.1	1379.8	1401.1	Mexique
Montserrat	0.6	0.7	0.7	0.7	0.7	0.7	0.7	0.7	0.7	0.7	Montserrat
Netherlands Antilles	0.2	0.0	0.0	0.0	0.0	0.0	0.0	0.0	0.0	0.0	Antilles néerlandaises
Nicaragua	57.3	45.1	47.7	52.5	51.3	49.1	49.8	51.9	45.8	47.9	Nicaragua
Panama	64.2	61.4	58.6	60.3	59.8	61.0	65.6	60.0	63.5	60.3	Panama
Puerto Rico	20.9	18.9	20.6	18.7	17.8	16.2	13.7	15.7	15.7	15.7	Porto Rico
St. Kitts-Nevis	0.1	0.1	0.1	0.1	0.1	0.1	0.1	0.1	0.1	0.1	St-Kitts-Nevis
St. Lucia	0.6	0.6	0.6	0.6	0.6	0.5	0.5	0.5	0.5	0.5	St-Lucie
St. Vincent-Grenadines	0.2	0.2	0.2	0.2	0.2	0.2	0.2	0.2	0.2	0.2	St. Vincent-Grenadines
Trinidad and Tobago	1.2	1.2	1.0	1.0	1.1	1.2	1.2	1.1	0.9	1.0	Trinité-et-Tobago
United States	10465.0	10534.0	10612.0	10584.0	11194.0	11585.0	11749.0	11714.0	11803.0	12123.0	Etats-Unis
United States Virgin Is.	0.5	0.5	0.5	0.5	0.5	0.5	0.5	0.5	0.5	0.5	Iles Vierges américaines
America, South	**9369**	**9598**	**9578**	**9739**	**10114**	**10639**	**11265**	**11181**	**10794**	**11331**	**Amérique du Sud**
Argentina	3007.0	2918.0	2784.0	2808.0	2783.0	2688.0	2694.0	2712.0	2451.5	2652.6	Argentine
Bolivia	130.4	132.2	126.1	130.3	135.9	139.6	143.2	147.3	151.0	155.3	Bolivie
Brazil	4115.0	4510.8	4715.5	4806.9	5136.0	5710.2	6186.9	5921.5	5794.3	6182.4	Brésil
Chile	242.5	229.8	200.0	224.1	239.6	257.8	259.5	262.1	256.3	226.4	Chili
Colombia	746.1	701.0	594.6	602.6	646.3	702.3	730.0	763.0	766.0	724.0	Colombie
Ecuador	100.0	113.3	113.2	126.0	127.5	148.7	153.3	155.6	158.2	164.3	Equateur
Falkland Is. (Malvinas)	0.2	0.2	0.2	0.1	0.1	0.1	0.1	0.1	0.1	0.1	Iles Falkland (Malvinas)
French Guiana	0.6	0.5	0.5	0.4	0.4	0.4	0.4	0.4	0.4	0.4	Guyane française
Guyana	2.2	3.0	4.2	3.8	4.6	3.8	3.5	3.2	2.9	2.9	Guyana
Paraguay	189.0	219.0	233.0	225.0	225.0	226.0	226.0	226.0	231.0	246.0	Paraguay
Peru	117.1	109.5	110.7	106.6	101.7	107.1	110.1	118.2	123.9	133.5	Pérou
Suriname	2.3	2.7	2.6	2.5	1.7	1.8	1.6	2.0	2.1	2.2	Suriname
Uruguay	334.6	320.4	328.6	309.7	361.4	337.6	407.0	454.4	449.9	457.7	Uruguay
Venezuela	381.9	337.2	365.3	393.5	351.2	315.6	349.6	415.2	405.9	383.6	Venezuela
Asia	**7401**	**9069**	**9517**	**10424**	**11024**	**11806**	**11765**	**12865**	**13266**	**13561**	**Asie**
Afghanistan	86.4	86.4	86.4	97.2	113.4	130.2	142.6	156.3	171.4	187.2	Afghanistan
Armenia	..	...	32.6	30.4	28.8	29.7	33.1	34.8	34.9	32.0	Arménie
Azerbaijan	..	...	50.0	44.0	43.6	41.0	43.6	48.4	50.0	51.6	Azerbaïdjan
Bahrain	0.7	0.6	0.7	0.7	0.7	0.6	0.7	0.7	0.8	0.8	Bahreïn
Bangladesh	142.8	143.1	144.5	147.2	149.9	151.2	155.5	168.5	164.5	173.5	Bangladesh
Bhutan	5.4	5.5	5.6	5.7	5.8	5.8	5.8	5.8	5.8	5.8	Bhoutan
Brunei Darussalam	1.8	2.0	1.6	1.4	1.8	1.2	1.6	1.6	2.1	4.9	Brunéi Darussalam
Cambodia	38.8	41.0	44.8	46.9	47.9	52.2	53.1	53.7	54.9	55.2	Cambodge
China [1]	1301.9	1579.1	1845.3	2374.5	2806.0	3598.0	3585.1	4431.0	4824.8	5078.2	Chine [1]
Cyprus	4.1	4.6	4.6	4.8	4.4	5.0	4.9	5.4	4.0	4.0	Chypre
Gaza Strip (Palestine)	1.1	1.3	1.3	1.3	1.4	1.4	1.4	1.4	1.4	1.4	Bande de Gaza (Palestine)
Georgia	..	...	40.3	40.0	43.6	52.7	54.2	56.0	42.8	41.3	Géorgie
India	2403.3	2452.1	2534.7	2632.5	2681.8	2716.3	2751.3	2781.6	2780.8	2831.8	Inde
Indonesia	303.5	309.7	342.0	397.5	384.7	359.5	395.9	401.0	388.9	399.6	Indonésie
Iran(Islamic Rep. of)	219.9	227.9	236.9	245.8	255.9	265.1	287.1	308.5	325.7	305.7	Iran(Rép. islamique)
Iraq	50.8	32.7	44.9	54.9	50.5	42.5	37.2	45.9	47.3	47.5	Iraq
Israel	35.9	38.0	37.0	35.5	41.0	40.5	44.0	46.3	43.8	44.4	Israël
Japan	549.5	575.2	591.7	594.3	602.3	600.9	554.5	530.2	529.3	540.4	Japon
Jordan	2.5	2.8	2.3	2.6	3.9	3.9	3.3	3.5	3.1	3.9	Jordanie
Kazakhstan	..	...	596.2	661.5	641.6	548.2	463.0	398.2	350.5	349.2	Kazakhstan
Korea,Dem.Ppl's.Rep.	34.5	30.0	30.3	31.1	31.5	30.6	21.8	18.8	19.5	20.0	Corée,Rép.pop.dém.de
Korea, Republic of	127.8	132.2	174.0	204.0	214.0	221.0	248.0	338.0	375.7	305.0	Corée, République de
Kuwait	1.4	0.1	0.9	0.8	1.5	1.5	1.6	1.8	2.1	1.6	Koweït
Kyrgyzstan	..	...	87.8	87.8	82.3	84.7	86.4	95.1	94.6	95.1	Kirghizistan

For general note and footnotes, see end of table.

Voir la fin du tableau pour la remarque générale et les notes.

Beef and veal, fresh (Total production) (continued)
Viande de boeuf ou de veau, non préparée (Production totale) (suite)

ISIC-BASED CODE - CODE BASE CITI

3111-01

Unit : Thousand metric tons   Unité : Milliers de tonnes métriques

Country or area	1990	1991	1992	1993	1994	1995	1996	1997	1998	1999	Pays ou zone
Lao People's Dem. Rep.	15.7	18.2	19.4	20.6	21.7	28.4	27.7	29.8	31.0	37.7	Rép. dém. pop. lao
Lebanon	10.1	14.6	16.2	16.3	14.9	12.3	10.5	20.3	22.4	25.0	Liban
Malaysia	15.2	17.5	17.7	18.7	19.4	20.7	21.7	22.5	21.7	23.8	Malaisie
Mongolia	66.2	83.8	75.7	64.5	64.4	69.4	89.9	86.6	86.0	93.5	Mongolie
Myanmar	106.9	107.7	109.2	110.2	111.1	113.4	116.5	119.0	120.5	121.0	Myanmar
Nepal	135.6	136.8	137.4	137.9	143.8	150.0	151.9	161.3	165.2	167.3	Népal
Oman	2.7	2.7	2.7	2.7	2.7	2.8	2.8	2.8	2.9	2.9	Oman
Pakistan	667.0	696.0	731.0	768.0	807.0	847.0	811.0	830.0	853.0	875.0	Pakistan
Philippines	124.6	127.0	130.0	137.4	135.7	147.5	160.8	188.9	211.5	223.2	Philippines
Qatar	0.2	0.2	0.2	0.2	0.2	0.2	0.3	0.4	0.4	0.5	Qatar
Saudi Arabia	28.0	27.0	28.0	29.0	30.0	26.0	18.0	16.0	19.0	19.0	Arabie saoudite
Singapore	0.3	0.3	0.3	0.3	0.2	0.1	0.0	0.1	0.0	0.0	Singapour
Sri Lanka	25.8	27.9	30.8	28.9	30.7	31.9	28.7	29.6	29.0	27.8	Sri Lanka
Syrian Arab Republic	32.4	32.7	28.7	28.7	30.6	33.9	40.1	41.9	43.5	46.9	Rép. arabe syrienne
Tajikistan	..	..	41.0	34.0	36.0	30.5	34.0	26.0	15.0	15.0	Tadjikistan
Thailand	316.7	320.3	317.7	337.6	348.3	337.2	329.0	299.6	274.9	244.3	Thaïlande
Turkey	372.1	348.3	308.6	303.1	324.7	298.5	305.0	385.2	363.8	354.3	Turquie
Turkmenistan	..	...	46.0	50.0	51.0	51.0	52.4	54.6	61.1	63.0	Turkménistan
United Arab Emirates	5.4	5.5	5.8	6.3	7.4	8.8	9.9	12.5	14.3	15.0	Emirats arabes unis
Uzbekistan	..	...	323.3	378.0	390.0	392.0	362.0	387.0	400.0	403.0	Ouzbékistan
Viet Nam	164.2	165.4	173.0	170.8	175.7	179.8	175.5	175.2	167.4	175.8	Viet Nam
Yemen	..	36.8	37.6	38.7	39.8	40.6	41.6	43.1	45.3	47.1	Yémen
Europe	**9144**	**16699**	**17033**	**15613**	**14843**	**13959**	**13643**	**13179**	**12512**	**12131**	**Europe**
Albania	22.0	21.1	23.4	24.3	28.3	30.8	32.6	32.5	32.0	33.7	Albanie
Austria	223.8	236.1	246.7	223.3	211.9	195.9	221.1	206.0	196.9	203.3	Autriche
Belarus	..	...	495.1	410.7	384.0	315.6	276.6	255.8	270.7	262.1	Bélarus
Belgium-Luxembourg	322.6	381.5	359.4	373.3	355.3	356.6	361.5	339.6	303.4	281.2	Belgique-Luxembourg
Bosnia and Herzegovina	..	...	30.0	30.0	23.0	15.9	13.0	10.0	12.4	12.4	Bosnie-Herzégovine
Bulgaria	121.4	108.4	134.9	116.5	89.2	64.8	79.5	57.0	56.3	52.8	Bulgarie
Croatia	..	...	36.8	33.8	28.3	25.8	21.5	26.3	25.7	23.5	Croatie
Denmark	201.7	212.5	217.0	203.1	189.3	181.7	178.0	174.8	161.8	156.6	Danemark
Czechoslovakia(former)	403.3	354.4	..	..	..	..	..	..	..	..	Tchécoslovaquie(anc.)
Czech Republic	..	...	..	216.2	170.2	169.5	163.5	155.7	134.5	135.7	République tchèque
Estonia	..	...	45.4	42.6	31.0	25.8	22.1	19.0	19.3	21.7	Estonie
Finland	118.2	121.7	117.3	106.4	107.6	96.2	96.6	99.6	93.8	90.2	Finlande
France	1911.7	2026.1	1876.8	1703.8	1626.8	1683.3	1737.0	1720.0	1632.0	1609.0	France
Germany	..	2180.7	1789.7	1570.3	1420.3	1407.8	1481.8	1447.6	1367.0	1446.7	Allemagne
Greece	79.4	79.2	75.8	72.7	70.9	72.3	71.0	70.1	69.5	66.6	Grèce
Hungary	113.8	122.8	123.2	97.1	72.1	57.5	50.2	55.3	47.0	44.7	Hongrie
Iceland	2.9	3.0	3.4	3.4	3.5	3.1	3.1	3.4	3.4	3.7	Islande
Ireland	515.0	554.0	564.5	526.2	445.3	477.3	534.5	567.6	589.7	639.6	Irlande
Italy	1165.4	1181.6	1217.5	1187.7	1171.2	1180.9	1182.0	1161.1	1112.7	1164.8	Italie
Latvia	..	...	119.6	107.0	68.1	48.0	26.5	25.5	25.8	20.5	Lettonie
Lithuania	..	...	226.1	161.8	116.1	86.9	83.0	89.6	81.4	77.3	Lituanie
Malta	1.7	1.7	1.6	1.6	1.7	1.7	1.8	1.7	1.6	1.6	Malte
Netherlands	521.0	623.0	635.0	611.0	603.0	580.0	580.1	564.7	534.7	508.0	Pays-Bas
Norway	82.8	80.3	84.9	84.3	87.9	85.5	86.4	89.4	90.8	91.0	Norvège
Poland	725.4	662.5	544.1	480.4	421.3	385.7	414.9	429.1	429.9	384.6	Pologne
Portugal	116.4	126.9	123.6	116.7	95.2	103.6	98.9	109.0	96.0	97.4	Portugal
Republic of Moldova	..	...	72.8	68.3	61.8	46.7	38.9	34.9	24.4	23.5	Rép. de Moldova
Romania	316.5	317.0	249.5	252.0	258.0	201.8	177.4	185.1	183.0	170.0	Roumanie
Russian Federation	..	...	3632.0	3359.0	3240.0	2733.0	2629.8	2394.2	2247.3	1868.0	Fédération de Russie
Slovakia	..	..	...	92.8	67.1	59.3	61.1	65.6	58.8	50.2	Slovaquie
Slovenia	..	...	38.2	51.5	52.2	51.2	53.7	54.0	44.6	43.1	Slovénie
Spain	513.9	509.3	539.4	488.0	483.7	508.5	564.6	592.3	650.7	677.6	Espagne
Sweden	145.3	137.1	130.1	141.7	142.4	143.4	137.5	148.9	142.8	143.0	Suède
Switzerland	165.2	173.7	165.4	156.0	142.0	147.4	158.6	151.8	147.2	146.5	Suisse
Ukraine	..	...	1655.6	1379.0	1427.0	1185.9	1047.8	929.6	793.3	791.2	Ukraine
United Kingdom	1001.7	1019.6	971.0	881.0	943.0	996.0	708.0	696.0	697.0	678.0	Royaume-Uni
Yugoslavia	..	...	201.3	230.9	196.5	226.6	242.2	208.6	127.0	104.0	Yougoslavie
T.F.Yug.Rep. Macedonia	..	...	7.5	8.4	7.5	6.9	6.7	8.0	7.1	7.0	L'ex-RY Macédoine
Yugoslavia, SFR	352.5	..	..	..	..	..	..	..	..	..	Yougoslavie, RSF

For general note and footnotes, see end of table.   Voir la fin du tableau pour la remarque générale et les notes.

Beef and veal, fresh (Total production) (continued)
Viande de boeuf ou de veau, non préparée (Production totale) (suite)

ISIC-BASED CODE - CODE BASE CITI

3111-01

Unit : Thousand metric tons

Unité : Milliers de tonnes métriques

Country or area	1990	1991	1992	1993	1994	1995	1996	1997	1998	1999	Pays ou zone
USSR (former)	8814.0	..	..	..	..	..	..	..	..	..	URSS (anc.)
Oceania	2176	2320	2347	2418	2383	2452	2398	2477	2610	2593	Océanie
Australia	1676.7	1759.6	1790.9	1825.8	1824.8	1803.4	1744.7	1810.3	1955.3	2010.5	Australie
Fiji	10.6	10.5	9.9	8.9	8.6	8.6	8.9	9.1	9.3	9.5	Fidji
French Polynesia	0.3	0.2	0.1	0.1	0.1	0.2	0.1	0.1	0.2	0.2	Polynésie française
New Caledonia	2.7	3.0	3.3	3.8	4.1	3.7	4.3	4.0	4.1	4.1	Nouvelle-Calédonie
New Zealand	478.6	540.0	536.0	572.0	537.0	629.0	633.0	646.3	634.1	561.3	Nouvelle-Zélande
Papua New Guinea	2.1	2.1	2.0	2.0	2.2	1.9	1.8	2.0	1.8	1.8	Papouasie-Nvl-Guinée
Samoa	0.9	0.9	0.9	0.9	0.9	0.9	0.9	0.9	0.9	0.9	Samoa
Solomon Islands	0.5	0.5	0.5	0.5	0.5	0.5	0.5	0.5	0.5	0.5	Iles Salomon
Tonga	0.3	0.3	0.3	0.3	0.3	0.3	0.3	0.3	0.3	0.3	Tonga
Vanuatu	3.0	3.4	3.3	3.7	4.1	3.9	3.7	3.8	3.6	3.9	Vanuatu
Total	53748	54702	55714	55341	56156	57143	57650	58495	58267	59236	Total

General Note.

Fresh, chilled or frozen meat of bovine animals, irrespective of the origin of the animals, expressed in terms of carcass weight, excluding edible offals and tallow. Includes non-industrial production. (SITC, Rev.3: 01100-0).
Source: Food and Agriculture Organization of the United Nations (FAO), Rome.

Remarque générale.

Poids net de viande fraîche, réfrigérée ou congelée, provenant de bovins abattus, quelle que soit la provenance de ces animaux, à l'exclusion des abats comestibles et du suif. Y compris production non-industrielle. (CTCI, Rev.3: 01100-0).
Source: Organisation des Nations Unies pour l'alimentation et l'agriculture (FAO), Rome.

[1] Including Hong-Kong, Macao and Taiwan.

[1] Y compris Hong-Kong, Macao et Taïwan.

Beef and veal, fresh (Industrial production)
Viande de boeuf ou de veau, non préparée (Production industrielle)

ISIC-BASED CODE - CODE BASE CITI

3111-011

Unit : Thousand metric tons

Unité : Milliers de tonnes métriques

Country or area	1990	1991	1992	1993	1994	1995	1996	1997	1998	1999	Pays ou zone
Africa	**456**	**486**	**503**	**483**	**384**	**366**	**362**	**320**	**297**	**274**	**Afrique**
South Africa	456	486	503	483	384	366	362	...	...	...	Afrique du Sud
America, North	**10557**	**10643**	**10701**	**10734**	**11385**	**11783**	**11945**	**11940**	**12037**	**12810**	**Amérique du Nord**
Belize	1	1	2	1	1	1	1	1	1	...	Belize
Dominican Republic	82	84	83	86	81	80	80	79	80	83	Rép. dominicaine
Mexico	8	8	8	61	57	69	71	72	72	64	Mexique
Panama	24	...	22	55	52	48	44	...	...	...	Panama
United States	10442	10509	10586	10531	11194	11585	11749	11714	11803	...	Etats-Unis
America, South	**3020**	**3072**	**3222**	**3273**	**3510**	**3880**	**4232**	**3514**	**3555**	**3980**	**Amérique du Sud**
Bolivia	101	96	101	93	116	*114	...	...	...	...	Bolivie
Brazil	2836	2921	3062	3124	3333	3707	4053	3335	3398	3807	Brésil
Colombia	...	...	14	11	32	32	...	34	35	...	Colombie
Ecuador	67	...	45	45	29	27	42	33	8	...	Equateur
Asia	**613**	**1139**	**988**	**1026**	**936**	**855**	**752**	**714**	**681**	**675**	**Asie**
Armenia	..	13	2	1	1	0	0	...	...	...	Arménie
Azerbaijan	..	21	12	8	6	3	2	1	1	0	Azerbaïdjan
Cyprus	4	5	5	4	4	5	5	5	4	4	Chypre
Georgia	..	...	4	1	0	0	0	0	0	0	Géorgie
Indonesia	2	0	1	3	1	1	...	5	12	...	Indonésie
Japan	549	575	592	594	602	600	554	530	528	539	Japon
Kazakhstan	..	402	270	309	232	169	111	105	68	52	Kazakhstan
Kyrgyzstan	..	25	14	18	8	5	3	2	2	2	Kirghizistan
Tajikistan	..	21	10	8	5	4	3	1	1	1	Tadjikistan
Turkey	58	63	66	68	63	62	67	61	59	63	Turquie
Turkmenistan	..	13	12	12	14	6	4	4	6	...	Turkménistan
Europe	**7782**	**12466**	**11275**	**10014**	**8978**	**7476**	**7370**	**6806**	**6211**	**6210**	**Europe**
Austria	...	...	...	...	...	96	109	106	108	117	Autriche
Belarus	..	405	374	296	271	219	195	170	198	192	Bélarus
Belgium	316	373	352	367	# [1]43	[1]37	[1]35	[1]36	[1]33	[1]36	Belgique
Bulgaria	99	64	56	42	14	7	9	4	4	5	Bulgarie
Croatia	..	45	44	36	31	28	26	26	21	...	Croatie
Denmark[2]	178	188	207	183	163	164	138	163	145	161	Danemark[2]
Czechoslovakia(former)	363	286		..	..	..	..	..	..	..	Tchécoslovaquie(anc.)
Czech Republic	..	..	168	136	113	101	103	103	88	89	République tchèque
Estonia	..	49	43	26	18	17	12	10	10	11	Estonie
Finland	127	140	131	140	129	130	137	80	75	66	Finlande
France	1710	1819	1832	1662	1587	1647	1694	1677	1591	...	France
Germany	..	2133	1784	1560	1406	566	675	753	792	...	Allemagne
Germany(Fed.Rep.)[3]	1759	..	..	..	..	..	..	..	..	..	Allemagne(Rép.féd.)[3]
German D.R.(former)	307	..	..	..	..	..	..	..	..	..	R.D.A. (anc.)
Greece	...	...	...	16	17	17	23	...	17	...	Grèce
Hungary	97	96	89	59	46	42	38	38	33	35	Hongrie
Iceland	...	...	...	...	...	...	3	3	3	4	Islande
Ireland	569	...	...	...	...	...	488	...	176	473	Irlande
Latvia	..	95	82	67	29	15	9	8	7	9	Lettonie
Lithuania	..	167	160	93	56	47	47	47	37	37	Lituanie
Luxembourg	[1]14	17	15	16	15	16	18	17	17	17	Luxembourg
Netherlands[2][5]	227	262	266	351	348	347	366	385	382	388	Pays-Bas[2][5]
Norway	82	79	84	84	...	108	...	111	110	...	Norvège
Poland	446	338	221	181	181	137	161	202	214	179	Pologne
Portugal	...	...	19	16	14	10	8	17	21	25	Portugal
Republic of Moldova	..	69	49	[6]40	[6]33	[6]21	[6]15	[6]15	[6]6	[6]8	Rép. de Moldova
Romania[3]	274	226	136	120	106	88	67	54	45	40	Roumanie[3]
Russian Federation	..	2503	2123	1864	1507	1106	901	705	553	404	Fédération de Russie
Slovakia	..	..	65	51	29	25	13	9	24	20	Slovaquie
Slovenia	..	45	35	31	26	22	27	25	25	26	Slovénie
Spain	...	...	...	271	373	426	462	459	537	595	Espagne
Sweden	135	128	119	128	131	136	258	192	174	182	Suède
Ukraine	..	1351	1231	951	907	671	540	428	292	296	Ukraine
United Kingdom	...	...	...	663	715	757	664	496	451	...	Royaume-Uni

For general note and footnotes, see end of table.

Voir la fin du tableau pour la remarque générale et les notes.

Beef and veal, fresh (Industrial production) (continued)
Viande de boeuf ou de veau, non préparée (Production industrielle) (suite)

ISIC-BASED CODE - CODE BASE CITI

3111-011

Unit : Thousand metric tons

Unité : Milliers de tonnes métriques

Country or area	1990	1991	1992	1993	1994	1995	1996	1997	1998	1999	Pays ou zone
Yugoslavia	..	54	46	40	49	42	34	22	21	18	Yougoslavie
T.F.Yug.Rep. Macedonia	..	3	2	3	2	1	1	1	1	1	L'ex-RY Macédoine
USSR (former)	6018	..	..	..	..	..	..	..	..	..	URSS (anc.)
Total	28446	27806	26689	25529	25193	24360	24661	23293	22780	23949	Total

General Note.

Fresh, chilled or frozen meat of bovine animals, irrespective of the origin of the animals, expressed in terms of carcass weight, excluding edible offals and tallow. Data refer to industrial production only. (SITC, Rev.3: 01100-0).

Remarque générale.

Poids net de viande fraîche, réfrigérée ou congelée, provenant de bovins abattus, quelle que soit la provenance de ces animaux, à l'exclusion des abats comestibles et du suif. Les données se rapportent à la production industrielle seulement. (CTCI, Rev.3: 01100-0).

[1] Incomplete coverage.
[2] Sales.
[3] Including edible offals.
[4] Including unrendered fats.
[5] Production by establishments employing 20 or more persons.
[6] Excluding Transnistria region.

[1] Couverture incomplète.
[2] Ventes.
[3] Y compris les abats comestibles.
[4] Y compris les graisses non fondues.
[5] Production des établissements occupant 20 personnes ou plus.
[6] Non compris la région de Transnistria.

Mutton and lamb, fresh (Total production)
Viande d'ovins et de caprins, non préparée (Production totale)

ISIC-BASED CODE - CODE BASE CITI

3111-04

Unit : Thousand metric tons

Unité : Milliers de tonnes métriques

Country or area	1990	1991	1992	1993	1994	1995	1996	1997	1998	1999	Pays ou zone
Africa	**1689**	**1729**	**1769**	**1815**	**1859**	**1910**	**1954**	**2011**	**2089**	**2085**	**Afrique**
Algeria	142.4	152.2	163.8	177.6	178.1	178.5	190.0	178.9	179.2	175.5	Algérie
Angola	4.6	5.2	5.3	5.6	5.9	6.4	7.5	8.7	9.4	10.2	Angola
Benin	5.7	5.8	6.1	6.4	6.5	6.5	6.0	6.1	6.9	6.3	Bénin
Botswana	7.0	8.7	8.3	6.5	6.1	9.3	7.7	8.4	7.2	7.5	Botswana
Burkina Faso	29.3	30.1	30.6	30.7	30.7	31.5	33.2	34.5	35.1	35.7	Burkina Faso
Burundi	5.0	5.3	5.5	5.8	5.5	5.2	4.6	3.7	3.5	4.4	Burundi
Cameroon	26.9	28.0	28.1	30.1	30.3	30.6	30.8	31.0	31.1	31.3	Cameroun
Cape Verde	0.4	0.5	0.5	0.5	0.5	0.5	0.5	0.5	0.6	0.5	Cap-Vert
Central African Rep.	5.1	5.9	6.1	6.2	6.8	7.6	8.0	8.4	8.5	8.6	Rép. centrafricaine
Chad	17.0	18.8	19.7	20.8	21.4	22.1	24.1	24.6	25.7	26.6	Tchad
Comoros	0.3	0.3	0.3	0.3	0.4	0.4	0.4	0.4	0.4	0.4	Comores
Congo	1.1	1.1	1.1	1.1	1.1	1.1	1.1	1.1	1.0	1.0	Congo
Côte d'Ivoire	8.5	8.5	8.5	9.1	9.3	9.5	9.7	10.0	10.2	10.3	Côte d'Ivoire
Dem. Rep. of Congo	19.9	20.3	21.3	21.9	23.1	23.3	22.5	23.9	24.4	22.2	Rép. dém. du Congo
Djibouti	4.1	4.5	4.5	4.4	4.4	4.4	4.4	4.4	4.4	4.5	Djibouti
Egypt	82.0	74.0	78.3	82.5	87.5	91.2	90.7	93.2	95.0	112.7	Egypte
Equatorial Guinea	0.1	0.1	0.1	0.1	0.1	0.1	0.1	0.1	0.1	0.1	Guinée équatoriale
Eritrea	...	...	...	9.3	9.9	10.1	10.2	10.4	10.9	11.5	Erythrée
Ethiopia,incl.Eritrea	148.3	148.9	149.2	...	...	...	...	...	...	...	Ethiopie,incl.Erythrée
Ethiopia	...	...	...	139.0	143.0	143.2	143.5	143.9	144.2	144.8	Ethiopie
Gabon	0.8	0.8	0.8	0.9	0.9	0.9	0.9	0.9	0.9	1.0	Gabon
Gambia	1.0	0.9	1.2	1.2	1.2	1.2	1.3	1.4	1.5	1.6	Gambie
Ghana	10.9	11.2	11.0	10.9	11.5	11.5	11.9	12.6	13.1	13.3	Ghana
Guinea	3.0	3.1	3.2	3.2	3.3	4.1	4.2	4.3	4.6	4.8	Guinée
Guinea-Bissau	1.2	1.2	1.3	1.4	1.4	1.4	1.5	1.5	1.6	1.6	Guinée-Bissau
Kenya	56.4	59.5	59.5	59.5	58.9	58.3	58.3	58.3	60.5	59.3	Kenya
Lesotho	6.8	7.1	6.6	6.8	7.3	6.3	5.7	5.8	4.7	4.9	Lesotho
Liberia	1.3	1.3	1.3	1.3	1.3	1.3	1.3	1.3	1.3	1.3	Libéria
Libyan Arab Jamah.	28.8	29.6	29.5	35.5	31.0	36.2	44.9	42.6	87.3	33.8	Jamah. arabe libyenne
Madagascar	9.0	9.2	9.4	9.8	9.9	10.1	9.5	9.6	9.7	9.8	Madagascar
Malawi	3.5	3.7	4.0	3.6	4.0	4.3	4.9	4.9	4.9	4.9	Malawi
Mali	43.7	46.2	48.0	43.5	44.9	48.2	50.2	55.3	58.5	56.0	Mali
Mauritania	20.6	21.2	20.0	20.2	21.0	21.2	24.6	24.6	23.9	22.6	Mauritanie
Mauritius	0.2	0.2	0.2	0.2	0.3	0.2	0.2	0.2	0.2	0.3	Maurice
Morocco	121.8	120.0	128.3	122.5	124.6	132.0	112.0	142.0	135.0	141.0	Maroc
Mozambique	2.6	2.5	2.6	2.6	2.6	2.6	2.7	2.7	2.7	2.7	Mozambique
Namibia	15.9	18.2	16.2	17.7	17.5	12.7	12.8	15.2	11.1	11.8	Namibie
Niger	31.2	31.6	33.2	33.0	33.9	34.8	36.2	36.7	37.6	38.6	Niger
Nigeria	164.7	170.5	174.1	177.6	180.1	180.1	218.0	234.1	239.7	245.7	Nigéria
Réunion	0.1	0.1	0.1	0.1	0.1	0.1	0.1	0.1	0.1	0.1	Réunion
Rwanda	4.7	4.8	4.8	4.9	4.9	3.4	3.8	4.0	4.6	4.8	Rwanda
Senegal	22.1	24.8	27.1	27.9	29.0	29.3	28.9	29.2	29.5	29.5	Sénégal
Sierra Leone	1.4	1.4	1.4	1.4	1.4	1.4	1.4	1.5	1.6	1.6	Sierra Leone
Somalia	88.3	72.8	52.0	53.3	54.6	57.2	59.8	61.1	72.8	72.8	Somalie
South Africa	167.6	168.0	167.0	159.0	154.6	146.4	134.8	127.6	127.6	147.5	Afrique du Sud
Sudan	104.6	129.1	153.0	179.0	204.9	236.9	242.3	255.0	263.8	266.4	Soudan
Swaziland	3.0	3.0	3.0	3.0	3.1	3.1	3.1	3.4	3.4	3.7	Swaziland
Togo	7.0	7.3	7.3	7.3	7.1	7.0	4.8	4.0	4.7	4.7	Togo
Tunisia	46.3	46.4	47.4	50.5	51.9	54.0	55.6	55.0	58.1	58.0	Tunisie
Uganda	20.3	20.6	21.7	22.9	23.5	24.0	24.3	24.5	24.7	25.0	Ouganda
United Rep.Tanzania	31.3	32.0	33.1	34.2	35.3	35.6	35.9	36.1	36.4	36.6	Rép. Unie de Tanzanie
Zambia	2.1	2.2	2.2	2.5	2.6	2.7	2.8	2.9	3.7	4.4	Zambie
Zimbabwe	11.0	11.1	11.2	10.7	11.1	11.3	12.1	12.0	12.5	12.7	Zimbabwe
America, North	**251**	**257**	**256**	**250**	**235**	**224**	**214**	**211**	**209**	**208**	**Amérique du Nord**
Antigua and Barbuda	0.1	0.1	0.1	0.1	0.1	0.1	0.1	0.1	0.1	0.1	Antigua-et-Barbuda
Bahamas	0.1	0.1	0.1	0.1	0.1	0.1	0.1	0.1	0.1	0.1	Bahamas
Barbados	0.2	0.2	0.2	0.2	0.2	0.2	0.2	0.2	0.2	0.2	Barbade
British Virgin Islands	0.1	0.1	0.1	0.1	0.1	0.1	0.1	0.1	0.1	0.1	Iles Vierges britanniques
Canada	9.3	10.4	11.3	10.9	10.5	10.2	10.7	10.2	9.9	10.8	Canada
Cuba	2.0	2.0	1.6	1.5	1.5	1.5	1.5	1.5	1.6	1.7	Cuba
Dominica	0.1	0.1	0.1	0.1	0.1	0.1	0.1	0.1	0.1	0.1	Dominique
Dominican Republic	2.5	2.5	2.5	2.6	2.6	2.6	2.6	2.6	1.6	1.0	Rép. dominicaine

For general note and footnotes, see end of table.

Voir la fin du tableau pour la remarque générale et les notes.

Mutton and lamb, fresh (Total production) (continued)
Viande d'ovins et de caprins, non préparée (Production totale) (suite)

ISIC-BASED CODE - CODE BASE CITI

3111-04

Unit : Thousand metric tons   Unité : Milliers de tonnes métriques

Country or area	1990	1991	1992	1993	1994	1995	1996	1997	1998	1999	Pays ou zone
El Salvador	0.1	0.1	0.1	0.1	0.1	0.1	0.1	0.1	0.1	0.1	El Salvador
Greenland	0.4	0.4	0.4	0.4	0.4	0.4	0.4	0.4	0.4	0.4	Groënland
Grenada	0.1	0.1	0.1	0.1	0.1	0.1	0.1	0.1	0.1	0.1	Grenade
Guadeloupe	0.3	0.3	0.3	0.3	0.3	0.3	0.2	0.2	0.2	0.2	Guadeloupe
Guatemala	2.5	2.5	2.4	2.5	2.8	2.9	3.0	3.0	3.0	3.0	Guatemala
Haiti	4.1	4.1	4.1	4.1	4.1	3.9	4.5	5.3	6.0	6.0	Haïti
Honduras	0.2	0.2	0.2	0.2	0.2	0.2	0.2	0.3	0.3	0.3	Honduras
Jamaica	1.7	1.7	1.7	1.7	1.7	1.7	1.7	1.7	1.7	1.7	Jamaïque
Martinique	0.5	0.5	0.5	0.4	0.4	0.3	0.3	0.3	0.3	0.3	Martinique
Mexico	60.8	65.6	70.8	70.2	69.0	67.6	65.3	65.4	68.7	68.2	Mexique
Netherlands Antilles	0.1	0.1	0.1	0.1	0.1	0.1	0.1	0.1	0.1	0.1	Antilles néerlandaises
Nicaragua	0.0	0.0	0.0	0.1	0.0	0.1	0.0	0.0	0.0	0.0	Nicaragua
Puerto Rico	0.3	0.3	0.3	0.3	0.3	0.2	0.2	0.2	0.2	0.2	Porto Rico
St. Kitts-Nevis	0.1	0.1	0.1	0.1	0.1	0.1	0.1	0.1	0.1	0.1	St-Kitts-Nevis
St. Lucia	0.2	0.2	0.2	0.2	0.2	0.1	0.1	0.1	0.1	0.1	St-Lucie
St. Vincent-Grenadines	0.1	0.1	0.1	0.1	0.1	0.1	0.1	0.1	0.1	0.1	St. Vincent-Grenadines
Trinidad and Tobago	0.5	0.5	0.5	0.5	0.5	0.5	0.5	0.5	0.5	0.5	Trinité-et-Tobago
United States	164.7	164.7	157.9	152.9	139.7	130.2	121.6	118.0	113.9	112.5	Etats-Unis
America, South	**365**	**361**	**346**	**351**	**372**	**358**	**327**	**328**	**316**	**329**	**Amérique du Sud**
Argentina	91.6	91.5	72.7	72.2	92.5	88.3	71.3	65.3	56.9	54.0	Argentine
Bolivia	19.0	17.0	17.2	17.4	18.6	19.6	20.0	20.4	20.6	21.0	Bolivie
Brazil	111.8	114.0	115.3	119.0	120.0	125.0	96.7	101.1	102.1	109.7	Brésil
Chile	19.2	17.8	17.2	17.7	16.5	14.5	13.5	15.1	16.6	18.1	Chili
Colombia	12.5	11.9	12.5	13.4	13.4	13.6	16.1	16.9	15.6	16.5	Colombie
Ecuador	4.9	4.9	4.9	6.1	6.5	7.2	7.3	7.5	6.7	9.2	Equateur
Falkland Is. (Malvinas)	1.0	1.0	1.1	1.0	1.1	1.1	0.6	0.8	0.8	0.8	Iles Falkland (Malvinas)
Guyana	0.8	0.8	0.8	0.8	0.8	0.8	0.8	0.8	0.8	0.8	Guyana
Paraguay	3.4	3.3	3.2	3.3	3.3	3.1	3.1	3.1	3.4	3.4	Paraguay
Peru	32.6	27.5	28.1	26.3	25.6	26.1	26.6	27.8	28.8	36.7	Pérou
Suriname	0.1	0.1	0.1	0.1	0.1	0.1	0.1	0.1	0.1	0.1	Suriname
Uruguay	61.2	62.5	64.4	64.0	66.0	52.0	64.0	60.0	55.0	51.0	Uruguay
Venezuela	6.7	9.1	8.4	9.6	7.5	6.9	6.8	9.1	8.9	7.5	Venezuela
Asia	**3732**	**4411**	**4540**	**4802**	**5003**	**5272**	**5118**	**5282**	**5648**	**5939**	**Asie**
Afghanistan	131.4	132.6	129.1	125.5	126.7	127.2	140.8	155.5	171.7	186.9	Afghanistan
Armenia	..	...	8.2	8.4	7.4	7.1	5.5	4.9	5.1	4.5	Arménie
Azerbaijan	..	...	27.0	26.0	22.0	23.0	25.6	25.8	32.4	33.2	Azerbaïdjan
Bahrain	6.9	7.3	7.4	7.3	9.1	8.8	8.6	8.8	7.1	7.2	Bahreïn
Bangladesh	75.2	79.8	85.6	92.6	100.0	107.2	117.6	125.6	128.6	129.6	Bangladesh
Bhutan	0.3	0.3	0.4	0.4	0.4	0.4	0.4	0.4	0.4	0.4	Bhoutan
China[1]	1068.6	1180.6	1250.8	1374.7	1482.5	1748.7	1814.6	1935.4	2255.5	2495.0	Chine[1]
Cyprus	8.1	7.0	6.6	7.4	7.4	7.8	7.7	8.1	9.8	10.8	Chypre
Gaza Strip (Palestine)	1.5	1.1	1.0	1.1	1.3	1.2	1.2	1.2	1.2	1.2	Bande de Gaza (Palestine)
Georgia	..	..	6.1	6.7	7.4	8.3	9.4	6.5	8.3	6.9	Géorgie
India	611.2	618.8	626.4	635.2	654.8	663.3	671.8	680.5	687.6	694.0	Inde
Indonesia	90.0	94.4	99.0	111.3	99.7	94.3	98.6	107.2	81.7	83.7	Indonésie
Iran(Islamic Rep. of)	337.5	344.0	358.0	366.0	372.0	377.0	380.5	406.0	418.0	397.0	Iran(Rép. islamique)
Iraq	35.8	21.7	29.4	37.5	33.5	30.6	22.2	27.1	28.2	28.4	Iraq
Israel	6.0	6.0	6.0	6.6	6.6	6.7	6.6	6.5	6.2	6.2	Israël
Japan	0.4	0.4	0.5	0.5	0.5	0.4	0.3	0.3	0.3	0.3	Japon
Jordan	10.9	14.9	14.2	16.0	11.9	12.0	12.7	11.7	18.7	16.8	Jordanie
Kazakhstan	..	...	242.9	275.3	251.8	205.8	167.4	142.7	116.8	116.0	Kazakhstan
Korea,Dem.Ppl's.Rep.	5.6	6.0	5.8	5.8	6.4	4.5	4.5	5.7	7.6	10.1	Corée,Rép.pop.dém.de
Korea, Republic of	1.0	1.6	2.3	2.6	2.7	3.1	3.2	3.6	3.3	3.1	Corée, République de
Kuwait	17.1	8.6	17.2	25.2	48.8	38.3	39.4	39.0	38.4	38.3	Koweït
Kyrgyzstan	..	...	70.0	81.6	76.4	54.1	54.2	44.6	43.4	46.6	Kirghizistan
Lao People's Dem. Rep.	0.3	0.3	0.2	0.3	0.3	0.3	0.4	0.4	0.4	0.4	Rép. dém. pop. lao
Lebanon	10.7	12.5	13.7	16.3	17.0	14.5	13.6	14.5	16.0	16.1	Liban
Malaysia	0.7	0.7	0.7	0.7	0.7	0.6	0.6	0.6	0.5	0.6	Malaisie
Mongolia	132.3	135.9	116.3	112.6	111.9	111.5	121.3	104.4	112.4	116.5	Mongolie
Myanmar	6.6	6.5	6.9	7.1	7.1	7.5	7.9	8.2	8.5	8.7	Myanmar
Nepal	31.9	32.4	32.9	33.4	33.8	34.0	34.9	37.5	38.5	39.1	Népal
Oman	15.3	16.2	15.7	16.0	16.3	15.0	15.1	15.4	15.6	15.7	Oman

For general note and footnotes, see end of table.   Voir la fin du tableau pour la remarque générale et les notes.

Mutton and lamb, fresh (Total production) (continued)
Viande d'ovins et de caprins, non préparée (Production totale) (suite)

ISIC-BASED CODE - CODE BASE CITI

3111-04

Unit : Thousand metric tons

Unité : Milliers de tonnes métriques

Country or area	1990	1991	1992	1993	1994	1995	1996	1997	1998	1999	Pays ou zone
Pakistan	484.0	519.0	556.0	595.0	637.0	683.0	464.0	476.5	488.5	500.0	Pakistan
Philippines	26.8	24.9	25.8	28.3	29.6	30.6	30.3	30.6	31.1	31.9	Philippines
Qatar	11.6	14.2	11.8	12.2	12.6	14.0	7.5	7.9	8.0	8.0	Qatar
Saudi Arabia	82.7	79.0	83.8	85.1	88.5	87.5	87.9	85.0	85.0	91.0	Arabie saoudite
Singapore	0.8	0.7	0.7	0.7	0.5	0.4	0.2	0.2	0.2	0.2	Singapour
Sri Lanka	1.8	1.7	2.2	2.4	2.8	2.5	2.2	2.1	1.8	1.8	Sri Lanka
Syrian Arab Republic	119.8	129.2	117.7	98.0	125.5	136.6	150.3	153.7	160.1	182.0	Rép. arabe syrienne
Tajikistan	..	...	20.0	20.0	21.0	19.0	11.0	3.3	13.0	13.0	Tadjikistan
Thailand	1.2	1.3	1.6	1.3	1.1	1.0	0.7	0.8	0.8	0.8	Thaïlande
Turkey	370.0	367.0	365.0	363.0	372.0	372.0	366.0	378.0	374.0	368.0	Turquie
Turkmenistan	..	...	35.0	45.0	45.0	49.5	53.3	51.2	61.1	63.3	Turkménistan
United Arab Emirates	25.6	31.3	29.8	35.0	36.3	37.5	38.5	37.3	30.4	31.3	Emirats arabes unis
Uzbekistan	..	...	67.5	74.0	73.0	83.0	76.0	80.0	82.0	84.0	Ouzbékistan
Viet Nam	2.8	2.3	2.3	2.6	3.2	4.1	4.6	4.6	4.7	4.7	Viet Nam
Yemen	..	40.2	41.0	40.0	38.0	38.0	39.3	42.5	44.6	45.8	Yémen
Europe	**1507**	**1888**	**1889**	**1899**	**1817**	**1750**	**1707**	**1574**	**1578**	**1505**	**Europe**
Albania	12.0	12.5	14.8	15.2	18.5	18.3	16.6	15.7	16.7	18.1	Albanie
Austria	5.7	5.8	6.2	5.7	6.2	6.5	6.9	7.3	7.3	6.9	Autriche
Belarus	..	...	5.7	5.8	5.2	3.9	4.0	3.0	3.2	3.0	Bélarus
Belgium-Luxembourg	7.5	8.2	5.8	4.3	5.4	4.9	4.7	4.3	4.2	4.5	Belgique-Luxembourg
Bosnia and Herzegovina	..	..	4.0	3.0	2.4	2.6	2.7	2.7	2.7	2.7	Bosnie-Herzégovine
Bulgaria	63.2	73.3	59.9	56.2	46.8	44.9	55.6	50.2	53.0	53.3	Bulgarie
Croatia	..	...	2.6	2.3	2.1	1.9	1.9	1.9	1.9	1.8	Croatie
Denmark	1.5	1.8	1.9	2.0	1.7	1.5	1.6	1.5	1.5	1.4	Danemark
Czechoslovakia(former)	9.9	8.9	..	..	..	..	..	..	..	..	Tchécoslovaquie(anc.)
Czech Republic	..	..	..	5.3	4.3	4.0	3.6	3.5	3.3	3.3	République tchèque
Estonia	..	...	1.8	1.2	1.3	0.8	0.5	0.5	0.4	0.4	Estonie
Finland	1.1	1.0	1.2	1.3	1.5	1.6	1.4	1.3	1.2	0.9	Finlande
France	194.2	169.6	155.8	155.4	147.1	147.7	154.5	149.9	144.4	138.3	France
Germany	..	49.9	43.9	40.8	40.0	41.7	43.0	44.2	44.5	44.0	Allemagne
Greece	140.4	139.9	139.5	140.7	141.7	143.5	145.2	143.3	148.5	126.5	Grèce
Hungary	5.4	6.0	6.0	1.8	1.1	1.9	1.6	1.9	2.5	2.6	Hongrie
Iceland	9.5	9.3	8.6	8.9	8.8	8.7	8.1	7.9	8.2	8.6	Islande
Ireland	86.0	92.0	94.5	98.7	92.6	89.4	90.0	78.9	83.1	86.4	Irlande
Italy	84.7	84.8	86.0	80.8	78.9	76.5	77.6	75.8	73.3	73.4	Italie
Latvia	..	...	3.9	3.8	2.2	1.1	0.7	0.4	0.3	0.3	Lettonie
Lithuania	..	...	1.7	1.6	1.7	1.6	1.4	1.2	1.2	1.2	Lituanie
Netherlands	14.9	17.7	17.7	18.4	17.2	16.0	18.1	15.5	16.0	16.0	Pays-Bas
Norway	24.8	24.2	24.8	25.6	26.7	26.9	27.5	26.2	23.6	24.5	Norvège
Poland	28.7	33.0	22.5	17.6	8.3	5.6	4.6	2.9	1.3	1.6	Pologne
Portugal	27.8	30.2	27.5	27.2	27.3	26.8	26.2	27.2	25.6	24.9	Portugal
Republic of Moldova	..	...	3.9	3.5	3.8	3.2	3.4	3.3	3.6	3.6	Rép. de Moldova
Romania	108.5	94.0	99.5	91.5	80.5	75.2	71.5	64.2	59.8	54.0	Roumanie
Russian Federation	..	...	329.6	359.0	316.0	261.0	230.2	199.6	178.1	143.3	Fédération de Russie
Slovakia	..	..	...	3.1	2.2	2.2	1.9	2.0	1.8	1.6	Slovaquie
Slovenia	..	..	0.2	0.2	0.1	0.1	0.3	0.6	0.7	1.0	Slovénie
Spain	233.8	243.6	233.0	240.6	241.3	242.1	237.8	245.1	249.7	238.8	Espagne
Sweden	5.0	4.2	4.4	4.2	4.2	3.5	3.7	3.5	3.5	3.7	Suède
Switzerland	5.1	5.7	6.1	6.0	5.7	5.8	6.2	6.4	6.4	6.6	Suisse
Ukraine	..	...	35.0	30.0	44.0	39.5	31.8	24.4	20.7	18.5	Ukraine
United Kingdom	370.2	385.5	398.0	399.0	391.0	401.0	382.0	321.0	351.0	361.0	Royaume-Uni
Yugoslavia	..	...	22.9	25.1	26.2	28.8	30.7	30.7	29.7	22.7	Yougoslavie
T.F.Yug.Rep. Macedonia	..	...	12.4	12.9	13.1	10.0	9.5	6.6	5.6	5.7	L'ex-RY Macédoine
Yugoslavia, SFR	67.3	..	..	..	..	..	..	..	..	..	Yougoslavie, RSF
USSR (former)	1007.6	..	..	..	..	..	..	..	..	..	URSS (anc.)
Oceania	**1174**	**1243**	**1242**	**1144**	**1184**	**1167**	**1095**	**1120**	**1172**	**1141**	**Océanie**
Australia	641.0	682.9	680.8	654.8	658.4	631.1	583.4	575.0	624.2	621.8	Australie
Fiji	0.6	0.7	0.7	0.7	0.8	0.8	0.9	1.0	1.0	1.0	Fidji
French Polynesia	0.1	0.1	0.1	0.1	0.1	0.1	0.1	0.1	0.1	0.1	Polynésie française
New Caledonia	0.1	0.1	0.1	0.1	0.1	0.1	0.0	0.0	0.0	0.0	Nouvelle-Calédonie
New Zealand	532.0	559.2	560.1	488.2	524.9	534.8	511.1	544.4	546.7	518.5	Nouvelle-Zélande

For general note and footnotes, see end of table.

Voir la fin du tableau pour la remarque générale et les notes.

93

Mutton and lamb, fresh (Total production) (continued)
Viande d'ovins et de caprins, non préparée (Production totale) (suite)

ISIC-BASED CODE - CODE BASE CITI

3111-04

Unit : Thousand metric tons   Unité : Milliers de tonnes métriques

Country or area	1990	1991	1992	1993	1994	1995	1996	1997	1998	1999	Pays ou zone
Total	9725	9888	10042	10260	10470	10681	10416	10526	11012	11208	Total

General Note.
Fresh, chilled or frozen meat of sheep, lambs, goats and kids irrespective of the origin of the animals, expressed in terms of carcass weight, excluding edible offals and tallow. Includes non-industrial production. (SITC, Rev.3: 01210-0).
Source: Food and Agriculture Organization of the United Nations (FAO), Rome.

Remarque générale.
Poids net de viande fraîche, réfrigérée ou congelée, provenant de moutons, d'agneaux, de chèvres et de chevreaux abattus, quelle que soit la provenance de ces animaux, à l'exclusion des abats comestibles et du suif. Y compris production non-industrielle. (CTCI, Rev.3: 01210-0).
Source: Organisation des Nations Unies pour l'alimentation et l'agriculture (FAO), Rome.

[1] Including Hong-Kong, Macao and Taiwan.

[1] Y compris Hong-Kong, Macao et Taïwan.

Mutton and lamb, fresh (Industrial production)
Viande d'ovins et de caprins, non préparée (Production industrielle)

ISIC-BASED CODE - CODE BASE CITI

3111-041

Unit : Thousand metric tons   Unité : Milliers de tonnes métriques

Country or area	1990	1991	1992	1993	1994	1995	1996	1997	1998	1999	Pays ou zone
Africa	**146**	**153**	**141**	**125**	**83**	**79**	**84**	**46**	**32**	**18**	**Afrique**
South Africa	146	153	141	125	83	79	84	...	...	...	Afrique du Sud
America, North	**165**	**165**	**158**	**152**	**142**	**132**	**123**	**120**	**116**	**93**	**Amérique du Nord**
Dominican Republic	2	2	2	*2	2	2	2	2	2	2	Rép. dominicaine
United States	163	163	156	150	140	130	121	118	114	...	Etats-Unis
America, South	**25**	**29**	**16**	**29**	**24**	**23**	**23**	**32**	**22**	**27**	**Amérique du Sud**
Brazil	21	24	12	24	21	20	20	...	...	...	Brésil
Ecuador	4	...	4	5	3	3	3	12	2	...	Equateur
Asia	**19**	**193**	**175**	**161**	**107**	**67**	**44**	**37**	**40**	**48**	**Asie**
Armenia	..	3	0	0	0	0	0	...	13	20	Arménie
Azerbaijan	..	5	4	4	2	1	1	0	0	0	Azerbaïdjan
Cyprus	8	7	7	7	7	5	5	5	5	6	Chypre
Kazakhstan	..	140	133	123	78	43	28	20	14	13	Kazakhstan
Kyrgyzstan	..	18	11	9	5	2	0	0	0	0	Kirghizistan
Tajikistan	..	4	4	2	1	0	0	0	0	0	Tadjikistan
Turkey	11	6	10	9	7	9	6	5	6	7	Turquie
Turkmenistan	..	10	6	7	7	7	4	3	2	...	Turkménistan
Europe	**647**	**780**	**777**	**756**	**717**	**722**	**667**	**660**	**637**	**677**	**Europe**
Belarus	..	2	1	1	0	0	0	0	0	...	Bélarus
Belgium	7	8	6	4	# [1]1	[1]1	[1]1	[1]1	[1]1	[1]1	Belgique
Bulgaria	31	9	8	6	5	1	4	3	3	3	Bulgarie
Croatia	..	1	0	0	0	0	0	0	0	...	Croatie
Denmark[2]	1	1	1	1	0	0	0	1	0	0	Danemark[2]
Czechoslovakia(former)	3	1	..	..	..	..	..	..	..	..	Tchécoslovaquie(anc.)
Czech Republic	..	..	1	1	0	0	0	0	0	0	République tchèque
Estonia	..	2	1	1	1	0	0	0	0	0	Estonie
Finland	1	1	1	1	1	1	1	1	1	1	Finlande
France	156	149	138	131	124	119	123	120	115	...	France
Germany	..	21	17	16	16	...	...	...	...	...	Allemagne
Germany(Fed.Rep.)[3]	21	..	..	..	..	..	..	..	..	..	Allemagne(Rép.féd.)[3]
Greece	...	...	...	6	8	8	8	7	6	...	Grèce
Hungary	0	1	2	2	...	...	...	...	...	...	Hongrie
Iceland	...	...	...	...	...	...	7	8	7	10	Islande
Ireland	66	...	...	...	...	...	71	55	52	55	Irlande
Latvia	..	2	1	0	0	0	0	0	0	0	Lettonie
Netherlands[2][4]	7	1	1	1	1	1	2	1	...	...	Pays-Bas[2][4]
Norway	24	24	24	26	...	...	...	27	27	...	Norvège
Poland	1	2	1	0	0	0	0	0	0	0	Pologne
Portugal	...	...	2	1	1	1	1	4	5	3	Portugal
Republic of Moldova	..	1	1	[5]1	[5]1	[5]1	[5]1	[5]1	[5]0	[5]0	Rép. de Moldova
Romania	19	[6]6	[6]4	[6]3	[6]2	[6]3	[6]3	[6]3	[6]1	[6]1	Roumanie
Russian Federation	..	135	137	99	70	37	21	13	8	7	Fédération de Russie
Slovakia	..	..	1	0	0	0	0	0	...	0	0	Slovaquie
Spain	...	...	...	37	69	103	103	87	106	119	Espagne
Sweden	4	4	4	4	4	3	3	3	3	2	Suède
Ukraine	..	17	17	13	19	19	8	5	3	2	Ukraine
United Kingdom	...	...	...	332	...	309	262	300	278	...	Royaume-Uni
Yugoslavia	..	3	3	1	1	1	1	1	0	0	Yougoslavie
T.F.Yug.Rep. Macedonia	..	3	3	1	2	2	2	1	1	...	L'ex-RY Macédoine
USSR (former)	458	..	..	..	..	..	..	..	..	..	URSS (anc.)
Total	**1460**	**1319**	**1267**	**1224**	**1073**	**1023**	**941**	**896**	**846**	**862**	**Total**

General Note.
Fresh, chilled or frozen meat of sheep, lambs, goats and kids, irrespective of the origin of the animals, expressed in terms of carcass weight, excluding edible offals and tallow. Data refer to industrial production only. (SITC, Rev.3: 01210-0).

Remarque générale.
Poids net de viande fraîche, réfrigérée ou congelée, provenant de moutons, d'agneaux, de chèvres et de chevreaux abattus, guelle que soit la provenance de ces animaux, à l'exclusion des abats comestibles et du suif. Les données se rapportent à la production industrielle seulement. (CTCI, Rev.3: 01210-0).

For footnotes, see end of table.

Voir la fin du tableau pour les notes.

Mutton and lamb, fresh (Industrial production) (continued)
Viande d'ovins et de caprins, non préparée (Production industrielle) (suite)

ISIC-BASED CODE - CODE BASE CITI
3111-041

Footnotes
[1] Incomplete coverage.
[2] Sales.
[3] Including edible offals.
[4] Production by establishments employing 20 or more persons.
[5] Excluding Transnistria region.
[6] Including by-products.

Notes.
[1] Couverture incomplète.
[2] Ventes.
[3] Y compris les abats comestibles.
[4] Production des établissements occupant 20 personnes ou plus.
[5] Non compris la région de Transnistria.
[6] Y compris les sous-produits.

Pork, fresh (Total production)
Viande de porc, non préparée (Production totale)

ISIC-BASED CODE - CODE BASE CITI

3111-07

Unit : Thousand metric tons   Unité : Milliers de tonnes métriques

Country or area	1990	1991	1992	1993	1994	1995	1996	1997	1998	1999	Pays ou zone
Africa	**590**	**579**	**549**	**541**	**543**	**602**	**579**	**590**	**607**	**614**	**Afrique**
Algeria	0.1	0.1	0.1	0.1	0.1	0.1	0.1	0.1	0.1	0.1	Algérie
Angola	22.0	23.0	24.0	24.5	25.0	26.0	28.0	29.0	29.0	28.6	Angola
Benin	5.2	5.8	5.9	6.2	6.3	7.0	7.6	7.5	6.0	6.0	Bénin
Botswana	0.7	0.7	0.5	0.2	0.2	0.2	0.5	0.3	0.6	0.7	Botswana
Burkina Faso	6.0	6.1	6.2	6.3	6.3	6.3	7.0	7.5	8.0	8.5	Burkina Faso
Burundi	6.2	4.8	5.1	5.4	5.2	4.9	4.6	4.2	4.4	4.3	Burundi
Cameroon	16.4	16.5	16.8	17.1	17.4	17.7	17.8	17.9	17.9	18.0	Cameroun
Cape Verde	3.7	3.8	3.9	7.3	4.7	8.4	3.1	5.0	6.5	7.0	Cap-Vert
Central African Rep.	8.0	8.0	8.1	8.7	9.3	9.9	11.3	11.8	12.0	12.1	Rép. centrafricaine
Chad	0.3	0.3	0.3	0.3	0.3	0.3	0.3	0.4	0.4	0.4	Tchad
Congo	2.0	2.1	2.0	2.1	2.1	2.1	2.1	2.0	2.0	2.0	Congo
Côte d'Ivoire	14.4	14.8	15.2	15.7	16.2	18.5	13.5	12.3	12.5	12.6	Côte d'Ivoire
Dem. Rep. of Congo	38.5	39.2	41.2	41.9	42.9	44.0	41.5	42.5	43.0	41.0	Rép. dém. du Congo
Egypt	2.5	2.5	2.9	2.9	2.8	2.8	2.9	2.9	3.0	3.0	Egypte
Equatorial Guinea	0.1	0.1	0.1	0.1	0.1	0.1	0.1	0.1	0.1	0.1	Guinée équatoriale
Ethiopia,incl.Eritrea	1.1	1.1	1.2	...	...	...	...	...	...	...	Ethiopie,incl.Erythrée
Ethiopia	...	...	...	1.2	1.2	1.2	1.3	1.3	1.4	1.4	Ethiopie
Gabon	2.3	2.5	2.8	2.9	3.0	3.0	3.1	3.1	3.1	3.1	Gabon
Gambia	0.4	0.4	0.4	0.4	0.4	0.4	0.4	0.4	0.4	0.4	Gambie
Ghana	10.6	10.2	9.3	9.1	9.4	7.8	7.1	8.0	8.0	8.0	Ghana
Guinea	0.6	0.7	0.9	1.0	1.1	1.3	1.3	1.5	1.7	1.7	Guinée
Guinea-Bissau	8.9	8.9	9.2	9.5	9.8	10.0	10.2	10.3	10.5	10.6	Guinée-Bissau
Kenya	5.2	6.5	7.2	7.8	8.8	8.8	10.4	10.4	10.4	9.1	Kenya
Lesotho	3.0	2.4	2.2	3.0	2.3	3.3	3.2	2.9	3.1	3.2	Lesotho
Liberia	4.0	4.0	4.0	4.0	4.0	4.0	4.0	4.0	4.0	4.0	Libéria
Madagascar	54.0	56.9	58.2	60.5	61.8	67.9	70.0	72.1	72.1	73.5	Madagascar
Malawi	10.3	10.5	10.8	11.3	11.8	12.4	11.0	12.0	11.3	11.8	Malawi
Mali	1.8	2.1	2.4	2.0	2.0	2.0	2.0	2.1	2.8	2.8	Mali
Mauritius	0.9	0.9	1.0	1.1	1.1	1.1	1.2	1.0	0.8	0.7	Maurice
Morocco	0.7	0.7	0.7	0.7	0.7	0.7	0.7	0.8	0.6	0.6	Maroc
Mozambique	12.4	11.7	12.2	12.2	12.1	12.2	12.4	12.5	12.7	12.8	Mozambique
Namibia	2.5	2.5	2.4	2.1	2.6	2.7	2.4	2.5	1.7	2.1	Namibie
Niger	1.3	1.4	1.4	1.4	1.4	1.4	1.4	1.4	1.4	1.4	Niger
Nigeria	106.9	106.3	47.3	39.2	34.0	66.8	47.4	56.0	65.3	77.9	Nigéria
Réunion	7.6	8.5	9.5	10.2	10.3	10.3	10.3	12.4	12.5	12.5	Réunion
Rwanda	2.6	2.6	2.7	2.7	2.7	1.8	1.8	1.9	2.0	2.0	Rwanda
Sao Tome and Principe	0.1	0.1	0.1	0.1	0.1	0.1	0.1	0.1	0.1	0.1	Sao Tomé-et-Principe
Senegal	6.6	6.8	7.0	7.2	7.2	7.3	7.3	7.4	7.4	7.4	Sénégal
Seychelles	1.1	1.1	1.1	1.1	1.1	1.1	1.1	1.1	1.1	1.1	Seychelles
Sierra Leone	2.2	2.2	2.2	2.2	2.2	2.2	2.2	2.2	2.2	2.3	Sierra Leone
Somalia	0.3	0.2	0.1	0.1	0.1	0.1	0.1	0.1	0.1	0.1	Somalie
South Africa	130.8	112.7	129.6	119.6	119.0	126.5	127.8	120.0	124.0	117.0	Afrique du Sud
Swaziland	0.9	1.0	1.0	1.0	1.1	1.2	1.4	1.5	1.6	1.6	Swaziland
Togo	9.9	9.9	11.2	11.9	11.9	11.9	12.0	12.2	12.5	12.5	Togo
Tunisia	0.2	0.2	0.2	0.2	0.2	0.2	0.2	0.2	0.2	0.2	Tunisie
Uganda	44.5	45.9	47.5	48.6	50.4	51.0	51.4	52.3	53.0	53.6	Ouganda
United Rep.Tanzania	9.0	9.2	9.2	9.4	9.4	9.5	9.2	9.4	9.5	9.7	Rép. Unie de Tanzanie
Zambia	9.5	9.5	9.5	9.7	10.1	9.7	10.3	10.3	10.4	10.6	Zambie
Zimbabwe	11.4	11.1	11.4	8.2	10.0	13.1	12.7	11.9	12.9	12.8	Zimbabwe
America, North	**9104**	**9434**	**10071**	**10024**	**10392**	**10571**	**10183**	**10319**	**11288**	**11632**	**Amérique du Nord**
Antigua and Barbuda	0.1	0.1	0.1	0.1	0.1	0.1	0.1	0.1	0.1	0.1	Antigua-et-Barbuda
Bahamas	0.2	0.2	0.2	0.2	0.2	0.2	0.2	0.2	0.2	0.2	Bahamas
Barbados	3.8	3.9	3.9	3.9	3.9	3.9	3.9	4.0	4.4	4.4	Barbade
Belize	1.3	1.3	1.3	1.2	1.2	1.1	1.2	1.2	1.2	1.2	Belize
Bermuda	0.1	0.1	0.1	0.1	0.1	0.1	0.1	0.1	0.1	0.1	Bermudes
Canada	1123.8	1096.2	1207.7	1194.3	1229.4	1275.8	1227.8	1256.7	1389.7	1562.0	Canada
Costa Rica	14.3	17.3	19.2	20.5	23.1	23.6	20.1	21.2	24.8	26.6	Costa Rica
Cuba	101.1	91.2	47.4	63.4	68.6	71.6	74.4	78.3	97.8	103.4	Cuba
Dominica	0.4	0.4	0.4	0.4	0.4	0.4	0.4	0.4	0.4	0.4	Dominique
Dominican Republic	20.7	38.0	43.0	53.0	57.0	62.0	63.0	64.0	64.0	57.7	Rép. dominicaine
El Salvador	11.0	10.7	11.0	11.3	8.1	10.9	11.2	9.9	10.4	11.3	El Salvador
Grenada	0.1	0.1	0.1	0.2	0.2	0.2	0.2	0.2	0.2	0.2	Grenade

For general note and footnotes, see end of table.   Voir la fin du tableau pour la remarque générale et les notes.

Pork, fresh (Total production) (continued)
Viande de porc, non préparée (Production totale) (suite)

ISIC-BASED CODE - CODE BASE CITI

3111-07

Unit : Thousand metric tons

Unité : Milliers de tonnes métriques

Country or area	1990	1991	1992	1993	1994	1995	1996	1997	1998	1999	Pays ou zone
Guadeloupe	1.9	1.0	1.1	1.1	1.0	1.2	1.0	1.1	1.1	1.1	Guadeloupe
Guatemala	14.2	13.4	14.1	16.6	15.5	16.1	16.4	17.0	17.5	17.5	Guatemala
Haiti	12.8	15.0	18.2	19.1	21.0	23.0	24.1	25.4	26.9	26.9	Haïti
Honduras	13.0	13.1	13.2	13.4	13.6	14.1	14.7	15.4	16.1	16.9	Honduras
Jamaica	7.4	4.7	5.9	7.0	7.2	6.5	6.6	6.6	6.8	6.9	Jamaïque
Martinique	2.0	2.1	2.0	1.8	1.8	1.5	1.5	1.5	1.5	1.5	Martinique
Mexico	757.4	811.9	819.8	821.6	872.9	921.6	910.3	939.2	960.7	992.4	Mexique
Montserrat	0.1	0.1	0.1	0.1	0.1	0.1	0.1	0.1	0.1	0.1	Montserrat
Netherlands Antilles	0.2	0.2	0.2	0.2	0.2	0.2	0.2	0.1	0.1	0.2	Antilles néerlandaises
Nicaragua	10.5	9.4	8.5	8.0	4.9	5.1	5.3	5.5	5.6	5.7	Nicaragua
Panama	11.5	12.3	14.6	15.6	16.0	16.8	18.8	18.9	18.7	20.5	Panama
Puerto Rico	28.4	30.3	18.0	17.1	15.4	15.4	14.9	13.2	13.2	13.2	Porto Rico
St. Kitts-Nevis	0.1	0.1	0.1	0.1	0.1	0.1	0.2	0.2	0.2	0.2	St-Kitts-Nevis
St. Lucia	0.6	0.6	0.6	0.7	0.7	0.7	0.7	0.7	0.7	0.7	St-Lucie
St. Vincent-Grenadines	0.6	0.5	0.6	0.6	0.6	0.6	0.6	0.6	0.6	0.6	St. Vincent-Grenadines
Trinidad and Tobago	2.4	2.4	2.5	1.9	1.6	1.6	1.6	2.1	1.9	1.9	Trinité-et-Tobago
United States	6964.0	7257.5	7817.0	7751.0	8027.0	8097.0	7764.0	7835.0	8623.0	8758.0	Etats-Unis
United States Virgin Is.	0.1	0.1	0.1	0.1	0.1	0.1	0.1	0.1	0.1	0.1	Iles Vierges américaines
America, South	**1900**	**1992**	**2124**	**2214**	**2274**	**2412**	**2572**	**2514**	**2701**	**2867**	**Amérique du Sud**
Argentina	140.5	141.6	157.2	181.9	181.8	178.4	148.5	137.0	155.6	181.4	Argentine
Bolivia	65.3	65.3	66.8	57.7	59.6	62.3	65.8	68.7	72.3	73.6	Bolivie
Brazil	1050.0	1120.0	1188.0	1250.0	1300.0	1430.0	1600.0	1518.0	1652.3	1751.6	Brésil
Chile	123.2	128.8	137.6	147.3	160.8	172.4	184.7	208.7	235.0	243.7	Chili
Colombia	133.5	133.4	134.7	134.0	133.2	133.2	135.0	135.0	135.0	150.3	Colombie
Ecuador	70.7	76.3	81.8	81.1	82.3	88.8	103.2	106.7	99.9	110.3	Equateur
French Guiana	0.9	0.8	0.8	0.9	0.8	1.1	1.1	1.2	1.2	1.2	Guyane française
Guyana	0.9	0.9	0.6	1.1	0.5	0.5	0.5	0.5	0.5	0.5	Guyana
Paraguay	118.1	120.5	126.5	126.8	127.8	130.0	115.7	117.4	118.8	120.0	Paraguay
Peru	66.5	68.7	72.8	75.7	77.7	80.1	83.0	86.6	90.7	92.9	Pérou
Suriname	1.7	2.0	1.5	1.4	1.6	0.9	0.8	1.1	1.1	1.0	Suriname
Uruguay	22.1	21.8	22.5	22.8	22.9	22.0	20.5	21.7	25.8	27.0	Uruguay
Venezuela	107.1	111.4	132.9	133.2	124.7	112.5	112.8	111.1	113.1	114.1	Venezuela
Asia	**29562**	**31692**	**33887**	**36245**	**39145**	**39843**	**39643**	**43969**	**46865**	**48258**	**Asie**
Armenia	..	...	16.8	4.5	6.1	4.8	5.6	5.4	7.2	8.3	Arménie
Azerbaijan	..	...	5.0	3.0	2.0	2.0	1.7	1.6	1.3	1.4	Azerbaïdjan
Bhutan	1.1	1.2	1.2	1.2	1.2	1.2	1.2	1.2	1.2	1.2	Bhoutan
Brunei Darussalam	0.3	0.3	0.1	0.1	0.1	0.1	0.1	0.1	0.1	0.2	Brunéi Darussalam
Cambodia	60.6	62.0	81.7	84.9	81.0	81.5	86.0	97.0	100.0	102.5	Cambodge
China [1]	24015.7	25824.1	27647.2	29836.5	32613.2	33401.3	33014.7	37154.9	39898.9	41047.9	Chine [1]
Cyprus	31.4	31.9	33.5	39.2	42.5	42.8	45.6	46.1	47.2	49.2	Chypre
Georgia	..	...	56.5	44.8	47.3	44.3	45.5	46.7	42.3	40.8	Géorgie
India	416.5	434.0	444.5	469.0	477.1	495.2	514.0	533.4	542.5	560.0	Inde
Indonesia	544.5	572.0	583.0	621.5	660.0	572.0	599.5	632.5	621.5	748.0	Indonésie
Israel	9.2	9.4	9.4	8.7	8.9	10.6	11.0	12.3	12.1	12.1	Israël
Japan	1555.2	1482.8	1434.1	1439.6	1390.3	1322.1	1266.4	1283.3	1285.9	1277.1	Japon
Kazakhstan	..	...	217.3	194.3	158.2	113.4	109.8	81.9	78.9	82.5	Kazakhstan
Korea,Dem.Ppl's.Rep.	225.0	235.0	175.0	150.0	135.0	115.0	105.1	83.8	111.5	133.8	Corée,Rép.pop.dém.de
Korea, Republic of	550.0	530.0	752.0	770.0	786.0	799.0	886.9	895.8	939.4	940.8	Corée, République de
Kyrgyzstan	..	...	35.6	24.8	18.0	28.0	28.7	25.7	30.4	28.6	Kirghizistan
Lao People's Dem. Rep.	20.9	21.9	22.6	24.6	25.6	28.8	29.6	30.5	31.4	31.6	Rép. dém. pop. lao
Lebanon	3.7	3.9	4.3	5.3	6.1	6.6	8.0	8.0	8.3	8.5	Liban
Malaysia	226.6	233.3	250.9	262.8	284.8	283.4	278.3	282.3	262.4	250.0	Malaisie
Mongolia	7.9	3.8	1.8	0.7	0.7	0.6	0.3	0.2	0.8	1.0	Mongolie
Myanmar	55.0	57.8	60.5	61.3	63.3	68.8	71.5	89.1	91.3	133.1	Myanmar
Nepal	9.9	10.2	10.4	10.4	10.6	11.0	11.8	12.4	13.1	13.9	Népal
Philippines	684.0	701.6	658.0	731.0	765.0	805.0	860.0	901.1	932.8	973.0	Philippines
Singapore	76.3	81.2	83.5	85.5	87.4	86.2	83.9	84.2	84.1	50.0	Singapour
Sri Lanka	1.6	2.2	2.0	1.6	2.0	2.3	2.3	2.2	1.9	1.7	Sri Lanka
Tajikistan	..	...	4.0	1.0	1.0	1.2	0.2	0.1	0.2	0.2	Tadjikistan
Thailand	337.5	401.9	433.3	458.8	489.4	488.9	511.3	548.7	474.6	425.9	Thaïlande
Turkey	0.3	0.1	0.1	0.1	0.1	0.4	1.4	0.1	0.3	0.3	Turquie
Turkmenistan	..	...	7.0	5.0	4.0	3.0	1.4	0.7	0.5	0.7	Turkménistan

For general note and footnotes, see end of table.

Voir la fin du tableau pour la remarque générale et les notes.

Pork, fresh (Total production) (continued)
Viande de porc, non préparée (Production totale) (suite)

ISIC-BASED CODE - CODE BASE CITI

3111-07

Unit : Thousand metric tons   Unité : Milliers de tonnes métriques

Country or area	1990	1991	1992	1993	1994	1995	1996	1997	1998	1999	Pays ou zone
Uzbekistan	..	...	36.1	27.0	20.0	16.0	9.0	4.0	15.0	16.0	Ouzbékistan
Viet Nam	728.6	715.5	820.0	878.0	957.7	1007.0	1052.0	1104.0	1228.0	1318.2	Viet Nam
Europe	**17184**	**24825**	**25754**	**25586**	**24740**	**24649**	**25010**	**24310**	**25717**	**26015**	**Europe**
Albania	13.3	9.0	10.6	12.5	13.6	13.6	6.4	6.6	6.5	6.2	Albanie
Austria	517.0	516.6	527.3	538.2	538.5	521.1	538.0	556.1	592.2	499.0	Autriche
Belarus	..	...	323.0	284.0	252.0	262.8	273.0	297.6	319.7	305.0	Bélarus
Belgium-Luxembourg	784.0	915.0	951.1	1000.8	1019.3	1043.0	1069.8	1033.1	1085.2	1004.7	Belgique-Luxembourg
Bosnia and Herzegovina	..	..	14.3	14.5	15.0	17.0	11.4	11.0	11.6	11.7	Bosnie-Herzégovine
Bulgaria	405.8	361.5	311.4	276.8	207.1	256.4	252.4	226.7	247.0	258.0	Bulgarie
Croatia			65.0	59.6	60.4	55.6	56.4	54.5	60.1	64.2	Croatie
Denmark	1208.5	1271.9	1369.7	1503.7	1521.0	1494.0	1493.7	1520.6	1629.3	1641.8	Danemark
Czechoslovakia(former)	912.6	826.9	..	..						..	Tchécoslovaquie(anc.)
Czech Republic	..	..	...	614.9	470.6	502.2	502.4	463.6	475.7	451.6	République tchèque
Estonia	..	...	50.1	34.7	30.4	35.4	31.7	29.5	32.4	31.3	Estonie
Finland	187.0	177.0	176.0	169.2	170.7	167.6	171.8	179.7	184.5	181.9	Finlande
France	1726.8	1772.7	1903.0	2033.9	2116.4	2144.0	2161.0	2219.0	2328.0	2377.0	France
Germany	..	3812.6	3584.9	3645.8	3604.0	3602.4	3635.0	3563.8	3834.1	4113.4	Allemagne
Greece	139.8	140.2	144.7	136.2	136.8	136.9	135.5	142.1	142.6	138.3	Grèce
Hungary	1017.7	930.5	764.3	672.4	608.3	578.3	670.7	580.7	569.9	664.2	Hongrie
Iceland	2.5	2.6	2.6	2.9	3.2	3.3	3.7	3.9	3.9	4.7	Islande
Ireland	157.0	179.0	201.9	212.0	214.6	212.1	211.0	219.9	239.3	250.7	Irlande
Italy	1333.1	1332.8	1341.6	1371.3	1369.3	1345.6	1410.3	1395.8	1412.2	1471.7	Italie
Latvia	..	...	100.5	68.1	53.8	62.6	39.5	37.1	36.5	34.6	Lettonie
Lithuania	..	...	155.3	90.2	81.6	93.1	88.5	87.1	95.6	91.0	Lituanie
Malta	7.8	8.3	8.4	8.5	9.3	8.5	8.6	10.2	10.4	10.3	Malte
Netherlands	1661.0	1591.0	1585.0	1747.0	1673.3	1622.1	1624.0	1375.6	1715.2	1711.0	Pays-Bas
Norway	83.3	85.5	91.1	90.1	91.1	95.8	103.3	105.4	106.4	108.6	Norvège
Poland	1854.5	1947.3	2035.6	1903.0	1681.3	1962.3	2063.7	1891.3	2026.2	2043.0	Pologne
Portugal	279.3	262.5	264.6	307.3	315.6	305.0	324.6	305.6	332.0	345.6	Portugal
Republic of Moldova	..	...	113.8	79.1	61.2	59.6	63.5	65.5	57.8	60.8	Rép. de Moldova
Romania	787.8	833.9	788.8	761.3	775.3	673.0	630.6	666.7	619.5	610.0	Roumanie
Russian Federation	..	...	2784.0	2432.0	2103.0	1865.0	1705.1	1545.9	1505.1	1485.4	Fédération de Russie
Slovakia	..	..	...	241.5	244.3	242.8	250.8	254.8	227.0	175.5	Slovaquie
Slovenia	..	...	41.1	65.3	71.1	60.8	62.7	59.2	60.5	67.3	Slovénie
Spain	1788.8	1877.4	1917.8	2088.8	2124.1	2174.8	2356.2	2401.1	2744.4	2893.0	Espagne
Sweden	290.8	267.9	277.9	291.1	307.6	308.8	318.9	329.3	330.4	325.4	Suède
Switzerland	269.6	265.4	264.1	260.5	246.1	250.7	219.9	214.4	231.5	225.7	Suisse
Ukraine	..	...	1179.8	1013.0	916.0	806.9	789.3	710.0	668.2	656.3	Ukraine
United Kingdom	946.1	979.0	992.0	1012.0	1053.0	1012.0	1004.0	1094.0	1142.0	1047.0	Royaume-Uni
Yugoslavia	..	...	591.7	533.7	571.1	644.0	713.0	644.0	625.0	640.0	Yougoslavie
T.F.Yug.Rep. Macedonia	..	...	10.4	9.6	9.7	9.3	9.4	8.7	8.8	8.8	L'ex-RY Macédoine
Yugoslavia, SFR	810.1	..	..	..	..	..	..	..	..	..	Yougoslavie, RSF
USSR (former)	6653.9	..	..	..	..	..	..	..	..	..	URSS (anc.)
Oceania	**404**	**400**	**430**	**428**	**447**	**459**	**441**	**445**	**470**	**482**	**Océanie**
American Samoa	0.3	0.3	0.3	0.3	0.3	0.3	0.3	0.3	0.3	0.3	Samoa américaines
Australia	317.1	312.1	335.8	328.3	344.3	351.3	334.0	335.6	358.5	369.9	Australie
Cook Islands	0.4	0.3	0.3	0.4	0.4	0.5	0.6	0.6	0.6	0.6	Iles Cook
Fiji	3.2	3.3	3.2	3.4	3.5	3.2	3.4	3.9	3.5	3.6	Fidji
French Polynesia	1.2	1.2	1.2	1.2	1.3	1.3	1.2	1.1	1.1	1.2	Polynésie française
Guam	0.1	0.1	0.1	0.1	0.1	0.1	0.1	0.1	0.1	0.1	Guam
Kiribati	0.7	0.7	0.7	0.7	0.7	0.7	0.7	0.7	0.7	0.7	Kiribati
Nauru	0.1	0.1	0.1	0.1	0.1	0.1	0.1	0.1	0.1	0.1	Nauru
New Caledonia	1.1	1.2	1.3	1.3	1.3	1.3	1.3	1.4	1.5	1.4	Nouvelle-Calédonie
New Zealand	43.2	44.0	47.0	49.0	49.0	51.0	49.8	49.5	49.7	50.0	Nouvelle-Zélande
Papua New Guinea	27.1	27.1	29.9	33.0	36.0	39.0	39.9	42.0	43.5	43.5	Papouasie-Nvl-Guinée
Samoa	4.1	3.7	3.5	3.6	3.6	3.6	3.6	3.6	3.6	3.6	Samoa
Solomon Islands	1.8	1.8	1.8	1.8	1.8	1.8	1.9	1.9	1.9	2.0	Iles Salomon
Tonga	1.5	1.5	1.5	1.5	1.5	1.5	1.5	1.5	1.5	1.5	Tonga
Tuvalu	0.1	0.1	0.1	0.1	0.1	0.1	0.1	0.1	0.1	0.1	Tuvalu
Vanuatu	2.2	2.5	2.6	2.6	2.6	2.6	2.7	2.7	2.8	2.8	Vanuatu
Wallis and Funtuna Is	0.3	0.3	0.3	0.3	0.3	0.3	0.3	0.3	0.3	0.3	Iles Wallis et Futuna

For general note and footnotes, see end of table.   Voir la fin du tableau pour la remarque générale et les notes.

Pork, fresh (Total production) (continued)
Viande de porc, non préparée (Production totale) (suite)

ISIC-BASED CODE - CODE BASE CITI

3111-07

Unit : Thousand metric tons
Unité : Milliers de tonnes métriques

Country or area	1990	1991	1992	1993	1994	1995	1996	1997	1998	1999	Pays ou zone
Total	65399	68922	72814	75038	77539	78535	78427	82147	87648	89868	Total

General Note.

Fresh, chilled or frozen meat of swine, irrespective of the origin of the animals, expressed in terms of carcass weight, excluding edible offals and lard. Bacon and ham are not included. Includes non-industrial production. (SITC, Rev.3: 01220-0).
Source: Food and Agriculture Organization of the United Nations (FAO), Rome.

Remarque générale.

Poids net de viande fraîche, réfrigérée ou congelée, provenant de porcs abattus, quelle que soit la provenance de ces animaux, à l'exclusion des abats comestibles et du saindoux, bacon et jambon non compris. Y compris production non-industrielle. (CTCI, Rev.3: 01220-0).
Source: Organisation des Nations Unies pour l'alimentation et l'agriculture (FAO), Rome.

[1] Including Hong-Kong, Macao and Taiwan.

[1] Y compris Hong-Kong, Macao et Taïwan.

Pork, fresh (Industrial production)
Viande de porc, non préparée (Production industrielle)

ISIC-BASED CODE - CODE BASE CITI

3111-071

Unit : Thousand metric tons

Unité : Milliers de tonnes métriques

Country or area	1990	1991	1992	1993	1994	1995	1996	1997	1998	1999	Pays ou zone
Africa	**119**	**114**	**112**	**112**	**97**	**108**	**113**	**103**	**101**	**99**	**Afrique**
Kenya	1	2	1	1	2	2	2	...	...	...	Kenya
South Africa	118	112	111	111	95	106	111	...	...	...	Afrique du Sud
America, North	**6999**	**7287**	**7853**	**7832**	**8142**	**8197**	**7867**	**7932**	**8727**	**8929**	**Amérique du Nord**
Belize	1	0	1	1	1	1	1	1	1	...	Belize
Dominican Republic	6	4	4	5	6	6	6	6	6	8	Rép. dominicaine
Mexico	30	27	29	100	108	94	96	90	97	122	Mexique
United States	6962	7256	7819	7726	8027	8096	7764	7835	8623	...	Etats-Unis
America, South	**745**	**833**	**916**	**908**	**995**	**1188**	**1265**	**1046**	**1154**	**1280**	**Amérique du Sud**
Bolivia	2	4	6	6	6	*8	...	...	...	...	Bolivie
Brazil	730	812	893	885	977	1155	1240	1010	1119	1237	Brésil
Colombia	...	...	4	3	2	12	...	13	7	...	Colombie
Ecuador	10	...	13	14	10	13	11	15	20	...	Equateur
Asia	**1586**	**1672**	**1578**	**1565**	**1464**	**1379**	**1316**	**1333**	**1338**	**1331**	**Asie**
Armenia	..	4	1	0	0	0	0	...	6	6	Arménie
Azerbaijan	..	2	2	1	0	0	0	0	0	0	Azerbaïdjan
Cyprus	31	32	34	32	33	34	36	36	36	41	Chypre
Georgia	..	...	2	2	0	0	0	0	...	...	Géorgie
Indonesia	0	0	2	0	...	1	...	0	0	...	Indonésie
Japan	1555	1483	1434	1440	1390	1322	1266	1283	1289	1277	Japon
Kazakhstan	..	130	91	75	35	19	12	12	7	7	Kazakhstan
Kyrgyzstan	..	9	4	11	3	2	1	0	0	0	Kirghizistan
Tajikistan	..	4	2	0	0	0	0	0	0	0	Tadjikistan
Turkmenistan	..	6	6	4	2	1	0	0	0	...	Turkménistan
Europe	**13314**	**16210**	**15145**	**14221**	**13523**	**12279**	**12541**	**11706**	**11711**	**12036**	**Europe**
Austria	...	...	...	...	...	220	240	229	298	336	Autriche
Belarus	..	217	167	136	104	89	78	97	112	112	Bélarus
Belgium	778	908	944	993	# [1]175	[1]273	[1]285	[1]302	[1]330	[1]320	Belgique
Bulgaria	300	191	129	97	61	71	65	25	37	40	Bulgarie
Croatia	..	68	55	56	57	48	46	44	41	...	Croatie
Denmark[2]	468	487	515	563	610	149	146	160	181	211	Danemark[2]
Czechoslovakia(former)	601	498	..	..	..	..	..	..	..		Tchécoslovaquie(anc.)
Czech Republic	..	..	296	252	229	227	239	249	237	255	République tchèque
Estonia	..	57	43	20	15	18	15	14	18	17	Estonie
Finland	237	234	215	216	213	237	266	117	96	103	Finlande
France	1622	1665	1734	1772	1854	1872	1910	1945	2026	...	France
Germany		3770	3559	3620	3540	1945	...	...	...	...	Allemagne
Germany(Fed.Rep.)[3]	3241	..	..	..	..	..	...	...	...	...	Allemagne(Rép.féd.)[3]
German D.R.(former)	854	..	..	..	..	..	..	..	..		R.D.A. (anc.)
Greece	...	...	...	26	32	30	36	32	40	...	Grèce
Hungary	497	470	301	287	255	253	292	292	271	335	Hongrie
Iceland	...	...	...	...	...	...	3	3	3	5	Islande
Latvia	..	62	40	16	12	9	7	7	7	12	Lettonie
Lithuania	..	121	72	22	17	26	29	26	26	26	Lituanie
Luxembourg	8	8	7	9	9	9	10	10	9	12	Luxembourg
Netherlands[2] [4]	1052	1105	1124	1330	1311	1277	1271	1197	1274	1346	Pays-Bas[2] [4]
Norway	83	85	91	90	...	103	...	110	110	113	Norvège
Poland	963	844	823	718	654	728	727	720	785	815	Pologne
Portugal	...	...	131	140	159	159	173	177	157	165	Portugal
Republic of Moldova	..	84	53	[5]16	[5]10	[5]7	[5]12	[5]15	[5]11	[5]9	Rép. de Moldova
Romania[6]	485	493	378	408	390	374	397	331	245	241	Roumanie[6]
Russian Federation	..	1615	1244	942	772	612	484	366	288	232	Fédération de Russie
Slovakia	..	..	119	81	61	56	30	22	64	64	Slovaquie
Slovenia	..	38	29	26	...	...	31	27	27	30	Slovénie
Spain	...	...	...	1074	1389	2208	2124	2068	2248	2599	Espagne
Sweden	276	264	267	271	285	290	413	435	473	440	Suède
Ukraine	..	642	440	277	209	156	123	72	54	79	Ukraine
United Kingdom	749	798	808	539	...	...	...	...	...	...	Royaume-Uni
Yugoslavia	..	129	106	69	65	74	79	69	65	67	Yougoslavie
T.F.Yug.Rep. Macedonia	..	4	3	3	3	2	2	2	2	3	L'ex-RY Macédoine

For general note and footnotes, see end of table.

Voir la fin du tableau pour la remarque générale et les notes.

Pork, fresh (Industrial production) (continued)
Viande de porc, non préparée (Production industrielle) (suite)

ISIC-BASED CODE - CODE BASE CITI

3111-071

Unit : Thousand metric tons

Unité : Milliers de tonnes métriques

Country or area	1990	1991	1992	1993	1994	1995	1996	1997	1998	1999	Pays ou zone
USSR (former)	3473	..	..	..	..	..	..	..	..	..	URSS (anc.)
Total	26236	26116	25604	24639	24221	23150	23101	22120	23031	23675	Total

General Note.

Fresh, chilled or frozen meat of swine, irrespective of the origin of the animals, expressed in terms of carcass weight, excluding edible offals and lard. Bacon and ham are not included. Data refer to industrial production only.(SITC,Rev.3: 01220-0).

Remarque générale.

Poids net de viande fraîche, réfrigérée ou congelée, provenant de porcs abattus, quelle que soit la provenance de ces animaux, à l'exclusion des abats comestibles et du saindoux, bacon et jambon non compris. Les données se rapportent à la production industrielle seulement. (CTCI, Rev.3: 01220-0).

[1] Incomplete coverage.
[2] Sales.
[3] Including edible offals.
[4] Production by establishments employing 20 or more persons.
[5] Excluding Transnistria region.
[6] Including edible offals and lard.

[1] Couverture incomplète.
[2] Ventes.
[3] Y compris les abats comestibles.
[4] Production des établissements occupant 20 personnes ou plus.
[5] Non compris la région de Transnistria.
[6] Y compris les abats comestibles et le saindoux.

Poultry, dressed, fresh (Total production)
Volailles plumées et vidées, non préparées (Production totale)

ISIC-BASED CODE - CODE BASE CITI

3111-10

Unit : Thousand metric tons　　　　　　　　　　　　　　　　　　　　　　　　　　　Unité : Milliers de tonnes métriques

Country or area	1990	1991	1992	1993	1994	1995	1996	1997	1998	1999	Pays ou zone
Africa	**1965**	**2020**	**2069**	**2105**	**2203**	**2349**	**2476**	**2646**	**2668**	**2695**	**Afrique**
Algeria	185.3	189.3	193.3	198.3	202.3	202.3	205.3	220.3	220.5	220.3	Algérie
Angola	7.1	7.2	7.2	7.3	7.3	7.3	7.4	7.4	7.5	7.6	Angola
Benin	25.6	25.6	24.0	20.8	22.4	24.8	28.0	30.4	33.0	21.7	Bénin
Botswana	3.8	4.0	4.8	4.2	4.6	7.4	7.1	8.2	6.8	6.2	Botswana
Burkina Faso	18.0	18.8	19.8	20.0	20.0	20.8	22.0	23.0	24.0	25.6	Burkina Faso
Burundi	5.9	6.2	6.5	6.7	6.6	6.4	6.3	6.1	6.2	6.1	Burundi
Cameroon	18.3	18.7	19.3	20.0	20.0	20.8	21.6	22.4	23.2	24.0	Cameroun
Cape Verde	0.5	0.5	0.5	0.5	0.6	0.5	0.6	0.6	0.6	0.5	Cap-Vert
Central African Rep.	2.5	2.5	2.5	2.6	2.6	2.6	3.2	3.3	2.7	2.6	Rép. centrafricaine
Chad	3.8	3.9	3.9	4.1	4.1	4.2	4.3	4.4	4.5	4.7	Tchad
Comoros	0.4	0.4	0.4	0.5	0.5	0.5	0.5	0.5	0.5	0.5	Comores
Congo	5.3	5.3	5.4	5.5	5.6	5.7	5.8	5.8	5.7	5.8	Congo
Côte d'Ivoire	42.7	44.4	45.0	48.0	48.4	48.4	48.8	55.0	51.0	52.8	Côte d'Ivoire
Dem. Rep. of Congo	25.0	20.2	22.7	22.2	23.4	21.1	19.7	19.2	19.5	18.8	Rép. dém. du Congo
Egypt	271.5	303.0	317.3	330.5	358.7	406.8	422.7	541.6	534.9	536.8	Egypte
Equatorial Guinea	0.2	0.2	0.2	0.2	0.2	0.2	0.2	0.2	0.2	0.2	Guinée équatoriale
Eritrea	...	...	...	3.1	3.9	4.3	4.9	1.5	1.7	1.7	Erythrée
Ethiopia,incl.Eritrea	76.3	76.6	77.2	...	...	...	...	...	...	...	Ethiopie,incl.Erythrée
Ethiopia	...	...	...	72.0	72.0	72.4	72.8	73.0	73.3	73.6	Ethiopie
Gabon	2.6	2.7	2.8	3.0	3.0	3.2	3.3	3.4	3.6	3.7	Gabon
Gambia	0.8	0.9	1.0	1.1	1.3	1.1	0.8	1.0	1.1	1.2	Gambie
Ghana	9.0	9.6	10.4	11.3	11.5	11.7	11.9	14.5	16.0	16.4	Ghana
Guinea	1.7	1.7	1.8	1.9	2.0	2.3	2.5	2.6	2.9	3.0	Guinée
Guinea-Bissau	0.7	0.7	0.7	0.7	0.7	0.8	0.8	0.8	1.0	1.0	Guinée-Bissau
Kenya	47.9	48.0	49.2	39.0	45.5	54.6	55.9	59.8	59.8	56.4	Kenya
Lesotho	1.3	1.3	1.1	1.0	1.4	1.4	1.5	1.6	1.5	1.7	Lesotho
Liberia	4.8	4.8	4.8	4.8	4.8	4.8	5.4	5.6	5.8	5.8	Libéria
Libyan Arab Jamah.	65.0	66.3	67.6	71.5	83.8	102.8	100.0	99.0	98.0	98.2	Jamah. arabe libyenne
Madagascar	41.4	42.4	42.6	44.1	45.0	47.8	50.6	53.2	56.7	59.6	Madagascar
Malawi	11.8	12.9	11.8	12.6	13.1	13.6	14.2	14.3	14.6	15.0	Malawi
Mali	23.7	24.0	24.4	24.6	25.3	25.6	25.7	26.0	28.8	29.2	Mali
Mauritania	3.8	3.9	3.8	3.9	3.9	3.9	3.9	3.9	4.0	4.0	Mauritanie
Mauritius	12.6	13.3	15.5	17.1	18.9	19.4	20.6	20.9	18.4	21.0	Maurice
Morocco	147.2	143.4	152.1	141.0	160.0	180.0	230.0	230.0	230.0	230.0	Maroc
Mozambique	27.2	27.8	27.8	27.8	29.6	30.5	31.4	33.2	34.1	35.9	Mozambique
Namibia	2.0	2.2	2.3	2.4	2.6	2.7	2.8	3.0	3.1	3.0	Namibie
Niger	21.4	21.8	22.9	23.2	23.2	23.2	23.2	23.2	23.2	23.2	Niger
Nigeria	174.0	165.0	162.0	165.0	168.0	169.0	170.0	171.0	172.0	172.0	Nigéria
Réunion	10.4	11.9	12.0	12.5	13.4	14.5	14.8	16.5	16.6	16.6	Réunion
Rwanda	1.4	1.4	1.5	1.5	1.4	1.3	1.4	1.4	1.5	1.5	Rwanda
Sao Tome and Principe	0.2	0.3	0.4	0.4	0.4	0.4	0.4	0.5	0.5	0.5	Sao Tomé-et-Principe
Senegal	27.8	38.2	43.3	52.0	55.0	58.0	60.0	62.0	64.1	64.1	Sénégal
Seychelles	0.5	0.5	0.6	0.6	0.7	1.0	1.0	1.1	0.9	0.9	Seychelles
Sierra Leone	8.6	8.7	8.7	8.7	8.7	8.7	9.1	9.1	9.1	9.1	Sierra Leone
Somalia	3.2	2.4	1.6	2.6	2.9	3.1	3.2	3.4	3.2	3.3	Somalie
South Africa	373.9	379.0	379.0	384.0	394.1	414.2	454.4	444.5	444.6	451.8	Afrique du Sud
Sudan	21.6	22.4	23.1	23.6	24.0	25.0	26.0	28.0	28.5	29.5	Soudan
Swaziland	1.2	1.2	1.2	1.3	1.1	1.2	1.2	2.3	2.7	5.3	Swaziland
Togo	7.4	7.4	7.5	7.5	7.2	7.4	7.5	8.5	9.4	9.4	Togo
Tunisia	51.2	52.0	55.8	59.0	61.3	65.8	67.5	77.7	88.6	98.0	Tunisie
Uganda	29.6	31.5	33.0	34.7	36.0	36.4	36.4	36.1	36.1	40.1	Ouganda
United Rep.Tanzania	25.2	29.3	30.4	35.5	31.4	35.5	32.9	36.4	39.5	41.5	Rép. Unie de Tanzanie
Zambia	18.9	20.8	22.9	25.2	24.3	25.0	27.5	30.0	32.3	33.5	Zambie
Zimbabwe	16.9	17.9	17.4	17.4	17.9	19.1	20.8	21.9	23.4	23.7	Zimbabwe
America, North	**12849**	**13561**	**14281**	**14920**	**15923**	**16734**	**17508**	**18161**	**18575**	**19669**	**Amérique du Nord**
Antigua and Barbuda	0.2	0.2	0.2	0.2	0.2	0.2	0.2	0.2	0.2	0.2	Antigua-et-Barbuda
Bahamas	5.8	6.5	5.2	4.8	4.4	7.5	8.8	9.7	10.7	9.5	Bahamas
Barbados	10.2	10.1	8.8	8.7	9.8	11.0	12.3	11.7	11.5	11.9	Barbade
Belize	6.2	6.6	7.9	7.6	7.0	7.1	7.6	7.5	7.2	7.3	Belize
Bermuda	0.2	0.1	0.1	0.1	0.1	0.1	0.1	0.1	0.1	0.1	Bermudes
Canada	733.3	737.4	738.7	772.9	860.9	870.1	900.1	924.9	970.8	1020.7	Canada
Costa Rica	43.0	47.6	49.6	49.9	54.3	63.7	65.9	62.8	72.1	76.8	Costa Rica

For general note and footnotes, see end of table.　　　　　　　　　　　　Voir la fin du tableau pour la remarque générale et les notes.

Poultry, dressed, fresh (Total production) (continued)
Volailles plumées et vidées, non préparées (Production totale) (suite)

ISIC-BASED CODE - CODE BASE CITI

3111-10

Unit : Thousand metric tons

Unité : Milliers de tonnes métriques

Country or area	1990	1991	1992	1993	1994	1995	1996	1997	1998	1999	Pays ou zone
Cuba	91.3	89.0	51.7	51.2	55.6	66.8	61.9	63.2	59.6	60.1	Cuba
Dominica	0.2	0.2	0.3	0.3	0.3	0.3	0.3	0.3	0.3	0.3	Dominique
Dominican Republic	109.7	111.9	122.0	127.8	131.1	137.0	148.7	156.3	157.7	176.7	Rép. dominicaine
El Salvador	32.5	35.6	40.0	44.2	37.6	40.0	40.6	43.5	47.9	46.2	El Salvador
Grenada	0.4	0.5	0.5	0.5	0.5	0.5	0.5	0.5	0.6	0.6	Grenade
Guadeloupe	0.9	1.0	1.1	1.2	0.9	0.6	0.4	0.6	0.6	0.6	Guadeloupe
Guatemala	66.9	70.6	86.9	91.3	100.6	103.7	108.9	114.5	120.2	129.0	Guatemala
Haiti	6.7	6.4	6.1	6.1	8.5	6.7	5.8	5.8	7.6	7.6	Haïti
Honduras	28.1	31.4	35.3	38.5	45.9	49.6	53.8	58.4	54.2	58.5	Honduras
Jamaica	51.9	53.4	52.5	45.2	44.9	45.4	55.1	59.3	63.2	72.9	Jamaïque
Martinique	1.0	1.3	1.3	1.3	0.9	0.6	0.9	0.9	0.9	0.9	Martinique
Mexico	792.5	896.5	930.0	1071.0	1154.7	1314.5	1295.4	1475.4	1633.4	1767.0	Mexique
Montserrat	0.1	0.1	0.1	0.1	0.1	0.1	0.1	0.1	0.1	0.1	Montserrat
Netherlands Antilles	0.2	0.3	0.3	0.5	0.6	0.7	0.4	0.4	0.4	0.3	Antilles néerlandaises
Nicaragua	7.1	10.5	16.9	23.4	26.7	28.8	28.8	29.7	32.0	36.8	Nicaragua
Panama	25.3	36.3	34.1	43.2	41.4	58.6	53.4	48.0	58.5	58.5	Panama
Puerto Rico	51.3	56.7	57.6	59.3	61.3	61.7	59.8	59.9	59.9	59.9	Porto Rico
St. Kitts-Nevis	0.2	0.2	0.2	0.2	0.2	0.2	0.2	0.2	0.2	0.2	St-Kitts-Nevis
St. Lucia	0.6	0.6	0.6	0.6	0.6	0.6	0.6	0.6	0.7	0.7	St-Lucie
St. Vincent-Grenadines	0.4	0.4	0.4	0.4	0.4	0.4	0.4	0.4	0.4	0.4	St. Vincent-Grenadines
Trinidad and Tobago	24.4	25.7	24.6	29.9	26.5	30.1	30.0	26.6	26.2	26.2	Trinité-et-Tobago
United States	10758.6	11324.5	12007.6	12439.6	13247.4	13827.2	14566.9	14999.4	15177.9	16039.0	Etats-Unis
United States Virgin Is.	0.0	0.1	0.1	0.1	0.1	0.1	0.1	0.1	0.1	0.1	Iles Vierges américaines
America, South	**3915**	**4485**	**5062**	**5547**	**6032**	**6926**	**6916**	**7422**	**8041**	**8920**	**Amérique du Sud**
Argentina	385.8	427.1	603.9	714.2	723.8	786.3	760.4	792.0	895.8	952.6	Argentine
Bolivia	43.0	52.2	54.2	71.9	88.9	96.9	106.1	116.6	135.7	144.8	Bolivie
Brazil	2421.6	2703.9	2957.0	3235.1	3511.6	4153.7	4152.5	4571.0	4969.1	5646.8	Brésil
Chile	124.3	140.7	207.6	246.8	278.7	289.2	304.9	313.6	339.2	344.0	Chili
Colombia	297.6	386.1	408.2	445.1	498.8	553.1	464.5	432.8	507.0	504.0	Colombie
Ecuador	70.0	76.3	80.5	80.5	102.4	105.3	149.0	177.5	107.8	146.3	Equateur
French Guiana	0.5	0.7	0.6	0.5	0.6	0.6	0.6	0.6	0.6	0.6	Guyane française
Guyana	2.1	1.5	3.1	4.1	6.2	7.3	10.7	12.0	11.3	12.4	Guyana
Paraguay	24.7	18.6	20.2	21.7	30.6	33.6	34.1	36.6	37.6	37.6	Paraguay
Peru	245.8	291.8	320.2	302.8	353.7	410.8	410.5	443.9	490.3	553.6	Pérou
Suriname	11.7	9.6	8.9	7.5	4.4	4.0	3.8	4.2	3.1	3.9	Suriname
Uruguay	27.8	29.7	30.1	34.7	35.7	40.5	43.2	43.8	52.6	57.7	Uruguay
Venezuela	259.6	346.3	367.6	382.2	396.9	444.9	476.0	477.6	491.5	516.0	Venezuela
Asia	**9905**	**11183**	**12525**	**14268**	**15246**	**16987**	**17527**	**19504**	**20049**	**21176**	**Asie**
Afghanistan	13.2	13.3	13.4	13.4	13.5	13.7	13.7	13.7	13.7	13.7	Afghanistan
Armenia	..	...	9.6	3.2	3.3	6.8	4.2	4.0	4.1	4.3	Arménie
Azerbaijan	..	...	30.9	19.9	16.7	13.0	14.9	14.7	16.5	17.1	Azerbaïdjan
Bahrain	3.4	4.0	4.6	4.4	4.5	5.0	4.9	4.9	5.3	5.4	Bahreïn
Bangladesh	80.3	82.8	87.2	94.0	98.1	103.4	117.8	124.2	109.7	111.5	Bangladesh
Bhutan	0.3	0.3	0.3	0.3	0.3	0.3	0.3	0.3	0.3	0.3	Bhoutan
Brunei Darussalam	3.1	3.9	4.3	4.3	4.5	4.2	4.2	5.6	6.7	6.2	Brunéi Darussalam
Cambodia	16.3	17.5	19.4	20.7	19.8	19.8	22.0	23.3	24.1	25.0	Cambodge
China [1]	3728.0	4467.2	5114.1	6402.8	7168.8	8670.3	8999.1	10584.9	11349.1	11943.1	Chine [1]
Cyprus	22.2	21.0	25.3	26.6	28.0	29.5	31.2	33.1	32.6	34.5	Chypre
Gaza Strip (Palestine)	10.7	14.0	15.8	13.5	13.5	13.5	13.5	13.5	13.5	13.5	Bande de Gaza (Palestine)
Georgia	..	...	10.2	8.8	9.3	10.0	8.6	11.4	10.5	11.3	Géorgie
India	342.0	360.0	405.0	453.6	467.7	478.8	478.8	526.5	540.0	558.9	Inde
Indonesia	508.7	583.5	546.6	698.6	822.7	875.7	946.9	898.5	621.2	699.9	Indonésie
Iran(Islamic Rep. of)	395.2	436.9	538.6	580.3	634.6	658.7	672.6	717.1	716.5	744.8	Iran(Rép. islamique)
Iraq	192.3	8.9	24.4	22.3	34.0	37.0	38.0	33.0	28.0	49.0	Iraq
Israel	182.5	196.7	215.9	235.0	257.9	253.2	262.5	265.3	269.5	281.5	Israël
Japan	1391.3	1356.9	1365.0	1318.0	1256.0	1251.7	1235.8	1234.0	1211.7	1185.2	Japon
Jordan	50.0	60.0	70.1	83.5	94.1	107.7	100.1	97.9	93.2	110.8	Jordanie
Kazakhstan	..	...	139.0	114.1	80.2	53.0	39.4	23.9	24.1	22.0	Kazakhstan
Korea,Dem.Ppl's.Rep.	47.3	49.5	37.4	30.8	23.7	22.0	22.6	17.1	20.4	23.4	Corée,Rép.pop.dém.de
Korea, Republic of	260.7	314.2	350.2	366.2	373.5	382.4	401.4	378.7	357.6	400.4	Corée, République de
Kuwait	28.7	1.1	10.9	20.1	25.3	25.1	29.7	31.7	36.1	38.3	Koweït
Kyrgyzstan	..	...	22.2	9.3	7.2	2.7	3.0	3.1	4.0	4.5	Kirghizistan

For general note and footnotes, see end of table.

Voir la fin du tableau pour la remarque générale et les notes.

Poultry, dressed, fresh (Total production) (continued)
Volailles plumées et vidées, non préparées (Production totale) (suite)

ISIC-BASED CODE - CODE BASE CITI

3111-10

Unit : Thousand metric tons

Unité : Milliers de tonnes métriques

Country or area	1990	1991	1992	1993	1994	1995	1996	1997	1998	1999	Pays ou zone
Lao People's Dem. Rep.	6.9	7.4	7.9	9.0	9.5	10.1	10.7	11.0	11.3	10.9	Rép. dém. pop. lao
Lebanon	56.0	55.0	54.8	56.0	42.0	58.0	58.2	65.0	69.0	71.3	Liban
Malaysia	384.9	473.5	558.8	644.2	684.1	706.7	684.9	765.3	788.6	809.6	Malaisie
Mongolia	0.3	0.4	0.1	0.1	0.0	0.0	0.0	0.0	0.0	0.0	Mongolie
Myanmar	79.8	83.5	91.0	95.7	100.0	117.4	131.1	144.1	154.2	176.5	Myanmar
Nepal	9.1	9.4	9.4	9.5	9.6	9.7	10.0	11.0	11.7	12.4	Népal
Oman	3.0	3.1	3.4	3.6	3.8	3.9	3.9	4.0	4.1	4.2	Oman
Pakistan	160.7	154.9	173.2	269.3	300.4	312.6	359.7	391.7	288.7	314.7	Pakistan
Philippines	241.7	287.2	307.3	363.5	380.5	418.6	474.1	515.7	511.3	520.7	Philippines
Qatar	2.9	3.7	3.8	3.7	4.0	3.8	4.1	3.3	2.7	2.7	Qatar
Saudi Arabia	265.3	285.4	303.7	286.0	297.0	310.0	341.0	452.0	396.0	419.0	Arabie saoudite
Singapore	68.0	66.7	63.7	60.9	59.1	61.2	61.2	69.6	69.6	69.6	Singapour
Sri Lanka	23.5	24.2	29.0	39.0	50.3	54.1	56.5	57.7	59.0	57.0	Sri Lanka
Syrian Arab Republic	66.8	68.2	90.1	84.1	82.6	92.8	89.5	100.5	105.1	112.5	Rép. arabe syrienne
Tajikistan	..	..	5.0	3.0	4.0	1.5	0.8	0.6	1.8	1.8	Tadjikistan
Thailand	667.8	872.7	1039.9	1056.6	996.4	1007.2	1044.7	1057.2	1189.7	1190.3	Thaïlande
Turkey	415.0	414.0	439.0	460.0	489.8	516.2	436.4	486.4	509.1	659.9	Turquie
Turkmenistan	..	...	7.0	5.0	4.0	4.0	1.8	1.6	4.3	4.6	Turkménistan
United Arab Emirates	15.9	16.5	16.1	16.6	22.1	22.5	29.1	29.3	26.4	29.3	Emirats arabes unis
Uzbekistan	..	...	38.8	36.0	24.0	16.0	12.0	10.0	16.5	17.5	Ouzbékistan
Viet Nam	161.2	163.2	174.6	168.7	170.4	175.8	196.7	211.6	260.2	323.6	Viet Nam
Yemen	..	35.1	48.1	54.0	55.0	47.2	55.5	56.3	61.4	63.1	Yémen
Europe	7896	9961	10784	10608	10683	10853	11026	11289	11700	11681	Europe
Albania	6.7	6.3	2.5	3.3	3.7	3.9	3.5	3.7	5.1	4.7	Albanie
Austria	87.4	93.0	99.2	102.2	102.6	98.7	98.3	102.5	106.0	101.7	Autriche
Belarus	..	...	120.9	131.0	96.8	69.2	63.6	69.3	73.9	70.0	Bélarus
Belgium-Luxembourg	190.1	200.1	226.8	243.6	271.9	315.4	337.8	336.8	375.2	368.9	Belgique-Luxembourg
Bosnia and Herzegovina	..	..	18.0	15.1	13.4	14.8	11.2	8.2	8.9	8.9	Bosnie-Herzégovine
Bulgaria	181.8	100.3	88.9	97.1	81.7	92.2	99.1	100.8	107.0	100.0	Bulgarie
Croatia	..	..	40.1	36.2	40.2	38.9	37.4	36.8	33.1	32.4	Croatie
Denmark	131.1	138.9	155.2	167.4	172.4	173.0	170.2	175.7	190.3	202.5	Danemark
Czechoslovakia(former)	245.6	229.3	..	..	..	..	..	..	..	..	Tchécoslovaquie(anc.)
Czech Republic	..	..	...	131.3	120.2	148.7	144.4	173.7	197.5	200.4	République tchèque
Estonia	..	...	10.3	5.1	6.5	5.7	4.3	4.4	7.9	7.7	Estonie
Finland	32.7	36.5	35.8	34.7	39.4	42.6	49.4	52.7	61.1	66.1	Finlande
France	1604.6	1717.6	1772.7	1820.8	1972.4	2071.5	2203.5	2251.4	2292.6	2188.1	France
Germany	..	523.6	593.0	604.0	634.0	641.7	692.8	733.6	789.7	806.9	Allemagne
Greece	159.9	160.6	146.6	146.8	148.8	163.4	153.6	157.6	148.1	153.4	Grèce
Hungary	450.5	352.7	340.0	319.3	341.2	387.0	377.3	402.1	451.5	399.5	Hongrie
Iceland	1.5	1.6	1.6	1.5	1.3	2.0	1.7	2.1	2.7	3.0	Islande
Ireland	91.3	99.4	91.6	90.3	99.6	99.8	104.1	108.8	110.4	111.4	Irlande
Italy	1102.8	1093.0	1098.7	1104.0	1092.1	1090.8	1115.7	1134.2	1154.2	1177.0	Italie
Latvia	..	...	21.1	12.7	11.4	10.8	8.7	7.6	7.9	6.3	Lettonie
Lithuania	..	...	31.6	21.9	23.9	26.0	27.4	28.0	23.6	23.0	Lituanie
Malta	4.4	4.4	4.5	4.5	4.8	5.1	5.2	5.3	5.1	5.4	Malte
Netherlands	532.6	547.0	575.0	581.0	613.0	641.0	700.0	715.0	709.0	718.0	Pays-Bas
Norway	19.8	20.2	22.7	22.8	25.6	28.6	32.4	33.4	24.9	29.5	Norvège
Poland	333.0	344.2	323.8	305.8	380.7	383.6	438.0	478.0	522.5	576.0	Pologne
Portugal	129.4	150.0	161.0	178.3	192.4	188.5	209.3	261.3	279.5	268.2	Portugal
Republic of Moldova	..	..	39.1	26.6	24.0	24.6	18.6	17.0	16.2	15.8	Rép. de Moldova
Romania	386.4	331.8	295.4	300.8	260.0	286.1	292.6	254.3	257.5	280.0	Roumanie
Russian Federation	..	..	1428.0	1277.0	1068.0	859.0	678.3	621.3	680.9	736.7	Fédération de Russie
Slovakia	..	..	...	58.4	64.1	71.6	64.2	73.4	83.9	82.8	Slovaquie
Slovenia	..	...	64.5	57.9	54.3	67.0	69.9	72.7	71.7	67.5	Slovénie
Spain	836.0	880.1	858.0	835.6	873.8	924.3	887.4	906.3	900.0	897.0	Espagne
Sweden	51.1	56.9	62.0	67.1	77.2	82.2	84.5	91.9	89.1	94.2	Suède
Switzerland	33.1	35.0	36.7	35.8	37.8	39.8	40.5	43.9	44.2	45.6	Suisse
Ukraine	..	...	498.2	362.0	264.0	235.2	217.8	186.0	200.0	204.2	Ukraine
United Kingdom	989.0	1037.2	1229.9	1296.0	1364.0	1402.0	1462.0	1510.0	1552.0	1522.5	Royaume-Uni
Yugoslavia	..	...	108.1	96.9	91.7	106.5	109.8	117.0	104.6	93.6	Yougoslavie
T.F.Yug.Rep. Macedonia	..	...	5.5	13.4	14.2	12.4	12.0	12.0	12.0	12.0	L'ex-RY Macédoine
Yugoslavia, SFR	295.0	..	..	..	..	..	..	..	..	..	Yougoslavie, RSF

For general note and footnotes, see end of table.

Voir la fin du tableau pour la remarque générale et les notes.

105

Poultry, dressed, fresh (Total production) (continued)
Volailles plumées et vidées, non préparées (Production totale) (suite)

ISIC-BASED CODE - CODE BASE CITI

3111-10

Unit : Thousand metric tons   Unité : Milliers de tonnes métriques

Country or area	1990	1991	1992	1993	1994	1995	1996	1997	1998	1999	Pays ou zone
USSR (former)	3284.0	..	..	..	..	..	..	..	..	..	URSS (anc.)
Oceania	**483**	**490**	**527**	**553**	**580**	**596**	**614**	**624**	**687**	**711**	**Océanie**
Australia	412.6	416.6	443.4	464.3	488.8	489.0	507.4	515.9	572.9	593.4	Australie
Cook Islands	0.0	0.0	0.0	0.0	0.0	0.0	0.0	0.0	0.1	0.1	Iles Cook
Fiji	5.6	6.0	6.2	5.9	8.3	8.9	9.8	9.3	7.9	8.3	Fidji
French Polynesia	0.7	0.8	0.7	0.7	0.6	0.6	0.6	0.6	0.6	0.6	Polynésie française
Kiribati	0.3	0.3	0.3	0.3	0.3	0.3	0.3	0.3	0.3	0.3	Kiribati
New Caledonia	0.5	0.5	0.4	0.5	0.5	0.6	0.6	0.7	0.7	0.8	Nouvelle-Calédonie
New Zealand	57.9	60.5	69.9	75.1	75.5	90.7	88.7	90.8	98.3	100.7	Nouvelle-Zélande
Papua New Guinea	4.2	4.4	4.5	4.8	4.9	5.0	5.1	5.2	5.3	5.3	Papouasie-Nvl-Guinée
Samoa	0.3	0.3	0.3	0.3	0.3	0.3	0.3	0.3	0.3	0.3	Samoa
Solomon Islands	0.1	0.2	0.2	0.2	0.2	0.2	0.2	0.2	0.2	0.2	Iles Salomon
Tonga	0.2	0.2	0.2	0.2	0.2	0.2	0.2	0.2	0.2	0.2	Tonga
Vanuatu	0.4	0.5	0.4	0.5	0.5	0.5	0.5	0.5	0.5	0.5	Vanuatu
Total	**40297**	**41700**	**45247**	**48001**	**50668**	**54445**	**56067**	**59646**	**61720**	**64852**	**Total**

General Note.
Fresh, chilled or frozen meat of fowls, ducks, geese, turkeys and guinea fowls and edible offals thereof, except liver. Includes non-industrial production. (SITC, Rev.3: 01231-0, 01232-0, 01234-0, 01235-0).
Source: Food and Agriculture Organization of the United Nations (FAO), Rome.

Remarque générale.
Viande fraîche, réfrigérée ou congelée, de poulet, de canard, d'oie, de dinde et de pintade, y compris les abats comestibles, à l'exclusion du foie. Y compris production non-industrielle. (CTCI, Rev.3: 01231-0, 01232-0, 01234-0, 01235-0).
Source: Organisation des Nations Unies pour l'alimentation et l'agriculture (FAO), Rome.

[1] Including Hong-Kong, Macao and Taiwan.

[1] Y compris Hong-Kong, Macao et Taïwan.

Poultry, dressed, fresh (Industrial production)
Volailles plumées et vidées, non préparées (Production industrielle)

ISIC-BASED CODE - CODE BASE CITI

3111-101

Unit : Thousand metric tons   Unité : Milliers de tonnes métriques

Country or area	1990	1991	1992	1993	1994	1995	1996	1997	1998	1999	Pays ou zone
Africa	**2**	**2**	**2**	**2**	**2**	**3**	**3**	**3**	**3**	**4**	**Afrique**
Kenya	2	2	2	2	2	3	3	...	...	...	Kenya
America, North	**11239**	**11841**	**12548**	**13418**	**13994**	**14618**	**15375**	**15859**	**16112**	**18223**	**Amérique du Nord**
Dominican Republic	110	112	122	128	131	137	149	156	158	177	Rép. dominicaine
Mexico	82	90	110	434	476	508	479	481	546	661	Mexique
Panama	33	...	41	37	51	48	51	...	...	...	Panama
United States	11014	11596	12275	12819	13336	13925	14696	15150	15331	...	Etats-Unis
America, South	**1750**	**2011**	**2073**	**2257**	**2658**	**3014**	**3232**	**4150**	**4733**	**5138**	**Amérique du Sud**
Bolivia	7	8	9	9	10	*10	...	...	...	...	Bolivie
Brazil[1]	1605	1801	1912	2074	2459	2793	3011	3891	4196	4681	Brésil[1]
Colombia	...	...	118	121	143	163	...	200	221	...	Colombie
Ecuador	24	...	34	53	46	48	50	49	305	...	Equateur
Asia	**1044**	**1195**	**1288**	**1228**	**1167**	**1176**	**1238**	**1299**	**1294**	**1410**	**Asie**
Armenia	..	23	...	...	...	...	...	...	...	...	Arménie
Azerbaijan	..	18	9	2	1	1	1	0	0	0	Azerbaïdjan
Cyprus	21	20	6	5	6	7	9	8	9	11	Chypre
Indonesia	0	4	7	4	5	5	...	7	9	...	Indonésie
Japan	962	950	1046	1027	972	966	950	950	942	949	Japon
Kazakhstan	..	113	92	65	41	23	10	7	8	13	Kazakhstan
Kyrgyzstan	..	14	9	4	1	0	0	0	0	0	Kirghizistan
Tajikistan	..	7	3	1	1	0	0	0	0	0	Tadjikistan
Turkey	...	42	86	95	116	151	240	304	303	405	Turquie
Turkmenistan	..	4	7	2	1	0	0	0	0	...	Turkménistan
Europe	**5800**	**7604**	**7408**	**7168**	**7642**	**7930**	**8103**	**8194**	**8652**	**9183**	**Europe**
Austria	...	...	...	...	...	...	73	77	...	72	Autriche
Belarus	..	122	96	91	72	52	44	53	56	54	Bélarus
Belgium	190	200	227	243	249	334	490	387	473	466	Belgique
Bulgaria	121	49	46	34	45	47	39	20	24	25	Bulgarie
Croatia	..	47	42	39	36	31	33	32	28	...	Croatie
Denmark[2]	12	13	17	29	29	17	83	90	109	127	Danemark[2]
Czechoslovakia(former)	262	217	..	..	..	..	..	..	..	..	Tchécoslovaquie(anc.)
Czech Republic	..	..	130	109	113	148	149	163	185	203	République tchèque
Estonia	..	15	5	3	5	5	3	4	7	7	Estonie
Finland	29	36	35	33	19	28	15	18	20	22	Finlande
France	1455	1569	1696	1765	1822	1916	2015	2061	2104	...	France
Germany	..	510	541	553	582	580	597	659	689	...	Allemagne
Germany(Fed.Rep.)[3]	415	..	..	..	..	..	..	..	..	..	Allemagne(Rép.féd.)[3]
German D.R.(former)	102	..	..	..	..	..	..	..	..	..	R.D.A. (anc.)
Greece	62	70	68	79	82	70	64	80	81	...	Grèce
Hungary	232	153	164	136	155	188	246	265	288	280	Hongrie
Latvia	..	28	16	6	5	4	5	4	3	5	Lettonie
Lithuania	..	26	11	14	13	16	16	13	13	13	Lituanie
Netherlands[2][4]	263	254	306	442	423	743	766	799	884	894	Pays-Bas[2][4]
Norway	20	20	23	23	...	14	...	...	54	63	Norvège
Poland	201	197	199	187	247	276	342	418	478	539	Pologne
Portugal	...	...	111	143	168	171	194	198	200	208	Portugal
Republic of Moldova	..	33	13	[5]4	[5]3	[5]5	[5]8	[5]4	[5]3	[5]1	Rép. de Moldova
Romania[6]	147	125	99	95	96	138	139	107	82	79	Roumanie[6]
Russian Federation	..	1189	955	868	738	497	378	333	363	427	Fédération de Russie
Slovakia	..	..	46	39	43	57	8	12	90	98	Slovaquie
Slovenia	..	62	54	42	40	44	46	44	40	18	Slovénie
Spain	...	...	...	767	907	990	1004	1102	1079	1163	Espagne
Sweden	43	46	52	57	63	59	80	99	91	90	Suède
Ukraine	..	292	251	167	92	66	49	23	29	24	Ukraine
United Kingdom	...	...	...	1107	1475	1351	1175	1086	1093	...	Royaume-Uni
Yugoslavia	..	40	29	19	14	9	11	11	12	10	Yougoslavie
T.F.Yug.Rep. Macedonia	..	0	1	...	...	...	...	...	...	...	L'ex-RY Macédoine
USSR (former)	**2166**	..	..	..	..	..	..	..	..	..	**URSS (anc.)**

For general note and footnotes, see end of table.   Voir la fin du tableau pour la remarque générale et les notes.

Poultry, dressed, fresh (Industrial production) (continued)
Volailles plumées et vidées, non préparées (Production industrielle) (suite)

ISIC-BASED CODE - CODE BASE CITI

3111-101

Unit : Thousand metric tons   Unité : Milliers de tonnes métriques

Country or area	1990	1991	1992	1993	1994	1995	1996	1997	1998	1999	Pays ou zone
Oceania	**6**	**6**	**6**	**6**	**6**	**6**	**6**	**6**	**6**	**6**	**Océanie**
Fiji	6	6	...	...	...	...	...	...	...	...	Fidji
Total	**22008**	**22660**	**23324**	**24079**	**25469**	**26748**	**27957**	**29511**	**30801**	**33964**	**Total**

General Note.

Fresh, chilled or frozen meat of fowls, ducks, geese, turkeys and guinea fowls and edible offals thereof, except liver. Data refer to industrial production only. (SITC, Rev.3: 01231-0, 01232-0, 01234-0, 01235-0).

Remarque générale.

Viande fraîche, réfrigérée ou congelée, de poulet, de canard, d'oie, de dinde et de pintade, y compris les abats comestibles, à l'exclusion du foie. Les données se rapportent à la production industrielle seulement. (CTCI, Rev.3: 01230-0, 01232-0, 01234-0, 01235-0).

[1] Incomplete coverage.
[2] Sales.
[3] Production of establishments with monthly capacity of 2000 fowls or more.
[4] Production by establishments employing 20 or more persons.
[5] Excluding Transnistria region.
[6] Including liver.

[1] Couverture incomplète.
[2] Ventes.
[3] Production des établissements d'un débit mensuel de 2000 volailles ou plus.
[4] Production des établissements occupant 20 personnes ou plus.
[5] Non compris la région de Transnistria.
[6] Y compris les foies.

Other meat, fresh (Total production)
Autres viandes, non préparées (Production totale)

ISIC-BASED CODE - CODE BASE CITI

3111-13

Unit : Thousand metric tons

Unité : Milliers de tonnes métriques

Country or area	1990	1991	1992	1993	1994	1995	1996	1997	1998	1999	Pays ou zone
Africa	**1182**	**1201**	**1208**	**1210**	**1231**	**1248**	**1264**	**1274**	**1287**	**1307**	**Afrique**
Algeria	9.7	9.8	9.8	9.7	9.7	9.7	9.8	9.8	9.9	9.9	Algérie
Angola	6.0	6.0	6.0	6.5	6.8	7.0	7.2	7.4	7.5	7.5	Angola
Benin	6.0	6.0	6.0	6.0	6.0	6.0	6.0	6.0	6.0	6.0	Bénin
Botswana	6.1	6.5	6.7	8.4	8.7	11.0	10.4	10.3	11.2	12.2	Botswana
Burkina Faso	7.7	7.7	7.8	7.8	7.9	7.9	8.0	8.1	8.1	8.1	Burkina Faso
Burundi	0.4	0.5	0.6	0.6	0.4	0.4	0.3	0.3	0.3	0.3	Burundi
Cameroon	44.3	44.3	45.3	46.3	46.3	46.3	46.3	46.4	46.4	46.4	Cameroun
Central African Rep.	7.5	7.6	7.7	7.8	7.8	7.8	8.0	8.2	8.4	8.6	Rép. centrafricaine
Chad	4.2	4.3	4.3	4.3	4.3	4.4	4.4	4.4	4.5	4.5	Tchad
Congo	11.0	11.2	11.5	11.8	12.0	12.2	12.4	13.0	15.0	16.0	Congo
Côte d'Ivoire	28.0	28.0	28.0	28.0	28.0	28.0	28.0	28.0	28.0	28.0	Côte d'Ivoire
Dem. Rep. of Congo	119.0	120.0	124.0	126.0	129.0	132.0	136.0	140.0	143.0	144.5	Rép. dém. du Congo
Djibouti	0.6	0.6	0.6	0.6	0.6	0.6	0.6	0.6	0.6	0.6	Djibouti
Egypt	79.2	85.7	88.5	81.8	91.0	96.1	100.7	101.8	102.4	112.7	Egypte
Eritrea	...	...	...	0.7	0.7	0.7	0.7	0.7	0.7	0.7	Erythrée
Ethiopia,incl.Eritrea	130.8	133.4	134.0	...	...	...	...	...	...	...	Ethiopie,incl.Erythrée
Ethiopia	...	...	...	133.4	133.4	133.5	133.6	133.7	133.7	133.7	Ethiopie
Gabon	20.1	20.2	20.2	20.2	20.2	20.7	21.2	21.7	22.3	22.8	Gabon
Gambia	1.0	1.0	1.0	1.0	1.0	1.0	1.0	1.0	1.0	1.0	Gambie
Ghana	90.0	90.0	90.0	90.0	90.0	90.0	90.0	90.0	90.0	90.0	Ghana
Guinea	4.0	4.0	4.0	4.0	4.0	4.0	4.0	4.0	4.0	4.0	Guinée
Kenya	31.3	32.2	32.1	32.3	32.3	32.4	32.5	33.6	34.9	35.5	Kenya
Lesotho	3.5	3.5	3.5	3.5	3.5	3.5	3.5	3.6	3.7	3.8	Lesotho
Liberia	6.0	6.0	6.0	6.0	6.0	6.0	6.0	6.0	6.0	6.0	Libéria
Libyan Arab Jamah.	10.0	10.6	10.0	7.6	6.7	7.5	7.8	5.0	3.1	3.6	Jamah. arabe libyenne
Madagascar	3.4	3.6	3.7	3.9	4.1	3.9	4.1	4.2	4.4	4.6	Madagascar
Mali	23.0	23.1	23.2	23.0	23.4	23.9	24.4	25.0	23.9	23.9	Mali
Mauritania	21.2	19.4	18.5	16.4	19.4	19.4	19.5	19.7	19.7	19.9	Mauritanie
Mauritius	0.5	0.3	0.6	0.6	0.6	0.6	0.6	0.6	0.6	0.6	Maurice
Morocco	32.0	33.9	34.4	36.3	37.1	37.0	36.9	36.8	36.7	37.0	Maroc
Namibia	3.6	3.7	3.8	3.9	3.9	3.9	3.8	4.0	4.1	4.0	Namibie
Niger	16.8	17.8	18.8	19.9	21.1	21.2	21.3	21.6	21.8	21.9	Niger
Nigeria	100.0	100.0	100.0	100.0	100.0	100.0	100.0	100.0	100.0	100.0	Nigéria
Réunion	3.3	3.1	3.3	3.3	3.3	3.3	3.3	3.3	3.3	3.3	Réunion
Rwanda	7.6	7.7	7.8	7.8	7.8	7.8	7.8	7.8	7.8	7.8	Rwanda
Senegal	11.2	11.4	11.4	12.2	12.2	12.4	12.5	12.7	13.0	13.2	Sénégal
Sierra Leone	2.0	2.0	2.0	2.0	2.0	2.0	2.0	2.0	2.0	2.0	Sierra Leone
Somalia	30.6	34.0	32.3	34.0	34.0	34.9	35.7	34.0	35.7	34.0	Somalie
South Africa	11.0	11.0	11.0	11.2	11.4	11.6	12.7	14.4	15.4	16.4	Afrique du Sud
Sudan	67.1	66.9	67.9	66.7	67.7	68.8	71.8	73.3	75.1	77.0	Soudan
Togo	4.0	4.0	4.0	4.0	4.0	4.0	4.0	4.0	4.0	4.0	Togo
Tunisia	8.0	8.5	8.7	8.8	8.8	8.8	8.8	8.8	8.8	8.8	Tunisie
Uganda	17.0	17.1	17.2	17.3	17.4	17.5	17.6	17.7	17.8	17.9	Ouganda
United Rep.Tanzania	12.2	12.4	12.6	12.7	12.8	12.8	12.9	13.0	13.1	13.2	Rép. Unie de Tanzanie
Zambia	28.5	29.0	29.5	30.0	30.5	31.0	31.5	32.0	32.5	33.0	Zambie
Zimbabwe	18.5	19.0	16.0	19.0	20.0	22.0	22.0	23.0	24.0	25.0	Zimbabwe
America, North	**408**	**399**	**385**	**365**	**343**	**344**	**344**	**345**	**339**	**339**	**Amérique du Nord**
Canada	29.3	32.0	24.4	23.0	17.8	18.2	19.5	24.6	21.9	21.9	Canada
Cuba	1.7	1.7	1.6	1.3	1.3	1.2	1.2	1.1	1.0	1.1	Cuba
Greenland	0.2	0.2	0.2	0.2	0.2	0.2	0.2	0.2	0.2	0.2	Groënland
Grenada	0.1	0.1	0.1	0.1	0.1	0.1	0.1	0.1	0.1	0.1	Grenade
Guadeloupe	0.2	0.2	0.2	0.2	0.2	0.1	0.1	0.0	0.0	0.0	Guadeloupe
Guatemala	2.0	2.1	2.1	2.1	2.1	2.1	2.2	2.2	2.2	2.2	Guatemala
Haiti	8.8	8.7	8.0	8.1	8.2	8.3	8.4	8.4	8.4	8.4	Haïti
Honduras	0.5	0.5	0.5	0.5	0.5	0.5	0.5	0.5	0.5	0.6	Honduras
Martinique	0.1	0.1	0.1	0.1	0.1	0.1	0.1	0.1	0.1	0.1	Martinique
Mexico	76.3	78.2	80.4	80.9	81.9	82.9	83.5	83.5	83.5	83.5	Mexique
Nicaragua	2.0	2.0	2.0	2.0	1.9	1.9	1.9	1.9	1.9	1.9	Nicaragua
Puerto Rico	...	...	...	...	...	...	0.1	0.1	0.1	0.1	Porto Rico
United States	286.5	273.3	265.8	246.5	228.5	228.3	226.0	222.5	219.3	218.8	Etats-Unis
America, South	**180**	**191**	**201**	**202**	**199**	**199**	**200**	**202**	**198**	**203**	**Amérique du Sud**

For general note and footnotes, see end of table.

Voir la fin du tableau pour la remarque générale et les notes.

Other meat, fresh (Total production) (continued)
Autres viandes, non préparées (Production totale) (suite)

ISIC-BASED CODE - CODE BASE CITI

3111-13

Unit : Thousand metric tons

Unité : Milliers de tonnes métriques

Country or area	1990	1991	1992	1993	1994	1995	1996	1997	1998	1999	Pays ou zone
Argentina	90.5	94.6	97.8	101.4	102.0	103.0	104.0	104.0	104.0	110.2	Argentine
Bolivia	7.1	7.0	7.1	7.2	7.3	7.4	7.5	7.6	7.7	7.9	Bolivie
Brazil	10.7	16.4	23.6	24.5	21.5	18.7	16.2	16.3	16.4	17.5	Brésil
Chile	10.8	11.5	9.5	6.6	7.2	10.8	11.5	12.0	11.2	11.2	Chili
Colombia	8.3	8.3	8.4	8.4	8.4	8.4	8.4	8.4	8.4	8.6	Colombie
Ecuador	7.7	7.7	7.8	8.0	8.1	8.2	8.3	8.4	8.5	8.5	Equateur
Paraguay	0.4	0.4	0.3	0.4	0.6	0.6	0.8	0.7	0.7	0.7	Paraguay
Peru	38.2	37.2	37.8	36.9	36.7	35.8	35.5	35.5	33.1	30.7	Pérou
Uruguay	6.3	7.6	8.2	8.5	7.8	6.7	7.7	8.8	8.0	7.8	Uruguay
Asia	**621**	**746**	**982**	**985**	**1087**	**1255**	**1340**	**1230**	**1270**	**1278**	**Asie**
Afghanistan	11.2	11.2	11.2	11.2	11.2	11.2	11.4	11.6	11.8	12.0	Afghanistan
Armenia	..	...	0.2	0.3	0.4	0.5	0.6	0.7	0.8	0.8	Arménie
Bahrain	0.1	0.1	0.1	0.1	0.1	0.1	0.1	0.1	0.1	0.1	Bahreïn
Bangladesh	9.3	8.5	8.5	9.0	9.0	9.0	9.0	9.0	9.0	9.0	Bangladesh
China[1]	295.3	311.1	540.9	554.3	649.8	825.5	886.8	778.9	826.4	836.7	Chine[1]
Cyprus	1.2	1.1	1.2	1.1	1.5	1.2	1.2	1.3	1.3	1.4	Chypre
Gaza Strip (Palestine)	0.1	0.1	0.2	0.1	0.1	0.1	0.1	0.1	0.1	0.1	Bande de Gaza (Palestine)
Georgia			0.3	0.1	0.1	0.1	0.1	0.1	0.3	0.2	Géorgie
India	127.0	129.0	130.0	131.0	132.0	132.0	132.0	132.0	132.0	132.0	Inde
Indonesia	1.7	1.5	1.8	1.6	1.3	1.2	1.2	1.5	1.9	1.3	Indonésie
Iran(Islamic Rep. of)	23.3	24.3	30.3	33.4	30.2	28.0	17.4	5.5	5.7	5.7	Iran(Rép. islamique)
Iraq	2.3	0.5	0.4	0.3	0.2	0.2	0.2	0.3	0.3	0.3	Iraq
Israel	0.1	0.1	0.1	0.1	0.1	0.1	0.1	0.1	0.1	0.1	Israël
Japan	6.7	6.9	7.3	8.3	9.6	11.4	10.4	10.0	9.8	10.4	Japon
Jordan	0.6	0.5	0.4	0.4	0.3	0.4	0.4	0.4	0.4	0.4	Jordanie
Kazakhstan	..	...	62.1	66.6	74.8	64.6	74.9	70.9	68.2	68.7	Kazakhstan
Korea,Dem.Ppl's.Rep.	...	...	...	...	...	...	0.1	0.1	0.1	0.2	Corée,Rép.pop.dém.de
Korea, Republic of	4.0	4.3	4.7	4.3	4.1	5.0	5.4	5.4	4.8	5.4	Corée, République de
Kuwait	0.2	0.1	0.0	0.1	0.1	0.3	0.3	0.4	0.5	0.3	Koweït
Kyrgyzstan	..	...	12.1	10.8	13.3	10.5	13.3	18.4	18.1	20.6	Kirghizistan
Malaysia	0.1	0.1	0.1	0.1	0.1	0.1	0.1	0.1	0.0	0.1	Malaisie
Maldives	0.8	0.8	0.8	0.8	0.9	0.9	0.9	0.9	0.9	1.0	Maldives
Mongolia	42.3	57.1	57.3	38.2	26.9	30.1	48.5	49.3	46.6	42.4	Mongolie
Oman	4.0	4.2	4.3	4.5	4.6	4.6	4.7	4.8	4.9	5.0	Oman
Pakistan	13.0	13.3	13.5	13.7	14.0	14.5	14.8	15.2	15.5	15.5	Pakistan
Philippines	12.3	12.3	12.4	12.4	12.7	12.9	13.1	13.3	13.3	13.5	Philippines
Qatar	0.7	0.8	1.0	1.0	1.0	1.0	1.1	1.1	1.0	1.0	Qatar
Saudi Arabia	39.9	41.3	41.3	43.0	48.0	48.0	49.0	56.0	53.0	50.0	Arabie saoudite
Syrian Arab Republic	0.6	0.6	0.6	0.8	0.8	0.8	0.8	0.8	0.8	0.9	Rép. arabe syrienne
Tajikistan	..	...	4.0	1.0	...	...	...	...	...	...	Tadjikistan
Turkey	3.4	3.8	3.9	4.2	4.2	3.6	4.0	4.1	3.5	3.5	Turquie
Turkmenistan	..	...	3.0	4.0	3.0	3.0	3.0	2.0	2.0	1.9	Turkménistan
United Arab Emirates	6.8	7.2	7.4	8.0	8.8	9.4	10.1	10.8	11.5	12.3	Emirats arabes unis
Uzbekistan	..	...	3.0	2.0	2.0	2.0	2.0	2.0	2.0	1.5	Ouzbékistan
Viet Nam	13.8	13.9	14.9	15.7	16.4	16.9	17.5	17.5	17.7	18.3	Viet Nam
Yemen	..	2.5	2.5	2.6	2.6	2.6	2.6	2.6	2.7	2.7	Yémen
Europe	**892**	**1082**	**1130**	**1138**	**1124**	**1176**	**1210**	**1208**	**1208**	**1206**	**Europe**
Austria	6.8	6.8	6.9	6.9	6.8	7.3	6.8	6.9	7.0	6.7	Autriche
Belarus	..	...	5.9	6.0	5.0	5.3	6.0	5.8	5.8	6.2	Bélarus
Belgium-Luxembourg	29.1	30.3	28.9	30.3	31.0	31.1	30.3	29.7	33.2	30.6	Belgique-Luxembourg
Bulgaria	2.6	3.2	4.1	4.7	4.7	5.0	6.5	12.7	5.0	5.0	Bulgarie
Croatia	..	...	4.0	3.8	3.3	3.2	3.3	3.3	3.5	3.2	Croatie
Denmark	3.9	4.0	3.9	4.0	4.9	4.3	4.1	4.3	3.7	3.8	Danemark
Czechoslovakia(former)	37.5	36.5	..	..	..	..	..	..	..	..	Tchécoslovaquie(anc.)
Czech Republic	..	..	...	34.5	34.7	33.7	35.2	35.3	38.7	38.9	République tchèque
Estonia	..	...	0.4	0.2	0.2	0.1	0.0	0.0	0.0	0.0	Estonie
Finland	4.7	5.0	4.1	4.2	3.7	3.1	2.5	2.4	2.7	2.5	Finlande
France	306.4	309.7	310.8	311.2	304.3	301.1	301.4	296.3	295.2	295.2	France
Germany	..	53.3	67.5	65.5	65.4	128.3	128.0	128.5	128.7	128.5	Allemagne
Greece	9.0	10.1	9.9	9.9	10.6	10.6	10.4	12.7	9.7	9.7	Grèce
Hungary	24.2	23.8	26.2	27.4	25.0	21.4	23.4	22.5	21.3	19.8	Hongrie
Iceland	2.6	2.7	2.8	2.8	2.8	3.0	2.6	2.7	2.8	3.1	Islande

For general note and footnotes, see end of table.

Voir la fin du tableau pour la remarque générale et les notes.

Other meat, fresh (Total production) (continued)
Autres viandes, non préparées (Production totale) (suite)

ISIC-BASED CODE - CODE BASE CITI

3111-13

Unit : Thousand metric tons   Unité : Milliers de tonnes métriques

Country or area	1990	1991	1992	1993	1994	1995	1996	1997	1998	1999	Pays ou zone
Ireland	0.0	0.1	0.5	0.5	0.6	0.5	0.7	1.4	0.7	1.3	Irlande
Italy	261.6	270.3	285.5	285.5	288.4	288.7	291.2	292.9	291.4	296.4	Italie
Latvia	..	...	1.4	1.2	0.4	0.2	0.2	0.3	0.3	0.2	Lettonie
Lithuania	..	...	1.1	1.1	0.9	1.0	0.9	1.1	1.1	1.0	Lituanie
Malta	0.4	0.4	0.4	0.4	0.4	0.4	0.7	1.4	1.4	1.4	Malte
Netherlands	1.0	1.0	1.0	1.0	1.0	0.8	0.9	1.0	0.9	0.9	Pays-Bas
Norway	6.4	7.1	6.8	6.7	5.4	5.5	9.3	5.7	5.7	5.7	Norvège
Poland	23.1	26.1	25.1	21.1	22.5	20.3	21.1	19.1	23.2	24.8	Pologne
Portugal	12.1	12.1	12.1	12.2	12.0	11.8	10.5	10.2	10.3	10.5	Portugal
Republic of Moldova	..	...	1.6	1.5	1.5	1.1	1.0	0.9	0.8	0.8	Rép. de Moldova
Romania	20.3	17.5	14.5	14.6	15.0	15.5	15.6	15.4	15.6	16.4	Roumanie
Russian Federation	..	...	87.0	86.0	82.9	78.2	93.0	93.4	92.2	79.5	Fédération de Russie
Slovakia	..	..	...	11.0	10.7	4.7	4.6	4.6	4.6	4.3	Slovaquie
Slovenia	..	..	0.2	0.1	0.2	0.2	0.3	0.3	0.3	0.3	Slovénie
Spain	94.1	92.8	103.1	111.7	116.2	125.2	136.5	136.5	142.8	149.1	Espagne
Sweden	22.1	25.1	23.3	23.6	20.5	20.4	20.0	19.0	20.0	20.1	Suède
Switzerland	4.4	4.5	4.3	4.6	4.6	4.4	4.5	4.3	4.2	4.1	Suisse
Ukraine	..	...	30.0	30.0	25.0	26.2	26.0	24.9	24.2	25.1	Ukraine
United Kingdom	11.5	11.7	12.0	12.1	12.3	11.8	10.8	10.8	9.8	9.8	Royaume-Uni
Yugoslavia	..	...	1.3	1.3	1.3	1.4	1.4	1.4	1.4	1.4	Yougoslavie
Yugoslavia, SFR	8.3	..	..	..	..	..	..	..	..	..	Yougoslavie, RSF
USSR (former)	246.7	..	..	..	..	..	..	..	..	..	URSS (anc.)
Oceania	**46**	**51**	**64**	**61**	**65**	**65**	**61**	**61**	**65**	**69**	**Océanie**
Australia	20.7	21.8	21.8	22.4	22.4	22.4	21.8	21.8	21.3	21.3	Australie
New Zealand	7.4	12.0	24.9	21.0	24.8	24.9	20.6	20.6	25.2	28.9	Nouvelle-Zélande
Papua New Guinea	17.4	17.4	17.6	17.7	18.0	18.0	18.2	18.3	18.5	18.5	Papouasie-Nvl-Guinée
Total	**3575**	**3670**	**3970**	**3961**	**4049**	**4287**	**4418**	**4319**	**4367**	**4401**	**Total**

General Note.
Fresh, chilled or frozen meat of other animals, irrespective of the origin of the animals, in carcass weight, excluding edible offals and tallow. Includes non-industrial production. (SITC, Rev.3: 01240-0, 01290-1).
Source: Food and Agriculture Organization of the United Nations (FAO), Rome.

Remarque générale.
Poids net de viande fraîche, réfrigérée ou congelée, d'autres animaux abattus, quelle que soit leur provenance, à l'exclusion des abats comestibles et du suif. Y compris production non-industrielle. (CTCI, Rev.3: 01240-0, 01290-1).
Source: Organisation des Nations Unies pour l'alimentation et l'agriculture (FAO), Rome.

[1] Including Hong-Kong, Macao and Taiwan.

[1] Y compris Hong-Kong, Macao et Taïwan.

Other meat, fresh (Industrial production)
Autres viandes, non préparées (Production industrielle)

ISIC-BASED CODE - CODE BASE CITI
3111-131

Unit : Thousand metric tons   Unité : Milliers de tonnes métriques

Country or area	1990	1991	1992	1993	1994	1995	1996	1997	1998	1999	Pays ou zone
America, North	**8**	**12**	**12**	**11**	**12**	**15**	**17**	**14**	**11**	**8**	**Amérique du Nord**
Mexico	8	12	12	11	12	15	17	14	11	8	Mexique
America, South	**12**	**19**	**25**	**21**	**26**	**27**	**25**	**32**	**34**	**36**	**Amérique du Sud**
Brazil	12	19	25	21	26	27	25	...	...	...	Brésil
Asia	**5**	**27**	**32**	**25**	**24**	**20**	**20**	**24**	**30**	**27**	**Asie**
Armenia	..	1	0	0	0	0	0	...	6	6	Arménie
Hong Kong SAR	...	2	...	...	...	6	9	8	16	13	Hong-Kong RAS
Indonesia	2	0	...	...	...	2	...	...	0	...	Indonésie
Kazakhstan	..	20	18	11	11	8	8	10	7	5	Kazakhstan
Kyrgyzstan	..	1	1	0	0	0	0	0	0	0	Kirghizistan
Tajikistan	..	1	0	0	0	0	0	0	0	0	Tadjikistan
Turkmenistan	..	2	3	3	3	4	2	3	1	...	Turkménistan
Europe	**122**	**739**	**614**	**500**	**405**	**368**	**345**	**297**	**338**	**258**	**Europe**
Belarus	..	45	38	32	27	22	23	22	25	24	Bélarus
Belgium	29	30	29	30	...	# [1]5	[1]6	[1]6	[1]5	[1]5	Belgique
Bulgaria	0	1	1	1	0	5	1	...	...	...	Bulgarie
Croatia	..	8	2	0	0	0	0	0	0	...	Croatie
Czech Republic	..	..	0	1	...	...	...	...	...	...	République tchèque
Estonia	..	0	0	0	0	1	0	0	0	0	Estonie
Finland	2	2	3	2	1	1	1	2	5	6	Finlande
France	13	14	13	12	10	10	11	11	10	...	France
Germany	..	5	5	5	4	39	...	...	38	...	Allemagne
Germany(Fed.Rep.)	4	..	..	..	..	..	..	..	..	..	Allemagne(Rép.féd.)
Greece	...	...	...	...	...	0	0	...	2	...	Grèce
Hungary	1	7	15	12	8	8	6	7	10	6	Hongrie
Iceland	...	...	...	...	...	...	1	1	1	1	Islande
Latvia	..	1	0	1	1	0	0	0	0	3	Lettonie
Netherlands[2][3]	8	1	1	0	0	0	0	0	0	...	Pays-Bas[2][3]
Poland	17	14	12	7	8	4	5	7	6	10	Pologne
Portugal	...	...	6	6	3	4	5	8	10	6	Portugal
Russian Federation	..	373	325	268	196	164	153	117	124	60	Fédération de Russie
Slovakia	..	..	...	0	...	...	...	...	1	1	Slovaquie
Slovenia	..	0	0	0	...	0	0	1	1	0	Slovénie
Spain	...	...	...	30	51	47	64	57	64	66	Espagne
Sweden	2	1	1	1	1	1	3	2	2	2	Suède
Ukraine	..	186	111	80	65	45	39	25	18	20	Ukraine
United Kingdom	10	10	11	...	...	...	...	...	...	...	Royaume-Uni
Yugoslavia	..	0	0	0	0	0	0	0	1	0	Yougoslavie
Yugoslavia, SFR	1	..	..	..	..	..	..	..	..	..	Yougoslavie, RSF
USSR (former)	839	..	..	..	..	..	..	..	..	...	URSS (anc.)
Total	**986**	**797**	**683**	**556**	**467**	**430**	**407**	**367**	**413**	**330**	**Total**

General Note.
Fresh, chilled or frozen meat of other animals, irrespective of the origin of
the animals, in carcass weight, excluding edible offals and tallow. Data refer
to industrial production only. (SITC, Rev.3: 01240-0, 01290-1).

Remarque générale.
Poids net de viande fraîche, réfrigérée ou congelée, d'autres animaux abattus,
quelle que soit leur provenance, à l'exclusion des abats comestibles et du suif.
Les données se rapportent à la production industrielle seulement. (CTCI, Rev.3:
01240-0, 01290-1).

[1] Incomplete coverage.
[2] Sales.
[3] Production by establishments employing 20 or more persons.

[1] Couverture incomplète.
[2] Ventes.
[3] Production des établissements occupant 20 personnes ou plus.

Bacon, ham and other dried, salted or smoked pig meat
Lard entrelardé, jambon et autres viandes de porc, séchées, salées ou fumées

ISIC-BASED CODE - CODE BASE CITI

3111-16

Unit : Thousand metric tons | Unité : Milliers de tonnes métriques

Country or area	1990	1991	1992	1993	1994	1995	1996	1997	1998	1999	Pays ou zone
Africa	**16**	**16**	**16**	**15**	**16**	**16**	**16**	**16**	**16**	**16**	**Afrique**
Kenya	1	1	1	1	2	1	...	...	...	...	Kenya
South Africa	15	15	15	14	14	15	15	15	15	...	Afrique du Sud
America, North	**396**	**498**	**302**	**366**	**517**	**577**	**543**	**819**	**799**	**875**	**Amérique du Nord**
Jamaica[1]	334	429	222	234	373	436	394	645	606	...	Jamaïque[1]
Mexico	60	67	78	130	142	139	148	172	191	199	Mexique
Panama	2	...	2	2	2	2	1	...	...	...	Panama
America, South	**16**	**15**	**12**	**15**	**17**	**17**	**13**	**15**	**12**	**12**	**Amérique du Sud**
Colombia	...	...	8	10	11	11	...	10	8	...	Colombie
Ecuador	2	...	2	3	3	3	1	...	1	...	Equateur
Peru[2]	...	...	...	...	...	2	3	3	3	3	Pérou[2]
Asia	**264**	**269**	**288**	**297**	**270**	**262**	**257**	**242**	**246**	**241**	**Asie**
Hong Kong SAR	13	16	17	15	12	13	8	7	11	7	Hong-Kong RAS
Cyprus	*2	*2	4	*4	*4	3	4	4	4	4	Chypre
Indonesia	0	3	20	35	...	2	...	0	0	...	Indonésie
Japan	249	248	247	243	245	244	236	231	231	230	Japon
Europe	**1152**	**1488**	**1331**	**1536**	**1666**	**1637**	**1688**	**1686**	**1774**	**1820**	**Europe**
Austria	...	...	...	...	...	22	24	28	29	30	Autriche
Belgium	...	...	...	...	44	43	47	48	54	44	Belgique
Croatia	..	7	7	7	7	7	8	6	6	...	Croatie
Denmark[3]	106	137	112	106	119	119	116	128	135	112	Danemark[3]
Finland	10	10	7	6	7	6	6	6	6	5	Finlande
France	95	104	104	115	120	125	128	127	136	...	France
Germany	..	...	...	...	...	257	264	383	402	...	Allemagne
Greece	4	4	4	4	5	6	6	7	7	...	Grèce
Hungary	13	14	14	14	14	11	15	17	13	15	Hongrie
Iceland	...	...	...	...	...	...	1	1	1	1	Islande
Ireland	...	...	...	...	...	47	46	138	167	71	Irlande
Latvia	..	8	5	3	3	4	4	5	6	6	Lettonie
Netherlands[3][4]	78	80	71	48	60	55	69	71	91	59	Pays-Bas[3][4]
Norway	...	...	...	...	...	...	...	20	22	20	Norvège
Poland[5]	4	3	2	2	1	4	3	3	3	5	Pologne[5]
Portugal	66	82	10	14	12	10	13	10	10	9	Portugal
Romania[6]	365	260	184	168	175	179	150	125	129	147	Roumanie[6]
Slovakia	..	..	...	12	10	9	8	9	8	6	Slovaquie
Slovenia	..	10	8	7	7	6	6	5	5	5	Slovénie
Spain				[7]122	[7]150	[7]177	205	187	202	236	Espagne
Sweden	[6]52	[6]52	[6]58	[6]62	[6]90	[6]63	[6]46	[6]45	44	46	Suède
United Kingdom	180	176	168	400	422	456	492	308	290	...	Royaume-Uni
Yugoslavia	..	16	13	8	7	9	10	9	8	9	Yougoslavie
T.F.Yug.Rep. Macedonia	..	1	0	...	...	...	...	...	...	...	L'ex-RY Macédoine
Oceania	**98**	**104**	**108**	**116**	**112**	**111**	**116**	**126**	**142**	**136**	**Océanie**
Australia[8]	...	...	...	97	94	93	99	102	119	111	Australie[8]
New Zealand[9]	14	16	17	19	18	18	17	24	23	...	Nouvelle-Zélande[9]
Total	**1941**	**2390**	**2058**	**2345**	**2597**	**2619**	**2633**	**2905**	**2989**	**3101**	**Total**

General Note.
Edible pig meat, salted, in brine, dried or smoked. Including streaky pork with similar meats interlarded with a high proportion of fat, and fat with an adhering layer of meat. Hams enclosed in sausage casings are excluded. (SITC, Rev.3: 01610-0).

Remarque générale.
Viandes comestibles de porc, salées, en saumure, séchées ou fumées, y compris le lard maigre et les autres viandes analogues entrelardées de gras en proportion élevée et le lard gras avec couche de viande adhérente, mais à l'exclusion des jambons fermés dans des boyaux, vessies ou enveloppes similaires. (CTCI, Rev.3:01610-0).

For footnotes, see end of table.

Voir la fin du tableau pour les notes.

Bacon, ham and other dried, salted or smoked pig meat (continued)
Lard entrelardé, jambon et autres viandes de porc, séchées, salées ou fumées (suite)

ISIC-BASED CODE - CODE BASE CITI

3111-16

Footnotes

[1] Data refer to bacon and ham.
[2] Data refer to ham only.
[3] Sales.
[4] Production by establishments employing 20 or more persons.
[5] Bacon only.
[6] Including other meat and edible offals and sausages.

[7] Excluding bacon.
[8] Twelve months ending 30 June of year stated.
[9] Twelve months ending 30 September of year stated.

Notes.

[1] Données se rapportant au bacon et au jambon.
[2] Les données se rapportent au jambon seulement.
[3] Ventes.
[4] Production des établissements occupant 20 personnes ou plus.
[5] Bacon seulement.
[6] Y compris les autres viandes et abats comestibles et les saucisses et saucissons.
[7] Non compris le bacon.
[8] Période de douze mois finissant le 30 juin de l'année indiquée.
[9] Période de douze mois finissant le 30 septembre de l'année indiquée.

Other meat and edible offals, dried, salted or smoked
Autres viandes et abats comestibles, séchés, salés ou fumés

ISIC-BASED CODE - CODE BASE CITI

3111-19

Unit : Thousand metric tons

Unité : Milliers de tonnes métriques

Country or area	1990	1991	1992	1993	1994	1995	1996	1997	1998	1999	Pays ou zone
America, North	**12**	**12**	**13**	**30**	**27**	**28**	**30**	**31**	**30**	**31**	**Amérique du Nord**
Mexico	12	12	13	30	27	28	30	31	30	31	Mexique
America, South	**1**	**1**	**1**	**1**	**1**	**1**	**0**	**1**	**1**	**1**	**Amérique du Sud**
Ecuador	...	...	...	...	...	...	0	1	...	...	Equateur
Asia	**6**	**8**	**8**	**9**	**9**	**11**	**9**	**5**	**10**	**11**	**Asie**
Hong Kong SAR	5	4	4	5	5	7	5	1	6	7	Hong-Kong RAS
Indonesia	...	...	1	...	...	...	...	...	...	...	Indonésie
Turkmenistan	..	3	3	3	...	...	...	...	...	...	Turkménistan
Europe	**196**	**266**	**293**	**272**	**226**	**207**	**152**	**191**	**172**	**147**	**Europe**
Belgium	[1]78	[1]91	[1]91	[1]96	#6	7	6	6	4	3	Belgique
Croatia	..	...	...	...	...	...	...	1	0	...	Croatie
Denmark[2]	7	2	1	1	1	1	1	1	1	1	Danemark[2]
Finland	1	1	1	0	...	1	1	2	1	1	Finlande
France	5	4	5	2	2	3	7	...	...	...	France
Germany	..	...	...	...	...	22	27	74	70	...	Allemagne
Greece	30	27	28	...	...	...	...	...	...	...	Grèce
Iceland	...	...	...	...	...	...	1	1	1	1	Islande
Latvia	..	5	4	4	4	3	3	3	3	1	Lettonie
Lithuania	..	7	3	2	2	3	5	6	9	9	Lituanie
Netherlands[2][3]	4	4	5	2	3	7	6	6	4	...	Pays-Bas[2][3]
Norway	...	...	...	...	...	...	...	3	...	...	Norvège
Portugal	...	...	2	2	2	2	3	10	8	8	Portugal
Republic of Moldova	..	5	3	[4]2	[4]2	[4]1	[4]1	[4]1	[4]1	[4]1	Rép. de Moldova
Slovakia	..	..	0	63	61	1	1	1	0	Slovaquie
Spain	...	...	2	2	10	7	7	6	3	Espagne
Sweden	9	11	9	22	19	11	...	...	3	2	Suède
United Kingdom	...	...	...	56	38	42	40	26	24	...	Royaume-Uni
Oceania	**16**	**18**	**18**	**17**	**18**	**15**	**12**	**13**	**16**	**13**	**Océanie**
New Zealand[5]	16	18	18	17	18	15	12	13	16	...	Nouvelle-Zélande[5]
Total	**231**	**304**	**333**	**329**	**281**	**261**	**203**	**241**	**228**	**202**	**Total**

General Note.
Meat (except pork) and edible meat offals (except poultry liver and poultry fat) salted, in brine, dried or smoked. Meat and offals cooked, prepared or preserved by other processes, and meat flours and meals suitable only for feeding animals are excluded.(SITC, Rev.3: 01681-0, 01689-1).

Remarque générale.
Viandes (autres que la viande de porc) et abats comestibles (autres que les foies de volailles et la graisse de volailles), salés, en saumure, séchés ou fumés, à l'exclusion des viandes et des abats cuits, préparés ou mis en conserve par d'autres moyens et des farines et poudres de viande uniquement propres à l'alimentation des animaux. (CTCI, Rev.3: 01681-0,01689-1).

[1] Edible offals only.
[2] Sales.
[3] Production by establishments employing 20 or more persons.
[4] Excluding Transnistria region.
[5] Twelve months ending 30 September of year stated.

[1] Abats comestibles seulement.
[2] Ventes.
[3] Production des établissements occupant 20 personnes ou plus.
[4] Non compris la région de Transnistria.
[5] Période de douze mois finissant le 30 septembre de l'année indiquée.

Sausages
Saucissons

ISIC-BASED CODE - CODE BASE CITI

3111-22

Unit : Thousand metric tons

Unité : Milliers de tonnes métriques

Country or area	1990	1991	1992	1993	1994	1995	1996	1997	1998	1999	Pays ou zone
Africa	**48**	**45**	**44**	**43**	**45**	**45**	**44**	**45**	**46**	**49**	**Afrique**
Kenya	2	2	3	3	3	3	3	...	...	...	Kenya
South Africa	46	43	41	40	42	42	41	41	42	45	Afrique du Sud
America, North	**68**	**80**	**83**	**124**	**124**	**133**	**154**	**173**	**192**	**209**	**Amérique du Nord**
Jamaica	2	3	1	1	2	3	2	3	3	...	Jamaïque
Mexico	62	72	78	119	117	124	146	162	180	196	Mexique
Panama	4	...	4	4	5	6	6	...	...	...	Panama
America, South	**89**	**98**	**104**	**113**	**125**	**131**	**150**	**169**	**179**	**203**	**Amérique du Sud**
Bolivia	2	2	2	2	2	*2	...	...	...	...	Bolivie
Chile	54	59	63	71	78	86	94	97	100	...	Chili
Colombia	...	...	29	30	35	28	...	55	58	...	Colombie
Ecuador	8	...	8	7	6	10	9	8	10	...	Equateur
Peru	...	...	...	...	...	5	6	7	9	10	Pérou
Asia	**337**	**634**	**539**	**516**	**483**	**465**	**444**	**434**	**411**	**399**	**Asie**
Armenia	..	12	4	1	0	0	0	...	0	0	Arménie
Azerbaijan	..	14	8	10	4	2	1	1	0	0	Azerbaïdjan
Hong Kong SAR	5	5	3	7	10	7	8	6	8	6	Hong-Kong RAS
Cyprus	*1	*1	2	*2	*2	1	1	1	1	1	Chypre
Georgia	..	..	4	1	0	0	0	1	1	1	Géorgie
Indonesia	0	0	0	1	1	0	...	1	1	...	Indonésie
Iran(Islamic Rep. of)[1]	13	28	24	...	...	...	...	...	...	...	Iran(Rép. islamique)[1]
Japan	277	289	299	303	304	310	308	300	297	293	Japon
Kazakhstan	..	152	97	83	55	35	22	16	12	10	Kazakhstan
Korea, Republic of	27	32	33	38	45	59	59	64	51	49	Corée, République de
Kyrgyzstan	..	16	9	6	3	2	1	0	1	1	Kirghizistan
Mongolia	6	6	4	1	1	1	1	1	1	...	Mongolie
Tajikistan	..	10	4	2	1	0	0	0	0	0	Tadjikistan
Turkey	8	8	8	11	10	11	11	12	13	14	Turquie
Turkmenistan	..	16	13	12	7	3	2	3	3	...	Turkménistan
Uzbekistan	..	44	26	16	18	12	8	5	...	...	Ouzbékistan
Europe	**3769**	**7238**	**6851**	**6481**	**6529**	**6139**	**6320**	**6382**	**6389**	**6083**	**Europe**
Austria	...	...	...	...	...	136	144	148	151	151	Autriche
Belarus	..	210	220	196	164	141	149	154	164	150	Bélarus
Belgium	...	...	...	...	66	75	89	133	123	80	Belgique
Bulgaria	134	91	93	68	50	52	42	22	36	41	Bulgarie
Croatia	..	33	29	31	31	31	33	37	34	...	Croatie
Denmark[2]	86	86	89	100	107	99	100	100	93	89	Danemark[2]
Czech Republic	...	...	216	194	196	199	227	241	230	233	République tchèque
Estonia	..	43	35	34	32	33	32	36	39	35	Estonie
Finland	133	134	132	136	128	127	155	132	129	119	Finlande
France	274	282	287	305	305	317	332	332	345	...	France
Germany	..	1256	1297	1321	1315	1222	1219	1258	1274	...	Allemagne
Germany(Fed.Rep.)	1029	..	..	..	..	..	..	..	..	..	Allemagne(Rép.féd.)
German D.R.(former)	232	..	..	..	..	..	..	..	..	..	R.D.A. (anc.)
Greece	11	11	11	28	31	33	29	32	36	...	Grèce
Hungary	159	146	129	129	138	132	171	184	192	179	Hongrie
Iceland	1	1	1	1	1	...	2	2	2	2	Islande
Ireland	13	...	...	...	...	...	...	...	...	...	Irlande
Latvia	..	41	34	34	29	27	24	24	24	26	Lettonie
Lithuania	..	70	58	47	38	40	46	45	44	45	Lituanie
Netherlands[2 3]	88	92	101	130	141	150	152	146	144	158	Pays-Bas[2 3]
Norway	...	...	...	56	...	51	...	56	54	...	Norvège
Poland[4]	714	676	669	676	703	756	845	945	888	873	Pologne[4]
Portugal	11	10	17	17	17	18	20	22	22	18	Portugal
Republic of Moldova	..	45	30	[5]12	[5]7	[5]7	[5]7	[5]8	[5]7	[5]9	Rép. de Moldova
Russian Federation	..	2077	1547	1493	1545	1293	1296	1147	1113	948	Fédération de Russie
Slovakia	..	...	...	...	...	...	...	...	10	10	Slovaquie
Slovenia	..	39	29	27	31	30	36	35	33	34	Slovénie
Spain	...	...	...	275	308	345	350	397	419	375	Espagne
Sweden	107	111	112	105	119	114	121	124	119	128	Suède

For general note and footnotes, see end of table.

Voir la fin du tableau pour la remarque générale et les notes.

Sausages (continued)
Saucissons (suite)

ISIC-BASED CODE - CODE BASE CITI
3111-22

Unit : Thousand metric tons | | | | | | | | | | | Unité : Milliers de tonnes métriques

Country or area	1990	1991	1992	1993	1994	1995	1996	1997	1998	1999	Pays ou zone
Ukraine	..	852	758	500	437	276	213	206	155	160	Ukraine
United Kingdom	...	...	...	275	317	344	337	328	438	...	Royaume-Uni
Yugoslavia	..	100	75	51	59	65	70	64	58	55	Yougoslavie
T.F.Yug.Rep. Macedonia	..	2	3	3	2	1	1	1	1	3	L'ex-RY Macédoine
Oceania	8	8	7	9	10	11	13	19	18	22	Océanie
New Zealand[6]	8	8	7	9	10	11	13	19	18	...	Nouvelle-Zélande[6]
Total	4318	8103	7628	7286	7316	6923	7125	7222	7234	6965	Total

General Note.
Sausages and the like of meat, meat offal or animal blood, whether or not tinned. (SITC, Rev.3: 01720-1).

Remarque générale.
Saucissons, saucisses et préparations similaires faites de viande, d'abats ou de sang, contenues ou non dans des récipients fermés hermétiquement. (CTCI, Rev.3:01720-1).

[1] Twelve months beginning 21 March of year stated.
[2] Sales.
[3] Production by establishments employing 20 or more persons.
[4] Excluding sausages of horse, poultry and rabbit meat and venison.

[5] Excluding Transnistria region.
[6] Twelve months ending 30 September of year stated.

[1] Période de douze mois commençant le 21 mars de l'année indiquée.
[2] Ventes.
[3] Production des établissements occupant 20 personnes ou plus.
[4] Non compris les saucisses faites de viande de cheval, de volaille, de lapin et de venaison.
[5] Non compris la région de Transnistria.
[6] Période de douze mois finissant le 30 septembre de l'année indiquée.

Meals, frozen prepared
Repas préparés, congelés

ISIC-BASED CODE - CODE BASE CITI

3111-25

Unit : Metric tons

Unité : Tonnes métriques

Country or area	1990	1991	1992	1993	1994	1995	1996	1997	1998	1999	Pays ou zone
America, North	**712**	**1468**	**2223**	**2781**	**2888**	**3581**	**3696**	**5162**	**6262**	**7055**	**Amérique du Nord**
Mexico	...	...	...	2781	2888	3581	3696	5162	6262	7055	Mexique
America, South	**7628**	**7628**	**4898**	**6042**	**7539**	**12031**	**7628**	**7628**	**7628**	**7628**	**Amérique du Sud**
Colombia	...	...	4898	6042	7539	12031	...	...	...	...	Colombie
Asia	**598**	**598**	**598**	**598**	**598**	**598**	**598**	**598**	**598**	**598**	**Asie**
Indonesia	...	...	598	...	...	...	...	...	...	...	Indonésie
Europe	**1739718**	**1765190**	**1753250**	**1670130**	**1773794**	**1857924**	**1755852**	**1793044**	**1796082**	**1786123**	**Europe**
Austria	5785	7310	8499	8213	9335	[1]31307	[1]33102	[1]33816	[1]40098	[1]44192	Autriche
Belgium	...	...	...	...	...	189519	198455	204753	208377	195480	Belgique
Croatia	..	57	35	15	15	2	5	5	...	...	Croatie
Czechoslovakia(former)	13437	...	..	..	..	..	..	..	..	..	Tchécoslovaquie(anc.)
Czech Republic	..	..	5254	5401	..	..	..	..	..	..	République tchèque
Estonia	..	20362	13667	12265	8638	9010	5558	5352	5811	6901	Estonie
Finland	5395	3911	3420	2787	3870	3552	7887	...	...	...	Finlande
German D.R.(former)	554	..	..	..	..	..	..	..	..	..	R.D.A. (anc.)
Hungary	737	167	356	1683	2057	3649	...	...	...	...	Hongrie
Latvia	..	2334	1935	2303	...	...	...	...	...	...	Lettonie
Netherlands[2][3]	...	..	...	226319	212469	206422	213316	221132	...	...	Pays-Bas[2][3]
Slovakia	..	..	734	865	807	818	...	167	...	...	Slovaquie
Slovenia	..	1392	738	839	941	1043	628	...	...	...	Slovénie
United Kingdom[1]	...	...	...	1217036	1332713	1402446	1284160	...	...	...	Royaume-Uni[1]
Yugoslavia	..	1160	2317	1779	2650	2606	1832	...	...	7	Yougoslavie
T.F.Yug.Rep. Macedonia	..	18	22	46	17	32	39	6	16	32	L'ex-RY Macédoine
Total	**1748656**	**1774883**	**1760969**	**1679551**	**1784819**	**1874134**	**1767773**	**1806431**	**1810570**	**1801404**	**Total**

General Note.

More than one food arranged on a shaped container, so as to constitute the main element of a meal, such as mixed frozen dinners and frozen pies of beef, pork and poultry. (SITC, Rev.3: 01720-2, 01730-1, 01740-1, 01750-1, 01760-1, 01790-1).

Remarque générale.

Plusieurs plats disposés dans un récipient de forme appropriée, de façon à constituer l'élément principal d'un repas, tels que les repas congelés assortis et les pâtés congelés de viande de boeuf, de porc ou de volaille. (CTCI, Rev.3: 01720-2, 01730-1, 01740-1, 01750-1, 01760-1, 01790-1).

[1] Including canned meat.
[2] Sales.
[3] Production by establishments employing 20 or more persons.

[1] Y compris les conserves de viande.
[2] Ventes.
[3] Production des établissements occupant 20 personnes ou plus.

Meat, tinned
Conserves de Viande
ISIC-BASED CODE - CODE BASE CITI

3111-28

Unit : Metric tons | Unité : Tonnes métriques

Country or area	1990	1991	1992	1993	1994	1995	1996	1997	1998	1999	Pays ou zone
Africa	**10161**	**12777**	**12904**	**10782**	**15492**	**14906**	**13162**	**8930**	**7743**	**7791**	**Afrique**
Botswana	785	1356	1793	871	1400	1085	509	1274	1262	1608	Botswana
Kenya	282	...	446	90	64	69	79	...	...	...	Kenya
Madagascar	15	57	50	50	34	42	18	23	21	...	Madagascar
South Africa	9053	11180	10596	9752	13975	13691	12537	7595	6441	6147	Afrique du Sud
United Rep.Tanzania	26	12	...	...	...	...	...	...	...	...	Rép. Unie de Tanzanie
America, North	**352**	**358**	**320**	**186**	**232**	**166**	**125**	**84**	**42**	**1**	**Amérique du Nord**
Mexico	352	358	320	186	232	...	...	...	...	...	Mexique
America, South	**64678**	**116525**	**147233**	**110462**	**107364**	**94905**	**77826**	**65007**	**70846**	**88760**	**Amérique du Sud**
Bolivia	42	48	55	128	121	*124	...	...	...	...	Bolivie
Brazil	[1]58695	[1]110662	[1]141610	[1]106044	[1]101309	89388	71807	59181	65229	83797	Brésil
Colombia	...	...	5399	4070	5832	5333	...	5200	4990	...	Colombie
Ecuador	...	...	169	220	102	60	755	490	...	...	Equateur
Asia	**259268**	**327069**	**326829**	**302118**	**299384**	**299605**	**297461**	**297373**	**294372**	**294102**	**Asie**
China	234500	300300	301600	...	...	...	...	...	...	...	Chine
Indonesia	...	...	822	1292	1477	...	...	1967	564	...	Indonésie
Japan	22111	20053	18917	18334	16188	16627	15918	15186	14146	13830	Japon
Kyrgyzstan	..	3360	4080	2680	2353	2168	877	494	224	71	Kirghizistan
Mongolia	1109	1055	569	358	243	400	339	651	322	72	Mongolie
Myanmar[2]	195	155	...	...	...	...	...	...	...	...	Myanmar[2]
Tajikistan[3]	..	420	423	253	102	131	7	1	44	39	Tadjikistan[3]
Turkey	0	0	...	...	1	...	...	...	...	...	Turquie
Turkmenistan	..	405	243	226	45	79	120	99	97	...	Turkménistan
Europe	**756615**	**1039113**	**1033186**	**1004672**	**1027740**	**1593795**	**1652464**	**1734025**	**2018029**	**2239413**	**Europe**
Austria	17556	15181	16292	17459	21292	21812	[4]33102	[4]33816	[4]40098	[4]44192	Autriche
Belarus	..	[5]32757	29563	25724	21701	10731	9404	17602	22289	20494	Bélarus
Belgium[6]	15747	18476	18342	16725	...	...	...	...	...	...	Belgique[6]
Bulgaria[7]	39463	17688	9899	4537	14781	12671	13247	9940	...	...	Bulgarie[7]
Croatia	..	21153	17898	16511	17054	17896	15678	16328	16217	...	Croatie
Czechoslovakia(former)	50044	38799	..	..	..	..	..	..	..	..	Tchécoslovaquie(anc.)
Czech Republic	..	..	23466	20610	28207	32452	39963	49554	49720	50287	République tchèque
Estonia	..	12019	12127	3077	4194	4607	4708	4486	4899	2165	Estonie
Finland	13099	11601	11023	4858	4890	3255	3810	...	...	...	Finlande
France	#85859	87198	85086	85790	92488	84422	114800	121700	131100	...	France
Germany	..	84742	84144	70844	72547	[4]713754	[4]712008	[4]713247	...	...	Allemagne
Germany(Fed.Rep.)	64197	..	..	..	..	..	..	..	..	..	Allemagne(Rép.féd.)
German D.R.(former)[8]	35591									..	R.D.A. (anc.)[8]
Greece	683	757	816	...	...	...	...	...	...	...	Grèce
Hungary[9]	60892	53246	46919	42467	45986	50128	...	...	...	...	Hongrie[9]
Iceland	...	...	...	...	...	...	5165	5143	5963	7501	Islande
Ireland	9329	...	...	...	...	...	...	...	...	...	Irlande
Italy	30527	39140	49051	61169	56873	38256	28179	30314	33129	31420	Italie
Latvia	..	...	...	1799	1274	561	849	1407	1206	6950	Lettonie
Lithuania	..	12190	10849	6432	4736	5715	5374	3815	2972	1603	Lituanie
Netherlands[10][11]	5339	...	...	...	...	...	...	...	...	...	Pays-Bas[10][11]
Poland[12]	117934	104109	102317	97681	89133	83622	99952	104615	101278	89185	Pologne[12]
Portugal	14512	14561	...	...	...	...	...	...	...	...	Portugal
Romania	47938	41841	25239	25100	20462	19758	18260	13593	10271	9877	Roumanie
Russian Federation	..	164225	194885	183737	140499	137945	151996	129117	139000	223657	Fédération de Russie
Slovakia	..	..	10376	10891	6319	7092	6992	82294	33270	29643	Slovaquie
Slovenia	..	6096	4635	4700	4885	...	4018	7559	8791	...	Slovénie
Spain[13]	141962	147386	150279	196974	252888	227610	...	...	...	...	Espagne[13]
Ukraine[5]	..	66322	70863	61620	64509	50538	48591	43769	30042	27072	Ukraine[5]
Yugoslavia	..	28893	23666	9949	9726	11716	12230	11412	9538	11728	Yougoslavie
T.F.Yug.Rep. Macedonia	..	122	29	118	74	220	85	99	175	303	L'ex-RY Macédoine
USSR (former)[5]	420711	..	..	..	..	..	..	..	..	..	URSS (anc.)[5]
Oceania	**32237**	**17380**	**16113**	**16124**	**16817**	**16780**	**19822**	**24772**	**18319**	**16140**	**Océanie**
Australia[14]	32237	17380	16113	16124	16817	16780	19822	24772	18319	16140	Australie[14]

For general note and footnotes, see end of table. | Voir la fin du tableau pour la remarque générale et les notes.

Meat, tinned (continued)
Conserves de Viande (suite)

ISIC-BASED CODE - CODE BASE CITI
3111-28

Unit : Metric tons   Unité : Tonnes métriques

Country or area	1990	1991	1992	1993	1994	1995	1996	1997	1998	1999	Pays ou zone
Total	1544022	1513222	1536586	1444344	1467029	2020157	2060859	2130192	2409351	2646207	Total

General Note.

Meat and meat products (other than meat extracts, soups and broths), packed and heat-processed in hermetically-sealed containers. Tinned meat preparations such as sausages and meat paste are excluded. (SITC, Rev.3: 01730-2, 01740-2, 01752-2, 01760-2, 01790-2).

[1] Beef only.
[2] Twelve months ending 31 March of year stated.
[3] Original data in conventional cans.
[4] Including frozen prepared meals.
[5] Including canned sausages, meat pies and vegetable stew.
[6] Production by establishments employing 5 or more persons.
[7] Including canned meat and vegetables.
[8] Including canned sausages and meat and sausage preserves.
[9] Including meat pies.
[10] Source: Industrial Statistics, Statistical Office of the European Communities, (Luxembourg).
[11] Production by establishments employing 20 or more persons.
[12] Excluding sausages of horse, poultry and rabbit meat and venison.
[13] Beginning 1979, including sausages.
[14] Twelve months ending 30 June of year stated.

Remarque générale.

Viandes et produits de viande (autres que les extraits de viande, les soupes et les bouillons) mis et traités à chaud dans des récipients fermés hermétiquement. Cette rubrique ne comprend pas les produits de viande en boîte, ni les préparations telles que les saucisses, les saucissons et les pâtés de viande. (CTCI, Rev.3: 01730-2, 01740-2, 01750-2, 01760-2, 01790-2).

[1] Boeuf seulement.
[2] Période de douze mois finissant le 31 mars de l'année indiquée.
[3] Données d'origine exprimées en boîte de type classique.
[4] Y compris les repas préparés congelés.
[5] Y compris les saucisses, les pâtés de viande et les ragoûts de légumes en boîte.
[6] Production des établissements occupant 5 personnes ou plus.
[7] Y compris les conserves de viande et de légumes.
[8] Y compris les saucisses en boîte et les viandes et saucisses en conserve.
[9] Y compris les pâtés de viande.
[10] Source: Statistiques industrielles, Office statistique des Communautés européennes, (Luxembourg).
[11] Production des établissements occupant 20 personnes ou plus.
[12] Non compris les saucisses faites de viande de cheval, de volaille, de lapin et de venaison.
[13] A partir de 1979, y compris les saucisses.
[14] Période de douze mois finissant le 30 juin de l'année indiquée.

Lard (Industrial production)
Saindoux (Production industrielle)

ISIC-BASED CODE - CODE BASE CITI

3111-311

Unit : Thousand metric tons   Unité : Milliers de tonnes métriques

Country or area	1990	1991	1992	1993	1994	1995	1996	1997	1998	1999	Pays ou zone
America, North	**15**	**15**	**15**	**14**	**16**	**15**	**15**	**16**	**16**	**16**	**Amérique du Nord**
Mexico	15.0	15.0	15.0	14.0	16.0	...	...	...	...	...	Mexique
America, South	**35**	**34**	**31**	**38**	**52**	**49**	**53**	**57**	**61**	**65**	**Amérique du Sud**
Peru	35.0	34.0	31.0	38.0	52.0	...	...	...	...	...	Pérou
Asia	**239**	**183**	**197**	**176**	**172**	**173**	**161**	**155**	**166**	**175**	**Asie**
Hong Kong SAR[1]	20.0	5.0	26.0	4.0	4.0	15.0	9.0	2.0	...	23.0	Hong-Kong RAS[1]
China, Macao, SAR[2]	...	...	...	0.2	...	...	0.0	0.2	0.0	0.2	Chine, Macao PAS[2]
Japan	219.0	178.0	171.0	172.0	168.0	158.0	152.0	153.0	154.0	152.0	Japon
Europe	**621**	**742**	**661**	**598**	**483**	**573**	**560**	**539**	**571**	**540**	**Europe**
Austria	...	...	...	...	...	9.0	5.8	6.2	18.5	17.0	Autriche
Belarus	..	32.9	26.9	20.3	17.2	12.5	10.0	12.0	10.0	9.0	Bélarus
Belgium	...	...	...	...	26.0	27.0	21.0	22.0	...	15.0	Belgique
Bulgaria	45.0	25.0	21.0	7.0	3.0	2.0	2.0	0.4	1.0	1.0	Bulgarie
Croatia	..	4.0	3.0	2.0	2.0	2.0	2.0	2.0	2.0	...	Croatie
Czechoslovakia(former)	93.0	74.0	..	..	..	..	..	..	..	..	Tchécoslovaquie(anc.)
Czech Republic	..	..	35.0	27.0	15.0	12.0	12.0	11.0	11.0	10.0	République tchèque
Finland[3]	3.0	4.0	4.0	3.0	2.0	2.0	2.0	2.0	1.0	1.0	Finlande[3]
France	0.9	1.0	1.0	0.9	0.8	1.0	1.0	...	...	...	France
Germany	..	...	...	...	...	129.0	124.0	122.0	153.0	...	Allemagne
German D.R.(former)	32.0	..	..	..	..	..	..	..	..	..	R.D.A. (anc.)
Hungary	77.0	71.0	44.0	39.0	33.0	29.0	37.0	30.0	27.0	32.0	Hongrie
Ireland	2.0	...	...	...	...	...	...	...	...	...	Irlande
Lithuania	..	...	4.0	1.0	1.0	1.0	1.0	1.0	1.0	1.0	Lituanie
Netherlands[4][5]	...	...	...	114.0	50.0	94.0	91.0	94.0	85.0	90.0	Pays-Bas[4][5]
Poland	82.0	90.0	87.0	63.0	47.0	53.0	43.0	40.0	41.0	36.0	Pologne
Portugal	...	...	0.0	...	8.0	6.0	13.0	7.0	8.0	0.0	Portugal
Republic of Moldova	..	7.0	5.0	[6]2.0	[6]1.0	[6]1.0	[6]1.0	[6]1.0	[6]0.0	[6]0.0	Rép. de Moldova
Slovakia	..	..	16.0	12.0	5.0	6.0	6.0	7.0	3.0	2.0	Slovaquie
Slovenia	..	24.0	18.0	16.0	15.0	10.0	15.0	1.0	2.0	2.0	Slovénie
Spain	[7]99.0	[7]104.0	[7]108.0	[8]85.0	[8]82.0	[8]149.0	[8]144.0	...	...	...	Espagne
Sweden	28.0	31.0	27.0	34.0	35.0	21.0	22.0	28.0	25.0	22.0	Suède
Yugoslavia	..	12.0	9.0	4.0	3.0	4.0	5.0	4.0	4.0	5.0	Yougoslavie
T.F.Yug.Rep. Macedonia	..	0.3	0.2	...	...	...	...	...	...	...	L'ex-RY Macédoine
Yugoslavia, SFR	32.0	..	..	..	..	..	..	..	..	..	Yougoslavie, RSF
Total	**910**	**974**	**905**	**827**	**723**	**811**	**790**	**767**	**813**	**795**	**Total**

General Note.
Lard and other rendered pig fat, crude or refined. Data refer to industrial production only. (SITC, Rev.3: 41120-1).

Remarque générale.
Saindoux et autres graisses de porc, pressées ou fondues, brutes ou raffinées. Les données se rapportent à la production industrielle seulement. (CTCI, Rev.3: 41120-1).

[1] 1998 data are confidential.
[2] 1995 data are confidential.
[3] Including small quantities of rendered poultry fats.
[4] Sales.
[5] Production by establishments employing 20 or more persons.
[6] Excluding Transnistria region.
[7] Including bacon.
[8] Including lard and other prepared fat of pork or poultry.

[1] Pour 1998, les données sont confidentielles.
[2] Pour 1995, les données sont confidentielles.
[3] Y compris de petites quantités de graisse de volaille fondue.
[4] Ventes.
[5] Production des établissements occupant 20 personnes ou plus.
[6] Non compris la région de Transnistria.
[7] Y compris le bacon.
[8] Y compris le saindoux et autres graisses de porc ou de volailles.

Hides, cattle and horse, undressed (Total production)
Peaux de bovins et d'équidés, non préparées (Production totale)

ISIC-BASED CODE - CODE BASE CITI

3111-34

Unit : Thousand metric tons

Unité : Milliers de tonnes métriques

Country or area	1990	1991	1992	1993	1994	1995	1996	1997	1998	1999	Pays ou zone
Africa	**555**	**573**	**593**	**603**	**580**	**589**	**596**	**604**	**630**	**637**	**Afrique**
Algeria	11.7	11.8	12.0	12.2	12.3	11.3	11.8	11.3	11.2	13.0	Algérie
Angola	8.8	9.0	9.9	9.9	9.9	9.9	10.6	11.4	12.5	12.5	Angola
Benin	2.5	2.6	2.7	2.7	2.9	3.0	3.2	3.3	3.2	3.5	Bénin
Botswana	4.9	5.5	6.6	6.5	4.9	6.1	5.8	4.9	4.8	4.9	Botswana
Burkina Faso	5.9	6.1	6.3	6.5	6.5	6.6	7.7	8.1	8.3	8.5	Burkina Faso
Burundi	2.4	2.4	2.6	2.6	2.4	2.4	2.5	2.0	2.1	1.8	Burundi
Cameroon	10.3	10.6	10.9	11.2	11.5	11.9	12.2	12.5	12.8	12.8	Cameroun
Cape Verde	0.1	0.1	0.1	0.1	0.1	0.1	0.1	0.1	0.1	0.1	Cap-Vert
Central African Rep.	6.9	6.8	6.8	7.0	7.2	7.3	8.8	7.5	7.7	7.7	Rép. centrafricaine
Chad	10.5	10.7	11.2	11.1	9.0	10.8	11.7	11.6	13.1	12.9	Tchad
Comoros	0.2	0.2	0.2	0.2	0.2	0.2	0.2	0.2	0.2	0.2	Comores
Congo	0.3	0.2	0.2	0.2	0.2	0.2	0.2	0.3	0.3	0.2	Congo
Côte d'Ivoire	4.1	4.3	4.5	4.5	4.5	4.8	4.9	5.0	5.0	5.1	Côte d'Ivoire
Dem. Rep. of Congo	3.5	3.1	3.1	3.2	3.0	3.0	2.8	2.6	2.3	2.2	Rép. dém. du Congo
Djibouti	0.4	0.5	0.5	0.6	0.6	0.6	0.6	0.6	0.7	0.7	Djibouti
Egypt	35.0	38.4	39.2	41.4	42.0	44.1	42.5	46.4	48.9	49.9	Egypte
Eritrea	...	...	...	1.9	1.9	1.9	2.4	2.8	3.0	3.6	Erythrée
Ethiopia,incl.Eritrea	47.0	47.0	48.8	...	...	...	...	...	...	...	Ethiopie,incl.Erythrée
Ethiopia	...	...	...	45.9	45.9	46.2	50.0	51.5	54.2	55.7	Ethiopie
Gabon	0.2	0.2	0.2	0.2	0.2	0.2	0.2	0.2	0.2	0.2	Gabon
Gambia	0.4	0.4	0.3	0.3	0.3	0.3	0.4	0.4	0.4	0.4	Gambie
Ghana	2.5	2.6	2.5	2.5	2.6	2.6	2.6	1.6	1.7	1.7	Ghana
Guinea	1.6	1.7	1.8	1.9	2.1	2.4	2.5	2.5	2.6	2.6	Guinée
Guinea-Bissau	0.8	0.8	0.8	0.9	0.9	0.9	0.9	0.9	0.9	1.0	Guinée-Bissau
Kenya	39.4	38.9	37.2	37.2	38.0	38.9	41.0	40.5	36.4	37.8	Kenya
Lesotho	1.7	1.7	1.9	2.0	1.7	1.8	1.6	2.0	1.6	2.3	Lesotho
Liberia	0.2	0.2	0.2	0.2	0.2	0.2	0.2	0.2	0.2	0.2	Libéria
Libyan Arab Jamah.	3.3	4.3	3.7	3.6	2.9	3.6	2.4	6.6	7.2	2.5	Jamah. arabe libyenne
Madagascar	20.2	20.3	20.3	20.4	20.5	20.6	20.7	20.8	20.9	20.9	Madagascar
Malawi	1.7	1.7	1.7	1.8	1.4	1.4	1.6	1.8	1.7	1.7	Malawi
Mali	11.0	11.4	12.0	12.4	12.8	13.0	13.2	13.6	14.0	14.4	Mali
Mauritania	2.2	2.5	1.8	1.4	1.4	1.4	1.5	1.5	1.5	1.6	Mauritanie
Mauritius	0.3	0.4	0.3	0.3	0.3	0.3	0.3	0.3	0.4	0.4	Maurice
Morocco	17.8	18.2	27.0	28.5	20.5	19.8	16.1	17.8	16.8	17.5	Maroc
Mozambique	5.4	5.2	4.8	5.0	4.8	4.9	4.9	5.0	5.0	5.1	Mozambique
Namibia	4.5	5.0	5.2	5.5	5.4	5.4	5.5	3.4	4.2	4.5	Namibie
Niger	5.1	4.4	5.7	5.6	5.7	5.9	5.9	6.0	6.0	6.2	Niger
Nigeria	28.9	30.1	24.3	29.5	31.0	32.0	35.0	36.0	36.3	36.5	Nigéria
Réunion	0.1	0.1	0.1	0.1	0.1	0.1	0.1	0.1	0.1	0.1	Réunion
Rwanda	2.0	2.1	1.9	1.7	1.5	1.5	1.7	2.0	2.3	2.6	Rwanda
Senegal	8.5	8.7	8.8	9.0	9.1	9.2	9.3	9.5	9.6	9.6	Sénégal
Sierra Leone	1.2	1.2	1.3	1.4	1.4	1.4	1.4	1.5	1.5	1.6	Sierra Leone
Somalia	8.4	7.4	6.6	7.6	8.0	9.0	9.8	11.0	11.2	10.6	Somalie
South Africa	88.1	93.8	97.5	93.2	78.0	75.0	69.9	67.5	83.0	82.5	Afrique du Sud
Sudan	33.4	35.5	37.8	41.4	43.1	45.2	47.3	48.3	50.4	52.7	Soudan
Swaziland	1.3	1.5	1.6	1.6	1.6	1.7	1.6	1.7	1.8	1.6	Swaziland
Togo	0.7	0.7	0.8	0.8	0.8	0.9	1.0	0.9	1.0	1.0	Togo
Tunisia	3.7	3.8	4.2	4.2	4.6	4.8	4.9	5.1	5.0	5.3	Tunisie
Uganda	11.4	11.8	12.0	12.8	11.8	12.1	12.2	12.4	13.0	13.4	Ouganda
United Rep.Tanzania	39.7	40.0	40.5	41.4	41.8	42.0	42.6	43.1	43.5	43.7	Rép. Unie de Tanzanie
Zambia	4.7	4.9	5.3	5.7	5.7	5.3	5.3	3.8	3.8	4.0	Zambie
Zimbabwe	8.2	8.4	10.5	8.2	6.9	7.7	6.7	7.0	7.4	8.7	Zimbabwe
America, North	**1303**	**1270**	**1281**	**1273**	**1330**	**1368**	**1386**	**1393**	**1411**	**1442**	**Amérique du Nord**
Antigua and Barbuda	0.1	0.1	0.1	0.1	0.1	0.1	0.1	0.1	0.1	0.1	Antigua-et-Barbuda
Barbados	0.1	0.1	0.2	0.1	0.1	0.1	0.1	0.1	0.1	0.1	Barbade
Belize	0.2	0.2	0.2	0.2	0.2	0.2	0.1	0.2	0.1	0.1	Belize
Canada	83.9	78.8	80.8	75.8	76.6	78.7	87.6	90.8	94.2	99.3	Canada
Costa Rica	13.8	14.8	14.2	14.4	14.5	14.6	15.2	14.7	10.7	11.7	Costa Rica
Cuba	19.8	15.9	15.0	11.7	9.4	9.8	10.0	9.8	10.1	11.0	Cuba
Dominica	0.1	0.1	0.1	0.1	0.1	0.1	0.1	0.1	0.1	0.1	Dominique
Dominican Republic	8.1	7.5	7.3	7.4	7.4	7.6	7.6	9.2	9.3	8.7	Rép. dominicaine
El Salvador	5.3	4.6	4.3	4.8	4.9	5.5	5.4	6.9	6.8	6.8	El Salvador

For general note and footnotes, see end of table.

Voir la fin du tableau pour la remarque générale et les notes.

122

Hides, cattle and horse, undressed (Total production) (continued)
Peaux de bovins et d'équidés, non préparées (Production totale) (suite)

ISIC-BASED CODE - CODE BASE CITI

3111-34

Unit : Thousand metric tons

Unité : Milliers de tonnes métriques

Country or area	1990	1991	1992	1993	1994	1995	1996	1997	1998	1999	Pays ou zone
Guadeloupe	0.6	0.6	0.6	0.5	0.5	0.6	0.6	0.6	0.6	0.6	Guadeloupe
Guatemala	9.2	7.2	5.6	6.6	7.1	7.4	7.5	7.5	7.6	8.0	Guatemala
Haiti	3.7	3.9	4.2	4.5	4.4	3.8	4.4	4.4	4.8	4.8	Haïti
Honduras	7.8	7.8	7.8	7.8	7.8	3.9	4.4	4.5	7.9	3.6	Honduras
Jamaica	1.5	1.7	1.8	1.9	1.6	1.6	1.5	1.4	1.4	1.4	Jamaïque
Martinique	0.3	0.3	0.3	0.2	0.2	0.2	0.3	0.3	0.3	0.3	Martinique
Mexico	181.0	155.0	160.0	161.0	165.0	170.0	160.0	161.0	170.0	170.0	Mexique
Montserrat	0.1	0.1	0.1	0.1	0.1	0.1	0.1	0.1	0.1	0.1	Montserrat
Nicaragua	8.9	7.0	7.4	8.1	7.9	7.6	7.8	8.2	7.1	7.1	Nicaragua
Panama	7.1	6.8	6.4	6.7	6.5	6.6	7.1	7.7	8.1	7.7	Panama
Puerto Rico	2.4	2.2	2.1	1.9	1.7	1.6	1.4	1.6	1.6	1.6	Pórto Rico
St. Lucia	0.1	0.1	0.1	0.1	0.1	0.1	0.1	0.1	0.1	0.1	St-Lucie
Trinidad and Tobago	0.2	0.2	0.2	0.2	0.2	0.2	0.2	0.2	0.1	0.1	Trinité-et-Tobago
United States	949.0	955.4	962.2	959.0	1013.6	1048.0	1064.7	1063.3	1069.6	1099.1	Etats-Unis
United States Virgin Is.	0.1	0.1	0.1	0.1	0.1	0.1	0.1	0.1	0.1	0.1	Iles Vierges américaines
America, South	**1118**	**1148**	**1110**	**1137**	**1140**	**1159**	**1310**	**1339**	**1302**	**1360**	**Amérique du Sud**
Argentina	402.7	414.6	393.3	399.5	396.0	385.7	387.5	383.8	338.2	364.2	Argentine
Bolivia	15.4	15.7	16.2	15.9	16.2	16.4	17.8	17.2	17.7	18.2	Bolivie
Brazil	411.5	448.0	442.0	454.5	448.0	475.0	605.0	622.0	637.0	667.0	Brésil
Chile	36.4	33.9	28.6	32.1	34.7	38.0	38.7	39.4	37.8	36.3	Chili
Colombia	87.4	84.0	70.1	71.7	77.1	81.0	84.3	81.3	80.8	85.5	Colombie
Ecuador	22.3	21.9	22.7	25.0	25.5	29.0	30.6	31.1	31.6	32.8	Equateur
French Guiana	0.1	0.1	0.1	0.0	0.0	0.0	0.0	0.0	0.0	0.0	Guyane française
Guyana	0.4	0.5	0.7	0.6	0.7	0.6	0.6	0.5	0.5	0.5	Guyana
Paraguay	29.4	34.0	36.4	35.0	35.0	35.3	35.0	35.0	35.8	38.4	Paraguay
Peru	17.1	15.7	14.1	13.3	12.1	12.5	12.6	14.1	14.8	14.9	Pérou
Suriname	0.3	0.4	0.4	0.3	0.3	0.3	0.3	0.3	0.3	0.3	Suriname
Uruguay	49.3	39.1	41.4	42.7	50.0	46.7	57.0	65.4	60.4	58.0	Uruguay
Venezuela	45.5	40.2	43.7	46.6	44.3	38.1	40.4	49.4	47.4	44.0	Venezuela
Asia	**1691**	**1890**	**1968**	**2145**	**2403**	**2571**	**2555**	**2848**	**2939**	**2998**	**Asie**
Afghanistan	9.6	9.6	9.6	10.8	12.6	14.5	15.8	17.4	19.0	20.8	Afghanistan
Armenia	..	...	4.6	4.3	3.9	4.1	4.4	4.7	4.7	4.3	Arménie
Azerbaijan	..	...	7.9	7.2	7.2	7.1	7.5	8.2	8.4	8.7	Azerbaïdjan
Bahrain	0.1	0.1	0.1	0.1	0.1	0.1	0.1	0.1	0.2	0.1	Bahreïn
Bangladesh	31.1	31.1	31.4	31.7	32.1	32.3	31.7	32.3	31.5	31.8	Bangladesh
Bhutan	1.1	1.2	1.2	1.2	1.2	1.2	1.2	1.2	1.2	1.2	Bhoutan
Brunei Darussalam	0.3	0.3	0.3	0.2	0.3	0.2	0.3	0.3	0.3	0.8	Brunéi Darussalam
Cambodia	9.2	9.8	10.7	11.2	11.5	12.5	12.7	12.9	13.1	13.2	Cambodge
China [1]	285.0	339.9	396.2	511.9	722.2	887.4	854.6	1107.1	1210.2	1269.6	Chine [1]
Cyprus	0.6	0.6	0.6	0.6	0.6	0.7	0.7	0.8	0.7	0.7	Chypre
Georgia	..	...	4.3	4.3	4.7	5.7	5.8	6.0	4.6	4.5	Géorgie
India	857.4	851.2	871.9	900.9	917.4	930.8	944.3	953.0	942.0	954.0	Inde
Indonesia	42.6	43.5	48.0	55.8	54.3	50.9	56.7	57.2	55.7	57.1	Indonésie
Iran(Islamic Rep. of)	37.5	37.1	37.0	36.9	38.4	38.2	41.2	44.4	46.9	44.0	Iran(Rép. islamique)
Iraq	6.1	3.6	5.0	6.1	5.6	4.7	4.1	5.1	5.3	5.3	Iraq
Israel	3.8	4.0	3.9	3.7	4.3	4.3	4.6	4.9	4.6	4.7	Israël
Japan	43.0	45.0	38.0	39.0	39.0	38.0	36.0	34.0	33.0	34.0	Japon
Jordan	0.6	0.6	0.5	0.6	0.9	0.9	0.8	0.8	0.7	0.9	Jordanie
Kazakhstan	..	...	61.4	66.2	75.9	65.4	57.7	50.4	44.0	37.8	Kazakhstan
Korea,Dem.Ppl's.Rep.	4.8	4.2	4.2	4.3	4.4	4.3	3.0	2.6	2.7	2.8	Corée,Rép.pop.dém.de
Korea, Republic of	18.3	19.1	29.6	34.4	34.2	36.7	40.8	56.3	61.6	50.4	Corée, République de
Kuwait	0.2	0.0	0.2	0.1	0.2	0.2	0.2	0.4	0.3	0.2	Koweït
Kyrgyzstan	..	...	11.5	10.5	9.3	9.3	9.9	10.8	12.2	9.3	Kirghizistan
Lao People's Dem. Rep.	2.3	2.6	2.8	3.0	3.0	3.7	3.9	4.0	4.2	4.3	Rép. dém. pop. lao
Lebanon	1.4	1.9	2.2	2.2	2.0	1.6	1.4	2.7	3.0	3.3	Liban
Malaysia	2.3	2.7	2.7	2.9	3.0	3.2	3.4	3.5	3.4	3.7	Malaisie
Mongolia	14.7	19.2	17.1	13.4	12.9	14.7	19.0	19.5	21.2	21.8	Mongolie
Myanmar	22.9	23.0	23.2	23.3	23.5	23.7	24.3	24.7	25.2	25.3	Myanmar
Nepal	31.2	30.7	30.8	33.1	33.6	33.8	33.9	36.7	36.7	37.5	Népal
Oman	0.3	0.3	0.3	0.3	0.3	0.3	0.3	0.3	0.3	0.3	Oman
Pakistan	100.4	104.2	110.2	114.8	121.2	122.8	121.9	124.9	127.8	130.4	Pakistan
Philippines	15.0	14.6	15.2	16.0	16.9	17.9	19.4	21.3	22.2	23.4	Philippines

For general note and footnotes, see end of table.

Voir la fin du tableau pour la remarque générale et les notes.

Hides, cattle and horse, undressed (Total production) (continued)
Peaux de bovins et d'équidés, non préparées (Production totale) (suite)

ISIC-BASED CODE - CODE BASE CITI
3111-34

Unit : Thousand metric tons

Unité : Milliers de tonnes métriques

Country or area	1990	1991	1992	1993	1994	1995	1996	1997	1998	1999	Pays ou zone
Qatar	0.0	0.0	0.0	0.0	0.0	0.0	0.0	0.1	0.1	0.1	Qatar
Saudi Arabia	4.0	3.9	4.0	4.2	4.3	3.8	2.6	2.3	2.7	2.7	Arabie saoudite
Sri Lanka	4.7	4.9	5.4	5.0	5.2	5.4	4.9	5.0	4.9	4.8	Sri Lanka
Syrian Arab Republic	5.0	5.1	4.4	4.4	4.7	5.2	6.2	6.5	6.7	7.3	Rép. arabe syrienne
Tajikistan	..	...	6.8	3.6	3.9	3.3	3.7	2.8	1.3	1.3	Tadjikistan
Thailand	51.0	57.6	53.2	56.7	60.6	58.9	56.5	50.7	47.7	46.7	Thaïlande
Turkey	53.4	41.5	36.2	36.5	39.4	31.7	31.3	41.2	37.9	36.2	Turquie
Turkmenistan	..	...	4.9	5.3	5.4	5.4	5.5	5.8	6.5	6.7	Turkménistan
United Arab Emirates	0.4	0.4	0.5	0.5	0.6	0.7	0.8	1.0	1.1	1.2	Emirats arabes unis
Uzbekistan	..	...	30.4	38.0	41.0	43.7	40.3	42.8	44.1	44.4	Ouzbékistan
Viet Nam	30.6	30.8	32.8	32.3	33.4	34.2	33.2	33.1	30.8	31.9	Viet Nam
Yemen		6.9	7.0	7.2	7.4	7.6	7.8	8.1	8.5	8.8	Yémen
Europe	**974**	**1860**	**1861**	**1777**	**1702**	**1678**	**1575**	**1536**	**1427**	**1379**	**Europe**
Albania	4.0	4.2	4.6	5.1	5.7	6.2	6.9	6.6	6.7	7.0	Albanie
Austria	23.8	24.0	24.0	24.0	24.0	25.0	25.0	25.0	22.0	22.0	Autriche
Belarus	..	...	52.7	48.1	41.7	34.3	30.4	28.3	29.9	29.4	Bélarus
Belgium-Luxembourg	29.3	34.6	32.7	34.0	32.4	32.5	32.9	31.0	27.6	25.6	Belgique-Luxembourg
Bosnia and Herzegovina	..	..	5.4	5.3	4.3	3.0	2.5	1.9	2.4	2.4	Bosnie-Herzégovine
Bulgaria	18.4	16.5	20.4	18.9	14.4	10.2	12.7	9.2	9.0	8.5	Bulgarie
Croatia	..	...	7.3	6.7	6.3	5.1	5.1	5.3	2.2	1.9	Croatie
Denmark	19.7	20.9	25.7	24.0	23.2	22.4	22.0	21.7	19.9	19.2	Danemark
Czechoslovakia(former)	54.4	45.5	..	..	..	..	..	..	..	..	Tchécoslovaquie(anc.)
Czech Republic	..	..	...	32.0	25.9	26.0	25.1	23.6	21.6	21.5	République tchèque
Estonia			5.3	5.6	3.7	3.5	3.1	2.9	2.9	3.0	Estonie
Finland	12.5	12.6	12.2	11.6	11.0	11.0	11.0	11.0	10.0	10.5	Finlande
France	165.0	175.0	171.0	162.0	154.0	159.0	164.0	163.0	154.0	151.0	France
Germany	..	245.8	197.6	197.0	180.0	176.0	176.0	176.0	160.7	160.5	Allemagne
Greece	14.9	15.4	15.4	14.4	13.8	13.2	13.2	12.9	12.9	12.7	Grèce
Hungary	12.2	11.4	9.6	6.5	4.9	4.2	4.0	3.6	3.4	3.6	Hongrie
Iceland	0.4	0.4	0.5	0.4	0.4	0.4	0.4	0.4	0.4	0.4	Islande
Ireland	63.2	68.3	67.8	63.0	53.4	57.6	64.0	68.9	68.0	73.7	Irlande
Italy	148.1	150.3	154.4	151.1	148.6	150.1	150.2	148.2	142.2	148.2	Italie
Latvia	..	...	11.6	13.3	7.3	4.1	3.4	3.0	3.4	2.8	Lettonie
Lithuania	..	...	26.0	18.3	13.4	11.7	11.3	11.8	9.6	9.2	Lituanie
Malta	0.3	0.3	0.3	0.3	0.3	0.3	0.3	0.3	0.3	0.3	Malte
Netherlands	47.3	54.1	55.0	52.7	52.1	50.4	50.9	53.0	53.0	53.0	Pays-Bas
Norway	5.4	5.2	5.2	5.4	5.4	5.2	5.2	5.3	5.3	5.3	Norvège
Poland	74.0	70.0	55.0	49.0	42.0	40.0	43.0	45.0	45.0	43.0	Pologne
Portugal	13.2	14.2	13.9	13.0	10.0	10.4	10.2	12.1	10.7	10.8	Portugal
Republic of Moldova	..	...	6.8	6.8	6.9	6.6	5.6	4.1	3.2	3.1	Rép. de Moldova
Romania	47.5	50.6	37.8	35.1	34.6	32.7	28.2	29.0	28.8	28.6	Roumanie
Russian Federation	..	...	382.6	373.9	375.6	375.6	324.9	294.2	275.0	229.3	Fédération de Russie
Slovakia	..	..	...	12.7	8.4	8.4	8.7	9.6	7.9	5.2	Slovaquie
Slovenia	..	...	4.7	7.1	6.3	6.1	6.5	6.8	5.9	5.7	Slovénie
Spain	44.5	44.1	46.4	42.5	40.1	42.1	46.1	45.5	47.8	51.0	Espagne
Sweden	11.7	10.9	10.3	10.6	10.6	10.5	10.5	11.5	10.5	11.3	Suède
Switzerland	21.0	23.0	21.0	19.0	18.0	19.0	20.0	20.0	20.0	19.0	Suisse
Ukraine	..	...	207.9	184.5	198.6	182.0	158.6	152.0	122.0	120.5	Ukraine
United Kingdom	98.9	101.0	105.9	97.0	102.0	106.7	67.1	67.0	67.0	67.0	Royaume-Uni
Yugoslavia	..	...	21.9	24.4	21.2	24.5	24.7	24.4	14.5	11.5	Yougoslavie
T.F.Yug.Rep. Macedonia	..	...	1.5	1.7	1.6	1.8	1.4	1.5	1.3	1.3	L'ex-RY Macédoine
Yugoslavia, SFR	44.1	..	..	..	..	..	..	..	..	..	Yougoslavie, RSF
USSR (former)	818.9	..	..	..	..	..	..	..	..	..	URSS (anc.)
Oceania	**260**	**272**	**273**	**273**	**268**	**273**	**261**	**269**	**288**	**284**	**Océanie**
Australia	201.0	211.0	215.0	212.0	207.0	207.0	198.0	211.0	230.0	230.0	Australie
Fiji	1.6	1.5	1.5	1.3	1.3	1.3	1.3	1.3	1.4	1.4	Fidji
New Caledonia	0.3	0.4	0.4	0.5	0.5	0.4	0.5	0.5	0.5	0.5	Nouvelle-Calédonie
New Zealand	56.0	58.0	55.0	58.0	58.0	63.0	60.0	55.0	55.0	51.0	Nouvelle-Zélande
Papua New Guinea	0.4	0.4	0.3	0.3	0.4	0.3	0.3	0.3	0.3	0.3	Papouasie-Nvl-Guinée
Samoa	0.2	0.2	0.2	0.2	0.2	0.2	0.2	0.2	0.2	0.2	Samoa
Solomon Islands	0.1	0.1	0.1	0.1	0.1	0.1	0.1	0.1	0.1	0.1	Iles Salomon

For general note and footnotes, see end of table.

Voir la fin du tableau pour la remarque générale et les notes.

Hides, cattle and horse, undressed (Total production) (continued)
Peaux de bovins et d'équidés, non préparées (Production totale) (suite)

ISIC-BASED CODE - CODE BASE CITI

3111-34

Unit : Thousand metric tons — Unité : Milliers de tonnes métriques

Country or area	1990	1991	1992	1993	1994	1995	1996	1997	1998	1999	Pays ou zone
Vanuatu	0.5	0.5	0.5	0.6	0.6	0.6	0.6	0.6	0.6	0.6	Vanuatu
Total	6719	7013	7085	7208	7422	7638	7682	7989	7997	8101	Total

General Note.
Raw hides of bovines and equines, from which the hair has not been removed, in terms of fresh weight. Includes non-industrial production. (SITC, Rev.3: 21110-1).
Source: Food and Agriculture Organization of the United Nations (FAO), Rome.

Remarque générale.
Peaux brutes, non épilées, de bovins et d'équidés (poids des cuirs verts). Y compris production non-industrielle. (CTCI, Rev.3: 21110-1).
Source: Organisation des Nations Unies pour l'alimentation et l'agriculture (FAO), Rome.

[1] Including Hong-Kong, Macao and Taiwan.

[1] Y compris Hong-Kong, Macao et Taïwan.

Hides, cattle and horse, undressed (Industrial production)
Peaux de bovins et d'équidés, non préparées (Production industrielle)

ISIC-BASED CODE - CODE BASE CITI

3111-341

Unit : Thousand metric tons

Unité : Milliers de tonnes métriques

Country or area	1990	1991	1992	1993	1994	1995	1996	1997	1998	1999	Pays ou zone
America, North	**3**	**2**	**3**	**3**	**3**	**3**	**3**	**3**	**3**	**4**	**Amérique du Nord**
Mexico	3	2	3	3	3	...	...	...	...	...	Mexique
America, South	**3**	**4**	**2**	**4**	**6**	**5**	**6**	**8**	**7**	**8**	**Amérique du Sud**
Colombia	...	...	2	4	6	5	...	8	7	...	Colombie
Asia	**9**	**9**	**8**	**6**	**10**	**9**	**8**	**7**	**9**	**8**	**Asie**
Turkey	9	9	8	6	10	9	8	7	9	8	Turquie
Europe	**459**	**665**	**603**	**521**	**593**	**550**	**637**	**544**	**572**	**516**	**Europe**
Bulgaria	32	20	16	21	6	3	3	2	0	1	Bulgarie
Croatia	..	[1]6	[1]7	4	3	3	3	3	2	...	Croatie
Denmark[2]	...	...	...	...	...	13	18	16	9	15	Danemark[2]
Czechoslovakia(former)	53	45	..	..	..	..	..	..	..	..	Tchécoslovaquie(anc.)
Czech Republic	..	..	13	14	...	...	...	7	9	9	République tchèque
Finland	9	10	10	11	10	9	10	10	9	10	Finlande
France	108	110	105	91	95	105	119	...	...	...	France
Germany	..	...	...	...	...	25	35	42	...	...	Allemagne
Hungary	12	11	10	7	5	4	5	4	3	3	Hongrie
Ireland	...	...	...	...	...	40	104	39	74	33	Irlande
Latvia	..	...	...	...	...	...	...	...	...	1	Lettonie
Lithuania	..	...	...	...	...	2	3	4	4	4	Lituanie
Netherlands[2][3]	...	...	...	19	28	24	34	40	...	...	Pays-Bas[2][3]
Norway	...	...	...	...	...	...	...	10	9	7	Norvège
Portugal	...	...	7	5	2	2	7	20	20	15	Portugal
Romania[4]	29	25	16	12	6	5	4	2	2	2	Roumanie[4]
Slovakia	..	..	10	7	3	3	3	2	2	2	Slovaquie
Slovenia	..	...	3	3	3	3	2	2	2	2	Slovénie
Spain	...	...	...	26	46	68	78	89	109	100	Espagne
Sweden[1]	14	13	13	13	13	13	13	15	13	10	Suède[1]
United Kingdom	...	...	...	35	62	47	50	...	...	...	Royaume-Uni
Yugoslavia	..	191	154	116	168	161	126	80	70	62	Yougoslavie
Yugoslavia, SFR	20	..	..	..	..	..	..	..	..	..	Yougoslavie, RSF
Total	**474**	**680**	**616**	**534**	**612**	**567**	**654**	**562**	**591**	**536**	**Total**

General Note.

Raw hides of bovines and equines, from which the hair has not been removed, in terms of fresh weight. Data refer to industrial production only. (SITC, Rev.3: 21110-1).

Remarque générale.

Peaux brutes, non épilées, de bovins et d'équidés (poids des cuirs verts). Les données se rapportent à la production industrielle seulement. (CTCI, Rev.3: 21110-1).

[1] Including calf hides.
[2] Sales.
[3] Production by establishments employing 20 or more persons.
[4] Including by-products.

[1] Y compris les peaux de veau.
[2] Ventes.
[3] Production des établissements occupant 20 personnes ou plus.
[4] Y compris les sous-produits.

Skins, calf, goat and sheep, undressed (Total production)
Peaux de veaux, de caprins et d'ovins, non préparées (Production totale)

ISIC-BASED CODE - CODE BASE CITI

3111-37

Unit : Thousand metric tons   Unité : Milliers de tonnes métriques

Country or area	1990	1991	1992	1993	1994	1995	1996	1997	1998	1999	Pays ou zone
Africa	**293**	**301**	**313**	**314**	**319**	**321**	**336**	**337**	**351**	**350**	**Afrique**
Algeria	25.6	26.4	28.5	29.2	27.9	26.7	27.1	25.8	24.0	26.5	Algérie
Angola	0.6	0.6	0.6	0.6	0.5	0.5	0.6	0.6	0.7	0.8	Angola
Benin	1.0	1.0	1.1	1.1	1.2	1.2	1.1	1.1	1.2	1.1	Bénin
Botswana	1.2	1.4	1.4	1.1	1.0	1.5	1.3	1.4	1.2	1.2	Botswana
Burkina Faso	7.4	7.6	7.8	7.8	7.8	8.0	8.4	8.8	8.9	9.1	Burkina Faso
Burundi	1.2	1.3	1.4	1.4	1.4	1.3	1.1	0.9	0.8	1.1	Burundi
Cameroon	3.7	3.8	3.8	4.1	4.1	4.2	4.2	4.2	4.2	4.3	Cameroun
Cape Verde	0.1	0.1	0.1	0.1	0.1	0.1	0.1	0.1	0.1	0.1	Cap-Vert
Central African Rep.	0.6	0.8	0.8	0.8	0.9	1.0	1.0	1.1	1.1	1.1	Rép. centrafricaine
Chad	3.4	3.5	3.6	3.7	3.8	3.9	4.3	4.3	4.5	4.7	Tchad
Comoros	0.1	0.1	0.1	0.1	0.1	0.1	0.1	0.1	0.1	0.1	Comores
Congo	0.2	0.2	0.2	0.2	0.2	0.2	0.2	0.2	0.2	0.2	Congo
Côte d'Ivoire	2.1	2.1	2.1	2.3	2.3	2.4	2.4	2.5	2.5	2.6	Côte d'Ivoire
Dem. Rep. of Congo	3.8	3.9	4.1	4.2	4.4	4.4	4.4	4.5	4.6	4.3	Rép. dém. du Congo
Djibouti	0.8	0.9	0.9	0.9	0.9	0.9	0.9	0.9	0.9	0.9	Djibouti
Egypt	10.6	9.7	10.1	10.6	11.1	11.7	11.7	12.0	12.2	14.4	Egypte
Eritrea	...	...	...	1.0	1.1	1.1	1.1	1.1	1.2	1.3	Erythrée
Ethiopia,incl.Eritrea	28.8	28.9	29.3	...	...	...	...	...	...	...	Ethiopie,incl.Erythrée
Ethiopia	...	...	...	27.3	27.7	27.8	27.8	27.9	28.0	28.1	Ethiopie
Gabon	0.2	0.2	0.2	0.2	0.2	0.2	0.2	0.2	0.2	0.2	Gabon
Gambia	0.1	0.1	0.1	0.1	0.1	0.1	0.1	0.2	0.2	0.2	Gambie
Ghana	1.9	2.0	1.9	1.9	2.0	2.0	2.1	2.2	2.3	2.3	Ghana
Guinea	0.4	0.4	0.4	0.4	0.4	0.5	0.6	0.6	0.6	0.6	Guinée
Guinea-Bissau	0.3	0.3	0.3	0.4	0.4	0.4	0.4	0.4	0.4	0.4	Guinée-Bissau
Kenya	14.9	15.5	15.7	15.7	15.6	15.5	15.5	15.5	16.1	15.9	Kenya
Lesotho	1.4	1.4	1.3	1.4	1.5	1.3	1.1	1.2	0.9	0.9	Lesotho
Liberia	0.3	0.3	0.3	0.3	0.3	0.3	0.3	0.3	0.3	0.3	Libéria
Libyan Arab Jamah.	6.4	6.5	6.5	7.9	6.8	8.0	10.0	9.3	16.1	7.3	Jamah. arabe libyenne
Madagascar	1.3	1.3	1.4	1.4	1.4	1.5	1.4	1.4	1.4	1.4	Madagascar
Malawi	0.6	0.6	0.7	0.6	0.7	0.7	0.8	0.9	0.8	0.9	Malawi
Mali	8.1	8.6	8.9	7.7	8.0	8.6	8.9	10.0	10.7	10.1	Mali
Mauritania	2.6	2.7	2.6	2.6	2.7	2.7	3.2	3.2	3.1	2.9	Mauritanie
Mauritius	0.1	0.1	0.1	0.1	0.1	0.1	0.1	0.1	0.1	0.1	Maurice
Morocco	14.3	13.5	14.8	13.0	14.4	15.1	14.9	15.9	15.4	15.7	Maroc
Mozambique	0.6	0.6	0.6	0.6	0.6	0.6	0.6	0.6	0.6	0.6	Mozambique
Namibia	2.1	2.4	2.2	2.3	2.2	1.8	1.7	2.0	1.5	1.6	Namibie
Niger	4.7	4.8	5.0	5.0	5.1	5.3	5.5	5.5	5.7	5.8	Niger
Nigeria	27.0	28.0	28.6	29.2	29.6	29.6	35.9	39.0	39.9	40.9	Nigéria
Rwanda	1.1	1.1	1.1	1.1	1.1	0.8	0.9	0.9	1.1	1.1	Rwanda
Senegal	4.6	5.1	5.6	5.8	6.0	6.1	6.0	6.1	6.1	6.1	Sénégal
Sierra Leone	0.3	0.3	0.3	0.3	0.3	0.3	0.3	0.3	0.3	0.4	Sierra Leone
Somalia	14.9	12.4	8.9	9.2	9.4	9.9	10.3	10.6	12.6	12.6	Somalie
South Africa	26.3	27.5	32.2	27.3	25.8	19.0	22.0	16.4	17.6	18.6	Afrique du Sud
Sudan	17.2	21.8	25.9	30.4	34.7	40.2	41.1	43.4	45.7	46.1	Soudan
Swaziland	0.3	0.3	0.3	0.3	0.4	0.4	0.4	0.4	0.4	0.4	Swaziland
Togo	0.9	1.0	1.0	1.0	1.0	0.9	0.7	0.5	0.6	0.6	Togo
Tunisia	7.8	8.0	7.8	7.9	8.2	8.8	8.9	8.8	9.6	9.7	Tunisie
Uganda	4.0	4.0	4.2	4.5	4.6	4.7	4.7	4.8	4.8	4.8	Ouganda
United Rep.Tanzania	6.9	7.1	7.3	7.6	7.8	7.9	7.9	8.0	8.1	8.1	Rép. Unie de Tanzanie
Zambia	0.4	0.4	0.4	0.4	0.5	0.5	0.5	0.5	0.7	0.8	Zambie
Zimbabwe	1.8	1.8	1.9	1.8	1.8	1.9	2.0	2.0	2.1	2.1	Zimbabwe
America, North	**34**	**34**	**34**	**34**	**32**	**31**	**29**	**28**	**28**	**28**	**Amérique du Nord**
Canada	1.7	1.8	2.0	1.8	1.8	1.8	1.8	1.7	1.6	1.8	Canada
Cuba	0.5	0.5	0.4	0.4	0.4	0.4	0.4	0.4	0.4	0.4	Cuba
Dominican Republic	0.5	0.5	0.5	0.5	0.5	0.5	0.5	0.5	0.3	0.2	Rép. dominicaine
Guatemala	0.4	0.4	0.4	0.4	0.5	0.5	0.5	0.5	0.5	0.5	Guatemala
Haiti	0.5	0.5	0.5	0.5	0.5	0.5	0.6	0.7	0.8	0.8	Haïti
Jamaica	0.3	0.3	0.3	0.3	0.3	0.3	0.3	0.3	0.3	0.3	Jamaïque
Martinique	0.1	0.1	0.1	0.1	0.1	0.0	0.0	0.0	0.0	0.0	Martinique
Mexico	12.2	12.5	12.8	13.8	13.3	12.5	12.0	12.0	12.0	12.1	Mexique
Puerto Rico	0.1	0.1	0.1	0.1	0.1	0.1	0.1	0.1	0.1	0.1	Porto Rico
Trinidad and Tobago	0.1	0.1	0.1	0.1	0.1	0.1	0.1	0.1	0.1	0.1	Trinité-et-Tobago

For general note and footnotes, see end of table.   Voir la fin du tableau pour la remarque générale et les notes.

Skins, calf, goat and sheep, undressed (Total production) (continued)
Peaux de veaux, de caprins et d'ovins, non préparées (Production totale) (suite)

ISIC-BASED CODE - CODE BASE CITI

3111-37

Unit : Thousand metric tons

Unité : Milliers de tonnes métriques

Country or area	1990	1991	1992	1993	1994	1995	1996	1997	1998	1999	Pays ou zone
United States	17.3	17.4	16.8	15.9	15.0	13.9	12.7	11.9	11.6	11.3	Etats-Unis
America, South	**96**	**91**	**92**	**94**	**93**	**86**	**88**	**89**	**89**	**88**	**Amérique du Sud**
Argentina	28.4	26.7	27.2	27.7	27.7	24.5	24.6	25.4	25.1	26.0	Argentine
Bolivia	6.7	5.8	5.0	5.7	5.8	6.2	6.3	6.3	6.6	6.6	Bolivie
Brazil	19.6	19.9	20.2	20.8	21.0	22.0	19.7	20.0	20.1	20.3	Brésil
Chile	4.4	3.9	3.7	4.0	3.8	3.2	2.9	3.3	3.7	4.1	Chili
Colombia	2.1	2.0	2.1	2.3	2.3	2.3	2.7	2.8	2.6	2.8	Colombie
Ecuador	0.7	0.7	0.7	0.9	0.9	1.0	1.0	1.1	0.9	1.3	Equateur
Falkland Is. (Malvinas)	0.2	0.2	0.2	0.2	0.2	0.2	0.1	0.1	0.1	0.1	Iles Falkland (Malvinas)
Guyana	0.2	0.2	0.2	0.2	0.2	0.2	0.2	0.2	0.2	0.2	Guyana
Paraguay	0.6	0.6	0.6	0.6	0.6	0.5	0.5	0.5	0.6	0.6	Paraguay
Peru	10.7	8.5	8.8	8.7	8.2	8.5	8.9	9.2	9.3	9.5	Pérou
Uruguay	21.3	21.9	22.5	21.7	21.9	17.0	20.6	19.8	18.8	16.5	Uruguay
Venezuela	0.7	0.7	0.8	0.9	0.8	0.8	0.7	0.7	0.7	0.6	Venezuela
Asia	**826**	**949**	**975**	**1026**	**1069**	**1135**	**1116**	**1155**	**1198**	**1251**	**Asie**
Afghanistan	21.1	21.4	20.9	20.3	20.6	20.7	23.0	25.5	28.3	30.8	Afghanistan
Armenia	..	...	1.0	1.0	0.9	0.8	0.7	0.6	0.6	0.5	Arménie
Azerbaijan	..	...	3.1	3.0	2.6	2.7	3.0	3.0	3.7	3.8	Azerbaïdjan
Bahrain	1.0	1.1	1.1	1.1	1.4	1.3	1.3	1.3	1.1	1.1	Bahreïn
Bangladesh	23.9	25.4	27.3	29.5	31.9	34.5	37.8	39.2	38.1	38.5	Bangladesh
Bhutan	0.1	0.1	0.1	0.1	0.1	0.1	0.1	0.1	0.1	0.1	Bhoutan
China [1]	246.8	270.8	286.8	309.4	332.5	393.4	406.6	440.2	476.3	518.4	Chine [1]
Cyprus	2.1	1.7	1.8	1.9	1.8	1.9	1.8	1.8	2.3	2.4	Chypre
Georgia	..	...	1.1	1.2	1.3	1.4	1.6	1.1	1.3	1.2	Géorgie
India	149.2	161.8	162.7	166.3	168.3	171.2	174.1	176.8	178.1	179.6	Inde
Indonesia	20.7	21.7	22.8	25.6	22.9	21.7	22.7	24.6	18.8	19.2	Indonésie
Iran(Islamic Rep. of)	62.4	63.6	66.2	67.7	68.8	69.8	70.4	75.2	77.4	73.5	Iran(Rép. islamique)
Iraq	6.9	4.2	5.7	7.2	6.4	5.9	4.3	5.2	5.5	5.5	Iraq
Israel	1.0	1.0	1.0	1.0	1.0	1.0	1.0	1.0	1.0	1.0	Israël
Japan	0.1	0.1	0.1	0.1	0.1	0.1	0.1	0.1	0.1	0.1	Japon
Jordan	3.1	4.1	3.9	4.2	3.2	3.2	3.4	3.0	5.0	4.4	Jordanie
Kazakhstan	..	...	28.0	31.4	32.9	29.2	24.1	17.3	13.3	13.3	Kazakhstan
Korea,Dem.Ppl's.Rep.	0.9	1.0	0.9	0.9	1.0	0.7	0.7	0.8	1.1	1.4	Corée,Rép.pop.dém.de
Korea, Republic of	0.2	0.3	0.4	0.4	0.5	0.5	0.5	0.6	0.6	0.5	Corée, République de
Kuwait	6.0	3.0	6.0	8.9	17.2	13.5	13.8	13.7	13.5	13.4	Koweït
Kyrgyzstan	..	...	10.5	12.2	11.5	7.8	7.6	6.2	5.9	6.4	Kirghizistan
Lao People's Dem. Rep.	0.1	0.1	0.0	0.1	0.1	0.1	0.1	0.1	0.1	0.1	Rép. dém. pop. lao
Lebanon	1.6	1.8	2.0	2.4	2.5	2.2	2.1	2.2	2.4	2.4	Liban
Malaysia	0.2	0.2	0.2	0.2	0.2	0.1	0.1	0.1	0.1	0.2	Malaisie
Mongolia	38.0	43.9	37.3	33.4	32.0	32.6	36.3	31.6	34.1	34.7	Mongolie
Myanmar	0.9	0.9	1.0	1.0	1.0	1.1	1.1	1.2	1.2	1.2	Myanmar
Nepal	5.9	6.0	6.1	6.1	6.2	6.3	6.4	6.8	6.9	7.0	Népal
Oman	1.2	1.2	1.2	1.2	1.2	1.1	1.1	1.1	1.1	1.1	Oman
Pakistan	124.1	135.2	143.5	156.0	160.0	166.3	126.8	129.8	133.6	137.9	Pakistan
Philippines	5.4	5.7	5.9	6.5	6.7	7.0	7.0	7.1	6.7	6.9	Philippines
Qatar	1.6	1.9	1.6	1.6	1.7	1.9	1.0	1.1	1.1	1.1	Qatar
Saudi Arabia	14.3	13.6	14.5	14.7	15.4	15.2	15.2	14.7	14.7	15.8	Arabie saoudite
Singapore	0.1	0.1	0.1	0.1	0.1	0.0	0.0	0.0	0.0	0.0	Singapour
Sri Lanka	0.1	0.1	0.2	0.2	0.2	0.2	0.2	0.2	0.1	0.1	Sri Lanka
Syrian Arab Republic	20.1	21.6	19.7	16.4	21.0	22.9	25.2	25.7	26.8	30.4	Rép. arabe syrienne
Tajikistan	..	...	2.6	2.6	2.7	2.5	1.5	0.5	1.5	1.6	Tadjikistan
Thailand	0.2	0.2	0.2	0.2	0.2	0.2	0.1	0.1	0.1	0.1	Thaïlande
Turkey	62.6	62.2	61.9	61.6	63.2	63.4	62.4	64.7	64.0	62.4	Turquie
Turkmenistan	..	...	4.7	6.0	6.0	6.6	7.1	6.9	8.2	8.5	Turkménistan
United Arab Emirates	4.1	5.0	4.8	5.6	5.8	6.0	6.2	5.9	4.8	4.9	Emirats arabes unis
Uzbekistan	..	...	7.7	8.5	8.3	9.3	8.6	9.0	9.2	9.4	Ouzbékistan
Viet Nam	0.5	0.4	0.4	0.4	0.5	0.7	0.8	0.8	0.8	0.8	Viet Nam
Yemen	..	8.0	8.2	8.0	7.6	7.6	7.8	8.5	8.9	9.1	Yémen
Europe	**285**	**628**	**703**	**692**	**617**	**532**	**507**	**428**	**404**	**388**	**Europe**
Albania	3.1	3.3	3.9	4.1	5.5	6.2	4.9	4.7	4.8	4.8	Albanie
Austria	1.3	1.4	1.4	1.3	1.5	1.6	1.6	1.7	1.7	1.6	Autriche

For general note and footnotes, see end of table.

Voir la fin du tableau pour la remarque générale et les notes.

Skins, calf, goat and sheep, undressed (Total production) (continued)
Peaux de veaux, de caprins et d'ovins, non préparées (Production totale) (suite)

ISIC-BASED CODE - CODE BASE CITI

3111-37

Unit : Thousand metric tons   Unité : Milliers de tonnes métriques

Country or area	1990	1991	1992	1993	1994	1995	1996	1997	1998	1999	Pays ou zone
Belarus	..	...	228.0	230.4	208.0	156.0	160.0	120.0	100.0	95.7	Bélarus
Belgium-Luxembourg	2.0	2.3	1.6	1.2	1.5	1.5	1.4	1.3	1.3	1.4	Belgique-Luxembourg
Bosnia and Herzegovina	..	..	0.8	0.6	0.5	0.5	0.5	0.5	0.5	0.5	Bosnie-Herzégovine
Bulgaria	24.7	28.2	23.3	22.6	18.2	17.8	21.7	19.5	20.5	20.5	Bulgarie
Croatia	..	...	0.8	0.7	0.6	0.6	0.6	0.6	0.6	0.6	Croatie
Denmark	0.4	0.5	0.5	0.6	0.5	0.4	0.5	0.4	0.4	0.4	Danemark
Czechoslovakia(former)	0.8	0.6	..	..	..	..	..	..	..	..	Tchécoslovaquie(anc.)
Czech Republic	..	..	...	0.1	0.1	0.1	0.0	0.0	0.0	0.0	République tchèque
Estonia	..	...	0.2	0.2	0.1	0.1	0.1	0.1	0.1	0.0	Estonie
Finland	0.1	0.1	0.1	0.1	0.1	0.1	0.1	0.1	0.1	0.1	Finlande
France	22.1	19.4	17.0	16.2	16.4	16.4	16.4	17.2	16.6	16.0	France
Germany	..	10.8	10.2	9.9	9.8	9.4	9.8	9.9	9.9	9.9	Allemagne
Greece	30.7	30.7	30.7	28.9	28.9	28.3	28.9	28.9	28.5	27.0	Grèce
Hungary	0.1	0.4	0.5	0.4	0.3	0.5	0.4	0.5	0.7	0.7	Hongrie
Iceland	2.0	2.0	1.9	1.9	1.9	2.0	1.8	1.8	1.8	2.0	Islande
Ireland	19.0	20.2	21.0	21.6	20.3	19.3	19.6	16.9	16.5	17.2	Irlande
Italy	19.2	19.3	19.5	18.4	18.0	17.4	18.1	17.6	17.0	16.9	Italie
Latvia	..	...	111.7	104.2	64.3	35.2	25.4	14.5	11.1	9.4	Lettonie
Lithuania	..	...	0.2	0.2	0.2	0.2	0.2	0.1	0.1	0.1	Lituanie
Netherlands	1.4	1.7	1.6	1.7	1.5	1.4	1.6	1.5	1.5	1.5	Pays-Bas
Norway	7.4	7.4	7.7	7.6	8.0	8.1	8.3	7.9	7.0	7.4	Norvège
Poland	7.0	8.0	5.5	4.5	2.0	1.3	1.1	0.7	0.4	0.4	Pologne
Portugal	6.1	6.7	6.1	6.1	5.8	5.7	5.6	6.0	5.5	5.3	Portugal
Republic of Moldova	..	...	1.4	1.6	1.7	1.7	1.5	1.7	1.5	1.4	Rép. de Moldova
Romania	22.9	20.5	23.9	22.4	19.5	24.3	19.7	17.8	16.3	15.1	Roumanie
Russian Federation	..	...	44.3	48.5	42.9	39.0	28.6	24.3	21.4	16.4	Fédération de Russie
Slovakia	..	...	...	0.5	0.3	0.3	0.3	0.3	0.2	0.2	Slovaquie
Slovenia	..	...	0.0	0.0	0.0	0.0	0.0	0.1	0.1	0.2	Slovénie
Spain	23.5	23.2	23.8	23.3	23.0	23.0	22.5	22.8	23.2	22.3	Espagne
Sweden	2.5	2.5	3.2	2.5	2.4	2.1	2.2	2.1	2.1	2.1	Suède
Switzerland	0.7	0.9	0.9	1.0	0.7	0.9	1.1	1.1	1.1	1.3	Suisse
Ukraine	..	...	14.2	11.5	14.9	14.1	11.3	9.0	7.3	6.1	Ukraine
United Kingdom	84.0	87.9	88.5	89.5	89.0	89.0	83.6	69.9	77.8	77.8	Royaume-Uni
Yugoslavia	..	...	5.6	5.7	5.6	5.7	5.8	5.8	5.8	4.4	Yougoslavie
T.F.Yug.Rep. Macedonia	..	...	2.4	2.6	2.7	2.1	2.0	1.4	1.2	1.2	L'ex-RY Macédoine
Yugoslavia, SFR	4.1		..	..	..	..	..	..	..	..	Yougoslavie, RSF
Oceania	262	271	269	245	251	256	231	235	250	240	Océanie
Australia	152.0	159.8	159.6	151.7	151.2	150.4	132.4	132.7	143.2	139.5	Australie
Fiji	0.1	0.1	0.1	0.1	0.1	0.1	0.1	0.1	0.1	0.1	Fidji
New Zealand	110.3	111.0	109.4	93.4	99.3	105.3	98.2	102.3	106.3	100.3	Nouvelle-Zélande
Total	1796	2274	2386	2405	2381	2361	2306	2274	2320	2345	Total

General Note.
Raw skins of sheep and goats from which the hair has not been removed,
in terms of fresh weight. Includes non-industrial production.
(SITC, Rev.3:21110-2, 21120-0, 21140-0, 21160-0).
Source: Food and Agriculture Organization of the United Nations (FAO), Rome.

Remarque générale.
Peaux brutes, non épilées, d'ovins et de caprins (poids des cuirs verts).
Y compris production non-industrielle. (CTCI, Rev.3: 21110-2, 21120-0, 21140-0, 21160-0).
Source: Organisation des Nations Unies pour l'alimentation et l'agriculture (FAO), Rome.

[1] Including Hong-Kong, Macao and Taiwan.

[1] Y compris Hong-Kong, Macao et Taïwan.

Milk and cream, condensed (Total production)
Lait et crème, concentrés (Production totale)

ISIC-BASED CODE - CODE BASE CITI

3112-01

Unit : Thousand metric tons   Unité : Milliers de tonnes métriques

Country or area	1990	1991	1992	1993	1994	1995	1996	1997	1998	1999	Pays ou zone
Africa	**47**	**48**	**45**	**44**	**47**	**48**	**44**	**51**	**47**	**48**	**Afrique**
Kenya	0.1	0.1	0.1	0.2	0.2	0.2	0.2	0.2	0.2	0.2	Kenya
Madagascar	1.4	1.4	1.5	1.5	1.5	1.5	1.5	1.6	1.6	1.6	Madagascar
South Africa	37.9	39.3	37.8	37.5	40.0	41.8	36.9	43.8	40.3	41.3	Afrique du Sud
Zimbabwe	8.1	7.6	5.7	5.1	4.9	4.9	4.9	4.9	5.0	5.0	Zimbabwe
America, North	**1281**	**1297**	**1343**	**1315**	**1324**	**1232**	**1199**	**1256**	**1178**	**1206**	**Amérique du Nord**
Canada	69.2	98.1	94.4	87.2	84.2	86.6	94.7	107.1	95.3	79.7	Canada
Cuba	59.0	59.0	48.0	43.0	43.0	43.0	43.0	43.0	43.0	43.0	Cuba
Jamaica	26.0	19.4	18.8	21.9	16.8	17.1	17.3	16.6	18.1	16.4	Jamaïque
Mexico	132.0	133.1	133.0	132.6	132.8	136.8	136.8	136.8	136.8	136.8	Mexique
Panama	25.2	23.8	25.2	26.7	27.9	28.6	29.1	32.1	34.7	29.2	Panama
Trinidad and Tobago	0.1	0.8	0.7	0.6	1.3	1.3	1.3	1.3	0.3	0.2	Trinité-et-Tobago
United States	969.5	962.6	1022.9	1003.4	1017.6	918.9	877.1	919.4	850.3	900.6	Etats-Unis
America, South	**189**	**192**	**185**	**187**	**203**	**213**	**212**	**218**	**233**	**250**	**Amérique du Sud**
Argentina	9.6	9.5	9.6	9.6	9.6	9.7	9.7	9.8	10.5	10.2	Argentine
Brazil	36.0	36.0	36.0	30.0	30.0	20.0	20.0	25.0	25.0	25.0	Brésil
Chile	9.1	9.5	11.0	10.2	11.4	9.6	9.8	10.9	13.7	16.2	Chili
Colombia	6.0	6.0	6.0	6.0	6.0	6.1	5.6	5.6	5.6	5.6	Colombie
Peru	117.4	121.5	112.0	116.8	133.9	155.3	154.8	154.4	165.8	180.9	Pérou
Uruguay	...	...	...	5.5	...	0.1	0.6	0.0	1.4	0.7	Uruguay
Venezuela	7.0	6.0	7.8	9.2	10.4	12.2	11.2	12.6	10.6	11.4	Venezuela
Asia	**323**	**420**	**466**	**474**	**499**	**469**	**447**	**434**	**421**	**432**	**Asie**
China[1]	69.7	72.9	76.0	78.9	84.3	84.0	84.8	88.3	89.6	93.5	Chine[1]
Indonesia	8.1	8.5	8.8	9.0	9.9	10.1	10.3	9.9	8.9	9.6	Indonésie
Japan	62.3	65.9	63.3	57.8	56.5	58.9	52.8	45.7	43.7	43.1	Japon
Kazakhstan	..	...	62.7	73.0	56.3	39.5	29.5	27.8	46.3	46.8	Kazakhstan
Korea, Republic of	3.4	4.0	3.1	2.9	3.3	2.9	5.6	4.5	4.4	3.0	Corée, République de
Lebanon	1.9	2.5	2.6	2.7	2.9	3.0	3.2	2.8	4.0	4.0	Liban
Malaysia	157.6	169.8	192.1	203.3	234.5	222.2	212.6	196.7	176.1	184.4	Malaisie
Mongolia	..	...	...	...	...	0.3	0.4	0.4	0.4	0.4	Mongolie
Sri Lanka	3.9	4.4	4.0	4.2	4.2	4.4	3.9	4.1	4.2	4.2	Sri Lanka
Tajikistan	..	...	17.5	10.5	7.0	3.5	0.7	0.7	0.7	0.7	Tadjikistan
Thailand	16.4	14.9	18.5	18.4	21.9	27.6	32.7	43.1	32.6	32.4	Thaïlande
Uzbekistan	..	...	17.2	13.3	17.5	12.6	10.5	9.8	10.5	10.3	Ouzbékistan
Europe	**1032**	**2235**	**2439**	**2288**	**2103**	**2038**	**2050**	**2006**	**1913**	**1835**	**Europe**
Austria	17.9	18.0	18.1	19.5	18.5	18.1	44.2	15.6	16.5	16.0	Autriche
Belarus	..	...	7.6	11.4	11.4	13.3	36.1	38.0	33.2	37.4	Bélarus
Belgium-Luxembourg	27.9	23.5	22.0	21.6	40.7	50.0	57.4	63.4	76.0	64.3	Belgique-Luxembourg
Croatia	..	...	...	...	...	...	2.5	0.3	0.3	0.3	Croatie
Denmark	10.2	13.3	11.0	13.1	13.8	12.6	9.1	9.2	5.7	9.3	Danemark
Czechoslovakia(former)	147.8	116.7	..	..	..	..	..	..	..	..	Tchécoslovaquie(anc.)
Czech Republic	...	...	...	118.5	107.9	108.0	110.9	91.5	89.0	94.0	République tchèque
Estonia	..	...	73.7	61.8	61.6	51.4	39.8	31.8	29.4	25.2	Estonie
France	69.7	70.1	77.0	72.2	59.0	56.3	49.2	42.1	70.0	58.2	France
Germany	..	570.4	522.8	598.2	623.0	644.7	641.9	667.2	547.1	522.6	Allemagne
Hungary	4.7	15.0	26.4	9.6	4.3	3.9	8.1	6.9	8.7	8.7	Hongrie
Ireland	11.4	18.2	33.5	1.5	2.1	1.4	...	2.9	...	4.5	Irlande
Italy	12.8	21.3	30.7	39.9	45.5	45.1	50.1	50.1	70.7	76.1	Italie
Latvia	..	...	11.8	11.4	11.2	11.1	15.2	18.5	16.8	6.3	Lettonie
Lithuania	..	...	11.7	8.4	8.1	13.5	12.7	18.2	23.5	28.5	Lituanie
Netherlands	402.4	407.1	387.0	374.5	339.8	359.6	333.6	332.0	308.5	297.4	Pays-Bas
Norway	39.0	34.0	31.0	31.0	31.0	30.0	30.1	30.1	17.3	17.4	Norvège
Poland	14.1	12.4	12.7	13.0	13.4	14.8	15.1	15.4	15.4	15.4	Pologne
Portugal	5.9	6.6	6.6	8.0	7.6	8.1	7.8	8.4	9.3	9.2	Portugal
Republic of Moldova	...	...	63.7	61.5	29.4	12.1	11.4	11.4	11.4	11.4	Rép. de Moldova
Romania	...	...	0.8	0.4	0.4	0.4	0.4	0.4	0.4	0.4	Roumanie
Russian Federation	..	...	582.9	434.0	299.0	225.3	205.6	202.6	186.1	178.6	Fédération de Russie
Slovakia	..	..	...	4.6	3.6	3.7	3.7	3.7	6.6	6.3	Slovaquie
Slovenia	..	...	...	0.1	0.2	0.3	0.8	0.8	0.5	0.5	Slovénie
Spain	36.8	58.0	43.4	57.8	56.1	56.0	65.6	61.5	66.0	61.8	Espagne

For general note and footnotes, see end of table.   Voir la fin du tableau pour la remarque générale et les notes.

Milk and cream, condensed (Total production) (continued)
Lait et crème, concentrés (Production totale) (suite)

ISIC-BASED CODE - CODE BASE CITI

3112-01

Unit : Thousand metric tons

Unité : Milliers de tonnes métriques

Country or area	1990	1991	1992	1993	1994	1995	1996	1997	1998	1999	Pays ou zone
Sweden	11.0	9.1	10.9	10.6	11.5	10.8	9.6	11.0	11.0	11.0	Suède
Switzerland	3.3	3.3	2.8	0.6	0.6	0.5	0.3	0.5	0.5	0.5	Suisse
Ukraine	..	...	110.8	107.0	98.3	98.3	81.1	68.5	85.4	87.0	Ukraine
United Kingdom	217.0	233.9	219.0	197.0	204.1	188.0	199.0	204.0	198.0	186.6	Royaume-Uni
USSR (former)	619.5	..	..	..	..	..	..	..	..	..	URSS (anc.)
Oceania	88	97	91	106	108	100	95	89	90	112	Océanie
Australia	86.9	95.4	89.5	104.2	106.5	98.6	94.1	88.0	88.0	105.0	Australie
New Zealand	1.3	1.3	1.3	1.3	1.4	1.4	1.3	1.4	2.0	6.5	Nouvelle-Zélande
Total	3581	4288	4568	4415	4282	4101	4047	4054	3882	3883	Total

General Note.

Milk and cream (including buttermilk, skim milk and whey), evaporated or condensed (in liquid or semi-solid form). In terms of net weight. (SITC, Rev.3: 02223-0, 02224-0, 02232-1, 02241-1).
Source: Food and Agriculture Organization of the United Nations (FAO), Rome.

Remarque générale.

Lait et crème (y compris le babeurre, le lait écrémé et le petit lait), évaporés ou concentrés (à l'état liquide ou pâteux). Poids net. (CTCI, Rev.3: 02223-0, 02224-0, 02232-1, 02241-1).
Source: Organisation des Nations Unies pour l'alimentation et l'agriculture (FAO), Rome.

[1] Including Hong-Kong, Macao and Taiwan.

[1] Y compris Hong-Kong, Macao et Taïwan.

Milk and cream, condensed (Industrial production)
Lait et crème, concentrés (Production industrielle)

ISIC-BASED CODE - CODE BASE CITI
3112-011

Unit : Thousand metric tons

Unité : Milliers de tonnes métriques

Country or area	1990	1991	1992	1993	1994	1995	1996	1997	1998	1999	Pays ou zone
America, North	**988**	**973**	**958**	**1026**	**952**	**908**	**843**	**888**	**850**	**850**	**Amérique du Nord**
Mexico	...	...	...	24	30	31	29	33	37	39	Mexique
United States	...	...	...	1002	922	877	814	855	813	...	Etats-Unis
America, South	**6**	**11**	**21**	**12**	**12**	**16**	**12**	**6**	**8**	**9**	**Amérique du Sud**
Colombia	5	...	19	10	10	15	...	4	5	...	Colombie
Peru	2	1	2	2	2	2	2	2	3	2	Pérou
Asia	**414**	**650**	**525**	**488**	**496**	**777**	**701**	**718**	**695**	**783**	**Asie**
Armenia	..	128	[1]26	[1]10	[1]10	251	253	...	264	269	Arménie
Indonesia	103	95	102	110	156	229	...	235	104	...	Indonésie
Kyrgyzstan	..	1	1	1	0	0	0	1	0	0	Kirghizistan
Tajikistan	..	139	77	48	36	19	6	2	1	2	Tadjikistan
Thailand	...	...	...	...	...	...	164	168	...	...	Thaïlande
Turkey	145	121	153	153	128	112	136	161	160	165	Turquie
Europe	**1430**	**2004**	**1794**	**2080**	**1918**	**2634**	**2430**	**2845**	**3275**	**3227**	**Europe**
Austria	...	...	...	...	...	...	21	17	16	16	Autriche
Belgium	28	23	22	12	...	...	...	...	...	...	Belgique
Croatia	..	16	10	9	10	13	14	6	8	...	Croatie
Estonia	..	296	124	131	133	163	127	176	169	123	Estonie
Finland	7	6	7	5	...	...	...	...	...	...	Finlande
France	70	70	77	64	51	47	42	39	37	...	France
Germany	..	474	503	514	528	*1242	1222	1547	...	...	Allemagne
Germany(Fed.Rep.)	440	..	..	..	..	..	..	..	...	..	Allemagne(Rép.féd.)
German D.R.(former)	158	..	..	..	..	..	..	..	..	..	R.D.A. (anc.)
Greece	...	...	...	...	33	...	...	...	...	...	Grèce
Hungary	7	5	5	5	4	4	7	4	4	5	Hongrie
Latvia	..	...	...	7	8	7	12	15	17	6	Lettonie
Lithuania	..	31	18	9	5	13	11	15	12	9	Lituanie
Netherlands[2][3]	413	445	428	697	568	525	487	455	571	456	Pays-Bas[2][3]
Poland	14	12	13	13	13	15	15	19	21	22	Pologne
Russian Federation	..	133	134	171	154	148	128	150	185	158	Fédération de Russie
Slovenia	..	0	0	0	...	0	1	0	1	0	Slovénie
Sweden	10	10	20	20	22	21	17	17	8	20	Suède
Switzerland	109	114	107	117	98	117	...	...	...	...	Suisse
Ukraine[4]	..	140	98	92	77	71	61	53	69	57	Ukraine[4]
United Kingdom	...	...	...	...	...	...	78	144	147	...	Royaume-Uni
Yugoslavia	..	0	14	...	...	...	...	...	...	...	Yougoslavie
T.F.Yug.Rep. Macedonia	..	48	32	33	38	40	9	9	8	...	L'ex-RY Macédoine
Oceania	**87**	**95**	**89**	**104**	**94**	**94**	**94**	**94**	**94**	**94**	**Océanie**
Australia[5]	87	95	89	104	...	...	...	...	...	...	Australie[5]
Total	**2925**	**3733**	**3386**	**3709**	**3472**	**4430**	**4079**	**4551**	**4921**	**4964**	**Total**

General Note.
Industrial production of milk and cream (including buttermilk, skim milk and whey), evaporated or condensed (in liquid or semi-solid form), in terms of net weight. (SITC, Rev.3: 02223-0, 02224-0, 02232-1, 02241-1).

[1] Incomplete coverage.
[2] Sales.
[3] Production by establishments employing 20 or more persons.
[4] Tinned milk and cream.
[5] Twelve months ending 30 June of year stated.

Remarque générale.
Production industrielle de lait et de crème (y compris la babeurre, le lait écrémé et le petit lait), evaporés ou concentrés (à l'état liquide ou pâteux), poids net. (CTCI, Rev.3: 02223-0, 02224-0, 02232-1, 02241-1).

[1] Couverture incomplète.
[2] Ventes.
[3] Production des établissements occupant 20 personnes ou plus.
[4] Conserves de lait et de crème.
[5] Période de douze mois finissant le 30 juin de l'année indiquée.

Milk and cream, dried (Total production)
Lait et crème, séchés (Production totale)

ISIC-BASED CODE - CODE BASE CITI

3112-04

Unit : Thousand metric tons

Unité : Milliers de tonnes métriques

Country or area	1990	1991	1992	1993	1994	1995	1996	1997	1998	1999	Pays ou zone
Africa	**54**	**42**	**48**	**43**	**45**	**51**	**35**	**36**	**45**	**48**	**Afrique**
Kenya	4.4	4.0	3.7	2.8	4.4	5.6	3.3	3.4	3.5	3.5	Kenya
South Africa	39.6	28.3	36.8	31.0	27.5	31.4	17.5	27.4	34.2	37.2	Afrique du Sud
Zimbabwe	10.3	10.1	7.2	9.2	13.0	14.1	13.9	5.4	7.4	7.4	Zimbabwe
America, North	**1265**	**1259**	**1287**	**1304**	**1517**	**1502**	**1363**	**1424**	**1401**	**1509**	**Amérique du Nord**
Canada	165.5	154.0	137.7	133.1	144.9	157.5	152.2	145.1	138.2	138.1	Canada
Costa Rica	3.5	3.5	6.0	6.0	8.6	6.0	6.0	6.0	6.0	6.0	Costa Rica
Cuba	2.3	2.3	2.0	1.7	1.7	1.7	1.7	1.7	1.7	1.7	Cuba
El Salvador	0.3	0.3	0.3	0.4	0.4	0.4	0.4	0.5	0.4	0.5	El Salvador
Guatemala	1.0	0.8	0.8	1.0	1.0	1.0	1.2	1.4	1.4	1.4	Guatemala
Honduras	0.3	0.3	0.3	0.3	0.3	0.3	0.3	0.3	0.3	0.3	Honduras
Mexico	56.5	88.7	72.0	90.3	150.1	131.5	122.0	116.0	116.3	116.3	Mexique
Panama	2.7	2.7	2.7	2.7	2.7	4.9	4.8	4.6	4.6	4.6	Panama
United States	1032.7	1006.4	1065.4	1068.6	1207.4	1198.6	1074.0	1148.1	1132.4	1239.7	Etats-Unis
America, South	**435**	**398**	**416**	**459**	**455**	**491**	**548**	**627**	**687**	**727**	**Amérique du Sud**
Argentina	119.0	101.0	103.0	103.0	129.0	142.0	157.0	206.0	243.0	270.0	Argentine
Bolivia	7.0	5.0	7.0	7.0	7.0	7.0	7.0	7.0	7.0	10.0	Bolivie
Brazil	165.0	140.0	160.0	186.0	175.0	200.0	220.0	231.0	240.0	244.0	Brésil
Chile	50.4	49.1	50.8	56.1	59.7	67.4	69.3	73.5	79.1	79.7	Chili
Colombia	14.5	14.5	14.5	13.5	13.5	12.0	30.0	35.0	37.9	38.6	Colombie
Ecuador	4.4	5.6	4.1	4.1	4.1	4.1	4.1	4.1	4.1	4.1	Equateur
Uruguay	13.3	12.8	12.7	20.8	19.7	23.0	21.5	24.5	33.3	42.0	Uruguay
Venezuela	61.8	70.4	64.1	68.6	46.6	35.0	39.3	46.0	43.0	38.6	Venezuela
Asia	**329**	**388**	**423**	**448**	**375**	**371**	**364**	**341**	**343**	**329**	**Asie**
Israel	7.2	11.3	8.6	11.1	11.6	14.0	12.8	10.7	11.1	10.6	Israël
Japan	269.8	272.4	294.9	313.5	264.1	262.2	261.7	256.4	254.9	244.9	Japon
Jordan	1.6	2.6	1.8	1.6	...	...	1.6	...	...	...	Jordanie
Kazakhstan	..	...	64.0	65.6	47.2	36.5	23.5	17.7	17.5	17.7	Kazakhstan
Korea, Republic of	47.7	43.3	42.7	44.9	39.1	44.9	50.4	44.6	48.8	44.3	Corée, République de
Sri Lanka	2.7	8.3	8.5	8.4	8.9	10.2	11.7	9.9	8.6	9.5	Sri Lanka
Uzbekistan	..	...	2.7	3.2	2.3	1.8	1.8	1.6	1.5	1.4	Ouzbékistan
Europe	**3293**	**4696**	**4421**	**4309**	**4233**	**4272**	**4223**	**4109**	**4085**	**4084**	**Europe**
Austria	37.0	37.9	35.7	32.7	31.6	37.4	30.0	31.7	25.2	25.7	Autriche
Belarus		...	106.7	89.6	66.6	48.1	45.7	47.5	47.9	40.5	Bélarus
Belgium-Luxembourg	132.0	131.1	97.0	114.2	122.8	128.1	125.8	138.5	140.1	157.2	Belgique-Luxembourg
Bulgaria	8.0	7.6	7.0	4.1	0.8	0.7	0.6	1.0	0.5	0.5	Bulgarie
Croatia	..	...	5.5	5.5	5.3	5.5	5.2	4.9	5.9	3.4	Croatie
Denmark	146.9	142.8	142.3	148.2	160.6	159.7	165.3	160.6	161.8	167.9	Danemark
Czechoslovakia(former)	140.0	129.2	..	..	..	..	..	..	..	..	Tchécoslovaquie(anc.)
Czech Republic	..	..	...	101.4	107.5	104.1	94.5	70.0	81.1	83.1	République tchèque
Estonia	..	...	22.5	27.1	22.5	20.5	16.4	19.8	11.5	15.6	Estonie
Finland	64.1	46.9	32.2	28.3	31.3	27.2	20.1	31.9	29.8	36.8	Finlande
France	1212.8	1176.8	1153.7	1097.7	1160.4	1176.0	1191.3	1168.1	1174.3	1180.2	France
Germany		860.7	736.8	676.3	626.6	657.5	663.4	615.2	617.9	610.3	Allemagne
Hungary	43.9	28.2	16.7	21.8	23.5	23.0	22.6	24.2	21.8	23.2	Hongrie
Iceland	2.1	1.9	2.0	1.9	2.1	2.2	2.2	2.3	2.3	2.3	Islande
Ireland	237.7	226.3	190.2	201.0	197.5	193.8	187.7	172.1	165.3	156.7	Irlande
Italy	11.2	7.0	5.6	4.3	5.5	5.7	4.8	3.7	2.9	2.9	Italie
Latvia	..	...	11.1	9.6	6.8	6.8	6.8	6.8	5.2	4.3	Lettonie
Lithuania	..	...	48.9	27.9	80.2	71.6	69.0	73.6	74.4	74.4	Lituanie
Netherlands	506.3	471.5	456.8	489.5	423.9	432.6	459.6	431.5	422.0	414.7	Pays-Bas
Norway	14.0	15.0	15.0	10.9	11.2	9.3	7.9	8.8	7.8	13.5	Norvège
Poland	216.1	212.1	182.0	195.0	152.1	166.1	158.7	167.5	171.3	154.9	Pologne
Portugal	20.9	19.8	19.5	17.5	17.4	21.0	17.0	21.1	18.5	22.3	Portugal
Republic of Moldova	..	...	11.6	7.7	5.6	6.7	5.4	3.8	2.7	4.1	Rép. de Moldova
Romania	29.3	18.9	10.2	11.0	12.0	13.0	12.0	11.0	6.7	6.8	Roumanie
Russian Federation	..	...	474.9	457.9	420.3	416.0	397.0	377.5	349.5	337.0	Fédération de Russie
Slovakia	..	...	...	16.0	12.0	12.0	12.0	15.8	29.4	29.7	Slovaquie
Slovenia	..	...	8.5	6.1	4.5	4.8	4.8	4.7	4.5	5.7	Slovénie
Spain	56.7	46.9	41.2	29.6	23.5	29.1	25.4	24.9	21.6	20.3	Espagne

For general note and footnotes, see end of table.

Voir la fin du tableau pour la remarque générale et les notes.

Milk and cream, dried (Total production) (continued)
Lait et crème, séchés (Production totale) (suite)

ISIC-BASED CODE - CODE BASE CITI

3112-04

Unit : Thousand metric tons   Unité : Milliers de tonnes métriques

Country or area	1990	1991	1992	1993	1994	1995	1996	1997	1998	1999	Pays ou zone
Sweden	63.4	44.9	39.6	46.7	44.8	36.2	38.2	38.4	39.3	41.0	Suède
Switzerland	40.2	41.7	39.0	40.1	41.1	42.6	40.2	40.2	41.3	46.4	Suisse
Ukraine	..	...	168.0	157.6	157.4	155.3	144.5	140.3	132.6	131.8	Ukraine
United Kingdom	280.9	254.8	219.3	229.4	254.7	258.0	245.0	250.0	267.7	268.6	Royaume-Uni
Yugoslavia	..	...	4.9	2.7	1.5	1.2	3.4	2.3	2.3	2.1	Yougoslavie
Yugoslavia, SFR	29.6	..	..	..	..	..	..	..	..	..	Yougoslavie, RSF
USSR (former)	1037.0	..	..	..	..	..	..	..	..	..	URSS (anc.)
Oceania	616	670	703	768	870	894	946	1044	1112	1137	Océanie
Australia	220.1	234.3	255.7	295.7	351.1	361.7	388.6	419.6	441.0	488.2	Australie
New Zealand	395.7	435.3	447.8	472.0	519.0	531.9	557.7	624.4	671.5	648.7	Nouvelle-Zélande
Total	7030	7454	7299	7331	7495	7580	7478	7582	7674	7833	Total

General Note.

Milk and cream (including buttermilk and skim milk), dry (in solid form, such as blocks or powder). (SITC, Rev.3: 02221-0, 02222-0, 02232-2, 02241-2).
Source: Food and Agriculture Organization of the United Nations (FAO), Rome.

Remarque générale.

Lait et crème (y compris le babeurre et le lait écrémé), secs (sous forme solide: morceaux ou poudre). (CTCI, Rev.3: 02221-0, 02222-0, 02232-2, 02241-2).
Source: Organisation des Nations Unies pour l'alimentation et l'agriculture (FAO), Rome.

Milk and cream, dried (Industrial production)
Lait et crème, séchés (Production industrielle)

ISIC-BASED CODE - CODE BASE CITI

3112-041

Unit : Metric tons   Unité : Tonnes métriques

Country or area	1990	1991	1992	1993	1994	1995	1996	1997	1998	1999	Pays ou zone
America, North	**731494**	**734815**	**738135**	**670287**	**786905**	**806394**	**707365**	**772262**	**745365**	**761378**	**Amérique du Nord**
Mexico	...	...	...	...	...	...	...	...	...	139840	Mexique
United States	...	...	...	530447	647065	666554	567525	632422	605525	...	Etats-Unis
America, South	**64847**	**59797**	**58667**	**50804**	**54584**	**57130**	**54644**	**60000**	**60595**	**58020**	**Amérique du Sud**
Brazil	22020	15282	14840	11305	10546	7614	5065	...	...	...	Brésil
Colombia	...	...	43827	39499	44038	49516	...	60000	60595	...	Colombie
Asia	**410347**	**593433**	**631639**	**730582**	**725611**	**820509**	**816621**	**878793**	**941454**	**971089**	**Asie**
Azerbaijan	..	..	43304	...	...	...	...	...	...	...	Azerbaïdjan
Bangladesh	4491	46497	12511	...	...	...	...	...	...	...	Bangladesh
China	241525	293856	336545	417368	424600	525665	504100	564800	...	...	Chine
India	...	...	...	88642	81586	85809	98379	94431	132928	165880	Inde
Indonesia	49537	56301	59479	49425	53356	52198	...	75752	122293	...	Indonésie
Japan	33363	35715	33464	30635	29037	30561	23656	18890	18665	17833	Japon
Kazakhstan	..	17597	25106	25014	16809	7597	3550	1721	937	518	Kazakhstan
Kyrgyzstan	..	..	..	..	..	599	408	779	441	555	Kirghizistan
Malaysia	35819	41711	50532	54391	55122	53552	57207	57892	49221	54188	Malaisie
Turkey	58	58	...	...	...	...	...	...	...	...	Turquie
Europe	**2747471**	**2894759**	**2519394**	**2862257**	**2553397**	**2832536**	**2961248**	**3102362**	**2965670**	**3037046**	**Europe**
Belarus	..	32915	22211	20501	16798	13129	12495	13117	11960	11183	Bélarus
Belgium	34626	49694	39624	49731	...	...	...	...	...	...	Belgique
Croatia	..	3623	3737	3860	3439	3623	3215	2737	3969	...	Croatie
Czechoslovakia(former)	140040	129188	..	..	...	...	...	...	...	..	Tchécoslovaquie(anc.)
Czech Republic	..	..	95675	136273	104999	109577	100802	64867	64339	66356	République tchèque
Estonia	..	4328	1367	994	179	168	104	592	1083	1358	Estonie
Finland	52783	35629	19525	13432	16276	15964	16893	53958	49126	51293	Finlande
France	796000	739000	653000	637000	661000	651000	739000	769000	761000	...	France
Germany	...	764696	627712	644102	588594	753827	807122	820348	789280	...	Allemagne
Germany(Fed.Rep.)	604578									..	Allemagne(Rép.féd.)
German D.R.(former)	178973	..	..	..	..	..	..	..	..	..	R.D.A. (anc.)
Hungary	48145	33771	26400	20420	21954	21517	16493	16742	15117	17139	Hongrie
Iceland	...	...	...	...	...	...	547	676	620	492	Islande
Latvia	..	8262	6612	3382	1056	737	2011	3570	4816	13011	Lettonie
Lithuania	..	..	..	..	..	21679	28673	35852	32923	26640	Lituanie
Netherlands[1][2]	220290	201522	182812	#492000	321000	389000	465000	507000	496000	567735	Pays-Bas[1][2]
Poland	216451	212664	181649	194610	151372	165622	156675	161108	170822	144628	Pologne
Portugal	16474	13776	43193	37561	52410	48258	49731	51483	49111	54511	Portugal
Romania	29345	19064	10486	11152	13873	14705	13783	10745	6981	6281	Roumanie
Russian Federation	..	158634	149982	133870	115039	124570	82880	89340	76289	83774	Fédération de Russie
Slovakia	..	..	6898	19432	7773	2868	13943	15917	17764	16373	Slovaquie
Slovenia	..	5007	4807	3555	2520	2466	1762	1755	2881	2838	Slovénie
Sweden	61279	54827	37106	52639	49484	48465	25891	37338	32231	38227	Suède
Ukraine[3]	..	51727	29365	25352	19913	21442	12012	9284	8307	8562	Ukraine[3]
United Kingdom	...	...	...	335609	335149	378653	365274	390375	325092	...	Royaume-Uni
Yugoslavia	..	5871	3830	2714	1665	1263	3523	3139	2540	3115	Yougoslavie
Oceania	**200205**	**215454**	**224867**	**258628**	**224789**	**224789**	**224789**	**224789**	**224789**	**224789**	**Océanie**
Australia[4]	200205	215454	224867	258628	...	...	...	...	...	...	Australie[4]
Total	**4154364**	**4498258**	**4172702**	**4572558**	**4345286**	**4741357**	**4764666**	**5038206**	**4937872**	**5052322**	**Total**

General Note.
Industrial production of milk and cream (including buttermilk, skim milk and whey), dry (in solid form, such as blocks or powder). (SITC, Rev.3: 02221-0, 02222-0, 02232-2, 02241-2).

Remarque générale.
Production industrielle de lait et de crème (y compris la babeurre, le lait écrémé et le petit lait), secs (sous forme solide: morceau ou poudre). (CTCI, Rev.3: 02221-0, 0222-0, 02232-2, 02241-2).

[1] Sales.
[2] Production by establishments employing 20 or more persons.
[3] Including dried mixtures.
[4] Twelve months ending 30 June of year stated.

[1] Ventes.
[2] Production des établissements occupant 20 personnes ou plus.
[3] Y compris les mélanges séchés.
[4] Période de douze mois finissant le 30 juin de l'année indiquée.

Butter (Total production)
Beurre (Production totale)

ISIC-BASED CODE - CODE BASE CITI

3112-07

Unit : Thousand metric tons   Unité : Milliers de tonnes métriques

Country or area	1990	1991	1992	1993	1994	1995	1996	1997	1998	1999	Pays ou zone
Africa	**190**	**187**	**191**	**193**	**185**	**186**	**186**	**202**	**208**	**215**	**Afrique**
Algeria	1.0	1.0	1.1	1.0	1.1	1.2	1.1	1.2	1.2	1.2	Algérie
Angola	0.4	0.4	0.4	0.4	0.4	0.4	0.4	0.4	0.5	0.5	Angola
Botswana	1.5	1.5	1.2	1.0	1.0	1.1	1.0	1.0	1.0	1.0	Botswana
Burkina Faso	0.7	0.9	0.9	0.9	1.0	1.0	1.1	1.2	1.2	1.2	Burkina Faso
Burundi	0.2	0.2	0.2	0.2	0.2	0.1	0.1	0.1	0.1	0.1	Burundi
Chad	0.3	0.3	0.3	0.3	0.3	0.3	0.3	0.4	0.4	0.4	Tchad
Egypt	78.3	82.7	85.6	89.7	81.6	77.2	84.4	91.1	91.4	96.1	Egypte
Eritrea	...	...	...	0.4	0.4	0.4	0.5	0.6	0.6	0.7	Erythrée
Ethiopia,incl.Eritrea	9.9	10.4	10.8	...	...	...	...	...	...	...	Ethiopie,incl.Erythrée
Ethiopia	...	...	...	10.4	10.4	10.4	10.8	11.3	11.7	11.7	Ethiopie
Guinea	0.1	0.1	0.1	0.1	0.1	0.1	0.1	0.1	0.1	0.2	Guinée
Kenya	4.6	3.5	3.1	2.4	2.4	3.1	2.3	2.2	2.3	2.3	Kenya
Mauritania	0.7	0.7	0.6	0.7	0.7	0.7	0.7	0.7	0.7	0.7	Mauritanie
Morocco	14.2	14.7	15.0	13.4	13.5	13.6	13.9	15.5	16.5	17.6	Maroc
Namibia	0.3	0.3	0.3	0.3	0.3	0.3	0.3	0.3	0.3	0.3	Namibie
Niger	3.9	4.1	4.2	4.3	4.4	4.5	4.6	4.6	4.6	4.6	Niger
Nigeria	8.3	8.5	8.7	8.8	8.6	9.0	8.6	7.9	8.3	8.7	Nigéria
Rwanda	0.3	0.4	0.4	0.3	0.3	0.3	0.3	0.3	0.3	0.3	Rwanda
Senegal	0.4	0.4	0.4	0.4	0.4	0.4	0.4	0.5	0.5	0.5	Sénégal
Somalia	8.3	7.1	6.8	9.0	11.0	11.2	11.4	11.6	11.0	10.4	Somalie
South Africa	22.9	15.4	17.1	14.9	12.0	14.8	6.7	13.8	17.6	18.5	Afrique du Sud
Sudan	13.5	13.7	14.0	14.2	14.4	14.6	14.9	15.1	15.3	15.5	Soudan
Swaziland	0.2	0.2	0.2	0.2	0.2	0.2	0.2	0.1	0.2	0.1	Swaziland
Tunisia	1.7	1.7	1.7	1.7	2.3	2.5	4.2	5.0	5.0	5.0	Tunisie
Uganda	...	...	...	...	...	...	...	...	0.1	0.0	Ouganda
United Rep.Tanzania	4.5	4.6	4.7	4.8	4.8	4.9	4.9	5.0	5.1	5.1	Rép. Unie de Tanzanie
Zambia	0.3	0.3	0.3	0.3	0.3	0.3	0.3	0.2	0.2	0.2	Zambie
Zimbabwe	3.9	3.8	2.7	2.4	2.7	2.3	1.8	1.8	1.8	1.8	Zimbabwe
America, North	**769**	**767**	**795**	**764**	**761**	**730**	**682**	**667**	**694**	**753**	**Amérique du Nord**
Canada	104.4	101.1	90.2	87.5	92.7	96.8	97.6	94.1	90.6	92.1	Canada
Costa Rica	3.5	3.5	3.5	3.5	3.5	3.5	3.5	3.5	3.5	3.5	Costa Rica
Cuba	8.7	8.7	8.0	7.5	7.5	7.5	7.5	7.5	7.5	7.5	Cuba
Dominican Republic	1.5	1.5	1.5	1.5	1.5	1.5	1.5	1.5	1.5	1.5	Rép. dominicaine
El Salvador	0.2	0.2	0.2	0.2	0.2	0.2	0.2	0.2	0.2	0.2	El Salvador
Guatemala	0.5	0.4	0.5	0.4	0.4	0.4	0.5	0.5	0.5	0.6	Guatemala
Honduras	4.1	4.1	4.1	3.8	3.3	3.7	3.9	4.3	4.3	8.3	Honduras
Mexico	38.0	25.3	38.0	34.3	30.2	30.9	30.0	32.9	55.0	60.0	Mexique
Nicaragua	0.9	0.9	0.9	0.9	0.9	1.0	0.8	0.7	0.9	0.9	Nicaragua
Panama	0.0	0.0	0.0	0.0	0.0	0.1	0.1	0.1	0.1	0.1	Panama
United States	607.7	621.5	648.4	624.5	620.5	584.3	536.1	522.0	529.8	578.4	Etats-Unis
America, South	**154**	**147**	**140**	**141**	**151**	**159**	**161**	**166**	**174**	**181**	**Amérique du Sud**
Argentina	35.4	38.0	37.0	36.0	43.5	51.3	52.0	49.0	52.0	55.0	Argentine
Bolivia	0.6	0.6	0.6	0.6	0.6	0.6	0.6	0.6	0.6	0.6	Bolivie
Brazil	75.0	70.0	65.0	68.0	70.0	65.1	66.4	67.6	68.3	69.2	Brésil
Chile	6.4	7.3	7.3	7.7	7.0	6.7	6.5	9.6	11.2	11.5	Chili
Colombia	14.8	14.8	14.8	14.8	14.8	14.8	14.8	17.4	18.2	18.4	Colombie
Ecuador	4.6	4.6	4.6	4.6	4.6	4.6	4.6	4.6	4.6	4.6	Equateur
Peru	1.6	1.4	1.2	1.0	0.6	0.6	0.7	0.6	0.8	0.8	Pérou
Uruguay	13.6	8.4	8.5	7.5	10.1	14.5	12.1	15.0	16.4	19.2	Uruguay
Venezuela	1.8	2.2	1.2	0.4	0.2	0.5	3.4	1.4	1.7	1.6	Venezuela
Asia	**1787**	**1919**	**1999**	**2091**	**2156**	**2267**	**2388**	**2476**	**2641**	**2815**	**Asie**
Afghanistan	16.0	16.8	17.4	19.7	23.3	26.4	32.5	37.0	42.0	48.0	Afghanistan
Armenia	...	...	0.2	0.2	0.2	0.1	0.1	0.1	0.1	0.1	Arménie
Azerbaijan	..	...	2.9	2.3	1.4	1.5	0.3	0.5	0.4	0.4	Azerbaïdjan
Bangladesh	13.6	13.6	13.7	14.0	15.0	15.0	15.0	15.0	14.5	15.0	Bangladesh
China [1]	63.7	67.1	70.0	72.9	74.3	74.6	74.9	77.4	78.6	79.4	Chine [1]
Georgia	..	...	0.2	0.0	0.0	0.0	0.0	0.9	0.3	1.4	Géorgie
India	1020.0	1050.0	1060.0	1110.0	1200.0	1300.0	1400.0	1470.0	1600.0	1750.0	Inde
Iran(Islamic Rep. of)	89.7	93.4	96.1	99.8	104.3	109.9	119.3	120.8	128.0	139.4	Iran(Rép. islamique)
Iraq	8.0	6.4	3.7	4.2	5.4	5.1	7.2	7.7	7.9	7.9	Iraq

For general note and footnotes, see end of table.   Voir la fin du tableau pour la remarque générale et les notes.

Butter (Total production) (continued)
Beurre (Production totale) (suite)

ISIC-BASED CODE - CODE BASE CITI

3112-07

Unit : Thousand metric tons

Unité : Milliers de tonnes métriques

Country or area	1990	1991	1992	1993	1994	1995	1996	1997	1998	1999	Pays ou zone
Israel	7.1	5.4	5.1	5.7	4.5	6.2	6.9	6.9	8.2	7.9	Israël
Japan	76.3	75.9	95.1	108.0	79.7	80.3	86.3	87.2	88.9	85.3	Japon
Kazakhstan	..	...	61.6	69.9	46.5	30.4	15.3	7.2	4.7	3.6	Kazakhstan
Korea, Republic of	43.5	44.7	47.2	47.4	51.0	53.8	51.7	53.6	49.0	50.1	Corée, République de
Kyrgyzstan	..	...	8.6	7.0	3.9	2.0	1.1	1.5	1.3	1.2	Kirghizistan
Mongolia	4.4	3.1	1.3	0.7	0.5	1.0	0.7	0.7	0.8	1.0	Mongolie
Myanmar	9.3	9.4	9.5	9.6	9.7	9.9	10.1	10.3	10.5	10.7	Myanmar
Nepal	15.9	16.1	16.4	16.7	17.1	17.4	17.7	17.9	18.2	18.8	Népal
Oman	0.1	0.1	0.1	0.1	0.1	0.1	0.1	0.1	0.1	0.1	Oman
Pakistan	284.1	300.0	316.7	334.4	353.0	372.7	393.5	415.4	438.6	450.7	Pakistan
Saudi Arabia	1.0	1.1	2.1	2.5	2.7	2.8	2.7	2.8	3.1	3.6	Arabie saoudite
Sri Lanka	0.3	0.4	0.4	0.4	0.4	0.3	0.8	0.4	0.6	0.4	Sri Lanka
Syrian Arab Republic	15.7	15.9	15.8	11.4	12.6	13.1	13.6	14.5	17.1	14.0	Rép. arabe syrienne
Tajikistan	..	...	3.8	2.0	1.5	0.7	0.2	0.2	0.1	0.1	Tadjikistan
Turkey	117.6	125.2	125.5	126.2	127.5	126.9	128.4	119.6	118.1	117.0	Turquie
Turkmenistan	..	...	4.2	4.1	3.2	1.9	1.0	1.1	1.2	1.3	Turkménistan
United Arab Emirates	0.2	0.2	0.2	0.3	0.3	0.3	0.3	0.3	0.4	0.4	Emirats arabes unis
Uzbekistan	..	...	17.3	17.9	14.4	10.5	4.4	2.8	3.5	3.0	Ouzbékistan
Yemen	..	3.8	3.9	3.9	3.8	3.9	4.0	4.1	4.4	4.5	Yémen
Europe	**2151**	**3402**	**3557**	**3391**	**2967**	**2921**	**2769**	**2711**	**2668**	**2582**	**Europe**
Albania	2.4	1.8	1.5	1.2	1.3	1.5	1.5	1.5	1.5	1.6	Albanie
Austria	40.6	41.9	42.7	43.1	42.5	40.7	41.6	41.8	42.4	36.8	Autriche
Belarus	..	...	98.5	87.0	73.6	65.1	61.5	71.7	74.2	62.8	Bélarus
Belgium-Luxembourg	93.1	80.9	75.7	72.9	73.3	91.0	97.4	107.2	112.4	117.1	Belgique-Luxembourg
Bosnia and Herzegovina	..	..	0.1	0.1	0.1	0.1	0.1	0.1	0.1	0.1	Bosnie-Herzégovine
Bulgaria	21.6	12.4	8.8	4.6	2.2	2.9	2.3	1.7	1.7	1.4	Bulgarie
Croatia	..	...	1.7	2.3	2.4	2.2	2.6	2.6	2.4	1.7	Croatie
Denmark	93.3	70.5	62.2	59.4	59.3	54.4	56.6	50.4	48.7	47.9	Danemark
Czechoslovakia(former)	157.7	132.8	..	..	..	..	..	..	..	..	Tchécoslovaquie(anc.)
Czech Republic	..	..	...	83.2	69.5	72.3	68.9	61.9	63.5	68.2	République tchèque
Estonia	..	...	26.8	23.1	18.9	15.6	16.9	16.8	11.4	9.5	Estonie
Finland	62.2	59.4	56.7	55.2	53.2	52.5	54.2	50.0	50.0	52.0	Finlande
France	527.4	486.3	451.2	434.2	444.0	452.7	473.2	466.1	462.6	447.6	France
Germany	..	556.5	552.6	482.2	461.3	486.2	480.2	442.4	426.4	427.0	Allemagne
Greece	3.9	4.1	4.2	4.4	4.8	3.9	3.8	4.8	5.1	4.4	Grèce
Hungary	38.8	28.9	23.3	18.5	15.3	15.2	13.5	12.8	16.1	15.3	Hongrie
Iceland	1.7	1.6	1.6	1.7	1.7	1.7	1.6	1.6	1.6	1.6	Islande
Ireland	148.2	140.0	133.6	127.5	126.8	142.4	142.2	138.8	131.3	135.4	Irlande
Italy	102.9	103.5	102.0	94.2	92.8	108.3	115.9	141.6	136.0	105.4	Italie
Latvia	..	...	31.8	18.8	9.7	6.4	7.5	7.8	9.2	7.4	Lettonie
Lithuania	..	...	49.2	45.3	31.2	32.3	34.8	34.7	35.7	26.2	Lituanie
Netherlands	178.0	163.3	148.5	146.8	128.6	131.8	127.6	134.5	149.0	139.9	Pays-Bas
Norway	21.6	20.5	19.2	18.4	16.2	16.3	14.4	12.7	13.0	13.2	Norvège
Poland	300.0	220.0	185.0	176.0	160.0	162.0	160.0	178.0	174.0	166.0	Pologne
Portugal	15.5	16.0	16.6	16.7	16.9	19.4	19.3	21.2	19.6	24.7	Portugal
Republic of Moldova	..	...	16.7	9.3	8.2	5.6	3.9	2.6	2.6	1.9	Rép. de Moldova
Romania	33.3	22.7	20.5	17.5	14.3	16.1	13.4	9.2	6.4	9.2	Roumanie
Russian Federation	..	...	761.6	732.3	487.8	421.3	323.3	292.0	276.2	257.0	Fédération de Russie
Slovakia	..	...	...	15.1	16.1	16.0	15.0	13.5	15.0	16.1	Slovaquie
Slovenia	..	...	2.5	1.9	1.5	2.0	2.3	2.2	3.5	4.3	Slovénie
Spain	45.5	38.2	29.9	25.2	18.8	24.8	23.4	23.5	22.0	30.0	Espagne
Sweden	71.6	59.6	59.8	62.0	56.3	57.0	56.6	59.1	52.9	49.6	Suède
Switzerland	37.9	39.8	38.6	38.0	40.5	41.9	39.9	39.7	40.8	38.0	Suisse
Ukraine	..	...	302.9	311.8	253.7	221.9	163.0	116.5	112.7	108.0	Ukraine
United Kingdom	138.2	111.7	127.0	151.6	155.0	127.0	120.0	138.7	137.0	144.0	Royaume-Uni
Yugoslavia	..	...	3.7	1.7	1.5	1.7	2.7	3.3	2.0	1.7	Yougoslavie
T.F.Yug.Rep. Macedonia	..	...	8.0	7.8	7.7	8.5	8.0	8.0	9.3	9.3	L'ex-RY Macédoine
Yugoslavia, SFR	15.9	..	..	..	..	..	..	..	..	..	Yougoslavie, RSF
USSR (former)	1739.0	..	..	..	..	..	..	..	..	..	URSS (anc.)
Oceania	**363**	**358**	**371**	**380**	**417**	**401**	**444**	**500**	**506**	**522**	**Océanie**
Australia	104.2	105.9	108.0	126.5	142.8	134.4	145.0	147.0	161.0	200.0	Australie

For general note and footnotes, see end of table.

Voir la fin du tableau pour la remarque générale et les notes.

Butter (Total production) (continued)
Beurre (Production totale) (suite)

Butter (Total production) (continued)
Beurre (Production totale) (suite)

ISIC-BASED CODE - CODE BASE CITI

3112-07

Unit : Thousand metric tons

Unité : Milliers de tonnes métriques

Country or area	1990	1991	1992	1993	1994	1995	1996	1997	1998	1999	Pays ou zone
Fiji	1.2	1.5	1.5	1.5	1.7	1.7	1.7	1.7	1.8	1.8	Fidji
New Zealand	257.8	250.9	261.7	252.3	272.1	265.3	297.4	350.9	343.7	320.0	Nouvelle-Zélande
Total	**7153**	**6780**	**7054**	**6960**	**6637**	**6663**	**6630**	**6722**	**6891**	**7068**	**Total**

General Note.

Natural fresh butter, whether salted or not, including melted. Includes non-industrial production. (SITC, Rev.3: 02300-0).

Source: Food and Agriculture Organization of the United Nations (FAO), Rome.

Remarque générale.

Beurre, frais, salé ou non, y compris le beurre fondu. Y compris production non-industrielle. (CTCI, Rev.3: 02300-0).

Source: Organisation des Nations Unies pour l'alimentation et l'agriculture (FAO), Rome.

[1] Including Hong-Kong, Macao and Taiwan.

[1] Y compris Hong-Kong, Macao et Taïwan.

Butter (Industrial production)
Beurre (Production industrielle)

ISIC-BASED CODE - CODE BASE CITI

3112-071

Unit : Thousand metric tons   Unité : Milliers de tonnes métriques

Country or area	1990	1991	1992	1993	1994	1995	1996	1997	1998	1999	Pays ou zone
Africa	**431**	**438**	**444**	**450**	**332**	**780**	**224**	**543**	**487**	**494**	**Afrique**
Egypt	1.8	1.9	2.0	1.7	1.1	2.1	5.0	3.2	...	...	Egypte
Kenya	3.2	3.0	2.2	2.0	2.4	4.0	2.0	...	...	...	Kenya
Madagascar	...	...	...	...	328.7	773.4	217.0	537.3	481.5	...	Madagascar
America, North	**595**	**610**	**623**	**611**	**602**	**588**	**545**	**600**	**504**	**515**	**Amérique du Nord**
Mexico	4.2	4.3	4.1	#14.9	14.4	15.2	12.7	12.1	13.3	15.3	Mexique
United States	590.7	605.9	619.2	596.4	587.9	573.0	532.7	587.8	490.7	...	Etats-Unis
America, South	**77**	**73**	**83**	**72**	**77**	**88**	**91**	**92**	**95**	**100**	**Amérique du Sud**
Argentina	40.1	37.0	36.6	35.8	43.5	51.3	52.2	49.1	48.8	55.0	Argentine
Bolivia	0.1	0.1	0.1	0.0	0.0	*0.0	...	...	...	...	Bolivie
Brazil	32.7	30.6	41.4	31.4	26.9	29.5	31.8	35.7	34.5	33.3	Brésil
Colombia	3.9	...	3.9	4.2	5.6	6.0	...	6.2	5.8	...	Colombie
Ecuador	...	...	0.6	0.4	0.4	0.3	...	0.8	5.0	...	Equateur
Peru	0.1	0.4	0.4	0.4	0.6	0.6	0.7	0.6	0.8	*0.9	Pérou
Asia	**83**	**197**	**203**	**222**	**162**	**141**	**124**	**119**	**111**	**111**	**Asie**
Armenia	..	0.2	0.2	0.1	0.1	0.0	0.0	0.0	0.0	0.0	Arménie
Azerbaijan	..	3.1	2.9	2.3	1.4	0.8	0.3	0.0	0.1	0.0	Azerbaïdjan
Bangladesh	0.3	0.2	0.4	...	...	...	...	...	...	...	Bangladesh
Cyprus	*0.0	*0.0	0.0	*0.0	*0.1	0.1	0.1	0.1	0.2	0.4	Chypre
Georgia	..	...	0.2	...	0.0	0.0	0.0	...	...	1.5	Géorgie
Indonesia	0.6	0.8	0.3	1.3	1.1	1.8	...	7.3	1.6	...	Indonésie
Israel	2.8	3.4	3.9	4.0	4.5	4.2	4.2	...	...	...	Israël
Japan	76.3	75.9	95.1	108.0	79.7	80.3	86.3	87.2	88.9	85.3	Japon
Kazakhstan	..	76.0	61.6	69.9	46.5	30.4	15.3	6.9	4.4	3.6	Kazakhstan
Kyrgyzstan	..	10.1	8.6	7.0	3.9	2.0	1.1	1.5	1.3	1.2	Kirghizistan
Syrian Arab Republic	0.4	...	...	...	...	...	...	...	...	...	Rép. arabe syrienne
Tajikistan	..	4.7	3.8	2.0	1.5	...	...	0.2	0.1	0.2	Tadjikistan
Turkey	2.4	3.5	4.4	4.5	5.2	6.4	6.4	6.3	7.5	7.8	Turquie
Turkmenistan	..	4.3	4.2	4.1	3.2	1.9	1.1	0.6	0.6	...	Turkménistan
Uzbekistan	..	14.6	17.3	17.9	14.4	10.4	4.4	2.8	...	...	Ouzbékistan
Europe	**2527**	**3552**	**3224**	**3262**	**2765**	**2688**	**2486**	**2425**	**2381**	**2294**	**Europe**
Austria	...	...	...	...	...	38.5	44.1	44.2	43.0	41.2	Autriche
Belarus	..	137.0	98.5	87.0	73.6	65.1	61.5	71.7	74.2	62.8	Bélarus
Belgium	77.4	67.1	63.3	61.0	...	...	...	...	...	...	Belgique
Bulgaria	21.6	12.4	8.7	4.6	2.2	2.9	2.3	1.7	1.7	1.3	Bulgarie
Croatia		2.0	1.7	2.3	2.4	2.2	2.6	2.6	2.4	...	Croatie
Czechoslovakia(former)	157.5	132.8	..	..	..	..	..	..	..	..	Tchécoslovaquie(anc.)
Czech Republic	..	..	83.2	83.2	70.5	70.5	67.0	60.3	65.1	68.2	République tchèque
Estonia	..	28.4	23.5	23.1	18.1	12.1	12.4	15.0	11.4	7.4	Estonie
Finland	65.7	60.0	55.6	49.8	55.5	65.6	54.7	62.2	49.7	52.8	Finlande
France	451.0	414.0	392.0	377.0	376.0	381.0	404.0	383.0	377.0	...	France
Germany		552.6	473.7	482.2	461.3	479.7	478.3	438.4	429.6	...	Allemagne
Germany(Fed.Rep.)	393.1	..	..	..	..	..	..	..	..	..	Allemagne(Rép.féd.)
German D.R.(former)	282.9	..	..	..	..	..	..	..	..	..	R.D.A. (anc.)
Greece	2.4	2.3	2.1	1.5	1.5	1.9	...	...	1.8	...	Grèce
Hungary	38.8	28.9	21.7	18.4	15.3	15.2	13.4	7.3	9.7	10.5	Hongrie
Iceland	1.0	1.0	0.8	0.9	1.0	0.9	1.6	1.6	1.6	1.8	Islande
Ireland	148.5	...	...	...	...	151.7	156.9	145.0	146.0	147.0	Irlande
Latvia	..	38.3	31.8	18.9	9.8	6.5	7.5	7.8	9.4	7.6	Lettonie
Lithuania	..	67.2	49.2	45.3	31.2	32.4	34.8	34.8	35.9	26.2	Lituanie
Luxembourg	4.6	3.5	2.6	3.4	3.2	3.7	3.1	...	...	...	Luxembourg
Netherlands [1,2]	172.5	139.2	135.4	#206.0	164.0	178.0	179.0	203.0	219.0	211.4	Pays-Bas [1,2]
Norway	23.9	22.8	21.5	19.4	...	15.9	14.0	13.7	...	...	Norvège
Poland	271.6	191.6	155.1	146.4	119.8	122.3	131.7	139.0	146.0	134.6	Pologne
Portugal	14.1	7.6	17.3	16.9	14.8	20.2	17.3	21.2	18.8	24.3	Portugal
Republic of Moldova [3]	...	...	...	9.3	8.2	5.6	3.9	2.6	2.6	1.9	Rép. de Moldova [3]
Romania	33.3	22.7	20.5	17.5	14.3	16.1	13.4	13.8	7.5	6.9	Roumanie
Russian Federation	..	729.0	761.6	732.3	487.8	421.3	323.3	292.0	276.2	261.7	Fédération de Russie
Slovakia	..	..	18.6	18.3	15.8	15.2	13.1	13.1	13.7	13.6	Slovaquie
Slovenia	..	2.0	2.5	1.8	1.5	1.8	2.3	2.2	3.5	4.3	Slovénie

For general note and footnotes, see end of table.   Voir la fin du tableau pour la remarque générale et les notes.

Butter (Industrial production) (continued)
Beurre (Production industrielle) (suite)

ISIC-BASED CODE - CODE BASE CITI

3112-071

Unit : Thousand metric tons   Unité : Milliers de tonnes métriques

Country or area	1990	1991	1992	1993	1994	1995	1996	1997	1998	1999	Pays ou zone
Spain	45.3	37.7	29.0	31.3	...	...	...	...	...	...	Espagne
Sweden	51.0	49.0	35.1	46.7	44.9	42.8	28.2	44.4	41.0	31.3	Suède
Ukraine	..	376.4	302.9	311.8	253.7	221.9	162.8	116.5	112.7	108.3	Ukraine
United Kingdom	...	...	...	254.9	204.7	192.0	145.2	176.4	160.7	...	Royaume-Uni
Yugoslavia	..	4.1	3.6	1.6	1.5	1.7	2.7	3.3	2.0	2.2	Yougoslavie
USSR (former)	1738.8	..	..	..	..	..	..	..	..	..	URSS (anc.)
Oceania	**370**	**367**	**381**	**392**	**428**	**414**	**467**	**458**	**471**	**500**	**Océanie**
Australia[4]	104.2	105.9	108.0	126.5	142.8	134.4	154.4	146.9	153.6	175.0	Australie[4]
Fiji	1.2	1.5	1.5	1.5	1.7	1.7	1.7	1.7	1.8	...	Fidji
New Zealand	264.3	259.3	271.4	263.6	283.9	277.5	310.5	...	...	...	Nouvelle-Zélande
Total	**5821**	**5237**	**4959**	**5010**	**4367**	**4698**	**3936**	**4237**	**4049**	**4014**	**Total**

General Note.
Natural fresh butter, whether salted or not, including melted. Data refer to industrial production only. (SITC, Rev.3: 02300-0).

Remarque générale.
Beurre, frais, salé ou non, y compris le beurre fondu. Les données se rapportent à la production industrielle seulement. (CTCI, Rev.3: 02300-0).

[1] Sales.
[2] Production by establishments employing 20 or more persons.
[3] Excluding Transnistria region.
[4] Twelve months ending 30 June of year stated.

[1] Ventes.
[2] Production des établissements occupant 20 personnes ou plus.
[3] Non compris la région de Transnistria.
[4] Période de douze mois finissant le 30 juin de l'année indiquée.

Cheese (Total production)
Fromage (Production totale)

ISIC-BASED CODE - CODE BASE CITI

3112-10

Unit : Thousand metric tons

Unité : Milliers de tonnes métriques

Country or area	1990	1991	1992	1993	1994	1995	1996	1997	1998	1999	Pays ou zone
Africa	**427**	**457**	**459**	**478**	**561**	**596**	**578**	**605**	**641**	**702**	**Afrique**
Algeria	1.0	1.0	1.0	1.0	1.0	1.0	1.0	1.0	1.0	1.0	Algérie
Angola	0.9	1.0	1.0	1.0	0.9	0.9	1.0	1.1	1.2	1.2	Angola
Botswana	2.3	2.3	2.1	2.0	1.9	2.3	2.4	3.1	2.3	2.2	Botswana
Egypt	268.3	272.8	275.5	281.5	323.0	343.8	371.3	400.0	427.0	464.3	Egypte
Eritrea	...	...	...	0.2	0.2	0.2	0.2	0.3	0.3	0.3	Erythrée
Ethiopia,incl.Eritrea	3.3	3.5	3.6	...	...	...	...	...	...	...	Ethiopie,incl.Erythrée
Ethiopia	...	...	...	3.5	3.5	3.5	3.6	3.8	3.9	3.9	Ethiopie
Kenya	0.2	0.3	0.2	0.2	0.1	0.2	0.2	0.2	0.2	0.2	Kenya
Mauritania	1.8	1.8	1.7	2.0	1.9	1.9	1.9	2.0	2.0	1.8	Mauritanie
Morocco	7.3	7.2	7.4	7.3	7.0	7.0	7.1	7.3	7.5	7.7	Maroc
Namibia	0.1	0.1	0.1	0.1	0.1	0.1	0.1	0.1	0.1	0.1	Namibie
Niger	11.4	11.8	12.0	12.5	12.8	13.5	13.6	13.6	13.6	13.6	Niger
Nigeria	6.6	6.8	7.0	7.0	6.9	7.2	6.8	6.3	6.6	7.0	Nigéria
South Africa	42.3	39.2	32.6	35.5	38.2	37.7	39.5	35.8	38.0	36.0	Afrique du Sud
Sudan	66.8	94.1	100.5	109.3	148.7	162.5	114.4	116.5	122.3	148.2	Soudan
Tunisia	5.4	5.9	6.4	6.7	6.6	6.2	6.4	6.4	6.4	6.4	Tunisie
United Rep.Tanzania	1.3	1.4	1.5	1.6	1.6	1.8	1.8	1.9	2.0	2.0	Rép. Unie de Tanzanie
Zambia	0.9	1.0	1.0	1.0	1.0	1.0	0.9	0.7	0.7	0.7	Zambie
Zimbabwe	3.3	3.2	2.3	2.1	2.1	2.1	2.1	2.1	2.1	2.1	Zimbabwe
America, North	**3582**	**3581**	**3776**	**3781**	**3877**	**3991**	**4120**	**4192**	**4272**	**4488**	**Amérique du Nord**
Canada	286.2	292.0	290.1	292.7	307.0	313.4	311.3	358.2	351.6	353.0	Canada
Costa Rica	5.9	5.9	5.9	5.9	3.1	5.7	5.6	5.3	5.4	5.8	Costa Rica
Cuba	16.3	16.3	15.0	14.5	14.5	14.5	14.5	14.5	14.5	14.5	Cuba
Dominican Republic	2.5	2.5	2.5	2.5	2.5	2.5	2.5	2.5	2.5	2.5	Rép. dominicaine
El Salvador	2.4	2.4	2.5	2.6	2.6	2.6	2.6	2.6	2.6	2.6	El Salvador
Guatemala	11.3	11.3	11.3	11.5	11.5	11.5	11.1	11.1	11.1	11.1	Guatemala
Honduras	8.3	8.3	8.3	7.9	7.1	7.6	8.1	8.7	8.6	8.7	Honduras
Mexico	114.5	114.5	130.5	131.4	131.7	126.3	122.9	129.8	130.2	138.4	Mexique
Nicaragua	4.6	4.7	4.9	5.2	5.3	7.2	7.7	7.4	7.9	11.3	Nicaragua
Panama	4.3	4.9	5.1	5.8	6.0	6.4	6.8	6.7	8.8	9.5	Panama
United States	3126.1	3118.0	3299.9	3301.0	3385.6	3493.5	3626.8	3645.0	3728.5	3931.0	Etats-Unis
America, South	**514**	**545**	**615**	**640**	**637**	**632**	**651**	**721**	**711**	**703**	**Amérique du Sud**
Argentina	243.6	283.0	336.2	350.0	385.0	369.0	376.0	445.0	420.0	425.0	Argentine
Bolivia	7.0	6.5	6.7	6.7	6.8	6.8	6.8	6.8	6.8	6.8	Bolivie
Brazil	60.5	59.8	59.8	60.2	33.2	22.8	33.2	33.5	38.5	38.5	Brésil
Chile	32.2	34.9	39.1	42.5	45.3	47.5	48.9	50.4	53.2	52.7	Chili
Colombia	51.0	51.0	51.0	51.0	51.0	51.0	51.0	51.0	51.0	51.0	Colombie
Ecuador	6.8	6.4	6.1	6.3	6.4	7.1	7.1	7.2	7.2	7.2	Equateur
Peru	17.6	15.5	11.0	7.8	5.3	5.8	6.1	5.4	6.0	6.1	Pérou
Uruguay	16.5	18.2	17.1	19.0	22.6	25.4	24.7	28.0	29.0	27.3	Uruguay
Venezuela	79.0	69.5	88.4	96.8	81.5	97.1	97.8	93.7	99.8	88.7	Venezuela
Asia	**803**	**921**	**953**	**957**	**981**	**938**	**953**	**974**	**994**	**1019**	**Asie**
Afghanistan	17.3	17.8	17.4	17.4	17.8	17.9	20.2	22.6	25.6	28.1	Afghanistan
Armenia	..	...	10.0	9.9	9.0	9.0	8.7	8.9	9.7	9.9	Arménie
Azerbaijan	..	...	15.5	11.6	6.6	3.9	1.8	1.2	1.1	0.9	Azerbaïdjan
Bangladesh	1.0	1.0	1.0	1.0	1.0	1.0	1.0	1.0	1.0	1.0	Bangladesh
China[1]	160.2	162.1	166.9	177.3	199.6	184.7	185.1	190.6	173.6	185.3	Chine[1]
Cyprus	5.3	5.3	5.3	5.4	5.6	5.5	5.5	5.6	4.4	4.5	Chypre
Georgia	..	...	4.0	2.8	1.5	0.4	0.3	0.1	0.0	0.1	Géorgie
Iran(Islamic Rep. of)	188.0	192.4	195.9	201.0	206.4	191.8	191.0	190.4	199.2	212.9	Iran(Rép. islamique)
Iraq	31.1	24.9	13.7	15.4	19.8	18.2	27.6	29.6	30.3	30.4	Iraq
Israel	75.6	76.7	81.7	84.9	89.0	92.0	94.3	94.9	95.1	96.7	Israël
Japan	82.2	88.5	92.2	100.4	101.8	105.4	109.0	114.0	123.8	123.7	Japon
Jordan	2.8	4.6	3.9	5.2	4.0	4.0	4.3	3.9	3.5	2.3	Jordanie
Kazakhstan	..	...	25.5	25.3	20.6	13.6	10.2	7.5	5.9	6.3	Kazakhstan
Kyrgyzstan	..	...	12.7	10.8	7.0	3.8	2.1	2.1	2.7	2.8	Kirghizistan
Lebanon	9.9	13.2	13.9	14.4	15.4	16.1	17.4	14.9	21.0	21.1	Liban
Mongolia	0.9	1.1	1.4	1.2	1.0	1.0	0.9	1.2	1.2	1.3	Mongolie
Myanmar	26.6	26.8	27.0	27.3	27.6	28.1	28.8	29.4	29.9	30.6	Myanmar
Oman	0.4	0.4	0.4	0.4	0.4	0.4	0.4	0.4	0.4	0.4	Oman

For general note and footnotes, see end of table.

Voir la fin du tableau pour la remarque générale et les notes.

Cheese (Total production) (continued)
Fromage (Production totale) (suite)

ISIC-BASED CODE - CODE BASE CITI

3112-10

Unit : Thousand metric tons

Unité : Milliers de tonnes métriques

Country or area	1990	1991	1992	1993	1994	1995	1996	1997	1998	1999	Pays ou zone
Syrian Arab Republic	65.3	74.9	72.3	58.2	64.2	65.6	75.1	86.4	96.6	87.9	Rép. arabe syrienne
Tajikistan	..	...	10.6	8.6	8.0	3.0	0.9	4.2	5.6	6.0	Tadjikistan
Turkey	136.6	142.1	140.7	140.8	140.3	139.8	141.4	133.1	132.1	130.9	Turquie
Turkmenistan	..	...	5.0	3.5	3.1	2.4	1.8	1.8	1.5	1.6	Turkménistan
Uzbekistan	..	...	27.0	25.4	22.5	21.7	16.1	19.7	18.8	23.5	Ouzbékistan
Yemen	..	9.0	9.2	9.4	9.2	9.3	9.6	10.1	10.6	10.9	Yémen
Europe	**5785**	**7561**	**7743**	**7889**	**7942**	**7960**	**8105**	**8167**	**8330**	**8290**	**Europe**
Albania	13.3	9.7	8.3	7.5	7.6	9.9	15.2	11.2	11.2	11.4	Albanie
Austria	114.1	109.2	108.7	110.8	127.3	120.3	119.8	127.0	134.8	136.8	Autriche
Belarus	..	...	59.3	56.1	53.0	35.8	39.5	51.1	61.5	56.9	Bélarus
Belgium-Luxembourg	67.2	69.8	74.6	74.8	75.6	73.2	74.8	78.2	75.3	65.0	Belgique-Luxembourg
Bosnia and Herzegovina	..	..	17.9	16.0	13.5	13.5	13.5	13.5	14.0	11.0	Bosnie-Herzégovine
Bulgaria	196.9	158.2	120.3	96.0	87.3	81.5	75.9	66.1	71.6	58.0	Bulgarie
Croatia	..	...	16.2	16.0	17.3	17.9	19.5	21.5	19.2	19.0	Croatie
Denmark	295.0	286.7	291.4	323.3	288.1	311.2	299.2	290.6	289.3	290.0	Danemark
Czechoslovakia(former)	217.7	170.5	..	..	..	..	..	..	..	..	Tchécoslovaquie(anc.)
Czech Republic	..	..	...	116.5	102.2	95.7	117.4	127.4	143.1	145.1	République tchèque
Estonia	..	...	19.7	17.8	21.7	16.0	14.1	18.3	17.3	15.5	Estonie
Finland	93.3	84.8	88.3	89.1	92.2	95.7	94.8	87.9	92.9	92.6	Finlande
France	1458.6	1490.2	1504.6	1537.1	1568.9	1593.0	1605.3	1621.6	1653.4	1675.6	France
Germany	..	1236.7	1291.9	1341.2	1367.4	1419.9	1497.2	1558.0	1569.3	1562.7	Allemagne
Greece	228.6	216.3	214.9	216.1	214.5	224.4	231.5	235.8	231.5	242.4	Grèce
Hungary	92.8	85.7	79.3	84.3	83.0	83.3	88.6	90.9	88.8	92.5	Hongrie
Iceland	2.6	2.7	2.9	3.2	3.4	3.5	3.5	3.7	3.7	3.7	Islande
Ireland	70.8	76.0	95.8	95.0	95.3	82.3	100.2	98.7	98.3	108.5	Irlande
Italy	917.4	889.8	905.8	882.2	900.3	981.8	984.5	948.8	1012.5	981.5	Italie
Latvia	..	...	15.4	12.6	10.5	9.8	9.7	11.5	11.0	11.2	Lettonie
Lithuania	..	...	24.7	24.7	23.1	22.3	30.5	38.2	49.3	39.4	Lituanie
Malta	0.1	0.1	0.1	0.1	0.1	0.1	0.3	0.3	0.3	0.3	Malte
Netherlands	585.6	602.5	626.0	627.9	648.3	680.1	688.1	693.0	638.0	645.6	Pays-Bas
Norway	87.6	82.0	81.3	83.6	81.8	84.6	86.0	87.1	90.9	85.9	Norvège
Poland	332.7	294.4	288.3	315.3	352.2	354.2	397.2	445.1	473.1	476.1	Pologne
Portugal	58.0	64.1	65.1	64.9	64.7	66.1	66.3	68.4	70.4	72.8	Portugal
Republic of Moldova	..	...	5.1	5.5	4.3	3.7	3.3	4.9	5.1	5.1	Rép. de Moldova
Romania	105.8	84.3	61.4	62.0	58.6	62.3	58.9	41.8	47.8	49.4	Roumanie
Russian Federation	..	...	638.9	662.5	613.4	476.9	428.0	387.0	385.0	363.0	Fédération de Russie
Slovakia	..	..	...	34.4	37.4	38.6	41.6	45.4	54.3	55.0	Slovaquie
Slovenia	..	...	12.4	14.0	15.3	15.8	16.9	18.4	20.9	21.1	Slovénie
Spain	166.1	165.9	167.7	174.0	177.0	166.0	164.0	167.1	186.3	175.4	Espagne
Sweden	116.0	115.0	117.0	126.0	133.0	129.0	127.0	118.0	130.8	133.5	Suède
Switzerland	132.0	136.4	134.7	138.2	142.1	137.3	139.2	136.2	134.9	135.6	Suisse
Ukraine	..	...	125.2	115.3	117.8	87.8	70.1	57.8	63.0	63.0	Ukraine
United Kingdom	311.9	298.1	327.0	331.0	330.0	354.0	369.0	377.0	366.0	376.0	Royaume-Uni
Yugoslavia	..	...	19.8	13.1	12.1	10.6	13.5	17.8	13.6	11.5	Yougoslavie
T.F.Yug.Rep. Macedonia	..	...	0.6	0.9	1.5	1.7	1.5	1.3	1.5	1.5	L'ex-RY Macédoine
Yugoslavia, SFR	120.6	..	..	..	..	..	..	..	..	..	Yougoslavie, RSF
USSR (former)	2074.0	..	..	..	..	..	..	..	..	..	URSS (anc.)
Oceania	**293**	**304**	**335**	**355**	**427**	**432**	**493**	**539**	**561**	**522**	**Océanie**
Australia	175.3	179.4	198.0	210.9	233.6	234.4	264.0	285.0	295.0	308.0	Australie
New Zealand	118.1	124.8	137.4	144.5	193.3	197.4	229.1	253.6	265.6	214.0	Nouvelle-Zélande
	13478	**13368**	**13882**	**14101**	**14425**	**14550**	**14901**	**15197**	**15508**	**15724**	**Total**

General Note.

Cheese made by coagulating animal milk either from a natural process or by addition of rennet or another curdling agent and then removing the whey. Curd and processed cheese are excluded. Includes non-industrial production. (SITC, Rev.3: 02410-0, 02430-0,02491-1, 02499-0).
Source: Food and Agriculture Organization of the United Nations (FAO), Rome.

[1] Including Hong-Kong, Macao and Taiwan.

Remarque générale.

Fromage résultant de la coagulation du lait animal soit par un procédé naturel soit par l'addition de présure ou d'une autre substance coagulante, après enlè-vement du petit lait. Ne compris pas la caillebotte et les fromages fondus. Y compris la production non-industrielle.
(CTCI, Rev.3: 02410-0, 02430-0, 02491-1, 02499-0). Source: Organisation des Nations Unies pour l'alimentation et l'agriculture (FAO), Rome.

[1] Y compris Hong-Kong, Macao et Taïwan.

Cheese (Industrial production)
Fromage (Production industrielle)

ISIC-BASED CODE - CODE BASE CITI

3112-101

Unit : Thousand metric tons

Unité : Milliers de tonnes métriques

Country or area	1990	1991	1992	1993	1994	1995	1996	1997	1998	1999	Pays ou zone
Africa	**887**	**827**	**769**	**706**	**538**	**746**	**516**	**370**	**447**	**353**	**Afrique**
Egypt	206.0	216.5	229.6	236.5	240.6	241.0	277.8	283.3	290.0	306.0	Egypte
Kenya	0.6	0.6	0.3	0.6	0.3	0.4	0.4	...	...	...	Kenya
Madagascar	...	...	...	...	291.5	499.5	232.0	78.7	146.0	...	Madagascar
Tunisia	4.1	4.1	4.4	6.1	6.0	4.8	6.0	7.3	10.5	11.0	Tunisie
America, North	**2760**	**2760**	**2957**	**3068**	**3165**	**3245**	**3381**	**3441**	**3518**	**3794**	**Amérique du Nord**
Mexico	7.2	7.7	8.9	#102.5	103.7	100.7	99.4	105.8	104.2	110.5	Mexique
Panama	3.9	...	4.7	5.4	6.1	6.4	7.9	...	...	...	Panama
United States	2748.5	2746.4	2943.0	2960.5	3054.8	3137.5	3273.8	3325.0	3402.8	...	Etats-Unis
America, South	**368**	**459**	**518**	**508**	**537**	**522**	**561**	**587**	**606**	**620**	**Amérique du Sud**
Argentina	271.0	289.0	336.2	350.0	385.2	368.9	395.6	418.0	426.5	442.6	Argentine
Brazil	45.7	65.6	68.1	66.3	53.2	54.5	67.2	67.8	67.4	61.3	Brésil
Colombia	8.7	...	11.9	13.7	17.2	18.0	...	19.2	22.2	...	Colombie
Ecuador	...	...	1.1	1.2	3.3	2.4	2.1	2.0	8.7	...	Equateur
Peru	...	...	...	...	...	1.4	2.6	2.4	3.6	4.7	Pérou
Venezuela	42.4	88.3	100.9	...	...	...	...	...	...	...	Venezuela
Asia	**195**	**241**	**230**	**234**	**228**	**231**	**231**	**248**	**257**	**254**	**Asie**
Armenia	..	9.2	3.3	1.5	1.6	0.8	1.2	4.4	4.4	4.4	Arménie
Azerbaijan	..	16.1	9.5	7.6	5.3	2.5	1.8	0.4	0.0	0.0	Azerbaïdjan
Cyprus	*8.4	*9.1	7.0	*7.6	*7.9	8.6	8.7	9.6	9.8	9.4	Chypre
Georgia	..		2.8	0.9	0.4	0.4	0.3	0.1	0.0	0.1	Géorgie
Indonesia	1.5	2.1	2.4	2.7	3.0	3.3	...	3.9	0.1	...	Indonésie
Israel	76.4		...	...	...	...	...	...	...	...	Israël
Japan	82.2	88.5	92.2	100.4	101.8	105.4	109.0	114.0	123.8	123.5	Japon
Kyrgyzstan	..	5.1	2.7	2.3	1.5	0.8	0.7	1.0	1.3	1.4	Kirghizistan
Tajikistan		3.1	1.3	0.4	0.4	0.3	0.0	0.0	0.1	0.0	Tadjikistan
Turkey	26.0	26.9	29.2	29.9	25.0	29.8	29.0	36.7	39.2	35.4	Turquie
Turkmenistan	..	1.2	1.0	0.5	0.7	0.4	0.2	0.3	0.3	...	Turkménistan
Uzbekistan	..	2.3	2.6	3.6	3.7	2.3	1.5	1.4	...	...	Ouzbékistan
Europe	**5559**	**6318**	**6170**	**6145**	**6252**	**6398**	**6535**	**6644**	**6683**	**6782**	**Europe**
Austria	...	...	...	...	...	90.6	96.7	101.6	107.6	105.0	Autriche
Belarus	..	¹57.3	39.4	35.0	34.6	24.7	29.7	37.9	43.3	40.6	Bélarus
Belgium	62.6	64.3	68.7	69.1	...	...	...	...	...	...	Belgique
Bulgaria	146.6	120.6	87.4	67.5	59.9	52.9	48.1	38.4	42.1	28.2	Bulgarie
Croatia	..	18.5	15.7	15.5	16.7	17.4	19.0	20.9	18.5	...	Croatie
Denmark[2]	331.6	315.1	321.3	340.7	309.2	254.1	254.5	273.5	284.9	271.6	Danemark[2]
Czechoslovakia(former)	157.4	124.0	..	..	..	..	..	..	..	..	Tchécoslovaquie(anc.)
Czech Republic	..		88.2	82.4	86.7	..	..	..	..	..	République tchèque
Estonia	..	13.8	9.7	8.8	10.2	8.6	9.1	11.0	12.3	10.2	Estonie
Finland	127.9	79.1	83.2	82.6	86.1	88.3	85.5	86.7	96.6	103.8	Finlande
France	1538.0	1571.0	1590.0	1635.0	1674.0	1711.0	1732.0	1748.0	1789.0	...	France
Germany	..	1247.9	1293.4	1336.6	1399.1	1691.3	1744.5	1802.2	1822.1	...	Allemagne
Germany(Fed.Rep.)	1115.1		..	..	..	..	..	..	..	..	Allemagne(Rép.féd.)
German D.R.(former)	79.5										R.D.A. (anc.)
Greece	47.2	43.8	40.8	39.0	43.2	47.4	...	...	59.1	...	Grèce
Hungary	59.3	52.4	46.8	49.6	50.4	51.0	46.6	50.2	48.3	49.7	Hongrie
Iceland	3.0	3.0	3.0	3.0	3.9	3.8	3.5	4.0	4.2	4.4	Islande
Ireland	75.0	...	...	...	...	...	...	...	...	...	Irlande
Latvia	..	21.3	14.8	12.0	9.9	9.4	9.3	11.1	11.2	16.3	Lettonie
Lithuania	..	24.5	17.6	19.7	18.5	17.2	22.3	29.9	35.8	35.5	Lituanie
Luxembourg	3.3	3.7	3.8	3.2	3.5	3.3	3.0	...	...	...	Luxembourg
Netherlands[2][3]	646.5	663.3	702.4	618.0	631.0	608.0	666.0	746.0	662.0	702.9	Pays-Bas[2][3]
Norway	88.6	83.6	81.9	83.6	...	82.6	...	77.8	...	...	Norvège
Poland	125.8	113.5	101.5	113.4	129.5	122.2	136.8	158.3	163.5	154.8	Pologne
Portugal	42.8	42.4	45.5	44.3	47.4	45.6	48.5	47.9	52.9	54.5	Portugal
Republic of Moldova	..	...	4.6	⁴3.8	⁴2.5	⁴1.7	⁴1.4	⁴1.1	⁴1.2	⁴1.1	Rép. de Moldova
Romania	93.6	71.2	49.4	49.6	46.8	50.6	47.6	42.4	36.7	31.0	Roumanie
Russian Federation	..	394.0	298.9	312.5	285.4	217.7	193.0	173.6	163.1	185.2	Fédération de Russie
Slovakia	..		30.8	34.7	34.4	34.9	34.6	32.2	32.2	34.9	Slovaquie
Slovenia	..	12.3	12.6	13.9	15.2	15.8	16.5	18.0	19.9	20.5	Slovénie

For general note and footnotes, see end of table.

Voir la fin du tableau pour la remarque générale et les notes.

Cheese (Industrial production) (continued)
Fromage (Production industrielle) (suite)

ISIC-BASED CODE - CODE BASE CITI
3112-101

Unit : Thousand metric tons   Unité : Milliers de tonnes métriques

Country or area	1990	1991	1992	1993	1994	1995	1996	1997	1998	1999	Pays ou zone
Spain	172.8	266.3	261.8	243.4	...	...	...	...	...	...	Espagne
Sweden	106.5	105.1	106.4	107.3	123.0	123.8	125.8	119.3	129.7	117.4	Suède
Ukraine [1]	..	161.5	112.7	101.8	104.7	73.5	59.0	46.3	52.0	52.5	Ukraine [1]
United Kingdom	...	...	...	445.0	464.2	475.3	495.5	434.4	450.4	...	Royaume-Uni
Yugoslavia	..	25.8	19.2	13.3	12.2	10.7	13.7	18.0	14.8	12.8	Yougoslavie
T.F.Yug.Rep. Macedonia	..	1.2	0.6	0.9	1.5	1.7	1.5	1.3	1.5	1.7	L'ex-RY Macédoine
USSR (former) [1]	886.9	..	..	..	..	..	..	..	..	..	URSS (anc.) [1]
Oceania	295	306	335	356	429	432	497	543	577	607	Océanie
Australia [5]	175.3	179.4	198.0	210.9	235.6	234.4	267.8	285.0	300.0	311.7	Australie [5]
New Zealand	119.7	127.0	137.4	145.5	193.3	197.4	229.1	...	...	...	Nouvelle-Zélande
Total	10950	10911	10980	11018	11149	11573	11721	11833	12087	12410	Total

General Note.
Cheese made by coagulating animal milk either from a natural process or by addition of rennet or another curdling agent and then removing the whey. Curd and processed cheese are excluded. Data refer to industrial production only. (SITC, Rev.3: 02410-0, 02430-0, 02491-1, 02499-0).

[1] Including processed cheese containing not less than 20 per cent fat.

[2] Sales.
[3] Production by establishments employing 20 or more persons.
[4] Excluding Transnistria region.
[5] Twelve months ending 30 June of year stated.

Remarque générale.
Fromage résultant de la coagulation du lait animal soit par un procédé naturel soit par l'addition de présure ou d'une autre substance coagulante, après enlèvement du petit lait. Cette rubrique ne comprend pas la caillebotte et les fromages fondus. Les données se rapportent à la production industrielle seulement.

[1] Y compris les fromages fondus contenant moins de 20 p. 100 de matières grasses.
[2] Ventes.
[3] Production des établissements occupant 20 personnes ou plus.
[4] Non compris la région de Transnistria.
[5] Période de douze mois finissant le 30 juin de l'année indiquée.

Ice-cream
Crème glacée
ISIC-BASED CODE - CODE BASE CITI
3112-13

Unit : Thousand kilolitres

Unité : Milliers de kilolitres

Country or area	1990	1991	1992	1993	1994	1995	1996	1997	1998	1999	Pays ou zone
Africa											**Afrique**
Egypt[1]	2.7	1.9	1.8	2.7	1.2	1.3	0.5	0.4	...	...	Egypte[1]
Kenya	0.6	0.7	0.7	0.8	0.8	0.9	0.9	...	...	...	Kenya
South Africa	60.2	69.1	68.9	72.2	74.5	87.0	87.4	85.6	86.3	89.3	Afrique du Sud
America, North											**Amérique du Nord**
Panama	10.9	9.0	9.3	11.9	14.6	11.2	15.1	...	...		Panama
United States	3412.3	3496.1	3514.1	3338.9	3317.7	3243.9	3325.8	3428.0	3276.4	...	Etats-Unis
America, South											**Amérique du Sud**
Bolivia	391.8	413.1	166.4	1088.8	1224.3	*1356.1	...	...	...	...	Bolivie
Brazil[1]	111.7	139.8	109.1	115.5	113.7	167.7	145.2	132.9	151.9	131.7	Brésil[1]
Chile	33.5	38.6	45.3	51.8	54.9	58.7	63.8	74.2	78.7	65.6	Chili
Colombia[1]	22.1	...	24.0	24.8	34.4	25.2	...	23.0	24.5	...	Colombie[1]
Paraguay[1]	2.3	3.0	2.9	...	...	...	...	...	...	...	Paraguay[1]
Asia											**Asie**
Armenia[1]	..	3.4	0.7	0.3	0.3	0.1	0.4	0.4	0.6	0.7	Arménie[1]
Azerbaijan[1]	..	3.6	2.0	1.0	0.6	0.5	0.3	0.3	0.2	0.1	Azerbaïdjan[1]
Bangladesh	105.0	...	...	...	...	...	...	...	...	...	Bangladesh
Hong Kong SAR	20.7	19.0	15.7	16.5	15.2	13.6	12.2	10.6	11.1	15.7	Hong-Kong RAS
China, Macao, SAR[1]	...	...	...	0.1	0.1	0.2	0.2	0.1	0.1	0.1	Chine, Macao PAS[1]
Georgia	..	...	...	79.0	5.0	59.7	...	...	...	...	Géorgie
Indonesia[1]	3.9	2.4	1.3	1.1	1.9	1.3	...	...	9.2	...	Indonésie[1]
Iran(Islamic Rep. of)[1][2]	11.0	13.2	11.7	...	...	...	...	...	...	...	Iran(Rép. islamique)[1][2]
Japan[3]	144.4	154.9	154.0	140.0	153.2	151.2	153.0	117.7	105.7	109.8	Japon[3]
Kazakhstan[1]	..	25.6	10.9	9.4	9.0	4.7	3.4	3.2	3.8	4.2	Kazakhstan[1]
Korea, Republic of	110.6	132.7	127.0	133.9	121.4	[1]259.0	[1]270.8	[1]266.8	[1]231.8	[1]270.9	Corée, République de
Kyrgyzstan	..	7.0	2.1	[1]2.0	[1]1.3	[1]1.2	[1]1.1	[1]1.0	[1]0.7	[1]0.9	Kirghizistan
Tajikistan[1]	..	3.3	1.3	0.6	0.4	0.1	0.1	0.0	0.0	0.0	Tadjikistan[1]
Turkey[1]	...	6.8	...	17.5	...	17.8	18.4	27.3	37.3	44.3	Turquie[1]
Turkmenistan[1]	..	3.8	2.4	1.4	2.2	0.8	0.6	0.4	0.4	...	Turkménistan[1]
Uzbekistan[1]	..	15.0	8.0	5.8	5.8	3.2	2.5	2.7	...	...	Ouzbékistan[1]
Europe											**Europe**
Austria	...	...	...	45.1	43.1	44.6	30.9	36.5	6.3	5.4	Autriche
Belarus[1]	..	34.0	31.2	21.3	22.7	20.1	26.1	32.0	39.5	43.7	Bélarus[1]
Belgium	110.8	125.3	116.7	73.8	124.0	125.0	124.9	134.7	147.5	133.4	Belgique
Croatia	..	[1]6.7	[1]4.7	[1]4.9	[1]8.5	[1]6.6	[1]6.8	[1]8.5	[1]8.2	...	Croatie
Denmark[4]	62.2	71.7	86.5	75.3	82.4	86.3	75.7	79.5	40.9		Danemark[4]
Czechoslovakia(former)	65.5	60.6	..	..	..	..	..	..	..		Tchécoslovaquie(anc.)
Czech Republic	..	..	35.5	27.6	23.9	33.0	36.8	30.4	31.5	27.9	République tchèque
Estonia	..	2.8	1.3	0.9	1.3	1.6	2.5	5.6	8.8	12.3	Estonie
Finland[5]	53.7	49.6	57.5	69.2	91.2	68.5	66.2	67.7	64.5	59.9	Finlande[5]
France	291.5	286.9	302.0	323.3	355.6	338.0	309.0	313.0	315.0	...	France
Germany	...	...	311.7	280.6	316.3	435.3	430.1	440.9	512.8	...	Allemagne
Germany(Fed.Rep.)[1]	238.3	..	..	..	..	..	..	..	..		Allemagne(Rép.féd.)[1]
German D.R.(former)[1]	7.6	..	..	..	..	..	..	..	..		R.D.A. (anc.)[1]
Greece	[1]22.9	[1]22.9	[1]23.2	39.7	46.8	44.2	38.8	37.5	41.0	...	Grèce
Hungary	5.3	1.6	6.0	6.4	9.7	12.0	11.7	13.9	15.2	41.4	Hongrie
Iceland	[1]1.0	[1]1.0	[1]1.0	...	...	...	2.5	2.5	2.4	3.1	Islande
Ireland	...	...	...	...	...	31.6	...	...	...	...	Irlande
Latvia	..	[1]10.1	[1]6.5	[1]4.5	[1]5.6	[1]6.1	[1]5.6	[1]6.2	[1]4.7	9.8	Lettonie
Lithuania[1]	..	15.3	8.5	7.4	10.4	8.3	10.7	11.1	13.8	13.0	Lituanie[1]
Netherlands[4][6]	37.2	39.5	48.6	58.0	55.3	53.0	49.0	76.0	79.0	79.0	Pays-Bas[4][6]
Norway	45.3	42.9	47.3	44.5	...	53.8	...	...	...	...	Norvège
Poland	19.8	29.4	28.7	35.7	50.0	74.8	87.2	136.9	118.8	100.4	Pologne
Portugal	[1]19.6	[1]21.1	[1]29.0	[1]24.3	[1]25.2	[1]28.7	25.2	26.7	29.2	26.0	Portugal
Republic of Moldova[1]	..	8.5	7.2	[7]2.9	[7]2.5	[7]2.4	[7]3.0	[7]3.3	[7]4.4	[7]4.3	Rép. de Moldova[1]
Russian Federation[1]	..	425.1	251.1	263.2	253.3	231.7	222.9	259.6	314.8	362.7	Fédération de Russie[1]
Slovakia	..	..	..	..	..	..	..	..	4.8	67.8	Slovaquie
Slovenia	..	[1]2.7	[1]3.8	[1]3.6	[1]3.2	[1]2.8	6.2	5.8	6.3	5.0	Slovénie
Spain	110.0	129.1	119.4	262.9	...	...	...	...	...	...	Espagne
Sweden	[1]58.1	[1]57.2	[1]66.0	[1]62.5	[1]75.0	[1]71.6	136.8	140.5	132.2	128.3	Suède

For general note and footnotes, see end of table.

Voir la fin du tableau pour la remarque générale et les notes.

Ice-cream (continued)
Crème glacée (suite)

ISIC-BASED CODE - CODE BASE CITI

3112-13

Unit : Thousand kilolitres   Unité : Milliers de kilolitres

Country or area	1990	1991	1992	1993	1994	1995	1996	1997	1998	1999	Pays ou zone
Switzerland	51.6	52.6	51.8	50.5	52.5	50.7	...	...	...	...	Suisse
Ukraine	..	125.0	84.9	77.4	79.9	60.1	51.3	56.9	67.0	89.7	Ukraine
United Kingdom	338.7	343.7	...	413.7	469.0	517.4	557.5	506.4	486.3	...	Royaume-Uni
Yugoslavia	..	9.0	8.5	6.5	9.7	10.1	8.4	6.6	5.9	3.1	Yougoslavie
T.F.Yug.Rep. Macedonia [1]	..	0.6	0.5	0.4	0.5	0.3	0.2	0.3	0.0	0.0	L'ex-RY Macédoine [1]
USSR (former) [1]	807.9	..	..	..	..	..	..	..	..	..	URSS (anc.) [1]
Oceania											**Océanie**
Australia [8]	197.1	192.4	194.9	193.1	...	...	...	...	...	...	Australie [8]
Fiji	3.0	2.5	2.5	2.8	2.9	2.8	2.1	2.5	2.3	...	Fidji

General Note.

Mixture containing 80 per cent cream and milk products, 15 per cent sweeteners and no less than 5 per cent butter fat, with some amounts of colour and flavour. (SITC. Rev.3: 02233-1).

Remarque générale.

Mélange contenant 80 p. 100 de crème et de produits laitiers, 15 p. 100 d'édulcorant et au moins 5 p. 100 de butyrine, ainsi qu'une certaine quantité de colorant et de parfum. (CTCI, Rev.3: 02233-1).

[1] In thousand metric tons.
[2] Production by establishments employing 50 or more persons.
[3] Milk fat content, 8 per cent.
[4] Sales.
[5] Ice-cream containing cocoa.
[6] Production by establishments employing 20 or more persons.
[7] Excluding Transnistria region.
[8] Twelve months ending 30 June of year stated.

[1] En milliers de tonnes métriques.
[2] Production des établissements occupant 50 personnes ou plus.
[3] Teneur en matières grasses lactiques, 8 p. 100.
[4] Ventes.
[5] Crème glacée contenant du cacao.
[6] Production des établissements occupant 20 personnes ou plus.
[7] Non compris la région de Transnistrie.
[8] Période de douze mois finissant le 30 juin de l'année indiquée.

Fruits, dried
Fruits secs
ISIC-BASED CODE - CODE BASE CITI
3113-01

Unit : Metric tons   Unité : Tonnes métriques

Country or area	1990	1991	1992	1993	1994	1995	1996	1997	1998	1999	Pays ou zone
Africa	**826**	**666**	**535**	**689**	**689**	**616**	**775**	**714**	**689**	**689**	**Afrique**
Egypt	826	666	535	...	...	616	775	714	...	...	Egypte
America, South	**11551**	**7738**	**6805**	**7523**	**7147**	**6406**	**8111**	**8287**	**6222**	**5577**	**Amérique du Sud**
Chile	11186	7355	6565	7211	6666	5748	7677	7851	5744	...	Chili
Colombia	...	...	240	312	481	658	...	436	478	...	Colombie
Asia	**158897**	**167798**	**140659**	**165100**	**206180**	**206645**	**193797**	**200012**	**199034**	**175080**	**Asie**
Armenia	..	115	70	2	21	0	0	0	0	...	Arménie
Azerbaijan	..	0	0	7	0	20	0	0	0	...	Azerbaïdjan
Hong Kong SAR	236	...	...	...	...	...	...	...	...	...	Hong-Kong RAS
China, Macao, SAR[1]	...	...	...	422	301	238	256	185	178	...	Chine, Macao PAS[1]
Cyprus	850	480	330	330	600	162	93	61	145	105	Chypre
Indonesia	...	...	191	...	...	...	...	...	...	...	Indonésie
Kazakhstan	..	30	71	...	63	115	295	124	...	3	Kazakhstan
Kyrgyzstan	..	1196	2188	945	236	75	29	14	8	11	Kirghizistan
Tajikistan	..	4716	1354	2102	695	2521	1012	726	390	...	Tadjikistan
Turkey	157246	140525	123726	143596	187347	189909	181064	190262	191372	168999	Turquie
Turkmenistan	..	...	1	62	47	40	126	37	94	...	Turkménistan
Uzbekistan	..	19932	12162	17107	16443	13138	10495	8176	...	...	Ouzbékistan
Europe	**169507**	**165649**	**210513**	**175015**	**182145**	**204248**	**209870**	**240802**	**251177**	**242174**	**Europe**
Austria	...	...	...	...	...	27733	33422	38652	41431	39672	Autriche
Belarus	..	27	54	84	44	17	81	88	49	112	Bélarus
Bulgaria	1770	1329	1080	652	626	294	686	786	123	301	Bulgarie
Croatia	..	...	...	...	...	...	...	4	4	...	Croatie
Finland	89	72	78	84	548	530	519	...	...	18	Finlande
France	[2]36745	[2]24800	[2]50970	[2]37150	[2]43100	61300	66696	...	...	...	France
Germany	..	...	...	...	...	12206	...	...	...	...	Allemagne
Greece	[3]98294	[3]68163	[3]68036	...	...	57206	44961	53756	51309	...	Grèce
Hungary[4]	385	207	...	#2669	2815	1784	...	...	...	...	Hongrie[4]
Poland	550	5188	6665	3558	4089	2101	2465	4229	2687	6453	Pologne
Portugal	1179	787	...	...	...	...	...	...	...	...	Portugal
Republic of Moldova	..	10724	6089	[5]2423	[5]1916	[5]1609	[5]1680	[5]1229	[5]437	[5]373	Rép. de Moldova
Romania	2974	2271	1131	436	896	324	382	261	80	51	Roumanie
Russian Federation	..	1097	3766	3437	#343	640	385	309	125	149	Fédération de Russie
Slovakia	..	..	...	...	...	...	...	9	...	...	Slovaquie
Slovenia	..	...	...	...	...	...	26	107	0	...	Slovénie
Spain	[6]13660	[6]17290	[6]31211	21334	23053	35511	41838	50126	58484	55753	Espagne
Ukraine	..	3069	3428	2215	727	1327	265	406	146	103	Ukraine
Yugoslavia	..	754	2468	672	499	102	167	566	234	105	Yougoslavie
T.F.Yug.Rep. Macedonia	..	567	480	...	...	...	...	...	...	...	L'ex-RY Macédoine
USSR (former)	49409	..	..	..	..	..	..	..	..	..	URSS (anc.)
Total	**390191**	**341851**	**358512**	**348326**	**396161**	**417915**	**412553**	**449815**	**457122**	**423519**	**Total**

General Note.
Fruits prepared either by direct drying in the sun or by industrial processes, whether or not containing added sugar. Drained, glace or crystallized fruit as well as dried citrus fruit are excluded. (SITC, Rev.3: 05730-1, 05752-0, 05760-1, 05795-1, 05796-1, 05797-1, 05799-1).

Remarque générale.
Fruits séchés, soit par action directe du soleil, soit par des procédés industriels, avec ou sans addition de sucre. Cette rubrique ne comprend ni les fruits confits au sucre (égouttés, glacés ou candis) ni les agrumes séchés. (CTCI, Rev.3: 05730-1, 05752-0, 05760-1, 05795-1, 05796-1, 05797-1, 05799-1).

[1] 1999 data are confidential.
[2] Prunes only.
[3] Pasteurized dried figs and raisins.
[4] Including crystallised fruit.
[5] Excluding Transnistria region.
[6] Including dried vegetables.

[1] Pour 1999, les données sont confidentielles.
[2] Pruneaux seulement.
[3] Figues et raisins secs pasteurisés.
[4] Y compris les fruits candis.
[5] Non compris la région de Transnistria.
[6] Y compris les légumes secs.

Jams, marmalades and fruit jellies
Confitures, marmelades et gelées de fruits

ISIC-BASED CODE - CODE BASE CITI

3113-04

Unit : Thousand metric tons

Unité : Milliers de tonnes métriques

Country or area	1990	1991	1992	1993	1994	1995	1996	1997	1998	1999	Pays ou zone
Africa	**73**	**65**	**64**	**67**	**48**	**54**	**56**	**51**	**50**	**53**	**Afrique**
Algeria	10.8	10.9	7.9	13.3	12.7	10.2	7.3	9.7	13.1	9.8	Algérie
Egypt	23.1	16.7	13.4	11.9	5.1	11.3	8.8	3.3	...	...	Egypte
Ethiopia[1]	2.3	1.6	1.1	1.1	0.0	0.2	0.8	1.1	0.7	2.9	Ethiopie[1]
Kenya	1.1	1.1	1.1	0.9	1.2	1.1	1.2	...	...	...	Kenya
South Africa	35.2	34.4	40.5	40.2	28.6	30.7	38.1	35.4	30.6	35.5	Afrique du Sud
America, North	**8**	**5**	**6**	**40**	**38**	**34**	**42**	**46**	**49**	**58**	**Amérique du Nord**
Mexico	7.5	5.4	6.1	#39.5	37.8	33.9	42.4	46.4	49.1	58.1	Mexique
America, South	**24**	**35**	**41**	**37**	**32**	**38**	**39**	**46**	**53**	**54**	**Amérique du Sud**
Bolivia	0.0	0.1	0.1	0.1	0.1	*0.1	...	...	...	...	Bolivie
Chile[1]	14.8	15.4	20.1	16.5	16.3	18.3	18.6	18.3	20.4	16.8	Chili[1]
Colombia	...	...	8.8	10.2	5.8	9.4	...	12.0	14.1	...	Colombie
Ecuador	0.3	...	#11.6	10.2	9.3	9.9	10.3	15.1	18.3	...	Equateur
Peru	...	...	...	...	...	0.3	0.3	0.3	0.2	0.2	Pérou
Asia	**72**	**120**	**79**	**66**	**66**	**67**	**65**	**63**	**72**	**68**	**Asie**
Azerbaijan	..	9.3	8.1	2.0	0.4	0.3	0.3	0.5	0.6	0.5	Azerbaïdjan
Bangladesh	0.1	0.1	0.1	...	...	...	...	...	...	...	Bangladesh
China, Macao, SAR	...	...	..	0.1	0.1	0.1	0.1	0.1	0.1	0.1	Chine, Macao PAS
Cyprus	1.1	1.0	1.0	1.1	0.9	0.9	0.9	0.8	0.9	0.8	Chypre
Georgia	..	...	0.2	0.2	0.1	0.0	0.1	0.0	...	0.0	Géorgie
Indonesia	0.0	0.0	0.2	0.2	0.1	0.3	...	0.7	3.7	...	Indonésie
Iran(Islamic Rep. of)	[2][3]8.5	[2][3]36.5	[3]6.0	[3]5.1	[3]6.0	[4]8.0	[4]8.9	[4]8.5	[4]12.0	...	Iran(Rép. islamique)
Japan	56.8	59.1	54.1	47.1	49.2	47.9	45.1	45.0	45.9	45.2	Japon
Kyrgyzstan	..	0.1	0.2	0.2	0.0	0.0	...	...	...	...	Kirghizistan
Tajikistan[5]	..	7.4	2.2	3.2	1.7	0.3	0.6	0.1	0.4	0.7	Tadjikistan[5]
Turkey	5.1	5.5	6.3	5.9	7.0	8.6	8.1	7.1	7.6	13.4	Turquie
Turkmenistan	..	0.4	0.4	0.7	0.5	0.1	0.0	0.0	0.6	...	Turkménistan
Europe	**1037**	**1247**	**1211**	**1165**	**1153**	**1357**	**1435**	**1456**	**1502**	**1628**	**Europe**
Austria	20.4	21.5	21.3	23.1	22.9	23.9	24.2	22.9	22.6	23.4	Autriche
Belarus	..	13.5	11.2	11.1	7.1	2.9	4.5	5.6	7.4	8.9	Bélarus
Belgium	27.0	30.0	28.6	30.4	65.5	69.9	71.8	73.9	69.7	67.6	Belgique
Bulgaria	12.4	9.1	6.2	6.2	4.1	3.6	5.2	6.5	...	14.3	Bulgarie
Croatia	..	11.0	11.7	7.8	6.8	5.9	3.3	4.2	3.6	...	Croatie
Denmark[6]	36.4	39.6	44.8	45.4	48.7	46.2	48.8	47.9	50.2	52.8	Danemark[6]
Czechoslovakia(former)	24.5	22.3	..	..	..	..	..	..	..	..	Tchécoslovaquie(anc.)
Czech Republic	..	..	13.6	16.0	18.1	18.2	19.6	24.2	24.2	23.3	République tchèque
Finland	19.3	17.7	18.1	20.7	20.6	15.7	14.0	18.4	20.1	19.3	Finlande
France	151.2	161.8	154.8	153.0	160.1	158.3	156.3	155.9	160.3	...	France
Germany	..	219.0	217.2	216.5	232.2	472.5	498.8	528.1	511.3	...	Allemagne
Germany(Fed.Rep.)	256.0	..	..	..	..	..	..	..	..	..	Allemagne(Rép.féd.)
German D.R.(former)	18.0	..	..	..	..	..	..	..	..	..	R.D.A. (anc.)
Greece	10.5	9.4	9.6	30.5	34.6	34.9	47.1	40.1	56.0	...	Grèce
Hungary	60.6	25.7	22.1	13.4	15.3	17.3	14.3	13.3	13.9	13.2	Hongrie
Latvia	..	..	...	0.4	0.1	0.3	0.3	0.3	0.0	1.7	Lettonie
Lithuania	..	7.2	4.8	2.1	1.0	1.7	2.0	2.6	2.7	2.3	Lituanie
Netherlands[6][7]	21.8	27.4	24.8	22.5	48.2	56.8	58.0	58.0	94.0	92.9	Pays-Bas[6][7]
Norway	[8]22.5	[8]21.7	[8]26.2	...	...	28.3	25.9	25.0	23.4	22.9	Norvège
Poland	52.1	43.0	43.0	46.8	51.8	57.2	65.1	60.9	55.7	75.3	Pologne
Portugal	5.3	2.5	7.9	6.3	6.9	7.3	8.1	7.4	7.9	8.7	Portugal
Romania[9]	1.7	1.1	1.2	0.9	0.6	0.6	0.8	0.6	0.4	0.6	Roumanie[9]
Russian Federation	..	117.1	85.2	69.5	24.1	13.5	16.5	13.4	11.5	19.6	Fédération de Russie
Slovakia	..	..	5.5	4.8	5.5	4.9	7.1	7.7	5.3	5.7	Slovaquie
Slovenia	..	1.6	1.5	1.4	1.7	1.2	1.4	1.3	1.6	1.6	Slovénie
Spain	126.8	149.7	152.1	92.6	74.6	90.9	90.7	95.8	101.0	107.0	Espagne
Sweden	32.2	32.9	29.1	33.1	33.8	37.6	55.4	57.2	60.7	52.5	Suède
Ukraine	..	113.2	92.3	89.9	39.0	15.4	17.2	12.1	10.4	13.2	Ukraine
United Kingdom	138.3	138.2	...	188.5	197.7	165.2	164.4	168.0	175.1	...	Royaume-Uni
Yugoslavia	..	10.4	11.0	7.5	7.1	6.3	13.7	4.1	5.5	6.5	Yougoslavie
T.F.Yug.Rep. Macedonia	..	0.2	0.5	0.6	0.4	0.2	0.3	0.2	0.2	0.2	L'ex-RY Macédoine

For general note and footnotes, see end of table.

Voir la fin du tableau pour la remarque générale et les notes.

Jams, marmalades and fruit jellies (continued)
Confitures, marmelades et gelées de fruits (suite)

ISIC-BASED CODE - CODE BASE CITI

3113-04

Unit : Thousand metric tons

Unité : Milliers de tonnes métriques

Country or area	1990	1991	1992	1993	1994	1995	1996	1997	1998	1999	Pays ou zone
USSR (former)	436.7	..	..	..	..	..	..	..	..	..	URSS (anc.)
Oceania	31	30	32	32	36	36	42	46	37	37	Océanie
Australia[10]	31.3	30.2	32.0	32.4	...	...	41.6	45.7	...	...	Australie[10]
Total	1681	1502	1434	1408	1372	1584	1679	1707	1763	1897	Total

General Note.
Cooked preparations of fruits, whether or not containing added sugar, including jams made with vegetables or with products such as ginger. In terms of net weight. (SITC, Rev.3: 05810-1, 09813-0).

[1] Marmalade only.
[2] Including canned or bottled fruits.
[3] Production by establishments employing 50 or more persons.
[4] Production by establishments employing 10 or more persons.
[5] Original data in conventional cans.
[6] Sales.
[7] Production by establishments employing 20 or more persons.
[8] Including compotes.
[9] Fruit jam only.
[10] Twelve months ending 30 June of year stated.

Remarque générale.
Préparations de fruits obtenues par cuisson, avec ou sans addition de sucre, y compris les confitures faites de légumes ou d'autres ingrédients tels que le gingembre. Poids net. (CTCI, Rev.3: 05810-1, 09813-0).

[1] Marmelades seulement.
[2] Y compris les conserves de fruits (en boîtes ou en bocaux).
[3] Production des établissements occupant 50 personnes ou plus.
[4] Production des établissements occupant 10 personnes ou plus.
[5] Données d'origine exprimées en boîte de type classique.
[6] Ventes.
[7] Production des établissements occupant 20 personnes ou plus.
[8] Y compris les compotes.
[9] Confitures de fruits seulement.
[10] Période de douze mois finissant le 30 juin de l'année indiquée.

Fruit and vegetable juices, concentrated, frozen or not
Jus concentrés de fruits et de légumes, congelés ou non

ISIC-BASED CODE - CODE BASE CITI

3113-07

Unit : Thousand metric tons

Unité : Milliers de tonnes métriques

Country or area	1990	1991	1992	1993	1994	1995	1996	1997	1998	1999	Pays ou zone
Africa											**Afrique**
Algeria	46.0	47.0	29.0	19.0	4.0	...	...	...	...	...	Algérie
Ethiopia[1]	0.4	1.3	1.0	1.2	1.0	1.6	1.9	0.8	1.0	1.9	Ethiopie[1]
Kenya	0.2	0.2	0.2	0.2	0.2	0.1	...	...	...	...	Kenya
South Africa[2]	200.1	226.7	249.7	244.7	268.5	291.2	290.8	277.9	256.1	223.7	Afrique du Sud[2]
America, North											**Amérique du Nord**
Belize[2]	7.4	5.6	8.6	7.3	7.7	12.6	12.9	13.7	12.5	...	Belize[2]
Mexico	...	...	...	12.1	14.3	15.7	15.4	17.3	21.1	17.4	Mexique
America, South											**Amérique du Sud**
Brazil[2][3]	973.2	736.2	750.8	884.9	814.0	605.6	888.8	1073.3	865.2	835.6	Brésil[2][3]
Colombia	...	...	1.0	1.0	...	0.7	...	...	...	...	Colombie
Peru[1]	...	...	...	...	...	1.3	1.7	3.0	1.8	1.0	Pérou[1]
Asia											**Asie**
Azerbaijan	...	...	137.1	...	...	...	...	...	...	...	Azerbaïdjan
Hong Kong SAR[2][4]	13.6	7.0	9.3	4.7	5.0	4.7	4.2	4.3	5.3	5.9	Hong-Kong RAS[2][4]
China, Macao, SAR[2][5]	...	...	...	0.9	...	1.1	...	1.1	1.6	1.6	Chine, Macao PAS[2][5]
Cyprus	0.3	0.3	0.7	1.3	1.6	2.4	1.7	1.5	1.2	1.0	Chypre
Japan	65.7	73.5	69.4	45.2	34.5	39.2	29.5	56.1	31.1	50.0	Japon
Tajikistan[6]	..	37.8	30.9	28.2	9.1	6.1	7.0	7.4	7.5	9.1	Tadjikistan[6]
Turkey	19.4	24.2	24.4	38.2	34.2	60.0	66.3	63.0	44.6	34.8	Turquie
Europe											**Europe**
Austria[2]	33.0	26.2	39.1	46.3	49.9	56.6	61.6	72.2	75.2	63.4	Autriche[2]
Bulgaria	64.1	35.7	22.5	10.5	15.0	32.0	23.7	15.1	15.8	...	Bulgarie
Croatia	..	1.7	1.6	1.8	19.3	14.1	13.6	36.5	51.7	...	Croatie
Denmark[7]	...					14.9	30.5	19.6	27.8	22.6	Danemark[7]
Czechoslovakia(former)	170.9	141.0	..	..	..					..	Tchécoslovaquie(anc.)
Czech Republic	..	..	115.4	103.3	...	40.4	44.5	58.2	60.9	48.9	République tchèque
Finland[2]	2.3	#44.2	46.2	62.3	45.9	28.1	28.7	26.2	24.2	24.7	Finlande[2]
France	18.2	10.5	24.8	16.1	13.9	...	...	...	...	...	France
Germany[2]	..	82.9	59.7	68.4	85.7	...	197.3	219.6	224.1	...	Allemagne[2]
Germany(Fed.Rep.)[2]	89.6	..	..	..	..					..	Allemagne(Rép.féd.)[2]
German D.R.(former)	25.8		..	..	..			..	..	..	R.D.A. (anc.)
Greece	32.1	20.7	17.5	[2]21.0	[2]17.0	[2]23.0	[2]21.0	[2]24.0	[2]24.6	...	Grèce
Hungary	97.6	92.0	77.9	74.3	86.2	84.7	46.2	61.6	42.3	43.5	Hongrie
Ireland	...	...	...	...	...	2.9	...	...	...	...	Irlande
Latvia[8]	..	...	...	...	...	18.9	47.1	43.8	53.5	[2]1.7	Lettonie[8]
Lithuania[2]						11.6	1.0	5.8	0.3	1.9	Lituanie[2]
Netherlands[2]	...	...	...	263.4	279.2	209.4	...	...	...	...	Pays-Bas[2]
Portugal	...	...	30.8	29.0	36.4	44.7	48.6	55.5	61.5	76.4	Portugal
Romania[3]	6.4	3.8	2.8	2.5	1.6	3.0	8.6	8.1	0.7	1.0	Roumanie[3]
Russian Federation	..	99.2	62.9	37.2	42.4	19.8	30.3	35.4	13.4	18.9	Fédération de Russie
Slovakia	..	..	41.6	[2]21.4	[2]19.9	[2]18.5	[2]17.6	[2]16.8	[2]10.3	[2]10.7	Slovaquie
Slovenia[2]	..	2.6	1.8	1.6	1.8	1.7	8.6	5.6	6.1	4.4	Slovénie[2]
Spain[2]	...	...	...	66.8	84.5	93.6	86.4	107.4	149.8	139.1	Espagne[2]
Ukraine	..	7.9	29.9	41.8	9.8	38.8	56.0	114.2	19.1	59.7	Ukraine
United Kingdom	...	...	...	243.1	345.9	332.7	386.4	...	...	...	Royaume-Uni
Yugoslavia	..	12.4	6.8	5.4	3.9	6.3	1.3	1.1	1.1	1.6	Yougoslavie
T.F.Yug.Rep. Macedonia	..	0.9	1.0	0.9	0.3	0.3	0.3	...	0.1	...	L'ex-RY Macédoine

General Note.

Unfermented juice of fruit or vegetables, concentrated or in the form of crystals or powder, containing added sugar (but not containing added alcohol) and intended for consumption as beverages. Unfermented grape juice is included. In terms of net weight. (SITC, Rev.3: 05900-1).

[1] Tomato paste only.
[2] In thousand kilolitres.
[3] Fruit juices only.
[4] Including unconcentrated juices.
[5] 1996 data are confidential.
[6] Original data in conventional cans.
[7] Sales.
[8] Including unconcentrated fruit and vegetable juices.

Remarque générale.

Jus non fermentés de fruits ou de légumes, concentrés ou sous forme de cristaux ou de poudre, additionnés ou non de sucre (mais sans addition d'alcool), qu'ils puissent ou non être employés comme boissons. Cette position comprend les moûts de raisins non fermentés. Poids net. (CTCI, Rev.3: 05900-1).

[1] Purée de tomate seulement.
[2] En milliers de kilolitres.
[3] Jus de fruits seulement.
[4] Y compris les jus non concentrés
[5] Pour 1996, les données sont confidentielles.
[6] Données d'origine exprimées en boîte de type classique.
[7] Ventes.
[8] Y compris les jus non concentrés de fruits et de légumes.

Fruit and vegetable juices, unconcentrated, frozen or not
Jus non concentrés de fruits et de légumes, congelés ou non

ISIC-BASED CODE - CODE BASE CITI

3113-10

Unit : Thousand metric tons — Unité : Milliers de tonnes métriques

Country or area	1990	1991	1992	1993	1994	1995	1996	1997	1998	1999	Pays ou zone
Africa											**Afrique**
Algeria	11.5	20.2	10.0	14.5	17.8	19.5	13.9	20.2	23.8	24.3	Algérie
Kenya	5.2	5.2	5.3	5.3	5.3	5.0	...	...	...	...	Kenya
Madagascar[1][2]	...	...	...	...	19.6	16.9	16.9	18.2	17.9	...	Madagascar[1][2]
Seychelles[2][3]	...	...	...	0.4	1.8	2.1	2.6	2.7	3.0	2.8	Seychelles[2][3]
America, North											**Amérique du Nord**
Martinique[4]	3.5	3.6	3.1	2.8	3.2	...	...	...	...	...	Martinique[4]
Mexico	[3]148.8	[3]139.1	[3]124.2	[3]338.0	[3]365.1	[3]355.0	[3]359.6	[3]438.2	[3]508.0	563.6	Mexique
Panama[2][3]	24.6	...	28.2	23.0	28.0	26.0	26.0	...	...	...	Panama[2][3]
Trinidad and Tobago[2]	3.3	2.9	3.0	3.4	3.5	...	...	...	...	...	Trinité-et-Tobago[2]
America, South											**Amérique du Sud**
Bolivia	4.5	2.3	2.1	2.1	2.6	*3.0	...	...	...	...	Bolivie
Colombia[2]	...	...	38.7	57.8	43.0	57.8	...	103.4	190.2	...	Colombie[2]
Ecuador	5.1	...	8.9	10.7	9.9	11.0	11.7	45.1	36.9	...	Equateur
Asia											**Asie**
Azerbaijan	..	123.1	94.7	56.0	28.5	12.3	13.4	1.4	1.5	5.9	Azerbaïdjan
Bangladesh	0.2	...	...	...	...	...	...	...	...	...	Bangladesh
Cyprus	43.6	30.7	28.7	31.2	44.8	41.1	41.0	42.1	39.4	38.4	Chypre
Indonesia	...	...	0.7	1.1	...	...	...	...	...	...	Indonésie
Kyrgyzstan	..	4.1	2.9	1.6	0.4	0.0	...	...	...	...	Kirghizistan
Malaysia[4]	1.8	...	...	...	...	...	...	...	...	...	Malaisie[4]
Turkey	52.9	66.7	94.3	143.0	146.3	174.9	178.1	215.6	250.1	212.4	Turquie
Turkmenistan	..	2.0	0.9	0.5	1.3	0.1	0.3	0.0	0.0	...	Turkménistan
Europe											**Europe**
Austria[2]	112.3	115.7	130.9	168.6	223.8	...	...	...	...	...	Autriche[2]
Belarus	..	[3]65.8	56.5	51.7	29.6	17.2	22.3	21.5	25.4	25.7	Bélarus
Belgium[2]	...	...	...	...	203.0	215.0	215.0	222.0	225.0	200.0	Belgique[2]
Bulgaria	[1]103.0	[1]35.4	[1]3.5	[1]6.4	[1]7.6	[1]3.0	[1]3.7	18.5	21.0	...	Bulgarie
Croatia	..	15.5	12.5	14.4	16.5	22.8	17.8	10.3	13.8	...	Croatie
Denmark[2][6]	[5]151.1	...	[5]140.3	...	[5]135.8	161.7	133.7	129.9	131.9	143.5	Danemark[2][6]
Czechoslovakia(former)[2]	44.8	16.6	..	..	..	..	..	..	..	..	Tchécoslovaquie(anc.)[2]
Czech Republic	..	..	[2]10.0	15.2	14.8	24.7	22.6	17.6	5.0	...	République tchèque
Estonia	..	0.5	0.3	0.1	0.1	0.1	0.1	0.1	0.1	0.1	Estonie
Finland[2][3]	130.7	106.0	106.0	131.0	165.0	154.0	180.0	168.0	149.0	113.0	Finlande[2][3]
France[2]	167.8	163.0	164.0	161.7	157.4	...	...	...	...	...	France[2]
Germany[2]	..	3411.0	3424.7	3521.0	3680.0	2317.0	2389.0	2529.0	2608.0	...	Allemagne[2]
Germany(Fed.Rep.)[2]	2983.0										Allemagne(Rép.féd.)[2]
German D.R.(former)[7]	136.8	..	..	..	..	..	..	..	..	..	R.D.A. (anc.)[7]
Greece	69.8	76.5	91.9	[2]88.0	[2]156.0	[2]191.0	[2]205.0	[2]209.0	209.7	...	Grèce
Hungary	104.0	178.7	201.2	206.2	336.3	298.5	164.0	182.8	209.3	144.0	Hongrie
Iceland[2]	7.5	7.6	6.6	7.6	14.0	...	9.0	9.0	8.0	8.0	Islande[2]
Latvia[2]	..	...	...	...	...	...	...	...	...	30.3	Lettonie[2]
Lithuania[2]	...	...	...	...	...	1.9	1.5	9.1	9.8	7.7	Lituanie[2]
Poland	140.6	153.2	212.6	257.2	354.6	430.6	576.5	831.4	818.9	841.7	Pologne
Portugal[2]	20.7	26.1	13.0	8.0	4.0	5.0	9.0	5.0	12.0	12.0	Portugal[2]
Russian Federation	..	393.0	264.5	165.7	86.8	79.7	95.6	125.5	171.7	140.7	Fédération de Russie
Slovakia[2]	..	..	7.5	7.0	16.0	16.0	...	...	90.0	67.0	Slovaquie[2]
Slovenia[2]	..	5.1	3.2	3.6	4.6	4.7	4.9	5.1	5.7	59.1	Slovénie[2]
Spain	[3]312.0	[3]387.9	[3]361.0	[2][8]775.8	[2][8]730.5	[2][8]692.1	[2][8]650.4	[2][8]864.1	[2][8]1100.0	[2][8]992.7	Espagne
Sweden[2][3]	157.0	152.0	176.0	169.0	174.0	169.0	...	...	...	...	Suède[2][3]
Ukraine[3]	..	333.6	286.3	303.5	148.5	97.9	63.7	91.7	105.0	96.0	Ukraine[3]
United Kingdom	...	...	...	655.5	707.0	645.3	655.4	...	...	...	Royaume-Uni
Yugoslavia	..	69.8	66.1	29.2	28.2	39.7	36.2	47.2	38.2	32.5	Yougoslavie
T.F.Yug.Rep. Macedonia	..	14.6	3.2	3.6	3.9	4.3	5.1	5.3	2.4	19.0	L'ex-RY Macédoine
USSR (former)[3]	1981.0	..	..	..	..	..	..	..	..	..	**URSS (anc.)[3]**

For general note and footnotes, see end of table. — Voir la fin du tableau pour la remarque générale et les notes.

Fruit and vegetable juices, unconcentrated, frozen or not (continued)
Jus non concentrés de fruits et de légumes, congelés ou non (suite)

ISIC-BASED CODE - CODE BASE CITI
3113-10

General Note.

Unfermented juice of fruit or vegetables presented in liquid form, whether or not containing added sugar (but not containing added alcohol) and whether or not intended for consumption as beverages. Unfermented grape juice is included. In terms of net weight. (SITC, Rev.3: 05900-2).

[1] Fruit juices only.
[2] In thousand kilolitres.
[3] Including concentrated fruit and vegetable juices.
[4] Pineapple juice only.
[5] Including concentrated fruit juices.
[6] Sales.
[7] Pasteurized fruit juice and drinkable fruit juice.
[8] Excluding frozen orange juice.

Remarque générale.

Jus non fermentés de fruits ou de légumes se présentant sous forme liquide, additionnés ou non de sucre (mais sans addition d'alcool), qu'ils puissent ou non être employés comme boissons. Cette position comprend les moûts de raisins non fermentés. Poids net. (CTCI, Rev.3: 05900-2).

[1] Jus de fruits seulement.
[2] En milliers de kilolitres.
[3] Y compris les jus concentrés de fruits et de légumes.
[4] Jus d'ananas seulement.
[5] Y compris les jus concentrés de fruits.
[6] Ventes.
[7] Jus de fruits pasteurisés et jus de fruits buvables.
[8] Non compris le jus d'orange congelé.

Fruits, frozen
Fruits congelés

ISIC-BASED CODE - CODE BASE CITI

3113-13

Unit : Metric tons   Unité : Tonnes métriques

Country or area	1990	1991	1992	1993	1994	1995	1996	1997	1998	1999	Pays ou zone
America, North	**1760**	**2106**	**2645**	**34959**	**25501**	**47609**	**28080**	**22350**	**31183**	**36599**	**Amérique du Nord**
Mexico	1760	2106	2645	#34959	25501	47609	28080	22350	31183	36599	Mexique
America, South	**5734**	**5734**	**5702**	**7623**	**1986**	**7623**	**5734**	**5734**	**5734**	**5734**	**Amérique du Sud**
Colombia	...	...	5702	7623	1986	7623	...	...	...	...	Colombie
Asia	**8090**	**1723**	**816**	**4801**	**4847**	**7144**	**10737**	**6183**	**10841**	**13161**	**Asie**
Indonesia	44	63	...	...	...	...	...	...	...	...	Indonésie
Turkey	8046	1660	762	4747	4793	7090	10683	6129	10787	13107	Turquie
Europe	**310179**	**446595**	**440437**	**391892**	**387405**	**382201**	**431670**	**444786**	**457426**	**507160**	**Europe**
Belarus	..	133	204	1321	1109	972	2002	3553	2991	539	Bélarus
Belgium	..	...	..	...	...	20217	21942	3464	23487	...	Belgique
Bulgaria	4380	3079	1356	988	4235	3327	5974	6182	5773	6727	Bulgarie
Croatia	..	982	871	73	25	15	0	25	...	...	Croatie
Denmark[1]	5144	6137	5203	5079	6370	5458	5460	4988	5581	...	Danemark[1]
Czechoslovakia(former)	15865		..	..	..	..	..	..		..	Tchécoslovaquie(anc.)
Czech Republic	..	..	6358	4492	...	...	...	...	...	...	République tchèque
Finland	2981	6066	5067	5007	6997	4022	6302	6704	6271	4940	Finlande
France	44235	50860	30928	...	...	...	...	...	...	...	France
Germany	..	..	..	...	...	4720	3466	13732	17415	...	Allemagne
German D.R.(former)	1294		..	..	..	..	..	..	..	..	R.D.A. (anc.)
Greece	2545	4334	10581	9996	11392	12385	12732	13291	11498	...	Grèce
Hungary	15137	16446	26385	·20621	20579	15474	23128	26031	28586	30988	Hongrie
Latvia	..	...	...	[2]2192	3177	18749	...	...	...	...	Lettonie
Lithuania	..	...	...				496	653	361	259	Lituanie
Netherlands[1 3]	...	...	...	19982	22260	20546	...	...	...	...	Pays-Bas[1 3]
Poland	145551	212776	232225	188827	187601	179451	217823	239702	224506	280414	Pologne
Portugal[4]	122	102	522	...	1113	...	1504	...	...	...	Portugal[4]
Republic of Moldova	..	2002	1528	[5 6]937	[5 6]764	[5 6]957	[5 6]369	[5 6]136	...	[6]772	Rép. de Moldova
Romania	92	0	0	0	0	0	90	24	23	13	Roumanie
Russian Federation	..	6997	7060	6292	1958	921	653	300	78	286	Fédération de Russie
Slovakia	..	..	2851	1307	2464	6891	3999	1939	3469	623	Slovaquie
Slovenia	..	...	...	...	...	...	...	24	0	...	Slovénie
Spain	...	...	...	2753	3867	5736	3632	2926	4252	4820	Espagne
Sweden	6515	521	292	412	251	118	7679	7212	8359	8566	Suède
Ukraine	..	3222	3053	2317	#265	116	47	170	474	956	Ukraine
United Kingdom	...	...	...	22778	12209	12153	12092	12283	...	...	Royaume-Uni
Yugoslavia	..	33972	25043	26071	24909	20996	25449	23146	26935	32297	Yougoslavie
T.F.Yug.Rep. Macedonia	..	...	189	202	862	...	...	...	...	...	L'ex-RY Macédoine
Total	**325763**	**456157**	**449599**	**439275**	**419738**	**444577**	**476220**	**479052**	**505183**	**562653**	**Total**

General Note.
Fruits, whether or not cooked, frozen by ordinary refrigeration or by the "quick-freezing" process. (SITC, Rev.3: 05830-0).

Remarque générale.
Fruits, cuits ou non, congelés ou surgelés. (CTCI, Rev.3: 05830-0).

[1] Sales.
[2] Source: Food and Agriculture Organization of the United Nations (FAO), (Rome).
[3] Production by establishments employing 20 or more persons.
[4] Beginning 1997, data are confidential.
[5] Including frozen vegetables.
[6] Excluding Transnistria region.

[1] Ventes.
[2] Source: Organisation des Nations Unies pour l'alimentation et l'agriculture (FAO), (Rome).
[3] Production des établissements occupant 20 personnes ou plus.
[4] A partir de 1997, les données sont confidentielles
[5] Y compris les légumes congelés.
[6] Non compris la région de Transnistria.

Fruits, tinned or bottled
Fruits en boîtes ou en bocaux

ISIC-BASED CODE - CODE BASE CITI

3113-16

Unit : Thousand metric tons

Unité : Milliers de tonnes métriques

Country or area	1990	1991	1992	1993	1994	1995	1996	1997	1998	1999	Pays ou zone
Africa	**457**	**399**	**423**	**414**	**409**	**502**	**529**	**575**	**514**	**567**	**Afrique**
Egypt	20.7	21.5	22.9	19.6	22.6	11.1	10.2	12.4	...	...	Egypte
Kenya	209.1	175.0	180.5	184.5	204.3	287.9	287.0	...	...	...	Kenya
Madagascar[1]	...	...	...	...	0.0	0.1	0.0	0.0	0.0	...	Madagascar[1]
South Africa	212.0	184.7	204.3	197.6	167.6	183.8	216.0	242.6	164.4	200.5	Afrique du Sud
Swaziland	14.0	17.0	14.0	11.0	13.0	14.9	...	...	...	...	Swaziland
United Rep.Tanzania	1.0	1.1	1.6	1.5	1.3	3.9	2.0	2.0	...	...	Rép. Unie de Tanzanie
America, North	**34**	**28**	**37**	**31**	**28**	**29**	**28**	**27**	**26**	**25**	**Amérique du Nord**
Martinique	13.4	16.2	16.2	17.5	18.4	...	...	...	...	...	Martinique
Mexico[2]	20.2	11.9	20.4	13.2	9.2	...	...	...	...	...	Mexique[2]
America, South	**64**	**61**	**59**	**63**	**76**	**74**	**88**	**95**	**88**	**115**	**Amérique du Sud**
Bolivia	0.1	0.1	0.1	0.1	0.1	*0.1	...	...	...	...	Bolivie
Brazil	31.1	28.2	26.0	23.8	17.8	17.3	19.6	25.6	21.1	34.8	Brésil
Chile	30.2	26.0	28.8	36.1	53.9	48.7	58.8	54.7	45.8	59.0	Chili
Colombia	...	...	3.0	2.7	3.7	5.0	...	6.0	7.3	...	Colombie
Ecuador	0.8	...	1.2	0.2	0.6	2.9	4.9	8.3	13.3	...	Equateur
Asia	**911**	**1153**	**1394**	**1249**	**1188**	**1186**	**1196**	**1766**	**1003**	**1428**	**Asie**
Azerbaijan	..	5.5	3.2	0.5	0.1	0.0	0.0	0.0	0.0	0.1	Azerbaïdjan
Bangladesh	0.1	0.0	0.0	...	...	...	...	...	...	...	Bangladesh
China	581.0	754.3	942.1	...	...	...	...	...	...	...	Chine
Hong Kong SAR[3]	1.1	2.8	1.7	2.3	0.3	0.9	2.0	2.2	0.7	1.0	Hong-Kong RAS[3]
Cyprus	2.4	2.4	3.5	3.7	3.9	4.4	4.1	3.6	2.9	2.9	Chypre
Indonesia	25.4	47.7	136.6	...	189.3	200.7	...	787.4	28.8	...	Indonésie
Iran(Islamic Rep. of)	[4]10.3	[4]14.5	[4]7.7	[4]7.4	[4]6.0	[5]10.9	[5]11.8	[5]6.6	[5]10.6	...	Iran(Rép. islamique)
Japan	211.7	201.2	194.7	172.5	140.5	126.3	119.1	101.2	99.4	94.4	Japon
Kyrgyzstan	..	9.5	4.3	1.1	1.1	0.5	0.8	0.9	0.9	0.8	Kirghizistan
Malaysia[6]	43.5	...	...	...	...	...	...	...	...	...	Malaisie[6]
Syrian Arab Republic[1]	14.0	14.9	18.2	15.2	17.6	18.1	20.1	22.3	18.6	...	Rép. arabe syrienne[1]
Tajikistan[7]	..	40.8	24.7	21.9	2.1	4.8	2.7	0.8	1.0	1.0	Tadjikistan[7]
Turkey	0.6	2.2	1.9	2.0	6.9	3.9	14.4	16.6	16.8	19.7	Turquie
Viet Nam	20.6	13.7	11.9	...	...	[8]12.8	[8]16.3	[8]21.4	[8]20.0	* [8]20.3	Viet Nam
Europe	**1368**	**1837**	**1761**	**1846**	**1449**	**1510**	**1609**	**1503**	**1504**	**1562**	**Europe**
Austria	4.7	7.7	5.6	6.2	3.2	2.7	...	...	...	...	Autriche
Belarus	..	30.8	31.1	31.0	14.6	9.6	7.8	6.4	6.6	8.9	Bélarus
Belgium	44.6	46.7	50.7	44.9	...	...	...	...	...	...	Belgique
Bulgaria[9]	65.9	21.3	21.8	19.4	9.0	6.1	17.4	18.9	12.0	6.9	Bulgarie[9]
Croatia	..	2.6	1.4	0.7	1.2	0.7	0.7	2.2	2.9	...	Croatie
Czechoslovakia(former)	41.7	20.9	..	..	...	...	...	...	...	..	Tchécoslovaquie(anc.)
Czech Republic	..	..	19.0	17.2	...	...	...	...	...	...	République tchèque
Estonia	..	9.6	4.0	4.0	6.8	7.6	8.9	9.0	8.1	8.0	Estonie
Finland	0.5	1.2	1.6	1.5	1.5	8.2	7.7	...	...	...	Finlande
France	116.4	97.0	111.0	96.2	81.0	70.3	78.8	74.0	54.1	...	France
Germany	..	140.9	...	136.4	154.3	215.6	219.3	...	176.1	...	Allemagne
Germany(Fed.Rep.)	96.2	..	..	..	..	..	..	..	..	..	Allemagne(Rép.féd.)
German D.R.(former)	23.6	..	..	..	..	..	..	..	..	..	R.D.A. (anc.)
Greece	...	...	...	...	...	362.8	382.9	243.2	301.4	...	Grèce
Hungary	86.6	23.0	39.7	22.4	27.8	22.0	...	...	...	...	Hongrie
Latvia	..	...	...	0.7	0.4	0.8	0.9	0.2	0.7	0.0	Lettonie
Netherlands[10] [11]	8.7	9.7	12.1	#104.0	66.0	74.0	82.0	78.0	46.0	51.0	Pays-Bas[10] [11]
Poland	34.6	35.6	13.7	9.7	5.1	7.0	13.7	7.0	7.4	5.8	Pologne
Portugal	139.6	111.1	#5.4	2.3	5.8	4.9	0.0	0.1	0.1	0.1	Portugal
Romania	124.1	71.3	47.6	47.0	47.8	48.2	52.5	47.6	40.4	40.9	Roumanie
Russian Federation	..	321.9	278.4	263.4	#68.4	33.4	46.8	52.0	68.2	77.3	Fédération de Russie
Slovakia	..	..	6.0	4.4	2.9	1.3	2.8	1.7	1.3	0.4	Slovaquie
Slovenia	..	1.2	0.6	0.9	0.7	0.5	3.1	2.7	2.8	2.7	Slovénie
Spain	219.6	249.6	255.4	384.8	367.0	390.0	460.3	541.4	579.6	525.6	Espagne
Sweden	6.0	6.6	7.2	9.5	10.3	10.9	10.3	12.9	12.2	11.6	Suède
Ukraine	..	272.5	260.6	206.1	#82.3	47.8	27.3	19.0	10.1	11.8	Ukraine
United Kingdom	32.7	26.1	...	109.6	104.3	120.0	98.3	121.1	85.9	...	Royaume-Uni
Yugoslavia	..	6.1	3.5	1.1	1.5	0.7	0.9	0.7	0.3	0.4	Yougoslavie

For general note and footnotes, see end of table.

Voir la fin du tableau pour la remarque générale et les notes.

Fruits, tinned or bottled (continued)
Fruits en boîtes ou en bocaux (suite)

ISIC-BASED CODE - CODE BASE CITI

3113-16

Unit : Thousand metric tons   Unité : Milliers de tonnes métriques

Country or area	1990	1991	1992	1993	1994	1995	1996	1997	1998	1999	Pays ou zone
T.F.Yug.Rep. Macedonia	..	0.6	0.6	0.4	0.1	0.0	0.1	0.0	0.0	0.1	L'ex-RY Macédoine
USSR (former)	702.1	..	..	..	..	..	..	..	..	..	URSS (anc.)
Oceania	164	164	164	164	164	164	160	162	163	172	Océanie
Australia [12] [13]	...	...	...	...	...	...	159.5	161.7	162.7	172.4	Australie [12] [13]
Total	3700	3643	3839	3767	3314	3464	3609	4127	3297	3870	Total

General Note.
Fruits preserved in syrup, in water, in chemicals or in alcohol, and put in hermetically-sealed containers or bottles. In terms of net weight. (SITC, Rev.3: 05890-1).

[1] Including canned vegetables.
[2] Including fruit and vegetable juices.
[3] Including jams, marmalades and fruit jellies.
[4] Production by establishments employing 50 or more persons.
[5] Production by establishments employing 10 or more persons.
[6] Canned pineapple only.
[7] Original data in conventional cans.
[8] Canned fruits only.
[9] Excluding marinated and cocktail fruits.
[10] Sales.
[11] Production by establishments employing 20 or more persons.
[12] Including frozen fruits
[13] Twelve months ending 30 June of year stated.

Remarque générale.
Fruits conservés dans le sirop, l'eau, les produits chimiques ou l'alcool et contenus dans des récipients ou des bocaux fermés hermétiquement. Poids net. (CTCI, Rev.3: 05890-1).

[1] Y compris les conserves de légumes.
[2] Y compris les jus de fruits et de légumes.
[3] Y compris les confitures, marmelades et gelées de fruits.
[4] Production des établissements occupant 50 personnes ou plus.
[5] Production des établissements occupant 10 personnes ou plus.
[6] Conserves d'ananas seulement.
[7] Données d'origine exprimées en boîte de type classique.
[8] Conserves de fruits seulement.
[9] Non compris les fruits marinés et les fruits pour cocktails.
[10] Ventes.
[11] Production des établissements occupant 20 personnes ou plus.
[12] Y compris les fruits congelés.
[13] Période de douze mois finissant le 30 juin de l'année indiquée.

Vegetables, frozen
Légumes congelés

ISIC-BASED CODE - CODE BASE CITI

3113-19

Unit : Thousand metric tons

Unité : Milliers de tonnes métriques

Country or area	1990	1991	1992	1993	1994	1995	1996	1997	1998	1999	Pays ou zone
Africa	**68**	**62**	**66**	**57**	**68**	**80**	**74**	**92**	**92**	**112**	**Afrique**
South Africa	67.8	62.2	66.0	56.6	67.8	79.7	73.5	91.7	92.1	112.0	Afrique du Sud
America, South	**0**	**0**	**1**	**1**	**2**	**3**	**4**	**5**	**5**	**6**	**Amérique du Sud**
Peru[1]	...	...	...	...	...	2.8	3.7	4.7	5.3	5.7	Pérou[1]
Asia	**111**	**101**	**109**	**122**	**123**	**123**	**122**	**117**	**110**	**115**	**Asie**
Japan	101.1	93.0	102.6	112.1	110.0	102.0	89.5	86.4	86.9	90.4	Japon
Kazakhstan	..	0.1	0.0	..	...	...	...	...	...	...	Kazakhstan
Turkey	10.2	7.6	5.9	10.0	13.0	20.8	32.5	31.0	22.7	24.1	Turquie
Europe	**2136**	**2578**	**2639**	**2688**	**2652**	**2906**	**3134**	**2791**	**2918**	**3450**	**Europe**
Belarus	..	0.1	0.0	0.0	0.0	0.0	0.0	0.0	...	...	Bélarus
Belgium	487.3	555.2	655.4	654.2	441.6	503.8	536.3	623.4	701.6	713.2	Belgique
Bulgaria	2.2	2.8	1.7	0.9	3.6	4.0	5.5	5.7	6.6	4.7	Bulgarie
Croatia	..	0.5	0.4	0.6	0.4	0.5	0.2	0.0	0.2	...	Croatie
Denmark[2]	60.0	69.8	59.6	57.3	48.2	40.7	83.2	49.8	46.7	...	Danemark[2]
Czechoslovakia(former)	41.3	...	..	..	..	..	..	..	..	..	Tchécoslovaquie(anc.)
Czech Republic	..	..	14.6	18.1	17.0	18.3	23.0	21.6	25.6	18.3	République tchèque
Finland	34.2	34.0	35.8	38.4	45.0	45.4	48.3	28.0	26.8	25.0	Finlande
France	345.3	376.7	405.9	...	...	...	...	...	...	...	France
Germany	..	168.1	165.7	...	186.3	312.5	276.3	212.1	196.0	...	Allemagne
German D.R.(former)	17.6	..	..	..	..	..	..	..	..	..	R.D.A. (anc.)
Greece	22.9	28.0	25.7	31.0	32.3	28.7	26.1	24.0	23.5	...	Grèce
Hungary	84.8	92.7	80.6	82.2	103.4	115.2	91.5	101.6	145.9	153.3	Hongrie
Latvia	..	...	...	...	1.4	1.3	0.9	0.0	0.0	...	Lettonie
Lithuania	..	...	...	...	...	...	0.0	0.0	0.1	0.0	Lituanie
Netherlands[2][3]	104.2	121.3	106.2	102.9	120.0	113.0	122.0	127.0	131.0	170.3	Pays-Bas[2][3]
Norway	...	...	...	33.8	...	19.8	...	36.9	42.4	90.0	Norvège
Poland	93.1	142.4	110.2	125.8	125.8	137.7	163.0	175.8	213.7	233.6	Pologne
Portugal	11.5	6.5	19.3	21.0	29.2	31.4	12.8	14.9	17.5	27.9	Portugal
Republic of Moldova	..	1.1	0.2	0.0	...	...	...	...	...	...	Rép. de Moldova
Romania	0.0	0.1	0.0	0.4	0.2	0.3	0.1	0.0	0.4	0.4	Roumanie
Russian Federation	..	5.6	3.1	2.0	0.5	0.6	0.2	0.1	0.5	1.9	Fédération de Russie
Slovakia	..	..	7.4	3.4	2.9	2.7	2.9	4.0	3.5	4.6	Slovaquie
Slovenia	..	..	..	..	..	..	..	0.8	0.8	0.8	Slovénie
Spain	[4]164.6	[4]202.4	[4]193.3	154.3	251.7	272.8	252.9	316.9	369.2	362.0	Espagne
Sweden	103.5	95.7	81.1	87.9	84.4	84.6	169.3	177.1	161.8	171.4	Suède
Ukraine	..	0.2	0.1	0.1	0.0	0.0	0.3	0.0	0.0	0.2	Ukraine
United Kingdom	563.5	585.5	...	663.3	721.8	778.1	875.7	475.9	404.8	...	Royaume-Uni
Yugoslavia	..	38.2	20.5	15.3	14.8	17.4	21.6	19.0	23.1	17.7	Yougoslavie
T.F.Yug.Rep. Macedonia	..	0.7	0.2	0.2	0.1	...	...	...	...	...	L'ex-RY Macédoine
USSR (former)	**4.2**	..	..	..	..	..	..	..	..	..	**URSS (anc.)**
Oceania	**541**	**545**	**550**	**527**	**552**	**577**	**579**	**582**	**559**	**570**	**Océanie**
Australia[5]	...	...	...	...	...	...	406.8	420.1	425.4	...	Australie[5]
New Zealand	...	...	...	109.7	134.6	159.3	172.4	161.5	133.3	152.2	Nouvelle-Zélande
Total	**2860**	**3287**	**3365**	**3396**	**3397**	**3688**	**3913**	**3586**	**3684**	**4252**	**Total**

General Note.

Vegetables, whether or not cooked, frozen by ordinary refrigeration or by the "quick-freezing" process. (SITC, Rev.3: 05460-0, 05660-0, 05672-1, 05673-1, 05674-1).

Remarque générale.

Légumes, cuits ou non, congelés ou surgelés. (CTCI, Rev.3: 05460-0, 05660-0, 05672-1, 05673-1, 05674-1).

[1] Data refer to asparagus only.
[2] Sales.
[3] Production by establishments employing 20 or more persons.
[4] Including frozen fruits.
[5] Twelve months ending 30 June of year stated.

[1] Les données se rapportent aux asperges seulement.
[2] Ventes.
[3] Production des établissements occupant 20 personnes ou plus.
[4] Y compris les fruits congelés.
[5] Période de douze mois finissant le 30 juin de l'année indiquée.

Vegetables, tinned or bottled
Légumes en boîtes ou en bocaux

ISIC-BASED CODE - CODE BASE CITI

3113-22

Unit : Thousand metric tons

Unité : Milliers de tonnes métriques

Country or area	1990	1991	1992	1993	1994	1995	1996	1997	1998	1999	Pays ou zone
Africa	**97**	**102**	**98**	**81**	**88**	**92**	**103**	**107**	**88**	**93**	**Afrique**
Algeria	1.4	2.6	1.0	1.3	3.8	2.1	1.2	2.2	0.9	0.6	Algérie
Egypt	9.3	10.7	10.2	10.9	11.5	10.6	16.8	12.6	15.5	14.2	Egypte
Kenya	0.4	0.5	0.5	0.5	0.4	0.5	0.3	...	...	...	Kenya
South Africa	85.7	88.7	86.4	67.9	71.9	79.1	84.3	91.5	71.6	78.2	Afrique du Sud
America, North	**328**	**348**	**402**	**548**	**575**	**589**	**404**	**441**	**488**	**550**	**Amérique du Nord**
Mexico	328.4	347.6	401.9	548.4	574.9	589.0	403.5	440.7	488.1	549.7	Mexique
America, South	**25**	**22**	**27**	**40**	**49**	**49**	**48**	**44**	**65**	**69**	**Amérique du Sud**
Chile	20.4	16.1	19.9	26.8	29.0	18.1	13.6	8.0	9.6	10.6	Chili
Colombia	...	...	4.2	4.4	6.3	5.8	...	7.2	6.8	...	Colombie
Ecuador	...	...	2.3	3.7	4.1	9.7	8.9	14.4	16.1	...	Equateur
Peru[1]	...	...	...	...	...	15.0	20.2	14.8	32.6	31.1	Pérou[1]
Asia	**807**	**967**	**971**	**891**	**856**	**845**	**833**	**829**	**849**	**841**	**Asie**
Azerbaijan	..	59.0	43.4	27.5	25.3	11.1	4.9	3.5	3.6	3.2	Azerbaïdjan
China	546.0	648.0	651.5	...	...	...	...	...	...	...	Chine
Hong Kong SAR	11.3	6.1	...	8.8	3.3	5.4	3.4	4.4	1.7	3.9	Hong-Kong RAS
Cyprus	1.1	1.0	1.3	1.1	1.0	0.8	1.5	0.7	0.6	0.5	Chypre
Indonesia	0.2	0.4	...	...	0.6	0.9	...	1.0	36.1	...	Indonésie
Iran(Islamic Rep. of)[2]	12.6	2.8	0.6	...	...	...	...	...	...	...	Iran(Rép. islamique)[2]
Japan	168.1	151.3	153.3	140.2	138.7	121.8	113.7	116.3	107.6	103.9	Japon
Korea, Republic of[3]	38.1	39.0	39.2	20.1	16.8	24.7	20.1	25.2	15.5	24.1	Corée, République de[3]
Kyrgyzstan	..	26.5	17.7	13.3	4.8	1.5	2.1	1.9	3.3	4.2	Kirghizistan
Myanmar[4]	0.2	0.1	0.0	...	...	...	...	...	...	...	Myanmar[4]
Tajikistan[5]	..	10.8	11.2	8.1	3.8	5.0	1.6	1.0	1.1	2.1	Tadjikistan[5]
Turkey	29.5	22.3	41.4	45.2	41.5	52.9	58.8	54.3	58.5	54.8	Turquie
Europe	**4490**	**5561**	**5821**	**6349**	**5617**	**7842**	**7892**	**7313**	**7190**	**8806**	**Europe**
Austria	32.7	51.1	70.9	75.9	69.8	77.0	87.0	86.4	91.3	87.2	Autriche
Belarus	..	67.5	62.3	54.9	57.6	36.2	21.3	27.1	39.7	48.8	Bélarus
Belgium	233.3	285.5	276.5	254.4	185.5	347.1	319.6	362.2	399.9	460.4	Belgique
Bulgaria	[6]244.4	[6]185.0	[6]81.3	[6]86.8	[6]143.2	[6]134.4	[6]127.3	[6]136.1	[6]63.3	28.8	Bulgarie
Croatia	..	17.9	21.4	17.8	20.8	20.7	15.6	14.9	21.5	...	Croatie
Czechoslovakia(former)	141.4	128.2	..	..	..	..	..	..	..	..	Tchécoslovaquie(anc.)
Czech Republic	..	..	51.3	79.4	78.7	67.3	84.7	77.6	74.5	84.3	République tchèque
Estonia	..	8.1	5.6	1.9	2.5	1.6	1.4	2.5	1.8	2.7	Estonie
Finland	20.7	18.6	19.0	19.7	20.3	24.6	24.6	36.1	39.5	46.2	Finlande
France	1271.0	1384.9	1449.5	1315.0	1323.7	1387.1	1444.5	1362.1	1489.1	...	France
Germany	..	203.1	178.7	87.9	87.8	#1208.8	1241.0	1325.3	1306.4	...	Allemagne
Germany(Fed.Rep.)	158.1	..	..	..	..	..	..	..	..	..	Allemagne(Rép.féd.)
German D.R.(former)	102.5	..	..	..	..	..	..	..	..	..	R.D.A. (anc.)
Greece	12.3	13.0	14.9	...	...	#293.9	326.0	328.9	34.7	...	Grèce
Hungary	225.2	145.3	46.5	59.8	99.3	144.3	...	...	...	...	Hongrie
Iceland	...	...	...	...	...	...	1.1	0.8	0.8	0.7	Islande
Latvia	...	...	...	5.4	5.0	3.6	2.9	6.9	10.0	5.0	Lettonie
Lithuania	..	...	12.8	7.1	3.8	1.8	2.0	3.0	3.8	3.4	Lituanie
Netherlands[7][8]	386.5	426.6	454.1	...	...	...	...	...	...	...	Pays-Bas[7][8]
Norway	26.8	30.7	32.4	11.5	...	...	...	...	...	...	Norvège
Poland	136.9	96.4	55.9	70.9	68.4	57.6	84.4	119.5	116.9	126.1	Pologne
Portugal	10.3	10.6	107.4	115.1	165.1	184.3	206.7	184.1	239.7	242.5	Portugal
Romania	189.7	138.9	117.6	98.1	122.5	131.5	110.4	91.9	75.4	65.1	Roumanie
Russian Federation	..	380.7	352.6	343.6	182.4	149.2	86.5	86.6	91.5	129.0	Fédération de Russie
Slovakia	..	..	18.4	23.6	18.5	13.1	12.7	10.8	15.4	16.2	Slovaquie
Slovenia	..	16.1	7.9	9.1	10.4	10.2	7.2	11.2	10.5	12.0	Slovénie
Spain	464.5	507.8	518.3	952.3	969.1	1216.2	1271.6	1030.5	...	1295.2	Espagne
Sweden	58.7	57.9	49.5	43.5	51.5	51.9	61.6	48.4	62.9	75.3	Suède
Ukraine	..	566.5	516.6	493.2	323.3	205.3	73.9	70.0	135.4	153.8	Ukraine
United Kingdom	774.5	758.0	...	1522.8	982.9	1594.3	1709.4	1339.6	1398.6	...	Royaume-Uni
Yugoslavia	..	42.6	29.3	23.9	25.0	25.5	23.5	19.0	25.1	18.2	Yougoslavie
T.F.Yug.Rep. Macedonia	..	9.2	5.2	5.5	5.1	5.6	7.8	2.0	5.7	4.7	L'ex-RY Macédoine
USSR (former)	**2097.4**	..	..	..	..	..	..	..	..	..	**URSS (anc.)**

For general note and footnotes, see end of table.

Voir la fin du tableau pour la remarque générale et les notes.

Vegetables, tinned or bottled (continued)
Légumes en boîtes ou en bocaux (suite)

ISIC-BASED CODE - CODE BASE CITI
3113-22

Unit : Thousand metric tons   Unité : Milliers de tonnes métriques

Country or area	1990	1991	1992	1993	1994	1995	1996	1997	1998	1999	Pays ou zone
Oceania	78	78	53	54	166	173	169	213	234	255	Océanie
New Zealand	77.5	77.9	52.9	54.1	165.9	173.3	168.9	...	...	...	Nouvelle-Zélande
Total	7923	7079	7372	7963	7351	9590	9449	8947	8914	10613	Total

General Note.

Vegetables prepared or preserved and put in hermetically-sealed containers or bottles. In terms of net weight. (SITC, Rev.3: 05672-2, 05673-2, 05674-2, 05675-1, 05676-1, 05677-1, 05679-1, 09812-1).

[1] Data refer to asparagus only.
[2] Production by establishments employing 50 or more persons.
[3] Including fruits.
[4] Twelve months ending 31 March of year stated.
[5] Original data in conventional cans.
[6] Including vegetable juices.
[7] Sales.
[8] Production by establishments employing 20 or more persons.

Remarque générale.

Légumes préparés ou conservés, contenus dans des récipients ou des bocaux fermés hermétiquement. Poids net. (CTCI, Rev.3: 05672-2, 05673-2, 05674-2, 05675-1, 05676-1, 05677-1, 05679-1, 09812-1).

[1] Les données se rapportent aux asperges seulement.
[2] Production des établissements occupant 50 personnes ou plus.
[3] Y compris les fruits.
[4] Période de douze mois finissant le 31 mars de l'année indiquée.
[5] Données d'origine exprimées en boîte de type classique.
[6] Y compris les jus de légumes.
[7] Ventes.
[8] Production des établissements occupant 20 personnes ou plus.

Fish, frozen
Poisson congelé

ISIC-BASED CODE - CODE BASE CITI

3114-01

Unit : Thousand metric tons   Unité : Milliers de tonnes métriques

Country or area	1990	1991	1992	1993	1994	1995	1996	1997	1998	1999	Pays ou zone
Africa	**291**	**262**	**258**	**286**	**325**	**332**	**366**	**429**	**405**	**415**	**Afrique**
Angola[1]	14.0	10.0	10.0	10.0	10.0	10.9	10.6	12.9	...	...	Angola[1]
Benin[1]	0.0	0.0	0.0	0.1	0.1	0.0	0.0	0.0	...	...	Bénin[1]
Cape Verde[1]	1.6	2.1	1.1	1.0	0.9	0.9	0.9	0.9	...	...	Cap-Vert[1]
Côte d'Ivoire[1]	0.0	0.0	0.0	0.0	0.0	0.0	0.1	0.0	...	...	Côte d'Ivoire[1]
Djibouti[1]	0.1	0.0	0.0	0.0	0.0	0.0	0.0	0.0	...	...	Djibouti[1]
Egypt[1]	3.3	2.1	1.6	1.0	1.0	0.8	0.6	0.0	...	...	Egypte[1]
Equatorial Guinea[1]	0.0	0.0	0.0	0.0	0.0	0.0	0.0	0.3	...	...	Guinée équatoriale[1]
Eritrea[1]	...	...	...	0.0	0.0	0.0	0.0	0.1	...	...	Erythrée[1]
Gabon[1]	0.0	0.0	0.0	0.0	0.0	0.4	0.0	0.1	...	...	Gabon[1]
Gambia[1]	0.0	0.1	0.0	0.1	0.5	0.5	0.1	1.8	...	...	Gambie[1]
Ghana[1]	68.1	66.5	52.1	56.7	70.0	70.0	67.1	69.2	...	...	Ghana[1]
Guinea[1]	0.0	0.0	0.0	0.9	1.1	2.4	2.7	7.0	...	...	Guinée[1]
Guinea-Bissau[1]	1.1	1.9	0.1	0.9	1.3	1.0	4.9	3.7	...	...	Guinée-Bissau[1]
Kenya	5.6	5.8	5.3	14.8	5.4	0.3	0.1	...	...	...	Kenya
Liberia[1]	1.0	2.6	0.7	0.7	1.1	1.1	1.2	1.8	...	...	Libéria[1]
Madagascar[1]	0.6	0.6	0.2	0.6	1.5	0.5	0.5	0.5	...	...	Madagascar[1]
Malawi[1]	0.0	0.0	0.0	0.1	0.0	0.0	0.0	0.0	...	...	Malawi[1]
Mauritania[1]	25.0	13.3	8.3	11.3	10.8	16.0	17.5	13.6	...	...	Mauritanie[1]
Mauritius	7.5	*6.9	8.2	9.1	5.5	5.3	4.4	4.4	3.6	3.9	Maurice
Morocco	6.0	...	...	1.9	3.3	2.2	3.3	14.4	22.0	37.0	Maroc
Namibia[1]	15.3	16.2	26.9	35.5	52.9	60.7	70.9	109.9	...	...	Namibie[1]
Réunion	1.7	1.6	1.7	1.9	3.6	3.9	3.6	4.1	4.7	...	Réunion
Sao Tome and Principe[1]	0.0	0.0	0.0	0.0	0.0	0.0	0.1	0.5	...	...	Sao Tomé-et-Principe[1]
Senegal[1]	66.8	53.8	49.8	36.6	45.6	44.8	53.1	59.9	...	...	Sénégal[1]
Seychelles[1]	0.9	1.2	0.8	0.1	0.2	0.2	0.4	0.4	...	...	Seychelles[1]
Sierra Leone[1]	0.0	0.0	0.0	10.5	13.5	11.5	11.3	6.1	...	...	Sierra Leone[1]
Somalia[1]	4.7	2.1	3.2	3.0	2.3	3.3	2.3	3.4	...	...	Somalie[1]
South Africa	62.0	55.9	68.5	75.5	65.9	64.5	68.4	67.8	76.6	64.9	Afrique du Sud
Togo[1]	0.0	0.0	0.0	0.2	0.1	0.0	0.0	0.1	...	...	Togo[1]
Tunisia	[1]0.0	[1]0.1	[1]0.1	[1]0.1	[2]11.7	[2]8.5	[2]10.8	[2]13.7	[2]13.9	[2]10.4	Tunisie
Uganda	[1]1.7	[1]4.7	[1]4.9	[1]5.1	[1]6.0	[1]7.0	[1]7.9	5.9	8.5	8.4	Ouganda
United Rep.Tanzania[1]	1.0	0.7	0.5	6.6	9.2	13.4	21.0	24.2	...	...	Rép. Unie de Tanzanie[1]
Zambia[1]	0.0	0.0	0.2	0.0	0.0	0.0	0.0	0.0	...	...	Zambie[1]
Zimbabwe[1]	2.6	2.2	2.2	2.2	2.0	1.7	1.6	1.5	...	...	Zimbabwe[1]
America, North	**1088**	**1552**	**1427**	**1554**	**1450**	**1278**	**1378**	**1501**	**1542**	**1573**	**Amérique du Nord**
Antigua and Barbuda	[1]0.1	[1]0.1	[1]0.0	[1]0.0	[1]0.0	[1]0.0	1.0	1.2	...	...	Antigua-et-Barbuda
Bahamas[1]	0.0	0.0	0.1	0.1	0.1	0.1	0.1	0.1	...	...	Bahamas[1]
Belize	0.8	1.1	1.3	1.3	1.2	1.5	1.4	1.7	2.2	...	Belize
Canada[1]	234.0	208.4	196.0	228.8	165.6	135.2	141.3	110.5	...	...	Canada[1]
Costa Rica[1]	0.0	0.0	0.0	0.0	2.7	3.3	10.1	11.4	...	...	Costa Rica[1]
Cuba[1]	90.6	72.3	6.5	5.7	6.6	35.0	...	...	...	...	Cuba[1]
Dominican Republic[1]	0.4	0.4	0.2	0.0	0.0	0.0	0.0	0.0	...	...	Rép. dominicaine[1]
El Salvador[1]	0.0	0.4	0.3	0.6	0.1	0.1	0.0	0.0	...	...	El Salvador[1]
Greenland[1]	25.8	13.3	12.8	11.4	11.1	13.4	13.2	15.1	...	...	Groënland[1]
Grenada[1]	0.0	0.1	0.0	0.0	0.0	0.1	0.0	0.1	...	...	Grenade[1]
Guatemala[1]	0.0	0.0	0.0	0.1	0.0	0.0	0.0	0.1	...	...	Guatemala[1]
Honduras[1]	2.5	3.5	2.6	4.6	3.4	3.4	1.0	0.0	...	...	Honduras[1]
Jamaica[1]	0.0	0.0	0.0	0.0	0.0	0.1	0.0	0.4	...	...	Jamaïque[1]
Mexico	2.6	1.3	0.2	5.0	6.6	7.4	6.3	7.0	5.2	4.7	Mexique
Nicaragua[1]	0.0	1.2	1.2	1.5	2.5	4.0	3.4	2.4	...	...	Nicaragua[1]
Panama[1]	4.0	3.5	4.1	6.3	6.2	7.7	6.2	16.8	...	...	Panama[1]
St.Pierre-Miquelon	5.9	5.9	4.8	#0.0	0.0	0.0	0.1	0.1	0.1	...	St-Pierre-Miquelon
St. Vincent-Grenadines	[1]3.2	[1]2.4	[1]0.5	[1]0.4	[1]0.4	[1]0.4	0.6	0.8	0.9	0.7	St. Vincent-Grenadines
Trinidad and Tobago[1]	0.3	0.3	1.0	0.5	0.5	0.5	0.7	1.5	...	...	Trinité-et-Tobago[1]
United States[3]	717.8	1238.2	1195.6	1287.3	1243.0	1066.4	1183.7	...	...	...	Etats-Unis[3]
America, South	**757**	**777**	**740**	**771**	**892**	**995**	**901**	**1010**	**937**	**940**	**Amérique du Sud**
Argentina[1]	210.5	239.1	244.9	268.3	315.9	423.4	368.5	400.8	...	...	Argentine[1]
Bolivia[1]	0.0	0.0	0.4	0.4	0.1	0.0	0.0	0.0	...	...	Bolivie[1]
Brazil[4]	36.6	63.4	59.5	59.6	62.3	52.5	39.7	47.4	46.2	52.0	Brésil[4]
Chile[1]	116.8	112.6	158.1	151.2	171.0	210.0	227.9	297.2	...	...	Chili[1]
Colombia	[1]35.2	[1]55.4	15.7	13.1	15.3	12.9	...	23.8	12.7	...	Colombie

For general note and footnotes, see end of table.   Voir la fin du tableau pour la remarque générale et les notes.

Fish, frozen (continued)
Poisson congelé (suite)

ISIC-BASED CODE - CODE BASE CITI

3114-01

Unit : Thousand metric tons   Unité : Milliers de tonnes métriques

Country or area	1990	1991	1992	1993	1994	1995	1996	1997	1998	1999	Pays ou zone
Ecuador	[1]47.6	[1]25.3	[1]14.9	[1]10.8	[1]10.5	16.3	20.7	35.0	38.9	...	Equateur
Falkland Is. (Malvinas)	...	53.9	...	...	...	...	...	...	...	...	Iles Falkland (Malvinas)
French Guiana [1]	0.8	0.9	0.8	1.0	1.0	1.1	1.3	1.3	...	...	Guyane française [1]
Guyana [1]	0.0	0.0	0.0	0.0	0.0	0.9	1.1	1.0	...	...	Guyana [1]
Peru	176.1	129.0	91.0	135.0	171.8	128.6	84.1	80.6	49.1	*45.9	Pérou
Suriname [1]	1.0	0.5	0.7	1.1	1.1	3.3	1.0	1.7	...	...	Suriname [1]
Uruguay [1]	49.0	68.2	67.9	53.1	60.6	63.7	58.0	52.8	...	...	Uruguay [1]
Venezuela [1]	29.4	28.3	31.9	23.8	27.8	28.7	21.8	14.8	...	...	Venezuela [1]
Asia	**6850**	**6676**	**6886**	**7016**	**7225**	**7388**	**7566**	**7764**	**7453**	**7330**	**Asie**
Azerbaijan	..	6.2	6.3	3.0	4.5	3.2	2.9	3.4	2.4	3.2	Azerbaïdjan
Bahrain [1]	0.0	1.0	0.5	0.0	0.1	0.2	0.2	0.2	...	...	Bahreïn [1]
Bangladesh	29.4	18.1	15.9	[1]2.7	[1]3.1	[1]4.7	...	...	...	...	Bangladesh
China [1]	1566.9	1579.9	1706.8	1906.0	2689.1	3168.0	3293.8	3361.6	...	...	Chine [1]
Hong Kong SAR [1]	4.3	4.7	5.2	2.8	3.0	2.8	...	...	...	...	Hong-Kong RAS [1]
China, Macao, SAR	0.8	0.4	0.1	0.2	0.2	0.2	0.1	0.1	0.0	0.0	Chine, Macao PAS
Georgia	..	...	1.6	0.2	0.2	0.5	0.6	1.5	0.0	0.0	Géorgie
India [1]	164.2	102.5	161.8	141.7	180.0	178.3	257.8	218.3	...	...	Inde [1]
Indonesia	14.0	19.8	28.6	40.0	45.7	48.1	...	89.9	155.3	...	Indonésie
Iran(Islamic Rep. of)	[1]0.5	[5]2.2	[5]9.7	[5]4.9	[5]4.3	[6]1.6	[6]2.0	[6]2.4	[6]2.1	...	Iran(Rép. islamique)
Israel [1]	2.3	0.0	0.0	0.0	0.0	0.0	0.0	0.0	...	...	Israël [1]
Japan	3907.2	3999.0	3925.4	3878.0	3608.5	3279.2	3232.3	3328.2	3047.8	2794.1	Japon
Kazakhstan	..	...	[1]7.7	4.8	5.0	6.4	7.3	6.9	6.2	5.9	Kazakhstan
Korea,Dem.Ppl's.Rep. [1]	631.6	453.1	420.2	435.5	140.4	109.1	89.6	60.7	...	...	Corée,Rép.pop.dém.de [1]
Korea, Republic of	87.4	87.0	74.7	63.5	64.7	57.9	67.7	40.1	38.0	41.8	Corée, République de
Kyrgyzstan [1]	..	...	0.6	0.3	0.1	0.1	0.1	0.1	...	...	Kirghizistan [1]
Malaysia [1]	4.3	2.2	0.0	0.0	0.1	1.1	5.8	9.6	...	...	Malaisie [1]
Maldives	17.1	10.1	5.5	9.9	7.4	3.0	4.6	6.9	3.6	9.5	Maldives
Mongolia [1]	0.0	0.0	0.0	0.1	0.2	0.2	0.2	0.2	...	...	Mongolie [1]
Myanmar [1]	11.6	10.3	13.5	1.5	4.0	4.9	4.5	4.9	...	...	Myanmar [1]
Oman [1]	32.2	28.0	28.1	45.0	43.5	57.7	54.8	52.9	...	...	Oman [1]
Pakistan [1]	7.4	7.1	24.8	31.1	12.8	12.8	19.0	22.5	...	...	Pakistan [1]
Philippines [1]	14.2	14.6	11.7	33.3	38.0	38.8	36.2	48.2	...	...	Philippines [1]
Saudi Arabia [1]	0.5	5.9	5.8	6.0	4.1	5.1	4.4	4.4	...	...	Arabie saoudite [1]
Singapore [1]	13.2	9.0	7.3	7.3	11.4	13.7	11.4	12.1	...	...	Singapour [1]
Sri Lanka [1]	0.2	0.3	1.2	1.8	1.4	0.2	0.2	0.1	...	...	Sri Lanka [1]
Thailand [1]	325.4	277.8	387.8	354.1	308.5	342.3	357.9	432.0	...	...	Thaïlande [1]
Turkey	3.1	3.4	4.6	2.1	1.4	1.6	1.4	3.3	2.3	2.3	Turquie
Turkmenistan [1]	..	...	0.0	0.0	1.1	0.6	0.2	0.2	...	...	Turkménistan [1]
United Arab Emirates [1]	8.6	6.3	5.8	5.4	3.8	3.5	3.0	0.0	...	...	Emirats arabes unis [1]
Uzbekistan [1]	..	...	0.4	0.9	0.1	0.2	0.2	0.2	...	...	Ouzbékistan [1]
Viet Nam [1]	3.7	14.6	20.1	29.7	34.3	38.5	43.2	47.1	...	...	Viet Nam [1]
Yemen [1]	..	4.0	3.9	4.2	4.0	4.0	3.9	3.5	...	...	Yémen [1]
Europe	**1906**	**4482**	**4227**	**3753**	**3492**	**3921**	**4082**	**3917**	**3589**	**3827**	**Europe**
Albania	[1]0.4	[1]0.7	[1]0.4	[1]0.9	[1]0.7	[1]0.1	[1]0.2	[1]0.2	...	0.0	Albanie
Belarus [1]	..	...	0.0	0.0	0.7	0.3	0.1	0.0	...	...	Bélarus [1]
Belgium	[1]9.9	[1]10.2	[1]10.1	[1]9.6	[7]3.8	[7]4.3	[7]4.0	[7]4.0	[7]4.1	[7]4.4	Belgique
Bulgaria	[1]37.4	35.6	20.6	6.5	0.2	20.3	19.2	1.6	0.8	0.7	Bulgarie
Croatia	..	...	[1]0.2	[1]0.2	[1]0.0	[1]0.0	[1]0.0	0.7	1.1	...	Croatie
Denmark [8]	..	...	...	20.7	23.6	14.7	13.0	16.2	19.6	21.6	Danemark [8]
Czech Republic [1]	..	...	...	0.0	0.0	0.3	1.0	1.0	...	...	République tchèque [1]
Estonia	..	107.2	60.2	71.1	59.4	53.2	20.6	29.0	28.6	22.5	Estonie
Finland	18.3	7.7	15.6	17.0	21.1	5.9	16.3	12.4	13.3	8.6	Finlande
France [1]	148.2	153.5	154.6	167.1	191.4	175.7	187.5	155.3	...	...	France [1]
Germany	..	[1]172.4	34.3	35.4	37.6	[1]211.7	[1]214.5	[1]172.1	38.2	...	Allemagne
German D.R.(former)	12.8		..	..	..	..	..	..	..	..	R.D.A. (anc.)
Greece	[8]8.3	[8]8.0	[1]10.2	[1]10.1	[7]7.7	7.2	2.3	...	2.2	...	Grèce
Hungary [1]	4.1	3.0	3.0	2.0	1.0	1.0	1.0	1.2	...	...	Hongrie [1]
Iceland	171.5	173.6	159.6	174.0	214.6	187.2	228.6	236.1	218.2	166.6	Islande
Ireland	[1]95.0	[1]84.8	[1]82.7	[1]111.7	[1]181.3	[1]177.6	[1]176.5	[1]144.0	87.0	75.0	Irlande
Italy [1]	62.5	73.7	80.7	73.5	77.7	35.1	19.8	11.0	...	...	Italie [1]
Latvia	..	163.9	78.7	72.0	7.0	8.5	10.3	10.6	5.2	5.2	Lettonie
Lithuania	..	...	[1]33.8	[1]4.2	[1]6.7	3.4	5.2	4.3	4.8	9.4	Lituanie

For general note and footnotes, see end of table.   Voir la fin du tableau pour la remarque générale et les notes.

160

Fish, frozen (continued)
Poisson congelé (suite)

ISIC-BASED CODE - CODE BASE CITI

3114-01

Unit : Thousand metric tons

Unité : Milliers de tonnes métriques

Country or area	1990	1991	1992	1993	1994	1995	1996	1997	1998	1999	Pays ou zone
Netherlands[8][9]	53.0	60.5	58.7	54.5	54.4	56.1	51.0	54.0	50.0	50.4	Pays-Bas[8][9]
Norway	[1]348.2	[1]449.4	[1]474.5	[1]577.6	[1]792.3	[1]887.7	[1]1030.1	837.7	...	993.9	Norvège
Poland	124.6	101.7	101.9	95.5	116.5	107.3	115.0	106.3	97.6	68.3	Pologne
Portugal	42.1	24.8	24.0	16.3	21.2	26.9	28.7	32.6	35.1	35.7	Portugal
Romania	134.3	86.5	38.2	1.0	0.0	0.0	0.0	0.0	0.0	0.3	Roumanie
Russian Federation	..	1874.9	1850.9	1693.8	1350.6	1391.0	1555.0	1625.8	1598.7	1762.3	Fédération de Russie
Slovakia	..	..	...	[1]1.5	[1]1.7	[1]1.4	[1]0.9	[1]1.1	3.6	2.9	Slovaquie
Slovenia	..	0.3	[1]0.4	[1]0.4	[1]0.5	[1]0.3	0.5	0.5	0.5	0.4	Slovénie
Spain	[1]349.5	[1]341.3	[1]445.1	63.3	73.3	67.2	70.4	76.7	97.8	...	Espagne
Sweden	[1]17.3	[1]14.2	[1]8.6	[1]14.3	[1]19.4	[1]24.8	[1]18.5	[1]14.9	13.3	5.1	Suède
Switzerland[1]	0.9	0.9	0.9	0.9	0.7	0.8	0.9	0.9	...	...	Suisse[1]
Ukraine	..	248.3	152.8	162.5	125.6	173.7	181.3	205.7	181.2	162.0	Ukraine
United Kingdom	245.7	253.8	306.1	295.1	101.4	[1]276.9	109.4	154.4	169.8	...	Royaume-Uni
Yugoslavia, SFR[1]	2.7	..	..	..	..	..	..	..	..	..	Yougoslavie, RSF[1]
USSR (former)[1]	3132.8	..	..	..	..	..	..	..	..	..	URSS (anc.)[1]
Oceania	**197**	**237**	**231**	**249**	**216**	**236**	**222**	**240**	**237**	**236**	**Océanie**
Australia[1]	13.3	15.1	10.4	11.6	10.8	11.0	8.7	8.3	...	...	Australie[1]
Fiji[1]	1.2	1.2	0.9	7.0	8.2	8.9	4.3	8.3	...	...	Fidji[1]
French Polynesia[1]	0.0	0.0	0.1	0.1	0.0	0.2	0.1	0.7	...	...	Polynésie française[1]
Kiribati[1]	0.9	0.1	0.4	0.3	0.1	0.1	0.1	0.1	...	...	Kiribati[1]
New Caledonia[1]	1.2	1.0	0.9	1.3	1.4	1.1	0.9	0.2	...	...	Nouvelle-Calédonie[1]
New Zealand[1]	153.4	181.6	190.0	212.4	172.0	175.4	184.6	199.6	...	...	Nouvelle-Zélande[1]
Papua New Guinea[1]	0.7	0.2	0.7	0.4	0.1	0.8	0.0	0.1	...	...	Papouasie-Nvl-Guinée[1]
Solomon Islands	[1]26.0	[1]37.6	[1]27.8	[1]15.4	[1]23.2	[1]38.9	[1]23.1	[1]23.1	26.1	...	Iles Salomon
Total	**14221**	**13986**	**13768**	**13629**	**13599**	**14151**	**14514**	**14862**	**14162**	**14321**	**Total**

General Note.
Frozen fish and fish products, including production on board fish factory ships.
(SITC, Rev.3: 03420-0, 03440-0, 03455-0).

Remarque générale.
Poisson et produits de poisson, congelés, y compris la production des navires-usines. (CTCI, Rev.3: 03420-0, 03440-0, 03455-0).

[1] Source: Food and Agriculture Organization of the United Nations (FAO), (Rome).

[2] Including salted, dried or smoked fish.

[3] Including chilled fish.

[4] Excluding sardines.

[5] Production by establishments employing 50 or more persons.

[6] Production by establishments employing 10 or more persons.

[7] Incomplete coverage.

[8] Sales.

[9] Production by establishments employing 20 or more persons.

[1] Source: Organisation des Nations Unies pour l'alimentation et l'agriculture (FAO), (Rome).

[2] Y compris le poisson salé, séché ou fumé.

[3] Y compris les poissons réfrigérés.

[4] Non compris les sardines.

[5] Production des établissements occupant 50 personnes ou plus.

[6] Production des établissements occupant 10 personnes ou plus.

[7] Couverture incomplète.

[8] Ventes.

[9] Production des établissements occupant 20 personnes ou plus.

Fish, salted, dried or smoked
Poisson salé, séché ou fumé

ISIC-BASED CODE - CODE BASE CITI

3114-04

Unit : Thousand metric tons   Unité : Milliers de tonnes métriques

Country or area	1990	1991	1992	1993	1994	1995	1996	1997	1998	1999	Pays ou zone
Africa	**380**	**349**	**341**	**335**	**376**	**421**	**430**	**445**	**425**	**431**	**Afrique**
Algeria[1]	0.0	0.1	0.1	0.1	0.0	0.0	0.0	0.0	...	...	Algérie[1]
Angola	18.0	11.0	10.0	[1]15.0	[1]15.0	[1]15.0	[1]16.0	[1]16.0	...	...	Angola
Benin[1]	2.1	2.0	2.0	2.0	2.0	2.0	2.0	2.0	...	...	Bénin[1]
Burkina Faso[1]	1.0	0.8	0.8	0.8	1.0	1.0	0.9	0.9	...	...	Burkina Faso[1]
Cameroon[1]	3.5	3.5	3.5	3.0	3.0	2.6	3.4	3.0	...	...	Cameroun[1]
Central African Rep.[1]	3.5	3.5	3.5	3.5	3.5	3.5	3.5	3.5	...	...	Rép. centrafricaine[1]
Chad	15.0	15.0	15.0	15.0	15.0	15.0	...	...	...	...	Tchad
Côte d'Ivoire[1]	15.2	15.2	15.2	15.0	15.0	15.0	15.0	15.0	...	...	Côte d'Ivoire[1]
Egypt[1]	10.8	10.8	9.0	9.0	15.0	17.0	16.1	16.0	...	...	Egypte[1]
Gabon[1]	4.5	4.5	4.5	5.0	5.0	5.0	5.0	5.0	...	...	Gabon[1]
Gambia[1]	0.6	0.5	0.8	0.9	1.1	1.0	1.0	1.1	...	...	Gambie[1]
Ghana[1]	58.0	57.0	57.0	52.0	54.2	54.5	54.5	52.5	...	...	Ghana[1]
Guinea[1]	10.0	10.0	11.0	11.0	11.0	11.0	10.8	10.8	...	...	Guinée[1]
Kenya	16.4	19.7	16.8	17.3	18.1	[1]35.6	[1]36.8	[1]39.4	...	...	Kenya
Liberia[1]	0.1	0.3	0.7	0.7	0.6	1.2	1.2	1.0	...	...	Libéria[1]
Madagascar[1]	2.0	2.0	4.7	2.9	2.5	2.5	2.2	2.0	...	...	Madagascar[1]
Malawi	[1]6.7	[1]6.0	[1]6.0	[1]6.0	[1]5.0	[1]4.0	[1]5.7	[1]5.0	4.3	3.7	Malawi
Mali	10.1	11.4	11.2	10.5	12.1	12.0	12.1	...	...	...	Mali
Mauritania[1]	0.9	0.7	0.9	2.7	6.6	11.5	12.5	5.8	...	...	Mauritanie[1]
Mauritius	[1]0.9	[1]1.1	1.4	1.5	0.9	1.7	2.1	1.8	1.5	1.6	Maurice
Morocco	0.0	0.0	[1]2.3	[1]0.5	[1]0.7	[1]0.6	[1]0.5	[1]1.3	...	...	Maroc
Mozambique[1]	3.1	3.0	3.0	2.8	2.8	2.8	2.8	2.8	...	...	Mozambique[1]
Namibia[1]	0.0	0.0	0.0	0.0	22.7	32.7	30.0	28.4	...	...	Namibie[1]
Niger	3.2	3.2	2.1	2.2	2.5	3.6	...	...	...	...	Niger
Nigeria[1]	48.0	28.5	18.3	17.6	25.4	30.5	38.0	38.9	...	...	Nigéria[1]
Rwanda[1]	0.1	0.2	0.3	0.3	0.3	0.3	0.3	0.3	...	...	Rwanda[1]
Senegal[1]	25.0	31.1	31.0	31.0	29.6	28.0	31.5	36.2	...	...	Sénégal[1]
Seychelles[1]	0.2	0.2	0.2	0.2	0.2	0.2	0.2	0.2	...	...	Seychelles[1]
Sierra Leone[1]	17.5	21.2	20.9	15.0	13.1	14.5	14.4	21.0	...	...	Sierra Leone[1]
Somalia[1]	1.2	1.0	1.0	1.0	1.0	1.0	1.0	1.0	...	...	Somalie[1]
South Africa	2.1	2.2	2.8	2.4	1.1	1.0	...	...	...	...	Afrique du Sud
Sudan[1]	3.3	3.3	3.3	3.3	3.3	3.8	4.0	4.0	...	...	Soudan[1]
Togo[1]	3.6	2.8	2.8	2.9	1.9	3.6	4.3	4.6	...	...	Togo[1]
Tunisia[1]	0.0	0.0	0.0	0.0	0.0	0.1	0.0	0.2	...	...	Tunisie[1]
Uganda[1]	0.0	0.0	0.0	1.2	1.2	1.5	0.4	0.4	...	...	Ouganda[1]
United Rep.Tanzania[1]	70.0	55.0	55.0	58.0	60.0	60.6	58.0	68.0	...	...	Rép. Unie de Tanzanie[1]
Zambia[1]	18.1	17.0	18.7	17.4	18.8	20.2	19.6	20.0	...	...	Zambie[1]
Zimbabwe[1]	5.1	5.0	5.0	5.0	5.0	5.0	5.0	5.0	...	...	Zimbabwe[1]
America, North	**99**	**112**	**102**	**93**	**53**	**68**	**87**	**59**	**56**	**60**	**Amérique du Nord**
Canada	[1][2]83.2	[1][2]72.4	[1][2]62.7	[1]60.2	[1]38.5	26.9	32.6	...	...	...	Canada
Costa Rica[1]	0.1	0.1	0.1	0.2	0.1	0.1	0.2	0.2	...	...	Costa Rica[1]
Cuba[1]	0.0	0.0	0.0	0.3	0.2	0.4	0.4	0.3	...	...	Cuba[1]
El Salvador[1]	0.0	0.1	0.1	0.0	0.1	0.0	0.1	0.1	...	...	El Salvador[1]
Greenland[1]	2.5	1.8	1.2	0.2	0.0	0.0	0.0	0.1	...	...	Groënland[1]
Guatemala[1]	0.6	0.2	0.1	0.1	0.3	0.2	0.0	0.0	...	...	Guatemala[1]
Mexico[1]	0.4	0.4	0.6	0.5	0.8	1.2	1.1	1.6	...	...	Mexique[1]
Nicaragua[1]	0.0	0.1	0.0	0.0	0.1	0.7	0.1	0.2	...	...	Nicaragua[1]
Panama[1]	0.0	0.0	0.0	0.0	0.0	0.0	0.0	0.2	...	...	Panama[1]
St.Pierre-Miquelon	1.4	1.6	1.5	0.0	0.0	0.1	0.1	0.1	0.2	...	St-Pierre-Miquelon
United States	10.5	34.9	35.6	31.3	12.6	38.5	51.9	...	...	...	Etats-Unis
America, South	**67**	**72**	**66**	**77**	**69**	**76**	**80**	**76**	**73**	**92**	**Amérique du Sud**
Argentina[1]	9.2	11.5	11.0	11.5	11.5	12.5	11.2	13.1	...	...	Argentine[1]
Brazil[1]	21.9	22.1	22.1	22.5	22.5	23.0	24.1	22.2	...	...	Brésil[1]
Chile[1]	3.4	2.3	1.9	5.6	6.4	8.2	11.0	12.4	...	...	Chili[1]
Colombia[1]	14.3	11.7	...	10.1	...	...	9.8	7.5	...	...	Colombie[1]
Ecuador[1]	0.1	0.1	0.2	0.2	0.2	...	0.2	0.9	...	...	Equateur[1]
Guyana[1]	0.1	0.4	0.4	0.3	0.4	0.4	0.4	0.4	...	...	Guyana[1]
Peru	8.7	14.0	13.0	18.0	8.7	12.6	14.9	11.0	9.3	*27.6	Pérou
Suriname[1]	0.5	0.6	0.7	0.9	1.0	1.0	1.0	1.0	...	...	Suriname[1]
Uruguay[1]	0.0	0.0	0.0	0.0	0.0	0.0	0.3	0.3	...	...	Uruguay[1]
Venezuela[1]	9.2	9.4	6.5	7.6	7.3	7.5	7.2	7.2	...	...	Venezuela[1]

For general note and footnotes, see end of table.   Voir la fin du tableau pour la remarque générale et les notes.

Fish, salted, dried or smoked (continued)
Poisson salé, séché ou fumé (suite)

ISIC-BASED CODE - CODE BASE CITI

3114-04

Unit : Thousand metric tons   Unité : Milliers de tonnes métriques

Country or area	1990	1991	1992	1993	1994	1995	1996	1997	1998	1999	Pays ou zone
Asia	**2314**	**2281**	**2335**	**2348**	**2403**	**3396**	**2801**	**2738**	**2667**	**2883**	**Asie**
Azerbaijan	..	6.6	3.6	1.2	1.0	0.5	0.2	0.3	0.2	0.2	Azerbaïdjan
Bangladesh[1]	...	...	...	52.9	47.9	44.7	46.6	52.1	...	...	Bangladesh[1]
Cambodia[1]	3.9	4.4	3.1	2.8	2.7	2.7	3.5	3.3	...	...	Cambodge[1]
China[1]	188.8	208.7	208.1	206.7	408.9	544.1	604.2	689.3	...	...	Chine[1]
Hong Kong SAR[1]	1.4	1.1	0.5	0.3	0.2	0.3	0.6	0.2	...	...	Hong-Kong RAS[1]
India[1]	186.0	197.1	222.9	252.4	294.4	290.0	314.5	353.1	...	...	Inde[1]
Indonesia	55.9	20.3	70.7	45.6	53.5	[1]892.0	...	122.0	126.2	...	Indonésie
Iran(Islamic Rep. of)[1]	0.0	2.5	3.0	3.1	3.1	4.1	4.3	4.3	...	...	Iran(Rép. islamique)[1]
Japan	916.7	908.7	839.7	843.7	805.7	831.1	831.2	811.7	771.9	753.2	Japon
Kazakhstan[1]	..	...	11.0	8.7	6.1	5.2	5.0	4.0	...	...	Kazakhstan[1]
Korea,Dem.Ppl's.Rep.[1]	136.1	105.0	94.0	90.4	28.5	21.5	21.1	15.0	...	...	Corée,Rép.pop.dém.de[1]
Korea, Republic of	33.8	26.0	[1]27.9	[1]37.9	[1]32.0	[1]36.1	[1]79.2	[1]64.8	...	...	Corée, République de
Kyrgyzstan	..	0.8	0.5	0.1	0.1	0.1	0.0	0.0	0.0	0.0	Kirghizistan
Lao People's Dem. Rep.[1]	136.1	105.0	94.0	90.4	28.5	21.5	21.1	15.0	...	...	Rép. dém. pop. lao[1]
Malaysia[1]	12.2	7.8	13.0	9.0	8.8	8.5	9.2	6.5	...	...	Malaisie[1]
Maldives	5.4	6.8	5.5	6.6	8.0	7.3	6.8	6.6	7.0	6.5	Maldives
Myanmar[1]	63.4	62.6	62.8	66.4	68.0	68.4	70.4	71.0	...	...	Myanmar[1]
Oman[1]	13.0	14.1	8.7	8.2	6.5	8.3	6.7	6.6	...	...	Oman[1]
Pakistan[1]	22.8	22.7	32.3	40.5	33.1	31.2	37.9	42.0	...	...	Pakistan[1]
Philippines[1]	244.2	259.7	248.9	234.1	239.3	244.9	241.7	155.5	...	...	Philippines[1]
Sri Lanka	177.1	198.1	206.2	200.9	...	...	...	...	...	...	Sri Lanka
Thailand[1]	29.9	31.4	91.7	107.8	92.8	98.6	87.7	83.9	...	...	Thaïlande[1]
Turkey[1]	2.0	2.5	3.0	3.5	3.6	4.1	4.0	3.5	...	...	Turquie[1]
United Arab Emirates[1]	21.5	20.6	22.3	23.3	23.0	22.0	23.0	20.5	...	...	Emirats arabes unis[1]
Uzbekistan	..	...	2.9	2.0	[1]1.5	[1]1.0	[1]0.4	[1]0.0	...	...	Ouzbékistan
Viet Nam[1]	7.2	7.3	9.5	9.5	10.0	12.0	13.0	10.5	...	...	Viet Nam[1]
Dem. Yemen (former)[1]	6.3	..	..	..	..	..	..	..	..	..	Yémen dém. (anc.)[1]
Yemen[1]	..	0.0	0.0	0.0	0.0	0.0	0.1	0.2	...	...	Yémen[1]
Europe	**428**	**989**	**691**	**649**	**635**	**609**	**667**	**639**	**623**	**582**	**Europe**
Austria[1]	0.6	0.5	0.5	0.5	0.5	0.5	0.5	0.5	...	...	Autriche[1]
Belarus	..	2.8	2.4	0.0	0.0	2.2	2.2	1.5	1.7	1.6	Bélarus
Belgium	4.4	4.3	4.2	4.3	[3]2.8	[3]2.9	[3]3.0	[3]2.9	[3]2.8	[3]3.9	Belgique
Bulgaria	[1]2.1	[1]2.1	[1]1.9	[1]1.7	...	[1]2.0	...	[1]1.9	[4]0.1	[4]0.1	Bulgarie
Croatia	..	0.1	0.1	0.1	0.0	0.0	0.1	0.0	...	...	Croatie
Denmark	37.0	[1]25.1	30.0	[5]28.5	[5]25.6	[5]23.6	[5]27.9	[5]26.5	[5]20.4	[5]24.0	Danemark
Czechoslovakia(former)	[6]6.5	[1]2.4	..	..	..	..	..	..	..	..	Tchécoslovaquie(anc.)
Czech Republic	..	..	3.0	2.5	[1]0.3	10.4	10.8	9.3	5.6	4.6	République tchèque
Estonia	..	4.5	1.7	3.6	2.2	2.3	2.5	3.9	3.7	1.2	Estonie
Finland	2.9	7.2	6.7	6.8	3.2	2.0	2.1	2.8	2.4	1.6	Finlande
France[1]	14.1	14.1	13.5	12.5	12.5	13.0	13.1	12.3	...	...	France[1]
Germany	..	[1]30.6	26.8	[1]24.8	25.9	[1]27.1	23.8	20.4	19.8	..	Allemagne
Germany(Fed.Rep.)	22.2	..	..	..	..	..	..	..	..	..	Allemagne(Rép.féd.)
German D.R.(former)	12.1	..	..	..	..	..	..	..	..	..	R.D.A. (anc.)
Greece	[1]8.0	[7]7.0	[1]1.2	6.5	0.7	6.3	6.5	...	6.5	...	Grèce
Iceland	72.7	69.4	56.2	61.9	69.6	66.3	74.9	71.9	73.3	75.0	Islande
Ireland	[1]8.6	[1]8.0	[6]6.3	[1]7.5	[1]5.6	[1]6.0	[1]6.6	[1]6.3	2.0	2.0	Irlande
Italy[1]	7.0	7.8	9.1	13.2	13.6	14.2	14.2	14.2	...	...	Italie[1]
Latvia	..	20.3	6.1	4.8	5.0	3.8	6.6	5.8	6.4	6.6	Lettonie
Lithuania	..	...	[1]1.4	[1]0.0	[1]2.2	3.2	4.1	4.2	5.3	4.9	Lituanie
Netherlands[1]	26.6	27.4	25.0	24.7	26.4	19.1	21.1	21.9	...	...	Pays-Bas[1]
Norway	[2]68.5	[2]114.3	[2]107.5	[1]126.8	[1]166.3	[1]162.5	[1]164.7	[1]160.3	...	127.2	Norvège
Poland	36.5	24.2	27.6	37.1	48.4	47.6	46.2	45.0	43.0	42.8	Pologne
Portugal	22.4	26.9	15.3	12.9	7.5	11.1	51.7	57.6	54.3	42.4	Portugal
Romania	16.6	6.5	4.0	3.7	2.3	3.9	2.3	1.8	0.9	0.6	Roumanie
Russian Federation	..	409.2	227.8	196.8	147.2	107.2	102.7	88.1	99.1	80.4	Fédération de Russie
Slovakia	..	..	...	0.6	1.1	1.3	1.1	0.8	1.1	0.8	Slovaquie
Slovenia	..	0.0	[1]0.1	[1]0.1	[1]0.0	[1]0.0	[1]0.0	[1]0.0	0.0	..	Slovénie
Spain	31.6	43.0	40.9	23.4	24.5	26.7	28.8	33.3	33.8	28.8	Espagne
Sweden	[1]0.0	[1]1.8	[1]0.0	[1]1.9	[1]0.0	[1]0.6	[2]2.8	[1]1.9	1.7	2.4	Suède
Switzerland[1]	0.1	0.1	0.1	0.1	0.1	0.1	0.1	0.1	...	...	Suisse[1]
Ukraine	..	101.0	44.9	15.1	12.0	15.6	13.4	11.9	25.3	25.8	Ukraine
United Kingdom	27.1	26.6	26.3	[1]27.3	[1]27.9	[1]27.8	[1]31.5	26.0	30.6	...	Royaume-Uni

For general note and footnotes, see end of table.   Voir la fin du tableau pour la remarque générale et les notes.

Fish, salted, dried or smoked (continued)
Poisson salé, séché ou fumé (suite)

ISIC-BASED CODE - CODE BASE CITI
3114-04

Unit : Thousand metric tons

Unité : Milliers de tonnes métriques

Country or area	1990	1991	1992	1993	1994	1995	1996	1997	1998	1999	Pays ou zone
Yugoslavia, SFR	0.2	..	..	..	..	..	..	..	..	..	Yougoslavie, RSF
USSR (former)[1]	730.4	..	..	..	..	..	..	..	..	..	URSS (anc.)[1]
Oceania	**8**	**7**	**2**	**2**	**2**	**2**	**2**	**2**	**2**	**2**	**Océanie**
Australia[1]	0.1	0.1	0.0	0.1	0.2	0.2	0.2	0.4	...	...	Australie[1]
Fiji[1]	0.1	0.2	0.0	0.0	0.0	0.0	0.1	0.0	...	...	Fidji[1]
New Zealand[1]	7.8	6.0	0.9	0.8	0.7	1.0	0.5	0.9	...	...	Nouvelle-Zélande[1]
Papua New Guinea[1]	0.0	0.0	0.1	0.0	0.0	0.0	0.0	0.0	...	...	Papouasie-Nvl-Guinée[1]
Solomon Islands	[1]0.5	[1]0.4	[1]0.4	[1]0.6	0.8	0.8	0.9	0.9	1.5	...	Iles Salomon
Total	**4026**	**3809**	**3537**	**3503**	**3537**	**4572**	**4067**	**3959**	**3847**	**4050**	**Total**

General Note.

Salted, dried or smoked edible fish (whole, in pieces or filleted) including those preserved in brine. Production on fish factory ships is included. (SITC, Rev.3: 03500-0).

Remarque générale.

Poisson comestible salé, séché ou fumé (poissons entiers ou tronçonnés, et filets de poissons), y compris le poisson conservé dans la saumure. Cette rubrique comprend la production des navires-usines. (CTCI, Rev.3: 03500-0).

[1] Source: Food and Agriculture Organization of the United Nations (FAO), (Rome).

[2] Excluding shellfish.
[3] Incomplete coverage.
[4] Excluding dried fish.
[5] Sales.
[6] Smoked fish only.

[1] Source: Organisation des Nations Unies pour l'alimentation et l'agriculture (FAO), (Rome).
[2] Non compris les coquillages.
[3] Couverture incomplète.
[4] Non compris le poisson séché.
[5] Ventes.
[6] Poisson fumé seulement.

Fish, tinned
Conserves de poisson
ISIC-BASED CODE - CODE BASE CITI

3114-07

Unit : Thousand metric tons

Unité : Milliers de tonnes métriques

Country or area	1990	1991	1992	1993	1994	1995	1996	1997	1998	1999	Pays ou zone
Africa	**269**	**253**	**291**	**313**	**275**	**382**	**337**	**365**	**380**	**386**	**Afrique**
Algeria[1]	6.5	6.8	6.3	6.0	5.5	4.5	4.5	4.0	...	...	Algérie[1]
Angola[1]	5.0	2.8	2.4	2.4	2.7	2.7	2.8	3.1	...	...	Angola[1]
Cape Verde	[1]0.4	[1]0.2	[1]0.3	[1]0.2	0.3	0.3	[1]0.3	[1]0.3	...	...	Cap-Vert
Côte d'Ivoire[1]	41.4	47.2	41.4	49.9	43.6	57.1	61.0	51.1	...	...	Côte d'Ivoire[1]
Egypt	3.2	4.0	2.3	3.0	1.6	1.7	2.7	2.7	...	...	Egypte
Ghana[1]	4.1	3.7	3.1	3.7	5.4	9.9	12.4	9.1	...	...	Ghana[1]
Kenya[1]	0.0	0.2	0.0	0.2	0.2	0.1	0.2	0.5	...	...	Kenya[1]
Libyan Arab Jamah.	1.4	1.8	2.2	2.7	2.2	1.9	1.6	1.2	1.8	1.8	Jamah. arabe libyenne
Madagascar[1]	0.0	0.0	7.7	8.8	11.1	14.1	14.0	5.9	...	...	Madagascar[1]
Mauritius	[1]10.0	[1]13.8	10.0	10.4	11.6	15.7	17.4	17.7	17.2	19.0	Maurice
Morocco	91.7	57.3	[1]101.2	95.6	100.7	149.3	126.4	141.8	147.2	169.7	Maroc
Mozambique[1]	0.2	0.2	0.2	0.0	0.0	0.2	0.2	0.1	...	...	Mozambique[1]
Namibia[1]	33.0	25.5	32.0	46.5	25.7	28.1	6.0	17.8	...	...	Namibie[1]
Senegal	[1]20.7	[1]34.7	[1]29.2	[1]17.6	20.6	24.1	19.8	14.3	18.7	14.4	Sénégal
Seychelles	2.8	3.6	3.0	4.5	5.1	7.5	12.7	15.1	18.9	33.2	Seychelles
South Africa	45.2	48.1	46.0	59.1	34.4	59.7	42.8	53.8	53.1	21.2	Afrique du Sud
Tunisia	3.4	2.9	2.9	2.4	3.6	3.2	1.6	2.6	3.9	5.7	Tunisie
Uganda[1]	0.0	0.0	0.0	0.1	0.1	0.0	0.0	0.0	...	...	Ouganda[1]
United Rep.Tanzania	[1]0.1	[1]0.1	[1]0.1	[1]0.2	[1]0.4	2.4	11.1	24.4	...	...	Rép. Unie de Tanzanie
Zimbabwe[1]	0.2	0.2	0.2	0.0	0.0	0.0	0.0	0.0	...	...	Zimbabwe[1]
America, North	**556**	**772**	**705**	**926**	**1026**	**1190**	**637**	**586**	**819**	**831**	**Amérique du Nord**
Canada[1]	71.1	60.9	45.1	59.6	56.5	53.1	48.3	38.0	...	...	Canada[1]
Costa Rica[1]	3.7	2.8	4.8	1.1	9.9	13.1	17.0	13.6	...	...	Costa Rica[1]
Cuba[1]	5.5	2.2	1.8	0.8	0.7	0.7	0.4	0.2	...	...	Cuba[1]
El Salvador[1]	0.1	0.4	0.9	0.2	0.5	0.8	0.9	0.8	...	...	El Salvador[1]
Greenland[1]	0.4	0.3	0.2	0.1	0.1	0.1	0.1	0.3	...	...	Groënland[1]
Mexico	40.6	46.3	42.6	88.8	96.6	86.6	98.9	108.4	87.7	97.8	Mexique
Trinidad and Tobago[1]	0.0	0.0	0.0	0.0	0.1	0.2	0.3	0.1	...	...	Trinité-et-Tobago[1]
United States	434.2	659.5	609.2	775.2	862.0	1035.2	[1]471.4	[1]424.8	...	...	Etats-Unis
America, South	**236**	**255**	**315**	**323**	**317**	**374**	**370**	**493**	**408**	**466**	**Amérique du Sud**
Argentina[1]	13.2	21.0	26.4	42.4	35.6	40.3	41.9	35.9	...	...	Argentine[1]
Brazil[1]	24.3	40.7	41.0	34.3	32.4	33.1	33.2	31.2	...	...	Brésil[1]
Chile[1]	71.0	52.9	75.0	79.7	95.8	100.3	93.4	140.6	...	...	Chili[1]
Colombia	[1]0.5	[1]1.6	4.0	2.1	3.7	#23.0	[1]13.0	18.6	13.3	...	Colombie
Ecuador	[1]34.3	[1]31.2	[1]33.3	[1]41.5	[1]56.8	75.2	86.5	103.5	104.3	...	Equateur
Peru	39.6	31.2	34.5	35.7	49.7	57.4	59.4	124.8	54.5	63.6	Pérou
Uruguay[1]	0.0	0.0	0.0	0.1	2.0	2.1	4.0	1.8	...	...	Uruguay[1]
Venezuela[1]	53.1	76.1	101.2	87.6	41.3	43.0	38.3	36.2	...	...	Venezuela[1]
Asia	**1108**	**1354**	**1303**	**1251**	**1286**	**1249**	**1325**	**1337**	**1319**	**1335**	**Asie**
Armenia[1]	..	...	0.0	0.1	0.1	0.1	0.1	0.1	...	...	Arménie[1]
Azerbaijan	..	23.2	12.8	#0.6	0.1	0.0	0.0	0.0	0.0	0.0	Azerbaïdjan
Bangladesh[1]	0.1	0.1	0.3	0.2	0.3	0.6	0.5	0.6	...	...	Bangladesh[1]
Cambodia[1]	9.2	8.7	5.5	7.2	7.8	8.5	5.8	7.1	...	...	Cambodge[1]
China[1]	122.6	141.1	138.8	137.6	126.7	124.1	153.9	187.9	...	...	Chine[1]
Hong Kong SAR[1]	0.7	1.8	2.9	8.6	10.3	18.6	37.8	40.9	...	...	Hong-Kong RAS[1]
Georgia	..	...	0.6	0.2	0.0	0.0	0.0	...	...	...	Géorgie
India[1]	17.7	18.2	15.7	6.2	5.6	7.1	11.4	11.0	...	...	Inde[1]
Indonesia	18.7	43.7	50.4	29.9	40.8	[1]61.4	[1]69.8	72.0	...	...	Indonésie
Iran(Islamic Rep. of)	[2]2.9	[2]3.2	[2]6.4	[2]7.3	[2]7.6	[3]7.9	[3]9.3	[3]10.6	[3]10.8	...	Iran(Rép. islamique)
Israel[1]	7.3	7.3	6.4	6.2	5.3	3.6	3.3	3.0	...	...	Israël[1]
Japan	194.2	193.7	198.1	189.3	176.3	158.4	147.4	154.1	150.7	147.8	Japon
Kazakhstan[1]	..	...	11.8	10.6	8.0	8.1	7.9	7.9	...	...	Kazakhstan[1]
Korea,Dem.Ppl's.Rep.[1]	3.7	2.4	1.5	1.5	2.5	1.2	1.3	1.2	...	...	Corée,Rép.pop.dém.de[1]
Korea, Republic of	85.8	86.5	68.7	63.7	66.2	66.7	[1]108.1	[1]135.1	...	...	Corée, République de
Malaysia	8.9	12.1	12.1	15.7	16.9	15.5	19.4	19.5	18.9	16.4	Malaisie
Maldives	6.9	7.2	7.5	4.9	6.8	7.8	7.2	6.8	6.7	4.6	Maldives
Myanmar[1]	114.9	113.6	114.0	120.5	123.4	120.0	120.0	128.8	...	...	Myanmar[1]
Pakistan[1]	1.0	3.2	4.9	5.6	3.9	5.9	10.6	11.3	...	...	Pakistan[1]
Philippines[1]	71.3	73.5	75.3	88.3	91.2	80.0	102.0	88.9	...	...	Philippines[1]
Saudi Arabia[1]	1.0	4.4	4.9	3.9	3.2	5.4	5.8	7.5	...	...	Arabie saoudite[1]

For general note and footnotes, see end of table.

Voir la fin du tableau pour la remarque générale et les notes.

Fish, tinned (continued)
Conserves de poisson (suite)

ISIC-BASED CODE - CODE BASE CITI

3114-07

Unit : Thousand metric tons

Unité : Milliers de tonnes métriques

Country or area	1990	1991	1992	1993	1994	1995	1996	1997	1998	1999	Pays ou zone
Singapore[1]	2.6	1.8	3.2	4.1	1.3	1.2	1.2	2.0	...	...	Singapour[1]
Sri Lanka[1]	0.0	0.0	0.0	0.0	0.0	0.1	0.1	0.0	...	...	Sri Lanka[1]
Thailand[1]	330.7	436.6	394.8	366.8	409.1	367.4	331.0	270.1	...	...	Thaïlande[1]
Turkey	0.2	0.1	4.3	12.6	7.6	14.7	8.0	17.2	13.5	24.2	Turquie
Turkmenistan	..	6.7	2.8	1.6	1.1	0.7	0.2	0.3	0.5	...	Turkménistan
Uzbekistan	..	5.6	4.6	2.8	1.9	2.1	[1]0.6	[1]0.5	...	...	Ouzbékistan
Viet Nam[1]	107.2	148.3	154.7	155.6	160.5	160.5	161.1	151.4	...	...	Viet Nam[1]
Yemen[1]	..	0.0	0.0	0.0	1.2	1.2	1.0	1.0	...	...	Yémen[1]
Europe	**758**	**1700**	**1362**	**1226**	**1138**	**1216**	**1253**	**1724**	**1717**	**1648**	**Europe**
Albania	[1]1.5	[1]0.5	[1]0.2	[1]0.0	[1]0.1	[1]0.2	[1]0.0	...	0.2	0.0	Albanie
Belarus	..	1.9	1.7	1.4	1.3	1.2	1.7	3.0	3.3	3.2	Bélarus
Belgium	6.6	5.7	6.0	5.4	13.1	14.0	13.1	13.0	14.5	15.5	Belgique
Bulgaria	7.7	3.9	3.5	2.3	1.8	2.3	1.8	1.4	1.8	1.4	Bulgarie
Croatia	..	18.5	18.0	13.5	11.4	12.5	14.8	13.4	12.0		Croatie
Denmark[1]	101.7	111.1	106.6	103.7	104.2	103.6	85.6	90.0	...	...	Danemark[1]
Czechoslovakia(former)[1]	21.3	11.0	..	..	..	..	..	..	..	..	Tchécoslovaquie(anc.)[1]
Czech Republic	..	..	2.6	[1]2.0	[1]3.3	[1]3.3	[1]3.3	[1]3.3	...	...	République tchèque
Estonia	..	68.3	29.5	21.2	31.2	35.4	43.5	67.5	63.7	38.4	Estonie
Finland	0.9	0.8	0.8	0.7	0.8	0.7	1.0	4.5	4.2	3.4	Finlande
France	[1]65.3	[1]68.8	[1]64.4	[1]66.3	68.7	67.7	74.8	70.4	68.5	...	France
Germany	..	56.8	55.9	57.8	52.3	[1]141.3	[1]127.7	343.2	334.3	...	Allemagne
Germany(Fed.Rep.)	45.7	..	..	..	..	..	..	..	..	..	Allemagne(Rép.féd.)
German D.R.(former)	17.3	..	..	..	..	..	..	..	..	..	R.D.A. (anc.)
Greece	[1]0.7	[1]0.7	[1]0.8	[1]1.3	[1]1.8	[1]4.2	[1]3.9	[1]2.8	1.2	...	Grèce
Hungary	0.7	0.3	0.9	0.8	0.5	0.4	[1]0.6	[1]0.6	...	...	Hongrie
Iceland	[1]2.7	1.5	1.6	1.7	1.6	1.7	2.5	3.1	3.2	3.9	Islande
Ireland	[1]3.0	[1]3.5	[1]4.8	[1]5.3	[1]4.9	[1]10.1	[1]18.8	[1]11.3	4.0	6.0	Irlande
Italy[1]	119.3	121.5	125.6	116.5	111.5	103.2	97.0	98.1	...	...	Italie[1]
Latvia	..	...	[1]31.0	[1]22.9	30.1	38.9	59.2	91.1	78.7	62.8	Lettonie
Lithuania	..	24.2	10.6	4.8	5.0	4.7	6.6	7.0	5.9	2.7	Lituanie
Netherlands[4 5]	15.9	16.3	15.8	12.1	7.7	7.5	...	...	...	...	Pays-Bas[4 5]
Norway	[1]54.8	[1]56.9	[1]57.9	[1]63.4	[1]60.3	[1]58.3	[1]58.8	[1]53.4	...	61.8	Norvège
Poland	22.5	29.7	34.4	30.4	37.9	35.1	45.9	52.0	49.4	40.4	Pologne
Portugal	43.5	40.2	39.3	43.6	47.8	52.1	43.8	37.7	48.2	45.6	Portugal
Romania	18.0	15.7	7.0	6.0	2.5	2.2	2.1	1.4	0.6	0.7	Roumanie
Russian Federation	..	700.4	470.7	321.1	206.9	200.8	164.9	178.0	144.5	170.1	Fédération de Russie
Slovakia	..	..	...	4.3	7.4	9.1	...	...	10.4	10.4	Slovaquie
Slovenia	..	3.5	2.9	2.5	2.7	2.2	2.3	[1]1.7	...	...	Slovénie
Spain	122.8	137.6	140.6	[6]207.2	[6]233.1	[6]235.6	[1]258.8	[1]264.4	...	...	Espagne
Sweden	42.2	42.2	[1]43.2	[1]59.3	[1]42.7	[1]20.6	[1]42.8	[1]25.1	66.5	63.7	Suède
Switzerland[1]	0.2	0.2	0.2	0.2	0.2	0.0	0.0	0.0	...	...	Suisse[1]
Ukraine	..	106.6	65.9	31.6	27.9	29.6	39.3	46.4	48.0	34.8	Ukraine
United Kingdom	11.7	12.4	12.7	[1]16.4	[1]16.9	[1]17.5	[1]21.2	#224.7	223.3	...	Royaume-Uni
Yugoslavia	..	0.0	0.0	0.3	0.4	0.5	0.6	0.4	0.7	0.8	Yougoslavie
Yugoslavia, SFR	32.3	..	..	..	..	..	..	..	..	..	Yougoslavie, RSF
USSR (former)	1130.6	..	..	..	..	..	..	..	..	..	URSS (anc.)
Oceania	**24**	**34**	**37**	**33**	**34**	**39**	**34**	**30**	**31**	**34**	**Océanie**
American Samoa[7]	0.2	0.2	0.2	0.2	...	...	...	...	...	...	Samoa américaines[7]
Australia	[8]7.6	[8]6.5	[8]7.0	[1]1.4	[1]0.7	[1]2.7	[8]7.2	[8]7.1	[8]7.7	...	Australie
Fiji	8.9	13.7	14.0	15.6	15.7	15.7	12.7	6.8	7.0	...	Fidji
New Zealand[1]	4.7	8.7	9.9	9.8	10.0	11.0	8.1	8.1	...	...	Nouvelle-Zélande[1]
Solomon Islands	2.8	5.1	5.4	5.8	7.7	9.9	5.9	7.5	6.4	...	Iles Salomon
Total	**4082**	**4368**	**4012**	**4073**	**4077**	**4451**	**3956**	**4536**	**4675**	**4700**	**Total**

General Note.

Edible fish products packed and heat-processed in hermetically-sealed containers. Prior to packing, the products may have been smoked, dried, seasoned or otherwise prepared. In terms of net weight. (SITC, Rev.3: 03710-1).

Remarque générale.

Produits de poisson comestibles, traités par la chaleur et mis dans des récipients fermés hermétiquement. Avant le conditionnement, les produits peuvent avoir été fumés, séchés, assaisonnés ou autrement préparés. Poids net.(CTCI, Rev.3: 03710-1).

For footnotes, see end of table.

Voir la fin du tableau pour les notes.

Fish, tinned (continued)
Conserves de poisson (suite)

ISIC-BASED CODE - CODE BASE CITI

3114-07

Footnotes

[1] Source: Food and Agriculture Organization of the United Nations (FAO), (Rome).

[2] Production by establishments employing 50 or more persons.

[3] Production by establishments employing 10 or more persons.

[4] Sales.

[5] Production by establishments employing 20 or more persons.

[6] Including fish preserved otherwise than by tinning.

[7] Twelve months beginning 21 March of year stated.

[8] Twelve months ending 30 June of year stated.

Notes.

[1] Source: Organisation des Nations Unies pour l'alimentation et l'agriculture (FAO), (Rome).

[2] Production des établissements occupant 50 personnes ou plus.

[3] Production des établissements occupant 10 personnes ou plus.

[4] Ventes.

[5] Production des établissements occupant 20 personnes ou plus.

[6] Y compris le poisson préservé autrement qu'en conserve.

[7] Période de douze mois commençant le 21 mars de l'année indiquée.

[8] Période de douze mois finissant le 30 juin de l'année indiquée.

Margarine, imitation lard and other prepared fats
Margarine, simili-saindoux et autres graisses alimentaires préparées

ISIC-BASED CODE - CODE BASE CITI

3115-01

Unit : Thousand metric tons

Unité : Milliers de tonnes métriques

Country or area	1990	1991	1992	1993	1994	1995	1996	1997	1998	1999	Pays ou zone
Africa	**265**	**304**	**267**	**301**	**298**	**345**	**359**	**376**	**392**	**402**	**Afrique**
Algeria	17.0	15.6	20.3	23.0	22.0	16.4	16.9	17.0	18.8	15.3	Algérie
Kenya	112.1	102.3	71.7	93.5	61.8	102.6	94.3	...	...	...	Kenya
Mozambique	0.7	0.7	0.5	0.4	0.5	0.4	0.3	0.0	...	...	Mozambique
South Africa	132.7	167.7	165.7	172.3	198.6	207.9	228.5	...	...	...	Afrique du Sud
Tunisia	[1]2.1	...	8.5	11.5	14.7	17.5	19.0	26.0	27.5	29.2	Tunisie
America, North	**809**	**826**	**880**	**938**	**947**	**879**	**922**	**929**	**926**	**895**	**Amérique du Nord**
Canada	...	...	...	...	...	488.8	532.2	...	...	...	Canada
Jamaica[2]	10.6	9.1	8.4	6.3	7.3	6.6	6.6	6.4	6.3	5.5	Jamaïque[2]
Mexico	279.8	299.1	353.8	413.9	422.1	375.9	374.3	403.2	399.7	369.8	Mexique
Trinidad and Tobago	7.7	7.2	7.0	7.2	7.0	7.2	9.1	9.4	9.4	9.2	Trinité-et-Tobago
America, South	**118**	**101**	**105**	**95**	**90**	**97**	**98**	**102**	**101**	**106**	**Amérique du Sud**
Colombia[1]	101.0	...	89.2	83.7	76.7	81.2	...	89.6	93.5	...	Colombie[1]
Ecuador	17.0	...	15.7	11.4	13.6	15.7	9.9	12.1	7.2	...	Equateur
Asia	**1239**	**1351**	**1324**	**1297**	**1281**	**1330**	**1338**	**1386**	**1313**	**1298**	**Asie**
Armenia	..	5.8	2.0	0.1	0.0	0.1	0.1	0.4	0.3	0.3	Arménie
Azerbaijan	..	18.3	10.2	6.0	3.6	1.0	0.3	0.4	0.0	0.9	Azerbaïdjan
Georgia	..	...	2.3	2.3	0.1	0.0	...	...	...	...	Géorgie
Israel[1]	30.9	...	...	...	...	...	...	...	...	...	Israël[1]
Japan	696.7	684.0	683.1	700.9	700.7	707.2	710.7	709.9	704.0	707.7	Japon
Kyrgyzstan	..	...	4.8	0.4	0.2	0.0	0.0	0.0	...	...	Kirghizistan
Malaysia	19.4	18.8	25.0	25.2	25.0	25.6	28.1	26.6	25.8	23.9	Malaisie
Syrian Arab Republic	6.0	[3]5.2	[3]5.5	[3]4.0	[3]4.8	[3]5.2	2.9	1.4	0.9	0.9	Rép. arabe syrienne
Turkey[1]	485.8	553.9	530.9	492.8	481.0	535.2	535.1	587.2	522.0	504.8	Turquie[1]
Uzbekistan	..	30.9	29.4	34.5	35.1	24.8	...	...	...	...	Ouzbékistan
Europe	**2754**	**3909**	**3859**	**3751**	**3538**	**3576**	**3397**	**3524**	**3319**	**3335**	**Europe**
Austria	61.8	77.5	69.4	68.9	63.9	66.3	...	...	...	86.5	Autriche
Belarus	..	71.5	36.5	35.6	19.2	17.0	25.3	22.7	15.0	22.4	Bélarus
Bulgaria	...	...	...	1.5	3.0	5.0	5.3	6.2	10.5	11.5	Bulgarie
Croatia	..	21.0	17.7	14.7	13.1	14.3	16.6	14.7	15.4	...	Croatie
Denmark[4]	109.0	108.0	103.0	93.0	88.0	86.0	87.0	88.1	103.0	68.0	Danemark[4]
Czechoslovakia(former)	194.8	165.4	..	..	..	..	..	..	..	..	Tchécoslovaquie(anc.)
Czech Republic	..	..	140.0	150.8	235.0	..	..	...	...	...	République tchèque
Finland	42.0	45.6	53.8	61.9	62.4	81.8	102.5	...	...	44.9	Finlande
France	155.8	152.5	152.5	147.4	134.8	131.2	138.3	...	...	...	France
Germany	..	834.7	850.6	827.7	744.4	708.9	710.8	787.2	...	...	Allemagne
Germany(Fed.Rep.)	692.5	..	..	..	..	..	..	..	..	..	Allemagne(Rép.féd.)
Greece	51.3	56.2	71.3	44.2	34.4	44.0	43.8	[1]36.8	44.4	...	Grèce
Hungary	68.6	58.9	75.7	...	...	...	...	...	...	...	Hongrie
Iceland	[1]2.3	[1]2.5	[1]2.4	[1]2.4	[1]2.2	[1]1.9	2.3	2.3	2.1	2.3	Islande
Ireland	26.6	...	...	...	...	...	...	...	...	...	Irlande
Italy[1]	95.8	101.0	101.0	99.6	121.2	135.4	124.8	127.9	122.1	127.6	Italie[1]
Latvia	..	7.4	4.5	2.8	1.9	1.1	0.6	0.5	0.4	0.2	Lettonie
Netherlands[4][5]	[1]256.2	267.0	270.9	#470.0	453.0	494.0	451.0	521.0	443.0	404.3	Pays-Bas[4][5]
Norway	71.8	70.0	66.5	64.3	[1]63.4	[1]65.2	[1]59.4	[1]57.2	[1]57.1	...	Norvège
Portugal[6]	71.4	63.3	66.8	68.9	76.7	71.1	60.1	58.9	57.5	...	Portugal[6]
Russian Federation	..	627.3	560.5	438.4	278.0	197.6	199.9	222.3	238.7	379.4	Fédération de Russie
Slovakia	..	..	...	51.6	57.5	63.6	77.2	7.6	...	...	Slovaquie
Slovenia	..	..	..	..	..	..	0.1	..	0.1	0.1	Slovénie
Spain	91.3	95.5	78.9	116.6	159.6	116.7	116.1	112.7	106.8	118.4	Espagne
Sweden	164.3	170.8	158.2	...	205.6	294.6	243.9	290.8	236.9	237.3	Suède
Ukraine	..	266.5	249.2	172.9	105.5	108.5	89.2	84.7	96.8	120.4	Ukraine
United Kingdom	598.9	577.6	592.1	468.0	489.1	565.5	469.9	523.9	492.1	...	Royaume-Uni
Yugoslavia	..	42.1	37.9	32.6	32.2	36.7	32.5	32.0	39.2	39.1	Yougoslavie
Total	**5185**	**6490**	**6434**	**6382**	**6155**	**6226**	**6114**	**6318**	**6050**	**6036**	**Total**

For general note and footnotes, see end of table.

Voir la fin du tableau pour la remarque générale et les notes

Margarine, imitation lard and other prepared fats (continued)
Margarine, simili-saindoux et autres graisses alimentaires préparées (suite)

ISIC-BASED CODE - CODE BASE CITI
3115-01

General Note.
Solid edible preparations of fats, consisting of mixtures of different animal fats and oils, different vegetable fats and oils, or both. Fats and oils simply refined, or both hydrogenated and refined without further treatment and liquid mixtures of vegetable oils, are excluded. (SITC, Rev.3: 09100-0).

[1] Margarine only.
[2] Including lard.
[3] Including butter.
[4] Sales.
[5] Production by establishments employing 20 or more persons.
[6] 1999 data are confidential.

Remarque générale.
Mélanges solides comestibles de corps gras, composés de mélanges de diverses graisses et huiles animales, de diverses graisses et huiles végétales, soit entre elles, soit les unes avec les autres. Cette position ne comprend pas les graisses et les huiles ayant subi un simple raffinage, ou un raffinage suivi d'une hydrogénation, sans autre traitement, ni les mélanges liquides d'huiles végétales. (CTCI, Rev.3: 09100-0).

[1] Margarine seulement.
[2] Y compris le saindoux.
[3] Y compris les beurre.
[4] Ventes.
[5] Production des établissements occupant 20 personnes ou plus.
[6] Pour 1999, les données sont confidentielles.

Margarine
Margarine

ISIC-BASED CODE - CODE BASE CITI

3115-011

Unit : Thousand metric tons   Unité : Milliers de tonnes métriques

Country or area	1990	1991	1992	1993	1994	1995	1996	1997	1998	1999	Pays ou zone
Africa	**258**	**238**	**219**	**256**	**244**	**249**	**259**	**291**	**268**	**301**	**Afrique**
Egypt	132	103	87	120	103	101	82	101	96	130	Egypte
Mozambique	1	1	0	0	0	0	0	0	...	...	Mozambique
South Africa	124	129	126	130	133	139	168	175	161	156	Afrique du Sud
Tunisia	2	6	5	6	8	9	...	15	11	14	Tunisie
America, North	**1298**	**1261**	**1322**	**1356**	**1239**	**1288**	**1288**	**1285**	**1282**	**1279**	**Amérique du Nord**
Barbados	3	2	4	4	4	4	4	4	4	4	Barbade
Mexico	34	29	35	35	40	...	...	...	...	...	Mexique
Trinidad and Tobago	6	6	5	6	6	6	8	8	8	7	Trinité-et-Tobago
United States	1256	1224	1278	1312	1190	...	...	...	...	...	Etats-Unis
America, South	**526**	**497**	**500**	**485**	**515**	**488**	**512**	**473**	**493**	**520**	**Amérique du Sud**
Brazil	368	349	353	348	383	350	365	325	340	364	Brésil
Chile	39	40	40	32	34	34	35	35	36	37	Chili
Colombia	101	...	89	84	77	81	...	90	93	...	Colombie
Guyana	1	1	1	1	1	...	...	...	...	...	Guyana
Peru	16	19	16	19	19	18	18	18	17	17	Pérou
Suriname	1	0	1	1	2	3	3	...	...	...	Suriname
Asia	**698**	**812**	**846**	**796**	**794**	**1041**	**845**	**841**	**816**	**853**	**Asie**
Indonesia	5	30	93	86	114	293	...	45	85	...	Indonésie
Israel	31	34	35	34	25	36	35	...	...	...	Israël
Japan	176	171	177	183	175	176	181	174	175	175	Japon
Kyrgyzstan	..	12	5	0	0	0	0	0	...	...	Kirghizistan
Tajikistan	..	11	5	0	0	0	0	0	0	0	Tadjikistan
Turkey	486	554	531	493	481	535	535	587	522	505	Turquie
Europe	**2509**	**3185**	**3226**	**3322**	**3207**	**3307**	**3140**	**3320**	**3190**	**3393**	**Europe**
Austria	48	48	50	50	47	...	...	...	...	...	Autriche
Belgium	189	196	207	217	...	...	248	...	...	238	Belgique
Bulgaria	3	1	2	2	3	5	5	6	10	11	Bulgarie
Croatia	..	13	12	10	9	10	12	12	13	...	Croatie
Czechoslovakia(former)	40	36	..	..	..	..	..	..	..	..	Tchécoslovaquie(anc.)
Czech Republic	..	..	35	63	98	115	122	128	130	126	République tchèque
Estonia	..	6	2	1	0	0	0	...	...	...	Estonie
Finland	38	42	49	57	57	76	98	...	...	...	Finlande
France	148	143	143	139	131	130	137	140	138	...	France
Germany	..	721	746	722	648	656	657	731	...	...	Allemagne
Germany(Fed.Rep.)	578	..	..	..	..	..	..	..	..	..	Allemagne(Rép.féd.)
German D.R.(former)	105	..	..	..	..	..	..	..	..	..	R.D.A. (anc.)
Greece	30	33	34	...	...	36	36	37	39	...	Grèce
Hungary	33	35	39	...	...	...	...	...	...	...	Hongrie
Iceland	2	2	2	2	2	2	2	2	2	2	Islande
Ireland	23	...	...	...	...	36	54	48	33	...	Irlande
Italy	96	101	101	100	121	135	125	128	122	128	Italie
Lithuania	..	...	...	...	...	...	...	...	0	2	Lituanie
Netherlands[1][2]	256	209	201	#314	293	335	297	349	310	282	Pays-Bas[1][2]
Norway	69	68	66	59	63	65	59	57	57	55	Norvège
Poland	179	194	234	276	320	374	368	395	363	367	Pologne
Portugal[3]	53	43	59	58	61	59	44	50	50	...	Portugal[3]
Romania	29	26	20	21	16	17	22	26	36	36	Roumanie
Russian Federation	..	408	387	305	188	125	136	148	181	264	Fédération de Russie
Slovakia	..	..	...	...	...	...	...	8	...	...	Slovaquie
Spain	82	83	71	83	126	85	81	73	64	64	Espagne
Sweden	160	167	154	189	194	190	76	90	87	100	Suède
Ukraine	..	203	201	142	90	99	81	78	90	108	Ukraine
United Kingdom	348	344	342	371	383	424	366	387	359	...	Royaume-Uni
Yugoslavia	..	20	21	20	18	21	19	18	22	21	Yougoslavie
T.F.Yug.Rep. Macedonia	..	2	2	2	2	2	2	3	2	3	L'ex-RY Macédoine
USSR (former)	1403	..	..	..	..	..	..	..	..	..	URSS (anc.)
Oceania	**157**	**162**	**162**	**160**	**163**	**163**	**174**	**163**	**166**	**160**	**Océanie**

For general note and footnotes, see end of table.   Voir la fin du tableau pour la remarque générale et les notes.

Margarine (continued)
Margarine (suite)

ISIC-BASED CODE - CODE BASE CITI

3115-011

Unit : Thousand metric tons   Unité : Milliers de tonnes métriques

Country or area	1990	1991	1992	1993	1994	1995	1996	1997	1998	1999	Pays ou zone
Australia[4]	157	162	162	160	...	...	174	163	166	160	Australie[4]
Total	6849	6155	6275	6375	6163	6536	6218	6373	6216	6505	Total

General Note.
Margarine (excluding liquid margarine).(SITC, Rev.3: 09100-0)

Remarque générale.
Margarine (à l'exclusion de la margarine liquide). (CTCI, Rev.3: 09100-0)

[1] Sales.
[2] Production by establishments employing 20 or more persons.
[3] 1999 data are confidential.
[4] Twelve months ending 30 June of year stated.

[1] Ventes.
[2] Production des établissements occupant 20 personnes ou plus.
[3] Pour 1999, les données sont confidentielles.
[4] Période de douze mois finissant le 30 juin de l'année indiquée.

Oils and fats of aquatic animal origin
Huiles et graisses d'animaux aquatiques

ISIC-BASED CODE - CODE BASE CITI

3115-04

Unit : Thousand metric tons   Unité : Milliers de tonnes métriques

Country or area	1990	1991	1992	1993	1994	1995	1996	1997	1998	1999	Pays ou zone
Africa	**18**	**20**	**27**	**29**	**31**	**43**	**38**	**30**	**37**	**39**	**Afrique**
Angola[1]	1.4	1.0	1.0	1.0	1.0	1.0	1.0	1.0	...	...	Angola[1]
Morocco[1]	6.3	6.7	9.5	10.8	22.1	31.0	27.8	17.0	...	...	Maroc[1]
Namibia[1]	6.5	3.6	7.4	10.1	2.8	6.8	1.0	5.1	...	...	Namibie[1]
Senegal[1]	0.0	0.0	0.0	0.0	0.0	0.2	0.2	0.0	...	...	Sénégal[1]
South Africa[1]	4.3	8.6	8.8	7.2	5.3	3.9	8.0	7.0	...	...	Afrique du Sud[1]
United Rep.Tanzania[1]	0.0	0.0	0.0	0.0	0.0	0.0	0.0	0.1	...	...	Rép. Unie de Tanzanie[1]
America, North	**164**	**155**	**113**	**165**	**164**	**139**	**132**	**152**	**143**	**142**	**Amérique du Nord**
Canada[1]	9.6	14.6	11.6	10.5	10.0	10.2	5.7	4.6	...	...	Canada[1]
Greenland[1]	0.0	0.0	0.0	0.0	0.1	0.0	0.0	0.0	...	...	Groënland[1]
Mexico[1]	9.1	10.6	6.3	5.0	7.0	9.8	10.2	11.0	...	...	Mexique[1]
Panama	8.2	6.0	11.0	11.0	14.0	9.0	3.0	...	...	...	Panama
United States[1]	136.7	124.1	83.8	137.9	132.5	109.8	112.9	128.9	...	...	Etats-Unis[1]
America, South	**395**	**436**	**327**	**436**	**782**	**577**	**549**	**585**	**643**	**685**	**Amérique du Sud**
Argentina[1]	4.1	4.0	4.1	4.2	6.2	4.3	4.3	4.2	...	...	Argentine[1]
Brazil[1]	2.9	3.0	2.9	3.0	3.1	3.1	3.0	3.0	...	...	Brésil[1]
Chile[1]	188.3	241.2	153.0	191.2	289.5	326.1	291.8	206.0	...	...	Chili[1]
Colombia	0.0	0.0	1.4	[1]0.0	0.0	0.0	[1]0.0	[1]0.0	...	...	Colombie
Ecuador	[1]8.0	[1]5.3	[1]4.5	[1]2.9	[1]8.2	[1]8.3	15.0	29.0	1.0	...	Equateur
Peru	192.0	182.0	161.0	235.0	475.0	235.0	235.0	...	...	...	Pérou
Uruguay[1]	0.1	0.3	0.3	0.1	0.0	0.1	0.0	0.0	...	...	Uruguay[1]
Asia	**405**	**312**	**163**	**116**	**61**	**75**	**84**	**84**	**90**	**87**	**Asie**
Bahrain[1]	0.0	0.0	0.0	0.0	0.0	0.0	0.0	0.3	...	...	Bahreïn[1]
China[1]	11.3	10.6	10.1	10.1	9.1	10.1	10.7	8.4	...	...	Chine[1]
India[1]	7.3	8.1	1.3	0.6	0.4	0.3	0.2	0.1	...	...	Inde[1]
Indonesia[1]	4.4	4.3	1.5	0.6	0.3	0.1	0.3	...	...	...	Indonésie[1]
Iran(Islamic Rep. of)[1]	0.0	0.0	0.0	0.0	0.0	0.1	0.0	0.0	...	...	Iran(Rép. islamique)[1]
Japan[2]	370.0	280.0	145.0	98.0	45.0	59.0	67.0	70.0	76.0	73.0	Japon[2]
Korea, Republic of[1]	7.5	5.2	2.7	1.4	0.5	2.6	4.7	4.5	...	...	Corée, République de[1]
Malaysia[1]	0.3	0.9	0.0	0.0	0.0	0.0	0.0	0.0	...	...	Malaisie[1]
Oman[1]	0.0	0.0	0.0	0.0	0.0	0.0	0.1	0.0	...	...	Oman[1]
Philippines[1]	0.1	0.0	0.0	0.0	0.0	0.0	0.0	0.0	...	...	Philippines[1]
Turkey[1]	4.0	3.0	2.0	5.0	5.5	3.0	0.9	1.1	...	...	Turquie[1]
Europe	**317**	**480**	**492**	**554**	**509**	**676**	**626**	**574**	**632**	**692**	**Europe**
Austria[1]	0.0	0.0	0.0	0.0	0.0	0.0	0.0	0.2	...	...	Autriche[1]
Belgium[3]	25.0	19.0	14.0	...	...	...	...	...	...	...	Belgique[3]
Bulgaria[1]	0.1	0.1	0.1	0.1	0.0	0.0	0.0	0.0	...	...	Bulgarie[1]
Croatia	..	...	[1]0.2	[1]0.1	[1]0.1	[1]0.1	[1]0.1	0.0	0.0	...	Croatie
Denmark[4]	10.0	14.0	14.0	16.0	13.0	15.0	6.0	8.0	4.0	1.0	Danemark[4]
Estonia	..	4.0	2.0	2.0	1.0	1.0	1.0	1.0	...	...	Estonie
France[1]	4.5	4.0	4.3	4.4	4.3	4.1	4.3	4.1	...	...	France[1]
Germany	..	[1]10.1	[1]9.9	[1]9.8	[1]8.6	133.0	116.0	116.0	...	...	Allemagne
Iceland	75.0	35.0	85.0	116.0	85.0	85.0	136.0	132.0	90.0	90.0	Islande
Ireland[1]	5.6	7.2	9.0	8.1	10.4	11.0	11.0	6.3	...	...	Irlande[1]
Latvia	..	...	[1]0.6	[1]0.4	[1]0.3	[1]0.4	[1]0.3	[1]0.2	...	0.0	Lettonie
Netherlands	[1]4.3	[1]3.3	[1]2.7	[1]1.4	[1]0.8	[1]0.2	[1]4.0	0.0	0.0	...	Pays-Bas
Norway	[1]52.4	[1]91.2	[1]118.7	[1]131.2	[1]120.4	121.0	85.0	[1]92.6	...	...	Norvège
Poland[1]	0.4	0.4	0.0	0.0	0.0	0.0	0.0	0.0	...	...	Pologne[1]
Portugal	[1]3.0	[1]5.9	[1]4.0	[1]2.7	[1]2.3	[1]2.5	1.0	1.0	1.0	1.0	Portugal
Republic of Moldova	..	118.0	58.0	[5]39.0	[5]31.0	[5]32.0	[5]23.0	[5]19.0	[5]18.0	[5]17.0	Rép. de Moldova
Romania[1]	0.1	0.2	0.1	0.0	0.0	0.0	0.0	0.0	...	...	Roumanie[1]
Russian Federation[1]	..	...	46.2	21.4	11.9	11.5	7.0	2.4	...	...	Fédération de Russie[1]
Spain	[1]7.5	[1]6.0	9.0	20.0	16.0	9.0	17.0	16.4	20.0	18.0	Espagne
Sweden	[1]4.6	4.0	[1]5.4	7.0	8.0	8.0	[1]10.0	6.0	7.0	9.0	Suède
United Kingdom	[1]124.1	129.0	109.0	155.0	177.0	223.0	185.0	149.0	172.0	...	Royaume-Uni
Yugoslavia, SFR[1]	0.3		..		..		..		..		Yougoslavie, RSF[1]
USSR (former)	132.0									..	URSS (anc.)
Oceania	**1**	**2**	**2**	**1**	**2**	**2**	**2**	**3**	**3**	**3**	**Océanie**

For general note and footnotes, see end of table.   Voir la fin du tableau pour la remarque générale et les notes.

Oils and fats of aquatic animal origin (continued)
Huiles et graisses d'animaux aquatiques (suite)

ISIC-BASED CODE - CODE BASE CITI

3115-04

Unit : Thousand metric tons   Unité : Milliers de tonnes métriques

Country or area	1990	1991	1992	1993	1994	1995	1996	1997	1998	1999	Pays ou zone
Australia[1]	0.0	0.4	0.7	0.7	0.5	0.3	0.3	0.2	...	...	Australie[1]
New Zealand[1]	1.4	1.2	1.1	0.6	1.1	1.8	2.1	3.0	...	...	Nouvelle-Zélande[1]
Papua New Guinea[1]	0.0	0.0	0.2	0.0	0.0	0.0	0.0	0.0	...	...	Papouasie-Nvl-Guinée[1]
Total	**1433**	**1404**	**1123**	**1301**	**1549**	**1512**	**1431**	**1429**	**1548**	**1647**	**Total**

General Note.

Oils and fats of fish and marine mammals, edible or inedible, crude and refined, but not further prepared, extracted from the body of the aquatic animal or from its liver, viscera or any other part (for example, whale oil, sperm oil, whale liver oil, fish liver oils, fish body oils). Processed products on the basis of these oils are excluded. (SITC, Rev.3: 41110-0).

Remarque générale.

Huiles et graisses de poissons et de mammifères marins, comestibles ou non, brutes et raffinées, mais n'ayant subi aucun autre traitement, extraites du corps d'animaux aquatiques ou de leurs foies, viscères ou autres parties du corps (par exemple huile de baleine, huile de cachalot ou huile de spermaceti, huile de foie de baleine, huiles de foie de poisson, huiles de poissons). Cette rubrique ne comprend pas les produits dérivés de ces huiles. (CTCI, Rev.3: 41110-0).

[1] Source: Food and Agriculture Organization of the United Nations (FAO), (Rome).

[2] Twelve months beginning 1 April of year stated.
[3] Crude oils only.
[4] Sales.
[5] Excluding Transnistria region.

[1] Source: Organisation des Nations Unies pour l'alimentation et l'agriculture (FAO), (Rome).
[2] Période de douze mois commençant le 1er avril de l'année indiquée.
[3] Huiles brutes seulement.
[4] Ventes.
[5] Non compris la région de Transnistria.

Oils and fats of animals, unprocessed
Huiles et graisses d'origine animale, non traitées

ISIC-BASED CODE - CODE BASE CITI
3115-07

Unit : Thousand metric tons   Unité : Milliers de tonnes métriques

Country or area	1990	1991	1992	1993	1994	1995	1996	1997	1998	1999	Pays ou zone
Africa	**219**	**230**	**237**	**245**	**237**	**246**	**248**	**252**	**251**	**254**	**Afrique**
Algeria	5.9	6.2	6.6	7.0	7.0	6.9	7.0	6.7	...	...	Algérie
Angola	3.4	3.4	3.4	3.4	3.3	3.3	3.5	3.6	...	...	Angola
Benin	1.1	1.2	1.2	1.2	1.3	1.4	1.4	1.5	...	...	Bénin
Botswana	5.0	5.3	5.6	6.3	5.5	5.5	5.0	5.0	...	...	Botswana
Burkina Faso	2.6	2.7	2.8	2.8	2.8	2.9	3.2	3.3	...	...	Burkina Faso
Burundi	1.1	0.9	1.0	1.1	1.0	1.0	1.0	0.9	...	...	Burundi
Cameroon	4.4	4.5	4.6	4.7	4.8	4.9	5.0	5.1	...	...	Cameroun
Cape Verde	0.3	0.3	0.4	0.6	0.4	0.6	0.3	0.4	...	...	Cap-Vert
Central African Rep.	2.5	2.5	2.5	2.6	2.7	2.8	3.1	3.0	...	...	Rép. centrafricaine
Chad	1.4	1.4	1.5	1.5	1.5	1.5	1.7	1.7	...	...	Tchad
Comoros	0.1	0.1	0.1	0.1	0.1	0.1	0.1	0.1	...	...	Comores
Congo	[1]3.0	[1]2.0	[1]2.0	[1]3.0	0.2	[1]2.0	[1]1.0	[1]0.0	[1]0.0	[1]0.0	Congo
Côte d'Ivoire	2.0	2.1	2.2	2.2	2.3	2.5	2.2	2.2	...	...	Côte d'Ivoire
Dem. Rep. of Congo	5.3	5.3	5.5	5.6	5.7	5.8	5.7	5.7	...	...	Rép. dém. du Congo
Djibouti	0.3	0.3	0.3	0.3	0.4	0.4	0.4	0.4	...	...	Djibouti
Egypt	13.1	14.1	14.4	14.7	15.3	15.5	16.0	17.7	...	...	Egypte
Eritrea	...	...	...	0.7	0.8	0.8	0.8	0.8	...	...	Erythrée
Ethiopia,incl.Eritrea	16.1	16.1	16.5	...	...	...	...	...	...	...	Ethiopie,incl.Erythrée
Ethiopia	...	...	...	15.5	15.6	15.7	16.5	16.8	...	...	Ethiopie
Gabon	0.2	0.2	0.2	0.2	0.2	0.2	0.2	0.2	...	...	Gabon
Gambia	0.1	0.1	0.1	0.1	0.1	0.1	0.1	0.2	...	...	Gambie
Ghana	1.9	1.9	1.8	1.8	1.8	1.8	1.8	1.8	...	...	Ghana
Guinea	0.4	0.4	0.4	0.5	0.5	0.6	0.6	0.6	...	...	Guinée
Guinea-Bissau	0.6	0.6	0.6	0.6	0.7	0.7	0.7	0.7	...	...	Guinée-Bissau
Kenya	10.8	10.9	10.6	10.4	10.8	11.1	11.6	11.4	...	...	Kenya
Lesotho	0.8	0.8	0.7	0.9	0.8	0.9	0.9	0.9	...	...	Lesotho
Liberia	0.3	0.3	0.3	0.3	0.3	0.3	0.3	0.3	...	...	Libéria
Libyan Arab Jamah.	1.6	1.8	1.7	1.7	[1]1.0	[1]2.0	[1]2.0	[1]2.0	[1]2.0	[1]2.0	Jamah. arabe libyenne
Madagascar	9.3	9.5	9.6	9.7	9.8	9.9	10.0	10.1	...	...	Madagascar
Malawi	1.1	1.1	1.1	1.1	1.1	1.2	1.1	1.2	...	...	Malawi
Mali	3.1	3.2	3.4	3.3	3.4	3.5	3.6	3.7	...	...	Mali
Mauritania	1.4	1.5	1.2	1.1	1.2	1.2	1.3	1.3	...	...	Mauritanie
Mauritius	0.1	0.1	0.1	0.1	0.1	0.1	0.1	0.1	...	...	Maurice
Morocco	6.0	5.9	6.8	6.6	5.8	5.9	5.9	[1]6.0	...	...	Maroc
Mozambique	2.0	1.9	1.9	1.9	1.9	1.9	1.9	2.0	...	...	Mozambique
Namibia	4.9	6.0	6.2	7.3	6.9	6.2	6.2	6.3	...	...	Namibie
Niger	1.9	1.8	2.1	2.0	2.1	2.1	2.2	2.2	...	...	Niger
Nigeria	17.9	20.2	21.2	25.3	26.3	27.1	29.2	30.5	...	...	Nigéria
Rwanda	0.7	0.7	0.7	0.6	0.5	0.5	0.6	0.6	...	...	Rwanda
Senegal	1.8	1.9	2.0	2.0	2.1	2.1	2.1	2.1	...	...	Sénégal
Sierra Leone	0.3	0.3	0.4	0.4	0.4	0.4	0.4	0.4	...	...	Sierra Leone
Somalia	5.2	4.9	4.2	4.5	4.7	5.0	5.2	5.6	...	...	Somalie
South Africa	31.4	32.2	33.3	31.4	27.7	28.0	26.9	27.2	...	...	Afrique du Sud
Sudan	7.1	8.0	9.0	10.1	11.1	12.3	12.7	12.9	...	...	Soudan
Swaziland	0.4	0.4	0.4	0.4	0.4	0.4	0.4	0.4	...	...	Swaziland
Togo	1.2	1.2	1.4	1.6	1.4	1.4	1.5	1.9	...	...	Togo
Tunisia	4.8	4.8	4.8	4.9	5.1	5.5	5.5	5.5	...	...	Tunisie
Uganda	5.9	6.1	6.3	6.5	6.6	6.7	6.7	6.8	...	...	Ouganda
United Rep.Tanzania	6.4	6.5	6.6	6.8	6.9	6.9	7.0	7.1	...	...	Rép. Unie de Tanzanie
Zambia	1.8	1.9	2.0	2.1	2.1	2.0	2.1	2.1	...	...	Zambie
Zimbabwe	5.5	9.0	9.5	8.8	6.5	7.9	7.3	7.3	...	...	Zimbabwe
America, North	**5961**	**6107**	**6430**	**6401**	**6613**	**6709**	**6632**	**6663**	**6746**	**6797**	**Amérique du Nord**
Barbados	1.4	1.4	1.4	1.4	1.4	1.5	1.4	1.4	[1]1.0	[1]1.0	Barbade
Belize	0.2	0.2	0.2	0.2	0.2	0.2	0.2	0.2	...	...	Belize
Canada	494.1	484.3	531.6	521.8	534.0	550.0	569.0	585.0	...	...	Canada
Costa Rica	12.8	14.1	14.3	14.9	17.4	17.5	17.2	16.0	...	...	Costa Rica
Cuba	11.4	9.4	6.2	7.0	7.0	7.4	7.6	7.4	...	...	Cuba
Dominican Republic	8.7	14.0	15.4	18.6	19.9	21.5	21.8	22.2	...	...	Rép. dominicaine
El Salvador	4.7	4.4	4.6	4.5	3.6	4.5	4.6	4.7	...	...	El Salvador
Guatemala	9.0	8.8	7.7	8.1	[1]8.0	[1]8.0	[1]8.0	[1]8.0	...	...	Guatemala
Haiti	1.7	1.9	2.1	2.3	2.4	2.3	2.6	2.7	...	...	Haïti
Honduras	5.2	5.0	5.0	4.9	4.6	3.0	3.2	3.6	...	...	Honduras

For general note and footnotes, see end of table.   Voir la fin du tableau pour la remarque générale et les notes.

Oils and fats of animals, unprocessed (continued)
Huiles et graisses d'origine animale, non traitées (suite)

ISIC-BASED CODE - CODE BASE CITI

3115-07

Unit : Thousand metric tons

Unité : Milliers de tonnes métriques

Country or area	1990	1991	1992	1993	1994	1995	1996	1997	1998	1999	Pays ou zone
Jamaica	3.9	2.7	3.2	3.7	3.7	3.8	3.4	3.4	...	...	Jamaïque
Mexico	188.6	200.6	207.8	208.7	220.6	241.7	230.3	230.6	...	...	Mexique
Nicaragua	8.0	6.7	6.6	6.6	5.8	5.6	5.6	6.1	...	...	Nicaragua
Panama	13.2	12.8	13.3	13.7	14.0	14.5	15.8	16.8	...	...	Panama
St. Lucia	0.3	0.3	0.2	0.2	0.2	0.2	0.2	0.2	...	...	St-Lucie
Trinidad and Tobago	0.4	0.4	0.4	0.3	0.2	0.2	0.3	0.2	...	...	Trinité-et-Tobago
United States	5197.8	5340.5	5610.3	5583.8	5770.3	5826.8	5740.7	5754.9	...	...	Etats-Unis
America, South	**1071**	**1084**	**1103**	**1155**	**1165**	**1177**	**1206**	**1258**	**1192**	**1226**	**Amérique du Sud**
Argentina	248.1	241.0	230.1	237.4	242.4	235.7	229.9	225.8	...	...	Argentine
Bolivia	25.0	24.9	25.4	23.1	23.7	24.6	26.1	26.6	...	...	Bolivie
Brazil	599.0	628.4	651.1	694.4	694.1	718.6	733.2	[1]772.0	...	...	Brésil
Chile	15.7	15.1	14.0	15.2	16.2	17.4	18.2	20.2	...	...	Chili
Colombia	29.5	29.0	25.8	25.9	27.2	28.1	29.1	27.7	...	...	Colombie
Ecuador	26.3	28.6	30.4	30.8	31.5	34.1	38.8	[1]40.0	[1]1.0	...	Equateur
Guyana	0.2	0.2	0.2	0.2	0.2	0.2	0.2	0.2	...	...	Guyana
Paraguay[1]	3.7	4.4	4.3	3.6	3.3	3.0	2.7	2.7	2.5	2.5	Paraguay[1]
Peru	13.7	13.2	13.2	12.9	12.4	12.8	12.9	14.0	...	...	Pérou
Suriname	0.3	0.3	0.3	0.3	0.3	0.2	0.2	0.2	...	...	Suriname
Uruguay	38.1	31.1	33.6	33.4	40.1	36.8	46.4	53.3	...	...	Uruguay
Venezuela	71.7	68.0	74.9	78.0	73.6	65.8	68.3	74.8	...	...	Venezuela
Asia	**2795**	**3065**	**3248**	**3439**	**3637**	**3656**	**3624**	**3827**	**3755**	**3842**	**Asie**
Afghanistan	9.1	9.2	9.2	9.2	9.2	9.3	9.3	9.3	...	...	Afghanistan
Armenia	..	1.0	2.5	1.6	1.6	1.5	1.7	[1]0.3	[1]0.3	...	Arménie
Bangladesh	10.2	10.5	11.0	11.6	12.1	12.7	13.4	13.5	...	...	Bangladesh
Brunei Darussalam	0.1	0.1	0.1	0.1	0.1	0.1	0.1	0.1	...	...	Brunéi Darussalam
Cambodia	6.1	6.3	8.0	8.3	8.1	8.2	8.6	8.8	...	...	Cambodge
China	1611.4	1732.6	1853.6	2000.7	2177.3	2284.4	2246.6	2431.4	...	...	Chine
Hong Kong SAR	41.1	39.9	39.8	41.2	42.9	42.6	42.0	41.6	...	...	Hong-Kong RAS
China, Macao, SAR	0.4	0.4	0.4	0.4	0.4	0.4	0.5	0.4	...	...	Chine, Macao PAS
Cyprus	5.9	6.0	6.2	7.0	7.5	7.6	8.0	8.1	...	...	Chypre
Georgia[1]	..	...	18.9	14.8	16.0	17.0	19.0	17.0	...	...	Géorgie[1]
India[1]	196.7	201.8	206.4	213.8	213.0	216.0	219.0	229.4	...	...	Inde[1]
Indonesia	74.5	78.3	82.1	87.4	91.4	82.4	85.1	88.1	[1]51.0	...	Indonésie
Iran(Islamic Rep. of)	40.6	41.7	44.1	45.3	46.4	48.0	49.3	53.0	...	...	Iran(Rép. islamique)
Iraq	5.1	3.0	4.1	4.4	4.6	3.6	3.5	3.7	...	...	Iraq
Israel	3.2	3.3	3.2	3.2	3.3	3.4	3.5	3.5	...	...	Israël
Japan[1]	419.6	401.5	401.2	401.0	394.0	318.5	302.1	303.8	309.0	305.0	Japon[1]
Jordan	0.4	0.7	0.6	0.7	0.6	0.6	0.6	0.6	...	...	Jordanie
Kazakhstan	..	...	99.2	93.2	85.2	67.0	60.7	46.9	...	...	Kazakhstan
Korea,Dem.Ppl's.Rep.	16.9	17.4	13.3	11.5	10.5	8.9	8.1	6.6	...	...	Corée,Rép.pop.dém.de
Korea, Republic of	26.7	25.4	42.8	43.6	44.4	45.9	48.7	49.2	...	...	Corée, République de
Kuwait[1]	1.5	0.8	1.5	2.2	14.0	15.0	16.0	17.0	18.0	19.0	Koweït[1]
Kyrgyzstan	..	...	16.6	13.7	11.2	13.3	13.6	12.5	...	...	Kirghizistan
Lao People's Dem. Rep.	2.7	2.8	2.9	3.2	3.3	3.6	3.7	3.8	...	...	Rép. dém. pop. lao
Lebanon	1.6	1.8	1.9	2.2	2.2	1.8	1.7	2.0	...	...	Liban
Malaysia	18.7	19.3	19.0	18.9	19.9	...	...	...	...	...	Malaisie
Mongolia	9.6	10.9	9.0	8.3	6.9	7.2	8.6	8.0	...	...	Mongolie
Myanmar	9.5	10.2	10.6	10.7	10.9	11.5	12.4	13.0	...	...	Myanmar
Nepal[1][2]	6.0	6.0	6.1	6.4	6.5	6.4	6.8	6.9	...	...	Népal[1][2]
Pakistan	76.4	82.1	87.5	95.5	102.1	113.6	117.7	124.6	...	...	Pakistan
Philippines	71.6	73.3	85.5	114.5	119.8	111.7	119.4	120.4	...	...	Philippines
Saudi Arabia	9.6	9.3	9.7	10.0	10.3	10.5	10.8	10.9	...	...	Arabie saoudite
Sri Lanka	1.2	1.3	1.4	1.3	1.4	1.5	1.3	1.3	...	...	Sri Lanka
Syrian Arab Republic	17.0	18.4	16.7	13.8	17.8	19.4	21.3	22.0	...	...	Rép. arabe syrienne
Tajikistan	..	...	3.1	2.0	2.1	[1]1.0	[1]0.0	[1]0.0	[1]0.0	[1]0.0	Tadjikistan
Thailand	24.5	25.0	25.2	26.1	26.2	25.5	25.7	27.6	...	...	Thaïlande
Turkey	29.3	27.5	26.6	26.5	27.6	26.5	26.2	28.5	...	...	Turquie
Turkmenistan	..	...	3.5	3.9	3.9	4.1	3.7	3.8	...	...	Turkménistan
United Arab Emirates	1.7	1.9	1.9	2.2	2.3	2.4	2.5	2.5	...	...	Emirats arabes unis
Uzbekistan	..	...	15.1	16.4	16.2	16.5	14.8	15.6	...	...	Ouzbékistan
Viet Nam	46.4	47.1	53.4	57.5	59.6	62.2	63.3	66.5	...	...	Viet Nam
Yemen	..	4.4	4.5	4.4	4.3	4.3	4.4	4.7	...	...	Yémen

For general note and footnotes, see end of table.

Voir la fin du tableau pour la remarque générale et les notes.

Oils and fats of animals, unprocessed (continued)
Huiles et graisses d'origine animale, non traitées (suite)

ISIC-BASED CODE - CODE BASE CITI

3115-07

Unit : Thousand metric tons

Unité : Milliers de tonnes métriques

Country or area	1990	1991	1992	1993	1994	1995	1996	1997	1998	1999	Pays ou zone
Europe	**4280**	**6629**	**6790**	**6538**	**6242**	**6163**	**6076**	**5860**	**5658**	**5568**	**Europe**
Albania	2.3	2.1	2.0	2.1	2.7	2.8	2.6	2.5	...	[1]0.0	Albanie
Austria	144.6	146.0	144.0	142.0	147.1	162.6	158.2	162.3	...	...	Autriche
Belarus	..	...	116.2	104.3	93.2	93.3	94.9	96.6	...	...	Bélarus
Belgium-Luxembourg	233.7	261.8	266.7	269.2	311.5	315.8	317.2	300.5	...	...	Belgique-Luxembourg
Bosnia and Herzegovina	..	..	8.7	6.5	4.2	2.8	3.0	2.1	...	...	Bosnie-Herzégovine
Bulgaria	108.2	100.2	90.5	83.1	62.5	72.3	70.3	63.2	[1]69.0	...	Bulgarie
Croatia	..	5.0	23.0	19.9	19.6	19.7	19.3	[1]9.0	[1]4.0	...	Croatie
Denmark[1][3]	155.4	160.3	169.5	168.6	168.0	114.0	114.0	130.0	116.0	118.0	Danemark[1][3]
Czechoslovakia(former)[1]	208.0	183.9	..	..	..	..	..	..	..	..	Tchécoslovaquie(anc.)[1]
Czech Republic[1]	..	..	..	181.9	151.5	157.9	155.4	143.3	...	...	République tchèque[1]
Estonia	..	...	9.5	7.2	7.1	7.1	7.0	5.6	...	...	Estonie
Finland	16.3	16.2	15.9	15.1	14.4	14.2	14.0	14.2	[1]9.0	[1]13.0	Finlande
France	481.4	502.7	486.0	492.2	490.0	504.7	516.7	524.2	...	...	France
Germany	..	1134.5	1077.0	1053.8	1017.4	1007.6	1035.8	1000.6	...	...	Allemagne
Greece[1]	83.2	77.9	86.9	76.4	79.1	83.8	88.4	94.5	7.9	...	Grèce[1]
Hungary	299.4	272.5	265.1	246.5	225.0	219.2	237.2	208.6	...	...	Hongrie
Iceland	0.6	0.6	0.6	0.6	0.6	0.6	0.6	0.6	[1]1.0	[1]0.0	Islande
Ireland	106.3	123.3	124.4	124.4	113.3	119.1	131.1	137.1	...	...	Irlande
Italy	345.3	339.6	361.1	369.9	371.7	359.9	373.8	381.1	...	...	Italie
Latvia	..	...	30.4	28.8	25.6	26.4	14.6	13.4	...	[1]0.0	Lettonie
Lithuania	..	...	36.8	22.3	20.2	...	...	...	...	...	Lituanie
Malta	3.4	4.4	4.2	3.7	3.5	3.4	3.2	3.1	...	...	Malte
Netherlands[1]	414.6	396.9	358.4	383.1	343.0	340.0	355.0	324.0	...	...	Pays-Bas[1]
Norway	19.8	20.3	20.8	20.9	22.1	21.9	22.3	[1]23.0	...	[1]79.0	Norvège
Poland	421.1	435.3	436.4	406.9	355.2	380.9	389.2	365.6	...	...	Pologne
Portugal[1]	77.0	76.0	79.1	86.2	88.1	85.7	15.0	18.0	23.0	11.0	Portugal[1]
Republic of Moldova	..	..	37.3	27.6	20.7	19.8	19.5	18.7	...	...	Rép. de Moldova
Romania[1]	31.0	23.0	19.0	14.0	13.0	6.0	7.0	4.0	0.0	0.0	Roumanie[1]
Russian Federation	..	...	1009.0	908.2	825.5	774.6	699.5	673.1	...	...	Fédération de Russie
Slovakia	..	...	...	66.2	61.7	60.2	62.0	63.7	[1]8.0	[1]8.0	Slovaquie
Slovenia	..	...	22.0	33.8	34.4	31.5	28.7	28.4	[1]14.0	[1]14.0	Slovénie
Spain	390.9	408.9	415.1	434.9	434.4	442.6	460.8	488.0	...	...	Espagne
Sweden	59.2	57.3	58.0	59.3	61.6	64.0	64.2	[1]66.0	[1]41.0	[1]33.0	Suède
Switzerland	48.7	50.1	48.3	46.4	42.7	44.4	45.1	43.8	...	...	Suisse
Ukraine	..	...	413.3	354.3	328.6	287.0	278.4	252.0	...	...	Ukraine
United Kingdom	276.3	283.6	274.4	254.6	259.2	265.6	220.1	[1]151.0	[1]195.0	...	Royaume-Uni
Yugoslavia[1]	..	36.0	18.7	19.0	18.1	20.0	20.7	17.0	15.0	16.0	Yougoslavie[1]
T.F.Yug.Rep. Macedonia	..	...	5.2	4.7	5.3	5.0	5.0	5.0	...	...	L'ex-RY Macédoine
Yugoslavia, SFR[1]	353.0	..	..	..	..	..	..	..	...	...	Yougoslavie, RSF[1]
USSR (former)[1]	2540.7	..	..	..	..	..	..	..	..	..	URSS (anc.)[1]
Oceania	**631**	**668**	**683**	**686**	**686**	**706**	**678**	**694**	**699**	**702**	**Océanie**
Australia	475.3	496.5	510.2	510.5	518.1	515.8	490.3	501.8	...	...	Australie
Fiji	0.7	0.7	0.7	0.7	0.7	0.7	0.7	0.7	...	...	Fidji
French Polynesia	0.1	0.1	0.1	0.1	0.1	0.1	0.1	0.0	...	...	Polynésie française
New Caledonia	0.1	0.1	0.1	0.2	0.2	0.2	0.2	0.2	...	...	Nouvelle-Calédonie
New Zealand	152.3	167.6	168.6	171.5	164.0	186.0	183.0	187.8	...	...	Nouvelle-Zélande
Papua New Guinea	1.9	1.9	2.1	2.3	2.5	2.7	2.7	2.9	...	...	Papouasie-Nvl-Guinée
Solomon Islands	0.3	0.3	0.3	0.3	0.3	0.3	0.3	0.3	[1]0.0	...	Iles Salomon
Vanuatu	0.4	0.4	0.4	0.4	0.5	0.4	0.4	0.5	...	...	Vanuatu
Total	**17499**	**17783**	**18491**	**18463**	**18580**	**18657**	**18463**	**18555**	**18301**	**18389**	**Total**

General Note.
Crude, refined or purified oils, unrendered fats of pigs, poultry, bovine
cattle, sheep or goats, tallow, lard stearine, and lard oil, wool grease and
degras. Processed products on the basis of these oils are excluded. (SITC,
Rev.3: 41120-1, 41130-1).
Main source: Food and Agriculture Organization of the United Nations
(FAO), Rome.

Remarque générale.
Huiles brutes, raffinées ou épurées, graisses de porc, de volaille, de bovins,
d'ovins et de caprins, non pressées ni fondues, suif, stéarine solaire et huile
de saindoux, graisses de suint et dégras. Cette rubrique ne comprend pas les
produits fabriqués dérivés de ces huiles ou graisses. (CTCI, Rev.3: 41120-1,
41130-1).
Source principale: Organisation des Nations Unies pour l'alimentation et
l'agriculture (FAO, Rome).

[1] Official figures.
[2] Twelve months beginning 16 July of year stated.
[3] Sales.

[1] Données officielles.
[2] Période de douze mois commençant le 16 juillet de l'année indiquée.
[3] Ventes.

Oil, soya bean, crude
Huile de fèves de soya, brute

ISIC-BASED CODE - CODE BASE CITI

3115-10

Unit : Thousand metric tons

Unité : Milliers de tonnes métriques

Country or area	1990	1991	1992	1993	1994	1995	1996	1997	1998	1999	Pays ou zone
America, North	**6234**	**6208**	**6464**	**6254**	**6503**	**7092**	**7006**	**7398**	**8206**	**8235**	**Amérique du Nord**
United States	...	6208	6464	6254	6503	7092	7006	7398	8206	8235	Etats-Unis
America, South	**2437**	**3360**	**3323**	**3533**	**3694**	**4105**	**4320**	**4580**	**5154**	**5289**	**Amérique du Sud**
Argentina	352	1255	1402	1460	1541	1599	1838	...	...	...	Argentine
Bolivia	10	2	0	0	9	*12	...	...	...	...	Bolivie
Brazil	2073	2101	1918	2071	2144	2493	2473	2279	2661	2609	Brésil
Colombia	...	...	3	2	0	1	...	0	3	...	Colombie
Asia	**1882**	**1926**	**1851**	**1987**	**1818**	**2160**	**2005**	**2052**	**2170**	**2347**	**Asie**
China	665	708	555	...	...	...	...	...	...	...	Chine
India[1]	...	...	...	...	502	821	687	716	853	985	Inde[1]
Japan[1]	665	629	671	683	664	680	673	690	667	697	Japon[1]
Turkey	9	...	...	...	...	16	2	3	7	22	Turquie
Europe	**1159**	**1522**	**1451**	**1295**	**1196**	**1408**	**1270**	**1229**	**1273**	**1301**	**Europe**
Bulgaria	1	1	0	0	0	1	1	0	...	...	Bulgarie
Croatia	..	...	10	2	11	11	15	22	31	...	Croatie
Denmark[2]	1	...	0	0	0	...	...	...	...	...	Danemark[2]
Finland	23	27	26	25	17	21	23	...	...	...	Finlande
France	46	29	43	68	67	122	93	90	103	...	France
Germany	..	...	...	...	...	338	287	287	360	...	Allemagne
Greece	47	54	54	48	42	45	38	...	31	...	Grèce
Hungary	3	1	...	...	...	...	...	...	...	...	Hongrie
Latvia	..	4	2	2	0	...	...	...	...	...	Lettonie
Netherlands[2][3]	621	608	508	434	381	357	...	...	...	...	Pays-Bas[2][3]
Portugal	81	80	65	62	75	122	106	96	80	66	Portugal
Republic of Moldova	..	5	4	[4]1	[4]0	[4]0	[4]0	[4]0	[4]0	[4]0	Rép. de Moldova
Russian Federation	..	76	109	47	33	40	20	13	23	45	Fédération de Russie
Spain	...	...	...	198	163	261	...	...	...	299	Espagne
Sweden	0	1	0	0	...	1	1	0	0	0	Suède
Ukraine	..	8	7	2	1	0	0	0	0	...	Ukraine
United Kingdom	106	77	73	...	...	...	...	...	...	...	Royaume-Uni
USSR (former)	49	..	..	..	..	..	..	..	..	..	URSS (anc.)
Total	**11762**	**13016**	**13089**	**13069**	**13212**	**14765**	**14601**	**15258**	**16803**	**17172**	**Total**

General Note.
Data refer to crude soya bean oil. (SITC, Rev.3: 42111-0).

[1] Including refined soybean oil.
[2] Sales.
[3] Production by establishments employing 20 or more persons.
[4] Excluding Transnistria region.

Remarque générale.
Les données se rapportent à la production d'huile brute de fèves de soya. CTCI, Rev.3 42111-0).

[1] Y compris l'huile de soja raffinée.
[2] Ventes.
[3] Production des établissements occupant 20 personnes ou plus.
[4] Non compris la région de Transnistria.

Oil, soya bean, refined
Huile de fèves de soya, raffinée

ISIC-BASED CODE - CODE BASE CITI

3115-13

Unit : Thousand metric tons

Unité : Milliers de tonnes métriques

Country or area	1990	1991	1992	1993	1994	1995	1996	1997	1998	1999	Pays ou zone
Africa	**8**	**11**	**18**	**25**	**25**	**13**	**23**	**18**	**22**	**22**	**Afrique**
Egypt	8	11	18	25	25	13	23	18	...	...	Egypte
America, North	**5260**	**5525**	**5773**	**6044**	**6131**	**6208**	**6220**	**6382**	**6698**	**6807**	**Amérique du Nord**
Dominican Republic*	...	...	...	...	211	239	268	296	324	...	Rép. dominicaine*
Mexico	178	203	239	276	299	345	385	362	341	468	Mexique
United States	4985	5196	5380	5586	5621	5624	5567	5724	6033	5986	Etats-Unis
America, South	**1193**	**1264**	**1287**	**1249**	**1273**	**1326**	**1299**	**1407**	**1685**	**1708**	**Amérique du Sud**
Argentina	17	26	49	54	48	53	35	...	...	...	Argentine
Bolivia	25	30	33	29	44	*45	...	...	...	...	Bolivie
Brazil	1083	1126	1102	1055	1088	1116	1125	1222	1491	1502	Brésil
Colombia	...	...	34	45	43	53	...	44	48	...	Colombie
Ecuador	7	...	24	16	17	25	19	4	3	...	Equateur
Paraguay	16	23	45	50	...	...	...	...	...	...	Paraguay
Asia	**345**	**409**	**241**	**330**	**314**	**330**	**333**	**325**	**328**	**331**	**Asie**
Armenia	..	4	2	...	...	1	1	0	0	...	Arménie
Bangladesh	285	341	186	...	...	...	...	...	...	...	Bangladesh
Israel	55	55	44	49	37	53	59	...	...	...	Israël
Kyrgyzstan	..	3	4	0	0	0	0	0	0	2	Kirghizistan
Turkey	...	...	...	9	5	5	2	4	7	8	Turquie
Europe	**22446**	**23037**	**22978**	**22952**	**22978**	**66391**	**1444**	**23202**	**1548**	**23091**	**Europe**
Austria	...	...	...	...	...	65125	36	...	34	...	Autriche
Belarus	..	...	...	0	1	1	0	0	0	...	Bélarus
Belgium	...	...	...	...	[1]50	[1]39	...	65	75	54	Belgique
Bulgaria	3	2	2	1	1	0	1	0	...	...	Bulgarie
Croatia	..	6	4	2	1	4	0	...	0	...	Croatie
Denmark[2]	10	10	7	5	5	3	2	1	1	3	Danemark[2]
Finland	7	6	7	9	6	1	5	...	...	...	Finlande
France	17	28	25	27	26	19	29	37	29	...	France
Germany	..	...	...	...	...	328	344	381	406	...	Allemagne
Greece	25	33	53	46	48	51	39	51	58	...	Grèce
Netherlands[2][3]	263	...	290	322	329	381	468	552	573	486	Pays-Bas[2][3]
Norway	38	40	37	2	...	...	...	...	...	...	Norvège
Poland	10	17	48	71	71	63	52	55	62	38	Pologne
Portugal	25	26	44	37	59	59	60	29	20	11	Portugal
Slovenia	...	...	...	...	...	...	...	6	6	6	Slovénie
Spain	...	...	...	128	180	214	234	219	210	228	Espagne
Sweden	32	29	10	27	11	8	5	4	2	2	Suède
United Kingdom	...	137	139	123	59	59	77	36	40	...	Royaume-Uni
Total	**29253**	**30246**	**30297**	**30600**	**30722**	**74267**	**9319**	**31335**	**10281**	**31960**	**Total**

General Note.

Soya bean once-refined (e.g. refined by deacidifying, filtering, washing, decolorizing or deodorizing) and before use in end products. (SITC,Rev.3: 42119-0).

Remarque générale.

Huile de soya, ayant subi un premier raffinage (notamment par désacidification, filtration, lavage, décoloration ou désodorisation) et avant emploi dans les produits définitifs. (CTCI, Rev.3: 42119-0).

[1] Incomplete coverage.

[2] Sales.

[3] Production by establishments employing 20 or more persons.

[1] Couverture incomplète.

[2] Ventes.

[3] Production des établissements occupant 20 personnes ou plus.

Oil, cotton-seed, crude
Huile de graines de coton, brute

ISIC-BASED CODE - CODE BASE CITI

3115-16

Unit : Thousand metric tons

Unité : Milliers de tonnes métriques

Country or area	1990	1991	1992	1993	1994	1995	1996	1997	1998	1999	Pays ou zone
Africa	**2**	**1**	**3**	**2**	**2**	**2**	**2**	**2**	**2**	**2**	**Afrique**
Burkina Faso	...	1	3	2	...	...	...	...	...	...	Burkina Faso
America, North	**564**	**570**	**548**	**518**	**519**	**586**	**553**	**555**	**510**	**395**	**Amérique du Nord**
United States	...	570	548	518	519	586	553	555	510	395	Etats-Unis
America, South	**287**	**218**	**183**	**102**	**124**	**150**	**111**	**52**	**59**	**68**	**Amérique du Sud**
Argentina	161	62	56	31	48	65	67	...	...	...	Argentine
Brazil	126	156	127	71	76	85	44	33	50	68	Brésil
Asia	**208**	**302**	**368**	**312**	**304**	**281**	**268**	**214**	**252**	**239**	**Asie**
China	120	126	193	...	...	...	...	...	...	...	Chine
India	...	...	...	...	12	9	11	8	7	7	Inde
Japan [1]	6	8	8	7	7	6	7	7	8	7	Japon [1]
Turkey	70	53	71	63	69	73	68	31	58	54	Turquie
Turkmenistan	..	104	85	85	70	47	36	22	33	...	Turkménistan
Europe	**34**	**21**	**30**	**10**	**13**	**13**	**13**	**9**	**7**	**0**	**Europe**
Greece	34	21	30	10	13	13	13	9	7	...	Grèce
Total	**1094**	**1112**	**1132**	**944**	**962**	**1032**	**947**	**832**	**830**	**704**	**Total**

General Note.
Data refer to crude cotton-seed oil. (SITC, Rev.3: 42121-0).

Remarque générale.
Les données se rapportent à la production d'huile brute de graines de coton. (CTCI, Rev.3: 42121-0).

[1] Including refined cotton-seed oil.

[1] Y compris l'huile de coton raffinée.

Oil, cotton-seed, refined
Huile de graines de coton, raffinée

ISIC-BASED CODE - CODE BASE CITI

3115-19

Unit : Thousand metric tons

Unité : Milliers de tonnes métriques

Country or area	1990	1991	1992	1993	1994	1995	1996	1997	1998	1999	Pays ou zone
Africa	**343**	**396**	**345**	**354**	**349**	**337**	**298**	**319**	**337**	**321**	**Afrique**
Burkina Faso	14	19	11	9	...	...	...	...	...	...	Burkina Faso
Egypt	317	357	312	329	318	306	267	288	306	290	Egypte
Mali	12	20	22	16	...	...	...	...	...	...	Mali
America, North	**459**	**450**	**462**	**449**	**468**	**448**	**398**	**361**	**310**	**233**	**Amérique du Nord**
Mexico	19	8	9	11	6	...	...	...	...	...	Mexique
United States	440	442	453	438	462	444	397	361	310	233	Etats-Unis
America, South	**56**	**103**	**91**	**56**	**54**	**56**	**44**	**26**	**29**	**33**	**Amérique du Sud**
Brazil	27	65	62	34	40	41	25	13	16	20	Brésil
Colombia	...	...	20	12	0	2	...	0	0	...	Colombie
Paraguay	11	23	9	10	...	...	...	...	...	...	Paraguay
Asia	**593**	**773**	**776**	**755**	**801**	**853**	**868**	**895**	**1086**	**1137**	**Asie**
Azerbaijan	..	36	22	14	9	12	5	5	8	5	Azerbaïdjan
Indonesia	0	1	...	...	...	...	...	...	...	...	Indonésie
Iran(Islamic Rep. of)	[1]559	[1]620	[1]633	[1]613	[1]691	[2]766	[2]787	[2]824	[2]994	...	Iran(Rép. islamique)
Israel	7	6	3	3	2	2	2	...	...	...	Israël
Kyrgyzstan	..	6	3	3	2	2	2	4	6	3	Kirghizistan
Tajikistan	..	74	43	34	26	21	28	22	23	22	Tadjikistan
Turkey	· 27	22	13	23	16	10	13	21	28	27	Turquie
Turkmenistan	..	8	58	65	55	39	30	18	26	...	Turkménistan
Europe	**29**	**16**	**12**	**20**	**27**	**34**	**38**	**31**	**30**	**41**	**Europe**
Greece	28	15	11	20	27	34	38	31	30	...	Grèce
United Kingdom	...	1	1	...	0	0	0	0	0	...	Royaume-Uni
Total	**1480**	**1737**	**1685**	**1634**	**1698**	**1727**	**1645**	**1631**	**1792**	**1764**	**Total**

General Note.

Once-refined cotton-seed oil (for example, refined by deacidifying, filtering, washing, decolourizing or deodorizing) and before use in end products. (SITC, Rev.3: 42129-0).

[1] Production by establishments employing 50 or more persons.
[2] Production by establishments employing 10 or more persons.

Remarque générale.

Huile de graines de coton, ayant subi un premier raffinage (notamment par désacidification, filtration, lavage, décoloration ou désodorisation) et avant emploi dans les produits définitifs. (CTCI, Rev.3: 42129-0).

[1] Production des établissements occupant 50 personnes ou plus.
[2] Production des établissements occupant 10 personnes ou plus.

Oil, groundnut, crude
Huile d'arachides, brute

ISIC-BASED CODE - CODE BASE CITI
3115-22

Unit : Thousand metric tons   Unité : Milliers de tonnes métriques

Country or area	1990	1991	1992	1993	1994	1995	1996	1997	1998	1999	Pays ou zone
Africa	**236**	**112**	**144**	**90**	**125**	**138**	**131**	**83**	**101**	**120**	**Afrique**
Congo*	1	...	...	...	...	...	...	...	...	...	Congo*
Mali	15	20	18	17	29	23	24	...	...	...	Mali
Senegal	200	76	114	57	80	99	91	38	54	72	Sénégal
South Africa	20	15	11	...	...	...	...	...	...	...	Afrique du Sud
America, North	**137**	**119**	**173**	**106**	**104**	**151**	**159**	**76**	**61**	**99**	**Amérique du Nord**
United States	...	119	173	106	104	151	159	76	61	99	Etats-Unis
America, South	**43**	**78**	**96**	**44**	**40**	**49**	**61**	**48**	**46**	**44**	**Amérique du Sud**
Argentina	43	78	96	44	40	49	61	...	...	...	Argentine
Asia	**407**	**414**	**309**	**370**	**422**	**320**	**325**	**356**	**333**	**309**	**Asie**
China	275	292	193	...	...	...	...	...	...	...	Chine
Hong Kong SAR[1]	21	19	20	29	22	16	24	50	...	18	Hong-Kong RAS[1]
India	...	...	...	...	146	50	47	52	54	37	Inde
Japan[2]	...	1	1	...	...	...	...	...	...	...	Japon[2]
Europe	**0**	**0**	**0**	**0**	**6**	**7**	**8**	**3**	**15**	**15**	**Europe**
France	0	0	0	0	6	7	8	3	15	...	France
Total	**823**	**723**	**722**	**611**	**698**	**666**	**685**	**566**	**555**	**587**	**Total**

General Note.
Data refer to crude groundnut oil. (SITC, Rev.3: 42131-0).

Remarque générale.
Les données se rapportent à la production d'huile brute d'arachide. (CTCI, Rev.3: 42131-0).

[1] 1998 data are confidential.
[2] Including refined groundnut oil.

[1] Pour 1998, les données sont confidentielles.
[2] Y compris l'huile d'arachide raffinée.

Oil, olive, crude
Huile d'olives, brute

ISIC-BASED CODE - CODE BASE CITI

3115-28

Unit : Thousand metric tons   Unité : Milliers de tonnes métriques

Country or area	1990	1991	1992	1993	1994	1995	1996	1997	1998	1999	Pays ou zone
Africa	**291**	**358**	**232**	**307**	**160**	**127**	**473**	**210**	**291**	**350**	**Afrique**
Algeria	25	10	46	28	24	16	50	49	16	58	Algérie
Libyan Arab Jamah.	9	9	10	8	8	6	7	9	10	10	Jamah. arabe libyenne
Morocco	78	58	43	45	51	41	87	55	66	67	Maroc
Tunisia	179	281	133	226	77	65	329	96	200	215	Tunisie
America, North	**3**	**1**	**2**	**2**	**2**	**2**	**2**	**2**	**2**	**2**	**Amérique du Nord**
El Salvador	1	1	1	1	1	1	1	1	1	1	El Salvador
Mexico	1	0	0	0	0	0	0	0	0	...	Mexique
United States	1	0	1	1	1	1	1	1	1	1	Etats-Unis
America, South	**9**	**24**	**11**	**10**	**11**	**9**	**5**	**14**	**10**	**8**	**Amérique du Sud**
Argentina	8	23	10	8	10	8	4	12	9	7	Argentine
Chile	1	1	1	1	1	1	1	2	1	1	Chili
Asia	**204**	**127**	**205**	**137**	**318**	**164**	**398**	**158**	**392**	**181**	**Asie**
Cyprus	2	1	3	2	2	2	2	1	2	2	Chypre
Iran(Islamic Rep. of)	2	2	2	1	2	2	2	3	3	2	Iran(Rép. islamique)
Jordan	8	5	15	9	16	12	25	18	19	19	Jordanie
Lebanon	5	6	9	2	6	6	7	6	6	7	Liban
Syrian Arab Republic	94	41	112	66	111	93	140	85	160	89	Rép. arabe syrienne
Turkey	92	72	65	58	182	51	222	45	203	62	Turquie
Europe	**1123**	**1989**	**1538**	**1620**	**1476**	**1494**	**1942**	**2440**	**1799**	**1943**	**Europe**
Albania	1	4	2	3	3	5	3	3	4	4	Albanie
Croatia	..	...	3	1	3	6	2	2	3	2	Croatie
France	2	2	3	2	2	2	2	3	3	3	France
Greece	214	428	357	356	324	387	433	457	435	436	Grèce
Italy	176	836	469	608	523	678	420	704	500	747	Italie
Portugal	26	69	26	36	36	49	46	42	38	52	Portugal
Slovenia	..	...	0	0	0	0	0	0	1	0	Slovénie
Spain	703	647	678	613	585	367	1036	1230	814	699	Espagne
Yugoslavia	..	...	0	0	0	0	0	0	1	0	Yougoslavie
Yugoslavia, SFR	1	..	..	..	..	..	..	..	..	..	Yougoslavie, RSF
Total	**1630**	**2499**	**1988**	**2076**	**1967**	**1796**	**2821**	**2824**	**2494**	**2484**	**Total**

General Note.
Data refer to crude olive oil. Processed products based on olive oil such as mayonnaise, salad dressings etc. are excluded.(SITC, Rev.3: 42141-0, 42149-1).
Source: Food and Agriculture Organization of the United Nations (FAO), Rome.

Remarque générale.
Les données se rapportent à la production d'huile brute d'olives. (CTCI, Rev.3: 42141-0, 42149-1).
Source: Organisation des Nations Unies pour l'alimentation et l'agriculture (FAO), Rome.

Oils, other, of vegetable origin, crude
Autres huiles brutes d'origine végétale

ISIC-BASED CODE - CODE BASE CITI

3115-34

Unit : Thousand metric tons　　　　　　　　　　　　　　　　　　　　　　　　Unité : Milliers de tonnes métriques

Country or area	1990	1991	1992	1993	1994	1995	1996	1997	1998	1999	Pays ou zone
Africa	**1851**	**1932**	**1938**	**2010**	**2007**	**2034**	**2092**	**2090**	**2064**	**2094**	**Afrique**
Angola	2	2	1	[1][2]50	[1][2]52	[1][2]53	[1][2]54	[1][2]53	[1][2]54	[1][2]50	Angola
Benin[1][2]	20	14	14	14	9	11	10	10	10	10	Bénin[1][2]
Burundi[1][2]	2	2	2	2	2	2	2	2	2	2	Burundi[1][2]
Cameroon[1][2]	158	130	120	123	125	125	161	135	136	133	Cameroun[1][2]
Central African Rep.[1][2]	7	6	6	7	7	7	7	7	7	3	Rép. centrafricaine[1][2]
Congo	3	[1][2]16	[1][2]15	[1][2]15	[1][2]16	[1][2]16	[1][2]17	[1][2]16	[1][2]16	[1][2]17	Congo
Côte d'Ivoire[1][2]	250	264	290	283	285	249	267	249	240	242	Côte d'Ivoire[1][2]
Dem. Rep. of Congo[1][2]	179	180	181	182	183	186	188	166	157	157	Rép. dém. du Congo[1][2]
Equatorial Guinea[1][2]	5	5	5	5	5	5	5	4	4	5	Guinée équatoriale[1][2]
Gabon[1][2]	4	7	7	8	8	7	7	7	6	6	Gabon[1][2]
Gambia[1][2]	3	3	3	3	3	3	3	3	3	3	Gambie[1][2]
Ghana[1][2]	85	90	100	95	100	102	84	92	111	105	Ghana[1][2]
Guinea[1][2]	41	43	40	48	50	50	55	55	50	50	Guinée[1][2]
Guinea-Bissau[1][2]	4	5	5	4	5	5	5	5	4	5	Guinée-Bissau[1][2]
Liberia[1][2]	24	25	25	30	33	37	35	36	41	42	Libéria[1][2]
Madagascar[1][2]	4	4	4	4	3	4	3	4	4	4	Madagascar[1][2]
Mozambique	4	3	1	2	2	4	...	3	3	2	Mozambique
Nigeria[1][2]	730	760	792	825	837	860	776	810	845	896	Nigéria[1][2]
Sao Tome and Principe[1][2]	0	1	1	1	1	1	1	1	1	1	Sao Tomé-et-Principe[1][2]
Senegal[1][2]	5	3	3	3	4	6	5	5	6	6	Sénégal[1][2]
Sierra Leone[1][2]	50	51	48	47	50	45	48	51	40	36	Sierra Leone[1][2]
South Africa	251	262	254	241	215	244	327	336	312	309	Afrique du Sud
Togo[1][2]	7	7	7	7	7	8	9	7	7	7	Togo[1][2]
United Rep.Tanzania	13	19	15	11	6	5	24	35	[1][2]6	[1][2]6	Rép. Unie de Tanzanie
America, North	**283**	**363**	**352**	**454**	**457**	**376**	**347**	**360**	**455**	**483**	**Amérique du Nord**
Costa Rica[1][2]	73	76	75	85	89	93	97	101	109	109	Costa Rica[1][2]
Dominica	...	...	...	...	[3]1	[3]1	[3]1	...	0	0	Dominique
Dominican Republic[1][2]	9	13	16	20	23	24	25	25	25	24	Rép. dominicaine[1][2]
Guatemala[1][2]	8	10	13	16	22	25	36	50	47	52	Guatemala[1][2]
Honduras[1][2]	78	80	82	80	76	76	76	77	88	80	Honduras[1][2]
Jamaica	15	13	7	8	7	...	...	...	...	...	Jamaïque
Mexico	92	162	152	237	230	146	102	95	177	209	Mexique
Nicaragua[1][2]	4	4	3	4	6	6	8	8	8	8	Nicaragua[1][2]
St. Lucia[3]	3	3	2	3	2	1	...	3	1	2	St-Lucie[3]
America, South	**2063**	**2191**	**2055**	**2055**	**2130**	**2151**	**2236**	**2184**	**2104**	**2435**	**Amérique du Sud**
Argentina[4]	1524	1600	...	...	...	...	...	...	...	...	Argentine[4]
Bolivia	...	0	0	0	2	*2	...	...	...	...	Bolivie
Brazil[1][2]	66	70	60	54	71	76	80	80	89	93	Brésil[1][2]
Colombia	[1][2]252	[1][2]291	163	183	200	230	[1]410	337	289	[1]500	Colombie
Ecuador	[1][2]150	[1][2]161	[1][2]166	[1][2]171	[1][2]195	[1][2]180	74	79	81	[1][2]171	Equateur
Paraguay	26	29	27	[1][2]4	[1][2]4	[1][2]2	[1][2]2	[1][2]2	[1][2]2	[1][2]2	Paraguay
Peru	25	23	50	49	56	58	61	66	[1][2]34	[1][2]42	Pérou
Suriname	16	11	15	12	7	2	[1][2]0	[1][2]0	[1][2]0	[1][2]0	Suriname
Venezuela[1][2]	4	7	12	21	34	39	45	54	44	60	Venezuela[1][2]
Asia	**21058**	**21615**	**22411**	**23323**	**23429**	**24729**	**25782**	**24526**	**34121**	**32028**	**Asie**
Bangladesh	21	77	...	...	...	...	...	...	...	...	Bangladesh
China	4382	5317	5609	...	...	...	...	...	...	...	Chine
Georgia	..	...	1	1	0	0	0	1	1	0	Géorgie
India	...	...	...	...	5929	5540	5889	5678	6179	5699	Inde
Indonesia	2544	2019	2280	2539	2766	3701	...	1849	11642	...	Indonésie
Iraq	...	...	7	...	...	...	...	...	...	...	Iraq
Japan	[5]1049	1083	1056	1055	1052	1070	1092	1133	1138	1176	Japon
Malaysia[1][2][6]	6095	6141	6373	7403	7221	7811	8386	9069	8320	10554	Malaisie[1][2][6]
Pakistan[7][8]	683	656	639	725	671	711	733	714	719	773	Pakistan[7][8]
Philippines[1][2]	45	52	54	55	54	53	52	52	48	52	Philippines[1][2]
Sri Lanka[9]	75	74	76	56	...	...	...	...	...	...	Sri Lanka[9]
Syrian Arab Republic	26	28	29	22	28	33	33	51	64	...	Rép. arabe syrienne
Thailand[1][2]	226	234	270	265	300	370	400	450	475	707	Thaïlande[1][2]
Turkey	[10]124	[10]141	177	196	127	173	223	213	212	215	Turquie
Viet Nam	10	6	4	...	...	[8][11]39	[8][11]78	[8][11]88	[8][11]95	*[8][11]103	Viet Nam

For general note and footnotes, see end of table.　　　　　　　　　　　Voir la fin du tableau pour la remarque générale et les notes.

Oils, other, of vegetable origin, crude (continued)
Autres huiles brutes d'origine végétale (suite)

ISIC-BASED CODE - CODE BASE CITI

3115-34

Unit : Thousand metric tons   Unité : Milliers de tonnes métriques

Country or area	1990	1991	1992	1993	1994	1995	1996	1997	1998	1999	Pays ou zone
Europe	**4536**	**6721**	**6474**	**5304**	**5321**	**5539**	**5540**	**5545**	**5751**	**5646**	**Europe**
Austria [12]	74	76	81	72	68	...	...	...	...	116	Autriche [12]
Belarus	..	[5]12	...	5	5	7	10	11	11	16	Bélarus
Croatia		21	22	27	23	19	12	21	17	...	Croatie
Czechoslovakia(former) [12]	187	168	..	..	..	..	..	..	..	..	Tchécoslovaquie(anc.) [12]
Czech Republic	..	..	144	...	...	177	186	203	166	165	République tchèque
Finland	46	41	38	57	48	52	61	...	...	3	Finlande
France	876	931	979	739	878	961	985	1028	1003	...	France
Germany	..	...	...	...	...	964	857	874	840	...	Allemagne
German D.R.(former)	134	..	..	..	..	..	..	..	..	..	R.D.A. (anc.)
Greece	38	32	46	...	...	23	28	...	33	...	Grèce
Hungary	330	275	340	...	...	...	...	...	...	...	Hongrie
Latvia	..	...	...	...	...	...	...	...	...	5	Lettonie
Netherlands [13] [14]	638	641	648	584	560	522	...	...	...	...	Pays-Bas [13] [14]
Poland	260	222	200	227	227	299	304	317	320	368	Pologne
Portugal	...	...	138	110	130	119	128	141	122	117	Portugal
Republic of Moldova	..	113	54	[15]38	[15]31	[15]32	[15]23	[15]19	[15]18	[15]17	Rép. de Moldova
Romania [16]	26	16	13	8	7	10	13	25	11	13	Roumanie [16]
Slovakia	..	..	...	[12]52	..	...	..	25	27	23	Slovaquie
Slovenia	..	0	1	0	1	2	2	0	0	...	Slovénie
Spain	[17]1105	[17]1283	[17]1086	298	216	195	167	220	...	143	Espagne
Sweden	169	150	137	163	168	173	153	23	8	4	Suède
Ukraine	..	995	857	802	633	696	705	510	511	577	Ukraine
United Kingdom	526	518	566	551	716	711	766	949	1048	...	Royaume-Uni
Yugoslavia	..	204	184	148	165	139	155	160	120	112	Yougoslavie
T.F.Yug.Rep. Macedonia	..	8	10	12	3	5	4	6	5	5	L'ex-RY Macédoine
Oceania	**187**	**218**	**246**	**266**	**269**	**272**	**318**	**299**	**332**	**353**	**Océanie**
Fiji	12	9	9	6	5	6	6	7	7	...	Fidji
French Polynesia [3]	7	6	5	...	...	...	...	...	...	...	Polynésie française [3]
Papua New Guinea [1] [2]	145	180	202	223	225	223	272	249	283	299	Papouasie-Nvl-Guinée [1] [2]
Solomon Islands	23	23	30	31	34	37	34	37	36	...	Iles Salomon
Total	**29978**	**33039**	**33477**	**33411**	**33614**	**35100**	**36315**	**35003**	**44826**	**43040**	**Total**

General Note.
Data refer to crude oils of other vegetable origin and include linseed oil, palm oil, coconut (copra) oil, palm kernel oil, castor oil and those oils covered under SITC 4229. (SITC, Rev.3: 42151-0, 42161-0, 42171-0, 42180-1, 42211-0, 42221-0, 42231-0, 42241-0, 42250-1, 42291-1, 42299-1).

Remarque générale.
Les autres huiles brutes d'origine végétale comprises dans cette position sont les suivantes: huile de lin, huile de palme, huile de coprah, huile de palmiste, huile de ricin et les huiles énumérées dans la rubrique 4229 de la CTCI. (CTCI, Rev.3: 42151-0, 42161-0, 42171-0, 42180-1, 42211-0, 42221-0, 42231-0, 42241-0, 42250-1, 42291-1, 42299-1).

[1] Source: Food and Agriculture Organization of the United Nations (FAO), (Rome).
[2] Palm oil only.
[3] Coconut oil only.
[4] Edible and inedible vegetable oils.
[5] Including refined oils.
[6] Data refer to Peninsular Malaysia and Sabah.
[7] Twelve months ending 30 June of year stated.
[8] All vegetable oils.
[9] Crude and refined coconut oil only.
[10] Sunflower seed oil.
[11] Official figures.
[12] Comestible vegetable oils.
[13] Sales.
[14] Production by establishments employing 20 or more persons.
[15] Excluding Transnistria region.
[16] Vegetable oils for industrial use.
[17] Including cotton-seed, groundnut and soya bean oil.

[1] Source: Organisation des Nations Unies pour l'alimentation et l'agriculture (FAO), (Rome).
[2] Huile de palme seulement.
[3] Huile de coco seulement.
[4] Huiles végétales comestibles ou non.
[5] Y compris les huiles raffinées.
[6] Données se rapportant à la Malaisie péninsulaire et au Sabah.
[7] Période de douze mois finissant le 30 juin de l'année indiquée.
[8] Huiles végétales de toutes catégories.
[9] Huile de coco brute et raffinée seulement.
[10] Huile de tournesol.
[11] Données officielles.
[12] Huiles végétales comestibles.
[13] Ventes.
[14] Production des établissements occupant 20 personnes ou plus.
[15] Non compris la région de Transnistria.
[16] Huiles végétales pour usage industriel.
[17] Y compris huile de graines de coton, huile d'arachides et huile de fèves de soya.

Oils, other, of vegetable origin, refined
Autres huiles d'origine végétale, raffinées

ISIC-BASED CODE - CODE BASE CITI

3115-37

Unit : Thousand metric tons

Unité : Milliers de tonnes métriques

Country or area	1990	1991	1992	1993	1994	1995	1996	1997	1998	1999	Pays ou zone
Africa	**347**	**307**	**282**	**300**	**307**	**291**	**296**	**301**	**326**	**293**	**Afrique**
Algeria[1]	338	301	277	296	303	285	291	289	311	280	Algérie[1]
Ethiopia	9	6	5	4	4	6	5	12	15	13	Ethiopie
America, North	**387**	**391**	**357**	**751**	**771**	**713**	**765**	**760**	**766**	**723**	**Amérique du Nord**
Mexico	380	385	352	744	765	708	760	754	761	718	Mexique
St. Lucia[2]	3	2	2	3	2	1	1	2	1	1	St-Lucie[2]
Trinidad and Tobago[3]	4	4	3	4	4	4	4	...	...	...	Trinité-et-Tobago[3]
America, South	**363**	**449**	**404**	**474**	**471**	**505**	**452**	**565**	**575**	**587**	**Amérique du Sud**
Chile	100	97	87	115	101	92	...	...	...	...	Chili
Colombia	...	...	180	208	228	260	...	233	221	...	Colombie
Ecuador	33	...	137	151	142	153	132	...	...	...	Equateur
Asia	**1136**	**891**	**1502**	**1585**	**1805**	**3692**	**1936**	**2262**	**2361**	**2857**	**Asie**
Hong Kong SAR[4]	41	42	46	37	6	36	57	68	...	53	Hong-Kong RAS[4]
Indonesia	627	280	971	993	1324	3164	...	1570	1751	...	Indonésie
Iraq	...	...	2	...	...	...	...	...	...	...	Iraq
Israel	...	20	10	6	6	12	16	...	...	...	Israël
Kyrgyzstan	..	5	1	1	1	1	1	1	1	2	Kirghizistan
Malaysia[2]	25	18	17	15	20	21	16	14	13	10	Malaisie[2]
Tajikistan	..	0	1	0	0	0	0	0	0	0	Tadjikistan
Turkey	[5]429	524	455	531	445	456	509	596	540	442	Turquie
Europe	**3960**	**5231**	**5548**	**5297**	**4946**	**5184**	**5271**	**5679**	**5352**	**5084**	**Europe**
Belgium	...	...	...	...	314	497	544	656	351	[6]140	Belgique
Bulgaria[7]	140	106	129	151	141	192	161	156	...	...	Bulgarie[7]
Croatia	..	37	28	22	25	31	34	36	26	...	Croatie
Czech Republic	..	..	...	...	...	208	202	244	256	243	République tchèque
Finland	34	40	36	37	34	15	17	12	19	24	Finlande
France	445	501	533	455	420	505	572	621	566	...	France
Germany	...	...	...	...	...	1014	1092	1288	1373	...	Allemagne
German D.R.(former)	115	..	..	..	..	..	..	..	..	..	R.D.A. (anc.)
Greece	38	68	69	...	...	...	...	...	...	...	Grèce
Hungary	84	65	114	...	...	...	...	...	...	...	Hongrie
Iceland[3]	...	...	...	...	...	...	1	0	...	...	Islande[3]
Latvia	..	7	2	2	1	1	0	2	...	0	Lettonie
Lithuania	..	0	0	0	0	1	3	4	6	11	Lituanie
Netherlands[7][8][9]	881	580	616	765	700	677	...	...	...	...	Pays-Bas[7][8][9]
Poland	67	53	46	53	43	86	119	152	146	209	Pologne
Portugal	66	45	111	53	85	78	89	120	119	110	Portugal
Romania[7]	270	236	216	213	194	224	236	246	173	245	Roumanie[7]
Slovakia	..	..	...	...	...	...	...	0	3	4	Slovaquie
Slovenia	..	44	27	29	29	30	36	40	37	38	Slovénie
Spain	[10]470	[10]492	[10]522	606	623	653	671	717	636	623	Espagne
Sweden	57	62	59	61	61	67	69	83	74	77	Suède
Ukraine	..	97	73	57	50	39	28	27	59	103	Ukraine
United Kingdom	...	969	1004	692	577	602	465	340	411	...	Royaume-Uni
Yugoslavia	..	119	101	99	96	103	88	101	103	77	Yougoslavie
T.F.Yug.Rep. Macedonia	..	16	13	12	19	12	22	21	19	11	L'ex-RY Macédoine
Oceania	**6**	**6**	**6**	**7**	**7**	**7**	**7**	**7**	**8**	**8**	**Océanie**
Fiji[11]	6	6	6	7	7	7	...	...	...	...	Fidji[11]
Total	**6199**	**7277**	**8100**	**8414**	**8307**	**10391**	**8728**	**9574**	**9387**	**9551**	**Total**

General Note.
Linseed oil, palm oil, coconut (copra) oil, palm kernel oil, castor oil and those oils covered under SITC 4229, refined (for description of refining see 3115-19) and before use in end products. (SITC, Rev.3: 42159-0, 42169-0, 42179-0, 42180-2, 42219-0, 42229-0, 42239-0, 42249-0, 42250-2, 42291-2, 42299-2,).

Remarque générale.
Huile de lin, huile de palme, huile de coprah, huile de palmiste, huile de ricin et huiles énumérées dans la rubrique 4229 de la CTCI, raffinées (notamment par désacidification, filtration, lavage, décoloration ou désodorisation) et avant emploi dans les produits définitifs. (CTCI, Rev.3: 42159-0, 42169-0, 42179-0, 42180-2, 42219-0, 42229-0, 42239-0, 42249-0, 42250-2, 42291-2, 42299-2).

For footnotes, see end of table.

Voir la fin du tableau pour les notes.

Oils, other, of vegetable origin, refined (continued)
Autres huiles d'origine végétale, raffinées (suite)

Footnotes
[1] Including refined olive oil.
[2] Coconut oil only.
[3] All refined vegetable oils.
[4] 1998 data are confidential.
[5] Sunflower seed oil.
[6] Incomplete coverage.
[7] Comestible vegetable oils.
[8] Sales.
[9] Production by establishments employing 20 or more persons.
[10] Including cotton-seed and groundnut oil.
[11] Data refer to edible oil.

Notes.
[1] Y compris l'huile d'olive raffinée.
[2] Huile de coco seulement.
[3] Huiles végétales raffinées de toutes catégories.
[4] Pour 1998, les données sont confidentielles.
[5] Huile de tournesol.
[6] Couverture incomplète.
[7] Huiles végétales comestibles.
[8] Ventes.
[9] Production des établissements occupant 20 personnes ou plus.
[10] Y compris huile de graines de coton et huile d'arachides.
[11] Les données se rapportent à l'huile comestible.

Flour, wheat
Farines de froment

ISIC-BASED CODE - CODE BASE CITI

3116-01

Unit : Thousand metric tons

Unité : Milliers de tonnes métriques

Country or area	1990	1991	1992	1993	1994	1995	1996	1997	1998	1999	Pays ou zone
Africa	14796	14678	15445	15627	16134	16836	18169	18635	16266	18123	Afrique
Algeria[1]	2873	2810	2610	2890	3120	3410	3562	3770	1450	...	Algérie[1]
Angola	22	19	10	[2]17	[2]15	[2]39	[2]37	...	...	...	Angola
Benin[2]	22	19	17	18	16	12	7	...	...	...	Bénin[2]
Botswana[2]	26	30	40	56	57	46	36	47	57	56	Botswana[2]
Burkina Faso	23	21	21	28	[2]20	[2]29	[2]31	...	...	...	Burkina Faso
Burundi	0	0	7	3	[2]8	[2]9	[2]9	...	...	...	Burundi
Cameroon	13	8	26	52	62	54	[2]26	...	...	...	Cameroun
Cape Verde	[2]13	11	14	14	14	14	[2]16	...	...	...	Cap-Vert
Central African Rep.[2]	2	0	0	0	0	0	0	...	...	...	Rép. centrafricaine[2]
Chad[2]	1	2	2	4	2	2	1	...	...	...	Tchad[2]
Congo	12	12	13	15	[2]13	35	17	...	...	...	Congo
Côte d'Ivoire[2]	161	177	165	160	162	165	140			...	Côte d'Ivoire[2]
Dem. Rep. of Congo[2]	91	91	118	101	79	122	109	...	...	...	Rép. dém. du Congo[2]
Egypt	3532	3392	3510	3352	3662	3767	4657	4739		...	Egypte
Eritrea[2]	...	...	...	151	122	145	140	...	...	...	Erythrée[2]
Ethiopia,incl.Eritrea[2]	1160	1316	1465	...	...	...					Ethiopie,incl.Erythrée[2]
Ethiopia[3]	177	158	88	62	75	116	121	140	105	168	Ethiopie[3]
Gabon	29	30	31	[2]26	[2]31	[2]27	[2]26	...	...	...	Gabon
Ghana[2]	120	123	97	159	135	90	69	...	...	...	Ghana[2]
Kenya	172	186	222	143	219	237	227	[1]251	[1]345	...	Kenya
Lesotho[2]	59	53	38	34	36	35	42	...	...	...	Lesotho[2]
Liberia[2]	2	0	8	0	0	43	55	...	...	...	Libéria[2]
Libyan Arab Jamah.	[2]365	[2]400	[2]532	[2]492	543	480	372	416	479	464	Jamah. arabe libyenne
Madagascar	[2]57	[2]38	[2]32	[2]51	47	46	26	33	42	...	Madagascar
Malawi	[2]14	[2]11	[2]2	[2]1	[2]22	[2]13	[2]20	10	8	...	Malawi
Mali	23	15	23	23	19	24	25	...	...	...	Mali
Mauritania[2]	49	138	50	59	89	41	43	...	...	...	Mauritanie[2]
Mauritius[2]	62	42	63	88	95	79	87	...	...	...	Maurice[2]
Morocco[4]	1832	1769	2055	2030	2130	2210	2353	2332	2404	...	Maroc[4]
Mozambique	49	60	51	28	40	39	38	82	115	125	Mozambique
Namibia[2]	11	17	22	23	33	35	29	...	...	...	Namibie[2]
Niger[2]	26	22	10	7	5	10	8	...	...	...	Niger[2]
Nigeria	[2]52	[2]95	153	362	265	251	[2]561	...	...	...	Nigéria
Réunion[2]	8	19	16	19	20	16	16	...	...	...	Réunion[2]
Rwanda[2]	17	16	11	8	10	5	5	...	...	...	Rwanda[2]
Senegal	125	124	137	139	138	146	142	159	168	171	Sénégal
Seychelles[2]	0	0	0	0	0	1	1	...	...	...	Seychelles[2]
Sierra Leone[2]	6	16	12	13	7	10	12	...	...	...	Sierra Leone[2]
Somalia[2]	36	47	59	53	12	12	6	...	...	...	Somalie[2]
South Africa	1773	1734	1833	1867	1872	1997	2027	1909	1893	1784	Afrique du Sud
Sudan[2]	728	618	747	807	632	736	684	...	...	...	Soudan[2]
Swaziland[2]	1	0	0	0	0	0	0	...	...	...	Swaziland[2]
Togo[2]	60	35	56	21	26	36	31	...	...	...	Togo[2]
Tunisia	564	566	613	627	657	670	679	697	708	721	Tunisie
Uganda	13	11	12	10	8	[2]11	[2]11	...	...	...	Ouganda
United Rep.Tanzania	12	3	16	7	13	12	34	78	...	...	Rép. Unie de Tanzanie
Zambia[2]	51	66	80	71	47	49	57	...	...	...	Zambie[2]
Zimbabwe[2]	211	220	217	222	243	195	261	...	...	...	Zimbabwe[2]
America, North	22171	22597	22875	24022	24626	24091	26343	26886	24915	25333	Amérique du Nord
Barbados	15	15	15	14	15	15	16	18	19	15	Barbade
Belize	10	11	12	12	12	12	13	12	11	...	Belize
Canada[1][5]	1801	1771	1749	1910	2039	2001	2094	2208	2237	2332	Canada[1][5]
Costa Rica	[2]90	[2]110	[2]72	[2]61	[2]110	[2]117	[1]133	[1]139	...	...	Costa Rica
Cuba[2]	400	450	420	380	440	380	350	...	...	...	Cuba[2]
Dominican Republic	426	483	500	511	509	374	447	438	498	391	Rép. dominicaine
El Salvador	[2]128	[2]133	[2]145	[2]176	[2]176	[2]192	124	...	...	...	El Salvador
Grenada	8	8	8	7	7	[2]6	[2]4	...	...	...	Grenade
Guadeloupe[2]	28	34	40	37	40	38	38	...	...	...	Guadeloupe[2]
Guatemala	[2]150	104	131	111	122	128	137	141	238	...	Guatemala
Haiti	78	71	# [2]7	[2]1	[2]0	[2]7	[2]7	...	...	...	Haïti
Honduras[2]	83	100	95	104	105	99	100	...	147	136	Honduras[2]
Jamaica	140	147	145	148	148	146	141	147	136	131	Jamaïque

For general note and footnotes, see end of table.

Voir la fin du tableau pour la remarque générale et les notes.

187

ISIC-BASED CODE - CODE BASE CITI

3116-01

Unit : Thousand metric tons

Unité : Milliers de tonnes métriques

Country or area	1990	1991	1992	1993	1994	1995	1996	1997	1998	1999	Pays ou zone
Martinique[2]	3	1	3	3	1	1	1	...	...	...	Martinique[2]
Mexico	2511	2489	2482	2736	2857	2696	2597	2603	2581	2457	Mexique
Netherlands Antilles[2]	10	10	10	9	10	8	12	...	...	...	Antilles néerlandaises[2]
Nicaragua[2]	47	66	56	57	67	66	76	...	...	...	Nicaragua[2]
Panama	[6]58	[2]58	[6]63	[6]72	[6]68	[2]71	67	...	...	...	Panama
St. Vincent-Grenadines	[2]21	[2]20	[2]22	[2]23	[2]24	[2]24	23	24	21	17	St. Vincent-Grenadines
Trinidad and Tobago	[2]91	[2]82	[2]81	[2]79	[2]71	[2]80	[2]77	96	96	97	Trinité-et-Tobago
United States	16073	16434	16820	17571	17805	[2]17631	19888	20207	18094	18691	Etats-Unis
America, South	**10957**	**12023**	**12371**	**12313**	**12844**	**13058**	**13723**	**14310**	**14717**	**15457**	**Amérique du Sud**
Argentina	3102	3314	3118	3137	3292	3283	3538	3640	3739	3605	Argentine
Bolivia	138	183	200	195	163	*159	[1]211	[1]198	[1]165	...	Bolivie
Brazil	[2]4791	[2]4933	[2]5070	[2]4929	[2]5243	[2]5448	[2]5662	[1]6194	[1]6308	...	Brésil
Chile	1026	1007	1105	1087	[1]1087	[1]1110	[1]1120	[1]1133	[1]1146	[1]1129	Chili
Colombia	463	[2]600	571	575	649	702	[2]778	649	747	...	Colombie
Ecuador	[2]312	[2]210	313	291	195	[2]238	[2]283	276	283	265	Equateur
Guyana	33	35	35	36	36	[1]38	[1]37	[1]35	[1]33	[1]35	Guyana
Paraguay	97	67	59	54	48	52	55	50	54	55	Paraguay
Peru	464	624	687	751	812	793	820	805	847	903	Pérou
Suriname[2]	15	17	22	21	19	13	14	...	...	...	Suriname[2]
Uruguay[2]	205	206	220	191	178	187	226	...	...	...	Uruguay[2]
Venezuela	310	# [1]827	[1]972	[1]1046	[1]1123	[1]1035	[1]979	[1]1116	[1]1182	...	Venezuela
Asia	**118644**	**125732**	**128392**	**136960**	**138767**	**134026**	**134015**	**135391**	**133328**	**133561**	**Asie**
Afghanistan[2]	1403	1408	1521	1762	1832	2029	2145	...	...	...	Afghanistan[2]
Armenia	..	362	299	290	290	265	156	143	104	148	Arménie
Azerbaijan	..	804	698	656	461	408	190	90	79	52	Azerbaïdjan
Bahrain	[2]22	[2]26	[2]36	[2]34	[2]49	[2]52	[2]52	...	49	49	Bahreïn
Bangladesh	43	46	50	56	70	69	60	61	[1]67	[1]68	Bangladesh
Bhutan[2]	14	19	13	12	9	16	16	...	...	...	Bhoutan[2]
Cambodia[2]	0	0	0	0	4	6	6	...	...	...	Cambodge[2]
China[1]	70500	67500	69000	71250	73125	75000	75375	75750	77250	78000	Chine[1]
Hong Kong SAR	80	110	[2]75	79	83	[2]43	[2]40	...	...	...	Hong-Kong RAS
Cyprus	*72	*75	65	*65	*70	54	59	61	64	54	Chypre
Georgia	..	...	578	463	420	334	211	180	148	114	Géorgie
India[7]	4732	4775	4607	4800	4800	4800	4800	5040	3625	2323	Inde[7]
Indonesia	1285	1578	1306	7683	7006	2812	[1]2964	2623	710	[1]2074	Indonésie
Iran(Islamic Rep. of)[2]	7815	8338	8936	8942	9639	9517	9339	...	...	...	Iran(Rép. islamique)[2]
Iraq[2]	2623	1602	1396	1348	1336	1238	1298	...	...	...	Iraq[2]
Israel	[2]446	[2]462	[2]483	[2]503	[2]538	[2]573	[2]573	[1]600	...	[1]570	Israël
Japan[8]	4652	4677	4668	4791	4999	4947	4970	4902	4873	4640	Japon[8]
Jordan	[2]370	[2]459	[2]445	[2]380	[2]458	[2]522	[2]536	[1]72	[1]52	...	Jordanie
Kazakhstan	..	2013	1970	1940	1960	1575	1593	1528	1546	1262	Kazakhstan
Korea,Dem.Ppl's.Rep.[2]	377	454	244	536	494	384	137	...	...	...	Corée,Rép.pop.dém.de[2]
Korea, Republic of	1616	1564	1553	1554	1591	1679	[2]1695	1750	1722	1834	Corée, République de
Kuwait	[2]85	[2]30	105	127	136	133	141	156	155	157	Koweït
Kyrgyzstan	..	475	321	426	320	267	252	292	298	280	Kirghizistan
Lebanon[2]	244	252	294	310	328	336	344	...	...	...	Liban[2]
Malaysia	539	587	602	621	672	713	692	720	714	761	Malaisie
Mongolia	[2]190	174	182	176	127	159	92	64	66	67	Mongolie
Myanmar	[2]83	[2]82	[2]97	[2]94	[2]73	[2]60	[2]52	1	1	1	Myanmar
Nepal[2]	575	666	666	634	705	732	755	...	...	...	Népal[2]
Oman[2]	90	84	112	98	116	118	89	...	...	...	Oman[2]
Pakistan[2]	14712	14801	16481	16005	15860	14841	15326	...	...	...	Pakistan[2]
Philippines[1]	874	1347	1367	1330	1589	1555	1300	1350	1301	1349	Philippines[1]
Qatar[9]	40	36	33	45	42	43	39	44	50	40	Qatar[9]
Saudi Arabia[2]	1613	1692	1717	1743	1775	1760	1600	...	...	...	Arabie saoudite[2]
Singapore[2]	113	158	151	127	148	101	77	...	...	...	Singapour[2]
Sri Lanka	526	537	556	[1]584	[1]634	[1]731	[1]627	[1]617	[1]633	...	Sri Lanka
Syrian Arab Republic	1177	1253	1251	1218	1211	1398	1492	1646	1621	1649	Rép. arabe syrienne
Tajikistan	..	756	628	667	360	303	271	322	416	341	Tadjikistan
Thailand[1]	220	317	339	401	470	428	486	485	...	...	Thaïlande[1]
Turkey	1364	1361	1362	1465	1256	1436	1585	1908	1868	1879	Turquie
Turkmenistan	..	446	453	429	439	442	329	303	339	...	Turkménistan

For general note and footnotes, see end of table.

Voir la fin du tableau pour la remarque générale et les notes.

Flour, wheat (continued)
Farines de froment (suite)

ISIC-BASED CODE - CODE BASE CITI

3116-01

Unit : Thousand metric tons   Unité : Milliers de tonnes métriques

Country or area	1990	1991	1992	1993	1994	1995	1996	1997	1998	1999	Pays ou zone
United Arab Emirates[2]	128	76	59	79	100	90	138	...	...	...	Emirats arabes unis[2]
Uzbekistan[1]	..	...	2925	2940	2942	1770	1812	1713	1566	...	Ouzbékistan[1]
Viet Nam[2]	20	43	22	33	9	82	49	...	...	...	Viet Nam[2]
Yemen	..	[2]820	[2]726	265	220	204	251	253	...	...	Yémen
Europe	**40265**	**64560**	**63095**	**56745**	**52370**	**50979**	**54004**	**55776**	**54170**	**54284**	**Europe**
Albania	352	313	208	115	44	36	89	68	83	0	Albanie
Austria	259	266	273	271	269	288	298	277	278	293	Autriche
Belarus	..	[10]3013	2188	1886	1698	1417	1397	1274	1153	1137	Bélarus
Belgium	[11]1158	[11]1221	[11]1278	...	1243	1201	1319	1343	1332	[12]1417	Belgique
Bosnia and Herzegovina[2]			247	229	203	187	157	...	...	...	Bosnie-Herzégovine[2]
Bulgaria	[10]1293	[10]1206	[10]1004	[10]1051	[10]988	[10]977	[10]876	[10]757	[1]473	[1]760	Bulgarie
Croatia	..	433	420	346	323	324	315	305	298	[1]294	Croatie
Denmark[13]	247	266	261	275	295	314	323	327	300	...	Danemark[13]
Czechoslovakia(former)	1256	1107	..	..	..	..	..	..	..	..	Tchécoslovaquie(anc.)
Czech Republic	..	..	879	773	820	909	792	858	837	797	République tchèque
Estonia	..	166	48	48	35	20	11	17	12	5	Estonie
Finland[14][15]	213	223	245	242	244	269	314	329	315	286	Finlande[14][15]
France	[16]5170	[16]5391	[16]5123	[16]5354	[16]5186	[16]5282	[16]5400	[1]6080	[1]6183	[1]6800	France
Germany	..	3117	3237	3158	3113	3221	3392	3660	3678	..	Allemagne
Germany(Fed.Rep.)	2617	..	..	..	..	..	..	..	..	..	Allemagne(Rép.féd.)
German D.R.(former)	680	..	..	..	..	..	..	..	..	..	R.D.A. (anc.)
Greece	[2]1089	[2]1105	[2]1091	705	680	641	660	705	738	...	Grèce
Hungary	1191	1131	1245	896	864	1168	1050	1110	962	999	Hongrie
Iceland[2]	11	9	9	8	9	10	8	...	...	...	Islande[2]
Ireland	[2]204	[2]197	[2]197	[2]197	[2]212	[2]212	[2]190	[1]195	...	...	Irlande
Italy[2]	7838	8549	8666	7960	7716	7880	8132	...	...	...	Italie[2]
Latvia	..	214	153	69	130	103	107	96	86	99	Lettonie
Lithuania	..	202	188	167	164	142	141	150	166	145	Lituanie
Luxembourg[1]	41	42	40	41	43	42	...	...	...	...	Luxembourg[1]
Malta	[2]36	[2]35	[2]38	[2]36	[2]37	[2]32	[2]32	[1]37	[1]36	[1]35	Malte
Netherlands[10][17]	[13]1135	[13]1151	[13]1233	[13]1138	[13]1181	[13]1218	[1]1240	[1]1250	[1]1300	...	Pays-Bas[10][17]
Norway[2]	273	283	284	287	288	288	288	...	...	...	Norvège[2]
Poland	1807	1835	1782	1724	1810	1848	1969	2104	2065	2055	Pologne
Portugal	[10]570	[10]487	542	594	631	624	647	630	701	645	Portugal
Republic of Moldova	..	577	500	[18]406	[18]313	[18]283	[18]284	[18]252	[18]229	[18]150	Rép. de Moldova
Romania	2195	1984	1844	1783	1923	2153	2406	2596	2101	1976	Roumanie
Russian Federation	..	15458	14803	12439	9346	7498	9508	10400	10112	10789	Fédération de Russie
Slovakia	..	..	409	419	361	375	357	328	350	319	Slovaquie
Slovenia	..	102	106	102	120	112	133	128	116	116	Slovénie
Spain	2691	2534	2661	1784	1973	2466	2578	2624	2570	2643	Espagne
Sweden	[14][15]459	[14][15]514	[14][15]519	[14][15]477	[14][15]510	[14][15]494	[2]475	[14][15]526	[14][15]506	[14][15]481	Suède
Switzerland	451	435	441	438	442	439	[1]400	[1]370	[1]388	[1]395	Suisse
Ukraine	..	[10]6794	[10]6066	5047	4442	3554	3859	3986	3608	3036	Ukraine
United Kingdom	3880	3851	3844	3865	3796	3794	3869	3698	3740	...	Royaume-Uni
Yugoslavia	..	213	886	999	779	992	807	796	838	725	Yougoslavie
T.F.Yug.Rep. Macedonia	..	135	137	137	139	165	140	162	150	136	L'ex-RY Macédoine
Yugoslavia, SFR[2]	3150	..	..	..	..	..	..	..	..	..	Yougoslavie, RSF[2]
USSR (former)	32842	..	..	..	..	..	..	..	..	..	URSS (anc.)
Oceania	**1532**	**1523**	**1574**	**1635**	**1737**	**1753**	**1801**	**2016**	**2250**	**2356**	**Océanie**
Australia[5]	1237	1218	1249	1304	1376	1355	1414	1556	1762	1857	Australie[5]
Fiji	25	27	28	33	38	41	43	46	51	...	Fidji
French Polynesia[2]	1	1	0	0	0	0	0	...	...	...	Polynésie française[2]
New Caledonia[2]	14	13	13	13	16	19	14	...	...	...	Nouvelle-Calédonie[2]
New Zealand	207	214	223	185	208	235	205	[1]247	[1]256	[1]244	Nouvelle-Zélande
Papua New Guinea[2]	45	43	56	94	95	96	119	...	...	...	Papouasie-Nvl-Guinée[2]
Solomon Islands[2]	4	6	5	7	5	6	6	...	...	...	Iles Salomon[2]
Total	**241208**	**241113**	**243751**	**247302**	**246478**	**240744**	**248056**	**253015**	**245647**	**249113**	**Total**

General Note.
Sifted (bolted) flour made from wheat or meslin. (SITC, Rev.3: 04610-0).

Remarque générale.
Farines tamisées (blutées) de froment ou de méteil. (CTCI, Rev.3: 04610-0).

For footnotes, see end of table.

Voir la fin du tableau pour les notes.

Flour, wheat (continued)
Farines de froment (suite)

ISIC-BASED CODE - CODE BASE CITI

3116-01

Meal and groats of all cereals
Semoules et gruaux de toutes céréales

ISIC-BASED CODE - CODE BASE CITI

3116-04

Unit : Thousand metric tons

Unité : Milliers de tonnes métriques

Country or area	1990	1991	1992	1993	1994	1995	1996	1997	1998	1999	Pays ou zone
Africa	**3597**	**3613**	**3602**	**3690**	**3712**	**3746**	**3743**	**3772**	**3800**	**3769**	**Afrique**
Algeria	2588	2634	2539	...	...	...	...	...	...	...	Algérie
South Africa	543	510	583	598	...	...	...	...	...	...	Afrique du Sud
Tunisia	466	469	480	505	566	600	597	626	654	623	Tunisie
America, North	**11**	**3**	**4**	**7**	**13**	**10**	**11**	**12**	**12**	**13**	**Amérique du Nord**
Mexico	11	3	4	7	13	...	...	...	...	...	Mexique
America, South	**169**	**145**	**148**	**139**	**139**	**141**	**147**	**145**	**150**	**138**	**Amérique du Sud**
Chile[1]	127	129	135	...	...	...	...	...	...	...	Chili[1]
Colombia	33	...	6	1	1	4	...	8	11	...	Colombie
Ecuador	2	...	...	...	...	...	0	...	...	...	Equateur
Peru	7	6	6	7	6	6	7	6	8	6	Pérou
Asia	**131**	**3403**	**3287**	**3415**	**3395**	**2153**	**2135**	**2016**	**1454**	**1191**	**Asie**
Armenia	..	12	5	2	3	3	1	1	1	0	Arménie
Cyprus	*93	*96	100	...	...	...	...	...	...	...	Chypre
Kuwait[2]	...	...	34	31	40	36	64	41	39	42	Koweït[2]
Tajikistan	..	27	24	4	3	1	2	0	0	0	Tadjikistan
Turkmenistan	..	26	27	34	38	34	11	7	9	...	Turkménistan
Uzbekistan	..	3203	3097	3248	3215	1983	1961	1871	...	...	Ouzbékistan
Europe	**1914**	**6128**	**5223**	**5091**	**4700**	**4744**	**3628**	**3516**	**3522**	**3477**	**Europe**
Belarus	..	229	166	136	92	73	59	97	84	60	Bélarus
Belgium	...	...	...	...	50	16	16	17	18	47	Belgique
Bulgaria	2	2	3	1	6	8	0	0	2	2	Bulgarie
Croatia	..	43	45	31	35	41	42	28	44	...	Croatie
Denmark[4]	[3]15	[3]24	[3]22	20	17	17	11	10	8	8	Danemark[4]
Estonia	..	20	14	3	4	3	2	1	2	1	Estonie
Finland[5]	30	42	33	46	46	52	36	17	15	14	Finlande[5]
France	[6][7]458	[6][7]477	[6][7]475	[6][7]479	469	504	495	499	470	...	France
Germany	..	...	...	...	...	389	...	351	326	...	Allemagne
Greece	...	...	...	71	71	79	96	99	77	...	Grèce
Hungary[8]	520	505	501	389	385	470	54	39	43	65	Hongrie[8]
Latvia	..	35	34	4	5	3	5	4	4	14	Lettonie
Lithuania	..	...	35	17	15	18	17	10	17	21	Lituanie
Netherlands[4][9]	...	...	...	60	61	60	...	...	...	...	Pays-Bas[4][9]
Poland	77	90	75	69	55	64	60	67	68	58	Pologne
Portugal	121	103	94	79	84	82	91	85	95	93	Portugal
Republic of Moldova	..	13	18	[10]10	[10]9	[10]9	[10]9	[10]7	[10]8	[10]6	Rép. de Moldova
Russian Federation	..	2679	2011	1877	1597	1418	988	992	1085	899	Fédération de Russie
Slovakia	..	..	...	...	...	...	...	...	5	4	Slovaquie
Slovenia	..	7	8	4	3	3	4	5	6	5	Slovénie
Spain	280	322	314	[11]417	[11]438	[11]436	332	364	299	294	Espagne
Sweden	18	16	7	6	4	4	2	3	3	2	Suède
Ukraine	..	944	804	695	605	532	456	366	409	342	Ukraine
United Kingdom	...	38	39	...	...	#458	433	390	374	...	Royaume-Uni
Yugoslavia, SFR	48	..	..	...	...	...	...	...	...	..	Yougoslavie, RSF
USSR (former)	4122	..	..	..	..	..	..	..	..	..	URSS (anc.)
Total	**9944**	**13292**	**12264**	**12342**	**11959**	**10794**	**9663**	**9461**	**8938**	**8588**	**Total**

General Note.
Small fragments of floury kernels obtained by the rough grinding of grains of all cereals (groats) and granules obtained either from the first sifting after the initial milling operation, or by regrinding and resifting the groats resulting from that initial milling (meal). (SITC, Rev.3: 04620-0, 04720-0).

For footnotes, see end of table.

Remarque générale.
Petits fragments de grains farineux obtenus par mouture grossière de toutes céréales (gruaux) et granules résultant soit d'un blutage après la première mouture, soit d'un nouveau blutage après remouture des gruaux issus de la première opération (semoule). (CTCI, Rev.3: 04620-0, 04702-0).

Voir la fin du tableau pour les notes.

Meal and groats of all cereals (continued)
Semoules et gruaux de toutes céréales (suite)

ISIC-BASED CODE - CODE BASE CITI

3116-04

Footnotes
[1] Wheat meal and groats only.
[2] Bran only
[3] Oat meal and barley groats only.
[4] Sales.
[5] Including meslin flour.
[6] Crop year production.
[7] Shipments.
[8] Low-grade flour and bran.
[9] Production by establishments employing 20 or more persons.
[10] Excluding Transnistria region.
[11] Including boiled wheat and semolina.

Notes.
[1] Farine et gruau de blé seulement.
[2] Sons seulement.
[3] Farine d'avoine et gruau d'orge seulement.
[4] Ventes.
[5] Y compris les farines de méteil.
[6] Production par campagne.
[7] Expéditions.
[8] Farines et sons de qualité inférieure.
[9] Production des établissements occupant 20 personnes ou plus.
[10] Non compris la région de Transnistria.
[11] Y compris le froment boulli et la semoule.

Flour, cereal, other than wheat
Farines de céréales autres que le froment

ISIC-BASED CODE - CODE BASE CITI

3116-07

Unit : Thousand metric tons

Unité : Milliers de tonnes métriques

Country or area	1990	1991	1992	1993	1994	1995	1996	1997	1998	1999	Pays ou zone
Africa	**344**	**328**	**176**	**179**	**264**	**326**	**270**	**309**	**321**	**333**	**Afrique**
Ethiopia	49	57	21	4	9	2	0	0	0	0	Ethiopie
Kenya	241	227	121	168	253	313	267	...	...	...	Kenya
Madagascar[1]	...	...	...	...	0	1	1	1	1	...	Madagascar[1]
Mozambique	54	44	34	7	2	10	2	13	11	9	Mozambique
America, North	**1008**	**989**	**1036**	**1762**	**2043**	**2392**	**2655**	**2309**	**2308**	**1951**	**Amérique du Nord**
Mexico	932	914	959	1687	1968	2319	2581	2235	2235	1878	Mexique
Panama	3	...	4	2	2	0	1	...	...	...	Panama
United States[2]	...	...	73	...	...	...	...	...	...	...	Etats-Unis[2]
America, South	**260**	**194**	**113**	**192**	**264**	**279**	**314**	**403**	**454**	**433**	**Amérique du Sud**
Bolivia	108	115	86	169	240	*253	...	...	...	...	Bolivie
Colombia	152	...	24	20	20	21	...	145	172	...	Colombie
Ecuador	...	...	3	3	4	5	5	12	19	...	Equateur
Asia	**136**	**175**	**173**	**169**	**149**	**151**	**180**	**178**	**160**	**188**	**Asie**
Cyprus	*13	*13	1	...	...	6	8	5	5	5	Chypre
Indonesia	...	17	...	...	...	...	...	...	...	...	Indonésie
Japan	106	114	123	116	96	99	119	127	107	135	Japon
Kyrgyzstan	..	...	28	...	...	...	...	...	...	...	Kirghizistan
Turkmenistan	..	3	4	1	1	1	8	1	...	...	Turkménistan
Europe	**3194**	**6687**	**6285**	**5683**	**5027**	**5165**	**5288**	**3902**	**3926**	**3872**	**Europe**
Austria	72	79	67	68	64	59	59	51	52	53	Autriche
Belgium	...	...	...	...	11	...	...	15	14	15	Belgique
Bulgaria	19	10	7	6	8	10	2	1	2	1	Bulgarie
Croatia	..	6	6	30	34	7	5	7	6	...	Croatie
Denmark[3]	87	75	62	78	85	25	3	3	1	1	Danemark[3]
Czechoslovakia(former)	271	237		..	..	..	..	..	..	..	Tchécoslovaquie(anc.)
Czech Republic	..	..	158	120	...	106	111	107	131	126	République tchèque
Estonia	..	...	105	38	29	17	13	12	16	13	Estonie
Finland	84	93	71	71	67	64	65	87	62	59	Finlande
France	24	24	26	25	24	24	24	...	...	...	France
Germany	..	640	631	595	538	500	459	435	446	...	Allemagne
Germany(Fed.Rep.)	452	..	..	..	..	..	..	..	..	..	Allemagne(Rép.féd.)
German D.R.(former)	243	..	..	..	..	..	..	..	..	..	R.D.A. (anc.)
Greece	...	...	...	246	201	226	136	141	...	...	Grèce
Hungary	41	21	25	16	12	26	11	8	7	12	Hongrie
Latvia	..	181	117	41	43	40	46	36	31	30	Lettonie
Lithuania	..	204	208	128	90	95	98	82	72	66	Lituanie
Netherlands[3][4]	...	...	...	35	29	26	...	...	...	...	Pays-Bas[3][4]
Poland	576	492	454	362	319	280	321	331	313	259	Pologne
Portugal	19	11	46	66	63	66	49	49	45	52	Portugal
Russian Federation	..	2747	2450	1856	1563	1347	2277	1780	1929	1898	Fédération de Russie
Slovakia	..	..	53	51	47	46	50	42	39	36	Slovaquie
Slovenia	..	4	4	3	2	2	3	3	5	3	Slovénie
Spain	621	584	602	66	78	91	98	78	104	100	Espagne
Sweden	50	52	72	50	37	46	45	47	49	51	Suède
Ukraine	..	588	559	1540	1273	1765	1106	334	282	318	Ukraine
United Kingdom	...	...	...	175	285	279	258	193	153	...	Royaume-Uni
Yugoslavia	..	3	4	3	2	4	5	6	5	4	Yougoslavie
Yugoslavia, SFR	11	..	..	..	..	..	..	..	..	..	Yougoslavie, RSF
Total	**4942**	**8373**	**7782**	**7985**	**7746**	**8312**	**8706**	**7101**	**7169**	**6776**	**Total**

General Note.
Sifted (bolted) flour of cereals other than wheat or meslin. (SITC, Rev.3: 04710-0).

Remarque générale.
Farines tamisées (blutées) de céréales autres que le froment ou le méteil. (CTCI, Rev.3: 04710-0).

[1] Corn meal only.
[2] Rye flour only.
[3] Sales.
[4] Production by establishments employing 20 or more persons.

[1] Farine de maïs seulement.
[2] Farine de seigle seulement.
[3] Ventes.
[4] Production des établissements occupant 20 personnes ou plus.

Cereal breakfast food
Aliments à base de céréales, pour le petit déjeûner

ISIC-BASED CODE - CODE BASE CITI

3116-10

Unit : Thousand metric tons
Unité : Milliers de tonnes métriques

Country or area	1990	1991	1992	1993	1994	1995	1996	1997	1998	1999	Pays ou zone
Africa	**25**	**30**	**27**	**33**	**37**	**37**	**34**	**35**	**31**	**36**	**Afrique**
Kenya	0.3	0.4	0.4	0.4	0.4	0.4	...	...	...	...	Kenya
South Africa	24.3	29.7	26.6	32.2	36.2	36.5	33.8	34.4	30.1	35.5	Afrique du Sud
America, South	**12**	**12**	**11**	**14**	**2**	**20**	**12**	**12**	**12**	**12**	**Amérique du Sud**
Colombia	...	...	11.2	14.3	2.0	20.1	...	...	...	...	Colombie
Europe	**386**	**632**	**659**	**850**	**880**	**852**	**935**	**984**	**1062**	**1213**	**Europe**
Austria	...	...	...	...	...	18.3	22.7	24.4	25.4	26.3	Autriche
Belgium	...	...	...	...	5.9	9.1	14.7	15.1	18.9	22.8	Belgique
Croatia	..	...	0.0	0.0	0.0	0.3	0.3	1.0	0.5	...	Croatie
Denmark[1]	32.9	39.0	41.9	44.6	46.8	0.1	0.1	0.1	0.0	0.0	Danemark[1]
Finland	0.1	0.1	0.6	0.9	0.1	0.1	0.2	...	...	...	Finlande
France	24.7	25.2	35.6	46.1	55.5	72.9	82.6	...	...	...	France
Germany	..	...	...	...	...	144.3	157.9	156.0	163.0	...	Allemagne
Greece	...	...	...	7.3	7.3	7.6	8.5	5.8	5.5	...	Grèce
Hungary	...	...	...	...	...	...	...	2.2	0.8	2.1	Hongrie
Latvia	..	...	...	0.1	0.8	1.4	1.7	2.2	0.2	0.2	Lettonie
Norway	5.3	...	1.8	...	...	...	...	0.8	...	...	Norvège
Portugal[2]	...	...	2.5	2.5	3.0	3.9	4.4	...	...	...	Portugal[2]
Russian Federation	..	59.2	51.1	45.1	38.3	34.6	34.2	32.5	33.2	28.8	Fédération de Russie
Slovenia	..	1.8	2.2	4.5	1.8	1.8	1.9	2.1	2.2	2.2	Slovénie
Spain	...	...	...	31.1	30.6	48.4	53.8	65.1	...	...	Espagne
Sweden	18.1	18.9	15.9	15.6	16.9	18.6	26.5	24.5	23.2	21.8	Suède
United Kingdom	[3]278.7	[3]290.3	[3]301.5	467.7	495.6	486.4	520.9	547.0	596.4	...	Royaume-Uni
Oceania	**110**	**118**	**119**	**119**	**103**	**100**	**100**	**101**	**110**	**112**	**Océanie**
Australia[4]	109.7	118.5	119.2	119.4	103.0	100.3	100.0	100.8	109.8	112.1	Australie[4]
Total	**532**	**792**	**816**	**1017**	**1022**	**1009**	**1081**	**1132**	**1214**	**1373**	**Total**

General Note.
Prepared foods (ready to serve or to be cooked before serving) obtained by swelling or roasting of cereals or cereal products such as puffed rice, corn flakes and similar products. (SITC, Rev.3: 04811-0).

Remarque générale.
Produits alimentaires (pour consommation immédiate, ou après cuisson) obtenus par gonflage, le soufflage ou le grillage de céréales ou de produits à base de céréales (riz soufflé, flocons de maïs et produits similaires). (CTCI,Rev.3: 04811-0).

[1] Sales.
[2] Beginning 1997, data are confidential.
[3] Data refer to 53-week period.
[4] Twelve months ending 30 June of year stated.

[1] Ventes.
[2] A partir de 1997, les données sont confidentielles
[3] Données se rapportant à une période de 53 semaines.
[4] Période de douze mois finissant le 30 juin de l'année indiquée.

Macaroni and noodle products, uncooked
Pâtes alimentaires

ISIC-BASED CODE - CODE BASE CITI

3117-01

Unit : Thousand metric tons

Unité : Milliers de tonnes métriques

Country or area	1990	1991	1992	1993	1994	1995	1996	1997	1998	1999	Pays ou zone
Africa	**228**	**244**	**228**	**234**	**246**	**254**	**266**	**280**	**287**	**297**	**Afrique**
Algeria	89	98	92	...	...	...	...	...	...	...	Algérie
Cameroon	...	4	4	4	4	4	...	...	...	...	Cameroun
Egypt	...	...	...	26	27	...	...	...	...	...	Egypte
Ethiopia[1]	15	15	3	5	11	19	15	18	20	24	Ethiopie[1]
Madagascar	...	...	...	...	1	1	1	1	1	...	Madagascar
Mauritania	7	8	9	10	...	...	...	...	...	...	Mauritanie
Tunisia	86	92	93	94	102	102	118	129	134	140	Tunisie
America, North	**177**	**186**	**161**	**187**	**210**	**223**	**250**	**259**	**257**	**252**	**Amérique du Nord**
Barbados	2	1	1	1	1	1	2	1	0	1	Barbade
Mexico	169	177	153	179	200	214	240	246	244	237	Mexique
Panama	6	...	7	7	9	8	8	...	...	...	Panama
America, South	**787**	**823**	**819**	**829**	**884**	**869**	**892**	**968**	**1035**	**943**	**Amérique du Sud**
Bolivia	18	19	21	24	24	*24	...	...	...	...	Bolivie
Brazil	546	545	524	528	589	561	565	620	689	610	Brésil
Chile	112	122	136	129	142	150	167	175	157	132	Chili
Colombia	68	...	98	94	89	95	...	104	112	...	Colombie
Ecuador	...	...	40	54	40	39	41	44	51	...	Equateur
Asia	**2161**	**2439**	**2636**	**2654**	**2548**	**2723**	**2727**	**3077**	**3540**	**3249**	**Asie**
Armenia	..	15	8	7	9	3	1	0	1	1	Arménie
Azerbaijan	..	23	17	14	10	5	7	1	2	1	Azerbaïdjan
Hong Kong SAR	83	79	73	93	75	126	76	93	99	127	Hong-Kong RAS
China, Macao, SAR	...	...	...	2	1	2	2	2	3	3	Chine, Macao PAS
Cyprus	*4	*4	4	*5	*5	5	5	5	4	5	Chypre
Georgia	..	...	19	8	5	4	1	0	1	0	Géorgie
Indonesia	294	180	333	366	338	...	...	860	1441	...	Indonésie
Japan[2]	1407	1441	1458	1445	1451	1456	1464	1442	1424	1426	Japon[2]
Kazakhstan	..	136	137	130	123	79	69	61	63	32	Kazakhstan
Kuwait	...	...	5	5	6	6	6	6	6	6	Koweït
Kyrgyzstan	..	6	6	14	7	8	9	12	11	8	Kirghizistan
Myanmar[3]	22	23	23	23	25	...	...	...	...	...	Myanmar[3]
Syrian Arab Republic	9	9	9	7	7	6	6	6	6	...	Rép. arabe syrienne
Tajikistan	..	29	20	18	8	8	2	1	2	1	Tadjikistan
Thailand[4]	...	...	...	...	...	...	132	136	125	...	Thaïlande[4]
Turkey	205	233	268	270	258	274	312	360	297	260	Turquie
Turkmenistan		21	22	16	14	17	12	9	8	...	Turkménistan
Uzbekistan	..	94	101	100	75	23	53	56	...	...	Ouzbékistan
Europe	**2975**	**4715**	**4725**	**4482**	**3942**	**4184**	**4806**	**4667**	**4724**	**5010**	**Europe**
Albania	26	19	10	6	4	...	...	...	...	...	Albanie
Austria	21	20	22	20	20	22	23	23	23	21	Autriche
Belarus	..	65	67	55	42	36	36	44	53	50	Bélarus
Bulgaria	17	16	16	17	22	29	22	17	11	9	Bulgarie
Croatia	..	16	14	9	9	8	9	7	7	...	Croatie
Denmark[5]	...	...	...	...	...	5	8	6	6	7	Danemark[5]
Czechoslovakia(former)	52	42	..	..	..	..	..	..	..	..	Tchécoslovaquie(anc.)
Czech Republic	..	..	26	21	33	45	64	76	67	56	République tchèque
Estonia	..	7	6	1	2	1	0	0	...	...	Estonie
Finland	10	12	13	13	15	23	17	...	...	...	Finlande
France	292	304	289	284	278	289	286	...	...	...	France
Germany	..	274	286	272	288	285	294	299	262	...	Allemagne
Germany(Fed.Rep.)	232	..	..	..	..	..	..	..	..	..	Allemagne(Rép.féd.)
German D.R.(former)	39	..	..	..	..	..	..	..	..	..	R.D.A. (anc.)
Greece	75	77	80	95	101	112	127	119	116	...	Grèce
Hungary	65	46	43	38	50	73	77	66	38	44	Hongrie
Italy	...	...	...	...	1675	1937	2672	2534	2546	2647	Italie
Latvia	..	12	8	1	3	3	2	4	3	3	Lettonie
Lithuania	..	13	11	7	6	5	3	3	3	3	Lituanie
Poland	65	66	70	60	68	74	105	112	119	109	Pologne
Portugal	65	62	17	19	19	14	13	19	17	39	Portugal
Republic of Moldova	..	27	16	[6]13	[6]8	[6]11	[6]12	[6]10	[6]11		Rép. de Moldova

For general note and footnotes, see end of table.

Voir la fin du tableau pour la remarque générale et les notes.

195

Macaroni and noodle products, uncooked (continued)
Pâtes alimentaires (suite)

ISIC-BASED CODE - CODE BASE CITI
3117-01

Unit : Thousand metric tons

Unité : Milliers de tonnes métriques

Country or area	1990	1991	1992	1993	1994	1995	1996	1997	1998	1999	Pays ou zone
Romania	55	48	31	26	31	39	38	37	42	41	Roumanie
Russian Federation	..	1115	1102	836	680	603	444	453	554	707	Fédération de Russie
Slovakia	..	..	34	16	21	22	26	22	19	18	Slovaquie
Slovenia	..	1	5	6	7	6	15	13	13	13	Slovénie
Spain	94	110	127	156	185	200	221	238	233	228	Espagne
Sweden	21	24	20	21	22	20	28	32	24	23	Suède
Switzerland	67	69	68	70	70	70	...	...	...	...	Suisse
Ukraine	..	365	350	340	253	224	172	142	165	154	Ukraine
Yugoslavia	..	31	26	19	23	27	20	18	20	20	Yougoslavie
T.F.Yug.Rep. Macedonia	..	2	1	1	1	1	1	1	1	1	L'ex-RY Macédoine
USSR (former)	1842	..	..	..	..	..	..	..	..	..	URSS (anc.)
Total	**8169**	**8408**	**8568**	**8385**	**7829**	**8252**	**8941**	**9250**	**9842**	**9751**	**Total**

General Note.

Uncooked products made generally from semolina or wheat flour doughs by extrusion, moulding or rolling. "Couscous" made of hard wheat semolina, steamed and dried, is included. Stuffed dough products (for example, ravioli, tortellini etc.) and cooked macaroni, spaghetti etc. are excluded. (SITC, Rev.3: 04830-0).

Remarque générale.

Produits non cuits généralement préparés par extrusion, pressage ou laminage à partir de pâte de semoule ou de farine de blé. Cette rubrique comprend le couscous, préparé à partir de semoule de blé dur traitée à la vapeur et séchée, mais non les produits farcis (raviolis, tortellinis etc.) ni les pâtes cuites. (CTCI, Rev.3: 04830-0).

[1] Twelve months ending 7 July of the year stated.
[2] Twelve months beginning 1 April of year stated.
[3] Twelve months ending 31 March of year stated.
[4] Beginning 1999, series discontinued.
[5] Sales.
[6] Excluding Transnistria region.

[1] Période de douze mois finissant le 7 juillet de l'année indiquée.
[2] Période de douze mois commençant le 1er avril de l'année indiquée.
[3] Période de douze mois finissant le 31 mars de l'année indiquée.
[4] A partir de 1999, série abandonnée.
[5] Ventes.
[6] Non compris la région de Transnistria.

Bread, ships' biscuits and other ordinary bakers' wares
Pain, biscuits de mer et autres produits de boulangerie ordinaire

ISIC-BASED CODE - CODE BASE CITI

3117-04

Unit : Thousand metric tons

Unité : Milliers de tonnes métriques

Country or area	1990	1991	1992	1993	1994	1995	1996	1997	1998	1999	Pays ou zone
Africa	**1325**	**1351**	**1390**	**1373**	**1383**	**1329**	**1315**	**1362**	**1348**	**1373**	**Afrique**
Algeria	3	4	3	...	...	...	...	...	...	...	Algérie
Angola	45	38	21	...	...	...	...	...	...	...	Angola
Cape Verde	4	4	...	...	...	...	...	...	...	...	Cap-Vert
Ethiopia[1]	...	56	35	22	12	19	20	21	27	19	Ethiopie[1]
Gabon	...	...	8	6	6	5	...	...	...	...	Gabon
Kenya[1]	99	95	99	96	156	66	67	...	...	...	Kenya[1]
South Africa[1]	1134	1148	1221	1207	1167	1197	1180	1213	1197	1233	Afrique du Sud[1]
America, North	**425**	**452**	**478**	**474**	**483**	**530**	**529**	**554**	**584**	**590**	**Amérique du Nord**
Mexico	...	...	...	446	454	503	506	527	557	563	Mexique
Panama	21	...	32	28	29	...	23	...	...	...	Panama
America, South	**74**	**118**	**105**	**119**	**115**	**145**	**126**	**149**	**116**	**178**	**Amérique du Sud**
Bolivia	1	1	2	2	2	*2	...	...	...	...	Bolivie
Colombia	56	...	77	83	84	88	...	97	97	...	Colombie
Ecuador	17	...	26	34	29	55	41	50	17	...	Equateur
Asia	**1763**	**6782**	**7075**	**7111**	**6729**	**5218**	**4744**	**4617**	**4236**	**4035**	**Asie**
Armenia	..	441	424	334	360	296	372	374	373	372	Arménie
Azerbaijan	..	699	872	947	854	752	652	659	663	669	Azerbaïdjan
Cyprus	*55	*55	55	55	57	59	58	59	59	58	Chypre
Georgia	..	...	760	639	498	296	262	199	173	114	Géorgie
Indonesia	118	198	132	30	50	40	...	81	45	...	Indonésie
Japan[2]	1193	1193	1180	1182	1221	1220	1230	1221	1232	1250	Japon[2]
Kazakhstan	..	1351	1518	1591	1508	853	631	559	515	451	Kazakhstan
Korea, Republic of	265	287	260	266	254	258	270	244	216	224	Corée, République de
Kuwait	...	...	64	70	71	72	74	76	76	77	Koweït
Kyrgyzstan	..	259	274	287	154	91	72	70	70	135	Kirghizistan
Mongolia	63	61	61	46	34	37	30	20	19	15	Mongolie
Tajikistan	..	247	217	194	176	372	287	342	411	370	Tadjikistan
Turkmenistan	..	171	208	232	248	267	206	143	126	...	Turkménistan
Uzbekistan	..	1235	1041	1231	1237	598	506	563	...	...	Ouzbékistan
Yemen	..	9	9	7	7	7	7	7	...	...	Yémen
Europe	**17320**	**46059**	**41129**	**36321**	**32542**	**31127**	**29564**	**27738**	**26930**	**27044**	**Europe**
Albania	378	377	263	138	32	20	147	87	61	0	Albanie
Austria	...	...	...	...	...	232	253	257	298	296	Autriche
Belarus	..	1547	1506	1494	1345	1037	992	955	949	966	Bélarus
Belgium	...	...	...	...	186	195	205	229	249	290	Belgique
Bulgaria	1527	1359	1093	1152	1077	1066	1042	890	817	447	Bulgarie
Croatia	..	206	203	185	172	166	149	160	144	...	Croatie
Denmark[3]	290	...	...	344	...	155	214	183	168	149	Danemark[3]
Czechoslovakia(former)	1351	1199	..	..	..	..	..	..	..	..	Tchécoslovaquie(anc.)
Czech Republic	..	..	586	566	576	591	636	631	625	623	République tchèque
Estonia	..	149	139	112	109	99	94	87	81	77	Estonie
Finland	191	191	180	182	185	174	180	198	211	214	Finlande
Germany	..	2086	2032	2015	2047	2560	2704	...	...	...	Allemagne
Germany(Fed.Rep.)[1]	1644	..	..	..	..	..	..	..	..	..	Allemagne(Rép.féd.)[1]
Greece	...	...	...	43	46	57	94	105	122	...	Grèce
Hungary	831	725	584	452	340	353	294	296	...	...	Hongrie
Iceland	11	11	11	...	...	...	...	...	...	...	Islande
Latvia	..	293	239	179	161	145	137	132	125	126	Lettonie
Lithuania	..	320	295	280	240	215	203	192	192	186	Lituanie
Netherlands[3][4]	301	191	212	230	...	...	...	...	...	...	Pays-Bas[3][4]
Poland	3129	2775	2634	2707	2750	2750	2915	3194	3449	3674	Pologne
Portugal	325	309	350	375	403	325	291	279	284	307	Portugal
Republic of Moldova	..	513	450	[5]350	[5]251	[5]195	[5]195	[5]179	[5]139	[5]103	Rép. de Moldova
Romania	2988	2558	2504	2145	2129	2271	2425	2258	1987	2130	Roumanie
Russian Federation	..	18845	16834	15030	12417	11336	9851	8832	8459	9160	Fédération de Russie
Slovakia	..	..	236	230	188	260	196	204	149	151	Slovaquie
Slovenia	..	99	97	93	88	86	89	80	87	82	Slovénie
Spain	[6]1603	[6]1718	[6]1685	679	767	844	916	875	922	1007	Espagne
Sweden	302	299	346	335	297	317	...	...	475	479	Suède

For general note and footnotes, see end of table.

Voir la fin du tableau pour la remarque générale et les notes.

Bread, ships' biscuits and other ordinary bakers' wares (continued)
Pain, biscuits de mer et autres produits de boulangerie ordinaire (suite)

ISIC-BASED CODE - CODE BASE CITI

3117-04

Unit : Thousand metric tons   Unité : Milliers de tonnes métriques

Country or area	1990	1991	1992	1993	1994	1995	1996	1997	1998	1999	Pays ou zone
Ukraine	..	6685	6441	5444	4816	4114	3452	3060	2676	2505	Ukraine
United Kingdom	2103	2115	...	658	776	853	856	882	812	...	Royaume-Uni
Yugoslavia	..	797	332	400	374	376	360	310	312	328	Yougoslavie
T.F.Yug.Rep. Macedonia	..	96	112	99	95	90	73	73	71	72	L'ex-RY Macédoine
USSR (former)	32599	..	..	..	..	..	..	..	..	..	URSS (anc.)
Total	**53506**	**54762**	**50177**	**45399**	**41252**	**38348**	**36278**	**34421**	**33215**	**33221**	**Total**

General Note.

Ordinary bakers' wares (including wholemeal bread and ships' biscuits), that is, containing only normal bread ingredients (cereal flours, leavens, salt) in terms of baked weight. Bakers' wares containing added sugar, honey, eggs, fats, cheeses, fruit or cocoa are excluded. (SITC, Rev.3: 04849-1).

Remarque générale.

Produits de boulangerie ordinaire (y compris le pain entier et les biscuits de mer), c'est-à-dire contenant seulement les ingrédients normaux du pain (farines de céréales, levures, sel). Cette position ne comprend pas les produits de boulangerie additionnés de sucre, de miel, d'oeufs, de matières grasses, de fromage, de fruits ou de cacao. Poids en tonnes métriques de produits cuits. (CTCI, Rev.3: 04849-1).

[1] Bread only.
[2] Quantity of wheat flour used for making bread.
[3] Sales.
[4] Production by establishments employing 20 or more persons.
[5] Excluding Transnistria region.
[6] Including bakery products containing added eggs, milk and some other ingredients.

[1] Pain seulement.
[2] Quantité de farine de froment destinée à la panification.
[3] Ventes.
[4] Production des établissements occupant 20 personnes ou plus.
[5] Non compris la région de Transnistria.
[6] Y compris les produits de boulangerie contenant des oeufs, du lait et autres ingrédients.

Biscuits
Biscuits

ISIC-BASED CODE - CODE BASE CITI

3117-07

Unit : Thousand metric tons   Unité : Milliers de tonnes métriques

Country or area	1990	1991	1992	1993	1994	1995	1996	1997	1998	1999	Pays ou zone
Africa	**134**	**132**	**139**	**144**	**104**	**149**	**151**	**152**	**158**	**151**	**Afrique**
Algeria	2.2	3.9	2.3	...	...	...	...	...	...	...	Algérie
Egypt[1]	55.6	59.0	61.7	64.2	24.7	66.4	68.3	65.3	...	...	Egypte[1]
Ethiopia[2]	0.1	0.3	0.3	0.2	6.8	9.7	7.8	6.7	10.6	9.1	Ethiopie[2]
Kenya	2.4	3.8	2.1	2.3	3.9	5.0	5.1	...	...	...	Kenya
Madagascar	...	...	...	...	1.2	1.1	1.4	2.0	1.2	...	Madagascar
Mali	...	...	...	0.1	...	...	...	...	...	...	Mali
Mauritania	2.7	2.8	3.5	4.4	...	...	...	...	...	...	Mauritanie
Nigeria	21.4	20.6	29.6	30.0	22.4	22.7					Nigéria
South Africa	47.6	39.9	37.8	39.1	38.9	37.9	37.0	40.2	47.2	40.1	Afrique du Sud
United Rep.Tanzania	1.1	0.7	0.5	0.4	0.2	0.2	0.1	0.3	...	...	Rép. Unie de Tanzanie
America, North	**276**	**268**	**266**	**349**	**392**	**407**	**391**	**376**	**398**	**428**	**Amérique du Nord**
Barbados	3.8	3.4	3.4	3.8	3.5	4.6	4.4	4.7	5.6	6.2	Barbade
Mexico	265.6	256.8	256.1	336.5	379.4	395.1	379.3	360.8	381.5	409.5	Mexique
Panama	6.2	...	6.1	8.9	8.7	7.0	6.9	...	...	...	Panama
America, South	**212**	**231**	**207**	**205**	**221**	**232**	**238**	**250**	**249**	**247**	**Amérique du Sud**
Bolivia	2.7	3.1	3.2	3.5	2.5	*2.3	...	...	...	...	Bolivie
Chile	36.8	46.7	40.9	43.3	44.9	41.0	45.8	43.5	43.3	42.4	Chili
Colombia	...	...	85.7	85.2	99.2	112.8	...	120.0	117.5	...	Colombie
Ecuador	18.3	...	3.0	2.2	3.4	4.7	15.0	12.3	14.3	...	Equateur
Guyana	1.1	0.9	1.2	1.9	1.8	...	...	...	...	...	Guyana
Paraguay	59.1	74.7	72.8	...	...	...	...	...	...	...	Paraguay
Asia	**1477**	**1724**	**2054**	**1583**	**1577**	**1619**	**1596**	**1424**	**1387**	**1576**	**Asie**
Armenia	..	3.9	2.3	0.7	1.6	1.3	0.3	0.2	0.2	0.3	Arménie
Azerbaijan	..	37.8	15.7	9.9	3.6	0.2	0.0	0.1	0.3	0.2	Azerbaïdjan
Hong Kong SAR[3]	21.0	14.2	16.1	12.3	...	10.5	10.3	...	6.1	6.4	Hong-Kong RAS[3]
Cyprus	...		1.2	...		1.8	1.9	2.0	2.6	2.1	Chypre
India[4]	664.2	635.5	619.1	630.2	652.3	672.7	621.2	607.8	704.5	780.3	Inde[4]
Indonesia	168.3	213.2	604.4	119.2	143.2	138.7	...	183.1	72.4	...	Indonésie
Iran(Islamic Rep. of)	...	82.6	...	...	...	...	...	...	...	...	Iran(Rép. islamique)
Japan	245.0	250.0	250.0	250.0	231.0	225.0	...	22.6	21.9	219.0	Japon
Kazakhstan	..	64.0	55.6	35.8	23.6	8.3	9.1	9.2	14.9	17.0	Kazakhstan
Kuwait	...	...	1.0	2.0	2.0	1.7	2.0	1.9	1.9	1.5	Koweït
Kyrgyzstan	..	18.6	11.0	10.6	5.5	5.4	2.0	1.2	1.6	1.4	Kirghizistan
Malaysia	75.0	83.3	92.6	93.8	99.5	108.8	114.9	107.0	109.3	122.4	Malaisie
Mongolia	41.6	33.4	17.0	12.0	10.8	10.8	11.3	12.5	10.6	8.0	Mongolie
Myanmar[5]	8.6	8.7	9.1	9.4	8.8	8.6	1.4	1.1	1.6	1.1	Myanmar[5]
Nepal[6]	...	...	5.5	6.5	6.3	6.8	6.1	6.9	9.1	11.8	Népal[6]
Syrian Arab Republic	17.0	19.8	16.8	14.3	13.9	14.0	12.6	11.6	11.5	...	Rép. arabe syrienne
Tajikistan	..	8.0	2.0	3.0	0.9	0.4	...	...	...	...	Tadjikistan
Thailand	9.5	10.6	...	...	...	...	...	...	...	...	Thaïlande
Turkey	134.9	154.2	162.3	184.1	193.6	239.9	266.2	300.3	283.4	255.8	Turquie
Turkmenistan	..	4.0	2.0	4.0	5.2	3.4	0.8	4.4	4.4	...	Turkménistan
Yemen	..	73.0	77.0	91.0	69.0	67.7	47.0	47.0	...	...	Yémen
Europe	**2201**	**3379**	**3134**	**2981**	**2863**	**2880**	**2924**	**2962**	**3064**	**2921**	**Europe**
Austria	52.9	63.5	54.3	51.7	54.5	49.2	53.0	43.6	44.3	55.1	Autriche
Belarus	..	25.5	27.7	23.7	18.7	14.3	16.0	23.6	28.1	30.9	Bélarus
Belgium	190.1	203.9	198.5	201.9	171.1	185.7	198.3	200.4	200.1	170.1	Belgique
Bulgaria	28.1	16.3	17.3	18.0	18.1	16.2	13.6	9.0	19.5	24.6	Bulgarie
Croatia		20.3	13.5	11.5	11.5	11.5	11.8	21.7	21.4	...	Croatie
Czechoslovakia(former)	98.8	89.5	..	..	..	..	..	..	..	..	Tchécoslovaquie(anc.)
Estonia	..	5.1	2.4	1.8	2.2	1.8	2.2	1.9	1.8	1.9	Estonie
Finland	17.6	17.8	19.2	24.6	23.8	24.8	20.0	17.0	16.8	14.4	Finlande
France	460.8	476.8	477.2	472.3	468.3	487.1	511.3	521.0	517.0	...	France
Germany	..	...	...	...	...	383.3	392.8	400.6	...	...	Allemagne
German D.R.(former)	40.8	..	..	..	..	..	..	..	..	..	R.D.A. (anc.)
Greece	22.9	22.3	22.9	21.0	23.2	18.5	18.5	23.4	24.8	...	Grèce
Iceland	0.7	0.6	0.6	0.7	0.8	...	0.8	0.7	0.8	0.8	Islande
Latvia	..	12.9	...	4.0	5.0	4.9	6.0	7.0	7.4	4.5	Lettonie
Lithuania	..	12.0	9.0	5.4	4.0	4.8	5.3	8.1	9.9	10.1	Lituanie

For general note and footnotes, see end of table.   Voir la fin du tableau pour la remarque générale et les notes.

Biscuits (continued)
Biscuits (suite)

ISIC-BASED CODE - CODE BASE CITI

3117-07

Unit : Thousand metric tons   Unité : Milliers de tonnes métriques

Country or area	1990	1991	1992	1993	1994	1995	1996	1997	1998	1999	Pays ou zone
Netherlands [7] [8]	[9]236.7	[9]190.6	[9]200.5	161.0	172.0	166.0	176.0	190.0	199.0	181.4	Pays-Bas [7] [8]
Norway	6.9	6.6	6.2	8.1	...	...	...	...	...	...	Norvège
Portugal	38.3	35.6	19.2	18.5	20.6	19.8	26.7	23.8	26.2	25.4	Portugal
Republic of Moldova	..	14.5	6.5	[10]4.8	[10]1.6	[10]1.4	[10]1.2	[10]1.3	[10]5.0	[10]4.0	Rép. de Moldova
Romania	66.2	53.5	40.2	39.9	54.1	66.6	62.7	54.2	71.7	65.9	Roumanie
Russian Federation	..	554.5	430.6	394.4	338.9	289.6	258.0	264.8	276.6	333.1	Fédération de Russie
Slovakia	..	..	22.8	23.6	27.2	24.8	28.9	...	21.0	20.9	Slovaquie
Slovenia	..	1.2	1.5	1.8	3.2	3.2	3.6	3.4	3.3	3.4	Slovénie
Spain	225.3	206.7	228.3	211.8	215.1	220.8	227.9	272.7	280.6	281.1	Espagne
Sweden	28.2	27.6	27.3	27.6	30.5	30.7	28.8	30.2	29.3	32.0	Suède
Switzerland	[7]36.4	[7]35.1	[7]36.8	[7]38.0	[7]35.8	[7]35.6	[7]35.3	36.5	41.0	45.3	Suisse
Ukraine	..	177.9	152.6	143.2	90.5	64.4	52.0	59.3	80.7	106.7	Ukraine
United Kingdom	649.9	670.7	674.9	653.6	641.3	707.8	726.6	...	688.5	...	Royaume-Uni
Yugoslavia	..	41.9	41.1	22.8	28.4	35.9	36.1	36.7	47.5	50.8	Yougoslavie
T.F.Yug.Rep. Macedonia	..	3.9	4.0	3.1	3.7	3.7	3.6	2.9	2.8	2.7	L'ex-RY Macédoine
USSR (former)	1053.3	..	..	..	..	..	..	..	..	..	URSS (anc.)
Oceania	137	140	146	141	139	145	144	146	147	148	Océanie
Australia	132.7	136.4	142.2	139.3	135.9	141.8	139.5	...	...	...	Australie
Fiji	4.2	3.9	3.8	1.4	3.5	3.7	4.0	3.0	3.6	...	Fidji
Total	5489	5874	5945	5404	5297	5432	5443	5309	5405	5470	Total

General Note.
Fine bakers' wares without leavening made from flour, sugar and shortening, usually crisp, dry and hard and in the form of small flat thin cakes, in terms of baked weight. Ships' biscuits, crisp bread, matzos and rusks are excluded. (SITC, Rev.3: 04842-1).

Remarque générale.
Produits de boulangerie fine préparés sans levain à partir de farine, sucre et corps gras, généralement croustillants, secs et durs et se présentant sous forme de petits gâteaux plats. Cette rubrique ne comprend pas les biscuits de mer, le pain dur, le pain azyme et les biscottes. Poids en tonnes métriques de produits cuits. (CTCI, Rev.3: 04842-1).

[1] Including biscuits with chocolate and rusk.
[2] Twelve months ending 7 July of the year stated.
[3] 1997 data are confidential.
[4] Production by large and medium scale establishments only.
[5] Twelve months ending 31 March of year stated.
[6] Twelve months beginning 16 July of year stated.
[7] Sales.
[8] Production by establishments employing 20 or more persons.
[9] Including pastry, cakes and other fine bakers" wares.
[10] Excluding Transnistria region.

[1] Y compris les biscuits et les biscottes.
[2] Période de douze mois finissant le 7 juillet de l'année indiquée.
[3] Pour 1997, les données sont confidentielles.
[4] Production des grandes et moyennes entreprises seulement.
[5] Période de douze mois finissant le 31 mars de l'année indiquée.
[6] Période de douze mois commençant le 16 juillet de l'année indiquée.
[7] Ventes.
[8] Production des établissements occupant 20 personnes ou plus.
[9] Y compris pâtisseries, gâteaux, et autres produits de boulangerie.
[10] Non compris la région de Transnistria.

Pastry, cakes, and other fine bakers' wares
Pâtisseries, gâteaux et autres produits de boulangerie

ISIC-BASED CODE - CODE BASE CITI

3117-10

Unit : Thousand metric tons

Unité : Milliers de tonnes métriques

Country or area	1990	1991	1992	1993	1994	1995	1996	1997	1998	1999	Pays ou zone
Africa	**0**	**0**	**0**	**0**	**0**	**0**	**0**	**0**	**0**	**0**	**Afrique**
Kenya	0.1	0.1	0.1	0.2	0.2	0.2	...	...	...	...	Kenya
America, North	**131**	**138**	**145**	**149**	**168**	**147**	**154**	**163**	**192**	**194**	**Amérique du Nord**
Mexico	...	...	...	148.9	167.6	146.5	153.5	163.4	191.7	193.8	Mexique
America, South	**33**	**46**	**41**	**41**	**45**	**47**	**45**	**56**	**58**	**66**	**Amérique du Sud**
Colombia	24.5	...	32.8	33.3	37.8	39.2	...	47.8	50.1	...	Colombie
Peru	...	...	...	...	...	7.5	7.1	8.0	7.6	6.7	Pérou
Asia	**341**	**592**	**455**	**456**	**430**	**393**	**404**	**408**	**362**	**370**	**Asie**
Armenia	..	6.8	1.7	1.2	2.6	3.9	1.9	1.5	1.0	0.8	Arménie
Azerbaijan	..	11.4	3.4	2.8	1.1	0.1	0.2	0.0	0.0	0.0	Azerbaïdjan
Georgia	..	...	1.1	0.9	0.3	0.2	0.2	0.1	0.1	0.1	Géorgie
Indonesia	52.5	...	25.2	...	...	17.1	...	17.5	13.9	...	Indonésie
Korea, Republic of[1]	287.8	299.0	299.7	318.4	330.0	327.2	...	...	...	...	Corée, République de[1]
Kyrgyzstan	..	11.8	11.4	2.9	2.7	2.1	2.3	1.1	1.3	1.2	Kirghizistan
Tajikistan	..	48.8	12.6	12.1	4.3	1.0	0.6	0.4	0.3	0.1	Tadjikistan
Turkey	0.2	...	0.0	0.3	1.1	3.7	3.3	5.0	4.8	16.0	Turquie
Turkmenistan	..	20.0	14.0	16.0	5.0	3.0	2.3	2.5	4.2	...	Turkménistan
Uzbekistan	..	164.0	86.1	76.2	57.9	34.8	39.6	47.4	...	...	Ouzbékistan
Europe	**2815**	**5141**	**4603**	**4705**	**4097**	**3978**	**4038**	**4218**	**4318**	**4436**	**Europe**
Austria	29.7	32.5	35.4	36.6	39.0	#68.5	68.3	65.5	73.0	83.7	Autriche
Belarus	..	17.7	9.6	9.8	8.9	6.4	6.9	7.6	10.3	9.4	Bélarus
Belgium	...	...	...	...	35.0	42.5	41.5	42.4	48.7	57.4	Belgique
Croatia	..	3.1	2.8	2.4	2.9	3.2	3.0	5.3	5.8	...	Croatie
Czechoslovakia(former)	43.5	25.4	..	..	..	..	..	..	..	..	Tchécoslovaquie(anc.)
Czech Republic	..	..	14.7	15.1	...	...	...	...	...	...	République tchèque
Estonia	..	5.3	2.6	1.8	3.2	2.3	3.4	3.4	2.4	2.7	Estonie
Finland	72.3	69.6	68.0	69.9	72.2	68.7	72.1	43.4	45.9	43.1	Finlande
France	115.2	122.2	124.2	125.7	120.1	129.9	130.9	...	...	...	France
Germany	...	...	...	...	...	557.9	578.9	677.9	...	...	Allemagne
Greece	...	...	...	7.0	7.5	8.4	8.6	9.2	11.1	...	Grèce
Hungary	34.1	66.0	64.0	53.2	54.2	53.3	76.4	82.2	84.7	107.3	Hongrie
Iceland	3.7	3.4	3.6	...	...	...	...	#0.0	...	...	Islande
Latvia	..	1.3	...	2.7	5.1	5.9	7.1	9.3	9.6	11.4	Lettonie
Netherlands[2][3]	...	...	...	148.0	180.0	183.0	188.0	204.0	...	...	Pays-Bas[2][3]
Portugal	...	...	22.4	46.0	48.3	32.8	35.7	35.6	35.4	40.2	Portugal
Republic of Moldova	..	9.0	4.2	[4]3.1	[4]1.4	[4]1.8	[4]2.5	[4]3.1	[4]3.1	[4]3.3	Rép. de Moldova
Romania	98.7	53.8	23.7	10.5	10.2	18.8	28.3	35.9	15.8	11.1	Roumanie
Russian Federation	..	1446.7	998.5	906.3	815.1	391.5	346.0	374.1	444.1	471.9	Fédération de Russie
Slovakia	..	..	4.1	13.9	9.4	11.8	28.9	31.7	73.5	...	Slovaquie
Slovenia	..	2.3	1.7	1.7	1.9	2.1	4.8	6.2	7.1	8.2	Slovénie
Spain	[5]290.0	[5]314.0	[5]307.9	241.1	335.6	375.2	407.4	443.1	477.4	496.1	Espagne
Sweden	...	...	...	...	...	...	...	...	420.7	425.3	Suède
Ukraine	..	220.6	183.3	131.4	94.2	65.5	50.9	57.7	65.5	80.8	Ukraine
United Kingdom	...	...	...	1808.6	1206.7	...	...	...	...	...	Royaume-Uni
Yugoslavia	..	0.3	0.1	0.1	0.1	0.1	0.1	0.1	0.1	0.1	Yougoslavie
T.F.Yug.Rep. Macedonia	..	0.9	0.6	0.4	0.3	0.2	0.1	0.1	0.1	0.1	L'ex-RY Macédoine
Oceania	**210**	**210**	**210**	**210**	**210**	**210**	**210**	**210**	**210**	**210**	**Océanie**
Australia	209.6	...	...	...	...	...	...	...	...	...	Australie
Total	**3528**	**6126**	**5453**	**5560**	**4950**	**4774**	**4850**	**5055**	**5139**	**5276**	**Total**

General Note.

Bakery products containing sugar, honey, eggs, fats, cheese, fruit, or cocoa, in terms of baked weight. Products containing meat and fish are excluded. (SITC, Rev.3: 04849-2).

Remarque générale.

Produits de boulangerie contenant un ou plusieurs des ingrédients suivants: sucre, miel, oeufs, matières grasses, fromage, fruits, cacao, à l'exclusion des produits contenant de la viande ou du poisson. Poids en tonnes métriques de produits cuits. (CTCI, Rev.3: 04849-2).

[1] Including biscuits.
[2] Sales.
[3] Production by establishments employing 20 or more persons.
[4] Excluding Transnistria region.
[5] Excluding bakery products containing eggs, milk and some other ingredients.

[1] Y compris les biscuits.
[2] Ventes.
[3] Production des établissements occupant 20 personnes ou plus.
[4] Non compris la région de Transnistrie.
[5] Non compris les produits de boulangerie contenant des oeufs, du lait et autres ingrédients.

Farinaceous preparations (ravioli, tortellini etc.)
Préparations à base de pâtes alimentaires

ISIC-BASED CODE - CODE BASE CITI
3117-13

Unit : Metric tons   Unité : Tonnes métriques

Country or area	1990	1991	1992	1993	1994	1995	1996	1997	1998	1999	Pays ou zone
Africa	**1080**	**1094**	**1159**	**1175**	**1127**	**1127**	**1127**	**1127**	**1127**	**1127**	**Afrique**
Burkina Faso	1080	1094	1159	1175	...	...	...	...	...	...	Burkina Faso
America, North	**31998**	**33308**	**26745**	**27134**	**25545**	**23222**	**21314**	**19406**	**17498**	**15590**	**Amérique du Nord**
Mexico	31998	33308	26745	27134	25545	...	...	...	...	...	Mexique
America, South	**60870**	**116504**	**134807**	**130374**	**125577**	**130891**	**129119**	**172854**	**178671**	**177699**	**Amérique du Sud**
Colombia	24052	...	97989	93556	88759	94073	...	...	...	...	Colombie
Ecuador	...	...	...	...	...	...	14465	49457	46532	...	Equateur
Asia	**1068**	**9068**	**2876**	**4068**	**1950**	**1702**	**1068**	**1068**	**1068**	**1068**	**Asie**
Cyprus	...	...	876	...	...	1260	...	...	...	...	Chypre
Tajikistan	..	8000	2000	3000	882	442	...	...	...	...	Tadjikistan
Europe	**547301**	**882850**	**937700**	**1010820**	**847677**	**897296**	**1239207**	**1440193**	**1535530**	**1659690**	**Europe**
Austria	...	...	...	...	...	4818	5162	5173	5121	6884	Autriche
Belarus	..	76114	58083	51432	44055	31982	38258	54126	67005	69120	Bélarus
Belgium	...	...	...	...	34168	23184	32422	33621	39583	36246	Belgique
Croatia	..	1830	1141	3449	4633	3325	2615	#68	44	...	Croatie
Finland	3582	3979	3071	2397	2550	3007	3316	3809	3788	3879	Finlande
France	93651	94509	96912	94212	95700	95841	101487	...	...	...	France
Germany	..	...	...	...	...	...	...	...	99662	...	Allemagne
Greece	718	666	38	...	...	...	...	...	...	...	Grèce
Hungary	...	...	...	...	...	...	...	7328	40716	10060	Hongrie
Italy	...	...	...	...	253322	290971	631375	823054	823443	861001	Italie
Latvia	..	...	...	...	...	...	...	...	...	1844	Lettonie
Norway	...	...	...	...	...	7622	11870	12200	11243	...	Norvège
Portugal	...	...	44317	48982	39886	41338	49679	55581	60171	37989	Portugal
Republic of Moldova	..	8955	...	...	...	...	...	...	...	...	Rép. de Moldova
Slovakia	..	...	...	...	...	...	...	...	5033	320	Slovaquie
Slovenia	..	8869	7173	7178	8044	6549	#181	192	680	761	Slovénie
Spain	...	...	...	7463	13785	16186	17800	21920	...	...	Espagne
Sweden	1317	1463	1379	1460	1380	1632	3804	4713	4818	6246	Suède
United Kingdom	141648	...	...	209171	202236	237861	208258	204295	236247	...	Royaume-Uni
Oceania	**19462**	**19462**	**19462**	**19462**	**19462**	**19462**	**19462**	**19462**	**19462**	**19462**	**Océanie**
Australia	19462	...	...	...	...	...	...	...	...	...	Australie
Total	**661779**	**1062286**	**1122749**	**1193033**	**1021338**	**1073700**	**1411297**	**1654110**	**1753355**	**1874635**	**Total**

General Note.
Cooked stuffed dough products, such as ravioli, tortellini, cannelloni and the like, consisting of pastas of the macaroni type, ready for consumption after heating. (SITC 09909-2).

Remarque générale.
Produits cuits de pâte farcie, tels que raviolis, tortellinis, cannellonis et autres produits analogues, faits en pâtes alimentaires, prêts à la consommation après chauffage. (CTCI 09909-2).

Raw sugar
Sucre brut

ISIC-BASED CODE - CODE BASE CITI

3118-01

Unit : Thousand metric tons

Unité : Milliers de tonnes métriques

Country or area	1990	1991	1992	1993	1994	1995	1996	1997	1998	1999	Pays ou zone
Africa	**6678**	**6787**	**5868**	**5382**	**6255**	**6559**	**7572**	**7812**	**8438**	**8204**	**Afrique**
Angola* [1]	25	30	25	20	20	30	25	28	32	32	Angola* [1]
Benin [1]	3	3	4	3	3	2	3	4	5	4	Bénin [1]
Burkina Faso [1]	*27	*31	*31	*34	*31	31	31	31	31	31	Burkina Faso [1]
Burundi* [1]	11	16	18	16	13	17	19	20	22	23	Burundi* [1]
Cameroon [1]	69	60	65	*57	*60	*53	*44	*46	*52	*54	Cameroun [1]
Central African Rep. [1]	7	5	*3	*8	*8	*9	*9	*9	*10	10	Rép. centrafricaine [1]
Chad	47	27	26	25	27	26	[1]30	[1]30	[1]28	[1]28	Tchad
Congo	23	20	27	28	26	38	42	39	43	40	Congo
Côte d'Ivoire [1]	141	150	151	141	128	119	121	131	115	115	Côte d'Ivoire [1]
Dem. Rep. of Congo [1]	99	103	89	86	79	90	81	*50	*51	*65	Rép. dém. du Congo [1]
Egypt [1]	*971	*1064	*1077	*1093	*1195	*1230	*1222	1170	1242	1350	Egypte [1]
Ethiopia,incl.Eritrea [1]	186	155	162	...	...	...	...	...	...	...	Ethiopie,incl.Erythrée [1]
Ethiopia [2]	171	143	150	137	123	129	172	172	173	235	Ethiopie [2]
Gabon* [1]	20	22	18	17	16	15	16	17	16	17	Gabon* [1]
Guinea [1]	*20	*20	*16	*20	*19	19	19	19	19	19	Guinée [1]
Kenya	443	426	377	375	303	384	401	[1]391	[3]488	[3]512	Kenya
Liberia [1]	5	4	4	4	4	4	4	4	4	4	Libéria [1]
Madagascar	111	108	92	71	79	90	102	74	60	...	Madagascar
Malawi	189	191	200	114	185	132	95	105	107	113	Malawi
Mali	22	31	31	24	27	25	25	* [3]26	* [3]32	* [3]31	Mali
Mauritius	580	556	572	502	460	533	[1]589	[3]658	[3]667	[3]396	Maurice
Morocco	244	239	221	254	241	455	400	406	459	448	Maroc
Mozambique	34	27	[1]30	[1]17	[1]21	[1]34	[1]32	* [3]42	[3]39	[3]46	Mozambique
Niger [1]	9	8	10	6	6	10	14	17	13	15	Niger [1]
Nigeria [1]	*59	45	*45	*50	35	32	35	35	35	35	Nigéria [1]
Réunion [1]	193	215	227	184	177	195	205	207	*195	*234	Réunion [1]
Rwanda [1]	3	3	2	*5	*1	*1	*1	*1	*1	4	Rwanda [1]
Senegal [1]	*90	*90	*90	*86	96	96	98	96	99	99	Sénégal [1]
Sierra Leone [1]	6	*6	*4	*2	*5	2	2	2	2	2	Sierra Leone [1]
Somalia* [1]	25	30	28	15	20	20	21	18	19	21	Somalie* [1]
South Africa	1153	1366	757	568	883	804	1828	1735	2140	1778	Afrique du Sud
Sudan [1]	*421	443	470	423	428	459	500	*544	610	644	Soudan [1]
Swaziland	497	490	495	432	497	414	[1]471	[1]476	[1]475	[1]534	Swaziland
Togo [3]	5	5	5	5	5	5	3	3	3	3	Togo [3]
Tunisia	18	15	21	19	18	20	17	26	14	8	Tunisie
Uganda	29	42	54	49	59	*104	* [1]109	* [1]120	* [1]111	* [1]137	Ouganda
United Rep.Tanzania [1]	96	119	108	121	124	105	117	116	*80	114	Rép. Unie de Tanzanie [1]
Zambia* [1]	135	134	155	147	158	151	166	174	184	197	Zambie* [1]
Zimbabwe [1]	*493	*346	*9	56	*507	*512	337	602	595	583	Zimbabwe [1]
America, North	**20608**	**20420**	**20852**	**17262**	**16912**	**15358**	**16979**	**17910**	**17190**	**18105**	**Amérique du Nord**
Barbados	69	66	54	48	52	39	59	65	48	53	Barbade
Belize	102	104	102	102	107	107	111	126	121	...	Belize
Canada [1]	138	160	118	113	182	164	157	105	93	122	Canada [1]
Costa Rica [1]	230	259	284	300	319	326	349	328	376	*379	Costa Rica [1]
Cuba	8050	7233	[1]7013	[1]4302	[1]3997	[1]3328	[1]4446	[1]4252	[1]3229	[1]3783	Cuba
Dominican Republic	511	604	560	587	584	508	619	689	514	376	Rép. dominicaine
El Salvador [1]	213	273	346	324	323	311	310	399	502	500	El Salvador [1]
Guadeloupe [1]	26	53	38	63	58	33	49	57	38	38	Guadeloupe [1]
Guatemala	726	712	*943	[1]1049	1130	487	617	689	653	...	Guatemala
Haiti	20	22	[1]23	* [1]20	* [1]15	* [1]5	* [1]8	* [1]9	* [1]10	* [1]10	Haïti
Honduras [1]	185	177	182	177	160	187	227	241	247	190	Honduras [1]
Jamaica	208	234	228	219	224	249	236	233	183	...	Jamaïque
Martinique	6	6	6	7	7	7	[1]8	[1]7	...	...	Martinique
Mexico	[1]3278	[1]3365	[1]3290	2471	1990	2332	2596	2719	2907	2804	Mexique
Nicaragua [1]	201	220	224	200	244	298	348	353	331	390	Nicaragua [1]
Panama	50	60	82	93	76	58	110	* [3]166	* [3]181	* [3]177	Panama
Puerto Rico	68	74	67	64	50	46	33	27	15	3	Porto Rico
St. Kitts-Nevis	15	19	22	23	22	22	[1]20	* [1]30	* [1]24	[1]18	St-Kitts-Nevis
St. Vincent-Grenadines	[1]2	[1]2	[1]2	[1]2	[1]2	0	0	0	0	0	St. Vincent-Grenadines
Trinidad and Tobago	118	100	[1]110	105	131	117	92	[1]90	65	69	Trinité-et-Tobago
Turks and Caicos Islands	...	...	49	...	...	...	...	...	...	...	Iles Turques et Caiques
United States [1]	6344	6628	7110	6944	7191	6685	6536	7276	7596	8197	Etats-Unis [1]

For general note and footnotes, see end of table.

Voir la fin du tableau pour la remarque générale et les notes.

Raw sugar (continued)
Sucre brut (suite)

ISIC-BASED CODE - CODE BASE CITI

3118-01

Unit : Thousand metric tons

Unité : Milliers de tonnes métriques

Country or area	1990	1991	1992	1993	1994	1995	1996	1997	1998	1999	Pays ou zone
America, South	**13082**	**14349**	**12703**	**13307**	**15083**	**16941**	**17265**	**18285**	**20636**	**21232**	**Amérique du Sud**
Argentina	1243	1473	1282	1008	1110	1493	1290	[1]1649	[1]1749	[1]1578	Argentine
Bolivia	258	303	226	212	277	*332	[1]387	[1]382	[1]396	[1]390	Bolivie
Brazil	7900	8755	8655	8744	10952	11986	12231	13418	15321	16460	Brésil
Chile[1]	343	334	485	451	464	535	442	357	471	448	Chili[1]
Colombia	[1]1589	[1]1702	269	1197	459	662	...	508	565	...	Colombie
Ecuador[1]	*332	*326	*349	*341	*362	396	412	252	530	556	Equateur[1]
Guyana	130	145	247	247	257	*260	[1]280	[1]276	[1]256	[1]321	Guyana
Paraguay[1]	113	148	145	121	120	123	135	127	145	151	Paraguay[1]
Peru	592	558	439	401	541	643	603	674	449	*550	Pérou
Suriname[1]	3	*5	*5	*5	*7	*10	*7	*7	7	7	Suriname[1]
Uruguay*[1]	80	77	75	35	22	17	15	20	12	8	Uruguay*[1]
Venezuela	499	523	525	[1]545	[1]512	[1]484	[1]594	[1]614	[1]736	[1]763	Venezuela
Asia	**29097**	**33143**	**38254**	**34903**	**33804**	**37855**	**42034**	**39502**	**40487**	**42571**	**Asie**
Afghanistan[1]	*1	*1	*1	*1	*1	*1	*1	*1	*1	1	Afghanistan[1]
Bangladesh	* [1]200	224	165	* [1]204	* [1]241	* [1]294	* [1]200	* [1]147	* [1]181	* [1]166	Bangladesh
Cambodia[1]	16	12	9	9	15	14	11	12	8	9	Cambodge[1]
China	5820	6950	8309	7713	5921	5586	6402	7026	8260	8610	Chine
Georgia[1]	..	...	*3	2	1	2	0	0	0	0	Géorgie[1]
India	[3]12068	[3]13113	[3]13873	[3]11750	[3]11745	[3]15337	[1]18225	[1]14616	...	...	Inde
Indonesia	2253	2758	[1]2300	2483	[1]2421	[1]2105	[1]2160	[1]2187	1846	* [1]1600	Indonésie
Iran(Islamic Rep. of)*[1]	626	799	949	920	899	935	696	823	896	986	Iran(Rép. islamique)*[1]
Iraq[1]	*26	*6	*6	*2	*2	*2	*2	*2	2	2	Iraq[1]
Japan	422	352	387	790	767	844	716	808	175	188	Japon
Kazakhstan	..	307	213	164	97	113	120	148	230	228	Kazakhstan
Kyrgyzstan*[1]	..	...	13	20	15	18	25	26	36	42	Kirghizistan*[1]
Lebanon[1]	1	6	*27	*22	23	*29	*31	*32	*37	*40	Liban[1]
Malaysia[1]	105	95	*104	*106	*114	*102	*105	*108	*100	*105	Malaisie[1]
Myanmar[1]	36	21	58	54	47	43	45	52	61	*62	Myanmar[1]
Nepal[4]	30	45	55	64	34	49	67	63	67	76	Népal[4]
Pakistan*[1]	2017	2100	2528	2603	3177	3212	2643	2560	3817	3791	Pakistan*[1]
Philippines	1629	1847	1854	2020	* [1]1873	* [1]1705	* [1]1854	* [1]1893	* [1]1866	* [1]1682	Philippines
Sri Lanka	26	22	25	16	40	88	85	63	63	66	Sri Lanka
Syrian Arab Republic[1]	*51	*76	*99	*99	*113	*124	*80	86	96	95	Rép. arabe syrienne[1]
Thailand	1869	2192	5106	3750	[3]4168	[3]5447	[1]6087	[1]6188	[1]3921	[1]5630	Thaïlande
Turkey[1]	1579	1824	1805	1743	1727	1290	1842	2012	2530	2400	Turquie[1]
Uzbekistan[1]	..	...	0	0	0	0	0	0	*11	*23	Ouzbékistan[1]
Viet Nam	323	372	*365	[1]369	[1]364	[1]517	[1]637	[1]649	[1]736	[1]937	Viet Nam
Europe	**21417**	**29315**	**29040**	**29663**	**25458**	**23741**	**25251**	**25004**	**24246**	**26576**	**Europe**
Albania	15	3	1	0	0	*3	[1]4	0	0	0	Albanie
Austria[1]	*451	466	437	*520	*438	*481	*535	*529	*533	*545	Autriche[1]
Belarus*[1]	..	...	111	148	107	139	150	158	192	150	Bélarus*[1]
Belgium-Luxembourg[1]	1146	1049	1039	1118	1005	999	1036	1106	863	*1186	Belgique-Luxembourg[1]
Bosnia and Herzegovina[1]	..	..	*61	*52	*4	3	2	0	0	0	Bosnie-Herzégovine[1]
Bulgaria	201	181	165	187	298	258	318	124	132	272	Bulgarie
Croatia[1]	..	...	55	86	115	155	195	141	139	114	Croatie[1]
Denmark[5]	506	510	471	484	273	444	432	509	557	535	Danemark[5]
Czechoslovakia(former)	134	115	..	..	..	..	..	..	..	..	Tchécoslovaquie(anc.)
Czech Republic	..	..	124	103	54	59	72	51	36	...	République tchèque
Finland	42	14	29	27	28	20	8	...	...	...	Finlande
France[1]	4736	4413	4723	4724	4364	4564	4543	5134	4637	4914	France[1]
Germany	..	...	[1]4251	[1]4359	[1]3672	#148	186	327	160	...	Allemagne
Germany(Fed.Rep.)[1]	3396	..	..	..	..	..	..	..	..	..	Allemagne(Rép.féd.)[1]
German D.R.(former)	249	..	..	..	..	..	..	..	..	..	R.D.A. (anc.)
Greece[1]	304	262	320	*333	*271	*312	*288	*396	*220	*252	Grèce[1]
Hungary	564	666	399	393	440	480	[1]607	[1]520	[1]486	[1]368	Hongrie
Ireland*[1]	245	232	242	191	232	242	247	223	238	235	Irlande*[1]
Italy[1]	1585	1641	2032	1542	1621	1621	1561	1891	*1735	*1853	Italie[1]
Latvia	..	...	* [1]35	* [1]24	[1]27	* [1]33	* [1]33	41	[1]68	[1]67	Lettonie
Lithuania[1]	..	...	*85	*75	*55	*97	*97	*128	122	117	Lituanie[1]
Netherlands*[1]	1304	1137	1295	1232	1051	1074	1125	1120	896	1215	Pays-Bas*[1]
Poland	2190	1818	1631	2202	1537	1772	2466	2384	2336	2025	Pologne

For general note and footnotes, see end of table.

Voir la fin du tableau pour la remarque générale et les notes.

Raw sugar (continued)
Sucre brut (suite)

ISIC-BASED CODE - CODE BASE CITI

3118-01

Unit : Thousand metric tons | Unité : Milliers de tonnes métriques

Country or area	1990	1991	1992	1993	1994	1995	1996	1997	1998	1999	Pays ou zone
Portugal* [1]	2	1	2	4	6	6	3	71	66	76	Portugal* [1]
Republic of Moldova	..	237	208	⁶209	⁶154	⁶197	⁶252	⁶204	⁶187	⁶99	Rép. de Moldova
Romania [1]	*467	379	273	185	231	267	396	260	*190	*109	Roumanie [1]
Russian Federation	..	3425	3923	3918	2736	3155	3294	3778	4745	6808	Fédération de Russie
Slovakia	..	..	...	139	122	157	220	¹218	70	154	Slovaquie
Slovenia [1]	..	...	34	41	45	65	60	55	*55	70	Slovénie [1]
Spain [1]	994	949	1032	1237	1116	1111	1228	1142	1327	1071	Espagne [1]
Sweden [1]	444	266	333	414	369	357	398	396	400	*467	Suède [1]
Switzerland [1]	160	*136	*137	*153	*128	*140	*203	*199	*191	*192	Suisse [1]
Ukraine	..	4786	3647	3993	3368	3894	3296	2034	1984	1858	Ukraine
United Kingdom [1]	1349	1326	1476	1436	1373	*1326	1605	1592	1439	1540	Royaume-Uni [1]
Yugoslavia	..	470	314	127	210	¹156	¹382	240	216	¹248	Yougoslavie
T.F.Yug.Rep. Macedonia	..	...	...	7	6	7	8	25	...	...	L'ex-RY Macédoine
Yugoslavia, SFR* [1]	933	..	..	..	..	..	..	..	..	..	Yougoslavie, RSF* [1]
USSR (former) [1]	9130	..	..	..	..	..	..	..	..	..	URSS (anc.) [1]
Oceania	4008	3621	4721	4974	5767	5625	5227	5675	6046	6100	Océanie
Australia	⁷3570	⁷3195	* ⁷4260	³4488	³5217	³5129	4833	5267	5732	5778	Australie
Fiji	408	389	426	443	517	454	¹351	¹363	¹266	* ¹270	Fidji
Papua New Guinea* [1]	30	37	35	43	33	42	43	45	48	52	Papouasie-Nvl-Guinée* [1]
Total	104020	107635	111438	105492	103279	106079	114328	114188	117043	122788	Total

General Note.
Crude beet and cane sugars in crystalline form. Aqueous solutions of raw sugar are excluded. (SITC, Rev.3: 06110-0).

Remarque générale.
Sucre brut de betterave ou de canne sous forme cristallisée. Cette rubrique ne comprend pas les solutions aqueuses de sucre brut. (CTCI, Rev.3: 06110-0).

[1] Source: Food and Agriculture Organization of the United Nations (FAO), (Rome).

[2] Twelve months ending 7 July of the year stated.
[3] Source: International Sugar Organization, (London).
[4] Twelve months beginning 16 July of year stated.
[5] Sales.
[6] Excluding Transnistria region.
[7] Twelve months ending 30 June of year stated.

[1] Source: Organisation des Nations Unies pour l'alimentation et l'agriculture (FAO), (Rome).
[2] Période de douze mois finissant le 7 juillet de l'année indiquée.
[3] Source: Organisation Internationale du Sucre, (Londres).
[4] Période de douze mois commençant le 16 juillet de l'année indiquée.
[5] Ventes.
[6] Non compris la région de Transnistria.
[7] Période de douze mois finissant le 30 juin de l'année indiquée.

Refined sugar
Sucre raffiné

ISIC-BASED CODE - CODE BASE CITI

3118-04

Unit : Thousand metric tons — Unité : Milliers de tonnes métriques

Country or area	1990	1991	1992	1993	1994	1995	1996	1997	1998	1999	Pays ou zone
Africa	**5411**	**5637**	**5490**	**5213**	**5641**	**5990**	**5927**	**5622**	**5812**	**5453**	**Afrique**
Algeria	209	211	192	201	193	169	170	68	58	48	Algérie
Angola[1]	23	28	23	18	18	28	23	...	...	...	Angola[1]
Benin[1]	2	2	3	3	3	1	3	...	...	...	Bénin[1]
Botswana[1]	0	0	32	40	41	34	43	89	54	50	Botswana[1]
Burkina Faso	42	47	45	35	[1]29	[1]29	[1]29	...	...	...	Burkina Faso
Burundi[1]	10	14	17	14	12	14	8	...	...	...	Burundi[1]
Cameroon	[1]71	*69	*70	64	*72	*57	[1]40	...	...	...	Cameroun
Central African Rep.[1]	6	4	3	8	8	9	9	...	...	...	Rép. centrafricaine[1]
Chad	47	27	26	25	27	26	[1]28	...	...	...	Tchad
Côte d'Ivoire[1]	108	122	125	108	101	113	100	...	...	...	Côte d'Ivoire[1]
Dem. Rep. of Congo[1]	104	101	83	78	78	74	46	...	...	...	Rép. dém. du Congo[1]
Egypt	331	366	419	437	481	661	745	823	982	706	Egypte
Ethiopia,incl.Eritrea[1]	172	143	149	...	...	...	...	...	...	...	Ethiopie,incl.Erythrée[1]
Ethiopia[1]	...	...	...	170	121	129	168	...	...	...	Ethiopie[1]
Gabon	[1]18	[1]13	14	15	14	14	[1]15	...	...	...	Gabon
Ghana[1]	0	0	0	0	13	6	79	...	...	...	Ghana[1]
Guinea[1]	18	18	15	18	17	17	17	...	...	...	Guinée[1]
Kenya[1]	511	469	430	399	452	419	349	...	...	...	Kenya[1]
Liberia[1]	4	4	4	3	3	3	3	...	...	...	Libéria[1]
Madagascar[1]	65	69	81	85	59	95	110	...	...	...	Madagascar[1]
Malawi	[1]128	[1]144	[1]172	[1]94	[1]169	255	235	88	80	155	Malawi
Mali[1]	20	29	27	24	28	31	23	...	...	...	Mali[1]
Mauritania[1]	0	66	38	37	58	68	69	...	...	...	Mauritanie[1]
Mauritius	44	55	70	63	40	70	...	...	...	...	Maurice
Morocco	746	785	807	851	906	901	917	936	961	920	Maroc
Mozambique	[1]2	[1]2	[1]1	[1]1	[1]1	[1]1	[1]7	...	6	3	Mozambique
Niger[1]	12	12	12	12	12	12	12	...	...	...	Niger[1]
Nigeria[1]	76	51	51	51	51	40	40	...	...	...	Nigéria[1]
Réunion[1]	29	28	21	22	20	28	27	...	...	...	Réunion[1]
Rwanda	2	3	2	3	1	[1]1	[1]1	...	...	2	Rwanda
Senegal	[1]83	[1]83	[1]83	[1]79	[1]88	49	37	39	42	47	Sénégal
Seychelles[1]	1	0	0	0	0	0	0	...	...	...	Seychelles[1]
Sierra Leone[1]	6	6	4	2	5	2	2	...	...	...	Sierra Leone[1]
Somalia[1]	23	28	26	14	18	18	19	...	...	...	Somalie[1]
South Africa	1306	1359	1316	1098	1246	1303	1246	1120	1151	1034	Afrique du Sud
Sudan[1]	387	446	471	470	394	423	485	...	...	...	Soudan[1]
Swaziland[1]	58	73	68	55	55	55	58	...	...	...	Swaziland[1]
Tunisia	49	61	69	67	72	70	73	75	101	115	Tunisie
Uganda	[1]23	[1]42	[1]53	[1]50	[1]44	[1]70	[1]100	103	104	127	Ouganda
United Rep.Tanzania	107	122	117	106	112	114	104	81	...	...	Rép. Unie de Tanzanie
Zambia[1]	124	123	132	135	146	93	91	...	...	...	Zambie[1]
Zimbabwe[1]	294	265	72	101	280	334	181	...	...	...	Zimbabwe[1]
America, North	**15006**	**14075**	**14963**	**12617**	**13228**	**12771**	**14002**	**13631**	**13755**	**13650**	**Amérique du Nord**
Barbados[1]	15	17	14	15	25	6	10	...	...	...	Barbade[1]
Belize[1]	7	8	11	10	12	12	17	...	...	...	Belize[1]
Canada[1]	951	931	1020	1055	1091	1091	1131	...	...	...	Canada[1]
Costa Rica[1]	137	156	164	196	214	170	209	...	...	...	Costa Rica[1]
Cuba[1]	1521	653	1251	577	766	604	524	...	...	...	Cuba[1]
Dominica	[1]1	[1]0	[1]0	[1]2	[1]0	[1]1	[1]1	0	0	0	Dominique
Dominican Republic	79	90	89	117	102	98	112	113	299	79	Rép. dominicaine
El Salvador[1]	155	177	168	207	204	202	210	...	...	...	El Salvador[1]
Grenada[1]	3	2	0	2	0	0	2	...	...	...	Grenade[1]
Guadeloupe[1]	9	5	5	4	5	6	18	...	...	...	Guadeloupe[1]
Guatemala	[1]399	[1]317	[1]261	[1]356	[1]401	[1]391	[1]457	597	519	...	Guatemala
Honduras[1]	146	145	162	166	157	164	215	...	...	...	Honduras[1]
Jamaica[1]	65	75	82	64	89	95	52	...	...	...	Jamaïque[1]
Martinique[1]	6	7	6	7	5	7	6	...	...	...	Martinique[1]
Mexico	[1]3647	[1]3412	[1]3076	1531	1609	1873	2011	1808	1786	1699	Mexique
Netherlands Antilles[1]	0	0	0	0	0	4	3	...	...	...	Antilles néerlandaises[1]
Nicaragua[1]	92	109	137	124	142	147	179	...	...	...	Nicaragua[1]
Panama	71	62	69	66	64	63	61	...	...	...	Panama
Puerto Rico[1]	58	63	58	55	43	39	29	...	...	...	Porto Rico[1]

For general note and footnotes, see end of table.　　　Voir la fin du tableau pour la remarque générale et les notes.

Refined sugar (continued)
Sucre raffiné (suite)

ISIC-BASED CODE - CODE BASE CITI

3118-04

Unit : Thousand metric tons

Unité : Milliers de tonnes métriques

Country or area	1990	1991	1992	1993	1994	1995	1996	1997	1998	1999	Pays ou zone
St. Kitts-Nevis[1]	1	1	1	1	0	0	0	...	...	...	St-Kitts-Nevis[1]
St. Lucia[1]	3	2	3	3	3	4	2	...	...	...	St-Lucie[1]
St. Vincent-Grenadines[1]	5	5	5	4	6	5	...	...	...	...	St. Vincent-Grenadines[1]
Trinidad and Tobago	[1]56	[1]55	[1]52	[1]54	[1]73	[1]69	[1]93	46	36	42	Trinité-et-Tobago
United States[1]	7580	7784	8330	8001	8218	7720	8656	...	...	...	Etats-Unis[1]
America, South	**6672**	**6745**	**7301**	**6109**	**6379**	**7552**	**7508**	**7592**	**7789**	**8216**	**Amérique du Sud**
Argentina[1]	1014	...	1048	880	1000	1259	1115	...	...	...	Argentine[1]
Bolivia[1]	238	346	271	198	255	319	339	...	...	...	Bolivie[1]
Brazil	2252	2296	2572	2079	1949	2075	2070	2208	1997	2208	Brésil
Chile	354	334	487	453	463	549	423	358	470	434	Chili
Colombia	...	[1]1399	1537	1359	1491	1425	[1]1685	1359	1313	...	Colombie
Ecuador	126	[1]280	401	234	242	322	[1]351	123	570	...	Equateur
French Guiana[1]	1	1	1	1	1	0	0	...	...	...	Guyane française[1]
Guyana[1]	20	33	23	11	17	26	23	...	...	...	Guyana[1]
Paraguay	104	136	133	111	111	118	103	109	119	90	Paraguay
Peru	[1]469	111	81	48	109	642	608	674	450	605	Pérou
Suriname[1]	4	9	10	4	6	8	8	...	...	...	Suriname[1]
Uruguay	[1]74	[1]95	[1]106	[1]77	[1]93	[1]89	[1]95	119	102	...	Uruguay
Venezuela[1]	561	653	630	655	643	720	688	...	...	...	Venezuela[1]
Asia	**30654**	**36392**	**37950**	**32876**	**36291**	**40589**	**41642**	**40082**	**43566**	**47202**	**Asie**
Afghanistan[1]	1	1	1	1	1	1	1	...	...	...	Afghanistan[1]
Armenia[1]	..	...	78	59	13	48	57	...	...	...	Arménie[1]
Azerbaijan	..	...	...	...	...	...	1	0	0	0	Azerbaïdjan
Bangladesh[2]	184	246	195	187	221	270	184	135	...	...	Bangladesh[2]
Cambodia[1]	15	11	8	8	14	12	10	...	...	...	Cambodge[1]
China[1]	7208	8777	8650	6354	6769	8573	7839	...	...	...	Chine[1]
Hong Kong SAR[1]	3	12	9	5	3	1	7	...	...	...	Hong-Kong RAS[1]
Georgia	..	...	2	1	0	0	26	20		20	Géorgie
India	11241	12989	12531	9973	12665	14806	15307	13250	14308	17467	Inde
Indonesia	1028	2010	1509	2294	2224	[1]2202	[1]2564		1793	...	Indonésie
Iran(Islamic Rep. of)	[3]572	[3]742	[3]1200	[3]1060	[3]1052	[4]845	[4]832	[4]1055	[4]1050	...	Iran(Rép. islamique)
Iraq[1]	33	6	6	2	2	2	2	...	...	...	Iraq[1]
Israel[1]	13	6	4	4	4	4	4	...	...	...	Israël[1]
Japan	2563	2575	2523	1932	1902	1887	1848	1782	2245	2242	Japon
Kazakhstan	..	94	27	38	14	16	23	...	...	...	Kazakhstan
Korea, Republic of	1008	999	1077	1038	1140	1131	[1]1166	...	...	...	Corée, République de
Kyrgyzstan	..	371	114	116	82	70	167	90	88	70	Kirghizistan
Lebanon[1]	10	37	45	40	47	40	42	...	...	...	Liban[1]
Malaysia	801	895	951	957	1002	1052	1117	1155	1073	1226	Malaisie
Myanmar[5]	29	35	50	47	48	42	43	53	53	43	Myanmar[5]
Nepal[1]	30	43	52	43	39	40	40	...	...	...	Népal[1]
Pakistan[2]	1857	1934	2322	2384	2841	2964	2426	2383	3555	3542	Pakistan[2]
Philippines[1]	1440	1344	1704	1661	1554	1644	1743	...	...	...	Philippines[1]
Singapore[1]	130	139	147	114	145	167	184	...	...	...	Singapour[1]
Sri Lanka[1]	264	346	353	257	259	298	351	...	...	...	Sri Lanka[1]
Syrian Arab Republic	135	179	178	183	180	158	181	176	89	158	Rép. arabe syrienne
Thailand	484	578	# [1]2419	[1]1942	[1]1938	[1]2495	[1]3088	...	...	...	Thaïlande
Turkey	1579	1798	1640	1737	1717	1293	1842	2012	2530	2100	Turquie
Turkmenistan[1]	..	...	82	72	6	0	0	...	...	...	Turkménistan[1]
Viet Nam	27	49	72	# [1]365	[1]409	[1]527	[1]545	...	...	...	Viet Nam
Europe	**15674**	**20349**	**19403**	**16332**	**14558**	**14912**	**17179**	**16174**	**16005**	**15655**	**Europe**
Albania	[1]14	[1]3	[1]1	[1]0	[1]2	[1]3	[1]4	0	0	0	Albanie
Austria	447	430	421	[1]479	[1]404	[1]447	[1]494	...	...	...	Autriche
Belarus	..	335	233	153	144	140	226	352	476	501	Bélarus
Belgium-Luxembourg[1]	1058	967	959	1032	928	922	870	...	...	...	Belgique-Luxembourg[1]
Bosnia and Herzegovina[1]	..	..	10	6	4	2	2	...	...	...	Bosnie-Herzégovine[1]
Bulgaria	185	167	152	172	274	237	292	114	121	250	Bulgarie
Croatia	..	94	95	79	115	175	195	141	139	...	Croatie
Denmark[7]	[6]506	[6]510	[6]471	[6]484	#5	7	13	12	11	12	Danemark[7]
Czechoslovakia(former)	740	722	..	..	..	..	..	...	...	..	Tchécoslovaquie(anc.)
Czech Republic	..	..	555	518	433	506	602	598	492	420	République tchèque

For general note and footnotes, see end of table.

Voir la fin du tableau pour la remarque générale et les notes.

Refined sugar (continued)
Sucre raffiné (suite)

ISIC-BASED CODE - CODE BASE CITI

3118-04

Unit : Thousand metric tons

Unité : Milliers de tonnes métriques

Country or area	1990	1991	1992	1993	1994	1995	1996	1997	1998	1999	Pays ou zone
Estonia[1]	..	...	4	15	22	13	5	...	...	...	Estonie[1]
Finland	238	300	267	285	242	259	254	...	...	301	Finlande
France	#385	423	399	386	331	331	329	...	...	...	France
Germany	..	[1]3747	[1]3970	[1]3964	[1]3382	[1]3497	4603	...	...	...	Allemagne
German D.R.(former)	831	..	..	..	..	..	..	...	..	..	R.D.A. (anc.)
Greece	304	262	320	354	307	249	287	265	364	...	Grèce
Hungary	512	605	397	393	440	479	562	487	...	438	Hongrie
Ireland[1]	225	213	223	177	215	226	228	...	...	...	Irlande[1]
Italy	1490	1329	1789	1505	1556	1720	1481	1835	1701	1752	Italie
Latvia	..	21	2	0	2	27	40	44	42	66	Lettonie
Lithuania	..	150	88	91	52	105	126	113	123	121	Lituanie
Malta[1]	0	0	0	0	2	0	2	...	...	...	Malte[1]
Netherlands	[7][8]1232	[7][8]1131	[7][8]1080	[7][8]1143	[7][8]1136	[7][8]1048	[1]975	...	...	...	Pays-Bas
Norway[1]	2	2	2	5	5	4	5	...	...	...	Norvège[1]
Poland	1971	1636	1468	1982	1383	1595	2220	2145	2102	1821	Pologne
Portugal	305	408	298	303	294	296	300	339	381	359	Portugal
Republic of Moldova[1]	..	...	201	197	75	122	167	...	...	...	Rép. de Moldova[1]
Romania	538	348	290	185	231	266	396	243	321	246	Roumanie
Russian Federation	..	886	747	443	214	126	127	139	100	70	Fédération de Russie
Slovakia	..	..	149	143	128	159	223	202	82	43	Slovaquie
Slovenia	..	50	34	41	45	37	71	67	48	90	Slovénie
Spain	1002	913	889	914	1299	1165	1027	1163	1172	1109	Espagne
Sweden	359	300	379	383	378	357	[1]366	301	303	301	Suède
Switzerland	146	129	131	135	121	123	[1]190	...	...	...	Suisse
Ukraine	..	1491	493	190	133	51	42	13	7	13	Ukraine
United Kingdom	[1]2326	[1]2325	[1]2545	#41	39	54	54	...	...	...	Royaume-Uni
Yugoslavia	..	...	333	127	212	156	382	240	216	250	Yougoslavie
T.F.Yug.Rep. Macedonia	..	9	8	7	6	7	18	35	40	43	L'ex-RY Macédoine
Yugoslavia, SFR[1]	857	..	..	..	..	..	..	..	..	..	Yougoslavie, RSF[1]
USSR (former)	12137	..	..	..	..	..	..	..	..	..	URSS (anc.)
Oceania	836	684	2136	1426	1795	1275	1973	2215	2361	2516	Océanie
Australia[1]	637	477	1926	1208	1568	1051	1757	...	...	...	Australie[1]
Fiji[1]	34	36	23	26	25	25	25	...	...	...	Fidji[1]
Kiribati[1]	2	3	3	3	3	3	3	...	...	...	Kiribati[1]
New Caledonia[1]	6	5	6	4	4	7	4	...	...	...	Nouvelle-Calédonie[1]
New Zealand	130	134	142	153	153	153	153	...	...	...	Nouvelle-Zélande
Papua New Guinea	21	23	30	26	33	28	23	39	34	38	Papouasie-Nvl-Guinée
Samoa[1]	4	5	4	5	7	6	6	...	...	...	Samoa[1]
Tonga[1]	1	2	2	2	2	2	2	...	...	...	Tonga[1]
Total	86389	83883	87244	74572	77893	83089	88231	85317	89289	92692	Total

General Note.
Beet sugar and cane sugar, refined, in solid form or powder, including white sugar derived directly from the processing of sugar beet. Aqueous solutions of sugar with added flavouring or colouring matter are excluded. (SITC, Rev.3: 06120-0).

Remarque générale.
Sucre de betterave et sucre de canne, raffiné, à l'état solide (même en poudre), y compris le sucre blanc obtenu directement par traitement des betteraves sucrières. Cette rubrique ne comprend pas les solutions aqueuses de sucre aromatisées ou additionnées de colorants. (CTCI, Rev.3: 06120-0).

[1] Source: Food and Agriculture Organization of the United Nations (FAO), (Rome).

[2] Twelve months ending 30 June of year stated.
[3] Production by establishments employing 50 or more persons.
[4] Production by establishments employing 10 or more persons.
[5] Government production only.
[6] Solid beet and cane sugar.
[7] Sales.
[8] Production by establishments employing 20 or more persons.

[1] Source: Organisation des Nations Unies pour l'alimentation et l'agriculture (FAO), (Rome).

[2] Période de douze mois finissant le 30 juin de l'année indiquée.
[3] Production des établissements occupant 50 personnes ou plus.
[4] Production des établissements occupant 10 personnes ou plus.
[5] Production de l'Etat seulement.
[6] Sucres de betterave et de canne, à l'état solide.
[7] Ventes.
[8] Production des établissements occupant 20 personnes ou plus.

Fruit, glace or crystalized
Fruits glacés ou cristallisés

ISIC-BASED CODE - CODE BASE CITI

3119-01

Unit : Metric tons

Unité : Tonnes métriques

Country or area	1990	1991	1992	1993	1994	1995	1996	1997	1998	1999	Pays ou zone
America, South	**367**	**367**	**255**	**356**	**438**	**418**	**367**	**367**	**367**	**367**	**Amérique du Sud**
Colombia	...	...	255	356	438	418	...	...	...	...	Colombie
Asia	**114**	**295**	**908**	**429**	**456**	**439**	**433**	**439**	**439**	**439**	**Asie**
China, Macao, SAR[1][2]	...	...	...	24	51	...	28	...	...	...	Chine, Macao PAS[1][2]
Indonesia	80	261	874	...	...	...	...	...	...	...	Indonésie
Europe	**10600**	**21193**	**25380**	**25096**	**27163**	**24573**	**30208**	**29804**	**29214**	**28584**	**Europe**
Austria	351		...	...	...	...				...	Autriche
Croatia	..	32	53	32	25	15	10	0	0	...	Croatie
Denmark[3]	218	26	68	23	297	372	391	22	3	...	Danemark[3]
Finland	9	11	5	25	37	27	30	...	...	...	Finlande
France	17	17	16	15	15	15	14	14	15	...	France
Germany	...	...	...	...	...	8865	10353	10560	10356	...	Allemagne
Greece	1815	2091	2029	2535	2519	1664	2860	1670	2220	...	Grèce
Netherlands	...	...	...	80	...	...	...			...	Pays-Bas
Portugal	561	#139	3406	4044	3159	2414	3550	3507	3097	2786	Portugal
Spain	...	...	...	5899	9846	9833	11665	12135	12115	11946	Espagne
Sweden	193	216	302	285	234	158	66	44	18	...	Suède
United Kingdom	...	...	...	1773	566	779	838	1378	...	...	Royaume-Uni
Oceania	**715**	**715**	**715**	**715**	**715**	**715**	**715**	**715**	**715**	**715**	**Océanie**
Australia	715	...	...	...	...	...	...	...	...	...	Australie
Total	**11796**	**22570**	**27259**	**26596**	**28772**	**26145**	**31723**	**31325**	**30735**	**30105**	**Total**

General Note.
Fruit, fruit-peel and parts of plants, preserved by sugar either drained, glace or crystallized.·(SITC, Rev.3: 06210-1).

Remarque générale.
Fruits, peaux de fruits et parties de plantes conservés au sucre, égouttés, glacés ou cristallisés. (CTCI, Rev.3: 06210-1).

[1] 1995 data are confidential.
[2] Beginning 1997, data are confidential.
[3] Sales.

[1] Pour 1995, les données sont confidentielles.
[2] A partir de 1997, les données sont confidentielles
[3] Ventes.

Sugar confectionery
Sucreries

ISIC-BASED CODE - CODE BASE CITI

3119-04

Unit : Thousand metric tons

Unité : Milliers de tonnes métriques

Country or area	1990	1991	1992	1993	1994	1995	1996	1997	1998	1999	Pays ou zone
Africa	**137**	**146**	**147**	**151**	**110**	**118**	**136**	**131**	**145**	**130**	**Afrique**
Cameroon	...	1.3	1.0	1.2	0.9	*1.1	...	...	...	...	Cameroun
Ethiopia[1]	2.5	1.6	1.0	1.0	1.7	1.5	1.8	0.8	1.9	1.3	Ethiopie[1]
Kenya	4.5	3.0	2.5	7.5	10.3	10.5	11.0	...	...	...	Kenya
Mali	...	...	...	2.0	...	...	...	...	...	...	Mali
Mozambique[2]	1.6	0.9	...	0.4	0.3	...	...	...	...	...	Mozambique[2]
Nigeria	24.3	43.5	58.3	61.2	14.6	15.8	...	...	...	...	Nigéria
South Africa[3]	100.8	94.2	81.9	77.8	79.7	86.6	90.6	84.3	98.1	83.6	Afrique du Sud[3]
America, North	**928**	**1031**	**1151**	**1197**	**1236**	**1312**	**1382**	**1539**	**1608**	**1683**	**Amérique du Nord**
Mexico	...	...	...	30.7	34.8	26.7	30.9	37.0	35.3	39.4	Mexique
Panama	2.8	...	5.2	6.0	5.5	...	...	...	...	...	Panama
United States	898.7	998.0	1116.5	1160.2	1195.7	1280.5	1346.2	...	...	...	Etats-Unis
America, South	**10**	**11**	**11**	**11**	**10**	**10**	**10**	**10**	**10**	**10**	**Amérique du Sud**
Bolivia	1.1	1.7	1.5	2.0	1.0	*0.8	...	...	...	...	Bolivie
Colombia	...	...	2.0	1.6	1.3	1.8	...	...	...	...	Colombie
Paraguay	1.0	1.4	1.3	...	...	...	...	...	...	...	Paraguay
Peru	...	...	...	...	...	6.5	5.9	5.5	5.7	6.5	Pérou
Asia	**334**	**559**	**500**	**474**	**419**	**388**	**413**	**409**	**410**	**393**	**Asie**
Armenia	..	15.0	7.6	3.0	1.2	0.8	0.6	0.9	0.6	0.3	Arménie
Azerbaijan	..	38.3	18.8	11.7	3.5	0.6	0.3	0.3	0.2	0.3	Azerbaïdjan
Hong Kong SAR[2]	8.5	10.7	12.6	4.0	8.7	13.7	13.3	12.4	14.7	15.2	Hong-Kong RAS[2]
Cyprus	*0.9	*1.1	1.4	...	...	1.5	...	...	...	...	Chypre
Indonesia	34.4	39.1	72.6	81.9	61.9	59.6	...	65.9	82.0	...	Indonésie
Japan	165.0	165.5	164.8	162.0	160.0	156.0	155.5	155.0	154.2	152.0	Japon
Kazakhstan	..	96.7	63.2	56.2	36.6	12.5	19.0	27.7	17.4	14.6	Kazakhstan
Korea, Republic of	104.1	126.0	124.1	121.2	114.6	114.1	120.7	99.6	93.1	102.0	Corée, République de
Kyrgyzstan	..	26.8	11.6	8.1	4.8	1.9	1.8	1.4	1.4	1.4	Kirghizistan
Myanmar[4]	3.1	3.6	3.5	1.6	1.9	0.7	...	...	...	...	Myanmar[4]
Turkey	[5]18.4	[5]17.3	13.6	16.9	18.0	25.0	34.7	41.8	42.6	31.5	Turquie
Turkmenistan		19.0	6.0	6.3	6.7	1.0	2.6	2.2	1.9	...	Turkménistan
Europe	**2245**	**4683**	**4173**	**3454**	**3156**	**3221**	**3224**	**3308**	**3218**	**2961**	**Europe**
Austria[2]	14.8	17.5	18.8	21.4	17.9	18.9	20.9	16.7	10.0	10.0	Autriche[2]
Belarus	..	77.8	51.7	47.2	41.9	31.8	33.8	47.7	60.2	64.6	Bélarus
Belgium	[6]65.8	[6]63.9	[6]64.0	[6]73.3	80.3	83.0	82.3	85.9	90.4	94.5	Belgique
Bulgaria[2][7]	91.2	59.9	63.9	63.9	68.0	77.0	60.7	52.7	...	...	Bulgarie[2][7]
Croatia		12.3	10.5	9.7	9.5	8.8	9.0	5.7	5.3	...	Croatie
Denmark[8]		60.0	64.3	69.8	73.7	71.5	...	...	...	...	Danemark[8]
Czechoslovakia(former)	48.0	35.3	..							..	Tchécoslovaquie(anc.)
Estonia	..	16.1	8.7	7.3	3.7	2.7	3.8	5.8	6.0	4.4	Estonie
Finland	21.2	25.9	20.0	21.4	20.4	20.9	22.6	24.0	29.0	27.5	Finlande
France	175.1	174.5	178.1	190.5	196.3	206.1	207.3	213.1	211.3	...	France
Germany	..	604.8	609.4	...	...	...	...	...	...	...	Allemagne
German D.R.(former)	40.1	..	..	...	...	...	...	...	...	..	R.D.A. (anc.)
Greece	21.4	23.0	24.5	19.9	19.8	19.9	18.4	...	17.4	...	Grèce
Hungary	23.0	21.7	16.5	16.4	13.1	12.3	13.9	17.0	15.9	17.7	Hongrie
Iceland	0.8	0.9	0.7	0.7	0.6	...	0.4	0.5	0.8	0.8	Islande
Latvia	..	22.6	118.1	47.8	8.1	10.5	13.4	15.8	10.6	4.7	Lettonie
Lithuania	..	13.3	9.0	6.7	5.9	11.1	12.6	9.1	6.4	5.9	Lituanie
Netherlands[8][9]	127.3	133.3	133.7	152.2	158.1	166.7	...	...	...	...	Pays-Bas[8][9]
Norway	12.2	10.6	9.4	...	...	...	...	...	...	...	Norvège
Poland[10]	88.6	90.2	85.5	87.8	114.5	108.8	119.3	118.5	96.4	73.6	Pologne[10]
Portugal	18.8	13.6	11.0	10.0	9.5	7.7	8.2	9.8	9.3	9.9	Portugal
Republic of Moldova	..	35.0	22.0	[11]26.2	[11]10.7	[11]9.9	[11]8.7	[11]7.9	[11]7.1	[11]5.1	Rép. de Moldova
Romania[2]	306.0	174.8	107.4	85.3	80.4	90.6	105.3	96.3	80.6	82.6	Roumanie[2]
Russian Federation	..	1193.9	850.5	840.0	715.2	691.1	656.1	730.4	678.7	699.9	Fédération de Russie
Slovakia	..	..	9.3	13.5	12.8	7.9	21.5	21.9	4.7	4.4	Slovaquie
Slovenia	..	8.1	6.4	7.3	8.3	7.7	6.6	6.5	6.1	5.8	Slovénie
Spain[12]	139.0	156.6	163.4	245.5	242.8	269.9	298.8	301.1	...	...	Espagne[12]
Sweden	44.2	44.1	39.6	42.1	43.7	39.3	50.2	49.5	51.1	51.6	Suède
Switzerland	[8]22.5	[8]23.3	[8]22.9	[8]23.9	[8]23.7	[8]21.4	[8]22.1	20.9	20.9	23.5	Suisse

For general note and footnotes, see end of table.

Voir la fin du tableau pour la remarque générale et les notes.

Sugar confectionery (continued)
Sucreries (suite)

ISIC-BASED CODE - CODE BASE CITI

3119-04

Unit : Thousand metric tons   Unité : Milliers de tonnes métriques

Country or area	1990	1991	1992	1993	1994	1995	1996	1997	1998	1999	Pays ou zone
Ukraine	..	611.6	490.1	331.1	193.5	153.3	141.1	145.9	178.5	246.1	Ukraine
United Kingdom	[13]927.0	[13]929.0	[13]935.2	360.4	349.1	432.2	408.7	399.7	363.5	...	Royaume-Uni
Yugoslavia	..	29.6	28.4	14.6	16.2	21.8	21.2	20.1	22.0	19.7	Yougoslavie
USSR (former)	2162.6	..	..	..	..	..	..	..	..	..	URSS (anc.)
Oceania	65	65	68	67	71	72	72	76	77	78	Océanie
Australia	64.8	64.7	68.1	67.4	71.5	71.9	71.9	...	...	...	Australie
Total	5882	6495	6051	5354	5001	5121	5238	5472	5468	5256	Total

General Note.
Sugar preparations marketed in a solid or semi-solid form and collectively referred to as sweetmeats or confectionery. Sugar preparations containing cocoa are excluded. (SITC, Rev.3: 06220-0).

[1] Twelve months ending 7 July of the year stated.
[2] Including chocolate and chocolate products.
[3] Including drinking chocolate, cocoa powder, cocoa butter and grindings from cocoa beans.
[4] Twelve months ending 31 March of year stated.
[5] Including jams, marmalades and fruit jellies.
[6] Production by establishments employing 5 or more persons.
[7] Including biscuits, waffles, halva and Turkish delight.
[8] Sales.
[9] Production by establishments employing 20 or more persons.
[10] Excluding chocolate confectionery.
[11] Excluding Transnistria region.
[12] Including nougats, marzipans, mantecados, polvorons, chewing gum and similar products.
[13] Sugar produced from home-grown sugar beet.

Remarque générale.
Préparations au sucre, solides ou semi-solides, et généralement désignées sous le nom de sucreries ou de confiseries. Cette rubrique ne comprend pas les préparations sucrées contenant du cacao. (CTCI, Rev.3: 06220-0).

[1] Période de douze mois finissant le 7 juillet de l'année indiquée.
[2] Y compris le chocolat et les produits à base de chocolat.
[3] Y compris le chocolat à boire, le cacao en poudre, le beurre de cacao et les brisures de fèves de cacao.
[4] Période de douze mois finissant le 31 mars de l'année indiquée.
[5] Y compris les confitures, marmelades et gelées de fruits.
[6] Production des établissements occupant 5 personnes ou plus.
[7] Y compris les biscuits, les gaufres, le halva et le rahat loukoum.
[8] Ventes.
[9] Production des établissements occupant 20 personnes ou plus.
[10] Non compris les confiseries au chocolat.
[11] Non compris la région de Transnistria.
[12] Y compris les nougats, les massepains, les mantecados, les polvorons, les chewing-gums et produits similaires.
[13] Sucre provenant de betteraves récoltées localement.

Cocoa powder
Cacao en poudre

ISIC-BASED CODE - CODE BASE CITI

3119-07

Unit : Metric tons   Unité : Tonnes métriques

Country or area	1990	1991	1992	1993	1994	1995	1996	1997	1998	1999	Pays ou zone
Africa	**621**	**825**	**617**	**507**	**342**	**574**	**965**	**662**	**667**	**673**	**Afrique**
Kenya	...	825	617	507	342	574	965	...	...	...	Kenya
America, South	**53707**	**60624**	**48889**	**45650**	**42999**	**35112**	**21432**	**38624**	**26953**	**35439**	**Amérique du Sud**
Bolivia	41	63	75	0	18	*9	...	...	...	...	Bolivie
Brazil	29472	30907	21670	18945	...	2219	0	0	0	...	Brésil
Colombia	...	...	3419	2870	3465	1946	...	1617	998	...	Colombie
Ecuador	4223	...	5921	6964	10314	14441	2523	20285	9362	...	Equateur
Peru	166	568	704	652	81	278	291	495	...	...	Pérou
Venezuela	15529	16028	17100	...	...	...	...	...	...	...	Venezuela
Asia	**10239**	**7312**	**14550**	**28177**	**30955**	**28945**	**41239**	**64418**	**33661**	**53154**	**Asie**
Indonesia	4832	1486	9299	22901	22474	18676	...	49020	16578	...	Indonésie
Japan[1]	4877	5139	4719	4575	7451	9384	22173	14207	16134	15261	Japon[1]
Turkey	530	687	532	701	1030	885	908	1191	949	279	Turquie
Europe	**241119**	**262932**	**259826**	**249378**	**256671**	**273821**	**276712**	**293265**	**294583**	**287782**	**Europe**
Austria	6995	7510	9364	9685	7173	2817	1527	...	...	...	Autriche
Belarus	..	...	...	22	98	113	136	213	125	128	Bélarus
Croatia	..	1748	1177	968	752	780	738	302	353	...	Croatie
Denmark[2]	380	362	474	189	140	36	0	0	1	1	Danemark[2]
Czechoslovakia(former)	5781	3046	..	..	..	..	..	..	..		Tchécoslovaquie(anc.)
Finland	7	3	3	...	...	...	...	...	...	...	Finlande
France[3]	22482	28000	24039	...	...	...	...	...	...	...	France[3]
Germany	..	...	73768	46917	50161	44547	34348	34736	32135	...	Allemagne
Germany(Fed.Rep.)	66028	..	..	..	..	..	..	..	..	..	Allemagne(Rép.féd.)
German D.R.(former)	1400	..	..	..	..	..	..	..	..	..	R.D.A. (anc.)
Greece	1146	1237	1274	1217	1144	1132	1178	...	704	...	Grèce
Hungary	3860	2945	2065	1726	...	...	...	...	...	...	Hongrie
Latvia	..	53	...	91	380	285	263	443	109	32	Lettonie
Lithuania	..	...	...	0	86	83	99	64	80	52	Lituanie
Netherlands[2][4]	111139	120652	116894	123000	133000	161900	175000	180000	183000	185800	Pays-Bas[2][4]
Poland	4331	4410	5391	5198	3280	2845	3065	2285	6746	7563	Pologne
Portugal	1059	501	436	302	361	235	149	49	98	170	Portugal
Russian Federation	..	5373	2920	7562	5351	4318	4452	4391	3987	3781	Fédération de Russie
Slovenia	..	688	1579	1591	1193	611	13	15	18	21	Slovénie
Spain	15960	22257	19245	25210	25220	25787	27133	38773	37786	45155	Espagne
Sweden	551	569	452	581	551	477	722	954	710	313	Suède
Ukraine	..	...	87	124	213	296	368	960	728	680	Ukraine
Yugoslavia	..	263	273	81	19	15	16	5	23	17	Yougoslavie
T.F.Yug.Rep. Macedonia	..	35	56	69	55	50	11	10	44	41	L'ex-RY Macédoine
Total	**305686**	**331693**	**323882**	**323712**	**330966**	**338452**	**340348**	**396968**	**355865**	**377047**	**Total**

General Note.

Unsweetened powder obtained by pulverising the partly defatted cocoa paste.
Sweetened cocoa powder and cocoa powder to which milk powder or peptones
have been added are excluded. (SITC, Rev.3: 07220-0).

Remarque générale.

Poudre non sucrée provenant de la pulvérisation de la pâte de cacao
partiellement dégraissée. Cette rubrique ne comprend pas le cacao en poudre sucré
et le cacao additionné de poudre de lait ou de peptones. (CTCI, Rev.3: 07220-0).

[1] Including sweetened cocoa powder.
[2] Sales.
[3] Cocoa powder for sale.
[4] Production by establishments employing 20 or more persons.

[1] Y compris le cacao en poudre sucré.
[2] Ventes.
[3] Cacao en poudre pour vente en l'état.
[4] Production des établissements occupant 20 personnes ou plus.

Cocoa butter
Beurre de cacao

ISIC-BASED CODE - CODE BASE CITI

3119-10

Unit : Metric tons

Unité : Tonnes métriques

Country or area	1990	1991	1992	1993	1994	1995	1996	1997	1998	1999	Pays ou zone
America, North	**11776**	**12010**	**13796**	**12908**	**10557**	**11029**	**10176**	**8290**	**16755**	**19598**	**Amérique du Nord**
Mexico	222	136	125	68	130	...	...	...	...	...	Mexique
United States[1]	...	...	13671	12840	10427	10968	10141	8280	16755	19598	Etats-Unis[1]
America, South	**64105**	**77738**	**60675**	**63771**	**50534**	**44095**	**79702**	**44205**	**40438**	**52988**	**Amérique du Sud**
Bolivia	59	48	51	58	62	*89	...	...	...	...	Bolivie
Brazil	51693	63053	48038	46097	38726	31242	40907	37036	36147	34802	Brésil
Colombia	3133	...	2714	2894	3439	3998	...	2880	3406	...	Colombie
Ecuador	9220	...	9872	14722	8307	8766	35513	4214	807	...	Equateur
Asia	**10895**	**6532**	**12215**	**17614**	**23878**	**24552**	**19745**	**24090**	**30810**	**33708**	**Asie**
Indonesia	6363	3066	8663	14358	20647	20989	...	20913	27394	...	Indonésie
Japan	4532	3466	3552	3256	3231	3563	4446	3177	3416	3596	Japon
Europe	**193440**	**255027**	**274921**	**268233**	**266842**	**265105**	**269524**	**283484**	**282687**	**263451**	**Europe**
Austria	85	...	...	...	...	...	...	...	...	...	Autriche
Denmark[2]	...	...	0	0	0	0	0	0	3	3	Danemark[2]
France	9850	15102	14101	...	...	...	...	...	...	...	France
Germany	..	...	61862	39456	36589	29240	26483	24799	19296	...	Allemagne
Germany(Fed.Rep.)	57257		..	..	..	..	..	..	..	...	Allemagne(Rép.féd.)
Hungary	2119	1205	530	...	...	...	...	...	...	...	Hongrie
Latvia	..	...	...	1	1	1	2	1	...	0	Lettonie
Netherlands[2][3]	118706	130661	142284	151470	153108	156354	164000	178000	179000	177200	Pays-Bas[2][3]
Portugal[4]	62	55	22	22	22	8	1	...	...	...	Portugal[4]
Romania	15	5	2	0	0	0	0	0	0	0	Roumanie
Russian Federation	..	...	...	...	...	...	50436	...	...	...	Fédération de Russie
Spain	5344	5562	5550	12414	...	14631	14167	15813	19516	17259	Espagne
Sweden	2	...	...	1	...	...	...	...	...	...	Suède
Yugoslavia	..	...	46	...	...	...	...	...	...	...	Yougoslavie
Total	**280216**	**351307**	**361607**	**362526**	**351811**	**344780**	**379147**	**360069**	**370690**	**369745**	**Total**

General Note.
Fat and oil contained in cocoa beans. (SITC, Rev.3: 07240-0).

[1] Shipments.
[2] Sales.
[3] Production by establishments employing 20 or more persons.
[4] Beginning 1997, data are confidential.

Remarque générale.
Graisse et huile contenues dans les fèves de cacao. (CTCI, Rev.3: 07240-0).

[1] Expéditions.
[2] Ventes.
[3] Production des établissements occupant 20 personnes ou plus.
[4] A partir de 1997, les données sont confidentielles

Chocolate and chocolate products
Chocolat et produits à base de chocolat

ISIC-BASED CODE - CODE BASE CITI

3119-13

Unit : Thousand metric tons

Unité : Milliers de tonnes métriques

Country or area	1990	1991	1992	1993	1994	1995	1996	1997	1998	1999	Pays ou zone
Africa	**62**	**62**	**59**	**58**	**64**	**61**	**65**	**65**	**61**	**58**	**Afrique**
Egypt	8.3	7.2	7.3	7.2	6.8	6.7	6.8	7.5	7.1	7.3	Egypte
Kenya	0.7	0.6	0.6	0.3	0.5	0.6	...	...	...	...	Kenya
Madagascar	...	...	...	...	0.1	0.1	0.8	0.7	1.1	...	Madagascar
South Africa	48.9	49.9	47.6	46.4	52.3	49.3	52.4	51.4	47.2	43.4	Afrique du Sud
Tunisia	...	4.1	4.0	4.3	4.4	4.6	4.8	5.0	5.0	5.2	Tunisie
America, North	**1281**	**1231**	**1292**	**1378**	**1378**	**1400**	**1424**	**1447**	**1470**	**1519**	**Amérique du Nord**
Mexico	39.8	44.6	49.0	78.5	81.0	79.2	80.0	81.0	80.9	107.7	Mexique
United States	1240.8	1186.0	1243.4	1299.4	1297.2	...	...	...	...	...	Etats-Unis
America, South	**180**	**197**	**195**	**183**	**183**	**204**	**208**	**214**	**217**	**220**	**Amérique du Sud**
Bolivia	0.2	0.2	0.2	0.1	0.2	*0.2	...	...	...	...	Bolivie
Brazil	62.3	83.1	63.4	65.0	67.1	89.5	81.5	71.0	73.2	70.8	Brésil
Chile	20.7	27.0	30.1	34.9	31.4	33.6	39.7	40.0	45.8	47.6	Chili
Colombia	58.2	...	67.3	70.6	74.6	67.5	...	72.1	65.3	...	Colombie
Ecuador	34.7	...	26.9	4.2	0.2	0.2	9.0	17.6	13.9	...	Equateur
Peru	...	...	...	...	...	12.8	10.2	13.4	18.9	15.5	Pérou
Asia	**256**	**293**	**280**	**301**	**291**	**305**	**365**	**368**	**348**	**370**	**Asie**
Armenia	..	0.7	...	...	0.0	0.0	0.0	0.0	0.0	0.0	Arménie
Azerbaijan	..	0.1	0.0	0.0	0.0	0.0	0.0	0.1	0.1	0.1	Azerbaïdjan
Cyprus	*0.7	*0.8	0.6	...	...	0.6	0.5	0.6	0.5	0.5	Chypre
India[1][2]	10.3	10.9	12.5	11.8	15.9	17.9	21.0	19.7	20.2	24.5	Inde[1][2]
Indonesia	12.9	20.5	19.0	41.0	35.0	12.7	...	40.1	...	...	Indonésie
Japan	180.0	197.0	195.0	191.1	181.5	187.0	191.7	189.5	190.5	200.6	Japon
Kazakhstan	..	0.0	...	0.7	0.6	0.0	0.0	0.1	...	10.2	Kazakhstan
Syrian Arab Republic	4.7	6.0	5.8	6.1	5.9	5.9	5.9	5.1	5.9	...	Rép. arabe syrienne
Tajikistan	..	0.1	0.0	...	...	...	...	...	...	...	Tadjikistan
Turkey	47.4	56.5	45.0	49.8	51.6	80.8	119.4	113.1	101.0	99.6	Turquie
Turkmenistan	..	...	...	...	0.2	0.1	0.0	0.1	0.0	...	Turkménistan
Europe	**2290**	**3109**	**3052**	**3789**	**3557**	**3638**	**4118**	**4209**	**3967**	**4020**	**Europe**
Austria	51.6	49.7	46.9	64.7	64.4	...	#93.3	...	...	...	Autriche
Belarus	..	[3]5.9	3.0	6.5	7.7	8.8	10.6	15.4	15.0	16.3	Bélarus
Belgium	[4]278.8	[4]293.0	[4]313.2	[4]340.7	[5]136.1	[5]175.3	[5]199.9	[5]206.1	[5]158.7	[5]158.2	Belgique
Bulgaria	14.5	8.6	13.2	13.9	15.1	15.2	14.9	11.2	21.4	16.6	Bulgarie
Croatia	..	17.7	9.7	9.8	10.0	10.6	10.1	12.3	12.5	...	Croatie
Denmark[6]	26.6	32.7	30.2	32.4	32.9	31.0	32.9	39.7	32.5	31.8	Danemark[6]
Czechoslovakia(former)	59.7	52.6	..	...	...	...	...	...	...		Tchécoslovaquie(anc.)
Estonia	..	1.8	1.2	3.6	5.8	5.2	7.4	8.4	6.7	4.9	Estonie
Finland	36.6	37.8	39.0	54.2	55.4	49.8	49.1	52.5	42.3	42.5	Finlande
France	443.5	490.1	496.0	544.3	554.0	569.9	576.8	629.7	685.8	...	France
Germany	..	650.2	639.1	...	...	...	1241.2	1232.4	...	...	Allemagne
German D.R.(former)	34.1	...	..	..	..	..	..	..	..	...	R.D.A. (anc.)
Greece	26.5	25.6	28.1	25.9	30.1	29.4	37.0	...	33.6	...	Grèce
Hungary	33.6	31.3	25.3	27.6	36.1	19.9	38.8	42.6	42.6	45.1	Hongrie
Iceland	1.3	1.3	1.6	1.5	...	...	1.4	1.5	1.6	1.6	Islande
Ireland[7]	46.2	46.9	...	...	...	...	...	...	...	...	Irlande[7]
Latvia	..	2.3	...	3.5	8.2	7.2	9.1	10.1	7.1	4.9	Lettonie
Lithuania	..	0.0	0.0	0.1	0.7	18.4	20.6	23.6	19.2	13.5	Lituanie
Netherlands[6][8]	218.4	224.5	243.7	351.5	259.9	287.4	...	...	...	...	Pays-Bas[6][8]
Norway[9]	34.3	33.2	32.4	40.4	...	...	...	...	...	...	Norvège[9]
Poland	66.0	96.8	105.5	127.7	131.0	144.3	184.2	193.0	211.7	214.2	Pologne
Portugal	6.3	7.9	7.6	6.4	7.1	6.3	6.5	5.2	5.9	6.1	Portugal
Republic of Moldova	..	0.0	0.0	[10]0.4	[10]0.1	[10]0.1	[10]0.1	[10]0.1	[10]0.1	[10]0.1	Rép. de Moldova
Romania	29.7	18.7	15.2	15.7	16.9	15.8	20.6	14.8	15.5	21.8	Roumanie
Russian Federation	..	41.8	11.0	38.2	47.3	49.2	50.4	74.6	79.0	90.8	Fédération de Russie
Slovakia	..	..	15.4	16.5	12.4	20.0	5.8	7.0	22.4	20.0	Slovaquie
Slovenia	..	4.6	3.7	3.9	4.3	3.3	3.2	4.4	4.2	4.0	Slovénie
Spain	[11]56.5	[11]53.1	[11]57.5	190.8	201.0	212.7	202.0	211.5	210.4	203.5	Espagne
Sweden	70.7	75.3	69.0	62.1	74.6	84.4	93.5	89.2	87.1	82.2	Suède
Switzerland	[6]108.9	[6]111.5	[6]115.9	[6]119.2	[6]121.0	[6]128.3	[6]128.2	[6]135.1	[6]130.9	130.6	Suisse
Ukraine	..	29.7	16.8	41.2	32.1	31.2	38.6	65.2	76.1	81.0	Ukraine

For general note and footnotes, see end of table.

Voir la fin du tableau pour la remarque générale et les notes.

Chocolate and chocolate products (continued)
Chocolat et produits à base de chocolat (suite)

ISIC-BASED CODE - CODE BASE CITI

3119-13

Unit : Thousand metric tons

Unité : Milliers de tonnes métriques

Country or area	1990	1991	1992	1993	1994	1995	1996	1997	1998	1999	Pays ou zone
United Kingdom	...	...	...	646.2	652.9	609.3	645.1	620.0	619.8	...	Royaume-Uni
Yugoslavia	..	15.2	12.8	8.3	11.9	15.3	15.1	14.8	16.1	15.3	Yougoslavie
T.F.Yug.Rep. Macedonia	..	5.9	5.0	4.3	4.5	4.3	3.8	3.8	3.7	3.5	L'ex-RY Macédoine
USSR (former)	595.2	..	..	..	..	..	..	..	..	..	URSS (anc.)
Oceania	95	97	102	110	112	114	111	122	125	128	Océanie
Australia	95.4	97.5	102.1	109.7	111.7	113.5	111.4	...	...	...	Australie
Total	4760	4989	4981	5819	5586	5722	6291	6426	6189	6315	Total

General Note.
Chocolate and food preparations containing cocoa or chocolate, including all sugar confectionery containing cocoa in any proportion, sweetened cocoa powder, chocolate powder and chocolate spreads. The product known as "white chocolate" (composed of cocoa butter, sugar and powdered milk) is excluded. (SITC, Rev.3: 07300-0).

[1] Production by large and medium scale establishments only.
[2] Including sugar confectionery.
[3] Including soft candies glazed with chocolate.
[4] Production by establishments employing 5 or more persons.
[5] Incomplete coverage.
[6] Sales.
[7] Including sugar confectionary and chewing gum.
[8] Production by establishments employing 20 or more persons.
[9] Including pudding powder without cocoa.
[10] Excluding Transnistria region.
[11] Including substitutes; excluding sweetened cocoa powder.

Remarque générale.
Chocolat et préparations alimentaires contenant du cacao ou du chocolat, y compris toutes les sucreries contenant du cacao, en proportion quelconque, les cacaos en poudre sucrés, les chocolats en poudre et les produits pâteux à base de chocolat. La préparation dite "chocolat blanc" (composée de beurre de cacao, de sucre et de lait en poudre) n'est pas comprise dans cette position. (CTCI, Rev.3: 07300-0).

[1] Production des grandes et moyennes entreprises seulement.
[2] Y compris les sucreries.
[3] Y compris les bonbons mous glacés au chocolat.
[4] Production des établissements occupant 5 personnes ou plus.
[5] Couverture incomplète.
[6] Ventes.
[7] Y compris les sucreries et les chewing-gums.
[8] Production des établissements occupant 20 personnes ou plus.
[9] Y compris les flans en poudre sans cacao.
[10] Non compris la région de Transnistria.
[11] Y compris les succédanés; non compris les cacaos en poudre sucrés.

Coffee extracts, including instant coffee
Les extraits et essences de café, y compris le café soluble

ISIC-BASED CODE - CODE BASE CITI
3121-01

Unit : Metric tons

Unité : Tonnes métriques

Country or area	1990	1991	1992	1993	1994	1995	1996	1997	1998	1999	Pays ou zone
Africa	**117637**	**115656**	**101693**	**127028**	**120909**	**109224**	**119677**	**113585**	**116935**	**117192**	**Afrique**
Kenya	86302	85805	69942	94487	86367	80170	88824	...	...	...	Kenya
South Africa	31093	29524	31411	32120	34313	28738	30561	26471	...	...	Afrique du Sud
United Rep.Tanzania [1]	242	327	340	421	229	316	292	286	...	...	Rép. Unie de Tanzanie [1]
America, North	**26263**	**29630**	**37018**	**156833**	**190434**	**178757**	**191686**	**174416**	**154948**	**169753**	**Amérique du Nord**
Jamaica	7158	9437	...	10524	9134	15398	15288	17146	16873	13110	Jamaïque
Mexico	19105	20193	24344	#146309	181300	163359	176398	157270	138075	156643	Mexique
America, South	**162693**	**141828**	**139216**	**143270**	**157392**	**135668**	**126706**	**87689**	**77412**	**59173**	**Amérique du Sud**
Bolivia	463	363	565	655	664	*831	...	...	...	...	Bolivie
Brazil	53702	44695	61661	64587	66420	62878	62562	60372	46805	53124	Brésil
Chile	2580	2825	3469	4199	4273	4198	5306	5520	4061	3695	Chili
Colombia	...	...	72472	72475	84690	66531	...	19687	24241	...	Colombie
Peru	1414	1374	1049	1354	1345	1230	1403	1317	1472	1481	Pérou
Asia	**79089**	**83963**	**88493**	**102971**	**105639**	**113314**	**97803**	**118293**	**108054**	**111827**	**Asie**
Cyprus	*1560	*1730	1656	*1640	*1680	1717	1785	1622	1601	1446	Chypre
Indonesia	9485	13548	15464	24922	25667	34954	...	38169	...	...	Indonésie
Japan	33993	33977	33651	35217	33669	32486	35055	33157	31410	32067	Japon
Korea, Republic of	22735	23392	26406	29876	33307	32841	28457	33062	32671	35814	Corée, République de
Thailand [1]	...	...	...	...	...	...	9333	12283	12333	...	Thaïlande [1]
Europe	**216727**	**217818**	**241448**	**119651**	**123699**	**109238**	**135624**	**131584**	**122031**	**121404**	**Europe**
Austria	...	...	...	...	...	4227	3926	...	...	7407	Autriche
Croatia	..	55	25	17	20	15	5	0	...	...	Croatie
Denmark [2]	...	...	0	0	0	0	0	11	11	15	Danemark [2]
Finland	...	...	...	14	30	...	...	...	...	...	Finlande
Germany	..	26365	...	31131	35819	31586	57284	54224	58860	...	Allemagne
Germany(Fed.Rep.)	24372	..	..	..	..	..	..	..	..	..	Allemagne(Rép.féd.)
German D.R.(former)	3	..	..	..	..	..	..	..	..	..	R.D.A. (anc.)
Hungary	179	859	1834	...	...	...	2090	2193	1922	2192	Hongrie
Latvia	..	1644	1238	918	492	480	646	720	534	461	Lettonie
Netherlands [2][3]	10408	9871	12216	12392	12799	12920	...	...	...	...	Pays-Bas [2][3]
Poland	4607	3485	3782	4107	5183	6874	4674	3606	5635	3138	Pologne
Portugal [4]	3481	3138	125	115	3	3	32	...	...	...	Portugal [4]
Russian Federation	..	3592	2788	2601	831	244	340	335	667	1745	Fédération de Russie
Slovakia	..	..	...	...	...	...	...	5333	...	...	Slovaquie
Slovenia	..	322	257	213	233	226	178	0	0	...	Slovénie
Spain	115686	110770	118505	11352	12636	12723	13707	19479	...	...	Espagne
Ukraine [1]	..	1419	1135	1424	569	312	247	553	1007	1306	Ukraine [1]
United Kingdom	...	...	...	...	42641	32504	34025	26463	29138	...	Royaume-Uni
T.F.Yug.Rep. Macedonia		1610	647	369	313	159	118	154	103	138	L'ex-RY Macédoine
Total	**602409**	**588895**	**607869**	**649753**	**698073**	**646201**	**671496**	**625567**	**579380**	**579350**	**Total**

General Note.
Data under this heading relate to coffee extracts, essences and concentrates. These may be made from real coffee (whether or not caffeine has been removed) or from a mixture of real coffee and coffee substitutes in any proportion. They may be in liquid or powder form, usually highly concentrated. The heading includes instant or pulverized coffee. (SITC, Rev.3: 07131-0, 07132-0).

Remarque générale.
Les données se rapportent aux extraits et essences de café. Ils peuvent être préparés à partir de véritable café, décaféiné ou non, ou à partir d'un mélange, en toutes proportions, de véritable café et de succédanés de café. Ces extraits ou essences se présentent à l'état liquide ou en poudre et sont généralement très concentrés. Cette rubrique comprend le café soluble. (CTCI, Rev.3: 07131-0, 07132-0).

[1] Instant coffee only.
[2] Sales.
[3] Production by establishments employing 20 or more persons.
[4] Beginning 1997, data are confidential.

[1] Café soluble seulement.
[2] Ventes.
[3] Production des établissements occupant 20 personnes ou plus.
[4] A partir de 1997, les données sont confidentielles

Vinegar
Vinaigres
ISIC-BASED CODE - CODE BASE CITI
3121-04

Unit : Thousand hectolitres
Unité : Milliers de hectolitres

Country or area	1990	1991	1992	1993	1994	1995	1996	1997	1998	1999	Pays ou zone
Africa	**5**	**5**	**5**	**5**	**5**	**5**	**5**	**5**	**5**	**5**	**Afrique**
Mali	...	...	...	4	...	...	...	...	...	...	Mali
Mauritius	1	1	1	1	1	1	1	1	1	1	Maurice
America, North	**7**	**8**	**6**	**8**	**10**	**8**	**8**	**8**	**8**	**8**	**Amérique du Nord**
Panama	7	...	6	8	10	...	...	...	...	...	Panama
America, South	**48**	**80**	**58**	**126**	**67**	**74**	**79**	**116**	**62**	**103**	**Amérique du Sud**
Colombia	28	...	35	104	45	52	...	94	40	...	Colombie
Paraguay	20	23	23	...	...	...	...	...	...	...	Paraguay
Asia	**3892**	**4238**	**4035**	**4092**	**4093**	**4194**	**4299**	**4378**	**4582**	**4445**	**Asie**
Cyprus	...	...	16	...	...	9	11	16	12	13	Chypre
Indonesia	63	366	107	162	127	160	...	...	364	...	Indonésie
Japan	3818	3861	3912	3917	3953	4025	4095	4169	4206	4252	Japon
Europe	**5278**	**6420**	**6329**	**5038**	**5258**	**5344**	**4866**	**5029**	**5114**	**4605**	**Europe**
Austria	72	79	78	77	80	#172	159	190	191	167	Autriche
Belarus	..	47	47	41	41	43	42	37	44	41	Bélarus
Belgium	[1]250	[1]258	[1]265	[1]218	...	...	112	104	117	...	Belgique
Bulgaria	324	248	262	247	225	210	158	160	109	78	Bulgarie
Croatia	..	228	164	139	143	120	116	125	67	...	Croatie
Denmark[2]	193	214	206	151	160	154	147	62	39	0	Danemark[2]
Czechoslovakia(former)	418	481	..	..	..	..	..	..	..	..	Tchécoslovaquie(anc.)
Czech Republic	..	..	228	274	239	155	116	99	96	100	République tchèque
Finland[3]	26	25	30	28	31	32	26	29	28	33	Finlande[3]
Germany	..	1628	...	1729	1826	1796	1696	1789	1994	..	Allemagne
Germany(Fed.Rep.)	1360	..	..	..	..	..	..	..	..	..	Allemagne(Rép.féd.)
German D.R.(former)	174	..	..	..	..	..	..	..	..	..	R.D.A. (anc.)
Greece	118	96	111	58	57	60	59	61	50	...	Grèce
Hungary	327	325	299	...	222	217	230	...	...	...	Hongrie
Latvia	..	...	...	...	...	...	...	...	...	1	Lettonie
Lithuania	..	37	34	19	18	20	21	21	19	23	Lituanie
Poland	324	337	312	259	316	342	252	293	235	315	Pologne
Portugal	...	...	...	0	...	...	87	110	97	96	Portugal
Republic of Moldova	..	15	17	[4]0	...	[4]1	[4]1	[4]0	[4]1	[4]2	Rép. de Moldova
Romania	635	357	327	279	266	269	232	243	305	248	Roumanie
Russian Federation	..	209	164	141	119	132	119	91	58	46	Fédération de Russie
Slovakia	..	..	155	183	199	193	188	178	117	197	Slovaquie
Slovenia	..	85	60	78	79	72	60	74	75	75	Slovénie
Spain	932	826	801	124	278	303	371	447	775	...	Espagne
Sweden	39	37	47	59	58	67	68	117	13	13	Suède
Ukraine	..	684	692	487	473	560	460	451	360	334	Ukraine
United Kingdom	...	...	...	...	...	84	85	90	87	...	Royaume-Uni
Yugoslavia	..	91	132	77	59	68	56	76	88	58	Yougoslavie
T.F.Yug.Rep. Macedonia	..	25	16	13	10	6	4	16	3	9	L'ex-RY Macédoine
Total	**9230**	**10751**	**10433**	**9269**	**9433**	**9626**	**9257**	**9536**	**9770**	**9166**	**Total**

General Note.
Wine vinegar, beer and malt vinegar, fermented fruit vinegar, spirit vinegar and substitutes for vinegar (obtained by diluting acetic acid with water), in terms of 10 per cent of vinegar. Toilet vinegar is excluded. (SITC, Rev.3: 09844-0).

Remarque générale.
Vinaigres de vin, de bière ou de malt, vinaigres de fruits fermentés, vinaigres d'alcools et succédanés du vinaigre (obtenus par dilution d'acide acétique dans l'eau) exprimés en vinaigre à 10 p. 100. Cette rubrique ne comprend pas le vinaigre de toilette. (CTCI, Rev.3: 09844-0).

[1] Including data for Luxembourg.
[2] Sales.
[3] Including grape must.
[4] Excluding Transnistria region.

[1] Y compris les données relatives au Luxembourg.
[2] Ventes.
[3] Y compris les moûts de raisin.
[4] Non compris la région de Transnistria.

Prepared animal feeds
Aliments préparés pour animaux

ISIC-BASED CODE - CODE BASE CITI

3122-01

Unit : Thousand metric tons

Unité : Milliers de tonnes métriques

Country or area	1990	1991	1992	1993	1994	1995	1996	1997	1998	1999	Pays ou zone
Africa	**6873**	**6574**	**6258**	**5996**	**5976**	**6077**	**5892**	**4931**	**4939**	**4649**	**Afrique**
Algeria	1663	1553	1412	1485	1331	1291	1127	1265	1274	1008	Algérie
Egypt	1700	1617	1273	1006	1122	914	901	802	...	...	Egypte
Ethiopia	28	21	11	7	7	11	5	5	5	5	Ethiopie
Kenya	146	151	153	102	96	143	181	...	...	...	Kenya
Mali	75	89	93	89	63	66	...	...	...	...	Mali
Mauritius	61	68	74	81	85	107	108	111	107	110	Maurice
Mozambique	20	14	6	0	0	0	...	0	3	2	Mozambique
Nigeria	...	8	31	...	52	47	...	...	...	...	Nigéria
Seychelles	...	...	...	12	12	10	11	13	13	13	Seychelles
South Africa	3108	3010	3168	3160	3172	3434	3369	2444	2486	2526	Afrique du Sud
Uganda	15	22	20	18	35	54	46	10	2	0	Ouganda
United Rep.Tanzania	12	10	6	2	2	1	33	32		...	Rép. Unie de Tanzanie
America, North	**3150**	**3328**	**3362**	**7198**	**7463**	**6709**	**6228**	**6442**	**7398**	**8098**	**Amérique du Nord**
Barbados	59	66	60	58	57	60	69	65	67	65	Barbade
Grenada	3	3	4	4	5	...	...	...	...	...	Grenade
Jamaica	230	221	206	224	206	182	174	187	192	232	Jamaïque
Mexico	2475	2633	2697	6498	6826	6049	5626	5725	6536	7053	Mexique
Panama	154	...	190	211	217	229	176	...	...	...	Panama
Trinidad and Tobago	229	209	205	203	152	184	177	164	282	407	Trinité-et-Tobago
America, South	**4780**	**5442**	**5468**	**5634**	**5889**	**6499**	**6496**	**6854**	**6782**	**8266**	**Amérique du Sud**
Bolivia	32	36	20	25	14	*15	...	...	...	...	Bolivie
Brazil	2171	2203	2044	2205	2399	2581	2812	2743	2664	2645	Brésil
Chile	21	26	36	40	64	69	76	109	96	134	Chili
Colombia	1446	...	...	...	2088	2365	...	2490	2594	...	Colombie
Ecuador	230	...	342	320	334	333	268	284	243	...	Equateur
Guyana	10	6	6	10	15	...	...	...	...	...	Guyana
Paraguay	126	34	24	...	...	...	...	...	...	...	Paraguay
Peru	664	614	775	759	898	1049	1038	1137	...	...	Pérou
Suriname	80	32	24	17	16	12	14	...	...	...	Suriname
Asia	**42954**	**46677**	**48366**	**48041**	**46695**	**47581**	**47756**	**50268**	**46856**	**49726**	**Asie**
Armenia	..	398	240	109	108	84	54	56	38	50	Arménie
Azerbaijan		689	365	208	132	116	86	27	4	1	Azerbaïdjan
Hong Kong SAR	81	59	88	16	3	25	7	14	16	13	Hong-Kong RAS
Cyprus	*195	*184	177	176	188	274	350	355	353	339	Chypre
Indonesia	1361	1633	2866	2978	3081	3301	...	5447	...	...	Indonésie
Iran(Islamic Rep. of)	[1]207	[1]224	[1]308	[1]286	[1]282	[2]881	[2]823	[2]670	[2]656	...	Iran(Rép. islamique)
Israel[3]	1625	...	...	...	...	...	...	...	...	...	Israël[3]
Japan	25862	26018	26024	26136	25256	24866	24702	24769	24516	24392	Japon
Korea, Republic of	10107	11092	12008	12003	12106	12248	12992	12908	11314	...	Corée, République de
Kyrgyzstan	..	738	457	212	77	59	37	20	24	14	Kirghizistan
Lao People's Dem. Rep.	...	...	...	...	3	3	...	...	...	...	Rép. dém. pop. lao
Malaysia	1166	1331	1302	1294	1288	1408	1441	1674	1750	1969	Malaisie
Nepal[4]	...	...	22	15	18	20	22	24	22	*23	Népal[4]
Turkey	2328	2126	2386	2450	2122	2483	2566	2625	2756	3039	Turquie
Turkmenistan	..	537	495	530	406	188	96	51	46	...	Turkménistan
Europe	**104009**	**108127**	**109095**	**92529**	**91481**	**97312**	**99628**	**99293**	**102282**	**103632**	**Europe**
Austria	720	1375	851	887	877	1068	...	...	1136	1101	Autriche
Belgium	5498	5226	5242	5372	4855	5777	5955	6104	6274	...	Belgique
Bulgaria	4525	2973	2353	1699	1359	1503	938	619	624	491	Bulgarie
Croatia	..	785	696	646	526	516	474	465	528	...	Croatie
Denmark[5]	...	...	...	...	...	180	181	217	232	230	Danemark[5]
Czech Republic	..	...	...	...	1649	1706	1860	2795	2808	2521	République tchèque
Estonia	..	632	304	201	185	163	98	131	150	132	Estonie
Finland	1517	1360	1237	1221	1318	1443	1458	1531	1701	1667	Finlande
France	18178	18983	19383	20269	20797	21230	22003	22601	22875	...	France
Germany	...	...	...	14991	14649	16029	16497	15351	15372	...	Allemagne
Germany(Fed.Rep.)	12392										Allemagne(Rép.féd.)
German D.R.(former)	4606	..	..	..	..	..	..	..	..	..	R.D.A. (anc.)
Greece	925	887	834	745	882	834	868	873	926	...	Grèce

For general note and footnotes, see end of table.

Voir la fin du tableau pour la remarque générale et les notes.

218

Prepared animal feeds (continued)
Aliments préparés pour animaux (suite)

ISIC-BASED CODE - CODE BASE CITI

3122-01

Unit : Thousand metric tons   Unité : Milliers de tonnes métriques

Country or area	1990	1991	1992	1993	1994	1995	1996	1997	1998	1999	Pays ou zone
Hungary	2829	2465	2821	2564	2182	2274	2521	2040	2423	...	Hongrie
Iceland	...	...	...	...	...	...	48	56	80	83	Islande
Latvia	..	1402	719	255	182	220	206	205	203	144	Lettonie
Lithuania	..	...	...	...	...	524	465	455	394	284	Lituanie
Netherlands[5][6]	13211	13469	13894	15603	15941	15922	15748	15294	15381	14965	Pays-Bas[5][6]
Norway	...	1759	1733	...	...	...	...	1998	...	2040	Norvège
Poland	4968	4372	4164	2941	3121	3634	4023	4248	4029	3928	Pologne
Portugal	3676	3028	3360	3523	3672	3504	3684	3742	3812	3674	Portugal
Republic of Moldova	..	1729	1022	[7]431	[7]302	[7]326	[7]344	[7]226	[7]217	[7]106	Rép. de Moldova
Russian Federation	..	538	446	392	359	303	245	192	198	174	Fédération de Russie
Slovakia	..	..	...	...	501	568	662	655	730	638	Slovaquie
Slovenia	..	554	388	429	426	343	443	435	451	444	Slovénie
Spain	14694	14870	15822	10486	10586	12820	13618	13912	15551	16514	Espagne
Sweden	2170	1810	1717	2160	2120	2121	2169	1998	2419	2265	Suède
Switzerland	1148	1173	1155	1120	1133	1098	...	...	...	...	Suisse
Ukraine[8]	..	202	163	121	100	81	59	46	32	33	Ukraine[8]
United Kingdom	10900	10900	11000	#284	173	256	242	282	...	...	Royaume-Uni
Yugoslavia	..	1304	1172	874	759	793	690	605	652	560	Yougoslavie
T.F.Yug.Rep. Macedonia	..	167	140	143	126	127	130	106	98	98	L'ex-RY Macédoine
Oceania	**22**	**25**	**25**	**23**	**29**	**28**	**29**	**29**	**30**	**33**	**Océanie**
Fiji	22	25	25	23	29	28	29	29	30	...	Fidji
Total	**161787**	**170174**	**172574**	**159421**	**157534**	**164207**	**166030**	**167816**	**168287**	**174404**	**Total**

General Note.
Preparations of vegetable or animal origin with or without added mineral or chemical materials. They may be ready for direct consumption or may be in concentrated form requiring dilution before use. Inorganic esters and their salts, medicaments and simple mixtures of cereal grain, of cereal flours or of flours of leguminous vegetables are excluded. Biscuits for dogs and other animals, bird foods, fish foods and chemical preparations, such as egg-laying mixtures, are included. (SITC, Rev.3: 08195-0, 08199-0).

Remarque générale.
Produits d'origine végétale ou animale additionnés ou non de produits chimiques ou de sels minéraux, soit tout préparés et prêts à la consommation, soit présentés sous forme concentrée et devant être dilués avant consommation. Cette position ne comprend pas les esters et les sels d'acides minéraux, les médicaments, et les simples mélanges de céréales en grain ou en farine et de farines de légumineuses. Toutefois, elle inclut les biscuits pour chiens ou autres animaux, les nourritures pour oiseaux et poissons et les produits minéraux ou chimiques comme par exemple les pâtées servant à favoriser la ponte. (CTCI, Rev.3: 08195-0, 08199-0).

[1] Production by establishments employing 50 or more persons.
[2] Production by establishments employing 10 or more persons.
[3] Twelve months ending 30 September of year stated.
[4] Twelve months beginning 16 July of year stated.
[5] Sales.
[6] Production by establishments employing 20 or more persons.
[7] Excluding Transnistria region.
[8] Dried animal feeds only.

[1] Production des établissements occupant 50 personnes ou plus.
[2] Production des établissements occupant 10 personnes ou plus.
[3] Période de douze mois finissant le 30 septembre de l'année indiquée.
[4] Période de douze mois commençant le 16 juillet de l'année indiquée.
[5] Ventes.
[6] Production des établissements occupant 20 personnes ou plus.
[7] Non compris la région de Transnistria.
[8] Aliments séchés pour animaux seulement.

Distilled alcoholic beverages, excluding ethyl alcohol
Boissons alcooliques distillées, à l'exclusion de l'alcool éthylique

ISIC-BASED CODE - CODE BASE CITI
3131-01

Unit : Thousand hectolitres

Unité : Milliers de hectolitres

Country or area	1990	1991	1992	1993	1994	1995	1996	1997	1998	1999	Pays ou zone
Africa	**220**	**233**	**215**	**236**	**225**	**297**	**273**	**285**	**285**	**317**	**Afrique**
Cape Verde	2	2	4	4	4	5	...	...	...	...	Cap-Vert
Ethiopia[1]	62	51	35	33	47	29	17	30	29	31	Ethiopie[1]
Kenya	12	16	15	13	17	21	23	...	...	...	Kenya
Madagascar[2]	...	...	...	...	18	91	80	83	87	...	Madagascar[2]
Mauritius	69	66	66	61	56	55	52	47	47	45	Maurice
Réunion[2]	59	72	53	70	58	71	72	72	68	...	Réunion[2]
Uganda	4	4	3	3	5	5	6	6	2	2	Ouganda
United Rep.Tanzania	12	15	19	19	20	20	18	18	...	...	Rép. Unie de Tanzanie
America, North	**6506**	**6013**	**6398**	**6159**	**5423**	**6047**	**6186**	**6324**	**6483**	**6488**	**Amérique du Nord**
Barbados[2]	55	63	48	68	75	80	78	94	84	96	Barbade[2]
Belize	0	1	0	0	0	1	1	1	1	...	Belize
Dominican Republic	414	393	444	*424	*437	...	...	...	...	...	Rép. dominicaine
Grenada[2]	2	2	4	3	3	...	...	...	...	...	Grenade[2]
Guatemala	...	153	345	170	308	340	201	181	178	...	Guatemala
Haiti[2]	5	5	...	...	...	...	...	...	...	...	Haïti[2]
Jamaica[2]	181	185	162	206	211	204	204	224	222	197	Jamaïque[2]
Martinique[2]	85	67	74	99	78	...	...	...	...	...	Martinique[2]
Mexico	2170	2293	2250	2311	2263	1995	2177	2269	2397	2323	Mexique
Panama	77	84	95	103	103	101	119	...	...	...	Panama
St. Lucia[2][3]	6	7	7	7	8	8	8	9	8	9	St-Lucie[2][3]
St. Vincent-Grenadines[2]	6	3	4	3	4	4	4	4	4	5	St. Vincent-Grenadines[2]
Trinidad and Tobago[2]	112	116	100	72	58	132	202	213	245	281	Trinité-et-Tobago[2]
United States	3149	...	2860	2687	[4]1870	...	...	...	...	...	Etats-Unis
America, South	**2830**	**2812**	**2814**	**2899**	**2853**	**2574**	**2643**	**2354**	**2240**	**2001**	**Amérique du Sud**
Argentina	572	716	745	792	777	*677	657	764	731	674	Argentine
Colombia	...	...	1441	1492	1520	...	...	1187	1064	...	Colombie
Ecuador	269	...	410	363	290	240	305	32	32	...	Equateur
Guyana	183	163	218	252	258	...	...	...	...	...	Guyana
Peru[2]	...	...	...	...	...	29	30	37	54	82	Pérou[2]
Asia	**9880**	**9118**	**9868**	**10740**	**10323**	**9899**	**10303**	**11124**	**10260**	**11267**	**Asie**
Azerbaijan	..	436	270	149	85	22	33	12	19	55	Azerbaïdjan
Cyprus	44	41	48	43	43	42	38	38	39	41	Chypre
Georgia	..	...	200	221	51	26	27	33	15	49	Géorgie
Israel[5]	21	...	...	...	...	...	...	...	...	...	Israël[5]
Japan[6]	8360	7092	7927	8519	8422	8336	8530	9108	8147	9073	Japon[6]
Kyrgyzstan	..	16	10	6	7	5	6	8	9	5	Kirghizistan
Lao People's Dem. Rep.	...	...	...	...	1	2	...	...	...	...	Rép. dém. pop. lao
Mongolia	6	68	68	53	36	37	4	4	5	6	Mongolie
Nepal[7]	...	...	30	35	21	25	26	28	31	*33	Népal[7]
Turkey	[8]616	733	717	799	733	775	871	839	912	925	Turquie
Turkmenistan	..	174	178	187	198	94	74	96	100	...	Turkménistan
Viet Nam	804	392	397	...	...	514	671	936	961	969	Viet Nam
Europe	**20214**	**35060**	**33761**	**32835**	**30470**	**34467**	**28042**	**28226**	**27111**	**32839**	**Europe**
Austria	[9]295	[9]327	[9]274	[9]280	[9]250	111	91	92	81	74	Autriche
Belgium	...	...	...	...	326	296	168	94	77	68	Belgique
Croatia	..	787	353	315	300	282	280	262	242	...	Croatie
Denmark[10]	200	197	187	...	...	...	...	...	...	...	Danemark[10]
Czechoslovakia(former)	1331	1434	..	...	...	...	...	...	..	..	Tchécoslovaquie(anc.)
Czech Republic	..	...	926	889	809	779	759	736	638	680	République tchèque
Estonia	..	161	121	168	123	173	96	109	102	66	Estonie
Finland[11]	725	615	617	588	720	849	816	987	1033	804	Finlande[11]
France	3115	3599	3571	4008	4239	3989	4448	4655	4449	...	France
Germany	..	1636	1651	1802	1858	5532	5122	4364	4022	...	Allemagne
Germany(Fed.Rep.)	3519	..	..	..	..	..	..	..	..	..	Allemagne(Rép.féd.)
German D.R.(former)	1486	..	..	..	..	..	..	..	..	..	R.D.A. (anc.)
Greece	480	399	434	380	396	540	503	487	229	...	Grèce
Hungary	981	832	646	607	876	1204	708	334	336	428	Hongrie
Iceland	7	3	2	...	...	...	2	2	3	2	Islande
Latvia	..	218	163	130	144	162	169	206	195	[12]168	Lettonie

For general note and footnotes, see end of table.

Voir la fin du tableau pour la remarque générale et les notes.

Distilled alcoholic beverages, excluding ethyl alcohol (continued)
Boissons alcooliques distillées, à l'exclusion de l'alcool éthylique (suite)

ISIC-BASED CODE - CODE BASE CITI

3131-01

Unit : Thousand hectolitres

Unité : Milliers de hectolitres

Country or area	1990	1991	1992	1993	1994	1995	1996	1997	1998	1999	Pays ou zone
Lithuania	..	355	270	240	217	262	283	272	159	142	Lituanie
Luxembourg	1	1	1	1	1	1	1	1	1	1	Luxembourg
Netherlands[10][12][13]	789	830	832	933	961	926	...	...	...	...	Pays-Bas[10][12][13]
Poland	1510	1457	1357	1495	1566	1539	1223	1104	937	860	Pologne
Portugal	79	73	397	262	209	198	157	214	241	270	Portugal
Romania	343	408	416	834	390	397	330	254	55	35	Roumanie
Russian Federation	..	15769	15382	15865	12677	12389	7176	8393	8811	13400	Fédération de Russie
Slovakia	..	..	575	539	453	489	448	420	160	126	Slovaquie
Slovenia	..	90	122	63	59	43	16	12	8	9	Slovénie
Spain	2796	2804	2908	1193	1014	987	1389	1618	1672	1364	Espagne
Sweden[14]	609	578	609	733	1089	744	658	642	679	739	Suède[14]
Switzerland	52	52	54	61	67	57	...	...	...	...	Suisse
United Kingdom	...	...	...	953	1327	2120	1803	...	...	...	Royaume-Uni
Yugoslavia	..	550	13	2	...	...	...	...	...	...	Yougoslavie
T.F.Yug.Rep. Macedonia	..	19	42	38	13	12	6	9	4	17	L'ex-RY Macédoine
Total	**39651**	**53237**	**53055**	**52868**	**49294**	**53283**	**47446**	**48314**	**46379**	**52911**	**Total**

General Note.
Spirits produced by distilling wine, cides etc., or fermented grain or other vegetable products, without adding flavouring; spirits, liqueurs and cordials containing added flavouring and other spirituous beverages. The average alcoholic content should be indicated. (SITC, Rev.3: 11241-0, 11242-0, 11244-0, 11245-0, 11249-0).

Remarque générale.
Eaux de vie obtenues par distillation du vin, du cidre etc., ou de grains fermentés ou d'autres produits végétaux, non additionnés d'aromates; alcools et liqueurs additionnés d'aromates et toutes autres boissons spiritueuses. Indiquer le degré moyen d'alcool. (CTCI, Rev.3: 11241-0, 11242-0,11244-0, 11245-0, 11249-0).

[1] Twelve months ending 7 July of the year stated.
[2] Rum only.
[3] Original data in proof gallons.
[4] Twelve months ending 30 September of year stated.
[5] Marketed quantities.
[6] Twelve months beginning 1 April of year stated.
[7] Twelve months beginning 16 July of year stated.
[8] Government production only.
[9] Including ethyl alcohol.
[10] Sales.
[11] Including beverages from imported spirits.
[12] In terms of 100 per cent alcohol.
[13] Production by establishments employing 20 or more persons.
[14] Vermouths, blended from imported wines.

[1] Période de douze mois finissant le 7 juillet de l'année indiquée.
[2] Rhum seulement.
[3] Données d'origine exprimées en gallons d'alcool de titre normal.
[4] Période de douze mois finissant le 30 septembre de l'année indiquée.
[5] Quantités commercialisées.
[6] Période de douze mois commençant le 1er avril de l'année indiquée.
[7] Période de douze mois commençant le 16 juillet de l'année indiquée.
[8] Production de l'Etat seulement.
[9] Y compris l'alcool éthylique.
[10] Ventes.
[11] Y compris les boissons mises en bouteille à partir d'eaux de vie importées
[12] Sur la base de 100 p. 100 d'alcool.
[13] Production des établissements occupant 20 personnes ou plus.
[14] Vermouths constitués à partir de vins importés.

Ethyl alcohol for all purposes
Alcool éthylique pour tous usages

ISIC-BASED CODE - CODE BASE CITI

3131-04

Unit : Thousand hectolitres   Unité : Milliers de hectolitres

Country or area	1990	1991	1992	1993	1994	1995	1996	1997	1998	1999	Pays ou zone
Africa	**13**	**13**	**13**	**13**	**13**	**13**	**13**	**13**	**13**	**13**	**Afrique**
Ethiopia[1]	13	...	...	...	...	...	...	...	...	...	Ethiopie[1]
America, North	**28071**	**31689**	**38164**	**34097**	**26409**	**31728**	**31783**	**31790**	**31806**	**31823**	**Amérique du Nord**
Panama	71	93	87	70	129	132	187	...	...	...	Panama
United States	[2]28000	...	[2]38077	[2]34027	[3]26280	...	...	...	...	...	Etats-Unis
America, South	**2245**	**2452**	**2148**	**1704**	**1976**	**1756**	**1602**	**1307**	**1109**	**1075**	**Amérique du Sud**
Argentina	1390	1391	1187	931	1020	...	...	...	...	...	Argentine
Colombia	...	...	246	277	257	317	...	197	156	...	Colombie
Ecuador	49	...	161	174	203	107	172	18	13	...	Equateur
Paraguay	238	405	325	92	...	...	...	...	...	...	Paraguay
Peru	...	...	...	...	...	242	218	242	210	250	Pérou
Suriname	1	1	1	1	1	...	...	...	...	...	Suriname
Asia	**7690**	**7645**	**5711**	**6725**	**6970**	**7016**	**6774**	**7288**	**7460**	**7702**	**Asie**
Armenia	..	12	9	8	7	2	0	1	1	6	Arménie
Azerbaijan	..	1225	685	54	45	26	19	15	1	0	Azerbaïdjan
Cyprus	5	6	5	5	4	4	5	6	4	5	Chypre
Georgia	..	..	...	...	1	4	6	6	6	1	Géorgie
Indonesia[4]	3494	2253	815	...	...	...	...	...	...	...	Indonésie[4]
Japan[5]	2122	1997	1944	2081	2237	2232	1936	...	...	...	Japon[5]
Korea, Republic of	2026	1972	2048	2155	2276	2315	2313	2528	2685	2875	Corée, République de
Kyrgyzstan	..	6	6	18	22	23	20	12	12	4	Kirghizistan
Syrian Arab Republic	17	18	23	21	17	16	19	13	21	...	Rép. arabe syrienne
Tajikistan	..	29	30	36	34	21	20	30	28	28	Tadjikistan
Turkey	26	42	46	47	29	0	0	16	8	20	Turquie
Turkmenistan	..	1	2	2	1	5	2	2	1	...	Turkménistan
Uzbekistan	..	81	94	107	110	181	247	357	...	...	Ouzbékistan
Europe	**10177**	**35143**	**33184**	**33615**	**31339**	**32499**	**30246**	**25911**	**19179**	**20162**	**Europe**
Belarus	..	860	846	853	827	985	1025	1312	1046	959	Bélarus
Belgium	72	38	27	27	...	...	...	...	...	...	Belgique
Croatia	..	248	219	201	129	131	129	96	75	...	Croatie
Denmark[6]	0	331	356	288	202	27	29	29	28	23	Danemark[6]
Czechoslovakia(former)	1242	902	..	..	..	..	..	..	..	..	Tchécoslovaquie(anc.)
Czech Republic	..	..	926	817	912	893	1000	1121	872	762	République tchèque
Estonia	..	83	71	94	76	91	79	77	59	32	Estonie
Finland	402	361	338	511	362	182	190	...	...	...	Finlande
Germany	..	...	...	...	...	1708	1911	1975	1187	...	Allemagne
German D.R.(former)	376	...	...	...	...	..	..	..	..	..	R.D.A. (anc.)
Greece	[7]233	[7]215	[7]211	165	175	128	169	127	134	...	Grèce
Hungary	939	852	831	683	749	826	633	440	405	513	Hongrie
Latvia	..	112	97	87	109	98	110	118	82	128	Lettonie
Lithuania	..	176	158	163	178	165	264	214	142	74	Lituanie
Netherlands[6][8][9]	805	876	1091	1134	1063	1048	...	...	...	...	Pays-Bas[6][8][9]
Poland	2304	1766	1036	1256	1336	1326	1470	1335	1126	903	Pologne
Portugal	86	72	29	46	30	15	26	50	29	26	Portugal
Republic of Moldova	..	88	79	[10]23	[10]71	[10]71	[10]65	[10]113	[10]146	[10]135	Rép. de Moldova
Romania	1117	752	818	726	782	889	866	840	473	218	Roumanie
Russian Federation	..	15000	14500	15000	12800	12400	8340	8220	5090	6340	Fédération de Russie
Slovakia	..	..	...	...	...	...	...	...	231	190	Slovaquie
Slovenia	..	780	66	78	...	72	0	0	0	2	Slovénie
Spain	[11]1579	[12]2157	[11]1619	1357	967	1004	1231	1729	1841	1514	Espagne
Sweden	709	676	604	650	708	748	446	595	351	398	Suède
Ukraine	..	4833	4569	4658	4825	6224	6432	2461	1576	1360	Ukraine
United Kingdom	...	...	...	298	342	267	285	201	286	...	Royaume-Uni
Yugoslavia	..	391	376	320	254	257	184	131	195	148	Yougoslavie
T.F.Yug.Rep. Macedonia	..	1572	2111	2274	2371	2692	4004	3180	2479	3007	L'ex-RY Macédoine
USSR (former)	**22060**	..	..	..	..	..	..	..	..	..	**URSS (anc.)**
Total	**70255**	**76942**	**79220**	**76154**	**66708**	**73012**	**70419**	**66308**	**59568**	**60775**	**Total**

For general note and footnotes, see end of table.   Voir la fin du tableau pour la remarque générale et les notes.

Ethyl alcohol for all purposes (continued)
Alcool éthylique pour tous usages (suite)

ISIC-BASED CODE - CODE BASE CITI

3131-04

General Note.
Ethyl alcohol of any strength, denatured or undenatured, irrespective of its use, in terms of 100 per cent spirit. (SITC, Rev.3: 11243-0, 51215-0, 51216-0).

[1] Twelve months ending 7 July of the year stated.
[2] Twelve months ending 30 June of year stated.
[3] Twelve months ending 30 September of year stated.
[4] Including distilled alcoholic beverages.
[5] Twelve months beginning 1 April of year stated.
[6] Sales.
[7] Original data in metric tons.
[8] Production by establishments employing 20 or more persons.
[9] In terms of 100 per cent alcohol.
[10] Excluding Transnistria region.
[11] Including household production.

Remarque générale.
Alcool éthylique, quel que soit son degré alcoolique, dénaturé ou non, et quel que soit son usage, exprimé en alcool à 100 p. 100. (CTCI, Rev.3: 11243-0, 51215-0 51216-0).

[1] Période de douze mois finissant le 7 juillet de l'année indiquée.
[2] Période de douze mois finissant le 30 juin de l'année indiquée.
[3] Période de douze mois finissant le 30 septembre de l'année indiquée.
[4] Y compris les boissons alcooliques distillées.
[5] Période de douze mois commençant le 1er avril de l'année indiquée.
[6] Ventes.
[7] Données d'origine exprimées en tonnes.
[8] Production des établissements occupant 20 personnes ou plus.
[9] Sur la base de 100 p. 100 d'alcool.
[10] Non compris la région de Transnistria.
[11] Y compris la production ménagère.

Wine
Vins
ISIC-BASED CODE - CODE BASE CITI
3132-04

Unit : Thousand hectolitres

Unité : Milliers de hectolitres

Country or area	1990	1991	1992	1993	1994	1995	1996	1997	1998	1999	Pays ou zone
Africa	**8489**	**8853**	**6999**	**6608**	**7018**	**6043**	**5418**	**5030**	**4500**	**4108**	**Afrique**
Egypt[1]	20	20	...	...	...	...	...	...	...	...	Egypte[1]
Ethiopia[2]	95	70	61	69	57	71	58	35	26	20	Ethiopie[2]
Madagascar	8	3	19	6	24	49	20	9	17	...	Madagascar
Mauritius	27	33	34	31	25	27	21	29	32	30	Maurice
Morocco	300	300	...	...	...	...	...	...	...	...	Maroc
Nigeria	...	53	75	72	75	68	...	...	...	...	Nigéria
South Africa	7706	7946	6153	5765	6220	...	...	...	...	...	Afrique du Sud
Tunisia	267	425	333	344	294	292	221	372	352	469	Tunisie
United Rep.Tanzania	6	3	4	1	...	...	...	...	...	...	Rép. Unie de Tanzanie
America, North	**18817**	**19574**	**19479**	**16557**	**17524**	**18935**	**22808**	**20873**	**21206**	**21584**	**Amérique du Nord**
Canada* [1]	460	500	...	...	...	...	...	...	...	...	Canada* [1]
Mexico	400	1017	679	503	457	397	476	558	535	558	Mexique
Panama	2	1	2	2	2	2	2	...	...	...	Panama
United States	[3]17955	...	[3]18318	[3]15572	[4]16585	...	[4]21850	...	...	...	Etats-Unis
America, South	**25539**	**25381**	**24538**	**22865**	**22451**	**21813**	**21831**	**21711**	**20713**	**21117**	**Amérique du Sud**
Argentina	17131	17111	16193	14558	14179	13491	13542	13435	12428	12809	Argentine
Bolivia	7	13	15	15	17	*19	...	...	...	...	Bolivie
Brazil[1]	3110	3110	...	...	...	...	...	...	...	...	Brésil[1]
Chile[1]	3980	3900	...	...	...	...	...	...	...	...	Chili[1]
Colombia	...	...	195	...	130	204	...	153	164	...	Colombie
Ecuador	...	...	5	3	5	2	1	...	...	...	Equateur
Paraguay[5]	147	181	180	...	...	...	...	...	...	...	Paraguay[5]
Peru	[1]100	[1]100	...	...	...	27	31	34	31	33	Pérou
Uruguay[1]	900	800	...	...	...	...	...	...	...	...	Uruguay[1]
Asia	**1865**	**12928**	**10091**	**6684**	**4990**	**4628**	**4251**	**4465**	**3688**	**3626**	**Asie**
Armenia	..	433	258	274	227	102	48	32	14	49	Arménie
Azerbaijan	..	976	670	306	126	71	26	49	26	47	Azerbaïdjan
China, Macao, SAR	4	2	4	4	4	4	4	5	6	6	Chine, Macao PAS
Cyprus	663	532	464	350	610	590	569	442	329	421	Chypre
Georgia	...	...	1797	1043	630	367	228	312	230	194	Géorgie
Indonesia	127	91	...	...	49	122	...	89	41	...	Indonésie
Israel[6]	128	130	...	...	...	...	...	...	...	...	Israël[6]
Japan[7][8]	452	467	402	510	520	652	675	934	1159	1002	Japon[7][8]
Kazakhstan	..	7831	4723	2378	1217	1094	879	902	163	218	Kazakhstan
Korea, Republic of	145	131	84	72	66	65	60	89	66	83	Corée, République de
Kyrgyzstan	..	22	11	10	6	4	3	4	4	3	Kirghizistan
Lebanon[1]	100	110	...	...	...	...	...	...	...	...	Liban[1]
Syrian Arab Republic	3	3	2	3	3	35	38	3	34	...	Rép. arabe syrienne
Tajikistan	..	182	193	149	141	66	129	81	65	51	Tadjikistan
Thailand	7	...	...	...	...	...	...	...	...	...	Thaïlande
Turkey	236	216	251	288	299	319	363	336	341	260	Turquie
Turkmenistan	..	141	149	87	88	95	53	152	133	...	Turkménistan
Uzbekistan	..	761	755	883	763	801	848	794	...	...	Ouzbékistan
Europe	**194608**	**203083**	**194062**	**171782**	**176395**	**179349**	**178991**	**177275**	**168633**	**167193**	**Europe**
Albania	35	11	12	9	5	...	...	0	0	7	Albanie
Austria	3166	3093	5377	4610	4723	...	...	...	#205	246	Autriche
Belarus	..	650	537	556	606	548	869	1257	1922	2306	Bélarus
Bulgaria	2458	2572	2125	1659	1838	2625	2346	2096	2333	1715	Bulgarie
Croatia	..	745	808	685	657	606	551	624	639	...	Croatie
Czechoslovakia(former)	859	828	...	...	...	...	...	...	...	..	Tchécoslovaquie(anc.)
Czech Republic	..	..	525	591	497	786	647	688	676	694	République tchèque
Estonia	..	51	21	13	13	14	22	19	31	24	Estonie
Finland[9]	141	161	170	165	150	136	130	...	...	104	Finlande[9]
France[10]	65530	62000	...	...	...	...	...	...	...	...	France[10]
Germany	...	...	...	...	...	4047	4068	4071	4233	...	Allemagne
Germany(Fed.Rep.)[1]	9490	...	...	...	...	...	...	...	...	..	Allemagne(Rép.féd.)[1]
Greece	[1]3530	[1]4500	...	1846	1486	1586	1783	1455	1465	...	Grèce
Hungary	1692	1028	1179	1089	1087	992	2031	1529	1387	2334	Hongrie
Italy[1]	54870	59150	...	...	...	...	...	...	...	...	Italie[1]

For general note and footnotes, see end of table.

Voir la fin du tableau pour la remarque générale et les notes.

Wine (continued)
Vins (suite)

ISIC-BASED CODE - CODE BASE CITI
3132-04

Unit : Thousand hectolitres   Unité : Milliers de hectolitres

Country or area	1990	1991	1992	1993	1994	1995	1996	1997	1998	1999	Pays ou zone
Latvia	..	170	144	71	109	112	119	100	89	66	Lettonie
Lithuania	..	135	121	86	77	123	94	94	80	65	Lituanie
Luxembourg	151	86	271	169	175	150	128	75	160	184	Luxembourg
Malta[1]	30	30	...	...	...	...	...	...	...	...	Malte[1]
Poland	2114	2970	2285	2469	2498	2474	3482	3817	4498	4494	Pologne
Portugal	10970	9910	3351	3235	3522	3555	4712	4409	3463	4479	Portugal
Republic of Moldova	..	2390	1411	[11]1029	[11]886	[11]930	[11]1422	[11]1909	[11]1196	[11]652	Rép. de Moldova
Romania	4705	5009	4707	5499	7341	7193	7217	2137	954	1356	Roumanie
Russian Federation	..	7210	4740	3350	2960	2340	2050	2230	2180	1830	Fédération de Russie
Slovakia	..	..	335	429	549	469	555	772	519	548	Slovaquie
Slovenia	..	368	542	679	557	399	542	501	466	365	Slovénie
Spain	32958	28773	31687	13832	16267	21891	17780	20892	...	...	Espagne
Sweden	709	[9][12]816	[9][12]766	[9][12]925	[9][12]1380	[9][12]624	[9][12]288	[9][12]286	[9][12]234	[9][12]210	Suède
Switzerland	1200	1240	1249	1169	1188	1181	...	...	...	...	Suisse
Ukraine	..	2656	2088	1438	1156	1381	1199	990	771	856	Ukraine
Yugoslavia	..	1293	1293	872	947	746	881	963	882	653	Yougoslavie
T.F.Yug.Rep. Macedonia	..	1133	1202	397	811	566	1015	1171	1057	695	L'ex-RY Macédoine
USSR (former)	16237	..	..	..	..	..	..	..	..	..	URSS (anc.)
Oceania	4940	4531	4778	4811	4793	4826	4825	4795	4793	4777	Océanie
Australia	4450	4000	...	...	...	...	...	...	...	...	Australie
New Zealand[3]	490	531	553	586	568	601	600	570	568	552	Nouvelle-Zélande[3]
Total	270495	274350	259947	229307	233171	235593	238124	234150	223533	222406	Total

General Note.
Ordinary wine of fresh grapes produced in wineries (red, white, rose), sparkling wines, dessert wines (malaga, port, sherry, mistelles), vermouth and other wines flavoured with aromatic extracts. Unfermented grape juice and grape must are excluded. (SITC,Rev.3: 11210-0).

Remarque générale.
Vins ordinaires (vins rouges, rosés ou blancs), vins mousseux, vins de dessert (malaga, porto, sherry, mistelle), vermouths et autres vins de raisins frais aromatisés. Cette rubrique ne comprend pas les moûts de raisin ni les jus de raisin non fermentés. (CTCI, Rev.3: 11210-0).

[1] Source: Food and Agriculture Organization of the United Nations (FAO), (Rome).
[2] Twelve months ending 7 July of the year stated.
[3] Twelve months ending 30 June of year stated.
[4] Twelve months ending 30 September of year stated.
[5] Including cider.
[6] Marketed quantities.
[7] Including liqueurs of apples and other fruits.
[8] Twelve months beginning 1 April of year stated.
[9] Wines blended from imported wines.
[10] Including grape must.
[11] Excluding Transnistria region.
[12] Vermouths, blended from imported wines.

[1] Source: Organisation des Nations Unies pour l'alimentation et l'agriculture (FAO), (Rome).
[2] Période de douze mois finissant le 7 juillet de l'année indiquée.
[3] Période de douze mois finissant le 30 juin de l'année indiquée.
[4] Période de douze mois finissant le 30 septembre de l'année indiquée.
[5] Y compris le cidre.
[6] Quantités commercialisées.
[7] Y compris les liqueurs de pomme et d'autres fruits.
[8] Période de douze mois commençant le 1er avril de l'année indiquée.
[9] Vins constitués à partir de vins importés.
[10] Y compris les moûts de raisin.
[11] Non compris la région de Transnistria.
[12] Vermouths constitués à partir de vins importés.

Malt

Malt

ISIC-BASED CODE - CODE BASE CITI

3133-01

Unit : Thousand metric tons

Unité : Milliers de tonnes métriques

Country or area	1990	1991	1992	1993	1994	1995	1996	1997	1998	1999	Pays ou zone
Africa	**395**	**422**	**426**	**410**	**415**	**421**	**427**	**430**	**430**	**432**	**Afrique**
Ethiopia [1]	13	8	7	6	6	8	12	12	10	9	Ethiopie [1]
Kenya	23	30	39	30	35	...	...	...	...	...	Kenya
South Africa	359	384	380	...	...	...	...	...	...	...	Afrique du Sud
America, North	**2466**	**2431**	**2410**	**2468**	**2503**	**2452**	**2500**	**2534**	**2539**	**2462**	**Amérique du Nord**
Mexico	243	242	221	286	257	263	297	345	350	373	Mexique
United States	2223	...	2189	2182	[2]2246	...	[2]2203	...	...	[2]2089	Etats-Unis
America, South	**423**	**485**	**426**	**422**	**494**	**572**	**515**	**515**	**491**	**517**	**Amérique du Sud**
Argentina	66	...	...	...	...	...	...	...	...	...	Argentine
Brazil	152	215	163	169	244	263	241	249	220	246	Brésil
Colombia	...	...	196	182	180	236	...	...	...	...	Colombie
Ecuador	7	...	1	...	4	7	10	2	...	...	Equateur
Asia	**1166**	**1477**	**1453**	**1358**	**1383**	**1363**	**1359**	**1320**	**1299**	**1305**	**Asie**
Azerbaijan	..	5	0	1	1	0	0	0	0	0	Azerbaïdjan
Indonesia	863	1172	1188	...	...	...	...	...	...	...	Indonésie
Israel	68	...	...	...	...	...	...	...	...	...	Israël
Japan [3][4]	150	115	109	126	144	116	101	77	51	57	Japon [3][4]
Turkey [5]	85	117	88	89	96	105	116	101	106	106	Turquie [5]
Europe	**6548**	**7807**	**7742**	**7163**	**7405**	**7720**	**7499**	**7593**	**7543**	**8150**	**Europe**
Austria	155	152	150	152	76	190	162	...	156	...	Autriche
Belarus	..	125	124	78	60	74	65	70	77	72	Bélarus
Belgium	581	598	600	551	665	589	679	809	780	751	Belgique
Bulgaria	98	83	77	65	69	59	62	42	64	63	Bulgarie
Croatia	..	17	15	9	13	9	8	20	17	...	Croatie
Denmark [6]	109	117	133	116	123	133	124	119	211	229	Danemark [6]
Czechoslovakia(former)	644	606	..	..	..	..	..	..	..	..	Tchécoslovaquie(anc.)
Czech Republic	..	..	383	385	387	435	403	419	409	407	République tchèque
Estonia	..	...	...	...	...	13	11	10	12	6	Estonie
Finland	95	101	105	115	119	124	143	...	...	165	Finlande
France	[7]1287	[7]1335	[7]1318	[7]1265	[7]1216	[7]1269	[7]1274	1158	1148	...	France
Germany	..	...	...	1601	1786	1762	1693	1792	1774	...	Allemagne
Germany(Fed.Rep.)	1296										Allemagne(Rép.féd.)
German D.R. (former)	209	..	..	..	..	..	..	..	..	..	R.D.A. (anc.)
Greece	57	43	46	44	...	42	40	...	43	...	Grèce
Hungary	98	106	89	83	71	74	71	...	...	50	Hongrie
Ireland	126	...	...	...	...	51	165	184	...	...	Irlande
Latvia	..	6	6	6	7	5	1	2	1	2	Lettonie
Lithuania	..		24	12	16	19	13	10	11	12	Lituanie
Poland	190	184	191	164	165	169	161	188	160	215	Pologne
Portugal	55	58	62	67	...	...	...	...	...	...	Portugal
Romania	151	153	149	137	133	151	125	113	120	108	Roumanie
Russian Federation	..	475	448	376	276	292	212	273	257	327	Fédération de Russie
Slovakia	..		150	143	116	196	137	115	119	151	Slovaquie
Slovenia	..	4	5	4	5	5	5	4	4	3	Slovénie
Spain	[8]122	[8]212	[8]195	210	213	...	201	207	202	219	Espagne
Sweden	61	64	61	59	59	77	54	54	66	139	Suède
Ukraine	..	208	177	176	162	152	125	81	77	84	Ukraine
United Kingdom	1214	1178	...	1148	1347	1496	1408	1383	1343	...	Royaume-Uni
Yugoslavia	..	110	64	44	60	66	86	74	89	93	Yougoslavie
T.F.Yug.Rep. Macedonia	..	17	7	6	...	...	...	...	...	...	L'ex-RY Macédoine
Oceania	**603**	**604**	**561**	**518**	**557**	**554**	**586**	**571**	**597**	**566**	**Océanie**
Australia	603	604	561	518	557	554	586	571	597	566	Australie
Total	**11601**	**13225**	**13018**	**12339**	**12758**	**13082**	**12887**	**12963**	**12899**	**13432**	**Total**

General Note.

Roasted malt (most frequently roasted barley) as whole malt, ground malt or malt flour. Malt extracts are excluded. (SITC,Rev.3: 04820-0).

Remarque générale.

Malt grillé (en général obtenu à partir de l'orge), en grains, en semoule ou en farine, à l'exclusion des extraits de malt. (CTCI, Rev.3: 04820-0).

For footnotes, see end of table.

Voir la fin du tableau pour les notes.

Malt (continued)
Malt (suite)

ISIC-BASED CODE - CODE BASE CITI

3133-01

Footnotes

[1] Twelve months ending 7 July of the year stated.

[2] Twelve months ending 30 September of year stated.

[3] Twelve months beginning 1 April of year stated.

[4] For use in alcoholic liquors only.

[5] Government production only.

[6] Sales.

[7] Including grape must.

[8] Beer malt only.

Notes.

[1] Période de douze mois finissant le 7 juillet de l'année indiquée.

[2] Période de douze mois finissant le 30 septembre de l'année indiquée.

[3] Période de douze mois commençant le 1er avril de l'année indiquée.

[4] Pour emploi dans les boissons alcooliques seulement.

[5] Production de l'Etat seulement.

[6] Ventes.

[7] Y compris les moûts de raisin.

[8] Malt de bière seulement.

Beer
Bières

ISIC-BASED CODE - CODE BASE CITI

3133-04

Unit : Thousand hectolitres   Unité : Milliers de hectolitres

Country or area	1990	1991	1992	1993	1994	1995	1996	1997	1998	1999	Pays ou zone
Africa	**42786**	**42156**	**45843**	**52027**	**34350**	**35475**	**37561**	**36895**	**35653**	**35769**	**Afrique**
Algeria	325	301	337	421	398	402	377	379	382	383	Algérie
Angola	410	484	345	...	...	...	...	...	...	...	Angola
Botswana	1214	1211	1289	1374	1305	1366	1351	1005	1019	1591	Botswana
Burkina Faso	350	394	71	258	...	...	...	...	...	...	Burkina Faso
Burundi	1107	981	1007	1044	...	...	...	...	...	...	Burundi
Cameroon	...	4324	3834	4373	2073	2933	...	...	...	...	Cameroun
Central African Rep.	...	270	285	124	450	269	...	...	...	...	Rép. centrafricaine
Chad	116	144	129	117	110	95	...	...	...	...	Tchad
Congo	566	686	708	759	...	...	...	...	...	...	Congo
Egypt	500	440	420	350	360	360	380	...	...	...	Egypte
Ethiopia[1]	500	435	428	522	634	724	876	843	831	921	Ethiopie[1]
Gabon	819	814	785	905	801	816	...	...	...	...	Gabon
Kenya	3311	3140	3686	3589	3250	3474	2759	...	...	...	Kenya
Madagascar	298	236	226	228	219	246	347	234	297	...	Madagascar
Malawi	752	763	774	763	811	289	277	292	206	684	Malawi
Mali	34	38	41	40	43	52	60	...	...	...	Mali
Mauritius	281	291	295	292	283	309	312	339	376	358	Maurice
Mozambique	353	227	211	204	118	244	374	631	75	95	Mozambique
Nigeria	7877	8108	11438	16860	1561	1461	...	...	...	...	Nigéria
Seychelles	53	59	70	65	58	58	63	71	72	68	Seychelles
South Africa	17750	17710	18290	...	...	...	...	...	...	...	Afrique du Sud
Tunisia	426	407	494	601	689	659	662	780	813	912	Tunisie
Uganda	194	195	187	239	308	512	642	896	1105	1178	Ouganda
United Rep.Tanzania	450	498	493	570	568	893	125	148	...	...	Rép. Unie de Tanzanie
America, North	**281221**	**283370**	**285602**	**287361**	**289190**	**287186**	**286544**	**293059**	**296558**	**300154**	**Amérique du Nord**
Barbados	77	66	58	67	73	74	76	75	87	76	Barbade
Belize	34	36	38	68	56	49	41	37	42	...	Belize
Dominica	...	...	...	...	...	3	14	11	11	8	Dominique
Dominican Republic	1376	1459	1956	1992	2190	2082	447	2593	2993	3484	Rép. dominicaine
Grenada	25	25	26	18	24	...	...	...	...	...	Grenade
Guatemala	...	974	1172	1327	805	1471	1655	1303	1363	...	Guatemala
Jamaica	887	715	828	786	760	662	690	674	670	656	Jamaïque
Mexico	38734	41092	42262	43630	45060	44205	48111	51315	54569	57905	Mexique
Panama	1066	1219	1163	1204	1291	1274	1206	...	...	...	Panama
Puerto Rico	751	773	654	477	438	397	360	317	263	259	Porto Rico
St. Kitts-Nevis	17	17	16	17	17	17	20	19	...	...	St-Kitts-Nevis
Trinidad and Tobago	412	487	395	424	482	428	419	407	517	522	Trinité-et-Tobago
United States[2]	236670	...	237029	237345	237987	...	233485	...	...	...	Etats-Unis[2]
America, South	**78737**	**94346**	**82989**	**88530**	**94536**	**117173**	**108630**	**112587**	**109838**	**111434**	**Amérique du Sud**
Argentina	6170	7979	9518	10305	11272	10913	11615	12687	12395	12133	Argentine
Bolivia	1031	1278	1333	1121	1262	*1429	...	...	...	...	Bolivie
Brazil	43849	54545	43509	45336	52556	67284	63559	66582	66453	62491	Brésil
Chile	2658	2791	3349	3623	3303	3551	3459	3640	3666	3343	Chili
Colombia	15098	...	14574	...	15739	20525	...	18290	16461	...	Colombie
Ecuador	...	...	1826	1525	1131	3201	2163	238	633	...	Equateur
Guyana	109	124	143	145	97	...	...	...	...	...	Guyana
Paraguay	1070	1150	1140	1710	...	...	...	...	...	...	Paraguay
Peru	5685	6774	6764	7060	6957	7817	7435	7431	6557	6168	Pérou
Suriname	122	122	71	107	69	65	72	...	...	...	Suriname
Uruguay	...	...	...	817	...	998	815	921	860	...	Uruguay
Asia	**148312**	**207768**	**212524**	**206895**	**235018**	**241600**	**253765**	**269374**	**271196**	**313660**	**Asie**
Armenia	..	419	149	70	70	53	29	50	133	84	Arménie
Azerbaijan	..	5159	1855	148	114	22	13	16	12	69	Azerbaïdjan
China[3]	56657	68590	83536	97565	115752	128406	137664	154610	162693	...	Chine[3]
Cyprus	342	331	370	341	359	352	331	333	365	405	Chypre
Georgia	..	...	235	120	63	65	48	79	97	126	Géorgie
India[4]	1915	2136	2233	3053	2778	3700	4255	4331	4332	3632	Inde[4]
Indonesia	1042	1043	1145	871	779	1136	...	531	...	...	Indonésie
Israel	567	532	511	587	508	...	...	...	...	...	Israël
Japan[5]	65636	69157	70106	69642	71007	67971	69082	66370	61759	58901	Japon[5]

For general note and footnotes, see end of table.   Voir la fin du tableau pour la remarque générale et les notes.

Beer (continued)
Bières (suite)

ISIC-BASED CODE - CODE BASE CITI

3133-04

Unit : Thousand hectolitres   Unité : Milliers de hectolitres

Country or area	1990	1991	1992	1993	1994	1995	1996	1997	1998	1999	Pays ou zone
Kazakhstan	..	31330	23011	1692	...	812	636	693	850	824	Kazakhstan
Korea, Republic of	13045	15928	15673	15252	17176	17554	17210	16907	14080	14866	Corée, République de
Kyrgyzstan	...	45	31	19	12	12	14	14	13	12	Kirghizistan
Lao People's Dem. Rep.	...	...	...	...	102	151	...	...	...	...	Rép. dém. pop. lao
Lebanon*	130	...	...	...	...	...	...	...	...	...	Liban*
Malaysia	1401	1413	...	...	...	...	...	...	...	...	Malaisie
Myanmar[6]	24	30	19	24	13	...	...	...	...	...	Myanmar[6]
Nepal[7]	...	...	123	144	149	168	183	215	139	188	Népal[7]
Syrian Arab Republic	99	99	102	104	102	102	102	97	97	121	Rép. arabe syrienne
Tajikistan	..	364	135	82	67	47	6	6	9	7	Tadjikistan
Thailand	2635	2840	3252	4153	5230	6473	7591	8742	9770	10422	Thaïlande
Turkey	3544	4188	4843	5524	6019	6946	7381	7656	7130	7188	Turquie
Turkmenistan	..	465	372	287	218	113	17	44	29	...	Turkménistan
Uzbekistan	..	1759	1434	1363	1291	724	677	619	...	...	Ouzbékistan
Viet Nam	1000	1312	1685	...	...	4650	5330	5810	6700	*6480	Viet Nam
Yemen	..	100	40	...	...	...	...	...	...	...	Yémen
Europe	**389925**	**444100**	**438333**	**419322**	**431478**	**420905**	**418743**	**433236**	**435324**	**509227**	**Europe**
Albania	187	76	18	5	72	89	9	151	92	82	Albanie
Austria	9799	9971	10176	11465	10070	9767	9445	9303	8837	8884	Autriche
Belarus	..	3389	2736	2146	1489	1518	2013	2413	2604	2730	Bélarus
Belgium	14141	13799	14259	...	15055	15110	14648	14758	14763	15166	Belgique
Bulgaria	6507	4880	4695	4247	4792	4331	4402	3031	3796	4045	Bulgarie
Croatia	..	2248	2720	2481	3122	3166	3292	3607	3759	..	Croatie
Denmark[8]	9362	...	9775	9435	9410	9903	9591	9181	8044	8205	Danemark[8]
Czechoslovakia(former)	21966	20579	..	..	..	..	..	..	..	..	Tchécoslovaquie(anc.)
Czech Republic	..	..	18982	17366	17876	17687	18057	18558	18290	17946	République tchèque
Estonia	..	675	426	419	477	492	459	543	744	957	Estonie
Finland	4151	4418	4685	4579	4524	4702	4980	4840	4341	4733	Finlande
France	19109	18654	18512	18291	17688	18311	17140	17010	16551	...	France
Germany	..	112071	114089	111075	113428	111875	108938	108729	106993	..	Allemagne
Germany(Fed.Rep.)	99150	..	..	..	..	..	..	..	..	..	Allemagne(Rép.féd.)
German D.R.(former)	15885	..	..	..	..	..	..	..	..	..	R.D.A. (anc.)
Greece	3961	3772	4025	4088	4376	4024	3766	3950	3886	...	Grèce
Hungary	9918	9570	9162	7877	8082	7697	7270	6973	7163	6996	Hongrie
Iceland	35	30	32	41	54	52	63	64	71	77	Islande
Ireland	[2]5236	...	...	...	...	8132	10765	12095	12580	..	Irlande
Italy	11248	11049	10489	9873	10258	10616	9559	10379	11073	11123	Italie
Latvia	..	1295	859	546	638	653	645	715	721	953	Lettonie
Lithuania	..	1412	1426	1164	1353	1093	1139	1413	1559	1847	Lituanie
Luxembourg	600	572	569	558	531	518	484	481	469	450	Luxembourg
Netherlands[8][9]	20055	19863	20419	19720	21200	22380	22670	23780	23040	23799	Pays-Bas[8][9]
Norway	2281	..	2273	...	...	2255	...	2396	1833	2651	Norvège
Poland	11294	13633	14139	12585	14099	15205	16667	19281	21017	23360	Pologne
Portugal	6919	6309	6923	6662	6902	7220	6958	6766	7072	6947	Portugal
Republic of Moldova	..	660	410	[10]297	[10]233	[10]276	[10]226	[10]238	[10]278	[10]214	Rép. de Moldova
Romania	10527	9803	10014	9929	9047	8768	8118	7651	9989	11133	Roumanie
Russian Federation	..	33300	27900	24700	21800	21400	20800	26100	33600	44500	Fédération de Russie
Slovakia	..	..	3686	3967	4974	4369	4666	5577	4478	4473	Slovaquie
Slovenia	..	2203	1783	1978	2075	2087	2223	2138	2000	2022	Slovénie
Spain	27940	26482	24279	21353	25587	25396	24520	24786	22428	26007	Espagne
Sweden	4711	4663	4969	5087	5379	5471	5318	5078	4763	4718	Suède
Switzerland[8]	4143	4137	4020	3804	3828	3672	...	...	...	...	Suisse[8]
Ukraine	..	13093	10997	9086	9087	7102	6025	6125	6842	8407	Ukraine
United Kingdom	70800	...	...	...	66161	59337	61262	64736	60806	...	Royaume-Uni
Yugoslavia	..	5460	4413	3019	5043	5611	5987	6106	6630	6786	Yougoslavie
T.F.Yug.Rep. Macedonia	..	928	861	952	725	620	622	600	578	652	L'ex-RY Macédoine
USSR (former)	62507	..	..	..	..	..	..	..	..	..	URSS (anc.)
Oceania	**23745**	**22904**	**21979**	**21571**	**21693**	**21463**	**20848**	**21124**	**21071**	**20715**	**Océanie**
Australia	19540	18970	18040	17760	17840	17700	17118	17615	17570	17290	Australie
Fiji	194	183	173	167	160	150	170	170	170	...	Fidji
French Polynesia	121	124	129	...	...	...	...	...	...	...	Polynésie française

For general note and footnotes, see end of table.   Voir la fin du tableau pour la remarque générale et les notes.

Beer (continued)
Bières (suite)

ISIC-BASED CODE - CODE BASE CITI
3133-04

Unit : Thousand hectolitres   Unité : Milliers de hectolitres

Country or area	1990	1991	1992	1993	1994	1995	1996	1997	1998	1999	Pays ou zone
New Zealand[8]	3890	3627	3637	3519	3568	3488	3435	3214	3206	3148	Nouvelle-Zélande[8]
Total	1027233	1094644	1087271	1075706	1106266	1123801	1126091	1166275	1169639	1290959	Total

General Note.
Beer made from malt (including ale, stout, porter). (SITC, Rev.3: 11230-0).

Remarque générale.
Bières obtenues à partir du malt (y compris l'ale, le stout et le porter). (CTCI, Rev.3: 11230-0).

[1] Twelve months ending 7 July of the year stated.
[2] Twelve months ending 30 September of year stated.
[3] Original data in metric tons.
[4] Production by large and medium scale establishments only.
[5] Twelve months beginning 1 April of year stated.
[6] Government production only.
[7] Twelve months beginning 16 July of year stated.
[8] Sales.
[9] Production by establishments employing 20 or more persons.
[10] Excluding Transnistria region.

[1] Période de douze mois finissant le 7 juillet de l'année indiquée.
[2] Période de douze mois finissant le 30 septembre de l'année indiquée.
[3] Données d'origine exprimées en tonnes.
[4] Production des grandes et moyennes entreprises seulement.
[5] Période de douze mois commençant le 1er avril de l'année indiquée.
[6] Production de l'Etat seulement.
[7] Période de douze mois commençant le 16 juillet de l'année indiquée.
[8] Ventes.
[9] Production des établissements occupant 20 personnes ou plus.
[10] Non compris la région de Transnistria.

Mineral waters
Eaux minérales

ISIC-BASED CODE - CODE BASE CITI

3134-01

Unit : Thousand hectolitres

Unité : Milliers de hectolitres

Country or area	1990	1991	1992	1993	1994	1995	1996	1997	1998	1999	Pays ou zone
Africa	**3253**	**2895**	**3267**	**3331**	**3549**	**3166**	**3762**	**4277**	**4579**	**5064**	**Afrique**
Algeria	873	657	830	742	662	424	498	603	652	670	Algérie
Congo	59	30	31	32	...	...	...	...	...	...	Congo
Ethiopia[1]	237	125	128	159	199	298	358	374	390	421	Ethiopie[1]
Kenya	1491	1445	1333	1324	1314	1223	1403	...	...	...	Kenya
Seychelles	8	8	8	9	8	8	8	10	13	15	Seychelles
Tunisia	585	630	937	1065	1328	1175	1457	2020	2280	2740	Tunisie
America, North	**2829**	**2706**	**2630**	**4649**	**3663**	**3354**	**3235**	**3452**	**3977**	**3485**	**Amérique du Nord**
Dominica	...	...	...	1	...	1	3	2	6	5	Dominique
Mexico	2829	2706	2630	4648	3660	3353	3232	3450	3971	3480	Mexique
America, South	**3008**	**4159**	**4071**	**7863**	**6529**	**6116**	**7958**	**11208**	**10588**	**13576**	**Amérique du Sud**
Bolivia	79	71	84	76	32	*16	...	...	...	...	Bolivie
Colombia	...	...	2795	...	5267	4957	...	9821	9434	...	Colombie
Ecuador	...	...	320	418	484	215	516	59	126	...	Equateur
Paraguay	147	107	93	...	...	...	...	...	...	...	Paraguay
Peru	...	...	...	...	630	812	837	1184	890	*787	Pérou
Asia	**7583**	**31072**	**39879**	**30787**	**35861**	**52794**	**48988**	**83729**	**42452**	**48424**	**Asie**
Armenia	..	...	77	38	48	78	114	129	109	106	Arménie
Azerbaijan	..	488	685	32	7	5	6	16	18	16	Azerbaïdjan
China	...	...	...	...	...	...	1456	1945	...	...	Chine
Cyprus	*150	*150	146	*160	*230	252	287	344	398	555	Chypre
Georgia	..	...	...	133	45	47	180	332	306	248	Géorgie
Indonesia	2751	4163	18825	8342	12093	26367	...	33987	...	...	Indonésie
Japan	1500	2440	3000	3464	4123	4522	4859	6460	7140	9564	Japon
Kazakhstan	..	18665	11275	11848	11631	13925	17812	30609	475	549	Kazakhstan
Korea, Republic of	...	...	...	...	...	4883	8039	8370	7731	9746	Corée, République de
Kyrgyzstan	..	104	60	34	31	55	38	64	98	86	Kirghizistan
Pakistan	...	...	...	...	...	...	180	...	...	...	Pakistan
Tajikistan	..	46	16	9	8	4	2	2	25	8	Tadjikistan
Turkey	140	125	128	143	147	212	146	151	139	150	Turquie
Turkmenistan	..	115	198	196	197	68	62	105	77	...	Turkménistan
Uzbekistan	..	699	482	521	492	495	589	1035	...	...	Ouzbékistan
Europe	**171728**	**195675**	**197574**	**194731**	**203073**	**219443**	**217846**	**229958**	**243078**	**253854**	**Europe**
Austria	4859	5008	6087	5839	6246	6335	5880	6259	6585	6517	Autriche
Belarus	..	462	294	270	236	175	296	548	1082	1392	Bélarus
Belgium	9364	9450	10030	...	8205	8526	7753	8228	8097	...	Belgique
Bulgaria	206	218	227	376	471	578	590	311	596	893	Bulgarie
Croatia	..	876	154	572	957	1299	1454	1748	1932	...	Croatie
Denmark[2]	1246	3030	3174	2572	2082	3435	3698	3926	3708	4058	Danemark[2]
Czechoslovakia(former)	3162	2501		..	..	..	..	..	..		Tchécoslovaquie(anc.)
Czech Republic	..	..	1130	1815	2850	3583	3997	5597	6000	6294	République tchèque
Estonia	..	157	55	20	36	36	46	50	41	42	Estonie
Finland	359	333	297	268	278	406	454	431	458	569	Finlande
France[2]	52170	51920	53000	51000	53000	61540	61230	...	...	...	France[2]
Germany	..	65945	72249	...	...	...	...	...	...	...	Allemagne
Germany(Fed.Rep.)	52916	..	..	..	..	..	..	..	..	..	Allemagne(Rép.féd.)
German D.R.(former)	1952	..	..	..	..	..	..	..	..	..	R.D.A. (anc.)
Greece	1665	1699	2093	3457	3246	3240	3386	3629	4663	...	Grèce
Hungary	316	335	449	533	900	1206	1416	1786	2204	2631	Hongrie
Iceland	...	5	2	...	...	...	48	50	48	51	Islande
Ireland	149	...	...	...	...	...	1173	668	60	71	Irlande
Latvia	..	152	58	40	63	159	201	289	445	547	Lettonie
Lithuania	..	300	98	76	103	136	133	151	235	260	Lituanie
Netherlands[2][3]	724	863	1082	1005	1215	1303	1200	1360	1330	1300	Pays-Bas[2][3]
Norway	...	...	...	...	...	#214	...	43	41	107	Norvège
Poland	17359	11978	8324	9080	10767	11374	12182	14014	14516	11337	Pologne
Portugal	3411	3020	3720	4176	4244	5183	5641	6098	6475	6719	Portugal
Republic of Moldova	..	330	137	[4]76	[4]75	[4]81	[4]85	[4]93	[4]176	[4]238	Rép. de Moldova
Romania	1985	1472	1015	1057	1364	2148	2797	2976	3308	3830	Roumanie
Russian Federation	..	3800	2200	1540	2000	2760	3030	4110	5120	7450	Fédération de Russie

For general note and footnotes, see end of table.

Voir la fin du tableau pour la remarque générale et les notes.

Mineral waters (continued)
Eaux minérales (suite)

ISIC-BASED CODE - CODE BASE CITI

3134-01

Unit : Thousand hectolitres

Unité : Milliers de hectolitres

Country or area	1990	1991	1992	1993	1994	1995	1996	1997	1998	1999	Pays ou zone
Slovakia	..	..	...	2513	...	...	760	1219	1632	1759	Slovaquie
Slovenia	..	1500	1402	1085	1073	930	1033	1157	1343	1185	Slovénie
Spain	14250	16976	17470	19900	20537	23703	20866	22783	27598	32949	Espagne
Sweden	956	912	...	1009	1158	1119	924	732	440	446	Suède
Switzerland[2]	4090	4398	4659	4791	5129	4942	4557	4533	4298	4340	Suisse[2]
Ukraine	..	4591	3042	1802	1798	1627	1494	2146	3432	4243	Ukraine
United Kingdom	...	...	...	369	530	625	482	449	478	...	Royaume-Uni
Yugoslavia	..	2344	1823	990	3145	1530	1693	2170	2619	3009	Yougoslavie
T.F.Yug.Rep. Macedonia	..	95	102	137	132	118	149	181	237	290	L'ex-RY Macédoine
Total	**188401**	**236507**	**247421**	**241361**	**252675**	**284873**	**281789**	**332624**	**304673**	**324403**	**Total**

General Note.

Natural and artificial spa waters, aerated waters. Ordinary natural waters, sweetened and flavoured waters are excluded. (SITC, Rev.3: 11101-1).

Remarque générale.

Eaux minérales naturelles et artificielles, eaux gazeuses, à l'exclusion des eaux naturelles ordinaires et des eaux sucrées ou aromatisées. (CTCI, Rev.3: 11101-1).

[1] Twelve months ending 7 July of the year stated.
[2] Sales.
[3] Production by establishments employing 20 or more persons.
[4] Excluding Transnistria region.

[1] Période de douze mois finissant le 7 juillet de l'année indiquée.
[2] Ventes.
[3] Production des établissements occupant 20 personnes ou plus.
[4] Non compris la région de Transnistria.

Soft drinks
Boissons non alcooliques
ISIC-BASED CODE - CODE BASE CITI
3134-04

Unit : Thousand hectolitres

Unité : Milliers de hectolitres

Country or area	1990	1991	1992	1993	1994	1995	1996	1997	1998	1999	Pays ou zone
Africa	**39156**	**32586**	**33714**	**32501**	**22171**	**24042**	**26130**	**28669**	**26852**	**26526**	**Afrique**
Algeria	1067	938	1048	1007	901	755	621	599	375	315	Algérie
Angola	80	59	73	...	...	...	...	...	...	...	Angola
Botswana	283	275	255	276	278	293	308	348	411	410	Botswana
Burkina Faso	108	99	27	...	...	...	...	...	...	...	Burkina Faso
Burundi	142	148	160	179	...	...	...	...	...	...	Burundi
Cameroon	...	1098	974	900	622	676	...	...	...	...	Cameroun
Cape Verde	7	1	1	1	1	1	...	...	...	...	Cap-Vert
Central African Rep.	...	46	46	21	39	59	...	...	...	...	Rép. centrafricaine
Chad	35	37	35	35	26	27	...	...	...	...	Tchad
Congo	218	261	294	300	...	...	...	...	...	...	Congo
Ethiopia[1]	599	668	570	554	546	710	741	669	655	667	Ethiopie[1]
Gabon	413	439	410	390	351	416	...	...	...	...	Gabon
Ghana[2]	587	...	...	...	...	...	...	...	...	...	Ghana[2]
Mali	69	65	67	66	66	79	92	...	...	...	Mali
Mozambique	64	46	20	20	97	235	320	419	51	100	Mozambique
Niger	75	60	54	47	61	56	...	...	...	...	Niger
Nigeria[2]	18013	12034	13472	13458	3452	3756	...	...	...	...	Nigéria[2]
Seychelles	50	56	61	70	80	85	79	83	103	106	Seychelles
South Africa[2]	14920	14740	14580	13370	13970	15030	15820	19880	20440	21230	Afrique du Sud[2]
Uganda	243	260	218	269	410	586	704	654	364	808	Ouganda
United Rep.Tanzania	934	669	762	802	109	118	119	113	...	...	Rép. Unie de Tanzanie
America, North	**69884**	**71866**	**72962**	**98241**	**103554**	**99678**	**103313**	**104493**	**115586**	**122203**	**Amérique du Nord**
Antigua and Barbuda[3]	...	...	...	...	1	...	...	...	...	...	Antigua-et-Barbuda[3]
Barbados	221	246	223	274	265	283	...	...	...	...	Barbade
Dominican Republic	...	...	104	144	182	173	182	159	...	...	Rép. dominicaine
Jamaica	563	499	520	486	557	490	341	280	201	379	Jamaïque
Mexico	67645	69562	70831	95786	100992	97545	100923	101752	112776	119083	Mexique
Panama	1264	...	1241	1511	1512	1141	1550	...	...	...	Panama
St. Kitts-Nevis	55	47	42	40	45	45	41	41	...	...	St-Kitts-Nevis
America, South	**91320**	**103841**	**98508**	**102098**	**105924**	**119261**	**115784**	**123677**	**126176**	**131178**	**Amérique du Sud**
Argentina	10065	15561	19545	20565	22528	20025	20665	23109	25240	25960	Argentine
Bolivia	929	1004	908	1069	1171	*1493	...	...	...	...	Bolivie
Brazil	37704	42128	34093	34904	38973	50985	50289	54602	56499	54783	Brésil
Chile	7625	7567	8838	9623	9362	10212	11116	11947	11969	11535	Chili
Colombia	21921	...	22423	...	22310	24427	...	25924	23943	...	Colombie
Ecuador	...	...	6449	6728	5000	6063	3129	319	305	...	Equateur
Paraguay	1495	1731	1847	1644	...	...	...	...	...	...	Paraguay
Peru	2683	4546	4303	3981	4725	4183	3890	4556	4946	*4446	Pérou
Suriname	167	265	102	93	176	193	230	...	...	...	Suriname
Asia	**91895**	**123911**	**109965**	**116322**	**120313**	**123300**	**134834**	**147477**	**133344**	**143606**	**Asie**
Armenia	..	286	30	16	13	12	6	164	241	221	Arménie
Azerbaijan	..	3011	930	70	18	13	65	495	569	326	Azerbaïdjan
China	...	...	...	...	...	...	8831	10501	9589	11860	Chine
China, Macao, SAR	...	...	...	102	108	106	105	102	109	101	Chine, Macao PAS
Cyprus	472	538	555	561	622	569	575	583	593	600	Chypre
Georgia	..	...	274	58	36	60	161	404	290	219	Géorgie
India[4][5]	1034	774	833	1630	1756	2194	2740	3334	3800	4518	Inde[4][5]
Indonesia	[6]4404	[6]5170	[6]2905	[6]9885	4911	5904	...	6815	...	...	Indonésie
Iran(Islamic Rep. of)	[7]6198	[7]7680	[7]6729	[7]7737	[7]8802	[8]9717	[8]11790	[8]12266	[8]12424	...	Iran(Rép. islamique)
Japan[2]	31450	32840	32750	31964	35743	33922	33839	36520	35670	38484	Japon[2]
Kazakhstan	..	18968	8719	6385	4639	2638	8353	10463	1375	1091	Kazakhstan
Korea, Republic of	18265	20809	20853	19592	23137	22715	24704	25144	...	...	Corée, République de
Kyrgyzstan	..	42	14	8	8	9	12	25	33	22	Kirghizistan
Lao People's Dem. Rep.	...	...	...	...	92	105	...	...	...	...	Rép. dém. pop. lao
Malaysia[2]	2797	2794	3088	3361	3899	4170	5047	5133	4183	3513	Malaisie[2]
Nepal[9]	...	...	134	130	145	206	240	258	256	256	Népal[9]
Pakistan	1034	811	1023	1678	1364	1716	1573	1390	1798	2220	Pakistan
Tajikistan	..	177	84	39	22	4	12	21	29	19	Tadjikistan
Thailand	11160	11960	12570	13490	15530	17220	17990	17690	15920	13840	Thaïlande
Turkey	4523	5145	6135	7428	7401	10426	11041	13005	13645	17819	Turquie

For general note and footnotes, see end of table.

Voir la fin du tableau pour la remarque générale et les notes.

Soft drinks (continued)
Boissons non alcooliques (suite)

ISIC-BASED CODE - CODE BASE CITI

3134-04

Unit : Thousand hectolitres											Unité : Milliers de hectolitres
Country or area	1990	1991	1992	1993	1994	1995	1996	1997	1998	1999	Pays ou zone
Turkmenistan	..	355	300	368	400	230	176	203	257	...	Turkménistan
Uzbekistan	..	1206	740	766	861	658	1422	2512	...	...	Ouzbékistan
Yemen	..	624	900	760	610	510	340	350	...	...	Yémen
Europe	**185224**	**228979**	**208296**	**210356**	**227991**	**265241**	**277447**	**292507**	**311798**	**333580**	**Europe**
Austria	7353	7969	8779	8345	9368	10421	10175	10460	11257	12294	Autriche
Belarus	..	2621	1420	942	786	1264	1627	2031	2196	1935	Bélarus
Belgium	10452	10275	10199	...	7483	9470	9267	10299	[10]8282	[10]8162	Belgique
Bulgaria	6457	4767	5509	6198	5315	5401	4686	2842	3867	4100	Bulgarie
Croatia	..	786	754	729	1094	1397	1667	1739	2098	...	Croatie
Denmark[11]	2759	2882	3301	3417	4018	5036	4673	5233	5661	6527	Danemark[11]
Czechoslovakia(former)	6856	4953		..	..	..	..	..	..	..	Tchécoslovaquie(anc.)
Czech Republic	..	..	3042	4717	6163	7768	9092	9961	10421	13017	République tchèque
Estonia		327	156	224	368	435	544	638	666	840	Estonie
Finland	1958	1804	2072	1912	2138	2547	3042	2728	2710	2959	Finlande
France	13275	13700	14870	15810	16930	20404	20008	21460	21640		France
Germany	..	61725	64719	64144	68264	87817	90560	95953	96814	...	Allemagne
Germany(Fed.Rep.)	56118	..	..	..	..	..	..	..	..	..	Allemagne(Rép.féd.)
German D.R.(former)	7210	..	..	..	..	..	..	..	..	..	R.D.A. (anc.)
Greece	4415	4532	4597	6018	6227	6228	6388	6512	7177	...	Grèce
Hungary	3104	3239	472	604	489	513	589	864	906	911	Hongrie
Iceland	317	351	379	359	376	360	397	386	429	437	Islande
Ireland	...	...	...	...	...	...	5343	1603	148	159	Irlande
Latvia	..	579	280	159	195	242	168	195	264	449	Lettonie
Lithuania	..	807	484	299	133	252	197	580	772	764	Lituanie
Netherlands[11][12]	12026	12942	12624	15910	17280	16850	16340	16450	15670	15368	Pays-Bas[11][12]
Norway	...	...	..	..	..	5009	..	...	5036	4875	Norvège
Poland	4383	4423	6613	8216	12374	11372	14552	16107	17724	24160	Pologne
Portugal	3180	3230	3682	3517	3643	3565	4143	4395	4914	5354	Portugal
Republic of Moldova	..	864	294	[13]160	[13]159	[13]204	[13]147	[13]139	[13]295	[13]337	Rép. de Moldova
Romania	4296	2485	1772	3441	3865	5416	4109	4533	4910	4495	Roumanie
Russian Federation	..	22800	7900	7700	6760	8470	11400	14400	21500	18900	Fédération de Russie
Slovakia	..	..	...	213	889	575	943	1064	2342	2696	Slovaquie
Slovenia	..	1067	839	939	1209	1146	1472	1481	1451	1532	Slovénie
Spain	25259	29310	29442	26050	30673	35139	33982	36428	43223	48534	Espagne
Sweden	4225	4290	4157	4216	4283	5046	5899	6066	5471	6955	Suède
Switzerland[11]	4794	5179	5014	4959	5497	5521	5533	5898	6293	6640	Suisse[11]
Ukraine	..	11438	5870	3753	3623	3711	3568	4456	4453	5969	Ukraine
Yugoslavia	..	2471	1785	887	1095	1222	1335	1691	2391	1814	Yougoslavie
T.F.Yug.Rep. Macedonia	..	376	400	410	507	627	628	942	817	737	L'ex-RY Macédoine
USSR (former)	58270	..	..	..	..	..	..	..	..	..	URSS (anc.)
Oceania	**16436**	**16770**	**16895**	**17095**	**21535**	**21694**	**25223**	**25246**	**27054**	**28435**	**Océanie**
Australia[2][14]	14695	14949	15009	14955	...	...	22510	22200	23796	25010	Australie[2][14]
Fiji	70	82	92	103	90	99	98	106	147	...	Fidji
New Zealand	1671	1739	1794	2037	2305	2454	2615	...	...	...	Nouvelle-Zélande
Total	**552185**	**577953**	**540339**	**576613**	**601487**	**653215**	**682731**	**722070**	**740810**	**785528**	**Total**

General Note.
Sweetened and flavoured spa waters (natural or artificial), lemonade, orangeade etc. (SITC, Rev.3: 11102-0).

Remarque générale.
Eaux minérales sucrées ou aromatisées, naturelles et artificielles, limonades, orangeades, etc. (CTCI, Rev.3: 11102-0).

For footnotes, see end of table.

Voir la fin du tableau pour les notes.

Soft drinks (continued)
Boissons non alcooliques (suite)

ISIC-BASED CODE - CODE BASE CITI

3134-04

Footnotes
[1] Twelve months ending 7 July of the year stated.
[2] Including mineral waters.
[3] Twelve months beginning 21 March of year stated.
[4] Production by large and medium scale establishments only.
[5] Original data in million bottles converted on the basis of 200 ml per bottle.
[6] Including fruit juice.
[7] Production by establishments employing 50 or more persons.
[8] Production by establishments employing 10 or more persons.
[9] Twelve months beginning 16 July of year stated.
[10] Incomplete coverage.
[11] Sales.
[12] Production by establishments employing 20 or more persons.
[13] Excluding Transnistria region.
[14] Twelve months ending 30 June of year stated.

Notes.
[1] Période de douze mois finissant le 7 juillet de l'année indiquée.
[2] Y compris les eaux minérales.
[3] Période de douze mois commençant le 21 mars de l'année indiquée.
[4] Production des grandes et moyennes entreprises seulement.
[5] Données d'origine exprimées en millions de bouteilles converties sur la base de 200 ml par bouteille.
[6] Y compris les jus de fruits.
[7] Production des établissements occupant 50 personnes ou plus.
[8] Production des établissements occupant 10 personnes ou plus.
[9] Période de douze mois commençant le 16 juillet de l'année indiquée.
[10] Couverture incomplète.
[11] Ventes.
[12] Production des établissements occupant 20 personnes ou plus.
[13] Non compris la région de Transnistria.
[14] Période de douze mois finissant le 30 juin de l'année indiquée.

Tobacco, prepared leaf
Feuilles de tabac, traitées

ISIC-BASED CODE - CODE BASE CITI

3140-01

Unit : Thousand metric tons
Unité : Milliers de tonnes métriques

Country or area	1990	1991	1992	1993	1994	1995	1996	1997	1998	1999	Pays ou zone
Africa	**290**	**358**	**405**	**401**	**340**	**384**	**419**	**451**	**467**	**418**	**Afrique**
Angola	1	1	1	...	...	...	...	...	...	...	Angola
Malawi	[1]101	[1]113	[1]127	[1]130	[1]99	[1]129	[1]142	[1]158	[1]125	71	Malawi
Morocco[1]	7	7	4	4	4	4	6	9	11	4	Maroc[1]
Nigeria[1]	9	9	9	9	9	9	9	9	9	9	Nigéria[1]
South Africa[1]	27	30	35	30	20	21	22	26	31	30	Afrique du Sud[1]
Uganda[1]	3	5	7	5	7	7	6	7	7	...	Ouganda[1]
United Rep.Tanzania	11	13	11	16	18	15	24	25	...	...	Rép. Unie de Tanzanie
Zimbabwe[1]	130	179	211	205	182	198	209	215	260	...	Zimbabwe[1]
America, North	**821**	**842**	**836**	**839**	**885**	**723**	**861**	**990**	**875**	**890**	**Amérique du Nord**
Canada[1]	63	79	66	77	70	74	69	76	73	70	Canada[1]
Costa Rica[1]	2	1	2	2	2	1	1	0	1	0	Costa Rica[1]
Cuba	41	[1]30	[1]25	[1]20	[1]17	[1]25	[1]31	[1]31	[1]38	[1]31	Cuba
Dominican Republic	18	24	20	15	19	19	29	39	43	16	Rép. dominicaine
Mexico[1]	34	29	21	64	60	27	43	32	49	51	Mexique[1]
United States	663	679	703	660	[1]718	[1]576	[1]689	[1]811	[1]671	...	Etats-Unis
America, South	**561**	**558**	**707**	**810**	**621**	**550**	**612**	**755**	**664**	**784**	**Amérique du Sud**
Argentina[1]	68	95	109	112	82	79	98	123	117	113	Argentine[1]
Brazil[1]	445	414	576	656	520	456	473	597	505	626	Brésil[1]
Chile[1]	14	15	16	20	16	12	11	11	12	12	Chili[1]
Colombia	[1]33	[1]34	6	...	3	3	[1]30	[1]23	[1]30	[1]33	Colombie
Asia	**3591**	**4014**	**4451**	**4580**	**3761**	**3727**	**2843**	**3320**	**3138**	**3077**	**Asie**
Bangladesh	35	35	36	*36	[1]39	[1]38	[1]39	[1]38	[1]37	...	Bangladesh
China	[2]2393	[2]2742	[2]3084	[2]3214	...	...	1682	2056	...	...	Chine
Georgia	..	..	..	2	1	1	1	0	...	1	Géorgie
India[1]	552	556	584	597	563	567	535	618	646	702	Inde[1]
Indonesia	75	38	38	...	...	...	...	...	...	...	Indonésie
Japan	72	67	*70	*70	[1]72	[1]70	[1]66	[1]69	[1]64	[1]65	Japon
Korea, Republic of	48	40	48	61	66	62	[1]61	[1]54	[1]56	[1]65	Corée, République de
Kyrgyzstan	..	49	37	29	23	17	11	24	40	38	Kirghizistan
Malaysia[1]	10	9	11	10	6	10	12	11	11	10	Malaisie[1]
Myanmar[1]	40	45	56	52	52	38	44	47	57	42	Myanmar[1]
Pakistan[1]	68	81	97	102	100	81	80	92	99	109	Pakistan[1]
Philippines[1]	82	85	115	105	57	64	65	65	62	52	Philippines[1]
Thailand	67	85	94	51	49	49	60	72	74	79	Thaïlande
Turkey	149	181	178	202	154	152	137	123	132	134	Turquie
Europe	**659**	**726**	**666**	**600**	**554**	**529**	**534**	**557**	**559**	**573**	**Europe**
Belgium	35	37	34	32	...	...	...	...	...	...	Belgique
Bulgaria[1]	77	72	66	46	33	19	40	61	39	34	Bulgarie[1]
Croatia	..	12	12	8	7	7	11	12	9	...	Croatie
Czechoslovakia(former)	5	4	..	..	..	..	..	..	..	..	Tchécoslovaquie(anc.)
France[1]	28	29	24	26	27	26	28	25	26	26	France[1]
Greece[1]	136	162	187	168	142	149	134	137	137	140	Grèce[1]
Hungary	13	16	[1]13	[1]11	[1]12	[1]11	[1]10	[1]11	[1]13	10	Hongrie
Italy[1]	215	193	151	136	121	124	131	131	133	131	Italie[1]
Netherlands[3,4]	16	13	10	...	...	...	...	...	...	...	Pays-Bas[3,4]
Poland[1]	59	57	45	36	43	40	38	32	38	44	Pologne[1]
Portugal	...	...	1	0	0	0	...	...	...	...	Portugal
Republic of Moldova	..	57	40	[5]33	[5]33	[5]24	[5]18	[5]17	[5]22	[5]26	Rép. de Moldova
Romania	17	16	14	12	13	14	11	13	16	10	Roumanie
Russian Federation	..	7	6	2	1	1	0	3	4	1	Fédération de Russie
Spain	18	24	26	[1]45	[1]44	[1]43	[1]44	[1]46	[1]45	...	Espagne
Yugoslavia	..	10	14	7	10	8	7	6	8	8	Yougoslavie
T.F.Yug.Rep. Macedonia	..	17	22	26	21	16	14	15	23	26	L'ex-RY Macédoine
Yugoslavia, SFR	42	..	..	..	..	..	..	..	..	..	Yougoslavie, RSF
Oceania	**12**	**13**	**11**	**11**	**8**	**7**	**9**	**9**	**8**	**7**	**Océanie**
Australia[1]	12	13	11	11	8	7	9	9	8	7	Australie[1]
Total	**5934**	**6511**	**7077**	**7241**	**6169**	**5920**	**5278**	**6081**	**5711**	**5750**	**Total**

For general note and footnotes, see end of table.　　　　Voir la fin du tableau pour la remarque générale et les notes.

Tobacco, prepared leaf (continued)
Feuilles de tabac, traitées (suite)

ISIC-BASED CODE - CODE BASE CITI
3140-01

General Note.
Tobacco leaves cured, stripped and cut to shape in industrial establishments. (SITC, Rev.3: 12120-0).

Remarque générale.
Feuilles de tabac séchées ou fermentées, écotées et découpées à la forme voulue dans des établissements industriels. (CTCI, Rev.3: 12120-0).

[1] Source: Food and Agriculture Organization of the United Nations (FAO), (Rome).

[2] Source: U. S. Department of Agriculture , (Washington, D. C.).
[3] Sales.
[4] Production by establishments employing 20 or more persons.
[5] Excluding Transnistria region.

[1] Source: Organisation des Nations Unies pour l'alimentation et l'agriculture (FAO), (Rome).
[2] Source: U.S. Department of Agriculture, (Washington, D.C.).
[3] Ventes.
[4] Production des établissements occupant 20 personnes ou plus.
[5] Non compris la région de Transnistria.

Cigars
Cigares

ISIC-BASED CODE - CODE BASE CITI

3140-04

Unit : Million units — Unité : En millions

Country or area	1990	1991	1992	1993	1994	1995	1996	1997	1998	1999	Pays ou zone
Africa	**18**	**18**	**18**	**18**	**18**	**18**	**18**	**18**	**18**	**18**	**Afrique**
South Africa[1]	18	...	...	...	...	...	...	...	...	...	Afrique du Sud[1]
America, North	**3159**	**3073**	**3058**	**3084**	**3338**	**3488**	**3932**	**3819**	**4481**	**5261**	**Amérique du Nord**
Jamaica	9	8	7	9	11	17	16	18	19	6	Jamaïque
Panama	1	0	0	0	1	1	1	...	...	...	Panama
United States	[2]3149	[2]3065	[2]3051	[2]3075	[3]3326	[3]3470	[3]3915	[3]3800	[3]4461	[3]5254	Etats-Unis
America, South	**32**	**33**	**33**	**32**	**30**	**32**	**32**	**33**	**35**	**32**	**Amérique du Sud**
Colombia	...	...	...	...	22	...	...	25	27	...	Colombie
Paraguay	7	8	8	...	...	...	...	...	...	...	Paraguay
Asia	**3404**	**3428**	**3384**	**3378**	**3379**	**3376**	**3405**	**3380**	**3377**	**3343**	**Asie**
China	...	...	...	...	...	...	3402	3377	3374	3340	Chine
Indonesia	28	53	9	3	3	...	...	...	...	...	Indonésie
Myanmar[4]	3	2	2	2	3	...	...	...	...	...	Myanmar[4]
Europe	**5562**	**5712**	**5712**	**5239**	**6616**	**6817**	**8308**	**8837**	**8647**	**8915**	**Europe**
Austria	36	...	...	...	...	...	...	...	...	...	Autriche
Belgium	[5]362	[5]381	[5]337	[5]308	...	...	#2673	2905	...	...	Belgique
Czechoslovakia(former)	19	6	..	..	..	..	...	...	...	...	Tchécoslovaquie(anc.)
Finland	64	61	57	51	51	49	49	...	...	...	Finlande
France	666	677	718	712	580	615	703	644	695	...	France
Germany	..	1356	...	1024	1187	1168	1343	1559	1948	...	Allemagne
Germany(Fed.Rep.)	1127	..	..	..	..	..	..	..	..	..	Allemagne(Rép.féd.)
German D.R.(former)	214	..	..	..	..	..	..	..	..	..	R.D.A. (anc.)
Hungary	7	4	2	...	...	...	...	...	...	...	Hongrie
Italy	[1]162	[1]161	[1]175	[1]182	[1]163	[1]143	[1]140	[1]128	121	111	Italie
Netherlands[6][7]	1436	1426	1391	1372	1790	1759	1776	1889	2015	2195	Pays-Bas[6][7]
Poland	3	2	...	...	#208	401	56	44	20	1	Pologne
Portugal	[1]3	...	7	6	4	6	6	7	13	...	Portugal
Spain	535	675	619	592	601	624	664	736	771	850	Espagne
Sweden	173	178	171	147	140	146	141	120	...	...	Suède
Switzerland	230	205	204	185	163	176	190	195	172	206	Suisse
United Kingdom[1][8]	519	...	...	...	...	...	...	...	...	...	Royaume-Uni[1][8]
Yugoslavia	..	2	1	0	0	0	0	0	0	0	Yougoslavie
T.F.Yug.Rep. Macedonia	..	17	14	10	9	11	8	10	7	9	L'ex-RY Macédoine
Yugoslavia, SFR	7	..	..	..	..	..	..	..	..	..	Yougoslavie, RSF
Total	**12174**	**12264**	**12204**	**11752**	**13380**	**13731**	**15694**	**16085**	**16557**	**17569**	**Total**

General Note.
Cigars of all sizes, cigarillos and cheroots. (SITC, Rev.3: 12210-0, 12231-1).

Remarque générale.
Cigares de toutes dimensions, cigarillos et cigares à bouts coupés (cheroots). (CTCI, Rev.3: 12210-0, 12231-1).

[1] Original data in units of weight. Computed on the basis of 250000 cigars per ton.

[2] Twelve months ending 30 June of year stated.

[3] Twelve months ending 30 September of year stated.

[4] Twelve months ending 31 March of year stated.

[5] Excluding cigarillos.

[6] Sales.

[7] Production by establishments employing 20 or more persons.

[8] Sales by manufacturers employing 25 or more persons.

[1] Données d'origine exprimées en poids. Calcul sur la base de 250 000 cigares par tonne.

[2] Période de douze mois finissant le 30 juin de l'année indiquée.

[3] Période de douze mois finissant le 30 septembre de l'année indiquée.

[4] Période de douze mois finissant le 31 mars de l'année indiquée.

[5] Non compris les cigarillos.

[6] Ventes.

[7] Production des établissements occupant 20 personnes ou plus.

[8] Ventes des fabricants employant 25 personnes ou plus.

Cigarettes
Cigarettes
ISIC-BASED CODE - CODE BASE CITI
3140-07

Unit : Million units   Unité : En millions

Country or area	1990	1991	1992	1993	1994	1995	1996	1997	1998	1999	Pays ou zone
Africa	**170043**	**170289**	**165599**	**161302**	**154850**	**158196**	**163432**	**167690**	**170241**	**170019**	**Afrique**
Algeria[1]	18775	17848	16426	16260	16345	...	...	...	...	...	Algérie[1]
Angola[2]	2400	2400	2400	...	...	...	...	...	...	...	Angola[2]
Burkina Faso	822	983	979	943	...	...	...	...	...	...	Burkina Faso
Burundi	384	450	453	517	...	...	...	...	...	...	Burundi
Cameroon[2]	4900	5000	5000	...	...	...	...	...	...	...	Cameroun[2]
Central African Rep.	25	26	21	12	21	30	...	...	...	...	Rép. centrafricaine
Chad	248	476	415	499	508	569	...	...	...	...	Tchad
Congo[1]	*645	581	431	...	...	...	...	...	...	...	Congo[1]
Côte d'Ivoire[2]	4500	4500	4500	...	...	...	...	...	...	...	Côte d'Ivoire[2]
Dem. Rep. of Congo[2]	5200	5200	5200	...	...	...	...	...	...	...	Rép. dém. du Congo[2]
Egypt	39837	40154	42516	38844	39145	42469	46000	50000	52000	51000	Egypte
Ethiopia[3]	2258	2416	1879	1932	1468	1583	1862	2024	2029	1829	Ethiopie[3]
Gabon	328	358	399	334	288	297	...	...	...	...	Gabon
Ghana	1805	*2100	*2100	...	...	...	...	...	...	...	Ghana
Kenya	6647	6473	7193	7267	7319	7932	8436	...	...	...	Kenya
Liberia[2]	22	22	22	...	...	...	...	...	...	...	Libéria[2]
Libyan Arab Jamah.[2]	3500	3500	3500	...	...	...	...	...	...	...	Jamah. arabe libyenne[2]
Madagascar[1]	1476	1950	2223	2304	...	...	...	...	...	...	Madagascar[1]
Malawi	1061	951	1000	1020	1127	1160	975	731	501	...	Malawi
Mali	17	23	24	23	20	22	21	...	...	...	Mali
Mauritius	1000	1034	1060	1269	1300	1215	1193	1144	1034	979	Maurice
Morocco	640	602	515	...	...	...	...	...	...	...	Maroc
Mozambique	1030	217	124	377	343	106	250	250	950	1084	Mozambique
Nigeria	10380	9405	8608	9384	338	256	...	...	...	...	Nigéria
Senegal[2]	3350	3350	3350	...	...	...	...	...	...	...	Sénégal[2]
Seychelles	67	69	62	65	49	56	62	70	61	60	Seychelles
Sierra Leone[2]	1200	1200	1200	...	...	...	...	...	...	...	Sierra Leone[2]
South Africa	40792	40163	35563	34499	...	...	...	...	...	...	Afrique du Sud
Sudan[2]	750	750	750	...	...	...	...	...	...	...	Soudan[2]
Tunisia	6852	7790	7797	6965	7128	7421	7159	7735	9813	11066	Tunisie
Uganda	1290	1688	1575	1412	1459	1576	1702	1864	1866	1688	Ouganda
United Rep.Tanzania	3742	3870	3789	3893	3383	3699	3733	4710	...	...	Rép. Unie de Tanzanie
Zambia[2]	1500	1500	1500	...	...	...	...	...	...	...	Zambie[2]
Zimbabwe[2]	2600	3240	3025	...	...	...	...	...	...	...	Zimbabwe[2]
America, North	**830804**	**813459**	**838611**	**779111**	**843224**	**871639**	**880263**	**841474**	**808372**	**739343**	**Amérique du Nord**
Barbados	[1]135	[1]124	[1]115	[1]133	[1]150	65	...	...	...	...	Barbade
Belize	101	104	104	105	101	95	79	88	94	...	Belize
Canada	[2]46111	[2]46815	[2]45500	...	...	50775	49362	47263	...	...	Canada
Costa Rica	[2]2030	[2]2000	[2]2000	[1][4]16	[1][4]16	[1][4]16	[1][4]16	...	...	...	Costa Rica
Dominican Republic	4535	4170	4432	4356	4696	4092	4192	3972	4098	4005	Rép. dominicaine
El Salvador	[2]1655	[2]1620	[2]1620	...	...	1701	1756	...	...	...	El Salvador
Grenada	22	20	20	19	15	...	...	...	...	...	Grenade
Guatemala	[2]1955	870	[2]2001	2010	1390	2616	1725	2198	4184	...	Guatemala
Haiti	1027	985	970	1110	722	...	...	...	...	...	Haïti
Honduras[2]	2862	2300	2200	...	...	...	...	...	...	...	Honduras[2]
Jamaica	1380	1219	1299	1224	1273	1216	1219	1175	1160	1078	Jamaïque
Mexico	55380	54680	55988	53435	53402	56821	59907	57618	60407	59492	Mexique
Nicaragua[2]	2400	2400	2400	...	...	...	...	...	...	...	Nicaragua[2]
Panama	810	771	806	903	1204	1136	663	...	...	...	Panama
Trinidad and Tobago	[1]701	[1]881	[1]656	638	593	920	1102	1386	1680	1945	Trinité-et-Tobago
United States	709700	694500	718500	661000	725500	746500	754500	719600	679700	611929	Etats-Unis
America, South	**236800**	**237972**	**232320**	**233383**	**233352**	**230384**	**236103**	**236405**	**240393**	**235694**	**Amérique du Sud**
Argentina	1657	1727	1845	1929	1975	1963	1971	1940	1967	1996	Argentine
Bolivia	97	102	116	119	...	*170	...	...	...	...	Bolivie
Brazil[2]	173987	175396	169000	...	...	...	...	...	...	...	Brésil[2]
Chile	10198	10259	11167	10793	10801	10891	11569	12522	12904	13271	Chili
Colombia	[2]14490	[2]13585	14877	...	11566	10491	...	11662	12472	...	Colombie
Ecuador	*4600	*4600	3000	3079	2515	1734	1745	1678	1997	...	Equateur
Guyana	247	307	318	302	314	...	...	...	...	...	Guyana
Paraguay	992	827	777	...	...	...	...	...	...	...	Paraguay
Peru	2585	2696	2501	2511	2752	3041	3358	3028	3115	3580	Pérou

For general note and footnotes, see end of table.   Voir la fin du tableau pour la remarque générale et les notes.

Cigarettes (continued)
Cigarettes (suite)

ISIC-BASED CODE - CODE BASE CITI

3140-07

Unit : Million units

Unité : En millions

Country or area	1990	1991	1992	1993	1994	1995	1996	1997	1998	1999	Pays ou zone
Suriname	487	337	419	454	443	472	483	...	...	...	Suriname
Uruguay	²3900	²3900	²3900	3736	...	3561	6044	6870	9209	...	Uruguay
Venezuela²	23560	24236	24400	...	...	...	...	...	...	...	Venezuela²
Asia	**2378860**	**2413549**	**2461038**	**2480335**	**2469269**	**2460397**	**2560730**	**2694288**	**2728510**	**2744163**	**Asie**
Armenia	..	6614	3927	1878	2014	1043	...	815	2489	3132	Arménie
Azerbaijan	..	7256	4855	5277	3179	1926	766	827	241	416	Azerbaïdjan
Bangladesh⁵	12289	13604	12535	11516	12655	17379	16222	18601	...	...	Bangladesh⁵
Cambodia²	4200	4200	4200	...	...	...	...	...	...	...	Cambodge²
China	1648765	1613245	1642340	1655630	...	...	...	...	...	...	Chine
Hong Kong SAR⁶ ⁷	21700	32721	36513	25759	24747	22767	21386	20929	13470	...	Hong-Kong RAS⁶ ⁷
China, Macao, SAR¹ ⁴ ⁸	500	500	500	500	450	450	450	...	...	...	Chine, Macao PAS¹ ⁴ ⁸
Cyprus	4601	5497	6177	3530	2493	2528	2728	3662	4362	4783	Chypre
Georgia	..	...	4953	3593	3256	1840	1183	917	601	1327	Géorgie
India⁹	61162	65130	61413	71842	71038	69589	73841	83162	...	82504	Inde⁹
Indonesia	..	...	34382	34757	36421	38768	...	220157	271177	...	Indonésie
Iran(Islamic Rep. of)	¹⁰12319	* ¹⁰11565	¹⁰10171	¹⁰7835	¹⁰7939	¹¹9787	¹¹11860	¹¹10304	¹¹14335	...	Iran(Rép. islamique)
Iraq²	26000	13000	5794	...	...	...	...	...	...	...	Iraq²
Israel	5440	¹5590	¹5742	¹5525	¹5638	¹4933	¹4793	...	...	...	Israël
Japan¹²	268100	275000	279000	...	...	...	...	...	...	...	Japon¹²
Jordan	3185	3719	3091	3465	4191	3675	4738	...	...	...	Jordanie
Kazakhstan	..	9536	8997	10664	9393	12080	19121	24109	21747	18773	Kazakhstan
Korea, Republic of	91923	94336	96648	96887	90774	87959	94709	96725	101011	95995	Corée, République de
Kyrgyzstan	..	4015	3120	3428	1943	1332	975	716	862	2103	Kirghizistan
Lao People's Dem. Rep.	²1200	²1200	²1200	...	936	1062	...	...	...	...	Rép. dém. pop. lao
Lebanon	²4000	²4000	²4000	...	...	# ¹535	¹539	...	...	...	Liban
Malaysia¹	17331	17498	16574	15568	15762	15918	16896	20236	18410	15504	Malaisie¹
Myanmar¹³	979	682	396	426	440	752	1727	1991	2040	2270	Myanmar¹³
Nepal¹⁴	..	...	6963	7846	6894	7430	8067	7944	8127	7315	Népal¹⁴
Pakistan⁵	32279	29887	29673	29947	35895	32747	45506	46101	48215	51579	Pakistan⁵
Philippines¹ ⁴	7175	7071	6771	7135	7300	7440	7440	...	...	...	Philippines¹ ⁴
Singapore²	9620	10500	11760	...	...	...	...	...	...	...	Singapour²
Sri Lanka	5621	5789	5359	5649	5656	5822	6160	*5712	5797	5412	Sri Lanka
Syrian Arab Republic¹	6855	7974	8093	7185	7773	9699	8528	10137	10398	10991	Rép. arabe syrienne¹
Tajikistan	..	4467	2607	1901	1644	964	604	153	191	209	Tadjikistan
Thailand	38180	39697	40691	42043	45359	43020	48173	43387	34585	31146	Thaïlande
Turkey¹	63055	71106	67549	74845	85093	80700	73787	74984	81616	75135	Turquie¹
Uzbekistan	..	4897	4150	4151	3379	2742	5172	8521	...	...	Ouzbékistan
Viet Nam	24990	25960	*24600	...	...	...	...	...	...	...	Viet Nam
Yemen	..	¹ ⁴6790	¹ ⁴6294	¹ ⁴8844	¹ ⁴5423	6540	6740	6800	...	...	Yémen
Europe	**1035640**	**1261669**	**1178711**	**1132557**	**1212313**	**1223235**	**1221119**	**1240451**	**1266327**	**1353184**	**Europe**
Albania¹	4947	1703	1393	1395	929	685	4830	414	764	63	Albanie¹
Austria	14961	16406	15836	16247	16429	16297	...	...	...	...	Autriche
Belarus	..	15009	8847	8670	7378	6228	6267	6787	7296	9259	Bélarus
Belgium	⁶27758	⁶27303	⁶29576	⁶27173	21366	18826	17471	18061	17519	14712	Belgique
Bulgaria	73000	79749	48558	32098	53664	74603	57238	43315	33181	25715	Bulgarie
Croatia	..	11655	12833	11585	12672	12110	11548	11416	11987	...	Croatie
Denmark¹⁵	11387	11407	11439	10980	11448	11902	11804	12262	12392	11749	Danemark¹⁵
Czechoslovakia(former)	26708	28190	...	...	...	...	...	..	..	..	Tchécoslovaquie(anc.)
Estonia	..	3577	1780	2630	2287	1864	954	...	...	...	Estonie
Finland	8974	8180	8106	7237	7232	6542	5910	...	...	...	Finlande
France	55495	50311	*53312	47912	48188	46361	46931	44646	43304	...	France
Germany	..	...	...	204730	222791	...	...	...	...	...	Allemagne
Germany(Fed.Rep.)	177905	..	..	...	...	...	...	...	...	...	Allemagne(Rép.féd.)
German D.R.(former)	22469	...	...	...	...	...	...	...	...	...	R.D.A. (anc.)
Greece	26175	27700	*29250	30427	32843	39291	38268	36909	21427	...	Grèce
Hungary	28212	26124	26835	28728	29518	25709	27594	26057	26849	22985	Hongrie
Ireland	6218	6377	*7850	¹ ⁴7300	¹ ⁴7000	¹ ⁴7500	¹ ⁴7500	4605	6452	6176	Irlande
Italy	¹61736	¹57634	¹53799	¹54943	¹55175	¹50247	¹51489	¹51894	50785	45159	Italie
Latvia	..	4765	3435	2589	2093	2101	1876	1775	2018	1916	Lettonie
Lithuania	..	6438	5269	3435	3860	4876	4538	5755	7427	8217	Lituanie
Malta²	1475	1475	1475	...	...	...	...	...	...	...	Malte²
Netherlands¹⁵ ¹⁶	71992	74767	78479	71254	88069	97727	...	...	...	...	Pays-Bas¹⁵ ¹⁶

For general note and footnotes, see end of table.

Voir la fin du tableau pour la remarque générale et les notes.

Unit : Million units   Unité : En millions

Country or area	1990	1991	1992	1993	1994	1995	1996	1997	1998	1999	Pays ou zone
Norway[2]	1480	1730	1825	...	...	...	...	...	...	...	Norvège[2]
Poland	91497	90407	86571	90713	98394	100627	95293	95798	96741	95056	Pologne
Portugal	17547	17361	15619	15335	13610	13215	12780	13234	15781	17742	Portugal
Republic of Moldova	..	9164	8582	[17]8790	[17]8001	[17]7108	[17]9657	[17]9539	[17]7512	[17]8731	Rép. de Moldova
Romania[18]	18090	17722	17781	15222	14532	14747	16536	25943	...	...	Roumanie[18]
Russian Federation	..	112326	107763	100162	91601	99545	112319	140077	195806	266031	Fédération de Russie
Slovenia	..	4798	5278	4851	4722	4543	4909	5767	7555	8032	Slovénie
Spain	75995	81843	76696	80103	81886	78676	77675	77315	81940	74873	Espagne
Sweden	9648	9594	9841	7420	8032	7193	7251	6237	5692	6060	Suède
Switzerland	31771	32943	33740	34713	39906	41976	42955	37638	34453	32139	Suisse
Ukraine	..	66645	60990	40571	47083	48033	44900	54488	59275	54105	Ukraine
United Kingdom	112000	127000	*126538	146138	165479	155103	166496	167670	152998	...	Royaume-Uni
Yugoslavia	..	17605	15654	16053	12972	12686	13176	10988	14597	13126	Yougoslavie
Yugoslavia, SFR	58200	..	..	..	..	..	..	..	..	..	Yougoslavie, RSF
USSR (former)	313082	..	..	..	..	..	..	..	..	..	URSS (anc.)
Oceania	41283	39505	37950	38967	38959	38855	39179	38979	38753	38465	Océanie
Australia[18]	36263	34977	*34000	...	...	...	...	...	...	...	Australie[18]
Fiji	531	514	484	506	483	437	439	450	410	...	Fidji
New Zealand	4489	4014	3466	3381	[15]3396	[15]3338	[15]3660	[15]3449	[15]3263	[15]3010	Nouvelle-Zélande
Total	5006512	4936442	4914228	4825655	4951967	4982706	5100826	5219286	5252595	5280869	Total

General Note.
Cigarettes only. (SITC, Rev.3: 12220-0, 12231-2).

[1] Original data in units of weight. Computed on the basis of one million cigarettes per ton.
[2] Source: U. S. Department of Agriculture , (Washington, D. C.).
[3] Twelve months ending 7 July of the year stated.
[4] Source: Food and Agriculture Organization of the United Nations (FAO), (Rome).
[5] Twelve months ending 30 June of year stated.
[6] Including cigarillos.
[7] 1999 data are confidential.
[8] Beginning 1997, data are confidential.
[9] Production by large and medium scale establishments only.
[10] Production by establishments employing 50 or more persons.
[11] Production by establishments employing 10 or more persons.
[12] Twelve months beginning 1 April of year stated.
[13] Government production only.
[14] Twelve months beginning 16 July of year stated.
[15] Sales.
[16] Production by establishments employing 20 or more persons.
[17] Excluding Transnistria region.
[18] Including cigars.

Remarque générale.
Cigarettes seulement. (CTCI, Rev.3: 12220-0, 12231-2).

[1] Données d'origine exprimées en poids. Calcul sur la base d'un million de cigarettes par tonne.
[2] Source: U.S. Department of Agriculture, (Washington, D.C.).
[3] Période de douze mois finissant le 7 juillet de l'année indiquée.
[4] Source: Organisation des Nations Unies pour l'alimentation et l'agriculture (FAO), (Rome).
[5] Période de douze mois finissant le 30 juin de l'année indiquée.
[6] Y compris les cigarillos.
[7] Pour 1999, les données sont confidentielles.
[8] A partir de 1997, les données sont confidentielles
[9] Production des grandes et moyennes entreprises seulement.
[10] Production des établissements occupant 50 personnes ou plus.
[11] Production des établissements occupant 10 personnes ou plus.
[12] Période de douze mois commençant le 1er avril de l'année indiquée.
[13] Production de l'Etat seulement.
[14] Période de douze mois commençant le 16 juillet de l'année indiquée.
[15] Ventes.
[16] Production des établissements occupant 20 personnes ou plus.
[17] Non compris la région de Transnistria.
[18] Y compris les cigares.

Tobacco, manufactured
Tabacs manufacturés

ISIC-BASED CODE - CODE BASE CITI

3140-10

Unit : Metric tons | Unité : Tonnes métriques

Country or area	1990	1991	1992	1993	1994	1995	1996	1997	1998	1999	Pays ou zone
Africa	**53340**	**52814**	**53553**	**57980**	**65291**	**48465**	**54198**	**54641**	**54026**	**53559**	**Afrique**
Algeria	8730	8222	7253	7740	7173	7807	8307	8382	8497	8326	Algérie
Cape Verde	90	94	94	94	94	70	...	...	...	...	Cap-Vert
Congo	175	230	97	68	...	...	...	...	...	...	Congo
Egypt	35423	37265	37771	41427	49991	32520	37564	38290	37356	37356	Egypte
Kenya	2	2	1	2	2	1	1	...	...	...	Kenya
Madagascar	630	580	441	360	194	224	438	177	299	...	Madagascar
South Africa[1]	7757	5832	7451	7759	...	...	...	...	...	...	Afrique du Sud[1]
Tunisia	533	589	445	530	495	501	462	367	450	395	Tunisie
America, North	**57013**	**59683**	**60122**	**59025**	**60042**	**59683**	**58226**	**59683**	**59683**	**63673**	**Amérique du Nord**
United States	57013	...	60122	59025	[2]60042	...	[2]58226	...	...	63673	Etats-Unis
America, South	**4**	**4**	**2**	**4**	**4**	**6**	**4**	**4**	**4**	**4**	**Amérique du Sud**
Colombia	...	...	2	...	4	6	...	...	...	...	Colombie
Asia	**74128**	**133029**	**64112**	**172818**	**223084**	**140334**	**135569**	**172022**	**171677**	**197081**	**Asie**
Azerbaijan	..	46999	46794	38137	20369	13585	8539	10134	5317	7761	Azerbaïdjan
Bangladesh	5123	6439	4160	...	...	...	...	...	...	...	Bangladesh
China, Macao, SAR[3][4][5]	...	...	...	684	808	...	...	1107	...	...	Chine, Macao PAS[3][4][5]
Indonesia	62689	72589	8932	124110	190998	112448	...	141838	144589	...	Indonésie
Iran(Islamic Rep. of)	[6]4846	[7]4703	[7]1822	[7]3200	[7]3869	[7]3546	[7]2520	[7]3754	[7]2509	...	Iran(Rép. islamique)
Kyrgyzstan	..	611	403	309	317	506	551	641	715	574	Kirghizistan
Turkey[8]	604	369	487	379	422	315	331	241	127	122	Turquie[8]
Uzbekistan	..	453	648	758	1060	3827	10247	9066	...	...	Ouzbékistan
Europe	**130835**	**150084**	**146885**	**144127**	**143773**	**145683**	**143669**	**152161**	**166899**	**166420**	**Europe**
Austria	185	188	175	...	...	...	...	...	...	...	Autriche
Belgium	4811	4445	4197	4131	...	...	...	...	...	...	Belgique
Croatia	..	8	9	26	20	17	0	0	...	...	Croatie
Denmark[9]	5472	6205	6073	4531	4343	4321	4066	4032	4119	4015	Danemark[9]
Czechoslovakia(former)	188	346	..	...	...	...	...	...	...	...	Tchécoslovaquie(anc.)
Finland	587	705	846	1060	1000	980	1094	...	...	...	Finlande
France	3786	3574	3747	3618	4212	4086	4362	3407	3781	...	France
Germany	..	13834	15069	...	...	...	16510	23401	29835	...	Allemagne
German D.R.(former)[10]	78	..	..	...	...	...	...	...	...	...	R.D.A. (anc.)[10]
Greece	11	11	10	#593	771	799	206	...	2282	...	Grèce
Hungary[10]	0	0	1162	...	...	...	...	...	...	...	Hongrie[10]
Iceland[11]	11	11	9	11	14	...	...	...	...	...	Islande[11]
Italy	273	176	255	150	162	214	162	59	149	41	Italie
Netherlands[9][12]	31511	27477	30282	42222	41651	41750	...	...	...	...	Pays-Bas[9][12]
Poland	58	58	45	49	44	41	23	13	8	5	Pologne
Portugal	157	125	144	134	134	139	151	176	157	...	Portugal
Romania[13]	44000	42000	41000	23273	21920	22538	25440	25945	28576	30802	Roumanie[13]
Russian Federation	..	384	357	107	#9	3	23	1	...	...	Fédération de Russie
Slovenia	..	1163	528	956	321	123	0	...	0	...	Slovénie
Spain[14]	17200	26774	20274	...	...	...	...	...	...	...	Espagne[14]
Sweden	6881	7010	7121	7320	7564	7690	7969	7651	9966	9039	Suède
Switzerland[10]	299	294	272	255	214	189	141	135	110	125	Suisse[10]
United Kingdom	...	...	...	13877	...	16643	...	...	...	...	Royaume-Uni
Yugoslavia	..	36	50	98	22	25	13	2	12	59	Yougoslavie
Yugoslavia, SFR[15]	67	..	..	..	..	..	..	..	..	..	Yougoslavie, RSF[15]
USSR (former)[10]	1972	..	..	..	..	..	..	..	..	..	URSS (anc.)[10]
Oceania	**27921**	**27486**	**25307**	**24812**	**23968**	**23892**	**23649**	**23260**	**22821**	**22329**	**Océanie**
Australia	27318	26833	24538	[16]24001	[16]23273	[16]23083	...	...	...	...	Australie
Fiji	1	...	...	...	...	...	...	...	...	...	Fidji
New Zealand	602	652	768	810	[9]694	[9]808	[9]658	[9]732	[9]756	[9]727	Nouvelle-Zélande
Total	**345213**	**423100**	**349981**	**458765**	**516161**	**418063**	**415314**	**461771**	**475110**	**503066**	**Total**

General Note.
Smoking tobacco, chewing tobacco, snuff. (SITC, Rev.3: 12232-0, 12239-0,).

Remarque générale.
Tabac à fumer, tabac à chiquer, tabac à priser. (CTCI, Rev.3: 12232-0, 12239-0).

Footnotes

[1] Pipe tobacco only.

[2] Twelve months ending 30 September of year stated.

[3] 1995 data are confidential.

[4] 1996 data are confidential.

[5] Beginning 1998, data are confidential.

[6] Production by establishments employing 10 or more persons.

[7] Production by establishments employing 50 or more persons.

[8] Twelve months beginning 21 March of year stated.

[9] Sales.

[10] Smoking tobacco only.

[11] Snuff tobacco only.

[12] Production by establishments employing 20 or more persons.

[13] Including prepared tobacco leaves.

[14] Excluding snuff.

[15] Fermented tobacco only.

[16] Twelve months ending 30 June of year stated.

Notes.

[1] Tabacs à pipe seulement.

[2] Période de douze mois finissant le 30 septembre de l'année indiquée.

[3] Pour 1995, les données sont confidentielles.

[4] Pour 1996, les données sont confidentielles.

[5] A partir de 1998, les données sont confidentielles.

[6] Production des établissements occupant 10 personnes ou plus.

[7] Production des établissements occupant 50 personnes ou plus.

[8] Période de douze mois commençant le 21 mars de l'année indiquée.

[9] Ventes.

[10] Tabac à fumer seulement.

[11] Tabac à priser seulement.

[12] Production des établissements occupant 20 personnes ou plus.

[13] Y compris les feuilles de tabac traitées.

[14] Non compris le tabac à priser.

[15] Tabac à fermenter seulement.

[16] Période de douze mois finissant le 30 juin de l'année indiquée.

Wool yarn, pure and mixed (total)
Filés de laine pure et mélangée (production totale)

ISIC-BASED CODE - CODE BASE CITI

3211-03

Unit : Thousand metric tons   Unité : Milliers de tonnes métriques

Country or area	1990	1991	1992	1993	1994	1995	1996	1997	1998	1999	Pays ou zone
Africa	**29**	**31**	**31**	**24**	**24**	**23**	**21**	**14**	**20**	**18**	**Afrique**
Algeria	5.1	4.9	5.9	3.9	4.0	3.6	2.0	1.6	3.0	1.5	Algérie
Egypt	15.8	20.4	20.0	19.2	15.2	14.1	14.1	7.3	...	...	Egypte
South Africa	8.1	6.2	4.8	1.3	...	...	...	...	...	...	Afrique du Sud
America, North	**50**	**61**	**61**	**58**	**63**	**58**	**51**	**49**	**42**	**35**	**Amérique du Nord**
United States	49.8	61.1	61.3	58.2	62.7	58.3	51.2	49.3	42.2	35.4	Etats-Unis
America, South	**6**	**5**	**5**	**5**	**5**	**5**	**5**	**5**	**5**	**5**	**Amérique du Sud**
Bolivia	0.7	0.5	...	...	...	...	...	...	...	...	Bolivie
Brazil	4.1	4.5	...	...	...	...	...	...	...	...	Brésil
Colombia	0.7		0.1	0.1	0.1	0.0	...	...	...	...	Colombie
Ecuador	...	...	0.2	0.3	0.2	0.3	0.4	0.3	0.4	0.3	Equateur
Asia	**442**	**522**	**579**	**536**	**444**	**494**	**485**	**495**	**466**	**450**	**Asie**
Armenia	..	2.1	2.0	0.5	0.2	0.2	0.2	0.1	0.1	0.0	Arménie
Azerbaijan	..	10.2	7.2	4.8	1.6	0.6	0.2	0.1	0.2	0.1	Azerbaïdjan
China	238.0	282.8	350.6	343.5	250.6	325.2	...	...	...	...	Chine
Hong Kong SAR	4.8	...	...	...	...	...	...	...	...	...	Hong-Kong RAS
China, Macao, SAR[1]	...	...	...	2.6	5.2	...	9.5	9.7	3.2	5.0	Chine, Macao PAS[1]
Georgia	..		2.4	1.5	0.3	0.3	0.2	0.1	0.1	0.0	Géorgie
Japan	105.1	106.9	105.5	84.1	89.5	71.7	64.7	62.4	46.6	42.0	Japon
Korea, Republic of	28.3	29.2	26.1	23.2	23.6	21.5	...	...	...	...	Corée, République de
Kyrgyzstan	..	12.7	10.3	8.3	4.7	3.0	2.3	2.1	1.3	0.5	Kirghizistan
Syrian Arab Republic	0.8	1.3	1.5	1.3	1.6	1.4	1.6	0.9	0.8	1.7	Rép. arabe syrienne
Tajikistan	..	4.6	4.3	4.0	1.5	0.6	0.3	0.8	1.1	0.8	Tadjikistan
Turkey	61.8	54.8	52.4	49.2	52.8	52.2	55.7	64.9	55.1	38.8	Turquie
Turkmenistan	..	3.0	2.6	...	...	...	...	...	...	...	Turkménistan
Uzbekistan	..	4.3	4.8	5.3	4.9	3.3	2.7	2.3	...	...	Ouzbékistan
Europe	**754**	**1045**	**945**	**842**	**869**	**804**	**760**	**774**	**682**	**810**	**Europe**
Austria	5.2	5.4	5.3	3.3	...	...	...	...	...	...	Autriche
Belarus	..	34.8	30.3	28.2	22.0	11.8	12.8	15.5	16.3	16.4	Bélarus
Belgium	88.2	87.8	80.6	70.5	#12.8	14.0	12.5	13.1	14.9	14.3	Belgique
Bulgaria[2]	29.8	18.4	15.8	15.2	14.1	14.0	12.9	11.6	7.3	7.8	Bulgarie[2]
Croatia	..	3.6	3.7	3.9	3.6	3.2	2.5	1.9	1.5	...	Croatie
Denmark[3]	2.7	2.4	...	...	3.3	...	...	...	...	...	Danemark[3]
Czechoslovakia(former)	52.3	33.1	..	..	...	...	...	...	...	..	Tchécoslovaquie(anc.)
Czech Republic	..	..	21.9	21.4	17.8	16.8	17.2	15.9	12.1	9.8	République tchèque
Estonia	..	3.1	1.6	0.2	0.2	0.1	0.2	0.3	0.4	0.5	Estonie
Finland	0.9	0.9	1.0	1.3	1.6	1.1	1.5	...	...	...	Finlande
France	19.3	20.2	19.9	16.5	15.8	...	...	...	...	...	France
Germany	..	42.8	45.0	34.6	34.3	30.9	25.8	26.2	23.1	...	Allemagne
Germany(Fed.Rep.)	39.6	..	..	...	...	...	...	...	...	...	Allemagne(Rép.féd.)
Greece	11.0	9.7	9.6	6.5	4.8	6.4	13.9	12.8	4.9	...	Grèce
Hungary	4.0	3.3	1.5	1.3	1.1	1.3	...	...	...	...	Hongrie
Iceland	0.8	0.1	0.4	0.4	0.4	...	0.4	0.6	0.4	0.4	Islande
Italy	284.7	306.9	323.6	318.9	496.4	477.4	448.6	468.9	419.3	...	Italie
Latvia	..	10.1	6.4	7.1	5.3	2.0	3.6	3.1	3.2	0.5	Lettonie
Lithuania	..	10.9	7.7	5.2	3.8	3.5	4.1	3.7	3.8	3.3	Lituanie
Netherlands[4]	2.6	1.9	1.7	...	...	...	...	...	...	...	Pays-Bas[4]
Norway	2.4	2.6	1.5	1.6	1.9	1.3	1.5	...	...	1.9	Norvège
Poland	55.0	37.4	33.8	35.8	36.9	34.4	35.5	32.5	27.1	18.2	Pologne
Portugal	13.5	13.1	11.4	11.4	12.6	#4.9	6.2	7.5	5.8	5.7	Portugal
Republic of Moldova	..	5.9	3.2	[5]2.9	[5]2.8	[5]1.7	[5]1.5	[5]1.2	[5]1.2	[5]0.8	Rép. de Moldova
Romania	58.9	49.1	40.2	42.7	35.6	31.7	31.7	27.8	20.2	17.4	Roumanie
Russian Federation	..	206.8	152.9	116.9	56.3	44.0	29.4	27.7	23.5	29.2	Fédération de Russie
Slovakia	..		4.5	1.3	3.7	3.3	2.6	...	1.8	...	Slovaquie
Slovenia	..	4.5	5.1	5.0	4.9	2.9	0.9	...	1.1	1.0	Slovénie
Spain	[6]23.1	[6]24.8	[6]25.4	20.2	21.6	19.0	...	...	...	...	Espagne
Sweden	0.2	...	...	0.0	...	...	...	...	...	...	Suède
Switzerland	9.9	6.3	6.3	4.9	5.4	4.3	...	...	...	...	Suisse
Ukraine	..	41.2	35.8	29.6	15.8	8.8	4.5	4.5	3.2	3.0	Ukraine
United Kingdom	[7]49.8	[7]41.7	...	19.8	18.3	...	...	...	...	...	Royaume-Uni

For general note and footnotes, see end of table.   Voir la fin du tableau pour la remarque générale et les notes

Wool yarn, pure and mixed (total) (continued)
Filés de laine pure et mélangée (production totale) (suite)

ISIC-BASED CODE - CODE BASE CITI

3211-03

Unit : Thousand metric tons   Unité : Milliers de tonnes métriques

Country or area	1990	1991	1992	1993	1994	1995	1996	1997	1998	1999	Pays ou zone
Yugoslavia	..	8.4	6.2	4.3	4.6	3.7	3.6	5.6	6.7	4.8	Yougoslavie
T.F.Yug.Rep. Macedonia	..	8.1	7.0	5.9	4.9	3.9	4.0	4.4	3.8	3.0	L'ex-RY Macédoine
USSR (former)	426.7	..	..	..	..	..	..	..	..	..	URSS (anc.)
Oceania	**37**	**37**	**37**	**38**	**45**	**43**	**41**	**39**	**38**	**41**	**Océanie**
Australia[8]	19.2	19.0	18.1	18.5	23.5	21.3	18.9	18.3	18.1	17.7	Australie[8]
New Zealand	18.3	17.6	18.9	19.7	21.1	21.4	22.4	20.9	...	23.5	Nouvelle-Zélande
Total	**1745**	**1702**	**1658**	**1503**	**1450**	**1427**	**1363**	**1377**	**1254**	**1359**	**Total**

General Note.
Data refer to total production of pure yarn of carded and combed (worsted) wool, and mixed yarn in which wool is predominant material by weight, containing less than 10 per cent by weight of silk, noil or other waste silk or any combination thereof. (SITC, Rev.3: 65112-0, 65113-0, 65116-1).

Remarque générale.
Les données se rapportent à la production totale de filés de laine pure (cardée ou peignée) et de filés mélangés dans lesquels le poids de laine prédomine, qui contiennent moins de 10 p. 100 en poids de soie, de bourre de soie ou d'autres déchets de soie, ou de mélange de ces fibres. (CTCI, Rev.3: 65112-0, 65113-0, 65116-1).

[1] 1995 data are confidential.
[2] Including yarn of man-made staple.
[3] Sales.
[4] Including hand-knit wool yarn.
[5] Excluding Transnistria region.
[6] Including household production.
[7] Estimated production in the woollen system and deliveries in the worsted system. Including man-made fibres and yarn of wholly wool and hair.
[8] Twelve months ending 30 June of year stated.

[1] Pour 1995, les données sont confidentielles.
[2] Y compris les filés de fibres synthétiques discontinues.
[3] Ventes.
[4] Y compris filés de laine tricotés à la main.
[5] Non compris la région de Transnistria.
[6] Y compris la production ménagère.
[7] Production estimative du cardage et quantités obtenues par peignage. Y compris les fibres artificielles et les filés entièrement constitués de laine et de poils.
[8] Période de douze mois finissant le 30 juin de l'année indiquée.

Wool yarn, mixed
Filés de laine mélangée

ISIC-BASED CODE - CODE BASE CITI

3211-04

Unit : Thousand metric tons   Unité : Milliers de tonnes métriques

Country or area	1990	1991	1992	1993	1994	1995	1996	1997	1998	1999	Pays ou zone
Africa	**7**	**5**	**4**	**5**	**5**	**5**	**5**	**5**	**5**	**5**	**Afrique**
South Africa	7.2	5.0	3.8	...	...	...	...	...	...	...	Afrique du Sud
America, South	**5**	**4**	**4**	**4**	**4**	**4**	**4**	**4**	**4**	**4**	**Amérique du Sud**
Brazil	3.8	3.9	...	...	...	...	...	...	...	...	Brésil
Colombia	0.7	...	0.1	0.1	0.1	0.0	...	0.0	0.0	...	Colombie
Asia	**279**	**299**	**326**	**287**	**293**	**292**	**291**	**286**	**278**	**275**	**Asie**
China	208.0	234.8	265.4	231.2	...	...	...	...	...	...	Chine
Indonesia	0.3	0.1	0.2	...	...	...	...	...	...	...	Indonésie
Japan	26.6	25.0	25.4	22.1	21.9	19.8	17.0	17.9	15.0	13.2	Japon
Korea, Republic of	18.8	18.0	16.8	15.8	...	...	...	...	...	...	Corée, République de
Turkey	25.7	21.3	18.4	17.5	18.6	19.9	21.5	15.7	10.3	9.1	Turquie
Europe	**339**	**354**	**354**	**350**	**608**	**579**	**553**	**571**	**516**	**698**	**Europe**
Austria	3.6	3.3	3.1	...	...	...	...	...	...	...	Autriche
Croatia	..	2.7	2.8	2.6	2.4	2.2	1.7	1.2	1.1	...	Croatie
Finland	0.4	0.5	0.6	0.8	1.0	0.6	0.7	...	...	...	Finlande
France [1]	19.3	20.2	19.9	16.5	15.8	...	...	...	...	...	France [1]
Germany	..	...	...	...	...	4.7	4.1	5.3	6.8	...	Allemagne
Greece	5.3	5.2	4.4	...	...	...	...	...	...	...	Grèce
Hungary	3.5	2.8	1.1	1.0	0.9	1.1	...	...	...	...	Hongrie
Italy	215.0	228.7	236.7	237.0	496.4	477.4	448.6	468.9	419.3	...	Italie
Poland	52.9	35.3	32.0	32.7	32.7	29.3	33.9	30.6	25.6	17.3	Pologne
Portugal	10.5	10.7	7.9	7.3	7.5	...	...	...	...	...	Portugal
Slovakia	..	..	...	1.3	1.0	0.9	0.8	...	...	...	Slovaquie
Slovenia	..	3.0	3.6	3.2	3.2	1.7	...	...	...	...	Slovénie
United Kingdom	28.2	...	...	...	...	...	...	...	...	...	Royaume-Uni
Yugoslavia	..	...	1.8	1.4	1.5	1.2	1.5	3.9	5.2	3.7	Yougoslavie
T.F.Yug.Rep. Macedonia	..	6.0	5.4	4.5	3.5	2.6	3.0	3.2	3.0	2.4	L'ex-RY Macédoine
Oceania	**15**	**12**	**11**	**15**	**15**	**26**	**17**	**16**	**16**	**16**	**Océanie**
Australia [2]	8.6	7.6	6.4	...	...	21.3	...	...	...	...	Australie [2]
New Zealand	6.2	4.7	4.4	4.4	4.2	4.9	6.3	5.2	...	5.5	Nouvelle-Zélande
Total	**645**	**674**	**699**	**662**	**925**	**907**	**870**	**882**	**819**	**999**	**Total**

General Note.

Mixed yarn in which wool is the predominant material by weight, containing less than 10 per cent by weight of silk, noil or other waste silk or any combination thereof. (SITC, Rev.3: 65112-1, 65113-1, 65116-1).

[1] More than 50 per cent wool.
[2] Twelve months ending 30 June of year stated.

Remarque générale.

Filés de laine mélangée dans lesquels la laine prédomine en poids et contenant moins de 10 p. 100 en poids de soie, de bourre de soie (schappe) ou de bourette de soie, ou de mélange de ces fibres. (CTCI, Rev.3: 65112-1, 65113-1, 65116-1).

[1] Plus de 50 p. 100 de laine.
[2] Période de douze mois finissant le 30 juin de l'année indiquée.

Wool yarn, pure
Filés de laine pure

ISIC-BASED CODE - CODE BASE CITI

3211-07

Unit : Thousand metric tons

Unité : Milliers de tonnes métriques

Country or area	1990	1991	1992	1993	1994	1995	1996	1997	1998	1999	Pays ou zone
Africa	**1**	**1**	**1**	**1**	**1**	**1**	**1**	**1**	**1**	**1**	**Afrique**
South Africa	0.9	1.2	1.0	...	...	...	...	...	...	...	Afrique du Sud
America, South	**1**	**1**	**1**	**1**	**1**	**1**	**1**	**1**	**1**	**1**	**Amérique du Sud**
Bolivia	0.7	0.4	0.9	0.3	...	*0.4	...	...	...	...	Bolivie
Brazil	0.3	0.6	...	...	...	...	...	...	...	...	Brésil
Asia	**159**	**183**	**216**	**221**	**185**	**169**	**165**	**177**	**160**	**142**	**Asie**
China	30.0	48.0	85.2	112.2	...	...	...	...	...	...	Chine
Hong Kong SAR	4.8	...	...	...	...	...	...	...	...	...	Hong-Kong RAS
Japan	78.4	81.9	80.1	61.9	67.7	51.9	47.8	44.6	31.6	28.8	Japon
Korea, Republic of	9.5	11.1	9.3	7.4	...	...	...	...	...	...	Corée, République de
Turkey	36.1	33.6	34.0	31.7	34.3	32.3	34.2	49.2	44.8	29.7	Turquie
Turkmenistan	..	3.0	2.6	2.5	0.3	2.0	0.3	0.5	0.5	...	Turkménistan
Europe	**127**	**175**	**183**	**175**	**176**	**177**	**168**	**167**	**160**	**166**	**Europe**
Austria	1.6	2.2	2.2	...	...	...	...	...	...	...	Autriche
Croatia	..	0.9	0.9	1.3	1.2	1.1	0.8	0.7	0.5	...	Croatie
Finland	0.5	0.4	0.4	0.5	0.7	0.5	0.8	...	...	...	Finlande
France	...	...	...	...	15.8	12.7	10.5	10.3	8.8	10.3	France
Germany	..	...	...	...	...	26.2	21.7	20.9	16.3	...	Allemagne
Greece	5.7	4.5	5.2	...	...	...	...	...	...	...	Grèce
Hungary	0.5	0.5	0.4	0.3	0.3	0.2	...	0.3	0.5	0.5	Hongrie
Italy	69.7	78.2	87.0	81.9	...	...	...	...	...	...	Italie
Lithuania	..	10.9	7.7	5.2	3.8	3.5	4.1	3.7	3.8	3.3	Lituanie
Poland	2.1	2.1	1.9	3.1	4.2	5.1	1.7	1.9	1.4	0.8	Pologne
Portugal	3.0	2.4	3.5	4.1	5.1	...	...	...	...	...	Portugal
Slovakia	..	..	...	...	2.7	2.4	1.8	...	...	...	Slovaquie
Slovenia	..	1.5	1.6	1.8	1.7	1.2	...	...	...	...	Slovénie
United Kingdom	29.0	...	...	...	...	...	...	...	...	...	Royaume-Uni
Yugoslavia	..	5.3	4.3	2.8	3.1	2.5	2.2	1.7	1.5	1.1	Yougoslavie
T.F.Yug.Rep. Macedonia	..	2.1	1.6	1.4	1.3	1.3	1.0	1.1	0.8	0.6	L'ex-RY Macédoine
Oceania	**24**	**24**	**25**	**27**	**28**	**28**	**27**	**27**	**27**	**29**	**Océanie**
Australia [1]	11.2	11.2	11.0	11.5	...	...	...	...	...	...	Australie [1]
New Zealand	13.2	12.9	14.5	15.3	16.8	16.6	16.1	15.6	...	18.0	Nouvelle-Zélande
Total	**312**	**384**	**426**	**424**	**391**	**376**	**362**	**373**	**349**	**339**	**Total**

General Note.
Pure yarn of carded and combed (worsted) wool. (SITC, Rev.3: 65112-2, 65113-2, 65116-1).

Remarque générale.
Filés de pure laine cardée ou peignée. (CTCI, Rev.3: 65112-2, 65113-2, 65116-1).

[1] Twelve months ending 30 June of year stated.

[1] Période de douze mois finissant le 30 juin de l'année indiquée.

Cotton yarn, pure and mixed (total)
Filés de coton pur et mélangé (production totale)

ISIC-BASED CODE - CODE BASE CITI

3211-09

Unit : Thousand metric tons   Unité : Milliers de tonnes métriques

Country or area	1990	1991	1992	1993	1994	1995	1996	1997	1998	1999	Pays ou zone
Africa	**456**	**415**	**438**	**421**	**421**	**423**	**384**	**349**	**377**	**375**	**Afrique**
Algeria	27.4	26.6	27.0	...	...	...	...	...	...	...	Algérie
Burkina Faso	95.4	54.3	68.2	...	...	...	...	...	...	...	Burkina Faso
Egypt	259.0	260.3	273.0	253.9	251.5	250.3	211.6	170.5	...	...	Egypte
Ethiopia[1]	9.0	4.5	3.8	3.4	5.7	4.9	4.4	3.1	2.7	3.4	Ethiopie[1]
Kenya	3.4	...	...	3.3	3.3	...	...	...	...	...	Kenya
South Africa	62.1	66.5	62.6	60.9	60.7	65.2	65.4	72.7	63.4	65.8	Afrique du Sud
America, North	**1356**	**1547**	**1689**	**1796**	**2025**	**2033**	**1989**	**2028**	**2038**	**1855**	**Amérique du Nord**
Mexico	14.6	13.0	10.7	31.6	35.4	27.8	24.1	24.3	24.1	21.1	Mexique
United States	1341.6	1533.8	1678.0	1764.6	1989.1	2004.8	1965.2	2003.3	2014.0	1833.9	Etats-Unis
America, South	**748**	**752**	**690**	**711**	**762**	**713**	**701**	**710**	**653**	**683**	**Amérique du Sud**
Bolivia	1.4	2.0	1.9	0.4	...	...	...	...	...	...	Bolivie
Brazil	498.8	506.5	509.2	532.5	545.6	491.4	483.0	486.6	438.0	468.1	Brésil
Chile	9.5	15.6	14.4	12.8	12.7	15.3	19.3	18.2	14.7	11.1	Chili
Colombia	...	...	#16.7	7.2	14.4	15.3	...	...	...	...	Colombie
Ecuador	...	...	3.8	6.0	7.3	8.3	3.4	9.0	4.9	7.9	Equateur
Paraguay	218.8	209.0	144.0	152.1	...	...	...	...	...	...	Paraguay
Asia	**9189**	**8752**	**9443**	**9571**	**9816**	**10348**	**10188**	**10636**	**10362**	**10594**	**Asie**
Armenia	..	5.9	5.4	1.0	0.4	0.2	0.3	0.0	0.1	0.1	Arménie
Azerbaijan	..	27.1	24.2	25.0	21.9	19.9	13.7	8.6	2.6	0.9	Azerbaïdjan
Bangladesh[2]	145.4	67.5	123.8	60.5	57.8	49.1	50.5	53.1	...	...	Bangladesh[2]
China	4625.9	4104.9	4458.8	4447.7	4894.7	5421.8	5122.1	5598.3	5420.0	5670.0	Chine
Hong Kong SAR	216.6	178.0	179.8	166.0	169.6	147.9	125.2	163.3	101.1	...	Hong-Kong RAS
Georgia	..	...	5.0	2.6	0.8	0.6	0.4	0.2	0.1	0.0	Géorgie
India	1690.7	1687.4	1734.5	1919.6	...	...	...	...	...	...	Inde
Indonesia	218.8	218.8	360.5	391.0	271.0	...	...	108.1	...	...	Indonésie
Japan[3]	425.6	373.3	338.2	284.1	234.8	215.0	195.8	183.5	173.4	171.0	Japon[3]
Kazakhstan	..	36.9	38.6	35.0	19.8	4.2	3.1	2.3	1.9	1.8	Kazakhstan
Korea, Republic of	330.1	317.9	301.6	295.5	315.7	308.9	297.3	277.1	251.8	282.6	Corée, République de
Kyrgyzstan	..	24.9	25.0	13.8	8.5	2.7	4.2	3.1	2.4	2.1	Kirghizistan
Malaysia	37.7	30.4	28.7	39.5	55.7	71.3	80.8	80.2	88.9	92.9	Malaisie
Myanmar[4]	9.3	5.4	3.3	3.7	4.1	4.9	4.8	3.7	3.9	4.8	Myanmar[4]
Pakistan[2][5]	911.6	1041.2	1170.7	1219.0	1309.6	1369.7	1495.1	1520.8	1532.3	1540.3	Pakistan[2][5]
Sri Lanka	8.5	3.3	2.1	...	...	...	...	...	...	...	Sri Lanka
Syrian Arab Republic	37.2	39.1	38.1	32.6	37.3	40.4	43.2	53.7	...	...	Rép. arabe syrienne
Tajikistan	..	24.7	18.7	17.8	12.7	13.2	19.5	8.5	14.4	14.7	Tadjikistan
Thailand[6]	133.1	123.7	...	...	...	...	...	...	...	...	Thaïlande[6]
Turkey	340.0	299.2	298.8	320.9	349.5	369.2	421.1	513.5	471.2	449.7	Turquie
Turkmenistan	..	5.3	5.8	...	...	...	...	...	...	...	Turkménistan
Uzbekistan	..	94.3	108.9	109.5	107.9	103.2	105.2	114.3	...	...	Ouzbékistan
Viet Nam	58.3	40.3	43.6	...	...	...	...	...	...	...	Viet Nam
Europe	**1699**	**2905**	**2289**	**1960**	**1716**	**1565**	**1604**	**1634**	**1476**	**1503**	**Europe**
Austria	16.7	18.1	19.2	23.2	22.2	...	...	...	...	...	Autriche
Belarus	..	50.5	44.9	35.2	13.0	9.7	11.4	10.2	18.6	15.1	Bélarus
Belgium	50.7	47.8	46.0	47.2	[7]21.0	[7]19.0	[7]16.8	[7]19.4	[7]17.3	[7]16.6	Belgique
Bulgaria	72.2	31.0	25.5	24.2	23.7	27.6	26.0	28.2	26.9	19.8	Bulgarie
Croatia	..	13.7	10.7	10.3	10.6	8.9	5.3	5.6	5.2	...	Croatie
Denmark[8]	...	...	3.0	...	3.0	3.0	2.9	3.0	3.0	2.7	Danemark[8]
Czechoslovakia(former)	146.0	99.2	..	..	...	...	...	..	..	..	Tchécoslovaquie(anc.)
Czech Republic	..	..	71.2	59.8	59.5	63.5	57.8	62.4	66.5	56.4	République tchèque
Estonia	..	37.8	21.5	12.6	13.9	16.0	20.1	23.1	23.9	20.0	Estonie
Finland	1.4	2.1	2.0	2.1	2.7	2.7	2.1	2.1	...	...	Finlande
France[9]	170.5	153.8	149.9	154.4	179.7	...	...	...	...	...	France[9]
Germany	..	185.1	168.9	154.1	152.8	98.6	98.3	106.5	96.2	...	Allemagne
Germany(Fed.Rep.)[9]	189.9	..	..	..	..	..	..	..	..	..	Allemagne(Rép.féd.)[9]
Greece	[10]134.1	[10]127.7	[10]111.9	122.4	120.1	120.7	223.9	222.4	109.7	...	Grèce
Hungary[6]	54.6	29.9	24.3	22.4	19.5	20.7	...	...	...	...	Hongrie[6]
Italy	271.3	260.8	245.1	244.2	262.5	260.1	262.0	266.4	262.4	239.3	Italie
Latvia	..	13.3	6.3	5.2	2.3	3.4	3.5	3.8	4.7	5.2	Lettonie
Lithuania	..	28.4	24.0	12.0	8.9	8.5	8.2	11.3	14.3	11.8	Lituanie

For general note and footnotes, see end of table.   Voir la fin du tableau pour la remarque générale et les notes.

Cotton yarn, pure and mixed (total) (continued)
Filés de coton pur et mélangé (production totale) (suite)

ISIC-BASED CODE - CODE BASE CITI

3211-09

Unit : Thousand metric tons

Unité : Milliers de tonnes métriques

Country or area	1990	1991	1992	1993	1994	1995	1996	1997	1998	1999	Pays ou zone
Netherlands	3.5	2.5	2.5	...	...	...	...	...	...	...	Pays-Bas
Poland	126.7	73.2	84.4	94.3	102.8	96.2	95.9	95.0	82.2	67.3	Pologne
Portugal	[9]148.7	[9]137.9	96.3	102.0	122.1	119.3	121.0	122.8	120.6	112.9	Portugal
Republic of Moldova		32.6	26.1	[11]0.4	[11]0.2	[11]0.1	[11]0.1	[11]0.1	[11]0.1	[11]0.0	Rép. de Moldova
Romania[9]	130.1	92.4	64.7	62.6	62.0	60.8	62.1	43.2	35.7	27.7	Roumanie[9]
Russian Federation	..	1118.4	709.3	513.9	265.1	198.7	146.9	175.1	149.1	191.4	Fédération de Russie
Slovakia	..	..	17.0	2.0	2.7	1.7	11.5	9.2	5.6	4.0	Slovaquie
Slovenia	..	11.0	9.8	9.0	10.5	9.8	8.8	...	...	7.2	Slovénie
Spain	103.2	96.5	95.8	105.8	129.0	146.3	...	...	...	...	Espagne
Sweden	4.4	4.6	3.9	...	...	...	...	2.2	1.6	1.5	Suède
Switzerland	50.1	45.1	41.0	39.6	38.3	31.1	...	...	...	...	Suisse
Ukraine	..	145.6	124.4	58.9	30.2	17.5	9.1	6.4	10.6	5.4	Ukraine
United Kingdom	22.6	12.6	8.7	14.6	13.3	12.6	12.8	10.0	8.8	...	Royaume-Uni
Yugoslavia	..	22.2	22.2	11.6	11.5	5.6	8.1	8.6	9.8	8.5	Yougoslavie
T.F.Yug.Rep. Macedonia	..	8.9	8.8	7.5	7.3	4.8	5.9	3.6	4.1	2.2	L'ex-RY Macédoine
USSR (former)	1704.8	..	..	..	..	..	..	..		..	URSS (anc.)
Oceania	22	24	25	30	36	38	39	40	37	37	Océanie
Australia[2]	21.8	24.2	25.5	30.4	36.1	37.9	38.6	39.9	36.9	36.8	Australie[2]
Total	15175	14396	14574	14490	14776	15119	14906	15397	14943	15046	Total

General Note.
Data refer to pure cotton yarn including yarn from cotton waste and mixed yarn in which cotton or cotton waste is predominant material by weight, containing less than 10 per cent by weight of silk, noil or other waste silk or any combination thereof. (SITC, Rev.3: 651310-0, 65133-0).

Remarque générale.
Les données se rapportent à la production totale de filés de coton pur ou mélangé à d'autres matières textiles dans lesquelles le poids de coton et les déchets de coton prédominent, et où le poids de la soie, de la bourrette et autres déchets de soie ou mélangé de ces textiles représente moins de 10 p. 100 du poids total. (CTCI, Rev.3: 65131-0, 65133-0).

[1] Twelve months ending 7 July of the year stated.
[2] Twelve months ending 30 June of year stated.
[3] Including condenser cotton yarn.
[4] Government production only.
[5] Factory production only.
[6] Excluding yarn made from waste.
[7] Incomplete coverage.
[8] Sales.
[9] Including tire-cord yarn.
[10] Including all mixed yarns, irrespective of predominant raw material.
[11] Excluding Transnistria region.

[1] Période de douze mois finissant le 7 juillet de l'année indiquée.
[2] Période de douze mois finissant le 30 juin de l'année indiquée.
[3] Y compris les filés de coton obtenus sur carde fileuse.
[4] Production de l'Etat seulement.
[5] Production des fabriques seulement.
[6] Non compris les filés à base de déchets de coton.
[7] Couverture incomplète.
[8] Ventes.
[9] Y compris les filés de coton pour pneumatiques à cordes.
[10] Y compris les filés mélangés, quelle que soit la matière première principale.
[11] Non compris la région de Transnistria.

Cotton yarn, mixed
Filés de coton mélangé

ISIC-BASED CODE - CODE BASE CITI

3211-10

Unit : Thousand metric tons

Unité : Milliers de tonnes métriques

Country or area	1990	1991	1992	1993	1994	1995	1996	1997	1998	1999	Pays ou zone
Africa	**17**	**20**	**20**	**21**	**24**	**22**	**24**	**24**	**22**	**20**	**Afrique**
South Africa	16.5	19.6	20.3	21.2	23.8	22.3	23.6	24.0	22.3	20.5	Afrique du Sud
America, North	**190**	**194**	**172**	**176**	**183**	**183**	**183**	**183**	**183**	**183**	**Amérique du Nord**
United States	189.5	194.1	172.1	176.1	...	...	...	...	...	...	Etats-Unis
America, South	**293**	**297**	**232**	**238**	**276**	**274**	**272**	**288**	**283**	**294**	**Amérique du Sud**
Brazil	66.7	76.5	74.9	79.0	83.8	81.5	80.9	92.3	87.7	97.2	Brésil
Chile	...	...	4.5	3.9	3.4	3.0	2.4	3.0	1.9	1.1	Chili
Colombia	4.4	...	9.1	3.3	8.6	8.9	...	12.1	12.5	...	Colombie
Paraguay	218.4	208.5	143.4	151.5	...	...	...	...	...	...	Paraguay
Asia	**2253**	**1681**	**1822**	**2037**	**2063**	**2246**	**2422**	**2512**	**2361**	**2446**	**Asie**
China	1542.4	983.3	1081.1	1135.0	1306.2	1447.7	1536.5	1701.1	...	...	Chine
India	202.0	225.7	241.1	291.5	...	...	...	...	...	...	Inde
Indonesia	...	109.4	117.4	170.7	#16.7	...	...	13.3	...	...	Indonésie
Japan [1]	36.0	33.5	29.9	29.6	26.1	13.2	13.7	14.4	13.0	13.1	Japon [1]
Korea, Republic of	54.5	57.6	59.7	58.0	...	...	...	...	...	...	Corée, République de
Malaysia	18.0	12.8	11.8	24.1	34.8	52.1	56.4	54.5	67.1	68.6	Malaisie
Pakistan	122.7	152.1	176.2	191.5	237.6	213.9	263.3	293.6	340.5	390.0	Pakistan
Turkey	118.0	106.1	104.5	136.5	144.6	136.0	169.5	137.3	117.7	120.5	Turquie
Europe	**192**	**180**	**184**	**188**	**208**	**200**	**197**	**186**	**182**	**187**	**Europe**
Austria	5.9	0.7	1.0	0.3	...	...	...	...	...	...	Autriche
Croatia	..	1.6	1.8	3.1	3.6	2.2	1.1	0.2	0.1	...	Croatie
Finland	0.5	...	...	...	...	...	...	...	...	...	Finlande
France	66.0	61.3	63.6	60.2	69.3	...	...	...	...	...	France
Germany	...	...	...	...	...	9.0	7.6	8.7	8.6	...	Allemagne
Greece [2]	6.5	7.3	8.2	...	...	...	...	...	...	...	Grèce [2]
Hungary	11.1	4.7	4.4	3.6	3.6	6.4	...	...	...	...	Hongrie
Italy	42.1	39.4	36.9	37.2	42.5	42.0	40.2	41.2	40.5	39.2	Italie
Poland	37.0	23.5	23.9	30.4	35.1	31.0	32.7	23.9	20.6	23.1	Pologne
Portugal	20.8	24.2	...	...	...	...	...	...	...	...	Portugal
Slovakia	..	..	...	2.0	1.7	1.2	...	...	...	...	Slovaquie
Slovenia	..	1.1	1.1	1.0	0.9	0.6	...	...	...	...	Slovénie
United Kingdom	2.2	1.4	2.3	7.3	8.0	7.1	7.0	5.2	4.9	...	Royaume-Uni
Yugoslavia	..	4.3	6.5	3.0	1.6	1.1	1.8	1.6	2.0	1.4	Yougoslavie
T.F.Yug.Rep. Macedonia	..	1.1	1.4	0.9	1.0	0.9	1.5	0.7	0.7	0.3	L'ex-RY Macédoine
Total	**2945**	**2371**	**2430**	**2660**	**2755**	**2924**	**3098**	**3193**	**3032**	**3130**	**Total**

General Note.

Mixed yarn in which cotton or cotton waste is the predominant material by weight, containing less than 10 per cent by weight of silk, noil or other waste silk or any combination thereof. (SITC, Rev.3: 65131-1, 65133-1).

Remarque générale.

Filés de coton mélangé dans lesquels le coton ou les déchets de coton prédominent en poids et contenant moins de 10 p. 100 en poids de soie, de bourre de soie ou d'autres déchets de soie, ou de mélange de ces fibres. (CTCI, Rev.3: 65131-1, 65133-1).

[1] Including condenser cotton yarn.
[2] Including all mixed yarns, irrespective of predominant raw material.

[1] Y compris les filés de coton obtenus sur carde fileuse.
[2] Y compris les filés mélangés, quelle que soit la matière première principale.

Cotton yarn, pure
Filés de coton pur

ISIC-BASED CODE - CODE BASE CITI

3211-13

Unit : Thousand metric tons   Unité : Milliers de tonnes métriques

Country or area	1990	1991	1992	1993	1994	1995	1996	1997	1998	1999	Pays ou zone
Africa	**314**	**317**	**325**	**303**	**297**	**303**	**263**	**229**	**258**	**257**	**Afrique**
Burkina Faso	0.3	0.3	0.5	0.4	...	...	...	...	...	...	Burkina Faso
Egypt	259.0	260.3	273.0	253.9	251.0	250.3	211.6	170.5	...	...	Egypte
Ethiopia[1][2]	9.0	...	...	...	...	...	...	...	...	...	Ethiopie[1][2]
South Africa	45.5	47.0	42.3	39.7	36.9	43.0	41.8	48.7	41.0	45.3	Afrique du Sud
America, North	**1167**	**1353**	**1517**	**1620**	**1432**	**1424**	**1421**	**1421**	**1421**	**1418**	**Amérique du Nord**
Mexico	14.6	13.0	10.7	31.6	35.4	27.8	24.1	24.3	24.1	21.1	Mexique
United States	1152.1	1339.7	1505.9	1588.5	...	...	...	...	...	...	Etats-Unis
America, South	**449**	**448**	**454**	**467**	**478**	**429**	**426**	**416**	**370**	**387**	**Amérique du Sud**
Bolivia	1.4	2.0	1.9	0.4	0.5	*0.4	...	...	...	...	Bolivie
Brazil	432.2	429.9	434.4	453.5	461.8	409.9	402.1	394.3	350.3	371.0	Brésil
Chile	9.5	9.7	9.8	8.9	9.3	12.2	16.9	15.2	12.8	10.0	Chili
Colombia	...	...	#7.6	3.9	5.8	6.3	...	...	...	...	Colombie
Paraguay	0.4	0.6	1.0	0.6	...	...	...	...	...	...	Paraguay
Asia	**6706**	**6625**	**7108**	**7110**	**6854**	**7310**	**7304**	**7467**	**7537**	**7767**	**Asie**
Bangladesh[3]	50.6	55.9	60.4	60.5	57.0	48.6	49.9	52.5	...	...	Bangladesh[3]
China	3083.5	3121.6	3377.7	3312.8	2907.5	3158.5	2763.1	2840.0	...	...	Chine
India[1]	1488.7	1461.7	1493.4	1622.3	1695.7	1894.2	2148.0	2218.4	2058.0	...	Inde[1]
Indonesia	...	109.4	243.1	220.3	253.5	155.4	...	89.9	312.0	...	Indonésie
Japan[4]	389.6	339.8	308.3	254.5	208.7	201.8	182.1	169.1	160.4	157.9	Japon[4]
Korea, Republic of	275.6	260.3	241.9	237.5	...	...	...	...	...	...	Corée, République de
Malaysia	19.8	17.7	17.0	15.4	21.0	19.2	24.5	25.7	21.8	24.3	Malaisie
Myanmar[5]	9.3	5.4	3.3	3.7	4.1	4.9	4.8	3.7	3.9	4.8	Myanmar[5]
Pakistan	788.9	889.1	994.5	1027.5	1072.1	1155.8	1231.8	1227.2	1191.8	1150.3	Pakistan
Sri Lanka	8.5	3.3	2.1	...	...	...	...	...	...	...	Sri Lanka
Syrian Arab Republic	37.2	39.1	38.1	32.6	37.3	40.4	43.2	53.7	59.9	61.7	Rép. arabe syrienne
Thailand[6]	133.1	123.7	...	...	...	...	...	...	...	...	Thaïlande[6]
Turkey	222.0	193.1	194.3	184.4	204.9	233.2	251.6	376.2	353.5	329.2	Turquie
Turkmenistan	..	5.3	5.4	5.1	5.3	11.4	20.8	23.1	28.7	...	Turkménistan
Europe	**755**	**821**	**758**	**761**	**765**	**739**	**767**	**776**	**758**	**695**	**Europe**
Austria	10.8	17.4	18.3	22.9	22.2	22.0	...	...	...	...	Autriche
Croatia	..	12.1	8.9	7.2	6.9	6.7	4.2	5.4	5.1	...	Croatie
Finland	0.9	2.1	2.0	2.1	2.7	2.7	2.1	2.1	...	...	Finlande
France	[7]104.5	[7]92.5	[7]86.3	[7]94.2	75.4	83.7	98.7	98.6	111.2	103.0	France
Germany	..	...	...	...	...	89.6	90.7	97.8	87.6	...	Allemagne
Greece	127.6	120.4	103.7	...	...	...	...	...	...	...	Grèce
Hungary[6]	43.5	25.2	19.9	18.9	15.9	14.3	...	16.6	14.6	11.6	Hongrie[6]
Italy	229.3	221.5	208.2	207.0	220.0	218.1	221.7	225.3	221.9	200.2	Italie
Lithuania	..	28.4	24.0	12.0	8.9	8.5	8.2	11.3	14.3	11.8	Lituanie
Poland	89.7	49.7	60.4	63.9	67.7	65.2	63.2	71.2	61.6	44.2	Pologne
Portugal	[7]127.9	[7]113.7	95.6	94.1	104.4	...	...	...	...	...	Portugal
Slovakia	..	..	...	0.0	1.0	0.5	11.5	9.2	5.6	4.0	Slovaquie
Slovenia	..	9.9	8.8	8.1	9.6	9.2	...	...	...	...	Slovénie
United Kingdom	20.4	11.2	6.4	7.3	5.3	5.5	5.8	4.8	3.9	...	Royaume-Uni
Yugoslavia	..	17.9	15.7	8.7	9.8	4.5	6.3	7.0	7.8	7.0	Yougoslavie
T.F.Yug.Rep. Macedonia	..	7.8	7.4	6.6	6.3	3.9	4.4	2.9	3.4	1.9	L'ex-RY Macédoine
Total	**9391**	**9564**	**10162**	**10261**	**9826**	**10205**	**10180**	**10308**	**10343**	**10524**	**Total**

General Note.
Pure cotton yarn, including yarn from cotton waste. (SITC, Rev.3: 65131-2, 65133-2).

Remarque générale.
Filés de coton pur, y compris les filés obtenus à partir de déchets de coton. (CTCI, Rev.3: 65131-2, 65133-2).

[1] Factory production only.
[2] Twelve months ending 7 July of the year stated.
[3] Twelve months ending 30 June of year stated.
[4] Including condenser cotton yarn.
[5] Production by government-owned enterprises only.
[6] Excluding yarn made from waste.
[7] Including tire-cord yarn.

[1] Production des fabriques seulement.
[2] Période de douze mois finissant le 7 juillet de l'année indiquée.
[3] Période de douze mois finissant le 30 juin de l'année indiquée.
[4] Y compris les filés de coton obtenus sur carde fileuse.
[5] Production des établissements d'Etat seulement.
[6] Non compris les filés à base de déchets de coton.
[7] Y compris les filés de coton pour pneumatiques à cordes.

Flax, ramie and true hemp yarn
Filés de lin, de ramie et de chanvre

ISIC-BASED CODE - CODE BASE CITI

3211-16

Unit : Thousand metric tons   Unité : Milliers de tonnes métriques

Country or area	1990	1991	1992	1993	1994	1995	1996	1997	1998	1999	Pays ou zone
Africa	**0**	**0**	**0**	**0**	**0**	**0**	**0**	**0**	**0**	**0**	**Afrique**
Egypt[1][2]	0.4	0.4	0.3	0.2	0.3	0.4	0.3	0.1	...	...	Egypte[1][2]
Asia	**3**	**2**	**2**	**4**	**2**	**2**	**2**	**2**	**1**	**1**	**Asie**
Indonesia	0.3	0.1	...	...	0.2	0.3	...	...	0.6	...	Indonésie
Japan	2.6	2.0	1.4	3.3	2.2	2.0	1.4	1.4	0.7	1.0	Japon
Europe	**84**	**230**	**209**	**173**	**127**	**114**	**102**	**95**	**76**	**76**	**Europe**
Austria[3]	2.7	*3.1	...	...	...	...	...	...	...	...	Autriche[3]
Belarus	..	[1]24.4	27.2	20.8	15.1	16.1	16.1	16.8	17.4	16.5	Bélarus
Belgium[1]	6.5	5.2	4.6	5.2	5.1	3.3	...	...	3.0	2.9	Belgique[1]
Bulgaria[3]	7.3	3.9	1.6	0.6	0.8	0.8	0.8	0.5	0.4	0.3	Bulgarie[3]
Croatia	..	0.4	0.4	0.2	0.2	0.2	0.0	...	...	...	Croatie
Czechoslovakia(former)[3]	15.3	9.9	..	..	..	..	..	..	..	..	Tchécoslovaquie(anc.)[3]
Czech Republic[4]	..	..	9.4	9.0	9.2	10.5	4.1	4.4	4.5	5.0	République tchèque[4]
Estonia	..	0.7	0.5	0.3	0.0	0.4	0.1	0.1	0.6	1.0	Estonie
Finland[1]	0.3	0.3	0.2	0.3	0.3	0.2	0.2	...	...	...	Finlande[1]
France	5.3	5.3	5.1	6.8	5.6	...	...	...	...	...	France
Germany[4]	..	...	...	...	...	2.4	1.9	2.5	...	...	Allemagne[4]
German D.R.(former)	0.3	..	..	..	..	..	..	..	..	..	R.D.A. (anc.)
Greece	0.1	0.1	0.1	...	...	...	...	...	...	...	Grèce
Hungary	5.7	3.7	2.6	2.2	2.8	2.7	...	1.5	1.9	2.0	Hongrie
Latvia	..	2.3	1.6	0.3	0.8	0.4	0.2	0.7	0.8	0.8	Lettonie
Lithuania	..	4.8	4.2	3.0	3.5	3.2	3.0	2.9	2.9	3.1	Lituanie
Poland	14.9	9.5	9.6	9.4	12.8	8.3	5.1	5.1	5.0	3.8	Pologne
Romania[3]	24.4	22.0	15.4	9.3	7.7	8.4	7.0	5.2	4.6	4.3	Roumanie[3]
Russian Federation	..	107.8	97.0	78.6	40.9	36.3	36.6	31.6	17.1	20.1	Fédération de Russie
Slovakia	..	..	1.1	0.9	1.6	0.8	0.6	...	0.5	0.5	Slovaquie
Slovenia	..	0.2	0.2	0.2	0.0	...	...	...	...	...	Slovénie
Ukraine[1]	..	19.5	18.7	18.0	13.7	8.8	8.0	6.5	2.9	1.7	Ukraine[1]
United Kingdom	...	...	...	1.3	0.9	...	...	...	...	...	Royaume-Uni
Yugoslavia	..	3.4	2.8	1.6	0.8	0.3	0.3	0.3	0.4	0.2	Yougoslavie
USSR (former)[1]	200.3	..	..	..	..	..	..	..	..	..	URSS (anc.)[1]
Total	**287**	**232**	**211**	**177**	**130**	**116**	**104**	**96**	**77**	**78**	**Total**

General Note.
Flax, ramie and true hemp yarn, including yarns put up for retail sale. (SITC, Rev.3: 65196-0, 65199-1).

[1] Flax yarn only.
[2] Including waste.
[3] Yarn of flax and true hemp.
[4] Including jute yarn and yarn of other vegetable textile fibres.

Remarque générale.
Filés de lin, de ramie et de chanvre, y compris les fils conditionnés pour la vente au détail. (CTCI, Rev.3: 65196-0, 65199-1).

[1] Filés de lin seulement.
[2] Y compris les déchets.
[3] Filés de lin et de chanvre.
[4] Y compris les filés de jute et les filés d'autres fibres textiles végétales.

Yarn of man-made staple
Filés de fibres synthétiques et artificielles

ISIC-BASED CODE - CODE BASE CITI

3211-19

Unit : Thousand metric tons / Unité : Milliers de tonnes métriques

Country or area	1990	1991	1992	1993	1994	1995	1996	1997	1998	1999	Pays ou zone
America, North	**1480**	**1447**	**1524**	**1485**	**1625**	**1600**	**1644**	**1587**	**1428**	**1383**	**Amérique du Nord**
Mexico	26.4	26.8	27.8	74.9	69.8	63.4	77.9	83.2	78.0	73.8	Mexique
United States	1454.1	1420.5	1496.0	1410.4	1554.9	1537.0	1566.3	1503.6	1349.7	1309.3	Etats-Unis
America, South	**15**	**29**	**36**	**38**	**39**	**30**	**38**	**28**	**32**	**39**	**Amérique du Sud**
Chile	8.6	10.0	10.1	10.2	8.4	7.8	6.5	5.8	6.0	5.8	Chili
Colombia	1.2	...	#16.5	18.9	20.2	...	...	8.1	5.1	...	Colombie
Ecuador	...	...	9.0	8.9	10.4	10.2	20.1	14.0	20.4	...	Equateur
Asia	**1412**	**1361**	**1387**	**1329**	**1281**	**1260**	**1236**	**1234**	**1174**	**1155**	**Asie**
Hong Kong SAR	3.6	3.8	2.5	2.0	0.4	1.3	1.4	1.2	0.8	...	Hong-Kong RAS
India	108.6	114.0	127.8	134.5	...	...	...	...	...	...	Inde
Indonesia	0.8	1.4	...	...	5.8	8.8	...	...	1.4	...	Indonésie
Japan	470.2	454.2	431.8	356.0	328.7	296.9	265.0	257.6	209.9	186.2	Japon
Korea, Republic of	805.4	769.8	...	...	...	...	...	...	...	...	Corée, République de
Turkey	23.8	18.2	33.7	45.0	37.2	43.9	56.7	62.4	53.2	55.3	Turquie
Europe	**1007**	**991**	**909**	**820**	**836**	**914**	**857**	**912**	**624**	**734**	**Europe**
Austria	4.7	4.1	4.8	...	...	...	...	...	...	...	Autriche
Belgium	16.3	13.9	17.1	16.0	36.6	49.0	41.1	50.6	42.3	[1]25.0	Belgique
Croatia	..	7.1	4.8	4.0	4.1	3.5	2.1	0.4	0.3	...	Croatie
Denmark[3]	[2]13.3	[2]12.4	[2]10.4	...	[2]11.8	16.3	18.0	21.5	21.5	20.1	Danemark[3]
Finland	0.4	0.3	1.4	1.5	1.5	1.2	1.1	...	...	...	Finlande
France	101.5	...	66.1	79.5	85.9	...	...	...	...	...	France
Germany	..	391.2	368.9	322.7	333.7	401.4	365.8	398.9	136.8	...	Allemagne
Germany(Fed.Rep.)	409.3	...	..	..	..	...	...	...	...	...	Allemagne(Rép.féd.)
Greece	...	...	...	8.9	9.2	5.7	9.5	...	11.4	...	Grèce
Hungary	20.3	11.1	8.0	8.4	8.0	5.9	12.6	15.7	20.7	17.7	Hongrie
Latvia	..	...	...	...	...	...	...	...	...	2.0	Lettonie
Netherlands	9.1	8.5	8.3	...	...	...	...	...	...	...	Pays-Bas
Portugal	48.8	45.6	60.6	52.0	51.1	45.2	41.4	40.7	39.1	33.8	Portugal
Romania	209.2	142.1	112.6	100.4	83.3	92.0	78.5	74.5	47.7	28.3	Roumanie
Russian Federation	..	81.3	62.5	52.4	20.1	25.2	15.6	16.9	14.4	14.9	Fédération de Russie
Slovakia	..	...	...	...	...	...	...	...	0.9	0.5	Slovaquie
Slovenia	..	5.5	9.0	7.4	6.6	6.1	4.7	4.8	6.0	5.0	Slovénie
Spain	124.3	123.4	108.3	87.5	114.6	111.8	117.4	128.2	132.2	140.4	Espagne
Sweden	0.4	0.3	0.2	0.1	...	...	...	0.1	0.1	0.0	Suède
Switzerland	39.8	38.8	41.6	41.3	47.2	45.6	...	...	...	...	Suisse
Yugoslavia	..	10.4	11.8	5.9	5.9	5.5	3.8	3.6	3.0	2.1	Yougoslavie
T.F.Yug.Rep. Macedonia	..	0.3	0.3	0.2	0.2	0.2	0.2	0.2	0.2	0.2	L'ex-RY Macédoine
USSR (former)	173.6									..	URSS (anc.)
Oceania	**10**	**11**	**10**	**8**	**10**	**10**	**10**	**10**	**10**	**10**	**Océanie**
Australia[4]	9.9	11.2	10.0	8.4	...	...	...	...	...	...	Australie[4]
Total	**4099**	**3840**	**3865**	**3681**	**3790**	**3814**	**3785**	**3770**	**3267**	**3321**	**Total**

General Note.

Yarns obtained by converting discontinuous man-made fibres other than textile glass fibres into slivers, rovings and yarnsby processes generally similar to those used for cotton and wool. Monofils, yarns obtained by grouping together a number of filaments as they emerge from the spinnerets, either reeled parallel without twist or twisted, and continuous filament tow are excluded. (SITC, 65181-0, 65182-0, 65183-0, 65184-0, 65185-0, 65186-0, 65187-0).

Remarque générale.

Filés obtenus à partir de fibres artificielles ou synthétiques discontinues autres que les fibres de verre par transformation en rubans, mèches et filés par des procédés en général analogues à ceux que l'on emploie pour le coton et la laine. Cette rubrique ne comprend pas les monofils, les fils constitués par la juxtaposition d'un certain nombre de filaments simples à la sortie des filières, moulinés ou non moulinés, et les câbles de fibres continues. (CTCI, Rev.3: 65181-0, 65182-0, 65183-0, 65184-0, 65185-0, 65186-0, 65187-0).

[1] Incomplete coverage.
[2] Yarns containing at least 50 per cent discontinuous man-made fibres.
[3] Sales.
[4] Twelve months ending 30 June of year stated.

[1] Couverture incomplète.
[2] Filés contenant au moins 50 p. 100 de fibres synthétiques discontinues.
[3] Ventes.
[4] Période de douze mois finissant le 30 juin de l'année indiquée.

Jute yarn
Filés de jute

ISIC-BASED CODE - CODE BASE CITI

3211-22

Unit : Thousand metric tons   Unité : Milliers de tonnes métriques

Country or area	1990	1991	1992	1993	1994	1995	1996	1997	1998	1999	Pays ou zone
Africa	**28**	**27**	**28**	**27**	**21**	**21**	**22**	**17**	**17**	**13**	**Afrique**
Algeria	3.2	3.3	3.1	5.2	0.3	0.9	2.4	1.8	2.2	3.3	Algérie
Egypt	25.1	24.1	25.0	21.6	20.8	19.8	20.0	14.9	15.0	10.0	Egypte
America, South	**26**	**22**	**24**	**24**	**24**	**24**	**24**	**24**	**24**	**24**	**Amérique du Sud**
Brazil[1]	25.9	21.2	...	...	...	...	...	...	...	...	Brésil[1]
Colombia	...	...	...	0.3	...	...	...	...	...	...	Colombie
Asia	**32**	**28**	**43**	**47**	**84**	**65**	**85**	**123**	**88**	**85**	**Asie**
India	32.1	28.0	42.9	46.7	84.2	65.1	84.3	122.9	88.0	85.0	Inde
Indonesia	...	0.0	0.2	...	0.0	...	...	...	...	...	Indonésie
Japan[2]	0.2	0.1	0.0	...	...	...	...	...	...	...	Japon[2]
Europe	**36**	**50**	**42**	**56**	**41**	**41**	**41**	**40**	**39**	**38**	**Europe**
Belgium	7.1	5.4	4.9	4.3	...	...	...	...	...	...	Belgique
Croatia	..	...	...	...	...	...	...	...	0.1	...	Croatie
Czechoslovakia(former)[3]	4.2	2.7	..	..	..	..	..	..	..	...	Tchécoslovaquie(anc.)[3]
Hungary	0.2	...	...	...	...	...	...	...	...	...	Hongrie
Poland	10.3	8.6	4.9	3.3	4.0	4.0	3.0	2.5	1.2	0.3	Pologne
United Kingdom	14.3	...	...	48.0	...	...	...	...	...	...	Royaume-Uni
Yugoslavia	..	1.5	0.8	0.1	0.1	0.6	0.6	0.6	0.7	0.4	Yougoslavie
Total	**123**	**127**	**137**	**154**	**170**	**151**	**171**	**204**	**168**	**160**	**Total**

General Note.
Jute yarns obtained by spinning slivers of jute. (SITC, Rev.3: 65197-1).

Remarque générale.
Filé de jute résultant du filage de rubans de jute. (CTCI, Rev.3: 65197-1).

[1] Including mixed yarn.
[2] Shipments.
[3] Including yarn made from tow.

[1] Y compris les filés mélangés.
[2] Expéditions.
[3] Y compris les filés d'étoupe.

Yarn of other vegetable textile fibres
Filés d'autres fibres textiles végétales

ISIC-BASED CODE - CODE BASE CITI

3211-25

Unit : Thousand metric tons

Unité : Milliers de tonnes métriques

Country or area	1990	1991	1992	1993	1994	1995	1996	1997	1998	1999	Pays ou zone
America, North	**18**	**5**	**12**	**7**	**7**	**5**	**7**	**6**	**5**	**5**	**Amérique du Nord**
Mexico	18.5	5.1	12.4	6.9	7.1	4.7	6.7	6.2	5.5	5.2	Mexique
America, South	**0**	**0**	**0**	**0**	**0**	**0**	**0**	**0**	**0**	**0**	**Amérique du Sud**
Colombia	...	...	0.1	...	0.1	0.1	...	...	...	...	Colombie
Asia	..	**0**	**0**	**0**	**0**	**0**	**0**	**0**	**0**	**0**	**Asie**
Tajikistan	..	0.4	0.2	0.2	0.2	0.1	0.1	0.1	0.1	0.1	Tadjikistan
Europe	**10**	**13**	**12**	**11**	**11**	**12**	**11**	**11**	**11**	**11**	**Europe**
Austria	0.5	0.7	0.7	...	...	...	...	...	...	...	Autriche
Belgium	7.3	8.1	8.5	8.9	...	...	...	...	...	...	Belgique
Croatia	..	0.6	0.7	0.2	0.1	0.1	0.0	0.0	...	...	Croatie
Czechoslovakia(former) [1]	0.7	0.6	..	..	..	..	..	..		..	Tchécoslovaquie(anc.) [1]
Hungary	...	...	...	...	...	...	...	...	0.7	0.5	Hongrie
Spain [3]	[2]1.2	[2]0.7	[2]0.9	1.0	1.4	2.1	...	...	...	...	Espagne [3]
Yugoslavia	..	1.3	0.6	0.0	0.0	0.2	0.0	0.0	0.0	0.0	Yougoslavie
Total	**29**	**18**	**25**	**19**	**18**	**17**	**18**	**18**	**17**	**17**	**Total**

General Note.
Yarns obtained by spinning vegetable textile fibres other than cotton, flax, ramie, true hemp and jute. (SITC, Rev.3: 65197-2, 65199-2).

[1] Yarn of sisal.
[2] Including continuous fibres.
[3] Including flax, ramie and ture hemp yarn.

Remarque générale.
Filés obtenus par filage de fibres textiles végétales autres que le coton, le lin, la ramie, le chanvre et le jute. (CTCI, Rev.3: 65197-2, 65199-2).

[1] Filés de sisal.
[2] Y compris de fibres continues.
[3] Y compris filés de lin, de ramie et de chanvre.

Cotton woven fabrics
Tissus de coton

ISIC-BASED CODE - CODE BASE CITI
3211-28

Unit : Million square metres

Unité : Millions de mètres carrés

Country or area	1990	1991	1992	1993	1994	1995	1996	1997	1998	1999	Pays ou zone
Africa	**1401**	**1422**	**1449**	**1127**	**1081**	**972**	**977**	**941**	**876**	**814**	**Afrique**
Cameroon[1]	...	18	21	18	35	24	...	...	...	...	Cameroun[1]
Chad	58	60	81	...	...	...	...	...	...	...	Tchad
Congo[1]	11	7	6	2	...	...	...	...	...	...	Congo[1]
Egypt	603	609	613	329	494	414	321	290	...	...	Egypte
Ethiopia[2]	65	32	30	36	61	50	48	35	38	43	Ethiopie[2]
Kenya	45	27	31	28	27	22	28	...	...	...	Kenya
Madagascar[1]	59	57	50	42	44	34	27	32	23	...	Madagascar[1]
Nigeria	316	395	420	393	124	113	...	...	...	...	Nigéria
South Africa	175	170	138	166	195	228	246	269	223	224	Afrique du Sud
Uganda[3]	[4]8	[4]9	[4]10	[4]7	4	...	...	...	...	...	Ouganda[3]
United Rep.Tanzania	46	38	49	40	24	10	13	27	...	...	Rép. Unie de Tanzanie
America, North	**4103**	**4017**	**4130**	**4095**	**4031**	**4029**	**4266**	**4492**	**4247**	**3980**	**Amérique du Nord**
Mexico[5]	371	335	284	413	291	276	256	246	273	259	Mexique[5]
United States	3732	3682	3846	3682	3740	3753	4010	4246	3974	3721	Etats-Unis
America, South	**1951**	**1727**	**1664**	**1624**	**1616**	**1405**	**1374**	**1331**	**1257**	**1313**	**Amérique du Sud**
Bolivia[1]	2	1	1	0	0	*0	...	...	...	...	Bolivie[1]
Brazil[1]	[6][7]1901	[6][7]1679	[6][7]1616	[6][7]1568	[6]1566	1354	1318	1278	1209	1270	Brésil[1]
Chile[1]	31	24	23	32	28	29	34	31	27	21	Chili[1]
Paraguay[1]	18	23	23	24	...	...	...	...	...	...	Paraguay[1]
Asia	**42662**	**43624**	**45613**	**48746**	**46877**	**52333**	**46066**	**50897**	**49850**	**50904**	**Asie**
Armenia	..	10	5	2	0	0	1	0	0	0	Arménie
Azerbaijan	..	95	77	98	78	58	24	17	7	1	Azerbaïdjan
Bangladesh[8]	63	63	63	63	63	63	63	63	...	...	Bangladesh[8]
China[1]	22557	21719	22783	24263	25243	31091	24987	29730	28800	29875	Chine[1]
Hong Kong SAR[9]	*818	753	807	755	692	658	540	506	...	...	Hong-Kong RAS[9]
China, Macao, SAR	...	...	...	15	10	8	9	9	10	11	Chine, Macao PAS
Georgia	..	...	13	7	2	1	1	0	0	0	Géorgie
India	15177	16478	17582	19648	...	...	...	...	...	...	Inde
Japan	1765	1603	1465	1205	1180	1029	916	917	842	774	Japon
Kazakhstan	..	134	135	136	85	21	21	14	10	9	Kazakhstan
Korea, Republic of[3]	620	608	483	480	447	379	...	...	...	...	Corée, République de[3]
Kyrgyzstan	..	119	119	65	49	21	25	20	13	12	Kirghizistan
Myanmar[1][10]	47	27	22	16	13	16	118	112	130	214	Myanmar[1][10]
Pakistan[11]	[12]295	[12]293	[12]308	[12]325	315	322	327	333	340	385	Pakistan[11]
Syrian Arab Republic[5]	[13]214	221	205	222	213	184	186	198	199	...	Rép. arabe syrienne[5]
Tajikistan	..	102	58	57	34	28	17	8	13	11	Tadjikistan
Turkey[1]	[14]715	626	648	532	432	414	395	580	479	471	Turquie[1]
Turkmenistan	..	28	29	29	20	17	18	14	15	...	Turkménistan
Uzbekistan	..	392	474	482	433	456	445	425	...	...	Ouzbékistan
Viet Nam	380	[1]335	[1]325	...	...	...	...	...	...	...	Viet Nam
Europe	**7999**	**14284**	**10947**	**9060**	**7712**	**7249**	**6810**	**7121**	**7022**	**6587**	**Europe**
Austria	108	100	86	83	83	101	...	...	...	74	Autriche
Belarus	..	144	119	92	25	34	45	48	72	50	Bélarus
Belgium	399	379	337	331	#[5]232	[5]232	[5]267	[5]270	[5]283	[5]274	Belgique
Bulgaria	[3]254	[3]138	[3]102	[3]83	[3]86	[3]93	[3]85	[3]98	[1]96	[1]62	Bulgarie
Croatia	..	30	29	29	23	22	19	34	39	...	Croatie
Czechoslovakia(former)[3]	629	464	..	..	..	..	..	..	..	..	Tchécoslovaquie(anc.)[3]
Czech Republic	..	..	293	337	340	358	330	346	331	267	République tchèque
Estonia	..	168	111	55	74	90	120	130	127	95	Estonie
Finland[3]	41	24	20	20	19	8	9	...	...	...	Finlande[3]
France[5]	836	760	753	761	691	...	...	...	...	...	France[5]
Germany	..	929	763	687	635	444	466	489	506	...	Allemagne
Germany(Fed.Rep.)[3]	896	..	..	..	..	..	..	..	..	..	Allemagne(Rép.féd.)[3]
German D.R.(former)	213	..	..	..	..	..	..	..	..	..	R.D.A. (anc.)
Greece	...	...	...	[6]119	[6]94	[6]72	...	...	29	...	Grèce
Hungary[3]	206	133	86	78	76	66	...	79	44	48	Hongrie[3]
Italy[5]	1618	1529	1352	1293	1383	1441	1413	1462	1506	1427	Italie[5]
Latvia	..	45	22	0	0	2	6	9	12	12	Lettonie
Lithuania	..	106	89	48	42	35	35	62	64	57	Lituanie

For general note and footnotes, see end of table.

Voir la fin du tableau pour la remarque générale et les notes.

Cotton woven fabrics (continued)
Tissus de coton (suite)

ISIC-BASED CODE - CODE BASE CITI
3211-28

Unit : Million square metres

Unité : Millions de mètres carrés

Country or area	1990	1991	1992	1993	1994	1995	1996	1997	1998	1999	Pays ou zone
Netherlands[5]	83	81	70	...	...	...	...	...	...	...	Pays-Bas[5]
Norway[5]	*13	11	10	7	8	6	6	...	...	...	Norvège[5]
Poland[3][15]	474	332	290	284	321	263	295	303	275	234	Pologne[3][15]
Portugal	[5]544	[5]511	367	388	421	418	401	412	444	405	Portugal
Republic of Moldova	..	165	150	[16]1	[16]0	[16]0	[16]0	[16]0	[16]0	[16]0	Rép. de Moldova
Romania[3]	536	437	289	271	294	275	212	173	170	143	Roumanie[3]
Russian Federation	..	5949	3799	2822	1631	1401	1120	1374	1241	1455	Fédération de Russie
Slovakia	..			78	76	90	57	...	[5]125	[5]32	Slovaquie
Slovenia	..	[15]102	[15]78	81	81	71	53	...	...	...	Slovénie
Spain	[5][17]766	[5][17]773	[5][17]748	523	622	689	...	...	...	...	Espagne
Switzerland[1]	103	81	77	74	82	70	...	...	...	...	Suisse[1]
Ukraine	..	561	509	262	145	87	54	28	57	27	Ukraine
United Kingdom[1]	202	184	170	130	103	96	99	93	88	...	Royaume-Uni[1]
Yugoslavia[4][7]	..	45	39	27	24	19	22	18	23	21	Yougoslavie[4][7]
T.F.Yug.Rep. Macedonia	..	25	21	19	23	15	16	8	12	6	L'ex-RY Macédoine
USSR (former)[3]	8647	..	..	..	..	..	..	..	..	..	URSS (anc.)[3]
Oceania	38	36	40	41	50	52	64	61	62	56	Océanie
Australia[8]	38	[18]36	40	41	50	52	64	61	62	56	Australie[8]
Total	66801	65110	63843	64693	61368	66040	59558	64842	63313	63654	Total

General Note.

Woven cotton fabrics (at loom stage) before undergoing finishing processes such as bleaching, dyeing, printing, mercerizing, lazing etc. (SITC, Rev.3: 65211-0, 65212-0, 65220-0).

Remarque générale.

Tissus de coton sortant du métier à tisser, avant les opérations de finition, c'est-à-dire avant d'être blanchis, teints, imprimés, mercerisés, glacés etc. (CTCI, Rev.3: 65211-0, 65212-0, 65220-0).

[1] Original data in metres.
[2] Twelve months ending 7 July of the year stated.
[3] After undergoing finishing processes.
[4] Including cellulosic fabrics.
[5] Original data in metric tons.
[6] Including cotton fabrics after undergoing finishing processes.
[7] Including mixed cotton fabrics.
[8] Twelve months ending 30 June of year stated.
[9] 1998 data are confidential.
[10] Production by government-owned enterprises only.
[11] Factory production only.
[12] Including finished fabrics and blanketing made of synthetic fibers.
[13] Including silk fabrics.
[14] Government production only.
[15] Including fabrics of cotton substitutes.
[16] Excluding Transnistria region.
[17] Including household production.
[18] Including pile and chenille fabrics of non-cellulosic fibres.

[1] Données d'origine exprimées en mètres.
[2] Période de douze mois finissant le 7 juillet de l'année indiquée.
[3] Après opérations de finition.
[4] Y compris les tissus en fibres cellulosiques.
[5] Données d'origine exprimées en tonnes.
[6] Y compris les tissus de coton, après opérations de finition.
[7] Y compris les tissus de coton mélangé.
[8] Période de douze mois finissant le 30 juin de l'année indiquée.
[9] Pour 1998, les données sont confidentielles.
[10] Production des établissements d'Etat seulement.
[11] Production des fabriques seulement.
[12] Y compris les tissus finis et les couvertures en fibres synthétiques.
[13] Y compris les tissus de soie.
[14] Production de l'Etat seulement.
[15] Y compris les tissus de succédanés de coton.
[16] Non compris la région de Transnistria.
[17] Y compris la production ménagère.
[18] Y compris les tissus bouclés et les tissus chenille en fibres non-cellulosiques.

Cotton woven fabrics
Tissus de coton

ISIC-BASED CODE - CODE BASE CITI

3211-28A

Unit : Million metres

Unité : Millions de mètres

Country or area	1990	1991	1992	1993	1994	1995	1996	1997	1998	1999	Pays ou zone
Africa	**150**	**150**	**140**	**118**	**138**	**119**	**118**	**123**	**117**	**107**	**Afrique**
Algeria	63.1	53.7	69.7	...	...	...	...	...	...	...	Algérie
Cameroon	...	15.5	17.6	14.9	29.5	19.9	...	...	...	...	Cameroun
Chad	3.4	1.9	0.0	0.0	0.2	0.2	...	...	...	...	Tchad
Congo	8.8	5.6	5.1	1.8	...	...	...	...	...	...	Congo
Madagascar	49.1	47.4	41.9	35.1	37.1	28.4	22.4	27.0	19.6	...	Madagascar
Niger	12.0	25.5	6.0	4.0	3.8	3.0	...	...	...	...	Niger
America, North	**2**	**3**	**2**	**2**	**1**	**2**	**2**	**2**	**2**	**2**	**Amérique du Nord**
Jamaica	2.3	3.2	2.3	...	1.0	...	...	...	...	...	Jamaïque
America, South	**1913**	**1696**	**1629**	**1584**	**1555**	**1276**	**1316**	**1217**	**1146**	**1130**	**Amérique du Sud**
Bolivia	1.3	1.1	1.1	0.1	0.3	*0.3	...	...	...	...	Bolivie
Brazil	[1][2]1590.8	[1][2]1405.3	[1][2]1352.6	[1][2]1311.8	[1]1310.2	1133.1	1103.1	1069.6	1011.4	1063.2	Brésil
Chile	25.6	20.1	19.2	26.9	23.8	24.3	28.3	25.6	22.3	17.5	Chili
Colombia	...	...	208.0	199.1	175.7	75.7	...	73.8	63.6	...	Colombie
Ecuador	...	...	29.1	25.8	26.3	24.2	33.6	...	...	...	Equateur
Paraguay	14.8	19.1	19.2	20.1	...	...	...	...	...	...	Paraguay
Asia	**33411**	**34975**	**36817**	**39780**	**38087**	**42869**	**37694**	**41770**	**40892**	**41750**	**Asie**
Armenia	..	13.0	5.6	1.0	0.2	0.1	0.6	0.1	0.2	0.1	Arménie
Azerbaijan	..	110.8	88.8	110.0	85.1	60.1	25.4	17.6	7.4	0.8	Azerbaïdjan
Bangladesh	68.7	59.8	58.7	45.0	31.6	17.0	10.3	10.9	...	...	Bangladesh
China	18876.0	18175.0	19065.0	20303.8	21124.0	26018.0	20910.0	24879.0	24100.0	25000.0	Chine
India	13319.5	14826.0	15819.8	17678.8	...	...	...	...	...	...	Inde
Indonesia	26.2	75.0	...	...	...	...	...	...	...	...	Indonésie
Kyrgyzstan	..	112.0	112.6	60.6	45.5	19.0	22.5	18.2	12.5	10.7	Kirghizistan
Myanmar[3]	39.2	23.0	18.6	13.2	10.8	13.1	9.8	9.4	10.9	17.9	Myanmar[3]
Nepal[4]	...	...	7.2	7.1	5.6	5.1	5.2	4.0	3.3	2.7	Népal[4]
Sri Lanka	22.4	16.1	4.3	...	...	...	...	...	...	...	Sri Lanka
Syrian Arab Republic[5]	178.8	185.3	171.3	185.9	178.3	153.6	155.3	166.0	166.3	...	Rép. arabe syrienne[5]
Tajikistan	..	110.1	61.8	60.7	39.0	30.9	16.6	7.9	12.5	10.2	Tadjikistan
Turkey	[6]597.9	524.0	542.6	445.2	361.5	346.1	330.2	485.3	401.2	394.2	Turquie
Turkmenistan	..	30.2	31.0	30.2	20.1	17.2	18.5	14.8	15.2	...	Turkménistan
Uzbekistan	..	428.5	506.4	496.9	433.4	437.0	437.8	404.6	...	...	Ouzbékistan
Viet Nam	...	280.4	272.2	...	...	...	...	...	...	...	Viet Nam
Europe	**1626**	**8034**	**5626**	**3949**	**2637**	**2306**	**1996**	**2195**	**2069**	**2098**	**Europe**
Austria	72.3	69.3	69.0	55.1	55.0	59.2	13.8	15.7	...	...	Autriche
Belarus	..	116.5	96.9	74.7	19.9	23.0	30.2	31.5	48.8	33.4	Bélarus
Bulgaria	290.5	126.1	89.6	71.5	69.9	76.6	68.8	75.7	80.2	52.0	Bulgarie
Czechoslovakia(former)	579.7	408.2	...	..	..	..	..	..	..	..	Tchécoslovaquie(anc.)
Czech Republic	..	..	362.4	282.0	...	...	...	...	...	...	République tchèque
Estonia	..	0.2	0.1	0.0	0.1	0.1	0.1	0.1	0.1	0.1	Estonie
Latvia	..	35.1	16.1	0.1	0.1	1.1	3.8	5.5	6.9	...	Lettonie
Lithuania	..	96.9	79.7	40.3	32.3	30.4	[7]29.3	...	...	...	Lituanie
Poland[8][9]	427.5	286.2	238.5	229.3	255.8	205.2	236.0	229.4	206.7	179.0	Pologne[8][9]
Republic of Moldova	..	150.8	135.3	[10]0.4	[10]0.3	[10]0.0	[10]0.1	[10]0.1	[10]0.1	[10]0.1	Rép. de Moldova
Russian Federation	..	5996.4	3745.3	2686.5	1506.2	1296.7	1044.1	1279.9	1144.3	1359.9	Fédération de Russie
Slovakia	..	..	...	100.9	89.4	75.2	57.0	51.4	...	...	Slovaquie
Switzerland	86.6	68.2	64.5	61.7	68.7	58.2	...	...	...	...	Suisse
Ukraine	..	526.3	471.9	237.6	130.9	77.7	47.5	24.3	52.4	24.4	Ukraine
United Kingdom	169.0	154.0	142.0	109.0	86.0	80.0	83.0	78.0	74.0	...	Royaume-Uni
Total	**37102**	**44858**	**44214**	**45433**	**42418**	**46572**	**41127**	**45308**	**44227**	**45089**	**Total**

General Note.
Woven cotton fabrics (at loom stage) before undergoing finishing processes such as bleaching, dyeing, printing, mercerizing, lazing etc. (SITC, Rev.3: 65211-0A, 65212-0A, 65220-0A).

For footnotes, see end of table.

Remarque générale.
Tissus de coton sortant du métier à tisser, avant les opérations de finition, c'est-à-dire avant d'être blanchis, teints, imprimés, mercerisés, glacés etc. (CTCI, Rev.3: 65211-0A, 65212-0A, 65220-0A).

Voir la fin du tableau pour les notes.

Cotton woven fabrics (continued)
Tissus de coton (suite)

ISIC-BASED CODE - CODE BASE CITI

3211-28A

Footnotes
[1] Including cotton fabrics after undergoing finishing processes.
[2] Including mixed cotton fabrics.
[3] Production by government-owned enterprises only.
[4] Twelve months beginning 16 July of year stated.
[5] Original data in metric tons.
[6] Government production only.
[7] Original data in square metres.
[8] After undergoing finishing processes.
[9] Including fabrics of cotton substitutes.
[10] Excluding Transnistria region.

Notes.
[1] Y compris les tissus de cotton, après opérations de finition.
[2] Y compris les tissus de cotton mélangé.
[3] Production des établissements d'Etat seulement.
[4] Période de douze mois commençant le 16 juillet de l'année indiquée.
[5] Données d'origine exprimées en tonnes.
[6] Production de l'Etat seulement.
[7] Données d'origine exprimées en mètres carrés.
[8] Après opérations de finition.
[9] Y compris les tissus de succédanés de coton.
[10] Non compris la région de Transnistria.

Cotton woven fabrics
Tissus de coton

ISIC-BASED CODE - CODE BASE CITI

3211-28B

Unit : Thousand metric tons   Unité : Milliers de tonnes métriques

Country or area	1990	1991	1992	1993	1994	1995	1996	1997	1998	1999	Pays ou zone
Africa	68	69	69	69	69	69	69	76	72	73	**Afrique**
Egypt	68	69	69	69	69	69	69	76	...		Egypte
America, North	570	558	574	569	560	558	556	555	559	557	**Amérique du Nord**
Mexico	52	47	40	57	40	38	36	34	38	36	Mexique
United States[1]	519	512	535	512	520	...	...	...	...	...	Etats-Unis[1]
America, South	278	240	257	258	260	260	261	254	257	256	**Amérique du Sud**
Brazil*	264	227	...	...	...	...	...	...	...	...	Brésil*
Chile	4	...	...	...	...	...	...	...	...	...	Chili
Colombia	...	...	2	3	4	3	...	...	...	...	Colombie
Ecuador	...	...	5	5	6	7	8	2	4	...	Equateur
Asia	6311	6098	6325	6433	6276	6266	6228	6266	6266	6264	**Asie**
China*	3135	3019	3067	3266	...	...	...	...	...	...	Chine*
India*	2255	2132	2283	...	...	...	...	...	...	...	Inde*
Indonesia	...	...	684	...	...	...	...	...	...	...	Indonésie
Japan[1][2]	...	...	204	167	164	...	127	...	...	...	Japon[1][2]
Kazakhstan[1]	..	...	19	19	12	3	3	...	...	...	Kazakhstan[1]
Pakistan[1][3]	...	...	[4]43	[4]45	44	45	45	46	...	...	Pakistan[1][3]
Syrian Arab Republic	[5]27	28	26	28	27	23	23	25	25	...	Rép. arabe syrienne
Europe	945	915	867	844	822	804	806	826	819	775	**Europe**
Austria	17	17	18	14	14	17	14	15	16	13	Autriche
Belgium	[6]58	[6]56	[6]52	[6]52	#32	32	37	38	39	38	Belgique
Croatia	..	..	[1]4	[1]4	[1]3	[1]3	[1]3	4	4	...	Croatie
Czech Republic	..	..	[1]41	...	47	49	47	51	53	43	République tchèque
Finland[7]	7	4	3	3	3	2	2	...	...	...	Finlande[7]
France	106	96	95	96	91	86	85	87	83	89	France
Germany	..	178	148	136	131	94	118	125	133	...	Allemagne
Germany(Fed.Rep.)	170										Allemagne(Rép.féd.)
Greece	...	...	...	32	29	26	...	...	6	...	Grèce
Hungary[7]	...	...	[1]12	[1]11	[1]11	[1]9	...	12	7	9	Hongrie[7]
Italy	225	212	188	180	192	200	196	203	209	198	Italie
Latvia	..	...	...	...	...	...	...	...	...	2	Lettonie
Netherlands	11	10	9	...	...	...	...	...	...	...	Pays-Bas
Norway	*2	1	1	1	1	1	1	...	...	*1	Norvège
Poland[7][8]	71	45	41	41	43	40	43	41	41	36	Pologne[7][8]
Portugal	76	71	49	...	...	...	...	...	...	...	Portugal
Romania[1][7]	...	...	40	38	41	38	29	...	...	...	Roumanie[1][7]
Slovakia	..	..	...	...	...	...	...	...	17	4	Slovaquie
Slovenia[1]	..	..	[8]11	11	11	10	7	...	...	...	Slovénie[1]
Spain	[9]97	[9]98	[9]95	66	79	87	...	...	...	...	Espagne
United Kingdom[10]	*28	*26	...	...	2	...	...	...	...	...	Royaume-Uni[10]
Yugoslavia[1]	..	...	5	4	3	3	3	...	...	...	Yougoslavie[1]
Total	8172	7881	8092	8173	7987	7957	7920	7978	7972	7924	**Total**

General Note.

Woven cotton fabrics (at loom stage) before undergoing finishing processes such as bleaching, dyeing, printing, mercerizing, lazing etc. (SITC, Rev.3: 65211-0B, 65212-0B, 65220-0B).

Remarque générale.

Tissus de coton sortant du métier à tisser, avant les opérations de finition, c'est-à-dire avant d'être blanchis, teints, imprimés, mercerisés, glacés etc. (CTCI, Rev.3: 65211-0B, 65212-0B, 65 220-0B).

[1] Original data in square metres.
[2] Shipments.
[3] Factory production only.
[4] Including finished fabrics and blanketing made of synthetic fibers.
[5] Including silk fabrics.
[6] Including cotton blankets and carpets.
[7] After undergoing finishing processes.
[8] Including fabrics of cotton substitutes.
[9] Including household production.
[10] Production in cotton spinning sector only.

[1] Données d'origine exprimées en mètres carrés.
[2] Expéditions.
[3] Production des fabriques seulement.
[4] Y compris les tissus finis et les couvertures en fibres synthétiques.
[5] Y compris les tissus de soie.
[6] Y compris les couvertures et les tapis en coton.
[7] Après opérations de finition.
[8] Y compris les tissus de succédanés de coton.
[9] Y compris la production ménagère.
[10] Production du secteur des filatures de coton seulement.

Silk fabrics
Tissus de soie

ISIC-BASED CODE - CODE BASE CITI

3211-31

Unit : Thousand square metres   Unité : Milliers de mètres carrés

Country or area	1990	1991	1992	1993	1994	1995	1996	1997	1998	1999	Pays ou zone
Africa	**22964**	**23126**	**23809**	**17355**	**20523**	**19931**	**18549**	**17736**	**17235**	**17235**	**Afrique**
Algeria	18062	17680	19104	14092	...	...	...	...	...	...	Algérie
Egypt	4902	5446	4705	3263	3288	2696	1314	...	...	...	Egypte
America, North	**636**	**686**	**810**	**595**	**487**	**461**	**519**	**519**	**382**	**274**	**Amérique du Nord**
United States	636	686	810	595	487	461	519	519	382	274	Etats-Unis
Asia	**2450321**	**3713125**	**3839289**	**4153665**	**4500174**	**9266245**	**6892985**	**9037974**	**5200995**	**5371388**	**Asie**
Armenia	..	9257	3681	4016	653	370	191	172	262	21	Arménie
Azerbaijan	..	30050	21203	11010	4457	801	190	49	0	0	Azerbaïdjan
China[1]	2345549	3296015	3481293	3866140	4285913	9125570	6774650	8935140	5135818	5313289	Chine[1]
Hong Kong SAR[2]	444	1040	2192	2832	2431	1689	789	417	...	...	Hong-Kong RAS[2]
China, Macao, SAR	...	...	...	0	...	1638	1918	8804	...	...	Chine, Macao PAS
Georgia	..	...	...	4722	881	888	503	318	121	61	Géorgie
Indonesia	...	...	[3]189	[1]101	[1]96	...	...	[1]271	[1]951	...	Indonésie
Japan	83664	80669	76971	71364	65444	59577	58371	55381	40440	34564	Japon
Kazakhstan	..	57667	45551	14106	3699	4007	2933	1744	...	...	Kazakhstan
Korea, Republic of	14956	13882	13381	13626	13698	11127	...	...	...	...	Corée, République de
Kyrgyzstan	..	13707	13885	10480	3430	1029	1040	164	21	26	Kirghizistan
Syrian Arab Republic	[1]2618	[3]3345	[3]3048	[3]4968	[3]5302	[3]2705	[3]3246	[3]2164	[3]1984	...	Rép. arabe syrienne
Tajikistan	..	68570	65708	54194	24120	8389	3887	446	642	386	Tadjikistan
Turkmenistan	..	6543	6787	5709	3556	4153	4468	4479	4529	...	Turkménistan
Uzbekistan	..	125872	99517	90397	83404	43980	28144	16369	...	...	Ouzbékistan
Europe	**176214**	**1207159**	**970035**	**788438**	**389866**	**345731**	**275039**	**259308**	**218114**	**212122**	**Europe**
Austria	182	106	48	...	...	...	...	...	...	...	Autriche
Bulgaria	46134	23840	19889	22080	23378	26641	26747	22931	[1]22469	[1]16311	Bulgarie
Czechoslovakia(former)	159	53	..	..	..	...	...	...			Tchécoslovaquie(anc.)
Czech Republic	..	...	...	...	...	...	...	4667	4273	3792	République tchèque
Estonia	..	5341	787	76	42	34	28	...	...	...	Estonie
France	3897	3445	3383	3355	2923	...	...	...	...	...	France
Germany	..	...	...	...	...	751	505	452	...	...	Allemagne
German D.R.(former)	10	..	..	..	..	..	..	..	..	..	R.D.A. (anc.)
Greece	[3]252	[3]433	[3]162	113	...	180	379	502	237	...	Grèce
Latvia	..	24000	12574	6461	...	...	...	...	...	...	Lettonie
Poland[4]	170	133	108	81	80	31	19	10	...	...	Pologne[4]
Romania[4]	107453	98399	80958	73624	59645	53790	56741	51871	40461	31869	Roumanie[4]
Russian Federation	..	1019268	822521	656750	263729	222538	148981	144620	114172	125894	Fédération de Russie
Slovenia	..	[5]6859	[5]7366	9694	9927	10363	...	...	...	...	Slovénie
Switzerland[1][5]	17957	6797	6650	5722	3118	3062	...	...	...	...	Suisse[1][5]
Ukraine[1]	..	2134	1877	1867	1207	708	532	153	179	179	Ukraine[1]
Yugoslavia	..	15782	8898	3689	6264	6143	5830	3550	5481	2135	Yougoslavie
Total	**2650135**	**4944096**	**4833943**	**4960054**	**4911049**	**9632368**	**7187092**	**9315537**	**5436725**	**5601018**	**Total**

General Note.
Woven fabrics of silk with more than 10 per cent by weight of silk or of waste silk (noil silk and other) at loom stage. (SITC, Rev.3: 65410-0).

[1] Original data in metres.
[2] 1998 data are confidential.
[3] Original data in metric tons.
[4] After undergoing finishing processes.
[5] Including rayon fabrics.

Remarque générale.
Tissus contenant plus de 10 p. 100 en poids de soie, de bourre de soie ou d'autres déchets de soie, au sortir du métier à tisser. (CTCI, Rev.3: 65410-0).

[1] Données d'origine exprimées en mètres.
[2] Pour 1998, les données sont confidentielles.
[3] Données d'origine exprimées en tonnes.
[4] Après opérations de finition.
[5] Y compris les tissus de rayonne.

Silk fabrics
Tissus de soie

ISIC-BASED CODE - CODE BASE CITI

3211-31A

Unit : Thousand metres   Unité : Milliers de mètres

Country or area	1990	1991	1992	1993	1994	1995	1996	1997	1998	1999	Pays ou zone
America, South	**16**	**0**	**0**	**0**	**0**	**0**	**0**	**0**	**0**	**0**	**Amérique du Sud**
Bolivia	16	0	0	0	0	*0	...	...	...	...	Bolivie
Asia	**1714153**	**2700913**	**2783162**	**3012305**	**3259530**	**6726932**	**4987114**	**6546442**	**3756061**	**3884612**	**Asie**
Armenia	..	8163	3097	3597	587	307	154	138	235	18	Arménie
Azerbaijan	..	27411	19695	10203	3933	745	183	48	0	0	Azerbaïdjan
China	1712080	2405850	2541090	2822353	3128404	6661000	4945000	6522000	3748772	3878313	Chine
Indonesia	...	150	...	74	70	...	...	198	694	...	Indonésie
Kazakhstan	..	38605	30334	9599	2522	2703	1969	1162	...	...	Kazakhstan
Kyrgyzstan	..	11801	11818	9056	3033	903	877	137	19	18	Kirghizistan
Syrian Arab Republic [1]	1911	2352	2143	3493	3727	1902	2282	1521	1395	...	Rép. arabe syrienne [1]
Tajikistan	..	65419	62175	51439	22875	7978	3250	441	540	307	Tadjikistan
Turkey	5	4	4	3	1	2	1	1	1	2	Turquie
Turkmenistan	..	6208	6375	5387	3552	4048	4366	4367	4405	...	Turkménistan
Uzbekistan	..	134950	106194	97101	90826	47107	28795	16429	...	...	Ouzbékistan
Europe	**50818**	**926219**	**734648**	**589515**	**266114**	**246302**	**199662**	**182522**	**159591**	**160141**	**Europe**
Austria	211	129	67	30	...	...	...	...	...	...	Autriche
Bulgaria	36330	18014	15245	15739	16731	19216	19331	16541	16401	11906	Bulgarie
Czechoslovakia(former)	150	53	..	..	...	..	..	..	..	..	Tchécoslovaquie(anc.)
Estonia	..	3782	714	69	38	31	25	...	...	...	Estonie
Lithuania	..	30927	22284	15252	6966	15255	[2]26449	...	...	...	Lituanie
Poland [3]	189	147	121	90	89	34	21	11	...	...	Pologne [3]
Republic of Moldova	..	39872	...	...	...	...	...	...	...	...	Rép. de Moldova
Russian Federation	..	825945	649290	512092	198321	168202	110973	107720	86411	92206	Fédération de Russie
Switzerland [4]	13107	4961	4854	4177	2276	2235	...	...	...	...	Suisse [4]
Ukraine	..	1558	1370	1363	881	517	388	112	131	131	Ukraine
United Kingdom	831	...	...	...	...	...	...	...	...	...	Royaume-Uni
Total	**1764987**	**3627132**	**3517810**	**3601820**	**3525645**	**6973234**	**5186777**	**6728965**	**3915652**	**4044752**	**Total**

General Note.

Woven fabrics of silk with more than 10 per cent by weight of silk or of waste silk (noil silk and other) at loom stage. (SITC, Rev.3: 65410-0A).

Remarque générale.

Tissus contenant plus de 10 p. 100 en poids de soie, de bourre de soie ou d'autres déchets de soie, au sortir du métier à tisser. (CTCI, Rev.3: 65410-0A).

[1] Original data in metric tons.
[2] Original data in square metres.
[3] After undergoing finishing processes.
[4] Including rayon fabrics.

[1] Données d'origine exprimées en tonnes.
[2] Données d'origine exprimées en mètres carrés.
[3] Après opérations de finition.
[4] Y compris les tissus de rayonne.

Woollen woven fabrics
Tissus de laine

ISIC-BASED CODE - CODE BASE CITI

3211-34

Unit : Million square metres   Unité : Millions de mètres carrés

Country or area	1990	1991	1992	1993	1994	1995	1996	1997	1998	1999	Pays ou zone
Africa	**55**	**55**	**48**	**33**	**39**	**38**	**32**	**32**	**30**	**25**	**Afrique**
Algeria[1]	13.3	16.3	13.1	...	...	...	...	...	...	...	Algérie[1]
Egypt	23.2	23.5	23.0	8.7	13.8	13.7	7.6	8.4	...	...	Egypte
Kenya	0.3	...	...	0.0	...	0.5	0.7	...	...	...	Kenya
South Africa[2]	18.7	15.1	11.2	10.3	10.6	9.9	9.0	9.0	7.5	...	Afrique du Sud[2]
America, North	**126**	**150**	**158**	**166**	**158**	**148**	**143**	**159**	**130**	**83**	**Amérique du Nord**
Mexico[3]	8.8	8.4	10.5	12.5	8.8	12.0	16.4	20.3	19.3	18.6	Mexique[3]
United States	117.6	141.8	147.4	153.8	149.3	135.6	127.1	138.4	110.5	64.7	Etats-Unis
America, South	**3**	**3**	**3**	**2**	**3**	**4**	**2**	**0**	**2**	**3**	**Amérique du Sud**
Bolivia[1]	0.2	0.2	0.2	0.1	0.1	*0.1	...	...	...	...	Bolivie[1]
Ecuador[1]	...	...	3.0	2.2	2.5	3.4	1.7	0.0	2.1	2.5	Equateur[1]
Paraguay[1]	0.1	0.1	0.1	0.1	...	...	...	...	...	...	Paraguay[1]
Asia	**887**	**979**	**990**	**778**	**781**	**1412**	**1095**	**995**	**758**	**752**	**Asie**
Armenia	..	3.8	2.9	0.8	0.3	0.1	0.1	0.1	0.1	0.0	Arménie
Azerbaijan	..	9.2	6.7	5.3	2.1	0.6	0.2	0.0	0.1	0.1	Azerbaïdjan
China[1]	486.8	513.8	557.6	387.7	413.5	1079.0	758.2	640.1	441.8	450.7	Chine[1]
Georgia	..	...	0.0	1.9	0.6	0.5	0.2	0.1	0.0	0.1	Géorgie
Japan[4]	334.9	344.9	325.7	286.8	285.5	249.3	246.9	247.0	212.9	199.1	Japon[4]
Kazakhstan	..	31.1	22.9	20.1	9.8	3.5	2.2	1.6	0.7	0.1	Kazakhstan
Korea, Republic of	[5]19.5	[5]19.5	[5]19.7	[5]18.9	19.6	17.8	17.2	14.0	7.3	6.1	Corée, République de
Kyrgyzstan	..	12.9	10.9	9.4	4.3	2.5	2.8	3.1	1.9	0.9	Kirghizistan
Mongolia[1]	1.8	1.3	1.2	0.5	0.1	0.1	0.1	0.0	0.0	0.0	Mongolie[1]
Syrian Arab Republic[3]	1.5	0.2	1.4	1.9	2.3	4.2	5.1	7.7	13.8	...	Rép. arabe syrienne[3]
Tajikistan	..	2.4	2.8	2.7	1.0	0.3	0.0	0.0	0.0	0.0	Tadjikistan
Turkey[1]	41.9	35.6	34.7	38.4	37.9	50.2	59.1	78.1	76.7	78.1	Turquie[1]
Turkmenistan	..	3.3	3.0	3.0	3.3	3.1	2.8	3.2	2.5	...	Turkménistan
Uzbekistan	..	0.6	0.9	1.2	1.1	0.8	0.6	0.4	...	...	Ouzbékistan
Europe	**1040**	**1667**	**1433**	**1239**	**1048**	**990**	**934**	**933**	**844**	**852**	**Europe**
Austria	8.8	7.8	7.6	5.1	2.7	2.4	11.6	13.3	17.1	12.5	Autriche
Belarus	..	49.4	39.4	40.0	19.7	7.7	7.7	9.4	9.9	9.9	Bélarus
Belgium[6]	5.3	5.8	4.1	3.6	...	...	...	...	...	...	Belgique[6]
Bulgaria[5]	47.3	26.0	22.3	23.4	20.7	19.6	17.9	17.4	[1]10.2	[1]8.0	Bulgarie[5]
Croatia	..	5.2	5.7	7.0	7.2	6.7	4.5	3.1	2.0	...	Croatie
Denmark[7]	[4]1.2	[4]1.2	[4]0.9	0.8	0.8	0.8	0.8	0.9	0.1	0.1	Danemark[7]
Czechoslovakia(former)[5]	76.7	56.5	..	..	..	..	..	..	..	..	Tchécoslovaquie(anc.)[5]
Czech Republic	..	..	45.9	43.0	34.2	31.8	29.6	28.5	27.8	20.1	République tchèque
Estonia	..	6.6	3.5	0.8	0.1	0.0	0.0	0.1	0.1	0.0	Estonie
Finland*[5]	0.4	0.2	0.1	0.1	...	...	...	...	...	...	Finlande*[5]
France	15.9	14.5	12.6	9.1	36.6	...	...	...	...	...	France
Germany	..	120.7	118.9	...	...	86.8	87.2	86.6	79.0	...	Allemagne
Germany(Fed.Rep.)[5]	107.7	..	..	..	..	..	..	..	..	..	Allemagne(Rép.féd.)[5]
German D.R.(former)	37.9	..	..	..	..	..	..	..	..	..	R.D.A. (anc.)
Greece	[3][5]2.3	[3][5]2.9	[3][5]2.5	3.1	1.6	1.9	2.2	2.8	3.0	...	Grèce
Hungary[5]	10.7	6.6	3.7	2.7	1.4	1.2	...	0.1	...	...	Hongrie[5]
Iceland	0.1	0.1	0.1	0.0	0.0	...	...	...	...	...	Islande
Ireland[5]	1.7	...	...	...	...	...	...	...	...	...	Irlande[5]
Italy[3]	417.8	428.3	445.1	426.0	443.4	432.6	430.8	444.5	396.1	...	Italie[3]
Latvia	..	11.2	8.0	2.0	[5]0.1	[5]0.2	[5]0.0	[5]0.0	[5]0.0	...	Lettonie
Lithuania	..	21.5	16.9	12.4	9.4	9.9	12.6	11.9	14.3	10.5	Lituanie
Netherlands[5]	4.4	4.2	4.4	...	...	...	...	...	...	...	Pays-Bas[5]
Norway[3]	...	1.3	1.6	1.5	1.6	1.8	1.6	1.7	1.6	...	Norvège[3]
Poland[5][8]	98.0	67.2	50.0	48.2	50.7	49.7	50.1	48.6	44.9	34.7	Pologne[5][8]
Portugal	[3]33.7	[3]28.6	11.8	9.5	9.1	8.1	6.4	6.5	7.7	9.0	Portugal
Republic of Moldova	..	0.0	0.2	[9]0.1	[9]0.0	[9]0.0	[9]0.1	[9]0.1	[9]0.0	[9]0.0	Rép. de Moldova
Romania[5]	107.3	100.0	69.0	68.2	64.7	67.5	50.4	34.1	21.8	17.6	Roumanie[5]
Russian Federation	..	492.3	351.4	269.5	114.0	107.1	66.9	62.6	51.8	61.1	Fédération de Russie
Slovakia	..	..	[5]11.1	[5]10.4	[5]9.8	[1]9.7	[1]10.7	[1]11.5	[3]9.8	[3]7.0	Slovaquie
Slovenia	..	14.7	15.1	12.8	9.5	6.9	2.6	...	...	1.2	Slovénie
Spain[3]	[10]30.7	[10]31.5	[10]27.7	17.0	13.6	14.6	...	...	...	...	Espagne[3]
Sweden	0.6	...	...	[3]0.0	...	...	...	...	...	...	Suède

For general note and footnotes, see end of table.   Voir la fin du tableau pour la remarque générale et les notes.

Woollen woven fabrics (continued)
Tissus de laine (suite)

ISIC-BASED CODE - CODE BASE CITI

3211-34

Unit : Million square metres | | | | | | | | | | | Unité : Millions de mètres carrés

Country or area	1990	1991	1992	1993	1994	1995	1996	1997	1998	1999	Pays ou zone
Switzerland[2]	9.5	9.8	8.5	7.2	6.9	5.1	...	...	...	...	Suisse[2]
Ukraine	..	79.0	76.5	59.7	26.0	18.8	11.6	13.6	7.7	6.3	Ukraine
United Kingdom	[11]20.1	*39.0	*37.0	*33.0	*38.0	...	...	...	...	...	Royaume-Uni
Yugoslavia[12][13]	..	24.1	20.8	13.3	12.6	11.3	11.1	10.1	9.1	6.8	Yougoslavie[12][13]
T.F.Yug.Rep. Macedonia	..	9.6	8.7	6.8	5.3	5.7	4.1	3.9	4.0	3.3	L'ex-RY Macédoine
USSR (former)	864.6	..	..	..	..	..	..	..	..	..	URSS (anc.)
Oceania	8	8	8	8	8	8	7	6	7	6	Océanie
Australia[14]	7.8	7.6	8.2	8.3	7.9	8.2	6.5	6.3	6.6	6.3	Australie[14]
Total	2983	2862	2640	2228	2037	2600	2212	2126	1771	1721	Total

General Note.
Woollen and worsted fabrics in the piece (at loom stage) before undergoing finishing processes such as bleaching, dyeing, making up etc. Fabrics of fine hair are excluded. (SITC, Rev.3: 65420-1, 65430-1).

Remarque générale.
Tissus de laine cardée ou peignée, en pièces, sortant du métier à tisser, avant les opérations de finition, c'est-à-dire avant d'être blanchis, teints, confectionnés etc., à l'exclusion des tissus de poils fins. (CTCI, Rev.3:65420-1, 65430-1).

[1] Original data in metres.
[2] Pure woollen fabrics only.
[3] Original data in metric tons.
[4] Including finished fabrics and blanketing made of synthetic fibers.
[5] After undergoing finishing processes.
[6] Including woollen blankets and carpets.
[7] Sales.
[8] Including fabrics of wool substitutes.
[9] Excluding Transnistria region.
[10] Including household production.
[11] Deliveries of woollen and worsted fabrics, except blankets, containing, by weight, more than 15 per cent wool or animal fibres. Including finished fabrics.
[12] Including cellulosic fabrics.
[13] Including mixed wool fabrics.
[14] Twelve months ending 30 June of year stated.

[1] Données d'origine exprimées en mètres.
[2] Tissus de laine pure seulement.
[3] Données d'origine exprimées en tonnes.
[4] Y compris les tissus finis et les couvertures en fibres synthétiques.
[5] Après opérations de finition.
[6] Y compris les couvertures et tapis en laine.
[7] Ventes.
[8] Y compris les tissus de succédanés de laine.
[9] Non compris la région de Transnistria.
[10] Y compris la production ménagère.
[11] Quantités livrées de tissus de laine cardée et peignée, à l'exception des couvertures, contenant, en poids, plus de 15 p. 100 de laine ou de fibres animales. Y compris les tissus finis.
[12] Y compris les tissus en fibres cellulosiques.
[13] Y compris les tissus de laine mélangée.
[14] Période de douze mois finissant le 30 juin de l'année indiquée.

Woollen woven fabrics
Tissus de laine

ISIC-BASED CODE - CODE BASE CITI
3211-34A

Unit : Million metres   Unité : Millions de mètres

Country or area	1990	1991	1992	1993	1994	1995	1996	1997	1998	1999	Pays ou zone
Africa	**10**	**12**	**10**	**11**	**11**	**11**	**11**	**11**	**11**	**11**	**Afrique**
Algeria	8.1	9.9	7.9	...	...	...	...	...	...	...	Algérie
South Africa*	2.2	2.6	2.3	...	...	...	...	...	...	...	Afrique du Sud*
America, South	**2**	**2**	**3**	**2**	**2**	**3**	**2**	**1**	**2**	**2**	**Amérique du Sud**
Bolivia	0.1	0.1	0.1	0.0	0.1	*0.1	...	...	...	...	Bolivie
Colombia	...	...	0.9	0.9	0.8	0.8	...	...	...	...	Colombie
Ecuador	...	...	1.8	1.3	1.5	2.0	1.1	0.0	1.3	1.5	Equateur
Paraguay	0.0	0.1	0.1	0.0	...	...	...	...	...	...	Paraguay
Asia	**323**	**460**	**681**	**1397**	**1683**	**3247**	**3590**	**5080**	**8662**	**9018**	**Asie**
Armenia	..	2.4	2.0	0.5	0.2	0.1	0.1	0.1	0.1	0.1	Arménie
Azerbaijan	..	7.3	5.0	3.9	1.6	0.5	0.1	0.0	0.1	0.0	Azerbaïdjan
China	295.1	311.4	337.9	235.0	250.6	653.9	459.5	387.9	267.8	273.2	Chine
Indonesia	...	...	...	0.8	...	...	...	...	...	...	Indonésie
Kyrgyzstan	..	7.0	5.9	4.9	2.3	1.3	1.5	1.6	1.0	0.5	Kirghizistan
Mongolia	1.1	0.8	0.7	0.3	0.1	0.1	0.0	0.0	0.0	0.0	Mongolie
Syrian Arab Republic[1]	0.9	104.0	302.0	1123.0	1402.0	2559.0	3092.0	4639.0	8343.0	...	Rép. arabe syrienne[1]
Tajikistan	..	1.7	2.0	2.2	0.8	0.3	0.0	0.0	0.0	0.0	Tadjikistan
Turkey	25.4	21.6	21.0	23.3	22.9	30.4	35.8	47.3	46.5	47.3	Turquie
Turkmenistan	..	2.8	2.5	2.2	0.6	0.2	0.1	2.5	1.9	...	Turkménistan
Uzbekistan	..	0.5	0.6	0.8	0.8	0.6	0.5	0.3	...	...	Ouzbékistan
Europe	**169**	**524**	**401**	**312**	**194**	**167**	**148**	**145**	**126**	**120**	**Europe**
Austria	6.9	6.2	6.0	3.9	2.3	2.1	3.3	3.3	...	...	Autriche
Belarus	..	30.5	24.5	24.9	12.1	4.7	4.7	5.7	6.0	6.0	Bélarus
Bulgaria[2]	31.4	17.3	15.1	15.7	14.0	13.2	12.1	11.2	6.2	4.8	Bulgarie[2]
Czechoslovakia(former)	58.8	44.3	..	..	..	..	..	..	..	..	Tchécoslovaquie(anc.)
Czech Republic	..	..	33.9	29.6	...	...	...	...	...	...	République tchèque
Estonia	..	4.9	2.5	0.6	0.1	0.0	0.0	0.1	0.0	0.0	Estonie
Latvia	..	8.8	5.8	1.9	[2]0.1	[2]0.1	[2]0.0	[2]0.0	[2]0.0	...	Lettonie
Lithuania	..	14.5	11.2	8.2	6.1	6.4	[3]7.7	...	...	...	Lituanie
Poland[2][4]	64.7	44.3	32.9	31.8	33.4	32.6	32.8	31.8	29.5	22.4	Pologne[2][4]
Republic of Moldova	..	0.0	0.2	[5]0.1	[5]0.0	[5]0.0	[5]0.1	[5]0.0	[5]0.0	[5]0.0	Rép. de Moldova
Russian Federation	..	295.1	207.6	145.2	64.7	54.1	37.2	34.9	28.5	33.9	Fédération de Russie
Slovakia	..	..	..	..	..	5.9	6.5	7.0	...	...	Slovaquie
Switzerland	6.8	7.2	6.3	5.4	5.3	4.4	...	...	...	...	Suisse
Ukraine	..	50.7	48.8	38.0	17.2	12.0	6.8	8.2	5.8	3.8	Ukraine
USSR (former)	529.0	..	..	..	..	..	..	..	..	..	URSS (anc.)
Total	**1034**	**999**	**1095**	**1722**	**1890**	**3428**	**3751**	**5236**	**8801**	**9152**	**Total**

General Note.
Woollen and worsted fabrics in the piece (at loom stage) before undergoing finishing processes such as bleaching, dyeing, making up etc. Fabrics of fine hair are excluded. (SITC, Rev.3: 65420-1A, 65430-1A).

Remarque générale.
Tissus de laine cardée ou peignée, en pièces, sortant du métier à tisser, avant les opérations de finition, c'est-à-dire avant d'être blanchis, teints, confectionnés etc., à l'exclusion des tissus de poils fins. (CTCI, Rev.3:65420-1A, 65430-1A).

[1] Original data in metric tons.
[2] After undergoing finishing processes.
[3] Original data in square metres.
[4] Including fabrics of wool substitutes.
[5] Excluding Transnistria region.

[1] Données d'origine exprimées en tonnes.
[2] Après opérations de finition.
[3] Données d'origine exprimées en mètres carrés.
[4] Y compris les tissus de succédanés de laine.
[5] Non compris la région de Transnistrie.

Woollen woven fabrics
Tissus de laine

ISIC-BASED CODE - CODE BASE CITI

3211-34B

Unit : Metric tons   Unité : Tonnes métriques

Country or area	1990	1991	1992	1993	1994	1995	1996	1997	1998	1999	Pays ou zone
Africa	**9125**	**5488**	**8197**	**3083**	**4912**	**4895**	**2717**	**3217**	**2763**	**2308**	**Afrique**
Egypt	9125	...	[1]8197	[1]3083	[1]4912	[1]4895	[1]2717	...	...	...	Egypte
America, North	**45060**	**53528**	**56259**	**59267**	**56333**	**62945**	**67173**	**71261**	**73587**	**76030**	**Amérique du Nord**
Mexico	3142	2991	3743	4451	3129	4291	5834	7237	6878	6636	Mexique
United States[1]	41918	50537	52516	54816	53204	...	...	...	...	...	Etats-Unis[1]
Asia	**232509**	**235461**	**229509**	**199454**	**225814**	**196339**	**195334**	**185994**	**181213**	**174188**	**Asie**
China	...	...	...	89206	119916	...	...	...	...	...	Chine
Indonesia	...	...	228	...	...	...	...	...	...	...	Indonésie
Japan[1 2 3]	...	...	116063	102191	101740	88812	87960	...	...	...	Japon[1 2 3]
Kazakhstan[1]	..	...	8159	7169	3506	1234	767	...	...	...	Kazakhstan[1]
Syrian Arab Republic	533	61	498	660	424	1504	1818	2727	4905	...	Rép. arabe syrienne
Europe	**340413**	**348051**	**354375**	**312719**	**327324**	**311299**	**296474**	**295375**	**269702**	**271770**	**Europe**
Austria[4]	2497	2202	2157	1451	765	...	3192	3326	4327	3359	Autriche[4]
Belgium[5]	34207	31467	31892	28289	...	...	...	...	...	...	Belgique[5]
Croatia	..	...	[1]2048	[1]2500	[1]2583	[1]2379	[1]1607	712	568	...	Croatie
Czech Republic	..	...	[1]16340	...	9475	9199	7916	7627	7371	5573	République tchèque
Finland	*104	*70	*44	18	...	...	...	...	...	...	Finlande
France	33096	32604	30266	23952	25850	...	...	...	...	...	France
Germany	..	34352	32963	...	...	22526	22531	22385	20728	...	Allemagne
Germany(Fed.Rep.)	30409										Allemagne(Rép.féd.)
Greece	[6]835	[6]1016	[6]881	867	434	563	1322	1670	792	...	Grèce
Hungary[1 6]	...	...	1302	974	492	433	...	...	...	...	Hongrie[1 6]
Italy	148836	152594	158584	151772	165541	158332	153650	158358	141116	...	Italie
Netherlands	1658	1574	1857	...	...	...	...	...	...	...	Pays-Bas
Norway	*491	452	566	524	584	627	574	...	...	479	Norvège
Poland[6 7]	28976	19287	14241	13610	14226	13669	14033	13581	11805	8514	Pologne[6 7]
Portugal	12014	10179	4211	3049	2756	...	...	...	...	...	Portugal
Romania[1 6]	...	...	24584	24312	23049	24060	17963	...	...	...	Roumanie[1 6]
Slovakia	..	..	...	...	...	...	...	...	3491	2494	Slovaquie
Slovenia[1]	..	...	5366	4568	3402	2451	942	...	...	...	Slovénie[1]
Spain	[8]10939	[8]11218	[8]9854	6056	4858	5211	...	...	...	...	Espagne
Sweden	196	...	...	0	...	...	...	...	...	...	Suède
United Kingdom[2]	7164	...	...	6367	6595	...	...	...	...	...	Royaume-Uni[2]
Yugoslavia[1]	..	...	7420	4735	4490	4034	3951	...	...	...	Yougoslavie[1]
USSR (former)	**308045**	..	..	..	..	..	..	..	..		**URSS (anc.)**
Oceania	**3353**	**3194**	**2930**	**2866**	**2928**	**2600**	**2271**	**2244**	**2085**	**1927**	**Océanie**
Australia[1]	...	...	2930	2866	2928	2600	2271	...	...	...	Australie[1]
Total	**938505**	**645723**	**651270**	**577389**	**617311**	**578077**	**563969**	**558090**	**529350**	**526224**	**Total**

General Note.

Woollen and worsted fabrics in the piece (at loom stage) before undergoing finishing processes such as bleaching, dyeing, making up etc. Fabrics of fine hair are excluded. (SITC, Rev.3: 65420-1B, 65430-1B).

Remarque générale.

Tissus de laine cardée ou peignée, en pièces, sortant du métier à tisser, avant les opérations de finition, c'est-à-dire avant d'être blanchis, teints, confectionnés etc., à l'exclusion des tissus de poils fins. (CTCI, Rev.3:65420-1B, 65430-1B).

[1] Original data in square metres.
[2] Shipments.
[3] Including finished fabrics and blanketing made of synthetic fibers.
[4] 1995 data are confidential.
[5] Including woollen blankets and carpets.
[6] After undergoing finishing processes.
[7] Including fabrics of wool substitutes.
[8] Including household production.

[1] Données d'origine exprimées en mètres carrés.
[2] Expéditions.
[3] Y compris les tissus finis et les couvertures en fibres synthétiques.
[4] Pour 1995, les données sont confidentielles.
[5] Y compris les couvertures et tapis en laine.
[6] Après opérations de finition.
[7] Y compris les tissus de succédanés de laine.
[8] Y compris la production ménagère.

Linen fabrics
Tissus de lin

ISIC-BASED CODE - CODE BASE CITI

3211-37

Unit : Million square metres

Unité : Millions de mètres carrés

Country or area	1990	1991	1992	1993	1994	1995	1996	1997	1998	1999	Pays ou zone
Africa	**14**	**13**	**14**	**14**	**14**	**14**	**14**	**14**	**14**	**14**	**Afrique**
Egypt[1]	13.9	13.2	...	...	...	...	...	...	...	...	Egypte[1]
America, South	**1**	**1**	**0**	**1**	**0**	**1**	**1**	**1**	**1**	**1**	**Amérique du Sud**
Colombia[2]	...	...	0.0	0.6	0.5	1.0	...	...	...	...	Colombie[2]
Asia	**15**	**12**	**11**	**12**	**8**	**7**	**6**	**5**	**4**	**4**	**Asie**
Japan	15.4	12.4	11.3	11.9	8.1	7.1	5.8	4.6	3.7	4.0	Japon
Europe	**296**	**921**	**770**	**571**	**405**	**335**	**283**	**269**	**212**	**219**	**Europe**
Austria[3]	1.5	1.3	1.3	2.4	3.0	...	...	...	...	...	Autriche[3]
Belarus	..	84.4	87.0	68.4	41.9	43.6	44.1	47.5	51.5	49.5	Bélarus
Belgium	10.9	8.8	7.9	7.0	[1 4]2.3	[1 4]3.0	[1 4]2.0	[1 4]1.4	[1 4]1.6	[1 4]1.5	Belgique
Bulgaria[5 6]	10.1	4.2	3.7	2.5	2.7	2.7	2.4	1.2	[2]1.2	[2]1.2	Bulgarie[5 6]
Croatia	..	0.0	0.0	0.3	0.2	0.0	0.0	...	...	...	Croatie
Czechoslovakia(former)[5]	114.3	72.1	..	..	..	..	..	..	..	..	Tchécoslovaquie(anc.)[5]
Czech Republic	. ..		70.2	43.4	49.0	44.4	27.3	27.5	23.6	20.9	République tchèque
Estonia	..	10.2	4.9	1.9	0.2	0.0	0.0	0.0	1.4	3.9	Estonie
Finland	*0.0	0.1	*0.0	*0.1	...	...	...	...	...	...	Finlande
France	12.4	8.9	6.9	3.3	9.9	...	...	...	...	...	France
Germany	..	3.8	3.6	3.6	4.4	4.1	2.7	2.3	1.8	...	Allemagne
Germany(Fed.Rep.)	3.6	..	..	..	..						Allemagne(Rép.féd.)
Hungary[5]	5.1	3.4	3.1	1.8	2.3	1.6	...	...	...	...	Hongrie[5]
Latvia	..	12.3		0.8	2.4	1.1	0.9	1.0	3.2	3.7	Lettonie
Lithuania	..	27.1	23.1	13.7	15.4	13.1	13.6	13.9	17.9	20.0	Lituanie
Poland[5 7]	36.7	28.9	23.5	21.9	28.7	22.4	13.2	11.8	10.9	9.1	Pologne[5 7]
Portugal	[1]0.2	[1]0.3	#1.3	2.0	3.5	3.2	2.3	2.4	3.0	3.2	Portugal
Romania[5 8]	95.1	76.1	41.5	25.2	26.9	28.0	22.8	17.3	8.5	6.7	Roumanie[5 8]
Russian Federation	..	486.7	403.4	301.2	155.6	124.1	111.7	106.4	61.2	74.9	Fédération de Russie
Slovakia	..	..	[5]6.2	[5]5.2	[5]5.1	[2]5.0	[2]1.4	[2]0.8	[1]1.2	[1]0.4	Slovaquie
Slovenia	..	...	...	0.3	0.3	...	1.3	...	...	2.8	Slovénie
Spain[1]	...	...	...	1.4	2.3	2.8	...	...	...	...	Espagne[1]
Ukraine	..	84.3	71.6	61.7	43.1	21.8	21.8	19.7	9.9	5.5	Ukraine
United Kingdom[1 9]	...	...	...	2.9	5.9	...	...	...	...	...	Royaume-Uni[1 9]
USSR (former)	845.3	..	..	..	..	..	..	..	..	..	URSS (anc.)
Total	**1172**	**947**	**795**	**597**	**427**	**356**	**303**	**288**	**230**	**237**	**Total**

General Note.
Woven fabrics of flax or ramie yarn (at loom stage) before undergoing finishing processes. (SITC, Rev.3: 65440-1).

Remarque générale.
Tissus de fil de lin ou de ramie sortant du métier à tisser, avant les opérations de finition. (CTCI, Rev.3: 65440-1).

[1] Original data in metric tons.
[2] Original data in metres.
[3] Beginning 1995, data are confidential.
[4] Incomplete coverage.
[5] After undergoing finishing processes.
[6] Including jute fabrics.
[7] Including fabrics of hemp.
[8] Including fabrics of flax, hemp, jute and mixed yarns.
[9] Deliveries of woollen and worsted fabrics, except blankets, containing, by weight, more than 15 per cent wool or animal fibres. Including finished fabrics.

[1] Données d'origine exprimées en tonnes.
[2] Données d'origine exprimées en mètres.
[3] A partir de 1995, les données sont confidentielles
[4] Couverture incomplète.
[5] Après opérations de finition.
[6] Y compris les tissus de jute.
[7] Y compris les tissus de chanvre.
[8] Y compris les tissus de lin, de chanvre, de jute et de filés mélangés.
[9] Quantités livrées de tissus de laine cardée et peignée, à l'exception des couvertures, contenant, en poids, plus de 15 p. 100 de laine ou de fibres animales. Y compris les tissus finis.

Linen fabrics
Tissus de lin

ISIC-BASED CODE - CODE BASE CITI

3211-37A

Unit : Thousand metres | | | | | | | | | | Unité : Milliers de mètres

Country or area	1990	1991	1992	1993	1994	1995	1996	1997	1998	1999	Pays ou zone
America, South	**746**	**746**	**746**	**672**	**534**	**1032**	**746**	**746**	**746**	**746**	**Amérique du Sud**
Colombia	...	...	...	672	534	1032	...	...	...	...	Colombie
Europe	**145221**	**697713**	**605625**	**475779**	**310909**	**267966**	**251734**	**235435**	**188539**	**187961**	**Europe**
Austria	1208	1084	1150	1990	2598	2052	988	893	...	...	Autriche
Belarus	..	64786	68689	52406	32775	35400	35078	36598	38609	36140	Bélarus
Bulgaria[1][2]	8985	3590	3338	2159	2088	2230	1873	958	1249	1288	Bulgarie[1][2]
Czechoslovakia(former)	99481	65852	..	..	..	..	..	..	..	..	Tchécoslovaquie(anc.)
Czech Republic	..	..	66529	60591	...	...	...	...	...	...	République tchèque
Estonia	..	7140	3296	1353	173	0	2	6	881	2384	Estonie
Latvia	..	10384	...	680	1765	790	715	737	2024	...	Lettonie
Lithuania	..	20093	17571	10741	11014	9614	[3]14632	...	...	...	Lituanie
Poland[1][4]	35547	26609	20331	18801	23195	18613	11321	10444	8609	7017	Pologne[1][4]
Russian Federation	..	430291	357635	271496	130973	111392	102801	93493	51168	59858	Fédération de Russie
Slovakia	..	..	7437	5816	6960	5377	1527	877	..	..	Slovaquie
Ukraine	..	67884	57207	49746	35808	18938	19237	16834	8647	4868	Ukraine
USSR (former)	729778	..	..	..	..	..	..	..	..	..	URSS (anc.)
Total	**875745**	**698459**	**606371**	**476451**	**311443**	**268998**	**252480**	**236181**	**189285**	**188707**	**Total**

General Note.

Woven fabrics of flax or ramie yarn (at loom stage) before undergoing finishing processes. (SITC, Rev.3: 65440-1A).

[1] After undergoing finishing processes.
[2] Including jute fabrics.
[3] Original data in square metres.
[4] Including fabrics of hemp.

Remarque générale.

Tissus de fil de lin ou de ramie sortant du métier à tisser, avant les opérations de finition. (CTCI, Rev.3: 65440-1A).

[1] Après opérations de finition.
[2] Y compris les tissus de jute.
[3] Données d'origine exprimées en mètres carrés.
[4] Y compris les tissus de chanvre.

Linen fabrics
Tissus de lin

ISIC-BASED CODE - CODE BASE CITI
3211-37B

Unit : Metric tons

Unité : Tonnes métriques

Country or area	1990	1991	1992	1993	1994	1995	1996	1997	1998	1999	Pays ou zone
Africa	**5100**	**4850**	**4975**	**4975**	**4975**	**4975**	**4975**	**4975**	**4975**	**4975**	**Afrique**
Egypt	5100	4850	...	...	...	...	...	...	...	...	Egypte
Europe	**39921**	**34382**	**59186**	**36270**	**43033**	**40785**	**31180**	**29600**	**27069**	**24471**	**Europe**
Austria[1]	480	413	425	770	994	...	...	...	...	...	Autriche[1]
Belgium	3005	2454	2165	2000	[2]830	[2]1093	[2]746	[2]519	[2]575	[2]542	Belgique
Bulgaria*	3711	1544	1360	...	...	...	...	...	...	...	Bulgarie*
Croatia[3]	..	...	3	106	65	0	0	...	...	...	Croatie[3]
Czech Republic	..	..	[3]25810	...	12064	11683	7500	7928	6646	5446	République tchèque
Finland*	12	32	28	22	...	...	...	...	...	...	Finlande*
France	[4]4548	[4]3283	[4]2532	[4]1224	[4]3636	2440	2100	2720	2868	3060	France
Germany	..	...	...	...	...	1271	930	554	422	...	Allemagne
Hungary[3 5]	..	...	1154	675	840	576	...	...	...	...	Hongrie[3 5]
Latvia										734	Lettonie
Poland[5 6]	9155	7057	5898	5398	7433	6189	3292	2971	2645	2135	Pologne[5 6]
Portugal	62	97	...	...	...	...	...	...	...	...	Portugal
Romania[3 5 7]	..	...	15246	9266	9895	10272	8372	...	...	...	Roumanie[3 5 7]
Slovakia	..	..	...	...	...	...	...	...	438	154	Slovaquie
Slovenia[3]	..	...	...	100	103	...	491	...	...	...	Slovénie[3]
Spain	...	...	...	521	858	1034	...	...	...	...	Espagne
United Kingdom[8]	...	...	...	1068	2183	...	...	...	...	...	Royaume-Uni[8]
USSR (former)	310658	..	..	..	..	..	..	..	..	..	URSS (anc.)
Total	**355679**	**39232**	**64161**	**41245**	**48008**	**45760**	**36155**	**34575**	**32044**	**29446**	**Total**

General Note.	**Remarque générale.**
Woven fabrics of flax or ramie yarn (at loom stage) before undergoing finishing processes. (SITC, Rev.3: 65440-1B).	Tissus de fil de lin ou de ramie sortant du métier à tisser, avant les opérations de finition. (CTCI, Rev.3: 65440-1B).

[1] Beginning 1995, data are confidential.

[2] Incomplete coverage.

[3] Original data in square metres.

[4] Woven fabrics of flax or ramie yarn, or mixed yarn (50 percent cotton and 50 per cent flax).

[5] After undergoing finishing processes.

[6] Including fabrics of hemp.

[7] Including fabrics of flax, hemp, jute and mixed yarns.

[8] Deliveries of woollen and worsted fabrics, except blankets, containing, by weight, more than 15 per cent wool or animal fibres. Including finished fabrics.

[1] A partir de 1995, les données sont confidentielles

[2] Couverture incomplète.

[3] Données d'origine exprimées en mètres carrés.

[4] Tissus de filés de lin ou de ramie ou filés mélangés (50 p. 100 de lin).

[5] Après opérations de finition.

[6] Y compris les tissus de chanvre.

[7] Y compris les tissus de lin, de chanvre, de jute et de filés mélangés.

[8] Quantités livrées de tissus de laine cardée et peignée, à l'exception des couvertures, contenant, en poids, plus de 15 p. 100 de laine ou de fibres animales. Y compris les tissus finis.

Jute fabrics
Tissus de jute
ISIC-BASED CODE - CODE BASE CITI
3211-40

Unit : Million square metres

Unité : Millions de mètres carrés

Country or area	1990	1991	1992	1993	1994	1995	1996	1997	1998	1999	Pays ou zone
Africa	**49**	**46**	**48**	**45**	**41**	**47**	**48**	**33**	**34**	**25**	**Afrique**
Algeria*	6.5	5.7	...	...	...	...	...	...	...	...	Algérie*
Egypt[1]	42.3	40.5	42.3	38.4	35.0	40.6	42.2	27.2	27.4	19.0	Egypte[1]
Asia	**4672**	**4490**	**3872**	**4466**	**4219**	**4117**	**4043**	**4001**	**4011**	**3962**	**Asie**
Bangladesh[1][2]	1113.8	914.7	877.7	940.3	889.1	896.7	852.8	860.9	...	...	Bangladesh[1][2]
India[1]	3013.2	3048.0	2459.0	3033.8	...	...	...	...	...	...	Inde[1]
Indonesia[1]	...	0.5	...	...	...	...	...	...	...	...	Indonésie[1]
Iran(Islamic Rep. of)	...	16.1	26.8	...	...	...	...	...	...	...	Iran(Rép. islamique)
Japan[3]	0.2	0.1	0.0	0.1	0.0	...	...	...	...	...	Japon[3]
Kyrgyzstan	..	9.2	7.1	3.7	1.7	0.4	1.0	1.4	0.8	0.5	Kirghizistan
Pakistan[1]	201.9	204.2	212.7	205.4	161.1	144.5	148.8	144.8	201.2	180.2	Pakistan[1]
Thailand[1]	321.0	287.8	278.5	250.7	247.2	159.8	129.8	82.6	53.9	38.9	Thaïlande[1]
Uzbekistan	..	9.5	9.2	9.9	9.4	5.0	0.5	0.4	...	...	Ouzbékistan
Europe	**139**	**217**	**85**	**77**	**57**	**76**	**59**	**54**	**49**	**50**	**Europe**
Belgium	0.1	0.0	0.0	0.0	...	...	...	...	...	...	Belgique
Czechoslovakia(former)	92.7	84.4	...	...	..	...	...	..	..	..	Tchécoslovaquie(anc.)
France[1]	5.8	7.8	8.0	8.2	7.8	...	...	...	...	...	France[1]
Germany	..	[1]12.6	[1]12.1	[1]11.5	[1]10.4	33.7	29.1	29.4	28.9	...	Allemagne
Germany(Fed.Rep.)[1]	11.6				..	..	..	..	..	..	Allemagne(Rép.féd.)[1]
Greece[1]	1.0	0.9	0.9	...	...	...	...	...	...	...	Grèce[1]
Hungary[4]	0.6	0.1	0.1	0.0	0.1	0.0	...	...	...	...	Hongrie[4]
Poland[5]	25.0	21.1	9.6	5.6	6.2	5.3	5.2	5.4	3.6	1.9	Pologne[5]
Russian Federation[6]	..	29.8	28.1	26.0	14.2	10.5	5.2	2.4	0.4	...	Fédération de Russie[6]
Slovenia	..	2.5	0.0	0.0	...	...	...	...	...	...	Slovénie
Spain[1][7]	1.9	0.6	1.1	1.1	...	...	...	...	...	...	Espagne[1][7]
Ukraine	..	28.5	24.0	23.8	14.9	14.1	6.7	4.3	2.6	...	Ukraine
Yugoslavia	..	28.7	1.3	0.0	0.1	0.0	0.1	0.1	0.2	0.0	Yougoslavie
USSR (former)	89.7	..	..	..	..	..	..	..	..	..	URSS (anc.)
Total	**4949**	**4753**	**4005**	**4588**	**4317**	**4239**	**4150**	**4088**	**4093**	**4037**	**Total**

General Note.
Woven fabrics manufactured with yarns of jute at loom stage.
(SITC, Rev.3: 65450-1).

Remarque générale.
Tissus sortant du métier à tisser, fabriqués à partir de fils de jute. (CTCI, Rev.3: 65450-1).

[1] Original data in metric tons.
[2] Twelve months ending 30 June of year stated. Production of jute mills.

[3] Shipments.
[4] Finished fabrics.
[5] After undergoing finishing processes.
[6] Including hemp fabrics.
[7] Including fabrics of flax, hemp, jute and mixed yarns.

[1] Données d'origine exprimées en tonnes.
[2] Période de douze mois finissant le 30 juin de l'année indiquée. Production d'usines de jute.

[3] Expéditions.
[4] Tissus finis.
[5] Après opérations de finition.
[6] Y compris les tissus de chanvre.
[7] Y compris les tissus de lin, de chanvre, de jute et de filés mélangés.

Jute fabrics
Tissus de jute

ISIC-BASED CODE - CODE BASE CITI
3211-40A

Unit : Thousand metres   Unité : Milliers de mètres

Country or area	1990	1991	1992	1993	1994	1995	1996	1997	1998	1999	Pays ou zone
Africa	**7009**	**6161**	**9409**	**5237**	**6954**	**6954**	**6954**	**6954**	**6954**	**6954**	**Afrique**
Algeria	7009	6161	9409	5237	...	...	...	...	...	...	Algérie
Asia	**117**	**17752**	**15469**	**12943**	**10586**	**5267**	**1539**	**1804**	**904**	**599**	**Asie**
Indonesia	117	...	...	...	...	...	...	...	...	...	Indonésie
Kyrgyzstan	..	8656	6708	3445	1580	391	975	1341	787	482	Kirghizistan
Uzbekistan	..	8979	8644	9381	8889	4759	447	346	...	...	Ouzbékistan
Europe	**81826**	**122875**	**50720**	**45789**	**29197**	**24263**	**13222**	**8871**	**5069**	**4487**	**Europe**
Austria	5	...	...	...	...	...	...	...	...	...	Autriche
Czechoslovakia(former)	61745	57317	..	..	..	..	..	..	..	..	Tchécoslovaquie(anc.)
Poland[1]	20076	16884	6887	3524	3988	2925	3078	3398	2732	1592	Pologne[1]
Russian Federation[2]	..	26838	25310	23156	12677	9427	4708	2187	227	...	Fédération de Russie[2]
Ukraine	..	21831	18518	19104	12527	11906	5431	3281	2105	...	Ukraine
USSR (former)	78017	..	..	..	..	..	..	..	..	..	URSS (anc.)
Total	**166969**	**146788**	**75598**	**63969**	**46737**	**36484**	**21715**	**17629**	**12927**	**12040**	**Total**

General Note.
Woven fabrics manufactured with yarns of jute at loom stage.
(SITC, Rev.3: 65450-1A).

Remarque générale.
Tissus sortant du métier à tisser, fabriqués à partir de fils de jute. (CTCI, Rev.3: 65450-1A).

[1] After undergoing finishing processes.
[2] Including hemp fabrics.

[1] Après opérations de finition.
[2] Y compris les tissus de chanvre.

Jute fabrics
Tissus de jute

ISIC-BASED CODE - CODE BASE CITI

3211-40B

Unit : Metric tons   Unité : Tonnes métriques

Country or area	1990	1991	1992	1993	1994	1995	1996	1997	1998	1999	Pays ou zone
Africa	**20082**	**19191**	**20063**	**18219**	**16591**	**19256**	**20000**	**12890**	**13000**	**9000**	**Afrique**
Egypt	20082	19191	20063	18219	16591	19256	20000	12890	13000	9000	Egypte
Asia	**2206027**	**2113458**	**1816144**	**2101876**	**1985953**	**1940226**	**1907617**	**1886773**	**1892081**	**1869171**	**Asie**
Bangladesh[1]	528350	433923	416364	446069	421765	425376	404987	408412	...	...	Bangladesh[1]
India	1429400	1445900	1166500	1439200	...	...	...	...	...	...	Inde
Indonesia	...	240	...	...	...	...	...	...	...	...	Indonésie
Pakistan	95774	96872	100909	97454	76415	68540	70580	68703	95439	85472	Pakistan
Thailand	152263	136523	132131	118913	117283	75820	61560	39168	25550	18450	Thaïlande
Europe	**17595**	**16462**	**13162**	**11841**	**11434**	**12467**	**11596**	**11690**	**11709**	**11543**	**Europe**
Austria	2	...	...	...	...	...	...	...	...	...	Autriche
Belgium[2]	60	15	38	11	...	...	...	...	...	...	Belgique[2]
France	2733	3708	3792	3910	3720	...	...	...	...	...	France
Germany	..	5969	5747	5439	4926	5906	4792	4679	4883	...	Allemagne
Germany(Fed.Rep.)	5505	..	..	..	..	..	..	..	..	..	Allemagne(Rép.féd.)
Greece	484	434	446	...	...	...	...	...	...	...	Grèce
Hungary[3][4]	...	...	46	22	29	13	...	...	...	...	Hongrie[3][4]
Poland[5]	7901	6007	2522	1444	1667	1271	1242	1248	846	549	Pologne[5]
Spain[6]	882	272	542	543	...	...	...	...	...	...	Espagne[6]
Yugoslavia[3]	..	...	...	15	45	4	44	...	...	...	Yougoslavie[3]
USSR (former)	42611	..	..	..	..	..	..	..	..	..	URSS (anc.)
Total	**2286315**	**2149111**	**1849369**	**2131936**	**2013978**	**1971949**	**1939213**	**1911353**	**1916790**	**1889714**	**Total**

General Note.
Woven fabrics manufactured with yarns of jute at loom stage.
(SITC, Rev.3: 65450-1B).

Remarque générale.
Tissus sortant du métier à tisser, fabriqués à partir de fils de jute. (CTCI, Rev.3: 65450-1B).

[1] Twelve months ending 30 June of year stated. Production of jute mills.

[2] Including carpets of jute.
[3] Original data in square metres.
[4] Finished fabrics.
[5] After undergoing finishing processes.
[6] Including fabrics of flax, hemp, jute and mixed yarns.

[1] Période de douze mois finissant le 30 juin de l'année indiquée. Production d'usines de jute.
[2] Y compris les carpettes et tapis en jute.
[3] Données d'origine exprimées en mètres carrés.
[4] Tissus finis.
[5] Après opérations de finition.
[6] Y compris les tissus de lin, de chanvre, de jute et de filés mélangés.

Woven fabrics of cellulosic fibres
Tissus de fibres cellulosiques

ISIC-BASED CODE - CODE BASE CITI

3211-43

Unit : Million square metres | Unité : Millions de mètres carrés

Country or area	1990	1991	1992	1993	1994	1995	1996	1997	1998	1999	Pays ou zone
America, North	**4**	**5**	**5**	**6**	**5**	**6**	**6**	**6**	**7**	**7**	**Amérique du Nord**
Mexico[1]	4.2	4.7	4.9	6.3	4.9	...	...	...	...	...	Mexique[1]
America, South	**108**	**106**	**97**	**114**	**111**	**112**	**96**	**108**	**92**	**97**	**Amérique du Sud**
Bolivia[2]	0.5	0.7	0.9	1.7	1.5	*2.3	...	...	...	...	Bolivie[2]
Colombia[2]	...	...	...	...	...	...	...	78.0	69.3	...	Colombie[2]
Ecuador[2]	...	...	22.8	38.9	36.0	35.9	20.8	...	20.5	20.4	Equateur[2]
Asia	**816**	**782**	**738**	**674**	**692**	**635**	**691**	**701**	**639**	**578**	**Asie**
Hong Kong SAR[3][4]	0.0	0.6	1.5	2.7	2.9	1.0	...	21.1	...	...	Hong-Kong RAS[3][4]
Japan	707.9	671.0	585.7	493.1	435.1	408.8	440.8	455.7	389.8	352.4	Japon
Turkey[2]	107.8	109.8	151.1	178.5	254.3	225.1	245.5	224.3	240.0	215.2	Turquie[2]
Europe	**3415**	**3980**	**3994**	**3915**	**3761**	**4173**	**4200**	**4392**	**4590**	**4648**	**Europe**
Austria[5]	10.3	6.8	10.4	1.1	0.8	...	...	...	...	...	Autriche[5]
Belarus	..	175.2	146.9	135.1	79.8	35.1	39.5	66.7	77.2	72.2	Bélarus
Belgium	[6]353.8	[6]338.2	[6]334.8	[6]308.7	[1]327.9	[1]589.9	[1]602.2	[1]656.4	[1]712.3	[1]712.2	Belgique
Croatia	..	5.5	6.4	9.7	9.8	8.4	5.4	6.0	6.8	...	Croatie
Czechoslovakia(former)	52.2	36.0	..	..	..	..	..	..	..	...	Tchécoslovaquie(anc.)
Finland[7]	4.0	*0.9	*0.6	*0.7	*0.8	*0.4	*0.4	...	...	...	Finlande[7]
France	2339.0	2345.8	2596.7	2715.7	2758.1	...	...	...	...	...	France
Germany	..	521.1	461.9	340.9	324.5	387.1	324.7	311.3	334.7	...	Allemagne
Germany(Fed.Rep.)[7]	525.5	..	..	..	..	..	..	..	..	...	Allemagne(Rép.féd.)[7]
Greece	...	...	...	0.2	0.2	...	...	...	...	...	Grèce
Hungary[7]	23.3	21.8	14.1	13.5	12.4	12.4	...	...	2.4	0.3	Hongrie[7]
Lithuania	..	34.5	26.1	17.5	...	...	...	37.6	39.8	35.0	Lituanie
Netherlands[1]	21.7	25.6	21.9	...	...	...	...	...	...	...	Pays-Bas[1]
Poland[7]	37.5	28.3	21.2	22.8	21.8	24.5	26.5	27.6	27.0	17.6	Pologne[7]
Portugal	[1]15.2	[1]14.9	26.1	24.6	30.2	24.0	10.2	10.9	8.9	7.8	Portugal
Republic of Moldova[8]	..	43.9	21.6	...	...	...	...	...	...	...	Rép. de Moldova[8]
Russian Federation[2]	..	201.2	162.4	134.9	44.3	29.3	13.8	10.7	8.0	6.9	Fédération de Russie[2]
Slovenia	..	7.2	6.0	5.4	10.2	24.1	10.0	...	...	4.3	Slovénie
Sweden[1][9]	9.6	5.7	...	...	1.8	1.6	...	...	...	...	Suède[1][9]
Ukraine[2]	..	136.6	102.2	92.1	28.7	9.3	3.1	2.8	2.5	1.6	Ukraine[2]
United Kingdom[1]	...	...	...	25.8	18.7	...	...	...	...	...	Royaume-Uni[1]
Yugoslavia	..	4.0	4.5	3.6	2.3	2.2	0.9	1.2	0.8	0.2	Yougoslavie
T.F.Yug.Rep. Macedonia	..	4.5	3.1	2.4	1.0	0.9	1.3	0.7	0.7	0.5	L'ex-RY Macédoine
Oceania	**11**	**9**	**8**	**10**	**10**	**10**	**10**	**10**	**10**	**10**	**Océanie**
Australia[10][11]	11.1	9.1	8.5	10.1	...	...	...	...	...	...	Australie[10][11]
Total	**4353**	**4882**	**4843**	**4720**	**4579**	**4935**	**5002**	**5217**	**5337**	**5339**	**Total**

General Note.
Fabrics of continuous and discontinuous rayon and acetate fibres, including pile and chenille fabrics at loom stage. (SITC,Rev.3: 65350-1, 65360-1, 65380-1, 65390-1).

Remarque générale.
Tissus de fibres de rayonne et d'acétate, continues ou discontinues, sortant du métier à tisser, y compris les velours, peluches, tissus bouclés et tissus chenille. (CTCI, Rev.3: 65350-1, 65360-1, 65380-1, 65390-1).

[1] Original data in metric tons.
[2] Original data in metres.
[3] 1996 data are confidential.
[4] 1998 data are confidential.
[5] Beginning 1995, data are confidential.
[6] Including blankets and carpets of cellulosic fibres.
[7] After undergoing finishing processes.
[8] Including silk fabrics.
[9] Including woven non-cellulosic fabrics.
[10] Including pile and chenille fabrics of non-cellulosic fibres.
[11] Twelve months ending 30 June of year stated.

[1] Données d'origine exprimées en tonnes.
[2] Données d'origine exprimées en mètres.
[3] Pour 1996, les données sont confidentielles.
[4] Pour 1998, les données sont confidentielles.
[5] A partir de 1995, les données sont confidentielles
[6] Y compris les couvertures et les tapis en fibres cellulosiques.
[7] Après opérations de finition.
[8] Y compris les tissus de soie.
[9] Y compris les tissus en fibres non cellulosiques.
[10] Y compris les tissus bouclés et les tissus chenille en fibres non cellulosiques.
[11] Période de douze mois finissant le 30 juin de l'année indiquée.

Woven fabrics of cellulosic fibres
Tissus de fibres cellulosiques

ISIC-BASED CODE - CODE BASE CITI

3211-43A

Unit : Thousand metres   Unité : Milliers de mètres

Country or area	1990	1991	1992	1993	1994	1995	1996	1997	1998	1999	Pays ou zone
America, South	**78478**	**77642**	**71008**	**83350**	**81159**	**81593**	**70329**	**78808**	**67287**	**70474**	**Amérique du Sud**
Bolivia	343	511	630	1223	1098	*1663	...	...	...	...	Bolivie
Colombia	...	...	...	...	...	...	...	56900	50619	...	Colombie
Ecuador	...	...	16618	28367	26301	26170	15147	...	14989	14908	Equateur
Asia	**78660**	**80178**	**110327**	**130287**	**185633**	**164281**	**179217**	**163705**	**175165**	**157044**	**Asie**
Turkey	78660	80178	110327	130287	185633	164281	179217	163705	175165	157044	Turquie
Europe	**101239**	**484359**	**361953**	**312669**	**159268**	**101765**	**91571**	**104970**	**107889**	**98027**	**Europe**
Austria	30239	23819	30295	6636	5388	3390	...	...	...	...	Autriche
Belarus	..	[1]125483	103701	94485	55384	23377	26605	44658	51603	49892	Bélarus
Czechoslovakia(former)	40792	27051	..	..	..	..	..	..	..		Tchécoslovaquie(anc.)
Poland[2]	30208	21552	15419	16253	15599	17226	18562	19398	18935	12311	Pologne[2]
Republic of Moldova	..	39872	19374	...	...	...	...	...	...	...	Rép. de Moldova
Russian Federation	..	146870	118559	98478	32361	21360	10093	7828	5871	5055	Fédération de Russie
Ukraine	..	99712	74605	67194	20913	6789	2243	2064	1857	1146	Ukraine
Total	**258377**	**642179**	**543288**	**526306**	**426060**	**347639**	**341118**	**347484**	**350341**	**325545**	**Total**

General Note.

Fabrics of continuous and discontinuous rayon and acetate fibres, including pile and chenille fabrics at loom stage. (SITC,Rev.3: 65350-1A, 65360-1A, 65380-1A, 65390-1A).

[1] Including silk fabrics.
[2] After undergoing finishing processes.

Remarque générale.

Tissus de fibres de rayonne et d'acétate, continues ou discontinues, sortant du métier à tisser, y compris les velours, peluches, tissus bouclés et tissus chenille. (CTCI, Rev.3: 65350-1A, 65360-1A, 65380-1A, 65390-1A).

[1] Y compris les tissus de soie.
[2] Après opérations de finition.

Woven fabrics of cellulosic fibres
Tissus de fibres cellulosiques

ISIC-BASED CODE - CODE BASE CITI

3211-43B

Unit : Metric tons   Unité : Tonnes métriques

Country or area	1990	1991	1992	1993	1994	1995	1996	1997	1998	1999	Pays ou zone
America, North	**468**	**525**	**539**	**696**	**538**	**647**	**678**	**709**	**740**	**771**	**Amérique du Nord**
Mexico	468	525	539	696	538	...	...	...	...	...	Mexique
Europe	**386259**	**387091**	**406572**	**393453**	**394384**	**452449**	**462471**	**481814**	**504562**	**510744**	**Europe**
Austria[1]	3751	2464	3797	2015	1542	...	...	...	...	...	Autriche[1]
Belgium	[2]39242	[2]37512	[2]37141	[2]34248	36366	65418	66790	72799	78999	78979	Belgique
Croatia	...	...	...	...	...	...	...	465	640	...	Croatie
Finland	455	271	172	*153	*141	...	...	...	...	...	Finlande
France	259404	260148	287976	301200	305880	...	...	...	...	...	France
Germany	..	78031	69321	47122	42906	54690	50099	50607	53543	...	Allemagne
Germany(Fed.Rep.)	75252	..	..	..	..					..	Allemagne(Rép.féd.)
Greece	...	...	...	93	33	...	...	...	...	...	Grèce
Hungary[3]	...	...	...	...	...				785	151	Hongrie[3]
Netherlands	2408	2836	2432	...	...	...	...	...	...	...	Pays-Bas
Portugal	1681	1648	...	...	...	...	...	...	...	...	Portugal
Sweden[4]	1069	632	...	...	200	178	...	...	...	...	Suède[4]
United Kingdom	...	...	...	2859	2072	...	...	...	...	...	Royaume-Uni
Total	**386727**	**387616**	**407111**	**394149**	**394922**	**453096**	**463149**	**482523**	**505302**	**511515**	**Total**

General Note.

Fabrics of continuous and discontinuous rayon and acetate fibres, including pile and chenille fabrics at loom stage. (SITC,Rev.3: 65350-1B, 65360-1B, 65380-1B, 65390-1B).

Remarque générale.

Tissus de fibres de rayonne et d'acétate, continues ou discontinues, sortant du métier à tisser, y compris les velours, peluches, tissus bouclés et tissus chenille. (CTCI, Rev.3: 65350-1B, 65360-1B, 65380-1B, 65390-1B).

[1] Beginning 1995, data are confidential.
[2] Including blankets and carpets of cellulosic fibres.
[3] After undergoing finishing processes.
[4] Including woven non-cellulosic fabrics.

[1] A partir de 1995, les données sont confidentielles
[2] Y compris les couvertures et les tapis en fibres cellulosiques.
[3] Après opérations de finition.
[4] Y compris les tissus en fibres non cellulosiques.

Woven fabrics of non-cellulosic fibres
Tissus de fibres non cellulosiques

ISIC-BASED CODE - CODE BASE CITI

3211-46

Unit : Million square metres   Unité : Millions de mètres carrés

Country or area	1990	1991	1992	1993	1994	1995	1996	1997	1998	1999	Pays ou zone
Africa	**5**	**3**	**2**	**4**	**4**	**5**	**5**	**4**	**5**	**4**	**Afrique**
Ethiopia[1]	5.0	3.1	2.4	3.8	3.8	4.9	5.2	4.2	4.7	4.0	Ethiopie[1]
America, North	**509**	**447**	**448**	**552**	**522**	**489**	**624**	**638**	**623**	**626**	**Amérique du Nord**
Mexico[2]	509.0	447.5	448.0	551.8	521.9	489.3	623.5	638.5	622.8	626.4	Mexique[2]
America, South	**17**	**17**	**3**	**24**	**20**	**22**	**16**	**15**	**16**	**16**	**Amérique du Sud**
Colombia	...	...	[2]3.0	[2]23.9	[2]19.8	[2]22.0	...	14.5	15.7	...	Colombie
Asia	**6116**	**6091**	**5699**	**4742**	**4706**	**4664**	**4519**	**4454**	**4048**	**3776**	**Asie**
Hong Kong SAR	0.2	0.7	0.5	0.4	0.4	0.3	...	...	...	...	Hong-Kong RAS
Japan[3]	2667.9	2591.8	2589.4	2265.1	2142.8	2049.6	1996.7	2040.6	1743.2	1580.8	Japon[3]
Korea, Republic of	3428.3	3478.6	3093.7	2459.3	2540.3	2593.8	...	...	...	...	Corée, République de
Nepal[4]	...	...	15.7	17.5	22.8	20.1	24.8	24.9	25.6	24.4	Népal[4]
Europe	**5943**	**6858**	**7214**	**6915**	**2707**	**3078**	**2792**	**2832**	**2870**	**2979**	**Europe**
Austria	90.7	58.9	62.2	46.2	40.6	59.0	...	...	...	...	Autriche
Belgium	[5]3601.2	[5]3544.9	[5]3924.3	[5]4466.9	[2]315.5	[2]287.9	[2]297.5	[2]315.6	[2]304.6	[2]301.5	Belgique
Croatia	..	6.1	5.6	4.1	1.2	0.6	3.0	4.9	4.7	...	Croatie
Czechoslovakia(former)	61.1	46.8	..	..	..	..	..	..	..	..	Tchécoslovaquie(anc.)
Czech Republic	..		35.5	29.1	...	...	...	...	...	...	République tchèque
Finland	23.5	15.8	13.1	13.0	10.6	7.9	7.8	...	...	...	Finlande
France	328.8	417.1	920.2	175.4	126.5						France
Germany	..	955.5	897.2	813.0	791.8	941.6	850.7	913.6	934.4	...	Allemagne
Germany(Fed.Rep.)	945.8	..	..	..	..	..	..	..	..		Allemagne(Rép.féd.)
Greece[6][7]	...	...	...	19.0	29.0	15.5	...	...	...	...	Grèce[6][7]
Hungary[8]	22.0	13.4	8.0	6.4	6.4	6.2	...	...	#95.0	231.0	Hongrie[8]
Lithuania	..	...	...	...		7.6	6.0	5.0	7.2	5.3	Lituanie
Netherlands[2][9]	181.2	177.7	167.2	...	...	...	...	...	...	...	Pays-Bas[2][9]
Poland[8]	75.1	60.1	76.4	62.6	84.5	78.8	68.9	67.3	59.7	40.1	Pologne[8]
Portugal	...	[2]414.5	[2]115.8	108.6	99.2	102.7	120.7	127.2	142.0	126.2	Portugal
Russian Federation[4]	..	472.0	373.9	256.1	122.3	84.5	50.8	45.2	42.3	70.5	Fédération de Russie[4]
Slovakia	..	..	[4]17.7	...	13.4	...	...	...	...	...	Slovaquie
Slovenia	..	...	...	...	...	...	32.3	...	...	30.2	Slovénie
Spain[2][10]	[11]569.1	[11]533.2	[11]465.8	626.0	785.3	1003.2	...	...	...	...	Espagne[2][10]
Sweden[2]	23.3	23.8	20.6	18.1	21.0	22.6	37.7	27.9	27.8	21.4	Suède[2]
Ukraine[4]	..	57.2	50.2	40.2	13.7	5.7	2.7	1.9	2.9	1.8	Ukraine[4]
Oceania	**168**	**175**	**177**	**175**	**174**	**174**	**174**	**174**	**174**	**174**	**Océanie**
Australia[12][13]	168.0	175.4	177.1	174.9	...	...	...	...	...	...	Australie[12][13]
Total	**12757**	**13591**	**13543**	**12411**	**8133**	**8432**	**8130**	**8117**	**7736**	**7575**	**Total**

General Note.
Fabrics of continuous and discontinuous non-cellulosic fibres other than textile glass fibres, including pile and chenille fabrics at loom stage. (SITC, Rev.3: 65310-1, 65320-1, 65330-1, 65340-1, 65390-1).

Remarque générale.
Tissus sortant du métier à tisser, composés de fibres non cellulosiques, continues ou discontinues, autres que les fibres de verre. Cette rubrique comprend les velours, peluches, tissus bouclés et tissus chenille. (CTCI, Rev.3: 65310-1, 65320-1, 65330-1, 65340-1, 65390-1).

[1] Twelve months ending 7 July of the year stated.
[2] Original data in metric tons.
[3] Including finished fabrics and blanketing made of synthetic fibers.
[4] Original data in metres.
[5] Including blankets and carpets of non-cellulosic fibres.
[6] Including fabrics after undergoing finishing processes.
[7] Including mixed fabrics.
[8] After undergoing finishing processes.
[9] Including linen and jute fabrics.
[10] Including woven cellulosic fabrics.
[11] Including household production.
[12] Twelve months ending 30 June of year stated.
[13] Excluding pile and chenille fabrics.

[1] Période de douze mois finissant le 7 juillet de l'année indiquée.
[2] Données d'origine exprimées en tonnes.
[3] Y compris les tissus finis et les couvertures en fibres synthétiques.
[4] Données d'origine exprimées en mètres.
[5] Y compris les couvertures et les tapis en fibres non cellulosiques.
[6] Y compris les tissus, après opérations de finition.
[7] Y compris les tissus mélangés.
[8] Après opérations de finition.
[9] Y compris les tissus de lin et de jute.
[10] Y compris les tissus en fibres cellulosiques.
[11] Y compris la production ménagère.
[12] Période de douze mois finissant le 30 juin de l'année indiquée.
[13] Non compris les tissus bouclés et les tissus chenille.

Woven fabrics of non-cellulosic fibres
Tissus de fibres non cellulosiques

ISIC-BASED CODE - CODE BASE CITI

3211-46A

Unit : Thousand metres   Unité : Milliers de mètres

Country or area	1990	1991	1992	1993	1994	1995	1996	1997	1998	1999	Pays ou zone
Asia	**14097**	**14585**	**11445**	**12795**	**16657**	**14700**	**18123**	**18183**	**18685**	**17811**	**Asie**
Nepal[1]	...	...	11445	12795	16657	14700	18123	18183	18685	17811	Népal[1]
Europe	**162345**	**502724**	**431966**	**320866**	**212428**	**187042**	**146563**	**138306**	**129011**	**133162**	**Europe**
Austria	55212	38049	30762	28338	21650	31517	...	...	...	...	Autriche
Czechoslovakia(former)	50288	35816	..	..	..	..	..	..	..	..	Tchécoslovaquie(anc.)
Czech Republic	..	..	26535	22841	...	...	...	...	...	...	République tchèque
Poland[2]	56845	42614	52216	42420	57780	54047	47309	46232	40675	27497	Pologne[2]
Russian Federation	..	344499	272931	186949	89263	61682	37069	32903	30867	51480	Fédération de Russie
Slovakia	..	..	12906	...	9042	...	...	...	...	...	Slovaquie
Ukraine	..	41746	36616	29344	10005	4134	1988	1404	2132	1278	Ukraine
Total	**176442**	**517309**	**443411**	**333661**	**229085**	**201742**	**164686**	**156489**	**147696**	**150973**	**Total**

General Note.
Fabrics of continuous and discontinuous non-cellulosic fibres other than textile glass fibres, including pile and chenille fabrics at loom stage. (SITC, Rev.3, 65310-1A, 65320-1A, 65330-1A, 65340-1A).

Remarque générale.
Tissus sortant du métier à tisser, composés de fibres non cellulosiques, continues ou discontinues, autres que les fibres de verre. Cette rubrique comprend les velours, peluches, tissus bouclés et tissus chenille. (CTCI, Rev.3: 65310-1A, 65320-1A, 65330-1A, 65340-1A).

[1] Twelve months beginning 16 July of year stated.
[2] After undergoing finishing processes.

[1] Période de douze mois commençant le 16 juillet de l'année indiquée.
[2] Après opérations de finition.

Woven fabrics of non-cellulosic fibres
Tissus de fibres non cellulosiques

ISIC-BASED CODE - CODE BASE CITI

3211-46B

Unit : Metric tons — Unité : Tonnes métriques

Country or area	1990	1991	1992	1993	1994	1995	1996	1997	1998	1999	Pays ou zone
America, North	**56454**	**49626**	**49688**	**61191**	**57877**	**54266**	**69149**	**70808**	**69065**	**69468**	**Amérique du Nord**
Mexico	56454	49626	49688	61191	57877	54266	69149	70808	69065	69468	Mexique
America, South	**43070**	**43070**	**41495**	**43819**	**43362**	**43604**	**43070**	**43070**	**43070**	**43070**	**Amérique du Sud**
Argentina	41164	...	...	...	...	...	...	...	...	...	Argentine
Colombia	...	...	331	2655	2198	2440	...	...	...	...	Colombie
Europe	**602499**	**743654**	**829504**	**812709**	**377678**	**403537**	**365028**	**372225**	**374176**	**386748**	**Europe**
Austria	9925	7048	7438	7392	6679	9723	...	...	...	...	Autriche
Belgium	[1]401348	[1]394840	[1]436978	[1]496669	34990	31926	32988	35006	33784	33442	Belgique
Croatia	...	...	...	...	...	...	...	1042	963	...	Croatie
Finland	2486	1890	1510	1657	1286	993	852	...	...	...	Finlande
France	36460	55020	102047	8088	14028	...	...	...	...	...	France
Germany	...	...	...	...	...	135784	121982	130316	135745	...	Allemagne
Greece [2][3]	...	...	...	3594	7403	2844	...	...	...	...	Grèce [2][3]
Hungary [4]	...	...	...	...	...	...	...	...	8544	23268	Hongrie [4]
Netherlands [5]	20099	19706	18546	...	...	...	...	...	...	...	Pays-Bas [5]
Portugal	45967	50898	...	...	...	...	...	...	...	...	Portugal
Slovakia	...	...	...	...	...	...	...	...	8710	7541	Slovaquie
Spain [7]	[6]63113	[6]59134	[6]51663	69424	87091	111254	...	...	...	...	Espagne [7]
Sweden	2581	2639	2285	2011	2327	2506	4179	3098	3086	2377	Suède
Total	**702023**	**836350**	**920687**	**917719**	**478917**	**501407**	**477247**	**486103**	**486311**	**499286**	**Total**

General Note.
Fabrics of continuous and discontinuous non-cellulosic fibres other than textile glass fibres, including pile and chenille fabrics at loom stage. (SITC, Rev.3: 65310-1B, 65320-1B, 65330-1B, 65340-1B).

[1] Including blankets and carpets of non-cellulosic fibres.
[2] Including fabrics after undergoing finishing processes.
[3] Including mixed fabrics.
[4] After undergoing finishing processes.
[5] Including linen and jute fabrics.
[6] Including household production.
[7] Including woven cellulosic fabrics.

Remarque générale.
Tissus sortant du métier à tisser, composés de fibres non cellulosiques, continues ou discontinues, autres que les fibres de verre. Cette rubrique comprend les velours, peluches, tissus bouclés et tissus chenille. (CTCI, Rev.3: 65310-1B, 65320-1B, 65330-1B, 65340-1B).

[1] Y compris les couvertures et les tapis en fibres non cellulosiques.
[2] Y compris les tissus, après opérations de finition.
[3] Y compris les tissus mélangés.
[4] Après opérations de finition.
[5] Y compris les tissus de lin et de jute.
[6] Y compris la production ménagère.
[7] Y compris les tissus en fibres cellulosiques.

Blankets
Couvertures

ISIC-BASED CODE - CODE BASE CITI

3212-01

Unit : Thousand units   Unité : En milliers

Country or area	1990	1991	1992	1993	1994	1995	1996	1997	1998	1999	Pays ou zone
Africa											**Afrique**
Algeria	2397	2689	2895	3237	3034	2091	1887	1240	1428	1745	Algérie
Burundi	326	276	252	243	...	...	...	...	...	...	Burundi
Egypt	3025	3030	3008	2738	2691	2373	1259	3608	...	...	Egypte
Ethiopia[2]	[1]980	507	265	415	510	488	401	244	194	182	Ethiopie[2]
Kenya	3421	3191	2164	1257	1585	1960	2333	...	...	...	Kenya
Madagascar[3]	3209	2534	2309	3474	1526	2132	1355	1460	1675	...	Madagascar[3]
Malawi	988	1126	1300	894	895	612	725	838	799	478	Malawi
Mozambique	204	240	195	234	130	46	10	128	...	...	Mozambique
Uganda	69	38	50	81	118	177	41	28	178	215	Ouganda
United Rep.Tanzania	535	588	422	450	423	426	383	317	...	...	Rép. Unie de Tanzanie
America, North											**Amérique du Nord**
Mexico[3]	2667	2379	2319	8081	8179	8448	9104	11272	13190	13648	Mexique[3]
United States	...	...	...	...	...	48960	54768	39864	40692	62220	Etats-Unis
America, South											**Amérique du Sud**
Bolivia	107	169	163	392	619	*915	...	...	...	...	Bolivie
Brazil	10791	10454	9586	7938	8010	8645	7932	8495	5706	7005	Brésil
Colombia	...	...	279	531	1088	530	...	...	...	...	Colombie
Ecuador	679	...	2024	1042	1402	1297	615	1882	1708	...	Equateur
Paraguay	35	66	66	...	...	...	...	...	...	...	Paraguay
Asia											**Asie**
Azerbaijan	..	...	1	2	0	0	0	0	0	0	Azerbaïdjan
Bangladesh	4	6	...	...	...	...	...	...	...	...	Bangladesh
China	22956	24000	24571	...	...	...	...	...	...	...	Chine
Indonesia	4476	1891	2344	2151	3690	2342	...	2882	6427	...	Indonésie
Iran(Islamic Rep. of)	[4]3081	[4]3921	[4]4799	[4]4333	[4]3789	[5]4458	[5]5468	[5]6107	[5]5697	...	Iran(Rép. islamique)
Japan[6][7]	2861	2669	2277	1660	1610	1647	1762	1279	...	...	Japon[6][7]
Korea, Republic of[7]	16223	17212	17365	19165	15011	22446	19604	21473	25933	33269	Corée, République de[7]
Kyrgyzstan	..	190	110	103	57	29	8	14	9	6	Kirghizistan
Myanmar[8]	698	373	378	414	437	491	351	171	106	115	Myanmar[8]
Syrian Arab Republic	190	199	408	328	358	399	449	489	385	...	Rép. arabe syrienne
Turkey	1957	2226	2842	3193	2596	3008	2823	4022	5099	5327	Turquie
Turkmenistan	..	64	45	97	72	44	15	19	24	...	Turkménistan
Europe											**Europe**
Austria[9]	173	222	203	213	221	291	...	217	177	192	Autriche[9]
Belarus	..	473	347	318	347	181	216	430	550	583	Bélarus
Belgium[3]	725	1019	493	448	...	...	...	...	...	...	Belgique[3]
Bulgaria	2066	1898	1968	1337	1032	982	717	465	415	769	Bulgarie
Croatia	..	1167	156	138	75	54	57	299	282	...	Croatie
Denmark[10]	62	65	56	9	7	4	6	3	20	15	Danemark[10]
Czech Republic	..	..	..	...	2419	1890	1794	1912	2152	2199	République tchèque
Finland	107	116	126	95	31	54	46	...	...	...	Finlande
France[3]	6467	4934	4392	4044	4660	3800	3550	3430	3516	3624	France[3]
Germany	..	...	...	8392	8963	10926	7957	7553	7398	...	Allemagne
German D.R.(former)	6111	..	..	..	...	...	...	...	...	...	R.D.A. (anc.)
Greece	[3]2511	[3]1408	[3]1288	[3]1930	[3]1327	[3]941	[3]589	[3]737	907	...	Grèce
Hungary	243	190	201	141	231	238	498	458	381	...	Hongrie
Iceland	57	85	66	51	47	...	...	...	...	...	Islande
Latvia	...	...	...	384	194	138	183	178	222	268	Lettonie
Lithuania	...	...	...	...	...	288	327	261	295	296	Lituanie
Portugal	[3]1213	[3]1258	1898	1086	960	791	908	2574	1521	1836	Portugal
Republic of Moldova	..	162	80	[11]93	[11]8	[11]0	[11]0	...	...	...	Rép. de Moldova
Russian Federation	..	4026	2039	1629	1113	587	4511	524	635	384	Fédération de Russie
Slovakia	..	..	...	...	20	47	337	504	[3]252	[3]257	Slovaquie
Slovenia	..	1542	1068	1453	1310	1204	...	...	...	393	Slovénie
Spain	[12]11884	[12]11008	[12]11483	10070	11935	12373	7041	8329	7576	7396	Espagne
Sweden	...	53	...	[1]0	...	...	...	...	...	...	Suède
Switzerland	1011	1204	1197	1097	1135	1287	...	...	...	...	Suisse
United Kingdom	...	...	...	...	3413	3354	3698	3683	2978	...	Royaume-Uni
Yugoslavia	..	150	138	61	57	72	71	63	120	34	Yougoslavie

For general note and footnotes, see end of table.   Voir la fin du tableau pour la remarque générale et les notes.

Blankets (continued)
Couvertures (suite)

ISIC-BASED CODE - CODE BASE CITI

3212-01

Unit : Thousand units   Unité : En milliers

Country or area	1990	1991	1992	1993	1994	1995	1996	1997	1998	1999	Pays ou zone
T.F.Yug.Rep. Macedonia	..	2442	#534	749	764	489	527	468	270	435	L'ex-RY Macédoine

General Note.
Blankets, travelling rugs and coverlets. Specially-shaped rugs and blankets for animals, bedspreads and counterpanes, and quilted or stuffed bed coverings are excluded. (SITC, Rev.3: 65830-0, 77585-0).

[1] Including woollen blankets.
[2] Twelve months ending 7 July of the year stated.
[3] In metric tons.
[4] Production by establishments employing 50 or more persons.
[5] Production by establishments employing 10 or more persons.
[6] Shipments.
[7] In thousand square metres.
[8] Government production only.
[9] 1996 data are confidential.
[10] Sales.
[11] Excluding Transnistria region.
[12] Including household production.

Remarque générale.
Couvertures de lits, couvertures de voyage, couvertures de berceaux, de voitures d'enfants. Cette rubrique ne comprend pas les couvertures de forme spéciale pour animaux, les couvre-lits, les couvre-pieds et les articles de literie rembourrés ou garnis intérieurement de toutes matières. (CTCI. Rev.3: 65830-0, 77585-0).

[1] Y compris les couvertures en laine.
[2] Période de douze mois finissant le 7 juillet de l'année indiquée.
[3] En tonnes métriques.
[4] Production des établissements occupant 50 personnes ou plus.
[5] Production des établissements occupant 10 personnes ou plus.
[6] Expéditions.
[7] En milliers de mètres carrés.
[8] Production de l'Etat seulement.
[9] Pour 1996, les données sont confidentielles.
[10] Ventes.
[11] Non compris la région de Transnistria.
[12] Y compris la production ménagère.

Bed linen, articles
Linge de literie

ISIC-BASED CODE - CODE BASE CITI

3212-04

Unit : Thousand units   Unité : En milliers

Country or area	1990	1991	1992	1993	1994	1995	1996	1997	1998	1999	Pays ou zone
Africa	**12812**	**13583**	**12327**	**11198**	**10598**	**14095**	**11838**	**10751**	**11556**	**11443**	**Afrique**
Algeria	913	703	468	324	...	...	...	...	...	...	Algérie
Egypt	200	243	226	167	142	207	111	84	...	...	Egypte
Ethiopia	...	...	...	...	...	...	32	30	21	7	Ethiopie
South Africa	11676	12614	11610	10684	9831	13263	11093	10035	...	...	Afrique du Sud
America, North	**343551**	**311449**	**339275**	**354439**	**381415**	**397173**	**416199**	**393677**	**390507**	**403416**	**Amérique du Nord**
Mexico	...	...	...	1723	2047	1545	1467	977	879	876	Mexique
United States	341220	309312	337332	352716	379368	395628	414732	392700	389628	402540	Etats-Unis
America, South	**50161**	**48647**	**49537**	**48531**	**49398**	**48210**	**48217**	**48224**	**48041**	**48024**	**Amérique du Sud**
Bolivia	9	12	38	59	0	*0	...	...	...	...	Bolivie
Brazil	45482	44147	...	...	...	...	...	...	...	...	Brésil
Colombia	...	...	3594	3319	2787	3082	...	...	...	...	Colombie
Ecuador	...	...	1090	338	1796	313	191	...	...	...	Equateur
Asia	**17446**	**78798**	**35648**	**27444**	**28400**	**27149**	**24835**	**29571**	**32474**	**27937**	**Asie**
Armenia	..	10937	#137	129	120	41	15	20	5	...	Arménie
Azerbaijan	..	5167	2114	1722	691	283	79	178	146	...	Azerbaïdjan
Bangladesh	561	...	...	...	...	...	...	...	...	...	Bangladesh
Cyprus	*830	*950	1442	...	...	928	857	220	201	...	Chypre
Indonesia	1558	6718	3572	2736	4449	3765	...	...	1206	...	Indonésie
Kazakhstan	..	9543	5900	5786	3328	798	539	576	562	589	Kazakhstan
Kyrgyzstan	..	3163	2536	2964	1264	247	215	411	124	115	Kirghizistan
Syrian Arab Republic	423	131	#1675	2229	2966	2266	2432	2483	1926	...	Rép. arabe syrienne
Tajikistan	..	1912	500	228	957	118	0	0	0	...	Tadjikistan
Turkey	14074	38427	15993	9033	12856	17513	16076	21010	26906	22127	Turquie
Turkmenistan	..	1289	1218	1281	433	629	632	683	837	...	Turkménistan
Europe	**148272**	**330607**	**259653**	**244929**	**187738**	**147754**	**150539**	**140251**	**147058**	**134587**	**Europe**
Austria	1893	2258	2549	1874	1974	1080	1054	1096	1119	1750	Autriche
Belarus	..	13521	10731	7603	4000	3029	2266	3083	3725	3591	Bélarus
Bulgaria	2675	2492	2392	1671	2228	1842	1863	2776	7562	4778	Bulgarie
Croatia	..	1829	1560	1454	2034	1752	826	746	644	...	Croatie
Czech Republic	...	...	...	...	4688	4224	3151	3451	3549	3621	République tchèque
Finland	1825	1531	1556	1596	1115	1143	892	1816	...	1984	Finlande
Germany	..	55274	47994	45118	43972	36757	33963	30619	...	...	Allemagne
Germany(Fed.Rep.)	47128		..	..	..	..	..	..	..	..	Allemagne(Rép.féd.)
German D.R.(former)	16186		..	..	..	..	..	..	..	..	R.D.A. (anc.)
Greece	...	...	...	3910	6762	5876	9918	7170	7785	...	Grèce
Hungary	11279	10330	6955	5435	7564	6502	7861	5335	4111	6098	Hongrie
Iceland	14	7	9	...	...	...	...	...	...	...	Islande
Latvia	..	2351	1185	299	223	230	76	135	164	123	Lettonie
Lithuania	..	...	...	...	...	1989	1945	2441	2599	...	Lituanie
Portugal	...	...	47505	54364	42496	38658	40625	40542	47010	42302	Portugal
Republic of Moldova	..	4926	4171	[1]775	[1]390	[1]41	[1]245	[1]86	[1]32	...	Rép. de Moldova
Russian Federation	..	122532	59908	71901	35171	15136	14871	13572	15155	13617	Fédération de Russie
Slovakia	..	...	...	3470	3579	3314	2489	1866	...	...	Slovaquie
Slovenia	..	2242	1628	1477	1897	1623	835	657	397	...	Slovénie
Spain	13090	11597	11202	9710	11897	14213	18018	18779	22022	19651	Espagne
Sweden	2028	1868	1770	...	...	...	...	...	...	...	Suède
Switzerland	987	930	776	665	620	702	...	...	...	...	Suisse
Ukraine	..	34688	36427	21535	8946	3916	4152	2831	2851	2158	Ukraine
Yugoslavia	..	1188	585	142	386	153	298	153	190	242	Yougoslavie
T.F.Yug.Rep. Macedonia	..	7740	4242	3705	3654	3675	2653	594	282	...	L'ex-RY Macédoine
Total	**572242**	**783084**	**696439**	**686541**	**657549**	**634380**	**651628**	**622474**	**629636**	**625406**	**Total**

General Note.
Articles made of cotton, flax, hemp, ramie or man-made fibres, such as bed sheets, pillow cases, mattress covers etc. Table linens and other furnishing articles are excluded. (SITC, Rev.3: 65841-0, 65842-0, 65843-0).

[1] Excluding Transnistria region.

Remarque générale.
Articles fabriqués en coton, lin, chanvre, ramie ou fibres artificielles, tels que draps de lit, taies d'oreiller, couvre-matelas, etc. Cette rubrique ne comprend pas le linge de table et autres articles d'ameublement. (CTCI, Rev.3, 65841-0, 65842-0, 65843-0).

[1] Non compris la région de Transnistria.

Towelling
Serviettes

ISIC-BASED CODE - CODE BASE CITI

3212-07

Unit : Thousand units   Unité : En milliers

Country or area	1990	1991	1992	1993	1994	1995	1996	1997	1998	1999	Pays ou zone
Africa											**Afrique**
Algeria	387	433	256	143	130	171	163	342	177	181	Algérie
Kenya[1]	299	642	1082	1177	621	1170	3700	...	...	...	Kenya[1]
South Africa	8481	7172	8142	11191	10131	10381	11292	...	...	...	Afrique du Sud
America, North											**Amérique du Nord**
Mexico	...	...	...	11784	12164	11092	15574	21740	39003	43891	Mexique
United States	508512	517896	585468	582204	587688	591756	543444	539280	550392	484692	Etats-Unis
America, South											**Amérique du Sud**
Bolivia	59	50	83	72	78	*21	...	...	...	...	Bolivie
Colombia	...	...	20495	24665	17401	11547	...	24984	23904	...	Colombie
Ecuador	...	...	508	603	507	538	766	899	1064	...	Equateur
Asia											**Asie**
Bangladesh	3093	1466	1161	...	...	...	...	...	...	...	Bangladesh
China	1830000	2109000	2352000	...	...	...	...	...	...	...	Chine
Cyprus	*700	*710	516	...	...	584	387	428	191	217	Chypre
Indonesia	20602	24509	29160	39186	39173	37039	...	22244	19102	...	Indonésie
Japan[1][2]	61856	61899	57905	54088	54560	52380	49313	48746	45704	42798	Japon[1][2]
Korea, Republic of[1]	6453	6088	6427	6245	6496	6995	...	...	...	...	Corée, République de[1]
Myanmar[3]	1434	1156	1250	1306	1358	1416	1823	1343	1368	1263	Myanmar[3]
Syrian Arab Republic	3839	4773	7893	8248	8809	8050	8289	8151	7908	...	Rép. arabe syrienne
Viet Nam	108544	109224	209689	...	...	276000	278000	385000	337000	351000	Viet Nam
Europe											**Europe**
Austria[4]	...	...	...	...	...	...	2584	2644	1929	1528	Autriche[4]
Bulgaria	1201	701	523	477	1260	1004	1054	1037	650	333	Bulgarie
Denmark[5]	...	..	...	34	25	39	38	39	73	111	Danemark[5]
Czech Republic	...	..	...	...	17982	19575	22737	23322	22055	22076	République tchèque
Finland	1610	1424	2470	2273	1400	1706	1135	...	...	...	Finlande
France[1]	1253	1368	5549	1368	4500	4310	4310	4990	5004	4548	France[1]
Germany	..	...	42527	40423	47974	38627	32222	22662	22544	...	Allemagne
Germany(Fed.Rep.)	48993	..	..	..	..	..	..	..	..	..	Allemagne(Rép.féd.)
German D.R.(former)	37193	..	..	..	..	..	..	..	..	..	R.D.A. (anc.)
Greece[1]	1466	1349	1315	..	..	..	..	..	..	..	Grèce[1]
Hungary	5016	3955	1777	1357	722	4245	6200	4806	8104	10457	Hongrie
Iceland	1	1	1	...	...	...	...	...	...	...	Islande
Latvia	..	...	...	3431	10788	12393	12571	14505	14915	14264	Lettonie
Lithuania	..	...	...	...	...	12799	7076	8458	7286	7326	Lituanie
Russian Federation	..	73740	42224	22316	11535	5279	3736	3478	3951	6197	Fédération de Russie
Slovakia	..	...	...	5816	4508	4060	3365	6216	[1]1936	[2]2508	Slovaquie
Slovenia	..	10639	10302	8182	16696	10978	6371	...	...	7166	Slovénie
Spain	26038	20262	16641	10048	13675	17997	...	...	...	...	Espagne
Switzerland	1094	941	601	511	455	618	...	...	...	...	Suisse
T.F.Yug.Rep. Macedonia	..	...	2625	2686	2226	2655	2341	2768	4518	3612	L'ex-RY Macédoine

General Note.
Toilet linen, that is, hand and face towels (including roller towels), bath towels, face cloths and toilet gloves. (SITC, REv.3: 65847-1, 65848-1).

Remarque générale.
Linge de toilette, c'est-à-dire serviettes de toilette, essuie-mains (y compris les touailles), serviettes de bain, débarbouillettes et gants de toilette. (CTCI, Rev.3: 65847-1, 65848-1).

[1] In thousand square metres.
[2] Shipments.
[3] Government production only.
[4] 1995 data are confidential.
[5] Sales.

[1] En milliers de mètres carrés.
[2] Expéditions.
[3] Production de l'Etat seulement.
[4] Pour 1995, les données sont confidentielles.
[5] Ventes.

Knitted fabrics
Etoffes de bonneterie

ISIC-BASED CODE - CODE BASE CITI

3213-01

Unit : Thousand metric tons   Unité : Milliers de tonnes métriques

Country or area	1990	1991	1992	1993	1994	1995	1996	1997	1998	1999	Pays ou zone
Africa	**14**	**34**	**21**	**21**	**2**	**2**	**7**	**4**	**2**	**1**	**Afrique**
Madagascar	...	...	...	...	0.4	0.5	0.6	0.6	0.7	...	Madagascar
Nigeria	14.2	33.4	20.6	20.3	1.5	1.2	...	...	...	...	Nigéria
America, North	**863**	**891**	**944**	**993**	**1011**	**1027**	**890**	**909**	**884**	**854**	**Amérique du Nord**
Mexico	0.5	0.3	0.0	...	0.0	...	...	...	...	...	Mexique
United States	862.0	890.5	943.7	992.4	1011.3	1026.9	889.5	909.0	883.8	853.6	Etats-Unis
America, South	**344**	**332**	**322**	**309**	**347**	**295**	**279**	**264**	**233**	**229**	**Amérique du Sud**
Brazil	...	...	...	...	344.9	292.9	278.9	263.3	231.8	228.5	Brésil
Ecuador	...	...	3.8	2.0	1.7	2.3	0.3	1.1	0.7	...	Equateur
Asia	**212**	**264**	**258**	**273**	**245**	**189**	**277**	**199**	**391**	**273**	**Asie**
Armenia	..	2.6	1.1	0.1	0.1	0.0	0.0	...	0.0	0.0	Arménie
Azerbaijan	..	0.6	1.3	1.2	0.8	0.5	0.3	0.1	0.1	0.0	Azerbaïdjan
Bangladesh	0.6	...	...	...	...	...	...	...	...	...	Bangladesh
Indonesia	32.6	73.7	...	101.5	70.5	7.5	...	12.6	224.4	...	Indonésie
Japan	168.4	170.0	159.6	149.3	151.9	150.2	149.6	151.2	[1]136.4	118.8	Japon
Turkey	10.7	16.1	21.2	20.1	21.3	30.5	52.0	34.0	29.1	22.0	Turquie
Europe	**359**	**457**	**413**	**363**	**360**	**356**	**357**	**372**	**351**	**327**	**Europe**
Austria	13.5	15.2	14.5	15.0	17.3	10.1	11.9	13.5	13.4	12.9	Autriche
Belgium	9.5	10.0	9.2	7.8	...	...	[2]4.9	[2]5.7	[2]6.4	[2]6.5	Belgique
Bulgaria	7.8	4.0	3.4	2.2	1.6	1.7	1.8	1.6	1.3	1.9	Bulgarie
Croatia	..	...	...	...	...	...	...	2.6	2.6	...	Croatie
Czechoslovakia(former)	30.6	18.7	..	..	..	..	..	..	..	..	Tchécoslovaquie(anc.)
Czech Republic	..	..	13.0	13.2	11.5	10.8	9.9	10.1	10.2	10.0	République tchèque
Finland	5.9	5.2	4.6	3.9	5.5	5.0	4.3	2.6	2.5	2.3	Finlande
France	45.3	44.8	49.1	38.2	50.3	...	...	...	...	...	France
Germany	..	94.6	75.5	60.2	56.0	...	58.7	63.5	...	...	Allemagne
Germany(Fed.Rep.)	83.7										Allemagne(Rép.féd.)
Greece	26.3	34.1	38.2	[3]26.1	[3]36.8	41.8	35.0	...	29.5	...	Grèce
Hungary	11.8	7.7	5.6	4.3	6.3	3.4	...	5.3	3.9	4.1	Hongrie
Latvia	..	3.9	...	...	...	...	...	...	...	1.2	Lettonie
Netherlands[4]	6.6	5.6	5.4	...	...	...	...	...	...	...	Pays-Bas[4]
Norway	...	...	...	...	...	...	...	1.0	...	...	Norvège
Portugal	85.0	58.1	56.2	85.7	89.2	83.4	94.9	94.3	99.7	87.6	Portugal
Russian Federation	..	78.5	55.5	41.2	22.2	14.7	6.9	6.6	6.0	9.7	Fédération de Russie
Slovakia	..	..	*1.0	*0.8	*2.0	*2.8	*4.8	*3.0	1.3	1.0	Slovaquie
Slovenia	..	3.6	2.6	3.0	2.5	1.9	0.1	0.5	0.4	0.4	Slovénie
Spain	[5]27.1	[5]25.4	[5]33.3	23.2	25.7	38.9	53.2	63.0	74.3	71.8	Espagne
Sweden[4]	4.4	2.0	2.0	2.1	2.3	2.7	3.4	7.9	6.6	6.7	Suède[4]
Ukraine	..	39.0	35.2	22.0	9.6	3.3	1.6	1.0	0.6	0.5	Ukraine
Yugoslavia	..	0.2	0.0	0.0	0.1	0.1	0.0	0.0	0.0	...	Yougoslavie
T.F.Yug.Rep. Macedonia	..	2.7	2.2	1.6	1.3	1.0	1.0	0.8	0.9	0.7	L'ex-RY Macédoine
Oceania	**24**	**27**	**26**	**24**	**25**	**24**	**24**	**24**	**23**	**23**	**Océanie**
Australia[6]	18.1	20.3	19.3	17.5	...	...	...	...	...	...	Australie[6]
New Zealand	6.4	6.7	6.7	6.4	6.1	5.2	[7]5.2	[7]4.9	[7]4.2	[7]3.7	Nouvelle-Zélande
Total	**1816**	**2004**	**1984**	**1982**	**1990**	**1893**	**1834**	**1773**	**1884**	**1706**	**Total**

General Note.
Knitted or crocheted fabrics (of all textile fibres), neither elastic nor rubberized. Knitted garments are excluded. (SITC,Rev.3: 65500-0).

[1] Shipments.
[2] Incomplete coverage.
[3] Excluding socks for women and girls.
[4] Knitted fabrics for sale only.
[5] Including household production.
[6] Twelve months ending 30 June of year stated.
[7] Twelve months ending 30 September of year stated.

Remarque générale.
Etoffes de bonneterie (en tous textiles), ni élastiques ni caoutchoutées. Cette rubrique ne comprend pas les vêtements tricotés. (CTCI, Rev.3: 65500-0).

[1] Expéditions.
[2] Couverture incomplète.
[3] Non compris les bas de dames et de fillettes.
[4] Etoffes de bonneterie destinées à la vente seulement.
[5] Y compris la production ménagère.
[6] Période de douze mois finissant le 30 juin de l'année indiquée.
[7] Période de douze mois finissant le 30 septembre de l'année indiquée.

Socks and other stockings, except women's stockings
Bas, chaussettes et socquettes

ISIC-BASED CODE - CODE BASE CITI

3213-04

Unit : Million pairs

Unité : Millions de paires

Country or area	1990	1991	1992	1993	1994	1995	1996	1997	1998	1999	Pays ou zone
Africa	**29**	**48**	**48**	**47**	**41**	**44**	**46**	**38**	**28**	**30**	**Afrique**
Algeria	[1]1.7	[1]3.6	[1]3.6	[1]3.3	[1]2.2	[1]2.1	[1]1.4	[1]0.7	0.9	[1]1.0	Algérie
Egypt	4.4	3.4	4.3	2.7	1.5	0.8	0.2	0.1	...	...	Egypte
Mozambique	[1]0.3	[1]0.5	0.1	0.1	0.0	...	...	...	...	...	Mozambique
South Africa	22.0	40.2	39.7	40.5	36.6	41.2	43.7	36.9	26.6	28.8	Afrique du Sud
United Rep.Tanzania	0.4	0.3	0.3	0.3	...	...	...	...	...	...	Rép. Unie de Tanzanie
America, North	**60**	**52**	**51**	**96**	**101**	**78**	**97**	**106**	**104**	**97**	**Amérique du Nord**
Mexico	60.2	51.7	51.3	96.1	101.3	78.1	96.5	106.5	104.3	96.7	Mexique
America, South	**152**	**160**	**158**	**163**	**157**	**150**	**149**	**129**	**133**	**137**	**Amérique du Sud**
Bolivia	0.2	0.1	0.2	1.9	2.3	*2.6	...	...	...	...	Bolivie
Brazil	[2][3]66.1	[2][3]73.7	[2][3]71.5	[2][3]67.9	[2][3]68.0	69.4	61.2	39.6	42.1	47.5	Brésil
Chile	23.0	23.7	25.0	24.8	22.5	24.0	25.2	26.4	26.9	26.0	Chili
Colombia	...	...	59.2	67.3	62.9	53.1	...	...	...	...	Colombie
Ecuador	...	...	1.7	1.2	1.1	0.8	0.0	0.0	0.0	...	Equateur
Asia	**1920**	**2400**	**2212**	**2205**	**2162**	**2027**	**2084**	**2112**	**1935**	**1959**	**Asie**
Armenia	..	26.9	14.1	9.8	5.1	3.0	7.1	1.6	0.7	0.5	Arménie
Azerbaijan	..	35.1	32.3	28.4	20.0	8.3	2.1	3.4	1.8	1.0	Azerbaïdjan
Bangladesh	3.0	3.1	3.4	...	...	...	...	...	...	...	Bangladesh
China[1]	1120.0	1268.4	1112.7	...	...	...	...	...	...	...	Chine[1]
Hong Kong SAR	23.0	19.6	18.3	14.6	6.4	10.9	6.5	3.6	3.4	1.6	Hong-Kong RAS
China, Macao, SAR	..	..	..	1.4	...	...	...	...	...	...	Chine, Macao PAS
Cyprus	*2.2	*2.3	1.9	...	...	1.4	1.6	1.5	0.6	0.6	Chypre
Georgia	..	...	9.5	6.2	1.1	0.5	0.2	0.1	0.0	0.0	Géorgie
Indonesia	50.5	57.2	76.3	57.6	81.3	52.1	...	131.1	33.9	...	Indonésie
Iran(Islamic Rep. of)	[4]78.2	[4]33.4	[5]12.1	[4]15.7	[5]18.4	[4]31.0	[4]29.1	[4]35.4	[4]39.6	...	Iran(Rép. islamique)
Japan[6]	440.8	455.4	450.0	434.9	421.0	413.2	411.8	388.7	349.6	320.7	Japon[6]
Kazakhstan	..	83.2	74.4	71.5	41.0	11.5	6.0	4.1	2.0	1.3	Kazakhstan
Korea, Republic of	100.9	110.4	114.7	96.8	108.4	108.6	...	...	...	...	Corée, République de
Kyrgyzstan	..	25.6	29.0	24.2	15.3	8.8	12.6	7.5	5.4	4.1	Kirghizistan
Malaysia[1]	31.7	31.1	32.0	31.0	26.5	10.6	22.8	20.2	21.9	17.9	Malaisie[1]
Myanmar[7]	0.3	0.5	0.3	0.2	0.2	...	...	...	...	...	Myanmar[7]
Syrian Arab Republic[1]	30.1	32.3	39.0	40.7	44.5	52.1	61.8	59.9	57.9	...	Rép. arabe syrienne[1]
Tajikistan	..	49.2	35.8	34.7	16.8	4.5	3.5	1.5	2.1	2.1	Tadjikistan
Turkey	35.5	43.1	34.9	46.6	66.9	60.3	88.1	99.4	84.0	117.3	Turquie
Turkmenistan	..	12.7	10.8	7.6	6.3	10.0	13.2	10.0	3.4	...	Turkménistan
Uzbekistan	..	102.6	106.2	108.8	106.9	66.1	68.6	62.8	...	...	Ouzbékistan
Viet Nam	2.6	2.7	2.7	...	...	...	...	...	...	...	Viet Nam
Europe	**1651**	**2755**	**2568**	**2207**	**1889**	**2113**	**1867**	**1776**	**1752**	**1876**	**Europe**
Austria	...	...	...	...	...	34.8	46.3	17.8	13.8	14.5	Autriche
Belarus	..	97.9	87.1	80.3	44.1	30.2	33.1	37.1	51.2	60.2	Bélarus
Belgium	10.6	9.8	9.7	8.8	7.5	9.1	8.2	7.7	...	[8]4.3	Belgique
Bulgaria	36.7	18.0	19.0	17.9	27.0	25.4	24.0	21.2	[1]20.8	[1]19.0	Bulgarie
Croatia	..	14.9	11.6	9.3	9.5	9.3	9.2	5.7	6.0	...	Croatie
Czech Republic	..	..	66.2	56.8	52.8	...	...	...	...	...	République tchèque
Estonia	..	16.0	11.7	7.9	9.3	5.7	6.0	5.4	4.0	3.6	Estonie
Finland	14.4	12.0	11.7	11.2	11.9	12.4	15.1	13.9	13.5	11.9	Finlande
France[10]	[9]224.7	[9]213.0	[9]207.6	[9]184.9	#189.0	...	193.5	197.1	196.9	179.4	France[10]
Germany		109.4	90.8	77.2	88.7	419.5	309.4	297.8	293.6	...	Allemagne
Germany(Fed.Rep.)	59.8	..	..	..	..	..	..	..	..	..	Allemagne(Rép.féd.)
German D.R.(former)[1]	310.1	..	..	..	..	..	..	..	..	..	R.D.A. (anc.)[1]
Greece	18.7	19.6	16.4	[11]13.7	[11]13.8	[11]11.0	[11]24.0	[11]25.6	...	...	Grèce
Hungary[3]	32.4	31.5	22.2	18.1	14.0	8.2	...	...	...	...	Hongrie[3]
Iceland	0.5	0.5	0.4	...	...	...	0.4	0.4	0.4	0.5	Islande
Latvia	..	28.6	16.5	7.0	8.5	11.7	10.5	6.6	5.2	17.6	Lettonie
Lithuania	..	81.2	63.3	49.8	42.2	#29.0	21.4	11.3	20.8	25.5	Lituanie
Netherlands	11.0	8.3	7.6	8.4	5.9	5.5	5.0	...	...	...	Pays-Bas
Norway	1.2	1.4	1.4	1.4	...	1.1	...	1.1	1.1	*0.9	Norvège
Poland	262.3	216.9	169.3	132.6	142.3	147.5	149.8	177.7	176.9	167.4	Pologne
Portugal	77.6	44.5	90.0	106.7	135.7	...	...	...	...	...	Portugal
Republic of Moldova	..	37.1	26.8	[12]19.4	[12]6.8	[12]2.8	[12]2.4	[12]1.0	[12]0.6	[12]0.5	Rép. de Moldova

For general note and footnotes, see end of table.

Voir la fin du tableau pour la remarque générale et les notes.

Socks and other stockings, except women's stockings (continued)
Bas, chaussettes et socquettes (suite)

ISIC-BASED CODE - CODE BASE CITI
3213-04

Unit : Million pairs

Unité : Millions de paires

Country or area	1990	1991	1992	1993	1994	1995	1996	1997	1998	1999	Pays ou zone
Romania[1]	199.4	242.9	211.8	213.9	216.0	242.4	196.8	181.0	168.6	157.2	Roumanie[1]
Russian Federation	..	742.8	626.0	552.4	352.7	287.5	209.3	178.0	153.8	263.4	Fédération de Russie
Slovakia	..	..	...	19.6	20.2	23.8	27.4	23.1	17.2	15.4	Slovaquie
Slovenia	..	4.9	2.8	3.2	3.3	2.9	9.5	11.8	23.8	18.0	Slovénie
Spain	[1][13]258.5	[1][13]260.3	[1][13]265.0	[14]202.1	[14]227.0	[14]222.9	...	...	...	...	Espagne
Sweden[1]	12.7	13.0	11.3	11.8	...	...	...	...	...	...	Suède[1]
Switzerland	44.1	40.5	40.9	31.9	29.4	29.9	...	...	...	...	Suisse
Ukraine	..	392.6	380.9	297.1	161.5	118.6	66.8	45.7	38.9	36.6	Ukraine
Yugoslavia	..	25.8	13.3	7.2	7.6	7.3	4.5	3.4	4.0	2.8	Yougoslavie
T.F.Yug.Rep. Macedonia	..	2.4	1.3	0.9	0.7	0.2	0.1	...	...	...	L'ex-RY Macédoine
USSR (former)	1309.6	..	..	..	..	..	..	..	..	..	URSS (anc.)
Oceania	**80**	**80**	**75**	**79**	**76**	**75**	**77**	**77**	**77**	**77**	**Océanie**
Australia[15]	60.9	60.2	54.6	56.9	...	...	...	...	...	...	Australie[15]
New Zealand[16]	...	...	20.3	22.0	18.3	16.7	...	...	...	...	Nouvelle-Zélande[16]
Total	**5202**	**5494**	**5111**	**4797**	**4426**	**4487**	**4321**	**4239**	**4029**	**4177**	**Total**

General Note.

Knitted or crocheted socks for men, women and children, extending from the ankle to below the knee, and knitted or crocheted stockings for men and children extending above the knee, of man-made fibres, cotton, wool or other textile fibres, made in knitting mills. Elastic and rubberized socks of all kinds and stockings for men and children are excluded, but those having rubber threads or elastic forming merely a supporting band are included. (SITC, Rev.3: 84622-1, 84629-0).

Remarque générale.

Bas, chaussettes et socquettes en bonneterie, faits en usine, pour hommes, femmes et enfants, montant jusqu'à la cheville, à mi-jambe ou jusqu'au-dessous du genou, et bas en bonneterie, pour hommes et enfants montant plus haut que le genou, en fibres artificielles, en coton, en laine ou en d'autres fibres textiles. Cette rubrique ne comprend pas les chaussettes élastiques et caoutchoutées de tous types et les bas élastiques et caoutchoutés pour hommes et enfants, mais comprend les chaussettes et les bas possédant des fils de caoutchouc ou des élastiques qui ne constituent qu'une bande de serrage. (CTCI, Rev.3: 84622-1,84629-0).

[1] Including women's stockings.
[2] Men's socks and stockings only.
[3] Including elastic socks and stockings.
[4] Production by establishments employing 10 or more persons.
[5] Production by establishments employing 50 or more persons.
[6] Including seamless stockings.
[7] Socks only.
[8] Incomplete coverage.
[9] Put up for sale. Excluding own consumption.
[10] 1995 data are confidential.
[11] Excluding socks for women and girls.
[12] Excluding Transnistria region.
[13] Including household production.
[14] Including pantyhose.
[15] Twelve months ending 30 June of year stated.
[16] Twelve months ending 30 September of year stated.

[1] Y compris les bas de dames.
[2] Bas, chaussettes et socquettes en bonneterie pour hommes seulement.
[3] Y compris les bas et chaussettes élastiques.
[4] Production des établissements occupant 10 personnes ou plus.
[5] Production des établissements occupant 50 personnes ou plus.
[6] Y compris les bas sans couture.
[7] Chaussettes seulement.
[8] Couverture incomplète.
[9] Pour la vente au mètre, auto-consommation exclue.
[10] Pour 1995, les données sont confidentielles.
[11] Non compris les bas de dames et de fillettes.
[12] Non compris la région de Transnistria.
[13] Y compris la production ménagère.
[14] Y compris les bas-culottes.
[15] Période de douze mois finissant le 30 juin de l'année indiquée.
[16] Période de douze mois finissant le 30 septembre de l'année indiquée.

Women's stockings
Bas de dames

ISIC-BASED CODE - CODE BASE CITI

3213-07

Unit : Million pairs | | | | | | | | | | Unité : Millions de paires

Country or area	1990	1991	1992	1993	1994	1995	1996	1997	1998	1999	Pays ou zone
Africa	**84**	**86**	**62**	**83**	**77**	**79**	**89**	**72**	**51**	**48**	**Afrique**
South Africa	84.3	86.5	62.3	82.7	77.0	78.9	88.9	72.1	51.5	47.6	Afrique du Sud
America, North	**170**	**188**	**190**	**219**	**214**	**184**	**231**	**210**	**180**	**174**	**Amérique du Nord**
Mexico	169.5	188.0	189.7	219.2	214.3	184.5	230.8	210.5	179.6	173.8	Mexique
America, South	**182**	**178**	**183**	**200**	**195**	**168**	**152**	**144**	**131**	**144**	**Amérique du Sud**
Bolivia	3.3	2.8	2.9	2.5	2.1	*2.7	...	...	...	...	Bolivie
Brazil	81.5	81.6	89.3	101.5	102.4	87.0	87.2	83.4	73.6	86.6	Brésil
Chile	44.0	45.6	52.3	49.9	45.6	44.3	44.8	40.7	38.0	37.7	Chili
Colombia	...	...	14.5	19.7	16.4	20.1	...	...	...	...	Colombie
Ecuador	...	...	24.2	26.5	29.0	14.4	0.0	0.0	0.0	...	Equateur
Asia	**1689**	**1555**	**1597**	**1458**	**1270**	**1119**	**1067**	**935**	**803**	**743**	**Asie**
Armenia	..	1.6	0.1	0.0	0.3	0.0	0.0	0.0	...	0.0	Arménie
Azerbaijan	..	3.1	2.1	0.9	0.4	0.3	0.1	0.2	0.0	0.1	Azerbaïdjan
Hong Kong SAR[1][2][3]	75.9	27.8	31.7	...	2.0	1.3	0.5	...	...	...	Hong-Kong RAS[1][2][3]
Japan[4]	1089.6	978.2	999.0	937.2	842.6	734.4	714.4	629.1	550.2	499.2	Japon[4]
Kazakhstan	..	5.1	2.2	1.1	0.4	0.1	0.0	...	...	...	Kazakhstan
Korea, Republic of	391.2	400.4	421.5	344.3	314.8	257.0	223.6	164.4	115.6	116.1	Corée, République de
Kyrgyzstan	..	0.9	0.6	0.7	0.3	0.3	0.5	0.2	0.1	0.0	Kirghizistan
Tajikistan	..	0.5	0.3	0.2	0.1	0.0	0.0	0.0	0.0	0.0	Tadjikistan
Turkey[1]	131.9	137.4	139.5	150.6	109.5	125.6	127.9	141.3	136.4	127.6	Turquie[1]
Europe	**977**	**1307**	**1155**	**1087**	**1042**	**990**	**864**	**866**	**844**	**748**	**Europe**
Austria	[5]26.5	[5]32.6	[5]30.6	[5]32.0	[5]30.2	15.3	14.4	17.4	12.6	5.5	Autriche
Belarus	..	6.8	10.0	4.7	1.9	2.3	1.1	1.6	2.2	2.1	Bélarus
Belgium	13.2	12.0	10.0	8.8	...	...	...	...	...	...	Belgique
Bulgaria	7.3	5.2	8.4	7.5	4.7	3.4	4.2	4.4	...	...	Bulgarie
Croatia		17.2	16.0	12.0	12.5	10.9	12.7	12.1	10.8	...	Croatie
Czechoslovakia(former)[5]	109.8	107.2	..	..	..	..	..	..	..	..	Tchécoslovaquie(anc.)[5]
Czech Republic	..	..	66.2	..	..	..	..	..	...	...	République tchèque
Estonia	..	6.3	4.6	2.5	2.0	1.2	0.9	0.6	0.5	0.4	Estonie
Finland	5.2	3.2	3.2	2.8	2.4	2.8	1.6	...	...	2.6	Finlande
France[6]	325.0	341.5	328.1	304.8	296.2	...	203.3	164.3	141.2	119.9	France[6]
Germany	..	114.0	92.9	96.8	88.9	110.8	65.8	77.4	89.1	...	Allemagne
Germany(Fed.Rep.)	99.7	...	...	...	...	...	...	...	...	...	Allemagne(Rép.féd.)
Greece	5.0	4.4	3.4	[2]5.8	[2]4.8	[2]4.4	[2]12.5	[2]29.4	...	...	Grèce
Hungary	7.4	3.9	1.0	0.8	1.3	0.6	...	...	...	...	Hongrie
Ireland[7]	77.7	...	...	...	...	...	...	...	...	...	Irlande[7]
Latvia	..	7.6	2.9	4.7	11.4	14.5	15.4	16.8	16.2	16.2	Lettonie
Lithuania	..	...	...	...	...	9.3	6.2	1.5	10.1	12.9	Lituanie
Poland	7.1	3.9	2.7	1.8	1.2	1.4	1.1	1.2	4.7	3.0	Pologne
Portugal	103.9	81.3	32.4	31.6	33.9	...	...	...	...	...	Portugal
Republic of Moldova	..	2.4	1.1	[8]0.4	[8]0.2	[8]0.1	[8]0.1	[8]0.0	[8]0.0	...	Rép. de Moldova
Romania	65.3	117.9	113.0	110.6	107.5	140.2	98.3	94.9	79.2	62.7	Roumanie
Russian Federation	..	33.2	28.0	20.4	10.5	9.5	3.8	3.5	3.1	5.2	Fédération de Russie
Slovakia	..	..	21.1	...	...	...	...	...	...	...	Slovaquie
Slovenia	..	122.1	120.5	123.0	106.4	94.0	93.4	...	...	48.3	Slovénie
Spain[9]	123.5	124.2	129.1	...	...	...	...	...	...	...	Espagne[9]
Ukraine	..	23.5	15.6	9.7	2.5	2.8	1.9	1.1	0.8	0.9	Ukraine
Yugoslavia	..	57.6	33.6	12.1	17.4	17.4	26.1	34.0	47.5	54.3	Yougoslavie
USSR (former)	132.4	..	..	..	..	..	..	..	..	..	URSS (anc.)
Oceania	**92**	**81**	**83**	**85**	**70**	**59**	**67**	**55**	**48**	**43**	**Océanie**
Australia[10]	92.4	80.7	83.3	85.4	[11]70.3	[11]58.7	[11]66.9	[11]55.4	[11]48.3	[11]43.0	Australie[10]
Total	**3326**	**3395**	**3270**	**3132**	**2869**	**2599**	**2470**	**2283**	**2058**	**1900**	**Total**

For general note and footnotes, see end of table.   Voir la fin du tableau pour la remarque générale et les notes.

Women's stockings (continued)
Bas de dames (suite)

General Note.

Knitted or crocheted women's stockings extending above the knee, of man-made fibres, silk, cotton, wool or other textile fibres, made in knitting mills.
Elastic and rubberized stockings are excluded, but those having rubber threads or elastic forming merely a supporting band are included.
(SITC, Rev.3: 84622-2).

[1] Including pantyhose.
[2] Including socks for women and girls.
[3] Beginning 1997, data are confidential.
[4] Including seamless stockings.
[5] Including socks and other stockings.
[6] 1995 data are confidential.
[7] Including tights.
[8] Excluding Transnistria region.
[9] Including household production.
[10] Twelve months ending 30 June of year stated.
[11] Including pantyhose and tights.

Remarque générale.

Bas en bonneterie, pour dames, faits en usine, montant plus haut que le genou, en fibres artificielles, en soie, en coton, en laine ou en d'autres fibres textiles. Cette rubrique ne comprend pas les bas élastiques ou caoutchoutés, mais comprend les bas possédant des fils de caoutchouc ou des élastiques qui ne constituent qu'une bande de serrage. (CTCI, Rev.3: 84622-2).

[1] Y compris les bas-culottes.
[2] Y compris les bas de dames et de fillettes.
[3] A partir de 1997, les données sont confidentielles
[4] Y compris les bas sans couture.
[5] Y compris les bas, chaussettes et socquettes.
[6] Pour 1995, les données sont confidentielles.
[7] Y compris les collants.
[8] Non compris la région de Transnistria.
[9] Y compris la production ménagère.
[10] Période de douze mois finissant le 30 juin de l'année indiquée.
[11] Y compris les bas-culottes et les collants.

Knitted undergarments
Sous-vêtements en bonneterie

ISIC-BASED CODE - CODE BASE CITI

3213-10

Unit : Thousand units   Unité : En milliers

Country or area	1990	1991	1992	1993	1994	1995	1996	1997	1998	1999	Pays ou zone
Africa	**5622**	**5798**	**5172**	**3114**	**3134**	**3037**	**2295**	**1581**	**1753**	**1759**	**Afrique**
Algeria	[1]5622	[1]5798	[1]5172	3114	3134	3037	2295	1581	1753	1759	Algérie
America, North	**12631**	**13540**	**14449**	**10281**	**23211**	**13286**	**14936**	**20288**	**18986**	**19248**	**Amérique du Nord**
Mexico	...	...	...	10281	23211	13286	14936	20288	18986	19248	Mexique
America, South	**8811**	**30816**	**38134**	**36746**	**30862**	**35220**	**31788**	**35989**	**30381**	**44335**	**Amérique du Sud**
Bolivia	135	175	29	149	0	*0	...	...	...	...	Bolivie
Colombia	4807	...	33631	31592	26967	33122	...	31816	24606	...	Colombie
Ecuador	...	...	4474	5005	3895	2098	5120	4169	5775	...	Equateur
Asia	**691192**	**864578**	**813862**	**713721**	**640808**	**661247**	**607612**	**552909**	**501357**	**483665**	**Asie**
Azerbaijan	..	18923	7092	6335	6624	2934	402	679	1255	333	Azerbaïdjan
Bangladesh	213		...	...	...	...	...	...	...	...	Bangladesh
Georgia	..	...	3504	1930	209	218	151	69	...	...	Géorgie
Indonesia	6190	22085	...	...	...	...	...	...	...	...	Indonésie
Japan[2][3]	341021	350491	336785	329766	306911	321115	299679	286198		...	Japon[2][3]
Kazakhstan	..	80196	47526	29902	19715	6731	2261	1358	295	224	Kazakhstan
Korea, Republic of	343768	365393	384550	315447	284915	309677	285707	247381	186724	174132	Corée, République de
Kyrgyzstan	..	13482	12988	8609	3061	1027	549	503	136	57	Kirghizistan
Tajikistan	..	4641	3527	3575	2470	1589	696	76	248	391	Tadjikistan
Turkmenistan	..	7176	3539	3806	2552	3605	3816	2294	2127	...	Turkménistan
Europe	**1044276**	**1753592**	**1401075**	**1220042**	**940957**	**782893**	**762739**	**722828**	**699003**	**669255**	**Europe**
Austria[4]	21071	17792	18093	16530	11245	#42616	40989	34474	...	25589	Autriche[4]
Belarus	..	120431	98079	64791	32112	21659	21513	25352	37177	39530	Bélarus
Belgium	12972	11664	9874	10068	[5]3788	[5]4050	[5]3871	[5]3101	[5]3145	[5]2844	Belgique
Bulgaria	60091	24053	18856	13451	13696	11178	10199	6519	8218	6894	Bulgarie
Croatia	..	34820	25476	26228	23765	21641	22956	10815	14546	...	Croatie
Czechoslovakia(former)	61042	41851			..	..	..	..	...	..	Tchécoslovaquie(anc.)
Czech Republic	..	...	19248	18723	17614	...	...	...	...	...	République tchèque
Estonia	..	17327	12558	4746	2884	3575	3147	4167	4064	3347	Estonie
Finland	22188	18025	16690	16902	16379	15443	17047	3581	3383	3990	Finlande
France	137694	127542	119512	124497	76984					...	France
Germany	..	220792	192555	201297	155425	57551	56260	59147	55790	...	Allemagne
Germany(Fed.Rep.)	178528		..	..	..	..	..	..	...	...	Allemagne(Rép.féd.)
German D.R.(former)	129124		..	..	..	..	..	..	...	..	R.D.A. (anc.)
Greece[6]	84483	78826	77746	53341	46127	48234	79623	...	47315	...	Grèce[6]
Hungary	31076	27027	34064	38963	48040	49627	...	45492	42376	43779	Hongrie
Iceland	43	32	24							...	Islande
Latvia	..	19473	9132	2195	2645	1756	2979	3303	3823	2604	Lettonie
Lithuania	..	36819	22195	12073	11080	10082	12010	11449	19020	15501	Lituanie
Netherlands	44700	47390	45130	43135	34118	31706	...	...	...	...	Pays-Bas
Norway	...	...	...	...	...	1169	1057	1463	...	...	Norvège
Poland	81843	53338	38817	36698	57439	57691	66927	70909	73754	70355	Pologne
Portugal	...	...	49975	60853	55580	49420	45404	55169	61428	67619	Portugal
Russian Federation	..	ꞏ446318	281555	201239	124123	73261	41455	38244	31412	53424	Fédération de Russie
Slovakia	..	..	10203	17250	6930	5897	...	...	2755	1900	Slovaquie
Slovenia	..	4058	4562	1302	1334	1069	1279	757	862	1395	Slovénie
Spain	[7]97133	[7]102306	[7]100089	135800	134740	137086	...	...	...	...	Espagne
Sweden	11392	8733	1037	948	775	717	...	...	1	93	Suède
Ukraine	..	210611	168348	95061	41032	18807	7899	5120	3346	5165	Ukraine
United Kingdom[8]	16869	18481	...	...	...	...	...	...	...	...	Royaume-Uni[8]
Yugoslavia	..	11135	8352	5013	4164	2515	2124	2572	2918	1620	Yougoslavie
Oceania	**74926**	**74926**	**74926**	**74926**	**74926**	**74926**	**74926**	**74926**	**74926**	**74926**	**Océanie**
Australia[9][10]	...	...	74926	...	...	...	...	...	...	...	Australie[9][10]
Total	**1837458**	**2743250**	**2347618**	**2058829**	**1713897**	**1570608**	**1494295**	**1408521**	**1326406**	**1293188**	**Total**

For general note and footnotes, see end of table.   Voir la fin du tableau pour la remarque générale et les notes.

Knitted undergarments (continued)
Sous-vêtements en bonneterie (suite)

ISIC-BASED CODE - CODE BASE CITI
3213-10

General Note.
Knitted or crocheted undergarments made in knitting mills, such as undershirts, pyjamas, night-gowns, drawers, slips, petticoats, camisoles, theatrical flesh tights. Elastic and rubberized undergarments (corsets, brassieres, braces etc.) are excluded. (SITC, Rev.3: 84381-0, 84382-0, 84481-0, 84482-0, 84483-0, 84512-1, 84621-0).

[1] Including knitted sports shirts.
[2] Excluding night gowns.
[3] Shipments.
[4] 1998 data are confidential.
[5] Incomplete coverage.
[6] Excluding knitted under-shirts, men's and boys'.
[7] Including household production.
[8] Including knitted sports shirts and underwear for children.
[9] Twelve months ending 30 June of year stated.
[10] Excluding shirts.

Remarque générale.
Sous-vêtements en bonneterie, faits en usine, tels que gilets, pyjamas, chemises de nuit, caleçons, combinaisons, jupons, chemises américaines, collants. Cette rubrique ne comprend pas les sous-vêtements élastiques ou caoutchoutés (corsets, soutien-gorge, bretelles etc.). (CTCI, Rev.3: 84381-0, 84382-0, 84481-0, 84482-0, 84483-0, 84512-1, 84621-0).

[1] Y compris les chemisettes en bonneterie.
[2] Non compris les chemises de nuit.
[3] Expéditions.
[4] Pour 1998, les données sont confidentielles.
[5] Couverture incomplète.
[6] Non compris les chemisettes en bonneterie pour hommes et garçonnets.
[7] Y compris la production ménagère.
[8] Y compris les chemisettes en bonneterie et les sous-vêtements pour enfants.
[9] Période de douze mois finissant le 30 juin de l'année indiquée.
[10] Non compris les chemises et chemisettes.

Knitted sports shirts
Chemisettes en bonneterie

ISIC-BASED CODE - CODE BASE CITI

3213-13

Unit : Thousand units

Unité : En milliers

Country or area	1990	1991	1992	1993	1994	1995	1996	1997	1998	1999	Pays ou zone
Africa	**6500**	**6410**	**4452**	**5196**	**4258**	**4394**	**4274**	**4042**	**3809**	**3577**	**Afrique**
South Africa	6500	6410	4452	5196	4258	4394	...	...	...	...	Afrique du Sud
America, North	**1358146**	**1221394**	**1412386**	**1194596**	**1283081**	**1240926**	**1223070**	**1205365**	**1187702**	**1170063**	**Amérique du Nord**
Mexico	...	...	...	476	581	614	448	432	458	508	Mexique
United States	1357584	1220844	1411848	1194120	1282500	...	...	...	...	...	Etats-Unis
America, South	**393**	**372**	**291**	**299**	**544**	**154**	**307**	**249**	**222**	**200**	**Amérique du Sud**
Colombia	...	...	291	299	544	154	...	249	...	...	Colombie
Asia	**43757**	**43061**	**53049**	**46449**	**45741**	**45340**	**42183**	**35995**	**30672**	**27000**	**Asie**
Georgia	..	...	[1]7798	[1]3244	[1]992	[1]429	[1]188	[1]76	[1]59	14	Géorgie
Indonesia	565	...	...	...	...	...	...	...	...	...	Indonésie
Japan[2]	31130	28593	31406	30835	31903	34526	33222	27660	25733	20979	Japon[2]
Malaysia	12062	10992	13280	11805	12281	9820	8208	7694	4315	5442	Malaisie
Europe	**77269**	**92572**	**88847**	**88530**	**77421**	**84333**	**85758**	**85849**	**88132**	**88949**	**Europe**
Austria	0	...	...	...	...	#1838	1516	1165	2058	2334	Autriche
Belgium	2287	2022	1915	1884	...	...	...	...	...	...	Belgique
Croatia	..	...	...	...	...	...	...	164	172	...	Croatie
Denmark[3]	...	...	4	39	57	262	143	23	21	...	Danemark[3]
Germany	..	12852	14970	14729	10663	...	...	...	...	...	Allemagne
Germany(Fed.Rep.)	15025	..	...	..	...	..	...	..	...	..	Allemagne(Rép.féd.)
Greece[4]	...	...	...	1880	2097	3212	6434	6916	...	...	Grèce[4]
Hungary	...	...	...	...	...	...	...	947	720	798	Hongrie
Latvia	..	...	...	...	...	...	...	...	...	330	Lettonie
Norway	156	237	232	227	...	...	...	...	...	...	Norvège
Portugal	...	...	39334	41713	36125	...	...	...	...	...	Portugal
Slovakia	..	...	...	...	...	...	54	45	266	573	Slovaquie
Slovenia	..	1498	1922	3356	1340	1443	...	...	...	48	Slovénie
Spain[4]	...	...	...	18716	19959	20898	...	...	...	...	Espagne[4]
Ukraine	..	14176	7573	2946	1901	525	232	199	75	271	Ukraine
Oceania	**15745**	**12084**	**10531**	**12787**	**12787**	**12787**	**12787**	**12787**	**12787**	**12787**	**Océanie**
Australia[4][5]	15745	12084	10531	...	...	...	...	...	...	...	Australie[4][5]
Total	**1501809**	**1375893**	**1569556**	**1347856**	**1423832**	**1387933**	**1368379**	**1344286**	**1323324**	**1302576**	**Total**

General Note.
Knitted and crocheted sports shirts for men, women and children, made in knitting mills. (SITC, Rev.3: 84370-1).

[1] All knitted outer garments.
[2] Including knitted sweaters and other knitted outer garments.
[3] Sales.
[4] All knitted shirts, men's and boys.
[5] Twelve months ending 30 June of year stated.

Remarque générale.
Chemisettes de bonneterie, pour hommes, femmes et enfants, faites en usine. (CTCI, Rev.3: 84370-1).

[1] Vêtements de dessus tricotés de toutes catégories.
[2] Y compris les chandails tricotés et autres vêtements de dessus en bonneterie.
[3] Ventes.
[4] Chemisettes en bonneterie de tous types pour hommes et garçonnets.
[5] Période de douze mois finissant le 30 juin de l'année indiquée.

Knitted sweaters
Tricots

ISIC-BASED CODE - CODE BASE CITI

3213-16

Unit : Thousand units · Unité : En milliers

Country or area	1990	1991	1992	1993	1994	1995	1996	1997	1998	1999	Pays ou zone
Africa	**1314**	**1310**	**1306**	**1302**	**1291**	**1305**	**1310**	**1308**	**1272**	**1255**	Afrique
Ethiopia	...	...	...	...	45	59	64	62	26	9	Ethiopie
Kenya	1246	...	...	...	...	...	...	...	...	...	Kenya
America, North	**67118**	**60637**	**63742**	**77499**	**76702**	**73216**	**66558**	**71873**	**61772**	**70690**	Amérique du Nord
Mexico	1818	1777	1822	#4311	5302	5252	4693	3833	4365	3307	Mexique
United States	...	58860	61920	73188	71400	67964	61865	68040	57407	67383	Etats-Unis
Asia	**319011**	**334475**	**306470**	**313575**	**303830**	**312067**	**298881**	**337936**	**301106**	**257782**	Asie
Hong Kong SAR	170445	182154	159606	185702	166935	166467	151502	176766	146438	117738	Hong-Kong RAS
Indonesia	10798	34793	34351	22581	24787	28228	...	24643	6108	...	Indonésie
Japan	53800	48224	46887	43833	39764	35277	34182	37710	33588	25465	Japon
Korea, Republic of	64411	52860	41090	40268	40933	39098	...	...	...	...	Corée, République de
Turkey	19557	16444	24536	21191	31411	42997	52791	64029	82514	74264	Turquie
Europe	**534016**	**501729**	**456892**	**408703**	**404407**	**399232**	**367978**	**309626**	**268590**	**296795**	Europe
Austria	0	...	...	...	...	3153	2289	2399	1995	1292	Autriche
Belgium	[1]8835	[1]8710	[1]8202	[1]7219	4888	4717	4624	4631	4439	4222	Belgique
Bulgaria[2]	55458	28587	21166	13980	11429	10893	10205	12202	3001	4151	Bulgarie[2]
Croatia	..	...	...	...	...	...	...	673	734	...	Croatie
Czech Republic	..	..	...	...	5577	5049	9905	10272	3948	3780	République tchèque
Finland	1498	1252	1178	1293	1992	1263	1032	1145	1196	955	Finlande
France[3]	37392	37692	40332	37488	40392		28368	27983	27353	24085	France[3]
Germany	..	47811	44710	...	...	25712	22514	20258	17302	...	Allemagne
Germany(Fed.Rep.)	42077	..	..	...	...	..	..	..	..	..	Allemagne(Rép.féd.)
Greece	...	...	...	50583	44360	37011	30849	29780	28819	...	Grèce
Hungary	6804	4388	4353	4006	3463	4910	5855	8044	6548	13916	Hongrie
Iceland	353	152	144	...	...	...	145	140	95	89	Islande
Latvia	..	..	...	...	...	...	...	...	...	1286	Lettonie
Lithuania	..	[1]17307	[1]14487	[1]10140	[1]5328	#2429	2795	3866	5289	5864	Lituanie
Netherlands	5710	5390	5580	6490	6601	5295	...	...	...	...	Pays-Bas
Norway	...	...	...	594	...	...	...	755	591	598	Norvège
Portugal	...	...	53435	26404	22081	18015	13990	13991	13926	13183	Portugal
Romania[1]	202537	173900	103000	101159	113530	124046	111054	46016	33305	35999	Roumanie[1]
Slovakia	..	..	...	...	...	...	5049	3557	3959	2629	Slovaquie
Slovenia	..	234	237	583	647	608	603	1712	1715	1727	Slovénie
Spain	...	...	...	21657	23582	23075	25346	29224	37603	45025	Espagne
Sweden	...	1284	1216	1069	797	3298	1133	1084	1012	729	Suède
United Kingdom	...	...	...	...	...	89722	83613	84587	68418	...	Royaume-Uni
Oceania	**13612**	**11634**	**12681**	**12529**	**12808**	**12474**	**12623**	**12623**	**12623**	**12623**	Océanie
Australia[4]	11361	9383	...	...	...	...	...	...	...	...	Australie[4]
New Zealand[5]	...	...	2309	2157	2436	2102	...	...	...	...	Nouvelle-Zélande[5]
Total	**935072**	**909786**	**841091**	**813608**	**799038**	**798294**	**747350**	**733366**	**645362**	**639145**	Total

General Note.
Knitted and crocheted sweaters, cardigans, pull-overs and jackets for men, women and children, made in knitting mills. (SITC, Rev.3: 84530-0).

Remarque générale.
Sweaters, cardigans, pull-overs et gilets en bonneterie, faits en usine. (CTCI, Rev.3: 84530-0).

[1] Including other knitted outer garments.
[2] Including knitted sports shirts and other knitted outer garments.
[3] 1995 data are confidential.
[4] Twelve months ending 30 June of year stated.
[5] Twelve months ending 30 September of year stated.

[1] Y compris autres vêtements de dessus en bonneterie.
[2] Y compris les chemisettes et autres vêtements de dessus en bonneterie.
[3] Pour 1995, les données sont confidentielles.
[4] Période de douze mois finissant le 30 juin de l'année indiquée.
[5] Période de douze mois finissant le 30 septembre de l'année indiquée.

Other knitted outer garments
Autres vêtements de dessus, en bonneterie

ISIC-BASED CODE - CODE BASE CITI

3213-19

Unit : Thousand units   Unité : En milliers

Country or area	1990	1991	1992	1993	1994	1995	1996	1997	1998	1999	Pays ou zone
Africa	**11635**	**10012**	**9500**	**8645**	**9776**	**10359**	**9030**	**9720**	**8932**	**8754**	**Afrique**
South Africa	11635	10012	9500	8645	9776	10359	9030	9720	8932	8754	Afrique du Sud
America, North	**397**	**393**	**603**	**12928**	**15946**	**19701**	**26739**	**30963**	**34842**	**33977**	**Amérique du Nord**
Mexico	397	393	603	12928	15946	19701	26739	30963	34842	33977	Mexique
Asia	**30214**	**52384**	**19917**	**35788**	**41363**	**33387**	**33378**	**32449**	**29297**	**42568**	**Asie**
Bangladesh	7649	...	...	...	...	...	...	...	...	...	Bangladesh
Hong Kong SAR	1819	511	2840	3174	11140	4093	4769	3725	664	14553	Hong-Kong RAS
Cyprus	*2100	*2540	2330	...	...	2313	2135	2335	2242	1611	Chypre
Indonesia	18646	35094	2470	...	...	...	...	...	...	...	Indonésie
Tajikistan	..	6590	4628	4028	1637	595	88	3	5	18	Tadjikistan
Europe	**432377**	**442972**	**404435**	**275163**	**255916**	**255907**	**299609**	**330925**	**436967**	**359531**	**Europe**
Albania [1]	9	5	3	4	3	0	0	0	0	...	Albanie [1]
Austria [2]	816	1022	1158	1015	533	#3890	3054	2051	...	2363	Autriche [2]
Belgium	...	...	...	...	6142	4504	4414	4085	3404	3407	Belgique
Croatia	..	...	...	...	...	...	...	272	464	...	Croatie
Czechoslovakia(former)	66885	38647	..	..	..	..	..	..	..	..	Tchécoslovaquie(anc.)
Czech Republic	..	..	21775	13022	12302	9524	7965	8396	8306	13451	République tchèque
Estonia	..	5073	3802	1519	1334	1273	1771	2917	2679	3253	Estonie
Finland	3861	2627	2277	2146	2183	2029	1891	5509	4587	4560	Finlande
France	23856	22297	18335	26408	25488	...	...	...	...	...	France
Germany	..	8193	5153	5159	4656	...	...	...	...	...	Allemagne
Germany(Fed.Rep.)	8411	..	..	..	..	..	..	..	..	..	Allemagne(Rép.féd.)
German D.R.(former)	44396	..	..	..	..	..	..	..	..	..	R.D.A. (anc.)
Greece	[1]56741	[1]54445	[1]55102	8575	11655	14157	...	...	154850	...	Grèce
Hungary	12036	9069	7307	5341	5217	5251	...	40891	37442	37994	Hongrie
Iceland	[3]805	[3]185	[3]161	...	...	...	209	201	176	184	Islande
Latvia [1]	..	16378	9506	4842	4148	2071	3304	4194	4944	8553	Lettonie [1]
Lithuania	..	...	...	...	...	11100	14544	18745	29499	29879	Lituanie
Netherlands	4150	4940	4430	...	...	...	...	...	...	...	Pays-Bas
Poland	71630	49853	36561	39804	41594	51308	54782	60983	59956	60363	Pologne
Slovakia	..	..	17752	11308	10171	9480	2123	1838	2296	1341	Slovaquie
Slovenia	..	3513	3592	2488	2011	1737	4333	...	...	...	Slovénie
Spain	[4][5]50478	[4][5]56113	[4][5]57584	6862	8416	10093	...	...	...	...	Espagne
Ukraine [1]	..	82188	71760	58239	24578	8203	5153	4140	3297	4493	Ukraine [1]
United Kingdom	...	...	...	78214	85336	84858	81569	...	...	...	Royaume-Uni
Total	**474623**	**505761**	**434455**	**332524**	**323001**	**319353**	**368756**	**404057**	**510037**	**444829**	**Total**

General Note.
Other knitted and crocheted outer garments made in knitting mills, such as dresses, coats, minor articles of apparel, curtains etc. (SITC, Rev.3: 84310-0, 84320-0, 84370-2, 84410-0, 84420-0, 84470-0, 84512-0, 84524-0, 84540-0, 84562-0, 84564-0, 84590-0, 84690-0).

Remarque générale.
Autres vêtements de dessus, en bonneterie, faits en usine, tels que robes, manteaux, divers articles d'habillement, rideaux etc. (CTCI, Rev.3: 84310-0, 84320-0, 84370-2, 84410-0, 84420-0, 84470-0, 84512-0, 84524-0, 84540-0, 84562-0, 84564-0, 84590-0, 84690-0,).

[1] All knitted outer garments.
[2] 1998 data are confidential.
[3] Including children's garments.
[4] Including household production.
[5] All knitted outer garments except uniforms, sombreros and gloves.

[1] Vêtements de dessus tricotés de toutes catégories.
[2] Pour 1998, les données sont confidentielles.
[3] Y compris les vêtements pour enfants.
[4] Y compris la production ménagère.
[5] Vêtements de dessus tricotés, sauf les sombreros et les gants.

Carpets and rugs of wool, knotted
Tapis de laine à points noués

ISIC-BASED CODE - CODE BASE CITI

3214-01

Unit : Thousand square metres   Unité : Milliers de mètres carrés

Country or area	1990	1991	1992	1993	1994	1995	1996	1997	1998	1999	Pays ou zone
Africa	**1035**	**857**	**585**	**912**	**793**	**771**	**704**	**686**	**624**	**638**	**Afrique**
Ethiopia[1]	...	2	6	12	13	17	18	13	6	0	Ethiopie[1]
Morocco	1025	855	579	900	780	754	686	673	618	638	Maroc
America, South	**998**	**935**	**1095**	**739**	**671**	**661**	**564**	**557**	**494**	**466**	**Amérique du Sud**
Colombia	...	...	671	502	289	402	...	...	...	...	Colombie
Ecuador	...	...	424	237	382	259	98	...	...	...	Equateur
Asia	**22710**	**36426**	**28607**	**33385**	**28810**	**28676**	**28545**	**32031**	**19316**	**26152**	**Asie**
Armenia	..	947	404	200	35	29	23	14	19	18	Arménie
Hong Kong SAR	202	150	57	67	41	133	80	22	...	...	Hong-Kong RAS
Georgia	..	..	128	89	24	1	6	15	...	...	Géorgie
Indonesia	4534	5166	1004	6800	...	6145	...	9393	2108	...	Indonésie
Japan[2]	8908	8179	7195	6247	5754	...	...	...	...	...	Japon[2]
Kazakhstan	..	2048	1700	1440	685	198	204	196	172	154	Kazakhstan
Korea, Republic of	6132	6649	6995	7875	9931	10369	12900	13576	10335	12736	Corée, République de
Kyrgyzstan	..	1628	1701	1609	1083	979	768	326	232	1675	Kirghizistan
Mongolia	1971	1400	1037	1000	682	596	667	644	588	629	Mongolie
Syrian Arab Republic[3]	630	818	810	656	819	2332	2370	2393	2347	...	Rép. arabe syrienne[3]
Tajikistan	..	2515	2354	1840	754	344	220	386	505	372	Tadjikistan
Turkey[4]	108	101	92	120	95	100	93	102	79	39	Turquie[4]
Turkmenistan	..	725	642	815	442	423	417	326	315	...	Turkménistan
Uzbekistan	..	5750	4203	4367	3184	1982	1555	1241	...	...	Ouzbékistan
Viet Nam	225	270	285	...	...	...	...	...	...	...	Viet Nam
Europe	**21695**	**41113**	**40002**	**39957**	**38976**	**34691**	**31970**	**28176**	**29454**	**30490**	**Europe**
Austria	519	362	414	...	...	...	...	...	...	...	Autriche
Belarus	..	5370	5110	4816	3707	2092	2108	2580	2823	3256	Bélarus
Bulgaria[3]	1801	1282	1772	1056	1039	913	817	633	848	854	Bulgarie[3]
Croatia	..	111	135	256	344	206	250	105	100	...	Croatie
Czechoslovakia(former)	613	200	..	..	..	..	..	..	..	..	Tchécoslovaquie(anc.)
France[3]	4068	6528	7128	7721	8268	...	...	...	...	...	France[3]
Greece	1258	1620	1334	...	...	...	...	...	...	...	Grèce
Hungary	377	341	290	164	250	163	...	...	...	...	Hongrie
Lithuania[5]	..	2739	2615	2226	867	286	186	136	85	67	Lituanie[5]
Poland	[3]11059	[3]6096	[3]7066	8514	9275	9521	8431	5442	5323	4655	Pologne
Republic of Moldova	..	3482	2234	[6]2560	[6]1718	[6]970	[6]986	[6]737	[6]666	[6]461	Rép. de Moldova
Russian Federation	..	7922	7635	7387	4854	5816	3230	1373	1356	1309	Fédération de Russie
Slovakia	..	..	...	...	214	...	...	...	...	...	Slovaquie
Ukraine[3]	..	363	222	185	65	60	44	106	86	39	Ukraine[3]
United Kingdom	2000	2000	...	...	...	...	...	...	...	...	Royaume-Uni
Yugoslavia	..	2694	1824	1014	4531	990	1104	1312	1477	2046	Yougoslavie
T.F.Yug.Rep. Macedonia	..	3	9	8	8	4	4	4	...	...	L'ex-RY Macédoine
USSR (former)[5]	115082	..	..	..	..	..	..	..	..	..	URSS (anc.)[5]
Oceania	**53913**	**51830**	**49973**	**51039**	**52822**	**53079**	**53272**	**52811**	**53104**	**53797**	**Océanie**
Australia[3][7]	45101	42854	42262	42618	...	...	...	...	...	...	Australie[3][7]
New Zealand[8]	...	...	[3]7711	[3]8421	9613	9870	10063	9602	[9]9895	[9]10588	Nouvelle-Zélande[8]
Total	**215432**	**131161**	**120262**	**126032**	**122072**	**117878**	**115054**	**114260**	**102992**	**111542**	**Total**

General Note.
Knotted wool carpets and rugs made up or not, composed of a taut warp around which the pile threads are knotted (giordes or Turkish knot, Senna or Persian knot, and single warp knots) in a complete turn. (SITC, Rev.3: 65921-0).

Remarque générale.
Tapis de laine à points noués, même confectionnés, constitués par une chaîne de fond tendue sur laquelle les fils de poil sont noués ou enroulés (noeud "ghiordès" ou point de Smyrne, noeud "senneh" ou point de Perse, noeud sur un seul fil de chaîne). (CTCI, Rev.3: 65921-0).

For footnotes, see end of table.   Voir la fin du tableau pour les notes.

Carpets and rugs of wool, knotted (continued)
Tapis de laine à points noués (suite)

ISIC-BASED CODE - CODE BASE CITI

3214-01

[1] Twelve months ending 7 July of the year stated.
[2] Shipments.
[3] Including other carpets.
[4] Government production only.
[5] Including other carpets and rugs.
[6] Excluding Transnistria region.
[7] Twelve months ending 30 June of year stated.
[8] Twelve months ending 30 September of year stated.
[9] Excluding rugs.

[1] Période de douze mois finissant le 7 juillet de l'année indiquée.
[2] Expéditions.
[3] Y compris les autres tapis.
[4] Production de l'Etat seulement.
[5] Y compris les autres tapis et carpettes.
[6] Non compris la région de Transnistria.
[7] Période de douze mois finissant le 30 juin de l'année indiquée.
[8] Période de douze mois finissant le 30 septembre de l'année indiquée.
[9] A l'exclusion des carpettes.

Carpets and rugs, other
Autres tapis
ISIC-BASED CODE - CODE BASE CITI
3214-04

Unit : Thousand square metres   Unité : Milliers de mètres carrés

Country or area	1990	1991	1992	1993	1994	1995	1996	1997	1998	1999	Pays ou zone
Africa											**Afrique**
Egypt	722	631	686	514	530	461	740	67	...	...	Egypte
Nigeria[1]	839000	1759000	1759000	2032000	691000	624000	...	...	...	...	Nigéria[1]
South Africa	18881	15621	14476	28984	17996	17995	26203	28774	30025	26784	Afrique du Sud
United Rep.Tanzania	37	28	22	3	...	...	21	0	...	...	Rép. Unie de Tanzanie
America, North											**Amérique du Nord**
Mexico	10300	8153	8016	14865	14843	12859	14729	16569	15804	15793	Mexique
United States[3]	[2]1137132	[2]1068550	1186565	1247003	1370268	1328600	1328600	1418000	1555500	1594800	Etats-Unis[3]
America, South											**Amérique du Sud**
Bolivia	37	40	54	49	0	*0	...	...	...	...	Bolivie
Colombia	...	...	2618	3285	4751	5687	...	...	...	...	Colombie
Ecuador	...	...	...	...	...	...	164	10	1	...	Equateur
Asia											**Asie**
Azerbaijan	..	2446	1417	539	241	77	41	40	35	20	Azerbaïdjan
Bangladesh	1405	2184	2113	...	...	...	...	...	...	...	Bangladesh
Hong Kong SAR	...	172	...	35	...	...	...	...	...	...	Hong-Kong RAS
Indonesia	910	78	5151	772	...	1195	...	1254	4008	...	Indonésie
Iran(Islamic Rep. of)	[4]19696	[4]26373	[4]29026	[4]30085	[4]28064	[5]50223	[5]59487	[5]84457	[5]85163	...	Iran(Rép. islamique)
Japan[3 6]	100971	98511	92893	87370	88458	...	...	...	...	...	Japon[3 6]
Tajikistan	..	5080	6170	3862	1313	323	349	607	576	673	Tadjikistan
Turkey	11011	9984	8527	9579	10249	16216	18797	15971	15881	16495	Turquie
Turkmenistan		599	418	118	...	...	...	...	...	...	Turkménistan
Viet Nam	2988	604	235	...	...	...	...	...	...	...	Viet Nam
Europe											**Europe**
Austria[7]	11616	13510	13613	[2]12662	[2]11437	[2]6942	[2]9481	[2]9442	[2]9480		Autriche[7]
Belarus		8365	6314	6925	2405	453	1220	1835	2793	3589	Bélarus
Belgium	[1]340633	[1]332442	[1]376218	[1 2]796793	[1 2]796205	[1 2]809402	[2]540959	[2]567147	[2]517235	[2]531143	Belgique
Croatia	..	2	2	...	...	...	...	202	146	...	Croatie
Czechoslovakia(former)	27957	17675	..	..	...	...	...	...	...	...	Tchécoslovaquie(anc.)
Czech Republic	..	..	12315	9833	6734	...	...	...	...	...	République tchèque
Estonia	..	5617	2400	2731	2943	2350	2256	2434	2199	1352	Estonie
France	80796	75924	71616	75408	91872	93120	101490	95850	97284	102672	France
Germany		185157	186611	172889	168652	[2]181405	[2]173797	[2]177221	[2]170664	...	Allemagne
Germany(Fed.Rep.)	166000										Allemagne(Rép.féd.)
German D.R.(former)[2]	38138			..	..						R.D.A. (anc.)[2]
Greece	[8]3134	[8]2981	[8]2698	# [2]6331	[2]6369	[2]5266	[2]6681	...	[2]6346	...	Grèce
Hungary	5274	3599	1998	1309	1142	1199	...	2036	2030	2295	Hongrie
Ireland[2]	4494		...	...	...	...	...	...	...	...	Irlande[2]
Latvia	..	473	189	28	...	...	...	...	...	...	Lettonie
Netherlands[2 9 10]	82630	85210	77819	96991	90102	...	...	...	...	...	Pays-Bas[2 9 10]
Portugal	2946	3067	8992	7201	6108	5503	5616	5572	7045	7193	Portugal
Republic of Moldova	..	749	572	[11]36	[11]4	[11]6	[11]20	[11]89	[11]25	[11]91	Rép. de Moldova
Russian Federation	..	26126	26894	34827	21549	12886	6055	2786	7304	8488	Fédération de Russie
Slovakia	..	..	4297	...	...	...	...	...	[1]248	[1]247	Slovaquie
Spain[2]	22931	24541	22105	24558	35922	35384	...	...	...	...	Espagne[2]
United Kingdom	[12]131123	[12]140355	...	202718	181600	202495	168927	...	...	...	Royaume-Uni
T.F.Yug.Rep. Macedonia	..	384	324	201	171	164	126	162	142	153	L'ex-RY Macédoine

General Note.
Other carpets, carpeting and rugs, mats and matting, kelem, "schumacks" and "karamanic" rugs and the like, made up or not. (SITC, Rev.3: 65929-0, 65930-0, 65940-0, 65950-0, 65960-0).

Remarque générale.
Autres tapis et moquettes, tissus et matières pour tapis, paillassons, dessous de tapis, tissus kilim, soumack, karamanic ou similaires, même confectionnés. (CTCI, Rev.3: 65929-0, 65930-0, 65940-0, 65950-0, 65960-0).

For footnotes, see end of table.

Voir la fin du tableau pour les notes.

Carpets and rugs, other (continued)
Autres tapis (suite)

ISIC-BASED CODE - CODE BASE CITI
3214-04

Footnotes
[1] In metric tons.
[2] Including carpets and rugs of wool.
[3] Shipments.
[4] Production by establishments employing 50 or more persons.
[5] Production by establishments employing 10 or more persons.
[6] Excluding tufted carpets.
[7] 1999 data are confidential.
[8] Machine-woven carpets and rugs only.
[9] Sales.
[10] Production by establishments employing 20 or more persons.
[11] Excluding Transnistria region.
[12] Manufacturers' sales, including carpets and rugs of wool.

Notes.
[1] En tonnes métriques.
[2] Y compris les carpettes et les tapis de laine.
[3] Expéditions.
[4] Production des établissements occupant 50 personnes ou plus.
[5] Production des établissements occupant 10 personnes ou plus.
[6] Non compris les tapis tuftés.
[7] Pour 1999, les données sont confidentielles.
[8] Tapis et carpettes tissés à la machine seulement.
[9] Ventes.
[10] Production des établissements occupant 20 personnes ou plus.
[11] Non compris la région de Transnistria.
[12] Ventes des fabricants, y compris les tapis et carpettes de laine.

Cordage, rope and twine
Cordes, câbles, cordages et ficelles

ISIC-BASED CODE - CODE BASE CITI

3215-01

Unit : Metric tons

Unité : Tonnes métriques

Country or area	1990	1991	1992	1993	1994	1995	1996	1997	1998	1999	Pays ou zone
Africa	**30360**	**29760**	**29453**	**33370**	**28904**	**25586**	**18049**	**11294**	**18758**	**17353**	Afrique
Algeria	1101	1499	856	...	...	...	...	...	...	...	Algérie
Egypt[1]	5478	4757	4194	4513	4035	4012	3618	2303	...	...	Egypte[1]
Kenya	848	848	848	848	1033	1256	1256	...	...	...	Kenya
Madagascar	1947	1433	1749	1702	1366	1450	1505	1500	1570	...	Madagascar
Uganda	66	10	8	5	6	3	0	32	30	27	Ouganda
United Rep.Tanzania	20920	21213	21798	25150	21312	17713	10518	4919	...	...	Rép. Unie de Tanzanie
America, North	**3478**	**4223**	**4969**	**5170**	**5814**	**5909**	**7380**	**7807**	**9083**	**9341**	Amérique du Nord
Jamaica	5	2	0	1	...	...	...	...	...	...	Jamaïque
Mexico	...	...	...	5169	5812	5907	7378	7805	9081	9339	Mexique
America, South	**4874**	**4856**	**4834**	**5345**	**3830**	**5342**	**4805**	**4741**	**4738**	**4738**	Amérique du Sud
Colombia	...	...	...	5290	3740	5183	...	...	...	...	Colombie
Ecuador	...	...	96	55	90	159	...	3	0	...	Equateur
Asia	**118592**	**106355**	**107518**	**109704**	**118248**	**122742**	**120392**	**120437**	**95733**	**108384**	Asie
Hong Kong SAR	5791	1101	3585	1051	824	...	1089	976	1175	451	Hong-Kong RAS
China, Macao, SAR	...	...	...	149	199	288	186	200	204	105	Chine, Macao PAS
Indonesia	8825	10404	...	14999	18374	...	...	16176	1055	...	Indonésie
Japan	39675	36258	33267	31544	31482	29948	29545	29359	26280	23810	Japon
Korea, Republic of	62666	57537	58501	61685	67320	79036	77883	73726	67019	75735	Corée, République de
Turkey	1407	835	314	276	49	49	50	0	0	0	Turquie
Europe	**206147**	**270896**	**259624**	**240922**	**203275**	**227207**	**246725**	**234699**	**231879**	**245204**	Europe
Austria	5958	7186	7086	7838	5130	9340	8414	7934	9148	8898	Autriche
Belarus	..	4337	2941	915	1041	858	1170	1465	1632	1730	Bélarus
Belgium	5617	4890	4465	4209	2723	4935	4819	4118	3847	3462	Belgique
Croatia	..	514	417	340	300	269	311	334	366	...	Croatie
Denmark[2]	...	...	...	...	...	...	...	3169	3218	...	Danemark[2]
Czechoslovakia(former)	10653	8084	..	..	..	..	..	..	..	...	Tchécoslovaquie(anc.)
Czech Republic	..	..	10862	9893	11366	13209	14499	14333	12656	14382	République tchèque
Finland	2747	2211	2202	2313	2609	2584	1530	2725	2212	2361	Finlande
France	36300	29004	26868	26856	19980	19240	20360	17440	18732	18600	France
Germany	..	...	...	...	...	...	11723	11696	11737	...	Allemagne
Germany(Fed.Rep.)	4234	..	..	..	..	..	..	..	..	...	Allemagne(Rép.féd.)
German D.R.(former)	3622	..	..	..	..	..	..	..	..	...	R.D.A. (anc.)
Greece	4899	4911	4860	2797	2845	2871	3876	...	3579	...	Grèce
Hungary	8137	5877	6415	4947	5917	4290	3331	...	...	...	Hongrie
Iceland	1999	1563	1445	1583	1581	...	...	661	...	...	Islande
Latvia	..	1211	...	...	298	223	220	392	409	424	Lettonie
Netherlands[2 3 4]	...	...	...	3692	3136	3452	...	...	...	...	Pays-Bas[2 3 4]
Poland	23256	15555	16781	19875	19642	21180	21484	19367	21886	23064	Pologne
Portugal	65978	58709	62909	62962	62558	75448	79971	78367	80675	83056	Portugal
Russian Federation	..	54717	42169	32546	12992	13023	12513	11287	9987	10961	Fédération de Russie
Slovakia	..	..	...	...	...	891	2600	992	890	366	Slovaquie
Slovenia	..	444	392	484	397	362	1773	1712	2047	2295	Slovénie
Spain	10250	14619	9597	6893	8480	12505	16503	17011	19316	19341	Espagne
Sweden	1187	945	430	410	484	...	903	793	866	894	Suède
Ukraine	..	21584	16913	15319	6340	4758	3273	2926	2136	1738	Ukraine
United Kingdom	14690	12919	...	17546	17328	...	28244	27029	19508	...	Royaume-Uni
Yugoslavia	..	3277	1942	1886	1240	1008	1116	1363	1219	768	Yougoslavie
USSR (former)	106385	..	..	..	..	..	..	..	..	..	URSS (anc.)
Total	**469835**	**416090**	**406398**	**394511**	**360071**	**386787**	**397351**	**378978**	**360190**	**385020**	Total

For general note and footnotes, see end of table.

Voir la fin du tableau pour la remarque générale et les notes.

Cordage, rope and twine (continued)
Cordes, câbles, cordages et ficelles (suite)

ISIC-BASED CODE - CODE BASE CITI
3215-01

General Note.

Twine, cordage, ropes and cables of all fibres produced by twisting or by plaiting. Textile yarns reinforced with metal are included. Twine, cordage, ropes and cables of paper yarn are included only if plaited or reinforced with metal. Fancy cords, cords of a kind commonly used in machinery or plant as packing or lubricating materials, abrasives, coated twine, cord etc. Gymnasium apparatus and articles of twine, cordage, ropes and cables are excluded. (SITC, Rev.3: 65751-0).

[1] Products of flax only.
[2] Sales.
[3] Production by establishments employing 20 or more persons.
[4] Including carpets and rugs of wool.

Remarque générale.

Ficelles, cordages, cordes et câbles en toutes fibres fabriqués par commettage ou tressage, y compris les fils textiles armés de métal. Cette rubrique comprend aussi les ficelles en papier et les cordages, cordes et câbles en ficelle de papier, à condition qu'ils soient armés de métal ou obtenus par tressage. Elle ne comprend pas les cordonnets employés comme ficelles de fantaisie, les cordons du type généralement utilisé dans la mécanique ou l'industrie pour le bourrage ou le graissage, les cordes et ficelles revêtues de poudres abrasives, les agrès de gymnastique et les articles fabriqués en ficelles, cordes ou cordages. (CTCI, Rev.3: 65751-0).

[1] Produits en lin seulement.
[2] Ventes.
[3] Production des établissements occupant 20 personnes ou plus.
[4] Y compris les carpettes et les tapis de laine.

Floor covering
Couvre-parquets

ISIC-BASED CODE - CODE BASE CITI

3219-01

Unit : Thousand square metres

Unité : Milliers de mètres carrés

Country or area	1990	1991	1992	1993	1994	1995	1996	1997	1998	1999	Pays ou zone
America, South											**Amérique du Sud**
Brazil	21229	28706	26175	31394	31468	31582	33393	35177	31644	30959	Brésil
Colombia	...	...	2619	3285	4751	5687	...	...	...	...	Colombie
Asia											**Asie**
Armenia	..	1292	412	85	23	18	1	...	11	0	Arménie
Cyprus	...	...	13	...	...	11	13	12	10	11	Chypre
Indonesia	5046	...	...	9981	...	...	...	...	...	...	Indonésie
Thailand [1] [2]	486	604	...	...	...	...	...	...	...	...	Thaïlande [1] [2]
Turkey	5123	5411	9266	12825	11225	10877	13804	18785	20879	20193	Turquie
Europe											**Europe**
Belarus	..	[3]4546	4432	4123	2502	1969	1730	2289	2530	2077	Bélarus
Bulgaria	9487	3837	3770	4435	4422	3902	3715	1629	1736	...	Bulgarie
Germany	...	...	...	...	...	17593	15944	...	...	...	Allemagne
Hungary [4]	757	1073	1317	1273	1153	1189	...	...	...	...	Hongrie [4]
Latvia	..	4878	1703	714	285	233	107	32	...	43	Lettonie
Poland	5134	5117	4882	5899	5614	4132	4972	7525	5939	4744	Pologne
Portugal	[2]8	[2]4	...	#12886	14878	...	...	...	...	...	Portugal
Republic of Moldova	..	2428	1596	[5]11	[5]0	[5]0	[5]289	[5]373	[5]176	[5]138	Rép. de Moldova
Russian Federation	..	89501	93107	91877	64094	57061	41099	45897	50202	55673	Fédération de Russie
Slovakia	..	...	...	2701	589	...	...	...	...	...	Slovaquie
Sweden [2]	2	2	3	3	3	4	...	...	...	...	Suède [2]
Ukraine [3]	..	29784	23608	19632	9037	7572	6012	5211	4598	3411	Ukraine [3]
Yugoslavia	..	11334	7440	3463	4987	4769	5754	5880	6720	5874	Yougoslavie
USSR (former) [3]	157681	..	..	..	..	..	..	..	..	..	URSS (anc.) [3]
Oceania											**Océanie**
Australia	42937	41487	42018	43116	49028	43538	43924	43982	44494	45142	Australie

General Note.

Floor covering (other than carpets and blankets) on base of paper, paperboard or felt paper (whether or not coated with linoleum); and linoleum; and linoleum textile base, cut in sheets or tiles. (SITC, Rev.3: 65911-0, 65912-0).

Remarque générale.

Couvre-parquets (autres que les tapis et les couvertures) à support de papier, de carton ou de feutre cellulosique, revêtu ou non de linoléum; linoléum à support de matières textiles; découpés en feuilles ou en carreaux. (CTCI, Rev.3: 65911-0, 65912-0).

[1] Vinyl floor and wall tiles.
[2] In thousand metric tons.
[3] Including linoleum without base.
[4] Wooden floor covering.
[5] Excluding Transnistria region.

[1] Revêtements de sol et de murs en vinyle.
[2] En milliers de tonnes métriques.
[3] Y compris les linoléums sans semelle.
[4] Revêtements de sol en bois.
[5] Non compris la région de Transnistria.

Jackets, men's and boys'
Vestes pour hommes et garçonnets

ISIC-BASED CODE - CODE BASE CITI

3220-01

Unit : Thousand units

Unité : En milliers

Country or area	1990	1991	1992	1993	1994	1995	1996	1997	1998	1999	Pays ou zone
Africa	**1942**	**1773**	**1867**	**2767**	**2583**	**3024**	**2522**	**2848**	**2405**	**2022**	**Afrique**
Kenya	73	...	...	...	...	...	...	...	...	...	Kenya
South Africa	1869	1700	1794	2694	2510	2951	2449	2775	2332	1949	Afrique du Sud
America, North	**15056**	**14839**	**14623**	**14165**	**15345**	**14193**	**12597**	**13303**	**12111**	**11569**	**Amérique du Nord**
Mexico	...	...	...	1029	1481	1178	1329	1519	1480	1335	Mexique
United States	13945	13683	13422	13136	13864	...	11268	11784	...	...	Etats-Unis
America, South	**1329**	**1352**	**1251**	**1385**	**1517**	**1373**	**1720**	**1769**	**1978**	**1898**	**Amérique du Sud**
Brazil	191	148	...	...	...	...	...	...	...	...	Brésil
Colombia	...	...	1013	1124	1245	1172	...	1565	1777	...	Colombie
Ecuador	...	...	68	91	102	31	234	34	31	...	Equateur
Asia	**44176**	**62112**	**70375**	**80780**	**64494**	**58571**	**61187**	**67007**	**60135**	**61561**	**Asie**
Armenia	..	120	117	8	60	31	59	166	635	655	Arménie
Azerbaijan	..	14	0	0	0	0	0	0	0	0	Azerbaïdjan
Hong Kong SAR	16444	17556	21130	14930	13708	13552	14843	7419	10117	6414	Hong-Kong RAS
China, Macao, SAR	...	...	...	5717	4717	4941	6534	7348	6441	6061	Chine, Macao PAS
Cyprus	...	...	624	...	...	143	103	126	81	70	Chypre
Indonesia	10122	27142	[1]30972	[1]49712	37294	32333	...	43101	34768	...	Indonésie
Japan	11275	10767	10436	8979	7175	5903	5202	6029	4735	3492	Japon
Tajikistan	..	32	66	13	3	0	0	0	0	0	Tadjikistan
Turkey	1334	1249	1800	1228	1342	1662	1265	2816	3356	3854	Turquie
Turkmenistan	..	3	2	2	4	6	0	2	2	...	Turkménistan
Europe	**29426**	**35536**	**38825**	**37465**	**38312**	**36259**	**36973**	**34792**	**32342**	**35228**	**Europe**
Austria[2][3]	608	553	467	446	501	570	...	...	481	420	Autriche[2][3]
Belgium	905	895	594	489	[4]293	[4]318	[4]304	[4]294	[4]278	[4]164	Belgique
Croatia	..	1422	1420	1442	1271	1382	1295	1998	1924	...	Croatie
Denmark[5]	21	25	23	27	8	0	0	0	1	5	Danemark[5]
Czech Republic	..	..	...	...	3586	3256	2923	2967	2784	2751	République tchèque
Estonia	..	26	81	135	148	142	171	216	213	198	Estonie
Finland	350	215	200	153	184	171	161	200	269	322	Finlande
France	2304	2467	2287	2184	2760	3161	2354	[4]1952	1864	1640	France
Germany	..	5864	5315	...	...	3857	3462	3136	2824	...	Allemagne
Germany(Fed.Rep.)	5147	..	..	..	..	..	..	..	..	..	Allemagne(Rép.féd.)
German D.R.(former)	1614										R.D.A. (anc.)
Greece	1270	1181	1000	1236	1021	716	885	996	1095	...	Grèce
Hungary[6]	1074	1341	1676	1852	1913	1840	2092	619	2198	1950	Hongrie[6]
Iceland	4	3	3	...	...	...	9	7	3	3	Islande
Ireland	172				...	...	...	...	...	...	Irlande
Latvia	..	..	...	193	269	281	211	264	267	781	Lettonie
Lithuania	..	...	...	...	...	735	1009	1177	1296	1478	Lituanie
Netherlands[5][7][8]	352	394	417	580	541	368	...	...	...	...	Pays-Bas[5][7][8]
Norway	...				...	...	...	320	365	372	Norvège
Portugal	6917	4216	2974	3357	2927	2844	3216	2845	2707	2572	Portugal
Russian Federation	..	539	308	574	662	704	563	536	563	687	Fédération de Russie
Slovakia	..	...	...	...	...	...	4240	3789	742	401	Slovaquie
Slovenia	..	1792	1442	1065	2072	1028	520	401	304	467	Slovénie
Spain	[9][10]5477	[9][10]5657	[9][10]5278	4936	5417	5758	5894	5436	5892	5764	Espagne
Sweden	226	164	152	104	...	78	199	203	194	283	Suède
Ukraine[9]	..	5337	3998	2720	1753	1375	968	936	939	1219	Ukraine[9]
United Kingdom	[11]2633	[11]1611	...	4962	4877	4442	4469	4751	4010	...	Royaume-Uni
Yugoslavia	..	975	482	202	186	182	290	301	311	120	Yougoslavie
T.F.Yug.Rep. Macedonia	..	185	170	198	240	229	227	279	145	273	L'ex-RY Macédoine
Oceania	**1476**	**1175**	**960**	**831**	**822**	**715**	**642**	**590**	**545**	**480**	**Océanie**
Australia[12]	1029	822	826	695	652	589	537	516	...	...	Australie[12]
New Zealand[13]	447	353	134	136	170	126	...	...	...	...	Nouvelle-Zélande[13]
Total	**93406**	**116787**	**127900**	**137393**	**123073**	**114134**	**115640**	**120308**	**109516**	**112758**	**Total**

For general note and footnotes, see end of table.

Voir la fin du tableau pour la remarque générale et les notes.

Jackets, men's and boys' (continued)
Vestes pour hommes et garçonnets (suite)

ISIC-BASED CODE - CODE BASE CITI
3220-01

General Note.

Jackets produced for sale as individual garments rather than as a part of a combined costume. Waistcoats, blazers, sports jackets and jackets of battledress type are included. Smoking-jackets designed primarily for indoor wear are excluded. (SITC, Rev.3:84130-0).

[1] Including jackets for women and girls.
[2] 1996 data are confidential.
[3] 1997 data are confidential.
[4] Incomplete coverage.
[5] Sales.
[6] Excluding work jackets.
[7] Production by establishments employing 20 or more persons.
[8] Jackets and sports jackets only.
[9] Excluding children's clothing.
[10] Including household production.
[11] Manufacturers' sales.
[12] Twelve months ending 30 June of year stated.
[13] Twelve months ending 30 September of year stated.

Remarque générale.

Ces vêtements sont fabriqués pour être vendus séparément et non comme partie d'un costume complet. Cette rubrique comprend les gilets, les blazers, les sahariennes, les blousons, les vestes de sport, mais non les vestons d'intérieur. (CTCI, Rev.3: 84130-0).

[1] Y compris les vestes pour dames et fillettes.
[2] Pour 1996, les données sont confidentielles.
[3] Pour 1997, les données sont confidentielles.
[4] Couverture incomplète.
[5] Ventes.
[6] Non compris les vestes de travail.
[7] Production des établissements occupant 20 personnes ou plus.
[8] Vestons et vestes de sport seulement.
[9] Non compris les vêtements d'enfants.
[10] Y compris la production ménagère.
[11] Ventes des fabricants.
[12] Période de douze mois finissant le 30 juin de l'année indiquée.
[13] Période de douze mois finissant le 30 septembre de l'année indiquée.

Overcoats, men's and boys'
Vêtements de dessus pour hommes et garçonnets

ISIC-BASED CODE - CODE BASE CITI

3220-04

Unit : Thousand units
Unité : En milliers

Country or area	1990	1991	1992	1993	1994	1995	1996	1997	1998	1999	Pays ou zone
Africa	189	120	127	67	90	115	116	71	61	51	**Afrique**
Cameroon	...	24	22	24	26	18	...	...	...	...	Cameroun
South Africa	164	96	105	43	64	97	95	...	...	...	Afrique du Sud
America, North	986	735	658	882	1017	1136	974	1029	1279	1238	**Amérique du Nord**
Mexico	10	11	14	11	2	...	...	...	...	...	Mexique
United States	976	724	644	871	1015	1131	971	1027	1279	1238	Etats-Unis
America, South	3	3	4	7	12	13	20	55	44	59	**Amérique du Sud**
Colombia	...	...	1	4	9	10	...	51	41	...	Colombie
Ecuador	...	...	...	...	...	...	1	4	3	...	Equateur
Asia	4565	2924	5651	2622	1896	4945	1908	3168	2746	623	**Asie**
Armenia	..	97	5	1	4	2	0	0	0	0	Arménie
Hong Kong SAR[1]	2062	1044	3637	1010	381	3450	612	2099	...	123	Hong-Kong RAS[1]
China, Macao, SAR[1][2]	...	...	...	...	...	306	...	67	...	20	Chine, Macao PAS[1][2]
Cyprus	...	...	9	...	...	6	4	6	8	4	Chypre
Indonesia	25	14	...	38	...	...	...	...	...	...	Indonésie
Japan[3][4]	2209	1438	1703	1261	1283	1110	1008	...	...	...	Japon[3][4]
Tajikistan	..	91	38	77	23	8	0	0	0	0	Tadjikistan
Turkey	132	102	101	97	41	36	126	375	551	189	Turquie
Turkmenistan	...	...	...	1	...	...	1	...	...	...	Turkménistan
Europe	5452	18029	14827	14569	12121	11484	11193	11673	12972	12291	**Europe**
Austria[5]	182	173	235	185	132	...	...	...	...	...	Autriche[5]
Belgium	426	414	251	389	...	[6]153	[6]189	[6]390	[6]234	[6]372	Belgique
Croatia	..	261	289	128	107	259	285	289	112	...	Croatie
Denmark[7]	122	181	37	23	57	66	57	59	109	63	Danemark[7]
Czech Republic	..	..	...	...	332	557	432	406	321	303	République tchèque
Estonia	..	9	12	10	25	28	16	13	32	41	Estonie
Finland	1108	762	561	372	605	644	452	664	604	326	Finlande
Germany	..	...	...	262	177	644	604	728	730	...	Allemagne
German D.R.(former)[6]	898	..	..	..	..	..	..	..	..	...	R.D.A. (anc.)[6]
Greece	51	90	101	463	254	293	...	...	...	...	Grèce
Hungary[8]	496	372	352	478	500	546	...	509	1058	580	Hongrie[8]
Iceland	0	#0	0	...	...	...	29	29	...	...	Islande
Ireland	107	...	...	...	...	...	...	...	...	...	Irlande
Latvia[9]	..	...	...	...	77	23	27	34	30	288	Lettonie[9]
Lithuania	..	[10]854	[10]476	[10]535	[10]309	#376	387	310	414	328	Lituanie
Portugal	58	53	3091	2879	2393	1821	2380	2272	2501	2270	Portugal
Russian Federation	..	4287	1807	1340	554	61	226	189	178	267	Fédération de Russie
Slovakia	..	...	...	...	...	...	2	30	249	119	Slovaquie
Slovenia	..	1902	1543	1307	1130	965	313	265	227	308	Slovénie
Spain	[3][11][12]1632	[3][11][12]2112	[3][11][12]1790	3465	3718	3830	...	...	...	...	Espagne
Sweden[9]	118	164	201	...	#15	24	...	...	...	...	Suède[9]
Ukraine	..	4155	1826	1133	354	186	155	253	344	354	Ukraine
United Kingdom[13]	254	84	...	...	...	...	...	...	...	...	Royaume-Uni[13]
Yugoslavia	..	1505	684	258	197	136	173	190	242	115	Yougoslavie
T.F.Yug.Rep. Macedonia	..	243	381	387	484	329	376	242	508	263	L'ex-RY Macédoine
Oceania	56	36	117	116	108	100	114	120	126	132	**Océanie**
New Zealand[9][14]	56	36	117	116	108	100	...	...	...	...	Nouvelle-Zélande[9][14]
Total	11251	21847	21384	18263	15243	17792	14324	16115	17229	14395	**Total**

General Note.
Men's and boys' overcoats of all types other than raincoats, such as overcoats, topcoats, greatcoats, duffel coats (with or without hoods), capes and cloaks. Dressing-gowns, bath-robes and similar indoor wear are excluded. (SITC, Rev.3: 84110-1).

Remarque générale.
Vêtements de tous types autres que les imperméables, tels que pardessus, manteaux, capotes, trois-quarts, paletots, redingotes, jaquettes, capes, pèlerines et duffel-coats. Cette rubrique ne comprend pas les robes de chambre, les peignoirs de bain et autres vêtements d'intérieur analogues. (CTCI, Rev.3: 84110-1).

For footnotes, see end of table.

Voir la fin du tableau pour les notes.

Overcoats, men's and boys' (continued)
Vêtements de dessus pour hommes et garçonnets (suite)

ISIC-BASED CODE - CODE BASE CITI

3220-04

Footnotes	**Notes.**
[1] 1998 data are confidential.	[1] Pour 1998, les données sont confidentielles.
[2] 1996 data are confidential.	[2] Pour 1996, les données sont confidentielles.
[3] Excluding children's clothing.	[3] Non compris les vêtements d'enfants.
[4] Shipments.	[4] Expéditions.
[5] Beginning 1995, data are confidential.	[5] A partir de 1995, les données sont confidentielles
[6] Incomplete coverage.	[6] Couverture incomplète.
[7] Sales.	[7] Ventes.
[8] Excluding overcoats for work and for uniforms.	[8] Non compris les pardessus de travail et d'uniformes.
[9] Including raincoats for men and boys.	[9] Y compris les imperméables pour hommes et garçonnets.
[10] Including coats for women and girls.	[10] Y compris les manteaux de dames et de fillettes.
[11] Including household production.	[11] Y compris la production ménagère.
[12] Including raincoats.	[12] Y compris les imperméables.
[13] Manufacturers' sales.	[13] Ventes des fabricants.
[14] Twelve months ending 30 September of year stated.	[14] Période de douze mois finissant le 30 septembre de l'année indiquée.

Raincoats, men's and boys'
Imperméables pour hommes et garçonnets
ISIC-BASED CODE - CODE BASE CITI
3220-07

Unit : Thousand units · Unité : En milliers

Country or area	1990	1991	1992	1993	1994	1995	1996	1997	1998	1999	Pays ou zone
Africa	**568**	**471**	**319**	**154**	**116**	**117**	**72**	**2**	**10**	**15**	**Afrique**
Algeria	15	22	48	4	5	5	3	2	10	15	Algérie
South Africa	553	449	271	150	111	112	69	...	...	...	Afrique du Sud
America, North	**2923**	**2725**	**2535**	**2731**	**2731**	**2734**	**2735**	**2737**	**2739**	**2740**	**Amérique du Nord**
Mexico	4	3	10	9	9	...	...	...	...	...	Mexique
United States	2919	...	2525	...	...	...	...	...	...	...	Etats-Unis
America, South	**114**	**114**	**132**	**125**	**93**	**105**	**114**	**114**	**114**	**114**	**Amérique du Sud**
Colombia	...	...	132	125	93	105	...	...	...	...	Colombie
Asia	**1672**	**2086**	**1110**	**1360**	**2911**	**1836**	**2662**	**4652**	**5655**	**6008**	**Asie**
Armenia	..	6	...	...	1	8	5	0	0	25	Arménie
Hong Kong SAR[1][2]	1648	2039	...	...	310	223	...	...	...	...	Hong-Kong RAS[1][2]
Cyprus	...	...	2	...	...	16	13	17	21	11	Chypre
Indonesia	15	31	44	284	2585	...	...	3579	4578	...	Indonésie
Turkmenistan	..	0	3	1	...	...	...	...	...	...	Turkménistan
Europe	**3899**	**4031**	**3291**	**2641**	**1567**	**2090**	**2022**	**1891**	**1385**	**1207**	**Europe**
Austria[1][3]	59	76	61	19	13	...	...	...	...	...	Autriche[1][3]
Belgium	[1]1036	[1]1046	[1]778	[1]626	# [4]69	[4]104	...	...	[4]34	[4]9	Belgique
Estonia	..	2	1	0	10	15	5	5	23	22	Estonie
Finland	245	267	244	212	125	112	157	...	...	4	Finlande
France	...	...	...	...	...	98	78	68	50	92	France
Germany	..	99	...	81	56	...	...	...	...	...	Allemagne
Germany(Fed.Rep.)[1]	145	..	..	..	..	..	...	...	...	..	Allemagne(Rép.féd.)[1]
Greece	85	110	70	20	59	43	...	...	...	...	Grèce
Hungary[5]	66	56	29	45	61	79	...	...	...	...	Hongrie[5]
Iceland[1]	18	2	3	...	...	...	...	...	...	...	Islande[1]
Netherlands[6][7][8]	230	304	356	230	179	574	...	...	...	...	Pays-Bas[6][7][8]
Portugal	402	230	370	333	205	394	212	193	205	260	Portugal
Russian Federation	..	397	172	291	128	94	56	53	35	51	Fédération de Russie
Slovakia	..	..	...	...	...	...	...	...	249	119	Slovaquie
Spain	[1][9]1508	[1][9]1114	[1][9]759	452	350	269	...	...	...	...	Espagne
Ukraine	..	227	88	47	31	37	57	57	22	41	Ukraine
Oceania	**67**	**67**	**74**	**95**	**0**	**98**	**67**	**67**	**67**	**67**	**Océanie**
New Zealand[10]	...	...	74	95	0	98	...	...	...	...	Nouvelle-Zélande[10]
Total	**9242**	**9494**	**7461**	**7106**	**7418**	**6980**	**7672**	**9463**	**9969**	**10151**	**Total**

General Note.
Men's and boys' raincoats of all types and materials, except rubber. (SITC, Rev.3: 84110-2).

Remarque générale.
Imperméables de tous types et en toutes matières pour hommes et garçonnets, sauf ceux en caoutchouc. (CTCI, Rev.3:84110-2).

[1] Including raincoats for women and girls.
[2] Beginning 1996, data are confidential.
[3] Beginning 1995, data are confidential.
[4] Incomplete coverage.
[5] Excluding work raincoats.
[6] Sales.
[7] Production by establishments employing 20 or more persons.
[8] Including overcoats for men and boys.
[9] Including household production.
[10] Twelve months ending 30 September of year stated.

[1] Y compris les imperméables pour dames et fillettes.
[2] A partir de 1996, les données sont confidentielles.
[3] A partir de 1995, les données sont confidentielles
[4] Couverture incomplète.
[5] Non compris les imperméables de travail.
[6] Ventes.
[7] Production des établissements occupant 20 personnes ou plus.
[8] Y compris les vêtements de dessus pour hommes et garçonnets.
[9] Y compris la production ménagère.
[10] Période de douze mois finissant le 30 septembre de l'année indiquée.

Suits, men's and boys'
Costumes pour hommes et garçonnets

ISIC-BASED CODE - CODE BASE CITI

3220-10

Unit : Thousand units
Unité : En milliers

Country or area	1990	1991	1992	1993	1994	1995	1996	1997	1998	1999	Pays ou zone
Africa	**1920**	**1295**	**1157**	**1103**	**935**	**883**	**749**	**721**	**643**	**596**	**Afrique**
Kenya	293	267	204	185	108	80	93	...	...	...	Kenya
South Africa[1]	1627	1028	953	918	827	803	656	721	643	596	Afrique du Sud[1]
America, North	**12150**	**10315**	**10839**	**11131**	**12911**	**10502**	**10713**	**10626**	**9935**	**6638**	**Amérique du Nord**
Mexico	759	722	723	836	876	903	1114	1257	1453	1124	Mexique
Panama	89	...	84	...	...	...	...	...	...	...	Panama
United States	11302	9506	10032	10208	11948	...	...	9282	8395	5427	Etats-Unis
America, South	**2552**	**2455**	**2276**	**2084**	**2452**	**2806**	**2329**	**2423**	**2645**	**2487**	**Amérique du Sud**
Bolivia	...	1	0	1	1	*1	...	...	...	...	Bolivie
Brazil	641	625	491	639	799	937	913	1033	1094	1241	Brésil
Colombia	...	...	1465	848	1083	1000	...	1375	1528	...	Colombie
Ecuador	...	...	320	596	569	868	198	14	22	...	Equateur
Asia	**29814**	**28463**	**28201**	**23836**	**23223**	**20911**	**22347**	**21469**	**18232**	**16484**	**Asie**
Armenia	..	91	66	49	15	54	...	43	86	15	Arménie
Azerbaijan	..	87	306	248	128	38	5	2	15	7	Azerbaïdjan
Hong Kong SAR	1201	2475	1598	433	250	219	516	197	199	116	Hong-Kong RAS
China, Macao, SAR	...	...	...	766	838	1036	658	938	106	149	Chine, Macao PAS
Cyprus	...	...	149	...	...	103	102	102	85	59	Chypre
Indonesia	6258	1782	3536	...	...	529	...	821	506	...	Indonésie
Japan[2]	14458	13621	13466	11984	12381	11994	11752	12370	10032	8701	Japon[2]
Kazakhstan	..	854	782	762	264	88	68	45	44	74	Kazakhstan
Korea, Republic of[2]	5885	5356	5323	5830	6024	6134	...	...	...	...	Corée, République de[2]
Kyrgyzstan	..	1132	755	457	110	58	40	49	35	129	Kirghizistan
Tajikistan	..	641	276	167	117	31	17	31	30	19	Tadjikistan
Turkey	663	522	633	610	558	554	799	604	921	1012	Turquie
Turkmenistan	..	674	304	191	199	73	126	240	92	...	Turkménistan
Europe	**12818**	**29824**	**27695**	**25087**	**17323**	**16761**	**16350**	**15711**	**14964**	**16757**	**Europe**
Austria	546	538	438	392	303	437	241	231	133	151	Autriche
Belarus	..	2891	2356	1796	1340	674	761	911	977	999	Bélarus
Belgium	487	508	486	346	[3]35	[3]30	[3]61	[3]60	[3]21	[3]47	Belgique
Croatia	..	856	664	1359	1217	857	791	823	832	...	Croatie
Denmark[4]	0	0	0	0	0	2	0	0	1	1	Danemark[4]
Czech Republic	..	..	...	...	398	479	436	457	534	578	République tchèque
Estonia	..	167	99	45	56	52	81	39	49	54	Estonie
Finland	1678	1143	1020	888	143	137	103	120	141	133	Finlande
Germany	...	...	...	...	...	1743	1245	1163	1186	...	Allemagne
German D.R.(former)	2451	...	...	...	...	...	...	...	...	..	R.D.A. (anc.)
Greece	503	520	526	494	374	391	308	312	317	...	Grèce
Hungary[5]	1184	958	922	807	838	876	857	241	1042	1130	Hongrie[5]
Iceland	2	1	1	...	...	...	...	...	...	...	Islande
Ireland	81	...	...	...	...	...	...	...	...	...	Irlande
Latvia	..	...	...	72	45	37	78	36	15	33	Lettonie
Lithuania	..	632	392	236	277	#123	266	180	240	289	Lituanie
Netherlands[4][6]	143	132	115	87	79	73	...	...	...	...	Pays-Bas[4][6]
Norway	...	...	46	47	...	...	...	...	...	...	Norvège
Portugal	2826	1196	1055	773	769	839	932	1334	1439	1595	Portugal
Republic of Moldova	..	627	457	[7]341	[7]80	[7]68	[7]126	[7]90	[7]211	[7]247	Rép. de Moldova
Russian Federation	..	8169	7345	6978	4307	3835	4028	3794	2643	2722	Fédération de Russie
Slovakia	..	...	...	...	...	...	793	860	353	223	Slovaquie
Slovenia	..	1761	1855	1493	822	552	438	447	144	425	Slovénie
Spain	[2][8]1203	[2][8]1347	[2][8]1358	1328	1157	1233	1230	1155	1351	1438	Espagne
Sweden	150	93	88	70	79	84	42	22	27	30	Suède
Ukraine[2]	..	3559	3186	2695	1055	618	667	875	583	797	Ukraine[2]
United Kingdom	[9]1517	[9]1725	...	...	1349	2367	2119	1801	1899	...	Royaume-Uni
Yugoslavia	..	1255	800	383	434	413	314	382	419	291	Yougoslavie
T.F.Yug.Rep. Macedonia	..	214	206	224	146	155	230	183	219	192	L'ex-RY Macédoine
Oceania	**421**	**322**	**285**	**289**	**262**	**271**	**252**	**262**	**237**	**201**	**Océanie**
Australia[10][11]	360	258	222	221	199	213	190	200	175	139	Australie[10][11]
New Zealand[12]	61	64	63	68	63	58	...	...	...	...	Nouvelle-Zélande[12]

For general note and footnotes, see end of table.
Voir la fin du tableau pour la remarque générale et les notes.

Suits, men's and boys' (continued)
Costumes pour hommes et garçonnets (suite)

ISIC-BASED CODE - CODE BASE CITI
3220-10

Unit : Thousand units   Unité : En milliers

Country or area	1990	1991	1992	1993	1994	1995	1996	1997	1998	1999	Pays ou zone
Total	59674	72674	70454	63530	57106	52134	52740	51212	46655	43163	Total

General Note.

Men's and boys' suits of all types, such as lounge suits, dress suits, dinner-jacket suits, morning suits, clerical suits, plus-fours, siren suits, skiing, hunting and other sports suits and uniforms of all kinds (including liveries). They consist of a jacket and a pair of trousers (usually matching) and may include a vest and an extra pair of trousers. Suits for small boys consisting of a jacket and a pair of short pants are included. (SITC, Rev.3: 84120-0, 84321-0).

[1] Lounge suits only.
[2] Excluding children's clothing.
[3] Incomplete coverage.
[4] Sales.
[5] Excluding work suits and uniforms.
[6] Production by establishments employing 20 or more persons.
[7] Excluding Transnistria region.
[8] Including household production.
[9] Manufacturers' sales.
[10] Men's suits only.
[11] Twelve months ending 30 June of year stated.
[12] Twelve months ending 30 September of year stated.

Remarque générale.

Costumes de tous types pour hommes et garçonnets, tels que complets de ville et costumes de sport (pour le ski, la chasse etc.), costumes de soirée ou de cérémonie (tels que smokings, spencers ou fracs), vêtements ecclésiastiques, uniformes militaires, administratifs et autres (y compris les livrées). Ils se composent d'une veste et d'un pantalon (habituellement du même tissu) et peuvent comprendre un gilet et un second pantalon. Cette rubrique comprend les costumes pour garçonnets composés d'une veste et d'une culotte courte. (CTCI, Rev.3: 84120-0, 84321-0).

[1] Complets vestons seulement.
[2] Non compris les vêtements d'enfants.
[3] Couverture incomplète.
[4] Ventes.
[5] Non compris les vêtements de travail et les uniformes.
[6] Production des établissements occupant 20 personnes ou plus.
[7] Non compris la région de Transnistria.
[8] Y compris la production ménagère.
[9] Ventes des fabricants.
[10] Costumes pour hommes seulement.
[11] Période de douze mois finissant le 30 juin de l'année indiquée.
[12] Période de douze mois finissant le 30 septembre de l'année indiquée.

Trousers, men's and boys'
Pantalons pour hommes et garçonnets

ISIC-BASED CODE - CODE BASE CITI

3220-13

Unit : Thousand units — Unité : En milliers

Country or area	1990	1991	1992	1993	1994	1995	1996	1997	1998	1999	Pays ou zone
Africa	**20409**	**19339**	**17150**	**22082**	**24254**	**26052**	**25841**	**24034**	**23541**	**25150**	**Afrique**
Algeria	2084	1967	1266	1473	...	...	...	...	...	...	Algérie
Kenya	1706	1523	1539	1198	655	530	613	...	...	...	Kenya
Malawi	47	77	59	51	38	...	...	...	...	...	Malawi
Mozambique	366	384	...	303	240	115	25	30	19	49	Mozambique
South Africa	16206	15388	14116	19057	21623	23668	23469	22263	21796	23380	Afrique du Sud
America, North	**123114**	**127945**	**121337**	**127717**	**133713**	**121873**	**133512**	**155753**	**138682**	**140427**	**Amérique du Nord**
Mexico	11718	10823	9043	18897	19231	15230	18101	17885	19580	18637	Mexique
Panama	3389	...	3769	1592	2101	1296	1548	...	...	...	Panama
United States	108007	114839	108525	107228	112381	105347	113863	136407	117805	120657	Etats-Unis
America, South	**37781**	**44491**	**35226**	**37676**	**37192**	**35087**	**35143**	**37477**	**36667**	**37712**	**Amérique du Sud**
Brazil	34515	40152	29921	32511	31422	30001	27714	26152	23843	24790	Brésil
Colombia	...	...	4540	4352	4790	4013	...	9956	11311	...	Colombie
Ecuador	...	...	765	813	980	1073	935	1369	1513	...	Equateur
Asia	**142510**	**165862**	**226064**	**223442**	**148117**	**117749**	**160875**	**138210**	**134692**	**131024**	**Asie**
Armenia	...	3074	287	36	116	111	...	8	2	115	Arménie
Azerbaijan	..	3524	1707	617	206	103	216	204	11	11	Azerbaïdjan
Hong Kong SAR[1]	93653	94004	120099	94388	61788	49499	...	44086	41953	32937	Hong-Kong RAS[1]
China, Macao, SAR	...	...	...	14049	13955	14582	21382	11633	12826	13786	Chine, Macao PAS
Cyprus	...	...	2230	...	...	1270	1097	1227	1036	845	Chypre
Indonesia	8950	15513	[2]58708	[2]88020	46210	28747	...	50883	49542	...	Indonésie
Korea, Republic of	6231	6036	...	...	...	...	...	...	...	...	Corée, République de
Kyrgyzstan	..	1534	884	471	109	129	212	202	229	402	Kirghizistan
Malaysia	13948	14565	14254	14338	14640	12544	13145	16554	15825	13463	Malaisie
Myanmar	10	21	43	...	...	...	...	...	...	...	Myanmar
Tajikistan	..	4499	1542	954	432	135	34	666	86	974	Tadjikistan
Turkey	2737	3570	3837	2279	2644	4255	4375	6454	5634	7997	Turquie
Turkmenistan	..	2762	1095	848	575	216	198	135	1390	...	Turkménistan
Europe	**205199**	**252516**	**245692**	**223352**	**202607**	**198077**	**194293**	**219868**	**237269**	**240931**	**Europe**
Austria	4544	3526	2694	2020	1512	1531	1471	1388	1523	1304	Autriche
Belgium	14850	13512	13084	13553	[3]7152	[3]6834	[3]6464	[3]5456	[3]1122	[3]1464	Belgique
Croatia	..	4700	4536	3420	3209	3717	3233	2422	2426	...	Croatie
Denmark[4]	75	79	138	268	467	10	13	140	174	1715	Danemark[4]
Czech Republic	..	...	...	...	3306	3349	3545	3453	3869	3648	République tchèque
Estonia	..	485	443	508	609	693	206	650	693	617	Estonie
Finland	2260	1840	1113	891	1099	1005	904	1115	885	1034	Finlande
France	...	...	...	...	...	18862	16845	13536	12840	8246	France
Germany	..	28461	22414	20297	17423	14068	13024	11778	11826	...	Allemagne
Germany(Fed.Rep.)	28354	..	..	..	..	..	..	..	..	..	Allemagne(Rép.féd.)
German D.R.(former)	11743	..	..	..	..	..	..	..	..	..	R.D.A. (anc.)
Greece	11510	10933	9197	7737	6880	7344	6361	6855	7504	...	Grèce
Hungary[5]	3683	4340	4859	5030	4969	4788	6540	7182	8383	8997	Hongrie[5]
Iceland	13	6	4	...	...	...	[2]32	[2]37	[2]32	[2]34	Islande
Ireland[6]	1986	...	...	...	...	...	...	...	...	...	Irlande[6]
Latvia	..	...	...	842	1150	1491	1258	1516	2241	2210	Lettonie
Lithuania	..	...	1563	1857	2341	#1783	2627	3372	4475	4212	Lituanie
Netherlands[4][7]	3026	2765	2676	3226	2816	3607	...	...	...	...	Pays-Bas[4][7]
Norway	...	...	...	...	...	...	...	701	723	602	Norvège
Portugal	22143	14216	14776	13392	11991	11602	11318	10269	11489	12916	Portugal
Republic of Moldova	..	1064	894	[8]311	[8]356	[8]254	[8]194	[8]48	[8]114	[8]619	Rép. de Moldova
Russian Federation	..	47635	30108	20924	12931	7882	5462	5622	5790	10013	Fédération de Russie
Slovakia	..	..	...	...	...	...	1070	1364	2808	1133	Slovaquie
Slovenia	..	2435	2341	1982	1796	1466	779	1119	724	784	Slovénie
Spain	[9][10]46771	[9][10]47370	[9][10]43078	37835	40504	43516	46091	48875	55450	53305	Espagne
Sweden	834	531	418	358	...	149	202	159	171	163	Suède
Ukraine[9]	..	10799	9870	5807	2355	2005	2416	2216	2537	3176	Ukraine[9]
United Kingdom	21000	16595	...	#48884	51558	55589	56270	...	...	...	Royaume-Uni
Yugoslavia	..	5707	3921	1726	1380	1229	1291	1219	1130	914	Yougoslavie
T.F.Yug.Rep. Macedonia	..	876	776	654	557	1025	790	436	943	753	L'ex-RY Macédoine

For general note and footnotes, see end of table.　　　　Voir la fin du tableau pour la remarque générale et les notes.

Trousers, men's and boys' (continued)
Pantalons pour hommes et garçonnets (suite)

3220-13

Unit : Thousand units   Unité : En milliers

Country or area	1990	1991	1992	1993	1994	1995	1996	1997	1998	1999	Pays ou zone
Oceania	**10501**	**7302**	**6791**	**5973**	**4639**	**4867**	**4534**	**4058**	**3572**	**3001**	**Océanie**
Australia[11]	6648	4536	4275	4011	3666	3792	3476	3283	3080	2792	Australie[11]
New Zealand[12]	3853	2766	2516	1962	973	1075	...	...	...	...	Nouvelle-Zélande[12]
Total	**539514**	**617455**	**652260**	**640242**	**550522**	**503705**	**554198**	**579401**	**574423**	**578245**	**Total**

General Note.

Trousers for men and boys produced for sale as individual garments rather than as part of a combined costume. Knickerbockers, breeches and shorts are included. (SITC, Rev.3: 84140-0, 84324-0).

[1] 1996 data are confidential.
[2] Including women's and girls' dresses.
[3] Incomplete coverage.
[4] Sales.
[5] Excluding work trousers.
[6] Excluding cotton jeans.
[7] Production by establishments employing 20 or more persons.
[8] Excluding Transnistria region.
[9] Excluding children's clothing.
[10] Including household production.
[11] Twelve months ending 30 June of year stated.
[12] Twelve months ending 30 September of year stated.

Remarque générale.

Pantalons pour hommes et garçonnets fabriqués pour être vendus séparément et non comme partie d'un costume complet. Cette rubrique comprend les pantalons de golf, les culottes et les shorts. (CTCI, Rev.3: 84140-0, 84324-0).

[1] Pour 1996, les données sont confidentielles.
[2] Y compris les robes de dames et de fillettes.
[3] Couverture incomplète.
[4] Ventes.
[5] Non compris les pantalons de travail.
[6] Non compris les 'jeans' en coton.
[7] Production des établissements occupant 20 personnes ou plus.
[8] Non compris la région de Transnistria.
[9] Non compris les vêtements d'enfants.
[10] Y compris la production ménagère.
[11] Période de douze mois finissant le 30 juin de l'année indiquée.
[12] Période de douze mois finissant le 30 septembre de l'année indiquée.

Blouses, women's and girls'
Blouses de dames et de fillettes

ISIC-BASED CODE - CODE BASE CITI

3220-16

Unit : Thousand units — Unité : En milliers

Country or area	1990	1991	1992	1993	1994	1995	1996	1997	1998	1999	Pays ou zone
Africa	**10085**	**10601**	**10291**	**7354**	**7724**	**7808**	**7835**	**8612**	**8444**	**7957**	**Afrique**
Kenya	21	...	...	...	...	...	...	...	...	...	Kenya
South Africa	10064	10580	10270	7333	7703	7787	7814	8591	8423	7936	Afrique du Sud
America, North	**208981**	**180097**	**192878**	**212908**	**247684**	**203458**	**199139**	**157511**	**158258**	**167362**	**Amérique du Nord**
Mexico	829	657	1058	#5531	5264	3587	2352	2535	3003	4134	Mexique
Panama	156	...	420	401	452	588	744	...	...	...	Panama
United States	207996	178980	191400	206976	241968	199283	196043	153985	154158	162025	Etats-Unis
America, South	**33575**	**35979**	**37224**	**41264**	**33264**	**31507**	**23787**	**23225**	**28236**	**31868**	**Amérique du Sud**
Bolivia	13	5	8	1	14	*14	...	...	...	...	Bolivie
Brazil	31201	33456	34713	39134	30502	28445	20821	19491	24418	28085	Brésil
Colombia	...	...	2446	2066	2628	3010	...	3633	3734	...	Colombie
Ecuador	...	...	57	63	120	38	36	90	73	...	Equateur
Asia	**342588**	**338417**	**311292**	**264706**	**237131**	**204058**	**207570**	**182340**	**159130**	**147332**	**Asie**
Armenia	..	285	88	24	50	85	24	0	0	0	Arménie
Azerbaijan	..	165	42	16	2	0	0	0	0	0	Azerbaïdjan
Hong Kong SAR	246406	247855	220638	168806	152823	119258	124535	94453	74571	63596	Hong-Kong RAS
China, Macao, SAR	...	...	...	33243	15566	16346	14895	15182	10906	11997	Chine, Macao PAS
Cyprus	...	...	7106	...	...	2911	3212	2657	2457	1875	Chypre
Indonesia	14372	8583	9245	7950	10239	10999	...	15481	14026	...	Indonésie
Japan[1]	21286	19817	18318	18341	20851	20584	20329	23483	21354	17274	Japon[1]
Kyrgyzstan	..	...	43	17	38	5	23	34	59	44	Kirghizistan
Malaysia	22746	26209	24987	26930	23328	19057	18547	17173	18547	24392	Malaisie
Tajikistan	..	...	32	42	49	16	8	0	0	0	Tadjikistan
Turkey	3895	4294	5945	5955	10789	14782	14632	13875	17209	16341	Turquie
Turkmenistan	..	15	19	12	26	15	3	2	...	...	Turkménistan
Europe	**137983**	**165520**	**167255**	**138719**	**134311**	**93310**	**117002**	**105311**	**113162**	**120903**	**Europe**
Austria	2044	1741	1541	1213	986	614	639	515	454	345	Autriche
Belarus	..	1634	1457	1791	1364	1000	842	773	757	944	Bélarus
Belgium	7124	7379	7407	6324	[2]3184	[2]2246	[2]2032	[2]466	[2]350	[2]538	Belgique
Croatia	..	1184	1279	1456	1377	952	812	949	937	...	Croatie
Denmark[3]	2510	2515	...	...	...	...	...	...	...	...	Danemark[3]
Czech Republic	..	..	...	218	1995	1588	981	398	432	326	République tchèque
Estonia	..	374	363	218	666	433	316	564	409	337	Estonie
Finland	904	483	419	377	401	460	367	373	396	335	Finlande
France	18702	19543	17576	17267	12200	10976	9572	8707	8445	8723	France
Germany	..	36530	32450	31787	26831	24650	20830	20355	20888	...	Allemagne
Germany(Fed.Rep.)	38471	..	..	..	..	..	..	..	..	..	Allemagne(Rép.féd.)
German D.R.(former)	3536	..	..	..	..	..	..	..	..	..	R.D.A. (anc.)
Greece	27823	29176	31451	12709	11757	7713	4642	7869	6133	...	Grèce
Hungary[4]	4252	4336	4395	4177	3572	3325	3215	3254	3215	3156	Hongrie[4]
Iceland	5	8	7	...	...	...	...	...	...	...	Islande
Ireland	2375	...	...	...	...	...	...	...	...	...	Irlande
Latvia	..	...	...	488	397	513	704	1037	1463	1176	Lettonie
Lithuania	..	...	...	...	...	2398	3166	3571	5030	5083	Lituanie
Netherlands[3][5]	2222	2475	2251	4185	4684	4328	4435	4893	3510	3528	Pays-Bas[3][5]
Norway	...	...	71	56	...	...	...	...	...	...	Norvège
Portugal	...	...	2809	2767	3400	2757	3237	4024	4238	3405	Portugal
Republic of Moldova	..	315	313	[6]82	[6]66	[6]300	[6]151	[6]174	[6]63	[6]206	Rép. de Moldova
Russian Federation	..	11553	10647	6704	3334	2086	2069	1966	2039	2555	Fédération de Russie
Slovakia	..	..	...	...	...	...	745	787	358	123	Slovaquie
Slovenia	..	2260	1795	1876	1545	1299	1075	1108	1191	897	Slovénie
Spain	[1][7]13326	[1][7]13008	[1][7]11868	7996	9205	9246	9795	12604	14135	15401	Espagne
Sweden	171	...	10	13	27	30	20	110	59	47	Suède
Ukraine	..	8831	7242	5607	2813	3127	2587	4004	4382	5038	Ukraine
United Kingdom	[8]11455	[8]10355	...	...	34384	5252	37407	19113	24837	...	Royaume-Uni
Yugoslavia	..	4357	2302	1036	897	757	1269	1888	1339	455	Yougoslavie
T.F.Yug.Rep. Macedonia	..	1737	1597	2352	2086	1799	1136	851	3144	3894	L'ex-RY Macédoine
Oceania	**11051**	**10314**	**8931**	**7714**	**6917**	**6776**	**7231**	**7315**	**5590**	**4796**	**Océanie**
Australia[9]	...	...	...	4778	4823	4676	3704	5007	4144	3697	Australie[9]

For general note and footnotes, see end of table. — Voir la fin du tableau pour la remarque générale et les notes.

Blouses, women's and girls' (continued)
Blouses de dames et de fillettes (suite)

ISIC-BASED CODE - CODE BASE CITI

3220-16

Unit : Thousand units

Unité : En milliers

Country or area	1990	1991	1992	1993	1994	1995	1996	1997	1998	1999	Pays ou zone
New Zealand [10] [11]	5884	5300	4069	2936	2094	2100	...	2308	...	...	Nouvelle-Zélande [10] [11]
Total	744262	740927	727871	672666	667031	546917	562564	484314	472820	480218	Total

General Note.
Women's and girls' blouses of all types, with or without sleeves, extending from the shoulders to the waist. They may button down the front or back or may be pulled on over the head and shoulders. (SITC, Rev.3: 84270-0).

[1] Excluding children's clothing.
[2] Incomplete coverage.
[3] Sales.
[4] Excluding blouses for work and for uniforms.
[5] Production by establishments employing 20 or more persons.
[6] Excluding Transnistria region.
[7] Including household production.
[8] Manufacturers' sales.
[9] Twelve months ending 30 June of year stated.
[10] Twelve months ending 30 September of year stated.
[11] Including work wear.

Remarque générale.
Blouses de tous types, pour dames et fillettes, avec ou sans manches, allant des épaules à la taille. Elles peuvent se boutonner devant ou derrière ou être enfilées par la tête. (CTCI, Rev.3: 84270-0).

[1] Non compris les vêtements d'enfants.
[2] Couverture incomplète.
[3] Ventes.
[4] Non compris les blouses de travail et d'uniformes.
[5] Production des établissements occupant 20 personnes ou plus.
[6] Non compris la région de Transnistria.
[7] Y compris la production ménagère.
[8] Ventes des fabricants.
[9] Période de douze mois finissant le 30 juin de l'année indiquée.
[10] Période de douze mois finissant le 30 septembre de l'année indiquée.
[11] Y compris les vêtements de travail.

Coats, women's and girls'
Manteaux de dames et de fillettes

ISIC-BASED CODE - CODE BASE CITI

3220-19

Unit : Thousand units

Unité : En milliers

Country or area	1990	1991	1992	1993	1994	1995	1996	1997	1998	1999	Pays ou zone
America, North	**8161**	**8167**	**8172**	**9049**	**8091**	**8292**	**7224**	**8164**	**8164**	**8163**	**Amérique du Nord**
Mexico	5	11	16	12	3	...	...	...	...	...	Mexique
United States	...	...	...	9037	8088	8283	7216	...	...	...	Etats-Unis
America, South	**90**	**76**	**125**	**5**	**46**	**5**	**31**	**3**	**4**	**0**	**Amérique du Sud**
Colombia	...	...	125	5	46	5	...	3	4	...	Colombie
Asia	**6099**	**8622**	**9050**	**10971**	**8522**	**6760**	**5736**	**7848**	**5851**	**5629**	**Asie**
Armenia	..	...	...	...	1	0	0	0	0	0	Arménie
Azerbaijan[1]	..	371	91	46	11	8	0	76	3	0	Azerbaïdjan[1]
Hong Kong SAR	728	1097	2753	4857	1473	1236	517	2334	287	268	Hong-Kong RAS
Cyprus	...	...	259	...	...	349	263	208	192	178	Chypre
Indonesia	...	...	1114	1849	2883	...	...	...	...	...	Indonésie
Japan[1,2]	3188	2914	3300	3103	3401	3028	2856	...	...	...	Japon[1,2]
Kazakhstan	..	907	787	459	217	33	9	31	212	136	Kazakhstan
Kyrgyzstan	..	1019	553	346	81	29	21	14	5	7	Kirghizistan
Tajikistan	..	96	98	9	6	0	0	0	0	0	Tadjikistan
Turkey	15	19	85	55	206	127	117	243	233	145	Turquie
Turkmenistan	..	25	10	5	1	1	4	...	...	...	Turkménistan
Europe	**21979**	**39639**	**34492**	**28511**	**24395**	**22390**	**23876**	**23343**	**22578**	**20297**	**Europe**
Austria[3,4]	590	504	465	271	232	...	168	166	...	145	Autriche[3,4]
Belgium	2851	2664	1928	1553	...	...	...	...	...	...	Belgique
Croatia	..	325	360	227	207	348	439	469	402	...	Croatie
Denmark[5]	215	145	131	128	114	83	162	228	71	50	Danemark[5]
Czech Republic	...	...	...	...	658	562	496	444	396	284	République tchèque
Estonia	...	245	145	153	202	194	206	225	222	184	Estonie
Finland	2108	1124	1144	530	656	679	628	...	...	...	Finlande
France[3]	...	...	...	...	...	...	485	405	385	458	France[3]
Germany	..	7024	...	5000	3947	3831	5064	4873	3678	...	Allemagne
Germany(Fed.Rep.)	6850	..	..	..	..	..	..	..	..	..	Allemagne(Rép.féd.)
German D.R.(former)[6]	1267	..	..	..	..	..	..	..	..	..	R.D.A. (anc.)[6]
Greece	572	678	594	546	523	383	...	...	...	...	Grèce
Hungary[7]	885	894	1080	898	723	727	...	...	...	79	Hongrie[7]
Iceland	1	0	1	...	...	...	2	...	...	...	Islande
Ireland	152	...	...	...	...	...	...	...	...	...	Irlande
Latvia[1]	..	...	...	...	64	40	47	47	49	265	Lettonie[1]
Lithuania	..	...	...	...	...	434	614	731	761	584	Lituanie
Netherlands[5,8]	208	170	159	489	786	1172	...	...	...	...	Pays-Bas[5,8]
Norway	...	...	...	106	...	...	...	...	...	...	Norvège
Portugal	207	207	1434	1632	1498	945	1030	1064	1210	971	Portugal
Republic of Moldova	..	386	198	[9]266	[9]156	[9]44	[9]39	[9]88	[9]134	[9]89	Rép. de Moldova
Russian Federation	..	11963	9034	7268	3035	2041	1402	1507	1793	1895	Fédération de Russie
Slovakia	..	...	...	...	...	...	963	864	123	94	Slovaquie
Slovenia	..	296	319	656	811	720	1428	1123	1139	541	Slovénie
Spain	[10,11]4345	[10,11]4625	[10,11]4694	2020	2703	2854	...	...	...	...	Espagne
Sweden[1]	...	3	8	...	...	18	...	...	23	23	Suède[1]
Ukraine[10]	..	4176	2740	1529	1572	1233	1335	1575	1792	1355	Ukraine[10]
United Kingdom	1180	1363	...	...	...	...	...	...	...	...	Royaume-Uni
Yugoslavia	..	1369	894	422	286	197	347	485	343	69	Yougoslavie
T.F.Yug.Rep. Macedonia	..	419	877	1369	992	844	477	652	1505	656	L'ex-RY Macédoine
Oceania	**568**	**657**	**822**	**776**	**642**	**633**	**634**	**654**	**560**	**621**	**Océanie**
Australia	424	573	636	[12]655	[12]495	[12]486	[12]488	[12]506	[12]410	[12]469	Australie
New Zealand[13,14]	144	84	186	121	147	147	...	...	...	...	Nouvelle-Zélande[13,14]
Total	**36897**	**57161**	**52662**	**49312**	**41695**	**38080**	**37501**	**40012**	**37156**	**34710**	**Total**

General Note.

Women's and girls' coats of all types other than raincoats, such as overcoats, spring coats, duffel coats (with or without hoods), capes and cloaks. Jackets, boleros and beach wraps are excluded as well as dressing-gowns, bathrobes, negligees, bed jackets, house coats and similar indoor wear. (SITC, Rev.3: 84211-1, 84219-0).

Remarque générale.

Manteaux de tous types pour dames et fillettes, autres que les imperméables, tels que manteaux d'hiver, manteaux d'été, capes, pèlerines et duffel-coats. Cette rubrique ne comprend pas les jaquettes, les boléros, les pyjamas de plage, les robes de chambre, les déshabillés, les négligés, les saut-de-lit, les liseuses, les peignoirs de bain et les autres vêtements d'intérieur de même genre. (CTCI, Rev.3: 84211-1, 84219-0).

For footnotes, see end of table.

Voir la fin du tableau pour les notes.

Coats, women's and girls' (continued)
Manteaux de dames et de fillettes (suite)

ISIC-BASED CODE - CODE BASE CITI
3220-19

Footnotes
[1] Including raincoats for women and girls.
[2] Shipments.
[3] 1995 data are confidential.
[4] 1998 data are confidential.
[5] Sales.
[6] Incomplete coverage.
[7] Excluding work coats and uniforms.
[8] Production by establishments employing 20 or more persons.
[9] Excluding Transnistria region.
[10] Excluding children's clothing.
[11] Including household production.
[12] Twelve months ending 30 June of year stated.
[13] Twelve months ending 30 September of year stated.
[14] Including raincoats.

Notes.
[1] Y compris les imperméables pour dames et fillettes.
[2] Expéditions.
[3] Pour 1995, les données sont confidentielles.
[4] Pour 1998, les données sont confidentielles.
[5] Ventes.
[6] Couverture incomplète.
[7] Non compris les blouses de travail et les uniformes.
[8] Production des établissements occupant 20 personnes ou plus.
[9] Non compris la région de Transnistria.
[10] Non compris les vêtements d'enfants.
[11] Y compris la production ménagère.
[12] Période de douze mois finissant le 30 juin de l'année indiquée.
[13] Période de douze mois finissant le 30 septembre de l'année indiquée.
[14] Y compris les imperméables.

Dresses, women's and girls'
Robes de dames et de fillettes

ISIC-BASED CODE - CODE BASE CITI

3220-22

Unit : Thousand units   Unité : En milliers

Country or area	1990	1991	1992	1993	1994	1995	1996	1997	1998	1999	Pays ou zone
Africa	**22965**	**21477**	**17080**	**14565**	**13689**	**13341**	**11496**	**11453**	**9012**	**8231**	**Afrique**
Algeria[1]	364	180	146	80	53	70	55	36	38	12	Algérie[1]
Kenya	1611	1270	1309	1124	306	260	222	...	...	...	Kenya
Mozambique	136	77	...	98	158	118	14	111	...	...	Mozambique
South Africa	20854	19950	15523	13263	13172	12893	11205	11306	8875	8120	Afrique du Sud
America, North	**174655**	**163396**	**159940**	**180807**	**202037**	**218793**	**194063**	**192168**	**211609**	**198193**	**Amérique du Nord**
Mexico	2338	2076	2042	#5290	4941	4007	3988	4036	4018	3821	Mexique
United States	172317	161320	157898	175517	197096	214786	190075	188132	207591	194372	Etats-Unis
America, South	**5995**	**8125**	**7465**	**9694**	**12035**	**12093**	**12625**	**10406**	**10289**	**11424**	**Amérique du Sud**
Brazil	[2][3]2090	[2][3]3765	[2][3]3380	[2][3]5147	[2][3]7094	8025	8160	5942	5775	6194	Brésil
Colombia	3891	...	4070	4529	4921	4046	...	4432	4491	...	Colombie
Ecuador	...	...	15	18	20	22	125	32	23	...	Equateur
Asia	**39319**	**69301**	**61123**	**46986**	**50099**	**50808**	**44693**	**39070**	**55745**	**50361**	**Asie**
Armenia	..	4440	1071	211	261	130	...	43	49	6	Arménie
Azerbaijan	..	4591	2264	1605	591	110	90	50	5	9	Azerbaïdjan
Hong Kong SAR	9184	18892	11788	10846	8103	10433	6585	6457	6612	5688	Hong-Kong RAS
China, Macao, SAR	...	...	...	1256	3517	4108	3664	3063	3294	3416	Chine, Macao PAS
Cyprus	..	..	2032	..	...	1092	881	860	890	580	Chypre
Indonesia	10382	11476	...	14703	18206	...	...	14304	31101	...	Indonésie
Japan[2][4]	8461	7722	7370	3110	3657	3635	3665	3771	3608	2802	Japon[2][4]
Kyrgyzstan	..	4547	2221	1556	861	307	234	371	290	327	Kirghizistan
Malaysia	5518	5745	7650	5782	7752	7456	6157	5449	4092	5278	Malaisie
Tajikistan	..	3642	1798	1601	964	310	65	9	4	8	Tadjikistan
Turkey	2341	2020	3761	3559	3769	5916	5465	4425	5651	6551	Turquie
Turkmenistan	..	2635	1819	1701	1362	616	415	268	149	...	Turkménistan
Europe	**76578**	**261654**	**166983**	**109362**	**86444**	**59045**	**63913**	**59367**	**57992**	**57673**	**Europe**
Austria	719	721	569	451	405	308	354	314	376	271	Autriche
Belarus	..	11722	8537	6163	3108	1222	1094	1198	1561	1376	Bélarus
Belgium	5022	4833	4144	3842	[5]1106	[5]1097	[5]1179	[5]967	[5]822	[5]964	Belgique
Croatia	..	725	380	288	333	404	332	303	...	...	Croatie
Denmark[6]	967	1152	1146	1022	1046	1549	1410	1176	1626	2584	Danemark[6]
Estonia	..	1237	713	102	135	168	93	99	203	175	Estonie
Finland	336	263	196	220	189	199	182	168	221	146	Finlande
France[7]	10416	9111	8584	10128	[5]8360	10540	8988	8437	8114	7335	France[7]
Germany	..	16067	12635	11486	8822	8202	6068	4452	4548	...	Allemagne
Germany(Fed.Rep.)	16593	..	..	..	..	..	..	..	..	..	Allemagne(Rép.féd.)
German D.R.(former)	3855										R.D.A. (anc.)
Greece	2919	2382	1977	1630	1668	1609	1489	1059	1122	...	Grèce
Hungary[8]	4655	2195	1666	1776	1593	1977	1591	1350	1601	1869	Hongrie[8]
Iceland	0	1	1	...	...	...	...	...	...	...	Islande
Ireland	251	...	...	...	...	...	...	...	...	...	Irlande
Latvia	..	869	408	149	314	353	447	397	690	711	Lettonie
Lithuania	..	2513	1269	409	297	691	771	752	1414	1580	Lituanie
Netherlands[6][9]	1514	1440	985	1417	1606	2763	...	...	...	...	Pays-Bas[6][9]
Portugal	1633	458	746	636	678	1005	1047	1638	1746	1986	Portugal
Republic of Moldova	..	7229	4713	[10]1211	[10]777	[10]307	[10]366	[10]156	[10]95	[10]125	Rép. de Moldova
Russian Federation	..	121064	57138	30781	22473	10733	8587	5997	5268	6304	Fédération de Russie
Slovakia	..	..	...	...	...	...	456	372	177	25	Slovaquie
Slovenia	..	811	718	640	620	558	159	212	497	222	Slovénie
Spain	[4][11]7272	[4][11]7344	[4][11]6415	4318	5879	7092	7386	7186	8527	9166	Espagne
Sweden	...	...	...	...	...	9	4	3	8	16	Suède
Ukraine	..	49557	36090	15606	4932	3218	2740	1920	1946	1806	Ukraine
United Kingdom	[12]20426	[12]17836	...	...	21125	4007	...	18165	...	...	Royaume-Uni
Yugoslavia	..	1746	1094	250	412	245	278	406	567	265	Yougoslavie
T.F.Yug.Rep. Macedonia	..	127	39	15	54	280	298	255	458	276	L'ex-RY Macédoine
Oceania	**872**	**623**	**425**	**382**	**472**	**493**	**498**	**216**	**233**	**189**	**Océanie**
New Zealand[13]	872	623	425	382	472	493	...	216	...	...	Nouvelle-Zélande[13]
Total	**320384**	**524576**	**413016**	**361796**	**364776**	**354574**	**327288**	**312680**	**344880**	**326070**	**Total**

For general note and footnotes, see end of table.   Voir la fin du tableau pour la remarque générale et les notes.

Dresses, women's and girls' (continued)
Robes de dames et de fillettes (suite)

General Note.

Women's and girls' dresses of all types, such as street dresses, cocktail dresses, evening dresses, house dresses and schoolgirls' tunics. They may include a matching jacket or bolero. Two-piece dresses consisting of a matching blouse and skirt are included. Knitted dresses made in knitting mills are excluded. (SITC, Rev.3: 84240-0, 84424-0).

[1] Including skirts.
[2] Including suits for women and girls.
[3] Including knitted dresses and suits.
[4] Excluding children's clothing.
[5] Incomplete coverage.
[6] Sales.
[7] Dresses for beach and street, and ensemble dresses.
[8] Excluding work dresses and uniforms.
[9] Production by establishments employing 20 or more persons.
[10] Excluding Transnistria region.
[11] Including household production.
[12] Manufacturers' sales.
[13] Twelve months ending 30 September of year stated.

Remarque générale.

Robes de tous types pour dames et fillettes, telles que robes de ville, robes de cocktail, robes du soir, robes de maison et uniformes d'écolière. Elles peuvent comprendre une jaquette ou un boléro du même tissu. Cette rubrique comprend les costumes deux-pièces, qui consistent en une blouse et une jupe du même tissu, mais ne comprend pas les robes en bonneterie faites en usine. (CTCI, Rev.3: 84240-0, 84424-0).

[1] Y compris les jupes.
[2] Y compris les costumes pour dames et fillettes.
[3] Y compris les robes et costumes en bonneterie.
[4] Non compris les vêtements d'enfants.
[5] Couverture incomplète.
[6] Ventes.
[7] Robes de ville, de plage et ensembles.
[8] Non compris les habits de travail et les uniformes.
[9] Production des établissements occupant 20 personnes ou plus.
[10] Non compris la région de Transnistrie.
[11] Y compris la production ménagère.
[12] Ventes des fabricants.
[13] Période de douze mois finissant le 30 septembre de l'année indiquée.

Raincoats, women's and girls'
Imperméables pour dames et fillettes

ISIC-BASED CODE - CODE BASE CITI

3220-25

Unit : Thousand units

Unité : En milliers

Country or area	1990	1991	1992	1993	1994	1995	1996	1997	1998	1999	Pays ou zone
Africa	**202**	**202**	**202**	**202**	**202**	**202**	**202**	**202**	**202**	**202**	**Afrique**
South Africa	202	...	...	...	...	...	...	...	...	...	Afrique du Sud
America, North	**4982**	**5169**	**4718**	**4956**	**4956**	**4956**	**4956**	**4956**	**4956**	**4956**	**Amérique du Nord**
Mexico	...	...	...	...	...	3587	...	...	...	...	Mexique
United States	1395	1582	1131	...	...	...	...	...	...	...	Etats-Unis
Asia	**351**	**635**	**600**	**636**	**512**	**363**	**358**	**388**	**377**	**371**	**Asie**
Armenia	..	38	35	7	11	3	0	0	0	0	Arménie
Indonesia	...	...	351	...	...	...	...	...	...	...	Indonésie
Kazakhstan	..	91	90	140	114	3	1	...	...	...	Kazakhstan
Kyrgyzstan	..	25	16	5	7	0	0	0	0	5	Kirghizistan
Tajikistan	..	130	103	121	22	0	0	0	0	0	Tadjikistan
Turkmenistan	..	0	5	12	7	...	...	...	5	...	Turkménistan
Europe	**2749**	**5839**	**5089**	**4838**	**3487**	**3473**	**2606**	**2907**	**2732**	**2233**	**Europe**
Austria [1] [2]	...	...	...	...	...	...	99	99	...	50	Autriche [1] [2]
Estonia	..	32	8	5	7	18	15	9	8	10	Estonie
Finland	16	15	18	17	78	86	67	218	112	78	Finlande
France	...	...	...	...	...	312	145	116	90	71	France
Greece	100	110	97	82	43	57	...	...	...	...	Grèce
Hungary [3]	28	14	22	17	10	17	...	...	...	...	Hongrie [3]
Portugal	...	...	762	738	703	877	492	629	378	126	Portugal
Republic of Moldova	..	43	2	[4]3	[4]1	[4]0	[4]0	...	...	...	Rép. de Moldova
Russian Federation	..	2548	1918	1855	636	351	193	229	427	336	Fédération de Russie
Slovakia	..	..	...	...	...	...	...	...	123	94	Slovaquie
Spain	...	...	...	150	204	308	...	...	...	...	Espagne
Ukraine [5]	..	566	407	390	278	228	167	186	206	170	Ukraine [5]
United Kingdom [6]	1028	...	...	...	...	...	...	...	...	...	Royaume-Uni [6]
Oceania	**73**	**73**	**116**	**94**	**0**	**80**	**73**	**73**	**73**	**73**	**Océanie**
New Zealand [7]	...	...	116	94	0	80	...	...	...	...	Nouvelle-Zélande [7]
Total	**8357**	**11917**	**10725**	**10726**	**9157**	**9074**	**8195**	**8526**	**8339**	**7834**	**Total**

General Note.
Women's and girls' raincoats of all types and materials, except rubber. (SITC, Rev.3: 84211-2).

Remarque générale.
Imperméables de tous types et en toutes matières pour dames et fillettes, sauf en caoutchouc. (CTCI, Rev.3: 84211-2).

[1] 1995 data are confidential.
[2] 1998 data are confidential.
[3] Excluding work raincoats.
[4] Excluding Transnistria region.
[5] Excluding children's clothing.
[6] Manufacturers' sales.
[7] Twelve months ending 30 September of year stated.

[1] Pour 1995, les données sont confidentielles.
[2] Pour 1998, les données sont confidentielles.
[3] Non compris les imperméables de travail.
[4] Non compris la région de Transnistria.
[5] Non compris les vêtements d'enfants.
[6] Ventes des fabricants.
[7] Période de douze mois finissant le 30 septembre de l'année indiquée.

Skirts, slacks and shorts, women's and girls'
Jupes, pantalons et shorts pour dames et fillettes

ISIC-BASED CODE - CODE BASE CITI

3220-28

Unit : Thousand units   Unité : En milliers

Country or area	1990	1991	1992	1993	1994	1995	1996	1997	1998	1999	Pays ou zone
Africa	**15112**	**13413**	**14040**	**18256**	**22398**	**22956**	**24156**	**21505**	**18384**	**21105**	**Afrique**
Angola[1]	861	673	325	...	...	...	...	...	...	...	Angola[1]
South Africa	14251	12740	13715	17636	21778	22336	23536	20885	17764	20485	Afrique du Sud
America, North	**453525**	**438635**	**493410**	**533723**	**484274**	**481694**	**481498**	**482324**	**482296**	**484076**	**Amérique du Nord**
Mexico	1748	1706	2112	#7733	7344	5417	4897	5421	5321	7029	Mexique
Panama	349	...	578	701	989	336	660	...	...	...	Panama
United States	451428	436327	490720	525289	...	...	...	...	...	...	Etats-Unis
America, South	**2664**	**3078**	**2063**	**5175**	**3416**	**2562**	**4892**	**7393**	**5915**	**6838**	**Amérique du Sud**
Colombia	...	...	2004	5140	3385	2539	...	7169	5620	...	Colombie
Ecuador	...	...	59	35	31	23	582	224	295	...	Equateur
Asia	**202409**	**211230**	**176930**	**152167**	**129324**	**123972**	**126100**	**112223**	**121701**	**125655**	**Asie**
Armenia	..	...	625	222	46	6	5	0	0	0	Arménie
Azerbaijan	..	47	250	133	40	6	59	29	11	6	Azerbaïdjan
Hong Kong SAR	143134	152739	116824	94072	74286	70013	74502	61336	[2]70136	[2]77344	Hong-Kong RAS
China, Macao, SAR	...	...	...	3151	2462	3861	4681	5168	5325	5858	Chine, Macao PAS
Cyprus	...	...	2393	...	...	1851	1855	1952	1786	1574	Chypre
Indonesia	8950	3934	...	5305	5826	6341	...	...	3786	...	Indonésie
Japan[3]	45628	48300	46588	45552	42514	38268	35897	34819	...	...	Japon[3]
Kyrgyzstan	..	87	76	72	34	9	11	28	40	53	Kirghizistan
Tajikistan	..	90	66	51	42	7	0	0	0	0	Tadjikistan
Turkey	1359	1839	1635	1688	2162	3592	3395	3200	4334	3503	Turquie
Turkmenistan	..	47	48	19	10	18	5	1	4	...	Turkménistan
Europe	**258948**	**276036**	**271554**	**255715**	**228828**	**233220**	**240768**	**228467**	**229665**	**236251**	**Europe**
Austria[4]	2303	2088	1865	1267	911	1538	1191	947	...	...	Autriche[4]
Belgium	10259	9460	8719	6726	[5]5473	[5]5337	[5]5164	[5]3988	[5]3199	[5]3250	Belgique
Croatia	..	2098	1608	1883	1621	1406	1320	1948	1803	...	Croatie
Estonia	..	259	169	140	308	279	246	298	287	302	Estonie
Finland	2010	1694	975	832	1176	1206	973	2250	2403	1861	Finlande
France	...	...	...	...	[5]27786	29574	28151	24361	22386	20707	France
Germany	..	68170	60780	51903	41806	38077	34778	31909	30226	...	Allemagne
Germany(Fed.Rep.)	62546	..	..	..	..	..	..	..	..	..	Allemagne(Rép.féd.)
German D.R.(former)	9518	..	..	..	..	..	..	..	..	..	R.D.A. (anc.)
Greece	17278	16304	13641	16452	10353	8403	9223	10801	9784	...	Grèce
Hungary[6]	5417	4587	4915	4910	4959	4367	...	3018	6228	9448	Hongrie[6]
Iceland	18	13	6	...	...	...	...	...	...	...	Islande
Ireland[1]	2443	...	...	...	...	...	...	...	...	...	Irlande[1]
Latvia	..	295	208	899	996	811	1200	1491	1759	1527	Lettonie
Lithuania	..	702	532	563	695	#3607	5249	8438	12057	13148	Lituanie
Netherlands[7][8][9]	3027	2827	2654	2681	2008	2657	...	...	...	...	Pays-Bas[7][8][9]
Norway	..	...	16	...	...	...	...	...	...	...	Norvège
Portugal	[10]3715	[10]1552	18330	16728	14720	13829	13507	13096	12923	12217	Portugal
Republic of Moldova	..	547	340	[11]39	[11]22	[11]85	[11]64	[11]41	[11]72	[11]241	Rép. de Moldova
Russian Federation	..	13469	10637	5924	2382	1607	1546	1316	1419	2082	Fédération de Russie
Slovakia	..	..	...	...	...	...	571	484	712	34	Slovaquie
Slovenia	..	956	823	911	769	720	3188	3151	3113	2882	Slovénie
Spain	[3][12]18463	[3][12]19602	[3][12]19635	18410	25207	27413	30237	38020	47710	51854	Espagne
Sweden	321	148	128	109	117	121	181	178	164	226	Suède
Ukraine[10]	..	6116	4628	3573	1777	1834	2183	2343	3059	3020	Ukraine[10]
United Kingdom	...	...	...	88637	81097	85397	90068	73490	62059	...	Royaume-Uni
Yugoslavia	..	2937	1586	457	551	461	599	994	966	458	Yougoslavie
T.F.Yug.Rep. Macedonia	..	1164	902	1652	1172	1569	943	1097	1622	1135	L'ex-RY Macédoine
Oceania	**5590**	**3328**	**3218**	**3979**	**2419**	**3358**	**3473**	**2422**	**2046**	**1809**	**Océanie**
New Zealand[13]	5590	3328	3218	3979	2419	3358	...	2422	...	...	Nouvelle-Zélande[13]
Total	**938248**	**945720**	**961214**	**969015**	**870658**	**867761**	**880887**	**854334**	**860007**	**875733**	**Total**

For general note and footnotes, see end of table.   Voir la fin du tableau pour la remarque générale et les notes.

Skirts, slacks and shorts, women's and girls' (continued)
Jupes, pantalons et shorts pour dames et fillettes (suite)

General Note.

Women's and girls' skirts, slacks or shorts of all types, produced for sale as individual garments rather than as part of a combined costume, other than those made in knitting mills. (SITC, Rev.3: 84250-0, 84260-0).

Remarque générale.

Jupes, pantalons et shorts de tous types pour dames et fillettes, fabriqués pour être vendus séparément en non comme partie d'un costume deux-pièces. Cette rubrique ne comprend pas les jupes en bonneterie faites en usine. (CTCI, Rev.3: 84250-0, 84260-0).

[1] Excluding shorts.
[2] Excluding women's and girls' slacks and shorts of corduroy, for confidentiality purposes.
[3] Excluding children's clothing.
[4] Beginning 1998, data are confidential.
[5] Incomplete coverage.
[6] Excluding skirts, slacks and shorts for work and for uniforms.
[7] Sales.
[8] Production by establishments employing 20 or more persons.
[9] Excluding shorts and slacks.
[10] Skirts only.
[11] Excluding Transnistria region.
[12] Including household production.
[13] Twelve months ending 30 September of year stated.

[1] Non compris les shorts.
[2] A l'exclusion des pantalons et shorts de corduroy pour dames et fillettes, pour raisons de confidentialité.
[3] Non compris les vêtements d'enfants.
[4] A partir de 1998, les données sont confidentielles.
[5] Couverture incomplète.
[6] Non compris les jupes, shorts et pantalons de travail ou d'uniformes.
[7] Ventes.
[8] Production des établissements occupant 20 personnes ou plus.
[9] Non compris les shorts et pantalons tout-aller.
[10] Jupes seulement.
[11] Non compris la région de Transnistria.
[12] Y compris la production ménagère.
[13] Période de douze mois finissant le 30 septembre de l'année indiquée.

Suits, women's and girls'
Costumes pour dames et fillettes

ISIC-BASED CODE - CODE BASE CITI

3220-31

Unit : Thousand units   Unité : En milliers

Country or area	1990	1991	1992	1993	1994	1995	1996	1997	1998	1999	Pays ou zone
Africa	**1758**	**1792**	**1719**	**1809**	**2132**	**1829**	**1650**	**858**	**758**	**806**	**Afrique**
South Africa	1758	1792	1719	1809	2132	1829	1650	858	758	806	Afrique du Sud
America, North	**8447**	**10790**	**9951**	**9637**	**9739**	**10131**	**9579**	**9949**	**9988**	**10027**	**Amérique du Nord**
Mexico	366	7	...	...	...	...	...	...	...	...	Mexique
Panama	353	...	332	262	364	756	204	...	...	...	Panama
United States [1]	7728	10404	9432	...	...	...	...	...	...	...	Etats-Unis [1]
America, South	**4826**	**4778**	**4644**	**4722**	**4803**	**4764**	**4621**	**4447**	**4441**	**4432**	**Amérique du Sud**
Colombia	...	...	...	...	...	...	...	4432	4441	...	Colombie
Ecuador	...	...	212	290	371	332	189	15	9	...	Equateur
Asia	**25106**	**25870**	**25413**	**24126**	**26307**	**20373**	**19701**	**18799**	**23847**	**14971**	**Asie**
Armenia		257	11	32	1	0	0	0	0	0	Arménie
Hong Kong SAR [2]	3975	2095	2973	3348	5168	880	1204	72	...	29	Hong-Kong RAS [2]
Cyprus	...	...	310	...	...	137	142	125	119	86	Chypre
Indonesia	...	...	8622	...	...	...	...	...	...	...	Indonésie
Tajikistan	..	81	49	43	32	8	49	0	0	0	Tadjikistan
Turkey	12342	14651	13439	11907	12321	10716	9674	9970	12902	6224	Turquie
Turkmenistan	..	0	9	21	10	...	...	...	...	...	Turkménistan
Europe	**12085**	**17332**	**17983**	**14517**	**13154**	**15286**	**15790**	**15180**	**15711**	**14586**	**Europe**
Austria	213	244	171	73	87	14	17	17	16	11	Autriche
Belgium	545	454	386	290	[3]38	[3]43	[3]28	[3]9	[3]7	[3]30	Belgique
Croatia	..	432	348	450	360	244	240	297	295	...	Croatie
Denmark [4]	279	108	71	874	850	1004	1311	1567	1037	694	Danemark [4]
Czech Republic	..	..	...	...	184	113	132	89	95	57	République tchèque
Estonia	..	6	...	3	1	6	5	4	7	3	Estonie
Finland	541	394	309	684	509	668	617	117	117	100	Finlande
Germany	..	2506	2060	1596	1765	3540	2655	2156	...	...	Allemagne
Germany(Fed.Rep.)	2091	..	..	..	..	..	..	..	..	..	Allemagne(Rép.féd.)
German D.R.(former)	659	..	..	..	..	..	..	..	..	..	R.D.A. (anc.)
Greece	670	616	470	489	180	187	244	325	349	...	Grèce
Hungary [5]	805	508	608	548	505	529	521	509	386	351	Hongrie [5]
Iceland	0	1	1	...	...	...	...	...	...	...	Islande
Ireland	70	...	...	...	...	...	...	...	...	...	Irlande
Latvia	..	...	...	18	100	55	50	96	602	614	Lettonie
Lithuania	..	...	...	...	...	93	76	217	434	426	Lituanie
Netherlands [4][6]	433	475	703	537	564	679	...	...	...	...	Pays-Bas [4][6]
Portugal	...	...	148	139	151	86	199	123	224	149	Portugal
Russian Federation		1807	2341	1953	1001	590	886	620	649	814	Fédération de Russie
Slovakia	...	...	...	...	...	...	1564	1502	242	65	Slovaquie
Slovenia	..	677	253	333	507	578	327	288	293	213	Slovénie
Spain	[7][8]2314	[7][8]2903	[7][8]3424	899	1232	1248	1342	1318	1768	1912	Espagne
Sweden	17	19	9	8	26	27	23	27	30	27	Suède
Ukraine [7]	..	1489	1390	981	257	511	398	377	448	401	Ukraine [7]
United Kingdom	...	...	...	3213	3657	3718	4071	4276	4406	...	Royaume-Uni
Yugoslavia		944	611	307	244	415	346	339	446	146	Yougoslavie
T.F.Yug.Rep. Macedonia		112	69	65	22	24	26	176	413	359	L'ex-RY Macédoine
Oceania	**168**	**152**	**589**	**631**	**64**	**514**	**308**	**35**	**219**	**204**	**Océanie**
New Zealand [9]	168	152	589	631	64	514	...	35	...	...	Nouvelle-Zélande [9]
Total	**52390**	**60714**	**60299**	**55442**	**56199**	**52896**	**51648**	**49268**	**54964**	**45026**	**Total**

General Note.

Women's and girls' suits of all types, consisting essentially of a jacket and skirt or a jacket and a pair of trousers (usually matching), including skiing, riding, hunting and other sports suits. Knitted suits made in knitting mills are excluded. (SITC,Rev.3: 84221-0).

Remarque générale.

Costumes de tous types pour dames et fillettes, comprenant essentiellement une jaquette et une jupe ou une jaquette et un pantalon (habituellement du même tissu), y compris les costumes de ski, d'équitation, de chasse et autres costumes pour le sport. Cette rubrique ne comprend pas les costumes en bonneterie faits en usine. (CTCI, Rev.3: 84221-0).

For footnotes, see end of table.   Voir la fin du tableau pour les notes.

Suits, women's and girls' (continued)
Costumes pour dames et fillettes (suite)

ISIC-BASED CODE - CODE BASE CITI

3220-31

Footnotes
[1] Including pants suits.
[2] 1998 data are confidential.
[3] Incomplete coverage.
[4] Sales.
[5] Excluding work suits and uniforms.
[6] Production by establishments employing 20 or more persons.
[7] Excluding children's clothing.
[8] Including household production.
[9] Twelve months ending 30 September of year stated.

Notes.
[1] Y compris les ensembles pantalon.
[2] Pour 1998, les données sont confidentielles.
[3] Couverture incomplète.
[4] Ventes.
[5] Non compris les vêtements de travail et les uniformes.
[6] Production des établissements occupant 20 personnes ou plus.
[7] Non compris les vêtements d'enfants.
[8] Y compris la production ménagère.
[9] Période de douze mois finissant le 30 septembre de l'année indiquée.

Shirts, men's and boys'
Chemises d'hommes et de garçonnets

ISIC-BASED CODE - CODE BASE CITI

3220-34

Unit : Thousand units Unité : En milliers

Country or area	1990	1991	1992	1993	1994	1995	1996	1997	1998	1999	Pays ou zone
Africa	**36041**	**40855**	**28034**	**33537**	**31380**	**33595**	**27774**	**30823**	**22717**	**26114**	**Afrique**
Algeria	1868	2028	1518	1331	1265	1040	498	330	519	598	Algérie
Angola	1081	523	234	...	...	...	...	...	...	...	Angola
Kenya	1697	2725	2566	2699	2364	1850	1450	...	...	...	Kenya
Malawi	174	653	472	364	268	...	...	...	...	...	Malawi
Mozambique	1365	1362		542	613	618	855	715	730	862	Mozambique
South Africa	29856	33564	22393	27988	26257	29118	24013	27118	18914	22206	Afrique du Sud
America, North	**120457**	**107602**	**121612**	**126891**	**127190**	**122740**	**122312**	**121067**	**121331**	**120689**	**Amérique du Nord**
Mexico	6034	5847	5695	#17219	16738	12224	12228	10362	10565	9863	Mexique
Panama	3975	...	2517	2072	2852	2916	2484	...	...	...	Panama
United States	110448	98952	113400	...	...	...	...	...	...	...	Etats-Unis
America, South	**80869**	**108207**	**119906**	**117383**	**129773**	**112365**	**95245**	**59805**	**66737**	**60762**	**Amérique du Sud**
Bolivia	131	121	211	632	490	*807	...	...	...	...	Bolivie
Brazil	68610	88728	91707	91950	99347	89400	74981	51109	56035	45773	Brésil
Colombia	10678	...	26402	23583	28670	20818	...	6735	8627	...	Colombie
Ecuador	...	...	1586	1218	1266	1340	1654	1212	1256	...	Equateur
Asia	**265560**	**324239**	**277510**	**261471**	**253261**	**233332**	**216750**	**239963**	**162731**	**176531**	**Asie**
Armenia	..	1285	726	174	138	101	...	#12	23	2	Arménie
Azerbaijan	..	4964	1988	1401	518	324	88	3	1	1	Azerbaïdjan
Hong Kong SAR	173282	171615	148344	132108	119456	96323	82157	85198	49139	41040	Hong-Kong RAS
China, Macao, SAR	...	...	...	15166	13418	11996	13487	10604	9914	9366	Chine, Macao PAS
Cyprus	...	...	1823	...	...	1266	1275	1090	961	878	Chypre
Indonesia	31234	72586	56104	...	64348	68052	...	87606	43490	...	Indonésie
Japan[1]	6831	6084	5707	4514	5313	4774	3898	3079	...	...	Japon[1]
Kyrgyzstan	..	4071	1766	1119	475	143	97	65	35	26	Kirghizistan
Malaysia	27110	29084	33187	33253	33688	33726	36431	33230	37250	36693	Malaisie
Myanmar[2]	2315	2050	2032	2490	4670	...	...	...	...	...	Myanmar[2]
Tajikistan	..	5793	2667	1976	658	329	18	12	50	91	Tadjikistan
Turkey	7007	6312	6262	5667	7919	10808	12378	13052	12360	12042	Turquie
Turkmenistan	..	3527	2147	1899	1444	1234	1353	726	81	...	Turkménistan
Europe	**181756**	**359115**	**288287**	**224330**	**184996**	**175173**	**155641**	**149759**	**148843**	**132027**	**Europe**
Austria	3195	2989	2802	2763	2439	1874	1707	1377	1299	996	Autriche
Belarus	..	9011	8477	7694	4673	3211	2547	2899	3366	3144	Bélarus
Belgium	3376	3342	3264	3144	771	736	703	778	[3]493	[3]365	Belgique
Croatia	..	3329	2582	2646	2237	1897	1651	1408	1306	...	Croatie
Denmark[4]	40	7	4	39	57	271	143	23	21	41	Danemark[4]
Czech Republic	...	...	...	...	2884	2701	2137	2095	1917	1626	République tchèque
Estonia	..	1734	1291	584	780	646	740	797	823	894	Estonie
Finland	470	308	306	142	185	197	219	162	200	153	Finlande
France	16535	14110	9519	9035	12327	...	...	...	...	...	France
Germany	...	...	...	6745	5457	...	...	...	...	...	Allemagne
Germany(Fed.Rep.)	7644	..	..	..	..	..	..	..	..	..	Allemagne(Rép.féd.)
German D.R.(former)	7139	..	..	..	..	..	..	..	..	..	R.D.A. (anc.)
Greece	3371	3114	2768	5090	4745	4774	3889	3607	2792	...	Grèce
Hungary	2389	2699	1962	2102	1813	1953	2192	2135	1642	2036	Hongrie
Iceland	3	3	3	...	...	...	10	...	...	...	Islande
Ireland	40225	...	...	...	...	...	...	...	...	...	Irlande
Latvia	..	1942	893	507	569	503	565	598	475	39	Lettonie
Lithuania	..	2630	2144	1913	1755	1936	2028	2096	2354	2018	Lituanie
Netherlands[4][5]	...	...	...	7928	5093	4270	...	...	...	...	Pays-Bas[4][5]
Norway	...	483	526	291	...	...	...	...	204	...	Norvège
Portugal	14943	11021	13569	14581	12329	12592	16474	14031	13770	12334	Portugal
Republic of Moldova	..	7824	7483	[6]155	[6]185	[6]97	[6]77	[6]18	[6]14	[6]24	Rép. de Moldova
Russian Federation	..	101570	57253	40512	25405	13550	7159	3220	2542	3848	Fédération de Russie
Slovakia	...	...	...	...	...	...	348	1915	637	389	Slovaquie
Slovenia	..	2098	2203	1797	1547	1223	1100	969	873	646	Slovénie
Spain	38981	43377	43118	18707	20579	25107	22524	25035	24633	21400	Espagne
Sweden[7]	530	360	324	271	172	185	264	410	368	379	Suède[7]
Ukraine	..	41545	36123	21489	11230	9684	4537	3349	4731	3220	Ukraine
United Kingdom	[8]36775	[8]31685	...	...	15780	...	15784	15060	15829	...	Royaume-Uni

For general note and footnotes, see end of table. Voir la fin du tableau pour la remarque générale et les notes.

Shirts, men's and boys' (continued)
Chemises d'hommes et de garçonnets (suite)

ISIC-BASED CODE - CODE BASE CITI

3220-34

Unit : Thousand units   Unité : En milliers

Country or area	1990	1991	1992	1993	1994	1995	1996	1997	1998	1999	Pays ou zone
Yugoslavia	..	13753	7005	3407	4149	3752	3062	4172	5528	2025	Yougoslavie
T.F.Yug.Rep. Macedonia	..	8091	7214	7318	6407	6408	6407	*5575	6721	5991	L'ex-RY Macédoine
Oceania	16755	24132	20199	14710	14112	11760	12285	10702	9645	9389	Océanie
Australia	[9]12798	21102	17942	12815	11936	10483	10046	9620	8761	[9]8730	Australie
New Zealand[10]	3957	3030	2257	1895	2176	1277	...	1082	...	...	Nouvelle-Zélande[10]
Total	701437	964149	855548	778321	740711	688965	630007	612120	532004	525512	Total

General Note.
Men's and boys' shirts of all types, with full length or short sleeves, designed to be worn with or without a tie, such as shirts for street wear, dress shirts, work shirts and sports shirts. Knitted sports shirts made in knitting mills are excluded. (SITC, Rev.3: 84150-0, 84370-0).

Remarque générale.
Chemises de tous types, pour hommes et garçonnets, à manches longues ou courtes, conçues pour être portées avec ou sans cravate, telles que les chemises de ville, les chemises habillées, les chemises de travail et les chemises de sport,à l'exclusion des chemisettes en bonneterie faites en usine. (CTCI, Rev.3: 84150-0, 84370-0).

[1] Shipments.
[2] Government production only.
[3] Incomplete coverage.
[4] Sales.
[5] Production by establishments employing 20 or more persons.
[6] Excluding Transnistria region.
[7] Including knitted or crocheted shirts.
[8] Source: Stataistical Office of the European Communities (Luxembourg).
[9] Twelve months ending 30 June of year stated.
[10] Twelve months ending 30 September of year stated.

[1] Expéditions.
[2] Production de l'Etat seulement.
[3] Couverture incomplète.
[4] Ventes.
[5] Production des établissements occupant 20 personnes ou plus.
[6] Non compris la région de Transnistria.
[7] Y compris les chemises en bonneterie.
[8] Source: Office de statistique des Communautés européennes (Luxembourg).
[9] Période de douze mois finissant le 30 juin de l'année indiquée.
[10] Période de douze mois finissant le 30 septembre de l'année indiquée.

Underwear, men's and boys'
Sous-vêtements pour hommes et garçonnets

ISIC-BASED CODE - CODE BASE CITI
3220-37

Unit : Thousand units

Unité : En milliers

Country or area	1990	1991	1992	1993	1994	1995	1996	1997	1998	1999	Pays ou zone
Africa	**16539**	**16043**	**12290**	**13920**	**15468**	**16921**	**14804**	**11615**	**11089**	**10982**	**Afrique**
Angola[1]	1199	299	485	...	...	...	...	...	...	...	Angola[1]
Kenya	985	...	...	...	...	...	...	...	...	...	Kenya
South Africa	14355	14759	10820	12274	13822	15275	13158	9969	9443	9336	Afrique du Sud
America, North	**1180279**	**1177747**	**1312033**	**1329064**	**1239379**	**1117670**	**1175780**	**1439984**	**1054346**	**1013793**	**Amérique du Nord**
Mexico	9961	12682	9110	#29270	41226	26260	34824	39472	42391	44304	Mexique
Panama	2886	...	3143	5750	3625	2760	2916	...	...	...	Panama
United States	[2]1167432	[2]1161552	[2]1299780	[2]1294044	1194528	1088650	1138040	1395911	1007136	964453	Etats-Unis
America, South	**526**	**2987**	**7823**	**7423**	**12370**	**11653**	**19359**	**30316**	**46724**	**46426**	**Amérique du Sud**
Bolivia	318	352	745	...	...	...	...	...	...	...	Bolivie
Colombia	...	...	6930	6780	11745	11086	...	29806	46247	...	Colombie
Ecuador	...	...	148	171	153	95	122	38	5	...	Equateur
Asia	**225739**	**154616**	**170705**	**272651**	**142023**	**163344**	**141887**	**312252**	**266873**	**285420**	**Asie**
Hong Kong SAR	122773	77932	89492	181873	45138	64775	30501	23042	23342	36498	Hong-Kong RAS
China, Macao, SAR	...	...	...	1486	798	816	3205	5075	4198	16998	Chine, Macao PAS
Cyprus	...	...	1871	...	...	1128	977	758	627	695	Chypre
Indonesia[1]	44217	13083	19560	29298	31970	25539	...	47053	18514	...	Indonésie[1]
Japan[3]	22243	20752	21080	20003	20248	17242	17384	164186	138684	120135	Japon[3]
Kyrgyzstan	..	2395	1743	707	431	69	34	28	6	31	Kirghizistan
Malaysia	3392	3754	5081	3058	6934	5379	8175	7892	8643	8271	Malaisie
Syrian Arab Republic	18624	19824	21600	24540	24216	34188	39276	50760	58644	...	Rép. arabe syrienne
Turkey	13410	13285	8776	9798	10432	13758	13277	13030	13571	11852	Turquie
Turkmenistan	..	2529	1502	879	847	450	404	428	644	...	Turkménistan
Europe	**131051**	**127587**	**121277**	**63000**	**63828**	**88353**	**88383**	**82300**	**89755**	**84749**	**Europe**
Austria	30	119	109	132	133	97	100	109	167	117	Autriche
Belgium[4]	374	208	93	32	...	...	...	...	...	...	Belgique[4]
Croatia	..	87	78	33	27	33	23	#1036	3859	...	Croatie
Denmark[5]	...	...	...	92	115	90	78	100	134	160	Danemark[5]
Czech Republic	..	..	...	...	962	944	983	1034	933	779	République tchèque
Finland	25	18	18	22	26	29	27	...	...	...	Finlande
France	5108	4617	3794	3218	14037	...	...	...	...	...	France
Germany	...	...	...	1712	1622	#26530	25030	...	20740	...	Allemagne
Germany(Fed.Rep.)	1990			..							Allemagne(Rép.féd.)
Greece	10584	8221	3736	3960	2549	2497	2081	2091	2864	...	Grèce
Hungary	743	2823	2373	2318	2767	3810	3258	2690	2117	2014	Hongrie
Iceland[1]	8	6	8	...	...	...	4	...	...	...	Islande[1]
Latvia	..	...	...	6	48	31	37	88	73	47	Lettonie
Lithuania	..	...	...	...	...	979	735	512	367	744	Lituanie
Netherlands[5][6]	...	...	...	11673	7812	8194	...	...	...	...	Pays-Bas[5][6]
Norway	...	...	823	...	...	857	738	...	...	...	Norvège
Portugal	...	...	15220	13719	11060	9250	8146	8151	10650	10606	Portugal
Republic of Moldova	..	426	201	...	...	...	...	...	...	...	Rép. de Moldova
Slovakia	..	..	...	...	...	...	1613	1112	318	109	Slovaquie
Slovenia	..	82	74	254	270	144	394	153	379	299	Slovénie
Spain	[3][7]70143	[3][7]58680	[3][7]52324	3408	3642	4242	4687	4347	4706	4712	Espagne
United Kingdom	19730	17070	...	17972	15070	...	...	20337	15397	...	Royaume-Uni
Yugoslavia	..	1930	1211	410	511	475	320	440	421	331	Yougoslavie
T.F.Yug.Rep. Macedonia	..	79	100	144	167	178	78	30	39	13	L'ex-RY Macédoine
Oceania	**34474**	**37464**	**34208**	**23535**	**32843**	**33447**	**32662**	**32662**	**32662**	**32662**	**Océanie**
Australia[8]	31773	34763	31711	21595	...	...	...	...	...	...	Australie[8]
New Zealand[9]	...	...	2497	1940	2882	3486	...	...	...	...	Nouvelle-Zélande[9]
Total	**1588609**	**1516445**	**1658336**	**1709592**	**1505910**	**1431387**	**1472875**	**1909129**	**1501448**	**1474033**	**Total**

General Note.
Underwear made from woven or knitted fabrics other than knitted garments made in knitting mills. Elastic or rubberized garments are excluded. (SITC, Rev.3: 84160-0, 84380-0).

Remarque générale.
Sous-vêtements faits d'étoffe tissée ou tricotée, autres que les articles de bonneterie faits en usine. Cette rubrique ne comprend pas les articles élastiques ou caoutchoutés. (CTCI, Rev.3: 84160-0, 84380-0).

For footnotes, see end of table.

Voir la fin du tableau pour les notes.

Underwear, men's and boys' (continued)
Sous-vêtements pour hommes et garçonnets (suite)

ISIC-BASED CODE - CODE BASE CITI

3220-37

Footnotes

[1] Including underwear for women and girls.
[2] Including knitted undergarments except body supporting garments.

[3] Excluding children's clothing.
[4] Including knitted undergarments.
[5] Sales.
[6] Production by establishments employing 20 or more persons.
[7] Including household production.
[8] Knitted underwear only.
[9] Twelve months ending 30 September of year stated.

Notes.

[1] Y compris les sous-vêtements pour dames et fillettes.
[2] Y compris les sous-vêtements en bonneterie autres que les sous-vêtements élastiques ou caoutchoutés.
[3] Non compris les vêtements d'enfants.
[4] Y compris les sous-vêtements en bonneterie.
[5] Ventes.
[6] Production des établissements occupant 20 personnes ou plus.
[7] Y compris la production ménagère.
[8] Sous vêtements en bonneterie seulement.
[9] Période de douze mois finissant le 30 septembre de l'année indiquée.

Underwear, women's and girls'
Sous-vêtements de dames et de fillettes

ISIC-BASED CODE - CODE BASE CITI

3220-40

Unit : Thousand units   Unité : En millier

Country or area	1990	1991	1992	1993	1994	1995	1996	1997	1998	1999	Pays ou zone
Africa	**36823**	**39939**	**34987**	**37379**	**44785**	**47314**	**42089**	**36227**	**31184**	**27242**	**Afrique**
South Africa	36823	39939	34987	37379	44785	47314	42089	36227	31184	27242	Afrique du Sud
America, North	**916024**	**964177**	**1028137**	**996053**	**982248**	**978539**	**975872**	**982134**	**983629**	**983743**	**Amérique du Nord**
Mexico	...	...	...	11545	17287	11405	11546	14384	15234	14702	Mexique
Panama	4253	...	3642	3952	5339	7512	4704	...	...	...	Panama
United States [1]	899532	946740	1011660	980556	...	...	...	...	...	...	Etats-Unis [1]
America, South	**74174**	**80912**	**62988**	**69499**	**64619**	**67760**	**67368**	**58202**	**60588**	**56539**	**Amérique du Sud**
Brazil	53024	60174	45896	47531	46329	49321	47105	37506	40811	39093	Brésil
Colombia	...	...	16460	21527	17977	17628	...	20691	19772	...	Colombie
Ecuador	...	...	632	441	313	811	1254	5	5	...	Equateur
Asia	**657246**	**308553**	**436189**	**235593**	**290322**	**284348**	**300801**	**255423**	**257867**	**260055**	**Asie**
Hong Kong SAR	558214	235285	355038	130499	176748	120307	167870	111702	87668	93529	Hong-Kong RAS
China, Macao, SAR [2]	...	...	...	12168	11237	19313	...	27551	31942	24233	Chine, Macao PAS [2]
Cyprus	...	...	1132	...	...	1116	1131	946	1208	1255	Chypre
Indonesia	42326	10420	10066	37587	39359	76183	...	53206	71478	...	Indonésie
Japan [3] [4]	40039	42199	42340	38753	42500	42258	38909	36330	...	...	Japon [3] [4]
Turkey	10023	10881	15736	15455	19347	25171	29239	25688	26545	28932	Turquie
Europe	**322287**	**344196**	**299722**	**192254**	**201940**	**257267**	**290990**	**259572**	**253742**	**222154**	**Europe**
Austria	33914	37040	43497	39745	43028	37000	74382	49259	41100	40000	Autriche
Belgium	[5]3114	[5]3185	[5]3397	[5]3056	...	# [6]1003	[6]729	[6]552	[6]528	[6]256	Belgique
Croatia	..	631	536	1348	1317	1238	2250	4167	10709	...	Croatie
Denmark [7]	1146	1292	...	...	...	...	...	...	...	...	Danemark [7]
Czech Republic	..	..	...	...	1625	1471	889	910	738	814	République tchèque
Finland	195	28	19	16	27	32	30	...	...	...	Finlande
France [8]	38459	35849	34901	29520	50829	...	...	...	...	...	France [8]
Germany	..	...	...	26118	22331	#96901	87739	79358	74437	..	Allemagne
Germany(Fed.Rep.)	29241	..	..	...	...	...	...	...	...	...	Allemagne(Rép.féd.)
Greece	8998	6579	5762	9323	2822	2552	3774	2568	1975	...	Grèce
Hungary	2114	1272	1066	3114	4266	6250	7112	2442	3518	3387	Hongrie
Iceland	7	9	12	...	...	...	...	...	...	...	Islande
Latvia	..	...	...	...	...	...	...	...	...	109	Lettonie
Lithuania	..	...	...	...	...	270	231	182	135	89	Lituanie
Netherlands [7] [9] [10]	35960	37300	37160	22338	21214	17982	...	...	...	...	Pays-Bas [7] [9] [10]
Portugal	[10]25055	[10]18562	7761	7518	6439	6278	11351	14132	13601	12035	Portugal
Republic of Moldova	..	453	106	...	...	...	...	...	...	...	Rép. de Moldova
Slovakia	..	..	...	...	...	...	3657	2725	247	51	Slovaquie
Slovenia	..	7940	6598	7622	7483	7169	2720	1478	1701	1264	Slovénie
Spain	[11] [12]6808	[11] [12]6407	[11] [12]6137	8807	9191	10007	10917	9156	...	...	Espagne
United Kingdom	76001	71649	...	#27973	24305	20854	17203	20268	31530	...	Royaume-Uni
Yugoslavia	..	16334	9245	654	1698	1429	1192	5901	6913	3527	Yougoslavie
T.F.Yug.Rep. Macedonia	..	8	35	...	2	...	3	*7	1	708	L'ex-RY Macédoine
Oceania	**55492**	**52944**	**49343**	**36029**	**46934**	**52578**	**48887**	**48887**	**48887**	**48887**	**Océanie**
Australia [13]	49502	46954	43215	31917	...	...	...	...	...	...	Australie [13]
New Zealand [14]	...	...	6128	4112	4037	9681	...	...	...	...	Nouvelle-Zélande [14]
Total	**2062045**	**1790721**	**1911366**	**1566808**	**1630849**	**1687806**	**1726006**	**1640444**	**1635898**	**1598619**	**Total**

General Note.

Underwear made from woven or knitted fabrics, other than knitted garments made in knitting mills. Elastic or rubberized garments are excluded. (SITC, Rev.3: 84280-0, 84480-0).

Remarque générale.

Sous-vêtements faits d'étoffe tissée ou tricotée, autres que la bonneterie. Cette rubrique ne comprend pas les sous-vêtements élastiques ou caoutchoutés. (CTCI, Rev.3: 84280-0, 84480-0).

For footnotes, see end of table.

Voir la fin du tableau pour les notes.

Underwear, women's and girls' (continued)
Sous-vêtements de dames et de fillettes (suite)

Footnotes

[1] Including knitted undergarments except body supporting garments.

[2] 1996 data are confidential.

[3] Excluding children's clothing.

[4] Shipments.

[5] Including knitted undergarments.

[6] Incomplete coverage.

[7] Sales.

[8] Ready-to-wear articles made from fabrics.

[9] Production by establishments employing 20 or more persons.

[10] Including underwear for men and boys.

[11] Underwear for women only.

[12] Including household production.

[13] Knitted underwear only.

[14] Twelve months ending 30 September of year stated.

Notes.

[1] Y compris les sous-vêtements en bonneterie autres que les sous-vêtements élastiques ou caoutchoutés.

[2] Pour 1996, les données sont confidentielles.

[3] Non compris les vêtements d'enfants.

[4] Expéditions.

[5] Y compris les sous-vêtements en bonneterie.

[6] Couverture incomplète.

[7] Ventes.

[8] Articles de confection en tissus.

[9] Production des établissements occupant 20 personnes ou plus.

[10] Y compris les sous-vêtements pour hommes et garçonnets.

[11] Sous-vêtements pour dames seulement.

[12] Y compris la production ménagère.

[13] Sous vêtements en bonneterie seulement.

[14] Période de douze mois finissant le 30 septembre de l'année indiquée.

Heavy leather
Cuirs forts

ISIC-BASED CODE - CODE BASE CITI

3231-01A

Unit : Metric tons

Unité : Tonnes métrique

Country or area	1990	1991	1992	1993	1994	1995	1996	1997	1998	1999	Pays ou zone
Africa	**1006**	**907**	**626**	**721**	**894**	**879**	**870**	**792**	**820**	**876**	**Afrique**
Algeria	408	163	94	27	202	185	161	69	83	114	Algérie
Ethiopia[1][2]	76	142	40	110	28	...	...	...	...	...	Ethiopie[1][2]
Kenya	87	82	82	...	...	...	...	...	...	...	Kenya
Tunisia	435	520	410	500	580	...	...	...	...	...	Tunisie
America, North	**29931**	**30414**	**30426**	**31244**	**29842**	**31367**	**33031**	**33597**	**34355**	**34123**	**Amérique du Nord**
Dominican Republic	300	...	...	...	...	...	...	...	...	...	Rép. dominicaine
El Salvador	100	...	...	...	...	...	...	...	...	...	El Salvador
Mexico	...	...	...	...	7217	8894	10807	10777	11431	11096	Mexique
Panama	806	...	530	963	1225	1073	824	...	...	...	Panama
United States	21000	...	...	...	...	...	...	...	...	...	Etats-Unis
America, South	**50140**	**43537**	**39825**	**52224**	**50102**	**47500**	**49727**	**50353**	**50980**	**51606**	**Amérique du Sud**
Brazil[3]	21000	...	...	...	...	...	...	...	...	...	Brésil[3]
Ecuador	300	...	753	#6771	6542	3940	...	...	...	...	Equateur
Paraguay	28840	18876	18072	24453	...	...	...	...	...	...	Paraguay
Asia	**170496**	**172137**	**168304**	**165335**	**170239**	**174623**	**177549**	**171006**	**168270**	**165797**	**Asie**
Azerbaijan	..	706	158	102	109	0	0	0	0	0	Azerbaïdjan
Cyprus	500	...	561	...	...	468	298	586	148	280	Chypre
Indonesia	...	...	...	79177	80037	...	...	...	...	...	Indonésie
Iran(Islamic Rep. of)[4]	1200	416	553	259	654	...	769	...	529	...	Iran(Rép. islamique)[4]
Japan[4][5]	1330	1075	817	790	...	...	...	...	...	...	Japon[4][5]
Jordan[1]	100	...	...	...	...	...	...	...	...	...	Jordanie[1]
Kazakhstan	..	3807	2422	1386	#212	130	86	10	...	...	Kazakhstan
Korea, Republic of	78942	...	...	...	...	...	...	...	...	...	Corée, République de
Lao People's Dem. Rep.	...	...	...	...	81	196	...	...	...	...	Rép. dém. pop. lao
Mongolia	1000	800	500	200	100	82	71	...	...	...	Mongolie
Sri Lanka	61	9	...	...	...	...	...	...	...	...	Sri Lanka
Syrian Arab Republic	79	48	45	71	72	42	6	...	...	...	Rép. arabe syrienne
Turkey	7500	6047	4394	3700	8463	13374	16481	9911	7754	5499	Turquie
Viet Nam	...	...	...	...	...	18	12	33	5	*4	Viet Nam
Europe	**83821**	**145642**	**125867**	**119017**	**112959**	**107748**	**106416**	**106427**	**108362**	**105339**	**Europe**
Belarus	..	4959	4308	2850	2503	929	528	994	1039	1269	Bélarus
Belgium	1557	1439	1339	1117	...	...	...	...	...	...	Belgique
Bulgaria	300	277	110	37	17	12	21	15	...	...	Bulgarie
Croatia	..	67	58	38	63	81	30	35	40	...	Croatie
Czechoslovakia(former)	2498	1243	..	..	..	..	..	...	...	..	Tchécoslovaquie(anc.)
Czech Republic	..	..	342	..	...	...	...	...	...	...	République tchèque
France	...	...	...	12000	12000	...	...	...	...	...	France
Germany	..	3486	2734	1949	1915	...	...	...	...	...	Allemagne
Germany(Fed.Rep.)	2200	..	..	..	..	...	...	...	...	...	Allemagne(Rép.féd.)
German D.R.(former)	1484	..	..	..	..	...	...	...	...	...	R.D.A. (anc.)
Greece	1174	1303	1219	...	...	...	...	...	...	...	Grèce
Hungary	407	311	237	225	242	246	...	...	...	...	Hongrie
Italy[3]	39600	...	...	...	...	...	...	...	...	..	Italie[3]
Latvia		1312								25	Lettonie
Poland	4005	2209	1796	1675	1801	#397	544	550	213	293	Pologne
Portugal	2340	1058	774	444	373	...	...	...	...	...	Portugal
Republic of Moldova	..	2309	605	[6]364	[6]155	[6]220	[6]253	[6]260	[6]261	[6]89	Rép. de Moldova
Romania	3456	2702	1916	1358	969	962	684	441	2621	229	Roumanie
Russian Federation	..	39939	28542	...	...	...	...	...	...	...	Fédération de Russie
Slovakia	..	..	...	...	...	...	...	...	1126	...	Slovaquie
Slovenia	..	...	...	...	...	...	4	...	...	...	Slovénie
Spain[3]	7500	...	...	...	...	...	...	...	...	...	Espagne[3]
Ukraine	..	20527	17890	9220	3901	1295	650	438	455	250	Ukraine
United Kingdom	2800	...	...	...	...	...	...	...	...	...	Royaume-Uni
Yugoslavia	..	597	298	...	144	209	90	92	146	239	Yougoslavie
Yugoslavia, SFR	2500	..	..	..	..	..	..	..	..	..	Yougoslavie, RSF
USSR (former)	**93861**	..	..	..	..	..	..	..	..	..	**URSS (anc.)**

For general note and footnotes, see end of table.

Voir la fin du tableau pour la remarque générale et les notes.

Heavy leather (continued)
Cuirs forts (suite)

ISIC-BASED CODE - CODE BASE CITI

3231-01A

Unit : Metric tons

Unité : Tonnes métriques

Country or area	1990	1991	1992	1993	1994	1995	1996	1997	1998	1999	Pays ou zone
Total	**429255**	**392637**	**365047**	**368540**	**364036**	**362117**	**367592**	**362175**	**362786**	**357740**	**Total**

General Note.

Hides and skins, tanned (including chamois-dressed), parchment dressed or otherwise prepared as leather, undressed or dressed, but excluding those tanned or dressed with the hair on. Reconstituted and artificial leather are excluded. The heavy and light leather together correspond to SITC 6113, 6114 and 6119. The headings include, inter alia, sole leather (in heavy leather), upper and lining leather, leather for hand-bags (in light leather). (SITC, Rev.3: 61130-1A, 61140-1A, 61150-1A, 61160-1A, 61170-1A, 61180-1A).

[1] Sole leather only.
[2] Twelve months ending 7 July of the year stated.
[3] Source: Food and Agriculture Organization of the United Nations (FAO), (Rome).
[4] Production by establishments employing 10 or more persons.
[5] Shipments.
[6] Excluding Transnistria region.

Remarque générale.

Peaux tannées, chamoisées, corroyées ou autrement préparées (parcheminées, vernies etc.), à l'exception de celles revêtues de leurs poils. Les cuirs artificiels ou reconstitués ne sont pas compris dans cette rubrique. L'ensemble des deux rubriques représente les positions 6113, 6114 et 6119 de la CTCI. Elles comprennent notamment le cuir pour semelles (cuir fort), les cuirs pour empeignes et doublures, le cuir pour sacs à main (cuir léger). (CTCI, Rev.3: 61130-1A, 61140-1A, 61150-1A, 61160-1A, 61170-1A, 61180-1A).

[1] Cuir pour semelles seulement.
[2] Période de douze mois finissant le 7 juillet de l'année indiquée.
[3] Source: Organisation des Nations Unies pour l'alimentation et l'agriculture (FAO), (Rome).
[4] Production des établissements occupant 10 personnes ou plus.
[5] Expéditions.
[6] Non compris la région de Transnistria.

Light leather
Cuirs légers

ISIC-BASED CODE - CODE BASE CITI

3231-04B

Unit : Thousand square metres

Country or area	1990	1991	1992	1993	1994	1995	1996	1997	1998	1999	Pays ou zone
Africa	**5642**	**5378**	**3728**	**5006**	**4635**	**4467**	**4611**	**5034**	**4745**	**5034**	**Afrique**
Algeria	2928	2583	924	1949	1520	970	786	811	830	1008	Algérie
Kenya	8	12	15	19	56	63	63	...	...	...	Kenya
Tunisia	2706	2783	2789	3038	3059	3434	3762	4134	...	...	Tunisie
America, North	**14253**	**14339**	**14425**	**14970**	**14703**	**13565**	**14126**	**15395**	**15156**	**14859**	**Amérique du Nord**
Cuba	2880	...	...	...	...	...	...	...	...	...	Cuba
Dominican Republic	780	...	...	...	...	...	...	...	...	...	Rép. dominicaine
Mexico	...	...	...	10490	10223	9085	9646	10915	10676	10379	Mexique
Panama	820	...	...	...	...	...	...	...	...	...	Panama
America, South	**58471**	**58471**	**58471**	**58471**	**58471**	**58471**	**58471**	**58471**	**58471**	**58471**	**Amérique du Sud**
Brazil[1]	58470	...	...	...	...	...	...	...	...	...	Brésil[1]
Ecuador	...	...	...	...	...	...	...	1	...	...	Equateur
Asia	**140124**	**140552**	**137098**	**132979**	**135275**	**137834**	**137822**	**135802**	**135647**	**135729**	**Asie**
Cyprus	120	...	31	...	...	200	...	...	...	...	Chypre
Georgia	..	...	...	81	42	6	7	3	4	5	Géorgie
Indonesia	...	...	...	12176	...	...	...	...	...	...	Indonésie
Iran(Islamic Rep. of)	[2]3960	[2]3938	[2]2700	[2]1620	[3]1530	[3]4197	[3]4382	[3]2448	[3]2374	...	Iran(Rép. islamique)
Japan[4]	35371	36851	34138	31960	...	...	...	...	...	...	Japon[4]
Jordan[5]	110	...	...	...	...	...	...	...	...	...	Jordanie[5]
Korea, Republic of	86260	85544	...	...	...	...	...	...	...	...	Corée, République de
Kyrgyzstan	..	684	665	399	175	142	199	134	57	64	Kirghizistan
Mongolia	1511	1030	995	287	316	194	22	5	...	...	Mongolie
Sri Lanka	616	37	...	...	...	...	...	...	...	...	Sri Lanka
Europe	**352223**	**428409**	**404847**	**371094**	**339983**	**331728**	**328933**	**325869**	**319791**	**316051**	**Europe**
Austria[6]	5331	5429	5686	5240	5638	...	...	...	...	...	Autriche[6]
Belarus	..	9924	8269	7381	6418	4989	4194	3912	3340	3926	Bélarus
Belgium	1324	1110	1078	943	...	...	...	...	...	...	Belgique
Bulgaria	203	118	122	101	122	136	114	111	...	...	Bulgarie
Croatia	..	2202	1460	1449	1463	1057	640	281	395	...	Croatie
Denmark[1][7]	1143	...	...	...	...	...	...	...	...	...	Danemark[1][7]
Czechoslovakia(former)	23615	15161								..	Tchécoslovaquie(anc.)
Czech Republic	..	..	12558	7512	...	..	..	...	...	...	République tchèque
Finland	4888	3205	3308	2853	2445	1414	915	...	...	...	Finlande
Germany	..	24577	21678	17385	16260	...	...	...	...	...	Allemagne
Germany(Fed.Rep.)	22101										Allemagne(Rép.féd.)
German D.R.(former)	11038	..	..	..	..	..	..	...	...	..	R.D.A. (anc.)
Greece[1]	6864	...	...	...	...	...	...	...	...	...	Grèce[1]
Hungary	6531	5041	3464	2977	2661	2002	...	...	...	493	Hongrie
Ireland[1]	2527	...	...	...	...	...	...	...	...	...	Irlande[1]
Italy[1]	149944										Italie[1]
Latvia	..	14861	9896	6403	2442	1736	1807	1209	518	22	Lettonie
Netherlands[7][8]	6499	6507	5331	4583	4603	4175	3615	4857	7195	...	Pays-Bas[7][8]
Norway[1]	827	...	...	...	...	...	...	...	...	...	Norvège[1]
Poland	20201	14013	11904	10765	10895	12213	12448	13367	11573	8861	Pologne
Portugal[1]	9550	...	...	...	...	...	...	...	...	...	Portugal[1]
Republic of Moldova	..	1676	1282	[9]873	[9]260	[9]204	[9]253	[9]305	[9]135	[9]57	Rép. de Moldova
Romania	13707	12879	9167	7830	6024	5638	6549	5405	3663	2353	Roumanie
Russian Federation	..	42014	37336	28543	11609	8996	6494	5248	3903	7865	Fédération de Russie
Slovakia	..	..	4151	...	...	...	...	...	309	...	Slovaquie
Slovenia	..	8186	8460	9353	7455	6646	6971	...	...	...	Slovénie
Spain[1]	52574	...	...	...	...	...	...	...	...	...	Espagne[1]
Sweden[10]	3344	...	...	...	...	...	...	...	...	...	Suède[10]
Ukraine	..	21151	19894	15772	9400	4738	3500	2992	3104	3381	Ukraine
United Kingdom	10012	...	...	...	...	...	...	...	...	...	Royaume-Uni
Yugoslavia	..	3399	2881	1950	1994	1924	2140	1826	1578	1418	Yougoslavie
T.F.Yug.Rep. Macedonia	..	171	137	166	130	129	210	151	146	58	L'ex-RY Macédoine
Total	**570713**	**647149**	**618568**	**582520**	**553066**	**546065**	**543963**	**540570**	**533809**	**530143**	**Total**

For general note and footnotes, see end of table.

Voir la fin du tableau pour la remarque générale et les notes.

Light leather (continued)
Cuirs légers (suite)

ISIC-BASED CODE - CODE BASE CITI

3231-04B

General Note.

Hides and skins, tanned (including chamois-dressed), parchment dressed or otherwise prepared as leather, undressed or dressed, but excluding those tanned or dressed with the hair on. Reconstituted and artificial leather are excluded. The heavy and light leather together correspond to SITC 6113, 6114 and 6119. The headings include, inter alia, sole leather (in heavy leather), upper and lining leather, leather for hand-bags (in light leather). (SITC, Rev.3: 61130-2B, 61140 -2B, 61150-2B, 61160-2B, 61170-2B, 61180-2B).

[1] Source: Food and Agriculture Organization of the United Nations (FAO), (Rome).

[2] Production by establishments employing 50 or more persons.

[3] Production by establishments employing 10 or more persons.

[4] Shipments.

[5] Upper leather only.

[6] Beginning 1995, data are confidential.

[7] Sales.

[8] Production by establishments employing 20 or more persons.

[9] Excluding Transnistria region.

[10] Including heavy leather.

Remarque générale.

Peaux tannées, chamoisées, corroyées ou autrement préparées (parcheminées, vernies etc.), à l'exception de celles revêtues de leurs poils. Les cuirs artificiels ou reconstitués ne sont pas compris dans cette rubrique. L'ensemble des deux rubriques représente les positions 6113, 6114 et 6119 de la CTCI. Elles comprennent notamment le cuir pour semelles (cuir fort), les cuirs pour empeignes et doublures, le cuir pour sacs à main (cuir léger). (CTCI, Rev.3: 61130-2B, 61140-2B, 61150-2B, 61160-2B, 61170-2B, 61180-2B).

[1] Source: Organisation des Nations Unies pour l'alimentation et l'agriculture (FAO), (Rome).

[2] Production des établissements occupant 50 personnes ou plus.

[3] Production des établissements occupant 10 personnes ou plus.

[4] Expéditions.

[5] Cuirs pour empeignes seulement.

[6] A partir de 1995, les données sont confidentielles

[7] Ventes.

[8] Production des établissements occupant 20 personnes ou plus.

[9] Non compris la région de Transnistria.

[10] Y compris les cuirs forts.

Footwear, total production, excluding rubber footwear
Chaussures, production totale, non compris les chaussures de caoutchouc

ISIC-BASED CODE - CODE BASE CITI

3240-00

Unit : Thousand pairs

Unité : Milliers de paires

Country or area	1990	1991	1992	1993	1994	1995	1996	1997	1998	1999	Pays ou zone
Africa	**149424**	**144045**	**132744**	**132978**	**126474**	**125854**	**126358**	**127765**	**118168**	**114884**	**Afrique**
Algeria	16376	11824	9040	7171	6467	3986	2320	2542	1249	1167	Algérie
Angola	143	95	48	...	...	...	...	...	...	...	Angola
Burkina Faso	500	1271	[1]1200	...	...	...	...	...	...	...	Burkina Faso
Cameroon	[2]1800	[1]1800	[1]1900	...	...	...	...	...	...	...	Cameroun
Cape Verde	...	...	...	...	...	192	...	...	...	...	Cap-Vert
Central African Rep.	200	[1]200	[1]200	...	...	...	...	...	...	...	Rép. centrafricaine
Congo	* [3]300	[1]300	[1]300	...	...	...	...	...	...	...	Congo
Côte d'Ivoire	1800	[1]1800	[1]1800	...	...	...	...	...	...	...	Côte d'Ivoire
Dem. Rep. of Congo[1]	900	900	900	...	...	...	...	...	...	...	Rép. dém. du Congo[1]
Egypt	48325	48311	48390	48385	48394	48444	48300	48131	...	...	Egypte
Ethiopia[4]	5367	3374	2419	3083	2871	3751	3773	6925	6252	[2]7477	Ethiopie[4]
Kenya	1605	1190	1480	1571	1774	2018	2089	...	...	...	Kenya
Madagascar	[5]807	[5]837	[5]702	[5]306	180	136	158	126	115	...	Madagascar
Mali	...	127	104	86	106	99	98	...	...	...	Mali
Mozambique	347	242	148	153	87	29	...	12	10	7	Mozambique
Nigeria	3779	7093	4538	4554	1182	1255	...	...	...	...	Nigéria
Senegal	302	153	644	508	...	...	...	...	...	...	Sénégal
South Africa[2]	51633	49318	42251	44492	41078	[6]39071	[6]38858	[6]35486	[6]29581	[6]24926	Afrique du Sud[2]
Sudan[1]	4000	3000	3000	...	...	...	...	...	...	...	Soudan[1]
Togo	100	[1]100	[1]100	...	...	...	...	...	...	...	Togo
Tunisia	10380	11590	13220	12870	14100	16580	18380	20300	...	...	Tunisie
United Rep.Tanzania	459	328	168	55	89	339	121	152	...	...	Rép. Unie de Tanzanie
America, North	**261507**	**244603**	**237522**	**272764**	**252187**	**229505**	**215946**	**218700**	**201045**	**169072**	**Amérique du Nord**
Canada[1]	15100	16000	16000	...	...	...	...	...	...	...	Canada[1]
Cuba	13400	[1]13000	[1]13400	...	...	...	...	...	...	...	Cuba
Dominican Republic[1]	2100	2000	2200	...	...	...	...	...	...	...	Rép. dominicaine[1]
El Salvador	3600	[1]3700	[1]3800	...	...	...	...	...	...	...	El Salvador
Haiti[1]	500	500	600	...	...	...	...	...	...	...	Haïti[1]
Jamaica[1]	700	700	800	...	...	...	...	...	...	...	Jamaïque[1]
Mexico	38931	36911	33141	62315	56948	44006	50340	52586	47072	43916	Mexique
Nicaragua	*1100	[1]1200	[1]1300	...	...	...	...	...	...	...	Nicaragua
Panama	1508	[1]1600	1377	1483	1294	1287	1058	...	...	...	Panama
United States	184568	168992	164904	171733	156712	146979	127315	127876	115808	87065	Etats-Unis
America, South	**203110**	**219118**	**215190**	**246499**	**203576**	**177658**	**219352**	**211728**	**192320**	**185205**	**Amérique du Sud**
Bolivia	833	862	1152	1308	1381	*1222	...	...	...	...	Bolivie
Brazil	141000	152925	156540	190026	146540	124272	163042	159861	142734	145393	Brésil
Chile	7577	9231	9311	9270	8317	7410	7134	7008	6777	6237	Chili
Colombia	[1]28100	[1]30000	20651	19471	20933	18277	...	[3]18736	[3]16635	...	Colombie
Ecuador	1500	[1]1600	1936	1691	1672	1744	1507	2	1	...	Equateur
Paraguay	5300	[1]5500	[1]5600	...	...	...	...	...	...	...	Paraguay
Peru[1]	18800	19000	20000	...	...	...	...	...	...	...	Pérou[1]
Asia	**1676821**	**1867885**	**2243116**	**2054887**	**2020729**	**2002978**	**1931285**	**1959113**	**2001668**	**2047159**	**Asie**
Armenia	..	11340	5661	3517	1612	656	305	87	65	24	Arménie
Azerbaijan	..	10491	5221	4329	3057	799	495	313	315	54	Azerbaïdjan
China	1202565	1328950	1613647	...	...	...	...	...	...	...	Chine
Hong Kong SAR	73496	...	8433	...	...	...	1499	[7]752	[7]178	[7]120	Hong-Kong RAS
Cyprus	10447	10591	6199	3835	[8]3820	[8]3444	[8]2507	[8]2309	[8]2100	[8]1710	Chypre
Georgia	...	...	2614	1046	224	50	48	101	95	101	Géorgie
India[9]	198404	201449	207181	188746	158263	181462	157095	137837	180490	134524	Inde[9]
Indonesia[5]	61657	87571	...	#250053	272529	249509	...	238335	258780	...	Indonésie[5]
Iran(Islamic Rep. of)	[10]23374	[10]20944	[10]25129	[10]21756	[10]17598	[11]29807	[11]28310	[11]27267	[11]22362	...	Iran(Rép. islamique)
Iraq	4400	[1]5000	4087	...	...	...	...	...	...	...	Iraq
Japan[11][12]	54054	53351	52455	47703	51503	49525	48819	47573	42573	37546	Japon[11][12]
Korea, Republic of	24440	28923	27617	19085	16806	15309	...	...	...	...	Corée, République de
Kyrgyzstan	..	9646	5757	3528	1512	755	605	332	135	85	Kirghizistan
Lao People's Dem. Rep.	...	...	...	...	240	150	...	...	...	...	Rép. dém. pop. lao
Mongolia	4223	3994	2245	1031	407	325	146	41	33	7	Mongolie
Nepal	[1]600	[1]700	[13]800	[13]823	[13]700	[13]685	[13]649	[13]550	[13]550	* [13]605	Népal
Philippines[1]	10000	12000	15000	...	...	...	...	...	...	...	Philippines[1]
Singapore	[3]2800	[1]3000	[1]3100	...	...	...	...	...	...	...	Singapour

For general note and footnotes, see end of table.

Voir la fin du tableau pour la remarque générale et les notes.

Footwear, total production, excluding rubber footwear (continued)
Chaussures, production totale, non compris les chaussures de caoutchouc (suite)

ISIC-BASED CODE - CODE BASE CITI
3240-00

Unit : Thousand pairs

Unité : Milliers de paires

Country or area	1990	1991	1992	1993	1994	1995	1996	1997	1998	1999	Pays ou zone
Sri Lanka	339	276	272	274	...	...	...	...	...	...	Sri Lanka
Tajikistan	..	8567	5476	4044	929	612	394	107	123	72	Tadjikistan
Turkmenistan	..	4246	3231	3358	1938	1910	1546	1108	561	...	Turkménistan
Uzbekistan	..	45443	40491	40466	28202	5654	5591	5547	...	...	Ouzbékistan
Viet Nam	5827	6188	5672	...	...	46440	61785	79289	77037	*81780	Viet Nam
Europe	**1334836**	**1730262**	**1453896**	**1287395**	**1144452**	**1133933**	**1078662**	**1050394**	**1007132**	**999492**	**Europe**
Albania	5990	1881	1214	1818	266	267				...	Albanie
Austria[14]	16553	16760	14842	13229	12767	...	...	...	...	...	Autriche[14]
Belarus	..	45343	37207	33412	26358	13004	11381	15587	16223	16534	Bélarus
Belgium	3562	3454	3190	2267	...	...	...	...	...	...	Belgique
Bulgaria	27214	17048	13421	10785	10244	11980	8915	6838	6401	4591	Bulgarie
Croatia	..	11717	11240	13449	12459	9521	9271	9598	8742	...	Croatie
Denmark[1]	4400	4400	4600	...	...	...	...	...	...	...	Danemark[1]
Czechoslovakia(former)	113596	72134	..	..	..	..	..	..	..	..	Tchécoslovaquie(anc.)
Czech Republic	..	..	36948	32293	23323	22115	21572	13455	10099	8373	République tchèque
Estonia	..	6301	3208	1035	827	682	711	793	803	840	Estonie
Finland	4752	3683	3606	3291	3421	3186	3220	2928	3499	2650	Finlande
France[2]	194700	169221	160320	151124	154898	151704	139442	135447	125524	114540	France[2]
Germany	..	84435	63672	55485	47193	45491	40675	36948	38441	...	Allemagne
Germany(Fed.Rep.)	64358										Allemagne(Rép.féd.)
German D.R.(former)	61822	..	..	..	..	..	..	..	..	..	R.D.A. (anc.)
Greece	12260	10712	9264	8166	6922	7032	6769	6202	5716	...	Grèce
Hungary	27426	20757	14752	12783	12499	12178	...	...	...	14386	Hongrie
Iceland	39	46	18	...	...	...	9	8	...	...	Islande
Ireland	1403	[1]3000	[1]3200	...	...	...	...	...	...	...	Irlande
Italy[1]	320200	310200	295000	...	...	...	...	...	...	...	Italie[1]
Latvia	..	7778	5764	2687	1633	1032	939	753	753	350	Lettonie
Lithuania	..	11154	7702	3657	1565	1961	2004	1663	1654	1686	Lituanie
Netherlands[2 15 16]	5598	5255	5289	6315	5455	5492	...	...	...	...	Pays-Bas[2 15 16]
Norway	[3]900	[1]900	[1]1000	...	...	...	...	...	...	...	Norvège
Poland	98200	66857	55181	47905	53236	59783	66620	68513	54491	48538	Pologne
Portugal	75378	39658	60463	75422	71648	68070	69439	71949	68179	75054	Portugal
Republic of Moldova	..	20751	14504	[17]4897	[17]2267	[17]1506	[17]1429	[17]1032	[17]739	[17]704	Rép. de Moldova
Romania	80670	63196	41237	41893	45666	48239	44838	34365	30341	30491	Roumanie
Russian Federation	..	356147	231005	153343	80776	54254	38428	34541	24998	30821	Fédération de Russie
Slovakia	..	..	22875	18332	13577	46438	13188	10300	9772	7643	Slovaquie
Slovenia	..	9124	9492	8923	8683	6951	5739	5976	5641	4779	Slovénie
Spain	117199	115190	106959	74883	104788	140141	155218	165417	177464	...	Espagne
Sweden	1904	[1]2500	[1]3000	1013	676	372	1104	1202	430	501	Suède
Switzerland	4039	3385	3065	3291	3232	2490	...	...	...	...	Suisse
Ukraine	..	183888	147703	105814	40309	20757	13175	10580	11389	11875	Ukraine
United Kingdom	[18]92673	[1]41000	[1]43000	70837	69637	61141	62157	54423	45155	...	Royaume-Uni
Yugoslavia	..	18149	16169	10590	8824	5982	6461	6848	6976	3892	Yougoslavie
T.F.Yug.Rep. Macedonia	..	4238	3786	2031	1760	1121	1200	1507	1382	1953	L'ex-RY Macédoine
USSR (former)	843245	..	..	..	..	..	..	..	..	..	URSS (anc.)
Oceania	**6852**	**5957**	**4148**	**3808**	**3905**	**3397**	**2781**	**2222**	**1484**	**1650**	**Océanie**
Australia[19 20]	1875	1935	383	283	315	278	...	...	...	...	Australie[19 20]
New Zealand[20]	[21]4977	[21]4022	[21]3765	[21]3525	[21]3590	[21]3119	[21]2676	[21]2222	[21]1484	[22]1650	Nouvelle-Zélande[20]
Total	**4475795**	**4211870**	**4286616**	**3998332**	**3751323**	**3673325**	**3574385**	**3569921**	**3521817**	**3517462**	**Total**

General Note.
Data refer to total production of leather footwear for children, men and women and all other footwear such as footwear with outer soles of wood or cork, sports footwear and orthopedic leather footwear. House slippers and sandals of various types are included. Rubber footwear, however, are excluded. (SITC, Rev.3: 85115-0, 85122-0, 85124-0, 85125-0, 85140-0, 85150-0, 85170-0).

Remarque générale.
Les données se rapportent à la production totale de chaussures de cuir pour enfants, hommes et dames et toutes les autres chaussures telles que chaussures à semelles en bois ou en liège, chaussures pour sports et chaussures orthopédiques en cuir. Les chaussures en caoutchouc ne sont pas comprises. (CTCI, Rev.3: 85115-0, 85122-0, 85124-0, 85125-0, 85140-0, 85150-0, 85170-0).

For footnotes, see end of table.

Voir la fin du tableau pour les notes.

Footwear, total production, excluding rubber footwear (continued)
Chaussures, production totale, non compris les chaussures de caoutchouc (suite)

ISIC-BASED CODE - CODE BASE CITI
3240-00

Footnotes

[1] Source: Food and Agriculture Organization of the United Nations (FAO), (Rome).

[2] Including rubber footwear.

[3] Including rubber and plastic footwear.

[4] Twelve months ending 7 July of the year stated.

[5] Including plastic footwear.

[6] Excluding children's footwear.

[7] Excluding other footwear for confidentiality purposes.

[8] Including other footwear, house footwear, sandals and other light footwear. Also including rubber footwear.

[9] Production by large and medium scale establishments only.

[10] Production by establishments employing 50 or more persons.

[11] Production by establishments employing 10 or more persons.

[12] Shipments.

[13] Twelve months beginning 16 July of year stated.

[14] Beginning 1995, data are confidential.

[15] Sales.

[16] Production by establishments employing 20 or more persons.

[17] Excluding Transnistria region.

[18] Manufacturers' sales.

[19] Excluding sporting footwear.

[20] Twelve months ending 30 June of year stated.

[21] Including non-leather footwear.

[22] Sports footwear only.

Notes.

[1] Source: Organisation des Nations Unies pour l'alimentation et l'agriculture (FAO), (Rome).

[2] Y compris les chaussures en caoutchouc.

[3] Y compris les chaussures en caoutchouc et en matière plastique.

[4] Période de douze mois finissant le 7 juillet de l'année indiquée.

[5] Y compris les chaussures en matière plastique.

[6] Non compris les chaussures d'enfants.

[7] A l'exclusion d'autres chaussures, pour raisons de confidentialité

[8] Y compris les autres chaussures, chaussures de maison, sandales et autres chaussures légères. Y compris également les chaussures en caoutchouc.

[9] Production des grandes et moyennes entreprises seulement.

[10] Production des établissements occupant 50 personnes ou plus.

[11] Production des établissements occupant 10 personnes ou plus.

[12] Expéditions.

[13] Période de douze mois commençant le 16 juillet de l'année indiquée.

[14] A partir de 1995, les données sont confidentielles

[15] Ventes.

[16] Production des établissements occupant 20 personnes ou plus.

[17] Non compris la région de Transnistria.

[18] Ventes des fabricants.

[19] Non compris les chaussures de sport.

[20] Période de douze mois finissant le 30 juin de l'année indiquée.

[21] Y compris les chaussures en toutes matières autres que le cuir.

[22] Chaussures de sport seulement.

Footwear, leather, children's
Chaussures de cuir pour enfants

ISIC-BASED CODE - CODE BASE CITI

3240-01

Unit : Thousand pairs　　　　　　　　　　　　　　　　　　　　　　　　　　　　　　　　　Unité : Milliers de paires

Country or area	1990	1991	1992	1993	1994	1995	1996	1997	1998	1999	Pays ou zone
Africa	**7004**	**7466**	**6359**	**5589**	**5377**	**4757**	**4253**	**3727**	**3201**	**2676**	**Afrique**
Kenya	371	275	342	363	410	339	...	...	...	...	Kenya
South Africa	6633	7191	6017	5226	4967	...	...	...	...	...	Afrique du Sud
America, North	**24557**	**23289**	**21818**	**24428**	**22445**	**18127**	**15045**	**14565**	**13422**	**10099**	**Amérique du Nord**
Mexico	6251	5715	5961	10074	10086	7431	6920	7932	7247	6941	Mexique
Panama	353	...	494	356	272	340	236	...	...	...	Panama
United States[1]	17953	17232	15363	13998	12087	10356	7889	6272	5810	2789	Etats-Unis[1]
America, South	**9499**	**11459**	**11619**	**11345**	**10943**	**9331**	**9761**	**9772**	**10430**	**12138**	**Amérique du Sud**
Bolivia	197	223	407	493	514	*486	...	...	...	...	Bolivie
Brazil	4800	4950	4954	3694	3268	2079	3103	2939	4051	4520	Brésil
Chile	1435	2226	2337	2749	2446	1959	2074	2337	2220	2220	Chili
Colombia	2787	...	3641	4129	4435	4527	...	3658	3286	...	Colombie
Peru	280	...	...	...	...	...	...	...	...	...	Pérou
Asia	**6805**	**26182**	**14451**	**10986**	**7037**	**4000**	**2052**	**2445**	**2680**	**1477**	**Asie**
Armenia	..	2964	1162	927	632	311	124	2	1	4	Arménie
Azerbaijan	..	4858	2178	2174	1880	335	123	20	0	0	Azerbaïdjan
Hong Kong SAR	4471	3246	474	...	...	...	19	91	...	1	Hong-Kong RAS
Cyprus	1221	1512	878	750	[2]770	[2]334	[2]232	[2]208	[2]191	[2]222	Chypre
Indonesia	624	234	1829	166	713	636	...	1616	867	...	Indonésie
Japan[3]	313	264	208	177	175	207	176	148	144	130	Japon[3]
Kyrgyzstan	..	5373	2904	1732	664	326	233	172	42	26	Kirghizistan
Tajikistan	..	5273	3114	2542	563	351	250	22	34	11	Tadjikistan
Turkey	176	...	...	5	39	40	0	116	10	22	Turquie
Turkmenistan	..	2407	1653	1129	217	76	59	50	7	...	Turkménistan
Europe	**65136**	**314103**	**200927**	**129843**	**86262**	**62001**	**51319**	**44954**	**45424**	**51291**	**Europe**
Austria[4]	1003	1039	1075	1214	1099	...	...	...	...	...	Autriche[4]
Belarus	..	[5]19604	13446	10662	7367	3103	2470	4036	4796	5186	Bélarus
Belgium	378	367	347	353	...	192	162	153	128	120	Belgique
Bulgaria	3329	2469	2697	2470	1963	1556	1945	1181	1298	1188	Bulgarie
Croatia	..	3417	2925	2965	2182	1674	1474	1493	1227	...	Croatie
Estonia	..	1789	875	200	158	78	59	45	36	27	Estonie
Finland	52	94	71	63	55	51	42	...	41	...	Finlande
France	[2]24548	[2]24644	[6]11090	[6]12590	[6]9880	...	...	...	...	...	France
Germany	..	4806	3416	2736	2553	2426	2268	2477	2346	...	Allemagne
Germany(Fed.Rep.)	3189	..	..	..	..	..	..	..	..	..	Allemagne(Rép.féd.)
Greece	1458	1239	1186	336	200	190	177	207	205	...	Grèce
Hungary	3720	3007	2239	2007	1828	764	...	...	...	1159	Hongrie
Ireland	...	...	...	...	...	102	95	13	...	...	Irlande
Latvia	..	3406	2043	618	259	213	118	122	98	66	Lettonie
Netherlands[7][8]	767	710	636	383	255	280	168	...	...	...	Pays-Bas[7][8]
Portugal	3631	2776	3415	4856	4241	3846	3687	4557	5175	5864	Portugal
Republic of Moldova	..	4185	3067	[9]905	[9]314	[9]94	[9]103	[9]118	...	...	Rép. de Moldova
Russian Federation	..	146405	77319	39692	20030	15014	10513	7133	5848	6991	Fédération de Russie
Slovakia	..	..	...	...	...	...	...	...	397	102	Slovaquie
Slovenia	..	835	1224	988	1008	218	393	153	535	...	Slovénie
Spain	10303	10500	9715	5592	7295	9927	11516	11841	12817	12862	Espagne
Switzerland	255	222	211	216	195	155	...	...	...	...	Suisse
Ukraine	..	[5]71003	[5]51302	[5]28395	[5]8796	3851	1995	1125	855	777	Ukraine
United Kingdom	[10]12433	...	...	#11309	15345	12016	9650	5915	5386	...	Royaume-Uni
Yugoslavia	..	845	1547	936	550	519	569	531	596	367	Yougoslavie
T.F.Yug.Rep. Macedonia	..	378	468	37	125	...	...	*5	1	55	L'ex-RY Macédoine
USSR (former)[5]	365778	..	...	...	...	...	...	...	...	..	URSS (anc.)[5]
Oceania	**2501**	**1808**	**1688**	**1344**	**1724**	**1758**	**1670**	**1581**	**1563**	**1563**	**Océanie**
Australia[11]	2090	1538	1450	1175	...	...	...	...	...	...	Australie[11]
New Zealand[1][11]	411	270	238	169	161	195	107	...	...	...	Nouvelle-Zélande[1][11]
Total	**481280**	**384308**	**256862**	**183534**	**133788**	**99973**	**84100**	**77045**	**76720**	**79242**	**Total**

For general note and footnotes, see end of table.　　　　　　　　　　　Voir la fin du tableau pour la remarque générale et les notes.

Footwear, leather, children's (continued)
Chaussures de cuir pour enfants (suite)

ISIC-BASED CODE - CODE BASE CITI
3240-01

General Note.

Boots and shoes with leather, rubber, composition leather or plastic soles, and with leather or mainly leather uppers. Rubber footwear is excluded. (SITC, Rev.3: 85115-1, 85140-1, 85170-1).

[1] Including non-leather footwear.
[2] Including other footwear, house footwear, sandals and other light footwear. Also including rubber footwear.
[3] Production by establishments employing 10 or more persons.
[4] Beginning 1995, data are confidential.
[5] Including sporting footwear of all types and orthopedic shoes.
[6] Including sandals.
[7] Sales.
[8] Production by establishments employing 20 or more persons.
[9] Excluding Transnistria region.
[10] Manufacturers' sales.
[11] Twelve months ending 30 June of year stated.

Remarque générale.

Bottes et chaussures à semelle en cuir naturel, en caoutchouc, en cuir artificiel ou reconstitué, ou en matière plastique, et à dessus en cuir ou principalement en cuir. Les chaussures en caoutchouc ne sont pas comprises. (CTCI. Rev.3: 85115-1, 85140-1, 85170-1).

[1] Y compris les chaussures en toutes matières autres que le cuir.
[2] Y compris les autres chaussures, chaussures de maison, sandales et autres chaussures légères. Y compris également les chaussures en caoutchouc.
[3] Production des établissements occupant 10 personnes ou plus.
[4] A partir de 1995, les données sont confidentielles
[5] Y compris les chaussures de sport de tous genres et les chaussures orthopédiques.
[6] Y compris les sandales.
[7] Ventes.
[8] Production des établissements occupant 20 personnes ou plus.
[9] Non compris la région de Transnistria.
[10] Ventes des fabricants.
[11] Période de douze mois finissant le 30 juin de l'année indiquée.

Footwear, leather, men's
Chaussures en cuir pour hommes
ISIC-BASED CODE - CODE BASE CITI

3240-04

Unit : Thousand pairs | | | | | | | | | | Unité : Milliers de paires

Country or area	1990	1991	1992	1993	1994	1995	1996	1997	1998	1999	Pays ou zone
Africa	**15258**	**15357**	**13805**	**13546**	**13406**	**14647**	**13409**	**11956**	**10212**	**9310**	**Afrique**
Kenya	692	513	638	677	764	468	...	...	...	...	Kenya
Mozambique	...	240	148	151	80	29	...	12	10	7	Mozambique
South Africa	14396	14604	13019	12718	12562	14150	12718	11342	9605	8710	Afrique du Sud
America, North	**51398**	**46318**	**46991**	**57800**	**56305**	**48865**	**47579**	**53069**	**47275**	**43164**	**Amérique du Nord**
Mexico	6327	5662	5316	11980	10441	9163	9977	11176	10850	10895	Mexique
Panama	450	...	405	463	501	364	391	...	...	...	Panama
United States[1]	44621	...	41270	45357	45363	39338	37211	41348	35857	31678	Etats-Unis[1]
America, South	**29896**	**30406**	**30187**	**30479**	**29445**	**25922**	**25871**	**24809**	**22484**	**22985**	**Amérique du Sud**
Bolivia	395	378	354	378	510	*412	...	...	...	...	Bolivie
Brazil	14187	14453	13979	14841	13016	10109	10667	9934	8748	8432	Brésil
Chile	3050	3393	3610	3168	2875	2843	2656	2593	2600	2193	Chili
Colombia	6158	...	5806	5840	6771	6162	...	5535	4381	...	Colombie
Ecuador	...	...	1623	1570	1591	1714	...	...	...	...	Equateur
Paraguay[2]	4287	4555	4620	...	...	...	...	...	...	...	Paraguay[2]
Peru	195	...	...	...	...	...	...	...	...	...	Pérou
Asia	**64050**	**79327**	**85341**	**70193**	**71005**	**67181**	**62729**	**74606**	**66425**	**78112**	**Asie**
Armenia	..	4433	3043	1532	448	220	107	84	58	16	Arménie
Azerbaijan	..	2358	1356	1238	737	324	288	281	315	53	Azerbaïdjan
Hong Kong SAR	1459	430	160	188	62	36	...	10	4	13	Hong-Kong RAS
China, Macao, SAR	...	...	...	55	147	382	684	636	588	1658	Chine, Macao PAS
Cyprus[4]	3273	3510	3003	2141	[3]2058	[3]478	[3]371	[3]350	[3]331	[3]280	Chypre
India[4]	8847	11808	9018	...	...	...	...	...	...	...	Inde[4]
Indonesia	[5]1360	[5]142	...	#13266	18416	20508	...	32154	27854	...	Indonésie
Iran(Islamic Rep. of)	[6]10915	[6]10211	[6]8083	7815	7381	5495	5041	...	...	...	Iran(Rép. islamique)
Japan[7]	21012	21196	20343	18186	18997	18535	17726	16982	15213	12967	Japon[7]
Korea, Republic of[2]	15946	19326	19253	12534	11160	10019	...	...	...	...	Corée, République de[2]
Kyrgyzstan	..	1698	984	766	342	147	...	...	...	...	Kirghizistan
Tajikistan	..	2396	1846	1245	212	224	123	82	62	49	Tadjikistan
Turkey	1238	1103	1271	1078	962	704	484	601	718	2998	Turquie
Yemen	..	716	738	258	192	218	280	283	...	...	Yémen
Europe	**195368**	**332468**	**256021**	**232058**	**191420**	**165138**	**151840**	**142112**	**128132**	**132558**	**Europe**
Austria	1732	2509	1381	1330	1137	1177	1187	1191	1138	1165	Autriche
Belarus	..	[8]11846	10364	9652	8048	5225	5159	6391	5979	6088	Bélarus
Belgium	527	388	412	267	[9]172	[9]169	[9]163	[9]123	[9]125	[9]109	Belgique
Bulgaria	5467	4326	3711	3385	3586	3549	3070	2436	1660	1009	Bulgarie
Croatia	..	3806	3443	3787	3811	2864	2344	2692	2249	...	Croatie
Estonia	..	2166	1096	439	286	255	265	212	198	268	Estonie
Finland	1458	1099	910	757	829	1102	972	...	...	...	Finlande
France	[3]58325	[3]56119	[10]11707	[10]10757	[10]10028	...	...	...	...	...	France
Germany	..	14607	9013	7256	6844	...	5911	5406	4781	...	Allemagne
Germany(Fed.Rep.)	12386	..	..	..	..	...	..	..	..	..	Allemagne(Rép.féd.)
Greece	3735	3380	3075	2588	1432	1415	1369	1212	1144	...	Grèce
Hungary	4917	4724	3998	4265	3887	4657	...	...	...	5134	Hongrie
Iceland	8	9	3	...	...	...	...	...	...	...	Islande
Ireland	...	...	...	...	...	358	345	315	235	...	Irlande
Latvia	..	1658	1619	975	620	398	406	281	380	199	Lettonie
Netherlands[11][12]	1047	1064	976	748	623	648	589	579	619	648	Pays-Bas[11][12]
Portugal	34748	14952	24099	29328	26677	26628	28696	27072	23658	24969	Portugal
Romania[2]	36434	35381	29465	30660	37300	40055	36335	27839	23901	24582	Roumanie[2]
Russian Federation	..	87566	65465	49772	30070	20197	14021	15659	11505	15150	Fédération de Russie
Slovakia	..	...	...	...	...	...	...	...	3420	3934	Slovaquie
Slovenia	..	542	1287	1099	1221	1168	778	937	1271	...	Slovénie
Spain	18556	18897	18514	...	...	...	...	...	...	...	Espagne
Switzerland	2641	2161	1861	2160	2192	1607	...	...	...	...	Suisse
Ukraine[8]	..	46267	41151	33850	13700	8550	6481	5268	5313	5728	Ukraine[8]
United Kingdom[13][14]	13074	...	...	...	...	...	...	...	...	...	Royaume-Uni[13][14]
Yugoslavia	..	5174	4713	2985	2714	1815	1731	1804	1716	1292	Yougoslavie
T.F.Yug.Rep. Macedonia	..	440	694	271	516	199	262	263	208	239	L'ex-RY Macédoine

For general note and footnotes, see end of table.　　　　　　　　　　Voir la fin du tableau pour la remarque générale et les notes.

Footwear, leather, men's (continued)
Chaussures en cuir pour hommes (suite)

ISIC-BASED CODE - CODE BASE CITI

3240-04

Unit : Thousand pairs

Unité : Milliers de paires

Country or area	1990	1991	1992	1993	1994	1995	1996	1997	1998	1999	Pays ou zone
USSR (former)[8]	217056	..	..	..	..	..	..	..	..	..	URSS (anc.)[8]
Oceania	6686	5609	5558	5953	5683	5765	5689	5480	5286	5253	Océanie
Australia[15]	5598	4783	4727	5003	...	...	...	...	...	...	Australie[15]
New Zealand[15]	[1]1088	[1]826	[1]831	[1]950	[1]655	[1]737	[1]661	[1]452	[1]258	[16]225	Nouvelle-Zélande[15]
Total	579712	509485	437903	410029	367264	327518	307117	312031	279813	291381	Total

General Note.

Boots and shoes with leather, rubber, composition leather or plastic soles, and with leather or mainly leather uppers. Rubber footwear is excluded. (SITC, Rev.3: 85115-2, 85140-2, 85170-2).

[1] Including non-leather footwear.
[2] Including footwear for women and children.
[3] Including other footwear, house footwear, sandals and other light footwear. Also including rubber footwear.
[4] Production by large and medium scale establishments only.
[5] Including footwear for women.
[6] Production by establishments employing 50 or more persons.
[7] Production by establishments employing 10 or more persons.
[8] Including sporting footwear of all types and orthopedic shoes.

[9] Incomplete coverage.
[10] Including sandals.
[11] Sales.
[12] Production by establishments employing 20 or more persons.
[13] Including sports shoes with leather uppers and excluding safety footwear with leather uppers.
[14] Manufacturers' sales.
[15] Twelve months ending 30 June of year stated.
[16] Sports footwear only.

Remarque générale.

Bottes et chaussures à semelle en cuir naturel, en caoutchouc, en cuir artificiel ou reconstitué, ou en matière plastique, et à dessus en cuir ou principalement en cuir. Les chaussures en caoutchouc ne sont pas comprises. (CTCI, Rev.3: 85115-2,85140-2, 85170-2).

[1] Y compris les chaussures en toutes matières autres que le cuir.
[2] Y compris les chaussures pour dames et enfants.
[3] Y compris les autres chaussures, chaussures de maison, sandales et autres chaussures légères. Y compris également les chaussures en caoutchouc.
[4] Production des grandes et moyennes entreprises seulement.
[5] Y compris les chaussures pour dames.
[6] Production des établissements occupant 50 personnes ou plus.
[7] Production des établissements occupant 10 personnes ou plus.
[8] Y compris les chaussures de sport de tous genres et les chaussures orthopédiques.
[9] Couverture incomplète.
[10] Y compris les sandales.
[11] Ventes.
[12] Production des établissements occupant 20 personnes ou plus.
[13] Y compris les chaussures de sport à empeigne en cuir et, à l'exclusion des chaussures de sécurité à empeigne en cuir.
[14] Ventes des fabricants.
[15] Période de douze mois finissant le 30 juin de l'année indiquée.
[16] Chaussures de sport seulement.

Footwear, leather, women's
Chaussures en cuir pour dames

ISIC-BASED CODE - CODE BASE CITI

3240-07

Unit : Thousand pairs   Unité : Milliers de paires

Country or area	1990	1991	1992	1993	1994	1995	1996	1997	1998	1999	Pays ou zone
Africa	**18408**	**17786**	**13904**	**19443**	**19716**	**22260**	**20804**	**17389**	**14791**	**10947**	**Afrique**
Kenya	542	402	500	531	600	202	...	...	...	...	Kenya
South Africa	17866	17384	13404	18912	19116	22058	20403	17003	14420	10592	Afrique du Sud
America, North	**67310**	**59247**	**57586**	**57640**	**55865**	**47003**	**45828**	**38897**	**29923**	**21705**	**Amérique du Nord**
Mexico	3671	3308	3293	5591	4748	4621	6107	6009	6300	6764	Mexique
Panama	557	...	477	576	441	507	343	...	...	...	Panama
United States[1]	63082	55455	53816	51473	50676	41875	39378	32344	23067	14373	Etats-Unis[1]
America, South	**70860**	**73545**	**74340**	**81244**	**70340**	**65849**	**73788**	**72072**	**59300**	**61244**	**Amérique du Sud**
Bolivia	222	217	318	342	353	*320	...	...	...	...	Bolivie
Brazil	64969	66873	68159	74967	64010	59696	68193	66546	54016	55459	Brésil
Chile	3092	3612	3364	3353	2996	2608	2404	2078	1957	1824	Chili
Colombia	2339	...	2261	2300	2739	3034	...	2848	2714	...	Colombie
Ecuador	...	...	...	121	81	30	...	...	...	...	Equateur
Peru	161	...	...	...	...	...	...	...	...	...	Pérou
Asia	**30668**	**37072**	**48496**	**48674**	**55744**	**50865**	**38720**	**44266**	**23285**	**43157**	**Asie**
Armenia	..	3748	1442	1058	532	125	74	1	6	4	Arménie
Azerbaijan	..	3047	1621	653	358	84	44	12	0	1	Azerbaïdjan
Hong Kong SAR	6360	3888	4616	1047	363	851	716	651	174	186	Hong-Kong RAS
China, Macao, SAR	...	...	...	610	595	975	266	326	293	973	Chine, Macao PAS
Cyprus	1498	1244	1236	944	[2]992	[2]449	[2]366	[2]346	[2]322	[2]158	Chypre
Indonesia	1482	1123	...	#23976	30193	27412	...	22352	4245	...	Indonésie
Japan[3]	20585	19921	20574	18669	21850	20456	21236	20381	18144	16769	Japon[3]
Kyrgyzstan	..	2436	1863	1030	506	282	...	...	...	...	Kirghizistan
Tajikistan	..	898	516	257	116	37	21	3	27	12	Tadjikistan
Turkey	137	167	207	430	239	194	171	194	74	107	Turquie
Europe	**325521**	**469132**	**352481**	**322937**	**275483**	**234685**	**209516**	**213941**	**207938**	**207075**	**Europe**
Austria	8368	9262	7848	7787	7996	6312	6473	6792	7131	6079	Autriche
Belarus	..	[4]13877	11304	13073	10943	4676	3744	5087	5390	5170	Bélarus
Belgium	552	485	556	391	[5]211	...	...	...	...	...	Belgique
Bulgaria	5768	3661	2918	3115	2419	4322	1850	1255	1889	1322	Bulgarie
Croatia	..	1536	1592	2414	2659	2302	2250	1976	2697	...	Croatie
Czechoslovakia(former)[6]	54217	39877	..	..	..	..	..	..	..	..	Tchécoslovaquie(anc.)[6]
Czech Republic	..	..	17520	15057	15960	...	...	...	...	...	République tchèque
Estonia	..	2346	1237	305	174	127	92	112	78	123	Estonie
Finland	2170	1467	1577	1356	1461	1121	1273	...	1227	1008	Finlande
France	[2]94618	[2]88458	[7]32350	[7]31844	[7]31462	...	...	...	...	...	France
Germany		20095	18089	15225	13432	...	11351	10825	10679	...	Allemagne
Germany(Fed.Rep.)	19192	..	..	..	..	...	...	...	...	...	Allemagne(Rép.féd.)
Greece	4775	4250	3566	2956	1358	2097	2122	1828	1309	...	Grèce
Hungary[7]	12549	7304	5257	4215	4206	3274	...	...	...	3732	Hongrie[7]
Iceland	9	9	4	...	...	...	...	...	...	...	Islande
Latvia	..	2674	2102	903	379	182	211	174	139	24	Lettonie
Netherlands[8][9]	2202	1885	2106	1546	916	777	389	373	411	416	Pays-Bas[8][9]
Poland[6]	43273	28538	22817	20935	22639	24630	26884	27652	24408	22594	Pologne[6]
Portugal	27756	18622	23535	30319	29665	26036	25153	27292	26049	30125	Portugal
Russian Federation		100451	76947	55144	26377	16407	11973	10258	6456	7714	Fédération de Russie
Slovakia[6]	..	..	10408	9266	6593	...	...	...	1957	1182	Slovaquie[6]
Slovenia	..	3801	3599	3700	3776	3666	3128	2529	2487	...	Slovénie
Spain	33723	33915	32376	[6]39354	[6]55940	[6]74854	...	...	...	...	Espagne
Switzerland	1062	894	885	834	771	669	...	...	...	...	Suisse
Ukraine[4]	..	60066	50298	42234	17377	8190	4640	4015	5182	5359	Ukraine[4]
United Kingdom[10]	15287	15978	...	...	...	...	...	...	...	...	Royaume-Uni[10]
Yugoslavia	..	6943	5703	3899	2532	1624	2166	2403	2457	1089	Yougoslavie
T.F.Yug.Rep. Macedonia	..	2738	2254	1425	597	402	*528	804	818	853	L'ex-RY Macédoine
USSR (former)[4]	232767	..	..	..	..	..	..	..	..	..	URSS (anc.)[4]
Oceania	**12037**	**10539**	**8868**	**8000**	**9170**	**9484**	**9225**	**9027**	**8586**	**8628**	**Océanie**
Australia[11]	9675	8523	6938	6221	...	...	...	...	...	...	Australie[11]
New Zealand[11]	[1]2362	[1]2016	[1]1930	[1]1779	[1]1331	[1]1645	[1]1386	[1]1188	[1]747	[1,2]789	Nouvelle-Zélande[11]

For general note and footnotes, see end of table.   Voir la fin du tableau pour la remarque générale et les notes.

Footwear, leather, women's (continued)
Chaussures en cuir pour dames (suite)

ISIC-BASED CODE - CODE BASE CITI
3240-07

Unit : Thousand pairs

Unité : Milliers de paires

Country or area	1990	1991	1992	1993	1994	1995	1996	1997	1998	1999	Pays ou zone
Total	757571	667321	555674	537938	486318	430146	397882	395591	343822	352755	Total

General Note.
Boots and shoes with leather, rubber, composition leather or plastic soles, and with leather or mainly leather uppers. Rubber footwear is excluded. (SITC, Rev.3: 85115-3, 85140-3, 85170-3).

[1] Including non-leather footwear.
[2] Including other footwear, house footwear, sandals and other light footwear. Also including rubber footwear.
[3] Production by establishments employing 10 or more persons.
[4] Including sporting footwear of all types and orthopedic shoes.

[5] Incomplete coverage.
[6] Including footwear for men and children.
[7] Including sandals.
[8] Sales.
[9] Production by establishments employing 20 or more persons.
[10] Industrial sales.
[11] Twelve months ending 30 June of year stated.
[12] Sports footwear only.

Remarque générale.
Bottes et chaussures à semelle en cuir naturel, en caoutchouc, en cuir artificiel ou reconstitué, ou en matière plastique, et à dessus en cuir ou principalement en cuir. Les chaussures en caoutchouc ne sont pas comprises. (CTCI, Rev.3: 85115-3,85140-3, 85170-3).

[1] Y compris les chaussures en toutes matières autres que le cuir.
[2] Y compris les autres chaussures, chaussures de maison, sandales et autres chaussures légères. Y compris également les chaussures en caoutchouc.
[3] Production des établissements occupant 10 personnes ou plus.
[4] Y compris les chaussures de sport de tous genres et les chaussures orthopédiques.
[5] Couverture incomplète.
[6] Y compris les chaussures pour hommes et enfants.
[7] Y compris les sandales.
[8] Ventes.
[9] Production des établissements occupant 20 personnes ou plus.
[10] Ventes industrielles.
[11] Période de douze mois finissant le 30 juin de l'année indiquée.
[12] Chaussures de sport seulement.

Footwear, other (sports, orthopedic etc.)
Autres chaussures (pour sports, orthopédiques etc.)

ISIC-BASED CODE - CODE BASE CITI

3240-10

Unit : Thousand pairs

Unité : Milliers de paires

Country or area	1990	1991	1992	1993	1994	1995	1996	1997	1998	1999	Pays ou zone
Africa	**12738**	**10139**	**9811**	**10894**	**7728**	**6663**	**5737**	**7141**	**5556**	**5624**	**Afrique**
South Africa[1]	12738	10139	9811	10894	7728	6663	5737	7141	5556	5624	Afrique du Sud[1]
America, North	**34892**	**32844**	**26285**	**43977**	**40652**	**30606**	**33847**	**33100**	**28332**	**22526**	**Amérique du Nord**
Mexico	22682	22226	18571	34670	31673	22791	27336	27469	22675	19316	Mexique
Panama	1	...	1	88	79	76	88	88	...	...	Panama
United States[2]	12209	10562	7713	9219	8900	7739	6423	5488	5496	3032	Etats-Unis[2]
America, South	**11593**	**8643**	**8489**	**10846**	**10692**	**16985**	**7497**	**6974**	**5061**	**5826**	**Amérique du Sud**
Bolivia	19	44	72	95	4	*4	...	...	...	...	Bolivie
Brazil[3]	10516	7541	7359	9693	9630	15923	6409	5858	4009	4746	Brésil[3]
Colombia	...	...	...	...	...	...	1089	1027	...	Colombie
Asia	**284792**	**309962**	**278450**	**432461**	**441055**	**422683**	**369856**	**393777**	**395768**	**438339**	**Asie**
Azerbaijan	..	228	...	264	82	8	19	0	0	0	Azerbaïdjan
Cyprus	*418	*410	155	...	...	#17	7	0	0	0	Chypre
India[4][5]	189557	189641	198163	...	...	...	...	...	...	...	Inde[4][5]
Indonesia	58191	86072	49854	#212645	223207	200953	...	176242	180266	...	Indonésie
Iran(Islamic Rep. of)	[6]12464	[6]10733	[6]7554	5067	3517	5130	5669	...	...	...	Iran(Rép. islamique)
Japan[7]	12143	11970	11329	10671	10481	10327	9681	10062	9072	7680	Japon[7]
Korea, Republic of	11150	9597	8364	...	...	...	...	...	...	...	Corée, République de
Kyrgyzstan	..	139	6	0	0	0	0	0	0	0	Kirghizistan
Syrian Arab Republic[8]	211	491	186	142	286	1737	1769	2459	2640	...	Rép. arabe syrienne[8]
Turkey	658	609	2434	941	915	2070	1842	1773	1349	778	Turquie
Turkmenistan	..	72	330	448	...	...	...	...	...	...	Turkménistan
Europe	**233951**	**190948**	**146947**	**136565**	**131855**	**135454**	**135175**	**120768**	**105587**	**99617**	**Europe**
Austria	1981	505	2399	1053	1193	340	454	468	171	131	Autriche
Belgium[9]	409	374	312	232	...	...	...	...	...	...	Belgique[9]
Croatia	..	1468	1094	1030	704	787	507	383	476	...	Croatie
Czechoslovakia(former)	55366	29750	..	..	..	...	..	..	..	..	Tchécoslovaquie(anc.)
Czech Republic	..	..	17486	15729	...	...	...	...	...	...	République tchèque
Finland	922	895	954	1034	1076	787	758	...	344	370	Finlande
Germany	..	41166	29774	28447	22030	...	...	6788	7297	...	Allemagne
Germany(Fed.Rep.)	26336	..	..	..	...	...	...	...	...	..	Allemagne(Rép.féd.)
German D.R.(former)[10]	30549	..	..	..	..	...	...	...	...	..	R.D.A. (anc.)[10]
Greece	524	369	338	544	2391	1893	1770	1960	...	...	Grèce
Hungary[11]	6240	3599	2493	1660	1993	1680	...	...	...	48	Hongrie[11]
Iceland	12	12	4	...	...	...	...	...	...	...	Islande
Latvia	..	...	...	73	65	29	121	52	54	...	Lettonie
Netherlands[12][13][14]	814	828	851	848	921	1049	...	...	...	...	Pays-Bas[12][13][14]
Poland	54927	38319	32364	26970	30597	35153	39736	40861	30083	25944	Pologne
Portugal	4038	1935	5136	4098	3679	3293	3253	3254	2796	3156	Portugal
Romania	39759	27815	11772	11233	8366	8184	8503	6526	5607	5342	Roumanie
Russian Federation	..	19736	10590	7454	4245	2636	1664	1491	1182	957	Fédération de Russie
Slovakia	..	..	11130	9066	6984	...	...	...	1118	722	Slovaquie
Slovenia	..	3274	3016	2802	2678	1899	875	974	927	...	Slovénie
Spain	11889	12505	12000	[8]22334	[8]26941	[8]31715	...	...	...	...	Espagne
Switzerland	185	108	108	81	74	59	...	...	...	...	Suisse
Ukraine[15]	..	6552	3733	1335	436	166	59	172	39	11	Ukraine[15]
Yugoslavia	..	1620	1299	506	529	421	260	222	216	368	Yougoslavie
T.F.Yug.Rep. Macedonia	..	50	...	...	4	...	...	...	...	...	L'ex-RY Macédoine
Oceania	**712**	**546**	**766**	**627**	**561**	**542**	**522**	**471**	**443**	**415**	**Océanie**
New Zealand[15][16]	712	546	766	627	561	542	522	...	...	...	Nouvelle-Zélande[15][16]
Total	**578678**	**553082**	**470749**	**635371**	**632542**	**612933**	**552634**	**562231**	**540746**	**572347**	**Total**

General Note.
All other footwear such as sports footwear equipped with spikes, studs, bars etc., and orthopedic leather footwear. Rubberfootwear is excluded. (SITC, Rev.3: 85122-0, 85124-0, 85125-0, 85140-4, 85150-1, 85170-4).

Remarque générale.
Toutes autres chaussures, telles que chaussures pour sports, équipées de pointes, de crampons, de barrettes, etc., et chaussures orthopédiques en cuir. Cette rubrique ne comprend pas les chaussures en caoutchouc. (CTCI, Rev.3: 85122-0, 85124-0, 85125-0, 85140-4, 85150-1, 85170-4).

For footnotes, see end of table.

Voir la fin du tableau pour les notes.

Footwear, other (sports, orthopedic etc.) (continued)
Autres chaussures (pour sports, orthopédiques etc.) (suite)

ISIC-BASED CODE - CODE BASE CITI
3240-10

Footnotes

[1] Including rubber footwear.
[2] Including non-leather footwear.
[3] Including boots for women.
[4] Indigenous-type footwear.
[5] Production by large and medium scale establishments only.
[6] Production by establishments employing 50 or more persons.
[7] Production by establishments employing 10 or more persons.
[8] Including rubber and plastic footwear.
[9] Including sandals and similar light footwear.
[10] Including footwear for men, women and children.
[11] Including leather top-boots, brogues, sports shoes and slippers.

[12] Sales.
[13] Production by establishments employing 20 or more persons.
[14] Including rubber footwear, slippers and sandals with leather uppers.
[15] Sports footwear only.
[16] Twelve months ending 30 June of year stated.

Notes.

[1] Y compris les chaussures en caoutchouc.
[2] Y compris les chaussures en toutes matières autres que le cuir.
[3] Y compris les bottes pour dames.
[4] Chaussures de type indigène.
[5] Production des grandes et moyennes entreprises seulement.
[6] Production des établissements occupant 50 personnes ou plus.
[7] Production des établissements occupant 10 personnes ou plus.
[8] Y compris les chaussures en caoutchouc et en matière plastique.
[9] Y compris les sandales et chaussures légères analogues.
[10] Y compris les chaussures pour hommes, dames et enfants.
[11] Y compris les bottes à revers, les brogues, les chaussures de sport et les pantoufles en cuir.
[12] Ventes.
[13] Production des établissements occupant 20 personnes ou plus.
[14] Y compris les pantoufles et sandales à empeigne en cuir.
[15] Chaussures de sport seulement.
[16] Période de douze mois finissant le 30 juin de l'année indiquée.

Footwear, house
Chaussures d'intérieur

ISIC-BASED CODE - CODE BASE CITI

3240-13

Unit : Thousand pairs   Unité : Milliers de paires

Country or area	1990	1991	1992	1993	1994	1995	1996	1997	1998	1999	Pays ou zone
America, North	**44718**	**42963**	**45692**	**51686**	**43625**	**46732**	**36401**	**41988**	**45578**	**35095**	**Amérique du Nord**
United States	44718	42963	45692	51686	43625	46732	36401	41988	45578	35095	Etats-Unis
America, South	**57896**	**68919**	**71244**	**94297**	**63819**	**50851**	**90318**	**75703**	**72985**	**72806**	**Amérique du Sud**
Brazil[1]	46528	59108	62089	86831	56616	46095	85190	74584	71910	72373	Brésil[1]
Colombia	...	...	8720	7033	6770	4323	...	#686	642	...	Colombie
Ecuador	...	...	305	...	...	...	...	...	...	...	Equateur
Paraguay[2]	125	128	130	...	...	...	...	...	...	...	Paraguay[2]
Asia	**81041**	**34904**	**11759**	**16185**	**16209**	**16598**	**15663**	**14909**	**15034**	**14852**	**Asie**
Armenia	..	853	387	232	137	70	0	35	0	0	Arménie
Azerbaijan	..	2828	738	391	448	64	72	5	0	0	Azerbaïdjan
Hong Kong SAR[3][4]	61206	17243	3183	1653	1116	1260	...	...	...	...	Hong-Kong RAS[3][4]
Cyprus	*117	*115	120	...	...	297	230	321	362	440	Chypre
Kazakhstan	...	344	117	92	100	2	...	3	20	14	Kazakhstan
Korea, Republic of	17561	10449	4486	...	...	...	...	...	...	...	Corée, République de
Lao People's Dem. Rep.	...	...	...	...	480	450	...	...	...	...	Rép. dém. pop. lao
Sri Lanka	60	24	...	...	...	...	...	...	...	...	Sri Lanka
Tajikistan	..	586	145	120	40	8	0	6	0	1	Tadjikistan
Turkey	1632	1703	1772	2108	2531	2660	3562	2959	3071	2685	Turquie
Turkmenistan	..	...	...	0	233	913	373	241	242	...	Turkménistan
Europe	**134732**	**225690**	**160252**	**116998**	**100719**	**92756**	**86559**	**83300**	**70173**	**65215**	**Europe**
Austria	2963	2867	1447	1335	909	803	659	577	1119	1192	Autriche
Belarus	..	7137	6280	5272	4534	1889	1106	2165	2330	2548	Bélarus
Belgium	1696	1830	1564	1256	...	...	...	...	...	...	Belgique
Bulgaria	4732	1858	1680	723	535	892	747	1032	130	161	Bulgarie
Croatia	..	825	1560	2513	2630	1374	1981	2308	2093	...	Croatie
Finland	70	53	33	33	30	30	24	...	...	...	Finlande
France	[5]61704	[5]54795	[5]41938	[5]41347	51811	52117	49044	48075	43505	39382	France
Germany	..	10586	6227	5179	4840	...	...	3926	...	...	Allemagne
Germany(Fed.Rep.)	5659	..	..	..	..	..	..	..	..	..	Allemagne(Rép.féd.)
German D.R.(former)	22224	..	..	..	..	..	..	..	..	..	R.D.A. (anc.)
Greece	3289	3057	3213	318	756	868	811	308	140	...	Grèce
Hungary	3119	2032	736	1024	838	776	...	...	...	752	Hongrie
Iceland[6]	10	17	7	...	...	...	...	...	...	...	Islande[6]
Latvia	..	1349	454	5	2	0	0	0	2	...	Lettonie
Portugal	155	...	905	1944	2651	2881	3081	3390	3292	3008	Portugal
Republic of Moldova	..	6573	4397	[7]1885	[7]1350	[7]937	[7]716	[7]254	...	...	Rép. de Moldova
Russian Federation	..	69954	34084	21232	10001	6811	4243	5374	2669	4089	Fédération de Russie
Slovakia	..	..	...	4785	...	...	...	...	...	...	Slovaquie
Slovenia	..	213	130	125	152	136	0	...	...	...	Slovénie
Spain	11699	11960	12329	#716	369	1011	1634	1927	1734	2443	Espagne
Switzerland	757	866	622	27	40	7	...	...	...	...	Suisse
Ukraine	..	41518	32322	24311	9232	5687	3991	2573	1709	1585	Ukraine
United Kingdom	[8]16655	...	...	2566	3082	3269	3962	2953	2892	...	Royaume-Uni
Yugoslavia	..	744	356	233	384	399	297	222	102	32	Yougoslavie
T.F.Yug.Rep. Macedonia	..	...	...	158	190	335	403	435	695	671	L'ex-RY Macédoine
Total	**318387**	**372475**	**288947**	**279166**	**224372**	**206937**	**228941**	**215900**	**203770**	**187968**	**Total**

General Note.

House slippers, underwedge slippers such as slip-on type, without laces, buckles, zippers or other closures, of underwedgeheel construction, or with leather upper and split leather tread sole and heel held together by a blown sponge rubber midsole created and simultaneously attached thereto. Slipper socks are excluded. (SITC, Rev.3: 85140-5, 85150-2, 85170-5).

Remarque générale.

Pantoufles, babouches, mules et autres chaussons, sans lacets, boucles, fermetures à glissière ni autres fermetures, du type à semelle compensée ou avec empeigne de cuir et semelle et talon en cuir refendu, réunis par un cambrion intégral en caoutchouc mousse. Cette rubrique ne comprend pas les chaussettes à semelle renforcée. (CTCI, Rev.3: 85140-5, 85150-2, 85170-5).

For footnotes, see end of table.   Voir la fin du tableau pour les notes.

Footwear, house (continued)
Chaussures d'intérieur (suite)

ISIC-BASED CODE - CODE BASE CITI

3240-13

<table>
<tr><td>

Footnotes

[1] Including plastic footwear.
[2] Slippers only.
[3] Including other footwear n.e.s.
[4] Beginning 1996, data are confidential.
[5] Also included with data for leather footwear for men, women and children.
[6] Including sandals and light footwear.
[7] Excluding Transnistria region.
[8] Sales.

</td><td>

Notes.

[1] Y compris les chaussures en matière plastique.
[2] Pantoufles seulement.
[3] Y compris les autres chaussures n.d.a.
[4] A partir de 1996, les données sont confidentielles.
[5] Aussi comptées dans les données concernant les chaussures en cuir pour hommes, pour dames et pour enfants.
[6] Y compris les sandales et chaussures légères.
[7] Non compris la région de Transnistria.
[8] Ventes.

</td></tr>
</table>

Sandals and similar light footwear
Sandales et autres chaussures légères

ISIC-BASED CODE - CODE BASE CITI

3240-16

Unit : Thousand pairs   Unité : Milliers de paires

Country or area	1990	1991	1992	1993	1994	1995	1996	1997	1998	1999	Pays ou zone
America, North	**118**	**163**	**315**	**93**	**125**	**163**	**163**	**163**	**163**	**163**	**Amérique du Nord**
Panama	118	...	315	93	125	...	...	...	...	...	Panama
America, South	**153244**	**170337**	**121157**	**127239**	**128098**	**130292**	**122909**	**122228**	**135693**	**131874**	**Amérique du Sud**
Bolivia	411	457	691	503	522	*453	...	...	...	...	Bolivie
Brazil[1]	150993	168040	118626	124896	125736	127999	119747	120095	133901	129506	Brésil[1]
Colombia	...	...	...	...	...	...	...	1599	1259	...	Colombie
Ecuador	...	...	...	...	...	...	1214	12	8	...	Equateur
Asia	**15587**	**11164**	**44134**	**52821**	**54883**	**32452**	**44875**	**57417**	**94706**	**98055**	**Asie**
China, Macao, SAR[2]	...	...	...	440	1266	1211	1153	1287	...	2526	Chine, Macao PAS[2]
Cyprus	*3920	*3800	807	...	...	1886	1301	1084	894	610	Chypre
Indonesia	11032	6592	...	#50592	51828	29354	...	55045	92497	...	Indonésie
Turkmenistan	..	...	...	...	...	1	...	...	...	...	Turkménistan
Europe	**45439**	**84840**	**56666**	**43917**	**38984**	**47245**	**48185**	**48977**	**40628**	**46024**	**Europe**
Austria[3 4 5]	506	596	692	510	433	...	...	...	363	507	Autriche[3 4 5]
Bulgaria	1330	454	314	556	458	260	232	176	120	385	Bulgarie
Croatia	..	665	626	740	473	520	715	746	608	...	Croatie
Finland[6]	77	66	61	49	40	77	28	...	58	40	Finlande[6]
Germany		19476	13740	14690	9091	13398	...	...	...	...	Allemagne
Germany(Fed.Rep.)	10870	..	..	..	..	..	...	...	..	..	Allemagne(Rép.féd.)
Greece	262	181	219	779	557	325	297	676	764	...	Grèce
Hungary	6112	3212	2153	1857	1472	1444	...	...	...	...	Hongrie
Latvia	..	...	...	238	195	144	98	53	54	61	Lettonie
Netherlands[7 8]	...	...	...	159	144	146	...	...	...		Pays-Bas[7 8]
Portugal	[9]1539	[9]1277	3970	5015	4889	5555	5569	6383	7209	7933	Portugal
Russian Federation	..	25197	9082	3383	1706	1473	1134	743	298	494	Fédération de Russie
Slovakia	..	...	...	758	...	...	...	...	831	562	Slovaquie
Slovenia	..	459	236	209	78	58	965	937	662	543	Slovénie
Spain	22723	20166	14749	8004	14094	19655	24761	25901	...	27341	Espagne
Ukraine	..	7476	5061	2361	682	301	219	93	48	40	Ukraine
United Kingdom	...	...	...	2438	1512	1268	991	1791	1544	...	Royaume-Uni
Yugoslavia	..	2773	2551	2031	2115	1204	1438	1666	1889	744	Yougoslavie
T.F.Yug.Rep. Macedonia	..	629	370	140	328	185	259	371	408	394	L'ex-RY Macédoine
Total	**214388**	**266504**	**222273**	**224070**	**222090**	**210152**	**216131**	**228785**	**271189**	**276115**	**Total**

General Note.
Sandals of various types, "espadrilles", "alpargatas" (shoes with canvas uppers and soles of plaited vegetable material) and similar light footwear. Rubber footwear is excluded. (SITC, Rev.3: 85115-6, 85140-6, 85150-3, 85170-6).

Remarque générale.
Sandales de types divers, "espadrilles", "alpargates" (chaussures avec dessus de toile et semelle de sparte tressée) et autres chaussures légères, à l'exclusion des chaussures en caoutchouc. (CTCI, Rev.3: 85115-6, 85140-6, 85150-3, 85170-6)

[1] Including rubber footwear.
[2] 1998 data are confidential.
[3] 1995 data are confidential.
[4] 1996 data are confidential.
[5] 1997 data are confidential.
[6] Sandals only.
[7] Sales.
[8] Production by establishments employing 20 or more persons.
[9] Tennis shoes only.

[1] Y compris les chaussures en caoutchouc.
[2] Pour 1998, les données sont confidentielles.
[3] Pour 1995, les données sont confidentielles.
[4] Pour 1996, les données sont confidentielles.
[5] Pour 1997, les données sont confidentielles.
[6] Sandales seulement.
[7] Ventes.
[8] Production des établissements occupant 20 personnes ou plus.
[9] Chaussures de tennis seulement.

Sawnwood, coniferous
Sciages de résineux

ISIC-BASED CODE - CODE BASE CITI

3311-04

Unit : Thousand cubic metres

Unité : Milliers de mètres cubes

Country or area	1990	1991	1992	1993	1994	1995	1996	1997	1998	1999	Pays ou zone
Africa	**2491**	**2437**	**2415**	**2297**	**2621**	**2704**	**2653**	**2642**	**2573**	**2612**	**Afrique**
Algeria	9	9	9	9	9	9	9	9	9	9	Algérie
Burundi	2	3	3	11	9	21	7	7	7	7	Burundi
Côte d'Ivoire	...	...	12	10	10	10	...	...	...	...	Côte d'Ivoire
Ethiopia,incl.Eritrea	16	9	9	...	...	...	...	...	...	...	Ethiopie,incl.Erythrée
Ethiopia	...	...	...	30	25	25	25	25	25	25	Ethiopie
Ghana	...	...	10	29	54	54	54	...	...	...	Ghana
Kenya	184	184	184	184	184	184	184	184	184	184	Kenya
Madagascar	2	...	5	5	10	20	20	20	20	20	Madagascar
Malawi	28	28	28	30	30	30	30	30	30	30	Malawi
Mauritius	3	5	4	5	4	2	3	3	4	4	Maurice
Morocco	43	43	43	43	43	43	43	43	43	43	Maroc
Mozambique	8	7	6	13	11	13	13	...	...	...	Mozambique
Nigeria	6	...	...	...	...	...	...	...	...	...	Nigéria
Rwanda	6	6	6	6	7	15	16	20	21	22	Rwanda
South Africa	1734	1619	1639	1251	1365	1439	1439	1439	1396	1396	Afrique du Sud
Sudan	2	...	...	...	1	1	1	1	1	1	Soudan
Swaziland	77	75	75	75	80	90	100	102	102	102	Swaziland
Tunisia	16	5	2	6	7	7	7	7	7	7	Tunisie
Uganda	10	10	20	30	40	50	54	57	61	67	Ouganda
United Rep.Tanzania	85	85	26	21	13	13	13	13	13	13	Rép. Unie de Tanzanie
Zambia	53	62	78	300	340	300	230	145	145	145	Zambie
Zimbabwe	168	221	221	221	361	361	377	419	375	395	Zimbabwe
America, North	**140776**	**132171**	**139976**	**139313**	**144316**	**138219**	**145037**	**149009**	**149835**	**159097**	**Amérique du Nord**
Bahamas	1	1	1	1	1	1	1	1	1	1	Bahamas
Belize	5	5	5	5	5	5	5	5	5	5	Belize
Canada	53702	51037	55512	58651	60648	59343	61828	63929	64082	68235	Canada
Costa Rica	12	12	12	12	11	12	12	12	12	12	Costa Rica
Cuba	59	59	59	59	59	59	59	59	59	66	Cuba
El Salvador	57	57	57	57	57	57	57	57	57	57	El Salvador
Guatemala	30	40	60	239	250	263	263	263	263	263	Guatemala
Haiti	8	8	8	8	8	8	8	8	8	8	Haïti
Honduras	327	300	403	359	356	230	321	357	352	404	Honduras
Mexico	2028	2345	2345	2146	2401	2206	2407	2751	3044	3044	Mexique
Nicaragua	34	34	20	29	12	38	67	104	104	104	Nicaragua
Trinidad and Tobago	...	...	...	11	15	15	5	10	10	10	Trinité-et-Tobago
United States	84500	78260	81481	77736	80493	75982	80004	81453	81838	86888	Etats-Unis
America, South	**11462**	**12019**	**12012**	**12037**	**12460**	**13312**	**13539**	**14291**	**14205**	**14279**	**Amérique du Sud**
Argentina	130	130	309	360	254	625	594	...	...	...	Argentine
Bolivia	2	5	10	10	10	10	15	15	15	15	Bolivie
Brazil	7923	8591	8591	8591	8591	8591	8591	8591	8591	8591	Brésil
Chile	2889	2751	2565	2663	2927	3394	3744	4274	4222	4222	Chili
Colombia	244	244	244	244	244	244	100	139	6	1	Colombie
Ecuador	...	...	8	39	320	340	377	416	416	416	Equateur
Peru	5	...	2	3	1	...	...	...	...	...	Pérou
Uruguay	77	67	84	84	84	84	84	84	84	84	Uruguay
Venezuela	21	27	199	43	29	21	31	10	...	...	Venezuela
Asia	**52157**	**47531**	**45749**	**48937**	**49953**	**48850**	**49883**	**43566**	**37153**	**37460**	**Asie**
Afghanistan	380	380	380	380	380	380	380	380	380	380	Afghanistan
Bhutan	...	...	13	12	12	12	12	12	12	12	Bhoutan
Cambodia	...	...	10	5	5	...	...	...	...	...	Cambodge
China[1]	15050	11798	11452	15566	15501	15501	16613	12346	10997	9787	Chine[1]
Cyprus	21	16	14	17	14	14	15	13	10	11	Chypre
India	2500	2500	2500	2500	2500	2500	2500	2500	2500	2500	Inde
Indonesia	138	138	138	138	138	138	138	138	...	...	Indonésie
Japan	26421	25075	24200	23298	24740	23391	22771	20719	17788	17270	Japon
Korea,Dem.Ppl's.Rep.	185	185	185	185	185	185	185	185	185	185	Corée,Rép.pop.dém.de
Korea, Republic of	2884	3152	2810	2696	3190	3048	3598	4059	1900	3648	Corée, République de
Kyrgyzstan	..	...	...	...	...	...	...	2	3	3	Kirghizistan
Lao People's Dem. Rep.	...	...	20	20	171	273	140	209	100	150	Rép. dém. pop. lao
Lebanon	13	11	9	9	9	9	9	9	9	9	Liban

For general note and footnotes, see end of table.

Voir la fin du tableau pour la remarque générale et les notes.

Sawnwood, coniferous (continued)
Sciages de résineux (suite)

ISIC-BASED CODE - CODE BASE CITI

3311-04

Unit : Thousand cubic metres

Unité : Milliers de mètres cubes

Country or area	1990	1991	1992	1993	1994	1995	1996	1997	1998	1999	Pays ou zone
Malaysia	69	69	69	85	100	150	150	150	150	150	Malaisie
Mongolia	509	270	124	84	50	61	170	200	300	300	Mongolie
Myanmar	...	...	20	30	38	38	38	38	38	38	Myanmar
Nepal	20	20	20	20	20	20	20	20	20	20	Népal
Pakistan	312	240	312	577	432	485	500	400	400	410	Pakistan
Philippines	5	3	4	...	...	...	...	...	...	...	Philippines
Singapore	5	10	5	5	5	5	5	5	5	5	Singapour
Syrian Arab Republic	7	7	7	7	7	7	7	7	7	7	Rép. arabe syrienne
Thailand	...	...	...	...	20	22	22	36	4	9	Thaïlande
Turkey	3354	3354	3330	3179	2334	2502	2502	2032	2101	2322	Turquie
Viet Nam	105	113	102	96	96	96	96	96	96	96	Viet Nam
Europe	58925	96706	110515	99934	99239	100040	95211	100607	102148	104821	Europe
Albania	86	86	86	1	2	2	2	2	2	2	Albanie
Austria	7212	6942	6774	6558	7316	7552	7950	8254	8534	9558	Autriche
Belarus	..	...	1031	938	938	938	938	938	938	938	Bélarus
Belgium-Luxembourg	930	960	900	900	925	880	830	880	1074	1005	Belgique-Luxembourg
Bulgaria	860	930	214	186	186	186	186	186	186	186	Bulgarie
Croatia	..	...	118	146	127	100	114	139	154	166	Croatie
Denmark	456	456	368	338	338	338	338	338	191	303	Danemark
Czechoslovakia(former)	4082	3037	..	..	..	..	..	..	..	..	Tchécoslovaquie(anc.)
Czech Republic	..	...	...	2770	2925	3220	3100	3100	3100	3251	République tchèque
Estonia	..	...	270	270	310	315	360	684	780	860	Estonie
Finland	7417	6430	7280	8500	10220	9860	9710	11360	12240	12710	Finlande
France	7049	6904	6650	6166	6649	6827	6506	6800	7197	7450	France
Germany	..	11599	11866	10358	12365	12925	13123	13682	13807	14770	Allemagne
Greece	185	198	210	210	210	210	210	81	85	87	Grèce
Hungary	331	201	149	122	87	83	102	110	103	98	Hongrie
Ireland	380	380	560	622	699	664	670	632	665	804	Irlande
Italy	875	825	800	800	808	800	750	788	700	730	Italie
Latvia	..	...	480	401	750	950	1510	2550	2800	3047	Lettonie
Lithuania	..	...	100	627	700	865	1350	1130	900	850	Lituanie
Netherlands	175	140	155	181	174	200	186	223	196	203	Pays-Bas
Norway	2401	2250	2350	2300	2400	2205	2400	2500	2525	2551	Norvège
Poland	3399	2644	3556	3694	4500	4600	4280	5010	5441	5275	Pologne
Portugal	1750	1650	1350	1300	1244	1250	1250	1250	1120	1080	Portugal
Republic of Moldova	..	...	...	...	31	25	25	25	25	25	Rép. de Moldova
Romania	1357	1019	860	860	867	877	924	1115	1456	1456	Roumanie
Russian Federation	..	...	43695	32800	24640	22525	17530	16675	15610	15130	Fédération de Russie
Slovakia	..	...	...	345	400	427	426	501	845	903	Slovaquie
Slovenia	..	...	386	381	386	344	335	367	535	535	Slovénie
Spain	2697	2559	1686	2159	1995	2507	2378	2378	2437	2373	Espagne
Sweden	11798	11250	11928	12538	13616	14737	14170	15419	14874	14608	Suède
Switzerland	1783	1555	1413	1300	1200	1342	1240	1100	1200	1300	Suisse
United Kingdom	1935	1894	1916	1950	2050	2106	2140	2214	2253	2387	Royaume-Uni
Yugoslavia	..	...	170	170	170	170	170	170	170	170	Yougoslavie
T.F.Yug.Rep. Macedonia	..	...	...	15	11	10	8	7	6	11	L'ex-RY Macédoine
Yugoslavia, SFR	1769	..	..	..	..	..	..	..	..	..	Yougoslavie, RSF
USSR (former)	92000	..	..	..	..	..	..	..	..	..	URSS (anc.)
Oceania	3651	3669	4091	4555	4837	5142	5159	5293	5603	6152	Océanie
Australia	1405	1337	1570	1660	1898	2121	2053	2063	2327	2331	Australie
Fiji	41	90	40	57	47	43	43	56	64	169	Fidji
New Zealand	2161	2198	2437	2794	2848	2934	3019	3130	3168	3608	Nouvelle-Zélande
Papua New Guinea	43	43	43	43	43	43	43	43	43	43	Papouasie-Nvl-Guinée
Tonga	1	1	1	1	1	1	1	1	1	1	Tonga
Total	361462	294532	314757	307072	313424	308266	311481	315407	311516	324421	Total

For general note and footnotes, see end of table.

Voir la fin du tableau pour la remarque générale et les notes.

Sawnwood, coniferous (continued)
Sciages de résineux (suite)

ISIC-BASED CODE - CODE BASE CITI
3311-04

General Note.

Sawnwood includes wood simply sawn lengthwise (for example, planks, beams, joists, boards, rafters, scantlings, laths etc.)and wood which has been sliced, peeled or rotary cut, and which is more than 5 mm thick. Rough sawnwood is often further processed in the same establishment into planed, tongued, grooved, chamfered, rabbeted, v-jointed and beaded wood etc. Where this occurs, production may be counted at the sawn stage or at a later stage, but steps should be taken to ensure that the sawn wood is not counted more than once. Boxes, whether assembled or not and sawn railway sleepers are excluded, as is wood sawn into sheets of a thickness of 5 mm or less (SITC, Rev.3: 24820-0, 24830-0).

Source: Food and Agriculture Organization of the United Nations (FAO), Rome.

[1] Including Hong-Kong, Macao and Taiwan.

Remarque générale.

Les sciages comprennent les bois simplement sciés longitudinalement (par exemple: madriers, poutres, solives, planches, chevrons, voliges, lattes etc.) et les bois tranchés ou déroulés, de plus de 5 mm d'épaisseur. Dans le même établissement, on fait souvent subir aux sciages bruts un traitement ultérieur pour en faire des bois rabotés, bouvetés, rainés, languetés, chamfreinés, feuillurés, chevronnés et moulurés etc. Dans ce cas, la production peut être comptée au stade du sciage ou à un stade ultérieur, mais on doit veiller à ne pas compter deux fois le même bois. N'entrent dans cette rubrique ni les caisses ni les planches de caisserie, ni les traverses de chemin de fer sciées, ni le bois scié en feuilles d'une épaisseur de 5 mm ou moins (CTCI, Rev.3: 24820-0, 24830-0).

Source: Organisation des Nations Unies pour l'alimentation et l'agriculture (FAO), Rome.

[1] Y compris Hong-Kong, Macao et Taïwan.

Sawnwood, broadleaved
Sciages de feuillus

ISIC-BASED CODE - CODE BASE CITI

3311-07

Unit : Thousand cubic metres

Unité : Milliers de mètres cubes

Country or area	1990	1991	1992	1993	1994	1995	1996	1997	1998	1999	Pays ou zone
Africa	**5918**	**5692**	**5840**	**5676**	**5992**	**5661**	**5347**	**5085**	**5166**	**5098**	**Afrique**
Algeria	3	3	3	3	3	3	3	3	3	3	Algérie
Angola	5	5	5	5	5	5	5	5	5	5	Angola
Benin	14	27	24	24	24	15	11	12	13	13	Bénin
Burkina Faso	2	2	2	2	1	1	1	2	1	1	Burkina Faso
Burundi	...	...	...	9	12	22	26	26	26	26	Burundi
Cameroon	591	563	577	579	647	676	685	560	588	600	Cameroun
Central African Rep.	63	60	68	60	73	70	61	72	91	79	Rép. centrafricaine
Chad	1	2	2	2	2	2	2	2	2	2	Tchad
Congo	50	54	52	52	57	62	59	64	73	74	Congo
Côte d'Ivoire	753	608	611	577	698	696	596	613	623	611	Côte d'Ivoire
Dem. Rep. of Congo	117	105	105	105	75	65	85	90	80	80	Rép. dém. du Congo
Egypt	...	...	...	...	...	...	...	...	101	101	Egypte
Equatorial Guinea	12	13	8	7	4	4	4	4	4	4	Guinée équatoriale
Ethiopia,incl.Eritrea	6	3	3	...	...	...	...	...	...	...	Ethiopie,incl.Erythrée
Ethiopia	...	...	...	3	20	15	8	35	35	35	Ethiopie
Gabon	37	85	155	153	173	100	50	30	60	98	Gabon
Gambia	1	1	1	1	1	1	1	1	1	1	Gambie
Ghana	472	400	410	475	747	558	550	575	590	475	Ghana
Guinea	70	70	63	65	72	85	85	25	26	26	Guinée
Guinea-Bissau	16	16	16	16	16	16	16	16	16	16	Guinée-Bissau
Kenya	1	1	1	1	1	1	1	1	1	1	Kenya
Liberia	85	75	125	90	90	90	90	90	90	90	Libéria
Libyan Arab Jamah.	31	31	31	31	31	31	31	31	31	31	Jamah. arabe libyenne
Madagascar	233	233	233	139	64	64	64	64	64	64	Madagascar
Malawi	15	15	15	15	15	15	15	15	15	15	Malawi
Mali	13	13	13	13	13	13	13	13	13	13	Mali
Mauritius	0	0	0	0	0	0	0	0	1	1	Maurice
Morocco	40	40	40	40	40	40	40	40	40	40	Maroc
Mozambique	18	10	10	17	19	29	29	33	28	28	Mozambique
Niger	...	...	1	4	4	4	4	4	4	4	Niger
Nigeria	2723	2719	2715	2711	2533	2356	2178	2000	2000	2000	Nigéria
Réunion	3	2	2	2	2	2	2	2	2	2	Réunion
Rwanda	30	30	30	30	19	39	43	54	55	57	Rwanda
Sao Tome and Principe	5	5	5	5	5	5	5	5	5	5	Sao Tomé-et-Principe
Senegal	22	23	23	23	23	23	23	23	23	23	Sénégal
Sierra Leone	11	9	9	5	5	5	5	5	5	5	Sierra Leone
Somalia	14	14	14	14	14	14	14	14	14	14	Somalie
South Africa	202	173	179	132	134	135	135	135	102	102	Afrique du Sud
Sudan	2	2	3	3	44	44	44	44	50	50	Soudan
Togo	6	2	3	3	8	14	15	17	18	21	Togo
Tunisia	1	12	4	14	14	14	14	14	14	14	Tunisie
Uganda	20	20	76	77	100	150	161	172	184	197	Ouganda
United Rep.Tanzania	71	71	22	18	11	11	11	11	11	11	Rép. Unie de Tanzanie
Zambia	28	32	34	18	27	20	15	12	12	12	Zambie
Zimbabwe	22	29	29	29	40	40	41	46	41	43	Zimbabwe
America, North	**27540**	**26112**	**28677**	**30490**	**31478**	**31678**	**31918**	**32123**	**34184**	**35176**	**Amérique du Nord**
Belize	9	9	9	9	15	30	30	30	30	30	Belize
Canada	1204	1003	806	1123	1002	1093	1000	835	1027	1051	Canada
Costa Rica	400	400	760	786	735	768	768	768	768	768	Costa Rica
Cuba	72	72	72	72	72	72	72	72	72	80	Cuba
El Salvador	14	14	14	14	14	14	14	14	14	14	El Salvador
Guadeloupe	1	1	1	1	1	1	1	1	1	1	Guadeloupe
Guatemala	7	15	30	159	167	92	92	92	92	92	Guatemala
Haiti	6	6	6	6	6	6	6	6	6	6	Haïti
Honduras	1	3	8	5	5	1	1	22	17	17	Honduras
Jamaica	40	32	27	24	20	12	12	12	12	12	Jamaïque
Martinique	1	1	1	1	1	1	1	1	1	1	Martinique
Mexico	339	351	351	414	292	123	136	210	216	216	Mexique
Nicaragua	46	46	41	36	15	36	93	44	44	44	Nicaragua
Panama	48	16	37	37	37	37	19	17	8	24	Panama
Trinidad and Tobago	53	42	59	24	43	49	24	28	17	17	Trinité-et-Tobago
United States	25300	24103	26456	27780	29054	29344	29650	29972	31860	32804	Etats-Unis

For general note and footnotes, see end of table.

Voir la fin du tableau pour la remarque générale et les notes.

Sawnwood, broadleaved (continued)
Sciages de feuillus (suite)

ISIC-BASED CODE - CODE BASE CITI

3311-07

Unit : Thousand cubic metres

Unité : Milliers de mètres cubes

Country or area	1990	1991	1992	1993	1994	1995	1996	1997	1998	1999	Pays ou zone
America, South	**13991**	**14115**	**14693**	**13437**	**14730**	**15081**	**16454**	**16158**	**15251**	**14626**	**Amérique du Sud**
Argentina	820	820	1163	638	826	704	1117	...	...	...	Argentine
Bolivia	100	120	220	258	175	152	166	165	500	244	Bolivie
Brazil	9256	10037	10037	10037	10100	10500	10500	10500	10000	10000	Brésil
Chile	438	467	455	450	437	408	396	387	329	329	Chili
Colombia	569	569	514	450	400	400	1034	946	154	179	Colombie
Ecuador	1641	865	900	157	1280	1356	1509	1663	1663	1663	Equateur
French Guiana	19	19	19	18	15	15	15	15	15	15	Guyane française
Guyana	50	50	50	50	77	101	97	57	24	25	Guyana
Paraguay	228	313	357	357	357	400	500	550	550	550	Paraguay
Peru	494	477	498	589	648	630	693	482	590	282	Pérou
Suriname	44	40	43	33	29	29	40	41	41	30	Suriname
Uruguay	152	138	185	185	185	185	185	185	185	185	Uruguay
Venezuela	180	200	252	215	201	201	202	240	261	174	Venezuela
Asia	**52737**	**52729**	**51478**	**52693**	**48099**	**46931**	**48378**	**45167**	**36506**	**35864**	**Asie**
Afghanistan	20	20	20	20	20	20	20	20	20	20	Afghanistan
Bangladesh	79	79	79	79	79	70	70	70	70	70	Bangladesh
Bhutan	35	35	8	6	6	6	6	6	6	6	Bhoutan
Brunei Darussalam	90	90	90	90	90	90	90	90	90	90	Brunéi Darussalam
Cambodia	71	122	122	150	190	140	100	71	40	10	Cambodge
China [1]	8531	9144	8304	10143	10102	10102	10797	8636	7736	6930	Chine [1]
Cyprus	1	0	0	0	1	1	1	1	1	0	Chypre
India	14960	14960	14960	14960	14960	14960	14960	14960	14960	14960	Inde
Indonesia	9008	8500	8300	8200	6700	6500	7200	7100	2523	2427	Indonésie
Iran(Islamic Rep. of)	169	173	187	170	178	159	144	141	129	97	Iran(Rép. islamique)
Iraq	8	8	8	8	8	8	8	8	12	12	Iraq
Japan	3360	3189	3077	2962	1166	1102	1073	990	837	682	Japon
Korea,Dem.Ppl's.Rep.	95	95	95	95	95	95	95	95	95	95	Corée,Rép.pop.dém.de
Korea, Republic of	1013	889	703	553	672	392	693	700	340	652	Corée, République de
Lao People's Dem. Rep.	100	300	150	242	160	192	180	351	150	200	Rép. dém. pop. lao
Malaysia	8780	8924	9300	9310	8758	8232	8232	7176	5091	5091	Malaisie
Myanmar	296	282	282	309	309	309	313	334	299	267	Myanmar
Nepal	550	600	600	600	600	600	600	600	600	600	Népal
Pakistan	1138	1280	1138	926	695	781	780	624	651	665	Pakistan
Philippines	841	726	643	440	407	286	313	351	216	216	Philippines
Singapore	50	20	20	20	20	20	20	20	20	20	Singapour
Sri Lanka	10	5	5	5	5	6	5	5	5	5	Sri Lanka
Syrian Arab Republic	2	2	2	2	2	2	2	2	2	2	Rép. arabe syrienne
Thailand	1170	939	1076	715	548	404	285	390	99	186	Thaïlande
Turkey	1569	1574	1561	2062	1703	1829	1766	1801	1889	1935	Turquie
Viet Nam	791	772	747	625	625	625	625	625	625	625	Viet Nam
Europe	**14463**	**22124**	**24259**	**20401**	**18579**	**16879**	**16444**	**15880**	**16582**	**17144**	**Europe**
Albania	296	296	296	3	3	3	3	3	3	3	Albanie
Austria	297	297	246	228	256	252	250	196	203	228	Autriche
Belarus	..	...	662	607	607	607	607	607	607	607	Bélarus
Belgium-Luxembourg	264	284	284	284	284	270	270	270	193	184	Belgique-Luxembourg
Bosnia and Herzegovina	..	..	20	20	20	20	20	20	20	20	Bosnie-Herzégovine
Bulgaria	248	184	110	67	67	67	67	67	67	67	Bulgarie
Croatia	..	...	533	553	474	478	484	505	522	519	Croatie
Denmark	406	406	252	245	245	245	245	245	47	47	Danemark
Czechoslovakia(former)	682	584	..	..	..	..	..	..	..	..	Tchécoslovaquie(anc.)
Czech Republic	..	..	...	255	230	270	305	293	327	333	République tchèque
Estonia	..	...	30	30	31	35	40	45	70	85	Estonie
Finland	87	30	50	70	70	80	70	70	60	60	Finlande
France	3911	4070	3838	2966	3000	3021	3094	2807	3023	3050	France
Germany	..	1723	1630	1164	1202	1180	1144	1048	1165	1559	Allemagne
Greece	170	189	127	127	127	127	127	49	52	53	Grèce
Hungary	767	735	518	358	330	147	183	207	195	210	Hongrie
Ireland	6	6	15	15	10	14	17	10	10	7	Irlande
Italy	1075	1025	1023	900	1000	1050	900	963	900	900	Italie
Latvia	..	...	260	45	200	350	104	150	400	593	Lettonie
Lithuania	..	...	5	72	60	75	100	120	250	300	Lituanie

For general note and footnotes, see end of table.

Voir la fin du tableau pour la remarque générale et les notes.

348

Sawnwood, broadleaved (continued)
Sciages de feuillus (suite)

ISIC-BASED CODE - CODE BASE CITI

3311-07

Unit : Thousand cubic metres

Unité : Milliers de mètres cubes

Country or area	1990	1991	1992	1993	1994	1995	1996	1997	1998	1999	Pays ou zone
Netherlands	280	285	250	208	209	226	173	178	153	159	Pays-Bas
Norway	12	12	12	15	15	5	20	20	...	...	Norvège
Poland	730	561	526	566	800	1050	780	900	1080	1120	Pologne
Portugal	340	320	200	194	426	481	481	481	370	350	Portugal
Republic of Moldova	...	...	...	...	...	...	4	5	5	6	Rép. de Moldova
Romania	1554	1214	1600	1600	860	900	769	746	744	744	Roumanie
Russian Federation	..	...	9675	8090	6080	3975	4383	3925	3970	3850	Fédération de Russie
Slovakia	..	..	...	205	300	219	203	266	420	405	Slovaquie
Slovenia	..	...	17	132	127	167	161	143	129	129	Slovénie
Spain	570	603	782	558	760	755	702	702	741	715	Espagne
Sweden	220	213	200	200	200	207	200	250	250	250	Suède
Switzerland	203	173	113	110	120	137	115	180	200	200	Suisse
United Kingdom	336	347	181	162	175	189	151	142	129	115	Royaume-Uni
Yugoslavia	..	...	320	300	240	240	240	240	240	240	Yougoslavie
T.F.Yug.Rep. Macedonia	..	...	...	48	46	32	32	27	21	20	L'ex-RY Macédoine
Yugoslavia, SFR	2010	..	..	..	..	..	..	..	..	..	Yougoslavie, RSF
USSR (former)	13000	..	..	..	..	..	..	..	..	..	URSS (anc.)
Oceania	**1960**	**1758**	**1816**	**1714**	**1830**	**1864**	**1768**	**1720**	**1681**	**1600**	**Océanie**
Australia	1746	1521	1471	1527	1533	1570	1477	1418	1384	1339	Australie
Fiji	53	51	51	54	65	59	59	77	67	30	Fidji
New Caledonia	5	3	2	2	3	3	3	3	3	3	Nouvelle-Calédonie
New Zealand	37	65	107	11	13	16	13	6	10	11	Nouvelle-Zélande
Papua New Guinea	74	74	140	75	175	175	175	175	175	175	Papouasie-Nvl-Guinée
Samoa	21	21	21	21	21	21	21	21	21	21	Samoa
Solomon Islands	16	16	16	16	12	12	12	12	12	12	Iles Salomon
Tonga	1	1	1	1	1	1	1	1	1	1	Tonga
Vanuatu	7	7	7	7	7	7	7	7	7	7	Vanuatu
Total	**129607**	**122531**	**126763**	**124411**	**120708**	**118094**	**120310**	**116133**	**109370**	**109508**	**Total**

General Note.

Sawnwood includes wood simply sawn lengthwise (for example, planks, beams, joists, boards, rafters, scantlings, laths etc.)and wood which has been sliced, peeled or rotary cut, and which is more than 5 mm thick. Rough sawnwood is often further processed in the same establishment into planed, tongued, grooved, chamfered, rabbeted, v-jointed and beaded wood etc. Where this occurs, production may be counted at the sawn stage or at a later stage, but steps should be taken to ensure that the sawn wood is not counted more than once. Boxes, whether assembled or not and sawn railway sleepers are excluded, as is wood sawn into sheets of a thickness of 5 mm or less (SITC, Rev.3: 24840-0, 24850-0).

Source: Food and Agriculture Organization of the United Nations (FAO), Rome.

Remarque générale.

Les sciages comprennent les bois simplement sciés longitudinalement (par exemple: madriers, poutres, solives, planches, chevrons, voliges, lattes etc.) et les bois tranchés ou déroulés, de plus de 5 mm d'épaisseur. Dans le même établissement, on fait souvent subir aux sciages bruts un traitement ultérieur pour en faire des bois rabotés, bouvetés, rainés, languetés, chamfreinés, feuillurés, chevronnés et moulurés etc. Dans ce cas, la production peut être comptée au stade du sciage ou à un stade ultérieur, mais on doit veiller à ne pas compter deux fois le même bois. N'entrent dans cette rubrique ni les caisses ni les planches de caisserie, ni les traverses de chemin de fer sciées, ni le bois scié en feuilles d'une épaisseur de 5 mm ou moins (CTCI, Rev.3: 24840-0, 24850-0).

Source: Organisation des Nations Unies pour l'alimentation et l'agriculture (FAO), Rome.

[1] Including Hong-Kong, Macao and Taiwan.

[1] Y compris Hong-Kong, Macao et Taïwan.

Veneer sheets
Feuilles de placage

ISIC-BASED CODE - CODE BASE CITI

3311-10

Unit : Thousand cubic metres

Unité : Milliers de mètres cubes

Country or area	1990	1991	1992	1993	1994	1995	1996	1997	1998	1999	Pays ou zone
Africa	**563**	**436**	**390**	**407**	**496**	**469**	**491**	**615**	**682**	**860**	**Afrique**
Algeria	2	2	2	2	2	2	2	2	2	2	Algérie
Angola	1	1	1	1	1	1	1	1	1	1	Angola
Cameroon	32	32	32	31	31	31	31	61	59	53	Cameroun
Congo	60	36	35	35	47	49	50	76	52	19	Congo
Côte d'Ivoire	206	185	195	195	205	215	222	252	274	269	Côte d'Ivoire
Dem. Rep. of Congo	15	14	14	14	8	8	10	10	10	10	Rép. dém. du Congo
Egypt	28	28	28	28	28	28	28	28	12	12	Egypte
Equatorial Guinea	10	10	7	8	8	9	9	9	9	9	Guinée équatoriale
Gabon	65	12	9	2	2	2	5	...	76	133	Gabon
Ghana	46	21	25	33	105	58	67	75	80	245	Ghana
Liberia	5	5	5	5	5	5	5	...	...	...	Libéria
Malawi	4	4	4	4	4	4	4	4	4	4	Malawi
Morocco	25	4	7	7	7	7	7	7	7	7	Maroc
Mozambique	...	0	1	1	1	1	2	3	3	3	Mozambique
South Africa	29	34	8	25	28	35	35	35	75	75	Afrique du Sud
Tunisia	4	4	4	4	4	4	4	4	4	4	Tunisie
Zambia	26	30	1	1	1	1	1	1	1	1	Zambie
Zimbabwe	4	13	13	13	8	8	8	8	8	8	Zimbabwe
America, North	**605**	**617**	**639**	**651**	**671**	**678**	**689**	**700**	**710**	**721**	**Amérique du Nord**
Canada	501	501	501	501	501	501	501	501	501	501	Canada
Costa Rica	10	15	20	21	21	21	21	21	21	21	Costa Rica
Guatemala	3	5	5	17	17	19	19	19	19	19	Guatemala
Honduras	...	...	...	...	...	1	1	1	...	...	Honduras
Mexico	5	10	20	29	49	...	...	...	...	...	Mexique
Panama	...	...	...	...	...	...	...	...	...	2	Panama
United States	...	...	90	80	80	80	80	80	80	80	Etats-Unis
America, South	**496**	**517**	**578**	**657**	**704**	**719**	**719**	**650**	**630**	**623**	**Amérique du Sud**
Argentina	26	26	3	4	1	1	1	13	2	...	Argentine
Bolivia	2	2	2	2	2	2	1	1	8	1	Bolivie
Brazil	234	234	234	300	310	300	265	265	240	240	Brésil
Chile	9	13	28	40	46	69	88	87	104	104	Chili
Colombia	7	7	5	5	5	5	5	1	1	2	Colombie
Ecuador	1	9	120	110	143	151	168	185	185	185	Equateur
Paraguay	102	102	60	60	60	60	60	60	60	60	Paraguay
Peru	3	2	1	7	8	2	2	4	1	1	Pérou
Venezuela	112	123	125	129	129	129	129	34	29	30	Venezuela
Asia	**1176**	**1461**	**1904**	**2784**	**2608**	**2347**	**2409**	**1891**	**2541**	**2250**	**Asie**
Bangladesh	1	1	1	1	1	1	1	1	1	1	Bangladesh
Cambodia	...	...	...	...	9	29	29	182	181	68	Cambodge
China[1]	16	30	48	51	82	86	86	86	86	86	Chine[1]
India	27	24	18	7	7	7	7	7	7	7	Inde
Indonesia	56	50	55	55	50	50	50	50	1110	927	Indonésie
Iran(Islamic Rep. of)	4	4	7	7	8	11	6	3	2	3	Iran(Rép. islamique)
Japan	307	303	274	268	242	242	242	242	242	242	Japon
Malaysia	480	705	1200	2122	2067	1800	1800	1165	760	760	Malaisie
Myanmar	0	0	1	1	0	0	0	0	...	2	Myanmar
Philippines	49	54	80	65	39	19	82	62	59	59	Philippines
Singapore	75	64	65	65	65	65	65	65	65	65	Singapour
Sri Lanka	0	0	0	0	0	5	5	5	5	5	Sri Lanka
Syrian Arab Republic	10	10	10	10	10	10	10	10	10	10	Rép. arabe syrienne
Thailand	136	154	71	72	14	8	8	2	2	2	Thaïlande
Turkey	10	44	44	17	15	15	18	11	10	14	Turquie
Europe	**1498**	**1621**	**1623**	**1644**	**1772**	**1763**	**1931**	**2053**	**1807**	**1843**	**Europe**
Albania	10	10	10	10	10	10	10	10	10	10	Albanie
Austria	21	22	25	24	27	27	27	27	28	23	Autriche
Belgium-Luxembourg	45	45	45	45	45	45	45	46	46	46	Belgique-Luxembourg
Bulgaria	30	30	30	20	20	20	20	20	20	20	Bulgarie
Croatia	..	...	25	30	31	28	27	26	28	31	Croatie
Denmark	6	6	6	8	14	14	14	2	11	12	Danemark

For general note and footnotes, see end of table.

Voir la fin du tableau pour la remarque générale et les notes.

Veneer sheets (continued)
Feuilles de placage (suite)

ISIC-BASED CODE - CODE BASE CITI

3311-10

Unit : Thousand cubic metres

Unité : Milliers de mètres cubes

Country or area	1990	1991	1992	1993	1994	1995	1996	1997	1998	1999	Pays ou zone
Czechoslovakia(former)	47	27	..	..	..	..	..	..	..	..	Tchécoslovaquie(anc.)
Czech Republic	..	..	...	13	8	9	9	8	12	12	République tchèque
Estonia	..	...	5	6	6	1	1	21	20	21	Estonie
Finland	20	20	21	50	74	74	74	74	74	74	Finlande
France	58	58	58	58	154	113	123	140	149	150	France
Germany	..	442	419	380	392	392	392	392	392	392	Allemagne
Greece	20	20	8	8	8	8	8	5	6	7	Grèce
Hungary	14	14	14	16	12	9	15	13	11	7	Hongrie
Italy	622	436	483	500	500	500	500	500	500	450	Italie
Latvia	..	...	5	8	10	10	12	13	15	15	Lettonie
Lithuania	..	...	5	6	6	6	...	3	1	1	Lituanie
Netherlands	20	15	19	21	23	25	19	17	17	19	Pays-Bas
Poland	15	15	11	11	12	13	15	17	45	48	Pologne
Portugal	140	110	110	110	110	110	110	110	...	...	Portugal
Romania	50	44	35	35	50	37	36	33	25	25	Roumanie
Russian Federation	..	...	92	32	65	56	33	136	25	27	Fédération de Russie
Slovakia	..	..	...	...	21	17	19	22	20	10	Slovaquie
Slovenia	..	...	23	21	21	27	21	18	22	22	Slovénie
Spain	80	80	50	119	60	119	300	300	95	186	Espagne
Sweden	13	13	13	13	13	13	13	...	50	50	Suède
Switzerland	30	30	30	30	30	30	30	30	30	30	Suisse
Ukraine	..	...	...	...	...	...	32	27	27	27	Ukraine
United Kingdom	22	22	...	...	...	...	...	...	...	...	Royaume-Uni
Yugoslavia, SFR	235	..	..	..	..	..	..	..	..	..	Yougoslavie, RSF
USSR (former)	400	..	..	..	..	..	..	..	..	..	URSS (anc.)
Oceania	77	92	104	85	118	144	158	331	282	382	Océanie
Australia	29	29	29	29	29	29	29	5	5	5	Australie
Fiji	11	10	10	10	10	10	10	10	10	3	Fidji
New Zealand	4	20	32	41	74	100	114	311	262	369	Nouvelle-Zélande
Papua New Guinea	33	33	33	5	5	5	5	5	5	5	Papouasie-Nvl-Guinée
Total	**4814**	**4743**	**5238**	**6228**	**6369**	**6120**	**6397**	**6239**	**6652**	**6679**	**Total**

General Note.

Thin sheets of wood of a uniform thickness not exceeding 5 mm (excluding any reinforcing material), produced by a sawing, slicing or peeling (rotary cutting) process for use in making plywood and other types of laminated boards, furniture, veneer containers etc. (SITC, Rev.3: 63410-0).
Source: Food and Agriculture Organization of the United Nations (FAO), Rome.

Remarque générale.

Minces feuilles de bois d'épaisseur uniforme ne dépassant pas 5 mm (à l'exclusion de tout matériau de renforcement), sciées, tranchées ou déroulées pour être utilisées dans la fabrication du contreplaqué, des bois laminés, des meubles, des emballages, etc. (CTCI, Rev.3: 63410-0).
Source: Organisation des Nations Unies pour l'alimentation et l'agriculture (FAO), Rome.

[1] Including Hong-Kong, Macao and Taiwan.

[1] Y compris Hong-Kong, Macao et Taïwan.

Blockboard
Contreplaqués à âme épaisse

ISIC-BASED CODE - CODE BASE CITI

3311-13

Unit : Thousand cubic metres   Unité : Milliers de mètres cubes

Country or area	1990	1991	1992	1993	1994	1995	1996	1997	1998	1999	Pays ou zone
America, North	**135**	**111**	**94**	**157**	**165**	**205**	**205**	**215**	**209**	**203**	**Amérique du Nord**
Mexico	135	111	94	157	165	205	205	215	209	203	Mexique
Asia	**37230**	**26770**	**42400**	**69048**	**48459**	**78333**	**158902**	**202223**	**150653**	**124838**	**Asie**
Indonesia	542	345	768	1022	...	206	...	872	935	...	Indonésie
Korea, Republic of	334	392	658	763	923	...	...	...	...	...	Corée, République de
Malaysia	36354	25578	40762	67153	46826	77028	156998	199962	148175	122376	Malaisie
Uzbekistan	..	455	212	110	40	20	...	...	...	...	Ouzbékistan
Europe	**6043**	**20493**	**20288**	**19402**	**19599**	**19571**	**19426**	**19974**	**19771**	**19807**	**Europe**
Austria[1]	61	65	37	36	40	#250	266	204	...	...	Autriche[1]
Belarus	..	1442	1188	794	361	201	140	258	290	244	Bélarus
Croatia	..	1	0	...	...	...	...	...	...	...	Croatie
Czechoslovakia(former)	83	36	..	..	..	..	..	..	..	..	Tchécoslovaquie(anc.)
Czech Republic	..	..	28	33	72	45	58	62	54	56	République tchèque
Finland	4	*5	*9	*8	*7	*8	*8	...	...	...	Finlande
France	5113	4472	4232	3746	...	...	...	...	...	...	France
Germany	..	...	...	...	...	...	13418	13867	...	...	Allemagne
Greece	24	26	33	...	...	...	...	...	...	...	Grèce
Hungary	0	0	1	1	...	...	...	...	...	...	Hongrie
Latvia	..	44	48	58	65	74	100	120	151	203	Lettonie
Poland	15	19	25	32	38	50	61	95	66	87	Pologne
Portugal	21	17	30	...	45	...	...	...	...	...	Portugal
Slovakia	..	..	...	...	...	...	234	246	...	...	Slovaquie
Slovenia	..	17	8	9	6	45	52	...	...	...	Slovénie
Switzerland	722	699	762	742	656	564	...	...	...	...	Suisse
Yugoslavia	..	7	4	4	7	4	4	2	2	2	Yougoslavie
Total	**43408**	**47374**	**62782**	**88607**	**68223**	**98109**	**178532**	**222412**	**170634**	**144848**	**Total**

General Note.

Blockboard, laminboard and battenboard consist of a thick core composed of blocks, laths or battens of wood glued together and surfaced with outer plies. (SITC 63121-1).

Remarque générale.

Panneaux en bois contreplaqué dont le centre est constitué de planches brutes ou lamelles de bois juxtaposées et collées ensemble. (CTCI 63121-1).

[1] Beginning 1998, data are confidential.

[1] A partir de 1998, les données sont confidentielles.

Plywood
Contreplaqués
ISIC-BASED CODE - CODE BASE CITI
3311-16

Unit : Thousand cubic metres

Unité : Milliers de mètres cubes

Country or area	1990	1991	1992	1993	1994	1995	1996	1997	1998	1999	Pays ou zone
Africa	**493**	**503**	**461**	**422**	**395**	**432**	**418**	**537**	**771**	**803**	**Afrique**
Algeria	23	23	23	23	23	23	23	23	23	23	Algérie
Angola	10	10	10	10	10	10	10	10	10	10	Angola
Cameroon	48	48	48	43	43	43	43	90	89	92	Cameroun
Central African Rep.	2	1	2	2	2	2	2	1	1	2	Rép. centrafricaine
Congo	...	...	1	1	1	3	5	3	2	3	Congo
Côte d'Ivoire	42	37	39	41	41	58	43	61	67	59	Côte d'Ivoire
Dem. Rep. of Congo	17	13	12	13	8	8	10	10	10	10	Rép. dém. du Congo
Egypt	7	5	7	7	7	7	7	7	122	122	Egypte
Ethiopia,incl.Eritrea	3	2	2	...	...	...	...	...	...	...	Ethiopie,incl.Erythrée
Ethiopia	...	...	...	2	3	3	2	4	3	1	Ethiopie
Gabon	80	80	20	20	20	25	25	25	115	134	Gabon
Ghana	29	35	32	32	23	35	35	65	71	90	Ghana
Kenya	36	36	36	36	36	36	36	36	36	36	Kenya
Liberia	3	3	3	3	3	3	3	30	48	48	Libéria
Malawi	10	10	14	14	14	14	14	14	14	14	Malawi
Morocco	44	22	25	25	25	25	25	25	25	25	Maroc
Mozambique	0	0	0	0	0	0	1	1	1	1	Mozambique
Nigeria	67	70	72	65	63	60	58	55	55	55	Nigéria
South Africa	24	15	39	20	21	25	25	25	27	27	Afrique du Sud
Swaziland	8	8	8	8	8	8	8	8	8	8	Swaziland
Tunisia	26	26	30	30	30	30	30	30	30	30	Tunisie
Uganda	3	3	4	4	4	4	4	4	4	4	Ouganda
United Rep.Tanzania	3	3	1	1	0	0	0	0	0	0	Rép. Unie de Tanzanie
Zambia	1	1	1	1	1	1	1	1	1	1	Zambie
Zimbabwe	3	48	30	20	7	7	7	7	7	7	Zimbabwe
America, North	**20962**	**18462**	**19168**	**19129**	**19422**	**19177**	**18985**	**19535**	**17674**	**17868**	**Amérique du Nord**
Canada	1971	1705	1838	1824	1834	1831	1814	1830	1760	1928	Canada
Costa Rica	22	22	22	22	22	22	22	22	22	22	Costa Rica
Cuba	2	2	2	2	2	2	2	2	2	2	Cuba
Guatemala	...	...	7	12	12	20	20	20	20	20	Guatemala
Honduras	9	10	14	15	14	14	14	15	19	20	Honduras
Mexico	157	184	150	136	132	...	...	...	...	...	Mexique
Nicaragua	9	5	5	5	5	5	5	5	5	5	Nicaragua
Panama	8	13	21	21	21	21	21	21	21	21	Panama
United States	18771	16508	17109	17093	17380	17140	16975	17517	15732	15767	Etats-Unis
America, South	**1605**	**1549**	**1750**	**1929**	**2346**	**2494**	**2183**	**2139**	**2114**	**2114**	**Amérique du Sud**
Argentina	37	48	68	59	50	38	54	63	62	...	Argentine
Bolivia	7	10	29	15	7	8	1	1	4	4	Bolivie
Brazil	1300	1150	1300	1575	1870	1900	1600	1600	1500	1500	Brésil
Chile	40	55	57	59	64	73	69	65	129	129	Chili
Colombia	64	64	49	55	64	65	35	28	25	26	Colombie
Ecuador	20	91	94	22	88	93	99	109	109	109	Equateur
Guyana	...	...	...	30	57	96	98	67	76	87	Guyana
Paraguay	10	10	19	30	50	100	100	100	100	100	Paraguay
Peru	24	26	30	36	40	64	70	53	57	57	Pérou
Suriname	6	6	8	6	7	7	9	8	7	4	Suriname
Uruguay	4	4	3	3	3	3	3	3	3	3	Uruguay
Venezuela	52	39	39	39	46	46	46	...	...	30	Venezuela
Asia	**19911**	**21521**	**22530**	**23071**	**23797**	**28467**	**25989**	**28944**	**21084**	**21447**	**Asie**
Bangladesh	1	1	1	1	1	1	1	1	1	1	Bangladesh
Bhutan	5	5	5	5	5	5	5	5	5	5	Bhoutan
Cambodia	2	2	2	2	9	29	29	20	16	15	Cambodge
China[1]	1273	1568	2079	2639	3124	8104	5414	8098	4979	7790	Chine[1]
Cyprus	2	2	2	2	2	2	2	2	2	3	Chypre
India	258	250	231	245	245	245	245	245	245	245	Inde
Indonesia	8250	9600	10100	10050	9836	9500	9575	9600	7015	4437	Indonésie
Iran(Islamic Rep. of)	53	57	23	19	19	20	16	16	17	19	Iran(Rép. islamique)
Israel	109	109	109	109	109	109	109	109	109	109	Israël
Japan	6415	6174	5954	5263	4865	4421	4311	4257	3267	3261	Japon
Korea, Republic of	1124	1134	948	898	886	974	896	1014	641	774	Corée, République de

For general note and footnotes, see end of table.

Voir la fin du tableau pour la remarque générale et les notes.

Plywood (continued)
Contreplaqués (suite)

ISIC-BASED CODE - CODE BASE CITI
3311-16

Unit : Thousand cubic metres

Unité : Milliers de mètres cubes

Country or area	1990	1991	1992	1993	1994	1995	1996	1997	1998	1999	Pays ou zone
Lao People's Dem. Rep.	10	10	10	10	10	9	117	125	125	125	Rép. dém. pop. lao
Lebanon	34	34	34	34	34	34	34	34	34	34	Liban
Malaysia	1363	1670	2100	2821	3613	3996	4100	4447	3904	3904	Malaisie
Mongolia	3	2	1	1	1	1	1	1	1	1	Mongolie
Myanmar	15	15	15	15	10	18	8	10	8	8	Myanmar
Pakistan	13	15	13	15	20	25	30	35	36	38	Pakistan
Philippines	414	312	331	273	380	290	508	484	244	244	Philippines
Singapore	328	280	280	280	280	280	280	280	280	280	Singapour
Sri Lanka	7	7	7	7	7	7	7	7	7	7	Sri Lanka
Syrian Arab Republic	8	8	8	8	8	8	8	8	8	8	Rép. arabe syrienne
Thailand	122	164	166	260	220	278	195	44	53	60	Thaïlande
Turkey	65	65	74	77	77	75	61	66	50	43	Turquie
Viet Nam	37	37	37	37	37	37	37	37	37	37	Viet Nam
Europe	2839	4133	4336	4299	4258	4550	4579	4678	5702	5582	Europe
Albania	6	6	6	6	6	6	6	6	6	6	Albanie
Austria	120	140	150	150	150	150	150	150	150	155	Autriche
Belarus	..	...	157	127	104	104	103	122	122	122	Bélarus
Belgium-Luxembourg	65	67	68	68	68	66	65	60	60	59	Belgique-Luxembourg
Bosnia and Herzegovina	..	..	31	34	34	34	34	34	34	34	Bosnie-Herzégovine
Bulgaria	49	25	22	23	23	23	23	23	23	23	Bulgarie
Croatia	..	..	6	8	7	7	8	7	8	9	Croatie
Denmark	30	14	11	18	11	11	11	16	14	15	Danemark
Czechoslovakia(former)	234	157	..	..	..	..	..	..	..	..	Tchécoslovaquie(anc.)
Czech Republic	..	..	...	75	76	77	100	110	108	110	République tchèque
Estonia	..	...	7	8	10	11	18	20	17	20	Estonie
Finland	643	477	462	621	700	778	869	987	992	1076	Finlande
France	518	470	484	460	594	559	537	566	541	543	France
Germany	..	424	429	416	397	498	512	448	428	363	Allemagne
Greece	98	87	70	70	70	70	70	31	32	34	Grèce
Hungary	14	13	11	9	8	7	7	7	7	7	Hongrie
Italy	445	450	427	415	427	418	402	414	420	450	Italie
Latvia	..	...	52	58	63	73	103	120	150	155	Lettonie
Lithuania	..	...	16	15	15	15	21	30	36	32	Lituanie
Netherlands	15	15	18	15	15	15	15	15	5	3	Pays-Bas
Norway	7	8	4	4	4	4	20	...	20	28	Norvège
Poland	126	111	132	133	124	115	109	132	178	172	Pologne
Portugal	21	23	24	25	27	23	23	23	25	26	Portugal
Romania	123	51	100	100	97	83	83	81	76	76	Roumanie
Russian Federation	..	...	1268	1042	890	939	972	943	1102	1320	Fédération de Russie
Slovakia	..	..	...	20	26	27	25	32	33	31	Slovaquie
Slovenia	..	...	65	63	64	75	17	24	32	32	Slovénie
Spain	141	140	120	200	119	210	110	110	382	382	Espagne
Sweden	68	67	55	73	85	108	119	113	114	105	Suède
Switzerland	22	7	5	2	3	3	3	3	3	3	Suisse
Ukraine	..	...	...	...	...	...	11	7	7	7	Ukraine
United Kingdom	15	14	7	5	5	5	5	5	5	5	Royaume-Uni
Yugoslavia	..	...	27	27	27	27	27	27	27	27	Yougoslavie
T.F.Yug.Rep. Macedonia	..	...	...	...	...	1	1	1	545	153	L'ex-RY Macédoine
Yugoslavia, SFR	79	..	..	..	..	..	..	..	..	..	Yougoslavie, RSF
USSR (former)	1744	..	..	..	..	..	..	..	..	..	URSS (anc.)
Oceania	212	174	207	235	291	325	318	362	369	419	Océanie
Australia	125	101	107	122	138	145	131	151	170	169	Australie
Fiji	6	6	10	6	6	6	6	6	11	10	Fidji
New Zealand	68	54	77	97	137	164	171	195	178	230	Nouvelle-Zélande
Papua New Guinea	13	13	13	10	10	10	10	10	10	10	Papouasie-Nvl-Guinée
Total	47766	46342	48452	49084	50509	55445	52472	56194	47713	48234	Total

For general note and footnotes, see end of table.

Voir la fin du tableau pour la remarque générale et les notes.

Plywood (continued)
Contreplaqués (suite)

ISIC-BASED CODE - CODE BASE CITI
3311-16

General Note.
A wooden sheet material consisting of three or more layers of veneers glued or cemented together, the grains of adjoining plies usually being at right angles to one another. This item includes veneered panels, that is, sheets or panels consisting of a thin veneer of wood affixed to a base, usually of inferior wood, by gluing under pressure. (SITC, Rev.3: 63430-0, 63440-2).
Source: Food and Agriculture Organization of the United Nations (FAO), Rome.

[1] Including Hong-Kong, Macao and Taiwan.

Remarque générale.
Panneaux de bois faits de trois couches au moins de feuilles de placage assemblées à la colle ou à l'adhesif et généralement superposées de façon que le fil de chaque feuille soit perpendiculaire à celui de la feuille contiguë. Cette rubrique comprend les panneaux de bois plaqué, c'est-à-dire des feuilles ou des panneaux constitués par des feuilles de placage appliquées par collage et pressage sur un support normalement en bois de qualité inférieure. (CTCI, Rev.3: 63430-0, 63440-2).
Source: Organisation des Nations Unies pour l'alimentation et l'agriculture (FAO), Rome.

[1] Y compris Hong-Kong, Macao et Taïwan.

Particle board
Panneaux de particules

ISIC-BASED CODE - CODE BASE CITI

3311-22

Unit : Thousand cubic metres

Unité : Milliers de mètres cubes

Country or area	1990	1991	1992	1993	1994	1995	1996	1997	1998	1999	Pays ou zone
Africa	**443**	**421**	**523**	**340**	**724**	**787**	**786**	**796**	**464**	**464**	**Afrique**
Algeria	24	24	24	24	24	24	24	24	24	24	Algérie
Dem. Rep. of Congo	1	1	1	1	1	1	1	1	1	1	Rép. dém. du Congo
Egypt	24	34	41	41	41	41	41	41	6	6	Egypte
Ethiopia,incl.Eritrea	6	6	4	...	...	...	...	...	...	...	Ethiopie,incl.Erythrée
Ethiopia	...	...	...	5	6	7	7	8	7	7	Ethiopie
Ghana	5	3	3	3	3	3	3	3	8	8	Ghana
Kenya	10	10	10	10	10	10	10	10	10	10	Kenya
Morocco	32	4	3	3	3	3	3	3	3	3	Maroc
Mozambique	4	2	1	1	1	1	...	...	...	...	Mozambique
Nigeria	35	35	40	40	40	40	40	40	40	40	Nigéria
South Africa	202	202	296	112	489	551	551	551	224	224	Afrique du Sud
Sudan	2	2	2	2	2	2	2	2	2	2	Soudan
Tunisia	52	52	55	55	55	55	55	55	55	55	Tunisie
Uganda	1	1	1	1	1	1	1	1	1	1	Ouganda
United Rep.Tanzania	6	6	2	3	2	2	2	2	2	2	Rép. Unie de Tanzanie
Zambia	16	16	16	16	16	16	16	16	16	16	Zambie
Zimbabwe	19	19	19	19	26	26	26	35	60	60	Zimbabwe
America, North	**10432**	**9936**	**11276**	**12182**	**19651**	**20257**	**23267**	**24760**	**27229**	**29101**	**Amérique du Nord**
Canada	3112	2650	3557	4173	4493	5309	6754	7961	8621	10076	Canada
Costa Rica	23	23	30	31	31	31	31	31	31	31	Costa Rica
Cuba	62	62	62	62	62	62	62	62	62	62	Cuba
Guatemala	6	6	6	3	4	5	5	5	5	5	Guatemala
Mexico	352	414	414	407	397	...	...	...	...	...	Mexique
United States	6877	6781	7207	7506	14664	14429	15985	16263	18064	18472	Etats-Unis
America, South	**1165**	**1268**	**1391**	**1587**	**1326**	**1475**	**1590**	**1759**	**1660**	**1657**	**Amérique du Sud**
Argentina	142	133	178	376	199	288	383	445	442	442	Argentine
Bolivia	10	10	10	10	3	3	1	1	7	1	Bolivie
Brazil	660	660	660	660	660	660	660	660	660	660	Brésil
Chile	178	166	234	255	299	348	379	425	321	321	Chili
Colombia	93	93	93	93	93	93	70	72	69	78	Colombie
Ecuador	25	81	84	88	60	71	85	94	94	94	Equateur
Paraguay	1	1	1	1	1	1	1	1	1	1	Paraguay
Suriname	1	0	0	0	0	0	0	0	0	0	Suriname
Uruguay	4	3	1	1	1	1	1	1	1	1	Uruguay
Venezuela	52	121	130	103	10	10	10	60	65	59	Venezuela
Asia	**3465**	**3836**	**4955**	**5799**	**6019**	**9367**	**8375**	**8943**	**7527**	**7352**	**Asie**
Afghanistan	1	1	1	1	1	1	1	1	1	1	Afghanistan
Bangladesh	2	2	2	2	2	2	2	2	2	2	Bangladesh
Bhutan	8	8	8	8	8	8	8	8	8	8	Bhoutan
Cambodia	...	...	...	...	...	...	...	...	...	228	Cambodge
China [1]	501	697	1242	1654	1763	4433	3463	3687	2746	2493	Chine [1]
Cyprus	12	10	10	20	20	19	19	18	17	18	Chypre
Georgia	..	...	...	10	10	10	10	10	10	10	Géorgie
India	53	59	60	60	60	60	60	60	60	60	Inde
Indonesia	310	320	350	380	330	296	430	440	274	213	Indonésie
Iran(Islamic Rep. of)	220	234	265	240	310	330	330	377	498	344	Iran(Rép. islamique)
Iraq	3	3	3	3	3	3	3	3	5	5	Iraq
Israel	58	58	58	58	58	58	58	58	58	58	Israël
Japan	987	1097	1163	1265	1299	1310	1332	1249	1084	1084	Japon
Korea, Republic of	165	155	276	435	524	548	659	721	507	672	Corée, République de
Lao People's Dem. Rep.	...	...	4	4	4	...	...	...	...	...	Rép. dém. pop. lao
Lebanon	12	12	12	12	12	12	12	12	12	12	Liban
Malaysia	110	130	150	150	150	500	300	150	250	250	Malaisie
Mongolia	6	1	1	1	1	1	1	1	1	1	Mongolie
Pakistan	54	57	54	55	50	55	60	50	51	54	Pakistan
Philippines	6	6	6	6	6	6	6	6	6	6	Philippines
Singapore	15	30	10	10	10	10	10	10	10	10	Singapour
Sri Lanka	3	3	3	3	3	3	3	3	3	3	Sri Lanka
Syrian Arab Republic	9	9	9	9	9	9	9	9	9	9	Rép. arabe syrienne
Thailand	60	64	81	300	258	216	172	106	156	162	Thaïlande

For general note and footnotes, see end of table.

Voir la fin du tableau pour la remarque générale et les notes.

Particle board (continued)
Panneaux de particules (suite)

ISIC-BASED CODE - CODE BASE CITI

3311-22

Unit : Thousand cubic metres   Unité : Milliers de mètres cubes

Country or area	1990	1991	1992	1993	1994	1995	1996	1997	1998	1999	Pays ou zone
Turkey	636	636	947	883	898	1243	1193	1728	1525	1643	Turquie
Viet Nam	2	2	2	2	2	2	2	2	2	2	Viet Nam
Europe	**19943**	**31081**	**31556**	**31301**	**31217**	**32539**	**32293**	**33917**	**35995**	**36026**	**Europe**
Austria	1529	1689	1606	1595	1666	1700	1700	1771	1800	1800	Autriche
Belarus	..	...	417	349	270	270	270	270	270	270	Bélarus
Belgium-Luxembourg	2222	2323	2350	2350	2400	2876	3087	2565	2632	2586	Belgique-Luxembourg
Bulgaria	231	205	128	124	124	124	124	124	124	124	Bulgarie
Croatia	..	...	59	70	45	40	38	47	48	50	Croatie
Denmark	270	244	230	321	328	328	328	320	322	324	Danemark
Czechoslovakia(former)	950	665	..	..	..	..	..	..	..	..	Tchécoslovaquie(anc.)
Czech Republic	..	..	...	501	536	587	635	737	790	700	République tchèque
Estonia	..	...	61	90	85	155	143	179	177	169	Estonie
Finland	526	385	354	439	477	475	510	475	455	439	Finlande
France	2464	2638	2668	2461	2567	2733	3030	3275	3483	3588	France
Germany	..	7441	7451	7961	8639	8902	8584	9152	9487	8894	Allemagne
Greece	275	264	250	250	250	250	250	257	268	283	Grèce
Hungary	317	295	330	336	396	407	383	429	440	457	Hongrie
Ireland	80	80	84	85	85	90	160	200	320	510	Irlande
Italy	3050	3030	2265	2250	2202	2450	2205	2750	2300	2300	Italie
Latvia	..	...	118	101	148	130	143	149	152	129	Lettonie
Lithuania	..	...	149	90	75	70	110	170	159	100	Lituanie
Netherlands	40	40	34	32	36	43	35	44	37	39	Pays-Bas
Norway	458	400	398	313	372	390	384	397	419	420	Norvège
Poland	718	941	1008	1129	1336	1466	1747	2072	2474	2637	Pologne
Portugal	805	787	630	575	757	650	695	695	748	719	Portugal
Republic of Moldova	..	...	...	47	14	10	10	10	10	10	Rép. de Moldova
Romania	581	470	430	430	241	228	226	229	173	173	Roumanie
Russian Federation	..	...	4522	3941	2626	2206	1472	1490	1568	1969	Fédération de Russie
Slovakia	..	..	...	200	233	243	216	221	220	195	Slovaquie
Slovenia	..	...	205	216	222	249	246	351	384	384	Slovénie
Spain	1790	1795	1680	1660	1730	1863	1970	1970	2843	2897	Espagne
Sweden	843	762	581	597	609	632	577	612	650	618	Suède
Switzerland	722	699	762	742	656	564	530	501	524	525	Suisse
Ukraine	..	...	...	..	...	...	240	199	199	199	Ukraine
United Kingdom	1517	1569	1737	1757	1803	2118	2164	2175	2287	2287	Royaume-Uni
Yugoslavia	..	...	80	80	80	80	80	80	80	80	Yougoslavie
T.F.Yug.Rep. Macedonia	..	...	...	...	...	1	1	1	152	152	L'ex-RY Macédoine
Yugoslavia, SFR	555	..	..	..	..	..	..	..	..	..	Yougoslavie, RSF
USSR (former)	6397	..	..	..	..	..	..	..	..	..	URSS (anc.)
Oceania	**895**	**794**	**804**	**888**	**1001**	**1031**	**992**	**1005**	**1047**	**1078**	**Océanie**
Australia	723	636	642	711	828	864	826	790	882	902	Australie
New Zealand	172	158	162	177	173	167	166	215	165	176	Nouvelle-Zélande
Total	**42739**	**47336**	**50506**	**52098**	**59937**	**65456**	**67303**	**71179**	**73922**	**75677**	**Total**

General Note.

Sheet material manufactured from small pieces of wood or other ligno-cellulosic materials (for example, chips, flakes, splinters, strands, shreds, shives etc.) agglomerated by use of an organic binder together with one or more of the following agents - heat, pressure, humidity, a catalyst etc. Wood wool or other particle boards agglomerated by means of an inorganic binder such as cement or plaster are excluded. (SITC, Rev.3: 63422-0, 63423-0).
Source: Food and Agriculture Organization of the United Nations (FAO), Rome.

Remarque générale.

Matériaux en feuilles, fabriqués à partir de petits fragments de bois ou d'autres substances ligno-cellulosiques (copeaux, flocons, éclats, fils, brins etc.) agglomérés sous l'action d'un liant organique, ainsi que d'un ou plusieurs des agents suivants: chaleur, pression, humidité, catalyseur, etc. Cette rubrique ne comprend pas les panneaux faits de fibres de bois ou autres particules agglomérées au moyen de liants inorganiques tels que le ciment ou le plâtre. (CTCI, Rev.3: 63422-0, 63423-0).
Source: Organisation des Nations Unies pour l'alimentation et l'agriculture (FAO), Rome.

[1] Including Hong-Kong, Macao and Taiwan.

[1] Y compris Hong-Kong, Macao et Taïwan.

Mattresses
Matelas

ISIC-BASED CODE - CODE BASE CITI

3320-01

Unit : Thousand units   Unité : En milliers

Country or area	1990	1991	1992	1993	1994	1995	1996	1997	1998	1999	Pays ou zone
Africa	**869**	**781**	**758**	**724**	**847**	**738**	**890**	**853**	**797**	**739**	**Afrique**
Algeria	129	82	53	53	72	82	90	76	144	62	Algérie
South Africa	740	699	705	671	775	656	800	777	653	677	Afrique du Sud
America, North	**1849**	**1964**	**2081**	**2138**	**2411**	**2009**	**2254**	**2529**	**2732**	**2788**	**Amérique du Nord**
Mexico	...	...	...	1990	2289	1873	2118	2393	2596	2652	Mexique
Panama	133	...	142	148	122	...	...	...	...	...	Panama
America, South	**844**	**1090**	**1184**	**1260**	**1457**	**1587**	**1879**	**1912**	**1955**	**2164**	**Amérique du Sud**
Bolivia	6	8	7	5	6	*13	...	...	...	...	Bolivie
Chile	508	649	805	886	948	1063	1081	1131	1100	1082	Chili
Colombia	256	...	290	280	363	377	...	452	486	...	Colombie
Ecuador	...	...	6	14	65	59	356	245	284	...	Equateur
Paraguay	74	75	76	...	...	...	...	...	...	...	Paraguay
Asia	**193**	**432**	**512**	**616**	**643**	**402**	**392**	**291**	**198**	**310**	**Asie**
Cyprus	*53	*56	59	*50	*45	37	37	36	38	39	Chypre
Indonesia	140	...	402	520	524	...	...	228	117	...	Indonésie
Turkmenistan	..	...	...	46	74	43	33	27	43	...	Turkménistan
Europe	**17434**	**19709**	**21581**	**21385**	**21321**	**21664**	**25185**	**26273**	**30268**	**34307**	**Europe**
Austria	452	504	970	665	485	359	509	478	459	474	Autriche
Belgium	...	...	...	...	2934	2967	3126	4019	4890	4555	Belgique
Bulgaria	91	96	103	94	87	64	59	24	25	9	Bulgarie
Croatia	..	76	64	71	117	104	111	127	123	...	Croatie
Denmark[1]	569	530	538	594	640	607	#3353	4126	6264	9076	Danemark[1]
Finland	331	335	507	555	558	554	544	362	420	444	Finlande
Germany	..	6039	6401	6315	6626	6946	7788	7373	6977	...	Allemagne
Germany(Fed.Rep.)	5324	..	..	..	..	..	..	..	..	..	Allemagne(Rép.féd.)
Greece	[2]282	[2]283	[2]333	240	216	164	201	198	214	...	Grèce
Hungary	12	7	5	2	30	8	49	119	71	77	Hongrie
Latvia	..	...	...	...	...	...	...	...	...	1	Lettonie
Lithuania	..	...	...	...	...	32	106	127	178	234	Lituanie
Netherlands[1][3]	...	...	...	699	751	687	641	648	660	639	Pays-Bas[1][3]
Portugal	671	723	617	561	458	488	609	616	615	631	Portugal
Slovakia	..	...	...	...	...	...	179	260	44	31	Slovaquie
Slovenia	..	169	143	143	123	150	32	29	30	17	Slovénie
Spain	...	...	...	2537	2723	2573	2674	2702	3167	3358	Espagne
Sweden	...	...	...	...	...	...	...	630	1205	1294	Suède
Ukraine	..	819	577	551	329	173	94	80	51	59	Ukraine
United Kingdom	[4]3232	[4]3226	...	...	...	4601	...	4345	4866	...	Royaume-Uni
Yugoslavia	..	84	5	1	3	1	...	...	...	...	Yougoslavie
T.F.Yug.Rep. Macedonia		26	22	15	15	13	12	9	8	16	L'ex-RY Macédoine
Oceania	**1083**	**993**	**1069**	**1093**	**1060**	**1060**	**1060**	**1060**	**1060**	**1060**	**Océanie**
Australia[5][6]	1083	993	1069	1093	...	...	...	...	...	...	Australie[5][6]
Total	**22272**	**24968**	**27185**	**27216**	**27739**	**27459**	**31659**	**32918**	**37010**	**41368**	**Total**

General Note.
Mattresses fitted with inner springs or filled with any material (cotton,wool, horsehair, down etc.) or of expended foam or sponge rubber or artificial materials (whether or not covered with woven fabrics, plastic materials etc.). Box-mattresses are excluded. (SITC, Rev.3: 82123-0, 82125-0).

Remarque générale.
Matelas qui sont, soit pourvus de ressorts ou rembourrés ou garnis intérieurement de toutes matières (coton, laine, crin, duvet etc.), soit en caoutchouc ou en matières artificielles à l'état spongieux ou cellulaire, recouverts ou non de tissu, de matière plastique etc. Cette rubrique ne comprend pas les sommiers. (CTCI, Rev. 3: 82123-0, 82125-0).

[1] Sales.
[2] Mattresses filled with springs only.
[3] Beginning 1986, production by establishments employing 20 or more persons.
[4] Inner spring only.
[5] Twelve months ending 30 June of year stated.
[6] Excluding mattresses of rubber and of a thickness of less than 7.5 cm.

[1] Ventes.
[2] Matelas garnis de ressorts seulement.
[3] A partir de 1986, production des éstablissements occupant 20 prsonnes ou plus.
[4] Ressorts intérieurs seulement.
[5] Période de douze mois finissant le 30 juin de l'année indiquée.
[6] Non compris les matelas de caoutchouc et d'une épaisseur inférieure à 7.5 cm.

Wood pulp, mechanical
Pâte de bois mécanique

ISIC-BASED CODE - CODE BASE CITI

3411-01

Unit : Thousand metric tons · Unité : Milliers de tonnes métriques

Country or area	1990	1991	1992	1993	1994	1995	1996	1997	1998	1999	Pays ou zone
Africa	**403**	**401**	**319**	**321**	**289**	**401**	**401**	**400**	**300**	**300**	**Afrique**
Madagascar	3	1	1	1	1	1	1	0	0	0	Madagascar
South Africa	370	370	288	290	258	370	370	370	270	270	Afrique du Sud
United Rep.Tanzania	10	10	10	10	10	10	10	10	10	10	Rép. Unie de Tanzanie
Zimbabwe	20	20	20	20	20	20	20	20	20	20	Zimbabwe
America, North	**16443**	**16555**	**16156**	**16195**	**16906**	**17169**	**16388**	**16773**	**15792**	**16372**	**Amérique du Nord**
Canada	10537	10630	10212	10589	11000	11550	10979	11355	10481	11213	Canada
Costa Rica	4	3	3	3	3	3	3	3	3	3	Costa Rica
Honduras	...	...	...	...	...	...	...	...	4	4	Honduras
Mexico	126	108	39	13	15	20	33	10	14	42	Mexique
United States	5772	5810	5898	5586	5884	5593	5369	5401	5291	5110	Etats-Unis
America, South	**594**	**631**	**627**	**742**	**718**	**753**	**753**	**967**	**857**	**978**	**Amérique du Sud**
Argentina	6	3	1	59	63	68	12	273	116	116	Argentine
Brazil	418	425	421	475	448	466	492	443	466	445	Brésil
Chile	160	179	181	183	184	184	214	209	230	369	Chili
Ecuador	...	...	...	...	1	2	2	2	2	2	Equateur
Uruguay	1	1	2	2	2	2	2	2	2	2	Uruguay
Venezuela	8	21	21	21	20	31	31	...	...	...	Venezuela
Asia	**3122**	**3085**	**2904**	**2706**	**2808**	**3014**	**2932**	**2726**	**2629**	**2513**	**Asie**
Bangladesh	48	45	45	45	45	38	30	24	8	8	Bangladesh
China[1]	417	410	435	500	575	640	540	440	450	450	Chine[1]
India	204	198	163	210	222	223	223	223	223	223	Inde
Indonesia	33	36	49	60	60	...	...	...	...	...	Indonésie
Japan	2048	2072	1861	1644	1636	1673	1705	1674	1598	1473	Japon
Korea,Dem.Ppl's.Rep.	13	13	13	13	13	13	13	13	13	13	Corée,Rép.pop.dém.de
Korea, Republic of	159	167	161	142	170	181	229	197	169	174	Corée, République de
Philippines	50	39	53	30	20	28	28	28	28	28	Philippines
Turkey	148	94	112	47	52	132	70	25	31	27	Turquie
Viet Nam	2	11	12	15	15	15	15	15	15	15	Viet Nam
Europe	**11097**	**13276**	**13044**	**12991**	**13295**	**14143**	**12709**	**13594**	**14450**	**14418**	**Europe**
Albania	2	2	2	2	2	2	2	2	2	2	Albanie
Austria	352	371	376	375	399	390	344	378	376	369	Autriche
Belgium-Luxembourg	260	237	238	203	210	210	173	173	207	207	Belgique-Luxembourg
Bulgaria	12	8	2	2	2	2	2	2	2	2	Bulgarie
Croatia	..	...	36	35	34	37	36	34	37	39	Croatie
Denmark	...	...	68	67	75	75	75	75	...	...	Danemark
Czechoslovakia(former)	148	90	..	..	..	..	..	..	..	..	Tchécoslovaquie(anc.)
Czech Republic	..	..	...	58	68	78	75	59	79	62	République tchèque
Estonia	..	..	7	7	7	7	7	...	...	...	Estonie
Finland	3293	3156	3170	3401	3631	3797	3489	3940	4637	4602	Finlande
France	667	810	922	823	886	934	757	845	762	760	France
Germany	..	1531	1461	1331	1236	1266	1133	1220	1191	1192	Allemagne
Greece	50	50	50	25	25	25	25	...	...	...	Grèce
Hungary	6	3	...	...	...	...	...	...	...	...	Hongrie
Italy	449	396	342	339	381	408	365	385	384	366	Italie
Latvia	..	..	6	4	1	2	1	...	...	...	Lettonie
Lithuania	..	...	20	4	1	8	3	1	1	0	Lituanie
Netherlands	190	175	135	119	119	148	125	138	129	117	Pays-Bas
Norway	1334	1293	1217	1418	1516	1627	1502	1534	1664	1644	Norvège
Poland	108	108	84	77	98	112	71	99	78	80	Pologne
Romania	100	70	70	70	43	38	23	28	30	30	Roumanie
Russian Federation	..	...	1396	1165	919	1245	976	899	981	1160	Fédération de Russie
Slovakia	..	...	...	28	30	7	6	5	5	...	Slovaquie
Slovenia	..	...	31	28	23	32	30	28	30	30	Slovénie
Spain	161	146	108	81	83	121	106	103	112	100	Espagne
Sweden	2953	2709	2525	2722	2858	2861	2753	2959	3026	3029	Suède
Switzerland	219	201	165	133	116	134	105	106	94	102	Suisse
Ukraine	..	...	...	...	...	...	18	10	10	10	Ukraine
United Kingdom	595	595	495	444	502	548	490	537	509	411	Royaume-Uni
Yugoslavia	..	...	...	...	...	...	...	13	13	13	Yougoslavie

For general note and footnotes, see end of table. · Voir la fin du tableau pour la remarque générale et les notes.

Wood pulp, mechanical (continued)
Pâte de bois mécanique (suite)

ISIC-BASED CODE - CODE BASE CITI

3411-01

Unit : Thousand metric tons   Unité : Milliers de tonnes métriques

Country or area	1990	1991	1992	1993	1994	1995	1996	1997	1998	1999	Pays ou zone
Yugoslavia, SFR	129	..	..	..	..	..	..	..	..	..	Yougoslavie, RSF
USSR (former)	2680	..	..	..	..	..	..	..	..	..	URSS (anc.)
Oceania	1006	1038	1141	1109	1027	1130	1079	1091	1106	1117	Océanie
Australia	431	422	459	436	363	430	364	364	345	350	Australie
New Zealand	575	616	682	673	664	700	715	727	761	767	Nouvelle-Zélande
Total	35346	34986	34192	34064	35042	36610	34262	35550	35135	35699	Total

General Note.

Fibrous material prepared from wood by mechanical disintegration. It includes exploded and defibrated pulp and mechanical screenings. In terms of air-dry weight (10 per cent moisture content). (SITC, Rev.3: 25120-0).

Source: Food and Agriculture Organization of the United Nations (FAO), Rome.

Remarque générale.

Matériaux fibreux préparés en soumettant le bois à la désintégration mécanique. Cette rubrique comprend le bois éclaté et défibré ainsi que les refus du traitement mécanique. Poids après séchage à l'air (pâte à 10 p. 100 d'humidité). (CTCI, Rev.3: 25120-0).

Source: Organisation des Nations Unies pour l'alimentation et l'agriculture (FAO), Rome.

[1] Including Hong-Kong, Macao and Taiwan.

[1] Y compris Hong-Kong, Macao et Taïwan.

Pulp of fibres other than wood
Pâtes de fibres autres que le bois

ISIC-BASED CODE - CODE BASE CITI

3411-04

Unit : Thousand metric tons   Unité : Milliers de tonnes métriques

Country or area	1990	1991	1992	1993	1994	1995	1996	1997	1998	1999	Pays ou zone
Africa	**235**	**195**	**196**	**196**	**209**	**209**	**209**	**229**	**216**	**217**	**Afrique**
Algeria	21	21	21	21	21	21	21	21	21	21	Algérie
Egypt	80	47	47	47	60	60	60	60	60	60	Egypte
Ethiopia	...	...	...	...	...	...	...	10	9	9	Ethiopie
Madagascar	2	2	2	2	2	2	2	2	2	2	Madagascar
Morocco	5	5	5	5	5	5	5	5	5	5	Maroc
South Africa	99	99	99	99	99	99	99	115	...	...	Afrique du Sud
Tunisia	18	12	12	12	12	12	12	16	14	14	Tunisie
America, North	**707**	**577**	**527**	**391**	**454**	**457**	**505**	**473**	**529**	**534**	**Amérique du Nord**
Canada	40	40	40	40	40	40	40	40	40	40	Canada
Costa Rica	7	7	7	7	7	7	7	7	7	7	Costa Rica
Cuba	52	52	52	52	52	52	52	52	52	52	Cuba
Honduras	...	...	...	...	...	...	...	1	1	1	Honduras
Mexico	254	237	240	121	117	117	154	134	182	189	Mexique
United States	353	240	187	170	237	240	251	239	247	245	Etats-Unis
America, South	**508**	**488**	**552**	**415**	**391**	**498**	**456**	**457**	**408**	**417**	**Amérique du Sud**
Argentina	117	78	112	49	48	166	128	124	108	108	Argentine
Brazil	146	125	127	119	106	75	75	77	80	83	Brésil
Colombia	97	101	129	131	147	142	138	141	137	144	Colombie
Ecuador	1	...	...	...	...	...	...	...	...	...	Equateur
Peru	59	116	116	23	23	48	48	48	17	17	Pérou
Venezuela	88	67	67	92	66	66	66	66	...	...	Venezuela
Asia	**13055**	**14000**	**15283**	**17174**	**19190**	**23903**	**14191**	**17657**	**17787**	**18074**	**Asie**
Bangladesh	32	33	33	33	33	38	38	31	18	18	Bangladesh
China[1]	11489	12232	13369	15307	17551	22206	12566	15986	15986	16432	Chine[1]
India	921	1009	1099	1096	900	920	920	930	1020	1020	Inde
Indonesia	84	84	116	120	100	89	79	79	79	79	Indonésie
Iran(Islamic Rep. of)	41	62	62	62	45	45	45	45	45	45	Iran(Rép. islamique)
Iraq	9	9	9	9	9	9	9	9	11	11	Iraq
Japan	17	7	4	11	4	4	4	19	19	19	Japon
Jordan	8	8	8	8	8	8	8	8	8	8	Jordanie
Korea,Dem.Ppl's.Rep.	50	50	50	50	50	50	50	50	50	50	Corée,Rép.pop.dém.de
Malaysia	1	1	1	1	1	1	1	1	1	1	Malaisie
Myanmar	2	2	2	1	9	9	9	19	17	17	Myanmar
Nepal	15	15	15	15	15	15	15	15	15	15	Népal
Pakistan	183	159	145	145	150	160	165	170	80	87	Pakistan
Philippines	22	22	27	27	27	27	27	27	27	27	Philippines
Sri Lanka	4	3	3	2	2	6	7	7	7	7	Sri Lanka
Thailand	44	148	180	178	177	134	94	108	228	80	Thaïlande
Turkey	87	87	89	35	35	108	80	79	102	84	Turquie
Viet Nam	47	70	72	74	74	74	74	74	74	74	Viet Nam
Europe	**373**	**392**	**403**	**376**	**270**	**320**	**323**	**328**	**308**	**330**	**Europe**
Austria	...	1	1	1	1	1	1	1	...	...	Autriche
Bulgaria	20	10	10	10	10	10	10	10	10	10	Bulgarie
Denmark	34	34	34	34	34	34	34	34	...	...	Danemark
Czechoslovakia(former)	2	2	..	..	..	..	..	..	..	..	Tchécoslovaquie(anc.)
Czech Republic	..	..	...	2	2	2	4	2	...	1	République tchèque
France	23	23	23	1	1	1	2	2	2	3	France
Germany	..	45	45	45	...	...	...	...	...	...	Allemagne
Greece	2	2	2	2	2	2	2	...	...	...	Grèce
Hungary	4	5	15	20	20	20	16	12	17	17	Hongrie
Italy	96	97	86	80	80	131	137	125	123	133	Italie
Latvia	..	...	6	6	6	6	..	...	...	...	Lettonie
Netherlands	3	3	3	3	3	3	3	...	...	...	Pays-Bas
Poland	1	1	1	1	1	1	...	...	...	...	Pologne
Portugal	13	13	13	13	13	13	13	...	...	...	Portugal
Romania	25	25	25	25	4	1	1	1	1	1	Roumanie
Slovakia	..	...	...	...	...	...	17	16	...	...	Slovaquie
Spain	122	108	99	97	11	11	11	35	12	24	Espagne
United Kingdom	21	14	...	...	...	...	...	...	...	...	Royaume-Uni

For general note and footnotes, see end of table.   Voir la fin du tableau pour la remarque générale et les notes.

Pulp of fibres other than wood (continued)
Pâtes de fibres autres que le bois (suite)

ISIC-BASED CODE - CODE BASE CITI
3411-04

Unit : Thousand metric tons   Unité : Milliers de tonnes métriques

Country or area	1990	1991	1992	1993	1994	1995	1996	1997	1998	1999	Pays ou zone
Yugoslavia	..	..	...	...	...	...	...	1	1	1	Yougoslavie
T.F.Yug.Rep. Macedonia	..	...	...	...	...	4	1	1	1	...	L'ex-RY Macédoine
Yugoslavia, SFR	6	..	..	..	..	..	..	..	..	..	Yougoslavie, RSF
USSR (former)	355	..	..	..	..	..	..	..	..	..	URSS (anc.)
Oceania	**12**	**12**	**9**	**6**	**6**	**7**	**7**	**3**	**2**	**1**	**Océanie**
Australia	12	12	9	6	6	7	7	...	...	...	Australie
Total	**15244**	**15664**	**16969**	**18557**	**20518**	**25393**	**15689**	**19146**	**19251**	**19573**	**Total**

General Note.

Pulp other than wood pulp, derived from fibrous materials such as straw, bagasse, cotton, flax, bamboo, esparto and other grasses, used for the manufacture of paper, paperboard and fibreboard. In terms of air-dry weight (10 per cent moisture content). (SITC, Rev.3: 25192-0).
Source: Food and Agriculture Organization of the United Nations (FAO), Rome.

[1] Including Hong-Kong, Macao and Taiwan.

Remarque générale.

Pâtes autres que la pâte de bois, dérivées de matières fibreuses telles que paille, bagasse, coton, lin, bambou, alfa, spart et autres herbes servant à la fabrication de papiers, de cartons et de panneaux de fibres. Poids après séchage à l'air (pâte à 10 p. 100 d'humidité). (CTCI, Rev.3: 25192-0).
Source: Organisation des Nations Unies pour l'alimentation et l'agriculture (FAO), Rome.

[1] Y compris Hong-Kong, Macao et Taïwan.

Wood pulp, dissolving grades
Pâte de bois chimiques, solubles

ISIC-BASED CODE - CODE BASE CITI

3411-07

Unit : Thousand metric tons   Unité : Milliers de tonnes métriques

Country or area	1990	1991	1992	1993	1994	1995	1996	1997	1998	1999	Pays ou zone
Africa	**470**	**470**	**568**	**521**	**521**	**490**	**490**	**590**	**556**	**546**	**Afrique**
Morocco	...	...	...	70	70	70	70	70	70	70	Maroc
South Africa	400	400	498	451	451	420	420	520	486	476	Afrique du Sud
America, North	**1399**	**1467**	**1501**	**1395**	**1325**	**1348**	**1246**	**1155**	**1136**	**1122**	**Amérique du Nord**
Canada	221	219	241	...	27	27	27	27	...	...	Canada
Honduras	...	...	...	...	...	...	...	...	1	1	Honduras
Mexico	4	4	4	4	4	123	123	123	123	123	Mexique
United States	1173	1243	1255	1277	1293	1197	1095	1004	1004	998	Etats-Unis
America, South	**92**	**73**	**75**	**61**	**72**	**72**	**145**	**159**	**137**	**129**	**Amérique du Sud**
Brazil	89	70	70	59	70	69	142	156	134	126	Brésil
Chile	...	...	5	2	2	...	...	...	...	...	Chili
Asia	**586**	**585**	**608**	**682**	**669**	**676**	**445**	**410**	**370**	**364**	**Asie**
China [1]	221	241	270	260	260	265	42	15	15	15	Chine [1]
India	160	160	160	255	255	255	255	255	255	255	Inde
Japan	187	172	166	153	140	142	134	126	86	80	Japon
Sri Lanka	9	3	3	...	...	...	...	...	...	...	Sri Lanka
Turkey	9	9	9	9	9	9	9	...	...	...	Turquie
Europe	**1054**	**1219**	**1270**	**1230**	**982**	**1019**	**886**	**937**	**867**	**869**	**Europe**
Austria	142	142	148	147	154	154	155	154	158	167	Autriche
Czechoslovakia(former)	46	34	..	..	..	..	..	..	..	..	Tchécoslovaquie(anc.)
Czech Republic	..	..	...	15	6	6	...	...	...	...	République tchèque
Finland	121	92	92	92	92	92	92	92	92	92	Finlande
France	4	4	4	4	4	4	4	...	...	...	France
Germany	..	...	23	19	23	34	36	25	23	9	Allemagne
Italy	30	67	46	34	24	...	...	...	...	...	Italie
Norway	158	148	143	143	72	72	72	72	72	72	Norvège
Poland	42	43	47	44	45	46	44	43	24	25	Pologne
Romania	74	74	74	74	3	4	3	1	...	...	Roumanie
Russian Federation	..	...	320	293	191	210	77	93	82	90	Fédération de Russie
Slovakia	..	..	...	...	13	15	17	67	20	20	Slovaquie
Spain	63	46	25	25	36	36	36	...	48	49	Espagne
Sweden	296	319	319	319	319	319	319	319	...	...	Suède
Yugoslavia, SFR	78	..	..	..	..	..	..	..	..	..	Yougoslavie, RSF
USSR (former)	668	..	..	..	..	..	..	..	..	..	URSS (anc.)
Oceania	**5**	**5**	**5**	**5**	**5**	**5**	**5**	**5**	**5**	**5**	**Océanie**
New Zealand	...	...	5	5	5	5	5	5	...	...	Nouvelle-Zélande
Total	**4274**	**3819**	**4027**	**3894**	**3574**	**3610**	**3217**	**3256**	**3071**	**3034**	**Total**

General Note.
Bleached hardwood or softwood chemical pulp (sulphite or sulphate), of high alpha-cellulose content readily adaptable for uses other than paper-making (rayon, cellophane, lacquers etc.). In terms of air-dry weight (10 per cent moisture content). (SITC, Rev.3: 25130-0).
Source: Food and Agriculture Organization of the United Nations (FAO), Rome.

Remarque générale.
Pâtes chimiques blanchies de bois feuillus ou résineux (au bisulfite ou au sulfate), à haute teneur en cellulose alfa, qui peuvent être facilement adaptées à des emplois autres que la fabrication du papier (rayonne, cellophane, laques etc.). Poids après séchage à l'air (pâte à 10 p. 100 d'humidité). (CTCI, Rev.3: 25130-0).
Source: Organisation des Nations Unies pour l'alimentation et l'agriculture (FAO), Rome.

[1] Including Hong-Kong, Macao and Taiwan.

[1] Y compris Hong-Kong, Macao et Taïwan.

Wood pulp, sulphate and soda
Pâte de bois chimiques, au sulfate

ISIC-BASED CODE - CODE BASE CITI

3411-10

Unit : Thousand metric tons

Unité : Milliers de tonnes métriques

Country or area	1990	1991	1992	1993	1994	1995	1996	1997	1998	1999	Pays ou zone
Africa	**1204**	**1238**	**1337**	**1354**	**994**	**1232**	**1252**	**1508**	**1596**	**1538**	**Afrique**
Angola	15	15	15	15	15	15	15	15	15	15	Angola
Morocco	100	91	103	92	103	99	99	110	113	107	Maroc
Nigeria	4	4	4	4	4	4	4	9	14	14	Nigéria
South Africa	955	950	1032	1043	672	914	914	1200	1304	1211	Afrique du Sud
Swaziland	130	178	183	200	200	200	220	174	150	191	Swaziland
America, North	**55519**	**57948**	**58251**	**57611**	**65668**	**61971**	**60575**	**61480**	**60908**	**60797**	**Amérique du Nord**
Canada	10097	10830	11013	11033	12457	12592	12237	12393	12181	13076	Canada
Honduras	...	...	...	...	...	...	...	...	1	1	Honduras
Mexico	393	359	280	209	160	279	324	303	410	307	Mexique
United States	45028	46758	46957	46368	53050	49099	48013	48783	48316	47413	Etats-Unis
America, South	**5032**	**5617**	**6721**	**7211**	**7640**	**7840**	**8182**	**8294**	**8731**	**9315**	**Amérique du Sud**
Argentina	393	362	379	515	477	437	472	449	423	423	Argentine
Brazil	3735	4158	4677	4853	5222	5311	5610	5777	6127	6620	Brésil
Chile	710	913	1479	1662	1754	1910	1918	1868	1980	2064	Chili
Colombia	131	131	134	129	130	131	131	139	142	145	Colombie
Peru	43	25	25	25	...	...	...	...	...	...	Pérou
Uruguay	20	28	27	27	27	21	21	31	29	33	Uruguay
Asia	**11998**	**12538**	**12669**	**12865**	**13650**	**14648**	**14814**	**16488**	**15176**	**15858**	**Asie**
Bangladesh	54	51	51	51	51	46	46	42	11	11	Bangladesh
China[1]	1290	1317	1393	1548	1725	1725	1195	1755	1775	2140	Chine[1]
India	625	628	664	682	719	727	727	970	1020	1080	Inde
Indonesia	593	634	873	1063	1500	1853	2266	2684	1816	1646	Indonésie
Iran(Islamic Rep. of)	74	80	80	80	200	200	200	...	...	...	Iran(Rép. islamique)
Japan	8731	9118	8850	8534	8576	9089	9155	9487	9066	9315	Japon
Korea, Republic of	159	160	162	305	361	373	396	394	249	413	Corée, République de
Malaysia	...	...	...	...	...	...	102	91	112	112	Malaisie
Philippines	103	113	98	90	79	94	94	94	94	94	Philippines
Sri Lanka	2	3	1	2	2	2	2	2	2	2	Sri Lanka
Thailand	...	...	...	...	64	160	385	439	489	489	Thaïlande
Turkey	153	175	196	160	225	230	202	223	209	197	Turquie
Viet Nam	...	...	40	44	44	44	44	44	44	44	Viet Nam
Europe	**17606**	**20053**	**20820**	**20459**	**20842**	**21835**	**20864**	**22551**	**23228**	**24588**	**Europe**
Albania	...	...	...	14	14	14	14	14	14	14	Albanie
Austria	550	568	565	567	638	656	639	663	691	713	Autriche
Belgium-Luxembourg	187	197	196	92	144	144	209	209	209	209	Belgique-Luxembourg
Bulgaria	110	110	79	79	79	79	79	79	79	79	Bulgarie
Czechoslovakia(former)	682	666	...	..	..	..	..	..	..	..	Tchécoslovaquie(anc.)
Czech Republic	..	..	...	260	208	213	194	239	280	275	République tchèque
Estonia	..	...	14	14	14	6	21	36	44	50	Estonie
Finland	4870	4763	4859	5465	5844	5782	5736	6620	6718	6977	Finlande
France	1339	1276	1428	1342	1520	1511	1417	1578	1517	1590	France
Germany	..	...	...	...	...	...	...	...	...	5	Allemagne
Norway	433	423	409	382	439	517	481	500	493	490	Norvège
Poland	429	416	462	493	534	595	610	707	722	700	Pologne
Portugal	1331	1487	1485	1421	1448	1532	1511	1628	1624	1670	Portugal
Romania	225	133	134	134	87	168	158	138	121	121	Roumanie
Russian Federation	..	...	3334	2558	2035	2617	2009	2066	2328	3062	Fédération de Russie
Slovakia	..	..	...	179	215	234	224	39	243	269	Slovaquie
Spain	1258	1332	1323	1155	1233	1367	1295	1432	1495	1568	Espagne
Sweden	5954	6035	6064	6252	6338	6348	6209	6552	6599	6751	Suède
Ukraine	..	...	...	...	...	...	32	25	25	25	Ukraine
Yugoslavia	..	...	...	...	...	...	...	21	21	21	Yougoslavie
Yugoslavia, SFR	224	..	..	..	..	..	..	..	..	..	Yougoslavie, RSF
USSR (former)	4509	..	..	..	..	..	..	..	..	..	URSS (anc.)
Oceania	**942**	**1010**	**974**	**1072**	**1047**	**1057**	**971**	**1009**	**985**	**962**	**Océanie**
Australia	331	334	403	402	382	382	365	362	361	306	Australie
New Zealand	611	676	571	670	665	675	606	647	624	656	Nouvelle-Zélande

For general note and footnotes, see end of table.

Voir la fin du tableau pour la remarque générale et les notes.

Wood pulp, sulphate and soda (continued)
Pâte de bois chimiques, au sulfate (suite)

ISIC-BASED CODE - CODE BASE CITI

3411-10

Unit : Thousand metric tons   Unité : Milliers de tonnes métriques

Country or area	1990	1991	1992	1993	1994	1995	1996	1997	1998	1999	Pays ou zone
Total	96809	98404	100772	100572	109841	108582	106657	111329	110623	113058	**Total**

General Note.

Wood pulp prepared by an alkaline process in which the liquor used for digestion contains a mixture of sodium hydroxide and sodium sulphide (sulphate method), and sodium hydroxide alone (soda method). Includes chemical sulphate screenings. In terms of air-dry weight (10 per cent moisture content). (SITC, Rev.3: 25140-0, 25150-0).
Source: Food and Agriculture Organization of the United Nations (FAO), Rome.

Remarque générale.

Pâtes de bois préparées par un procédé alcalin dans lequel la liqueur utilisée pour la délignification contient soit un mélange de soude caustique et de sulfure de sodium (procédé au sulfate) soit uniquement de la soude (procédé à la soude). Cette rubrique comprend les produits obtenus par tamisage après traitement chimique. Poids après séchage à l'air (pâte à 10 p. 100 d'humidité). (CTCI, REv.3: 25140-0, 25150-0).
Source: Organisation des Nations Unies pour l'alimentation et l'agriculture (FAO), Rome.

[1] Including Hong-Kong, Macao and Taiwan.

[1] Y compris Hong-Kong, Macao et Taïwan.

Wood pulp, sulphite
Pâte de bois chimiques, au bisulfite

ISIC-BASED CODE - CODE BASE CITI

3411-13

Unit : Thousand metric tons

Unité : Milliers de tonnes métriques

Country or area	1990	1991	1992	1993	1994	1995	1996	1997	1998	1999	Pays ou zone
Africa	**221**	**223**	**240**	**255**	**228**	**231**	**231**	**226**	**240**	**227**	**Afrique**
Kenya	56	58	75	90	63	66	66	66	66	66	Kenya
South Africa	...	...	...	...	...	...	...	160	174	161	Afrique du Sud
America, North	**2932**	**2504**	**2304**	**2278**	**2285**	**2273**	**2105**	**2192**	**1766**	**1740**	**Amérique du Nord**
Canada	1515	1132	853	815	822	904	766	682	459	532	Canada
Honduras	...	...	...	...	...	...	...	...	1	1	Honduras
United States	1416	1371	1450	1462	1462	1368	1338	1509	1306	1207	Etats-Unis
America, South	**215**	**223**	**225**	**231**	**221**	**193**	**243**	**216**	**202**	**187**	**Amérique du Sud**
Argentina	26	29	31	42	38	31	33	...	18	18	Argentine
Brazil	20	22	22	17	18	20	17	18	20	23	Brésil
Chile	22	19	20	20	15	19	14	...	...	...	Chili
Peru	30	34	34	34	...	...	...	...	...	...	Pérou
Uruguay	3	5	5	5	5	5	5	...	...	...	Uruguay
Venezuela	...	...	...	...	...	85	141	116	113	96	Venezuela
Asia	**172**	**167**	**165**	**170**	**176**	**171**	**178**	**184**	**274**	**280**	**Asie**
China[1]	75	72	76	87	100	...	...	...	...	...	Chine[1]
Japan	31	26	24	16	9	3	3	3	86	86	Japon
Korea,Dem.Ppl's.Rep.	43	43	43	43	43	43	43	43	43	43	Corée,Rép.pop.dém.de
Turkey	23	26	22	...	...	...	...	...	...	...	Turquie
Europe	**2812**	**4080**	**4413**	**3962**	**3810**	**4017**	**3700**	**3894**	**3739**	**3868**	**Europe**
Austria	415	401	399	364	404	419	412	434	425	439	Autriche
Belarus	..	...	37	26	31	31	31	31	31	31	Bélarus
Belgium-Luxembourg	31	31	31	15	24	24	...	...	16	16	Belgique-Luxembourg
Czechoslovakia(former)	394	303		..	..	..	..	..	..	..	Tchécoslovaquie(anc.)
Czech Republic	..	..	...	356	234	227	218	214	210	229	République tchèque
Estonia		...	21	21	21	...	...	...	...	...	Estonie
Finland	168	61	54	...	...	...	...	...	...	...	Finlande
France	272	225	258	261	262	263	241	290	276	285	France
Germany	..	829	720	682	698	684	683	738	759	701	Allemagne
Hungary	6	...	...	...	...	...	...	...	...	...	Hongrie
Italy	54	47	39	29	45	40	38	78	79	98	Italie
Latvia	..	...	31	6	1	2	1	...	...	...	Lettonie
Lithuania	..	...	20	6	6	6	...	...	...	...	Lituanie
Norway	192	163	159	148	170	244	221	255	191	165	Norvège
Poland	52	51	57	60	65	76	78	...	...	...	Pologne
Portugal	118	132	107	99	91	85	84	75	84	85	Portugal
Romania	70	59	59	59	48	42	36	34	30	30	Roumanie
Russian Federation	..	...	1110	756	557	735	556	429	394	560	Fédération de Russie
Slovakia	..	..	...	...	90	...	...	...	...	...	Slovaquie
Slovenia	..	..	72	41	93	81	74	105	112	112	Slovénie
Sweden	723	733	725	715	722	727	643	720	688	656	Suède
Switzerland	122	127	129	127	147	120	139	159	131	143	Suisse
T.F.Yug.Rep. Macedonia	..	...	...	...	...	...	...	...	0	1	L'ex-RY Macédoine
Yugoslavia, SFR	195	..	..	..	..	..	..	..	..	..	Yougoslavie, RSF
USSR (former)	1998	..	..	..	..	..	..	..	..	..	URSS (anc.)
Oceania	**43**	**43**	**52**	**52**	**49**	**77**	**83**	**81**	**108**	**85**	**Océanie**
Australia	43	43	52	52	49	77	83	81	108	85	Australie
Total	**8393**	**7240**	**7399**	**6947**	**6768**	**6962**	**6539**	**6793**	**6329**	**6388**	**Total**

General Note.
Wood pulp prepared by an acid pulping process. The liquor used is an aqueous solution of sulphurous acid in which lime or some other base has been dissolved. It may be bleached or not. Includes chemical sulphite screenings. In terms of air-dry weight (10 per cent moisture content). (SITC, Rev.3: 25160-0).
Source: Food and Agriculture Organization of the United Nations (FAO), Rome.

Remarque générale.
Pâtes de bois préparées par un procédé acide de délignification. La liqueur utilisée est une solution aqueuse de gaz sulfureux dans laquelle on a dissout de la chaux ou une autre base. Pâte blanchie ou écrue. Cette rubrique comprend les produits obtenus par tamisage après traitement chimique. Poids après séchage à l'air (pâte à 10 p. 100 d'humidité). (CTCI, Rev.3: 25160-0).
Source: Organisation des Nations Unies pour l'alimentation et l'agriculture (FAO), Rome.

[1] Including Hong-Kong, Macao and Taiwan.

[1] Y compris Hong-Kong, Macao et Taïwan.

Wood pulp, semi-chemical
Pâte de bois mi-chimiques

ISIC-BASED CODE - CODE BASE CITI

3411-16

Unit : Thousand metric tons   Unité : Milliers de tonnes métriques

Country or area	1990	1991	1992	1993	1994	1995	1996	1997	1998	1999	Pays ou zone
Africa	**166**	**165**	**124**	**112**	**145**	**189**	**189**	**184**	**192**	**197**	**Afrique**
Madagascar	1	0	0	0	0	0	0	0	0	0	Madagascar
Nigeria	3	3	3	3	3	3	3	6	9	9	Nigéria
South Africa	140	140	99	87	120	164	164	...	...	...	Afrique du Sud
Zimbabwe	22	22	22	22	22	22	22	22	22	22	Zimbabwe
America, North	**4484**	**4350**	**4238**	**4080**	**4478**	**3971**	**3884**	**4078**	**4095**	**4200**	**Amérique du Nord**
Canada	650	630	511	434	373	356	381	404	482	551	Canada
Mexico	...	...	...	...	...	...	...	6	...	...	Mexique
United States	3828	3714	3721	3640	4099	3609	3497	3668	3607	3643	Etats-Unis
America, South	**344**	**337**	**332**	**195**	**245**	**261**	**207**	**157**	**148**	**171**	**Amérique du Sud**
Argentina	180	185	181	62	119	121	108	67	59	59	Argentine
Brazil	45	39	51	37	37	37	31	27	27	33	Brésil
Colombia	38	38	32	34	34	40	38	37	34	44	Colombie
Uruguay	2	2	2	2	2	1	1	4	4	3	Uruguay
Venezuela	...	...	...	...	...	62	29	22	24	32	Venezuela
Asia	**666**	**687**	**668**	**630**	**616**	**559**	**672**	**648**	**624**	**560**	**Asie**
China [1]	54	62	54	...	...	...	...	...	...	...	Chine [1]
Indonesia	76	81	112	136	136	80	216	216	...	...	Indonésie
Japan	324	334	293	243	214	211	198	196	152	102	Japon
Malaysia	...	...	...	88	103	105	...	...	...	...	Malaisie
Pakistan	...	...	...	...	...	...	...	...	24	25	Pakistan
Thailand	...	...	...	...	...	...	23	26	55	55	Thaïlande
Turkey	...	...	...	42	42	42	55	30	50	26	Turquie
Europe	**1737**	**2033**	**1984**	**1873**	**1860**	**1895**	**1693**	**1946**	**1802**	**1808**	**Europe**
Austria	39	39	39	39	39	...	...	...	...	...	Autriche
Bulgaria	20	20	16	16	16	16	16	16	16	16	Bulgarie
Croatia	..	...	90	90	93	78	93	71	58	56	Croatie
Denmark	68	68	65	63	71	71	71	71	...	...	Danemark
Czechoslovakia(former)	80	62	..	..	..					..	Tchécoslovaquie(anc.)
Finland	434	433	458	472	487	509	468	529	529	539	Finlande
France	117	119	116	113	119	110	100	117	120	125	France
Germany	..	71	71	...	...	...	...	...	...	...	Allemagne
Hungary	34	29	14	5	5	5	5	...	...	...	Hongrie
Italy	88	67	46	34	24	...	...	...	79	78	Italie
Norway	86	81	78	76	90	97	66	73	72	55	Norvège
Poland	103	103	90	93	100	96	88	78	110	100	Pologne
Romania	12	27	27	27	39	46	29	47	36	36	Roumanie
Russian Federation	..	...	382	300	215	266	199	263	206	210	Fédération de Russie
Slovakia	..	..	...	5	5	5	5	76	76	85	Slovaquie
Spain	110	97	86	88	105	78	50	...	1	...	Espagne
Sweden	289	292	276	264	250	251	242	266	236	257	Suède
United Kingdom	148	148	123	110	124	91	85	86	75	63	Royaume-Uni
Yugoslavia	..	...	...	...	...	...	...	7	7	7	Yougoslavie
Yugoslavia, SFR	109	..	..	..	..	..	...	..	..	..	Yougoslavie, RSF
USSR (former)	539	..	..	..	..	..	..	..	..	..	URSS (anc.)
Oceania	**278**	**296**	**134**	**131**	**233**	**149**	**176**	**171**	**155**	**159**	**Océanie**
Australia	230	238	105	106	203	114	142	138	122	125	Australie
New Zealand	48	58	29	25	30	35	34	33	33	34	Nouvelle-Zélande
Total	**8213**	**7868**	**7480**	**7020**	**7577**	**7024**	**6821**	**7184**	**7016**	**7095**	**Total**

General Note.
Wood pulp in which the fibres are partly separated without material damage by a sequence of chemical and mechanical actions and where the conditions of the separation treatment are not sufficiently severe in themselves to bring about a complete separation of the fibres. In terms of air-dry weight (10 per cent moisture content). (SITC, Rev.3: 25191-0).
Source: Food and Agriculture Organization of the United Nations (FAO), Rome.

[1] Including Hong-Kong, Macao and Taiwan.

Remarque générale.
Pâtes de bois dans lesquelles les fibres sont partiellement séparées, sans dommage important, par une suite de traitements chimiques et mécaniques qui ne sont pas suffisamment vigoureux pour entraîner une séparation complète des fibres. Poids après séchage à l'air (pâte à 10 p. 100 d'humidité). (CTCI, Rev.3: 25191-0).
Source: Organisation des Nations Unies pour l'alimentation et l'agriculture (FAO), Rome.

[1] Y compris Hong-Kong, Macao et Taïwan.

Newsprint
Papier journal
ISIC-BASED CODE - CODE BASE CITI

3411-19

Unit : Thousand metric tons .

Unité : Milliers de tonnes métriques

Country or area	1990	1991	1992	1993	1994	1995	1996	1997	1998	1999	Pays ou zone
Africa	**423**	**413**	**390**	**394**	**424**	**498**	**497**	**391**	**405**	**386**	**Afrique**
Ethiopia	...	...	...	...	...	...	1	3	2	2	Ethiopie
Kenya	6	11	16	16	13	14	14	14	14	14	Kenya
Nigeria	31	21	13	3	...	...	...	...	...	...	Nigéria
South Africa	355	350	330	350	367	440	440	332	347	328	Afrique du Sud
United Rep.Tanzania	8	8	8	8	8	8	8	8	8	8	Rép. Unie de Tanzanie
Zimbabwe	21	21	21	15	17	17	17	17	17	17	Zimbabwe
America, North	**15483**	**15600**	**15661**	**15819**	**15889**	**15864**	**15605**	**16079**	**15489**	**15997**	**Amérique du Nord**
Canada	9069	8977	8931	9165	9321	9226	9015	9205	8581	9204	Canada
El Salvador	...	...	...	...	...	...	14	14	14	14	El Salvador
Honduras	...	...	...	...	...	8	8	11	12	12	Honduras
Mexico	398	401	289	216	214	265	265	305	308	250	Mexique
United States	6001	6206	6424	6419	6334	6351	6303	6544	6574	6517	Etats-Unis
America, South	**628**	**625**	**596**	**585**	**594**	**667**	**644**	**590**	**593**	**624**	**Amérique du Sud**
Argentina	208	198	206	129	142	176	166	138	154	154	Argentine
Brazil	246	253	226	268	263	282	277	265	273	242	Brésil
Chile	171	171	161	185	186	206	198	184	163	225	Chili
Colombia	...	...	...	...	...	1	1	...	...	...	Colombie
Ecuador	...	...	...	...	2	2	2	2	2	2	Equateur
Asia	**5316**	**5390**	**5392**	**5197**	**5520**	**6058**	**6537**	**6783**	**7160**	**7349**	**Asie**
Bangladesh	46	50	50	46	48	40	30	28	8	8	Bangladesh
China [1]	475	486	590	629	721	865	995	825	824	914	Chine [1]
India	310	300	320	320	350	400	400	380	440	450	Inde
Indonesia	157	151	169	195	239	243	267	390	478	532	Indonésie
Iran(Islamic Rep. of)	...	...	...	...	...	...	...	...	20	25	Iran(Rép. islamique)
Israel	1	...	...	...	...	...	...	...	...	...	Israël
Japan	3479	3515	3255	2917	2972	3098	3140	3192	3265	3295	Japon
Korea, Republic of	522	563	613	743	874	948	1305	1592	1700	1718	Corée, République de
Malaysia	...	...	...	...	2	2	2	3	2	2	Malaisie
Pakistan	...	...	...	...	...	...	...	...	14	17	Pakistan
Philippines	52	100	125	110	110	138	138	138	156	174	Philippines
Thailand	...	...	...	...	39	116	125	118	118	110	Thaïlande
Turkey	151	93	135	94	110	151	78	60	98	68	Turquie
Viet Nam	9	12	10	13	16	18	18	18	36	35	Viet Nam
Europe	**7781**	**9922**	**9934**	**10446**	**11102**	**11943**	**11196**	**11643**	**12162**	**12621**	**Europe**
Albania	8	8	8	8	8	8	8	8	8	8	Albanie
Austria	333	397	395	387	403	380	361	397	376	394	Autriche
Belgium-Luxembourg	102	106	119	119	122	122	104	104	105	112	Belgique-Luxembourg
Croatia	...	...	...	...	3	2	1	2	9	14	Croatie
Czechoslovakia(former)	75	27	..	..	..	..	..	..	..	..	Tchécoslovaquie(anc.)
Czech Republic	..	..	...	59	86	89	101	94	102	104	République tchèque
Finland	1430	1305	1257	1425	1446	1425	1327	1470	1483	1490	Finlande
France	422	509	670	802	844	890	783	909	923	950	France
Germany	..	1229	1222	1302	1499	1726	1572	1618	1630	1643	Allemagne
Greece	16	20	20	9	9	9	9	9	9	9	Grèce
Hungary	...	...	...	...	...	...	...	410	434	...	Hongrie
Italy	233	196	101	83	154	183	178	180	190	183	Italie
Latvia	..	...	0	3	2	2	3	3	1	...	Lettonie
Netherlands	300	309	306	326	311	361	338	373	349	376	Pays-Bas
Norway	910	955	934	1007	1007	973	913	798	914	870	Norvège
Poland	25	64	61	46	68	95	86	80	92	150	Pologne
Romania	67	57	57	57	57	47	31	42	44	44	Roumanie
Russian Federation	..	...	943	845	1038	1457	1245	1195	1395	1620	Fédération de Russie
Slovakia	..	..	...	20	20	20	5	2	...	...	Slovaquie
Slovenia	..	..	81	66	76	93	39	49	68	68	Slovénie
Spain	173	149	120	94	99	148	137	143	192	242	Espagne
Sweden	2273	2063	2124	2325	2415	2346	2283	2411	2478	2508	Suède
Switzerland	280	272	282	288	234	263	259	308	307	332	Suisse
Ukraine	..	...	...	...	...	...	15	8	8	8	Ukraine
United Kingdom	696	672	700	741	769	873	976	1030	1046	1071	Royaume-Uni

For general note and footnotes, see end of table.

Voir la fin du tableau pour la remarque générale et les notes.

Newsprint (continued)
Papier journal (suite)

ISIC-BASED CODE - CODE BASE CITI
3411-19

Unit : Thousand metric tons   Unité : Milliers de tonnes métriques

Country or area	1990	1991	1992	1993	1994	1995	1996	1997	1998	1999	Pays ou zone
Yugoslavia, SFR	16	..	..	..	..	..	..	..	..	..	Yougoslavie, RSF
USSR (former)	1780	..	..	..	..	..	..	..	..	..	URSS (anc.)
Oceania	**666**	**716**	**783**	**802**	**798**	**840**	**824**	**818**	**837**	**784**	Océanie
Australia	371	395	404	433	426	444	445	421	444	405	Australie
New Zealand	295	321	379	369	372	396	379	397	393	379	Nouvelle-Zélande
Total	**32077**	**32665**	**32756**	**33243**	**34327**	**35870**	**35303**	**36304**	**36646**	**37761**	**Total**

General Note.

Bleached, unsized or slack-sized printing paper, without coating, of the type usually used for newspapers, weight from 45 to 60 grammes per square metre, usually with at least 70 per cent of the weight of the fibrous material derived from mechanical pulp.(SITC, Rev.3: 64110-0).

Source: Food and Agriculture Organization of the United Nations (FAO), Rome.

Remarque générale.

Papier d'impression, blanchi, non encollé ou peu collé, non couché, du type utilisé d'ordinaire pour les journaux, poids de 45 à 60 g au m^2, contenant généralement au moins 70 p. 100 en poids de matière fibreuse tirée de la pâte mécanique. (CTCI, Rev.3: 64110-0).

Source: Organisation des Nations Unies pour l'alimentation et l'agriculture (FAO), Rome.

[1] Including Hong-Kong, Macao and Taiwan.

[1] Y compris Hong-Kong, Macao et Taïwan.

Other printing and writing paper
Autres papiers d'imprimerie et d'écriture

ISIC-BASED CODE - CODE BASE CITI

3411-22

Unit : Thousand metric tons   Unité : Milliers de tonnes métriques

Country or area	1990	1991	1992	1993	1994	1995	1996	1997	1998	1999	Pays ou zone
Africa	**626**	**603**	**546**	**642**	**606**	**516**	**507**	**615**	**643**	**661**	**Afrique**
Algeria	39	37	37	33	36	35	29	34	24	14	Algérie
Egypt	73	65	58	85	75	70	70	55	36	36	Egypte
Ethiopia,incl.Eritrea	7	5	2	...	...	...	...	...	...	...	Ethiopie,incl.Erythrée
Ethiopia	...	...	...	5	5	4	4	5	2	3	Ethiopie
Kenya	28	23	32	32	17	18	18	18	18	18	Kenya
Madagascar	3	3	3	4	4	3	2	3	3	1	Madagascar
Morocco	29	29	29	25	29	30	30	23	25	25	Maroc
Nigeria	...	...	...	...	...	3	1	1	1	1	Nigéria
South Africa	395	395	335	400	380	301	301	423	479	506	Afrique du Sud
Tunisia	29	23	28	36	39	33	33	34	36	38	Tunisie
United Rep.Tanzania	6	6	6	6	6	6	6	6	6	6	Rép. Unie de Tanzanie
Zambia	1	1	1	2	1	1	1	2	2	2	Zambie
Zimbabwe	...	...	...	...	...	...	...	...	7	7	Zimbabwe
America, North	**24283**	**24031**	**24435**	**26210**	**28207**	**28470**	**27789**	**29963**	**28469**	**29641**	**Amérique du Nord**
Canada	3599	3564	3567	4194	4444	4882	4689	4966	5155	5691	Canada
Cuba	39	37	15	14	14	14	14	14	14	14	Cuba
Dominican Republic	...	...	...	...	...	...	10	10	10	10	Rép. dominicaine
El Salvador	...	...	...	...	...	...	3	3	3	3	El Salvador
Guatemala	10	10	10	10	4	2	2	2	2	2	Guatemala
Honduras	...	...	...	...	...	8	9	14	13	13	Honduras
Mexico	528	532	545	462	402	509	509	623	625	692	Mexique
United States	20092	19872	20281	21511	23323	23042	22553	24331	22647	23216	Etats-Unis
America, South	**1869**	**1940**	**2031**	**2310**	**2594**	**2505**	**2524**	**2788**	**2830**	**2950**	**Amérique du Sud**
Argentina	170	176	197	209	233	246	228	261	272	272	Argentine
Brazil	1321	1348	1394	1670	1858	1791	1807	1996	1966	2070	Brésil
Chile	60	75	82	86	98	70	83	116	137	129	Chili
Colombia	128	135	187	184	211	197	205	214	208	233	Colombie
Ecuador	9	2	3	3	...	...	...	...	...	...	Equateur
Paraguay	2	2	...	...	...	...	...	...	...	...	Paraguay
Peru	45	50	12	12	9	22	22	22	11	11	Pérou
Uruguay	16	26	26	26	26	28	28	43	48	47	Uruguay
Venezuela	118	126	128	118	153	145	145	130	182	182	Venezuela
Asia	**17395**	**18291**	**18974**	**16586**	**18849**	**20188**	**22421**	**23613**	**23323**	**26034**	**Asie**
Bangladesh	38	34	34	45	50	40	30	28	30	30	Bangladesh
China[1]	4984	5199	5531	3009	4528	4677	6291	6611	6009	6715	Chine[1]
India	900	990	1060	1085	1112	1150	1150	1110	1280	1510	Inde
Indonesia	504	599	735	844	992	1061	1236	1510	1855	2733	Indonésie
Iran(Islamic Rep. of)	72	75	60	65	85	85	85	85	...	...	Iran(Rép. islamique)
Iraq	16	5	5	5	7	7	7	7	8	8	Iraq
Israel	61	69	69	61	62	95	95	95	95	95	Israël
Japan	9250	9727	9610	9543	9805	10565	10812	11092	10887	11330	Japon
Korea, Republic of	919	919	1040	1116	1350	1439	1640	1813	1625	1876	Corée, République de
Malaysia	130	131	201	201	159	162	145	126	123	123	Malaisie
Myanmar	5	5	5	8	8	8	8	31	20	18	Myanmar
Pakistan	55	62	55	52	62	99	110	120	180	200	Pakistan
Philippines	94	95	144	103	103	154	154	154	140	162	Philippines
Sri Lanka	12	12	11	15	15	13	11	11	11	11	Sri Lanka
Thailand	190	186	224	256	299	381	401	529	623	780	Thaïlande
Turkey	139	125	127	111	164	197	191	236	250	252	Turquie
Viet Nam	26	58	63	67	48	55	55	55	102	105	Viet Nam
Europe	**18566**	**24453**	**25580**	**25956**	**28742**	**28979**	**29141**	**32219**	**33096**	**34273**	**Europe**
Albania	5	5	5	5	5	5	5	5	5	5	Albanie
Austria	1377	1447	1546	1574	1728	1764	1787	1826	2002	2067	Autriche
Belgium-Luxembourg	733	678	666	666	610	610	991	991	1028	1245	Belgique-Luxembourg
Bulgaria	52	47	8	4	5	5	5	5	5	5	Bulgarie
Croatia	..	...	...	2	4	4	4	5	9	11	Croatie
Denmark	124	132	117	93	93	93	93	114	117	102	Danemark
Czechoslovakia(former)	152	104	..	...	...	...	...	...	...	..	Tchécoslovaquie(anc.)
Czech Republic	..	..	...	63	160	173	158	185	177	158	République tchèque

For general note and footnotes, see end of table.   Voir la fin du tableau pour la remarque générale et les notes.

Other printing and writing paper (continued)
Autres papiers d'imprimerie et d'écriture (suite)

ISIC-BASED CODE - CODE BASE CITI
3411-22

Unit : Thousand metric tons   Unité : Milliers de tonnes métriques

Country or area	1990	1991	1992	1993	1994	1995	1996	1997	1998	1999	Pays ou zone
Estonia	..	...	9	9	9	9	20	...	...	...	Estonie
Finland	4682	4705	4979	5502	6096	6315	5837	7121	7760	7902	Finlande
France	2773	2827	2948	2936	3268	3096	3141	3350	3102	3250	France
Germany	..	5114	5173	4928	5865	5872	5702	6367	6630	6757	Allemagne
Greece	75	76	76	125	125	125	125	21	23	23	Grèce
Hungary	127	88	107	64	80	83	142	169	...	202	Hongrie
Italy	2247	2252	2397	2381	2595	2594	2662	2751	2778	2886	Italie
Latvia	..	...	2	1	1	2	1	1	3	2	Lettonie
Lithuania	..	...	...	2	2	2	...	...	1	1	Lituanie
Netherlands	819	834	797	775	902	818	840	878	875	892	Pays-Bas
Norway	339	368	308	495	606	746	677	861	817	851	Norvège
Poland	243	230	262	284	336	389	431	485	410	368	Pologne
Portugal	167	282	353	385	435	438	486	533	552	572	Portugal
Romania	111	52	52	52	36	48	56	40	24	24	Roumanie
Russian Federation	..	...	845	665	430	486	433	441	474	569	Fédération de Russie
Slovakia	..	...	...	90	85	100	200	214	221	208	Slovaquie
Slovenia	..	...	60	45	44	32	80	183	240	240	Slovénie
Spain	832	853	850	812	874	858	844	901	885	938	Espagne
Sweden	1655	1793	1805	1884	2061	2047	2170	2459	2545	2617	Suède
Switzerland	370	360	373	381	413	444	441	461	479	557	Suisse
Ukraine	..	...	...	...	...	...	30	29	29	29	Ukraine
United Kingdom	1387	1478	1583	1675	1819	1766	1753	1779	1742	1745	Royaume-Uni
Yugoslavia	..	...	...	...	...	...	...	25	25	25	Yougoslavie
T.F.Yug.Rep. Macedonia	..	...	...	4	2	2	1	1	2	1	L'ex-RY Macédoine
Yugoslavia, SFR	296	..	..	..	..	..	..	..	..	..	Yougoslavie, RSF
USSR (former)	1365	..	..	..	..	..	..	..	..	..	URSS (anc.)
Oceania	**444**	**425**	**321**	**314**	**362**	**378**	**364**	**378**	**436**	**508**	Océanie
Australia	406	390	304	304	348	365	351	364	424	497	Australie
New Zealand	38	35	17	10	14	13	13	14	12	11	Nouvelle-Zélande
Total	**64547**	**69743**	**71887**	**72017**	**79360**	**81036**	**82746**	**89576**	**88798**	**94067**	Total

General Note.

Paper, except newsprint, suitable for printing and business purposes, writing sketching, drawing, etc. made from a variety of pulp blends and with various finishes. Included are such papers as those used for books and magazines, wallpaper base stock, box lining and covering, calculator paper, rotonews, duplicating, tablet or block, label, lithograth, banknote, tabulating card stock, bible or imitation bible, stationery, manifold, onionskin, typewriter, poster, etc. (SITC, Rev.3: 64120-1, 64132-0, 64133-0, 64134-0).
Source: Food and Agriculture Organization of the United Nations (FAO), Rome.

Remarque générale.

Papiers, autres que le papier journal, utilisés pour l'impression, les besoins commerciaux, l'écriture, les croquis, le dessin, etc., faits avec divers mélanges de pâte et soumis à divers procédés de finissage. Dans cette rubrique figurent des papiers tels que les papiers pour livres et revues, les supports de tentures (papier peint), le papier pour garnissage et habillage de boîtes, le papier pour machines à calculer, le papier pour impression sur rotatives, le papier pour reproduction ou duplicateur, le papier pour blocs-notes, le papier pour étiquettes, les papiers pour lithographie, le papier pour billets de banque, le papier pour cartes mécanographiques, le papier bible véritable ou imitation, le papier à lettres, le papier pour manifold, le papier pelure surglacé, le papier machine, le papier pour affiches, etc. (CTCI. Rev.3: 64120-1,64132-0, 64133-0, 64134-0).
Source: Organisation des Nations Unies pour l'alimentation et l'agriculture (FAO), Rome.

[1] Including Hong-Kong, Macao and Taiwan.

[1] Y compris Hong-Kong, Macao et Taïwan.

Household and sanitary paper
Papiers domestique et hygiénique

ISIC-BASED CODE - CODE BASE CITI

3411-24

Unit : Thousand metric tons											Unité : Milliers de tonnes métriques
Country or area	1990	1991	1992	1993	1994	1995	1996	1997	1998	1999	Pays ou zone
Africa	**152**	**150**	**147**	**128**	**164**	**181**	**179**	**202**	**194**	**218**	**Afrique**
Algeria	2	3	3	3	3	4	2	3	3	3	Algérie
Egypt	...	15	15	14	55	60	60	44	59	59	Egypte
Kenya	6	7	8	8	5	6	6	6	6	6	Kenya
Morocco	2	2	1	1	1	1	1	1	1	1	Maroc
South Africa	115	120	117	99	97	107	107	145	122	145	Afrique du Sud
Tunisia	...	...	...	...	...	...	...	3	3	4	Tunisie
America, North	**6252**	**6183**	**6304**	**6573**	**6710**	**6865**	**6899**	**7180**	**7356**	**7668**	**Amérique du Nord**
Canada	467	515	530	542	584	617	605	617	624	661	Canada
Costa Rica	19	19	19	19	20	20	20	20	20	20	Costa Rica
Cuba	9	9	5	5	5	5	5	5	5	5	Cuba
Dominican Republic	...	...	...	...	...	...	...	...	62	62	Rép. dominicaine
El Salvador	6	6	6	6	6	6	3	3	3	3	El Salvador
Guatemala	...	...	...	...	14	21	21	21	21	21	Guatemala
Honduras	...	...	...	...	...	4	4	5	6	6	Honduras
Jamaica	4	4	5	3	3	...	...	...	...	...	Jamaïque
Mexico	385	388	392	447	464	477	477	596	622	660	Mexique
Panama	18	18	18	18	18	18	18	18	...	...	Panama
United States	5264	5143	5247	5450	5530	5632	5681	5831	5973	6210	Etats-Unis
America, South	**774**	**827**	**847**	**867**	**928**	**977**	**1056**	**1150**	**987**	**1125**	**Amérique du Sud**
Argentina	38	44	67	42	79	66	86	114	90	90	Argentine
Brazil	376	406	414	452	458	496	517	565	576	572	Brésil
Chile	54	57	62	71	76	83	106	108	101	107	Chili
Colombia	82	90	86	87	98	101	110	113	129	125	Colombie
Ecuador	5	19	23	15	12	13	13	14	14	14	Equateur
Peru	55	58	29	29	32	38	38	38	...	...	Pérou
Uruguay	8	8	13	13	13	16	16	17	12	10	Uruguay
Venezuela	156	145	153	158	160	164	170	181	32	175	Venezuela
Asia	**2733**	**3104**	**3322**	**2617**	**3696**	**4204**	**4760**	**4858**	**4825**	**4958**	**Asie**
China [1]	885	1018	1170	380	1378	1820	2320	2300	2330	2351	Chine [1]
India	19	21	23	23	25	29	29	30	35	35	Inde
Indonesia	47	60	82	93	109	127	92	89	111	162	Indonésie
Israel	37	35	40	42	46	50	50	50	50	50	Israël
Japan	1366	1438	1475	1523	1548	1560	1649	1715	1660	1701	Japon
Jordan	15	15	15	29	31	31	31	20	20	20	Jordanie
Korea, Republic of	196	232	268	298	317	318	308	332	272	291	Corée, République de
Lebanon	2	6	6	6	6	6	6	6	6	6	Liban
Malaysia	62	68	81	68	73	91	87	115	115	115	Malaisie
Myanmar	...	...	...	...	...	...	...	1	1	1	Myanmar
Pakistan	10	8	10	6	10	10	12	14	14	14	Pakistan
Philippines	8	18	20	21	21	19	19	19	23	27	Philippines
Thailand	43	142	60	62	69	75	81	84	95	90	Thaïlande
Turkey	35	31	58	55	54	57	65	73	83	85	Turquie
Viet Nam	7	11	13	10	8	10	10	10	10	10	Viet Nam
Europe	**2761**	**4101**	**4213**	**4318**	**4722**	**4666**	**4743**	**5498**	**5507**	**5730**	**Europe**
Austria	101	95	93	86	96	95	102	108	111	110	Autriche
Belgium-Luxembourg	96	119	96	96	118	118	82	82	82	82	Belgique-Luxembourg
Bulgaria	...	14	10	9	9	10	10	10	10	10	Bulgarie
Croatia	..	...	...	...	...	156	129	178	181	179	Croatie
Denmark	16	17	...	...	...	...	...	...	...	...	Danemark
Czechoslovakia(former)	53	47	..	..	..	..	..	..	..	..	Tchécoslovaquie(anc.)
Czech Republic	..	..	...	16	16	18	23	25	24	29	République tchèque
Finland	164	159	167	176	193	184	188	204	171	185	Finlande
France	321	365	381	396	478	489	508	534	514	520	France
Germany	..	889	879	847	864	877	886	890	931	954	Allemagne
Greece	109	117	117	247	247	247	247	128	23	26	Grèce
Hungary	21	18	25	34	25	35	37	34	34	35	Hongrie
Italy	353	388	421	416	510	545	548	1026	1102	1182	Italie
Lithuania	..	...	...	...	...	...	...	8	12	8	Lituanie
Netherlands	167	174	171	166	167	161	159	169	169	144	Pays-Bas

For general note and footnotes, see end of table.

Voir la fin du tableau pour la remarque générale et les notes.

Household and sanitary paper (continued)
Papiers domestique et hygiénique (suite)

ISIC-BASED CODE - CODE BASE CITI

3411-24

Unit : Thousand metric tons

Unité : Milliers de tonnes métriques

Country or area	1990	1991	1992	1993	1994	1995	1996	1997	1998	1999	Pays ou zone
Norway	40	24	21	21	29	27	26	...	28	27	Norvège
Poland	120	116	91	92	86	100	103	113	122	130	Pologne
Portugal	53	51	63	58	61	59	63	64	65	63	Portugal
Romania	30	20	20	20	27	30	34	33	35	35	Roumanie
Russian Federation	..	...	93	88	75	82	82	93	94	100	Fédération de Russie
Slovakia	..	..	...	...	72	77	97	133	114	118	Slovaquie
Slovenia	..	..	61	65	64	61	63	56	52	52	Slovénie
Spain	232	245	260	264	293	239	284	329	393	416	Espagne
Sweden	283	291	296	298	295	293	297	292	299	294	Suède
Switzerland	150	146	151	154	197	83	88	215	198	205	Suisse
Ukraine	..	...	...	...	...	...	28	45	45	45	Ukraine
United Kingdom	441	455	473	445	551	567	586	639	635	718	Royaume-Uni
Yugoslavia	..	...	...	...	...	...	...	47	47	47	Yougoslavie
USSR (former)	195	..	..	..	..	..	..	..	..	..	URSS (anc.)
Oceania	**240**	**211**	**185**	**232**	**237**	**260**	**263**	**255**	**248**	**242**	**Océanie**
Australia	167	134	145	165	167	173	180	181	191	187	Australie
New Zealand	73	77	40	67	70	87	83	74	57	55	Nouvelle-Zélande
Total	**13107**	**14576**	**15018**	**14736**	**16456**	**17154**	**17900**	**19144**	**19116**	**19941**	**Total**

General Note.

Household and sanitary paper; special thin paper. Household and sanitary paper includes absorbent paper, creped or uncreped, sometimes embossed, made from bleached or unbleached chemical wood pulp, sometimes with a mixture of pulp from waste paper and mechanical pulp. Included are: towelling, napkins, facial tissue, toilet tissue, wadding, disposable tissues. (SITC, Rev.3: 64163-0). Source: Food and Agriculture Organization of the United Nations (FAO), Rome.

Remarque générale.

Papiers de ménage et papiers hygiéniques. Les papiers de ménage et les papiers hygiéniques comprennent les papiers absorbants, crêpes ou non, parfois gaufrés, faits avec de la pâte de bois chimique, blanchie ou écrue, parfois mélangée à de la pâte de vieux papiers et de la pâte mécanique. Font partie de cette catégorie les essuie-mains et serviettes, papiers à démaquiller, papiers hygiéniques, ouate de cellulose, articles en papier à jeter. (CTCI, Rev.3: 64163-0). Source: Organisation des Nations Unies pour l'alimentation et l'agriculture (FAO), Rome.

[1] Including Hong-Kong, Macao and Taiwan.

[1] Y compris Hong-Kong, Macao et Taïwan.

Wrapping and packaging paper and paperboard
Papiers et cartons d'empaquetage et d'emballage

ISIC-BASED CODE - CODE BASE CITI

3411-25

Unit : Thousand metric tons   Unité : Milliers de tonnes métriques

Country or area	1990	1991	1992	1993	1994	1995	1996	1997	1998	1999	Pays ou zone
Africa	**1443**	**1437**	**1441**	**1258**	**1073**	**1287**	**1306**	**1640**	**1705**	**1607**	**Afrique**
Algeria	50	51	51	57	48	39	25	28	28	24	Algérie
Cameroon	5	5	5	5	5	5	5	...	...	...	Cameroun
Egypt	128	128	128	121	83	85	85	183	248	248	Egypte
Ethiopia,incl.Eritrea	1	1	1	...	...	...	...	...	...	...	Ethiopie,incl.Erythrée
Ethiopia	...	...	...	2	2	2	2	3	2	2	Ethiopie
Kenya	51	49	120	120	73	75	91	91	91	91	Kenya
Libyan Arab Jamah.	6	6	6	6	6	6	6	6	6	6	Jamah. arabe libyenne
Madagascar	...	...	...	...	...	...	...	...	2	1	Madagascar
Morocco	87	86	72	73	73	75	75	83	84	83	Maroc
Mozambique	1	2	2	1	1	1	1	...	...	...	Mozambique
Nigeria	12	8	8	2	3	3	20	18	18	18	Nigéria
South Africa	1035	1035	988	811	710	923	923	1147	1157	1062	Afrique du Sud
Sudan	3	1	1	1	1	1	1	1	1	1	Soudan
Tunisia	49	49	43	44	53	57	57	60	49	52	Tunisie
United Rep.Tanzania	11	11	11	11	11	11	11	11	11	11	Rép. Unie de Tanzanie
Zambia	...	...	...	...	...	1	1	1	1	1	Zambie
America, North	**41885**	**43126**	**44522**	**44980**	**9852**	**9766**	**10010**	**10246**	**49979**	**51574**	**Amérique du Nord**
Canada	3331	3503	3557	3656	3999	3988	4105	4181	4365	4591	Canada
Cuba	49	48	26	25	25	25	25	25	25	25	Cuba
Dominican Republic	10	10	10	7	7	7	11	11	58	58	Rép. dominicaine
El Salvador	11	11	11	11	11	11	19	19	19	19	El Salvador
Guatemala	4	4	4	4	7	8	8	8	8	8	Guatemala
Honduras	...	...	...	...	...	66	72	54	62	62	Honduras
Mexico	1524	1537	1567	1322	1438	1772	1772	1944	2094	2161	Mexique
Panama	10	10	10	10	10	10	10	10	...	...	Panama
United States	36870	37929	39265	39874	4286	3879	3988	3994	43338	44640	Etats-Unis
America, South	**3710**	**4327**	**4127**	**4049**	**4158**	**4499**	**4529**	**4893**	**4652**	**5138**	**Amérique du Sud**
Argentina	434	498	425	409	408	500	463	607	437	437	Argentine
Brazil	2267	2680	2683	2779	2923	3057	3070	3386	3401	3668	Brésil
Chile	164	174	184	169	188	197	280	196	233	324	Chili
Colombia	284	296	325	306	342	367	363	352	347	346	Colombie
Ecuador	25	80	99	63	53	56	59	62	62	62	Equateur
Paraguay	7	8	11	11	11	11	11	11	11	11	Paraguay
Peru	163	171	100	38	51	77	77	77	41	41	Pérou
Uruguay	30	40	43	43	43	42	42	27	23	29	Uruguay
Venezuela	336	380	257	231	139	192	164	175	97	220	Venezuela
Asia	**23260**	**24578**	**26279**	**27481**	**30836**	**37033**	**38298**	**40880**	**40842**	**43103**	**Asie**
Bangladesh	8	7	7	32	34	30	20	14	8	8	Bangladesh
China[1]	6043	6387	7010	7648	9978	15240	15370	15975	17131	17451	Chine[1]
India	918	1010	1081	1152	1282	1354	1354	1390	1480	1675	Inde
Indonesia	567	734	992	1140	1331	1549	2407	2590	2831	3417	Indonésie
Iraq	39	8	8	8	11	11	11	11	12	12	Iraq
Israel	95	96	106	110	121	130	130	130	130	130	Israël
Japan	11716	12023	11755	11618	11986	12255	12295	13855	12093	12285	Japon
Jordan	...	...	...	...	...	...	...	12	12	12	Jordanie
Korea, Republic of	2503	2725	3063	3128	3330	3566	3802	3729	3690	4358	Corée, République de
Lebanon	35	36	36	36	36	36	36	36	36	36	Liban
Malaysia	30	64	350	390	309	352	431	457	518	518	Malaisie
Myanmar	6	6	6	7	7	7	7	7	20	18	Myanmar
Pakistan	100	83	100	240	230	178	185	180	180	180	Pakistan
Philippines	78	250	267	270	270	269	269	269	453	522	Philippines
Sri Lanka	4	11	15	14	16	11	9	9	9	9	Sri Lanka
Syrian Arab Republic	...	1	1	1	1	1	1	1	1	1	Rép. arabe syrienne
Thailand	557	630	757	877	1082	1167	1157	1309	1285	1495	Thaïlande
Turkey	538	474	688	766	770	830	767	871	918	941	Turquie
Viet Nam	10	22	25	32	30	35	35	35	35	35	Viet Nam
Europe	**22572**	**29579**	**30903**	**30885**	**32665**	**32864**	**32879**	**34971**	**35594**	**36737**	**Europe**
Austria	1067	1110	1172	1210	1330	1315	1359	1438	1449	1503	Autriche
Belgium-Luxembourg	214	266	214	214	202	202	216	216	492	402	Belgique-Luxembourg

For general note and footnotes, see end of table.   Voir la fin du tableau pour la remarque générale et les notes.

Wrapping and packaging paper and paperboard (continued)
Papiers et cartons d'empaquetage et d'emballage (suite)

ISIC-BASED CODE - CODE BASE CITI
3411-25

Unit : Thousand metric tons   Unité : Milliers de tonnes métriques

Country or area	1990	1991	1992	1993	1994	1995	1996	1997	1998	1999	Pays ou zone
Bulgaria	...	197	135	126	134	135	135	135	135	135	Bulgarie
Croatia	..	...	...	...	...	74	76	137	135	138	Croatie
Denmark	195	207	200	246	252	252	252	269	254	272	Danemark
Czechoslovakia(former)	671	598	..	..	..	..	..	..	..	..	Tchécoslovaquie(anc.)
Czech Republic	..	..	...	317	406	426	430	450	434	451	République tchèque
Estonia	..	...	33	33	33	33	33	35	43	48	Estonie
Finland	2324	2252	2373	2492	2740	2605	2667	2895	2869	2970	Finlande
France	3131	3356	3342	3477	3838	3767	3842	4074	4347	4500	France
Germany	..	4685	5019	5024	5275	5348	5562	5953	5983	6168	Allemagne
Greece	109	117	117	325	325	325	325	320	462	480	Grèce
Hungary	223	195	198	175	207	173	182	202	...	217	Hongrie
Ireland	35	36	...	...	...	...	...	...	42	42	Irlande
Italy	2638	2706	2816	2826	3120	3136	3207	3702	3812	3945	Italie
Latvia	..	...	43	6	1	2	4	10	14	17	Lettonie
Lithuania	..	...	...	...	...	...	...	7	25	28	Lituanie
Netherlands	1484	1545	1561	1588	1631	1627	1650	1739	1787	1844	Pays-Bas
Norway	470	371	370	394	466	471	438	398	501	494	Norvège
Poland	656	636	710	734	692	726	697	747	886	815	Pologne
Portugal	455	442	475	428	444	471	463	469	511	518	Portugal
Romania	289	196	196	196	145	152	199	198	181	181	Roumanie
Russian Federation	..	...	2664	1996	1398	1515	1046	1199	1242	1605	Fédération de Russie
Slovakia	..	...	...	20	76	81	103	119	205	210	Slovaquie
Slovenia	..	...	209	224	254	242	252	133	120	120	Slovénie
Spain	1812	1911	1905	1918	1985	2052	2201	2293	1709	1788	Espagne
Sweden	3974	3986	3949	4067	4495	4456	4246	4447	4429	4527	Suède
Switzerland	445	431	449	479	586	540	563	599	608	661	Suisse
Ukraine	..	...	...	...	...	...	105	77	77	77	Ukraine
United Kingdom	2024	2106	2148	2137	2375	2534	2513	2617	2590	2527	Royaume-Uni
Yugoslavia	..	...	...	...	...	...	..	42	42	42	Yougoslavie
T.F.Yug.Rep. Macedonia	..	...	...	11	14	19	12	12	12	13	L'ex-RY Macédoine
Yugoslavia, SFR	204	..	..	..	..	..	..	..	..	..	Yougoslavie, RSF
USSR (former)	4796	..	..	..	..	..	..	..	..	..	URSS (anc.)
Oceania	**1406**	**1469**	**1427**	**1514**	**1592**	**1603**	**1720**	**1850**	**1855**	**1835**	Océanie
Australia	1067	1099	1135	1135	1196	1210	1344	1452	1482	1475	Australie
New Zealand	339	370	292	379	396	393	376	398	373	360	Nouvelle-Zélande
Total	**99072**	**104516**	**108699**	**110166**	**80175**	**87051**	**88741**	**94479**	**134626**	**139994**	**Total**

General Note.
Machine-made paper and paperboard of high mechanical strength, consisting
mainly of soda or sulphate pulp. It may be coloured in the mass and may contain
a certain amount of bleached pulp. This heading applies only to kraft paper when
in strips or rolls exceeding 15 cm in width or in rectangular sheets of which
one side exceeds 36 cm. (SITC, Rev.3: 64140-0).
Source: Food and Agriculture Organization of the United Nations (FAO), Rome.

Remarque générale.
Papier et carton fabriqués à la machine, ayant une résistance mécanique élevée,
fabriqués principalement à partir de pâte à la soude ou au sulfate, éventuellement
teintés dans la masse et contenant une certaine quantité de pâte blanchie. Cette
rubrique ne comprend que le papier kraft en rouleaux dont la largeur est
supérieure à 15 cm ou en feuilles dont la dimension d'un côté au moins est
supérieure à 36 cm. (CTCI, Rev.3: 64140-0).
Source: Organisation des Nations Unies pour l'alimentation et l'agriculture
(FAO), Rome.

[1] Including Hong-Kong, Macao and Taiwan.

[1] Y compris Hong-Kong, Macao et Taïwan.

Cigarette paper
Papier à cigarettes

ISIC-BASED CODE - CODE BASE CITI

3411-28

Unit : Metric tons

Unité : Tonnes métriques

Country or area	1990	1991	1992	1993	1994	1995	1996	1997	1998	1999	Pays ou zone
America, North	**3258**	**2884**	**2706**	**2812**	**2578**	**2418**	**2275**	**2132**	**1988**	**1845**	**Amérique du Nord**
Mexico	3258	2884	2706	2812	2578	...	...	...	...	...	Mexique
America, South	**2031**	**3766**	**1907**	**9900**	**7921**	**2057**	**3766**	**1243**	**1301**	**2500**	**Amérique du Sud**
Colombia	2031	...	1907	9900	7921	2057	...	1243	1301	...	Colombie
Asia	**31127**	**29639**	**57831**	**38083**	**36037**	**46571**	**34692**	**32954**	**35309**	**31198**	**Asie**
Indonesia	8915	6272	38233	19115	22894	32725	...	19688	...	...	Indonésie
Japan [1]	18348	19322	15967	13947	10973	11130	11562	...	...	...	Japon [1]
Turkey	3864	4045	3631	5021	2170	2716	2010	6255	7550	4743	Turquie
Europe	**45193**	**46419**	**41618**	**35867**	**34889**	**40632**	**35038**	**34450**	**35743**	**36915**	**Europe**
Belarus	..	996	800	115	161	271	100	0	0	...	Bélarus
Croatia	..	8090	5357	5846	3280	5123	1066	0	...	...	Croatie
Czechoslovakia(former)	4071	3642		..	..	..	..	..	..	..	Tchécoslovaquie(anc.)
Finland	8626	8506	9225	9479	10754	13272	14436	...	...	...	Finlande
Germany	..	...	...	...	...	30	...	...	...	...	Allemagne
Poland	3461	2180	559	723	432	404	236	179	148	36	Pologne
Russian Federation	..	...	868	662	352	396	187	280	496	905	Fédération de Russie
Spain	18377	18637	20025	15057	...	...	...	...	...	...	Espagne
Ukraine	..	3802	4754	3955	1856	3112	959	235	326	183	Ukraine
Yugoslavia, SFR	10658	..	..	..	..	..	..	..	..	..	Yougoslavie, RSF
Total	**81609**	**82708**	**104062**	**86662**	**81425**	**91678**	**75771**	**70779**	**74342**	**72458**	**Total**

General Note.

Cigarette paper in rolls exceeding 15 cm in width or in rectangular sheets of which at least one side exceeds 36 cm. It is a specially made tissue, strong, opaque, generally white but occasionally coloured, containing fillers such as calcium or magnesium carbonate. Its rate of combustion varies. The pulp from which this paper is made is very carefully refined and is drawn on narrow gauge machines. (SITC, Rev.3: 64155-1).

[1] Shipments.

Remarque générale.

Papier à cigarettes en rouleaux d'une largeur supérieure à 15 cm ou en feuilles rectangulaires dont une dimension au moins est supérieure à 36 cm. C'est un papier de soie spécial, solide, opaque, généralement blanc mais parfois coloré, contenant une charge d'un produit tel que le carbonate de calcium ou de magnésium. Sa vitesse de combustion est variable. Le papier est fabriqué sur des machines étroites, à partir d'une pâte raffinée avec soin. (CTCI, Rev.3: 64155-1).

[1] Expéditions.

Other machine-made paper and paperboard, simply finished
Autres papiers et cartons fabriqués à la machine simplement finis

ISIC-BASED CODE - CODE BASE CITI

3411-31

Unit : Thousand metric tons

Unité : Milliers de tonnes métriques

Country or area	1990	1991	1992	1993	1994	1995	1996	1997	1998	1999	Pays ou zone
Africa	**104**	**92**	**120**	**134**	**214**	**184**	**184**	**252**	**260**	**284**	**Afrique**
Algeria	...	...	...	...	...	...	...	...	...	3	Algérie
Dem. Rep. of Congo	1	1	3	3	3	3	3	3	3	3	Rép. dém. du Congo
Egypt	22	...	...	...	6	6	6	...	...	...	Egypte
Madagascar	3	2	2	2	1	1	1	1	...	...	Madagascar
Morocco	1	...	...	...	...	...	...	...	...	...	Maroc
South Africa	4	4	30	50	130	100	100	...	...	...	Afrique du Sud
Sudan	1	2	2	2	2	2	2	2	2	2	Soudan
Uganda	3	3	3	3	3	3	3	3	3	3	Ouganda
Zambia	1	1	1	2	1	...	...	1	1	1	Zambie
Zimbabwe	65	65	65	58	64	64	64	64	52	56	Zimbabwe
America, North	**3832**	**3666**	**4016**	**4063**	**41538**	**46680**	**43510**	**45633**	**7243**	**7515**	**Amérique du Nord**
Cuba	26	25	14	13	13	13	13	13	13	13	Cuba
El Salvador	...	...	...	...	...	...	17	17	17	17	El Salvador
Honduras	...	...	...	...	...	4	10	4	2	2	Honduras
Mexico	38	38	32	...	...	24	24	23	24	21	Mexique
United States	3738	3574	3943	3996	41472	46622	43446	45576	7187	7462	Etats-Unis
America, South	**921**	**473**	**491**	**407**	**547**	**565**	**503**	**556**	**434**	**440**	**Amérique du Sud**
Argentina	41	47	82	61	99	37	48	13	25	25	Argentine
Bolivia	...	...	...	...	...	2	2	2	2	2	Bolivie
Brazil	634	201	196	183	228	230	214	263	308	337	Brésil
Chile	13	9	19	15	5	17	13	10	8	11	Chili
Colombia	55	...	31	18	21	24	14	25	28	29	Colombie
Ecuador	5	28	35	22	11	12	12	13	13	13	Equateur
Paraguay	3	3	2	2	2	2	2	2	2	2	Paraguay
Peru	...	...	...	...	2	3	3	3	11	11	Pérou
Uruguay	7	1	1	1	1	...	...	3	5	6	Uruguay
Venezuela	...	...	121	100	176	235	192	222	32	4	Venezuela
Asia	**8389**	**9227**	**9264**	**14008**	**12866**	**9946**	**9592**	**9123**	**9497**	**12858**	**Asie**
Bangladesh	20	20	6	27	28	10	10	...	...	...	Bangladesh
China[1]	5022	5550	5748	10411	9022	5915	5937	6052	6009	9251	Chine[1]
India	38	41	44	46	90	92	92	90	115	125	Inde
Indonesia	163	211	285	328	383	445	119	243	212	134	Indonésie
Iran(Islamic Rep. of)	139	160	130	195	120	120	120	120	...	...	Iran(Rép. islamique)
Japan	2277	2350	2229	2163	2216	2186	2118	1160	1981	2020	Japon
Korea, Republic of	384	483	520	519	564	607	626	868	463	632	Corée, République de
Malaysia	53	30	4	4	31	58	9	10	3	3	Malaisie
Nepal	13	13	13	13	13	13	13	13	13	13	Népal
Pakistan	64	53	64	64	101	133	140	186	206	220	Pakistan
Philippines	13	10	14	14	14	33	33	33	8	9	Philippines
Singapore	80	85	85	96	97	87	87	87	87	87	Singapour
Sri Lanka	...	...	...	...	...	4	5	5	5	5	Sri Lanka
Thailand	87	...	109	111	175	231	272	231	246	217	Thaïlande
Turkey	28	24	5	6	4	5	4	6	8	5	Turquie
Viet Nam	5	7	4	7	4	7	7	7	7	7	Viet Nam
Europe	**3228**	**4737**	**4858**	**4586**	**3949**	**4392**	**4079**	**4371**	**4772**	**4950**	**Europe**
Albania	31	31	31	31	31	31	31	31	31	31	Albanie
Austria	54	41	46	44	46	45	44	47	71	68	Autriche
Belgium-Luxembourg	51	64	52	52	36	36	39	39	123	130	Belgique-Luxembourg
Croatia	..	...	100	112	241	89	94	71	69	75	Croatie
Denmark	..	...	...	...	...	...	...	...	8	23	Danemark
Czechoslovakia(former)	349	311	..	..	..	...	...	..	..	..	Tchécoslovaquie(anc.)
Czech Republic	..	..	...	188	32	32	2	18	31	28	République tchèque
Finland	368	357	376	395	434	413	423	459	420	400	Finlande
France	402	385	350	364	273	377	282	276	276	280	France
Germany	..	987	921	933	954	1004	1011	1102	1137	1170	Allemagne
Greece	52	57	57	44	44	44	44	...	...	...	Grèce
Hungary	72	63	18	19	16	30	2	5	250	2	Hongrie
Italy	261	253	305	313	326	352	359	373	373	373	Italie
Latvia	..	..	...	...	...	...	...	2	...	...	Lettonie

For general note and footnotes, see end of table.

Voir la fin du tableau pour la remarque générale et les notes.

Other machine-made paper and paperboard, simply finished (continued)
Autres papiers et cartons fabriqués à la machine simplement finis (suite)

ISIC-BASED CODE - CODE BASE CITI

3411-31

Unit : Thousand metric tons

Unité : Milliers de tonnes métriques

Country or area	1990	1991	1992	1993	1994	1995	1996	1997	1998	1999	Pays ou zone
Lithuania	..	...	50	29	21	27	31	10	...	0	Lituanie
Norway	60	66	50	41	40	44	42	72	...	0	Norvège
Poland	20	20	23	27	144	167	211	235	208	367	Pologne
Portugal	105	102	68	7	9	9	14	14	8	10	Portugal
Romania	50	34	34	34	23	87	12	11	10	10	Roumanie
Russian Federation	..	...	1220	865	471	533	418	411	390	574	Fédération de Russie
Slovakia	..	..	...	173	46	49	62	58	57	66	Slovaquie
Slovenia	..	...	2	1	22	21	22	9	11	11	Slovénie
Spain	397	418	313	260	252	387	302	302	366	423	Espagne
Sweden	234	216	204	207	18	17	22	147	128	125	Suède
Switzerland	50	50	50	30	20	105	110	...	...	...	Suisse
Ukraine	..	...	...	...	...	...	110	102	102	102	Ukraine
United Kingdom	276	240	248	284	315	353	361	415	464	515	Royaume-Uni
Yugoslavia	..	...	...	...	...	...	...	3	3	3	Yougoslavie
T.F.Yug.Rep. Macedonia	..	...	...	7	8	13	8	8	0	...	L'ex-RY Macédoine
Yugoslavia, SFR	378	..	..	..	..	..	..	..	..	..	Yougoslavie, RSF
USSR (former)	2582	..	..	..	..	..	..	..	..	..	URSS (anc.)
Oceania	43	43	12	13	72	74	45	38	40	40	Océanie
Australia	...	...	2	2	60	60	...	...	...	...	Australie
New Zealand	12	12	10	11	12	14	14	7	9	9	Nouvelle-Zélande
Total	19099	18237	18760	23211	59186	61841	57913	59973	22246	26088	Total

General Note.

Includes: kraft papers for waxing, asphalting, waterprofing, laminating, impregnating, spinning or twisting, gumming, etc., papers manufactured principally from furnishes other than sulphate pulp and not included elsewhere, such as rope and jute paper, folder stock, blotting paper, filter paper, photographic sensitizing paper, etc. and paperboards not included elsewhere, such as shoe board, gasket board, transformer board, press textile board, index pressboard, panel board (car), trunk and suitcase board and matrix board. (SITC, Rev.3: 64151-0, 64152-0, 64154-0, 64156-0, 64157-0, 64158-0, 64159-0).

Source: Food and Agriculture Organization of the United Nations (FAO), Rome.

Remarque générale.

Cette rubrique comprend: les papiers kraft destinés à être paraffinés, asphaltés ou imperméabilisés, laminés, imprégnés, filés ou tordus, gommés, etc., les papiers faits principalement avec des matières premières autres que la pâte au sulfate et non décrits ailleurs, tels que les papiers de chanvre et de jute, le papier pour dossier, le papier buvard, le papier fitre, le papier support photographique, etc., et les cartons non décrits ailleurs, notamment les cartons pour l'industrie de la chaussure, les cartons pour joints, les cartons pour transformateurs, les cartons pour apprêts textiles, les cartons pour classeurs, les cartons pour carrosserie automobile, les cartons pour valises et malles, les cartons pour flans de clicherie, etc. (CTCI, Rev.3: 64151-0, 64152-0, 64154-0, 64156-0, 64157-0, 64158-0,64159-0).

Source: Organisation des Nations Unies pour l'alimentation et l'agriculture (FAO), Rome.

[1] Including Hong-Kong, Macao and Taiwan.

[1] Y compris Hong-Kong, Macao et Taïwan.

Fibreboard, compressed
Panneaux de fibres, comprimés

ISIC-BASED CODE - CODE BASE CITI

3411-34A

Unit : Thousand cubic metres   Unité : Milliers de mètres cubes

Country or area	1990	1991	1992	1993	1994	1995	1996	1997	1998	1999	Pays ou zone
Africa	**110**	**109**	**111**	**109**	**87**	**89**	**90**	**83**	**183**	**184**	**Afrique**
Kenya	6	6	6	6	6	6	6	6	6	6	Kenya
Liberia	...	...	...	...	...	...	...	18	30	30	Libéria
Madagascar	5	5	5	5	5	5	5	5	5	5	Madagascar
Mozambique	0	0	3	2	2	...	...	...	...	...	Mozambique
South Africa	52	51	51	51	31	32	32	32	120	120	Afrique du Sud
Tunisia	15	15	15	15	15	15	15	15	15	15	Tunisie
United Rep.Tanzania	6	6	5	4	2	2	2	2	2	2	Rép. Unie de Tanzanie
America, North	**3693**	**3667**	**3943**	**4037**	**4244**	**3814**	**4189**	**4462**	**4666**	**4848**	**Amérique du Nord**
Canada	288	308	290	320	353	292	469	631	820	1029	Canada
Cuba	85	85	85	85	85	85	85	85	85	85	Cuba
Mexico	39	45	35	29	28	...	...	...	...	...	Mexique
United States	3281	3229	3533	3603	3778	3413	3615	3730	3749	3726	Etats-Unis
America, South	**857**	**882**	**943**	**1198**	**1251**	**1126**	**1274**	**1348**	**1374**	**1372**	**Amérique du Sud**
Argentina	53	59	96	250	250	104	181	170	248	248	Argentine
Bolivia	...	...	...	...	...	...	15	11	4	5	Bolivie
Brazil	637	637	637	637	637	637	637	637	637	637	Brésil
Chile	122	140	161	255	309	329	391	464	417	417	Chili
Colombia	15	10	10	10	10	10	10	18	18	13	Colombie
Ecuador	...	...	...	...	...	25	28	31	31	31	Equateur
Peru	0	5	7	13	11	11	11	...	...	...	Pérou
Uruguay	3	1	1	1	1	1	1	1	1	1	Uruguay
Asia	**874**	**1011**	**1348**	**2026**	**2770**	**3505**	**4234**	**5870**	**5160**	**7113**	**Asie**
Bangladesh	5	5	5	5	5	5	5	5	5	5	Bangladesh
China[1]	...	...	...	...	...	1709	1957	2660	2214	3911	Chine[1]
India	46	42	45	33	33	33	33	33	33	33	Inde
Indonesia	1	1	13	13	13	23	23	23	85	85	Indonésie
Iran(Islamic Rep. of)	10	22	16	18	19	22	22	24	23	23	Iran(Rép. islamique)
Israel	...	...	...	...	...	...	25	67	67	67	Israël
Japan	392	385	385	447	448	453	510	838	690	690	Japon
Korea, Republic of	167	293	354	407	506	614	744	750	584	844	Corée, République de
Malaysia	0	0	10	80	200	260	370	700	1000	1000	Malaisie
Pakistan	8	11	8	8	8	11	20	22	22	25	Pakistan
Philippines	36	36	36	36	36	...	...	...	...	...	Philippines
Thailand	82	90	160	201	234	151	189	138	44	46	Thaïlande
Turkey	70	70	100	95	120	131	301	574	357	348	Turquie
Europe	**3329**	**4767**	**5030**	**5283**	**5455**	**6426**	**6353**	**7624**	**9612**	**10217**	**Europe**
Austria	83	81	74	78	94	95	95	119	131	143	Autriche
Belgium-Luxembourg	...	...	...	...	...	...	...	...	501	522	Belgique-Luxembourg
Bulgaria	98	80	45	59	59	59	59	59	59	59	Bulgarie
Denmark	0	0	40	67	79	79	79	79	97	80	Danemark
Czechoslovakia(former)	121	82	..	..	..	..	..	..	..	..	Tchécoslovaquie(anc.)
Czech Republic	..	..	...	89	95	112	98	105	105	70	République tchèque
Estonia	..	...	20	29	35	48	67	13	177	170	Estonie
Finland	88	62	67	76	81	80	72	99	111	121	Finlande
France	200	215	350	375	475	469	475	540	751	813	France
Germany	..	526	538	634	804	804	850	1790	1875	2368	Allemagne
Greece	12	25	30	30	30	30	30	...	...	...	Grèce
Hungary	50	42	35	35	41	54	57	62	61	56	Hongrie
Ireland	160	160	162	162	180	246	274	340	330	369	Irlande
Italy	240	250	250	240	207	800	800	700	1450	1260	Italie
Latvia	..	..	20	20	17	23	23	27	26	24	Lettonie
Lithuania	..	...	50	33	42	51	46	55	55	29	Lituanie
Norway	56	45	43	36	38	36	32	31	32	30	Norvège
Poland	411	400	278	296	339	464	481	556	789	861	Pologne
Portugal	275	325	237	288	334	387	387	387	426	430	Portugal
Romania	184	127	107	107	62	85	84	70	41	41	Roumanie
Russian Federation	..	...	1270	1088	733	715	570	685	605	758	Fédération de Russie
Slovakia	..	..	...	30	20	23	22	23	25	24	Slovaquie
Slovenia	..	...	27	33	54	39	34	63	100	100	Slovénie

For general note and footnotes, see end of table.   Voir la fin du tableau pour la remarque générale et les notes.

Fibreboard, compressed (continued)
Panneaux de fibres, comprimés (suite)

ISIC-BASED CODE - CODE BASE CITI

3411-34A

Unit : Thousand cubic metres

Unité : Milliers de mètres cubes

Country or area	1990	1991	1992	1993	1994	1995	1996	1997	1998	1999	Pays ou zone
Spain	350	360	400	480	550	600	590	590	1140	1135	Espagne
Sweden	191	146	80	67	71	110	106	125	149	177	Suède
Switzerland	44	40	49	36	38	32	30	29	34	33	Suisse
Ukraine	..	...	...	...	...	...	35	42	42	42	Ukraine
United Kingdom	148	163	156	318	400	408	420	460	435	435	Royaume-Uni
Yugoslavia	..	...	...	...	...	25	25	25	25	25	Yougoslavie
Yugoslavia, SFR	106	..	..	..	..	..	..	..	..	..	Yougoslavie, RSF
USSR (former)	2200	..	..	..	..	..	..	..	..	..	URSS (anc.)
Oceania	438	482	495	511	591	596	837	907	950	1068	Océanie
Australia	95	86	86	86	86	86	377	434	501	495	Australie
New Zealand	343	396	409	425	505	510	460	473	449	573	Nouvelle-Zélande
Total	11500	10918	11871	13163	14399	15555	16977	20294	21946	24801	Total

General Note.
Sheet material manufactured from fibres of wood or other ligno-cellulosic
materials, with the primary bond deriving from the arrangement of the fibres and
their inherent adhesive properties, with a density over 0.40 gr./cubic
centimetre (25 lb./cubic foot). It includes semi-hardboard, hardboard and super
hardboard as variously defined. (SITC, Rev.3: 63450-1).
Source: Food and Agriculture Organization of the United Nations (FAO), Rome.

Remarque générale.
Panneaux d'une densité supérieure à 0.4 g/cm^3 (25 livres par pied cube), fabriqués
à partir de fibres de bois ou d'autres matières ligneuses ou cellulosiques, dont
la cohésion est due principalement à l'arrangement des fibres et à leur
adhérence propre. Cette rubrique comprend les panneaux semi-durs, durs et
extra-durs définis ailleurs. (CTCI, Rev.3: 63450-1).
Source: Organisation des Nations Unies pour l'alimentation et l'agriculture
(FAO), Rome.

[1] Including Hong-Kong, Macao and Taiwan.

[1] Y compris Hong-Kong, Macao et Taïwan.

Insulating board
Panneaux isolants

ISIC-BASED CODE - CODE BASE CITI

3411-37A

Unit : Thousand cubic metres · Unité : Milliers de mètres cubes

Country or area	1990	1991	1992	1993	1994	1995	1996	1997	1998	1999	Pays ou zone
Africa	**16**	**16**	**14**	**17**	**14**	**20**	**21**	**21**	**54**	**54**	**Afrique**
Egypt	...	...	3	5	5	5	5	5	18	18	Egypte
Ethiopia,incl.Eritrea	3	3	3	...	...	...	...	...	...	...	Ethiopie,incl.Erythrée
Ethiopia	...	...	...	3	3	3	3	3	...	...	Ethiopie
South Africa	6	6	6	6	4	10	10	10	30	30	Afrique du Sud
America, North	**3643**	**3540**	**3648**	**3433**	**3550**	**3520**	**3225**	**2957**	**3676**	**3676**	**Amérique du Nord**
Canada	486	384	382	430	474	425	425	425	425	425	Canada
United States	3157	3156	3266	3003	3076	3095	2800	2532	3251	3251	Etats-Unis
America, South	**89**	**97**	**101**	**95**	**95**	**106**	**106**	**106**	**108**	**110**	**Amérique du Sud**
Argentina	14	21	...	...	...	...	...	...	...	...	Argentine
Brazil	61	61	61	61	61	61	61	61	61	61	Brésil
Chile	...	...	10	4	4	15	15	...	...	...	Chili
Colombia	4	3	3	3	3	3	3	...	...	...	Colombie
Venezuela	9	9	9	9	9	9	9	...	...	...	Venezuela
Asia	**714**	**721**	**676**	**804**	**757**	**834**	**788**	**904**	**770**	**785**	**Asie**
China[1]	...	...	...	...	8	120	80	22	18	32	Chine[1]
India	3	3	3	3	3	3	3	3	3	3	Inde
Indonesia	...	...	40	50	50	50	50	50	...	...	Indonésie
Israel	10	10	10	10	10	10	10	10	10	10	Israël
Japan	531	544	544	642	640	617	605	779	648	648	Japon
Pakistan	8	5	8	12	16	4	...	...	...	...	Pakistan
Thailand	49	49	10	30	30	30	30	30	30	30	Thaïlande
Europe	**1008**	**1146**	**1325**	**1134**	**918**	**982**	**1022**	**1006**	**1014**	**1055**	**Europe**
Austria	20	20	19	20	24	24	25	31	34	38	Autriche
Belgium-Luxembourg	48	52	48	48	48	48	48	28	30	30	Belgique-Luxembourg
Bulgaria	...	...	7	7	7	7	7	7	7	7	Bulgarie
Croatia	..	..	...	...	...	...	0	2	2	3	Croatie
Czechoslovakia(former)	56	40	..	..	..	..	..	..	..	..	Tchécoslovaquie(anc.)
Estonia	...	...	18	36	44	60	83	4	...	...	Estonie
Finland	60	47	34	38	37	37	40	40	40	42	Finlande
France	75	75	75	75	8	8	37	...	50	60	France
Germany	..	50	50	50	50	50	50	105	110	138	Allemagne
Greece	...	...	...	5	5	5	5	...	...	...	Grèce
Italy	...	...	...	15	15	15	...	...	...	...	Italie
Lithuania	..	...	13	15	17	15	20	15	19	21	Lituanie
Netherlands	22	35	40	39	36	31	27	25	...	...	Pays-Bas
Norway	137	120	114	148	156	130	108	103	106	93	Norvège
Poland	125	110	194	168	176	186	172	177	186	199	Pologne
Portugal	1	1	7	2	2	...	...	...	...	...	Portugal
Romania	156	156	156	156	2	4	4	4	4	4	Roumanie
Russian Federation	..	...	295	71	34	33	19	64	13	13	Fédération de Russie
Slovakia	..	...	...	3	28	31	30	41	41	41	Slovaquie
Spain	80	80	...	...	...	...	...	...	...	...	Espagne
Sweden	135	120	83	67	55	116	116	67	59	44	Suède
Switzerland	39	35	33	67	70	75	110	115	110	120	Suisse
United Kingdom	27	17	...	...	...	...	...	...	...	...	Royaume-Uni
USSR (former)	1940	..	..	..	..	..	..	..	..	..	URSS (anc.)
Oceania	**113**	**128**	**133**	**138**	**161**	**164**	**155**	**156**	**150**	**187**	**Océanie**
Australia	13	13	13	13	13	13	20	...	...	...	Australie
New Zealand	100	115	120	125	148	151	135	138	131	167	Nouvelle-Zélande
Total	**7522**	**5649**	**5896**	**5620**	**5495**	**5626**	**5316**	**5149**	**5771**	**5866**	**Total**

General Note.

Sheet material manufactured from fibres of wood or other ligno-cellulosic materials, with the primary bond deriving from the arrangement of the fibres and their inherent adhesive properties, with a density 0.40 gr./cubic centimetre (25 lb./cubic foot) or less. (SITC. Rev. 3: 63450-2).
Source: Food and Agriculture Organization of the United Nations (FAO), Rome.

Remarque générale.

Panneaux d'une densité inférieure à 0.4 g/cm^3 (25 livres par pied cube), fabriqués à partir de fibres de bois ou autres matières ligneuses ou cellulosiques, dont la cohésion est due principalement à l'arrangement des fibres et à leur adhérence propre. (CTCI, Rev.3: 63450-2).
Source: Organisation des Nations Unies pour l'alimentation et l'agriculture (FAO), Rome.

[1] Including Hong-Kong, Macao and Taiwan.

[1] Y compris Hong-Kong, Macao et Taïwan.

Packing containers of paper or paperboard
Récipients d'emballage en papier ou en carton

ISIC-BASED CODE - CODE BASE CITI

3412-01

Unit : Thousand metric tons
Unité : Milliers de tonnes métriques

Country or area	1990	1991	1992	1993	1994	1995	1996	1997	1998	1999	Pays ou zone
Africa	**1045**	**1069**	**969**	**1086**	**1108**	**1185**	**1183**	**1173**	**1150**	**1267**	**Afrique**
Algeria	127	121	106	118	108	...	...	...	...	...	Algérie
Madagascar	1	1	1	1	...	...	...	...	...	...	Madagascar
Nigeria	...	...	...	...	6	6	...	...	...	...	Nigéria
South Africa	880	911	822	925	957	1035	1044	1036	1016	...	Afrique du Sud
Tunisia	31	30	34	36	36	40	32	35	36	42	Tunisie
America, North	**577**	**646**	**677**	**1526**	**1613**	**1610**	**1731**	**1899**	**2030**	**2169**	**Amérique du Nord**
Mexico	563	572	587	#1446	1525	1515	1656	1759	1877	2003	Mexique
Panama	14	...	90	80	88	95	75	...	...	...	Panama
America, South	**9**	**9**	**9**	**9**	**9**	**9**	**9**	**10**	**7**	**9**	**Amérique du Sud**
Colombia	...	...	...	...	...	...	...	10	7	...	Colombie
Asia	**11045**	**11118**	**11242**	**11392**	**11529**	**11799**	**11829**	**12207**	**11742**	**11959**	**Asie**
Armenia	..	4	2	1	0	0	0	0	0	0	Arménie
Bangladesh	418	75	...	...	...	...	...	...	...	...	Bangladesh
India	2348	2467	2563	2745	...	...	...	...	...	...	Inde
Japan[1]	8275	8568	8426	8394	8748	9019	9048	9425	8961	9180	Japon[1]
Turkey	4	4	4	5	4	3	4	5	4	2	Turquie
Europe	**13781**	**156621**	**156756**	**156947**	**157323**	**158161**	**158076**	**159484**	**139783**	**180163**	**Europe**
Austria	451	301	200	202	208	483	477	500	521	556	Autriche
Belgium	679	742	800	760	691	790	834	892	937	974	Belgique
Croatia	..	99	73	66	69	71	76	76	71	...	Croatie
Czechoslovakia(former)	419	303	..	..	..	..	..	..	..	..	Tchécoslovaquie(anc.)
Czech Republic	..	..	207	182	239	255	271	298	334	297	République tchèque
Finland	249	207	201	214	238	243	257	272	261	246	Finlande
Germany	..	4996	4930	4797	4928	4761	4713	4846	4995	...	Allemagne
Germany(Fed.Rep.)	4705										Allemagne(Rép.féd.)
German D.R.(former)[2]	131	..	..	..	..	..	..	..	..	..	R.D.A. (anc.)[2]
Greece	238	220	334	190	208	237	230	[3]213	228	...	Grèce
Hungary	301	218	188	184	181	202	168	203	218	...	Hongrie
Iceland	10	10	7	...	...	...	...	...	...	...	Islande
Latvia	..	...	...	3	3	3	5	9	11	16	Lettonie
Netherlands[4][5]	...	...	...	1061	1050	1346	1320	1394	1420	1423	Pays-Bas[4][5]
Poland	330	295	284	310	350	409	442	507	584	583	Pologne
Portugal	[6]45	[6]41	312	296	297	293	326	347	330	338	Portugal
Russian Federation	..	...	...	1621	1126	1272	870	1030	1044	1445	Fédération de Russie
Slovakia	..	..	...	44	...	...	233	96	87	70	Slovaquie
Slovenia	..	62	59	63	71	70	73	76	88	84	Slovénie
Spain	1448	1481	1351	1860	2208	2290	2238	2525	2765	2933	Espagne
Sweden	...	...	...	...	...	372	...	591	526	546	Suède
Ukraine	...	...	...	...	...	...	...	...	121247	161193	Ukraine
United Kingdom	...	...	...	3272	3527	3648	3724	4286	4009	...	Royaume-Uni
Yugoslavia	..	145	124	73	71	69	70	77	78	63	Yougoslavie
T.F.Yug.Rep. Macedonia	..	19	14	11	14	12	11	17	20	20	L'ex-RY Macédoine
Oceania	**666**	**666**	**666**	**666**	**666**	**666**	**666**	**666**	**666**	**666**	**Océanie**
Australia	666	...	...	...	...	...	...	...	...	...	Australie
Total	**27123**	**170128**	**170318**	**171625**	**172248**	**173430**	**173493**	**175440**	**155379**	**196233**	**Total**

General Note.
Bags, boxes, cartons and other containers made of paper or paperboard used for the packing, transport, storage or sale of merchandise. (SITC, Rev.3: 64210-0).

Remarque générale.
Sacs, boîtes, cartons et autres récipients fabriqués en papier ou en carton, utilisés pour l'emballage, le transport, l'entreposage ou la vente de marchandises. (CTCI, Rev.3: 64210-0).

[1] Packing containers of paperboard only.
[2] Paper bags and paperboard boxes only.
[3] Incomplete coverage.
[4] Sales.
[5] Beginning 1986, production by establishments employing 20 or more persons.
[6] Paper bags only, including envelopes.

[1] Emballages en carton seulement.
[2] Sacs en papier et boîtes seulement.
[3] Couverture incomplète.
[4] Ventes.
[5] A partir de 1986, production des établissements occupant 20 prsonnes ou plus.
[6] Sacs en papier seulement, y compris les enveloppes.

Sulphur, recovered as by-product
Soufre en tant que sous-produit

ISIC-BASED CODE - CODE BASE CITI

3511-01

Unit : Thousand metric tons

Unité : Milliers de tonnes métriques

Country or area	1990	1991	1992	1993	1994	1995	1996	1997	1998	1999	Pays ou zone
Africa	**375**	**360**	**355**	**370**	**492**	**421**	**445**	**411**	**397**	**383**	**Afrique**
Algeria* [1]	20	20	20	20	20	20	23	23	...	...	Algérie* [1]
Dem. Rep. of Congo* [1]	24	16	11	2	1	...	...	...	...	...	Rép. dém. du Congo* [1]
Egypt* [1]	8	8	8	4	8	10	8	4	...	...	Egypte* [1]
Libyan Arab Jamah.	* [1]14	* [1]14	* [1]14	* [1]13	13	13	13	13	...	...	Jamah. arabe libyenne
South Africa [1]	*233	*228	*222	*252	*372	300	323	293	*278	*264	Afrique du Sud [1]
Zambia* [1]	71	69	75	75	...	...	...	...	...	...	Zambie* [1]
Zimbabwe* [1]	5	5	5	4	5	5	5	5	...	...	Zimbabwe* [1]
America, North	**15379**	**15625**	**16041**	**15104**	**15168**	**17526**	**18332**	**18556**	**19383**	**19726**	**Amérique du Nord**
Bahamas [1]	48	...	...	...	...	...	...	...	...	...	Bahamas [1]
Canada	7753	7821	7309	6077	6731	[1]8953	[1]9490	[1]9480	[1]9694	* [1]10116	Canada
Cuba* [1]	5	4	5	5	4	5	5	5	...	...	Cuba* [1]
Mexico [1]	972	1054	1592	1217	1177	1241	1280	1340	*1387	*1310	Mexique [1]
Netherlands Antilles* [1]	60	43	32	32	43	24	24	28	...	...	Antilles néerlandaises* [1]
Trinidad and Tobago* [1]	5	5	5	5	5	5	5	5	...	...	Trinité-et-Tobago* [1]
United States	6536	6650	7050	7720	7160	7250	7480	7650	8220	8220	Etats-Unis
America, South	**663**	**784**	**827**	**846**	**820**	**1068**	**1177**	**1427**	**1649**	**1813**	**Amérique du Sud**
Brazil* [1]	265	264	279	242	236	213	252	252	...	...	Brésil* [1]
Chile [1]	*187	278	306	385	*350	*588	*587	*768	*899	*1040	Chili [1]
Colombia* [1]	8	9	9	12	12	15	16	16	...	...	Colombie* [1]
Ecuador* [1]	10	10	10	10	10	10	10	10	...	...	Equateur* [1]
Peru* [1]	66	66	66	60	60	60	60	60	...	...	Pérou* [1]
Uruguay* [1]	2	2	2	2	2	2	2	2	...	...	Uruguay* [1]
Venezuela	* [1]125	* [1]155	* [1]155	* [1]135	*150	* [1]180	* [1]250	* [1]319	[1]425	* [1]450	Venezuela
Asia	**8307**	**13769**	**11128**	**12827**	**11657**	**12972**	**13443**	**14488**	**17659**	**16755**	**Asie**
Bahrain	4	3	4	4	4	4	35	31	29	31	Bahreïn
China* [1]	650	650	650	700	820	940	1100	1400	1450	1580	Chine* [1]
India* [1]	106	118	142	154	213	235	225	...	...	...	Inde* [1]
Indonesia	1481	6836	4109	4205	[1]3500	[1]3500	[1]3500	[1]3500	6427	...	Indonésie
Iran(Islamic Rep. of)* [1]	680	700	750	800	880	890	890	900	900	910	Iran(Rép. islamique)* [1]
Iraq* [1]	380	50	100	200	225	225	225	220	200	...	Iraq* [1]
Israel* [1]	64	66	60	60	60	60	60	60	...	...	Israël* [1]
Japan [1]	2580	2590	2710	2893	*2900	*3022	*3104	*3341	*3402	*3423	Japon [1]
Kazakhstan* [1]	..	...	...	458	480	386	654	917	1150	1320	Kazakhstan* [1]
Korea,Dem.Ppl's.Rep.* [1]	30	30	30	30	...	...	...	...	...	...	Corée,Rép.pop.dém.de* [1]
Korea, Republic of* [1]	286	294	360	463	450	455	460	465	470	480	Corée, République de* [1]
Kuwait [1]	*350	*30	*50	*175	*200	*559	*595	675	*665	*675	Koweït [1]
Pakistan* [1]	25	26	26	27	27	27	27	27	...	...	Pakistan* [1]
Philippines [1]	120	119	111	147	125	125	125	125	...	...	Philippines [1]
Saudi Arabia [1]	1435	2000	1630	2400	1630	*2400	*2300	*2400	*2300	*2400	Arabie saoudite [1]
Singapore* [1]	65	75	75	75	...	...	...	...	...	...	Singapour* [1]
Syrian Arab Republic* [1]	30	30	10	10	10	10	10	...	...	...	Rép. arabe syrienne* [1]
Turkey* [1]	21	22	22	26	30	31	30	...	...	...	Turquie* [1]
Europe	**4782**	**7335**	**6922**	**7255**	**7001**	**7758**	**7615**	**8456**	**9564**	**10069**	**Europe**
Austria* [1]	18	18	17	17	16	11	10	9	...	...	Autriche* [1]
Belgium* [1]	310	300	300	300	300	347	406	430	428	408	Belgique* [1]
Bulgaria* [1]	60	50	50	50	50	...	...	...	...	...	Bulgarie* [1]
Denmark [1]	[2]12	[2]6	7	[2]10	10	8	7	11	...	...	Danemark [1]
Czechoslovakia(former) [1]	40	...	..	..	..	..	..	..	..	..	Tchécoslovaquie(anc.) [1]
Estonia	..	1	1	2	2	2	2	2	1	...	Estonie
Finland	46	40	38	34	43	39	51	...	...	...	Finlande
France	[3]919	[3]1056	[3]1034	* [1]1260	* [1]1180	* [1]1170	* [1]1090	* [1]1060	* [1]1110	* [1]1100	France
Germany	..	1187	1139	1171	1121	* [1]1110	* [1]1110	* [1]1160	* [1]1180	* [1]1190	Allemagne
Germany(Fed.Rep.)	1140	..	..	..	..	..	..	..	..	..	Allemagne(Rép.féd.)
German D.R.(former)	100	..	..	..	..	..	..	..	..	..	R.D.A. (anc.)
Greece* [1]	140	131	125	125	125	...	...	...	...	...	Grèce* [1]
Hungary	22	18	27	30	31	...	...	...	...	...	Hongrie
Italy* [1]	297	280	280	300	300	530	551	609	624	678	Italie* [1]
Netherlands* [1]	410	415	415	415	425	484	499	577	563	574	Pays-Bas* [1]
Norway [1]	*90	*90	*90	*90	90	...	...	...	...	...	Norvège [1]

For general note and footnotes, see end of table.

Voir la fin du tableau pour la remarque générale et les notes.

Sulphur, recovered as by-product (continued)
Soufre en tant que sous-produit (suite)

ISIC-BASED CODE - CODE BASE CITI
3511-01

Unit : Thousand metric tons   Unité : Milliers de tonnes métriques

Country or area	1990	1991	1992	1993	1994	1995	1996	1997	1998	1999	Pays ou zone
Poland* [1]	228	228	225	249	162	166	133	300	318	334	Pologne* [1]
Portugal* [1]	3	4	4	4	4	4	4	3	...	...	Portugal* [1]
Romania	7	5	9	8	31	35	24	26	30	14	Roumanie
Russian Federation	..	2695	2383	2424	2334	2764	2519	2988	3986	4455	Fédération de Russie
Spain* [1]	399	359	350	352	352	382	505	543	563	567	Espagne* [1]
Sweden* [1]	165	165	165	165	165	...	...	...	...	...	Suède* [1]
Switzerland* [1]	4	4	3	3	3	...	...	...	...	...	Suisse* [1]
Ukraine	..	38	25	33	44	36	37	30	32	21	Ukraine
United Kingdom [1]	199	205	235	...	...	...	...	...	...	...	Royaume-Uni [1]
Yugoslavia, SFR [1]	173	..	..	..	..	..	..	..	..	..	Yougoslavie, RSF [1]
USSR (former) [1]	4125	..	..	..	..	..	..	..	..	..	URSS (anc.) [1]
Oceania	**296**	**301**	**373**	**391**	**392**	**298**	**362**	**509**	**542**	**475**	**Océanie**
Australia* [1]	293	298	370	384	390	298	362	509	542	475	Australie* [1]
New Zealand	[1]3	[1]3	...	[1]7	2	0	0	...	...	...	Nouvelle-Zélande
Total	**33927**	**38173**	**35645**	**36793**	**35529**	**40042**	**41373**	**43847**	**49194**	**49221**	**Total**

General Note.

Sulphur recovered as by-product in the purification of coal-gas, in petroleum refineries and gas plants and from copper, lead and zinc sulphide ores. (SITC, Rev.3: 27411-2).

Remarque générale.

Soufre récupéré comme sous-produit lors de la purification du gaz de houille, dans les raffineries de pétrole et les usines à gaz et lors du traitement des minerais sulfurés de cuivre, de plomb et de zinc. (CTCI, Rev.3: 27411-2).

[1] Source: U. S. Geological Survey, (Washington, D. C.).
[2] Sales.
[3] Crude sulfur and sulfur recovered in petroleum refineries.

[1] Source: U.S. Geological Survey, (Washington, D.C.).
[2] Ventes.
[3] Soufre sorti des raffineries françaises et des vapocraqueurs intégrés.

Sulphur, recovered from pyrites etc.
Soufre de récupération

ISIC-BASED CODE - CODE BASE CITI

3511-02

Unit : Thousand metric tons

Unité : Milliers de tonnes métriques

Country or area	1990	1991	1992	1993	1994	1995	1996	1997	1998	1999	Pays ou zone
Africa	**721**	**547**	**601**	**559**	**487**	**395**	**406**	**374**	**355**	**335**	**Afrique**
Namibia[1]	209	192	244	171	182	...	...	...	...	...	Namibie[1]
South Africa[1]	452	293	296	323	252	159	184	167	152	141	Afrique du Sud[1]
Zambia*[1]	31	31	32	33	22	28	26	...	...	...	Zambie*[1]
Zimbabwe*[1]	29	31	29	32	31	31	26	21	...	...	Zimbabwe*[1]
America, South	**46**	**66**	**25**	**2**	**0**	**4**	**4**	**4**	**0**	**0**	**Amérique du Sud**
Brazil[1]	46	66	25	2	0	4	4	4	...	...	Brésil[1]
Asia	**10383**	**11885**	**11123**	**12011**	**12434**	**12544**	**12496**	**12653**	**10955**	**10313**	**Asie**
China*[1]	4400	4940	4500	5330	5870	5930	5990	6040	4490	3860	Chine*[1]
India[1]	41	30	30	36	38	40	40	...	...	...	Inde[1]
Japan[1]	53	30	31	29	4	*88	*45	*39	*23	*41	Japon[1]
Kazakhstan*[1]	..	...	...	219	200	71	71	...	...	...	Kazakhstan*[1]
Korea,Dem.Ppl's.Rep.*[1]	230	240	240	240	250	...	...	...	...	...	Corée,Rép.pop.dém.de*[1]
Pakistan	5468	5757	5612	...	...	...	...	...	...	...	Pakistan
Philippines[1]	[2]158	[2]155	[2]64	[2]114	100	100	100	100	...	...	Philippines[1]
Turkey	33	39	40	*27	*27	[1]130	[1]130	...	...	...	Turquie
Uzbekistan	..	554	466	404	333	321	252	278	...	...	Ouzbékistan
Europe	**3162**	**2740**	**2160**	**2204**	**2512**	**2270**	**2143**	**2224**	**2123**	**2173**	**Europe**
Bulgaria	16	14	14	17	15	25	26	25	...	...	Bulgarie
Czechoslovakia(former)[1]	50	...	..	..	..	..	..	..	..	..	Tchécoslovaquie(anc.)[1]
Finland	659	568	667	665	840	875	813	...	...	...	Finlande
Germany(Fed.Rep.)[1]	290	..	..	..	..	..	..	..	..	..	Allemagne(Rép.féd.)[1]
Greece[1]	41	35	*25	*20	*20	...	...	...	...	...	Grèce[1]
Hungary*[1]	1	1	1	1	1	...	...	...	...	...	Hongrie*[1]
Italy[1]	290	214	174	145	130	...	...	...	...	...	Italie[1]
Norway	149	159	125	44	...	...	...	...	...	...	Norvège
Portugal[1]	45	6	5	5	5	5	5	5	...	...	Portugal[1]
Romania[1]	300	300	...	...	...	...	...	...	...	...	Roumanie[1]
Russian Federation*[1]	..	...	390	640	700	450	400	400	254	300	Fédération de Russie*[1]
Spain	[3]950	[3]800	[1]406	[1]327	[1]342	[1]404	[1]438	[1]424	[1]430	* [1]388	Espagne
Sweden[1]	121	89	53	*40	*40	...	...	...	...	...	Suède[1]
Yugoslavia, SFR[1]	250	..	..	..	..	..	..	..	..	..	Yougoslavie, RSF[1]
USSR (former)[1]	1900	..	..	..	..	..	..	..	..	..	URSS (anc.)[1]
Total	**16212**	**15239**	**13909**	**14776**	**15434**	**15213**	**15049**	**15255**	**13433**	**12820**	**Total**

General Note.
Sulphur content of iron and copper pyrites, including pyrite concentrates obtained from copper, lead and zinc ores. (SITC,Rev.3: 27411-3).

Remarque générale.
Soufre contenu dans les pyrites de fer et de cuivre, y compris celui des concentrés de pyrites obtenus à partir des minerais de cuivre, de plomb et de zinc. (CTCI, Rev.3: 27411-3).

[1] Source: U. S. Geological Survey, (Washington, D. C.).
[2] Twelve months ending 30 June of year stated.
[3] Sulphur from iron pyrites only.

[1] Source: U. S. Geological Survey, (Washington, D.C.).
[2] Période de douze mois finissant le 30 juin de l'année indiquée.
[3] Soufre provenant de pyrites de fer seulement.

Styrene
Styrène

ISIC-BASED CODE - CODE BASE CITI

3511-03

Unit : Thousand metric tons

Unité : Milliers de tonnes métriques

Country or area	1990	1991	1992	1993	1994	1995	1996	1997	1998	1999	Pays ou zone
America, North	**4416**	**4461**	**4862**	**5132**	**5908**	**5949**	**6171**	**5936**	**5947**	**7051**	**Amérique du Nord**
Canada	780.0	...	...	...	...	...	...	...	...	...	Canada
United States	3636.3	3680.5	4082.2	4352.0	[1]5127.6	[1]5169.3	[1]5391.0	[1]5155.6	[1]5166.6	...	Etats-Unis
America, South	**71**	**77**	**78**	**81**	**85**	**103**	**105**	**94**	**104**	**112**	**Amérique du Sud**
Argentina	71.3	77.0	78.0	81.2	84.9	103.3	105.0	94.3	104.3	112.2	Argentine
Asia	**2642**	**3205**	**3537**	**3512**	**3995**	**4374**	**4776**	**5164**	**5024**	**5370**	**Asie**
Azerbaijan	..	22.9	8.7	2.3	0.0	0.0	0.5	0.7	0.0	0.0	Azerbaïdjan
India	25.4	20.6	28.2	6.2	1.7	12.9	4.8	...	...	...	Inde
Japan	2161.1	2227.0	2182.3	2166.8	2621.6	2939.1	3085.4	3035.3	2770.1	3054.7	Japon
Kazakhstan	..	203.9	92.3	77.8	32.1	46.5	25.7	7.3	...	...	Kazakhstan
Korea, Republic of	436.1	727.5	1215.0	1248.5	1329.0	1365.1	1648.5	2110.2	2243.5	2304.6	Corée, République de
Turkey	18.9	2.6	...	...	...	...	...	...	...	...	Turquie
Europe	**2584**	**3860**	**3756**	**3678**	**3973**	**3167**	**3215**	**3850**	**3291**	**3443**	**Europe**
Bulgaria	32.5	25.0	19.9	24.4	24.2	31.3	28.7	28.6	...	...	Bulgarie
Croatia	..	6.4	1.4	0.0	0.0	0.0	0.0	...	...	...	Croatie
Czechoslovakia(former)	100.5	...	..	..	..	..	..	...	...	...	Tchécoslovaquie(anc.)
Czech Republic	..	..	...	...	88.3	87.2	88.4	90.5	97.5	113.0	République tchèque
France	740.2	...	...	...	...	...	...	...	...	...	France
Germany	..	...	...	...	[1]1150.7	409.2	474.3	[1]1100.0	505.8	...	Allemagne
German D.R.(former)	61.8	..	..	..	..	..	...	...	...	..	R.D.A. (anc.)
Italy	365.0	334.9	374.5	449.0	471.7	426.4	...	...	...	...	Italie
Netherlands[2][3]	...	...	...	...	...	784.9	...	...	...	...	Pays-Bas[2][3]
Poland	70.0	[1]46.0	[1]50.0	...	...	...	...	...	...	...	Pologne
Romania	34.0	21.7	13.7	2.2	6.1	9.0	4.0	2.0	0.0	0.0	Roumanie
Russian Federation	..	387.7	329.2	292.8	254.1	241.2	170.2	162.0	170.6	245.0	Fédération de Russie
Spain	116.4	105.4	109.6	57.5	[1]121.2	[1]105.6	[1]143.0	[1]150.3	[1]161.0	...	Espagne
United Kingdom	270.0	[1]280.0	[1]280.0	...	...	...	...	...	...	...	Royaume-Uni
Yugoslavia, SFR	8.9	..	..	..	..	..	..	...	...	..	Yougoslavie, RSF
USSR (former)	718.8	..	..	..	..	..	..	..	..	..	URSS (anc.)
Total	**10432**	**11602**	**12234**	**12404**	**13961**	**13594**	**14266**	**15045**	**14366**	**15976**	**Total**

General Note.
Pure $C_6H_5.CH=CH_2$. (SITC, Rev.3: 51125-0).

Remarque générale.
$C_6H_5.CH=CH_2$ pur. (CTCI, Rev.3: 51125-0).

[1] Source: United Nations Economic Commission for Europe (ECE), (Geneva).

[2] Sales.

[3] Production by establishments employing 20 or more persons.

[1] Source: Commission économique des Nations Unies pour l'Europe (CEE), (Genève).

[2] Ventes.

[3] Production des établissements occupant 20 personnes ou plus.

Acetylene
Acétylène

ISIC-BASED CODE - CODE BASE CITI

3511-05

Unit : Thousand metric tons

Unité : Milliers de tonnes métriques

Country or area	1990	1991	1992	1993	1994	1995	1996	1997	1998	1999	Pays ou zone
Africa	**8**	**9**	**8**	**7**	**18**	**19**	**21**	**24**	**27**	**30**	**Afrique**
Algeria	[1]1.2	[1]1.3	[1]1.1	[1]1.2	[1]1.3	1.2	1.0	0.9	0.9	0.9	Algérie
Central African Rep.	...	0.9	0.8	0.3	11.0	11.9	...	...	...	...	Rép. centrafricaine
Congo[1]	0.1	0.1	0.1	0.0	...	...	...	...	...	...	Congo[1]
Egypt	[1]1.1	1.0	0.9	1.0	0.9	0.9	0.8	0.8	0.8	1.0	Egypte
Gabon	0.1	0.1	0.1	0.1	0.1	0.1	...	...	...	...	Gabon
Kenya	0.4	0.3	0.4	0.3	0.3	0.3	0.4	...	...	...	Kenya
Madagascar[1]	0.2	0.1	0.1	0.1	...	...	...	...	...	...	Madagascar[1]
Mozambique	[1]0.2	[1]0.2	[1]0.2	[1]0.1	0.1	0.1	0.1	0.2	0.0	0.0	Mozambique
South Africa	4.4	4.3	3.4	2.9	3.2	3.5	3.4	3.5	3.2	3.0	Afrique du Sud
Tunisia	0.5	0.6	0.6	0.6	0.6	0.5	0.5	0.5	0.5	...	Tunisie
America, North	**130**	**139**	**137**	**136**	**129**	**132**	**132**	**131**	**131**	**130**	**Amérique du Nord**
Antigua and Barbuda	0.2	0.2	...	...	...	...	...	...	...	...	Antigua-et-Barbuda
Jamaica	0.3	0.3	0.3	0.2	0.2	0.2	0.2	0.2	0.2	0.2	Jamaïque
Mexico	2.1	2.1	2.0	1.8	1.3	1.2	1.2	1.2	1.2	1.2	Mexique
United States[2]	127.6	136.6	134.6	133.4	126.8	...	...	...	...	...	Etats-Unis[2]
America, South	**10**	**12**	**3**	**6**	**5**	**2**	**3**	**3**	**2**	**1**	**Amérique du Sud**
Argentina	8.1	10.3	1.7	4.2	3.6	0.8	...	...	...	...	Argentine
Chile	0.5	0.5	0.5	0.5	...	...	...	...	...	...	Chili
Colombia	...	...	0.7	0.7	0.6	0.6	...	0.7	0.7	...	Colombie
Peru	...	...	...	...	...	0.4	0.4	0.4	0.4	0.4	Pérou
Asia	**22**	**58**	**49**	**38**	**35**	**32**	**28**	**23**	**21**	**21**	**Asie**
India[1]	11.4	11.2	11.1	...	...	...	...	...	...	...	Inde[1]
Indonesia	1.6	1.7	2.2	2.3	2.2	3.4	...	3.3	1.8	...	Indonésie
Kazakhstan	..	37.4	24.3	15.9	[3]13.0	[3]9.7	6.6	1.0	...	...	Kazakhstan
Korea, Republic of	5.4	5.2	5.4	4.5	4.3	3.5	...	...	...	...	Corée, République de
Myanmar[1][4]	0.1	0.1	0.1	...	...	...	...	...	...	...	Myanmar[1][4]
Sri Lanka	0.3	...	...	...	...	...	...	...	...	...	Sri Lanka
Thailand	0.4	0.4	...	...	...	...	...	...	...	...	Thaïlande
Viet Nam	2.4	1.8	5.3	...	...	...	...	...	...	...	Viet Nam
Europe	**485**	**501**	**570**	**402**	**385**	**474**	**352**	**416**	**433**	**464**	**Europe**
Austria[5][6][7]	...	...	...	...	...	...	...	...	...	2.0	Autriche[5][6][7]
Belgium[8]	1.9	1.9	0.9	0.7	...	...	...	...	...	...	Belgique[8]
Bosnia and Herzegovina[3]	..	..	...	...	0.0	0.1	...	0.3	...	...	Bosnie-Herzégovine[3]
Bulgaria	5.7	3.0	0.3	...	...	...	...	...	...	...	Bulgarie
Croatia	..	1.2	1.2	1.1	[3]1.0	[3]0.9	[3]0.9	0.9	1.0	...	Croatie
Denmark	...	[3][9]2.2	[3][9]1.9	...	...	...	[3]1.4	[3]1.2	[3]1.2	[9]0.0	Danemark
Czechoslovakia(former)	14.5	12.6	..	..	..	..	..	..	..	..	Tchécoslovaquie(anc.)
Czech Republic	..	..	..	..	0.8	2.4	2.7	2.6	3.5	2.8	République tchèque
France	...	...	[1]8.6	[1]6.7	[1][3]6.7	[3]6.8	[3]6.5	[3]6.2	[3]5.9	...	France
Germany	...	...	155.9	102.7	[3]119.2	[3]248.9	[3]164.1	...	...	...	Allemagne
Germany(Fed.Rep.)	226.4	..	..	..	..	..	..	..	..	...	Allemagne(Rép.féd.)
Greece	[1]1.1	[1]0.8	[1]0.9	...	...	...	[3]0.8	[3]0.7	...	...	Grèce
Hungary	4.6	3.5	3.0	2.9	[3]2.9	...	...	...	...	...	Hongrie
Italy	49.3	38.8	15.9	17.1	[3]19.1	[3]19.9	[3]18.6	19.2	19.5	16.9	Italie
Netherlands	...	...	...	...	[3]18.4	[3]7.6	9.0	...	...	...	Pays-Bas
Poland	13.4	13.2	12.6	[10]11.4	[10]10.2	[10]8.6	[10]9.8	[10]10.4	[10]10.9	[10]11.3	Pologne
Portugal	[1]1.2	[1]1.2	1.2	1.0	1.0	[3]1.2	0.9	1.0	...	...	Portugal
Romania	37.8	26.6	12.8	8.9	4.8	4.4	3.9	3.8	3.2	2.0	Roumanie
Russian Federation	..	123.1	198.9	100.7	76.5	51.3	28.0	28.8	31.7	53.1	Fédération de Russie
Slovakia	..	..	3.1	2.8	[3]2.3	[3]2.2	[3]2.2	[3]2.0	9.3	9.1	Slovaquie
Slovenia	..	0.7	0.5	0.4	[3]0.4	[3]0.4	[3]0.5	[3]0.4	0.3	0.3	Slovénie
Sweden	2.3	2.0	2.2	2.1	2.1	2.1	2.1	2.1	2.0	1.7	Suède
Ukraine	..	39.6	35.5	24.4	[3]13.5	[3]8.0	[3]3.9	[3]2.0	[3]2.4	[3]3.2	Ukraine
United Kingdom[3]	...	...	...	...	...	...	87.1	106.8	...	...	Royaume-Uni[3]
Yugoslavia		2.1	1.7	0.9	0.9	1.0	1.2	1.2	0.9	0.7	Yougoslavie
T.F.Yug.Rep. Macedonia	..	0.4	0.3	0.2	0.2	0.2	0.2	0.2	0.2	0.1	L'ex-RY Macédoine
Yugoslavia, SFR	6.4	..	..	..	..	..	..	..	..	..	Yougoslavie, RSF
USSR (former)[3]	256.3	..	..	..	..	..	..	..	..	..	URSS (anc.)[3]

For general note and footnotes, see end of table.

Voir la fin du tableau pour la remarque générale et les notes.

Acetylene (continued)
Acétylène (suite)

ISIC-BASED CODE - CODE BASE CITI

3511-05

Unit : Thousand metric tons

Unité : Milliers de tonnes métriques

Country or area	1990	1991	1992	1993	1994	1995	1996	1997	1998	1999	Pays ou zone
Total	911	719	767	588	572	658	536	597	613	647	Total

General Note.

Pure C_2H_2. (SITC, Rev.3: 51119-1).

Remarque générale.

C_2H_2 pur. (CTCI, Rev.3: 51119-1).

[1] Original data in units of volume.

[2] For chemical use only.

[3] Source: United Nations Economic Commission for Europe (ECE), (Geneva).

[4] Government production only.

[5] 1995 data are confidential.

[6] 1996 data are confidential.

[7] 1997 and 1998 data are confidential

[8] Production by establishments employing 5 or more persons.

[9] Sales.

[10] Compressed acetylene for welding use.

[1] Données d'origine exprimées en unités de volume.

[2] A usage chimique seulement.

[3] Source: Commission économique des Nations Unies pour l'Europe (CEE), (Genève).

[4] Production de l'Etat seulement.

[5] Pour 1995, les données sont confidentielles.

[6] Pour 1996, les données sont confidentielles.

[7] Pour 1997 et 1998, les données sont confidentielles.

[8] Production des établissements occupant 5 personnes ou plus.

[9] Ventes.

[10] Acétylène comprimé pour la soudure.

Benzene (Benzol)
Benzène (Benzol)

ISIC-BASED CODE - CODE BASE CITI

3511-07

Unit : Thousand metric tons   Unité : Milliers de tonnes métriques

Country or area	1990	1991	1992	1993	1994	1995	1996	1997	1998	1999	Pays ou zone
America, North	**6412**	**5925**	**5798**	**6234**	**7652**	**7920**	**7779**	**8513**	**8137**	**9524**	**Amérique du Nord**
Canada	765.0	712.5	685.7	684.8	[1]770.2	726.8	757.6	*715.1	717.9	...	Canada
Mexico	3.0	3.5	2.3	1.3	0.7	...	...	...	...	...	Mexique
United States	[2]5644.1	[2]5209.2	[2]5110.3	[2]5547.6	[2]6881.0	7193.4	7021.7	[1]7797.6	[1]7418.8	...	Etats-Unis
America, South	**752**	**728**	**718**	**688**	**793**	**832**	**804**	**860**	**858**	**1016**	**Amérique du Sud**
Argentina	146.3	152.1	145.0	116.7	112.4	126.0	124.0	118.8	118.9	128.9	Argentine
Brazil	[3]605.7	[3]575.9	[3]572.6	[3]571.1	[4]680.5	[4]705.7	[4]680.1	[4]741.1	[4]739.0	[4]886.8	Brésil
Asia	**3562**	**4041**	**4696**	**4654**	**5122**	**5539**	**5878**	**6601**	**6906**	**7313**	**Asie**
India	60.8	68.4	69.0	73.2	#125.0	141.0	152.0	138.0	144.0	143.0	Inde
Indonesia	...	5.6	...	...	...	...	...	...	...	...	Indonésie
Japan	3011.9	3284.6	3527.1	3327.0	[1]3620.2	4012.7	4176.6	4502.0	4203.1	4458.9	Japon
Kazakhstan	..	39.6	30.0	11.7	[2]2.6	[1]5.5	14.1	16.5	6.3	4.9	Kazakhstan
Korea, Republic of	381.0	560.8	964.4	1138.9	1254.7	1284.6	1406.6	1818.6	2412.2	2572.5	Corée, République de
Turkey	103.1	82.0	99.5	97.2	[1]113.4	[1]89.5	[1]123.1	120.7	134.6	128.6	Turquie
Europe	**6341**	**7855**	**7408**	**5918**	**6236**	**6460**	**6072**	**6123**	**5988**	**6370**	**Europe**
Austria	17.0	[1]18.0	[1]18.0	...	39.8	55.0	34.7	35.9	16.7	...	Autriche
Belarus	..	143.8	84.4	49.2	39.8	55.0	34.7	35.9	16.7	23.4	Bélarus
Belgium	[5]44.0	[5]40.1	[5]39.6	[5]42.2	...	183.0	203.9	168.2	177.4	164.0	Belgique
Bulgaria	77.7	44.9	40.4	37.4	[1]39.3	[1]47.5	51.0	52.2	...	...	Bulgarie
Croatia	..	0.4	...	...	...	[1]10.8	[1]5.6	0.3	0.2	...	Croatie
Czechoslovakia(former)	350.4	256.0	..	..	..	..	..	..	..	..	Tchécoslovaquie(anc.)
Czech Republic	..	..	185.1	206.9	269.1	277.8	303.6	271.4	294.7	296.1	République tchèque
Estonia	..	88.1	59.8	43.4	[1]16.3	[1]49.3	34.3	37.5	23.8	14.5	Estonie
France	647.6	701.6	735.6	728.7	[1]765.3	[1]791.7	[1]895.3	[1]882.4	[1]917.6	...	France
Germany	..	...	...	1518.5	[1]1944.3	1598.8	1597.8	1618.2	1425.0	...	Allemagne
Germany(Fed.Rep.)	1490.7									..	Allemagne(Rép.féd.)
German D.R. (former)	256.1	..	..	..	..	..	..	..	..	..	R.D.A. (anc.)
Hungary	99.0	101.7	99.6	104.6	[1]104.1	...	...	...	205.2	168.5	Hongrie
Italy	612.5	615.3	517.0	496.0	[1]322.0	[1]374.3	...	...	...	...	Italie
Netherlands[6]	1331.0	1201.1	1337.7	# [7]610.0	[7]644.0	[7]789.0	[7]729.0	[7]717.0	[7]739.0	[7]781.0	Pays-Bas[6]
Poland	[1]225.8	[1]162.0	[1]173.0	133.3	[1]128.8	[1]140.9	[1]141.2	147.6	145.9	145.0	Pologne
Portugal[1]	...	...	...	...	56.2	48.1	46.1	43.9	51.0	...	Portugal[1]
Romania	129.4	74.1	51.0	38.7	33.6	38.9	19.1	18.6	18.5	17.1	Roumanie
Russian Federation	..	1173.6	1129.6	941.3	667.2	737.8	492.1	580.5	537.3	748.7	Fédération de Russie
Slovakia	..	..	...	...	[1]51.0	[1]51.3	[1]49.2	45.8	60.8	54.9	Slovaquie
Spain	280.0	239.5	279.6	231.9	[1]299.3	[1]250.1	[1]263.2	[1]279.4	[1]284.4	...	Espagne
Ukraine	..	326.0	258.0	237.8	[1]192.3	[1]183.3	[1]112.9	[1]170.9	[1]171.5	[1]143.9	Ukraine
United Kingdom	702.1	910.9	...	371.7	[1][7]522.4	[1][7]686.7	[1]578.6	[1]565.5	543.9	...	Royaume-Uni
Yugoslavia	...	...	...	..	...	...	[1]1.1	[1]4.0	[1]2.9	0.0	Yougoslavie
Yugoslavia, SFR	20.0	..	..	..	..	..	..	..	..	..	Yougoslavie, RSF
USSR (former)	2135.0	..	..	..	..	..	..	..	..	..	URSS (anc.)
Total	**19202**	**18549**	**18619**	**17494**	**19802**	**20751**	**20534**	**22097**	**21888**	**24223**	**Total**

General Note.
Pure C_6H_6. Includes benzene obtained by dealkylation. (SITC, Rev.3: 51122-0).

Remarque générale.
C_6H_6 pur. Comprend le benzène obtenu par desalkylation. (CTCI , Rev.3: 51122-0).

[1] Source: United Nations Economic Commission for Europe (ECE), (Geneva).

[2] Production by petroleum refiners only.
[3] Production by main establishments only.
[4] Incomplete coverage.
[5] Production by establishments employing 5 or more persons.
[6] Production by establishments employing 20 or more persons.
[7] Sales.

[1] Source: Commission économique des Nations Unies pour l'Europe (CEE), (Genève).

[2] Production des raffineurs de pétrole seulement.
[3] Production des principaux établissements seulement.
[4] Couverture incomplète.
[5] Production des établissements occupant 5 personnes ou plus.
[6] Production des établissements occupant 20 personnes ou plus.
[7] Ventes.

Butylenes, butadiene
Butylènes, butadiène

ISIC-BASED CODE - CODE BASE CITI

3511-09

Unit : Thousand metric tons | Unité : Milliers de tonnes métriques

Country or area	1990	1991	1992	1993	1994	1995	1996	1997	1998	1999	Pays ou zone
America, North	**2944**	**3011**	**3078**	**3145**	**3238**	**3267**	**3288**	**3459**	**3476**	**3546**	**Amérique du Nord**
Canada	...	...	...	...	344.1	373.7	394.6	*565.5	582.6	...	Canada
United States [1]	2893.6	...	...	...	...	...	...	...	...	...	Etats-Unis [1]
America, South	**259**	**220**	**246**	**304**	**333**	**370**	**385**	**433**	**446**	**469**	**Amérique du Sud**
Argentina	54.3	33.7	43.1	74.2	65.9	105.3	119.4	...	...	...	Argentine
Brazil	204.7	186.4	203.2	229.9	267.1	264.4	265.9	297.9	297.7	307.7	Brésil
Asia	**3246**	**3456**	**3671**	**3616**	**3874**	**4355**	**4494**	**4665**	**4487**	**4811**	**Asie**
Azerbaijan	..	42.7	7.1	3.0	[2]2.1	[2]0.0	0.6	[2]0.6	0.2	0.0	Azerbaïdjan
Japan	3070.2	3200.9	3280.1	3111.8	3310.0	3784.5	3867.6	3979.1	3733.9	4024.2	Japon
Korea, Republic of	168.0	204.8	375.9	486.0	546.7	555.3	600.8	658.3	730.9	763.6	Corée, République de
Turkey	8.0	8.0	8.0	...	...	...	[2]25.1	[2]26.9	...	...	Turquie
Europe	**3486**	**4214**	**3903**	**3725**	**3885**	**3866**	**3893**	**3344**	**3395**	**3626**	**Europe**
Bulgaria	[2]17.2	[2]16.2	[2]16.8	17.7	[2]20.2	[2]23.4	27.5	28.5	...	...	Bulgarie
Croatia	..	4.6	5.0	1.6	0.0	0.0	0.0	...	...	...	Croatie
Czechoslovakia(former)	79.3	20.3	..	..	..	..	..	..	..	..	Tchécoslovaquie(anc.)
Czech Republic	..	..	...	...	67.5	117.6	175.2	165.3	[2]135.6	...	République tchèque
France	279.6	283.5	332.7	320.5	349.5	...	[2]474.3	...	...	...	France
Germany	..	[2]1545.5	1504.2	1670.5	[2]1965.2	[2]1657.7	[2]1570.7	1213.4	1343.8	...	Allemagne
Germany(Fed.Rep.)	1503.4	..	...	...	..	...	..	...	...	...	Allemagne(Rép.féd.)
Hungary	...	...	...	...	...	...	[2]93.4	[2]85.1	[2]20.5	17.6	Hongrie
Italy	99.4	142.7	210.4	218.4	182.8	228.0	...	...	...	...	Italie
Netherlands	[3]807.9	[3]771.6	...	[3][4]538.1	[2]592.8	[2]618.2	[2]507.3	[2]470.2	[2]466.5	[3][4]536.1	Pays-Bas
Poland	76.5	36.9	36.4	36.3	31.6	38.1	40.8	43.6	46.8	37.4	Pologne
Portugal [2]	...	...	...	...	101.6	89.5	85.2	95.5	131.3	...	Portugal [2]
Romania	51.3	4.4	...	0.0	0.0	0.0	0.0	0.0	0.0	0.0	Roumanie
Russian Federation	..	783.6	618.9	342.7	236.8	332.1	301.3	222.5	194.4	266.7	Fédération de Russie
Spain	189.6	233.2	...	...	...	...	...	...	...	...	Espagne
United Kingdom	198.1	197.5	...	...	70.4	...	...	...	...	...	Royaume-Uni
Yugoslavia	..	51.7	28.2	0.0	1.5	0.0	26.6	71.4	68.6	25.4	Yougoslavie
Yugoslavia, SFR	67.8	..	..	..	..	..	..	..	..		Yougoslavie, RSF
Total	**9935**	**10902**	**10898**	**10790**	**11330**	**11858**	**12061**	**11901**	**11804**	**12452**	**Total**

General Note.
Pure C_4H_8. Including butene-1, cisbutene-2, transbutene-2 and isobutene. (SITC, Rev.3: 51113-0).

Remarque générale.
C_4H_8 pur. Comprend le butène-1, le cisbutène-2, le transbutène-2 et l'isobutène. (CTCI, Rev.3: 51113-0).

[1] Butadiene and butylene fractions, 1, 3-butadiene, grade for rubber (elastomers) and isobutylene.
[2] Source: United Nations Economic Commission for Europe (ECE), (Geneva).
[3] Production by establishments employing 20 or more persons.
[4] Sales.

[1] Fractions de butadiène et butylène, butadiène -1,3, caoutchouc calibre, et l'isobutylène.
[2] Source: Commission économique des Nations Unies pour l'Europe (CEE), (Genève).
[3] Production des établissements occupant 20 personnes ou plus.
[4] Ventes.

Ethylene
Ethylène

ISIC-BASED CODE - CODE BASE CITI

3511-10

Unit : Thousand metric tons
Unité : Milliers de tonnes métriques

Country or area	1990	1991	1992	1993	1994	1995	1996	1997	1998	1999	Pays ou zone
Africa	**41**	**70**	**53**	**50**	**79**	**95**	**79**	**96**	**68**	**92**	**Afrique**
Algeria	41.0	69.6	53.4	49.6	78.7	95.4	79.4	96.0	68.0	91.8	Algérie
America, North	**18966**	**20549**	**21084**	**20685**	**22965**	**24184**	**25472**	**26410**	**27171**	**30366**	**Amérique du Nord**
Canada	2425.0	2425.3	2521.2	2536.0	2715.7	2861.8	3201.7	*3241.3	3556.7	...	Canada
United States	16541.3	18123.5	18562.9	18149.4	[1]20249.2	[1]21322.4	[1]22270.1	[1]23168.6	[1]23614.4	...	Etats-Unis
America, South	**1786**	**1714**	**1803**	**1995**	**2164**	**2187**	**2200**	**2400**	**2532**	**2721**	**Amérique du Sud**
Argentina	286.4	265.2	297.1	285.2	268.7	306.1	324.1	273.6	276.9	304.6	Argentine
Brazil	1499.7	1448.8	1505.6	1709.5	1895.8	1881.1	1875.7	2126.3	2254.7	2416.0	Brésil
Asia	**9360**	**10461**	**11860**	**12227**	**13198**	**14349**	**15447**	**16898**	**17937**	**19000**	**Asie**
Azerbaijan	..	103.5	8.7	30.3	[1]22.9	[1]31.0	[1]38.8	18.4	24.7	30.0	Azerbaïdjan
China	1572.1	1761.1	2003.4	2027.3	2129.4	2400.5	3039.6	3586.2	3787.0	4350.0	Chine
India	189.5	188.9	225.1	366.6	463.6	495.7	505.0	509.2	994.6	1377.3	Inde
Indonesia	...	...	...	14.0	14.5	...	...	...	...	...	Indonésie
Japan	5809.6	6141.8	6103.2	5772.6	[1]6125.0	6944.5	7137.5	7416.2	7075.5	7086.6	Japon
Kazakhstan	..	65.3	22.2	24.5	...	...	...	...	...	...	Kazakhstan
Korea, Republic of	1054.1	1565.6	2768.7	3273.0	3667.1	3720.9	3967.6	4450.0	5110.0	5216.4	Corée, République de
Qatar	293.9	234.7	332.7	351.6	357.2	293.6	314.9	486.2	490.5	479.0	Qatar
Turkey	426.2	386.0	382.1	367.3	[1]381.2	[1]411.3	[1]392.3	380.4	402.9	408.5	Turquie
Europe	**12829**	**16021**	**16750**	**14751**	**16162**	**14995**	**14108**	**14987**	**15520**	**15474**	**Europe**
Austria	320.0	[1]360.0	[1]340.0	...	...	...	...	...	...	...	Autriche
Belarus	..	135.2	92.7	65.2	80.3	111.3	78.9	104.0	108.1	115.4	Bélarus
Belgium	...	...	...	...	...	700.8	740.5	850.6	947.7	900.1	Belgique
Bulgaria	175.0	111.6	122.1	131.6	[1]151.0	[1]164.3	184.4	184.4	...	...	Bulgarie
Croatia	..	66.9	68.3	68.6	[1]65.3	[1]67.5	[1]64.8	63.5	60.1	...	Croatie
Czechoslovakia(former)	619.5	498.5	..	..	..	..	..	..	..	..	Tchécoslovaquie(anc.)
Czech Republic	..	..	..	..	390.8	373.3	429.9	399.0	452.3	466.3	République tchèque
France	[2]2252.5	[2]2421.4	[2]2654.4	[2]2535.8	[2]2796.9	[2]2667.3	[2]2722.5	[2]2874.0	[1]3003.6	...	France
Germany	...	...	...	3904.8	[1]4182.7	2496.8	2163.2	2368.3	2479.9	...	Allemagne
Germany(Fed.Rep.)	3071.8	..	..	..	..	..	..	..	..	..	Allemagne(Rép.féd.)
German D.R.(former)	325.5	..	..	..	..	..	..	..	..	..	R.D.A. (anc.)
Greece	10.3	11.0	10.4	...	...	...	...	...	...	...	Grèce
Hungary	234.4	254.0	280.9	276.4	[1]274.6	[1]270.4	270.1	299.6	314.9	300.1	Hongrie
Italy	1463.2	1507.4	2316.7	1294.0	1774.5	2255.2	...	...	...	...	Italie
Poland	308.2	271.4	283.1	289.1	[1]235.0	[1]260.0	[1]298.8	307.9	330.2	295.8	Pologne
Portugal[1]	...	...	...	...	291.7	283.6	238.7	336.6	322.4	...	Portugal[1]
Romania	243.0	162.1	127.1	125.7	142.7	161.0	158.6	147.1	153.1	167.4	Roumanie
Russian Federation	..	2149.3	1960.3	1726.4	1405.9	1596.3	1199.7	1255.4	1165.8	1630.6	Fédération de Russie
Slovakia	..	..	..	157.7	[1]209.5	[1]200.3	[1]190.0	188.5	[1]148.2	...	Slovaquie
Spain	1043.1	988.0	1014.9	...	[1]1196.1	[1]1201.3	[1]1239.6	[1]1189.1	[1]1296.1	...	Espagne
Sweden[2]	378.3	337.0	357.4	325.5	[1]379.1	394.5	397.0	384.9	373.2	228.8	Suède[2]
Ukraine	..	432.6	286.5	157.5	[1]187.7	[1]164.7	[1]82.9	[1]138.6	[1]135.5	[1]58.7	Ukraine
United Kingdom	[3]1498.1	[3]1810.1	[1][3]1933.5	[3]849.4	[1][3]1294.2	[1][3]1168.5	[1]1246.6	[1]1350.6	1456.2	...	Royaume-Uni
Yugoslavia	..	133.3	69.7	...	...	...	68.8	159.4	159.4	55.3	Yougoslavie
Yugoslavia, SFR	256.1	..	..	..	..	..	..	..	..	..	Yougoslavie, RSF
USSR (former)[1]	3065.2	..	..	..	..	..	..	..	..	..	URSS (anc.)[1]
Total	**46047**	**48815**	**51551**	**49708**	**54569**	**55811**	**57306**	**60792**	**63227**	**67653**	**Total**

General Note.
Pure C_2H_4. (SITC, Rev.3: 51111-0).

Remarque générale.
C_2H_4 pur. (CTCI, Rev.3: 51111-0).

[1] Source: United Nations Economic Commission for Europe (ECE), (Geneva).

[2] Including acetylene used partly for welding.

[3] Produced from oil base, other than for use as fuel.

[1] Source: Commission économique des Nations Unies pour l'Europe (CEE), (Genève).

[2] Y compris l'acétylène utilisé en partie pour la soudure.

[3] Obtenu à partir de pétrole autre que celui servant de combustible.

Naphthalene
Naphtalène

ISIC-BASED CODE - CODE BASE CITI

3511-11

Unit : Thousand metric tons Unité : Milliers de tonnes métriques

Country or area	1990	1991	1992	1993	1994	1995	1996	1997	1998	1999	Pays ou zone
America, North	**165**	**165**	**165**	**165**	**165**	**165**	**165**	**165**	**165**	**165**	**Amérique du Nord**
Canada	20.0	...	...	...	...	...	...	...	...	...	Canada
United States [1]	145.0	...	...	...	...	...	...	...	...	...	Etats-Unis [1]
America, South	**16**	**20**	**17**	**16**	**15**	**17**	**16**	**14**	**13**	**14**	**Amérique du Sud**
Brazil	14.9	18.9	16.6	15.0	14.7	16.4	15.9	13.3	13.2	13.8	Brésil
Colombia	...	...	0.7	0.6	0.3	0.2	...	0.3	0.3	...	Colombie
Asia	**202**	**210**	**201**	**186**	**190**	**194**	**199**	**207**	**184**	**180**	**Asie**
Japan	202.2	207.7	199.2	184.4	188.0	192.7	197.5	204.7	181.7	177.7	Japon
Kazakhstan [2]	..	...	...	...	2.0	1.4	...	...	...	...	Kazakhstan [2]
Turkey	0.1	0.2	0.2	0.2	[2]0.1	...	...	...	...	...	Turquie
Europe	**794**	**838**	**832**	**807**	**839**	**846**	**846**	**646**	**859**	**991**	**Europe**
Bulgaria	0.8	0.5	0.4	0.3	[2]0.3	[2]0.8	0.7	0.4	...	...	Bulgarie
Croatia	..	0.3	0.1	0.0	0.0	0.0	0.0	...	...	...	Croatie
Czechoslovakia(former)	36.9	...	..	..	..	..	..	..	...	..	Tchécoslovaquie(anc.)
Czech Republic	..	..	...	...	29.1	22.8	20.3	21.3	24.1	23.7	République tchèque
Germany	..	...	80.8	71.9	90.8	...	...	...	...	...	Allemagne
Germany(Fed.Rep.)	92.5	..	..	..	..	..	..	..	..	..	Allemagne(Rép.féd.)
Netherlands [3][4]	...	...	...	...	697.0	722.0	736.0	537.0	746.0	875.0	Pays-Bas [3][4]
Poland	4.6	3.2	4.2	1.8	[2]0.6	...	[2]0.3	0.0	...	...	Pologne
Romania	3.2	1.2	1.8	1.3	0.8	2.7	1.4	1.2	0.6	2.0	Roumanie
Russian Federation	..	...	...	1.4	0.9	1.1	0.4	0.1	0.0	...	Fédération de Russie
Ukraine	..	48.9	43.3	20.0	[2]19.0	[2]13.3	[2]6.1	[2]4.7	[2]6.4	[2]8.7	Ukraine
Yugoslavia, SFR	2.4	..	..	..	..	..	..	..	..	..	Yougoslavie, RSF
USSR (former) [2]	97.8	..	..	..	..	..	..	..	..	..	URSS (anc.) [2]
Total	**1275**	**1232**	**1215**	**1174**	**1209**	**1222**	**1227**	**1031**	**1221**	**1350**	**Total**

General Note.
Pure $C_{10}H_8$ hydrocarbon with two condensed rings. Crude naphthalene is excluded. (SITC, Rev.3: 51129-1).

[1] Petroleum naphthalene only.
[2] Source: United Nations Economic Commission for Europe (ECE), (Geneva).
[3] Production by establishments employing 20 or more persons.
[4] Sales.

Remarque générale.
$C_{10}H_8$. Hydrocarbure résultant de la condensation de deux noyaux. A l'état pur, à l'exclusion du naphtalène brut. (CTCI, Rev.3: 51129-1).

[1] Naphtalène de pétrole seulement.
[2] Source: Commission économique des Nations Unies pour l'Europe (CEE), (Genève).
[3] Production des établissements occupant 20 personnes ou plus.
[4] Ventes.

Propylene
Propylène

ISIC-BASED CODE - CODE BASE CITI

3511-13

Unit : Thousand metric tons | | | | | | | | | | Unité : Milliers de tonnes métriques

Country or area	1990	1991	1992	1993	1994	1995	1996	1997	1998	1999	Pays ou zone
America, North	**10674**	**10491**	**11377**	**10505**	**11587**	**12420**	**12212**	**13348**	**14017**	**14826**	**Amérique du Nord**
Canada	765.0	716.6	753.5	765.8	[1]716.3	756.2	822.4	*859.1	1038.0	...	Canada
United States	9909.4	9774.4	10623.9	9738.9	[1]10870.2	[1]11663.8	[1]11390.1	[1]12488.6	[1]12978.7	...	Etats-Unis
America, South	**891**	**887**	**974**	**1152**	**1280**	**1281**	**1309**	**1495**	**1568**	**1619**	**Amérique du Sud**
Argentina	97.0	108.2	148.0	176.8	194.0	203.8	224.3	...	...	...	Argentine
Brazil	[2]793.5	779.2	826.5	975.0	1086.3	1076.8	1085.0	1219.5	1271.0	1299.3	Brésil
Asia	**5027**	**5523**	**6173**	**6259**	**6708**	**7284**	**7583**	**8358**	**8547**	**9008**	**Asie**
Azerbaijan	..	51.9	4.9	17.7	[1]14.0	[1]20.4	22.6	14.6	14.7	16.4	Azerbaïdjan
Japan	4214.5	4431.4	4535.9	4272.1	[1]4435.0	4956.1	5143.3	5408.6	5100.6	5519.8	Japon
Korea, Republic of	608.3	854.9	1481.7	1808.0	2095.1	2131.4	2244.4	2760.4	3246.9	3281.7	Corée, République de
Turkey	204.3	184.4	150.6	160.8	[1]164.0	[1]176.3	[1]172.7	174.8	185.3	190.0	Turquie
Europe	**7819**	**8973**	**9263**	**9160**	**9644**	**9161**	**8548**	**9104**	**9711**	**9738**	**Europe**
Austria	185.0	[1]210.0	[1]210.0	...	...	...	...	...	...	...	Autriche
Belarus	..	95.9	62.0	42.4	50.3	72.4	55.1	69.8	70.5	74.2	Bélarus
Belgium	...	...	...	...	...	852.9	513.3	[1]563.0	[1]619.6	...	Belgique
Bulgaria	112.1	77.6	75.6	98.2	[1]106.8	[1]117.0	132.5	130.4	...	...	Bulgarie
Croatia	..	15.3	13.3	9.0	[1]7.1	[1]8.2	[1]7.8	7.6	6.5	...	Croatie
Czechoslovakia(former)	288.7	246.0	..	..	..						Tchécoslovaquie(anc.)
Czech Republic	..				197.1	186.8	199.3	195.9	224.5	227.3	République tchèque
France	1437.2	1691.0	1804.7	1651.2	[1]1866.2	[1]1946.9	[2]2044.0	[2]2182.0	[2]2267.4	...	France
Germany	..	[1]1837.1	2220.3	2439.0	[1]2668.1	1608.0	1561.9	1738.2	1952.7	...	Allemagne
Germany(Fed.Rep.)	1826.9	..	..	..	..	..	..	..	..	..	Allemagne(Rép.féd.)
German D.R.(former)	219.5	..	..	..	..	..	..	..	..	..	R.D.A. (anc.)
Greece [1]	7.0	7.0	7.0	...	...	...	...	...	...	...	Grèce [1]
Hungary	167.2	173.3	195.8	195.2	[1]192.8	[1]200.4	[1]211.6	224.9	228.2	207.8	Hongrie
Italy	773.9	778.5	764.4	701.9	698.2	970.2	..				Italie
Poland	192.8	176.9	189.6	187.5	[1]163.5	[1]175.6	[1]194.1	201.6	189.1	197.8	Pologne
Portugal [1]	...	...	...	...	143.2	140.2	112.9	155.5	167.5	...	Portugal [1]
Romania	180.6	109.8	85.4	84.7	120.9	137.4	129.6	149.7	138.4	123.9	Roumanie
Russian Federation	..	929.4	854.1	778.0	582.5	680.6	494.6	543.1	543.2	740.5	Fédération de Russie
Slovakia	..	..	...	...	[1]90.3	[1]93.3	[1]91.1	93.0	...	...	Slovaquie
Spain	643.7	625.0	547.5	..	[1]806.5	[1]810.6	[1]827.2	[1]852.7	[1]930.9	876.7	Espagne
Sweden	170.8	166.0	172.9	147.4	[1]186.9	203.8	217.6	213.3	205.2	120.9	Suède
Ukraine	..	215.7	149.9	77.0	[1]93.9	[1]80.7	[1]35.8	[1]60.6	[1]59.9	[1]25.1	Ukraine
United Kingdom	[3]751.3	[3]792.7	[1][3]832.1	...	773.3	617.6	658.5	596.8	759.1	...	Royaume-Uni
Yugoslavia	..	77.2	40.4	0.0	...	...	32.3	87.9	83.1	29.3	Yougoslavie
Yugoslavia, SFR	119.5	..	..	..	..	..	..	..	..	..	Yougoslavie, RSF
USSR (former) [1]	1345.9	..	..	..	..	..	..	..	..	..	URSS (anc.) [1]
Total	**25757**	**25874**	**27788**	**27075**	**29219**	**30146**	**29652**	**32305**	**33843**	**35190**	**Total**

General Note.
Pure C_3H_6 should be shown at 100 per cent. However, the tonnage of the C_3 cuts should be counted as pure propylene when thepropylene content is at least 90 per cent. (SITC, Rev.3: 51112-0).

Remarque générale.
Exprimé en C_3H_6 pur à 100 p. 100. Néanmoins, les fractions à 3 atomes de carbone seront à compter comme du propylène pur si la concentration de propylène est au moins égale à 90 p. 100. (CTCI, Rev.3: 51112-0).

[1] Source: United Nations Economic Commission for Europe (ECE), (Geneva).

[2] Production by establishments employing 5 or more persons.

[3] Produced from oil base, other than for use as fuel.

[1] Source: Commission économique des Nations Unies pour l'Europe (CEE), (Genève).

[2] Production des établissements occupant 5 personnes ou plus.

[3] Obtenu à partir de pétrole autre que celui servant de combustible.

Toluene
Toluène

ISIC-BASED CODE - CODE BASE CITI

3511-14

Unit : Thousand metric tons
Unité : Milliers de tonnes métriques

Country or area	1990	1991	1992	1993	1994	1995	1996	1997	1998	1999	Pays ou zone
America, North	**3236**	**3220**	**2714**	**2614**	**3356**	**2910**	**2945**	**2954**	**2848**	**2807**	**Amérique du Nord**
Canada	420.0	363.8	371.8	337.1	[1]288.0	[1]260.4	303.1	*320.5	221.9	...	Canada
United States[2]	2816.4	2856.5	2342.4	2276.6	[1]3068.2	...	...	...	...	...	Etats-Unis[2]
America, South	**237**	**231**	**220**	**296**	**314**	**303**	**315**	**410**	**417**	**469**	**Amérique du Sud**
Argentina	67.2	56.3	56.2	117.6	128.3	105.6	112.8	...	...	...	Argentine
Brazil	170.2	174.8	164.2	178.6	[3]185.2	[3]197.8	[3]202.7	[3]262.9	[3]259.4	[3]300.5	Brésil
Asia	**1537**	**1748**	**1976**	**2071**	**2186**	**2355**	**2493**	**2716**	**2558**	**2835**	**Asie**
Japan	1110.5	1150.5	1181.4	1190.7	1219.1	1373.6	1370.3	1418.7	1349.5	1488.0	Japon
Kazakhstan	..	12.6	8.1	5.5	0.5	0.6	1.5	2.6	1.0	0.6	Kazakhstan
Korea, Republic of	407.5	569.2	773.8	859.8	953.7	979.1	1110.9	1294.3	1207.2	1345.8	Corée, République de
Turkey	19.2	16.0	12.5	15.4	[1]12.9	[1]2.1	[1]9.8	0.8	0.4	0.7	Turquie
Europe	**1678**	**2469**	**2326**	**2023**	**2089**	**2092**	**2004**	**2034**	**1965**	**2048**	**Europe**
Belarus	..	113.4	67.3	36.5	14.4	7.7	13.2	9.3	0.2	0.8	Bélarus
Belgium	...	...	...	...	[1]55.8	[1]92.4	92.6	[1]94.4	[1]92.1	78.7	Belgique
Bulgaria	41.4	19.5	28.4	30.5	[1]29.4	[1]34.0	[1]38.4	39.5	...	...	Bulgarie
Croatia	..	...	...	...	...	[1]32.9	[1]18.0	0.0	0.0	...	Croatie
Denmark[4]	...	..	...	0.1	[1]0.1	[1]0.2	0.2	0.3	0.2	0.0	Danemark[4]
Czechoslovakia(former)	53.1	49.0	..	..						..	Tchécoslovaquie(anc.)
Czech Republic	..	..	...	...	35.2	37.7	39.8	28.4	34.4	29.3	République tchèque
Estonia	..	37.4	24.0	18.2	[1]5.1	[1]21.1	11.2	10.8	4.6	4.5	Estonie
France	40.4	34.9	32.0	51.5	[1]56.6	[1]58.2	[1]55.4	[1]55.1	[1]78.8	...	France
Germany	..	[1]595.7	...	449.1	[1]596.9	514.6	[1]703.0	[1]723.6	[1]736.2	...	Allemagne
Germany(Fed.Rep.)	537.1	..	..	..	..	..	..	..	..	..	Allemagne(Rép.féd.)
German D.R.(former)	42.6	..	..	..	..	..	..	..	..	..	R.D.A. (anc.)
Hungary	101.8	90.4	70.4	67.4	[1]74.4	[1]73.3	[1]69.4	58.9	44.2	36.9	Hongrie
Italy	191.9	186.4	129.4	195.7	[1]357.6	[1]440.7	...	...	...	...	Italie
Poland	88.2	64.8	46.3	50.8	[1]43.5	[1]54.9	[1]48.6	53.8	44.3	51.4	Pologne
Portugal[1]	...	...	...	...	144.9	145.2	121.7	113.9	111.3	...	Portugal[1]
Romania	127.7	71.5	53.9	40.3	34.5	36.3	10.3	12.3	10.2	8.3	Roumanie
Russian Federation	..	616.0	589.0	477.1	344.9	289.9	200.1	204.2	162.3	168.0	Fédération de Russie
Slovakia	..	..	...	...	[1]47.5	[1]35.9	[1]43.4	44.9	51.6	42.3	Slovaquie
Spain	95.1	183.6	211.6	...	[1]123.7	[1]101.1	99.8	109.3	[1]110.0	...	Espagne
Ukraine	..	68.9	48.4	32.3	[1]26.9	[1]20.5	[1]20.0	[1]28.4	[1]30.0	[1]29.5	Ukraine
United Kingdom	81.9	70.0	70.0	116.0	84.1	94.5	63.5	[1]65.4	[1]11.3	...	Royaume-Uni
Yugoslavia	..	1.5	0.7	0.0	0.3	0.5	1.0	1.5	1.1	0.1	Yougoslavie
Yugoslavia, SFR	15.8		..	..	..	..	..	..	..	..	Yougoslavie, RSF
USSR (former)[1]	1027.0	..	..	..	..	..	..	..	..	..	URSS (anc.)[1]
Total	**7716**	**7668**	**7236**	**7004**	**7944**	**7660**	**7757**	**8115**	**7789**	**8160**	**Total**

General Note.
Pure methylbenzene $C_6H_5CH_3$ excluding toluene intended for dealkylation. (SITC, Rev.3: 51123-0).

Remarque générale.
Méthylbenzène pur $C_6H_5CH_3$, à l'exclusion du toluène destiné à la desalkylation. (CTCI, Rev.3: 51123-0).

[1] Source: United Nations Economic Commission for Europe (ECE), (Geneva).

[2] Production by petroleum refiners only.
[3] Incomplete coverage.
[4] Sales.

[1] Source: Commission économique des Nations Unies pour l'Europe (CEE), (Genève).

[2] Production des raffineurs de pétrole seulement.
[3] Couverture incomplète.
[4] Ventes.

Xylenes
Xylènes
ISIC-BASED CODE - CODE BASE CITI
3511-15

Unit : Thousand metric tons | | | | | | | | | | | Unité : Milliers de tonnes métriques

Country or area	1990	1991	1992	1993	1994	1995	1996	1997	1998	1999	Pays ou zone
America, North	**3326**	**3257**	**3321**	**3315**	**3596**	**3675**	**3759**	**3835**	**3880**	**3960**	**Amérique du Nord**
Canada	510.0	390.7	339.5	310.9	356.4	398.3	383.9	*361.7	307.6	...	Canada
United States[1]	2815.7	*2866.3	*2981.6	*3003.8	3239.2	...	...	...	...	...	Etats-Unis[1]
America, South	**468**	**412**	**400**	**413**	**420**	**420**	**375**	**416**	**358**	**467**	**Amérique du Sud**
Argentina	137.8	125.6	119.4	114.2	82.9	...	...	...	...	...	Argentine
Brazil[2 3]	330.0	286.5	280.9	299.0	336.8	340.8	307.1	360.1	314.6	435.7	Brésil[2 3]
Asia	**3454**	**3928**	**4715**	**5026**	**5481**	**6335**	**7061**	**8818**	**7579**	**9558**	**Asie**
India	119.5	173.7	164.3	156.5	168.6	194.0	146.9	...	...	...	Inde
Japan	2651.5	2917.7	3208.8	3462.2	3627.2	4154.2	3991.1	4634.0	4339.6	5519.8	Japon
Korea, Republic of	572.6	750.2	1236.4	1296.5	1552.9	1863.8	2779.5	3854.5	2917.6	3714.3	Corée, République de
Turkey	110.5	86.7	105.7	111.3	132.0	122.8	143.4	146.2	133.8	131.8	Turquie
Europe	**2259**	**2829**	**2814**	**2281**	**2585**	**2643**	**2295**	**2295**	**2059**	**2273**	**Europe**
Belarus	..	68.5	48.2	30.6	25.4	21.5	7.6	9.3	0.0	7.5	Bélarus
Belgium	...		...	...	...	...	...	27.9	13.0		Belgique
Bulgaria	22.3	10.3	15.6	16.0	20.9	25.9	26.1	24.8	...	...	Bulgarie
Croatia	..	1.3	...	...	...	26.3	17.1	0.3	0.2	...	Croatie
Czechoslovakia(former)	99.7	63.8	..	..		..	..	..	..	..	Tchécoslovaquie(anc.)
Czech Republic	..	..	..	..	30.5	31.1	29.3	17.4	21.4	17.1	République tchèque
France[4]	189.5	183.6	183.8	173.0	...	...	...	...	...	...	France[4]
Germany	..	[4]544.1	...	561.2	669.7	680.8	713.9	720.2	636.8	...	Allemagne
Germany(Fed.Rep.)	578.8	..	...	..	..	..	..	..	..	..	Allemagne(Rép.féd.)
German D.R.(former)	120.6	..	..	..	..	..	..	..	..	..	R.D.A. (anc.)
Hungary	95.8	81.7	66.0	71.7	69.8	67.8	59.8	53.6	47.6	45.7	Hongrie
Italy	381.2	397.5	322.6	147.9	301.8	341.8	...	...	...	...	Italie
Poland	48.7	51.4	40.4	32.0	28.3	35.8	29.5	36.7	30.9	37.1	Pologne
Portugal	148.3	123.7	126.3	124.7	[4]155.5	[4]150.8	[4]132.4	[4]118.2	[4]126.3	...	Portugal
Romania[5]	174.7	82.5	48.4	24.2	28.7	51.8	20.3	4.3	2.3	2.5	Roumanie[5]
Russian Federation	..	835.2	805.9	652.1	650.7	620.5	525.5	457.6	413.2	435.6	Fédération de Russie
Slovakia	..	..	...	...	[4]68.2	[4]55.2	[4]66.6	71.5	57.8	51.6	Slovaquie
Spain	62.9	62.9	72.4	...	[4]73.4	[4]80.3	[4]73.4	[4]75.2	[4]77.8	...	Espagne
Ukraine	..	2.4	2.1	1.9	0.7	0.4	0.2	0.0	0.0	0.0	Ukraine
United Kingdom	300.0	[4]300.0	[4]310.0	...	...	...	112.4	[4]226.9	...	...	Royaume-Uni
Yugoslavia, SFR	15.5	..	..	..	..	..	..	..	..	..	Yougoslavie, RSF
USSR (former)	943.4	..	..	..	..	..	..	..	..	..	URSS (anc.)
Total	**10449**	**10427**	**11251**	**11035**	**12081**	**13073**	**13489**	**15364**	**13875**	**16257**	**Total**

General Note.
Pure dimethylbenzene ($C_6H_4(CH_3)_2$) total of three isomers: orthoxylene, metaxylene and paraxylene. (SITC, Rev.3: 51124-1).

Remarque générale.
Diméthyl benzène pur ($C_6H_4(CH_3)_2$). Poids total des trois isomères: l'orthoxylène, le métaxylène et le paraxylène. (CTCI, Rev.3: 51124-1).

[1] High purity only.
[2] Excluding metaxylene.
[3] Including mixed xylene isomers.
[4] Source: United Nations Economic Commission for Europe (ECE), (Geneva).
[5] Including ethylbenzene.

[1] De grande pureté seulement.
[2] Non compris le métaxylène.
[3] Y compris les isomers de xylène mélangé.
[4] Source: Commission économique des Nations Unies pour l'Europe (CEE), (Genève).
[5] Y compris ethylbenzène.

Methanol (methyl alcohol)
Méthanol (Alcool méthylique)

ISIC-BASED CODE - CODE BASE CITI
3511-21

Unit : Thousand metric tons   Unité : Milliers de tonnes métriques

Country or area	1990	1991	1992	1993	1994	1995	1996	1997	1998	1999	Pays ou zone
Africa	**93**	**81**	**95**	**84**	**80**	**98**	**72**	**76**	**69**	**94**	**Afrique**
Algeria	93.0	81.0	94.9	84.0	80.2	97.9	71.8	76.0	69.2	93.8	Algérie
America, North	**6298**	**6762**	**6478**	**7692**	**8821**	**8956**	**9923**	**10338**	**11256**	**11786**	**Amérique du Nord**
Canada	2000.0	2222.5	2154.0	2253.2	...	...	...	...	...	...	Canada
Mexico	110.1	139.0	176.0	180.7	122.0	...	...	...	...	...	Mexique
Trinidad and Tobago	402.5	452.9	481.7	492.8	1019.5	1008.1	1539.4	1518.8	2001.3	2095.5	Trinité-et-Tobago
United States	3785.0	3948.0	3666.1	4765.3	5522.2	...	...	...	...	...	Etats-Unis
America, South	**230**	**304**	**301**	**334**	**335**	**338**	**313**	**335**	**274**	**303**	**Amérique du Sud**
Argentina	45.8	61.8	62.3	67.1	69.8	86.6	53.8	65.4	43.5	42.5	Argentine
Brazil	168.6	206.6	204.4	223.5	220.3	205.1	223.8	226.4	210.2	215.5	Brésil
Colombia	15.7	...	34.0	43.5	44.9	45.8	...	43.4	20.3	...	Colombie
Asia	**222**	**330**	**262**	**311**	**273**	**459**	**438**	**466**	**478**	**440**	**Asie**
India	107.0	216.8	189.0	215.6	180.5	326.8	376.1	396.1	413.1	361.0	Inde
Indonesia	...	...	6.1	7.5	9.1	...	...	...	...	...	Indonésie
Japan	84.4	77.1	34.2	57.7	42.8	75.5	7.7	...	...	...	Japon
Turkey	...	...	...	30.6	40.9	49.5	46.9	48.1	51.1	71.7	Turquie
Europe	**1606**	**5007**	**4796**	**4321**	**4582**	**3626**	**3034**	**3474**	**3112**	**2729**	**Europe**
Czechoslovakia(former)	8.3	5.3	..	..	..	..	..	..	..	..	Tchécoslovaquie(anc.)
Czech Republic	..	..	..	...	...	...	5.0	6.2	5.6	4.7	République tchèque
Finland	...	...	...	0.0	0.1	0.0	...	...	...	...	Finlande
Germany	..	1231.5	1291.0	1202.2	1438.3	1014.5	1045.7	801.7	979.7	...	Allemagne
German D.R.(former)	595.7	..	..	..	..	..	..	..	..	..	R.D.A. (anc.)
Italy	90.0	89.5	51.5	15.8	0.0	0.0	0.0	...	...	...	Italie
Lithuania	..	..	..	...	[1]32.2	39.0	18.2	23.5	10.9	0.0	Lituanie
Poland	155.4	102.0	59.3	29.5	21.6	81.7	71.8	93.1	31.7	2.0	Pologne
Romania	231.8	140.4	104.0	133.8	287.5	223.9	188.8	321.4	135.8	105.8	Roumanie
Russian Federation	..	...	...	...	1909.0	1523.0	[1]1076.3	[1]1495.2	[1]1179.0	...	Fédération de Russie
Slovakia	..	..	..	...	...	...	[1]3.2	[1]5.0	[1]4.5	3.1	Slovaquie
Slovenia	..	78.2	...	...	43.4	92.8	81.7	125.6	127.6	136.2	Slovénie
Ukraine	..	605.5	619.2	481.7	404.4	204.0	79.1	60.8	59.9	77.1	Ukraine
United Kingdom	400.0	[1]450.0	[1]450.0	...	...	...	...	...	...	...	Royaume-Uni
Yugoslavia	..	81.9	43.8	0.0	0.0	0.0	29.6	107.1	142.2	33.2	Yougoslavie
T.F.Yug.Rep. Macedonia	..	...	...	...	[1]2.6	[1]4.0	[1]1.1	1.2	1.2	...	L'ex-RY Macédoine
Yugoslavia, SFR	125.2	..	..	..	..	..	..	..	..	..	Yougoslavie, RSF
USSR (former)[1]	3233.2	..	..	..	..	..	..	..	..	...	URSS (anc.)[1]
Total	**11682**	**12484**	**11932**	**12742**	**14091**	**13476**	**13779**	**14689**	**15188**	**15352**	**Total**

General Note.
Pure CH$_3$OH. Crude methyl alcohol (wood naphtha) is excluded.
(SITC, Rev.3: 51211-0).

Remarque générale.
CH$_3$OH pur, à l'exclusion de l'alcool méthylique brut (esprit de bois). (CTCI, Rev.3: 51211-0).

[1] Source: United Nations Economic Commission for Europe (ECE), (Geneva).

[1] Source: Commission économique des Nations Unies pour l'Europe (CEE), (Genève).

Butyl alcohol (butanol)
Alcools butyliques (butanols)

ISIC-BASED CODE - CODE BASE CITI

3511-22

Unit : Thousand metric tons   Unité : Milliers de tonnes métriques

Country or area	1990	1991	1992	1993	1994	1995	1996	1997	1998	1999	Pays ou zone
America, South	**52**	**54**	**52**	**51**	**53**	**38**	**51**	**51**	**50**	**55**	**Amérique du Sud**
Argentina	8.1	8.5	8.8	9.9	11.1	10.9	12.1	10.7	9.7	10.5	Argentine
Brazil	43.1	44.1	42.7	40.0	41.2	25.1	38.0	39.3	39.4	43.7	Brésil
Colombia	...	...	0.8	1.1	1.1	1.8	...	...	...	...	Colombie
Asia	**316**	**351**	**385**	**402**	**395**	**441**	**430**	**462**	**439**	**510**	**Asie**
India	15.9	16.7	14.0	14.0	14.3	16.8	15.4	...	...	...	Inde
Japan	300.1	334.0	371.2	388.1	380.3	424.2	415.0	447.0	424.2	494.9	Japon
Europe	**681**	**859**	**805**	**776**	**811**	**784**	**857**	**896**	**510**	**829**	**Europe**
Bulgaria	5.4	1.0	...	...	...	...	...	...	...	...	Bulgarie
Czechoslovakia(former)	26.9	26.6	..	..	...						Tchécoslovaquie(anc.)
Czech Republic	..		25.6	...	27.5	27.7	27.1	27.0	27.9	28.4	République tchèque
Germany	..	[1]470.8	...	382.0	465.1	[1]404.2	[1]537.4	[1]579.7	252.8	..	Allemagne
Germany(Fed.Rep.)	494.4	..	..	..	..	..	..	..	..	..	Allemagne(Rép.féd.)
German D.R.(former)	42.4	..	..	..	..	..	..	..	..	..	R.D.A. (anc.)
Poland	38.4	40.1	32.2	29.1	27.1	32.4	30.2	36.6	27.1	27.3	Pologne
Romania	25.6	22.9	18.2	16.1	14.6	21.1	17.5	3.0	0.0	0.0	Roumanie
Russian Federation	..	...	...	263.8	205.6	239.0	159.4	170.5	126.6	202.8	Fédération de Russie
Spain	15.8	16.9	17.4	18.1	[1]18.1	[1]15.1	[1]20.5	[1]16.2	[1]14.2	...	Espagne
Sweden	32.2	27.2	27.6	36.7	50.1	41.0	61.8	59.7	58.2	45.7	Suède
USSR (former)[1]	342.6	..	..	..	..	..	..	..	..	..	URSS (anc.)[1]
Total	**1392**	**1264**	**1243**	**1229**	**1259**	**1262**	**1339**	**1409**	**999**	**1394**	**Total**

General Note.
Including n-butyl, isobutyl, sec-butyl and tert-butyl alcohols. Methyl, ethyl alcohols and glycerol are excluded. (SITC, Rev.3: 51213-0).

Remarque générale.
Y compris les alcools n-butylique, isobutylique et les alcools butyliques secondaires et tertiaires, mais à l'exclusion du méthanol, de l'éthanol et du glycérol. (CTCI, Rev.3: 51213-0).

[1] Source: United Nations Economic Commission for Europe (ECE), (Geneva).

[1] Source: Commission économique des Nations Unies pour l'Europe (CEE), (Genève).

Ethanediol (ethylene glycol)
Ethane-diol (ethylène-glycol)

ISIC-BASED CODE - CODE BASE CITI

3511-23

Unit : Thousand metric tons

Unité : Milliers de tonnes métriques

Country or area	1990	1991	1992	1993	1994	1995	1996	1997	1998	1999	Pays ou zone
America, North	**2300**	**2182**	**2326**	**2359**	**2762**	**2716**	**2826**	**2936**	**3046**	**3156**	**Amérique du Nord**
United States	2299.9	2181.6	2326.2	2358.8	2761.5	...	...	...	...	...	Etats-Unis
America, South	**99**	**115**	**99**	**111**	**114**	**124**	**97**	**179**	**229**	**248**	**Amérique du Sud**
Brazil	99.5	114.8	99.2	111.5	114.1	123.8	97.5	178.7	229.4	248.3	Brésil
Asia	**637**	**859**	**1099**	**1065**	**1159**	**1412**	**1385**	**1850**	**2369**	**2371**	**Asie**
India	18.4	32.7	116.0	137.4	138.5	178.3	178.9	327.4	454.9	473.0	Inde
Japan	500.6	608.9	560.5	526.8	567.1	709.4	750.8	885.9	919.7	922.3	Japon
Korea, Republic of	69.9	151.1	371.2	356.4	400.7	434.8	379.3	562.9	914.4	886.1	Corée, République de
Turkey	48.0	66.1	50.8	44.1	53.0	89.8	76.5	73.7	80.0	89.8	Turquie
Europe	**585**	**620**	**714**	**781**	**856**	**950**	**930**	**1185**	**1190**	**1291**	**Europe**
Belgium	...	...	...	...	...	351.0	361.3	501.8	[1]498.3	481.6	Belgique
Bulgaria	30.1	25.9	34.7	49.7	55.6	57.7	74.1	73.1	...	...	Bulgarie
Czechoslovakia(former)	88.7	72.3	..	..	..	..	..	..	..	..	Tchécoslovaquie(anc.)
Czech Republic	..	..	...	...	...	...	8.7	9.1	9.0	8.2	République tchèque
Germany	..	[1]200.9	...	231.6	222.3	[1]277.8	[1]242.6	[1]286.3	[1]296.5	...	Allemagne
Germany(Fed.Rep.)	209.7	..	..	..	..	..	..	..	..		Allemagne(Rép.féd.)
German D.R.(former)	43.7	..	..	..	..	..	..	..	..		R.D.A. (anc.)
Romania [1]	...	...	...	...	...	22.6	17.6	18.4	14.3	...	Roumanie [1]
Russian Federation	..	...	...	103.3	140.0	120.7	131.2	188.3	189.4	253.0	Fédération de Russie
Slovakia	..	..	...	...	...	...	...	[1]48.6	38.8	33.1	Slovaquie
Spain	31.5	27.4	23.0	...	[1]48.9	[1]67.8	[1]51.5	[1]56.6	[1]68.8	...	Espagne
Sweden	3.2	3.0	3.0	3.0	3.0	3.3	...	...	...	...	Suède
Total	**3622**	**3776**	**4238**	**4316**	**4891**	**5201**	**5239**	**6150**	**6835**	**7067**	**Total**

General Note.
Ethylene glycol, glycol CH_2OHCH_2OH. (SITC, Rev.3: 51221-0).

Remarque générale.
Ethylène-glycol, glycol CH_2OHCH_2OH. (CTCI, Rev.3: 51221-0).

[1] Source: United Nations Economic Commission for Europe (ECE), (Geneva).

[1] Source: Commission économique des Nations Unies pour l'Europe (CEE), (Genève).

Glycerine (Glycerol)
Glycérine (Glycérol)

ISIC-BASED CODE - CODE BASE CITI

3511-25

Unit : Metric tons   Unité : Tonnes métriques

Country or area	1990	1991	1992	1993	1994	1995	1996	1997	1998	1999	Pays ou zone
Africa	**11268**	**9091**	**9239**	**9336**	**7465**	**5922**	**4230**	**2756**	**2884**	**0**	**Afrique**
Egypt	11268	9091	9239	9336	7465	5922	4230	2756	2884	...	Egypte
America, North	**10424**	**8203**	**5541**	**9379**	**12309**	**12694**	**12040**	**13338**	**14597**	**17647**	**Amérique du Nord**
Dominica	...	...	...	120	278	228	238	...	0	103	Dominique
Mexico	10114	7923	5290	9259	12031	12466	11802	13177	14597	17544	Mexique
America, South	**30798**	**33115**	**27894**	**22732**	**24682**	**21678**	**27012**	**27082**	**29949**	**21967**	**Amérique du Sud**
Brazil[1]	25395	27805	22553	17846	21376	16691	21981	20445	25289	17400	Brésil[1]
Colombia	...	...	5341	4886	3306	4987	...	6637	...	...	Colombie
Asia	**78959**	**75422**	**96805**	**70901**	**82277**	**85013**	**101826**	**123994**	**172732**	**166837**	**Asie**
Azerbaijan	..	623	531	153	132	121	113	0	0	0	Azerbaïdjan
India[2]	16991	17769	16685	14257	14647	14168	14521	15369	16519	19409	Inde[2]
Indonesia	2860	1538	...	6818	13763	14240	...	42842	92157	...	Indonésie
Japan	52279	48959	47406	41831	48247	48825	51421	54893	51791	51736	Japon
Kazakhstan	..	535	412	348	339	281	433	317	147	50	Kazakhstan
Myanmar[3]	107	199	156	...	...	...	...	...	...	...	Myanmar[3]
Turkey	6722	5799	6727	7340	4995	7224	10296	10419	11964	13605	Turquie
Europe	**135902**	**181257**	**166821**	**154927**	**169773**	**155030**	**144607**	**140003**	**139571**	**152729**	**Europe**
Bulgaria	153	88	64	20	9	4	...	...	...	...	Bulgarie
Croatia	..	101	37	20	14	2	0	4	6	...	Croatie
Denmark[4]	1790	779	1000	1	18	1	...	...	...	...	Danemark[4]
Czechoslovakia(former)	6151	7575	..	..	..	...	...	...	...	..	Tchécoslovaquie(anc.)
Czech Republic	..	..	...	...	...	...	...	3956	2864	8179	République tchèque
France[5]	18660	25100	23028	20616	21180	...	...	...	...	...	France[5]
Germany	..	...	80226	84543	96350	...	...	...	...	...	Allemagne
Germany(Fed.Rep.)	91332	..	..	..	..	...	...	...	...	...	Allemagne(Rép.féd.)
Greece	229	204	...	...	...	...	...	...	...	...	Grèce
Hungary	1311	652	724	...	...	...	70	...	...	...	Hongrie
Latvia	..	277	54	0	...	...	...	...	...	...	Lettonie
Lithuania	..	...	...	...	...	0	1	1	0	0	Lituanie
Poland	1641	1433	1097	1706	813	822	502	602	660	1045	Pologne
Portugal	1211	935	...	...	...	...	...	...	...	...	Portugal
Romania	405	304	286	263	186	224	141	108	95	106	Roumanie
Russian Federation	..	32548	30207	20430	23027	19143	9522	6727	4726	11413	Fédération de Russie
Slovenia	..	..	...	...	...	...	27	...	...	...	Slovénie
Spain	3924	4000	4357	2111	2286	1940	2226	2279	3765	4207	Espagne
Sweden	114	6306	6010	6208	6654	5987	6401	5529	...	...	Suède
Ukraine	..	4547	4195	3320	2702	1774	1305	571	366	422	Ukraine
United Kingdom[6]	...	...	...	8631	9331	...	...	...	...	...	Royaume-Uni[6]
Yugoslavia	..	348	206	30	65	91	31	73	95	77	Yougoslavie
T.F.Yug.Rep. Macedonia		11	32	...	...	...	...	...	...	...	L'ex-RY Macédoine
Total	**267351**	**307088**	**306300**	**267275**	**296506**	**280337**	**289716**	**307173**	**359733**	**359180**	**Total**

General Note.

Glycerol and glycerol lyes, including both synthetic and chemically pure glycerol. Glycerol put up as a medicament, perfumed glycerol and glycerol with added pharmaceutical substances or cosmetics are excluded. (SITC, Rev.3: 51222-0).

Remarque générale.

Glycérol, y compris les eaux et lessives glycérinées ainsi que le glycérol synthétique chimiquement pur. Cette rubrique ne comprend pas le glycérol présenté sous conditionnement pharmaceutique, le glycérol parfumé et le glycérol additionné de substances médicamenteuses ou de cosmétiques. (CTCI, Rev.3: 51222-0).

[1] Production by main establishments only.

[2] Production by large and medium scale establishments only.

[3] Government production only.

[4] Sales.

[5] Crude glycerine (100 per cent glycerol).

[6] Crude natural glycerol plus glycerine processed into distilled glycerine.

[1] Production des principaux établissements seulement.

[2] Production des grandes et moyennes entreprises seulement.

[3] Production de l'Etat seulement.

[4] Ventes.

[5] Glycérine brute (100 pour cent glycérol).

[6] Glycérol naturel brut et glycérine épurée.

Phenol
Phénol
ISIC-BASED CODE - CODE BASE CITI
3511-26

Unit : Thousand metric tons

Unité : Milliers de tonnes métriques

Country or area	1990	1991	1992	1993	1994	1995	1996	1997	1998	1999	Pays ou zone
America, North	**1664**	**1691**	**1821**	**1603**	**1951**	**1892**	**1941**	**1989**	**2038**	**2087**	**Amérique du Nord**
Canada	59.0	...	...	...	...	...	...	...	...	...	Canada
United States	1604.6	1631.6	1762.5	1544.2	1891.7	...	...	...	...	...	Etats-Unis
America, South	**97**	**98**	**91**	**105**	**113**	**115**	**112**	**123**	**119**	**132**	**Amérique du Sud**
Brazil	[1]97.1	98.4	91.4	105.3	112.8	114.8	112.1	122.9	118.7	132.0	Brésil
Asia	**518**	**639**	**717**	**704**	**850**	**984**	**983**	**1068**	**1092**	**1131**	**Asie**
India	48.6	52.8	54.0	52.4	56.0	63.8	64.2	72.5	77.1	79.3	Inde
Indonesia	...	...	51.6	46.8	14.8	...	...	...	...	...	Indonésie
Japan	403.1	495.0	538.1	512.5	669.8	771.4	767.6	832.7	851.4	888.3	Japon
Korea, Republic of	28.8	53.4	72.9	91.9	108.8	110.5	113.8	125.0	125.7	125.3	Corée, République de
Europe	**1273**	**1484**	**1610**	**1517**	**1325**	**1439**	**1716**	**1590**	**1629**	**1847**	**Europe**
Bulgaria	31.0	15.9	19.1	13.1	18.8	25.0	24.9	28.0			Bulgarie
Croatia	..	3.4	...	...	...	...	...	...	...	...	Croatie
Czechoslovakia(former)	40.4	34.5								..	Tchécoslovaquie(anc.)
Czech Republic	..	..	17.7	20.6	29.1	24.7	27.9	23.1	19.4	13.8	République tchèque
Germany[2]	..	469.7	...	...	497.6	586.9	929.6	763.7	801.5	...	Allemagne[2]
Germany(Fed.Rep.)	482.0	..	...	...	..	..	...	..	..	...	Allemagne(Rép.féd.)
German D.R.(former)	56.3	..	..	..	..	..	..	..	..	...	R.D.A. (anc.)
Italy	[2]370.0	[2]350.9	337.6	345.5	368.0	351.3	...	...	...	...	Italie
Poland	44.1	24.9	33.3	24.4	35.7	42.6	46.6	46.7	47.3	48.5	Pologne
Romania	63.4	40.7	25.9	17.2	9.5	23.1	13.1	31.0	23.5	7.1	Roumanie
Russian Federation	..	352.5	280.7	202.2	135.3	172.8	100.0	100.6	104.4	127.0	Fédération de Russie
Slovakia	..	..	...	...	[2]31.6	[2]33.1	[2]34.5	[2]31.7	34.9	30.9	Slovaquie
Spain	96.0	84.2	77.1	96.1	[2]109.9	[2]113.7	[2]110.5	[2]152.4	[2]136.0	...	Espagne
Ukraine	..	4.1	4.2	3.4	3.0	2.0	1.1	1.4	1.4	1.1	Ukraine
United Kingdom	[3]80.0	[2][3]80.0	[2][3]80.0	...	...	...	...	[2]0.5	...	...	Royaume-Uni
Yugoslavia[2]	..	...	...	...	...	0.0	12.5	56.2	...	...	Yougoslavie[2]
Yugoslavia, SFR	9.8	..	..	..	..	..	..	..	..		Yougoslavie, RSF
USSR (former)[2]	454.9	..	..	..	..	...	..	..	..	..	URSS (anc.)[2]
Total	**4007**	**3912**	**4239**	**3929**	**4238**	**4429**	**4752**	**4770**	**4878**	**5196**	**Total**

General Note.
Pure $C_6H_5.OH$ obtained by fractional distillation of coal tars or by synthesis. Crude phenol is excluded. (SITC, Rev.3: 51241-0).

[1] Production by main establishments only.
[2] Source: United Nations Economic Commission for Europe (ECE), (Geneva).

[3] Synthetic phenol only.

Remarque générale.
$C_6H_5.OH$ pur, obtenu par distillation fractionnée des goudrons de houille, ou par synthèse, à l'exclusion du phénol brut. (CTCI, Rev.3: 51241-0).

[1] Production des principaux établissements seulement.
[2] Source: Commission économique des Nations Unies pour l'Europe (CEE), (Genève).
[3] Phénol synthétique seulement.

Ethylene oxide
Oxide d'éthylène

ISIC-BASED CODE - CODE BASE CITI

3511-29

Unit : Thousand metric tons

Unité : Milliers de tonnes métriques

Country or area	1990	1991	1992	1993	1994	1995	1996	1997	1998	1999	Pays ou zone
America, North	**3448**	**2780**	**3044**	**2818**	**3056**	**3860**	**3686**	**4170**	**4092**	**4498**	**Amérique du Nord**
Canada	400.0	...	...	...	...	...	...	...	...	...	Canada
United States	3048.1	2380.4	2643.8	2417.5	2656.0	[1]3460.0	[1]3286.3	[1]3770.3	[1]3692.3	...	Etats-Unis
America, South	**127**	**150**	**143**	**149**	**163**	**161**	**149**	**218**	**259**	**261**	**Amérique du Sud**
Brazil	127.2	150.3	142.6	149.5	163.5	161.3	149.1	218.0	259.0	261.3	Brésil
Colombia	...	...	0.1	0.0	0.0	0.0	...	...	...	...	Colombie
Asia	**739**	**892**	**827**	**792**	**825**	**912**	**952**	**1071**	**1074**	**1100**	**Asie**
India	24.7	25.3	33.1	38.7	35.5	36.0	39.4	...	...	...	Inde
Japan	674.0	760.1	720.9	680.3	716.1	802.5	839.5	952.3	952.5	976.4	Japon
Turkey	40.0	106.8	...	...	...	...	...	...	...	...	Turquie
Europe	**1165**	**1434**	**1349**	**1267**	**1147**	**669**	**571**	**718**	**672**	**643**	**Europe**
Bulgaria [1]	...	...	...	...	46.7	50.3	67.9	66.6	...	...	Bulgarie [1]
Czechoslovakia(former)	14.6	9.2	..	..	..	..	..	..	..	..	Tchécoslovaquie(anc.)
Germany	..	...	...	623.3	656.9	148.3	131.0	182.2	191.3	...	Allemagne
Germany(Fed.Rep.)	628.4	..	..	..	..	..	..	..	..	..	Allemagne(Rép.féd.)
German D.R.(former)	76.3	..	..	..	..	..	..	..	..		R.D.A. (anc.)
Poland	18.6	15.2	16.2	15.8	14.3	12.1	12.6	16.8	14.1	12.6	Pologne
Romania	49.1	31.3	19.5	17.5	16.8	22.6	19.6	20.0	15.4	12.0	Roumanie
Russian Federation	..	474.4	434.6	350.5	280.7	284.0	199.2	265.7	215.2	260.1	Fédération de Russie
Slovakia	..	..	...	...	[1]7.7	[1]9.0	...	...	10.3	10.9	Slovaquie
Spain	62.9	67.7	61.8	61.2	[1]70.5	[1]87.7	[1]80.7	[1]87.5	[1]99.6	...	Espagne
Sweden	47.0	50.5	53.2	53.0	53.1	55.2	[1]50.9	69.6	68.6	66.5	Suède
United Kingdom	[2]210.0	[1][2]200.0	[1][2]220.0	...	0.0	0.0	0.0	0.0	0.0	...	Royaume-Uni
USSR (former) [1]	513.6	..	..	..	..	..	..	..		..	URSS (anc.) [1]
Total	**5993**	**5257**	**5363**	**5027**	**5191**	**5602**	**5359**	**6177**	**6097**	**6503**	**Total**

General Note.

Pure CH_2CH_2O. (SITC, Rev.3: 51613-0).

Remarque générale.

CH_2CH_2O pur. (CTCI, Rev.3: 51613-0).

[1] Source: United Nations Economic Commission for Europe (ECE), (Geneva).

[2] Including ethylene oxide used in the production of ethylene glycols.

[1] Source: Commission économique des Nations Unies pour l'Europe (CEE), (Genève).

[2] Y compris l'oxyde d'éthylène utilisé pour la production d'éthylène glycols.

Acetaldehyde (ethanal)
Aldéhyde acétique (éthanal)

ISIC-BASED CODE - CODE BASE CITI

3511-30

Country or area	1990	1991	1992	1993	1994	1995	1996	1997	1998	1999	Pays ou zone
America, South	**74**	**93**	**89**	**76**	**63**	**62**	**46**	**20**	**18**	**24**	**Amérique du Sud**
Argentina	...	9.4	8.3	3.5	...	7.1	9.4	...	...	...	Argentine
Brazil	66.2	83.3	80.5	72.3	55.1	54.5	36.1	12.4	11.1	17.0	Brésil
Asia	**383**	**384**	**391**	**350**	**369**	**395**	**419**	**436**	**414**	**415**	**Asie**
Japan	383.5	384.1	391.2	349.7	369.4	395.3	418.7	435.8	414.1	414.7	Japon
Europe	**459**	**548**	**525**	**565**	**513**	**553**	**467**	**447**	**467**	**477**	**Europe**
Bulgaria	45.1	12.9	7.5	...	...	4.5	8.7	11.8	...	...	Bulgarie
Czechoslovakia(former)	17.0	13.9	..	..	..	..	..	..	..	..	Tchécoslovaquie(anc.)
Czech Republic	..	..	...	...	...	...	1.5	1.6	[1]0.8	...	République tchèque
Germany	..	[1]337.4	327.7	348.2	358.9	385.9	346.8	328.2	...	...	Allemagne
Germany(Fed.Rep.)	349.7	..	..	..	..	..	..	..	..	..	Allemagne(Rép.féd.)
Russian Federation	..	...	..	98.5	49.3	64.2	18.1	3.8	4.7	13.6	Fédération de Russie
Slovakia[1]	..	..	...	...	...	...	21.6	...	...	...	Slovaquie[1]
Spain	24.9	24.9	28.5	32.9	[1]33.9	[1]48.5	[1]48.3	[1]56.2	...	...	Espagne
Sweden	22.0	23.4	22.9	24.6	24.4	24.8	21.5	24.0	26.1	24.9	Suède
Ukraine	..	41.4	36.2	22.6	8.2	2.3	0.1	0.0	0.0	0.0	Ukraine
USSR (former)[1]	300.3	..	..	..	..	..	..	..	..	..	URSS (anc.)[1]
Total	**1217**	**1025**	**1005**	**990**	**945**	**1010**	**931**	**903**	**899**	**916**	**Total**

General Note.
Pure CH$_3$.CHO (ethanal), saturated acyclic aldehyde. (SITC, Rev.3: 51621-1).

Remarque générale.
Aldéhyde acyclique saturé pur CH$_3$.CHO (éthanal). (CTCI, Rev.3: 51621-1).

[1] Source: United Nations Economic Commission for Europe (ECE), (Geneva).

[1] Source: Commission économique des Nations Unies pour l'Europe (CEE), (Genève).

Methanal (formaldehyde)
Méthanal (formaldéhyde)

ISIC-BASED CODE - CODE BASE CITI

3511-31

Unit : Thousand metric tons   Unité : Milliers de tonnes métriques

Country or area	1990	1991	1992	1993	1994	1995	1996	1997	1998	1999	Pays ou zone
America, North	**3044**	**3113**	**3862**	**3868**	**3871**	**4243**	**4473**	**4704**	**4934**	**5164**	**Amérique du Nord**
Canada	...	114.0	106.9	154.1	167.6	...	...	...	...	...	Canada
United States	2908.5	2999.2	3755.0	3713.9	3703.1	...	...	...	...	...	Etats-Unis
America, South	**194**	**211**	**222**	**262**	**278**	**293**	**299**	**309**	**365**	**412**	**Amérique du Sud**
Argentina	9.7	9.4	8.3	...	...	...	...	...	...	...	Argentine
Brazil	177.4	194.6	206.4	244.9	261.8	276.4	282.2	292.0	348.2	395.8	Brésil
Colombia	...	...	6.4	7.8	6.7	7.1	...	...	...	...	Colombie
Ecuador	...	...	0.5	0.5	0.3	...	...	...	...	...	Equateur
Asia	**1118**	**1810**	**1836**	**1725**	**2067**	**2105**	**2136**	**2262**	**2108**	**2061**	**Asie**
India	110.9	108.2	132.9	150.1	180.5	326.8	376.1	396.1	413.1	361.0	Inde
Indonesia	...	...	...	48.7	290.8	...	...	...	...	...	Indonésie
Japan	534.2	...	...	...	1358.4	1386.9	1358.2	1408.8	1232.1	1263.9	Japon
Korea, Republic of	183.8	...	...	...	...	...	...	...	...	...	Corée, République de
Turkey	119.0	128.0	129.6	122.4	54.0	37.9	48.4	103.8	109.0	82.2	Turquie
Europe	**1833**	**3062**	**2794**	**2567**	**2692**	**2306**	**2128**	**2209**	**2343**	**2255**	**Europe**
Belgium	...	...	...	...	...	...	...	[1]42.4	[1]62.6	70.5	Belgique
Denmark[2]	10.0	7.8	7.8	7.0	9.5	8.8	9.3	10.4	11.2	13.8	Danemark[2]
Czechoslovakia(former)	268.9	206.2	..	..	..	..	..			..	Tchécoslovaquie(anc.)
Czech Republic	..	..	...	...	35.9	40.4	8.1	4.4	3.7	5.5	République tchèque
Estonia	..	200.2	60.5	15.3	18.1	11.0	13.5	31.8	31.8	14.4	Estonie
Finland	47.9	36.0	34.8	43.6	49.7	55.2	62.0	...	...	...	Finlande
France	99.8	43.5	48.7	41.4	120.3	[1]117.8	[1]110.7	[1]119.1	[1]120.4	...	France
Germany	...	...	...	...	[1]725.0	159.1	144.8	153.9	138.6	...	Allemagne
German D.R.(former)	95.4	..	..	..	..	..	..	..	..	..	R.D.A. (anc.)
Hungary	13.3	18.1	7.5	...	[1]3.8	...	...	...	...	...	Hongrie
Italy	113.9	103.8	86.8	58.0	59.2	48.2	47.6	43.1	52.5	50.7	Italie
Lithuania	..	...	...	...	[1]13.5	11.9	21.6	21.2	12.1	12.0	Lituanie
Poland	[1]112.7	[1]106.0	[1]99.4	[1]121.0	[1]123.3	[1]177.1	[1]91.9	89.9	83.1	81.7	Pologne
Portugal[1]	36.1	37.5	29.9	29.1	36.8	34.2	37.5	41.1	44.2	...	Portugal[1]
Romania	330.6	...	...	...	...	...	...	...	...	...	Roumanie
Russian Federation	...	...	...	...	231.0	219.0	[1]188.0	[1]158.0	[1]161.0	...	Fédération de Russie
Slovakia[1]	..	..	...	...	...	...	148.2	169.7	167.7	...	Slovaquie[1]
Slovenia	..	43.4	47.1	36.0	23.4	76.4	79.8	88.8	93.1	105.0	Slovénie
Spain	271.2	248.9	279.4	250.6	242.6	330.4	353.8	369.6	417.3	493.2	Espagne
Sweden	244.5	219.7	202.9	237.4	260.1	279.2	266.5	313.5	389.7	300.7	Suède
Ukraine	...	169.7	186.2	150.6	99.1	57.0	50.4	41.2	36.6	50.4	Ukraine
United Kingdom	42.8	59.6	...	97.1	[1][2]84.9	[1][2]113.8	92.3	104.4	108.0	...	Royaume-Uni
Yugoslavia	..	6.7	4.4	3.0	2.0	0.9	0.8	0.2	0.2	0.3	Yougoslavie
T.F.Yug.Rep. Macedonia	..	4.4	5.0	2.8	2.6	4.0	1.1	1.2	...	...	L'ex-RY Macédoine
Yugoslavia, SFR	87.9	..	..	..	..	..	..	..	..	..	Yougoslavie, RSF
Total	**6190**	**8196**	**8714**	**8423**	**8908**	**8947**	**9036**	**9484**	**9749**	**9892**	**Total**

General Note.
Formaldehyde H.CHO saturated acyclic aldehyde also known as formalin or formol. (SITC, Rev.3: 51621-2).

Remarque générale.
Aldéhyde formique H.CHO, aldéhyde acyclique saturé, appelé aussi formal ou formol. (CTCI, Rev.3: 51621-2).

[1] Source: United Nations Economic Commission for Europe (ECE), (Geneva).

[2] Sales.

[1] Source: Commission économique des Nations Unies pour l'Europe (CEE), (Genève).
[2] Ventes.

Acetone
Acétone

ISIC-BASED CODE - CODE BASE CITI
3511-33

Unit : Thousand metric tons   Unité : Milliers de tonnes métriques

Country or area	1990	1991	1992	1993	1994	1995	1996	1997	1998	1999	Pays ou zone
America, North	**1083**	**1086**	**1129**	**1127**	**1232**	**1233**	**1267**	**1301**	**1335**	**1369**	**Amérique du Nord**
Mexico	26.1	21.7	25.2	...	...	...	...	...	...	...	Mexique
United States	1056.7	1064.7	1104.3	1102.4	1207.7	...	...	...	...	...	Etats-Unis
America, South	**76**	**80**	**77**	**83**	**81**	**88**	**85**	**89**	**74**	**95**	**Amérique du Sud**
Argentina	15.5	19.2	19.8	18.2	15.6	17.5	18.5	...	...	...	Argentine
Brazil[1]	60.5	61.2	57.0	64.4	65.7	70.6	66.6	70.7	55.8	76.7	Brésil[1]
Asia	**374**	**413**	**419**	**388**	**394**	**443**	**461**	**503**	**505**	**553**	**Asie**
India	40.5	43.7	41.7	38.1	40.9	47.1	43.6	...	...	...	Inde
Japan	333.7	369.1	377.3	350.3	352.8	396.1	417.1	458.1	459.0	507.1	Japon
Europe	**294**	**508**	**415**	**352**	**312**	**330**	**289**	**335**	**310**	**317**	**Europe**
Bulgaria	18.5	9.5	11.2	7.5	11.1	14.6	15.1	17.2	...	...	Bulgarie
Croatia	..	1.9	0.0	0.0	0.0	0.0	0.0	0.2	0.2	...	Croatie
Denmark	...	...	0.0	[2]0.3	[2]0.3	[2]0.2	[2]0.2	[2]0.2	[2]0.2	[2]0.2	Danemark
Czechoslovakia(former)	20.0	16.9	..	..	..	..				..	Tchécoslovaquie(anc.)
Czech Republic	..	..	...	..	..	..	0.0	0.1	0.1	0.1	République tchèque
Poland	22.3	14.6	20.1	15.3	22.9	27.1	29.8	29.7	29.7	30.2	Pologne
Romania	36.7	23.6	15.7	10.0	5.6	13.8	7.9	18.3	13.6	4.0	Roumanie
Russian Federation	..	255.7	198.9	137.4	90.8	110.6	66.7	65.1	68.7	84.2	Fédération de Russie
Spain	67.4	59.3	56.8	...	...	...	72.8	93.0	...	...	Espagne
Sweden	0.2	...	...	...	...	0.1	0.1	0.1	0.2	0.2	Suède
Ukraine	..	...	0.9	0.7	0.6	0.3	0.0	0.0	0.0	0.0	Ukraine
United Kingdom	128.5	125.9	...	...	...	93.1	96.0	...	...	...	Royaume-Uni
Total	**1827**	**2088**	**2040**	**1950**	**2019**	**2094**	**2102**	**2228**	**2224**	**2335**	**Total**

General Note.
Propanone $CH_3.CO.CH_3$. (SITC, Rev.3: 51623-0).

Remarque générale.
Propanone $CH_3.CO.CH_3$. (CTCI, Rev.3: 51623-0).

[1] Production by main establishments only.
[2] Sales.

[1] Production des principaux établissements seulement.
[2] Ventes.

Acetates (methyl, ethyl, butyl)
Acétates de méthyle, d'éthyle et de butyle

ISIC-BASED CODE - CODE BASE CITI

3511-34

Unit : Thousand metric tons   Unité : Milliers de tonnes métriques

Country or area	1990	1991	1992	1993	1994	1995	1996	1997	1998	1999	Pays ou zone
America, North	**238**	**286**	**249**	**241**	**289**	**277**	**283**	**289**	**294**	**300**	**Amérique du Nord**
United States[1][2]	238.1	*285.8	*248.8	*241.0	288.7	...	...	...	...	...	Etats-Unis[1][2]
America, South	**43**	**55**	**57**	**66**	**60**	**59**	**62**	**68**	**59**	**82**	**Amérique du Sud**
Brazil[3]	42.6	54.8	57.4	65.7	59.9	58.9	[4]61.7	[4]67.6	[4]59.2	[4]82.3	Brésil[3]
Asia	**201**	**201**	**201**	**201**	**201**	**201**	**201**	**201**	**201**	**201**	**Asie**
Japan	201.2	...	...	...	...	...	...	...	...	...	Japon
Europe	**656**	**634**	**618**	**615**	**640**	**599**	**607**	**617**	**686**	**725**	**Europe**
Czechoslovakia(former)	8.8	7.8	..	..	..	..	..	..	..	..	Tchécoslovaquie(anc.)
Germany	..	..	...	377.7	431.7	..	..	..	..	..	Allemagne
Germany(Fed.Rep.)	474.3	..	..	..	..	..	..	..	..	..	Allemagne(Rép.féd.)
Hungary	6.9	6.7	5.2	...	...	...	...	...	...	...	Hongrie
Italy	114.1	145.3	142.5	128.1	126.4	113.4	124.7	...	...	...	Italie
Latvia	..	...	...	...	...	...	...	...	...	0.2	Lettonie
Spain	33.8	51.5	43.4	79.1	49.2	51.4	46.9	58.0	126.4	167.5	Espagne
Sweden[3]	18.3	17.9	21.8	23.5	26.3	22.8	24.4	29.0	30.7	30.3	Suède[3]
Total	**1138**	**1176**	**1125**	**1123**	**1190**	**1136**	**1153**	**1175**	**1241**	**1308**	**Total**

General Note.
Esters of acetic acid responding to the formula in which the hydrogen atom of the carboxyl group (COOH) is replaced by an alkyl or aryl radical. (SITC, Rev.3: 51372-0).

Remarque générale.
Esters de l'acide acétique dans la formule desquels l'atome d'hydrogène du groupement carboxyde (COOH) est remplacé par un radical alkyle ou aryle. (CTCI, Rev.3: 51372-0).

[1] Ethyl acetate only.
[2] High purity only.
[3] Ethyl and butyl acetates only.
[4] Production by main establishments only.

[1] Acétate d'éthyle seulement.
[2] De grande pureté seulement.
[3] Acétates d'éthyle et de butyle seulement.
[4] Production des principaux établissements seulement.

Acetic acid
Acide acétique

ISIC-BASED CODE - CODE BASE CITI

3511-35

Unit : Thousand metric tons   Unité : Milliers de tonnes métriques

Country or area	1990	1991	1992	1993	1994	1995	1996	1997	1998	1999	Pays ou zone
America, North	**1770**	**1715**	**1673**	**1544**	**1852**	**1709**	**1708**	**1708**	**1707**	**1714**	**Amérique du Nord**
Mexico	68.5	75.0	43.4	35.3	44.7	...	...	...	...	...	Mexique
United States	1701.3	1639.9	1630.1	1508.9	1807.4	...	...	...	...	...	Etats-Unis
America, South	**101**	**124**	**117**	**107**	**83**	**86**	**90**	**26**	**24**	**30**	**Amérique du Sud**
Argentina	12.1	11.8	10.0	4.3	...	8.9	11.8	...	...	...	Argentine
Brazil	87.9	109.9	104.3	99.5	[1]71.2	[1]72.2	[1]75.7	[1]15.6	[1]15.5	[1]20.2	Brésil
Colombia	0.6	...	2.4	2.9	2.1	5.1	...	3.8	2.0	...	Colombie
Asia	**554**	**575**	**568**	**596**	**624**	**753**	**793**	**832**	**860**	**857**	**Asie**
Armenia	..	13.9	4.2	...	0.1	0.0	0.0	0.0	0.0	0.0	Arménie
India	77.0	87.5	98.7	94.8	83.9	148.6	180.4	199.5	189.2	200.4	Inde
Indonesia	...	15.6	14.3	15.3	16.5	29.4	...	...	19.4	...	Indonésie
Japan	456.9	453.6	446.1	479.3	514.2	568.7	593.1	613.8	647.4	637.1	Japon
Kazakhstan[2]	..	...	...	...	9.3	6.6	1.0	0.1	...	...	Kazakhstan[2]
Europe	**510**	**715**	**542**	**579**	**603**	**276**	**211**	**305**	**250**	**220**	**Europe**
Bulgaria	0.2	0.1	0.1	0.0	...	...	...	...	...	...	Bulgarie
Croatia	..	0.4	0.3	0.4	0.3	0.2	0.1	0.1	0.1	...	Croatie
Denmark[3]	...	...	...	4.9	4.7	4.5	4.8	5.7	5.6	...	Danemark[3]
Czechoslovakia(former)	21.0	16.7	..	..	..	..	..	..	..	..	Tchécoslovaquie(anc.)
Czech Republic	..	..	..	...	2.4	1.9	0.9	0.6	0.7	0.6	République tchèque
Finland	4.9	4.6	3.5	0.6	0.0	0.5	0.2	...	...	...	Finlande
Germany	..	[2]321.0	...	340.6	405.6	56.7	43.6	71.8	...	...	Allemagne
Germany(Fed.Rep.)	323.3	..	..	..	..	..	..	..	..	..	Allemagne(Rép.féd.)
German D.R.(former)	58.9	..	..	..	..	..	..	..	..	..	R.D.A. (anc.)
Italy	9.6	9.6	8.8	8.4	9.4	5.4	...	...	...	...	Italie
Netherlands[2]	...	...	...	...	3.0	1.7	2.7	...	...	...	Pays-Bas[2]
Poland	20.1	23.5	18.6	19.9	19.6	19.6	17.5	12.5	8.4	4.4	Pologne
Romania	22.6	14.1	10.3	5.5	3.0	3.1	3.7	2.7	1.7	0.0	Roumanie
Russian Federation	..	96.2	83.6	75.4	35.2	21.7	20.3	56.6	50.2	112.4	Fédération de Russie
Spain	4.1	5.2	0.1	...	[2]5.6	[2]12.5	5.7	1.6	0.4	2.4	Espagne
Sweden	15.2	18.4	19.1	21.8	21.1	23.5	20.5	21.6	23.7	20.5	Suède
Ukraine	..	166.5	161.9	93.1	92.7	123.9	71.3	65.5	36.0	47.2	Ukraine
Yugoslavia	..	32.2	19.6	0.0	0.0	0.0	12.5	56.2	76.2	13.9	Yougoslavie
Yugoslavia, SFR	23.3		..	..	..	..	..	..	..	..	Yougoslavie, RSF
USSR (former)[2]	299.6	..	..	..	..	..	..	..	..	..	URSS (anc.)[2]
Total	**3234**	**3130**	**2899**	**2826**	**3162**	**2824**	**2803**	**2870**	**2841**	**2822**	**Total**

General Note.
CH$_3$.COOH in terms of 100 per cent obtained by the dry distillation of wood or by synthesis. (SITC, Rev.3: 51371-1).

Remarque générale.
Acide obtenu par synthèse ou par distillation sèche du bois. Poids exprimé sur la base de CH$_3$.COOH pur. (CTCI, Rev.3: 51371-1).

[1] Production by main establishments only.
[2] Source: United Nations Economic Commission for Europe (ECE), (Geneva).

[3] Sales.

[1] Production des principaux établissements seulement.
[2] Source: Commission économique des Nations Unies pour l'Europe (CEE), (Genève).

[3] Ventes.

Formic acid
Acide formique
ISIC-BASED CODE - CODE BASE CITI
3511-37

Unit : Thousand metric tons   Unité : Milliers de tonnes métriques

Country or area	1990	1991	1992	1993	1994	1995	1996	1997	1998	1999	Pays ou zone
America, South	**1**	**1**	**0**	**1**	**1**	**1**	**1**	**1**	**1**	**1**	**Amérique du Sud**
Argentina	...	0.7	0.4	...	...	...	...	...	...	...	Argentine
Asia	**20**	**19**	**20**	**21**	**23**	**18**	**19**	**18**	**18**	**18**	**Asie**
Indonesia	8.2	7.3	...	9.1	11.9	6.9	...	7.1	7.5	...	Indonésie
Japan[1]	11.7	12.2	12.0	11.6	10.8	10.7	10.8	11.1	10.8	...	Japon[1]
Europe	**55**	**148**	**131**	**145**	**146**	**140**	**144**	**142**	**147**	**149**	**Europe**
Denmark	...	...	0.0	[2]0.0	[2]0.0	[2]0.1	[2]0.0	...	...	...	Danemark
Czechoslovakia(former)	10.4	10.5	..	..	..	..	..	..	..	..	Tchécoslovaquie(anc.)
Finland	35.7	34.6	33.5	35.1	37.4	32.1	39.0	...	...	...	Finlande
Germany	..	92.3	87.1	98.6	...	...	...	...	...	...	Allemagne
Hungary	...	...	...	...	...	...	...	0.5	...	...	Hongrie
Russian Federation	..	0.3	0.2	0.1	0.0	0.1	0.0	...	0.1	0.2	Fédération de Russie
Sweden	8.9	9.5	9.6	10.7	15.2	14.4	11.8	12.3	16.4	17.8	Suède
Total	**76**	**168**	**152**	**166**	**169**	**158**	**164**	**161**	**166**	**167**	**Total**

General Note.
H.COOH in terms of 100 per cent either native or obtained by synthesis. (SITC, Rev.3: 51374-1).

Remarque générale.
Sur la base de H.COOH pur, naturel ou synthétique. (CTCI, Rev.3: 51374-1).

[1] Beginning 1999, series discontinued.
[2] Sales.

[1] A partir de 1999, série abandonnée.
[2] Ventes.

Phthalic anhydride
Anhydride phtalique

ISIC-BASED CODE - CODE BASE CITI

3511-38

Unit : Thousand metric tons

Unité : Milliers de tonnes métriques

Country or area	1990	1991	1992	1993	1994	1995	1996	1997	1998	1999	Pays ou zone
America, North	**463**	**301**	**441**	**421**	**476**	**464**	**479**	**494**	**509**	**523**	**Amérique du Nord**
Canada	9.0	...	...	...	...	...	...	...	...	...	Canada
Mexico	27.4	25.5	24.5	25.1	32.0	...	...	...	...	...	Mexique
United States	426.5	266.3	407.4	387.1	435.1	...	...	...	...	...	Etats-Unis
America, South	**88**	**82**	**102**	**104**	**119**	**102**	**117**	**115**	**106**	**123**	**Amérique du Sud**
Argentina	...	1.8	21.4	22.8	25.3	26.4	26.9	...	...	...	Argentine
Brazil	65.6	77.4	77.2	76.0	91.4	74.8	87.3	85.5	74.3	89.8	Brésil
Colombia	7.7	...	3.4	5.4	2.5	0.5	...	0.4	0.2	...	Colombie
Asia	**559**	**603**	**621**	**617**	**658**	**704**	**768**	**842**	**768**	**815**	**Asie**
India	40.7	53.9	53.9	47.3	56.5	67.2	92.9	139.5	108.3	121.0	Inde
Indonesia	...	...	...	50.1	...	...	...	...	...	...	Indonésie
Japan	301.2	308.0	309.0	276.6	307.9	316.0	342.2	330.1	301.5	301.4	Japon
Korea, Republic of	136.9	164.1	180.9	216.4	212.8	237.9	250.5	288.4	271.6	305.1	Corée, République de
Turkey	30.2	26.6	26.7	26.1	30.3	32.9	31.9	33.6	36.3	37.7	Turquie
Europe	**846**	**1054**	**906**	**920**	**938**	**716**	**706**	**707**	**630**	**680**	**Europe**
Austria	36.0	[1]18.0	[1]18.0	...	...	...	...	...	...	...	Autriche
Belarus [1]	..			...	...	12.5	15.1	11.6	16.1	13.7	Bélarus [1]
Belgium	123.1	172.3	185.3	152.8	161.0	113.3	137.6	134.2	126.1	124.4	Belgique
Bulgaria	8.3	3.0	3.2	6.4	15.2	16.3	16.3	17.2	...	...	Bulgarie
Czechoslovakia(former)	31.3	27.5		..	..	..	..	..	..		Tchécoslovaquie(anc.)
Czech Republic	..	..	20.9	...	23.5	22.6	23.5	19.8	22.8	23.6	République tchèque
Germany	..	[1]198.7	...	208.9	206.1	41.2	44.5	62.4	49.1	...	Allemagne
Germany(Fed.Rep.)	229.9	..	..	..	..	..	..	..	..		Allemagne(Rép.féd.)
German D.R.(former)	13.0										R.D.A. (anc.)
Hungary	19.7	20.9	20.7	19.3	20.4	...	...	...	...	...	Hongrie
Italy	136.4	144.9	119.6	132.4	131.8	118.0	...	...	...	...	Italie
Poland	28.5	21.5	17.5	17.1	25.2	28.4	29.0	30.5	19.7	19.7	Pologne
Portugal [1]	18.0	18.3	16.7	15.9	18.8	16.0	16.9	18.6	15.9	...	Portugal [1]
Romania	21.9	16.1	13.3	9.0	12.3	11.2	6.5	0.0	0.0	0.0	Roumanie
Russian Federation	..	146.7	133.4	114.0	111.5	104.8	55.2	59.6	23.6	60.9	Fédération de Russie
Slovenia	..	18.4	23.3	10.4	22.8	21.1	27.3	28.0	16.2	23.8	Slovénie
Spain	53.4	68.0	56.3	...	[1]37.4	[1]39.8	[1]39.0	[1]44.7	[1]43.3	...	Espagne
Sweden	26.8	24.3	24.6	26.1	28.3	28.3	31.1	31.0	31.6	33.1	Suède
Ukraine	..	68.1	50.4	26.5	12.3	23.7	20.8	8.2	9.2	6.9	Ukraine
United Kingdom	75.0	[1]75.0	[1]75.0	...	...	...	...	...	...	...	Royaume-Uni
Yugoslavia, SFR	24.9	..	..	..	..	..	..	..	..	..	Yougoslavie, RSF
USSR (former) [1]	249.9	..	..	..	..	..	..	..	..	..	URSS (anc.) [1]
Total	**2206**	**2039**	**2069**	**2062**	**2191**	**1987**	**2069**	**2157**	**2012**	**2141**	**Total**

General Note.
Pure $C_6H_4(CO)_2O$. (SITC, Rev.3: 51382-0).

Remarque générale.
$C_6H_4(CO)_2O$, pur. (CTCI, Rev.3: 51382-0).

[1] Source: United Nations Economic Commission for Europe (ECE), (Geneva).

[1] Source: Commission économique des Nations Unies pour l'Europe (CEE), (Genève).

Aniline
Aniline
ISIC-BASED CODE - CODE BASE CITI
3511-42

Unit : Metric tons
Unité : Tonnes métriques

Country or area	1990	1991	1992	1993	1994	1995	1996	1997	1998	1999	Pays ou zone
America, North	448620	436021	457867	449509	572913	475778	489736	362626	339996	317366	**Amérique du Nord**
United States	448620	436021	457867	449509	572913	...	[1]489736	...	...	...	Etats-Unis
Asia	160757	177551	208269	197837	218043	262194	247387	269615	233009	242362	**Asie**
India	13027	14014	15780	13836	14020	20726	25013				Inde
Japan	147730	163537	192489	184001	204023	241468	222374	244480	206173	213826	Japon
Europe	427676	431193	452266	431965	451323	462091	437263	453340	475796	477460	**Europe**
Belgium[1]	...	...	...	...	175416	...	...	...	...	...	Belgique[1]
Bulgaria	4107	584	96	...	...	...	...	...	...	...	Bulgarie
Denmark[2]	...	...	9	0	0	0	0	0	0	0	Danemark[2]
Czechoslovakia(former)	62602	68077	..	..	..						Tchécoslovaquie(anc.)
Czech Republic	..	..			66576	75135	60808	66060	67941	60651	République tchèque
Germany		...	135500	113984	130977						Allemagne
Germany(Fed.Rep.)	137511	..						..	..	..	Allemagne(Rép.féd.)
Hungary	372	0	...	...	...	...	...	...	...	...	Hongrie
Poland	4683	852	0	0	0	...	...	...	...	...	Pologne
Portugal	38595	33386	46773	46869	[1]51258	[1]55359	[1]59887	...	...	...	Portugal
Romania	4387	2923	2333	2618	2182	4447	3509	1751	25	89	Roumanie
Russian Federation	..	...	...	...	...	...	9041	14009	32299	37179	Fédération de Russie
Total	1037053	1044765	1118402	1079311	1242279	1200063	1174386	1085581	1048800	1037188	**Total**

General Note.
$C_6H_5NH_2$, phenylamine, aromatic monoamine. (SITC, Rev.3: 51454-1).

Remarque générale.
$C_6H_5NH_2$, phénylamine, monoamine aromatique. (CTCI, Rev.3: 51454-1).

[1] Source: United Nations Economic Commission for Europe (ECE), (Geneva).

[2] Sales.

[1] Source: Commission économique des Nations Unies pour l'Europe (CEE), (Genève).

[2] Ventes.

Acrylonitrile
Acrylonitrile

ISIC-BASED CODE - CODE BASE CITI

3511-43

Unit : Thousand metric tons   Unité : Milliers de tonnes métriques

Country or area	1990	1991	1992	1993	1994	1995	1996	1997	1998	1999	Pays ou zone
America, North	**1214**	**1201**	**1283**	**1129**	**1353**	**1456**	**1531**	**1493**	**1415**	**1634**	**Amérique du Nord**
United States	1213.9	1200.9	1283.2	1129.1	1352.6	[1]1456.1	[1]1531.2	[1]1493.0	[1]1415.2	...	Etats-Unis
America, South	**78**	**63**	**74**	**74**	**77**	**80**	**78**	**87**	**64**	**80**	**Amérique du Sud**
Brazil	78.0	63.5	74.2	74.3	76.5	79.8	78.4	87.1	64.1	79.7	Brésil
Asia	**745**	**736**	**790**	**794**	**835**	**893**	**903**	**1085**	**1104**	**1188**	**Asie**
Japan	592.5	603.8	621.0	593.8	610.2	663.2	674.7	730.1	667.1	737.7	Japon
Korea, Republic of	86.6	79.6	104.5	123.9	135.7	145.6	144.9	284.9	357.9	371.7	Corée, République de
Turkey	65.6	52.2	64.1	76.0	89.1	83.7	83.5	69.6	78.7	78.6	Turquie
Europe	**312**	**820**	**814**	**790**	**820**	**902**	**841**	**826**	**818**	**859**	**Europe**
Belarus[1]	..	...	..	..	...	62.5	47.6	56.5	63.6	61.9	Bélarus[1]
Bulgaria	21.2	18.3	23.3	27.3	24.4	28.5	28.9	32.0	...	...	Bulgarie
Germany	..	...	...	358.7	413.0	[1]427.7	[1]443.6	[1]456.6	[1]429.9	...	Allemagne
German D.R.(former)	55.3	..	..	..	..	..	..	..	..	..	R.D.A. (anc.)
Poland	1.3	0.0	0.0	0.0	0.0	...	0.3	0.3	0.2	0.2	Pologne
Romania	52.8	45.6	41.0	48.3	59.4	73.9	66.9	78.6	70.4	80.8	Roumanie
Russian Federation	..	...	...	109.9	71.2	92.0	36.6	22.6	4.3	14.0	Fédération de Russie
Spain	84.1	96.5	98.6	96.6	[1]101.0	[1]120.2	[1]120.5	[1]82.6	[1]122.0	...	Espagne
Sweden	0.0	0.0	0.1	0.0	...	...	...	...	...	...	Suède
United Kingdom[1]	...	...	...	...	...	...	...	...	97.0	...	Royaume-Uni[1]
Total	**2348**	**2820**	**2961**	**2787**	**3084**	**3331**	**3354**	**3491**	**3401**	**3760**	**Total**

General Note.
Pure CH_2=CHCN. Acrylonitrile polymers and co-polymers are excluded. (SITC, Rev.3: 51483-0).

Remarque générale.
CH_2=CHCN pur, à l'exclusion des polymères et copolymères de l'acrylonitrile. (CTCI, Rev.3: 51483-0).

[1] Source: United Nations Economic Commission for Europe (ECE), (Geneva).

[1] Source: Commission économique des Nations Unies pour l'Europe (CEE), (Genève).

Chlorine
Chlore
ISIC-BASED CODE - CODE BASE CITI
3511-45

Unit : Thousand metric tons　　　　　　　　　　　　　　　　　　　　　Unité : Milliers de tonnes métriques

Country or area	1990	1991	1992	1993	1994	1995	1996	1997	1998	1999	Pays ou zone
Africa	**33**	**33**	**35**	**35**	**33**	**33**	**31**	**30**	**36**	**39**	**Afrique**
Algeria	23	23	23	...	...	...	...	...	...	...	Algérie
Egypt	10	10	12	12	10	10	8	7	13	16	Egypte
America, North	**13374**	**13228**	**12276**	**12318**	**12365**	**12632**	**12805**	**13221**	**13075**	**13522**	**Amérique du Nord**
Canada	...	1402	1364	1170	1074	1032	1118	*1061	989	...	Canada
Mexico	332	254	307	302	335	356	384	437	437	421	Mexique
United States	11809	11572	10605	10846	10956	11244	11303	11723	11649	12114	Etats-Unis
America, South	**1195**	**1268**	**1257**	**1294**	**1304**	**1317**	**1338**	**1384**	**1357**	**1353**	**Amérique du Sud**
Argentina	210	185	142	139	153	163	...	...	...	...	Argentine
Brazil	950	1041	1072	1110	1106	1102	1147	1194	1173	1167	Brésil
Chile	28	28	33	33	...	...	...	...	...	...	Chili
Colombia	7	...	10	12	...	21	...	18	17	...	Colombie
Asia	**1479**	**1587**	**1627**	**1519**	**1516**	**1750**	**1685**	**1710**	**1691**	**1773**	**Asie**
Azerbaijan	..	...	...	5	[1]5	[1]2	3	3	2	1	Azerbaïdjan
Bangladesh[2]	5	5	5	4	4	4	5	4	...	...	Bangladesh[2]
Cyprus	*1	*1	1	*1	*1	1	1	1	1	1	Chypre
India	339	398	485	501	541	709	689	676	705	794	Inde
Israel	36	36	34	35	38	38	35	...	...	...	Israël
Japan[3]	1042	1027	978	900	875	942	894	928	881	875	Japon[3]
Kazakhstan[1]	..	...	...	...	1	1	4	3	2	...	Kazakhstan[1]
Kuwait	...	...	11	14	14	16	15	18	19	18	Koweït
Pakistan[2]	7	7	6	6	6	8	9	9	10	11	Pakistan[2]
Tajikistan[1][3]	..	...	...	...	3	1	...	...	...	...	Tadjikistan[1][3]
Thailand	21	23	...	...	...	...	...	...	...	...	Thaïlande
Turkey	14	68	77	27	7	5	5	7	6	4	Turquie
Europe	**10078**	**8727**	**8406**	**7675**	**8525**	**8679**	**8255**	**8915**	**8773**	**9097**	**Europe**
Belgium	452	430	439	426	[1]663	[1]707	[1]542	[1]547	[1]538	...	Belgique
Bulgaria	[1]63	[1]50	[1]51	[1]36	55	50	57	61	...	...	Bulgarie
Denmark	...	...	[4]3	[4]2	[4]2	[1][4]1	[1][4]0	[1]0	[1][4]0	...	Danemark
Czechoslovakia(former)[3]	305	269	..	..	..	..	..	..	..		Tchécoslovaquie(anc.)[3]
Czech Republic	..	..	...	...	134	130	53	46	50	47	République tchèque
Finland	137	100	52	21	12	9	7	...	...	...	Finlande
France	1340	1268	1405	1388	1476	[1]1420	[1]1470	[1]1479	[1]1500	...	France
Germany	..	[1]3033	...	2852	3135	3281	3100	3529	3428	...	Allemagne
Germany(Fed.Rep.)	3254		..	..	..				..	..	Allemagne(Rép.féd.)
German D.R.(former)	430	..	..	..	..						R.D.A. (anc.)
Greece	34	35	34	...	...	...	...	...	...		Grèce
Hungary	20	35	...	...	[1]111	[1]124	142	142	132	129	Hongrie
Italy[5]	1043	865	885	864	891	869	827	1018	890	...	Italie[5]
Norway[1]	241	193	185	...	...	...	...	...	...	...	Norvège[1]
Poland	340	295	294	261	259	289	313	322	329	313	Pologne
Portugal[1]	...	...	...	...	57	62	63	63	61	...	Portugal[1]
Romania	346	259	206	192	218	312	229	251	225	206	Roumanie
Russian Federation[1]	..	..	...	...	...	...	46	54	...	...	Fédération de Russie[1]
Slovakia	..	..	95	...	...	...	[1]86	[1]4	[1]82	...	Slovaquie
Slovenia	..	10	10	8	[1]10	[1]9	14	16	11	3	Slovénie
Spain	607	580	572	426	497	551	570	559	577	568	Espagne
Sweden	295	247	148	206	254	212	202	207	241	239	Suède
Ukraine[3]	..	20	19	12	12	11	9	8	8	6	Ukraine[3]
United Kingdom	940	879	...	350	378	277	266	[1]313	301	...	Royaume-Uni
Yugoslavia	..	47	21	2	2	5	16	56	54	11	Yougoslavie
T.F.Yug.Rep. Macedonia	..	2	2	2	2	2	2	0	1	...	L'ex-RY Macédoine
Yugoslavia, SFR	172	..	..	..	..	..	..	..	..		Yougoslavie, RSF
Total	**26159**	**24844**	**23601**	**22840**	**23743**	**24410**	**24114**	**25260**	**24932**	**25784**	**Total**

General Note.
Gas usually obtained by electrolysis of alkali chlorides, especially sodium chloride. (SITC, Rev.3: 52224-0).

Remarque générale.
Gaz généralement obtenu par électrolyse des chlorures alcalins, particulièrement du chlorure de sodium. (CTCI,Rev.3: 52224-0).

For footnotes, see end of table.　　　　　　　　　　　　　　　　Voir la fin du tableau pour les notes.

Chlorine (continued)
Chlore (suite)

ISIC-BASED CODE - CODE BASE CITI
3511-45

Footnotes
[1] Source: United Nations Economic Commission for Europe (ECE), (Geneva).

[2] Twelve months ending 30 June of year stated.
[3] Liquid chlorine only.
[4] Sales.
[5] Excluding chlorine used in production of calcium hypochlorite and sodium hypochlorite.

Notes.
[1] Source: Commission économique des Nations Unies pour l'Europe (CEE), (Genève).
[2] Période de douze mois finissant le 30 juin de l'année indiquée.
[3] Chlore liquide seulement.
[4] Ventes.
[5] Non compris le chlore utilisé pour fabriquer de l'hypochlorite de calcium et de l'hypochlorite de sodium.

Hydrochloric acid
Acide chlorhydrique

ISIC-BASED CODE - CODE BASE CITI

3511-46

Unit : Thousand metric tons

Unité : Milliers de tonnes métriques

Country or area	1990	1991	1992	1993	1994	1995	1996	1997	1998	1999	Pays ou zone
Africa	**205**	**210**	**213**	**209**	**206**	**214**	**174**	**158**	**177**	**169**	**Afrique**
Egypt	12.0	13.0	14.1	15.4	13.7	14.6	6.0	8.9	...	...	Egypte
South Africa	193.0	197.1	198.7	193.1	192.4	199.0	168.1	149.2	167.1	159.6	Afrique du Sud
America, North	**3049**	**3302**	**3426**	**3330**	**3547**	**3683**	**3890**	**4292**	**4375**	**4326**	**Amérique du Nord**
Canada	...	193.4	167.8	133.9	134.5	125.6	145.8	*141.5	149.1	...	Canada
Mexico	45.2	41.9	22.9	28.4	24.6	...	...	...	...	...	Mexique
United States	2847.9	3067.1	3234.8	3167.5	3387.6	3541.5	3733.5	4145.4	4226.3	4191.4	Etats-Unis
America, South	**188**	**149**	**123**	**140**	**164**	**183**	**204**	**229**	**235**	**267**	**Amérique du Sud**
Bolivia	0.1	0.0	0.0	0.0	0.0	*0.0	...	...	...	...	Bolivie
Brazil	116.2	74.8	80.8	96.4	105.7	106.0	119.8	115.5	119.7	111.4	Brésil
Colombia	[1]11.2	...	9.1	6.0	0.3	13.8	...	21.7	...	...	Colombie
Peru	60.2	63.5	32.7	37.3	57.6	62.9	74.1	91.6	102.1	141.7	Pérou
Asia	**3620**	**3931**	**4086**	**3876**	**3860**	**3905**	**3890**	**3951**	**3903**	**3914**	**Asie**
Azerbaijan	..	40.1	32.5	9.8	9.9	6.9	6.5	7.6	5.6	4.4	Azerbaïdjan
Bangladesh[2]	2.2	2.5	3.0	3.5	3.7	3.4	3.9	3.7	...	...	Bangladesh[2]
China	2622.8	2851.7	3028.0	...	...	...	...	...	...	...	Chine
Japan	798.9	823.2	819.7	824.1	829.7	864.1	845.7	888.8	843.0	856.8	Japon
Kuwait	...	...	2.7	2.0	...	...	...	...	...	...	Koweït
Thailand[1]	122.1	174.8	...	...	...	...	...	...	...	...	Thaïlande[1]
Turkey[1]	71.6	36.5	52.1	54.0	31.4	46.0	49.2	65.6	65.6	64.0	Turquie[1]
Europe	**3850**	**4530**	**4502**	**4266**	**4261**	**3867**	**3781**	**3732**	**3615**	**3337**	**Europe**
Belgium	347.6	369.0	335.4	337.1	...	...	...	...	...	...	Belgique
Bulgaria	77.6	62.7	45.7	34.1	37.9	42.0	45.2	35.0	...	...	Bulgarie
Croatia				1.6	1.3	1.5	1.1	1.0	0.5	...	Croatie
Denmark[3]	10.2	6.4	0.0	0.1	0.0	0.1	0.1	0.1	0.1	...	Danemark[3]
Czechoslovakia(former)	75.6	65.0	..	..	..				..	..	Tchécoslovaquie(anc.)
Czech Republic	..	..	...	...	83.0	82.1	75.3	57.1	60.5	58.9	République tchèque
Finland[4]	22.6	38.7	48.8	53.4	58.2	59.5	59.9	74.7	75.6	*72.1	Finlande[4]
France	679.5	653.4	620.8	572.3	600.0	...	...	...	...	...	France
Germany	...	...	878.2	826.6	865.3	328.9	334.1	372.1	399.1	...	Allemagne
Germany(Fed.Rep.)	899.0									..	Allemagne(Rép.féd.)
German D.R.(former)	103.6		..	..	..	..	..	..	..	..	R.D.A. (anc.)
Greece	37.6	43.4	31.7	34.0	24.7	42.4	90.6	66.7	53.1	...	Grèce
Hungary	32.1	28.0	29.7	31.2	32.9	36.2	32.5	35.2	31.6	33.9	Hongrie
Italy	739.2	561.4	575.0	553.3	562.4	609.3	563.0	524.3	512.0	499.8	Italie
Netherlands	245.2	239.4	254.9	...	...	...	...	...	...	...	Pays-Bas
Poland	62.6	48.1	44.0	46.9	49.5	56.9	62.1	59.4	66.4	67.8	Pologne
Romania	106.2	93.1	71.4	60.4	57.3	54.9	55.0	58.3	56.8	54.3	Roumanie
Russian Federation	..	...	...	732.0	583.8	608.8	478.5	504.2	430.2	561.0	Fédération de Russie
Slovenia	..	17.7	17.6	16.8	...	...	18.9	20.6	22.1	6.6	Slovénie
Spain	169.4	178.4	247.7	142.4	230.5	292.6	359.2	379.8	402.5	347.3	Espagne
Sweden	79.7	87.2	92.5	73.2	88.8	90.2	89.7	94.6	81.7	78.5	Suède
Ukraine	...	279.8	256.7	201.4	173.8	172.9	171.6	107.6	81.7	47.7	Ukraine
United Kingdom	[5]162.6	[5]153.4	...	206.6	179.6	206.8	199.3	210.7	203.9	...	Royaume-Uni
Yugoslavia	..	18.6	11.0	7.3	7.2	10.2	13.3	25.8	24.8	11.4	Yougoslavie
T.F.Yug.Rep. Macedonia		15.6	11.8	10.8	13.5	8.0	8.2	5.4	4.3	3.3	L'ex-RY Macédoine
Oceania	**60**	**56**	**59**	**62**	**59**	**59**	**59**	**59**	**59**	**59**	**Océanie**
Australia[2]	60.5	55.7	...	62.2	...	...	...	...	...	...	Australie[2]
Total	**10973**	**12179**	**12408**	**11883**	**12096**	**11912**	**11999**	**12421**	**12366**	**12072**	**Total**

General Note.
HCl in all forms, in terms of 100 per cent HCl. Chloro-sulphuric acids are excluded. (SITC, Rev.3: 52231-1).

[1] Strength of acid not known.
[2] Twelve months ending 30 June of year stated.
[3] Sales.
[4] Original data in 33 per cent HCl.
[5] Sales by manufacturers employing 25 or more persons.

Remarque générale.
HCl sous toutes ses formes sur la base de 100 p. 100 de HCl, à l'exclusion de l'acide chlorosulfonique. (CTCI, Rev.3: 52231-1).

[1] Titre de l'acide inconnu.
[2] Période de douze mois finissant le 30 juin de l'année indiquée.
[3] Ventes.
[4] Données d'origine en HCl de 33 p. 100.
[5] Ventes des fabricants employant 25 personnes ou plus.

Sulphuric acid
Acide sulfurique

ISIC-BASED CODE - CODE BASE CITI

3511-47

Unit : Thousand metric tons

Unité : Milliers de tonnes métriques

Country or area	1990	1991	1992	1993	1994	1995	1996	1997	1998	1999	Pays ou zone
Africa	**3556**	**3568**	**3807**	**3724**	**4313**	**4417**	**4764**	**4395**	**4869**	**5079**	**Afrique**
Algeria	39	46	52	55	40	45	42	55	45	48	Algérie
Egypt	92	101	111	122	112	133	299	84	...	...	Egypte
Tunisia	3425	3421	3644	3547	4161	4239	4423	4256	4657	4858	Tunisie
America, North	**44507**	**16880**	**16311**	**15791**	**15734**	**15554**	**15353**	**14941**	**15040**	**14944**	**Amérique du Nord**
Canada	3830	3676	3776	3713	4059	3844	4278	*4100	4333	...	Canada
Mexico	455	362	195	178	375	...	...	...	...	...	Mexique
United States	[1]40222	[2]12842	[2]12340	[2]11900	[2]11300	[2]11500	[2]10900	[2]10700	[2]10600	[2]10400	Etats-Unis
America, South	**4466**	**5255**	**4850**	**5404**	**6057**	**6246**	**6812**	**7472**	**7704**	**8482**	**Amérique du Sud**
Argentina	209	243	219	206	204	226	220	...	...	...	Argentine
Bolivia	1	1	0	1	3	*1	...	...	...	...	Bolivie
Brazil	3451	3634	3257	3724	4112	4043	4308	4638	4624	4882	Brésil
Chile	347	804	887	920	1174	1427	1518	1864	1983	2436	Chili
Colombia	76	...	91	77	103	86	...	95	93	...	Colombie
Peru	172	207	143	229	215	216	429	411	541	592	Pérou
Venezuela	210	277	253	...	...	...	...	...	...	...	Venezuela
Asia	**23218**	**31777**	**30865**	**28080**	**28443**	**32346**	**33696**	**35077**	**36234**	**38308**	**Asie**
Azerbaijan	..	552	269	141	56	24	31	53	24	26	Azerbaïdjan
Bangladesh[3]	3	10	8	7	6	5	9	4	...	...	Bangladesh[3]
China	11969	13329	14087	13365	15365	18110	18836	20369	21710	23560	Chine
India	3272	3904	4183	3730	3745	4402	4988	4830	5366	5686	Inde
Indonesia	40	52	52	42	35	35	...	224	314	...	Indonésie
Israel	154	...	...	...	...	...	...	...	...	...	Israël
Japan	6887	7057	7100	6937	6594	6888	6851	6828	6739	6943	Japon
Kazakhstan	..	2815	2349	1179	681	695	653	635	605	685	Kazakhstan
Pakistan[3]	90	93	98	100	102	80	69	31	28	27	Pakistan[3]
Syrian Arab Republic	8	8	10	10	...	...	...	...	...	...	Rép. arabe syrienne
Thailand[4]	72	82	...	...	...	...	...	...	...	...	Thaïlande[4]
Turkey	716	532	642	757	730	765	[5]798	947	913	828	Turquie
Turkmenistan	..	788	353	206	70	76	120	31	47	...	Turkménistan
Uzbekistan	..	2393	1476	1361	805	1016	984	870	...	...	Ouzbékistan
Viet Nam	8	9	7	...	...	10	18	15	23	*24	Viet Nam
Europe	**25215**	**39493**	**32359**	**27056**	**25355**	**27626**	**26102**	**28081**	**27166**	**27504**	**Europe**
Albania	68	21	11	6	4	...	0	0	0	0	Albanie
Belarus	..	998	616	399	291	437	549	698	640	614	Bélarus
Belgium	[6]1906	[6]1936	[6]1906	[6]1593	[7]717	[7]673	[7]678	[7]668	[7]596	[7]709	Belgique
Bulgaria	522	356	404	409	428	454	525	556	499	456	Bulgarie
Croatia	..	187	278	178	206	233	223	202	164	...	Croatie
Denmark[9]	[8]90	[8]37	[8]38	...	5	25	19	2	...	...	Danemark[9]
Czechoslovakia(former)	1089	682	..	...	...	...	...	...	...	...	Tchécoslovaquie(anc.)
Czech Republic	..	..	522	383	337	340	345	333	327	318	République tchèque
Estonia	..	460	46	...	0	...	...	...	...	...	Estonie
Finland	1010	1015	1087	1179	1084	1159	1288	2182	2496	2857	Finlande
France	3771	3627	2871	2357	2227	[5]2382	[5]2263	[5]2243	[5]2231	...	France
Germany	..	3064	...	...	[5]2781	1387	1225	1370	1601	...	Allemagne
Germany(Fed.Rep.)	3221	..	..	..	..	...	...	...	...	...	Allemagne(Rép.féd.)
German D.R.(former)	431	..	...	..	..	...	...	...	..	..	R.D.A. (anc.)
Greece	950	841	617	550	623	753	1544	1655	814	...	Grèce
Hungary[10]	263	141	99	77	80	114	94	89	62	53	Hongrie[10]
Italy	2038	1853	1733	1430	1975	2161	2214	2214	2013	1627	Italie
Lithuania	..	368	141	129	212	344	425	504	619	800	Lituanie
Netherlands	...	...	...	...	...	[5]500	[5]418	[5]356	[5]429	[9] [11]487	Pays-Bas
Norway	...	...	615	...	...	...	...	...	...	...	Norvège
Poland	1721	1088	1244	1145	1452	1861	1761	1741	1707	1505	Pologne
Portugal	260	51	...	...	[5]2	[5]3	[5]10	[5]11	[5]15	...	Portugal
Romania	1111	745	572	527	491	477	422	329	229	234	Roumanie
Russian Federation	..	11597	9704	8243	6334	6946	5764	6247	5840	7148	Fédération de Russie
Slovakia	..	..	...	...	...	...	[5]62	73	68	16	Slovaquie
Slovenia	..	86	121	114	123	116	103	109	128	126	Slovénie
Spain	2848	1628	1724	1199	1375	2847	2265	2817	[5]3134	...	Espagne

For general note and footnotes, see end of table.

Voir la fin du tableau pour la remarque générale et les notes.

Sulphuric acid (continued)
Acide sulfurique (suite)

ISIC-BASED CODE - CODE BASE CITI

3511-47

Unit : Thousand metric tons

Unité : Milliers de tonnes métriques

Country or area	1990	1991	1992	1993	1994	1995	1996	1997	1998	1999	Pays ou zone
Sweden	855	928	...	...	487	507	[5]572	566	383	415	Suède
Ukraine	..	4186	3000	1843	1646	1593	1577	1438	1354	1393	Ukraine
United Kingdom	1997	1852	1568	1268	1266	1293	[5]643	[5]613	716	...	Royaume-Uni
Yugoslavia	..	582	302	80	24	87	231	177	211	30	Yougoslavie
T.F.Yug.Rep. Macedonia	..	102	95	89	72	82	99	105	101	88	L'ex-RY Macédoine
USSR (former)	27267	..	..	..	..	..	..	..	..	..	URSS (anc.)
Oceania	1464	986	816	868	833	579	441	303	165	27	Océanie
Australia[3]	1464	986	816	868	833	...	...	...	...	...	Australie[3]
Total	129693	97959	89008	80923	80735	86768	87169	90269	91177	94345	Total

General Note.

H_2SO_4 in terms of pure monohydrate sulphuric acid, including the sulphuric acid equivalent of oleum or fuming sulphuric acid (H_2SO_4 + NSO_3). (SITC, Rev.3: 52232-1).

[1] Including data for government-owned, but privately-operated plants.

[2] Sold or used by producers.
[3] Twelve months ending 30 June of year stated.
[4] Strength of acid not known.
[5] Source: United Nations Economic Commission for Europe (ECE), (Geneva).

[6] Production by establishments employing 5 or more persons.
[7] Incomplete coverage.
[8] Excluding quantities consumed by superphosphate industry.
[9] Sales.
[10] Including regenerated sulphuric acid.
[11] Production by establishments employing 20 or more persons.

Remarque générale.

H_2SO_4 sur la base de l'acide sulfurique monohydraté, y compris l'équivalent en acide sulfurique de l'oléum ou acide sulfurique fumant (H_2SO_4 + NSO_3). (CTCI, Rev.3: 52232-1).

[1] Y compris les données relatives à des usines appartenant à l'Etat mais exploitées par des entreprises privées.
[2] Vendu ou utilisé par les producteurs.
[3] Période de douze mois finissant le 30 juin de l'année indiquée.
[4] Titre de l'acide inconnu.
[5] Source: Commission économique des Nations Unies pour l'Europe (CEE), (Genève).
[6] Production des établissements occupant 5 personnes ou plus.
[7] Couverture incomplète.
[8] Non compris les quantités utilisées par l'industrie des superphosphates.
[9] Ventes.
[10] Y compris l'acide sulfurique régénéré.
[11] Production des établissements occupant 20 personnes ou plus.

Nitric acid
Acide nitrique

ISIC-BASED CODE - CODE BASE CITI

3511-49

Unit : Thousand metric tons   Unité : Milliers de tonnes métriques

Country or area	1990	1991	1992	1993	1994	1995	1996	1997	1998	1999	Pays ou zone
Africa	**4**	**2**	**5**	**5**	**2**	**2**	**2**	**2**	**2**	**2**	**Afrique**
Egypt	4	2	5	5	2	2	2	2	...	...	Egypte
America, North	**8124**	**2529**	**2606**	**8411**	**8820**	**8924**	**9395**	**9563**	**9364**	**9095**	**Amérique du Nord**
Canada	...	912	919	916	910	899	1039	*1000	935	...	Canada
Mexico	5	7	7	7	5	...	...	...	...	...	Mexique
United States	7194	1610	1680	7488	7905	8019	8350	8557	8423	8115	Etats-Unis
America, South	**516**	**515**	**513**	**533**	**685**	**729**	**725**	**742**	**586**	**609**	**Amérique du Sud**
Argentina	28	26	26	24	30	29	26	33	...	...	Argentine
Brazil	387	405	399	417	554	574	612	612	533	525	Brésil
Colombia	39	...	32	36	50	63	...	69	18	...	Colombie
Peru	62	...	56	56	51	63	43	28	5	*0	Pérou
Asia	**1056**	**1220**	**1549**	**1694**	**1513**	**1990**	**1893**	**1698**	**1955**	**1919**	**Asie**
China	318	343	444	561	493	560	642	670	755	751	Chine
Indonesia	50	...	...	29	...	59	...	10	27	...	Indonésie
Japan	683	698	691	678	675	698	660	668	631	620	Japon
Turkey	[1]5	[1]7	192	217	134	541	418	224	397	382	Turquie
Turkmenistan	..	89	154	194	167	122	121	109	145	...	Turkménistan
Uzbekistan	..	48	33	15	9	10	17	17	...	...	Ouzbékistan
Europe	**9709**	**11072**	**11040**	**9628**	**9988**	**10923**	**10162**	**9291**	**9103**	**8803**	**Europe**
Belarus	..	936	874	849	935	837	707	833	978	998	Bélarus
Belgium[2]	1453	1434	1626	1320	...	...	...	...	...	...	Belgique[2]
Bulgaria	1213	874	712	609	719	1033	1055	812	521	394	Bulgarie
Croatia	..	292	382	288	311	299	279	293	221	...	Croatie
Denmark	[3]41	[3]18	[3]16	[3]5	2	[3]8	[3]12	[3]9	[3]13	...	Danemark
Czech Republic	..	..	...	...	422	485	414	404	433	369	République tchèque
Finland	551	482	433	465	501	217	223	...	...	...	Finlande
Germany	..	483	445	443	450	1357	1522	...	...	...	Allemagne
German D.R.(former)	753	..	..	..	..	..	...	...	...	..	R.D.A. (anc.)
Greece	511	421	441	...	...	...	...	...	...	...	Grèce
Hungary	726	366	211	310	...	...	...	...	...	...	Hongrie
Italy	1037	988	937	724	532	588	545	...	...	...	Italie
Poland	1577	1438	1388	1608	1701	1931	1929	1808	1671	1635	Pologne
Portugal	297	247	...	...	...	...	...	...	...	...	Portugal
Russian Federation	..	541	380,	299	209	228	147	155	160	171	Fédération de Russie
Slovakia	..	..	...	...	...	...	123	...	...	...	Slovaquie
Spain	1203	1070	935	...	...	...	229	245	465	480	Espagne
Sweden	347	639	247	259	350	390	122	86	90	85	Suède
Ukraine	..	654	1009	380	325	26	35	17	11	11	Ukraine
Yugoslavia	..	189	163	116	156	149	229	240	185	79	Yougoslavie
Total	**19409**	**15338**	**15713**	**20271**	**21009**	**22568**	**22177**	**21296**	**21010**	**20428**	**Total**

General Note.

HNO$_3$ in terms of 100 per cent HNO$_3$. Sulpho-nitric acids are excluded. (SITC. Rev.3: 52233-1).

Remarque générale.

HNO$_3$ sur la base de HNO$_3$ à 100 p. 100, à l'exclusion des acides sulfonitriques. (CTCI, Rev.3: 52233-1).

[1] State sector only.
[2] Production by establishments employing 5 or more persons.
[3] Sales.

[1] Secteur public seulement.
[2] Production des établissements occupant 5 personnes ou plus.
[3] Ventes.

Phosphoric acid
Acide phosphorique

ISIC-BASED CODE - CODE BASE CITI

3511-50

Unit : Thousand metric tons

Unité : Milliers de tonnes métriques

Country or area	1990	1991	1992	1993	1994	1995	1996	1997	1998	1999	Pays ou zone
Africa	**424**	**440**	**469**	**468**	**530**	**552**	**576**	**607**	**632**	**908**	**Afrique**
Morocco	3.9	4.7	3.9	5.1	4.6	2.6	2.6	2.7	2.7	2.7	Maroc
Tunisia	419.7	435.2	465.0	463.3	525.4	549.4	573.9	604.0	629.0	905.0	Tunisie
America, North	**11503**	**11321**	**11872**	**11230**	**12343**	**12801**	**12993**	**12944**	**13495**	**13910**	**Amérique du Nord**
Canada[1]	402.0	348.0	...	...	...	...	...	...	...	...	Canada[1]
Mexico	183.8	165.7	148.4	...	363.2	510.8	634.0	631.0	518.0	526.3	Mexique
United States	10917.5	10807.0	11349.0	10446.0	11605.0	11915.0	11984.0	11938.0	12601.9	...	Etats-Unis
America, South	**616**	**671**	**493**	**605**	**724**	**738**	**786**	**803**	**827**	**904**	**Amérique du Sud**
Brazil	609.2	664.3	487.2	600.6	[2]716.8	[2]727.2	[2]778.4	[2]795.9	[2]819.8	[2]897.0	Brésil
Colombia	...	...	6.3	4.4	7.5	11.0	...	6.6	7.5	...	Colombie
Asia	**236**	**1404**	**1289**	**1128**	**385**	**420**	**436**	**382**	**256**	**294**	**Asie**
Japan	165.2	164.2	151.3	147.8	139.5	147.8	143.1	145.2	138.2	173.8	Japon
Kazakhstan	..	537.8	322.7	142.6	69.9	53.0	27.9	14.6	8.0	11.1	Kazakhstan
Turkey	70.7	61.3	222.1	189.6	63.7	67.6	78.1	108.2	109.3	108.8	Turquie
Turkmenistan	..	117.9	291.0	401.8	1.3	2.9	...	...	...	...	Turkménistan
Uzbekistan	..	523.0	302.0	246.0	110.3	149.0	179.7	113.6	...	...	Ouzbékistan
Europe	**4447**	**4812**	**4162**	**3559**	**3209**	**3474**	**3959**	**3866**	**3321**	**3107**	**Europe**
Belarus	..	199.4	102.9	69.2	35.4	36.4	78.4	93.4	87.3	75.9	Bélarus
Belgium	535.9	647.8	682.8	694.9	[2]283.4	[2]283.2	[2]324.5	[2]326.6	[2]286.6	[2]240.5	Belgique
Bulgaria	66.0	52.2	43.8	45.6	52.6	58.0	85.2	100.0	...	...	Bulgarie
Croatia	..	56.6	71.5	49.3	55.2	62.0	54.8	58.8	44.7	...	Croatie
Czechoslovakia(former)	68.3	47.1	..	...	...	...	...	...	...	..	Tchécoslovaquie(anc.)
Czech Republic	..	..	[1]35.5	...	25.3	25.4	23.4	24.8	16.0	1.1	République tchèque
Finland	175.3	156.6	180.4	204.9	215.2	232.2	235.4	...	...	...	Finlande
France	[3]424.0	[3]453.6	[3]470.0	[3]277.8	[1]238.5	...	...	...	...	...	France
Germany	..	[1]271.4	259.5	219.4	105.9	...	...	[1]73.3	...	...	Allemagne
Germany(Fed.Rep.)	327.9	..	..	..	..	..	..	..	..	..	Allemagne(Rép.féd.)
Greece	341.5	319.1	164.9	136.5	140.1	165.9	376.1	428.2	155.7	...	Grèce
Hungary	48.4	27.8	17.3	14.8	[1]11.8	...	...	...	...	...	Hongrie
Italy	225.3	168.8	87.0	1.8	0.0	0.0	0.0	0.0	0.0	0.0	Italie
Lithuania	..	93.5	36.9	39.7	75.0	123.4	150.7	183.8	235.5	294.0	Lituanie
Netherlands	...	...	...	156.1	199.3	264.8	290.7	271.0	[1]231.2	[4][5]270.9	Pays-Bas
Poland	[1]317.2	[1]226.1	[1]306.1	[3]259.3	[3]366.3	[3]449.1	[3]493.0	[3]509.9	[3]490.0	[3]438.0	Pologne
Romania	247.1	93.9	111.5	164.4	165.8	197.7	164.3	103.3	63.8	62.5	Roumanie
Russian Federation	..	..	..	11.6	35.3	32.7	21.5	23.7	21.0	28.0	Fédération de Russie
Slovenia	..	17.5	16.3	17.8	7.7	0.1	0.1	0.1	0.1	0.0	Slovénie
Spain	597.5	463.3	383.3	393.7	[1]448.1	[1]432.0	[1]506.5	[1]493.2	[1]490.4	360.6	Espagne
Sweden	[6]168.7	[6]170.0	...	...	59.0	[6]36.3	...	64.4	64.1	0.0	Suède
Ukraine	..	509.0	408.8	211.1	213.6	196.9	216.1	230.6	220.3	169.5	Ukraine
United Kingdom[1]	...	508.0	404.0	...	...	...	...	...	...	...	Royaume-Uni[1]
Yugoslavia		104.3	53.4	9.1	0.2	3.8	41.0	44.2	31.8	10.8	Yougoslavie
T.F.Yug.Rep. Macedonia	..	20.9	26.0	23.8	19.8	23.9	20.8	16.1	24.1	21.7	L'ex-RY Macédoine
Yugoslavia, SFR	280.9	..	..	..	..	..	..	..	..		Yougoslavie, RSF
USSR (former)[1]	5042.7	..	..	..	..	..	..	..	..	..	URSS (anc.)[1]
Total	**22269**	**18648**	**18286**	**16990**	**17192**	**17986**	**18750**	**18601**	**18530**	**19122**	**Total**

General Note.

In terms of phosphorus pentoxide (P_2O_5), orthophosphoric acid (H_3PO_4), pyrophosphoric acid ($H_4P_2O_7$) and metaphosphoric acid(HPO_3) produced by the thermal process, by sulphuric acid reaction or by other processes. (SITC, Rev.3: 52234-2).

[1] Source: United Nations Economic Commission for Europe (ECE), (Geneva).

[2] Incomplete coverage.

[3] In terms of P_2O_5, coloured or not, for industrial use.

[4] Production by establishments employing 20 or more persons.

[5] Sales.

[6] Orthophosphoric acid.

Remarque générale.

Acide orthophosphorique (H_3PO_4), acide pyrophosphorique ($H_4P_2O_7$) et acide métaphosphorique (HPO_3) obtenus par l'action de la chaleur, par réaction avec l'acide sulfurique ou par d'autres procédés. Exprimé sur la base d'anhydride phosphorique (P_2O_5). (CTCI, Rev.3:: 52234-2).

[1] Source: Commission économique des Nations Unies pour l'Europe (CEE), (Genève).

[2] Couverture incomplète.

[3] En poids de P_2O_5, coloré ou non, pour usages industriels.

[4] Production des établissements occupant 20 personnes ou plus.

[5] Ventes.

[6] Acide orthophosphorique.

Carbon bisulphide
Sulfure de carbone

ISIC-BASED CODE - CODE BASE CITI

3511-53

Country or area	1990	1991	1992	1993	1994	1995	1996	1997	1998	1999	Pays ou zone
America, North	**272**	**272**	**272**	**272**	**272**	**272**	**272**	**272**	**272**	**272**	**Amérique du Nord**
Mexico	...	...	...	271.6	...	...	...	...	...	...	Mexique
America, South	**22**	**19**	**19**	**20**	**20**	**18**	**17**	**17**	**15**	**17**	**Amérique du Sud**
Argentina	7.8	8.9	9.3	...	...	...	...	...	...	...	Argentine
Brazil	14.3	9.9	10.2	11.8	11.5	9.4	8.5	8.5	6.9	8.4	Brésil
Asia	**73**	**68**	**59**	**58**	**50**	**48**	**45**	**46**	**44**	**42**	**Asie**
Japan[1]	72.5	68.2	59.5	57.6	49.7	47.9	45.3	45.9	...	...	Japon[1]
Europe	**140**	**115**	**106**	**100**	**105**	**108**	**92**	**85**	**88**	**86**	**Europe**
Bulgaria	17.3	20.4	20.8	13.5	10.5	13.3	13.6	12.6	...	...	Bulgarie
Poland	99.7	70.1	62.9	64.3	73.0	71.9	56.4	50.2	54.1	53.0	Pologne
Spain	23.4	21.4	19.6	...	...	...	...	...	...	...	Espagne
Yugoslavia	..	3.0	2.3	0.5	0.4	1.1	0.7	1.0	0.7	0.0	Yougoslavie
Total	**507**	**473**	**456**	**449**	**447**	**445**	**426**	**420**	**419**	**416**	**Total**

General Note.
CS_2. (SITC, Rev.3: 52242-1).

Remarque générale.
CS_2. (CTCI, Rev.3: 52242-1).

[1] Beginning 1999, series discontinued.

[1] A partir de 1999, série abandonnée.

Zinc oxide
Oxyde de zinc

ISIC-BASED CODE - CODE BASE CITI

3511-54

Unit : Thousand metric tons   Unité : Milliers de tonnes métriques

Country or area	1990	1991	1992	1993	1994	1995	1996	1997	1998	1999	Pays ou zone
Africa	**0**	**0**	**0**	**0**	**0**	**0**	**0**	**0**	**0**	**0**	**Afrique**
Kenya	0.3	0.3	0.4	0.4	...	0.3	0.4	...	...	...	Kenya
America, North	**101**	**98**	**107**	**142**	**150**	**144**	**169**	**180**	**177**	**156**	**Amérique du Nord**
Mexico	2.8	2.9	2.6	#39.8	44.1	40.1	43.5	50.7	38.5	42.0	Mexique
United States	98.0	94.6	103.9	102.0	106.0	104.0	125.0	129.0	138.0	114.0	Etats-Unis
America, South	**23**	**25**	**24**	**29**	**29**	**27**	**27**	**7**	**30**	**35**	**Amérique du Sud**
Brazil	19.9	22.3	23.0	25.8	25.6	22.8	24.5	2.7	29.2	32.5	Brésil
Colombia	...	...	1.3	3.3	3.0	3.7	...	4.7	0.8	...	Colombie
Asia	**96**	**98**	**100**	**93**	**96**	**89**	**94**	**93**	**98**	**97**	**Asie**
Indonesia	4.3	4.1	9.6	9.3	13.7	4.6	...	4.7	13.9	...	Indonésie
Japan	83.2	84.9	82.3	75.2	73.9	76.0	76.0	79.7	77.2	78.9	Japon
Thailand [1]	...	...	...	...	...	...	9.8	8.3	7.4	...	Thaïlande [1]
Europe	**251**	**244**	**232**	**232**	**233**	**237**	**241**	**208**	**193**	**202**	**Europe**
Belgium	...	...	...	...	...	47.2	50.8	52.0	32.0	32.9	Belgique
Czech Republic	..	...	...	...	...	...	0.6	0.8	0.7	0.8	République tchèque
Finland	1.7	1.2	1.4	1.5	1.9	1.8	2.2	...	...	...	Finlande
France	44.6	40.1	32.5	...	...	...	...	...	...	...	France
Germany	..	...	...	49.2	46.7	...	...	...	...	...	Allemagne
Germany(Fed.Rep.)	44.2	..	..	..	..	..	..	..	..		Allemagne(Rép.féd.)
German D.R.(former)	4.4	..	..	..	..	..	..	..	..	..	R.D.A. (anc.)
Greece	0.2	0.2	0.2	...	...	...	...	...	...		Grèce
Romania	8.9	2.8	3.4	4.5	4.5	5.3	5.9	3.4	2.1	1.7	Roumanie
Slovenia	..	1.0	0.6	0.0	0.0	...	...	...	...		Slovénie
Spain	8.5	16.3	19.3	...	...	...	32.2	...	39.2	36.1	Espagne
Sweden	2.4	1.8	...	0.0	...	...	0.4	...	...	...	Suède
United Kingdom	...	...	...	47.8	54.3	65.9	58.9	34.0	25.9	...	Royaume-Uni
Yugoslavia	..	1.7	1.3	0.2	0.4	0.7	0.7	0.4	0.5	0.2	Yougoslavie
T.F.Yug.Rep. Macedonia	..	1.1	1.6	...	...	...	...	...	...	...	L'ex-RY Macédoine
Total	**472**	**464**	**464**	**496**	**508**	**497**	**531**	**488**	**498**	**491**	**Total**

General Note.
ZnO zinc white including zinc peroxide (ZnO_2). Natural zinc oxide or zincite is excluded. (SITC, Rev.3: 52251-0).

Remarque générale.
Blanc de zinc ZnO, y compris le peroxyde de zinc (ZnO_2), mais non compris l'oxyde de zinc naturel ou zincite. (CTCI, Rev.3: 52251-0).

[1] Beginning 1999, series discontinued.

[1] A partir de 1999, série abandonnée.

Titanium oxides
Oxydes de titane

ISIC-BASED CODE - CODE BASE CITI

3511-55

Unit : Thousand metric tons   Unité : Milliers de tonnes métriques

Country or area	1990	1991	1992	1993	1994	1995	1996	1997	1998	1999	Pays ou zone
America, North	**979**	**992**	**1140**	**1160**	**1250**	**1250**	**1230**	**1330**	**1323**	**1355**	**Amérique du Nord**
United States	978.7	992.0	1140.0	1160.0	1250.0	1250.0	1230.0	1330.2	1323.3	1354.7	Etats-Unis
America, South	**46**	**42**	**43**	**59**	**59**	**59**	**65**	**79**	**92**	**86**	**Amérique du Sud**
Brazil	46.0	41.7	42.6	59.4	58.9	58.6	65.1	78.9	91.8	85.8	Brésil
Asia	**296**	**296**	**270**	**270**	**268**	**265**	**251**	**257**	**273**	**292**	**Asie**
India[1]	[2]16.5	[2]16.9	[2]18.0	[2]23.7	[2]30.4	[2]15.6	[2]13.3	[2]15.7	[2]22.1	23.0	Inde[1]
Japan	279.8	279.1	252.3	246.0	238.0	249.3	237.9	241.4	251.3	269.2	Japon
Europe	**157**	**367**	**537**	**527**	**555**	**673**	**895**	**878**	**994**	**1056**	**Europe**
Belgium	57.5	69.5	77.3	76.2	...	...	...	...	[3]87.4	...	Belgique
Czechoslovakia(former)[3]	23.3	13.6	..	..	..	..	..	..	..	..	Tchécoslovaquie(anc.)[3]
Czech Republic[3]	..	..	20.0	...	22.1	23.0	23.6	22.2	27.9	..	République tchèque[3]
Germany	..	...	317.2	300.1	332.4	[3]431.2	[3]656.1	...	...	...	Allemagne
Slovenia[2]	..	...	...	20.2	26.6	30.0	26.8	29.3	35.0	36.5	Slovénie[2]
Spain	[2]54.4	[2]54.2	[2]54.1	60.2	61.3	53.8	[3]64.5	[3]65.7	[3]62.8	...	Espagne
Ukraine[3]	..	...	...	...	39.5	61.8	50.8	36.8	49.7	66.9	Ukraine[3]
Yugoslavia, SFR[3]	21.8	..	..	..	..	..	..	..	..	..	Yougoslavie, RSF[3]
USSR (former)[3]	113.1	..	..	..	..	..	..	..	..	..	URSS (anc.)[3]
Total	**1591**	**1696**	**1990**	**2016**	**2133**	**2247**	**2442**	**2544**	**2682**	**2788**	**Total**

General Note.
TiO$_2$ and TiO$_3$. Natural titanium dioxide is excluded. (SITC, Rev.3: 52256-0).

[1] Production by large and medium scale establishments only.
[2] Titanium dioxide only.
[3] Source: United Nations Economic Commission for Europe (ECE), (Geneva).

Remarque générale.
TiO$_2$ et TiO$_3$, à l'exclusion du bioxyde de titane naturel. (CTCI, Rev.3: 52256-0).

[1] Production des grandes et moyennes entreprises seulement.
[2] Bioxyde de titane seulement.
[3] Source: Commission économique des Nations Unies pour l'Europe (CEE), (Genève).

Lead oxides
Oxydes de plomb

ISIC-BASED CODE - CODE BASE CITI

3511-57

Unit : Thousand metric tons

Unité : Milliers de tonnes métriques

Country or area	1990	1991	1992	1993	1994	1995	1996	1997	1998	1999	Pays ou zone
Africa	**3**	**3**	**2**	**2**	**1**	**1**	**1**	**1**	**1**	**0**	**Afrique**
Egypt	2.6	2.9	2.4	1.6	1.1	0.8	0.7	0.9	...	...	Egypte
America, North	**364**	**458**	**310**	**322**	**350**	**664**	**705**	**767**	**778**	**765**	**Amérique du Nord**
Mexico	29.9	29.7	28.7	46.2	57.8	52.2	50.3	54.8	41.6	37.4	Mexique
United States	...	428.5	280.9	276.0	292.0	612.0	655.0	712.0	736.0	728.0	Etats-Unis
America, South	**5**	**4**	**2**	**3**	**5**	**4**	**3**	**0**	**1**	**0**	**Amérique du Sud**
Colombia	...	...	2.5	3.0	4.8	3.6	...	0.3	1.2	...	Colombie
Asia	**74**	**78**	**68**	**68**	**65**	**59**	**53**	**49**	**44**	**34**	**Asie**
India[1]	11.2	13.6	10.8	11.0	10.0	10.5	9.2	...	...	...	Inde[1]
Japan	63.0	64.4	56.8	57.1	55.3	48.1	44.0	40.2	35.5	...	Japon
Europe	**32**	**300**	**303**	**496**	**503**	**299**	**92**	**103**	**298**	**297**	**Europe**
Germany	..	...	...	468.2	472.5	...	62.9	71.9	...	...	Allemagne
Portugal	8.1	9.3	...	...	...	...	...	...	...	...	Portugal
Spain	18.1	15.8	22.3	...	...	...	...	...	...	...	Espagne
Sweden	5.9	6.1	...	0.0	...	...	1.6	3.3	1.5	0.9	Suède
Total	**478**	**843**	**685**	**891**	**924**	**1026**	**854**	**920**	**1121**	**1097**	**Total**

General Note.
Such as oxide, dioxide, litharge, massicot, minium, orange lead, puce oxide etc.
(SITC, Rev.3: 52257-0).

Remarque générale.
Notamment le protoxyde de plomb (litharge, massicot), le minium, la mine orange,
le bioxyde de plomb (oxyde puce de plomb) etc. (CTCI, Rev.3: 52257-0).

[1] Production by large and medium scale establishments only.

[1] Production des grandes et moyennes entreprises seulement.

Ammonia
Ammoniac

ISIC-BASED CODE - CODE BASE CITI

3511-58

Unit : Thousand metric tons

Unité : Milliers de tonnes métriques

Country or area	1990	1991	1992	1993	1994	1995	1996	1997	1998	1999	Pays ou zone
Africa	**1281**	**1140**	**1422**	**1426**	**1279**	**1161**	**1112**	**1355**	**1328**	**1431**	**Afrique**
Algeria	377	305	533	462	310	217	176	458	426	487	Algérie
Egypt	...	...	...	...	15	15	2	...	...	...	Egypte
Nigeria[1]	...	367	337	270	*200	*170	*164	*134	*168	*148	Nigéria[1]
South Africa[1]	...	457	541	683	754	759	770	752	723	785	Afrique du Sud[1]
America, North	**23435**	**20425**	**21408**	**20444**	**21783**	**21432**	**21982**	**21825**	**22722**	**23273**	**Amérique du Nord**
Canada	...	3669	3770	4181	4368	4246	4282	*4779	4737	...	Canada
Cuba*[1]	...	140	135	135	130	135	135	135	135	135	Cuba*[1]
Mexico[1]	...	2221	2203	1760	2030	1992	2054	1448	1449	1003	Mexique[1]
Trinidad and Tobago	...	[1]1595	1900	1768	1955	2059	2111	2163	2601	3327	Trinité-et-Tobago
United States	15424	12800	13400	12600	13300	13000	13400	13300	13800	14100	Etats-Unis
America, South	**1981**	**1737**	**1602**	**1782**	**1751**	**1918**	**1908**	**1992**	**1800**	**1964**	**Amérique du Sud**
Argentina	88	86	72	93	89	96	102	127	102	111	Argentine
Brazil	1153	1012	1038	1153	1157	1222	1201	1253	1176	1331	Brésil
Colombia	...	[1]92	1	1	0	0	...	...	...	...	Colombie
Venezuela	666	547	491	[1]535	[1]505	[1]600	[1]605	[1]612	[1]522	* [1]522	Venezuela
Asia	**37246**	**40189**	**41886**	**41506**	**42290**	**48445**	**52762**	**55409**	**54623**	**57949**	**Asie**
Afghanistan*[1]	...	...	...	15	15	10	5	5	5	5	Afghanistan*[1]
Bahrain	...	...	...	...	...	...	...	443	130	186	Bahreïn
China	21290	22016	22981	21925	24368	27659	30942	30003	31342	34317	Chine
Georgia[2]	..	...	117	91	53	66	93	102	78	127	Géorgie[2]
India[1][3]	...	...	...	7176	7503	8287	8549	9328	10240	10376	Inde[1][3]
Indonesia	...	...	...	...	767	2031	...	4939	2389	...	Indonésie
Iran(Islamic Rep. of)[1]	...	468	664	723	696	715	882	880	1034	*865	Iran(Rép. islamique)[1]
Israel	76	[1]35	[1]37	[1]41	[1]46	[1]70	[1]65	[1]57	[1]1		Israël
Japan	1831	1855	1788	1708	1713	1831	1811	1836	1689	1685	Japon
Kazakhstan[4]	..	...	...	...	42	59	91	70	7	...	Kazakhstan[4]
Korea, Republic of	...	[1]407	[1]442	[1]450	[1]460	729	704	617	594	560	Corée, République de
Kuwait	...	...	170	385	474	599	501	526	550	...	Koweït
Malaysia[1]	...	...	...	334	313	333	329	243	351	*432	Malaisie[1]
Pakistan[1]	...	...	...	1446	1505	1493	1606	1549	1797	1999	Pakistan[1]
Qatar	708	691	756	763	785	794	783	1148	1371	1374	Qatar
Saudi Arabia[1]	...	827	904	1097	1340	1327	1386	1405	1418	1402	Arabie saoudite[1]
Syrian Arab Republic	...	...	[1]81	[1]67	[1]67	30	36	22	46	43	Rép. arabe syrienne
Tajikistan	...	...	...	...	[4]13	[4]22	[4]19	[4]19	21	10	Tadjikistan
Turkey	446	424	405	639	503	586	605	624	357	100	Turquie
Turkmenistan	...	22	39	122	102	86	85	74	93	...	Turkménistan
United Arab Emirates[1]	...	286	275	306	287	363	331	373	331	380	Emirats arabes unis[1]
Uzbekistan	..	1736	1593	1344	985	1102	1155	1147	...	...	Ouzbékistan
Europe	**19614**	**35748**	**33040**	**30118**	**28693**	**30760**	**31396**	**29091**	**25303**	**28007**	**Europe**
Albania	...	...	* [1]15	* [1]15	* [1]15	* [1]15	* [1]15	...	...	0	Albanie
Belarus	...	1233	1115	753	656	813	824	718	833	931	Bélarus
Belgium	...	[1]272	[1]514	[1]535	[4]774	[4]365	...	[4]315	[4]287	...	Belgique
Bulgaria	1309	1093	905	885	995	1203	1194	982	527	378	Bulgarie
Croatia	..	286	350	283	288	310	307	293	220	...	Croatie
Denmark[5]	5	5	6	2	2	2	2	2	1	1	Danemark[5]
Czechoslovakia(former)	971	677	..	..	..	..	..	..	..	..	Tchécoslovaquie(anc.)
Czech Republic	..	..	...	...	345	310	339	312	324	275	République tchèque
Estonia	...	...	...	...	[4]114	[4]138	[4]137	153	175	199	Estonie
Finland	30	30	12	4	5	2	0	0	0	...	Finlande
France	1608	1697	1340	1769	1475	[1]1480	[1]1559	[1]1520	[1]1508	...	France
Germany	..	2123	2113	2100	2170	[2]2593	[2]2565	[2]2547	1076	...	Allemagne
Germany(Fed.Rep.)	1671	..	..	..	..	..	..	..	..	..	Allemagne(Rép.féd.)
German D.R.(former)	984										R.D.A. (anc.)
Greece	313	256	168	...	...	[1]65	[1]90	* [1]83	[1]178	[1]160	Grèce
Hungary	445	262	185	237	[1]250	* [1]250	* [1]250	[4]344	[4]293	264	Hongrie
Iceland[4]	...	...	...	...	9	8	*9	*9	...	...	Islande[4]
Ireland[1]	...	...	...	367	380	408	377	465	458	405	Irlande[1]
Italy	1455	1392	1358	885	612	592	[1]397	[1]446	[1]409	[1]367	Italie
Lithuania	..	620	334	158	277	442	561	467	496	487	Lituanie

For general note and footnotes, see end of table.

Voir la fin du tableau pour la remarque générale et les notes.

Ammonia (continued)
Ammoniac (suite)

ISIC-BASED CODE - CODE BASE CITI

3511-58

Unit : Thousand metric tons

Unité : Milliers de tonnes métriques

Country or area	1990	1991	1992	1993	1994	1995	1996	1997	1998	1999	Pays ou zone
Netherlands	3879	3689	3148	[1]2472	[1]2479	[1]2580	[1]2652	[1]2478	* [1]2350	* [1]2430	Pays-Bas
Norway[1]	...	384	343	315	271	289	295	279	245	122	Norvège[1]
Poland[2]	1962	1531	1490	1419	1500	1726	1752	1739	1299	1151	Pologne[2]
Portugal	...	[1]198	[1]100	[1]91	[1]100	[4]189	[4]243	[4]240	[4]251	...	Portugal
Romania	2178	1375	1733	1620	1443	1809	1841	951	468	834	Roumanie
Russian Federation	..	11936	10529	9900	8838	9657	9650	8737	7965	9280	Fédération de Russie
Slovakia	..	..	...	...	...	...	[4]356	349	311	278	Slovaquie
Spain	521	402	292	400	547	471	438	619	[4]579	...	Espagne
Sweden	...	...	...	...	[4]0		[4]4	0	...	4	Suède
Ukraine[2]	..	4642	4821	3938	3655	3782	4018	4142	3984	4515	Ukraine[2]
United Kingdom	...	[1]1011	[1]869	[1]873	966	[1]799	[1]849	[1]642	[1]871	[1]902	Royaume-Uni
Yugoslavia	..	...	...	...	[4]40	[4]135	[4]235	[4]235	171	57	Yougoslavie
Oceania	476	484	460	476	494	512	514	512	529	541	Océanie
Australia[1]	...	414	392	398	413	433	446	*432	435	431	Australie[1]
New Zealand[1]	...	70	68	78	81	79	68	80	94	110	Nouvelle-Zélande[1]
Total	84032	99723	99817	95752	96291	104228	109674	110184	106305	113164	Total

General Note.
Ammonia obtained from impure ammoniacal gas liquors in coal gas purification and coke works or by synthesis from hydrogen and nitrogen, expressed in terms of 100 per cent N. (SITC, Rev.3: 52261-0).

[1] Source: U. S. Geological Survey, (Washington, D. C.).
[2] Synthetic ammonia only.
[3] Twelve months beginning 1 April of year stated.
[4] Source: United Nations Economic Commission for Europe (ECE), (Geneva).

[5] Sales.

Remarque générale.
Ammoniac obtenu à partir d'eaux ammoniacales impures provenant de l'épuration du gaz d'éclairage et des cokeries, ou par synthèse de l'hydrogène et de l'azote. Exprimé sur la base d'azote pur. (CTCI, Rev.3: 52261-0).

[1] Source: U.S. Geological Survey, (Washington, D.C.).
[2] Ammoniac synthétique seulement.
[3] Période de douze mois commençant le 1er avril de l'année indiquée.
[4] Source: Commission économique des Nations Unies pour l'Europe (CEE), (Genève).
[5] Ventes.

Caustic soda
Soude caustique

ISIC-BASED CODE - CODE BASE CITI

3511-59

Unit : Thousand metric tons

Unité : Milliers de tonnes métriques

Country or area	1990	1991	1992	1993	1994	1995	1996	1997	1998	1999	Pays ou zone
Africa	**70**	**75**	**75**	**76**	**66**	**65**	**67**	**54**	**68**	**75**	**Afrique**
Algeria	17	17	16	...	...	...	...	...	...	...	Algérie
Egypt	53	58	59	59	49	48	50	37	51	58	Egypte
America, North	**12809**	**12923**	**13080**	**12889**	**12954**	**12978**	**13161**	**13182**	**13170**	**13220**	**Amérique du Nord**
Canada	...	1498	1428	1225	1153	1078	1151	*1092	1015	...	Canada
Cuba[1]	12	18	12	9	5	11	8	12	11	...	Cuba[1]
Mexico	380	293	348	347	408	424	463	465	458	439	Mexique
United States	11116	11114	11292	11308	11388	...	...	...	...	...	Etats-Unis
America, South	**1515**	**1566**	**1580**	**1569**	**1578**	**1620**	**1637**	**1673**	**1665**	**1660**	**Amérique du Sud**
Argentina	230	210	160	156	172	186	[1]155	[1]149	...	...	Argentine
Brazil	1105	1211	1238	1271	1273	1270	1322	1379	1356	1352	Brésil
Chile	46	44	53	53	58	58	58	51	49	50	Chili
Colombia	39	...	46	0	0	26	...	...	...	...	Colombie
Peru	60	51	29	30	45	50	56	48	66	72	Pérou
Venezuela	35	28	54	59	30	[1]30	[1]30	...	...	...	Venezuela
Asia	**8946**	**9448**	**9894**	**10040**	**10388**	**11936**	**12708**	**13317**	**13063**	**13780**	**Asie**
Armenia	..	15	15	5	4	4	4	4	4	5	Arménie
Azerbaijan	..	171	92	49	40	36	33	23	21	21	Azerbaïdjan
Bangladesh[2]	6	8	8	8	8	7	8	7	...	...	Bangladesh[2]
China	3354	3541	3795	3954	4295	5318	5738	5744	5394	5801	Chine
India	964	1027	1078	1109	1121	1357	1456	1426	1431	1425	Inde
Indonesia	...	19	40	165	134	...	...	...	...	...	Indonésie
Iran(Islamic Rep. of)	5	5	5	19	33	35	39	...	180	...	Iran(Rép. islamique)
Israel	32	32	29	30	33	45	41	...	...	...	Israël
Japan	3800	3788	3751	3664	3672	3885	3940	4259	4124	4215	Japon
Kazakhstan	..	48	36	15	...	1	...	...	...	...	Kazakhstan
Korea, Republic of	340	385	524	507	496	627	766	959	1069	1163	Corée, République de
Kuwait	...	...	12	16	16	18	17	20	22	21	Koweït
Pakistan[2]	74	78	82	81	89	93	109	118	116	120	Pakistan[2]
Tajikistan	..	31	16	6	6	2	0	1	1	1	Tadjikistan
Thailand[3]	158	194	...	...	...	...	338	455	417	...	Thaïlande[3]
Turkey	100	85	93	92	96	99	95	94	105	91	Turquie
Viet Nam	8	5	5	...	...	7	9	8	10	*13	Viet Nam
Europe	**11099**	**12956**	**12167**	**11436**	**11632**	**11740**	**11089**	**11296**	**10671**	**10938**	**Europe**
Albania	32	11	0	0	0	0	0	0	...	0	Albanie
Belgium	...	...	...	...	621	638	593	657	634	660	Belgique
Bosnia and Herzegovina[4]	..	..	...	...	...	...	...	1	...	...	Bosnie-Herzégovine[4]
Bulgaria	104	77	71	49	71	70	81	80	58	53	Bulgarie
Croatia	..	1	0	0	...	0	0	0	0	...	Croatie
Denmark[5]	...	...	0	0	22	0	0	0	0	0	Danemark[5]
Czechoslovakia(former)	335	298	..	..	..	..	..	..	..	..	Tchécoslovaquie(anc.)
Czech Republic	..	..	...	...	151	136	152	149	144	144	République tchèque
Finland	174	137	108	82	75	77	57	63	59	57	Finlande
France	1426	1333	1476	1473	1561	[4]1501	[4]1552	[4]1548	[4]1574	...	France
Germany	...	...	3187	3121	3367	[4]3445	...	[4]3040	...	...	Allemagne
Germany(Fed.Rep.)	3383	..	..	..	..	..	..	..	..	..	Allemagne(Rép.féd.)
German D.R.(former)	488	..	..	..	..	..	..	..	..	..	R.D.A. (anc.)
Greece	38	39	38	...	...	...	...	...	...	...	Grèce
Hungary	181	165	132	124	131	159	159	160	148	143	Hongrie
Italy	1101	1045	965	934	953	922	876	855	772	810	Italie
Netherlands[4]	...	...	...	...	437	393	450	522	638	...	Pays-Bas[4]
Norway	215	...	...	202	...	...	...	...	...	...	Norvège
Poland	397	319	322	284	284	314	340	349	349	362	Pologne
Portugal	86	85	80	58	[4]69	[4]75	[4]77	[4]77	[4]71	...	Portugal
Romania	552	461	372	331	298	383	326	324	310	297	Roumanie
Russian Federation	..	2042	1836	1423	1137	1156	871	946	847	1036	Fédération de Russie
Slovakia	..	..	...	...	...	[4]145	[4]77	[4]66	78	77	Slovaquie
Slovenia	..	10	11	10	11	...	13	14	12	9	Slovénie
Spain	569	536	537	585	600	652	722	660	689	788	Espagne
Sweden	330	281	290	274	286	288	280	308	281	347	Suède

For general note and footnotes, see end of table.

Voir la fin du tableau pour la remarque générale et les notes.

424

Caustic soda (continued)
Soude caustique (suite)

ISIC-BASED CODE - CODE BASE CITI

3511-59

Unit : Thousand metric tons

Unité : Milliers de tonnes métriques

Country or area	1990	1991	1992	1993	1994	1995	1996	1997	1998	1999	Pays ou zone
Ukraine	..	443	402	292	266	213	157	156	127	99	Ukraine
United Kingdom[4]	...	...	...	...	...	...	801	1004	901	...	Royaume-Uni[4]
Yugoslavia	..	51	23	4	5	7	20	65	63	14	Yougoslavie
T.F.Yug.Rep. Macedonia	..	7	6	6	6	4	4	4	3	1	L'ex-RY Macédoine
USSR (former)	2974	..	..	..	..	..	..	..	..	..	URSS (anc.)
Total	**37413**	**36968**	**36796**	**36009**	**36618**	**38339**	**38661**	**39521**	**38637**	**39673**	**Total**

General Note.
NaOH. This item excludes soda lyes obtained as residual products from the manufacture of wood pulp by the alkali or sulphate processes, and mixtures of sodium hydroxide and lime known as soda lime. (SITC, Rev.3: 52262-0, 52263-0).

[1] Source: United Nations Economic Commission for Latin America and the Caribbean (ECLAC), (Santiago).
[2] Twelve months ending 30 June of year stated.
[3] Beginning 1999, series discontinued.
[4] Source: United Nations Economic Commission for Europe (ECE), (Geneva).

[5] Sales.

Remarque générale.
NaOH. Cette rubrique ne comprend pas les lessives sodiques résiduaires du traitement à la soude ou au sulfate des pâtes de bois ni les mélanges de soude caustique et de chaux appelés chaux sodées. (CTCI, Rev.3: 52262-0, 52263-0).

[1] Source: Commission économique des Nations Unies pour l'Amérique Latine et les Caraïbes (CEPAL), (Santiago).
[2] Période de douze mois finissant le 30 juin de l'année indiquée.
[3] A partir de 1999, série abandonnée.
[4] Source: Commission économique des Nations Unies pour l'Europe (CEE), (Genève).

[5] Ventes.

Aluminium oxide
Oxyde d'aluminium

ISIC-BASED CODE - CODE BASE CITI

3511-61

Unit : Thousand metric tons   Unité : Milliers de tonnes métriques

Country or area	1990	1991	1992	1993	1994	1995	1996	1997	1998	1999	Pays ou zone
America, North	**4801**	**4621**	**4459**	**4493**	**4055**	**4321**	**4303**	**4601**	**4537**	**4016**	**Amérique du Nord**
United States	4801.3	4621.0	4459.3	4493.5	4054.7	4321.4	4303.3	4601.4	4536.9	4015.8	Etats-Unis
Asia	**627**	**312**	**308**	**459**	**310**	**210**	**501**	**351**	**436**	**198**	**Asie**
Turkey	627.0	311.7	308.3	459.4	310.1	210.3	501.3	351.0	436.1	197.9	Turquie
Europe	**2991**	**2718**	**2394**	**2478**	**2470**	**2514**	**2451**	**2470**	**2441**	**2468**	**Europe**
Czechoslovakia(former)	209.2	186.6	..	...	...	..	..	...	..	..	Tchécoslovaquie(anc.)
France	466.5	403.8	365.6	...	...	...	...	...	...	...	France
Germany	..	863.2	857.0	840.0	823.6	...	...	...	...	...	Allemagne
Germany(Fed.Rep.)	921.6	..	..	...	..	..	..	...	..	..	Allemagne(Rép.féd.)
Romania	440.4	309.8	279.7	293.2	301.6	322.8	260.6	279.5	250.3	277.4	Roumanie
Spain	952.8	954.5	891.4	...	...	...	...	...	...	...	Espagne
Total	**8419**	**7651**	**7161**	**7431**	**6835**	**7045**	**7256**	**7423**	**7414**	**6682**	**Total**

General Note.

Al_2O_3 anhydrous or calcined alumina. Natural alumina is excluded. (SITC, Rev.3: 28520-0).

Remarque générale.

Alumine anhydre ou calcinée Al_2O_3, à l'exclusion de l'alumine naturelle. (CTCI, Rev.3: 28520-0).

Aluminium sulphate
Sulfate d'aluminium

ISIC-BASED CODE - CODE BASE CITI

3511-63

Unit : Thousand metric tons

Unité : Milliers de tonnes métriques

Country or area	1990	1991	1992	1993	1994	1995	1996	1997	1998	1999	Pays ou zone
Africa	**13**	**11**	**11**	**8**	**10**	**9**	**10**	**7**	**9**	**12**	**Afrique**
Tunisia	13.5	11.0	11.4	7.7	9.9	8.5	9.7	6.8	8.9	12.0	Tunisie
America, North	**1420**	**1414**	**1314**	**1302**	**1337**	**1350**	**1378**	**1216**	**1249**	**1257**	**Amérique du Nord**
Canada	...	191.6	170.2	192.7	173.4	157.4	171.8	*162.3	190.9	...	Canada
United States	1241.2	1222.1	1143.9	1109.3	1163.7	1192.2	1206.1	1053.4	1057.6	1084.8	Etats-Unis
America, South	**257**	**286**	**218**	**139**	**259**	**268**	**171**	**151**	**230**	**233**	**Amérique du Sud**
Brazil	194.3	219.9	159.8	129.6	[1]162.4	[1]153.9	[1]103.8	[1]104.2	[1]150.4	[1]144.4	Brésil
Colombia	56.6	...	51.2	3.0	90.1	107.4	...	38.6	71.9		Colombie
Peru	...	...	...	...	...	6.7	7.8	7.9	8.1	7.5	Pérou
Asia	**1026**	**1045**	**1024**	**989**	**1064**	**1094**	**1110**	**1186**	**1089**	**1111**	**Asie**
Indonesia	52.1	71.4	79.8	86.7	109.1	119.9	...	168.1	108.3	...	Indonésie
Japan	959.7	953.9	924.2	881.6	942.8	954.0	984.8	992.8	950.5	935.0	Japon
Turkey	14.1	19.8	19.6	20.6	12.6	20.3	25.7	24.7	30.6	31.6	Turquie
Europe	**868**	**784**	**794**	**813**	**802**	**808**	**734**	**810**	**810**	**727**	**Europe**
Bulgaria	16.3	5.6	1.1	2.5	2.8	1.2	0.8	0.9	...	...	Bulgarie
Czechoslovakia(former)	55.5	51.8	..	..	..	..	..	..	..	..	Tchécoslovaquie(anc.)
Czech Republic	..	..	...	...	...	...	35.1	29.8	27.1	18.4	République tchèque
Finland	61.4	67.2	70.8	71.1	88.2	102.3	96.9	...	...	...	Finlande
Germany	..	...	...	90.8	94.1	...	...	...	...	...	Allemagne
Germany(Fed.Rep.)	93.5	..	..	..	..	..	..	..	..	..	Allemagne(Rép.féd.)
German D.R.(former)	28.7	..	..	..	..	..	..	..	..	..	R.D.A. (anc.)
Greece	8.3	9.7	8.7	...	...	...	...	...	...	...	Grèce
Romania	68.2	64.4	49.8	37.2	49.6	58.2	56.6	39.5	31.7	21.1	Roumanie
Slovenia	..	21.3	21.7	18.8	19.4	21.3	22.8	26.2	29.9	24.3	Slovénie
Spain	118.0	50.6	94.6	...	...	...	...	...	...	22.5	Espagne
Sweden	...	...	...	...	...	...	...	202.4	206.2	192.2	Suède
United Kingdom	...	...	...	279.7	235.4	216.3	141.3	...	...	...	Royaume-Uni
Yugoslavia	..	2.7	8.6	5.0	4.5	7.9	7.5	5.7	2.9	1.0	Yougoslavie
Total	**3585**	**3540**	**3360**	**3251**	**3473**	**3528**	**3403**	**3369**	**3387**	**3340**	**Total**

General Note.
$Al_2(SO_4)_3$ ordinary or pure, in terms of Al_2O_3. (SITC, Rev.3: 52349-1).

Remarque générale.
$Al_2(SO_4)_3$ ordinaire ou pur, exprimé en poids de Al_2O_3. (CTCI, Rev.3: 52349-1).

[1] Production by main establishments only.

[1] Production des principaux établissements seulement.

Copper sulphate
Sulfate de cuivre

ISIC-BASED CODE - CODE BASE CITI

3511-65

Unit : Metric tons

Unité : Tonnes métriques

Country or area	1990	1991	1992	1993	1994	1995	1996	1997	1998	1999	Pays ou zone
America, North	**34286**	**40200**	**46800**	**46400**	**48400**	**52000**	**43400**	**48400**	**51800**	**52700**	**Amérique du Nord**
United States	34286	40200	46800	46400	48400	52000	43400	48400	51800	52700	Etats-Unis
America, South	**8967**	**11537**	**13484**	**14798**	**15784**	**22975**	**26847**	**30618**	**33667**	**31118**	**Amérique du Sud**
Brazil	2856	4074	5295	6051	[1]5954	14226	14675	16207	19626	19072	Brésil
Colombia	334	...	898	699	1026	1363	...	773	1410	...	Colombie
Peru	...	...	...	...	...	7386	11243	13638	12631	10476	Pérou
Asia	**88**	**88**	**88**	**88**	**88**	**88**	**88**	**88**	**88**	**88**	**Asie**
Indonesia	88	...	...	...	...	...	...	...	...	...	Indonésie
Europe	**23652**	**40623**	**37325**	**30047**	**27978**	**27389**	**36266**	**35259**	**33404**	**31247**	**Europe**
Bulgaria	2489	2128	2171	464	434	344	481	231	...	...	Bulgarie
Denmark	...	...	0	[2]0	[2]0	[2]0	[2]0	[2]0	[2]0	[2]1	Danemark
Czechoslovakia(former)	5411	4337	..	..	..	..	..	..	..	..	Tchécoslovaquie(anc.)
Finland	1112	747	868	1073	1149	1566	2673	...	...	...	Finlande
Poland	7645	7588	7925	6068	7089	6894	6213	5594	5881	6232	Pologne
Romania	...	1885	1937	1345	1376	1456	2733	3005	4082	4082	Roumanie
Slovakia	..	..	...	...	...	...	...	...	7648	5182	Slovaquie
Spain	5557	6249	9042	...	...	...	...	...	...	...	Espagne
Ukraine	..	8853	3997	5149	2913	2302	8200	6687	2756	2497	Ukraine
Yugoslavia	..	8836	4970	2584	1653	1463	2602	3886	3323	3341	Yougoslavie
Total	**66993**	**92448**	**97697**	**91333**	**92251**	**102452**	**106601**	**114365**	**118959**	**115153**	**Total**

General Note.

$CuSO_4.5H_2O$ (cupric sulphate). Cuprous sulphate Cu_2SO_4 is excluded. (SITC, Rev.3: 52349-2).

Remarque générale.

$CuSO_4.5H_2O$ (sulfate cuivrique). Cette rubrique ne comprend pas le sulfate cuivreux Cu_2SO_4. (CTCI, Rev.3: 52349-2).

[1] Production by main establishments only.
[2] Sales.

[1] Production des principaux établissements seulement.
[2] Ventes.

Soda ash
Cendres sodiques

ISIC-BASED CODE - CODE BASE CITI
3511-66

Unit : Thousand metric tons
Unité : Milliers de tonnes métriques

Country or area	1990	1991	1992	1993	1994	1995	1996	1997	1998	1999	Pays ou zone
Africa	**354**	**307**	**305**	**342**	**398**	**426**	**343**	**458**	**439**	**480**	**Afrique**
Botswana	...	62	124	126	174	202	119	200	196	234	Botswana
Kenya	[1][2]244	[1][2]245	181	216	224	224	224	[1][2]258	[1][2]243	[1][2]246	Kenya
America, North	**9605**	**9459**	**9820**	**9400**	**9610**	**10390**	**10490**	**10990**	**10390**	**10490**	**Amérique du Nord**
Mexico[1]	[3]449	[3]449	[3]440	[3]440	290	290	290	290	290	290	Mexique[1]
United States[2]	9156	9010	9380	8960	9320	10100	10200	10700	10100	10200	Etats-Unis[2]
America, South	**317**	**329**	**342**	**352**	**340**	**325**	**332**	**327**	**323**	**330**	**Amérique du Sud**
Brazil	196	208	221	231	219	204	211	206	202	209	Brésil
Colombia[1]	121	121	121	121	121	121	...	...	...	...	Colombie[1]
Asia	**7124**	**7326**	**7919**	**8899**	**9293**	**9532**	**10143**	**10674**	**10684**	**11097**	**Asie**
China	3795	3936	4549	5349	5814	5977	6693	7258	7440	7660	Chine
India	1392	1408	1391	1545	1452	1464	1488	1568	1392	1515	Inde
Japan	1129	1098	1052	1051	1044	1044	921	797	718	[1]722	Japon
Korea, Republic of	335	345	331	331	357	369	[1]320	[1]320	[1]300	[1]310	Corée, République de
Pakistan[4]	149	147	186	196	197	196	221	247	240	239	Pakistan[4]
Turkey	324	392	410	427	429	482	500	484	594	651	Turquie
Europe	**8609**	**11147**	**10457**	**9628**	**9150**	**10109**	**9648**	**9684**	**9412**	**9799**	**Europe**
Albania	23	5	...	0	0	0	0	0	...	0	Albanie
Belgium[1]	380	380	375	300	300	300	...	...	...	...	Belgique[1]
Bulgaria	1025	893	517	...	...	...	[5]866	[5]841	...	...	Bulgarie
Czechoslovakia(former)	104	55	..	..	..	..					Tchécoslovaquie(anc.)
France[1]	1180	1140	1100	1222	1123	1120	1100	1053	1000	1000	France[1]
Germany	..	...	...	1586	1380	[5]1526	[5]1592	[5]1589	1642	...	Allemagne
Germany(Fed.Rep.)	1436		..		..		..			...	Allemagne(Rép.féd.)
German D.R.(former)	723		..		..		..				R.D.A. (anc.)
Italy[1]	610	600	600	500	500	1070	1100	1000	1000	1000	Italie[1]
Netherlands[1]	400	400	400	400	400	400	400	400	400	400	Pays-Bas[1]
Poland	948	943	910	799	977	998	891	931	980	908	Pologne
Portugal	...	* [1]150	* [1]150	* [1]150	[5]191	[5]199	[5]204	[5]205	[5]187	...	Portugal
Romania	632	471	452	376	456	505	537	548	482	431	Roumanie
Russian Federation	..	3048	2679	1992	1585	1823	1449	1652	1538	1918	Fédération de Russie
Slovakia	..	..	...	0	...	...	[5]2	[5]1	[5]1	...	Slovaquie
Spain	816	500	668	700	[5]753	[5]864	[5]832	[5]808	[5]789	...	Espagne
Ukraine	..	1065	1091	775	656	475	376	368	390	456	Ukraine
Yugoslavia, SFR	165	..	..	..	...	..	..	..	..	..	Yougoslavie, RSF
USSR (former)	4472	..	..	..	..	..	..	..	..	..	URSS (anc.)
Total	**30481**	**28568**	**28843**	**28621**	**28791**	**30782**	**30956**	**32133**	**31248**	**32196**	**Total**

General Note.
Na$_2$CO$_3$. Sodium bicarbonate (NaHCO$_3$) and natural sodium carbonate are excluded. (SITC, Rev.3: 52372-0).

Remarque générale.
Na$_2$CO$_3$. Cette rubrique ne comprend pas le bicarbonate de sodium (NaHCO$_3$) ni le carbonate de sodium naturel. (CTCI, Rev.3: 52372-0).

[1] Source: U. S. Geological Survey, (Washington, D. C.).
[2] Natural sodium carbonate (Na$_2$CO$_3$).
[3] Including natural sodium carbonate (Na$_2$CO$_3$).
[4] Twelve months ending 30 June of year stated.
[5] Source: United Nations Economic Commission for Europe (ECE), (Geneva).

[1] Source: U.S. Geological Survey, (Washington, D.C.).
[2] Le carbonate de sodium naturel (Na$_2$CO$_3$).
[3] Y compris le carbonate de sodium naturel (Na$_2$CO$_3$).
[4] Période de douze mois finissant le 30 juin de l'année indiquée.
[5] Source: Commission économique des Nations Unies pour l'Europe (CEE), (Genève).

Sodium silicates
Silicate de sodium

ISIC-BASED CODE - CODE BASE CITI

3511-69

Unit : Thousand metric tons

Unité : Milliers de tonnes métriques

Country or area	1990	1991	1992	1993	1994	1995	1996	1997	1998	1999	Pays ou zone
Africa	**6**	**5**	**8**	**8**	**8**	**14**	**18**	**19**	**21**	**23**	**Afrique**
Kenya	5.6	5.4	7.5	8.5	7.6	14.0	18.3	...	...	...	Kenya
America, North	**1061**	**1156**	**1181**	**1249**	**1246**	**1337**	**1437**	**1441**	**1435**	**1327**	**Amérique du Nord**
Mexico	223.8	251.4	252.9	247.4	246.2	...	...	...	...	...	Mexique
United States	837.1	904.7	927.6	1001.7	999.8	1080.8	1176.4	1176.6	1166.2	1054.5	Etats-Unis
America, South	**90**	**137**	**99**	**106**	**212**	**241**	**247**	**191**	**204**	**210**	**Amérique du Sud**
Brazil	74.5	111.0	63.3	84.6	[1]187.2	[1]211.0	[1]213.7	[1]156.2	[1]166.9	[1]171.5	Brésil
Colombia	15.8	...	36.0	21.9	24.5	29.9	...	...	...	...	Colombie
Asia	**846**	**847**	**799**	**845**	**938**	**922**	**940**	**917**	**939**	**953**	**Asie**
Indonesia	4.0	15.2	32.0	61.7	51.6	24.1	...	17.8	84.0	...	Indonésie
Japan	788.3	786.1	721.5	728.6	830.7	836.2	799.5	795.1	765.5	769.4	Japon
Turkey	53.5	45.7	45.1	54.9	56.1	62.0	104.3	103.9	89.3	121.0	Turquie
Europe	**346**	**373**	**329**	**363**	**416**	**385**	**382**	**419**	**399**	**407**	**Europe**
Hungary	17.2	14.1	14.7	9.6	10.0	6.5	...	...	...	...	Hongrie
Lithuania	..	...	...	...	...	1.4	1.5	1.2	0.7	0.4	Lituanie
Romania	49.6	42.1	25.7	37.7	15.7	15.0	26.7	21.1	22.5	18.1	Roumanie
Slovenia	..	12.5	31.3	53.5	49.7	38.3	39.9	...	...	...	Slovénie
Spain	66.0	89.9	51.7	...	...	...	...	...	...	...	Espagne
Sweden	41.0	39.4	31.2	32.4	93.3	82.5	...	82.5	91.4	91.9	Suède
United Kingdom	...	...	...	158.7	176.3	...	...	192.1	160.9	...	Royaume-Uni
Total	**2348**	**2518**	**2415**	**2573**	**2820**	**2899**	**3025**	**2988**	**2998**	**2921**	**Total**

General Note.
In terms of SiO_2. (SITC, Rev.3: 52383-1).

Remarque générale.
En poids de SiO_2 . (CTCI, Rev.3: 52383-1).

[1] Production by main establishments only.

[1] Production des principaux établissements seulement.

Hydrogen peroxide
Péroxyde d'hydrogène

ISIC-BASED CODE - CODE BASE CITI

3511-71

Unit : Thousand metric tons   Unité : Milliers de tonnes métriques

Country or area	1990	1991	1992	1993	1994	1995	1996	1997	1998	1999	Pays ou zone
America, North	**345**	**323**	**380**	**409**	**439**	**462**	**474**	**491**	**529**	**532**	**Amérique du Nord**
Canada	...	83.1	118.9	128.4	142.6	132.8	155.9	*179.1	199.4	...	Canada
Mexico	7.9	9.3	7.3	7.0	7.5	...	...	...	...	...	Mexique
United States	216.1	230.5	254.0	273.6	288.8	322.0	311.0	305.9	323.7	341.7	Etats-Unis
America, South	**33**	**34**	**33**	**33**	**34**	**34**	**34**	**34**	**35**	**35**	**Amérique du Sud**
Argentina	4.0	3.9	4.1	4.4	4.7	...	...	...	...	...	Argentine
Brazil	26.6	29.2	...	...	...	...	...	...	...	...	Brésil
Colombia	2.6	...	0.8	0.9	1.4	1.5	...	...	...	...	Colombie
Asia	**167**	**180**	**182**	**166**	**164**	**165**	**166**	**164**	**162**	**167**	**Asie**
Indonesia	...	...	...	22.2	22.8	...	...	...	...	...	Indonésie
Japan	144.6	157.8	159.0	143.8	141.6	142.6	143.1	141.2	139.8	144.6	Japon
Europe	**73**	**214**	**177**	**163**	**169**	**181**	**181**	**190**	**204**	**233**	**Europe**
Finland	36.1	36.4	32.2	37.5	53.4	75.5	75.9	...	...	...	Finlande
Germany	..	...	...	...	...	...	26.4	...	...	...	Allemagne
Hungary	2.9	2.3	1.6	...	...	...	...	...	...	...	Hongrie
Russian Federation	..	87.8	59.6	34.6	21.3	14.1	13.7	12.2	17.2	18.7	Fédération de Russie
Slovenia	..	18.8	16.5	17.8	21.5	21.6	21.8	20.8	21.8	20.4	Slovénie
Spain	33.8	31.2	32.7	...	...	...	...	...	...	60.8	Espagne
Ukraine	..	10.8	7.7	4.3	4.7	1.6	0.8	0.2	0.4	0.1	Ukraine
Total	**618**	**751**	**771**	**771**	**807**	**842**	**854**	**880**	**930**	**967**	**Total**

General Note.

H$_2$O$_2$ including solid hydrogen peroxide combined with urea, whether or not stabilized. Hydrogen peroxide put up as a pharmaceutical preparation is excluded. (SITC, Rev.3: 52491-0).

Remarque générale.

H$_2$O$_2$, y compris le péroxyde d'hydrogène sous forme solide en combinaison avec l'urée, stabilisé ou non, à l'exclusion de l'eau oxygénée pharmaceutique. (CTCI, Rev.3: 52491-0).

Calcium carbide
Carbure de calcium

ISIC-BASED CODE - CODE BASE CITI

3511-73

Unit : Thousand metric tons   Unité : Milliers de tonnes métriques

Country or area	1990	1991	1992	1993	1994	1995	1996	1997	1998	1999	Pays ou zone
America, North	**20**	**20**	**19**	**29**	**32**	**34**	**37**	**41**	**44**	**47**	**Amérique du Nord**
Mexico	20	20	19	29	32	...	...	...	...	...	Mexique
America, South	**56**	**63**	**47**	**64**	**44**	**37**	**27**	**23**	**18**	**12**	**Amérique du Sud**
Argentina	41	59	46	60	...	37	*23	...	...	...	Argentine
Colombia	15	...	1	...	0	0	...	...	...	...	Colombie
Asia	**2768**	**3087**	**3122**	**3192**	**3425**	**3990**	**3596**	**3896**	**3266**	**3172**	**Asie**
Armenia	..	3	8	1	1	1	1	0	0	0	Arménie
China	2280	2358	2425	2642	2920	3457	3092	3447	2813	2731	Chine
India	91	94	93	97	104	95	91	83	83	93	Inde
Indonesia	27	25	27	28	...	...	...	...	...	...	Indonésie
Japan	294	303	270	245	246	273	263	256	...	...	Japon
Kazakhstan	..	244	234	122	70	89	67	29	29	16	Kazakhstan
Korea, Republic of	38	40	40	43	39	39	...	...	...	...	Corée, République de
Turkey	38	20	25	14	18	9	15	14	21	15	Turquie
Europe	**2319**	**2798**	**2714**	**2658**	**2586**	**2631**	**2616**	**2500**	**2500**	**2495**	**Europe**
Bulgaria	44	28	20	14	14	16	15	14	...	...	Bulgarie
Czechoslovakia(former)	36	41	..	..	..	..	..	..	..	..	Tchécoslovaquie(anc.)
Germany	..	...	...	300	285	[1]293	...	...	...	...	Allemagne
Greece[1]	72	91	78	...	...	...	...	...	...	...	Grèce[1]
Norway	...	...	...	...	...	[1]131	[1]129	...	...	94	Norvège
Poland[2]	297	283	221	180	174	178	145	121	70	53	Pologne[2]
Romania	129	94	87	84	68	95	113	96	73	54	Roumanie
Russian Federation	..	236	228	229	170	153	134	148	160	197	Fédération de Russie
Slovakia	..	..	...	...	...	...	[1]91	[1]16	84	77	Slovaquie
Slovenia	..	20	18	14	22	24	25	...	...	49	Slovénie
Spain	44	36	38	24	[1]37	[1]44	[1]43	[1]41	[1]44	...	Espagne
Sweden	60	56	42	44	46	46	...	47	43	43	Suède
Ukraine	..	8	10	9	10	9	6	6	6	7	Ukraine
United Kingdom	...	...	...	1494	...	...	...	...	...	...	Royaume-Uni
Yugoslavia, SFR	25	..	..	..	..	..	..	..	..	..	Yougoslavie, RSF
USSR (former)[1]	540	..	..	..	..	...	..	...	..	..	URSS (anc.)[1]
Total	**5704**	**5968**	**5902**	**5943**	**6087**	**6691**	**6277**	**6459**	**5828**	**5726**	**Total**

General Note.
CaC$_2$ in terms of 75 per cent of C. (SITC, Rev.3: 52493-0).

Remarque générale.
CaC$_2$ rapporté à une teneur de 75 p. 100 de C. (CTCI, Rev.3: 52493-0).

[1] Source: United Nations Economic Commission for Europe (ECE), (Geneva).

[1] Source: Commission économique des Nations Unies pour l'Europe (CEE), (Genève).

[2] In terms of 75 per cent calcium carbide.

[2] Sur la base de 75 p. 100 de carbure de calcium.

Dyestuffs, synthetic
Colorant synthétiques

ISIC-BASED CODE - CODE BASE CITI

3511-74

Unit : Metric tons

Unité : Tonnes métriques

Country or area	1990	1991	1992	1993	1994	1995	1996	1997	1998	1999	Pays ou zone
America, North	**81456**	**87289**	**93122**	**93183**	**110259**	**97243**	**100028**	**117261**	**125758**	**130620**	Amérique du Nord
Mexico	...	...	...	93183	110259	97243	100028	117261	125758	130620	Mexique
America, South	**9510**	**10980**	**10245**	**10245**	**10245**	**10245**	**10245**	**10245**	**10245**	**10245**	Amérique du Sud
Brazil	9510	10980	...	...	...	...	...	...	...	...	Brésil
Asia	**102794**	**106801**	**107359**	**109508**	**117764**	**122574**	**131994**	**143425**	**128910**	**131742**	Asie
Indonesia	582	...	...	...	...	...	...	...	...	...	Indonésie
Japan[1]	74880	77114	73707	67395	71161	70818	69081	69014	62553	56011	Japon[1]
Korea, Republic of	26380	27825	31462	39595	43536	49440	58629	70451	62472	71245	Corée, République de
Turkey[2]	...	...	...	...	2485	1734	3702	3378	3303	...	Turquie[2]
Europe	**350816**	**532860**	**532029**	**418914**	**470360**	**544666**	**564271**	**610538**	**578091**	**689235**	Europe
Austria[3]	...	...	...	...	...	...	2592	9274	9642	9306	Autriche[3]
Belgium	...	...	...	...	7579	7988	8742	9523	10012	10702	Belgique
Bulgaria[4]	653	338	226	122	147	117	99	87	...	...	Bulgarie[4]
Croatia	...	...	...	...	273	162	162	218	222	...	Croatie
Denmark[5]	8104	9604	12404	15240	21904	25	27	6	0	20	Danemark[5]
Czechoslovakia(former)	15436	10148								...	Tchécoslovaquie(anc.)
Czech Republic	..	..	9956	7470	9303	8204	7503	10150	9312	6720	République tchèque
Estonia				...	[2]8961	[2]11409	14025	17048	16842	15003	Estonie
Finland	1282	1562	1131	969	867	1243	1562	836	1302	1523	Finlande
France	45967	47183	52104	60155	57600	...	[2]55791	[2]62071	[2]51456	...	France
Germany	..	..	..	110580	119081	241121	244275	246025	238072	...	Allemagne
Germany(Fed.Rep.)[6]	93453	..	..	..	..	..	..	..	..	..	Allemagne(Rép.féd.)[6]
German D.R.(former)	6754	..	..	..	..	..	..	..	..	..	R.D.A. (anc.)
Greece	[7]1828	[7]1462	[7]1639	880	3703	3952	8794	9670	5126	...	Grèce
Hungary	97	71	46	...	[2]28	[2]27	...	...	...	...	Hongrie
Italy	15815	15935	17957	21206	24234	23037	23708	27115	27448	27828	Italie
Lithuania	...	...	...	...	...	78	16	4	2	1	Lituanie
Netherlands	...	...	...	...	...	...	[2]20121	[2]24547	[5][8]26393	[5][8]26319	Pays-Bas
Poland[9]	10089	7093	7788	7032	6786	5199	4556	4388	3691	3641	Pologne[9]
Romania[10]	10634	7273	4688	1809	1520	1199	1099	750	656	489	Roumanie[10]
Russian Federation	..	45840	31182	16624	13474	8699	7569	8503	8457	10520	Fédération de Russie
Slovenia					[2]27	[2]7	[2]12	11	11	12	Slovénie
Spain	[10]47091	[10]51909	[10]54115	33843	30775	34276	34186	38643	34916	38538	Espagne
Sweden	...	...	...	1062	1842	917	3525	2929	3961	4260	Suède
Ukraine	..	24985	17924	9899	6962	2446	2037	2122	1155	525	Ukraine
United Kingdom	[11]54399	...	...	[11]74790	114049	100980	113003	124062	117145	...	Royaume-Uni
Yugoslavia	..	17565	12812	4919	9126	7491	10843	12539	12233	7292	Yougoslavie
USSR (former)	83959	..	..	..	..	..	..	..	..	..	URSS (anc.)
Oceania	**5**	**5**	**5**	**5**	**5**	**5**	**5**	**5**	**5**	**5**	Océanie
Australia	5	...	...	...	...	...	...	...	...	...	Australie
Total	**628540**	**737936**	**742760**	**631855**	**708633**	**774733**	**806543**	**881474**	**843009**	**961847**	Total

General Note.
Synthetic organic dyestuffs (including pigment dyestuffs), synthetic organic products of a kind used as luminophores, products of the kind known as optical bleaching agents, substantive to the fibre, natural indigo, colour lakes, in terms of 60 per cent concentration basis. (SITC, Rev.3: 53110-0, 53120-0).

Remarque générale.
Colorants organiques synthétiques (y compris les pigments), produits organiques synthétiques du genre de ceux utilisés comme "luminophores", produits des types dits "agents de blanchiment optique" fixables sur la fibre, indigo naturel, laques colorantes, dont le poids est ramené à une concentration de 60 p. 100. (CTCI, Rev.3: 53110-0, 53120-0).

Dyestuffs, synthetic (continued)
Colorant synthétiques (suite)

Footnotes

[1] Excluding pigment resin colours and lakes.

[2] Source: United Nations Economic Commission for Europe (ECE), (Geneva).

[3] 1995 data are confidential.

[4] In terms of 100 per cent synthetic dyestuffs.

[5] Sales.

[6] Excluding luminophores, optical bleaching agents, natural indigo and colour lakes.

[7] Including organic colours.

[8] Production by establishments employing 20 or more persons.

[9] Data relate to gross weight of organic dyestuffs.

[10] Organic dyestuffs only.

[11] Sales by manufacturers employing 25 or more persons.

Notes.

[1] Non compris les couleurs et laques à base de pigments et de résines.

[2] Source: Commission économique des Nations Unies pour l'Europe (CEE), (Genève).

[3] Pour 1995, les données sont confidentielles.

[4] Sur la base de 100 p. 100 de matières colorantes synthétiques.

[5] Ventes.

[6] Non compris les luminophores, les agents de blanchiment optique, l'indigo naturel et les laques colorantes.

[7] Y compris les colorants organiques.

[8] Production des établissements occupant 20 personnes ou plus.

[9] Données se rapportant au poids brut des colorants organiques.

[10] Colorants organiques seulement.

[11] Ventes des fabricants employant 25 personnes ou plus.

Vegetable tanning extracts
Extraits tannants d'origine végétale

ISIC-BASED CODE - CODE BASE CITI
3511-75

Unit : Metric tons | Unité : Tonnes métriques

Country or area	1990	1991	1992	1993	1994	1995	1996	1997	1998	1999	Pays ou zone
America, South	**7370**	**6551**	**4001**	**8052**	**6494**	**6494**	**6494**	**6494**	**6494**	**6494**	**Amérique du Sud**
Paraguay	7370	6551	4001	8052	...	...	...	...	...	...	Paraguay
Europe	**1353**	**44355**	**31620**	**13855**	**6409**	**6143**	**5598**	**5402**	**4892**	**7752**	**Europe**
Denmark	...	...	0	[1]0	[1]0	[1]0	[1]0	[1]1	[1]0	[1]0	Danemark
Finland	93	89	...	...	...	...	...	...	...	...	Finlande
Poland	352	55	...	0	...	...	...	...	...	...	Pologne
Romania	908	640	456	298	121	174	190	93	106	0	Roumanie
Russian Federation	..	36333	25490	8424	2073	1496	1504	1044	579	1056	Fédération de Russie
Slovenia	..	2810	3465	3908	3408	4123	3596	...	...	6469	Slovénie
Ukraine	..	4428	1982	1134	580	123	81	69	12	0	Ukraine
Total	**8723**	**50906**	**35621**	**21907**	**12902**	**12636**	**12091**	**11896**	**11386**	**14245**	**Total**

General Note.
Tannin content (Shake method) of various tannin extracts of vegetable origin from oak, chestnut, quebracho, pines, wattle, sumach, myrobolans, vallonia, gambier, mangrove and divi-divi. Tannin, tannin extracts mixed with synthetic tannin substances and concentrated sulphite lye are excluded. (SITC, Rev.3: 53221-1).

Remarque générale.
Teneur en tanin (déterminée par la méthode Shake) des divers extraits d'origine végétale provenant du chêne, du marronnier, du quebracho, de certains pins et acacias, du sumac, du myrobalan, de la vallonée, du gambier, du palétuvier, du dividivi. Cette rubrique ne comprend ni les tanins et extraits tannants mélangés à des produits tannants synthétiques ni les lignosulfites. (CTCI, Rev.3: 53221-1).

[1] Sales.

[1] Ventes.

Lithopone
Lithopone

ISIC-BASED CODE - CODE BASE CITI

3511-78

Unit : Metric tons   Unité : Tonnes métriques

Country or area	1990	1991	1992	1993	1994	1995	1996	1997	1998	1999	Pays ou zone
America, South	**10**	**10**	**10**	**10**	**10**	**10**	**10**	**10**	**10**	**10**	**Amérique du Sud**
Colombia	...	...	...	10	...	...	...	...	...	...	Colombie
Asia	**102642**	**101921**	**101160**	**97186**	**101294**	**98568**	**89895**	**81075**	**71169**	**81601**	**Asie**
Georgia	..	...	3901	2619	587	57	1761	1859	0	391	Géorgie
Korea, Republic of	...	...	...	...	100707	98511	88134	79216	71169	81210	Corée, République de
Europe	**25172**	**270215**	**164097**	**125864**	**68485**	**85259**	**77329**	**54942**	**67916**	**91708**	**Europe**
Belarus	..	...	...	...	...	...	56	236	209	125	Bélarus
Denmark[1]	89	61	31	44	23	23	26	16	13	14	Danemark[1]
Czechoslovakia(former)	18900	13940	..	..	..	..	..	..	..	..	Tchécoslovaquie(anc.)
Finland*	177	170	187	...	...	...	...	...	...	...	Finlande*
Poland	5903	3434	2288	1068	1761	420	...	...	...	...	Pologne
Russian Federation	..	105196	53989	36805	19641	14886	15326	11833	11125	16806	Fédération de Russie
Slovenia	..	4043	4185	1574	...	...	...	...	...	...	Slovénie
Spain	3	7	8	..	...	...	...	...	...	...	Espagne
Sweden	100	250	56	16	...	...	...	...	...	...	Suède
Ukraine	..	142957	103196	86016	43347	66217	57808	39225	53012	71206	Ukraine
USSR (former)	352562	..	..	..	..	..	..	..	..	..	URSS (anc.)
Total	**480386**	**372146**	**265266**	**223059**	**169789**	**183837**	**167234**	**136027**	**139095**	**173319**	**Total**

General Note.
Lithopone and other pigments with a basis of zinc sulphide, such as white pigments consisting of mixtures in varying proportions of zinc sulphide and barium sulphate. (SITC, Rev.3: 53315-0).

Remarque générale.
Lithopone et produits similaires à base de sulfure de zinc, tels que les pigments blancs constitués par un mélange en proportions variables de sulfure de zinc et de sulfate de baryum. (CTCI, Rev.3: 53315-0).

[1] Sales.

[1] Ventes.

Activated carbon
Charbons activés

ISIC-BASED CODE - CODE BASE CITI

3511-79

Unit : Thousand metric tons   Unité : Milliers de tonnes métriques

Country or area	1990	1991	1992	1993	1994	1995	1996	1997	1998	1999	Pays ou zone
America, North	**118**	**117**	**120**	**130**	**143**	**142**	**154**	**150**	**150**	**151**	**Amérique du Nord**
United States	117.7	116.9	119.6	130.4	142.9	141.8	154.4	150.1	150.1	151.2	Etats-Unis
Asia	**68**	**71**	**79**	**78**	**95**	**91**	**95**	**94**	**113**	**102**	**Asie**
Indonesia	3.4	4.5	10.6	12.7	12.7	10.0	...	11.0	25.8	...	Indonésie
Japan	64.6	66.8	68.7	65.1	82.8	80.5	83.5	83.4	86.7	80.6	Japon
Europe	**601**	**153**	**107**	**124**	**121**	**121**	**118**	**117**	**117**	**118**	**Europe**
Bulgaria	0.1	0.0	0.0	0.1	0.1	0.0	0.1	0.0	...	...	Bulgarie
Germany	..	...	...	...	...	14.7	...	...	...	...	Allemagne
Germany(Fed.Rep.)	484.2	..	..	..	..	..	..	..	..	..	Allemagne(Rép.féd.)
German D.R.(former)	1.2	..	..	..	..	..	..	..	..	..	R.D.A. (anc.)
Hungary	0.2	0.2	0.3	...	...	...	...	...	...	...	Hongrie
Russian Federation	..	29.6	20.8	10.3	7.2	7.8	4.3	3.9	3.2	4.4	Fédération de Russie
Spain	115.7	108.8	71.2	...	...	...	...	...	...	...	Espagne
Total	**787**	**342**	**306**	**332**	**359**	**354**	**367**	**362**	**379**	**371**	**Total**

General Note.

Activated carbon and activated natural mineral products (that is, activated diatomite, certain volcanic minerals, activated clays and earths, activated bauxite). Activated carbons having the character of medicament, catalysts consisting of chemical products are excluded. (SITC, Rev.3: 59864-0).

Remarque générale.

Charbons activés et produits minéraux naturels activés (silices fossiles activées, certaines roches volcaniques, argiles et terres activées, bauxite activée). Cette rubrique ne comprend pas les charbons activés à caractère médicamenteux et les catalyseurs constitués par un produit chimique fixé sur une matière activée. (CTCI, Rev.3: 59864-0).

Nitrogenous fertilizers (total production)
Engrais azotés (production totale)

ISIC-BASED CODE - CODE BASE CITI

3512-00

Unit : Thousand metric tons

Unité : Milliers de tonnes métriques

Country or area	1990	1991	1992	1993	1994	1995	1996	1997	1998	1999	Pays ou zone
Africa	**6860**	**6757**	**7790**	**8029**	**8354**	**8430**	**5614**	**5339**	**7134**	**6191**	**Afrique**
Algeria	[1]263	[1]230	[1]230	*105	*83	*12	*8	*28	*41	57	Algérie
Egypt[1][2]	.4600	4339	5342	5588	5918	6136	3337	2813	...	...	Egypte[1][2]
Libyan Arab Jamah.	89	125	286	269	347	410	399	383	408	387	Jamah. arabe libyenne
Mauritius[2]	[1]12	[1]12	[1]12	[1]13	[1]12	[1]14	16	14	14	[1]16	Maurice[2]
Morocco	*344	*340	*296	*370	*266	*269	*258	*262	*271	[1]200	Maroc
Nigeria*	284	261	287	267	151	138	114	41	71	81	Nigéria*
Senegal[2]	14	27	*25	*24	*26	*29	*25	*30	*25	*24	Sénégal[2]
South Africa[1]	947	1088	1010	1116	1335	1142	1178	1508	1839	1026	Afrique du Sud[1]
Tunisia	209	[1]244	[1]219	[1]182	[1]113	[1]193	[1]186	[1]165	[1]156	[1]172	Tunisie
United Rep.Tanzania	3	3	...	...	...	...	...	...	...	...	Rép. Unie de Tanzanie
Zambia	*6	5	*14	*11	*6	*4	*4	*4	*2	*2	Zambie
Zimbabwe	89	83	*67	*82	*94	80	*86	*88	*74	*81	Zimbabwe
America, North	**19262**	**19660**	**19589**	**21143**	**21209**	**21924**	**23271**	**20778**	**19922**	**18730**	**Amérique du Nord**
Canada[2]	2706	2904	2972	3851	3801	4019	*3864	*3654	*3737	*3981	Canada[2]
Costa Rica*	30	39	40	49	41	44	56	41	32	35	Costa Rica*
Cuba	146	*120	*100	*70	*15	*55	*60	*62	*50	*50	Cuba
El Salvador	...	10	8	0	0	[1]10	[1]11	...	...	...	El Salvador
Guatemala	* [2]7	[1] [2]5	* [2]8	* [2]9	29	24	[1] [2]35	[1] [2]37	[1] [2]41	...	Guatemala
Mexico[1]	3011	2784	2245	2507	2808	2956	3439	2596	2042	1342	Mexique[1]
Trinidad and Tobago	*232	*241	210	*242	[1]498	[1]572	[1]580	[1]595	[1]514	[1]589	Trinité-et-Tobago
United States[2]	13124	13557	14006	14415	14017	14244	15226	13786	13499	12669	Etats-Unis[2]
America, South	**1386**	**1357**	**1245**	**1329**	**1434**	**1610**	**1604**	**1672**	**1366**	**1527**	**Amérique du Sud**
Argentina	41	42	33	48	43	58	*81	*97	*68	64	Argentine
Brazil	737	704	665	709	768	795	779	808	728	848	Brésil
Chile*	126	98	126	116	97	111	111	115	94	95	Chili*
Colombia*	100	99	86	82	95	93	109	92	69	67	Colombie*
Ecuador	...	...	[1]8	[1]1	...	[1]81	...	96	2	...	Equateur
Peru	32	20	10	11	*14	*16	*13	*12	[1]3	* [1]1	Pérou
Venezuela*	337	375	317	362	379	456	473	452	402	384	Venezuela*
Asia	**32938**	**35651**	**36560**	**35454**	**38320**	**41556**	**44688**	**45800**	**47750**	**49906**	**Asie**
Afghanistan[2]	55	*49	*42	*40	*14	*10	*5	*5	*5	*5	Afghanistan[2]
Bangladesh[2]	678	759	925	*996	910	982	*966	868	*1010	*1027	Bangladesh[2]
China[1]	14636	15101	15705	15256	17363	18592	21361	20749	22257	24720	Chine[1]
Georgia	..	...	[1]76	59	34	[1]43	[1]68	[1]81	[1]55	[1]95	Géorgie
India[1]	[2]7063	7697	7797	7786	8040	9228	8764	10469	10796	10913	Inde[1]
Indonesia[1]	2369	2348	2302	2513	2357	2428	2986	...	...	...	Indonésie[1]
Iran(Islamic Rep. of)	[2]308	* [2]451	* [2]572	* [2]467	[2]466	* [2]500	[1]523	[1]688	[2]579	[2]661	Iran(Rép. islamique)
Iraq*	409	95	130	218	218	218	235	235	235	255	Iraq*
Israel*[2]	75	76	64	75	65	75	76	88	87	82	Israël*[2]
Japan[1]	1318	1275	1260	1208	1198	1193	1186	1157	1018	986	Japon[1]
Jordan	107	108	100	85	*135	*131	121	128	*150	*136	Jordanie
Kazakhstan	..	410	[1]253	[1]91	[1]41	[1]57	[1]71	[1]60	[1]9	[1]10	Kazakhstan
Korea,Dem.Ppl's.Rep.*	660	660	660	660	314	75	72	72	72	72	Corée,Rép.pop.dém.de*
Korea, Republic of	554	*577	*623	*621	*669	[1]950	[1]975	[1]923	[1]823	*584	Corée, République de
Kuwait	204	...	118	*293	*324	*391	*356	*349	361	331	Koweït
Malaysia*[2]	249	270	348	342	284	290	290	232	317	385	Malaisie*[2]
Myanmar[3]	*70	*69	*45	*50	69	66	74	56	52	64	Myanmar[3]
Pakistan[2]	[1]1155	[1]1119	[1]1042	[1]1	[1]1566	[1]1544	1682	[1]1682	[1]1660	[1]1774	Pakistan[2]
Philippines	*146	*153	*142	*158	169	215	256	213	165	163	Philippines
Qatar[1]	761	799	826	825	858	886	870	1440	1668	1645	Qatar[1]
Saudi Arabia*	568	598	714	831	1051	1027	1064	981	1080	1064	Arabie saoudite*
Syrian Arab Republic[1]	93	40	57	90	96	67	84	50	112	101	Rép. arabe syrienne[1]
Tajikistan[1]	..	84	53	20	8	13	11	10	12	5	Tadjikistan[1]
Turkey[1]	1208	1100	1310	1434	1040	1402	1395	1194	1229	790	Turquie[1]
Turkmenistan[1]	..	59	71	83	74	54	50	49	62	...	Turkménistan[1]
United Arab Emirates	228	238	232	*260	*230	*294	*258	*300	*259	272	Emirats arabes unis
Uzbekistan	..	[1]1109	[1]1012	[1]946	[1]679	[1]775	[1]835	[1]826	*732	*700	Ouzbékistan
Viet Nam	[1]24	[1]45	[1]82	*46	*48	*50	*54	*54	*30	*22	Viet Nam
Europe	**17608**	**34971**	**34281**	**29721**	**29285**	**31505**	**32523**	**29850**	**27837**	**28621**	**Europe**

For general note and footnotes, see end of table.

Voir la fin du tableau pour la remarque générale et les notes.

Nitrogenous fertilizers (total production) (continued)
Engrais azotés (production totale) (suite)

ISIC-BASED CODE - CODE BASE CITI

3512-00

Unit : Thousand metric tons   Unité : Milliers de tonnes métriques

Country or area	1990	1991	1992	1993	1994	1995	1996	1997	1998	1999	Pays ou zone
Albania[1]	183	55	110	21	9	4	...	...	...	...	Albanie[1]
Austria	* [2]230	#227	[2]1183	[2]1251	[2]1223	[2]1136	...	...	...	...	Autriche
Belarus[1]	..	2382	2112	1481	1134	1395	1571	1378	1485	1642	Bélarus[1]
Belgium[2]	64	59	70	...	...	...	...	...	...	...	Belgique[2]
Bulgaria[1]	2648	2157	1808	1687	1844	2291	2263	1846	...	...	Bulgarie[1]
Croatia[1]	..	610	719	567	592	616	629	684	497	...	Croatie[1]
Denmark[4]	* [2]200	* [2]185	* [2]173	* [2]171	* [2]179	[1]142	[1]164	[1]152	[1]154	[1]75	Danemark[4]
Czechoslovakia(former)[1]	514	357		..	..	..	..	..	..	..	Tchécoslovaquie(anc.)[1]
Czech Republic[1]	..		240	194	358	414	389	337	348	311	République tchèque[1]
Estonia[1]	..	482	241	65	245	263	245	197	149	197	Estonie[1]
Finland* [2]	268	192	224	237	235	247	231	238	230	225	Finlande* [2]
France	[1]2282	[1]2045	[1]2144	[1]1942	[1]1896	* [2]1490	* [2]1616	* [2]1484	* [2]1470	* [2]1450	France
Germany*	..	1095	1191	1131	1167	1174	1269	1125	1175	1195	Allemagne*
Germany(Fed.Rep.)[1][2]	959		..	..	..	..	..	..	..		Allemagne(Rép.féd.)[1][2]
Greece	[1]412	[1]293	[1]306	[1]292	[1]317	*275	[1]316	*240	[1]231	[1]229	Grèce
Hungary	[1]541	[1]288	[1]189	[1]167	[1]228	220	261	...	[1]655	[1]532	Hongrie
Iceland	10	13	11	*10	11	9	12	*12	*12	*12	Islande
Ireland* [2]	279	305	307	315	320	307	288	326	311	277	Irlande* [2]
Italy[2]	862	917	991	*654	*621	*660	*535	*537	*456	*390	Italie[2]
Latvia[1]	..	31	7	0	...	...	16	4	2	...	Lettonie[1]
Lithuania[1]	..	319	233	174	188	274	327	330	541	557	Lituanie[1]
Netherlands[2]	*1928	1821	1817	1756	1785	*1595	*1513	*1586	*1576	*1425	Pays-Bas[2]
Norway[2]	[1]439	[1]518	[1]446	[1]491	558	*595	*595	*570	*570	*575	Norvège[2]
Poland[1]	1303	1148	1167	1224	1385	1619	1615	1604	1406	1272	Pologne[1]
Portugal* [2]	158	109	88	100	99	124	135	143	148	138	Portugal* [2]
Romania[1]	1518	2109	2749	2511	2240	2998	3003	1779	912	1298	Roumanie[1]
Russian Federation[1]	..	6680	5815	4770	4050	4879	4900	4272	4135	5159	Fédération de Russie[1]
Slovakia	..	..	[1]200	...	[1]213	[1]229	[1]262	284	219	202	Slovaquie
Slovenia[1]	..	6	..	4	5	6	..	..	..	...	Slovénie[1]
Spain	[2]870	[2]862	[2]655	[1]658	[1]828	[1]1220	[2]882	[2]919	* [2]791	[2]917	Espagne
Sweden[5]	176	148	107	111	118	123	[1]120	[1]103	[1]104	...	Suède[5]
Switzerland[2]	27	*23	*21	21	*14	*22	*13	*13	*18	*18	Suisse[2]
Ukraine[1]	..	8110	7723	6230	6024	5813	6515	6445	...	...	Ukraine[1]
United Kingdom[1][6]	1183	1000	888	977	1017	1024	1036	985	1040	1040	Royaume-Uni[1][6]
Yugoslavia[1]	..	411	329	203	297	259	415	422	359	163	Yougoslavie[1]
T.F.Yug.Rep. Macedonia[1]	..	15	12	12	11	8	9	7	8	9	L'ex-RY Macédoine[1]
Yugoslavia, SFR[1]	554	..	..	..	..	..	..	..	..	..	Yougoslavie, RSF[1]
USSR (former)[1]	13208	..	..	..	..	..	..	..	..	..	URSS (anc.)[1]
Oceania	285	293	300	356	305	358	310	321	392	411	Océanie
Australia[2]	225	230	224	[1]280	229	281	[1]240	[1]240	*299	*303	Australie[2]
New Zealand	[1]60	[1]63	[1]76	[1]76	[1]76	77	70	81	93	108	Nouvelle-Zélande
Total	**91546**	**98688**	**99765**	**96032**	**98907**	**105383**	**108010**	**103761**	**104401**	**105386**	**Total**

General Note.
Data refer to N content of nitrogenous fertilizer materials (other than natural), of multinutrient fertilizers (physical mixtures and chemical combinations), containing two or three different minerals or chemical fertilizing substances (nitrogen, phosphorus or potassium). Intermediary products such as ammonia for further processing into fertilizers and part of separate chemically defined compounds and compounds of a high degree of purity are excluded. (SITC, Rev.3: 56210-0, 56291-1, 56293-1, 56294-1, 56295-1, 56296-1, 56299-1).
Main source: Food and Agriculture Organization of the United Nations (FAO), Rome.

[1] Official figures.
[2] Fertilizer year ending 30 June of year stated.
[3] Twelve months ending 30 September of year stated.
[4] Sales.
[5] Fertilizer year ending 30 April of year stated.
[6] Deliveries.
[7] Twelve months ending 30 June of year stated.

Remarque générale.
Les données se rapportent au poids de l'azote contenu dans les produits fertilisants azotés (autres que naturels), engrais composés (mélanges physiques et combinaisons chimiques) contenant deux ou trois minéraux ou éléments chimiques fertilisants différents (azote, phosphore ou potassium). Les produits intermédiaires, tels que l'ammoniac devant servir à la fabrication d'engrais, les composés chimiques définis séparément et les corps composés d'une grande pureté ne sont pas compris dans cette rubrique. (CTCI, Rev.3: 56210-0, 56291-1, 56293-1, 56294-1, 56295-1, 56296-1, 56299-1).
Source principale: Organisation des Nations Unies pour l'alimentation et l'agriculture (FAO), Rome.

[1] Données officielles.
[2] Campagne d'engrais se terminant le 30 juin de l'année indiquée.
[3] Période de douze mois finissant le 30 septembre de l'année indiquée.
[4] Ventes.
[5] Campagne d'engrais se terminant le 30 avril de l'année indiquée.
[6] Livraisons.
[7] Période de douze mois finissant le 30 juin de l'année indiquée.

Nitrogenous fertilizers, N content
Engrais azotés, N contenu

ISIC-BASED CODE - CODE BASE CITI

3512-01

Unit : Thousand metric tons

Unité : Milliers de tonnes métriques

Country or area	1990	1991	1992	1993	1994	1995	1996	1997	1998	1999	Pays ou zone
Africa	**5986**	**5774**	**6696**	**7058**	**7578**	**7775**	**8190**	**8889**	**9606**	**9188**	**Afrique**
Algeria	87	71	88	80	62	31	8	...	...	...	Algérie
Egypt[1]	4600	4339	5342	5588	5918	...	...	...	...	...	Egypte[1]
Mauritius	1	1	1	1	1	2	...	...	...	...	Maurice
Nigeria	*200	125	125	...	...	...	...	...	...	...	Nigéria
Senegal	14	16	27	25	24	12	29	25		...	Sénégal
South Africa	947	1088	1010	1116	[1]1335	[1]1142	[1]1178	[1]1508	[1]1839	[1]1026	Afrique du Sud
Tunisia	70	[1]82	[1]74	[1]46	[1]38	[1]65	[1]62	[1]55	[1]52	[1]58	Tunisie
United Rep.Tanzania	2	0	...	...	...	...	...	...	...	...	Rép. Unie de Tanzanie
Zambia	...	1	...	...	...	...	...	...	...	...	Zambie
Zimbabwe	64	51	*27	*50	...	...	...	...	...	...	Zimbabwe
America, North	**16056**	**16485**	**16262**	**16894**	**18368**	**17668**	**18975**	**19518**	**18194**	**17731**	**Amérique du Nord**
Canada[2]	2570	2777	2810	2884	3391	3060	[1]3936	* [1]4451	...	...	Canada[2]
Costa Rica*	30	39	42	38	38	...	...	...	...	...	Costa Rica*
Cuba[1]	136	...	...	...	...	...	...	...	...	...	Cuba[1]
Mexico	3011	[1]2784	[1]2245	[1]2507	[1]2808	[1]2956	[1]3439	[1]2596	[1]2042	[1]1342	Mexique
Trinidad and Tobago	232	240	209	...	...	...	...	...	...	...	Trinité-et-Tobago
United States[2]	10077	10509	10820	11102	11768	11247	11194	12063	...	...	Etats-Unis[2]
America, South	**1053**	**1012**	**983**	**1027**	**1076**	**1071**	**1067**	**1093**	**1106**	**1120**	**Amérique du Sud**
Argentina	*41	42	33	48	58	...	...	...	...	...	Argentine
Brazil	614	584	571	601	640	[1]645	[1]641	...	...	...	Brésil
Colombia	...	26	...	...	...	...	...	...	...	...	Colombie
Peru	32	20	13	12	12	...	...	...	...	...	Pérou
Venezuela	...	...	...	...	340	...	...	...	...	...	Venezuela
Asia	**26221**	**28188**	**28494**	**28682**	**30707**	**32439**	**36272**	**36206**	**37481**	**40114**	**Asie**
Afghanistan[2]	55	*53	*49	*42	*40	*49	50	50	...	...	Afghanistan[2]
Bangladesh[2]	678	654	749	912	997	905	975	1003	...	...	Bangladesh[2]
China[3]	14636	15101	*15505	*15030	*17119	*18346	*21089	*20410	*21943	...	Chine[3]
Georgia	..	...	77	59	34	43	68	81	[1]55	[1]95	Géorgie
India	[2]5991	[2]6148	[2]6154	6321	6376	6657	7431	7357	...	...	Inde
Iran(Islamic Rep. of)[2]	267	344	389	499	402	427	...	...	...	...	Iran(Rép. islamique)[2]
Israel	...	...	48	50	58	63	65	...	...	...	Israël
Japan[1][2]	957	922	920	878	860	881	895	876	763	752	Japon[1][2]
Kazakhstan[4]	..	...	...	...	41	57	...	...	...	...	Kazakhstan[4]
Kuwait	204	...	118	293	188	274	327	...	...	...	Koweït
Myanmar[5]	88	60	47	54	80	78	...	...	...	...	Myanmar[5]
Pakistan[2]	1078	1045	971	1159	1508	1478	1617	[1]1602	[1]1593	[1]1708	Pakistan[2]
Qatar[1]	761	799	826	825	858	886	870	1440	1668	1645	Qatar[1]
Saudi Arabia	584	658	662	...	...	...	...	...	...	...	Arabie saoudite
Syrian Arab Republic[1]	93	40	57	90	96	67	84	50	112	101	Rép. arabe syrienne[1]
Tajikistan[1]	..	84	53	20	8	13	11	10	12	5	Tadjikistan[1]
Turkey[1]	563	549	576	561	489	566	514	563	459	150	Turquie[1]
United Arab Emirates	228	238	232	*260	...	...	...	...	...	...	Emirats arabes unis
Uzbekistan	..	1109	1012	946	679	775	[1]835	[1]826	...	...	Ouzbékistan
Europe	**13391**	**22458**	**21516**	**19428**	**19723**	**21804**	**21901**	**20621**	**20439**	**21841**	**Europe**
Albania	[1]183	[1]55	[1]110	[1]21	[1]9	*4	...	...	...	...	Albanie
Belarus	..	720	668	498	424	[1]502	[1]565	[1]490	[1]559	[1]615	Bélarus
Belgium	...	...	...	...	944	[1]1130	[1]1297	[1]1235	[1]1332	[1]1398	Belgique
Bulgaria[1]	911	760	654	611	676	827	835	677	629	529	Bulgarie[1]
Croatia[1]	..	228	264	208	214	227	237	255	189	...	Croatie[1]
Denmark	[2][6]63	[2][6]58	...	...	[4]45	[4]52	[6]67	[6]59	[6]52	[6]75	Danemark
Czechoslovakia(former)[1]	514	357	...	..	..	..	...	...	...	..	Tchécoslovaquie(anc.)[1]
Czech Republic[1]	..	...	240	194	234	265	253	245	247	220	République tchèque[1]
Estonia[1]	..	101	50	14	51	55	51	41	31	41	Estonie[1]
Finland[2]	26	25	21	...	[4]12	[4]6	[4]35	...	...	...	Finlande[2]
France[1][2]	2002	1756	1851	1575	1720	...	...	...	...	...	France[1][2]
Germany	..	1299	1227	...	[4]1199	1229	1187	1103	[1]1116	...	Allemagne
German D.R.(former)[1]	955	..	..	..	..	..	...	...	..	..	R.D.A. (anc.)[1]
Greece	...	...	...	...	...	...	...	...	126	...	Grèce
Hungary[1]	470	250	185	167	228	178	275	262	225	188	Hongrie[1]

For general note and footnotes, see end of table.

Voir la fin du tableau pour la remarque générale et les notes.

Nitrogenous fertilizers, N content (continued)
Engrais azotés, N contenu (suite)

ISIC-BASED CODE - CODE BASE CITI

3512-01

Unit : Thousand metric tons   Unité : Milliers de tonnes métriques

Country or area	1990	1991	1992	1993	1994	1995	1996	1997	1998	1999	Pays ou zone
Iceland	2	3	2	2	2	2	[4]1	...	...	...	Islande
Ireland* [2]	297	279	...	...	...	...	...	...	...	...	Irlande* [2]
Italy	[2]956	[2]650	[2]733	[2]807	[4]1610	[4]1597	[4]1518	...	...	...	Italie
Lithuania[1]	..	...	...	...	...	274	327	330	541	557	Lituanie[1]
Netherlands[2]	1614	...	1597	1638	1598	...	...	...	...	...	Pays-Bas[2]
Norway[1] [2]	131	128	110	120	...	...	...	...	...	...	Norvège[1] [2]
Poland	[1]1233	[1]1105	[1]1081	1143	1269	1469	1458	1434	[1]1240	[1]1121	Pologne
Portugal	[1]141	[1]102	...	...	[4]53	[4]98	[4]117	...	...	...	Portugal
Romania[1]	1249	824	1086	1011	905	1200	1215	669	318	612	Roumanie[1]
Russian Federation[1]	..	6680	5815	4770	4050	4879	4807	4272	4082	5159	Fédération de Russie[1]
Slovakia	..	..	...	...	213	229	262	226	[1]721	[1]206	Slovaquie
Spain	[2]748	[2]682	[2]673	658	828	1220	786	725	[1]808	[1]907	Espagne
Sweden[7]	83	111	94	79	78	75	77	251	240	[1]255	Suède[7]
Switzerland[2]	28	25	25	21	19	...	...	...	...	...	Suisse[2]
Ukraine[1]	..	2819	2544	2072	1935	1871	2083	2022	1675	2060	Ukraine[1]
United Kingdom[1] [8]	678	595	526	526	607	615	672	588	638	608	Royaume-Uni[1] [8]
Yugoslavia	..	86	78	58	91	78	129	[1]131	[1]109	[1]48	Yougoslavie
USSR (former)[1]	13208	..	..	..	..	..	..	..	..	..	URSS (anc.)[1]
Oceania	59	63	57	63	61	61	61	61	61	61	Océanie
New Zealand[2]	59	63	57	63	...	...	...	...	...	...	Nouvelle-Zélande[2]
Total	75974	73980	74007	73153	77512	80817	86466	86388	86887	90054	**Total**

General Note.

N content of nitrogenous fertilizer materials (other than natural). Intermediary products such as ammonia for further processing into fertilizers and part of separate chemically defined compounds and compounds of a high degree of purity are excluded. (SITC, Rev.3: 56210-0).
Main source: Food and Agriculture Organization of the United Nations (FAO), Rome.

[1] Official figures.
[2] Fertilizer year ending 30 June of year stated.
[3] Including Hong-Kong, Macao and Taiwan.
[4] Source: United Nations Economic Commission for Europe (ECE), (Geneva).
[5] Twelve months ending 30 September of year stated.
[6] Sales.
[7] Fertilizer year ending 30 April of year stated.
[8] Deliveries.

Remarque générale.

Poids de l'azote contenu dans les produits fertilisants azotés (autres que naturels). Les produits intermédiaires, tels que l'ammoniac devant servir à la fabrication d'engrais, les composés chimiques définis séparément et les corps composés d'une grande pureté ne sont pas compris dans cette rubrique. (CTCI, Rev.3: 56210-0).
Source principale: Organisation des Nations Unies pour l'alimentation et l'agriculture (FAO), Rome.

[1] Données officielles.
[2] Campagne d'engrais se terminant le 30 juin de l'année indiquée.
[3] Y compris Hong-Kong, Macao et Taïwan.
[4] Source: Commission économique des Nations Unies pour l'Europe (CEE), (Genève).
[5] Période de douze mois finissant le 30 septembre de l'année indiquée.
[6] Ventes.
[7] Campagne d'engrais se terminant le 30 avril de l'année indiquée.
[8] Livraisons.

Phosphate fertilizers (total production)
Engrais phosphatés (production totale)

ISIC-BASED CODE - CODE BASE CITI
3512-03

Unit : Thousand metric tons

Unité : Milliers de tonnes métriques

Country or area	1990	1991	1992	1993	1994	1995	1996	1997	1998	1999	Pays ou zone
Africa	**3312**	**2990**	**3037**	**2700**	**3002**	**3324**	**2937**	**2718**	**2732**	**2814**	**Afrique**
Algeria[1]	173	155	154	204	179	80	46	118	183	201	Algérie[1]
Côte d'Ivoire*	3	3	3	3	3	1	...	...	...	...	Côte d'Ivoire*
Egypt[1]	1095	1060	825	689	779	956	377	419	365	378	Egypte[1]
Morocco[1]	582	422	535	434	461	530	667	488	542	481	Maroc[1]
Nigeria	50	58	84	63	6	1	10	5	11	5	Nigéria
Senegal	[2]27	*[2]50	*[2]46	*[2]33	[1]131	[1]193	[1]177	[1]222	[1]220	[1]178	Sénégal
South Africa[1]	490	407	498	550	530	701	775	643	557	663	Afrique du Sud[1]
Tunisia[1]	849	787	843	682	868	819	844	786	814	866	Tunisie[1]
United Rep.Tanzania	2	3	...	...	...	...	...	...	...	...	Rép. Unie de Tanzanie
Zimbabwe	41	45	46	39	42	40	36	33	36	38	Zimbabwe
America, North	**11861**	**12705**	**11717**	**11153**	**12208**	**11709**	**12272**	**10265**	**10273**	**9673**	**Amérique du Nord**
Canada[2]	[1]440	[1]354	[1]478	[1]395	[1]368	[1]364	[1]395	[1]400	358	273	Canada[2]
Cuba	[1]14	*7	*7	*6	*6	...	...	...	...	...	Cuba
El Salvador	...	0	9	10	...	...	[1]10	...	...	...	El Salvador
Guatemala[2]	7	7	7	2	...	...	...	...	...	...	Guatemala[2]
Mexico[1]	1256	1200	533	517	766	829	960	847	901	917	Mexique[1]
United States[2]	10137	11137	10683	10223	11055	10500	10900	9005	9001	8470	Etats-Unis[2]
America, South	**1234**	**1276**	**1208**	**1295**	**1498**	**1358**	**1400**	**1419**	**1457**	**1447**	**Amérique du Sud**
Brazil	[1]1056	[1]1087	[1]1062	[1]1218	[1]1378	1265	1305	1354	1369	1358	Brésil
Chile	*5	*4	*4	*5	5	5	4	0	0	0	Chili
Colombia	99	95	75	12	11	9	10	9	9	9	Colombie
Peru	5	*3	*4	*1	2	1	2	3	3	3	Pérou
Uruguay	*12	*17	*17	*17	10	5	9	9	9	10	Uruguay
Venezuela	57	70	46	42	92	73	70	44	67	67	Venezuela
Asia	**10478**	**12310**	**12390**	**11231**	**12304**	**13700**	**13863**	**14707**	**14257**	**15891**	**Asie**
Azerbaijan[1]	..	146	74	23	4	2	0	1	1	0	Azerbaïdjan[1]
Bangladesh[2]	51	41	40	49	50	[1]50	[1]60	[1]52	41	53	Bangladesh[2]
China*	4240	4723	4771	4283	5145	6730	6628	7270	6804	...	Chine*
India[1]	2237	2973	2804	2098	2912	2781	2803	3191	3227	3374	Inde[1]
Indonesia[1]	551	589	948	1179	...	...	...	...	...	...	Indonésie[1]
Iran(Islamic Rep. of)[2]	81	161	185	109	110	83	136	93	105	101	Iran(Rép. islamique)[2]
Iraq	*207	*30	*80	*90	*90	90	90	90	90	90	Iraq
Israel	200	185	210	190	190	216	222	244	250	285	Israël
Japan[1]	642	615	582	566	559	532	498	472	422	399	Japon[1]
Jordan	596	600	554	470	750	729	671	[1]586	[1]642	...	Jordanie
Korea,Dem.Ppl's.Rep.	*137	*137	*130	*130	*20	*20	*20	*20	*10	10	Corée,Rép.pop.dém.de
Korea, Republic of	516	368	*422	*438	*447	421	409	[1]450	[1]421	425	Corée, République de
Lebanon	*34	*40	65	64	89	81	95	115	86	75	Liban
Pakistan[2]	106	105	106	105	93	92	96	[1]81	[1]67	[1]66	Pakistan[2]
Philippines	199	190	183	185	205	264	273	217	...	181	Philippines
Saudi Arabia	*27	*200	*182	*132	*148	123	130	120	137	150	Arabie saoudite
Syrian Arab Republic	14	21	25	...	...	56	[1]201	[1]183	[1]209	[1]144	Rép. arabe syrienne
Turkey	595	428	547	542	305	302	371	[1]435	[1]426	[1]266	Turquie
Turkmenistan	..	131	33	45	[1]13	[1]14	[1]13	[1]5	[1]6	5	Turkménistan
Uzbekistan	..	551	349	327	132	168	[1]194	[1]129	141	147	Ouzbékistan
Viet Nam	[1]45	[1]76	[1]100	99	119	129	136	136	144	179	Viet Nam
Europe	**8591**	**15383**	**9744**	**9881**	**7493**	**8183**	**7805**	**7660**	**6527**	**6056**	**Europe**
Albania	[1]141	[1]43	[1]22	[1]9	[1]11	[1]14	[1]27	[1]27	[1]26	0	Albanie
Austria[2]	70	77	79	77	58	44	72	64	70	65	Autriche[2]
Belarus[1]	..	212	101	68	84	104	200	474	471	457	Bélarus[1]
Belgium	[1]423	[1]382	[1]342	[1]284	[3]84	[3]140	[3]108	[3]130	[3]128	[3]132	Belgique
Bulgaria[1]	88	47	69	86	98	92	173	224	...	...	Bulgarie[1]
Denmark[4]	*136	*81	*75	1764	153	[1]1414	[1]991	[1]779	[1]622	[1]112	Danemark[4]
Czechoslovakia(former)[1]	257	169								..	Tchécoslovaquie(anc.)[1]
Czech Republic	..	..	[1]45	[1]28	25	30	[1]26	[1]26	[1]26	[1]18	République tchèque
Estonia[1]	..	425	52	1	19	7	...	...	...	...	Estonie[1]
Finland	172	117	127	132	130	122	105	95	96	97	Finlande
France[1]	3669	3420	2117	1867	1831	...	...	...	...	...	France[1]
Germany	..	250	224	130	19	110	203	194	184	185	Allemagne

For general note and footnotes, see end of table.

Voir la fin du tableau pour la remarque générale et les notes.

Phosphate fertilizers (total production) (continued)
Engrais phosphatés (production totale) (suite)

ISIC-BASED CODE - CODE BASE CITI

3512-03

Unit : Thousand metric tons   Unité : Milliers de tonnes métriques

Country or area	1990	1991	1992	1993	1994	1995	1996	1997	1998	1999	Pays ou zone
Germany(Fed.Rep.)[1]	304	..	..	..	..	..	..	..	..	..	Allemagne(Rép.féd.)[1]
German D.R.(former)[1]	106	..	..	..	..	..	..	..	..	..	R.D.A. (anc.)[1]
Greece	211	202	164	107	114	146	162	125	132	134	Grèce
Hungary	[1]141	[1]51	[1]5	[1]2	13	26	29	27	16	15	Hongrie
Iceland	5	6	5	5	5	5	...	...	...	...	Islande
Italy[2]	325	389	166	167	282	216	198	170	170	170	Italie[2]
Latvia[1]	..	103	23	0	...	...	...	...	...	...	Lettonie[1]
Lithuania[1]	..	149	52	52	83	139	164	193	242	300	Lituanie[1]
Netherlands[2]	365	424	292	321	382	338	271	402	405	355	Pays-Bas[2]
Norway[2]	229	221	215	203	207	236	265	236	236	240	Norvège[2]
Poland[1]	467	252	329	282	415	523	570	596	593	535	Pologne[1]
Portugal	63	31	52	61	56	56	57	56	56	56	Portugal
Romania[1]	388	216	260	246	208	197	456	327	223	214	Roumanie[1]
Russian Federation[1]	..	4275	3015	2512	1718	1929	1584	1787	1703	2044	Fédération de Russie[1]
Spain[2]	293	271	296	365	422	413	*447	*557	*540	382	Espagne[2]
Sweden	108	72	30	26	20	18	[1]20	15	15	18	Suède
Switzerland	[2]3	[2]3	[2]3	[2]2	[2]3	[2]3	0	2	2	...	Suisse
Ukraine[1]	..	2967	1164	716	732	551	746	685	...	...	Ukraine[1]
United Kingdom[1][5]	307	233	211	292	223	219	254	304	270	277	Royaume-Uni[1][5]
Yugoslavia[1]	..	286	200	68	48	31	133	111	77	15	Yougoslavie[1]
T.F.Yug.Rep. Macedonia[1]	..	9	9	8	8	6	8	7	8	8	L'ex-RY Macédoine[1]
Yugoslavia, SFR[1]	320	..	..	..	..	..	..	..	..	..	Yougoslavie, RSF[1]
USSR (former)	9434	..	..	..	..	..	..	..	..	..	URSS (anc.)
Oceania	**2519**	**1617**	**2386**	**2942**	**2834**	**3560**	**3952**	**4141**	**4465**	**4798**	**Océanie**
Australia[6]	[1]2351	*1406	*1463	*1416	*1568	[1]1688	[1]1729	[1]1567	...	...	Australie[6]
New Zealand[7]	168	211	[1]923	[1]1526	[1]1266	...	...	...	...	...	Nouvelle-Zélande[7]
Total	**47429**	**46281**	**40482**	**39201**	**39338**	**41834**	**42229**	**40911**	**39711**	**40679**	**Total**

General Note.
Data refer to P_2O_5 content of single, double and concentrated superphosphates, of phosphatic fertilizers and fertilizing materials (other than natural, superphosphates and Thomas basic slag), of multinutrient fertilizers (physical mixtures and chemical combinations), containing two or three different minerals or fertilizing substances (nitrogen, phosphorus or potassium). Intermediary products such as liquid phosphoric and superphosphoric acids are excluded. (SITC, Rev.3: 56222-0, 56229-0, 56291-2, 56292-1, 56293-2, 56294-2, 56295-2, 56296-2, 56299-2).
Main source: Food and Agriculture Organization of the United Nations (FAO), Rome.

Remarque générale.
Les données se rapportent au poids de P_2O_5 contenu dans les superphosphates simples, doubles et composés, engrais phosphatés et les produits fertilisants (autres que les engrais phosphatés naturels, les superphosphates et les scories de déphosphoration Thomas), engrais composés (mélanges physiques et combinaisons chimiques) contenant deux ou trois minéraux ou éléments chimiques fertilisants (azote, phosphore ou potassium). Cette rubrique ne comprend pas les produits intermédiaires tels que les solutions d'acide phosphorique et l'acide superphosphorique. (CTCI, Rev.3: 56222-0, 56229-0, 56291-2, 56292-1, 56293-2, 56294-2, 56295-2, 56296-2, 56299-2).
Source principale: Organisation des Nations Unies pour l'alimentation et l'agriculture (FAO), Rome.

[1] Official figures.
[2] Fertilizer year ending 30 June of year stated.
[3] Data refer to Belgium and Luxembourg.
[4] Sales.
[5] Deliveries.
[6] In terms of single superphosphates (9 per cent P equivalent).
[7] Twelve months ending 30 June of year stated.

[1] Données officielles.
[2] Campagne d'engrais se terminant le 30 juin de l'année indiquée.
[3] Données se rapportant à la Belgique et au Luxembourg.
[4] Ventes.
[5] Livraisons.
[6] En termes des superphosphates simples (9 p. 100 P d'équivalent).
[7] Période de douze mois finissant le 30 juin de l'année indiquée.

Superphosphates, P2O5 content
Superphosphates, P2O5 contenu

ISIC-BASED CODE - CODE BASE CITI

3512-04

Unit : Thousand metric tons / Unité : Milliers de tonnes métriques

Country or area	1990	1991	1992	1993	1994	1995	1996	1997	1998	1999	Pays ou zone
Africa	**1167**	**1042**	**1160**	**975**	**1101**	**1169**	**1356**	**1129**	**1169**	**1107**	**Afrique**
Algeria	20	11	16	15	8	0	0	0	5	9	Algérie
Egypt[1]	170	142	130	114	*145	163	202	*195	174	173	Egypte[1]
Morocco	...	422	535	434	461	530	667	[2]488	[2]542	[2]481	Maroc
Nigeria	4	4	5	0	6	1	0	0	11	5	Nigéria
Senegal[1]	11	9	...	...	...	...	3	5	2	3	Sénégal[1]
South Africa	...	71	48	62	43	59	73	58	36	13	Afrique du Sud
Tunisia[2]	377	339	373	304	389	369	374	349	362	384	Tunisie[2]
United Rep.Tanzania	1	1	...	...	...	...	...	...	...	...	Rép. Unie de Tanzanie
Zimbabwe		43	46	39	42	40	36	33	36	38	Zimbabwe
America, North	**2143**	**2067**	**1463**	**1211**	**1540**	**1562**	**1706**	**1507**	**1497**	**1436**	**Amérique du Nord**
Mexico[2]	1256	1200	533	517	766	829	960	847	901	917	Mexique[2]
United States[2]	887	867	930	694	774	733	746	660	596	...	Etats-Unis[2]
America, South	**621**	**641**	**660**	**731**	**834**	**710**	**776**	**879**	**875**	**859**	**Amérique du Sud**
Brazil	[2]607	629	648	718	820	697	763	869	865	849	Brésil
Chile	5	4	4	5	5	5	4	0	0	0	Chili
Peru	2	*1	1	1	2	1	2	3	3	3	Pérou
Uruguay	...	...	...	...	...	...	*7	*7	*7	7	Uruguay
Asia	**6114**	**7057**	**6783**	**6207**	**6969**	**8243**	**8188**	**8714**	**8099**	**9736**	**Asie**
Azerbaijan[2]	..	146	74	23	4	2	0	1	1	0	Azerbaïdjan[2]
Bangladesh[1]	51	41	40	49	50	[2]50	[2]60	[2]52	41	53	Bangladesh[1]
China[2]	4114	4597	4622	4190	5044	6626	6512	7146	6668	...	Chine[2]
India[1]	502	584	478	361	484	512	510	595	580	580	Inde[1]
Indonesia	551	500	437	542	541	325	355	238	238	308	Indonésie
Iraq	105	...	43	...	...	...	...	...	...	...	Iraq
Israel[2]	...	...	16	17	15	17	19	...	...	...	Israël[2]
Japan	104	[2]95	[2]83	[2]84	[2]85	[2]76	[2]67	[2]69	[2]60	...	Japon
Jordan	...	...	...	...	...	...	...	1	1	1	Jordanie
Korea, Republic of	...	...	...	...	...	52	38	...	...	...	Corée, République de
Lebanon	...	40	65	65	89	81	95	115	86	75	Liban
Pakistan	[1][2]29	31	[1][2]35	36	[1][2]35	[1][2]26	[1][2]19	[1][2]0	[1][2]0	[1][2]4	Pakistan
Philippines	...	...	...	1	1	2	3	0	2	2	Philippines
Syrian Arab Republic[1]	15	21	25	...	...	28	92	84	97	66	Rép. arabe syrienne[1]
Turkey	238	215	195	186	88	98	80	[2]52	[2]48	[2]30	Turquie
Uzbekistan[2]	..	336	300	296	176	169	152	117	...	...	Ouzbékistan[2]
Viet Nam	[2]280	[2]315	[2]323	...	...	104	111	106	111	121	Viet Nam
Europe	**1796**	**8014**	**5023**	**5646**	**3287**	**5645**	**5425**	**5144**	**4730**	**4088**	**Europe**
Albania[2]	141	43	22	9	11	14	12	12	12	0	Albanie[2]
Austria	...	4	3	3	3	0	2	0	2	0	Autriche
Belarus[2]	..	212	101	68	42	52	100	136	130	120	Bélarus[2]
Belgium	[2]35	[2]36	[2]29	[2]24	[3]12	[3]11	[3]1	[3]21	[3]20	[3]22	Belgique
Bulgaria[2]	47	37	37	45	51	53	90	110	...	...	Bulgarie[2]
Denmark[2][5]	[4]37	...	[4]9	1714	82	1356	946	734	577	112	Danemark[2][5]
Czechoslovakia(former)[2]	82	27	..	..	..	..	..	..	..	..	Tchécoslovaquie(anc.)[2]
Czech Republic	..	...	...	...	7	...	...	...	...	...	République tchèque
Estonia[2]	..	80	10	0	4	1	...	...	...	...	Estonie[2]
France	[2]640	[2]524	[2]464	[2]452	[2]439	...	...	155	135	136	France
Germany	...	41	23	12	17	...	...	...	...	...	Allemagne
German D.R.(former)[2]	65	..	..	..	..	...	...	...	..	..	R.D.A. (anc.)[2]
Greece	11	13	10	7	0	7	6	5	2	2	Grèce
Hungary	[2]56	[2]13	[2]1	[2]2	3	26	29	27	16	0	Hongrie
Italy[1]	53	112	80	83	122	74	48	30	40	40	Italie[1]
Lithuania[2]	..	...	111	33	77	43	36	29	0	0	Lituanie[2]
Netherlands[1]	51	107	75	85	62	75	90	100	100	50	Pays-Bas[1]
Poland[2]	277	138	118	61	87	94	109	104	107	87	Pologne[2]
Portugal	[2]58	[2]43	...	...	8	6	5	3	3	3	Portugal
Romania[2]	111	108	139	86	121	123	122	136	99	101	Roumanie[2]
Russian Federation[2]	..	4275	3015	2512	1718	...	...	...	...	...	Fédération de Russie[2]
Spain[1]	58	44	25	44	29	[2]72	[2]123	[2]217	[2]180	[2]117	Espagne[1]
Sweden[1][2]	37	46	19	0	3	...	...	...	...	...	Suède[1][2]

For general note and footnotes, see end of table. — Voir la fin du tableau pour la remarque générale et les notes.

Superphosphates, P2O5 content (continued)
Superphosphates, P2O5 contenu (suite)

ISIC-BASED CODE - CODE BASE CITI

3512-04

Unit : Thousand metric tons   Unité : Milliers de tonnes métriques

Country or area	1990	1991	1992	1993	1994	1995	1996	1997	1998	1999	Pays ou zone
Switzerland[1]	1	1	...	...	...	...	...	...	...	...	Suisse[1]
Ukraine[2]	..	1282	592	325	324	295	327	305	240	238	Ukraine[2]
United Kingdom[2]	...	...	...	18	46	47	39	58	33	...	Royaume-Uni[2]
Yugoslavia[2]	..	114	80	39	18	17	61	50	37	13	Yougoslavie[2]
USSR (former)[2]	9434	..	..	..	..	..	..	..	..	..	URSS (anc.)[2]
Oceania	**2519**	**1579**	**1672**	**1626**	**1761**	**1869**	**1893**	**1781**	**1730**	**1708**	**Océanie**
Australia[2][6]	2351	1368	1422	1374	1518	1622	1653	1511	...	...	Australie[2][6]
New Zealand[1]	168	211	250	252	243	247	240	270	260	260	Nouvelle-Zélande[1]
Total	**23794**	**20400**	**16761**	**16396**	**15492**	**19198**	**19344**	**19153**	**18100**	**18934**	**Total**

General Note.

P_2O_5 content of single, double and concentrated superphosphates. (SITC, Rev.3: 56222-0).

Main source: Food and Agriculture Organization of the United Nations (FAO), Rome.

Remarque générale.

Poids de P_2O_5 contenu dans les superphosphates simples, doubles et composés. (CTCI, Rev.3: 56222-0).

Source principale: Organisation des Nations Unies pour l'alimentation et l'agriculture (FAO), Rome.

[1] Fertilizer year ending 30 June of year stated.
[2] Official figures.
[3] Data refer to Belgium and Luxembourg.
[4] Fertilizer year ending 31 July of year stated.
[5] Sales.
[6] Twelve months ending 30 June of year stated.

[1] Campagne d'engrais se terminant le 30 juin de l'année indiquée.
[2] Données officielles.
[3] Données se rapportant à la Belgique et au Luxembourg.
[4] Campagne d'engrais se terminant le 31 juillet de l'année indiquée.
[5] Ventes.
[6] Période de douze mois finissant le 30 juin de l'année indiquée.

Phosphatic fertilizers, other, P2O5 content
Autres engrais phosphatés, P2O5 contenu

ISIC-BASED CODE - CODE BASE CITI
3512-07

Unit : Thousand metric tons　　　　　　　　　　　　　　　　　　　　　　　　　Unité : Milliers de tonnes métriques

Country or area	1990	1991	1992	1993	1994	1995	1996	1997	1998	1999	Pays ou zone
Africa	**8**	**13**	**10**	**7**	**7**	**6**	**9**	**9**	**10**	**11**	**Afrique**
Tunisia[1]	8	13	10	7	7	6	9	9	10	11	Tunisie[1]
America, North	**7260**	**7212**	**7620**	**7289**	**8300**	**2801**	**2206**	**2252**	**2991**	**2554**	**Amérique du Nord**
United States	[1]7260	[1]7212	[1]7620	[1]7289	[1]8300	[2]2801	[2]2206	[2]2252	...	...	Etats-Unis
America, South	**18**	**26**	**30**	**31**	**36**	**34**	**31**	**26**	**26**	**33**	**Amérique du Sud**
Brazil	18	*26	*30	*31	*36	*34	*31	26	26	...	Brésil
Asia	**468**	**197**	**453**	**444**	**304**	**231**	**187**	**386**	**369**	**285**	**Asie**
Bangladesh	9	...	...	...	...	...	...	...	...	...	Bangladesh
Japan	[2]102	[2]105	[2]92	[2]79	[2]78	78	68	63	[1]60	...	Japon
Turkey	357	83	352	356	217	144	110	314	[1]300	[1]236	Turquie
Europe	**1424**	**1326**	**907**	**988**	**808**	**793**	**726**	**636**	**552**	**468**	**Europe**
Belgium[1]	246	224	175	160	...	...	...	...	...	...	Belgique[1]
Czechoslovakia(former)[1]	175	142	..	..	..	..	..	..	..	..	Tchécoslovaquie(anc.)[1]
Czech Republic	..	..	26	[1]18	...	...	...	...	...	...	République tchèque
France[2]	[3]888	[3]772	[3]605	[3]765	497	...	...	...	...	...	France[2]
Germany	..	...	...	...	...	36	37	41	...	...	Allemagne
Germany(Fed.Rep.)[1][2]	74	..	..	..	..	..	..	..	..	..	Allemagne(Rép.féd.)[1][2]
German D.R.(former)[1]	39	..	..	..	..	..	..	..	..	..	R.D.A. (anc.)[1]
Latvia	..	103	23	0	...	...	...	...	...	...	Lettonie
Slovakia	..	..	...	...	...	...	...	3	...	...	Slovaquie
Ukraine	..	3	3	2	[1]2	[1]1	[1]0	[1]0	[1]0	...	Ukraine
United Kingdom[1]	...	...	...	2	...	...	...	...	...	...	Royaume-Uni[1]
Yugoslavia	..	42	32	0	1	...	29	[1]14	[1]12	[1]6	Yougoslavie
USSR (former)	144	..	..	..	..	..	..	..	..	..	URSS (anc.)
Total	**9322**	**8774**	**9020**	**8759**	**9455**	**3865**	**3159**	**3309**	**3949**	**3351**	**Total**

General Note.

P$_2$O$_5$ content of phosphatic fertilizers and fertilizing materials other than natural, superphosphates and Thomas basic slag. Intermediary products such as liquid phosphoric and superphosphoric acids are excluded. (SITC, Rev.3: 56229-0).
Main source: Food and Agriculture Organization of the United Nations (FAO), Rome.

Remarque générale.

Poids de P$_2$O$_5$ contenu dans les engrais phosphatés et les produits fertilisants autres que les engrais phosphatés naturels, les superphosphates et les scories de déphosphoration Thomas. Cette rubrique ne comprend pas les produits intermédiaires tels que les solutions d'acide phosphorique et l'acide superphosphorique. (CTCI, Rev.3: 56229-0).
Source principale: Organisation des Nations Unies pour l'alimentation et l'agriculture (FAO), Rome.

[1] Official figures.
[2] Fertilizer year ending 30 June of year stated.
[3] Crude weight.

[1] Données officielles.
[2] Campagne d'engrais se terminant le 30 juin de l'année indiquée.
[3] Poids brut.

Potassic fertilizers (total production)
Engrais potassiques (production totale)

ISIC-BASED CODE - CODE BASE CITI
3512-09

Unit : Thousand metric tons

Unité : Milliers de tonnes métriques

Country or area	1990	1991	1992	1993	1994	1995	1996	1997	1998	1999	Pays ou zone
America, North	**10134**	**10966**	**10355**	**10671**	**10675**	**12486**	**11452**	**12273**	**12535**	**12797**	**Amérique du Nord**
Canada[1]	6774	7520	7014	7289	7293	9104	[2]8070	...	...	...	Canada[1]
United States[1][2]	3360	3446	3341	...	...	...	...	...	...	...	Etats-Unis[1][2]
America, South	**75**	**108**	**90**	**175**	**242**	**224**	**248**	**288**	**333**	**355**	**Amérique du Sud**
Brazil	68	101	77	174	229	[2]224	[2]241	281	326	348	Brésil
Colombia	...	...	13	1	13	0	...	...	...	...	Colombie
Asia	**2593**	**2590**	**2639**	**2607**	**2879**	**2963**	**2928**	**2865**	**2747**	**2929**	**Asie**
Azerbaijan[2]	..	43	8	10	3	0	2	5	0	0	Azerbaïdjan[2]
Bangladesh[2]	965	...	...	...	...	...	...	...	...	...	Bangladesh[2]
China[2]	46	47	153	117	327	263	...	...	...	...	Chine[2]
Israel[2]	...	...	25	29	28	32	35	...	...	...	Israël[2]
Japan[1][2]	327	315	313	310	304	292	272	264	233	217	Japon[1][2]
Jordan	842	818	808	822	930	1068	1059	987	916	1080	Jordanie
Korea, Republic of[2]	...	...	...	...	322	343	328	314	273	...	Corée, République de[2]
Europe	**9940**	**27087**	**23024**	**16845**	**18934**	**19174**	**18292**	**20313**	**20364**	**21199**	**Europe**
Belarus[2]	..	12128	9161	5288	6733	7502	7298	8761	9226	9681	Bélarus[2]
Belgium[2]	152	130	140	100	...	...	...	...	...	...	Belgique[2]
Croatia[2]	..	90	128	88	97	101	98	105	72	...	Croatie[2]
Denmark[2][3]	...	...	...	...	18	85	0	2	1	...	Danemark[2][3]
Czechoslovakia(former)[2]	106	35	..	...	...	...	...	...	...	...	Tchécoslovaquie(anc.)[2]
Finland[2]	...	160	96	156	176	163	176	...	...	...	Finlande[2]
France[2]	[1]4950	[1]4439	[1]4450	[1]3397	3595	...	...	...	...	...	France[2]
Germany	...	3902	3525	2860	*3454	3278	3334	3423	3582	3545	Allemagne
Germany(Fed.Rep.)	2611	..	..	...	...	...	...	..	...	...	Allemagne(Rép.féd.)
Hungary[2]	80	37	6	...	...	...	...	...	...	...	Hongrie[2]
Iceland	4	4	4	4	4	4	...	...	...	...	Islande
Italy[1]	131	6	126	13	...	...	...	...	...	...	Italie[1]
Lithuania[2]	..	...	...	...	...	...	...	...	...	28	Lituanie[2]
Poland[2]	...	...	...	159	234	272	294	309	299	274	Pologne[2]
Republic of Moldova	..	...	...	...	...	...	...	5	5	...	Rép. de Moldova
Romania[2]	213	111	115	152	149	112	104	100	76	109	Roumanie[2]
Russian Federation[2]	..	4086	3470	2628	2498	2831	2685	3487	3596	4294	Fédération de Russie[2]
Spain[1]	729	642	543	960	890	873	680	640	496	550	Espagne[1]
Sweden	...	...	...	...	164	142	...	...	...	...	Suède
Ukraine[2]	..	459	440	306	266	118	122	162	71	69	Ukraine[2]
United Kingdom[2][4]	406	312	268	361	291	289	315	341	332	345	Royaume-Uni[2][4]
Yugoslavia[2]	...	...	84	...	...	...	...	...	...	...	Yougoslavie[2]
T.F.Yug.Rep. Macedonia[2]	..	7	6	6	8	6	6	6	8	8	L'ex-RY Macédoine[2]
USSR (former)[2]	9037	..	..	...	..	..	...	...	...	..	URSS (anc.)[2]
Total	**31778**	**40752**	**36108**	**30298**	**32731**	**34848**	**32920**	**35739**	**35978**	**37280**	**Total**

General Note.
Data refer to K$_2$O content of potassic fertilizers and potassic fertilizer materials (except crude potash salts), of multinutrient fertilizers (physical mixtures and chemical combinations), containing two or three different minerals or fertilizing substances (nitrogen, phosphorus or potassium).(SITC, Rev.3: 56230-0, 56291-3, 56292-2).
Main source: Food and Agriculture Organization of the United Nations (FAO), Rome.

Remarque générale.
Les données se rapportent au poids de K$_2$O contenu dans les engrais potassiques et les produits potassiques fertilisants (à l'exception des sels bruts de potassium), engrais composés (mélanges physiques et combinaisons chimiques) contenant deux ou trois minéraux ou éléments chimiques fertilisants (azote, phosphore ou potassium). (CTCI, Rev.3: 56230-0, 56291-3,56292-2).
Source principale: Organisation des Nations Unies pour l'alimentation et l'agriculture (FAO), Rome.

[1] Fertilizer year ending 30 June of year stated.
[2] Official figures.
[3] Sales.
[4] Deliveries.

[1] Campagne d'engrais se terminant le 30 juin de l'année indiquée.
[2] Données officielles.
[3] Ventes.
[4] Livraisons.

Potassic fertilizers, K2O content
Engrais potassiques, K2O contenu

ISIC-BASED CODE - CODE BASE CITI

3512-10

Unit : Thousand metric tons   Unité : Milliers de tonnes métriques

Country or area	1990	1991	1992	1993	1994	1995	1996	1997	1998	1999	Pays ou zone
America, North	**8487**	**9269**	**8719**	**9011**	**9015**	**10826**	**9792**	**10613**	**10875**	**11137**	**Amérique du Nord**
Canada	6774	7520	7014	7289	7293	9104	[1]8070	...	...	...	Canada
United States[1]	1713	1749	1705	...	...	...	...	...	...	...	Etats-Unis[1]
America, South	**68**	**101**	**77**	**174**	**229**	**224**	**241**	**281**	**326**	**348**	**Amérique du Sud**
Brazil	68	101	77	174	229	[2]224	[2]241	281	326	348	Brésil
Asia	**909**	**931**	**994**	**978**	**1288**	**1363**	**1363**	**1184**	**1276**	**1469**	**Asie**
Azerbaijan[2]	..	43	8	10	3	0	2	5	0	0	Azerbaïdjan[2]
China[2]	46	47	153	117	327	263	...	...	...	...	Chine[2]
Israel	...	...	25	29	28	32	35	...	...	...	Israël
Jordan	842	818	808	822	930	1068	1059	849	916	1080	Jordanie
Europe	**7159**	**14046**	**12533**	**10267**	**10363**	**10766**	**10436**	**11726**	**12100**	**12789**	**Europe**
Belarus[2]	..	4238	3311	1947	2515	2796	2716	3247	3451	3613	Bélarus[2]
Croatia	..	...	...	...	[3]97	[3]101	[3]98	[2]57	[2]39	..	Croatie
Denmark[2] [4]	...	...	...	...	18	85	0	2	1	...	Danemark[2] [4]
Czechoslovakia(former)[2]	106	35	..	..	..	..	..	..	..	..	Tchécoslovaquie(anc.)[2]
Czech Republic[2]	..	..	...	...	22	28	25	24	25	16	République tchèque[2]
Finland[3]	...	...	...	...	176	163	176	...	...	...	Finlande[3]
France[2]	[1]1296	[1]1128	[1]1142	[1]890	870	...	...	...	...	...	France[2]
Germany	..	...	...	...	3286	3278	3334	3423	3582	3545	Allemagne
Germany(Fed.Rep.)[2]	2216										Allemagne(Rép.féd.)[2]
German D.R.(former)[2]	2326	..	..	..	..	..	..	..	..	..	R.D.A. (anc.)[2]
Italy[1]	67	6	121	13	...	...	...	...	...	...	Italie[1]
Poland[2]	...	...	...	0	0	1	1	1	1	1	Pologne[2]
Romania[2]	107	50	52	60	50	51	47	45	34	50	Roumanie[2]
Russian Federation[2]	..	4086	3470	2628	2498	2831	2685	3487	3596	4294	Fédération de Russie[2]
Spain	[1]729	[1]642	[1]543	[2]838	[2]588	[2]482	[2]457	[2]442	...	[2]502	Espagne
Ukraine[2]	..	135	122	100	80	56	39	49	21	21	Ukraine[2]
United Kingdom[2]	...	...	...	...	85	89	133	153	107	...	Royaume-Uni[2]
Yugoslavia	..	...	...	...	[3]26	[3]15	[3]45	[2]52	[2]28	...	Yougoslavie
USSR (former)[2]	9037	..	..	..	..	..	..	..	..	..	URSS (anc.)[2]
Total	**25659**	**24347**	**22323**	**20431**	**20896**	**23179**	**21832**	**23804**	**24576**	**25743**	**Total**

General Note.

K₂O content of potassic fertilizers and potassic fertilizer materials, except crude potash salts. (SITC, Rev.3: 56230-0).
Main source: Food and Agriculture Organization of the United Nations (FAO), Rome.

Remarque générale.

Poids de K₂O contenu dans les engrais potassiques et les produits potassiques fertilisants à l'exception des sels bruts de potassium. (CTCI, Rev.3: 56230-0).
Source principale: Organisation des Nations Unies pour l'alimentation et l'agriculture (FAO), Rome.

[1] Fertilizer year ending 30 June of year stated.
[2] Official figures.
[3] Source: United Nations Economic Commission for Europe (ECE), (Geneva).

[4] Sales.

[1] Campagne d'engrais se terminant le 30 juin de l'année indiquée.
[2] Données officielles.
[3] Source: Commission économique des Nations Unies pour l'Europe (CEE), (Genève).

[4] Ventes.

Multinutrient fertilizers, N content
Engrais composés, N contenu

ISIC-BASED CODE - CODE BASE CITI

3512-13A

Unit : Thousand metric tons

Unité : Milliers de tonnes métriques

Country or area	1990	1991	1992	1993	1994	1995	1996	1997	1998	1999	Pays ou zone
Africa	**621**	**553**	**589**	**562**	**584**	**553**	**572**	**493**	**535**	**550**	**Afrique**
Algeria	3	*17	...	*26	*22	*12	...	...	...	3	Algérie
Mauritius	11	11	13	11	14	14	14	13	*11	[1]14	Maurice
Morocco	344	...	[1]226	[1]212	[1]250	[1]209	[1]212	[1]179	[1]206	[1]200	Maroc
Nigeria	84	106	146	*118	...	...	...	...	...	...	Nigéria
Senegal	16	25	*24	*19	*20	*23	*20	*29	*10	*20	Sénégal
Tunisia	134	[1]130	[1]131	[1]136	[1]136	[1]152	[1]169	[1]139	[1]167	[1]189	Tunisie
United Rep.Tanzania	1	2	...	...	...	...	...	...	...	...	Rép. Unie de Tanzanie
Zambia	*4	4	*4	*6	*3	...	...	...	...	...	Zambie
Zimbabwe	24	32	*30	*32	...	...	...	0	...	...	Zimbabwe
America, North	**2806**	**2875**	**3050**	**2784**	**2912**	**3240**	**3012**	**3073**	**3146**	**2877**	**Amérique du Nord**
Canada[2]	136	66	95	88	78	[1]140	[1]84	...	...	...	Canada[2]
Cuba	[1]10	10	10	8	...	...	...	...	...	...	Cuba
El Salvador	2	3	8	8	9	[1]10	[1]11	...	...	...	El Salvador
Mexico*	...	59	33	33	45	30	30	20	25	25	Mexique*
United States	2615	2737	2904	2647	2770	3050	2877	2935	3002	2733	Etats-Unis
America, South	**232**	**227**	**180**	**173**	**182**	**199**	**225**	**191**	**154**	**143**	**Amérique du Sud**
Brazil	[1]123	[1]120	[1]94	96	[1]100	[1]103	[1]101	...	...	...	Brésil
Colombia	74	77	61	60	61	60	80	75	40	40	Colombie
Peru	...	...	2	2	1	...	...	...	...	...	Pérou
Venezuela	33	28	23	15	20	34	42	26	27	20	Venezuela
Asia	**2888**	**2921**	**3397**	**3405**	**3220**	**3498**	**3478**	**3399**	**3368**	**2805**	**Asie**
China[3]	181	*181	*200	*226	*244	*246	*272	*292	*323	80	Chine[3]
India[4]	502	628	642	530	653	693	642	617	662	*661	Inde[4]
Indonesia	...	...	572	...	...	...	...	...	...	...	Indonésie
Iran(Islamic Rep. of)	19	32	62	73	42	34	...	...	...	...	Iran(Rép. islamique)
Israel*[2]	32	27	24	27	32	38	37	37	52	52	Israël*[2]
Japan[1]	[2]361	[2]353	[2]341	[2]330	320	312	291	281	255	234	Japon[1]
Jordan	...	...	...	...	...	...	...	9	13	*13	Jordanie
Korea, Republic of	*361	*349	*376	*419	*431	428	414	*360	*324	*324	Corée, République de
Pakistan[2]	77	74	71	68	58	66	77	[1]81	[1]67	[1]66	Pakistan[2]
Philippines	*120	*136	*125	*150	155	187	189	155	128	24	Philippines
Saudi Arabia*	...	...	...	...	...	...	8	8	5	5	Arabie saoudite*
Turkey[1]	645	551	966	992	695	904	914	935	913	719	Turquie[1]
Europe	**3038**	**10207**	**10000**	**8462**	**7933**	**8122**	**8796**	**8297**	**8209**	**9601**	**Europe**
Austria	*68	*70	*51	*66	*55	*52	*64	*57	*62	[1]362	Autriche
Belarus[1]	..	1662	1444	983	710	893	1006	888	926	1027	Bélarus[1]
Belgium*[2 5]	208	207	176	174	117	140	112	130	130	130	Belgique*[2 5]
Croatia[1]	..	70	93	62	73	71	66	67	59	...	Croatie[1]
Denmark	[6 7]137	[6 7]127	*132	*139	*110	*90	*97	*83	*85	*86	Danemark
Czech Republic	..	..	...	*18	*16	*26	*27	24	28	*20	République tchèque
Finland*[2]	250	181	209	224	226	231	208	211	203	205	Finlande*[2]
France[1]	280	289	293	367	285	...	...	...	...	...	France[1]
Germany*	..	109	127	109	74	110	188	170	160	160	Allemagne*
Germany(Fed.Rep.)[1 2]	142	..	..	..	..	..	..	..	..	..	Allemagne(Rép.féd.)[1 2]
German D.R.(former)[1]	8	..	..	..	..	..	..	..	..	..	R.D.A. (anc.)[1]
Hungary[1]	71	38	4	...	...	...	...	...	...	...	Hongrie[1]
Iceland	9	10	9	*8	10	7	9	*11	*11	*12	Islande
Italy[2]	212	184	184	*133	*74	*101	*69	*55	*50	*50	Italie[2]
Netherlands[2]	*214	198	157	136	143	*173	*148	*169	*170	*170	Pays-Bas[2]
Norway[2]	[1]308	[1]390	[1]356	[1]371	428	*446	*455	*436	*436	*440	Norvège[2]
Poland[1]	70	44	85	80	116	150	158	169	167	150	Pologne[1]
Portugal*	32	16	22	26	18	25	28	32	32	32	Portugal*
Romania[1]	269	152	173	74	73	68	70	41	101	101	Roumanie[1]
Russian Federation	...	...	...	...	...	...	...	0	*516	*634	Fédération de Russie
Slovakia[1]	..	..	...	...	...	248	274	...	...	...	Slovaquie[1]
Spain[2]	188	189	137	124	141	142	153	153	*212	241	Espagne[2]
Sweden	65	54	28	33	43	*25	*57	*66	*66	*70	Suède
Switzerland[2]	2	*3	*2	3	*1	*1	...	...	...	...	Suisse[2]
Ukraine[1]	..	5291	5179	4158	4089	3942	4432	4423	3695	4531	Ukraine[1]

For general note and footnotes, see end of table.

Voir la fin du tableau pour la remarque générale et les notes.

Multinutrient fertilizers, N content (continued)
Engrais composés, N contenu (suite)

ISIC-BASED CODE - CODE BASE CITI

3512-13A

Unit : Thousand metric tons   Unité : Milliers de tonnes métriques

Country or area	1990	1991	1992	1993	1994	1995	1996	1997	1998	1999	Pays ou zone
United Kingdom[1][8]	505	404	362	451	410	409	364	397	402	433	Royaume-Uni[1][8]
Yugoslavia[1]	..	120	101	29	28	14	42	62	35	11	Yougoslavie[1]
T.F.Yug.Rep. Macedonia[1]	..	15	12	12	11	8	9	7	8	9	L'ex-RY Macédoine[1]
Oceania	**17**	**34**	**37**	**37**	**42**	**55**	**60**	**47**	**47**	**49**	**Océanie**
Australia	*17	*34	*37	*37	*42	[1]55	[1]60	[1]47	[1]47	*49	Australie
Total	**9603**	**16816**	**17254**	**15423**	**14872**	**15666**	**16142**	**15500**	**15457**	**16026**	**Total**

General Note.

N content of multinutrient fertilizers (physical mixtures and chemical combinations), containing two or three different minerals or chemical fertilizing substances (nitrogen, phosphorus or potassium). (SITC, Rev.3: 56291-1, 56293-1, 56294-1, 56295-1, 56296-1, 56299-1).
Main source: Food and Agriculture Organization of the United Nations (FAO), Rome.

Remarque générale.

Poids de l'azote contenu dans les engrais composés (mélanges physiques et combinaisons chimiques) contenant deux ou trois minéraux ou éléments chimiques fertilisants différents (azote, phosphore ou potassium). (CTCI, Rev.3: 56291-1, 56293-1, 56294-1, 56295-1, 56296-1, 56299-1).
Source principale: Organisation des Nations Unies pour l'alimentation et l'agriculture (FAO), Rome.

[1] Official figures.
[2] Fertilizer year ending 30 June of year stated.
[3] Including Hong-Kong, Macao and Taiwan.
[4] Twelve months ending 31 March of year stated.
[5] Data refer to Belgium and Luxembourg.
[6] Fertilizer year ending 31 July of year stated.
[7] Sales.
[8] Deliveries.

[1] Données officielles.
[2] Campagne d'engrais se terminant le 30 juin de l'année indiquée.
[3] Y compris Hong-Kong, Macao et Taïwan.
[4] Période de douze mois finissant le 31 mars de l'année indiquée.
[5] Données se rapportant à la Belgique et au Luxembourg.
[6] Campagne d'engrais se terminant le 31 juillet de l'année indiquée.
[7] Ventes.
[8] Livraisons.

Multinutrient fertilizers, P205 content
Engrais composés, P2O5 contenu

ISIC-BASED CODE - CODE BASE CITI

3512-13B

Unit : Thousand metric tons

Unité : Milliers de tonnes métriques

Country or area	1990	1991	1992	1993	1994	1995	1996	1997	1998	1999	Pays ou zone
Africa	**361**	**392**	**424**	**333**	**269**	**284**	**248**	**227**	**237**	**232**	**Afrique**
Algeria	34	20	18	26	22	12	...	...	...	...	Algérie
Morocco	75	81	89	76	76	71	62	61	63	66	Maroc
Nigeria	46	54	76	39	22	...	10	5	6	...	Nigéria
Senegal[1]	37	33	30	25	20	25	20	46	26	33	Sénégal[1]
South Africa	...	*155	*181	*138	*100	*115	*111	92	*99	...	Afrique du Sud
Tunisia	...	...	...	...	...	...	...	...	7	7	Tunisie
United Rep.Tanzania	1	1	2	...	...	...	...	...	...	...	Rép. Unie de Tanzanie
Zimbabwe	...	41	...	...	...	...	...	0	...	...	Zimbabwe
America, North	**499**	**430**	**526**	**444**	**428**	**410**	**422**	**406**	**405**	**399**	**Amérique du Nord**
Canada[2]	440	354	478	395	368	364	...	...	...	...	Canada[2]
Cuba	...	7	6	6	...	...	...	...	...	...	Cuba
El Salvador	...	...	9	10	...	...	[2]10	...	...	...	El Salvador
Mexico	...	59	33	33	44	30	30	20	25	25	Mexique
America, South	**273**	**270**	**309**	**314**	**340**	**269**	**248**	**210**	**174**	**150**	**Amérique du Sud**
Brazil	136	165	205	198	200	141	103	90	71	54	Brésil
Colombia	78	80	64	...	...	...	...	...	...	...	Colombie
Peru	2	2	2	0	...	...	...	...	...	...	Pérou
Venezuela	57	23	38	42	64	52	69	44	27	20	Venezuela
Asia	**2464**	**2969**	**3309**	**2883**	**2780**	**2986**	**2985**	**2871**	**2782**	**2745**	**Asie**
China[3]	126	126	149	93	101	104	116	124	136	137	Chine[3]
India[1]	317	762	753	615	725	862	797	777	817	818	Inde[1]
Iran(Islamic Rep. of)	50	81	162	187	...	...	...	...	...	...	Iran(Rép. islamique)
Israel[1]	20	20	20	30	20	21	21	39	47	...	Israël[1]
Japan[1]	436	415	407	403	396	378	363	[2]340	[2]302	[2]284	Japon[1]
Jordan	274	276	...	...	...	...	...	...	13	13	Jordanie
Korea, Republic of	298	322	349	388	408	398	391	316	281	283	Corée, République de
Pakistan[1]	77	74	71	68	58	66	77	[2]81	[2]67	[2]66	Pakistan[1]
Philippines	...	...	...	185	204	202	202	164	157	138	Philippines
Saudi Arabia*	27	200	146	132	165	...	...	...	...	...	Arabie saoudite*
Thailand	...	...	...	...	...	...	...	43	85	110	Thaïlande
Turkey[2]	532	396	821	559	360	415	457	485	498	452	Turquie[2]
Europe	**4611**	**6553**	**4824**	**4451**	**4560**	**4187**	**4424**	**4524**	**4382**	**4186**	**Europe**
Belarus	..	0	...	...	[2]42	[2]52	[2]100	[2]338	[2]341	[2]337	Bélarus
Belgium	[2]143	[2]122	[2]138	[2]100	[4]62	[4]121	[4]107	[4]108	[4]108	[4]110	Belgique
Bulgaria	...	...	...	...	...	...	...	9	8	...	Bulgarie
Croatia	..	88	119	79	87	90	87	[2]91	[2]76	81	Croatie
Denmark	[5][6]99	71	40	50	71	58	45	46	46	47	Danemark
Czech Republic	..	..	...	28	18	30	25	25	26	16	République tchèque
Finland	172	117	127	132	130	122	105	95	96	97	Finlande
France[2]	2141	2124	1500	1570	1516	...	...	...	...	...	France[2]
Germany	..	170	169	109	...	110	203	194	184	185	Allemagne
Germany(Fed.Rep.)[1][2]	229	..	..	..	..	..	..	..	..	..	Allemagne(Rép.féd.)[1][2]
German D.R.(former)[2]	5	..	..	..	..	..	..	..	..	..	R.D.A. (anc.)[2]
Hungary[2]	85	38	4	...	...	...	...	...	...	...	Hongrie[2]
Iceland	5	6	5	5	5	5	...	...	...	...	Islande
Italy[1]	272	276	86	84	160	137	150	140	130	130	Italie[1]
Netherlands[1]	314	317	217	236	320	263	181	302	305	305	Pays-Bas[1]
Norway[1]	229	221	215	203	207	236	265	236	236	240	Norvège[1]
Poland[2]	190	115	211	221	328	429	461	492	487	448	Pologne[2]
Portugal	51	17	[2]35	55	48	50	51	52	52	52	Portugal
Romania[2]	277	159	184	96	87	74	80	43	96	101	Roumanie[2]
Russian Federation	..	...	...	...	...	...	...	441	441	618	Fédération de Russie
Slovakia	..	...	...	18	12	37	37	16	26	26	Slovaquie
Spain[1]	249	246	252	195	219	209	324	340	360	360	Espagne[1]
Sweden	62	58	28	26	20	18	16	15	15	18	Suède
Switzerland	2	2	3	2	3	3	...	2	2	...	Suisse
Ukraine[2]	..	1682	569	389	406	255	419	380	386	232	Ukraine[2]
United Kingdom[7]	78	76	96	92	66	88	111	190	190	200	Royaume-Uni[7]
Yugoslavia[2]	..	130	88	29	29	14	43	47	28	10	Yougoslavie[2]

For general note and footnotes, see end of table.

Voir la fin du tableau pour la remarque générale et les notes.

Multinutrient fertilizers, P205 content (continued)
Engrais composés, P2O5 contenu (suite)

ISIC-BASED CODE - CODE BASE CITI

3512-13B

Unit : Thousand metric tons   Unité : Milliers de tonnes métriques

Country or area	1990	1991	1992	1993	1994	1995	1996	1997	1998	1999	Pays ou zone
T.F.Yug.Rep. Macedonia[2]	..	9	9	8	8	6	7	7	8	8	L'ex-RY Macédoine[2]
Oceania	43	38	41	42	50	66	76	56	65	70	**Océanie**
Australia	...	38	41	42	50	[2]66	[2]76	[2]56	[2]65	70	Australie
Total	8251	10652	9433	8467	8427	8201	8402	8294	8044	7781	**Total**

General Note.

P_2O_5 content of multinutrient fertilizers (physical mixtures and chemical combinations), containing two or three different minerals or fertilizing substances (nitrogen, phosphorus or potassium). (SITC, Rev.3, 56291-2, 56292-1, 56293-2, 56294-2, 56295-2, 56296-2, 56299-2).
Main source: Food and Agriculture Organization of the United Nations (FAO), Rome.

Remarque générale.

Poids de P_2O_5 contenu dans les engrais composés (mélanges physiques et combinaisons chimiques) contenant deux ou trois minéraux ou éléments chimiques fertilisants (azote, phosphore ou potassium). (CTCI, Rev.3: 56291-2, 56292-1, 56293-2. 56294-2, 56295-2, 56296-2, 56299-2).
Source principale: Organisation des Nations Unies pour l'alimentation et l'agriculture (FAO), Rome.

[1] Fertilizer year ending 30 June of year stated.
[2] Official figures.
[3] Including Hong-Kong, Macao and Taiwan.
[4] Data refer to Belgium and Luxembourg.
[5] Fertilizer year ending 31 July of year stated.
[6] Sales.
[7] Fertilizer year ending 31 May of year stated.

[1] Campagne d'engrais se terminant le 30 juin de l'année indiquée.
[2] Données officielles.
[3] Y compris Hong-Kong, Macao et Taïwan.
[4] Données se rapportant à la Belgique et au Luxembourg.
[5] Campagne d'engrais se terminant le 31 juillet de l'année indiquée.
[6] Ventes.
[7] Campagne d'engrais se terminant le 31 mai de l'année indiquée.

Multinutrient fertilizers, K2O content
Engrais composés, K2O contenu

ISIC-BASED CODE - CODE BASE CITI

3512-13C

Unit : Thousand metric tons   Unité : Milliers de tonnes métriques

Country or area	1990	1991	1992	1993	1994	1995	1996	1997	1998	1999	Pays ou zone
Asia	**327**	**315**	**313**	**310**	**304**	**292**	**272**	**264**	**233**	**217**	**Asie**
Japan[1][2]	327	315	313	310	304	292	272	264	233	217	Japon[1][2]
Europe	**4614**	**12388**	**10403**	**6850**	**8077**	**8047**	**7708**	**8418**	**8350**	**8349**	**Europe**
Belarus[2]	..	7890	5850	3341	4218	4706	4582	5514	5775	6068	Bélarus[2]
Belgium[2]	152	130	140	100	...	...	...	...	...	...	Belgique[2]
Croatia	..	90	128	88	97	101	98	...	...	...	Croatie
France[2]	[1]3654	[1]3311	[1]3308	[1]2507	2725	...	...	...	...	...	France[2]
Germany[2]	...	...	...	166	168	...	...	...	...	...	Allemagne[2]
Germany(Fed.Rep.)[2]	312	..	..	..	..	..	..	..	..	..	Allemagne(Rép.féd.)[2]
German D.R.(former)[2]	9	..	..	..	..	..	..	..	..	..	R.D.A. (anc.)[2]
Hungary[2]	80	37	6	...	...	...	...	...	...	...	Hongrie[2]
Iceland	4	4	4	4	4	4	...	...	...	...	Islande
Italy[1]	64	...	...	...	...	...	...	...	...	...	Italie[1]
Poland[2]	84	60	127	158	235	271	294	308	297	274	Pologne[2]
Romania[2]	106	50	52	19	17	9	8	2	34	50	Roumanie[2]
Spain[1]	...	...	...	122	157	168	...	...	...	...	Espagne[1]
Ukraine	..	324	318	206	186	62	[2]83	[2]113	[2]50	[2]48	Ukraine
Yugoslavia	..	105	84	28	26	15	45	[2]51	[2]29	[2]10	Yougoslavie
T.F.Yug.Rep. Macedonia[2]	..	7	6	6	8	6	6	6	8	8	L'ex-RY Macédoine[2]
Total	**4941**	**12703**	**10716**	**7160**	**8381**	**8339**	**7980**	**8682**	**8583**	**8566**	**Total**

General Note.

K₂O content of multinutrient fertilizers (physical mixtures and chemical combinations), containing two or three different minerals or fertilizing substances (nitrogen, phosphorus or potassium). (SITC, Rev.3: 56291-3, 56292-2, 56296-3, 56299-3).
Main source: Food and Agriculture Organization of the United Nations (FAO), Rome.

Remarque générale.

Poids de K₂O contenu dans les engrais composés (mélanges physiques et combinaisons chimiques) contenant deux ou trois minéraux ou éléments chimiques fertilisants (azote, phosphore ou potassium). (CTCI, Rev.3: 56291-3, 56292-2, 56296-3, 56299-3).
Source principale: Organisation des Nations Unies pour l'alimentation et l'agriculture (FAO), Rome.

[1] Fertilizer year ending 30 June of year stated.
[2] Official figures.

[1] Campagne d'engrais se terminant le 30 juin de l'année indiquée.
[2] Données officielles.

Insecticides, fungicides, disinfectants etc.
Insecticides, fongicides, désinfectants etc.

ISIC-BASED CODE - CODE BASE CITI

3512-16

Unit : Thousand metric tons

Unité : Milliers de tonnes métriques

Country or area	1990	1991	1992	1993	1994	1995	1996	1997	1998	1999	Pays ou zone
Africa	**60**	**61**	**53**	**57**	**66**	**75**	**83**	**80**	**82**	**85**	**Afrique**
Algeria	8.0	11.0	7.3	...	...	...	...	...	...	...	Algérie
Burundi	3.8	3.4	2.0	2.7	...	...	...	...	...	...	Burundi
Egypt	21.1	21.1	19.2	20.4	21.7	25.3	33.2	...	...	...	Egypte
Kenya	3.0	0.9	0.7	0.8	1.0	1.1	1.2	...	...	...	Kenya
South Africa[1]	22.7	23.8	23.3	23.8	31.0	36.0	36.2	35.0	...	...	Afrique du Sud[1]
United Rep.Tanzania	1.2	0.9	0.6	0.5	...	...	...	...	...	...	Rép. Unie de Tanzanie
America, North	**127**	**139**	**131**	**169**	**202**	**169**	**174**	**209**	**235**	**228**	**Amérique du Nord**
Mexico	126.7	138.8	130.9	168.8	201.7	169.2	174.4	208.7	235.1	227.8	Mexique
America, South	**88**	**86**	**92**	**85**	**87**	**85**	**86**	**89**	**86**	**88**	**Amérique du Sud**
Brazil	63.7	61.4	...	...	...	...	...	...	...	...	Brésil
Colombia	...	...	29.6	20.7	20.6	21.1	...	...	...	...	Colombie
Ecuador	...	...	0.1	1.4	3.9	1.6	0.8	3.4	0.5	...	Equateur
Asia	**461**	**532**	**533**	**572**	**496**	**665**	**713**	**771**	**787**	**847**	**Asie**
China	227.8	255.0	280.8	257.1	289.5	416.5	447.5	526.7	559.0	625.0	Chine
Cyprus	...	...	0.4	...	...	0.3	...	...	...	...	Chypre
Indonesia	19.0	10.3	13.0	15.8	10.6	18.4	...	...	10.7	...	Indonésie
Korea, Republic of	181.9	190.0	171.0	221.2	141.4	167.6	189.0	185.8	170.7	173.0	Corée, République de
Turkey	23.2	28.9	27.8	30.4	26.6	32.3	32.8	24.2	25.6	26.0	Turquie
Uzbekistan	..	34.6	28.3	31.6	12.0	14.7	9.2	1.2	...	...	Ouzbékistan
Viet Nam[2]	9.2	12.8	11.5	...	...	15.6	20.0	19.1	20.2	*18.8	Viet Nam[2]
Europe	**1377**	**1390**	**1284**	**1215**	**1175**	**1051**	**1076**	**1119**	**963**	**1006**	**Europe**
Albania	9.0	1.5	1.6	1.6	0.0	0.0	0.0	0.0	0.0	0.0	Albanie
Austria	16.6	17.5	17.2	13.2	19.8	12.4	26.2	20.5	16.7	12.4	Autriche
Belgium	100.3	87.1	114.0	114.7	...	[3]3.2	[3]5.5	[3]66.8	[3]3.8	[3]6.2	Belgique
Bulgaria	10.0	9.7	7.2	5.1	6.3	7.6	5.7	5.3	5.7	8.0	Bulgarie
Croatia	..	9.2	8.6	7.0	7.1	6.8	8.1	10.2	8.7	...	Croatie
Denmark[4]	...	...	...	...	...	17.7	16.8	16.7	17.2	18.8	Danemark[4]
Czechoslovakia(former)	17.2	7.1	..	..	..	..	..	..	..		Tchécoslovaquie(anc.)
Czech Republic	..	..	3.9	1.9	18.1	21.8	23.3	20.9	21.4	19.1	République tchèque
Finland	13.9	14.5	13.7	10.3	13.2	14.1	7.2	...	...	3.6	Finlande
France	326.4	314.7	303.5	301.9	...	...	...	...	...	...	France
Germany	..	251.7	204.8	191.5	204.4	127.5	105.9	109.1	106.5	..	Allemagne
Germany(Fed.Rep.)[5]	280.6	..	..	..	..	..	..	..	..	..	Allemagne(Rép.féd.)[5]
German D.R.(former)	61.6	..	..	..	..	..	..	..	..	..	R.D.A. (anc.)
Greece	[6]6.6	[6]6.4	[6]6.8	6.4	7.5	11.1	21.5	22.2	11.4	...	Grèce
Hungary	56.0	37.9	30.4	31.4	22.7	19.4	21.2	21.7	18.1	14.5	Hongrie
Lithuania	...	...	...	...	...	0.6	0.7	0.3	0.4	0.3	Lituanie
Poland	19.7	17.0	21.8	22.3	20.7	24.2	27.7	27.9	29.9	30.2	Pologne
Portugal	24.5	16.6	13.2	14.7	13.5	14.9	20.8	19.4	19.9	20.9	Portugal
Romania	23.5	16.7	16.9	19.2	13.1	15.1	15.0	8.3	5.2	4.2	Roumanie
Russian Federation	..	87.4	65.4	38.7	19.1	15.9	12.5	11.3	5.8	9.8	Fédération de Russie
Slovakia	..	..	2.2	...	...	...	2.2	2.6	3.4	2.8	Slovaquie
Slovenia	..	9.5	6.8	5.6	5.3	6.1	1.4	1.4	1.5	1.2	Slovénie
Spain	[7]82.6	[7]102.1	[7]80.2	78.6	94.5	91.1	96.3	89.4	92.8	98.7	Espagne
Sweden	...	6.9	7.2	4.5	6.1	8.6	...	3.4	2.3	2.0	Suède
Ukraine	..	38.9	21.7	16.7	4.0	4.1	4.6	2.7	1.9	1.8	Ukraine
United Kingdom	...	...	...	...	...	306.9	327.8	327.3	259.1	...	Royaume-Uni
Yugoslavia	..	13.3	13.4	4.4	6.1	7.3	8.3	8.8	8.6	5.6	Yougoslavie
T.F.Yug.Rep. Macedonia	..	2.4	1.0	0.5	0.3	0.2	0.2	0.1	0.2	0.1	L'ex-RY Macédoine
USSR (former)	204.8	..	..	..	..	..	..	..	..	..	URSS (anc.)
Total	**2318**	**2208**	**2093**	**2098**	**2026**	**2046**	**2132**	**2268**	**2153**	**2253**	**Total**

For general note and footnotes, see end of table.

Voir la fin du tableau pour la remarque générale et les notes.

Insecticides, fungicides, disinfectants etc. (continued)
Insecticides, fongicides, désinfectants etc. (suite)

ISIC-BASED CODE - CODE BASE CITI

3512-16

General Note.
Preparations, other than solutions, dilutions and suspensions of single chemical compounds in a liquid (unless the liquid plays an active part in the preparations) of products intended to destroy or combat pathogenic germs, insects, mosses and moulds, weeds, rodents, wild birds etc., to disinfect seeds or to prevent vegetables from sprouting. Excluded are separately-defined chemical compounds, medicaments, fumigants, deodorizers and disinfectant soaps. (SITC, Rev.3: 59100-0).

[1] Excluding products usually measured in units of volume.
[2] Insecticides only.
[3] Incomplete coverage.
[4] Sales.
[5] Excluding disinfectants.
[6] Insecticides for household use.
[7] Including insecticides for household use.

Remarque générale.
Préparations autres que les solutions, dilutions et suspensions de composés chimiques uniques dans un liquide (à moins que le liquide ne joue un rôle actif dans les préparations) de produits conçus pour détruire ou pour repousser les germes pathogènes, les insectes, les mousses et moisissures, les mauvaises herbes, les rongeurs, les oiseaux, etc., pour désinfecter les semences ou prévenir la germination des végétaux. Cette rubrique ne comprend pas les composés chimiques définis sous d'autres rubriques, les médicaments, les produits pour fumigation, les désodorisants et les savons désinfectants.(CTCI, Rev.3: 59100-0).

[1] Non compris les produits normalement mesurés en unités de volume.
[2] Insecticides seulement.
[3] Couverture incomplète.
[4] Ventes.
[5] Non compris les désinfectants.
[6] Insecticides pour usage domestique.
[7] Y compris les insecticides pour usage domestique.

Rubber, synthetic
Caoutchoucs synthétiques

ISIC-BASED CODE - CODE BASE CITI

3513-01

Unit : Thousand metric tons   Unité : Milliers de tonnes métriques

Country or area	1990	1991	1992	1993	1994	1995	1996	1997	1998	1999	Pays ou zone
Africa	**46**	**35**	**34**	**35**	**49**	**57**	**58**	**62**	**63**	**52**	**Afrique**
South Africa[1]	45.9	34.9	33.5	35.1	48.6	56.5	57.5	62.3	62.9	52.4	Afrique du Sud[1]
America, North	**2429**	**2477**	**2482**	**2451**	**2709**	**2842**	**2853**	**2959**	**2964**	**2705**	**Amérique du Nord**
Canada*[1]	195.0	180.0	206.0	187.0	197.0	170.0	220.0	216.0	191.0	180.0	Canada*[1]
Mexico	119.5	107.2	126.1	93.5	122.2	[1]141.5	[1]147.4	[1]154.0	[1]173.1	[1]171.3	Mexique
United States[1]	2114.5	2190.0	2150.0	2170.0	2390.0	*2530.0	2486.0	2589.0	*2600.0	*2354.0	Etats-Unis[1]
America, South	**314**	**294**	**298**	**295**	**323**	**341**	**368**	**403**	**364**	**416**	**Amérique du Sud**
Argentina	57.2	40.9	41.8	43.7	48.8	54.3	58.0	55.8	54.0	52.4	Argentine
Brazil	256.2	253.0	256.0	[1]251.5	[1]273.9	[1]286.3	*[1]310.0	[1]347.0	[1]310.0	[1]363.0	Brésil
Ecuador	...	...	...	...	...	...	...	...	0.2	...	Equateur
Asia	**2153**	**2213**	**2249**	**2212**	**2333**	**2720**	**2838**	**3000**	**2869**	**3264**	**Asie**
Armenia	..	10.6	11.7	0.4	2.1	1.5	2.8	3.8	2.2	3.6	Arménie
Azerbaijan		78.1	27.7	9.3	3.0	1.5	1.4	1.3	0.7	0.0	Azerbaïdjan
China	317.6	334.7	372.6	392.6	443.5	585.6	599.7	642.3	589.0	732.8	Chine
India	51.4	53.4	49.5	53.6	61.3	59.2	57.5	53.6	53.3	61.6	Inde
Indonesia[1]	...	...	...	...	...	...	...	...	17.0	35.0	Indonésie[1]
Iran(Islamic Rep. of)[1]	...	...	...	...	14.5	49.5	45.7	59.8	*62.0	*65.0	Iran(Rép. islamique)[1]
Japan	1425.8	1377.3	1389.9	1309.8	1350.8	1497.6	1519.9	1591.9	1520.1	1576.9	Japon
Korea, Republic of	227.7	224.2	264.2	299.9	342.0	399.0	472.9	564.5	547.4	654.9	Corée, République de
Thailand[1]	...	...	...	...	...	...	...	10.0	30.0	100.0	Thaïlande[1]
Turkey	34.0	34.4	28.7	37.8	42.7	53.7	65.0	46.7	47.0	33.9	Turquie
Europe	**2573**	**3274**	**3263**	**3481**	**3474**	**3518**	**3578**	**3409**	**3411**	**3510**	**Europe**
Austria*[1]	5.0	5.0	5.0	5.0	5.0	5.0	5.0	5.0	5.0	5.0	Autriche*[1]
Belgium	[1]125.0	[1]114.0	[1]120.0	[1]120.0	290.2	254.6	276.9	299.0	303.3	327.0	Belgique
Bulgaria	15.5	10.6	16.1	17.2	20.6	24.4	30.0	34.4	[1]28.4	*[1]22.9	Bulgarie
Denmark[2]	...	0.2	0.3	0.3	0.4	0.3	0.2	0.2	0.0	0.0	Danemark[2]
Czechoslovakia(former)	69.4	44.7	..		..					..	Tchécoslovaquie(anc.)
Czech Republic	..	..	...	...	71.6	74.5	90.1	87.8	91.9	90.5	République tchèque
Finland*[1]	29.0	30.0	32.0	32.0	33.0	36.0	36.0	38.0	39.0	40.0	Finlande*[1]
France	514.6	470.7	498.6	486.4	518.4	[1]618.1	[1]582.5	[1]594.9	[1]605.5	[1]592.4	France
Germany	...	...	556.8	583.7	643.1	478.5	563.1	450.1	512.4	...	Allemagne
Germany(Fed.Rep.)	523.3	..	..	..	..	..	..	..	..	..	Allemagne(Rép.féd.)
German D.R.(former)	124.1	..	..	..	..	..	..	..	..	..	R.D.A. (anc.)
Italy[1]	300.0	305.0	310.0	300.0	305.0	310.0	303.0	295.0	290.0	279.0	Italie[1]
Netherlands	243.9	230.9	233.0	[1]176.4	[1]209.3	[1]177.6	[1]198.3	[1]193.5	[1]184.1	[2][3]161.5	Pays-Bas
Poland	103.1	79.5	88.9	75.1	83.4	104.7	106.5	100.7	95.0	95.9	Pologne
Romania	102.0	54.6	35.9	29.7	26.7	41.3	37.0	29.4	22.5	16.2	Roumanie
Russian Federation	..	...	...	1102.5	631.9	836.9	796.0	703.9	621.7	736.3	Fédération de Russie
Slovakia	..	...	...	8.2	10.2	9.4	...	...	...	...	Slovaquie
Slovenia	..	...	...	...	...	...	1.8	2.1	1.0	0.1	Slovénie
Spain	70.3	64.9	65.0	93.9	126.3	105.9	133.7	123.1	117.4	...	Espagne
Sweden	55.8	45.5	44.7	24.4	51.5	82.8	...	52.6	48.0	55.9	Suède
United Kingdom	292.1	251.3	253.0	346.4	445.2	357.1	346.4	356.1	403.0	...	Royaume-Uni
Yugoslavia	..	18.7	7.4	0.0	1.1	0.0	10.6	34.0	33.9	12.4	Yougoslavie
USSR (former)*[1]	2365.0	..					..		..	..	URSS (anc.)*[1]
Oceania	**41**	**36**	**40**	**46**	**45**	**48**	**42**	**39**	**35**	**31**	**Océanie**
Australia[1]	40.8	35.5	39.9	46.4	44.6	48.2	41.5	38.5	34.6	31.3	Australie[1]
Total	**9920**	**8329**	**8366**	**8520**	**8932**	**9526**	**9736**	**9872**	**9706**	**9978**	**Total**

General Note.
Copolymers of butadiene with styrene and acrylonitrile, and neoprene and butyl-type rubber. Latices should be included (dryweight). (SITC, Rev.3: 23210-0).

Remarque générale.
Copolymères du butadiène associé au styrène ou à l'acrylonitrile, néoprène et caoutchouc butyle, y compris les latex (poids du produit sec). (CTCI, Rev.3: 23210-0).

[1] Source: International Rubber Study Group, (London).
[2] Sales.
[3] Production by establishments employing 20 or more persons.

[1] Source: International Rubber Study Group, (Londres).
[2] Ventes.
[3] Production des établissements occupant 20 personnes ou plus.

Non-cellulosic staple and tow
Fibres discontinues et câbles non cellulosiques

ISIC-BASED CODE - CODE BASE CITI

3513-04

Unit : Thousand metric tons

Unité : Milliers de tonnes métriques

Country or area	1990	1991	1992	1993	1994	1995	1996	1997	1998	1999	Pays ou zone
Africa	**74**	**76**	**60**	**73**	**95**	**98**	**106**	**106**	**105**	**108**	**Afrique**
Egypt[1]	40.0	40.8	24.0	24.5	25.3	26.1	27.9	28.1	...	...	Egypte[1]
Kenya	1.0	1.2	1.2	1.4	2.5	2.0	*2.0	...	...	...	Kenya
Nigeria[1]	1.1	1.3	3.7	3.7	6.4	8.5	8.5	8.4	...	...	Nigéria[1]
South Africa[1]	32.2	32.4	31.5	43.6	60.4	61.3	68.0	67.1	...	...	Afrique du Sud[1]
America, North	**1832**	**1828**	**1891**	**1899**	**2059**	**2008**	**2047**	**2092**	**2054**	**2053**	**Amérique du Nord**
Canada[1]	57.6	61.1	61.2	50.0	84.7	86.5	84.3	82.7	...	...	Canada[1]
Mexico	148.1	167.7	174.0	225.9	263.4	279.9	315.7	330.3	297.5	290.3	Mexique
United States[1]	1626.3	1599.2	1655.7	1622.7	1711.1	1641.7	1647.4	1678.7	...	...	Etats-Unis[1]
America, South	**183**	**207**	**218**	**215**	**228**	**200**	**200**	**219**	**203**	**214**	**Amérique du Sud**
Argentina[1]	20.2	21.5	15.2	11.7	11.8	8.6	14.7	21.0	...	...	Argentine[1]
Brazil[1]	86.9	94.7	101.3	100.0	101.9	82.6	79.2	90.6	...	...	Brésil[1]
Chile[1]	6.5	6.2	6.3	6.4	4.8	5.6	7.7	8.2	...	...	Chili[1]
Colombia	[1]14.0	[1]29.2	29.0	29.9	34.4	36.1	[1]28.2	27.7	21.2	...	Colombie
Peru[1]	32.2	32.1	34.3	35.6	38.3	33.5	34.7	35.3	...	...	Pérou[1]
Uruguay[1]	4.4	4.4	4.3	4.4	1.8	1.7	1.8	1.9	...	...	Uruguay[1]
Venezuela[1]	19.0	19.0	28.0	27.0	34.6	31.6	33.9	34.6	...	...	Venezuela[1]
Asia	**3616**	**3892**	**4529**	**4290**	**4844**	**5088**	**4329**	**4880**	**4928**	**5016**	**Asie**
Armenia[2]	..	..	..	...	0.1	0.2	0.4	...	...	...	Arménie[2]
China[1]	811.6	889.9	911.8	905.2	1121.0	1115.0	1425.2	1501.4	...	...	Chine[1]
India	[1]177.3	[1]176.5	[1]215.1	[1]237.4	[1]302.1	[3]300.6	[3]348.1	[1]508.0	...	...	Inde
Indonesia[1]	115.0	140.5	164.9	189.7	210.0	225.7	302.5	355.1	...	...	Indonésie[1]
Iran(Islamic Rep. of)[1]	32.0	36.1	394.0	38.1	51.6	52.5	57.1	57.3	...	...	Iran(Rép. islamique)[1]
Japan[1]	722.9	714.7	729.7	694.2	708.2	731.2	737.3	764.8	...	...	Japon[1]
Kazakhstan[2]	..	...	...	...	0.8	0.0	0.1	...	...	...	Kazakhstan[2]
Korea, Republic of	1391.9	1492.9	1615.3	1672.9	1838.7	1953.5	658.1	815.8	...	...	Corée, République de
Malaysia[1]	41.9	45.0	62.1	58.2	55.3	58.9	59.6	94.5	...	...	Malaisie[1]
Pakistan[1]	40.2	64.5	85.1	117.0	134.6	163.5	218.0	223.6	...	...	Pakistan[1]
Philippines[1]	17.5	17.0	17.6	16.8	16.8	16.5	0.0	0.0	...	...	Philippines[1]
Thailand[1]	91.5	126.8	157.2	182.2	199.6	228.3	259.5	267.5	...	...	Thaïlande[1]
Turkey	[1]174.5	187.8	176.0	177.9	204.9	242.1	263.0	292.0	286.3	303.9	Turquie
Europe	**2276**	**2287**	**2306**	**2437**	**2503**	**2234**	**2153**	**2243**	**2138**	**2128**	**Europe**
Austria[1]	17.8	17.2	20.1	17.3	22.3	...	...	...	...	...	Autriche[1]
Belarus	..	...	...	203.5	165.9	157.3	124.0	123.2	116.1	117.5	Bélarus
Belgium[1][4]	39.5	35.8	37.9	35.7	45.7	...	...	...	...	...	Belgique[1][4]
Bulgaria[1]	41.4	35.6	23.4	22.3	31.3	27.1	28.1	29.1	...	...	Bulgarie[1]
Croatia	..	7.8	9.4	6.3	4.1	2.7	0.0	0.0	0.4	...	Croatie
Denmark[2]	...	...	...	...	56.3	55.6	...	...	...	...	Danemark[2]
Czechoslovakia(former)	48.0	37.7									Tchécoslovaquie(anc.)
Czech Republic	..	..	[1]17.4	13.9	17.0	16.6	16.0	23.9	23.5	22.7	République tchèque
Finland	0.1	0.1	0.1	0.3	0.4	0.3	0.2	...	...	...	Finlande
France[1]	80.3	55.1	54.2	56.0	61.6	...	...	...	...	...	France[1]
Germany	..	469.1	472.3	446.4	470.7	396.7	392.6	419.6	...	...	Allemagne
Germany(Fed.Rep.)	439.7	..	..	..	..	..	..	..	...	..	Allemagne(Rép.féd.)
German D.R.(former)	132.7	..	..	..	..	..	..	..	..		R.D.A. (anc.)
Hungary	21.4	25.0	21.9	20.7	24.5	21.2	25.0	29.1	32.4	19.5	Hongrie
Ireland[1]	77.8	75.2	89.9	86.6	93.1	...	...	...	...	...	Irlande[1]
Italy	691.6	672.8	693.2	641.2	714.0	649.1	663.1	659.4	631.4	582.7	Italie
Latvia	..	2.7	2.7	1.7	1.1	0.9	0.5	0.5	0.7	0.6	Lettonie
Poland	34.2	23.7	27.9	30.9	42.9	37.4	26.9	34.5	34.1	31.7	Pologne
Portugal	94.2	88.3	66.5	68.8	75.4	59.1	80.0	84.7	89.6	81.9	Portugal
Romania	149.2	105.6	86.5	85.8	72.3	80.9	67.2	66.6	41.6	28.3	Roumanie
Russian Federation	..	...	...	...	25.8	27.2	13.2	...	...	...	Fédération de Russie
Slovakia	..	...	...	...	[2]79.9	[2]75.0	35.1	...	...	...	Slovaquie
Slovenia	..	...	...	...	[2]11.9	[2]15.8	14.5	16.2	21.7	19.5	Slovénie
Spain	[1]177.9	[1]174.8	[1]175.5	177.7	195.8	138.5	158.7	176.2	173.3	186.1	Espagne
Switzerland[1]	17.1	14.7	17.3	14.2	16.5	...	...	...	...	...	Suisse[1]
Ukraine	..	16.1	11.4	8.7	4.3	1.6	0.3	0.5	0.2	0.1	Ukraine
United Kingdom	[1]92.7	[1]102.9	[1]107.2	319.1	240.9	219.0	203.5	185.9	183.6		Royaume-Uni
Yugoslavia	..	10.9	7.7	3.3	3.3	4.0	5.0	2.5	2.1	0.9	Yougoslavie

For general note and footnotes, see end of table.

Voir la fin du tableau pour la remarque générale et les notes.

Non-cellulosic staple and tow (continued)
Fibres discontinues et câbles non cellulosiques (suite)

ISIC-BASED CODE - CODE BASE CITI

3513-04

Unit : Thousand metric tons   Unité : Milliers de tonnes métriques

Country or area	1990	1991	1992	1993	1994	1995	1996	1997	1998	1999	Pays ou zone
T.F.Yug.Rep. Macedonia	..	...	...	...	26.5	20.3	13.6	16.8	10.5	3.9	L'ex-RY Macédoine
Yugoslavia, SFR	64.3	..	..	..	..	..	..	..	..	..	Yougoslavie, RSF
USSR (former)	427.7	..	..	..	..	..	..	..	..	..	URSS (anc.)
Oceania	**2**	**2**	**0**	**0**	**0**	**0**	**3**	**14**	**6**	**6**	**Océanie**
Australia [1]	[5]2.0	[5]2.1	0.0	0.0	0.0	0.0	2.8	13.6	...	...	Australie [1]
Total	**8412**	**8292**	**9005**	**8914**	**9728**	**9627**	**8839**	**9554**	**9434**	**9525**	**Total**

General Note.

Non-cellulosic (synthetic) discontinuous fibres ranging from around 3/4 inch to 18 inches and tow (a collection of many parallel, continuous filaments without twist grouped together in rope-like form) made of natural polymers based on materials such as casein, or of synthetic polymers mainly from coal and oil distillation products. Waste, spun yarns and other manufactures are excluded. (SITC, Rev.3: 26650-0, 26660-0).

Remarque générale.

Fibres discontinues longues d'environ 2 à 45 centimètres et câbles (ensemble filaments continus, parallèles, sans torsion) de matières non cellulosiques artificielles ou synthétiques. Polymères naturels obtenus à partir de produits tels que la caséine ou polymères synthétiques obtenus principalement à partir de produits de la distillation du charbon ou du pétrole. Cette rubrique ne comprend pas les déchets, les filés de fibres discontinues et les autres produits non cellulosiques. (CTCI, Rev.3: 26650-0, 26660-0).

[1] Source: Fiber Economics Bureau, Inc. (U.S.A.).

[2] Source: United Nations Economic Commission for Europe (ECE), (Geneva).

[3] Official figures.

[4] Including production in Netherlands and Luxembourg.

[5] Including production in New Zealand.

[1] Source: Fiber Economics Bureau, Inc. (Etats-Unis).

[2] Source: Commission économique des Nations Unies pour l'Europe (CEE), (Genève).

[3] Données officielles.

[4] Y compris la production des Pays-Bas et du Luxembourg.

[5] Y compris la production de la Nouvelle-Zélande.

Cellulosic staple and tow
Fibres et câbles cellulosiques

ISIC-BASED CODE - CODE BASE CITI

3513-07

Unit : Thousand metric tons   Unité : Milliers de tonnes métriques

Country or area	1990	1991	1992	1993	1994	1995	1996	1997	1998	1999	Pays ou zone
Africa	**5**	**5**	**5**	**5**	**5**	**5**	**5**	**5**	**5**	**5**	**Afrique**
Egypt[1]	5.2	5.2	5.2	5.2	5.3	5.2	5.3	5.2	...	...	Egypte[1]
America, North	**185**	**177**	**173**	**148**	**147**	**160**	**142**	**149**	**149**	**149**	**Amérique du Nord**
Canada[1]	28.5	29.5	24.8	0.0	0.0	0.0	0.0	0.0	...	...	Canada[1]
Cuba[1]	*7.9	*8.3	8.3	8.5	9.0	13.5	...	...	...	...	Cuba[1]
Mexico	12.4	14.9	14.9	13.8	14.2	...	...	...	...	...	Mexique
United States[1]	135.7	124.0	124.8	126.1	123.8	131.5	116.2	122.7	...	...	Etats-Unis[1]
America, South	**44**	**46**	**79**	**77**	**76**	**79**	**24**	**29**	**50**	**49**	**Amérique du Sud**
Brazil[1]	39.6	41.3	43.9	43.3	46.3	41.1	24.1	29.3	...	...	Brésil[1]
Chile[1 2]	4.3	4.3	2.2	2.2	0.0	0.0	0.0	0.0	...	...	Chili[1 2]
Colombia	[1]0.0	[1]0.0	33.1	31.0	30.0	37.5	[1]0.0	[1]0.0	...	...	Colombie
Asia	**602**	**654**	**694**	**748**	**819**	**937**	**914**	**948**	**950**	**977**	**Asie**
Bangladesh[1]	1.2	0.0	0.0	0.0	0.0	0.0	0.0	0.0	...	...	Bangladesh[1]
China[1]	157.6	185.0	189.2	212.1	270.9	365.2	359.0	378.0	...	...	Chine[1]
India[1]	158.5	156.4	161.1	178.0	173.3	192.9	184.6	179.2	...	...	Inde[1]
Indonesia[1]	60.0	90.0	110.0	130.0	167.0	177.0	179.6	212.9	...	...	Indonésie[1]
Iraq[1]	5.6	5.6	5.6	5.5	5.5	5.5	5.3	5.8	...	...	Iraq[1]
Japan[1]	176.7	169.9	168.0	162.0	140.7	134.9	124.0	110.8	...	...	Japon[1]
Thailand[1]	41.5	45.3	58.6	58.6	60.0	60.0	61.0	60.2	...	...	Thaïlande[1]
Turkey	1.2	1.6	1.4	1.6	1.5	1.1	0.8	0.6	0.0	0.0	Turquie
Europe	**1045**	**883**	**918**	**769**	**797**	**729**	**664**	**627**	**597**	**545**	**Europe**
Austria[1 3]	135.0	120.0	128.3	131.2	134.3	139.4	127.9			...	Autriche[1 3]
Czechoslovakia(former)[2]	40.8	31.7	..	..	..	..	..	..	..	..	Tchécoslovaquie(anc.)[2]
Czech Republic	..	..	[1]35.4	37.8	37.1	29.5	24.1	21.8	21.4	12.8	République tchèque
Finland[2]	62.2	50.4	56.4	57.5	59.2	55.8	50.9	...	...	...	Finlande[2]
France	259.4	260.1	288.0	184.5	171.7					...	France
Germany	..	...	183.4	178.4	197.0	141.7	142.6	136.9	...	...	Allemagne
Germany(Fed.Rep.)[3 4]	177.9	..	..	..	..	..	..	..	..	..	Allemagne(Rép.féd.)[3 4]
German D.R.(former)[2]	53.3	..	..	..	..	..	..	..	..	..	R.D.A. (anc.)[2]
Greece	...	...	[1]5.0	[1]5.0	[1]5.5	[1 3]5.5	...	...	14.8	...	Grèce
Hungary	4.1	2.5									Hongrie
Italy[5]	35.5	31.9	35.2	32.8	28.8	31.8	32.3	32.2	32.2	25.8	Italie[5]
Poland	21.8	17.4	16.0	17.1	17.6	16.6	10.7	2.5	0.1		Pologne
Portugal	[2]0.9	* [2]0.8	*0.0	*0.0	0.0	[1]0.0	...	...	...	...	Portugal
Romania	60.0	36.5	26.1	14.7	11.0	11.2	11.3	7.9	6.1	0.0	Roumanie
Spain[1]	[3]36.0	[3]30.0	[3]22.5	8.5	[3]27.5	36.1	...	...	...	...	Espagne[1]
Sweden	24.2	19.5	[1 3]17.6	13.1	24.1	24.2	[1]23.8	...	11.8	22.6	Suède
Ukraine	..	13.2	23.4	14.3	12.6	4.3	0.3	0.0	0.0		Ukraine
United Kingdom[1 3]	71.0	63.0	65.0	...	...	...	...	...	...	...	Royaume-Uni[1 3]
Yugoslavia	..	19.6	12.8	4.3	1.3	5.7	5.6	8.7	5.2	0.2	Yougoslavie
Yugoslavia, SFR[2]	57.5	..	..	..	..	..	..	..	..	..	Yougoslavie, RSF[2]
USSR (former)	322.7	..	..	..	..	..	..	..	..	..	URSS (anc.)
Total	**2203**	**1764**	**1869**	**1747**	**1845**	**1909**	**1750**	**1758**	**1750**	**1725**	**Total**

General Note.

Rayon and acetate (artificial) discontinuous fibres ranging from around 3/4 inch to 18 inches and tow (a collection of many parallel, continuous filaments without twist grouped together in rope-like form) produced by chemical transformation of natural organic polymers from cellulose. Waste of these fibres, spun yarn and other manufactures of rayon and acetate are excluded. (SITC, Rev.3: 26711-0; 26712-0).

Remarque générale.

Fibres discontinues de rayonne et d'acétate longues d'environ 2 à 45 centimètres, et câbles (ensemble de filaments continus parallèles, sans torsion) artificiels obtenus par transformation chimique de polymères organiques naturels cellulosiques. Cette rubrique ne comprend pas les déchets de ces fibres, les fils de fibres discontinues et les autres produits fabriqués à partir de rayonne ou d'acétate. (CTCI, Rev.3: 26711-0, 26712-0).

[1] Source: Fiber Economics Bureau, Inc. (U.S.A.).
[2] Production of acetate fibres is nil or negligible.
[3] Including cellulosic continuous filaments.
[4] Including cigarette filtration tow.
[5] Including continuous fibres.

[1] Source: Fiber Economics Bureau, Inc. (Etats-Unis).
[2] Production de fibres d'acétate nulle ou négligeable.
[3] Y compris les filaments cellulosiques continus.
[4] Y compris l'étoupe pour filtres de cigarettes.
[5] Y compris de fibres continues.

Alkyd resins
Résines alkyliques

ISIC-BASED CODE - CODE BASE CITI

3513-10

Unit : Thousand metric tons   Unité : Milliers de tonnes métriques

Country or area	1990	1991	1992	1993	1994	1995	1996	1997	1998	1999	Pays ou zone
America, North	**10**	**12**	**12**	**17**	**18**	**17**	**21**	**22**	**23**	**26**	**Amérique du Nord**
Mexico	9.8	11.5	12.0	17.4	17.7	17.2	21.1	22.5	23.5	25.9	Mexique
America, South	**21**	**21**	**19**	**21**	**30**	**24**	**27**	**27**	**27**	**26**	**Amérique du Sud**
Chile	7.7	8.0	9.6	10.2	9.9	12.0	14.1	14.2	14.2	13.2	Chili
Colombia	...	...	9.6	10.9	19.7	11.6	...	...	...	...	Colombie
Asia	**476**	**504**	**456**	**432**	**435**	**436**	**445**	**400**	**427**	**392**	**Asie**
Indonesia	19.3	...	17.2	26.8	39.1	22.2	...	2.5	92.4	...	Indonésie
Japan	441.6	426.9	410.2	386.0	383.3	400.4	400.9	384.8	328.3	317.4	Japon
Turkey	14.8	17.6	...	...	...	...	...	...	[1]6.7	...	Turquie
Uzbekistan	..	27.9	15.3	6.4	0.0	0.0	0.0	0.0	...	...	Ouzbékistan
Europe	**680**	**760**	**739**	**686**	**663**	**681**	**657**	**696**	**683**	**679**	**Europe**
Albania	...	...	...	...	...	...	...	[1]0.1	...	0.0	Albanie
Austria	33.3	...	...	...	...	...	...	...	...	...	Autriche
Belarus	..	33.8	26.5	14.1	7.1	7.7	10.0	11.5	10.9	10.7	Bélarus
Belgium	8.3	8.4	7.4	7.5	...	22.7	22.4	28.1	30.1	26.6	Belgique
Croatia	..	7.0	2.0	4.8	2.0	1.8	2.6	3.4	4.8	...	Croatie
Denmark[2]	5.7	5.4	5.5	5.0	5.2	5.3	5.5	5.7	5.5	7.7	Danemark[2]
Czechoslovakia(former)	40.8	14.4	..	..	..	..	..	..	..	..	Tchécoslovaquie(anc.)
Czech Republic	..	..	..	...	32.2	33.8	36.2	38.7	42.5	29.2	République tchèque
Finland[3]	3.0	3.1	0.9	1.3	2.1	2.0	...	...	...	...	Finlande[3]
France	50.0	47.0	47.3	42.7	43.8	...	...	...	...	...	France
Germany	..	...	...	154.0	156.8	140.2	138.7	142.7	132.4	...	Allemagne
Germany(Fed.Rep.)	131.3	..	..	..	..	..	..	..	..	..	Allemagne(Rép.féd.)
German D.R.(former)	37.5	..	..	..	..	..	..	..	..	..	R.D.A. (anc.)
Greece[1]	...	...	...	...	...	...	12.0	13.7	...	...	Grèce[1]
Hungary	9.7	6.4	6.6	5.6	6.1	6.4	...	8.0	6.1	6.3	Hongrie
Italy	29.5	28.2	28.2	22.9	17.3	22.2	23.2	25.8	22.3	21.3	Italie
Latvia	..	5.0	...	...	...	...	...	...	...	...	Lettonie
Netherlands	51.8	49.6	60.9	...	...	...	...	...	...	...	Pays-Bas
Poland	43.3	...	...	...	...	...	...	...	...	...	Pologne
Portugal	7.8	6.3	...	...	...	[1]7.4	[1]7.7	[1]7.8	[1]8.2	...	Portugal
Romania	28.7	19.9	12.4	10.7	9.6	12.3	9.1	6.6	13.8	11.7	Roumanie
Russian Federation	..	112.6	87.3	72.2	42.8	47.6	45.9	48.6	38.9	31.2	Fédération de Russie
Slovenia	..	...	...	...	...	...	12.1	13.1	12.4	11.9	Slovénie
Spain	25.8	28.6	22.3	29.8	41.2	58.9	47.8	53.9	59.1	56.6	Espagne
Sweden	24.9	20.7	26.4	22.6	29.9	29.4	[1]21.0	24.4	25.5	21.6	Suède
Ukraine	..	29.0	26.4	17.6	12.8	10.8	9.9	10.0	9.2	9.1	Ukraine
United Kingdom	122.6	...	...	71.8	67.5	71.0	69.4	[1]79.2	75.4	...	Royaume-Uni
Yugoslavia, SFR	13.1	..	..	..	..	..	..	..	..	..	Yougoslavie, RSF
USSR (former)	292.5	..	..	..	..	..	..	..	..	..	URSS (anc.)
Oceania	**2**	**2**	**2**	**2**	**2**	**2**	**2**	**2**	**2**	**2**	**Océanie**
Australia	1.7	...	...	...	...	...	...	...	...	...	Australie
Total	**1480**	**1297**	**1228**	**1158**	**1147**	**1159**	**1152**	**1148**	**1163**	**1125**	**Total**

General Note.
Polycondensation products of polyhydric alcohols (glycerol) with polybasic organic acids (glycerophthalic resins) and maleic acids (glyceromaleic resins). Dry weight of resins. (SITC, Rev.3: 57432-0).

Remarque générale.
Produits de la polycondensation des polyalcools (glycérol) avec des acides organiques polybasiques (résines glycéro-phtaliques) ou l'acide maléique (résines glycéro-maléiques). Poids sec des résines. (CTCI, Rev.3: 57432-0).

[1] Source: United Nations Economic Commission for Europe (ECE), (Geneva).

[2] Sales.

[3] Wet weight of resins and plastic materials.

[1] Source: Commission économique des Nations Unies pour l'Europe (CEE), (Genève).

[2] Ventes.

[3] Poids mouillé des résines et câbles non cellulosiques.

Amino plastics
Aminoplastes

ISIC-BASED CODE - CODE BASE CITI

3513-13

Unit : Thousand metric tons   Unité : Milliers de tonnes métriques

Country or area	1990	1991	1992	1993	1994	1995	1996	1997	1998	1999	Pays ou zone
America, North	**14**	**15**	**16**	**15**	**17**	**18**	**22**	**21**	**20**	**24**	**Amérique du Nord**
Mexico	...	...	...	15.5	17.4	17.5	22.4	21.3	20.2	23.6	Mexique
Asia	**627**	**611**	**556**	**544**	**523**	**492**	**503**	**485**	**390**	**380**	**Asie**
Indonesia	...	...	...	1.2	...	...	...	...	...	...	Indonésie
Japan	625.7	610.0	555.0	542.6	521.4	490.5	502.3	483.7	388.5	379.1	Japon
Europe	**1805**	**1981**	**1697**	**1778**	**1945**	**1724**	**1928**	**2028**	**1925**	**2146**	**Europe**
Belgium	21.7	23.8	26.5	25.4	...	...	...	...	...	...	Belgique
Bulgaria	26.7	15.9	10.5	10.2	8.0	7.5	7.7	6.3	...	...	Bulgarie
Croatia	..	1.5	1.0	0.5	0.3	0.1	0.0	0.0	0.0	...	Croatie
Denmark[1]	37.1	36.0	35.1	39.3	46.7	41.5	43.9	50.5	50.4	...	Danemark[1]
Czechoslovakia(former)	1.7	1.2	..	..	..	..	..	..	..	..	Tchécoslovaquie(anc.)
Finland[2]	76.8	52.1	42.5	54.8	62.6	57.6	75.1	...	...	67.6	Finlande[2]
France	159.8	179.0	160.2	148.6	184.2	...	...	...	...	...	France
Germany	..	1073.9	...	874.7	884.8	620.4	627.1	802.4	747.2	...	Allemagne
Germany(Fed.Rep.)[3]	811.4	..	..	..	..	..	..	..	..	..	Allemagne(Rép.féd.)[3]
German D.R.(former)	27.1	..	..	..	..	..	..	..	..	..	R.D.A. (anc.)
Hungary	4.4	2.9	2.5	1.9	1.9	3.5	3.6	1.6	3.2	32.5	Hongrie
Latvia	..	0.7	...	...	...	...	...	...	...	15.2	Lettonie
Poland	5.4	3.8	3.4	3.5	3.6	4.1	2.8	2.9	...	...	Pologne
Portugal	86.9	80.3	77.8	78.1	94.9	108.7	127.7	146.8	149.6	147.7	Portugal
Russian Federation	..	13.7	8.3	2.7	1.1	0.8	0.6	0.2	0.4	0.2	Fédération de Russie
Slovenia	..	1.4	1.0	0.5	0.7	1.3	#88.0	98.8	102.7	117.1	Slovénie
Spain	210.9	181.6	213.3	256.0	322.7	325.3	335.2	364.5	...	...	Espagne
Sweden	131.3	104.4	88.4	101.4	119.7	114.1	43.5	50.4	53.0	51.4	Suède
United Kingdom	...	...	...	172.3	181.9	234.5	366.9	234.4	184.0	...	Royaume-Uni
Total	**2446**	**2607**	**2269**	**2337**	**2485**	**2233**	**2454**	**2534**	**2335**	**2550**	**Total**

General Note.
Materials derived by condensation of amines or amides with formaldehyde, furfuraldehyde etc., such as urea-formal-dehyde, thiourea-formaldehyde, melamine-formaldehyde, aniline-formaldehyde etc. Dry resin content of moulding powders. (SITC, Rev.3: 57541-0,57542-0, 57543-0).

Remarque générale.
Matières dérivées par condensation des amines ou des amides avec des aldéhydes (formaldéhyde, furfural, etc.) telles que les résines urée-formol, thiourée-formol, mélamine-formol, aniline-formol etc. Teneur des poudres de moulageen résine sèche. (CTCI, Rev.3: 57541-0, 57542-0, 57543-0).

[1] Sales.
[2] Wet weight of resins and plastic materials.
[3] Including phenolic and cresylic plastics.

[1] Ventes.
[2] Poids mouillé des résines et câbles non cellulosiques.
[3] Y compris les résines phénoliques et crésyliques.

Phenolic and cresylic plastics
Phénoplastes

ISIC-BASED CODE - CODE BASE CITI

3513-16

Unit : Thousand metric tons

Unité : Milliers de tonnes métriques

Country or area	1990	1991	1992	1993	1994	1995	1996	1997	1998	1999	Pays ou zone
America, North	**15**	**16**	**17**	**17**	**16**	**16**	**22**	**25**	**24**	**18**	**Amérique du Nord**
Mexico	...	...	...	17.4	15.6	15.6	21.8	24.8	24.3	17.9	Mexique
Asia	**385**	**396**	**360**	**329**	**331**	**327**	**294**	**303**	**260**	**250**	**Asie**
Armenia	..	13.1	4.1	0.7	0.9	0.2	0.1	0.2	0.3	0.2	Arménie
Japan	384.9	383.0	355.8	328.2	330.0	327.0	293.8	302.6	259.5	249.9	Japon
Europe	**518**	**2200**	**2042**	**1955**	**1760**	**1901**	**1559**	**1687**	**1900**	**2324**	**Europe**
Austria [1]	...	...	...	...	...	34.0	41.2	49.2	42.5	42.1	Autriche [1]
Belgium [1]	...	...	...	...	...	...	...	16.7	16.1	...	Belgique [1]
Croatia	..	2.1	1.6	0.7	0.3	0.2	0.1	0.0	...	...	Croatie
Czechoslovakia(former)	11.9	6.1						..	..	..	Tchécoslovaquie(anc.)
Finland [2]	80.2	62.2	73.6	83.1	104.6	100.6	110.0	...	...	...	Finlande [2]
France	72.1	67.0	65.5	60.8	74.3	...	...	...	...	...	France
Germany	..	...	...	...	...	...	258.6	272.6	279.5	...	Allemagne
German D.R.(former)	57.4	..	..	..	..	..	..	..	..	..	R.D.A. (anc.)
Hungary	4.7	3.2	2.4	2.5	...	...	...	...	...	...	Hongrie
Italy	67.0	63.1	57.2	63.5	58.1	75.0	74.2	71.7	78.1	66.1	Italie
Latvia	..	...	...	...	...	...	...	...	...	10.7	Lettonie
Netherlands	...	...	...	22.5	11.7	9.4	9.0	6.0	...	...	Pays-Bas
Poland	2.7	2.4	1.8	2.1	1.4	1.6	2.0	1.9	1.5	1.0	Pologne
Portugal	4.8	3.3	...	...	...	[1]7.0	[1]8.7	[1]10.5	[1]12.6	...	Portugal
Romania [1]	...	...	...	...	...	...	6.7	6.6	4.7	...	Roumanie [1]
Russian Federation	..	1491.5	1336.4	1240.2	1007.2	1130.7	780.7	878.4	1088.4	1514.9	Fédération de Russie
Slovenia	..	7.1	4.7	5.7	8.2	11.1	13.6	14.6	18.6	21.0	Slovénie
Spain	29.9	38.3	39.6	41.2	49.8	53.6	72.1	74.6	64.6	68.5	Espagne
Sweden	39.9	23.5	22.4	23.5	24.9	25.5	0.9	1.1	1.2	1.0	Suède
United Kingdom	...	...	...	62.8	67.6	78.5	83.0	79.1	80.2	...	Royaume-Uni
T.F.Yug.Rep. Macedonia	..	1.9	0.5	0.4	0.5	0.4	0.2	0.2	0.1	0.1	L'ex-RY Macédoine
Total	**918**	**2612**	**2419**	**2301**	**2106**	**2244**	**1874**	**2015**	**2184**	**2592**	**Total**

General Note.

Material derived from condensation of phenol, cresol, xylenol etc. or substituted phenols with aldehydes, such as, resins (novolaks), thermosetting phenol-formaldehyde resins, oil-soluble resins prepared from butylphenol, amyphenol, parahydroxydiphenyl or other substituted phenol, and modified phenolic resins. Dry resin content of moulding powders. (SITC, Rev.3: 57544-0).

Remarque générale.

Matières dérivées de la condensation, avec des aldéhydes, du phénol, du crésol, du xylénol etc., ou de phénols de substitution, telles que: résines "novolaques", résines formophénoliques thermodurcissables, résines oléosolubles préparées à partir du butylphénol, de l'amylphénol, du paraphénylphénol ou d'autres phénols de substitution, résines phénoliques modifiées. Teneur en résine sèche des poudres de moulage. (CTCI, Rev.3: 57544-0).

[1] Source: United Nations Economic Commission for Europe (ECE), (Geneva).

[2] Wet weight of resins and plastic materials.

[1] Source: Commission économique des Nations Unies pour l'Europe (CEE), (Genève).

[2] Poids mouillé des résines et câbles non cellulosiques.

Polyethylene
Polyéthylène

ISIC-BASED CODE - CODE BASE CITI

3513-19

Unit : Thousand metric tons

Unité : Milliers de tonnes métriques

Country or area	1990	1991	1992	1993	1994	1995	1996	1997	1998	1999	Pays ou zone
Africa	**38**	**35**	**33**	**27**	**40**	**37**	**40**	**40**	**44**	**32**	**Afrique**
Algeria	34.5	31.7	29.0	23.3	37.6	33.7	34.5	31.5	37.1	29.0	Algérie
Burundi	0.4	0.4	0.4	0.3	...	...	...	...	...	...	Burundi
Egypt	2.7	2.7	2.5	2.4	1.9	1.7	2.3	2.1	...	...	Egypte
Ethiopia	0.7	0.4	0.6	0.5	0.3	1.8	3.2	5.7	4.2	0.5	Ethiopie
America, North	**12564**	**12325**	**12412**	**12500**	**12666**	**12692**	**12952**	**12948**	**13041**	**12947**	**Amérique du Nord**
Canada	...	1566.7	1654.1	1742.1	1907.8	...	2194.1	2189.6	2282.6	...	Canada
United States[1]	...	...	...	...	10758.0	...	...	...	...	...	Etats-Unis[1]
America, South	**1268**	**1267**	**1246**	**1478**	**1567**	**1623**	**1643**	**1856**	**1899**	**2067**	**Amérique du Sud**
Argentina	227.4	241.8	268.3	238.6	246.6	278.1	274.2	257.6	279.5	260.8	Argentine
Brazil	948.2	924.6	881.6	1142.3	1221.2	1239.3	1260.9	1484.6	1515.9	1689.1	Brésil
Chile	35.7	42.2	41.0	39.3	45.8	45.4	49.9	43.4	49.5	47.4	Chili
Colombia	56.5	...	54.9	57.2	53.5	60.4	...	70.8	54.0	...	Colombie
Asia	**5000**	**5615**	**6426**	**6316**	**6672**	**7083**	**7465**	**7854**	**7839**	**8342**	**Asie**
Azerbaijan	..	65.6	6.3	19.2	11.1	18.8	27.7	15.0	18.2	23.2	Azerbaïdjan
China	783.5	911.8	1080.7	...	...	...	...	...	...	...	Chine
Hong Kong SAR[2]	16.0	1.2	14.2	15.7	28.6	25.6	16.9	19.7	30.4	...	Hong-Kong RAS[2]
India	123.2	109.1	174.3	...	...	...	...	...	...	...	Inde
Israel	106.6	124.6	128.7	144.1	127.0	...	...	...	...	...	Israël
Japan	2887.6	2982.4	2980.9	2761.5	2944.1	3193.0	3313.2	3366.0	3142.7	3368.8	Japon
Kazakhstan[1]	..	...	...	...	0.0	0.2	0.2	0.0	...	...	Kazakhstan[1]
Korea, Republic of	841.3	1163.8	1780.7	2042.4	2216.5	2340.6	2596.7	2943.0	3132.9	3398.7	Corée, République de
Turkey	241.9	256.0	260.6	271.8	283.9	300.1	299.5	292.6	291.4	288.6	Turquie
Europe	**9417**	**10603**	**10952**	**10531**	**10481**	**10852**	**10695**	**9736**	**9996**	**10548**	**Europe**
Belarus	..	129.7	89.0	60.7	74.3	103.9	76.6	96.5	103.7	110.5	Bélarus
Belgium	1031.7	1210.8	1341.8	1227.1	...	[3]672.7	[3]731.7	[3]719.3	[3]625.9	[3]615.1	Belgique
Bulgaria	88.4	59.5	67.1	74.1	81.9	86.9	88.3	86.9	80.2	...	Bulgarie
Croatia	..	136.0	141.6	144.4	130.7	145.2	144.0	145.3	144.0	...	Croatie
Denmark[4]	11.5	13.2	16.4	16.4	17.1	20.4	26.1	24.5	23.1	26.7	Danemark[4]
Czechoslovakia(former)	154.5	150.2	..	..	..	..	..	..	..	..	Tchécoslovaquie(anc.)
Czech Republic	..	..	..	..	113.7	107.5	124.1	120.8	134.0	131.0	République tchèque
France	1115.6	1199.4	1340.9	1307.9	1427.7	[1]1416.8	[1]1354.6	[1]1155.9	[1]1249.0	...	France
Germany	..	...	...	1623.4	1766.7	1790.7	1757.8	1724.9	1795.1	...	Allemagne
Germany(Fed.Rep.)	1475.7	..	..	..	..	..	..	..	..	..	Allemagne(Rép.féd.)
German D.R.(former)	217.0	..	..	..	..	..	..	..	..	..	R.D.A. (anc.)
Hungary	221.3	248.6	247.6	258.6	273.3	273.8	244.2	283.4	289.5	261.8	Hongrie
Italy	931.1	949.4	926.6	950.4	972.1	1052.4	1055.4	1065.1	1176.5	1165.3	Italie
Lithuania	..	..	..	..	...	0.1	0.1	0.1	0.1	0.2	Lituanie
Netherlands	...	...	...	...	[1]1771.3	[1]2007.3	[1]1806.4	[1]1117.0	[1]1232.0	[4][5]1228.1	Pays-Bas
Poland	158.5	149.9	163.1	162.2	141.9	151.1	163.5	159.7	173.4	133.6	Pologne
Portugal	...	...	...	...	[1]243.0	[1]230.3	226.7	281.0	264.1	247.4	Portugal
Republic of Moldova[6]	..	..	..	1.6	[1]0.9	[1]0.7	1.6	1.2	1.2	0.7	Rép. de Moldova[6]
Romania	120.3	91.7	70.6	61.9	59.5	75.7	80.8	70.1	80.9	91.0	Roumanie
Russian Federation	..	..	635.4	649.1	509.7	684.7	572.5	585.9	596.5	801.3	Fédération de Russie
Slovakia	..	..	...	133.5	169.2	169.9	172.5	[1]174.4	[1]178.6	161.8	Slovaquie
Slovenia	..	0.4	0.2	0.0	...	...	...	...	...	...	Slovénie
Spain	793.7	601.1	794.7	784.1	840.2	842.8	955.5	900.0	...	...	Espagne
Sweden	422.0	409.7	419.8	447.7	481.0	483.9	440.5	460.2	483.8	431.3	Suède
Ukraine	..	210.0	102.4	26.7	24.9	2.3	0.8	0.0	0.0	2.7	Ukraine
United Kingdom	423.5	...	...	...	...	[1]533.1	[1]614.5	[1]452.8	[1]340.3	...	Royaume-Uni
Yugoslavia	..	82.6	48.0	0.0	0.0	0.0	56.2	110.2	113.0	46.4	Yougoslavie
Total	**28287**	**29845**	**31069**	**30851**	**31426**	**32288**	**32796**	**32433**	**32818**	**33935**	**Total**

General Note.
Dry resin content of polymerized ethylene. (SITC, Rev.3: 57110-0).

[1] Source: United Nations Economic Commission for Europe (ECE), (Geneva).

[2] 1999 data are confidential.

[3] Incomplete coverage.

[4] Sales.

[5] Production by establishments employing 20 or more persons.

[6] Excluding Transnistria region.

Remarque générale.
Teneur en résine sèche de l'éthylène polymérisé. (CTCI, Rev.3: 57110-0).

[1] Source: Commission économique des Nations Unies pour l'Europe (CEE), (Genève).

[2] Pour 1999, les données sont confidentielles.

[3] Couverture incomplète.

[4] Ventes.

[5] Production des établissements occupant 20 personnes ou plus.

[6] Non compris la région de Transnistria.

Polypropylene
Polypropylène

ISIC-BASED CODE - CODE BASE CITI

3513-22

Unit : Thousand metric tons   Unité : Milliers de tonnes métriques

Country or area	1990	1991	1992	1993	1994	1995	1996	1997	1998	1999	Pays ou zone
America, North	**4604**	**4606**	**4605**	**4605**	**4606**	**4606**	**4608**	**4608**	**4609**	**4609**	**Amérique du Nord**
Canada	270.0	...	...	...	...	...	...	...	...	...	Canada
Mexico	[1]7.2	[1]8.7	[1]8.2	[1]7.9	[1]9.3	[1]8.6	[1]10.9	[1]10.6	[1]12.2	11.7	Mexique
United States[2]	...	...	...	...	4327.0	...	...	...	...	...	Etats-Unis[2]
America, South	**360**	**416**	**476**	**597**	**666**	**723**	**770**	**866**	**960**	**8162**	**Amérique du Sud**
Argentina	55.7	59.6	101.0	118.5	144.3	164.7	180.8	...	...	...	Argentine
Brazil	303.8	356.3	375.0	478.3	521.5	558.3	589.6	635.9	707.9	7887.3	Brésil
Colombia	0.0	...	0.0	0.1	0.1	0.2	...	0.1	0.1	...	Colombie
Asia	**2995**	**3239**	**3799**	**3996**	**4383**	**4682**	**5036**	**5515**	**5488**	**5674**	**Asie**
China	377.9	361.9	398.3	...	...	...	...	...	...	...	Chine
Hong Kong SAR[3]	11.8	29.3	...	2.3	1.8	8.1	22.7	14.0	...	...	Hong-Kong RAS[3]
India	27.4	27.3	32.9	68.8	81.5	82.3	79.4	...	...	...	Inde
Japan	1942.1	1955.2	2038.2	2031.1	2224.8	2501.9	2730.2	2854.3	2520.4	2626.3	Japon
Kazakhstan	...	30.3	28.1	9.8	15.8	10.7	3.7	...	...	0.1	Kazakhstan
Korea. Republic of	571.4	769.9	1222.6	1435.8	1607.1	1619.2	1738.0	2055.9	2355.2	2439.7	Corée, République de
Turkey	64.3	64.9	66.5	69.0	72.5	80.4	82.6	83.6	81.2	79.6	Turquie
Europe	**4390**	**4447**	**4488**	**4523**	**5224**	**4873**	**5004**	**5780**	**6549**	**6870**	**Europe**
Belarus	..	...	...	0.6	0.5	1.9	1.7	2.3	3.1	3.1	Bélarus
Belgium	813.8	794.9	825.9	888.9	...	1041.0	1084.6	1269.0	1298.5	1384.4	Belgique
Bulgaria	53.8	30.7	27.0	48.5	57.4	61.2	71.1	74.0	...	...	Bulgarie
Denmark[4]	0.9	1.0	0.9	0.7	0.8	0.8	1.0	1.7	1.6	2.0	Danemark[4]
Czechoslovakia(former)	190.0	167.5	..	..	..	..	..	..	..	..	Tchécoslovaquie(anc.)
Czech Republic	..	..	...	...	113.7	105.1	115.5	119.1	124.0	130.5	République tchèque
Finland[5]	124.2	112.6	124.8	135.1	150.4	153.4	148.0	139.4	152.5	...	Finlande[5]
France	780.2	818.9	897.3	972.1	1124.0	[2]1065.2	[2]1107.4	[2]1238.8	[2]1320.6	...	France
Germany	..	...	...	...	[2]706.9	668.5	699.2	...	884.3	...	Allemagne
Germany(Fed.Rep.)[2]	549.2	..	..	..	..	..	..	..	..	..	Allemagne(Rép.féd.)[2]
Hungary	155.4	150.0	147.6	136.1	137.3	137.0	135.6	143.5	137.9	131.3	Hongrie
Italy	507.0	454.6	467.2	427.4	520.8	548.9	438.7	541.7	534.7	570.7	Italie
Netherlands	...	...	...	315.8	501.6	352.7	...	...	...	...	Pays-Bas
Poland	[2]86.2	[2]88.6	[2]85.7	75.2	[2]75.8	76.4	80.2	95.1	101.7	121.9	Pologne
Portugal	25.9	22.9	...	0.7	...	0.8	1.1	1.0	1.3	2.3	Portugal
Romania	7.0	2.2	2.3	4.6	16.6	26.1	30.7	31.3	25.4	15.7	Roumanie
Russian Federation	..	77.2	66.5	52.5	38.5	62.2	82.0	102.7	147.9	201.4	Fédération de Russie
Slovakia	..	..	...	45.4	...	...	[2]71.3	68.4	...	71.7	Slovaquie
Slovenia	..	0.1	0.0	0.0	...	...	0.6	0.9	0.7	0.7	Slovénie
Spain	316.9	304.7	251.5	307.3	415.3	386.5	429.4	542.0	747.7	913.4	Espagne
Sweden	9.1	10.2	9.4	8.3	10.9	10.6	[2]11.2	12.9	12.4	12.8	Suède
Ukraine	..	...	...	...	10.6	13.2	19.7	30.0	18.8	34.0	Ukraine
United Kingdom	349.5	...	...	...	224.9	[2]96.1	[2]69.1	[2]205.2	[2]478.5	...	Royaume-Uni
Yugoslavia	..	33.3	21.1	0.2	1.4	0.4	16.0	31.3	34.3	13.2	Yougoslavie
Yugoslavia, SFR	31.2	..	..	..	..	..	..	..	..	..	Yougoslavie, RSF
USSR (former)	202.9	..	..	..	..	..	..	..	..	..	URSS (anc.)
Total	**12552**	**12708**	**13369**	**13721**	**14879**	**14884**	**15419**	**16769**	**17607**	**25315**	**Total**

General Note.
Dry resin content of polymerized propylene. (SITC, Rev.3: 57511-0).

Remarque générale.
Teneur en résine sèche du propylène polymérisé. (CTCI, Rev.3: 57511-0).

[1] Incomplete coverage.
[2] Source: United Nations Economic Commission for Europe (ECE), (Geneva).

[3] 1998 data are confidential.
[4] Sales.
[5] Wet weight of resins and plastic materials.

[1] Couverture incomplète.
[2] Source: Commission économique des Nations Unies pour l'Europe (CEE), (Genève).

[3] Pour 1998, les données sont confidentielles.
[4] Ventes.
[5] Poids mouillé des résines et câbles non cellulosiques.

Polystyrene
Polystyrène

ISIC-BASED CODE - CODE BASE CITI

3513-25

Unit : Thousand metric tons   Unité : Milliers de tonnes métriques

Country or area	1990	1991	1992	1993	1994	1995	1996	1997	1998	1999	Pays ou zone
America, North	**6**	**6**	**7**	**175**	**223**	**290**	**332**	**384**	**553**	**614**	**Amérique du Nord**
Mexico	6.3	6.4	7.5	#175.3	223.2	290.1	332.0	383.5	552.7	614.1	Mexique
America, South	**198**	**248**	**230**	**247**	**284**	**302**	**275**	**285**	**290**	**341**	**Amérique du Sud**
Argentina	34.3	46.0	52.4	49.2	62.9	65.4	*67.9	...	...	...	Argentine
Brazil	134.1	154.7	136.6	154.4	168.2	186.2	159.4	143.1	152.6	180.4	Brésil
Chile	1.2	1.3	1.4	1.4	...	...	...	...	...	...	Chili
Colombia	28.9	...	39.4	41.9	51.4	49.5	...	59.5	50.1	...	Colombie
Asia	**3020**	**3169**	**3014**	**3156**	**3358**	**3491**	**3687**	**3731**	**3468**	**3693**	**Asie**
China	87.8	41.0	46.8	...	...	...	...	...	...	...	Chine
Hong Kong SAR[1]	226.5	216.5	175.4	285.8	...	337.0	392.0	335.7	368.3	...	Hong-Kong RAS[1]
Japan	2092.2	2121.4	2005.0	1965.6	2098.5	2149.1	2177.7	2201.0	1974.8	2037.6	Japon
Kazakhstan[2]	...	...	...	...	...	...	30.1	2.5	3.1	...	Kazakhstan[2]
Korea, Republic of	592.0	758.5	754.3	809.0	869.4	904.6	999.6	1104.1	1037.8	1105.1	Corée, République de
Turkey	21.9	19.6	20.5	25.0	27.4	29.8	29.5	29.1	25.1	23.5	Turquie
Europe	**2693**	**3610**	**3452**	**3392**	**3372**	**3245**	**2906**	**2583**	**2622**	**2633**	**Europe**
Belgium	408.8	383.3	388.6	453.1	[3]328.6	[3]554.7	[3]266.2	[3]275.9	[3]232.3	[3]319.2	Belgique
Bulgaria	18.6	...	13.1	13.4	12.9	13.4	11.6	9.0	...	...	Bulgarie
Croatia	..	61.2	63.8	64.3	67.5	55.8	64.1	61.3	64.2	...	Croatie
Denmark[4]	0.7	...	0.1	0.1	0.2	0.2	0.2	0.3	0.3	0.4	Danemark[4]
Czechoslovakia(former)	83.2	62.6	..	..	..	..	..	..	..	..	Tchécoslovaquie(anc.)
Czech Republic	..	..	...	...	65.2	70.3	79.6	84.1	86.0	101.1	République tchèque
France	[5]541.8	[5]529.6	[5]509.1	[5]481.1	[5]533.4	...	[2]441.0	...	...	...	France
Germany	..	...	...	...	[2]656.2	627.6	554.5	532.2	629.7	...	Allemagne
German D.R.(former)	29.4	..	..	..	..	..	..	..	..	..	R.D.A. (anc.)
Hungary	...	...	...	...	...	271.9	[2]106.2	[2]82.6	89.0	90.8	Hongrie
Italy	352.7	337.0	306.2	252.3	277.0	271.9	279.0	290.8	287.0	290.8	Italie
Netherlands	...	...	...	...	[2]402.5	[2]388.3	[2]449.6	[2]232.4	[2]197.3	[4] [6]225.5	Pays-Bas
Poland	19.1	20.8	25.8	31.5	33.8	46.2	46.5	48.9	51.5	70.6	Pologne
Portugal	...	...	...	...	[2]0.1	[2]0.1	[2]0.1	[2]0.1	[2]0.1	8.0	Portugal
Romania	17.3	13.8	8.2	6.7	5.1	4.7	4.2	3.5	2.0	0.7	Roumanie
Russian Federation	..	190.8	166.9	151.5	104.5	98.6	53.9	48.2	35.1	68.3	Fédération de Russie
Slovakia[2]	..	..	...	...	...	...	0.5	0.8	...	...	Slovaquie[2]
Slovenia	..	0.0	0.0	0.0	0.5	0.0	0.0	...	...	...	Slovénie
Spain	132.5	144.3	146.2	130.3	157.6	139.6	156.8	196.7	165.8	168.6	Espagne
Sweden	22.1	23.8	23.9	22.6	27.7	29.7	[2]31.1	58.4	68.0	71.5	Suède
Ukraine	..	125.8	81.2	41.3	20.7	8.3	11.4	4.0	10.1	23.8	Ukraine
United Kingdom	...	...	...	548.3	585.3	336.6	349.4	[2]386.6	470.4	...	Royaume-Uni
Total	**5919**	**7033**	**6703**	**6971**	**7237**	**7328**	**7200**	**6982**	**6932**	**7282**	**Total**

General Note.
Dry resin content of polymerized styrene. (SITC, Rev.3: 57210-0).

Remarque générale.
Teneur en résine sèche du styrène polymérisé. (CTCI, Rev.3: 57210-0).

[1] 1999 data are confidential.
[2] Source: United Nations Economic Commission for Europe (ECE), (Geneva).

[3] Incomplete coverage.
[4] Sales.

[5] Polystyrene and its copolymers.
[6] Production by establishments employing 20 or more persons.

[1] Pour 1999, les données sont confidentielles.
[2] Source: Commission économique des Nations Unies pour l'Europe (CEE), (Genève).

[3] Couverture incomplète.
[4] Ventes.

[5] Polystyrène et ses copolymères.
[6] Production des établissements occupant 20 personnes ou plus.

Polyvinylchloride
Chlorure de polyvinyle

ISIC-BASED CODE - CODE BASE CITI
3513-28

Unit : Thousand metric tons · Unité : Milliers de tonnes métriques

Country or area	1990	1991	1992	1993	1994	1995	1996	1997	1998	1999	Pays ou zone
Africa	**14**	**12**	**7**	**12**	**17**	**19**	**15**	**13**	**16**	**9**	**Afrique**
Algeria	14.2	12.1	7.0	12.0	17.2	19.0	14.8	13.5	16.1	8.6	Algérie
America, North	**5724**	**5618**	**5730**	**5778**	**5835**	**5811**	**5866**	**5916**	**5922**	**5986**	**Amérique du Nord**
Canada	...	286.9	385.4	419.2	470.1	...	496.8	539.5	528.8	...	Canada
Mexico	...	...	...	373.2	378.7	378.5	382.8	390.6	407.3	473.9	Mexique
United States[1]	...	...	...	...	4986.0	...	...	...	...	...	Etats-Unis[1]
America, South	**750**	**747**	**716**	**730**	**821**	**1031**	**968**	**978**	**983**	**1014**	**Amérique du Sud**
Argentina	104.5	105.7	90.9	85.3	91.0	104.8	102.2	102.6	105.2	96.8	Argentine
Brazil	504.3	500.3	488.9	510.8	[2]691.5	[2]671.0	[2]724.9	[2]734.3	[2]736.6	[2]776.0	Brésil
Colombia	...	...	135.9	134.1	38.3	255.2	...	...	...	...	Colombie
Asia	**3643**	**3819**	**3965**	**3941**	**4103**	**4383**	**4689**	**4878**	**4641**	**4794**	**Asie**
China	785.3	813.1	904.2	...	...	...	...	...	...	...	Chine
Hong Kong SAR	60.3	95.3	83.4	70.0	68.8	58.1	15.0	19.3	15.4	16.8	Hong-Kong RAS
Indonesia	85.7	...	...	137.6	141.0	...	...	...	...	...	Indonésie
Japan	2048.8	2055.1	1982.9	1979.8	2110.7	2274.2	2511.0	2626.0	2457.2	2460.5	Japon
Korea, Republic of	526.5	602.1	725.5	760.3	791.4	914.2	1004.6	1087.5	1012.8	1169.9	Corée, République de
Turkey	136.7	131.6	147.8	159.3	156.5	181.0	202.6	189.3	199.6	191.1	Turquie
Europe	**5252**	**5925**	**5875**	**5854**	**6487**	**6287**	**6563**	**6735**	**6658**	**7397**	**Europe**
Belgium	278.8	266.0	284.5	307.7	797.0	792.4	829.1	824.9	768.7	860.9	Belgique
Bulgaria	17.5	6.8	5.5	2.7	3.5	1.1	2.0	1.4	...	...	Bulgarie
Croatia	..	67.9	70.8	44.3	78.3	93.4	44.6	47.8	43.6	...	Croatie
Denmark[3]	0.1	0.1	0.4	0.3	0.1	0.1	0.1	...	0.6	...	Danemark[3]
Czechoslovakia(former)	197.6	187.8	..	..	..	..	..	..	..	..	Tchécoslovaquie(anc.)
Czech Republic	..	..	...	...	128.3	89.7	125.4	130.1	118.7	130.2	République tchèque
France	1061.7	1050.5	1124.1	1203.0	1177.9	[1][2]1061.7	[1][2]1181.3	[1][2]1200.3	[1][2]1151.4	...	France
Germany	..	1328.2	1280.3	1209.7	1263.6	1228.4	1294.2	1415.8	1305.4	...	Allemagne
Germany(Fed.Rep.)	1320.9	..	..	..	..	..	..	..	..	..	Allemagne(Rép.féd.)
German D.R.(former)	258.8	..	..	..	..	..	..	..	..	..	R.D.A. (anc.)
Greece	79.1	77.7	79.3	...	...	...	[1]94.8	[1]105.9	108.3	...	Grèce
Hungary	185.6	171.4	177.0	183.5	118.2	194.0	226.6	283.0	249.1	276.6	Hongrie
Italy	617.6	621.5	617.4	611.8	599.1	575.6	628.1	629.1	598.9	446.6	Italie
Netherlands	...	...	...	...	[1]5.1	[1]4.3	[1]3.4	...	...	5.6	Pays-Bas
Poland	203.4	194.8	220.0	212.1	202.3	225.3	254.4	285.3	266.0	259.4	Pologne
Portugal	...	...	145.9	159.9	174.4	165.2	179.2	181.4	183.8	207.7	Portugal
Romania	154.9	112.6	91.5	96.6	138.2	130.9	123.1	132.3	123.3	130.4	Roumanie
Russian Federation	..	480.9	426.3	352.8	332.5	283.3	158.1	266.0	296.6	419.4	Fédération de Russie
Slovakia	..	..	72.8	57.9	63.0	70.9	71.5	66.3	68.2	65.6	Slovaquie
Spain	346.6	366.6	372.2	449.5	491.6	458.5	508.9	505.5	503.2	526.4	Espagne
Ukraine	..	114.9	107.0	59.2	57.3	60.5	14.6	15.1	11.7	0.4	Ukraine
United Kingdom	165.4	...	...	689.1	756.1	750.6	810.8	[1]585.2	790.3	...	Royaume-Uni
Yugoslavia	..	34.5	22.3	0.0	0.0	0.1	9.3	44.3	50.0	8.0	Yougoslavie
T.F.Yug.Rep. Macedonia	..	24.5	9.2	2.1	...	...	4.0	10.3	15.7	5.1	L'ex-RY Macédoine
Yugoslavia, SFR	198.7	..	..	..	..	..	..	..	..	..	Yougoslavie, RSF
USSR (former)[1]	605.6	..	..	..	..	..	..	..	..	..	URSS (anc.)[1]
Total	**15989**	**16121**	**16293**	**16315**	**17263**	**17531**	**18101**	**18520**	**18220**	**19200**	**Total**

General Note.
Dry resin content of polyvinylchloride (PVC) derived from polymerisation of vinylchloride monomer and peroxide catalysts. (SITC, Rev.3: 57310-0).

Remarque générale.
Teneur en résine sèche du chlorure de polyvinyle obtenu par polymérisation du chlorure de vinyle en présence de catalyseurs (péroxydes). (CTCI, Rev.3: 57310-0).

[1] Source: United Nations Economic Commission for Europe (ECE), (Geneva).

[2] Including other polyvinyl resins.

[3] Sales.

[1] Source: Commission économique des Nations Unies pour l'Europe (CEE), (Genève).

[2] Y compris les autres résines de polyvinyle.

[3] Ventes.

Regenerated cellulose
Cellulose régénérée

ISIC-BASED CODE - CODE BASE CITI

3513-31

Unit : Thousand metric tons — Unité : Milliers de tonnes métriques

Country or area	1990	1991	1992	1993	1994	1995	1996	1997	1998	1999	Pays ou zone
America, North	**15**	**14**	**12**	**10**	**10**	**8**	**7**	**5**	**4**	**2**	**Amérique du Nord**
Mexico	14.8	14.1	11.9	9.7	10.1	...	...	...	...	...	Mexique
Asia	..	**3**	**3**	**4**	**2**	**1**	**1**	**1**	**0**	**0**	**Asie**
Azerbaijan	..	...	...	4.1	[1]1.6	[1]1.2	[1]1.0	0.5	0.5	0.3	Azerbaïdjan
Europe	**481**	**617**	**594**	**574**	**481**	**593**	**553**	**504**	**478**	**491**	**Europe**
Belgium[1]	...	...	...	...	19.7	21.9	26.9	24.9	24.8	...	Belgique[1]
Bulgaria[1]	...	...	...	...	2.0	1.9	2.3	2.4	...	...	Bulgarie[1]
Czechoslovakia(former)	13.7	10.7	..	...	..	...	...	...	..	..	Tchécoslovaquie(anc.)
Czech Republic	..	..	...	...	7.9	7.5	7.2	7.1	[1]1.4	...	République tchèque
Finland[2]	32.9	33.8	...	...	...	...	...	...	...	...	Finlande[2]
Germany[1]	..	...	...	...	...	145.4	140.0	...	...	...	Allemagne[1]
Hungary	[1]9.8	[1]3.8	[1]5.0	[1]5.3	[1]5.1	[1]6.6	...	7.5	...	...	Hongrie
Netherlands	...	...	...	...	[1]20.1	[1]24.2	[1]18.0	[1]19.6	[1]18.0	[3] [4]18.8	Pays-Bas
Poland[1]	6.6	3.4	3.1	2.5	2.1	1.6	1.1	0.3	0.2	...	Pologne[1]
Romania[1]	...	...	...	...	162.9	234.5	203.3	154.5	129.4	...	Roumanie[1]
Russian Federation	..	20.8	20.2	13.4	2.2	1.8	0.6	1.2	[1]2.3	...	Fédération de Russie
Slovakia	..	..	...	6.3	...	...	...	...	...	...	Slovaquie
Slovenia	..	3.6	2.0	2.7	2.6	1.9	...	...	...	...	Slovénie
Spain	30.0	23.6	12.1	12.2	...	5.4	5.9	1.8	1.1	1.2	Espagne
Sweden	22.1	14.7	10.1	20.2	11.0	12.0	11.4	13.8	28.4	30.1	Suède
Ukraine	..	4.9	3.3	1.7	0.3	0.2	0.0	0.1	0.0	0.0	Ukraine
United Kingdom	...	...	...	59.7	51.7	87.6	88.1	86.4	80.8	...	Royaume-Uni
Yugoslavia	..	...	...	...	[1]0.6	[1]0.4	[1]0.6	0.2	0.5	...	Yougoslavie
Total	**495**	**635**	**609**	**588**	**492**	**602**	**560**	**509**	**482**	**494**	**Total**

General Note.
Net dry content of regenerated cellulose, cellulose nitrate, cellulose acetate and other cellulose derivatives. Collodions and vulcanized fibres are excluded. (SITC, Rev.3: 57550-1).

[1] Source: United Nations Economic Commission for Europe (ECE), (Geneva).

[2] Wet weight of resins and plastic materials.
[3] Production by establishments employing 20 or more persons.
[4] Sales.

Remarque générale.
Teneur en cellulose sèche de la cellulose régénérée, du nitrate de cellulose, de l'acétate de cellulose et d'autres dérivés de la cellulose. Cette rubrique ne comprend pas les collodions et les fibres vulcanisées. (CTCI, Rev.3:57550-1).

[1] Source: Commission économique des Nations Unies pour l'Europe (CEE), (Genève).

[2] Poids mouillé des résines et câbles non cellulosiques.
[3] Production des établissements occupant 20 personnes ou plus.
[4] Ventes.

Non-cellulosic continuous fibres
Fibres continues non cellulosiques

ISIC-BASED CODE - CODE BASE CITI

3513-37

Unit : Thousand metric tons

Unité : Milliers de tonnes métriques

Country or area	1990	1991	1992	1993	1994	1995	1996	1997	1998	1999	Pays ou zone
Africa	**92**	**92**	**103**	**120**	**116**	**123**	**124**	**127**	**128**	**131**	**Afrique**
Egypt[1]	10.7	9.7	9.1	11.7	14.7	14.2	14.3	14.8	...	...	Egypte[1]
Kenya[1]	*6.3	*6.3	8.8	8.8	9.8	12.0	*12.0	12.5	...	...	Kenya[1]
Morocco[1]	...	...	...	...	11.3	13.2	14.4	14.9	...	...	Maroc[1]
Nigeria[1]	*4.7	*4.8	9.6	20.9	10.2	10.5	9.9	9.6	...	...	Nigéria[1]
South Africa[1]	57.3	57.5	61.8	64.8	70.0	73.3	73.6	75.2	...	...	Afrique du Sud[1]
America, North	**1495**	**1546**	**1567**	**1602**	**1836**	**1917**	**1972**	**2087**	**2031**	**2061**	**Amérique du Nord**
Canada[1]	65.4	65.6	59.9	56.9	90.3	96.5	103.6	103.4	...	...	Canada[1]
Costa Rica[1]	6.1	6.3	6.5	6.4	7.7	7.7	7.8	7.9	...	...	Costa Rica[1]
Mexico	163.4	170.2	175.7	185.6	199.2	215.5	228.0	250.8	243.1	235.0	Mexique
United States[1]	1259.7	1303.7	1324.9	1353.4	1539.2	1597.2	1632.9	1725.0	...	...	Etats-Unis[1]
America, South	**227**	**241**	**236**	**257**	**239**	**252**	**264**	**282**	**268**	**272**	**Amérique du Sud**
Argentina	28.0	33.7	32.0	34.9	37.0	[1]38.3	[1]43.2	[1]48.7	...	...	Argentine
Bolivia[1]	...	...	...	...	2.6	2.7	2.7	2.7	...	...	Bolivie[1]
Brazil[1]	120.9	124.4	118.9	133.3	141.3	144.0	150.2	155.5	...	...	Brésil[1]
Chile[1]	5.4	5.2	5.3	5.6	2.6	2.4	4.0	4.5	...	...	Chili[1]
Colombia[1]	41.5	43.8	44.7	47.9	34.6	40.0	39.4	44.6	...	...	Colombie[1]
Ecuador[1]	5.2	5.1	5.3	5.4	4.6	5.6	5.2	5.6	...	...	Equateur[1]
Peru[1]	10.2	10.4	10.7	10.5	5.7	7.5	7.5	7.6	...	...	Pérou[1]
Uruguay[1]	1.8	1.9	1.5	1.5	0.6	0.8	0.7	0.9	...	...	Uruguay[1]
Venezuela[1]	11.5	13.6	14.7	15.0	9.9	10.5	11.2	11.6	...	...	Venezuela[1]
Asia	**2588**	**2786**	**3578**	**3903**	**4134**	**4613**	**5099**	**5851**	**5627**	**5856**	**Asie**
Armenia	..	2.1	0.4	0.3	0.2	0.3	0.4	0.3	0.1	0.0	Arménie
Bangladesh[1]	0.8	0.6	1.0	1.8	4.2	11.8	14.6	14.3	...	...	Bangladesh[1]
China[1]	531.2	599.0	821.9	966.7	988.0	1168.7	1286.3	1446.7	...	...	Chine[1]
India	[1]259.3	[1]263.1	[1]315.4	[1]357.1	[1]378.9	[2]429.9	[2]549.5	[1]759.5	...	...	Inde
Indonesia[1]	148.0	167.5	235.0	340.2	402.8	417.6	477.1	523.9	...	...	Indonésie[1]
Iran(Islamic Rep. of)[1]	12.2	23.8	24.2	24.5	24.6	26.7	27.8	28.0	...	...	Iran(Rép. islamique)[1]
Israel[1]	10.8	8.8	8.9	7.9	10.2	11.1	10.6	11.2	...	...	Israël[1]
Japan[1]	702.1	715.1	719.1	670.9	661.8	668.8	661.7	668.8	...	...	Japon[1]
Korea, Republic of[1]	*670.7	*736.0	...	...	1116.0	1224.2	1367.1	1586.4	...	...	Corée, République de[1]
Malaysia[1]	0.0	0.0	0.0	7.7	28.4	71.0	71.7	100.5	...	...	Malaisie[1]
Pakistan[1]	31.5	36.8	34.1	49.0	92.9	91.5	94.8	99.1	...	...	Pakistan[1]
Philippines[1]	14.2	16.5	20.5	14.1	22.3	22.7	11.1	9.2	...	...	Philippines[1]
Saudi Arabia[1]	...	...	...	...	0.0	0.0	9.4	11.8	...	...	Arabie saoudite[1]
Singapore[1]	...	...	...	...	1.6	3.3	3.6	4.2	...	...	Singapour[1]
Sri Lanka[1]	*2.1	*2.5	3.3	2.6	2.9	5.0	5.4	5.3	...	...	Sri Lanka[1]
Thailand[1]	69.9	89.2	116.1	176.1	220.5	250.9	273.5	307.9	...	...	Thaïlande[1]
Turkey	127.2	116.3	153.3	158.5	178.3	209.8	234.9	273.4	298.6	287.4	Turquie
Europe	**1276**	**1595**	**1607**	**1415**	**1416**	**1431**	**1354**	**1389**	**1373**	**1374**	**Europe**
Belarus	..	115.6	102.7	69.8	41.2	43.5	46.6	63.4	66.2	66.9	Bélarus
Belgium[1 3]	84.8	80.0	92.5	83.7	86.3	...	...	...	...	...	Belgique[1 3]
Bulgaria[1]	22.0	20.1	16.4	14.2	10.0	9.6	9.5	10.3	...	...	Bulgarie[1]
Czechoslovakia(former)	78.0	59.9	..	..	..	..	..	..	...	..	Tchécoslovaquie(anc.)
Czech Republic[1]	..	..	0.4	0.3	0.6	0.4	0.4	0.2	...	...	République tchèque[1]
Finland	2.3	2.0	1.5	2.1	2.8	2.8	2.2	...	...	...	Finlande
France[1]	56.9	51.9	51.0	47.7	63.1	...	...	...	...	...	France[1]
Germany	..	[1]375.0	[1]376.6	368.9	410.7	427.6	407.8	448.7	434.0	...	Allemagne
Germany(Fed.Rep.)	401.4	..	..	..	..	..	..	..	..	...	Allemagne(Rép.féd.)
German D.R.(former)[1]	57.0	..	..	..	..	..	..	..	..	..	R.D.A. (anc.)[1]
Greece[1]	7.0	6.0	6.1	5.6	9.5	8.5	...	...	...	...	Grèce[1]
Hungary	5.6	2.9	3.0	[1]2.2	2.9	2.5	[1]2.8	[1]3.9	6.5	5.5	Hongrie
Ireland[1]	17.8	21.2	18.8	22.8	24.4	...	...	...	...	...	Irlande[1]
Italy[1]	201.1	186.8	195.7	176.9	202.2	...	...	...	...	...	Italie[1]
Latvia	..	[4]39.5	[4]36.6	26.7	17.3	19.1	16.1	12.9	15.7	6.2	Lettonie
Poland	63.8	47.4	52.5	52.1	62.2	66.1	65.0	67.7	48.7	43.1	Pologne
Portugal[1]	0.0	1.0	1.5	1.6	1.9	1.3	...	...	...	...	Portugal[1]
Romania[1]	39.2	45.1	34.1	27.9	21.6	22.8	21.7	23.3	...	...	Roumanie[1]
Russian Federation	..	285.3	266.8	181.1	102.1	104.5	75.6	54.1	62.7	73.2	Fédération de Russie
Slovakia	..	..	...	66.4	79.9	75.0	65.1	[1]55.6	...	...	Slovaquie

For general note and footnotes, see end of table.

Voir la fin du tableau pour la remarque générale et les notes.

Non-cellulosic continuous fibres (continued)
Fibres continues non cellulosiques (suite)

ISIC-BASED CODE - CODE BASE CITI

3513-37

Unit : Thousand metric tons   Unité : Milliers de tonnes métriques

Country or area	1990	1991	1992	1993	1994	1995	1996	1997	1998	1999	Pays ou zone
Slovenia	..	10.1	8.5	7.5	8.7	10.7	2.0	0.0	0.0	...	Slovénie
Spain	[1]77.1	[1]66.3	[1]81.5	82.1	93.4	91.1	...	...	...	...	Espagne
Sweden	0.7	0.6	0.9	0.9	1.3	1.2	0.9	...	...	...	Suède
Switzerland[1]	73.7	68.6	72.1	67.6	72.6	85.0	...	...	...	...	Suisse[1]
Ukraine	..	16.1	11.4	8.7	4.3	1.6	0.3	0.5	0.2	0.1	Ukraine
United Kingdom[1]	87.1	76.4	80.2	...	...	...	...	...	...	...	Royaume-Uni[1]
Yugoslavia[1]	..	...	...	...	15.9	17.1	17.4	18.1	...	...	Yougoslavie[1]
USSR (former)	527.3	..	..	..	..	..	..	..	..	..	URSS (anc.)
Oceania	15	14	12	13	12	13	13	20	15	15	Océanie
Australia[1]	15.3	14.1	11.8	12.5	11.6	12.5	13.4	20.3	...	...	Australie[1]
Total	6221	6273	7103	7309	7753	8349	8827	9756	9443	9709	Total

General Note.

Non-cellulosic (synthetic) continuous fibres made of natural polymers based on materials such as casein, or of synthetic polymers mainly from coal and oil distillation products. Textile glass fibres are excluded. They comprise filament yarn composed of two or more grouped, continuous, fine filaments, usually slightly twisted together, monofilaments other than those for use as bristle, and slit film mainly an olefin product made by slitting attenuated film to desired widths and often fibrillated by twisting. Waste, spun yarns and other manufactures are excluded. (SITC, Rev.3: 65141-0, 65150-0, 65160-0, 65188-0).

Remarque générale.

Fibres continues non cellulosiques artificielles ou synthétiques de polymères naturels obtenus à partir de matériaux comme la caséine, ou de polymères synthétiques obtenus principalement à partir de produits de la distillation du charbon ou du pétrole. Cette rubrique comprend les filés constitués d'un ensemble d'au moins deux filaments fins et continus soumis en général à une légère torsion. Les monofils autres que ceux servant à la fabrication des soies de brosserie, les lames obtenues en refendant à la largeur désirée un film fin de matière à base d'oléfines et en leur donnant souvent par torsion le crochet désiré. Cette rubrique ne comprend pas les fibres textiles de verre, les déchets, les filés de fibres discontinues et les autres produits non cellulosiques. (CTCI, Rev.3: 65141-0, 65150-0, 65160-0, 65188-0).

[1] Source: Fiber Economics Bureau, Inc. (U.S.A.).
[2] Official figures.
[3] Including production in Netherlands and Luxembourg.
[4] Including discontinuous fibres.

[1] Source: Fiber Economics Bureau, Inc. (Etats-Unis).
[2] Données officielles.
[3] Y compris la production des Pays-Bas et du Luxembourg.
[4] Y compris fibres discontinues.

Cellulosic continuous filaments
Filaments cellulosiques continus

ISIC-BASED CODE - CODE BASE CITI

3513-40

Unit : Thousand metric tons

Unité : Milliers de tonnes métriques

Country or area	1990	1991	1992	1993	1994	1995	1996	1997	1998	1999	Pays ou zone
Africa	**8**	**8**	**8**	**8**	**8**	**8**	**8**	**7**	**7**	**7**	**Afrique**
Egypt[1]	7.9	7.9	7.5	7.6	7.6	7.5	7.5	7.4	...	...	Egypte[1]
America, North	**115**	**118**	**120**	**128**	**128**	**123**	**128**	**114**	**124**	**124**	**Amérique du Nord**
Canada[1]	11.2	11.3	11.5	15.6	15.3	15.1	15.2	14.2	...	...	Canada[1]
Cuba	0.5	0.3	0.3	[1]0.0	[1]0.0	[1]0.0	...	...	...	...	Cuba
Mexico	10.3	10.0	8.9	9.4	11.8	[1]13.5	[1]13.5	[1]14.4	...	...	Mexique
United States[1]	93.5	96.7	99.7	102.7	101.2	94.5	99.1	85.6	...	...	Etats-Unis[1]
America, South	**25**	**23**	**21**	**24**	**24**	**25**	**24**	**21**	**23**	**21**	**Amérique du Sud**
Argentina	2.7	3.3	3.2	3.5	3.9	4.1	4.7	4.1	3.8	2.0	Argentine
Brazil[1]	14.9	11.7	10.3	13.4	12.3	12.0	10.3	8.6	...	...	Brésil[1]
Chile[1]	1.3	1.4	1.4	1.0	1.1	2.0	2.0	2.0	...	...	Chili[1]
Colombia[1]	2.0	1.9	1.8	1.8	1.9	2.0	2.0	1.1	...	...	Colombie[1]
Peru[1]	1.4	1.4	1.4	1.3	1.4	1.4	...	...	...	...	Pérou[1]
Uruguay[1]	1.6	1.4	1.0	1.5	2.0	2.0	2.0	1.8	...	...	Uruguay[1]
Venezuela[1]	1.4	1.5	1.5	1.6	1.6	1.7	2.0	2.0	...	...	Venezuela[1]
Asia	**237**	**231**	**220**	**220**	**225**	**233**	**232**	**225**	**227**	**226**	**Asie**
Bangladesh[1]	1.3	1.2	0.8	1.0	3.0	4.0	5.0	4.4	...	...	Bangladesh[1]
China[1]	56.7	57.0	59.9	64.1	65.2	70.2	73.0	72.0	...	...	Chine[1]
India[1]	58.2	59.0	58.8	60.9	66.4	69.3	67.3	63.2	...	...	Inde[1]
Iraq[1]	3.0	3.0	2.0	2.1	2.1	2.5	2.4	2.8	...	...	Iraq[1]
Japan[1]	99.1	96.5	85.8	82.4	78.2	77.7	74.2	73.3	...	...	Japon[1]
Korea, Republic of[1]	15.8	10.9	9.2	6.1	6.6	6.6	6.8	6.3	...	...	Corée, République de[1]
Pakistan[1]	2.8	3.0	3.1	3.1	3.1	3.0	3.2	3.2	...	...	Pakistan[1]
Europe	**93**	**417**	**356**	**290**	**220**	**244**	**195**	**214**	**207**	**190**	**Europe**
Belarus	..	39.4	28.2	13.1	8.1	9.5	10.7	13.2	14.3	13.0	Bélarus
Belgium[2]	8.0	7.7	8.2	6.8	...	...	...	...	...	...	Belgique[2]
Bulgaria[1]	4.3	4.2	4.1	4.0	4.9	4.6	4.7	4.2	...	...	Bulgarie[1]
Czechoslovakia(former)[3]	16.1	9.2	..	..	..	..	..	..	..	..	Tchécoslovaquie(anc.)[3]
Czech Republic	..	..	[1]3.9	3.2	4.6	5.5	6.3	5.7	5.5	5.1	République tchèque
Germany	..	...	...	...	...	...	...	59.9	...	...	Allemagne
German D.R.(former)	26.1	...	..	..	..	..	..	..	..	..	R.D.A. (anc.)
Lithuania	..	6.1	4.2	3.4	4.6	8.3	11.2	13.1	10.7	6.6	Lituanie
Poland	13.8	8.1	6.0	6.4	5.8	5.5	5.0	3.9	3.6	2.4	Pologne
Romania[1]	9.8	6.2	4.4	1.6	6.6	6.1	6.3	7.4	...	...	Roumanie[1]
Russian Federation	..	243.3	207.2	167.4	96.0	111.3	58.8	74.8	70.8	62.5	Fédération de Russie
Slovakia	..	..	...	6.5	[1]6.9	7.5	6.0	6.8	...	...	Slovaquie
Ukraine	..	23.5	19.7	17.3	14.4	17.3	16.1	15.4	15.2	15.4	Ukraine
Yugoslavia	..	9.0	3.7	0.0	0.7	1.1	2.2	1.5	1.8	0.7	Yougoslavie
Yugoslavia, SFR[1]	15.2	..	..	..	..	..	..	..	..	..	Yougoslavie, RSF[1]
USSR (former)	199.4	..	...	...	...	...	...	...	...	..	URSS (anc.)
Total	**678**	**796**	**724**	**669**	**605**	**633**	**586**	**581**	**587**	**569**	**Total**

General Note.

Rayon and acetate (artificial) continuous filaments produced by chemical transformation of natural organic polymers from cellulose. They comprise filament yarn composed of two or more grouped, continuous, fine filaments, usually slightly twisted together, and monofilaments other than those for use as bristle. Waste of these fibres, spun yarn and other manufactures of rayon and acetate are excluded. (SITC, Rev.3: 65170-1).

Remarque générale.

Filaments artificiels continus de rayonne ou d'acétate obtenus par une transformation chimique de polymères organiques naturels cellulosiques. Cette rubrique comprend les filés constitués d'un ensemble d'au moins deux filaments fins continus, soumis en général à une légère torsion, ainsi que les monofils autres que ceux servant à la fabrication des soies de brosserie, mais non les déchets de ces fibres, les filés de fibres discontinues et les autres produits fabriqués à partir de rayonne ou d'acétate. (CTCI, Rev.3: 65170-1).

[1] Source: Fiber Economics Bureau, Inc. (U.S.A.).
[2] Excluding acetate fibres.
[3] Production of acetate fibres is nil or negligible.

[1] Source: Fiber Economics Bureau, Inc. (Etats-Unis).
[2] Non compris les fibres d'acétate.
[3] Production de fibres d'acétate nulle ou négligeable.

Paints, cellulose
Peintures cellulosiques

ISIC-BASED CODE - CODE BASE CITI

3521-01A

Unit : Thousand metric tons
Unité : Milliers de tonnes métriques

Country or area	1990	1991	1992	1993	1994	1995	1996	1997	1998	1999	Pays ou zone
Africa											**Afrique**
Burundi[1]	0.9	1.0	1.0	0.8	...	...	...	...	...	...	Burundi[1]
Kenya[2]	9.3	7.9	*3.9	4.8	4.9	4.8	*4.8	...	...	...	Kenya[2]
Madagascar[1][3]	2.4	2.0	1.6	2.8	2.2	2.1	2.0	2.3	1.8	...	Madagascar[1][3]
Nigeria[1][2]	13.7	21.5	19.1	20.0	5.5	4.4	...	...	...	...	Nigéria[1][2]
America, North											**Amérique du Nord**
Antigua and Barbuda	...	...	...	[4]1.0	0.2	0.2	0.2	...	...	...	Antigua-et-Barbuda
America, South											**Amérique du Sud**
Bolivia	0.1	0.1	0.1	0.0	0.0	*0.0	...	...	...	...	Bolivie
Asia											**Asie**
India[5]	320.3	302.0	300.8	310.9	410.8	500.8	473.8	483.9	569.8	633.2	Inde[5]
Indonesia	..	0.2	0.3	0.6	...	...	...	...	...	...	Indonésie
Japan	49.1	45.6	41.9	37.7	36.5	35.4	33.9	33.1	28.8	27.6	Japon
Korea, Republic of[2][6]	246.8	247.2	271.8	240.4	...	...	...	...	...	...	Corée, République de[2][6]
Pakistan	11.2	14.3	19.0	16.6	9.4	6.9	8.0	8.0	5.9	6.5	Pakistan
Turkey	7.0	11.1	9.6	12.2	9.3	10.7	19.3	22.1	10.7	8.6	Turquie
Europe											**Europe**
Belarus	..	[1]178.1	125.4	80.3	45.9	47.6	56.4	80.5	82.4	77.0	Bélarus
Bulgaria	[1]94.8	[1]36.4	[1]34.7	[1]29.1	[1]31.6	[1]36.5	[1]42.1	[1]40.4	26.8	[1]21.3	Bulgarie
Croatia	..	1.4	0.8	0.7	0.5	0.3	0.3	0.3	0.3	...	Croatie
Denmark[7]	...	73.6	72.9	79.2	81.0	84.9	79.6	81.3	74.1	71.7	Danemark[7]
Czech Republic	..	..	...	...	24.1	29.4	28.8	27.8	26.0	26.0	République tchèque
Germany	..	72.3	68.7	61.2	62.4	# [1]635.5	[1]687.2	[1]692.4	[1]710.7	...	Allemagne
Germany(Fed.Rep.)	58.7	..	..	..	..	..	..	..	..	..	Allemagne(Rép.féd.)
German D.R.(former)	29.5	..	..	..	..	..	..	..	..	..	R.D.A. (anc.)
Greece[8]	72.6	73.9	82.2	...	...	...	...	...	...	...	Grèce[8]
Hungary	8.5	10.7	10.1	9.9	10.1	8.9	...	...	1.5	1.2	Hongrie
Lithuania	..	...	...	...	...	0.1	0.1	0.2	0.1	0.1	Lituanie
Norway	36.5	30.3	30.4	...	...	...	...	...	...	...	Norvège
Portugal	7.6	4.6	29.0	24.2	24.8	25.2	29.3	30.5	29.5	29.5	Portugal
Romania[1]	134.6	94.6	58.5	55.8	45.8	49.0	43.6	37.5	35.5	33.6	Roumanie[1]
Russian Federation	..	284.2	173.9	122.4	88.3	66.5	51.8	56.1	51.1	51.8	Fédération de Russie
Slovakia	..	..	...	...	...	...	27.6	20.2	19.2	10.3	Slovaquie
Slovenia	..	3.8	2.6	2.3	1.8	1.6	23.3	...	...	...	Slovénie
Spain	8.4	8.3	6.9	...	...	...	...	...	...	...	Espagne
Ukraine	..	73.0	55.6	21.5	8.9	5.5	4.3	3.2	2.9	2.4	Ukraine
Yugoslavia	..	1.7	1.5	0.7	0.8	0.7	0.9	0.9	1.1	0.8	Yougoslavie
Oceania											**Océanie**
Australia[2][9]	5.4	4.4	4.9	5.3	...	...	...	...	...	...	Australie[2][9]

General Note.
Paints, enamels and varnishes with cellulose derivative bases. (SITC, Rev.3: 53342-1A, 53343-1A).

Remarque générale.
Peintures, laques et vernis à base de dérivés de la cellulose. (CTCI, Rev.3: 53342-1A, 53343-1A).

[1] Including other paints.
[2] In thousand kilolitres.
[3] Including water paints.
[4] Twelve months beginning 21 March of year stated.
[5] Production by large and medium scale establishments only.
[6] Varnishes and lacquers with cellulose derivative base.
[7] Sales.
[8] Varnishes only.
[9] Twelve months ending 30 June of year stated.

[1] Y compris les autres peintures.
[2] En milliers de kilolitres.
[3] Y compris les peintures à l'eau.
[4] Période de douze mois commençant le 21 mars de l'année indiquée.
[5] Production des grandes et moyennes entreprises seulement.
[6] Vernis et laques à base de dérivés de la cellulose.
[7] Ventes.
[8] Vernis seulement.
[9] Période de douze mois finissant le 30 juin de l'année indiquée.

Paints, water
Peintures à l'eau

ISIC-BASED CODE - CODE BASE CITI

3521-04A

Unit : Thousand metric tons

Unité : Milliers de tonnes métriques

Country or area	1990	1991	1992	1993	1994	1995	1996	1997	1998	1999	Pays ou zone
Africa											**Afrique**
Congo	1.4	1.3	1.4	1.3	...	...	...	...	...	...	Congo
Ethiopia [1]	1.1	0.1	0.1	0.4	0.3	0.2	0.3	0.3	0.4	...	Éthiopie [1]
Kenya	0.4	0.1	0.0	0.1	0.0	0.0	0.1	...	...	...	Kenya
South Africa [1]	45.6	55.4	48.9	52.1	52.5	60.4	74.9	74.2	64.4	64.7	Afrique du Sud [1]
United Rep.Tanzania [1]	2.2	2.5	2.4	2.1	2.0	3.2	5.2	5.0	...	...	Rép. Unie de Tanzanie [1]
America, North											**Amérique du Nord**
Jamaica	3.1	2.1	2.6	[1]0.0	[1]0.0	[1]0.0	[1]0.0	[1]0.0	[1]0.0	0.0	Jamaïque
Mexico	61.6	64.7	69.8	69.1	68.2	[1]87.3	[1]98.4	[1]113.6	[1]120.3	[1]122.6	Mexique
America, South											**Amérique du Sud**
Argentina	49.2	...	...	...	...	...	...	...	...	...	Argentine
Bolivia	1.4	1.9	1.4	2.0	3.7	*3.0	...	...	...	...	Bolivie
Chile	17.1	19.2	23.2	26.5	29.5	30.3	31.3	34.0	39.3	34.9	Chili
Ecuador	...	...	[1]13.8	[1]18.2	[1]25.3	[1]28.8	[1]22.9	21.6	4.2	...	Equateur
Asia											**Asie**
Indonesia	70.3	...	148.3	154.4	192.4	184.6	...	...	194.8	...	Indonésie
Japan	398.6	382.1	374.2	363.6	373.8	377.0	411.3	413.4	364.8	373.5	Japon
Korea, Republic of [1]	74.6	102.9	108.4	97.6	...	...	...	...	...	...	Corée, République de [1]
Malaysia [1]	41.8	47.8	54.8	58.5	66.1	69.0	76.1	84.9	66.3	67.4	Malaisie [1]
Turkey	95.8	116.0	121.7	123.5	102.7	131.3	172.2	205.6	166.5	150.1	Turquie
Europe											**Europe**
Belgium	...	...	...	...	32.0	32.6	31.8	...	40.9	39.5	Belgique
Croatia	..	8.3	7.6	8.1	10.0	10.2	9.9	11.5	11.3	...	Croatie
Denmark [2]	37.1	35.6	44.4	47.5	42.9	44.9	47.3	51.7	49.6	52.7	Danemark [2]
Czech Republic	..	..	..	..	9.8	14.3	14.2	19.0	19.4	19.8	République tchèque
Finland	29.9	26.8	23.4	22.9	22.9	21.4	23.4	34.1	28.5	30.3	Finlande
Germany	..	...	695.6	812.9	854.8	908.0	...	1064.7	1073.1	...	Allemagne
Germany(Fed.Rep.)	538.6	..	..	..	..	..	..	..	..	..	Allemagne(Rép.féd.)
German D.R.(former)	47.5	..	..	..	..	..	..	..	..	..	R.D.A. (anc.)
Greece	...	...	...	45.8	50.1	51.4	101.9	119.1	59.4	...	Grèce
Hungary	0.0	0.0	...	...	...	...	...	...	34.2	41.3	Hongrie
Iceland	2.0	2.0	2.0	2.0	2.0	2.0	1.8	1.8	1.8	1.9	Islande
Latvia	..	0.4	0.2	0.1	0.1	0.5	0.5	1.1	0.8	2.1	Lettonie
Lithuania	..	...	...	...	...	0.1	0.1	0.1	0.0	0.0	Lituanie
Norway	16.9	16.0	14.7	14.6	...	...	...	18.2	...	...	Norvège
Portugal	78.4	75.1	77.1	64.9	72.5	67.6	81.9	90.8	104.1	100.5	Portugal
Russian Federation	..	47.4	37.1	25.9	21.6	15.7	12.3	13.0	11.6	7.6	Fédération de Russie
Slovakia	..	..	..	..	..	..	7.0	14.0	13.2	12.8	Slovaquie
Slovenia	..	31.9	15.7	15.9	22.3	26.2	5.8	4.9	4.1	6.4	Slovénie
Spain	382.3	408.2	371.9	228.0	240.4	249.5	260.4	278.3	...	...	Espagne
Sweden	66.4	52.4	49.0	61.5	59.6	68.7	54.7	53.7	60.6	59.6	Suède
Ukraine	..	32.9	29.6	14.6	8.0	4.8	3.4	2.3	2.0	2.4	Ukraine
United Kingdom	...	...	...	354	370	373	413	555	438	...	Royaume-Uni
Yugoslavia	..	1.7	1.7	0.5	0.6	0.5	0.4	0.5	0.2	0.1	Yougoslavie
Oceania											**Océanie**
Australia [1][3]	79.2	77.5	79.8	85.0	...	...	...	...	...	...	Australie [1][3]
Fiji [1][4]	2.2	2.3	2.6	2.8	2.6	2.4	2.4	2.6	2.8	...	Fidji [1][4]

General Note.

Water paints including aqueous emulsions and distempers in paste form or ready for use. (SITC, Rev.3: 53341-0A).

Remarque générale.

Peintures à l'eau, y compris les émulsions aqueuses et les détrempes à l'état pâteux ou prêtes à l'emploi. (CTCI, Rev.3: 53341-0A).

[1] In thousand kilolitres.
[2] Sales.
[3] Twelve months ending 30 June of year stated.
[4] Including cellulose paints and other paints.

[1] En milliers de kilolitres.
[2] Ventes.
[3] Période de douze mois finissant le 30 juin de l'année indiquée.
[4] Y compris les peintures cellulosiques et les autres peintures.

Paints, other
Autres peintures

ISIC-BASED CODE - CODE BASE CITI

3521-07A

Unit : Thousand metric tons

Unité : Milliers de tonnes métriques

Country or area	1990	1991	1992	1993	1994	1995	1996	1997	1998	1999	Pays ou zone
Africa											**Afrique**
Algeria[1]	103.0	83.0	91.0	84.0	102.0	94.0	89.0	90.0	91.0	97.0	Algérie[1]
Angola	2.6	1.9	1.0	...	...	...	...	...	...	...	Angola
Cameroon	...	6.0	5.7	4.7	7.3	3.1	...	...	...	...	Cameroun
Cape Verde[2]	...	0.0	0.0	0.0	0.0	0.1	...	...	...	...	Cap-Vert[2]
Central African Rep.	...	0.4	0.3	0.2	0.4	0.3	...	...	...	...	Rép. centrafricaine
Congo	1.4	1.3	...	...	...	...	...	...	...	...	Congo
Ethiopia	0.1	0.1	...	0.4	0.3	0.2	0.3	0.3	0.4	...	Ethiopie
Gabon	2.2	2.4	2.4	2.2	1.9	1.9	...	...	...	...	Gabon
Mali	0.8	0.5	0.7	0.6	0.5	0.3	0.6	...	...	...	Mali
Senegal	3.0	3.0	3.0	4.0	...	...	...	...	...	...	Sénégal
Seychelles[2]	...	...	...	0.4	0.4	0.3	0.4	0.5	0.6	0.5	Seychelles[2]
South Africa[2]	73.8	76.8	75.3	81.7	82.8	83.1	86.2	84.7	78.0	75.2	Afrique du Sud[2]
Uganda[2]	0.1	[1]0.3	[1]0.9	[1]1.2	[1]1.5	[1]1.9	[1]1.3	[2]2.4	2.4	2.5	Ouganda[2]
America, North											**Amérique du Nord**
Barbados[1 2]	2.6	2.6	2.2	2.3	2.0	2.5	2.3	2.9	2.1	2.5	Barbade[1 2]
Dominican Republic	12.2	13.9	16.3	16.7	17.7	18.8	18.8	21.0	22.6	25.9	Rép. dominicaine
Mexico[2]	18.3	20.0	22.0	29.0	29.3	21.3	28.0	34.3	37.0	38.4	Mexique[2]
America, South											**Amérique du Sud**
Argentina[3]	87.0	118.0	...	171.0	...	...	...	...	...	...	Argentine[3]
Bolivia	143.0	29.0	122.0	150.0	1.0	*0.0	...	...	...	...	Bolivie
Chile[4]	24.0	...	...	...	...	...	...	...	...	...	Chili[4]
Colombia	...	...	0.5	1.2	0.9	0.7	...	...	...	...	Colombie
Ecuador	...	...	...	...	...	[2]5.5	[2]5.5	9461.0	22762.0	...	Equateur
Guyana[2]	0.5	0.6	...	1.1	1.1	...	...	...	...	...	Guyana[2]
Asia											**Asie**
Armenia	..	[1]7.0	3.0	1.0	0.0	0.3	0.1	0.1	0.5	0.8	Arménie
Azerbaijan	..	11.9	4.8	2.0	2.0	2.0	1.0	0.0	0.0	...	Azerbaïdjan
Bangladesh	3.0	3.0	9.0	3.0	3.0	4.0	5.0	7.0	...	...	Bangladesh
Cyprus	*3.0	*3.0	4.0	*5.0	*5.0	5.0	5.0	4.0	4.0	5.0	Chypre
Indonesia[1]	63.1	...	149.0	37.0	...	...	...	...	...	...	Indonésie[1]
Iran(Islamic Rep. of)	[5]54.0	[5]58.0	[5]50.0	[5]46.0	[5]36.0	[6]32.0	[6]33.0	[6]39.0	[6]41.0	...	Iran(Rép. islamique)
Israel[1 7]	46.0	48.2	59.0	57.4	53.3	57.7	58.0	...	...	...	Israël[1 7]
Japan	1753.0	1688.0	1647.0	1554.0	1597.0	1581.0	1623.0	1636.0	1497.0	1597.0	Japon
Korea, Republic of[2 4]	200.0	...	...	...	...	...	...	...	...	...	Corée, République de[2 4]
Malaysia[2]	16.7	18.1	15.3	15.7	17.3	19.0	19.0	20.9	14.2	16.4	Malaisie[2]
Myanmar[2]	1.6	1.4	1.6	1.3	...	...	...	...	...	...	Myanmar[2]
Pakistan[1 8]	11.0	14.0	19.0	17.0	9.0	7.0	7.0	...	...	...	Pakistan[1 8]
Syrian Arab Republic	11.0	14.0	20.0	19.0	20.0	20.0	21.0	26.0	31.0	...	Rép. arabe syrienne
Tajikistan	..	9.0	4.0	2.0	1.0	1.0	0.0	0.0	0.0	0.0	Tadjikistan
Turkey	7.0	7.0	7.0	7.0	6.0	13.0	15.0	18.0	19.0	21.0	Turquie
Yemen	..	2.5	2.7	2.7	2.8	3.2	[2]2.0	[2]2.0	...	...	Yémen
Europe											**Europe**
Austria[9]	...	...	...	...	...	93.0	...	...	...	...	Autriche[9]
Belgium	[1 10]514.0	[1 10]312.0	[1 10]162.0	[1 10]155.0	[3]99.0	[3]100.0	[3]76.0	[3]74.0	[3]77.0	[3]110.0	Belgique
Croatia	..	31.0	16.0	15.0	16.0	17.0	18.0	17.0	16.0	...	Croatie
Denmark[11]	1.0	1.0	0.6	0.8	0.8	1.0	1.0	1.0	1.0	0.0	Danemark[11]
Czechoslovakia(former)[3]	178.0	92.0	..	..	..	..	..	..	..	..	Tchécoslovaquie(anc.)[3]
Czech Republic	..	..	46.0	37.0	19.0	22.0	33.0	32.0	30.0	30.0	République tchèque
Finland[3]	55.0	46.0	43.0	46.0	53.0	47.0	52.0	...	...	...	Finlande[3]
Germany	..	728.0	722.0	634.0	669.0	...	...	...	...	...	Allemagne
Germany(Fed.Rep.)	660.0	..	..	..	..	..	..	..	..	..	Allemagne(Rép.féd.)
German D.R.(former)	158.0	..	..	..	..	..	..	..	..	..	R.D.A. (anc.)
Greece[3]	...	...	...	24.0	26.0	24.0	55.0	61.0	...	...	Grèce[3]
Hungary	80.0	62.0	66.0	60.0	65.0	57.0	...	...	89.0	75.0	Hongrie
Iceland	1.0	1.0	1.0	1.0	...	...	2.0	2.0	2.0	2.0	Islande
Ireland[1]	17.0	...	...	...	...	...	...	...	...	...	Irlande[1]
Latvia	..	36.0	13.0	8.0	11.0	9.0	10.0	9.0	9.0	8.0	Lettonie
Lithuania	..	1.0	0.2	0.4	0.2	0.2	0.0	0.0	...	...	Lituanie
Netherlands[1]	289.0	312.0	307.0	...	...	...	...	...	...	...	Pays-Bas[1]

For general note and footnotes, see end of table.

Voir la fin du tableau pour la remarque générale et les notes.

Paints, other (continued)
Autres peintures (suite)

ISIC-BASED CODE - CODE BASE CITI

3521-07A

Unit : Thousand metric tons

Unité : Milliers de tonnes métriques

Country or area	1990	1991	1992	1993	1994	1995	1996	1997	1998	1999	Pays ou zone
Norway[1]	0.0	9.0	7.0	7.0	...	...	...	...	...	...	Norvège[1]
Portugal	30.0	28.0	6.0	6.0	5.0	5.0	6.0	7.0	11.0	13.0	Portugal
Slovakia	..	..	38.0	38.0	44.0	203.0	28.0	...	19.0	10.0	Slovaquie
Slovenia	..	21.0	14.0	16.0	14.0	17.0	3.0	...	...	...	Slovénie
Sweden[3]	86.0	77.0	78.0	80.0	85.0	...	...	...	...	...	Suède[3]
Yugoslavia	..	11.0	14.0	9.0	9.0	7.0	8.0	7.0	6.0	2.0	Yougoslavie
USSR (former)[3]	3543.0	..	..	..	..	..	..	..	..	..	URSS (anc.)[3]
Oceania											**Océanie**
Australia[2][8]	101.6	92.2	88.8	91.3	197.3	185.6	191.4	...	...	...	Australie[2][8]

General Note.

Other paints, enamels, pigments and extenders, varnishes, lacquers and stains other than cellulose, siccatives and other ancillary products ready for use, responding to products based on glycerophthalic resins, epoxy, acrylic or vinyl resin polyesters, polyurethanes, rubber derivatives, bituminous protective products, and products based on other resins and oils. Artists' colours, printing inks and printers' colours, theatrical grease paint and other make-up and coloured crayons and pastels are excluded. (SITC, Rev.3: 53342-2A, 53343-2A, 53344-0A).

Remarque générale.

Autres peintures, peintures-émaux, pigments et diluants, vernis, laques et teintures autres que celles à base de cellulose, siccatifs et autres produits connexes prêts à l'emploi, correspondant aux produits à base de résines glycérophtaliques, polyesters des résines époxiques, acryliques ou vinyliques, polyuréthanes, dérivés du caoutchouc, enduits protecteurs bitumineux, produits à base d'autres résines et huiles. Cette rubrique ne comprend pas les couleurs pour la peinture artistique, les encres et les couleurs d'imprimerie, les fards et autres produits de maquillage et les pastels. (CTCI, Rev.3: 53342-2A, 53343-2A, 53344-0A).

[1] Including water paints and cellulose paints.
[2] In thousand kilolitres.
[3] Including cellulose paints.
[4] Oil paints and enamels only.
[5] Production by establishments employing 50 or more persons.
[6] Production by establishments employing 10 or more persons.
[7] Production of establishments employing 15 or more persons.
[8] Twelve months ending 30 June of year stated.
[9] Beginning 1996, data are confidential.
[10] Excluding enamels.
[11] Sales.

[1] Y compris les peintures à l'eau et les peintures cellulosiques.
[2] En milliers de kilolitres.
[3] Y compris les peintures cellulosiques.
[4] Peintures à l'huile et peintures-émaux seulement.
[5] Production des établissements occupant 50 personnes ou plus.
[6] Production des établissements occupant 10 personnes ou plus.
[7] Production des établissements occupant 15 personnes ou plus.
[8] Période de douze mois finissant le 30 juin de l'année indiquée.
[9] A partir de 1996, les données sont confidentielles.
[10] Non compris les émaux.
[11] Ventes.

Mastics
Mastics

ISIC-BASED CODE - CODE BASE CITI

3521-10

Unit : Thousand metric tons
Unité : Milliers de tonnes métriques

Country or area	1990	1991	1992	1993	1994	1995	1996	1997	1998	1999	Pays ou zone
Africa	**1**	**2**	**2**	**1**	**1**	**2**	**1**	**1**	**1**	**1**	**Afrique**
Algeria	1.3	2.3	2.0	1.2	1.2	1.6	1.0	1.1	0.8	0.8	Algérie
America, South	**0**	**0**	**0**	**0**	**0**	**0**	**0**	**0**	**0**	**0**	**Amérique du Sud**
Bolivia	0.0	0.0	0.0	0.1	0.1	*0.2	...	...	...	...	Bolivie
Asia	**0**	**0**	**0**	**0**	**0**	**0**	**0**	**0**	**0**	**0**	**Asie**
Hong Kong SAR[1]	...	...	0.0	0.0	0.3	0.1	...	...	...	...	Hong-Kong RAS[1]
Europe	**793**	**876**	**966**	**1030**	**1178**	**1543**	**1785**	**1818**	**1893**	**2092**	**Europe**
Austria	0.5	0.5	...	...	...	#24.4	22.3	21.6	30.0	33.1	Autriche
Belgium	...	...	...	...	40.0	47.5	43.5	51.3	59.0	75.2	Belgique
Bulgaria	[2]2.0	[2]1.6	[2]0.7	[2]0.4	[2]0.2	[2]0.1	[2]0.1	[2]0.3	5.1	2.9	Bulgarie
Croatia	..	1.3	0.7	0.7	1.0	1.2	1.2	7.9	10.0	...	Croatie
Denmark[3]	40.6	37.4	49.5	37.6	30.3	30.1	30.8	36.3	9.7	...	Danemark[3]
Czechoslovakia(former)	15.0	12.7	..	..	..	..	..	..	..	..	Tchécoslovaquie(anc.)
Czech Republic	..	..	...	...	11.2	9.0	3.7	11.3	12.1	12.7	République tchèque
Finland	18.3	15.7	14.2	12.2	14.6	16.8	17.3	19.1	14.4	16.8	Finlande
Germany	..	340.9	377.9	421.3	476.1	851.3	887.6	894.9	904.0	...	Allemagne
Germany(Fed.Rep.)	298.3	..	..	..	..	..	..	..	..	..	Allemagne(Rép.féd.)
German D.R.(former)	6.8	..	..	..	..	..	..	..	..	..	R.D.A. (anc.)
Greece	...	...	...	15.6	[2]7.2	10.2	18.7	16.2	10.9	...	Grèce
Hungary	11.3	10.6	9.7	7.5	5.9	6.4	2.4	0.7	...	...	Hongrie
Latvia	..	...	...	...	...	...	...	...	...	0.5	Lettonie
Lithuania	..	...	...	...	...	0.6	1.4	3.0	4.9	6.0	Lituanie
Netherlands	...	...	...	67.2	80.5	80.3	87.3	101.5	...	...	Pays-Bas
Norway	3.8	...	...	...	...	...	...	...	...	...	Norvège
Portugal	3.4	1.6	1.6	8.8	10.4	10.5	12.8	13.9	31.7	40.9	Portugal
Russian Federation		1.9	1.2	0.9	0.6	0.6	0.5	0.5	0.5	0.5	Fédération de Russie
Slovakia	..	..	...	...	...	...	...	0.1	1.9	1.1	Slovaquie
Slovenia	..	5.4	8.8	5.9	8.1	8.2	#54.8	63.8	67.2	77.7	Slovénie
Spain	41.7	57.4	48.5	60.7	54.0	49.8	44.4	47.5	50.2	59.6	Espagne
Sweden	...	...	...	...	...	26.0	136.0	135.9	130.3	183.3	Suède
United Kingdom	...	...	...	313.0	...	362.5	413.5	386.3	436.9	...	Royaume-Uni
Yugoslavia	..	4.3	2.3	1.2	1.7	2.0	1.5	1.7	1.6	1.0	Yougoslavie
Yugoslavia, SFR	7.4	..	..	..	..	..	..	..	..	..	Yougoslavie, RSF
Total	**794**	**879**	**968**	**1031**	**1180**	**1545**	**1787**	**1820**	**1894**	**2093**	**Total**

General Note.
Glazier's putty, grafting putty, painters' fillings and stopping, sealing and similar mastics, including resin mastics and cements. This heading covers mastics based on: oil, sodium silicate, zinc oxychloride, magnesium oxychloride, sulphur, plaster, artificial plastic materials, zinc oxide, glycerol, rubber and luting wax. Plasters, lime and cement are excluded, as well as bituminous mastic, dental cements, brewers' pitch, factory cements and mortars. (SITC, Rev.3: 53354-0).

Remarque générale.
Mastic de vitrier, mastic de jardinier, mastic de peintre en bâtiment et autres mastics pour l'obturation, le colmatage et autres fonctions, y compris les résines et les ciments. Cette rubrique comprend les mastics à base des produits suivants: huile, silicate de sodium, oxychlorure de zinc, oxychlorure de magnésium, soufre, plâtre, matières plastiques artificielles, oxyde de zinc, glycérine, caoutchouc, cire à luter. Elle ne comprend pas le plâtre, la chaux et le ciment, ni les mastics bitumineux, les ciments dentaires, le brai des brasseurs, les ciments et mortiers produits en usines. (CTCI, Rev.3: 53354-0).

[1] Beginning 1996, data are confidential.
[2] Incomplete coverage.
[3] Sales.

[1] A partir de 1996, les données sont confidentielles.
[2] Couverture incomplète.
[3] Ventes.

Soap
Savons
ISIC-BASED CODE - CODE BASE CITI
3523-01

Unit : Thousand metric tons

Unité : Milliers de tonnes métriques

Country or area	1990	1991	1992	1993	1994	1995	1996	1997	1998	1999	Pays ou zone
Africa	**1040**	**1002**	**1000**	**1104**	**867**	**871**	**857**	**903**	**925**	**841**	**Afrique**
Algeria	123.0	105.0	91.5	91.6	84.6	97.9	71.1	82.0	82.1	76.5	Algérie
Angola	7.6	4.7	4.2	...	...	...	...	...	...	...	Angola
Burkina Faso	14.5	25.6	13.6	14.1	...	...	...	...	...	...	Burkina Faso
Burundi	2.6	3.5	3.0	5.2	...	...	...	...	...	...	Burundi
Cameroon	...	...	14.4	29.0	*28.6	32.9	...	...	...	...	Cameroun
Cape Verde	...	...	...	1.0	1.0	1.5	...	...	...	...	Cap-Vert
Chad	4.3	3.1	3.1	3.4	2.8	4.7	...	...	...	...	Tchad
Congo	3.1	4.6	3.2	1.5	...	...	...	...	...	...	Congo
Egypt	327.9	289.3	290.1	318.2	257.0	198.1	168.0	185.0	224.0	...	Egypte
Ethiopia[1]	8.6	0.4	5.5	17.3	15.0	15.2	18.4	14.3	10.9	26.1	Ethiopie[1]
Gabon	1.6	2.3	2.1	3.1	3.4	3.4	...	...	...	...	Gabon
Kenya	37.2	38.8	38.8	40.0	47.8	55.7	62.5	...	...	...	Kenya
Madagascar	14.2	16.3	16.2	19.3	16.9	16.0	15.6	15.1	14.5	...	Madagascar
Mali	9.9	11.1	9.8	8.6	11.0	13.2	16.4	...	...	...	Mali
Mauritania	3.0	4.5	5.5	3.7	...	...	...	...	...	...	Mauritanie
Mozambique	8.8	9.4	6.6	11.0	10.7	12.6	14.4	8.5	14.6	1.4	Mozambique
Nigeria[2]	241.2	242.7	262.2	302.9	123.8	110.9	...	...	...	...	Nigéria[2]
Senegal	37.1	36.9	42.0	35.7	22.7	44.4	38.2	40.5	38.6	40.9	Sénégal
Sierra Leone	...	1.4	1.9	2.6	...	...	...	...	...	...	Sierra Leone
South Africa	112.3	117.7	126.7	120.8	138.1	149.4	155.2	163.5	152.0	166.5	Afrique du Sud
Uganda	30.8	33.3	38.7	47.6	48.5	55.2	43.7	66.6	72.8	83.7	Ouganda
United Rep.Tanzania[2]	23.2	23.9	20.3	22.2	20.3	25.0	24.8	29.7	...	...	Rép. Unie de Tanzanie[2]
America, North	**395**	**419**	**411**	**365**	**359**	**330**	**334**	**357**	**365**	**357**	**Amérique du Nord**
Dominica	...	...	...	10.6	10.6	10.8	14.4	12.1	14.5	11.8	Dominique
Haiti	44.5	49.1	34.3	34.8	29.3	...	...	...	...	...	Haïti
Jamaica	7.9	6.5	2.6	#0.0	0.0	0.0	...	...	...	...	Jamaïque
Mexico	327.1	345.2	342.6	313.5	314.0	290.3	294.1	323.0	332.8	332.0	Mexique
Panama	3.9	...	18.5	4.3	3.3	2.7	3.6	...	...	...	Panama
St. Lucia	0.0	0.0	0.0	0.1	0.0	0.0	0.0	0.0	...	...	St-Lucie
Trinidad and Tobago	2.0	1.9	1.9	1.9	1.6	1.6	1.6	2.0	2.3	2.3	Trinité-et-Tobago
America, South	**347**	**342**	**316**	**316**	**326**	**369**	**382**	**392**	**401**	**449**	**Amérique du Sud**
Argentina[3]	37.1	40.6	45.7	44.3	45.2	41.7	51.2	52.4	46.7	49.1	Argentine[3]
Bolivia	5.6	2.9	2.9	3.2	5.2	*3.9	...	...	...	...	Bolivie
Chile	8.5	9.0	10.2	9.0	9.1	8.4	7.6	6.9	5.8	6.0	Chili
Colombia	179.5	...	185.1	174.1	190.8	213.9	...	249.5	242.8	...	Colombie
Ecuador	68.2	...	29.0	38.1	22.7	48.5	59.1	21.3	42.2	...	Equateur
Guyana	0.4	0.7	0.6	0.4	0.2	...	...	...	...	...	Guyana
Paraguay	8.4	6.8	6.2	...	...	...	...	...	...	...	Paraguay
Peru	39.4	35.5	35.8	39.9	45.5	44.9	47.5	...	...	...	Pérou
Asia	**3451**	**3490**	**3310**	**3265**	**3347**	**3741**	**3263**	**3428**	**3595**	**4714**	**Asie**
Armenia	..	9.2	...	...	...	...	...	...	...	...	Arménie
Azerbaijan	..	6.2	2.4	0.3	0.0	0.0	0.0	0.0	0.0	0.0	Azerbaïdjan
China	1067.1	904.5	840.2	844.7	798.6	826.5	733.3	643.3	514.2	561.4	Chine
Cyprus	*4.7	*5.3	6.3	5.5	4.8	4.1	3.9	3.8	3.8	3.4	Chypre
Georgia	..	...	1.2	1.4	1.0	0.4	0.1	0.1	0.1	0.1	Géorgie
India[4]	1551.1	1547.8	1469.9	1464.8	1569.6	1862.5	1480.0	1586.1	1969.4	2993.8	Inde[4]
Indonesia	111.2	111.1	102.0	123.8	97.1	186.7	...	313.4	257.7	...	Indonésie
Israel	4.4	...	...	...	...	...	...	...	...	...	Israël
Japan	183.3	194.2	187.2	167.8	170.1	168.8	164.7	167.7	149.2	155.6	Japon
Kazakhstan	..	37.5	24.2	18.7	17.2	11.9	14.7	9.8	4.8	2.7	Kazakhstan
Korea, Republic of	181.6	144.9	142.5	122.3	120.0	103.7	...	...	...	...	Corée, République de
Kyrgyzstan	..	0.1	0.1	0.0	0.0	0.0	0.0	0.0	0.0	0.0	Kirghizistan
Malaysia[5]	23.8	28.4	27.2	23.6	34.0	39.2	46.6	25.1	28.1	30.8	Malaisie[5]
Mongolia	5.0	3.6	1.2	0.8	0.4	0.6	0.5	0.4	0.2	0.3	Mongolie
Myanmar[6]	14.8	23.1	17.6	12.5	25.4	35.6	29.9	26.9	35.3	39.9	Myanmar[6]
Nepal[7]	...	...	20.9	23.0	20.6	23.5	25.1	29.0	39.1	47.7	Népal[7]
Pakistan[5]	35.1	46.1	55.1	58.2	53.6	53.2	60.1	68.9	73.1	76.2	Pakistan[5]
Syrian Arab Republic	15.0	16.0	16.6	16.5	18.1	18.3	18.0	18.3	21.3	...	Rép. arabe syrienne
Tajikistan	..	15.9	11.0	2.9	2.2	1.8	1.0	0.6	0.8	0.6	Tadjikistan
Thailand[8]	41.6	39.7	...	...	...	...	48.6	55.8	58.9	...	Thaïlande[8]

For general note and footnotes, see end of table.

Voir la fin du tableau pour la remarque générale et les notes.

Soap (continued)
Savons (suite)

ISIC-BASED CODE - CODE BASE CITI

3523-01

Unit : Thousand metric tons

Unité : Milliers de tonnes métriques

Country or area	1990	1991	1992	1993	1994	1995	1996	1997	1998	1999	Pays ou zone
Turkey	135.8	112.6	119.9	136.9	182.4	172.5	199.8	225.4	210.5	209.3	Turquie
Turkmenistan	..	8.5	7.7	4.0	3.2	2.0	1.7	0.4	0.7	...	Turkménistan
Uzbekistan	..	97.9	84.0	73.4	70.7	70.6	61.2	50.6	...	...	Ouzbékistan
Viet Nam	54.7	68.5	71.7	...	...	...	...	...	...	...	Viet Nam
Yemen	..	41.0	39.0	36.0	30.0	32.0	24.0	23.0	...	...	Yémen
Europe	**885**	**1596**	**1400**	**1188**	**1053**	**1042**	**1030**	**1014**	**908**	**1030**	**Europe**
Albania	[9]21.0	[9]5.0	[9]2.0	[9]4.0	[9]3.0	[9]2.0	[9]2.0	[9]2.0	[9]2.0	0.0	Albanie
Austria	8.4	13.1	13.4	5.5	5.4	#1.1	1.1	0.7	0.4	0.4	Autriche
Belarus[10]	..	45.8	35.1	29.7	19.2	18.1	29.7	33.7	26.3	33.7	Bélarus[10]
Belgium	19.1	36.7	26.5	33.0	[11]11.1	[11]12.4	[11]18.0	[11]18.6	[11]12.1	[11]14.1	Belgique
Bulgaria	24.3	16.9	14.6	4.1	2.1	3.3	2.8	1.3	1.8	3.4	Bulgarie
Croatia	..	1.6	0.9	0.8	0.5	0.3	0.3	0.4	0.3	...	Croatie
Czechoslovakia(former)	35.0	25.1	..	..	..	..	..	..	..	..	Tchécoslovaquie(anc.)
Czech Republic	..	..	24.2	28.4	35.5	36.1	44.4	34.0	30.7	26.9	République tchèque
Finland	7.4	6.7	5.7	4.5	4.3	11.1	11.9	13.8	12.1	7.2	Finlande
France	117.4	122.0	108.2	95.2	101.5	106.0	105.0	104.0	103.0	100.0	France
Germany	..	122.4	113.1	104.0	106.4	...	...	123.0	...	...	Allemagne
Germany(Fed.Rep.)	126.1	..	..	..	..	..	..	..	..	..	Allemagne(Rép.féd.)
German D.R.(former)	22.4	..	..	..	..	..	..	..	..	..	R.D.A. (anc.)
Greece	9.2	10.3	9.0	8.9	6.9	7.1	11.8	11.4	6.3	...	Grèce
Hungary	20.0	12.7	9.2	7.5	7.0	11.3	9.2	7.0	7.1	6.7	Hongrie
Iceland	...	...	...	...	...	...	0.5	0.4	0.3	0.4	Islande
Latvia[10]	..	16.3	7.4	2.5	2.8	1.8	1.2	0.2	0.0	0.0	Lettonie[10]
Lithuania	..	15.3	7.5	2.9	3.0	4.9	5.0	4.3	4.7	3.8	Lituanie
Norway	6.5	...	5.6	...	...	...	...	...	...	...	Norvège
Poland	56.9	37.2	33.9	27.3	28.9	28.3	32.3	37.9	39.6	41.4	Pologne
Portugal	56.8	37.2	10.0	3.8	3.8	4.6	4.2	11.4	14.1	13.0	Portugal
Republic of Moldova	..	13.0	4.8	[12]2.7	[12]0.7	[12]0.6	[12]0.5	[12]0.6	[12]0.3	[12]0.2	Rép. de Moldova
Romania	35.9	27.1	14.4	19.1	14.2	18.0	10.2	9.8	6.9	2.5	Roumanie
Russian Federation	..	410.9	344.3	257.7	173.4	167.7	139.5	129.5	100.5	163.2	Fédération de Russie
Slovakia	..	..	...	...	...	...	0.0	...	2.1	2.5	Slovaquie
Slovenia	..	3.0	2.1	1.8	2.4	1.7	1.2	0.5	0.5	0.5	Slovénie
Spain	50.1	51.2	46.9	46.5	50.1	53.6	51.7	63.6	82.8	126.0	Espagne
Sweden	...	...	...	...	17.8	13.4	8.2	7.4	7.4	6.9	Suède
Switzerland[13][14]	167.7	165.3	156.0	151.7	143.6	154.4	...	...	...	...	Suisse[13][14]
Ukraine[10]	..	272.5	265.0	188.2	158.9	94.4	70.5	41.5	33.3	44.9	Ukraine[10]
United Kingdom	...	...	...	...	138.6	163.9	195.3	197.0	201.5	...	Royaume-Uni
Yugoslavia	..	6.8	7.8	4.3	3.3	3.9	4.3	5.5	5.4	3.5	Yougoslavie
T.F.Yug.Rep. Macedonia	..	0.8	0.5	0.6	0.7	0.7	0.8	0.8	0.7	1.3	L'ex-RY Macédoine
USSR (former)[10]	1705.1	..	..	..	..	..	..	..	..	...	URSS (anc.)[10]
Oceania	**7**	**7**	**7**	**7**	**7**	**7**	**6**	**8**	**9**	**9**	**Océanie**
Fiji	6.6	7.1	6.9	7.0	7.2	7.1	6.2	8.3	9.2	...	Fidji
Total	**7830**	**6857**	**6444**	**6245**	**5959**	**6361**	**5872**	**6103**	**6203**	**7399**	**Total**

General Note.
Normal soaps of commerce, including both hard and soft soaps. Included are, in particular, household soaps, toilet soaps, transparent soaps, shaving soaps, medicated soaps, disinfectant soaps, abrasive soaps, resin and naphthenate soaps, and industrial soaps. (SITC, Rev.3: 55410-0).

Remarque générale.
Produits commercialement désignés sous le nom de savon, y compris les savons durs et les savons mous. Cette rubrique comprend notamment: les savons de ménage, les savons de toilette, les savons translucides, les savons à barbe, les savons médicinaux, les savons désinfectants, les savons abrasifs, les savons de résines ou de naphténates et les savons industriels. (CTCI, Rev.3: 55410-0).

For footnotes, see end of table.

Voir la fin du tableau pour les notes.

Soap (continued)
Savons (suite)

ISIC-BASED CODE - CODE BASE CITI

3523-01

Footnotes

[1] Twelve months ending 7 July of the year stated.
[2] Including washing powder and detergents.
[3] Excluding liquid toilet soap.
[4] Production by large and medium scale establishments only.
[5] Toilet soap only.
[6] Government production only.
[7] Twelve months beginning 16 July of year stated.
[8] Beginning 1999, series discontinued.
[9] Including washing powder.
[10] In terms of 40 per cent fat content.
[11] Incomplete coverage.
[12] Excluding Transnistria region.
[13] Sales.
[14] Including other cleaning products.

Notes.

[1] Période de douze mois finissant le 7 juillet de l'année indiquée.
[2] Y compris les poudres pour lessives et les détersifs.
[3] Non compris le savon liquide de toilette.
[4] Production des grandes et moyennes entreprises seulement.
[5] Savons de toilette seulement.
[6] Production de l'Etat seulement.
[7] Période de douze mois commençant le 16 juillet de l'année indiquée.
[8] A partir de 1999, série abandonnée.
[9] Y compris les poudres pour lessives.
[10] Sur la base de 40 p. 100 de matières grasses.
[11] Couverture incomplète.
[12] Non compris la région de Transnistria.
[13] Ventes.
[14] Y compris les autres produits de nettoyage.

Washing powders and detergents
Poudres pour lessives et détersifs

ISIC-BASED CODE - CODE BASE CITI

3523-04

Unit : Thousand metric tons · Unité : Milliers de tonnes métriques

Country or area	1990	1991	1992	1993	1994	1995	1996	1997	1998	1999	Pays ou zone
Africa	**548**	**561**	**509**	**516**	**529**	**498**	**495**	**469**	**532**	**528**	**Afrique**
Algeria	137.9	142.4	93.1	114.0	138.0	99.7	85.2	86.0	107.1	113.6	Algérie
Egypt	89.0	81.1	68.2	64.0	49.9	45.2	42.0	29.0	66.0	64.0	Egypte
Gabon	134.7	150.6	167.5	...	...	...	...	...	...	...	Gabon
Kenya	36.2	24.1	21.1	22.0	16.4	20.5	27.3	...	...	...	Kenya
South Africa[1]	150.4	162.5	158.7	164.9	174.0	181.3	189.7	185.8	192.0	184.8	Afrique du Sud[1]
America, North	**859**	**913**	**936**	**849**	**898**	**867**	**870**	**892**	**973**	**1007**	**Amérique du Nord**
Haiti[2]	1.0	1.2	0.9	1.0	0.8	...	...	...	...	...	Haïti[2]
Jamaica	8.0	6.5	8.1	#0.0	0.0	0.0	0.0	0.0	0.0	...	Jamaïque
Mexico	839.2	886.0	914.3	823.8	876.1	844.6	845.6	856.6	934.4	965.7	Mexique
Panama	10.5	...	12.5	23.9	21.4	21.3	23.2	...	...	...	Panama
America, South	**376**	**396**	**406**	**429**	**474**	**469**	**512**	**648**	**550**	**621**	**Amérique du Sud**
Argentina	115.6	121.1	132.1	145.1	169.4	169.2	195.6	180.5	178.6	203.7	Argentine
Bolivia	1.5	1.5	1.5	1.1	1.8	*2.6					Bolivie
Chile	60.5	63.8	62.6	67.6	67.7	71.5	70.1	70.3	80.4	75.2	Chili
Colombia	...	...	133.2	136.5	143.0	160.9	...	284.4	178.3	...	Colombie
Ecuador	26.9	...	28.0	21.4	31.1	1.5	6.5	35.9	42.4	...	Equateur
Guyana	...	0.2	0.2	0.2	0.2	...	...	...	...	...	Guyana
Peru	39.9	43.6	48.8	56.8	60.8	63.1	64.9	74.9	68.3	79.2	Pérou
Asia	**4481**	**4559**	**4902**	**5063**	**5642**	**6224**	**6226**	**6787**	**7050**	**7009**	**Asie**
Armenia		2.9	1.2	0.5	0.3	0.2	0.0	0.1	0.0	0.1	Arménie
Azerbaijan	..	76.1	51.6	39.6	9.6	3.2	1.9	0.2	0.6	0.3	Azerbaïdjan
China	1513.9	1462.0	1660.0	1883.3	2174.8	2998.0	2622.0	2799.1	2803.4	2865.3	Chine
Hong Kong SAR	83.9	56.4	45.6	41.6	278.1	65.8	46.4	116.3	[3]49.5	[3]44.3	Hong-Kong RAS
Cyprus	*8.0	*9.9	7.5	*7.4	*8.6	8.9	8.2	6.2	6.1	6.2	Chypre
Georgia	..	...	...	0.8	[4]0.2	[4]0.1	[4]0.0	0.0	0.0	0.0	Géorgie
India[5]	242.5	246.6	281.7	307.7	382.1	452.3	513.1	517.6	535.9	646.9	Inde[5]
Indonesia	391.0	344.2	466.4	429.3	332.5	217.9	...	455.7	906.8	...	Indonésie
Iran(Islamic Rep. of)	[6]212.0	[6]192.0	[6]170.0	[6]181.0	[6]191.0	[7]225.0	[7]226.8	[7]245.8	[7]304.1	...	Iran(Rép. islamique)
Japan[8]	1127.3	1176.3	1207.1	1142.0	1176.6	1132.9	1085.9	1113.1	1040.3	...	Japon[8]
Kazakhstan[4]	..	...	...	...	26.4	15.3	0.6	0.1	0.2	...	Kazakhstan[4]
Korea, Republic of	341.6	362.7	360.4	338.7	364.8	367.1	369.4	375.1	327.0	379.3	Corée, République de
Kuwait	...	...	0.7	1.4	0.8	0.9	...	...	...	...	Koweït
Lao People's Dem. Rep.	...	...	...	...	0.7	0.9	...	...	...	...	Rép. dém. pop. lao
Malaysia	56.1	59.6	74.5	80.9	101.8	84.9	78.9	112.6	90.9	95.3	Malaisie
Pakistan	24.1	29.1	31.1	30.7	28.4	30.9	38.1	35.1	39.6	41.0	Pakistan
Syrian Arab Republic	24.8	22.1	27.4	39.8	39.4	40.6	39.5	41.0	50.6	...	Rép. arabe syrienne
Thailand[9]	148.5	155.9	...	...	...	...	209.1	224.6	213.8	...	Thaïlande[9]
Turkey	306.0	267.0	258.4	297.2	323.4	376.8	537.1	738.5	678.8	650.1	Turquie
Turkmenistan	..	15.9	13.0	5.4	5.2	5.1	1.1	0.8	0.8	...	Turkménistan
Uzbekistan	..	35.9	18.1	16.1	7.6	6.6	3.2	3.0	...	...	Ouzbékistan
Europe	**8291**	**11467**	**11426**	**11697**	**11558**	**11750**	**12195**	**11794**	**11896**	**12511**	**Europe**
Albania	...	...	...	...	...	...	[4]0.2	[4]0.0	[4]0.0	0.0	Albanie
Austria[10]	145.0	149.3	174.8	149.5	117.5	...	...	...	...	...	Autriche[10]
Belarus		25.4	23.1	15.0	5.1	4.8	3.7	6.1	6.0	7.7	Bélarus
Belgium	398.1	402.9	396.5	386.6	466.5	514.7	569.2	623.4	576.6	597.7	Belgique
Bosnia and Herzegovina[4]	..	..	...	...	0.3	0.9	...	0.7	...	...	Bosnie-Herzégovine[4]
Bulgaria	...	...	5.1	3.4	3.8	4.5	6.4	4.5	12.9	17.2	Bulgarie
Croatia	..	65.1	51.2	43.3	30.7	31.0	30.8	39.8	40.1	...	Croatie
Denmark[11]	...	...	...	...	97.0	188.0	198.0	181.0	187.0	226.0	Danemark[11]
Czechoslovakia(former)	103.4	80.3	..	..	..			..		..	Tchécoslovaquie(anc.)
Czech Republic	..				158.8	193.9	245.2	326.5	427.0	374.8	République tchèque
Estonia	..	28.0	4.1	2.5	4.1	1.9	1.1	1.3	1.1	0.8	Estonie
Finland	85.9	74.6	66.4	70.4	68.9	63.1	64.0	63.1	78.0	85.5	Finlande
France	693.5	658.9	714.2	683.1	727.7	...	...	...	...	...	France
Germany	..	...	...	...	[4]2392.3	2130.4	2166.1	2270.1	2237.3	...	Allemagne
German D.R.(former)	268.5	..	..	..	..			..		..	R.D.A. (anc.)
Greece	149.4	140.0	144.6	231.3	250.0	266.7	532.9	506.7	242.4	...	Grèce
Hungary	123.6	90.5	82.7	84.6	84.1	79.8	109.9	88.6	85.3	123.1	Hongrie
Iceland	3.0	1.0	2.0	2.0	2.0	[4]2.0	3.3	3.4	3.8	3.4	Islande

For general note and footnotes, see end of table. · Voir la fin du tableau pour la remarque générale et les notes.

Washing powders and detergents (continued)
Poudres pour lessives et détersifs (suite)

ISIC-BASED CODE - CODE BASE CITI

3523-04

Unit : Thousand metric tons Unité : Milliers de tonnes métriques

Country or area	1990	1991	1992	1993	1994	1995	1996	1997	1998	1999	Pays ou zone
Italy[4]	...	...	...	...	1748.7	1712.1	1807.8	2041.1	...	...	Italie[4]
Latvia	..	1.9	0.7	0.5	1.0	0.8	0.9	1.0	0.9	4.4	Lettonie
Lithuania	..	[12]12.6	[12]5.8	[12]2.3	[12]0.4	[12]0.6	#0.7	0.9	1.2	1.6	Lituanie
Malta[4]	...	...	...	...	...	...	9.7	...	...	...	Malte[4]
Netherlands	...	..	...	...	[4]331.4	[4]384.5	[4]436.5	[4]461.5	[4]423.5	[11][13]450.3	Pays-Bas
Norway								[4]103.3	...	87.3	Norvège
Poland[12]	158.3	161.6	140.5	167.3	193.2	183.3	229.8	262.9	276.9	231.6	Pologne[12]
Portugal	156.2	140.5	195.0	198.9	177.4	179.6	211.6	208.8	318.5	326.7	Portugal
Republic of Moldova	..	10.1	7.3	[14]4.0	[14]0.9	[14]1.2	[14]1.5	[14]0.3	[14]0.2	[14]0.5	Rép. de Moldova
Romania[15]	13.0	9.8	5.6	7.6	5.3	6.6	6.2	3.7	5.8	6.6	Roumanie[15]
Russian Federation	..	695.5	531.9	441.5	344.1	334.0	313.0	305.6	252.7	385.9	Fédération de Russie
Slovakia				27.6	22.8	[4]25.4	31.9	42.0	[4]42.4	52.5	Slovaquie
Slovenia	..	60.8	45.3	43.6	47.0	43.1	43.8	37.2	38.4	29.2	Slovénie
Spain	[1]1326.1	[1]1363.2	[1]1442.1	1853.5	1961.8	2040.0	1764.8	1772.1	1983.5	2130.8	Espagne
Sweden	158.5	127.3	121.3	...	...	...	164.9	130.1	129.8	128.9	Suède
Switzerland[4]	...	...	...	...	153.2	154.4	...	...	...	...	Suisse[4]
Ukraine	..	257.6	216.8	133.1	107.9	76.4	45.7	37.9	35.6	61.5	Ukraine
United Kingdom	...	...	...	1815.3	1742.5	1948.2	1999.7	1138.1	1437.7	...	Royaume-Uni
Yugoslavia	..	91.0	84.3	52.4	49.7	59.9	68.4	85.2	77.1	63.4	Yougoslavie
T.F.Yug.Rep. Macedonia	..	18.6	15.4	20.1	19.6	21.5	20.2	22.9	22.0	20.4	L'ex-RY Macédoine
USSR (former)	1503.5	..	..	..	..	..	..	..	..	..	URSS (anc.)
Total	**16059**	**17896**	**18179**	**18554**	**19102**	**19806**	**20298**	**20590**	**21001**	**21676**	**Total**

General Note.

Organic surface-active agents, surface-active preparations and washing preparations, whether or not containing soap. (SITC,Rev.3: 55420-0).

Remarque générale.

Produits organiques tensio-actifs, préparations tensio-actives et préparations pour lessives contenant ou non du savon. (CTCI, Rev.3: 55420-0).

[1] Synthetic detergents in powder form only.

[2] Detergents only.

[3] Excluding washing and cleaning powder, for confidentiality purposes.

[4] Source: United Nations Economic Commission for Europe (ECE), (Geneva).

[5] Production by large and medium scale establishments only.

[6] Production by establishments employing 50 or more persons.

[7] Production by establishments employing 10 or more persons.

[8] Surface-active agents only.

[9] Beginning 1999, series discontinued.

[10] Beginning 1995, data are confidential.

[11] Sales.

[12] Washing powder only.

[13] Production by establishments employing 20 or more persons.

[14] Excluding Transnistria region.

[15] On the basis of 100 per cent active substances.

[1] Détersifs synthétiques en poudre seulement.

[2] Détersifs seulement.

[3] A l'exclusion des poudres à laver et à récurer, pour raisons de confidentialité.

[4] Source: Commission économique des Nations Unies pour l'Europe (CEE), (Genève).

[5] Production des grandes et moyennes entreprises seulement.

[6] Production des établissements occupant 50 personnes ou plus.

[7] Production des établissements occupant 10 personnes ou plus.

[8] Produits tensio-actifs seulement.

[9] A partir de 1999, série abandonnée.

[10] A partir de 1995, les données sont confidentielles

[11] Ventes.

[12] Poudres pour lessive seulement.

[13] Production des établissements occupant 20 personnes ou plus.

[14] Non compris la région de Transnistria.

[15] Sur la base de 100 p. 100 de substances actives.

Carbon black
Noirs de carbone

ISIC-BASED CODE - CODE BASE CITI

3529-01

Unit : Thousand metric tons | | | | | | | | | | Unité : Milliers de tonnes métriques

Country or area	1990	1991	1992	1993	1994	1995	1996	1997	1998	1999	Pays ou zone
America, North	**1629**	**1602**	**1603**	**1577**	**1598**	**1606**	**1616**	**1622**	**1627**	**1626**	**Amérique du Nord**
Mexico	124.9	97.0	98.6	72.5	93.6	101.4	111.2	117.7	122.4	121.0	Mexique
United States[1]	...	...	...	...	1504.5	...	...	...	...	...	Etats-Unis[1]
America, South	**215**	**225**	**226**	**237**	**247**	**254**	**259**	**272**	**274**	**269**	**Amérique du Sud**
Argentina	36.7	42.9	39.4	39.3	42.5	53.4	56.9	63.9	63.3	47.4	Argentine
Brazil	178.4	182.6	186.4	197.2	204.3	200.6	202.2	207.8	211.1	221.5	Brésil
Asia	**1177**	**1220**	**1249**	**1230**	**1252**	**1385**	**1435**	**1488**	**1433**	**1535**	**Asie**
India	118.7	130.7	164.8	164.4	177.8	234.2	255.3	218.3	258.7	281.6	Inde
Indonesia	...	...	...	22.2	26.3	...	...	...	...	...	Indonésie
Japan	788.0	792.9	770.7	701.9	703.5	756.6	756.9	776.1	722.7	761.0	Japon
Korea, Republic of	215.5	231.8	247.9	300.1	310.6	323.4	354.8	425.6	384.3	438.1	Corée, République de
Turkey	30.6	32.2	34.8	34.9	28.0	40.0	39.3	39.1	40.0	26.4	Turquie
Turkmenistan	..	8.3	6.2	6.1	6.3	6.3	4.7	4.7	3.3	...	Turkménistan
Europe	**1380**	**1579**	**1586**	**1570**	**1565**	**1667**	**1573**	**1689**	**1775**	**1709**	**Europe**
Bulgaria[1]	...	...	...	...	0.6	0.9	1.1	1.2	...	...	Bulgarie[1]
Croatia	..	18.8	13.5	17.1	21.5	27.2	26.7	24.2	22.2	...	Croatie
Czechoslovakia(former)	46.4	39.3	..	..	...	...	...	...	...	..	Tchécoslovaquie(anc.)
Czech Republic	..	,	..	...	[1]21.5	[1]55.5	53.2	53.1	59.8	65.4	République tchèque
Finland	...	...	...	...	1.6	...	...	...	...	...	Finlande
France	254.3	226.2	232.1	205.0	235.2	[1]259.2	[1]245.9	[1]251.6	[1]263.6	...	France
Germany	..	...	...	334.6	299.2	[1]330.8	[1]315.6	[1]337.6	[1]343.3	...	Allemagne
Germany(Fed.Rep.)	394.4	..	..	..	..	..	..	..	..	...	Allemagne(Rép.féd.)
German D.R.(former)	7.4	..	..	..	..	..	..	..	..	...	R.D.A. (anc.)
Italy	183.5	185.5	182.9	171.3	190.5	207.6	196.7	200.2	220.7	212.8	Italie
Netherlands	112.1	111.2	117.8	...	...	...	...	...	...	...	Pays-Bas
Poland	22.7	17.1	25.9	26.4	25.5	23.3	24.8	25.0	22.6	15.3	Pologne
Portugal[1]	20.9	20.1	19.9	22.1	24.0	25.3	29.6	34.2	33.6	...	Portugal[1]
Romania	58.5	47.4	27.4	27.5	19.3	21.6	26.0	21.4	18.5	12.5	Roumanie
Russian Federation[1]	..	...	...	...	...	...	310.1	315.6	...	...	Fédération de Russie[1]
Slovakia[1]	..	...	...	...	...	...	3.8	...	...	...	Slovaquie[1]
Spain	87.9	95.4	105.9	97.5	[1]102.8	[1]90.0	[1]95.0	[1]107.0	[1]108.0	...	Espagne
Sweden	32.9	25.7	24.4	27.7	34.0	34.8	[1]35.1	...	...	...	Suède
Ukraine[1]	..	...	...	...	1.2	1.3	1.1	1.2	0.8	0.9	Ukraine[1]
United Kingdom	...	...	...	164.1	...	...	[1]91.6	[1]159.3	[1]210.3	...	Royaume-Uni
Yugoslavia[1]	..	...	...	...	1.0	1.4	...	...	...	...	Yougoslavie[1]
Total	**4401**	**4627**	**4664**	**4613**	**4662**	**4912**	**4883**	**5071**	**5110**	**5139**	**Total**

General Note.
All forms of carbon, other than natural and artificial graphite, natural carbons in the form of solid fuels, black mineral colouring matter, animal black, activated carbon, wood charcoal and crystalline carbon in the form of diamonds. (SITC, Rev.3: 52210-1).

Remarque générale.
Toutes les formes de carbone autres que le graphite naturel et artificiel, les charbons naturels constituant des combustibles solides, les pigments noirs minéraux, les noirs d'origine animale, les charbons activés, le charbon de bois et le carbone cristallisé sous forme de diamant. (CTCI, Rev.3: 52210-1).

[1] Source: United Nations Economic Commission for Europe (ECE), (Geneva).

[1] Source: Commission économique des Nations Unies pour l'Europe (CEE), (Genève).

Printers' ink
Encre d'imprimerie

ISIC-BASED CODE - CODE BASE CITI

3529-04

Unit : Thousand metric tons   Unité : Milliers de tonnes métriques

Country or area	1990	1991	1992	1993	1994	1995	1996	1997	1998	1999	Pays ou zone
America, North	**1629**	**1602**	**1603**	**1577**	**1598**	**1606**	**1616**	**1622**	**1627**	**1626**	**Amérique du Nord**
Mexico	124.9	97.0	98.6	72.5	93.6	101.4	111.2	117.7	122.4	121.0	Mexique
United States[1]	...	...	...	...	1504.5	...	...	...	...	...	Etats-Unis[1]
America, South	**215**	**225**	**226**	**237**	**247**	**254**	**259**	**272**	**274**	**269**	**Amérique du Sud**
Argentina	36.7	42.9	39.4	39.3	42.5	53.4	56.9	63.9	63.3	47.4	Argentine
Brazil	178.4	182.6	186.4	197.2	204.3	200.6	202.2	207.8	211.1	221.5	Brésil
Asia	**1177**	**1220**	**1249**	**1230**	**1252**	**1385**	**1435**	**1488**	**1433**	**1535**	**Asie**
India	118.7	130.7	164.8	164.4	177.8	234.2	255.3	218.3	258.7	281.6	Inde
Indonesia	...	...	...	22.2	26.3	...	...	...	...	...	Indonésie
Japan	788.0	792.9	770.7	701.9	703.5	756.6	756.9	776.1	722.7	761.0	Japon
Korea, Republic of	215.5	231.8	247.9	300.1	310.6	323.4	354.8	425.6	384.3	438.1	Corée, République de
Turkey	30.6	32.2	34.8	34.9	28.0	40.0	39.3	39.1	40.0	26.4	Turquie
Turkmenistan	..	8.3	6.2	6.1	6.3	6.3	4.7	4.7	3.3	...	Turkménistan
Europe	**1380**	**1579**	**1586**	**1570**	**1565**	**1667**	**1573**	**1689**	**1775**	**1709**	**Europe**
Bulgaria[1]	...	...	...	...	0.6	0.9	1.1	1.2	...	...	Bulgarie[1]
Croatia	..	18.8	13.5	17.1	21.5	27.2	26.7	24.2	22.2	...	Croatie
Czechoslovakia(former)	46.4	39.3	...	...	..	..	...	...	...	..	Tchécoslovaquie(anc.)
Czech Republic	...	...	...	...	[1]21.5	[1]55.5	53.2	53.1	59.8	65.4	République tchèque
Finland	...	...	...	...	1.6	...	...	...	...	...	Finlande
France	254.3	226.2	232.1	205.0	235.2	[1]259.2	[1]245.9	[1]251.6	[1]263.6	...	France
Germany	...	...	...	334.6	299.2	[1]330.8	[1]315.6	[1]337.6	[1]343.3	...	Allemagne
Germany(Fed.Rep.)	394.4	..	..	..	..	..	..	..	..	..	Allemagne(Rép.féd.)
German D.R.(former)	7.4	..	..	..	..	..	..	..	..	..	R.D.A. (anc.)
Italy	183.5	185.5	182.9	171.3	190.5	207.6	196.7	200.2	220.7	212.8	Italie
Netherlands	112.1	111.2	117.8	...	...	...	...	...	...	...	Pays-Bas
Poland	22.7	17.1	25.9	26.4	25.5	23.3	24.8	25.0	22.6	15.3	Pologne
Portugal[1]	20.9	20.1	19.9	22.1	24.0	25.3	29.6	34.2	33.6	...	Portugal[1]
Romania	58.5	47.4	27.4	27.5	19.3	21.6	26.0	21.4	18.5	12.5	Roumanie
Russian Federation[1]	..	..	...	...	...	...	310.1	315.6	...	...	Fédération de Russie[1]
Slovakia[1]	..	..	...	...	...	..	3.8	...	...	...	Slovaquie[1]
Spain	87.9	95.4	105.9	97.5	[1]102.8	[1]90.0	[1]95.0	[1]107.0	[1]108.0	...	Espagne
Sweden	32.9	25.7	24.4	27.7	34.0	34.8	[1]35.1	...	...	...	Suède
Ukraine[1]	..	...	...	...	1.2	1.3	1.1	1.2	0.8	0.9	Ukraine[1]
United Kingdom	...	...	...	164.1	...	...	[1]91.6	[1]159.3	[1]210.3	...	Royaume-Uni
Yugoslavia[1]	...	...	...	...	1.0	1.4	...	...	...	...	Yougoslavie[1]
Total	**4401**	**4627**	**4664**	**4613**	**4662**	**4912**	**4883**	**5071**	**5110**	**5139**	**Total**

General Note.
Printing ink, including printing colours. (SITC, Rev.3: 53320-0).

Remarque générale.
Encres d'imprimerie, y compris les couleurs d'imprimerie. (CTCI, Rev.3: 53320-0).

[1] Source: United Nations Economic Commission for Europe (ECE), (Geneva).

[1] Source: Commission économique des Nations Unies pour l'Europe (CEE), (Genève).

Explosives
Explosifs
ISIC-BASED CODE - CODE BASE CITI
3529-07

Unit : Thousand metric tons Unité : Milliers de tonnes métriques

Country or area	1990	1991	1992	1993	1994	1995	1996	1997	1998	1999	Pays ou zone
America, North	**1629**	**1602**	**1603**	**1577**	**1598**	**1606**	**1616**	**1622**	**1627**	**1626**	**Amérique du Nord**
Mexico	124.9	97.0	98.6	72.5	93.6	101.4	111.2	117.7	122.4	121.0	Mexique
United States [1]	...	...	...	...	1504.5	...	...	...	...	...	Etats-Unis [1]
America, South	**215**	**225**	**226**	**237**	**247**	**254**	**259**	**272**	**274**	**269**	**Amérique du Sud**
Argentina	36.7	42.9	39.4	39.3	42.5	53.4	56.9	63.9	63.3	47.4	Argentine
Brazil	178.4	182.6	186.4	197.2	204.3	200.6	202.2	207.8	211.1	221.5	Brésil
Asia	**1177**	**1220**	**1249**	**1230**	**1252**	**1385**	**1435**	**1488**	**1433**	**1535**	**Asie**
India	118.7	130.7	164.8	164.4	177.8	234.2	255.3	218.3	258.7	281.6	Inde
Indonesia	...	...	...	22.2	26.3	...	...	...	...	...	Indonésie
Japan	788.0	792.9	770.7	701.9	703.5	756.6	756.9	776.1	722.7	761.0	Japon
Korea, Republic of	215.5	231.8	247.9	300.1	310.6	323.4	354.8	425.6	384.3	438.1	Corée, République de
Turkey	30.6	32.2	34.8	34.9	28.0	40.0	39.3	39.1	40.0	26.4	Turquie
Turkmenistan	..	8.3	6.2	6.1	6.3	6.3	4.7	4.7	3.3	...	Turkménistan
Europe	**1380**	**1579**	**1586**	**1570**	**1565**	**1667**	**1573**	**1689**	**1775**	**1709**	**Europe**
Bulgaria [1]	...	...	...	...	0.6	0.9	1.1	1.2	...	...	Bulgarie [1]
Croatia	..	18.8	13.5	17.1	21.5	27.2	26.7	24.2	22.2	...	Croatie
Czechoslovakia(former)	46.4	39.3	..	..	..	..	..	..	..		Tchécoslovaquie(anc.)
Czech Republic	...	...	...	...	[1]21.5	[1]55.5	53.2	53.1	59.8	65.4	République tchèque
Finland	...	...	...	...	1.6	...	...	...	...	...	Finlande
France	254.3	226.2	232.1	205.0	235.2	[1]259.2	[1]245.9	[1]251.6	[1]263.6	...	France
Germany	..	...	...	334.6	299.2	[1]330.8	[1]315.6	[1]337.6	[1]343.3	...	Allemagne
Germany(Fed.Rep.)	394.4	..	..	..	..	..	..	..	..	..	Allemagne(Rép.féd.)
German D.R.(former)	7.4	..	..	..	..	..	..	..	..	..	R.D.A. (anc.)
Italy	183.5	185.5	182.9	171.3	190.5	207.6	196.7	200.2	220.7	212.8	Italie
Netherlands	112.1	111.2	117.8	...	...	...	...	...	...	...	Pays-Bas
Poland	22.7	17.1	25.9	26.4	25.5	23.3	24.8	25.0	22.6	15.3	Pologne
Portugal [1]	20.9	20.1	19.9	22.1	24.0	25.3	29.6	34.2	33.6	...	Portugal [1]
Romania	58.5	47.4	27.4	27.5	19.3	21.6	26.0	21.4	18.5	12.5	Roumanie
Russian Federation [1]	..	...	...	...	...	...	310.1	315.6	...	...	Fédération de Russie [1]
Slovakia [1]	..	...	...	...	...	...	...	3.8	...	...	Slovaquie [1]
Spain	87.9	95.4	105.9	97.5	[1]102.8	[1]90.0	[1]95.0	[1]107.0	[1]108.0	...	Espagne
Sweden	32.9	25.7	24.4	27.7	34.0	34.8	[1]35.1	...	...	...	Suède
Ukraine [1]	...	...	...	...	1.2	1.3	1.1	1.2	0.8	0.9	Ukraine [1]
United Kingdom	...	...	...	164.1	...	...	[1]91.6	[1]159.3	[1]210.3	...	Royaume-Uni
Yugoslavia [1]	..	...	...	...	1.0	1.4	...	...	...	...	Yougoslavie [1]
Total	**4401**	**4627**	**4664**	**4613**	**4662**	**4912**	**4883**	**5071**	**5110**	**5139**	**Total**

General Note.
Mixtures based on nitric esters of polyhydric alcohols, other organic nitrated derivatives, ammonium nitrate, chlorate or perchlorates. Initiatory explosives are included. (SITC, Rev.3: 59312-0).

Remarque générale.
Mélanges à base des produits suivants: esters nitriques de polyalcools, autres dérivés nitrés organiques, nitrate d'ammonium, chlorates et perchlorates. Cette rubrique comprend les explosifs d'amorçage. (CTCI, Rev.3: 59312-0).

[1] Source: United Nations Economic Commission for Europe (ECE), (Geneva).

[1] Source: Commission économique des Nations Unies pour l'Europe (CEE), (Genève).

Photographic film, sensitized, in rolls
Pellicules photographiques sensibilisées, en rouleaux

ISIC-BASED CODE - CODE BASE CITI

3529-16

Unit : Thousand square metres   Unité : Milliers de mètres carrés

Country or area	1990	1991	1992	1993	1994	1995	1996	1997	1998	1999	Pays ou zone
Asia	**265696**	**283250**	**298604**	**294559**	**309287**	**323200**	**317999**	**320548**	**308383**	**340522**	**Asie**
Indonesia	...	...	...	24607	...	...	...	...	...	...	Indonésie
Japan	241089	258643	273997	269952	284680	298593	293392	295941	283776	315915	Japon
Europe	**107585**	**745099**	**421714**	**312618**	**226705**	**191110**	**120663**	**101901**	**294397**	**103943**	**Europe**
Croatia	..	48	37	26	68	72	94	139	60	...	Croatie
Czechoslovakia(former)	1619	1555	..	..	..	..	..	..	..	..	Tchécoslovaquie(anc.)
German D.R.(former)[1]	18651	..	..	..	..	..	..	..	..	..	R.D.A. (anc.)[1]
Hungary	318	471	373	...	...	...	...	...	...	...	Hongrie
Poland	1993	2581	2801	2749	2883	2770	2764	2522	2320	1691	Pologne
Romania	6415	6376	4818	4674	4543	4042	2305	2186	1644	757	Roumanie
Russian Federation	..	654000	332300	231300	130900	96300	24200	24900	...	9900	Fédération de Russie
Spain	75	19	14	..	..	..	..	..	..	...	Espagne
United Kingdom	...	...	...	73395	87810	87239	90730	71561	101780	...	Royaume-Uni
Yugoslavia	..	154	95	51	78	264	147	170	195	132	Yougoslavie
Total	**373281**	**1028349**	**720318**	**607177**	**535992**	**514310**	**438662**	**422449**	**602780**	**444465**	**Total**

General Note.

Unexposed, sensitized films in rolls (as opposed to plates in the flat), usually of celluloid, cellulose acetate or similar flexible materials, which normally provide for a number of exposures. Cinematographic film (raw stock) is included. (SITC, Rev.3: 88230-0).

Remarque générale.

Pellicules sensibilisées non impressionnées, en rouleaux (par opposition aux films plans), habituellement en celluloïd, en acétate de cellulose ou en d'autres matières flexibles analogues, qui servent normalement à prendre un certain nombre d'images. Cette rubrique comprend les films cinématographiques vierges. (CTCI, Rev.3: 88230-0).

[1] Incomplete coverage.

[1] Couverture incomplète.

Photographic paper
Papiers photographiques

ISIC-BASED CODE - CODE BASE CITI

3529-19

Unit : Thousand square metres

Unité : Milliers de mètres carrés

Country or area	1990	1991	1992	1993	1994	1995	1996	1997	1998	1999	Pays ou zone
Asia											**Asie**
India	170	134	120	...	...	...	...	...	...	...	Inde
Indonesia	...	...	...	526	...	...	...	...	...	...	Indonésie
Japan[1]	344308	352734	343354	345157	328259	327258	334874	324038	293886	305774	Japon[1]
Europe											**Europe**
Bulgaria	8766	1923	375	296	580	314	266	239	...	...	Bulgarie
Croatia	..	1166	550	485	595	212	360	457	160	...	Croatie
Czechoslovakia(former)	6484	1888	..	..	..	..	..	..	..	..	Tchécoslovaquie(anc.)
Finland[2]	1256	1551	1668	1560	1598	660	...	...	...	...	Finlande[2]
Germany	..	...	...	348805	375832	541106	502815	380666	332895	...	Allemagne
German D.R.(former)	4541	..	..	..	..	..	..	..	..	..	R.D.A. (anc.)
Hungary	5329	3863	3571	...	...	...	...	...	...	...	Hongrie
Poland	1995	1104	506	442	255	209	167	116	47	12	Pologne
Romania	2187	5027	4066	...	...	314	316	226	...	...	Roumanie
Russian Federation	..	48225	27154	8566	5060	3489	2254	1973	1145	12822	Fédération de Russie
Ukraine	..	7362	5464	1860	912	914	201	330	252	166	Ukraine

General Note.

Sensitized paper, unexposed, not developed, for the production of positive photographic prints (amateur, professional, recording, x-ray, photo-copying etc. work) for the production of negatives by exposure in a camera, and papers used to produce blue-prints, tracings etc. Sensitized paperboard and cloth are excluded. (SITC, Rev.3: 88240-0).

Remarque générale.

Papiers sensibilisés, non impressionnés, non développés, pour la production de positifs (papiers pour photographie d'amateurs, photographie d'art, photocopie, radiographie, appareils enregistreurs, etc.), et la production de négatifs par exposition dans un appareil photographique, et papiers utilisés pour la production de calques photographiques, la reproduction de plans et de dessins, etc. Cette rubrique ne comprend pas les cartons et les tissus sensibilisés. (CTCI, Rev.3: 88240-0).

[1] Excluding sensitized paper for blue-prints and office use.
[2] In metric tons.

[1] Non compris les papiers sensibilisés pour bleus et usages de bureau.
[2] En tonnes métriques.

Aviation gasolene
Essence aviation

ISIC-BASED CODE - CODE BASE CITI
3530-01A

Unit : Thousand metric tons

Unité : Milliers de tonnes métriques

Country or area	1990	1991	1992	1993	1994	1995	1996	1997	1998	1999	Pays ou zone
Africa	**188**	**195**	**193**	**195**	**198**	**262**	**288**	**204**	**205**	**255**	**Afrique**
Cameroon*	11	12	12	14	14	15	17	17	17	...	Cameroun*
Congo	53	*53	*54	*54	*55	*55	*57	*57	*57	...	Congo
Egypt*	5	7	5	5	5	5	5	5	5	...	Egypte*
Gabon	*1	*1	1	1	1	1	1	1	*1	...	Gabon
Senegal*	92	94	95	98	98	99	99	99	101	...	Sénégal*
South Africa	*23	*23	*21	18	20	*82	*104	*20	*19	...	Afrique du Sud
Sudan*	3	5	5	5	5	5	5	5	5	...	Soudan*
America, North	**1148**	**1154**	**1118**	**1117**	**1145**	**1142**	**1040**	**1032**	**1045**	**999**	**Amérique du Nord**
Canada	93	87	80	88	107	110	89	83	*107	...	Canada
Mexico	*44	124	99	125	107	109	118	*120	*121	...	Mexique
Netherlands Antilles*	10	7	7	9	9	9	10	10	12	...	Antilles néerlandaises*
Trinidad and Tobago	10	4	*5	*5	6	*5	*5	*5	*5	...	Trinité-et-Tobago
United States	991	932	927	890	916	909	818	814	*800	...	Etats-Unis
America, South	**138**	**154**	**112**	**125**	**142**	**130**	**117**	**119**	**132**	**119**	**Amérique du Sud**
Argentina	14	12	*12	5	8	8	5	2	*2	...	Argentine
Bolivia	7	*6	5	4	4	4	4	4	*4	...	Bolivie
Brazil	51	42	29	63	73	64	60	54	77	...	Brésil
Chile	14	12	13	10	16	11	9	8	11	...	Chili
Colombia	32	35	33	25	*18	*21	*21	20	*20	...	Colombie
Uruguay	1	1	0	...	...	...	...	...	...	...	Uruguay
Venezuela	19	46	*20	17	22	21	17	30	*17	...	Venezuela
Asia	**262**	**217**	**242**	**307**	**238**	**237**	**233**	**253**	**294**	**251**	**Asie**
Azerbaijan	..	...	4	1	1	1	1	1	*0	...	Azerbaïdjan
China	*77	*80	*88	*92	*95	*81	81	77	*126	...	Chine
Indonesia	11	4	11	5	11	10	2	7	*4	...	Indonésie
Iran(Islamic Rep. of)[1]	*150	*106	*110	*73	*76	*76	78	99	*96	...	Iran(Rép. islamique)[1]
Japan	9	8	9	8	8	7	7	7	*6	...	Japon
Jordan	*15	14	17	21	*20	30	32	*32	*32	...	Jordanie
Myanmar[2]	0	1	1	0	0	0	0	0	*0	...	Myanmar[2]
Philippines	0	0	0	107	...	...	...	...	...	...	Philippines
Uzbekistan	..	...	...	*0	*0	5	5	3	*3	...	Ouzbékistan
Europe	**236**	**329**	**377**	**350**	**270**	**241**	**217**	**208**	**206**	**151**	**Europe**
Belgium	8	1	0	0	0	0	2	0	*0	...	Belgique
Czech Republic	..	..	12	8	12	9	6	2	*1	...	République tchèque
Finland	...	15	31	36	29	29	20	23	*32	...	Finlande
France incl. Monaco	97	97	73	17	77	53	68	71	*63	...	France y compris Monaco
Italy and San Marino	*36	36	44	64	25	26	6	9	*6	...	Italie y comp. St. Marin
Netherlands	64	50	46	80	68	68	65	61	*63	...	Pays-Bas
Romania	...	...	...	5	4	4	5	3	*6	...	Roumanie
Russian Federation	..	...	159	113	48	45	38	39	*31	...	Fédération de Russie
Slovakia	..	..	*8	*8	*7	*7	*7	0	...	...	Slovaquie
Spain	0	0	0	19	0	0	0	0	*0	...	Espagne
USSR (former)	**451**	..	..	..	..	..	..	..	..		**URSS (anc.)**
Oceania	**159**	**124**	**99**	**125**	**107**	**109**	**118**	**96**	**107**	**85**	**Océanie**
Australia[3]	159	124	99	125	107	109	118	96	*107	...	Australie[3]
Total	**2582**	**2173**	**2141**	**2219**	**2099**	**2120**	**2012**	**1911**	**1988**	**1859**	**Total**

General Note.

Motor spirit prepared especially for aviation piston engines, with an octane number varying from 80 to 145 RON and a freezing point of -60°C. (SITC, Rev.3: 33411-1A).

Remarque générale.

Carburant fabriqué spécialment pour les moteurs d'avion, à pistons avec un indice d'octane variant de 80 à 145 IOR et dont le point de congélation est de -60°C. (CTCI, Rev.3: 33411-1A).

[1] Twelve months beginning 21 March of year stated.
[2] Twelve months beginning 1 April of year stated.
[3] Twelve months ending 30 June of year stated.

[1] Période de douze mois commençant le 21 mars de l'année indiquée.
[2] Période de douze mois commençant le 1er avril de l'année indiquée.
[3] Période de douze mois finissant le 30 juin de l'année indiquée.

Jet fuels
Carburéacteurs
ISIC-BASED CODE - CODE BASE CITI
3530-04A

Unit : Thousand metric tons — Unité : Milliers de tonnes métriques

Country or area	1990	1991	1992	1993	1994	1995	1996	1997	1998	1999	Pays ou zone
Africa	**4341**	**4100**	**4068**	**4513**	**5518**	**5652**	**6091**	**6029**	**5952**	**7204**	**Afrique**
Algeria*	530	300	350	559	1080	977	1104	1197	970	...	Algérie*
Angola*	157	155	160	316	294	283	302	306	285	...	Angola*
Cameroon*	8	9	9	9	9	10	10	10	10	...	Cameroun*
Congo*	12	14	14	15	15	16	16	17	17	...	Congo*
Côte d'Ivoire*	51	53	58	59	61	62	62	63	63	...	Côte d'Ivoire*
Dem. Rep. of Congo*	5	4	3	5	2	3	3	3	3	...	Rép. dém. du Congo*
Egypt	363	378	414	506	780	860	850	854	*900	...	Egypte
Ethiopia,incl.Eritrea	*62	*63	*60	*53	37	*28	*8	*5	*5	...	Ethiopie,incl.Erythrée
Gabon	*68	*70	64	64	40	17	28	23	*26	...	Gabon
Ghana	*48	47	*48	*51	*51	*52	*52	*52	*54	...	Ghana
Kenya	344	294	319	298	295	262	*265	218	231	...	Kenya
Libyan Arab Jamah.*	1460	1535	1245	1183	1375	1403	1423	1339	1339	...	Jamah. arabe libyenne*
Madagascar*	1	1	1	1	1	1	1	1	1	...	Madagascar*
Morocco	250	183	206	223	238	239	231	241	*272	...	Maroc
Nigeria*	38	40	40	40	30	30	30	25	25	...	Nigéria*
Senegal*	92	92	92	92	92	93	93	94	94	...	Sénégal*
Sierra Leone*	14	14	14	16	15	16	17	17	17	...	Sierra Leone*
South Africa	*698	*700	*817	866	947	1139	1432	*1409	*1488	...	Afrique du Sud
Sudan*	75	82	85	88	88	90	91	91	92	...	Soudan*
United Rep.Tanzania*	28	28	31	32	32	33	33	34	34	...	Rép. Unie de Tanzanie*
Zambia	*37	*38	*38	*37	*36	*38	*40	*30	26	...	Zambie
America, North	**80278**	**77481**	**75710**	**76481**	**77753**	**76452**	**82515**	**83666**	**82915**	**84298**	**Amérique du Nord**
Canada	4388	3827	3659	3274	2777	3096	3711	4140	*4277	...	Canada
Costa Rica	23	19	36	28	43	*37	30	35	*0	...	Costa Rica
Cuba*	51	12	3	8	7	0	0	0	0	...	Cuba*
Dominican Republic*	23	20	20	18	18	17	17	16	16	...	Rép. dominicaine*
El Salvador	29	23	29	49	40	33	64	*50	*57	...	El Salvador
Guatemala	33	38	34	*40	*39	*14	*4	*5	*5	...	Guatemala
Honduras*	12	10	10	...	...	...	...	...	...	...	Honduras*
Jamaica	76	94	*107	*64	*44	*24	*27	*31	*33	...	Jamaïque
Mexico	2402	2557	2688	2884	3110	3074	2538	2401	*2563	...	Mexique
Netherlands Antilles*	800	750	800	812	818	820	820	822	825	...	Antilles néerlandaises*
Nicaragua	26	23	16	11	12	18	19	18	*22	...	Nicaragua
Panama*	67	46	55	42	21	0	0	0	21	...	Panama*
Puerto Rico*	705	727	710	730	750	760	760	762	765	...	Porto Rico*
Trinidad and Tobago	236	230	146	*170	469	*420	*465	*470	*638	...	Trinité-et-Tobago
United States	69957	67605	65932	66840	68044	66548	72464	73315	*72087	...	Etats-Unis
United States Virgin Is.*	1450	1500	1465	1500	1550	1580	1585	1590	1595	...	Iles Vierges américaines*
America, South	**7430**	**7391**	**6146**	**7882**	**7667**	**9133**	**9182**	**9530**	**9509**	**10818**	**Amérique du Sud**
Argentina	696	627	*670	811	986	1235	1268	1235	*1240	...	Argentine
Bolivia	*85	*81	86	94	96	106	124	169	*134	...	Bolivie
Brazil	2467	2457	2359	2294	2298	2541	2805	2787	3051	...	Brésil
Chile	248	277	278	309	360	359	373	543	502	...	Chili
Colombia	509	524	600	651	*653	*702	*550	527	*535	...	Colombie
Ecuador	179	185	197	193	174	206	218	*215	*256	...	Equateur
Paraguay	35	*20	*20	*22	*7	*6	*3	*3	*3	...	Paraguay
Uruguay	24	35	34	7	0	25	41	37	*66	...	Uruguay
Venezuela	3187	3185	*1902	*3501	*3093	*3953	3800	4014	*3722	...	Venezuela
Asia	**28361**	**27915**	**30747**	**31859**	**35962**	**40094**	**42230**	**45153**	**46885**	**54519**	**Asie**
Azerbaijan	..	...	442	470	419	504	527	450	*526	...	Azerbaïdjan
Bahrain	*1210	*1100	*840	556	896	784	772	1208	*1172	...	Bahreïn
Bangladesh[1]	13	27	3	4	0	1	1	5	*6	...	Bangladesh[1]
Brunei Darussalam	35	44	54	53	68	73	64	72	*78	...	Brunéi Darussalam
Cyprus	19	27	24	30	34	16	3	5	*4	...	Chypre
India[2]	1649	1656	1680	1706	1992	*2035	2165	2155	*2224	...	Inde[2]
Indonesia	634	763	661	576	686	838	1167	990	*1150	...	Indonésie
Iran(Islamic Rep. of)*[3]	600	900	1000	1100	1200	1250	1300	1325	1350	...	Iran(Rép. islamique)*[3]
Iraq*	410	250	458	505	565	553	541	549	567	...	Iraq*
Israel*	490	486	...	...	...	...	...	...	...	...	Israël*
Japan	3479	4076	4707	5053	5625	6168	5872	7226	*8245	...	Japon

For general note and footnotes, see end of table. — Voir la fin du tableau pour la remarque générale et les notes.

Jet fuels (continued)
Carburéacteurs (suite)

ISIC-BASED CODE - CODE BASE CITI

3530-04A

Unit : Thousand metric tons   Unité : Milliers de tonnes métriques

Country or area	1990	1991	1992	1993	1994	1995	1996	1997	1998	1999	Pays ou zone
Jordan	250	96	193	220	198	244	298	267	*221	...	Jordanie
Kazakhstan	..	...	982	525	420	327	314	200	*200	...	Kazakhstan
Korea, Republic of	2109	2261	2690	2604	3371	4502	4996	5462	8211	...	Corée, République de
Kuwait,part Ntl.Zone	1977	49	1090	1149	1268	*1389	606	1595	*1880	...	Koweït et prt.Zne.N.
Malaysia	365	390	400	502	951	*1537	*1839	*1937	*1926	...	Malaisie
Myanmar[2]	29	38	37	42	52	63	52	56	*50	...	Myanmar[2]
Oman	261	274	182	150	*163	166	156	170	*186	...	Oman
Pakistan[1]	490	518	559	572	567	527	585	594	*583	...	Pakistan[1]
Philippines	441	445	524	*394	*561	*632	815	827	*584	...	Philippines
Qatar	387	360	399	354	422	*401	456	413	*437	...	Qatar
S.Arabia,pt.Ntrl.Zn*	2450	2560	2660	2700	2750	2740	2900	2770	2440	...	Arab.saoud,p.Zn.neut*
Singapore	*6370	*6425	*6460	*7575	*8198	*7895	9029	7995	*6463	...	Singapour
Sri Lanka	101	79	67	89	60	67	69	74	*54	...	Sri Lanka
Syrian Arab Republic	490	*324	284	*290	336	209	203	*230	*230	...	Rép. arabe syrienne
Thailand	2120	1503	1596	1781	2073	2407	2731	2917	*2721	...	Thaïlande
Turkey	621	553	687	812	978	1146	1026	1440	*1588	...	Turquie
United Arab Emirates	*1100	*1110	*1110	*1170	*1210	*2585	2474	2980	*2550	...	Emirats arabes unis
Uzbekistan	..	...	69	51	73	209	300	272	*270	...	Ouzbékistan
Viet Nam	1	*1	*1	*1	*1	*1	*1	*1	*1	...	Viet Nam
Dem. Yemen (former)*	260	..	..	..	..	..	..	..	..		Yémen dém. (anc.)*
Yemen	..	*360	*400	*337	*337	*337	480	*480	*480	...	Yémen
Europe	**34423**	**46090**	**49126**	**47867**	**47281**	**47467**	**50523**	**50486**	**52022**	**52203**	Europe
Austria	305	*367	389	375	376	421	478	505	*533	...	Autriche
Belarus	..	...	1278	917	768	*0	*0	*0	*0	...	Bélarus
Belgium	1438	1547	1715	1514	1618	1268	1739	1644	*2067	...	Belgique
Bulgaria	209	60	28	196	194	220	184	152	*165	...	Bulgarie
Croatia	..	...	29	85	101	96	83	95	*87	...	Croatie
Denmark	249	187	147	200	224	276	411	431	*378	...	Danemark
Czech Republic	..	..	224	226	155	170	153	145	*108	...	République tchèque
Finland	493	548	421	410	473	797	722	593	*804	...	Finlande
France incl. Monaco	4997	4723	4645	4907	5297	5649	6397	6598	*6689	...	France y compris Monaco
Germany	..	2345	*2219	2579	2842	3079	3281	3596	*3660	...	Allemagne
Germany(Fed.Rep.)	2302	..	..	..	..	..	..	..	..		Allemagne(Rép.féd.)
Greece	1800	1488	1479	1279	1583	1714	1942	1949	*1934	...	Grèce
Hungary	161	126	196	161	250	176	191	173	*206	...	Hongrie
Ireland	0	0	0	69	11	51	69	48	*43	...	Irlande
Italy and San Marino	2703	2572	2738	3105	3162	3329	3525	3657	*3822	...	Italie y comp. St. Marin
Lithuania	..	...	...	177	226	211	260	225	*373	...	Lituanie
Netherlands	4940	4730	4978	4938	5500	5997	6321	5921	*6340	...	Pays-Bas
Norway,Svlbd.J.Myn. I	918	678	862	905	844	902	1032	973	*762	...	Norvège,Svalbd,J.May
Poland	201	136	128	229	265	220	231	225	*263	...	Pologne
Portugal	891	773	883	710	1061	1051	932	1023	*1048	...	Portugal
Romania	...	...	...	255	210	178	92	88	*84	...	Roumanie
Russian Federation	..	...	13681	11126	9184	9015	9189	9189	*9189	...	Fédération de Russie
Slovakia	..	..	...	...	141	97	70	62	*50	...	Slovaquie
Spain	4230	3667	3560	3427	3648	3339	3600	3577	*4190	...	Espagne
Sweden	269	220	142	66	57	125	215	150	*101	...	Suède
Switzrld,Liechtenstein	231	260	243	281	313	317	381	410	*417	...	Suisse,Liechtenstein
Ukraine	..	...	831	1200	1043	890	665	620	*651	...	Ukraine
United Kingdom	7541	7037	7681	8341	7697	7837	8305	8342	*7963	...	Royaume-Uni
Yugoslavia	..	...	*50	*40	38	42	55	95	*95	...	Yougoslavie
Yugoslavia, SFR*	300	..	..	..	..	..	..	..	..		Yougoslavie, RSF*
Oceania	**3417**	**3480**	**3764**	**4090**	**4262**	**4286**	**4659**	**5053**	**5138**	**5825**	Océanie
Australia[1]	2611	2744	3043	3322	3428	3515	3882	4208	*4311	...	Australie[1]
New Zealand[2]	786	716	701	748	814	751	757	825	*809	...	Nouvelle-Zélande[2]
Papua New Guinea*	...	20	20	20	20	20	20	20	18	...	Papouasie-Nvl-Guinée*
Total	**158250**	**166457**	**169561**	**172692**	**178443**	**183084**	**195200**	**199917**	**202421**	**214867**	Total

For general note and footnotes, see end of table.   Voir la fin du tableau pour la remarque générale et les notes.

Jet fuels (continued)
Carburéacteurs (suite)

ISIC-BASED CODE - CODE BASE CITI

3530-04A

General Note.

Fuel meeting the required properties for use in jet engines and aircraft-turbine engines, mainly refined from kerosene. Gasolene-type jet fuel (light hydrocarbons, also naphtha type, intended for use in aviation gas-turbine units) is included. (SITC, Rev.3: 33412-0A).

[1] Twelve months ending 30 June of year stated.
[2] Twelve months beginning 1 April of year stated.
[3] Twelve months beginning 21 March of year stated.

Remarque générale.

Carburants ayant les propriétés requises pour l'emploi dans les moteurs à réaction et les moteurs d'avion à turbine, obtenus principalement par raffinage du kérosène, y compris les carburéacteurs analogues à l'essence (hydrocarbures légers, y compris ceux analogues au naphta, devant servir dans les moteurs d'avion à turbine à gaz). (CTCI, Rev.3: 33412-0A).

[1] Période de douze mois finissant le 30 juin de l'année indiquée.
[2] Période de douze mois commençant le 1er avril de l'année indiquée.
[3] Période de douze mois commençant le 21 mars de l'année indiquée.

Motor gasolene
Essence auto

ISIC-BASED CODE - CODE BASE CITI

3530-07A

Unit : Thousand metric tons

Unité : Milliers de tonnes métriques

Country or area	1990	1991	1992	1993	1994	1995	1996	1997	1998	1999	Pays ou zone
Africa	**20597**	**21070**	**20809**	**21152**	**20902**	**22303**	**21760**	**21674**	**21976**	**22656**	**Afrique**
Algeria	2083	2233	2272	2477	2903	2546	2336	1989	*2037	...	Algérie
Angola*	108	105	110	110	119	118	111	97	102	...	Angola*
Cameroon	*285	*292	*294	414	296	*298	*301	*303	*304	...	Cameroun
Congo	51	58	53	*55	*56	*53	*55	*55	*56	...	Congo
Côte d'Ivoire	*375	464	472	414	*425	*428	*432	434	*437	...	Côte d'Ivoire
Dem. Rep. of Congo	58	42	28	31	8	*9	*9	*9	*9	...	Rép. dém. du Congo
Egypt[1]	3714	3783	3638	4073	4356	*4520	4784	5065	*5242	...	Egypte[1]
Ethiopia,incl.Eritrea	*128	*131	*90	*85	82	*25	*7	*5	*5	...	Ethiopie,incl.Erythrée
Gabon	84	83	90	85	74	78	76	71	60	...	Gabon
Ghana	204	284	192	192	260	196	200	200	*205	...	Ghana
Kenya	335	328	348	329	329	305	*300	273	294	...	Kenya
Libyan Arab Jamah.	1743	*1800	*1810	*1820	*1890	*1929	1957	1970	*1970	...	Jamah. arabe libyenne
Madagascar*	25	35	37	38	57	64	71	103	68	...	Madagascar*
Mauritania*	203	210	225	228	229	230	232	234	234	...	Mauritanie*
Morocco	392	352	403	397	408	366	394	409	*354	...	Maroc
Nigeria	3745	3594	3233	3178	1675	1718	*1700	*1720	*1800	...	Nigéria
Senegal	109	*112	*115	*117	*118	*118	*120	*120	*120	...	Sénégal
Sierra Leone*	23	25	26	28	27	28	28	28	29	...	Sierra Leone*
South Africa	*6385	*6596	*6792	6524	6998	*8653	*7995	*7898	*8024	...	Afrique du Sud
Sudan*	95	98	95	97	95	98	101	103	105	...	Soudan*
Tunisia	241	228	268	238	280	302	326	362	*294	...	Tunisie
United Rep.Tanzania*	96	98	98	102	102	104	105	106	106	...	Rép. Unie de Tanzanie*
Zambia	*115	119	120	*120	*115	*117	*120	*120	121	...	Zambie
America, North	**352030**	**352244**	**354856**	**368693**	**367876**	**381078**	**385706**	**391720**	**398895**	**416897**	**Amérique du Nord**
Barbados	59	59	59	61	57	61	56	68	*0	...	Barbade
Canada	26357	25827	25507	26555	27077	27567	28636	28353	*28578	...	Canada
Costa Rica	61	55	61	63	102	100	77	81	*4	...	Costa Rica
Cuba[2]	1306	880	940	939	939	958	978	440	*310	...	Cuba[2]
Dominican Republic	399	448	427	343	349	356	363	370	*221	...	Rép. dominicaine
El Salvador	112	124	152	195	182	175	197	149	*134	...	El Salvador
Guatemala	104	94	117	125	121	131	131	137	*124	...	Guatemala
Honduras	70	66	68	...	...	...	...	...	...	...	Honduras
Jamaica	146	131	173	95	139	152	166	180	*195	...	Jamaïque
Martinique*	122	124	137	143	148	151	152	152	153	...	Martinique*
Mexico	*17734	17904	16870	17175	17613	17360	16062	15525	*16435	...	Mexique
Netherlands Antilles*	1450	1700	1700	1775	1785	1788	1790	1795	1810	...	Antilles néerlandaises*
Nicaragua	77	105	111	114	98	102	102	97	*101	...	Nicaragua
Panama[1]	168	154	215	217	112	113	256	289	*313	...	Panama[1]
Puerto Rico*	1930	1950	1670	1910	2068	1700	1720	1745	1750	...	Porto Rico*
Trinidad and Tobago	721	664	667	760	841	917	812	670	*1466	...	Trinité-et-Tobago
United States	298814	299534	303897	316055	313977	327079	331830	339281	*344908	...	Etats-Unis
United States Virgin Is.*	2400	2425	2085	2100	2200	2300	2310	2320	2325	...	Iles Vierges américaines*
America, South	**36328**	**36201**	**38071**	**40532**	**42303**	**40568**	**42551**	**45284**	**48552**	**51088**	**Amérique du Sud**
Argentina	5267	5677	5870	5937	6057	6444	5160	4815	*4183	...	Argentine
Bolivia	380	380	349	356	362	404	433	466	*456	...	Bolivie
Brazil	8546	8530	9320	11003	10913	10803	11822	13193	14581	...	Brésil
Chile	1439	1451	1480	1685	1746	1849	1847	1964	2040	...	Chili
Colombia	3558	3785	3856	3768	3802	3972	4886	4579	*4578	...	Colombie
Ecuador	1229	1305	1338	1273	1281	1218	1505	1324	*1345	...	Equateur
Paraguay	76	70	*57	74	63	53	26	27	*23	...	Paraguay
Peru	1233	1210	1116	1160	1250	1000	1188	1175	*1552	...	Pérou
Uruguay	197	237	187	62	0	257	235	265	*356	...	Uruguay
Venezuela	14403	13556	14498	15214	16829	14568	15449	17476	*19438	...	Venezuela
Asia	**104847**	**115338**	**124862**	**133914**	**136035**	**140822**	**151262**	**157167**	**159028**	**180166**	**Asie**
Azerbaijan	..	...	1024	1066	1269	1128	737	800	*630	...	Azerbaïdjan
Bahrain	*924	*959	*1040	1086	906	1050	957	1061	*746	...	Bahreïn
Bangladesh[3]	71	79	88	101	88	102	122	144	*90	...	Bangladesh[3]
Brunei Darussalam	181	152	147	161	171	183	190	194	*184	...	Brunéi Darussalam
China	21734	24037	27261	31600	28541	30516	32636	35060	*35010	...	Chine
Cyprus	122	121	102	94	122	102	95	141	*142	...	Chypre

For general note and footnotes, see end of table.

Voir la fin du tableau pour la remarque générale et les notes.

Motor gasolene (continued)
Essence auto (suite)

ISIC-BASED CODE - CODE BASE CITI

3530-07A

Unit : Thousand metric tons   Unité : Milliers de tonnes métriques

Country or area	1990	1991	1992	1993	1994	1995	1996	1997	1998	1999	Pays ou zone
Georgia	..	...	22	52	34	7	0	5	*4	...	Géorgie
India[4]	3536	3453	3440	3545	4097	4367	4597	4876	*5247	...	Inde[4]
Indonesia	4455	4820	5005	5330	5264	4942	7155	7950	*7302	...	Indonésie
Iran(Islamic Rep. of)[5]	5105	6400	7416	7574	*7796	*7831	7643	7893	*9025	...	Iran(Rép. islamique)[5]
Iraq	2500	2117	2856	*2960	*2970	*2990	*2927	*2968	*3066	...	Iraq
Israel	1463	1305	1801	2428	2373	2294	2155	2184	*2109	...	Israël
Japan	31067	32678	34013	35295	36671	37409	38452	39389	*40709	...	Japon
Jordan	400	427	421	430	471	483	500	531	*524	...	Jordanie
Kazakhstan	..	..	3375	2896	2207	2180	2296	1787	*1732	...	Kazakhstan
Korea,Dem.Ppl's.Rep.*	1000	990	990	980	970	960	950	885	841	...	Corée,Rép.pop.dém.de*
Korea, Republic of	2816	3357	3806	4855	5966	7113	8345	9253	8944	...	Corée, République de
Kuwait,part Ntl.Zone	1880	900	1107	1307	1751	1902	1954	1822	*2057	...	Koweït et prt.Zne.N.
Lebanon	87	93	63	...	...	...	...	...	...	...	Liban
Malaysia	1339	1584	1642	1730	2206	2244	2315	2395	*2392	...	Malaisie
Myanmar[4]	136	137	155	168	192	213	175	255	*271	...	Myanmar[4]
Oman	483	497	558	368	561	555	710	648	*679	...	Oman
Pakistan[3]	891	926	993	1031	998	923	1031	976	*1055	...	Pakistan[3]
Philippines	1678	1396	1574	*1536	*1432	*1898	2056	2207	*2242	...	Philippines
Qatar	470	414	403	411	551	*530	*608	525	*603	...	Qatar
S.Arabia,pt.Ntrl.Zn	10709	9869	10442	10900	11386	10622	11844	11309	*12242	...	Arab.saoud,p.Zn.neut
Singapore	3377	3391	*3420	*3600	*4077	*4676	5231	5032	*4920	...	Singapour
Sri Lanka	179	148	122	173	181	153	201	171	*198	...	Sri Lanka
Syrian Arab Republic	1306	1197	1166	1352	1360	1372	1591	1591	*1591	...	Rép. arabe syrienne
Thailand	2248	2295	2577	2988	3281	3889	5550	6462	*6038	...	Thaïlande
Turkey	3103	3014	3172	3535	3754	3973	3759	3916	*3677	...	Turquie
Turkmenistan	..	...	931	727	699	641	677	766	*693	...	Turkménistan
United Arab Emirates	*1250	1258	1270	*1091	*1200	1200	1468	1507	*1539	...	Emirats arabes unis
Uzbekistan	..	...	1506	1642	1545	1213	1202	1344	*1406	...	Ouzbékistan
Viet Nam	7	*7	*7	*7	*7	*7	*7	*7	*7	...	Viet Nam
Dem. Yemen (former)*	220									...	Yémen dém. (anc.)*
Yemen (former)*	110	..	..	..	..	..	..	..	..	...	Yémen (anc.)*
Yemen	..	634	947	814	857	1073	1045	1032	*1032	...	Yémen
Europe	**149223**	**185769**	**196118**	**191741**	**188689**	**189979**	**191118**	**194363**	**195688**	**196274**	**Europe**
Albania	81	121	85	87	74	74	74	74	*74	...	Albanie
Austria	2631	2399	2461	2329	2541	2271	2298	2410	*2157	...	Autriche
Belarus	..		2222	1687	1744	1849	1816	1954	*1907	...	Bélarus
Belgium	5263	5883	6162	5614	5686	5259	5947	6103	*6431	...	Belgique
Bulgaria	1297	540	451	1544	1239	1477	1266	1112	*925	...	Bulgarie
Croatia	..	...	802	1038	1080	1177	1057	1089	*1158	...	Croatie
Denmark	1318	1551	1537	1477	1597	2132	2559	2343	*2176	...	Danemark
Czechoslovakia(former)	1440	1536	..	..	..	..	..	..	..	...	Tchécoslovaquie(anc.)
Czech Republic	..		1152	1052	970	1046	1237	1202	*1056	...	République tchèque
Finland	2971	3160	3539	3394	4116	4150	4297	3788	*4056	...	Finlande
France incl. Monaco	17690	17631	18015	17966	17696	17951	18094	18894	*19717	...	France y compris Monaco
Germany	..	24622	*25330	26848	26419	25875	26105	25354	*26222	...	Allemagne
Germany(Fed.Rep.)	21124	..	..	..	..	..	..	..	..		Allemagne(Rép.féd.)
German D.R. (former)*	4700	..	..	..	..	..	..	..	..		R.D.A. (anc.)*
Greece	3379	3128	3581	3445	3543	3545	3383	3607	*3671	...	Grèce
Hungary	1447	1371	1307	1280	1246	1396	1351	1392	*1471	...	Hongrie
Ireland	340	333	361	367	354	382	379	452	*468	...	Irlande
Italy and San Marino	18488	18243	19451	19443	19888	19802	20065	21384	*21239	...	Italie y comp. St. Marin
Lithuania	..	...	848	1320	1037	858	1295	1664	*2112	...	Lituanie
Netherlands[6]	12842	13248	12794	14794	14391	14857	14882	14121	*14913	...	Pays-Bas[6]
Norway,Svlbd.J.Myn. I	3203	2766	3242	3233	3155	2767	3086	3413	*3215	...	Norvège,Svalbd,J.May
Poland	2192	2172	2933	3144	3212	2994	3132	3193	*3347	...	Pologne
Portugal	1704	1623	1860	1687	2354	2757	2591	2835	*2792	...	Portugal
Romania	4666	3122	2923	2620	3420	3451	3125	3205	*3197	...	Roumanie
Russian Federation	..	...	35289	30147	26903	28140	26780	27178	*25923	...	Fédération de Russie
Slovakia	..	..	*700	692	*673	*811	800	832	*912	...	Slovaquie
Slovenia	..	...	135	138	74	120	79	89	14	...	Slovénie
Spain	9230	8932	9441	8950	9570	9696	9260	9235	*9930	...	Espagne
Sweden	3741	3796	4363	4361	3814	4103	4345	4571	*4336	...	Suède
Switzrld,Liechtenstein	752	1153	988	1084	1096	1037	1131	1181	*1211	...	Suisse,Liechtenstein

For general note and footnotes, see end of table.   Voir la fin du tableau pour la remarque générale et les notes.

Motor gasolene (continued)
Essence auto (suite)

ISIC-BASED CODE - CODE BASE CITI

3530-07A

Unit : Thousand metric tons Unité : Milliers de tonnes métriques

Country or area	1990	1991	1992	1993	1994	1995	1996	1997	1998	1999	Pays ou zone
Ukraine	..	...	5388	3324	3052	2610	2138	2803	*2943	...	Ukraine
United Kingdom	26724	27793	28126	28135	27562	27254	28048	28260	*27392	...	Royaume-Uni
Yugoslavia	..	...	462	110	104	116	440	590	*570	...	Yougoslavie
T.F.Yug.Rep. Macedonia	..	...	*170	431	79	22	58	35	*153	...	L'ex-RY Macédoine
Yugoslavia, SFR*	2000	..	..	..	..	..	..	..	..	..	Yougoslavie, RSF*
USSR (former)	63596	..	..	..	..	..	..	..	..	..	URSS (anc.)
Oceania	13782	13824	14431	14829	14730	14747	14978	14805	15223	15728	Océanie
Australia[3]	11969	12098	12640	13020	13023	13164	13495	13256	*13633	...	Australie[3]
New Zealand[4]	1813	1726	1791	1809	1707	1583	1483	1549	*1590	...	Nouvelle-Zélande[4]
Total	740403	724446	749147	770861	770535	789497	807375	825013	839362	882808	Total

General Note.

Light hydrocarbon oil used in positive ignition engines other than aircraft, distilling between 35 and 200°C, and treated to reach a sufficiently high-octane number of generally between 80 and 100 RON. Treatment may be done by reforming, blending with an aromatic fraction or addition of benzole or other additives (such as tetraethyl lead). (SITC, Rev.3: 33411-2A).

Remarque générale.

Hydrocarbure léger utilisé dans les moteurs à allumage par étincelle autres que les moteurs d'avion dont les températeurs de distillation se situent entre 35 et 200°C et qui est traité de façon à atteindre un indice d'octane suffisamment élevé, généralement entre 80 et 100 IOR. Le traitement peut consister en reformage, mélange avec une fraction aromatique, ou adjonction de benzol ou d'autres additifs (tels que du plomb tétraéthyl). (CTCI, Rev.3: 33411-2A).

[1] Including naphthas.
[2] Including alcohol.
[3] Twelve months ending 30 June of year stated.
[4] Twelve months beginning 1 April of year stated.
[5] Twelve months beginning 21 March of year stated.
[6] Including other light oils.

[1] Y compris les naphthas.
[2] Y compris l'alcool.
[3] Période de douze mois finissant le 30 juin de l'année indiquée.
[4] Période de douze mois commençant le 1er avril de l'année indiquée.
[5] Période de douze mois commençant le 21 mars de l'année indiquée.
[6] Y compris les autres huiles légères.

Naphthas
Naphtas

ISIC-BASED CODE - CODE BASE CITI

3530-10A

Unit : Thousand metric tons

Unité : Milliers de tonnes métriques

Country or area	1990	1991	1992	1993	1994	1995	1996	1997	1998	1999	Pays ou zone
Africa	**6949**	**7112**	**6812**	**6463**	**5758**	**5998**	**6001**	**6803**	**6488**	**5929**	**Afrique**
Algeria*	4200	4250	3837	3614	2813	3330	3464	4043	3855	...	Algérie*
Angola*	7	7	130	75	153	155	153	170	137	...	Angola*
Gabon	*1	3	3	4	4	5	4	3	*3	...	Gabon
Libyan Arab Jamah.	*2080	*2220	*2130	*2100	*2300	*1958	1984	1998	*1998	...	Jamah. arabe libyenne
Morocco	522	465	542	449	359	416	275	303	*385	...	Maroc
Sierra Leone*	7	8	8	8	8	8	8	8	8	...	Sierra Leone*
South Africa	...	*40	*40	50	50	*40	*30	*20	*20	...	Afrique du Sud
Sudan*	20	22	22	22	23	23	24	24	24	...	Soudan*
Tunisia	70	97	100	141	48	63	59	234	*58	...	Tunisie
America, North	**13719**	**12545**	**13960**	**12606**	**13608**	**14252**	**15063**	**15808**	**16695**	**17295**	**Amérique du Nord**
Canada	3699	3851	3917	3478	3300	3865	3893	3701	*3787	...	Canada
Costa Rica	22	14	22	8	6	5	12	7	*1	...	Costa Rica
Cuba*	292	215	63	62	61	70	83	56	45	...	Cuba*
Mexico	1620	1583	1424	1381	1947	1906	1835	1096	*1226	...	Mexique
Puerto Rico*	600	500	500	520	500	590	595	600	600	...	Porto Rico*
Trinidad and Tobago	45	*40	*40	*35	111	*30	*35	*30	*30	...	Trinité-et-Tobago
United States	7441	6342	7994	7122	7683	7786	8610	10318	*11006	...	Etats-Unis
America, South	**6865**	**6000**	**5783**	**5830**	**5956**	**5654**	**5701**	**6484**	**6845**	**6229**	**Amérique du Sud**
Argentina	871	664	*650	*640	663	*650	785	937	*940	...	Argentine
Brazil	5926	5260	5047	5096	5222	4903	4715	5257	5603	...	Brésil
Chile	41	42	46	78	51	55	133	197	242	...	Chili
Peru	...	...	...	*15	*20	*30	*52	82	*50	...	Pérou
Uruguay	13	14	15	1	0	16	16	11	*10	...	Uruguay
Asia	**47620**	**49612**	**54525**	**57981**	**63337**	**69222**	**73791**	**82324**	**83783**	**96633**	**Asie**
Bahrain	1740	1790	1832	1523	*1587	1720	1765	1713	*1735	...	Bahreïn
Bangladesh [1]	59	61	34	48	35	34	30	13	*14	...	Bangladesh [1]
Brunei Darussalam	*6	78	95	99	100	100	98	*98	*98	...	Brunéi Darussalam
China	...	...	...	11285	12310	14032	15892	17439	*17412	...	Chine
India [2]	4730	4423	*4475	4783	5466	*5630	6157	6015	*6006	...	Inde [2]
Indonesia	1592	1213	1075	1002	1138	1115	1673	929	*522	...	Indonésie
Iran(Islamic Rep. of) [3]	*260	*280	*300	*400	*300	*684	692	679	*1871	...	Iran(Rép. islamique) [3]
Iraq*	600	450	600	500	500	492	482	489	505	...	Iraq*
Israel	159	292	453	431	546	643	485	695	*887	...	Israël
Japan	8004	10386	11793	12794	12869	13136	12230	14176	*13270	...	Japon
Korea, Republic of	4060	6069	7467	7492	7777	10105	11800	17657	17601	...	Corée, République de
Kuwait,part Ntl.Zone	*3200	*63	*1200	*4397	*6812	*7416	7302	7936	*7872	...	Koweït et prt.Zne.N.
Malaysia*	350	281	290	340	375	395	405	420	1259	...	Malaisie*
Pakistan [1]	58	196	151	99	108	148	105	81	*71	...	Pakistan [1]
Philippines	226	387	366	*373	*499	*643	690	648	*585	...	Philippines
S.Arabia,pt.Ntrl.Zn*	4390	4294	4306	4724	4908	4578	5182	4948	5356	...	Arab.saoud,p.Zn.neut*
Singapore	4242	4953	*5100	*5500	*5650	*5700	*5850	*5100	*5200	...	Singapour
Sri Lanka	74	87	72	120	115	120	107	99	*121	...	Sri Lanka
Syrian Arab Republic	196	231	243	197	301	367	238	311	*276	...	Rép. arabe syrienne
Tajikistan	..	...	56	39	30	22	18	23	*12	...	Tadjikistan
Turkey	1466	1118	1241	1207	1220	1451	1607	1605	*1874	...	Turquie
United Arab Emirates	900	920	700	628	691	691	983	1250	*1236	...	Emirats arabes unis
Europe	**36312**	**41852**	**44332**	**45099**	**45438**	**49919**	**49620**	**52020**	**51825**	**55025**	**Europe**
Belgium	1391	1078	715	820	906	696	1148	1407	*1524	...	Belgique
Bulgaria	...	...	220	*400	484	599	642	615	*624	...	Bulgarie
Croatia	..	...	...	236	279	353	307	292	*274	...	Croatie
Denmark	251	152	131	149	137	145	197	65	*12	...	Danemark
Czech Republic	..	...	594	513	526	505	467	402	*443	...	République tchèque
Finland	286	260	149	149	300	344	311	344	*336	...	Finlande
France incl. Monaco	3480	3704	3194	3381	3516	4252	4282	5744	*5398	...	France y compris Monaco
Germany	..	7179	*7588	8393	9531	9685	9366	8733	*9638	...	Allemagne
Germany(Fed.Rep.)	6535	..	..	..	..	..	..	..	..	..	Allemagne(Rép.féd.)
Greece	550	223	404	145	549	755	977	970	*932	...	Grèce
Hungary	928	749	489	589	627	665	662	757	*798	...	Hongrie
Ireland	70	46	41	32	54	65	59	94	*121	...	Irlande

For general note and footnotes, see end of table.

Voir la fin du tableau pour la remarque générale et les notes.

Naphthas (continued)
Naphtas (suite)

ISIC-BASED CODE - CODE BASE CITI

3530-10A

Unit : Thousand metric tons   Unité : Milliers de tonnes métriques

Country or area	1990	1991	1992	1993	1994	1995	1996	1997	1998	1999	Pays ou zone
Italy and San Marino	4129	3613	3682	3532	3648	4465	4087	4370	*5132	...	Italie y comp. St. Marin
Netherlands	9790	9601	9773	8579	11227	11215	10680	11265	*9646	...	Pays-Bas
Norway,Svlbd.J.Myn. I	564	699	740	651	843	652	636	567	*744	...	Norvège,Svalbd,J.May
Poland	985	773	852	850	705	604	729	837	*781	...	Pologne
Portugal	811	691	728	749	909	865	820	900	*904	...	Portugal
Romania	...	...	...	455	355	466	541	433	*424	...	Roumanie
Russian Federation	..	...	6379	8260	3547	...	...	...	...	...	Fédération de Russie
Slovakia	..	..	...	560	626	670	670	670	*670	...	Slovaquie
Slovenia	..	...	133	108	78	99	125	74	53	...	Slovénie
Spain	2190	2409	2551	2308	2235	2471	2303	2694	*2940	...	Espagne
Sweden	574	770	1358	1355	1399	1402	1491	1452	*1613	...	Suède
Switzrld,Liechtenstein	13	14	6	0	0	0	8	17	*19	...	Suisse,Liechtenstein
United Kingdom	2165	2545	3069	2721	2810	2711	2824	2871	*2352	...	Royaume-Uni
Yugoslavia	..	...	200	164	147	173	226	385	*385	...	Yougoslavie
Yugoslavia, SFR*	910	..	..	..	..	..	..	..	..	..	Yougoslavie, RSF*
Oceania	**217**	**298**	**199**	**260**	**187**	**249**	**203**	**247**	**153**	**176**	Océanie
Australia [1]	217	298	199	260	187	249	203	247	*153	...	Australie [1]
Total	**111682**	**117418**	**125612**	**128239**	**134284**	**145294**	**150379**	**163686**	**165789**	**181288**	Total

General Note.

Light or medium oil distilling between 30 and 210°C, for which there is no official definition, but which does not meet the the standards laid down for motor spirit. The properties depend on consumer specifications; the C:H ratio is usually 84:14 or 84:16, with a very low sulphur content. Naphtha may be further blended or mixed with other materials to make high-grade motor gasolene or jet fuel, used as raw materials for town gas or feedstocks to make various kinds of chemical products, or used as various solvents (SITC, Rev.3: 33419-1A).

Remarque générale.

Huiles légères ou lourdes, dont les températures de distillation se situent entre 30 et 210°C et pour lequelles il n'existe pas de définition officielle, mais qui ne satisfont pas aux normes fixées pour le carburant auto. Leurs propriétés peuvent être adaptées aux spécifications des utilisateurs; le rapport C/H est habituellement de 84/14 ou 84/16, avec une très faible teneur en soufre. Les naphtas peuvent être coupés ou mélangés avec d'autres produits en vue d'obtenir de l'essence auto de haute qualité ou du carburéacteur, ou servir de matières premières dans la fabrication du gaz de ville ou de charge de départ pour la fabrication de divers produits chimiques, ou encore être utilisés comme solvants. (CTCI, Rev.3: 33419-1A).

[1] Twelve months ending 30 June of year stated.
[2] Twelve months beginning 1 April of year stated.
[3] Twelve months beginning 21 March of year stated.

[1] Période de douze mois finissant le 30 juin de l'année indiquée.
[2] Période de douze mois commençant le 1er avril de l'année indiquée.
[3] Période de douze mois commençant le 21 mars de l'année indiquée.

Kerosene
Pétrole lampant
ISIC-BASED CODE - CODE BASE CITI
3530-13A

Unit : Thousand metric tons

Unité : Milliers de tonnes métriques

Country or area	1990	1991	1992	1993	1994	1995	1996	1997	1998	1999	Pays ou zone
Africa	**6924**	**6765**	**6348**	**5988**	**4875**	**4530**	**4958**	**4846**	**4906**	**3624**	**Afrique**
Algeria*	120	100	110	129	200	250	300	325	317	...	Algérie*
Angola*	52	52	50	22	24	22	17	24	28	...	Angola*
Cameroon	*238	*240	*242	*203	245	*243	*245	*247	*248	...	Cameroun
Congo	53	50	49	*50	*50	*48	*50	*50	*51	...	Congo
Côte d'Ivoire	*535	541	670	484	*488	*490	*491	*493	*495	...	Côte d'Ivoire
Dem. Rep. of Congo	63	53	27	27	9	*10	*10	*10	*10	...	Rép. dém. du Congo
Egypt	2327	2271	1983	1930	1405	1169	1328	1227	*1084	...	Egypte
Ethiopia,incl.Eritrea	*12	*13	*8	*9	8	*8	*8	*8	*8	...	Ethiopie,incl.Erythrée
Gabon	103	100	113	108	89	55	68	81	*85	...	Gabon
Ghana	118	82	59	74	81	98	100	*101	*103	...	Ghana
Kenya	148	127	136	128	126	112	*115	117	124	...	Kenya
Libyan Arab Jamah.	*240	*242	*252	*240	*250	*255	*259	274	*274	...	Jamah. arabe libyenne
Madagascar*	20	21	22	24	46	45	54	76	57	...	Madagascar*
Mauritania*	52	55	58	61	62	62	64	65	65	...	Mauritanie*
Morocco	45	47	45	43	43	49	38	62	*79	...	Maroc
Nigeria	1941	1899	1636	1603	799	649	650	*655	*780	...	Nigéria
Senegal*	14	15	15	17	17	18	18	20	20	...	Sénégal*
Sierra Leone*	5	6	6	7	8	8	8	8	8	...	Sierra Leone*
South Africa	*612	*609	*620	582	689	703	902	*780	*842	...	Afrique du Sud
Sudan*	15	21	22	24	25	25	26	26	27	...	Soudan*
Tunisia	142	150	153	147	137	134	131	119	*127	...	Tunisie
United Rep.Tanzania*	40	41	42	44	44	45	45	46	46	...	Rép. Unie de Tanzanie*
Zambia	*29	*30	*30	*32	*30	*32	*31	*32	28	...	Zambie
America, North	**5915**	**6070**	**5887**	**6765**	**7240**	**6437**	**6950**	**6647**	**6192**	**7167**	**Amérique du Nord**
Barbados	3	4	4	3	4	4	2	3	*0	...	Barbade
Canada	1876	2085	2045	2297	2590	2474	2405	2177	*1705	...	Canada
Costa Rica	10	6	4	5	6	3	3	6	*1	...	Costa Rica
Cuba*	577	495	152	196	208	156	222	168	75	...	Cuba*
Dominican Republic	85	151	162	184	208	223	236	251	*0	...	Rép. dominicaine
El Salvador	15	18	16	16	16	16	15	*19	*24	...	El Salvador
Guatemala	9	6	7	10	*5	*5	*5	*5	*5	...	Guatemala
Honduras*	23	23	19	...	...	...	...	...	...	...	Honduras*
Jamaica*	34	17	37	45	51	60	69	78	85	...	Jamaïque*
Martinique*	126	125	126	124	128	130	132	132	133	...	Martinique*
Mexico	744	867	974	1138	1048	638	601	363	*169	...	Mexique
Netherlands Antilles*	25	25	30	32	36	37	38	40	43	...	Antilles néerlandaises*
Nicaragua	9	10	12	17	18	13	17	16	*18	...	Nicaragua
Panama*	6	7	12	8	8	6	8	10	10	...	Panama*
Puerto Rico*	45	50	70	72	68	70	70	70	70	...	Porto Rico*
Trinidad and Tobago	*184	*324	*283	*290	52	*50	*55	*55	*60	...	Trinité-et-Tobago
United States	2097	1797	1902	2256	2722	2470	2988	3170	*3707	...	Etats-Unis
United States Virgin Is.*	47	60	32	50	50	60	62	62	65	...	Iles Vierges américaines*
America, South	**2738**	**2379**	**2577**	**2464**	**2274**	**2333**	**2154**	**1901**	**1873**	**1646**	**Amérique du Sud**
Argentina	480	432	*465	357	346	263	200	164	*180	...	Argentine
Bolivia	38	34	28	29	35	29	32	35	*33	...	Bolivie
Brazil	198	176	150	208	131	127	109	68	55	...	Brésil
Chile	176	235	266	266	266	273	315	271	288	...	Chili
Colombia	270	226	261	*246	*150	*162	*159	154	*120	...	Colombie
Ecuador	264	131	90	83	71	77	67	*60	*50	...	Equateur
Paraguay*	7	6	6	7	4	4	3	3	4	...	Paraguay*
Peru	996	980	967	996	999	1077	1102	1001	*1000	...	Pérou
Uruguay	50	56	49	1	0	30	36	21	*24	...	Uruguay
Venezuela	259	103	*295	*271	*272	*291	*131	*124	*119	...	Venezuela
Asia	**52243**	**54391**	**61525**	**64301**	**68050**	**69827**	**74322**	**76741**	**75816**	**88348**	**Asie**
Azerbaijan	..	...	472	541	562	594	150	150	*178	...	Azerbaïdjan
Bahrain	*1040	*1239	*1614	1587	1345	1463	1502	999	*1050	...	Bahreïn
Bangladesh [1]	258	283	302	408	288	295	275	304	*187	...	Bangladesh [1]
Brunei Darussalam	4	...	...	...	...	...	...	...	...	...	Brunéi Darussalam
China	3925	4062	3945	3729	4072	4458	5383	6129	*6161	...	Chine
Cyprus	12	12	14	14	15	14	17	20	*23	...	Chypre

For general note and footnotes, see end of table.

Voir la fin du tableau pour la remarque générale et les notes.

Kerosene (continued)
Pétrole lampant (suite)

ISIC-BASED CODE - CODE BASE CITI

3530-13A

Unit : Thousand metric tons   Unité : Milliers de tonnes métriques

Country or area	1990	1991	1992	1993	1994	1995	1996	1997	1998	1999	Pays ou zone
Georgia	..	...	34	24	16	3	0	0	*1	...	Géorgie
India[2]	5686	5270	5397	5376	5206	5325	5969	6357	*6003	...	Inde[2]
Indonesia	5956	6178	6396	6197	6694	6193	6894	6159	*6956	...	Indonésie
Iran(Islamic Rep. of)* [3]	3454	3800	4000	4400	4500	4600	4655	4700	4750	...	Iran(Rép. islamique)* [3]
Iraq*	600	560	690	900	1027	998	977	991	1023	...	Iraq*
Israel	*323	397	1013	1128	1166	1076	1163	1207	*1330	...	Israël
Japan	18819	19918	21168	21945	22138	22218	22982	22482	*22536	...	Japon
Jordan	205	228	297	237	222	215	202	196	*195	...	Jordanie
Kazakhstan	..	...	1001	525	250	249	268	231	*229	...	Kazakhstan
Korea,Dem.Ppl's.Rep.*	232	220	220	215	210	205	200	186	177	...	Corée,Rép.pop.dém.de*
Korea, Republic of	1742	1750	3772	4107	4158	5395	6603	9253	8044	...	Corée, République de
Kuwait,part Ntl.Zone	1128	104	1478	2946	5999	*6396	6309	6641	*6655	...	Koweït et prt.Zne.N.
Lebanon	1	6	4	...	...	...	...	...	...	...	Liban
Malaysia	497	527	525	562	698	*372	*315	*292	*276	...	Malaisie
Myanmar[2]	2	2	1	1	1	1	1	1	*0	...	Myanmar[2]
Oman	*11	*10	0	*5	*5	0	0	0	*0	...	Oman
Pakistan[1]	411	531	480	511	488	463	507	413	*478	...	Pakistan[1]
Philippines	502	425	551	*550	*504	*517	597	580	*538	...	Philippines
Qatar	96	0	10	13	*20	*20	21	21	*21	...	Qatar
S.Arabia,pt.Ntrl.Zn*	3900	4100	4574	4610	4770	4760	5200	5066	4420	...	Arab.saoud,p.Zn.neut*
Singapore*	2500	2600	2700	2800	2900	2975	3025	3100	3250	...	Singapour*
Sri Lanka	165	147	123	186	190	186	191	143	*198	...	Sri Lanka
Syrian Arab Republic	192	184	187	186	190	180	169	169	*169	...	Rép. arabe syrienne
Thailand	164	85	100	103	100	94	156	101	*95	...	Thaïlande
Turkey	165	157	150	166	115	88	100	76	*87	...	Turquie
United Arab Emirates	*80	*85	*80	*78	*90	*150	144	174	*148	...	Emirats arabes unis
Uzbekistan	..	...	...	...	0	63	56	62	*100	...	Ouzbékistan
Viet Nam	3	*3	*3	*3	*3	*3	3	3	*3	...	Viet Nam
Dem. Yemen (former)*	170				..	..	..	..	..		Yémen dém. (anc.)*
Yemen	..	*172	*220	*240	*100	*250	280	527	*527	...	Yémen
Europe	**6999**	**7352**	**7483**	**6492**	**6535**	**5890**	**6402**	**6658**	**6694**	**6462**	**Europe**
Albania	55	61	41	29	29	74	69	57	*57	...	Albanie
Austria	13	*12	8	2	2	0	1	1	*9	...	Autriche
Belarus	..	...	46	21	30	15	22	86	*100	...	Bélarus
Belgium	79	89	74	14	84	88	100	112	*128	...	Belgique
Bulgaria	*145	1	2	2	2	1	0	0	*0	...	Bulgarie
Croatia	..	...	6	13	10	10	6	5	*3	...	Croatie
Denmark	76	27	22	11	25	4	12	10	*10	...	Danemark
Czechoslovakia(former)	315	272	..	..	..	..	..	..	..		Tchécoslovaquie(anc.)
Czech Republic	..	..	159	169	50	11	4	10	*13	...	République tchèque
Finland	1	2	2	2	3	0	0	0	*0	...	Finlande
France incl. Monaco	60	85	82	62	51	45	54	78	*66	...	France y compris Monaco
Germany	..	28	*29	16	62	49	31	29	*39	...	Allemagne
Germany(Fed.Rep.)	40										Allemagne(Rép.féd.)
German D.R.(former)*	11	..	..	..	..	..	..	..	..		R.D.A. (anc.)*
Greece	22	0	13	10	27	14	30	24	*61	...	Grèce
Hungary	307	125	61	90	82	84	109	93	*3	...	Hongrie
Ireland	0	*0	0	0	96	70	85	176	*168	...	Irlande
Italy and San Marino	2458	2179	2095	1831	1787	1473	1246	1518	*1522	...	Italie y comp. St. Marin
Lithuania	..	..	*150	177	226	211	260	225	..	...	Lituanie
Netherlands	225	263	229	262	196	216	209	233	*189	...	Pays-Bas
Norway,Svlbd.J.Myn. l	148	129	161	165	165	150	228	154	*118	...	Norvège,Svalbd,J.May
Poland	1	4	7	12	6	39	6	11	*8	...	Pologne
Portugal	26	22	23	13	20	15	13	28	*30	...	Portugal
Romania	453	407	385	101	126	46	67	66	*80	...	Roumanie
Russian Federation	..	...	1053	475	253	122	124	107	*51	...	Fédération de Russie
Slovakia	..	..	*97	85	*70	50	34	26	*26	...	Slovaquie
Spain	238	189	170	176	124	137	131	207	*235	...	Espagne
Sweden	15	5	5	2	0	0	2	0	*0	...	Suède
Switzrld,Liechtenstein	2	3	2	2	3	*2	1	1	*1	...	Suisse,Liechtenstein
Ukraine	..	...	75	16	14	12	11	11	*11	...	Ukraine
United Kingdom	2309	2446	2450	2707	2967	2924	3510	3336	*3471	...	Royaume-Uni
Yugoslavia	..	...	36	27	25	28	37	54	*52	...	Yougoslavie

For general note and footnotes, see end of table.   Voir la fin du tableau pour la remarque générale et les notes.

Kerosene (continued)
Pétrole lampant (suite)

ISIC-BASED CODE - CODE BASE CITI

3530-13A

Unit : Thousand metric tons   Unité : Milliers de tonnes métriques

Country or area	1990	1991	1992	1993	1994	1995	1996	1997	1998	1999	Pays ou zone
USSR (former)	35500	..	..	..	..	..	..	..	..	..	URSS (anc.)
Oceania	249	241	230	243	225	235	317	350	228	305	Océanie
Australia[1]	247	240	230	243	225	235	317	346	*224	...	Australie[1]
New Zealand[2]	2	1	0	0	0	0	0	4	*4	...	Nouvelle-Zélande[2]
Total	110568	77198	84050	86252	89198	89251	95102	97142	95708	107553	Total

General Note.

Medium oil distilling between 150 and 300°C; at least 65% in volume distills at 250°C. Its specific gravity is around 0.80 and the flash point above 38°C. It is used as an illuminant and as a fuel in certain types of spark-ignition engines, such as those used for agricultural tractors and stationary engines. Other names for this product are burning oil, vaporizing oil, power kerosene and illuminating oil. (SITC, Rev.3: 33421-0A).

Remarque générale.

Huile moyennement visqueuse dont les températures de distillation se situent entre 150 et 300°C, et qui donne au moins 65% en volume de distillat à 250°C. Sa densité se situe aux alentours de 0.80 et son point d'éclair est supérieur à 38°C. Elle sert à l'éclairage et aussi de carburant dans certains moteurs à allumage par étincelle, tels que ceux utilisés dans les tracteurs agricoles et les installations stationaires. Les données concernent les produits couramment appelés kérosène, pétrole carburant ou "power kerosene", et huile d'éclairage. (CTCI, Rev.3: 33421-0A).

[1] Twelve months ending 30 June of year stated.
[2] Twelve months beginning 1 April of year stated.
[3] Twelve months beginning 21 March of year stated.

[1] Période de douze mois finissant le 30 juin de l'année indiquée.
[2] Période de douze mois commençant le 1er avril de l'année indiquée.
[3] Période de douze mois commençant le 21 mars de l'année indiquée.

White spirit/industrial spirit
White spirit/essences spéciales

ISIC-BASED CODE - CODE BASE CITI

3530-16A

Unit : Thousand metric tons   Unité : Milliers de tonnes métrique

Country or area	1990	1991	1992	1993	1994	1995	1996	1997	1998	1999	Pays ou zone
Africa	**12**	**13**	**14**	**14**	**14**	**15**	**15**	**15**	**15**	**17**	**Afrique**
Cameroon*	7	7	8	8	8	9	9	9	9	...	Cameroun*
Tunisia	5	6	6	6	6	6	*6	6	*6	...	Tunisie
America, North	**2598**	**2546**	**2806**	**2494**	**2405**	**2238**	**2262**	**2379**	**2975**	**2432**	**Amérique du Nord**
Canada	281	262	265	168	133	103	125	127	*129	...	Canada
Trinidad and Tobago	1	1	1	2	2	0	3	*2	*2	...	Trinité-et-Tobago
United States	...	2283	2540	2324	2270	2135	2134	2250	*2844	...	Etats-Unis
America, South	**434**	**482**	**555**	**520**	**563**	**489**	**501**	**502**	**510**	**535**	**Amérique du Sud**
Brazil	215	271	309	286	304	250	269	310	317	...	Brésil
Chile	38	38	44	42	49	42	49	45	51	...	Chili
Colombia	169	134	160	*145	*170	*150	*140	*100	*100	...	Colombie
Ecuador	4	27	33	36	33	37	31	*30	*30	...	Equateur
Uruguay	3	6	3	5	0	3	5	10	*6	...	Uruguay
Venezuela*	5	6	6	6	7	7	7	7	6	...	Venezuela*
Asia	**603**	**665**	**733**	**791**	**821**	**842**	**839**	**862**	**830**	**980**	**Asie**
Azerbaijan	..	...	7	5	0	0	0	0	*0	...	Azerbaïdjan
Indonesia*	40	41	41	41	42	42	42	43	44	...	Indonésie*
Iran(Islamic Rep. of)* [1]	160	200	250	300	300	300	300	320	320	...	Iran(Rép. islamique)* [1]
Japan	79	73	74	66	66	65	64	58	*53	...	Japon
Korea, Republic of	68	52	58	55	90	95	86	81	65	...	Corée, République de
Philippines	*59	100	*100	*105	*110	*115	*120	*130	*135	...	Philippines
Singapore*	160	165	170	190	200	200	194	194	194	...	Singapour*
Sri Lanka	4	2	4	3	2	1	1	0	*0	...	Sri Lanka
Syrian Arab Republic	1	2	2	2	2	2	2	2	*2	...	Rép. arabe syrienne
Turkey	32	22	23	24	9	9	17	20	*3	...	Turquie
Uzbekistan	..	...	...	0	0	13	13	14	*14	...	Ouzbékistan
Europe	**2216**	**2147**	**1972**	**1867**	**1896**	**1774**	**1554**	**1725**	**1698**	**1498**	**Europe**
Austria	0	*0	8	18	7	5	5	0	*0	...	Autriche
Belgium	352	361	371	361	391	334	145	164	*157	...	Belgique
Bulgaria	14	7	4	7	4	4	7	5	*10	...	Bulgarie
Croatia	..	...	119	2	3	3	2	3	*4	...	Croatie
Czech Republic	..	..	28	17	15	11	10	8	*13	...	République tchèque
Finland	63	54	71	70	144	77	61	71	*92	...	Finlande
France incl. Monaco	394	409	82	92	115	112	103	106	*114	...	France y compris Monaco
Germany	..	176	*138	119	102	87	81	89	*46	...	Allemagne
Germany(Fed.Rep.)	153	..	..	..	..	..	..	..	..	...	Allemagne(Rép.féd.)
Hungary	539	333	420	396	368	223	214	277	*287	...	Hongrie
Italy and San Marino	69	21	21	125	52	39	21	34	*36	...	Italie y comp. St. Marin
Netherlands	255	244	211	182	181	220	230	465	*320	...	Pays-Bas
Norway,Svlbd.J.Myn. I	23	52	48	0	0	0	0	0	...	...	Norvège,Svalbd,J.May
Poland	46	44	36	33	66	61	71	70	*53	...	Pologne
Portugal	25	22	22	27	28	37	35	28	*30	...	Portugal
Romania	...	...	...	32	25	24	26	14	*17	...	Roumanie
Russian Federation	..	...	76	74	74	220	204	56	*161	...	Fédération de Russie
Slovenia	..	...	9	4	3	2	4	2	2	...	Slovénie
Spain	117	94	111	142	171	167	199	205	*220	...	Espagne
Sweden	0	*3	0	0	0	0	0	0	...	...	Suède
Ukraine	..	...	19	7	4	*5	0	0	*0	...	Ukraine
United Kingdom	121	136	150	159	143	143	136	128	*136	...	Royaume-Uni
Yugoslavia, SFR*	14	..	..	..	..	..	..	..	..	..	Yougoslavie, RSF*
USSR (former)	336		..	..	..	..	..	..	..	..	URSS (anc.)
Oceania	**40**	**44**	**42**	**51**	**45**	**136**	**144**	**139**	**141**	**201**	**Océanie**
Australia [2]	40	44	42	51	45	136	144	139	*141	...	Australie [2]
Total	**6238**	**5896**	**6122**	**5737**	**5744**	**5494**	**5315**	**5622**	**6169**	**5663**	**Total**

General Note.
A highly-refined distillate with a boiling-point range about 135 to 200 degrees centigrade used as a paint solvent and for dry-cleaning purposes. (SITC, Rev.3: 33429-1A).

[1] Twelve months beginning 21 March of year stated.
[2] Twelve months ending 30 June of year stated.

Remarque générale.
Distillats hautement raffinés dont le point d'ébullition se situe entre 135° C et 200° C, utilisés comme diluants pour peinture et comme solvants pour le nettoyage à sec. (CTCI, Rev.3: 33429-1A).

[1] Période de douze mois commençant le 21 mars de l'année indiquée.
[2] Période de douze mois finissant le 30 juin de l'année indiquée.

Gas-diesel oil (distillate fuel oil)
Gazole/carburant diesel (mazout distillé)

ISIC-BASED CODE - CODE BASE CITI

3530-19A

Unit : Thousand metric tons / Unité : Milliers de tonnes métriques

Country or area	1990	1991	1992	1993	1994	1995	1996	1997	1998	1999	Pays ou zone
Africa	**30280**	**30329**	**30555**	**29822**	**28429**	**30077**	**29827**	**30370**	**30588**	**30123**	**Afrique**
Algeria	8052	7800	7960	7538	6545	6864	6143	6523	*6198	...	Algérie
Angola*	323	325	330	438	474	496	479	486	474	...	Angola*
Cameroon	*280	*282	*284	*258	287	*288	*290	*291	*295	...	Cameroun
Congo	103	108	90	*92	*92	*90	*92	*95	*96	...	Congo
Côte d'Ivoire	*695	840	847	665	567	430	696	706	*708	...	Côte d'Ivoire
Dem. Rep. of Congo	118	92	53	37	21	*19	*18	*19	*19	...	Rép. dém. du Congo
Egypt	3943	4146	4332	4747	5246	5792	5652	5870	*6072	...	Egypte
Ethiopia,incl.Eritrea	*214	*217	*215	*210	169	*170	*45	*43	*45	...	Ethiopie,incl.Erythrée
Gabon	219	210	242	230	209	169	165	230	213	...	Gabon
Ghana	205	297	234	224	316	264	270	270	*272	...	Ghana
Kenya	563	542	580	529	539	476	*480	412	429	...	Kenya
Libyan Arab Jamah.	*4100	*4110	*4110	*4000	*4100	*4184	4244	4272	*4272	...	Jamah. arabe libyenne
Madagascar*	43	45	45	47	47	48	48	50	50	...	Madagascar*
Mauritania*	135	140	152	148	145	147	148	148	149	...	Mauritanie*
Morocco	1786	1797	2080	1919	2167	2019	2122	2394	*2236	...	Maroc
Nigeria	3019	3029	2761	2928	1413	1767	*1770	*1775	*2430	...	Nigéria
Senegal*	285	287	292	294	295	295	296	298	299	...	Sénégal*
Sierra Leone*	58	64	65	67	67	68	68	70	70	...	Sierra Leone*
South Africa	*4919	*4792	*4701	4275	4504	5223	5535	*5147	*5030	...	Afrique du Sud
Sudan*	331	329	325	326	325	327	328	330	331	...	Soudan*
Tunisia	542	522	499	493	539	576	571	571	*560	...	Tunisie
United Rep.Tanzania*	142	145	146	147	147	148	148	150	151	...	Rép. Unie de Tanzanie*
Zambia	*205	*210	*212	*210	*215	*217	*219	*220	189	...	Zambie
America, North	**194041**	**195880**	**196667**	**204940**	**209577**	**205514**	**216864**	**222689**	**222781**	**235477**	**Amérique du Nord**
Barbados	53	53	35	47	39	43	31	36	*0	...	Barbade
Canada	23045	22316	21509	22852	23493	23114	25259	27541	*25389	...	Canada
Costa Rica	109	84	150	151	162	203	175	176	*17	...	Costa Rica
Cuba	1041	782	191	206	164	159	210	220	*200	...	Cuba
Dominican Republic	261	382	443	404	418	433	448	464	*400	...	Rép. dominicaine
El Salvador	214	254	271	291	256	211	103	122	*146	...	El Salvador
Guatemala	195	241	277	245	294	309	258	331	*338	...	Guatemala
Honduras	126	123	98	...	...	...	...	...	...	...	Honduras
Jamaica	210	175	224	155	262	267	275	282	*289	...	Jamaïque
Martinique*	142	145	152	155	156	158	158	160	160	...	Martinique*
Mexico	13055	14260	15355	14816	14874	13304	13447	13506	*13976	...	Mexique
Netherlands Antilles*	2075	2000	2100	2115	2203	2215	2218	2220	2225	...	Antilles néerlandaises*
Nicaragua	169	199	210	206	231	217	174	220	*224	...	Nicaragua
Panama	312	280	481	373	262	209	573	457	*632	...	Panama
Puerto Rico*	1250	1140	985	1000	1100	1334	1335	1337	1340	...	Porto Rico*
Trinidad and Tobago	651	771	915	884	897	1035	1069	1078	*1536	...	Trinité-et-Tobago
United States	147653	149525	150536	158124	161790	159307	168130	171533	*172898	...	Etats-Unis
United States Virgin Is.*	3480	3150	2735	2800	2860	2880	2885	2890	2895	...	Iles Vierges américaines*
America, South	**48475**	**50215**	**48436**	**50914**	**52407**	**54186**	**57256**	**61422**	**60983**	**65888**	**Amérique du Sud**
Argentina	8228	8622	9401	9502	8793	8627	9487	10394	*10957	...	Argentine
Bolivia	326	363	329	344	363	*345	332	338	*411	...	Bolivie
Brazil	20914	20652	21029	20291	22764	22445	23229	24264	25494	...	Brésil
Chile	2009	2041	2023	2227	2450	2698	2823	2937	3415	...	Chili
Colombia	2080	2254	2384	3146	2803	2850	3340	3353	*3111	...	Colombie
Ecuador	1327	1428	1459	1531	1534	1447	1678	1912	*1344	...	Equateur
Paraguay	137	*123	*150	114	123	92	73	58	*62	...	Paraguay
Peru	1187	1327	1311	1793	1790	1705	1769	1869	*2079	...	Pérou
Uruguay	390	413	327	118	0	413	608	431	*615	...	Uruguay
Venezuela	11877	12992	10023	11848	11787	13564	13917	15866	*13495	...	Venezuela
Asia	**211413**	**231280**	**248545**	**263230**	**277197**	**290983**	**311310**	**330142**	**324639**	**378141**	**Asie**
Azerbaijan	..	...	2900	2200	2331	2213	2111	1900	*2057	...	Azerbaïdjan
Bahrain	3898	3840	4214	4062	*4065	4195	4443	4436	*4369	...	Bahreïn
Bangladesh[1]	174	209	174	*248	284	300	277	300	*231	...	Bangladesh[1]
Brunei Darussalam	98	109	128	130	129	143	131	142	*147	...	Brunéi Darussalam
China	26090	28533	31709	35428	34795	39726	44190	49245	*48977	...	Chine
Cyprus	230	278	252	253	324	300	258	365	*382	...	Chypre

For general note and footnotes, see end of table.

Voir la fin du tableau pour la remarque générale et les notes.

499

Gas-diesel oil (distillate fuel oil) (continued)
Gazole/carburant diesel (mazout distillé) (suite)

ISIC-BASED CODE - CODE BASE CITI

3530-19A

Unit : Thousand metric tons   Unité : Milliers de tonnes métriques

Country or area	1990	1991	1992	1993	1994	1995	1996	1997	1998	1999	Pays ou zone
Georgia	..	...	111	80	53	11	4	7	*15	...	Géorgie
India[2]	17121	17249	*17600	18262	19676	*20225	21643	23304	*24984	...	Inde[2]
Indonesia	10037	11548	10959	*11737	*10474	*10364	*12492	*12275	*13423	...	Indonésie
Iran(Islamic Rep. of)[3]	11571	12120	*13100	*14155	*14571	*15000	15500	16000	*16850	...	Iran(Rép. islamique)[3]
Iraq	*5100	*4500	5600	*6150	*6882	*6750	*6608	*6701	*6921	...	Iraq
Israel	2019	2210	2541	2976	3054	2817	2636	2796	*2958	...	Israël
Japan	48996	54510	56785	58276	60841	62640	63609	64036	*61396	...	Japon
Jordan	745	717	753	880	859	872	853	923	*928	...	Jordanie
Kazakhstan	..	...	4546	4334	3471	3303	3295	2838	*2495	...	Kazakhstan
Korea,Dem.Ppl's.Rep.*	1075	1055	1055	1050	1045	1040	1035	965	917	...	Corée,Rép.pop.dém.de*
Korea, Republic of	13078	17603	21103	23232	23380	25022	29937	36538	32158	...	Corée, République de
Kuwait,part Ntl.Zone	6639	571	2841	4968	10549	11925	11006	12704	*12302	...	Koweït et prt.Zne.N.
Kyrgyzstan	..	...	...	...	...	...	5	28	36	...	Kirghizistan
Lebanon	*102	*133	92	...	...	...	...	...	...	...	Liban
Malaysia	3427	3730	3969	4190	5101	*5918	*6325	*6792	*5974	...	Malaisie
Myanmar[2]	320	349	323	331	405	440	345	465	*450	...	Myanmar[2]
Oman	610	634	581	448	792	738	715	740	*818	...	Oman
Pakistan[1]	1584	1725	1718	1648	1761	1615	1694	1596	*1602	...	Pakistan[1]
Philippines	3282	3341	3698	*3488	*3643	*4760	5301	5557	*5112	...	Philippines
Qatar	737	702	810	677	757	*673	*684	*646	*668	...	Qatar
S.Arabia,pt.Ntrl.Zn	22360	20391	21340	21609	22775	22359	25735	24514	*23352	...	Arab.saoud,p.Zn.neut
Singapore	14564	15715	*16000	*17100	*18200	*18800	*19200	*19500	*19650	...	Singapour
Sri Lanka	532	474	370	575	657	598	605	543	*695	...	Sri Lanka
Syrian Arab Republic	3405	3632	3692	3882	4031	4095	4227	4301	*4435	...	Rép. arabe syrienne
Thailand	3056	4176	5021	6053	7014	8348	11521	14327	*13679	...	Thaïlande
Turkey	6566	6397	6590	7272	7421	8070	7691	7269	*7969	...	Turquie
Turkmenistan	..	..	1942	1399	1357	1240	1253	1520	*1575	...	Turkménistan
United Arab Emirates	*2700	*2750	*2745	*2750	*3333	3333	3210	3309	*3258	...	Emirats arabes unis
Uzbekistan	..	...	2006	2257	2053	2105	1861	2035	*2318	...	Ouzbékistan
Viet Nam	17	*17	*17	*17	*17	*17	17	17	*17	...	Viet Nam
Dem. Yemen (former)*	1150	..	..	..	..	..	..	..	..	...	Yémen dém. (anc.)*
Yemen (former)*	130	..	..	..	..	..	..	..	..	...	Yémen (anc.)*
Yemen	..	1237	1229	973	957	888	784	1399	*1412	...	Yémen
Europe	**214289**	**290663**	**304982**	**302185**	**297122**	**295298**	**306686**	**311483**	**317232**	**321463**	**Europe**
Albania	238	180	116	148	111	106	108	107	*107	...	Albanie
Austria	2770	3198	3245	3605	3648	3374	3604	3916	*3892	...	Autriche
Belarus	..	...	4499	3316	3053	3465	3170	3115	*3318	...	Bélarus
Belgium	10229	10980	10795	10707	11438	10993	12619	12520	*12447	...	Belgique
Bulgaria	1889	1062	559	1235	2079	2564	2351	2040	*1957	...	Bulgarie
Croatia	..	..	1105	1281	1383	1533	1493	1492	*1522	...	Croatie
Denmark	3290	3735	4000	3929	4111	4270	4466	3651	*3244	...	Danemark
Czechoslovakia(former)	3524	3218	..	..	..	..	..	..	..	...	Tchécoslovaquie(anc.)
Czech Republic	..	..	1511	1943	1818	2377	2581	2455	*2481	...	République tchèque
Finland	3663	4044	4036	3881	4628	4028	4663	4374	*5263	...	Finlande
France incl. Monaco	27919	30320	29388	31559	30501	30877	33396	35172	*36050	...	France y compris Monaco
Germany	..	41685	*45527	47324	48840	45288	47387	45467	*47821	...	Allemagne
Germany(Fed.Rep.)	35046	..	..	..	..	..	..	..	..	...	Allemagne(Rép.féd.)
German D.R.(former)*	6200										R.D.A. (anc.)*
Greece	3883	3289	3786	3259	3723	3987	4760	5144	*5544	...	Grèce
Hungary	2736	2620	2591	2846	2538	2562	2468	2586	*2586	...	Hongrie
Ireland	*540	706	796	737	840	826	769	1000	*1122	...	Irlande
Italy and San Marino	29133	30517	31642	32215	31817	31460	31732	34562	*36272	...	Italie y comp. St. Marin
Lithuania	..	...	839	1523	1028	1000	1242	1632	*2055	...	Lituanie
Netherlands	15524	17479	18316	18749	19165	20495	21354	21201	*21251	...	Pays-Bas
Norway,Svlbd.J.Myn. l	5904	5847	6337	6445	6852	5973	6683	7070	*6824	...	Norvège,Svalbd,J.May
Poland	3963	3675	4401	4955	5031	5183	5275	5099	*5612	...	Pologne
Portugal	2984	2345	2987	3281	4186	3963	3684	3970	*4368	...	Portugal
Romania	6399	3951	3702	3742	4706	4698	4201	3953	*4035	...	Roumanie
Russian Federation	..	...	65131	56702	46721	47282	46682	47226	*45102	...	Fédération de Russie
Slovakia	..	..	*1000	1260	*1300	1681	1724	1782	*1898	...	Slovaquie
Slovenia	..	..	83	78	45	194	190	200	95	...	Slovénie
Spain	14871	15691	16119	15329	16312	16636	17280	18532	*19969	...	Espagne
Sweden	6213	6017	6503	6875	6747	6650	7126	7618	*7510	...	Suède

For general note and footnotes, see end of table.   Voir la fin du tableau pour la remarque générale et les notes.

Gas-diesel oil (distillate fuel oil) (continued)
Gazole/carburant diesel (mazout distillé) (suite)

ISIC-BASED CODE - CODE BASE CITI

3530-19A

Unit : Thousand metric tons   Unité : Milliers de tonnes métriques

Country or area	1990	1991	1992	1993	1994	1995	1996	1997	1998	1999	Pays ou zone
Switzrld,Liechtenstein	1167	1815	1706	2001	2061	2011	2292	2085	*2111	...	Suisse,Liechtenstein
Ukraine	..	...	8091	5337	4950	4275	3793	3779	*3968	...	Ukraine
United Kingdom	23404	26058	25651	27361	27137	27169	28926	28778	*27934	...	Royaume-Uni
Yugoslavia	..	...	270	236	298	338	390	784	*600	...	Yougoslavie
T.F.Yug.Rep. Macedonia	..	...	*250	326	55	40	277	173	*274	...	L'ex-RY Macédoine
Yugoslavia, SFR*	2800	..	..	..	..	..	..	..	..	..	Yougoslavie, RSF*
USSR (former)	112080	..	..	..	..	..	..	..	..	..	URSS (anc.)
Oceania	10081	10164	10229	10829	11348	11606	12212	12956	13378	14491	Océanie
Australia[1]	8700	8702	8794	9311	9748	10027	10727	11310	*11580	...	Australie[1]
New Zealand[2]	1351	1432	1405	1488	1570	1549	1455	1614	*1768	...	Nouvelle-Zélande[2]
Papua New Guinea*	...	30	30	30	30	30	30	32	30	...	Papouasie-Nvl-Guinée*
Total	820659	808531	839414	861919	876079	887663	934155	969062	969601	1045583	Total

General Note.
Heavy oils distilling between 200 and 380°C, but distilling less than 65% in volume at 250°C, including losses, and 85% or more at 350°C. Their flash point is always above 50°C and their specific gravity higher than 0.82. Heavy oils obtained by blending are grouped together with gas oils on the condition that their kinematic viscosity does not exceed 27.5 cST at 38°C. Included are middle distillates for the petrochemical industry. Gas-diesel oils are used as a fuel for internal combustion in diesel engines, as a burner fuel in heating installations such as furnaces and for enriching water gas to increase its luminosity. Other names for this product are diesel fuel, diesel oil, gas oil and solar oil. (SITC, Rev.3: 33430-0A).

[1] Twelve months ending 30 June of year stated.
[2] Twelve months beginning 1 April of year stated.
[3] Twelve months beginning 21 March of year stated.

Remarque générale.
Huiles lourdes dont les températures de distillation se situent entre 200 et 380°C, mais qui donnent moins de 65% en volme de distillat à 250°C (y compris les pertes) et 85% ou davantage à 350°C. Leur point d'éclair est toujours supérieur à 50°C et leur densité supérieure à 0.82. Les huiles lourdes obtenues par mélange sont classées dans la même catégorie que les gazoles à condition que leur viscosité cinématique ne dépasse pas 27.5 cST à 38°C. Sont compris dans cette rubrique les distillats moyens destinés à l'industrie pétrochimique. Les gazoles servent de carburant pour la combustion interne, dans les moteurs Diesel, de combustible dans les installations de chauffrage telles que les chaudières, et d'additifs destinés à augmenter la luminosité de la flamme du gaz à l'eau. Ce produit est aussi connu sous les appellations de gazole, gasoil, carburant ou combustible Diesel, et huile solaire. (CTCI, Rev.3: 33430-0A).

[1] Période de douze mois finissant le 30 juin de l'année indiquée.
[2] Période de douze mois commençant le 1er avril de l'année indiquée.
[3] Période de douze mois commençant le 21 mars de l'année indiquée.

Residual fuel oils
Mazout résiduel

ISIC-BASED CODE - CODE BASE CITI

3530-22A

Unit : Thousand metric tons

Unité : Milliers de tonnes métriques

Country or area	1990	1991	1992	1993	1994	1995	1996	1997	1998	1999	Pays ou zone
Africa	**34030**	**33679**	**32988**	**33959**	**33581**	**34029**	**33790**	**33449**	**34084**	**33946**	**Afrique**
Algeria	5948	5645	5700	5522	5085	5304	4983	5556	*5061	...	Algérie
Angola*	653	655	547	517	601	638	680	699	644	...	Angola*
Cameroon*	147	150	132	130	135	153	155	155	157	...	Cameroun*
Congo	316	311	267	*275	*268	*258	*260	*262	*262	...	Congo
Côte d'Ivoire	*468	*410	468	*470	*474	*477	*479	*482	*484	...	Côte d'Ivoire
Dem. Rep. of Congo	70	55	34	33	9	*7	*8	*8	*8	...	Rép. dém. du Congo
Egypt	11315	11675	11258	11735	12071	12044	12745	12928	*13123	...	Egypte
Ethiopia,incl.Eritrea	*301	*302	*297	*301	296	*268	*11	*70	*73	...	Ethiopie,incl.Erythrée
Gabon	282	284	295	280	278	315	308	285	*298	...	Gabon
Ghana	*279	281	*283	*288	*283	*284	*286	*286	*288	...	Ghana
Kenya	670	648	671	664	630	527	*530	498	506	...	Kenya
Libyan Arab Jamah.	*4800	*4810	*4190	3990	*4636	*4731	*4799	*4834	*4834	...	Jamah. arabe libyenne
Madagascar*	65	67	70	72	73	73	74	74	74	...	Madagascar*
Mauritania*	312	315	352	354	355	355	358	360	362	...	Mauritanie*
Morocco	2046	2027	2143	2459	2540	2331	1755	1711	*1918	...	Maroc
Nigeria	2900	2724	2569	2480	1257	1312	1310	*1315	*1600	...	Nigéria
Senegal*	218	221	224	225	226	226	227	227	229	...	Sénégal*
Sierra Leone*	48	50	51	50	52	53	53	54	54	...	Sierra Leone*
South Africa	*1983	*1878	*2368	3014	3078	3371	3464	*2337	*2819	...	Afrique du Sud
Sudan*	304	314	315	315	318	318	320	320	322	...	Soudan*
Tunisia	580	527	422	450	581	645	643	646	*635	...	Tunisie
United Rep.Tanzania	235	*238	*240	*242	*245	*246	*247	*247	*248	...	Rép. Unie de Tanzanie
Zambia	*90	*92	*92	*93	*90	*93	*95	*95	85	...	Zambie
America, North	**105447**	**101052**	**109460**	**101619**	**99748**	**94950**	**92338**	**92044**	**97209**	**88261**	**Amérique du Nord**
Barbados	152	150	131	142	143	155	165	169	*0	...	Barbade
Canada	8197	7564	6946	6727	6299	5935	6363	6792	*7234	...	Canada
Costa Rica	227	172	237	253	221	*320	310	325	*149	...	Costa Rica
Cuba	3495	2515	713	884	743	671	871	967	*420	...	Cuba
Dominican Republic	752	831	876	928	984	1013	1044	1106	*681	...	Rép. dominicaine
El Salvador	224	272	268	279	251	219	312	382	*497	...	El Salvador
Guatemala	203	245	284	277	270	262	267	230	*250	...	Guatemala
Honduras	164	160	153	...	...	...	...	...	...	...	Honduras
Jamaica	572	444	650	344	469	482	495	509	*523	...	Jamaïque
Martinique*	277	280	282	285	272	273	275	275	275	...	Martinique*
Mexico	23987	22832	24836	25574	25757	25602	24341	24760	*26227	...	Mexique
Netherlands Antilles*	4800	4500	4700	5005	5008	5010	5013	5015	5018	...	Antilles néerlandaises*
Nicaragua	297	247	252	223	255	184	250	355	*452	...	Nicaragua
Panama	554	585	966	1020	677	541	1129	667	*1286	...	Panama
Puerto Rico*	1875	1700	1760	1800	1900	1770	1790	1800	1810	...	Porto Rico*
Trinidad and Tobago	2525	3294	3359	2966	2432	2231	2550	2511	*3015	...	Trinité-et-Tobago
United States	52346	51516	59262	50953	50048	46313	43192	42207	*45395	...	Etats-Unis
United States Virgin Is.*	4800	3745	3785	3800	3860	3810	3812	3815	3818	...	Iles Vierges américaines*
America, South	**42210**	**43817**	**40917**	**39426**	**40529**	**37772**	**39536**	**38993**	**42307**	**38318**	**Amérique du Sud**
Argentina	4239	3654	3370	3089	2748	2282	1924	2555	*2445	...	Argentine
Bolivia	13	16	31	3	4	*4	3	1	*2	...	Bolivie
Brazil	11937	11386	12034	11700	11909	11756	13473	14988	17183	...	Brésil
Chile	1562	1451	1581	1554	1601	1737	1655	1663	1576	...	Chili
Colombia	3753	4120	3639	*3120	3002	3027	2890	2979	*2817	...	Colombie
Ecuador	2669	2485	2392	2361	2736	3095	3253	3728	*3486	...	Equateur
Paraguay	50	61	*78	65	71	62	51	57	*43	...	Paraguay
Peru	3745	3803	3529	3401	3018	2599	2656	2561	*3314	...	Pérou
Uruguay	367	322	404	143	0	496	587	487	*548	...	Uruguay
Venezuela	13875	16519	13859	13990	15440	12714	13044	9974	*10893	...	Venezuela
Asia	**218122**	**230514**	**251008**	**251318**	**256411**	**259109**	**257936**	**262844**	**256155**	**276794**	**Asie**
Azerbaijan	..	...	4100	5104	4000	4220	3961	3900	*4028	...	Azerbaïdjan
Bahrain	*3443	*3593	*3650	3332	3138	3124	3214	2881	*2979	...	Bahreïn
Bangladesh[1]	277	309	288	301	0	0	0	0	*0	...	Bangladesh[1]
Brunei Darussalam	37	48	50	53	69	68	60	*60	*60	...	Brunéi Darussalam
China	32679	32440	32322	*31959	30490	29607	25045	23112	*21004	...	Chine
Cyprus	174	249	264	313	316	317	316	422	*442	...	Chypre

For general note and footnotes, see end of table.

Voir la fin du tableau pour la remarque générale et les notes.

Residual fuel oils (continued)
Mazout résiduel (suite)

ISIC-BASED CODE - CODE BASE CITI

3530-22A

Unit : Thousand metric tons   Unité : Milliers de tonnes métriques

Country or area	1990	1991	1992	1993	1994	1995	1996	1997	1998	1999	Pays ou zone
Georgia	..	...	189	136	90	18	7	10	*18	...	Géorgie
India[2]	9310	9416	10580	10432	9860	9601	10088	10775	*10953	...	Inde[2]
Indonesia	*10690	*10755	10820	*10900	*11000	*11600	*10200	*12000	*11560	...	Indonésie
Iran(Islamic Rep. of)[3]	12729	16800	*16100	*16800	*17300	*18250	*18500	*19000	*19500	...	Iran(Rép. islamique)[3]
Iraq	*7200	*5000	6210	*7000	*7833	*7656	*7495	*7601	*7850	...	Iraq
Israel	3111	3027	3529	3554	3589	3567	3157	2957	*3166	...	Israël
Japan	41023	40956	43488	43556	47357	44321	40762	41840	*40519	...	Japon
Jordan	772	590	901	962	901	995	1020	1199	*1253	...	Jordanie
Kazakhstan	..	...	5846	5263	4200	3272	3146	3000	*3052	...	Kazakhstan
Korea,Dem.Ppl's.Rep.*	635	620	620	615	610	605	600	559	531	...	Corée,Rép.pop.dém.de*
Korea, Republic of	15550	22384	27096	28568	29665	31609	32463	35965	31737	...	Corée, République de
Kuwait,part Ntl.Zone	7011	1527	9342	6703	9511	10056	9583	11555	*10742	...	Koweït et prt.Zne.N.
Lebanon	226	283	156	..	..	..	..	..	..	...	Liban
Malaysia	3241	2655	2110	2375	2887	2307	2794	3153	*2390	...	Malaisie
Myanmar[2]	115	136	144	139	96	110	98	103	*101	...	Myanmar[2]
Oman	1687	1823	1345	1314	2055	2101	2128	1914	*1899	...	Oman
Pakistan[1]	1730	2094	2015	1797	1878	1722	1916	1794	*2014	...	Pakistan[1]
Philippines	3992	3645	3800	*3932	*4091	*6009	6406	5556	*5612	...	Philippines
Qatar	1003	943	1016	850	932	*898	1009	899	*983	...	Qatar
S.Arabia,pt.Ntrl.Zn	27768	24422	25932	*25758	23440	23889	27114	24834	*26500	...	Arab.saoud,p.Zn.neut
Singapore	11845	11930	*13000	*14000	*15000	*15700	*16200	*17000	*17800	...	Singapour
Sri Lanka	605	617	498	580	657	602	775	690	*742	...	Sri Lanka
Syrian Arab Republic	5390	5731	5246	5028	5019	4993	5158	5250	*5237	...	Rép. arabe syrienne
Thailand	3388	3449	4270	4686	5703	5905	8239	8570	*7631	...	Thaïlande
Turkey	8723	8905	8902	9283	8620	9415	8952	8790	*8213	...	Turquie
Turkmenistan	..	...	1667	1234	1246	1139	1301	1600	*2214	...	Turkménistan
United Arab Emirates	1822	2052	2125	2185	2403	2403	2269	2113	*1845	...	Emirats arabes unis
Uzbekistan	..	...	1595	1428	1314	2082	2181	1979	*1801	...	Ouzbékistan
Viet Nam	10	*10	*10	*10	*10	*10	10	10	*10	...	Viet Nam
Dem. Yemen (former)*	1800	..	..	..	..	..	..	..	..	..	Yémen dém. (anc.)*
Yemen (former)*	136	..	..	..	..	..	..	..	..	..	Yémen (anc.)*
Yemen	..	1293	1782	*946	909	716	1547	1531	*1547	...	Yémen
Europe	146403	252839	257818	244098	217646	208076	206068	204689	202764	173643	Europe
Albania	231	350	236	195	153	43	46	39	*39	...	Albanie
Austria	1727	1813	1821	1678	1472	1512	1421	1540	*1347	...	Autriche
Belarus	..	...	9006	6285	4962	5592	4812	4524	*4253	...	Bélarus
Belgium	5636	7283	6733	6599	5379	4923	6843	7444	*8042	...	Belgique
Bulgaria	2478	1732	746	*2500	2268	2056	1735	1477	*1327	...	Bulgarie
Croatia	..	...	1418	1674	1367	1365	1366	1484	*1395	...	Croatie
Denmark	2220	2065	2189	2360	2283	2395	2422	1718	*1560	...	Danemark
Czechoslovakia(former)	4394	3454	..	..	..	..	..	..	..	...	Tchécoslovaquie(anc.)
Czech Republic	..		1772	1562	1356	1466	1634	1523	*1512	...	République tchèque
Estonia[4]	..	...	273	266	301	313	343	367	*220	...	Estonie[4]
Finland	1610	1449	1147	1085	770	1032	1220	1105	*1297	...	Finlande
France incl. Monaco	12421	12474	12456	12637	10668	10658	10536	11073	*12171	...	France y compris Monaco
Germany		12319	14162	14318	13968	13641	13427	12271	*13591	...	Allemagne
Germany(Fed.Rep.)	8746	..	..	..	..	..	..	..	..	...	Allemagne(Rép.féd.)
German D.R.(former)*	4000	..	..	..	..	..	..	..	..	...	R.D.A. (anc.)*
Greece	5596	5374	5284	4419	5308	6061	7424	7149	*6959	...	Grèce
Hungary	1541	1789	1756	1955	1598	1522	1313	1358	*1233	...	Hongrie
Ireland	*505	623	682	681	819	785	793	1022	*1099	...	Irlande
Italy and San Marino	23653	24508	22001	22012	21802	19395	18283	19418	*20486	...	Italie y comp. St. Marin
Lithuania	..	...	1533	1798	1375	831	943	1374	*1515	...	Lituanie
Netherlands	12673	13772	14711	14850	12638	12876	14491	13245	*14448	...	Pays-Bas
Norway,Svlbd.J.Myn. I	1125	1452	1732	1463	1589	1608	1628	1768	*1868	...	Norvège,Svalbd,J.May
Poland	3631	3480	2983	3340	3259	3452	3929	4344	*4662	...	Pologne
Portugal	3816	3438	4220	3834	3855	3765	3116	3023	*3185	...	Portugal
Romania	8121	4951	3855	3711	3376	2984	2402	2079	*1941	...	Roumanie
Russian Federation	..	...	89262	85789	72294	67891	65594	63887	*56701	...	Fédération de Russie
Slovakia	..	..	*1200	1456	*1500	1061	1144	1146	*1217	...	Slovaquie
Slovenia	..	...	229	227	170	174	120	174	78	...	Slovénie
Spain	14980	15989	16593	14828	14252	13815	12546	13623	*15058	...	Espagne
Sweden	5070	5307	5689	5975	5725	5478	5824	6230	*5959	...	Suède

For general note and footnotes, see end of table.   Voir la fin du tableau pour la remarque générale et les notes.

Residual fuel oils (continued)
Mazout résiduel (suite)

ISIC-BASED CODE - CODE BASE CITI
3530-22A

Unit : Thousand metric tons

Unité : Milliers de tonnes métriques

Country or area	1990	1991	1992	1993	1994	1995	1996	1997	1998	1999	Pays ou zone
Switzrld,Liechtenstein	504	944	860	892	842	772	896	763	*709	...	Suisse,Liechtenstein
Ukraine	..	...	17678	9259	8082	6910	5141	4326	*4542	...	Ukraine
United Kingdom	15825	15422	14651	15539	13826	13287	13780	14062	*13476	...	Royaume-Uni
Yugoslavia	..	...	500	465	347	365	563	959	*584	...	Yougoslavie
T.F.Yug.Rep. Macedonia	..	...	*440	446	42	48	333	174	*290	...	L'ex-RY Macédoine
Yugoslavia, SFR*	5900	..	..	..	..	..	..	..	..	..	Yougoslavie, RSF*
USSR (former)	169041	..	..	..	..	..	..	..	..	..	URSS (anc.)
Oceania	2830	2992	3060	2951	2801	2876	2523	2296	2214	2062	Océanie
Australia [1]	2440	2611	2645	2567	2293	2476	2077	1808	*1715	...	Australie [1]
New Zealand [2]	390	381	415	384	508	400	446	488	*499	...	Nouvelle-Zélande [2]
Total	**718083**	**664893**	**695251**	**673371**	**650716**	**636812**	**632191**	**634315**	**634733**	**613024**	Total

General Note.

Heavy oils that make up the distillation residue. It comprises all fuels (including those obtained by blending) with a viscosity above 27.5 cST at 38°C. Their flash point is always above 50°C and their specific gravity higher than 0.90. It is commonly used by ships and industrial large-scale heating installatios as a fuel in furnaces or boilers. It is also called mazout. (SITC, Rev.3: 33440-0A).

Remarque générale.

Huiles lourdes constituant le résidu de la distillation. La rubrique comprend tous les combustibles (y compris ceux obtenus par mélange) d'une viscosité supérieure à 27.5 cST à 38°C. Leur point d'éclair est toujours supérieur à 50°C et leur densité supérieure à 0.90. Ces produits sont couramment utilisés comme combustible dans les chaudières des navires et des grandes installations de chauffage industriel. Ils sont également connus sous le nom de fuel oil.(CTCI, Rev.: 33440-0A).

[1] Twelve months ending 30 June of year stated.
[2] Twelve months beginning 1 April of year stated.
[3] Twelve months beginning 21 March of year stated.
[4] Data refer to production from oil shale.

[1] Période de douze mois finissant le 30 juin de l'année indiquée.
[2] Période de douze mois commençant le 1er avril de l'année indiquée.
[3] Période de douze mois commençant le 21 mars de l'année indiquée.
[4] Les données se rapportent à la production du schiste bitumineux.

Lubricants
Lubrifiants

ISIC-BASED CODE - CODE BASE CITI

3530-25A

Unit : Thousand metric tons | Unité : Milliers de tonnes métriques

Country or area	1990	1991	1992	1993	1994	1995	1996	1997	1998	1999	Pays ou zone
Africa	**914**	**927**	**914**	**929**	**976**	**1105**	**1034**	**956**	**949**	**1042**	**Afrique**
Algeria*	120	125	130	138	124	126	116	98	104	...	Algérie*
Cameroon*	39	37	35	27	28	38	40	42	42	...	Cameroun*
Congo	3	3	3	3	3	3	3	3	*3	...	Congo
Côte d'Ivoire*	6	5	7	8	8	8	9	9	9	...	Côte d'Ivoire*
Egypt	249	237	243	235	*242	*254	235	247	*283	...	Egypte
Gabon	7	7	7	7	7	8	8	8	*8	...	Gabon
Ghana*	21	23	23	25	25	26	26	26	26	...	Ghana*
Madagascar*	4	5	5	5	5	5	5	5	5	...	Madagascar*
Morocco	81	111	98	83	137	126	125	127	*118	...	Maroc
Senegal*	3	3	3	3	3	3	3	3	3	...	Sénégal*
Sierra Leone*	12	14	14	15	15	15	15	15	15	...	Sierra Leone*
South Africa*	349	338	326	360	357	471	427	351	311	...	Afrique du Sud*
Sudan*	20	19	20	20	22	22	22	22	22	...	Soudan*
America, North	**11140**	**10247**	**10417**	**10380**	**11165**	**11304**	**11655**	**12284**	**12369**	**12901**	**Amérique du Nord**
Canada	937	884	915	746	880	809	884	1181	*1098	...	Canada
Cuba*	130	125	125	110	110	100	90	60	87	...	Cuba*
Jamaica*	12	11	10	8	8	7	7	6	6	...	Jamaïque*
Mexico	390	...	...	...	...	...	...	...	...	...	Mexique
Netherlands Antilles*	400	300	350	365	372	375	377	380	385	...	Antilles néerlandaises*
Puerto Rico*	520	345	375	400	450	500	502	505	505	...	Porto Rico*
Trinidad and Tobago	0	36	*5	*5	71	*10	*13	*12	*12	...	Trinité-et-Tobago
United States	8751	8156	8247	8356	8884	9113	9392	9750	*9886	...	Etats-Unis
America, South	**1401**	**1423**	**1521**	**1489**	**1538**	**1428**	**1375**	**1408**	**1419**	**1420**	**Amérique du Sud**
Argentina	218	225	251	239	293	278	233	254	*260	...	Argentine
Bolivia	11	9	10	5	6	*7	7	5	*5	...	Bolivie
Brazil	680	636	727	661	712	625	681	662	662	...	Brésil
Chile	75	77	101	122	101	106	104	106	104	...	Chili
Colombia	*2	*2	*2	1	1	*1	*1	*1	*1	...	Colombie
Ecuador	36	37	32	36	36	*36	0	*0	*0	...	Equateur
Peru	*5	*7	*5	*5	*10	*17	*28	78	*60	...	Pérou
Uruguay*	8	...	...	...	...	...	...	...	...	...	Uruguay*
Venezuela	366	422	385	412	371	350	313	294	*319	...	Venezuela
Asia	**8225**	**9136**	**9489**	**9587**	**10145**	**11396**	**11721**	**12034**	**11790**	**13749**	**Asie**
Azerbaijan	..	...	391	208	230	127	128	128	*82	...	Azerbaïdjan
Bahrain	*290	*340	*350	*250	*300	26	*26	*26	*26	...	Bahreïn
Bangladesh[1]	32	17	23	22	34	0	0	0	*0	...	Bangladesh[1]
China	*1800	*1850	*2000	*2100	*2150	3936	*4000	*4100	*4200	...	Chine
India[2]	548	410	425	515	529	*545	601	588	*644	...	Inde[2]
Indonesia	230	205	241	224	253	236	*240	*220	*211	...	Indonésie
Iran(Islamic Rep. of)*[3]	560	600	580	600	610	610	650	675	695	...	Iran(Rép. islamique)*[3]
Iraq*	180	175	200	200	224	225	220	223	230	...	Iraq*
Israel	*10	44	58	52	42	55	47	42	*42	...	Israël
Japan	2232	2213	2209	2260	2422	2437	2466	2526	*2343	...	Japon
Jordan	*12	14	21	*21	24	25	27	*28	*29	...	Jordanie
Korea, Republic of	599	608	649	684	776	840	935	931	727	...	Corée, République de
Malaysia*	79	54	58	62	68	75	80	85	90	...	Malaisie*
Myanmar*[2]	15	14	14	13	13	13	13	13	10	...	Myanmar*[2]
Oman	*12	*15	*16	28	*25	0	0	0	*0	...	Oman
Pakistan[1]	191	191	191	193	196	198	189	180	*163	...	Pakistan[1]
Philippines	0	120	0	...	...	...	...	...	...	...	Philippines
S.Arabia,pt.Ntrl.Zn*	400	510	600	620	760	750	750	752	755	...	Arab.saoud,p.Zn.neut*
Singapore*	700	730	750	694	664	668	648	849	849	...	Singapour*
Sri Lanka	22	21	19	19	24	27	28	29	*34	...	Sri Lanka
Turkey	282	257	263	309	280	294	305	302	*325	...	Turquie
United Arab Emirates*	30	20	40	60	60	60	60	65	65	...	Emirats arabes unis*
Uzbekistan	..	...	390	412	420	208	267	231	*229	...	Ouzbékistan
Viet Nam	1	*1	*1	*1	*1	*1	*1	*1	*1	...	Viet Nam
Europe	**9737**	**12340**	**12958**	**12048**	**11546**	**12574**	**12273**	**11995**	**11500**	**11442**	**Europe**
Albania	16	8	3	3	1	0	0	0	*0	...	Albanie

For general note and footnotes, see end of table.   Voir la fin du tableau pour la remarque générale et les notes.

Lubricants (continued)
Lubrifiants (suite)

ISIC-BASED CODE - CODE BASE CITI

3530-25A

Unit : Thousand metric tons

Unité : Milliers de tonnes métriques

Country or area	1990	1991	1992	1993	1994	1995	1996	1997	1998	1999	Pays ou zone
Austria	69	*0	27	13	4	27	85	113	*107	...	Autriche
Belarus	..	...	266	199	163	180	191	208	*197	...	Bélarus
Belgium	3	0	0	0	0	0	0	0	...	...	Belgique
Bulgaria	139	70	72	85	68	64	0	0	*0	...	Bulgarie
Croatia	..	...	37	42	44	35	30	36	*31	...	Croatie
Czechoslovakia(former)*	330	275	..	..	..	..	..	..	..	..	Tchécoslovaquie(anc.)*
Czech Republic	..	..	186	116	176	112	95	87	*160	...	République tchèque
Finland	0	0	0	0	0	0	0	0	*50	...	Finlande
France incl. Monaco	1652	1769	1794	1857	1910	2342	2418	2660	*2270	...	France y compris Monaco
Germany	..	1551	*1534	1421	1539	1552	1565	1491	*1542	...	Allemagne
Germany(Fed.Rep.)	1561	..	..	..	..	..	..	..	..	..	Allemagne(Rép.féd.)
German D.R.(former)*	490	..	..	..	..	..	..	..	..	..	R.D.A. (anc.)*
Greece	189	158	169	132	154	166	182	154	*157	...	Grèce
Hungary	165	233	154	308	371	537	286	369	*342	...	Hongrie
Italy and San Marino	1279	1133	1246	1163	1295	1380	1473	1266	*1297	...	Italie y comp. St. Marin
Netherlands	597	569	499	443	549	617	624	562	*624	...	Pays-Bas
Poland	425	245	219	206	210	209	209	200	*205	...	Pologne
Portugal	128	131	132	136	147	156	144	84	*108	...	Portugal
Romania	*500	314	265	230	230	208	213	168	*155	...	Roumanie
Russian Federation	..	...	4069	3315	2200	2550	2440	2145	*1885	...	Fédération de Russie
Slovakia	..	..	...	42	70	75	75	75	*75	...	Slovaquie
Spain	375	323	318	345	422	400	348	380	*400	...	Espagne
Sweden	265	183	131	226	163	157	179	238	*233	...	Suède
Ukraine	..	...	388	321	...	...	...	...	...	...	Ukraine
United Kingdom	974	973	1163	1264	1296	1261	1111	1231	*1134	...	Royaume-Uni
Yugoslavia	..	...	225	181	179	191	250	173	*173	...	Yougoslavie
Yugoslavia, SFR*	580	..	..	..	..	..	..	..	..	..	Yougoslavie, RSF*
USSR (former)	7143	..	..	..	..	..	..	..	..	..	URSS (anc.)
Oceania	**560**	**622**	**610**	**603**	**626**	**686**	**716**	**697**	**682**	**762**	**Océanie**
Australia [1]	560	622	610	603	626	686	716	697	*682	...	Australie [1]
Total	**39120**	**34695**	**35909**	**35036**	**35996**	**38493**	**38774**	**39374**	**38709**	**41317**	**Total**

General Note.

Viscous, liquid hydrocarbons rich in paraffin waxes, distilling between 380°C and 500°C and obtained by vacuum distillation of oil residues from atmospheric distillation. Additives may be included to alter their characteristics. The main characteristics are as follows: Flash point greater than 125°C; pour point between -25 and +5°C depending on the grade; strong acid number normally 0.5 mg/g; ash content less than or equal to 0.3%; water content less than or equal to 0.2%. Included are cutting oils, white oils, insulating oils, spindle oils and lubricating greases. (SITC, Rev.3: 33450-1A).

Remarque générale.

Hydrocarbures liquides et visqueux, riches en paraffines, dont les températures de distillation se situent entre 380 et 500°C et qui sont obtenus par distillation sous vide des résidus de la distillation atmosphérique du pétrole. Des additifs peuvent y être incorporés pour modifier leurs caractéristiques. Leurs principales caractéristiques sont les suivantes: point d'éclair supérieur à 125°C; point d'écoulement compris entre -25 et +5°C selon la qualité; indice d'acide fort normalement égal à 0.5 mg/g; teneur en cendres inférieure ou égale à 0.3%, et teneur en eau inférieure ou égale à 0.2%. Figurent dans cette rubrique les huiles de coupe, les huiles blanches, les huiles isolantes, les huiles à broches et les graisses lubrifiantes. (CTCI, Rev.3: 33450-1A).

[1] Twelve months ending 30 June of year stated.
[2] Twelve months beginning 1 April of year stated.
[3] Twelve months beginning 21 March of year stated.

[1] Période de douze mois finissant le 30 juin de l'année indiquée.
[2] Période de douze mois commençant le 1er avril de l'année indiquée.
[3] Période de douze mois commençant le 21 mars de l'année indiquée.

Petroleum wax (paraffin)
Cires de pétrole (paraffines)

ISIC-BASED CODE - CODE BASE CITI

3530-28

Unit : Thousand metric tons   Unité : Milliers de tonnes métriques

Country or area	1990	1991	1992	1993	1994	1995	1996	1997	1998	1999	Pays ou zone
Africa	**89**	**93**	**105**	**100**	**102**	**100**	**100**	**102**	**112**	**113**	**Afrique**
Mauritania*	84	87	95	94	94	95	95	96	96	...	Mauritanie*
Morocco	5	6	10	6	8	5	5	6	*16	...	Maroc
America, North	**871**	**933**	**940**	**1011**	**1054**	**1064**	**1352**	**1240**	**1227**	**1453**	**Amérique du Nord**
Mexico	83	...	...	...	...	...	...	...	...	...	Mexique
United States	788	850	857	928	971	981	1269	1157	*1144	...	Etats-Unis
America, South	**50**	**55**	**59**	**61**	**58**	**63**	**42**	**65**	**61**	**62**	**Amérique du Sud**
Argentina	11	13	*13	*12	*11	*10	*10	*10	*12	...	Argentine
Bolivia	1	1	2	1	1	*1	*1	1	*1	...	Bolivie
Chile	11	15	18	18	19	23	24	25	21	...	Chili
Venezuela*	27	26	26	30	27	29	7	29	27	...	Venezuela*
Asia	**881**	**879**	**979**	**1040**	**1103**	**1099**	**1090**	**1164**	**1211**	**1353**	**Asie**
China*	550	560	610	670	710	750	780	850	900	...	Chine*
India	93	89	92	90	102	*108	84	91	*84	...	Inde
Indonesia	10	15	11	15	20	21	20	20	*22	...	Indonésie
Iraq*	70	10	70	80	90	88	86	87	90	...	Iraq*
Japan	137	129	129	113	111	118	107	103	*105	...	Japon
Myanmar	2	3	1	3	3	3	3	3	*2	...	Myanmar
Pakistan	3	3	4	4	4	3	4	5	*3	...	Pakistan
Syrian Arab Republic	*1	*1	*1	*1	*2	2	*2	2	*2	...	Rép. arabe syrienne
Turkey	15	12	10	10	6	5	2	2	*2	...	Turquie
Uzbekistan	..	...	51	54	55	1	2	1	*1	...	Ouzbékistan
Europe	**684**	**1361**	**1624**	**1213**	**955**	**985**	**1168**	**1021**	**1220**	**1190**	**Europe**
Belarus	..	...	161	68	35	4	2	1	*0	...	Bélarus
Bulgaria	8	5	3	4	3	3	0	0	*0	...	Bulgarie
Croatia	..	...	13	12	14	17	15	11	*9	...	Croatie
Czechoslovakia(former)*	8	5	..	..	..	..	..	..	..		Tchécoslovaquie(anc.)*
Czech Republic	..	..	8	7	6	4	5	3	*6	...	République tchèque
France incl. Monaco	124	126	126	132	116	140	174	177	*199	...	France y compris Monaco
Germany	..	252	*231	205	187	196	202	195	*194	...	Allemagne
Germany(Fed.Rep.)	209	..	..	..	..	..	..	..	..		Allemagne(Rép.féd.)
Greece	3	3	4	4	3	2	2	1	*1	...	Grèce
Hungary	29	42	46	45	55	60	55	29	*50	...	Hongrie
Italy and San Marino	49	31	39	36	55	38	53	44	*45	...	Italie y comp. St. Marin
Netherlands	75	51	73	74	84	85	89	92	*110	...	Pays-Bas
Poland	18	21	20	20	21	111	158	93	*117	...	Pologne
Portugal	11	15	10	9	13	12	14	7	*12	...	Portugal
Romania	19	13	15	7	10	8	11	7	*12	...	Roumanie
Russian Federation	..	...	*700	461	191	163	78	70	*157	...	Fédération de Russie
Spain	61	61	46	45	52	50	223	180	*203	...	Espagne
Ukraine	..	...	67	25	...	...	...	...	...		Ukraine
United Kingdom	40	37	62	59	64	46	41	65	*59	...	Royaume-Uni
Yugoslavia, SFR*	30	..	..	..	..	..	..	..	..		Yougoslavie, RSF*
USSR (former)	1688	..	..	..	..	..	..	..	..		URSS (anc.)
Oceania	**20**	**18**	**15**	**18**	**18**	**23**	**22**	**23**	**22**	**25**	**Océanie**
Australia	20	18	15	18	18	23	22	23	*22	...	Australie
Total	**4283**	**3339**	**3722**	**3443**	**3290**	**3334**	**3774**	**3615**	**3853**	**4196**	**Total**

General Note.

Saturated aliphatic hydrocarbon obtained as residues extracted when dewaxing lubricant oils, with a crystalline structure with C greater than 12. Their main characteristics are as follows: they are colourless, in most cases odourless and translucent, with a melting point above 45°C, specific gravity of 0.76 to 0.78 at 80°C, kinematic viscosity between 3.7 and 5.5 cST at 99°C. These waxes are used for candle manufacture polishes and waterproofing of containers, wrappings, etc.(SITC, Rev.3: 33512-1).

Remarque générale.

Hydrocarbures alipatiques saturés obtenus comme résidu lors du déparaffinage des huiles lubrifiantes et ayant une structure cristalline, avec un nombre d'atomes de carbone supérieur à 12. Leurs principales caractéristiques sont les suivantes: incolores, la plupart du temps inodores et translucides; point de fusion supérieur à 45°C, densité comprise entre 0.76 et 0.78 à 80°C, et viscosité cinématique comprise entre 3.7 et 5.5 cST à 99°C. Ces cires servent à la fabrication des bougies et des encaustiques, à l'imperméabilisation de récipients et d'emballages, etc. (CTCI, Rev.3: 33512-1).

Petroleum coke
Coke de pétrole

ISIC-BASED CODE - CODE BASE CITI

3530-31

Unit : Thousand metric tons

Unité : Milliers de tonnes métriques

Country or area	1990	1991	1992	1993	1994	1995	1996	1997	1998	1999	Pays ou zone
Africa	**128**	**124**	**134**	**137**	**141**	**156**	**155**	**122**	**181**	**173**	**Afrique**
Egypt	128	124	134	137	141	156	155	122	*181	...	Egypte
America, North	**37596**	**38860**	**41760**	**43279**	**43493**	**44670**	**48612**	**50008**	**52180**	**56964**	**Amérique du Nord**
Canada	978	1032	2091	2264	2244	2854	3006	2881	*3461	...	Canada
Cuba	22	19	15	15	15	16	16	18	*15	...	Cuba
Mexico	46	123	56	41	81	122	1491	1443	*1506	...	Mexique
United States	36550	37686	39598	40959	41153	41678	44099	45666	*47198	...	Etats-Unis
America, South	**2088**	**1998**	**2354**	**2194**	**2049**	**2835**	**3775**	**4472**	**3928**	**4985**	**Amérique du Sud**
Argentina	1248	1284	*1675	1508	1215	1213	1310	1397	*1400	...	Argentine
Brazil	600	549	516	522	722	823	977	1079	1006	...	Brésil
Uruguay	15	15	13	4	0	15	0	16	*0	...	Uruguay
Venezuela*	225	150	150	160	112	784	1488	1980	1522	...	Venezuela*
Asia	**1904**	**1979**	**2068**	**2385**	**2644**	**2722**	**2747**	**3182**	**3235**	**3748**	**Asie**
Azerbaijan	..	...	96	60	40	4	59	50	*30	...	Azerbaïdjan
China*	1100	1150	1220	1380	1400	1435	1450	1470	1500	...	Chine*
India[1]	246	229	236	215	258	*265	243	266	*287	...	Inde[1]
Indonesia	29	26	31	55	95	124	*130	*445	*463	...	Indonésie
Japan	314	311	300	603	669	657	711	753	*749	...	Japon
Myanmar[1]	36	29	26	24	28	27	25	26	*29	...	Myanmar[1]
Syrian Arab Republic	179	164	159	40	154	148	129	*126	*131	...	Rép. arabe syrienne
Uzbekistan	..	...	...	...	0	62	0	46	*46	...	Ouzbékistan
Europe	**6291**	**7560**	**7816**	**7919**	**7775**	**8103**	**7929**	**8591**	**9242**	**9284**	**Europe**
Belgium	230	404	441	444	286	233	300	297	*301	...	Belgique
Croatia	..	...	11	35	63	53	46	28	*58	...	Croatie
France incl. Monaco	879	899	907	875	901	933	961	975	*999	...	France y compris Monaco
Germany	..	1574	1561	1626	1735	1624	1739	1746	*1777	...	Allemagne
Germany(Fed.Rep.)	1498		..	..	..	..	..	..	..		Allemagne(Rép.féd.)
Greece	136	132	148	148	146	140	154	157	*163	...	Grèce
Hungary	...	...	...	...	0	0	22	48	*69	...	Hongrie
Italy and San Marino	1091	1156	1217	1236	1252	1264	913	1311	*1164	...	Italie y comp. St. Marin
Norway,Svlbd.J.Myn. I	161	143	165	198	204	167	151	191	*193	...	Norvège,Svalbd,J.May
Romania	370	286	267	264	404	514	551	422	*684	...	Roumanie
Russian Federation	..	...	1000	960	650	753	625	794	*997	...	Fédération de Russie
Spain	305	428	441	428	463	448	591	796	*907	...	Espagne
Sweden	0	*0	0	0	0	23	0	0	*0	...	Suède
Ukraine	..	...	76	14	...	...	...	...	...	...	Ukraine
United Kingdom	1562	1598	1582	1691	1626	1906	1831	1781	*1885	...	Royaume-Uni
Yugoslavia, SFR*	59	..	..	..	..	..	..	..	..	..	Yougoslavie, RSF*
USSR (former)	1685	..	..	..	..	..	..	..	..		URSS (anc.)
Oceania	**431**	**460**	**516**	**506**	**607**	**595**	**636**	**623**	**670**	**767**	**Océanie**
Australia[2]	431	460	516	506	607	595	636	623	*670	...	Australie[2]
Total	**50123**	**50981**	**54648**	**56420**	**56709**	**59081**	**63854**	**66998**	**69436**	**75922**	**Total**

General Note.

Shiny-black solid residue, obtained by cracking and carbonization in furnaces, consisting mainly of carbon (90 to 95%) and generally burning without leaving any ash. It is used mainly in metallurgical processes. It excludes those solid residues obtained from carbonization of coal. (SITC, Rev.3: 33542-0).

Remarque générale.

Résidu solide d'un noir brillant, obtenu par craquage et carbonisation au four, constitué essentiellement de carbon (90 à 95%) et dont la combustion ne laisse généralement aucune cendre. Il est utilisé surtout en métallurgie. Cette rubrique ne comprend pas les résidus solides obtenus par carbonisation du charbon.(CTCI, Rev.3: 33542-0).

[1] Twelve months beginning 1 April of year stated.
[2] Twelve months ending 30 June of year stated.

[1] Période de douze mois commençant le 1er avril de l'année indiquée.
[2] Période de douze mois finissant le 30 juin de l'année indiquée.

Bitumen (asphalt)
Bitume (brai)

ISIC-BASED CODE - CODE BASE CITI

3530-34A

Unit : Thousand metric tons
Unité : Milliers de tonnes métriques

Country or area	1990	1991	1992	1993	1994	1995	1996	1997	1998	1999	Pays ou zone
Africa	**1458**	**1380**	**1388**	**1400**	**1460**	**1517**	**1465**	**1476**	**1537**	**1561**	**Afrique**
Algeria*	210	220	230	258	223	233	208	183	171	...	Algérie*
Angola*	14	14	11	8	0	0	1	5	5	...	Angola*
Cameroon*	7	7	7	9	10	10	10	12	12	...	Cameroun*
Egypt	655	613	581	617	683	740	696	766	*857	...	Egypte
Ethiopia,incl.Eritrea*	8	10	10	10	9	7	2	2	2	...	Ethiopie,incl.Erythrée*
Gabon	2	2	2	3	4	10	14	10	*12	...	Gabon
Kenya	31	24	27	9	20	26	*26	10	13	...	Kenya
Libyan Arab Jamah.*	90	90	100	90	100	102	103	106	106	...	Jamah. arabe libyenne*
Morocco	99	114	116	101	136	137	123	126	*125	...	Maroc
South Africa*	333	277	294	285	265	242	272	248	229	...	Afrique du Sud*
Zambia	*9	*9	*10	*10	*10	*10	*10	*8	5	...	Zambie
America, North	**31585**	**30119**	**29369**	**31692**	**32147**	**33031**	**32487**	**34913**	**35885**	**36927**	**Amérique du Nord**
Barbados	7	6	2	5	6	5	5	5	*0	...	Barbade
Canada	2793	2633	2517	2938	3376	3305	3229	4112	*4288	...	Canada
Costa Rica	14	6	1	10	16	25	23	26	*12	...	Costa Rica
Cuba*	182	73	30	30	14	36	42	59	68	...	Cuba*
El Salvador	13	14	20	16	17	20	28	*35	*31	...	El Salvador
Jamaica*	13	12	10	10	10	9	10	8	8	...	Jamaïque*
Mexico	953	...	...	...	...	...	...	...	...	...	Mexique
Netherlands Antilles*	454	451	455	460	462	463	464	465	468	...	Antilles néerlandaises*
Nicaragua	9	6	15	15	15	*14	*14	*14	*14	...	Nicaragua
Panama	7	4	13	16	*10	*10	*10	*10	*10	...	Panama
Trinidad and Tobago	28	28	23	21	21	17	15	*15	*15	...	Trinité-et-Tobago
United States	27112	25933	25330	27218	27247	28174	27694	29211	*30018	...	Etats-Unis
America, South	**3683**	**3059**	**3623**	**3557**	**3824**	**3906**	**4252**	**4630**	**4873**	**5177**	**Amérique du Sud**
Argentina	203	229	*250	451	544	*525	467	591	*590	...	Argentine
Bolivia	*4	*2	2	2	2	*2	2	2	*2	...	Bolivie
Brazil	1266	986	1230	1104	1316	1252	1454	1484	1919	...	Brésil
Chile	7	3	0	0	0	0	0	0	0	...	Chili
Colombia	219	194	235	289	*276	*280	*280	*294	*285	...	Colombie
Ecuador	82	72	64	81	105	102	85	*90	*80	...	Equateur
Peru	...	...	...	*0	*50	*70	*95	182	*120	...	Pérou
Uruguay	35	51	52	15	0	30	61	66	*60	...	Uruguay
Venezuela	1854	1494	*1748	1615	1531	*1645	1808	1921	*1817	...	Venezuela
Asia	**17390**	**17937**	**19124**	**20322**	**20518**	**21577**	**23072**	**24126**	**24006**	**27173**	**Asie**
Azerbaijan	..	...	0	84	66	54	40	40	*25	...	Azerbaïdjan
Bahrain	76	92	69	*75	*70	180	253	336	*286	...	Bahreïn
Bangladesh[1]	52	*53	43	*45	71	0	0	0	*0	...	Bangladesh[1]
China*	2300	2350	2550	2650	2730	2800	2850	2900	3000	...	Chine*
Cyprus	38	28	24	34	35	37	30	37	*37	...	Chypre
India[2]	1598	1676	1740	1844	1904	*1960	2229	2214	*2339	...	Inde[2]
Indonesia	500	519	536	538	540	503	547	389	*319	...	Indonésie
Iran(Islamic Rep. of)*[3]	2000	2200	2100	2200	2200	2455	2806	2839	2841	...	Iran(Rép. islamique)*[3]
Iraq*	450	350	400	410	459	461	451	457	472	...	Iraq*
Israel	128	131	198	284	231	281	268	268	*268	...	Israël
Japan	6185	5989	6150	6086	6078	5963	6092	5896	*5644	...	Japon
Jordan	120	134	124	140	136	129	141	*129	*143	...	Jordanie
Korea, Republic of	846	1136	1599	1585	1727	1786	2012	2470	2117	...	Corée, République de
Kuwait,part Ntl.Zone	*40	1	10	45	59	*54	*47	*53	*42	...	Koweït et prt.Zne.N.
Malaysia*	163	215	225	235	250	260	270	280	57	...	Malaisie*
Pakistan[1]	163	175	170	260	205	218	237	224	*204	...	Pakistan[1]
Philippines	*59	55	44	*39	*38	*49	*46	*47	*33	...	Philippines
S.Arabia,pt.Ntrl.Zn*	900	920	1000	1100	1310	1400	1460	1480	1500	...	Arab.saoud,p.Zn.neut*
Singapore*	610	510	670	700	850	1166	1132	1480	1480	...	Singapour*
Sri Lanka	26	35	28	46	46	43	40	38	*60	...	Sri Lanka
Syrian Arab Republic	217	196	218	241	274	316	417	443	*496	...	Rép. arabe syrienne
Thailand	198	210	279	303	291	281	342	592	*654	...	Thaïlande
Turkey	721	871	879	1283	890	980	1152	1325	*1801	...	Turquie
Uzbekistan	..	...	...	...	0	143	150	130	*129	...	Ouzbékistan
Yemen	..	43	56	58	58	58	60	59	*59	...	Yémen

For general note and footnotes, see end of table.
Voir la fin du tableau pour la remarque générale et les notes.

Bitumen (asphalt) (continued)
Bitume (brai) (suite)

ISIC-BASED CODE - CODE BASE CITI

3530-34A

Unit : Thousand metric tons

Unité : Milliers de tonnes métriques

Country or area	1990	1991	1992	1993	1994	1995	1996	1997	1998	1999	Pays ou zone
Europe	**21199**	**29064**	**29768**	**26896**	**27048**	**26488**	**24566**	**24723**	**26704**	**23855**	**Europe**
Albania	54	21	11	19	34	40	36	14	*14	...	Albanie
Austria	268	293	280	294	311	255	264	327	*300	...	Autriche
Belarus	..	...	700	480	395	454	487	546	*571	...	Bélarus
Belgium	851	834	806	805	817	893	772	951	*957	...	Belgique
Bulgaria	384	109	63	70	60	0	0	0	*94	...	Bulgarie
Croatia	..	..	164	125	181	146	127	192	*144	...	Croatie
Denmark	27	*10	*0	0	0	0	0	0	...	...	Danemark
Czechoslovakia(former)*	1050	910	..	..	..	..	..	..			Tchécoslovaquie(anc.)*
Czech Republic	..	..	322	200	348	337	354	329	*469	...	République tchèque
Finland	509	357	356	252	283	227	225	289	*283	...	Finlande
France incl. Monaco	3067	3319	3215	3142	3348	3132	3116	3376	*3448	...	France y compris Monaco
Germany	..	3859	*4089	3804	4200	3707	3419	3467	*3425	...	Allemagne
Germany(Fed.Rep.)	2844	..	..	..	..	..	..	..	..	..	Allemagne(Rép.féd.)
German D.R.(former)*	730	..	..	..	..	..	..	..	..		R.D.A. (anc.)*
Greece	244	338	253	272	288	324	353	378	*427	...	Grèce
Hungary	473	391	301	285	351	331	308	332	*446	...	Hongrie
Italy and San Marino	2455	2243	2333	2128	2286	2359	2431	2626	*2693	...	Italie y comp. St. Marin
Lithuania	..	..	*25	31	51	28	25	35	*82	...	Lituanie
Netherlands	816	781	723	593	695	751	657	525	*474	...	Pays-Bas
Norway,Svlbd.J.Myn. I	58	102	212	103	8	0	0	0	*0	...	Norvège,Svalbd,J.May
Poland	609	524	552	523	435	285	314	648	*590	...	Pologne
Portugal	108	75	128	167	186	226	190	296	*396	...	Portugal
Romania	414	379	367	319	340	347	350	305	*241	...	Roumanie
Russian Federation	..	...	7394	6333	5138	5281	4255	3139	*4294	...	Fédération de Russie
Slovakia*			300	162	204	318	318	318	318	...	Slovaquie*
Spain	2180	2564	2400	2496	2345	2354	2134	2136	*2517	...	Espagne
Sweden	813	*750	788	904	878	929	922	873	*953	...	Suède
Switzrld,Liechtenstein	141	151	138	119	140	149	128	121	*140	...	Suisse,Liechtenstein
Ukraine	..	...	1458	788	...	...	...	...	...	...	Ukraine
United Kingdom	2454	2302	2336	2450	2569	2459	2189	2258	*2190	...	Royaume-Uni
Yugoslavia	..	...	54	32	34	33	69	119	*115	...	Yougoslavie
Yugoslavia, SFR*	650	..	..	..	..	..	..	..	..	..	Yougoslavie, RSF*
USSR (former)	17710	..	..	..	..	..	..	..	..	..	URSS (anc.)
Oceania	**705**	**697**	**723**	**780**	**853**	**793**	**821**	**818**	**867**	**926**	**Océanie**
Australia[1]	571	592	578	637	678	638	652	656	*708	...	Australie[1]
New Zealand[2]	134	105	145	143	175	155	169	162	*159	...	Nouvelle-Zélande[2]
Total	**93730**	**82257**	**83996**	**84647**	**85850**	**87312**	**86663**	**90686**	**93872**	**95618**	**Total**

General Note.

Solid or viscous hydrocarbon with a colloidal structure, brown or black in colour, often soluble in carbon bisulphite, non-volatile, thermoplastic (generally between 150 and 200°C), with insulating and adhesive prperties, obtained as a residue by vacuum distillation of oil residues from atmospheric distillation. It is used mainly in road construction. Natural asphalt is excluded. (SITC, Rev.3: 33541-1A).

Remarque générale.

Hydrocarbure solide ou visqueux de structure colloidale, de couleur brune ou noire, souvent soluble dans le bisulphite de carbone, non volatil, thermoplastique (généralement entre 150 et 200°C), ayant des propriétés isolantes et adhésives, obtenu comme résidu de la distillation sous vide des résidus de la distillation atmosphérique du pétrole. Il est utilisé principalement pour la construction des routes. Cette rubrique ne comprend pas l'asphalte naturel. (CTCI. Rev.3: 33541-1A).

[1] Twelve months ending 30 June of year stated.
[2] Twelve months beginning 1 April of year stated.
[3] Twelve months beginning 21 March of year stated.

[1] Période de douze mois finissant le 30 juin de l'année indiquée.
[2] Période de douze mois commençant le 1er avril de l'année indiquée.
[3] Période de douze mois commençant le 21 mars de l'année indiquée.

Liquefied petroleum gas from natural gas plants
Gaz de pétrole liquéfiés provenant du gaz naturel

ISIC-BASED CODE - CODE BASE CITI

3530-371A

Unit : Thousand metric tons   Unité : Milliers de tonnes métriques

Country or area	1990	1991	1992	1993	1994	1995	1996	1997	1998	1999	Pays ou zone
Africa	**5360**	**5451**	**5516**	**5779**	**5862**	**6107**	**6685**	**7839**	**8774**	**9115**	**Afrique**
Algeria	4533	4580	4530	4681	4569	4609	5039	*6186	*7089	...	Algérie
Egypt	567	571	676	758	823	853	976	971	*1000	...	Egypte
Libyan Arab Jamah.	*260	*300	*310	*340	*470	645	*670	*682	*685	...	Jamah. arabe libyenne
America, North	**55140**	**58239**	**59568**	**62541**	**63492**	**65364**	**62624**	**67559**	**68767**	**73252**	**Amérique du Nord**
Canada	9405	9687	9930	11712	12240	13462	14234	*18955	*20535	...	Canada
Mexico	6567	6698	6733	6895	7374	7164	5964	5354	*5917	...	Mexique
United States	39168	41854	42905	43934	43878	44738	42426	43250	*42315	...	Etats-Unis
America, South	**4562**	**4623**	**4791**	**5792**	**5667**	**6152**	**6402**	**6756**	**6761**	**7914**	**Amérique du Sud**
Argentina	850	802	813	913	681	1009	1054	1170	*1135	...	Argentine
Bolivia	161	163	159	158	170	198	237	240	*270	...	Bolivie
Brazil	479	489	452	396	288	272	239	286	319	...	Brésil
Chile	227	178	177	193	179	157	143	121	127	...	Chili
Colombia	76	37	138	132	133	70	*93	*93	*85	...	Colombie
Ecuador	73	85	84	118	108	89	114	*115	*110	...	Equateur
Peru	8	7	8	16	10	12	13	21	*15	...	Pérou
Venezuela	2688	2862	2960	3866	4098	4345	4509	4710	*4700	...	Venezuela
Asia	**22041**	**20513**	**23358**	**26781**	**31811**	**35397**	**35096**	**35868**	**38514**	**46492**	**Asie**
Bahrain	162	221	244	*227	*228	*219	*203	*195	*191	...	Bahreïn
Brunei Darussalam	*23	*15	15	14	9	11	12	*16	*16	...	Brunéi Darussalam
India	...	...	1312	1367	1408	1714	1780	1788	*2182	...	Inde
Iran(Islamic Rep. of)[1]	*400	*700	*1220	*1500	*1600	1786	*1800	*1790	*1880	...	Iran(Rép. islamique)[1]
Iraq*	900	0	2	486	700	1560	1590	1620	1650	...	Iraq*
Japan	12	0	12	12	12	12	12	12	*12	...	Japon
Kuwait,part Ntl.Zone	*2410	*100	580	*2014	*2463	2760	*2306	*2665	*3124	...	Koweït et prt.Zne.N.
Malaysia	352	325	360	485	870	*1745	*1113	*1156	*1402	...	Malaisie
Myanmar[2]	4	6	7	9	9	6	4	4	*5	...	Myanmar[2]
Oman	126	130	*4	*4	*24	17	26	32	*38	...	Oman
Pakistan[3]	86	102	86	76	39	91	121	114	*121	...	Pakistan[3]
Qatar	721	722	1080	1101	1067	1134	*1231	*1227	*1285	...	Qatar
S.Arabia,pt.Ntrl.Zn	12699	*13530	*14830	*15550	*17030	*17100	*17200	*17200	*17203	...	Arab.saoud,p.Zn.neut
Syrian Arab Republic	*42	*50	*60	*78	*80	*168	105	*110	*110	...	Rép. arabe syrienne
Thailand	530	793	863	897	808	912	1051	1350	*1336	...	Thaïlande
United Arab Emirates	*2470	*2500	*2600	*2700	*5165	*5840	6147	6149	*7509	...	Emirats arabes unis
Uzbekistan	..	...	...	...	...	24	27	32	*32	...	Ouzbékistan
Yemen	..	50	54	232	*270	*298	*368	*408	*418	...	Yémen
Europe	**2948**	**3401**	**3358**	**3365**	**3549**	**3629**	**3628**	**3731**	**3396**	**3832**	**Europe**
Croatia	..	...	*160	181	190	203	102	104	*94	...	Croatie
France incl. Monaco	145	256	229	228	460	410	406	352	*251	...	France y compris Monaco
Hungary	218	209	209	214	221	241	204	*200	*200	...	Hongrie
Norway,Svlbd.J.Myn. I	948	924	832	927	926	819	943	972	*753	...	Norvège,Svalbd,J.May
Spain	349	355	329	228	141	131	*135	*142	*188	...	Espagne
United Kingdom	1184	1462	1599	1587	1611	1825	1838	1961	*1910	...	Royaume-Uni
Yugoslavia, SFR	104	..	..	..	..	..	..	..	..	..	Yougoslavie, RSF
USSR (former)*	1000	..	..	..	..	..	..	..	..	..	URSS (anc.)*
Oceania	**2143**	**2031**	**1014**	**1162**	**1229**	**1223**	**1135**	**465**	**849**	**198**	**Océanie**
Australia[3]	2028	1901	872	1015	1083	1089	976	284	*670	...	Australie[3]
New Zealand[2]	115	130	142	147	146	134	159	181	*179	...	Nouvelle-Zélande[2]
Total	**93194**	**94258**	**97605**	**105420**	**111610**	**117872**	**115570**	**122218**	**127061**	**140803**	**Total**

For general note and footnotes, see end of table.   Voir la fin du tableau pour la remarque générale et les notes.

Liquefied petroleum gas from natural gas plants (continued)
Gaz de pétrole liquéfiés provenant du gaz naturel (suite)

General Note.

Hydrocarbons which are gaseous under conditions of normal temperature and pressure but are liquified by compression or cooling to facilitate storage, handling and transportation, and extracted by stripping of natural gas at crude petroleum and natural gas sources. It comprises propane (C_3H_8), butane (C_4H_{10}), or a mixture of these two hudrocarbons. Also included is ethane (C_2H_6) from petroleum or natural gas producers' separation and stabilization plants. (SITC, Rev.3: 34200-1A).

[1] Twelve months beginning 21 March of year stated.
[2] Twelve months beginning 1 April of year stated.
[3] Twelve months ending 30 June of year stated.

Remarque générale.

Hydrocarbures qui sont à l'état gazeux dans des conditions de température et de pression normales mais liquéfiés par compression ou refroidissement pour en faciliter l'entreposage, la manipulation et le transport et extraits par désessenciement du gaz naturel sur les sites de production de pétrole brut et de gaz naturel. Dans cette rubrique figurent les gaz propane (C_3H_8) et butane (C_4H_{10}) et les mélanges de ces deux hydrocarbures. Est également inclus l'éthane (C_2H_6) produit dans les installations de séparation et de stabilisation des producteurs de pétrole et de gaz naturel.(CTCI, Rev.3: 34200-1A).

[1] Période de douze mois commençant le 21 mars de l'année indiquée.
[2] Période de douze mois commençant le 1er avril de l'année indiquée.
[3] Période de douze mois finissant le 30 juin de l'année indiquée.

Liquefied petroleum gas from petroleum refineries
Gaz de pétrole liquéfiés, des raffineries de pétrole

ISIC-BASED CODE - CODE BASE CITI

3530-372A

Unit : Thousand metric tons

Unité : Milliers de tonnes métriques

Country or area	1990	1991	1992	1993	1994	1995	1996	1997	1998	1999	Pays ou zone
Africa	**1734**	**1783**	**1874**	**1977**	**2160**	**2182**	**2194**	**2164**	**2091**	**2416**	**Afrique**
Algeria	450	550	530	497	461	*465	*466	*477	*466	...	Algérie
Angola*	18	17	17	18	38	33	33	35	29	...	Angola*
Cameroon*	18	19	19	21	20	21	22	22	22	...	Cameroun*
Congo*	3	4	4	4	4	4	4	4	4	...	Congo*
Côte d'Ivoire*	14	17	15	17	17	18	18	19	19	...	Côte d'Ivoire*
Dem. Rep. of Congo	0	0	*1	0	0	0	0	0	*0	...	Rép. dém. du Congo
Egypt	337	330	328	385	409	459	443	459	*431	...	Egypte
Ethiopia,incl.Eritrea	*6	*6	*7	*7	6	*5	*2	*3	*3	...	Ethiopie,incl.Erythrée
Gabon	10	9	11	10	9	11	11	10	10	...	Gabon
Ghana*	16	16	17	17	17	18	18	18	18	...	Ghana*
Kenya	28	26	28	27	30	32	*32	24	29	...	Kenya
Libyan Arab Jamah.	*160	*170	*180	*200	*230	*235	*238	263	*263	...	Jamah. arabe libyenne
Madagascar*	1	1	1	1	4	5	5	5	6	...	Madagascar*
Mauritania*	28	32	38	36	36	37	38	38	38	...	Mauritanie*
Morocco	233	225	234	247	263	235	243	239	*252	...	Maroc
Nigeria*	100	55	60	60	159	169	202	119	70	...	Nigéria*
Senegal*	2	3	3	3	3	3	3	3	3	...	Sénégal*
South Africa	*134	*139	*200	269	300	279	*256	*286	*284	...	Afrique du Sud
Sudan*	7	6	6	6	6	7	7	7	7	...	Soudan*
Tunisia	154	143	159	136	132	130	142	122	*127	...	Tunisie
United Rep.Tanzania	5	5	*6	*6	*6	*6	*6	*6	*6	...	Rép. Unie de Tanzanie
Zambia	*10	*10	*10	*10	*10	*10	*5	*5	4	...	Zambie
America, North	**19725**	**20937**	**21985**	**22095**	**22707**	**23235**	**23487**	**24295**	**24094**	**26205**	**Amérique du Nord**
Barbados	1	2	2	2	2	2	1	1	*2	...	Barbade
Canada	1721	1848	2002	2028	1969	1223	1350	2197	*2251	...	Canada
Costa Rica	4	2	3	3	4	2	2	2	*0	...	Costa Rica
Cuba	104	83	70	42	23	62	60	56	*47	...	Cuba
Dominican Republic	24	27	25	30	35	37	39	36	*41	...	Rép. dominicaine
El Salvador	32	26	26	24	17	16	14	14	*16	...	El Salvador
Guatemala	5	5	8	10	10	7	7	5	*5	...	Guatemala
Honduras	6	5	4	...	...	...	...	...	...	...	Honduras
Jamaica	14	7	15	5	11	8	8	9	*10	...	Jamaïque
Martinique*	15	17	17	18	20	20	21	21	21	...	Martinique*
Mexico	1679	1611	1382	1956	2243	2071	1998	1182	*887	...	Mexique
Netherlands Antilles*	45	45	50	58	60	61	63	64	68	...	Antilles néerlandaises*
Nicaragua	16	16	20	16	18	13	15	13	*11	...	Nicaragua
Panama	8	7	8	8	6	3	19	15	*26	...	Panama
Puerto Rico*	94	90	70	110	90	110	112	115	115	...	Porto Rico*
Trinidad and Tobago	67	125	126	259	259	303	314	291	*330	...	Trinité-et-Tobago
United States	15640	16791	17967	17321	17800	19152	19317	20124	*20113	...	Etats-Unis
United States Virgin Is.*	250	230	190	200	135	140	142	145	146	...	Iles Vierges américaines*
America, South	**4881**	**4976**	**5339**	**5515**	**5878**	**5771**	**6090**	**6160**	**6516**	**7082**	**Amérique du Sud**
Argentina	601	696	816	752	869	758	830	883	*975	...	Argentine
Bolivia	*36	50	45	45	47	55	53	54	*50	...	Bolivie
Brazil	3044	2946	3178	3388	3511	3336	3281	3163	3208	...	Brésil
Chile	205	224	265	278	257	299	324	348	377	...	Chili
Colombia	386	438	366	352	505	518	*590	*594	*561	...	Colombie
Ecuador	149	189	219	255	253	215	253	206	*219	...	Equateur
Paraguay	11	9	*2	2	2	1	1	1	*0	...	Paraguay
Peru	135	134	140	146	139	165	165	196	*272	...	Pérou
Uruguay	65	56	55	19	0	42	37	62	*83	...	Uruguay
Venezuela	249	234	253	278	295	382	556	653	*771	...	Venezuela
Asia	**18034**	**18886**	**19332**	**20361**	**21731**	**24031**	**25630**	**26622**	**27245**	**31326**	**Asie**
Azerbaijan	..	...	0	2	20	10	4	3	*56	...	Azerbaïdjan
Bahrain	*25	*30	*25	24	*26	31	33	31	*26	...	Bahreïn
Bangladesh[1]	9	8	8	9	13	15	13	16	*14	...	Bangladesh[1]
Brunei Darussalam	*2	*2	12	12	11	10	9	*2	*1	...	Brunéi Darussalam
China	2616	3071	3501	*4126	4445	5408	6059	6679	*7474	...	Chine
Cyprus	25	29	28	27	32	27	26	32	*30	...	Chypre
India[2]	2075	2404	1254	1295	1394	1539	1966	1661	*1676	...	Inde[2]

For general note and footnotes, see end of table.

Voir la fin du tableau pour la remarque générale et les notes.

ISIC-BASED CODE - CODE BASE CITI

3530-372A

Unit : Thousand metric tons

Unité : Milliers de tonnes métriques

Country or area	1990	1991	1992	1993	1994	1995	1996	1997	1998	1999	Pays ou zone
Indonesia	2996	2642	2785	2777	3122	2941	3179	2945	*2344	...	Indonésie
Iran(Islamic Rep. of)* [3]	900	1000	1100	1300	1500	1924	1950	1940	2040	...	Iran(Rép. islamique)* [3]
Iraq*	210	170	400	600	600	600	600	610	610	...	Iraq*
Israel	227	216	290	383	430	460	442	493	*498	...	Israël
Japan	4450	4576	4724	4601	4585	4921	4881	5095	*4777	...	Japon
Jordan	102	99	122	127	126	138	133	143	*133	...	Jordanie
Kazakhstan	..	...	300	100	80	62	60	60	*60	...	Kazakhstan
Korea, Republic of	1030	1094	1259	1200	1263	1377	1377	1790	2361	...	Corée, République de
Lebanon	4	4	2	...	...	...	...	...		...	Liban
Malaysia	235	196	183	224	293	*396	*341	*341	*413	...	Malaisie
Myanmar [2]	3	3	4	3	2	4	4	6	*12	...	Myanmar [2]
Oman	36	61	39	33	34	61	35	36	*36	...	Oman
Pakistan [1]	41	45	45	36	40	37	36	41	*55	...	Pakistan [1]
Philippines	232	239	250	*224	*241	*374	414	454	*427	...	Philippines
Qatar	93	*60	*50	74	87	*79	89	69	*78	...	Qatar
S.Arabia,pt.Ntrl.Zn*	890	910	970	950	900	910	920	920	922	...	Arab.saoud,p.Zn.neut*
Singapore	*460	*475	*490	*564	*737	*699	875	965	*965	...	Singapour
Sri Lanka	19	19	14	17	15	14	18	14	*18	...	Sri Lanka
Syrian Arab Republic	153	152	164	163	*170	139	137	*140	*142	...	Rép. arabe syrienne
Thailand	211	207	323	412	479	708	935	1054	*973	...	Thaïlande
Turkey	700	675	677	710	726	775	800	777	*799	...	Turquie
United Arab Emirates	*240	*256	*260	*300	*297	*297	258	272	*272	...	Emirats arabes unis
Uzbekistan	..	...	...	...	0	14	14	10	*10	...	Ouzbékistan
Dem. Yemen (former)*	50	..	..	..	..	..	..	..	..	..	Yémen dém. (anc.)*
Yemen	..	*50	*50	*60	60	*58	*19	*20	*20	...	Yémen
Europe	16122	23579	24204	23964	23985	24039	24523	24984	24597	25155	Europe
Austria	41	*42	18	1	37	60	20	45	*30	...	Autriche
Belarus	..	...	262	214	177	203	200	138	*129	...	Bélarus
Belgium	443	458	374	409	501	458	544	595	*693	...	Belgique
Bulgaria	77	42	31	80	78	85	93	84	*75	...	Bulgarie
Croatia	..	...	113	151	122	191	165	158	*196	...	Croatie
Denmark	143	144	129	134	145	148	161	186	*137	...	Danemark
Czechoslovakia(former)	127	119	..	..	..	..	..	..	..	..	Tchécoslovaquie(anc.)
Czech Republic	..	..	170	170	128	136	176	169	*148	...	République tchèque
Finland	134	212	271	280	295	224	328	295	*353	...	Finlande
France incl. Monaco	2543	2682	2530	2694	2488	2459	2802	2758	*2828	...	France y compris Monaco
Germany	..	2468	*2655	2873	3425	3281	3004	2806	*2794	...	Allemagne
Germany(Fed.Rep.)	2272	..	..	..	..	..	..	..	..	..	Allemagne(Rép.féd.)
German D.R.(former)*	260	..	..	..	..	..	..	..	..	..	R.D.A. (anc.)*
Greece	395	426	423	401	470	476	555	561	*650	...	Grèce
Hungary	113	100	104	102	82	87	84	*98	*94	...	Hongrie
Ireland	32	29	34	28	30	36	40	43	*44	...	Irlande
Italy and San Marino	2131	2186	1701	2412	2550	2332	2271	2352	*2164	...	Italie y comp. St. Marin
Lithuania	..	...	123	160	153	166	234	256	*213	...	Lituanie
Netherlands	2640	2485	2698	2729	3112	3164	3759	3817	*3652	...	Pays-Bas
Norway,Svlbd.J.Myn. l	245	258	251	230	297	295	338	357	*327	...	Norvège,Svalbd,J.May
Poland	141	142	158	170	194	185	165	181	*225	...	Pologne
Portugal	357	312	369	346	477	422	380	454	*410	...	Portugal
Romania	217	224	229	239	259	280	264	242	*304	...	Roumanie
Russian Federation	..	...	7165	6113	4886	5039	4883	5041	*4808	...	Fédération de Russie
Slovakia	..	..	*30	*56	*52	*66	53	53	*31	...	Slovaquie
Spain	1498	1848	1854	1606	1710	1814	1507	1634	*1560	...	Espagne
Sweden	220	254	291	298	273	231	260	271	*294	...	Suède
Switzrld,Liechtenstein	139	195	169	190	188	170	207	221	*251	...	Suisse,Liechtenstein
Ukraine	..	...	423	275	239	204	158	147	*154	...	Ukraine
United Kingdom	1616	1681	1599	1575	1605	1815	1838	1972	*1979	...	Royaume-Uni
Yugoslavia	..	...	15	10	10	11	27	47	*45	...	Yougoslavie
T.F.Yug.Rep. Macedonia	..	...	*15	18	2	1	7	3	*9	...	L'ex-RY Macédoine
Yugoslavia, SFR	338	..	..	..	..	..	..	..	..	..	Yougoslavie, RSF
USSR (former)*	9136	..	..	..	..	..	..	..	..	..	URSS (anc.)*
Oceania	521	583	640	772	834	933	977	1007	838	1183	Océanie

For general note and footnotes, see end of table.

Voir la fin du tableau pour la remarque générale et les notes.

Liquefied petroleum gas from petroleum refineries (continued)
Gaz de pétrole liquéfiés, des raffineries de pétrole (suite)

ISIC-BASED CODE - CODE BASE CITI

3530-372A

Unit : Thousand metric tons

Unité : Milliers de tonnes métriques

Country or area	1990	1991	1992	1993	1994	1995	1996	1997	1998	1999	Pays ou zone
Australia [1]	521	583	640	772	834	933	977	1007	*838	...	Australie [1]
Total	70153	70744	73374	74684	77295	80191	82901	85232	85381	93367	Total

General Note.

Hydrocarbons which are gaseous under conditions of normal temperature and pressure but are liquified by compression or cooling to facilitate storage, handling and transportation. They are (i) extracted by stripping of natural gas at crude petroleum and natural gas sources; (ii) extracted by stripping of imported natural gas in installations of the importing country; and (iii) produced both in refineries and outside of refineries in the course of processing crude petroleum or its derivatives. It comprises propane (C_3H_8), butane (C_4H_{10}), or a mixture of these two hydrocarbons. Also included is ethane (C_2H_6) from petroleum or natural gas producers' separation and stabilization plants. (SITC, Rev.3: 34200-2A).

Remarque générale.

Hydrocarbures qui sont à l'état gazeux dans des conditions de température et de pression normales mais liquéfiés par compression ou refroidissement pour en faciliter l'entreposage, la manipulation et le transport. Ils sont (i) extraits par désessenciement du gaz naturel sur les sites de production de pétrole brut et de gaz naturel; (ii) extraits par désessenciement du gaz naturel importé dans les installations du pays importateur; et (iii) produits aussi bien à l'intérieur qu'en dehors des raffineries, au cours du traitement du pétrole brut ou de ses dérivés. Dans cette rubrique figurent les gaz propane (C_3H_8) et butane (C_4H_{10}) et les mélanges de ces deux hydrocarbures. Est également inclus l'éthane (C_2H_6) produit dans les installations de séparation et de stabilisation des producteurs de pétrole et de gaz naturel. (CTCI, Rev.3: 34200-2A).

[1] Twelve months ending 30 June of year stated.
[2] Twelve months beginning 1 April of year stated.
[3] Twelve months beginning 21 March of year stated.

[1] Période de douze mois finissant le 30 juin de l'année indiquée.
[2] Période de douze mois commençant le 1er avril de l'année indiquée.
[3] Période de douze mois commençant le 21 mars de l'année indiquée.

Hard-coal briquettes
Agglomérés (briquettes de houille)

ISIC-BASED CODE - CODE BASE CITI

3540-01

Unit : Thousand metric tons

Unité : Milliers de tonnes métriques

Country or area	1990	1991	1992	1993	1994	1995	1996	1997	1998	1999	Pays ou zone
Asia	**18939**	**15131**	**11181**	**7969**	**4802**	**3106**	**2063**	**1480**	**1311**	**61**	**Asie**
Afghanistan [1]	*37	*35	0	...	...	...	...	...	...	...	Afghanistan [1]
Japan	123	100	112	108	94	77	78	67	*58	...	Japon
Korea, Republic of	18779	14996	11069	7837	4684	3005	1961	1389	1229	...	Corée, République de
Europe	**2342**	**9565**	**10835**	**8116**	**4814**	**5029**	**3910**	**4203**	**3866**	**1505**	**Europe**
Austria	*0	0	0	0	0	0	0	62	*70	...	Autriche
Belgium	1	5	9	25	19	21	21	12	*10	...	Belgique
France incl. Monaco	554	634	526	427	336	287	273	231	*194	...	France y compris Monaco
Germany	..	*860	*677	585	460	379	357	318	*185	...	Allemagne
Germany(Fed.Rep.)	773	..	..	..	..	..	..	..	..	...	Allemagne(Rép.féd.)
Hungary	104	82	32	...	...	...	...	...	...	...	Hongrie
Ireland	...	...	...	0	0	0	28	31	*32	...	Irlande
Poland	77	1	0	0	0	0	0	0	*1	...	Pologne
Romania	332	181	157	69	0	0	0	0	*0	...	Roumanie
Russian Federation	..	...	300	300	267	702	...	...	...	...	Fédération de Russie
Spain	5	5	5	0	0	0	0	0	...	...	Espagne
Ukraine	..	...	8571	5972	3057	3057	2265	2270	*2293	...	Ukraine
United Kingdom	496	582	555	665	602	510	501	814	*616	...	Royaume-Uni
USSR (former)	773	..	..	..	..	..	..	..	..	..	URSS (anc.)
Total	**22054**	**24696**	**22016**	**16085**	**9616**	**8135**	**5973**	**5683**	**5177**	**1567**	**Total**

General Note.

Briquettes, ovoids and similar solid fuels manufactured from hard coal by agglomerating the particles of coal with pitch. Solid smokeless patent fuels are included. (SITC, Rev.3: 32210-0).

[1] Twelve months beginning 21 March of year stated.

Remarque générale.

Briquettes, boulets et combustibles solides analogues fabriqués à partir de la houille par agglomération du poussier de houille avec du brai. Cette rubrique comprend les agglomérés solides brûlant sans fumée. (CTCI, Rev.3: 32210-0).

[1] Période de douze mois commençant le 21 mars de l'année indiquée.

Brown-coal briquettes
Briquettes de lignite

ISIC-BASED CODE - CODE BASE CITI

3540-04

Unit : Thousand metric tons   Unité : Milliers de tonnes métriques

Country or area	1990	1991	1992	1993	1994	1995	1996	1997	1998	1999	Pays ou zone
Asia	**234**	**239**	**174**	**196**	**202**	**212**	**222**	**232**	**242**	**252**	**Asie**
India [1]	197	208	143	185	*200	*210	*220	*230	*240	...	Inde [1]
Turkey	37	31	31	11	2	2	2	2	*2	...	Turquie
Europe	**57713**	**60933**	**24665**	**21018**	**16578**	**13298**	**12519**	**10240**	**8380**	**3131**	**Europe**
Albania	267	144	37	38	2	0	0	0	*0	...	Albanie
Bulgaria	1451	1317	1412	1627	1168	1011	1201	1082	*1152	...	Bulgarie
Czechoslovakia(former)	1067	892	..	..	..	..	..	..	..	...	Tchécoslovaquie(anc.)
Czech Republic	..	..	586	625	499	499	724	506	*325	...	République tchèque
Germany	..	*52011	*16936	14060	11424	8943	8482	6953	*5601	...	Allemagne
Germany(Fed.Rep.)	5535	..	..	..	..	..	..	..	..	..	Allemagne(Rép.féd.)
German D.R.(former)*	46000		..	..	..	..	..	..	..	..	R.D.A. (anc.)*
Greece	127	122	62	40	107	93	88	99	*77	...	Grèce
Hungary	1791	1924	683	611	487	344	355	213	*151	...	Hongrie
Ireland	395	354	432	364	371	334	285	253	*264	...	Irlande
Poland	122	124	95	102	92	100	93	79	*63	...	Pologne
Romania	0	0	0	0	9	0	0	0	*0	...	Roumanie
Russian Federation	..	...	2506	2307	1619	934	604	443	*276	...	Fédération de Russie
Ukraine	..	...	1916	1244	800	1040	687	612	*471	...	Ukraine
Yugoslavia, SFR	958	..	..	..	..	..	..	..	..	..	Yougoslavie, RSF
USSR (former)	5217		..	..	..	..	..	..	..	..	URSS (anc.)
Oceania	**706**	**715**	**721**	**516**	**580**	**572**	**458**	**553**	**550**	**412**	**Océanie**
Australia [2]	706	715	721	516	580	572	458	553	*550	...	Australie [2]
Total	**63870**	**61887**	**25560**	**21730**	**17360**	**14082**	**13199**	**11025**	**9172**	**3796**	**Total**

General Note.

A solid fuel manufactured from brown coal by a process in which the brown coal is partly dried, warmed to expel additionalwater, and then compressed in moulds into briquettes, usually without the use of a binding substance. (SITC, Rev.3: 32222-0).

Remarque générale.

Combustible solide fabriqué à partir du lignite par un procédé qui consiste à sécher partiellement le lignite, à le chauffer pour en éliminer l'eau en excédent, et à le presser ensuite dans des moules pour en faire des briquettes, habituellement sans addition de liants. (CTCI, Rev.3: 32222-0).

[1] Twelve months beginning 1 April of year stated.
[2] Twelve months ending 30 June of year stated.

[1] Période de douze mois commençant le 1er avril de l'année indiquée.
[2] Période de douze mois finissant le 30 juin de l'année indiquée.

Coke

Coke

ISIC-BASED CODE - CODE BASE CITI

3540-07

Unit : Thousand metric tons   Unité : Milliers de tonnes métriques

Country or area	1990	1991	1992	1993	1994	1995	1996	1997	1998	1999	Pays ou zone
Africa	**3647**	**3854**	**4294**	**5217**	**4770**	**4977**	**4817**	**4873**	**4191**	**5228**	**Afrique**
Egypt	1210	1234	1180	1447	1464	1468	*1470	1489	*1550	...	Egypte
South Africa	*1835	*2000	*2500	3214	3053	*3010	*2839	*2839	*2141	...	Afrique du Sud
Zambia*	36	36	36	35	33	32	15	5	0	...	Zambie*
Zimbabwe	566	584	578	521	220	467	493	540	*500	...	Zimbabwe
America, North	**31151**	**27682**	**26981**	**26629**	**26250**	**26976**	**26475**	**25572**	**23526**	**22430**	**Amérique du Nord**
Canada	3708	3622	3711	3657	3684	3283	3357	3370	*3142	...	Canada
Mexico	2389	2246	2033	1942	1985	2148	2184	2139	*2203	...	Mexique
United States	25054	21814	21237	21030	20581	21545	20934	20063	*18181	...	Etats-Unis
America, South	**9314**	**9925**	**10289**	**10188**	**10113**	**10061**	**10277**	**9997**	**9640**	**10138**	**Amérique du Sud**
Argentina	952	785	950	549	709	602	741	758	*750	...	Argentine
Brazil	7635	8086	8160	8503	8265	8331	8357	8156	7911	...	Brésil
Chile	346	471	484	509	507	468	496	473	521	...	Chili
Colombia	381	583	695	626	631	660	683	610	*458	...	Colombie
Uruguay	0	0	0	1	1	0	0	0	*0	...	Uruguay
Asia	**144961**	**150665**	**154006**	**166707**	**172642**	**208521**	**209086**	**210910**	**202939**	**244918**	**Asie**
China	73283	73516	79839	94548	98762	132531	134322	*134782	*128991	...	Chine
India[1]	9735	10492	10571	10640	10836	*10950	11867	12446	*11879	...	Inde[1]
Iran(Islamic Rep. of)[2]	*220	213	23	37	443	172	127	*55	*55	...	Iran(Rép. islamique)[2]
Japan	45887	45458	43403	41767	41287	42010	40728	41089	*39554	...	Japon
Kazakhstan	..	...	3166	2494	...	...	...	...	...	...	Kazakhstan
Korea,Dem.Ppl's.Rep.*	3600	3600	3600	3600	3550	3500	3450	3215	3054	...	Corée,Rép.pop.dém.de*
Korea, Republic of	8410	10496	9452	9824	11188	12620	11756	12458	12687	...	Corée, République de
Pakistan[3]	668	724	737	716	764	...	...	...	...	...	Pakistan[3]
Tajikistan	..	...	11	4	2	0	0	4	*1	...	Tadjikistan
Turkey	3158	3329	3204	3077	2980	3131	3211	3217	*3056	...	Turquie
Europe	**87528**	**121020**	**129562**	**115217**	**109453**	**113888**	**99058**	**99503**	**94839**	**81884**	**Europe**
Albania	230	137	22	0	0	0	0	0	*0	...	Albanie
Austria	1725	1540	1470	1402	1432	1448	1559	1566	*1598	...	Autriche
Belgium	5420	4888	4575	3975	3736	3696	3550	3401	*3003	...	Belgique
Bulgaria	1193	653	730	794	1049	1237	1087	1165	*868	...	Bulgarie
Croatia	..	...	407	422	277	0	0	0	*0	...	Croatie
Czechoslovakia(former)	9625	8572	..	..	..	..	..	..	..	...	Tchécoslovaquie(anc.)
Czech Republic	..	..	5701	5272	5173	4963	4854	4290	*4009	...	République tchèque
Estonia	..	...	31	34	38	40	44	42	*27	...	Estonie
Finland	487	471	498	710	922	920	910	879	*912	...	Finlande
France incl. Monaco	7197	6915	6795	6197	5880	5566	5580	5441	*5500	...	France y compris Monaco
Germany	..	*6521	15296	12270	10919	11102	10662	10744	*10324	...	Allemagne
Germany(Fed.Rep.)*	18000	..	..	..	..	..	..	..	..	...	Allemagne(Rép.féd.)*
German D.R.(former)*	1100	..	..	..	..	..	..	..	..	...	R.D.A. (anc.)*
Hungary	672	671	694	641	993	1033	986	932	*966	...	Hongrie
Italy and San Marino	6356	6057	5413	4929	5293	5185	4962	5219	*5192	...	Italie y comp. St. Marin
Netherlands	2736	2932	2922	2879	2886	2895	2921	2905	*2837	...	Pays-Bas
Poland	13671	11411	11094	10282	11456	11579	10340	10536	*9747	...	Pologne
Portugal	230	240	268	268	290	331	331	340	*352	...	Portugal
Romania	3965	2581	2903	2601	2884	3384	3153	3316	*3132	...	Roumanie
Russian Federation	..	...	31110	27370	25392	33541	21465	21879	*19772	...	Fédération de Russie
Slovakia	..	..	*2000	1858	1875	1861	1708	1730	*1515	...	Slovaquie
Spain	3211	3180	2952	3055	2993	2438	2413	2646	*2631	...	Espagne
Sweden	1084	1112	1146	1137	1141	1149	1150	1160	*1148	...	Suède
Ukraine	..	...	26667	22582	18190	15500	14800	15000	*15150	...	Ukraine
United Kingdom	8350	7703	6868	6539	6634	6020	6583	6312	*6156	...	Royaume-Uni
Yugoslavia, SFR	2276	..	..	..	..	..	..	..	..	..	Yougoslavie, RSF
USSR (former)	77647	..	..	..	..	..	..	..	..	..	URSS (anc.)
Oceania	**4496**	**4236**	**4250**	**4101**	**4547**	**4617**	**4587**	**4287**	**4728**	**4693**	**Océanie**
Australia[3]	4495	4235	4250	4101	4547	4617	4587	4287	*4728	...	Australie[3]
New Zealand[1]	*1	*1	0	0	0	0	0	0	...	...	Nouvelle-Zélande[1]

For general note and footnotes, see end of table.   Voir la fin du tableau pour la remarque générale et les notes.

Coke (continued)
Coke (suite)

ISIC-BASED CODE - CODE BASE CITI

3540-07

Unit : Thousand metric tons   Unité : Milliers de tonnes métriques

Country or area	1990	1991	1992	1993	1994	1995	1996	1997	1998	1999	Pays ou zone
Total	358744	317381	329382	328059	327775	369040	354300	355142	339863	369291	Total

General Note.

The solid residue obtained from the distillation of hard coal or lignite in the total absence of air (carbonization). The data include: gas coke - a by-product of coal used for the production of manufactured or town gas in gasworks; and coke-oven coke - all other coke produced from hard coal; brown coal coke - a solid product obtained from carbonization of brown coal briquettes. (SITC, Rev.3: 32500-1).

[1] Twelve months beginning 1 April of year stated.
[2] Twelve months beginning 21 March of year stated.
[3] Twelve months ending 30 June of year stated.

Remarque générale.

Résidu solide obtenu lors de la distillation de houille ou de lignite en l'absence totale d'air (carbonisation). Les données comprennent le coke de gaz, sous-produit de l'utilisation du charbon pour la production de gaz manufacturé ou gaz de ville dans les usines à gaz; le coke de four, tous les autres types de coke produits à partir de la houille; et le coke de lignite, produit solide obtenu par carbonisation de briquettes de lignite. (CTCI 32500-1)

[1] Période de douze mois commençant le 1er avril de l'année indiquée.
[2] Période de douze mois commençant le 21 mars de l'année indiquée.
[3] Période de douze mois finissant le 30 juin de l'année indiquée.

Coke-oven gas
Gaz de cokerie

ISIC-BASED CODE - CODE BASE CITI

3540-13B

Unit : Terajoules — Unité : Terajoules

Country or area	1990	1991	1992	1993	1994	1995	1996	1997	1998	1999	Pays ou zone
Africa	**47000**	**45023**	**38949**	**28555**	**30131**	**27880**	**26832**	**24375**	**19024**	**8786**	**Afrique**
South Africa	*44000	*40000	*35000	26138	25563	*23985	*22937	*22576	*17024	...	Afrique du Sud
Zimbabwe	*3000	5023	3949	2417	4568	3895	3895	1799	*2000	...	Zimbabwe
America, North	**258539**	**207289**	**196164**	**133245**	**118506**	**109689**	**120731**	**107410**	**105365**	**23983**	**Amérique du Nord**
Canada	32917	32289	32154	30733	24307	21346	24014	26038	*26288	...	Canada
United States	*225622	175000	164010	102512	94199	88343	96717	81372	*79077	...	Etats-Unis
America, South	**73345**	**77599**	**78925**	**81275**	**79800**	**80377**	**83728**	**80315**	**79296**	**84150**	**Amérique du Sud**
Argentina	6815	5855	*5800	4703	5106	5250	7090	7133	*7000	...	Argentine
Brazil	59874	63885	64676	67406	66126	66747	67764	65052	63866	...	Brésil
Chile	4360	5539	6040	6888	6334	5878	6375	5739	5999	...	Chili
Colombia	*2021	2045	2084	*2000	*1959	*2224	*2219	*2109	*2151	...	Colombie
Peru*	275	275	325	278	275	278	280	282	280	...	Pérou*
Asia	**655374**	**682745**	**710274**	**736627**	**767215**	**759670**	**750350**	**774331**	**807116**	**871317**	**Asie**
China	307001	334621	324665	*380593	417404	*400792	399668	424655	*471632	...	Chine
India [1]	24340	26230	27000	0	0	0	0	0	*0	...	Inde [1]
Japan	299939	297592	335618	332730	327130	337011	327592	326168	*312619	...	Japon
Turkey	24094	24302	22991	23304	22681	21867	23090	23508	*22865	...	Turquie
Europe	**652596**	**840320**	**858856**	**711688**	**652615**	**690072**	**696967**	**669058**	**639720**	**568161**	**Europe**
Austria	*13000	11793	11164	10636	10790	10906	11784	11804	*12166	...	Autriche
Belgium	39627	32333	31631	29856	27721	27421	26889	24311	*23828	...	Belgique
Bulgaria	10099	5392	6274	6829	8264	8599	8256	8663	*6813	...	Bulgarie
Croatia	..	...	3187	3342	2618	*2500	*2500	*2500		...	Croatie
Czechoslovakia(former)	63511	56290		..	..	..	..	..	...		Tchécoslovaquie(anc.)
Czech Republic	..	..	39585	35657	28214	33000	35240	31884	*32872	...	République tchèque
Estonia	..	...	674	647	0	0	0	0	*0	...	Estonie
Finland	4507	4407	4322	6704	7832	7656	7682	7621	*7771	...	Finlande
France incl. Monaco	56140	51390	52000	46516	45292	49090	47527	47581	*46620	...	France y compris Monaco
Germany	..	*162000	126021	104993	96000	96000	96000	89376	*93762	...	Allemagne
Germany(Fed.Rep.)*	162000	..	..	..	..	..	..	..	..	...	Allemagne(Rép.féd.)*
Hungary	6106	6491	6735	3215	4024	4800	3877	3842	*4152	...	Hongrie
Italy and San Marino	48926	48800	46791	44853	40157	41184	42812	44804	*38564	...	Italie y comp. St. Marin
Netherlands	26479	28052	27849	27274	26978	26925	27115	26383	*24098	...	Pays-Bas
Poland	99782	94159	91452	84170	93336	94185	84484	88096	*81619	...	Pologne
Portugal	*2200	2244	2549	2265	1940	2606	2593	3047	*3059	...	Portugal
Romania	23411	16195	18297	15785	18084	23310	19045	19883	*18881	...	Roumanie
Russian Federation	..	...	*300000	193109	148546	173542	193170	165277	*151454	...	Fédération de Russie
Slovakia	..	..	*13900	12810	13368	14270	11788	12919	*10659	...	Slovaquie
Spain	*22704	22941	23607	25765	21863	19239	18102	21908	*22255	...	Espagne
Sweden	8625	8625	8926	9731	9020	9058	9341	9238	*9209	...	Suède
United Kingdom	50481	47399	43892	47531	48568	45781	48762	49921	*49511	...	Royaume-Uni
Yugoslavia, SFR	14998	..	..	..	..	..	..	..	..	..	Yougoslavie, RSF
USSR (former)	524944	..	..	..	..	..	..	..	..		URSS (anc.)
Oceania	**34658**	**31606**	**35703**	**34932**	**35165**	**35210**	**34264**	**34863**	**34481**	**35296**	**Océanie**
Australia [2]	34658	31606	35703	34932	35165	35210	34264	34863	*34481	...	Australie [2]
Total	**2246456**	**1884582**	**1918871**	**1726322**	**1683432**	**1702898**	**1712872**	**1690352**	**1685002**	**1591693**	**Total**

General Note.
By-product of the carbonization process in the production of coke at coke ovens. (SITC, Rev.3: 34500-1B).

Remarque générale.
Sous-produit du processus de carbonisation dans la production de coke dans les fours à coke. (CTCI, Rev.3: 34500-1B).

[1] Twelve months beginning 1 April of year stated.
[2] Twelve months ending 30 June of year stated.

[1] Période de douze mois commençant le 1er avril de l'année indiquée.
[2] Période de douze mois finissant le 30 juin de l'année indiquée.

Tars
Goudrons

ISIC-BASED CODE - CODE BASE CITI

3540-16

Unit : Thousand metric tons   Unité : Milliers de tonnes métriques

Country or area	1990	1991	1992	1993	1994	1995	1996	1997	1998	1999	Pays ou zone
Africa	**66**	**58**	**123**	**111**	**82**	**50**	**50**	**45**	**49**	**41**	**Afrique**
Libyan Arab Jamah.	66	58	123	111	82	50	50	45	49	41	Jamah. arabe libyenne
America, North	**56**	**53**	**42**	**59**	**68**	**73**	**69**	**70**	**79**	**83**	**Amérique du Nord**
Mexico	56	53	42	59	68	73	69	70	79	83	Mexique
Asia	**455**	**450**	**451**	**451**	**453**	**454**	**448**	**443**	**442**	**453**	**Asie**
Bangladesh	10	6	7	...	...	...	...	...	...	...	Bangladesh
Korea, Republic of	...	...	...	...	446	447	441	435	434	445	Corée, République de
Europe	**1698**	**1729**	**1812**	**1693**	**1792**	**1837**	**1750**	**1730**	**1613**	**1468**	**Europe**
Belgium	...	177	160	112	...	...	...	...	...	...	Belgique
Bulgaria	384	109	63	65	66	108	82	66	...	...	Bulgarie
Croatia	..	19	...	...	...	...	...	...	...	...	Croatie
Czech Republic	..	..	...	...	...	...	...	...	141	132	République tchèque
France	278	264	256	230	215	...	...	...	...	...	France
Germany	..	...	...	...	...	...	...	447	420	...	Allemagne
Poland	647	550	554	514	578	585	526	521	476	434	Pologne
Romania	179	114	130	122	136	149	153	161	156	80	Roumanie
Sweden	...	...	...	...	46	46	55	50	49	48	Suède
Switzerland	13	14	12	13	12	10	...	...	...	...	Suisse
Total	**2276**	**2290**	**2428**	**2314**	**2395**	**2415**	**2318**	**2287**	**2183**	**2044**	**Total**

General Note.

Tars obtained from coal, lignite, peat and water gas. Tars extracted from non-mineral sources are excluded. (SITC, Rev.3: 33521-0).

Remarque générale.

Goudrons obtenus à partir de la houille, du lignite, de la tourbe et du gaz à l'eau. Cette rubrique ne comprend pas les goudrons de provenance non minérale. (CTCI, Rev.3: 33521-0).

Inner tubes, rubber, for motor vehicles
Chambres à air en caoutchouc pour véhicules à moteur

ISIC-BASED CODE - CODE BASE CITI

3551-01

Unit : Thousand units   Unité : En milliers

Country or area	1990	1991	1992	1993	1994	1995	1996	1997	1998	1999	Pays ou zone
Africa	**5505**	**5303**	**4711**	**4229**	**5320**	**4630**	**5773**	**4632**	**4784**	**4776**	**Afrique**
Egypt	991	1235	1112	1107	1989	1759	2161	1769	2004	2172	Egypte
Ethiopia	78	28	4	25	43	10	452	45	64	63	Ethiopie
Kenya	494	467	407	416	407	458	468	...	...	...	Kenya
South Africa	3341	2959	2809	2095	2233	2080	...	...	...	...	Afrique du Sud
Tunisia	490	515	301	475	433	233	508	323	357	314	Tunisie
United Rep.Tanzania	111	99	78	111	215	90	123	138	...	...	Rép. Unie de Tanzanie
America, North	**2693**	**2483**	**2222**	**3271**	**3420**	**3327**	**4258**	**4527**	**4730**	**3853**	**Amérique du Nord**
Mexico	2693	2483	2222	3271	3420	3327	4258	4527	4730	3853	Mexique
America, South	**3154**	**3131**	**2997**	**3105**	**3125**	**2996**	**2807**	**2848**	**2314**	**2316**	**Amérique du Sud**
Argentina[1]	2220	...	...	...	...	...	...	...	...	...	Argentine[1]
Chile	724	772	747	885	905	776	587	628	94	96	Chili
Peru	210	139	30	0	0	0	0	...	...	...	Pérou
Asia	**104689**	**110514**	**114313**	**105726**	**107796**	**113555**	**120882**	**110411**	**112034**	**99933**	**Asie**
India	7572	6899	7076	8503	9468	8839	9541	...	...	...	Inde
Indonesia	...	...	7436	5248	7896	9213	...	9140	20573	...	Indonésie
Iran(Islamic Rep. of)	[2]3423	[2]3592	[2]2506	[2]1991	[2]1970	[3]4018	[3]3028	[3]2779	[3]2274	...	Iran(Rép. islamique)
Israel	111	...	...	...	...	...	...	...	...	...	Israël
Japan	18363	18584	15737	12320	10614	11725	12168	10967	8825	...	Japon
Korea, Republic of	53772	55702	61655	56104	56457	57557	61464	55968	52832	47197	Corée, République de
Malaysia	12224	13918	12775	14035	14753	14681	17434	15135	11836	11466	Malaisie
Pakistan[4]	648	646	618	550	706	833	909	643	665	586	Pakistan[4]
Sri Lanka	253	256	22	...	...	...	...	...	...	...	Sri Lanka
Thailand[5]	1871	1853	...	...	...	...	2882	2729	2099	...	Thaïlande[5]
Turkey	2148	3246	4090	4400	3357	4114	3250	2316	1761	1156	Turquie
Europe	**32714**	**81432**	**73081**	**62909**	**44704**	**41899**	**45275**	**48444**	**43976**	**43125**	**Europe**
Bulgaria[6]	3290	1725	930	795	702	616	477	303	...	...	Bulgarie[6]
Croatia	..	24	...	...	...	...	...	...	...	...	Croatie
Czechoslovakia(former)	4176	2136	..	..	..	..	..	..	..	..	Tchécoslovaquie(anc.)
France	5117	4536	2496	1911	1488	...	...	...	...	...	France
Germany	..	...	208	123	54	...	...	...	...	...	Allemagne
Hungary	701	477	420	...	...	...	...	...	...	...	Hongrie
Italy	11045	13578	14773	12134	12003	10381	10899	10506	7832	6017	Italie
Poland	4663	3958	4109	4179	4378	4332	5881	6422	6009	4382	Pologne
Romania	2625	2147	2086	2152	1908	1986	2095	1639	1501	1006	Roumanie
Russian Federation	..	44788	41816	36541	19770	18843	21164	24715	23510	28005	Fédération de Russie
Slovakia	..	..	...	...	...	...	...	...	509	384	Slovaquie
Slovenia	..	3245	3261	2699	2130	2672	1733	1485	1604	1064	Slovénie
Spain	1097	1074	703	...	...	...	...	...	...	...	Espagne
Yugoslavia		3616	1808	414	310	835	936	1284	1270	624	Yougoslavie
Total	**148755**	**202863**	**197323**	**179240**	**164365**	**166407**	**178994**	**170862**	**167838**	**154003**	**Total**

General Note.

Rubber inner tubes for motor vehicles other than bicycles and motorcycles. (Part of SITC, Rev.3: 62591-1).

Remarque générale.

Chambres à air en caoutchouc pour véhicules à moteur, à l'exclusion des chambres à air pour bicyclettes et motocyclettes. (Partie de CTCI, Rev.3: 62591-1).

[1] Including inner tubes for agricultural vehicles and aircraft.
[2] Production by establishments employing 50 or more persons.
[3] Production by establishments employing 10 or more persons.
[4] Twelve months ending 30 June of year stated.
[5] Beginning 1999, series discontinued.
[6] Including inner tubes for motorcycles.

[1] Y compris les chambres à air pour véhicules agricoles et pour aéronefs.
[2] Production des établissements occupant 50 personnes ou plus.
[3] Production des établissements occupant 10 personnes ou plus.
[4] Période de douze mois finissant le 30 juin de l'année indiquée.
[5] A partir de 1999, série abandonnée.
[6] Y compris les chambres à air pour motocyclettes.

Inner tubes, rubber, for bicycles and motorcycles
Chambres à air en caoutchouc pour bicyclettes et motocyclettes

ISIC-BASED CODE - CODE BASE CITI
3551-02

Unit : Thousand units   Unité : En milliers

Country or area	1990	1991	1992	1993	1994	1995	1996	1997	1998	1999	Pays ou zone
Africa	**2070**	**2112**	**2233**	**1852**	**1858**	**1688**	**1903**	**1940**	**2350**	**2212**	**Afrique**
Egypt	585	560	819	704	886	635	634	757	...	...	Egypte
Kenya[1]	319	311	393	354	224	212	341	...	...	...	Kenya[1]
Mozambique	...	77	...	40	15	...	2	4	1	0	Mozambique
Tunisia	1087	1142	970	723	702	790	895	894	1334	1201	Tunisie
United Rep.Tanzania	40	22	...	...	...	...	...	...	...	...	Rép. Unie de Tanzanie
America, North	**1728**	**2432**	**3336**	**3388**	**2727**	**3608**	**3904**	**4199**	**4495**	**4790**	**Amérique du Nord**
Mexico	1728	2432	3336	3388	2727	...	...	...	...	...	Mexique
America, South	**18973**	**18973**	**18973**	**18973**	**18973**	**18973**	**18973**	**18973**	**18973**	**18973**	**Amérique du Sud**
Argentina[2]	18973	...	...	...	...	...	...	...	...	...	Argentine[2]
Asia	**153590**	**153607**	**154046**	**165057**	**158854**	**153171**	**162470**	**184773**	**129117**	**158249**	**Asie**
India[3]	22806	22878	25826	25788	24300	25056	25394	[1]23009	[1]15891	[1]15650	Inde[3]
Indonesia	...	...	30326	40793	45958	49229	...	75638	35434	...	Indonésie
Japan	26824	26415	24653	24019	20302	17724	16746	11279	8748	1	Japon
Korea, Republic of[1]	28573	24720	22999	24851	18109	12022	...	...	...	...	Corée, République de[1]
Pakistan[1]	5501	5468	5757	5612	6191	5146	5594	5205	4978	5529	Pakistan[1]
Thailand[5]	[4]20887	[4]23548	...	...	...	...	43697	46272	42135	...	Thaïlande[5]
Viet Nam	8349	8533	9177	...	...	...	...	...	...	...	Viet Nam
Europe	**19365**	**38357**	**38516**	**38584**	**30640**	**30940**	**30356**	**32082**	**28209**	**30382**	**Europe**
Bulgaria	1700	832	201	278	373	352	304	173	...	...	Bulgarie
France	16749	17328	19860	17288	16368	...	...	...	...	...	France
Hungary	224	202	67	...	...	...	...	...	...	...	Hongrie
Portugal	446	270	...	...	...	...	...	...	...	...	Portugal
Romania	245	70	709	748	691	828	876	464	443	285	Roumanie
Russian Federation	..	...	...	15083	7460	7416	7092	9736	5931	8258	Fédération de Russie
Slovenia	..	5620	4326	4474	4590	3862	3618	3165	3250	3820	Slovénie
Spain	1	...	...	...	...	...	...	...	...	...	Espagne
Yugoslavia	..	2293	2010	190	635	681	745	903	954	538	Yougoslavie
Total	**195727**	**215481**	**217103**	**227854**	**213052**	**208381**	**217606**	**241967**	**183143**	**214605**	**Total**

General Note.	Remarque générale.
Rubber inner tubes for bicycles and motorcycles. (SITC, Rev3: 62591-2).	Les données se rapportent à la production de chambres à air en caoutchouc pour bicyclettes et motocyclettes. (CTCI, Rev.3: 62591-2).

[1] For bicycles only.
[2] Including inner tubes for baby carriages and tricycles used for transporting goods.
[3] Production by large and medium scale establishments only.
[4] Inner tubes of all types , except inner tubes for motor vehicles.
[5] Beginning 1999, series discontinued.

[1] Pour bicyclettes seulement.
[2] Y compris les chambres à air pour voitures d'enfant et pour triporteurs.
[3] Production des grandes et moyennes entreprises seulement.
[4] Chambres à air de tous genres, sauf chambres à air pour véhicules à moteur.
[5] A partir de 1999, série abandonnée.

Tires for agricultural and other off-the-road vehicles
Pneumatiques et bandages pour véhicules agricoles et autres véhicules tous terrains

ISIC-BASED CODE - CODE BASE CITI

3551-04

Unit : Thousand units

Unité : En milliers

Country or area	1990	1991	1992	1993	1994	1995	1996	1997	1998	1999	Pays ou zone
Africa	**328**	**267**	**285**	**349**	**411**	**391**	**350**	**358**	**331**	**293**	**Afrique**
South Africa	230	181	198	255	300	312	285	274	251	207	Afrique du Sud
Tunisia	98	86	87	94	111	79	65	84	80	86	Tunisie
America, North	**101**	**82**	**99**	**56**	**49**	**39**	**26**	**14**	**1**	**1**	**Amérique du Nord**
Jamaica[1]	1	2	0	0	...	...	...	...	...	...	Jamaïque[1]
Mexico[1]	100	80	99	56	48	...	...	...	...	...	Mexique[1]
America, South	**302**	**193**	**289**	**225**	**264**	**256**	**318**	**416**	**348**	**187**	**Amérique du Sud**
Argentina	278	171	263	205	246	234	296	394	326	165	Argentine
Colombia	24	...	26	20	18	...	...	...	...	...	Colombie
Asia	**3208**	**3993**	**2581**	**3593**	**3599**	**3470**	**3753**	**3415**	**5756**	**4495**	**Asie**
Armenia	..	429	95	36	16	3	19	0	0	0	Arménie
Azerbaijan	..	303	145	57	48	17	9	11	0	0	Azerbaïdjan
India	1724	1761	1792	1825	1874	1787	1933	2046	2478	2542	Inde
Indonesia	...	...	282	...	...	...	...	985	2892	...	Indonésie
Sri Lanka	16	13	...	...	...	...	...	...	...	...	Sri Lanka
Thailand[2]	76	84	...	...	...	...	371	343	354	...	Thaïlande[2]
Turkey	#6	17	7	29	15	17	20	15	17	0	Turquie
Europe	**5829**	**12392**	**9800**	**7667**	**6840**	**7285**	**6397**	**6733**	**7081**	**7485**	**Europe**
Belarus	..	482	249	248	178	128	183	177	226	216	Bélarus
Bulgaria	29	17	16	13	20	23	21	18	...	...	Bulgarie
Czechoslovakia(former)	653	513	..	..	..	..	..	..	..	..	Tchécoslovaquie(anc.)
Czech Republic	..	..	...	...	...	...	572	602	709	837	République tchèque
Germany	..	...	335	...	...	691	528	466	388	...	Allemagne
Germany(Fed.Rep.)	125	..	..	..	..	..	..	..	..	..	Allemagne(Rép.féd.)
German D.R.(former)	1098	..	..	..	..	..	..	..	..	..	R.D.A. (anc.)
Hungary	457	360	445	182	549	659	...	...	...	...	Hongrie
Italy	311	235	187	170	194	188	215	205	213	216	Italie
Poland	995	569	795	874	1148	1186	1028	1140	1349	1196	Pologne
Romania	368	336	377	475	317	445	468	411	474	389	Roumanie
Russian Federation		6133	4028	2037	782	546	751	883	770	896	Fédération de Russie
Slovakia	..	..	0	...	28	20	30	...	12	10	Slovaquie
Spain	770	545	471	606	780	855	804	...	...	...	Espagne
Sweden	..	436	454	483	749	1036	288	287	348	380	Suède
Ukraine	..	1439	940	826	325	254	293	347	279	310	Ukraine
United Kingdom	...	...	...	425	479	...	470	...	...	...	Royaume-Uni
Yugoslavia	..	561	365	150	129	116	229	312	371	267	Yougoslavie
Total	**9769**	**16928**	**13054**	**11891**	**11163**	**11442**	**10844**	**10935**	**13517**	**12462**	**Total**

General Note.
Solid rubber tires, cushion tires, reinforced tires, tires not requiring inner tubes and tire cases (outer covers) for all types of agricultural and other off-the-road tractors, construction machinery and aircraft. Excluding inner tubes, tires for bicycles and motorcycles, tires for road vehicles other than bicycles and motorcycles, tires for wheeled toys, articles of furniture etc. (SITC, Rev.3: 62550-0).

[1] For agricultural vehicles only.
[2] Beginning 1999, series discontinued.

Remarque générale.
Bandages pleins ou creux ("mi-pleins"), chambres à air renforcées, pneumatiques ne nécessitant pas de chambre à air et enveloppes pour machines de tous types tels que les tracteurs agricoles et autres tracteurs tous terrains, le matériel de travaux publics et les aérodynes. Cette rubrique ne comprend pas les chambres à air, les pneumatiques pour bicyclettes, motocyclettes et autres véhicules routiers, les pneumatiques pour jouets ou meubles etc. (CTCI, Rev.3: 62550-0).

[1] Pour véhicules agricoles seulement.
[2] A partir de 1999, série abandonnée.

Tires for bicycles and motorcycles
Pneumatiques pour bicyclettes et motocyclettes

ISIC-BASED CODE - CODE BASE CITI
3551-07

Unit : Thousand units   Unité : En milliers

Country or area	1990	1991	1992	1993	1994	1995	1996	1997	1998	1999	Pays ou zone
Africa	**4837**	**4284**	**3463**	**3245**	**4041**	**4021**	**3446**	**3397**	**3585**	**3517**	**Afrique**
Burkina Faso[1]	3483	2967	2457	2217	...	...	...	...	...	...	Burkina Faso[1]
Egypt	587	571	254	395	693	657	238	257	...	...	Egypte
Kenya	273	255	344	244	179	212	15	...	...	...	Kenya
Tunisia	433	472	386	355	354	337	378	291	402	348	Tunisie
United Rep.Tanzania	61	19	22	...	...	...	...	...	...	...	Rép. Unie de Tanzanie
America, North	**1676**	**2319**	**3412**	**3091**	**2575**	**3386**	**3643**	**3900**	**4157**	**4414**	**Amérique du Nord**
Mexico	1676	2319	3412	3091	2575	...	...	...	...	...	Mexique
America, South	**5274**	**4789**	**5142**	**4919**	**4548**	**4693**	**4789**	**4577**	**4368**	**4254**	**Amérique du Sud**
Argentina	4179	...	...	...	...	...	...	...	...	...	Argentine
Colombia	1095	...	963	740	369	514	...	398	189	...	Colombie
Asia	**137857**	**141929**	**155509**	**156464**	**137837**	**126974**	**157538**	**154693**	**233635**	**226089**	**Asie**
Azerbaijan	..	297	112	58	105	11	7	96	0	0	Azerbaïdjan
Bangladesh[1][2]	1390	844	563	560	563	...	...	...	...	...	Bangladesh[1][2]
India[3]	32403	28558	25275	19963	18941	18270	18240	19682	23026	25229	Inde[3]
Indonesia	...	...	36744	43553	30541	30173	...	44759	119719	...	Indonésie
Japan	29409	30207	28353	26247	23519	20638	19806	18545	18709	17090	Japon
Korea, Republic of[4]	24637	23930	20385	19189	17228	12625	...	...	...	...	Corée, République de[4]
Pakistan[2][4]	4000	3828	3751	3826	3872	3523	3988	4112	3445	3665	Pakistan[2][4]
Thailand[5]	17369	18373	...	...	...	...	40901	43400	39099	...	Thaïlande[5]
Viet Nam	9276	8634	8498	...	...	[4]9703	[4]8656	[4]10245	[4]16945	* [4]17961	Viet Nam
Europe	**17051**	**28098**	**21049**	**18855**	**17885**	**17113**	**15131**	**15251**	**13710**	**11332**	**Europe**
Bulgaria	1099	623	132	177	203	220	195	138	...	...	Bulgarie
Czechoslovakia(former)[6]	4244	4232	..	..	..	..	..	..	..	..	Tchécoslovaquie(anc.)[6]
Germany	...	...	...	...	...	4244	4039	3500	3586	...	Allemagne
German D.R.(former)[7]	3629	..	..	..	..	..	..	..	..	..	R.D.A. (anc.)[7]
Italy[1][8]	1237	286	317	...	...	...	...	...	...	...	Italie[1][8]
Poland	4083	4184	4640	4371	4966	5919	4407	4865	4363	2767	Pologne
Portugal	391	275	...	...	...	...	...	...	...	...	Portugal
Romania	1441	1540	370	528	460	435	436	349	356	220	Roumanie
Russian Federation	..	5132	4106	3296	1539	835	681	878	732	955	Fédération de Russie
Slovakia	..	..	..	..	..	..	..	..	52	0	Slovaquie
Slovenia	..	3840	3665	3621	3773	2946	2635	2396	1885	1323	Slovénie
Spain	751	741	874	...	...	...	...	...	...	...	Espagne
Sweden	176	142	155	158	201	23	15	15	26	15	Suède
Ukraine[9]	..	979	1110	1075	669	176	259	257	204	158	Ukraine[9]
Yugoslavia	..	2281	1479	26	471	554	703	1092	729	317	Yougoslavie
USSR (former)[8]	19508	..	..	..	..	..	..	..	..	..	URSS (anc.)[8]
Total	**186202**	**181418**	**188576**	**186574**	**166886**	**156187**	**184546**	**181818**	**259455**	**249606**	**Total**

General Note.
Data refer to bicycle and motorcycle tires, excluding inner tubes. (SITC, Rev.3: 62540-0).

Remarque générale.
Les données se rapportent à la production de pneumatiques pour bicyclettes et motocyclettes, à l'exclusion des chambres à air. (CTCI. Rev.3: 62540-0).

[1] Including inner tubes.
[2] Twelve months ending 30 June of year stated.
[3] Production by large and medium scale establishments only.
[4] For bicycles only.
[5] Beginning 1999, series discontinued.
[6] For motorcycles only.
[7] Incomplete coverage.
[8] Excluding tires for motorcycles and scooters.
[9] Tires for motorcycles and scooters only.

[1] Y compris les chambres à air.
[2] Période de douze mois finissant le 30 juin de l'année indiquée.
[3] Production des grandes et moyennes entreprises seulement.
[4] Pour bicyclettes seulement.
[5] A partir de 1999, série abandonnée.
[6] Pour motocyclettes seulement.
[7] Couverture incomplète.
[8] Non compris les pneumatiques pour motocyclettes et scooters.
[9] Pneumatiques pour motocyclettes et scooters seulement.

Tires for road motor vehicles
Pneumatiques pour véhicules à moteur

ISIC-BASED CODE - CODE BASE CITI

3551-10

Unit : Thousand units   Unité : En milliers

Country or area	1990	1991	1992	1993	1994	1995	1996	1997	1998	1999	Pays ou zone
Africa	**11262**	**10741**	**10392**	**10807**	**11992**	**12980**	**12716**	**12795**	**13640**	**14312**	**Afrique**
Angola[1]	46	20	...	...	...	...	...	...	...	...	Angola[1]
Egypt	1171	1243	1186	1162	1869	1932	1763	1277	1498	1426	Egypte
Ethiopia	118	65	66	100	171	168	80	151	152	148	Ethiopie
Kenya[2]	813	462	474	456	478	469	530	...	...	...	Kenya[2]
Morocco	...	1015	886	863	976	1073	1206	1254	1268	1339	Maroc
Mozambique	23	5	...	...	...	...	...	...	...	...	Mozambique
South Africa	7478	7236	7136	7421	7811	8635	8429	8958	9602	10318	Afrique du Sud
Tunisia	480	510	439	568	463	505	502	563	567	560	Tunisie
United Rep.Tanzania	208	185	158	190	177	151	159	167	...	...	Rép. Unie de Tanzanie
America, North	**244943**	**239683**	**270926**	**277107**	**287550**	**296587**	**300939**	**310939**	**322038**	**322073**	**Amérique du Nord**
Canada[3]	21692	24700	27637	28718	32656	31402	33416	33359	33979	36532	Canada[3]
Cuba[4]	373	88	126	63	112	194	212	233	165	...	Cuba[4]
Jamaica	347	326	308	359	352	146	782	0	...	...	Jamaïque
Mexico	11855	12148	12568	10490	10787	9292	10772	13450	16646	17386	Mexique
Panama	16	[4]30	31	33	43	32	34	[4]37	...	...	Panama
United States	210660	202391	230256	237444	243600	[3]255521	* [3]255723	[3]263860	[3]270905	[3]267652	Etats-Unis
America, South	**41569**	**42344**	**45014**	**47631**	**51089**	**52209**	**52385**	**56598**	**58326**	**59866**	**Amérique du Sud**
Argentina	4677	4568	5365	6038	7083	6940	7297	8138	9190	8085	Argentine
Brazil	[5]29162	[5]28926	[5]30306	[5]31795	[5]33395	[4]35076	[4]34539	...	...	...	Brésil
Chile	1632	1825	2002	2198	2285	2330	2269	2509	2350	2551	Chili
Colombia	1408	1437	1159	927	1234	769	...	605	...	...	Colombie
Ecuador	[4]102	[4]115	[4]894	837	924	920	1244	1247	1141	...	Equateur
Peru	637	686	575	717	783	813	797	868	1033	*969	Pérou
Venezuela	3951	4787	4713	[4]5119	[4]5385	[4]5361	[4]5162	[4]5717	[4]5383	...	Venezuela
Asia	**255849**	**272268**	**295290**	**249811**	**263458**	**280084**	**296007**	**312616**	**311375**	**320784**	**Asie**
Armenia	..	485	97	65	104	90	54	1	17	5	Arménie
Azerbaijan	..	271	222	134	65	21	6	5	0	0	Azerbaïdjan
China[1]	32091	38723	51834	6391	9302	7945	...	...	...	...	Chine[1]
Cyprus	*99	*72	38	*38	*42	56	60	46	47	29	Chypre
India	8460	8312	8756	9702	10456	12333	12434	[3]11948	[3]13780	[3]12995	Inde
Indonesia	7848	6396	8460	14376	20842	12033	...	23388	25701	...	Indonésie
Iran(Islamic Rep. of)	[6]6012	[6]6255	[6]6170	[6]5284	[6]5942	[7]5956	[7]5624	[7]6319	[7]7033	...	Iran(Rép. islamique)
Israel	778	786	892	854	966	918	900	...	...	...	Israël
Japan	153226	153677	154900	142595	139172	152040	157819	163006	158999	163705	Japon
Korea, Republic of	28129	33710	38120	42285	47105	53558	57835	59380	60192	67120	Corée, République de
Malaysia[1]	6764	7970	8540	9486	10156	11368	12221	13716	13567	13518	Malaisie[1]
Pakistan[8]	915	952	784	712	783	912	1003	525	767	845	Pakistan[8]
Philippines	2208	...	...	...	...	...	...	...	...	...	Philippines
Sri Lanka	382	392	276	184	* [3]286	* [3]269	[3]284	...	...	[3]60	Sri Lanka
Thailand[9]	4183	4518	[3]5530	[3]6360	[3]7300	[3]9000	8818	10945	11602	...	Thaïlande[9]
Turkey	4754	7541	8463	9137	8729	11377	12019	13659	13602	11454	Turquie
Europe	**224342**	**262200**	**270669**	**250055**	**254264**	**262741**	**269436**	**282466**	**305727**	**307155**	**Europe**
Belarus	..	3367	2862	1916	1027	1163	1733	2178	2098	2046	Bélarus
Bulgaria	1795	1125	1034	783	553	642	532	391	124	...	Bulgarie
Croatia	..	34	...	...	...	...	...	...	...	...	Croatie
Czechoslovakia(former)	5315	4733	..	..	..	..	..	..	..	..	Tchécoslovaquie(anc.)
Czech Republic	..	..	3123	3572	* [3]3924	* [3]5184	...	...	[3]9528	...	République tchèque
France	54536	57876	59928	53390	66744	[3]63765	[3]62720	[3]65242	[3]67458	[3]66870	France
Germany	..	...	50993	45595	46415	48534	48703	53605	57745	[3]59449	Allemagne
Germany(Fed.Rep.)	48247										Allemagne(Rép.féd.)
German D.R.(former)	4052	..	..	..	..	..	..	..	..	..	R.D.A. (anc.)
Hungary	605	425	355	146	...	...	391	429	464	415	Hongrie
Italy	30767	32447	29978	29138	31520	33551	33600	32761	36072	36268	Italie
Poland	4704	4516	5607	6479	7612	9502	10930	11939	14410	14660	Pologne
Portugal	2976	2184	...	1824	...	...	...	...	...	...	Portugal
Romania[10]	3702	2822	2877	3294	2781	3038	3304	2761	2646	2614	Roumanie[10]
Russian Federation	..	33522	33682	31208	17449	17462	19732	22954	22008	26155	Fédération de Russie
Slovakia	..	..	...	...	3797	4387	4528	...	3984	3282	Slovaquie
Slovenia	..	3289	4133	4371	4627	5184	5679	6472	6320	4924	Slovénie

For general note and footnotes, see end of table.   Voir la fin du tableau pour la remarque générale et les notes.

Tires for road motor vehicles (continued)
Pneumatiques pour véhicules à moteur (suite)

ISIC-BASED CODE - CODE BASE CITI

3551-10

Unit : Thousand units   Unité : En milliers

Country or area	1990	1991	1992	1993	1994	1995	1996	1997	1998	1999	Pays ou zone
Spain	23361	23812	25670	24116	[3]25539	[3]26430	28161	...	30441	32053	Espagne
Sweden	*2162	2158	2517	2336	2406	2543	2943	3507	3942	4152	Suède
Ukraine	..	7859	7886	7699	5726	5356	5832	6940	7941	7477	Ukraine
United Kingdom	29376	28500	30408	[3]29257	[3]30412	[3]32047	[3]30965	[3]32139	[3]34517	...	Royaume-Uni
Yugoslavia	..	4680	2782	544	965	1186	2254	3103	3666	2931	Yougoslavie
T.F.Yug.Rep. Macedonia	..	1	...	...	...	...	...	...	...	...	L'ex-RY Macédoine
Yugoslavia, SFR[11]	12744	..	..	..	..	..	..	..	..	..	Yougoslavie, RSF[11]
Oceania	**9150**	**9150**	**9150**	**9150**	**9150**	**9150**	**9150**	**9150**	**9150**	**9150**	**Océanie**
Australia[8][11]	7600	...	...	...	...	...	...	...	...	...	Australie[8][11]
New Zealand[10]	1550	...	...	...	...	...	...	...	...	...	Nouvelle-Zélande[10]
Total	**787115**	**836386**	**901441**	**844561**	**877503**	**913750**	**940633**	**984564**	**1020256**	**1033341**	**Total**

General Note.
Solid rubber tires, cushion tires, reinforced tires, tires not requiring inner tubes, tire cases (outer covers) for motor cars, lorries and all types of road vehicles other than bicycles and motorcycles. Inner tubes are excluded. (SITC, Rev.3: 62510-0, 62520-0).

Remarque générale.
Bandages pleins ou creux ("mi-pleins"), chambres à air renforcées, pneumatiques ne nécessitant pas de chambre à air, enveloppes pour voitures automobiles, camions et autres types de véhicules routiers à l'exception des bicyclettes et des motocyclettes. (CTCI, Rev.3: 62510-0, 62520-0).

[1] Tires of all types.
[2] Including retreaded tires.
[3] Source: International Rubber Study Group, (London).
[4] Source: United Nations Economic Commission for Latin America and the Caribbean (ECLAC), (Santiago).
[5] Including tires for motorcycles and bicycles.
[6] Production by establishments employing 50 or more persons.
[7] Production by establishments employing 10 or more persons.
[8] Twelve months ending 30 June of year stated.
[9] Beginning 1999, series discontinued.
[10] Including tires for vehicles operating off-the-road.
[11] Including motorcycle tires.

[1] Pneumatiques de tous genres.
[2] Y compris les pneumatiques rechapés.
[3] Source: International Rubber Study Group, (Londres).
[4] Source: Commission économique des Nations Unies pour l'Amérique Latine et les Caraïbes (CEPAL), (Santiago).
[5] Y compris les pneumatiques pour motocyclettes et bicyclettes.
[6] Production des établissements occupant 50 personnes ou plus.
[7] Production des établissements occupant 10 personnes ou plus.
[8] Période de douze mois finissant le 30 juin de l'année indiquée.
[9] A partir de 1999, série abandonnée.
[10] Y compris les pneumatiques pour véhicules tous terrains.
[11] Y compris les pneumatiques pour motocyclettes.

Rubber, reclaimed
Caoutchouc régénéré

ISIC-BASED CODE - CODE BASE CITI
3559-01

Unit : Metric tons   Unité : Tonnes métriques

Country or area	1990	1991	1992	1993	1994	1995	1996	1997	1998	1999	Pays ou zone
America, South	**1740**	**1666**	**733**	**2427**	**1057**	**2010**	**1447**	**1305**	**1151**	**1082**	**Amérique du Sud**
Colombia	...	...	733	2427	1057	2010	...	1305	1151	...	Colombie
Asia	**46392**	**45678**	**44528**	**39273**	**35715**	**35606**	**34242**	**33207**	**28549**	**24764**	**Asie**
Indonesia	...	...	3868	1566	2794	...	...	...	...	...	Indonésie
Japan	42091	41377	39102	36149	31363	31305	29941	28906	24248	20463	Japon
Turkey	1558	...	...	...	...	...	...	...	...	...	Turquie
Europe	**49405**	**133594**	**97393**	**73838**	**65163**	**60465**	**57974**	**56411**	**54709**	**57481**	**Europe**
Belarus	..	14984	10261	6908	4093	2101	2038	2106	2229	2012	Bélarus
Czechoslovakia(former)	12848	8898	..	..	..	..	..	..	..	..	Tchécoslovaquie(anc.)
Hungary	3680	2946	500	...	...	...	...	...	...	...	Hongrie
Poland	3912	...	1435	3202	3454	4123	4227	4108	3786	2618	Pologne
Romania	3630	2552	2513	3634	3011	2963	3307	3667	3292	2525	Roumanie
Russian Federation	..	57565	41376	22201	20374	20402	18208	17623	16528	18929	Fédération de Russie
Slovakia	..	..	..	8202	10165	9412	...	...	...	...	Slovaquie
Slovenia	..	532	502	523	627	579	...	...	...	...	Slovénie
Spain	14091	8736	5257	...	...	...	...	...	...	...	Espagne
Switzerland	11244	9865	8007	6614	7693	6405	...	...	...	...	Suisse
Ukraine	..	20734	17064	10466	3936	2311	1501	516	993	4086	Ukraine
Yugoslavia	..	3353	1218	351	73	432	608	743	670	536	Yougoslavie
Total	**97536**	**180939**	**142654**	**115538**	**101935**	**98080**	**93663**	**90923**	**84409**	**83326**	**Total**

General Note.
Rubber obtained from old rubber articles, or from waste or scrap of vulcanized rubber. (SITC, Rev.3: 23221-0).

Remarque générale.
Caoutchouc provenant du traitement de vieux ouvrages en caoutchouc ou de déchets et rognures de caoutchouc vulcanisé.(CTCI, Rev.3: 23221-0).

Rubber, unhardened vulcanized plates, sheets etc.
Plaques, feuilles etc. en caoutchouc vulcanisé non durci

ISIC-BASED CODE - CODE BASE CITI

3559-04

Unit : Metric tons

Unité : Tonnes métriques

Country or area	1990	1991	1992	1993	1994	1995	1996	1997	1998	1999	Pays ou zone
Asia	**7042**	**7603**	**8790**	**8722**	**8095**	**7205**	**5896**	**4646**	**4788**	**5365**	**Asie**
Georgia	..	...	1796	202	81	117	42	33	13	10	Géorgie
Malaysia	7042	7072	6994	8520	8014	7088	5854	4613	4775	5355	Malaisie
Europe	**384561**	**405140**	**407773**	**401716**	**404757**	**294403**	**376752**	**317039**	**343888**	**324703**	**Europe**
Austria[2][3]	[1]142083	[1]133554	[1]131130	[1]114941	[1]122807	#7015	...	8427	...	...	Autriche[2][3]
Belgium	...	...	...	33452	36650	33855	34566	36342	36037		Belgique
Croatia	..	4151	2699	2620	2731	1628	1687	211	98	...	Croatie
Finland	332	*340	282	*453	*440	*312	*565	...	...	2248	Finlande
Germany	..	...	...	137624	141306					...	Allemagne
Germany(Fed.Rep.)	115277	..	..	..	..	..	..	..	..	..	Allemagne(Rép.féd.)
Greece	1302	942	852	1058	[4]549	1472	1492	...	889	...	Grèce
Hungary	...	...	...	...	...	...	...	3467	3647	1308	Hongrie
Portugal	789	893	3872	4262	1008	4581	4346	4622	4326	4434	Portugal
Romania	5348	4850	2879	3539	4022	4893	5238	4786	5487	4916	Roumanie
Slovakia	..								15192	15829	Slovaquie
Slovenia	..	1306	1564	1455	1457	1737	2077	2614	2522	3389	Slovénie
Spain	46977	55613	48428	58321	54219	54453	55561	77168	85529	80239	Espagne
Sweden	31315	...	14983	19496	...	...	13100	14238	15308	14167	Suède
United Kingdom	...	...	...	4191	6013	5571	5019	8795	8409	...	Royaume-Uni
Yugoslavia	..	4779	3782	833	920	793	1750	1478	2053	1275	Yougoslavie
Total	**391603**	**412743**	**416563**	**410438**	**412852**	**301608**	**382648**	**321685**	**348676**	**330068**	**Total**

General Note.
Unhardened vulcanized plates, sheets, strips, rods and profile shapes of rubber including covered rubber material without further working. (SITC, Rev.3: 62132-0, 62133-0).

Remarque générale.
Plaques, feuilles, bandes, fils et profilés en caoutchouc vulcanisé non durci, découpés en rectangles ou se présentant sous la forme de fils ou de profilés, y compris les matières en caoutchouc recouvert mais n'ayant pas subi d'autre façon. (CTCI, Rev.3: 62132-0, 62133-0).

[1] All hardened and unhardened rubber products.
[2] 1996 data are confidential.
[3] 1998 data are confidential.
[4] Incomplete coverage.

[1] Produits de caoutchouc durci et non durci de toutes catégories.
[2] Pour 1996, les données sont confidentielles.
[3] Pour 1998, les données sont confidentielles.
[4] Couverture incomplète.

Rubber, unhardened vulcanized piping and tubing
Tubes et tuyaux en caoutchouc vulcanisé non durci

ISIC-BASED CODE - CODE BASE CITI

3559-07

Unit : Metric tons   Unité : Tonnes métriques

Country or area	1990	1991	1992	1993	1994	1995	1996	1997	1998	1999	Pays ou zone
Asia	**38985**	**38019**	**35485**	**52884**	**48915**	**62724**	**57064**	**61064**	**59186**	**63871**	**Asie**
Japan	31382	32226	30290	28888	31733	31699	32213	33783	29476	...	Japon
Turkey	7603	5793	5195	23996	17182	31025	...	...	...	...	Turquie
Europe	**157422**	**174990**	**182662**	**165151**	**188926**	**207172**	**198778**	**208013**	**229315**	**226474**	**Europe**
Austria[1][2]	...	...	...	...	...	10376	...	11534	...	...	Autriche[1][2]
Belgium	6770	6199	6217	4902	...	...	...	...	...	...	Belgique
Croatia	..	144	95	105	40	47	61	240	173	...	Croatie
Finland	812	638	533	591	691	789	855	878	911	863	Finlande
France	24741	31572	33456	36209	51408	...	...	...	...	...	France
Germany	..	56751	64889	52139	54544	70491	58738	63479	74837	...	Allemagne
Germany(Fed.Rep.)	51772	..	..	..	..	..	..	..	..	..	Allemagne(Rép.féd.)
Greece	145	134	...	...	107	81	157	...	142	...	Grèce
Hungary	414	252	203	376	250	279	1390	1728	3163	4779	Hongrie
Portugal	...	...	114	249	292	1132	1211	987	139	142	Portugal
Romania	11832	11762	6759	6406	5402	5436	5523	3487	3702	2849	Roumanie
Slovakia	..	..	..	...	...	...	...	...	1134	777	Slovaquie
Slovenia	..	1394	1499	1555	1522	1432	601	0	0	222	Slovénie
Spain	11152	12755	13721	12669	14632	20573	14292	14201	17045	...	Espagne
Sweden	...	...	...	...	...	...	3637	3863	4921	1829	Suède
United Kingdom	...	...	...	34017	37873	32438	...	...	...	...	Royaume-Uni
Yugoslavia	..	3595	4799	332	670	689	939	1272	1135	535	Yougoslavie
Total	**196407**	**213009**	**218147**	**218035**	**237841**	**269896**	**255842**	**269077**	**288501**	**290346**	**Total**

General Note.

Piping and tubing consisting wholly of vulcanized rubber and vulcanized piping and tubing reinforced by stratification of textile fabric. Inner rubber tubes for tires are excluded. (SITC, Rev.3: 62140-0).

Remarque générale.

Tubes et tuyaux entièrement constitués de caoutchouc vulcanisé, et tubes et tuyaux vulcanisés renforcés par une stratification d'un ou plusieurs plis textiles. Cette rubrique ne comprend pas les chambres à air pour pneumatiques. (CTCI, Rev.3: 62140-0).

[1] 1996 data are confidential.
[2] Beginning 1998, data are confidential.

[1] Pour 1996, les données sont confidentielles.
[2] A partir de 1998, les données sont confidentielles.

Rubber, hardened (ebonite and vulcanite in blocks, plates, sheets etc.)
Caoutchouc durci (en blocs, plaques, feuilles etc.)

ISIC-BASED CODE - CODE BASE CITI

3559-10

Unit : Metric tons

Unité : Tonnes métriques

Country or area	1990	1991	1992	1993	1994	1995	1996	1997	1998	1999	Pays ou zone
Asia	**79**	**84**	**89**	**94**	**98**	**107**	**108**	**114**	**120**	**125**	**Asie**
Japan	...	...	...	...	98	107	108	114	120	...	Japon
Europe	**60019**	**64209**	**60506**	**52334**	**47063**	**45419**	**45117**	**22040**	**21292**	**22545**	**Europe**
Croatia	..	421	180	102	15	0	0	3	...	...	Croatie
Germany	..	47621	45114	34067	31416	...	...	5694	5655	...	Allemagne
Germany(Fed.Rep.)	42611	..	..	..	..	..	..	..	..	...	Allemagne(Rép.féd.)
Hungary	274	239	109	110	75	...	26	3	...	...	Hongrie
Portugal	...	...	185	...	...	...	...	...	...	...	Portugal
Romania	4420	3381	2452	2667	3246	3007	2787	2679	2191	1985	Roumanie
Slovenia	..	...	...	...	...	...	252	196	0	...	Slovénie
Spain	862	546	650	1316	1821	2590	1939	1613	1593	...	Espagne
United Kingdom	...	...	...	13738	10156	11107	...	...	...	...	Royaume-Uni
Total	**60098**	**64293**	**60595**	**52428**	**47161**	**45526**	**45225**	**22154**	**21412**	**22670**	**Total**

General Note.
Ebonite and vulcanite in blocks, plates, sheets, strips, rods, profile shapes, powder and manufacturing waste. Articles of hardened rubber are excluded. (SITC, Rev.3: 62991-1).

Remarque générale.
Ebonite ou autre caoutchouc durci, en blocs, plaques, feuilles, bandes, bâtons, profilés et poudres, y compris les déchets de fabrication. Cette rubrique ne comprend pas les articles en caoutchouc durci. (CTCI, Rev.3: 62991-1).

Rubber, transmission, conveyor, elevator belts etc.
Courroies transporteuses, de transmission etc., en caoutchouc

ISIC-BASED CODE - CODE BASE CITI

3559-13

Unit : Metric tons

Unité : Tonnes métriques

Country or area	1990	1991	1992	1993	1994	1995	1996	1997	1998	1999	Pays ou zone
America, South											**Amérique du Sud**
Colombia	841	...	581	#65	30	82	...	35	...	...	Colombie
Asia											**Asie**
India[1]	16468	15664	12209	11382	9584	10926	16067	13606	13305	12669	Inde[1]
Indonesia	...	...	...	166	...	...	...	...	...	...	Indonésie
Japan	35838	36506	31494	28958	28195	29414	30964	32970	30321	27685	Japon
Korea, Republic of[2][3]	4146	3726	3368	3756	4425	5327	5219	5149	4314	5031	Corée, République de[2][3]
Europe											**Europe**
Belgium	4296	3381	3479	2551	...	[2]2915	[2]2389	[2]2033	[2]2158	[2]1504	Belgique
Croatia	..	131	...	...	...	...	...	...	...	...	Croatie
Czech Republic	..	...	...	...	...	...	...	1066	1376	848	République tchèque
Finland	2097	2131	1884	2286	2226	791	726	...	2311	2140	Finlande
France	13684	...	...	...	...	...	...	...	...	...	France
Germany	..	50412	42463	31362	39614	...	...	...	...	...	Allemagne
Germany(Fed.Rep.)	45641	...	...	..	..	...	...	...	...	..	Allemagne(Rép.féd.)
Greece	1175	1286	1294	...	1549	1589	1593	1590	1876	..	Grèce
Hungary	4571	3213	1984	2338	3249	4851	5241	6498	7230	8385	Hongrie
Latvia	..	[3]806000	...	...	...	...	...	...	...	30	Lettonie
Netherlandsμ	11919	11967	11656	...	...	...	...	...	...	...	Pays-Basμ
Poland	33739	24675	21969	24858	25841	30251	28524	29009	27708	23685	Pologne
Portugal	909	891	...	...	...	...	...	...	...	...	Portugal
Romania	5476	4406	2549	2153	1991	1836	1654	1420	1179	893	Roumanie
Slovakia	..	...	...	...	...	...	[3]766000	...	...	8094	Slovaquie
Slovenia	..	2765	2310	2771	2582	3641	3765	3864	3921	3549	Slovénie
Spain	12368	12006	10345	8814	8387	10289	13923	12279	13195	16248	Espagne
Sweden	...	661	312	565	338	389	...	...	...	0	Suède
United Kingdom	...	...	...	15981	11257	13643	13318	15813	18153	...	Royaume-Uni
Yugoslavia	..	4220	2716	809	1513	1943	2270	3732	4199	377	Yougoslavie

General Note.

Transmission, conveyor or elevator belts or belting of vulcanized rubber. Data represent belting and belts of wholly vulcanized rubber or of fabric impregnated, coated, covered or laminated with rubber or made from textile yarns or cord impregnated or coated with rubber. (SITC, Rev.3: 62920-0).

[1] Production by large and medium scale establishments only.
[2] Transmission belts only.
[3] In thousand units.
μ Including production in Belgium and Luxembourg.

Remarque générale.

Courroies et matières pour courroies transporteuses, élévatrices, de transmission, entièrement en caoutchouc vulcanisé ou en tissu imprégné, enduit ou recouvert de caoutchouc ou laminé avec du caoutchouc, ou faites en fils ou ficelles textiles imprégnés ou enduits de caoutchouc. (CTCI, Rev.3: 62920-0).

[1] Production des grandes et moyennes entreprises seulement.
[2] Courroies de transmission seulement.
[3] En milliers d'unités.
μ Y compris la production de la Belgique et du Luxembourg.

Rubber footwear
Chaussures en caoutchouc

ISIC-BASED CODE - CODE BASE CITI

3559-16

Unit : Thousand pairs

Unité : Milliers de paires

Country or area	1990	1991	1992	1993	1994	1995	1996	1997	1998	1999	Pays ou zone
Africa	**7897**	**5353**	**3639**	**4483**	**4031**	**3424**	**6089**	**3328**	**2997**	**2660**	**Afrique**
Burundi[1]	192	296	451	405	...	...	...	...	...	...	Burundi[1]
Kenya	7691	5045	3178	4046	3682	3074	5747	...	...	...	Kenya
Mozambique	14	12	10	32	13	14	6	10	10	4	Mozambique
America, North	**128862**	**139752**	**133763**	**103660**	**100754**	**93073**	**92309**	**87164**	**75267**	**57998**	**Amérique du Nord**
Mexico	23154	26568	24953	23339	23791	19573	27009	21464	20567	15698	Mexique
United States[2]	105708	113184	108810	80321	76963	73500	65300	65700	54700	42300	Etats-Unis[2]
America, South	**104473**	**116519**	**82789**	**86769**	**88661**	**101119**	**104062**	**112943**	**126722**	**128665**	**Amérique du Sud**
Bolivia	442	492	247	651	678	*613	...	...	...	...	Bolivie
Brazil	100889	109925	76669	79487	81511	95117	94312	100749	113585	114466	Brésil
Colombia	...	...	281	331	386	91	...	593	485	...	Colombie
Ecuador	2888	...	5592	6300	6086	5298	8765	...	...	...	Equateur
Asia	**1098154**	**1130288**	**1159883**	**1256909**	**1255886**	**1997855**	**1689532**	**1409646**	**982747**	**920819**	**Asie**
Armenia	..	2307	515	350	205	79	56	23	30	12	Arménie
Azerbaijan	..	266	204	134	111	49	12	3	0	0	Azerbaïdjan
China	897580	929960	904165	1103438	...	1832450	1521910	1247094	832871	781426	Chine
Georgia	..	...	109	40	11	10	1	0	0	0	Géorgie
India[3]	33130	24700	28400	35460	31724	27819	28334	27899	27214	23662	Inde[3]
Indonesia	...	...	140148	40048	31817						Indonésie
Iran(Islamic Rep. of)	[4]3318	[4]2540	[4]1587	[4]1105	[4]1083	[5]1125	[5]1151	[5]2846	[5]2373	...	Iran(Rép. islamique)
Japan	50827	46529	39376	33797	31565	29777	28348	22598	16998	15480	Japon
Kazakhstan		1058	1174	1344	808	259	87	22	243	340	Kazakhstan
Korea, Republic of	14633	9705	6402	4490	...	...	...	...	...	...	Corée, République de
Kyrgyzstan	..	...	...	...	...	...	...	104	62	3	Kirghizistan
Malaysia	21632	22128	19823	18624	18491	17068	16947	12832	8092	8282	Malaisie
Syrian Arab Republic	117	446	155	131	266	305	362	409	...	...	Rép. arabe syrienne
Tajikistan	..	6346	3287	2250	1262	464	455	244	108	22	Tadjikistan
Turkey	6246	7930	9552	10025	8105	6608	8545	11078	11658	7274	Turquie
Turkmenistan	..	...	...	...	...	...	...	...	205	...	Turkménistan
Uzbekistan	..	5401	4725	5412	4603	2102	3584	4810	...	...	Ouzbékistan
Europe	**45223**	**187666**	**157557**	**115092**	**81395**	**72190**	**68248**	**68037**	**65449**	**61208**	**Europe**
Belarus	..	8962	7619	5022	3035	2180	3054	4376	5036	4781	Bélarus
Bulgaria	3243	3039	2745	1946	1745	1291	957	654	1014	812	Bulgarie
Croatia	..	807	30	16	24	29	35	0	0	...	Croatie
Czechoslovakia(former)	4013	2507	..	..	..	..	..	..	..		Tchécoslovaquie(anc.)
Czech Republic	..	..	...	...	3096	2793	2924	3563	2872	2446	République tchèque
Estonia	..	973	628	472	504	472	159	139	102	76	Estonie
Finland	1041	829	[1]738	[1]605	[1]572	[1]577	[1]409	...	[1]604	[1]544	Finlande
German D.R.(former)	2686	..	..	..	..	..	..	..	..	..	R.D.A. (anc.)
Greece	147	119	277	...	68	...	...	...	...	...	Grèce
Hungary	706	564	401	355	312	318	...	...	...	...	Hongrie
Italy	...	...	...	...	...	...	...	...	138	139	Italie
Latvia	..	7571	3599	1536	1308	807	1312	499	605	114	Lettonie
Lithuania	..	7623	3858	1587	953	313	420	826	988	451	Lituanie
Poland	6388	4236	3391	2797	3024	2998	3252	3319	2624	1825	Pologne
Portugal	478	125	143	116	8	...	...	...	...	...	Portugal
Romania[6]	7307	5407	2988	3196	2936	3733	2635	2042	968	658	Roumanie[6]
Russian Federation	..	90458	72372	52544	28420	22667	20184	20447	20687	20085	Fédération de Russie
Slovakia	..	..	1337	1075	941	865	1870	2504	1378	1362	Slovaquie
Spain	18982	22980	28561	...	...	...	...	...	...	...	Espagne
Sweden	93	...	21	0	...	...	...	...	...	...	Suède
Ukraine	..	26838	22793	15287	7991	7288	4706	3060	2390	2207	Ukraine
Yugoslavia	..	4451	2833	1688	2774	2022	2208	1867	2137	1841	Yougoslavie
USSR (former)	203038	..	..	..	..	..	..	..	..	..	URSS (anc.)
Total	**1587647**	**1579577**	**1537631**	**1566913**	**1530727**	**2267661**	**1960240**	**1681118**	**1253182**	**1171350**	**Total**

For general note and footnotes, see end of table.

Voir la fin du tableau pour la remarque générale et les notes.

Rubber footwear (continued)
Chaussures en caoutchouc (suite)

ISIC-BASED CODE - CODE BASE CITI
3559-16

General Note.

Footwear, including overshoes, with both outer soles and uppers of rubber. (SITC, Rev.3: 85111-1, 85113-1, 85121-1, 85123-1, 85130-1).

[1] Including plastic footwear.

[2] Including plastic overshoes and footwear with rubber or plastic soles and fabric uppers.

[3] Production by large and medium scale establishments only.

[4] Production by establishments employing 50 or more persons.

[5] Production by establishments employing 10 or more persons.

[6] Excluding production of private workshops and small-scale private industry.

Remarque générale.

Chaussures, y compris les couvre-chaussures, dont la semelle extérieure et le dessus sont en caoutchouc. (CTCI, Rev.3: 85111-1, 85113-1, 85121-1, 85123-1, 85130-1).

[1] Y compris les chaussures en matière plastique.

[2] Y compris les couvre-chaussures en matière plastique et les chaussures à semelles en caoutchouc ou en matière plastique et à dessus en tissus.

[3] Production des grandes et moyennes entreprises seulement.

[4] Production des établissements occupant 50 personnes ou plus.

[5] Production des établissements occupant 10 personnes ou plus.

[6] Non compris la production des ateliers privés et de la petite industrie privée.

Plastic footwear
Chaussures en matière plastique

ISIC-BASED CODE - CODE BASE CITI

3560-03

Unit : Thousand pairs

Unité : Milliers de paires

Country or area	1990	1991	1992	1993	1994	1995	1996	1997	1998	1999	Pays ou zone
Africa	**94603**	**58062**	**82247**	**114980**	**32107**	**31794**	**33671**	**23936**	**12262**	**12557**	**Afrique**
Madagascar	...	...	...	...	659	493	410	420	396	...	Madagascar
Nigeria	...	48987	73732	105825	22098	20531	...	...	...	...	Nigéria
Tunisia	6970	8300	7800	8500	9350	10770	11590	12700	...	...	Tunisie
America, North	**14836**	**13579**	**14618**	**12831**	**11938**	**9126**	**12546**	**12983**	**15035**	**14187**	**Amérique du Nord**
Mexico	14836	13579	14618	12831	11938	9126	12546	12983	15035	14187	Mexique
America, South	**9011**	**8996**	**8960**	**7964**	**7326**	**5321**	**6394**	**4667**	**4639**	**2259**	**Amérique du Sud**
Bolivia	134	149	218	190	199	*181	...	...	...	...	Bolivie
Chile	1392	2195	2331	2263	...	...	...	...	...	...	Chili
Colombia	...	...	6411	5511	5082	3095	...	2418	2385	...	Colombie
Asia	**122336**	**118776**	**110389**	**104096**	**104293**	**106452**	**104331**	**109687**	**101389**	**87136**	**Asie**
Hong Kong SAR [1]	...	6015	...	1200	182	...	78	...	...	...	Hong-Kong RAS [1]
Cyprus	26	25	35	35	35	32	30	24	14	10	Chypre
Indonesia	...	...	35420	32429	28821	...	...	...	...	...	Indonésie
Iran(Islamic Rep. of)	18725	14213	9492	8874	6700	[2]5493	[2]5519	[2]4522	[2]5878	...	Iran(Rép. islamique)
Japan	...	...	...	...	63637	54946	52192	48027	39121	35509	Japon
Turkey	4106	3421	3441	4173	4679	#11650	14050	22783	22045	17286	Turquie
Turkmenistan	..	...	...	...	...	...	...	239	...	...	Turkménistan
Europe	**33494**	**20035**	**17255**	**17018**	**16924**	**15530**	**17237**	**16449**	**15421**	**17211**	**Europe**
Bulgaria	3243	684	885	401	401	354	370	244	292	478	Bulgarie
Croatia	..	685	730	453	548	181	217	271	120	...	Croatie
Czechoslovakia(former)	10729	2623		..	..	..	..	..	..	..	Tchécoslovaquie(anc.)
Finland	1041	829		...	...	...	...	...	...	...	Finlande
Germany	..	...	...	642	...	1548	1358	1140	1252	...	Allemagne
Greece	...	...	...	4549	3746	3174	...	...	1556	...	Grèce
Hungary	1109	293	293	...	...	...	...	...	60	...	Hongrie
Latvia	..	..	...	...	...	...	...	...	...	72	Lettonie
Netherlands [3][4]	...	...	...	1584	1631	...	...	...	...	...	Pays-Bas [3][4]
Portugal	2644	783	1198	1218	1781	...	...	...	...	...	Portugal
Romania	5206	3599	1856	1637	804	633	2517	2542	2854	2366	Roumanie
Slovakia	..	..	...	758	942	770	777	384	1243	1071	Slovaquie
Spain	2523	1744	2245	...	...	...	...	...	...	...	Espagne
Sweden	93	...	...	0	...	...	...	...	...	...	Suède
United Kingdom [5]	2042	...	...	...	...	...	...	...	...	...	Royaume-Uni [5]
Yugoslavia	..	942	444	118	178	...	...	...	...	...	Yougoslavie
Total	**274280**	**219448**	**233468**	**256890**	**172588**	**168224**	**174179**	**167723**	**148747**	**133350**	**Total**

General Note.
Footwear with both outer soles and uppers of plastic. (SITC, Rev.3: 85111-2, 85113-2, 85121-2, 85123-2, 85130-2).

Remarque générale.
Chaussures dont la semelle extérieure et le dessus sont en matière plastique. (CTCI, Rev.3: 85111-2, 85113-2, 85121-2, 85123-2, 85130-2).

[1] Beginning 1997, data are confidential.
[2] Production by establishments employing 10 or more persons.
[3] Sales.
[4] Production by establishments employing 20 or more persons.
[5] Including rubber footwear.

[1] A partir de 1997, les données sont confidentielles
[2] Production des établissements occupant 10 personnes ou plus.
[3] Ventes.
[4] Production des établissements occupant 20 personnes ou plus.
[5] Y compris les chaussures en caoutchouc.

Household ware of porcelain or china
Articles de ménage en porcelaine

ISIC-BASED CODE - CODE BASE CITI

3610-01A

Unit : Thousand units

Unité : En milliers

Country or area	1990	1991	1992	1993	1994	1995	1996	1997	1998	1999	Pays ou zone
Africa	**1134**	**961**	**589**	**459**	**444**	**447**	**445**	**67**	**5**	**0**	**Afrique**
Kenya	1089	926	551	421	421	430	*430	...	...	...	Kenya
Nigeria [1]	...	35	38	38	23	17	...	...	...	...	Nigéria [1]
America, South	**18361**	**18361**	**18361**	**18361**	**18361**	**17574**	**21593**	**21317**	**12959**	**18361**	**Amérique du Sud**
Ecuador	...	...	...	...	...	17574	21593	21317	12959	...	Equateur
Asia	**595891**	**686390**	**532700**	**441325**	**468539**	**338712**	**437279**	**366936**	**371490**	**274801**	**Asie**
Armenia	..	2114	1095	685	299	504	392	108	52	66	Arménie
Azerbaijan	..	26058	17693	15933	10316	2841	4650	4818	3963	2368	Azerbaïdjan
China, Macao, SAR	...	...	...	4			...	...	...	...	Chine, Macao PAS
Georgia	..	...	789	117	106	260	273	192	274	321	Géorgie
Indonesia [1]	176672	249659	162890	94276	142490	23952	...	66407	83681	...	Indonésie [1]
Korea, Republic of	246171	194854	171462	145704	126671	121943	...	...	...	...	Corée, République de
Syrian Arab Republic	32744	35637	36140	32639	39055	39228	39528	40012	...	...	Rép. arabe syrienne
Tajikistan	..	15000	13000	7747	5378	5760	4062	4192	4532	4709	Tadjikistan
Viet Nam	140300	162733	129627	...	...	...	...	...	...	...	Viet Nam
Europe	**180958**	**1024773**	**1035916**	**1024355**	**802169**	**703064**	**584861**	**543213**	**505705**	**609420**	**Europe**
Belarus	..	28431	29273	29308	24799	21211	23487	27731	29637	30356	Bélarus
Finland	3	...	...	...	...	...	...	...	...	...	Finlande
Greece	23462	24004	23579	...	...	...	...	...	5855	...	Grèce
Latvia	..	28296		13253	9212	6344	2313	1195	840	...	Lettonie
Lithuania		563	648	659	527	389	149	97	133	128	Lituanie
Poland	113065	96421	87067	99976	108314	119751	128824	127987	128650	127588	Pologne
Romania	44428	42047	43090	45487	50841	52475	60691	63806	37982	64960	Roumanie
Russian Federation	..	531779	551898	541774	340600	278961	200224	178016	179690	238816	Fédération de Russie
Ukraine	..	273229	291579	274670	248648	204705	149945	125153	122915	127490	Ukraine
USSR (former)	1064879	..		..	..		..		..	..	URSS (anc.)
Total	**1861223**	**1730485**	**1587565**	**1484499**	**1289513**	**1059797**	**1044178**	**931533**	**890160**	**902582**	**Total**

General Note.

Tableware and other articles of a kind commonly used for domestic purposes, of porcelain or china, including biscuit porcelain, parain and bone china. (SITC, Rev.3: 66611-0A, 66612-0A).

Remarque générale.

Vaisselle et autres articles du type communément utilisé à des fins ménagères, faits en porcelaine, y compris le biscuit, le parian et la porcelaine phosphatique. (CTCI, Rev.3: 66611-0A, 66612-0A).

[1] Including household ware of other ceramic materials.

[1] Y compris les articles de ménage faits d'autres matières céramiques.

Household ware of porcelain or china-
Articles de ménage en porcelaine

ISIC-BASED CODE - CODE BASE CITI

3610-01B

Unit : Metric tons

Unité : Tonnes métriques

Country or area	1990	1991	1992	1993	1994	1995	1996	1997	1998	1999	Pays ou zone
Africa	**4026**	**3659**	**5424**	**3477**	**3507**	**3765**	**3672**	**3667**	**4556**	**4222**	**Afrique**
Egypt	1478	1492	3178	1192	1156	1393	1088	1061	...	...	Egypte
Tunisia	2548	2167	2246	2285	2351	2372	2584	2606	3420	3148	Tunisie
Asia	**555068**	**538124**	**500197**	**472033**	**448396**	**427881**	**436953**	**423620**	**410287**	**396955**	**Asie**
Japan[1]	555068	538124	500197	472033	448396	427881	...	...	...	...	Japon[1]
Europe	**320676**	**304523**	**282156**	**262074**	**252937**	**276271**	**282894**	**266638**	**272838**	**262663**	**Europe**
Belgium	9300	9595	14407	13579	...	...	...	...	...	...	Belgique
Croatia	..	...	...	...	...	...	...	2187	2572	...	Croatie
Denmark[2]	...	...	...	517	461	480	467	419	415	401	Danemark[2]
Czechoslovakia(former)	22529	18253	..	..	..	..	..	..	..	..	Tchécoslovaquie(anc.)
Czech Republic	..	..	17430	17617	18262	18263	19917	20950	21732	19442	République tchèque
France	15420	14196	11532	10572	13308	...	...	...	...	...	France
Germany	..	105969	91695	84126	70979	80535	74490	...	...	...	Allemagne
Germany(Fed.Rep.)	91061	..	..	..	..	..	...	...	...	...	Allemagne(Rép.féd.)
German D.R.(former)	31114	..	..	..	..	..	..	..	..	...	R.D.A. (anc.)
Hungary	6477	5632	5726	4548	4482	4690	4313	4243	7777	5627	Hongrie
Latvia	...	...	...	...	...	...	...	...	...	106	Lettonie
Netherlands[2][3]	...	...	...	1803	...	...	...	...	...	...	Pays-Bas[2][3]
Poland	33239	28274	25254	28417	30937	34266	37518	37710	39399	40593	Pologne
Portugal	20305	15832	14346	13264	12778	19218	24802	26265	26723	22747	Portugal
Slovakia	..	..	...	...	...	...	...	...	385	...	Slovaquie
Slovenia	..	..	...	...	...	...	13	12	12	...	Slovénie
Spain	15914	18876	18132	11074	12590	13155	12573	14477	14136	13090	Espagne
United Kingdom	...	...	...	69026	68955	75722	79424	61008	63733	...	Royaume-Uni
Yugoslavia	..	3159	2453	841	1210	899	1780	1758	1684	1070	Yougoslavie
T.F.Yug.Rep. Macedonia	..	7605	4348	3807	2569	1986	1337	1539	2285	1649	L'ex-RY Macédoine
Total	**879770**	**846306**	**787777**	**737584**	**704840**	**707917**	**723519**	**693925**	**687682**	**663841**	**Total**

General Note.

Tableware and other articles of a kind commonly used for domestic purposes, of porcelain or china, including biscuit porcelain, parian and bone china. (SITC, Rev.3: 66611-0B, 66612-0B).

Remarque générale.

Vaisselle et autres articles du type communément utilisé à des fins ménagères, faits en porcelaine, y compris le biscuit, le parian et la porcelaine phosphatique. (CTCI, Rev.3: 66611-0B, 66612-0B).

[1] Including household ware of other ceramic materials.
[2] Sales.
[3] Production by establishments employing 20 or more persons.

[1] Y compris les articles de ménage faits d'autres matières céramiques.
[2] Ventes.
[3] Production des établissements occupant 20 personnes ou plus.

Household ware of other ceramic materials
Articles de ménage en autres matières céramiques

ISIC-BASED CODE - CODE BASE CITI
3610-04B

Unit : Metric tons

Unité : Tonnes métriques

Country or area	1990	1991	1992	1993	1994	1995	1996	1997	1998	1999	Pays ou zone
Africa	**16198**	**17338**	**17909**	**17167**	**15501**	**13111**	**12911**	**11831**	**12317**	**11251**	**Afrique**
Algeria	9598	10138	10359	9367	7651	5132	7171	4831	4967	3533	Algérie
Egypt	6600	7200	7550	7800	7850	7979	5740	7000	7350	7718	Egypte
Asia	**4040**	**3889**	**3624**	**2870**	**3606**	**3606**	**3606**	**3606**	**3606**	**3606**	**Asie**
Sri Lanka[1]	4040	3889	3624	2870	...	...	...	...	...	...	Sri Lanka[1]
Europe	**480862**	**433914**	**384428**	**389849**	**377002**	**381640**	**385717**	**390678**	**356811**	**362361**	**Europe**
Austria[2]	4278	4674	2287	2117	2388	1763	2284	...	...	...	Autriche[2]
Belgium	14437	15749	10940	8696	...	...	...	...	...	...	Belgique
Croatia	..	2411	2282	2314	2524	2089	2655	0	...	...	Croatie
Czech Republic	..	..	2491	2532	2558	3059	3140	2855	2435	2177	République tchèque
France	79068	78864	72876	84359	...	...	...	...	...	...	France
Germany	..	...	...	12063	10559	...	10475	7805	...	...	Allemagne
Germany(Fed.Rep.)	20418	..	..	..	...	...	..	..	..	..	Allemagne(Rép.féd.)
German D.R.(former)	5882	..	..	..	..	..	..	..	..	..	R.D.A. (anc.)
Greece	...	...	...	7648	...	...	...	...	...	...	Grèce
Hungary	3604	2415	2497	1820	1081	724	1947	1353	2172	2713	Hongrie
Iceland	7	6	6	...	...	...	...	...	...	...	Islande
Latvia	..	...	...	...	...	...	...	...	...	1891	Lettonie
Poland	14470	10570	11024	11732	12713	14133	14613	11768	10395	11393	Pologne
Portugal	71222	56056	44022	52883	53086	57764	81934	90412	102168	107848	Portugal
Slovakia	..	...	...	...	...	...	...	...	542	468	Slovaquie
Slovenia	..	2091	1820	1522	...	...	1126	...	1276	1139	Slovénie
Spain	47737	42314	28223	23035	22332	34367	29442	27492	31925	32846	Espagne
Sweden	...	...	...	...	1998	2257	...	1516	1402	1054	Suède
United Kingdom	...	...	...	174789	164931	152415	135109	...	92277	...	Royaume-Uni
Yugoslavia	..	200	183	44	39	50	49	42	41	37	Yougoslavie
Total	**501100**	**455141**	**405961**	**409886**	**396109**	**398357**	**402234**	**406115**	**372734**	**377217**	**Total**

General Note.
Tableware and other utensils and articles of a kind commonly used for domestic purposes of other ceramic materials, such as common pottery, stoneware, earthenware and imitation porcelain. (SITC, Rev.3: 66613-0B).

Remarque générale.
Vaisselle et autres ustensiles et articles du type communément utilisé à des fins ménagères, faits en autres matières céramiques telles que la terre cuite, le grès, la faïence et la simili-porcelaine. (CTCI, REv.3: 66613-0B).

[1] State sector only.
[2] Beginning 1997, data are confidential.

[1] Secteur public seulement.
[2] A partir de 1997, les données sont confidentielles

Sanitary ceramic fittings
Appareils sanitaires en céramique

ISIC-BASED CODE - CODE BASE CITI

3610-07A

Unit : Thousand units

Unité : En milliers

Country or area	1990	1991	1992	1993	1994	1995	1996	1997	1998	1999	Pays ou zone
Africa	**228**	**268**	**304**	**335**	**335**	**391**	**405**	**291**	**309**	**347**	**Afrique**
Tunisia	228	268	304	335	335	391	405	291	309	347	Tunisie
America, North	**2757**	**2315**	**2705**	**6427**	**8016**	**7778**	**9251**	**10663**	**11221**	**11695**	**Amérique du Nord**
Mexico	2757	2315	2705	#6427	8016	7778	9251	10663	11221	11695	Mexique
America, South	**4647**	**4879**	**3109**	**5627**	**6991**	**3352**	**4899**	**5193**	**5217**	**5634**	**Amérique du Sud**
Colombia	...	...	2686	5048	6276	2488	...	...	...	...	Colombie
Ecuador	522	...	423	579	715	864	774	1068	1092	...	Equateur
Asia	**8384**	**10155**	**11351**	**12544**	**13476**	**11384**	**13560**	**15926**	**21868**	**20592**	**Asie**
Azerbaijan	..	64	53	52	34	6	13	7	7	3	Azerbaïdjan
Bangladesh	246	1800	1768	...	...	...	...	...	...	...	Bangladesh
Indonesia	23	52	806	1825	2182	213	...	4171	9704	...	Indonésie
Israel	321	395	418	360	382	430	425	...	...	...	Israël
Korea, Republic of	2539	2632	3191	3879	4465	4534	...	...	...	...	Corée, République de
Kyrgyzstan	..	6	17	30	7	0	0	0	3	...	Kirghizistan
Thailand	4680	4579	...	...	...	...	...	...	...	...	Thaïlande
Turkey	575	627	468	497	505	300	386	701	864	1099	Turquie
Europe	**20866**	**31330**	**30083**	**36525**	**33976**	**35657**	**34622**	**35540**	**38831**	**41330**	**Europe**
Belarus	..	631	635	631	552	434	552	587	591	479	Bélarus
Bulgaria	651	485	525	1231	608	655	614	661	...	1821	Bulgarie
Croatia	..	370	304	328	366	209	216	222	209	...	Croatie
Germany	...	...	...	...	...	...	4135	3995	4095	...	Allemagne
Greece	781	767	768	1154	1087	1797	1082	1015	1948	...	Grèce
Portugal	...	...	2974	3463	3514	4572	5000	5093	5872	6653	Portugal
Romania	2258	1961	1781	1711	1717	2137	2319	2932	2210	2117	Roumanie
Russian Federation	..	2135	1377	6529	4412	4403	3505	3519	3885	4803	Fédération de Russie
Slovakia	..	..	...	...	...	...	...	...	187	286	Slovaquie
Spain	...	...	...	6479	6871	7330	7037	7375	9019	8736	Espagne
Switzerland	510	511	497	527	569	535	...	...	...	...	Suisse
Ukraine	..	3009	3068	2932	2628	1902	1359	1406	1655	1804	Ukraine
United Kingdom	...	...	...	7052	7116	7105	7642	7613	7336	...	Royaume-Uni
Yugoslavia	..	435	321	176	224	266	381	337	465	350	Yougoslavie
Yugoslavia, SFR	417	..	..	..	..	..	..	...	...	..	Yougoslavie, RSF
Total	**36882**	**48947**	**47552**	**61457**	**62793**	**58561**	**62737**	**67613**	**77446**	**79598**	**Total**

General Note.
China or earthenware fittings designed to be permanently fixed in place, normally by connection to the water or sewage system (for example, sinks, wash basins, bidets, water closet pans, urinals and the like). Small accessory bathroom or sanitary fittings are excluded. (SITC, Rev.3: 81220-0A).

Remarque générale.
Appareils en porcelaine ou en faïence destinés à être fixés à demeure, généralement par branchement sur une conduite d'eau ou d'égout (par exemple, les éviers, les lavabos, les bidets, les cuvettes de cabinets d'aisances, les urinoirs etc.). Cette rubrique ne comprend pas les petits accessoires de salle de bain ou autres petits articles sanitaires. (CTCI, Rev.3: 81220-0A).

Sanitary ceramic fittings
Appareils sanitaires en céramique

ISIC-BASED CODE - CODE BASE CITI
3610-07B

Unit : Metric tons

Unité : Tonnes métriques

Country or area	1990	1991	1992	1993	1994	1995	1996	1997	1998	1999	Pays ou zone
Africa	**37205**	**45328**	**47193**	**47656**	**47662**	**49591**	**53903**	**54679**	**53158**	**54684**	**Afrique**
Algeria	10184	11404	10258	...	...	...	...	...	...	...	Algérie
Egypt	23941	30230	32673	32441	32407	33438	37677	39987	...	...	Egypte
Tunisia	3080	3694	4262	4600	4640	5538	5611	4077	4271	4894	Tunisie
America, South	**14364**	**13238**	**16885**	**19040**	**22559**	**22863**	**22030**	**23728**	**26293**	**22460**	**Amérique du Sud**
Chile	14364	13238	16885	19040	22559	22863	22030	23728	26293	22460	Chili
Asia	**351078**	**351444**	**330803**	**224637**	**225630**	**229696**	**154130**	**156851**	**143601**	**140011**	**Asie**
Japan	[1]188692	[1]192553	[1]177682	...	...	...	11445	10771	8843	7972	Japon
Korea, Republic of	...	...	...	...	...	75628	70690	72171	57869	57794	Corée, République de
Sri Lanka[2]	1285	1137	1053	1027	...	...	...	...	...	...	Sri Lanka[2]
Turkey	...	...	60993	51961	57705	67520	70869	72783	75763	73119	Turquie
Europe	**450613**	**461534**	**434780**	**438573**	**440738**	**439064**	**445479**	**446424**	**450372**	**447970**	**Europe**
Croatia		4225	3638	3815	3659	2304	2443	2874	2860	...	Croatie
Czechoslovakia(former)	24509	21409	..	..	..	..	..	..	..	..	Tchécoslovaquie(anc.)
Czech Republic	..	..	21222	24721	29821	30864	35785	36320	35296	33909	République tchèque
France	132000	132932	124800	115200	106320	...	...	...	...	...	France
Germany	..	...	...	72938	76772	...	...	...	...	...	Allemagne
Germany(Fed.Rep.)	61160	..	..	..	..	..	..	..	..	..	Allemagne(Rép.féd.)
German D.R.(former)	13082	..	..	..	..	..	..	..	..	..	R.D.A. (anc.)
Hungary	11403	11088	10158	10392	...	...	...	...	...	...	Hongrie
Netherlands[3][4]	...	..	..	922	...	...	...	...	...	...	Pays-Bas[3][4]
Poland	17165	15424	17032	19477	20075	24673	29401	34678	43064	48537	Pologne
Portugal	31059	34028	...	...	...	...	...	...	...	...	Portugal
Romania	16564	16364	14803	17660	18563	18939	20984	22035	23919	26067	Roumanie
Spain	128907	127267	114015	...	...	...	...	...	...	...	Espagne
Sweden	...	...	...	...	...	13842	...	...	...	...	Suède
Yugoslavia	..	5227	3863	1411	1796	2134	3054	2698	3722	2796	Yougoslavie
T.F.Yug.Rep. Macedonia		3951	3086	2255	2268	2308	2879	3796	4397	3902	L'ex-RY Macédoine
Total	**853260**	**871544**	**829660**	**729906**	**736590**	**741214**	**675542**	**681682**	**673423**	**665125**	**Total**

General Note.

China or earthenware fittings designed to be permanently fixed in place, normally by connection to the water or sewage system (for example, sinks, wash basins, bidets, water closet pans, urinals and the like). Small accessory bathroom or sanitary fittings are excluded. (SITC, Rev.3: 81220-0B).

Remarque générale.

Appareils en porcelaine ou en faïence destinés à être fixés à demeure, généralement par branchement sur une conduite d'eau ou d'égout (par exemple, les éviers, les lavabos, les bidets, les cuvettes de cabinets d'aisances, les urinoirs etc.). Cette rubrique ne comprend pas les petits accessoires de salle de bain ou autres petits articles sanitaires. (CTCI, Rev.3: 81220-0B).

[1] Shipments by establishments employing 5 or more persons.
[2] State sector only.
[3] Sales.
[4] Production by establishments employing 20 or more persons.

[1] Expéditions des establissements occupant 5 personnes ou plus.
[2] Secteur public seulement.
[3] Ventes.
[4] Production des établissements occupant 20 personnes ou plus.

Glass, drawn or blown, in rectangles, unworked
Verres étirés ou soufflés, de forme rectangulaire, non travaillés

ISIC-BASED CODE - CODE BASE CITI

3620-01A

Unit : Thousand metric tons

Unité : Milliers de tonnes métriques

Country or area	1990	1991	1992	1993	1994	1995	1996	1997	1998	1999	Pays ou zone
Africa	**30**	**19**	**14**	**6**	**17**	**17**	**17**	**17**	**17**	**17**	**Afrique**
Algeria	30	19	14	6	...	...	...	...	...	...	Algérie
America, North	**3958**	**3603**	**3925**	**4084**	**4039**	**4021**	**4033**	**4052**	**4094**	**4116**	**Amérique du Nord**
Mexico	256	294	394	452	495	477	489	508	550	572	Mexique
United States	3702	3309	3531	3632	...	...	...	...	...	...	Etats-Unis
Asia	**923**	**954**	**1157**	**1024**	**1023**	**1042**	**1096**	**1066**	**939**	**1048**	**Asie**
Indonesia	247	267	423	...	...	...	...	...	...	...	Indonésie
Iran(Islamic Rep. of)[1]	209	205	247	...	...	...	...	...	...	...	Iran(Rép. islamique)[1]
Korea, Republic of	31	30	35	36	39	41	...	...	...	...	Corée, République de
Syrian Arab Republic[2]	38	54	53	57	54	70	58	69	57	...	Rép. arabe syrienne[2]
Thailand[3]	...	...	...	...	...	...	465	423	307	...	Thaïlande[3]
Europe	**587**	**581**	**696**	**597**	**604**	**515**	**444**	**447**	**360**	**334**	**Europe**
Austria	85	91	95	91	100	109	...	...	...	...	Autriche
Croatia	..	19	2	5	9	9	4	...	...	...	Croatie
Germany	..	...	...	9	9	...	...	...	...	...	Allemagne
Germany(Fed.Rep.)	56	..	..	..	..	..	..	..	..	...	Allemagne(Rép.féd.)
Hungary	56	36	188	158	160	...	...	...	1	1	Hongrie
Poland[4][5]	285	267	252	231	213	189	122	116	106	86	Pologne[4][5]
Portugal	105	86	...	...	...	...	...	...	...	...	Portugal
Yugoslavia	..	73	54	7	17	18	24	30	37	29	Yougoslavie
Total	**5498**	**5157**	**5791**	**5711**	**5683**	**5595**	**5589**	**5581**	**5410**	**5514**	**Total**

General Note.
Unworked drawn or blown glass (including flashed glass) in rectangles, used mainly for windows, doors, display cases, greenhouses, clocks and pictures, and sometimes as parts of articles of furniture, for photographic plates, plain spectacle glasses etc. Glass cut otherwise than into rectangles is excluded. (SITC, Rev.3: 66430-0A).

Remarque générale.
Verres étirés ou soufflés, non travaillés (y compris les verres plaqués) de forme rectangulaire, utilisés principalement dans le garnissage des fenêtres, des portes, des vitrines, des serres, des horloges et des tableaux, et servant parfois de recouvrement de meubles, de plaques photographiques, de lunettes ordinaires etc. Cette rubrique ne comprend pas les verres qui ne sont pas de forme rectangulaire. (CTCI, Rev.3: 66430-0A).

[1] Production by establishments employing 50 or more persons.
[2] Including pottery products.
[3] Beginning 1999, series discontinued.
[4] Drawn window glass.
[5] In terms of 2 mm thickness.

[1] Production des établissements occupant 50 personnes ou plus.
[2] Y compris la poterie.
[3] A partir de 1999, série abandonnée.
[4] Verre à vitres étiré.
[5] Sur la base de 2 mm d'épaisseur.

Glass, drawn or blown, in rectangles, unworked
Verres étirés ou soufflés, de forme rectangulaire, non travaillés

ISIC-BASED CODE - CODE BASE CITI
3620-01B

Unit : Thousand square metres

Unité : Milliers de mètres carrés

Country or area	1990	1991	1992	1993	1994	1995	1996	1997	1998	1999	Pays ou zone
America, North	**491268**	**457635**	**507866**	**552195**	**532145**	**528582**	**531130**	**534851**	**543157**	**547536**	**Amérique du Nord**
Mexico	51181	58959	74833	91061	98912	95349	97897	101618	109924	114303	Mexique
United States[1]	440087	398676	433033	461134	...	...	...	...	...	...	Etats-Unis[1]
America, South	**5684**	**5730**	**6657**	**7078**	**7159**	**6935**	**10897**	**21475**	**21800**	**22096**	**Amérique du Sud**
Chile	5684	5730	6653	7069	7089	6536	10659	21074	21313	21523	Chili
Ecuador	...	...	4	9	70	399	238	...	...	...	Equateur
Asia	**6514**	**10805**	**21898**	**17894**	**18793**	**21729**	**21951**	**21934**	**24529**	**25621**	**Asie**
Indonesia	...	#710	3528	...	...	...	...	...	...	...	Indonésie
Israel	4395	3974	4525	3975	11656	13088	13510	...	...	...	Israël
Kyrgyzstan	..	23	7723	6492	3683	2119	2762	2193	2084		Kirghizistan
Turkmenistan	..	6098	6122	5308	1335	4403	3560	336	1158	1257	Turkménistan
Europe	**164189**	**337855**	**329520**	**282944**	**223931**	**208272**	**185293**	**166211**	**140107**	**132210**	**Europe**
Austria[2]	5245	5907	5807	5669	6653	...	...	...	...	...	Autriche[2]
Belarus	..	9268	10366	8845	6896	5566	5045	#12154	12627	9487	Bélarus
Bulgaria	15371	12904	9991	7877	11030	12001	12346	10462	9551	...	Bulgarie
Croatia	..	2069	238	475	989	...	419	...	806	...	Croatie
Czechoslovakia(former)	23322	14775	..	..	...	...	...	...	...	...	Tchécoslovaquie(anc.)
Estonia	..	1600	784	731	1134	1489	...	...	...	..	Estonie
Finland	84	78	63	...	...	...	...	...	...	...	Finlande
Germany	...	...	...	1067	917	921	937	969	965	...	Allemagne
Germany(Fed.Rep.)	7150					..	..	..	..	..	Allemagne(Rép.féd.)
Hungary	11132	7166	38021	33691	34383	...	...	...	56	72	Hongrie
Latvia	..	4150	3445	378	...	...	...	...	...	...	Lettonie
Lithuania	..	4044	3788	1059	...	2451	2890	3201	3219	2715	Lituanie
Poland[3][4]	57191	53412	50469	46326	42923	37829	24258	23176	21085	17006	Pologne[3][4]
Romania[4]	44683	35016	36038	37320	29630	36200	36805	26445	23796	21940	Roumanie[4]
Russian Federation		127462	117601	101271	58576	58830	44814	38191	36177	38050	Fédération de Russie
Spain	...	...	...	...	...	...	...	...	...	11	Espagne
Ukraine	..	50856	45943	37361	23366	22890	26477	18634	16766	18334	Ukraine
Yugoslavia	..	8155	5978	788	1769	2100	2696	3270	3701	2859	Yougoslavie
USSR (former)	213172	..	..	..	..	..	..	..	..	..	URSS (anc.)
Total	**880827**	**812025**	**865941**	**860111**	**782027**	**765517**	**749270**	**744471**	**729593**	**727462**	**Total**

General Note.
Unworked drawn or blown glass (including flashed glass) in rectangles, used mainly for windows, doors, display cases, greenhouses, clocks and pictures, and sometimes as parts of articles of furniture, for photographic plates, plain spectacle glasses etc. Glass cut otherwise than into rectangles is excluded. (SITC, Rev.3: 66430-0B).

Remarque générale.
Verres étirés ou soufflés, non travaillés (y compris les verres plauqés) de forme rectangulaire, utilisés principalement dans le garnissage des fenêtres, des portes, des vitrines, des serres, des horloges et des tableaux, et servant parfois de recouvrement de meubles, de plaques photographiques, de lunettes ordinaires etc. Cette rubrique ne comprend pas les verres qui ne sont pas de forme rectangulaire. (CTCI, Rev.3: 66430-0B).

[1] Flat glass only.
[2] Beginning 1995, data are confidential.
[3] Drawn window glass.
[4] In terms of 2 mm thickness.

[1] Verre plat seulement.
[2] A partir de 1995, les données sont confidentielles
[3] Verre à vitres étiré.
[4] Sur la base de 2 mm d'épaisseur.

Glass, cast, rolled, drawn or blown
Verres coulés, laminés, étirés ou soufflés

ISIC-BASED CODE - CODE BASE CITI

3620-04A

Unit : Thousand metric tons

Unité : Milliers de tonnes métriques

Country or area	1990	1991	1992	1993	1994	1995	1996	1997	1998	1999	Pays ou zone
Africa	**26**	**25**	**24**	**22**	**21**	**23**	**21**	**24**	**19**	**20**	**Afrique**
Egypt	26	25	24	22	21	23	21	24	19	20	Egypte
America, North	**58**	**55**	**26**	**94**	**92**	**85**	**96**	**104**	**116**	**125**	**Amérique du Nord**
Mexico	58	55	26	94	92	85	96	104	116	125	Mexique
Asia	**1116**	**1118**	**1156**	**1166**	**1170**	**1191**	**1198**	**1302**	**1345**	**1234**	**Asie**
Indonesia	...	...	...	...	637	...	...	...	...	...	Indonésie
Turkey	440	449	482	493	497	518	525	629	672	561	Turquie
Viet Nam	39	32	37	...	...	...	...	...	...	...	Viet Nam
Europe	**2405**	**2594**	**2639**	**2614**	**2710**	**2698**	**2602**	**2743**	**2773**	**2786**	**Europe**
Croatia	..	1	1	1	1	2	0	0	...	...	Croatie
Germany	..	1524	1646	1531	...	...	...	...	...	...	Allemagne
Germany(Fed.Rep.)	1317	..	..	..	..	..	..	..	..	..	Allemagne(Rép.féd.)
Greece	50	38	5	..	..	...	...	...	...	...	Grèce
Hungary	41	16	12	...	...	...	...	...	...	...	Hongrie
Italy	816	859	826	863	892	880	796	934	961	971	Italie
Sweden	181	156	149	165	196	195	...	...	...	...	Suède
Total	**3605**	**3792**	**3845**	**3896**	**3993**	**3997**	**3917**	**4173**	**4253**	**4165**	**Total**

General Note.

Cast, rolled, drawn or blown glass (including flashed or wired glass) in rectangles, surface ground or polished, but not further worked, used mainly in furniture, for the manufacture of mirrors etc., in bay windows and display windows, show cases, ships etc. Glass cut to shape other than rectangular, bent and curved glass are excluded. (SITC, Rev.3: 66440-0A).

Remarque générale.

Verres coulés, laminés, étirés ou soufflés (y compris les verres plaqués ou armés) de forme rectangulaire, simplement doucis ou polis, utilisés principalement dans l'ameublement, dans la fabrication d'articles de miroiterie, etc., dans la garniture de baies de maisons, de vitrines de magasins, de navires, etc. Cette rubrique ne comprend pas les verres qui ne sont pas de forme rectangulaire ou qui sont incurvés et bombés. (CTCI, Rev.3: 66440-0A).

Glass fibres (including glass wool)
Fibres de verre (y compris la laine de verre)

ISIC-BASED CODE - CODE BASE CITI

3620-05

Unit : Metric tons

Unité : Tonnes métriques

Country or area	1990	1991	1992	1993	1994	1995	1996	1997	1998	1999	Pays ou zone
America, North	**5000**	**5000**	**7000**	**14487**	**15104**	**19400**	**19904**	**22634**	**25978**	**28164**	**Amérique du Nord**
Mexico	5000	5000	7000	14487	15104	19400	19904	22634	25978	28164	Mexique
America, South	**1260**	**1260**	**703**	**1810**	**1665**	**860**	**1260**	**1260**	**1260**	**1260**	**Amérique du Sud**
Colombia	...	...	703	1810	1665	860	...	...	...	...	Colombie
Asia	**124796**	**204844**	**194124**	**88159**	**217703**	**435959**	**368168**	**343357**	**289129**	**340129**	**Asie**
China	86900	120800	115300	12100	124900	328057	254800	205700	153300	162200	Chine
Indonesia	...	...	297	3197	2411	...	...	...	...	...	Indonésie
Korea, Republic of	35928	44976	50027	59524	86767	104846	111400	135689	133861	175961	Corée, République de
Turkmenistan	..	37100	28500	13338	3625	1088	...	...	...	...	Turkménistan
Europe	**616868**	**602148**	**547771**	**466643**	**512883**	**542046**	**524768**	**489477**	**492593**	**481283**	**Europe**
Belarus	..	20852	17338	9407	7051	11305	13264	13228	13690	16500	Bélarus
Belgium	...		...	...	...	...	...	40122	...	...	Belgique
Bulgaria	14363	10182	5935	11190	8824	3844	3438	2560	1675	902	Bulgarie
Czechoslovakia(former)	28000	23000	..	..	..	..	..	..	..	..	Tchécoslovaquie(anc.)
Czech Republic	..	..	..	..	7172	10526	11876	12509	11605	10729	République tchèque
Finland	52651	60527	58036	55409	64583	63780	87030	...	...	...	Finlande
Germany	..	...	99158	96303	104767	51906	54836	54525	56625	..	Allemagne
Germany(Fed.Rep.)	100000	..	..	..	..	..	..	..	..	..	Allemagne(Rép.féd.)
Hungary	...	...	...	...	...	...	...	2415	2224	3060	Hongrie
Italy	105000	92000	94925	82000	78257	119120	115430	104373	124435	134452	Italie
Latvia	..	...	...	1725	1118	3182	3127	3349	4333	4327	Lettonie
Romania	...	3376	2999	...	...	...	...	...	...	...	Roumanie
Spain	82000	76000	67802	18925	29176	91581	...	...	...	...	Espagne
Sweden	113000	93000	70101	74558	...	54713	...	...	...	...	Suède
United Kingdom	...	...	...	60998	83653	83170	86873	76896	64341	...	Royaume-Uni
T.F.Yug.Rep. Macedonia	..	...	1828	444	1332	3043	1454	961	960	...	L'ex-RY Macédoine
Total	**747924**	**813252**	**749598**	**571099**	**747355**	**998265**	**914100**	**856728**	**808960**	**850836**	**Total**

General Note.
Glass fibres, including glass wool, and articles made therefrom, n.e.s.
(SITC, Rev.3: 66495-0).

Remarque générale.
Fibres de verre (y compris la laine de verre) et ouvrages en ces matières,
n.d.a. (CTCI, Rev.3: 66495-0).

Glass, safety, of toughened or laminated glass
Glaces ou verres de sécurité consistant en verre trempé ou feuilleté

ISIC-BASED CODE - CODE BASE CITI

3620-07A

Unit : Thousand metric tons   Unité : Milliers de tonnes métriques

Country or area	1990	1991	1992	1993	1994	1995	1996	1997	1998	1999	Pays ou zone
Africa	**2**	**2**	**1**	**1**	**2**	**3**	**2**	**2**	**2**	**2**	**Afrique**
Algeria	1	1	0	0	0	0	0	0	0	0	Algérie
Egypt	1	1	1	1	2	3	2	2	...	...	Egypte
America, North	**571**	**464**	**509**	**648**	**735**	**632**	**729**	**807**	**843**	**881**	**Amérique du Nord**
Mexico	45	51	54	56	57	51	57	69	70	72	Mexique
United States [1]	526	413	455	592	678	581	672	...	...	...	Etats-Unis [1]
Europe	**613**	**610**	**614**	**544**	**570**	**508**	**515**	**516**	**533**	**645**	**Europe**
Austria	...	...	21	23	27	29	...	...	...	...	Autriche
Belgium [2]	...	...	...	...	29	32	32	36	37	34	Belgique [2]
Croatia	..	3	2	1	2	3	2	2	2	...	Croatie
Germany	..	...	...	261	283	...	...	...	...	...	Allemagne
Germany(Fed.Rep.)	261	..	..	..	..	..	..	..	..	..	Allemagne(Rép.féd.)
German D.R.(former)	19	..	..	..	..	..	..	..	..	..	R.D.A. (anc.)
Greece	2	1	1	...	...	...	...	...	...	...	Grèce
Hungary	6	5	4	4	5	5	5	7	10	10	Hongrie
Italy	227	223	234	182	172	159	145	145	158	273	Italie
Sweden	43	42	40	39	47	5	...	...	...	...	Suède
Yugoslavia	..	7	8	0	3	1	6	3	6	9	Yougoslavie
T.F.Yug.Rep. Macedonia	..	1	1	1	1	1	...	...	...	...	L'ex-RY Macédoine
Total	**1186**	**1076**	**1124**	**1193**	**1308**	**1143**	**1246**	**1324**	**1379**	**1529**	**Total**

General Note.

Toughened or laminated glass, shaped or not, used for motor-car windscreens and windows, in doors, in ships' portholes, in protective goggles for industrial workers and drivers, and for eye-pieces for gas masks and divers' helmets. Ordinary wired glass and selective absorption glasses are excluded. (SITC, Rev.3: 66470-0A).

Remarque générale.

Glaces ou verres trempés ou feuilletés, façonnés ou non, utilisés dans la fabrication de pare-brise et de fenêtres d'automobiles, de portes, de hublots de navires, de lunettes de protection pour ouvriers et conducteurs, ainsi que des verres de masques à gaz et de casques de scaphandriers. Cette rubrique ne comprend pas les verres armés ordinaires et les verres à absorption sélective. (CTCI, REv.3: 66470-0A).

[1] Flat glass only.
[2] Incomplete coverage.

[1] Verre plat seulement.
[2] Couverture incomplète.

Glass bottles and other containers of common glass
Bouteilles et autres récipients en verre ordinaire

ISIC-BASED CODE - CODE BASE CITI

3620-10A

Unit : Million units   Unité : En millions

Country or area	1990	1991	1992	1993	1994	1995	1996	1997	1998	1999	Pays ou zone
Africa	**7**	**17**	**11**	**9**	**19**	**27**	**21**	**17**	**27**	**28**	**Afrique**
Burundi	5	5	5	3	...	...	...	...	...	...	Burundi
Ethiopia	2	12	5	6	14	22	16	12	22	23	Ethiopie
America, North	**46659**	**45621**	**46124**	**47252**	**47412**	**45377**	**43410**	**44087**	**44521**	**44327**	**Amérique du Nord**
Mexico	4942	5141	4933	5258	5858	6408	6853	7446	7911	7518	Mexique
United States	41717	40480	41191	41994	41554	38969	36557	36641	[1]36610	[1]36809	Etats-Unis
America, South	**867**	**1219**	**1221**	**1220**	**1386**	**1487**	**1642**	**1744**	**1846**	**1948**	**Amérique du Sud**
Bolivia	19	17	27	23	58	*46	...	...	...	...	Bolivie
Colombia	831	...	1176	1179	1311	1423		...	...	...	Colombie
Paraguay	17	18	18	...	...	...	...	...	...	...	Paraguay
Asia	**449**	**1434**	**2661**	**1545**	**1168**	**1214**	**1204**	**1490**	**570**	**799**	**Asie**
Armenia	..	85	10	11	8	5	2	20	22	50	Arménie
Azerbaijan	..	51	12	0	1	1	1	0	0	0	Azerbaïdjan
Indonesia	210	792	2146	951	778	...	...	1117	97	...	Indonésie
Iran(Islamic Rep. of)[2]	221	274	263	295	230	280	260	268	392	...	Iran(Rép. islamique)[2]
Kyrgyzstan	..	97	93	72	47	0	1	18	9	12	Kirghizistan
Myanmar[3]	18	16	14	13	16	9	28	32	18	...	Myanmar[3]
Tajikistan	..	105	110	188	74	39	35	26	26	33	Tadjikistan
Turkmenistan	..	...	...	15	14	10	7	9	6	...	Turkménistan
Europe	**14932**	**31734**	**31539**	**32975**	**33606**	**34435**	**34944**	**35914**	**37090**	**37145**	**Europe**
Belarus	..	246	287	263	206	180	237	260	323	341	Bélarus
Belgium	...	...	...	...	150	282	150	204	143	160	Belgique
Croatia	...	...	...	...	...	...	...	...	391	...	Croatie
Denmark[4]	...	...	...	...	...	609	569	568	555	615	Danemark[4]
Czechoslovakia(former)	1335	1389	..	..	..	..	..	..	..	..	Tchécoslovaquie(anc.)
Czech Republic	..	..	939	898	1135	1297	1394	1373	1467	1403	République tchèque
Estonia	..	13	9	29	54	73	80	120	134	107	Estonie
Finland	187	167	165	172	174	195	208	...	...	198	Finlande
Germany	...	...	...	...	...	...	...	15228	15447	...	Allemagne
German D.R.(former)	1277	..	..	..	..	..	..	..	..	..	R.D.A. (anc.)
Hungary	801	610	381	418	487	553	182	645	498	286	Hongrie
Latvia	..	93	49	75	16	41	60	58	108	55	Lettonie
Lithuania	..	56	46	61	90	129	156	112	130	88	Lituanie
Poland	3145	3205	2914	3190	3407	3611	3760	4095	4134	4272	Pologne
Portugal	1667	1853	[5]1936	[5]1947	2333	2599	3056	3133	3079	3464	Portugal
Russian Federation	..	1262	1372	2937	2227	2274	2310	2251	2636	3045	Fédération de Russie
Slovakia	..	..	..	..	...	...	640	407	509	383	Slovaquie
Slovenia	..	159	94	70	65	95	45	38	52	42	Slovénie
Spain	...	...	...	5276	5904	5712	5777	6280	6757	...	Espagne
Sweden	...	...	...	...	...	...	391	...	370	409	Suède
Yugoslavia	..	315	378	257	171	182	200	178	174	106	Yougoslavie
Total	**62914**	**80025**	**81556**	**83001**	**83591**	**82540**	**81220**	**83252**	**84054**	**84246**	**Total**

General Note.

Bottles of all shapes and sizes, jars, pots and similar containers, and stoppers and closures of common glass, blown, pressed or moulded, but not otherwise worked. Inners for vacuum vessels are excluded. (SITC, Rev.3: 66511-0A).

Remarque générale.

Bouteilles de toutes formes et de toutes dimensions, bocaux, pots et récipients similaires et bouchons, couvercles et autres dispositifs de fermeture en verre ordinaire fabriqués par soufflage, pressage ou moulage, mais n'ayant subi aucune autre ouvraison. Cette rubrique ne comprend pas les ampoules en verre pour récipients isolants. (CTCI, Rev.3: 66511-0A).

[1] Shipments.
[2] Production by establishments employing 50 or more persons.
[3] Government production only.
[4] Sales.
[5] Incomplete coverage.

[1] Expéditions.
[2] Production des établissements occupant 50 personnes ou plus.
[3] Production de l'Etat seulement.
[4] Ventes.
[5] Couverture incomplète.

Glass bottles and other containers of common glass
Bouteilles et autres récipients en verre ordinaire

ISIC-BASED CODE - CODE BASE CITI

3620-10B

Unit : Thousand metric tons

Unité : Milliers de tonnes métriques

Country or area	1990	1991	1992	1993	1994	1995	1996	1997	1998	1999	Pays ou zone
Africa	**227**	**227**	**221**	**232**	**241**	**255**	**259**	**278**	**278**	**284**	**Afrique**
Algeria	28	37	25	25	29	24	17	18	16	14	Algérie
Egypt	140	147	139	150	145	154	160	163	...	...	Egypte
Kenya	22	5	19	22	34	48	46	...	...	...	Kenya
Tunisia	24	24	24	22	25	17	26	24	26	27	Tunisie
United Rep.Tanzania	13	14	14	13	8	12	10	14	...	...	Rép. Unie de Tanzanie
America, North	**9940**	**9586**	**10024**	**10422**	**10278**	**10491**	**10647**	**10792**	**10922**	**11081**	**Amérique du Nord**
Jamaica	22	19	32	31	28	21	28	24	6	...	Jamaïque
United States	9918	9567	9992	10391	10250	...	...	...	...	...	Etats-Unis
America, South	**112**	**148**	**226**	**234**	**237**	**164**	**157**	**183**	**247**	**238**	**Amérique du Sud**
Chile	77	83	101	108	108	123	152	180	190	199	Chili
Ecuador	35	...	125	126	129	41	5	3	57	...	Equateur
Asia	**3744**	**3628**	**3299**	**3826**	**3402**	**3415**	**3356**	**3215**	**3096**	**2901**	**Asie**
Indonesia	...	...	198	766	78	...	...	178	223	...	Indonésie
Japan[1][2]	2610	2445	2370	2351	2440	2233	2210	2160	1975	1905	Japon[1][2]
Korea, Republic of	677	768	731	709	884	893	...	...	...	...	Corée, République de
Europe	**9125**	**9884**	**9524**	**9466**	**9862**	**10019**	**9960**	**10021**	**10203**	**10067**	**Europe**
Austria[3]	295	332	321	297	315	...	...	...	...	...	Autriche[3]
Bulgaria	281	207	178	204	252	312	335	222	...	...	Bulgarie
Croatia	..	223	136	125	147	146	134	112	133	...	Croatie
France	2793	2824	2861	2719	2894	...	...	...	...	...	France
Germany	..	...	...	...	...	571	608	603	608	...	Allemagne
German D.R.(former)	344	..	..	..	..	..	..	..	..	..	R.D.A. (anc.)
Greece	69	71	86	...	...	...	...	...	...	...	Grèce
Hungary	326	227	140	172	198	234	57	222	166	93	Hongrie
Italy	2610	2784	2734	2789	2863	2909	2908	2930	3046	3084	Italie
Poland	577	592	565	624	712	777	811	873	918	928	Pologne
Romania	307	250	206	165	181	203	216	185	160	95	Roumanie
Slovenia	..	10	11	6	9	10	...	0	15	12	Slovénie
Spain	1400	1464	1443	...	...	...	...	...	...	...	Espagne
Sweden	123	145	111	165	107	97	...	...	...	...	Suède
Yugoslavia	..	157	134	91	76	88	86	71	73	44	Yougoslavie
Total	**23148**	**23473**	**23294**	**24179**	**24021**	**24343**	**24379**	**24489**	**24745**	**24571**	**Total**

General Note.
Bottles of all shapes and sizes, jars, pots and similar containers, and stoppers and closures of common glass, blown, pressed or moulded, but not otherwise worked. Inners for vacuum vessels are excluded. (SITC, REv.3: 66511-0B).

Remarque générale.
Bouteilles de toutes formes et de toutes dimensions, bocaux, pots et récipients similaires et bouchons, couvercles et autres dispositifs de fermeture en verre ordinaire fabriqués par soufflage, pressage ou moulage, mais n'ayant subi aucune autre ouvraison. Cette rubrique ne comprend pas les ampoules en verre pour récipients isolants. (CTCI, Rev.3: 66511-0B).

[1] Production by establishments employing 10 or more persons.
[2] Shipments.
[3] Beginning 1995, data are confidential.

[1] Production des établissements occupant 10 personnes ou plus.
[2] Expéditions.
[3] A partir de 1995, les données sont confidentielles

Building bricks, made of clay
Briques de construction en argile
ISIC-BASED CODE - CODE BASE CITI

3691-01A

Unit : Million units   Unité : En millions

Country or area	1990	1991	1992	1993	1994	1995	1996	1997	1998	1999	Pays ou zone
Africa	**2080**	**1979**	**2185**	**2081**	**1945**	**1984**	**2143**	**2277**	**2093**	**1494**	**Afrique**
Egypt	70	95	105	...	142	...	...	...	...	...	Egypte
Ethiopia	19	22	21	20	20	19	16	20	20	19	Ethiopie
South Africa	1991	1862	2059	1958	1783	1862	2024	2154	1970	1372	Afrique du Sud
America, North	**7178**	**5977**	**6071**	**7060**	**7380**	**7390**	**7607**	**8038**	**8285**	**8782**	**Amérique du Nord**
Mexico	62	38	42	#256	227	146	181	200	204	229	Mexique
United States	7116	5939	6029	6804	7153	7244	7426	7838	8081	8553	Etats-Unis
America, South	**1068**	**1375**	**1320**	**1373**	**1367**	**1295**	**1410**	**1544**	**1473**	**1578**	**Amérique du Sud**
Bolivia	16	15	16	21	19	20	...	...	...	...	Bolivie
Brazil	378	656	592	624	602	566	550	567	546	537	Brésil
Chile	44	63	75	89	88	84	97	85	94	114	Chili
Colombia	...	...	444	...	468	435	...	...	...	...	Colombie
Ecuador	...	...	3	2	2	2	106	234	175	...	Equateur
Paraguay	181	192	190	...	...	...	...	...	...	...	Paraguay
Asia	**468063**	**477091**	**603896**	**669521**	**731553**	**791103**	**752085**	**742060**	**349015**	**241165**	**Asie**
Azerbaijan	..	129	81	64	62	26	11	11	14	10	Azerbaïdjan
China	448507	456041	591193	657446	720431	771043	731563	722735	330446	223030	Chine
Cyprus	57	60	62	62	55	55	54	49	44	50	Chypre
Georgia	..	...	47	23	9	7	9	13	13	8	Géorgie
Indonesia	246	109	127	176	175	...	...	221	252	...	Indonésie
Iran(Islamic Rep. of)	[1]12850	[1]10292	[2]2502	[2]2208	[2]2077	[1]11564	[1]12020	[1]10957	[1]11053	...	Iran(Rép. islamique)
Korea, Republic of	1215	1195	744	714	661	579	...	...	...	...	Corée, République de
Kyrgyzstan	..	804	433	192	94	92	99	100	103	88	Kirghizistan
Malaysia	489	542	575	592	719	819	912	983	774	757	Malaisie
Mongolia	151	108	54	33	34	22	25	16	19	17	Mongolie
Myanmar[3]	61	62	55	63	59	63	61	67	68	64	Myanmar[3]
Nepal[4][5]	...	...	35	27	24	23	26	32	28	*23	Népal[4][5]
Tajikistan	..	263	142	93	72	71	39	27	33	33	Tadjikistan
Turkey	983	1037	1032	1253	1209	1149	1251	1251	1190	1108	Turquie
Turkmenistan	..	545	473	404	368	375	371	278	245	...	Turkménistan
Uzbekistan	..	2083	2062	2328	1661	1185	1038	969	...	...	Ouzbékistan
Viet Nam	3476	3769	4274	...	...	...	...	...	...	...	Viet Nam
Yemen	..	2	5	...	...	...	...	...	...	...	Yémen
Europe	**16634**	**49960**	**45480**	**41136**	**35284**	**32974**	**27679**	**26017**	**25779**	**25981**	**Europe**
Austria	209	211	214	226	231	211	...	...	...	...	Autriche
Belarus	..	1074	1044	925	726	732	584	654	672	514	Bélarus
Belgium[6]	164	173	120	105	...	...	...	...	...	...	Belgique[6]
Bulgaria	959	646	633	637	666	668	622	412	361	259	Bulgarie
Croatia	..	702	536	481	475	555	688	438	409	...	Croatie
Denmark[7]	291	291	302	279	390	363	378	419	423	405	Danemark[7]
Czechoslovakia(former)	2203	1704		..	..	..	..	..	..	..	Tchécoslovaquie(anc.)
Czech Republic	..	..	1067	1326	1307	1356	1434	1522	1445	1332	République tchèque
Estonia	..	222	131	52	48	10	10	9	7	9	Estonie
Finland	113	90	66	61	57	52	40	60	...	127	Finlande
German D.R.(former)	1022		..	..	..	..	..	..	..	..	R.D.A. (anc.)
Greece	1326	1430	1415	...	871	812	813	901	1044	...	Grèce
Hungary	1828	1311	1012	1163	1220	1388	643	305	1260	1207	Hongrie
Latvia[8]	..	409	170	48	33	26	23	25	33	...	Lettonie[8]
Lithuania[9]	..	1087	817	420	344	240	196	160	154	142	Lituanie[9]
Netherlands[7][10]	1432	1366	1387	1435	1493	1366	...	...	...	...	Pays-Bas[7][10]
Poland	856	729	788	871	871	890	848	980	885	760	Pologne
Republic of Moldova	..	218	154	[11]150	[11]64	[11]39	[11]37	[11]48	[11]49	[11]45	Rép. de Moldova
Romania	691	633	512	618	473	499	626	493	410	447	Roumanie
Russian Federation	..	23668	21697	18959	14655	13893	10943	10052	9592	10771	Fédération de Russie
Slovakia	..	..	...	...	...	523	414	1371	...	...	Slovaquie
Slovenia	..	251	229	210	193	211	...	...	...	...	Slovénie
Sweden	6	3	...	0	...	...	...	...	...	...	Suède
Switzerland	153	134	...	...	...	...	...	...	...	...	Suisse
Ukraine	..	6662	5785	5142	4008	2735	1879	1606	1579	1629	Ukraine
United Kingdom*	...	...	...	5000	5000	5000	4000	3000	3000	...	Royaume-Uni*

For general note and footnotes, see end of table.   Voir la fin du tableau pour la remarque générale et les notes.

Building bricks, made of clay (continued)
Briques de construction en argile (suite)

ISIC-BASED CODE - CODE BASE CITI

3691-01A

Unit : Million units   Unité : En millions

Country or area	1990	1991	1992	1993	1994	1995	1996	1997	1998	1999	Pays ou zone
Yugoslavia	..	1701	1486	943	1001	1032	1291	1374	1424	999	Yougoslavie
T.F.Yug.Rep. Macedonia	..	107	104	96	102	86	98	86	95	102	L'ex-RY Macédoine
USSR (former)	33588	..	..	..	..	..	..	..	..	..	URSS (anc.)
Oceania	1922	1653	1652	1775	1869	1673	1416	1532	1593	1736	Océanie
Australia	1922	1653	1652	1775	1869	1673	1416	1532	1593	1736	Australie
Total	530534	538035	660604	722946	779399	836419	792340	781468	388238	280736	Total

General Note.

Clay bricks for building purposes, including common and facing bricks (solid, hollow, shaped or perforated). Glazed, refractory, paving, concrete, shale and sand-lime bricks are excluded. (SITC, Rev.3: 66241-1A).

[1] Production by establishments employing 10 or more persons.
[2] Production by establishments employing 50 or more persons.
[3] Government production only.
[4] Production by government-owned enterprises only.
[5] Twelve months beginning 16 July of year stated.
[6] Excluding hollow bricks.
[7] Sales.
[8] Standard size.
[9] Including concrete bricks.
[10] Production by establishments employing 20 or more persons.
[11] Excluding Transnistria region.

Remarque générale.

Briques en argile pour la construction, y compris les briques ordinaires et les briques de parement (pleines, creuses, faconnées ou perforées). Cette rubrique ne comprend pas les briques vernissées, les briques réfractaires, les briques de pavement, les briques en béton et en schiste et les briques silico-calcaires. (CTCI, Rev.3: 66241-1A).

[1] Production des établissements occupant 10 personnes ou plus.
[2] Production des établissements occupant 50 personnes ou plus.
[3] Production de l'Etat seulement.
[4] Production des établissements d'Etat seulement.
[5] Période de douze mois commençant le 16 juillet de l'année indiquée.
[6] Non compris les briques creuses.
[7] Ventes.
[8] De taille courante.
[9] Y compris les briques en béton.
[10] Production des établissements occupant 20 personnes ou plus.
[11] Non compris la région de Transnistria.

Building bricks, made of clay
Briques de construction en argile

ISIC-BASED CODE - CODE BASE CITI

3691-01B

Unit : Thousand cubic metres   Unité : Milliers de mètres cubes

Country or area	1990	1991	1992	1993	1994	1995	1996	1997	1998	1999	Pays ou zone
Africa											**Afrique**
Algeria[1]	1644	1617	1776	1691	1548	1488	1567	1507	1586	1581	Algérie[1]
Asia											**Asie**
Cyprus	344	362	374	374	332	332	326	296	266	302	Chypre
Kuwait	...	...	135	251	469	434	379	506	505	...	Koweït
Europe											**Europe**
Austria[2][3]	1164	1175	1192	1259	1286	...	...	...	...	...	Autriche[2][3]
Belarus	..	2148	2088	1850	1452	1464	1168	1308	1343	1027	Bélarus
Belgium	[1][4]2431	[1][4]2322	[1][4]2394	[1][4]2496	...	...	[5]2445	[5]2739	[5]2437	[5]2426	Belgique
Croatia	..	1369	1045	...	...	...	...	1591	1830	...	Croatie
Czechoslovakia(former)	4296	3323	..	..	...	...					Tchécoslovaquie(anc.)
Czech Republic	..	..	2081	2586	2508	2726	2876	3022	2787	2587	République tchèque
France[1]	2791	2611	2564	2394	2387	...	...	...	...	...	France[1]
Germany	..	10453	11534	12550	15051	14482	13049	13307	13114	...	Allemagne
Germany(Fed.Rep.)	9422		..	..	..	..	..	..	..	..	Allemagne(Rép.féd.)
German D.R.(former)[6]	1594		..	..	..	..	..	..	..		R.D.A. (anc.)[6]
Hungary	4142	2661	1502	1566	1625	2076	2369	2360	2430	2305	Hongrie
Latvia	..	..	...	...	...	...	...	...	...	71	Lettonie
Netherlands[7][8]	...	...	...	1761	1848	1692	1620	1789	1662	1405	Pays-Bas[7][8]
Poland[6]	1335	1137	1230	1359	1359	1388	1324	1528	1381	1186	Pologne[6]
Portugal	[1]3769	[1]3316	2017	1818	2045	2618	2758	[1]3	[1]4	[1]5	Portugal
Slovakia	..	..	...	...	...	...	...	...	516	312	Slovaquie
Slovenia	..	..	...	...	...	...	337	359	379	448	Slovénie
Spain	[1]9573	[1]10821	[1]10749	10883	12054	12967	13284	15129	...	...	Espagne
Sweden	12	5	...	0	...	...	34	30	30	25	Suède
Ukraine	..	13323	11571	10283	8016	5470	3757	3212	3158	3257	Ukraine
USSR (former)	59153	..	..	..	..	..	..	..	..	..	URSS (anc.)

General Note.

Clay bricks for building purposes, including common and facing bricks (solid, hollow, shaped or perforated). Glazed, refractory, paving, concrete, shale and sand-lime bricks are excluded. (SITC, Rev.3: 66241-1B).

[1] In thousand metric tons.
[2] Original data in thousand standard bricks of dimensions 0.25 x 0.12 x 0.065 m.

[3] Beginning 1995, data are confidential.
[4] Excluding hollow bricks for partitions and ceilings.
[5] Ceramic facing bricks only.
[6] Original data in pieces, 641 pieces = 1 cubic metre.
[7] Production by establishments employing 20 or more persons.
[8] Sales.

Remarque générale.

Briques en argile pour la construction, y compris les briques ordinaires et les briques de parement (pleines, creuses, façonnées ou perforées). Cette rubrique ne comprend pas les briques vernissées, les briques réfractaires, les briques de pavement, les briques en béton et en schiste et les briques silico-calcaires. (CTCI. Rev.3: 66241-1B).

[1] En milliers de tonnes métriques.
[2] Données d'origine exprimées en milliers de briques type des dimensions suivantes: 0,25 x 0,12 x 0,065 m.
[3] A partir de 1995, les données sont confidentielles
[4] Non compris les briques creuses pour hourdis.
[5] Briques de pavage, en céramique, seulement.
[6] Données d'origine exprimées en unités (641 unités = 1 mètre cube).
[7] Production des établissements occupant 20 personnes ou plus.
[8] Ventes.

Tiles, roofing, made of clay
Tuiles de couverture en argile

ISIC-BASED CODE - CODE BASE CITI

3691-04A

Unit : Million units   Unité : En millions

Country or area	1990	1991	1992	1993	1994	1995	1996	1997	1998	1999	Pays ou zone
Africa	**66**	**122**	**71**	**80**	**39**	**81**	**88**	**70**	**68**	**66**	**Afrique**
Kenya	66	122	71	80	39	81	88	...	...	...	Kenya
America, North	**16**	**13**	**14**	**24**	**25**	**18**	**15**	**19**	**23**	**24**	**Amérique du Nord**
Mexico	16	13	14	24	25	18	15	19	23	24	Mexique
America, South	**34**	**36**	**32**	**38**	**40**	**44**	**38**	**39**	**39**	**39**	**Amérique du Sud**
Bolivia	6	5	4	7	6	*9	...	...	...	...	Bolivie
Colombia	9	...	9	...	15	16	...	...	...	...	Colombie
Paraguay	19	19	19	...	...	...	...	...	...	...	Paraguay
Asia	**49179**	**50382**	**62669**	**54288**	**54599**	**54448**	**54444**	**54498**	**54562**	**54488**	**Asie**
China	48192	49321	61468	...	...	...	...	...	...	...	Chine
Cyprus	5	4	4	3	3	5	3	5	5	7	Chypre
Indonesia[1]	341	362	507	524	868	...	...	623	736	...	Indonésie[1]
Malaysia	52	64	71	96	88	83	134	149	119	116	Malaisie
Turkey	184	167	174	198	179	190	197	174	180	183	Turquie
Viet Nam	405	455	431	...	...	561	478	482	434	*420	Viet Nam
Yemen	..	9	14	15	9	49	72	71	...	...	Yémen
Europe	**1406**	**1817**	**1892**	**1735**	**1902**	**2113**	**2233**	**2262**	**2359**	**2367**	**Europe**
Austria[2]	25	37	45	39	38	...	...	...	...	...	Autriche[2]
Bulgaria	39	31	25	24	24	25	31	19	11	9	Bulgarie
Croatia	..	57	42	42	36	49	69	57	57	...	Croatie
Denmark[3]	...	...	...	...	22	23	26	29	27	25	Danemark[3]
Czechoslovakia(former)	44	45	..	..	..	..	..	..	..	..	Tchécoslovaquie(anc.)
Czech Republic	..	..	33	33	30	...	...	...	...	...	République tchèque
Finland	20	8	...	...	...	...	...	...	...	...	Finlande
Germany	..	556	633	671	746	822	865	840	886	...	Allemagne
Germany(Fed.Rep.)	493	..	..	..	..	..	..	..	..	..	Allemagne(Rép.féd.)
German D.R.(former)	9	..	..	..	..	..	..	..	..	..	R.D.A. (anc.)
Greece	108	115	112	90	68	85	111	115	111	...	Grèce
Hungary	96	73	66	55	73	80	84	88	80	72	Hongrie
Latvia	..	3	2	1	1	1	0	0	0	0	Lettonie
Netherlands[3] [4]	47	48	50	58	67	...	...	...	...	...	Pays-Bas[3] [4]
Poland	21	27	32	31	52	55	61	67	71	74	Pologne
Portugal	...	...	122	132	139	167	163	185	186	202	Portugal
Romania	49	48	60	61	54	53	53	38	33	36	Roumanie
Slovenia	..	26	35	45	35	31	18	16	17	12	Slovénie
Spain	195	234	243	184	255	277	268	285	331	363	Espagne
Sweden	9	8	7	8	8	8	9	10	10	10	Suède
United Kingdom	...	...	...	91	81	106	89	99	97	...	Royaume-Uni
Yugoslavia	..	224	239	116	143	154	200	219	239	198	Yougoslavie
T.F.Yug.Rep. Macedonia	..	19	17	16	16	17	18	19	19	22	L'ex-RY Macédoine
Total	**50701**	**52370**	**64677**	**56165**	**56605**	**56704**	**56818**	**56887**	**57050**	**56984**	**Total**

General Note.
Clay tiles for roofs, for topping walls etc. They may be flat, half cylinders, or of special shapes for eaves, ridges, hips or valleys. (SITC, Rev.3: 66242-1A).

Remarque générale.
Tuiles d'argile pour toitures, couronnement des murs etc. Elles peuvent être plates, demi-rondes ou de forme spéciale (tuiles pour pignons, tuiles faîtières, tuiles de rives, tuiles d'arêtiers). (CTCI, Rev.3: 66242-1A).

[1] Including concrete tiles.
[2] Beginning 1995, data are confidential.
[3] Sales.
[4] Production by establishments employing 20 or more persons.

[1] Y compris les tuiles en béton.
[2] A partir de 1995, les données sont confidentielles
[3] Ventes.
[4] Production des établissements occupant 20 personnes ou plus.

Tiles, roofing, made of clay
Tuiles de couverture en argile

ISIC-BASED CODE - CODE BASE CITI

3691-04B

Unit : Million square metres

Unité : Millions de mètres carrés

Country or area	1990	1991	1992	1993	1994	1995	1996	1997	1998	1999	Pays ou zone
Africa											**Afrique**
Algeria[1]	35	31	31	29	31	20	24	23	25	30	Algérie[1]
Egypt	17	17	19	19	20	21	22	28	29	30	Egypte
Asia											**Asie**
Azerbaijan	..	11	3	1	0	0	0	0	0	0	Azerbaïdjan
Europe											**Europe**
Belarus	..	2	1	2	33	45	264	425	115	141	Bélarus
Belgium[1]	123	126	118	108	...	...	...	...	...	...	Belgique[1]
Czechoslovakia(former)	3	3	..	..	..	..	..	..	..	..	Tchécoslovaquie(anc.)
Czech Republic	..	..	2	2	2	...	...	...	...	...	République tchèque
France[1]	2029	2041	1999	2069	2189	...	...	...	...	...	France[1]
Hungary	4	4	4	3	4	5	5	5	5	...	Hongrie
Netherlands[2][3]	2	...	...	...	...	...	...	...	...	...	Pays-Bas[2][3]
Portugal[1]	588	594	#47	...	...	...	...	...	...	...	Portugal[1]
Russian Federation	..	9	46	2412	727	772	518	413	331	545	Fédération de Russie
Ukraine[4]	..	315	467	1066	1151	906	444	168	127	122	Ukraine[4]
United Kingdom	3	2	1	...	...	...	...	...	...	...	Royaume-Uni
USSR (former)[4]	3	..	..	..	..	..	..	..	..	..	URSS (anc.)[4]
Oceania											**Océanie**
Australia[5]	4	4	4	4	...	...	...	...	...	...	Australie[5]

General Note.

Clay tiles for roofs, for topping walls etc. They may be flat, half cylinders, or of special shapes for eaves, ridges, hips or valleys. (SITC, Rev.3: 66242-1B).

[1] In thousand metric tons.
[2] Sales.
[3] Production by establishments employing 20 or more persons.
[4] Including tiles of cement and sand and lime.
[5] Twelve months ending 30 June of year stated.

Remarque générale.

Tuiles d'argile pour toitures, couronnement des murs etc. Elles peuvent être plates, demi-rondes ou de forme spéciale (tuiles pour pignons, tuiles faîtières, tuiles de rives, tuiles d'arêtiers). (CTCI, Rev.3: 66242-1B).

[1] En milliers de tonnes métriques.
[2] Ventes.
[3] Production des établissements occupant 20 personnes ou plus.
[4] Y compris les tuiles de ciment, sable et chaux.
[5] Période de douze mois finissant le 30 juin de l'année indiquée.

Tiles, floor and wall
Carreaux pour planchers et murs

ISIC-BASED CODE - CODE BASE CITI

3691-07A

Unit : Thousand units   Unité : En milliers

Country or area	1990	1991	1992	1993	1994	1995	1996	1997	1998	1999	Pays ou zone
America, North											**Amérique du Nord**
Mexico	...	...	...	348825	379853	411895	477366	541404	584141	686296	Mexique
America, South											**Amérique du Sud**
Colombia	...	...	275	194	68	180	...	...	...	...	Colombie
Ecuador	...	...	3174	...	1676	...	...	...	...	...	Equateur
Paraguay	635	649	641	...	...	...	...	...	...	...	Paraguay
Asia											**Asie**
Indonesia	...	...	528	29	...	...	...	...	...	...	Indonésie
Israel	109344	149226	147287	142846	129756	159697	167637	...	...	...	Israël
Malaysia	535224	656299	769571	920956	[1]46558	[1]45442	[1]47315	[1]53727	[1]42211	[1]50434	Malaisie
Thailand	486	604	...	...	...	...	...	...	...	...	Thaïlande
Europe											**Europe**
Bulgaria	...	...	286	318	324	339	310	371	...	...	Bulgarie
Finland	94884	92652	79575	79186	...	...	...	...	...	...	Finlande
Poland	16833	28385	33879	50369	43197	55976	68779	94168	142510	165190	Pologne
Portugal[2]	186	198	...	...	...	...	...	...	...	...	Portugal[2]
Sweden[2]	14	12	12	10	11	12	...	...	...	...	Suède[2]
Yugoslavia[2]	..	111	93	38	49	53	71	70	87	65	Yougoslavie[2]

General Note.

Setts, flags and other tiles commonly used for paving or for facing walls, hearths etc., whether or not glazed. Vitrified brick and roofing tiles are excluded. (SITC, Rev.3: 66244-0A, 66245-0A).

[1] In thousand square metres.
[2] In thousand metric tons.

Remarque générale.

Carreaux, pavés et dalles de pavement ou de revêtement, émaillés ou non, communément utilisés pour le pavement des sols et le revêtement des murs, foyers de cheminée, etc. Cette rubrique ne comprend pas les briques vitrifiées et les tuiles de toiture.(CTCI, Rev.3: 66244-0A, 66245-0A).

[1] En milliers de mètres carrés.
[2] En milliers de tonnes métriques.

Tiles, floor and wall
Carreaux pour planchers et murs

ISIC-BASED CODE - CODE BASE CITI

3691-07B

Unit : Thousand square metres   Unité : Milliers de mètres carrés

Country or area	1990	1991	1992	1993	1994	1995	1996	1997	1998	1999	Pays ou zone
Africa	**10012**	**9393**	**18638**	**18843**	**17517**	**18472**	**17435**	**18286**	**20427**	**21415**	**Afrique**
Algeria	2610	2549	2578	2379	2104	...	...	...	...	...	Algérie
Ethiopia	144	147	135	109	204	177	709	531	368	341	Ethiopie
Mali	4	2	2	7	1	1	2	...	...	...	Mali
Nigeria	1515	1251	1355	1318	416	338	...	...	...	...	Nigéria
South Africa	5739	5444	14568	15030	14792	15866	14202	15471	18014	19267	Afrique du Sud
America, North	**47668**	**45543**	**46596**	**50323**	**53487**	**53357**	**54409**	**58268**	**59976**	**64568**	**Amérique du Nord**
Panama	363	...	545	542	574	511	495	...	...	...	Panama
United States	[1][2]47305	45038	46051	49781	52913	52846	53914	57505	59161	...	Etats-Unis
America, South	**4207**	**4817**	**5209**	**5514**	**7020**	**6375**	**2471**	**6253**	**6492**	**6731**	**Amérique du Sud**
Bolivia	84	60	64	598	69	*76	...	...	...	...	Bolivie
Chile	707	779	896	977	988	1184	...	...	...	...	Chili
Ecuador	3416	...	4249	3939	5963	5115	1184	...	...	...	Equateur
Asia	**149043**	**157533**	**167317**	**165529**	**168366**	**180949**	**178996**	**179280**	**174238**	**179882**	**Asie**
Armenia	..	602	134	37	12	6	0	0	0	0	Arménie
Azerbaijan	..	1385	1148	839	470	170	117	66	18	5	Azerbaïdjan
Cyprus	2064	2168	2182	2046	1750	1597	1492	1297	1042	804	Chypre
Indonesia	1362	1558	6718	6791	...	...	...	...	...	...	Indonésie
Iran(Islamic Rep. of)	[3]23834	[3]24205	[3]30879	[3]32285	[3]35164	[4]44451	[4]47142	[4]46616	[4]53309	...	Iran(Rép. islamique)
Japan	...	...	...	...	74712	76483	72801	72697	60105	53794	Japon
Korea, Republic of	40166	48195	49034	48506	52151	54135	...	...	...	...	Corée, République de
Europe	**233072**	**303647**	**331934**	**529328**	**552022**	**606989**	**612480**	**669197**	**745965**	**794417**	**Europe**
Austria	2540	2646	2518	2449	2624	2531	...	...	...	...	Autriche
Belarus	..	7292	7051	6760	6259	8058	8081	9589	10637	11629	Bélarus
Croatia	..	2076	2971	1981	485	3149	3103	3164	3208	...	Croatie
Denmark[5]	..	...	...	...	...	...	...	1	24	...	Danemark[5]
Czechoslovakia(former)	22689	22743									Tchécoslovaquie(anc.)
Czech Republic	..	..	17118	18646	19462	21424	23259	27142	27751	27822	République tchèque
Estonia	..	469	142	80	81	84	43	21	2	...	Estonie
Finland	...	...	...	...	1606	1544	1188	...	...	974	Finlande
France	17278	17136	27355	...	...	...	...	...	...	...	France
Germany	..	71933	71798	70432	66056	...	...	...	...	...	Allemagne
Germany(Fed.Rep.)	68652	..	..	..	..	...	...	...	...	..	Allemagne(Rép.féd.)
German D.R.(former)	7866	..	..	..	..	...	...	...	...		R.D.A. (anc.)
Greece	5229	3914	4815	3875	3872	4147	4014	4089	5289	...	Grèce
Hungary	8072	7556	7164	7793	7645	8051	8145	10098	9367	9538	Hongrie
Latvia	..	494	318	218	220	94	150	124	132	176	Lettonie
Lithuania	..	702	314	152	82	325	553	1034	1477	1672	Lituanie
Netherlands[5][6]	13890	14172	14924	13900	15300	...	...	...	...	...	Pays-Bas[5][6]
Portugal	...	...	74236	42823	41080	46008	49121	47897	53868	58938	Portugal
Republic of Moldova	..	551	598	[7]628	[7]182	[7]202	[7]143	[7]109		[7]50	Rép. de Moldova
Russian Federation	..	...	...	40096	28114	27061	21226	20979	23023	31927	Fédération de Russie
Slovakia	..	..	...	...	...	...	6924	6594	6887	6815	Slovaquie
Slovenia	..	2347	1953	2213	2486	2516	2803	2703	2683	2908	Slovénie
Spain	20503	22557	20936	#256971	304762	346760	353442	400822	468483	502252	Espagne
Sweden	...	...	...	...	...	...	334	344	332	371	Suède
Ukraine	..	23319	21509	17386	9954	7908	7124	6708	7139	7828	Ukraine
United Kingdom	...	...	...	12616	12240	12163	11409	14843	12076	...	Royaume-Uni
Yugoslavia	..	4051	3335	969	1697	1900	2735	2692	2779	1927	Yougoslavie
T.F.Yug.Rep. Macedonia	..	128	159	260	63	55	29	22	26	28	L'ex-RY Macédoine
USSR (former)	82624	..	..	..	..	..	..	..	..	..	URSS (anc.)
Total	**526626**	**520932**	**569694**	**769537**	**798412**	**866142**	**865791**	**931285**	**1007099**	**1067013**	**Total**

General Note.
Setts, flags and other tiles commonly used for paving or for facing walls, hearths etc., whether or not glazed. Vitrified brick and roofing tiles are excluded. (SITC, Rev.3: 66244-0B, 66245-0B).

Remarque générale.
Carreaux, pavés et dalles de pavement ou de revêtement, émaillés ou non, communément utilisés pour le pavement des sols et le revêtement des murs, foyers de cheminée, etc. Cette rubrique ne comprend pas les briques vitrifiées et les tuiles de toiture. (CTCI, Rev.3: 66244-0B, 66245-0B)

For footnotes, see end of table.

Voir la fin du tableau pour les notes.

Tiles, floor and wall (continued)
Carreaux pour planchers et murs (suite)

ISIC-BASED CODE - CODE BASE CITI
3691-07B

Footnotes
[1] Shipments.
[2] Clay tiles only.
[3] Production by establishments employing 50 or more persons.
[4] Production by establishments employing 10 or more persons.
[5] Sales.
[6] Production by establishments employing 20 or more persons.
[7] Excluding Transnistria region.

Notes.
[1] Expéditions.
[2] Carreaux d'argile.
[3] Production des établissements occupant 50 personnes ou plus.
[4] Production des établissements occupant 10 personnes ou plus.
[5] Ventes.
[6] Production des établissements occupant 20 personnes ou plus.
[7] Non compris la région de Transnistria.

Quicklime
Chaux vive

ISIC-BASED CODE - CODE BASE CITI

3692-01

Unit : Thousand metric tons

Unité : Milliers de tonnes métriques

Country or area	1990	1991	1992	1993	1994	1995	1996	1997	1998	1999	Pays ou zone
Africa	**2896**	**3448**	**3382**	**3265**	**3180**	**3223**	**3273**	**3253**	**3233**	**3681**	**Afrique**
Algeria	33	44	47	50	43	52	47	49	39	52	Algérie
Dem. Rep. of Congo[1]	92	83	65	*50	*40	*20	...	...	...	...	Rép. dém. du Congo[1]
Egypt[1][2]	68	#749	*749	*748	*750	*750	...	...	...	...	Egypte[1][2]
Ethiopia[3]	3	4	4	4	3	5	7	7	7	14	Ethiopie[3]
Kenya	14	14	14	12	12	12	*12	...	...	...	Kenya
Libyan Arab Jamah.	2	14	17	14	9	9	...	...	...	...	Jamah. arabe libyenne
Mali	1	1	1	0	1	1	2	...	...	...	Mali
Mauritius	7	6	6	6	5	5	...	...	...	...	Maurice
South Africa[1][4]	1830	1765	1738	1599	1597	1743	1650	1585	1523	1920	Afrique du Sud[1][4]
Tunisia[2]	587	578	525	552	508	412	466	471	483	475	Tunisie[2]
Uganda[1]	*2	*2	2	2	2	2	...	...	...	...	Ouganda[1]
United Rep.Tanzania	3	4	*[1]2	1	0	2	1	1	...	...	Rép. Unie de Tanzanie
Zambia	254	[1]184	[1]212	[1]227	[1]210	[1]210	...	...	...	...	Zambie
America, North	**22092**	**22442**	**23004**	**17402**	**18082**	**18646**	**20263**	**20806**	**20996**	**20695**	**Amérique du Nord**
Canada	[5]2341	[5]2375	[5]2384	[5]2379	[5]2391	[5]1839	[1]2402	[1]2477	[1]2514	[1]2585	Canada
Costa Rica*[1]	13	9	9	10	10	10	...	...	...	...	Costa Rica*[1]
Cuba*[1]	...	180	160	180	170	180	...	...	...	...	Cuba*[1]
Dominican Republic*[1]	4	...	...	...	...	...	...	...	...	...	Rép. dominicaine*[1]
Guatemala*[1]	75	72	70	70	70	72	...	...	...	...	Guatemala*[1]
Jamaica[1][2]	*90	*95	170	*151	170	*175	...	...	...	...	Jamaïque[1][2]
Martinique*[1][2]	5	5	5	5	5	5	...	...	...	...	Martinique*[1][2]
Mexico	*[1][2]6000	*[1][2]6500	*[1][2]6500	399	460	557	614	572	515	533	Mexique
Nicaragua[1][2]	1	2	2	4	*2	4	...	...	...	...	Nicaragua[1][2]
United States[6]	13392	13200	13700	14200	14800	15800	16800	17300	17500	17100	Etats-Unis[6]
America, South	**4091**	**4051**	**4031**	**3919**	**4018**	**3836**	**3957**	**4286**	**4173**	**4147**	**Amérique du Sud**
Bolivia	4	8	9	0	0	*8	...	...	...	...	Bolivie
Brazil	2698	2751	2635	2543	2689	2721	2814	3193	3081	3055	Brésil
Chile*[1]	1300	1200	1297	1300	1250	1000	1050	1000	1000	1000	Chili*[1]
Colombia	...	...	42	37	34	62	...	...	...	...	Colombie
Paraguay	33	36	36	27	...	...	...	...	...	...	Paraguay
Uruguay*[1]	12	12	12	12	12	12	...	...	...	...	Uruguay*[1]
Asia	**12835**	**13963**	**12937**	**12769**	**12374**	**12218**	**12181**	**12544**	**11788**	**11550**	**Asie**
Armenia	..	8	6	3	3	3	2	1	3	4	Arménie
Azerbaijan	..	42	38	15	7	3	1	1	0	0	Azerbaïdjan
Hong Kong SAR	...	5	6	11	...	...	...	...	...	...	Hong-Kong RAS
Cyprus	7	7	6	6	7	6	6	6	6	7	Chypre
Georgia	..	...	11	5	2	4	15	0	3	0	Géorgie
India*[1]	800	820	850	860	860	900	...	...	...	...	Inde*[1]
Indonesia	...	...	...	...	5	...	...	...	...	...	Indonésie
Iran(Islamic Rep. of)	*[1]650	*[1]650	*[1]650	*[1]650	*[1]650	[7]496	[7]499	[7]356	[7]404	...	Iran(Rép. islamique)
Israel*[1]	230	208	208	208	210	210	...	...	...	...	Israël*[1]
Japan	8983	9045	8049	7958	7712	7871	7744	8104	7646	7594	Japon
Jordan[1]	5	5	7	*7	*7	*7	...	...	...	...	Jordanie[1]
Korea, Republic of	426	435	533	...	...	...	...	...	...	...	Corée, République de
Kuwait	[1][2]50	[1][2]5	26	42	84	89	...	...	...	...	Koweït
Kyrgyzstan	..	69	37	13	18	6	4	21	8	8	Kirghizistan
Lebanon*[1][2]	10	10	15	15	15	15	...	...	...	...	Liban*[1][2]
Mongolia	*[1]103	76	68	51	66	51	55	58	56	50	Mongolie
Philippines	21	17	6	3	1	1	0	...	4	7	Philippines
Qatar	16	16	16	19	16	18	20	19	19	19	Qatar
Saudi Arabia*[1]	12	12	12	12	12	12	...	...	...	...	Arabie saoudite*[1]
Tajikistan	..	98	56	21	16	14	7	8	6	28	Tadjikistan
Thailand	92	107	120	130	146	151	160	168	124	121	Thaïlande
Turkey	709	875	812	986	931	897	1023	1170	1066	975	Turquie
Turkmenistan	..	108	92	58	45	27	21	28	16	...	Turkménistan
United Arab Emirates[1][2]	45	45	45	*45	*45	*45	...	...	...	...	Emirats arabes unis[1][2]
Uzbekistan	..	623	570	507	370	241	227	185	...	...	Ouzbékistan
Viet Nam	664	665	693	...	...	...	...	...	...	...	Viet Nam
Europe	**29753**	**34669**	**32460**	**29545**	**29679**	**25912**	**24621**	**25252**	**24629**	**23924**	**Europe**

For general note and footnotes, see end of table.

Voir la fin du tableau pour la remarque générale et les notes.

Quicklime (continued)
Chaux vive (suite)

ISIC-BASED CODE - CODE BASE CITI

3692-01

Unit : Thousand metric tons
Unité : Milliers de tonnes métriques

Country or area	1990	1991	1992	1993	1994	1995	1996	1997	1998	1999	Pays ou zone
Austria	678	640	609	619	592	#223	231	269	288	285	Autriche
Belarus	..	1080	1057	939	589	453	450	551	684	663	Bélarus
Belgium	1796	2020	1869	1865	1971	2062	2022	1954	1971	1927	Belgique
Bulgaria	1557	1034	729	401	533	804	869	807	783	715	Bulgarie
Croatia	..	108	79	83	86	93	110	120	126	...	Croatie
Denmark[8]	127	86	104	107	112	101	95	103	89	95	Danemark[8]
Czechoslovakia(former)	3230	2140	..	..	..	..	..	..	..	..	Tchécoslovaquie(anc.)
Czech Republic	..	..	1337	1147	1212	1186	1176	1217	1151	1142	République tchèque
Estonia	..	207	92	21	19	17	17	19	32	23	Estonie
Finland	253	244	250	230	262	268	261	..	..	...	Finlande
France	3148	3022	2823	2796	3007	[1]2940	[1]2714	* [1]2360	* [1]2400	* [1]2400	France
Germany	..	7533	7542	7483	8511	5432	4958	5183	5117	...	Allemagne
Germany(Fed.Rep.)	6893	..	..	..	..	..	..	..	..	..	Allemagne(Rép.féd.)
German D.R. (former)	1710	..	..	..	..	..	..	..	..	..	R.D.A. (anc.)
Greece	281	263	218	314	337	334	317	452	301	...	Grèce
Hungary	831	571	508	476	520	538	468	633	649	444	Hongrie
Ireland[1]	112	110	110	*100	*100	*100	...	...	...	...	Irlande[1]
Italy	1423	1600	1711	1756	1749	1865	1685	1722	1642	1642	Italie
Latvia	..	55	25	14	17	14	11	10	9	8	Lettonie
Lithuania	..	291	161	48	38	88	62	45	70	42	Lituanie
Malta[1 2]	5	5	5	...	...	...	...	...	...	...	Malte[1 2]
Norway* [1]	100	100	100	100	100	100	...	...	...	...	Norvège* [1]
Portugal	* [1]200	* [1]200	42	58	77	107	153	144	185	182	Portugal
Republic of Moldova	..	179	73	[9]30	[9]16	[9]11	[9]20	[9]10	[9]13	[9]5	Rép. de Moldova
Romania	3028	2334	1946	1738	1621	1763	1748	1688	1813	1623	Roumanie
Slovakia	..	..	616	727	765	803	994	1213	644	664	Slovaquie
Slovenia	..	198	138	135	160	149	142	151	146	140	Slovénie
Spain	* [1]1200	* [1]1200	* [1]1200	1001	1092	1050	1077	1076	1110	1044	Espagne
Sweden	446	449	389	404	477	432	446	499	396	398	Suède
Switzerland	26	21	19	...	...	...	...	...	...	...	Suisse
Ukraine	..	7648	7484	5924	4663	3902	3339	3535	3358	3385	Ukraine
United Kingdom	713	790	...	...	...	...	...	...	...	...	Royaume-Uni
Yugoslavia	..	512	439	225	260	284	267	242	406	253	Yougoslavie
T.F.Yug.Rep. Macedonia	..	29	34	25	14	14	11	5	1	...	L'ex-RY Macédoine
Yugoslavia, SFR	1996	..	..	..	..	..	..	..	..	..	Yougoslavie, RSF
USSR (former)	30237	..	..	..	..	..	..	..	..	..	URSS (anc.)
Oceania	104	94	104	104	104	104	104	104	105	105	Océanie
Australia	4	4	4	...	...	...	...	...	...	...	Australie
New Zealand* [1 2]	100	90	100	100	100	100	...	...	...	...	Nouvelle-Zélande* [1 2]
Total	**102008**	**78666**	**75918**	**67004**	**67437**	**63939**	**64399**	**66245**	**64924**	**64102**	**Total**

General Note.

Impure calcium oxide obtained by calcining limestone containing very little or no clay. Hydraulic lime and slaked lime are excluded. (SITC, Rev.3: 66111-0).

Remarque générale.

Oxyde de calcium impur obtenu par calcination de pierres calcaires contenant très peu d'argile ou pas d'argile. Cette rubrique ne comprend pas la chaux hydraulique et la chaux éteinte. (CTCI, Rev.3: 66111-0).

[1] Source: U. S. Geological Survey, (Washington, D. C.).
[2] Including other types of lime.
[3] Twelve months ending 7 July of the year stated.
[4] Domestic sales plus exports.
[5] Shipments.
[6] Sold or used by producers.
[7] Production by establishments employing 10 or more persons.
[8] Sales.
[9] Excluding Transnistria region.

[1] Source: U.S. Geological Survey, (Washington, D.C.).
[2] Y compris les autres types de chaux.
[3] Période de douze mois finissant le 7 juillet de l'année indiquée.
[4] Ventes nationales plus exportations.
[5] Expéditions.
[6] Vendu ou utilisé par les producteurs.
[7] Production des établissements occupant 10 personnes ou plus.
[8] Ventes.
[9] Non compris la région de Transnistria.

Cement
Ciments

ISIC-BASED CODE - CODE BASE CITI

3692-04

Unit : Thousand metric tons   Unité : Milliers de tonnes métriques

Country or area	1990	1991	1992	1993	1994	1995	1996	1997	1998	1999	Pays ou zone
Africa	**48512**	**51057**	**51106**	**48762**	**48538**	**52141**	**54552**	**54965**	**54894**	**52328**	**Afrique**
Algeria	6337	6323	7093	6951	6093	6783	7470	7146	7836	7587	Algérie
Angola	305	314	370	* ¹250	* ¹240	* ¹200	* ¹270	¹301	* ¹350	* ¹350	Angola
Benin¹	300	320	370	506	465	579	*360	*450	*520	*520	Bénin¹
Cameroon	¹624	¹521	¹620	* ¹620	* ¹479	522	¹305	¹350	¹400	* ¹500	Cameroun
Congo	90	102	124	95	87	98	43	20	0	0	Congo
Côte d'Ivoire* ¹	500	500	510	500	1100	1000	1000	1100	650	650	Côte d'Ivoire* ¹
Dem. Rep. of Congo¹	461	*250	174	149	166	235	241	125	*100	*100	Rép. dém. du Congo¹
Egypt²	14111	16427	15454	12576	13544	14237	15569	15569	15480	11933	Egypte²
Ethiopia²	324	270	237	377	464	609	672	775	497	470	Ethiopie²
Gabon	112	126	¹116	¹132	¹126	¹154	¹185	* ¹200	¹196	* ¹200	Gabon
Ghana¹	675	750	1020	1200	1350	*1300	*1500	*1700	1630	1870	Ghana¹
Kenya	1515	1423	1507	1417	1470	1670	1575	1440	...	...	Kenya
Liberia	50	* ¹2	* ¹8	* ¹8	* ¹3	* ¹5	* ¹15	* ¹7	* ¹10	* ¹15	Libéria
Libyan Arab Jamah.	4	4	4	4	4	3	3	3	3	3	Jamah. arabe libyenne
Madagascar	29	32	30	36	8	38	44	36	44	...	Madagascar
Malawi	101	112	108	117	122	124	88	70	83	104	Malawi
Mali	4	11	16	14	14	13	21	...	...	...	Mali
Mauritania¹	...	105	122	111	374	120	*100	*80	*50	*50	Mauritanie¹
Morocco	5381	5777	6223	6175	6284	6399	6585	7236	7155	7194	Maroc
Mozambique	80	63	73	60	62	146	179	217	264	266	Mozambique
Niger	19	20	29	31	26	31	¹29	* ¹30	* ¹30	* ¹30	Niger
Nigeria	2974	3418	3367	3247	1275	1573	...	...	...	...	Nigéria
Réunion	336	350	344	325	321	313	290	268	275	...	Réunion
Rwanda	60	60	60	60	10	36	42	61	60	66	Rwanda
Senegal	471	503	602	591	697	694	810	854	847	1030	Sénégal
South Africa	6563	6147	5850	6135	7068	7437	7664	7891	7676	8211	Afrique du Sud
Sudan¹	*167	*170	*250	*250	*160	391	*380	291	*300	*350	Soudan¹
Togo¹	399	388	350	*350	*286	350	413	421	565	*560	Togo¹
Tunisia	4311	4195	4184	4508	4605	4998	4566	4378	4588	4864	Tunisie
Uganda	27	27	38	52	45	84	195	290	321	347	Ouganda
United Rep.Tanzania	664	1022	677	749	686	739	726	621	...	...	Rép. Unie de Tanzanie
Zambia	432	376	¹347	* ¹350	¹280	¹312	¹348	¹384	¹351	* ¹350	Zambie
Zimbabwe	924	949	829	816	624	948	996	954	...	...	Zimbabwe
America, North	**118382**	**110801**	**114487**	**121664**	**130694**	**123812**	**128507**	**136922**	**140108**	**144934**	**Amérique du Nord**
Barbados	213	144	71	64	76	76	108	176	257	257	Barbade
Canada	11745	9372	8592	9394	10584	10440	11587	*11736	12064	*12624	Canada
Costa Rica¹	...	*700	*700	860	940	865	830	940	1085	*1100	Costa Rica¹
Cuba	3696	³1851	³1134	³1049	³1085	³1456	³1438	³1701	³1713	* ¹1800	Cuba
Dominican Republic	1109	1235	1365	1271	1276	1450	1642	1822	1872	2295	Rép. dominicaine
El Salvador	³641	³694	³760	³659	³915	³914	³938	³1029	³988	*1032	El Salvador
Guadeloupe	291	339	292	276	283	*230	* ¹230	* ¹230	* ¹230	* ¹230	Guadeloupe
Guatemala	³897	450	³658	³1018	³1163	1257	1173	1480	1496	...	Guatemala
Haiti	180	211	³216	³228	³228	...	...	...	...	...	Haïti
Honduras	326	402	³760	³933	³1000	³995	³948	³1068	³1026	³1211	Honduras
Jamaica	421	390	480	441	445	518	559	588	558	503	Jamaïque
Martinique	277	291	262	234	231	*225	* ¹220	* ¹220	* ¹220	* ¹220	Martinique
Mexico	24683	25208	27114	28725	31594	25295	26174	29685	30915	31958	Mexique
Nicaragua	* ³140	¹239	¹277	¹255	¹309	¹324	¹360	¹377	¹377	* ¹350	Nicaragua
Panama	325	¹300	473	³620	³678	³658	651	³756	¹750	* ¹760	Panama
Puerto Rico	1305	1296	1266	1303	1356	1398	1508	1586	1646	1757	Porto Rico
Trinidad and Tobago	438	486	482	527	583	559	617	677	700	740	Trinité-et-Tobago
United States	70944	67193	69585	73807	77948	76906	79266	82582	83931	85952	Etats-Unis
America, South	**49302**	**52223**	**53182**	**64811**	**56037**	**62185**	**68860**	**75951**	**76726**	**72654**	**Amérique du Sud**
Argentina	3612	4399	5051	5647	6306	5477	5117	6769	7092	7187	Argentine
Bolivia	524	621	630	629	789	869	³859	³970	³1095	³1163	Bolivie
Brazil	25850	27491	23902	24845	25229	28256	34559	37995	39942	40248	Brésil
Chile	2115	2251	2660	3024	3001	3304	3627	3718	3890	2508	Chili
Colombia	6360	6389	9163	18205	9273	9908	...	10878	8673	*6720	Colombie
Ecuador	1792	1774	2072	2155	2452	2549	2601	...	2539	...	Equateur
Paraguay	344	343	476	476	529	624	627	603	586	556	Paraguay
Peru	2185	2137	2080	2327	3177	3645	3678	4092	4069	3327	Pérou

For general note and footnotes, see end of table.   Voir la fin du tableau pour la remarque générale et les notes.

Cement (continued)
Ciments (suite)

ISIC-BASED CODE - CODE BASE CITI
3692-04

Unit : Thousand metric tons   Unité : Milliers de tonnes métriques

Country or area	1990	1991	1992	1993	1994	1995	1996	1997	1998	1999	Pays ou zone
Suriname	55	24	11	17	18	* ¹60	* ¹60	* ¹65	* ¹65	* ¹65	Suriname
Uruguay	469	458	552	610	701	593	656	³753	³907	³866	Uruguay
Venezuela	5996	6336	6585	6876	4562	*6900	³7568	³7867	³7869	³7875	Venezuela
Asia	**531807**	**598123**	**678700**	**761558**	**838218**	**909307**	**952675**	**980906**	**976376**	**1029352**	**Asie**
Afghanistan	⁴100	⁴109	* ¹115	* ¹115	* ¹115	* ¹115	* ¹116	* ¹116	* ¹116	* ¹116	Afghanistan
Armenia	..	1507	368	198	122	228	281	293	314	287	Arménie
Azerbaijan	..	923	827	643	467	196	223	303	201	171	Azerbaïdjan
Bangladesh⁵	337	275	272	207	324	316	426	610	*588	*756	Bangladesh⁵
Bhutan¹	...	116	116	108	*120	*140	*160	*160	*150	*150	Bhoutan¹
China	209711	244656	308217	367878	421180	475606	491189	511738	536000	573000	Chine
Hong Kong SAR	1808	1677	1644	1712	1927	1913	2027	1925	1539	1387	Hong-Kong RAS
Cyprus	1133	1134	1132	1089	1053	1024	1021	910	1207	1157	Chypre
Georgia	..	...	426	278	89	59	85	94	199	341	Géorgie
India	46170	52013	53936	57326	63461	67722	73261	82873	87646	100230	Inde
Indonesia	14786	13480	14048	19610	24564	23136	*24648	20702	*22344	*24024	Indonésie
Iran(Islamic Rep. of)⁶	14429	13996	15094	16321	16250	16904	17703	18349	20049	...	Iran(Rép. islamique)⁶
Iraq	13000	*5000	2453	* ¹2000	* ¹2000	¹2108	* ¹1600	* ¹1700	* ¹2000	* ¹2000	Iraq
Israel	2868	3340	3960	4536	4800	6204	6723	5916	...	...	Israël
Japan	84445	89564	88252	88046	91624	90474	94492	91938	81328	80120	Japon
Jordan	1733	1675	2651	3437	3392	3415	3512	3250	2650	...	Jordanie
Kazakhstan	..	7575	6436	3963	2033	1772	1115	657	622	838	Kazakhstan
Korea,Dem.Ppl's.Rep.* ¹	16000	16000	17000	17000	17000	17000	17000	17000	17000	16000	Corée,Rép.pop.dém.de* ¹
Korea, Republic of	33914	39167	44444	47313	52088	56101	58434	60317	46791	48579	Corée, République de
Kuwait	800	¹300	534	956	1232	*1363	⁷1113	...	2310	...	Koweït
Kyrgyzstan	..	1320	1096	692	426	310	546	658	709	386	Kirghizistan
Lao People's Dem. Rep.	...	* ...	...	...	7	59	...	...	...	...	Rép. dém. pop. lao
Lebanon	* ¹900	* ¹900	2163	2591	2948	3470	3430	...	...	...	Liban
Malaysia	5881	7451	8366	8797	9928	10713	12349	12668	10397	10104	Malaisie
Mongolia	441	227	133	82	86	109	106	* ¹112	109	104	Mongolie
Myanmar⁸	420	443	472	400	477	525	513	524	371	343	Myanmar⁸
Nepal⁹	107	¹136	237	248	315	327	309	227	139	191	Népal⁹
Oman	⁷1000	⁷1100	⁷1120	⁷1128	⁷1163	⁷1174	¹1260	⁷1247	...	...	Oman
Pakistan⁵	7488	7762	8321	8558	8100	7913	9567	9536	9364	9635	Pakistan⁵
Philippines	6360	6804	6540	7932	9576	10566	¹12429	¹14681	¹12888	¹12556	Philippines
Qatar	267	367	354	400	470	475	486	584	857	959	Qatar
Saudi Arabia	⁷12696	⁷12106	⁷15301	16584	17013	15772	16391	15448	15776	16381	Arabie saoudite
Singapore	1848	2199	* ¹1900	* ²2980	* ³3100	* ³3200	* ³3300	* ³3300	* ³3300	* ³3250	Singapour
Sri Lanka	579	620	553	466	* ¹925	956	670	*966	* ¹1100	* ¹1150	Sri Lanka
Syrian Arab Republic	3049	3078	3515	3906	4344	4804	4817	4838	5016	5134	Rép. arabe syrienne
Tajikistan	..	1013	447	262	178	78	49	36	18	33	Tadjikistan
Thailand	18054	19164	21711	26300	29929	34051	38749	37136	22722	25354	Thaïlande
Turkey	24299	26029	28455	31134	29356	33153	35214	36035	38175	34258	Turquie
Turkmenistan	..	904	1050	1118	690	437	438	601	750	...	Turkménistan
United Arab Emirates	⁷3800	⁷3710	⁷4328	⁷4734	⁷4968	⁷5071	* ¹6000	* ⁵5250	* ¹6000	* ¹6000	Emirats arabes unis
Uzbekistan	..	6191	5934	5277	4780	3419	3277	3286	...	...	Ouzbékistan
Viet Nam	2534	3127	3926	* ¹4200	* ¹4700	5828	6585	8019	9738	*10381	Viet Nam
Yemen (former)*	700		..	...	..	..	..	..	...	...	Yémen (anc.)*
Yemen	..	718	820	1000	898	1100	1028	1038	...	...	Yémen
Europe	**249812**	**342648**	**311095**	**274859**	**271034**	**266057**	**253768**	**255805**	**259317**	**263283**	**Europe**
Albania	644	311	197	198	240	240	204	100	84	107	Albanie
Austria¹⁰	4903	5017	5029	4941	4828	...	3900	...	...	...	Autriche¹⁰
Belarus	..	2402	2263	1908	1488	1235	1467	1876	2035	1998	Bélarus
Belgium	6924	7184	8073	7569	7542	7501	6996	6996	6852	9252	Belgique
Bulgaria	4710	2374	2132	2007	1910	2070	2137	1654	1742	2060	Bulgarie
Croatia	..	1742	1771	1683	2055	1708	1842	2184	3873	...	Croatie
Denmark¹¹	1656	2019	2072	2270	2427	2584	2629	2683	2667	2534	Danemark¹¹
Czechoslovakia(former)	10215	8299	..	...	..	..	..	..	...	...	Tchécoslovaquie(anc.)
Czech Republic	..	..	6145	5393	5252	4831	5016	4874	4599	4241	République tchèque
Estonia	..	905	483	354	403	418	388	422	321	358	Estonie
Finland	1649	1343	1133	835	864	907	975	* ¹960	*1104	*1164	Finlande
France	26230	25089	21584	19222	20020	19724	18337	18309	19434	20302	France
Germany	..	...	37331	36649	40217	38858	37006	37210	38464	*38100	Allemagne

For general note and footnotes, see end of table.   Voir la fin du tableau pour la remarque générale et les notes.

Cement (continued)
Ciments (suite)

ISIC-BASED CODE - CODE BASE CITI

3692-04

Unit : Thousand metric tons

Unité : Milliers de tonnes métriques

Country or area	1990	1991	1992	1993	1994	1995	1996	1997	1998	1999	Pays ou zone
Germany(Fed.Rep.)	30456	..	..	..	..	..	..	..	..	..	Allemagne(Rép.féd.)
German D.R.(former)	7316	..	..	..	..	..	..	..	..	..	R.D.A. (anc.)
Greece	13142	13151	12761	12492	12633	10914	13391	13660	14207	...	Grèce
Hungary	3933	2529	2236	2533	2793	2875	2747	2811	2999	2980	Hongrie
Iceland	114	106	100	86	81	82	90	110	118	131	Islande
Ireland[1]	*1630	*1600	*1600	1450	1623	1730	1933	2100	*2000	*2000	Irlande[1]
Italy	40544	40301	41034	33771	32698	33716	33327	33718	35512	36827	Italie
Latvia	..	720	340	114	244	204	325	246	366	301	Lettonie
Lithuania	..	3126	1485	727	736	649	656	714	788	666	Lituanie
Luxembourg	636	688	695	719	711	714	667	683	699	742	Luxembourg
Netherlands	[11][12]3682	[11][12]3571	[11][12]3296	[11][12]3142	[1]3180	[1]3180	[1]3140	[1]3300	...	...	Pays-Bas
Norway	1260	1293	1242	1368	1464	1613	1690				Norvège
Poland	12518	12012	11908	12200	13834	13914	13959	15003	14970	15555	Pologne
Portugal	7188	7342	7728	7662	7756	8030	8444	9395	9784	10079	Portugal
Republic of Moldova	..	1809	705	[13]110	[13]39	[13]49	[13]40	[13]122	[13]74	[13]50	Rép. de Moldova
Romania	9468	6692	6271	6158	5998	6842	6956	6553	7300	6252	Roumanie
Russian Federation	..	77463	61699	49903	37220	36466	27791	26688	26018	28529	Fédération de Russie
Slovakia	..	..	3374	2656	2879	2981	4234	5856	3066	3084	Slovaquie
Slovenia	..	1801	1568	1291	1667	1807	1064	1113	1149	1222	Slovénie
Spain	28092	27576	24612	21658	25884	27220	26339	27860	...	...	Espagne
Sweden	5000	4493	2289	2152	2138	2550	2503	2272	2372	2307	Suède
Switzerland	5206	4716	4260	* [1]4000	* [1]4370	[1]4024	[1]3638	[1]3568	* [1]3600	* [1]3600	Suisse
Ukraine	..	21745	20121	15012	11435	7627	5021	5101	5591	5828	Ukraine
United Kingdom	14740	12297	11006	11039	12307	11805	12214	12638	12409	12697	Royaume-Uni
Yugoslavia	..	2411	2036	1088	1612	1696	2212	2011	2253	1575	Yougoslavie
T.F.Yug.Rep. Macedonia	..	606	516	499	486	523	490	610	461	563	L'ex-RY Macédoine
Yugoslavia, SFR	7956	..	..	..	..	..	..	..	..	..	Yougoslavie, RSF
USSR (former)	137321	..	..	..	..	..	..	..	..	..	URSS (anc.)
Oceania	7358	6453	6671	7492	8108	7745	7671	7857	7437	7791	Océanie
Australia	6535	5725	5897	6628	7017	6606	6524	6701	6277	6620	Australie
Fiji	78	79	85	80	94	91	84	96	89	...	Fidji
New Caledonia	64	*68	90	100	97	98	89	84	...	...	Nouvelle-Calédonie
New Zealand	681	581	599	684	* [1]900	* [1]950	[1]974	[1]976	* [1]975	* [1]975	Nouvelle-Zélande
Total	1142493	1161305	1215241	1279145	1352629	1421248	1466033	1512406	1514857	1570341	Total

General Note.
All hydraulic cements used for construction (portland, metallurgic, aluminous, natural etc.). (SITC, Rev.3: 66120-0).

[1] Source: U. S. Geological Survey, (Washington, D. C.).
[2] Twelve months ending 7 July of the year stated.
[3] Source: United Nations Economic Commission for Latin America and the Caribbean (ECLAC), (Santiago).
[4] Twelve months beginning 21 March of year stated.
[5] Twelve months ending 30 June of year stated.
[6] Production by establishments employing 50 or more persons.
[7] Source: Arab Gulf Cooperation Council (GCC).
[8] Government production only.
[9] Twelve months beginning 16 July of year stated.
[10] Beginning 1997, data are confidential.
[11] Sales.
[12] Production by establishments employing 20 or more persons.
[13] Excluding Transnistria region.

Remarque générale.
Tous les ciments hydrauliques utilisés dans la construction (ciments portland, métallurgique, alumineux, naturel, etc.). (CTCI, Rev.3: 66120-0).

[1] Source: U.S. Geological Survey, (Washington, D.C.).
[2] Période de douze mois finissant le 7 juillet de l'année indiquée.
[3] Source: Commission économique des Nations Unies pour l'Amérique Latine et les Caraïbes (CEPAL), (Santiago).
[4] Période de douze mois commençant le 21 mars de l'année indiquée.
[5] Période de douze mois finissant le 30 juin de l'année indiquée.
[6] Production des établissements occupant 50 personnes ou plus.
[7] Source: "Arab Gulf Cooperation Council (GCC)".
[8] Production de l'Etat seulement.
[9] Période de douze mois commençant le 16 juillet de l'année indiquée.
[10] A partir de 1997, les données sont confidentielles
[11] Ventes.
[12] Production des établissements occupant 20 personnes ou plus.
[13] Non compris la région de Transnistria.

Asbestos-cement articles
Ouvrages en amiante-ciment, cellulose-ciment et similaires

ISIC-BASED CODE - CODE BASE CITI

3699-01A

Unit : Thousand metric tons

Unité : Milliers de tonnes métriques

Country or area	1990	1991	1992	1993	1994	1995	1996	1997	1998	1999	Pays ou zone
Africa	**210**	**197**	**195**	**177**	**166**	**165**	**110**	**121**	**81**	**85**	**Afrique**
Algeria	169	158	157	141	129	133	77	99	69	75	Algérie
Burundi	3	3	3	2	...	...	...	...	...	...	Burundi
Tunisia	34	33	33	32	31	26	27	16	6	4	Tunisie
United Rep.Tanzania	4	3	2	2	...	...	...	...	...	...	Rép. Unie de Tanzanie
America, North	**256**	**258**	**291**	**281**	**259**	**174**	**227**	**194**	**212**	**214**	**Amérique du Nord**
Mexico	256	258	291	281	259	174	227	194	212	214	Mexique
America, South	**404**	**404**	**288**	**306**	**342**	**681**	**404**	**404**	**404**	**404**	**Amérique du Sud**
Colombia	...	...	288	306	342	681	...	...	...	...	Colombie
Asia	**2349**	**4399**	**4968**	**4224**	**4175**	**4809**	**5696**	**5698**	**5091**	**6488**	**Asie**
Azerbaijan	..	78	70	51	14	8	14	14	14	17	Azerbaïdjan
Cyprus	5	3	3	2	2	1	1	0	0	0	Chypre
India	802	690	495	681	758	980	1083	1163	1223	1302	Inde
Indonesia	500	488	565	267	...	...	...	...	...	...	Indonésie
Kuwait	...	...	14	...	...	...	...	...	...	...	Koweït
Kyrgyzstan	..	199	200	192	154	75	116	146	170	150	Kirghizistan
Thailand[1]	833	854	...	...	...	...	2673	2314	1509	...	Thaïlande[1]
Turkey	195	291	213	225	161	131	124	125	107	103	Turquie
Turkmenistan	..	1782	1771	1155	980	1508	1216	1467	1599	...	Turkménistan
Europe	**2165**	**1799**	**1545**	**1545**	**1912**	**1722**	**1677**	**1635**	**1534**	**1431**	**Europe**
Austria[2]	..	...	...	...	...	74	82	...	...	...	Autriche[2]
Croatia	..	36	31	22	17	19	25	26	24	...	Croatie
Czech Republic	..	..	...	...	41	33	27	...	...	...	République tchèque
Finland	33	29	*33	...	...	15	16	...	...	...	Finlande
France	648	583	457	391	720	...	...	...	...	...	France
Germany	..	...	...	...	...	...	...	...	33	...	Allemagne
German D.R.(former)	177	..	..	...	..	..	..	..	..	..	R.D.A. (anc.)
Greece	82	69	47	...	...	...	...	...	...	...	Grèce
Hungary	190	102	78	...	...	...	...	...	...	...	Hongrie
Poland	409	242	267	232	260	266	219	217	131	29	Pologne
Slovenia	..	71	32	30	36	33	33	0	0	9	Slovénie
Spain	523	492	404	...	...	...	...	...	...	...	Espagne
Sweden	1	1	...	...	...	...	...	...	...	...	Suède
United Kingdom	...	...	...	23	24	...	...	...	...	...	Royaume-Uni
Yugoslavia	..	16	5	1	0	2	1	4	9	...	Yougoslavie
T.F.Yug.Rep. Macedonia	..	24	22	13	14	15	13	15	6	11	L'ex-RY Macédoine
Total	**5384**	**7058**	**7287**	**6533**	**6853**	**7550**	**8114**	**8052**	**7322**	**8622**	**Total**

General Note.
Articles consisting essentially of an intimate mixture of fibres (asbestos, cellulose or other vegetable fibres) and cement or other hydraulic binders. Control panels of asbestos-cement are excluded. (SITC, Rev.3: 66183-0A).

Remarque générale.
Ouvrages consistant essentiellement en un mélange intime de fibres (amiante, cellulose ou autres fibres végétales) et de ciment ou autres liants hydrauliques. Cette rubrique ne comprend pas les tableaux de commande en amiante-ciment. (CTCI, Rev.3: 66183-0A).

[1] Beginning 1999, series discontinued.
[2] Beginning 1997, data are confidential.

[1] A partir de 1999, série abandonnée.
[2] A partir de 1997, les données sont confidentielles

Abrasives, agglomerated or not (millstones, grindstones, grinding wheels etc.)
Abrasifs, agglomérés ou non (meules et pierres à moudre, à aiguiser etc.)

ISIC-BASED CODE - CODE BASE CITI

3699-04

Unit : Metric tons

Unité : Tonnes métriques

Country or area	1990	1991	1992	1993	1994	1995	1996	1997	1998	1999	Pays ou zone
America, South	697	697	897	524	815	553	697	697	697	697	**Amérique du Sud**
Colombia	...	...	897	524	815	553	...	...	...	...	Colombie
Asia	70999	68859	60954	55848	56138	58169	55081	57355	48333	44841	**Asie**
Japan	70999	68859	60954	55848	56138	58169	55081	57355	48333	44841	Japon
Europe	45551	143751	160637	143245	149565	159114	158588	163427	193599	184944	**Europe**
Croatia	..	...	...	...	...	...	...	0	32	...	Croatie
Czech Republic	..	..	...	...	21159	20174	20641	21268	20687	18747	République tchèque
Germany	..	...	...	...	...	91604	84566	...	...	...	Allemagne
Hungary	3184	1562	996	...	...	...	...	...	1163	1210	Hongrie
Portugal	1160	938	1582	1409	1541	1379	1472	1741	2226	1460	Portugal
Romania	...	9790	5101	4154	3174	4520	4341	3614	3539	2518	Roumanie
Slovenia	..	6832	6307	6270	6215	7333	8065	10807	10466	10233	Slovénie
Spain	22432	23400	24157	7973	14971	19729	23069	24486	54240	50251	Espagne
Sweden	...	...	...	...	...	...	3094	3609	4780	3102	Suède
United Kingdom	...	...	...	...	...	...	11415	7535	7799	...	Royaume-Uni
Yugoslavia	..	565	819	282	218	173	286	659	582	406	Yougoslavie
Total	117247	213307	222488	199617	206518	217836	214366	221479	242629	230483	**Total**

General Note.
Millstones, grindstones, grinding wheels and the like made essentially of natural stone (agglomerated or not), of agglomerated natural or artificial abrasives or of pottery. This item does not include the natural or artificial abrasive powder or grain coated onto fabric, paper and dental burrs. (SITC, Rev.3: 66310-0).

Remarque générale.
Meules et pierres à moudre, à aiguiser, à polir et articles analogues, essentiellement fabriqués en pierre naturelle (agglomérée ou non), en abrasifs agglomérés naturels ou artificiels ou en poterie. Cette rubrique ne comprend ni les abrasifs naturels ou artificiels en poudre ou en grains appliqués sur tissu ou sur papier, ni les fraises dentaires. (CTCI, Rev.3: 66310-0).

Concrete blocks and bricks
Blocs et briques en béton

ISIC-BASED CODE - CODE BASE CITI

3699-10A

Unit : Thousand metric tons　　　　　　　　　　　　　　　　　　　　　　　　　　　　　　Unité : Milliers de tonnes métriques

Country or area	1990	1991	1992	1993	1994	1995	1996	1997	1998	1999	Pays ou zone
Africa	**372**	**172**	**205**	**229**	**217**	**342**	**515**	**433**	**461**	**488**	**Afrique**
Kenya	372	172	205	229	217	342	515	...	...	...	Kenya
America, North	**999**	**1013**	**1163**	**2817**	**2889**	**1739**	**2029**	**2189**	**2582**	**3045**	**Amérique du Nord**
Mexico	999	1013	1163	2817	2889	1739	2029	2189	2582	3045	Mexique
Asia	**93**	**98**	**93**	**93**	**94**	**94**	**94**	**94**	**94**	**94**	**Asie**
Thailand[1]	75	82	...	...	...	...	...	...	...	...	Thaïlande[1]
Turkey	18	16	14	14	...	...	...	...	...	...	Turquie
Europe	**37827**	**58086**	**58446**	**52683**	**55280**	**55651**	**52765**	**57487**	**60982**	**56891**	**Europe**
Austria	983	1323	1418	2285	2400	2528	935	815	833	...	Autriche
Belgium	1628	1498	...	...	2087	2267	2382	2199	1888	2181	Belgique
Croatia	..	..	...	...	...	...	...	140	142	...	Croatie
Finland*	707	346	245	247	195	182	211	363	469	595	Finlande*
France	2336	...	...	2041	2480	2569	2332	2423	2459	2632	France
Germany	..	...	...	...	...	20810	19108	17734	...	...	Allemagne
Greece	...	...	...	102	94	104	88	84	75	...	Grèce
Hungary	228	173	101	88	188	219	423	418	373	554	Hongrie
Ireland	...	...	...	...	...	2755	3134	5788	8601	2503	Irlande
Latvia	..	...	...	...	...	...	...	...	...	111	Lettonie
Netherlands[2][3]	...	...	...	3761	4307	3790	3623	3952	3462	3503	Pays-Bas[2][3]
Portugal	981	967	289	311	282	396	534	637	667	752	Portugal
Slovakia	..	...	...	...	...	...	...	...	155	181	Slovaquie
Slovenia	..	...	...	...	...	...	216	125	250	190	Slovénie
Spain	9772	9920	9844	3247	3128	3891	3960	4786	5567	6161	Espagne
Sweden	254	286	...	...	...	...	154	214	270	274	Suède
United Kingdom	...	...	...	...	16954	15248	15211	17496	16408	...	Royaume-Uni
Yugoslavia	..	...	57	23	23	...	...	...	...	...	Yougoslavie
Total	**39291**	**59369**	**59907**	**55822**	**58480**	**57826**	**55403**	**60203**	**64118**	**60518**	**Total**

General Note.	**Remarque générale.**
Structural blocks and bricks made of light or heavy weight aggregates. Decorative blocks are included. (SITC, Rev.3: 66332-1A).	Blocs et briques de construction faits en agrégats légers ou lourds, y compris les blocs décoratifs. (CTCI, Rev.3:66332-1A).

[1] Refractory bricks only.

[2] Sales.

[3] Production by establishments employing 20 or more persons.

[1] Briques réfractaires seulement.

[2] Ventes.

[3] Production des établissements occupant 20 personnes ou plus.

Concrete blocks and bricks
Blocs et briques en béton

ISIC-BASED CODE - CODE BASE CITI
3699-10B

Unit : Thousand cubic metres   Unité : Milliers de mètres cubes

Country or area	1990	1991	1992	1993	1994	1995	1996	1997	1998	1999	Pays ou zone
Africa											**Afrique**
Mozambique	2	3	3	0	0	0	0	0	0	0	Mozambique
South Africa[1]	229	201	167	141	296	489	396	442	461	552	Afrique du Sud[1]
America, North											**Amérique du Nord**
Antigua and Barbuda[1]	2	2	...	...	...	3	2	...	...	...	Antigua-et-Barbuda[1]
Panama[1]	15	...	22	18	17	24	14	...	...	...	Panama[1]
America, South											**Amérique du Sud**
Ecuador	...	...	[1][2]19	[1][2]12	[1][2]19	[1][2]17	[1][2]22	123	134	...	Equateur
Asia											**Asie**
Armenia	..	754	192	99	53	37	44	41	35	39	Arménie
Hong Kong SAR[3]	397	14	93	186	...	271	133	398	...	...	Hong-Kong RAS[3]
Cyprus	...	...	55	...	...	24	86	72	70	80	Chypre
Georgia	..	...	208	86	13	11	10	9	9	9	Géorgie
India[1]	...	...	...	...	[4]415	[4]461	[4]461	[4]452	[4]603	[4]1	Inde[1]
Indonesia[5]	...		13	13	...	...	...	...	...	...	Indonésie[5]
Israel	414	...	...	...	...	...	...	...	...	...	Israël
Korea, Republic of[1]	3582	3973	3445	1434	1339	1188	...	...	...	...	Corée, République de[1]
Kuwait	...	...	9	14	12	13	21	25	10	...	Koweït
Yemen	..	69	82	176	50	64	73	73	...	...	Yémen
Europe											**Europe**
Belarus	..	7134	6011	4431	2680	1719	1370	1996	2130	1760	Bélarus
Belgium	1402	1329	...	...	...	...	...	...	...	...	Belgique
Croatia	..	156	101	55	27	83	115	179	173	...	Croatie
Czechoslovakia(former)	4853	2337	..	..	..	..	..	..	..	..	Tchécoslovaquie(anc.)
Czech Republic	..	..	716	500	473	454	506	652	561	574	République tchèque
Estonia	..	768	252	161	147	107	76	104	133	92	Estonie
Finland[1]	...	83	65	49	33	28	27	88	84	124	Finlande[1]
Germany	..	13967	16108	...	21264	...	...	...	...	...	Allemagne
Germany(Fed.Rep.)	12233	..	..								Allemagne(Rép.féd.)
Greece[1]	28	29	26	...	...	...	...	...	...	...	Grèce[1]
Hungary	189	201	72	90	125	149	451	440	400	548	Hongrie
Latvia	..	...		114	90	53	40	45	51	...	Lettonie
Netherlands[6][7]	1743	1838	1837	...	...	...	...	...	...	...	Pays-Bas[6][7]
Poland[8]	5164	4358	4030	3698	4238	4014	4136	4432	4528	5463	Pologne[8]
Romania	311	587	495	1004	862	925	1058	892	691	689	Roumanie
Russian Federation	..	75100	58639	50426	32952	28085	20003	16649	14733	15788	Fédération de Russie
Slovakia	..	..	458	248	189	...	230	106	...	...	Slovaquie
Slovenia	..	93	70	87	90	106	...	...	...	...	Slovénie
Ukraine[9]	..	22494	20255	15281	8501	5630	3011	2451	2518	2345	Ukraine[9]
Yugoslavia	..	54	57	19	12	19	17	14	15	...	Yougoslavie
USSR (former)[10]	143543	..	..	..	..	..	..	..	..	..	URSS (anc.)[10]

General Note.

Structural blocks and bricks made of light or heavy weight aggregates. Decorative blocks are included. (SITC, Rev.3: 66332-1B).

Remarque générale.

Blocs et briques de construction faits en agrégats légers ou lourds, y compris les blocs décoratifs. (CTCI, Rev.3:66332-1B).

[1] In million units.
[2] Including other concrete products.
[3] 1998 data are confidential.
[4] Railway concrete sleepers only.
[5] In thousand square metres.
[6] Sales.
[7] Production by establishments employing 20 or more persons.
[8] Ferro-concrete and concrete wall materials in terms of full brick.
[9] Including concrete pipes and other concrete products.
[10] Metal reinforced concrete blocks, bricks, pipes and other concrete products.

[1] En millions d'unités.
[2] Y compris les autres produits en béton.
[3] Pour 1998, les données sont confidentielles.
[4] Traverses en béton pour voies ferrées seulement.
[5] En milliers de mètres carrés.
[6] Ventes.
[7] Production des établissements occupant 20 personnes ou plus.
[8] Béton armé et autres produits en béton pour murs exprimés en briques pleines.
[9] Y compris les conduites en béton et autres produits en béton.
[10] Dalles, briques et conduites en béton armé et autres articles en béton.

Concrete pipes
Conduites en béton

ISIC-BASED CODE - CODE BASE CITI

3699-13A

Unit : Thousand metric tons | Unité : Milliers de tonnes métriques

Country or area	1990	1991	1992	1993	1994	1995	1996	1997	1998	1999	Pays ou zone
Africa	**524**	**373**	**371**	**330**	**394**	**405**	**414**	**418**	**416**	**413**	**Afrique**
Egypt[1]	36	25	23	20	21	31	44	46	45	42	Egypte[1]
Kenya	11	11	12	11	11	12	8	...	...	...	Kenya
South Africa[2]	477	337	336	299	...	...	...	...	...	...	Afrique du Sud[2]
America, North	**758**	**440**	**344**	**621**	**662**	**396**	**310**	**288**	**282**	**239**	**Amérique du Nord**
Mexico	758	440	344	621	662	396	310	288	282	239	Mexique
America, South	**17**	**17**	**12**	**19**	**14**	**21**	**17**	**17**	**17**	**17**	**Amérique du Sud**
Colombia	...	...	12	19	14	21	...	...	...	...	Colombie
Asia	**578**	**621**	**475**	**644**	**457**	**485**	**465**	**310**	**348**	**233**	**Asie**
Hong Kong SAR	406	427	336	419	275	299	280	135	165	50	Hong-Kong RAS
Cyprus	...	...	16	...	...	...	...	...	...	...	Chypre
Indonesia	...	...	...	...	114	...	...	...	...	...	Indonésie
Kuwait	...	...	1	82	...	...	...	...	...	...	Koweït
Kyrgyzstan	..	5	1	0	0	0	0	0	...	...	Kirghizistan
Turkey	0	17	7	13	10	14	13	3	11	11	Turquie
Europe	**12376**	**14053**	**13528**	**13018**	**13589**	**11650**	**11585**	**11461**	**11786**	**11807**	**Europe**
Austria	410	524	579	475	532	576	555	524	524	493	Autriche
Belgium	[3]489	[3]495	...	...	607	566	465	455	481	566	Belgique
Croatia	..	62	58	55	61	74	70	103	78	...	Croatie
Finland	*377	*280	202	115	164	130	99	86	98	126	Finlande
France	2366	...	...	2065	2094	2113	2180	1836	1745	1807	France
Germany	...	...	...	5510	5598	3701	3469	3447	3489	...	Allemagne
Germany(Fed.Rep.)	3654	..	...	..	..	..	..	..	..	...	Allemagne(Rép.féd.)
Greece	...	...	...	97	78	109	105	141	98	...	Grèce
Hungary	60	31	76	70	90	78	91	99	119	151	Hongrie
Iceland	...	...	...	...	...	...	9	...	...	...	Islande
Ireland	...	...	...	...	...	332	188	204	236	269	Irlande
Latvia	..	...	...	...	...	...	...	...	...	20	Lettonie
Netherlands[4][5]	...	...	...	394	426	400	421	422	396	428	Pays-Bas[4][5]
Norway	...	...	...	...	...	...	...	107	131	127	Norvège
Portugal	582	453	192	318	264	302	407	484	524	449	Portugal
Slovakia	..	..	...	...	...	...	...	...	34	10	Slovaquie
Slovenia	..	50	44	54	59	68	42	80	65	64	Slovénie
Spain	1984	2419	2344	1303	1464	1535	1754	1907	1947	2239	Espagne
Sweden	467	...	...	...	...	...	498	433	499	465	Suède
United Kingdom	...	...	...	1080	1191	984	1024	1037	1251	...	Royaume-Uni
Yugoslavia	..	69	62	44	47	37	44	45	42	22	Yougoslavie
Total	**14252**	**15503**	**14730**	**14632**	**15116**	**12957**	**12790**	**12493**	**12849**	**12708**	**Total**

General Note.
Culvert, sewer, pressure, irrigation etc., reinforced or non-reinforced, concrete pipes. (SITC, Rev.3: 66334-1A).

[1] Including other concrete products.
[2] Cement pipes and fittings.
[3] Production by establishments employing 5 or more persons.
[4] Sales.
[5] Production by establishments employing 20 or more persons.

Remarque générale.
Tuyaux d'écoulement, conduites d'égouts, conduites forcées, conduites d'irrigation, en béton armé ou non. (CTCI, Rev.3: 66334-1A).

[1] Y compris les autres produits en béton.
[2] Conduits et accessoires en ciment.
[3] Production des établissements occupant 5 personnes ou plus.
[4] Ventes.
[5] Production des établissements occupant 20 personnes ou plus.

Concrete pipes
Conduites en béton

ISIC-BASED CODE - CODE BASE CITI

3699-13B

Unit : Thousand cubic metres — Unité : Milliers de mètres cubes

Country or area	1990	1991	1992	1993	1994	1995	1996	1997	1998	1999	Pays ou zone
America, North											**Amérique du Nord**
Panama[1]	3	...	25	33	63	29	50	...	...	...	Panama[1]
America, South											**Amérique du Sud**
Bolivia	3	2	2	2	0	*0	...	...	...	...	Bolivie
Ecuador	...	...	...	...	...	[1,2]1056	[1,2]390	3252	13041	...	Equateur
Asia											**Asie**
Armenia	..	1	...	...	28	31	39	0	0	0	Arménie
Azerbaijan	..	22	13	2	1	1	0	0	0	0	Azerbaïdjan
Kazakhstan	..	89	65	42	21	7	5	3	...	...	Kazakhstan
Kuwait[3]	...	...	13	82	97	73	111	100	105	...	Koweït[3]
Myanmar[1,4]	1	1	...	...	...	...	...	...	...	...	Myanmar[1,4]
Tajikistan	..	6	4	4	2	1	0	1	1	0	Tadjikistan
Uzbekistan	..	52	29	15	7	2	2	1	...	...	Ouzbékistan
Europe											**Europe**
Belarus	..	173	103	48	28	24	20	24	37	23	Bélarus
Bulgaria	[3]497	[3]312	[3]171	[3]111	[3]161	[3]158	[3]182	[3]138	[3]22	22	Bulgarie
Czechoslovakia(former)[3,5]	490	...	..	..	..	..	..	..	..	..	Tchécoslovaquie(anc.)[3,5]
Greece[3]	631	647	758	...	...	...	...	...	...	...	Grèce[3]
Hungary	30	32	47	54	59	55	38	41	50	65	Hongrie
Latvia	..	16	5	0	...	...	...	...	...	...	Lettonie
Netherlands[6,7]	268	246	245	...	...	...	...	...	...	...	Pays-Bas[6,7]
Romania[3]	4610	228	57	86	254	252	108	139	16	7	Roumanie[3]
Russian Federation	..	529	293	201	128	124	83	71	81	84	Fédération de Russie
Ukraine	..	358	200	58	36	31	9	4	3	6	Ukraine

General Note.
Culvert, sewer, pressure, irrigation etc., reinforced or non-reinforced, concrete pipes. (SITC, Rev.3: 66334-1B).

[1] In thousand units.
[2] Including other concrete products.
[3] In thousand metres.
[4] Government production only.
[5] 50 cm outside diameter.
[6] Sales.
[7] Production by establishments employing 20 or more persons.

Remarque générale.
Tuyaux d'écoulement, conduites d'égouts, conduites forcées, conduites d'irrigation, en béton armé ou non. (CTCI, Rev.3: 66334-1B).

[1] En milliers d'unités.
[2] Y compris les autres produits en béton.
[3] En milliers de mètres.
[4] Production de l'Etat seulement.
[5] 50 cm de diamètre extérieur.
[6] Ventes.
[7] Production des établissements occupant 20 personnes ou plus.

Concrete, other products
Autres produits en béton

ISIC-BASED CODE - CODE BASE CITI

3699-16A

Unit : Thousand metric tons

Unité : Milliers de tonnes métriques

Country or area	1990	1991	1992	1993	1994	1995	1996	1997	1998	1999	Pays ou zone
Africa	**176**	**109**	**183**	**124**	**148**	**148**	**148**	**148**	**148**	**148**	**Afrique**
South Africa [1]	176	109	183	124	...	...	...	...	...	...	Afrique du Sud [1]
America, South	**18054**	**16075**	**2912**	**13887**	**19914**	**23806**	**10137**	**151**	**150**	**240**	**Amérique du Sud**
Colombia	...	...	184	222	0	190	...	...	...	...	Colombie
Ecuador	...	...	2728	13665	19914	23616	...	2	1	...	Equateur
Asia	**263**	**266**	**353**	**551**	**523**	**377**	**612**	**883**	**646**	**537**	**Asie**
Hong Kong SAR	30	59	21	18	34	52	#280	413	214	200	Hong-Kong RAS
Turkey	233	207	332	533	489	325	332	470	432	337	Turquie
Europe	**51864**	**96327**	**90460**	**89596**	**91177**	**95895**	**98622**	**103497**	**96276**	**110692**	**Europe**
Austria	788	733	937	829	979	993	#2905	3030	...	...	Autriche
Belgium	[2][3]7901	[2][3]8336	...	...	5002	4951	5862	6140	6193	7421	Belgique
Croatia	..	218	163	154	139	147	193	297	284	...	Croatie
Finland	*3068	2282	1591	1549	1553	1715	1922	1433	1896	1916	Finlande
Germany	..		...	...	...	47325	46160	46813	36328	...	Allemagne
Greece	...	...	172	120	78	105	143	159	184	...	Grèce
Hungary	1199	683	499	474	616	876	921	964	1445	1505	Hongrie
Iceland	...	...	...	...	...	...	22	...	...	...	Islande
Ireland	...	...	...	...	...	536	741	959	795	898	Irlande
Latvia	...	...	...	...	...	...	...	...	...	133	Lettonie
Netherlands [4][5]	...	...	...	11012	12424	12460	12465	12885	12785	15205	Pays-Bas [4][5]
Poland [2]	14948	13149	10782	9908	10408	9197	9737	11726	12947	13676	Pologne [2]
Portugal	[2]2746	[2]2754	1728	1895	1831	2088	2344	3037	2974	3276	Portugal
Slovakia	..	..	...	...	...	...	...	...	919	812	Slovaquie
Slovenia	..	..	...	...	...	...	352	331	278	285	Slovénie
Spain	7684	7808	6960	7347	8669	10752	10549	11175	13095	15095	Espagne
Sweden	...	2858	...	...	...	...	...	...	...	...	Suède
Yugoslavia	..	1520	1003	882	498	471	361	594	706	434	Yougoslavie
T.F.Yug.Rep. Macedonia	..	138	129	129	81	89	88	75	75	67	L'ex-RY Macédoine
Total	**70357**	**112776**	**93908**	**104158**	**111762**	**120226**	**109518**	**104679**	**97220**	**111617**	**Total**

General Note.
Other moulded, pressed or centrifuged articles of cement except blocks, bricks and pipes. (SITC, Rev.3: 66332-2A, 66333-0A,66334-2A).

Remarque générale.
Autres ouvrages en béton obtenus par moulage, pressage ou centrifugation, à l'exception des blocs, des briques et des conduites. (CTCI, Rev.3: 66332-2A, 66333-0A, 66334-2A).

[1] Railway sleepers of concrete.
[2] Including concrete blocks, bricks and pipes.
[3] Production by establishments employing 5 or more persons.
[4] Sales.
[5] Production by establishments employing 20 or more persons.

[1] Traverses en béton pour voies ferrées.
[2] Y compris les blocs, briques et conduits en béton.
[3] Production des établissements occupant 5 personnes ou plus.
[4] Ventes.
[5] Production des établissements occupant 20 personnes ou plus.

Concrete, other products
Autres produits en béton

ISIC-BASED CODE - CODE BASE CITI

3699-16B

Unit : Thousand cubic metres

Unité : Milliers de mètres cubes

Country or area	1990	1991	1992	1993	1994	1995	1996	1997	1998	1999	Pays ou zone
America, North											**Amérique du Nord**
Panama[1]	4	...	...	...	...	...	...	...	...	...	Panama[1]
America, South											**Amérique du Sud**
Colombia[2]	...	...	154	34	2	57	...	...	...	...	Colombie[2]
Ecuador	...	...	276	486	545	644	...	...	...	...	Equateur
Asia											**Asie**
Kuwait	...	...	48	135	117	71	130	109	129	...	Koweït
Europe											**Europe**
Greece[1]	1767	1851	1964	...	...	...	...	...	...	...	Grèce[1]
Hungary	915	620	544	567	666	829	...	...	...	...	Hongrie
Latvia	..	...	...	14	28	10	5	10	24	...	Lettonie
Netherlands[3][4]	4177	4308	4179	...	...	...	...	...	...	...	Pays-Bas[3][4]
Poland	8683	7560	6913	6527	7118	6433	6922	8048	8743	9850	Pologne
Portugal	2429	2519	...	...	...	...	...	...	...	...	Portugal
Slovakia	..	..	...	...	...	...	307	323	...	...	Slovaquie

General Note.

Other moulded, pressed or centrifuged articles of cement except blocks, bricks and pipes. (SITC, Rev.3: 66332-2B, 66333-0B, 66334-2B).

[1] In thousand square metres.
[2] In thousand units.
[3] Sales.
[4] Production by establishments employing 20 or more persons.

Remarque générale.

Autres ouvrages en béton obtenus par moulage, pressage ou centrifugation, à l'exception des blocs, des briques et des conduites. (CTCI, Rev.3: 66332-2B, 66333-0B, 66334-2B).

[1] En milliers de mètres carrés.
[2] En milliers d'unités.
[3] Ventes.
[4] Production des établissements occupant 20 personnes ou plus.

Spiegeleisen and ferro-manganese
Fonte Spiegel et ferro-manganèse

ISIC-BASED CODE - CODE BASE CITI

3710-04

Unit : Thousand metric tons

Unité : Milliers de tonnes métriques

Country or area	1990	1991	1992	1993	1994	1995	1996	1997	1998	1999	Pays ou zone
Africa	**26**	**28**	**10**	**32**	**35**	**35**	**35**	**35**	**35**	**35**	**Afrique**
Egypt*[1][2]	...	...	10	30	35	35	35	35	35	35	Égypte*[1][2]
Zimbabwe[1][2]	0	0	0	2	0	0	0	0	...	...	Zimbabwe[1][2]
America, North	**321**	**140**	**77**	**146**	**130**	**176**	**201**	**175**	**177**	**190**	**Amérique du Nord**
Canada[1][2]	185	45	0	0	0	0	...	...	...	...	Canada[1][2]
Mexico[1]	136	95	77	146	130	176	201	175	177	190	Mexique[1]
America, South	**415**	**475**	**500**	**500**	**463**	**143**	**228**	**167**	**131**	**94**	**Amérique du Sud**
Argentina[1]	[2]24	[2]26	5	5	5	5	5	*[2]8	*[2]5	*[2]5	Argentine[1]
Brazil	[1]387	[1]441	[1]479	[1]486	[1]448	130	215	153	122	85	Brésil
Chile[1][2]	4	7	7	9	10	8	*8	*6	*4	*4	Chili[1][2]
Venezuela[1][2]	0	1	9	0	0	0	0	...	...	...	Venezuela[1][2]
Asia	**1283**	**1324**	**1194**	**1181**	**1166**	**1180**	**1220**	**1258**	**1207**	**1138**	**Asie**
China[1]	370	390	...	...	...	...	...	...	...	...	Chine[1]
Georgia*[1][2]	..	...	10	20	10	13	8	4	10	15	Géorgie*[1][2]
India[1]	*[2]230	*[2]211	*[2]198	104	156	146	163	144	156	146	Inde[1]
Indonesia*[1][2]	...	...	...	10	10	14	14	15	13	14	Indonésie*[1][2]
Japan	514	531	434	491	476	496	523	550	484	437	Japon
Korea,Dem.Ppl's.Rep.[1][2]	*70	*70	*70	*70	#9	*7	*6	*6	*6	*6	Corée,Rép.pop.dém.de[1][2]
Korea, Republic of[1][2]	84	95	86	101	120	119	126	159	158	*140	Corée, République de[1][2]
Philippines*[1][2]	...	5	5	5	5	5	5	0	0	0	Philippines*[1][2]
Europe	**1397**	**1582**	**1539**	**1256**	**1262**	**1424**	**1436**	**1489**	**1506**	**1361**	**Europe**
Belgium*[1][2]	25	25	25	25	25	25	25	25	20	0	Belgique*[1][2]
Bulgaria	17	11	4	4	5	8	8	11	...	...	Bulgarie
Croatia*[1][2]	..	...	10	10	1	0	0	0	0	...	Croatie*[1][2]
France	324	240	*[1][2]340	*[1][2]357	*[1][2]360	*[1][2]433	*[1][2]437	*[1][2]426	*[1][2]421	*[1][2]402	France
Germany[3][4]	..	381	346	264	291	413	382	478	457		Allemagne[3][4]
Germany(Fed.Rep.)	513	..	..	..	..	..	..	..	..	..	Allemagne(Rép.féd.)
German D.R. (former)	1	..	..	..	..	..	..	..	..		R.D.A. (anc.)
Italy	1	1	1	1	[3]0	[3]0	[3]0	[3]19	[3]33	[3]0	Italie
Norway	213	173	[1][2]203	[1][2]226	[1][2]249	[1][2]213	[1][2]215	*[1][2]235	*[1][2]235	*[1][2]235	Norvège
Poland	71	57	43	56	66	46	60	48	50	0	Pologne
Portugal[1][2]	12	12	0	0	0	...	...	...	...	...	Portugal[1][2]
Romania[1][2]	...	...	*27	*16	31	28	20	12	*4	*0	Roumanie[1][2]
Russian Federation	..	235	115	87	55	83	67	47	79	138	Fédération de Russie
Slovakia[1]	..	..	...	*[2]22	[2]25	[2]25	[2]25	2	38	29	Slovaquie[1]
Slovenia	..	29	29	17	22	31	33	20	15	...	Slovénie
Spain[1][2]	52	50	50	40	*35	*25	*30	*35	*35	*35	Espagne[1][2]
Ukraine	..	197	188	86	97	94	134	131	112	58	Ukraine
United Kingdom	143	140	[1][2]137	[1][2]45	[1][2]0	[1][2]0	[1][2]0	[1][2]0	[1]0	...	Royaume-Uni
USSR (former)	596		..	..	..	..	..	..	..	..	URSS (anc.)
Oceania	**60**	**45**	**55**	**75**	**100**	**110**	**110**	**95**	**110**	**95**	**Océanie**
Australia	60	*[1][2]45	*[1][2]55	*[1][2]75	*[1][2]100	*[1][2]110	*[1][2]110	*[1][2]95	*[1][2]110	*[1][2]95	Australie
Total	**4098**	**3594**	**3375**	**3190**	**3155**	**3068**	**3230**	**3219**	**3167**	**2913**	**Total**

General Note.

Spiegeleisen is a ferrous product containing, by weight, at least 6 per cent but not more than 25 per cent manganese and otherwise conforming to the definition of pig iron. Ferro-manganese is a ferro-alloy containing, by weight, more than 25 per cent manganese. (SITC, Rev.3: 67123-2, 67140-0).

Remarque générale.

La fonte Spiegel est un produit ferreux contenant en poids de 6 à 25 p. 100 de manganèse et répondant, en ce qui concerne les autres caractéristiques, à la définition de la fonte. Le ferro-manganèse est un ferro-alliage contenant en poids plus de 25 p. 100 de manganèse. (CTCI, Rev.3: 67123-2, 67140-0).

[1] Ferro-manganese only.

[2] Source: U. S. Geological Survey, (Washington, D. C.).

[3] Source: Annual Bulletin of Steel Statistics for Europe, America and Asia, United Nations Economic Commission of Europe (Geneva).

[4] Spiegeleisen only.

[1] Ferro-manganèse seulement.

[2] Source: U.S. Geological Survey, (Washington, D.C.).

[3] Source: Bulletin annuel de statistiques de l'acier pour l'Europe, l'Amérique et l'Asie. Commission économique des Nations Unies pour l'Europe (Genève).

[4] Fonte Spiegel seulement.

Pig iron, foundry
Fonte de moulage

ISIC-BASED CODE - CODE BASE CITI

3710-07

Unit : Thousand metric tons

Unité : Milliers de tonnes métriques

Country or area	1990	1991	1992	1993	1994	1995	1996	1997	1998	1999	Pays ou zone
Africa	**1265**	**1426**	**1223**	**1495**	**1308**	**1229**	**1210**	**1167**	**1438**	**1595**	**Afrique**
Algeria	17	14	14	...	...	...	...	...	...	...	Algérie
Egypt[1][2]	1100	1250	1062	1326	1148	1062	1050	1000	1300	1400	Egypte[1][2]
Tunisia	148	162	147	154	145	152	145	152	123	180	Tunisie
America, North	**37**	**37**	**37**	**37**	**37**	**37**	**37**	**37**	**37**	**37**	**Amérique du Nord**
Mexico*	37	...	...	...	...	...	...	...	...	...	Mexique*
America, South	**25**	**25**	**25**	**25**	**25**	**25**	**25**	**25**	**25**	**25**	**Amérique du Sud**
Argentina*	25	...	...	...	...	...	...	...	...	...	Argentine*
Asia	**3860**	**9230**	**8535**	**7071**	**6722**	**6745**	**7392**	**7992**	**6731**	**7722**	**Asie**
Georgia	..	...	...	8	1	2	2	3	1	1	Géorgie
India	...	...	...	2239	2785	2873	3304	3427	2976	3201	Inde
Japan	1105	1209	732	697	918	807	900	849	702	603	Japon
Kazakhstan	..	4953	4666	3552	2435	2530	2536	3089	2594	3438	Kazakhstan
Korea, Republic of	144	337	343	323	...	...	...	...	...	...	Corée, République de
Turkey	321	299	227	252	296	246	363	337	171	192	Turquie
Europe	**3846**	**6656**	**6153**	**4213**	**3623**	**3406**	**2832**	**3128**	**3260**	**3535**	**Europe**
Bulgaria	2	18	12	16	29	26	23	30	...	...	Bulgarie
Czechoslovakia(former)	379	227	..	..	..	..	..	..	..	..	Tchécoslovaquie(anc.)
Czech Republic	..	..	[3]121	[3]145	[3]234	[3]271	..	0	0	...	République tchèque
France	780	648	[3]793	516	564	588	561	646	710	[3]896	France
Germany[3]	..	730	625	383	430	320	168	183	190	580	Allemagne[3]
Germany(Fed.Rep.)	710	..	..	..	..	..	..	..	..	..	Allemagne(Rép.féd.)
German D.R.(former)	201	..	..	..	..	..	..	..	..	..	R.D.A. (anc.)
Greece[1][2]	160	160	...	...	...	...	...	...	...	...	Grèce[1][2]
Hungary	15	4	3	[3]0	[3]0	[3]0	[3]0	[3]0	[3]0	[3]0	Hongrie
Italy	367	283	212	120	109	74	214	245	275	165	Italie
Poland	511	298	294	206	204	227	219	263	288	197	Pologne
Romania	406	338	185	122	122	145	187	167	145	69	Roumanie
Russian Federation	..	1990	1969	1405	1026	1182	793	890	1061	1032	Fédération de Russie
Spain[3]	8	8	6	6	0	0	0	0	0	...	Espagne[3]
Switzerland[2]	129	105	102	82	88	97	[1]100	* [1]100	* [1]100	* [1]100	Suisse[2]
Ukraine	..	1797	1598	1052	657	316	278	444	302	305	Ukraine
United Kingdom	[3]102	[3]50	[3]73	[3]0	[3]0	[3]0	[3]0	[3]0	0	...	Royaume-Uni
Yugoslavia, SFR[3]	76	..	..	..	..	..	..	..	..	..	Yougoslavie, RSF[3]
Total	**9033**	**17374**	**15973**	**12841**	**11715**	**11442**	**11495**	**12349**	**11491**	**12914**	**Total**

General Note.

Pig iron is iron in liquid or solid form, containing at least 3 per cent of carbon and possibly one or more of the following elements within the weight limits specified : less than 6 per cent of silicon, less than 6 per cent of manganese, and less than 3 per cent of phosphorus. It may also contain small proportions of other elements, for example, chromium and nickel. Foundry pig iron is pig iron for use in making cast iron, including forge pig iron and pig iron for direct casting. (SITC, Rev.3: 67121-1, 67122-1).

Remarque générale.

La fonte est du fer à l'état liquide ou solide contenant au moins 3 p. 100 de carbone et pouvant contenir un ou plusieurs des éléments suivants dans les limites de poids indiquées: moins de 6 p. 100 de silicium, moins de 6 p. 100 de manganèse et moins de 3 p. 100 de phosphore. Elle peut aussi contenir de faibles proportions d'autres éléments, tels que le chrome et le nickel. La fonte de moulage est de la fonte servant à la fabrication de pièces moulées en fonte et comprend notamment la fonte pour forge et la fonte pour moulages de première coulé. (CTCI, Rev.3: 67121-1, 67122-1).

[1] Source: U. S. Geological Survey, (Washington, D. C.).
[2] Including pig-iron for steel making.
[3] Source: Annual Bulletin of Steel Statistics for Europe, America and Asia, United Nations Economic Commission of Europe (Geneva).

[1] Source: U.S. Geological Survey, (Washington, D.C.).
[2] Y compris la fonte d'affinage.
[3] Source: Bulletin annuel de statistiques de l'acier pour l'Europe, l'Amérique et l'Asie. Commission économique des Nations Unies pour l'Europe (Genève).

Pig iron, steel-making
Fonte d'affinage

ISIC-BASED CODE - CODE BASE CITI

3710-10

Unit : Thousand metric tons

Unité : Milliers de tonnes métriques

Country or area	1990	1991	1992	1993	1994	1995	1996	1997	1998	1999	Pays ou zone
Africa	**7830**	**8397**	**8804**	**8091**	**8016**	**8323**	**7951**	**6949**	**6639**	**5637**	**Afrique**
Algeria	1037	879	930	[1]925	[1]919	[1]962	[1]850	[1]526	[1]757	[1]807	Algérie
Morocco[2]	15	15	15	15	*15	*15	*15	*15	*15	*15	Maroc[2]
South Africa[1][2]	6257	6968	7352	6940	6982	7137	6876	6192	*5650	*4587	Afrique du Sud[1][2]
Zimbabwe	521	* [2]535	* [2]507	* [2]211	* [2]100	* [2]209	* [2]210	* [2]216	* [2]217	* [2]228	Zimbabwe
America, North	**59353**	**54704**	**58218**	**59343**	**60871**	**63020**	**62442**	**62734**	**61669**	**59905**	**Amérique du Nord**
Canada[1]	7344	8268	8621	8628	8112	8460	8638	8670	8937	[2]8783	Canada[1]
Mexico	2341	[1]2313	[1]2220	[1]2515	[1]3359	[1]3660	[1]4404	[1]4464	[1]4532	[1][2]4822	Mexique
United States[1]	49668	44123	47377	48200	49400	50900	49400	49600	48200	46300	Etats-Unis[1]
America, South	**24500**	**25268**	**25356**	**26182**	**27765**	**27929**	**27487**	**28555**	**28791**	**28095**	**Amérique du Sud**
Argentina	1883	[1]1366	[1]971	[1]980	[1]1392	[1]1524	[1][2]1966	[1][2]2066	* [1][2]2148	* [1][2]2010	Argentine
Brazil[1]	21141	22695	23057	23900	25092	25021	23978	24962	25111	24549	Brésil[1]
Chile	722	700	[2]873	[2]917	[2]886	[2]855	* [2]996	* [2]941	* [2]993	* [2]1033	Chili
Colombia[1]	347	300	[2]308	[2]238	[2]245	[2]282	[2]274	[2]322	* [2]256	* [2]266	Colombie[1]
Peru[1][2]	93	207	147	147	*150	*247	*273	*264	*283	*237	Pérou[1][2]
Venezuela[1]	314	[3]0	[3]0	[3]0	[3]0	[3]0	...	...	...	...	Venezuela[1]
Asia	**171395**	**181834**	**185795**	**200683**	**211783**	**222436**	**226207**	**237991**	**238605**	**245181**	**Asie**
China	[1]62380	[1]67000	[1]75890	87389	97410	105293	107225	115114	118629	125392	Chine
Georgia	..	[4]501	242	#4	0	2	2	1	0	..	Géorgie
India[2]	[1]12600	[1]14176	[1]15126	15674	17808	18626	19864	19898	20194	20139	Inde[2]
Iran(Islamic Rep. of)	*1000	[2]1952	[2]2053	[2]1961	[2]1883	[2]1532	[2]1867	[1][2]2053	* [1][2]2117	* [1][2]2112	Iran(Rép. islamique)
Japan	79124	78776	72412	73041	72858	74098	73697	77671	74279	73917	Japon
Korea,Dem.Ppl's.Rep.* [1][2]	...	...	...	...	...	500	500	500	250	250	Corée,Rép.pop.dém.de* [1][2]
Korea, Republic of	15333	18546	19238	21870	[1]21169	[1]22344	[1]23010	[1]22712	[1]23093	[1]23328	Corée, République de
Turkey	33	33	59	44	30	...	...	...	...	...	Turquie
Europe	**127237**	**198174**	**189539**	**176823**	**173030**	**175278**	**165942**	**176347**	**170667**	**172257**	**Europe**
Austria	3452	3439	[4]3074	[4]3070	[4]3320	[4]3878	[4]3416	[4]3966	[4]4021	[4]3913	Autriche
Belgium	9416	9353	8524	8179	8976	9204	8628	8076	8616	8436	Belgique
Bulgaria	1141	943	837	998	1441	1581	1481	1613	[1][2]1389	[1][2]1130	Bulgarie
Croatia	..	69	* [2]40	* [2]40	* [2]40	* [2]0	* [2]0	* [2]0	...	...	Croatie
Czechoslovakia(former)	9288	8253	..	..							Tchécoslovaquie(anc.)
Czech Republic	..	..	4889	4511	5040	5274	[4]4898	[4]5276	[4]5165	[4]4137	République tchèque
Finland	2283	2332	2452	2595	2597	2242	2457	2784	2916	[2]2954	Finlande
France	13320	12768	12264	11880	12444	12272	11547	12778	12892	12956	France
Germany[4]	..	29878	27577	26322	29202	29279	27172	30279	29515	27354	Allemagne[4]
Germany(Fed.Rep.)	28875	..	..	..	..	..	..	..	..	..	Allemagne(Rép.féd.)
German D.R. (former)	1927	..	..	..	..	..	..	..	..	..	R.D.A. (anc.)
Hungary	1682	1310	1176	1407	[4]1595	[4]1515	[4]1496	[4]1140	[4]1259	[4]1310	Hongrie
Italy	11485	10278	10220	11068	11052	11603	10107	11232	10516	10664	Italie
Luxembourg	2645	2463	2255	2412	1927	1028	829	438	0	0	Luxembourg
Netherlands	4960	4697	4849	5405	[5][6]5443	[5][6]5530	[5][6]5544	[5][6]5805	[5][6]5562	[4]5307	Pays-Bas
Norway[2]	54	61	70	73	*70	*70	*70	*70	*70	*60	Norvège[2]
Poland	7841	5999	6021	5899	6662	7146	6321	7032	5841	5036	Pologne
Portugal	336	252	408	396	420	408	420	[2]431	[2]365	* [2]389	Portugal
Romania	5949	4187	2925	3068	3374	4058	3838	4390	4396	2900	Roumanie
Russian Federation	..	46638	44021	39339	35454	38494	36286	36387	33521	39663	Fédération de Russie
Slovakia	..	..	[4]2952	3205	3330	3207	2928	[4]3072	[4]2756	[4]2897	Slovaquie
Spain[4]	5432	5389	4758	5388	5447	5106	4127	3927	4236	4058	Espagne[4]
Sweden[1]	2696	2851	2883	2844	3036	3020	3130	3072	3156	3816	Suède[1]
Ukraine	..	34638	35350	27108	20180	17998	17832	20616	20937	23010	Ukraine
United Kingdom	12218	11834	11469	11534	11943	12236	12830	13056	12746	12139	Royaume-Uni
Yugoslavia	..	526	512	62	17	109	565	[4]907	792	128	Yougoslavie
T.F.Yug.Rep. Macedonia	..	...	13	20	20	* [2]20	* [2]20	* [2]0	* [2]0	* [2]0	L'ex-RY Macédoine
Yugoslavia, SFR	2237	..	..	..	..	..	..	..	..	..	Yougoslavie, RSF
USSR (former)[7]	110166	..	..	..	..	..	..	..	..	..	URSS (anc.)[7]
Oceania	**6188**	**5600**	**6394**	**7209**	**7449**	**7449**	**7554**	**7545**	**7928**	**7513**	**Océanie**
Australia[8]	[1]6188	[1]5600	[1]6394	[1]7209	[1]7449	[1]7449	7554	7545	[1]7928	[1]7513	Australie[8]

For general note and footnotes, see end of table.

Voir la fin du tableau pour la remarque générale et les notes.

Pig iron, steel-making (continued)
Fonte d'affinage (suite)

ISIC-BASED CODE - CODE BASE CITI

3710-10

Unit : Thousand metric tons

Unité : Milliers de tonnes métriques

Country or area	1990	1991	1992	1993	1994	1995	1996	1997	1998	1999	Pays ou zone
Total	506669	473977	474106	478331	488914	504435	497583	520121	514299	518588	Total

General Note.

Pig iron is iron in liquid or solid form, containing at least 3 per cent of carbon and possibly one or more of the following elements within the weight limits specified : less than 6 per cent of silicon, less than 6 per cent of manganese, and less than 3 per cent of phosphorus. It may also contain small proportions of other elements, for example, chromium and nickel. Steel-making pig iron is distinguished from foundry pig iron on the basis of the uses to which it is put. Steel-making pig iron is pig iron for use in making crude steel. (SITC, Rev.3: 67121-2, 67122-2).

[1] Including foundry pig iron.
[2] Source: U. S. Geological Survey, (Washington, D. C.).
[3] Source: United Nations Economic Commission for Latin America and the Caribbean (ECLAC), (Santiago).
[4] Source: Annual Bulletin of Steel Statistics for Europe, America and Asia, United Nations Economic Commission of Europe (Geneva).
[5] Production by establishments employing 20 or more persons.
[6] Sales.
[7] Including foundry pig iron and other ferro-alloys.
[8] Twelve months ending 30 June of year stated.

Remarque générale.

La fonte est du fer à l'état liquide ou solide contenant au moins 3 p. 100 de carbone et pouvant contenir un ou plusieurs des éléments suivants dans les limites de poids indiquées: moins de 6 p. 100 de silicium, moins de 6 p. 100 de manganèse et moins de 3 p. 100 de phosphore. Elle peut aussi contenir de faibles proportions d'autres éléments, tels que le chrome et le nickel. La fonte d'affinage ne se distingue de la fonte de moulage que par sa destination. La fonte d'affinage est de la fonte servant à la fabrication d'acier brut. (CTCI, Rev.3: 67121-2, 67122-2).

[1] Y compris la fonte de moulage.
[2] Source: U.S. Geological Survey, (Washington, D.C.).
[3] Source: Commission économique des Nations Unies pour l'Amérique Latine et les Caraïbes (CEPAL), (Santiago).
[4] Source: Bulletin annuel de statistiques de l'acier pour l'Europe, l'Amérique et l'Asie. Commission économique des Nations Unies pour l'Europe (Genève).
[5] Production des établissements occupant 20 personnes ou plus.
[6] Ventes.
[7] Y compris la fonte de moulage et les autres ferro-alliages.
[8] Période de douze mois finissant le 30 juin de l'année indiquée.

Other ferro-alloys
Autres ferro-alliages

ISIC-BASED CODE - CODE BASE CITI

3710-13

Unit : Thousand metric tons   Unité : Milliers de tonnes métriques

Country or area	1990	1991	1992	1993	1994	1995	1996	1997	1998	1999	Pays ou zone
Africa	**2124**	**2118**	**1836**	**2242**	**2765**	**3377**	**3184**	**3281**	**3602**	**3505**	**Afrique**
Egypt	8	#42	40	40	40	45	46	49	[1]44	* [1]44	Egypte
South Africa[2]	1878	1861	1585	2066	2506	3031	2862	2982	3290	3201	Afrique du Sud[2]
Zimbabwe[1]	238	215	211	136	219	301	276	250	268	*260	Zimbabwe[1]
America, North	**1191**	**1077**	**1035**	**980**	**1068**	**1080**	**1083**	**934**	**811**	**786**	**Amérique du Nord**
Canada[1]	117	97	77	77	77	79	83	87	87	87	Canada[1]
Dominican Republic	72	[1]76	58	61	80	81	78	85	66	[1]61	Rép. dominicaine
Mexico	127	...	...	...	...	...	...	...	...	...	Mexique
United States	875	777	773	715	784	793	795	635	531	511	Etats-Unis
America, South	**711**	**601**	**631**	**647**	**607**	**613**	**531**	**539**	**491**	**532**	**Amérique du Sud**
Argentina	18	68	55	55	61	72	33	[1]58	[1]60	* [1]56	Argentine
Brazil	552	388	446	444	399	376	344	318	265	312	Brésil
Chile[1]	10	11	10	11	10	12	13	10	9	*9	Chili[1]
Colombia	[1]44	[1]49	47	47	48	53	[1]52	[1]55	[1]61	* [1]62	Colombie
Peru* [1]	1	1	1	1	1	1	1	1	1	1	Pérou* [1]
Venezuela[1]	86	84	72	89	88	98	88	97	95	*92	Venezuela[1]
Asia	**3175**	**3554**	**4044**	**4439**	**4633**	**5828**	**5415**	**5624**	**5017**	**5583**	**Asie**
Bhutan* [1]	...	...	...	...	2	12	13	15	18	18	Bhoutan* [1]
China	2442	2160	2650	2999	3361	4319	4180	4044	3538	[1]3800	Chine
Georgia	..	...	...	17	11	8	7	17	32	26	Géorgie
India	104	110	135	201	105	105	203	302	282	320	Inde
Indonesia[1]	*25	*27	*28	*26	29	61	55	57	*49	*57	Indonésie[1]
Iran(Islamic Rep. of)[1]	...	...	...	...	7	22	31	32	34	*34	Iran(Rép. islamique)[1]
Japan	203	218	148	114	111	103	109	111	102	90	Japon
Kazakhstan[3]	..	...	...	...	635	809	607	843	726	1000	Kazakhstan[3]
Korea,Dem.Ppl's.Rep.* [1]	50	50	50	50	25	#5	4	4	4	4	Corée,Rép.pop.dém.de* [1]
Korea, Republic of	[2]197	[2]197	[2]202	[2]188	[2]212	[2]218	[1]88	[1]79	[1]110	* [1]103	Corée, République de
Philippines[1]	66	34	37	22	26	60	7	*0	*0	*0	Philippines[1]
Thailand	5	5	5	2	1	[1]0	[1]0	[1]0	...	...	Thaïlande
Turkey	[1]67	87	90	100	108	106	112	120	122	131	Turquie
Europe	**2728**	**4442**	**3955**	**3845**	**3501**	**3831**	**3358**	**3244**	**3024**	**3050**	**Europe**
Albania	24	35	22	35	34	43	42	31	30	[1]29	Albanie
Austria[1]	12	12	16	14	11	11	11	11	10	*9	Autriche[1]
Bulgaria	17	11	4	6	5	8	8	11	* [1]10	* [1]10	Bulgarie
Croatia	..	73	56	36	54	26	11	24	[1]12	* [1]10	Croatie
Czechoslovakia(former)	169	162		..	..	..	..	..	..	..	Tchécoslovaquie(anc.)
Czech Republic* [1]	..	..	...	1	1	1	1	1	1	1	République tchèque* [1]
Finland	155	196	198	195	254	247	228	[1]237	[1]231	* [1]235	Finlande
France	294	342	360	387	[1]263	[1]270	[4]254	[4]296	[4]299	[4]270	France
Germany	..	97	79	56	42	[3]56	[3]58	[3]58	[3]54	[3]42	Allemagne
Germany(Fed.Rep.)	108	..	..	..	..	..	..	..	..		Allemagne(Rép.féd.)
Greece	[1]91	[1]87	[1]73	[1]52	[1]77	125	110	[1]70	63	* [1]52	Grèce
Hungary	18	6	* [1]9	* [1]9	[1]9	[1]8	[1]8	[1]8	[1]8	* [1]8	Hongrie
Iceland	63	50	54	67	66	70	87	84	82	83	Islande
Italy	207	160	142	128	105	129	184	154	150	93	Italie
Norway	717	773	684	[1]794	[1]871	[1]947	[1]905	742	791	824	Norvège
Poland	141	105	107	113	97	112	104	112	108	75	Pologne
Romania[5]	142	109	86	66	99	120	132	85	64	1	Roumanie[5]
Russian Federation[3]	..	1377	1087	978	765	876	481	496	400	600	Fédération de Russie[3]
Slovakia	..	..	...	211	174	133	115	[3]164	96	87	Slovaquie
Slovenia	..	...	...	...	...	...	33	27	20	16	Slovénie
Spain[1]	*105	*100	*95	*77	69	91	111	150	161	*176	Espagne[1]
Sweden	130	136	149	146	153	[1]152	[1]159	[1]124	145	129	Suède
Switzerland[1]	5	5	5	5	0	0	0	0	...	...	Suisse[1]
Ukraine	..	504	433	376	273	321	254	288	223	244	Ukraine
United Kingdom[1]	...	...	...	10	0	0	0	0	...	...	Royaume-Uni[1]
Yugoslavia		12	6	1	2	2	7	6	1	...	Yougoslavie
T.F.Yug.Rep. Macedonia	..	56	64	58	53	59	55	64	66	54	L'ex-RY Macédoine
Yugoslavia, SFR	318	..	..	..	..	..	..	..	..	..	Yougoslavie, RSF

For general note and footnotes, see end of table.   Voir la fin du tableau pour la remarque générale et les notes.

Other ferro-alloys (continued)
Autres ferro-alliages (suite)

ISIC-BASED CODE - CODE BASE CITI
3710-13

Unit : Thousand metric tons — Unité : Milliers de tonnes métriques

Country or area	1990	1991	1992	1993	1994	1995	1996	1997	1998	1999	Pays ou zone
Oceania	**150**	**157**	**154**	**142**	**170**	**172**	**167**	**169**	**293**	**293**	**Océanie**
Australia[1]	118	123	122	105	130	130	125	125	135	*135	Australie[1]
New Caledonia	32	34	32	37	40	42	42	44	[1]158	[1]158	Nouvelle-Calédonie
Total	**10079**	**11950**	**11655**	**12295**	**12745**	**14900**	**13738**	**13791**	**13237**	**13749**	**Total**

General Note.
All ferro-alloys, other than ferro-manganese, which are produced in blast furnaces, low-shaft furnaces, electric furnaces and other types of iron-making installations. (SITC, Rev.3: 67150-0).

[1] Source: U. S. Geological Survey, (Washington, D. C.).
[2] Including ferro-manganese.
[3] Source: Annual Bulletin of Steel Statistics for Europe, America and Asia, United Nations Economic Commission of Europe (Geneva).
[4] Deliveries.
[5] Ferro-alloys produced in electric furnaces.

Remarque générale.
Tous les ferro-alliages autres que le ferro-manganèse, produits au haut fourneau, au bas fourneau, au four électrique ou dans d'autres types d'installations pour la fabrication de la fonte. (CTCI, Rev.3: 67150-0).

[1] Source: U.S. Geological Survey, (Washington, D.C.).
[2] Y compris le ferromanganèse.
[3] Source: Bulletin annuel de statistiques de l'acier pour l'Europe, l'Amérique et l'Asie. Commission économique des Nations Unies pour l'Europe (Genève).
[4] Livraisons.
[5] Ferro-alliages produits dans les fourneaux électriques.

Ferro-chromium (including ferro-silico-chromium and charge chrome)
Ferro-chrome (y compris le ferro-silicochrome et chrome de charge)

ISIC-BASED CODE - CODE BASE CITI
3710-131

Unit : Thousand metric tons   Unité : Milliers de tonnes métriques

Country or area	1990	1991	1992	1993	1994	1995	1996	1997	1998	1999	Pays ou zone
Africa	**1289**	**1405**	**1035**	**1209**	**1641**	**2210**	**2006**	**2127**	**2376**	**2314**	**Afrique**
South Africa	1051	1190	824	1085	1458	1956	1763	1894	2129	2074	Afrique du Sud
Zimbabwe[1]	238	215	211	124	183	254	243	233	247	*240	Zimbabwe[1]
America, North	**109**	**68**	**61**	**63**	**67**	**73**	**37**	**61**	**51**	**48**	**Amérique du Nord**
United States[2][3]	109	68	61	63	67	73	37	61	...	...	Etats-Unis[2][3]
America, South	**91**	**90**	**100**	**89**	**87**	**104**	**80**	**76**	**75**	**93**	**Amérique du Sud**
Brazil[4]	89	87	98	88	85	101	77	74	73	91	Brésil[4]
Chile[1]	2	3	2	1	2	3	3	2	*2	*2	Chili[1]
Asia	**823**	**1223**	**1243**	**1068**	**1187**	**1637**	**1248**	**1615**	**1444**	**1607**	**Asie**
China[1]	340	380	410	372	*370	*500	*423	*480	*424	*400	Chine[1]
India	38	56	56	39	163	233	144	204	200	210	Inde
Iran(Islamic Rep. of)[1]	...	...	...	...	7	12	11	11	14	*14	Iran(Rép. islamique)[1]
Japan	319	297	296	225	216	236	211	200	147	120	Japon
Kazakhstan	..	372	350	315	312	512	346	605	542	732	Kazakhstan
Philippines[1]	56	24	27	12	16	50	7	0	0	*0	Philippines[1]
Turkey	[1]62	85	95	95	103	94	107	115	117	131	Turquie
Europe	**654**	**1182**	**1074**	**886**	**995**	**1039**	**751**	**858**	**848**	**858**	**Europe**
Albania	24	35	22	35	34	43	42	31	30	28	Albanie
Croatia	..	73	56	36	54	26	11	24	[1]12	[1]10	Croatie
Czechoslovakia(former)	32	34	..	..	..	..	..	..	..	..	Tchécoslovaquie(anc.)
Finland	155	196	197	195	253	244	225	[1]237	[1]231	[1]235	Finlande
France[1]	25	23	7	0	0	0	0	...	...	...	France[1]
Germany*[1]	..	...	...	...	17	22	25	26	21	17	Allemagne*[1]
Germany(Fed.Rep.)[1]	50	..	..	..	..	..	..	..	..	..	Allemagne(Rép.féd.)[1]
German D.R.(former)	18	..	..	..	..	..	..	..	..	..	R.D.A. (anc.)
Greece	[1]30	*[1]11	[1]0	[1]0	[1]0	[1]0	0	...	0	...	Grèce
Italy	53	47	41	38	7	19	28	12	[1]11	[1]12	Italie
Norway	30	90	[1]102	[1]80	[1]120	[1]148	[1]109	[1]145	[1]175	*[1]160	Norvège
Poland[1]	14	2	35	38	7	18	4	6	4	*4	Pologne[1]
Russian Federation	..	505	428	292	343	354	135	248	218	267	Fédération de Russie
Slovakia	..	..	...	...	...	...	...	...	8	4	Slovaquie
Slovenia	..	13	18	9	13	23	23	10	10	4	Slovénie
Spain[1]	15	6	0	2	2	1	1	0	1	*1	Espagne[1]
Sweden	120	118	133	128	[1]134	[1]130	[1]138	[1]102	[1]124	[1]113	Suède
Ukraine	..	2	1	0	0	0	0	0	0	0	Ukraine
T.F.Yug.Rep. Macedonia	..	5	7	6	4	4	4	5	...	...	L'ex-RY Macédoine
Yugoslavia, SFR	88	..	..	..	..	..	..	..	..	..	Yougoslavie, RSF
USSR (former)[1]	860	..	..	..	..	..	..	..	..	..	URSS (anc.)[1]
Total	**3826**	**3967**	**3513**	**3315**	**3977**	**5063**	**4121**	**4737**	**4794**	**4920**	**Total**

General Note.
Data refer to ferro-chromium and include ferro-silico-chromium and charge chrome. (SITC, Rev.3: 67153-0, 67154-0).

Remarque générale.
Les données se rapportent au ferro-chrome et comprennent le ferro-silico-chrome. (CTCI, Rev.3: 67153-0, 67154-0).

[1] Source: U. S. Geological Survey, (Washington, D. C.).
[2] Data refer to all chromium ferro-alloys.
[3] Beginning 1998, data are confidential.
[4] Ferro-chromium only.

[1] Source: U.S. Geological Survey, (Washington, D.C.).
[2] Les données se rapportent à tous les ferro-alliages.
[3] A partir de 1998, les données sont confidentielles.
[4] Ferro-chrome seulement.

Ferro-nickel
Ferro-nickel

ISIC-BASED CODE - CODE BASE CITI

3710-132

Unit : Thousand metric tons

Unité : Milliers de tonnes métriques

Country or area	1990	1991	1992	1993	1994	1995	1996	1997	1998	1999	Pays ou zone
America, North	**83**	**90**	**77**	**45**	**81**	**98**	**109**	**118**	**74**	**64**	**Amérique du Nord**
Dominican Republic	76	76	58	35	81	81	78	85	66	64	Rép. dominicaine
United States	7	14	18	10	0	17	31	32	9	0	Etats-Unis
America, South	**78**	**83**	**80**	**83**	**82**	**84**	**82**	**87**	**87**	**82**	**Amérique du Sud**
Brazil	34	34	33	36	34	31	30	32	26	20	Brésil
Colombia	[1]44	[1]49	47	47	48	53	[1]52	[1]55	[1]61	* [1]62	Colombie
Asia	**259**	**322**	**265**	**283**	**271**	**405**	**377**	**403**	**388**	**382**	**Asie**
Indonesia* [1]	25	27	28	26	29	54	48	50	42	50	Indonésie* [1]
Japan	234	295	237	257	242	351	329	353	346	332	Japon
Europe	**79**	**208**	**238**	**163**	**170**	**181**	**182**	**126**	**103**	**97**	**Europe**
Austria [1]	8	9	10	8	5	5	5	5	*5	*4	Autriche [1]
Greece	[1]61	[1]87	[1]73	[1]52	[1]77	[1]69	83	[1]70	63	* [1]52	Grèce
Russian Federation* [1]	..	...	46	47	59	77	75	40	30	33	Fédération de Russie* [1]
Ukraine	..	...	* [1]98	* [1]50	* [1]23	* [1]23	* [1]8	* [1]0	0	* [1]0	Ukraine
Yugoslavia	..	12	6	1	2	2	7	6	1	...	Yougoslavie
T.F.Yug.Rep. Macedonia	..	1	5	5	4	5	4	5	5	[1]5	L'ex-RY Macédoine
Yugoslavia, SFR*	10	..	..	..	..	..	..	..	..	..	Yougoslavie, RSF*
Oceania	**32**	**34**	**32**	**37**	**40**	**42**	**42**	**44**	**158**	**158**	**Océanie**
New Caledonia	32	34	32	37	40	42	42	44	[1]158	[1]158	Nouvelle-Calédonie
Total	**531**	**736**	**691**	**611**	**644**	**809**	**792**	**778**	**811**	**782**	**Total**

General Note.
Data refer to ferro-nickel. (SITC, Rev.3: 67155-0).

Remarque générale.
Les données se rapportent au ferro-nickel. (CTCI, Rev.3: 67155-0).

[1] Source: U. S. Geological Survey, (Washington, D. C.).

[1] Source: U.S. Geological Survey, (Washington, D.C.).

Ferro-silicon
Ferro-silicium

ISIC-BASED CODE - CODE BASE CITI

3710-134

Unit : Thousand metric tons   Unité : Milliers de tonnes métriques

Country or area	1990	1991	1992	1993	1994	1995	1996	1997	1998	1999	Pays ou zone
Africa	**140**	**158**	**162**	**235**	**241**	**185**	**152**	**184**	**188**	**183**	**Afrique**
Egypt	8	20	36	40	44	4	7	7	7	7	Egypte
South Africa	115	110	103	172	174	158	122	154	158	153	Afrique du Sud
Zimbabwe[1]	17	28	...	...	...	...	...	...	...	...	Zimbabwe[1]
America, North	**535**	**419**	**406**	**378**	**414**	**414**	**418**	**415**	**390**	**381**	**Amérique du Nord**
Canada[1]	95	75	55	55	55	56	56	56	*56	*56	Canada[1]
Mexico	6	6	[1]5	[1]0	* [1]0	* [1]0	* [1]0	* [1]0	* [1]0	...	Mexique
United States	434	338	346	323	359	358	362	359	334	325	Etats-Unis
America, South	**469**	**292**	**320**	**333**	**256**	**287**	**338**	**292**	**239**	**271**	**Amérique du Sud**
Argentina	18	*18	[1]8	10	10	10	33	* [1]18	* [1]11	* [1]11	Argentine
Brazil	389	213	267	267	[1]199	222	[1]237	[1]212	166	201	Brésil
Chile* [1]	6	6	4	8	6	4	5	1	1	1	Chili* [1]
Peru* [1]	1	1	1	1	1	1	1	1	1	1	Pérou* [1]
Venezuela* [1]	55	54	40	47	41	50	63	60	60	57	Venezuela* [1]
Asia	**904**	**1191**	**1240**	**1488**	**1429**	**1539**	**1638**	**1462**	**1519**	**1630**	**Asie**
Bhutan* [1]	...	...	...	...	2	12	13	15	18	18	Bhoutan* [1]
China	[1]727	[1]817	[1]834	[1]1040	[1]1100	1163	1375	1185	* [1]1290	* [1]1400	Chine
India	54	32	46	139	57	39	76	73	67	46	Inde
Iran(Islamic Rep. of)* [1]	...	...	...	...	0	10	20	20	20	20	Iran(Rép. islamique)* [1]
Japan	68	68	42	33	23	14	9	9	5	4	Japon
Kazakhstan* [1]	..	...	...	...	208	256	119	133	92	120	Kazakhstan* [1]
Korea,Dem.Ppl's.Rep.* [1]	30	30	30	30	#5	4	3	3	3	3	Corée,Rép.pop.dém.de* [1]
Korea, Republic of[1]	2	0	55	...	...	...	...	...	...	...	Corée, République de[1]
Philippines* [1]	10	10	10	10	10	10	0	0	0	0	Philippines* [1]
Turkey	[1]5	2	1	5	5	12	4	5	5	0	Turquie
Europe	**1118**	**1389**	**1203**	**1156**	**1149**	**1132**	**1042**	**1063**	**1011**	**1038**	**Europe**
Bulgaria	17	11	4	6	5	8	8	11	* [1]8	* [1]8	Bulgarie
Czechoslovakia(former) [1]	21	14	..	..	..	..	..	..	..	..	Tchécoslovaquie(anc.) [1]
Finland	...	...	1	0	0	...	...	...	...	...	Finlande
France	117	106	99	80	[1]111	[1]108	* [1]103	* [1]109	* [1]110	* [1]110	France
Germany* [1]	..	50	20	20	20	0	0	0	0	0	Allemagne* [1]
Germany(Fed.Rep.)* [1]	40	..	..	..	..	..	..	..	..	..	Allemagne(Rép.féd.)* [1]
German D.R.(former)	68	..	..	..	..	..	..	..	..	..	R.D.A. (anc.)
Hungary	11	4	* [1]7	* [1]7	* [1]7	* [1]7	* [1]7	* [1]7	* [1]7	* [1]7	Hongrie
Iceland	63	50	54	67	66	70	72	70	68	71	Islande
Italy	40	12	4	2	2	0	12	0	...	...	Italie
Norway	460	414	377	401	453	386	350	342	357	354	Norvège
Poland[1]	89	80	36	43	54	70	72	77	*75	*70	Pologne[1]
Romania	28	16	23	24	28	19	24	10	6	0	Roumanie
Slovakia	..	..	...	[1]22	* [1]30	* [1]30	* [1]30	* [1]30	37	44	Slovaquie
Slovenia	..	16	11	8	9	8	10	10	5	12	Slovénie
Spain* [1]	37	40	40	30	25	30	30	30	30	40	Espagne* [1]
Sweden	19	19	15	18	19	[1]22	[1]21	[1]22	* [1]22	* [1]22	Suède
Switzerland[1]	3	3	3	3	0	0	0	0	...	...	Suisse[1]
Ukraine	..	502	432	376	273	321	254	288	223	244	Ukraine
United Kingdom	...	...	...	2	2	2	2	...	...	...	Royaume-Uni
T.F.Yug.Rep. Macedonia	..	50	52	47	45	50	47	54	61	54	L'ex-RY Macédoine
Yugoslavia, SFR	103	..	..	..	..	..	..	..	..	..	Yougoslavie, RSF
USSR (former) [1]	1860	..	..	..	..	..	..	..	..	..	URSS (anc.) [1]
Oceania	**20**	**19**	**17**	**19**	**19**	**19**	**19**	**19**	**19**	**19**	**Océanie**
Australia[2]	20	19	17	...	...	...	...	...	...	...	Australie[2]
Total	**5046**	**3468**	**3348**	**3608**	**3508**	**3575**	**3607**	**3434**	**3366**	**3521**	**Total**

General Note.
Data refer to ferro-silicon. (SITC, Rev.3: 67151-0).

[1] Source: U. S. Geological Survey, (Washington, D. C.).
[2] Twelve months ending 30 November of the year stated.

Remarque générale.
Les données se rapportent au ferrosilicium. (CTCI, Rev.3: 67151-0).

[1] Source: U.S. Geological Survey, (Washington, D.C.).
[2] Période de douze mois finissant le 30 novembre de l'année indiquée.

Crude steel for castings
Acier brut pour moulages

ISIC-BASED CODE - CODE BASE CITI

3710-16

Unit : Thousand metric tons

Unité : Milliers de tonnes métriques

Country or area	1990	1991	1992	1993	1994	1995	1996	1997	1998	1999	Pays ou zone
Africa	**186**	**203**	**192**	**192**	**193**	**211**	**194**	**203**	**179**	**239**	**Afrique**
Algeria*	2	...	...	...	...	...	...	...	...	...	Algérie*
Egypt	1	...	...	...	...	...	...	...	...	...	Egypte
Morocco[1][2]	*7	*7	*7	*7	*7	*7	*5	5	*5	*5	Maroc[1][2]
Tunisia	176	193	182	182	183	201	186	195	171	231	Tunisie
America, North	**0**	**92**	**94**	**69**	**64**	**64**	**64**	**64**	**64**	**64**	**Amérique du Nord**
Canada	*0	92	94	*69	...	...	...	...	...	...	Canada
America, South	**64**	**51**	**53**	**46**	**38**	**17**	**11**	**15**	**16**	**21**	**Amérique du Sud**
Brazil	64	51	53	46	38	17	11	15	16	21	Brésil
Asia	**11943**	**14440**	**16380**	**14444**	**16488**	**16152**	**18282**	**19085**	**16714**	**17218**	**Asie**
Azerbaijan	..	573	413	236	#40	20	3	25	8	0	Azerbaïdjan
China	2508	2881	3312	...	...	...	...	...	...	...	Chine
Georgia	..	...	...	2	1	87	82	102	56	7	Géorgie
India	350	433	884	379	384	406	467	438	419	435	Inde
Indonesia[1][2]	2890	3250	3171	1948	3220	3500	4100	3800	*2700	*2800	Indonésie[1][2]
Iran(Islamic Rep. of)[1][2]	1430	2200	2940	3672	4498	4696	5415	6322	5600	*6071	Iran(Rép. islamique)[1][2]
Japan	791	734	614	569	580	594	594	580	461	415	Japon
Kazakhstan	..	465	383	261	119	67	81	64	0	0	Kazakhstan
Korea, Republic of	122	125	122	115	142	139	...	...	...	...	Corée, République de
Turkey	3852	3751	4508	4362	4604	3743	4505	4717	4431	4449	Turquie
Europe	**6918**	**13365**	**13908**	**10623**	**9350**	**8436**	**7913**	**8601**	**8277**	**8299**	**Europe**
Austria[3]	4291	4082	3846	[4]4018	[4]4246	*3719	*3359	*3831	*3858	...	Autriche[3]
Belarus	..	324	[4]277	[4]241	164	108	91	110	111	113	Bélarus
Belgium	93	71	55	59	...	...	...	...	...	...	Belgique
Croatia	..	...	...	...	...	[4]1	[4]1	1	1	[4]0	Croatie
Finland	20	17	15	18	21	25	20	23	[4]23	[4]19	Finlande
France	260	252	250	201	218	228	220	224	225	223	France
Germany	..	730	625	383	430	[4]319	[4]296	[4]295	[4]323	[4]296	Allemagne
Germany(Fed.Rep.)	378	...	...	...	...	...	...	...	...	..	Allemagne(Rép.féd.)
Hungary	[4]32	[4]15	[4]4	[4]4	[4]0	[4]0	7	[4]0	[4]0	[4]0	Hongrie
Italy	180	170	133	130	139	136	106	101	137	139	Italie
Latvia	..	9	7	4	4	4	3	3	2	[4]2	Lettonie
Lithuania	..	4	3	2	1	1	0	1	1	1	Lituanie
Netherlands	4	3	2	0	0	0	0	0	...	...	Pays-Bas
Norway[4]	8	7	6	4	5	6	6	0	0	0	Norvège[4]
Poland[4]	...	201	888	81	98	52	235	382	311	30	Pologne[4]
Republic of Moldova	..	623	653	#[5]1	[5]1	[5]0	[5]0	[5]0	[5]0	[5]0	Rép. de Moldova
Romania	863	379	238	183	143	140	133	115	69	39	Roumanie
Russian Federation	..	4330	5062	3888	2946	2834	2625	2758	2459	3125	Fédération de Russie
Slovenia	..	14	9	8	9	9	4	2	3	3	Slovénie
Spain	*160	[4]146	[4]109	[4]109	[4]100	[4]120	[4]128	[4]118	[4]121	[4]121	Espagne
Sweden[4]	20	18	18	18	22	29	28	31	29	28	Suède[4]
Ukraine	..	1772	1526	1099	554	452	385	343	342	480	Ukraine
United Kingdom	240	189	171	166	174	180	188	186	185	128	Royaume-Uni
Yugoslavia	..	7	9	4	4	3	8	7	7	4	Yougoslavie
Yugoslavia, SFR	32	..	..	..	..	..	..	..	..	..	Yougoslavie, RSF
USSR (former)	7890	..	..	..	..	..	..	..	..	..	URSS (anc.)
Total	**27001**	**28151**	**30627**	**25374**	**26133**	**24880**	**26463**	**27967**	**25249**	**25840**	**Total**

General Note.

Crude steel is steel (including alloy steel) in the form in which it emerges from the Bessemer, Thomas, open-hearth or electric process or from one of the various oxygen-blowing processes. Puddled iron is excluded. Steel for castings is crude steel whichis used directly in liquid form for producing steel castings. Steel for castings produced by independent foundries is included. Continuously-cast blooms, billets and slabs are included as ingots. (SITC, Rev.3: 67241-1, 67247-1, 67249-1, 67260-1, 67270-1).

Remarque générale.

On entend par acier brut l'acier (y compris l'acier allié) produit par les procédés Bessemer, Thomas, Martin ou électrique ou par les procédés à l'oxygène. Cette rubrique ne comprend pas le fer puddlé. L'acier pour moulage est de l'acier brut utilisé directement à l'état liquide pour la fabrication de pièces moulées en acier. Cette rubrique comprend l'acier pour moulages produit par les fonderies indépendantes. (CTCI, Rev.3: 67241-1, 67247-1, 67249-1, 67260-1, 67270-1).

For footnotes, see end of table.

Voir la fin du tableau pour les notes.

Crude steel for castings (continued)
Acier brut pour moulages (suite)

ISIC-BASED CODE - CODE BASE CITI

3710-16

Footnotes
[1] Source: U. S. Geological Survey, (Washington, D. C.).
[2] Including ingots.
[3] 1999 data are confidential.
[4] Source: Annual Bulletin of Steel Statistics for Europe, America and Asia, United Nations Economic Commission of Europe (Geneva).
[5] Excluding Transnistria region.

Notes.
[1] Source: U.S. Geological Survey, (Washington, D.C.).
[2] Y compris les lingots.
[3] Pour 1999, les données sont confidentielles.
[4] Source: Bulletin annuel de statistiques de l'acier pour l'Europe, l'Amérique et l'Asie. Commission économique des Nations Unies pour l'Europe (Genève).
[5] Non compris la région de Transnistria.

Crude steel, ingots
Acier brut (lingots)

ISIC-BASED CODE - CODE BASE CITI

3710-19

Unit : Thousand metric tons
Unité : Milliers de tonnes métriques

Country or area	1990	1991	1992	1993	1994	1995	1996	1997	1998	1999	Pays ou zone
Africa	**12593**	**13507**	**13039**	**12696**	**12183**	**12430**	**11440**	**11627**	**10825**	**10471**	**Afrique**
Algeria	767	[1]797	[1]768	[1]798	[1]772	[1]780	[1]590	[1]361	[1]581	[1]675	Algérie
Angola* [2]	10	10	10	9	9	9	9	9	9	9	Angola* [2]
Egypt[2]	2325	[1]2541	[1]2524	[1]2772	[1]2622	[1]2642	[1]2618	[1]2717	* [1]2500	* [1]2619	Egypte[2]
Nigeria	220	200	* [2]200	* [2]150	* [2]58	* [2]36	* [2]0	* [2]0	* [2]2	* [2]0	Nigéria
South Africa[1]	8691	9358	[2]8970	[2]8726	[2]8525	[2]8741	[2]7999	[2]8311	[2]7506	* [2]6925	Afrique du Sud[1]
Uganda[1]	0	* [2]20	* [2]20	* [2]20	* [2]10	* [2]12	* [2]12	* [2]15	* [2]15	* [2]15	Ouganda[1]
Zimbabwe[2]	580	581	547	221	187	210	212	214	212	*228	Zimbabwe[2]
America, North	**110498**	**100457**	**106237**	**111379**	**113918**	**119770**	**120318**	**124956**	**125626**	**126031**	**Amérique du Nord**
Canada	12281	12987	13933	[2]14300	[1][2]13897	[1][2]14415	[1][2]14735	[1][2]15554	[1][2]15930	[1][2]16300	Canada
Cuba	270	270	[2]134	[2]91	[2]131	[2]207	[2]231	[2]342	[2]284	* [2]300	Cuba
Mexico	[1]8221	[1]7462	[1]7848	[1]8188	[1]8690	[1]9948	[1]9852	[1]10560	10812	...	Mexique
United States[1]	89726	79738	84322	88800	91200	95200	95500	98500	98600	97400	Etats-Unis[1]
America, South	**29182**	**30440**	**31090**	**32814**	**34779**	**34468**	**35834**	**36896**	**36192**	**34533**	**Amérique du Sud**
Argentina[1]	3636	2972	2680	2870	3274	3575	4069	4157	4210	3797	Argentine[1]
Brazil	20567	22566	23881	25161	25709	25076	25237	26153	25760	24996	Brésil
Chile	768	804	1008	1020	996	948	[2]1178	[2]1167	[2]1171	[2]1288	Chili
Colombia[1]	733	700	657	715	702	[2]714	[2]677	[2]710	[2]622	* [2]523	Colombie[1]
Ecuador	20	20	[2]20	[2]27	[2]32	[2]35	* [2]20	[2]44	[2]46	[2]53	Equateur
Peru[1]	284	404	343	417	[2]506	* [2]512	* [2]678	* [2]607	* [2]631	* [2]568	Pérou[1]
Uruguay	34	[2]41	[2]55	[2]36	[2]36	[2]40	[2]34	[2]39	* [2]52	* [2]47	Uruguay
Venezuela[1]	3140	2933	2446	2568	[2]3524	[2]3568	[2]3941	[2]4019	[2]3700	[2]3261	Venezuela[1]
Asia	**235168**	**249778**	**253521**	**262971**	**264541**	**268492**	**274905**	**293671**	**294920**	**307800**	**Asie**
Azerbaijan	..	554	396	225	#37	19	0	0	0	0	Azerbaïdjan
Bangladesh	[3]90	[2][3]58	[2][3]36	[2][3]32	[2][3]34	[2][3]36	[3]27	[3]23	[2]35	[2]36	Bangladesh
China	66350	71000	80940	[1]89556	[1]92617	[1]95360	[1]100056	[1]108942	[1]115590	124260	Chine
Georgia	..	...	532	222	121	88	83	103	56	7	Géorgie
India	16129	17144	17839	12972	12972	12972	12972	12978	[2]23480	[2]24269	Inde
Iraq* [2]	150	20	100	300	300	300	300	200	200	800	Iraq* [2]
Israel* [1][2]	144	90	109	120	180	200	203	203	203	200	Israël* [1][2]
Japan	109548	108914	97518	99063	97715	101046	98207	103965	93087	93777	Japon
Kazakhstan	..	5912	5680	4296	2849	2959	3135	3816	3116	4105	Kazakhstan
Korea,Dem.Ppl's.Rep.* [1][2]	8000	8000	8100	8100	8100	1500	1500	1000	1000	1000	Corée,Rép.pop.dém.de* [1][2]
Korea, Republic of	23125	26001	28055	33026	33745	37500	[1]39643	[1]43405	[1]40299	[1]41502	Corée, République de
Philippines[1][2]	600	605	497	623	473	*923	*920	*950	*950	*900	Philippines[1][2]
Saudi Arabia[2]	1833	1785	1825	2318	2411	2451	2683	2539	2356	*2610	Arabie saoudite[2]
Thailand	[2]685	[2]711	[2]779	[2]972	[2]1391	[2]2134	[2]2143	2101	1619	1474	Thaïlande
Turkey	8373	8572	10879	10836	11257	10695	12684	13078	12571	12372	Turquie
United Arab Emirates[4]	40	30	40	40	...	...	...	...	...	...	Emirats arabes unis[4]
Viet Nam	101	149	196	* [2]270	* [2]301	* [2]271	* [2]311	*330	* [2]320	* [2]450	Viet Nam
Europe	**194159**	**296849**	**275479**	**259240**	**251463**	**258425**	**241076**	**223719**	**216025**	**251430**	**Europe**
Albania[1]	79	16	0	15	19	22	22	22	22	16	Albanie[1]
Austria	[5]104	[5]104	[5]107	[5]131	[5]152	#1271	1083	1350	1425	1406	Autriche
Belarus	..	799	[5]828	[5]705	716	636	795	1110	1300	1335	Bélarus
Belgium	11453	11348	10331	10178	[1]11268	[1]11544	[1]10752	[1]10716	[1]11400	[1]10908	Belgique
Bosnia and Herzegovina[5]	..	..	...	...	...	...	52	72	75	60	Bosnie-Herzégovine[5]
Bulgaria[1]	2184	1615	1551	1941	2491	2724	2457	2628	[2]2216	[2]1846	Bulgarie[1]
Croatia	..	214	102	[5]74	63	45	46	69	[5]100	[5]75	Croatie
Denmark[6]	...	...	...	...	2	6	4	3	3	10	Danemark[6]
Czechoslovakia(former)[1]	14775	12071								..	Tchécoslovaquie(anc.)[1]
Czech Republic[1]	..	..	7349	6732	7075	7003	6519	6593	6059	5453	République tchèque[1]
Finland	2840	2873	3062	3239	3399	3151	3281	3711	[5]3929	[5]3937	Finlande
France	19044	18456	17940	17112	18024	17872	17413	19543	19901	19977	France
Germany	..	41267	39337	37322	40533	[5]41732	[5]39496	10296	9895	[5]41766	Allemagne
Germany(Fed.Rep.)	38055	..	..	..	..	..	..	..	..	..	Allemagne(Rép.féd.)
German D.R.(former)	5339	..	..	..	..	..	..	..	..	..	R.D.A. (anc.)
Greece[1]	999	980	924	980	852	936	852	1020	1104	960	Grèce[1]
Hungary	2776	1845	1556	1748	1932	1860	[5]1871	[5]1690	1940	1920	Hongrie
Ireland[1]	325	293	257	326	288	312	336	[5]336	[5]355	[5]337	Irlande[1]
Italy	25467	25100	24791	25837	26073	27771	24285	25769	25645	24641	Italie

For general note and footnotes, see end of table.

Voir la fin du tableau pour la remarque générale et les notes.

Crude steel, ingots (continued)
Acier brut (lingots) (suite)

ISIC-BASED CODE - CODE BASE CITI

3710-19

Unit : Thousand metric tons   Unité : Milliers de tonnes métriques

Country or area	1990	1991	1992	1993	1994	1995	1996	1997	1998	1999	Pays ou zone
Latvia	..	365	239	296	328	276	290	462	469	⁵482	Lettonie
Luxembourg	3560	3379	3068	3293	3073	2613	2501	2580	2477	2600	Luxembourg
Netherlands	5408	5168	5437	6000	6172	6409	6326	6641	6377	6075	Pays-Bas
Norway	368	⁵431	⁵440	⁵501	⁵451	⁵497	⁵505	⁵564	⁵639	⁵595	Norvège
Poland	¹11501	10239	8976	9855	11014	11840	⁵10433	11210	⁵9605	⁵8729	Pologne
Portugal¹	744	576	768	780	744	828	⁵840	⁵879	⁵907	⁵1013	Portugal¹
Romania	9761	7130	5376	5446	5800	6557	6083	6675	6336	4392	Roumanie
Russian Federation	..	72770	61966	54458	45866	48756	46628	45744	41214	48392	Fédération de Russie
Slovakia	..	..	4498	3922	3974	3958	253	255	36	16	Slovaquie
Slovenia	..	275	392	349	415	399	90	97	95	76	Slovénie
Spain	*12658	12700	12491	12851	13340	13812	⁵12038	⁵13559	⁵14698	⁵14754	Espagne
Sweden	4435	4230	4338	4578	4934	4891	4880	5117	5143	⁵5038	Suède
Switzerland	⁵1105	⁵955	⁵1238	⁵1254	⁵1100	⁵850	⁵750	²1000	²1000	* ²1000	Suisse
Ukraine	..	44995	41759	32610	24081	22309	22333	25629	24447	27393	Ukraine
United Kingdom	17601	16286	16041	16459	17112	17424	17804	18313	17130	16156	Royaume-Uni
Yugoslavia	..	157	87	47	40	25	37	39	38	25	Yougoslavie
T.F.Yug.Rep. Macedonia	..	209	162	133	67	31	21	27	45	47	L'ex-RY Macédoine
Yugoslavia, SFR	3576	..	..	..	..	..	..	..	..	..	Yougoslavie, RSF
USSR (former)¹	154436	..	..	..	..	..	..	..	..	..	URSS (anc.)¹
Oceania	8295	7947	5964	8481	8573	8894	8624	8768	9112	8422	Océanie
Australia¹ ³	7576	7141	#5205	7628	7807	8052	7944	8088	8356	7678	Australie¹ ³
New Zealand²	719	806	759	853	766	842	680	680	*756	*744	Nouvelle-Zélande²
Total	744331	698978	685330	687581	685456	702478	692197	699637	692700	738686	Total

General Note.

Crude steel is steel (including alloy steel) in the form in which it emerges from the Bessemer, Thomas, open-hearth or electric process or from one of the various oxygen-blowing processes. Puddled iron is excluded. Steel ingots are primary products for rolling or forging obtained by casting the molten steel into moulds which are usually square, rectangular or octagonal in cross-section with one end thicker than the other, to facilitate removal from the mould. Continuously-cast blooms, billets and slabs are included as ingots. (SITC, Rev.3: 67241-2, 67247-2, 67249-2, 67260-2, 67270-2).

¹ Including crude steel for casting.
² Source: U. S. Geological Survey, (Washington, D. C.).
³ Twelve months ending 30 June of year stated.
⁴ Source: "Statistical Yearbook of the OIC countries".
⁵ Source: Annual Bulletin of Steel Statistics for Europe, America and Asia, United Nations Economic Commission of Europe (Geneva).
⁶ Sales.

Remarque générale.

On entend par acier brut l'acier (y compris l'acier allié) produit par les procédés Bessemer, Thomas, Martin ou électrique ou par les procédés à l'oxygène. Cette rubrique ne comprend pas le fer puddlé. Les lingots d'acier sont des produits de base destinés à être transformés par laminage ou forgeage et obtenus en coulant l'acier liquide dans des lingotières qui sont ordinairement de section carrée, rectangulaire ou octogonale et dont l'une des extrémités est plus épaisse que l'autre pour faciliter le démoulage. Les blooms, les billettes et les brames obtenus par coulée continue sont classés parmi les lingots. (CTCI, Rev.3: 67241-2, 67247-2, 67249-2, 67260-2, 67270-2).

¹ Y compris l'acier brut pour moulages.
² Source: U.S. Geological Survey, (Washington, D.C.).
³ Période de douze mois finissant le 30 juin de l'année indiquée.
⁴ Source: "Annuaire des statistiques des pays de OCI".
⁵ Source: Bulletin annuel de statistiques de l'acier pour l'Europe, l'Amérique et l'Asie. Commission économique des Nations Unies pour l'Europe (Genève).
⁶ Ventes.

Ingots for tubes
Lingots pour tubes

ISIC-BASED CODE - CODE BASE CITI

3710-22

Unit : Thousand metric tons Unité : Milliers de tonnes métriques

Country or area	1990	1991	1992	1993	1994	1995	1996	1997	1998	1999	Pays ou zone
America, North	**207**	**330**	**196**	**273**	**355**	**377**	**396**	**426**	**420**	**437**	**Amérique du Nord**
Canada[1 2 3]	63	186	34	88	149	159	162	175	153	153	Canada[1 2 3]
Mexico	144	144	162	185	206	...	...	...	...	...	Mexique
Asia	**1163**	**1107**	**1200**	**1076**	**1310**	**1052**	**1040**	**914**	**777**	**378**	**Asie**
Japan	19	18	17	16	21	39	60	67	67	...	Japon
Turkey	...	...	[1 2]1183	[1 2]1060	1289	1013	980	847	710	290	Turquie
Europe	**3823**	**5720**	**4982**	**4558**	**4985**	**5117**	**4754**	**4938**	**4551**	**3683**	**Europe**
Austria[1 2]	300	270	209	185	164	...	...	...	...	...	Autriche[1 2]
Belarus[2]	..	...	[1]11	[1]29	[1]40	[1]32	[1]39	57	45	18	Bélarus[2]
Croatia		[1 2]198	[1 2]98	[1 2]74	[1 2]63	[1 2]45	[1 2]49	68	[1 2]105	[1 2]77	Croatie
France	[1 2]678	[2]667	[2]628	[2]583	[2]742	[2]648	566	653	737	471	France
Germany[1 2]		2160	1378	1308	1990	2202	2139	2243	1973	1468	Allemagne[1 2]
Germany(Fed.Rep.)*	2118	..	..	..	..	..	..	..	..		Allemagne(Rép.féd.)*
Hungary	39	...	...	...	...	...	...	...	...	...	Hongrie
Italy	142	151	160	116	43	...	...	...	...	...	Italie
Russian Federation	..	1000	968	872	769	834	719	709	575	639	Fédération de Russie
Slovakia	..	..	...	...	...	...	253	255	[1]195	[1]165	Slovaquie
Slovenia	..	...	...	...	...	...	87	97	95	76	Slovénie
Spain[1 2]	546	380	...	...	...	500	...	...	...	...	Espagne[1 2]
Ukraine	..	736	710	571	354	340	276	289	300	255	Ukraine
USSR (former)	1868	..	..	..	..	..	..	..	..	..	URSS (anc.)
Total	**7061**	**7157**	**6378**	**5907**	**6650**	**6545**	**6191**	**6278**	**5748**	**4498**	**Total**

General Note.

Ingots which are used directly for making seamless tubes, and which do not, therefore, pass through the stage of being rolled into a semi-manufactured product. (SITC, Rev.3: 67241-3, 67247-3, 67249-3).

[1] Source: Annual Bulletin of Steel Statistics for Europe, America and Asia, United Nations Economic Commission of Europe (Geneva).
[2] Including semis for tubes.
[3] Shipments.

Remarque générale.

Lingots qui sont utilisés directement pour la fabrication de tubes sans soudure et qui ne sont donc pas laminés en un produit semi-fini. (CTCI, Rev.3: 67241-3, 67247-3, 67249-3).

[1] Source: Bulletin annuel de statistiques de l'acier pour l'Europe, l'Amérique et l'Asie. Commission économique des Nations Unies pour l'Europe (Genève).
[2] Y compris les demi-produits pour tubes.
[3] Expéditions.

Semis for tubes
Demi-produits pour tubes

ISIC-BASED CODE - CODE BASE CITI

3710-25

Unit : Thousand metric tons

Unité : Milliers de tonnes métriques

Country or area	1990	1991	1992	1993	1994	1995	1996	1997	1998	1999	Pays ou zone
America, North	**1670**	**2019**	**2080**	**2252**	**2296**	**2019**	**2289**	**2376**	**1847**	**1344**	**Amérique du Nord**
United States[1][2]	1670	...	[3]2080	[3]2252	[3]2296	...	[3]2289	[3]2376	[3]1847	[3]1344	Etats-Unis[1][2]
Asia	**3220**	**3492**	**2649**	**2804**	**2596**	**2339**	**2189**	**2401**	**2371**	**1844**	**Asie**
Japan	3220	3492	2649	2804	2596	2339	2189	2401	2371	1844	Japon
Europe	**3601**	**7122**	**6881**	**6202**	**5153**	**5422**	**5436**	**4762**	**4702**	**4143**	**Europe**
Belgium	191	226	...	...	...	...	...	...	...	...	Belgique
Czechoslovakia(former)	772	619	..	..	..	..	..	..	..	..	Tchécoslovaquie(anc.)
Czech Republic	..	..	503	[3][4]873	[3][4]1032	[3][4]897	[3][4]835	[3][4]449	[3][4]448	[3][4]301	République tchèque
Germany	..	139	...	...	...	...	...	...	...	...	Allemagne
Germany(Fed.Rep.)	156	..	...	...	...	..	..	..	..		Allemagne(Rép.féd.)
Hungary	50	36	23	[3]23	[3]30	...	...	...	...	...	Hongrie
Italy	748	795	708	749	908	[3][4]997	[3][4]921	[3][4]924	[3][4]918	[3][4]737	Italie
Poland	224	164	159	151	57	153	137	142	198	95	Pologne
Romania	477	329	262	258	255	213	227	214	152	78	Roumanie
Russian Federation	..	2213	2015	1733	1105	1246	1113	1061	943	1212	Fédération de Russie
Slovakia	..	..	...	136	145	173	222	...	...	...	Slovaquie
Sweden[3][4][5]	614	..	...	...	...	...	...	...	...	...	Suède[3][4][5]
Ukraine	..	1750	1904	1143	491	605	915	738	833	544	Ukraine
United Kingdom	*369	[3][4]237	[3][4]176	[3][4]174	[3][4]168	[3][4]160	[3][4]93	[3][4]98	[3][4]79	[3][4]45	Royaume-Uni
USSR (former)	6480	..	..	..	..	..	..	..	..	..	URSS (anc.)
Total	**14971**	**12633**	**11610**	**11258**	**10045**	**9780**	**9914**	**9539**	**8920**	**7331**	**Total**

General Note.

All semi-manufactured products for use in making seamless tubes. Output of these products should be measured at the stage at which they are still solids, that is, before piercing. (SITC, Rev.3: 67260-3, 67270-3, 67280-1).

[1] Including ingots for tubes; beginning 1996, also including ingots and semis for sales.
[2] Shipments.
[3] Source: Annual Bulletin of Steel Statistics for Europe, America and Asia, United Nations Economic Commission of Europe (Geneva).
[4] Including ingots for tubes.
[5] Deliveries.

Remarque générale.

Tous les produits semi-finis servant à la fabrication de tubes sans soudure. La quantité de ces produits doit être mesurée au stade où ils sont encore pleins, c'est'-à-dire avant le perçage. (CTCI, Rev.3: 67260-3, 67270-3, 67280-1).

[1] Y compris les lingots pour tubes; à partir de 1996, y compris les lingots at demi-produits destinés à la vente.
[2] Expéditions.
[3] Source: Bulletin annuel de statistiques de l'acier pour l'Europe, l'Amérique et l'Asie. Commission économique des Nations Unies pour l'Europe (Genève).
[4] Y compris les lingots pour tubes.
[5] Livraisons.

Wire rods
Fil machine

ISIC-BASED CODE - CODE BASE CITI

3710-28

Unit : Thousand metric tons

Unité : Milliers de tonnes métriques

Country or area	1990	1991	1992	1993	1994	1995	1996	1997	1998	1999	Pays ou zone
America, North	**5992**	**5455**	**6339**	**7005**	**7234**	**7581**	**7658**	**8063**	**7837**	**7781**	**Amérique du Nord**
Canada[2]	[1]1029	[1]436	[1]1194	[1]1209	[1]1171	[1]1203	1274	*1246	1237	[1]1360	Canada[2]
Cuba[3]	83	14	16	16	...	...	...	...	...	...	Cuba[3]
Mexico	715	664	594	905	1108	1276	1231	1270	1199	1150	Mexique
Panama	15	15	[3]18	39	34	29	36	...	...	...	Panama
Trinidad and Tobago	277	365	447	413	521	594	575	653	656	524	Trinité-et-Tobago
United States[1][2]	3873	3961	4070	4423	4368	4447	4510	4816	4663	4661	Etats-Unis[1][2]
America, South	**3193**	**3125**	**3520**	**3761**	**3602**	**3338**	**3477**	**3382**	**3357**	**3694**	**Amérique du Sud**
Argentina	440	428	[3]283	[3]333	[3]391	[3]437	[3]398	[3]364	[3]375	...	Argentine
Brazil	2131	2089	2408	2526	2544	2099	2201	2097	2011	2285	Brésil
Chile	54	55	[3]78	[3]89	[3]127	[3]116	[3]139	[3]141	[3]146	...	Chili
Colombia	135	138	356	420	[3]140	271	[3]263	[3]257		...	Colombie
Ecuador	[3]10	[3]1	[3]1	[3]14	[3]2	0	0	[3]2	[3]2	...	Equateur
Peru	25	17	[3]18	[3]20	[3]11	[3]20	[3]24	[3]51	[3]54	...	Pérou
Uruguay[3]	12	9	10	7	6	7	5	3	3	...	Uruguay[3]
Venezuela	386	388	[3]366	[3]352	[3]381	[3]388	[3]447	[3]467	[3]485	...	Venezuela
Asia	**20233**	**22575**	**24056**	**26458**	**28425**	**30119**	**32225**	**34582**	**35165**	**39819**	**Asie**
China	9990	10999	12571	13895	15713	16872	18340	19538	22029	25949	Chine
Indonesia	19	238	241	33	32	350	...	101	*497	...	Indonésie
Japan	7335	7023	6544	7123	6826	6820	6950	7445	6737	7005	Japon
Korea, Republic of	1798	1669	1938	2070	2127	2026	2091	2360	2377	2530	Corée, République de
Malaysia	297	#1293	1585	1913	2310	2462	3030	3374	1903	2261	Malaisie
Myanmar[4]	8	7	10	13	18	...	...	...	...	...	Myanmar[4]
Sri Lanka	2	2	2	2	3	3	5	...	...	...	Sri Lanka
Syrian Arab Republic	83	82	95	83	33	37	74	68	74	62	Rép. arabe syrienne
Thailand	153	146	138	255	236	326	279	372	219	310	Thaïlande
Turkey	548	...	932	1071	1127	1204	1246	1295	1297	1322	Turquie
Europe	**17978**	**21683**	**22441**	**22642**	**24357**	**23706**	**23167**	**24302**	**23075**	**23506**	**Europe**
Austria	[5]583	[1]512	[1]429	[1]386	[1]439	[1]441	[1]389	[1]483	[1]473	[1]473	Autriche
Belarus	..	30	46	42	30	22	31	21	34	48	Bélarus
Belgium	509	553	634	724	[1]851	[1]745	[1]805	[1]942	[1]802	[1]943	Belgique
Bulgaria	200	119	86	194	212	124	150	99	...	...	Bulgarie
Croatia	..	[1]106	[1]61	[1]42	[1]45	[1]15	[1]0	[1]0	44	[1]0	Croatie
Czechoslovakia(former)	1030	894	..	..	..	..	..	..	..	..	Tchécoslovaquie(anc.)
Czech Republic	..	..	970	923	1083	[1]1184	[1]1244	1063	1113	1162	République tchèque
Finland	257	216	247	268	283	265	294	[1]326	[1]324	[1]354	Finlande
France	2064	1981	1992	1944	1944	[1]1845	[1]1766	[1]1892	[1]1803	[1]1678	France
Germany	..	4626	4908	5073	5423	5369	5234	5784	5652	[1]5886	Allemagne
Germany(Fed.Rep.)	3765	..	..	..	..	..	..	..	..	..	Allemagne(Rép.féd.)
Greece	[6][7]1035	[1]103	[1]120	[1]107	[1]127	[1]161	[1]197	[1]228	[1]206	[1]219	Grèce
Hungary	273	124	29	33	59	111	[7]73	[1]52	[1]46	53	Hongrie
Italy	2813	3020	3199	3122	3585	3805	3484	3731	3628	3678	Italie
Latvia	..	48	[1]41	20	[1]20	15	[1]28	[1]26	[1]6	[1]0	Lettonie
Luxembourg	513	499	561	469	480	435	419	431	458	616	Luxembourg
Netherlands	227	215	214	218	242	235	152	195	207	[1]180	Pays-Bas
Poland	677	540	636	633	825	926	930	1097	969	947	Pologne
Portugal[1]	...	100	224	...	178	184	138	135	157	126	Portugal[1]
Republic of Moldova	..	21	...	...	...	...	...	...	...	...	Rép. de Moldova
Romania	477	311	231	263	318	393	362	455	361	210	Roumanie
Russian Federation	..	2513	2543	2776	2641	2232	2427	1899	1874	1831	Fédération de Russie
Slovenia	..	51	76	[1]15	[1]0	1	[1]0	[1]0	0	[1]0	Slovénie
Spain	[1]1221	1175	[1]1385	1566	1704	1865	1713	1894	1947	1819	Espagne
Sweden	[1][8]74	30	[1][8]69	11	[1][8]68	[1][8]85	[1][8]65	[1][8]81	[1][8]126	[1][8]107	Suède
Ukraine	..	2616	2386	2203	2246	1585	1709	1882	1199	1617	Ukraine
United Kingdom[9]	1407	1272	1327	1427	1524	1642	1536	1565	1492	1407	Royaume-Uni[9]
Yugoslavia	..	...	...	[1]7	[1]9	0	0	0	0	[1]0	Yougoslavie
Yugoslavia, SFR	704	..	..	..	..	..	..	..	..	..	Yougoslavie, RSF
USSR (former)	5995	..	..	..	..	..	..	..	..	..	URSS (anc.)
Total	**53391**	**52838**	**56356**	**59866**	**63618**	**64744**	**66528**	**70329**	**69434**	**74799**	**Total**

For general note and footnotes, see end of table.

Voir la fin du tableau pour la remarque générale et les notes.

Wire rods (continued)
Fil machine (suite)

ISIC-BASED CODE - CODE BASE CITI

3710-28

General Note.

Round, oval, hexagonal etc., hot-rolled products with a diameter of 13 mm and less, delivered in coils. Straightened rods are excluded. (SITC, Rev.3: 67610-1).

[1] Source: Annual Bulletin of Steel Statistics for Europe, America and Asia, United Nations Economic Commission of Europe (Geneva).

[2] Shipments.

[3] Source: United Nations Economic Commission for Latin America and the Caribbean (ECLAC), (Santiago).

[4] Government production only.

[5] 1999 data are confidential.

[6] Including concrete reinforcement bars.

[7] Including cold-drawn rods.

[8] Deliveries.

[9] Including other bars and rods in coil.

Remarque générale.

Produits ronds, ovales, hexagonaux etc., laminés à chaud, d'un diamètre maximal de 13 mm, livrés en couronnes ou en torches. Cette rubrique ne comprend pas le fil machine redressé. (CTCI, Rev.3: 67610-1).

[1] Source: Bulletin annuel de statistiques de l'acier pour l'Europe, l'Amérique et l'Asie. Commission économique des Nations Unies pour l'Europe (Genève).

[2] Expéditions.

[3] Source: Commission économique des Nations Unies pour l'Amérique Latine et les Caraïbes (CEPAL), (Santiago).

[4] Production de l'Etat seulement.

[5] Pour 1999, les données sont confidentielles.

[6] Y compris les barres d'armature pour béton.

[7] Y compris les ronds étirés à froid.

[8] Livraisons.

[9] Y compris les barres et tiges en rouleaux.

Angles, shapes and sections (total production)
Cornières, profilés et poutrelles (production totale)

ISIC-BASED CODE - CODE BASE CITI

3710-35

Unit : Thousand metric tons

Unité : Milliers de tonnes métriques

Country or area	1990	1991	1992	1993	1994	1995	1996	1997	1998	1999	Pays ou zone
Africa	**341**	**411**	**411**	**402**	**387**	**329**	**486**	**454**	**434**	**443**	**Afrique**
Algeria	8	9	8	16	19	18	13	17	17	21	Algérie
Egypt	333	402	403	386	368	311	473	437	...	...	Egypte
America, North	**15247**	**14567**	**12598**	**13496**	**14780**	**15432**	**15619**	**16881**	**16185**	**16944**	**Amérique du Nord**
Canada[1] [2]	1790	328	381	414	422	440	427	488	559	564	Canada[1] [2]
Mexico	594	548	577	745	926	852	1003	1149	1291	1342	Mexique
United States[1] [2]	12863	...	11640	12337	13432	14140	14189	15244	14335	15038	Etats-Unis[1] [2]
America, South	**445**	**485**	**456**	**536**	**573**	**534**	**519**	**615**	**760**	**824**	**Amérique du Sud**
Brazil	[3]263	[3]297	[3]291	[3]350	[3]387	[1]334	[1]283	[1]348	[1]555	[1]587	Brésil
Colombia	...	...	139	159	152	164	...	199	139	...	Colombie
Ecuador	...	...	26	27	34	36	77	68	66	...	Equateur
Asia	**24047**	**23234**	**21038**	**20723**	**20330**	**21610**	**23236**	**23930**	**20650**	**21046**	**Asie**
Japan[1]	21908	20814	18776	17940	17659	18440	19271	19717	17232	17050	Japon[1]
Korea, Republic of	1810	2003	2076	2560	[1]2542	[1]2872	[1]3634	[1]3814	[1]2987	[1]3456	Corée, République de
Nepal[4]	...	...	60	60	71	95	92	107	91	107	Népal[4]
Turkey	[1]258	[1]342	[1]126	[1]163	[1]58	203	239	292	340	433	Turquie
Europe	**36800**	**69637**	**63158**	**60132**	**55858**	**45810**	**39931**	**42187**	**42084**	**41487**	**Europe**
Austria[1]	132	83	88	81	107	140	90	107	110	99	Autriche[1]
Belgium	540	484	465	565	548	[1]297	[1]235	[1]248	[1]242	[1]248	Belgique
Bulgaria	805	557	537	583	763	1017	769	1093	403	234	Bulgarie
Croatia[1]	..	0	0	0	0	4	0	0	0	0	Croatie[1]
Denmark[1]	119	...	108	123	157	179	158	173	162	159	Danemark[1]
Czechoslovakia(former)	3314	2503	..	..	..	..	..	..	..	..	Tchécoslovaquie(anc.)
Czech Republic	..	..	2418	2189	2133	[1]1487	[1]1180	[1]1285	[1]1240	[1]1119	République tchèque
Finland	279	245	252	270	280	338	285	[1]214	[1]236	[1]221	Finlande
France	2796	2700	2556	2434	1687	1689	1518	1706	1806	1723	France
Germany	..	5416	4976	4503	4603	2672	2544	2998	3123	...	Allemagne
Germany(Fed.Rep.)	4444	..	..	..	..	..	..	..	..	...	Allemagne(Rép.féd.)
Greece	[1]45	[1]54	[1]43	[1]45	[1]53	[1]58	[1]56	[1]42	31	[1]42	Grèce
Hungary	616	317	229	386	365	359	[1]208	119	133	143	Hongrie
Ireland[1]	...	262	251	299	240	275	...	...	...	...	Irlande[1]
Italy	8791	9020	9860	9169	8711	9301	8301	8702	8860	8614	Italie
Latvia[1]	..	105	0	13	10	0	0	0	0	0	Lettonie[1]
Luxembourg	1832	1685	1464	1632	1623	1575	1504	1701	1638	1772	Luxembourg
Netherlands	338	379	387	363	428	423	453	473	403	...	Pays-Bas
Norway[1]	494	467	503	493	460	374	387	387	349	245	Norvège[1]
Poland	3381	2823	2441	2798	2944	3348	3111	1938	1872	1831	Pologne
Portugal	...	[1]410	[1]454	...	# [1]52	[1]47	41	42	46	52	Portugal
Romania	1498	1265	778	778	712	952	821	728	740	...	Roumanie
Russian Federation[1]	..	23347	19330	19709	16517	7907	5668	6200	6300	7100	Fédération de Russie[1]
Slovakia	..	..	...	...	...	...	...	...	9	2	Slovaquie
Slovenia	..	155	133	128	156	156	73	86	101	109	Slovénie
Spain[1]	2377	2229	2151	2205	2404	2868	2567	3137	3364	3506	Espagne[1]
Sweden[1] [5]	580	507	522	552	679	694	744	862	613	564	Suède[1] [5]
Ukraine	..	[1]10967	[1]9527	[1]6956	6420	5550	4927	5586	6025	6189	Ukraine
United Kingdom[1]	3886	3502	3673	3704	3795	4090	4007	4067	3995	3690	Royaume-Uni[1]
Yugoslavia	..	6	6	5	5	4	9	16	10	3	Yougoslavie
USSR (former)	43593	..	..	..	..	..	..	..	..	..	URSS (anc.)
Total	**120473**	**108333**	**97661**	**95289**	**91928**	**83715**	**79791**	**84067**	**80113**	**80744**	**Total**

General Note.

Angles, shapes and sections of iron and steel commonly known as H, I, T, capital omega, Z and U, obtuse and right (L) angles. Sheet piling is included but rails are excluded. (SITC, Rev.3: 67680-0).

[1] Source: Annual Bulletin of Steel Statistics for Europe, America and Asia, United Nations Economic Commission of Europe (Geneva).
[2] Shipments.
[3] Structural shapes only.
[4] Twelve months beginning 16 July of year stated.
[5] Deliveries.

Remarque générale.

Profilés en fer et en acier, communément désignés d'après leurs sections: profilés en H, I, T, Z et U, profilés zorès (à section en forme d'oméga), cornières et équerres à angle obtus, aigu ou droit (en forme d'L). Cette rubrique comprend les palplanches mais non les rails. (CTCI, Rev.3: 67680-0).

[1] Source: Bulletin annuel de statistiques de l'acier pour l'Europe, l'Amérique et l'Asie. Commission économique des Nations Unies pour l'Europe (Genève).
[2] Expéditions.
[3] Profilés de construction seulement.
[4] Période de douze mois commençant le 16 juillet de l'année indiquée.
[5] Livraisons.

Angles, shapes and sections of 80 mm or more (heavy sections)
Cornières, profilés et poutrelles de 80 mm ou plus (profilés lourds)

ISIC-BASED CODE - CODE BASE CITI

3710-36

Unit : Thousand metric tons

Unité : Milliers de tonnes métriques

Country or area	1990	1991	1992	1993	1994	1995	1996	1997	1998	1999	Pays ou zone
America, North	**6346**	**5788**	**5628**	**5808**	**6001**	**6312**	**6110**	**6057**	**5622**	**6132**	**Amérique du Nord**
Canada[1][3]	[2]652	...	...	...	...	...	0	0	0	0	Canada[1][3]
Mexico	258	280	312	409	481	487	539	588	676	693	Mexique
United States[1][3]	5436	...	5186	5269	5390	5695	5571	5469	4946	5439	Etats-Unis[1][3]
America, South	**117**	**117**	**143**	**174**	**205**	**25**	**1**	**0**	**8**	**56**	**Amérique du Sud**
Brazil	[4]117	[4]117	[4]143	[4]174	[4]205	# [1]25	[1]1	[1]0	[1]8	[1]56	Brésil
Asia	**12243**	**11495**	**10870**	**10225**	**9341**	**10198**	**12878**	**11780**	**11145**	**10170**	**Asie**
Japan[1]	10191	9362	8795	8045	7925	8353	9005	9221	8656	7447	Japon[1]
Korea, Republic of[1]	...	...	...	...	1359	1642	[6]3634	2267	2149	2290	Corée, République de[1]
Turkey	[1]241	[1]253	[1]126	[1]163	[1]57	203	239	292	340	433	Turquie
Europe	**10769**	**22664**	**22768**	**21718**	**23672**	**14638**	**13007**	**12770**	**12730**	**14178**	**Europe**
Belgium	358	288	251	283	302	# [1]63	[1]61	[1]68	[1]42	[1]63	Belgique
Bulgaria	283	92	71	132	137	206	133	186	...	...	Bulgarie
Croatia[1]	..	0	0	0	0	4	0	0	0	0	Croatie[1]
Czech Republic	..	..	1158	1015	...	[1]466	[1]407	[1]466	[1]459	[1]456	République tchèque
Finland	36	42	55	59	79	96	79	[1]91	[1]88	[1]78	Finlande
France	708	600	564	491	423	333	303	325	354	408	France
Germany(Fed.Rep.)	1755	..	..	..	..	..	..	..	..	..	Allemagne(Rép.féd.)
German D.R.(former)	694	..	..	..	..	..	..	..	..	..	R.D.A. (anc.)
Hungary	111	68	87	133	89	60	[1]74	...	43	35	Hongrie
Ireland[1]	...	262	251	299	240	275	...	...	...	...	Irlande[1]
Italy	926	1052	878	610	614	[1]972	527	1102	1098	1129	Italie
Latvia[1]	..	5	0	13	10	0	0	0	0	0	Lettonie[1]
Luxembourg	1190	1150	878	956	1022	1027	962	1045	985	1018	Luxembourg
Norway[1]	206	150	160	139	161	168	124	148	151	102	Norvège[1]
Portugal[1]	...	22	35	...	#0	0	0	0	0	...	Portugal[1]
Romania	395	314	204	175	204	262	218	188	198	121	Roumanie
Russian Federation[1]	..	10543	10458	11193	13360	#5584	4764	3300	3000	3600	Fédération de Russie[1]
Slovenia	..	20	26	19	36	38	58	...	...	90	Slovénie
Spain[1]	1339	1227	1163	1190	1123	1282	1180	1430	1230	1680	Espagne[1]
Sweden[1][7]	580	507	522	552	#70	88	78	80	...	...	Suède[1][7]
Ukraine	..	[1]4578	[1]4219	[1]2569	3310	1838	1828	2162	2442	2896	Ukraine
United Kingdom[1]	1913	1744	1788	1882	1860	1876	1941	1789	2129	2075	Royaume-Uni[1]
Total	**29475**	**40064**	**39409**	**37926**	**39220**	**31173**	**31996**	**30607**	**29505**	**30536**	**Total**

General Note.

Angles, shapes and sections of iron and steel commonly known as H, I, T, capital omega, Z and U, obtuse, acute and right (L) angles. Sheet piling is included but rails are excluded. This item relates to heavy sections of 80 mm or more. (SITC, Rev.3: 67682-0, 67683-1, 67684-1, 67685-1, 67686-1, 67687-1, 67688-1).

Remarque générale.

Profilés en fer et en acier, communément désignés d'après leurs sections: profilés en H, I, T, Z et U, profilés zorès (à section en forme d'oméga), cornières et équerres à angle obtus, aigu ou droit (en forme d'L). Cette rubrique comprend les palplanches mais non les rails. Les données se rapportent aux profilés lourds de 80 mm ou plus. (CTCI, Rev.3: 67682-0, 67683-1, 67684-1, 67685-1, 67686-1, 67687-1, 67688-1).

[1] Source: Annual Bulletin of Steel Statistics for Europe, America and Asia, United Nations Economic Commission of Europe (Geneva).

[2] Including railway track material.

[3] Shipments.

[4] Structural shapes only.

[5] Sales.

[6] Including light sections of less than 80 mm.

[7] Deliveries.

[1] Source: Bulletin annuel de statistiques de l'acier pour l'Europe, l'Amérique et l'Asie. Commission économique des Nations Unies pour l'Europe (Genève).

[2] Y compris le matériel de voie.

[3] Expéditions.

[4] Profilés de construction seulement.

[5] Ventes.

[6] Y compris les profilés légers de moins de 80 mm.

[7] Livraisons.

Angles, shapes and sections, less than 80 mm (light sections)
Cornières, profilés et poutrelles de moins de 80 mm (profilés légers)

ISIC-BASED CODE - CODE BASE CITI

3710-37

Unit : Thousand metric tons / Unité : Milliers de tonnes métriques

Country or area	1990	1991	1992	1993	1994	1995	1996	1997	1998	1999	Pays ou zone
America, North	**8901**	**8909**	**7100**	**7818**	**8909**	**9250**	**9509**	**10824**	**10563**	**10812**	**Amérique du Nord**
Canada[1]	1138	328	381	414	422	440	427	488	559	564	Canada[1]
Mexico	336	268	265	336	445	365	464	561	615	649	Mexique
United States[1][2]	7427	...	6454	7068	8042	8445	8618	9775	9389	9599	Etats-Unis[1][2]
America, South	**146**	**180**	**148**	**176**	**182**	**309**	**282**	**348**	**547**	**531**	**Amérique du Sud**
Brazil	[3]146	[3]180	[3]148	[3]176	[3]182	[1]309	[1]282	[1]348	[1]547	[1]531	Brésil
Asia	**12902**	**12713**	**11157**	**11076**	**10917**	**11317**	**11459**	**12043**	**9414**	**10769**	**Asie**
Japan[1]	11717	11452	9981	9895	9734	10087	10266	10496	8576	9603	Japon[1]
Korea, Republic of[1]	...	...	...	...	1183	1230	...	1547	838	1166	Corée, République de[1]
Turkey[1]	17	89	0	0	0	...	...	...	...	...	Turquie[1]
Europe	**22033**	**37810**	**33241**	**31380**	**23676**	**23858**	**20161**	**23246**	**23650**	**22467**	**Europe**
Austria[1]	132	83	88	81	107	140	90	107	110	99	Autriche[1]
Belgium	[4]182	[4]196	[4]214	[4]282	[4]246	[1]234	[1]174	[1]180	[1]200	[1]185	Belgique
Bulgaria	161	119	104	115	251	98	114	68	...	...	Bulgarie
Denmark[1]	119	...	108	123	157	179	158	173	162	159	Danemark[1]
Czechoslovakia(former)[5]	1758	1385	..	..	..	..	..	..	..	..	Tchécoslovaquie(anc.)[5]
Czech Republic	..	..	1260	1174	...	[1]1021	[1]773	[1]819	[1]781	[1]663	République tchèque
Finland	243	203	195	187	198	242	206	[1]123	[1]148	[1]143	Finlande
France	2088	2100	1992	1943	1264	1356	1215	1381	1452	1315	France
Germany(Fed.Rep.)	2689									..	Allemagne(Rép.féd.)
Greece	[1]45	[1]54	[1]43	[1]45	[1]53	[1]58	[1]56	[1]42	31	[1]42	Grèce
Hungary	505	249	141	253	276	299	[1]134	...	85	89	Hongrie
Italy	7865	7968	8982	8559	8097	*8329	*7774	7600	7762	7485	Italie
Luxembourg	643	535	586	676	601	548	542	656	653	754	Luxembourg
Netherlands	338	379	387	363	428	423	453	473	403	...	Pays-Bas
Norway[1]	288	317	343	354	299	206	263	239	198	143	Norvège[1]
Portugal[1]	...	388	419	...	#52	47	0	0	0	...	Portugal[1]
Romania	1103	951	574	603	508	690	603	540	542	379	Roumanie
Russian Federation[1]	..	12804	8872	8516	3157	2323	904	2900	3300	3500	Fédération de Russie[1]
Slovenia	..	135	107	109	120	118	15	...	...	17	Slovénie
Spain[1]	1038	1002	988	1015	1281	1586	1387	1707	2134	1826	Espagne[1]
Sweden[1][6]	...	...	...	...	609	606	666	782	613	564	Suède[1][6]
Ukraine	..	[6]6389	[5]5308	[4]4387	3110	3141	2568	2864	3013	2893	Ukraine
United Kingdom[1]	[7]1973	[7]1758	[7]1885	[7]1822	1935	2214	2066	2278	1866	1615	Royaume-Uni[1]
Total	**43982**	**59612**	**51646**	**50450**	**43684**	**44734**	**41411**	**46461**	**44174**	**44579**	**Total**

General Note.

Angles, shapes and sections of iron and steel commonly known as H, I, T, capital omega, Z and U, obtuse and right (L) angles. Sheet piling is included but rails are excluded. This item relates to light sections of less than 80 mm. (SITC, Rev.3: 67681-0, 67683-2, 67684-2, 67685-2, 67686-2, 67687-2, 67688-2).

Remarque générale.

Profilés en fer et en acier, communément désignés d'après leurs sections: profilés en H, I, T, Z et U, profilés zorès (à section en forme d'oméga), cornières et équerres à angle obtus, aigu ou droit (en forme d'L). Cette rubrique comprend les palplanches mais non les rails. Les données se rapportent aux profilés légers de moins de 80 mm.(CTCI, Rev.3: 67681-0, 67683-2, 67684-2, 67685-2, 67686-2, 67687-2, 67688-2).

[1] Source: Annual Bulletin of Steel Statistics for Europe, America and Asia, United Nations Economic Commission of Europe (Geneva).
[2] Shipments.
[3] Structural shapes only.
[4] Including rolled wrought-iron products.
[5] Cross-section up to and including 840 square millimetres.
[6] Deliveries.
[7] 13 mm and over.

[1] Source: Bulletin annuel de statistiques de l'acier pour l'Europe, l'Amérique et l'Asie. Commission économique des Nations Unies pour l'Europe (Genève).
[2] Expéditions.
[3] Profilés de construction seulement.
[4] Y compris les articles en fer laminé et forgé.
[5] Surface de section: jusqu' à 840 millimètres carrés.
[6] Livraisons.
[7] 13 mm et plus.

Plates (heavy), over 4.75 mm
Tôles fortes de plus de 4,75 mm

ISIC-BASED CODE - CODE BASE CITI

3710-40

Unit : Thousand metric tons

Unité : Milliers de tonnes métriques

Country or area	1990	1991	1992	1993	1994	1995	1996	1997	1998	1999	Pays ou zone
America, North	**1134**	**1061**	**1434**	**474**	**552**	**665**	**658**	**674**	**689**	**642**	**Amérique du Nord**
Mexico	1134	1061	1434	474	552	665	658	674	689	642	Mexique
America, South	**2275**	**2380**	**2535**	**2466**	**2740**	**2784**	**2886**	**2987**	**3089**	**3190**	**Amérique du Sud**
Brazil[1]	2275	2380	2535	2466	2740	...	...	...	...	...	Brésil[1]
Asia	**5457**	**5805**	**5825**	**6062**	**6050**	**6617**	**6368**	**6470**	**7027**	**7035**	**Asie**
China	[2]684	[2]719	[2]854	1003	...	...	...	...	...	...	Chine
India	...	...	...	...	1606	2059	1812	1772	1738	1512	Inde
Korea, Republic of[1]	2805	3140	3039	3153	3503	3660	3667	3799	4403	4667	Corée, République de[1]
Turkey	92	91	98	93	[3]126	83	74	84	71	41	Turquie
Europe	**20584**	**26349**	**22479**	**21412**	**22685**	**25414**	**26318**	**27989**	**27929**	**26597**	**Europe**
Austria[4]	2688	2503	2510	2529	2802	2998	2787	3207	3316	3391	Autriche[4]
Belgium	1704	1802	...	...	...	...	...	...	...	...	Belgique
Bulgaria[1]	923	588	558	605	875	1058	799	1122	...	...	Bulgarie[1]
Denmark	350	333	347	[5]295	[5]353	[5]384	[5]369	[5]434	...	...	Danemark
Czechoslovakia(former)[2]	2279	2107	..	..	..	..	..	..	..	...	Tchécoslovaquie(anc.)[2]
Finland	790	751	..	..	..	..	..	..	..	...	Finlande
France	1944	1812	1584	1500	...	[1]4238	[1]4422	[1]4903	[1]4769	[1]5148	France
Germany	..	920	823	623	670	...	...	...	...	..	Allemagne
Germany(Fed.Rep.)	3417	..	..	..	..	...	...	...	...	..	Allemagne(Rép.féd.)
German D.R.(former)[2]	859	..	..	..	..	...	...	...	...	..	R.D.A. (anc.)[2]
Hungary[1]	703	648	803	717	734	751	...	...	...	...	Hongrie[1]
Italy	1383	1348	1475	1389	1538	...	...	...	...	...	Italie
Netherlands	206	211	169	52	37	54	50	51	...	...	Pays-Bas
Poland	1263	920	827	859	1032	1232	1084	1181	1066	911	Pologne
Romania	[2]2075	[2]1521	[2]1210	[2]1229	[2]1454	[2]1722	[2]1706	[2]1955	[1]2361	[1]1898	Roumanie
Russian Federation	..	6071	4962	4678	3654	4120	4007	3989	3971	2871	Fédération de Russie
Slovakia	..	..	...	1470	1501	1324	2545	2646	...	...	Slovaquie
Slovenia	..	29	29	8	1	1	...	...	...	...	Slovénie
Ukraine	..	[6]4784	[6]3768	[6]2930	[6]2140	[6]2716	2943	[6]2853	[6]2461	[6]2000	Ukraine
Yugoslavia	..	1	12	4	1	2	7	8	6	1	Yougoslavie
USSR (former)	13511	..	..	..	..	..	..	..	..	..	URSS (anc.)
Total	**42961**	**35595**	**32273**	**30414**	**32027**	**35480**	**36230**	**38120**	**38734**	**37464**	**Total**

General Note.
Universals and plates which are more than 4.75 mm thick. (SITC, Rev.3: 67311-0, 67313-1, 67314-0. 67321-0, 67323-1, 67324-0, 67316-1, 67317-1, 67326-1, 67327-1, 67339-1, 67349-1. 67351-1, 67353-1, 67531-0, 67534-0, 67537-1, 67551-1, 67556-1, 67571-1. 67572-1, 67573-1, 67574-1).

Remarque générale.
Larges plats et tôles de plus de 4.75 mm d'épaisseur. (CTCI, Rev.3: 67311-0, 67313-1, 67314-0. 67321-0, 67323-1, 67324-0, 67316-1, 67317-1, 67326-1, 67327-1, 67339-1, 67349-1. 67351-1, 67353-1, 67531-0, 67534-0, 67537-1, 67551-1. 67556-1, 67571-1. 67572-1, 67573-1, 67574-1).

[1] Including medium plates 3 to 4.75 mm thick.
[2] Heavy plates of 4 mm and over.
[3] Source: Annual Bulletin of Steel Statistics for Europe, America and Asia, United Nations Economic Commission of Europe (Geneva).
[4] Sheets and plates of all kinds.
[5] Sales.
[6] Over 5 mm.

[1] Y compris les tôles moyennes de 3 à 4,75 mm d'épaisseur.
[2] Tôles fortes de 4 mm et plus.
[3] Source: Bulletin annuel de statistiques de l'acier pour l'Europe, l'Amérique et l'Asie. Commission économique des Nations Unies pour l'Europe (Genève).
[4] Tôles de tous types.
[5] Ventes.
[6] Plus de 5 mm.

Plates (medium) 3 to 4.75 mm
Tôles moyennes de 3 à 4,75 mm

ISIC-BASED CODE - CODE BASE CITI

3710-43

Unit : Thousand metric tons

Unité : Milliers de tonnes métriques

Country or area	1990	1991	1992	1993	1994	1995	1996	1997	1998	1999	Pays ou zone
America, South	**120**	**120**	**97**	**123**	**119**	**142**	**120**	**120**	**120**	**120**	**Amérique du Sud**
Ecuador	...	...	97	123	119	142	...	...	...	...	Equateur
Asia	**219**	**180**	**165**	**225**	**106**	**132**	**228**	**227**	**268**	**163**	**Asie**
Turkey	219	180	165	225	106	132	228	227	268	163	Turquie
Europe	**3732**	**13114**	**11970**	**10769**	**10592**	**11260**	**12199**	**13581**	**13612**	**13747**	**Europe**
Belgium	946	955	...	...	...	...	...	...	...	...	Belgique
Finland	375	374	...	...	...	...	...	...	...	...	Finlande
France	864	888	804	662	800	...	...	...	...	...	France
Germany	..	3301	3014	2771	2968	...	...	...	...	...	Allemagne
Italy	7	5	1	2	1	...	...	...	...	...	Italie
Netherlands	33	31	30	22	18	23	21	18	...	...	Pays-Bas
Poland	624	456	481	538	608	691	632	760	664	647	Pologne
Romania[1]	883	644	394	388	484	603	366	481	...	...	Roumanie[1]
Russian Federation	..	4357	3829	2666	2069	2405	2579	3199	3195	2894	Fédération de Russie
Slovakia	..	..	...	979	1027	1122	[2]2545	[2]2646	...	...	Slovaquie
Slovenia	..	16	21	32	108	60	55	...	...	...	Slovénie
Ukraine[3]	..	2087	1863	1384	1184	1320	1000	1441	1203	1223	Ukraine[3]
USSR (former)	8028	..	..	..	..	..	..	..	..	..	URSS (anc.)
Total	**12099**	**13414**	**12232**	**11117**	**10817**	**11534**	**12547**	**13928**	**14000**	**14030**	**Total**

General Note.

Plates which are at least 3 mm but not more than 4.75 mm thick, including strip which is more than 500 mm wide and 3 mm or more thick used as such. (SITC, Rev.3: 67312-1, 67313-2, 67315-1, 67316-2, 67322-1, 67323-1, 67325-1, 67326-2, 67331-0, 67335-0, 67339-2, 67341-0, 67345-0, 67349-2, 67351-2, 67352-1, 67353-2, 67532-0, 67535-0, 67538-1, 67552-0, 67556-2, 67571-2, 67572-2, 67573-2, 67574-2).

[1] Under 4 mm.
[2] Including heavy plates over 4.75 mm.
[3] From 3 mm to 5 mm.

Remarque générale.

Tôles de 3 mm au moins et de 4.75 mm au plus d'épaisseur, y compris les bandes de plus de 500 mm de largeur et de 3 mm d'épaisseur ou plus, utilisées en l'état. (CTCI, Rev.3: 67312-1, 67313-2, 67315-1, 67316-2, 67322-1, 67323-1, 67325-1, 67326-2, 67331-0, 67335-0, 67339-2, 67341-0, 67345-0, 67349-2, 67351-2, 67352-1, 67353-2, 67532-0, 67535-0, 67538-1, 67552-0, 67556-2, 67571-2, 67572-2, 67573-2, 67574-2).

[1] Moins de 4 mm.
[2] Y compris les tôles fortes de plus de 4,75 mm.
[3] De 3 à 5 mm.

Sheets, electrical
Tôles magnétiques

ISIC-BASED CODE - CODE BASE CITI

3710-46

Unit : Thousand metric tons   Unité : Milliers de tonnes métriques

Country or area	1990	1991	1992	1993	1994	1995	1996	1997	1998	1999	Pays ou zone
America, North	**2571**	**2458**	**2558**	**2615**	**2712**	**3858**	**4158**	**4636**	**4717**	**5216**	Amérique du Nord
Mexico	2130	2043	2162	2212	2313	3472	3741	4173	4184	4706	Mexique
United States [1]	441	415	396	[2]403	[2]399	[2]386	[2]417	[2]463	[2]533	[2]510	Etats-Unis [1]
America, South	**95**	**97**	**99**	**95**	**105**	**102**	**105**	**105**	**111**	**107**	Amérique du Sud
Brazil [2]	...	...	...	95	105	102	105	105	111	107	Brésil [2]
Asia	**1669**	**1939**	**1791**	**1877**	**1923**	**2265**	**2083**	**2197**	**1894**	**2281**	Asie
Japan [2]	1476	1730	1574	1631	1649	1981	1774	1884	1604	1820	Japon [2]
Korea, Republic of	193	209	217	246	274	284	[2]309	[2]313	[2]290	[2]461	Corée, République de
Europe	**1454**	**4001**	**3650**	**2667**	**2751**	**2722**	**2647**	**3423**	**4061**	**3506**	Europe
Austria [2]	41	35	57	80	121	123	116	169	187	207	Autriche [2]
Belarus	..	1123	1105	946	880	744	886	1220	1412	1448	Bélarus
Belgium	55	67	41	61	[2]18	[2]17	[2]49	[2]69	[2]527	[2]51	Belgique
Denmark	...	...	0	[3]0	...	...	[3]25	[3]33	[3]36	...	Danemark
Czechoslovakia(former)	133	89	..	..	..	..	..	..	..	..	Tchécoslovaquie(anc.)
Czech Republic [2]	..	..	9	6	11	11	13	13	14	5	République tchèque [2]
France	168	168	144	168	192	[2]223	[2]204	[2]206	[2]263	[2]235	France
Germany	..	460	512	466	539	342	344	559	604	[2]527	Allemagne
Germany(Fed.Rep.)	473	..	..	..	..	..	..	..	..	..	Allemagne(Rép.féd.)
Italy	191	180	193	203	213	218	210	236	214	232	Italie
Norway [2]	0	7	6	3	2	8	...	...	...	...	Norvège [2]
Poland	65	50	51	50	38	52	46	44	41	38	Pologne
Republic of Moldova	..	623	653	[4]1	[4]1	[4]0	[4]0	[4]0	[4]0	[4]0	Rép. de Moldova
Romania [2]	48	32	15	6	8	21	16	13	17	...	Roumanie [2]
Russian Federation	..	931	597	377	391	572	438	457	360	357	Fédération de Russie
Slovakia	..	..	...	31	36	44	42	[2]80	[2]89	[2]81	Slovaquie
Slovenia	..	36	41	51	61	65	10	[2]60	[2]52	55	Slovénie
Spain	31	25	19	...	...	...	...	...	...	...	Espagne
United Kingdom [2]	198	175	181	193	196	238	217	233	214	184	Royaume-Uni [2]
Yugoslavia, SFR	51	..	..	..	..	..	..	..	..	..	Yougoslavie, RSF
Total	**5789**	**8495**	**8098**	**7254**	**7491**	**8947**	**8993**	**10361**	**10783**	**11110**	Total

General Note.
Uncoated hot-rolled or cold-rolled sheets and strip of silicon steel for use in making electric equipment, notably motors, transformers and dynamos. (SITC, Rev.3: 67510-0).

Remarque générale.
Tôles sans revêtement laminées à chaud ou à froid et bandes d'acier au silicium, utilisées pour la fabrication d'outillage électrique, notamment de moteurs, de transformateurs et de dynamos. (CTCI, Rev.3: 67510-0).

[1] Shipments.
[2] Source: Annual Bulletin of Steel Statistics for Europe, America and Asia, United Nations Economic Commission of Europe (Geneva).
[3] Sales.
[4] Excluding Transnistria region.

[1] Expéditions.
[2] Source: Bulletin annuel de statistiques de l'acier pour l'Europe, l'Amérique et l'Asie. Commission économique des Nations Unies pour l'Europe (Genève).
[3] Ventes.
[4] Non compris la région de Transnistria.

Sheets under 3 mm, cold-rolled, uncoated
Tôles de moins de 3 mm, laminées à froid, sans revêtement

ISIC-BASED CODE - CODE BASE CITI

3710-49

Unit : Thousand metric tons

Unité : Milliers de tonnes métriques

Country or area	1990	1991	1992	1993	1994	1995	1996	1997	1998	1999	Pays ou zone
Africa	**234**	**213**	**248**	**232**	**232**	**232**	**232**	**232**	**232**	**232**	**Afrique**
Algeria	234	213	248	...	...	...	...	...	...	...	Algérie
America, North	**13491**	**13341**	**12957**	**13273**	**13460**	**12876**	**14628**	**13930**	**13658**	**14350**	**Amérique du Nord**
Canada[1][2]	1207	1110	1204	1313	..		1522	1548	1464	1553	Canada[1][2]
United States[1][2]	12284	...	11753	11960	12095	11511	13106	12382	12194	12797	Etats-Unis[1][2]
America, South	**326**	**301**	**434**	**385**	**390**	**431**	**452**	**473**	**494**	**516**	**Amérique du Sud**
Brazil	326	301	434	385	390	...	...	...	...	...	Brésil
Asia	**31995**	**27860**	**26519**	**27223**	**27047**	**27683**	**25908**	**27276**	**23335**	**23877**	**Asie**
China[3]	5524	640	750	...	...	...	...	...	...	...	Chine[3]
Japan[1]	26198	26977	25454	24582	24505	25230	23459	24826	20903	21489	Japon[1]
Korea, Republic of	268	237	314	332	233	144	140	141	123	79	Corée, République de
Turkey	5	6	1	...	...	...	...	...	...	...	Turquie
Europe	**37216**	**46215**	**45969**	**42901**	**46192**	**49136**	**47204**	**52709**	**52088**	**52378**	**Europe**
Austria[1]	1395	1365	1363	1390	1457	1456	1289	1450	1510	1640	Autriche[1]
Belgium	3650	3489	[1]3556	[1]3138	[1]3618	[1]3964	[1]3901	[1]4624	[1]4898	[1]4951	Belgique
Bulgaria[1]	...	...	...	104	291	408	315	369	...	...	Bulgarie[1]
Czech Republic[1]	..	..	...	...	...	...	...	134	123	87	République tchèque[1]
Finland[1]	378	397	...	978	1085	1145	893	1200	1193	1362	Finlande[1]
France	6372	6420	6132	5448	6408	[1]6486	[1]6499	[1]7426	[1]7602	[1]7795	France
Germany	..	[1]10944	10586	10098	11305	[1]11519	[1]10615	[1]11443	[1]11757	[1]11557	Allemagne
Germany(Fed.Rep.)	9752		..	..	..					..	Allemagne(Rép.féd.)
Greece[1]	357	383	429	268	358	418	380	386	399	401	Grèce[1]
Hungary	[1]384	[1]272	[1]220	[1]304	[1]346	[1]335	[1]343	[1]384	[1]368	342	Hongrie
Italy	4133	4173	4295	4200	4784	[1]4984	[1]4268	[1]4702	[1]4627	[1]4413	Italie
Luxembourg	[1]344	[1]356	378	379	375	360	357	320	117	98	Luxembourg
Netherlands	1722	1769	1775	1706	1876	1991	2028	[1]2377	[1]2180	[1]2115	Pays-Bas
Poland	998	702	718	775	884	1023	959	1047	892	849	Pologne
Romania[1]	756	659	437	383	372	483	401	410	389	396	Roumanie[1]
Russian Federation	..	6193	5555	4679	3829	4923	4844	5508	4711	5580	Fédération de Russie
Slovakia	..	..	...	...	...	...	618	740	...	...	Slovaquie
Slovenia	..	12	11	14	9	10	22	[1]22	[1]19	26	Slovénie
Spain[1]	2683	2649	2618	2628	2893	3073	3093	3254	3406	3282	Espagne[1]
Sweden[1][4]	523	518	554	589	625	636	811	841	...	...	Suède[1][4]
Ukraine	..	1985	1964	1542	1007	990	1057	1365	1327	1508	Ukraine
United Kingdom[1]	3749	3592	3303	3452	3852	4100	4222	4437	4288	3914	Royaume-Uni[1]
Yugoslavia	..	261	191	32	24	38	174	270	360	61	Yougoslavie
USSR (former)	10531	..	..	..	..	..	..	..	..		URSS (anc.)
Total	**93793**	**87930**	**86127**	**84013**	**87320**	**90357**	**88423**	**94620**	**89806**	**91352**	**Total**

General Note.

Uncoated sheets less than 3 mm thick, produced from hot-rolled products by a cold-rolling process to improve their technical properties. (SITC, Rev.3: 67332-0, 67333-0, 67334-0, 67336-0, 67337-0, 67338-0, 67339-3, 67342-0, 67343-0, 67344-0, 67346-0, 67347-0, 67348-0, 67349-3, 67352-2, 67353-0, 67553-0, 67554-0, 67555-0, 67556-3, 67561-1, 67562-1, 67571-3, 67572-3, 67573-3, 67574-3).

Remarque générale.

Tôles sans revêtement de moins de 3 mm d'épaisseur, fabriquées à partir de produits laminés à chaud et dont on a amélioré les propriétés techniques par laminage à froid. (CTCI, Rev.3: 67332-0, 67333-0, 67334-0, 67336-0, 67337-0, 67338-0, 67339-3, 67342-0, 67343-0, 67344-0, 67346-0, 67347-0, 67348-0, 67349-3, 67352-2, 67353-0, 67553-0, 67554-0, 67555-0, 67556-3, 67561-1, 67562-1, 67571-3, 67572-3, 67573-3, 67574-3).

[1] Source: Annual Bulletin of Steel Statistics for Europe, America and Asia, United Nations Economic Commission of Europe (Geneva).
[2] Shipments.
[3] Including hot-rolled sheets.
[4] Deliveries.

[1] Source: Bulletin annuel de statistiques de l'acier pour l'Europe, l'Amérique et l'Asie. Commission économique des Nations Unies pour l'Europe (Genève).
[2] Expéditions.
[3] Y compris les tôles laminées à chaud.
[4] Livraisons.

Sheets under 3 mm, hot-rolled
Tôles de moins de 3 mm, laminées à chaud

ISIC-BASED CODE - CODE BASE CITI

3710-52

Unit : Thousand metric tons   Unité : Milliers de tonnes métriques

Country or area	1990	1991	1992	1993	1994	1995	1996	1997	1998	1999	Pays ou zone
Africa	**564**	**628**	**439**	**502**	**397**	**368**	**322**	**276**	**230**	**184**	**Afrique**
Algeria	564	628	439	502	397	...	...	...	...	...	Algérie
America, North	**16631**	**18877**	**16032**	**16962**	**18964**	**20329**	**19568**	**21451**	**19331**	**20622**	**Amérique du Nord**
United States[1,2,3]	16631	...	16032	16962	18964	20329	19568	21451	19331	20622	Etats-Unis[1,2,3]
America, South	**208**	**214**	**203**	**286**	**262**	**227**	**251**	**228**	**253**	**247**	**Amérique du Sud**
Brazil	208	214	203	286	262	[1]227	[1]251	[1]228	[1]253	[1]247	Brésil
Asia	**12910**	**12756**	**11048**	**11203**	**10664**	**11147**	**12281**	**12701**	**11770**	**10959**	**Asie**
Japan[1,3]	11392	11360	9888	9964	9314	10080	10523	10964	10302	9304	Japon[1,3]
Korea, Republic of	454	328	93	60	51	69	153	98	65	14	Corée, République de
Turkey	1064	1068	1067	1179	1299	998	1605	1639	1403	1641	Turquie
Europe	**9194**	**12553**	**14588**	**13818**	**12662**	**14629**	**14677**	**15649**	**15939**	**16985**	**Europe**
Austria[1,3]	464	444	425	379	446	335	340	358	422	331	Autriche[1,3]
Belgium[1,3]	1009	1032	887	764	851	827	566	264	654	607	Belgique[1,3]
Bulgaria	270	86	67	125	135	183	122	177	...	...	Bulgarie
Denmark[1,3]	362	...	378	321	388	409	398	479	442	486	Danemark[1,3]
Czechoslovakia(former)[4]	1303	1054	..	..	..	..	..	..	..	..	Tchécoslovaquie(anc.)[4]
Czech Republic[1,3]	..	..	...	...	...	...	...	781	697	541	République tchèque[1,3]
Finland	317	322	...	[1,3]552	[1,3]566	[1,3]547	[1,3]576	[1,3]562	[1,3]596	[1,3]576	Finlande
France	1776	1824	1968	1850	[1]811	[1]904	[1]846	[1]936	[1]876	[1]718	France
Germany	..	...	107	110	117	...	...	...	...	...	Allemagne
Germany(Fed.Rep.)	71	..	..	..	..	..	..	..	..	..	Allemagne(Rép.féd.)
German D.R.(former)[5]	155	..	..	..	..	..	..	..	..	..	R.D.A. (anc.)[5]
Greece[1,3]	...	...	...	...	...	7	4	4	2	3	Grèce[1,3]
Hungary	556	449	600	722	...	896	...	...	...	...	Hongrie
Italy	24	...	35	2	...	...	...	...	...	...	Italie
Netherlands	14	10	10	7	7	7	6	6	...	...	Pays-Bas
Poland	699	492	539	577	617	696	616	632	531	527	Pologne
Romania	510	445	326	284	286	349	364	348	374	477	Roumanie
Russian Federation	..	1926	1910	1688	1714	2857	3416	3541	3741	4524	Fédération de Russie
Slovakia	..	..	...	...	...	...	2105	2245	...		Slovaquie
Slovenia	..	1	9	...	...	...	...	...	...	...	Slovénie
Spain[1,3]	621	599	501	547	591	641	575	589	581	606	Espagne[1,3]
Ukraine[6]	..	2410	2525	2121	1639	1914	2221	2839	2844	3541	Ukraine[6]
United Kingdom[1,3]	1032	910	931	908	969	1072	1041	1073	1035	898	Royaume-Uni[1,3]
USSR (former)[6]	13681	..	..	..	..	..	..	..	..	..	URSS (anc.)[6]
Total	**53188**	**45027**	**42310**	**42771**	**42949**	**46700**	**47099**	**50305**	**47523**	**48997**	**Total**

General Note.

Hot-rolled sheets which are less than 3 mm thick, including strip which is more than 500 mm wide and less than 3 mm thick, and which is used as such in the country concerned. Coils for re-rolling which are exported, are considered as semi-manufactured products for sale, and are therefore excluded from this item. (SITC, Rev.3: 67312-2, 67315-2, 67319-1, 67322-2, 67325-2, 67329-1, 67351-3, 67533-0, 67536-0, 67540-1, 67571-4, 67573-4, 67574-4).

Remarque générale.

Tôles laminées à chaud, de moins de 3 mm d'épaisseur, y compris les bandes qui ont plus de 500 mm de largeur et moins de 3 mm d'épaisseur et sont utilisées en l'état dans le pays déclarant. Les ébauches en rouleaux pour relaminage destinées à l'exportation sont considérées comme des demi-produits pour la vente et ne sont donc pas comprises dans cette rubrique. (CTCI, Rev.3: 67312-2, 67315-2, 67319-1, 67322-2, 67325-2, 67329-1, 67351-3, 67533-0, 67536-0, 67540-1, 67571-4, 67573-4, 67574-4).

[1] Source: Annual Bulletin of Steel Statistics for Europe, America and Asia, United Nations Economic Commission of Europe (Geneva).
[2] Shipments.
[3] Including hot-rolled plates.
[4] Plates and sheets under 4 mm.
[5] Sheets under 4 mm.
[6] Including cold-rolled sheets by weight of rolled products.

[1] Source: Bulletin annuel de statistiques de l'acier pour l'Europe, l'Amérique et l'Asie. Commission économique des Nations Unies pour l'Europe (Genève).
[2] Expéditions.
[3] Y compris les plats et tôles laminées à chaud.
[4] Tôles de moins de 4 mm.
[5] Tôles de moins de 4 mm.
[6] Y compris les tôles laminées à froid en fonction du poids de produits laminés.

Tinplate
Fer blanc

ISIC-BASED CODE - CODE BASE CITI

3710-55

Unit : Thousand metric tons | | | | | | | | | | Unité : Milliers de tonnes métriques

Country or area	1990	1991	1992	1993	1994	1995	1996	1997	1998	1999	Pays ou zone
Africa	**298**	**298**	**298**	**298**	**298**	**298**	**298**	**298**	**298**	**298**	**Afrique**
Kenya	17	...	...	...	...	...	...	...	...	...	Kenya
South Africa	281	...	...	...	...	...	...	...	...	...	Afrique du Sud
America, North	**3910**	**3872**	**3831**	**3953**	**3924**	**3620**	**3776**	**3719**	**3464**	**3522**	**Amérique du Nord**
Canada	[1][2]416	[1][2]414	[1][2]430	[1][2]423	[1][2]397	[1]308	307	*305	300	[1][2]301	Canada
Mexico	82	110	47	64	61	...	...	...	...	...	Mexique
United States [1][2]	3412	...	3354	3466	3466	3266	3431	3385	3144	3210	Etats-Unis [1][2]
America, South	**721**	**814**	**918**	**850**	**907**	**995**	**1004**	**1048**	**1061**	**1031**	**Amérique du Sud**
Argentina [3]	60	...	...	...	...	...	...	...	...	...	Argentine [3]
Brazil	[3]448	526	606	575	623	696	706	750	775	743	Brésil
Chile	31	32	38	27	33	39	45	54	40	40	Chili
Colombia	* [3]65	...	52	47	50	59	...	43	45	...	Colombie
Venezuela	117	144	162	...	...	...	...	...	...	...	Venezuela
Asia	**2608**	**2860**	**3097**	**2901**	**3023**	**3065**	**2949**	**2937**	**2737**	**2964**	**Asie**
India [4]	61	33	46	43	...	...	...	...	92	106	Inde [4]
Indonesia	* [3]130	...	...	129	119	28	...	109	12	...	Indonésie
Japan	1711	1820	1909	1650	1711	1695	1583	1559	1464	1469	Japon
Kazakhstan [1]	..	...	...	...	125	223	125	...	...	...	Kazakhstan [1]
Korea, Republic of	305	354	439	485	534	579	595	580	601	720	Corée, République de
Philippines* [3]	124	...	...	...	...	...	...	...	...	...	Philippines* [3]
Thailand	173	190	226	222	237	271	262	257	206	250	Thaïlande
Turkey	104	93	107	90	109	81	109	87	80	78	Turquie
Europe	**5269**	**5805**	**5563**	**4952**	**5187**	**5449**	**5320**	**5340**	**5399**	**5052**	**Europe**
Belgium	313	330	309	221	291	[1]290	[1]284	[1]317	[1]306	[1]224	Belgique
Bulgaria	48	31	36	12	10	41	37	21	...	...	Bulgarie
Denmark [5]	2	3	3	3	3	0	0	0	0	0	Danemark [5]
Czechoslovakia(former)	108	80	..	..	..	...	...	..	..	..	Tchécoslovaquie(anc.)
France	996	984	960	876	984	[1]1052	[1]1084	[1]1133	[1]1069	[1]990	France
Germany	...	1175	1079	895	974	[1]1027	[1]960	[1]949	[1]987	[1]925	Allemagne
Germany(Fed.Rep.)	1140	..	..	...	...	...	...	...	...	...	Allemagne(Rép.féd.)
Greece [1]	78	100	104	77	96	95	83	87	80	55	Grèce [1]
Italy	389	443	446	405	385	350	331	292	301	279	Italie
Netherlands	528	549	550	523	494	528	560	619	[1]660	[1]628	Pays-Bas
Norway [1]	103	114	114	110	90	111	...	...	...	...	Norvège [1]
Poland	63	49	60	66	79	83	81	56	37	40	Pologne
Portugal [1]	...	58	...	...	62	68	64	...	...	...	Portugal [1]
Romania	[1]2	[1]0	[1]0	[1]0	[1]0	0	0	0	...	...	Roumanie
Russian Federation	..	521	404	320	253	296	315	317	321	335	Fédération de Russie
Slovakia	..	..	...	[1]76	[1]99	[1]112	103	126	[1]119	[1]123	Slovaquie
Spain	[1]499	[1]574	[1]512	451	[1]581	[1]586	[1]553	[1]488	[1]543	[1]519	Espagne
Ukraine	..	38	19	19	17	18	17	12	6	6	Ukraine
United Kingdom	855	742	805	829	767	791	739	754	772	736	Royaume-Uni
Yugoslavia	..	14	12	[1]6	2	1	4	2	7	2	Yougoslavie
Yugoslavia, SFR* [3]	82	..	..	..	...	...	..	..	..	..	Yougoslavie, RSF* [3]
USSR (former)	590	..	..	...	...	...	...	..	...	...	URSS (anc.)
Oceania	**310**	**241**	**106**	**106**	**191**	**191**	**191**	**191**	**191**	**191**	**Océanie**
Australia [3][6]	310	241	106	106	...	...	...	...	...	...	Australie [3][6]
Total	**13706**	**13889**	**13813**	**13060**	**13529**	**13618**	**13537**	**13533**	**13150**	**13057**	**Total**

General Note.

A product made by coating hot-rolled or cold-rolled sheets and strip on both sides with commercially-pure tin. (SITC, Rev.3: 67420-0).

[1] Source: Annual Bulletin of Steel Statistics for Europe, America and Asia, United Nations Economic Commission of Europe (Geneva).
[2] Shipments.
[3] Source: International Tin Statistics, (Geneva).
[4] Twelve months beginning 1 April of year stated.
[5] Sales.
[6] Twelve months ending 30 June of year stated.

Remarque générale.

Produit que l'on obtient en revêtant d'étain commercialement pur les deux faces des tôles et des bandes laminées à chaud ou à froid. (CTCI, Rev.3: 67420-0).

[1] Source: Bulletin annuel de statistiques de l'acier pour l'Europe, l'Amérique et l'Asie. Commission économique des Nations Unies pour l'Europe (Genève).
[2] Expéditions.
[3] Source: International Tin Statistics, (Genève).
[4] Période de douze mois commençant le 1er avril de l'année indiquée.
[5] Ventes.
[6] Période de douze mois finissant le 30 juin de l'année indiquée.

Sheets, galvanized
Tôles galvanisées

ISIC-BASED CODE - CODE BASE CITI

3710-58

Unit : Thousand metric tons   Unité : Milliers de tonnes métriques

Country or area	1990	1991	1992	1993	1994	1995	1996	1997	1998	1999	Pays ou zone
Africa	**82**	**118**	**101**	**103**	**118**	**131**	**128**	**151**	**159**	**167**	Afrique
Congo	2	5	5	3	...	...	...	...	...	...	Congo
Kenya	55	88	70	72	88	106	114	...	...	...	Kenya
Madagascar	3	2	2	2	3	3	4	6	6	...	Madagascar
United Rep.Tanzania	22	23	24	26	23	18	6	15	...	...	Rép. Unie de Tanzanie
America, North	**11418**	**15928**	**12352**	**14943**	**16234**	**16175**	**17489**	**18009**	**18989**	**20220**	Amérique du Nord
Canada[1]	1247	1154	1519	1709	...	...	...	...	...	...	Canada[1]
Mexico	4	8	4	3	3	...	...	...	...	...	Mexique
United States[1][2]	10167	...	10829	13231	14824	14765	16080	16601	17582	18813	Etats-Unis[1][2]
America, South	**435**	**409**	**455**	**541**	**750**	**973**	**1032**	**1160**	**1137**	**1148**	Amérique du Sud
Brazil	361	335	398	492	656	878	958	1086	1063	1074	Brésil
Colombia	...	...	57	49	94	95	...	...	...	...	Colombie
Asia	**15916**	**17063**	**16391**	**15511**	**15542**	**16419**	**16313**	**17945**	**16239**	**17343**	Asie
India	219	180	230	200	...	...	...	...	...	...	Inde
Indonesia	...	...	...	...	344	371	...	424	...	...	Indonésie
Japan	12949	13551	12711	11539	11451	11704	11331	12699	11114	11298	Japon
Korea, Republic of	1820	2344	2559	2813	2825	3283	3525	3712	3858	4699	Corée, République de
Malaysia	112	143	126	142	204	279	273	338	235	269	Malaisie
Pakistan	47	42	42	62	62	63	59	49	62	62	Pakistan
Thailand	208	289	217	250	307	370	397	374	242	287	Thaïlande
Turkey	181	134	126	125	...	...	...	...	...	...	Turquie
Europe	**12090**	**13998**	**13808**	**13874**	**15328**	**19003**	**16336**	**21256**	**22601**	**22768**	Europe
Austria[1]	396	456	550	575	609	766	785	870	921	1022	Autriche[1]
Belgium	1792	1815	1852	1654	[1]1534	[1]1740	[1]1598	[1]2090	[1]2886	[1]2857	Belgique
Bulgaria	98	42	35	23	63	127	76	146	...	...	Bulgarie
Czechoslovakia(former)[3]	276	192	..	..	..	..	..	..	..	..	Tchécoslovaquie(anc.)[3]
Finland	331	332	...	[1]416	[1]448	[1]424	[1]465	[1]470	[1]461	[1]469	Finlande
France	2196	2292	2304	2016	2280	[1]3064	[1]3071	[1]3622	[1]3911	[1]4213	France
Germany	..	[1]3815	3455	3682	4390	[1]5854	[1]3202	[1]6322	[1]5935	[1]5966	Allemagne
Germany(Fed.Rep.)[4]	2731	..	..	..	..	..	..	..	..	..	Allemagne(Rép.féd.)[4]
German D.R.(former)	347	..	..	..	..	..	..	..	..	..	R.D.A. (anc.)
Greece[1]	108	100	104	77	96	111	105	92	141	162	Grèce[1]
Hungary	4	1	0	[1]1	[1]1	[1]1	...	[1]57	[1]84	[1]90	Hongrie
Italy	721	678	686	853	1019	1306	1423	1508	1581	1483	Italie
Luxembourg	...	69	62	54	61	60	59	59	68	63	Luxembourg
Netherlands[1]	180	255	283	301	341	381	378	370	364	338	Pays-Bas[1]
Poland	280	203	229	249	289	377	354	414	385	411	Pologne
Portugal	...	[1]92	44	48	50	[1]100	[1]94	...	...	...	Portugal
Romania[4]	64	35	41	42	46	61	63	65	67	41	Roumanie[4]
Russian Federation	..	804	654	571	626	894	787	895	994	910	Fédération de Russie
Slovakia[1]	..	..	233	237	257	282	214	282	266	220	Slovaquie[1]
Spain[1]	704	677	725	774	948	1041	1086	1148	1256	1453	Espagne[1]
Sweden[1][5]	418	420	465	507	526	530	523	555	705	711	Suède[1][5]
Ukraine[6]	..	361	226	301	128	66	124	124	172	157	Ukraine[6]
United Kingdom[1]	1319	1315	1408	1488	1612	1809	1869	2018	2126	2005	Royaume-Uni[1]
Yugoslavia	..	44	28	5	4	9	33	67	88	0	Yougoslavie
USSR (former)	1229	..	..	..	..	..	..	..	..	..	URSS (anc.)
Total	**41170**	**47515**	**43107**	**44972**	**47972**	**52700**	**51297**	**58520**	**59125**	**61646**	Total

General Note.
A product made by coating hot-rolled or cold-rolled sheets and strip on both sides with zinc containing small proportions of certain other metals. (SITC, Rev.3: 67410-0).

[1] Source: Annual Bulletin of Steel Statistics for Europe, America and Asia, United Nations Economic Commission of Europe (Geneva).
[2] Shipments.
[3] Including sheets coated with lead.
[4] Including galvanized strip.
[5] Deliveries.
[6] Including sheets coated with tin, lead and zinc.

Remarque générale.
Produits que l'on obtient en revêtant de zinc contenant de faibles proportions de certains autres métaux les deux faces des tôles et des bandes laminées à chaud ou à froid. (CTCI, Rev.3: 67410-0).

[1] Source: Bulletin annuel de statistiques de l'acier pour l'Europe, l'Amérique et l'Asie. Commission économique des Nations Unies pour l'Europe (Genève).
[2] Expéditions.
[3] Y compris les tôles à revêtement de plomb.
[4] Y compris les feuillards galvanisés.
[5] Livraisons.
[6] Y compris les tôles à revêtement d'étain, de plomb et de zinc.

Hoop and strip, cold-reduced
Feuillards laminés à froid

ISIC-BASED CODE - CODE BASE CITI

3710-61

Unit : Thousand metric tons   Unité : Milliers de tonnes métriques

Country or area	1990	1991	1992	1993	1994	1995	1996	1997	1998	1999	Pays ou zone
Africa	**115**	**147**	**169**	**118**	**131**	**160**	**144**	**141**	**146**	**147**	**Afrique**
Egypt	115	147	169	118	131	160	144	141	...	...	Egypte
America, North	**740**	**685**	**755**	**851**	**887**	**897**	**871**	**915**	**1635**	**1863**	**Amérique du Nord**
United States[1][2]	[3]740	685	755	[3]851	[3]887	[3]897	[3]871	[3]915	[3]1635	[3]1863	Etats-Unis[1][2]
America, South	**0**	**6**	**1**	**1**	**35**	**40**	**28**	**24**	**68**	**66**	**Amérique du Sud**
Colombia	...	...	1	1	35	40	...	24	68	...	Colombie
Asia	**4111**	**4689**	**4800**	**5802**	**6191**	**6743**	**6606**	**7161**	**7348**	**7581**	**Asie**
Indonesia	...	...	...	...	442	...	...	...	...	...	Indonésie
Japan[3]	[1]586	588	[1]543	[1]606	[1]603	[1]640	[1]603	[1]613	[1]543	[1]482	Japon[3]
Korea, Republic of	2649	3267	3395	4330	4618	5239	...	...	...	...	Corée, République de
Pakistan	128	112	135	164	165	171	155	159	159	149	Pakistan
Turkey	306	280	285	260	363	251	465	749	750	798	Turquie
Europe	**4109**	**4498**	**4057**	**3592**	**3840**	**4925**	**4639**	**5109**	**5283**	**5185**	**Europe**
Austria[4]	13	13	13	12	11	...	...	...	...	...	Autriche[4]
Czechoslovakia(former)	310	222	..	..	..	...	...	...	...	...	Tchécoslovaquie(anc.)
Czech Republic	..	..	165	125	135	[1][3]157	[1][3]126	[1][3]144	[1][3]137	[1][3]100	République tchèque
France	[5]108	[5]98	[5]92	[5]79	[5]94	...	90	102	106	100	France
Germany	..	2231	2180	1563	1796	2667	2394	2667	2747	...	Allemagne
Germany(Fed.Rep.)	2148		..	..	..	..	..	..	..	..	Allemagne(Rép.féd.)
German D.R.(former)	252		..	..	..	..	..	..	..	..	R.D.A. (anc.)
Hungary	66	37	23	...	31	60	...	...	32	32	Hongrie
Italy[3]	...	305	[1]267	[1]609	[1]702	[1]725	...	...	...	...	Italie[3]
Luxembourg	28	25	31	34	40	42	46	58	61	61	Luxembourg
Poland	192	145	128	133	140	159	146	141	112	72	Pologne
Romania	270	220	149	119	127	205	133	165	160	176	Roumanie
Russian Federation	..	526	358	150	33	45	38	36	25	30	Fédération de Russie
Slovakia[1][3]	..	..	52	55	55	53	...	40	41	34	Slovaquie[1][3]
Slovenia	..	32	10	34	32	28	22	[1][3]13	[1][3]29	[1][3]23	Slovénie
Spain[3]	...	245	[1]217	...	[1]233	...	...	...	...	...	Espagne[3]
Sweden[3][5]	114	[1]107	[1]119	[1]156	[1]163	[1]167	[1]153	[1]178	...	...	Suède[3][5]
Ukraine	..	37	24	21	4	8	8	8	3	0	Ukraine
United Kingdom[1][3]	...	...	222	229	243	267	246	241	254	233	Royaume-Uni[1][3]
Yugoslavia	..	16	7	1	1	3	4	3	2	1	Yougoslavie
USSR (former)	596	..	..	..	..	..	..	..	..	..	URSS (anc.)
Total	**9671**	**10024**	**9782**	**10364**	**11084**	**12765**	**12289**	**13350**	**14480**	**14842**	**Total**

General Note.
A flat, cold-rolled product which is not more than 500 mm wide and is normally delivered in coils. (SITC, Rev.3: 67339-4, 67349-4, 67353-4, 67556-4, 67562-2, 67572-4, 67574-5).

Remarque générale.
Produits plats laminé à froid, de moins de 500 mm de largeur et normalement livrés en rouleaux. (CTCI, Rev.3: 67339-4, 67349-4, 67353-4, 67556-4, 67562-2, 67572-4, 67574-5).

[1] Cold-reduced strip only.
[2] Shipments.
[3] Source: Annual Bulletin of Steel Statistics for Europe, America and Asia, United Nations Economic Commission of Europe (Geneva).
[4] Beginning 1995, data are confidential.
[5] Deliveries.

[1] Feuillards laminés à froid seulement.
[2] Expéditions.
[3] Source: Bulletin annuel de statistiques de l'acier pour l'Europe, l'Amérique et l'Asie. Commission économique des Nations Unies pour l'Europe (Genève).
[4] A partir de 1995, les données sont confidentielles
[5] Livraisons.

Hoop and strip, hot-rolled
Feuillards laminés à chaud

ISIC-BASED CODE - CODE BASE CITI

3710-64

Unit : Thousand metric tons · Unité : Milliers de tonnes métriques

Country or area	1990	1991	1992	1993	1994	1995	1996	1997	1998	1999	Pays ou zone
Africa	**208**	**242**	**222**	**231**	**259**	**289**	**309**	**331**	**312**	**321**	**Afrique**
Egypt	208	242	222	231	259	289	309	331	...	...	Egypte
America, North	**806**	**702**	**498**	**563**	**646**	**734**	**636**	**737**	**811**	**890**	**Amérique du Nord**
United States[1][2]	806	...	498	563	646	734	636	737	811	890	Etats-Unis[1][2]
Asia	**9913**	**11194**	**12124**	**13668**	**13751**	**13874**	**14992**	**15348**	**13633**	**13396**	**Asie**
Indonesia	...	...	...	...	1634	...	...	...	...	...	Indonésie
Japan[1]	1525	1355	1320	1438	1402	1470	1485	1463	1117	1097	Japon[1]
Korea, Republic of	6378	7770	8718	10073	10152	10256	11338	11737	10408	10162	Corée, République de
Pakistan	339	383	392	481	517	468	486	465	423	451	Pakistan
Sri Lanka	33	48	54	39	...	...	...	...	...	...	Sri Lanka
Turkey	...	...	6	3	2	2	5	5	7	8	Turquie
Europe	**6324**	**14144**	**11900**	**7587**	**6229**	**6491**	**6248**	**6785**	**6087**	**4735**	**Europe**
Austria[3]	...	...	337	319	363	...	...	...	...	...	Autriche[3]
Belgium	39	56	66	17	[1]14	[1]13	[1]8	[1]8	[1]6	[1]5	Belgique
Croatia	..	57	62	52	45	35	22	8	...	...	Croatie
Czechoslovakia(former)	933	724	..	..	..	..	..	..	..	..	Tchécoslovaquie(anc.)
Czech Republic[1]	..	..	...	...	...	...	...	515	512	460	République tchèque[1]
Finland[1]	63	40	...	24	33	32	28	32	27	24	Finlande[1]
France	156	156	144	99	156	223	201	204	206	207	France
Germany	..	[1]789	[1]792	[1]577	[1]682	741	721	863	824	[1]673	Allemagne
Germany(Fed.Rep.)	2310	..	..	..	..	..	..	..	..		Allemagne(Rép.féd.)
German D.R.(former)	301	..	..	..	..	..	..	..	..		R.D.A. (anc.)
Greece[1]	5	13	6	10	13	38	9	0	0	0	Grèce[1]
Hungary	6	2	4	...	[1]3	# [1]82	[1]89	[1]98	109	100	Hongrie
Italy	450	483	501	527	589	468	# [1]48	[1]55	[1]46	[1]42	Italie
Luxembourg	278	274	262	167	176	0	0	0	0	0	Luxembourg
Netherlands	261	220	195	153	165	125	104	[1]173	[1]183	[1]223	Pays-Bas
Poland	579	498	489	481	580	698	537	615	568	292	Pologne
Romania	28	13	11	7	7	9	9	4	...	1	Roumanie
Russian Federation	..	5523	4244	2410	1174	1626	1368	1305	910	1071	Fédération de Russie
Slovakia	..	..	[1]164	[1]111	[1]153	[1]131	112	117	[1]128	[1]128	Slovaquie
Slovenia	..	99	104	116	137	139	84	...	...	...	Slovénie
Spain[1]	245	177	136	163	207	211	190	242	253	267	Espagne[1]
Sweden	63	[1,2]83	[1,2]98	[1,2]110	[1,2]130	[1,2]143	[1,2]261	...	[1,2]31	[1,2]29	Suède
Ukraine	..	3680	2965	1470	906	686	945	924	640	456	Ukraine
United Kingdom[1]	267	248	160	150	146	155	144	166	152	151	Royaume-Uni[1]
Yugoslavia	..	669	631	74	52	103	533	895	1026	149	Yougoslavie
USSR (former)[4]	12190	..	..	..	..	..	..	..	..	..	URSS (anc.)[4]
Total	**29440**	**26282**	**24744**	**22049**	**20884**	**21388**	**22185**	**23201**	**20843**	**19341**	**Total**

General Note.
A flat, hot-rolled product which is not more than 500 mm wide and is normally delivered in coils, including strip for use in making welded tubes. (SITC, Rev.3: 67317-2, 67319-2, 67327-2, 67329-2, 67353-5, 67537-2, 67538-2, 67543-2, 67572-5, 67574-6).

Remarque générale.
Produits plats laminés à chaud, de moins de 500 mm de largeur et normalement livrés en rouleaux. Cette rubrique comprend les bandes pour la fabrication des tubes soudés. (CTCI, Rev.3: 67317-2, 67319-2, 67327-2, 67329-2, 67353-5, 67537-2, 67538-2, 67543-2, 67572-5, 67574-6).

[1] Source: Annual Bulletin of Steel Statistics for Europe, America and Asia, United Nations Economic Commission of Europe (Geneva).
[2] Deliveries.
[3] Beginning 1995, data are confidential.
[4] Including cold-reduced hoop and strip.

[1] Source: Bulletin annuel de statistiques de l'acier pour l'Europe, l'Amérique et l'Asie. Commission économique des Nations Unies pour l'Europe (Genève).
[2] Livraisons.
[3] A partir de 1995, les données sont confidentielles
[4] Y compris les feuillards laminés à froid.

Railway track material
Matériel de voie

ISIC-BASED CODE - CODE BASE CITI

3710-67

Unit : Thousand metric tons

Unité : Milliers de tonnes métriques

Country or area	1990	1991	1992	1993	1994	1995	1996	1997	1998	1999	Pays ou zone
Africa	**98**	**57**	**77**	**72**	**63**	**61**	**57**	**46**	**42**	**37**	**Afrique**
South Africa[1]	98	57	77	72	63	61	57	...	...	...	Afrique du Sud[1]
America, North	**486**	**960**	**844**	**992**	**961**	**1014**	**1094**	**1145**	**1130**	**811**	**Amérique du Nord**
Canada	[2][3]16	[2][3]353	[2][3]367	[2][3]406	[2][3]389	[2][3]443	488	*352	331	[2][3]225	Canada
United States[2][3]	470	...	477	586	572	571	606	793	799	586	Etats-Unis[2][3]
America, South	**22**	**30**	**10**	**40**	**49**	**14**	**6**	**0**	**0**	**0**	**Amérique du Sud**
Brazil	22	30	10	40	49	[2]14	[2]6	[2]0	[2]0	[2]0	Brésil
Asia	**2721**	**2721**	**2661**	**3138**	**3452**	**2759**	**2576**	**2723**	**2642**	**2517**	**Asie**
China	1661	1638	1550	2013	2262	1611	1455	1524	1544	1471	Chine
India	...	...	...	...	578	559	559	595	493	477	Inde
Japan	[2]389	413	441	451	471	455	412	461	475	427	Japon
Korea, Republic of	69	76	86	102	140	134	150	143	130	142	Corée, République de
Turkey	1	3	2	0	1	[2]0	0	0	0	0	Turquie
Europe	**1817**	**5229**	**4168**	**3523**	**3598**	**3601**	**3309**	**2911**	**2855**	**2693**	**Europe**
Albania[2]	...	...	...	...	17	19	21	21	...	...	Albanie[2]
Austria	191	[2]210	[2]261	[2]269	[2]290	[2]252	[2]237	[2]336	[2]335	[2]316	Autriche
Croatia[2]	..	...	...	...	...	12	0	0	0	0	Croatie[2]
Czechoslovakia(former)[4]	194	101			...	..	..	..	..	..	Tchécoslovaquie(anc.)[4]
Czech Republic	..	..	[2]67	[2]72	[2]79	[2]103	[2]103	117	175	114	République tchèque
Finland	3	5	3	2	5	7	5	...	...	...	Finlande
France	204	240	264	228	192	228	255	275	315	302	France
Germany	..	[2]372	335	266	250	292	259	267	308	[2]268	Allemagne
Germany(Fed.Rep.)	224		..	..	..	..	..	..	..		Allemagne(Rép.féd.)
German D.R.(former)	55	..	..	..	..	..	..	..	..	..	R.D.A. (anc.)
Hungary	25	23	4	13	19	11	[2]14	[2]9	10	8	Hongrie
Italy	225	259	178	104	97	134	134	157	30	182	Italie
Luxembourg	116	131	129	134	105	121	55	42	48	43	Luxembourg
Poland	127	110	69	80	73	72	63	53	41	21	Pologne
Romania[1]	22	13	10	8	11	9	7	8	10	6	Roumanie[1]
Russian Federation	..	2084	1527	1575	1668	1603	1424	948	690	818	Fédération de Russie
Slovenia	..	0	0	[2]4	[2]8	...	[2]0	[2]0	0	...	Slovénie
Spain	111	86	61	[2]56	[2]128	[2]114	[2]64	[2]123	[2]119	[2]91	Espagne
Sweden[2][5]	41	23	10	40	64	59	50	...	160	81	Suède[2][5]
Ukraine	..	1335	1060	492	429	353	408	303	371	187	Ukraine
United Kingdom[2]	232	201	156	148	153	210	210	187	217	228	Royaume-Uni[2]
Yugoslavia, SFR[2]	27	..	..	..	..	..	..	..	..	..	Yougoslavie, RSF[2]
USSR (former)	4249	..	..	..	..	..	..	..	..	..	URSS (anc.)
Total	**9392**	**8997**	**7760**	**7765**	**8123**	**7449**	**7042**	**6825**	**6669**	**6058**	**Total**

General Note.

Hot-rolled steel products for the construction of railway and tramway track, that is, rails (including check-rails and rackrails), sleepers and products used as accessories for track construction, such as fishplates, soleplates, bedplates etc. This item does not include fabricated steel products for railway and tramway track construction, such as the following: (a) assembled track, turntables, platform buffers and loading gauges, (b) switch blades, crossings (or frogs), crossing pieces and point rods, and (c) screws, bolts, nuts, rivets and spikes used for fixing track construction materials. (SITC, Rev.3: 67701-0, 67709-1).

Remarque générale.

Produits sidérurgiques laminés à chaud utilisés pour la construction de voies ferrées, rails (y compris les contre-rails et les crémaillères), traverses et produits utilisés accessoirement pour la construction de voies ferrées (éclisses, plaques de serrage, plaques d'écartement, etc.). Cette rubrique ne comprend pas les articles manufacturés en acier pour la construction de voies ferrées tels que: (a) voies assemblées, plaques tournantes, butoirs et gabarits, (b) aiguilles, pointes de coeur, croisements et changements de voies et tringles d'aiguillages, (c) tire-fonds, boulons, écrous, rivets, clous etc., utilisés pour fixer les éléments servant à la construction des voies ferrées. (CTCI, Rev.3: 67701-0, 67709-1).

[1] Rails only.
[2] Source: Annual Bulletin of Steel Statistics for Europe, America and Asia, United Nations Economic Commission of Europe (Geneva).
[3] Shipments.
[4] Heavy rails and tram rails only.
[5] Deliveries.

[1] Rails seulement.
[2] Source: Bulletin annuel de statistiques de l'acier pour l'Europe, l'Amérique et l'Asie. Commission économique des Nations Unies pour l'Europe (Genève).
[3] Expéditions.
[4] Rails lourds et rails à ornière seulement.
[5] Livraisons.

Wire, plain
Fil ordinaire

ISIC-BASED CODE - CODE BASE CITI

3710-70

Unit : Thousand metric tons

Unité : Milliers de tonnes métriques

Country or area	1990	1991	1992	1993	1994	1995	1996	1997	1998	1999	Pays ou zone
Africa	365	364	347	347	372	389	397	438	425	438	**Afrique**
Egypt	72	82	89	79	89	88	...	...	...	...	Egypte
South Africa	293	282	258	268	283	301	309	348	334	346	Afrique du Sud
America, North	882	730	827	857	847	669	678	642	694	659	**Amérique du Nord**
Mexico	47	67	28	138	133	76	86	80	100	104	Mexique
United States[1,2]	835	...	799	719	714	593	592	562	594	555	Etats-Unis[1,2]
America, South	484	462	418	514	501	644	553	635	602	669	**Amérique du Sud**
Colombia	...	...	58	152	139	282	...	273	240	...	Colombie
Venezuela[3]	386	341	360	...	...	...	...	...	...	...	Venezuela[3]
Asia	5538	5420	5241	5095	5305	5522	5390	5684	5043	5354	**Asie**
Indonesia	...	...	...	...	285	...	...	...	...	...	Indonésie
Japan[2]	4387	4292	4087	3894	3847	3887	3900	3907	3394	3381	Japon[2]
Korea, Republic of	726	719	735	794	[2]1069	[2]1206	...	[2]1281	[2]1192	[2]1545	Corée, République de
Malaysia	43	36	40	48	51	51	83	103	78	55	Malaisie
Turkey	[2]97	[2]88	[2]94	[2]74	[2]53	[2]93	92	108	94	88	Turquie
Europe	6423	9607	9058	7474	7133	6305	5944	6335	6432	6446	**Europe**
Albania[2]	...	...	...	1	...	...	...	...	...	...	Albanie[2]
Austria	132	141	114	88	110	127	126	132	128	136	Autriche
Belarus	..	57	51	17	9	39	46	64	69	48	Bélarus
Belgium	...	...	...	...	496	494	488	615	596	650	Belgique
Croatia	..	2	7	4	2	2	2	20	29	[2]19	Croatie
Denmark[4]	16	16	19	14	18	21	15	20	19	...	Danemark[4]
Czechoslovakia(former)	538	339	..	..	..	..	..	..	..	..	Tchécoslovaquie(anc.)
Czech Republic	..	..	222	232	278	312	338	402	427	440	République tchèque
Finland	29	19	21	17	22	10	8	[2]27	21	20	Finlande
France[5]	412	474	499	444	454	...	...	...	...	...	France[5]
Germany	..	2397	2376	2301	2570	1475	1338	1388	1340	...	Allemagne
Germany(Fed.Rep.)	2270	..	..	..	..	..	..	..	..	..	Allemagne(Rép.féd.)
German D.R.(former)	263	..	..	..	..	..	..	..	..	..	R.D.A. (anc.)
Greece	[6]152	[6]146	[6]151	77	52	112	136	...	104	...	Grèce
Hungary	144	85	62	36	55	71	65	70	72	83	Hongrie
Latvia	..	...	...	...	[2]25	[2]14	[2]19	[2]21	[2]36	17	Lettonie
Lithuania	..	16	5	6	6	7	7	7	7	14	Lituanie
Netherlands[7]	101	97	112	...	...	...	...	...	...	...	Pays-Bas[7]
Norway	30	...	...	22	...	...	...	...	...	...	Norvège
Poland	168	124	122	139	164	196	196	239	284	316	Pologne
Portugal	80	84	74	84	94	101	100	109	118	145	Portugal
Romania	411	321	204	192	185	222	224	205	220	190	Roumanie
Russian Federation	..	2485	1880	1234	747	821	655	614	632	728	Fédération de Russie
Slovakia[2]	..	..	...	...	...	130	123	125	104	88	Slovaquie[2]
Slovenia	..	30	29	25	25	25	14	14	14	18	Slovénie
Spain	304	279	282	260	305	323	351	385	449	...	Espagne
Sweden[8]	214	180	183	156	216	252	157	175	178	...	Suède[8]
Ukraine	..	1086	1261	728	394	334	347	349	315	263	Ukraine
United Kingdom	...	...	...	607	626	606	573	...	[2]642	[2]630	Royaume-Uni
Yugoslavia	..	25	15	5	5	8	8	10	9	6	Yougoslavie
USSR (former)	1161	..	..	..	..	..	..	..	..	..	URSS (anc.)
Total	14853	16582	15891	14287	14158	13529	12962	13734	13197	13566	**Total**

General Note.
A cold-drawn steel product of solid section of any cross-sectional shape, of which no cross-sectional dimension exceeds 13 mm, produced from wire rod by drawing it through a die. Fabricated wire products are excluded. (SITC, Rev.3: 67800-0).

Remarque générale.
Produit sidérurgique de section pleine, étiré ou tréfilé à froid, dont la coupe transversale, de forme quelconque, n'excède pas 13 mm dans sa plus grande dimension, obtenu par étirage du fil machine à travers une filière. Cette rubrique ne comprend pas les ouvrages en fil. (CTCI, Rev.3: 67800-0).

Wire, plain (continued)
Fil ordinaire (suite)

ISIC-BASED CODE - CODE BASE CITI

3710-70

Footnotes
[1] Shipments.
[2] Source: Annual Bulletin of Steel Statistics for Europe, America and Asia, United Nations Economic Commission of Europe (Geneva).
[3] Source: Instituto Latino Americano del Fierro y el Acero, (Santiago).
[4] Sales.
[5] Deliveries.
[6] Black wire and wire coated with zinc.
[7] Production by wire industry only.
[8] Excluding wire of iron or steel covered metal.

Notes.
[1] Expéditions.
[2] Source: Bulletin annuel de statistiques de l'acier pour l'Europe, l'Amérique et l'Asie. Commission économique des Nations Unies pour l'Europe (Genève).
[3] Source: Instituto Latino Americano del Fierro y el Acero, (Santiago).
[4] Ventes.
[5] Livraisons.
[6] Fils noirs et fils galvanisés.
[7] Production de l'industrie du fil métallique seulement.
[8] Non compris les fils métalliques recouverts de fer ou d'acier.

Tubes, seamless
Tubes sans soudure

ISIC-BASED CODE - CODE BASE CITI

3710-76

Unit : Thousand metric tons

Unité : Milliers de tonnes métriques

Country or area	1990	1991	1992	1993	1994	1995	1996	1997	1998	1999	Pays ou zone
Africa	**12**	**14**	**21**	**23**	**24**	**30**	**16**	**17**	**11**	**13**	**Afrique**
Algeria	12	14	21	23	24	30	16	17	11	13	Algérie
America, North	**1734**	**1755**	**1507**	**1915**	**2062**	**2429**	**2673**	**2880**	**2261**	**1697**	**Amérique du Nord**
Mexico	318	381	267	324	367	469	609	628	568	408	Mexique
United States [1] [2]	1416	1374	1240	1591	1695	1960	2064	2252	1693	1289	Etats-Unis [1] [2]
America, South	**843**	**991**	**858**	**944**	**930**	**1019**	**1102**	**1152**	**996**	**845**	**Amérique du Sud**
Argentina	526	661	568	588	607	694	741	755	649	486	Argentine
Brazil	239	283	252	302	269	[2]271	[2]307	[2]343	[2]293	[2]305	Brésil
Venezuela [3]	78	47	38	...	...	...	...	...	...	...	Venezuela [3]
Asia	**5038**	**5953**	**5385**	**5616**	**5405**	**4843**	**5203**	**5580**	**5742**	**5468**	**Asie**
Azerbaijan	..	411	260	146	31	10	3	13	3	0	Azerbaïdjan
China	2111	2314	2656	2831	3039	[2]2737	[2]3162	...	...	...	Chine
Georgia [2]	..	...	...	...	...	...	33	28	9	1	Géorgie [2]
Japan	2794	3084	2327	2484	2300	2061	1938	2050	2083	1661	Japon
Korea, Republic of	127	123	120	133	[2]13	[2]11	...	[2]10	[2]11	[2]15	Corée, République de
Turkey	6	3	4	4	4	6	4	4	4	3	Turquie
Europe	**5813**	**11102**	**10045**	**8674**	**7169**	**8028**	**7711**	**8061**	**7948**	**6533**	**Europe**
Austria	...	...	...	[2]207	[2]169	200	258	242	219	162	Autriche
Belgium	...	...	...		5	8	7	7	9	10	Belgique
Bulgaria	52	24	22	23	23	25	26	19	[2]16	...	Bulgarie
Croatia	..	96	48	38	26	13	17	32	57	[2]41	Croatie
Czechoslovakia(former)	962	733	..	..	..	..	..	..	..	..	Tchécoslovaquie(anc.)
Czech Republic	..	..	827	362	377	[2] [4]423	[2]418	360	[2]376	[2]288	République tchèque
France [2]	...	...	...	443	525	555	566	653	736	471	France [2]
Germany	..	...	1047	972	1146	1567	1406	1723	1701	[2]1076	Allemagne
Germany(Fed.Rep.)	1362	..	..	..	..	..	..	..	..	..	Allemagne(Rép.féd.)
Greece	...	...	...	22	25	26	27	40	14	...	Grèce
Hungary	113	75	50	...	35	47	39	[2]29	[2]10	...	Hongrie
Ireland	...	...	...	...	...	3	...	...	...	...	Irlande
Italy	726	770	709	736	756	792	722	759	777	603	Italie
Poland	300	253	247	230	237	254	256	247	219	192	Pologne
Romania	576	284	260	264	282	332	379	420	417	238	Roumanie
Russian Federation	..	3553	2967	2594	1857	1934	1669	1677	1462	1706	Fédération de Russie
Slovakia	..	..	...	[2]100	[2]97	[2]113	135	132	187	170	Slovaquie
Spain	351	314	241	232	231	248	260	275	286	254	Espagne
Sweden	[4]147	[4]120	[4]107	[4]92	[4]114	[4]133	[2] [5]121	[2] [5]134	[2] [5]138	[2] [5]113	Suède
Ukraine	..	2517	2402	1729	836	893	971	850	869	681	Ukraine
United Kingdom	...	...	[2]287	571	425	462	431	459	452	...	Royaume-Uni
Yugoslavia, SFR [2]	126	..	..	..	..	..	..	..	..	..	Yougoslavie, RSF [2]
USSR (former)	7966	..	..	..	..	..	..	..	..	..	URSS (anc.)
Total	**21406**	**19815**	**17816**	**17172**	**15590**	**16349**	**16705**	**17691**	**16959**	**14557**	**Total**

General Note.

Steel tubes produced from an ingot or a semi-manufactured product by a number of different methods involving piercing followed by a series of finishing operations. (SITC, Rev.3: 67912-0, 67913-0, 67914-0, 67915-0, 67916-0, 67917-0).

Remarque générale.

Tubes d'acier fabriqués à partir d'un lingot ou demi-produit par divers procédés comprenant un perçage suivi d'une série d'opérations de finition. (CTCI, Rev.3: 67912-0, 67913-0, 67914-0, 67915-0, 67916-0, 67917-0).

[1] Shipments.
[2] Source: Annual Bulletin of Steel Statistics for Europe, America and Asia, United Nations Economic Commission of Europe (Geneva).
[3] Source: Instituto Latino Americano del Fierro y el Acero, (Santiago).
[4] Primary production of hot-rolled seamless tubes.
[5] Deliveries.

[1] Expéditions.
[2] Source: Bulletin annuel de statistiques de l'acier pour l'Europe, l'Amérique et l'Asie. Commission économique des Nations Unies pour l'Europe (Genève).
[3] Source: Instituto Latino Americano del Fierro y el Acero, (Santiago).
[4] Production primaire de tubes sans soudure laminés à chaud.
[5] Livraisons.

Tubes, welded
Tubes soudés

ISIC-BASED CODE - CODE BASE CITI

3710-79

Unit : Thousand metric tons   Unité : Milliers de tonnes métriques

Country or area	1990	1991	1992	1993	1994	1995	1996	1997	1998	1999	Pays ou zone
Africa	**685**	**611**	**640**	**708**	**606**	**632**	**558**	**561**	**523**	**438**	**Afrique**
Algeria	121	94	102	131	48	37	28	15	12	17	Algérie
South Africa	564	517	538	577	558	595	530	546	511	421	Afrique du Sud
America, North	**4575**	**4715**	**4242**	**4685**	**5405**	**5275**	**5901**	**6848**	**6394**	**6089**	**Amérique du Nord**
Canada	[1][2]1469	[1][2]1710	[1][2]1356	[1][2]1758	[1][2]2048	[1][2]1941	[1][2]2141	*2524	2530	[1][2]2487	Canada
Mexico	302	307	318	484	548	362	476	636	650	561	Mexique
United States[2][3]	2804	2698	2568	2443	2809	2972	3284	3688	3214	3041	Etats-Unis[2][3]
America, South	**83**	**84**	**71**	**79**	**96**	**92**	**123**	**85**	**71**	**95**	**Amérique du Sud**
Argentina	57	...	...	...	...	...	...	...	...	...	Argentine
Ecuador	...	...	14	22	39	35	66	28	14	...	Equateur
Asia	**13722**	**14100**	**13129**	**13106**	**12839**	**13774**	**13680**	**14809**	**12152**	**13321**	**Asie**
China[2]	...	...	...	...	...	2059	1938	...	...	...	Chine[2]
Hong Kong SAR[4]	[1]61	88	39	52	65	25	34	...	24	...	Hong-Kong RAS[4]
Cyprus	*6	*6	11	[2]13	[2]15	[2]15	[2]16	15	16	19	Chypre
Japan	[2]7733	7802	7177	6939	6406	6617	6981	6946	6375	5998	Japon
Kazakhstan	..	9	3	...	...	...	...	...	...	...	Kazakhstan
Korea, Republic of	2942	3152	2840	2923	[2]3141	[2]3685	...	[2]3931	[2]2092	[2]3397	Corée, République de
Malaysia	308	372	396	410	478	503	685	758	501	637	Malaisie
Turkey	673	672	664	764	729	864	897	1106	1139	1265	Turquie
Europe	**8807**	**18654**	**16101**	**12150**	**11659**	**12295**	**12872**	**13925**	**13683**	**13048**	**Europe**
Austria[1]	113	120	100	76	89	#323	329	382	330	399	Autriche[1]
Belarus	..	92	76	44	10	12	19	31	51	38	Bélarus
Bulgaria	156	63	57	61	59	66	65	49	53	54	Bulgarie
Croatia	..	96	67	74	90	45	33	42	64	[2]45	Croatie
Czechoslovakia(former)	605	442	..	..	..	..	..	..	..	..	Tchécoslovaquie(anc.)
Czech Republic	..	..	347	190	[2]292	[2]344	[2]324	362	[2]370	[2]271	République tchèque
Finland	263	227	272	308	344	399	368	415	407	450	Finlande
France	...	...	...	[2]717	[2]843	[2]739	784	903	810	836	France
Germany	...	...	1757	1432	1628	2052	1954	[2]2228	2396	[2]2053	Allemagne
Germany(Fed.Rep.)[5]	1505	..	..	..	..	..	..	..	..	..	Allemagne(Rép.féd.)[5]
Greece	[6]286	[6]253	[6]199	162	145	165	189	230	283	...	Grèce
Hungary	71	47	47	49	48	72	191	212	214	215	Hongrie
Italy	1919	2062	2029	1937	2808	2800	2946	3197	3279	3278	Italie
Latvia	..	...	..	...	...	...	...	...	...	1	Lettonie
Luxembourg	107	128	134	130	127	100	95	120	104	105	Luxembourg
Poland	267	267	273	250	259	307	255	269	256	257	Pologne
Portugal	...	...	79	80	83	82	74	95	118	128	Portugal
Romania	465	343	189	150	190	212	212	214	244	113	Roumanie
Russian Federation	..	6938	5114	3210	1733	1801	1851	1797	1380	1594	Fédération de Russie
Slovakia	..	..	...	[2]43	[2]48	[2]50	6	33	56	58	Slovaquie
Slovenia	..	35	37	44	58	62	3	1	1	2	Slovénie
Spain	729	706	766	737	935	835	780	931	1062	1225	Espagne
Sweden[2][7]	88	83	80	85	89	91	100	111	105	103	Suède[2][7]
Ukraine	..	3044	2686	1377	824	702	1031	995	653	495	Ukraine
United Kingdom	...	...	[2]901	[2]908	[2]930	[2]996	[2]1215	1249	1358	[2]1084	Royaume-Uni
Yugoslavia	..	72	64	31	7	15	25	27	43	9	Yougoslavie
T.F.Yug.Rep. Macedonia	..	...	...	[2]54	[2]19	[2]24	22	31	45	34	L'ex-RY Macédoine
Yugoslavia, SFR	463	..	..	..	..	..	..	..	..	..	Yougoslavie, RSF
USSR (former)	11540	..	..	..	..	..	..	..	..	..	URSS (anc.)
Total	**39411**	**38163**	**34182**	**30728**	**30605**	**32068**	**33134**	**36228**	**32822**	**32990**	**Total**

General Note.

Steel tubes generally produced from strip or sheets by a number of different processes involving welding, which may be followed by a cold-drawing finishing operation. (SITC, Rev.3: 67931-1, 67933-0, 67943-0, 67944-0).

[1] Including seamless tubes.
[2] Source: Annual Bulletin of Steel Statistics for Europe, America and Asia, United Nations Economic Commission of Europe (Geneva).
[3] Shipments.
[4] 1997 data are confidential.
[5] Excluding welded precision tubes.
[6] Including seamless tubes and iron pipes of all kinds.
[7] Deliveries.

Remarque générale.

Tubes d'acier fabriqués généralement à partir de bandes ou de tôles par divers procédés comprenant la soudure et, éventuellement, une opération ultérieure de finition par étirage à froid. (CTCI, Rev.3: 67931-1, 67933-0, 67943-0, 67944-0).

[1] Y compris les tubes sans soudure.
[2] Source: Bulletin annuel de statistiques de l'acier pour l'Europe, l'Amérique et l'Asie. Commission économique des Nations Unies pour l'Europe (Genève).
[3] Expéditions.
[4] Pour 1997, les données sont confidentielles.
[5] Non compris les tuyaux de précision soudés.
[6] Y compris les tubes sans soudure et tuyaux en fonte de toutes sortes.
[7] Livraisons.

Steel castings in the rough state
Moulages d'acier non usinés

ISIC-BASED CODE - CODE BASE CITI

3710-85

Unit : Thousand metric tons

Unité : Milliers de tonnes métriques

Country or area	1990	1991	1992	1993	1994	1995	1996	1997	1998	1999	Pays ou zone
Africa	**92**	**89**	**75**	**59**	**63**	**57**	**59**	**39**	**33**	**27**	**Afrique**
South Africa	92	89	75	59	63	57	59	...	...	...	Afrique du Sud
America, North	**1028**	**868**	**930**	**942**	**942**	**942**	**942**	**942**	**942**	**942**	**Amérique du Nord**
United States	[1]1028	868	930	...	...	...	...	...	...	...	Etats-Unis
Asia	**964**	**1029**	**836**	**794**	**880**	**964**	**608**	**600**	**530**	**473**	**Asie**
Indonesia	...	...	...	...	3			...	...	...	Indonésie
Japan	[2]485	450	377	349	356	370	375	357	286	257	Japon
Korea, Republic of	423	515	387	373	458	504	[2]136	[2]124	[2]120	[2]120	Corée, République de
Turkey[2]	...	...	...	69	63	87	94	116	121	93	Turquie[2]
Europe	**1524**	**3298**	**3150**	**3769**	**3686**	**2709**	**2355**	**2576**	**3429**	**5118**	**Europe**
Austria	...	12	13	17	13	...	...	...	...	...	Autriche
Belarus	..	188	158	139	90	58	48	58	58	59	Bélarus
Bulgaria[2]	...	31	19	11	10	13	13	12	11	9	Bulgarie[2]
Croatia	..	2	2	2	1	1	1	[2]0	0	...	Croatie
Czechoslovakia(former)	271	186	..	..	..	..	..	..	..	..	Tchécoslovaquie(anc.)
Czech Republic	..	..	112	88	81	...	...	[2]122	[2]131	[2]113	République tchèque
Estonia	..	4	2	1	1	2	2	3	2	1	Estonie
Finland	15	12	12	14	18	21	19	[2]14	[2]15	[2]12	Finlande
France	115	252	250	201	218	...	...	...	...	...	France
Germany	..	266	210	165	168	[2]184	[2]173	13	14	..	Allemagne
Germany(Fed.Rep.)	221		..	..	..	..	..	..	..	..	Allemagne(Rép.féd.)
German D.R.(former)	169	..	..	..	..	..	..	..	..	..	R.D.A. (anc.)
Hungary	20	12	6	8	11	7	[2]2	...	[2]2	...	Hongrie
Italy	117	115	86	[2]79	[2]92	[2]92	[2]84	[2]80	[2]76	[2]76	Italie
Poland	179	100	69	69	73	78	77	74	64	49	Pologne
Romania	245	184	110	88	82	82	74	65	47	32	Roumanie
Russian Federation	..	...	...	1535	862	869	724	637	532	680	Fédération de Russie
Slovakia	..	..	[2]4	8	8	9	5	[2]24	[2]28	[2]15	Slovaquie
Slovenia	..	...	[2]23	[2]16	[2]18	[2]20	23	1	0	2	Slovénie
Sweden	23	...	...	...	...	...	...	[2][3]31	...	...	Suède
Ukraine	..	...	...	[2]1187	[2]1795	[2]748	[2]559	1034	1977	3549	Ukraine
United Kingdom	[2]116	[2]93	[2]94	[2]93	[2]100	[2]100	[2]111	81	[2]110	...	Royaume-Uni
Yugoslavia	..	23	27	21	18	23	22	20	21	14	Yougoslavie
Total	**3609**	**5283**	**4990**	**5564**	**5571**	**4672**	**3964**	**4157**	**4934**	**6559**	**Total**

General Note.
Steel castings at the black stage, after fettling. (SITC, Rev.3: 69963-2).

Remarque générale.
Moulages d'acier noirs après ébarbage. (CTCI, Rev.3: 69963-2).

[1] Shipments.
[2] Source: Annual Bulletin of Steel Statistics for Europe, America and Asia, United Nations Economic Commission of Europe (Geneva).
[3] Deliveries.

[1] Expéditions.
[2] Source: Bulletin annuel de statistiques de l'acier pour l'Europe, l'Amérique et l'Asie. Commission économique des Nations Unies pour l'Europe (Genève).
[3] Livraisons.

Steel forgings
Pièces de forge

ISIC-BASED CODE - CODE BASE CITI

3710-88

Unit : Thousand metric tons
Unité : Milliers de tonnes métriques

Country or area	1990	1991	1992	1993	1994	1995	1996	1997	1998	1999	Pays ou zone
America, North	**1**	**2**	**1**	**48**	**42**	**61**	**90**	**101**	**117**	**104**	**Amérique du Nord**
Mexico	1	2	1	#48	42	61	90	101	117	104	Mexique
America, South	**2**	**2**	**2**	**2**	**2**	**2**	**2**	**2**	**2**	**2**	**Amérique du Sud**
Colombia	...	...	2	...	...	...	...	...	...	...	Colombie
Asia	**1163**	**1127**	**1042**	**1041**	**1136**	**1215**	**1249**	**1289**	**1134**	**1164**	**Asie**
Azerbaijan	..	9	5	4	2	1	1	1	1	0	Azerbaïdjan
India	[1]166	[1]180	206	...	...	...	...	...	...	...	Inde
Japan	671	593	534	506	536	569	583	619	543	497	Japon
Korea, Republic of	282	301	253	303	370	417	[2]437	[2]441	[2]362	[2]439	Corée, République de
Turkey	...	...	...	44	...	...	...	...	...	...	Turquie
Europe	**2433**	**2787**	**2661**	**1874**	**2266**	**2754**	**2229**	**2224**	**2194**	**2288**	**Europe**
Austria	53	[2]46	[2]43	[2]39	[2]43	[2]50	...	...	...	...	Autriche
Belarus	..	...	[2]24	17	13	11	10	10	9	10	Bélarus
Belgium	...	...	...	...	6	6	7	7	8	...	Belgique
Bulgaria[2]	...	38	14	13	15	21	17	23	22	...	Bulgarie[2]
Croatia	..	..	..	...	...	...	[2]1	[2]1	1	[2]1	Croatie
Czechoslovakia(former)	563	346	..	..	..	..	..	..	..	..	Tchécoslovaquie(anc.)
Czech Republic	..	..	213	193	194	...	...	[2]180	[2]191	[2]179	République tchèque
Finland	1	1	1	...	...	...	...	2	...	...	Finlande
Germany	..	...	254	229	256	311	...	...	...	...	Allemagne
Germany(Fed.Rep.)	253	..	..	..	..	..	..	..	..	..	Allemagne(Rép.féd.)
German D.R.(former)	343	..	..	..	..	..	..	..	..	..	R.D.A. (anc.)
Hungary	73	45	42	42	46	56	...	...	...	...	Hongrie
Italy	333	349	617	288	...	[2]915	[2]495	[2]536	...	...	Italie
Poland	336	233	210	185	252	285	271	261	250	215	Pologne
Portugal	...	...	0	1	1	6	9	15	11	14	Portugal
Romania	423	293	186	188	163	164	192	145	98	86	Roumanie
Russian Federation	..	795	694	390	548	528	495	483	453	607	Fédération de Russie
Slovakia	..	..	...	23	28	37	19	[2]55	[2]58	[2]50	Slovaquie
Slovenia	..	14	12	13	16	21	[2]24	[2]20	[2]22	[2]16	Slovénie
Spain	...	...	...	6	10	7	9	6	7	11	Espagne
Sweden[3]	...	21	...	...	...	...	...	...	...	...	Suède[3]
Ukraine	..	289	286	215	145	118	110	103	84	78	Ukraine
Yugoslavia	..	23	10	3	3	3	4	5	5	4	Yougoslavie
USSR (former)	1280	..	..	..	..	..	..	..	..	..	URSS (anc.)
Total	**4879**	**3918**	**3706**	**2965**	**3446**	**4032**	**3570**	**3616**	**3447**	**3558**	**Total**

General Note.
Finished steel products produced by forging (including drop forging), hammering and pressing operations. (SITC, Rev.3: 69965-0).

Remarque générale.
Produits en acier obtenus par forgeage (y compris l'estampage), travail au marteau ou formage. (CTCI, Rev.3: 69965-0).

[1] Production by large and medium scale establishments only.
[2] Source: Annual Bulletin of Steel Statistics for Europe, America and Asia, United Nations Economic Commission of Europe (Geneva).
[3] Including forged bars.

[1] Production des grandes et moyennes entreprises seulement.
[2] Source: Bulletin annuel de statistiques de l'acier pour l'Europe, l'Amérique et l'Asie. Commission économique des Nations Unies pour l'Europe (Genève).
[3] Y compris les barres forgées.

Wheels, wheel centres, tires and axles
Roues, centres de roues, bandages et essieux

ISIC-BASED CODE - CODE BASE CITI

3710-91

Unit : Thousand metric tons

Unité : Milliers de tonnes métriques

Country or area	1990	1991	1992	1993	1994	1995	1996	1997	1998	1999	Pays ou zone
America, North	**464**	**371**	**395**	**410**	**410**	**410**	**410**	**410**	**410**	**410**	**Amérique du Nord**
United States[1]	464	371	395	...	...	...	...	...	...	...	Etats-Unis[1]
America, South	**5**	**5**	**5**	**4**	**4**	**6**	**5**	**5**	**5**	**5**	**Amérique du Sud**
Colombia	...	...	5	4	4	6	...	...	...	...	Colombie
Asia	**67**	**53**	**55**	**49**	**64**	**70**	**56**	**64**	**83**	**78**	**Asie**
Japan	[2]51	37	40	34	48	54	40	48	67	64	Japon
Korea, Republic of[2]	...	...	...	...	...	...	...	13	14	12	Corée, République de[2]
Turkey	...	...	2	2	3	3	3	3	2	2	Turquie
Europe	**273**	**1086**	**898**	**670**	**543**	**610**	**710**	**534**	**561**	**610**	**Europe**
Croatia	..	...	...	...	...	...	...	1		...	Croatie
France	6	6	8	7	10	[2]12	[2]10	[2]7	[2]9	[2]7	France
Germany	..	...	58	53	41	41	[2]50	[2]53	[2]55	[2]57	Allemagne
Germany(Fed.Rep.)	50	..	..	..	..	..	..	..	..	..	Allemagne(Rép.féd.)
German D.R.(former)	93		..	..	..	..	..	..	..	..	R.D.A. (anc.)
Hungary	9	14	5	[2]3	[2]1	1	...	...	...	...	Hongrie
Italy	[3]41	[3]37	[2]28	39	38	[2]35	[2]35	[2]134	[2]143	...	Italie
Poland	64	46	24	33	27	29	31	29	34	30	Pologne
Romania	[3]10	[3]6	[3]3	[3]3	[3]3	[3]2	[3]1	[3]3	4	[3]5	Roumanie
Russian Federation	..	607	439	309	295	379	415	199	225	266	Fédération de Russie
Ukraine	..	319	332	222	127	109	165	108	90	102	Ukraine
Yugoslavia	..	...	...	0	[2]0	[2]1	[2]1	[2]0	[2]0	...	Yougoslavie
USSR (former)	1114	..	..	..	..	..	..	..	..	..	URSS (anc.)
Total	**1922**	**1515**	**1353**	**1133**	**1021**	**1096**	**1181**	**1013**	**1059**	**1103**	**Total**

General Note.
Wheels, parts of wheels and axles of steel for use in constructing vehicles running on rails. Although this item is classified under transport equipment in the SITC, the products concerned are generally made in steel works. (SITC, Rev.3: 79199-1).

Remarque générale.
Roues, parties de roues et essieux en acier servant à la construction de véhicules se déplaçant sur rails. Bien que ces articles soient classés par la CTCI parmi le matériel de transport, il convient de noter qu'ils sont généralement fabriqués dans les établissements sidérurgiques. (CTCI, Rev.3: 79199-1).

[1] Shipments.
[2] Source: Annual Bulletin of Steel Statistics for Europe, America and Asia, United Nations Economic Commission of Europe (Geneva).
[3] Excluding axles.

[1] Expéditions.
[2] Source: Bulletin annuel de statistiques de l'acier pour l'Europe, l'Amérique et l'Asie. Commission économique des Nations Unies pour l'Europe (Genève).
[3] Non compris les essieux.

Copper, blister and other unrefined
Cuivre blister et autre cuivre non affiné

ISIC-BASED CODE - CODE BASE CITI

3720-01

Unit : Thousand metric tons — Unité : Milliers de tonnes métriques

Country or area	1990	1991	1992	1993	1994	1995	1996	1997	1998	1999	Pays ou zone
Africa	**945**	**760**	**730**	**595**	**509**	**468**	**495**	**502**	**474**	**380**	**Afrique**
Dem. Rep. of Congo[1][2]	355.8	237.5	131.0	#46.5	30.0	28.8	49.8	40.1	40.0	*10.0	Rép. dém. du Congo[1][2]
Namibia[2]	33.2	33.5	37.5	34.8	29.8	29.8	16.7	16.0	*8.7	*0.0	Namibie[2]
South Africa[1]	[2]176.0	[2]165.0	[2]158.7	[2]156.6	[2]165.9	[2]154.4	[2]148.4	[3]163.6	[2]152.3	[2]160.0	Afrique du Sud[1]
Zambia[3][4]	355.4	300.5	380.2	337.8	265.2	237.7	262.0	264.2	255.1	...	Zambie[3][4]
Zimbabwe[3]	24.4	23.8	22.4	18.9	18.2	17.5	18.0	18.0	18.0	...	Zimbabwe[3]
America, North	**1859**	**1828**	**2010**	**2146**	**2176**	**2203**	**2241**	**2411**	**2496**	**2021**	**Amérique du Nord**
Canada	525.2	532.8	552.4	576.3	560.0	612.7	[3]612.7	[2]626.5	[2]624.4	[2]609.8	Canada
Mexico	175.4	175.0	278.0	300.0	305.8	339.8	328.2	344.0	[2]382.0	321.0	Mexique
United States	1158.5	1120.0	1180.0	1270.0	1310.0	1250.0	1300.0	1440.0	1490.0	1090.0	Etats-Unis
America, South	**1458**	**1486**	**1589**	**1678**	**1692**	**2210**	**2575**	**2871**	**3077**	**3388**	**Amérique du Sud**
Brazil[2]	152.0	141.0	158.0	161.1	170.0	165.0	172.1	177.1	167.2	192.9	Brésil[2]
Chile[1]	1110.0	1076.4	1095.0	1173.6	1148.3	1666.2	1991.3	2270.6	2511.2	2835.3	Chili[1]
Peru[1][2]	196.0	269.0	336.0	343.4	373.3	378.5	412.0	423.1	398.9	360.0	Pérou[1][2]
Asia	**2362**	**2846**	**2952**	**3166**	**3160**	**3570**	**3449**	**3825**	**3937**	**4220**	**Asie**
China*[2]	530.0	556.0	546.0	626.0	694.0	1000.0	836.0	969.0	1010.0	1020.0	Chine*[2]
India	38.8	47.2	50.8	59.9	64.9	65.6	80.8	101.2	114.1	175.6	Inde
Iran(Islamic Rep. of)*[2][5]	59.4	88.2	92.8	92.0	130.6	122.0	132.0	137.0	140.0	125.0	Iran(Rép. islamique)*[2][5]
Japan	1351.4	1417.8	1492.4	1526.7	1434.6	1534.3	1568.0	1684.3	1614.6	1737.3	Japon
Kazakhstan*[2]	..	...	...	300.0	285.0	242.8	245.0	316.0	335.0	384.2	Kazakhstan*[2]
Korea,Dem.Ppl's.Rep.*[2]	18.0	25.0	26.0	28.0	28.0	29.0	29.0	29.0	27.5	25.0	Corée,Rép.pop.dém.de*[2]
Korea, Republic of[6]	192.2	200.8	209.8	219.5	222.0	234.8	246.2	265.0	368.8	450.5	Corée, République de[6]
Philippines[2]	*153.5	167.5	168.8	212.4	200.3	242.2	201.7	206.2	*198.1	*192.0	Philippines[2]
Turkey[1]	18.8	26.8	30.0	31.2	30.4	24.4	30.3	32.5	34.4	33.1	Turquie[1]
Uzbekistan*[2]	..	...	80.0	70.0	70.0	75.0	80.0	85.0	94.9	77.0	Ouzbékistan*[2]
Europe	**1305**	**1934**	**1883**	**1861**	**1983**	**2006**	**2347**	**2414**	**2406**	**2424**	**Europe**
Albania	11.0	5.0	2.0	2.0	2.0	3.0	1.0	0.0	2.0	0.1	Albanie
Austria	[3]41.0	[3]44.8	[3]49.0	[3]47.3	[3]49.6	[2]53.4	[2]65.4	[2]73.0	[2]54.8	[2]60.0	Autriche
Bulgaria	[3]30.3	[3]27.8	[3]50.6	[3]71.9	[3]89.4	[3]74.5	[3]90.0	[3]90.0	[3]119.5	[2]100.0	Bulgarie
Czechoslovakia(former)	33.0	27.7	..	..	..	..	..	..	..	..	Tchécoslovaquie(anc.)
Finland	112.8	114.3	136.8	136.6	129.3	120.6	178.7	168.7	172.0	*149.7	Finlande
Germany	..	256.2	228.4	201.3	292.2	[2]308.0	[2]385.0	[2]349.0	[2]338.6	[2]326.0	Allemagne
Germany(Fed.Rep.)[7]	183.6	..	..	..	..	..	..	..	..	..	Allemagne(Rép.féd.)[7]
German D.R.(former)*[7]	14.3	..	..	..	..	..	..	..	..	..	R.D.A. (anc.)*[7]
Hungary	0.3	0.1	[2]0.1	[2]0.1	[2]0.1	[2]0.1	[2]0.1	[2]0.1	* [2]0.0	* [2]0.0	Hongrie
Norway	36.5	38.4	39.3	37.3	39.5	58.9	33.9	[3]32.9	[3]31.7	...	Norvège
Poland	351.4	452.9	401.1	411.7	403.6	413.5	417.7	444.8	451.5	493.5	Pologne
Portugal	2.0	1.1	[2]1.0	[2]1.0	[2]0.0	[2]0.0	[2]0.0	[2]0.0	...	...	Portugal
Romania	28.3	27.8	28.2	26.2	23.5	23.4	32.6	25.0	18.7	24.0	Roumanie
Russian Federation*[2]	..	..	...	544.0	524.0	545.0	570.0	570.0	550.0	698.0	Fédération de Russie*[2]
Slovakia	..	..	...	...	...	...	...	...	21.6	1.4	Slovaquie
Spain	[3]150.4	[3]149.1	[3]150.0	[3]173.0	[3]188.4	[3]160.0	[3]270.9	359.3	373.3	[2]330.0	Espagne
Sweden	[3]108.0	[3]97.6	[3]98.4	[3]99.1	[3]102.7	[2]105.0	[2]125.0	[2]125.0	[2]125.0	[2]114.0	Suède
Switzerland	50.4	42.2	45.0	40.4	40.4	41.4	...	...	...	...	Suisse
Yugoslavia	..	154.5	127.9	57.4	86.6	87.4	125.2	125.0	108.5	53.9	Yougoslavie
Yugoslavia, SFR	151.4	..	..	..	..	..	..	..	..	..	Yougoslavie, RSF
USSR (former)*[7]	990.0	..	..	..	..	..	..	..	..	..	URSS (anc.)*[7]
Oceania	**200**	**189**	**199**	**221**	**282**	**142**	**171**	**208**	**236**	**246**	**Océanie**
Australia[8]	199.9	188.5	199.0	221.0	282.0	142.0	171.0	208.0	236.0	246.0	Australie[8]
Total	**9119**	**9043**	**9363**	**9667**	**9801**	**10598**	**11278**	**12230**	**12627**	**12679**	**Total**

General Note.
Unwrought product obtained by smelting (black or blister copper), by precipitation or concentration (cement copper or copper precipitate) of ores and concentrates. (SITC, Rev.3: 28322-0, 68211-0).

Remarque générale.
Produit non travaillé obtenu à partir des minerais ou concentrés par convertissage (cuivre noir ou cuivre blister), ou par précipitation ("cémentation") (cuivre de cément ou précipités de cuivre). (CTCI, Rev.3: 28322-0, 68211-0).

For footnotes, see end of table.

Voir la fin du tableau pour les notes.

Copper, blister and other unrefined (continued)
Cuivre blister et autre cuivre non affiné (suite)

ISIC-BASED CODE - CODE BASE CITI

3720-01

Footnotes
[1] Including some production at the refined stage.
[2] Source: U. S. Geological Survey, (Washington, D. C.).
[3] Source: World Metal Statistics, (London).
[4] Including copper obtained from ores by leaching in electrowinningplants.

[5] Twelve months beginning 21 March of year stated.
[6] Production at the refined stage.
[7] Source: Metallgesellschaft Aktiengesellschaft, (Frankfurt).
[8] Twelve months ending 30 June of year stated.

Notes.
[1] Y compris certaines productions au stade affiné.
[2] Source: U.S. Geological Survey, (Washington, D.C.).
[3] Source: World Metal Statistics,(Londres).
[4] Y compris le cuivre obtenu à partir des minerais après lixiviation dans les fabriques de récupération électrolytique.
[5] Période de douze mois commençant le 21 mars de l'année indiquée.
[6] Données se rapportant au cuivre affiné.
[7] Source: "Metallgesellschaft Aktiengesellschaft", (Francfort).
[8] Période de douze mois finissant le 30 juin de l'année indiquée.

Copper, refined, unwrought (total production)
Cuivre affiné, non travaillé (production totale)

ISIC-BASED CODE - CODE BASE CITI

3720-04

Unit : Thousand metric tons Unité : Milliers de tonnes métriques

Country or area	1990	1991	1992	1993	1994	1995	1996	1997	1998	1999	Pays ou zone
Africa	**721**	**651**	**627**	**603**	**526**	**498**	**519**	**510**	**495**	**391**	**Afrique**
Dem. Rep. of Congo[1]	140.9	104.0	47.5	34.1	29.0	33.0	42.0	40.1	*35.0	*10.0	Rép. dém. du Congo[1]
South Africa[1]	133.0	127.0	120.1	127.9	129.6	124.3	123.0	130.2	125.6	134.5	Afrique du Sud[1]
Zambia	424.8	398.4	441.6	424.8	[1]352.1	[1]328.0	[1]334.0	[1]332.3	[1]329.5	[1]233.0	Zambie
Zimbabwe*[1]	22.5	22.0	17.9	16.4	15.4	13.2	20.1	7.9	5.3	13.0	Zimbabwe*[1]
America, North	**2690**	**2728**	**2873**	**3009**	**2959**	**3062**	**3161**	**3191**	**3374**	**2923**	**Amérique du Nord**
Canada	515.8	538.0	539.3	561.6	527.5	572.6	559.2	560.3	562.5	548.6	Canada
Mexico	*157.1	*190.1	*191.0	197.8	199.5	207.5	246.3	160.5	321.7	254.5	Mexique
United States	2017.4	2000.0	2143.0	2250.0	2232.0	2282.0	2355.0	2470.0	2490.0	2120.0	Etats-Unis
America, South	**1421**	**1440**	**1653**	**1513**	**1515**	**1952**	**2258**	**2689**	**2909**	**3293**	**Amérique du Sud**
Brazil[1]	201.7	141.4	158.0	161.1	170.0	165.0	172.1	177.1	*167.2	*193.0	Brésil[1]
Chile	990.8	1012.8	1242.3	1093.2	1080.0	1491.5	1748.2	2116.6	2334.9	2665.7	Chili
Peru[1]	228.0	285.6	252.6	258.9	265.4	295.1	338.1	395.1	407.3	433.8	Pérou[1]
Asia	**2074**	**2566**	**2836**	**2941**	**2851**	**3266**	**3412**	**3545**	**3683**	**4026**	**Asie**
China	*[2]561.5	*[2]560.0	*[2]659.0	*[2]733.0	*[2]736.1	1079.7	1120.5	1152.9	1109.4	*[1]1210.0	Chine
India[1]	*41.6	*47.2	46.8	*36.8	49.0	39.6	39.3	36.2	107.0	*208.0	Inde[1]
Iran(Islamic Rep. of)	43.3	77.9	[1]105.0	[1]86.6	[1]90.2	[1]90.4	[1]100.6	[1]112.8	[1]122.0	[1]122.0	Iran(Rép. islamique)
Japan[3]	1008.0	1076.3	1160.9	1188.8	1119.2	1188.0	1251.4	1278.7	1277.4	1341.5	Japon[3]
Kazakhstan*[1]	..	...	300.0	317.0	280.0	255.6	267.1	301.1	324.9	361.9	Kazakhstan*[1]
Korea,Dem.Ppl's.Rep.*[1]	22.0	24.0	25.0	27.0	27.0	27.0	28.0	28.0	28.0	25.0	Corée,Rép.pop.dém.de*[1]
Korea, Republic of	*[1]185.6	201.9	210.0	218.4	222.0	232.8	*[1]248.3	*[1]267.4	*[1]375.2	*[1]454.0	Corée, République de
Philippines[1]	125.9	115.5	145.7	166.0	154.7	158.1	155.8	146.6	152.4	148.2	Philippines[1]
Turkey	86.4	84.2	[2]104.0	[2]92.4	[1]82.7	[1]100.3	[1]100.7	[1]111.4	[1]91.8	[1]78.0	Turquie
Uzbekistan*[1]	..	...	80.0	75.0	90.0	95.0	100.0	110.0	94.9	77.0	Ouzbékistan*[1]
Europe	**2470**	**2920**	**2960**	**2957**	**2828**	**2778**	**3043**	**3030**	**2840**	**3134**	**Europe**
Austria	49.5	52.8	*[1]54.7	*[1]52.7	*[1]52.5	*[1]53.5	*[1]58.0	*[1]67.0	*[1]78.0	*[1]77.0	Autriche
Belgium[4]	542.5	478.0	471.3	455.2	[1]375.2	[1]376.0	[1]354.0	[1]373.0	[1]368.0	[1]388.0	Belgique[4]
Bulgaria	[2]24.3	12.8	18.0	26.3	26.5	25.5	22.3	34.5	32.1	21.9	Bulgarie
Denmark[5]	0.0	0.0	0.0	0.0	0.0	0.2	0.2	0.2	0.2	0.2	Danemark[5]
Czechoslovakia(former)	24.6	25.3	..	..	..	..	..	..	..	..	Tchécoslovaquie(anc.)
Finland	178.0	170.0	182.1	197.9	199.3	211.2	241.0	132.4	157.7	126.1	Finlande
France	43.8	43.6	42.8	44.4	41.7	42.0	39.0	36.0	22.0	[6]2.0	France
Germany	..	521.5	581.5	632.1	591.9	483.9	535.7	544.1	547.9	[1]696.0	Allemagne
Germany(Fed.Rep.)	476.3	..	..	..	..	..	..	..	..	..	Allemagne(Rép.féd.)
German D.R.(former)*[7]	56.7	..	..	..	..	..	..	..	..	..	R.D.A. (anc.)*[7]
Greece	28.0	31.7	32.9	...	...	...	...	...	...	...	Grèce
Hungary	12.8	9.3	2.3	*[1]11.0	*[1]11.0	*[1]11.0	*[1]11.0	*[1]11.0	*[1]11.0	*[1]10.0	Hongrie
Italy	83.0	83.4	76.0	90.3	84.0	98.0	85.8	85.7	29.1	28.5	Italie
Norway	33.5	38.4	39.3	37.2	39.4	34.3	33.9	*[1]32.6	*[1]32.0	*[1]33.0	Norvège
Poland	346.1	378.5	387.0	404.2	405.1	406.7	424.7	440.6	446.8	470.5	Pologne
Portugal	*6.0	2.1	[2]0.0	[2]0.0	[2]0.0	[2]0.0	[2]0.0	[2]0.0	[2]0.0	...	Portugal
Romania	24.7	25.7	26.5	25.2	22.1	22.0	29.3	22.9	21.0	21.0	Roumanie
Russian Federation*[1]	..	...	575.4	526.0	502.0	560.0	600.0	600.0	620.0	750.0	Fédération de Russie*[1]
Slovakia	..	..	*[1]28.0	*[1]25.0	*[1]21.5	*[1]28.0	*[1]31.3	19.2	*[1]21.0		Slovaquie
Spain	[2]170.6	[2]189.9	[2]179.1	[2]179.2	[2]188.3	[2]164.2	[2]264.0	[2]292.0	152.4	...	Espagne
Sweden	*97.3	96.6	[2]101.6	118.1	114.8	[1]105.1	[1]125.0	[1]128.4	[1]125.0	[1]115.0	Suède
United Kingdom	121.5	70.1	42.1	46.6	46.7	55.0	56.6	60.4	[1]52.0	[1]50.0	Royaume-Uni
Yugoslavia	..	134.2	119.7	51.3	72.1	77.5	104.0	106.6	94.4	50.1	Yougoslavie
Yugoslavia, SFR	151.2	..	..	..	..	..	..	..	..	..	Yougoslavie, RSF
USSR (former)*[7]	1160.0	..	..	..	..	..	..	..	..	..	URSS (anc.)*[7]
Oceania	**245**	**270**	**336**	**336**	**355**	**281**	**300**	**305**	**284**	**310**	**Océanie**
Australia[8]	244.9	270.2	335.6	336.0	355.2	281.0	300.0	305.0	284.0	310.0	Australie[8]
Total	**10781**	**10575**	**11285**	**11359**	**11035**	**11838**	**12693**	**13270**	**13586**	**14076**	**Total**

For general note and footnotes, see end of table.   Voir la fin du tableau pour la remarque générale et les notes.

Copper, refined, unwrought (total production) (continued)
Cuivre affiné, non travaillé (production totale) (suite)

ISIC-BASED CODE - CODE BASE CITI

3720-04

General Note.
Refined copper obtained by fire-refining or electrolysis of primary crude metal (blister, black or cement copper). It can also be recovered from secondary materials (scrap). Electrolytic copper obtained directly from ores by leaching is included. (SITC, Rev.3: 68212-0).

Remarque générale.
Cuivre affiné par affinage thermique ou électrolytique de la matière première (métal brut), (cuivre blister, cuivre noir ou cuivre de cément) ou par récupération à partir de produits secondaires (déchets de cuivre). Cette rubrique comprend le cuivre électrolytique obtenu directement à partir des minerais après lixiviation. (CTCI, Rev.3: 68212-0).

[1] Source: U. S. Geological Survey, (Washington, D. C.).
[2] Source: World Metal Statistics, (London).
[3] Electrolytic cathode copper.
[4] Including alloys and processing of refined copper imported from Zaire.
[5] Sales.
[6] Beginning 1999, production was reduced due to the closing of C.G. Electrolyse du Palais.
[7] Source: Metallgesellschaft Aktiengesellschaft, (Frankfurt).
[8] Twelve months ending 30 June of year stated.

[1] Source: U.S. Geological Survey, (Washington, D.C.).
[2] Source: World Metal Statistics,(Londres).
[3] Cuivre électrolytique à cathode.
[4] Y compris les alliages et le traitement ultérieur du cuivre raffiné importé du Zaïre.
[5] Ventes.
[6] A partir de 1999, production réduite en raison de la fermeture de C.G. Electrolyse du Palais.
[7] Source: "Metallgesellschaft Aktiengesellschaft", (Francfort).
[8] Période de douze mois finissant le 30 juin de l'année indiquée.

Copper, primary, refined
Cuivre, neuf, affiné

ISIC-BASED CODE - CODE BASE CITI

3720-041

Unit : Thousand metric tons / Unité : Milliers de tonnes métriques

Country or area	1990	1991	1992	1993	1994	1995	1996	1997	1998	1999	Pays ou zone
Africa	**713**	**643**	**619**	**595**	**520**	**492**	**513**	**510**	**495**	**391**	**Afrique**
Dem. Rep. of Congo[1]	140.9	104.0	47.5	34.1	29.0	33.0	42.0	40.1	35.0	*10.0	Rép. dém. du Congo[1]
South Africa[1]	133.0	127.0	120.1	127.9	129.6	124.3	123.0	130.2	125.6	134.5	Afrique du Sud[1]
Zambia	424.8	398.4	441.6	424.8	[1]352.1	[1]328.0	[1]334.0	[1]332.3	[1]329.5	[1]233.0	Zambie
Zimbabwe*[1]	14.1	13.8	9.7	8.2	9.4	7.1	14.1	7.9	5.3	13.0	Zimbabwe*[1]
America, North	**2171**	**2228**	**2322**	**2499**	**2508**	**2586**	**2716**	**2677**	**2937**	**2608**	**Amérique du Nord**
Canada	468.4	511.2	501.9	521.2	495.5	481.7	475.9	*461.0	*489.9	*477.3	Canada
Mexico	125.9	137.1	110.5	*187.8	*173.0	*174.8	*229.8	*145.7	*306.7	*240.5	Mexique
United States	1576.6	1580.0	1710.0	1790.0	1840.0	1930.0	2010.0	2070.0	2140.0	1890.0	Etats-Unis
America, South	**1371**	**1440**	**1653**	**1513**	**1515**	**1952**	**2258**	**2689**	**2909**	**3293**	**Amérique du Sud**
Brazil[1]	152.1	141.4	158.0	161.1	170.0	165.0	172.1	177.1	167.2	*193.0	Brésil[1]
Chile	990.8	1012.8	1242.3	1093.2	1080.0	1491.5	1748.2	2116.6	2334.9	2665.7	Chili
Peru[1]	228.0	285.6	252.6	258.9	265.4	295.1	338.1	395.1	407.3	433.8	Pérou[1]
Asia	**1446**	**1913**	**2078**	**2121**	**2016**	**2074**	**2179**	**2281**	**2450**	**2692**	**Asie**
India[1]	41.6	38.6	38.3	30.1	40.1	33.9	29.1	30.2	100.0	*200.0	Inde[1]
Iran(Islamic Rep. of)	43.3	77.9	[1]105.0	[1]86.6	[1]90.2	[1]90.4	[1]100.6	[1]112.8	[1]122.0	[1]122.0	Iran(Rép. islamique)
Japan	947.7	1005.4	1087.0	1126.3	1064.7	1112.8	1181.1	1194.7	1181.9	1248.7	Japon
Kazakhstan*[1]	..	...	300.0	317.0	280.0	255.6	267.1	301.1	324.9	361.9	Kazakhstan*[1]
Korea,Dem.Ppl's.Rep.*[1]	18.0	19.0	20.0	22.0	22.0	22.0	23.0	23.0	23.0	20.0	Corée,Rép.pop.dém.de*[1]
Korea, Republic of	183.0	200.9	208.0	216.0	220.0	230.8	[1]246.3	[1]265.4	[1]373.2	* [1]450.4	Corée, République de
Philippines[1]	126.0	115.5	145.7	166.0	154.7	158.1	155.8	146.6	152.4	148.2	Philippines[1]
Turkey	86.4	84.2	[1]104.0	[1]92.4	[1]59.1	[1]80.3	[1]80.7	[1]102.1	[1]82.8	[1]69.0	Turquie
Uzbekistan[1]	..	...	*70.0	*65.0	*85.0	*90.0	*95.0	105.0	*89.9	*72.0	Ouzbékistan[1]
Europe	**1852**	**2214**	**2228**	**2213**	**1998**	**1980**	**2102**	**2173**	**2104**	**2163**	**Europe**
Austria	8.7	8.1	[1]5.7	[1]5.9	[1]2.9	[1]0.5	[1]1.0	[1]2.0	[1]2.0	[1]2.0	Autriche
Belgium	[2][3]542.5	[2][3]478.0	[2][3]471.3	[2][3]455.2	[1]215.2	[1]216.0	[1]191.0	[1]190.0	[1]185.0	[1]201.0	Belgique
Czechoslovakia(former)	24.6	25.3	..	..	..	..	..	..	..	..	Tchécoslovaquie(anc.)
Finland	178.0	#131.9	142.0	155.4	193.9	...	...	...	...	...	Finlande
France	43.8	43.6	42.8	44.4	41.7	42.0	39.0	36.0	22.0	[4]2.0	France
Germany		203.2	242.2	270.4	252.9	...	...	...	...	...	Allemagne
Germany(Fed.Rep.)*	197.0	..	..	..	..	...	...	...	...	...	Allemagne(Rép.féd.)*
German D.R.(former)[3][5]	56.7		..	..	..	..	..	..	..	..	R.D.A. (anc.)[3][5]
Greece	28.0	31.7	32.9	...	...	...	...	...	...	...	Grèce
Hungary	6.9	4.9	1.3	[1][3]11.0	[1][3]11.0	[1][3]11.0	[1][3]11.0	[1][3]11.0	[1][3]11.0	[1][3]10.0	Hongrie
Norway	33.5	38.4	39.3	37.2	39.4	34.3	33.9	* [1]32.6	* [1]32.0	* [1]33.0	Norvège
Poland	346.1	378.5	387.0	404.2	405.1	406.7	424.7	440.6	446.8	470.5	Pologne
Portugal	*6.0	2.1	[6]0.0	[6]0.0	[6]0.0	[6]0.0	[6]0.0	[6]0.0	[6]0.0	...	Portugal
Romania[3]	24.7	...	...	...	...	...	...	...	...	...	Roumanie[3]
Russian Federation[1]	..	...	*525.0	*486.0	*452.0	*504.0	543.0	535.0	543.0	600.0	Fédération de Russie[1]
Spain[6]	140.6	161.9	147.1	131.2	148.3	130.2	205.0	268.0	...	...	Espagne[6]
Sweden	*66.3	66.1	77.6	102.2	102.8	* [1]78.0	* [1]100.0	* [1]105.0	* [1]100.0	* [1]95.0	Suède
United Kingdom	46.8	16.6	10.4	10.7	11.1	12.0	13.0	9.1	[1]8.0	[1]5.0	Royaume-Uni
Yugoslavia	..	95.1	78.6	43.4	66.3	70.8	59.9	58.1	58.4	36.2	Yougoslavie
Yugoslavia, SFR	102.2	..	..	..	..	..	..	..	..	..	Yougoslavie, RSF
Oceania	**218**	**235**	**304**	**312**	**331**	**250**	**300**	**305**	**284**	**310**	**Océanie**
Australia[7]	217.9	235.2	303.6	312.0	331.2	249.6	300.0	305.0	284.0	310.0	Australie[7]
Total	**7771**	**8674**	**9204**	**9253**	**8889**	**9334**	**10068**	**10635**	**11180**	**11456**	**Total**

General Note.
Refined copper obtained by fire-refining or electrolysis of primary crude metal (blister, black or cement copper). Electrolytic copper obtained directly from ores by leaching is included. (SITC, Rev.3: 68212-1).

[1] Source: U. S. Geological Survey, (Washington, D. C.).
[2] Including alloys and processing of refined copper imported from Zaire.
[3] Including secondary metal production.
[4] Beginning 1999, production was reduced due to the closing of C.G. Electrolyse du Palais.
[5] Source: Metallgesellschaft Aktiengesellschaft, (Frankfurt).
[6] Source: World Metal Statistics, (London).
[7] Twelve months ending 30 June of year stated.

Remarque générale.
Cuivre affiné par affinage thermique ou électrolytique de la matière première (métal brut), (cuivre blister, cuivre noir ou cuivre de cément). Le cuivre électrolytique obtenu directement à partir des minerais après lixiviation est compris. (CTCI, Rev.3: 68212-1).

[1] Source: U.S. Geological Survey, (Washington, D.C.).
[2] Y compris les alliages et le traitement ultérieur du cuivre raffiné importé du Zaïre.
[3] Y compris la production de métal de deuxième fusion.
[4] A partir de 1999, production réduite en raison de la fermeture de C.G. Electrolyse du Palais.
[5] Source: "Metallgesellschaft Aktiengesellschaft", (Francfort).
[6] Source: World Metal Statistics,(Londres).
[7] Période de douze mois finissant le 30 juin de l'année indiquée.

Copper, secondary, refined
Cuivre, récupéré, affiné

ISIC-BASED CODE - CODE BASE CITI

3720-042

Unit : Thousand metric tons   Unité : Milliers de tonnes métriques

Country or area	1990	1991	1992	1993	1994	1995	1996	1997	1998	1999	Pays ou zone
Africa	**8**	**8**	**8**	**8**	**6**	**6**	**6**	**0**	**0**	**0**	**Afrique**
Zimbabwe* [1]	8.4	8.2	8.2	8.2	6.0	6.0	6.0	0.0	0.0	0.0	Zimbabwe* [1]
America, North	**519**	**498**	**551**	**510**	**451**	**476**	**445**	**510**	**437**	**315**	**Amérique du Nord**
Canada	47.4	26.8	37.4	40.4	32.0	90.9	83.3	[1]99.3	[1]72.6	[1]71.3	Canada
Mexico	31.2	53.0	80.5	[1]10.0	[2]26.5	[1]32.8	[1]16.5	* [1]14.8	[1]15.0	[1]14.0	Mexique
United States	440.8	418.0	433.0	460.0	392.0	352.0	345.0	396.0	349.0	230.0	Etats-Unis
America, South	**50**	**0**	**0**	**17**	**17**	**17**	**17**	**17**	**17**	**17**	**Amérique du Sud**
Brazil [1]	49.6	0.0	0.0	...	...	...	...	...	...	...	Brésil [1]
Asia	**100**	**116**	**121**	**106**	**99**	**113**	**113**	**111**	**123**	**122**	**Asie**
India [1]	...	8.6	8.5	6.7	*8.9	*5.7	*10.2	*6.0	*7.0	*8.0	Inde [1]
Japan	60.3	70.9	73.8	62.5	54.4	75.2	70.3	84.0	95.4	92.9	Japon
Korea,Dem.Ppl's.Rep.* [1]	4.0	5.0	5.0	5.0	5.0	5.0	5.0	5.0	5.0	5.0	Corée,Rép.pop.dém.de* [1]
Korea, Republic of* [1]	2.6	1.0	2.0	2.0	2.0	2.0	2.0	2.0	2.0	2.0	Corée, République de* [1]
Turkey* [1]	...	...	...	...	23.6	20.0	20.0	9.3	9.0	9.0	Turquie* [1]
Uzbekistan* [1]	..	...	10.0	10.0	5.0	5.0	5.0	5.0	5.0	5.0	Ouzbékistan* [1]
Europe	**779**	**848**	**844**	**856**	**785**	**853**	**909**	**920**	**886**	**936**	**Europe**
Austria	40.9	44.7	* [1]49.0	* [1]46.9	* [1]49.6	* [1]53.0	* [1]57.0	* [1]65.0	* [1]76.0	* [1]75.0	Autriche
Belgium [1]	...	...	...	...	160.0	160.0	163.0	183.0	183.0	*187.0	Belgique [1]
Finland	...	38.2	40.2	42.3	5.4	...	...	...	...	...	Finlande
Germany	...	318.3	339.3	361.7	339.0	...	...	...	...	...	Allemagne
Germany(Fed.Rep.)*	279.3	..	..	..	..	..	..	..	..	..	Allemagne(Rép.féd.)*
Hungary	6.0	4.4	1.0	...	...	...	...	...	...	...	Hongrie
Italy	83.0	83.4	76.0	90.3	84.0	98.0	85.8	85.7	29.1	28.5	Italie
Russian Federation* [1]	..	...	50.0	40.0	50.0	56.0	57.0	65.0	77.0	150.0	Fédération de Russie* [1]
Spain [2]	30.0	28.0	32.0	48.0	40.0	34.0	59.0	24.0	...	...	Espagne [2]
Sweden	*31.0	30.5	[2]24.0	15.9	12.0	* [1]27.1	* [1]25.0	* [1]23.0	* [1]25.0	* [1]20.0	Suède
United Kingdom	74.6	53.5	31.7	35.9	35.6	43.0	43.6	51.3	* [1]44.0	[1]45.0	Royaume-Uni
Yugoslavia	..	39.1	41.1	7.9	5.8	6.7	44.1	48.5	36.0	13.9	Yougoslavie
Yugoslavia, SFR	49.0	..	..	..	..	..	..	..	..	..	Yougoslavie, RSF
Oceania	**27**	**35**	**32**	**24**	**24**	**23**	**22**	**20**	**18**	**17**	**Océanie**
Australia [3]	27.0	[2]35.0	[2]32.0	[2]24.0	[2]24.0	...	...	...	...	...	Australie [3]
Total	**1483**	**1506**	**1556**	**1521**	**1381**	**1487**	**1511**	**1578**	**1480**	**1406**	**Total**

General Note.
Secondary refined copper recovered from scrap and other similar materials.
(SITC, Rev.3: 68212-2).

Remarque générale.
Cuivre de deuxième fusion récupéré à partir de produits secondaires (déchets de cuivre). (CTCI, REv.3: 68212-2).

[1] Source: U. S. Geological Survey, (Washington, D. C.).
[2] Source: World Metal Statistics, (London).
[3] Twelve months ending 30 June of year stated.

[1] Source: U.S. Geological Survey, (Washington, D.C.).
[2] Source: World Metal Statistics,(Londres).
[3] Période de douze mois finissant le 30 juin de l'année indiquée.

Copper-base alloys
Alliages à base de cuivre

ISIC-BASED CODE - CODE BASE CITI

3720-07

Unit : Thousand metric tons   Unité : Milliers de tonnes métriques

Country or area	1990	1991	1992	1993	1994	1995	1996	1997	1998	1999	Pays ou zone
America, North	**704**	**704**	**775**	**776**	**873**	**828**	**872**	**936**	**932**	**1035**	**Amérique du Nord**
Mexico	48.8	49.3	51.0	27.6	32.1	31.7	43.6	73.0	70.5	61.4	Mexique
United States	655.0	655.0	724.0	[1]748.0	[1]841.0	[1]796.5	[1]828.3	[1]863.0	[1]861.9	...	Etats-Unis
America, South	**0**	**0**	**1**	**0**	**0**	**0**	**0**	**0**	**0**	**0**	**Amérique du Sud**
Colombia	...	...	0.6	0.2	0.3	0.3	...	...	...	...	Colombie
Asia	**94**	**107**	**100**	**91**	**91**	**102**	**100**	**99**	**100**	**101**	**Asie**
Armenia	..	10.9	13.1	4.1	3.9	...	9.1	6.8	9.2	9.8	Arménie
Indonesia	...	...	...	...	0.4	6.9	...	*6.2	...	...	Indonésie
Japan	89.2	92.0	82.6	82.0	...	...	...	...	...	...	Japon
Europe	**345**	**452**	**369**	**347**	**402**	**385**	**350**	**381**	**359**	**331**	**Europe**
Austria[2]	9.8	11.7	9.4	8.5	9.8	9.9	[1]4.2	[1]5.4	[1]7.1	...	Autriche[2]
France	14.4	12.8	12.5	9.3	...	...	...	...	...	...	France
Germany	..	59.2	58.2	52.3	57.5	36.7	33.6	38.7	...	...	Allemagne
German D.R.(former)	7.3	..	..	..	..	..	..	..	..	..	R.D.A. (anc.)
Hungary	3.8	2.1	0.8	0.9	1.3	0.9	19.0	20.9	22.8	22.8	Hongrie
Italy	80.3	75.7	76.4	81.3	89.1	106.5	106.1	114.8	117.1	116.4	Italie
Slovenia	..	10.4	11.2	7.6	5.9	6.4	8.1	7.6	10.0	10.2	Slovénie
Spain	[3]6.0	[3]9.2	[3]6.2	7.5	...	...	6.6	...	...	6.9	Espagne
Sweden	73.6	67.5	18.0	26.6	39.7	36.7	10.5	14.5	14.9	...	Suède
United Kingdom	[1]149.5	[1]134.8	[1]128.1	130.4	158.4	[1]146.7	[1]126.7	[1]131.1	[1]115.9	...	Royaume-Uni
Yugoslavia	..	67.7	47.4	21.2	20.8	21.1	23.3	28.7	26.5	16.9	Yougoslavie
T.F.Yug.Rep. Macedonia	..	...	1.0	1.2	0.5	0.4	0.1	...	...	...	L'ex-RY Macédoine
Total	**1143**	**1264**	**1245**	**1213**	**1366**	**1315**	**1323**	**1417**	**1392**	**1467**	**Total**

General Note.
Copper-base alloys in which copper predominates by weight over each of the other metals. (SITC, Rev.3: 68214-0).

Remarque générale.
Alliages à base de cuivre dans lesquels le cuivre prédomine en poids sur tous les autres métaux. (CTCI, Rev.3: 68214-0).

[1] Source: World Metal Statistics, (London).
[2] 1999 data are confidential.
[3] Including other copper alloys.

[1] Source: World Metal Statistics,(Londres).
[2] Pour 1999, les données sont confidentielles.
[3] Y compris les autres alliages de cuivre.

Copper bars, rods, angles, shapes, sections
Barres, cornières et profilés de cuivre

ISIC-BASED CODE - CODE BASE CITI

3720-10

Unit : Thousand metric tons   Unité : Milliers de tonnes métriques

Country or area	1990	1991	1992	1993	1994	1995	1996	1997	1998	1999	Pays ou zone
Africa	**5**	**4**	**4**	**4**	**4**	**3**	**3**	**3**	**3**	**3**	**Afrique**
Egypt	5.3	4.3	4.4	3.8	3.5	3.4	3.4	2.6	...	...	Egypte
America, North	**61**	**57**	**60**	**84**	**91**	**93**	**91**	**108**	**107**	**123**	**Amérique du Nord**
Mexico	0.7	0.8	1.0	13.6	14.6	13.5	9.2	9.3	9.1	8.7	Mexique
United States	59.9	56.3	58.5	[1]70.8	[1]76.2	[1]79.4	[1]81.6	[1]99.1	[1]97.9	...	Etats-Unis
America, South	**54**	**54**	**54**	**54**	**54**	**55**	**54**	**54**	**53**	**54**	**Amérique du Sud**
Brazil[1]	...	...	...	...	...	54.0	53.5	52.7	52.6	...	Brésil[1]
Colombia	...	...	0.3	0.5	0.5	0.6	...	0.9	0.8	...	Colombie
Asia	**164**	**187**	**216**	**238**	**231**	**262**	**262**	**283**	**243**	**294**	**Asie**
Japan	40.3	51.7	44.4	43.1	39.8	43.6	45.6	46.2	39.6	36.9	Japon
Korea, Republic of[2]	61.3	65.6	71.3	82.0	99.3	118.6	126.4	133.3	111.1	139.7	Corée, République de[2]
Turkey	[1]62.1	[1]69.4	[1]100.1	[1]112.5	[1]92.2	99.7	90.2	103.4	92.4	117.4	Turquie
Europe	**554**	**574**	**579**	**574**	**692**	**634**	**563**	**753**	**825**	**827**	**Europe**
Austria[3]	[1]4.9	[1]5.6	[1]6.4	[1]4.4	[1]6.2	[1]7.5	8.1	[1]6.9	[1]6.9	...	Autriche[3]
Belgium	...	...	...	...	...	0.5	0.8	0.9	0.5	0.4	Belgique
Denmark[4]	...	...	...	0.0	0.0	0.0	0.1	0.1	0.1	0.1	Danemark[4]
Czechoslovakia(former)	1.8	1.1	..	..	..	..	..	..	..	..	Tchécoslovaquie(anc.)
Finland	9.7	7.7	9.9	11.3	12.9	19.6	10.7	...	...	...	Finlande
France	[5]105.2	[5]108.7	[5]108.8	[5]100.2	[5]153.7	[1]47.4	[1]47.7	[1]180.8	[1]190.1	...	France
Germany	..	221.4	218.4	187.9	223.3	225.3	182.5	216.8	224.0	...	Allemagne
Germany(Fed.Rep.)[6]	203.9	..	..	..	..	..	..	..	..	..	Allemagne(Rép.féd.)[6]
Greece	21.9	25.6	26.7	61.9	61.3	82.2	83.3	87.8	100.9	...	Grèce
Hungary	1.1	0.7	0.5	...	...	...	15.5	...	...	17.9	Hongrie
Italy	19.5	11.6	18.4	14.9	17.1	18.5	17.5	17.0	18.6	17.8	Italie
Portugal	...	...	2.5	4.5	5.0	6.8	...	...	...	...	Portugal
Romania	6.1	5.2	3.0	3.2	2.5	3.1	2.8	1.7	12.1	9.3	Roumanie
Slovakia	..	..	...	5.2	3.9	3.4	7.3	7.7	6.5	5.1	Slovaquie
Slovenia	..	[7]8.2	[7]9.6	8.7	7.9	8.9	7.8	8.0	9.4	9.3	Slovénie
Spain	[1]34.4	[1]33.9	[1]33.8	[1]27.9	39.3	41.1	36.2	45.6	54.8	67.6	Espagne
Sweden	23.5	13.6	18.1	23.8	31.1	34.6	28.6	33.5	37.7	34.2	Suède
Switzerland[1]	28.1	24.6	26.1	24.4	27.4	30.7	25.8	27.6	...	...	Suisse[1]
United Kingdom	[1]88.5	[1]85.8	[1]82.6	[1]85.4	[1]87.4	[1]93.6	[1]79.3	[1]84.3	99.8	...	Royaume-Uni
Yugoslavia	..	14.4	8.3	2.8	4.8	4.0	4.1	5.0	5.7	4.6	Yougoslavie
Oceania	**60**	**19**	**21**	**59**	**12**	**70**	**68**	**68**	**67**	**82**	**Océanie**
Australia[1]	[8]60.2	[8]19.5	[8]20.9	[8]59.1	[8]11.8	70.0	68.0	68.0	67.0	...	Australie[1]
Total	**898**	**895**	**933**	**1013**	**1083**	**1117**	**1041**	**1268**	**1298**	**1383**	**Total**

General Note.

Rolled, extruded, drawn or forged copper products of solid section, of which the maximum cross-sectional dimension exceeds 6 mm and which, if they are flat, have a thickness exceeding one-tenth of the width. (SITC, Rev.3: 68230-0).

Remarque générale.

Produits en cuivre de section pleine, laminés, filés, étirés ou forgés, dont la plus grande dimension transversale est supérieure à 6 mm et, en ce qui concerne les produits plats, dont l'épaisseur dépasse le dixième de la largeur. (CTCI, Rev.3: 68230-0).

[1] Source: World Metal Statistics, (London).
[2] Excluding copper bars and sections.
[3] 1999 data are confidential.
[4] Sales.
[5] Products of copper and copper alloys (brass or bronze).
[6] Including products of copper alloys, except alloys with aluminium.
[7] Products of copper and brass.
[8] Twelve months ending 30 June of year stated.

[1] Source: World Metal Statistics,(Londres).
[2] Non compris les barres et profilés de cuivre.
[3] Pour 1999, les données sont confidentielles.
[4] Ventes.
[5] Produits en cuivre et en alliages à base de cuivre (laiton ou bronze).
[6] Y compris les produits en alliages de cuivre, autres que les alliages contenant de l'aluminum.
[7] Produits en cuivre et en laiton.
[8] Période de douze mois finissant le 30 juin de l'année indiquée.

Copper wire
Fil de cuivre
ISIC-BASED CODE - CODE BASE CITI
3720-13

Unit : Thousand metric tons

Unité : Milliers de tonnes métriques

Country or area	1990	1991	1992	1993	1994	1995	1996	1997	1998	1999	Pays ou zone
Africa	95	93	89	89	83	88	76	87	74	77	Afrique
Egypt	13.5	12.6	9.8	10.7	7.9	7.8	4.6	4.0	...	...	Egypte
South Africa[1]	...	...	...	...	75.2	79.8	71.7	82.6	69.3	...	Afrique du Sud[1]
America, North	1553	1490	1555	1671	1752	1689	1765	1887	2220	2253	Amérique du Nord
Mexico	51.9	39.5	40.8	25.9	29.8	28.1	29.8	49.2	57.6	63.0	Mexique
United States	1500.9	1450.6	1514.0	[1]1644.8	[1]1722.7	[1]1661.1	[1]1735.0	[1]1838.0	[2]2162.0	...	Etats-Unis
America, South	195	190	210	123	226	129	142	158	166	135	Amérique du Sud
Brazil[1]	182.1	178.5	195.1	116.9	219.4	123.6	135.3	152.0	161.8	...	Brésil[1]
Chile	11.2	10.1	12.7	5.6	5.9	5.6	...	...	...	...	Chili
Colombia	...	...	2.0	0.5	0.7	0.3	...	...	0.0	...	Colombie
Asia	379	367	356	368	489	633	667	694	607	698	Asie
India[1]	28.4	25.4	22.8	*24.0	25.9	20.1	44.5	21.8	...	...	Inde[1]
Indonesia	67.7	51.6	41.5	41.7	2.1	6.9	...	...	...	...	Indonésie
Japan	12.7	9.7	7.2	7.0	7.6	7.3	7.4	7.1	6.2	7.0	Japon
Kazakhstan	..	0.2	0.3	0.2	0.2	0.0	...	...	...	...	Kazakhstan
Korea, Republic of	235.6	245.6	240.7	262.8	426.2	561.3	569.0	615.1	518.2	601.6	Corée, République de
Turkey	34.8	34.6	43.5	32.0	27.3	37.4	37.0	47.3	54.2	60.7	Turquie
Europe	1926	1978	2165	2002	1969	2061	2099	2247	2339	2251	Europe
Albania	8.7	2.2	0.5	0.5	0.4	0.0	0.0	0.1	0.0	0.2	Albanie
Austria[2]	62.2	52.8	56.0	52.4	57.9	#11.0	18.6	17.5	18.5	14.0	Autriche[2]
Croatia	..	...	...	...	...	...	...	...	5.7	...	Croatie
Czechoslovakia(former)	28.8	11.5	..	..	..	..	..	..	..	..	Tchécoslovaquie(anc.)
Czech Republic	..	..	..	..	...	8.6	8.8	9.9	9.5	11.0	République tchèque
Finland	26.1	17.8	16.9	22.6	32.8	25.7	28.0	...	...	...	Finlande
France	[3]494.5	[3]476.0	[3]615.5	[3]460.8	[3]338.6	[1]319.7	[1]311.4	[1]351.7	[1]346.3	...	France
Germany	..	582.9	585.2	512.7	518.5	[1]595.7	619.6	693.6	737.6	...	Allemagne
Germany(Fed.Rep.)[4]	505.9	..	..	..	..	..	..	..	..	..	Allemagne(Rép.féd.)[4]
Hungary	22.6	14.2	14.8	...	...	...	...	...	...	...	Hongrie
Italy	294.0	275.0	287.0	302.0	308.2	344.3	334.0	340.0	361.5	370.8	Italie
Romania	25.5	14.3	15.1	16.9	14.3	15.7	14.5	12.8	6.8	4.3	Roumanie
Russian Federation[1]	..	...	...	...	0.6	3.1	4.5	0.7	0.3	...	Fédération de Russie[1]
Slovakia	..	...	...	...	...	...	...	14.0	17.8	1.5	Slovaquie
Spain	[1]115.5	[1]127.4	[1]120.2	165.0	174.3	179.4	205.8	219.6	[1]203.9	...	Espagne
Sweden	77.7	75.8	83.5	103.4	102.9	120.3	118.0	132.7	155.5	154.5	Suède
Switzerland[1]	48.0	43.9	45.2	43.9	47.0	48.3	47.6	46.5	94.0	...	Suisse[1]
United Kingdom	216.7	[1]193.1	[1]250.0	[1]256.7	[1]305.8	[1]325.3	[1]320.6	[1]320.9	[1]295.2	...	Royaume-Uni
Yugoslavia	..	82.5	48.0	21.3	25.8	29.6	33.5	33.7	37.0	26.8	Yougoslavie
T.F.Yug.Rep. Macedonia	..	0.2	0.0	0.0	0.0	0.0	...	...	...	...	L'ex-RY Macédoine
Oceania	23	20	14	9	20	130	125	125	120	187	Océanie
Australia[5]	22.7	20.1	13.7	9.4	[1]19.9	# [1]130.0	[1]125.0	[1]125.0	[1]119.5	...	Australie[5]
Total	4171	4139	4388	4262	4539	4730	4874	5198	5525	5600	Total

General Note.
Rolled, extruded or drawn copper products of solid section of any cross-sectional shape, of which no cross-sectional dimension exceeds 6 mm. (SITC, Rev.3: 68240-0).

Remarque générale.
Produits en cuivre de section pleine, laminés, filés, étirés ou tréfilés, dont la coupe transversale, de forme quelconque, n'excède pas 6 mm dans sa plus grande dimension. (CTCI, Rev.3: 68240-0).

[1] Source: World Metal Statistics, (London).
[2] Including all other copper products.
[3] Products of copper and copper alloys (brass or bronze).
[4] Including products of copper alloys, except alloys with aluminium.

[5] Twelve months ending 30 June of year stated.

[1] Source: World Metal Statistics,(Londres).
[2] Y compris tous les autres produits en cuivre.
[3] Produits en cuivre et en alliages à base de cuivre (laiton ou bronze).
[4] Y compris les produits en alliages de cuivre, autres que les alliages contenant de l'aluminum.

[5] Période de douze mois finissant le 30 juin de l'année indiquée.

Copper plates, sheets, strip, foil
Tôles, bandes et feuilles et papier de cuivre

ISIC-BASED CODE - CODE BASE CITI

3720-16

Unit : Thousand metric tons

Unité : Milliers de tonnes métriques

Country or area	1990	1991	1992	1993	1994	1995	1996	1997	1998	1999	Pays ou zone
Africa	**2**	**4**	**1**	**9**	**2**	**5**	**4**	**3**	**4**	**4**	**Afrique**
Egypt	2.3	4.3	1.1	9.4	2.0	5.1	...	3.5	...	...	Egypte
America, North	**135**	**121**	**129**	**141**	**180**	**181**	**197**	**359**	**427**	**465**	**Amérique du Nord**
Mexico	4.4	5.4	4.5	8.4	24.7	16.1	23.1	#178.0	232.3	244.5	Mexique
United States	130.2	116.1	124.3	[1]132.9	[1]155.6	[1]165.1	[1]173.7	[1]180.8	[1]194.4	...	Etats-Unis
America, South	**26**	**26**	**26**	**26**	**26**	**25**	**26**	**26**	**26**	**26**	**Amérique du Sud**
Brazil[1]	...	...	...	...	...	24.9	25.2	26.0	25.7	...	Brésil[1]
Colombia	...	...	0.4	0.4	0.3	0.3	...	*0.3	0.4	...	Colombie
Asia	**353**	**367**	**340**	**340**	**365**	**409**	**409**	**439**	**400**	**439**	**Asie**
Armenia	..	0.9	0.1	0.0	0.1	...	0.1	0.0	0.0	0.0	Arménie
India	31.7	29.0	22.6	...	...	...	...	...	...	...	Inde
Japan[2]	213.0	225.7	204.8	214.1	230.9	249.8	242.1	256.6	232.8	246.9	Japon[2]
Korea, Republic of[3]	103.6	107.3	100.4	91.3	102.0	126.5	133.9	148.0	132.0	160.1	Corée, République de[3]
Turkey[1]	4.4	4.6	12.4	6.3	4.7	4.7	4.8	6.7	7.0	4.7	Turquie[1]
Europe	**621**	**676**	**663**	**617**	**708**	**921**	**886**	**1004**	**1044**	**1026**	**Europe**
Austria	[1]0.1	[1]0.1	[1]0.6	[1]0.5	[1]0.5	1.6	2.0	0.2	0.1	0.1	Autriche
Czechoslovakia(former)	8.6	6.4	..	..	..	..	..	..	..	..	Tchécoslovaquie(anc.)
Finland	27.6	27.3	30.8	33.3	34.5	37.3	38.9	...	...	...	Finlande
France[1]	...	...	...	43.6	50.9	57.6	51.2	59.4	59.6	...	France[1]
Germany	..	325.9	340.0	336.4	391.2	564.0	539.7	634.8	663.5	...	Allemagne
Germany(Fed.Rep.)[4]	320.1	..	..	..	..	..	..	..	..	...	Allemagne(Rép.féd.)[4]
Greece	...	..	...	17.9	24.5	30.5	33.9	38.4	41.4	...	Grèce
Hungary	1.7	2.0	1.6	...	...	...	...	...	...	...	Hongrie
Italy	79.1	87.8	90.3	85.6	87.1	89.3	83.2	86.0	90.4	87.0	Italie
Russian Federation[1]	..	...	...	...	2.3	4.8	5.9	1.9	2.8	...	Fédération de Russie[1]
Slovakia	...	...	...	...	...	...	...	...	0.4	0.3	Slovaquie
Spain[1]	21.8	20.4	15.8	19.0	26.4	28.8	26.7	29.0	34.1	...	Espagne[1]
Sweden	66.5	54.7	42.9	34.5	43.4	46.7	46.7	47.9	49.5	47.6	Suède
Switzerland[1]	11.4	10.7	11.8	8.1	7.6	5.6	5.8	5.6	...	...	Suisse[1]
United Kingdom	18.0	[1]48.0	[1]40.1	27.0	30.9	[1]46.5	[1]43.1	[1]46.2	39.2	...	Royaume-Uni
Yugoslavia	..	18.6	10.3	5.0	6.1	5.7	6.9	9.2	10.6	7.9	Yougoslavie
Total	**1137**	**1195**	**1159**	**1134**	**1281**	**1541**	**1521**	**1831**	**1900**	**1960**	**Total**

General Note.

Flat-surfaced, wrought copper products (coiled or not), of which the maximum cross-sectional dimension exceeds 6 mm, and of which the thickness exceeds 0.15 mm but does not exceed one-tenth of the width (plates, sheets, strip), thin sheets, not exceeding 0.15 mm in thickness, whether or not embossed, cut to shape, perforated, coated, printed or backed with paper or other reinforcing material (copper foil). (SITC, Rev.3: 68250-0, 68261-0).

Remarque générale.

Produits plats en cuivre (enroulés ou non), dont la plus grande dimension transversale est supérieure à 6 mm et dont l'épaisseur, supérieure à 0.15 mm, ne dépasse pas le dixième de la largeur (tôles, feuilles et bandes), feuilles et bandes minces d'une épaisseur de 0.15 mm au maximum, même gaufrées, découpées, perforées, revêtues, imprimées ou fixées sur papier ou support similaire (feuilles minces ou papier de cuivre). (CTCI, Rev.3: 68250-0, 68261-0).

[1] Source: World Metal Statistics, (London).
[2] Excluding copper foil.
[3] Including copper bars and sections.
[4] Including products of copper alloys, except alloys with aluminium.

[1] Source: World Metal Statistics,(Londres).
[2] Non compris les feuilles de cuivre.
[3] Y compris les barres et profilés de cuivre.
[4] Y compris les produits en alliages de cuivre, autres que les alliages contenant de l'aluminum.

Copper tubes and pipes
Tuyaux et tubes de cuivre

ISIC-BASED CODE - CODE BASE CITI

3720-19

Unit : Thousand metric tons   Unité : Milliers de tonnes métriques

Country or area	1990	1991	1992	1993	1994	1995	1996	1997	1998	1999	Pays ou zone
Africa	**1**	**0**	**0**	**0**	**0**	**0**	**0**	**0**	**0**	**0**	**Afrique**
Egypt	0.6	0.0	0.4	...	...	...	...	...	...	...	Egypte
America, North	**371**	**396**	**433**	**456**	**543**	**543**	**607**	**633**	**655**	**763**	**Amérique du Nord**
Mexico	25.4	31.8	43.0	45.6	49.1	47.4	62.3	61.5	56.2	59.0	Mexique
United States	346.0	364.2	390.1	[1]410.1	[1]493.5	[1]495.3	[1]544.4	[1]571.4	[1]598.5	...	Etats-Unis
America, South	**25**	**25**	**25**	**25**	**25**	**23**	**26**	**25**	**28**	**25**	**Amérique du Sud**
Brazil[1]	...	...	...	...	...	23.0	25.5	24.8	28.3	...	Brésil[1]
Asia	**262**	**297**	**279**	**271**	**320**	**367**	**369**	**363**	**305**	**348**	**Asie**
Japan	212.9	239.0	218.8	202.2	234.6	254.5	262.0	242.7	212.8	220.9	Japon
Korea, Republic of	49.3	57.9	60.1	68.9	85.4	112.8	106.8	120.2	91.7	127.5	Corée, République de
Turkey	[1]0.2	[1]0.2	[1]0.1	[1]0.0	[1]0.0	0.0	0.0	0.0	0.0	0.0	Turquie
Europe	**533**	**589**	**599**	**576**	**631**	**665**	**648**	**670**	**703**	**699**	**Europe**
Austria[1][2]	16.6	16.9	16.1	14.9	16.8	19.0	21.0	21.2	20.0	...	Autriche[1][2]
Czechoslovakia(former)	4.8	3.2	...	...	..	..	..	..	..	..	Tchécoslovaquie(anc.)
Finland	29.7	28.8	31.5	29.9	32.2	35.0	33.2	...	...	...	Finlande
France	[3]68.1	[3]75.2	[3]74.3	[3]66.1	[3]76.9	[1]75.9	[1]74.7	[1]75.3	[1]76.3	...	France
Germany	..	235.7	248.3	237.5	255.8	263.2	240.4	258.5	275.4	...	Allemagne
Germany(Fed.Rep.)[4]	211.9	..	..	..	..	..	..	..	..	..	Allemagne(Rép.féd.)[4]
Greece	...	...	...	19.3	21.8	26.9	29.7	30.9	37.2	...	Grèce
Hungary	1.8	2.2	2.3	...	...	...	...	...	...	...	Hongrie
Italy	56.0	65.6	74.8	76.5	84.1	94.4	96.2	98.0	95.9	94.4	Italie
Russian Federation[1]	...	...	...	...	0.2	0.6	0.5	0.3	2.9	...	Fédération de Russie[1]
Slovakia	..	..	..	...	...	...	...	...	0.9	0.8	Slovaquie
Spain	[1]29.0	[1]31.6	[1]34.2	[1]33.7	37.0	39.9	39.9	42.3	42.0	58.3	Espagne
Sweden	26.9	23.6	21.8	22.8	21.9	23.4	24.6	23.0	25.7	13.5	Suède
Switzerland[1]	1.9	2.0	2.0	1.7	2.1	2.1	1.9	1.9	...	...	Suisse[1]
United Kingdom	[5]66.8	[1]67.7	[1]63.6	[1]67.0	[1]76.0	[1]78.1	[1]77.6	[1]71.0	74.9	...	Royaume-Uni
Yugoslavia	..	15.3	7.0	3.2	3.3	3.7	5.5	9.4	10.6	7.3	Yougoslavie
Total	**1192**	**1307**	**1337**	**1328**	**1520**	**1598**	**1650**	**1691**	**1690**	**1837**	**Total**

General Note.
Seamless and welded tubes and pipes, including blanks therefore, but excluding tube and pipe fittings. (SITC, Rev.3: 68271-0).

[1] Source: World Metal Statistics, (London).
[2] 1999 data are confidential.
[3] Products of copper and copper alloys (brass or bronze).
[4] Including products of copper alloys, except alloys with aluminium.
[5] Copper tubes only.

Remarque générale.
Tuyaux et tubes sans soudure et soudés, y compris leurs ébauches mais non les accessoires de tuyauterie en cuivre. (CTCI, Rev.3: 68271--0).

[1] Source: World Metal Statistics,(Londres).
[2] Pour 1999, les données sont confidentielles.
[3] Produits en cuivre et en alliages à base de cuivre (laiton ou bronze).
[4] Y compris les produits en alliages de cuivre, autres que les alliages contenant de l'aluminum.
[5] Tubes et tuyaux de cuivre seulement.

Nickel unwrought
Nickel brut

ISIC-BASED CODE - CODE BASE CITI

3720-20

Unit : Metric tons   Unité : Tonnes métriques

Country or area	1990	1991	1992	1993	1994	1995	1996	1997	1998	1999	Pays ou zone
Africa	**39642**	**38212**	**37715**	**41789**	**44269**	**40666**	**43057**	**44563**	**39771**	**46303**	**Afrique**
South Africa	[1]28200	[1]26900	[1]27600	[1]29900	[1]30751	[1]29803	[1]33362	[1]33700	[2]31039	[1]35803	Afrique du Sud
Zimbabwe	11442	11312	10115	11889	13518	10863	9695	10863	[1]8732	[1]10500	Zimbabwe
America, North	**189738**	**186970**	**188407**	**167878**	**149831**	**185886**	**202312**	**214189**	**214886**	**172520**	**Amérique du Nord**
Canada[1]	135000	132000	135200	123140	105144	125311	130136	131639	146715	123944	Canada[1]
Cuba[1]	21100	18800	16717	15999	13930	21388	26700	33992	38661	38500	Cuba[1]
Dominican Republic[3]	29937	29100	[1]27530	[1]23859	[1]30757	[1]30897	[1]30376	[1]32558	[1]25220	10076	Rép. dominicaine[3]
United States[3]	3701	7070	8960	4880	0	8290	15100	16000	4290	0	Etats-Unis[3]
America, South	**31400**	**34000**	**34863**	**35886**	**37443**	**40241**	**39874**	**43370**	**49226**	**51276**	**Amérique du Sud**
Brazil[1]	13000	13800	14668	15705	16610	15676	16940	18199	21083	22931	Brésil[1]
Colombia[1 3]	18400	20200	20195	20181	20833	24565	22934	25171	28143	28345	Colombie[1 3]
Asia	**54785**	**56478**	**58298**	**58887**	**62378**	**76482**	**80717**	**77798**	**73464**	**84112**	**Asie**
China	[1]27500	[1]27500	30754	30513	31322	38923	44600	40900	41315	44426	Chine
Indonesia[1 3]	5010	5320	5506	5266	5745	10735	9553	9999	8452	9205	Indonésie[1 3]
Japan	[4]22275	[4]23658	22038	23108	25311	26824	26564	26899	23697	30481	Japon
Europe	**135573**	**338394**	**368235**	**306272**	**321517**	**331988**	**352094**	**397570**	**407691**	**425245**	**Europe**
Czechoslovakia(former)[1]	2970	2500	..	..	..	..	..	..	..	..	Tchécoslovaquie(anc.)[1]
Finland	17136	13146	14984	14577	16902	16025	29139	[1]39218	[1]46018	51948	Finlande
France	[5]8539	[5]7455	[5]6788	[2 5]9000	[2 5]10000	8000	9000	9000	10000	9000	France
German D.R.(former)[1]	2382	..	..	..	..	..	..	..	..	..	R.D.A. (anc.)[1]
Greece[1 3]	15727	16005	15420	10934	16197	17164	17801	17610	15005	12964	Grèce[1 3]
Norway	57811	58729	[2]55686	56818	67955	53237	61582	[1]62702	[1]70152	[1]74137	Norvège
Russian Federation*[1 6]	..	...	245000	186000	180900	201000	190000	230000	227000	238000	Fédération de Russie*[1 6]
Sweden	908	743	* [1]500	* [1]500	* [1]500	* [1]500	* [1]0	* [1]0	* [1]0	* [1]0	Suède
United Kingdom	[6]26500	[6]28600	[6]28000	[6]28000	[6]28400	[6]35100	[6]42000	[6]36600	[1]39050	[1]38086	Royaume-Uni
Yugoslavia	..	4198	1857	443	663	962	2572	2440	466	...	Yougoslavie
Yugoslavia, SFR[1 3]	3600	..	..	..	..	..	..	..	..	..	Yougoslavie, RSF[1 3]
USSR (former)*[1]	236000	..	..	..	..	..	..	..	..	..	URSS (anc.)*[1]
Oceania	**77300**	**83800**	**96870**	**102733**	**117129**	**129276**	**127425**	**128478**	**124069**	**130289**	**Océanie**
Australia[1]	*45000	49400	57500	55000	67000	76933	74013	73586	79578	85000	Australie[1]
New Caledonia	[2]32300	[2]34400	39370	47733	50129	52343	53412	54892	[1 3]44491	[1 3]45289	Nouvelle-Calédonie
Total	**764438**	**737854**	**784388**	**713445**	**732567**	**804539**	**845479**	**905968**	**909107**	**909745**	**Total**

General Note.
Production of refined nickel plus nickel content of ferro-nickel and nickel oxide. (SITC, Rev.3: 68310-0).

Remarque générale.
Production de nickel raffiné et nickel contenu dans les oxydes de nickel et dans le ferro-nickel. (CTCI, Rev.3: 68310-0).

[1] Source: U. S. Geological Survey, (Washington, D. C.).
[2] Source: World Metal Statistics, (London).
[3] Nickel content of ferronickel only.
[4] Source: Metallgesellschaft Aktiengesellschaft, (Frankfurt).
[5] Including nickel content of refined nickel, nickel oxide and nickel matte.
[6] Including ferro-nickel.

[1] Source: U.S. Geological Survey, (Washington, D.C.).
[2] Source: World Metal Statistics,(Londres).
[3] La teneur en nickel de ferro-nickel seulement.
[4] Source: "Metallgesellschaft Aktiengesellschaft", (Francfort).
[5] Y compris la teneur en nickel de nickel affiné, de l'oxyde de nickel et de mattes de nickel.
[6] Y compris le ferro-nickel.

Alumina, calcined equivalent
Alumine calcinée

ISIC-BASED CODE - CODE BASE CITI

3720-21

Unit : Thousand metric tons   Unité : Milliers de tonnes métriques

Country or area	1990	1991	1992	1993	1994	1995	1996	1997	1998	1999	Pays ou zone
Africa	**642**	**651**	**661**	**656**	**640**	**616**	**640**	**650**	**480**	**500**	**Afrique**
Guinea	642	651	661	656	[1]640	[1]616	* [1]640	* [1]650	* [1]480	* [1]500	Guinée
America, North	**9186**	**9376**	**9211**	**9481**	**9254**	**8653**	**9125**	**9649**	**10259**	**9733**	**Amérique du Nord**
Canada[1]	1087	1131	1104	1182	1170	1064	1060	*1165	1229	1233	Canada[1]
Jamaica	2869	3015	2917	3009	3224	3059	3365	3394	3440	3570	Jamaïque
United States	5230	5230	5190	5290	4860	4530	4700	5090	5590	4930	Etats-Unis
America, South	**4479**	**4548**	**4715**	**4860**	**4666**	**5391**	**6096**	**6418**	**6475**	**6441**	**Amérique du Sud**
Brazil	1655	[1]1743	[1]1833	[1]1853	[1]1868	[1]2141	[1]2752	[1]3088	[1]3322	[1]3506	Brésil
Suriname	1531	1510	1574	1507	1498	1589	1643	* [1]1600	* [1]1600	* [1]1600	Suriname
Venezuela[1]	1293	1295	1308	1500	*1300	1661	1701	1730	1553	1335	Venezuela[1]
Asia	**3759**	**4846**	**4728**	**4989**	**4714**	**5433**	**5910**	**6440**	**6833**	**7476**	**Asie**
Azerbaijan	..	...	240	183	27	26	1	13	7	76	Azerbaïdjan
China	* [1]1500	* [1]1520	* [1]1580	* [1]1820	* [1]1850	* [1]2200	* [1]2550	* [1]2940	3335	3837	Chine
India	[1]1601	*1700	[1]1484	[1]1490	[1]1456	[1]1650	* [1]1780	* [1]1860	* [1]1890	* [1]1900	Inde
Japan	481	438	316	327	[1]326	[1]363	[1]337	* [1]368	* [1]359	* [1]352	Japon
Kazakhstan[1]	..	...	...	*1000	*900	*1022	*1083	1095	1085	1152	Kazakhstan[1]
Turkey	177	159	156	169	155	172	159	164	157	159	Turquie
Europe	**7581**	**9600**	**9669**	**8972**	**8413**	**9032**	**9009**	**9329**	**9575**	**9730**	**Europe**
Croatia	..	53	2	1	0	0	0	0	...	...	Croatie
Czechoslovakia(former)[2]	*209	187	..	..	..	..	..	..	..	..	Tchécoslovaquie(anc.)[2]
France	478	404	366	*367	[1]344	425	440	477	444	472	France
Germany	..	863	857	840	824	[1]750	[1]755	738	* [1]750	[1]600	Allemagne
Germany(Fed.Rep.)	922	..	..	..	..	..	..	..	..	..	Allemagne(Rép.féd.)
German D.R.(former)[2]	27	..	..	..	..	..	..	..	..	..	R.D.A. (anc.)[2]
Greece	[1]625	[1]520	[1]612	[1]615	[1]548	[1]598	620	* [1]602	648	* [1]600	Grèce
Hungary	823	625	516	375	120	146	306	[1]76	* [1]138	* [1]150	Hongrie
Ireland[1]	...	...	...	1103	1140	1186	1234	1273	*1200	*1200	Irlande[1]
Italy[1]	752	760	762	549	557	857	881	*913	*930	*973	Italie[1]
Romania	440	310	280	293	302	323	261	280	250	277	Roumanie
Russian Federation[1]	..	...	*2718	*2500	*2254	*2300	*2105	2400	2465	*2657	Fédération de Russie[1]
Slovakia	..	..	[1]143	*140	* [1]75	* [1]100	* [1]100	* [1]100	* [1]100	* [1]104	Slovaquie
Slovenia	..	49	4	2	3	14	9	20	10	11	Slovénie
Spain[1]	1002	1003	959	1060	1071	1070	1095	1110	*1100	1200	Espagne[1]
Ukraine*[1]	..	...	...	1010	1070	1100	1000	1080	1291	1230	Ukraine*[1]
United Kingdom[1]	115	110	*120	*105	*105	*108	99	100	96	100	Royaume-Uni[1]
Yugoslavia	..	208	197	12	0	55	104	160	153	156	Yougoslavie
Yugoslavia, SFR[1]	1086	..	..	..	..	..	..	..	..	..	Yougoslavie, RSF[1]
USSR (former)*[1]	3300	..	..	..	..	..	..	..	..	..	URSS (anc.)*[1]
Oceania	**11231**	**11703**	**11783**	**12221**	**12761**	**12940**	**13293**	**13252**	**13581**	**14207**	**Océanie**
Australia	* [1]11231	[1]11703	[1]11783	12221	12761	12940	[3]13293	[3]13252	[3]13581	[3]14207	Australie
Total	**40178**	**40724**	**40767**	**41179**	**40448**	**42065**	**44073**	**45738**	**47203**	**48087**	**Total**

General Note.

Alumina (aluminium oxide - Al_2O_3) (anhydrous or calcined alumina) is obtained by calcining the aluminium hydroxide or from ammonium alum. Aluminium hydroxide (hydrated alumina) is recovered from bauxite during aluminium metallurgy. Most of the calcined oxide is used to make the metal. (SITC, Rev.3: 28520-0, 52266-0).

Remarque générale.

L'alumine (oxyde d'aluminium - Al_2O_3) (alumine anhydre ou calcinée) est obtenu par calcination de l'hydrate d'aluminium ou à partir de l'alun ammoniacal. L'hydroxide d'aluminium (alumine hydratée) est obtenu au cours de la métallurgie de l'aluminium par le traitement de la bauxite. La plus grande partie de l'oxyde calciné sert à la fabrication du métal. (CTCI, Rev.3: 28520-0, 52266-0).

[1] Source: U. S. Geological Survey, (Washington, D. C.).
[2] Source: Metallgesellschaft Aktiengesellschaft, (Frankfurt).
[3] Twelve months ending 30 June of year stated.

[1] Source: U.S. Geological Survey, (Washington, D.C.).
[2] Source: "Metallgesellschaft Aktiengesellschaft", (Francfort).
[3] Période de douze mois finissant le 30 juin de l'année indiquée.

Aluminium, unwrought (total production)
Aluminium non travaillé (production totale)

ISIC-BASED CODE - CODE BASE CITI

3720-22

Unit : Thousand metric tons | | | | | | | | | | Unité : Milliers de tonnes métriques

Country or area	1990	1991	1992	1993	1994	1995	1996	1997	1998	1999	Pays ou zone
Africa	**573**	**571**	**575**	**576**	**543**	**572**	**939**	**1034**	**1018**	**1080**	**Afrique**
Cameroon	[1]87.5	[1]85.6	[1]82.5	[1]86.5	[1]81.1	71.4	[1]82.3	[2]91.0	[2]82.0	[2]92.0	Cameroun
Egypt[3]	141.1	141.0	139.4	138.8	149.2	135.8	149.9	118.5	[1]187.2	[2]187.0	Egypte[3]
Ghana	174.0	175.0	[1]179.9	[1]175.4	[1]140.7	[1]135.4	[1]137.0	[1]151.6	[1]56.1	[2]114.0	Ghana
South Africa[2]	170.0	169.0	173.0	175.0	172.0	229.0	570.0	673.0	693.0	687.0	Afrique du Sud[2]
America, North	**8198**	**8423**	**8939**	**9133**	**8815**	**8926**	**9438**	**9770**	**9824**	**10114**	**Amérique du Nord**
Canada	[1]1635.1	[1]1889.3	[1]2057.8	[1]2398.9	[1]2351.7	[1]2269.0	[1]2384.2	[1]2433.2	[1]2485.1	2389.8	Canada
Mexico	122.4	122.4	79.2	99.6	74.4	92.4	166.8	183.6	186.0	195.6	Mexique
United States[4]	6441.0	6411.0	6802.0	6635.0	6389.0	6565.0	6887.0	7153.0	7153.0	7529.0	Etats-Unis[4]
America, South	**1805**	**2041**	**2007**	**2067**	**2108**	**2181**	**2229**	**2267**	**2209**	**2037**	**Amérique du Sud**
Argentina	169.0	184.4	172.1	185.0	187.8	193.2	200.3	*203.0	[1]202.7	[2]206.4	Argentine
Brazil	[1]995.6	[1]1206.0	[1]1260.4	[1]1248.8	[1]1275.6	[1]1304.8	[1]1343.0	[1]1369.2	[1]1371.4	[2]1250.0	Brésil
Colombia	...	...	0.3	0.5	...	0.4	...	...	...	...	Colombie
Suriname	31.3	30.7	32.4	30.1	26.7	28.1	28.8	[2]32.0	[2]29.0	[2]10.0	Suriname
Venezuela	608.8	620.0	542.2	602.4	[1]617.3	[1]654.1	[1]656.2	[1]662.2	[1]605.7	[2]570.0	Venezuela
Asia	**2974**	**3390**	**3807**	**3858**	**4317**	**4750**	**4699**	**5148**	**5151**	**5532**	**Asie**
Bahrain	212.5	213.7	292.5	448.0	450.9	448.8	455.8	[2]490.0	[2]501.0	502.3	Bahreïn
China	854.3	900.0	1096.4	1255.4	1498.3	1869.7	1896.2	2180.1	2361.6	2808.9	Chine
India	427.6	504.3	499.0	477.6	478.8	518.4	516.0	538.8	[2]542.0	[2]550.0	Inde
Indonesia	192.1	173.0	213.5	202.1	[1]221.9	[1]228.1	[1]223.2	[1]219.4	[1]133.4	* [2]100.0	Indonésie
Iran(Islamic Rep. of)	73.0	109.5	118.7	[1]106.6	[1]142.2	[1]145.4	[1]96.0	[1]125.3	[1]135.0	[2]109.0	Iran(Rép. islamique)
Japan[4]	1140.6	1148.5	1112.2	1044.2	1215.3	1227.3	1237.8	1329.9	1206.8	1157.7	Japon[4]
Korea, Republic of	13.3	13.6	...	...	...	...	...	...	...	...	Corée, République de
Tajikistan	..	...	* [2]400.0	252.3	236.5	237.0	198.4	188.9	195.6	229.1	Tadjikistan
Turkey	61.0	56.0	61.3	58.5	59.7	61.5	62.1	62.0	61.8	61.7	Turquie
Europe	**5655**	**8125**	**7705**	**7718**	**7585**	**7490**	**7955**	**8040**	**8560**	**8297**	**Europe**
Austria	246.3	205.9	*78.4	[1]43.3	[1]52.5	[1]93.5	[1]97.5	[1]118.8	[1]126.4	...	Autriche
Belgium[1]	3.0	3.0	0.0	0.0	0.0	0.0	0.0	0.0	0.0	...	Belgique[1]
Croatia	..	54.5	29.0	26.0	26.0	30.9	33.0	[2]35.0	16.1	[2]35.0	Croatie
Denmark	[1]10.6	[1]12.0	[5]16.0	[5]21.3	[5]21.9	[5]28.0	[5]27.4	[5]35.0	[5]34.3	[5]33.8	Danemark
Czechoslovakia(former)	69.8	66.3	..	..	..	..	..	..	..	..	Tchécoslovaquie(anc.)
Finland*	4.9	4.2	4.5	3.7	4.3	4.7	5.3	...	...	...	Finlande*
France	[4]533.4	[4]471.8	[4]636.7	[4]627.3	[4]708.9	364.0	380.0	399.0	424.0	455.0	France
Germany		739.9	654.6	610.4	559.0	576.0	577.2	572.4	612.0	633.6	Allemagne
Germany(Fed.Rep.)	759.6										Allemagne(Rép.féd.)
German D.R.(former)[4]	82.8	..	..	..	..	..	..	..	..	..	R.D.A. (anc.)[4]
Greece	225.9	175.1	174.5	147.7	141.6	132.0	141.3	132.0	160.6	160.8	Grèce
Hungary	81.1	63.3	26.9	28.9	30.6	35.0	93.8	98.2	92.2	88.5	Hongrie
Iceland	86.8	88.8	89.5	94.5	99.3	100.1	102.1	123.4	159.5	161.2	Islande
Italy	581.4	566.0	513.8	501.7	551.0	590.1	561.0	630.6	689.6	689.0	Italie
Netherlands	392.1	367.8	377.6	367.4	405.4	407.5	[1]298.0	[1]311.8	[1]365.7	* [2]265.0	Pays-Bas
Norway	*886.6	*889.4	878.1	*943.3	*906.2	*918.7	*923.0	[1]977.2	[1]1057.9	[2]1034.0	Norvège
Poland	46.0	45.8	43.6	46.9	49.5	55.7	51.9	53.6	54.2	51.0	Pologne
Portugal	9.3	8.1	11.9	11.8	11.6	[1]3.0	[1]3.0	[1]3.0	[1]3.2	...	Portugal
Romania[4][6]	178.3	167.5	119.5	116.5	122.4	143.9	144.6	164.0	175.2	174.3	Roumanie[4][6]
Russian Federation[2]	..	...	2700.0	2820.0	2670.0	2724.0	2874.0	2906.0	3005.0	3146.0	Fédération de Russie[2]
Slovakia	..	..	..	19.2	4.2	25.1	310.9	[1]110.1	120.7	109.2	Slovaquie
Slovenia	..	90.2	84.8	82.9	76.8	57.6	27.0	9.1	10.2	9.0	Slovénie
Spain	[1]442.0	[1]451.2	[1]455.5	[1]455.6	[1]441.6	[1]468.9	[1]515.3	[1]533.1	[1]570.4	[2]360.0	Espagne
Sweden	[1]126.3	115.5	[1]95.8	[1]101.4	[1]105.4	[1]117.5	[1]122.8	[1]123.4	[1]122.7	[2]96.0	Suède
Switzerland	*106.1	*101.7	*62.8	*40.6	*30.4	[1]26.0	[1]32.6	[1]35.2	[1]47.2	[2]30.0	Suisse
Ukraine* [2]	..	...	100.0	100.0	100.0	98.0	90.0	101.0	107.0	112.0	Ukraine* [2]
United Kingdom[4]	491.2	488.6	441.5	475.3	455.5	467.6	501.0	490.4	533.2	528.0	Royaume-Uni[4]
Yugoslavia	..	75.8	66.9	25.8	4.5	17.0	37.4	67.2	61.2	73.4	Yougoslavie
T.F.Yug.Rep. Macedonia	..	6.0	5.8	6.5	7.0	5.4	5.3	5.4	6.6	5.7	L'ex-RY Macédoine
Yugoslavia, SFR	291.0	..	..	..	..	..	..	..	..	..	Yougoslavie, RSF
USSR (former)* [2]	2800.0	..	..	..	..	..	..	..	..	..	URSS (anc.)* [2]
Oceania	**1533**	**1528**	**1484**	**1626**	**1716**	**1566**	**1624**	**1713**	**1915**	**1986**	**Océanie**

For general note and footnotes, see end of table. | Voir la fin du tableau pour la remarque générale et les notes.

Aluminium, unwrought (total production) (continued)
Aluminium non travaillé (production totale) (suite)

ISIC-BASED CODE - CODE BASE CITI

3720-22

Unit : Thousand metric tons   Unité : Milliers de tonnes métriques

Country or area	1990	1991	1992	1993	1994	1995	1996	1997	1998	1999	Pays ou zone
Australia[7]	*1268.0	1264.6	1234.0	1340.8	1439.0	1285.0	1331.0	1395.0	1589.0	1686.0	Australie[7]
New Zealand	[1]264.5	[1]263.2	[1]249.6	[1]284.7	[1]277.3	[1]281.3	[1]292.7	[1]318.2	[1]325.5	[2]300.0	Nouvelle-Zélande
Total	**23538**	**24078**	**24516**	**24978**	**25085**	**25485**	**26884**	**27971**	**28677**	**29047**	**Total**

General Note.

Aluminium obtained by electrolytic reduction of alumina (primary) and remelting metal waste or scrap (secondary). (SITC, Rev.3: 68411-0).

Remarque générale.

Aluminium obtenu par réduction électrolytique de l'alumine (formes primaires) ou refonte des déchets et débris de métal (formes secondaires). (CTCI, Rev.3: 68411-0).

[1] Source: World Metal Statistics, (London).
[2] Source: U. S. Geological Survey, (Washington, D. C.).
[3] Including aluminium plates, shapes and bars.
[4] Including alloys.
[5] Sales.
[6] Including pure content of virgin alloys.
[7] Twelve months ending 30 June of year stated.

[1] Source: World Metal Statistics,(Londres).
[2] Source: U.S. Geological Survey, (Washington, D.C.).
[3] Y compris les tôles, les profilés et les barres d'aluminium.
[4] Y compris les alliages.
[5] Ventes.
[6] Y compris la teneur pure des alliages de première fusion.
[7] Période de douze mois finissant le 30 juin de l'année indiquée.

Aluminium, unwrought, primary
Aluminium non travaillé, neuf

ISIC-BASED CODE - CODE BASE CITI

3720-221

Unit : Thousand metric tons   Unité : Milliers de tonnes métriques

Country or area	1990	1991	1992	1993	1994	1995	1996	1997	1998	1999	Pays ou zone
Africa	**573**	**571**	**575**	**576**	**543**	**572**	**939**	**1033**	**1018**	**1080**	**Afrique**
Cameroon	[1]87.5	[1]85.6	[1]82.5	[1]86.5	[1]81.1	71.4	[1]82.3	[1]90.0	[1]81.6	[2]92.0	Cameroun
Egypt[3]	141.1	141.0	139.4	138.8	149.2	135.8	149.8	118.5	[1]187.2	[2]187.0	Egypte[3]
Ghana	174.0	175.0	[1]179.9	[1]175.4	[1]140.7	[1]135.4	[1]137.0	[1]151.6	[1]56.1	[2]114.0	Ghana
South Africa[2]	170.0	169.0	173.0	175.0	172.0	229.0	570.0	673.0	693.0	687.0	Afrique du Sud[2]
America, North	**5672**	**5985**	**6031**	**6029**	**5583**	**5580**	**5929**	**6001**	**6156**	**6238**	**Amérique du Nord**
Canada	[1]1567.4	1821.6	[1]1971.8	[2]2308.9	[2]2254.7	[2]2172.0	[2]2283.2	[2]2327.2	[2]2374.1	2389.8	Canada
Mexico	56.8	42.8	17.4	25.1	28.9	33.1	69.3	71.2	68.5	69.7	Mexique
United States	4048.0	4121.0	4042.0	3695.0	3299.0	3375.0	3577.0	3603.0	3713.0	3779.0	Etats-Unis
America, South	**1724**	**1946**	**1886**	**1940**	**1970**	**2026**	**2046**	**2049**	**2008**	**2036**	**Amérique du Sud**
Argentina	163.0	166.3	153.0	170.6	173.4	183.2	184.5	187.2	186.7	206.4	Argentine
Brazil	[1]930.6	[1]1139.0	[1]1193.3	[1]1172.0	[1]1184.6	[1]1188.1	[1]1197.4	[1]1189.1	[1]1208.0	[2]1250.0	Brésil
Suriname	31.3	30.7	32.4	30.1	26.7	28.1	28.8	[2]32.0	[2]29.0	[2]10.0	Suriname
Venezuela	598.8	610.0	507.5	567.6	[1]585.4	[1]626.6	[1]634.8	[1]640.8	[1]584.3	[2]570.0	Venezuela
Asia	**1870**	**2255**	**2694**	**2837**	**3117**	**3543**	**3481**	**3845**	**3969**	**4424**	**Asie**
Bahrain	212.5	213.7	292.5	448.0	450.9	448.8	455.8	[2]490.0	[2]501.0	502.3	Bahreïn
China	854.3	900.0	1096.4	1255.4	1498.3	1869.7	1896.2	2180.1	2361.6	2808.9	Chine
India	427.6	504.3	499.0	477.6	478.8	518.4	516.0	538.8	[2]542.0	[2]550.0	Inde
Indonesia	192.1	173.0	213.5	202.1	[1]221.9	[1]228.1	[1]223.2	[1]219.4	[1]133.4	[2]100.0	Indonésie
Iran(Islamic Rep. of)	[1]59.4	[1]70.1	[1]79.3	[1]91.5	[1]116.2	[1]119.4	[1]70.0	[1]99.3	[1]109.0	[2]109.0	Iran(Rép. islamique)
Japan	50.5	52.1	38.5	38.5	40.8	46.4	46.3	52.8	51.4	...	Japon
Korea, Republic of	13.3	13.6	...	...	...	...	...	...	...	...	Corée, République de
Tajikistan	..	...	* [2]400.0	252.3	236.5	237.0	198.4	188.9	195.6	229.1	Tadjikistan
Turkey	60.0	56.0	61.3	58.5	59.7	61.5	62.1	62.0	61.8	61.7	Turquie
Europe	**4337**	**6843**	**6486**	**6464**	**6246**	**6311**	**6860**	**6839**	**7169**	**7501**	**Europe**
Austria	159.1	89.0	33.0	[1]0.0	[1]0.0	[1]0.0	[1]0.0	[1]0.0	[1]0.0	...	Autriche
Croatia	..	54.5	29.0	26.0	26.0	30.9	33.0	[2]35.0	16.1	[2]35.0	Croatie
Czechoslovakia(former)	30.1	49.4	..	..	..	..	..	..	..	..	Tchécoslovaquie(anc.)
France	325.2	254.6	414.3	424.5	481.5	364.0	380.0	399.0	424.0	455.0	France
Germany	..	690.3	602.8	551.9	503.4	576.0	577.2	572.4	[2]612.0	633.6	Allemagne
Germany(Fed.Rep.)[4]	720.3	..	..	..	..	..	..	..	..	..	Allemagne(Rép.féd.)[4]
German D.R. (former)[5]	41.2		..	..	..	..	..	..	..	..	R.D.A. (anc.)[5]
Greece	225.9	175.1	174.5	147.7	141.6	132.0	141.3	132.0	146.4	160.8	Grèce
Hungary	75.2	63.3	26.9	28.9	30.6	35.0	93.8	98.2	92.2	88.5	Hongrie
Iceland	86.8	88.8	89.5	94.5	99.3	100.1	102.1	123.4	159.5	161.2	Islande
Italy	231.8	218.0	160.7	155.6	175.0	177.8	184.0	187.7	187.0	187.2	Italie
Netherlands	257.9	253.6	227.3	228.3	230.1	216.0	[1]227.0	[1]231.8	[1]263.7	[2]265.0	Pays-Bas
Norway	867.1	858.2	838.1	887.5	857.0	846.8	863.3	[1]918.6	[1]995.5	[2]1034.0	Norvège
Poland	46.0	45.8	43.6	46.9	49.5	55.7	51.9	53.6	54.2	51.0	Pologne
Romania[5][6]	168.0	158.2	112.0	112.4	119.6	140.5	140.9	161.9	174.0	174.1	Roumanie[5][6]
Russian Federation[2]	..	...	2700.0	2820.0	2670.0	2724.0	2874.0	2906.0	3005.0	3146.0	Fédération de Russie[2]
Slovakia	..	...	...	17.8	4.2	25.1	310.9	[1]110.1	114.9	...	Slovaquie
Slovenia	..	90.2	84.8	82.9	76.8	57.6	27.0	9.1	10.2	9.0	Slovénie
Spain	[1]355.3	[1]355.2	[1]359.0	[1]355.9	[1]338.1	[1]361.9	[1]361.5	[1]359.9	[1]360.4	[2]360.0	Espagne
Sweden	[1]96.3	[1]96.9	[1]77.2	[1]82.4	[1]83.9	[1]94.5	[1]98.3	[1]98.4	[1]95.7	[2]96.0	Suède
Switzerland	71.6	65.9	52.1	36.4	24.2	20.7	[1]26.6	[1]27.3	[1]32.1	[2]30.0	Suisse
Ukraine* [2]	..	...	100.0	100.0	100.0	98.0	90.0	101.0	107.0	112.0	Ukraine* [2]
United Kingdom[5]	289.8	293.5	244.2	239.1	231.2	237.9	240.0	247.7	258.4	269.7	Royaume-Uni[5]
Yugoslavia	..	75.6	66.9	25.7	4.3	16.9	37.4	65.7	61.2	73.4	Yougoslavie
Yugoslavia, SFR*	290.0	..	..	..	..	..	..	..	..	..	Yougoslavie, RSF*
USSR (former)* [2]	2200.0	..	..	..	..	..	..	..	..	..	URSS (anc.)* [2]
Oceania	**1495**	**1494**	**1437**	**1583**	**1653**	**1558**	**1616**	**1705**	**1907**	**1986**	**Océanie**
Australia[7]	1235.1	1235.0	1194.0	1306.0	1384.0	1285.0	1331.0	1395.0	1589.0	1686.0	Australie[7]
New Zealand	[1]259.7	[1]258.5	[1]242.9	[1]277.4	[1]269.1	[1]273.3	[1]284.7	[1]310.2	[1]317.5	[2]300.0	Nouvelle-Zélande
Total	**17870**	**19093**	**19109**	**19430**	**19112**	**19590**	**20871**	**21472**	**22227**	**23266**	**Total**

For general note and footnotes, see end of table.   Voir la fin du tableau pour la remarque générale et les notes.

Aluminium, unwrought, primary (continued)
Aluminium non travaillé, neuf (suite)

ISIC-BASED CODE - CODE BASE CITI
3720-221

General Note.
Primary aluminium recovered by the electrolytic reduction of alumina from domestic and imported ores. (SITC, Rev.3: 68411-1).

[1] Source: World Metal Statistics, (London).
[2] Source: U. S. Geological Survey, (Washington, D. C.).
[3] Including aluminium plates, shapes and bars.
[4] Source: Metallgesellschaft Aktiengesellschaft, (Frankfurt).
[5] Including alloys.
[6] Including pure content of virgin alloys.
[7] Twelve months ending 30 June of year stated.

Remarque générale.
Aluminium de première fusion obtenu par réduction électrolytique de l'alumine contenue dans les minerais nationaux ou importés. (CTCI, Rev.3: 68411-1).

[1] Source: World Metal Statistics,(Londres).
[2] Source: U.S. Geological Survey, (Washington, D.C.).
[3] Y compris les tôles, les profilés et les barres d'aluminium.
[4] Source: "Metallgesellschaft Aktiengesellschaft", (Francfort).
[5] Y compris les alliages.
[6] Y compris la teneur pure des alliages de première fusion.
[7] Période de douze mois finissant le 30 juin de l'année indiquée.

Aluminium, unwrought, secondary
Aluminium non travaillé, récupéré

ISIC-BASED CODE - CODE BASE CITI

3720-222

Unit : Thousand metric tons   Unité : Milliers de tonnes métriques

Country or area	1990	1991	1992	1993	1994	1995	1996	1997	1998	1999	Pays ou zone
America, North	**2526**	**2437**	**2908**	**3104**	**3233**	**3346**	**3509**	**3768**	**3669**	**4005**	**Amérique du Nord**
Canada[1]	67.7	67.7	86.0	90.0	97.0	97.0	101.0	106.0	111.0	...	Canada[1]
Mexico[2]	65.6	79.6	61.8	74.5	45.5	59.3	97.5	112.4	117.5	125.9	Mexique[2]
United States[3]	2393.0	2290.0	2760.0	2940.0	3090.0	3190.0	3310.0	3550.0	3440.0	3750.0	Etats-Unis[3]
America, South	**81**	**95**	**121**	**126**	**137**	**154**	**183**	**217**	**201**	**263**	**Amérique du Sud**
Argentina[1]	6.0	18.1	19.1	14.4	14.4	10.0	15.8	15.8	16.0	...	Argentine[1]
Brazil[1]	65.0	66.4	67.1	76.8	91.0	116.7	145.6	180.1	163.4	...	Brésil[1]
Venezuela[1]	10.0	10.0	34.7	34.8	31.9	27.5	21.4	21.4	21.4	...	Venezuela[1]
Asia	**1104**	**1136**	**1113**	**1021**	**1201**	**1207**	**1217**	**1303**	**1181**	**1183**	**Asie**
Iran(Islamic Rep. of)[1]	13.6	39.4	39.4	15.1	26.0	26.0	26.0	26.0	26.0	...	Iran(Rép. islamique)[1]
Japan[3]	1090.1	1096.4	1073.7	1005.6	1174.6	1180.8	1191.5	1277.1	1155.4	1157.7	Japon[3]
Europe	**1278**	**1280**	**1236**	**1253**	**1341**	**1460**	**1378**	**1486**	**1659**	**1644**	**Europe**
Austria	[4]87.2	[4]116.9	[4]45.4	[4]43.3	[4]52.5	[4]93.5	[4]97.5	[4]118.8	[4]126.4	...	Autriche
Belgium[1]	3.0	3.0	0.0	0.0	0.0	0.0	0.0	0.0	0.0	...	Belgique[1]
Denmark	[1]10.6	[1]12.0	[5]16.0	[5]21.3	[5]21.9	[5]28.0	[5]27.4	[5]35.0	[5]34.3	[5]33.8	Danemark
Czechoslovakia(former)	39.7	16.9	..	..	..	..	..	..	..	..	Tchécoslovaquie(anc.)
Finland*	4.9	4.2	4.5	3.7	4.3	4.7	5.3	...	...	...	Finlande*
France[3]	208.3	217.2	222.4	202.8	227.4	...	...	...	...	...	France[3]
Germany	..	49.5	51.9	58.5	55.6	...	...	...	...	...	Allemagne
German D.R.(former)[3]	41.6	..	..	..	..	..	..	..	..	..	R.D.A. (anc.)[3]
Hungary	5.9	..	..	..	..	..	..	..	..	..	Hongrie
Italy	349.6	348.0	353.1	346.1	375.5	412.3	376.6	442.9	502.6	501.8	Italie
Netherlands	134.2	114.3	150.2	139.1	175.3	191.5	[1]71.0	[1]80.0	[1]102.0	...	Pays-Bas
Norway[1]	19.5	31.2	40.0	55.8	49.2	71.9	59.7	58.6	62.4	...	Norvège[1]
Portugal	9.3	8.1	11.9	11.8	11.6	[1]3.0	[1]3.0	[1]3.0	[1]3.2	...	Portugal
Romania[3]	10.3	9.2	7.5	4.1	2.8	3.4	3.7	2.1	[6]1.1	[6]0.2	Roumanie[3]
Slovakia	..	..	..	1.4	..	..	..	..	5.8	...	Slovaquie
Spain[1]	86.7	96.0	96.5	99.7	103.5	107.0	153.8	173.2	210.0	...	Espagne[1]
Sweden[1]	30.0	16.5	18.6	19.0	21.5	23.0	24.5	25.0	27.0	...	Suède[1]
Switzerland[1]	34.5	35.8	10.7	4.2	6.2	5.3	6.0	7.9	15.1	...	Suisse[1]
United Kingdom	201.4	195.1	197.3	236.2	224.3	229.7	261.0	242.7	274.8	258.3	Royaume-Uni
Yugoslavia	..	0.2	0.1	0.0	0.1	0.1	0.1	1.5	0.0	...	Yougoslavie
Yugoslavia, SFR*	1.0	..	..	..	..	..	..	..	..	..	Yougoslavie, RSF*
USSR (former)*[2]	600.0	..	..	..	..	..	..	..	..	..	URSS (anc.)*[2]
Oceania	**38**	**34**	**47**	**42**	**63**	**61**	**66**	**71**	**76**	**83**	**Océanie**
Australia[7]	32.9	29.6	[1]40.0	[1]34.8	[1]55.0	...	...	...	...	...	Australie[7]
New Zealand[1]	4.8	4.7	6.7	7.3	8.2	8.0	8.0	8.0	8.0	...	Nouvelle-Zélande[1]
Total	**5626**	**4982**	**5424**	**5546**	**5975**	**6228**	**6353**	**6846**	**6786**	**7179**	**Total**

General Note.
Secondary aluminium obtained by remelting metal waste or scrap. (SITC, Rev.3: 68411-2).

Remarque générale.
Aluminium de deuxième fusion récupéré à partir de déchets et de débris d'ouvrages. (CTCI, Rev.3: 68411-2).

[1] Source: World Metal Statistics, (London).
[2] Source: U. S. Geological Survey, (Washington, D. C.).
[3] Including alloys.
[4] Secondary aluminium produced from old scrap only.
[5] Sales.
[6] Including pure content of virgin alloys.
[7] Twelve months ending 30 June of year stated.

[1] Source: World Metal Statistics,(Londres).
[2] Source: U.S. Geological Survey, (Washington, D.C.).
[3] Y compris les alliages.
[4] Aluminium de deuxième fusion obtenu à partir de vieux déchets seulement.
[5] Ventes.
[6] Y compris la teneur pure des alliages de première fusion.
[7] Période de douze mois finissant le 30 juin de l'année indiquée.

Aluminium-base alloys
Alliages à base d'aluminium

ISIC-BASED CODE - CODE BASE CITI

3720-23

Unit : Thousand metric tons   Unité : Milliers de tonnes métriques

Country or area	1990	1991	1992	1993	1994	1995	1996	1997	1998	1999	Pays ou zone
America, South	**3**	**3**	**2**	**2**	**3**	**3**	**2**	**1**	**1**	**1**	**Amérique du Sud**
Colombia	...	...	1.6	2.4	2.6	3.4	...	1.3	1.1	...	Colombie
Asia	**549**	**797**	**599**	**525**	**442**	**625**	**647**	**674**	**530**	**652**	**Asie**
Azerbaijan	..	31.7	21.3	14.3	7.7	3.8	0.8	4.8	3.4	1.3	Azerbaïdjan
Indonesia	...	234.0	...	...	12.7	...	...	...	...	...	Indonésie
Japan	326.6	425.2	361.3	283.3	294.6	301.0	312.5	310.3	257.8	276.2	Japon
Korea, Republic of	99.0	106.5	93.6	104.4	126.6	196.9	210.0	235.6	145.6	...	Corée, République de
Europe	**2487**	**2550**	**2489**	**2548**	**2703**	**3252**	**3507**	**3721**	**3761**	**3896**	**Europe**
Austria	...	...	...	...	...	207.5	207.0	239.0	249.0	256.3	Autriche
Croatia	...	...	...	...	...	...	...	3.4	2.2	...	Croatie
Finland[1]	17.9	21.7	27.5	29.7	31.2	33.6	33.0	...	...	...	Finlande[1]
Germany	..	600.5	624.1	464.5	496.2	[1]745.0	[1]708.9	[1]734.2	[1]777.2	...	Allemagne
Germany(Fed.Rep.)	614.2	..	..	..	..	..	..	..	..	...	Allemagne(Rép.féd.)
Hungary	...	...	...	...	...	...	...	152.7	168.0	170.8	Hongrie
Latvia	..	...	...	...	...	...	...	...	...	18.0	Lettonie
Lithuania	...	...	...	...	...	0.7	1.2	0.9	0.5	0.5	Lituanie
Norway	...	...	[2]160.3	[2]194.3	[2]219.3	[3]560.0	[3]791.1	[3]892.6	[3]915.9	952.4	Norvège
Poland	41.5	32.9	26.1	33.2	35.7	35.6	38.9	42.1	63.7	74.0	Pologne
Portugal	...	...	11.9	11.8	11.6	14.3	16.2	16.1	18.1	17.2	Portugal
Slovakia	..	..	...	...	...	...	122.9	128.5	120.7	130.6	Slovaquie
Slovenia	...	14.4	12.4	14.4	18.5	37.9	75.6	98.2	97.6	123.1	Slovénie
Spain	[1]374.7	[1]369.9	[1]373.7	534.9	550.5	545.4	556.0	593.5	...	...	Espagne
Sweden	[1]159.6	[1]113.6	[1]114.1	[1]117.2	121.0	[1]97.1	...	...	...	...	Suède
United Kingdom	...	...	...	...	711.5	656.7	660.1	...	587.6	...	Royaume-Uni
Yugoslavia	..	12.1	9.0	5.0	4.2	6.0	5.5	4.6	7.6	2.3	Yougoslavie
T.F.Yug.Rep. Macedonia	..	2.0	...	...	...	...	...	...	...	...	L'ex-RY Macédoine
Total	**3038**	**3350**	**3090**	**3076**	**3147**	**3881**	**4156**	**4396**	**4293**	**4549**	**Total**

General Note.
Aluminium-base alloys in which aluminium predominates by weight over each of the other metals. (SITC, Rev.3: 68412-1).

Remarque générale.
Alliages à base d'aluminium dans lesquels l'aluminium prédomine en poids sur tous les autres métaux. (CTCI, Rev.3: 68412-1).

[1] Including other aluminium alloys.
[2] Source: World Metal Statistics, (London).
[3] Excluding aluminium alloys in secondary form.

[1] Y compris autres alliages d'aluminium.
[2] Source: World Metal Statistics,(Londres).
[3] Non compris les alliages d'aluminium sous forme secondaires

Aluminium bars, rods, angles, shapes, sections
Barres, cornières et profilés d'aluminium

ISIC-BASED CODE - CODE BASE CITI

3720-25

Unit : Thousand metric tons

Unité : Milliers de tonnes métriques

Country or area	1990	1991	1992	1993	1994	1995	1996	1997	1998	1999	Pays ou zone
Africa	**0**	**0**	**0**	**0**	**0**	**0**	**0**	**0**	**0**	**0**	**Afrique**
Egypt[1]	0.2	0.1	0.2	0.3	0.3	0.3	0.3	0.1	...	...	Egypte[1]
America, North	**1392**	**1283**	**1370**	**1577**	**1462**	**1582**	**1642**	**1836**	**1848**	**2003**	**Amérique du Nord**
Dominican Republic	...	...	103.0	109.6	105.4	127.4	153.5	185.7	...	...	Rép. dominicaine
Mexico	25.4	28.6	29.5	49.8	51.3	30.2	48.1	59.3	64.1	80.3	Mexique
Panama	1.6	...	2.3	1.3	1.4	1.3	1.4	...	...	...	Panama
United States	[2]1267.1	[2]1146.8	[2]1234.8	[3]1415.9	[3]1304.2	[3]1422.9	[3]1439.3	[3]1588.9	[3]1619.3	...	Etats-Unis
America, South	**15**	**15**	**13**	**14**	**15**	**13**	**14**	**16**	**16**	**14**	**Amérique du Sud**
Colombia	...	...	13.2	13.8	14.9	13.4	...	15.7	15.9	...	Colombie
Asia	**1341**	**1360**	**1268**	**1225**	**1290**	**1332**	**1376**	**1415**	**1255**	**1225**	**Asie**
Cyprus	2.9	2.9	3.0	2.9	2.9	3.4	...	...	...	...	Chypre
India	155.0	150.8	120.0	109.5	110.5	141.4	128.1	138.7	135.1	123.1	Inde
Indonesia	...		2.0	3.4	2.6	...	...	...	...	...	Indonésie
Japan[4]	1113.1	1127.9	1067.5	1039.6	1109.6	1108.1	1166.3	1176.7	981.6	982.4	Japon[4]
Turkey	67.0	76.0	75.0	70.0	64.0	76.0	76.0	94.0	132.0	114.0	Turquie
Europe	**1670**	**1717**	**1694**	**1870**	**2051**	**1936**	**1929**	**2110**	**2207**	**2360**	**Europe**
Austria	...	...	...	...	...	70.5	75.0	71.7	73.5	80.2	Autriche
Belgium	[3]92.3	[3]87.4	[3]90.2	[3]75.0	82.9	84.4	94.3	107.3	105.0	110.8	Belgique
Croatia	..	0.1	0.2	0.0	0.0	0.0	0.0	5.3	5.1	...	Croatie
Czechoslovakia(former)	29.2	17.2							..	...	Tchécoslovaquie(anc.)
Finland	5.4	4.2	5.1	4.5	11.3	11.8	11.0	...	...	...	Finlande
France	[5]159.1	[5]152.5	[5]146.7	[5]144.2	[5]161.3	[3]152.8	[3]154.3	[3]168.5	[3]177.1	...	France
Germany	..	369.3	367.0	344.7	382.7	416.0	403.1	441.8	457.8	...	Allemagne
Germany(Fed.Rep.)[4]	360.9	..	..	..	..	..	..	..	..	..	Allemagne(Rép.féd.)[4]
Greece	35.8	42.2	53.5	46.7	65.0	68.2	58.0	64.2	64.9	...	Grèce
Hungary	17.5	...	...	...	...	...	...	33.1	39.4	43.8	Hongrie
Iceland	...	...	...	...	...	...	...	...	11.1	58.3	Islande
Italy	301.8	338.8	349.3	335.4	370.8	367.2	337.5	396.3	414.0	440.4	Italie
Netherlands[6]	155.0	164.0	164.0	190.7	...	...	...	...	...	...	Pays-Bas[6]
Poland	12.7	10.1	9.7	15.3	14.8	20.1	21.6	32.8	34.3	39.9	Pologne
Portugal	...	...	39.8	42.2	48.3	45.7	50.0	57.1	61.4	72.9	Portugal
Romania[4]	44.3	33.8	24.0	24.6	24.7	26.0	23.6	23.6	21.7	21.7	Roumanie[4]
Slovakia	..		...	7.9	15.3	11.4	5.4	6.3	7.9	10.2	Slovaquie
Slovenia	..	20.8	20.1	14.4	28.8	29.4	19.9	24.1	26.5	30.3	Slovénie
Spain	73.3	79.6	67.9	139.0	145.8	157.5	168.8	195.0	222.7	253.1	Espagne
Sweden	28.9	24.6	24.5	25.9	31.8	31.3	32.1	36.0	38.5	39.7	Suède
Switzerland[3]	63.9	60.5	55.0	53.4	60.4	59.7	59.3	65.1	66.5	...	Suisse[3]
United Kingdom	[7]149.7	[3]121.8	[3]124.4	262.4	293.7	[3]137.6	[3]169.6	[3]154.0	184.8	...	Royaume-Uni
Yugoslavia	..	5.8	4.0	2.5	2.7	3.6	3.2	3.9	4.4	1.8	Yougoslavie
T.F.Yug.Rep. Macedonia	..	7.0	4.7	...	...	...	...	...	...	...	L'ex-RY Macédoine
Oceania	**106**	**92**	**95**	**103**	**99**	**99**	**99**	**99**	**99**	**99**	**Océanie**
Australia[8]	105.5	92.5	95.2	103.4	...	...	...	...	...	...	Australie[8]
Total	**4523**	**4468**	**4440**	**4789**	**4918**	**4962**	**5062**	**5476**	**5425**	**5702**	**Total**

General Note.

Rolled, extruded, drawn or forged aluminium products of solid section, of which the maximum cross-sectional dimension exceeds 6 mm and which, if they are flat, have a thickness exceeding one-tenth of the width. (SITC, Rev.3: 68421-0).

Remarque générale.

Produits en aluminium de section pleine, laminés, filés, étirés ou forgés, dont la plus grande dimension transversale est supérieure à 6 mm et, en ce qui concerne les produits plats, dont l'épaisseur dépasse le dixième de la largeur. (CTCI, Rev.3: 68421-0).

[1] Aluminium sections only.
[2] Including bare wire.
[3] Source: World Metal Statistics, (London).
[4] Including products of alloys containing aluminium.
[5] Aluminium and light alloys.
[6] Semi-finished products.
[7] Shipments.
[8] Twelve months ending 30 June of year stated.

[1] Profilés en aluminium seulement.
[2] Y compris les fils nus.
[3] Source: World Metal Statistics,(Londres).
[4] Y compris les produits en alliages contenant de l'aluminium.
[5] Aluminium et alliages légers.
[6] Produits semi-finis.
[7] Expéditions.
[8] Période de douze mois finissant le 30 juin de l'année indiquée.

Aluminium wire
Fil d'aluminium

ISIC-BASED CODE - CODE BASE CITI

3720-28

Unit : Thousand metric tons   Unité : Milliers de tonnes métriques

Country or area	1990	1991	1992	1993	1994	1995	1996	1997	1998	1999	Pays ou zone
Africa	**33**	**30**	**32**	**31**	**32**	**32**	**34**	**33**	**33**	**33**	**Afrique**
Egypt	32.6	29.8	31.6	31.2	31.7	32.5	34.0	33.3	...	...	Egypte
America, North	**265**	**266**	**264**	**272**	**285**	**349**	**361**	**381**	**395**	**462**	**Amérique du Nord**
Mexico	17.8	10.9	9.5	7.4	5.9	7.1	9.2	9.1	13.4	21.6	Mexique
United States	[1]246.8	[1]255.4	[1]254.6	[1]264.8	[1]278.8	[2]342.0	[2]352.0	[2]372.0	[2]381.4	...	Etats-Unis
Asia	**40**	**43**	**48**	**46**	**47**	**64**	**58**	**58**	**56**	**65**	**Asie**
Japan[3]	23.5	26.9	26.3	26.0	24.2	24.7	23.1	...	...	...	Japon[3]
Korea, Republic of	16.2	16.2	21.8	19.6	23.1	39.6	35.1	34.2	32.7	42.1	Corée, République de
Europe	**323**	**331**	**331**	**283**	**262**	**295**	**287**	**276**	**296**	**284**	**Europe**
Belgium[2][4]	38.8	40.0	48.4	45.3	36.0	45.8	33.9	...	...	...	Belgique[2][4]
Croatia	..	0.1	0.0	0.0	0.0	0.0	0.0	0.0	0.0	...	Croatie
Czechoslovakia(former)	13.3	8.1	..	..	..	..	..	..	..	..	Tchécoslovaquie(anc.)
Finland	0.5	0.5	0.3	0.5	0.7	1.3	0.5			...	Finlande
France	103.0	105.4	107.2	73.8	70.7	[2]108.5	[2]99.5	[2]99.8	108.0		France
Germany	..	46.1	45.2	40.5	33.6	16.7	15.9	17.5	25.9	...	Allemagne
Germany(Fed.Rep.)[3]	23.9	..	..	..	..	..	..	..	..	..	Allemagne(Rép.féd.)[3]
Greece	...	...	...	1.5	...	...	...	...	2.7	...	Grèce
Hungary	45.7	24.8	20.7	...	...	...	...	...	...	...	Hongrie
Italy	32.6	34.6	40.0	24.7	27.6	31.5	32.5	25.8	28.3	33.8	Italie
Latvia	..	..	...	...	...	...	0.5	0.4	0.6		Lettonie
Romania	14.7	8.0	1.1	2.7	3.2	3.5	3.6	3.5	0.2	0.1	Roumanie
Slovakia	..	..	...	...	...	...	11.0	11.2	...	9.8	Slovaquie
Slovenia	..	2.2	2.4	2.2	3.1	...	0.5	0.6	0.8	...	Slovénie
Spain	10.1	7.4	8.9	17.5	12.9	3.9	21.0	...	26.8	30.4	Espagne
Sweden[5]	18.4	15.7	17.0	16.4	14.8	24.5	23.0	19.2	15.9	16.6	Suède[5]
Switzerland[2]	1.9	1.4	1.2	1.6	2.8	1.6	1.3	2.4	2.3	...	Suisse[2]
United Kingdom[2]	18.5	20.6	20.2	13.5	10.4	...	...	...	...	...	Royaume-Uni[2]
Yugoslavia	..	13.0	5.1	1.5	2.9	2.4	3.9	2.8	2.4	1.6	Yougoslavie
Total	**660**	**670**	**675**	**632**	**626**	**740**	**740**	**748**	**780**	**845**	**Total**

General Note.
Rolled, extruded or drawn aluminium products of solid section of any cross-sectional shape, of which no cross-sectional dimension exceeds 6 mm. (SITC, Rev.3: 68422-0).

Remarque générale.
Produits en aluminium de section pleine laminés, filés, étirés ou tréfilés, dont la coupe transversale, de forme quelconque, n'excède pas 6 mm dans sa plus grande dimension. (CTCI, Rev.3: 68422-0).

[1] Excluding bare wire.
[2] Source: World Metal Statistics, (London).
[3] Including products of alloys containing aluminium.
[4] Including tubes.
[5] Aluminium wire, rolled only.

[1] Non compris les fils nus.
[2] Source: World Metal Statistics,(Londres).
[3] Y compris les produits en alliages contenant de l'aluminium.
[4] Y compris les tubes.
[5] Fils d'aluminium, laminés seulement.

Aluminium plates, sheets, strip, foil
Tôles, bandes et feuilles d'aluminium

ISIC-BASED CODE - CODE BASE CITI

3720-31

Unit : Thousand metric tons

Unité : Milliers de tonnes métriques

Country or area	1990	1991	1992	1993	1994	1995	1996	1997	1998	1999	Pays ou zone
Africa	**60**	**57**	**53**	**41**	**43**	**67**	**30**	**45**	**42**	**41**	**Afrique**
Cameroon	...	...	...	...	14.1	16.6	...	...	...	...	Cameroun
Egypt	42.5	39.1	35.2	22.9	26.0	49.1	14.5	29.4	...	...	Egypte
United Rep.Tanzania	2.5	2.6	2.8	3.2	2.7	1.2	0.4	0.1	...	...	Rép. Unie de Tanzanie
America, North	**3837**	**3820**	**4123**	**4086**	**4955**	**5111**	**5005**	**5283**	**5403**	**6186**	**Amérique du Nord**
Mexico	38.4	36.6	26.3	51.8	44.6	45.0	44.0	50.4	50.2	49.7	Mexique
United States	3798.6	3783.1	4097.1	4034.0	4910.0	[1]5065.8	[1]4960.5	[1]5232.6	[1]5352.9	...	Etats-Unis
America, South	**7**	**7**	**7**	**6**	**6**	**6**	**6**	**5**	**5**	**4**	**Amérique du Sud**
Colombia	...	...	6.6	6.0	5.9	6.3	...	5.4	5.4	...	Colombie
Asia	**1521**	**1714**	**1556**	**1621**	**1708**	**1970**	**1986**	**2137**	**2056**	**2266**	**Asie**
Armenia	..	18.0	7.3	0.7	1.1	1.4	0.4	0.1	0.1	0.0	Arménie
Azerbaijan	..	14.6	4.7	2.7	1.4	0.9	0.6	0.6	0.3	0.0	Azerbaïdjan
India	78.3	82.8	93.3	...	...	...	...	...	...	...	Inde
Indonesia	17.3	117.5	24.2	120.8	36.5	36.7	...	33.9	6.0	...	Indonésie
Iran(Islamic Rep. of)	[2]42.4	[2]39.3	[2]39.9	[2]46.1	[2]38.0	[3]148.6	[3]100.9	[3]157.4	[3]156.5	...	Iran(Rép. islamique)
Japan[4]	1197.8	1264.6	1208.6	1167.8	1301.5	1362.4	1381.9	1446.2	1418.7	1458.7	Japon[4]
Korea, Republic of	122.1	130.9	134.1	142.2	215.4	282.6	315.9	346.4	318.9	448.1	Corée, République de
Turkey	63.0	46.0	44.0	56.0	29.0	52.0	53.0	68.0	71.0	68.0	Turquie
Europe	**2244**	**2279**	**2368**	**2370**	**2501**	**3347**	**3244**	**3807**	**4001**	**4099**	**Europe**
Austria[5][6]	152.2	144.5	149.8	130.2	141.7	...	87.3	106.5	114.0	124.4	Autriche[5][6]
Belgium	[1]217.4	[1]205.0	[1]166.9	[1]149.0	35.2	[7]31.8	[7]28.4	[7]32.4	[7]35.8	[7]32.1	Belgique
Croatia	..	30.6	21.7	13.3	18.9	20.2	20.1	15.3	20.7	..	Croatie
Czechoslovakia(former)	24.4	17.1	..	..	..	..	..	..	..	..	Tchécoslovaquie(anc.)
Finland	*37.7	*21.3	*17.3	...	...	*19.5	*17.5	14.3	...	...	Finlande
France[8]	37.8	41.6	41.0	39.8	44.1	...	...	...	...	...	France[8]
Germany	..	895.0	951.1	888.3	1018.5	1828.8	1766.2	2124.6	2155.6	..	Allemagne
Germany(Fed.Rep.)[4]	876.0	..	..	..	..	..	..	..	..	..	Allemagne(Rép.féd.)[4]
Greece	56.6	58.3	64.5	78.1	65.8	114.0	113.5	...	141.8	...	Grèce
Hungary	63.2	66.0	74.6	75.7	88.6	72.2	0.0	104.2	96.1	102.1	Hongrie
Italy	255.6	259.5	294.8	300.5	330.1	357.4	346.4	396.3	414.0	440.4	Italie
Poland	4.5	3.9	3.1	7.5	7.5	7.5	7.5	7.5	7.3	12.0	Pologne
Slovakia	..	...	...	...	...	...	0.3	0.2	0.2	0.5	Slovaquie
Slovenia	..	26.0	22.7	23.6	18.4	20.7	35.7	41.2	44.4	51.1	Slovénie
Spain	86.1	94.5	101.4	227.3	246.7	221.6	251.0	256.8	276.9	...	Espagne
Sweden	...	...	...	...	...	3.3	...	...	...	...	Suède
Switzerland[1]	111.1	105.8	108.0	93.1	104.6	108.1	103.2	117.4	107.8	...	Suisse[1]
United Kingdom	[9]318.2	[1]269.4	[1]328.9	[1]309.3	[1]346.4	[1]359.2	[1]406.8	[1]440.7	506.0	...	Royaume-Uni
Yugoslavia	..	37.5	18.7	9.1	9.4	10.6	11.6	13.6	14.4	8.6	Yougoslavie
Oceania	**262**	**265**	**267**	**270**	**280**	**284**	**251**	**270**	**299**	**284**	**Océanie**
Australia[1]	...	...	...	...	279.7	284.2	250.8	270.4	298.5	...	Australie[1]
Total	**7932**	**8142**	**8374**	**8394**	**9492**	**10785**	**10522**	**11548**	**11806**	**12880**	**Total**

General Note.

Flat-surfaced, wrought aluminium products (coiled or not), of which the maximum cross-sectional dimension exceeds 6 mm and of which the thickness exceeds 0.15mm but does not exceed one-tenth of the width (plates, sheets, strip), thin sheets, not exceeding 0.15 mm in thickness, whether or not embossed, cut to shape, perforated, coated, printed or backed with paper or other reinforcing material (aluminium foil). (SITC, Rev.3: 68423-0, 68424-0).

[1] Source: World Metal Statistics, (London).
[2] Production by establishments employing 50 or more persons.
[3] Production by establishments employing 10 or more persons.
[4] Including products of alloys containing aluminium.
[5] Including all other aluminium products.
[6] 1995 data are confidential.
[7] Aluminium foil only.
[8] Aluminium and light alloys.
[9] Shipments.

Remarque générale.

Produits plats en aluminium (enroulés ou non), dont la plus grande dimension transversale est supérieure à 6 mm et dont l'épaisseur, supérieure à 0.15 mm, ne dépasse pas le dixième de la largeur (tôles, feuilles et bandes), feuilles et bandes minces d'une épaisseur de 0.15 mm au maximum, même gaufrées, découpées, perforées, revêtues, imprimées ou fixées sur papier ou support similaire (feuilles minces ou papier d'aluminium). (CTCI, Rev.3: 68423-0, 68424-0).

[1] Source: World Metal Statistics,(Londres).
[2] Production des établissements occupant 50 personnes ou plus.
[3] Production des établissements occupant 10 personnes ou plus.
[4] Y compris les produits en alliages contenant de l'aluminium.
[5] Y compris tous les autres produits en aluminium.
[6] Pour 1995, les données sont confidentielles.
[7] Papier d'aluminium seulement.
[8] Aluminium et alliages légers.
[9] Expéditions.

Aluminium tubes and pipes
Tubes et tuyaux d'aluminium

ISIC-BASED CODE - CODE BASE CITI

3720-34

Unit : Thousand metric tons

Unité : Milliers de tonnes métriques

Country or area	1990	1991	1992	1993	1994	1995	1996	1997	1998	1999	Pays ou zone
Africa	**2**	**2**	**2**	**2**	**2**	**2**	**2**	**2**	**2**	**2**	**Afrique**
Egypt	0.0	0.0	0.1	...	...	0.0	...	...	...	...	Egypte
South Africa	2.0	1.8	...	...	...	...	...	...	...	...	Afrique du Sud
America, North	**135**	**135**	**121**	**131**	**137**	**172**	**184**	**197**	**201**	**232**	**Amérique du Nord**
Mexico	2.3	2.3	2.3	1.3	1.1	0.6	0.9	3.0	3.5	4.9	Mexique
United States	132.2	132.3	118.8	129.9	136.2	[1]171.5	[1]183.3	[1]193.7	[1]197.8	...	Etats-Unis
America, South	**0**	**0**	**0**	**0**	**0**	**0**	**0**	**0**	**0**	**0**	**Amérique du Sud**
Colombia	...	...	0.1	0.1	0.1	0.0	...	0.1	0.1	...	Colombie
Asia	**66**	**66**	**62**	**64**	**66**	**102**	**120**	**127**	**101**	**138**	**Asie**
Japan[2]	58.0	60.8	56.5	54.4	56.0	56.9	60.7	68.6	62.8	62.1	Japon[2]
Korea, Republic of	7.6	5.3	5.3	9.4	10.3	#45.6	58.9	58.8	37.9	...	Corée, République de
Europe	**99**	**93**	**90**	**99**	**99**	**86**	**85**	**91**	**111**	**107**	**Europe**
Belgium[3]	...	...	...	...	...	...	0.1	0.1	0.9	...	Belgique[3]
Croatia	..	0.0	0.0	0.0	0.0	0.0	0.0	0.6	0.4	...	Croatie
Czechoslovakia(former)	5.2	2.1	..	..	..	..	..	..	..	..	Tchécoslovaquie(anc.)
Finland*	0.1	...	...	...	...	...	...	...	...	...	Finlande*
France[4][5]	4.5	4.1	7.8	6.4	7.8	...	...	...	...	...	France[4][5]
Germany	..	30.2	31.0	26.6	27.8	19.9	20.3	19.5	...	...	Allemagne
Germany(Fed.Rep.)[2]	29.9	..	..	..	..	..	..	..	..	..	Allemagne(Rép.féd.)[2]
Greece	1.7	1.5	...	1.9	2.1	2.2	2.2	...	3.3	...	Grèce
Hungary	5.5	...	...	...	...	...	...	6.2	...	...	Hongrie
Italy	17.0	20.0	20.0	20.0	20.0	18.9	17.2	17.4	21.3	24.6	Italie
Romania	4.8	0.0	0.0	0.0	0.3	0.0	0.1	0.0	0.0	0.0	Roumanie
Slovakia	..	..	...	...	...	...	...	...	0.3	0.4	Slovaquie
Slovenia	..	0.6	1.0	0.6	0.6	0.7	0.9	1.1	1.0	1.3	Slovénie
Spain	3.1	4.2	1.8	4.6	5.2	8.8	8.3	10.2	11.0	17.0	Espagne
Sweden	10.4	8.8	9.5	10.8	13.6	13.9	13.4	15.2	15.9	16.6	Suède
United Kingdom	[6]16.8	[6]13.6	[1]9.0	20.5	15.0	[1]5.3	[1]6.6	[1]7.4	24.6	...	Royaume-Uni
Yugoslavia	..	0.7	0.4	0.3	0.2	0.2	0.2	0.3	0.2	0.2	Yougoslavie
T.F.Yug.Rep. Macedonia	..	0.8	0.4	0.3	0.2	0.2	0.2	0.0	0.0	0.0	L'ex-RY Macédoine
Total	**301**	**295**	**274**	**296**	**305**	**362**	**391**	**417**	**415**	**479**	**Total**

General Note.
Seamless and welded tubes and pipes, including blanks therefore, but excluding tube and pipe fittings. (SITC, Rev.3: 68426-0).

Remarque générale.
Tuyaux et tubes sans soudure et soudés, y compris leurs ébauches mais non les accessoires de tuyauterie en aluminium.(CTCI, Rev.3: 68426-0).

[1] Source: World Metal Statistics, (London).
[2] Including products of alloys containing aluminium.
[3] Incomplete coverage.
[4] Aluminium and light alloys.
[5] Including hollow rods of aluminium.
[6] Shipments of aluminium tubes only.

[1] Source: World Metal Statistics,(Londres).
[2] Y compris les produits en alliages contenant de l'aluminium.
[3] Couverture incomplète.
[4] Aluminium et alliages légers.
[5] Y compris les barres creuses en aluminium.
[6] Expéditions de tubes d'aluminium seulement.

Lead, refined, unwrought (total production)
Plomb non travaillé, affiné (production totale)

ISIC-BASED CODE - CODE BASE CITI

3720-37

Unit : Thousand metric tons

Unité : Milliers de tonnes métriques

Country or area	1990	1991	1992	1993	1994	1995	1996	1997	1998	1999	Pays ou zone
Africa	**146**	**143**	**148**	**138**	**120**	**171**	**167**	**171**	**171**	**183**	**Afrique**
Morocco	[1]66.9	[1]72.7	[1]71.4	*70.4	*63.8	101.6	107.6	110.5	115.1	114.2	Maroc
Namibia[2]	35.1	33.4	31.7	31.2	23.8	26.8	8.6	1.5	0.2	0.0	Namibie[2]
Nigeria[1]	3.0	4.5	5.0	4.5	3.9	7.5	5.0	5.0	5.0	...	Nigéria[1]
South Africa	36.0	28.8	36.0	28.8	27.6	34.7	45.0	53.5	[2]50.0	62.4	Afrique du Sud
Zambia	4.8	[1]3.5	[1]3.4	[1]2.9	[1]0.5	[1]0.5	[1]0.4	[1]0.4	[1]0.3	...	Zambie
America, North	**1683**	**1618**	**1674**	**1667**	**1713**	**1867**	**1908**	**1966**	**1963**	**1949**	**Amérique du Nord**
Canada	*184.1	*212.8	*255.1	*220.3	*247.8	281.2	310.8	270.0	262.9	266.4	Canada
Mexico	172.7	174.2	198.7	216.6	185.2	195.6	197.0	245.9	250.1	222.2	Mexique
United States	1326.6	1231.0	1220.0	1230.0	1280.0	1390.0	1400.0	1450.0	1450.0	1460.0	Etats-Unis
America, South	**194**	**187**	**199**	**210**	**214**	**216**	**194**	**189**	**213**	**217**	**Amérique du Sud**
Argentina	*27.0	25.0	30.0	28.0	25.0	29.0	[2]28.1	[2]32.1	[2]30.4	[2]32.4	Argentine
Bolivia[3]	0.4	0.2	0.3	...	...	...	...	...	...	...	Bolivie[3]
Brazil[2]	75.4	64.0	62.8	74.7	84.0	79.0	45.0	44.5	*45.0	*45.0	Brésil[2]
Colombia	...	...	1.5	1.0	1.9	2.6	[2]10.0	[2]10.0	[2]12.0	[2]12.0	Colombie
Peru[2]	74.3	79.5	89.0	92.2	88.1	89.6	94.3	86.0	109.5	111.3	Pérou[2]
Venezuela* [2]	14.0	15.0	15.0	14.0	15.0	16.0	16.0	16.0	16.0	16.0	Venezuela* [2]
Asia	**777**	**957**	**1159**	**1283**	**1200**	**1312**	**1381**	**1436**	**1531**	**1749**	**Asie**
China	296.5	319.7	366.0	410.3	467.9	607.9	715.5	707.5	758.5	945.1	Chine
India* [2]	46.7	47.8	63.7	78.2	81.7	90.0	94.0	93.0	95.0	92.0	Inde* [2]
Indonesia	...	15.0	8.9	7.5	20.5	...	...	...	...	...	Indonésie
Iran(Islamic Rep. of)[2]	...	...	42.0	52.0	40.1	45.2	46.9	49.4	47.0	47.0	Iran(Rép. islamique)[2]
Japan	195.6	207.3	274.5	276.1	250.4	220.5	237.0	248.8	*240.7	227.1	Japon
Kazakhstan[2]	..	...	*210.0	255.0	137.7	*88.5	*70.0	*82.0	*118.6	*160.0	Kazakhstan[2]
Korea,Dem.Ppl's.Rep.* [2]	76.0	80.0	75.0	80.0	80.0	80.0	80.0	80.0	80.0	75.0	Corée,Rép.pop.dém.de* [2]
Korea, Republic of*	76.8	53.5	92.7	100.1	96.5	139.8	98.6	132.6	142.2	153.7	Corée, République de*
Myanmar[2]	1.7	2.2	2.1	1.6	1.8	1.8	2.0	1.8	1.9	1.7	Myanmar[2]
Thailand	16.3	15.7	19.2	17.1	16.9	19.1	17.7	19.1	22.1	26.8	Thaïlande
Turkey* [2]	9.0	8.5	5.1	5.0	6.1	6.0	6.0	9.0	12.0	8.0	Turquie* [2]
Europe	**1733**	**1748**	**1685**	**1630**	**1675**	**1423**	**1493**	**1556**	**1503**	**1391**	**Europe**
Austria[4]	23.2	22.4	[1]23.9	[1]22.6	[1]17.6	[1]21.9	[1]22.9	[1]22.7	[1]23.1	...	Autriche[4]
Belgium	[5]106.8	[5]110.7	[5]116.3	[5]131.1	[2]123.5	* [2]122.0	* [2]125.0	[2]110.8	* [2]120.0	67.8	Belgique
Bulgaria	66.6	56.2	53.1	57.0	64.0	60.1	74.7	72.6	79.9	83.3	Bulgarie
Denmark[6]	1.2	0.4	0.6	0.5	0.5	0.5	0.3	0.5	0.5	0.5	Danemark[6]
Czechoslovakia(former)	23.7	17.8	..	..	..	..	..	..	..	..	Tchécoslovaquie(anc.)
Czech Republic				[1]23.2	[1]25.0	[1]22.0	[1]21.8	[1]21.6	24.4	27.0	République tchèque
France	197.0	205.0	198.1	181.2	180.6	134.0	141.0	131.0	136.0	131.0	France
Germany	..	362.5	354.3	334.1	331.7	220.8	207.6	242.4	217.8	201.6	Allemagne
Germany(Fed.Rep.)* [7][8]	372.7	..	..	..	..	..	..	..	..	..	Allemagne(Rép.féd.)* [7][8]
German D.R.(former)* [3]	45.5	..	..	..	..	..	..	..	..	..	R.D.A. (anc.)* [3]
Greece	[1]0.8	[1]0.9	[1]0.9	..	[1]0.0	2.1	1.6	[1]4.8	1.5	...	Grèce
Italy	170.9	207.6	186.3	182.8	203.6	189.4	209.8	211.6	199.3	215.3	Italie
Netherlands[2]	44.1	33.7	24.3	24.2	25.0	25.0	22.0	19.5	13.2	16.0	Pays-Bas[2]
Poland	64.8	50.8	53.7	62.3	61.2	66.4	66.0	64.7	64.3	64.0	Pologne
Portugal[2]	6.0	5.0	7.4	8.3	12.0	7.7	5.9	6.0	6.0	5.0	Portugal[2]
Romania	20.7	17.2	14.9	18.1	20.3	23.0	19.4	17.7	19.9	17.5	Roumanie
Russian Federation* [2]	..	...	32.5	45.0	34.0	30.0	30.0	52.0	36.0	30.0	Fédération de Russie* [2]
Slovenia	..	22.3	20.7	19.4	17.9	19.5	5.7	6.0	7.3	8.2	Slovénie
Spain	[1]124.0	[1]110.4	[1]62.1	19.4	27.4	27.5	20.5	23.7	...	21.6	Espagne
Sweden[9]	53.4	65.8	72.1	66.1	59.2	62.2	63.0	66.2	64.5	54.4	Suède[9]
Ukraine* [2]	..	...	20.0	17.0	9.0	10.0	21.0	11.0	9.0	9.0	Ukraine* [2]
United Kingdom	[10]329.4	[10]311.0	[10]346.8	[10]363.8	*415.9	[2]320.7	[2]351.4	[2]391.0	[2]350.0	[2]348.0	Royaume-Uni
Yugoslavia	..	44.1	23.3	6.4	4.5	11.5	30.3	23.6	23.8	...	Yougoslavie
T.F.Yug.Rep. Macedonia	..	53.2	51.2	45.5	41.5	46.5	52.8	56.6	57.7	46.8	L'ex-RY Macédoine
Yugoslavia, SFR	82.8	..	..	..	..	..	..	..	..	..	Yougoslavie, RSF
USSR (former)[2]	700.0	..	..	..	..	..	..	..	..	..	URSS (anc.)[2]
Oceania	**214**	**216**	**247**	**244**	**240**	**205**	**224**	**202**	**185**	**197**	**Océanie**
Australia[11]	213.8	216.2	247.4	243.8	240.0	205.0	224.0	202.0	185.0	197.0	Australie[11]

For general note and footnotes, see end of table.

Voir la fin du tableau pour la remarque générale et les notes.

Lead, refined, unwrought (total production) (continued)
Plomb non travaillé, affiné (production totale) (suite)

ISIC-BASED CODE - CODE BASE CITI

3720-37

Unit : Thousand metric tons   Unité : Milliers de tonnes métriques

Country or area	1990	1991	1992	1993	1994	1995	1996	1997	1998	1999	Pays ou zone
Total	5447	4870	5112	5171	5161	5194	5366	5520	5565	5686	Total

General Note.

Soft lead and the lead content of antimonial lead recovered directly from lead ores and concentrates (primary) or from scrap (secondary). Unless otherwise stated, remelted lead (soft and hard lead produced by simple remelting without further processing),lead bullions produced for export and the amount of lead recovered in the form of alloys are excluded. (SITC, Rev.3: 68512-0).

[1] Source: World Metal Statistics, (London).
[2] Source: U. S. Geological Survey, (Washington, D. C.).
[3] Source: Metallgesellschaft Aktiengesellschaft, (Frankfurt).
[4] 1999 data are confidential.
[5] Including lead remelted and recovered in alloys.
[6] Sales.
[7] Including production from imported bullion.
[8] Excluding antimonial lead.
[9] Including secondary remelted soft lead.
[10] Excluding hard lead.
[11] Twelve months ending 30 June of year stated.

Remarque générale.

Plomb antimonieux obtenu directement à partir de minerais et des concentrés de plomb (formes primaires) ou des déchets de plomb (formes secondaires). Sauf avis contraire, le plomb refondu (plomb doux et antimonieux obtenu par simple refonte sans processus ultérieur), le plomb d'oeuvre pour l'exportation et les quantités de plomb obtenues sous forme d'alliages sont exclus. (CTCI, Rev.3: 68512-0).

[1] Source: World Metal Statistics,(Londres).
[2] Source: U.S. Geological Survey, (Washington, D.C.).
[3] Source: "Metallgesellschaft Aktiengesellschaft", (Francfort).
[4] Pour 1999, les données sont confidentielles.
[5] Y compris le plomb refondu et le plomb récupéré à partir des alliages.
[6] Ventes.
[7] Y compris la production obtenue à partir de gueuses importées.
[8] Non compris les plomb antimonieux.
[9] Y compris le plomb refondu de deuxième fusion doux.
[10] Non compris le plomb antimonié.
[11] Période de douze mois finissant le 30 juin de l'année indiquée.

Lead, primary, refined soft
Plomb, neuf, doux affiné

ISIC-BASED CODE - CODE BASE CITI

3720-371A

Unit : Thousand metric tons
Unité : Milliers de tonnes métriques

Country or area	1990	1991	1992	1993	1994	1995	1996	1997	1998	1999	Pays ou zone
Africa	**105**	**107**	**104**	**102**	**85**	**90**	**71**	**66**	**62**	**65**	**Afrique**
Morocco	65.2	70.6	68.6	68.1	60.7	62.4	61.7	64.2	62.0	65.2	Maroc
Namibia[1]	35.1	33.4	31.7	31.2	23.8	26.8	8.6	1.5	0.2	0.0	Namibie[1]
Zambia	4.8	[2]3.5	[2]3.4	[2]2.9	[2]0.5	[2]0.5	[2]0.4	[2]0.4	[2]0.3	...	Zambie
America, North	**660**	**622**	**650**	**672**	**662**	**724**	**689**	**711**	**691**	**662**	**Amérique du Nord**
Canada[3]	87.6	106.8	151.2	151.2	150.0	177.6	192.9	160.8	145.9	148.5	Canada[3]
Mexico	169.1	168.9	194.3	186.0	161.2	172.3	170.0	207.4	208.2	163.8	Mexique
United States	403.7	346.0	305.0	335.0	351.0	374.0	326.0	343.0	337.0	350.0	Etats-Unis
America, South	**113**	**108**	**123**	**127**	**119**	**106**	**95**	**89**	**110**	**112**	**Amérique du Sud**
Argentina	14.0	*11.0	*15.0	*12.0	*7.4	*2.7	[1]0.4	[1]3.3	[1]0.3	[1]0.4	Argentine
Brazil[1]	30.1	22.0	24.5	27.7	24.0	14.0	0.0	0.0	0.0	0.0	Brésil[1]
Peru[1]	69.3	74.5	84.0	87.2	88.1	89.6	94.3	86.0	109.5	111.3	Pérou[1]
Asia	**633**	**790**	**965**	**1057**	**1034**	**1176**	**1219**	**1259**	**1358**	**1567**	**Asie**
China[3]	266.5	279.7	326.0	370.3	427.9	[4]607.9	[4]715.5	[4]707.5	[4]758.5	[4]945.1	Chine[3]
India*[1]	29.9	30.6	40.8	60.0	60.0	62.0	67.0	69.0	70.0	72.0	Inde*[1]
Indonesia	...	5.0	...	...							Indonésie
Iran(Islamic Rep. of)	0.0	0.0	0.0		[2]10.1	* [1]4.0	* [1]7.0	* [1]8.4	* [1]9.0	* [1]9.0	Iran(Rép. islamique)
Japan	187.7	198.2	263.9	242.7	223.2	192.0	182.4	178.8	*178.5	154.8	Japon
Kazakhstan[1]	..	...	*180.0	200.0	* [4]137.7	* [4]88.5	* [4]70.0	* [4]81.5	* [4]118.6	* [4]160.0	Kazakhstan[1]
Korea,Dem.Ppl's.Rep.*[1]	70.0	75.0	70.0	75.0	75.0	75.0	75.0	75.0	75.0	70.0	Corée,Rép.pop.dém.de*[1]
Korea, Republic of	62.8	48.5	67.7	90.1	86.5	129.8	88.6	122.6	132.1	143.6	Corée, République de
Thailand	5.5	5.0	8.5	5.7	5.0	8.0	4.9	4.1	3.2	3.0	Thaïlande
Turkey*[1]	5.4	5.4	3.0	3.0	4.0	4.0	4.0	7.0	8.0	4.0	Turquie*[1]
Europe	**614**	**769**	**753**	**711**	**686**	**640**	**693**	**744**	**696**	**686**	**Europe**
Austria	12.6	6.1	[2]5.7	[2]4.7	[2]0.7	[2]5.5	[2]0.0	[2]0.0	[2]0.0	...	Autriche
France	138.9	153.4	138.6	112.3	105.3	134.0	141.0	131.0	136.0	131.0	France
Germany		158.9	171.1	169.7	161.9	...	...	...	...	...	Allemagne
Germany(Fed.Rep.)*	106.0	..	..	..	..						Allemagne(Rép.féd.)*
Greece	0.8	0.9	0.9	[2]0.0	[2]0.0	[2]0.0	[2]0.0	[2]0.0	[2]0.0	...	Grèce
Italy[3]	68.7	111.1	102.0	89.9	108.5	54.4	65.9	65.7	57.4	67.0	Italie[3]
Romania[3]	12.5	10.4	8.6	11.8	15.2	18.0	13.9	12.7	15.0	13.5	Roumanie[3]
Russian Federation*[1]	..	...	18.0	34.0	[4]34.0	[4]30.0	[4]30.0	[4]52.0	[4]36.0	[4]30.0	Fédération de Russie*[1]
Slovenia	..	9.6	7.8	6.4	7.4	7.2	...	...	...	...	Slovénie
Sweden	35.4	49.2	54.1	46.8	40.2	42.2	...	...	...	...	Suède
United Kingdom	155.9	[1]164.3	[1]198.8	[1]209.6	[1]191.0	[1]149.7	[1]168.1	[1]215.2	[1]185.0	[1]185.0	Royaume-Uni
Yugoslavia	..	44.1	23.3	6.4	4.5	11.5	30.3	23.6	23.8	...	Yougoslavie
T.F.Yug.Rep. Macedonia	..	30.5	24.6	19.4	17.3	22.3	27.2	28.3	27.8	26.3	L'ex-RY Macédoine
Yugoslavia, SFR	82.8	...	..	..	..	..	..	..	..	..	Yougoslavie, RSF
USSR (former)*[1]	420.0	..	..	..	..	..	..	..	..	..	URSS (anc.)*[1]
Oceania	**197**	**197**	**232**	**225**	**220**	**205**	**224**	**202**	**185**	**197**	**Océanie**
Australia[5]	196.8	196.8	231.6	225.0	220.0	205.0	224.0	202.0	185.0	197.0	Australie[5]
Total	**2742**	**2592**	**2828**	**2894**	**2807**	**2941**	**2990**	**3072**	**3103**	**3289**	**Total**

General Note.
Soft lead recovered directly from lead ores and concentrates. (SITC, Rev.3: 68512-1).

Remarque générale.
Plomb doux obtenu directement à partir des minerais et des concentrés de plomb. (CTCI, Rev.3: 68512-1).

[1] Source: U. S. Geological Survey, (Washington, D. C.).
[2] Source: World Metal Statistics, (London).
[3] Including antimonial lead.
[4] Including secondary metal production.
[5] Twelve months ending 30 June of year stated.

[1] Source: U.S. Geological Survey, (Washington, D.C.).
[2] Source: World Metal Statistics,(Londres).
[3] Y compris le plomb antimonié.
[4] Y compris la production de métal de deuxième fusion.
[5] Période de douze mois finissant le 30 juin de l'année indiquée.

Lead, secondary, refined, soft
Plomb, récupéré, doux affiné

ISIC-BASED CODE - CODE BASE CITI

3720-373A

Unit : Thousand metric tons

Unité : Milliers de tonnes métriques

Country or area	1990	1991	1992	1993	1994	1995	1996	1997	1998	1999	Pays ou zone
Africa	**5**	**7**	**8**	**7**	**7**	**47**	**51**	**51**	**58**	**55**	**Afrique**
Morocco	[1]1.7	[1]2.1	[1]2.8	[1]2.3	[1]3.1	39.3	45.8	46.3	53.1	49.0	Maroc
Nigeria[1]	3.0	4.5	5.0	4.5	3.9	7.5	5.0	5.0	5.0	...	Nigéria[1]
America, North	**558**	**528**	**557**	**513**	**625**	**688**	**743**	**772**	**784**	**753**	**Amérique du Nord**
Canada	96.5	105.9	103.9	69.1	97.8	103.6	117.9	109.2	117.0	117.9	Canada
United States	[2]461.5	422.0	453.0	444.0	527.0	584.0	625.0	663.0	667.0	635.0	Etats-Unis
America, South	**88**	**87**	**84**	**93**	**109**	**123**	**104**	**104**	**108**	**110**	**Amérique du Sud**
Argentina	13.0	[1]14.0	[1]15.0	[1]16.0	[1]17.6	[1]26.3	[3]27.7	[3]28.8	[3]30.1	[3]32.0	Argentine
Brazil[3]	45.3	42.0	38.3	47.0	60.0	65.0	45.0	44.5	45.0	45.0	Brésil[3]
Colombia[3]	...	...	...	...	...	...	10.0	10.0	12.0	12.0	Colombie[3]
Peru* [3]	5.0	5.0	5.0	5.0	...	...	...	...	...	...	Pérou* [3]
Venezuela* [3]	14.0	15.0	15.0	14.0	15.0	16.0	16.0	16.0	16.0	16.0	Venezuela* [3]
Asia	**125**	**169**	**188**	**210**	**180**	**212**	**240**	**258**	**256**	**267**	**Asie**
China	* [3]30.0	* [3]40.0	* [3]40.0	40.0	40.0	...	...	...	...	...	Chine
India* [3]	16.8	17.2	22.9	18.2	21.7	28.0	27.0	24.0	25.0	20.0	Inde* [3]
Iran(Islamic Rep. of)[3]	...	...	42.0	35.0	19.9	41.2	39.9	41.0	38.0	38.0	Iran(Rép. islamique)[3]
Japan	7.9	9.1	10.6	33.4	27.2	28.5	54.6	70.0	*62.2	72.0	Japon
Kazakhstan* [3]	..	...	30.0	55.0	...	...	...	...	...	...	Kazakhstan* [3]
Korea,Dem.Ppl's.Rep.* [3]	6.0	5.0	5.0	5.0	5.0	5.0	5.0	5.0	5.0	5.0	Corée,Rép.pop.dém.de* [3]
Korea, Republic of* [3]	14.0	5.0	25.0	10.0	10.0	10.0	10.0	10.0	10.0	10.0	Corée, République de* [3]
Thailand	10.7	10.7	10.7	11.3	12.0	11.2	12.8	15.0	18.9	23.7	Thaïlande
Turkey* [3]	3.6	3.1	2.1	2.0	2.1	2.0	2.0	2.0	4.0	4.0	Turquie* [3]
Europe	**664**	**604**	**570**	**581**	**587**	**698**	**718**	**748**	**702**	**704**	**Europe**
Austria	4.2	[1]16.3	[1]18.2	[1]17.9	[1]16.9	[1]16.4	[1]22.9	[1]22.7	[1]23.1	...	Autriche
Denmark[4]	1.2	0.4	0.6	0.5	0.5	0.5	0.3	0.4	0.5	0.5	Danemark[4]
France	58.1	51.6	59.5	68.9	75.4	...	...	...	...	...	France
Germany	..	203.6	171.1	164.4	161.9	220.8	207.6	242.4	217.8	201.6	Allemagne
Germany(Fed.Rep.)* [5]	266.8	..	..	..	..	..	..	..	..	..	Allemagne(Rép.féd.)* [5]
Greece	...	...	...	...	[1]0.0	2.1	1.6	[1]4.8	1.5	...	Grèce
Italy[6]	102.2	96.5	84.3	92.9	95.1	135.0	143.9	145.9	141.9	148.3	Italie[6]
Netherlands[3]	44.1	33.7	24.3	24.2	25.0	25.0	22.0	19.5	13.2	16.0	Pays-Bas[3]
Portugal[3]	6.0	5.0	7.4	8.3	12.0	7.7	5.9	6.0	6.0	5.0	Portugal[3]
Romania[6]	8.1	6.8	6.3	6.3	5.1	5.0	5.4	5.0	4.9	4.0	Roumanie[6]
Russian Federation* [3]	..	...	14.5	11.0	...	...	...	...	...	...	Fédération de Russie* [3]
Slovenia	..	12.7	12.9	12.9	10.5	12.3	...	...	...	...	Slovénie
Ukraine* [3]	..	...	20.0	17.0	9.0	10.0	21.0	11.0	9.0	9.0	Ukraine* [3]
United Kingdom	[6]173.5	[3]146.7	[3]148.0	[3]154.2	[3]161.4	[3]171.0	[3]177.5	[3]175.8	[3]165.0	[3]163.0	Royaume-Uni
T.F.Yug.Rep. Macedonia	..	3.4	3.2	2.1	1.6	1.7	2.1	2.2	1.4	0.8	L'ex-RY Macédoine
USSR (former)* [3]	280.0	..	..	..	..	..	..	..	..	..	URSS (anc.)* [3]
Oceania	**17**	**19**	**16**	**19**	**20**	**20**	**20**	**21**	**21**	**22**	**Océanie**
Australia* [6] [7]	17.0	19.4	15.8	18.8	20.0	...	...	...	...	...	Australie* [6] [7]
Total	**1737**	**1414**	**1423**	**1423**	**1528**	**1788**	**1875**	**1954**	**1929**	**1911**	**Total**

General Note.
Secondary soft lead recovered from scrap or other similar materials. (SITC, Rev.3: 68512-3).

Remarque générale.
Plomb doux de deuxième fusion récupéré à partir des déchets de plomb. (CTCI, Rev.3: 68512-3).

[1] Source: World Metal Statistics, (London).
[2] Including remelted lead.
[3] Source: U. S. Geological Survey, (Washington, D. C.).
[4] Sales.
[5] Including production from imported bullion.
[6] Including antimonial lead.
[7] Twelve months ending 30 June of year stated.

[1] Source: World Metal Statistics,(Londres).
[2] Y compris le plomb refondu.
[3] Source: U.S. Geological Survey, (Washington, D.C.).
[4] Ventes.
[5] Y compris la production obtenue à partir de gueuses importées.
[6] Y compris le plomb antimonié.
[7] Période de douze mois finissant le 30 juin de l'année indiquée.

Lead-base alloys
Alliages à base de plomb

ISIC-BASED CODE - CODE BASE CITI
3720-38

Unit : Thousand metric tons   Unité : Milliers de tonnes métriques

Country or area	1990	1991	1992	1993	1994	1995	1996	1997	1998	1999	Pays ou zone
Africa	**37**	**30**	**36**	**28**	**27**	**35**	**45**	**54**	**66**	**62**	**Afrique**
South Africa	37.2	30.3	36.2	28.4	26.9	34.7	45.0	53.5	65.7	61.9	Afrique du Sud
America, South	**5**	**5**	**4**	**3**	**3**	**8**	**3**	**2**	**1**	**1**	**Amérique du Sud**
Colombia	...	...	4.3	2.6	2.8	8.0	...	2.0	0.9	...	Colombie
Asia	**7**	**7**	**16**	**5**	**0**	**7**	**7**	**7**	**7**	**7**	**Asie**
Indonesia	...	...	16.4	4.9	0.0	...	...	...	...	...	Indonésie
Europe	**82**	**108**	**104**	**111**	**135**	**164**	**138**	**185**	**242**	**240**	**Europe**
Belgium [1]	...	...	...	...	50.0	45.0	36.7	38.7	32.9	57.4	Belgique [1]
Germany	..	1.0	0.9	0.5	0.5	...	...	...	[1]70.4	...	Allemagne
Germany(Fed.Rep.)	0.8	..	..	..	..	...	...	...	..	..	Allemagne(Rép.féd.)
Italy	4.5	4.4	3.9	3.5	3.2	3.8	3.9	19.6	19.9	18.2	Italie
Slovenia	..	...	7.2	7.1	6.5	6.7	8.0	8.5	6.8	6.0	Slovénie
Spain [1]	12.8	19.6	24.8	36.3	48.4	67.9	46.5	...	...	...	Espagne [1]
Sweden [1]	20.5	21.9	19.2	18.3	22.7	20.9	21.5	19.7	22.8	29.5	Suède [1]
Yugoslavia	..	5.7	2.6	0.1	1.0	1.8	4.2	4.4	2.3	...	Yougoslavie
T.F.Yug.Rep. Macedonia	..	4.7	2.5	1.6	...	...	...	...	...	...	L'ex-RY Macédoine
Total	**132**	**150**	**161**	**147**	**165**	**213**	**194**	**247**	**316**	**310**	**Total**

General Note.
Lead-base alloys in which lead predominates by weight over each of the other metals. (SITC, Rev.3: 68511-1).

Remarque générale.
Alliages à base de plomb dans lesquels le plomb prédomine en poids sur tous les autres métaux. (CTCI, Rev.3: 68511-1).

[1] Including other lead alloys.

[1] Y compris autres alliages de plomb.

Lead tubes and pipes
Tuyaux et tubes de plomb

ISIC-BASED CODE - CODE BASE CITI

3720-40

Unit : Metric tons

Unité : Tonnes métriques

Country or area	1990	1991	1992	1993	1994	1995	1996	1997	1998	1999	Pays ou zone
Africa	168	231	99	3	15	0	0	0	0	0	**Afrique**
Tunisia	168	231	99	3	15	0	0	0	0	0	Tunisie
Asia	5026	4432	4175	3563	3104	2936	3040	2983	2820	1690	**Asie**
Japan	5026	4432	4175	3563	3104	2936	3040	2983	2820	...	Japon
Europe	7231	7037	5107	4731	4387	4315	3953	3900	3483	2931	**Europe**
Croatia	..	350	205	216	251	256	174	156	55	...	Croatie
France	[1]1008	[1]780	[1]756	[1]607	...	...	...	[2]573	[2]521	...	France
Germany	..	711	451	409	329	352	172	372	...	...	Allemagne
Germany(Fed.Rep.)	616	..	..	..	..	..	..	..	..	...	Allemagne(Rép.féd.)
Greece	1188	965	668	...	...	...	...	...	...	...	Grèce
Italy	2900	3100	2200	1400	1000	900	800	700	700	500	Italie
Spain	1519	1131	827	...	...	...	...	...	...	...	Espagne
Total	12425	11700	9381	8297	7506	7251	6993	6883	6303	4620	**Total**

General Note.

Seamless and welded tubes and pipes, including blanks therefore, but excluding tube and pipe fittings. (SITC, Rev.3: 68524-1).

Remarque générale.

Tuyaux et tubes sans soudure ou soudés, y compris leurs ébauches mais non les accessoires de tuyauterie. (CTCI, Rev.3: 68524-1).

[1] Pipes, tubes and hollow rods of lead.
[2] Source: World Metal Statistics, (London).

[1] Tubes, tuyaux et barres creuses en plomb.
[2] Source: World Metal Statistics,(Londres).

Zinc, unwrought (total production)
Zinc non travaillé, affiné (production totale)

ISIC-BASED CODE - CODE BASE CITI

3720-43

Unit : Thousand metric tons   Unité : Milliers de tonnes métriques

Country or area	1990	1991	1992	1993	1994	1995	1996	1997	1998	1999	Pays ou zone
Africa	**64**	**61**	**56**	**39**	**22**	**22**	**26**	**31**	**24**	**25**	**Afrique**
Algeria	15.0	24.9	29.4	29.7	20.1	21.9	26.3	31.4	23.7	24.9	Algérie
Dem. Rep. of Congo* [1]	38.2	28.3	18.8	4.2	1.0	0.0	0.0	0.0	0.0	...	Rép. dém. du Congo* [1]
Zambia	10.4	7.3	7.3	[2]4.7	[2]1.0	[2]0.0	[2]0.0	[2]0.0	[2]0.0	...	Zambie
America, North	**1058**	**1128**	**1186**	**1258**	**1269**	**1309**	**1317**	**1307**	**1390**	**1369**	**Amérique du Nord**
Canada	591.8	660.6	671.7	661.9	692.9	720.4	716.5	699.8	780.8	776.9	Canada
Mexico	108.2	91.2	114.6	214.2	220.1	225.9	234.6	241.1	241.0	220.3	Mexique
United States	358.4	376.0	399.6	382.0	356.0	363.0	366.0	366.0	368.0	372.0	Etats-Unis
America, South	**309**	**354**	**349**	**385**	**414**	**403**	**406**	**406**	**410**	**399**	**Amérique du Sud**
Argentina*	33.4	36.3	37.3	33.6	38.0	38.5	39.6	41.8	43.1	42.6	Argentine*
Brazil	154.1	[1]163.0	[1]187.4	[1]194.8	[1]194.0	[1]206.0	[1]193.3	[1]192.7	* [1]192.7	* [1]175.3	Brésil
Peru [1]	121.0	154.6	124.0	157.0	182.0	159.0	173.1	171.7	174.7	180.8	Pérou [1]
Asia	**1872**	**2241**	**2445**	**2663**	**2720**	**2714**	**2753**	**3110**	**3280**	**3512**	**Asie**
China	551.8	612.1	718.9	891.4	1077.6	1076.7	1163.8	1434.4	1491.9	1669.8	Chine
India	79.1	85.8	[1]152.1	[1]165.7	* [1]180.4	* [1]171.0	* [1]168.0	* [1]183.0	* [1]197.0	* [1]200.0	Inde
Indonesia	...	...	23.1	37.3	24.2	...	...	...	...	...	Indonésie
Japan	687.5	730.8	729.5	695.7	665.5	663.6	599.1	603.1	607.9	633.4	Japon
Kazakhstan* [1]		260.0	263.0	172.4	169.2	190.0	189.0	241.6	247.0		Kazakhstan* [1]
Korea,Dem.Ppl's.Rep.* [1]	200.0	175.0	175.0	200.0	200.0	200.0	200.0	200.0	180.0	180.0	Corée,Rép.pop.dém.de* [1]
Korea, Republic of	257.0	258.8	255.9	276.4	271.9	279.3	286.6	335.4	390.1	429.8	Corée, République de
Thailand	63.3	63.6	61.3	58.9	58.5	56.2	72.4	84.1	91.0	97.3	Thaïlande
Uzbekistan* [1]	..	...	65.0	65.0	70.0	70.0	45.0	53.0	52.0	27.0	Ouzbékistan* [1]
Viet Nam* [1]	...	...	...	10.0	0.0	0.0	0.0	0.0	0.0	...	Viet Nam* [1]
Europe	**2439**	**2729**	**2821**	**2813**	**2621**	**2663**	**2684**	**2737**	**2712**	**2669**	**Europe**
Austria [3]	23.2	12.3	[2]0.6	[2]0.0	[2]0.0	[2]0.0	[2]0.0	[2]0.0	[2]0.0	...	Autriche [3]
Belgium	[4]356.5	[4]385.1	[4]310.6	[4]399.6	[1]306.2	[1]301.1	[1]234.4	* [1]244.0	[1]205.0	[1]232.4	Belgique
Bulgaria	75.5	58.7	57.8	54.0	64.0	68.8	68.0	70.4	72.6	70.2	Bulgarie
Denmark [5]	1.6	1.0	1.8	1.5	1.4	1.4	1.2	0.8	0.0	0.2	Danemark [5]
Czechoslovakia(former)	1.0	0.8	..	..	..	..	..	..	..		Tchécoslovaquie(anc.)
Czech Republic* [1]	..	...	...	1.1	1.0	1.0	1.0	1.0	1.0	1.0	République tchèque* [1]
Finland	163.1	170.4	170.5	171.1	173.2	178.6	176.3	175.3	199.0	225.2	Finlande
France	276.8	312.3	318.7	323.5	322.3	286.0	321.0	329.0	333.0	331.0	France
Germany	..	345.7	383.1	380.9	359.9	345.0	352.3	335.9	357.3	[1]330.0	Allemagne
Germany(Fed.Rep.)	337.6										Allemagne(Rép.féd.)
German D.R.(former)	13.0	..	..	..	..	..	..	..	..	..	R.D.A. (anc.)
Italy	248.1	256.0	252.6	253.6	255.9	260.2	268.7	268.3	231.6	145.3	Italie
Netherlands	208.5	212.1	218.4	[2]206.0	[2]212.6	[2]206.3	[2]207.4	[2]200.5	[2]217.1	...	Pays-Bas
Norway	124.8	129.3	129.5	133.7	131.9	121.4	125.6	[2]137.4	[2]128.1	* [1]130.0	Norvège
Poland	132.1	126.1	134.6	149.1	157.6	164.4	165.5	172.9	178.0	177.8	Pologne
Romania	11.5	8.7	11.6	14.1	18.5	28.3	28.2	30.2	29.3	28.7	Roumanie
Russian Federation* [1]	..	..	245.0	203.0	138.0	166.0	172.0	189.0	192.0	225.0	Fédération de Russie* [1]
Slovakia* [1]	..	..	...	1.0	1.0	1.0	1.0	1.0	1.0	1.0	Slovaquie* [1]
Slovenia	..	0.5	0.5	0.3	0.3	0.6	0.5	0.5	0.7	0.4	Slovénie
Spain	248.1	262.2	351.9	[2]327.6	[2]298.7	[2]358.2	[2]362.8	[2]377.8	[2]385.0	* [1]375.0	Espagne
Switzerland	10.3	9.4	9.3	9.6	8.9	8.9	...	...	...	...	Suisse
Ukraine* [1]	..	..	15.0	15.0	14.0	5.0	2.0	2.0	0.0	0.0	Ukraine* [1]
United Kingdom	93.3	100.7	96.8	102.4	101.3	106.0	96.9	107.7	[2]99.6	* [1]130.0	Royaume-Uni
Yugoslavia	..	41.4	15.9	9.2	4.5	6.3	31.1	31.4	15.6	0.8	Yougoslavie
T.F.Yug.Rep. Macedonia	..	93.7	95.1	57.0	49.6	46.7	59.2	53.1	57.2	49.6	L'ex-RY Macédoine
Yugoslavia, SFR [6]	113.8	..	..	..	..	..	..	..	..	..	Yougoslavie, RSF [6]
USSR (former)* [1]	890.0	..	..	..	..	..	..	..	..	..	URSS (anc.)* [1]
Oceania	**299**	**325**	**329**	**337**	**320**	**312**	**330**	**319**	**304**	**323**	**Océanie**
Australia [7]	299.2	324.9	329.5	336.5	320.0	312.0	330.0	319.0	304.0	323.0	Australie [7]
Total	**6931**	**6837**	**7186**	**7495**	**7366**	**7424**	**7517**	**7911**	**8119**	**8298**	**Total**

For general note and footnotes, see end of table.   Voir la fin du tableau pour la remarque générale et les notes.

General Note.

Zinc recovered from zinc ores and concentrates and distilled zinc and zinc produced directly from ores by electrolysis (primary), zinc recovered from scrap (secondary). Unless otherwise stated, remelted zinc (metal produced by simple remelting without further processing) and the amount of zinc recovered in the form of alloys are excluded. (SITC, Rev.3: 68611-0).

[1] Source: U. S. Geological Survey, (Washington, D. C.).
[2] Source: World Metal Statistics, (London).
[3] 1999 data are confidential.
[4] Including zinc remelted and recovered in alloys.
[5] Sales.
[6] Including zinc dust.
[7] Twelve months ending 30 June of year stated.

Remarque générale.

Zinc obtenu à partir des minerais et des concentrés de zinc, zinc distillé et zinc obtenu directement à partir de minerais par électrolyse (formes primaires), zinc obtenu à partir de déchets (formes secondaires). Sauf avis contraire, le zinc refondu (zinc obtenu par simple refonte sans processus ultérieur) et les quantités de zinc obtenues sous forme d'alliages sont exclus. (CTCI, REv.3: 68611-0).

[1] Source: U.S. Geological Survey, (Washington, D.C.).
[2] Source: World Metal Statistics,(Londres).
[3] Pour 1999, les données sont confidentielles.
[4] Y compris le zinc refondu et récupéré à partir des alliages.
[5] Ventes.
[6] Y compris la poudre de zinc.
[7] Période de douze mois finissant le 30 juin de l'année indiquée.

Zinc, unwrought, primary
Zinc, neuf, affiné

ISIC-BASED CODE - CODE BASE CITI

3720-431

Unit : Thousand metric tons

Unité : Milliers de tonnes métriques

Country or area	1990	1991	1992	1993	1994	1995	1996	1997	1998	1999	Pays ou zone
Africa	**64**	**61**	**56**	**39**	**22**	**22**	**26**	**31**	**24**	**25**	**Afrique**
Algeria	15.0	24.9	29.4	29.7	20.1	21.9	26.3	31.4	23.7	24.9	Algérie
Dem. Rep. of Congo* [1]	38.2	28.3	18.8	4.2	1.0	0.0	0.0	0.0	0.0	...	Rép. dém. du Congo* [1]
Zambia	10.4	7.3	7.3	[2]4.7	[2]1.0	[2]0.0	[2]0.0	[2]0.0	[2]0.0	...	Zambie
America, North	**963**	**1005**	**1058**	**1116**	**1130**	**1178**	**1177**	**1167**	**1256**	**1238**	**Amérique du Nord**
Canada	591.8	660.6	671.7	661.9	692.9	720.4	716.5	699.8	780.8	776.9	Canada
Mexico	108.2	91.2	114.6	214.2	220.1	225.9	234.6	241.1	241.0	220.3	Mexique
United States	262.7	253.0	272.0	240.0	217.0	232.0	226.0	226.0	234.0	241.0	Etats-Unis
America, South	**301**	**346**	**339**	**376**	**404**	**394**	**396**	**396**	**400**	**389**	**Amérique du Sud**
Argentina	30.7	33.5	34.5	31.1	35.2	35.7	36.7	38.7	39.9	40.1	Argentine
Brazil [1]	149.5	157.5	180.4	187.6	*187.0	199.0	186.3	185.7	*185.7	*168.3	Brésil [1]
Peru [1]	121.0	154.6	124.0	157.0	182.0	159.0	173.1	171.7	174.7	180.8	Pérou [1]
Asia	**1264**	**1349**	**1382**	**1408**	**1413**	**1394**	**1324**	**1412**	**1467**	**1489**	**Asie**
India	79.1	85.8	[1]128.1	[1]141.7	[1]156.4	[1]146.5	[1]143.6	* [1]159.0	[1]171.9	[1]175.0	Inde
Japan	664.2	702.8	696.9	666.4	656.3	652.7	589.2	592.6	597.1	601.9	Japon
Korea,Dem.Ppl's.Rep.* [1]	200.0	175.0	175.0	200.0	200.0	200.0	200.0	200.0	180.0	180.0	Corée,Rép.pop.dém.de* [1]
Korea, Republic of	257.0	258.8	255.9	276.4	271.9	279.3	286.6	335.4	390.1	429.8	Corée, République de
Thailand	63.3	63.6	61.3	58.9	58.5	45.7	59.7	72.0	75.9	75.6	Thaïlande
Uzbekistan* [1]	..	...	65.0	65.0	70.0	70.0	45.0	53.0	52.0	27.0	Ouzbékistan* [1]
Europe	**2079**	**2411**	**2463**	**2453**	**2299**	**2269**	**2267**	**2349**	**2255**	**2219**	**Europe**
Austria	22.2	...	...	...	...	...	...	...	...	...	Autriche
Belgium	[3]356.5	[3]385.1	[3]310.6	[3]399.6	[1][4]306.2	[1][4]301.1	[1][4]234.4	[1][4]244.0	[1][4]205.0	[1][4]232.4	Belgique
Bulgaria	75.5	58.7	57.8	54.0	64.0	68.8	68.0	70.4	72.6	70.2	Bulgarie
Czechoslovakia(former)	1.0	0.8									Tchécoslovaquie(anc.)
France	264.7	299.6	304.7	309.8	293.0	286.0	321.0	329.0	333.0	331.0	France
Germany	..	299.5	328.6	331.2	300.5	237.6	226.8	...	...	...	Allemagne
Germany(Fed.Rep.)	287.7	..	..	..	..	..	..	..	..	..	Allemagne(Rép.féd.)
German D.R.(former) [4]	13.0	..	..	..	..	..	..	..	..	..	R.D.A. (anc.) [4]
Italy	[4]248.1	[4]256.0	[4]252.6	221.4	224.1	230.2	233.7	237.5	189.9	107.6	Italie
Netherlands	208.5	212.1	218.4	[2]206.0	[2]212.6	[2]206.3	[2]207.4	[2]200.5	[2]217.1	...	Pays-Bas
Norway	124.8	129.3	129.5	133.7	131.9	121.4	125.6	[2]137.4	[2]128.1	* [1]130.0	Norvège
Poland [4]	132.1	126.1	134.6	149.1	157.6	166.4	165.5	172.9	178.0	177.8	Pologne [4]
Romania [4]	11.5	8.7	11.6	14.1	18.5	28.3	28.2	30.2	29.3	28.7	Roumanie [4]
Russian Federation* [1]	..	...	185.0	170.0	[4]138.0	[4]166.0	[4]172.0	[4]189.0	[4]192.0	[4]225.0	Fédération de Russie* [1]
Slovenia	..	0.5	0.5	0.3	0.3	0.6	0.5	0.5	0.7	0.4	Slovénie
Spain	*239.7	248.7	338.8	...	...	...	...	...	...	...	Espagne
United Kingdom [4]	93.3	100.7	96.8	102.4	101.3	106.0	96.9	107.7	99.6	* [1]130.0	Royaume-Uni [4]
Yugoslavia	..	38.4	14.2	7.0	3.9	6.0	30.0	29.8	14.4	0.7	Yougoslavie
T.F.Yug.Rep. Macedonia	..	54.8	56.9	57.0	49.6	46.7	59.2	53.1	57.2	49.6	L'ex-RY Macédoine
USSR (former)* [1]	780.0	..	..	..	..	..	..	..	..	..	URSS (anc.)* [1]
Oceania	**295**	**320**	**325**	**332**	**315**	**312**	**330**	**319**	**304**	**323**	**Océanie**
Australia [5]	294.7	320.4	325.0	332.0	315.0	312.0	330.0	319.0	304.0	323.0	Australie [5]
Total	**5744**	**5491**	**5623**	**5724**	**5584**	**5569**	**5521**	**5675**	**5705**	**5683**	**Total**

General Note.

Zinc recovered from zinc ores and concentrates and distilled zinc and zinc produced directly from ores by electrolysis. (SITC, Rev.3: 68611-1).

Remarque générale.

Zinc de première fusion obtenu à partir des minerais et concentrés de zinc, zinc distilé et zinc obtenu directement à partir des minerais par électrolyse. (CTCI, Rev.3: 68611-1).

[1] Source: U. S. Geological Survey, (Washington, D. C.).
[2] Source: World Metal Statistics, (London).
[3] Including zinc remelted and recovered in alloys.
[4] Including secondary metal production.
[5] Twelve months ending 30 June of year stated.

[1] Source: U.S. Geological Survey, (Washington, D.C.).
[2] Source: World Metal Statistics,(Londres).
[3] Y compris le zinc refondu et récupéré à partir des alliages.
[4] Y compris la production de métal de deuxième fusion.
[5] Période de douze mois finissant le 30 juin de l'année indiquée.

Zinc, unwrought, secondary
Zinc, récupéré, affiné

ISIC-BASED CODE - CODE BASE CITI

3720-432

Unit : Thousand metric tons

Unité : Milliers de tonnes métriques

Country or area	1990	1991	1992	1993	1994	1995	1996	1997	1998	1999	Pays ou zone
America, North	**96**	**122**	**128**	**141**	**139**	**131**	**140**	**140**	**134**	**131**	**Amérique du Nord**
United States	95.7	122.5	127.6	141.0	139.0	131.0	140.0	140.0	134.0	131.0	Etats-Unis
America, South	**7**	**8**	**10**	**10**	**10**	**10**	**10**	**10**	**10**	**10**	**Amérique du Sud**
Argentina[1]	2.7	2.8	2.8	2.5	2.8	2.8	2.9	3.1	3.1	2.5	Argentine[1]
Brazil[1]	4.6	5.5	7.0	7.2	*7.0	*7.0	*7.0	*7.0	*7.0	*7.0	Brésil[1]
Asia	**47**	**52**	**57**	**53**	**33**	**35**	**34**	**35**	**36**	**54**	**Asie**
India*[1]	...	...	24.0	24.0	24.0	24.0	24.0	24.0	25.0	25.0	Inde*[1]
Japan	23.3	28.1	32.6	29.3	9.2	10.9	9.8	10.5	10.8	29.3	Japon
Europe	**100**	**201**	**230**	**160**	**196**	**230**	**255**	**235**	**254**	**262**	**Europe**
Austria	0.2	...	...	...	...	...	...	...	...	...	Autriche
Denmark[2]	1.6	1.0	1.8	1.5	1.4	1.4	1.2	0.8	0.0	...	Danemark[2]
Czech Republic*[1]	..	...	...	1.1	1.0	1.0	1.0	1.0	1.0	1.0	République tchèque*[1]
France	12.1	12.6	14.1	13.6	29.3	...	...	...	...	...	France
Germany	..	46.2	54.5	49.8	59.3	107.4	125.5	...	...	...	Allemagne
Germany(Fed.Rep.)	49.9	..	..	..	..	..	..	..	..	..	Allemagne(Rép.féd.)
Italy	...	...	...	32.2	31.8	30.0	35.0	30.8	41.7	37.7	Italie
Russian Federation*[1]	..	...	60.0	33.0	...	...	...	...	...	...	Fédération de Russie*[1]
Spain	*8.4	13.5	13.1	...	...	...	...	...	...	...	Espagne
Ukraine*[1]	..	.,..	15.0	15.0	14.0	5.0	2.0	2.0	0.0	0.0	Ukraine*[1]
Yugoslavia	..	3.0	1.7	2.2	0.6	0.4	1.1	1.7	1.2	...	Yougoslavie
T.F.Yug.Rep. Macedonia	..	38.9	38.2	0.0	0.0	0.0	0.0	0.0	0.0	...	L'ex-RY Macédoine
USSR (former)*[1]	110.0	..	..	..	..	..	..	..	..	..	URSS (anc.)*[1]
Oceania	**5**	**5**	**5**	**5**	**5**	**5**	**5**	**5**	**5**	**5**	**Océanie**
Australia[3]	4.5	4.5	4.5	4.5	5.0	...	...	...	...	...	Australie[3]
Total	**364**	**389**	**428**	**369**	**383**	**411**	**443**	**425**	**439**	**462**	**Total**

General Note.

Secondary zinc recovered from waste and scrap. Remelted zinc (metal produced by simple remelting without further processing) and the amount of zinc recovered in the form of alloys are excluded. (SITC, Rev.3: 68611-2).

Remarque générale.

Zinc de deuxième fusion obtenu à partir de déchets et de débris d'ouvrages. Zinc refondu (le zinc obtenu par simple refonte sans processus ultérieur) et les quantités de zinc obtenues sous forme d'alliages sont exclus. (CTCI, Rev.3: 68611-2).

[1] Source: U. S. Geological Survey, (Washington, D. C.).
[2] Sales.
[3] Twelve months ending 30 June of year stated.

[1] Source: U.S. Geological Survey, (Washington, D.C.).
[2] Ventes.
[3] Période de douze mois finissant le 30 juin de l'année indiquée.

Zinc-base alloys
Alliages à base de zinc

ISIC-BASED CODE - CODE BASE CITI
3720-44

Unit : Thousand metric tons   Unité : Milliers de tonnes métriques

Country or area	1990	1991	1992	1993	1994	1995	1996	1997	1998	1999	Pays ou zone
America, South	**1**	**1**	**1**	**1**	**1**	**1**	**1**	**1**	**1**	**1**	**Amérique du Sud**
Colombia	...	...	0.6	0.7	1.0	1.3	...	1.2	1.1	...	Colombie
Europe	**163**	**279**	**264**	**248**	**304**	**297**	**315**	**332**	**365**	**296**	**Europe**
Austria	5.1	...	...	...	...	...	...	...	...	...	Autriche
Finland [1]	5.8	5.3	5.1	4.1	14.8	...	...	...	...	...	Finlande [1]
Germany	..	119.5	114.0	77.4	77.8	[1]53.2	[1]69.9	[1]77.2	[1]88.9	...	Allemagne
German D.R.(former) [1]	5.4	..	..	..	..	..	..	..	..	...	R.D.A. (anc.) [1]
Hungary	1.1	0.5	0.1	...	...	...	...	...	...	...	Hongrie
Italy	60.8	56.6	52.3	59.3	65.5	68.6	70.2	67.6	68.3	38.4	Italie
Norway [1]	5.0	4.9	5.3	5.4	...	...	...	...	...	...	Norvège [1]
Slovakia	..	..	...	...	...	...	...	...	0.1	0.1	Slovaquie
Slovenia	..	1.9	0.2	0.2	0.4	0.5	0.2	0.3	0.2	0.3	Slovénie
Spain	28.4	25.8	23.9	52.8	62.7	77.5	69.7	90.9	99.2	84.9	Espagne
United Kingdom	...	...	...	42.1	71.2	61.4	58.5	66.5	77.0	...	Royaume-Uni
Yugoslavia	..	0.7	0.8	0.3	0.1	0.2	0.3	0.6	0.6	0.0	Yougoslavie
T.F.Yug.Rep. Macedonia	..	4.6	0.9	0.7	0.5	12.2	21.4	2.7	2.4	1.9	L'ex-RY Macédoine
Total	**164**	**279**	**264**	**249**	**305**	**298**	**316**	**333**	**366**	**297**	**Total**

General Note.
Zinc-base alloys in which zinc predominates by weight over each of the other metals. (SITC, REv.3: 68612-1).

Remarque générale.
Alliages à base de zinc dans lesquels le zinc prédomine en poids sur tous les autres métaux. (CTCI, Rev.3: 68612-1).

[1] Including other zinc alloys.

[1] Y compris les autres alliages de zinc.

Zinc plates, sheets, strip, foil
Tôles, plaques, bandes et feuilles de zinc

ISIC-BASED CODE - CODE BASE CITI
3720-46

Unit : Thousand metric tons Unité : Milliers de tonnes métriques

Country or area	1990	1991	1992	1993	1994	1995	1996	1997	1998	1999	Pays ou zone
America, South	**8**	**8**	**0**	**8**	**15**	**8**	**8**	**8**	**8**	**8**	**Amérique du Sud**
Colombia	...	...	0.4	...	15.5	...	...	...	...	...	Colombie
Asia	**2**	**3**	**4**	**4**	**3**	**5**	**5**	**5**	**4**	**4**	**Asie**
Turkey	1.9	2.8	3.7	4.2	3.5	4.6	4.6	4.9	4.2	4.3	Turquie
Europe	**180**	**201**	**199**	**203**	**209**	**201**	**201**	**178**	**178**	**142**	**Europe**
France	93.7	94.9	89.5	92.4	92.1	...	...	[1]66.0	[1]65.8	...	France
Germany	..	78.3	...	...	...	...	...	...	...	...	Allemagne
Germany(Fed.Rep.)	68.3	..	..	..	..	..	..	..	..	..	Allemagne(Rép.féd.)
Hungary	2.8	2.3	5.0	...	5.5	...	...	...	...	...	Hongrie
Italy	...	[1]9.0	[1]10.8	[1]13.6	[1]14.9	[1]16.8	[1]16.1	[1]15.0	15.0	16.0	Italie
Slovenia		6.7	7.1	8.6	9.5	10.5	10.2	11.2	11.7	10.6	Slovénie
United Kingdom[1][2]	3.6	3.6	4.1	4.0	4.6	3.0	3.0	3.3	3.3	...	Royaume-Uni[1][2]
T.F.Yug.Rep. Macedonia	..	6.5	4.5	2.8	3.8	3.9	4.2	0.7	0.3	0.1	L'ex-RY Macédoine
Total	**190**	**212**	**203**	**216**	**228**	**214**	**213**	**191**	**190**	**154**	**Total**

General Note.

Flat-surfaced, wrought zinc products (coiled or not), of which the maximum cross-sectional dimension exceeds 6 mm, and of which the thickness exceeds 0.15 mm but does not exceed one-tenth of the width (plates, sheets, strip), thin sheets, not exceeding 0.15 mm in thickness, whether or not embossed, cut to shape, perforated, coated, printed or backed with paper or other reinforcing material (zinc foil). (SITC, Rev.3: 68632-0).

Remarque générale.

Produits plats en zinc (enroulés ou non), dont la plus grande dimension transversale est supérieure à 6 mm et dont l'épaisseur, supérieure à 0.15 mm, ne dépasse pas le dixième de la largeur (tôles, feuilles et bandes), feuilles et bandes minces d'une épaisseur de 0.15 mm au maximum, même gaufrées, découpées, perforées, revêtues, imprimées ou fixées sur papier ou support similaire (feuilles minces ou papier de zinc). (CTCI, Rev.3: 68632-0).

[1] Source: World Metal Statistics, (London).
[2] Including zinc wire.

[1] Source: World Metal Statistics,(Londres).
[2] Y compris le fil de zinc.

Tin, unwrought (total production)
Etain, non travaillé (production totale)

ISIC-BASED CODE - CODE BASE CITI

3720-49

Unit : Metric tons — Unité : Tonnes métriques

Country or area	1990	1991	1992	1993	1994	1995	1996	1997	1998	1999	Pays ou zone
Africa	**2459**	**2278**	**1718**	**2155**	**541**	**359**	**100**	**100**	**150**	**50**	**Afrique**
Dem. Rep. of Congo* [1]	90	70	50	700	100	100	0	0	0	0	Rép. dém. du Congo* [1]
Nigeria	320	300	300	300	316	259	[1]100	[1]100	[1]150	[1]50	Nigéria
South Africa* [1]	1210	1112	652	497	43	0	0	0	0	...	Afrique du Sud* [1]
Zimbabwe	839	796	716	658	[1]82	* [1]0	0	0	* [1]0	...	Zimbabwe
America, North	**17409**	**14916**	**16490**	**13840**	**12468**	**12370**	**12834**	**13588**	**17500**	**16800**	**Amérique du Nord**
Canada* [1]	200	200	200	200	0	0	0	...	...	...	Canada* [1]
Mexico [1]	5004	2262	2590	1640	768	770	1234	1188	*1200	*500	Mexique [1]
United States*	...	...	13700	12000	11700	11600	11600	12400	16300	16300	Etats-Unis*
America, South	**48478**	**40837**	**40541**	**41847**	**36084**	**29781**	**30532**	**31259**	**29002**	**24600**	**Amérique du Sud**
Argentina* [1]	280	300	240	245	100	100	100	100	100	100	Argentine* [1]
Bolivia	[2]13087	14507	13051	14452	15284	12641	11812	13359	11102	[1]11000	Bolivie
Brazil	35111	* [1]26030	* [1]27250	* [1]27150	* [1]20700	* [1]17040	* [1]18620	* [1]17800	* [1]17800	* [1]13500	Brésil
Asia	**149129**	**136941**	**140387**	**144838**	**158344**	**164950**	**174168**	**175462**	**181319**	**188873**	**Asie**
China	35800	36400	39600	51617	67764	67659	71500	67700	79313	90524	Chine
India* [1]	200	200	200	200	100	100	0	0	0	0	Inde* [1]
Indonesia*	[2]38000	[2]38000	[2]35975	[2]38300	[2]39000	[2]44218	[2]48960	[2]52577	[2]54000	[1]49105	Indonésie*
Japan	816	716	821	804	706	630	524	507	500	568	Japon
Korea, Republic of	1093	1237	[1]1000	[1]1000	[1]1100	[1]1100	[2]300	[2]300	[2]300	...	Corée, République de
Malaysia	48864	43008	[2]45598	[2]40079	[2]37990	[1]39433	[1]38051	[1]38400	[1]27900	[1]35800	Malaisie
Myanmar [1]	275	157	189	*170	*200	*190	*0	*0	*0	*0	Myanmar [1]
Singapore* [1]	2500	600	...	...	...	...	...	...	...	...	Singapour* [1]
Thailand	19979	14937	10910	8618	7634	8470	10983	12028	15356	...	Thaïlande
Viet Nam	1602	1686	4544	* [1]2500	* [1]2300	* [1]2400	* [1]2300	* [1]2400	* [1]2400	* [1]2400	Viet Nam
Europe	**31672**	**31747**	**32620**	**31612**	**29749**	**26645**	**27495**	**25105**	**21088**	**21622**	**Europe**
Belgium	6063	4426	5878	6835	[2]7800	[2]6300	[2]8200	[2]8000	[2]8000	[1]8000	Belgique
Bulgaria	64	22	23	23	22	13	8	8	...	...	Bulgarie
Denmark	* [1]100	* [1]100	* [1]100	* [1]100	* [1]100	[3]0	[3]0	[3]0	[3]0	[3]0	Danemark
Czechoslovakia(former)	613	118	..	..	..	..	..	..	..	..	Tchécoslovaquie(anc.)
Czech Republic	..	..	...	* [1]115	* [1]100	* [1]100	* [1]100	* [1]100	* [1]100	773	République tchèque
France	2652	2916	3180	3444	2676	...	...	...	...	...	France
Germany* [1]	..	700	127	179	100	100	100	100	100	0	Allemagne* [1]
German D.R.(former)	1874	..	..	..	..	..	..	..	..	..	R.D.A. (anc.)
Greece* [1]	700	200	200	200	150	150	100	150	200	200	Grèce* [1]
Netherlands*	6318	4277	...	...	...	...	...	...	...	...	Pays-Bas*
Norway	24	* [1]90	* [1]90	* [1]90	* [1]90	* [1]70	* [1]50	* [1]50	* [1]50	* [1]50	Norvège
Portugal	[2]100	[2]100	[2]100	[2]100	[2]100	[1]100	[1]100	[1]100	[1]100	[1]100	Portugal
Russian Federation* [1]	..	...	16700	14400	12500	10500	10000	7700	3500	3250	Fédération de Russie* [1]
Spain* [1]	800	800	800	700	700	600	200	200	150	100	Espagne* [1]
Sweden	364	23	24	28	13	168	35	38	216	472	Suède
United Kingdom	12000	5236	* [1][4]100	* [1][4]100	* [1][4]100	* [1][4]100	* [1][4]100	* [1][4]100	* [1][4]50	* [1][4]0	Royaume-Uni
USSR (former)* [5]	14000	..	..	..	..	..	..	..	..	..	URSS (anc.)* [5]
Oceania	**584**	**624**	**600**	**508**	**446**	**455**	**550**	**570**	**650**	**595**	**Océanie**
Australia [6]	*584	*624	*600	*508	*446	455	550	570	650	595	Australie [6]
Total	**263731**	**227343**	**232356**	**234800**	**237632**	**234560**	**245679**	**246084**	**249709**	**252540**	**Total**

General Note.
Production of virgin metal (primary) and tin derived from scrap (secondary). Tin alloys are included. (SITC, Rev.3: 68711-0).

Remarque générale.
Production de métal vierge (formes primaires) et d'étain de récupération (formes secondaires), y compris les alliages d'étain. (CTCI, Rev.3: 68711-0).

[1] Source: U. S. Geological Survey, (Washington, D. C.).
[2] Source: World Metal Statistics, (London).
[3] Sales.
[4] Secondary metal production only.
[5] Source: Metallgesellschaft Aktiengesellschaft, (Frankfurt).
[6] Twelve months ending 30 June of year stated.

[1] Source: U.S. Geological Survey, (Washington, D.C.).
[2] Source: World Metal Statistics,(Londres).
[3] Ventes.
[4] Production du métal de deuxième fusion seulement.
[5] Source: "Metallgesellschaft Aktiengesellschaft", (Francfort).
[6] Période de douze mois finissant le 30 juin de l'année indiquée.

Tin, unwrought, primary
Etain, non travaillé, neuf

ISIC-BASED CODE - CODE BASE CITI

3720-491

Unit : Metric tons

Unité : Tonnes métriques

Country or area	1990	1991	1992	1993	1994	1995	1996	1997	1998	1999	Pays ou zone
Africa	**2389**	**2208**	**1658**	**2110**	**541**	**359**	**100**	**100**	**150**	**50**	**Afrique**
Dem. Rep. of Congo* [1]	90	70	50	700	100	100	0	0	0	0	Rép. dém. du Congo* [1]
Nigeria	320	300	300	300	316	259	[1]100	[1]100	[1]150	[1]50	Nigéria
South Africa* [1]	1140	1042	592	452	#43	0	0	0	0	...	Afrique du Sud* [1]
Zimbabwe	839	796	716	658	# [1]82	[1]0	0	0	* [1]0	...	Zimbabwe
America, North	**5004**	**2262**	**2590**	**1640**	**768**	**770**	**1234**	**1188**	**1200**	**500**	**Amérique du Nord**
Mexico [1]	5004	2262	2590	1640	768	770	1234	1188	*1200	*500	Mexique [1]
America, South	**48378**	**40483**	**40191**	**41497**	**35784**	**29528**	**30273**	**30984**	**28702**	**24300**	**Amérique du Sud**
Argentina* [1]	180	200	140	145	100	100	100	100	100	100	Argentine* [1]
Bolivia	[2]13087	14507	13051	14452	15284	12641	11812	13359	11102	[1]11000	Bolivie
Brazil	35111	* [1]25776	* [1]27000	* [1]26900	* [1]20400	* [1]16787	* [1]18361	* [1]17525	* [1]17500	* [1]13200	Brésil
Asia	**143369**	**131822**	**139110**	**143636**	**157139**	**164547**	**173866**	**175120**	**181016**	**197253**	**Asie**
China	35800	36400	39600	51617	67764	67659	71500	67700	79313	90524	Chine
Indonesia*	[2]38000	[2]38000	[2]35900	[2]38300	[2]39000	[2]44218	[2]48960	[2]52577	[2]54000	[1]49105	Indonésie*
Japan	816	716	821	804	706	630	524	507	500	568	Japon
Malaysia	48864	43008	[2]45598	[2]40079	[2]37990	[1]39433	[1]38051	[1]38400	[1]27900	[1]35800	Malaisie
Myanmar [1]	275	157	189	*170	*200	*190	*0	*0	*0	*0	Myanmar [1]
Singapore [1]	*2500	600	...	...	...	...	...	...	...	...	Singapour [1]
Thailand	15512	11255	10908	8616	7629	8467	10981	11986	15353	17306	Thaïlande
Viet Nam	1602	1686	4544	* [1]2500	* [1]2300	* [1]2400	* [1]2300	* [1]2400	* [1]2400	* [1]2400	Viet Nam
Europe	**21529**	**23375**	**30944**	**30053**	**29039**	**25539**	**26589**	**24089**	**20339**	**19989**	**Europe**
Belgium [3]	6063	4426	5878	6835	[2]7800	[2]6300	[2]8200	[2]8000	[2]8000	[1]8000	Belgique [3]
Czechoslovakia(former)	613	118	..	..	..	..	..	..	..	..	Tchécoslovaquie(anc.)
Germany* [1][3]	..	700	127	179	100	100	100	100	100	0	Allemagne* [1][3]
German D.R.(former)	1874	..	..	..	..	..	..	..	..	..	R.D.A. (anc.)
Netherlands	6118	4077	...	...	...	...	...	...	...	...	Pays-Bas
Portugal	[2]100	[2]100	[2]100	[2]100	[2]100	[1]100	[1]100	[1]100	[1]100	[1]100	Portugal
Russian Federation* [1]	..	...	15200	13400	11500	9500	9000	6700	3000	2800	Fédération de Russie* [1]
Spain* [1]	600	600	600	500	500	500	150	150	100	50	Espagne* [1]
Sweden	61	...	...	...	...	...	...	...	...	...	Suède
United Kingdom* [1]	6100	1661	...	...	...	...	...	...	...	...	Royaume-Uni* [1]
USSR (former)* [4]	13000	..	..	..	..	..	..	..	..	..	URSS (anc.)* [4]
Oceania	**384**	**324**	**240**	**258**	**186**	**455**	**550**	**570**	**650**	**595**	**Océanie**
Australia [5]	384	324	240	258	186	455	550	570	650	595	Australie [5]
Total	**234053**	**200474**	**214733**	**219194**	**223457**	**221198**	**232612**	**232051**	**232057**	**242687**	**Total**

General Note.
Primary (virgin) metal recovered from tin ores and concentrates. (SITC, Rev.3: 68711-1).

Remarque générale.
Production de métal neuf (vierge) obtenu par l'affinage de concentrés d'étain. (CTCI, Rev.3: 68711-1).

[1] Source: U. S. Geological Survey, (Washington, D. C.).
[2] Source: World Metal Statistics, (London).
[3] Including secondary metal production.
[4] Source: Metallgesellschaft Aktiengesellschaft, (Frankfurt).
[5] Twelve months ending 30 June of year stated.

[1] Source: U.S. Geological Survey, (Washington, D.C.).
[2] Source: World Metal Statistics,(Londres).
[3] Y compris la production de métal de deuxième fusion.
[4] Source: "Metallgesellschaft Aktiengesellschaft", (Francfort).
[5] Période de douze mois finissant le 30 juin de l'année indiquée.

Tin, unwrought, secondary
Etain, non travaillé, récupéré

ISIC-BASED CODE - CODE BASE CITI

3720-492

Unit : Metric tons   Unité : Tonnes métriques

Country or area	1990	1991	1992	1993	1994	1995	1996	1997	1998	1999	Pays ou zone
Africa	**70**	**70**	**60**	**45**	**0**	**0**	**0**	**0**	**0**	**0**	**Afrique**
South Africa* [1]	70	70	60	45	0	0	0	0	0	...	Afrique du Sud* [1]
America, North	**12405**	**12654**	**13900**	**12200**	**11700**	**11600**	**11600**	**12400**	**16300**	**16300**	**Amérique du Nord**
Canada* [1]	200	200	200	200	0	0	0	0	...	...	Canada* [1]
United States*	...	...	13700	12000	11700	11600	11600	12400	16300	16300	Etats-Unis*
America, South	**350**	**350**	**350**	**350**	**350**	**350**	**350**	**350**	**350**	**350**	**Amérique du Sud**
Argentina* [1]	100	100	100	100	...	...	...	...	...	...	Argentine* [1]
Brazil* [1]	...	250	250	250	250	250	250	250	250	250	Brésil* [1]
Asia	**278**	**278**	**277**	**277**	**180**	**178**	**77**	**77**	**78**	**78**	**Asie**
India* [1]	200	200	200	200	100	100	0	0	0	0	Inde* [1]
Indonesia	...	...	75	...	...	...	...	...	...	...	Indonésie
Thailand	...	...	2	2	5	3	2	2	3	...	Thaïlande
Europe	**10079**	**8508**	**5728**	**5494**	**4650**	**5051**	**4850**	**4955**	**4685**	**4899**	**Europe**
Denmark	* [1]100	* [1]100	* [1]100	* [1]100	* [1]100	[2]0	[2]0	[2]0	[2]0	[2]0	Danemark
Czech Republic* [1]	..	..	...	115	100	100	100	100	100	100	République tchèque* [1]
France	2652	2916	3180	3444	2676	...	...	...	...	...	France
Greece* [1]	700	200'	200	200	150	150	100	150	200	200	Grèce* [1]
Latvia	..	97	27	17	21	17	11	...	...	...	Lettonie
Netherlands* [1]	200	200									Pays-Bas* [1]
Norway	24	* [1]90	* [1]90	* [1]90	* [1]90	* [1]70	* [1]50	* [1]50	* [1]50	* [1]50	Norvège
Russian Federation* [1]	..	...	1500	1000	1000	1000	1000	1000	500	450	Fédération de Russie* [1]
Spain* [1]	200	200	200	200	200	100	50	50	50	50	Espagne* [1]
Sweden	303	23	24	28	13	168	35	38	216	472	Suède
United Kingdom* [1]	5900	3575	#100	100	100	100	100	100	50	0	Royaume-Uni* [1]
Oceania	**200**	**300**	**360**	**250**	**260**	**295**	**302**	**309**	**316**	**323**	**Océanie**
Australia* [1]	200	300	360	250	260	...	...	...	...	...	Australie* [1]
Total	**23381**	**22159**	**20675**	**18616**	**17140**	**17474**	**17179**	**18091**	**21729**	**21950**	**Total**

General Note.
Secondary metal recovered from scrap waste or detinning.
(SITC, Rev.3: 68711-2).

Remarque générale.
Production de métal de deuxième fusion provenant du vieux métal ou du désétamage. (CTCI, Rev.3: 68711-2).

[1] Source: U. S. Geological Survey, (Washington, D. C.).
[2] Sales.

[1] Source: U.S. Geological Survey, (Washington, D.C.).
[2] Ventes.

Cadmium unwrought
Cadmium brut

ISIC-BASED CODE - CODE BASE CITI

3720-52

Unit : Metric tons

Unité : Tonnes métriques

Country or area	1990	1991	1992	1993	1994	1995	1996	1997	1998	1999	Pays ou zone
Africa	**261**	**210**	**173**	**43**	**79**	**90**	**89**	**77**	**75**	**75**	**Afrique**
Algeria	65	[1]78	[1]56	[1]18	[1]59	[1]75	[1]75	[1]75	[1]75	* [1]75	Algérie
Dem. Rep. of Congo* [1]	127	65	84	12	1	0	0	0	0	...	Rép. dém. du Congo* [1]
Namibia [1]	69	67	33	13	19	15	14	2	0	*0	Namibie [1]
America, North	**3821**	**3631**	**3679**	**3066**	**3181**	**4308**	**4851**	**4555**	**3876**	**3880**	**Amérique du Nord**
Canada	[1]1431	[1]1787	1963	1888	2129	[1]2349	[1]2537	[1]1272	* [1]1361	* [1]1390	Canada
Mexico	[1]712	[1]164	96	88	42	# [1]689	[1]784	[1]1223	* [1]1275	* [1]1300	Mexique
United States [2]	1678	1680	1620	1090	1010	1270	1530	2060	1240	1190	Etats-Unis [2]
America, South	**520**	**387**	**636**	**697**	**837**	**903**	**745**	**819**	**808**	**810**	**Amérique du Sud**
Argentina [1]	55	49	37	25	27	43	40	45	*34	*30	Argentine [1]
Brazil* [1]	200	200	200	200	300	300	300	300	300	300	Brésil* [1]
Peru [1]	265	138	399	472	510	560	405	474	474	*480	Pérou [1]
Asia	**5000**	**6177**	**6639**	**6027**	**6387**	**7303**	**6013**	**6748**	**7510**	**7488**	**Asie**
China* [1]	1100	1200	1150	1160	1280	1450	1570	1980	2130	2200	Chine* [1]
India [1]	277	271	313	255	216	254	271	298	*300	*300	Inde [1]
Japan	2451	2889	2986	2832	2629	2652	2344	2473	2337	2567	Japon
Kazakhstan [1]	..	...	...	800	1097	794	*800	*1000	*1450	*1061	Kazakhstan [1]
Korea,Dem.Ppl's.Rep.* [1]	100	100	100	100	100	100	100	100	100	100	Corée,Rép.pop.dém.de* [1]
Korea, Republic of [1]	...	...	...	*400	*400	1665	501	570	*884	*900	Corée, République de [1]
Thailand	...	373	635	449	643	365	385	238	* [1]240	* [1]300	Thaïlande
Turkey* [1]	46	22	23	31	22	23	42	89	69	60	Turquie* [1]
Europe	**6386**	**8786**	**7469**	**7022**	**6652**	**6955**	**6895**	**6882**	**6266**	**6434**	**Europe**
Austria	44	[1]19	[1]0	[1]0	[1]0	...	...	...	...	...	Autriche
Belgium [1]	1960	1810	1549	1573	1556	1710	1579	1420	*1318	*1400	Belgique [1]
Bulgaria	309	232	194	266	286	305	341	274	8	...	Bulgarie
Finland	484	471	580	332	876	534	648	* [1]540	* [1]520	* [1]500	Finlande
France	790	1085	838	595	# [1]6	* [1]0	[1]92	[1]309	[1]223	* [1]230	France
Germany [1]	..	...	961	1056	1145	*1150	*1150	*1145	*1020	*1100	Allemagne [1]
German D.R.(former)* [1]	17	..	..	..	..	..	..	..	..	..	R.D.A. (anc.)* [1]
Italy	[1]700	[1]658	742	517	475	308	296	287	470	359	Italie
Netherlands [1]	590	549	594	526	307	704	603	718	739	*750	Pays-Bas [1]
Norway [1]	286	227	247	213	288	317	274	290	*270	*250	Norvège [1]
Poland [1]	*373	*364	*132	149	#61	0	0	*22	*25	*25	Pologne [1]
Romania	[1]40	[1]10	[1]10	* [1]10	[1]4	[1]5	* [1]5	* [1]4	0	0	Roumanie
Russian Federation [1]	..	...	...	*700	600	725	730	*790	*800	*900	Fédération de Russie [1]
Spain [1]	355	344	361	365	387	397	307	301	*196	*0	Espagne [1]
Ukraine* [1]	...	...	5	7	10	15	25	25	25	25	Ukraine* [1]
United Kingdom	[1][2]438	[1][2]449	[1][2]383	[1][2]458	[1][2]469	[1][2]549	* [1][2]541	[1][2]455	390	* [1][2]500	Royaume-Uni
Yugoslavia	..	596	#8	6	...	11	79	45	17	...	Yougoslavie
T.F.Yug.Rep. Macedonia	..	286	230	249	73	...	...	257	245	236	L'ex-RY Macédoine
USSR (former)* [1]	2800	..	..	..	..	..	..	..	..	..	URSS (anc.)* [1]
Oceania	**638**	**1080**	**1001**	**951**	**910**	**838**	**639**	**632**	**600**	**600**	**Océanie**
Australia [1]	638	1080	1001	951	910	838	639	632	*600	*600	Australie [1]
Total	**19426**	**20271**	**19597**	**17806**	**18046**	**20397**	**19232**	**19713**	**19135**	**19287**	**Total**

General Note.

Production of refined cadmium recovered from ores and other materials, but not from cadmium cast directly from remelted secondary cadmium. (SITC, Rev.3: 68982-1).

Remarque générale.

Production de cadmium raffiné provenant de minerais ou autres matières, à l'exclusion du cadmium coulé directement à partir de cadmium refondu de deuxième fusion. (CTCI, Rev.3: 68982-1).

[1] Source: U. S. Geological Survey, (Washington, D. C.).
[2] Including secondary metal production.

[1] Source: U.S. Geological Survey, (Washington, D.C.).
[2] Y compris la production de métal de deuxième fusion.

Magnesium, unwrought (total production)
Magnésium, non travaillé (production totale)

ISIC-BASED CODE - CODE BASE CITI

3720-55

Unit : Metric tons   Unité : Tonnes métriques

Country or area	1990	1991	1992	1993	1994	1995	1996	1997	1998	1999	Pays ou zone
America, North	**220867**	**216343**	**220492**	**214000**	**219000**	**255200**	**258200**	**260300**	**260200**	**158300**	**Amérique du Nord**
Canada[1]	26726	34512	26500	[2]23000	* [2]28900	* [2]48100	* [2]54000	* [2]57700	* [2]77100	* [2]71000	Canada[1]
United States	194141	181831	193992	191000	190100	207100	204200	202600	183100	[3]87300	Etats-Unis
America, South	**10300**	**9400**	**8900**	**11300**	**11300**	**11300**	**10600**	**10600**	**10600**	**10600**	**Amérique du Sud**
Brazil* [2]	10300	9400	8900	11300	11300	11300	10600	10600	10600	10600	Brésil* [2]
Asia	**62018**	**62577**	**53564**	**55886**	**73607**	**134327**	**110242**	**116069**	**125000**	**126228**	**Asie**
China[1]	5900	8600	10500	13233	24009	93593	[2]73100	[2]75990	* [2]70500	* [2]83000	Chine[1]
India* [4]	1000	1000	1000	...	...	...	...	...	...	...	Inde* [4]
Israel[2]	...	...	...	...	...	...	...	7400	24500	*25000	Israël[2]
Japan	36151	28718	20097	20686	22421	11767	8175	22707	20000	...	Japon
Kazakhstan* [1][2]	..	...	3000	2000	...	9000	9000	8972	9000	9500	Kazakhstan* [1][2]
Europe	**75511**	**119238**	**110545**	**91414**	**95634**	**96684**	**96138**	**99805**	**93478**	**86354**	**Europe**
France[1]	14640	14051	13453	10983	[2]12280	[2]14450	* [2]14000	[2]13740	* [2]14000	* [2]14000	France[1]
Germany	..	...	...	...	...	5722	8127	7553	7966	...	Allemagne
Italy	5937	3919	1211	[2]0	[2]0	0	0	0	0	0	Italie
Norway	[5]48222	[5]44618	[5]32727	[5]27177	[5]27600	[1][2]28000	[1][2]28000	[1][2]28000	[1][2]28000	[1][2]28000	Norvège
Russian Federation* [1][2]	..	...	40000	30000	35400	37500	35000	39500	41500	35000	Fédération de Russie* [1][2]
Sweden	...	...	...	...	...	...	11	12	...	...	Suède
Ukraine* [1][2]	..	...	15000	14900	12000	10000	10000	10000	1000	1000	Ukraine* [1][2]
United Kingdom[2][3][6]	900	800	800	1000	1000	1000	1000	1000	1000	1000	Royaume-Uni[2][3][6]
Yugoslavia, SFR[4]	5800	..	..	...	..	..	..	..	..	..	Yougoslavie, RSF[4]
USSR (former)[2]	95500	..	..	..	..	..	..	..	..	..	URSS (anc.)[2]
Total	**464195**	**407558**	**393500**	**372599**	**399540**	**497510**	**475180**	**486774**	**489278**	**381482**	**Total**

General Note.
Magnesium recovered from both domestic and imported ores (primary) and metal derived from scrap and waste (secondary). (SITC, Rev.3: 68915-1).

Remarque générale.
Magnésium obtenu à partir des minerais et de concentrés nationaux ou importés (formes primaires) et le métal récupéré à partir de déchets et de débris d'ouvrages (formes secondaires). (CTCI, Rev.3: 68915-1).

[1] Primary metal production only.
[2] Source: U. S. Geological Survey, (Washington, D. C.).
[3] Secondary metal production only.
[4] Source: Metallgesellschaft Aktiengesellschaft, (Frankfurt).
[5] Including magnesium-based alloys.
[6] Including alloys.

[1] Production du métal de première fusion seulement.
[2] Source: U.S. Geological Survey, (Washington, D.C.).
[3] Production du métal de deuxième fusion seulement.
[4] Source: "Metallgesellschaft Aktiengesellschaft", (Francfort).
[5] Y compris les alliages à base de magnésium.
[6] Y compris les alliages.

Razor blades
Lames de rasoir

ISIC-BASED CODE - CODE BASE CITI

3811-01

Unit : Million units   Unité : En million

Country or area	1990	1991	1992	1993	1994	1995	1996	1997	1998	1999	Pays ou zone
Africa	**206**	**179**	**184**	**182**	**177**	**176**	**175**	**173**	**172**	**170**	**Afrique**
Algeria	169	153	166	...	177	176	...	...	...	...	Algérie
Kenya	23	19	9	9	9	9	...	...	...	...	Kenya
Tunisia	10	6	5	4	2	1	1	1	1	1	Tunisie
United Rep.Tanzania	4	1	4	6	...	...	...	...	...	...	Rép. Unie de Tanzanie
America, South	**225**	**206**	**266**	**113**	**149**	**101**	**148**	**139**	**117**	**50**	**Amérique du Sud**
Colombia	...	...	266	113	149	101	...	139	117	...	Colombie
Asia	**4160**	**3870**	**3432**	**3615**	**3583**	**3891**	**4219**	**4465**	**4983**	**5358**	**Asie**
Bangladesh	6	14	8	...	...	...	...	...	...	...	Bangladesh
India	3456	3384	3093	3442	3341	3685	3906	4101	4646	4897	Inde
Indonesia	...	...	...	7	...	...	...	...	...	...	Indonésie
Turkey	691	465	324	157	226	190	297	348	321	445	Turquie
Europe	**1889**	**4162**	**3900**	**3899**	**3219**	**3339**	**3595**	**3724**	**3851**	**3996**	**Europe**
Denmark[1]	4	3	1	1	1	0	0	0	0	0	Danemark[1]
Germany	..	...	...	...	...	2120	2411	2299	2350	...	Allemagne
Germany(Fed.Rep.)[2]	1533	..	...	..	..	..	..	..	..	..	Allemagne(Rép.féd.)[2]
Hungary	42	32	5	...	...	...	...	...	...	...	Hongrie
Russian Federation	..	1409	1369	1227	561	839	791	1083	1116	1279	Fédération de Russie
Spain	310	314	180	...	...	...	...	...	...	...	Espagne
Yugoslavia	..	109	50	81	68	85	99	48	91	128	Yougoslavie
USSR (former)	1523	..	..	..	..	..	..	..	..	...	URSS (anc.)
Total	**8003**	**8417**	**7782**	**7809**	**7129**	**7508**	**8137**	**8502**	**9124**	**9575**	**Total**

General Note.
Blades for safety razors. (SITC, Rev.3: 69635-0).

Remarque générale.
Lames pour rasoirs mécaniques dits de sûreté. (CTCI, Rev.3: 69635-0).

[1] Sales.
[2] 1987-89, data are confidential.

[1] Ventes.
[2] 1987-1989, les données sont confidentielles.

Locksmiths' wares - locks, padlocks, keys etc.
Articles de serrurerie - serrures, cadenas, clefs etc.

ISIC-BASED CODE - CODE BASE CITI
3811-04A

Unit : Metric tons   Unité : Tonnes métriques

Country or area	1990	1991	1992	1993	1994	1995	1996	1997	1998	1999	Pays ou zone
Asia	**9112**	**9978**	**11317**	**8494**	**11554**	**21619**	**15695**	**16615**	**17536**	**18456**	**Asie**
Korea, Republic of	9112	9978	11317	8494	11554	21619	...	...	...	...	Corée, République de
Europe	**360824**	**338472**	**345174**	**315206**	**339996**	**340491**	**344025**	**360269**	**371935**	**395369**	**Europe**
Austria	1950	2198	2451	2656	3140	3533	...	...	...	...	Autriche
Belgium[1][2]	2030	2322	1859	1733	...	...	...	...	...	...	Belgique[1][2]
Croatia	..	...	...	...	...	...	...	24	8	...	Croatie
Czech Republic	..	..	...	...	4385	4290	6716	10248	11031	13922	République tchèque
France[2]	35544	31226	34752	31855	28800	...	...	...	...	...	France[2]
Germany	..	244542	253987	225964	252547	...	...	...	...	...	Allemagne
Germany(Fed.Rep.)	221016	..	..	..	..	..	..	..	..	..	Allemagne(Rép.féd.)
Hungary	3842	3904	3982	3042	2388	2080	...	...	...	...	Hongrie
Poland	73075	33923	21863	22696	24860	33874	36212	50250	62482	84351	Pologne
Spain	23367	20341	21914	...	...	...	...	...	...	...	Espagne
Total	**369936**	**348450**	**356491**	**323700**	**351550**	**362110**	**359720**	**376885**	**389470**	**413825**	**Total**

General Note.
Locks, padlocks and keys therefore of base metal. (SITC, Rev.3: 69911-1A).

Remarque générale.
Serrures, cadenas et clefs pour ces articles, en métaux communs. (CTCI, Rev.3: 69911-1A).

[1] Production by establishments employing 5 or more persons.
[2] Shipments.

[1] Production des établissements occupant 5 personnes ou plus.
[2] Expéditions.

Locksmiths' wares - locks, padlocks, keys etc.
Articles de serrurerie - serrures, cadenas, clefs etc.

ISIC-BASED CODE - CODE BASE CITI

3811-04B

Unit : Thousand units

Unité : En milliers

Country or area	1990	1991	1992	1993	1994	1995	1996	1997	1998	1999	Pays ou zone
Africa	**11938**	**12656**	**14399**	**18514**	**16013**	**14850**	**18426**	**19688**	**23958**	**25444**	**Afrique**
Egypt	824	463	714	725	525	456	222	...	...	...	Egypte
Kenya	101	...	...	...	...	...	...	...	...	...	Kenya
South Africa [1]	11013	12092	13584	17688	15387	14293	18103	19384	23726	...	Afrique du Sud [1]
America, South	**781**	**692**	**728**	**728**	**634**	**432**	**258**	**223**	**225**	**211**	**Amérique du Sud**
Chile	781	692	728	728	634	432	258	223	225	211	Chili
Asia	**34561**	**32259**	**36019**	**32319**	**31115**	**28527**	**35002**	**51474**	**34518**	**46402**	**Asie**
Bangladesh	686	...	...	...	...	...	...	...	...	...	Bangladesh
Indonesia	...	...	14499	10727	10305	5395	...	23694	6918	...	Indonésie
Korea, Republic of	...	...	...	...	...	13173	11079	13115	11609	13756	Corée, République de
Turkey	9577	7359	9136	9038	8086	9273	11314	13979	15305	21307	Turquie
Europe	**220480**	**472441**	**511366**	**426390**	**428148**	**439273**	**476767**	**481004**	**516695**	**496416**	**Europe**
Austria [2]	...	...	...	...	...	6530	6734	...	6568	7911	Autriche [2]
Croatia	..	...	...	...	...	...	...	1	...	...	Croatie
Czech Republic	..	..	...	25337	25148	27147	44134	45478	66550	74788	République tchèque
Finland	14704	14197	13901	14448	20067	16295	16627	7792	7921	7673	Finlande
Germany	...	...	...	...	...	262331	232383	271158	276989	...	Allemagne
Greece	4242	4360	3726	2410	2805	2663	2704	2677	1331	...	Grèce
Hungary	20106	18776	21725	16266	8888	16691	55453	9049	6712	5625	Hongrie
Latvia	..	...	...	...	526	656	473	1750	1153	522	Lettonie
Lithuania	..	...	...	...	...	461	384	311	187	130	Lituanie
Portugal	...	...	7876	6113	4941	5630	7172	6113	8941	6583	Portugal
Slovakia	..	...	...	...	...	...	972	929	1315	1225	Slovaquie
Slovenia	..	...	...	...	...	...	4236	2488	2505	1616	Slovénie
Spain	117469	105449	121802	#38605	37737	46186	55237	62358	79647	73658	Espagne
Sweden	...	...	...	...	...	...	...	7551	1821	1350	Suède
United Kingdom	...	...	...	46796	52436	47286	46683	56413	55054	...	Royaume-Uni
Total	**267760**	**518048**	**562513**	**477951**	**475909**	**483082**	**530453**	**552388**	**575396**	**568473**	**Total**

General Note.
Locks, padlocks and keys therefore of base metal. (SITC, Rev.3: 69911-1B).

Remarque générale.
Serrures, cadenas et clefs pour ces articles, en métaux communs. (CTCI, Rev.3: 69911-1B).

[1] Locks only.
[2] 1997 data are confidential.

[1] Serrures seulement.
[2] Pour 1997, les données sont confidentielles.

Hardware, general
Articles de quincaillerie, en général

ISIC-BASED CODE - CODE BASE CITI

3811-07A

Unit : Metric tons
Unité : Tonnes métriques

Country or area	1990	1991	1992	1993	1994	1995	1996	1997	1998	1999	Pays ou zone
Europe	**882976**	**898459**	**892812**	**835761**	**917325**	**1155069**	**1192653**	**1274715**	**1104219**	**1303136**	Europe
Austria[1][2]	202	147	67	69	66	...	#85687	...	112624	133447	Autriche[1][2]
Belgium	[3][4]20000	[3][4]20508	[3][4]17106	[3][4]18222	13255	12328	14109	15688	21147	30976	Belgique
Croatia		4532	3309	2927	2357	2114	1943	2525	2683	...	Croatie
Czechoslovakia(former)	19437	13716	..	..	..	..	..	..	..	..	Tchécoslovaquie(anc.)
Czech Republic	..	..	6791	6303	5699	9196	10791	12676	13593	12774	République tchèque
France[4]	230316	193817	196392	172475	...	...	...	...	...	...	France[4]
Germany	..	449308	451337	453769	500241	672037	642991	751269	525073	...	Allemagne
Germany(Fed.Rep.)	403257	..	..	..	..	..	..	..	..	..	Allemagne(Rép.féd.)
Greece	...	...	...	4462	5734	5998	6415	[5]5893	6034	...	Grèce
Hungary	9538	7474	7638	5986	5217	6608	6134	8461	8038	7502	Hongrie
Latvia	..	...	...	...	...	...	...	...	...	782	Lettonie
Portugal	...	...	20925	21730	22489	22145	24187	21653	23540	24810	Portugal
Slovakia	..	..	...	...	...	...	...	...	3416	4797	Slovaquie
Slovenia	..	10523	7519	9794	15570	16533	15453	17986	20894	19098	Slovénie
Spain	76272	71126	70001	45833	49844	51040	54493	67181	74559	84661	Espagne
Sweden	...	...	...	...	...	...	...	20756	23463	31023	Suède
United Kingdom	...	...	...	64222	68634	87312	102231	105950	70123	...	Royaume-Uni
Total	**882976**	**898459**	**892812**	**835761**	**917325**	**1155069**	**1192653**	**1274715**	**1104219**	**1303136**	Total

General Note.
Base-metal fittings and mountings of a kind suitable for furniture, doors, windows, staircases, blinds, coachwork, saddlery, trunks, caskets and the like. Base-metal hat-racks, hat-pegs, baskets etc. (SITC, Rev.3: 69913-0A, 69914-0A, 69915-0A, 69916-0A, 69917-0A, 69919-0A).

Remarque générale.
Garnitures et ferrures en métaux communs utilisées pour les meubles, les portes, les fenêtres, les escaliers, les volets, la carrosserie, la sellerie, les coffres et autres boîtes. Porte-chapeaux (râteliers ou patères) et paniers etc., en métaux communs. (CTCI, Rev.3: 69913-0A, 69914-0A, 69915-0A, 69916-0A, 69917-0A, 69919-0A).

[1] 1995 data are confidential.
[2] 1997 data are confidential.
[3] Production by establishments employing 5 or more persons.
[4] Shipments.
[5] Incomplete coverage.

[1] Pour 1995, les données sont confidentielles.
[2] Pour 1997, les données sont confidentielles.
[3] Production des établissements occupant 5 personnes ou plus.
[4] Expéditions.
[5] Couverture incomplète.

Tanks and vats
Citernes et cuves

ISIC-BASED CODE - CODE BASE CITI
3813-01A

Unit : Thousand metric tons | | | | | | | | | | Unité : Milliers de tonnes métriques

Country or area	1990	1991	1992	1993	1994	1995	1996	1997	1998	1999	Pays ou zone
Asia	**61**	**147**	**103**	**68**	**107**	**146**	**119**	**56**	**41**	**21**	**Asie**
Japan	61.0	147.0	103.0	68.0	107.0	146.0	119.0	56.0	41.0	21.0	Japon
Europe	**310**	**372**	**420**	**515**	**352**	**597**	**595**	**615**	**688**	**721**	**Europe**
Austria	15.0	15.0	15.0	14.0	13.0	29.0	24.2	22.2	22.1	20.0	Autriche
Belgium	...	...	...	...	35.0	40.0	50.0	55.0	47.0	53.0	Belgique
Croatia	..	4.0	1.0	3.0	1.0	1.0	1.0	3.0	2.0	...	Croatie
Czech Republic	..	..	...	21.0	52.0	72.0	65.0	54.0	75.0	60.0	République tchèque
Germany	..	160.0	144.0	144.0	114.0	269.0	261.0	272.0	...	...	Allemagne
Greece	5.4	6.2	6.7	8.0	0.0	0.0	0.0	0.1	...	...	Grèce
Hungary	22.0	12.0	16.0	13.0	13.0	11.0	18.0	29.0	17.0	16.0	Hongrie
Poland	149.0	60.0	50.0	174.0	38.0	49.0	54.0	53.0	51.0	54.0	Pologne
Portugal	...	...	9.0	11.0	10.0	10.0	12.0	17.0	15.0	12.0	Portugal
Slovakia	..	..	...	...	...	...	...	...	15.3	12.6	Slovaquie
Slovenia	..	4.0	2.0	3.0	4.0	2.0	4.0	4.0	4.0	4.0	Slovénie
Spain	71.0	56.0	75.0	63.0	56.0	99.0	90.0	89.0	117.0	142.0	Espagne
Yugoslavia	..	5.0	5.0	5.0	2.0	1.0	1.0	2.0	3.0	2.0	Yougoslavie
T.F.Yug.Rep. Macedonia	..	0.2	0.4	...	...	...	...	...	...	...	L'ex-RY Macédoine
Total	**371**	**519**	**523**	**583**	**459**	**743**	**714**	**671**	**729**	**742**	**Total**

General Note.

Reservoirs, tanks, vats and similar containers, for any material, of iron and steel, copper or aluminium of a capacity exceeding 300 litres, whether or not lined or heat-insulated, but not fitted with mechanical or thermal equipment, normally installed as permanent fixtures for storage or manufacturing use, in chemical works, dye works, gasworks etc. (SITC, Rev.3: 69210-1A, 69973-1A).

Remarque générale.

Réservoirs, citernes, cuves et autres récipients analogues, pour toutes matières, en fonte ou acier, en cuivre ou en aluminium, d'une contenance supérieure à 300 litres, sans dispositifs mécaniques ou thermiques, même avec revêtement intérieur ou calorifuge, normalement installé en permanence pour le magasinage ou la fabrication, dans les usines de produits chimiques, de matières colorantes, les usines à gaz, etc. (CTCI, Rev.3: 69210-1A, 69973-1A).

Boilers, steam-generating
Chaudières à vapeur

ISIC-BASED CODE - CODE BASE CITI

3813-04A

Unit : Number of units   Unité : Nombre

Country or area	1990	1991	1992	1993	1994	1995	1996	1997	1998	1999	Pays ou zone
Africa											**Afrique**
Algeria	1500	1218	...	...	...	...	...	...	...	...	Algérie
Egypt	108	104	85	70	50	...	...	...	...	...	Egypte
America, South											**Amérique du Sud**
Brazil	343	244	199	253	...	...	...	...	...	...	Brésil
Colombia	...	...	...	273	240	434	...	...	...	...	Colombie
Asia											**Asie**
Indonesia	...	...	16	11	3	158	...	15	41	...	Indonésie
Japan[1][2]	21494	21492	18479	18097	18097	18081	17618	17404	15618	15035	Japon[1][2]
Turkey	6804	3678	3096	2329	1744	4377	3591	3712	3794	2713	Turquie
Europe											**Europe**
Austria[3]	...	...	47851	39484	43106	...	#705	769	685	713	Autriche[3]
Belgium	...	...	...	...	1088	924	...	...	...	641	Belgique
Bulgaria	143	124	143	82	84	79	48	51	79	40	Bulgarie
Croatia	..	101	34	57	58	24	28	36	2	...	Croatie
Czechoslovakia(former)	137	148	..	..	..	..	..	..	..	..	Tchécoslovaquie(anc.)
Czech Republic	..	..	65	97	66	70	113	117	78	51	République tchèque
Germany	..	[4]130	[4]105	[4]90	[4]109	2765	2527	1764	1660	...	Allemagne
Germany(Fed.Rep.)[4]	107	..	..	..	..	..	..	..	..	..	Allemagne(Rép.féd.)[4]
Greece	550	795	971	#3616	3494	3587	4714	4980	1308	...	Grèce
Hungary	180	84	86	135	182	54	186	123	115	180	Hongrie
Latvia	..	..	...	...	8	263	275	2045	1651	...	Lettonie
Lithuania	..	...	...	...	...	0	22	59	80	35	Lituanie
Poland	49	61	190	172	132	150	116	106	107	85	Pologne
Portugal	...	...	246	171	175	184	115	116	118	130	Portugal
Romania	117	92	124	133	93	176	234	290	39	55	Roumanie
Russian Federation	..	507	287	487	181	176	103	80	62	64	Fédération de Russie
Slovakia	..	..	0	0	0	...	...	...	747	7	Slovaquie
Slovenia	..	...	...	...	...	...	15	...	...	171	Slovénie
Spain	2781	3639	4992	2319	4361	4834	6055	5964	7037	12796	Espagne
Ukraine[5]	..	8701	7016	4465	1723	1043	403	315	119	52	Ukraine[5]
Yugoslavia	..	644	2111	444	6	9	6	12	9	1	Yougoslavie
USSR (former)	8846	..	..	..	..	..	..	..	..	..	URSS (anc.)

General Note.
Steam and other vapour generating boilers (excluding central heating hot water boilers capable of producing low pressure steam), tank boilers, firetube boilers, water-tube boilers. (SITC, Rev.3: 71110-1A).

Remarque générale.
Générateurs de vapeur d'eau ou d'autres vapeurs (à l'exclusion des chaudières pour le chauffage central conçues pour produire à la fois de l'eau chaude et de la vapeur à basse pression). Chaudières à bouilleurs et chaudières à tubes de fumée et chaudières à tubes d'eau. (CTCI, Rev.3: 71110-1A).

[1] Excluding steam-generating boilers for ships.
[2] Including central-heating boilers.
[3] 1995 data are confidential.
[4] In thousand metric tons.
[5] Boilers with a capacity of 0.1-10 tons of steam per hour.

[1] Non compris les chaudières de navire.
[2] Y compris les chaudières de chauffage central.
[3] Pour 1995, les données sont confidentielles.
[4] En milliers de tonnes métriques.
[5] Chaudières d'une capacité de 0.1-10 tonnes de vapeur par heure.

Boilers, steam-generating
Chaudières à vapeur

ISIC-BASED CODE - CODE BASE CITI

3813-04B

Unit : Tons of steam per hour
Unité : Tonnes vapeur/hr

Country or area	1990	1991	1992	1993	1994	1995	1996	1997	1998	1999	Pays ou zone
Asia	**42274**	**30921**	**28995**	**23759**	**28747**	**22813**	**33622**	**34236**	**42483**	**47894**	**Asie**
Japan[1][2]	42274	30921	28995	23759	28747	22813	33622	34236	42483	47894	Japon[1][2]
Europe	**11409**	**41928**	**28328**	**29235**	**19617**	**24256**	**16371**	**22135**	**18151**	**7013**	**Europe**
Bulgaria	614	620	663	315	433	334	193	227	...	...	Bulgarie
Croatia	..	1361	647	564	566	231	308	225	383	...	Croatie
Czechoslovakia(former)	4381	3571	..	..	..	..	..	..	..	..	Tchécoslovaquie(anc.)
Czech Republic	..	..	938	1770	...	...	...	...	...	...	République tchèque
Hungary	1499	1597	848	620	194	190	...	509	215	655	Hongrie
Poland	3336	794	2439	225	517	1334	2678	2422	2447	1220	Pologne
Romania	1579	1092	2524	384	446	416	410	2985	160	52	Roumanie
Russian Federation	..	24089	13083	20078	10076	13060	6213	6023	7198	3220	Fédération de Russie
Ukraine[3]	..	8642	7043	5074	2031	1337	512	390	173	77	Ukraine[3]
Yugoslavia	..	162	143	205	4000	6000	4000	8000	6000	72	Yougoslavie
USSR (former)	51839	..	..	..	..	..	..	..	..	..	URSS (anc.)
Total	**105522**	**72849**	**57323**	**52994**	**48364**	**47069**	**49993**	**56371**	**60634**	**54907**	**Total**

General Note.

Steam and other vapour generating boilers (excluding central heating hot water boilers capable of producing low pressure steam), tank boilers, firetube boilers, water-tube boilers. (SITC, Rev.3: 71110-1B).

Remarque générale.

Générateurs de vapeur d'eau ou d'autres vapeurs (à l'exclusion des chaudières pour le chauffage central conçues pour produire à la fois de l'eau chaude et de la vapeur à basse pression). Chaudières à bouilleurs et chaudières à tubes de fumée et chaudières à tubes d'eau. (CTCI, Rev.3: 71110-1B).

[1] Excluding steam-generating boilers for ships.
[2] Including central-heating boilers.
[3] Boilers with a capacity of 0.1-10 tons of steam per hour.

[1] Non compris les chaudières de navire.
[2] Y compris les chaudières de chauffage central.
[3] Chaudières d'une capacité de 0.1-10 tonnes de vapeur par heure.

Cans, metal
Récipients métalliques
ISIC-BASED CODE - CODE BASE CITI
3819-01

Unit : Thousand metric tons

Unité : Milliers de tonnes métriques

Country or area	1990	1991	1992	1993	1994	1995	1996	1997	1998	1999	Pays ou zone
Africa											**Afrique**
Algeria	12	12	15	...	...	...	...	...	...	...	Algérie
Kenya[1]	268	268	270	270	270	158	300	...	...	...	Kenya[1]
United Rep.Tanzania[1]	31	31	46	27	0	0	0	2	...	...	Rép. Unie de Tanzanie[1]
America, North											**Amérique du Nord**
Mexico[1]	2352	2249	2644	4663	5930	5263	5884	6565	7856	7920	Mexique[1]
America, South											**Amérique du Sud**
Colombia[1]	...	...	91	59	73	75	...	...	...	...	Colombie[1]
Ecuador[1]	...	...	338	510	351	110	...	...	...	...	Equateur[1]
Asia											**Asie**
Bangladesh	8	...	...	...	...	...	...	...	...	...	Bangladesh
Indonesia	...	...	...	1840	...	...	...	...	...	...	Indonésie
Korea, Republic of[1,2]	2935	4004	3988	4058	4977	5678	5743	5692	4076	4365	Corée, République de[1,2]
Malaysia[1]	803	1025	1221	1182	1319	1591	1364	1642	1299	1333	Malaisie[1]
Turkey[1]	193	273	374	326	253	1214	1195	1202	211	813	Turquie[1]
Europe											**Europe**
Austria	[3]27	[3]26	[3]27	[3]28	[3]24	[1,3]31	[1,3]1469	...	...	...	Autriche
Belgium[1]	...	...	...	...	1997	1987	1983	1306	[4]397	[4]40	Belgique[1]
Croatia	..	7	7	6	6	7	6	8	6	...	Croatie
Czech Republic	..	..	...	...	32	50	55	56	59	58	République tchèque
Finland[1]	251	232	224	214	345	297	291	259	259	214	Finlande[1]
Germany		745	719	705	724	#86	84	81	73	...	Allemagne
Germany(Fed.Rep.)	722	..	..	..	..	..	..	..	..	..	Allemagne(Rép.féd.)
Greece[1]	1262	1377	1547	1790	1774	1797	...	...	1979	...	Grèce[1]
Hungary	2	1	1	...	...	...	...	...	...	...	Hongrie
Latvia[1]	..	1	...	...	...	...	...	...	...	6	Lettonie[1]
Norway[1]	...	5	...	...	...	...	...	...	...	...	Norvège[1]
Portugal	32	32	[1]628	[1]647	[1]740	[1]663	[1]724	[1]676	[1]616	[1]629	Portugal
Slovakia[1]	..	..	...	...	...	...	0	1	0	0	Slovaquie[1]
Slovenia	..	8	5	5	4	5	[1]138	[1]164	[1]172	[1]123	Slovénie
Spain[5]	339	381	365	...	...	...	...	...	...	...	Espagne[5]
United Kingdom[1]	...	...	...	6741	6299	...	...	...	...	...	Royaume-Uni[1]
Yugoslavia	..	11	13	5	6	7	7	4	5	1	Yougoslavie
T.F.Yug.Rep. Macedonia	..	2	2	2	2	...	...	...	...	...	L'ex-RY Macédoine

General Note.
All types of metal cans made of tinplate, terneplate, blackplate or enamelled sheet metal used for packing food and non-food products, of a capacity not exceeding 300 litres. (SITC, Rev.3: 69241-0, 69242-0, 69973-2).

Remarque générale.
Boîtes métalliques de tous types, d'une capacité ne dépassant pas 300 litres, fabriquées en fer blanc, en tôle plombée, en fer noir ou en tôle émaillée, utilisées pour l'emballage de produits alimentaires ou autres. (CTCI,Rev.3: 69241-0, 69242-0, 69973-2).

[1] In million units.
[2] Metal cans for packing food only.
[3] Beginning 1997, data are confidential.
[4] Incomplete coverage.
[5] Made of aluminium and tin.

[1] En millions d'unités.
[2] Récipients métalliques pour les produits alimentaires seulement.
[3] A partir de 1997, les données sont confidentielles
[4] Couverture incomplète.
[5] En aluminium et en étain.

Compressed gas cylinders, made of metal
Récipients cylindriques pour gaz comprimés, en métal

ISIC-BASED CODE - CODE BASE CITI

3819-07A

Unit : Thousand units   Unité : En milliers

Country or area	1990	1991	1992	1993	1994	1995	1996	1997	1998	1999	Pays ou zone
America, North											**Amérique du Nord**
Mexico	[1]37922	[1]51351	[1]57167	2287	2374	743	1220	1202	1314	2379	Mexique
America, South											**Amérique du Sud**
Chile	295	287	547	699	697	938	983	762	734	477	Chili
Colombia	...	...	201	237	283	150	...	...	...	...	Colombie
Ecuador	635	...	419	613	930	1282	358	38	156	...	Equateur
Asia											**Asie**
Indonesia	58	53	25	...	...	...	...	...	...	...	Indonésie
Kazakhstan	..	350	287	150	30	17	...	...	...	...	Kazakhstan
Korea, Republic of[1]	...	...	...	...	...	54863	58553	47713	31724	...	Corée, République de[1]
Thailand	1296	1372	...	...	...	...	...	...	...	...	Thaïlande
Europe											**Europe**
Austria[1]	...	...	...	...	...	15805	15825	14787	19632	23553	Autriche[1]
Croatia	..	52	56	35	39	59	41	82	127	...	Croatie
Czech Republic[1]	..	...	...	...	6767	10559	12854	18188	23932	22662	République tchèque[1]
Greece	...	...	...	...	...	...	...	...	1	...	Grèce
Hungary	211	275	228	116	83	89	...	...	[1]4345	...	Hongrie
Lithuania	..	100	90	112	15	22	19	28	35	36	Lituanie
Portugal[1]	...	...	30111	31249	33938	29967	32348	36755	50014	43235	Portugal[1]
Slovenia[1]	..	...	...	...	...	...	508	687	738	1091	Slovénie[1]
Spain	1010	1319	1558	[1]25321	[1]28572	[1]47987	[1]25375	[1]32413	[1]27611	[1]28731	Espagne
Oceania											**Océanie**
Australia	473	...	...	...	...	...	...	...	...	...	Australie

General Note.
Cylinders made of iron, steel or aluminium which are used for the transport and storage of compressed gases (oxygen, hydrogen, carbon dioxide or butane). (SITC, Rev.3: 69243-0A, 69244-0A).

Remarque générale.
Bouteilles cylindriques en fer, en acier ou en aluminium, utilisées pour le transport et le magasinage de gaz comprimés (oxygène, hydrogène, gaz carbonique ou butane). (CTCI, Rev.3: 69243-0A, 69244-0A).

[1] In metric tons.

[1] En tonnes métriques.

Cables
Câbles

ISIC-BASED CODE - CODE BASE CITI

3819-10

Unit : Thousand metric tons

Unité : Milliers de tonnes métriques

Country or area	1990	1991	1992	1993	1994	1995	1996	1997	1998	1999	Pays ou zone
Africa	**77**	**59**	**65**	**68**	**67**	**67**	**65**	**67**	**67**	**67**	**Afrique**
Algeria	2.6	3.0	3.9	3.6	3.1	3.4	1.2	2.8	3.3	3.4	Algérie
South Africa	74.7	56.4	60.8	...	...	...	...	...	...	...	Afrique du Sud
America, North	**260**	**233**	**224**	**236**	**287**	**294**	**390**	**394**	**386**	**412**	**Amérique du Nord**
Mexico	260.0	233.0	224.4	236.5	286.7	293.5	389.5	394.2	386.5	411.6	Mexique
America, South	**9**	**9**	**6**	**15**	**9**	**7**	**9**	**9**	**9**	**9**	**Amérique du Sud**
Colombia	...	...	6.1	15.1	8.7	7.2	...	...	...	...	Colombie
Asia	**213**	**304**	**441**	**386**	**314**	**998**	**404**	**320**	**353**	**485**	**Asie**
Armenia	..	21.2	7.5	3.6	2.5	2.0	0.9	0.6	0.6	0.3	Arménie
Azerbaijan	..	18.0	3.5	2.1	1.2	0.2	0.7	0.4	0.3	0.1	Azerbaïdjan
Indonesia	73.3	54.1	230.2	176.3	135.2	800.0	...	123.3	150.9	...	Indonésie
Korea, Republic of[1]	130.2	120.1	126.4	123.9	123.2	146.7	139.4	140.0	150.1	142.0	Corée, République de[1]
Kyrgyzstan		17.4	5.9	3.5	1.1	1.0	0.7	0.3	0.3	0.1	Kirghizistan
Syrian Arab Republic	1.7	2.2	4.0	5.0	5.5	6.9	7.9	8.4	11.3	10.8	Rép. arabe syrienne
Tajikistan	..	12.0	8.0	11.2	7.7	7.1	5.2	5.1	3.0	1.5	Tadjikistan
Turkey	7.5	9.1	10.1	14.1	11.6	22.9	17.1	32.4	33.5	31.2	Turquie
Turkmenistan	..	9.3	3.5	4.4	3.2	1.5	3.0	3.0	3.2	...	Turkménistan
Uzbekistan	..	40.3	41.4	42.2	23.4	9.7	10.9	6.6	...	...	Ouzbékistan
Europe	**977**	**986**	**953**	**861**	**848**	**956**	**989**	**1019**	**1108**	**1001**	**Europe**
Belgium[2][3]	97.6	105.3	101.8	93.9	...	...	...	...	...	...	Belgique[2][3]
Bulgaria	14.2	4.5	7.3	7.9	6.4	7.3	6.9	5.4	...	...	Bulgarie
Croatia	..	2.0	1.3	1.3	1.3	2.0	0.8	7.7	4.0	...	Croatie
Czechoslovakia(former)	39.3	25.9	..	..	..	..	..	..	..	..	Tchécoslovaquie(anc.)
Czech Republic	..	...	...	...	...	...	19.3	15.4	17.0	15.8	République tchèque
Estonia	..	3.1	0.4	0.2	0.5	0.4	0.7	0.8	1.1	1.0	Estonie
Finland	14.5	14.5	17.4	17.6	16.9	13.6	18.0	20.8	17.6	18.6	Finlande
Germany	..	...	152.1	136.9	146.1	219.4	215.7	...	...	...	Allemagne
Germany(Fed.Rep.)	156.8	..	..	..	..	..	..	..	..	..	Allemagne(Rép.féd.)
German D.R.(former)	37.8	..	..	..	..	..	..	..	..	..	R.D.A. (anc.)
Greece	39.3	41.1	51.8	# [4]5.5	[4]6.5	[4]6.2	[4]7.0	[4]9.2	9.2	...	Grèce
Hungary	42.1	23.7	18.0	8.8	14.8	18.3	...	...	28.3	22.2	Hongrie
Latvia	..	...	...	...	...	...	...	...	...	0.5	Lettonie
Lithuania	..	12.5	5.3	...	...	...	...	...	...	...	Lituanie
Norway	14.6	20.3	16.9	...	...	...	...	...	...	...	Norvège
Poland	82.0	89.7	79.5	89.6	80.4	96.7	117.4	124.4	140.3	142.7	Pologne
Portugal	11.3	10.2	...	...	...	...	...	...	...	...	Portugal
Romania[5]	42.9	29.1	18.7	61.5	53.4	22.7	25.0	19.9	85.5	31.6	Roumanie[5]
Slovakia	..	...	...	19.3	...	29.8	24.5	23.4	23.9	17.5	Slovaquie
Slovenia	..	0.6	0.5	0.5	0.7	0.6	0.2	0.1	0.2	0.2	Slovénie
Spain	202.5	189.4	179.7	127.4	131.1	174.5	182.3	190.3	175.3	129.3	Espagne
Ukraine	..	114.3	66.2	47.5	24.4	22.2	21.4	21.2	20.6	13.6	Ukraine
United Kingdom	...	...	...	182.0	...	...	...	...	...	...	Royaume-Uni
Yugoslavia	..	5.3	3.5	1.2	1.7	1.5	2.4	2.2	1.6	1.4	Yougoslavie
T.F.Yug.Rep. Macedonia	..	0.6	3.4	6.1	5.0	5.1	6.1	0.4	0.6	0.2	L'ex-RY Macédoine
Oceania	**8**	**10**	**8**	**9**	**9**	**9**	**9**	**9**	**9**	**9**	**Océanie**
Australia[6]	8.0	9.9	8.5	...	...	...	...	...	...	...	Australie[6]
Total	**1544**	**1601**	**1697**	**1576**	**1534**	**2331**	**1865**	**1818**	**1933**	**1984**	**Total**

General Note.
Stranded wire, cables, cordage, ropes, plaited bands, strings and the like of iron and steel, copper or aluminium, but excluding insulated electric cables. Uninsulated stranded copper wire for electrical purposes is included. (SITC, Rev.3: 69310-0).

[1] Wire rope only.

[2] Production by establishments employing 5 or more persons.

[3] Shipments.

[4] Incomplete coverage.

[5] Electric cables and conductors.

[6] Beginning 1987-88, uninsulated aluminium cables only.

Remarque générale.
Câbles, cordages, tresses, élingues et similaires, en fil de fer, d'acier, de cuivre ou d'aluminium, à l'exclusion des articles isolés pour l'électricité mais y compris les câbles de cuivre non isolés pour l'électricité. (CTCI, Rev.3: 69310-0).

[1] Câbles fils seulement.

[2] Production des établissements occupant 5 personnes ou plus.

[3] Expéditions.

[4] Couverture incomplète.

[5] Conducteurs et câbles électriques.

[6] A partir de 1987-88, câbles en aluminum non isolés seulement.

Nails, screws, nuts, bolts, rivets etc.
Clous, vis, écrous, boulons, rivets et articles similaires

ISIC-BASED CODE - CODE BASE CITI

3819-13

Unit : Thousand metric tons | | | | | | | | | | Unité : Milliers de tonnes métriques

Country or area	1990	1991	1992	1993	1994	1995	1996	1997	1998	1999	Pays ou zone
Africa	**126**	**111**	**102**	**100**	**102**	**100**	**108**	**114**	**113**	**106**	**Afrique**
Algeria	6.1	5.5	6.1	6.2	4.0	4.1	3.0	3.4	4.0	3.8	Algérie
Burundi[1]	0.1	0.5	0.4	0.0	...	...	...	...	...	...	Burundi[1]
Congo	0.1	0.2	0.1	0.1	...	...	...	...	...	...	Congo
Egypt	51.0	53.0	53.0	54.0	54.0	51.0	57.0	...	...	...	Egypte
Ethiopia[2]	1.0	0.9	0.2	2.4	3.1	2.9	3.2	3.5	2.7	2.5	Ethiopie[2]
Kenya	0.2	0.2	0.2	0.2	0.2	0.2	0.2	...	...	...	Kenya
Madagascar	0.7	0.7	0.8	0.9	...	...	...	...	...	...	Madagascar
South Africa[3]	66.9	50.2	41.2	36.3	39.1	41.1	43.3	49.7	48.2	41.3	Afrique du Sud[3]
America, North	**34**	**34**	**37**	**86**	**91**	**81**	**94**	**108**	**97**	**86**	**Amérique du Nord**
Barbados	0.2	0.2	0.0	...	...	...	...	...	...	...	Barbade
Haiti[1]	0.8	0.7	0.8	0.9	0.6	...	...	...	...	...	Haïti[1]
Mexico	32.1	32.1	35.0	83.4	88.7	78.6	91.6	105.6	93.5	83.3	Mexique
Panama	0.9	...	1.3	1.5	1.6	1.2	1.5	...	...	...	Panama
America, South	**223**	**229**	**238**	**261**	**308**	**305**	**327**	**335**	**303**	**324**	**Amérique du Sud**
Bolivia	1.2	0.8	1.2	1.2	1.2	*1.3	...	...	...	...	Bolivie
Brazil[4]	185.8	190.3	192.2	217.8	262.7	252.4	256.7	270.6	248.1	253.2	Brésil[4]
Chile[1]	24.4	24.1	31.8	27.8	31.4	29.9	33.4	...	...	...	Chili[1]
Colombia	...	...	10.8	13.1	11.1	12.3	...	...	...	...	Colombie
Ecuador	...	...	[1]1.9	[1]0.6	[1]1.9	[1]8.7	[1]23.8	15.3	4.7	...	Equateur
Asia	**1825**	**1853**	**1748**	**1679**	**1805**	**1949**	**1839**	**1928**	**1884**	**1943**	**Asie**
Armenia	..	2.2	0.4	0.1	0.0	0.0	0.1	0.1	0.0	0.0	Arménie
Azerbaijan	..	0.7	0.5	0.3	0.1	0.0	0.0	0.1	0.0	0.0	Azerbaïdjan
Cyprus	* [1]0.7	* [1]0.7	1.0	*1.1	*1.2	1.2	1.2	1.8	0.9	0.8	Chypre
India[5]	360.2	354.4	351.2	358.1	...	...	...	...	...	...	Inde[5]
Indonesia	77.6	85.8	70.1	46.7	191.6	278.5	...	196.6	176.2	...	Indonésie
Japan	1014.9	1004.6	936.9	861.0	832.5	857.7	868.4	886.7	853.2	839.4	Japon
Korea, Republic of	...	362.8	335.6	367.1	396.4	420.9	...	...	...	...	Corée, République de
Lao People's Dem. Rep.	...	...	...	...	0.1	0.1	...	...	...	...	Rép. dém. pop. lao
Myanmar[1] [6]	1.2	1.1	0.1	...	...	...	...	...	...	...	Myanmar[1] [6]
Turkey	47.3	40.4	52.2	43.4	26.6	34.1	42.1	38.6	31.5	26.8	Turquie
Europe	**1775**	**2019**	**1867**	**1430**	**1436**	**1644**	**1569**	**1614**	**1736**	**1655**	**Europe**
Austria[7]	36.7	34.5	31.3	25.6	23.0	...	...	...	...	...	Autriche[7]
Belarus	..	29.8	25.4	9.7	5.4	4.0	4.8	9.2	10.4	6.3	Bélarus
Belgium	[8] [9]46.9	[8] [9]34.8	[8] [9]28.1	[8] [9]22.1	7.4	33.0	32.3	20.8	31.0	28.5	Belgique
Bulgaria	[10]42.3	[10]20.5	[10]15.2	[10]14.2	20.4	24.5	24.3	23.9	31.6	27.8	Bulgarie
Croatia	..	12.7	2.7	1.8	1.3	1.4	1.8	2.2	1.6	...	Croatie
Czechoslovakia(former)	128.2	98.3	..	..	..	..	..	..	..	..	Tchécoslovaquie(anc.)
Czech Republic	..	..	48.4	38.4	40.7	87.7	78.0	81.5	95.7	89.1	République tchèque
France[9] [11]	180.9	188.4	184.3	150.2	206.4	...	...	...	...	...	France[9] [11]
Germany	..	603.1	608.7	509.1	522.9	642.9	598.3	627.5	677.8	...	Allemagne
Germany(Fed.Rep.)	567.3	..	..	..	..	..	..	..	..	..	Allemagne(Rép.féd.)
German D.R.(former)	118.4	..	..	..	..	..	..	..	..	..	R.D.A. (anc.)
Greece	23.7	22.0	21.8	...	...	...	...	...	18.1	...	Grèce
Hungary	57.6	40.5	28.2	17.8	18.9	16.3	17.3	19.1	23.4	26.5	Hongrie
Latvia	..	8.8	...	4.7	6.1	6.4	5.2	4.3	4.9	5.7	Lettonie
Lithuania	..	10.1	5.7	4.7	7.2	6.3	5.9	3.9	2.8	6.7	Lituanie
Poland	100.7	94.7	97.6	102.6	110.7	129.2	114.9	133.6	167.4	149.6	Pologne
Portugal	38.6	36.8	17.1	13.8	13.9	14.9	13.3	14.6	17.1	20.0	Portugal
Slovakia	..	..	28.2	...	...	...	22.9	22.8	21.8	2.5	Slovaquie
Slovenia	..	13.2	10.6	8.3	11.6	11.6	8.7	4.1	4.4	4.7	Slovénie
Spain	203.2	202.2	167.2	97.9	111.7	137.7	137.8	141.3	153.4	161.5	Espagne
Ukraine	..	325.0	302.8	135.1	54.0	48.0	43.7	44.8	39.4	38.1	Ukraine
United Kingdom	...	...	...	...	230.7	...	...	...	...	...	Royaume-Uni
Yugoslavia	..	12.5	6.9	2.1	1.3	1.8	2.7	4.3	3.6	2.3	Yougoslavie
T.F.Yug.Rep. Macedonia	..	1.0	0.4	0.1	1.8	1.8	2.2	3.1	3.0	3.2	L'ex-RY Macédoine
Total	**3984**	**4246**	**3992**	**3555**	**3743**	**4080**	**3937**	**4099**	**4132**	**4114**	**Total**

For general note and footnotes, see end of table. | Voir la fin du tableau pour la remarque générale et les notes.

Nails, screws, nuts, bolts, rivets etc. (continued)
Clous, vis, écrous, boulons, rivets et articles similaires (suite)

ISIC-BASED CODE - CODE BASE CITI
3819-13

General Note.
Nails, tacks, staples, hook-nails, corrugated nails, spiked cramps, studs, spikes and drawing pins, bolts, nuts (including bolt ends and screw studs), whether or not threaded or tapped, screws (including screw hooks and screw rings), rivets, cotters, cotter pins, washers, and spring washers, or iron, steel or copper. (SITC, Rev.3: 69400-0).

[1] Nails only.
[2] Twelve months ending 7 July of the year stated.
[3] Excluding rivets.
[4] Iron and steel products only.
[5] Production by large and medium scale establishments only.
[6] Government production only.
[7] Beginning 1995, data are confidential.
[8] Production by establishments employing 5 or more persons.
[9] Shipments.
[10] Excluding pins, drawing pins, clasps etc.
[11] Steel products only.

Remarque générale.
Clous, semences, agrafes, crochets, clous cannelés, crampons appointés, clous d'ornementation, pointes et punaises, boulons, écrous (y compris ceux des boulons et des goujons), filetés ou non, taraudés ou non, vis (y compris les crochets à vis et les pitons à vis), rivets, clavettes, goupilles, rondelles, élastiques ou non, en fer, en acier ou en cuivre. (CTCI,Rev.3: 69400-0).

[1] Clous seulement.
[2] Période de douze mois finissant le 7 juillet de l'année indiquée.
[3] Non compris les rivets.
[4] Produits en fer et acier seulement.
[5] Production des grandes et moyennes entreprises seulement.
[6] Production de l'Etat seulement.
[7] A partir de 1995, les données sont confidentielles
[8] Production des établissements occupant 5 personnes ou plus.
[9] Expéditions.
[10] Non compris les épingles, punaises, agrafes, etc.
[11] Produits en acier seulement.

Containers, one cubic metre and over
Cadres et autres conteneurs d'un mètre cube et plus

ISIC-BASED CODE - CODE BASE CITI

3819-16A

Unit : Thousand units   Unité : En milliers

Country or area	1990	1991	1992	1993	1994	1995	1996	1997	1998	1999	Pays ou zone
Africa											**Afrique**
South Africa[1]	9590	9708	9662	9859	8270	8173	8162	8242	7694	5711	Afrique du Sud[1]
America, South											**Amérique du Sud**
Colombia	...	...	21	61	16	34		...	...	...	Colombie
Asia											**Asie**
Hong Kong SAR[2]	...	26	...	...	295	43	1	...	...	...	Hong-Kong RAS[2]
Japan[3]	57	37	45	42	35	30	17	17	15	8	Japon[3]
Korea, Republic of	334	331	354	163	111	114	...	...	...	...	Corée, République de
Europe											**Europe**
Austria	...	...	...	...	...	9	7	6	4	4	Autriche
Belarus	..	101	65	...	...	...	...	...	...	...	Bélarus
Bulgaria	5	4	2	1	2	2	2	1	1	1	Bulgarie
Denmark[4]	4	4	12	16	34	0	0	0	0	0	Danemark[4]
Czech Republic	..	...	...	...	3	2	1	2	2	2	République tchèque
Finland	1	1	1	2	...	4	5	5	...	1	Finlande
Germany	..	139	136	112	93	112	106	101	97	...	Allemagne
Germany(Fed.Rep.)	62	..	..	..	..	..	..	..	..		Allemagne(Rép.féd.)
Greece	...	...	...	...	...	...	...	...	1	...	Grèce
Hungary	0	0	0	[3]3	[3]1	2	...	12	33	...	Hongrie
Latvia	..	...	...	...	...	...	...	...	...	1	Lettonie
Poland	8	19	19	18	18	20	19	19	24	28	Pologne
Portugal	...	...	4	2	1	1	1	1	2	2	Portugal
Slovakia	..	..	...	...	77	119	23	15	21	13	Slovaquie
Slovenia	..	6	10	10	9	11	8	5	6	5	Slovénie
Spain	[3]19	[3]22	[3]20	29	48	105	80	76	64	75	Espagne
Sweden	...	...	...	...	...	...	...	39	42	11	Suède
Ukraine	..	44	26	16	10	5	4	2	9	6	Ukraine
United Kingdom	...	...	...	23	11	15	14	16	16	...	Royaume-Uni

General Note.

An article of transport equipment (lift-van, movable tank or other similar structure) with an internal volume of one cubicmetre or more, which is (a) of a permanent character and accordingly strong enough to be suitable for repeated use, (b) specially designed to facilitate the carriage of goods, by one or more modes of transport, without intermediate reloading, (c) fitted with devices permitting its ready handling, particularly its transfer from one mode of transport to another, and (d) so designed as to be easy to fill and empty. This item does not include vehicles of any kind or conventional packing. (SITC, Rev.3: 78630-0A).

Remarque générale.

Engin de transport (cadre, citerne amovible ou autre engin analogue) ayant un volume intérieur d'un mètre cube ou plus: (a) ayant un caractère permanent et étant de ce fait suffisamment résistant pour permettre son usage répété, (b) spécialement conçu pour faciliter le transport de marchandises sans rupture de charge par un ou plusieurs moyens de transport, (c) muni de dispositifs le rendant facile à manipuler, notamment lors de son transbordement d'un moyen de transport à un autre, et (d) conçu de façon à être facile à remplir et à vider. Cette rubrique ne comprend ni les véhicules de toute espèce ni les emballages conventionnels. (CTCI, Rev.3: 78630-0A).

[1] Drums only.
[2] Beginning 1997, data are confidential.
[3] In thousand metric tons.
[4] Sales.

[1] Fûts seulement.
[2] A partir de 1997, les données sont confidentielles
[3] En milliers de tonnes métriques.
[4] Ventes.

Central-heating apparatus, non-electric
Appareils de chauffage central, non électriques

ISIC-BASED CODE - CODE BASE CITI

3819-19

Unit : Thousand units

Unité : En milliers

Country or area	1990	1991	1992	1993	1994	1995	1996	1997	1998	1999	Pays ou zone
Asia											**Asie**
Indonesia	...	...	13	...	...	...	...	...	...	...	Indonésie
Turkey[1]	4678	3516	4678	5610	4222	5665	6737	8036	8277	7174	Turquie[1]
Europe											**Europe**
Austria	45	51	53	44	30	57	57	56	65	55	Autriche
Belgium	[2][3]15	[2][3]16	[2][3]15	[2][3]17	137	126	137	140	127	133	Belgique
Croatia	..	1514	712	524	682	130	3588	4007	3570	...	Croatie
Finland	836	850	809	1150	1218	1052	1224	3135	4238	4720	Finlande
France[2]	33	43	34	40	52	...	...	...	...	...	France[2]
Germany	..	1081	952	780	875	787	811	753	728	...	Allemagne
Germany(Fed.Rep.)	690	..	..	..	..	..	..	..	..	..	Allemagne(Rép.féd.)
Greece	56	47	54	...	...	...	...	...	[4]1	...	Grèce
Hungary	1588	...	1133	1729	1113	1079	...	3073	2361	1995	Hongrie
Lithuania	..	...	...	...	...	5	5	5	4	6	Lituanie
Netherlands[5][6][7]	172	220	252	220	242	254	293	352	358	401	Pays-Bas[5][6][7]
Slovakia	..	...	...	...	27	35	54	55	51	27	Slovaquie
Slovenia[3]	..	13	9	6	13	3	[4]7	[4]8	[4]6	[4]3	Slovénie[3]
Spain	3632	2677	3728	...	...	...	...	...	...	...	Espagne
United Kingdom[3]	...	...	...	4	6	...	...	...	...	...	Royaume-Uni[3]
Yugoslavia	..	22	18	7	4	3	4	6	7	10	Yougoslavie

General Note.

Boilers (excluding steam-generating boilers) and radiators for central heating, air heaters and hot-air distributors, not electric. (SITC, Rev.3: 81211-1, 81215-1, 81217-0).

[1] In thousand square metres.
[2] Shipments.
[3] In thousand metric tons.
[4] Incomplete coverage.
[5] Sales.
[6] Production by establishments employing 20 or more persons.
[7] Central heating radiators only.

Remarque générale.

Chaudières (à l'exclusion des générateurs de vapeur d'eau) et radiateurs de chauffage central. Générateurs et distributeurs d'air chaud. Cette rubrique ne comprend pas les appareils électriques. (CTCI, Rev.3: 81211-1, 81215-1, 81217-0).

[1] En milliers de mètres carrés.
[2] Expéditions.
[3] En milliers de tonnes métriques.
[4] Couverture incomplète.
[5] Ventes.
[6] Production des établissements occupant 20 personnes ou plus.
[7] Radiateurs pour le chauffage central seulement.

Steam turbines
Turbines à vapeur

ISIC-BASED CODE - CODE BASE CITI

3821-01A

Unit : Number of units   Unité : Nombre

Country or area	1990	1991	1992	1993	1994	1995	1996	1997	1998	1999	Pays ou zone
America, South											**Amérique du Sud**
Colombia	...	...	86	111	131	181	...	...	...	...	Colombie
Asia											**Asie**
Indonesia	...	...	...	...	2	...	...	...	...	...	Indonésie
Japan[1][2]	406	526	481	358	339	381	460	390	484	297	Japon[1][2]
Europe											**Europe**
Croatia	..	...	4	...	...	...	2	1	1	...	Croatie
Czechoslovakia(former)	67	46	..	..	..	..	..	..	..	..	Tchécoslovaquie(anc.)
Czech Republic	..	..	37	25	15	19	35	37	20	20	République tchèque
France[3][4]	823	180	921	782	...	...	...	...	...	...	France[3][4]
Germany	..	...	452	344	293	269	291	270	313	...	Allemagne
Germany(Fed.Rep.)[5]	426	..	..	..	..	..	..	..	..	..	Allemagne(Rép.féd.)[5]
German D.R.(former)	80	..	..	..	..	..	..	..	..	..	R.D.A. (anc.)
Hungary	2	6	1	...	...	...	...	...	...	...	Hongrie
Poland	...	1	...	1	1	1	2	2	1	1	Pologne
Romania[6]	4	1	3	3	0	0	0	0	0	0	Roumanie[6]
Russian Federation	..	90	95	92	81	59	37	39	26	25	Fédération de Russie
Sweden	18	14	5	14	10	9	...	...	...	...	Suède
USSR (former)[7]	428	..	..	..	..	..	..	..	..	..	URSS (anc.)[7]

General Note.

Impulse turbines, reaction turbines and compound turbines. Mercury-vapour turbines are excluded. Steam piston-valve engines and parts of steam turbines are also excluded. (SITC, Rev.3: 71210-1A).

[1] Including gas turbines.
[2] Excluding steam turbines for ships.
[3] Shipments.
[4] In metric tons.
[5] Marketable production.
[6] Steam turbines of over 500 kW.
[7] Including gas and hydraulic turbines.

Remarque générale.

Turbines à action, turbines à réaction et turbines compound. Cette rubrique ne comprend pas les turbines à vapeur de mercure, les machines à vapeur à piston et les pièces détachées de turbines à vapeur. (CTCI, Rev.3: 71210-1A).

[1] Y compris les turbines à gaz.
[2] Non compris les turbines à vapeur de marine.
[3] Expéditions.
[4] En tonnes métriques.
[5] Production commercialisable.
[6] Turbines à vapeur de plus de 500 kW.
[7] Y compris les turbines à gaz et les turbines hydrauliques.

Steam turbines
Turbines à vapeur

ISIC-BASED CODE - CODE BASE CITI

3821-01B

Unit : Thousand kilowatts   Unité : Milliers de kilowatts

Country or area	1990	1991	1992	1993	1994	1995	1996	1997	1998	1999	Pays ou zone
Asia	**11612**	**13593**	**7766**	**9292**	**9292**	**7588**	**7680**	**13018**	**15815**	**9412**	**Asie**
Japan[1]	11612	13593	7766	9292	9292	7588	7680	13018	15815	9412	Japon[1]
Europe	**5049**	**12728**	**11446**	**9642**	**8651**	**7742**	**6838**	**6765**	**5222**	**5296**	**Europe**
Croatia	..	...	4	...	...	...	0	1	...	...	Croatie
Czechoslovakia(former)	986	1501	..	..	..	..	..	..	..	..	Tchécoslovaquie(anc.)
Czech Republic	..	..	1613	797	596	482	464	418	394	586	République tchèque
Germany	..	...	3678	3309	2888	...	...	...	...	...	Allemagne
Germany(Fed.Rep.)	3525	..	..	..	..	..	..	..	..	..	Allemagne(Rép.féd.)
German D.R.(former)	47	..	..	..	..	..	..	..	..	..	R.D.A. (anc.)
Hungary	54	133	6	...	...	...	...	...	...	...	Hongrie
Poland	...	6	...	60	60	12	448	300	70	65	Pologne
Romania[2]	375	12	74	329	...	...	...	...	...	...	Roumanie[2]
Russian Federation	..	7783	5943	5081	4843	3693	2372	2492	1203	1090	Fédération de Russie
USSR (former)[1][3]	18350	..	..	..	..	..	..	..	..	..	URSS (anc.)[1][3]
Total	**35011**	**26321**	**19212**	**18934**	**17943**	**15330**	**14518**	**19783**	**21037**	**14708**	**Total**

General Note.
Impulse turbines, reaction turbines and compound turbines. Mercury-vapour turbines are excluded. Steam piston-valve engines and parts of steam turbines are also excluded. (SITC, Rev.3: 71210-1B).

[1] Including gas turbines.
[2] Steam turbines of over 500 kW.
[3] Including hydraulic turbines.

Remarque générale.
Turbines à action, turbines à réaction et turbines compound. Cette rubrique ne comprend pas les turbines à vapeur de mercure, les machines à vapeur à piston et les pièces détachées de turbines à vapeur. (CTCI, Rev.3: 71210-1B).

[1] Y compris les turbines à gaz.
[2] Turbines à vapeur de plus de 500 kW.
[3] Y compris les turbines hydrauliques.

Engines, diesel
Moteurs diesel

3821-04A

Unit : Number of units　　　　　　　　　　　　　　　　　　　　　　　　　　　　　　　Unité : Nombre

Country or area	1990	1991	1992	1993	1994	1995	1996	1997	1998	1999	Pays ou zone
America, North	**206106**	**184245**	**178215**	**196895**	**220276**	**245762**	**242472**	**229649**	**296249**	**344382**	Amérique du Nord
United States	206106	184245	178215	196895	220276	245762	242472	229649	296249	344382	Etats-Unis
America, South	**156**	**156**	**130**	**132**	**186**	**176**	**156**	**156**	**156**	**156**	Amérique du Sud
Colombia	...	...	130	132	186	176	...	...	...	...	Colombie
Asia	**2992318**	**2836575**	**2799325**	**2831897**	**2966227**	**3320921**	**3307281**	**3106270**	**3260473**	**4045567**	Asie
Bangladesh	4441	...	491	520	270	525	360	...	...	...	Bangladesh
India	1741154	1677178	1682273	1674407	1774224	1965612	1988303	1946255	2221194	2927538	Inde
Indonesia	43554	70621	59014	89797	106693	92676	...	26196	23608	...	Indonésie
Japan	1165266	1056628	1031287	1035724	1057982	1226173	1217144	1100594	987258	1072460	Japon
Turkey	33433	19544	16933	24466	20650	30628	32639	28522	23865	15442	Turquie
Uzbekistan	..	6207	5453	2669	1815	1219	307	0	...	...	Ouzbékistan
Viet Nam	4470	5296	3264	...	...	...	...	...	...	...	Viet Nam
Europe	**364125**	**362139**	**337913**	**296857**	**318136**	**275521**	**257127**	**267864**	**286569**	**272027**	Europe
Croatia	..	600	225	120	19	28	40	26	13	...	Croatie
Denmark[1]	680	621	695	660	543	...	...	...	...	...	Danemark[1]
Czechoslovakia(former)	6392	6478	..	..	..	..	..	..	..	..	Tchécoslovaquie(anc.)
Czech Republic	..	..	4129	...	...	...	...	...	...	...	République tchèque
Finland*	290	125	170	250	347	393	407	...	...	...	Finlande*
Germany	..	228132	213371	194114	222375	173353	158800	171433	187993	...	Allemagne
Germany(Fed.Rep.)	240652	..	..	..	..	..	..	..	..		Allemagne(Rép.féd.)
German D.R.(former)	1183	..	..	..	..	..	..	..	..		R.D.A. (anc.)
Greece	...	...	...	...	...	...	...	...	81	...	Grèce
Hungary	17	...	...	...	...	...	...	...	...	...	Hongrie
Latvia	..	5650	2177	585	1024	994	515	803	811	3	Lettonie
Norway	...	...	...	...	...	...	...	989	...	...	Norvège
Slovakia	..	...	...	...	...	...	5718	5589	...	...	Slovaquie
Slovenia	..	2942	1304	864	713	1435	...	...	...	...	Slovénie
Spain	35292	31711	25458	6419	5505	8692	6239	6016	8445	7719	Espagne
Sweden	...	...	...	...	...	...	...	21071	20811	24976	Suède
Ukraine	..	6244	5095	1587	1031	639	728	442	354	534	Ukraine
United Kingdom	...	...	...	59102	53423	...	...	...	...	...	Royaume-Uni
Total	**3562705**	**3383115**	**3315583**	**3325781**	**3504825**	**3842381**	**3807037**	**3603939**	**3843447**	**4662132**	Total

General Note.
Compression-ignition engines (Diesel, semi-Diesel and other heavy oil engines).
Diesel engines for motor vehicles are excluded. (SITC, Rev.3: 71382-0A).

Remarque générale.
Moteurs à allumage par compression (diesels, semi-diesels et autres moteurs à huile lourde), non compris les diesels pour véhicules automobiles. (CTCI, Rev.3: 71382-0A).

[1] Sales.

[1] Ventes.

Engines, internal combustion
Moteurs à explosion, à essence

ISIC-BASED CODE - CODE BASE CITI
3821-08A

Unit : Thousand units   Unité : En milliers

Country or area	1990	1991	1992	1993	1994	1995	1996	1997	1998	1999	Pays ou zone
America, North	**16326**	**16220**	**18216**	**20538**	**23287**	**22287**	**22621**	**23998**	**26352**	**29727**	**Amérique du Nord**
United States	16326	16220	18216	20538	23287	22287	22621	23998	26352	...	Etats-Unis
Asia	**6311**	**5829**	**5949**	**4980**	**4867**	**5278**	**5412**	**6076**	**6246**	**7957**	**Asie**
Indonesia	...	...	26	...	...	...	...	...	...	...	Indonésie
Japan	6285	5803	5923	4954	4841	5252	5386	6050	6220	7931	Japon
Europe	**545**	**399**	**337**	**351**	**330**	**327**	**230**	**183**	**145**	**154**	**Europe**
Bulgaria	30	6	6	3	3	4	2	1	...	...	Bulgarie
Croatia	..	4	2	3	2	2	3	1	2	...	Croatie
Germany	..	38	36	28	22	...	...	12	8	...	Allemagne
Germany(Fed.Rep.)	105	..	..	..	..	..	..	..	..	..	Allemagne(Rép.féd.)
Greece	6	6	7	...	...	...	...	...	...	...	Grèce
Hungary	3	9	13	...	...	...	...	...	...	...	Hongrie
Poland	209	100	105	111	122	114	121	103	69	93	Pologne
Romania [1]	178	136	110	143	113	115	20	15	12	...	Roumanie [1]
Slovakia	..	..	...	...	...	...	...	...	4	3	Slovaquie
Slovenia	..	23	10	5	7	8	7	0	0	...	Slovénie
Spain	14	46	27	...	...	...	...	...	...	...	Espagne
Yugoslavia	..	31	17	11	14	13	6	4	6	4	Yougoslavie
Total	**23182**	**22448**	**24502**	**25869**	**28484**	**27892**	**28263**	**30257**	**32743**	**37838**	**Total**

General Note.
Spark-ignition, internal combustion, piston engines, equipped with fuel injection pumps, ignition parts, fuel and oil reservoirs, water radiators, oil coolers, water, oil and fuel pumps, blowers, air and oil filters, starting devices etc. Automobile, bus, truck and aircraft engines are excluded. (SITC, Rev.3: 71381-0A).

[1] Including engines for motor vehicles and aircraft.

Remarque générale.
Moteurs à explosion à pistons, à allumage par étincelle, munis des appareils suivants: dispositif d'alimentation en carburant, accessoires d'allumage, réservoirs à essence et à huile, radiateur à eau, refroidisseur à huile, pompes à eau, à huile et à essence, compresseur d'air, filtres à air et huile, dispositif de démarrage, etc. Cette rubrique ne comprend pas les moteurs d'automobile, d'autocar et d'avion. (CTCI, Rev.3: 71381-0A).

[1] Y compris les moteurs d'automobile et d'avion.

Engines, internal combustion
Moteurs à explosion, à essence

ISIC-BASED CODE - CODE BASE CITI

3821-08B

Unit : Thousand horsepower

Unité : Milliers de CV

Country or area	1990	1991	1992	1993	1994	1995	1996	1997	1998	1999	Pays ou zone
Asia	**138875**	**150912**	**192099**	**177814**	**190825**	**186687**	**256409**	**247512**	**200092**	**231082**	**Asie**
China	72446	89583	132666	153016	165547	158190	221528	206419	160343	178016	Chine
Japan[1]	64932	59663	57870	22643	22601	25732	32113	37940	38551	51235	Japon[1]
Korea, Republic of	1497	1666	1563	2155	[2]2677	[2]2765	[2]2768	[2]3153	[2]1198	[2]1831	Corée, République de
Europe	**20001**	**12445**	**9452**	**11590**	**8624**	**9189**	**2804**	**2190**	**1670**	**1104**	**Europe**
Bulgaria	2049	442	447	243	202	266	119	224	...	...	Bulgarie
Croatia	..	7	5	5	5	5	5	1	...	...	Croatie
Germany	..	...	564	323	305	195	231	...	...	...	Allemagne
Germany(Fed.Rep.)	878	..	..	..	..	..	..	...	..	..	Allemagne(Rép.féd.)
Hungary	12	35	75	...	...	...	...	...	...	...	Hongrie
Poland	3059	1210	906	813	679	1021	1427	1048	958	726	Pologne
Romania[3]	13835	10079	7393	10152	7375	7642	981	791	664	336	Roumanie[3]
Slovenia	..	110	62	13	17	19	...	...	..	...	Slovénie
Yugoslavia, SFR	168	..	..	..	..	..	..	..	..	..	Yougoslavie, RSF
Total	**158876**	**163357**	**201551**	**189404**	**199449**	**195876**	**259213**	**249702**	**201762**	**232186**	**Total**

General Note.

Spark-ignition, internal combustion, piston engines, equipped with fuel injection pumps, ignition parts, fuel and oil reservoirs, water radiators, oil coolers, water, oil and fuel pumps, blowers, air and oil filters, starting devices etc. Automobile, bus, truck and aircraft engines are excluded. (SITC, Rev.3: 71381-0B).

Remarque générale.

Moteurs à explosion à pistons, à allumage par étincelle, munis des appareils suivants: dispositif d'alimentation en carburant, accessoires d'allumage, réservoirs à essence et à huile, radiateur à eau, refroidisseur à huile, pompes à eau, à huile et à essence, compresseur d'air, filtres à air et huile, dispositif de démarrage, etc. Cette rubrique ne comprend pas les moteurs d'automobile, d'autocar et d'avion. (CTCI, Rev.3: 71381-0B).

[1] Excluding internal-combustion engines for ships and gas engines.

[2] Excluding engines for marine.

[3] Including engines for motor vehicles and aircraft.

[1] Non compris les moteurs à combustion interne pour bateaux et les moteurs à essence.

[2] Non compris les moteurs pour usages marins.

[3] Y compris les moteurs d'automobile et d'avion.

Hydraulic turbines
Turbines hydrauliques

ISIC-BASED CODE - CODE BASE CITI

3821-16A

Unit : Number of units   Unité : Nombre

Country or area	1990	1991	1992	1993	1994	1995	1996	1997	1998	1999	Pays ou zone
America, South											**Amérique du Sud**
Colombia	...	...	...	...	3	144	...	...	...	...	Colombie
Asia											**Asie**
Japan	28	23	20	23	21	18	21	25	35	25	Japon
Europe											**Europe**
Austria	...	...	...	...	...	122	76	66	57	53	Autriche
Czechoslovakia(former)	112	60	..	..	..	..	..	..	..	..	Tchécoslovaquie(anc.)
Czech Republic	..	..	41	51	39	51	48	42	36	25	République tchèque
Finland	...	4	6	6	2	5	5	...	...	...	Finlande
France[1][2]	3763	6873	3298	7794	...	...	...	...	...	...	France[1][2]
Hungary	3	...	...	...	...	...	...	...	...	...	Hongrie
Latvia	..	...	...	...	...	...	...	...	...	13	Lettonie
Romania	41	16	9	8	3	3	1	3	4	1	Roumanie
Russian Federation	..	8	9	7	10	21	9	10	23	9	Fédération de Russie
Slovenia	..	5	5	5	3	2	...	...	...	...	Slovénie
Spain	39	34	42	...	49	38	22	...	52	78	Espagne
Sweden	...	...	...	...	3	6	5	4	5	2	Suède
Ukraine	..	4	5	6	9	6	8	8	2	5	Ukraine

General Note.

Turbines consisting of a rotor encased in a stator which directs jets of water on to the blades of the rotor. There are three types of hydraulic turbines - the Pelton type, the Francis type and the Kaplan type. Regulators for water engines are also included. (SITC, Rev.3: 71810-1A).

Remarque générale.

Turbines se composant d'un rotor enveloppé d'un stator destiné à orienter les filets d'eau sur les aubages du rotor. Il existe trois types de turbines hydrauliques: les turbines du type Pelton, les turbines du type Francis et les turbines du type Kaplan. Cette rubrique comprend les organes régulateurs chargés de régler le débit d'eau des tuyères. (CTCI, Rev.3: 71810-1A).

[1] Shipments.
[2] In metric tons.

[1] Expéditions.
[2] En tonnes métriques.

Cultivators, scarifiers, weeders, hoes etc.
Cultivateurs, scarificateurs, extirpateurs, houes etc.

ISIC-BASED CODE - CODE BASE CITI

3822-02

Unit : Number of units											Unité : Nombre
Country or area	1990	1991	1992	1993	1994	1995	1996	1997	1998	1999	Pays ou zone
Africa	**294404**	**294404**	**294404**	**294404**	**294404**	**294404**	**294404**	**294404**	**294404**	**294404**	**Afrique**
Congo	294404	...	...	...	...	...	...	...	...	...	Congo
America, North	**31708**	**23647**	**20037**	**17260**	**17946**	**18297**	**18930**	**21702**	**19098**	**10267**	**Amérique du Nord**
United States[1]	31708	23647	20037	17260	17946	18297	18930	21702	19098	10267	Etats-Unis[1]
Asia	**362335**	**377103**	**349062**	**324881**	**172493**	**211361**	**198550**	**208223**	**176805**	**119395**	**Asie**
Armenia	..	454	108	48	0	0	0	0	0	0	Arménie
Japan	269027	270714	245675	225564	77669	81349	86267	93195	83725	102757	Japon
Korea, Republic of	...	...	...	...	...	129506	111613	113790	...	16569	Corée, République de
Turkey	...	...	...	#218	673	60	53	31	210	69	Turquie
Uzbekistan	..	12677	10072	6181	1281	446	617	1207	...	...	Ouzbékistan
Europe	**164420**	**254956**	**335569**	**187938**	**162721**	**167244**	**153721**	**154429**	**159638**	**169877**	**Europe**
Belarus	..	1175	553	893	539	1195	753	351	520	496	Bélarus
Belgium	..	...	...	...	...	455	393	...	...	...	Belgique
Bulgaria	...	...	437	1284	1735	966	838	...	1406	2141	Bulgarie
Croatia	..	1554	295	399	...	246	324	224	564	...	Croatie
Czech Republic	..	..	...	...	...	...	...	2214	2525	4724	République tchèque
Finland	0	#1173	764	706	563	682	511	736	495	325	Finlande
France[2]	23671	15541	96068	18300	...	...	...	...	...	...	France[2]
Germany		33993	24233	24226	25230	26365	21854	21316	22742	...	Allemagne
Germany(Fed.Rep.)	45510	..	..	..	..	..	..	..	..	..	Allemagne(Rép.féd.)
Greece	[3]4245	[3]4213	[3]3313	[3]887	[3]444	[3]464	[3]638	[3]630	5319	...	Grèce
Hungary	2660	1458	2638	2858	5339	3915	...	...	6996	19318	Hongrie
Latvia	..	2372	2968	2149	1088	728	455	301	829	1616	Lettonie
Lithuania	..	...	...	...	...	1384	1463	296	233	182	Lituanie
Poland	32730	16272	16216	15725	19727	16957	19379	20121	13028	13144	Pologne
Portugal	7333	5227	5720	5443	5313	6344	8662	9278	11347	11806	Portugal
Romania[4]	1465	981	563	3123	2233	1694	1335	948	1018	826	Roumanie[4]
Russian Federation	..	71821	49126	38211	3691	1985	2882	2963	3247	3165	Fédération de Russie
Slovakia	..	..	...	...	...	...	22	27	...	772	Slovaquie
Slovenia	..	4006	2193	979	1566	1116	498	494	416	407	Slovénie
Spain	1163	1660	3060	463	477	1124	...	...	...	...	Espagne
Ukraine	..	13637	5452	20076	5734	1927	2024	1896	2094	2977	Ukraine
United Kingdom	...	...	...	35769	41655	56764	42341	...	...	...	Royaume-Uni
Yugoslavia	..	31295	71457	10430	2823	1110	1190	1905	2853	1820	Yougoslavie
USSR (former)[5]	150760	..	..	..	..	..	..	..	..	..	URSS (anc.)[5]
Total	**1003626**	**950109**	**999072**	**824483**	**647563**	**691306**	**665605**	**678758**	**649944**	**593943**	**Total**

General Note.
Animal- or tractor-operated. Cultivators, scarifiers, weeders, hoes and like machines usually consisting of a horizontal frame fitted with several rows of various types of tools (shares, discs, teeth etc.) which may be rigid or springy, fixed or movable, and are sometimes interchangeable, used for working, weeding or smoothing the soil after ploughing or during the growth of the crops. Corn and cotton-type cultivators are excluded. (SITC, Rev.3: 72113-1).

[1] Shipments.
[2] Excluding rollers.
[3] Incomplete coverage.
[4] Tractor-operated cultivators only.
[5] Tractor-drawn machines only.

Remarque générale.
Cultivateurs, scarificateurs, extirpateurs, houes, etc., consistant habituellement en un bâti horizontal garni de plusieurs rangées d'outils (dents, socs, disques) rigides ou flexibles, fixes ou mobiles, parfois interchangeables, utilisés pour ameublir, désherber ou niveler le sol après labour ou pour entretenir les cultures. Cette rubrique ne comprend pas les cultivateurs des types utilisés pour le maïs et le coton. (CTCI, Rev.3: 72113-1).

[1] Expéditions.
[2] Non compris les rouleaux.
[3] Couverture incomplète.
[4] Cultivateurs tractés seulement.
[5] Machines tractées seulement.

Harrows, rotary, animal- or tractor-operated
Herses rotatives, à traction animale ou tractées

ISIC-BASED CODE - CODE BASE CITI

3822-08

Unit : Number of units   Unité : Nombre

Country or area	1990	1991	1992	1993	1994	1995	1996	1997	1998	1999	Pays ou zone
America, North	**88840**	**69390**	**74313**	**94399**	**120410**	**99897**	**113191**	**123022**	**108036**	**106052**	**Amérique du Nord**
United States	88840	69390	74313	94399	120410	99897	113191	123022	[1]108036	[1]106052	Etats-Unis
Asia	**6301**	**15786**	**11854**	**8138**	**7987**	**6889**	**6476**	**6384**	**6424**	**6361**	**Asie**
Indonesia	...	...	6301	...	...	...	...	...	...	...	Indonésie
Kazakhstan	..	9485	5553	1837	1686	588	175	83	123	60	Kazakhstan
Europe	**81301**	**228719**	**160367**	**171217**	**72450**	**48540**	**35855**	**29528**	**28399**	**24022**	**Europe**
Austria[2][3][4]	...	...	...	...	...	...	...	743	...	...	Autriche[2][3][4]
Belarus	..	75	60	55	211	295	372	395	334	486	Bélarus
Belgium	...	13131	...	...	...	476	518	523	1277	1607	Belgique
Croatia	..	...	...	...	...	6287	6135	1558	4748	...	Croatie
Finland	5578	2187	#439	302	412	865	896	...	...	...	Finlande
France	15269	#8462	6584	9910	5741	...	...	...	...	...	France
Germany	...	...	12938	11152	13209	#4065	2370	1738	...	...	Allemagne
Germany(Fed.Rep.)	28937	..	..			..	..	..	..	..	Allemagne(Rép.féd.)
Greece	8085	8042	8393	[5]1114	[5]1443	[5]1305	[5]1435	[5]1764	...	...	Grèce
Hungary	...	...	...	...	...	...	...	7899	6218	7007	Hongrie
Latvia	..	...	...	302	255	268	241	...	...	...	Lettonie
Lithuania	..	...	3	145	376	366	579	654	25	333	Lituanie
Poland	1942	3094	6034	3639	4474	5731	4684	5058	2676	1833	Pologne
Portugal	3535	2743	2436	2264	2060		...	...	...	...	Portugal
Romania[6]	3591	3625	5077	10245	8170	6448	3946	3884	3732	2850	Roumanie[6]
Russian Federation	..	4033	112	1635	226	1422	80	289	504	263	Fédération de Russie
Spain	1623	2349	2419	532	568	602	...	...	...	...	Espagne
Ukraine	..	153527	98367	114081	19632	6716	2497	2196	3610	2271	Ukraine
Yugoslavia	..	2958	1850	453	285	420	288	810	633	314	Yougoslavie
USSR (former)	20713	..	..	..	..	..	..	..	..	..	URSS (anc.)
Total	**197155**	**313895**	**246534**	**273754**	**200847**	**155326**	**155522**	**158934**	**142859**	**136435**	**Total**

General Note.
Animal- or tractor-operated rotary harrows which are used for breaking up the soil after ploughing. (SITC, Rev.3: 72113-2).

[1] Shipments.
[2] 1995 data are confidential.
[3] 1996 data are confidential.
[4] Beginning 1998, data are confidential.
[5] Incomplete coverage.
[6] Tractor-operated harrows only.

Remarque générale.
Herses servant à émietter le sol après le labourage. (CTCI, Rev.3: 72113-2).

[1] Expéditions.
[2] Pour 1995, les données sont confidentielles.
[3] Pour 1996, les données sont confidentielles.
[4] A partir de 1998, les données sont confidentielles.
[5] Couverture incomplète.
[6] Herses tractées seulement.

Ploughs, animal- or tractor-operated
Charrues à traction animale ou tractées

ISIC-BASED CODE - CODE BASE CITI

3822-18

Unit : Number of units
Unité : Nombre

Country or area	1990	1991	1992	1993	1994	1995	1996	1997	1998	1999	Pays ou zone
Africa	**11837**	**9531**	**8318**	**7836**	**6730**	**5819**	**4812**	**3693**	**2663**	**2634**	**Afrique**
Kenya	1901	...	...	...	...	...	...	...	...	...	Kenya
Mali	633	80	50	410	143	232	225	...	...	...	Mali
South Africa	1303	550	367	525	...	...	...	...	...	...	Afrique du Sud
United Rep.Tanzania	...	...	...	5000	4000	3000	2000	1000	...	...	Rép. Unie de Tanzanie
America, North	**4453**	**4028**	**4417**	**4118**	**5800**	**3516**	**4950**	**9197**	**9047**	**8085**	**Amérique du Nord**
Mexico	4453	4028	4417	4118	5800	3516	4950	9197	9047	8085	Mexique
America, South	**615**	**256**	**166**	**129**	**172**	**200**	**165**	**142**	**120**	**97**	**Amérique du Sud**
Colombia	615	...	166	129	172	200	...	...	...	...	Colombie
Asia	**1654**	**1907**	**1465**	**2879**	**1806**	**1142**	**1437**	**1110**	**1003**	**1105**	**Asie**
Indonesia	...	...	600	1440	860	...	...	...	...	...	Indonésie
Kyrgyzstan	..	...	...	...	...	68	370	63	36	36	Kirghizistan
Turkey[1]	687	587	551	1165	712	107	100	80	0	102	Turquie[1]
Europe	**163881**	**323932**	**271018**	**191417**	**166455**	**136951**	**107438**	**104456**	**107052**	**98386**	**Europe**
Belarus	..	11300	6111	4420	5500	16	13	20	29	60	Bélarus
Belgium	...	51282	49061	...	...	...	...	...	...	...	Belgique
Bulgaria	2378	1949	3653	3802	2437	1252	800	614	1067	373	Bulgarie
Croatia	..	557	10	40	...	413	824	483	409	...	Croatie
Denmark[2]	502	231	...	...	...	...	...	...	...	...	Danemark[2]
Czechoslovakia(former)	768	...	..	..	..	..	..	..	..	..	Tchécoslovaquie(anc.)
Czech Republic	..	..	10490	8618	8325	...	...	725	320	82	République tchèque
Finland	4874	2600	#700	600	500	...	...	...	...	...	Finlande
France	23560	18178	15071	13240	5875	...	...	...	...	...	France
Germany	...	...	...	9183	7732	...	...	...	...	...	Allemagne
Germany(Fed.Rep.)	16214	..	..	..	..	..	..	..	..	..	Allemagne(Rép.féd.)
German D.R.(former)[3]	3563	..	..	..	..	..	..	..	..	..	R.D.A. (anc.)[3]
Greece	2933	3210	2987	2256	1784	1616	1694	2171	2032	...	Grèce
Hungary	1009	604	219	2336	5442	3924	4625	4635	4704	3434	Hongrie
Latvia	..	..	...	748	313	335	125	72	19	15	Lettonie
Lithuania	..	...	210	3074	1439	994	618	295	578	315	Lituanie
Poland	31794	14694	13485	14158	19696	19092	15128	13562	9690	5815	Pologne
Portugal	8013	5451	4668	4346	3513	4132	5323	5024	5537	6021	Portugal
Romania	8380	11089	7809	9337	7304	4422	2570	1825	2042	1926	Roumanie
Russian Federation	..	81684	68658	20794	13024	3981	1600	1319	1352	1808	Fédération de Russie
Slovakia	..	..	...	...	4111	5647	115	190	...	...	Slovaquie
Slovenia	..	220	654	703	672	666	2521	1181	476	340	Slovénie
Spain	4066	16296	4154	1279	1309	2237	1747	1753	5040	4945	Espagne
Sweden	4820	2990	...	...	1474	2246	2324	2366	2323	1698	Suède
Ukraine[3]	..	71935	58358	33417	6519	1712	1371	3947	4045	3026	Ukraine[3]
United Kingdom	...	...	...	835	...	...	...	...	...	...	Royaume-Uni
Yugoslavia	..	17548	9289	2548	17582	16565	1429	4443	5043	4507	Yougoslavie
T.F.Yug.Rep. Macedonia	..	167	167	99	140	18	...	...	...	...	L'ex-RY Macédoine
USSR (former)[3]	180533										URSS (anc.)[3]
Total	**362972**	**339654**	**285384**	**206379**	**180963**	**147628**	**118802**	**118597**	**119885**	**110306**	**Total**

General Note.
Implements which cut a furrow slice by means of sharp-edged steel discs, of saucer-like shape, set obliquely to the ground surface (disc ploughs, animal- and tractor-operated) and machines which by means of a coulter and a share detach a slice of soil vertically from the undersoil (mouldboard ploughs, animal - and tractor-operated). (SITC, Rev.3: 72111-0).

[1] State sector only.
[2] Sales.
[3] Tractor-drawn ploughs only.

Remarque générale.
Charrues qui découpent la bande de terre au moyen de disques d'acier à bord tranchant, en forme de soucoupes, inclinés par rapport à la surface du sol (charrues à disques, à traction animale et tractées), et machines qui detachent du sol une tranche verticale de terre au moyen d'un coutre et d'un soc (charrues à soc, à traction animale et tractées). (CTCI, Rev.3: 72111-0).

[1] Secteur public seulement.
[2] Ventes.
[3] Charrues tractées seulement.

Seeders, planters and transplanters
Semoirs, planteuses et repiqueuses

ISIC-BASED CODE - CODE BASE CITI

3822-26

Unit : Number of units — Unité : Nombre

Country or area	1990	1991	1992	1993	1994	1995	1996	1997	1998	1999	Pays ou zone
Africa	**199**	**0**	**7**	**169**	**17**	**377**	**198**	**274**	**301**	**328**	**Afrique**
Mali[1]	199	0	7	169	17	377	198	...	...	...	Mali[1]
America, North	**432082**	**491091**	**482641**	**467796**	**467861**	**467332**	**467012**	**466691**	**466370**	**466050**	**Amérique du Nord**
Mexico	3453	2871	2544	2147	2212	...	...	...	...	...	Mexique
United States[2]	428629	488220	480097	...	...	...	...	...	...	...	Etats-Unis[2]
America, South	**57**	**57**	**34**	**136**	**57**	**1**	**57**	**57**	**57**	**57**	**Amérique du Sud**
Colombia	...	...	34	136	...	1	...	...	...	...	Colombie
Asia	**135555**	**129262**	**120926**	**123224**	**122281**	**111545**	**110348**	**104715**	**75869**	**81712**	**Asie**
Japan[3]	91141	87019	80540	84980	85837	86713	70614	63367	53122	58137	Japon[3]
Korea, Republic of[4]	...	...	...	...	...	24820	39697	41298	22747	23575	Corée, République de[4]
Turkey	379	152	239	41	185	12	37	50	0	0	Turquie
Europe	**85424**	**165245**	**107889**	**84875**	**65744**	**62287**	**48479**	**44844**	**42512**	**29934**	**Europe**
Austria	...	...	...	...	...	1440	1021	2010	2024	1245	Autriche
Bulgaria	1088	413	130	397	502	574	713	675	587	166	Bulgarie
Croatia	..	1905	86	241	...	429	382	277	666	...	Croatie
Czechoslovakia(former)	3848	2206	..	..	..	..	..	..	..		Tchécoslovaquie(anc.)
Czech Republic					767	554	488	53	140	...	République tchèque
Finland	3931	3238	3823	2898	822	885	821	...	...	1246	Finlande
France	38227	30743	28823	22550	19859	...	...	...	...	...	France
Germany	..	...	...	5788	6520	19706	...	...	20254	...	Allemagne
Germany(Fed.Rep.)	8883	..	..	..	..	..	..	..	..	..	Allemagne(Rép.féd.)
Greece	1091	1365	1011	595	646	496	573	719	734	...	Grèce
Hungary	1020	449	415	525	1127	1540	428	610	516	286	Hongrie
Latvia	..	...		383	603	509	385	270	58	85	Lettonie
Lithuania	..	...	...	...	...	85	294	209	4	0	Lituanie
Poland	13794	3970	5118	6378	10425	6441	7054	5880	3392	1619	Pologne
Portugal	558	399	229	215	267	246	255	256	272	321	Portugal
Romania[5]	8597	6287	5125	9832	10823	7290	4631	4536	3445	2172	Roumanie[5]
Russian Federation	..	40953	21303	11495	1967	1636	1921	1528	1328	3270	Fédération de Russie
Slovenia	..	754	980	461	822	329	400	222	300	107	Slovénie
Spain	3046	6234	3863	1814	2274	2659	3396	3240	...	...	Espagne
Sweden	222	181	191	311	482	497	909	1011	906	1038	Suède
Ukraine[5]	..	48740	17613	17040	4210	1505	1080	1424	740	1240	Ukraine[5]
Yugoslavia	..	2121	2854	1420	1438	904	592	1073	1110	801	Yougoslavie
USSR (former)[5]	117175	..	..	..	..	..	..	..	..	..	URSS (anc.)[5]
Oceania	**2303**	**2303**	**2303**	**2303**	**2303**	**2303**	**2303**	**2303**	**2303**	**2303**	**Océanie**
Australia	2303	...	...	...	...	...	...	...	...	...	Australie
Total	**772795**	**787958**	**713800**	**678503**	**658263**	**643845**	**628396**	**618884**	**587413**	**580384**	**Total**

General Note.
Boxes or hoppers mounted on wheels and fitted with devices for setting seeds. They may include devices for opening or recovering the furrow. This item includes animal- or tractor-operated seeders, planters and transplanters. (SITC, Rev.3: 72112-1).

Remarque générale.
Bacs ou trémies sur roues, munis de mécanismes distributeurs. Ils peuvent être dotés d'outils traceurs ou de dispositifs de recouvrement. Cette rubrique comprend les semoirs, planteuses et repiqueuses, à traction animale ou tractés. (CTCI, Rev.3: 72112-1).

[1] Seeders only.
[2] Shipments.
[3] Including rice transplanters.
[4] Transplanters only.
[5] Tractor-drawn seeders only.

[1] Semoirs seulement.
[2] Expéditions.
[3] Y compris les appareils à repiquer le riz.
[4] Repiqueuses seulement.
[5] Semoirs tractés seulement.

Combine harvester-threshers
Moissonneuses-batteuses

ISIC-BASED CODE - CODE BASE CITI

3822-32

Unit : Number of units

Unité : Nombre

Country or area	1990	1991	1992	1993	1994	1995	1996	1997	1998	1999	Pays ou zone
Africa	**567**	**510**	**530**	**291**	**176**	**46**	**328**	**79**	**59**	**247**	**Afrique**
Algeria	567	510	530	291	176	46	328	79	59	247	Algérie
America, North	**14629**	**11555**	**9198**	**11794**	**11794**	**11794**	**11794**	**11794**	**11794**	**11794**	**Amérique du Nord**
United States [1]	14629	11555	9198	...	...	...	...	...	...	...	Etats-Unis [1]
America, South	**4694**	**3351**	**4216**	**5729**	**7807**	**5415**	**4814**	**5952**	**5186**	**4258**	**Amérique du Sud**
Brazil	4585	3242	4087	5480	7786	5378	4705	5843	5077	4149	Brésil
Colombia	...	...	129	249	21	37	...	...	...	...	Colombie
Asia	**84091**	**93404**	**90130**	**84385**	**78424**	**92420**	**118783**	**143713**	**99046**	**102202**	**Asie**
China	5173	10638	15370	9569	7310	17393	45700	76100	...	...	Chine
Iran(Islamic Rep. of)	[2]665	[2]559	[2]546	[2]458	[2]111	[3]199	[3]240	[3]262	[3]251	...	Iran(Rép. islamique)
Japan	68993	72913	65673	65192	61242	66767	63371	56709	40196	42173	Japon
Korea, Republic of	...	...	...	...	...	6524	6870	7805	8651	...	Corée, République de
Turkey	...	...	1078	1703	2298	1537	2602	2837	2412	1009	Turquie
Europe	**43579**	**79751**	**59288**	**48241**	**26911**	**22640**	**18300**	**19770**	**17952**	**19043**	**Europe**
Belgium	7007	...	5769	...	...	...	...	...	...	...	Belgique
Bulgaria	9735	2576	27	264	108	77	261	166	...	...	Bulgarie
Croatia	..	252	85	1	...	65	73	88	100	...	Croatie
Denmark [4]	690	574	441	...	...	...	...	...	...	...	Danemark [4]
Finland	840	478	319	264	331	274	260	...	...	...	Finlande
Germany	..	...	5543	4638	4539	5491	6445	8080	8245	...	Allemagne
Germany(Fed.Rep.)	8416	..	..	..	..	..	..	..	..	..	Allemagne(Rép.féd.)
German D.R.(former)	7248	..	..	..	..	..	..	..	...	..	R.D.A. (anc.)
Poland	5019	417	306	200	304	382	539	885	642	225	Pologne
Romania	4111	1274	590	441	588	764	308	220	32	0	Roumanie
Russian Federation	..	55356	42165	32989	12063	6241	2515	2326	1038	2049	Fédération de Russie
Slovenia	..	4100	2068	1515	708	1700	...	...	...	...	Slovénie
Spain	513	554	375	...	...	...	...	...	...	...	Espagne
Yugoslavia	..	3452	1600	492	738	209	292	554	458	107	Yougoslavie
USSR (former)	65736	..	..	..	..	..	..	..	..	..	URSS (anc.)
Total	**213296**	**188571**	**163362**	**150440**	**125111**	**132315**	**154019**	**181308**	**134037**	**137543**	**Total**

General Note.

Tractor-operated or self-propelled. Machines which successively reap, thresh, clean and bag the grain. (SITC, Rev.3: 72122-1).

[1] Shipments.
[2] Production by establishments employing 50 or more persons.
[3] Production by establishments employing 10 or more persons.
[4] Sales.

Remarque générale.

Tractées ou automotrices. Machines qui réalisent successivement la coupe, l'égrenage, le nettoyage et la mise en sacs du grain. (CTCI, Rev.3: 72122-1).

[1] Expéditions.
[2] Production des établissements occupant 50 personnes ou plus.
[3] Production des établissements occupant 10 personnes ou plus.
[4] Ventes.

Mowers, animal- or tractor-operated and self-propelled
Faucheuses, à traction animale ou tractées et automotrices

ISIC-BASED CODE - CODE BASE CITI

3822-38

Unit : Number of units   Unité : Nombre

Country or area	1990	1991	1992	1993	1994	1995	1996	1997	1998	1999	Pays ou zone
Africa	**3007**	**3000**	**1243**	**1003**	**636**	**500**	**514**	**290**	**11**	**497**	**Afrique**
Algeria	3007	3000	1243	1003	636	500	514	290	11	497	Algérie
America, North	**19784**	**21176**	**14985**	**17379**	**23081**	**20163**	**20457**	**20751**	**21045**	**21339**	**Amérique du Nord**
Mexico	286	0	...	...	...	...	...	...	...	...	Mexique
United States[1]	19498	21176	14842	17236	22938	...	...	...	...	...	Etats-Unis[1]
America, South	**6**	**6**	**6**	**6**	**6**	**6**	**6**	**6**	**6**	**6**	**Amérique du Sud**
Colombia	...	...	...	...	...	6	...	...	...	...	Colombie
Asia	**1450**	**896**	**823**	**394**	**965**	**962**	**1232**	**1291**	**1968**	**1383**	**Asie**
Turkey	1450	896	823	394	965	962	1232	1291	1968	1383	Turquie
Europe	**2066055**	**1947694**	**2057071**	**1986167**	**2094702**	**3429497**	**2652250**	**3132636**	**3200640**	**4173054**	**Europe**
Belarus	..	...	717	5189	8821	4151	2126	2626	3428	2431	Bélarus
Belgium	..	...	...	...	...	72439	68405	...	...	...	Belgique
Bulgaria	...	...	197	235	...	...	...	...	...	...	Bulgarie
Croatia	..	2925	1167	1727	...	1649	1358	1050	4162	...	Croatie
Denmark[2]	136071	...	157082	144196	141267	99825	65511	57887	30040	116240	Danemark[2]
Czech Republic	..	..	...	...	38812	75214	91725	57593	51296	65203	République tchèque
Finland	3681	1574	1768	1823	1419	1392	1848	...	...	1643	Finlande
France	22145	12445	17525	10300	...	...	...	...	...	...	France
Germany	..	...	17007	20816	18044	#1292654	998711	1126224	1187259	...	Allemagne
Germany(Fed.Rep.)	31607	..									Allemagne(Rép.féd.)
Greece	436	405	298	...	...	...	...	...	223	...	Grèce
Hungary	...	...	...	...	...	...	...	32566	4926	183342	Hongrie
Latvia	..	...	...	419	363	72	123	90	114	1375	Lettonie
Lithuania	..	...	...	...	...	564	918	788	567	219	Lituanie
Poland	30598	20047	13571	11088	14232	16092	14897	12105	12053	144719	Pologne
Russian Federation	..	20448	16120	16997	8226	5074	3311	4225	6089	6693	Fédération de Russie
Slovakia	..	...	...	...	...	...	...	...	210	202	Slovaquie
Slovenia	..	8204	4204	3899	5090	5877	7110	7077	5274	7984	Slovénie
Spain	372	219	727	1249	366	345	229	227	149	96	Espagne
Sweden	285989	205651	206250	165685	189251	258155	179766	382427	287004	304952	Suède
United Kingdom	...	...	...	1389174	1501081	1496775	1122651	1342134	1511889	...	Royaume-Uni
Yugoslavia	..	13407	9016	5573	4401	9241	3583	16935	7822	6029	Yougoslavie
USSR (former)	49828	..								..	URSS (anc.)
Oceania	**247000**	**213000**	**230000**	**230000**	**230000**	**230000**	**230000**	**230000**	**230000**	**230000**	**Océanie**
Australia	247000	213000	...	...	...	...	...	...	...	...	Australie
Total	**2387130**	**2185772**	**2304128**	**2234949**	**2349390**	**3681128**	**2904459**	**3384974**	**3453670**	**4426279**	**Total**

General Note.
Animal- or tractor-operated and self-propelled mowers for cutting hay etc., consisting of a wheeled frame, supporting a horizontal cutter bar and a toothed knife. (SITC, Rev.3: 72121-0, 72123-1).

Remarque générale.
Faucheuses (à traction animale, tractées ou automotrices) servant à couper les foins, etc., consistant en un cadre sur roues portant une barre de coupe horizontale et une lame à dents tranchantes. (CTCI, Rev.3: 72121-0, 72123-1).

[1] Shipments.
[2] Sales.

[1] Expéditions.
[2] Ventes.

Rakes, animal- or tractor-operated and self-propelled
Râteaux, à traction animale ou tractés et automotrices

ISIC-BASED CODE - CODE BASE CITI

3822-44

Unit : Number of units   Unité : Nombre

Country or area	1990	1991	1992	1993	1994	1995	1996	1997	1998	1999	Pays ou zone
America, North	**16670**	**11348**	**10779**	**10857**	**14533**	**9330**	**11563**	**13485**	**12491**	**10931**	**Amérique du Nord**
Mexico	4419	2610	3491	2929	4600	1736	4514	6980	6531	5516	Mexique
United States [1]	12251	8738	7288	7928	9933	...	...	...	...	...	Etats-Unis [1]
Asia	..	**148**	**148**	**148**	**148**	**148**	**148**	**148**	**148**	**148**	**Asie**
Kazakhstan	..	148	...	...	...	...	...	...	...	...	Kazakhstan
Europe	**68324**	**73257**	**50584**	**57880**	**51364**	**40382**	**33972**	**30782**	**19727**	**29679**	**Europe**
Austria	...	...	...	...	...	8271	6872	6617	8665	7948	Autriche
Belarus	..	2005	1439	1628	847	261	725	837	1020	621	Bélarus
Croatia	..	1305	1167	1525	...	1286	1130	268	327	...	Croatie
Finland	2151	812	600	128	245	212	160	...	...	...	Finlande
France	17556	11852	9881	14130	7565	...	...	...	...	...	France
Germany	..	...	17740	17725	26280	...	...	...	4855	...	Allemagne
Germany(Fed.Rep.)	40953				..	..					Allemagne(Rép.féd.)
Portugal	...	...	...	792	...	...	...	...	...	...	Portugal
Russian Federation	..	21254	2574	8475	2904	1241	570	680	620	1272	Fédération de Russie
Slovakia	..	..	...	...	...	...	459	...	...	...	Slovaquie
Slovenia	..	4512	3393	1796	2840	4173	1289	908	1230	1244	Slovénie
Ukraine	..	6701	5267	3818	604	52	56	54	106	8	Ukraine
Yugoslavia	..	388	171	188	496	99	154	172	79	85	Yougoslavie
USSR (former)	39087	..	..	..	..	..	..	..	..	..	URSS (anc.)
Total	**124081**	**84753**	**61511**	**68885**	**66045**	**49859**	**45683**	**44414**	**32366**	**40758**	**Total**

General Note.
Animal-operated, self-propelled or tractor-operated tedder-rakes, windrower-rakes and bundling rakes. (SITC, Rev.3: 72123-2).

Remarque générale.
Râteaux-faneurs, râteaux-daineurs et râteaux (à traction animale, ou tractés et automotrices). (CTCI, Rev.3:72123-2).

[1] Shipments.

[1] Expéditions.

Threshing machines
Batteuses

ISIC-BASED CODE - CODE BASE CITI

3822-49

Unit : Number of units   Unité : Nombre

Country or area	1990	1991	1992	1993	1994	1995	1996	1997	1998	1999	Pays ou zone
America, South	**614**	**575**	**675**	**724**	**805**	**147**	**76**	**50**	**72**	**55**	**Amérique du Sud**
Brazil	601	544	614	703	784	110	37	9	29	10	Brésil
Colombia	13	...	61	21	21	37	...	...	...	...	Colombie
Asia	**80693**	**75185**	**60744**	**56186**	**52399**	**56811**	**38542**	**33403**	**30740**	**29133**	**Asie**
Indonesia	1650	1625	557	479	450	989	...	1180	1279	...	Indonésie
Japan	22634	20337	12656	11663	11422	12422	11593	9042	5102	5508	Japon
Korea, Republic of	5506	5423	...	...	...	...	...	...	...	...	Corée, République de
Turkey	1691	2700	1078	1703	2298	1537	2602	2837	2412	1009	Turquie
Viet Nam	...	...	...	...	...	36398	17856	14879	16482	*16525	Viet Nam
Europe	**48142**	**2776**	**3928**	**1410**	**780**	**2072**	**2013**	**1908**	**1427**	**1064**	**Europe**
Croatia	..	...	...	...	...	...	...	43	34	...	Croatie
Denmark	...	...	0	[1]0	[1]0	[1]640	[1]808	[1]909	[1]671	[1]583	Danemark
Germany	..	...	...	...	...	...	146	...	...	...	Allemagne
German D.R.(former)	43459	..	..	...	...	..	..	..	..	..	R.D.A. (anc.)
Latvia	..	...	...	...	6	1	1	...	3	...	Lettonie
Lithuania	..	...	...	...	...	3	2	0	0	0	Lituanie
Poland	809	646	6	1	0	0	0	...	...	...	Pologne
Portugal	...	...	49	...	...	...	...	...	...	...	Portugal
Russian Federation	..	335	7	...	0	...	...	...	...	...	Fédération de Russie
Spain	3468	1145	3543	773	491	1064	...	...	...	...	Espagne
United Kingdom	...	...	...	282	46	16	64	93	99	...	Royaume-Uni
USSR (former)	405	..	..	..	..	..	..	..	..	..	URSS (anc.)
Total	**129854**	**78536**	**65347**	**58320**	**53983**	**59029**	**40630**	**35360**	**32239**	**30252**	**Total**

General Note.
Machines used in place of hand tools for threshing grain. They may be driven by a steam engine, tractor etc. (SITC, Rev.3: 72123-3).

Remarque générale.
Machines utilisées au lieu d'outils à main pour le battage du grain. Elles peuvent être actionnées par une locomobile, un tracteur, etc. (CTCI, Rev.3: 72123-3)

[1] Sales.

[1] Ventes.

Milking machines
Trayeuses

ISIC-BASED CODE - CODE BASE CITI

3822-55

Unit : Number of units   Unité : Nombre

Country or area	1990	1991	1992	1993	1994	1995	1996	1997	1998	1999	Pays ou zone
America, South	**673**	**791**	**909**	**1101**	**1201**	**971**	**1501**	**1541**	**1617**	**1735**	**Amérique du Sud**
Argentina	...	...	...	1100	1200	970	1500	1540	...	...	Argentine
Colombia	1	...	...	...	...	...	...	...	...	...	Colombie
Asia	**3354**	**5518**	**11318**	**10966**	**11427**	**12116**	**12600**	**12489**	**12534**	**11440**	**Asie**
Japan	2273	4244	10140	9788	10249	10938	11422	11311	11356	10262	Japon
Korea, Republic of	1081	1274	...	...	...	...	...	...	...	...	Corée, République de
Europe	**15259**	**66901**	**43513**	**42271**	**21547**	**22488**	**14991**	**21134**	**25974**	**23624**	**Europe**
Croatia	..	2213	903	743	...	754	775	855	1216	...	Croatie
Czechoslovakia(former)	2166	1192	..	..	..	..	..	..	..	..	Tchécoslovaquie(anc.)
Czech Republic	..	..	1332	996	1035	1042	619	584	...	...	République tchèque
France	5622	3352	2657	...	...	...	...	...	...	...	France
Germany	..	...	...	...	...	6846	3116	...	...	...	Allemagne
Hungary	702	15	53	...	...	...	...	...	...	...	Hongrie
Latvia	..	34546	13446	13121	7024	7090	4125	137	320	304	Lettonie
Poland	5802	1092	...	730	261	709	456	8693	13001	11150	Pologne
Portugal	...	...	...	475	433	...	...	...	...	...	Portugal
Russian Federation	..	17692	13716	16241	1006	528	496	459	381	369	Fédération de Russie
Slovenia	..	59	0	0	...	...	17	0	11	...	Slovénie
Spain	432	825	899	...	...	...	...	...	...	...	Espagne
Ukraine	..	...	...	51	794	117	0	38	20	3	Ukraine
United Kingdom	...	...	...	...	...	81	...	...	...	...	Royaume-Uni
USSR (former)	52538	..	..	..	..	..	..	..	..	..	URSS (anc.)
Total	**71824**	**73210**	**55739**	**54338**	**34175**	**35574**	**29092**	**35164**	**40125**	**36799**	**Total**

General Note.

Machines comprising a rust-proof milking pail with a special cover to which is fitted a pulsator for causing intermittent suction in the attached teat cup assembly. In the cases where the air pump for causing a comparative vacuum in the milk pails forms an integral part of the pail, the whole unit (machine plus pump) is included under this heading. (SITC, Rev.3: 72131-0).

Remarque générale.

Machines comprenant un pot collecteur en métal inoxydable, et des gobelets trayeurs, reliés à un organe pulsateur disposé sur le couvercle. Lorsque la motopompe destinée à créer un vide relatif dans les gobelets trayeurs fait corps avec le récipient collecteur, l'ensemble (machine et pompe) est compris dans cette rubrique. (CTCI, Rev.3: 72131-0).

Garden tractors
Tracteurs horticoles

ISIC-BASED CODE - CODE BASE CITI

3822-58A

Unit : Number of units   Unité : Nombre

Country or area	1990	1991	1992	1993	1994	1995	1996	1997	1998	1999	Pays ou zone
America, North	**162538**	**160331**	**158125**	**155918**	**161445**	**161099**	**138763**	**146136**	**156525**	**131823**	**Amérique du Nord**
United States[1]	...	...	...	...	161445	161099	138763	146136	156525	131823	Etats-Unis[1]
America, South	**2528**	**1974**	**1878**	**1487**	**1532**	**1603**	**968**	**844**	**690**	**778**	**Amérique du Sud**
Brazil[2]	2528	1974	1878	1487	1532	1603	968	844	690	778	Brésil[2]
Asia	**1370457**	**1620269**	**1639903**	**1189033**	**1491373**	**2188718**	**2225121**	**2148768**	**2003163**	**2206297**	**Asie**
China	1101400	1347800	1390700	961400	1355400	2062997	2096600	2016400	1874000	2055200	Chine
Georgia	..	..	3498	2039	1073	1282	56	304	307	7	Géorgie
Japan	269027	270714	245675	225564	134870	124409	128435	132034	128826	151060	Japon
Myanmar	...	...	...	...	...	...	30	...	...	...	Myanmar
Europe	**65866**	**91372**	**74494**	**52559**	**43638**	**81567**	**75832**	**63508**	**64942**	**85174**	**Europe**
Belgium[3]	5248	...	4364	...	...	...	...	...	...	...	Belgique[3]
Croatia	..	18005	5641	1947	...	1774	1120	1846	2962	...	Croatie
Germany	..	...	17435	13212	11009	#52502	53433	41609	42862	...	Allemagne
Germany(Fed.Rep.)[4]	23808	..	..	...	...	..	..	..	...	...	Allemagne(Rép.féd.)[4]
Greece	384	199	703	856	749	937	909	877	...	...	Grèce
Russian Federation	..	4191	5590	7846	1244	1231	588	353	134	287	Fédération de Russie
Slovenia	..	...	...	...	...	...	512	0	0	603	Slovénie
Spain	25287	14325	13144	5138	3536	2728	...	...	...	...	Espagne
Sweden	...	...	...	7433	12750	13233	...	...	...	...	Suède
Ukraine	..	...	...	3986	314	478	204	23	5	115	Ukraine
Yugoslavia	..	21536	14108	7056	4195	3599	1181	2855	2061	2423	Yougoslavie
Total	**1601389**	**1873946**	**1874400**	**1398997**	**1697988**	**2432987**	**2440684**	**2359256**	**2225320**	**2424072**	**Total**

General Note.
Small tractors and mechanical cultivators developing less than 10 horsepower, used mainly for horticultural purposes. Motor tillers are included. (SITC, Rev.3: 72249-1A).

Remarque générale.
Petits tracteurs et cultivateurs mécaniques de moins de 10 CV utilisés surtout en horticulture, y compris les motobineuses. (CTCI, Rev.3: 72249-1A).

[1] Shipments.
[2] Motor tillers only.
[3] Including motorized cultivators.
[4] 1982-1989, data are confidential.

[1] Expéditions.
[2] Motobineuses seulement.
[3] Y compris les motoculteurs.
[4] 1982-1989, les données sont confidentielles.

Tractors of 10 HP and over, other than industrial and road tractors
Tracteurs (autres que les tracteurs industriels et ceux pour train routier) de 10 CV et plus

ISIC-BASED CODE - CODE BASE CITI

3822-61A

Unit : Number of units — Unité : Nombre

Country or area	1990	1991	1992	1993	1994	1995	1996	1997	1998	1999	Pays ou zone
Africa	**5242**	**4306**	**4625**	**5041**	**3785**	**2888**	**2147**	**321**	**1703**	**2352**	**Afrique**
Algeria	3505	3203	3009	4632	3385	2712	1279	321	1703	2352	Algérie
Egypt	1737	1103	1616	409	400	176	868	...	...	...	Egypte
America, North	**1134432**	**1136372**	**1212768**	**1205348**	**1273561**	**1297720**	**1335776**	**1376621**	**1409680**	**1444245**	**Amérique du Nord**
Mexico	9235	7759	9898	5362	7578	7307	10068	15619	13383	12654	Mexique
United States[1]	1125197	1128613	1202870	1199986	1265983	...	...	...	...	...	Etats-Unis[1]
America, South	**4868**	**3099**	**3783**	**2926**	**3667**	**2551**	**2869**	**2715**	**2562**	**2409**	**Amérique du Sud**
Argentina[2]	4868	3099	3783	2926	3667	2551	...	...	...	...	Argentine[2]
Asia	**268059**	**311151**	**280292**	**275945**	**288175**	**318905**	**332608**	**346261**	**320138**	**292048**	**Asie**
China	39400	52700	57000	37718	46800	63253	83700	82400	67800	65400	Chine
Indonesia	268	155	38	83	...	10364	...	...	5153	...	Indonésie
Iran(Islamic Rep. of)[3]	9561	12361	8993	7619	16339	6398	5652	4957	4432	...	Iran(Rép. islamique)[3]
Japan[4]	174529	161842	156182	155497	167686	164685	164008	171077	154343	163322	Japon[4]
Kazakhstan	..	34100	13400	5643	1988	1803	2465	2058	404	678	Kazakhstan
Korea, Republic of	...	...	...	...	...	25965	20982	23756	27085	25248	Corée, République de
Myanmar	230	265	200	188	130	...	440	330	341	518	Myanmar
Syrian Arab Republic	...	...	...	401	1501	1111	1714	1521	1650	1665	Rép. arabe syrienne
Turkey	20470	3788	1296	32942	24581	39417	45609	53100	57347	24969	Turquie
Uzbekistan	..	21132	19256	11531	1684	4032	3778	2802	...	...	Ouzbékistan
Viet Nam[5]	1700	2279	770	...	...	...	...	...	...	...	Viet Nam[5]
Europe	**582569**	**865930**	**772265**	**657955**	**523490**	**502696**	**495776**	**491931**	**461891**	**486832**	**Europe**
Austria[6]	7529	6297	5286	4896	4573	...	...	...	...	...	Autriche[6]
Belarus	..	95502	96063	82371	42879	27953	26815	27421	26922	27397	Bélarus
Belgium	108885	108008	103208	...	...	...	...	...	...	...	Belgique
Bulgaria	3120	1729	889	598	465	289	310	315	...	...	Bulgarie
Croatia	..	4880	1978	1309	783	359	1263	1132	976	...	Croatie
Czechoslovakia(former)	33205	20830	..	..	..	..	..	..	..	..	Tchécoslovaquie(anc.)
Czech Republic	..	..	16043	8380	12933	11674	11182	13425	...	...	République tchèque
Finland	5587	3556	3019	3322	5294	6845	7903	...	...	...	Finlande
France[7]	108635	76293	93955	82540	75032	...	...	...	...	...	France[7]
Germany	..	66924	53533	44284	48556	...	...	...	...	...	Allemagne
Germany(Fed.Rep.)	76653	..	..	..	..	..	..	..	..	..	Allemagne(Rép.féd.)
German D.R.(former)[8]	1736	..	..	..	..	..	..	..	..	..	R.D.A. (anc.)[8]
Greece	820	504	320	...	...	...	...	...	...	...	Grèce
Hungary	108	9	186	...	...	...	...	...	...	...	Hongrie
Italy	75815	58323	55519	54184	61068	69653	76655	85539	80043	78062	Italie
Poland	36094	17642	7976	11560	15465	21510	25129	22862	14999	8793	Pologne
Republic of Moldova	..	6572	5356	[9]4173	[9]1211	[9]951	[9]706	[9]938	[9]706	[9]42	Rép. de Moldova
Romania[10]	25640	22453	21471	26455	14128	15458	13063	10537	9572	4497	Roumanie[10]
Russian Federation	..	178178	136598	89087	28695	21169	13964	12438	9771	15417	Fédération de Russie
Slovakia	..	..	...	2724	881	773	526	1159	...	...	Slovaquie
Slovenia	..	61	...	...	...	585	1704	667	897	1011	Slovénie
Spain	10611	10248	9366	4742	...	...	...	...	...	...	Espagne
Sweden	...	...	...	147	267	347	...	...	...	...	Suède
Ukraine	..	90163	71158	55462	15989	10386	5428	4645	3248	4984	Ukraine
United Kingdom	[11]82551	...	...	68103	73930	70848	74109	70317	68953	...	Royaume-Uni
Yugoslavia	..	24817	14321	5448	4429	1955	1652	4099	3530	1867	Yougoslavie
Yugoslavia, SFR	5326	..	..	..	..	..	..	..	..	..	Yougoslavie, RSF
USSR (former)	494817	..	..	..	..	..	..	..	..	..	URSS (anc.)
Total	**2489987**	**2320858**	**2273733**	**2147215**	**2092678**	**2124760**	**2169176**	**2217849**	**2195974**	**2227886**	**Total**

For general note and footnotes, see end of table. — Voir la fin du tableau pour la remarque générale et les notes.

Tractors of 10 HP and over, other than industrial and road tractors (continued)
Tracteurs (autres que les tracteurs industriels et ceux pour train routier) de 10 CV et plus (suite)
ISIC-BASED CODE - CODE BASE CITI

3822-61A

General Note.

Vehicles constructed essentially for hauling or pushing another vehicle, appliance or load, whether or not they contain subsidiary provision for the transport, in connection with the main use of the tractor, of tools, seeds, fertilizers or other goods etc., irrespective of their mode of propulsion (internal combustion engine, steam engine etc.). This heading includes agricultural as well as other tractors, for example, for use in forestry or in construction. Road tractors for tractor-trailer combinations and industrial tractors are, however, excluded. Walking tractors, equipped with a single driving axle carried on one or two wheels, the steering of which is effected by means of two handles, used like normal tractors and possibly with interchangeable implements, are also included. Tractors of less than 10 horsepower (garden tractors) are excluded. (SITC, Rev.3: 72230-1A, 72241-0A,

[1] Shipments.
[2] Agricultural tractors only.
[3] Production by establishments employing 50 or more persons.
[4] Including bulldozers.
[5] Tractors of 12 HP only.
[6] Beginning 1995, data are confidential.
[7] Agricultural tractors of all sizes.
[8] Tractors of all types.
[9] Excluding Transnistria region.
[10] Including tractors of less than 10 HP.
[11] Deliveries of wheeled and half-track tractors. Production of wheeled tractors.

Remarque générale.

Véhicules essentiellement conçus, soit pour remorquer ou pousser d'autres engins, véhicules ou charges. Ils peuvent cependant comporter un plateau accessoire ou un dispositif analogue permettant le transport, en corrélation avec leur usage principal, d'outils, de semences, d'engrais, etc., quelle que soit la source d'énergie qui les actionne (moteur à explosion, moteur à vapeur, etc.). Cette rubrique comprend les tracteurs agricoles et autres (tracteurs forestiers et tracteurs de travaux publics, par exemple). Elle ne comprend pas les tracteurs pour trains routiers ni les tracteurs industriels. Elle comprend aussi les moto-culteurs comportant un seul essieu moteur, à une ou deux roues, et guidés à la main au moyen de deux mancherons, qui sont utilisés comme les tracteurs proprement dits et sont munis éventuellement d'outils interchangeables. Elle ne comprend pas les tracteurs de moins de 10 CV (tracteurs horticoles). (CTCI, Rev.3: 72230-1A, 72241-0A, 72249-2A).

[1] Expéditions.
[2] Tracteurs agricoles seulement.
[3] Production des établissements occupant 50 personnes ou plus.
[4] Y compris les bouteurs.
[5] Tracteurs de 12 cv seulement.
[6] A partir de 1995, les données sont confidentielles
[7] Tracteurs agricoles de toutes dimensions.
[8] Tracteurs de tous types.
[9] Non compris la région de Transnistria.
[10] Y compris les tracteurs de moins de 10 cv.
[11] Livraisons de tracteurs à roues et semi-chenillés. Production de tracteurs à roues.

Fertilizer distributors, animal-, hand- or tractor-operated
Distributeurs d'engrais, à traction animale, à bras ou tractés

ISIC-BASED CODE - CODE BASE CITI
3822-63

Unit : Number of units | | | | | | | | | | Unité : Nombre

Country or area	1990	1991	1992	1993	1994	1995	1996	1997	1998	1999	Pays ou zone
Africa	**282**	**1045**	**664**	**664**	**664**	**664**	**664**	**664**	**664**	**664**	**Afrique**
Algeria	282	1045	...	...	...	...	...	...	...	...	Algérie
America, North	**227027**	**212686**	**253087**	**203108**	**251670**	**208350**	**319223**	**398034**	**353458**	**351230**	**Amérique du Nord**
Mexico	203686	192828	232711	180078	238943	195383	305829	383129	337152	331625	Mexique
United States	23341	19858	20376	23030	[1]12727	[1]12967	[1]13394	[1]14905	[1]16306	[1]19605	Etats-Unis
Asia	**8301**	**9184**	**8043**	**8946**	**7790**	**7175**	**7175**	**7175**	**7175**	**7175**	**Asie**
Indonesia	7453	6286	...	7785	...	...	...	...	...	...	Indonésie
Turkey	848	2898	868	1161	615	0	0	0	0	0	Turquie
Europe	**106124**	**151509**	**104826**	**93567**	**88262**	**98794**	**118600**	**120774**	**130493**	**119069**	**Europe**
Austria	3244	5237	2635	...	...	...	...	...	...	...	Autriche
Belarus	..	27723	6172	1698	1198	484	415	229	116	142	Bélarus
Belgium	47646	...	44941	...	...	...	...	...	...	...	Belgique
Bulgaria	368	218	12	193	131	41	36	144	121	47	Bulgarie
Croatia	..	49	11	31	...	16	30	61	400	...	Croatie
Finland	3883	1430	413	710	1048	778	775	...	798	692	Finlande
France	8403	5477	5535	5200	3973	...	...	...	...	...	France
Germany	..	24496	17756	14021	18297	#32215	53660	55674	65853	...	Allemagne
Germany(Fed.Rep.)	32660	..	..	..	..	..	..	..	..		Allemagne(Rép.féd.)
Greece	1823	1430	1361	...	716	734	652	696	529	...	Grèce
Hungary	...	...	...	...	...	...	...	140	103	242	Hongrie
Latvia	..	8050	2378	733	560	576	820	617	458	29	Lettonie
Lithuania	..	...	...	...	...	385	404	270	27	70	Lituanie
Portugal	441	463	...	...	...	...	392	...	...	...	Portugal
Slovenia	..	1395	2215	2319	2319	2332	962	1349	2168	1658	Slovénie
Spain	...	...	...	...	3958	4043	4889	4314	...	...	Espagne
Sweden	...	382	197	...	...	...	182	187	183	178	Suède
Ukraine	..	14853	8676	7316	1047	148	197	738	336	234	Ukraine
United Kingdom	...	...	...	...	2797	3157	2925	...	...	...	Royaume-Uni
Yugoslavia	..	5755	3935	1648	789	98	38	646	1474	750	Yougoslavie
Oceania	**4332**	**4332**	**4332**	**4332**	**4332**	**4332**	**4332**	**4332**	**4332**	**4332**	**Océanie**
Australia	4332	...	...	...	...	...	...	...	...	...	Australie
Total	**346066**	**378756**	**370951**	**310616**	**352718**	**319314**	**449993**	**530978**	**496121**	**482469**	**Total**

General Note.
Distributors for spreading manure or solid fertilizers, usually consisting of long box hoppers mounted on wheels and fitted with a distributing mechanism (animal-, hand- or tractor-operated). (SITC, Rev.3: 72112-2).

Remarque générale.
Distributeurs destinés à répandre le fumier ou les engrais solides, consistant en général en longues trémies-réservoirs montées sur roues et munies d'un mécanisme distributeur (à traction animale, à bras ou tracté). (CTCI, Rev.3: 72112-2).

[1] Shipments.

[1] Expéditions.

Drilling and boring machines
Perceuses

ISIC-BASED CODE - CODE BASE CITI

3823-01

Unit : Number of units   Unité : Nombre

Country or area	1990	1991	1992	1993	1994	1995	1996	1997	1998	1999	Pays ou zone
Africa	**412**	**210**	**122**	**30**	**194**	**194**	**194**	**194**	**194**	**194**	**Afrique**
Algeria	412	210	122	30	...	...	...	...	...	...	Algérie
America, North	**10966**	**9790**	**8397**	**7669**	**8827**	**11882**	**9344**	**7651**	**7229**	**6513**	**Amérique du Nord**
Mexico	2138	2187	855	487	...	...	...	...	...	...	Mexique
United States[1]	8828	7603	7542	7182	...	10465	7927	6234	5812	5096	Etats-Unis[1]
Asia	**48061**	**43347**	**32107**	**22222**	**24807**	**27140**	**26002**	**27389**	**19335**	**15631**	**Asie**
Azerbaijan	..	643	428	86	102	112	49	24	29	1	Azerbaïdjan
Bangladesh	131	...	...	...	...	...	...	...	...	...	Bangladesh
Indonesia	89	437	1000	52	...	...	...	...	5153	...	Indonésie
Japan	40171	33929	22973	14496	11936	14678	16414	17097	12531	9377	Japon
Korea, Republic of[2]	7662	8150	7336	7416	11107	10861	8025	8741	1491	2805	Corée, République de[2]
Turkey	8	57	239	41	185	12	37	50	0	0	Turquie
Europe	**34866**	**63752**	**53138**	**56796**	**38739**	**36486**	**30818**	**31902**	**27375**	**22139**	**Europe**
Bulgaria	4729	1959	996	759	850	864	953	906	955	906	Bulgarie
Croatia	..	458	346	255	...	4369	3212	1134	31	...	Croatie
Denmark[3]	348	394	223	197	...	...	...	...	...	...	Danemark[3]
Czechoslovakia(former)	901	1133	..	..	..	...	..	..	..	..	Tchécoslovaquie(anc.)
Czech Republic	..	..	...	...	...	...	1235	1263	1352	986	République tchèque
Finland	59	42	54	78	88	106	109	...	67	13	Finlande
France[4]	2500	1460	1212	...	...	...	...	...	...	...	France[4]
Germany	..	...	15085	21222	15955	13049	11730	...	11396	...	Allemagne
Germany(Fed.Rep.)	14158	..	..	..	..	..	..	..	..	..	Allemagne(Rép.féd.)
Hungary	1929	1257	#75	78	15	4	...	...	...	...	Hongrie
Lithuania	..	...	...	...	...	749	437	333	192	171	Lituanie
Poland	2238	2995	1858	1348	998	771	840	1253	917	624	Pologne
Portugal	...	...	75	52	...	...	...	...	...	...	Portugal
Russian Federation	..	16020	12835	10607	5291	5021	3088	2522	1877	1898	Fédération de Russie
Slovenia	..	114	60	0	...	...	...	4	0	...	Slovénie
Spain	3688	2567	2060	886	1738	2313	2185	2689	3317	4732	Espagne
Sweden	...	...	...	...	...	...	...	3158	3661	2996	Suède
Ukraine	..	7970	11113	12996	3745	1337	563	667	418	306	Ukraine
United Kingdom	...	...	...	901	1061	...	...	...	...	...	Royaume-Uni
Yugoslavia	..	924	607	276	206	328	100	106	133	111	Yougoslavie
Total	**94305**	**117099**	**93764**	**86717**	**72566**	**75702**	**66358**	**67135**	**54132**	**44476**	**Total**

General Note.
Metal-working machines fitted with a baseplate, stand or other device for mounting on the floor, or on a bench, wall or another machine. (SITC, Rev.3: 73140-0).

Remarque générale.
Machines-outils pour le travail des métaux, munies d'un socle, d'un pied ou d'un autre dispositif permettant de les fixer au sol, à un établi, à une paroi ou à une autre machine. (CTCI, Rev.3: 73140-0).

[1] Shipments.
[2] Drilling machines only.
[3] Sales.
[4] Limited coverage.

[1] Expéditions.
[2] Perceuses seulement.
[3] Ventes.
[4] Couverture limitée.

Forging, stamping and die-stamping machines
Marteaux, martinets et moutons

ISIC-BASED CODE - CODE BASE CITI

3823-07

Unit : Number of units   Unité : Nombre

Country or area	1990	1991	1992	1993	1994	1995	1996	1997	1998	1999	Pays ou zone
Asia	**689**	**2252**	**1742**	**1632**	**1291**	**1244**	**1051**	**991**	**890**	**772**	**Asie**
Japan	689	587	485	402	357	475	424	409	375	272	Japon
Kazakhstan	..	1165	757	730	434	269	127	82	15	...	Kazakhstan
Uzbekistan	..	500	...	...	...	...	...	...	...	...	Ouzbékistan
Europe	**5922**	**37389**	**26765**	**15940**	**7498**	**5742**	**3849**	**3618**	**3671**	**3323**	**Europe**
Belarus	..	¹858	469	193	191	232	204	107	149	134	Bélarus
Bulgaria	59	33	7	...	...	3	...	...	...	...	Bulgarie
Denmark²	...	1	0	0	0	0	...	...	...	...	Danemark²
Czechoslovakia(former)	7	24	..	..	..	..	..	..	..	..	Tchécoslovaquie(anc.)
Czech Republic	..		8	...	...	...	...	...	...	...	République tchèque
Finland	770	*667	...	...	...	...	...	...	...	...	Finlande
Germany	..	...	...	...	...	240	237	249	266	...	Allemagne
Germany(Fed.Rep.)³	256	..	..	..	..	..	..	..	..	..	Allemagne(Rép.féd.)³
German D.R.(former)¹	4124	..	..	..	..	..	..	..	..	..	R.D.A. (anc.)¹
Russian Federation	..	23936	16532	7451	3114	2184	1237	1239	1257	1063	Fédération de Russie
Slovakia	..	...	...	...	...	...	...	...	106	31	Slovaquie
Slovenia	..	547	429	176	136	235	...	...	...	...	Slovénie
Spain	153	174	171	966	464	619	...	...	...	...	Espagne
Ukraine	..	10813	7854	6078	2520	1379	614	492	319	270	Ukraine
Yugoslavia	..	...	260	7	4	...	...	1	...	1	Yougoslavie
Yugoslavia, SFR	552	..	..	..	..	..	..	..	..	..	Yougoslavie, RSF
Total	**6611**	**39641**	**28507**	**17572**	**8789**	**6986**	**4900**	**4609**	**4561**	**4095**	**Total**

General Note.
Mechanical, hydraulic, pneumatic and steam forge hammers and die-stamping hammers. Metal-working presses are excluded. (SITC, Rev.3: 73311-1).

Remarque générale.
Marteaux à forger, à estamper et à matricer, à commande mécanique, hydraulique, pneumatique ou à vapeur.Cette rubrique ne comprend pas les presses à former les métaux. (CTCI, Rev.3: 73311-1).

[1] Data refer to forging and pressing equipment.
[2] Sales.
[3] 1984-1989, data are confidential.

[1] Données se rapportant aux machines de forgeage et d'emboutissage.
[2] Ventes.
[3] 1984-1989, les données sont confidentielles.

Grinding and sharpening machines
Meuleuses et affûteuses

ISIC-BASED CODE - CODE BASE CITI

3823-10

Unit : Number of units | Unité : Nombre

Country or area	1990	1991	1992	1993	1994	1995	1996	1997	1998	1999	Pays ou zone
America, North	**58276**	**49187**	**54585**	**56068**	**61100**	**66439**	**65737**	**112443**	**68389**	**55129**	**Amérique du Nord**
United States [1]	58276	49187	54585	56068	61100	66439	65737	112443	68389	55129	Etats-Unis [1]
Asia	**16194**	**14534**	**8388**	**6356**	**6635**	**7883**	**7983**	**7943**	**6209**	**4869**	**Asie**
Indonesia	221	210	...	250	227	...	...	...	...	...	Indonésie
Japan	13062	11956	7014	4904	4767	6093	6661	6766	5657	4094	Japon
Korea, Republic of	2911	2368	1147	1202	1641	1563	1095	950	325	548	Corée, République de
Europe	**88121**	**87242**	**82138**	**137191**	**131608**	**107215**	**149908**	**67519**	**66988**	**51529**	**Europe**
Austria	93	131	104	51	...	...	...	...	...	...	Autriche
Belarus	..	5512	3562	2458	732	183	230	315	427	480	Bélarus
Bulgaria	58	42	65	48	16	9	30	24	...	...	Bulgarie
Croatia	..	193	183	147	...	15	97	41	70	...	Croatie
Denmark [2]	...	...	5287	...	...	17602	19034	19079	30193	21798	Danemark [2]
Czechoslovakia(former)	18903	18636	..	..	..	..	..	..	..	..	Tchécoslovaquie(anc.)
Czech Republic	..	..	16595	...	...	...	4884	4587	3181	2242	République tchèque
Finland	195	193	180	221	231	180	153	...	...	...	Finlande
Germany	..	...	26804	21715	20469	20285	16968	18745	23510	...	Allemagne
Germany(Fed.Rep.)	36212	..	..	..	..	..	..	..	..	..	Allemagne(Rép.féd.)
German D.R.(former)	3460	..	..	..	..	..	..	..	..	..	R.D.A. (anc.)
Greece	...	...	...	...	...	...	...	...	106	...	Grèce
Hungary	0	97	67	...	...	...	...	...	...	...	Hongrie
Lithuania	..	619	406	231	40	37	18	27	20	22	Lituanie
Poland	13048	5879	11065	5187	7471	4002	6042	6285	7030	6636	Pologne
Portugal	...	...	98	...	...	...	...	...	...	...	Portugal
Slovakia	..	..	...	...	...	...	250	156	79	92	Slovaquie
Spain	751	1088	1063	#70303	70322	55940	96602	#795	977	1139	Espagne
Sweden	...	...	...	...	...	72	...	16124	102	134	Suède
Ukraine	..	13692	12002	6975	2195	1953	969	681	722	575	Ukraine
Yugoslavia	..	539	299	214	290	142	170	131	133	65	Yougoslavie
Total	**162591**	**150963**	**145111**	**199615**	**199343**	**181537**	**223628**	**187905**	**141586**	**111527**	**Total**

General Note.
Metal-working grinding, filing and sharpening machines. Including machines for grinding metallic carbide or hard metal tooltips and machines with metal brushes and abrasives. (SITC, Rev.3: 73161-0, 73162-0, 73163-0, 73164-0, 73165-0, 73166-0).

Remarque générale.
Machines-outils pour le travail des métaux, destinées au meulage, au limage et à l'affûtage, y compris celles servant à meuler le tranchant en carbure métallique ou en métal dur des outils et les machines équipées de brosses et d'abrasifs. (CTCI, REv.3: 73161-0, 73162-0, 73163-0, 73164-0, 73165-0, 73166-0).

[1] Shipments.
[2] Sales.

[1] Expéditions.
[2] Ventes.

Lathes
Tours
ISIC-BASED CODE - CODE BASE CITI

3823-13

Unit : Number of units

Unité : Nombre

Country or area	1990	1991	1992	1993	1994	1995	1996	1997	1998	1999	Pays ou zone
Africa	**270**	**273**	**310**	**194**	**118**	**196**	**189**	**110**	**14**	**171**	**Afrique**
Algeria	270	273	310	194	118	196	189	110	14	171	Algérie
America, North	**3247**	**2658**	**2409**	**3042**	**3662**	**4643**	**4190**	**5058**	**5089**	**3807**	**Amérique du Nord**
United States[1]	3247	2658	2409	3042	3662	4643	4190	5058	5089	3807	Etats-Unis[1]
America, South	**117**	**117**	**97**	**103**	**155**	**112**	**117**	**117**	**117**	**117**	**Amérique du Sud**
Colombia	...	...	97	103	155	112	...	...	...	...	Colombie
Asia	**43305**	**40611**	**24925**	**20165**	**25886**	**33290**	**32765**	**31846**	**27557**	**23551**	**Asie**
Armenia	..	2633	1079	486	395	190	141	81	71	33	Arménie
Bangladesh[2]	4	13	3	1	1	...	...	...	...	...	Bangladesh[2]
Georgia	..	...	1001	348	109	57	18	28	21	2	Géorgie
Indonesia	2	45	42	46	96	166	...	23	4	...	Indonésie
Japan	32659	26216	16155	12343	14961	20339	21443	23357	22652	16924	Japon
Korea, Republic of	10597	11324	6643	6931	10265	12526	11094	8357	4809	6542	Corée, République de
Turkey	43	23	2	10	59	12	16	0	0	0	Turquie
Europe	**39146**	**45064**	**34804**	**25940**	**22516**	**28080**	**27214**	**24891**	**24858**	**24454**	**Europe**
Austria[3]	1726	1647	1421	915	709	1482	1452	801	1914	...	Autriche[3]
Belarus	..		162	332	57	70	93	117	131	96	Bélarus
Bulgaria	5014	4744	3587	2197	1979	2496	2513	2315	1761	1611	Bulgarie
Croatia	..	584	463	358	...	52	68	98	144	...	Croatie
Denmark[4]	545	384	279	374	...	...	...	...	...	...	Danemark[4]
Czechoslovakia(former)	6020	5853	..	..	..	..	..	..	..	..	Tchécoslovaquie(anc.)
Czech Republic	..	..	1017	709	685	735	943	932	994	989	République tchèque
Finland	4	1	1	1	2	3	2	...	...	...	Finlande
France[1]	1400	988	942	...	546	...	...	...	...	...	France[1]
Germany	..	...	7689	4755	5322	8232	6375	5542	6070	...	Allemagne
Germany(Fed.Rep.)	7612	..	..	..	..	..	..	..	..	..	Allemagne(Rép.féd.)
Hungary	663	304	63	135	33	7	...	...	...	...	Hongrie
Latvia	..	...	...	28	87	36	26	20	29	...	Lettonie
Lithuania	..	95	110	93	27	64	4	1	6	6	Lituanie
Poland	5178	2184	1105	910	900	1012	1037	900	963	732	Pologne
Portugal	101	87	...	...	...	...	...	...	...	...	Portugal
Romania	3702	2883	1583	489	312	471	587	681	573	330	Roumanie
Russian Federation	..	9850	7079	6506	3807	3269	2095	2135	1798	1681	Fédération de Russie
Slovakia	..	..	...	1637	1566	1549	3121	3084	1660	1786	Slovaquie
Spain	1353	1265	925	1237	1713	2475	2887	3080	3509	3559	Espagne
Sweden	...	...	...	...	...	...	259	40	22	23	Suède
Ukraine	..	3300	2420	1619	867	808	338	352	234	213	Ukraine
United Kingdom	5742	...	...	2429	2941	3568	3845	3077	3377	...	Royaume-Uni
Yugoslavia	..	514	338	67	135	206	110	256	213	231	Yougoslavie
Total	**86085**	**88723**	**62545**	**49444**	**52337**	**66321**	**64474**	**62022**	**57635**	**52100**	**Total**

General Note.

Metal-working lathes of all kinds, whether or not automatic, including slide lathes, vertical lathes, capstan and turret lathes, production (or copying) lathes. (SITC, Rev.3: 73130-0).

[1] Shipments.

[2] Twelve months ending 30 June of year stated.

[3] 1999 data are confidential.

[4] Sales.

Remarque générale.

Tours à métaux, de tous types, automatiques ou non, y compris les tours parallèles, les tours verticaux, les tours à revolver, les tours à reproduire. (CTCI, Rev.3: 73130-0).

[1] Expéditions.

[2] Période de douze mois finissant le 30 juin de l'année indiquée.

[3] Pour 1999, les données sont confidentielles.

[4] Ventes.

Milling machines
Fraiseuses

ISIC-BASED CODE - CODE BASE CITI

3823-16

Unit : Number of units

Unité : Nombre

Country or area	1990	1991	1992	1993	1994	1995	1996	1997	1998	1999	Pays ou zone
Africa	**267**	**150**	**103**	**81**	**124**	**119**	**124**	**75**	**80**	**72**	**Afrique**
Algeria	267	150	103	81	124	119	124	75	80	72	Algérie
America, North	**4787**	**2772**	**2581**	**3386**	**4087**	**4747**	**4102**	**4240**	**3416**	**2749**	**Amérique du Nord**
United States[1]	4787	2772	2581	3386	4087	4747	4102	4240	3416	2749	Etats-Unis[1]
Asia	**12601**	**12603**	**7051**	**5110**	**6808**	**7462**	**6546**	**5711**	**3107**	**3471**	**Asie**
Armenia	..	759	410	0	63	73	47	188	82	27	Arménie
Bangladesh	144	...	...	...	...	...	...	...	...	...	Bangladesh
Indonesia	21	...	...	50	...	...	...	...	...	...	Indonésie
Japan	8492	7584	3913	2007	1791	1832	2198	2368	2019	1022	Japon
Korea, Republic of	3775	3994	2509	2824	4667	5293	3952	2900	825	2242	Corée, République de
Turkey	169	86	39	85	107	84	169	75	1	0	Turquie
Europe	**31665**	**25472**	**23603**	**17136**	**14408**	**13439**	**12474**	**12432**	**12469**	**13189**	**Europe**
Austria[2]	458	526	844	223	209	625	362	284	279	...	Autriche[2]
Belarus	..	150	56	13	0	1	3	5	3	2	Bélarus
Bulgaria	1240	961	432	324	200	227	295	412	104	139	Bulgarie
Croatia	..	212	168	192	...	77	90	165	224	...	Croatie
Denmark[3]	...	201	200	0	0	0	...	...	...	...	Danemark[3]
Czechoslovakia(former)	1470	1176	..	..	..	..	..	..	..	..	Tchécoslovaquie(anc.)
Czech Republic	..	..	1358	...	...	...	1109	1039	1117	821	République tchèque
France[1]	700	496	401	...	394	...	...	...	...	...	France[1]
Germany	..	...	...	6680	6327	...	5213	5335	5348	...	Allemagne
Germany(Fed.Rep.)	12150	..	..	..	..	..	..	..	..	..	Allemagne(Rép.féd.)
German D.R.(former)	3051	..	..	..	..	..	..	..	..	..	R.D.A. (anc.)
Greece	1805	1452	...	...	...	...	...	...	4	...	Grèce
Hungary	136	297	256	50	3	...	...	...	...	...	Hongrie
Latvia	..	...	...	12	44	44	9	26	78	...	Lettonie
Lithuania	..	1303	1035	450	341	255	213	161	130	58	Lituanie
Poland	1196	834	500	248	260	274	281	354	257	222	Pologne
Romania	1196	1355	764	436	162	341	458	403	321	333	Roumanie
Russian Federation	..	4233	4144	3424	1560	897	622	591	641	724	Fédération de Russie
Slovenia	..	13	12	15	26	27	...	...	...	...	Slovénie
Spain	7062	4169	4553	788	1458	1600	1852	1605	2986	3075	Espagne
Sweden	98	...	48	22	27	25	...	...	...	...	Suède
Ukraine	..	1208	1040	752	195	90	48	161	168	45	Ukraine
United Kingdom	...	...	...	824	856	493	268	240	245	...	Royaume-Uni
Yugoslavia	..	15	...	...	...	...	...	...	...	3	Yougoslavie
Total	**49320**	**40996**	**33337**	**25713**	**25426**	**25767**	**23246**	**22458**	**19071**	**19481**	**Total**

General Note.
Metal-working machines designed to work a plane or profile surface by means of rotating tools, known as milling cutters. (SITC, Rev.3: 73151-0, 73152-0, 73153-0, 73154-0).

Remarque générale.
Machines-outils pour le travail des métaux conçues pour usiner une surface plane ou un profil au moyen d'outils tournant appelés fraises. (CTCI, Rev.3: 73151-0, 73152-0, 73153-0, 73154-0).

[1] Shipments.
[2] 1999 data are confidential.
[3] Sales.

[1] Expéditions.
[2] Pour 1999, les données sont confidentielles.
[3] Ventes.

Other metal-cutting machine-tools
Autres machines-outils pour le travail des métaux

ISIC-BASED CODE - CODE BASE CITI

3823-19

Unit : Number of units   Unité : Nombre

Country or area	1990	1991	1992	1993	1994	1995	1996	1997	1998	1999	Pays ou zone
Africa	**44**	**200**	**100**	**65**	**102**	**102**	**102**	**102**	**102**	**102**	**Afrique**
Algeria	44	200	100	65	...	...	...	...	...	...	Algérie
America, North	**14942**	**12796**	**11838**	**13347**	**14803**	**18696**	**17013**	**28760**	**25858**	**23836**	**Amérique du Nord**
United States[1][2]	14942	12796	11838	13347	14803	18696	17013	28760	25858	23836	Etats-Unis[1][2]
Asia	**206671**	**233025**	**201004**	**192623**	**191132**	**187973**	**188083**	**187765**	**177808**	**170641**	**Asie**
China	134500	163900	...	...	...	...	...	...	...	...	Chine
Japan	72163	65519	49347	41905	41401	38675	38736	38479	28579	21441	Japon
Kazakhstan	..	2381	1629	1193	429	57	114	42	17	...	Kazakhstan
Kyrgyzstan	..	1145	789	266	69	27	17	44	12	...	Kirghizistan
Turkey	8	57	20	50	26	12	16	0	0	0	Turquie
Uzbekistan	..	23	19	9	7	2	0	0	...	...	Ouzbékistan
Europe	**18607**	**67819**	**61202**	**46295**	**50877**	**57112**	**41593**	**37965**	**39406**	**39164**	**Europe**
Austria	93	131	104	51	48	53	74	43	183	140	Autriche
Belarus	..	8880	7159	5472	3082	3107	3099	2949	3047	2306	Bélarus
Bulgaria	4712	4722	3379	2174	1954	2420	2456	2248	1005	946	Bulgarie
Croatia	..	...	...	...	...	28	32	5	...	...	Croatie
Denmark[3]	1143	632	438	543	593	3765	2613	2434	1061	1398	Danemark[3]
Czech Republic	..	..	...	...	...	...	1037	1876	3314	3665	République tchèque
Finland	*150	*140	*120	*175	*61	*51	*16	29	17	19	Finlande
France[2][4]	1400	1539	1256	...	1264	...	...	...	...	...	France[2][4]
Germany	...	...	...	18428	21321	22719	14246	13003	14568	...	Allemagne
Greece	1228	1410	1568	...	...	...	...	...	225	...	Grèce
Hungary	917	268	38	35	20	34	...	...	...	...	Hongrie
Latvia	..	...	...	...	...	...	...	...	...	420	Lettonie
Lithuania[5]	..	10943	9308	3286	...	...	...	...	...	...	Lituanie[5]
Portugal	322	384	302	228	261	273	264	207	227	229	Portugal
Slovakia	..	...	...	...	...	...	229	185	47	169	Slovaquie
Slovenia	..	1741	1304	882	3470	5320	...	4	109	...	Slovénie
Spain	3684	2339	1570	1233	1607	1055	1090	965	1087	907	Espagne
Ukraine	..	10624	7323	5124	2215	1778	1032	445	443	231	Ukraine
United Kingdom	...	...	...	2890	...	2929	2788	2806	...	...	Royaume-Uni
Yugoslavia	..	377	1767	229	102	211	46	28	1568	9	Yougoslavie
Yugoslavia, SFR	2105	..	..	..	..	..	..	..	..	..	Yougoslavie, RSF
Total	**240264**	**313840**	**274144**	**252330**	**256914**	**263883**	**246791**	**254592**	**243175**	**233743**	**Total**

General Note.
Broaching, centering and dividing, sawing, gear cutting, engraving, polishing, lapping and honing machine-tools. (SITC 73167-0, 73169-2, 73173-0, 73175-0, 73177-0, 73179-1).

Remarque générale.
Machines à brocher, machines à pointer et à diviser, scies mécaniques, machines à tailler les engrenages, machines à graver, machines à polir, à roder et à affiler. (CTCI 73167-0, 73169-2, 73173-0, 73175-0, 73177-0, 73179-1)

[1] Including planing, shaping and slotting machines.
[2] Shipments.
[3] Sales.
[4] Sawing, cutting and straightening machines.
[5] All metal-cutting machines.

[1] Y compris les raboteuses, étaux-limeurs et mortaiseuses.
[2] Expéditions.
[3] Ventes.
[4] Machines à scier, à tronconner et à rectifier.
[5] Machines-outils tous types pour le travail des métaux.

Planing, shaping and slotting machines
Raboteuses, étaux-limeurs, mortaiseuses

ISIC-BASED CODE - CODE BASE CITI

3823-22

Unit : Number of units   Unité : Nombre

Country or area	1990	1991	1992	1993	1994	1995	1996	1997	1998	1999	Pays ou zone
Africa	**15**	**15**	**15**	**15**	**15**	**15**	**15**	**15**	**15**	**15**	**Afrique**
Algeria	...	15	...	...	...	...	...	...	...	...	Algérie
America, South	**26**	**26**	**11**	**24**	**34**	**35**	**26**	**26**	**26**	**26**	**Amérique du Sud**
Colombia	...	...	11	24	34	35	...	...	...	...	Colombie
Asia	**291**	**310**	**296**	**249**	**153**	**73**	**107**	**97**	**62**	**19**	**Asie**
Azerbaijan	..	6	5	93	58	0	25	34	11	4	Azerbaïdjan
Indonesia	...	10	20	...	...	...	...	...	...	...	Indonésie
Japan	276	294	271	141	80	58	67	48	36	...	Japon
Europe	**2021**	**1637**	**2229**	**2670**	**2289**	**2171**	**2265**	**2161**	**2158**	**2091**	**Europe**
Belarus	..	183	124	42	6	10	7	1	2	3	Bélarus
Denmark[1]	1141	...	438	543	593	673	379	791	759	762	Danemark[1]
Germany	..	363	199	176	146	35	43	48	...	...	Allemagne
Germany(Fed.Rep.)	286	..	..	..	..	..	..	..	..	..	Allemagne(Rép.féd.)
Poland	14	2	0	0	0	0	0	0	1	...	Pologne
Romania	398	0	1	147	10	33	21	9	68	25	Roumanie
Slovakia	..	..	...	...	...	789	1287	...	...	...	Slovaquie
Spain	173	225	209	...	...	...	...	...	...	...	Espagne
Ukraine	..	163	195	487	283	419	311	64	62	35	Ukraine
United Kingdom	...	...	...	28	6	2	...	0	...	...	Royaume-Uni
Yugoslavia	..	17	16	7	5	8	6	8	17	17	Yougoslavie
USSR (former)	415	..	..	..	..	..	..	..	..	..	URSS (anc.)
Total	**2768**	**1988**	**2551**	**2958**	**2491**	**2294**	**2413**	**2299**	**2261**	**2151**	**Total**

General Note.
Machines whose function is to remove metal. These machines are fitted with a baseplate, stand or other device for mounting on the floor or on a bench, wall or another machine. (SITC, Rev.3: 73171-0, 73178-0).

Remarque générale.
Machines-outils dont la fonction est d'enlever du métal. Ces machines sont équipées d'un socle, d'un pied ou d'un autre dispositif permettant de les fixer au sol, à un établi, à une paroi ou à une autre machine. (CTCI, Rev.3: 73171-0, 73178-0).

[1] Sales.

[1] Ventes.

Metal-working presses
Presses pour le travail des métaux

ISIC-BASED CODE - CODE BASE CITI

3823-28

Unit : Number of units

Unité : Nombre

Country or area	1990	1991	1992	1993	1994	1995	1996	1997	1998	1999	Pays ou zone
America, North	**7285**	**5912**	**5822**	**6236**	**10947**	**5045**	**11023**	**12084**	**12559**	**12301**	**Amérique du Nord**
United States[1]	7285	5912	5822	6236	10947	5045	11023	12084	12559	12301	Etats-Unis[1]
America, South	**21023**	**21694**	**18186**	**15129**	**24497**	**28202**	**21498**	**21519**	**21372**	**20943**	**Amérique du Sud**
Brazil	1182	1853	1194	1763	1836	1858	1657	1678	1531	1102	Brésil
Colombia	...	...	16992	13366	22661	26344	...	...	...	...	Colombie
Asia	**22625**	**19433**	**12557**	**9670**	**9614**	**10609**	**10156**	**11660**	**8618**	**7350**	**Asie**
Armenia	..	206	45	100	29	43	34	31	18	11	Arménie
Indonesia	...	...	...	54	...	...	...	...	...	...	Indonésie
Japan	22571	19173	12458	9516	9531	10512	10068	11575	8546	7285	Japon
Europe	**24210**	**25067**	**62675**	**24856**	**27086**	**27021**	**34787**	**30544**	**16717**	**13258**	**Europe**
Czechoslovakia(former)	1424	920	..	..	..	..	..	..	..	..	Tchécoslovaquie(anc.)
Czech Republic	..	..	106	47	60	114	231	239	...	..	République tchèque
Finland	126	98	17	6	180	1764	2159	2101	2285	2315	Finlande
France[1]	1300	1235	1385	970	605	...	...	...	...	...	France[1]
Germany	..	17726	55997	18939	23284	16399	...	21531	...	...	Allemagne
Germany(Fed.Rep.)	16643	..	..	..	..	..	..	..	..	..	Allemagne(Rép.féd.)
German D.R.(former)	1781	..	..	..	..	..	..	..	..	..	R.D.A. (anc.)
Greece	328	320	355	...	...	...	...	...	...	...	Grèce
Latvia	..	3	...	...	...	...	...	...	...	...	Lettonie
Poland	50	44	13	11	8	2	2	15	...	...	Pologne
Portugal	255	102	742	670	649	...	...	...	...	...	Portugal
Slovakia	..	..	261	184	301	282	199	73	276	195	Slovaquie
Slovenia	..	119	92	145	153	215	719	...	...	...	Slovénie
Spain	1600	2152	1687	2436	723	5452	...	...	...	...	Espagne
Ukraine	..	666	268	277	117	146	35	42	38	29	Ukraine
United Kingdom	...	...	...	667	615	...	...	827	...	...	Royaume-Uni
Yugoslavia	..	979	1046	167	54	114	53	47	66	29	Yougoslavie
Total	**75143**	**72106**	**99240**	**55891**	**72144**	**70877**	**77464**	**75806**	**59266**	**53851**	**Total**

General Note.
Mechanical, hydraulic and pneumatic presses used for forging, stamping, cutting out etc. Forge hammers are excluded. (SITC,Rev.3: 73311-2, 73312-1, 73313-1, 73314-1, 73315-1, 73316-1, 73317-1, 73318-2).

Remarque générale.
Presses à commande mécanique, hydraulique et pneumatique servant à forger, à estamper, à matricer, etc. Cette rubrique ne comprend pas les outils agissant par chocs. (CTCI, Rev.3: 73311-2, 73312-1, 73313-1, 73314-1, 73315-1, 73316-1, 73317-1, 73318-2).

[1] Shipments.

[1] Expéditions.

Other metal-forming machine-tools
Autres machines-outils à former les métaux

ISIC-BASED CODE - CODE BASE CITI

3823-31

Unit : Number of units   Unité : Nombre

Country or area	1990	1991	1992	1993	1994	1995	1996	1997	1998	1999	Pays ou zone
America, North	**44459**	**35600**	**39185**	**45408**	**55060**	**36241**	**42622**	**46653**	**52564**	**49968**	**Amérique du Nord**
United States [1]	44459	35600	39185	45408	55060	36241	42622	46653	52564	49968	Etats-Unis [1]
Asia	..	**1761**	**1069**	**644**	**67**	**0**	**0**	**0**	**0**	**0**	**Asie**
Armenia	..	1761	1069	644	67	0	0	0	0	0	Arménie
Europe	**84739**	**68545**	**69391**	**55199**	**52110**	**63873**	**53617**	**49299**	**48555**	**44973**	**Europe**
Austria	487	[2]1449	[2]534	[2]204	[2]560	[2]558	[2]2294	[2]674	[2]1321	[2]1152	Autriche
Croatia	..	32	192	179	...	1000	1250	28	...	...	Croatie
Czech Republic	..	..	...	...	63	159	247	251	...	...	République tchèque
Finland	1596	1925	*715	*970	*1878	...	...	...	...	...	Finlande
France [1]	1900	2335	2434	1585	2823	...	...	...	...	...	France [1]
Germany	..	...	29967	23981	23071	35316	22480	21813	23060	...	Allemagne
Germany(Fed.Rep.)	51998	..	..	..	..	..	..	..	..	..	Allemagne(Rép.féd.)
Hungary	1430	930	368	350	415	315	...	...	...	...	Hongrie
Portugal	173	185	63	40	45	...	...	...	...	...	Portugal
Slovakia	..	..	...	...	...	2383	1438	...	298	213	Slovaquie
Slovenia	..	3	...	...	17	...	133	...	...	18	Slovénie
Spain	26302	31851	32631	...	21327	19159	...	...	...	...	Espagne
United Kingdom	...	...	...	266	341	...	...	1953	...	...	Royaume-Uni
Yugoslavia	..	564	328	64	40	243	236	228	63	5	Yougoslavie
Total	**129198**	**105906**	**109645**	**101251**	**107237**	**100114**	**96239**	**95952**	**101119**	**94941**	**Total**

General Note.

Other machine-tools for changing the shape or form of the metal without removing any of it, such as: riveting machines, bending and straightening machines, drawing machines, plate-working machines, shearing and notching machines, wire-drawing machines, thread-rolling machines. (SITC, Rev.3: 73312-2, 73313-2, 73314--2, 73315-2, 73316-2, 73317-2, 73391-0,

[1] Shipments.
[2] Including metal-working presses, swaging machines and rolling milles.

Remarque générale.

Autres machines-outils travaillant par déformation sans enlèvement de métal, notamment: machines à river, à cintrer, à dresser, à étirer, machines à travailler les tôles, à cisailler et à grignoter, machines à tréfiler, machines à fileter par roulage. (CTCI, Rev.3: 73312-2, 73313-2, 73314-2, 73315-2, 73316-2, 73317-2, 73391-0, 73393-0, 73395-0, 73399-1).

[1] Expéditions.
[2] Y compris les presses pour le travail des métaux, les machines à rétreindre et les laminoirs à imprimer.

Rolling mills for rolling metals
Laminoirs à métaux

ISIC-BASED CODE - CODE BASE CITI

3823-37

Unit : Number of units   Unité : Nombre

Country or area	1990	1991	1992	1993	1994	1995	1996	1997	1998	1999	Pays ou zone
America, South	1	1	1	1	1	1	1	1	1	1	**Amérique du Sud**
Colombia	...	...	1	...	...	...	...	...	...	...	Colombie
Asia	456	325	252	133	127	125	157	185	147	189	**Asie**
Japan[1]	435	312	245	107	121	111	145	173	136	178	Japon[1]
Korea, Republic of	21	13	7	26	6	14	...	...	...	...	Corée, République de
Europe	183	4339	2628	3455	3378	2864	3655	3042	3093	3095	**Europe**
Denmark[2]	23	28	15	12	15	6	15	17	15	7	Danemark[2]
Germany	..	...	...	...	...	2025	2047	2029	2005	...	Allemagne
Hungary	38	33	17	...	...	...	56	...	...	...	Hongrie
Poland	24	4	14	4	4	28	25	25	23	24	Pologne
Slovenia	..	...	...	...	...	...	386	100	36	...	Slovénie
Spain	16	69	49	333	18	16	118	...	289	...	Espagne
United Kingdom	...	...	...	...	...	124	66	57	...	...	Royaume-Uni
Yugoslavia	..	1922	250	787	1022	455	942	...	...	...	Yougoslavie
Total	640	4665	2881	3589	3506	2990	3813	3228	3242	3285	**Total**

General Note.

Hot and cold rolling-mill machinery designed for rolling out to reduce the thickness with the corresponding increase in length, rolling of blooms, billets etc., to form a particular cross-section, rolling tubes, and rolling of wheel blanks or wheel-rim blanks. (SITC, Rev.3: 73721-0).

Remarque générale.

Machines pour laminage à chaud ou à froid destinées à réduire l'épaisseur du métal avec une augmentation correspondante de la longueur, laminoirs à blooms, à billettes, etc., donnant des barres ou profilés de la section désirée, laminoirs à tubes, laminoirs à roues et à bandages. (CTCI, Rev.3: 73721-0).

[1] Including auxiliary equipment.
[2] Sales.

[1] Y compris l'équipement auxiliaire.
[2] Ventes.

Machine-tools for working wood
Machines-outils pour le travail du bois

ISIC-BASED CODE - CODE BASE CITI

3823-40

Unit : Number of units   Unité : Nombre

Country or area	1990	1991	1992	1993	1994	1995	1996	1997	1998	1999	Pays ou zone
America, North											**Amérique du Nord**
Mexico	...	...	...	177	#9023	17090	20067	#136	97	94	Mexique
America, South											**Amérique du Sud**
Colombia	...	...	1063	1194	1436	1089	...	...	...	...	Colombie
Ecuador	29259	...	77000	68831	105296		...	107485	153890	...	Equateur
Asia											**Asie**
Hong Kong SAR[1]	...	294	...	...	318	...	...	...	...	...	Hong-Kong RAS[1]
China, Macao, SAR[2][3]	...	...	...	12	19	...	...	...	...	...	Chine, Macao PAS[2][3]
Indonesia	1029	135	128	148	102	109	...	16	...	...	Indonésie
Japan	140709	148551	101776	76372	70051	63592	51807	48085	32613	20892	Japon
Kazakhstan	..	87	996	788	511	414	495	16	29	2	Kazakhstan
Korea, Republic of	22117	19824	13945	14395	23390	20820	...	...	...	...	Corée, République de
Europe											**Europe**
Austria	23490	23918	23044	14988	16341	18119	14856	12702	14331	14195	Autriche
Belgium	[4][5]3548	[4][5]3480	[4][5]3402	[4][5]3775	[4]9045	6099	6624	7181	7244	...	Belgique
Bulgaria	12000	9012	3373	2412	2704	2111	2172	1633	2307	1371	Bulgarie
Croatia	..	4935	3771	3303	...	1075	2800	1298	3336	...	Croatie
Czechoslovakia(former)	21973		..	..	..	..	..	..	..	..	Tchécoslovaquie(anc.)
Czech Republic	..	..	43041	17295	...	...	8391	8044	8563	6496	République tchèque
France[4][6]	18000	15760	19069	15250	4741	...	...	...	...	...	France[4][6]
Germany[5]	..	183294	161815	150409	194988	...	188591	185823	...	...	Allemagne[5]
Germany(Fed.Rep.)[5]	196249	..	..	..	..	...	..	..	...	...	Allemagne(Rép.féd.)[5]
Greece	7925	7734	7687	...	...	...	...	...	...	...	Grèce
Hungary	1665	1303	236	66	74	59	27	27	37	171	Hongrie
Latvia	..	..	..	...	...	...	...	...	...	995	Lettonie
Lithuania	..	...	5890	5185	1585	1037	677	501	532	392	Lituanie
Poland	39349	26385	14728	13594	15267	14954	10877	9065	11241	7161	Pologne
Portugal	2821	1883	1830	2170	1725	1790	930	1197	1237	1313	Portugal
Republic of Moldova	..	4752	4168	[7]2486	[7]916	[7]252	[7]107	[7]77	[7]50	[7]50	Rép. de Moldova
Romania[5]	9940	5052	6445	7606	5457	5456	4740	2638	3128	3244	Roumanie[5]
Russian Federation	..	24553	30106	22038	12726	11192	5864	5654	5918	9736	Fédération de Russie
Slovakia	..	..	1009	724	4464	2175	2353	1872	7220	626	Slovaquie
Slovenia	..	13982	11055	14005	16130	17600	5335	4659	2600	1813	Slovénie
Spain	7008	7715	6404	...	3011	4043	4672	4859	6516	8949	Espagne
Sweden	...	...	...	...	...	...	...	4532	3874	2582	Suède
Ukraine	..	9006	11332	16711	9647	5547	4290	2563	1650	1045	Ukraine
United Kingdom	...	...	...	...	185356	160990	330045	325736	...	...	Royaume-Uni
Yugoslavia	..	11820	11765	1588	154	607	194	206	25	63	Yougoslavie
USSR (former)	38155	..	..	..	..	..	..	..	..	..	URSS (anc.)

General Note.

Machines for shaping or surface-working wood (and also cork, bone, ebonite, plastic materials etc.), generally power-driven and designed to be mounted on the floor, a bench or a wall, such as wood de-barking machinery, sawing machines, slicing and paring machines, planing, profiling, grooving, mortising and tenoning, drilling, sandpapering machines, lathes, machinery for the cooperage industry etc. Tools for working in the hand, pneumatic or with self-contained electric or non-electric motor, are excluded. (SITC,Rev.3: 72812-0).

Remarque générale.

Machines servant à façonner ou à travailler en surface le bois (et aussi le liège, l'os, l'ébonite, les matières plastiques, etc.), généralement actionnées mécaniquement et conçues pour être fixées au sol, à un établi ou à une paroi, telles que machines à écorcer le bois, scies, machines à trancher et à dérouler, machines à raboter, à profiler, à rainurer, à mortaiser, à faire les tenons, à percer, à poncer, à meuler ou à polir, tours de tous types, machines pour tonnellerie, etc. Cette rubrique ne comprend pas les outils à main pneumatiques ou à moteur électrique ou non électrique incorporé. (CTCI, Rev.3: 72812-0).

[1] 1997 and 1998 data are confidential
[2] 1995 data are confidential.
[3] 1997 data are confidential.
[4] Shipments.
[5] In metric tons.
[6] Machines over 150 kilogrammes.
[7] Excluding Transnistria region.

[1] Pour 1997 et 1998, les données sont confidentielles.
[2] Pour 1995, les données sont confidentielles.
[3] Pour 1997, les données sont confidentielles.
[4] Expéditions.
[5] En tonnes métriques.
[6] Machines de plus de 150 kilogrammes.
[7] Non compris la région de Transnistrie.

Electro-mechanical hand tools
Outils et machines-outils électromécaniques, pour emploi à la main

ISIC-BASED CODE - CODE BASE CITI

3823-43

Unit : Thousand units   Unité : En milliers

Country or area	1990	1991	1992	1993	1994	1995	1996	1997	1998	1999	Pays ou zone
America, South	**52**	**52**	**81**	**52**	**56**	**18**	**52**	**52**	**52**	**52**	**Amérique du Sud**
Colombia	...	...	81	...	56	18	...	...	...	...	Colombie
Asia	**12947**	**13908**	**13398**	**11206**	**11636**	**10900**	**10436**	**10279**	**8194**	**7713**	**Asie**
Japan	12759	13697	13141	10950	11302	10533	10098	9921	8041	7431	Japon
Korea, Republic of[1]	188	211	257	256	334	367	338	358	153	282	Corée, République de[1]
Europe	**25509**	**27926**	**29106**	**26954**	**27521**	**29056**	**25563**	**30818**	**32641**	**30622**	**Europe**
Croatia	..	13	8	...	...	17	5	4	4	...	Croatie
Czech Republic	..	..	...	...	...	...	...	254	232	237	République tchèque
Finland	2	2	2	2	1	1	1	...	...	...	Finlande
Germany	..	11577	11651	10568	10806	8447	7160	7910	8728	...	Allemagne
Germany(Fed.Rep.)	10923	..	..	..	..	..	..	..	..	..	Allemagne(Rép.féd.)
Hungary	55	14	5	...	...	...	...	0	...	...	Hongrie
Latvia	..	...	...	...	735	668	659	636	384	155	Lettonie
Lithuania	..	...	...	...	...	11	6	4	2	0	Lituanie
Slovenia	..	494	449	561	664	590	121	103	186	134	Slovénie
Spain	1038	633	741	810	795	613	572	655	717	952	Espagne
United Kingdom	...	...	...	14029	14240	18449	16779	21251	22369	...	Royaume-Uni
Total	**38508**	**41886**	**42585**	**38212**	**39213**	**39974**	**36050**	**41148**	**40887**	**38386**	**Total**

General Note.
Tools for working in the hand, with self-contained electric motor or vibrator. This heading excludes portable mechanical tools permanently fitted with a baseplate, stand or other device for mounting on the wall, bench or floor, electrical lawn mowers, electro-mechanical domestic appliances, and electric shavers and hair clippers. (SITC, Rev.3: 77841-0, 77843-0, 77845-0)

Remarque générale.
Outils et machines-outils pour emploi à la main, avec moteur électrique ou vibreur incorporé. Cette rubrique ne comprend pas les outils ou machines-outils portatifs munis en permanence d'un socle, d'un pied ou d'un autre dispositif permettant de les fixer sur une paroi, sur un établi ou sur le sol, les tondeuses à gazon électriques, les appareils ménagers électromécaniques, les rasoirs et tondeuses électriques. (CTCI, Rev.3: 77841-0, 77843-0, 77845-0)

[1] Grinding machine tools only.

[1] Meuleuses seulement.

Spinning machines
Machines à filer les textiles

ISIC-BASED CODE - CODE BASE CITI

3824-04

Unit : Number of spindles
Unité : Nombre de broches

Country or area	1990	1991	1992	1993	1994	1995	1996	1997	1998	1999	Pays ou zone
Asia											**Asie**
Japan	10963	13248	7960	4593	2834	3415	2040	2246	1660	1201	Japon
Pakistan[1]	5195	5493	6141	6768	8182	8307	8493	...	...	...	Pakistan[1]
Uzbekistan[2]	..	1620	1119	571	237	23	2	0	...	...	Ouzbékistan[2]
Europe											**Europe**
Belgium[3][4]	3526	2761	4165	3476	...	...	...	...	...	...	Belgique[3][4]
Czechoslovakia(former)	166384	53136	..	..	..	..	..	..	..	..	Tchécoslovaquie(anc.)
Czech Republic	..	..	61093	18264	...	...	...	...	...	...	République tchèque
France[3]	7816	8820	...	...	...	...	...	...	...	...	France[3]
Germany	...	...	...	...	...	2044	1557	1550	1288	...	Allemagne
Poland	37740	7412	5204	724	640	0	0	...	0	...	Pologne
Russian Federation[2]	..	1506	1106	493	204	133	71	30	3	5	Fédération de Russie[2]
United Kingdom	...	...	...	406	391	231	269	72	...	...	Royaume-Uni
Yugoslavia	..	102	...	5	10	...	...	...	...	...	Yougoslavie
USSR (former)[2]	3268	..	..	..	..	..	..	..	..	..	URSS (anc.)[2]

General Note.

Machines for working up the various textile fibres, after preparation or special preliminary treatment, into yarns; spinning frames, the essential feature of which is the spinning mechanism associated with a revolving vertical or oblique spindle; flax, hemp, jute etc., spinning machines, intermittent spinning frames and continuous spinning frames for cotton, wool; throwing machines for twisting together continuous filaments of silk or of man-made textiles and "tow-to-yarn" machines (for breaking the filaments of the tow of synthetic or artificial continuous fibres, drawing out into a roving, and spinning into yarn). Machines for extruding man-made textiles in the form of monofilaments or of several filaments from a chemical composition forced through nozzles, and twisting and doubling machines for giving a supplementary torsion to yarns, are excluded. (SITC, Rev.3: 72443-1).

Remarque générale.

Machines pour la transformation en filés des diverses matières textiles après préparation ou traitement préliminaire spécial; métiers à filer dont l'organe essentiel est le dispositif de torsion associé à un axe tournant vertical ou oblique (broche); métiers à filer le lin, le chanvre, le jute, etc.; métiers à filer intermittents et métiers à filer continus pour le coton, la laine, etc., machines à mouliner la soie ou à tordre les filaments continus de fibres synthétiques, machines dites "tow-to-yarn" ("câble-à-filé") (qui assurent la rupture des câbles de fibres snythétiques ou artificielles continues, l'étirage de la mèche de fibres discontinues ainsi formée et la filature). Cette rubrique ne comprend pas les machines à filer les matières textiles artificielles ou synthétiques sous la forme de fibres continues composées soit d'un monofilament ou de plusieurs filaments juxtaposés et obtenus par extrusion dans des presses à filer à partir d'une composition chimique, les métiers à retordre, les machines à doubler et à câbler et les assembleuses-retordeuses, qui ont pour fonction de donner aux fils une torsion supplémentaire. (CTCI, Rev.3: 72443-1).

[1] Machines installed in cotton mills only.
[2] In number of units.
[3] Shipments.
[4] In metric tons.

[1] Machines installées en filature de coton seulement.
[2] En nombre de d'unités.
[3] Expéditions.
[4] En tonnes métriques.

Knitting machines
Métiers à bonneterie

ISIC-BASED CODE - CODE BASE CITI

3824-07

Unit : Number of units   Unité : Nombre

Country or area	1990	1991	1992	1993	1994	1995	1996	1997	1998	1999	Pays ou zone
Asia											**Asie**
Hong Kong SAR	75555	10061	3262	...	869	19801	...	...	114	...	Hong-Kong RAS
Indonesia	...	...	...	1101	2077	1225	...	850	...	...	Indonésie
Japan	17836	18859	16231	13376	14919	11262	13319	13607	9309	8761	Japon
Korea, Republic of	4680	5460	5985	5365	4829	4693	5963	4833	3861	6251	Corée, République de
Europe											**Europe**
Belgium[1][2][3]	16822	14861	15987	13876	...	...	...	...	...	...	Belgique[1][2][3]
Czechoslovakia(former)	3891	1966	..	..	..	..	..	..	..	..	Tchécoslovaquie(anc.)
Germany	..	5500	4487	3473	3063	6667	6581	7796	10266	...	Allemagne
Germany(Fed.Rep.)	4061	..	..	..	..	..	..	..	..	...	Allemagne(Rép.féd.)
Hungary	...	1	...	...	...	...	...	...	...	...	Hongrie
Poland[3]	127	32	11	9	7	5	0	0	3	0	Pologne[3]
Russian Federation	..	...	...	380	130	131	59	10	16	14	Fédération de Russie
Spain	770	548	234	1053	...	...	...	...	...	...	Espagne
United Kingdom	...	...	...	311	359	...	385	589	...	...	Royaume-Uni

General Note.

Flat and circular knitting machines. Small domestic knitting machines are excluded. (SITC, Rev.3: 72452-1).

Remarque générale.

Métiers à bonneterie rectilignes ou circulaires. Cette rubrique ne comprend pas les petites machines domestiques. (CTCI, Rev.3: 72452-1).

[1] Including looms.
[2] Shipments.
[3] In metric tons.

[1] Y compris les métiers à tisser.
[2] Expéditions.
[3] En tonnes métriques.

Looms
Métiers à tisser

ISIC-BASED CODE - CODE BASE CITI

3824-10

Unit : Number of units   Unité : Nombre

Country or area	1990	1991	1992	1993	1994	1995	1996	1997	1998	1999	Pays ou zone
Asia	**41275**	**39684**	**33885**	**24064**	**27872**	**21609**	**17718**	**22567**	**15187**	**10322**	**Asie**
Indonesia	23	63	289	30	1668	519	...	1279	591	...	Indonésie
Japan	23458	25856	26799	19558	20167	17245	14451	20353	13610	8104	Japon
Korea, Republic of	17778	13750	6782	4462	6023	3831	2696	925	976	970	Corée, République de
Pakistan	16	15	15	14	14	14	13	10	10	10	Pakistan
Europe	**12313**	**25021**	**15840**	**8856**	**6495**	**7081**	**5639**	**5988**	**5204**	**5004**	**Europe**
Denmark [1]	904	690	693	576	525	537	522	323	299	214	Danemark [1]
Czechoslovakia(former)	4082	2578	..	..	..	..	..	..	..	..	Tchécoslovaquie(anc.)
Czech Republic	..	..	902	248	...	...	...	...	...	...	République tchèque
France	3221	875	0	0	...	...	...	...	...	...	France
Germany	..	...	...	1426	1886	...	...	2232	...	...	Allemagne
Germany(Fed.Rep.)	2031	..	..	..	..	...	...	..	..	..	Allemagne(Rép.féd.)
Poland	141	16	32	22	0	0	...	...	...	...	Pologne
Portugal	86	42	...	...	...	...	...	...	...	...	Portugal
Romania	163	12	34	0	0	0	0	0	17	4	Roumanie
Russian Federation	..	17608	11887	5377	1278	1890	685	465	170	136	Fédération de Russie
Spain	1326	982	10	...	...	...	...	...	...	...	Espagne
Sweden	...	...	...	...	...	...	...	9	5	1	Suède
United Kingdom	...	...	...	...	...	...	132	512	418	...	Royaume-Uni
Yugoslavia	..	...	11	...	...	...	...	...	...	...	Yougoslavie
USSR (former)	18341	..	..	..	..	..	..	..	..	..	URSS (anc.)
Total	**71929**	**64705**	**49725**	**32920**	**34367**	**28690**	**23356**	**28555**	**20391**	**15326**	**Total**

General Note.
Machines for interlacing warp and weft yarns at right angles to form a fabric. They usually produce a flat fabric, but there are circular looms which produce a tubular fabric. Knitting machines and machines for making knotted net, tulle, braid etc. are excluded. (SITC, Rev.3: 72451-0).

Remarque générale.
Machines servant à entrelacer à angle droit les fils de chaîne et les fils de trame de manière à former le tissu. Le plus souvent, elles produisent un tissu plat mais il existe des métiers circulaires qui produisent un tissu cylindrique. Cette rubrique ne comprend pas les machines à tricoter, les machines pour la fabrication des filets, des tulles, des tresses, etc. (CTCI, Rev.3: 72451-0).

[1] Sales.

[1] Ventes.

Machinery for making or finishing cellulosic pulp etc.
Machines pour la fabrication ou le finissage de pâte cellulosique etc.

ISIC-BASED CODE - CODE BASE CITI

3824-13

Unit : Number of units

Unité : Nombre

Country or area	1990	1991	1992	1993	1994	1995	1996	1997	1998	1999	Pays ou zone
Asia	**566**	**466**	**235**	**445**	**466**	**584**	**733**	**645**	**485**	**423**	**Asie**
Japan	566	466	235	445	466	584	733	645	485	423	Japon
Europe	**11971**	**38807**	**38521**	**42830**	**32744**	**37662**	**36462**	**39477**	**36930**	**37050**	**Europe**
Croatia	..	52	42	75	...	8	12	...	...	...	Croatie
Denmark [1]	...	...	...	...	32	29	31	6	24	56	Danemark [1]
Germany	..	...	...	34369	23847	...	...	...	...	...	Allemagne
Romania	...	...	...	...	...	0	...	...	90	160	Roumanie
Slovenia	..	6	110	219	43	...	...	...	...	...	Slovénie
Spain	4239	1907	1526	431	417	796	782	945	957	...	Espagne
United Kingdom	...	...	...	...	8284	...	6351	9224	6646	...	Royaume-Uni
Total	**12537**	**39273**	**38756**	**43275**	**33210**	**38246**	**37195**	**40122**	**37415**	**37473**	**Total**

General Note.

Machines for making pulp from various cellulosic materials (wood, esparto, grass, straw, rags, waste paper etc.). Including machinery for making paper or paper board, and machinery for finishing paper or paperboard ready for its various uses (that is, pulpmill machinery, papermill machinery, paper and paperboard converting equipment). (SITC, Rev.3: 72510-0).

Remarque générale.

Machines pour transformer en pâte diverses matières riches en cellulose (bois, alfa, paille, chiffons, déchets de papier, etc.). Y compris les machines à fabriquer ou à finir le papier ou le carton en vue de leurs diverses utilisations (c'est-à-dire machines pour usines de pâte à papier, machines de papeteries, matériel pour la transformation du papier et du carton). (CTCI, Rev.3: 72510-0).

[1] Sales.

[1] Ventes.

Paper-cutting machines etc.
Coupeuses à papier etc.

ISIC-BASED CODE - CODE BASE CITI

3824-16

Unit : Number of units

Unité : Nombre

Country or area	1990	1991	1992	1993	1994	1995	1996	1997	1998	1999	Pays ou zone
America, South	**157**	**157**	**177**	**140**	**139**	**171**	**157**	**157**	**157**	**157**	**Amérique du Sud**
Colombia	...	...	177	140	139	171	...	...	...	...	Colombie
Asia	**140**	**140**	**140**	**140**	**140**	**140**	**140**	**140**	**140**	**140**	**Asie**
Indonesia	140	...	...	...	...	...	...	...	...	...	Indonésie
Europe	**116297**	**533260**	**532838**	**543086**	**518038**	**513786**	**594281**	**506276**	**521829**	**540896**	**Europe**
Austria [1] [2] [3]	...	...	...	...	...	...	...	102	249	...	Autriche [1] [2] [3]
Croatia	..	...	...	...	...	...	...	3	6	...	Croatie
Finland	40	28	53	57	*90	...	...	...	...	...	Finlande
Germany	..	...	...	...	...	440763	393366	...	...	...	Allemagne
Hungary	881	135	112	...	...	...	...	...	2630	4168	Hongrie
Slovenia	..	...	...	...	...	...	82	31	95	83	Slovénie
Spain	1381	2347	2310	1788	1041	1977	1201	2140	2775	8936	Espagne
Sweden	...	...	...	...	...	...	...	114	137	99	Suède
United Kingdom	...	...	...	122222	97888	68999	197645	85118	98741	...	Royaume-Uni
Total	**116593**	**533556**	**533155**	**543366**	**518317**	**514097**	**594578**	**506573**	**522125**	**541193**	**Total**

General Note.
This heading includes paper cutting and paper trimming machines, slitter-reelers, stacking machines, machines for making envelopes, for die-cutting, for cutting or grooving paper, for folding, for making paper bags, for folding and gluing cartons and boxes, for stapling, for forming waxed paper cups etc., and for moulding articles in paper pulp, paper or paperboard.
(SITC, Rev.3: 72520-0).

Remarque générale.
Cette rubrique comprend les machines à découper et à rogner le papier, les coupeuses-bobineuses, les machines àtaquer et égaliser les feuilles, les machines à fabriquer les enveloppes, à découper à l'emporte-pièce, à couper ou à rainer le papier, les plieuses, les machines à fabriquer les sacs en papier, celles à plier et à coller les cartons et les boîtes, les machines à agrafer, les machines à former les gobelets en papier paraffiné etc., et les machines à mouler les articles en pâte à papier, papier ou carton. (CTCI, Rev.3: 72520-0).

[1] 1995 data are confidential.
[2] 1996 data are confidential.
[3] 1999 data are confidential.

[1] Pour 1995, les données sont confidentielles.
[2] Pour 1996, les données sont confidentielles.
[3] Pour 1999, les données sont confidentielles.

Printing presses
Presses à imprimer

ISIC-BASED CODE - CODE BASE CITI

3824-19

Unit : Number of units

Unité : Nombre

Country or area	1990	1991	1992	1993	1994	1995	1996	1997	1998	1999	Pays ou zone
Asia											**Asie**
Hong Kong SAR[1][2]	1816	15961	5876	7343	3696	2111	...	1213	1822	...	Hong-Kong RAS[1][2]
Japan	7751	6686	5196	4295	3823	4145	4683	6512	5726	4807	Japon
Korea, Republic of	425	370	1215	957	773	686	588	498	344	255	Corée, République de
Europe											**Europe**
Austria	[3]2269	[3]2557	...	...	...	879	520	381	360	360	Autriche
Czech Republic								1158	1222	817	République tchèque
France[3][4]	9178	8625	6668	6135	3844	...	...	...	...	...	France[3][4]
Germany	..	...	[3]161941	[3]142370	[3]141789	21161	15577	29916	27927	...	Allemagne
Germany(Fed.Rep.)[3]	195334	..	..	..	..	..	..	..	..	..	Allemagne(Rép.féd.)[3]
Hungary	111	27	1	...	...	...	...	...	...	...	Hongrie
Russian Federation	..	797	412	321	90	46	44	32	34	27	Fédération de Russie
Spain	482	360	341	642	870	1698	1629	1891	2666	1606	Espagne
Sweden	...	...	...				185	1370	1699	1886	Suède
United Kingdom	...	...	...	46596	36033	43174	44232	53184	53548	...	Royaume-Uni
USSR (former)	845	..	..	..	..	..	..	..	..	..	URSS (anc.)

General Note.

Sheet- and roll-fed ordinary and platen presses, cylinder printing presses, and rotary presses, used industrially for typography, offset printing, photogravure or rotogravure. (SITC, Rev.3: 72650-0, 72661-0, 72663-0, 72665-0, 72667-0).

[1] Including other printing machinery.
[2] 1999 data are confidential.
[3] In metric tons.
[4] Shipments.

Remarque générale.

Presses ordinaires et presses à platine, travaillant à plat ou sur rouleaux, presses à cylindre, presses rotatives, utilisées industriellement en typographie, en impression offset, en héliogravure et en rotogravure. (CTCI, Rev.3: 72650-0, 72661-0, 72663-0, 72665-0, 72667-0).

[1] Y compris autres machines et appareils à imprimer.
[2] Pour 1999, les données sont confidentielles.
[3] En tonnes métriques.
[4] Expéditions.

Bulldozers
Bulldozers

ISIC-BASED CODE - CODE BASE CITI

3824-22A

Unit : Number of units

Unité : Nombre

Country or area	1990	1991	1992	1993	1994	1995	1996	1997	1998	1999	Pays ou zone
Africa	**22**	**22**	**22**	**22**	**22**	**22**	**22**	**22**	**22**	**22**	**Afrique**
Algeria	...	22	...	...	...	...	...	...	...	...	Algérie
America, North	**8781**	**7193**	**5846**	**7273**	**7273**	**7273**	**7273**	**7273**	**7273**	**7273**	**Amérique du Nord**
United States[1][2]	8781	7193	5846	...	...	...	...	...	...	...	Etats-Unis[1][2]
Asia	**18743**	**25297**	**13854**	**13751**	**12183**	**11792**	**11584**	**12103**	**9602**	**7717**	**Asie**
Azerbaijan	..	1431	139	19	1	0	0	0	0	0	Azerbaïdjan
Indonesia	...	...	135	318	429	879	...	1837	127	...	Indonésie
Iran(Islamic Rep. of)[3][4]	13	178	173	64	23	45	41	3	496	...	Iran(Rép. islamique)[3][4]
Japan	17639	12666	9743	8940	10954	10240	10643	9990	8930	6350	Japon
Kazakhstan	..	10288	3494	4234	695	521	247	273	49	38	Kazakhstan
Korea, Republic of	839	390	170	176	81	107	...	...	...	...	Corée, République de
Europe	**138**	**20207**	**14918**	**7661**	**2294**	**2521**	**2822**	**2693**	**1798**	**2584**	**Europe**
Belarus	..	2242	1077	74	9	11	34	55	105	41	Bélarus
Bulgaria	81	6	...	2	...	2	...	...	...	...	Bulgarie
Czechoslovakia(former)	44	34	..	..	..	..	..	..	..	..	Tchécoslovaquie(anc.)
Finland	8	5	...	...	...	...	...	...	...	...	Finlande
Poland	2	10	3	10	3	5	2	...	...	...	Pologne
Romania	...	...	...	0	0	0	29	22	0	0	Roumanie
Russian Federation	..	12431	12226	6498	2161	2404	2669	2467	1575	2434	Fédération de Russie
Slovakia	..	..	...	...	...	...	33	69	...	...	Slovaquie
Ukraine	..	5375	1444	932	32	12	4	3	3	4	Ukraine
Yugoslavia	..	100	83	87	9	29	22	45	32	22	Yougoslavie
USSR (former)	37144	..	..	..	..	..	..	..	..	..	URSS (anc.)
Total	**64828**	**52719**	**34640**	**28707**	**21773**	**21608**	**21701**	**22092**	**18695**	**17596**	**Total**

General Note.

Machines with large blades mounted squarely in front of a tractor unit used to level or clear away excess soil, debris etc. Angle dozers (or bullgraders) with blades mounted at an angle, and bulldozers designed for pushing down trees or for cutting through brush are included. (SITC, Rev.3: 72311-0A).

Remarque générale.

Grandes lames conçues pour être montées sur tracteurs perpendiculairement au sens de la marche et destinées aux travaux de nivellement ou de déblaiement. Cette rubrique comprend les angledozers, ou lames montées obliquement et les bulldozers concus pour l'abattage des arbres par simple poussée sur le tronc ou pour le débroussaillage. (CTCI, Rev.3: 72311-0A).

[1] Shipments.
[2] Bulldozers to be mounted on tracklaying tractors.
[3] Production by establishments employing 10 or more persons.
[4] Including excavating machines, and graders and levellers.

[1] Expéditions.
[2] Bouteurs à monter sur tracteurs chenillés.
[3] Production des établissements occupant 10 personnes ou plus.
[4] Y compris les machines d'excavation et les niveleuses-régleuses.

Excavating machines
Machines d'excavation

ISIC-BASED CODE - CODE BASE CITI

3824-25

Unit : Number of units   Unité : Nombre

Country or area	1990	1991	1992	1993	1994	1995	1996	1997	1998	1999	Pays ou zone
America, North	**4503**	**3071**	**3445**	**3951**	**8954**	**12332**	**12953**	**15183**	**17516**	**17583**	**Amérique du Nord**
Mexico	1	...	...	...	...	...	...	...	...	...	Mexique
United States [1]	4502	3070	3444	3950	8953	12331	12952	15182	17515	17582	Etats-Unis [1]
America, South	**920**	**668**	**574**	**761**	**873**	**671**	**438**	**763**	**699**	**526**	**Amérique du Sud**
Brazil	920	668	574	761	873	671	438	763	699	526	Brésil
Asia	**158225**	**158051**	**122477**	**113212**	**127473**	**130677**	**132959**	**133177**	**90474**	**97798**	**Asie**
Indonesia	188	220	265	502	718	1076	...	1837	69	...	Indonésie
Japan	147370	143808	111704	102067	113103	113596	114847	110465	79762	86488	Japon
Kazakhstan	..	618	312	210	32	...	11	24	...	6	Kazakhstan
Korea, Republic of	10667	12441	9362	9961	13532	15762	17435	20795	10470	10179	Corée, République de
Uzbekistan	..	964	834	472	88	70	57	56	...	...	Ouzbékistan
Europe	**11303**	**61593**	**51914**	**48526**	**38544**	**41166**	**33867**	**31902**	**33068**	**31781**	**Europe**
Austria	...	...	...	...	...	2287	2094	2439	3294	3772	Autriche
Belarus	..	124	50	100	37	60	46	51	50	37	Bélarus
Croatia	..	31	17	25	...	10	16	2	10	...	Croatie
Czechoslovakia(former)	836	318	..	..	..	..	..	..	..	..	Tchécoslovaquie(anc.)
Czech Republic	..	..	197	92	...	...	...	...	...	...	République tchèque
Estonia	..	1235	103	17	14	8	6	5	10	2	Estonie
Finland	1648	1087	643	605	582	685	269	...	...	...	Finlande
Germany	..	..	...	...	...	23065	17414	16853	19206	...	Allemagne
Hungary	6	5	...	...	...	...	...	...	...	...	Hongrie
Poland	1035	463	263	258	197	246	234	239	256	112	Pologne
Romania	871	457	252	142	150	146	109	61	12	14	Roumanie
Russian Federation	..	21112	15378	12642	6510	5234	3504	4166	3264	2599	Fédération de Russie
Slovakia	..	..	...	...	...	...	3450	1205	697	476	Slovaquie
Slovenia	..	...	...	...	...	...	2	0	0	...	Slovénie
Spain	...	...	...	2005	395	84	...	...	44	574	Espagne
Sweden	...	...	...	...	...	...	...	5729	5740	4670	Suède
Ukraine	..	10367	7057	5511	2923	2316	534	330	289	201	Ukraine
Yugoslavia	..	258	120	42	72	38	39	52	46	32	Yougoslavie
USSR (former)	37732	..	..	..	..	..	..	..	..	..	URSS (anc.)
Total	**212683**	**223383**	**178410**	**166450**	**175844**	**184847**	**180217**	**181025**	**141757**	**147688**	**Total**

General Note.

Boom, jib and cable types which dig into the soil, above or below machine level, by means of an excavating bucket, grab etc., multi-bucket excavators in which the digging buckets are fitted on endless chains or on rotating wheels, dredgers (bucket or shovel type) other than floating dredgers, railroad ballast excavator -screening machines consisting essentially of a continuous chain of buckets which dig the ballast from under railway tracks. (SITC, Rev.3: 72320-0).

Remarque générale.

Pelles mécaniques et excavatrices à godet suspendu, creusant le sol en butte ou en fouille, au moyen d'un godet tranchant ou à griffes, etc., excavateurs continus à godets excavateurs disposés en chapelet sur une chaîne sans fin ou la périphérie d'une roue, engins de dragage non flottants (à godet ou à pelle), machines dégarnisseuses et cribleuses de ballast, se composant essentiellement d'un chapelet de godets piocheurs qui reprennent le ballast se trouvant sous la voie. (CTCI, Rev.3: 72320-0).

[1] Shipments.

[1] Expéditions.

Graders and levellers
Niveleuses-régleuses

ISIC-BASED CODE - CODE BASE CITI

3824-28

Unit : Number of units

Unité : Nombre

Country or area	1990	1991	1992	1993	1994	1995	1996	1997	1998	1999	Pays ou zone
America, North	**4136**	**3289**	**2894**	**3569**	**3569**	**3766**	**3762**	**3023**	**2913**	**2804**	**Amérique du Nord**
United States [1]	4136	3289	2894	...	...	3766	3762	...	...	...	Etats-Unis [1]
America, South	**1481**	**1202**	**1271**	**1099**	**1869**	**1282**	**1254**	**1806**	**2151**	**893**	**Amérique du Sud**
Brazil	1481	1202	1271	1099	1869	1282	1254	1806	2151	893	Brésil
Asia	**83613**	**88596**	**73579**	**77765**	**84031**	**81060**	**89259**	**88393**	**68375**	**76138**	**Asie**
Indonesia	73	53	162	182	424	174	...	193	...	...	Indonésie
Japan	83479	88510	73378	77540	83567	80838	89040	88161	68128	75886	Japon
Korea, Republic of	51	22	...	...	...	...	...	...	...	...	Corée, République de
Turkey	10	11	2	6	3	11	2	2	0	0	Turquie
Europe	**731**	**5657**	**4521**	**4323**	**2536**	**2025**	**2169**	**2068**	**2151**	**2470**	**Europe**
Denmark [2]	...	3	0	1	0	0	0	0	0	0	Danemark [2]
Finland	58	54	39	29	21	25	33	...	...	...	Finlande
Portugal	672	587	...	...	...	...	...	...	...	...	Portugal
Russian Federation	..	4135	3420	3415	1468	1187	1386	1377	1484	1818	Fédération de Russie
Slovenia	..	9	35	1	...	...	...	...	...	...	Slovénie
Ukraine	..	851	392	237	402	168	105	35	15	7	Ukraine
Yugoslavia	..	18	5	10	0	0	0	1	3	0	Yougoslavie
USSR (former)	4841	..	..	..	..	..	..	..	..	..	URSS (anc.)
Total	**94802**	**98744**	**82264**	**86755**	**92004**	**88132**	**96443**	**95289**	**75591**	**82305**	**Total**

General Note.
Machines, usually self-propelled, designed for earth-levelling or smoothing (on flat surfaces or banks) by means of an adjustable grading blade, usually mounted within the wheel base. (SITC, Rev.3: 72312-0).

Remarque générale.
Machines, généralement automotrices, conçues pour niveler et régulariser le terrain, même en talus, à l'aide d'une lame réglable et inclinable sur l'horizontale, généralement montée dans l'empattement des roues. (CTCI, Rev.3: 72312-0).

[1] Shipments.
[2] Sales.

[1] Expéditions.
[2] Ventes.

Scrapers
Décapeuses (scrapers)
ISIC-BASED CODE - CODE BASE CITI
3824-31

Unit : Number of units   Unité : Nombre

Country or area	1990	1991	1992	1993	1994	1995	1996	1997	1998	1999	Pays ou zone
America, North	**1885**	**1260**	**1106**	**1902**	**1709**	**2100**	**2013**	**2427**	**1902**	**2719**	**Amérique du Nord**
United States[1]	1885	1260	1106	...	1709	2100	2013	2427	...	2719	Etats-Unis[1]
America, South	**175**	**83**	**84**	**41**	**129**	**95**	**41**	**85**	**62**	**50**	**Amérique du Sud**
Brazil	175	83	84	41	129	95	41	85	62	50	Brésil
Europe	**69**	**5921**	**1070**	**797**	**195**	**477**	**418**	**168**	**190**	**164**	**Europe**
Belarus	..	1831	442	264	69	74	52	29	60	43	Bélarus
Bulgaria	...	27	...	...	...	...	...	...	...	...	Bulgarie
Denmark[2]	...	...	0	0	0	0	3	35	26	17	Danemark[2]
Romania	40	0	0	0	...	...	...	...	...	...	Roumanie
Russian Federation	..	1348	192	19	0	...	...	0	0	...	Fédération de Russie
Slovenia	..	...	0	...	...	80	...	...	...	...	Slovénie
Ukraine	..	2645	382	423	20	0	0	0	0	...	Ukraine
T.F.Yug.Rep. Macedonia	..	...	...	24	29	...	...	...	...	...	L'ex-RY Macédoine
USSR (former)	6031	..	..	..	..	..	..	..	..	..	URSS (anc.)
Total	**8160**	**7264**	**2260**	**2740**	**2033**	**2672**	**2472**	**2680**	**2154**	**2933**	**Total**

General Note.
Machines incorporating a sharp cutting edge designed to slice off a layer of top soil which is then passed into the scraperbody or discharged by a conveyor. Scrapers with incorporated tractor are included. (SITC, Rev.3: 72331-0, 72346-0).

[1] Shipments.
[2] Sales.

Remarque générale.
Machines munies d'une lame horizontale coupante travaillant en rabot par découpage d'une couche de terrain, les déblais étant évacués soit dans un chariot de charge incorporé soit au moyen d'un convoyeur à bande. Cette rubrique comprend les scrapers automoteurs. (CTCI, Rev.3: 72331-0, 72346-0).

[1] Expéditions.
[2] Ventes.

Concrete mixers for use at construction sites
Bétonnières pour chantiers de construction

ISIC-BASED CODE - CODE BASE CITI

3824-34

Unit : Number of units   Unité : Nombre

Country or area	1990	1991	1992	1993	1994	1995	1996	1997	1998	1999	Pays ou zone
Africa	**3689**	**6094**	**5268**	**2156**	**738**	**913**	**527**	**471**	**234**	**176**	**Afrique**
Algeria	3689	6094	5268	2156	738	913	527	471	234	176	Algérie
America, North	**9172**	**9172**	**9172**	**9172**	**9172**	**9172**	**8402**	**8750**	**9109**	**10428**	**Amérique du Nord**
United States[1]	...	...	...	...	...	...	8402	8750	9109	10428	Etats-Unis[1]
Asia	**737**	**1406**	**1863**	**1299**	**730**	**698**	**1009**	**1176**	**578**	**382**	**Asie**
Indonesia	167	473	...	438	116	...	...	...	...	...	Indonésie
Kazakhstan	..	529	1167	431	403	119	...	...	4	3	Kazakhstan
Turkey	570	404	397	430	211	280	331	498	275	80	Turquie
Europe	**239179**	**272516**	**270141**	**258559**	**265825**	**262054**	**242380**	**272790**	**289450**	**264646**	**Europe**
Austria[2][3]	...	...	...	...	...	13685	16888	...	10713	...	Autriche[2][3]
Bulgaria	185	116	46	293	340	316	116	43	...	...	Bulgarie
Croatia	..	7934	2347	930	...	922	630	395	862	...	Croatie
Czechoslovakia(former)	12904	...	..	..	..	..	..	..	..	..	Tchécoslovaquie(anc.)
Czech Republic	..	..	24625	20755	...	...	...	...	...	...	République tchèque
Finland*	18420	5310	7670	12330	11090	5922	8487	...	...	...	Finlande*
Germany	..	...	...	106941	116080	104860	85172	...	104212	...	Allemagne
Germany(Fed.Rep.)	113406	..	..	..	..	..	..	..	..	..	Allemagne(Rép.féd.)
German D.R.(former)	7288	..	..	..	..	..	..	..	..	..	R.D.A. (anc.)
Greece	2566	2676	1993	690	411	431	330	178	177	...	Grèce
Hungary	2550	2045	1445	2038	2155	1610	998	304	2547	1297	Hongrie
Latvia	..	...	...	204	41	34	53	30	82	60	Lettonie
Lithuania	..	...	...	...	...	390	239	20	61	67	Lituanie
Portugal	...	...	10887	12988	13979	13991	16835	17838	21037	21360	Portugal
Romania	1371	2702	2009	2556	2235	2113	1759	1548	1470	785	Roumanie
Russian Federation	..	11124	6170	4293	1977	1624	1208	816	652	645	Fédération de Russie
Slovakia	..	..	3578	151	6157	1734	889	1064	...	...	Slovaquie
Slovenia	..	2918	2511	3168	3503	3652	9022	11451	13883	14697	Slovénie
Spain	13199	11549	12512	26243	22217	41191	29182	44575	56516	56912	Espagne
Ukraine	..	2197	3343	6183	1781	1180	400	279	323	406	Ukraine
United Kingdom	...	...	...	...	40157	40765	...	...	...	...	Royaume-Uni
Yugoslavia	..	16959	16299	4088	4845	4944	7021	8485	7670	4871	Yougoslavie
USSR (former)	14669	..	..	..	..	..	..	..	..	..	URSS (anc.)
Total	**267447**	**289188**	**286444**	**271186**	**276466**	**272837**	**252318**	**283187**	**299371**	**275631**	**Total**

General Note.

Machines consisting essentially of a container, equipped with paddles or other stirring devices, for mixing concrete or mortar by stirring or agitation. The item is confined to mixers of the types used at construction sites. Mixers permanently mounted on a railway wagon or on a lorry chassis are excluded. (SITC, Rev.3: 72833-1).

Remarque générale.

Machines consistant essentiellement en un récipient dans lequel le malaxage du béton et du mortier est effectué à l'aide de palettes ou d'autres dispositifs appropriés. Cette rubrique ne comprend que les bétonnières de tous types utilisées sur les chantiers de construction. Elle ne comprend pas les bétonnières montées de façon permanente sur wagon de chemin de fer ou sur châssis de camion. (CTCI, Rev.3: 72833-1).

[1] Shipments.
[2] 1997 data are confidential.
[3] 1999 data are confidential.

[1] Expéditions.
[2] Pour 1997, les données sont confidentielles.
[3] Pour 1999, les données sont confidentielles.

Typewriters
Machines à écrire
ISIC-BASED CODE - CODE BASE CITI
3825-01

Unit : Thousand units   Unité : En milliers

Country or area	1990	1991	1992	1993	1994	1995	1996	1997	1998	1999	Pays ou zone
America, North	**512**	**598**	**627**	**655**	**916**	**828**	**899**	**957**	**792**	**580**	**Amérique du Nord**
Mexico	512	598	627	655	916	828	899	957	792	580	Mexique
America, South	**461**	**480**	**408**	**362**	**323**	**255**	**221**	**97**	**46**	**22**	**Amérique du Sud**
Brazil	461	480	408	362	323	255	221	97	46	22	Brésil
Asia	**3098**	**2779**	**2299**	**2612**	**2379**	**2235**	**2363**	**2324**	**2258**	**2206**	**Asie**
India	117	115	109	79	87	102	83	91	71	66	Inde
Indonesia	...	...	...	122	120	...	...	...	...	...	Indonésie
Japan	1942	1549	1064	...	...	...	...	...	...	...	Japon
Korea, Republic of	918	994	1005	893	654	494	...	...	...	...	Corée, République de
Europe	**3228**	**2861**	**2475**	**2124**	**1984**	**1634**	**1454**	**1321**	**1297**	**1064**	**Europe**
Bulgaria	154	150	170	172	150	61	42	51	...	...	Bulgarie
Czechoslovakia(former)	70	58	..	..	..	...	...	..	..	..	Tchécoslovaquie(anc.)
Germany	..	858	...	388	494	...	...	...	...	...	Allemagne
Germany(Fed.Rep.)	671	..	...	..	..	..	..	..	..	..	Allemagne(Rép.féd.)
German D.R.(former)[1]	515	..	..	..	..	..	..	..	..	..	R.D.A. (anc.)[1]
Italy	295	283	239	...	...	...	...	...	...	...	Italie
Poland	56	33	32	27	14	4	4	1	1	0	Pologne
Russian Federation	..	182	303	248	98	58	11	13	20	6	Fédération de Russie
Spain	77	51	49	...	...	...	...	...	...	...	Espagne
United Kingdom	...	...	...	...	896	600	486	345	304	...	Royaume-Uni
Total	**7299**	**6718**	**5809**	**5754**	**5602**	**4952**	**4937**	**4699**	**4393**	**3872**	**Total**

General Note.
Manual or electric typewriters except those incorporating calculating mechanisms. Excluding cheque-writing machines. (SITC,Rev.3: 75110-0).

Remarque générale.
Machines à écrire, mécaniques ou électriques, à l'exception de celles comprenant un dispositif de totalisation et des machines à écrire les chèques. (CTCI, Rev.3: 75110-0).

[1] Standard typewriters only.

[1] Machines à écrire ordinaires.

Calculating machines
Machines à calculer

ISIC-BASED CODE - CODE BASE CITI

3825-04

Unit : Thousand units   Unité : En milliers

Country or area	1990	1991	1992	1993	1994	1995	1996	1997	1998	1999	Pays ou zone
America, North	**95**	**50**	**5**	**50**	**50**	**50**	**50**	**50**	**50**	**50**	**Amérique du Nord**
Mexico	95	50	5	...	...	...	...	...	...	...	Mexique
America, South	**1935**	**1460**	**736**	**1044**	**758**	**897**	**629**	**661**	**87**	**29**	**Amérique du Sud**
Brazil[1]	1935	1460	736	1044	758	897	629	661	87	29	Brésil[1]
Asia	**85037**	**77229**	**58441**	**48942**	**21248**	**14224**	**6967**	**6006**	**4523**	**3382**	**Asie**
Azerbaijan	..	26	2	0	0	6	0	0	0	0	Azerbaïdjan
Hong Kong SAR[2][3]	15600	6397	1332	...	760	8267	...	...	...		Hong-Kong RAS[2][3]
Japan	67479	69371	55800	41576	20170	5565	3249	3238	2705	2402	Japon
Korea, Republic of	1958	1426	1304	894	316	386	...	...	...	...	Corée, République de
Uzbekistan	..	9	3	1	2	0	0	...	...	...	Ouzbékistan
Europe	**690**	**630**	**519**	**671**	**153**	**453**	**478**	**499**	**552**	**544**	**Europe**
Croatia	..	10	1	0	0	0	0	0	...	...	Croatie
Czechoslovakia(former)	136	...	..	..	..	..	..	..	..	..	Tchécoslovaquie(anc.)
Germany	..	...	502	660	138	...	...	...	...	..	Allemagne
Germany(Fed.Rep.)	23	..	..	..	..	..	..	..	..	..	Allemagne(Rép.féd.)
German D.R.(former)	366	..	..	..	..	..	..	..	..	..	R.D.A. (anc.)
Hungary	3	3	5	8	9	8	...	...	...	...	Hongrie
Poland	131	46	10	2	5	10	35	56	105	100	Pologne
Sweden	...	...	...	...	...	...	...	0	4	0	Suède
Yugoslavia, SFR	30	..	..	..	..	..	..	..	..		Yougoslavie, RSF
Oceania	**4**	**4**	**4**	**4**	**4**	**4**	**4**	**4**	**4**	**4**	**Océanie**
Australia	4	...	...	...	...	...	...	...	...	...	Australie
Total	**87761**	**79373**	**59706**	**50712**	**22213**	**15628**	**8129**	**7220**	**5216**	**4009**	**Total**

General Note.
Calculating machines involving a simple calculating device and usually designed to perform one or more of the four arithmetical operations. Excluding accounting machines and similar machines incorporating a calculating device. (SITC, Rev.3: 75121-0, 75122-0).

Remarque générale.
Machines à calculer mettant en jeu un simple dispositif de calcul et généralement conçues pour effectuer une ou plusieurs des quatre opérations arithmétiques. Cette rubrique ne comprend pas les machines comptables ou analogues dans lesquelles un tel dispositif est incorporé. (CTCI, Rev.3: 75121-0, 75122-0).

[1] Production by establishments employing 5 or more persons.
[2] 1996 data are confidential.
[3] 1997 data are confidential.

[1] Production des établissements occupant 5 personnes ou plus.
[2] Pour 1996, les données sont confidentielles.
[3] Pour 1997, les données sont confidentielles.

Scales, industrial
Balances et bascules industrielles

ISIC-BASED CODE - CODE BASE CITI

3825-13

Unit : Number of units   Unité : Nombre

Country or area	1990	1991	1992	1993	1994	1995	1996	1997	1998	1999	Pays ou zone
America, South											**Amérique du Sud**
Brazil	34560	37596	...	...	...	...	...	...	...	...	Brésil
Colombia	...	...	146748	138857	116380	119299	...	...	...	...	Colombie
Asia											**Asie**
Bangladesh	32	...	...	...	...	...	...	...	...	...	Bangladesh
Cyprus	*340	*340	...	...	...	709	...	...	...	...	Chypre
Japan	26956	19978	18543	18099	18278	18264	18772	19891	18401	18115	Japon
Korea, Republic of	740	494	656	377	...	...	...	...	...	...	Corée, République de
Turkey	56	186	205	367	425	994	...	2875	1182	715	Turquie
Europe											**Europe**
Austria	[1][2]793	[1][2]582	[1][2]475	[1][2]300	[1][2]373	[2]398	[1]1615	[1]3038	[1]1404	...	Autriche
Croatia	..	..	...	...	...	...	...	149	221	...	Croatie
France[3][4]	5998	11398	17259	17694	25000	...	...	...	...	...	France[3][4]
Germany	..	203107	183234	185104	203345	292725	217169	226558	241494	...	Allemagne
Germany(Fed.Rep.)	230957	..	..	..	..	..	..	..	..	..	Allemagne(Rép.féd.)
Greece	361	324	...	1217	1494	...	...	...	1466	...	Grèce
Hungary	0	7	...	...	...	...	...	...	...	...	Hongrie
Latvia	..	...	...	...	...	...	...	...	...	10	Lettonie
Lithuania	..	...	...	...	...	10	59	100	73	6	Lituanie
Portugal	9017	13583	2227	2024	2023	3418	3059	3485	3524	3048	Portugal
Slovenia	..	1058	...	6734	6981	4545	7688	...	...	...	Slovénie
Spain	16585	11424	9029	4186	5189	6411	...	...	...	...	Espagne
United Kingdom	...	...	...	35226	...	...	...	...	...	...	Royaume-Uni
Yugoslavia	..	20	...	...	...	21	113	62	70	72	Yougoslavie

General Note.

Machines for the direct determination of the weight of objects, such as floor scales, bulk material weighers, predetermined weighing and check-weighing scales, and miscellaneous industrial scales. Retail, commercial and household scales and balances are excluded. (SITC, Rev.3: 74531-1).

Remarque générale.

Machines pour la détermination directe du poids des objets, telles que les bascules à plate-forme, les balances pour matières en vrac, les balances vérificatrices indiquant les excédents ou déficits par rapport à un poids prédéterminé et diverses balances industrielles. Cette rubrique ne comprend pas les balances utilisées dans le commerce de détail ou de gros et les balances de ménage. (CTCI, Rev.3: 74531-1).

[1] 1999 data are confidential.
[2] In metric tons.
[3] Shipments.
[4] Scales and balances of all types with a capacity of more than 200 kilogrammes.

[1] Pour 1999, les données sont confidentielles.
[2] En tonnes métriques.
[3] Expéditions.
[4] Balances et bascules de tous types, d'une portée supérieure à 200 kilogrammes.

Scales, other than industrial
Autres balances et bascules

ISIC-BASED CODE - CODE BASE CITI

3825-16

Unit : Thousand units   Unité : En milliers

Country or area	1990	1991	1992	1993	1994	1995	1996	1997	1998	1999	Pays ou zone
America, South	**16**	**17**	**18**	**16**	**17**	**17**	**17**	**17**	**17**	**17**	**Amérique du Sud**
Chile	16	17	18	16	...	...	...	...	...	...	Chili
Asia	**595**	**696**	**648**	**470**	**399**	**402**	**380**	**438**	**341**	**210**	**Asie**
Indonesia	...	...	34	44	47	...	...	...	...	...	Indonésie
Korea, Republic of	539	644	614	416	[1]347	[1]359	[1]337	[1]394	[1]297	...	Corée, République de
Turkey	14	10	0	10	...	1	1	2	2	1	Turquie
Europe	**5471**	**8188**	**9031**	**9397**	**9864**	**11293**	**12145**	**12998**	**14789**	**15431**	**Europe**
Croatia	..	2	2	0	0	0	0	1	...	...	Croatie
Finland	1	1	1	1	0	0	0	...	...	1	Finlande
France[2][3]	2103	4539	5325	5830	5731	...	...	...	...	...	France[2][3]
Germany	..	2906	3162	3094	3192	...	...	...	...	...	Allemagne
Germany(Fed.Rep.)	2742	..	..	..	...	...	...	..	...	..	Allemagne(Rép.féd.)
Hungary	2	2	2	1	...	...	...	...	1367	1161	Hongrie
Portugal	...	...	6	4	4	4	3	4	3	2	Portugal
Slovenia	..	345	108	245	266	236	229	...	...	...	Slovénie
Spain	25	219	255	52	78	101	...	...	...	...	Espagne
United Kingdom	...	...	...	170	...	...	...	...	...	...	Royaume-Uni
Yugoslavia	..	0	0	0	0	1	0	0	0	0	Yougoslavie
Yugoslavia, SFR	423	..	..	..	..	..	..	..	..	..	Yougoslavie, RSF
Total	**6081**	**8901**	**9697**	**9883**	**10279**	**11711**	**12541**	**13452**	**15147**	**15657**	**Total**

General Note.
Machines for the direct determination of the weight of objects such as retail and commercial scales, person-weighing scales and miscellaneous household scales. (SITC, Rev.3: 74531-2, 74532-0).

[1] Including industrial scales.
[2] Shipments.
[3] Scales and balances of all types with a capacity of less than 200 kilogrammes.

Remarque générale.
Machines pour la détermination directe du poids des objets, telles que les balances utilisées dans le commerce de gros ou de détail, les bascules pour personnes et diverses balances de ménage. (CTCI, Rev.3: 74531-2, 74532-0).

[1] Y compris les balances et bascules industrielles.
[2] Expéditions.
[3] Balances et bascules de tous types, d'une portée inférieure à 200 kilogrammes.

Ovens, household
Fours pour usages domestiques
ISIC-BASED CODE - CODE BASE CITI

3829-01

Unit : Thousand units   Unité : En milliers

Country or area	1990	1991	1992	1993	1994	1995	1996	1997	1998	1999	Pays ou zone
America, North	**9947**	**9404**	**10259**	**10129**	**9405**	**8473**	**8422**	**9563**	**10491**	**10569**	**Amérique du Nord**
Mexico	0	...	...	1	1	1	1	1	2	1	Mexique
United States[1]	9947	9403	10258	10128	9404	8472	8421	9562	10489	10568	Etats-Unis[1]
America, South	**51**	**55**	**48**	**62**	**58**	**58**	**68**	**71**	**74**	**78**	**Amérique du Sud**
Colombia	51	...	48	62	58	58	...	...	...	...	Colombie
Asia	**7760**	**8677**	**8620**	**9633**	**11679**	**11666**	**11408**	**12497**	**10784**	**13971**	**Asie**
Indonesia	48	62	30	26	31	...	...	...	...	...	Indonésie
Iran(Islamic Rep. of)[2]	674	387	375	414	601	401	437	505	316	...	Iran(Rép. islamique)[2]
Iraq	...	...	5	...	...	...	...	...	...	...	Iraq
Japan	324	297	294	176	216	228	243	230	188	195	Japon
Korea, Republic of[3]	6061	7174	7172	8279	10209	10487	10100	10990	9586	...	Corée, République de[3]
Turkey	648	732	723	714	599	520	611	762	689	610	Turquie
Yemen	..	20	21	19	18	7	1	1	...	...	Yémen
Europe	**7263**	**9807**	**9644**	**9400**	**9292**	**11240**	**11335**	**14260**	**13627**	**13814**	**Europe**
Austria[4][5]	49	108	67	64	61	...	...	2987	3084	3200	Autriche[4][5]
Croatia	..	...	...	52	21	64	98	82	...	...	Croatie
Denmark[6]	183	...	...	...	...	...	...	...	...	...	Danemark[6]
Czechoslovakia(former)	132	64	..	..	...	...	...	...	...	..	Tchécoslovaquie(anc.)
Czech Republic	..	..	43	51	...	...	...	...	...	...	République tchèque
Finland	3	3	2	2	1	1	1	...	...	15	Finlande
France	1818	2576	2764	2797	2853	...	...	...	...	...	France
Germany	..	4638	4061	3577	3640	...	...	...	...	...	Allemagne
Germany(Fed.Rep.)	3315	...	...	..	..	..	...	...	...	...	Allemagne(Rép.féd.)
Greece	11	38	37	...	...	...	...	...	...	...	Grèce
Hungary	89	51	41	52	48	37	...	...	...	...	Hongrie
Latvia	..	...	...	...	...	...	...	...	...	4	Lettonie
Netherlands	223	193	187	...	...	...	...	...	...	...	Pays-Bas
Poland	193	188	158	175	271	272	331	238	204	151	Pologne
Portugal	34	31	148	81	172	147	112	126	148	156	Portugal
Romania	139	124	93	92	92	62	79	290	22	39	Roumanie
Slovakia	..	..	...	37	...	...	135	990	210	72	Slovaquie
Slovenia	..	32	43	57	58	48	185	124	202	...	Slovénie
Spain	452	467	453	578	...	643	...	...	...	...	Espagne
Ukraine[7]	..	354	490	537	277	111	67	66	68	121	Ukraine[7]
United Kingdom	...	...	...	771	473	...	...	...	...	...	Royaume-Uni
Yugoslavia	..	123	100	61	54	51	44	52	59	35	Yougoslavie
Total	**25021**	**27944**	**28571**	**29224**	**30434**	**31438**	**31234**	**36392**	**34977**	**38432**	**Total**

<table>
<tr><td>

General Note.
Domestic ovens of all types, electric and non-electric, including infra-red ovens and high-frequency induction ovens. (SITC, Rev.3: 69731-1, 69732-1, 69734-1, 77586-1).

[1] Shipments.
[2] Production by establishments employing 10 or more persons.
[3] Microwave ovens only.
[4] 1995 data are confidential.
[5] 1996 data are confidential.
[6] Sales.
[7] Electric only.

</td><td>

Remarque générale.
Fours domestiques de tous types, électriques ou non, y compris les fours à rayons infrarouges et les fours à induction à haute fréquence. (CTCI, Rev.3: 69731-1, 69732-1, 69734-1, 77586-1).

[1] Expéditions.
[2] Production des établissements occupant 10 personnes ou plus.
[3] Les fours à micro-onde seulement.
[4] Pour 1995, les données sont confidentielles.
[5] Pour 1996, les données sont confidentielles.
[6] Ventes.
[7] Electrique seulement.

</td></tr>
</table>

Stoves, ranges, cookers
Poêles, fourneaux, cuisinières

ISIC-BASED CODE - CODE BASE CITI

3829-04

Unit : Thousand units   Unité : En milliers

Country or area	1990	1991	1992	1993	1994	1995	1996	1997	1998	1999	Pays ou zone
Africa	**166**	**192**	**219**	**213**	**250**	**259**	**237**	**218**	**219**	**207**	**Afrique**
Algeria	2	30	52	55	55	57	47	58	62	45	Algérie
South Africa[1]	161	157	163	153	190	199	188	158	154	159	Afrique du Sud[1]
United Rep.Tanzania	3	5	4	5	5	3	2	2	...	...	Rép. Unie de Tanzanie
America, North	**11361**	**11647**	**12713**	**14176**	**14775**	**13978**	**15153**	**14577**	**13758**	**15064**	**Amérique du Nord**
Antigua and Barbuda[2]	...	...	...	2	2	...	...	...	...	...	Antigua-et-Barbuda[2]
Mexico	1143	1304	1286	2144	2461	2301	2632	3008	3000	3165	Mexique
Trinidad and Tobago[3]	15	17	21	19	12	12	10	...	...	...	Trinité-et-Tobago[3]
United States[4]	10201	10324	11404	12011	12300	11663	12509	11558	10748	11890	Etats-Unis[4]
America, South	**921**	**1277**	**1828**	**1558**	**1398**	**1129**	**1629**	**1978**	**2095**	**2070**	**Amérique du Sud**
Bolivia	1	1	1	0	0	*0					Bolivie
Chile[1]	135	164	231	320	349	310	281	...	...	...	Chili[1]
Colombia	533	...	1184	972	818	654	...	...	...	...	Colombie
Ecuador	...	...	338	196	163	107	...	465	501	...	Equateur
Guyana	4	4	2	1	1	...	...	...	...	...	Guyana
Peru[3]	...	...	...	...	...	58	58	70	81	36	Pérou[3]
Asia	**2906**	**3962**	**4247**	**4887**	**5357**	**5566**	**4060**	**4339**	**3785**	**4571**	**Asie**
Azerbaijan	..	45	23	9	3	4	1	0	1	1	Azerbaïdjan
Indonesia	455	1219	1164	925	1591	3107	...	2382	2223	...	Indonésie
Iraq	...	...	29	...	...	...	...	...	..	...	Iraq
Korea, Republic of[5]	2350	2496	2814	3778	3620	2308	2284	1832	1443	...	Corée, République de[5]
Syrian Arab Republic	72	78	134	97	98	102	105	86	83	...	Rép. arabe syrienne
Turkmenistan	..	95	83	49	16	16	8	10	6	...	Turkménistan
Europe	**18276**	**17939**	**20036**	**15593**	**15075**	**15356**	**18150**	**18211**	**17349**	**17445**	**Europe**
Austria	337	382	1007	1009	943	843	[6]2538	[6]2987	[6]3084	...	Autriche
Belarus	..	[7]541	508	510	440	359	377	425	423	451	Bélarus
Bulgaria	259	163	290	193	178	169	124	62	83	78	Bulgarie
Croatia	..	104	107	169	47	36	12	72	184	...	Croatie
Czechoslovakia(former)	334	308	..	..	..	..	..	..	..	..	Tchécoslovaquie(anc.)
Czech Republic	..		369	374	...	...	...	...	...		République tchèque
Finland	196	191	125	174	182	108	107	...	93	*99	Finlande
France[4][6]	3521	3380	3578	3761	3827	...	...	...	...	...	France[4][6]
Germany	..	3473	3396	3348	3433	...	[6]4684	...	...	...	Allemagne
Germany(Fed.Rep.)	3147	..	..	..	..	..	..	..	..	..	Allemagne(Rép.féd.)
German D.R. (former)[8]	302	..	..	..	..	..	..	..	..	..	R.D.A. (anc.)[8]
Greece[1]	123	99	96	...	...	...	...	...	...	...	Grèce[1]
Hungary	560	543	260	228	203	144	...	...	...	...	Hongrie
Netherlands[9][10]	228	214	220	...	...	...	...	...	...	...	Pays-Bas[9][10]
Norway	78	...	...	...	...	...	...	...	...	...	Norvège
Poland[11]	507	364	345	322	271	204	220	219	172	180	Pologne[11]
Portugal	...	...	178	144	178	272	305	380	348	253	Portugal
Slovakia	..	..	...	...	90	70	126	983	250	148	Slovaquie
Slovenia	..	406	372	389	346	320	410	344	505	...	Slovénie
Spain	7734	6459	7959	3358	3530	3761	...	...	...	...	Espagne
United Kingdom	745	...	...	817	468	565	545	...	...	...	Royaume-Uni
Yugoslavia	..	388	339	187	163	151	205	279	331	317	Yougoslavie
Oceania	**138**	**108**	**168**	**138**	**138**	**138**	**138**	**138**	**138**	**138**	**Océanie**
Australia[6][12]	...	108	168	...	...	...	...	...	...	...	Australie[6][12]
Total	**33768**	**35126**	**39211**	**36566**	**36993**	**36427**	**39368**	**39461**	**37344**	**39495**	**Total**

General Note.
Kitchen stoves, ranges and cookers for household use and similar apparatus of larger size suitable for hotels, restaurants etc., burning any type of fuel. Electrically-operated apparatus is included. (SITC, Rev.3: 69731-2, 69732-2, 69734-2, 77586-2).

For footnotes, see end of table.

Remarque générale.
Poêles, fourneaux de cuisine, cuisinières pour usage ménager et appareils plus grands du même genre convenant aux hôtels, restaurants, etc., quel que soit le combustible utilisé. Cette rubrique comprend les appareils fonctionnant à l'électricité. (CTCI, Rev.3: 69731-2, 69732-2, 69734-2, 77586-2).

Voir la fin du tableau pour les notes.

Stoves, ranges, cookers (continued)
Poêles, fourneaux, cuisinières (suite)

ISIC-BASED CODE - CODE BASE CITI
3829-04

Footnotes
[1] Stoves only.
[2] Twelve months beginning 21 March of year stated.
[3] Gas cookers only.
[4] Shipments.
[5] Gas ranges only.
[6] Including ovens.
[7] Gas stoves only.
[8] Electric ranges and cookers only.
[9] Industrial sales.
[10] Including gas ovens.
[11] Gas cookers with ovens only.
[12] Twelve months ending 30 June of year stated.

Notes.
[1] Poêles seulement.
[2] Période de douze mois commençant le 21 mars de l'année indiquée.
[3] Cuisinières à gaz seulement.
[4] Expéditions.
[5] Fourneaux à gaz seulement.
[6] Y compris les fours.
[7] Poêles seulement.
[8] Fourneaux et cuisinières électriques seulement.
[9] Ventes industrielles.
[10] Y compris les fourneaux à gaz.
[11] Cuisinières à gaz avec fours seulement.
[12] Période de douze mois finissant le 30 juin de l'année indiquée.

Drying machines for household use
Machines à sécher, à usage domestique

ISIC-BASED CODE - CODE BASE CITI

3829-07

Unit : Thousand units   Unité : En milliers

Country or area	1990	1991	1992	1993	1994	1995	1996	1997	1998	1999	Pays ou zone
America, North	**4195**	**4171**	**4500**	**4787**	**5016**	**4855**	**4934**	**4919**	**4206**	**6151**	**Amérique du Nord**
Mexico	8	6	4	5	4	...	...	...	...	...	Mexique
United States[1]	4187	4165	4496	4782	5012	4852	4932	4918	4206	6151	Etats-Unis[1]
America, South	**1**	**1**	**1**	**1**	**1**	**1**	**1**	**1**	**1**	**1**	**Amérique du Sud**
Colombia	...	...	1	1	1	1	...	...	...	...	Colombie
Asia	**665**	**674**	**630**	**590**	**478**	**488**	**424**	**448**	**461**	**410**	**Asie**
Indonesia	33	35	...	...	...	...	...	...	...	...	Indonésie
Japan	632	639	596	556	444	454	390	414	427	376	Japon
Europe	**1865**	**3774**	**3225**	**2726**	**2405**	**2213**	**2244**	**2571**	**2538**	**2213**	**Europe**
Denmark[2]	*9	*8	7	7	7	11	10	10	13	14	Danemark[2]
Germany	..	...	1078	980	975	729	817	902	941	...	Allemagne
Germany(Fed.Rep.)	920	...	..	..	..	..	..	..	..	..	Allemagne(Rép.féd.)
Lithuania	..	...	...	...	...	97	93	170	139	15	Lituanie
Russian Federation	..	1604	954	506	376	266	231	261	53	79	Fédération de Russie
Slovenia	..	...	12	11	18	23	27	15	0	44	Slovénie
Spain	...	...	2	...	...	...	...	...	...	...	Espagne
Sweden	...	...	...	...	...	...	59	48	50	59	Suède
United Kingdom	...	...	...	1015	834	1030	1005	1163	1340	...	Royaume-Uni
Yugoslavia	..	5	2	1	1	1	0	0	0	...	Yougoslavie
Oceania	**227**	**158**	**150**	**150**	**171**	**171**	**171**	**171**	**171**	**171**	**Océanie**
Australia	227	158	150	150	...	...	...	...	...	...	Australie
Total	**6953**	**8778**	**8506**	**8254**	**8071**	**7728**	**7774**	**8110**	**7377**	**8947**	**Total**

General Note.
Machines designed for the drying of textile fabrics or made-up articles consisting essentially of a closed chamber in which the goods to be dried are subjected to the action of hot air. (SITC, Rev.3: 77512-0).

Remarque générale.
Machines destinées à sécher des tissus ou des ouvrages en matières textiles, se composant essentiellement d'une enceinte fermée dans laquelle les articles à sécher sont soumis à l'action de l'air chaud. (CTCI, Rev.3: 77512-0).

[1] Shipments.
[2] Sales.

[1] Expéditions.
[2] Ventes.

Sewing machines
Machines à coudre

ISIC-BASED CODE - CODE BASE CITI

3829-10

Unit : Thousand units

Unité : En millier

Country or area	1990	1991	1992	1993	1994	1995	1996	1997	1998	1999	Pays ou zone
Africa	**3**	**3**	**3**	**3**	**3**	**3**	**3**	**3**	**3**	**3**	**Afrique**
Nigeria	...	3	3	3	3	3	...	...	...	...	Nigéria
America, South	**1128**	**1134**	**952**	**963**	**1076**	**1155**	**1048**	**664**	**502**	**445**	**Amérique du Sud**
Brazil	1128	1134	952	963	1076	1155	1048	664	502	445	Brésil
Asia	**11340**	**10798**	**11478**	**11204**	**11077**	**11898**	**8842**	**8786**	**7023**	**5930**	**Asie**
China	7610	7638	8332	8405	8612	9706	6837	7026	5696	4830	Chine
Hong Kong SAR[1]	36	4	21	3	...	...	43	37	...	...	Hong-Kong RAS[1]
India[2]	615	151	127	112	99	128	108	96	67	60	Inde[2]
Indonesia	93	86	199	185	280	...	...	5	4	...	Indonésie
Japan	2461	2416	2396	2107	1711	1577	1413	1336	1011	822	Japon
Korea, Republic of[3]	186	170	155	167	168	139	108	121	90	...	Corée, République de[3]
Pakistan[4]	107	81	85	72	77	68	84	61	36	30	Pakistan[4]
Turkey[5]	232	252	163	153	106	134	127	104	90	90	Turquie[5]
Europe	**1350**	**2689**	**2343**	**2143**	**1096**	**703**	**527**	**546**	**482**	**427**	**Europe**
Belarus	..	75	70	65	45	12	11	6	7	5	Bélarus
Croatia	..	25	18	1	1	1	4	1	0	...	Croatie
Germany	..	444	224	213	207	186	178	...	194	...	Allemagne
Germany(Fed.Rep.)	253	..	..	..	..	..	..	..	..	..	Allemagne(Rép.féd.)
German D.R.(former)[5]	424	..	..	..	..	..	..	..	..	..	R.D.A. (anc.)[5]
Hungary	2	0	1	...	...	...	...	...	...	...	Hongrie
Italy	77	45	...	...	...	...	...	...	...	...	Italie
Poland[5]	343	245	127	169	181	179	86	73	64	59	Pologne[5]
Romania[5]	39	30	26	32	14	6	0	3	1	1	Roumanie[5]
Russian Federation	..	1583	1624	1420	411	100	43	14	9	23	Fédération de Russie
Spain	72	93	42	...	...	16	9	10	5	5	Espagne
Sweden	...	...	...	...	...	...	127	137	133	138	Suède
Ukraine[3]	..	9	10	10	4	1	1	1	0	...	Ukraine[3]
United Kingdom	...	...	...	6	6	6	...	4	7	...	Royaume-Uni
Total	**13821**	**14624**	**14776**	**14313**	**13252**	**13758**	**10420**	**9999**	**8010**	**6805**	**Total**

General Note.

All types of sewing machines, whether operated by hand or fitted with a built-in electric motor, for household use or for industrial use (tailors, dressmakers, shoe industry etc.). (SITC, Rev.3: 72433-0, 72435-0).

[1] Beginning 1998, data are confidential.
[2] Production by large and medium scale establishments only.
[3] For industrial use only.
[4] Twelve months ending 30 June of year stated.
[5] For household use only.

Remarque générale.

Machines à coudre de tous types, mues à la main ou par un moteur électrique incorporé, utilisées pour les travaux domestiques ou dans l'industrie (tailleurs, couturières, industrie de la chaussure etc.). (CTCI, Rev.3: 72433-0, 72435-0).

[1] A partir de 1998, les données sont confidentielles.
[2] Production des grandes et moyennes entreprises seulement.
[3] Pour usages industriels seulement.
[4] Période de douze mois finissant le 30 juin de l'année indiquée.
[5] Pour usages domestiques seulement.

Air-conditioning machines
Groupes pour le conditionnement de l'air

ISIC-BASED CODE - CODE BASE CITI

3829-25A

Unit : Thousand units   Unité : En milliers

Country or area	1990	1991	1992	1993	1994	1995	1996	1997	1998	1999	Pays ou zone
Africa											**Afrique**
Algeria	46	29	11	7	4	13	15	2	21	10	Algérie
Egypt	21	12	7	9	4	7	4	5	1	2	Egypte
Nigeria	...	30	29	32	17	16	...	...	...	...	Nigéria
South Africa	42	19	27	26	22	18	14	...	...	...	Afrique du Sud
America, North											**Amérique du Nord**
Mexico	472	503	760	#1779	2008	1302	1575	1660	1615	1809	Mexique
America, South											**Amérique du Sud**
Brazil	598	388	324	493	487	635	587	454	474	490	Brésil
Asia											**Asie**
Azerbaijan	..	295	268	179	119	64	79	36	10	2	Azerbaïdjan
Hong Kong SAR	...	...	...	3	2	6	...	...	...	...	Hong-Kong RAS
Indonesia	122	117	...	117	113	130	...	405	491	...	Indonésie
Iraq	...	...	26	...	...	...	...	...	...	...	Iraq
Japan	18077	20047	18272	21615	25550	29259	30350	27957	24380	25305	Japon
Korea, Republic of	655	836	826	658	[1]850	[1]1487	[1]1929	[1]1955	[1]2237	...	Corée, République de
Pakistan	20	19	13	15	12	51	80	56	...	...	Pakistan
Turkey[2]	36	39	50	50	36	62	73	67	72	47	Turquie[2]
Europe											**Europe**
Austria	[3]14	[3]14	[3]15	[3]18	[3]17	[3]19	11	10	11	11	Autriche
Croatia	..	17	3	0	0	1	0	1	0	...	Croatie
Czech Republic	..	..	...	...	284	316	803	726	834	892	République tchèque
Germany	..	...	[3]522	[3]476	[3]429	240	241	...	...	...	Allemagne
Germany(Fed.Rep.)[3]	459	..	..	..	..	..	..	..	..	..	Allemagne(Rép.féd.)[3]
Greece	29	39	33	14	17	25	25	19	18	...	Grèce
Hungary	5	4	3	2	2	2	...	...	19	41	Hongrie
Italy[1]	317	305	294	273	276	494	636	471	408	656	Italie[1]
Portugal	...	...	1	1	...	...	...	...	...	...	Portugal
Slovenia	..	15	8	5	5	4	3	0	0	...	Slovénie
Spain	94	117	102	88	66	131	118	134	183	311	Espagne
United Kingdom	...	...	...	630	654	...	...	...	...	...	Royaume-Uni
Yugoslavia	..	2	1	1	1	1	0	0	0	0	Yougoslavie
T.F.Yug.Rep. Macedonia[3]	..	0	0	0	0	0	0	0	0	0	L'ex-RY Macédoine[3]

General Note.
Machines equipped with a motor-driven fan or blower, designed to change both the temperature and the humidity of air, self-contained on a common chassis or in a common housing. (SITC, Rev.3: 74151-0A, 74155-0A).

Remarque générale.
Machines comprenant un ventilateur à moteur et des dispositifs montés dans une enveloppe commune ou sur un châssis commun, propres à modifier la température et l'humidité de l'air. (CTCI, Rev.3: 74151-0A, 74155-0A).

[1] Room air-conditioners only.
[2] Central air-conditioning units only.
[3] In thousand metric tons.

[1] Climatiseurs individuels seulement.
[2] Les appareils de climatisation centrale.
[3] En milliers de tonnes métriques.

Industrial refrigerators and freezers
Réfrigérateurs et congélateurs industriels

ISIC-BASED CODE - CODE BASE CITI
3829-28

Unit : Number of units   Unité : Nombre

Country or area	1990	1991	1992	1993	1994	1995	1996	1997	1998	1999	Pays ou zone
America, North											**Amérique du Nord**
Mexico	81431	89686	83624	#183161	214683	166471	194963	262326	375370	320539	Mexique
America, South											**Amérique du Sud**
Argentina	502	...	...	...	...	...	...	...	...	...	Argentine
Colombia	...	...	6353	9355	10758	11500	...	...	...	...	Colombie
Ecuador	11747	...	#170	117	154	196	...	768	971	...	Equateur
Asia											**Asie**
Hong Kong SAR	6849	2546	10039	4325	543	32651	26892	1728	751	1216	Hong-Kong RAS
Cyprus	*12100	*12130	13000	*14240	*15600	18062	20820	17810	12450	12540	Chypre
Indonesia	16800	218922	124719	171810	469369	317762	...	540769	...	...	Indonésie
Japan	1312401	1363509	1356253	1222413	1327284	1298097	...	...	...	...	Japon
Korea, Republic of	140636	157662	85629	77220	165108	225663	200149	172999	133914	...	Corée, République de
Europe											**Europe**
Austria	...	[1]10546	[1]10760	[1]12410	[1]12651	[1]13355	23655	23370	24452	29600	Autriche
Belgium[1][2][3]	50526	46800	48454	63325	...	...	...	...	...	...	Belgique[1][2][3]
Croatia	..	373	259	244	267	5484	5280	5912	6612	...	Croatie
Czech Republic	..	..	...	...	8171	13858	21724	25885	27922	25835	République tchèque
Finland	94780	*80315	*85630	*76235	*93675	*107104	*117625	...	...	...	Finlande
France	3967299	3198659	3205554	2314558	979679	...	...	...	...	...	France
Germany		494648	399142	393290	390726	307355	269638	277893	308977	...	Allemagne
Germany(Fed.Rep.)	425052										Allemagne(Rép.féd.)
Greece	32640	42191	44635	59130	65032	85517	85640	91001	89080	...	Grèce
Hungary	21889	20057	13677	17151	10569	4661	...	...	40622	26000	Hongrie
Latvia	..	67378	30712	13336	8544	...	...	...	...	79	Lettonie
Poland	...	34250	29798	27197	30835	120125	227063	307166	271937	187110	Pologne
Portugal	...		52546	59956	69777	69303	68132	74565	90821	101891	Portugal
Republic of Moldova	..	838	253	[4]149	[4]27	[4]21	[4]20	[4]15	[4]13	[4]13	Rép. de Moldova
Romania[1]	1057	758	699	881	1365	729	583	226	8	7	Roumanie[1]
Russian Federation	..	136554	113059	82603	53251	44705	23189	30062	32683	38510	Fédération de Russie
Slovenia	..	2093	69	43	53	49	21	0	0	...	Slovénie
Spain	190761	173373	161437	173155	339073	300074	307655	285661	...	373613	Espagne
Sweden	...	...	...	...	...	16142	...	...	...	...	Suède
Ukraine	..	114704	81838	49627	20721	11954	7385	4540	3304	1753	Ukraine
United Kingdom	...			246777	...	...	...	...	...	...	Royaume-Uni
T.F.Yug.Rep. Macedonia[1]	..	2146	1598	1966	1671	1279	416	*302	133	73	L'ex-RY Macédoine[1]
Yugoslavia, SFR	1763				..	..	..	..	..	..	Yougoslavie, RSF
USSR (former)	391286	..	...	...	..	..	..	..	..	..	URSS (anc.)

General Note.

Installations comprising a compressor, a condenser and an evaporator (or a generator and an evaporator not mounted on a common base or in the form of self-contained units, but as separate elements designed to operate together), used industrially for cold-storage plants and for manufacturing operations, for example, for the manufacture of block ice, for quick-freezing food products etc. They may include associated cold brine circulation systems as well as ancillary apparatus such as freezing chambers or cold tables. (SITC 74143-0, 74145-0)

Remarque générale.

Installations comprenant un compresseur, un condenseur et un évaporateur (ou un générateur et un évaporateur non montés sur un socle commun ni groupés en un seul corps, mais cependant conçus pour fonctionner ensemble) utilisés pour l'équipement des entrepôts frigorifiques ou à des fins industrielles, par exemple la fabrication de blocs de glace, la surgélation de produits alimentaires, etc. Elles peuvent être munies de tuyauteries à saumure et de dispositifs auxiliares tels que chambres de congélation ou tables réfrigérantes. (CTCI, Rev.3: 74143-0, 74145-0).

[1] In metric tons.
[2] Production by establishments employing 5 or more persons.
[3] Shipments.
[4] Excluding Transnistria region.

[1] En tonnes métriques.
[2] Production des établissements occupant 5 personnes ou plus.
[3] Expéditions.
[4] Non compris la région de Transnistria.

Pumps for liquids, except liquid elevators
Pompes pour liquides, non compris élévateurs à liquides

ISIC-BASED CODE - CODE BASE CITI

3829-42

Unit : Thousand units — Unité : En milliers

Country or area	1990	1991	1992	1993	1994	1995	1996	1997	1998	1999	Pays ou zone
Africa	**39**	**39**	**37**	**29**	**19**	**20**	**8**	**7**	**8**	**10**	**Afrique**
Algeria	39	39	37	29	19	20	8	7	8	10	Algérie
America, North	**5355**	**5363**	**5725**	**5903**	**5731**	**7256**	**7568**	**9915**	**12337**	**12158**	**Amérique du Nord**
Mexico	169	240	231	136	121	93	122	144	164	198	Mexique
United States[2]	[1]5186	[1]5123	[1]5494	[1]5767	[1]5610	[1]7163	[1]7446	9771	12173	11960	Etats-Unis[2]
America, South	**52**	**52**	**49**	**56**	**45**	**58**	**52**	**52**	**52**	**52**	**Amérique du Sud**
Colombia	...	...	49	56	45	58	...	...	...	...	Colombie
Asia	**12053**	**12851**	**14087**	**14892**	**15586**	**20355**	**18407**	**20314**	**16240**	**16828**	**Asie**
Armenia	..	27	27	18	8	9	16	5	3	2	Arménie
Bangladesh[3]	10	34	26	27	40	33	...	...	...	...	Bangladesh[3]
China	3664	3992	5450	6632	6453	10606	8875	10166	6746	7368	Chine
Hong Kong SAR	10	9	20	1	...	...	...	...	...	...	Hong-Kong RAS
Cyprus	*8	*8	7	*7	*6	5	6	7	7	6	Chypre
India[4]	526	498	532	...	...	...	...	...	...	...	Inde[4]
Indonesia	...	...	...	2903	...	...	...	...	...	...	Indonésie
Japan	3468	3688	3407	3173	3615	3566	3798	4312	3561	3429	Japon
Kazakhstan	..	21	17	14	8	6	3	0	2	2	Kazakhstan
Korea, Republic of	1380	1506	1554	1451	[5]1898	[5]2582	...	...	...	...	Corée, République de
Kyrgyzstan	..	45	43	45	25	12	7	5	2	1	Kirghizistan
Myanmar[6]	2	2	2	3	2	...	2	2	2	2	Myanmar[6]
Thailand	76	110	...	...	...	...	...	...	...	...	Thaïlande
Turkey	...	...	5	5	5	8	6	20	17	15	Turquie
Turkmenistan	..	1	1	1	1	1	0	0	0	...	Turkménistan
Europe	**27075**	**29897**	**29587**	**29005**	**29472**	**42613**	**44379**	**47602**	**53905**	**52797**	**Europe**
Austria	19	20	[7]32	[7]43	[7]39	[7]30	...	[7]828	...	...	Autriche
Belarus	..	10	9	13	8	4	5	6	9	11	Bélarus
Belgium[8]	...	...	...	...	...	20	14	11	11	12	Belgique[8]
Bulgaria	88	61	26	18	19	19	18	10	15	17	Bulgarie
Croatia	..	2	2	2	2	0	0	14	12	...	Croatie
Czechoslovakia(former)	456	298	..	..	..	..	..	..	..	..	Tchécoslovaquie(anc.)
Czech Republic	..	..	230	202	163	216	267	237	199	192	République tchèque
Finland	82	68	56	47	42	47	48	53	49	*44	Finlande
France[2]	3848	3898	3611	4256	4306	...	...	...	...	...	France[2]
Germany	..	15538	15628	14002	14481	27460	28713	31373	33575	...	Allemagne
Germany(Fed.Rep.)	13761	..	..	..	..	..	..	..	..	..	Allemagne(Rép.féd.)
Greece	35	32	31	...	7	8	10	11	37	...	Grèce
Hungary	144	172	140	129	133	166	235	122	3107	3755	Hongrie
Latvia	..	3	7	6	2	2	3	3	2	...	Lettonie
Lithuania	..	306	273	223	125	78	48	11	9	10	Lituanie
Poland	186	184	175	182	205	203	224	225	196	235	Pologne
Portugal	...	...	...	28	27	32	41	41	44	49	Portugal
Republic of Moldova	..	85	85	[9]54	[9]31	[9]22	[9]11	[9]5	[9]5	[9]3	Rép. de Moldova
Romania	56	54	34	25	19	21	21	21	15	11	Roumanie
Russian Federation	..	695	575	458	216	213	170	178	164	203	Fédération de Russie
Slovakia	..	..	21	23	11	8	5	6	33	45	Slovaquie
Slovenia	..	48	257	103	392	32	46	30	155	4	Slovénie
Spain	534	459	455	1275	1387	1813	2037	...	...	...	Espagne
Sweden	...	...	...	...	...	...	...	455	476	504	Suède
Ukraine	...	154	128	125	89	68	54	43	41	28	Ukraine
United Kingdom	...	...	...	...	...	7304	7291	6703	7775	...	Royaume-Uni
Yugoslavia	..	16	16	2	2	3	2	3	2	1	Yougoslavie
Yugoslavia, SFR	74	..	..	..	..	..	..	..	..	..	Yougoslavie, RSF
USSR (former)	1136	..	..	..	..	..	..	..	..	..	URSS (anc.)
Total	**45710**	**48202**	**49485**	**49885**	**50853**	**70302**	**70414**	**77890**	**82542**	**81845**	**Total**

For general note and footnotes, see end of table.   Voir la fin du tableau pour la remarque générale et les notes.

Pumps for liquids, except liquid elevators (continued)
Pompes pour liquides, non compris élévateurs à liquides (suite)

General Note.
Machines for raising or otherwise continuously displacing volumes of liquids, whether they are operated by hand or by any kind of power unit, integral or otherwise, including reciprocating pumps, rotary pumps, centrifugal pumps, ejector pumps. This item excludes liquid elevators and delivery pumps equipped with measuring or price calculating mechanisms. (SITC, Rev.3: 74220-0, 74230-0,74240-0, 74250-0, 74260-0, 74271-0).

Remarque générale.
Machines et appareils - qu'ils soient actionnés à la main ou par une force motrice quelconque - destinés à élever ou à mettre en circulation des liquides, visqueux ou non. On y range aussi les machines et appareils de l'espèce avec moteur incorporé (motopompe, turbopompe, électropompe). Y compris pompes alternatives, pompes rotatives volumétriques, pompes centrifuges et turbopompes, et pompes par injection. Cette rubrique ne comprend pas les élévateurs à liquides et les pompes distributrices de liquides comportant un dispositif mesureur et compteur, avec ou sans détermination du prix de vente. (CTCI,Rev.3: 74220-0, 74230-0, 74240-0, 74250-0, 74260-0, 74271-0).

[1] Industrial types only.
[2] Shipments.
[3] Twelve months ending 30 June of year stated.
[4] Production by large and medium scale establishments only.
[5] Household pumps only.
[6] Government production only.
[7] Including liquid elevators.
[8] Incomplete coverage.
[9] Excluding Transnistria region.

[1] Types industriels seulement.
[2] Expéditions.
[3] Période de douze mois finissant le 30 juin de l'année indiquée.
[4] Production des grandes et moyennes entreprises seulement.
[5] Pompes de ménage seulement.
[6] Production de l'Etat seulement.
[7] Y compris les élévateurs à liquides.
[8] Couverture incomplète.
[9] Non compris la région de Transnistria.

Compressors
Compresseurs et ventilateurs

ISIC-BASED CODE - CODE BASE CITI

3829-46

Unit : Thousand units   Unité : En milliers

Country or area	1990	1991	1992	1993	1994	1995	1996	1997	1998	1999	Pays ou zone
Africa	**1**	**1**	**1**	**0**	**0**	**0**	**0**	**0**	**0**	**0**	**Afrique**
Algeria	1.4	1.0	0.9	0.4	0.0	0.1	0.2	0.0	0.1	0.0	Algérie
America, North	**1895**	**1921**	**2201**	**2293**	**2568**	**3314**	**3136**	**3514**	**3405**	**3814**	**Amérique du Nord**
Mexico	9.3	9.6	10.3	9.3	7.9	5.6	6.6	11.4	10.2	13.6	Mexique
United States[1][2]	1885.8	1911.8	2190.7	2283.2	2559.8	3308.4	3129.0	3502.4	3394.6	3800.6	Etats-Unis[1][2]
America, South	**1**	**1**	**0**	**1**	**2**	**1**	**1**	**1**	**1**	**1**	**Amérique du Sud**
Colombia	...	...	0.4	0.9	1.6	0.6	...	1.3	1.4	...	Colombie
Asia	**10486**	**12941**	**13044**	**15348**	**16902**	**21034**	**23119**	**24476**	**23011**	**30773**	**Asie**
Armenia	..	5.0	2.5	1.7	1.4	0.3	0.0	0.1	0.0	0.1	Arménie
Azerbaijan	..	1027.5	839.0	976.7	398.2	57.8	10.3	5.6	4.1	0.5	Azerbaïdjan
India[3]	45.8	39.6	45.1	52.0	#629.2	722.3	724.3	663.6	1148.3	1216.1	Inde[3]
Indonesia	58.0	52.5	61.8	39.4	28.1	1103.0	...	3267.0	3186.6	...	Indonésie
Japan	298.8	283.1	236.5	194.0	184.1	183.2	239.5	255.0	207.1	203.9	Japon
Korea, Republic of	4559.1	5920.1	6036.2	8212.6	9871.0	12764.1	14292.8	13620.3	13691.9	...	Corée, République de
Thailand[4]	...	...	...	...	...	...	5271.6	4827.8	3925.4	...	Thaïlande[4]
Turkey	849.6	926.0	1139.3	1191.8	1114.3	1527.5	1605.2	1836.7	847.3	1708.1	Turquie
Turkmenistan	..	1.2	0.8	0.7	0.0	0.1	0.0	0.0	0.0	...	Turkménistan
Uzbekistan	..	11.1	8.1	4.0	1.3	0.8	0.8	0.3	...	...	Ouzbékistan
Europe	**5246**	**17388**	**17708**	**23519**	**24394**	**25841**	**25325**	**26325**	**36285**	**33762**	**Europe**
Austria[5]	...	...	...	...	...	2419.3	2517.0	2662.0	...	...	Autriche[5]
Belgium[6]	...	...	...	...	...	49.7	160.9	...	64.4	...	Belgique[6]
Bulgaria[7]	33.3	21.1	4.0	4.7	4.5	5.5	4.2	2.5	...	...	Bulgarie[7]
Croatia	..	0.1	0.1	0.0	0.0	0.1	0.1	0.2	0.1	...	Croatie
Czech Republic	..	..	...	...	118.1	124.8	108.5	117.3	145.8	131.8	République tchèque
Finland	64.1	*57.1	*34.7	*45.9	*42.3	*53.9	*50.4	41.9	46.0	27.4	Finlande
Germany	...	...	...	...	...	8841.4	7518.2	8509.3	8116.4	...	Allemagne
Greece	5.3	5.1	5.2	4.6	3.8	3.8	3.0	3.0	...	...	Grèce
Hungary	509.9	598.4	579.4	266.6	412.3	616.0	...	554.5	9364.7	6764.6	Hongrie
Latvia	..	...	...	0.0	0.0	...	...	...	...	0.5	Lettonie
Lithuania	..	1027.0	1069.0	1058.0	541.0	294.0	185.3	106.2	97.3	99.8	Lituanie
Poland	2.0	1.1	1.4	1.4	1.9	2.1	2.1	1.8	1.8	1.7	Pologne
Romania	44.7	43.6	22.3	22.9	42.2	47.5	44.5	29.7	33.0	15.4	Roumanie
Russian Federation	..	28.6	23.2	19.0	14.9	13.9	9.2	10.7	10.0	18.2	Fédération de Russie
Slovakia	...	...	...	...	...	...	63.9	47.1	39.8	78.0	Slovaquie
Slovenia	..	...	...	...	...	...	1119.1	1808.7	3105.7	3123.4	Slovénie
Spain	38.9	46.6	31.0	#5940.5	6880.3	7732.2	7852.0	8603.8	8590.3	8300.2	Espagne
Sweden	...	...	...	...	...	...	...	1426.2	1102.4	1243.8	Suède
Ukraine	..	207.5	144.6	94.1	34.8	28.1	23.3	16.3	13.4	8.8	Ukraine
United Kingdom	...	...	...	...	1822.9	2004.4	2219.8	2291.4	*3017.7	...	Royaume-Uni
Yugoslavia	..	1.0	0.7	0.3	0.6	0.4	0.2	0.1	0.2	0.1	Yougoslavie
T.F.Yug.Rep. Macedonia	..	0.1	0.1	...	...	...	...	...	...	...	L'ex-RY Macédoine
USSR (former)	118.2	..	...	..	..	..	..	..	..	..	URSS (anc.)
Total	**17747**	**32252**	**32954**	**41161**	**43866**	**50190**	**51581**	**54316**	**62702**	**68350**	**Total**

General Note.
Motor-driven air and gas compressors whether or not stationary which draw air at atmospheric pressure, compress it and deliver it at a higher pressure (that is, pumps, compressors, free-piston generators, and fans and blowers). (SITC, Rev.3: 74311-0, 74315-0, 74317-0, 74319-0, 74340-0).

Remarque générale.
Machines fixes ou mobiles entraînées par moteur, servant à comprimer l'air ou d'autres gaz, qui aspirent l'air à la pression atmosphérique et le restituent à une pression plus élevée (c'est-à-dire pompes, compresseurs, générateurs à pistons libres et ventilateurs). (CTCI, Rev.3: 74311-0, 74315-0, 74317-0, 74319-0, 74340-0).

[1] Shipments.
[2] Excluding air-conditioning and refrigeration compressors.
[3] Production by large and medium scale establishments only.
[4] Beginning 1999, series discontinued.
[5] Beginning 1998, data are confidential.
[6] Incomplete coverage.
[7] Excluding compressors for painters.

[1] Expéditions.
[2] Non compris les compresseurs pour appareils de climatisation et de réfrigération.
[3] Production des grandes et moyennes entreprises seulement.
[4] A partir de 1999, série abandonnée.
[5] A partir de 1998, les données sont confidentielles.
[6] Couverture incomplète.
[7] Non compris les compresseurs pour peintres.

Cranes
Grues

ISIC-BASED CODE - CODE BASE CITI

3829-49

Unit : Number of units   Unité : Nombre

Country or area	1990	1991	1992	1993	1994	1995	1996	1997	1998	1999	Pays ou zone
Africa											**Afrique**
Algeria	385	392	373	329	141	232	113	88	18	27	Algérie
America, North											**Amérique du Nord**
Mexico	24	56	15	#144	184	237	219	233	348	455	Mexique
United States	5847	7143	7779	8410	10259	...	...	...	...	...	Etats-Unis
America, South											**Amérique du Sud**
Colombia	...	...	127	194	338	215	...	...	...	...	Colombie
Asia											**Asie**
Georgia	..	...	95	39	13	16	2	1	0	0	Géorgie
India [1]	19462	15700	10894	11364	14538	22068	25824	17905	15504	9449	Inde [1]
Indonesia	...	...	2	47	94	...	...	...	...	...	Indonésie
Japan	18333	16506	13192	10235	8370	9256	11346	12702	10405	7661	Japon
Kazakhstan	..	95	59	88	95	56	23	12	27	6	Kazakhstan
Korea, Republic of [1]	34400	36820	28077	38725	[2]43491	[2]53245	[2]54666	[2]51509	[2]19119		Corée, République de [1]
Turkey	...	...	576	301	210	245	284	287	188	165	Turquie
Uzbekistan	..	740	506	412	216	67	120	86	...	...	Ouzbékistan
Europe											**Europe**
Austria	[1]39632	[1]43801	[1]48882	[1]48726	[1]59516	[1]64021	9831	8947	9629	8029	Autriche
Belarus	..	33	27	18	10	1	1	3	2	2	Bélarus
Bulgaria	1467	679	156	94	136	220	118	90	86	45	Bulgarie
Croatia	..	2290	779	670	...	60	54	477	218	...	Croatie
Czechoslovakia(former)	2376	1886	..	..	..	..	..	...	..	..	Tchécoslovaquie(anc.)
Czech Republic	..	..	694	594	642	725	676	405	426	424	République tchèque
Finland	1150	756	*880	*630	*1445	*1264	*1365	*1615	...	...	Finlande
France [3]	6969	5958	3952	3417	2085	...	...	...	...	...	France [3]
Germany	..	[1]256367	[1]245840	[1]202165	[1]205033	43826	47826	54583	56576	...	Allemagne
Germany(Fed.Rep.) [1]	213028	..	..	..	..	..	..	...	..	...	Allemagne(Rép.féd.) [1]
Greece	595	449	398	...	773	972	1117	...	...	...	Grèce
Hungary	493	119	62	31	66	6	...	...	83	905	Hongrie
Latvia	..	...	...	...	...	...	...	...	...	10	Lettonie
Poland	1340	725	448	365	241	204	146	234	357	1004	Pologne
Portugal	...	...	242	668	632	447	290	245	259	332	Portugal
Romania [4]	145	51	10	23	24	26	32	40	43	136	Roumanie [4]
Russian Federation	..	19161	16168	14092	6246	4438	4433	3356	2462	2714	Fédération de Russie
Slovakia	..	..	830	168	763	1305	251	270	...	...	Slovaquie
Slovenia	..	715	807	588	466	348	175	0	0	...	Slovénie
Spain	5665	5456	5107	7501	7554	8800	9763	10876	...	...	Espagne
Ukraine	..	12594	9081	22072	2946	1358	465	464	323	171	Ukraine
Yugoslavia	..	3990	9266	27253	2666	1466	1190	270	211	68	Yougoslavie
T.F.Yug.Rep. Macedonia	..	864	1368	410	672	95	...	...	...	...	L'ex-RY Macédoine

General Note.

Fixed or stationary and mobile cranes whether or not self-propelled such as tower cranes, balance cranes, jib or derrick cranes etc. Cranes mounted on transport equipment are excluded. (SITC, Rev.3: 74430-0).

Remarque générale.

Grues fixes ou stationnaires et grues mobiles, automobiles ou non, telles que les grues à tour, les grues à contrepoids, les grues à flèche, les derricks, etc. Cette rubrique ne comprend pas les grues montées sur matériel de transport. (CTCI, Rev.3: 74430-0).

[1] In metric tons.
[2] Excluding cranes for construction.
[3] Shipments.
[4] Mobile lifting frames on tires and portal cranes only.

[1] En tonnes métriques.
[2] Non compris les grues utilisées dans la construction.
[3] Expéditions.
[4] Portiques mobiles sur pneumatiques et grues sur portiques.

Elevators, for lifting goods and persons
Ascenseurs et monte-charge

ISIC-BASED CODE - CODE BASE CITI

3829-52

Unit : Number of units

Unité : Nombre

Country or area	1990	1991	1992	1993	1994	1995	1996	1997	1998	1999	Pays ou zone
America, North											**Amérique du Nord**
Mexico	492	503	713	913	963	937	641	616	729	659	Mexique
America, South											**Amérique du Sud**
Brazil	7552	7618	7371	8525	8208	7891	8653	10119	10183	9696	Brésil
Colombia	...	...	511	642	823	1101	...	...	...	...	Colombie
Ecuador	...	...	5	91	32	24	31	...	...	...	Equateur
Asia											**Asie**
India	3170	2890	3413	3452	3451	2436	2393	2360	3482	4009	Inde
Indonesia	49	1	...	87	177	...	...	...	...	...	Indonésie
Japan	34653	37887	33109	30738	32774	35703	41468	53724	45741	44051	Japon
Korea, Republic of	8701	11368	12923	12537	14314	18497	21098	22199	17879	...	Corée, République de
Turkey	169	264	207	300	331	369	458	346	327	347	Turquie
Europe											**Europe**
Austria [1] [2]	[3]15893	[3]9648	[3]10338	[3]13324	[3]16273	...	52065	...	...	...	Autriche [1] [2]
Belarus	..	12585	8710	3906	2594	1935	1781	2003	2784	2510	Bélarus
Bulgaria	1319	786	781	580	362	385	342	453	337	388	Bulgarie
Croatia	..	326	155	182	...	198	168	63	69	...	Croatie
Denmark [4]	674	1528	1720	...	...	688	953	975	911	678	Danemark [4]
Czech Republic	..	..	...	...	1939	2059	2482	2318	4328	4123	République tchèque
Finland	7295	*8235	*7145	*5120	*8175	*7620	*4175	*2818	*3441	2798	Finlande
Germany	..	[3]42829	[3]44347	[3]23603	[3]35423	5985504	5834503	5756118	2969355	...	Allemagne
Germany(Fed.Rep.) [3]	42640	..	..	..	..	..	..	..	..	..	Allemagne(Rép.féd.) [3]
Greece	473	390	809	...	...	...	...	...	...	...	Grèce
Hungary	602	481	202	208	222	184	...	...	...	197	Hongrie
Poland	2985	2168	1163	1038	696	543	616	641	495	668	Pologne
Portugal	...	...	4051	3348	3350	2655	1871	2317	1606	1861	Portugal
Romania	868	743	611	532	428	282	167	192	154	173	Roumanie
Russian Federation	..	14267	10361	9122	5528	4787	3070	3516	3423	4548	Fédération de Russie
Slovakia	..	..	...	...	...	...	2612	766	560	555	Slovaquie
Slovenia	..	4307	3870	3092	2914	3923	7	155	77	...	Slovénie
Spain	19911	19364	22743	18507	17114	18860	20562	22763	29657	38876	Espagne
Sweden	...	...	...	...	...	...	...	6020	4417	4123	Suède
Ukraine	..	1706	1554	1385	515	307	160	176	200	198	Ukraine
United Kingdom	6853	6539	...	17326	19126	21351	16586	10301	*13534	...	Royaume-Uni
Yugoslavia	..	230	182	31	27	15	5	2	0	...	Yougoslavie
USSR (former)	37996	..	..	..	..	..	..	..	..	..	URSS (anc.)
Oceania											**Océanie**
Australia	3043	...	...	...	...	...	...	...	...	...	Australie

General Note.
Electric and hydraulic passenger and freight elevators. Automobile lifts, moving escalators, and other farm and non-farm elevators are excluded. (SITC, Rev.3: 74420-0, 74481-0, 74489-1).

Remarque générale.
Ascenseurs pour personnes, et monte-charge à commande électrique ou hydraulique. Cette rubrique ne comprend pas les monte-voitures, les escaliers mécaniques et d'autres appareils de levage agricoles ou non. (CTCI, Rev.3: 74420-0, 74481-0, 74489-1).

[1] 1995 data are confidential.
[2] Beginning 1997, data are confidential.
[3] In metric tons.
[4] Sales.

[1] Pour 1995, les données sont confidentielles.
[2] A partir de 1997, les données sont confidentielles
[3] En tonnes métriques.
[4] Ventes.

Fork-lift trucks
Chariots gerbeurs

ISIC-BASED CODE - CODE BASE CITI

3829-55

Unit : Number of units

Unité : Nombre

Country or area	1990	1991	1992	1993	1994	1995	1996	1997	1998	1999	Pays ou zone
Africa	**538**	**168**	**190**	**280**	**428**	**0**	**10**	**0**	**119**	**171**	**Afrique**
Algeria	538	168	...	280	428	0	10	0	119	171	Algérie
Asia	**188108**	**185135**	**155198**	**124852**	**130511**	**149045**	**147621**	**160687**	**129349**	**123275**	**Asie**
Indonesia	198	288	616	120	239	...	...	1040	253	...	Indonésie
Japan	160162	159564	128751	105726	109128	121688	121743	129400	105343	98412	Japon
Korea, Republic of	26873	24107	24989	18092	20519	26526	24652	25692	18680	...	Corée, République de
Turkey	...	...	842	914	625	438	833	4555	5073	3354	Turquie
Europe	**379851**	**366112**	**324480**	**276463**	**328192**	**298515**	**186878**	**198762**	**143849**	**124653**	**Europe**
Austria[1]	...	...	207	187	175	...	...	...	...	...	Autriche[1]
Bulgaria[2]	58075	27669	12316	6403	5711	11640	3903	3313	2366	1448	Bulgarie[2]
Croatia	..	56	7	9	...	403	420	6	15	...	Croatie
Denmark[3]	...	...	...	43584	46414	50839	33849	37239	32949	29210	Danemark[3]
Czechoslovakia(former)	5493	7218	..	..	...	..	...	..	..	...	Tchécoslovaquie(anc.)
Czech Republic	..	..	3779	2526	...	..	...	..	..	...	République tchèque
Finland	2828	*2615	*1540	*2060	*2315	...	...	...	...	...	Finlande
Germany	..	193202	181864	145833	196735	...	65632	66191	...	...	Allemagne
Germany(Fed.Rep.)	193007	..	..	..	..	..	..	..	..	..	Allemagne(Rép.féd.)
German D.R.(former)	1398	..	..	..	..	..	..	..	..	..	R.D.A. (anc.)
Hungary	0	55	142	75	...	...	...	...	...	...	Hongrie
Latvia	..	...	...	...	...	...	...	...	...	308	Lettonie
Poland	8385	2160	4484	11131	11454	9243	5492	8375	3644	1706	Pologne
Slovakia	..	..	...	...	...	...	...	...	6117	898	Slovaquie
Slovenia	..	712	862	437	297	259	457	586	457	463	Slovénie
Spain	6794	5295	4919	3251	3407	6282	6756	7664	11850	12333	Espagne
Sweden	20591	27434	21523	23922	24408	31939	23269	24621	27126	28922	Suède
Ukraine	..	18579	9560	4292	1599	1069	583	586	520	259	Ukraine
United Kingdom	...	...	...	28865	28436	36132	37554	41280	*47634	...	Royaume-Uni
Yugoslavia	..	510	428	72	74	110	98	194	148	56	Yougoslavie
Yugoslavia, SFR	1905	..	..	..	..	..	..	..	..	..	Yougoslavie, RSF
Total	**568498**	**551416**	**479868**	**401595**	**459131**	**447561**	**334509**	**359449**	**273317**	**248099**	**Total**

General Note.

Mechanically-propelled vehicles, generally of small dimensions, used in workshops, mines, warehouses, docks etc., for the handling of short-distance transport of luggage, parcels or other goods. They are not designed for the transport of passengers. (SITC, Rev.3: 74411-0, 74412-0).

Remarque générale.

Véhicules automobiles de dimensions généralement réduites utilisés dans les ateliers, les mines, les entrepôts, les ports, etc., pour la manutention ou le transport sur de courtes distances de bagages, de colis ou de marchandises. Ils ne sont pas conçus pour le transport des personnes. (CTCI, Rev.3: 74411-0, 74412-0).

[1] Beginning 1995, data are confidential.
[2] Including hoisting gears.
[3] Sales.

[1] A partir de 1995, les données sont confidentielles
[2] Y compris les palans.
[3] Ventes.

Refrigerators for household use
Réfrigérateurs ménagers

ISIC-BASED CODE - CODE BASE CITI

3829-58

Unit : Thousand units   Unité : En milliers

Country or area	1990	1991	1992	1993	1994	1995	1996	1997	1998	1999	Pays ou zone
Africa	**1161**	**1187**	**1066**	**923**	**849**	**939**	**1005**	**1021**	**1090**	**1115**	**Afrique**
Algeria	387	388	317	183	119	131	137	175	215	181	Algérie
Angola	1	2	2	...	...	...	...	...	...	...	Angola
Egypt	246	260	232	204	236	236	250	...	...	...	Egypte
Kenya	21	...	...	...	...	...	...	...	...	...	Kenya
Mozambique	1	...	...	...	...	...	...	...	...	...	Mozambique
Nigeria	...	77	52	53	20	19	...	...	...	...	Nigéria
South Africa [1]	352	356	318	318	321	365	411	388	399	440	Afrique du Sud [1]
Tunisia	64	82	123	141	129	...	...	...	...	...	Tunisie
America, North	**7428**	**8102**	**10230**	**11377**	**12638**	**12265**	**12582**	**14037**	**13268**	**13802**	**Amérique du Nord**
Antigua and Barbuda [2]	...	...	...	3	3	...	...	...	...	...	Antigua-et-Barbuda [2]
Mexico	396	487	541	#1065	1356	1256	1447	1942	1986	2083	Mexique
Trinidad and Tobago	14	13	10	3	3	1	0	...	...	...	Trinité-et-Tobago
United States [3] [4]	7015	7599	9676	10306	11276	11005	11132	12092	11279	11716	Etats-Unis [3] [4]
America, South	**3333**	**3538**	**2826**	**3508**	**4103**	**4349**	**4544**	**4906**	**4304**	**3953**	**Amérique du Sud**
Argentina	265	439	554	688	494	49	45	401	424	354	Argentine
Brazil	2441	2445	1704	2098	2721	3242	3776	3592	3034	2796	Brésil
Chile	89	86	136	192	221	272	213	268	229	242	Chili
Colombia	...	...	306	396	465	465	...	...	...	...	Colombie
Ecuador	...	...	66	72	111	156	17	133	88	...	Equateur
Guyana	6	8	6	5	5	...	...	...	...	...	Guyana
Peru	46	70	54	57	86	161	81	101	118	42	Pérou
Asia	**16699**	**18172**	**18258**	**19857**	**22766**	**24757**	**26382**	**27724**	**26684**	**30438**	**Asie**
Azerbaijan	..	313	223	228	97	25	7	0	3	1	Azerbaïdjan
China	4631	4699	4858	5967	7681	9185	9797	10444	10600	12100	Chine
India	1220	1133	997	1382	1668	1913	1705	1600	1902	2012	Inde
Indonesia	196	194	...	172	469	291	...	573	417	...	Indonésie
Iran(Islamic Rep. of)	[5]649	[5]829	[5]896	[5]789	[5]629	[6]575	[6]756	[6]702	[6]1104	...	Iran(Rép. islamique)
Iraq	...	...	35	...	...	...	...	...	...	...	Iraq
Japan	5048	5212	4425	4351	4952	5013	5163	5369	4851	4543	Japon
Kazakhstan	..	...	...	13	...	...	...	...	...	...	Kazakhstan
Korea, Republic of	2827	3228	3296	3585	3943	3975	4292	4257	3790	...	Corée, République de
Kyrgyzstan	..	0	1	0	3	1	0	0	...	...	Kirghizistan
Malaysia	212	266	288	250	266	295	257	249	206	194	Malaisie
Syrian Arab Republic	40	85	129	150	148	156	155	138	137	...	Rép. arabe syrienne
Tajikistan	..	145	61	18	3	0	1	2	1	2	Tadjikistan
Thailand [7]	855	789	...	...	...	...	2246	2384	1631	...	Thaïlande [7]
Turkey	986	1019	1040	1254	1258	1680	1612	1945	1993	2079	Turquie
Uzbekistan	..	212	85	82	20	19	13	13	...	...	Ouzbékistan
Europe	**16011**	**21946**	**20652**	**20325**	**20677**	**21452**	**18362**	**19811**	**20359**	**20963**	**Europe**
Belarus	..	743	740	738	742	746	754	795	802	802	Bélarus
Bulgaria	82	65	106	81	69	49	36	21	58	47	Bulgarie
Denmark [8]	278	269	294	261	808	1502	1276	1523	1589	1560	Danemark [8]
Czechoslovakia(former)	449	515	..	..	..	..	..	..	..	..	Tchécoslovaquie(anc.)
Finland	166	150	144	128	134	104	68	102	107	...	Finlande
France	596	556	566	487	554	...	...	...	...	...	France
Germany	..	4226	4298	3838	3794	...	2747	...	...	...	Allemagne
Germany(Fed.Rep.)	4037	..	..	..	...	...	...	..	..	..	Allemagne(Rép.féd.)
German D.R.(former)	1005	..	..	..	..	..	..	..	..	..	R.D.A. (anc.)
Greece	119	85	80	...	...	...	...	...	...	...	Grèce
Hungary	438	443	483	520	603	714	736	835	708	849	Hongrie
Italy	4199	4484	4285	4753	5033	5908	5402	5562	6280	6582	Italie
Lithuania	..	254	137	207	183	187	138	172	154	153	Lituanie
Poland	604	553	500	588	605	585	584	705	714	726	Pologne
Portugal	464	529	251	224	244	...	173	211	257	300	Portugal
Republic of Moldova	..	118	55	[9]58	[9]53	[9]24	[9]1	[9]2	[9]0	...	Rép. de Moldova
Romania [10]	393	389	402	435	383	435	446	429	366	323	Roumanie [10]
Russian Federation	..	3566	2972	3049	2283	1531	966	1108	956	1041	Fédération de Russie
Slovakia	..	...	552	482	371	330	393	258	228	206	Slovaquie
Slovenia	..	720	661	665	797	863	592	692	756	780	Slovénie

For general note and footnotes, see end of table.   Voir la fin du tableau pour la remarque générale et les notes.

719

Refrigerators for household use (continued)
Réfrigérateurs ménagers (suite)

ISIC-BASED CODE - CODE BASE CITI

3829-58

Unit : Thousand units   Unité : En milliers

Country or area	1990	1991	1992	1993	1994	1995	1996	1997	1998	1999	Pays ou zone
Spain	1285	1410	1322	1240	1461	1269	1260	1960	2415	2107	Espagne
Sweden	584	562	562	549	582	610	478	523	545	604	Suède
Ukraine	..	883	838	757	653	562	431	382	390	409	Ukraine
United Kingdom	1312	...	...	1033	1094	1256	1225	1249	1096	...	Royaume-Uni
Yugoslavia	..	109	85	39	41	50	51	81	48	5	Yougoslavie
T.F.Yug.Rep. Macedonia	..	136	139	98	95	51	20	12	7	...	L'ex-RY Macédoine
USSR (former)[10]	6499	..	..	..	..	..	..	..	..	..	URSS (anc.)[10]
Oceania	**329**	**389**	**363**	**421**	**444**	**423**	**403**	**398**	**441**	**427**	**Océanie**
Australia	329	389	363	421	444	423	403	398	441	427	Australie
Total	**51461**	**53334**	**53396**	**56411**	**61477**	**64186**	**63279**	**67898**	**66145**	**70697**	**Total**

General Note.

Refrigerators of the compression type or of the absorption type, of the sizes commonly used in private households. Insulated cabinets to contain an active refrigerating element (block ice) but no machine are excluded. (SITC, Rev.3: 77520-0).

[1] Including deep freezers and deep freeze-refrigerator combinations.

[2] Twelve months beginning 21 March of year stated.

[3] Electric domestic refrigerators only.

[4] Shipments.

[5] Production by establishments employing 50 or more persons.

[6] Production by establishments employing 10 or more persons.

[7] Beginning 1999, series discontinued.

[8] Sales.

[9] Excluding Transnistria region.

[10] Including freezers.

Remarque générale.

Appareils frigorifiques du type à compression ou à absorption de la taille des appareils communément utilisés dans les ménages. Cette rubrique ne comprend pas les glacières conçues pour contenir un élément frigorifique actif (glace en bloc) mais non un équipement frigorifique. (CTCI, Rev.3: 77520-0).

[1] Y compris congélateurs-conservateurs et congélateurs combinés avec un réfrigérateur.

[2] Période de douze mois commençant le 21 mars de l'année indiquée.

[3] Réfrigérateurs électriques de ménage seulement.

[4] Expéditions.

[5] Production des établissements occupant 50 personnes ou plus.

[6] Production des établissements occupant 10 personnes ou plus.

[7] A partir de 1999, série abandonnée.

[8] Ventes.

[9] Non compris la région de Transnistria.

[10] Y compris les congélateurs.

Washing machines for household use
Machines et appareils à laver, à usage domestique

ISIC-BASED CODE - CODE BASE CITI

3829-64

Unit : Thousand units   Unité : En milliers

Country or area	1990	1991	1992	1993	1994	1995	1996	1997	1998	1999	Pays ou zone
Africa	**288**	**289**	**242**	**252**	**264**	**255**	**255**	**245**	**248**	**250**	**Afrique**
Egypt	179	202	198	200	209	198	200	201	...	...	Egypte
South Africa	109	87	44	52	55	57	55	44	44	45	Afrique du Sud
America, North	**6986**	**7015**	**7212**	**7824**	**8266**	**7487**	**7964**	**8390**	**9016**	**9584**	**Amérique du Nord**
Mexico	558	611	646	1085	1185	882	1091	1448	1512	1593	Mexique
United States[1]	6428	6404	6566	6739	7081	6605	6873	6942	7504	7991	Etats-Unis[1]
America, South	**1438**	**1649**	**1964**	**2410**	**2677**	**2635**	**3053**	**3257**	**3002**	**3116**	**Amérique du Sud**
Argentina	...	436	756	801	702	458	524	603	...	...	Argentine
Brazil	552	948	849	1167	1461	1681	2160	2095	1851	1940	Brésil
Chile	177	203	301	386	447	434	310	...	...	...	Chili
Colombia	...	...	41	41	50	45	...	...	...	...	Colombie
Ecuador	...	...	...	...	...	11	12	...	...	...	Equateur
Peru	9	6	5	3	5	6	3	1	0	0	Pérou
Asia	**15914**	**16956**	**16340**	**18506**	**20218**	**19039**	**20503**	**22991**	**21702**	**23372**	**Asie**
Armenia	..	74	9	0	0	1	0	...	...	...	Arménie
China	6627	6872	7079	8959	10941	9484	10747	12545	12073	13422	Chine
Indonesia	17	19	27	32	44	13	...	86	33	...	Indonésie
Iran(Islamic Rep. of)	[2]19	[2]43	[2]63	[2]59	[2]79	[3]98	[3]159	[3]194	[3]190	...	Iran(Rép. islamique)
Israel[4]	13	...	...	...	...	...	...	...	...	...	Israël[4]
Japan	5576	5587	5225	5163	5042	4876	5006	4818	4468	4287	Japon
Kazakhstan	..	391	370	255	88	46	23	11	3	2	Kazakhstan
Korea, Republic of	2163	2157	1896	2199	2443	2827	2878	2967	2643	...	Corée, République de
Kyrgyzstan	..	209	94	77	17	4	3	2	0	...	Kirghizistan
Syrian Arab Republic	44	29	41	47	50	78	80	72	68	...	Rép. arabe syrienne
Thailand[5]	...	...	...	...	...	...	541	794	800	...	Thaïlande[5]
Turkey	743	837	802	980	780	873	1015	1485	1408	1249	Turquie
Uzbekistan	..	13	9	10	9	14	4	4	...	...	Ouzbékistan
Europe	**9830**	**20153**	**18185**	**18163**	**17361**	**16648**	**16383**	**17911**	**18499**	**17970**	**Europe**
Austria	77	...	...	...	...	...	...	...	...	...	Autriche
Belarus	..	57	62	71	77	37	61	88	91	92	Bélarus
Belgium[1][6]	60	99	138	49	...	...	...	...	...	...	Belgique[1][6]
Bulgaria	90	74	69	42	41	26	24	5	...	...	Bulgarie
Croatia	..	1	1	0	0	0	0	0	...	...	Croatie
Czechoslovakia(former)	451	376	..	..	..	..	..	..	..	..	Tchécoslovaquie(anc.)
France[1]	1637	1645	1713	1943	2244	2200	1868	1933	1941	2229	France[1]
Germany	..	...	...	...	...	2703	2816	3035	3370	...	Allemagne
German D.R.(former)	556	..	..	..	..	..	..	..	..	..	R.D.A. (anc.)
Greece	...	...	...	31	20	15	10	...	...	...	Grèce
Hungary	315	220	219	...	...	...	...	...	...	...	Hongrie
Italy	4372	5044	5140	5693	6251	6996	7135	7967	8119	7367	Italie
Latvia	..	427	18	18	10	8	3	3	2	2	Lettonie
Poland	482	336	363	402	449	419	445	412	416	448	Pologne
Portugal	34	7	...	...	...	...	...	...	...	...	Portugal
Republic of Moldova	..	194	102	[7]123	[7]81	[7]49	[7]54	[7]46	[7]43	[7]18	Rép. de Moldova
Romania	205	188	159	161	109	125	138	82	36	28	Roumanie
Russian Federation	..	5541	4289	3901	2122	1294	762	800	862	999	Fédération de Russie
Slovakia	..	..	122	100	...	...	...	...	...	...	Slovaquie
Slovenia	..	318	188	189	200	220	291	405	474	447	Slovénie
Spain	1425	1522	1540	1334	1632	1655	1945	2270	2281	...	Espagne
Sweden	107	103	91	94	113	106	103	120	119	122	Suède
Ukraine	..	830	805	643	422	213	149	147	138	127	Ukraine
Yugoslavia	..	94	68	39	63	36	33	33	30	12	Yougoslavie
USSR (former)	**7818**	..	..	..	..	..	..	..	..	..	**URSS (anc.)**
Oceania	**343**	**295**	**295**	**328**	**314**	**310**	**266**	**268**	**321**	**354**	**Océanie**
Australia	343	295	295	328	314	310	266	268	321	354	Australie
Total	**42617**	**46356**	**44237**	**47482**	**49100**	**46374**	**48424**	**53062**	**52788**	**54646**	**Total**

For general note and footnotes, see end of table.   Voir la fin du tableau pour la remarque générale et les notes.

Washing machines for household use (continued)
Machines et appareils à laver, à usage domestique (suite)

General Note.

These machines usually include electrically-driven paddles or rotating cylinders (for keeping the cleaning solution circulating through the fabrics) or alternative devices. Washing machines with attached wringers or centrifugal spin driers, and centrifugal spin driers designed as independent units, are included. (SITC, Rev.3: 77511-0).

[1] Shipments.
[2] Production by establishments employing 50 or more persons.
[3] Production by establishments employing 10 or more persons.
[4] Marketed local production.
[5] Beginning 1999, series discontinued.
[6] Production by establishments employing 5 or more persons.
[7] Excluding Transnistria region.

Remarque générale.

Ces machines comprennent généralement des pales ou des cylindres rotatifs (destinés à assurer le brassage continu du liquide et du linge) ou des dispositifs à mouvements alternés, mus électriquement. Cette rubrique comprend les machines à laver avec essoreuses à rouleau ou essoreuses centrifuges et les essoreuses centrifuges conçues comme des appareils indépendants. (CTCI, Rev.3: 77511-0).

[1] Expéditions.
[2] Production des établissements occupant 50 personnes ou plus.
[3] Production des établissements occupant 10 personnes ou plus.
[4] Production locale commercialisée.
[5] A partir de 1999, série abandonnée.
[6] Production des établissements occupant 5 personnes ou plus.
[7] Non compris la région de Transnistria.

Generators for hydraulic turbines
Génératrices pour entraînement par turbines hydrauliques

ISIC-BASED CODE - CODE BASE CITI
3831-01A

Unit : Number of units   Unité : Nombre

Country or area	1990	1991	1992	1993	1994	1995	1996	1997	1998	1999	Pays ou zone
Asia	**12214**	**12219**	**12217**	**14141**	**10287**	**12218**	**12214**	**12207**	**12206**	**12205**	**Asie**
Indonesia[1]	...	...	...	14106	10259	...	...	...	...	...	Indonésie[1]
Japan[2]	31	36	34	35	28	35	31	24	23	22	Japon[2]
Europe	**48030**	**46397**	**40345**	**30451**	**27712**	**34936**	**32747**	**32084**	**32563**	**32101**	**Europe**
Austria[3][4]	...	...	...	...	...	...	300	...	...	...	Autriche[3][4]
Bulgaria[5]	6766	9340	4972	3542	3575	3957	1735	1018	...	...	Bulgarie[5]
Croatia	..	1	0	0	0	0	0	0	...	...	Croatie
Czechoslovakia(former)	1	10	..	..	..	..	..	..	...	..	Tchécoslovaquie(anc.)
Finland[2]	220	183	109	247	281	328	332	...	...	...	Finlande[2]
Germany	..	36548	34803	26202	23371	...	...	...	...	...	Allemagne
Germany(Fed.Rep.)[1]	40723	..	..	..	..	..	..	..	..	..	Allemagne(Rép.féd.)[1]
Romania[5]	14	7	9	9	6	0	0	1	7	2	Roumanie[5]
Russian Federation	..	7	11	11	9	10	10	10	12	10	Fédération de Russie
Slovakia	..	..	...	..	169	109	..	...	...	...	Slovaquie
Ukraine	..	1	2	1	1	1	0	0	0	...	Ukraine
Yugoslavia, SFR	6	..	..	..	..	..	..	..	..	..	Yougoslavie, RSF
Total	**60244**	**58616**	**52562**	**44592**	**37999**	**47154**	**44961**	**44291**	**44769**	**44306**	**Total**

General Note.

Machines which transform mechanical power into electrical energy. There are two main classes - direct-current generators (dynamos) and alternating-current generators (alternators). Dynamos used in conjunction with internal-combustion engines or for lighting or signalling equipment on motor vehicles or cycles are excluded. Prime movers associated with the generators are also excluded.(SITC, Rev.3: 71632-1A).

Remarque générale.

Machines qui produisent de l'énergie électrique par transformation de l'énergie mécanique. On appelle dynamos les génératrices de courant continu et alternateurs les génératrices de courant alternatif. Cette rubrique ne comprend pas les dynamos utilisées avec les moteurs à explosion ou à combustion interne, ni les dispositifs d'éclairage et de signalisation des cycles et automobiles. Elle ne comprend pas non plus les machines motrices associées aux génératrices. (CTCI,Rev.3: 71632-1A).

[1] Including generators for steam turbines.
[2] A.C. type generators for general use.
[3] 1995 data are confidential.
[4] Beginning 1997, data are confidential.
[5] Including other generators.

[1] Y compris les génératrices pour entraînement par turbines à vapeur.
[2] Génératrices à courant alternatif, tous usages.
[3] Pour 1995, les données sont confidentielles.
[4] A partir de 1997, les données sont confidentielles
[5] Y compris les autres génératrices.

Generators for hydraulic turbines
Génératrices pour entraînement par turbines hydrauliques

ISIC-BASED CODE - CODE BASE CITI

3831-01B

Unit : Thousand kilowatts   Unité : Milliers de kilowatts

Country or area	1990	1991	1992	1993	1994	1995	1996	1997	1998	1999	Pays ou zone
Asia	**1809**	**1843**	**2726**	**4868**	**3465**	**2571**	**349**	**1139**	**989**	**1085**	**Asie**
Japan[1]	1809	1843	2726	4868	3465	2571	349	1139	989	1085	Japon[1]
Europe	**262**	**1083**	**1584**	**1648**	**829**	**528**	**960**	**776**	**895**	**387**	**Europe**
Bulgaria[2]	118	60	35	58	30	12	475	19	...	...	Bulgarie[2]
Croatia	..	37	0	0	0	0	0	0	...	...	Croatie
Czechoslovakia(former)	0	39	..	..	..	..	..	..	..	..	Tchécoslovaquie(anc.)
Romania	144	164	164	75	47	0	0	0	0	0	Roumanie
Russian Federation	..	778	1375	1315	738	502	485	757	748	227	Fédération de Russie
Ukraine	..	5	10	200	14	14	0	0	0	...	Ukraine
Total	**2071**	**2926**	**4310**	**6516**	**4294**	**3099**	**1309**	**1915**	**1884**	**1472**	**Total**

General Note.

Machines which transform mechanical power into electrical energy. There are two main classes - direct-current generators (dynamos) and alternating-current generators (alternators). Dynamos used in conjunction with internal-combustion engines or for lighting or signalling equipment on motor vehicles or cycles are excluded. Prime movers associated with the generators are also excluded.(SITC, Rev.3: 71632-1B).

[1] A.C. type generators for general use.
[2] Including other generators.

Remarque générale.

Machines qui produisent de l'énergie électrique par transformation de l'énergie mécanique. On appelle dynamos les génératrices de courant continu et alternateurs les génératrices de courant alternatif. Cette rubrique ne comprend pas les dynamos utilisées avec les moteurs à explosion ou à combustion interne, ni les dispositifs d'éclairage et de signalisation des cycles et automobiles. Elle ne comprend pas non plus les machines motrices associées aux génératrices. (CTCI,Rev.3: 71632-1B).

[1] Génératrices à courant alternatif, tous usages.
[2] Y compris les autres génératrices.

Generators for steam turbines
Génératrices pour entraînement par turbines à vapeur

ISIC-BASED CODE - CODE BASE CITI

3831-04B

Unit : Thousand kilowatts

Unité : Milliers de kilowatts

Country or area	1990	1991	1992	1993	1994	1995	1996	1997	1998	1999	Pays ou zone
Asia	**8649**	**13652**	**8626**	**9345**	**6890**	**10858**	**8421**	**10940**	**17320**	**11888**	**Asie**
Japan[1]	8649	13652	8626	9345	6890	10858	8421	10940	17320	11888	Japon[1]
Europe	**3314**	**9244**	**6953**	**6583**	**5187**	**5129**	**4213**	**5220**	**4681**	**4431**	**Europe**
Croatia	..	...	...	...	...	1	7	..	..	...	Croatie
Czechoslovakia(former)	487	400	..	..	..	..	..	..	..	..	Tchécoslovaquie(anc.)
Hungary	400	47	...	...	...	...	...	...	...	...	Hongrie
Romania	337	144	72	390	60	60	0	0	...	...	Roumanie
Russian Federation	..	5899	4163	3455	2389	2328	1886	2902	2136	1888	Fédération de Russie
Ukraine[2]	..	660	400	420	420	426	6	0	218	225	Ukraine[2]
United Kingdom*	...	...	...	...	...	...	...	...	2090	...	Royaume-Uni*
USSR (former)[3]	9879	..	..	..	..	..	..	..	..	..	URSS (anc.)[3]
Total	**21842**	**22896**	**15579**	**15928**	**12077**	**15987**	**12634**	**16160**	**22001**	**16319**	**Total**

General Note.
Machines which transform mechanical power into electrical energy. There are two main classes - direct-current generators (dynamos) and alternating-current generators (alternators). Dynamos used in conjunction with internal-combustion engines or for lighting or signalling equipment on motor vehicles or cycles are excluded. Prime movers associated with the generators are also excluded.(SITC, Rev.3: 71632-2B).

Remarque générale.
Machines qui produisent de l'énergie électrique par transformation de l'énergie mécanique. On appelle dynamos les génératrices de courant continu et alternateurs les génératrices de courant alternatif. Cette rubrique ne comprend pas les dynamos utilisées avec les moteurs à explosion ou à combustion interne, ni les dispositifs d'éclairage et de signalisation des cycles et automobiles. Elle ne comprend pas non plus les machines motrices associées aux génératrices. (CTCI,Rev.3: 71632-2B).

[1] A.C. type generators for general use.
[2] Including generators for gas turbines.
[3] Including generators for gas and hydraulic turbines.

[1] Génératrices à courant alternatif, tous usages.
[2] Y compris les génératrices à entraînement par turbines à gaz.
[3] Y compris les génératrices à entraînement par turbines à gaz et turbines hydrauliques.

Motors, electric, fractional horsepower
Moteurs électriques de moins d'un CV

ISIC-BASED CODE - CODE BASE CITI

3831-07A

Unit : Thousand units   Unité : En milliers

Country or area	1990	1991	1992	1993	1994	1995	1996	1997	1998	1999	Pays ou zone
Africa	477	491	856	1780	131	171	123	143	233	184	**Afrique**
Algeria	32	51	55	6	32	...	...	...	...	...	Algérie
United Rep.Tanzania	445	440	801	1774	99	149	106	130	...	...	Rép. Unie de Tanzanie
America, North	293264	292821	264689	366051	393045	305300	303929	332512	282189	310770	**Amérique du Nord**
Mexico	685	749	814	#5136	16112	1825	2280	2711	3246	3218	Mexique
United States[1]	292579	292072	263875	360915	376933	303475	301649	329801	278943	307552	Etats-Unis[1]
America, South	123	127	104	91	130	208	191	239	200	311	**Amérique du Sud**
Chile	41	45	34	20	42	108	109	157	118	229	Chili
Colombia[2]	...	...	70	71	88	100	...	...	...	...	Colombie[2]
Asia	33330	70302	112853	92658	37148	33393	33777	30373	27809	26835	**Asie**
Armenia	..	700	256	159	53	27	17	5	4	0	Arménie
Hong Kong SAR[2]	1424	...	...	...	...	...	...	...	...	...	Hong-Kong RAS[2]
Georgia	..	...	78356	63956	9260	4609	4023	251	20	0	Géorgie
Indonesia	...	...	...	...	516	27	...	114	78	...	Indonésie
Japan[3]	27828	28037	26603	21875	22348	22390	22701	21617	18807	19671	Japon[3]
Pakistan[2]	29	31	33	33	24	24	24	23	26	34	Pakistan[2]
Thailand[2]	1197	986	...	...	...	...	...	...	...	...	Thaïlande[2]
Turkey	2668	2885	4906	3936	2431	3800	4313	5847	6358	4431	Turquie
Europe	94182	97604	95083	95683	105407	97964	102192	117343	135259	121182	**Europe**
Austria[4]	3283	# [2]2394	[2]3147	[2]2621	[2]2866	...	[2]1458	[2]1753	[2]1919	[2]2057	Autriche[4]
Belarus	..	957	469	448	192	211	244	295	319	299	Bélarus
Czechoslovakia(former)[5]	3210	2559	..	..	..	..	..	..	..	..	Tchécoslovaquie(anc.)[5]
Czech Republic	..	..	330	595	1281	1010	940	1069	1004	763	République tchèque
Finland	47	31	34	37	42	42	30	...	...	...	Finlande
Germany		75107	77043	72756	81110	73244	75320	87287	105413	...	Allemagne
Germany(Fed.Rep.)	74904	..	..	..	..	..	..	..	..	..	Allemagne(Rép.féd.)
German D.R.(former)	5808	..	..	..	..	..	..	..	..	..	R.D.A. (anc.)
Greece[6]	2	1	1	...	...	..	..	..	..	..	Grèce[6]
Hungary	2274	1150	914	566	586	538	...	837	3504	3624	Hongrie
Lithuania	..	...	...	...	814	319	329	320	228	83	Lituanie
Republic of Moldova	..	49	54	[7]49	[7]29	[7]22	[7]11	[7]6	[7]0	[7]0	Rép. de Moldova
Romania[8]	...	2882	2383	2964	2919	3256	3292	3299	3306	3190	Roumanie[8]
Slovenia	..	6521	5865	6959	7136	8904	10277	8040	8159	...	Slovénie
Spain	681	923	668	4954	5878	5723	6986	12987	...	...	Espagne
Sweden	...	...	...	...	...	...	...	1000	1316	1195	Suède
Ukraine[9]	..	2533	2095	1896	1253	1056	339	242	213	141	Ukraine[9]
Yugoslavia	..	697	336	149	129	79	240	173	260	165	Yougoslavie
USSR (former)[9]	9098	..	..	..	..	..	..	..	..	..	URSS (anc.)[9]
Oceania	2528	2480	2421	2476	2476	2476	2476	2476	2476	2476	**Océanie**
Australia[10]	2528	2480	2421	...	...	...	...	...	...	...	Australie[10]
Total	433002	463826	476006	558740	538337	439512	442689	483086	448166	461759	**Total**

General Note.

Machines which transform electrical energy into mechanical power in the form of rotary motion, having a capacity of less than one horsepower. Starter motors for internal-combustion engines are excluded. (SITC, Rev.3: 71610-0A, 71620-1A, 71631-1A).

[1] Shipments.
[2] Including electric motors of 1 HP and over.
[3] Single-phase A.C. electric motors, not less than 35 W.
[4] 1995 data are confidential.
[5] Electric motors, 1 kW and under.
[6] Electric motors less than 1/4 horsepower.
[7] Excluding Transnistria region.
[8] Electric motors under 0.25 kW.
[9] A.C. electric motors, 0.25-100 kW.
[10] Twelve months ending 30 June of year stated.

Remarque générale.

Machines qui transforment l'énergie électrique en énergie mécanique sous forme de mouvement rotatif, dont la puissance est inférieure à un cheval-vapeur. Cette rubrique ne comprend pas les démarreurs des moteurs à explosion ou à combustion interne. (CTCI, Rev.3: 71610-0A, 71620-1A, 71631-1A).

[1] Expéditions.
[2] Y compris les moteurs électriques de 1 cv et plus.
[3] Moteurs électriques C.A. monophasés d'au moins 35 W.
[4] Pour 1995, les données sont confidentielles.
[5] Moteurs électriques de 1 kW et moins.
[6] Moteurs électriques de moins de 1/4 cv.
[7] Non compris la région de Transnistria.
[8] Moteurs électriques de moins de 0,25 kW.
[9] Alternateurs de 0.25 à 100 kW.
[10] Période de douze mois finissant le 30 juin de l'année indiquée.

Motors, electric, fractional horsepower
Moteurs électriques de moins d'un CV

ISIC-BASED CODE - CODE BASE CITI

3831-07B

Unit : Thousand kilowatts

Unité : Milliers de kilowatts

Country or area	1990	1991	1992	1993	1994	1995	1996	1997	1998	1999	Pays ou zone
Asia	**6150**	**6854**	**6293**	**4754**	**5104**	**5902**	**5842**	**5343**	**4484**	**4634**	**Asie**
Armenia	..	630	269	184	53	35	18	8	7	...	Arménie
Japan[1]	6150	6224	6024	4570	5051	5867	5824	5335	4477	4634	Japon[1]
Europe	**807**	**15167**	**9723**	**8544**	**6701**	**5876**	**6072**	**5139**	**5967**	**5144**	**Europe**
Belarus	..	2841	1316	1430	573	520	493	570	669	645	Bélarus
Czechoslovakia(former)[2]	607	522	..	..	..	..	..	..	..	..	Tchécoslovaquie(anc.)[2]
Czech Republic	..	..	57	70	...	...	...	...	...	...	République tchèque
Hungary	200	199	152	70	116	143	...	...	...	...	Hongrie
Republic of Moldova	..	547	426	[3]518	[3]375	[3]268	[3]147	[3]103	[3]2	[3]4	Rép. de Moldova
Slovenia	..	1595	2092	1769	2696	2724	...	...	...	...	Slovénie
Ukraine[4]	..	9067	5415	4612	2806	2085	1836	836	711	332	Ukraine[4]
Yugoslavia	..	396	265	75	71	72	387	144	821	122	Yougoslavie
USSR (former)[4]	43346	..	..	..	..	..	..	..	..	..	URSS (anc.)[4]
Total	**50303**	**22021**	**16016**	**13298**	**11805**	**11778**	**11914**	**10482**	**10451**	**9778**	**Total**

General Note.
Machines which transform electrical energy into mechanical power in the form of rotary motion, having a capacity of less than one horsepower. Starter motors for internal-combustion engines are excluded. (SITC, Rev.3: 71610-0B, 71620-1B, 71631-1B).

Remarque générale.
Machines qui transforment l'énergie électrique en énergie mécanique sous forme de mouvement rotatif, dont la puissance est inférieure à un cheval-vapeur. Cette rubrique ne comprend pas les démarreurs des moteurs à explosion ou à combustion interne. (CTCI, Rev.3: 71610-0B, 71620-1B, 71631-1B).

[1] Single-phase A.C. electric motors, not less than 35 W.
[2] Electric motors, 1 kW and under.
[3] Excluding Transnistria region.
[4] A.C. electric motors, 0.25-100 kW.

[1] Moteurs électriques C.A. monophasés d'au moins 35 W.
[2] Moteurs électriques de 1 kW et moins.
[3] Non compris la région de Transnistrie.
[4] Alternateurs de 0.25 à 100 kW.

Motors, electric, of one horsepower and over
Moteurs électriques d'un CV et plus

ISIC-BASED CODE - CODE BASE CITI

3831-10A

Unit : Thousand units   Unité : En milli

Country or area	1990	1991	1992	1993	1994	1995	1996	1997	1998	1999	Pays ou zone
America, North	**7163**	**6825**	**6655**	**8201**	**9604**	**9584**	**10179**	**10827**	**11480**	**12070**	**Amérique du Nord**
Mexico	137	163	172	160	138	171	140	162	189	153	Mexique
United States[1]	7026	6662	6483	8041	9466	...	...	...	...	...	Etats-Unis[1]
Asia	**12250**	**18843**	**20136**	**16406**	**14090**	**15522**	**13915**	**12417**	**9939**	**10418**	**Asie**
Bangladesh	2	0	0	1	0	...	...	...	...	...	Bangladesh
Georgia	..	...	9498	7449	4308	2503	1098	879	294	420	Géorgie
India[2]	921	978	971	992	1008	1064	1160	1226	1310	1669	Inde[2]
Indonesia	1487	1587	846	851	516	...	...	...	...	...	Indonésie
Japan[3]	9811	10818	8647	6954	8165	11602	11573	10237	8281	8246	Japon[3]
Myanmar[4]	2	1	1	0	0	...	0	...	...	...	Myanmar[4]
Syrian Arab Republic	27	40	53	60	62	77	70	63	54	...	Rép. arabe syrienne
Uzbekistan	..	131	120	99	31	21	14	12	...	...	Ouzbékistan
Europe	**26084**	**20855**	**23531**	**24405**	**23588**	**23542**	**27476**	**27933**	**24578**	**25950**	**Europe**
Austria[5][6]	[2]487	659	...	...	...	...	...	#7	9	9	Autriche[5][6]
Bulgaria[2]	1503	819	590	458	470	440	389	406	522	389	Bulgarie[2]
Croatia[2]	..	382	263	280	175	72	86	55	60	..	Croatie[2]
Czechoslovakia(former)[7]	1118	809	..	..	..	..	..	..	..	..	Tchécoslovaquie(anc.)[7]
Czech Republic	..	..	1466	1310	1626	1651	1755	1873	2077	1870	République tchèque
Estonia	..	202	66	20	8	2	3	1	...	...	Estonie
Finland	66	38	34	42	51	59	67	148	134	145	Finlande
Germany	..	4349	4229	3408	3651	...	#141	147	154	...	Allemagne
Germany(Fed.Rep.)	4297	..	..	..	..	..	..	..	..	..	Allemagne(Rép.féd.)
Greece[8]	27	25	23	...	..	..	..	..	..	..	Grèce[8]
Hungary	327	204	119	104	41	97	...	570	555	718	Hongrie
Lithuania	..	...	...	...	38	45	29	161	12	202	Lituanie
Poland	10434	6747	4918	5680	5632	5535	5633	5225	4649	4981	Pologne
Portugal[2]	318	100	...	...	..	...	...	...	...	...	Portugal[2]
Romania[9]	737	621	336	338	396	748	742	606	662	565	Roumanie[9]
Slovakia	..	..	...	...	...	...	...	...	5154	5081	Slovaquie
Slovenia	..	120	93	70	41	43	#3642	5559	2803	...	Slovénie
Spain	3164	2706	2785	3806	3176	4690	4889	5329	5111	5310	Espagne
Sweden	...	...	...	...	...	...	...	324	353	408	Suède
United Kingdom	...	...	...	2897	2336	1916	3849	2170	2089	...	Royaume-Uni
Yugoslavia, SFR	515	..	..	..	..	..	..	..	..	..	Yougoslavie, RSF
USSR (former)	239	..	..	..	..	..	..	..	..	..	URSS (anc.)
Total	**45736**	**46523**	**50322**	**49012**	**47282**	**48648**	**51570**	**51177**	**45997**	**48438**	**Total**

General Note.
Machines which transform electrical energy into mechanical power in the form of rotary motion. Starter motors for internal-combustion engines are excluded. (SITC, Rev.3: 71620-2A, 71631-2A).

Remarque générale.
Machines qui transforment l'énergie électrique en énergie mécanique sous forme de mouvement rotatif. Cette rubrique ne comprend pas les démarreurs des moteu à explosion ou à combustion interne. (CTCI, Rev.3: 71620-2A, 71631-2A).

[1] Shipments.
[2] Including fractional-horsepower electric motors.
[3] Three-phase A.C. electric motors, 200 W and over, for general use.
[4] Government production only.
[5] 1995 data are confidential.
[6] 1996 data are confidential.
[7] Electric motors over 1 kW.
[8] Electric motors over 1/4 horsepower.
[9] Electric motors, 0.25 kW and over.

[1] Expéditions.
[2] Y compris les moteurs électriques de moins de 1 cv.
[3] Moteurs électriques C.A. triphasés de 200 W et plus, à usages généraux.
[4] Production de l'Etat seulement.
[5] Pour 1995, les données sont confidentielles.
[6] Pour 1996, les données sont confidentielles.
[7] Moteurs électriques de plus de 1 kW.
[8] Moteurs électriques de plus de 1/4 cv.
[9] Moteurs électriques de 0,25 kW et plus.

Motors, electric, of one horsepower and over
Moteurs électriques d'un CV et plus

ISIC-BASED CODE - CODE BASE CITI

3831-10B

Unit : Thousand kilowatts

Unité : Milliers de kilowatts

Country or area	1990	1991	1992	1993	1994	1995	1996	1997	1998	1999	Pays ou zone
Asia	**63195**	**68886**	**76662**	**75208**	**80885**	**86763**	**88448**	**89404**	**88662**	**89951**	**Asie**
Armenia	..	8	12	...	...	...	...	...	...	...	Arménie
China	35278	38250	52435	54505	59460	60106	...	...	...	...	Chine
Japan[1]	27917	30215	23822	20343	21299	26579	27528	25784	22374	20951	Japon[1]
Uzbekistan	..	413	393	350	116	68	56	44	...	...	Ouzbékistan
Europe	**25186**	**19781**	**13118**	**10819**	**10361**	**13243**	**12592**	**13640**	**11840**	**12809**	**Europe**
Bulgaria[2]	4123	2436	1252	888	825	960	1063	1185	...	...	Bulgarie[2]
Croatia[2]	..	559	402	272	283	167	192	271	282	...	Croatie[2]
Czechoslovakia(former)[3]	6522	4776	..	..	..	..	..	..	..	..	Tchécoslovaquie(anc.)[3]
Czech Republic	..	..	2998	2998	...	...	...	...	...	...	République tchèque
Estonia	..	1444	460	156	59	11	...	...	...	...	Estonie
Hungary	1458	648	323	285	151	256	...	...	...	...	Hongrie
Poland	6489	5154	4901	4449	4265	6599	5860	7091	6441	7872	Pologne
Portugal[2]	301	457	...	...	...	...	...	...	...	...	Portugal[2]
Romania[4]	5115	4030	2185	1201	1302	1787	1987	1716	...	...	Roumanie[4]
Slovenia	..	277	218	191	99	86	...	...	...	...	Slovénie
Yugoslavia, SFR	1178	..	..	..	..	..	..	..	..	..	Yougoslavie, RSF
USSR (former)[5]	8123	..	..	..	..	..	..	..	..	..	URSS (anc.)[5]
Total	**96504**	**88667**	**89780**	**86027**	**91246**	**100006**	**101040**	**103044**	**100502**	**102760**	**Total**

General Note.
Machines which transform electrical energy into mechanical power in the form of rotary motion. Starter motors for internal-combustion engines are excluded. (SITC, Rev.3: 71620-2B, 71631-2B).

Remarque générale.
Machines qui transforment l'énergie électrique en énergie mécanique sous forme de mouvement rotatif. Cette rubrique ne comprend pas les démarreurs des moteurs à explosion ou à combustion interne. (CTCI, Rev.3: 71620-2B, 71631-2B).

[1] Three-phase A.C. electric motors, 200 W and over, for general use.
[2] Including fractional-horsepower electric motors.
[3] Electric motors over 1 kW.
[4] Electric motors, 0.25 kW and over.
[5] A.C. electric motors over 100 kW.

[1] Moteurs électriques C.A. triphasés de 200 W et plus, à usages généraux.
[2] Y compris les moteurs électriques de moins de 1 cv.
[3] Moteurs électriques de plus de 1 kW.
[4] Moteurs électriques de 0,25 kW et plus.
[5] Moteurs électriques C.A. de plus de 100 kW.

Transformers less than 5 KVA
Transformateurs de moins de 5 kVA

ISIC-BASED CODE - CODE BASE CITI

3831-13A

Unit : Thousand units

Unité : En milliers

Country or area	1990	1991	1992	1993	1994	1995	1996	1997	1998	1999	Pays ou zone
Africa	3	5	5	4	3	4	5	5	3	4	**Afrique**
Algeria	2	4	4	4	3	3	4	3	2	3	Algérie
United Rep.Tanzania[1]	1	1	1	0	0	1	1	2	...	...	Rép. Unie de Tanzanie[1]
America, South	148	148	117	118	172	183	148	148	148	148	**Amérique du Sud**
Colombia[1]	...	...	117	118	172	183	...	...	...	...	Colombie[1]
Asia	1251	2032	7040	7105	12256	6948	7632	8453	10219	7521	**Asie**
Indonesia	645	1262	...	...	10345	...	...	...	...	...	Indonésie
Pakistan[1]	23	21	21	22	18	23	23	14	7	15	Pakistan[1]
Syrian Arab Republic	160	311	337	303	297	264	314	206	246	...	Rép. arabe syrienne
Thailand[1]	36	215	...	...	...	...	...	...	...	...	Thaïlande[1]
Turkey	387	223	2472	2570	1470	2451	3085	4023	5756	3032	Turquie
Europe	69356	72110	73078	77745	84750	104922	117137	119466	131269	142377	**Europe**
Austria[2]	587	1666	[1]1344	[1]1398	[1]1224	...	...	...	...	...	Autriche[2]
Belgium	...	...	...	...	432	510	484	489	837	592	Belgique
Croatia[3]	..	40	24	16	12	7	8	17	13	...	Croatie[3]
Czechoslovakia(former)	56	47	..	..	..	..	..	..	..	..	Tchécoslovaquie(anc.)
Czech Republic	..	..	41	...	853	1270	3780	5206	5967	5736	République tchèque
Finland	4309	3322	3052	3403	8465	23100	34566	...	...	...	Finlande
Germany	..	55304	50894	44840	48493	...	...	...	...	...	Allemagne
Germany(Fed.Rep.)[4]	54251	..	..	..	..	..	..	..	..	...	Allemagne(Rép.féd.)[4]
Greece	82	42	26	...	..	...	...	...	...	...	Grèce
Hungary	19	3	1	...	...	...	...	...	...	...	Hongrie
Portugal	[4]117	[4]5	# [4]4008	[4]10934	11891	15246	15736	14570	17225	23448	Portugal
Slovakia	..	..	...	...	...	...	703	1551	4657	5075	Slovaquie
Slovenia	..	188	124	119	91	71	...	...	...	...	Slovénie
Spain	9531	11063	10112	...	...	...	...	...	...	...	Espagne
Total	70758	74294	80239	84972	97181	112056	124921	128071	141638	150050	**Total**

General Note.

Electrical appliances which, without any action of moving parts, transform an alternating current system into another system of alternating current of different voltage. (SITC, Rev.3: 77110-1A).

[1] Including transformers 5 kVA and over.
[2] Beginning 1995, data are confidential.
[3] Including transformers less than 10KVA.
[4] Including transformers less than 16 kVA.

Remarque générale.

Appareils électriques qui, sans l'intervention d'organes mobiles, transforment un courant alternatif en un autre courant alternatif d'intensité et de tension différentes. (CTCI, Rev.3: 77110-1A).

[1] Y compris les transformateurs de 5 kVA et plus.
[2] A partir de 1995, les données sont confidentielles
[3] Y compris transformateurs de moins de 10 KVA.
[4] Y compris transformateurs de moins de 16 kVA.

Transformers of 5 KVA and over
Transformateurs de 5 KVA et plus

ISIC-BASED CODE - CODE BASE CITI

3831-16A

Unit : Number of units   Unité : Nombre

Country or area	1990	1991	1992	1993	1994	1995	1996	1997	1998	1999	Pays ou zone
America, North	**20785**	**21309**	**14651**	**91187**	**76905**	**95568**	**64283**	**83847**	**86707**	**81044**	**Amérique du Nord**
Mexico	20785	21309	14651	#91187	76905	95568	64283	83847	86707	81044	Mexique
America, South	**37**	**24**	**26**	**26**	**0**	**0**	**0**	**0**	**0**	**0**	**Amérique du Sud**
Bolivia	...	24	26	26	0	*0	...	...	...	...	Bolivie
Asia	**1090355**	**1164293**	**1030813**	**1099122**	**1221184**	**1535986**	**1442822**	**1546639**	**1487265**	**1647491**	**Asie**
Azerbaijan	..	1883	760	241	108	71	160	198	741	445	Azerbaïdjan
India	332745	333257	340947	452225	639115	861489	847858	955593	946444	1110192	Inde
Iran(Islamic Rep. of)	[1]7934	[1]10087	[1]9598	[1]8432	[1]9784	[2]16073	[2]19662	[2]39302	[2]33665	...	Iran(Rép. islamique)
Japan	740310	803543	666804	623625	561843	644126	563629	538578	493590	484831	Japon
Tajikistan[3]	..	4205	860	572	72	102	61	30	55	67	Tadjikistan[3]
Turkey	9366	11318	11844	14027	10262	14125	11452	12938	12770	9312	Turquie
Europe	**2831805**	**251093**	**477871**	**452115**	**445066**	**463294**	**488227**	**468779**	**540065**	**434076**	**Europe**
Austria[4][5][6]	11782	10985	...	...	...	...	...	...	...	79946	Autriche[4][5][6]
Belarus	..	41376	25129	20251	10602	11815	8156	12745	11776	10974	Bélarus
Bulgaria[7]	4861	4642	2716	982	689	706	763	956	...	...	Bulgarie[7]
Croatia	..	1340	773	2060	1922	...	...	3527	2846	...	Croatie
Czechoslovakia(former)	9678	12401	..	..	..	..	..	...	...	..	Tchécoslovaquie(anc.)
Czech Republic	..	..	12221	8491	...	...	...	...	...	...	République tchèque
Finland	8541	5579	5846	5500	7309	9188	8839	...	...	...	Finlande
Germany	..	..	...	18434	19315	...	[3]62001	...	...	...	Allemagne
Germany(Fed.Rep.)	2644396	..	..	..	..	..	..	..	...	..	Allemagne(Rép.féd.)
Greece	104895	96137	98195	...	...	...	...	...	...	...	Grèce
Hungary	1277	637	486	...	...	...	...	...	...	...	Hongrie
Poland[8]	10810	9454	7127	8108	5626	5748	...	...	...	...	Pologne[8]
Portugal[9]	5970	5335	...	...	...	...	...	...	...	...	Portugal[9]
Romania	14316	8676	1728	1335	1437	1778	1814	2058	2015	1755	Roumanie
Slovakia	..	..	..	...	...	...	...	...	303257	152891	Slovaquie
Slovenia	..	...	101	152	286	429	...	...	...	...	Slovénie
Spain	15279	17330	19481	...	...	...	...	...	...	...	Espagne
Yugoslavia	..	2051	1449	124	998	1087	884	2852	2724	3135	Yougoslavie
T.F.Yug.Rep. Macedonia	..	1658	1405	808	656	989	1458	2702	1607	1430	L'ex-RY Macédoine
Total	**3942982**	**1436719**	**1523361**	**1642450**	**1743155**	**2094848**	**1995332**	**2099265**	**2114037**	**2162611**	**Total**

General Note.

Electrical appliances which, without any action of moving parts, transform an alternating current system into another system of alternating current of different voltage. (SITC, Rev.3: 77110-2A).

[1] Production by establishments employing 50 or more persons.
[2] Production by establishments employing 10 or more persons.
[3] Including transformers less than 5 kVA.
[4] 1995 data are confidential.
[5] 1996 data are confidential.
[6] 1997 and 1998 data are confidential
[7] Transformers over 1 kVA.
[8] Transformers over 20 kVA.
[9] Including transformers less than 16 kVA.

Remarque générale.

Appareils électriques qui, sans l'intervention d'organes mobiles, transforment un courant alternatif en un autre courant alternatif d'intensité et de tension différentes. (CTCI, Rev.3: 77110-2A).

[1] Production des établissements occupant 50 personnes ou plus.
[2] Production des établissements occupant 10 personnes ou plus.
[3] Y compris transformateurs de moins de 5 kVA.
[4] Pour 1995, les données sont confidentielles.
[5] Pour 1996, les données sont confidentielles.
[6] Pour 1997 et 1998, les données sont confidentielles.
[7] Transformateurs de plus de 1 kVA.
[8] Transformateurs de plus de 20 kVA.
[9] Y compris transformateurs de moins de 16 kVA.

Transformers of 5 KVA and over
Transformateurs de 5 kVA et plus

ISIC-BASED CODE - CODE BASE CITI

3831-16B

Unit : Thousand kVA   Unité : Milliers de kVA

Country or area	1990	1991	1992	1993	1994	1995	1996	1997	1998	1999	Pays ou zone
Asia	**251232**	**274742**	**282435**	**487905**	**552982**	**346647**	**334510**	**370297**	**343531**	**372313**	**Asie**
Armenia	..	1575	1027	239	208	134	72	6	...	0	Arménie
Azerbaijan	..	1616	651	228	97	56	125	117	80	23	Azerbaïdjan
China	74426	77477	99492	317625	393982	164486	151037	161338	149096	177192	Chine
India	[1]40063	[1]32410	[1]34440	...	42000	38000	35000	44000	43386	55712	Inde
Japan	113604	125058	110766	98951	83713	96573	95724	109980	118605	82638	Japon
Korea, Republic of	23139	28153	30949	27461	31847	46577	51993	54451	31937	...	Corée, République de
Tajikistan[2]	..	1682	489	254	29	41	24	12	19	19	Tadjikistan[2]
Uzbekistan	..	6771	4621	2590	1106	780	535	393	...	...	Ouzbékistan
Europe	**34284**	**139350**	**96626**	**67535**	**68432**	**60423**	**60588**	**51083**	**51027**	**49688**	**Europe**
Belarus	..	5847	4039	3778	1884	2493	1450	1992	2271	1862	Bélarus
Bulgaria[3]	2799	2051	2212	1330	1417	1091	1173	1098	...	...	Bulgarie[3]
Croatia	..	1429	1440	860	2587	...	...	4208	4700	...	Croatie
Czechoslovakia(former)	5060	6120	..	..	..	..	..	..	..	..	Tchécoslovaquie(anc.)
Czech Republic	..	..	3419	2861	...	...	...	...	...	...	République tchèque
Hungary	1085	288	319	...	...	...	...	...	...	...	Hongrie
Poland[4]	6685	7421	4569	4228	3410	2759	...	...	...	...	Pologne[4]
Portugal[5]	4283	3651	...	...	...	...	...	...	...	...	Portugal[5]
Republic of Moldova	..	256	26	[6]0	[6]0	[6]0	[6]0	...	...	...	Rép. de Moldova
Romania	5665	2161	1668	3026	4283	1874	1629	1449	1825	2872	Roumanie
Russian Federation	..	33720	20340	12420	12777	9550	11587	5356	4445	9364	Fédération de Russie
Slovenia	..	..	3	3	7	10	...	...	...	...	Slovénie
Spain	8707	10335	12508	...	...	...	...	...	...	...	Espagne
Ukraine	..	65257	41291	23729	23108	20982	20225	15383	15732	10325	Ukraine
Yugoslavia	..	808	825	252	771	939	777	844	811	931	Yougoslavie
USSR (former)	**135392**	..	..	..	..	..	..	..	..	..	**URSS (anc.)**
Oceania	**7254**	**6312**	**6316**	**6627**	**6627**	**6627**	**6627**	**6627**	**6627**	**6627**	**Océanie**
Australia[3][7]	7254	6312	6316	...	...	...	...	...	...	...	Australie[3][7]
Total	**428162**	**420404**	**385377**	**562067**	**628041**	**413697**	**401726**	**428007**	**401185**	**428628**	**Total**

General Note.

Electrical appliances which, without any action of moving parts, transform an alternating current system into another system of alternating current of different voltage. (SITC, Rev.3: 77110-2B).

Remarque générale.

Appareils électriques qui, sans l'intervention d'organes mobiles, transforment un courant alternatif en un autre courant alternatif d'intensité et de tension différentes. (CTCI, Rev.3: 77110-2B).

[1] Production by large and medium scale establishments only.
[2] Including transformers less than 5 kVA.
[3] Transformers over 1 kVA.
[4] Transformers over 20 kVA.
[5] Including transformers less than 16 kVA.
[6] Excluding Transnistria region.
[7] Twelve months ending 30 June of year stated.

[1] Production des grandes et moyennes entreprises seulement.
[2] Y compris transformateurs de moins de 5 kVA.
[3] Transformateurs de plus de 1 kVA.
[4] Transformateurs de plus de 20 kVA.
[5] Y compris transformateurs de moins de 16 kVA.
[6] Non compris la région de Transnistria.
[7] Période de douze mois finissant le 30 juin de l'année indiquée.

Meters, electricity-supply
Compteurs d'électricité

ISIC-BASED CODE - CODE BASE CITI

3831-19

Unit : Thousand units   Unité : En milliers

Country or area	1990	1991	1992	1993	1994	1995	1996	1997	1998	1999	Pays ou zone
Africa	**627**	**802**	**874**	**540**	**625**	**527**	**575**	**668**	**691**	**698**	**Afrique**
Algeria	231	174	202	136	174	99	144	111	215	225	Algérie
Egypt	396	628	672	404	451	428	431	557	...	...	Egypte
America, North	**5276**	**4848**	**4927**	**4914**	**5155**	**3119**	**3119**	**626**	**688**	**673**	**Amérique du Nord**
United States[1]	...	4848	4927	4914	5155	...	...	626	688	673	Etats-Unis[1]
America, South	**2321**	**1998**	**2303**	**2392**	**3050**	**3432**	**3491**	**4522**	**5047**	**4711**	**Amérique du Sud**
Brazil	2203	1919	2166	2260	2897	3240	3281	4264	4838	4618	Brésil
Chile	118	79	137	132	153	192	210	258	209	93	Chili
Asia	**30941**	**33540**	**36116**	**40209**	**47471**	**56334**	**56212**	**66210**	**62205**	**64953**	**Asie**
China	23033	25310	28698	30510	36940	45231	43656	52504	...	...	Chine
India	2868	3295	2760	5270	5490	5680	7180	...	...	...	Inde
Israel	...	79	64	54	52	56	34	...	...	...	Israël
Japan	3178	3159	2716	2500	2930	3301	3203	3157	2489	2327	Japon
Korea, Republic of	1739	1644	1815	1803	2021	...	...	...	...	...	Corée, République de
Turkey	...	...	63	72	38	45	45	43	31	35	Turquie
Europe	**9001**	**11875**	**10617**	**11482**	**11778**	**11708**	**11383**	**12545**	**12295**	**14034**	**Europe**
Austria[2]	299	259	213	218	258	...	...	...	...	...	Autriche[2]
Bulgaria	231	231	258	320	261	138	163	104	112	114	Bulgarie
Croatia	..	...	...	...	...	...	...	2	25	...	Croatie
Finland	106	116	133	135	159	195	232	...	...	...	Finlande
France	2002	2282	2165	2326	2736	...	...	...	...	...	France
Germany	..	1252	1429	1667	1710	1857	1673	1475	1415	...	Allemagne
Germany(Fed.Rep.)	966	..	..	..	..	..	..	..	..	..	Allemagne(Rép.féd.)
Hungary	611	582	377	...	...	...	...	...	...	...	Hongrie
Latvia	..	...	...	...	22	16	20	37	36	...	Lettonie
Lithuania	..	2593	1888	1718	1055	850	657	910	704	582	Lituanie
Slovenia	..	1106	1007	1716	2488	2477	1805	1966	2111	2404	Slovénie
Spain	1351	918	946	852	858	1038	1167	1187	857	1033	Espagne
United Kingdom	2243	...	...	1982	1694	1632	2022	2840	2853	...	Royaume-Uni
Yugoslavia	..	340	0	0	0	0	0	0	0	0	Yougoslavie
Yugoslavia, SFR	1192	..	..	..	..	..	..	..	..	..	Yougoslavie, RSF
Total	**48166**	**53063**	**54837**	**59537**	**68079**	**75120**	**74779**	**84571**	**80927**	**85069**	**Total**

General Note.
Meters for measuring the amount of electricity consumed (ampere-hours) or the amount of energy consumed (watt-hours). Apparatus such as voltmeters, ammeters and the like is excluded. (SITC, Rev.3: 87315-0).

[1] Shipments.
[2] Beginning 1995, data are confidential.

Remarque générale.
Compteurs servant à mesurer les quantités d'électricité consommées (ampères-heures) ou l'énergie consommée (watts-heures). Cette rubrique ne comprend pas les voltmètres, ampèremètres, etc. (CTCI, Rev.3: 87315-0).

[1] Expéditions.
[2] A partir de 1995, les données sont confidentielles

Television receivers
Récepteurs de télévision

ISIC-BASED CODE - CODE BASE CITI

3832-01

Unit : Thousand units   Unité : En milliers

Country or area	1990	1991	1992	1993	1994	1995	1996	1997	1998	1999	Pays ou zone
Africa	**5301**	**5252**	**5226**	**5180**	**5144**	**5170**	**5271**	**4989**	**5178**	**4902**	**Afrique**
Algeria	283	176	218	258	165	194	250	172	251	173	Algérie
Angola	11	16	33	...	...	...	...	...	...	...	Angola
Egypt	333	264	260	269	281	288	336	114	...	30	Egypte
Kenya	4186	...	...	...	...	...	...	...	...	...	Kenya
South Africa	373	486	376	321	...	...	...	...	...	...	Afrique du Sud
Tunisia	115	124	153	126	103	93	90	108	90	104	Tunisie
America, North	**14622**	**13368**	**14423**	**13790**	**14315**	**12316**	**11646**	**11488**	**10715**	**11122**	**Amérique du Nord**
Mexico	633	490	435	98	423	181	205	...	...	...	Mexique
Trinidad and Tobago	7	13	16	13	11	3	1	...	...	...	Trinité-et-Tobago
United States[1]	13982	12865	13972	13679	13881	12132	11440	11476	10715	11122	Etats-Unis[1]
America, South	**3739**	**4052**	**3904**	**5582**	**7311**	**7578**	**9920**	**9743**	**7429**	**5764**	**Amérique du Sud**
Argentina	310	607	1386	1612	1523	949	1096	1630	1592	1335	Argentine
Brazil	3196	3255	2322	3738	5522	6424	8644	7976	5711	4328	Brésil
Colombia	135	[2]94	114	150	141	129	...	58	50	...	Colombie
Ecuador	...	...	11	11	54	5	0	...	...	...	Equateur
Peru	71	...	...	...	...	...	...	...	...	...	Pérou
Asia	**69904**	**72252**	**73187**	**74486**	**76876**	**80965**	**83073**	**80774**	**83947**	**91529**	**Asie**
Azerbaijan	..	...	6	9	2	4	1	1	3	0	Azerbaïdjan
Bangladesh	136	104	46	61	77	79	64	94	...	...	Bangladesh
China	26847	26914	28678	30330	32833	34962	35418	36372	42809	49113	Chine
Hong Kong SAR	1177	749	...	...	...	...	...	...	...	...	Hong-Kong RAS
Georgia	..	39	8	1	0	0	2	2	1	1	Géorgie
India	1322	1217	1254	1536	1559	2190	1949	2370	2461	2561	Inde
Indonesia	674	641	700	1001	...	...	...	...	...	...	Indonésie
Iran(Islamic Rep. of)	[3]598	[3]736	[3]688	[3]502	[3]360	[4]253	[4]453	[4]751	[4]769	...	Iran(Rép. islamique)
Iraq	...	...	16	...	...	...	...	...	...	...	Iraq
Japan	15132	15640	14253	12840	11192	9022	7568	7559	6567	4386	Japon
Kazakhstan	..	5	36	20	43	47	74	61	103	112	Kazakhstan
Korea, Republic of	16201	16129	16311	15956	17102	18722	21469	16428	12763	15556	Corée, République de
Kyrgyzstan	..	8	2	2	43	7	0	0	4	1	Kirghizistan
Malaysia	3238	4838	5553	6629	7702	9461	8901	7774	8035	7611	Malaisie
Pakistan	200	182	145	274	185	101	278	186	107	128	Pakistan
Syrian Arab Republic	18	17	20	20	77	71	124	128	151	150	Rép. arabe syrienne
Thailand	2351	2426	...	...	...	...	...	...	...	...	Thaïlande
Turkey	1994	2567	2111	1922	1528	1859	2510	4657	5795	6941	Turquie
Uzbekistan	..	...	9	16	52	65	140	269	...	...	Ouzbékistan
Europe	**16466**	**24622**	**21433**	**21875**	**20596**	**19654**	**16989**	**18238**	**19192**	**20393**	**Europe**
Albania	18	5	1	0	0	0	0	0	0	0	Albanie
Belarus	..	1103	798	610	473	250	314	454	468	516	Bélarus
Belgium[1][5]	1084	886	620	559	...	...	...	...	...	...	Belgique[1][5]
Bulgaria	219	108	64	26	19	10	11	6	3	2	Bulgarie
Croatia	..	3	0	0	0	0	0	...	...	...	Croatie
Denmark[6]	122	117	...	...	...	...	...	...	...	...	Danemark[6]
Czechoslovakia(former)	504	208	...	...	...	...	...	...	...	..	Tchécoslovaquie(anc.)
Czech Republic	..	..	...	...	128	66	74	180	567	707	République tchèque
Finland	412	327	269	321	339	308	191	...	...	...	Finlande
France	2838	2549	2799	2523	2796	...	...	...	...	...	France
Germany	..	...	...	2800	3234	3218	1965	...	1269	...	Allemagne
Germany(Fed.Rep.)	3595	..	..	..	..	..	..	..	..	..	Allemagne(Rép.féd.)
German D.R.(former)	632	..	..	..	..	..	..	..	..	..	R.D.A. (anc.)
Greece	10	2	...	...	...	...	...	...	...	...	Grèce
Hungary	492	217	274	204	272	274	...	...	...	...	Hongrie
Italy	2312	2435	2151	2432	2780	2780	2677	1920	1659	1627	Italie
Lithuania	..	516	445	423	181	55	57	52	84	187	Lituanie
Poland	748	438	652	855	888	1138	1615	3020	4436	5121	Pologne
Portugal	329	318	238	...	...	...	...	...	...	...	Portugal
Republic of Moldova	..	173	176	[7]167	[7]108	[7]47	[7]31	[7]19	[7]10	[7]3	Rép. de Moldova
Romania	401	389	318	464	452	369	275	89	134	56	Roumanie
Russian Federation	..	4439	3672	3987	2240	1005	313	327	329	281	Fédération de Russie

For general note and footnotes, see end of table.   Voir la fin du tableau pour la remarque générale et les notes.

Television receivers (continued)
Récepteurs de télévision (suite)

ISIC-BASED CODE - CODE BASE CITI

3832-01

Unit : Thousand units   Unité : En milliers

Country or area	1990	1991	1992	1993	1994	1995	1996	1997	1998	1999	Pays ou zone
Slovakia	..	..	...	165	...	...	...	...	304	311	Slovaquie
Slovenia	..	101	55	42	124	130	179	0	231	244	Slovénie
Spain	2466	2807	2544	3840	4103	5392	...	...	...	...	Espagne
Sweden	284	224	13	0	...	...	...	...	...	...	Suède
Ukraine	..	3616	2570	1919	821	315	118	50	93	81	Ukraine
Yugoslavia	..	80	64	24	40	31	24	25	30	13	Yougoslavie
USSR (former)	10540	..	..	..	..	..	..	..	..	..	URSS (anc.)
Oceania	**158**	**158**	**158**	**158**	**158**	**158**	**158**	**158**	**158**	**158**	**Océanie**
Australia[8][9]	158	...	...	...	...	...	...	...	...	...	Australie[8][9]
Total	**120730**	**119704**	**118331**	**121072**	**124400**	**125841**	**127056**	**125390**	**126618**	**133868**	**Total**

General Note.
Household television receivers of all kinds (table models, consoles, television sets incorporating a radio receiver or a gramophone). (SITC, Rev.3: 76100-1).

Remarque générale.
Récepteurs de télévision de tous genres pour usage privé (récepteurs de table, récepteurs-meubles, etc., même avec appareils récepteur de radio diffusion, phonographe ou tourne-disques incorporés). (CTCI, Rev.3: 76100-1).

[1] Shipments.
[2] Source: United Nations Economic Commission for Latin America and the Caribbean (ECLAC), (Santiago).
[3] Production by establishments employing 50 or more persons.
[4] Production by establishments employing 10 or more persons.
[5] Production by establishments employing 5 or more persons.
[6] Sales.
[7] Excluding Transnistria region.
[8] Twelve months ending 30 June of year stated.
[9] Colour television receivers only.

[1] Expéditions.
[2] Source: Commission économique des Nations Unies pour l'Amérique Latine et les Caraïbes (CEPAL), (Santiago).
[3] Production des établissements occupant 50 personnes ou plus.
[4] Production des établissements occupant 10 personnes ou plus.
[5] Production des établissements occupant 5 personnes ou plus.
[6] Ventes.
[7] Non compris la région de Transnistria.
[8] Période de douze mois finissant le 30 juin de l'année indiquée.
[9] Récepteurs de télévision en couleur seulement.

Television receivers, black and white
Récepteurs de télévision, en noir et blanc

ISIC-BASED CODE - CODE BASE CITI

3832-011

Unit : Thousand units   Unité : En milliers

Country or area	1990	1991	1992	1993	1994	1995	1996	1997	1998	1999	Pays ou zone
Africa	**362**	**291**	**259**	**223**	**237**	**208**	**207**	**161**	**171**	**160**	**Afrique**
Algeria	159	57	77	101	71	44	47	1	16	5	Algérie
Egypt	11	0	0	1	...	...	...	...	...	...	Egypte
South Africa	168	201	138	99	...	...	...	...	...	...	Afrique du Sud
Tunisia	24	33	44	22	11	9	5	5	0	0	Tunisie
America, North	**180**	**128**	**51**	**29**	**11**	**0**	**0**	**0**	**0**	**0**	**Amérique du Nord**
Mexico	180	128	51	29	11	...	...	...	...	...	Mexique
America, South	**592**	**618**	**314**	**423**	**386**	**127**	**59**	**65**	**49**	**30**	**Amérique du Sud**
Brazil	562	588	284	393	356	97	29	35	19	0	Brésil
Peru	30	...	...	...	...	...	...	...	...	...	Pérou
Asia	**20696**	**18416**	**17495**	**17420**	**17049**	**16465**	**10054**	**9413**	**8225**	**6831**	**Asie**
Azerbaijan	..	...	1	6	2	1	0	0	1	0	Azerbaïdjan
Bangladesh	...	...	...	...	42	31	56	81	70	*78	Bangladesh
China	16517	14863	15347	15973	15941	15857	9567	9259	7839	6493	Chine
Georgia	..	...	...	...	...	0	1	1	1	1	Géorgie
Indonesia	338	311	363	575	805	343	...	4	...	...	Indonésie
Iran(Islamic Rep. of)	[1]502	[1]515	[1]422	[1]232	[1]141	[2]48	[2]17	[2]49	[2]34	...	Iran(Rép. islamique)
Korea, Republic of	3307	2680	1319	581	103	167	...	...	...	...	Corée, République de
Uzbekistan	..	...	2	7	15	18	21	19	...	...	Ouzbékistan
Europe	**1009**	**3816**	**3151**	**3335**	**2019**	**1102**	**572**	**368**	**287**	**240**	**Europe**
Belarus	..	...	...	25	126	75	93	103	94	83	Bélarus
Bulgaria	39	56	31	13	6	5	5	3	...	...	Bulgarie
Croatia	..	1	0	0	0	0	0	...	...	...	Croatie
Denmark[3]	8	108	108	108	98	0	82	93	95	85	Danemark[3]
Czechoslovakia(former)	119	4	..	..	..	..	..	..	..	..	Tchécoslovaquie(anc.)
Finland	1	1	1	1	1	...	...	...	...	...	Finlande
Hungary	65	13	8	...	...	...	...	...	...	...	Hongrie
Italy	2	1	1	0	0	0	...	...	...	...	Italie
Lithuania	..	...	...	147	67	27	2	4	3	1	Lituanie
Poland	410	134	33	14	6	2	0	...	...	...	Pologne
Republic of Moldova	..	0	2	[4]41	[4]39	[4]19	[4]5	[4]3	[4]4	[4]1	Rép. de Moldova
Romania	340	279	259	229	95	74	47	11	6	0	Roumanie
Russian Federation	..	1941	1633	1812	1088	635	211	75	36	16	Fédération de Russie
Slovenia	..	1	0	0	...	...	...	...	...	...	Slovénie
Spain	25	1	3	0	...	...	...	...	...	...	Espagne
Ukraine	..	1089	901	915	456	227	89	38	11	16	Ukraine
Yugoslavia	..	1	...	...	...	...	...	...	...	...	Yougoslavie
Total	**22840**	**23269**	**21271**	**21430**	**19702**	**17902**	**10892**	**10007**	**8732**	**7261**	**Total**

General Note.
Household television receivers, black and white or other monochrome, of all kinds (table models, consoles, television sets incorporating a radio receiver or a gramophone). (SITC, Rev.3: 72410-2).

Remarque générale.
Récepteurs de télévision de tous genres pour usage privé en noir et blanc ou en autres monochromes (récepteurs de table, recepteurs-meubles, etc., même avec appareils récepteur de radio diffusion, phonographe ou tourne-disques incorporés). (CTCI, Rev.3: 72410-2)

[1] Production by establishments employing 50 or more persons.
[2] Production by establishments employing 10 or more persons.
[3] Sales.
[4] Excluding Transnistria region.

[1] Production des établissements occupant 50 personnes ou plus.
[2] Production des établissements occupant 10 personnes ou plus.
[3] Ventes.
[4] Non compris la région de Transnistria.

Television receivers, colour
Récepteurs de télévision, en couleurs

ISIC-BASED CODE - CODE BASE CITI

3832-012

Unit : Thousand units — Unité : En milliers

Country or area	1990	1991	1992	1993	1994	1995	1996	1997	1998	1999	Pays ou zone
Africa	**742**	**759**	**748**	**720**	**740**	**859**	**891**	**668**	**830**	**575**	**Afrique**
Algeria	124	119	141	157	94	150	203	171	235	168	Algérie
Egypt	322	264	260	237	234	[1]288	[1]336	[1]114	...	[1]30	Egypte
South Africa	205	285	238	222	320	337	267	280	273	273	Afrique du Sud
Tunisia	91	91	109	104	92	84	85	103	90	104	Tunisie
America, North	**453**	**362**	**384**	**98**	**423**	**181**	**205**	**110**	**72**	**34**	**Amérique du Nord**
Mexico	453	362	384	98	423	181	205	...	...	...	Mexique
America, South	**2985**	**3315**	**3465**	**4998**	**6730**	**7317**	**9752**	**9612**	**7325**	**5704**	**Amérique du Sud**
Argentina	310	607	1386	1612	1523	949	1096	1630	1592	1335	Argentine
Brazil	2634	2667	2038	3345	5166	6327	8615	7941	5692	4328	Brésil
Peru	41	...	...	...	...	...	...	...	...	...	Pérou
Asia	**38923**	**42113**	**43116**	**43115**	**46186**	**50348**	**57200**	**57660**	**60845**	**71156**	**Asie**
Azerbaijan	..	...	5	3	0	3	1	1	2	0	Azerbaïdjan
Bangladesh	...	...	...	...	37	30	25	50	37	*39	Bangladesh
China	10330	12051	13331	14357	16892	20577	25376	27113	34970	42620	Chine
Georgia	..	..	8	1	0	0	1	1	0	0	Géorgie
Indonesia	336	330	337	426	986	1212	...	1787	804	...	Indonésie
Iran(Islamic Rep. of)	[2]96	[2]221	[2]266	[2]270	[2]219	[3]204	[3]436	[3]701	[3]734	...	Iran(Rép. islamique)
Japan	13243	13438	12024	10717	9445	7854	6486	6672	5569	3444	Japon
Korea, Republic of	12893	13449	14992	15375	16999	18555	21469	16428	12763	15556	Corée, République de
Kyrgyzstan	..	8	2	2	43	7	0	0	4	1	Kirghizistan
Turkey	1994	2567	2111	1922	1528	1859	2510	4657	5795	6941	Turquie
Uzbekistan	..	...	7	9	37	47	119	250	...	...	Ouzbékistan
Europe	**12113**	**17007**	**14733**	**15823**	**14710**	**15952**	**13881**	**15103**	**16151**	**18054**	**Europe**
Belarus	..	1103	798	585	347	175	221	351	374	433	Bélarus
Bulgaria	180	52	33	13	13	5	6	3	...	...	Bulgarie
Croatia	..	2	0	0	0	0	0	...	...	...	Croatie
Denmark[4]	114	108	108	102	...	...	...	...	...	...	Danemark[4]
Czechoslovakia(former)	385	205	..	...	..	..	..	..	...	...	Tchécoslovaquie(anc.)
Finland	411	326	268	320	338	308	191	...	...	...	Finlande
Germany	..	...	...	...	...	3218	1965	...	1269	...	Allemagne
Germany(Fed.Rep.)	3595	..	..	..	..	..	..	..	..	..	Allemagne(Rép.féd.)
Greece	10	2	...	...	...	...	...	...	...	...	Grèce
Hungary	427	204	266	197	244	273	...	...	...	...	Hongrie
Italy	2310	2434	2150	2432	2780	2780	2677	1920	1659	1627	Italie
Lithuania	..	264	166	276	114	28	55	48	81	185	Lituanie
Poland	338	304	619	841	881	1136	1615	3020	4436	5121	Pologne
Republic of Moldova	..	173	174	[5]126	[5]69	[5]28	[5]26	[5]16	[5]6	[5]2	Rép. de Moldova
Russian Federation	..	2498	2039	2175	1152	370	102	252	293	264	Fédération de Russie
Slovakia	..	..	...	159	...	...	129	171	304	311	Slovaquie
Slovenia	..	101	55	42	124	130	179	0	231	244	Slovénie
Spain	2441	2806	2541	3840	4102	5392	...	...	...	...	Espagne
Sweden	284	224	13	0	...	...	...	...	...	...	Suède
Ukraine	..	2527	1669	1004	365	88	29	12	82	65	Ukraine
United Kingdom	1618	1444	...	...	...	...	...	...	...	...	Royaume-Uni
Yugoslavia	..	79	64	24	40	31	24	25	30	13	Yougoslavie
USSR (former)	7175	..	...	...	...	...	...	...	...	..	URSS (anc.)
Oceania	**158**	**167**	**177**	**154**	**164**	**164**	**164**	**164**	**164**	**164**	**Océanie**
Australia	158	167	177	154	...	...	...	...	...	...	Australie
Total	**62549**	**63722**	**62622**	**64909**	**68952**	**74820**	**82093**	**83317**	**85387**	**95688**	**Total**

General Note.
Household television receivers, colour, of all kinds (table models, consoles, television sets incorporating a radio receiver or a gramophone). (SITC, Rev.3: 72410-1).

[1] Including black and white TV.
[2] Production by establishments employing 50 or more persons.
[3] Production by establishments employing 10 or more persons.
[4] Sales.
[5] Excluding Transnistria region.

Remarque générale.
Récepteurs de télévision de tous genres pour usage privé en noir et couleurs (récepteurs de table, recepteurs-meubles, etc., même avec appareils récepteur de radio diffusion, phonographe ou tourne-disques incorporés). (CTCI, Rev.3: 72410-1)

[1] Y compris les téléviseurs en noir et blanc.
[2] Production des établissements occupant 50 personnes ou plus.
[3] Production des établissements occupant 10 personnes ou plus.
[4] Ventes.
[5] Non compris la région de Transnistria.

Radio receivers
Récepteurs de radio

ISIC-BASED CODE - CODE BASE CITI

3832-04

Unit : Thousand units

Unité : En milliers

Country or area	1990	1991	1992	1993	1994	1995	1996	1997	1998	1999	Pays ou zone
Africa	**1371**	**1319**	**1236**	**1063**	**1075**	**986**	**939**	**937**	**937**	**930**	**Afrique**
Algeria	341	304	238	109	107	...	...	...	...	...	Algérie
Angola	78	52	29	...	...	...	...	...	...	...	Angola
Chad	13	7	7	0	0	0	...	...	...	...	Tchad
Egypt	59	39	36	13	52	...	...	...	...	...	Egypte
Mozambique	12	19	...	...	...	...	...	...	...	...	Mozambique
South Africa	775	...	...	...	...	...	...	...	...	...	Afrique du Sud
Tunisia	22	21	27	2	...	...	...	...	...	...	Tunisie
United Rep.Tanzania	71	102	108	95	54	76	54	56	...	...	Rép. Unie de Tanzanie
America, North	**3016**	**3507**	**4009**	**2724**	**3313**	**3311**	**3311**	**3311**	**3311**	**3311**	**Amérique du Nord**
Trinidad and Tobago	2	3	3	4	...	0	0	...	...	...	Trinité-et-Tobago
United States[1]	3014	3504	4006	2720	...	...	...	...	...	...	Etats-Unis[1]
America, South	**5151**	**5333**	**5478**	**4097**	**4665**	**4729**	**2941**	**4211**	**2753**	**2039**	**Amérique du Sud**
Brazil	5151	5333	5478	4097	4665	4729	2941	4211	2753	2039	Brésil
Asia	**85212**	**76351**	**68974**	**77871**	**93465**	**87480**	**79391**	**87324**	**83525**	**89948**	**Asie**
Armenia	..	167	50	8	0	0	0	0	0	0	Arménie
Azerbaijan	..	7	0	30	3	0	0	0	0	0	Azerbaïdjan
Bangladesh	34	133	80	7	3	4	11	20	10	13	Bangladesh
China	[2]21030	[2]19691	[2]16489	[2]17542	41320	...	...	...	...	...	Chine
Hong Kong SAR[3]	8182	6145	6508	11018	3390	1698	...	...	...	...	Hong-Kong RAS[3]
India	[4]647	[4]286	[4]245	[4]152	210	116	47	33	2	0	Inde
Indonesia[5]	4436	4659	2863	3882	3372	3805	...	4177	#80	...	Indonésie[5]
Iran(Islamic Rep. of)	[6][7][8]232	[6]102	[6]138	[6]174	[6]138	45	56	76	127	...	Iran(Rép. islamique)
Japan	10955	11213	9418	8739	7569	7181	2638	2434	2623	2678	Japon
Kazakhstan	..	86	97	72	4	12	3	3	3	...	Kazakhstan
Korea, Republic of	1468	836	619	550	28	0	...	...	...	...	Corée, République de
Malaysia	37019	31920	31360	34537	36310	38767	29431	33491	30265	32957	Malaisie
Myanmar[10]	4	1	1	...	...	...	...	...	...	...	Myanmar[10]
Thailand	1105	1062	...	...	...	...	...	...	...	...	Thaïlande
Turkey	100	43	22	74	32	...	...	...	...	...	Turquie
Europe	**14180**	**19646**	**18663**	**17747**	**16492**	**13718**	**14046**	**16435**	**19772**	**18033**	**Europe**
Albania	26	9	0	0	0	0	0	0	0	0	Albanie
Belarus	..	932	721	768	545	277	138	170	114	195	Bélarus
Belgium[1][11]	986	556	416	408	...	...	...	...	...	...	Belgique[1][11]
Bulgaria	43	16	5	1	2	2	0	...	...	...	Bulgarie
Croatia	..	3	1	0	0	0	0	...	...	...	Croatie
Czechoslovakia(former)[12]	187	73	..	..	..	..	..	..	..	..	Tchécoslovaquie(anc.)[12]
Finland	...	...	*4	71	70	82	...	...	...	..	Finlande
France	2059	1865	1679	2083	2804	...	...	3853	4586	2961	France
Germany	...	...	4703	4623	5404	3182	3342	3632	3884	...	Allemagne
Germany(Fed.Rep.)	5955	..	..	..	..	..	..	..	..	..	Allemagne(Rép.féd.)
German D.R.(former)	522	..	..	..	..	..	..	..	..	..	R.D.A. (anc.)
Hungary	83	14	1	...	126	103	310	528	2328	2412	Hongrie
Latvia	..	1230	630	125	33	9	10	10	2	2	Lettonie
Poland	1433	589	334	329	309	225	206	143	154	132	Pologne
Portugal	1435	1522	...	...	...	...	4372	4552	5076	5939	Portugal
Republic of Moldova	..	5	3	[13]5	[13]3	[13]16	[13]67	[13]94	[13]51	[13]7	Rép. de Moldova
Romania[5]	438	435	83	79	28	29	76	28	10	0	Roumanie[5]
Russian Federation	..	5537	4015	2806	1087	988	477	342	235	332	Fédération de Russie
Slovakia[12]	..	...	...	2	...	...	...	...	...	...	Slovaquie[12]
Spain	10	28	...	...	...	54	82	313	508	357	Espagne
Ukraine	..	892	860	803	302	125	47	25	10	27	Ukraine
United Kingdom	...	...	...	978	1176	1480	1531	2095	2164	...	Royaume-Uni
Yugoslavia	..	6	1	1	0	0	1	0	0	0	Yougoslavie
USSR (former)	9168	..	..	..	..	..	..	..	..	..	URSS (anc.)
Total	**118098**	**106156**	**98359**	**103501**	**119009**	**110224**	**100628**	**112219**	**110298**	**114262**	**Total**

For general note and footnotes, see end of table.

Voir la fin du tableau pour la remarque générale et les notes.

Radio receivers (continued)
Récepteurs de radio (suite)

General Note.
Complete receiving sets, irrespective of frequencies covered, made for home, automobile and general use, including battery sets. Radio-gramophone combinations are included. (SITC, Rev.3: 76200-0).

Remarque générale.
Récepteurs complets, quelles que soient les longueurs d'ondes captées, d'appartement, d'automobiles et d'usage général, y compris les postes à piles. Cette rubrique comprend les récepteurs avec phonographes ou tourne-disques incorporés. (CTCI, Rev.3: 76200-0).

[1] Shipments.
[2] Portable battery sets only.
[3] Beginning 1996, data are confidential.
[4] Production by large and medium scale establishments only.
[5] Including radio with tape recording unit.

[6] Production by establishments employing 50 or more persons.
[7] Including sound reproducers.
[8] Including tape recorders.
[9] Production by establishments employing 10 or more persons.
[10] Government production only.
[11] Production by establishments employing 5 or more persons.
[12] Including record players.
[13] Excluding Transnistria region.

[1] Expéditions.
[2] Appareils portatifs à piles seulement.
[3] A partir de 1996, les données sont confidentielles.
[4] Production des grandes et moyennes entreprises seulement.
[5] Y compris les récepteurs radio avec appareil enregistreur à bande magnétique incorporé.
[6] Production des établissements occupant 50 personnes ou plus.
[7] Y compris les lecteurs de son.
[8] Y compris les magnétophones.
[9] Production des établissements occupant 10 personnes ou plus.
[10] Production de l'Etat seulement.
[11] Production des établissements occupant 5 personnes ou plus.
[12] Y compris les tourne-disques.
[13] Non compris la région de Transnistria.

Telephones
Appareils téléphoniques

ISIC-BASED CODE - CODE BASE CITI

3832-10

Unit : Thousand units   Unité : En milliers

Country or area	1990	1991	1992	1993	1994	1995	1996	1997	1998	1999	Pays ou zone
Africa	**71**	**105**	**104**	**201**	**135**	**112**	**74**	**3**	**30**	**151**	**Afrique**
Algeria	71	105	104	201	135	112	74	3	30	151	Algérie
America, North	**1202**	**751**	**561**	**1624**	**1960**	**1577**	**1096**	**2278**	**2107**	**2276**	**Amérique du Nord**
Mexico	1202	751	561	1624	1960	1577	1096	2278	2107	2276	Mexique
America, South	**1662**	**1217**	**917**	**450**	**556**	**860**	**862**	**996**	**2613**	**3610**	**Amérique du Sud**
Argentina	...	91	300	85	137	335	328	484	423.	432	Argentine
Brazil	1341	997	528	255	304	408	405	308	2085	3026	Brésil
Colombia	166	...	89	110	115	117	...	204	105	...	Colombie
Asia	**49828**	**50467**	**58976**	**64260**	**92942**	**128932**	**111351**	**117546**	**105519**	**105899**	**Asie**
Azerbaijan	..	0	29	19	3	2	0	1	51	0	Azerbaïdjan
Bangladesh[1]	38	33	26	31	16	6	9	24	36	4	Bangladesh[1]
China	8800	14820	19820	26636	57229	99563	79608	86537	65205	71399	Chine
Hong Kong SAR	11268	...	5949	...	...	1053	830	91			Hong-Kong RAS
India	1615	1183	1430	1935	1910	3806	3891	4989	4534	4988	Inde
Indonesia	126	287	1537	2780	2393	960	...	4193	17335	...	Indonésie
Iran(Islamic Rep. of)	[2]189	[2]495	[2]497	[2]288	[2]218	[3]150	[3]224	[3]248	[3]318	...	Iran(Rép. islamique)
Japan[4]	15719	18164	19786	18398	17641	12779	11290	12625	11920	10904	Japon[4]
Korea, Republic of	11436	11241	9427	9809	9105	9986	10980	7994	4953	5402	Corée, République de
Syrian Arab Republic	...	13	5	27	125	40	24	9	3	...	Rép. arabe syrienne
Turkey	604	393	470	499	464	587	794	835	496	323	Turquie
Europe	**6798**	**24804**	**25129**	**25763**	**27135**	**28407**	**29074**	**49163**	**54065**	**47125**	**Europe**
Austria[5][6]	134	109	71	52	29	...	#396	538	...	850	Autriche[5][6]
Belarus	..	10	57	72	146	210	93	132	101	128	Bélarus
Bulgaria	915	520	140	139	74	67	97	44	56	33	Bulgarie
Denmark[7]	...	305	293	257	383	0	243	352	1492	1896	Danemark[7]
Finland	58	23	18	*25	...	...	...	...	...	...	Finlande
Germany	..	...	...	...	...	13801	13953	15387	15942	...	Allemagne
German D.R.(former)	699	...	..	..	..	..	..	..	..	..	R.D.A. (anc.)
Greece	296	395	...	...	...	...	...	...	...	...	Grèce
Hungary	239	131	103	167	229	495	227	285	174	167	Hongrie
Latvia	..	2019	896	311	121	64	185	88	362	219	Lettonie
Lithuania	..	0	0	0	0	1	0	0	0	0	Lituanie
Poland	1589	993	349	297	428	409	626	653	691	505	Pologne
Portugal	128	110	...	342	374	...	...	...	...	...	Portugal
Republic of Moldova	..	26	56	[8]35	[8]9	[8]4	[8]4	[8]1	[8]1	...	Rép. de Moldova
Romania	243	236	110	133	188	129	165	202	136	55	Roumanie
Russian Federation	..	2586	2427	2231	1272	1026	712	723	518	674	Fédération de Russie
Slovenia	..	160	123	172	316	749	304	268	234	405	Slovénie
Spain	2417	909	1029	3242	3751	4115	4847	5695	6337	4520	Espagne
Ukraine	..	38	34	489	328	208	78	108	110	111	Ukraine
United Kingdom	...	...	...	2668	4337	6240	6503	#24072	*27024	...	Royaume-Uni
Yugoslavia	..	13	29	14	3	2	26	0	0	12	Yougoslavie
USSR (former)	**15106**	..	..	..	..	..	..	..	..	..	**URSS (anc.)**
Oceania	**1491**	**1491**	**1491**	**1491**	**1728**	**1592**	**1153**	**1491**	**1491**	**1491**	**Océanie**
Australia	...	...	...	...	1728	1592	1153	...	...	...	Australie
Total	**76158**	**78836**	**87178**	**93789**	**124456**	**161480**	**143611**	**171477**	**165825**	**160552**	**Total**

General Note.

Units composed of a microphone, one or more receivers, a switching device, a bell and possibly a dial selector. (SITC, Rev.3: 76411-0).

Remarque générale.

Appareils contenant un microphone, un ou plusieurs récepteurs, un avertisseur, un commutateur-interrupteur et, le cas échéant, un cadran sélecteur. (CTCI, Rev.3: 76411-0).

[1] Twelve months ending 30 June of year stated.
[2] Production by establishments employing 50 or more persons.
[3] Production by establishments employing 10 or more persons.
[4] Dial-system telephones only.
[5] 1995 data are confidential.
[6] 1998 data are confidential.
[7] Sales.
[8] Excluding Transnistria region.

[1] Période de douze mois finissant le 30 juin de l'année indiquée.
[2] Production des établissements occupant 50 personnes ou plus.
[3] Production des établissements occupant 10 personnes ou plus.
[4] Téléphones automatiques seulement.
[5] Pour 1995, les données sont confidentielles.
[6] Pour 1998, les données sont confidentielles.
[7] Ventes.
[8] Non compris la région de Transnistria.

Electronic tubes
Tubes électroniques

ISIC-BASED CODE - CODE BASE CITI

3832-25

Unit : Thousand units · Unité : En milliers

Country or area	1990	1991	1992	1993	1994	1995	1996	1997	1998	1999	Pays ou zone
Asia	**83487**	**77487**	**74424**	**81824**	**92898**	**123347**	**104177**	**138526**	**121240**	**125302**	**Asie**
China	42470	36770	36069	44046	52035	80409	63358	97572	...	...	Chine
Korea, Republic of	41017	40717	38355	37778	40863	42938	...	...	...	...	Corée, République de
Europe	**5152**	**3934**	**8679**	**8584**	**8818**	**11495**	**8641**	**8747**	**7734**	**7690**	**Europe**
Czechoslovakia(former)	362	2	..	..	..	..	..	..	..	..	Tchécoslovaquie(anc.)
Czech Republic	..	..	...	...	3134	5279	2433	2007	355	4	République tchèque
Germany	..	...	...	34	44	8	...	...	...	...	Allemagne
Germany(Fed.Rep.)	74	..	..	..	..	..	..	..	..	..	Allemagne(Rép.féd.)
Greece	2229	2507	2951	...	...	...	...	...	...	...	Grèce
Hungary	81	18	6	...	...	...	...	...	...	...	Hongrie
Poland	1842	207	736	1812	2401	2988	2995	3417	3905	4294	Pologne
United Kingdom	...	...	...	564	...	...	...	...	...	...	Royaume-Uni
Yugoslavia	..	607	429	53	78	59	23	133	284	202	Yougoslavie
Total	**88639**	**81421**	**83103**	**90408**	**101716**	**134842**	**112818**	**147273**	**128974**	**132992**	**Total**

General Note.

Valves and tubes which utilize the effect of electrons emitted from a cathode either in a vacuum or in gas. The envelopes are usually of glass, but sometimes of metal. Cathode-ray tubes and television camera tubes and photocathode valves and tubes are excluded. However, the modified form of cathode-ray tube which is used as a tuning indicator in radio receivers (magic eyes) is included. (SITC, Rev.3: 77625-0, 77627-0).

Remarque générale.

Lampes, tubes et valves utilisant les effets des émissions d'électrons d'une cathode dans le vide ou en atmosphère gazeuse. Les enveloppes sont habituellement en verre, mais parfois aussi en métal. Cette rubrique ne comprend pas les tubes cathodiques et les tubes et valves pour caméras de télévision. Toutefois, les tubes cathodiques sous une forme modifiée qui sont utilisés comme indicateurs d'accord (oeil magique) dans les appareils récepteurs de radio y sont compris. (CTCI Rev.3: 77625-0, 77627-0).

Transistors
Transistors

ISIC-BASED CODE - CODE BASE CITI

3832-28

Unit : Million units   Unité : En millions

Country or area	1990	1991	1992	1993	1994	1995	1996	1997	1998	1999	Pays ou zone
America, North	**463**	**483**	**730**	**47**	**97**	**94**	**85**	**147**	**156**	**170**	**Amérique du Nord**
Mexico	463	483	730	47	97	94	85	147	156	170	Mexique
America, South	**280**	**162**	**89**	**114**	**90**	**51**	**56**	**51**	**11**	**1**	**Amérique du Sud**
Brazil	280	162	89	114	90	51	56	51	11	1	Brésil
Asia	**72801**	**79183**	**69150**	**69442**	**76577**	**93321**	**89800**	**103583**	**101297**	**116625**	**Asie**
Hong Kong SAR[1]	...	...	...	5825	...	...	...	...	...	...	Hong-Kong RAS[1]
India	338	314	381	483	...	...	...	...	...	...	Inde
Japan	59495	65147	53984	54323	59498	68239	63259	76267	73512	83935	Japon
Korea, Republic of	7143	7897	8960	8811	10875	18878	20337	21112	21581	26486	Corée, République de
Europe	**620**	**2541**	**2436**	**2253**	**2540**	**2001**	**1389**	**1222**	**1393**	**1256**	**Europe**
Croatia	..	1	0	0	0	0	0	...	...	...	Croatie
Czechoslovakia(former)	89	36	..	..	..	..	..	..	..	..	Tchécoslovaquie(anc.)
Germany	..	...	1852	1523	1779	...	632	440	...	...	Allemagne
German D.R.(former)	237	..	..	..	..	..	..	..	..	..	R.D.A. (anc.)
Hungary	18	1	3	...	...	...	...	...	...	...	Hongrie
Poland	176	66	35	20	10	8	8	4	1	0	Pologne
Slovenia	..	186	153	204	180	100	...	...	...	...	Slovénie
Spain	100	497	387	498	563	638	...	...	...	...	Espagne
Yugoslavia	..	15	6	1	1	2	2	3	1	1	Yougoslavie
Total	**74164**	**82369**	**72405**	**71856**	**79304**	**95467**	**91330**	**105003**	**102857**	**118052**	**Total**

General Note.

Semi-conductor crystal, usually of germanium or silicon, and two junctions, usually in an envelope of glass or plastic material. Crystal diodes (crystal plus one junction) are included. (SITC, Rev.3: 77632-0, 77633-0).

[1] 1996 data are confidential.

Remarque générale.

Cristal semi-conducteur, généralement de germanium ou de silicium, à deux jonctions, le plus souvent monté dans une enveloppe de verre ou de matière plastique. Cette rubrique comprend les diodes à cristal (cristal à une jonction). (CTCI, Rev.3: 77632-0, 77633-0).

[1] Pour 1996, les données sont confidentielles.

Sound recorders
Appareils d'enregistrement du son

ISIC-BASED CODE - CODE BASE CITI

3832-34

Unit : Thousand units   Unité : En milliers

Country or area	1990	1991	1992	1993	1994	1995	1996	1997	1998	1999	Pays ou zone
America, North	**916**	**908**	**894**	**859**	**832**	**831**	**831**	**831**	**831**	**831**	**Amérique du Nord**
Mexico	85	77	63	28	1	...	...	...	...	...	Mexique
United States[1]	831	...	...	...	...	...	...	...	...	...	Etats-Unis[1]
Asia	**84362**	**85139**	**76002**	**76644**	**122619**	**113782**	**119698**	**125214**	**133308**	**140751**	**Asie**
Armenia	..	99	78	54	44	10	0	0	0	0	Arménie
China	30235	28737	32318	36429	83956	...	...	...	...	...	Chine
India	1183	1535	1203	1114	1157	1066	1326	1300	1416	877	Inde
Indonesia	35	53	54	87	198	...	...	...	...	...	Indonésie
Japan	43670	48232	39402	36862	32049	30515	24636	...	...	...	Japon
Kazakhstan	..	131	114	124	115	23	18	3	...	...	Kazakhstan
Korea, Republic of	9171	6229	2751	1974	...	...	...	...	...	...	Corée, République de
Turkey	...	123	82	0	...	...	...	...	...	...	Turquie
Europe	**2014**	**7153**	**5419**	**4069**	**1754**	**1182**	**692**	**669**	**684**	**615**	**Europe**
Belarus	..	242	210	130	72	30	5	1	11	9	Bélarus
Croatia	..	2	0	0	0	0	0	...	...	...	Croatie
Denmark[2]	...	15	12	...	...	...	...	...	...	...	Danemark[2]
Czechoslovakia(former)	47	2	..	..	..	..	..	..	..	..	Tchécoslovaquie(anc.)
Germany	..	...	...	...	...	210	174	162	151	...	Allemagne
German D.R.(former)	67	..	..	..	..	..	..	..	..	..	R.D.A. (anc.)
Hungary	715	98	12	8	...	...	...	...	...	...	Hongrie
Latvia	..	67	38	6	3	8	3	...	...	7	Lettonie
Lithuania	..	174	86	37	13	7	3	2	1	0	Lituanie
Poland	299	108	59	22	14	12	13	17	15	3	Pologne
Russian Federation	..	3623	2775	2215	731	343	102	39	9	7	Fédération de Russie
Slovenia	..	436	40	31	63	85	...	...	...	...	Slovénie
Spain[3] [4]	...	...	...	...	...	...	...	23	...	4	Espagne[3] [4]
Ukraine	..	2028	1828	1246	218	106	44	25	13	10	Ukraine
United Kingdom	...	...	...	...	231	146	113	160	*230	...	Royaume-Uni
Yugoslavia, SFR	690	..	..	..	...	...	...	...	..	..	Yougoslavie, RSF
Total	**87292**	**93200**	**82315**	**81572**	**125205**	**115795**	**121221**	**126714**	**134823**	**142198**	**Total**

General Note.
Groove type in which a stylus cuts a groove and magnetic type in which the recording-head is essentially an electro-magnet.(SITC, Rev.3: 76384-0).

Remarque générale.
Enregistreurs mécaniques, dans lesquels un graveur creuse un sillon, et enregistreurs magnétiques, dans lesquels la tête d'enregistrement est essentiellement un électro-aimant. (CTCI, Rev.3: 76384-0).

[1] Shipments.
[2] Sales.
[3] 1994-1996 data are confidential.
[4] 1998 data are confidential.

[1] Expéditions.
[2] Ventes.
[3] Les donnée de 1994 à 1996 sont confidentielles.
[4] Pour 1998, les données sont confidentielles.

Sound reproducers
Appareils de reproduction du son

ISIC-BASED CODE - CODE BASE CITI

3832-37

Unit : Thousand units   Unité : En milliers

Country or area	1990	1991	1992	1993	1994	1995	1996	1997	1998	1999	Pays ou zone
America, North	**174**	**195**	**159**	**111**	**110**	**82**	**62**	**18**	**0**	**0**	**Amérique du Nord**
Mexico	174	195	159	111	110	82	62	...	...	...	Mexique
America, South	**121**	**121**	**148**	**115**	**117**	**102**	**121**	**121**	**121**	**121**	**Amérique du Sud**
Colombia	...	...	70	73	73	62	...	...	...	...	Colombie
Ecuador	...	...	78	42	44	40	...	...	...	...	Equateur
Asia	**11616**	**11538**	**10091**	**7286**	**8558**	**8076**	**7113**	**5874**	**5483**	**5483**	**Asie**
Japan	5379	5654	4234	3333	3075	2593	1630	...	...	...	Japon
Korea, Republic of	6237	5884	5857	3953	...	...	...	...	...	...	Corée, République de
Europe	**6428**	**8722**	**6798**	**4648**	**5078**	**6202**	**6284**	**6650**	**3426**	**2875**	**Europe**
Croatia	..	12	3	0	0	0	0	...	...	...	Croatie
Denmark[1]	53	36	29	19	11	5	0	0	0	0	Danemark[1]
Germany	..	7514	5830	3937	4122	5114	...	5836	...	...	Allemagne
Germany(Fed.Rep.)[2]	5203	..	..	..	..	..	..	..	..	..	Allemagne(Rép.féd.)[2]
Hungary	2	...	...	...	...	...	...	...	...	...	Hongrie
Latvia	..	185	72	3	...	...	...	...	...	...	Lettonie
Poland	127	52	24	20	13	14	9	8	1	0	Pologne
Spain[3]	329	182	120	...	...	...	...	3	1	5	Espagne[3]
United Kingdom	...	...	...	559	736	874	687	...	...	...	Royaume-Uni
Yugoslavia	..	25	4	1	0	0	0	0	0	0	Yougoslavie
Total	**18339**	**20576**	**17196**	**12160**	**13862**	**14462**	**13579**	**12663**	**9029**	**8478**	**Total**

General Note.
Gramophones, record-players, automatic record changers, electric gramophones and magnetic sound reproducers. (SITC, Rev.3:76330-0, 76382-0, 76383-0).

Remarque générale.
Phonographes, tourne-disques manuels ou automatiques, phonographes électriques et appareils magnétiques de reproduction du son. (CTCI, Rev.3: 76330-0, 76382-0, 76383-0).

[1] Sales.
[2] Including sound recorders.
[3] 1993-1996 data are confidential.

[1] Ventes.
[2] Y compris les appareils d'enregistrement sonore.
[3] Les donnée de 1993 à 1996 sont confidentielles.

Gramophone records
Disques phonographiques

ISIC-BASED CODE - CODE BASE CITI

3832-40

Unit : Thousand units   Unité : En milliers

Country or area	1990	1991	1992	1993	1994	1995	1996	1997	1998	1999	Pays ou zone
Africa	364	412	436	436	436	436	445	451	457	463	**Afrique**
Kenya	364	412	436	436	436	436	...	...	...	...	Kenya
America, North	18000	11963	6163	6541	28150	225	34	43	6	0	**Amérique du Nord**
Mexico	18000	11963	6163	6541	28150	225	34	43	6	0	Mexique
America, South	9306	6434	7087	7791	7387	6522	6987	4740	3561	3109	**Amérique du Sud**
Brazil	285	354	228	348	676	1011	907	903	386	258	Brésil
Colombia	7906	...	5415	6259	5756	4634	...	2722	2060	...	Colombie
Ecuador	...	...	1444	1184	955	877	...	...	...	...	Equateur
Asia	0	0	0	12015	24047	35387	156249	208533	516401	1063393	**Asie**
Hong Kong SAR[1]	...	...	...	12015	24047	35387	156249	208533	516401	1063393	Hong-Kong RAS[1]
Europe	470304	487591	400252	420741	469967	413759	417563	420566	421952	403512	**Europe**
Bulgaria	2849	67	66	14	29	7	...	...	...	...	Bulgarie
Croatia	..	365	120	25	6	0	0	...	...	...	Croatie
Czechoslovakia(former)	11747	6650	..	..	..	..	..	..	...	...	Tchécoslovaquie(anc.)
Finland	1050	1776	1057	260	104	...	...	...	...	...	Finlande
Germany	..	...	335339	368597	431967	...	...	...	...	...	Allemagne
Germany(Fed.Rep.)	341187	..	..	..	..	..	..	..	..	..	Allemagne(Rép.féd.)
German D.R.(former)	2220	..	..	..	..	..	..	..	..	..	R.D.A. (anc.)
Greece	3454	3836	3840	...	...	...	...	...	...	...	Grèce
Hungary	...	..	3	2	...	...	...	5522	...	...	Hongrie
Latvia	..	7477	...	...	...	...	...	...	...	...	Lettonie
Poland	[2]4295	[2]1825	[2]435	143	2	55	...	...	...	...	Pologne
Russian Federation	..	49029	18972	8056	1664	278	11	0	0	...	Fédération de Russie
Spain[3]	10561	5693	2665	...	...	...	...	...	...	...	Espagne[3]
Sweden	...	...	...	...	...	...	...	4507	4628	3738	Suède
United Kingdom	[4] [5]86808	...	...	21849	12567	11157	15291	14409	19354	...	Royaume-Uni
Yugoslavia	..	186	68	11	1	1	...	...	...	...	Yougoslavie
USSR (former)	100936	..	..	..	..	..	..	..	..	..	**URSS (anc.)**
Oceania	15349	15349	15349	15349	15349	15349	15349	15349	15349	15349	**Océanie**
Australia[6]	15349	...	...	...	...	...	...	...	...	...	Australie[6]
Total	614259	521748	429287	462873	545336	471678	596626	649682	957726	1485827	**Total**

General Note.
Commercial records manufactured from shellac or resins mixed with inert materials (chalk, fine sand, slate powder etc.) and colouring (animal black etc.), or made from resins or other plastic materials (particularly in the case of micro-groove, long-playing or stereophonic records). Master records are excluded. (SITC, Rev.3: 89871-0).

Remarque générale.
Disques du commerce faits en gomme laque ou en résine mélangées à des matières inertes (craie, sable fin, poudre d'ardoise, etc.), et à des colorants (noir animal, etc.), ou composés de résines ou d'autres matières plastiques (particulièrement dans le cas des disques microsillon, des disques de longue durée et des disques stéréophoniques). Cette rubrique ne comprend pas les enregistrements originaux sur disque. (CTCI, Rev.3: 89871-0).

[1] Including compact disc and laser video disc.
[2] Data refer to recorded disks.
[3] Beginning 1993, data are confidential.
[4] Gramophone records pressed.
[5] Sales.
[6] Twelve months ending 30 June of year stated.

[1] Y compris les disques compacts et laser vidéo.
[2] Données se rapportent aux disques enregistrés.
[3] A partir de 1993, les données sont confidentielles.
[4] Disques phonographiques enregistrés.
[5] Ventes.
[6] Période de douze mois finissant le 30 juin de l'année indiquée.

Vacuum cleaners
Aspirateurs

ISIC-BASED CODE - CODE BASE CITI

3833-01

Unit : Thousand units   Unité : En milliers

Country or area	1990	1991	1992	1993	1994	1995	1996	1997	1998	1999	Pays ou zone
America, North	37	36	32	6	3	0	0	0	0	0	**Amérique du Nord**
Mexico	37	36	32	6	3	...	...	...	...	...	Mexique
America, South	520	416	513	552	599	732	749	964	829	855	**Amérique du Sud**
Brazil	377	238	288	287	312	427	438	619	546	593	Brésil
Chile	120	142	189	229	251	257	275	309	247	226	Chili
Colombia	23	...	...	...	36	48	...	...	...	...	Colombie
Asia	9022	10870	9951	10261	9850	11017	10852	11217	10168	9821	**Asie**
Hong Kong SAR[1]	502	2330	...	...	943	...	...	...	...	...	Hong-Kong RAS[1]
Japan[2]	6851	6981	6465	6331	6355	6595	6708	6860	5871	5686	Japon[2]
Kazakhstan	..	15	22	49	21	6	3	0	...	...	Kazakhstan
Korea, Republic of	1114	939	1219	1357	1581	2037	...	...	...	...	Corée, République de
Kyrgyzstan	..	0	3	0	4	0	0	0	...	...	Kirghizistan
Turkey	555	605	984	1266	946	1121	1127	1247	1092	834	Turquie
Europe	17134	24638	22923	21533	19940	18947	18715	18936	17519	19196	**Europe**
Belarus	..	...	1	0	12	7	6	4	6	4	Bélarus
Bulgaria	1	12	14	5	5	4	3	1	...	...	Bulgarie
Denmark[3]	153	147	169	148	159	138	71	83	198	154	Danemark[3]
Czechoslovakia(former)	700	781	...	...	...	...	...	...	...	..	Tchécoslovaquie(anc.)
France	1925	2798	2865	2565	[4]2208	[4]2379	[4]2919	[4]2407	[4]2412	[4]1909	France
Germany	..	7155	6546	5793	...	6173	5984	6249	5577	...	Allemagne
Germany(Fed.Rep.)	5494	..	..	..	..	..	..	..	..	..	Allemagne(Rép.féd.)
German D.R.(former)	1581	..	..	..	..	..	..	..	..	..	R.D.A. (anc.)
Hungary	49	14	45	...	33	136	126	271	332	...	Hongrie
Italy	1373	1596	1743	1920	2331	2264	2024	1960	1780	1928	Italie
Lithuania	..	250	169	96	44	22	6	9	1	1	Lituanie
Poland	913	857	961	1001	1143	1156	1307	1297	1578	1996	Pologne
Romania[2]	132	147	154	171	115	145	231	202	206	165	Roumanie[2]
Russian Federation	..	4707	4319	3657	1553	1001	691	610	450	745	Fédération de Russie
Slovenia	..	252	255	287	271	352	465	390	470	467	Slovénie
Spain	657	703	684	...	...	...	...	...	...	...	Espagne
Sweden	686	698	636	692	757	731	614	894	1039	1155	Suède
Ukraine	..	1044	888	920	405	285	114	132	123	128	Ukraine
United Kingdom	...	...	...	[4]3467	[4]4010	...	...	3742	*2660	...	Royaume-Uni
Yugoslavia	..	1	1	1	1	1	1	1	1	1	Yougoslavie
T.F.Yug.Rep. Macedonia	..	2	3	3	1	...	...	...	...	...	L'ex-RY Macédoine
USSR (former)	5774	..	..	..	..	..	..	..	..	..	URSS (anc.)
Total	32487	35960	33419	32352	30392	30697	30317	31116	28517	29871	**Total**

General Note.
Vacuum cleaners of all types, including those with rotating brushes or carpet-beating devices and/or supplementary attachments. (SITC, Rev.3: 77571-1).

Remarque générale.
Aspirateurs de poussières de tous types, y compris les appareils comportant des dispositifs accessoires, tels que brosses rotatives et batteurs de tapis. (CTCI, Rev.3: 77571-1).

[1] 1996 data are confidential.
[2] For household use only.
[3] Sales.
[4] Shipments.

[1] Pour 1996, les données sont confidentielles.
[2] Pour usages domestiques seulement.
[3] Ventes.
[4] Expéditions.

Shavers and hair clippers, electric
Rasoirs et tondeuses, électriques

ISIC-BASED CODE - CODE BASE CITI

3833-04

Unit : Thousand units   Unité : En milliers

Country or area	1990	1991	1992	1993	1994	1995	1996	1997	1998	1999	Pays ou zone
Asia	**17062**	**16924**	**15582**	**13852**	**15033**	**13014**	**12441**	**11253**	**10830**	**11283**	**Asie**
Hong Kong SAR	5332	2485	...	...	...	88	...	...	...	...	Hong-Kong RAS
Japan[1]	11730	14439	12947	11217	12398	12926	9806	8618	8195	8648	Japon[1]
Europe	**9906**	**13802**	**13644**	**12627**	**9970**	**9881**	**9659**	**9741**	**9708**	**9967**	**Europe**
France[2]	552	510	273	485	279	...	...	...	...	...	France[2]
Germany	..	...	8415	8281	7682	...	8575	8771	8787	...	Allemagne
Germany(Fed.Rep.)	9354	..	..	..	..	..	..	..	..	..	Allemagne(Rép.féd.)
Russian Federation[1]	..	..	...	...	...	675	547	498	448	571	Fédération de Russie[1]
Slovenia	..	121	0	23	22	25	1	0	0	...	Slovénie
Ukraine[1]	..	4341	4255	3167	1347	514	345	338	396	424	Ukraine[1]
Total	**26968**	**30726**	**29226**	**26479**	**25003**	**22895**	**22100**	**20994**	**20538**	**21250**	**Total**

General Note.
Shavers and hair clippers which have a built-in electric motor, including those for shearing sheep or for grooming horses,clipping cattle etc. (SITC, Rev.3:, Rev.3: 77541-0, 77542-0).

Remarque générale.
Rasoirs et tondeuses entraînés par un moteur électrique incorporé, y compris les appareils utilisés pour tondre les moutons ou pour panser les chevaux, le bétail, etc. (CTCI, Rev.3: 77541-0, 77542-0).

[1] Electric shavers only.
[2] Including hairdryers.

[1] Rasoirs électriques seulement.
[2] Y compris les sèche-cheveux.

Heaters, electric space
Appareils électriques pour le chauffage des locaux

ISIC-BASED CODE - CODE BASE CITI

3833-07

Unit : Thousand units   Unité : En milliers

Country or area	1990	1991	1992	1993	1994	1995	1996	1997	1998	1999	Pays ou zone
America, North	**4251**	**3795**	**2861**	**3751**	**5233**	**5670**	**5360**	**5017**	**4276**	**4207**	**Amérique du Nord**
Mexico	65	20	58	45	21	55	102	13	80	187	Mexique
United States[2]	[1]4186	[1]3775	[1]2803	[1]3706	5212	5615	5258	5004	4196	4020	Etats-Unis[2]
Asia	**2564**	**2608**	**2267**	**2806**	**2633**	**3021**	**3739**	**3918**	**2796**	**3105**	**Asie**
Azerbaijan	..	106	74	71	32	10	0	0	0	0	Azerbaïdjan
Hong Kong SAR	...	633	...	...	...	...	...	...	...	...	Hong-Kong RAS
Georgia	..					26	0	2	0	0	Géorgie
Japan	1843	1617	1043	1422	1599	1936	1888	1367	1042	1160	Japon
Kazakhstan	..	130	128	142	55	32	4	10	...	...	Kazakhstan
Turkey	88	85	357	512	293	384	1214	1906	1121	1312	Turquie
Europe	**16102**	**17750**	**17247**	**23263**	**18792**	**14907**	**14781**	**14674**	**13602**	**14149**	**Europe**
Austria	283	...	...	...	...	448	436	447	289	270	Autriche
Belgium[3]	...	...	...	...	...	...	8	8	12	14	Belgique[3]
Bulgaria	324	137	201	152	110	117	82	84	45	48	Bulgarie
Croatia	..	67	60	34	34	43	51	69	31	...	Croatie
Denmark[4]	...	...	...	96	72	63	82	125	85	...	Danemark[4]
Czechoslovakia(former)	80	38	..	..	..	..	..	..	..	..	Tchécoslovaquie(anc.)
Estonia	..	91	43	21	42	28	66	68	81	85	Estonie
Finland	518	379	*315	*290	*245	*182	*224	*207	*208	*290	Finlande
France[2]	3350	3396	3073	2898	2593	2741	2929	2981	2782	2956	France[2]
Germany	..	3865	3350	3011	3232	...	...	...	...	...	Allemagne
Germany(Fed.Rep.)	2825	..	..	..	..						Allemagne(Rép.féd.)
Greece	120	102	94	56	56	42	52	48	59	...	Grèce
Hungary	31	34	34	...	...	...	...	316	383	159	Hongrie
Norway	1073	845	803	840	...	...	...	...	...	...	Norvège
Poland	359	174	123	150	144	120	187	190	152	144	Pologne
Portugal	617	620	476	368	521	667	844	1041	980	976	Portugal
Slovakia	..	...	...	...	54	35	45	98	51	61	Slovaquie
Slovenia	..	23	38	50	53	46	58	56	54	57	Slovénie
Spain	1436	1490	1701	863	1083	1198	1237	989	1090	1348	Espagne
Sweden	...	...	...	...	...	...	284	303	404	428	Suède
Ukraine	..	1154	1709	9340	4574	258	180	133	156	174	Ukraine
United Kingdom	...	...	...	4056	4107	4066	...	3140	*2398	...	Royaume-Uni
Yugoslavia	..	103	161	100	95	73	48	116	87	54	Yougoslavie
Oceania	**423**	**497**	**321**	**220**	**365**	**365**	**365**	**365**	**365**	**365**	**Océanie**
Australia[5]	423	497	321	220	...	...	...	...	...	...	Australie[5]
Total	**23340**	**24650**	**22695**	**30040**	**27024**	**23963**	**24245**	**23974**	**21039**	**21826**	**Total**

General Note.

Electric fires, including portable types with parabolic reflectors, sometimes with built-in fans, convection heaters, and electric heaters in which electric elements heat up oil which circulates in the radiator. (SITC, Rev.3: 77582-0).

[1] Portable electric heaters.
[2] Shipments.
[3] Incomplete coverage.
[4] Sales.
[5] Twelve months ending 30 June of year stated.

Remarque générale.

Radiateurs, y compris les appareils portatifs à réflecteur parabolique parfois muni d'un ventileur incorporé. Radiateurs par convection et radiateurs à circulation de liquide, dans lesquels les éléments chauffants agissent sur de l'huile circulant dans le radiateur. (CTCI, Rev.3: 77582-0).

[1] Radiateurs électriques portatifs seulement.
[2] Expéditions.
[3] Couverture incomplète.
[4] Ventes.
[5] Période de douze mois finissant le 30 juin de l'année indiquée.

Irons, electric smoothing
Fers à repasser électriques de tous types

ISIC-BASED CODE - CODE BASE CITI

3833-10

Unit : Thousand units

Unité : En milliers

Country or area	1990	1991	1992	1993	1994	1995	1996	1997	1998	1999	Pays ou zone
America, North	**7200**	**4018**	**3941**	**12356**	**9721**	**13391**	**13957**	**14605**	**17146**	**15191**	Amérique du Nord
Mexico	640	420	665	#7878	5243	8913	9479	10127	12668	10713	Mexique
United States[1]	6560	3598	3276	...	...	...	...	...	...	...	Etats-Unis[1]
America, South	**5356**	**4329**	**3750**	**5190**	**5055**	**5626**	**4957**	**6443**	**7057**	**7436**	Amérique du Sud
Brazil	4787	3300	2853	4066	3840	4498	3615	4997	5538	5804	Brésil
Chile	93	81	78	61	25	6	0	0	0	0	Chili
Colombia	423	...	762	1039	1147	1040	...	...	...	...	Colombie
Peru	54	66	57	24	43	82	71	78	54	*69	Pérou
Asia	**22377**	**23389**	**25443**	**30513**	**26738**	**43824**	**27617**	**24713**	**31653**	**31687**	Asie
Armenia	..	322	96	127	76	41	22	6	4	1	Arménie
China	14056	14490	17223	22292	19047	35322	19860	17014	...	...	Chine
Hong Kong SAR	...	...	2472	...	...	...	...	...	...	...	Hong-Kong RAS
Georgia	..	...	...	...	95	67	65	12	5	6	Géorgie
Indonesia	...	...	288	...	...	...	...	...	...	...	Indonésie
Japan	4624	4619	4556	4416	3950	3839	3390	3189	3108	2798	Japon
Kyrgyzstan	..	54	72	35	18	8	17	14	15	16	Kirghizistan
Myanmar[2] [3]	2	2	1	...	...	...	...	...	...	...	Myanmar[2] [3]
Turkey	...	...	637	764	713	1725	1451	1654	2233	1982	Turquie
Uzbekistan	..	1	17	46	77	60	50	62	...	...	Ouzbékistan
Europe	**23152**	**35879**	**34307**	**32279**	**25292**	**25096**	**23825**	**26712**	**24048**	**23877**	Europe
Belarus	..	50	210	441	360	243	239	274	241	279	Bélarus
Bulgaria	8	9	18	3	1	4	1	...	...	...	Bulgarie
Croatia	..	170	184	125	33	59	63	66	63	...	Croatie
France[1]	4308	6350	6768	6421	6865	7383	7934	10449	8419	8206	France[1]
Germany	..	...	...	5163	4318	...	...	...	...	...	Allemagne
Germany(Fed.Rep.)	5219	..	..	..	..	..	..	..	..	..	Allemagne(Rép.féd.)
German D.R.(former)	2429	..	..	..	..	..	..	..	..	..	R.D.A. (anc.)
Greece	1	...	...	...	...	...	...	...	...	...	Grèce
Hungary	185	84	73	...	...	...	...	...	...	...	Hongrie
Italy	878	938	773	548	486	770	460	615	821	921	Italie
Latvia	..	500	361	66	14	11	8	...	31	20	Lettonie
Poland	1189	1049	928	735	777	608	262	211	106	84	Pologne
Portugal	33	12	29	17	165	...	...	...	...	...	Portugal
Republic of Moldova	..	984	817	[4]439	[4]168	[4]65	[4]20	[4]2	[4]7	[4]5	Rép. de Moldova
Russian Federation	..	8444	7718	7647	2736	1981	1264	954	760	1134	Fédération de Russie
Slovenia	..	358	294	277	420	514	448	231	301	...	Slovénie
Spain	4360	3966	3377	2795	3070	3432	3449	4077	...	2937	Espagne
Ukraine	..	3661	3432	2838	1300	492	121	123	193	261	Ukraine
United Kingdom	...	...	...	4630	4454	...	...	...	...	...	Royaume-Uni
Yugoslavia	..	20	41	19	10	5	0	0	0	...	Yougoslavie
Total	**58086**	**67614**	**67440**	**80337**	**66806**	**87937**	**70356**	**72472**	**79904**	**78191**	Total

General Note.
Smoothing irons, whether for domestic use or for tailors, dressmakers etc.
(SITC, Rev.3: 77584-0).

Remarque générale.
Fers à repasser, pour usage domestique ou servant à des tailleurs, des couturières, etc. (CTCI, Rev.3: 77584-0).

[1] Shipments.
[2] Twelve months ending 30 September of year stated.
[3] Government production only.
[4] Excluding Transnistria region.

[1] Expéditions.
[2] Période de douze mois finissant le 30 septembre de l'année indiquée.
[3] Production de l'Etat seulement.
[4] Non compris la région de Transnistria.

Fuses, electrical
Coupe-circuits électriques

ISIC-BASED CODE - CODE BASE CITI

3839-01

Unit : Thousand units   Unité : En milliers

Country or area	1990	1991	1992	1993	1994	1995	1996	1997	1998	1999	Pays ou zone
America, South	**677**	**630**	**666**	**535**	**309**	**567**	**489**	**517**	**342**	**254**	**Amérique du Sud**
Colombia	...	...	666	535	309	567	...	517	342	...	Colombie
Asia	**27570**	**24295**	**19085**	**21353**	**17985**	**13357**	**13441**	**24907**	**22608**	**21418**	**Asie**
Indonesia	5962	7311	...	...	...	...	...	...	...	...	Indonésie
Turkey	21608	16984	12448	14716	11348	6720	6804	18270	15971	14781	Turquie
Europe	**652143**	**756669**	**819528**	**676822**	**806404**	**1153695**	**949006**	**1056538**	**1143194**	**1130195**	**Europe**
Austria	2516	2757	...	...	...	...	...	...	...	...	Autriche
Croatia	..	478	497	922	465	620	648	2639	2726	...	Croatie
Denmark [1]	524	501	513	561	648	766	...	...	...	...	Danemark [1]
Finland	2555	2111	516	771	948	775	860	...	...	...	Finlande
Germany	...	...	...	524482	650358	980805	787071	854793	935989	...	Allemagne
Germany(Fed.Rep.)	542979					..				..	Allemagne(Rép.féd.)
Greece	9755	7635	9701	...	6171	7170	8735	8765	7831	...	Grèce
Hungary	68196	47119	48511	47985	56626	58144	55772	71631	71396	71009	Hongrie
Latvia	..	...	...	...	...	...	...	...	76	55	Lettonie
Portugal	867	861	...	...	...	...	...	...	...	...	Portugal
Slovenia	..	15937	40911	44954	43887	41026	34515	47752	56648	49072	Slovénie
Spain	7619	13500	14221	...	25398	42486	38506	47433	...	...	Espagne
Sweden	...	...	...	...	...	...	...	18169	17672	15555	Suède
Yugoslavia	..	...	...	...	...	...	1518	1083	1247	972	Yougoslavie
Total	**680390**	**781594**	**839278**	**698709**	**824698**	**1167619**	**962935**	**1081961**	**1166144**	**1151867**	**Total**

General Note.
Cartridge and socket-type non-renewable or renewable fuses for the protection of electrical circuits. (SITC, Rev.3: 77241-0).

Remarque générale.
Coupe-circuits à fusible du type à cartouche ou à bouchon, renouvelables ou non, servant à protéger des circuits électriques. (CTCI, Rev.3: 77241-0).

[1] Sales.

[1] Ventes.

Switches, electric
Interrupteurs électriques

ISIC-BASED CODE - CODE BASE CITI

3839-04

Unit : Thousand units   Unité : En milliers

Country or area	1990	1991	1992	1993	1994	1995	1996	1997	1998	1999	Pays ou zone
America, South	**109582**	**152471**	**118647**	**130637**	**160633**	**175587**	**148578**	**148679**	**145927**	**152869**	**Amérique du Sud**
Brazil	80732	123640	89834	101843	131858	146842	119904	121585	115454	124261	Brésil
Colombia	...	...	...	...	...	...	...	24602	28023	...	Colombie
Peru	...	...	...	...	...	2433	2362	2492	2450	2295	Pérou
Asia	**1005254**	**978163**	**997835**	**1028952**	**1173617**	**1353729**	**1179359**	**1223082**	**913182**	**1207241**	**Asie**
Bangladesh	1127	23147	27540	...	...	...	...	...	...	...	Bangladesh
Indonesia	17766	3113	2321	6620	15606	...	...	...	...	...	Indonésie
Korea, Republic of	965997	935774	932735	970899	1119302	1294956	1127574	1156927	857332	...	Corée, République de
Turkey	20364	16129	35239	34162	21438	32660	25754	40205	29981	31325	Turquie
Europe	**568384**	**530411**	**462176**	**401216**	**418729**	**995703**	**1012872**	**1113935**	**1245946**	**1170934**	**Europe**
Austria[1]	6700	7664	6614	6974	6101	...	...	...	...	...	Autriche[1]
Belgium	...	...	...	...	34667	42864	36443	41109	40100	35488	Belgique
Croatia	..	2135	2735	811	415	1135	1005	2749	2251	...	Croatie
Denmark[2]	6673	4707	5852	5238	5219	6061	6267	7347	8317	7168	Danemark[2]
Czech Republic	..	...	...	...	478	390	383	7591	6653	13520	République tchèque
Finland	2636	4050	3673	4879	5106	6077	7977	8117	15384	11180	Finlande
Germany	..	382596	314372	253812	272429	851163	811085	916018	1014292	...	Allemagne
Germany(Fed.Rep.)	429878	..	..	..	..	..	..	..	..	..	Allemagne(Rép.féd.)
Greece	3543	2904	3031	4748	3722	4420	2791	3367	3238	...	Grèce
Hungary	5071	4479	2750	5571	4762	4134	16574	27803	20802	8955	Hongrie
Latvia	..	...	...	1432	696	777	590	960	396	2188	Lettonie
Portugal	...	...	#8168	7143	4127	3141	2919	2229	1990	1893	Portugal
Slovakia	..	..	...	...	...	...	...	...	2195	2237	Slovaquie
Slovenia	..	5903	3987	1925	2266	2590	3404	4623	4616	5998	Slovénie
Spain	67093	67589	65760	63501	73749	61582	112393	82492	116283	120361	Espagne
Sweden	...	...	...	...	...	...	...	1295	3594	3015	Suède
Yugoslavia	..	1296	1158	980	141	274	135	152	157	546	Yougoslavie
Total	**1683220**	**1661045**	**1578657**	**1560805**	**1752979**	**2525019**	**2340810**	**2485696**	**2305054**	**2531044**	**Total**

General Note.
Apparatus for making and breaking electric circuits of single, double or triple poles. (SITC, Rev.3: 77244-0).

Remarque générale.
Appareils uni-, bi- ou tri-polaires servant à établir ou interrompre des circuits électriques. (CTCI, Rev.3: 77244-0).

[1] Beginning 1995, data are confidential.
[2] Sales.

[1] A partir de 1995, les données sont confidentielles
[2] Ventes.

Wire and cable, insulated
Fils et câbles électriques isolés

ISIC-BASED CODE - CODE BASE CITI

3839-07

Unit : Metric tons   Unité : Tonnes métriques

Country or area	1990	1991	1992	1993	1994	1995	1996	1997	1998	1999	Pays ou zone
Africa											**Afrique**
Algeria	16679	17510	14235	11806	10189	14613	6680	9552	11095	12691	Algérie
Angola	327	112	223	...	...	...	...	...	...	...	Angola
Egypt[1]	72000	86000	82000	79000	89000	88000	...	...	...	...	Egypte[1]
Nigeria	...	...	...	...	585	594	...	...	...	...	Nigéria
United Rep.Tanzania	761	878	1029	940	963	710	590	734	...	...	Rép. Unie de Tanzanie
America, North											**Amérique du Nord**
Mexico	29229	28838	30291	60829	65946	51089	75951	97601	115592	122021	Mexique
United States[2][3]	1357238	1301447	1351940	1573266	1720951	2218907	2295223	2588495	2999956	2945774	Etats-Unis[2][3]
America, South											**Amérique du Sud**
Brazil	98061	112433	107919	111590	115641	119351	132014	146663	157392	149623	Brésil
Colombia	...	...	13029	10619	3435	7424	...	10100	12647	...	Colombie
Ecuador	...	...	4770	4916	7605	7099	8751	44816	36968	...	Equateur
Asia											**Asie**
Azerbaijan	..	17971	3543	2127	1189	222	686	385	337	68	Azerbaïdjan
Hong Kong SAR[4]	1140481	9235827	...	1126968	608151	93838	36553	32483	33671	76786	Hong-Kong RAS[4]
Georgia[4]	..	...	4222	3067	664	355	830	382	1145	430	Géorgie[4]
India[5]	23031	19109	19634	...	...	...	...	...	...	...	Inde[5]
Indonesia	...	...	89249	113064	334508	...	...	...	...	...	Indonésie
Korea, Republic of	207664	212870	235698	255207	290092	...	...	...	...	...	Corée, République de
Kyrgyzstan	..	15545	5082	2704	757	840	529	181	255	126	Kirghizistan
Lao People's Dem. Rep.[4]	...	...	...	...	2072	2192	...	...	...	...	Rép. dém. pop. lao[4]
Malaysia	44380	57791	69323	85245	72129	91384	99239	122293	80864	74841	Malaisie
Turkey	[4]239476	[4]226717	15836	22832	19251	30167	35474	50059	53636	53816	Turquie
Europe											**Europe**
Austria	[6]56375	[6]64970	[6]60924	[6]60583	[6]56692	113026	107235	105397	99517	82518	Autriche
Belgium	[2][7][8]152008	[2][7][8]158784	[2][7][8]183022	[2][7][8]168636	94982	103014	15990	105766	98114	107284	Belgique
Bulgaria	18771	7125	10101	10761	8784	9140	9039	6905	18933	14583	Bulgarie
Croatia	..	17441	16301	15751	18538	17864	16209	18377	17234	...	Croatie
Czechoslovakia(former)	147772	109775	..	..	..	..	..	..	..	..	Tchécoslovaquie(anc.)
Czech Republic			82599	85433	61683	64108	73952	71526	80750	92710	République tchèque
Finland	[4]472150	*[4]339978	[4]373229	*[4]365030	*[4]439570	*[4]286422	*[4]399482	97216	111216	101868	Finlande
Germany		1208143	1206971	1054884	1076559	931044	864960	915679	869857	...	Allemagne
Germany(Fed.Rep.)	1038195	..	..	..	..	..	..	..	..	..	Allemagne(Rép.féd.)
German D.R.(former)	192561	..	..	..	..	..	..	..	..	..	R.D.A. (anc.)
Greece	27345	31091	41263	95587	99994	100859	85402	96850	110011	...	Grèce
Hungary	36958	36217	44580	43486	34731	31383	47589	53483	31661	53616	Hongrie
Latvia	..	...	...	...	0	0	0	0	0	81	Lettonie
Lithuania	..	9070	2980	1592	368	710	2060	1236	787	2183	Lituanie
Poland	170030	162797	146167	156035	147673	179193	201032	217851	236154	255330	Pologne
Portugal	57286	47140	47660	40493	41352	55001	64381	79556	85848	115605	Portugal
Romania[4]	244000	100000	99000	111634	103545	78152	150094	100353	105255	125533	Roumanie[4]
Slovakia	..	..	14338	19305	22720	29781	27153	39479	33460	35806	Slovaquie
Slovenia	..	410	53	487	95	...	951	1539	1668	1842	Slovénie
Spain	...	...	...	186022	229964	258311	237358	269345	...	...	Espagne
Sweden	...	...	...	...	...	...	...	142745	143213	163248	Suède
United Kingdom	...	...	...	447769	533453	567376	512058	...	...	...	Royaume-Uni
Yugoslavia	..	80428	53307	20221	23020	23349	31515	29755	35702	24960	Yougoslavie
T.F.Yug.Rep. Macedonia	..	5084	6160	7715	6654	8335	8656	15662	16119	18070	L'ex-RY Macédoine
Oceania											**Océanie**
Australia	27562	45236	50644	58013	65060	74571	73409	...	...	...	Australie

General Note.
Wire, cable, braids, bars, strips etc. covered with an insulating material for use in conducting electric energy, whether or not covered with a metal sheath or fitted with connectors. Enamelled, lacquered or anodized wire and co-axial cable are included.(SITC, Rev.3: 77310-0).

Remarque générale.
Fils, câbles, tresses, barres, bandes, etc., recouverts de matière isolante et utilisés comme conducteurs électiques, qu'ils soient ou non recouverts d'une gaine en métal ou munis de connecteurs. Cette rubrique comprend les fils émaillés, laqués ou oxydés anodiquement et les câbles coaxiaux. (CTCI, Rev.3: 77310-0).

For footnotes, see end of table.   Voir la fin du tableau pour les notes.

Wire and cable, insulated (continued)
Fils et câbles électriques isolés (suite)

ISIC-BASED CODE - CODE BASE CITI

3839-07

Footnotes

[1] Including non-insulated cables.

[2] Shipments.

[3] Data refer to copper content of insulated wires and cables.

[4] In thousand metres.

[5] Production by large and medium scale establishments only.

[6] Excluding multi-polar insulated wire.

[7] Production by establishments employing 5 or more persons.

[8] Including conduits for interior electrical installations.

[9] Incomplete coverage.

Notes.

[1] Y compris fils et câbles non isolés.

[2] Expéditions.

[3] Données se rapportant à la teneur en cuivre des fils et câbles isolés.

[4] En milliers de mètres.

[5] Production des grandes et moyennes entreprises seulement.

[6] Non compris les fils isolés multipolaires.

[7] Production des établissements occupant 5 personnes ou plus.

[8] Y compris les canalisations pour installations électriques intérieures.

[9] Couverture incomplète.

Batteries and cells, primary
Piles et batteries de piles

ISIC-BASED CODE - CODE BASE CITI

3839-10

Unit : Million units   Unité : En million

Country or area	1990	1991	1992	1993	1994	1995	1996	1997	1998	1999	Pays ou zone
Africa											**Afrique**
Algeria	75	77	51	36	30	25	26	22	30	20	Algérie
Burkina Faso	37	25	30	24	...	...	...	...	...	...	Burkina Faso
Burundi	7	15	9	8	...	...	...	...	...	...	Burundi
Egypt	22	6	18	...	...	...	...	...	...	...	Egypte
Kenya	160	158	130	100	101	138	147	...	...	...	Kenya
Mali	18	19	11	8	7	9	10	...	...	...	Mali
Mozambique	6	5	...	2	3	1	...	...	...	...	Mozambique
Nigeria	...	65	66	74	81	81	...	...	...	...	Nigéria
United Rep.Tanzania	21	44	47	53	57	58	66	43	...	...	Rép. Unie de Tanzanie
America, North											**Amérique du Nord**
Jamaica	30	23	15	8	4	...	...	...	...	...	Jamaïque
Mexico	570	534	458	430	414	400	636	668	758	466	Mexique
America, South											**Amérique du Sud**
Colombia	...	...	239	222	185	126	...	...	...	...	Colombie
Ecuador	...	...	32	...	...	...	...	...	...	...	Equateur
Asia											**Asie**
Bangladesh	74	62	58	58	65	52	55	51	...	48	Bangladesh
China	645	693	793	1062	10071	12806	12212	13159	11899	12095	Chine
Hong Kong SAR [1]	1938	3713	882	1279	1155	1295	1590	1026	...	...	Hong-Kong RAS [1]
Georgia	..	...	5	2	0	0	0	0	0	0	Géorgie
India	1204	1319	1192	1284	1284	1442	1566	1931	1640	2007	Inde
Indonesia	1348	1407	1842	1920	2104	2718	...	1729	555	...	Indonésie
Iran(Islamic Rep. of) [2]	74	88	86	42	50	79	91	74	...	...	Iran(Rép. islamique) [2]
Iraq	...	...	33	...	...	...	...	...	...	...	Iraq
Japan	4113	4283	4385	4532	4479	4716	4523	4760	4921	4807	Japon
Korea, Republic of	492	525	527	574	647	732	696	638	654	648	Corée, République de
Myanmar [3]	8	6	3	4	1	1	2	3	1	2	Myanmar [3]
Nepal [4]	...	...	13	12	17	18	26	29	29	23	Népal [4]
Syrian Arab Republic	3	...	...	...	...	...	...	...	...	...	Rép. arabe syrienne
Thailand [5]	2	3	...	...	...	...	388	454	318	...	Thaïlande [5]
Turkey	25	26	24	31	24	15	10	8	5	0	Turquie
Viet Nam	66	72	72	...	...	...	...	...	...	...	Viet Nam
Yemen	..	5	5	28	13	34	24	0	...	...	Yémen
Europe											**Europe**
Austria [6]	38364	44049	44211	42002	42394	47036	...	...	...	...	Autriche [6]
Bulgaria	2	1	1	1	1	1	1	1	1	1	Bulgarie
Croatia	..	32	15	32	21	8	4	3	6	...	Croatie
Hungary	120	80	37	...	...	...	...	...	...	...	Hongrie
Italy [6]	9421	8983	6765	5016	6787	5671	4596	2760	2873	3038	Italie [6]
Lithuania	..	232	58	40	37	25	10	6	6	4	Lituanie
Poland	101	72	57	42	46	42	307	631	734	719	Pologne
Portugal	56	41	...	...	...	...	...	...	...	...	Portugal
Slovenia	..	22	16	15	12	10	4	4	1	0	Slovénie
Spain	437	463	575	636	647	403	432	471	533	490	Espagne
United Kingdom	...	...	...	302	353	347	166	71	*98	...	Royaume-Uni
Yugoslavia	..	2721	1082	68	1350	8110	12497	1565	750	...	Yougoslavie

General Note.
A primary cell consists basically of a container holding a solid or a liquid electrolyte (ammonium chloride) in which are immersed two electrodes. Cells may be grouped together in batteries, either in series or in parallel or a combination of both. The various types of cells include dry cells, wet cells, inert cells and concentration cells. (SITC, Rev.3: 77811-0).

[1] Beginning 1998, data are confidential.
[2] Production by establishments employing 50 or more persons.
[3] Government production only.
[4] Twelve months beginning 16 July of year stated.
[5] Beginning 1999, series discontinued.
[6] In metric tons.

Remarque générale.
Une pile consiste essentiellement en un récipient contenant un électrolyte solide ou liquide (chlorure d'ammonium) dans lequel deux électrodes sont immergées. Les piles peuvent être groupées en série ou en parallèle, ou en mixte, pour donner des batteries de piles. Les divers types de piles sonts: les piles sèches, les piles à liquide, les piles amorçables et les piles de concentration. (CTCI, Rev.3: 77811-0).

[1] A partir de 1998, les données sont confidentielles.
[2] Production des établissements occupant 50 personnes ou plus.
[3] Production de l'Etat seulement.
[4] Période de douze mois commençant le 16 juillet de l'année indiquée.
[5] A partir de 1999, série abandonnée.
[6] En tonnes métriques.

Accumulators, electric, for motor vehicles
Accumulateurs pour véhicules automobiles

ISIC-BASED CODE - CODE BASE CITI

3839-13

Unit : Thousand units

Unité : En milliers

Country or area	1990	1991	1992	1993	1994	1995	1996	1997	1998	1999	Pays ou zone
Africa	**1821**	**2080**	**2148**	**2054**	**1994**	**2181**	**2075**	**2177**	**2251**	**2173**	**Afrique**
Algeria	586	548	566	546	501	459	504	501	540	474	Algérie
Egypt	626	...	974	...	...	1063	...	...	...	...	Egypte
Kenya	177	...	...	170	127	133	138	...	...	...	Kenya
Madagascar	9	70	12	12	...	...	...	...	...	...	Madagascar
Mozambique	22	15	...	21	15	11	13	8	14	15	Mozambique
Tunisia	401	410	432	417	438	489	507	556	575	553	Tunisie
America, North	**5076**	**5667**	**5690**	**9594**	**12598**	**8976**	**10519**	**12091**	**12954**	**14593**	**Amérique du Nord**
Barbados	14	22	23	31	27	29	28	24	17	10	Barbade
Mexico	5062	5645	5667	9563	12571	8947	10491	12067	12937	14583	Mexique
America, South	**5152**	**5713**	**4894**	**6083**	**6741**	**7541**	**8225**	**8963**	**8673**	**8733**	**Amérique du Sud**
Bolivia	6	6	6	23	56	24	*18	...	...	...	Bolivie
Brazil	3978	4433	3653	4645	5280	6295	6601	6905	6969	6929	Brésil
Chile	249	288	322	320	304	317	342	373	274	249	Chili
Colombia	...	...	669	862	903	638	...	1362	1154	...	Colombie
Ecuador	...	...	227	200	230	273	320	290	241	...	Equateur
Asia	**66005**	**63709**	**58490**	**61344**	**65848**	**64694**	**68641**	**68874**	**60846**	**62701**	**Asie**
Cyprus	*90	*92	46	...	...	112	...	...	...	...	Chypre
India[1]	3818	3734	2968	...	...	...	...	...	...	...	Inde[1]
Indonesia	...	...	6083	9923	12538	7916	...	9747	2245	...	Indonésie
Israel	375	372	460	455	438	576	564	...	...	...	Israël
Japan	29387	28121	26692	23868	23814	24512	24811	24269	23409	24129	Japon
Korea, Republic of	8912	8948	10514	11206	12972	15083	17240	17827	17176	17570	Corée, République de
Thailand	...	...	...	...	...	...	11513	9868	...	...	Thaïlande
Turkey	1171	1061	1036	1610	1804	2298	2846	2938	3067	2301	Turquie
Europe	**71994**	**128558**	**126968**	**125461**	**121530**	**145241**	**124899**	**119350**	**109721**	**122039**	**Europe**
Austria	...	...	...	...	...	3016	3611	3758	3982	3628	Autriche
Bulgaria	1104	836	1025	1013	914	852	780	831	747	574	Bulgarie
Croatia	..	171	181	203	124	162	159	185	100	...	Croatie
Finland	619	644	599	264	293	228	...	...	...	...	Finlande
France	11316	12665	11664	11280	11870	...	...	...	...	...	France
Germany	...	...	...	...	...	65283	41397	36315	41214	...	Allemagne
Greece	501	661	790	[2]270	[2]273	[2]327	[2]379	...	437	...	Grèce
Hungary	486	584	499	...	605	585	...	...	...	...	Hongrie
Portugal[3]	1576	1544	...	...	...	...	...	...	...	...	Portugal[3]
Russian Federation	..	7050	6103	6870	4198	3729	2759	2773	2346	3709	Fédération de Russie
Slovakia	..	..	...	...	...	...	...	...	113	59	Slovaquie
Slovenia	..	416	800	...	789	...	974	1138	1114	1084	Slovénie
Spain	5277	5574	6195	5522	...	...	...	...	...	...	Espagne
Sweden	...	1026	309	1752	1894	875	1768	1905	1035	471	Suède
United Kingdom	...	...	...	45477	43375	49549	52346	51178	*38205	...	Royaume-Uni
Yugoslavia	..	1016	689	311	455	560	783	883	793	558	Yougoslavie
T.F.Yug.Rep. Macedonia	..	409	491	386	279	209	201	262	129	119	L'ex-RY Macédoine
Total	**150049**	**205727**	**198189**	**204536**	**208711**	**228633**	**214359**	**211454**	**194445**	**210239**	**Total**

General Note.

A battery composed of several cells connected together in series, each of which consist essentially of a container holding the electrolyte in which are immersed two electrodes. A direct current is passed through the accumulator producing certain chemical changes (charging). When the terminals of the accumulator are subsequently connected to an external circuit these chemical changes reverse and produce a direct current in the external circuit (discharging). (SITC, Rev.3: 77812-0).

[1] Production by large and medium scale establishments only.
[2] Incomplete coverage.
[3] Excluding recomposed batteries.

Remarque générale.

Batteries composées de plusieurs éléments reliés en série, dont chacun consiste essentiellement en un récipient contenant un électrolyte dans lequel plongent deux électrodes. Le passage d'un courant continu dans l'accumulateur produit certaines réactions chimiques (charge). Si l'on connecte ensuite les bornes de l'accumulateur à un circuit extérieur, ces réactions chimiques s'effectuent en sens inverse, engendrant ainsi un courant continu dans le circuit extérieur (décharge). (CTCI, Rev.3: 77812-0).

[1] Production des grandes et moyennes entreprises seulement.
[2] Couverture incomplète.
[3] Non compris les piles reconstituées.

Lamps, electric
Lampes électriques

ISIC-BASED CODE - CODE BASE CITI

3839-16

Unit : Million units   Unité : En million

Country or area	1990	1991	1992	1993	1994	1995	1996	1997	1998	1999	Pays ou zone
Africa	**111**	**115**	**108**	**19**	**26**	**31**	**33**	**34**	**36**	**39**	**Afrique**
Algeria	26	25	21	10	16	21	22	26	27	30	Algérie
Egypt	80	84	83	4	4	3	...	...	...	...	Egypte
Kenya	5	6	4	4	6	7	8	...	...	...	Kenya
United Rep.Tanzania	0	0	...	1	0	0	0	0	...	...	Rép. Unie de Tanzanie
America, North	**2918**	**2890**	**3043**	**3187**	**3089**	**3160**	**3247**	**3349**	**3486**	**3585**	**Amérique du Nord**
Mexico	167	166	177	206	159	125	151	191	267	304	Mexique
United States	2751	2724	2866	2981	2930	...	...	...	...	...	Etats-Unis
America, South	**463**	**606**	**602**	**609**	**682**	**657**	**698**	**726**	**814**	**853**	**Amérique du Sud**
Argentina	9	89	99	114	139	133	153	141	160	189	Argentine
Brazil	355	372	353	333	369	348	383	376	435	476	Brésil
Chile	38	40	45	52	63	64	59	68	75	63	Chili
Colombia	56	...	...	...	...	...	...	121	115	...	Colombie
Ecuador	...	...	8	13	14	15	6	20	29	...	Equateur
Asia	**2974**	**3423**	**3349**	**3864**	**3138**	**3213**	**3693**	**4051**	**3422**	**3501**	**Asie**
Armenia	..	78	54	52	24	29	16	1	...	0	Arménie
Bangladesh	...	...	...	...	25	25	23	23	22	*22	Bangladesh
China	245	280	330	...	...	...	...	...	...	...	Chine
China, Macao, SAR	...	...	...	120	...	...	...	...	...	...	Chine, Macao PAS
India	[1]254	[1]280	[1]308	...	375	384	395	396	458	502	Inde
Indonesia	245	296	209	722	227	53	...	422	31	...	Indonésie
Iran(Islamic Rep. of)[2]	43	41	48	50	43	48	69	62	73	...	Iran(Rép. islamique)[2]
Japan	1868	1964	1904	1878	1835	1999	2200	2280	2028	2030	Japon
Kyrgyzstan	..	197	231	224	71	110	136	146	163	174	Kirghizistan
Myanmar[3]	1	2	1	0	0	...	1	1	1	1	Myanmar[3]
Pakistan	[4]56	[4]49	[4]25	41	43	42	46	56	63	67	Pakistan
Syrian Arab Republic	3	1	4	2	1	2	2	4	...	...	Rép. arabe syrienne
Thailand	20	19	...	...	...	...	...	...	...	...	Thaïlande
Turkey	94	71	71	74	70	96	105	236	124	106	Turquie
Europe	**3537**	**6018**	**8644**	**4520**	**4583**	**5592**	**5936**	**6465**	**7120**	**6190**	**Europe**
Austria[5][6]	36	...	...	...	...	...	0	0	...	...	Autriche[5][6]
Belarus[7]	..	301	278	180	142	130	124	127	105	91	Bélarus[7]
Croatia	..	30	17	15	12	11	14	14	13	...	Croatie
Denmark[8]	...	...	1	1	1	6	3	3	4	4	Danemark[8]
Czechoslovakia(former)	131	117	..	..	..	..	..	..	..	..	Tchécoslovaquie(anc.)
Germany	..	999	957	896	896	944	1016	1112	1188	...	Allemagne
Germany(Fed.Rep.)	1059	..	..	..	..	..	..	..	..	..	Allemagne(Rép.féd.)
German D.R.(former)	150	..	..	..	..	..	..	..	..	..	R.D.A. (anc.)
Hungary	429	483	446	...	...	...	...	...	...	...	Hongrie
Italy	767	693	718	667	584	673	765	744	748	727	Italie
Latvia	..	24	24	18	19	16	21	24	22	18	Lettonie
Poland	451	389	345	356	435	486	517	576	674	537	Pologne
Romania[9]	160	161	143	139	143	140	151	134	107	101	Roumanie[9]
Russian Federation	..	1037	981	874	537	610	576	564	568	650	Fédération de Russie
Slovakia	..	..	...	...	...	44	55	76	...	...	Slovaquie
Slovenia	..	14	11	10	9	10	10	9	10	...	Slovénie
Spain	69	69	67	223	221	219	216	223	...	154	Espagne
Sweden	41	37	37	31	3	...	...	1	5	3	Suède
Ukraine[7]	..	346	320	275	224	186	148	167	112	114	Ukraine[7]
United Kingdom	...	...	...	204	285	269	347	305	293	...	Royaume-Uni
Yugoslavia	..	1045	3963	105	546	1360	1499	1931	2584	1839	Yougoslavie
T.F.Yug.Rep. Macedonia	..	8	7	3	3	4	2	...	...	...	L'ex-RY Macédoine
USSR (former)[7]	2279	..	..	..	..	..	..	..	..	..	URSS (anc.)[7]
Total	**12283**	**13052**	**15747**	**12200**	**11519**	**12654**	**13608**	**14625**	**14878**	**14167**	**Total**

General Note.
Electric filament lamps of all shapes and wattages. Fluorescent tubes and special types of electric lamps are excluded. (SITC, Rev.3: 77821-0).

For footnotes, see end of table.

Remarque générale.
Lampes électriques à incandescence de toutes formes et de toutes puissances. Cette rubrique ne comprend pas les tubes fluorescents et les types spéciaux de lampes électriques. (CTCI, Rev.3: 77821-0).

Voir la fin du tableau pour les notes.

Footnotes
[1] Excluding miniature lamps.
[2] Production by establishments employing 10 or more persons.
[3] Government production only.
[4] Twelve months ending 30 June of year stated.
[5] 1995 data are confidential.
[6] Beginning 1998, data are confidential.
[7] Including fluorescent tubes and special type electric lamps.
[8] Sales.
[9] Including special-type electric lamps.

Notes.
[1] Non compris les lampes miniatures.
[2] Production des établissements occupant 10 personnes ou plus.
[3] Production de l'Etat seulement.
[4] Période de douze mois finissant le 30 juin de l'année indiquée.
[5] Pour 1995, les données sont confidentielles.
[6] A partir de 1998, les données sont confidentielles.
[7] Y compris les tubes fluorescents et les lampes électriques de types spéciaux.
[8] Ventes.
[9] Y compris les lampes électriques de type spécial.

Tubes, fluorescent
Tubes fluorescents

ISIC-BASED CODE - CODE BASE CITI

3839-19A

Unit : Thousand units

Unité : En milliers

Country or area	1990	1991	1992	1993	1994	1995	1996	1997	1998	1999	Pays ou zone
America, North	**502108**	**524181**	**568304**	**607573**	**613589**	**656192**	**689212**	**724862**	**765931**	**802172**	**Amérique du Nord**
Mexico	24935	22147	13121	15781	14725	11241	10947	13283	21038	23965	Mexique
United States	477173	502034	555183	591792	598864	...	...	...	...	...	Etats-Unis
America, South	**57137**	**56669**	**63316**	**65692**	**73832**	**72112**	**74737**	**71638**	**72214**	**87225**	**Amérique du Sud**
Argentina	4000	6000	5400	7200	4600	5000	7400	5300	5500	5800	Argentine
Bolivia	1	0	0	1	7	10	*8	...	...	...	Bolivie
Brazil	42122	35947	42693	43321	48341	47622	47284	48211	43504	60030	Brésil
Chile	6084	6545	7209	8442	9957	9157	11867	11894	13093	10061	Chili
Colombia	4929	...	8013	6722	10924	10325	...	6223	10106	...	Colombie
Peru	1	0	0	0	0	0	...	...	...	...	Pérou
Asia	**634691**	**714001**	**664692**	**676797**	**682203**	**758086**	**811611**	**856185**	**796896**	**838046**	**Asie**
Armenia	..	10498	6597	5708	1328	1364	676	25	...	0	Arménie
Azerbaijan	..	13109	8695	2177	881	367	285	6	0	0	Azerbaïdjan
India	56904	71910	69450	76650	92500	117200	136300	153900	154247	157847	Inde
Indonesia	46096	84893	31233	...	49046	...	...	43270	21055	...	Indonésie
Japan	398039	403957	400361	375138	371201	390267	431934	450348	448342	477206	Japon
Korea, Republic of	81952	76658	98837	119148	115401	150015	142237	152905	113179	138620	Corée, République de
Myanmar[1]	266	132	105	76	20	26	115	156	152	98	Myanmar[1]
Thailand	37103	40437	...	...	...	...	...	...	...	...	Thaïlande
Turkey	14331	12407	10644	13198	13056	14145	15362	16805	17876	13114	Turquie
Europe	**485741**	**610238**	**635932**	**441002**	**411830**	**446462**	**433790**	**443862**	**536716**	**477797**	**Europe**
Croatia	..	1140	897	831	546	802	1159	1271	1307	...	Croatie
Germany	..	176086	193202	187798	218538	219326	199455	228752	262833	...	Allemagne
Germany(Fed.Rep.)	176380	..	..	..	..	..	..	..	..	..	Allemagne(Rép.féd.)
German D.R.(former)	39360	..	..	..	..	..	..	..	..	..	R.D.A. (anc.)
Hungary	23242	29394	35753	...	...	...	...	...	...	...	Hongrie
Italy	43267	28146	28820	...	...	...	...	...	...	...	Italie
Romania	4475	5365	7000	6847	5205	4430	5491	4431	2466	2503	Roumanie
Russian Federation	..	68896	70339	68805	30102	38052	35890	42625	48906	52242	Fédération de Russie
Slovakia	..	..	...	...	...	...	2994	1372	...	...	Slovaquie
Spain	121634	122002	119932	#549	2030	2235	1695	1845	...	4011	Espagne
Sweden	13509	10272	9514	...	7475	2813	2670	3191	3475	3349	Suède
Ukraine	..	36500	36577	31131	14057	8710	4858	4258	4400	4574	Ukraine
United Kingdom	63874	...	...	...	...	...	...	...	...	...	Royaume-Uni
Yugoslavia	..	68563	67841	9858	4946	41163	52830	29369	42628	40979	Yougoslavie
Total	**1679677**	**1905089**	**1932244**	**1791064**	**1781454**	**1932852**	**2009350**	**2096547**	**2171757**	**2205239**	**Total**

General Note.

Glass tubes in which a gas becomes luminous under the influence of an electric discharge, and the internal wall of which is coated with substances which transform ultra-violet rays into visible light. (SITC, Rev.3: 77822-0A).

Remarque générale.

Tubes en verre contenant un gaz qui devient luminescent sous l'effet d'une décharge électrique et dont la paroi intérieure est enduite de substances qui transforment les rayons ultraviolets en rayonnement visible. (CTCI, Rev.3: 77822 -0A).

[1] Government production only.

[1] Production de l'Etat seulement.

Tankers, launched
Navires-citernes, mis à flot

ISIC-BASED CODE - CODE BASE CITI

3841-13A

Unit : Number of units · Unité : Nombre

Country or area	1990	1991	1992	1993	1994	1995	1996	1997	1998	1999	Pays ou zone
Africa	2	2	2	2	2	2	2	2	2	2	**Afrique**
Egypt[1]	...	...	...	1	...	...	[2]1	...	...	...	Egypte[1]
South Africa[1,2]	...	...	...	...	...	...	1	...	...	...	Afrique du Sud[1,2]
America, North	3	3	3	3	3	3	3	1	5	2	**Amérique du Nord**
United States[1,2]	...	...	...	...	...	...	...	1	5	2	Etats-Unis[1,2]
America, South	2	4	7	4	5	2	5	2	4	4	**Amérique du Sud**
Argentina[1]	1	...	...	...	...	[2]1	...	[2]1	...	...	Argentine[1]
Brazil[1]	1	3	6	3	4	[2]1	[2]4	[2]1	...	...	Brésil[1]
Asia	222	265	333	324	273	260	230	165	234	258	**Asie**
China	8	5	[1]8	[1]7	[1]6	[1,2]6	[1,2]13	[1,2]12	[1,2]21	[1,2]25	Chine
Georgia	..	...	2	...	...	...	...	...	...	...	Géorgie
India[1]	0	0	1	...	...	...	[2]1	...	[2]1	[2]1	Inde[1]
Indonesia	[1]1	[1]1	...	1	4	[1,2]6	...	[1,2]1	[1,2]3	[1,2]5	Indonésie
Japan	181	203	258	264	163	171	128	91	124	107	Japon
Korea, Republic of[1]	8	23	37	28	62	[2]43	[2]50	[2]42	[2]64	[2]103	Corée, République de[1]
Malaysia[1]	5	2	3	2	4	[2]3	[2]1	[2]1	[2]4	[2]2	Malaisie[1]
Philippines[1]	2	...	...	...	...	[2]1	[2]6	[2]2	[2]2	[2]1	Philippines[1]
Singapore[1]	9	20	10	5	20	[2]19	[2]17	[2]5	[2]5	[2]3	Singapour[1]
Thailand[1,2]	...	...	...	...	...	...	...	6	...	...	Thaïlande[1,2]
Turkey	1	0	...	[1]5	...	[1,2]1	[1,2]2	[1,2]1	[1,2]1	...	Turquie
United Arab Emirates	...	...	1	...	...	...	...	...	...	...	Emirats arabes unis
Europe	50	76	88	76	60	69	81	68	74	84	**Europe**
Belgium[1]	...	...	...	3	...	[2]1	...	...	[2]1	...	Belgique[1]
Bulgaria	5	2	4	5	4	4	4	1	...	...	Bulgarie
Croatia	..	7	6	2	[1]4	3	6	[1,2]2	[1,2]8	[1,2]8	Croatie
Denmark[1]	[3]4	...	[3]3	[3]3	[3]4	[2]5	[2]4	[2]4	[2]5	[2]4	Danemark[1]
Czech Republic[1,2]	..	..	...	...	...	...	...	...	...	1	République tchèque[1,2]
Finland	[1]2	1	1	1	...	...	2	[1,2]2	...	...	Finlande
France[1,2]	...	...	...	...	...	2	1	1	...	1	France[1,2]
Germany[1]	..	2	5	5	3	[2]6	[2]1	[2]2	[2]4	[2]7	Allemagne[1]
Germany(Fed.Rep.)[1]	1	..	..	..	..	..	..	..	..	..	Allemagne(Rép.féd.)[1]
Greece[1]	1	...	...	...	...	...	...	...	...	...	Grèce[1]
Italy[1]	2	7	11	12	2	[2]7	[2]7	[2]6	[2]9	[2]12	Italie[1]
Malta[1,2]	...	...	...	...	...	1	1	...	...	...	Malte[1,2]
Netherlands	[3,4]4	[3,4]15	[3,4]11	[3,4]9	[3,4]2	[3,4]1	[2,4]3	[2]3	[2]4	[2]4	Pays-Bas
Norway[1]	1	1	2	2	...	[2]3	[2]5	[2]3	[2]4	[2]2	Norvège[1]
Poland[1]	2	3	1	...	4	...	[2]2	[2]5	[2]2	[2]8	Pologne[1]
Portugal[1,2]	...	...	...	...	...	...	2	4	2	...	Portugal[1,2]
Romania[1]	0	2	1	0	0	0	[2]3	...	[2]1	[2]4	Roumanie[1]
Russian Federation[1,2]	..	...	...	...	...	4	2	4	4	2	Fédération de Russie[1,2]
Slovakia[1,2]	...	...	...	...	...	...	...	...	...	8	Slovaquie[1,2]
Spain	[1]6	[1]5	[1]9	[1]4	[1]4	[1,2]5	11	[1,2]8	8	7	Espagne
Sweden[1,2]	...	...	...	...	...	...	...	...	...	4	Suède[1,2]
Ukraine[1]	..	...	6	3	...	[2]4	[2]6	[2]3	[2]1	[2]1	Ukraine[1]
United Kingdom	2	7	[1]3	[1]1	[1]1	[1,2]1	[1,2]5	[1,2]2	0	...	Royaume-Uni
Yugoslavia, SFR	9	..	..	..	..	..	..	..	..	..	Yougoslavie, RSF
USSR (former)	4	..	..	..	..	..	..	..	..	..	URSS (anc.)
Oceania	17	17	17	17	17	17	17	17	17	17	**Océanie**
Australia	...	...	16	...	...	...	...	...	...	...	Australie
New Zealand	...	...	1	...	...	...	...	...	...	...	Nouvelle-Zélande
Total	299	367	449	426	359	352	337	255	335	366	**Total**

General Note.
Merchant vessels specialized for the transport of liquids (petroleum, wine etc.), of 100 gross tons and over. (SITC, Rev.3:79322-0A).

For footnotes, see end of table.

Remarque générale.
Navires marchands spécialisés dans le transport de liquides (essence, vins, etc.), de 100 tonneaux de jauge brute ou davantage. (CTCI, Rev.3: 79322-0A).

Voir la fin du tableau pour les notes.

Tankers, launched (continued)
Navires-citernes, mis à flot (suite)

ISIC-BASED CODE - CODE BASE CITI

3841-13A

[1] Source: Lloyd's Register of Shipping, (London).
[2] Completions.
[3] Sales.
[4] Production by establishments employing 20 or more persons.

Notes.
[1] Source: Lloyd's Register of Shipping, (Londres).
[2] Achèvements.
[3] Ventes.
[4] Production des établissements occupant 20 personnes ou plus.

Tankers, launched
Navires-citernes, mis à flot

ISIC-BASED CODE - CODE BASE CITI

3841-13B

Unit : Thousand gross register tons   Unité : Milliers de GRT

Country or area	1990	1991	1992	1993	1994	1995	1996	1997	1998	1999	Pays ou zone
Africa	**2**	**2**	**2**	**2**	**2**	**2**	**2**	**2**	**2**	**2**	**Afrique**
South Africa[1][2]	...	...	...	...	...	...	2	...	...	...	Afrique du Sud[1][2]
America, North	**69**	**69**	**69**	**69**	**69**	**69**	**69**	**30**	**114**	**62**	**Amérique du Nord**
United States[1][2]	...	...	...	...	...	...	...	30	114	62	Etats-Unis[1][2]
America, South	**99**	**220**	**264**	**189**	**157**	**33**	**113**	**28**	**77**	**67**	**Amérique du Sud**
Argentina[2]	9	...	...	...	...	[1]7	...	[1]2	...	...	Argentine[2]
Brazil[2]	90	214	258	183	151	[1]26	[1]107	[1]26	...	...	Brésil[2]
Asia	**4285**	**7830**	**8312**	**7450**	**5555**	**5759**	**6214**	**4506**	**7977**	**11268**	**Asie**
China[2]	157	106	290	212	150	[1]80	[1]155	[1]237	[1]317	[1]568	Chine[2]
India[2]	...	...	52	...	...	...	...	...	...	[1]52	Inde[2]
Indonesia[2]	1	1	11	3	...	[1]15	...	[1]2	[1]22	[1]27	Indonésie[2]
Japan	2940	4663	5275	4827	1907	2650	2917	2105	3399	4270	Japon
Korea, Republic of[2]	1081	2941	2639	2320	3314	[1]2856	[1]2970	[1]2079	[1]4113	[1]6315	Corée, République de[2]
Malaysia	19	8	14	*10	...	[1][2]11	...	[1]7	[1][2]12	[1][2]10	Malaisie
Philippines[2]	2	...	...	...	...	[1]3	[1]9	[1]4	[1]3	[1]0	Philippines[2]
Singapore[2]	29	51	23	17	103	[1]87	[1]85	[1]17	[1]53	[1]19	Singapour[2]
Thailand[1][2]	...	...	...	...	...	...	...	3	...	...	Thaïlande[1][2]
Turkey	1	...	...	[2]3	...	[1][2]2	[1][2]1	[1]0	[1][2]3	...	Turquie
Europe	**1662**	**1543**	**2169**	**2041**	**1647**	**2165**	**2204**	**1473**	**1942**	**1525**	**Europe**
Belgium[2]	...	...	...	17	...	[1]10	...	...	[1]2	...	Belgique[2]
Bulgaria[1][2]	...	...	...	...	...	...	...	3	...	...	Bulgarie[1][2]
Croatia	..	272	317	112	[2]156	110	382	[1][2]52	209	[1][2]188	Croatie
Denmark[2]	[3]172	...	[3]163	[3]478	[3]284	[1]638	[1]51	[1]76	[1]62	[1]55	Danemark[2]
Czech Republic[1][2]	..	..	...	...	...	...	...	...	...	2	République tchèque[1][2]
Finland	[2]6	10	51	51	...	...	233	[1][2]233	...	...	Finlande
France[1][2]	...	...	...	...	...	172	86	86	...	25	France[1][2]
Germany	..	14	40	*42	[2]27	[1][2]55	[1][2]22	[1][2]20	[1][2]40	[1][2]66	Allemagne
Germany(Fed.Rep.)[2]	15	..	..	...	...	...	...	...	...	...	Allemagne(Rép.féd.)[2]
Italy[2]	27	27	144	279	54	[1]136	[1]180	[1]62	[1]98	[1]114	Italie[2]
Malta[1][2]	...	...	...	...	...	5	...	...	...	...	Malte[1][2]
Netherlands	[3][4]11	[3][4]43	[3][4]27	[3][4]35	[3][4]7	[1][4]3	[1][4]11	[1]8	[1]17	[1]13	Pays-Bas
Norway[2]	19	19	38	18	...	[1]57	[1]65	[1]57	[1]65	[1]33	Norvège[2]
Poland[2]	62	51	54	...	131	...	[1]40	[1]88	[1]32	[1]140	Pologne[2]
Portugal[1][2]	...	...	...	...	...	...	7	15	7	...	Portugal[1][2]
Romania[2]	0	51	24	0	0	0	[1]99	...	[1]4	[1]14	Roumanie[2]
Russian Federation[1][2]	..	...	...	...	...	33	25	51	52	10	Fédération de Russie[1][2]
Slovakia[1][2]	..	..	...	...	...	...	...	...	...	291	Slovaquie[1][2]
Spain	[2]271	[2]211	[2]468	[2]169	154	[1][2]168	197	[1][2]167	556	234	Espagne
Sweden	...	321	...	...	...	...	...	...	...	[1][2]10	Suède
Ukraine[2]	..	...	60	76	...	[1]112	[1]162	[1]53	[1]21	[1]31	Ukraine[2]
United Kingdom	4	...	[2]161	[2]79	[2]4	[1][2]23	[1][2]168	[1][2]8	[1][2]32	...	Royaume-Uni
Yugoslavia, SFR	790	..	..	..	..	..	..	..	..	..	Yougoslavie, RSF
USSR (former)[2]	96	..	..	...	...	...	...	...	...	..	URSS (anc.)[2]
Total	**6213**	**9663**	**10816**	**9751**	**7429**	**8028**	**8601**	**6039**	**10112**	**12923**	**Total**

General Note.
Merchant vessels specialized for the transport of liquids (petroleum, wine etc.), of 100 gross tons and over. (SITC, Rev.3:79322-0B).

Remarque générale.
Navires marchands spécialisés dans le transport de liquides (essence, vins, etc.), de 100 tonneaux de jauge brute ou davantage. (CTCI, Rev.3: 79322-0B).

[1] Completions.
[2] Source: Lloyd's Register of Shipping, (London).
[3] Sales.
[4] Production by establishments employing 20 or more persons.

[1] Achèvements.
[2] Source: Lloyd's Register of Shipping, (Londres).
[3] Ventes.
[4] Production des établissements occupant 20 personnes ou plus.

Other sea-going merchant vessels, launched
Autres navires marchands, mis à flot

ISIC-BASED CODE - CODE BASE CITI

3841-16A

Unit : Number of units   Unité : Nombre

Country or area	1990	1991	1992	1993	1994	1995	1996	1997	1998	1999	Pays ou zone
Africa	**11**	**7**	**7**	**9**	**5**	**5**	**6**	**4**	**6**	**4**	**Afrique**
Egypt[1]	7	3	...	5	2	[2]2	...	[2]1	...	[2]1	Egypte[1]
South Africa[1]	2	2	2	...	1	[2]1	...	...	...	...	Afrique du Sud[1]
Tunisia[1]	...	...	2	...	...	...	...	...	...	...	Tunisie[1]
America, North	**26**	**32**	**37**	**57**	**11**	**6**	**12**	**10**	**12**	**10**	**Amérique du Nord**
Canada[1]	11	7	10	9	1	[2]1	...	[2]2	...	[2]3	Canada[1]
Cuba[1 2]	...	...	...	...	...	...	1	1	...	1	Cuba[1 2]
Mexico[1]	...	2	1	3	...	...	...	...	...	...	Mexique[1]
United States[1]	12	22	25	44	7	[2]2	[2]3	[2]5	[2]3	[2]4	Etats-Unis[1]
America, South	**30**	**41**	**54**	**61**	**26**	**48**	**42**	**38**	**44**	**45**	**Amérique du Sud**
Argentina[1]	9	4	11	10	3	...	...	[2]1	...	...	Argentine[1]
Brazil[1]	[3]1	[3]6	[3]3	[3]5	[3]3	[2]5	[2]3	[2]1	[2]3	...	Brésil[1]
Chile[1]	11	8	9	16	3	...	[2]1	[2]1	...	...	Chili[1]
Peru[1]	5	19	25	29	13	...	...	...	...	...	Pérou[1]
Venezuela[1]	...	...	6	1	...	...	...	...	...	...	Venezuela[1]
Asia	**617**	**624**	**576**	**624**	**625**	**647**	**789**	**754**	**598**	**484**	**Asie**
Bangladesh[1]	1	1	1	...	...	...	...	...	...	...	Bangladesh[1]
Brunei Darussalam[1 2]	...	...	...	...	...	...	...	1	...	...	Brunéi Darussalam[1 2]
China[1]	30	38	30	59	...	[2]37	[2]62	[2]90	[2]86	[2]68	Chine[1]
Hong Kong SAR[1]	...	...	7	2	1	...	...	[2]1	...	[2]1	Hong-Kong RAS[1]
China, Macao, SAR	...	...	...	28	38	42	151	40	24	26	Chine, Macao PAS
Georgia[1]	...	...	2	...	...	...	...	...	...	...	Géorgie[1]
India[1]	4	9	10	16	8	[2]6	[2]6	[2]9	[2]6	[2]3	Inde[1]
Indonesia[1]	5	2	15	13	...	[2]1	[2]1	[2]5	[2]9	[2]2	Indonésie[1]
Iran(Islamic Rep. of)[1]	...	...	1	...	2	[2]1	...	[2]1	...	...	Iran(Rép. islamique)[1]
Israel[1]	...	...	...	3	...	...	...	...	...	...	Israël[1]
Japan[4]	387	335	303	351	413	417	386	399	339	276	Japon[4]
Korea, Republic of[1]	92	94	73	60	35	[2]100	[2]120	[2]149	[2]86	[2]55	Corée, République de[1]
Malaysia[1]	3	9	24	35	15	[2]3	[2]3	[2]6	[2]2	[2]3	Malaisie[1]
Myanmar[1 2]	...	...	...	...	...	...	...	...	...	1	Myanmar[1 2]
Pakistan[1]	1	...	...	...	...	...	...	...	...	...	Pakistan[1]
Philippines[1]	0	...	...	...	...	...	...	[2]5	[2]4	[2]7	Philippines[1]
Singapore[1]	15	31	33	22	24	[2]10	[2]24	[2]11	[2]7	[2]10	Singapour[1]
Sri Lanka[1]	...	...	1	...	...	...	...	...	...	...	Sri Lanka[1]
Thailand[1]	...	...	2	...	1	...	...	...	...	...	Thaïlande[1]
Turkey[1]	3	26	8	16	8	[2]7	[2]9	[2]21	[2]15	...	Turquie[1]
United Arab Emirates[1]	1	...	1	...	...	...	...	...	...	...	Emirats arabes unis[1]
Viet Nam[1]	...	...	1	...	...	...	[2]7	...	...	...	Viet Nam[1]
Dem. Yemen (former)	2	..	..	..	..	..	..	..	..	..	Yémen dém. (anc.)
Europe	**459**	**510**	**474**	**354**	**313**	**258**	**270**	**244**	**293**	**292**	**Europe**
Austria[1]	4	5	1	...	...	...	...	...	...	...	Autriche[1]
Belgium[1]	6	8	8	4	8	...	...	...	...	...	Belgique[1]
Bulgaria	4	7	4	4	3	6	6	5	9	[1 2]1	Bulgarie
Croatia	..	5	5	[1]4	...	[1 2]3	[1 2]5	[1 2]5	[1 2]4	[1 2]1	Croatie
Denmark[1]	[4 5]21	[4 5]28	[4 5]35	[4 5]23	[4 5]13	[2]18	[2]19	[2]11	[2]11	[2]9	Danemark[1]
Czechoslovakia(former)		7	..	..	..	..	..	..	..	..	Tchécoslovaquie(anc.)
Czech Republic[1 2]	..	..	..	...	...	1	1	2	2	3	République tchèque[1 2]
Finland	10	9	8	8	3	4	5	...	[1 2]6	[1 2]5	Finlande
France[1]	26	22	17	11	6	[2]4	[2]6	[2]5	[2]5	[2]4	France[1]
Germany	..	[1]99	[1]82	[1]76	84	21	13	18	20	[1 2]41	Allemagne
Germany(Fed.Rep.)	53	..	..	..	..	..	..	..	..	..	Allemagne(Rép.féd.)
German D.R. (former)[1 6]	17	..	..	..	..	..	..	..	..	..	R.D.A. (anc.)[1 6]
Greece[1]	9	5	1	1	...	...	[2]1	...	...	...	Grèce[1]
Hungary[1]	2	2	2	1	...	...	...	...	...	...	Hongrie[1]
Iceland[1]	2	1	...	...	...	...	...	...	[2]1	...	Islande[1]
Italy[1]	25	29	33	14	10	...	[2]15	[2]11	[2]23	[2]25	Italie[1]
Lithuania[1 2]	..	...	...	...	...	1	2	3	2	...	Lituanie[1 2]
Malta[1]	2	1	2	1	...	...	...	...	[2]1	...	Malte[1]
Netherlands	[1 7]36	[1 7]45	[7 8]29	[7 8]41	[7 8]45	[1 7]36	[1 7]47	[1]50	[1]42	[1]44	Pays-Bas
Norway	[1]36	[1]42	[1]53	[1]23	[1]25	[1 2]13	[1 2]8	27	37	40	Norvège

For general note and footnotes, see end of table.   Voir la fin du tableau pour la remarque générale et les notes.

Other sea-going merchant vessels, launched (continued)
Autres navires marchands, mis à flot (suite)

ISIC-BASED CODE - CODE BASE CITI

3841-16A

Unit : Number of units

Unité : Nombre

Country or area	1990	1991	1992	1993	1994	1995	1996	1997	1998	1999	Pays ou zone
Poland[1]	28	53	53	51	25	[2]32	[2]33	[2]34	[2]37	[2]26	Pologne[1]
Portugal[1]	16	12	11	7	3	[2]5	[2]3	[2]6	[2]5	[2]1	Portugal[1]
Romania	[1]7	8	16	11	4	18	25	8	11	12	Roumanie
Russian Federation[1,2]	..	...	...	...	...	5	20	10	2	6	Fédération de Russie[1,2]
Slovakia[1,2]	..	..	...	...	...	13	12	13	14	10	Slovaquie[1,2]
Spain	[1]92	[1]62	[1]49	8	11	21	20	[1,2]8	26	25	Espagne
Sweden[1]	9	8	4	4	...	[2]2	[2]3	[2]1	[2]3	[2]20	Suède[1]
Ukraine[1]	..	...	6	8	...	[2]5	[2]3	[2]2	[2]3	[2]1	Ukraine[1]
United Kingdom	29	24	[1]18	[1]16	[1]16	[1,2]9	[1,2]6	[1,2]3	12	[1,2]1	Royaume-Uni
Yugoslavia[1,2]	..	...	...	...	...	...	...	1	5	2	Yougoslavie[1,2]
Yugoslavia, SFR	18	..	..	..	..	..	..	..	..	..	Yougoslavie, RSF
Oceania	**24**	**23**	**18**	**35**	**22**	**22**	**18**	**30**	**20**	**22**	**Océanie**
Australia[1]	22	20	16	33	20	[2]20	[2]16	[2]28	[2]18	[2]20	Australie[1]
Fiji[1]	...	...	...	...	1	...	[2]1	...	...	...	Fidji[1]
New Zealand[1]	...	2	1	...	...	[2]1	...	...	...	...	Nouvelle-Zélande[1]
Total	**1167**	**1236**	**1166**	**1140**	**1002**	**986**	**1138**	**1079**	**973**	**857**	**Total**

General Note.

Passenger vessels, dry cargo vessels and combined cargo-passenger vessels, including refrigerator vessels of 100 gross tons and over. Tankers are excluded. (SITC, Rev.3: 79326-0A, 79327-5A, 79328-0A).

Remarque générale.

Paquebots, navires de charge pour le transport de marchandises solides et paquebots mixtes, y compris les navires frigorifiques, de 100 tonneaux de jauge brute ou davantage. Non compris navires-citernes. (CTCI, Rev.3: 79326-0A, 79327-5A, 79328-0A).

[1] Source: Lloyd's Register of Shipping, (London).
[2] Completions.
[3] Vessels over 200 DWT.
[4] Excluding wooden vessels.
[5] Excluding vessels under 100 GRT.
[6] Including tankers launched.
[7] Production by establishments employing 20 or more persons.
[8] Sales.

[1] Source: Lloyd's Register of Shipping, (Londres).
[2] Achèvements.
[3] Navires de plus de 200 tonnes de port en lourd.
[4] Non compris les embarcations en bois.
[5] Non compris les embarcations de moins de 100 tonneaux de jauge brute.
[6] Y compris les navires citernes mis à flot.
[7] Production des établissements occupant 20 personnes ou plus.
[8] Ventes.

Other sea-going merchant vessels, launched
Autres navires marchands, mis à flot

ISIC-BASED CODE - CODE BASE CITI
3841-16B

Unit : Thousand gross register tons

Unité : Milliers de GRT

Country or area	1990	1991	1992	1993	1994	1995	1996	1997	1998	1999	Pays ou zone
Africa	**24**	**5**	**25**	**21**	**1**	**10**	**7**	**7**	**9**	**5**	**Afrique**
Egypt[1]	19	1	...	15	1	[2]9	[2]4	[2]5	...	[2]5	Egypte[1]
South Africa[1]	5	4	18	...	0	[2]1	...	...	...	...	Afrique du Sud[1]
America, North	**21**	**10**	**69**	**54**	**8**	**6**	**19**	**16**	**35**	**38**	**Amérique du Nord**
Canada[1]	4	4	17	27	0	[2]0	...	[2]5	...	[2]31	Canada[1]
Cuba[1][2]	...	...	...	...	...	...	1	0	...	1	Cuba[1][2]
Mexico[1]	...	4	4	6	...	...	...	...	...	...	Mexique[1]
United States[1]	12	1	47	20	3	[2]1	[2]2	[2]6	[2]19	[2]2	Etats-Unis[1]
America, South	**86**	**100**	**102**	**100**	**85**	**165**	**72**	**46**	**101**	**95**	**Amérique du Sud**
Argentina[1]	1	1	9	1	0	...	...	[2]9	...	...	Argentine[1]
Brazil[1][2]	...	...	...	...	...	146	56	26	85	...	Brésil[1][2]
Chile[1]	5	10	6	10	2	...	[2]2	...	...	...	Chili[1]
Peru[1]	1	10	8	11	4	...	...	...	...	...	Pérou[1]
Venezuela	...	...	1	0	...	...	...	...	...	...	Venezuela
Asia	**6220**	**4597**	**5372**	**6341**	**8914**	**11511**	**15171**	**15198**	**11099**	**11961**	**Asie**
Bangladesh[1]	0	0	1	...	...	...	...	...	...	...	Bangladesh[1]
China	165	[1]227	[1]169	[1]471	...	[1][2]679	[1][2]985	[1][2]1143	[1][2]1114	[1][2]840	Chine
Hong Kong SAR[1]	...	...	2	1	1	...	...	[2]0	...	[2]0	Hong-Kong RAS[1]
India[1]	1	5	33	13	7	[2]36	[2]6	[2]36	...	[2]22	Inde[1]
Indonesia[1]	11	3	52	46	...	[2]3	[2]30	[2]20	[2]41	[2]10	Indonésie[1]
Iran(Islamic Rep. of)[1]	...	...	0	...	2	[2]1	...	[2]1	...	...	Iran(Rép. islamique)[1]
Israel[1]	...	...	...	1	...	...	...	...	...	...	Israël[1]
Japan[3]	3383	2602	2540	3451	6203	5829	6701	7064	6662	6808	Japon[3]
Korea, Republic of	2415	1382	2169	*1705	[1]663	[1][2]3403	[1][2]4399	[1][2]5958	[1][2]2981	[1][2]2662	Corée, République de
Malaysia[1]	20	2	11	11	2	[2]1	[2]10	[2]30	[2]10	[2]7	Malaisie[1]
Myanmar[1][2]	...	...	...	...	...	...	...	...	...	1	Myanmar[1][2]
Pakistan[1]	11	...	...	...	...	...	...	...	...	...	Pakistan[1]
Philippines[1][2]	...	...	...	...	...	...	...	32	59	72	Philippines[1][2]
Singapore[1]	15	77	47	10	9	[2]3	[2]97	[2]31	[2]109	[2]46	Singapour[1]
Thailand[1]	...	...	...	...	2	...	...	...	...	...	Thaïlande[1]
Turkey	135	224	275	559	1287	1482	2869	...	[1][2]85	...	Turquie
United Arab Emirates	1	...	...	...	...	...	...	...	...	...	Emirats arabes unis
Viet Nam	...	...	3	...	...	...	[1][2]2	...	...	...	Viet Nam
Europe	**2336**	**3162**	**3278**	**3188**	**2762**	**3683**	**4231**	**3187**	**3856**	**3281**	**Europe**
Austria[1]	10	12	2	...	1	...	...	...	...	...	Autriche[1]
Belgium[1]	56	47	66	8	45	...	...	...	...	...	Belgique[1]
Bulgaria	...	...	...	...	...	...	...	[1][2]79	94	[1][2]3	Bulgarie
Croatia		69	56	87	...	[1][2]34	[1][2]129	[1][2]69	30	[1][2]37	Croatie
Denmark[1]	[3][4]247	[3][4]416	[3][4]478	[3][4]265	[3][4]113	[2]362	[2]436	[2]389	[2]386	[2]375	Danemark[1]
Czechoslovakia(former)	...	37	...	...	...	...	...	...	...	...	Tchécoslovaquie(anc.)
Czech Republic[1][2]	..	..	...	...	...	1	1	2	3	5	République tchèque[1][2]
Finland	[1]169	[1]97	[1]126	[1]130	[1]76	174	249	...	[1][2]211	[1][2]224	Finlande
France[1]	108	81	83	241	172	[2]70	[2]124	[2]98	[2]144	[2]83	France[1]
Germany[1]	..	856	938	894	1002	[2]1050	[2]1178	[2]1064	[2]992	[2]691	Allemagne[1]
Germany(Fed.Rep.)	466	..	..	..	..	..	..	..	..	..	Allemagne(Rép.féd.)
German D.R.(former)[1]	210									..	R.D.A. (anc.)[1]
Greece[1]	4	4	0	9	...	...	[2]2	...	...	...	Grèce[1]
Hungary[1]	4	1	3	1	...	...	...	...	...	...	Hongrie[1]
Iceland[1]	1	...	...	...	...	...	...	...	...	[2]0	Islande[1]
Italy[1]	317	507	346	180	90	[2]255	[2]475	[2]106	[2]710	[2]661	Italie[1]
Lithuania[1][2]	...	...	...	...	...	3	7	12	8	...	Lituanie[1][2]
Malta[1]	0	6	7	6	...	...	...	...	[2]6	...	Malte[1]
Netherlands	[1][5]124	[1][5]137	[5][6]130	[5][6]103	[5][6]142	[1][5]186	[1][5]189	[1][5]229	[1]194	[1]199	Pays-Bas
Norway[1]	68	126	130	83	161	[2]54	[2]41	[2]80	[2]18	[2]5	Norvège[1]
Poland[1]	93	174	291	385	316	[2]522	[2]579	[2]545	[2]659	[2]442	Pologne[1]
Portugal[1]	24	11	18	...	11	[2]18	[2]8	[2]23	[2]16	[2]4	Portugal[1]
Romania	[1]5	144	183	234	177	404	375	43	58	231	Roumanie
Russian Federation[1][2]	...	...	...	...	...	51	79	36	8	52	Fédération de Russie[1][2]
Slovakia[1][2]	..	..	...	...	...	30	29	33	37	112	Slovaquie[1][2]
Spain	[1]113	[1]140	[1]111	119	103	166	162	134	153	95	Espagne

For general note and footnotes, see end of table.

Voir la fin du tableau pour la remarque générale et les notes.

Other sea-going merchant vessels, launched (continued)
Autres navires marchands, mis à flot (suite)

ISIC-BASED CODE - CODE BASE CITI
3841-16B

Unit : Thousand gross register tons

Unité : Milliers de GRT

Country or area	1990	1991	1992	1993	1994	1995	1996	1997	1998	1999	Pays ou zone
Sweden[1]	27	59	2	20	...	[2]29	[2]28	[2]31	[2]31	[2]19	Suède[1]
Ukraine[1]	..	...	63	124	...	[2]60	[2]26	[2]14	[2]54	[2]10	Ukraine[1]
United Kingdom	74	12	[1]89	[1]127	[1]50	[1][2]100	[1][2]10	[1][2]3	[1]7	[1][2]1	Royaume-Uni
Yugoslavia[1][2]	..	...	...	...	...	...	...	4	18	7	Yougoslavie[1][2]
Yugoslavia, SFR	120	..	..	..	..	..	..	..	..	..	Yougoslavie, RSF
Oceania	**29**	**28**	**29**	**25**	**16**	**28**	**35**	**40**	**42**	**41**	**Océanie**
Australia[1]	25	25	25	21	12	[2]24	[2]31	[2]36	[2]38	[2]37	Australie[1]
Fiji	...	...	...	...	3	...	[1][2]3	...	...	...	Fidji
New Zealand[1]	...	0	...	...	...	[2]1	...	...	...	...	Nouvelle-Zélande[1]
Total	**8715**	**7901**	**8875**	**9728**	**11787**	**15403**	**19534**	**18493**	**15142**	**15421**	**Total**

General Note.
Passenger vessels, dry cargo vessels and combined cargo-passenger vessels, including refrigerator vessels of 100 gross tons and over. Tankers are excluded. (SITC, Rev.3: 79326-0B, 79327-5B, 79328-0B).

Remarque générale.
Paquebots, navires de charge pour le transport de marchandises solides et paquebots mixtes, y compris les navires frigorifiques, de 100 tonneaux de jauge brute ou davantage. Non compris navires-citernes. (CTCI, Rev.3: 79326-0B, 79327-5B, 79328-0B).

[1] Source: Lloyd's Register of Shipping, (London).
[2] Completions.
[3] Excluding wooden vessels.
[4] Excluding vessels under 100 GRT.
[5] Production by establishments employing 20 or more persons.
[6] Sales.

[1] Source: Lloyd's Register of Shipping, (Londres).
[2] Achèvements.
[3] Non compris les embarcations en bois.
[4] Non compris les embarcations de moins de 100 tonneaux de jauge brute.
[5] Production des établissements occupant 20 personnes ou plus.
[6] Ventes.

Locomotives, electric
Locomotives électriques

ISIC-BASED CODE - CODE BASE CITI

3842-01A

Unit : Number of units   Unité : Nombre

Country or area	1990	1991	1992	1993	1994	1995	1996	1997	1998	1999	Pays ou zone
Asia	**684**	**775**	**768**	**1028**	**1222**	**1303**	**1146**	**1057**	**1123**	**1154**	**Asie**
China	165	173	200	...	...	...	...	...	...	...	Chine
Georgia	..	...	29	7	1	1	1	0	0	0	Géorgie
India	[1]289	[1]303	[1]302	[1]294	[1]300	[1]278	[1]312	[1]329	[1]326	259	Inde
Japan	23	13	19	4	1	...	1	1	18	9	Japon
Korea, Republic of	207	277	218	544	741	835	653	548	600	707	Corée, République de
Europe	**646**	**859**	**710**	**526**	**504**	**337**	**395**	**498**	**556**	**489**	**Europe**
Denmark[2]	...	...	...	21	92	48	...	...	...	...	Danemark[2]
Czechoslovakia(former)[3]	106	122	..	..	..	..	..	..	..	..	Tchécoslovaquie(anc.)[3]
France	...	108	120	156	120	...	...	...	...	...	France
Germany	..	...	237	222	158	15	83	176	191	...	Allemagne
German D.R.(former)	213	..	..	..	..	..	..	..	..	..	R.D.A. (anc.)
Italy[4]	28	92	100	20	27	61	50	66	107	119	Italie[4]
Poland	20	6	18	8	5	3	5	2	...	...	Pologne
Romania	30	11	0	0	0	0	...	...	...	...	Roumanie
Russian Federation	..	210	112	32	30	15	8	5	8	20	Fédération de Russie
Sweden	...	...	...	...	...	...	...	5	4	...	Suède
United Kingdom	...	...	...	62	67	...	...	...	...	...	Royaume-Uni
Total	**1330**	**1634**	**1478**	**1554**	**1726**	**1640**	**1541**	**1556**	**1679**	**1643**	**Total**

General Note.

An electric locomotive is a railway vehicle equipped with one or more electric motors, deriving current from overhead wires or conductor rails or from accumulators carried on the locomotive. It is used for hauling railway vehicles. A locomotive so equipped which also has an engine (diesel or other) to supply current to the electric motor when it cannot be obtained from an overhead wire or from a conductor rail is classed as an electric locomotive. (SITC, Rev.3: 79110-0A, 79121-0A).

[1] Including diesel and steam locomotives.
[2] Sales.
[3] Line electric locomotives only.
[4] Including diesel locomotives.

Remarque générale.

Une locomotive électrique est un véhicule ferroviaire pourvu d'un ou plusieurs moteurs électriques alimentés en énergie électrique par fil ou par rail ou à l'aide d'accumulateurs. La locomotive ainsi équipée, qui serait également pourvue d'une génératrice (diesel ou autre) fournissant du courant au moteur quand celui-ci ne peut s'alimenter à un fil ou à un rail, est classée parmi les locomotives électriques. (CTCI, Rev.3: 79110-0A, 79121-0A).

[1] Y compris les locomotives Diesel et les locomotives à vapeur.
[2] Ventes.
[3] Locomotives électriques de ligne seulement.
[4] Y compris les locomotives Diesel.

Locomotives, diesel
Locomotives diesel

ISIC-BASED CODE - CODE BASE CITI
3842-04A

Unit : Number of units   Unité : Nombre

Country or area	1990	1991	1992	1993	1994	1995	1996	1997	1998	1999	Pays ou zone
Asia	**516**	**584**	**620**	**545**	**543**	**585**	**557**	**556**	**626**	**553**	**Asie**
China	466	521	563	...	...	...	...	...	...	...	Chine
Japan	2	...	10	22	4	19	3	3	4	1	Japon
Korea, Republic of	18	24	35	5	21	45	25	22	105	19	Corée, République de
Turkey	30	31	12	1	1	4	12	14	0	16	Turquie
Europe	**684**	**621**	**299**	**261**	**234**	**193**	**175**	**192**	**179**	**175**	**Europe**
Croatia	..	2	...	...	...	...	...	...	...	...	Croatie
Czechoslovakia(former) [1]	348	282	...	...	..	..	..	..	..	..	Tchécoslovaquie(anc.) [1]
Finland	5	10	10	6	...	...	...	...	...	...	Finlande
Germany	..	173	149	141	123	85	75	...	...	...	Allemagne
Germany(Fed.Rep.)	173	..	..	..	..	..	..	..	..	..	Allemagne(Rép.féd.)
Hungary	0	13	...	...	...	...	...	...	...	...	Hongrie
Poland	31	15	4	4	0	...	...	...	...	...	Pologne
Romania	61	12	0	1	0	1	0	0	0	0	Roumanie
Russian Federation	..	39	33	22	16	12	5	13	10	16	Fédération de Russie
Spain	66	74	93	...	...	...	...	...	...	...	Espagne
Yugoslavia	..	1	...	...	...	...	...	...	...	...	Yougoslavie
Total	**1200**	**1205**	**919**	**806**	**777**	**778**	**732**	**748**	**805**	**728**	**Total**

General Note.

A diesel locomotive is a railway vehicle in which the source of power is a diesel engine, irrespective of the type of transmission installed. It is used for hauling railway vehicles. However, diesel-electric locomotives equipped to derive power from an overhead wire or from a conductor rail are classed as electric locomotives. (SITC, Rev.3: 79129-1A).

Remarque générale.

Une locomotive diesel est une locomotive actionnée par un moteur Diesel, quel que soit le type de transmission. Toutefois, les locomotives diesel-électrique, équipées pour être actionnées par l'énergie électrique transmise par un fil ou par un rail, sont classées parmi les locomotives électriques. (CTCI, Ref.3: 79129-1A).

[1] Locomotives over 800 kW.

[1] Locomotives de plus de 800 kW.

Rail motor passenger vehicles
Automotrices pour le transport de passagers

ISIC-BASED CODE - CODE BASE CITI

3842-07A

Unit : Number of units   Unité : Nombre

Country or area	1990	1991	1992	1993	1994	1995	1996	1997	1998	1999	Pays ou zone
Asia	**4315**	**3919**	**4054**	**4444**	**3575**	**3363**	**4211**	**3888**	**3290**	**4143**	**Asie**
India	...	...	...	2470	1625	1822	2436	...	...	...	Inde
Japan	2227	1831	1966	1974	1950	1541	1775	1800	1202	2055	Japon
Europe	**835**	**1508**	**1234**	**1151**	**1159**	**1493**	**1103**	**917**	**980**	**1209**	**Europe**
Austria[1]	...	...	...	...	...	122	104	154	...	227	Autriche[1]
Denmark[2]	9	10	10	...	...	0	...	...	...	...	Danemark[2]
Czechoslovakia(former)[3]	326	326	..	..	..	..	..	..	..	..	Tchécoslovaquie(anc.)[3]
France	...	156	216	144	156	...	...	...	...	...	France
Germany	..	...	...	...	...	1162	...	542	625	...	Allemagne
German D.R.(former)	71	..	..	..	..	..	..	..	..	..	R.D.A. (anc.)
Hungary	12	4	...	...	...	...	...	...	...	...	Hongrie
Poland	52	45	10	10	4	11	2	1	...	...	Pologne
Sweden	45	38	61	53	55	21	36	36	19	21	Suède
Yugoslavia	..	...	...	...	...	...	1	...	...	...	Yougoslavie
Total	**5150**	**5427**	**5288**	**5595**	**4734**	**4856**	**5314**	**4806**	**4270**	**5352**	**Total**

General Note.

Motor vehicles constructed for the conveyance of passengers by rail, irrespective of the type of power equipment installed. This item includes rail motor vehicles consisting of several articulated vehicles forming an indivisible set. Each of such sets is counted as one unit. (SITC, Rev.3: 79160-1A).

Remarque générale.

Véhicules automoteurs aménagés pour le transport sur rail de passagers, quel que soit le mode de propulsion. Cette rubrique comprend les automotrices consistant en plusieurs véhicules articulés formant une rame indivisible. Chaque rame est comptée comme une unité. (CTCI, Rev.3: 79160-1A).

[1] 1998 data are confidential.
[2] Sales.
[3] Trams only.

[1] Pour 1998, les données sont confidentielles.
[2] Ventes.
[3] Tramways seulement.

Goods wagons and vans
Wagons de marchandises et fourgons

ISIC-BASED CODE - CODE BASE CITI

3842-10A

Unit : Number of units / Unité : Nombre

Country or area	1990	1991	1992	1993	1994	1995	1996	1997	1998	1999	Pays ou zone
Africa	**557**	**403**	**605**	**575**	**413**	**581**	**440**	**368**	**365**	**365**	**Afrique**
Algeria	253	111	105	210	48	216	75	3	0	0	Algérie
Egypt	304	292	500	...	...	...	...	...	...	...	Egypte
America, North	**3**	**0**	**32**	**125**	**0**	**32**	**32**	**32**	**32**	**32**	**Amérique du Nord**
Mexico	3	0	...	125	0	...	...	...	...	...	Mexique
America, South	**110**	**110**	**110**	**361**	**110**	**61**	**110**	**15**	**4**	**110**	**Amérique du Sud**
Colombia	...	...	...	361	...	61	...	15	4	...	Colombie
Asia	**48845**	**47248**	**51560**	**43375**	**26281**	**26795**	**27197**	**28064**	**27872**	**26731**	**Asie**
China	18597	18500	21636	...	...	...	...	...	...	...	Chine
India	24157	25778	25350	19532	2584	3376	3648	4418	4678	3666	Inde
Indonesia	4952	1584	3650	...	...	...	...	...	...	...	Indonésie
Japan	825	646	411	439	508	354	494	673	221	92	Japon
Turkey	314	740	513	431	216	92	82	0	0	0	Turquie
Europe	**26214**	**45805**	**34184**	**27386**	**35792**	**23188**	**20548**	**12198**	**13175**	**12723**	**Europe**
Bulgaria	1257	446	288	153	204	170	44	39	...	...	Bulgarie
Croatia	..	...	9	20	3	10	0	...	...	...	Croatie
Denmark[1]	9	...	...	6	11	24	13	2	...	...	Danemark[1]
Czechoslovakia(former)	4910	7792	..	..	..	..	..	..	..	..	Tchécoslovaquie(anc.)
Czech Republic	..	..	1266	...	...	...	...	..	..	...	République tchèque
Finland	1493	385	149	358	206	255	243	...	...	...	Finlande
France	...	960	1068	696	504	...	...	...	...	...	France
Germany	..	6156	4520	3675	1938	3666	2088	1687	2088	...	Allemagne
German D.R.(former)	2656	..	..	..	..	..	..	..	..	..	R.D.A. (anc.)
Hungary	0	0	...	...	...	...	198	12	...	...	Hongrie
Italy	1847	173	224	813	1173	1536	350	553	516	106	Italie
Latvia	..	...	..	...	...	...	...	...	...	341	Lettonie
Poland	4154	2301	678	362	249	835	645	897	1295	1719	Pologne
Romania[2]	7495	3675	1916	566	446	174	357	223	383	...	Roumanie[2]
Russian Federation	..	22388	16895	12309	7785	7072	7417	4965	3914	4140	Fédération de Russie
Slovakia	..	..	...	...	20564	...	...	387	1246	1673	Slovaquie
Spain	974	794	509	...	...	...	...	...	...	...	Espagne
Sweden	[3]612	...	...	[3]0	...	...	25	...	...	...	Suède
Yugoslavia		154	78	42	78	41	27	48	281	36	Yougoslavie
Oceania	**22184**	**14864**	**14234**	**19417**	**25354**	**25405**	**27328**	**29761**	**31462**	**33164**	**Océanie**
Australia	22184	14864	14234	19417	25354	25405	27328	...	...	...	Australie
Total	**97913**	**108430**	**100725**	**91239**	**87950**	**76063**	**75655**	**70439**	**72911**	**73125**	**Total**

General Note.
Goods wagons comprise all types of railway vehicles without power equipment, normally intended for the transport of goods. Vans are railway vehicles without power equipment, forming part of a passenger or freight train, used by train crews and possibly for the transport of luggage, mail, parcels, bicycles etc. Freight-train vans (that is, vans used exclusively on freight trains) are included. (SITC, Rev.3: 79170-1A, 79182-0A).

[1] Sales.
[2] Equivalent of four axles.
[3] Wagons and vans for public railways and tramways only.

Remarque générale.
Les wagons de marchandises comprennent tous les types de véhicules ferroviaires sans engin moteur, normalement destinés au seul transport des marchandises. Les fourgons sont des véhicules ferroviaires sans engin moteur, entrant dans la composition des trains de voyageurs ou de marchandises et utilisés par le personnel d'accompagnement et pour le transport éventuel de bagages, de la poste, de colis, de bicyclettes, etc. Cette rubrique comprend les fourgons des trains de marchandises (c'est-à-dire ceux qui sont exclusivement utilisés dans ces trains). (CTCI, Rev.3: 79170-1A, 79182-0A).

[1] Ventes.
[2] En equivalent quatre essieux.
[3] Wagons et fourgons pour chemins de fer et tramways publics seulement.

Rail passenger carriages
Voitures de passagers, pour voie ferrée

ISIC-BASED CODE - CODE BASE CITI

3842-13

Unit : Number of units

Unité : Nombre

Country or area	1990	1991	1992	1993	1994	1995	1996	1997	1998	1999	Pays ou zone
America, North	**102**	**77**	**60**	**32**	**30**	**60**	**60**	**60**	**60**	**60**	**Amérique du Nord**
Mexico	102	77	...	32	30	...	...	...	...	...	Mexique
America, South	**1**	**1**	**1**	**1**	**1**	**1**	**1**	**1**	**1**	**1**	**Amérique du Sud**
Colombia	...	...	...	...	...	1	...	1	1	...	Colombie
Asia	**3664**	**3613**	**4547**	**4466**	**2870**	**2912**	**3075**	**4051**	**4443**	**4417**	**Asie**
China	1866	1674	1652	...	...	...	...	...	...	...	Chine
India	1502	1584	2615	2460	780	890	1011	2041	2446	2419	Inde
Indonesia	...	...	252	...	...	...	...	...	...	...	Indonésie
Japan	33	84	16	9	93	25	67	13	0	1	Japon
Viet Nam	11	19	12	...	...	...	...	...	...	...	Viet Nam
Europe	**4723**	**7656**	**6736**	**5684**	**4254**	**3932**	**3873**	**2534**	**2129**	**3418**	**Europe**
Bulgaria	59	30	21	13	11	10	5	...	...	...	Bulgarie
Croatia	..	...	..	..	..	...	2	1	...	...	Croatie
Czechoslovakia(former)	174	393	..	..	..	...	..	..	..	..	Tchécoslovaquie(anc.)
Finland	30	17	13	...	...	...	...	...	...	..	Finlande
France	...	252	228	528	504	...	...	...	...	...	France
Germany	...	...	4548	3353	2145	...	...	910	608	...	Allemagne
Germany(Fed.Rep.)[1]	1380	..	..	..	..	..	..	..	..	..	Allemagne(Rép.féd.)[1]
German D.R.(former)	1505	..	..	..	..	..	..	..	..	..	R.D.A. (anc.)
Italy	534	318	42	0	0	41	185	230	151	127	Italie
Latvia	..	500	263	123	202	174	92	5	7	...	Lettonie
Poland[2]	160	83	40	48	28	7	10	6	9	5	Pologne[2]
Romania	129	141	150	199	4	14	23	17	10	0	Roumanie
Russian Federation	..	1013	961	997	709	489	449	517	503	716	Fédération de Russie
Spain	284	332	343	...	...	...	...	...	...	...	Espagne
Sweden	...	100	84	74	64	161	76	130	100	105	Suède
Yugoslavia	..	143	41	8	...	4	1	0	22	1746	Yougoslavie
Total	**8490**	**11347**	**11344**	**10183**	**7154**	**6905**	**7009**	**6646**	**6633**	**7896**	**Total**

General Note.

Railway vehicles without power equipment intended for the conveyance of passengers, even if they comprise one or more compartments or spaces specially reserved for luggage, parcels, mail etc. This item includes special vehicles for the conveyance of passengers, such as sleeping-cars, saloons, dining-cars and ambulance cars. (SITC, Rev.3: 79170-2).

[1] Including rail motor passenger vehicles.
[2] Excluding narrow-gauge vehicles.

Remarque générale.

Véhicules ferroviaires sans engin moteur destinés au transport de passagers, même s'il y est réservé un ou plusieurs compartiments pour les bagages, les colis, la poste, etc. Cette rubrique comprend les véhicules spéciaux pour le transport de passagers, tels que wagons-lits, wagons-salons, wagons-restaurants et wagons sanitaires. (CTCI, Rev.3: 79170-2).

[1] Y compris les automotrices pour le transport de passagers.
[2] Non compris le matériel roulant pour voie étroite.

Engines, internal combustion (compression-ignition), for motor vehicles, diesel engines
Moteurs à combustion interne (à allumage par compression) pour véhicules automobiles, moteurs Diesel

ISIC-BASED CODE - CODE BASE CITI

3843-01A

Unit : Thousand units   Unité : En milliers

Country or area	1990	1991	1992	1993	1994	1995	1996	1997	1998	1999	Pays ou zone
Africa	8	7	6	6	5	6	4	2	3	5	**Afrique**
Algeria	8	7	6	6	5	6	4	2	3	5	Algérie
America, North	441	390	474	625	678	733	689	776	855	927	**Amérique du Nord**
Mexico	8	7	4	17	17	1	2	5	4	1	Mexique
United States	433	383	469	608	661	732	687	771	851	927	Etats-Unis
Asia	44	76	20	44	4	5	0	0	0	0	**Asie**
Indonesia	44	76	[1]20	[1]44	4	...	...	...	...	...	Indonésie
Europe	1833	2506	2845	2307	2820	3037	2974	3169	2924	3548	**Europe**
Austria[2]	29	[3]761	[3]821	[3]721	[3]798	...	...	...	...	...	Autriche[2]
Belarus	..	142	142	144	77	54	45	51	55	55	Bélarus
Bulgaria	30	7	7	4	6	4	4	3	...	...	Bulgarie
Croatia	..	...	...	...	...	...	...	1	1	...	Croatie
Czech Republic	..	..	...	...	...	...	2	4	3	2	République tchèque
Finland	8	5	5	6	10	12	13	...	...	...	Finlande
Germany	..	...	1104	910	1033	...	...	...	356	...	Allemagne
Germany(Fed.Rep.)	1067	..	..	..	..	...	...	..	..	..	Allemagne(Rép.féd.)
Hungary	7	3	3	...	...	...	...	...	...	...	Hongrie
Netherlands[4][5]	...	...	...	5	13	18	14	15	16	16	Pays-Bas[4][5]
Slovakia	..	..	...	...	...	...	7	13	...	...	Slovaquie
Slovenia	..	3	2	2	1	1	0	0	0	0	Slovénie
Spain	28	32	49	64	97	127	...	90	92	...	Espagne
Sweden	50	47	36	35	52	52	58	60	72	65	Suède
United Kingdom	...	...	...	394	709	822	...	680	769	...	Royaume-Uni
Yugoslavia	..	27	19	5	6	3	2	6	4	3	Yougoslavie
Total	2325	2979	3345	2984	3507	3781	3666	3948	3783	4480	**Total**

General Note.

Internal combustion (compression-ignition) piston engines for motor vehicles (passenger cars and commercial vehicles) equipped with cylinders, pistons, connecting-rods, crankshafts, flywheels, inlet and exhaust valves etc. Compression-ignition engines employ a somewhat heavier fuel than petrol engines. Included are semi-diesel engines that employ a heat source to heat the cylinder head. (SITC, Rev.3: 71323-0A).

[1] Including spark-ignition engines.
[2] Beginning 1995, data are confidential.
[3] Including compression-ignition engines.
[4] Sales.
[5] Production by establishments employing 20 or more persons.

Remarque générale.

Moteurs à piston à combustion interne (à allumage par compression) pour véhicules automobiles destinés au transport de voyageurs ou de marchandises, comportant cylindres, pistons, bielles, vilebrequins, volants, soupapes d'admission et d'échappement, etc. Les moteurs à allumage par compression utilisent un carburant un peu plus lourd que l'essence. Sont inclus les moteurs utilisant une source de chaleur pour le réchauffage de la culasse (moteurs semi-diesel). (CTCI, REv.3: 71323-0A).

[1] Y compris les moteurs à allumage commandé.
[2] A partir de 1995, les données sont confidentielles
[3] Y compris les moteurs à allumage par compression.
[4] Ventes.
[5] Production des établissements occupant 20 personnes ou plus.

Engines, internal-combustion (spark-ignition), for motor vehicles, gasolene fueled
Moteurs à explosion pour véhicules automobiles à essence

ISIC-BASED CODE - CODE BASE CITI

3843-04A

Unit : Thousand units   Unité : En milliers

Country or area	1990	1991	1992	1993	1994	1995	1996	1997	1998	1999	Pays ou zone
America, North	**1684**	**1533**	**1315**	**1810**	**2231**	**2184**	**2302**	**2123**	**2227**	**2336**	Amérique du Nord
Mexico	1684	1533	1315	1810	2231	2184	2302	2123	2227	2336	Mexique
America, South	**9**	**9**	**4**	**12**	**9**	**10**	**9**	**9**	**9**	**9**	Amérique du Sud
Colombia	...	...	4	12	9	10	...	...	...	...	Colombie
Asia	**2132**	**2278**	**2484**	**2687**	**2999**	**3189**	**3593**	**3539**	**2764**	**3546**	Asie
Indonesia	...	783	...	...	...	...	...	...	...	...	Indonésie
Korea, Republic of	1349	1495	1701	1904	[1]2216	[1]2406	[1]2810	[1]2756	[1]1981	[1]2763	Corée, République de
Europe	**6459**	**5170**	**5039**	**6543**	**6750**	**5178**	**3788**	**5524**	**4058**	**5526**	Europe
Austria	728	...	...	...	...	...	...	...	...	...	Autriche
Germany	..	...	...	4331	4449	...	1149	...	1302	...	Allemagne
Germany(Fed.Rep.)	4208	..	..								Allemagne(Rép.féd.)
Hungary	0	0	24	...	...	...	..	...	...	...	Hongrie
Slovakia	..	..	...	...	...	...	25	29	...	...	Slovaquie
Slovenia	..	...	20	29	34	56	...	10	5	2	Slovénie
Spain	490	558	508	515	544	597	815	847	914	872	Espagne
Sweden	346	255	207	207	258	248	336	393	371	385	Suède
United Kingdom	687	...	...	...	...	...	...	...	...	...	Royaume-Uni
Yugoslavia	..	105	30	11	15	19	18	14	16	9	Yougoslavie
Total	**10284**	**8989**	**8842**	**11052**	**11989**	**10561**	**9692**	**11195**	**9058**	**11417**	Total

General Note.

Internal-combustion piston engines (spark-ignition engines) for motor vehicles (passenger cars and commercial vehicles) equipped with cylinders, pistons, connecting-rods, crankshafts, flywheels, inlet and exhaust valves etc. Spark-ignition motor vehicle engines are usually petrol-fueled but some may employ other fuel, e.g. propane. Rotary engines of the spark-ignition type are included. Motorcycle engines are excluded. (SITC, Rev.3: 71321-0A, 71322-0A, 71381-0A).

Remarque générale.

Moteurs à piston à explosion (à allumage par etincelle électrique) pour véhicules automobiles destinés au transport de voyageurs ou de marchandises, comportant cylindres, pistons, bielles, vilebrequins, volants, soupapes d'admission et d'échappement, etc. Les moteurs de véhicules automobiles à explosion marchent en général à l'essence, mais certains peuvent consommer d'autres carburants, du propane par exemple. Les moteurs à piston rotatif du type à allumage par etincelle sont inclus. Les moteurs de motocycles sont exclus. (CTCI, Rev.3: 71321-0A, 71322-0A, 71381-0A).

[1] Including diesel engines.

[1] Y compris les moteurs diesel.

Passenger cars, assembled from imported parts
Automobiles destinées au transport de voyageurs, assemblées à partir de pièces importées

ISIC-BASED CODE - CODE BASE CITI

3843-07

Unit : Thousand units Unité : En milliers

Country or area	1990	1991	1992	1993	1994	1995	1996	1997	1998	1999	Pays ou zone
Africa	**280**	**273**	**279**	**302**	**275**	**333**	**328**	**332**	**264**	**291**	**Afrique**
Kenya	14	8	7	8	2	2	2	...	...	...	Kenya
Morocco	37	39	72	72	...	...	...	...	...	...	Maroc
Nigeria	...	3	3	2	1	1	...	...	...	...	Nigéria
South Africa	225	223	197	220	217	275	271	277	209	236	Afrique du Sud
America, North	**2**	**4**	**3**	**2**	**2**	**0**	**0**	**0**	**0**	**0**	**Amérique du Nord**
Trinidad and Tobago	2	4	3	2	2	0	0	...	...	...	Trinité-et-Tobago
America, South	**88**	**99**	**118**	**129**	**130**	**132**	**122**	**128**	**114**	**139**	**Amérique du Sud**
Chile	3	3	4	3	3	4	...	...	...	...	Chili
Colombia	36	35	40	63	65	66	63	64	47	...	Colombie
Ecuador	...	...	21	28	27	26	19	24	27	...	Equateur
Peru	1	2	11	1	1	2	...	...	...	...	Pérou
Venezuela	24	35	42	...	...	...	...	...	...	...	Venezuela
Asia	**456**	**578**	**646**	**800**	**704**	**833**	**882**	**989**	**647**	**904**	**Asie**
Indonesia	3	19	39	72	95	127	...	42	6	...	Indonésie
Iran(Islamic Rep. of)	[1]14	[1]43	[1]27	[1]35	[1]48	[2]75	[2]95	[2]154	[2]166	...	Iran(Rép. islamique)
Malaysia	131	152	137	145	173	241	[3]313	[3]362	[3]149	[3]258	Malaisie
Pakistan[4]	26	25	29	27	20	21	31	33	34	39	Pakistan[4]
Philippines	34	...	...	...	...	...	...	...	...	...	Philippines
Thailand[5]	82	110	115	144	126	...	163	128	34	...	Thaïlande[5]
Turkey	166	195	265	343	208	222	196	236	224	221	Turquie
Europe	**2778**	**2661**	**2803**	**2704**	**2949**	**2854**	**2781**	**2661**	**2376**	**2293**	**Europe**
Belgium	[6]1160	[6]1064	[6]1094	[6]1089	1211	1177	1153	1020	[7]652	[7]570	Belgique
Bulgaria	15	3	...	...	...	...	...	...	...	...	Bulgarie
Greece	16	14	15	...	...	...	...	...	...	...	Grèce
Hungary	...	...	...	...	...	...	...	...	2	...	Hongrie
Portugal	71	69	#113	...	...	...	...	...	...	...	Portugal
Slovakia	..	..	...	...	...	...	32	42	125	127	Slovaquie
Slovenia	..	3	0	0	...	...	...	...	...	...	Slovénie
United Kingdom	...	...	...	1424	1545	...	...	...	...	...	Royaume-Uni
Yugoslavia	..	22	4	0	0	0	0	...	...	0	Yougoslavie
Yugoslavia, SFR	30	..	...	...	...	...	...	...	...	..	Yougoslavie, RSF
Oceania	**44**	**56**	**31**	**44**	**44**	**44**	**44**	**44**	**44**	**44**	**Océanie**
New Zealand	44	56	31	...	...	...	...	...	...	...	Nouvelle-Zélande
Total	**3648**	**3671**	**3879**	**3981**	**4103**	**4195**	**4157**	**4154**	**3445**	**3670**	**Total**

General Note.

Three- and four-wheeled road motor vehicles, other than motor-cycle combinations, intended for the transport of passengers and seating not more than nine persons (including the driver), which are assembled wholly or mainly from imported parts. (SITC, Rev.3: 78100-1).

[1] Production by establishments employing 50 or more persons.
[2] Production by establishments employing 10 or more persons.
[3] Including vans and buses.
[4] Twelve months ending 30 June of year stated.
[5] Beginning 1999, series discontinued.
[6] Production by establishments employing 5 or more persons.
[7] Incomplete coverage.

Remarque générale.

Véhicules automobiles routiers à trois ou à quatre roues, autres que les motocycles, destinés au transport de voyageurs, dont le nombre de places assises (y compris celle du conducteur) est inférieur à dix, et qui sont montés entièrement ou principalement avec des pièces importées. (CTCI, Rev.3: 78100-1).

[1] Production des établissements occupant 50 personnes ou plus.
[2] Production des établissements occupant 10 personnes ou plus.
[3] Y compris les autobus et les camionnettes.
[4] Période de douze mois finissant le 30 juin de l'année indiquée.
[5] A partir de 1999, série abandonnée.
[6] Production des établissements occupant 5 personnes ou plus.
[7] Couverture incomplète.

Passenger cars, produced
Automobiles destinées au transport des voyageurs, fabriquées

ISIC-BASED CODE - CODE BASE CITI

3843-10

Unit : Thousand units

Unité : En milliers

Country or area	1990	1991	1992	1993	1994	1995	1996	1997	1998	1999	Pays ou zone
Africa	**10**	**9**	**7**	**4**	**7**	**8**	**14**	**13**	**13**	**12**	Afrique
Egypt	10	9	7	4	7	8	14	13	13	12	Egypte
America, North	**7632**	**7061**	**7384**	**7655**	**8393**	**8027**	**8282**	**8496**	**8743**	**8942**	Amérique du Nord
Canada	940	890	901	838	...	...	...	...	...	...	Canada
Mexico	[1]611	[1]730	[1]799	861	887	705	802	858	947	...	Mexique
United States[2]	6081	5441	5684	5956	*6614	...	...	...	...	...	Etats-Unis[2]
America, South	**375**	**434**	**586**	**706**	**732**	**525**	**541**	**646**	**622**	**473**	Amérique du Sud
Argentina[1]	81	114	221	287	338	227	269	366	353	225	Argentine[1]
Brazil[3]	267	293	338	392	367	271	245	253	242	221	Brésil[3]
Ecuador	...	...	...	...	...	...	...	...	27	...	Equateur
Asia	**11116**	**11102**	**10868**	**10292**	**9943**	**10000**	**10593**	**11239**	**10122**	**10914**	Asie
China*	...	40	...	...	...	...	...	...	...	...	Chine*
India[4]	177	164	162	210	262	331	400	384	393	577	Inde[4]
Indonesia	16	26	28	20	85	19	...	11	56	...	Indonésie
Japan	9948	9753	9379	8494	7801	7611	7864	8491	8056	8100	Japon
Korea, Republic of[1]	935	1119	1259	1528	1755	1999	2256	2313	1577	2158	Corée, République de[1]
Europe	**14280**	**14788**	**14736**	**13082**	**14339**	**14760**	**14888**	**14382**	**14026**	**14336**	Europe
Austria	15	14	...	...	...	...	...	...	...	...	Autriche
Czechoslovakia(former)	191	177	..	..	..	..	..	..	..	..	Tchécoslovaquie(anc.)
Finland[1]	30	39	13	7	...	...	0	...	..	...	Finlande[1]
France	3293	3190	3326	2837	3176	...	...	...	...	...	France
Germany	..	4647	4895	3875	4222	...	[1]4713	...	...	...	Allemagne
Germany(Fed.Rep.)	4634	..	..	..	..	..	..	..	..	..	Allemagne(Rép.féd.)
German D.R.(former)	145	..	..	..	..	..	..	..	..	..	R.D.A. (anc.)
Hungary	...	...	...	...	...	...	...	...	90	125	Hongrie
Italy[4]	1873	1632	1475	1116	1340	1422	1244	1563	1379	1384	Italie[4]
Netherlands[1][5][6]	122	84	95	80	92	98	...	...	...	...	Pays-Bas[1][5][6]
Poland	266	167	219	334	338	366	441	520	592	647	Pologne
Romania	100	84	74	93	56	70	97	109	104	89	Roumanie
Russian Federation	..	1030	963	956	798	835	868	986	840	954	Fédération de Russie
Slovakia	..	..	...	5	8	22	32	42	125	127	Slovaquie
Slovenia	..	79	84	58	74	88	89	...	...	119	Slovénie
Spain	1696	1787	1817	[1][5]1774	[1][5]2146	[1][5]2254	[1][5]2334	[1][5]2278	[1][5]2468	[1][5]2473	Espagne
Sweden	216	178	205	173	193	...	207	219	214	235	Suède
Ukraine	..	156	135	140	94	59	7	2	26	10	Ukraine
United Kingdom	1302	1340	1291	1504	1654	1735	1707	1818	1709	...	Royaume-Uni
Yugoslavia	..	76	22	8	8	8	9	10	12	...	Yougoslavie
Yugoslavia, SFR	289	..	..	..	..	..	..	..	..	..	Yougoslavie, RSF
USSR (former)	1259	..	..	..	..	..	..	..	..	..	URSS (anc.)
Oceania	**361**	**278**	**270**	**285**	**310**	**294**	**305**	**304**	**313**	**340**	Océanie
Australia	361	278	270	285	310	294	305	304	313	340	Australie
Total	**35032**	**33671**	**33851**	**32024**	**33724**	**33613**	**34623**	**35079**	**33838**	**35017**	Total

General Note.

Three- and four-wheeled road motor vehicles, other than motor-cycle combinations, intended for the transport of passengers and seating not more than nine persons (including the driver), which are manufactured wholly or mainly from domestically-produced parts. Passenger cars shipped in "knocked-down" form for assembly abroad are included. (SITC, Rev.3: 78100-2).

Remarque générale.

Véhicules automobiles routiers à trois ou quatre roues, autres que les motocycles, destinés au transport de voyageurs, dont le nombre de places assises (y compris celle du conducteur) est inférieur à dix, et qui sont construits entièrement ou principalement avec des pièces fabriquées dans le pays. Cette rubrique comprend les voitures destinées au transport des voyageurs, exportées en pièces détachées pour être montées à l'étranger. (CTCI, REv.3: 78100-2).

[1] Including assembly.
[2] Factory sales.
[3] Excluding station wagons.
[4] Excluding production for armed forces.
[5] Sales.
[6] Production by establishments employing 20 or more persons.

[1] Y compris le montage.
[2] Ventes des fabriques.
[3] Non compris les station-wagons.
[4] Non compris la production destinée aux forces armées.
[5] Ventes.
[6] Production des établissements occupant 20 personnes ou plus.

Buses and motor coaches, assembled from imported parts
Autocars et autobus, assemblés à partir de pièces importées

ISIC-BASED CODE - CODE BASE CITI

3843-12

Unit : Number of units

Unité : Nombre

Country or area	1990	1991	1992	1993	1994	1995	1996	1997	1998	1999	Pays ou zone
Africa	**18596**	**16913**	**11527**	**9192**	**11550**	**15729**	**11450**	**9508**	**9154**	**7811**	**Afrique**
Algeria	727	654	1008	596	468	1064	473	264	307	529	Algérie
Kenya	228	274	191	177	400	609	653	...	...	...	Kenya
South Africa	17098	15420	9883	8018	10347	13705	9942	8211	7711	6059	Afrique du Sud
Tunisia	543	565	445	401	335	351	382	287	313	323	Tunisie
Asia	**17029**	**20327**	**23673**	**25859**	**10974**	**14726**	**21927**	**26858**	**37299**	**34177**	**Asie**
Azerbaijan	..	...	734	877	201	9	2	40	29	0	Azerbaïdjan
Indonesia	..	...	...	...	311	...	...	...	...	...	Indonésie
Pakistan[1]	2207	3609	2888	2501	1243	1622	2712	1154	1082	1842	Pakistan[1]
Tajikistan	..	160	169	352	195	127	57	48	55	51	Tadjikistan
Turkey	14331	15584	19302	21585	8791	12424	18612	25072	35589	31740	Turquie
Viet Nam[2]	180	250	269	...	...	...	...	...	...	...	Viet Nam[2]
Europe	**4492**	**20846**	**19580**	**14014**	**9966**	**7880**	**4514**	**3491**	**3471**	**3270**	**Europe**
Belgium[3][4]	4304	1984	3355	2623	...	...	...	...	...	...	Belgique[3][4]
Croatia	..	..	7	11	22	25	7	19	...	...	Croatie
Greece	188	123	121	30	...	230	146	...	188	...	Grèce
Latvia	..	15849	15139	10579	6357	4343	1196	102	44	...	Lettonie
Slovenia	..	472	349	333	156	155	43	...	...	...	Slovénie
T.F.Yug.Rep. Macedonia	..	2405	609	438	218	60	55	72	111	50	L'ex-RY Macédoine
Total	**40117**	**58086**	**54780**	**49065**	**32490**	**38335**	**37891**	**39858**	**49925**	**45259**	**Total**

General Note.
Passenger road motor vehicles (including trolley-buses) seating more than nine persons (including the driver), which are assembled wholly or mainly from imported parts. Seating capacity should be measured as the number of seats or berths, including the driver's, available in the vehicle when performing the service for which it is primarily intended. (SITC. Rev.3: 78310-1).

[1] Twelve months ending 30 June of year stated.
[2] Including passenger cars.
[3] Production by establishments employing 5 or more persons.
[4] Shipments.

Remarque générale.
Véhicules automobiles routiers (y compris les trolleybus) dont le nombre de places assises (y compris celle du conducteur) est supérieur à neuf et qui sont montés entièrement ou principalement avec des pièces importées. Le nombre de places est donné par le nombre de sièges ou de couchettes (y compris la place du conducteur) du véhicule lorsqu'il assure le service auquel il est essentiellement destiné. (CTCI, Rev.3: 78310 -1).

[1] Période de douze mois finissant le 30 juin de l'année indiquée.
[2] Y compris les voitures de tourisme.
[3] Production des établissements occupant 5 personnes ou plus.
[4] Expéditions.

Buses and motor coaches, produced
Autocars et autobus, fabriqués

ISIC-BASED CODE - CODE BASE CITI

3843-13

Unit : Number of units — Unité : Nombre

Country or area	1990	1991	1992	1993	1994	1995	1996	1997	1998	1999	Pays ou zone
Africa	**1493**	**1128**	**760**	**701**	**652**	**740**	**696**	**680**	**870**	**874**	**Afrique**
Egypt	1493	1128	760	701	652	740	696	680	870	874	Egypte
America, North	**7894**	**11651**	**14217**	**3310**	**1035**	**155**	**422**	**1027**	**1500**	**1415**	**Amérique du Nord**
Mexico	[1]7894	[1]11651	[1]14217	3310	1035	155	422	1027	1500	1415	Mexique
America, South	**16694**	**25294**	**28807**	**23469**	**23835**	**29048**	**25903**	**31275**	**32336**	**26972**	**Amérique du Sud**
Argentina	1663	2457	4521	4575	6400	...	...	...	...	...	Argentine
Brazil[2]	15031	22837	24286	18894	17435	21647	17343	21556	21458	14934	Brésil[2]
Asia	**286397**	**286669**	**335650**	**415701**	**391828**	**411496**	**462427**	**465292**	**425653**	**644697**	**Asie**
India	146769	145804	149062	* [3]210419	...	...	...	...	...	...	Inde
Indonesia	...	...	3840	1542	...	...	...	...	...	...	Indonésie
Iran(Islamic Rep. of)	[4]3757	[4]9369	[4]8470	[4]3876	[4]1678	[5]6290	[5]9238	[5]3910	[5]2924	...	Iran(Rép. islamique)
Japan	40185	44449	52005	48074	49112	47266	53126	62234	56953	48395	Japon
Korea, Republic of[1]	92995	84356	122273	151790	175333	192235	234358	233443	200071	426935	Corée, République de[1]
Europe	**64097**	**118289**	**105331**	**93068**	**89112**	**99971**	**85671**	**92504**	**91345**	**99946**	**Europe**
Austria[1]	4064	...	...	...	...	...	...	...	...	...	Autriche[1]
Belarus	..	..	..	45	64	62	59	338	1033	...	Bélarus
Bulgaria	[1]1533	[1]666	[1]168	162	59	83	92	12	...	754	Bulgarie
Croatia	..	..	...	14	11	5	6	4	26	...	Croatie
Czechoslovakia(former)	3467	1937									Tchécoslovaquie(anc.)
Czech Republic	..	..	1127	1258	...	...	...	..	..	..	République tchèque
Finland[1]	22	18	12	9	12	4	5	...	...	...	Finlande[1]
France	3000	2808	3108	2952	2628	...	...	...	...	...	France
Germany	...	...	...	11165	10540	8494	8963	10020	8679	...	Allemagne
Germany(Fed.Rep.)	12288										Allemagne(Rép.féd.)
German D.R.(former)	1170	..	..	..	..	..	..	..	..	..	R.D.A. (anc.)
Hungary	7994	4970	3572	...	1625	1207	967	1951	1232	706	Hongrie
Italy	7083	9881	9687	4151	2682	11173	3418	2320	3847	3032	Italie
Netherlands[6][7]	2557	2644	2418	325	342	431	...	...	...	...	Pays-Bas[6][7]
Poland	3856	1938	1273	1000	1048	1419	1610	1961	1888	1772	Pologne
Romania[2]	1186	930	565	368	378	452	420	188	258	68	Roumanie[2]
Russian Federation	..	51598	48209	47866	50049	39773	38343	45970	45704	50021	Fédération de Russie
Slovenia	..	522	361	313	97	131	...	...	...	...	Slovénie
Spain	1412	1466	1358	...	...	...	...	...	...	...	Espagne
Sweden	2145	2076	1857	1694	2153	2801	242	178	340	319	Suède
Ukraine	..	12144	8509	9012	3483	2335	1103	1771	2454	2032	Ukraine
United Kingdom	12320	9837	8517	4530	7170	22123	20637	18332	16530	...	Royaume-Uni
Yugoslavia	..	365	294	36	102	90	147	141	146	59	Yougoslavie
USSR (former)[8]	66946	..	..	..	..	..	..	..	..	..	**URSS (anc.)[8]**
Total	**443521**	**443031**	**484765**	**536249**	**506461**	**541409**	**575118**	**590778**	**551704**	**773904**	**Total**

General Note.

Passenger road motor vehicles (including trolley-buses) seating more than nine persons (including the driver), which are manufactured wholly or mainly from domestically-produced parts. Seating capacity should be measured as the number of seats or berths, including the driver's, available in the vehicle when performing the service for which it is primarily intended. (SITC, Rev.3: 78310-2).

Remarque générale.

Véhicules automobiles routiers (y compris les trolleybus) dont le nombre de places assises (y compris celle du conducteur) est supérieur à neuf, et qui sont construits entièrement ou principalement avec des pièces fabriquées dans le pays. Le nombre de places est donné par le nombre de sièges ou de couchettes (y compris la place du conducteur) du véhicule lorsqu'il assure le service auquel il est essentiellement destiné. (CTCI, Rev.3: 78310-2).

[1] Including assembly.
[2] Buses only.
[3] Including trucks.
[4] Production by establishments employing 50 or more persons.
[5] Production by establishments employing 10 or more persons.
[6] Sales.
[7] Production by establishments employing 20 or more persons.
[8] Beginning 1983, production of trolley-buses by the U.S.S.R. and buses by the Ukrainian SSR only.

[1] Y compris le montage.
[2] Autobus seulement.
[3] Y compris les camions.
[4] Production des établissements occupant 50 personnes ou plus.
[5] Production des établissements occupant 10 personnes ou plus.
[6] Ventes.
[7] Production des établissements occupant 20 personnes ou plus.
[8] A partir de 1983, production de trolley bus de URSS et d'autobus de la RSS d'Ukraine seulement.

Lorries (trucks), including articulated vehicles, assembled from imported parts
Camions, y compris les véhicules articulés, assemblés à partir de pièces importées

ISIC-BASED CODE - CODE BASE CITI
3843-15

Unit : Number of units / Unité : Nombre

Country or area	1990	1991	1992	1993	1994	1995	1996	1997	1998	1999	Pays ou zone
Africa	**130340**	**120335**	**111946**	**111179**	**133091**	**164113**	**148220**	**146698**	**131931**	**127822**	**Afrique**
Algeria	3564	3164	2434	2304	1230	2570	2136	1293	1798	1583	Algérie
Kenya	1701	1296	315	310	428	1103	1430	...	...	...	Kenya
Morocco[1]	10784	12775	11976	9734	...	...	...	...	...	...	Maroc[1]
Nigeria	...	4378	2683	1097	696	715	...	...	...	...	Nigéria
South Africa	107922	97178	93599	96772	118221	147792	132383	132338	117092	113483	Afrique du Sud
Tunisia	1024	1065	768	922	1084	616	954	1003	1016	770	Tunisie
United Rep.Tanzania[2]	637	479	171	40	115	0	0	0	...	...	Rép. Unie de Tanzanie[2]
America, North	**1124**	**1711**	**1698**	**1083**	**621**	**0**	**0**	**0**	**0**	**0**	**Amérique du Nord**
Trinidad and Tobago[1]	1124	1711	1698	1083	621	0	0	...	...	...	Trinité-et-Tobago[1]
America, South	**35609**	**44300**	**55068**	**53344**	**55192**	**52347**	**54652**	**48697**	**51169**	**52571**	**Amérique du Sud**
Chile[1]	8028	9400	14352	16584	15960	...	...	...	...	...	Chili[1]
Colombia	[1]12660	[1]8900	[1]10116	[1]13992	[1]15660	...	...	736	903	...	Colombie
Peru[1]	2921	2000	600	768	...	...	...	...	...	...	Pérou[1]
Venezuela	12000	24000	30000	...	...	...	...	...	...	...	Venezuela
Asia	**374234**	**363719**	**345350**	**444440**	**414044**	**460556**	**542008**	**611080**	**579426**	**590351**	**Asie**
Bangladesh	504	1090	715	452	642	1047	922	1000	...	...	Bangladesh
Iran(Islamic Rep. of)	[3]22198	[3]32672	[3]34842	[3]21234	[3]15785	[4]8836	[4]19777	[4]16761	[4]38141	...	Iran(Rép. islamique)
Israel	1074	864	852	836	1260	1217	1199	...	...	...	Israël
Malaysia[5]	73733	78926	34711	34711	42618	55961	78571	94977	19693	44951	Malaisie[5]
Myanmar[6]	166	117	85	172	846	500	550	255	31	102	Myanmar[6]
Pakistan[7]	13324	13911	13270	13700	6522	5857	9864	12733	11736	9210	Pakistan[7]
Thailand[1]	236221	206172	223680	323508	324780	...	...	...	...	...	Thaïlande[1]
Turkey	27014	29967	37195	49827	21591	35930	50471	73946	67985	44457	Turquie
Europe	**67833**	**91087**	**73392**	**56941**	**72090**	**71342**	**72205**	**72170**	**71187**	**70728**	**Europe**
Belgium[8][9]	65667	88937	70532	56244	...	...	...	...	...	...	Belgique[8][9]
Greece	1715	1534	1920	62	...	57	128	...	219	...	Grèce
Latvia	..	...	...	...	...	...	...	...	...	5	Lettonie
Slovakia	..	...	...	...	...	...	1421	709	312	72	Slovaquie
Slovenia	..	611	...	1	...	...	...	...	...	...	Slovénie
Yugoslavia, SFR	451									..	Yougoslavie, RSF
Oceania	**13500**	**13500**	**10210**	**12403**	**12403**	**12403**	**12403**	**12403**	**12403**	**12403**	**Océanie**
New Zealand*[5]	13500	13500	10210	...	...	...	...	...	...	...	Nouvelle-Zélande*[5]
Total	**622640**	**634652**	**597664**	**679390**	**687441**	**760761**	**829488**	**891048**	**846116**	**853875**	**Total**

General Note.
Road motor vehicles designed for the conveyance of goods, including vehicles specially equipped for the transport of certain goods, which are assembled wholly or mainly from imported parts. Articulated vehicles (that is, units made up of a road motor vehicle and a semi-trailer) are included. Ambulances, prison vans, and special purpose lorries and vans, such as fire-engines, are excluded. (SITC, Rev.3: 78210-1).

Remarque générale.
Véhicules automobiles routiers conçus pour le transport des marchandises, y compris les véhicules spécialement équipés pour le transport de certaines marchandises, et qui sont montés entièrement ou principalement avec des pièces importées. Les véhicules articulés (c'est-à-dire les ensembles composés d'un véhicule automobile routier et d'une semi-remorque) sont compris dans cette rubrique. Cette rubrique ne comprend pas les ambulances, les voitures cellulaires et les camions à usages spéciaux, tels que les voitures-pompes à incendie. (CTCI, Rev.3: 78210-1).

[1] Including motor coaches and buses.
[2] Including buses.
[3] Production by establishments employing 50 or more persons.
[4] Production by establishments employing 10 or more persons.
[5] Including vans and buses.
[6] Government production only.
[7] Twelve months ending 30 June of year stated.
[8] Production by establishments employing 5 or more persons.
[9] Shipments.

[1] Y compris les autocars et autobus.
[2] Y compris les autobus.
[3] Production des établissements occupant 50 personnes ou plus.
[4] Production des établissements occupant 10 personnes ou plus.
[5] Y compris les autobus et les camionnettes.
[6] Production de l'Etat seulement.
[7] Période de douze mois finissant le 30 juin de l'année indiquée.
[8] Production des établissements occupant 5 personnes ou plus.
[9] Expéditions.

Lorries (trucks), including articulated vehicles, produced
Camions, y compris les véhicules articulés, fabriqués

ISIC-BASED CODE - CODE BASE CITI

3843-16

Unit : Number of units   Unité : Nomb

Country or area	1990	1991	1992	1993	1994	1995	1996	1997	1998	1999	Pays ou zone
Africa	**1371**	**1127**	**1529**	**1208**	**1379**	**1241**	**738**	**328**	**760**	**701**	**Afrique**
Egypt	1371	1127	1529	1208	1379	1241	738	328	...	...	Egypte
America, North	**4709055**	**4400404**	**5289169**	**4797666**	**4783851**	**4776564**	**4962869**	**5035423**	**5011617**	**5018372**	**Amérique du Nord**
Canada[1]	789932	789600	901000	838000	...	...	...	...	...	...	Canada[1]
Mexico	[2]199123	[2]238804	[2]269591	222807	217359	210072	396377	468931	445125	451880	Mexique
United States	3720000	3372000	4118578	...	...	...	...	...	...	...	Etats-Unis
America, South	**68466**	**71683**	**69024**	**98681**	**128159**	**145529**	**136018**	**163322**	**175623**	**179400**	**Amérique du Sud**
Argentina[2]	16869	22388	36999	50805	64022	...	...	...	...	...	Argentine[2]
Brazil[3]	51597	49295	32025	47876	64137	70495	48712	63744	63773	55277	Brésil[3]
Asia	**4160182**	**4241955**	**3984252**	**3806908**	**3851090**	**3612410**	**3615141**	**3450225**	**3405718**	**3143955**	**Asie**
Armenia	..	6823	3171	1247	446	232	114	27	51	2	Arménie
Azerbaijan	..	3246	402	93	8	2	1	0	0	0	Azerbaïdjan
China	289700	382500	476700	597897	662600	595997	625100	573600	...	...	Chine
Georgia	..	...	650	384	137	209	95	82	39	38	Géorgie
India[1][4]	145200	146400	141600	148800	163200	...	...	...	...	...	Inde[1][4]
Indonesia	1280	26	174	...	2890	4755	...	575	#465464	...	Indonésie
Japan	3486618	3433790	3053477	2674941	2689340	2519319	2417370	2410124	1930965	1742111	Japon
Korea, Republic of[2]	237384	245232	293260	310639	332263	331328	340179	297565	182218	264212	Corée, République de[2]
Kyrgyzstan	..	23621	14818	5026	206	8	1	12	...	...	Kirghizistan
Europe	**1882869**	**2336769**	**2269834**	**1753252**	**1653870**	**1494737**	**1348379**	**1667881**	**1716545**	**1705479**	**Europe**
Austria[5]	736	5168	4089	3565	3098	...	...	...	...	...	Autriche[5]
Belarus	..	38178	32951	30771	21264	12902	10671	13002	12799	13370	Bélarus
Bulgaria	[2]7285	[2]2778	[2]945	[2]406	321	259	66	43	...	...	Bulgarie
Croatia	..	...	4	7	...	5	8	10	96	...	Croatie
Czechoslovakia(former)	49006	26507	..	..							Tchécoslovaquie(anc.)
Czech Republic	..	...	14030	33873	30103	22052	27036	39537	39098	23113	République tchèque
Finland[2]	910	545	578	435	546	540	492	493	687	721	Finlande[2]
France	539796	461640	494124	373200	453344	...	...	...	...	...	France
Germany	..	356059	325901	240014	259575	...	[2]240604	[2]272916	[2]292581	...	Allemagne
Germany(Fed.Rep.)	315010	..	..	..	..	...	...	...	...	..	Allemagne(Rép.féd.)
German D.R.(former)	31360	..	..	..	..	...	...	...	...	..	R.D.A. (anc.)
Hungary[4]	840	480	360	...	...	...	...	...	...	...	Hongrie[4]
Italy	234393	229860	194616	155476	191288	234354	188852	256062	278322	288038	Italie
Netherlands[6][7]	11305	10316	10034	9538	13938	15818	...	...	...	...	Pays-Bas[6][7]
Poland[8]	38956	20100	17657	18811	21356	30662	44159	57254	56080	62719	Pologne[8]
Romania	8457	7592	4456	4433	3044	3098	3142	1956	1263	900	Roumanie
Russian Federation	..	615868	582963	466925	185018	142483	134130	145850	141484	174625	Fédération de Russie
Slovakia	..	...	...	744	369	663	1421	709	312	72	Slovaquie
Slovenia	..	1513	377	424	397	277	195	...	...	16	Slovénie
Spain	[1]302400	244164	256070	[2][6]17923	[2][6]32217	[2][6]50255	[2][6]73319	[2][6]280708	[2][6]343699	[2][6]366702	Espagne
Sweden	[1]74400	[1]75000	...	...	...	...	...	51378	30582	30399	Suède
Ukraine	..	25096	33386	23052	11741	6492	4164	3386	4768	7769	Ukraine
United Kingdom	258026	207304	239936	320456	372633	247022	188215	189464	185152	...	Royaume-Uni
Yugoslavia	..	8601	4169	287	685	708	824	1278	1139	407	Yougoslavie
Yugoslavia, SFR	9989	..	..	..	..	...	...	...	...	..	Yougoslavie, RSF
Oceania	**25958**	**17666**	**14550**	**15459**	**18408**	**18408**	**18408**	**18408**	**18408**	**18408**	**Océanie**
Australia[9][10]	25958	17666	14550	15459	...	...	...	...	...	...	Australie[9][10]
Total	**10847901**	**11069604**	**11628358**	**10473174**	**10436758**	**10048889**	**10081553**	**10335588**	**10328672**	**10066315**	**Total**

General Note.
Road motor vehicles designed for the conveyance of goods, including vehicles specially equipped for the transport of certain goods, which are manufactured wholly or mainly from domestically-produced parts. Articulated vehicles (that is, units made up of a road motor vehicle and a semi-trailer) are included. Ambulances, prison vans, and special purpose lorries and vans, such as fire-engines, are excluded. (SITC, Rev.3: 78210-2).

Remarque générale.
Véhicules automobiles routiers conçus pour le transport des marchandises, y compris les véhicules spécialement équipés pour le transport de certaines marchandises, et qui sont construits entièrement ou principalement avec des pièces fabriquées dans le pays. Les véhicules articulés (c'est-à-dire les ensembles composés d'un véhicule automobile routier et d'une semi-remorque) sont compris dans cette rubrique. Cette rubrique ne comprend pas les ambulances, les voitures cellulaires et les camions à usages spéciaux, tels que les voitures-pompes à incendie. (CTCI, Rev.3: 78210-2).

For footnotes, see end of table.

Voir la fin du tableau pour les notes.

Lorries (trucks), including articulated vehicles, produced (continued)
Camions, y compris les véhicules articulés, fabriqués (suite)

ISIC-BASED CODE - CODE BASE CITI

3843-16

Footnotes
[1] Excluding production for armed forces.
[2] Including assembly.
[3] Trucks only.
[4] Including motor coaches and buses.
[5] Beginning 1995, data are confidential.
[6] Sales.
[7] Beginning 1986, production by establishments employing 20 or more persons.
[8] Including special-purpose vehicles.
[9] Finished and partly finished.
[10] Twelve months ending 30 June of year stated.

Notes.
[1] Non compris la production destinée aux forces armées.
[2] Y compris le montage.
[3] Camions seulement.
[4] Y compris les autocars et autobus.
[5] A partir de 1995, les données sont confidentielles
[6] Ventes.
[7] A partir de 1986, production des établissements occupant 20 prsonnes ou plus.
[8] Y compris véhicules à usages spéciaux.
[9] Finis et semi-finis.
[10] Période de douze mois finissant le 30 juin de l'année indiquée.

Road tractors for tractor-trailer combinations, produced
Tracteurs routiers pour les ensembles tracteur-remorque, fabriqués

ISIC-BASED CODE - CODE BASE CITI

3843-19

Unit : Number of units   Unité : Nombre

Country or area	1990	1991	1992	1993	1994	1995	1996	1997	1998	1999	Pays ou zone
America, North	**3893**	**8736**	**7680**	**4802**	**5578**	**544**	**1513**	**4852**	**9213**	**8911**	**Amérique du Nord**
Mexico	[1]3893	[1]8736	[1]7680	4802	5578	544	1513	4852	9213	8911	Mexique
America, South	**4868**	**3099**	**4298**	**3830**	**4642**	**3490**	**5681**	**4631**	**3346**	**1673**	**Amérique du Sud**
Argentina	4868	3099	4298	3830	4642	3490	5681	4631	3346	1673	Argentine
Asia	**12021**	**14124**	**15108**	**10587**	**14350**	**18418**	**11527**	**11289**	**6111**	**4801**	**Asie**
Japan	12021	14124	15108	10587	14350	18418	11527	11289	6111	4801	Japon
Europe	**96557**	**155540**	**158347**	**122048**	**90891**	**82548**	**78776**	**75742**	**74530**	**74252**	**Europe**
Belarus	..	95502	96063	82371	42879	27953	26815	27421	26922	27397	Bélarus
Croatia	..	...	...	...	...	359	607	...	...	...	Croatie
Czechoslovakia(former)	4128	1808		..	..	..	..	..	..	..	Tchécoslovaquie(anc.)
Czech Republic	..	..	1840	506	379	652	288	413	129	38	République tchèque
France	11280	12108	8988	7200	10896	...	...	...	...	...	France
Germany		...	32146	20476	23269	...	[1]29846	...	...	...	Allemagne
Germany(Fed.Rep.)	26012	..	..	..	..	..	..	..	..	..	Allemagne(Rép.féd.)
Hungary	212	168	46	...	...	...	...	...	...	...	Hongrie
Italy	6349	6904	5335	1184	163	207	246	147	285	191	Italie
Netherlands[2][3]	...	...	...	6962	11799	17636	...	...	...	...	Pays-Bas[2][3]
Slovakia	..	..	...	2724	881	773	876	...	...	...	Slovaquie
Yugoslavia, SFR	36444	..	..	..	..	..	..	..	..	..	Yougoslavie, RSF
Total	**117339**	**181499**	**185433**	**141267**	**115461**	**105000**	**97497**	**96514**	**93200**	**89637**	**Total**

General Note.
Road motor vehicles designed, exclusively or primarily, to haul other road vehicles. (SITC, Rev.3: 78320-0).

[1] Including assembly.
[2] Sales.
[3] Production by establishments employing 20 or more persons.

Remarque générale.
Véhicules automobiles routiers conçus exclusivement ou principalement pour le remorquage d'autres véhicules routiers. (CTCI, Rev.3: 78320-0).

[1] Y compris le montage.
[2] Ventes.
[3] Production des établissements occupant 20 personnes ou plus.

Trailers and semi-trailers
Remorques et semi-remorques

ISIC-BASED CODE - CODE BASE CITI

3843-22

Unit : Number of units / Unité : Nombre

Country or area	1990	1991	1992	1993	1994	1995	1996	1997	1998	1999	Pays ou zone
Africa	**37833**	**34876**	**35294**	**30307**	**25935**	**25519**	**25299**	**22819**	**20417**	**13251**	**Afrique**
Algeria	6630	8823	9000	...	...	...	...	...	...	...	Algérie
Egypt	...	...	472	...	321	597	276	257	...	...	Egypte
South Africa	30820	25670	25822	21771	17463	16771	16872	14411	11880	...	Afrique du Sud
America, North	**150048**	**122708**	**165660**	**186167**	**235000**	**279664**	**203261**	**232516**	**275956**	**303974**	**Amérique du Nord**
Mexico	931	347	392	426	713	520	349	961	2140	3511	Mexique
United States[1]	149117	122361	165268	185741	234287	279144	202912	231555	273816	300463	Etats-Unis[1]
America, South	**3083**	**3071**	**3271**	**4632**	**4287**	**2842**	**4214**	**5539**	**4777**	**5569**	**Amérique du Sud**
Argentina	1376	1464	2094	2624	2871	1955	3215	3631	4025	...	Argentine
Colombia	...	...	944	1736	1023	581	...	628	536	...	Colombie
Ecuador	...	...	233	272	393	306	91	1280	216	...	Equateur
Asia	**10110**	**18529**	**13898**	**8166**	**13411**	**23230**	**12003**	**10254**	**6314**	**11913**	**Asie**
Azerbaijan	..	110	94	52	34	9	7	4	9	3	Azerbaïdjan
Georgia	..	...	274	...	...	122	8	18	0	0	Géorgie
Indonesia	437	447	332	289	...	242	...	264	...	...	Indonésie
Japan	8530	9468	8006	4713	10654	17035	8234	7680	5151	4509	Japon
Korea, Republic of	1136	1320	1290	1471	2211	5630	3331	2192	846	7203	Corée, République de
Kyrgyzstan	..	7069	3899	1567	96	192	84	96	116	30	Kirghizistan
Turkey	7	9	3	4	10	0	4	0	0	0	Turquie
Europe	**570645**	**694963**	**530633**	**441008**	**416342**	**418884**	**376123**	**396769**	**444688**	**438131**	**Europe**
Austria	11235	13503	11766	8923	9549	11300	13343	15913	15966	14913	Autriche
Belarus	..	11664	7579	13399	7552	4895	3891	4565	4655	5057	Bélarus
Belgium	...	...	...	...	8073	10174	10761	11815	14513	14335	Belgique
Bulgaria	11231	11024	15567	11539	6987	4242	1747	669	785	275	Bulgarie
Croatia	..	6998	2395	1123	556	160	149	1	...	...	Croatie
Denmark[2]	...	...	...	...	19916	50035	44889	48611	52249	50204	Danemark[2]
Czechoslovakia(former)	3539	1928	..	..	..	..	..	..	..	..	Tchécoslovaquie(anc.)
Czech Republic	..	..	2119	602	9943	10967	8790	13953	10341	10919	République tchèque
Finland	35313	41437	#9800	7289	7804	7235	8667	7056	10865	9629	Finlande
Germany	..	203174	179359	171457	178702	134912	129334	143002	161625	...	Allemagne
Germany(Fed.Rep.)	167595	..	..	..	..	..	..	..	..	..	Allemagne(Rép.féd.)
German D.R.(former)	96176	..	..	..	..	..	..	..	..	..	R.D.A. (anc.)
Greece	100	96	94	1378	1009	1378	1161	1131	919	...	Grèce
Hungary	9230	5034	2755	2208	818	2604	1527	...	1896	1298	Hongrie
Italy	13372	12120	10920	7110	7365	8128	7621	6628	8007	10138	Italie
Latvia	..	...	...	926	1258	780	502	816	677	691	Lettonie
Netherlands[2][3]	6950	6988	6914	6245	5964	6235	...	...	...	...	Pays-Bas[2][3]
Norway	...	...	...	...	...	...	283	280	292		Norvège
Poland	39775	29228	25845	17175	23785	17156	30513	26454	28263	34658	Pologne
Portugal	10275	6810	1029	876	678	836	653	455	518	751	Portugal
Republic of Moldova	..	19729	7041	[4]0	[4]0	[4]0	[4]0	...	...	...	Rép. de Moldova
Romania	26155	15583	11067	12498	9274	9359	9081	5416	3470	2223	Roumanie
Russian Federation	..	134256	75574	41303	11223	11508	7659	6255	4778	6141	Fédération de Russie
Slovakia	..	..	206	136	99	...	646	397	3249	292	Slovaquie
Slovenia	..	14542	7825	7120	4269	32690	637	687	1106	4674	Slovénie
Spain	20995	19826	24101	7115	8557	10070	14706	16968	22310	25016	Espagne
Sweden	...	...	...	...	...	...	9017	7447	10964	10968	Suède
Ukraine	..	17660	15572	24034	30822	7797	1158	1006	10341	17138	Ukraine
United Kingdom	...	...	...	37978	50024	63671	61663	64884	68080	...	Royaume-Uni
Yugoslavia	..	10108	6279	2541	2015	1738	1261	2979	2385	1781	Yougoslavie
T.F.Yug.Rep. Macedonia	..	14489	2407	1099	216	412	333	*313	512	638	L'ex-RY Macédoine
Yugoslavia, SFR	26724	..	..	..	..	..	..	..	..	..	Yougoslavie, RSF
USSR (former)	51573	..	..	..	..	..	..	..	..	..	URSS (anc.)
Total	**823291**	**874147**	**748756**	**670280**	**694975**	**750139**	**620900**	**667897**	**752153**	**772839**	**Total**

For general note and footnotes, see end of table.   Voir la fin du tableau pour la remarque générale et les notes.

Trailers and semi-trailers (continued)
Remorques et semi-remorques (suite)

ISIC-BASED CODE - CODE BASE CITI

3843-22

General Note.
Road vehicles for the conveyance of goods which are designed to be drawn by a road motor vehicle; semi-trailers are trailers without a front axle, which are coupled to the hauling vehicle in such a manner that part of the trailer rests on the tractor. Articulated vehicles are included in "lorries". (SITC, Rev.3: 78620-0).

[1] Shipments.
[2] Sales.
[3] Production by establishments employing 20 or more persons.
[4] Excluding Transnistria region.

Remarque générale.
Véhicules routiers pour le transport des marchandises, conçus pour être remorqués par un véhicule automobile routier; les semi-remorques sont des remorques sans essieu avant, accouplées aux véhicules qui les entraînent de telle manière qu'une partie desdites remorques repose sur le véhicule tracteur. Les véhicules articulés sont classés sous la rubrique "camions". (CTCI, Rev.3: 78620-0).

[1] Expéditions.
[2] Ventes.
[3] Production des établissements occupant 20 personnes ou plus.
[4] Non compris la région de Transnistria.

Motorcycles, scooters etc.
Motocycles, scooters etc.

ISIC-BASED CODE - CODE BASE CITI

3844-01

Unit : Thousand units — Unité : En milliers

Country or area	1990	1991	1992	1993	1994	1995	1996	1997	1998	1999	Pays ou zone
Africa	**77**	**60**	**44**	**42**	**42**	**40**	**36**	**36**	**35**	**29**	**Afrique**
Algeria	21	13	9	13	7	9	3	4	7	2	Algérie
Burkina Faso	24	19	19	15	...	...	...	...	...	...	Burkina Faso
Central African Rep.	...	2	1	0	1	0	...	...	...	...	Rép. centrafricaine
Egypt	19	15	7	4	8	4	8	8	...	...	Egypte
Mozambique	1	1	1	1	...	...	...	...	...	...	Mozambique
Nigeria	...	10	7	9	6	6	...	...	...	...	Nigéria
America, North	**12**	**7**	**9**	**6**	**4**	**2**	**1**	**0**	**0**	**0**	**Amérique du Nord**
Mexico	12	7	9	6	4	...	...	...	...	...	Mexique
America, South	**286**	**332**	**290**	**300**	**344**	**389**	**435**	**604**	**628**	**632**	**Amérique du Sud**
Argentina[1]	56	94	136	125	96	41	38	45	43	27	Argentine[1]
Brazil	145	147	101	87	131	208	290	426	468	468	Brésil
Colombia	...	...	45	81	111	135	...	128	114	...	Colombie
Peru	...	...	...	...	...	5	4	5	3	1	Pérou
Asia	**7371**	**8062**	**8820**	**10286**	**12325**	**16009**	**17764**	**19748**	**16140**	**18913**	**Asie**
Bangladesh[2]	19	17	13	9	6	8	11	10	10	10	Bangladesh[2]
China	979	1341	2052	3556	5354	8254	9168	10334	8291	9782	Chine
India	1889	1607	1500	1759	2189	2588	2886	3046	3197	3722	Inde
Indonesia	431	689	419	401	491	601	...	1443	580	...	Indonésie
Iran(Islamic Rep. of)	[3]38	[3]81	[3]142	[3]42	[3]31	[4]196	[4]253	[4]234	[4]260	...	Iran(Rép. islamique)
Japan	2807	3029	3197	3023	2725	2753	2584	2676	2636	2252	Japon
Korea, Republic of	283	334	322	295	359	362	346	369	250	353	Corée, République de
Malaysia	214	223	235	242	270	328	330	424	249	272	Malaisie
Pakistan	72	83	84	96	64	61	122	117	97	93	Pakistan
Thailand[5]	594	600	...	...	...	...	1345	929	488	...	Thaïlande[5]
Turkey	45	58	65	72	45	67	87	166	82	25	Turquie
Europe	**1498**	**2364**	**1974**	**1490**	**1223**	**1151**	**1165**	**1315**	**1344**	**1259**	**Europe**
Austria	21	...	...	...	...	...	...	...	...	...	Autriche
Belarus	..	214	165	128	55	42	30	23	20	24	Bélarus
Czechoslovakia(former)	109	32	..	..	..	..	..	..	..	..	Tchécoslovaquie(anc.)
Czech Republic	..	..	15	17	11	7	9	8	4	2	République tchèque
Germany	..	...	...	...	...	56	54	...	...	...	Allemagne
German D.R.(former)	193	..	..	..	..	..	..	..	..	..	R.D.A. (anc.)
Greece	1	1	1	...	...	...	...	...	...	...	Grèce
Italy[6]	721	622	571	558	749	837	896	1015	1063	949	Italie[6]
Latvia	..	158	62	21	6	3	3	2	1	...	Lettonie
Netherlands[7][8]	25	26	24	22	18	19	...	...	...	...	Pays-Bas[7][8]
Poland	18	7	1	2	1	1	0	0	0	0	Pologne
Portugal	41	24	27	14	9	...	...	...	...	...	Portugal
Romania	4	0	0	0	0	0	0	0	0	0	Roumanie
Russian Federation	..	714	604	540	200	71	41	61	22	32	Fédération de Russie
Slovakia	..	..	0	0	18	...	24	13	...	...	Slovaquie
Slovenia	..	38	20	30	38	56	...	...	...	...	Slovénie
Spain	364	349	325	14	20	19	11	38	57	68	Espagne
Sweden	...	...	...	...	...	...	...	1	1	1	Suède
Ukraine	..	102	82	66	20	5	2	1	0	1	Ukraine
USSR (former)	1267									..	URSS (anc.)
Total	**10511**	**10824**	**11138**	**12125**	**13939**	**17591**	**19400**	**21704**	**18148**	**20833**	**Total**

General Note.
Two-wheeled road motor vehicles with or without a side-car, and cycles with auxiliary engines exceeding 50 cc. Motorized delivery tricycles are included, provided their unladen weight does not exceed 400 kilogrammes. (SITC, Rev.3: 78513-0, 78515-0, 78516-0, 78517-0, 78519-1).

[1] Excluding motor bicycles.
[2] Twelve months ending 30 June of year stated.
[3] Production by establishments employing 50 or more persons.
[4] Production by establishments employing 10 or more persons.
[5] Beginning 1999, series discontinued.
[6] Including motorcycles with engines below 50 cc.
[7] Sales.
[8] Production by establishments employing 20 or more persons.

Remarque générale.
Véhicules automobiles routiers à deux roues, avec ou sans side-car, et cycles à moteur auxiliaire d'une cylindrée supérieure à 50 cm cube. Cette rubrique comprend les triporteurs automobiles dont le poids à vide n'excède pas 400 kg. (CTCI, Rev.3: 78513-0, 78515-0, 78516-0, 78517-0, 78519-1).

[1] Non compris les vélomoteurs.
[2] Période de douze mois finissant le 30 juin de l'année indiquée.
[3] Production des établissements occupant 50 personnes ou plus.
[4] Production des établissements occupant 10 personnes ou plus.
[5] A partir de 1999, série abandonnée.
[6] Y compris les motocyclettes ayant un moteur de moins de 50 cc de cylindrée.
[7] Ventes.
[8] Production des établissements occupant 20 personnes ou plus.

Bicycles
Cycles

ISIC-BASED CODE - CODE BASE CITI

3844-04

Unit : Thousand units   Unité : En milliers

Country or area	1990	1991	1992	1993	1994	1995	1996	1997	1998	1999	Pays ou zone
Africa	**164**	**131**	**86**	**72**	**92**	**87**	**72**	**98**	**86**	**61**	**Afrique**
Algeria	39	16	19	18	31	15	6	16	14	9	Algérie
Burkina Faso	39	28	31	13	...	...	...	...	...	...	Burkina Faso
Cameroon	...	*1	2	2	1	1	...	...	...	...	Cameroun
Central African Rep.	...	2	0	0	0	1	...	...	...	...	Rép. centrafricaine
Chad	2	3	1	2	2	2	...	...	...	...	Tchad
Egypt	77	78	30	32	24	36	36	52	40	...	Egypte
Mozambique	4	3	...	5	6	5	0	0	...	...	Mozambique
America, North	**577**	**539**	**672**	**1054**	**990**	**679**	**951**	**1240**	**1364**	**1336**	**Amérique du Nord**
Mexico	577	539	672	1054	990	679	951	1240	1364	1336	Mexique
America, South	**1883**	**2522**	**2855**	**4105**	**3753**	**3547**	**3349**	**3180**	**2430**	**2093**	**Amérique du Sud**
Brazil	1501	2208	2539	3781	3458	3200	2969	2780	2055	1743	Brésil
Chile	123	142	175	198	194	251	276	297	285	300	Chili
Colombia	131	...	40	38	26	39	...	[1]50	[1]79	...	Colombie
Peru	...	...	...	...	...	57	46	53	11	9	Pérou
Asia	**48705**	**54555**	**59537**	**59149**	**63018**	**64527**	**53257**	**48213**	**41458**	**45315**	**Asie**
Armenia	..	135	27	16	12	8	7	6	3	1	Arménie
Azerbaijan	..	103	43	280	213	4	2	0	0	0	Azerbaïdjan
Bangladesh[2]	12	16	32	13	13	13	13	13	13	13	Bangladesh[2]
China	31416	36768	40836	41496	43649	44722	33612	29993	23125	23976	Chine
Georgia	..	...	...	...	2	4	1	0	0	0	Géorgie
India	6684	7150	6964	7721	8907	9912	10881	9765	10615	13734	Inde
Indonesia	221	493	2039	454	1259	1343	...	760	416	...	Indonésie
Iran(Islamic Rep. of)	...	160	121	...	...	...	...	...	...	...	Iran(Rép. islamique)
Iraq	...	...	16	...	...	...	...	...	...	...	Iraq
Japan	7969	7448	7286	6858	6702	6580	6138	5979	5928	5591	Japon
Kazakhstan	..	178	143	100	56	18	6	9	3	5	Kazakhstan
Korea, Republic of	1513	1484	1258	1210	1236	944	846	741	522	426	Corée, République de
Myanmar[3]	5	6	4	...	...	...	...	2	2	1	Myanmar[3]
Pakistan[2]	530	429	478	589	564	473	545	432	452	504	Pakistan[2]
Turkey	...	110		...	...	...	...	...	...	...	Turquie
Turkmenistan	..	10	20	8	3	0	...	0	...	...	Turkménistan
Viet Nam	88	46	158	...	...	236	56	247	112	*112	Viet Nam
Europe	**13558**	**17803**	**15351**	**13860**	**12294**	**11678**	**11067**	**10928**	**10312**	**10298**	**Europe**
Austria	129	...	...	...	...	...	...	...	...	...	Autriche
Belarus	..	815	724	603	385	271	280	317	452	508	Bélarus
Belgium	[4][5][6]148	[4][5][6]135	[4][5][6]128	[4][5][6]114	84	108	404	348	239	205	Belgique
Bulgaria	78	79	65	24	19	16	14	19	19	30	Bulgarie
Croatia	..	69	33	22	22	11	18	15	37	...	Croatie
Denmark[7]	211	206	188	170	70	156	168	174	185	127	Danemark[7]
Czechoslovakia(former)	653	497		..	..	...	...	...	...	..	Tchécoslovaquie(anc.)
Czech Republic	..	..	478	433	418	519	501	474	395	182	République tchèque
Finland[8]	180	168	151	139	125	119	114	153	125	101	Finlande[8]
France	1458	1020	880	754	968	...	...	...	...	...	France
Germany	..	3918	3691	3388	2951	2631	2277	2440	2558	...	Allemagne
Germany(Fed.Rep.)	3936	..	..	..	..	..	..	..	..	..	Allemagne(Rép.féd.)
German D.R.(former)	525	..	..	..	..	..	..	..	..	..	R.D.A. (anc.)
Greece	...	...	...	105	83	111	103	88	98	...	Grèce
Hungary[9]	135	169	160	130	106	...	...	...	...	...	Hongrie[9]
Italy	1336	1178	1242	1300	1471	1514	1321	960	817	917	Italie
Latvia	..	233	105	17	21	13	13	0	6	8	Lettonie
Lithuania	..	391	173	128	101	123	143	171	150	188	Lituanie
Netherlands[7][10]	873	894	739	721	703	766	754	880	1019	1003	Pays-Bas[7][10]
Poland	1339	971	814	745	973	1090	1132	1225	1198	1352	Pologne
Portugal	124	144	238	320	324	382	490	474	474	444	Portugal
Romania	136	107	67	42	28	22	19	6	6	3	Roumanie
Russian Federation	..	3390	2402	1812	869	563	348	424	359	425	Fédération de Russie
Slovakia	..	..	...	...	...	...	22	...	3	9	Slovaquie
Slovenia	..	218	190	190	182	104	106	69	61	99	Slovénie
Spain	579	377	357	515	475	593	379	340			Espagne

For general note and footnotes, see end of table.   Voir la fin du tableau pour la remarque générale et les notes.

Bicycles (continued)
Cycles (suite)

ISIC-BASED CODE - CODE BASE CITI

3844-04

Unit : Thousand units   Unité : En milliers

Country or area	1990	1991	1992	1993	1994	1995	1996	1997	1998	1999	Pays ou zone
Sweden	264	230	143	155	156	145	150	160	187	138	Suède
Ukraine[11]	..	812	726	528	235	36	29	28	13	31	Ukraine[11]
United Kingdom	...	...	...	...	...	1449	1500	1501	*965	...	Royaume-Uni
Yugoslavia	..	200	64	11	31	43	34	37	50	18	Yougoslavie
USSR (former)	5865	..	..	..	..	..	..	..	..	..	URSS (anc.)
Total	**70751**	**75551**	**78502**	**78240**	**80146**	**80519**	**68695**	**63659**	**55649**	**59103**	**Total**

General Note.

Two-wheeled road vehicles, fitted with pedals and using human energy as the sole means of propulsion. (SITC, Rev.3: 78520-0).

[1] Including tricycles.
[2] Twelve months ending 30 June of year stated.
[3] Government production only.
[4] Including motorcycles with engines below 50 cc.
[5] Production by establishments employing 5 or more persons.
[6] Shipments.
[7] Sales.
[8] Including delivery tricycles.
[9] Including bath chairs and delivery tricycles.
[10] Production by establishments employing 20 or more persons.
[11] Excluding children's bicycles.

Remarque générale.

Véhicules routiers à deux roues, munis de pédales et dont le seul moyen de propulsion est l'énergie humaine. (CTCI, Rev.3: 78520-0).

[1] Y compris les tricycles.
[2] Période de douze mois finissant le 30 juin de l'année indiquée.
[3] Production de l'Etat seulement.
[4] Y compris les motocyclettes ayant un moteur de moins de 50 cc de cylindrée.
[5] Production des établissements occupant 5 personnes ou plus.
[6] Expéditions.
[7] Ventes.
[8] Y compris les triporteurs.
[9] Y compris les fauteuils roulants et les triporteurs.
[10] Production des établissements occupant 20 personnes ou plus.
[11] Non compris les bicyclettes pour les enfants.

Commercial passenger and cargo planes
Avions commerciaux pour le transport de passagers et de marchandises

ISIC-BASED CODE - CODE BASE CITI

3845-07

Unit : Number of units

Unité : Nombre

Country or area	1990	1991	1992	1993	1994	1995	1996	1997	1998	1999	Pays ou zone
America, North	**2341**	**2172**	**1847**	**1685**	**1775**	**1517**	**1649**	**2037**	**2752**	**2054**	**Amérique du Nord**
United States [1]	2341	2172	1847	1685	1775	1517	1649	2037	2752	...	Etats-Unis [1]
America, South	**151**	**151**	**151**	**151**	**151**	**151**	**151**	**151**	**151**	**151**	**Amérique du Sud**
Brazil	151	...	...	...	...	...	...	...	...	...	Brésil
Asia	**7**	**7**	**7**	**7**	**7**	**7**	**7**	**7**	**7**	**7**	**Asie**
Indonesia	7	...	...	...	...	...	...	...	...	...	Indonésie
Europe	**619**	**646**	**616**	**642**	**653**	**602**	**497**	**442**	**373**	**389**	**Europe**
Germany	..	...	...	...	...	212	188	188	179	...	Allemagne
Poland	136	#0	0	1	3	6	7	...	...	...	Pologne
Romania	...	1	0	0	0	0	0	0	0	...	Roumanie
Sweden	...	...	...	...	...	...	51	55	53	23	Suède
United Kingdom	...	...	...	404	413	338	251	199	*141	...	Royaume-Uni
Total	**3118**	**2976**	**2621**	**2485**	**2586**	**2277**	**2304**	**2637**	**3283**	**2601**	**Total**

General Note.
Commercial heavier-than-air aircraft which are designed for the transport of passengers or goods for civilian purposes. Helicopters are included. (SITC, Rev.3: 79210-0, 79220-0, 79230-0, 79240-0).

Remarque générale.
Aéronefs commerciaux plus lourds que l'air conçus pour le transport de voyageurs et de marchandises à des fins civiles. Cette rubrique comprend les hélicoptères. (CTCI, Rev.3: 79210-0, 79220-0, 79230-0, 79240-0).

[1] Shipments.

[1] Expéditions.

Perambulators and push-chairs for babies
Landaux et poussettes pour bébés

ISIC-BASED CODE - CODE BASE CITI

3849-01

Unit : Thousand units   Unité : En milliers

Country or area	1990	1991	1992	1993	1994	1995	1996	1997	1998	1999	Pays ou zone
America, South	**59**	**54**	**53**	**43**	**49**	**22**	**37**	**22**	**30**	**8**	**Amérique du Sud**
Colombia	...	...	53	43	49	22	...	22	30	...	Colombie
Asia	**26**	**564**	**479**	**217**	**256**	**161**	**154**	**173**	**10**	**32**	**Asie**
Armenia	..	22	7	12	12	12	10	0	0	0	Arménie
Azerbaijan	..	259	94	91	43	4	2	1	0	0	Azerbaïdjan
Indonesia	26	197	338	84	187	...	...	152	4	...	Indonésie
Kazakhstan	..	76	33	22	10	4	1	...	5	6	Kazakhstan
Kyrgyzstan	..	10	7	8	4	0	0	0	1	...	Kirghizistan
Europe	**3148**	**6953**	**4655**	**3021**	**1793**	**1742**	**1719**	**1811**	**1993**	**1583**	**Europe**
Austria	22	...	...	...	...	...	...	...	...	...	Autriche
Belarus	..	141	58	51	22	4	1	3	3	6	Bélarus
Czechoslovakia(former)	84	49	..	..	..	..	..	..	..	..	Tchécoslovaquie(anc.)
Finland	8	13	..	...	...	...	...	...	...	..	Finlande
Germany	..	...	756	315	284	235	251	274	222	...	Allemagne
Germany(Fed.Rep.)	838	..	..	..	..	..	..	..	..	..	Allemagne(Rép.féd.)
German D.R.(former)	476	..	..	..	..	..	..	..	..	..	R.D.A. (anc.)
Greece	23	21	24	...	...	...	...	...	...	...	Grèce
Hungary	21	14	5	3	...	...	...	...	...	...	Hongrie
Latvia	..	151	39	1	1	0	0	...	...	...	Lettonie
Lithuania	..	86	32	18	7	1	0	0	0	0	Lituanie
Poland	89	77	10	51	84	80	115	259	284	200	Pologne
Portugal	...	...	127	122	100	94	95	107	107	101	Portugal
Russian Federation	..	3087	1401	629	223	103	53	28	17	45	Fédération de Russie
Slovenia	..	11	1	1	...	...	...	...	...	...	Slovénie
Spain	570	688	631	...	203	...	384	440	...	481	Espagne
Sweden	156	...	...	0	...	...	...	...	...	...	Suède
Ukraine	..	1117	725	410	137	59	11	2	1	...	Ukraine
United Kingdom	...	...	...	875	580	512	...	529	705	...	Royaume-Uni
Yugoslavia	..	43	30	5	4	...	...	...	...	...	Yougoslavie
USSR (former)	5770	..	..	..	..	..	..	..	..	..	URSS (anc.)
Total	**9003**	**7571**	**5187**	**3281**	**2098**	**1925**	**1910**	**2005**	**2033**	**1623**	**Total**

General Note.

Vehicles used for transporting babies, which have two or more wheels and are designed to be pushed by hand. Perambulators cover those in which the baby can lie down, and push-chairs refer to those in which the baby sits up or reclines at an angle. Either type may be designed so that it can be folded when not in use. Toy perambulators are excluded. (SITC, Rev.3: 89410-1).

Remarque générale.

Véhicules à deux ou plusieurs roues, servant au transport des bébés et conçus pour être poussés à la main. Dans les landaux, le bébé peut être couché alors que dans les poussettes il est assis en position droite ou inclinée. Les deux types peuvent être conçus pour être pliés lorsqu'ils ne sont pas en service. Les jouets en forme de landaux ne sont pas compris dans cette rubrique. (CTCI, Rev.3: 89410-1).

Binoculars and refracting telescopes
Jumelles et longues-vues

ISIC-BASED CODE - CODE BASE CITI

3852-01

Unit : Thousand units   Unité : En millier

Country or area	1990	1991	1992	1993	1994	1995	1996	1997	1998	1999	Pays ou zone
America, North	**14**	**12**	**10**	**5**	**18**	**4**	**0**	**0**	**0**	**0**	**Amérique du Nord**
Mexico	...	...	...	5	18	4	0	0	0	0	Mexique
Asia	**3945**	**4518**	**4288**	**4605**	**4185**	**5379**	**4494**	**4203**	**4098**	**3519**	**Asie**
Hong Kong SAR	...	638	...	...	...	...	...	...	...	...	Hong-Kong RAS
China, Macao, SAR	...	...	...	248	...	...	...	...	...	...	Chine, Macao PAS
Japan	2290	2679	2530	2895	2471	2178	2023	1795	1579	1299	Japon
Korea, Republic of	769	953	872	824	828	2315	1585	1522	1633	1334	Corée, République de
Europe	**404**	**183**	**182**	**186**	**186**	**185**	**180**	**179**	**199**	**186**	**Europe**
Germany	..	...	...	...	...	159	154	153	173	...	Allemagne
Germany(Fed.Rep.)	200	..	..	..	..	..	..	..	..	..	Allemagne(Rép.féd.)
German D.R.(former)[1]	171	..	..	..	..	..	..	..	..	..	R.D.A. (anc.)[1]
Hungary	11	1	0	...	...	...	...	...	...	...	Hongrie
United Kingdom	...	...	...	...	22	...	...	...	...	...	Royaume-Uni
Total	**4363**	**4713**	**4480**	**4796**	**4389**	**5568**	**4674**	**4382**	**4297**	**3705**	**Total**

General Note.

Monocular or binocular instruments normally used for obversation only, such as opera glasses, binoculars for touring or hunting, telescopes for hunting, touring, for use at sea etc. Astronomical telescopes are excluded. Telescopic sights for firearms, periscopes for submarines and telescopes for fitting to other instruments or apparatus are also excluded. (SITC, Rev.3: 87111-0, 87115-1).

Remarque générale.

Instruments monoculaires ou binoculaires ne servant normalement qu'à l'observation visuelle, tels que jumelles de spectacle, jumelles de tourisme ou de chasse, longues-vues de chasse, de tourisme, de marine, etc. Cette rubrique ne comprend pas les télescopes astronomiques, les lunettes de visée pour armes à feu, les périscopes pour sous-marins et les viseurs destinés à être montés sur d'autres instruments ou appareils. (CTCI, Rev.3: 87111-0, 87115-1).

[1] Telescopes only.

[1] Télescopes seulement.

Cameras, photographic
Appareils photographiques

ISIC-BASED CODE - CODE BASE CITI

3852-07

Unit : Thousand units   Unité : En milliers

Country or area	1990	1991	1992	1993	1994	1995	1996	1997	1998	1999	Pays ou zone
America, North	**3054**	**3007**	**2959**	**2950**	**2815**	**1994**	**3263**	**3565**	**3811**	**1319**	**Amérique du Nord**
Mexico	...	...	...	2950	2815	1994	3263	3565	3811	1319	Mexique
Asia	**28005**	**32185**	**29016**	**41634**	**49868**	**55466**	**61504**	**69250**	**75775**	**67939**	**Asie**
China	2132	4782	5265	19305	28300	33261	41208	46869	55219	48323	Chine
Hong Kong SAR[1]	5339	5999	5814	6377	6079	7216	4537	6599	5068	...	Hong-Kong RAS[1]
China, Macao, SAR	...	...	...	41	...	...	...	...	...	...	Chine, Macao PAS
Indonesia	...	...	1605	...	...	...	...	...	...	...	Indonésie
Japan	16955	17903	14637	12546	11942	11403	12256	12275	11977	10326	Japon
Korea, Republic of	1933	1855	1654	1760	1901	1940	...	...	...	...	Corée, République de
Europe	**576**	**3625**	**3285**	**1959**	**1105**	**847**	**737**	**677**	**570**	**591**	**Europe**
Austria[2]	6	...	...	...	...	...	...	...	...	...	Autriche[2]
Belarus	..	[3]965	949	495	128	34	35	16	5	8	Bélarus
Denmark[4]	7	5	2	1	1	0	0	1	0	0	Danemark[4]
Germany	..	138	155	138	182	226	197	234	232	...	Allemagne
Germany(Fed.Rep.)	125	..	..	..	..	..	..	..	..	..	Allemagne(Rép.féd.)
German D.R.(former)	425	..	..	..	..	..	..	..	..	..	R.D.A. (anc.)
Russian Federation	..	1905	1607	852	442	296	217	143	60	81	Fédération de Russie
Sweden	13	...	10	10	12	13	12	14	13	10	Suède
Ukraine[3]	..	342	304	205	82	20	18	11	2	1	Ukraine[3]
Yugoslavia	..	...	252	...	...	...	...	...	...	...	Yougoslavie
USSR (former)[3]	3079	..	..	..	..	..	..	..	..	..	URSS (anc.)[3]
Total	**34714**	**38817**	**35261**	**46544**	**53788**	**58308**	**65504**	**73492**	**80156**	**69849**	**Total**

General Note.
All kinds of photographic cameras other than cinematographic cameras. (SITC, Rev.3: 88111-0).

Remarque générale.
Appareils photographiques de tous types, autres que les appareils cinématographiques. (CTCI, Rev.3: 88111-0).

[1] 1999 data are confidential.
[2] Including cinematographic cameras.
[3] Excluding industrial still cameras.
[4] Sales.

[1] Pour 1999, les données sont confidentielles.
[2] Y compris les appareils cinématographiques.
[3] Non compris les appareils photographiques industriels.
[4] Ventes.

Watches
Montres

ISIC-BASED CODE - CODE BASE CITI

3853-01

Unit : Thousand units　　　　　　　　　　　　　　　　　　　　　　　　　　　　　　　　　　　　　　Unité : En millier

Country or area	1990	1991	1992	1993	1994	1995	1996	1997	1998	1999	Pays ou zone
Asia	**653665**	**704661**	**616086**	**718682**	**1007794**	**1049813**	**987348**	**909969**	**904207**	**821171**	Asie
Armenia	..	30	6	1	3	1	2	3	3	4	Arménie
China	86713	78248	86105	151830	453937	481913	479756	295046	236422	240515	Chine
Hong Kong SAR	186743	202202	...	147856	133651	140714	68317	81452	75402	[1]31926	Hong-Kong RAS
India	11311	9665	10661	8559	7561	10990	8508	6951	9611	9254	Inde
Indonesia	...	3387	6540	486	2679	2649	...	1387	231	...	Indonésie
Japan[2]	344398	389789	374146	390596	393187	396802	413746	511694	571117	531289	Japon[2]
Korea, Republic of	21139	21223	19883	19306	16744	16742	14539	13435	11420	7465	Corée, République de
Kyrgyzstan	..	117	48	48	30	1	0	0	...	...	Kirghizistan
Turkmenistan	..	...	...	0	2	1	0	..	...	...	Turkménistan
Europe	**13377**	**86509**	**79443**	**84460**	**47490**	**31872**	**19512**	**16381**	**15124**	**18340**	Europe
Austria	5017	...	...	...	...	...	...	...	...	...	Autriche
Belarus	..	14901	14108	16859	14311	6603	4809	4956	4848	5218	Bélarus
Denmark[3]	...	2	2	7	8	11	10	11	9	9	Danemark[3]
Czechoslovakia(former)[4]	499	323	...	..	..	..	..	..	..	..	Tchécoslovaquie(anc.)[4]
Germany	..	4488	...	2237	2125	2302	1975	1300	1392	...	Allemagne
Germany(Fed.Rep.)	3687	..	..	..	..	..	..	..	..	..	Allemagne(Rép.féd.)
German D.R.(former)[4]	4063	..	..	..	..	..	..	..	..	..	R.D.A. (anc.)[4]
Poland	...	7	3	1	0	0	0	0	0	0	Pologne
Russian Federation	..	61553	57842	60093	25879	17800	7563	4983	3763	6304	Fédération de Russie
Spain	...	3	...	...	...	...	...	...	34	...	Espagne
Ukraine[4]	..	...	...	133	65	47	17	4	0	3	Ukraine[4]
United Kingdom	...	...	...	92	63	72	101	88	*54	...	Royaume-Uni
Yugoslavia	..	13	12	2	3	1	1	3	7	1	Yougoslavie
USSR (former)	77363	..	..	..	..	..	..	..	..	..	URSS (anc.)
Total	**744405**	**791171**	**695529**	**803142**	**1055284**	**1081685**	**1006859**	**926349**	**919331**	**839511**	Total

General Note.
Pocket watches, wrist-watches and other watches including stop-watches. (SITC, Rev.3: 88530-0, 88540-0).

Remarque générale.
Montres de poche, montres-bracelets et autres montres, y compris les chronomètres. (CTCI, Rev.3: 88530-0, 88540-0).

[1] Excluding other electronic watches (quartz digital-analogue, pen-watches), for confidentiality purposes.
[2] Excluding stop-watches.
[3] Sales.
[4] Wrist-watches only.

[1] Non compris autres montres électroniques (quartz, à affichage numérique-analogique, stylos-montres), pour raisons de confidentialité.
[2] Non compris les chronomètres.
[3] Ventes.
[4] Montres-bracelets seulement.

Clocks, with watch movements
Pendulettes à mouvements de montres

ISIC-BASED CODE - CODE BASE CITI

3853-04

Unit : Thousand units   Unité : En milliers

Country or area	1990	1991	1992	1993	1994	1995	1996	1997	1998	1999	Pays ou zone
Africa	39	38	50	41	46	46	49	50	52	54	**Afrique**
Mozambique	...	...	15	6	...	...	...	...	...	...	Mozambique
Nigeria	...	27	35	35	35	35	...	...	...	...	Nigéria
Asia	32364	41231	45300	72823	93681	129379	92394	84227	104205	109526	**Asie**
Armenia	..	2095	1119	375	344	377	216	108	34	0	Arménie
China	30557	36601	40222	69252	90544	126265	89600	81826	...	...	Chine
Indonesia	1807	2535	3959	3196	2793	2737	...	2293	1302	...	Indonésie
Europe	27460	23889	18350	15324	15510	17538	17320	17164	17007	17002	**Europe**
Belarus	..	400	406	225	165	54	45	62	46	58	Bélarus
France[1][2]	1460	884	776	632	827	...	...	...	...	...	France[1][2]
Germany	..	21759	...	13267	13597	...	...	...	...	...	Allemagne
Germany(Fed.Rep.)	21570	..	..	..	..	..	..	..	..	..	Allemagne(Rép.féd.)
German D.R.(former)	3736	..	..	..	..	..	..	..	..	..	R.D.A. (anc.)
Hungary	...	544	...	...	...	...	...	...	...	...	Hongrie
Spain	122	182	168	...	...	...	...	...	...	...	Espagne
Sweden	...	...	...	...	...	...	...	6	2	1	Suède
Ukraine[3]	..	46	171	459	182	83	24	7	7	5	Ukraine[3]
United Kingdom	...	...	...	...	...	20	...	19	35	...	Royaume-Uni
Yugoslavia	..	46	50	12	10	9	6	4	3	4	Yougoslavie
Total	59863	65157	63700	88188	109237	146963	109763	101441	121264	126581	**Total**

General Note.
Clocks equipped with movements regulated by a balance-wheel and hair-spring not more than 12 mm in thickness, other than instrument-panel clocks or clocks of similar type. (SITC, Rev.3: 88572-0, 88573-0).

Remarque générale.
Pendulettes équipées de mouvements à balancier à ressort spiral de moins de 12 mm d'épaisseur, autres que les montres de tableau de bord ou analogues. (CTCI, Rev.3: 88572-0, 88573-0).

[1] Including other clocks.
[2] Shipments.
[3] Desktop clocks only.

[1] Y compris les autres appareils d'horlogerie.
[2] Expéditions.
[3] Appareils d'horlogerie de bureau seulement.

Clocks, other, electric and non-electric
Autres appareils d'horlogerie, électriques et non électriques

ISIC-BASED CODE - CODE BASE CITI

3853-10

Unit : Thousand units   Unité : En milliers

Country or area	1990	1991	1992	1993	1994	1995	1996	1997	1998	1999	Pays ou zone
Asia	**134286**	**97422**	**90562**	**97872**	**86987**	**86321**	**84365**	**83570**	**93607**	**85193**	**Asie**
Armenia	..	67	30	9	18	15	0	0	0	0	Arménie
Hong Kong SAR[1]	44475	7848	16775	13885	3230	2751	726	35	...	1868	Hong-Kong RAS[1]
Japan	87221	87427	71699	...	...	...	...	...	...	...	Japon
Korea, Republic of[2]	2590	2080	2058	1862	1623	1439	...	...	...	...	Corée, République de[2]
Europe	**1337**	**20061**	**19182**	**21209**	**18401**	**11967**	**9999**	**9565**	**9487**	**9570**	**Europe**
Belarus	..	11984	11408	13647	11010	4847	2662	2034	1893	2233	Bélarus
Croatia	..	12	2	0	0	0	0	...	...	...	Croatie
Denmark[3]	2	2	2	0	0	23	25	27	27	35	Danemark[3]
Germany	..	...	...	...	...	...	...	...	5962	...	Allemagne
Latvia	..	278	108	59	18	12	9	7	3	0	Lettonie
Slovenia	..	93	43	13	13	9	8	5	8	1	Slovénie
Spain	1	...	...	...	...	...	...	10	...	...	Espagne
Sweden	...	...	...	...	1	...	...	...	...	...	Suède
United Kingdom	...	...	...	...	...	1039	1258	1499	1535	...	Royaume-Uni
Yugoslavia	..	391	318	189	59	68	68	20	52	0	Yougoslavie
Total	**135623**	**117483**	**109744**	**119081**	**105388**	**98287**	**94364**	**93135**	**103094**	**94764**	**Total**

General Note.
Clocks having movements other than watch movements, driven by weights, spring or electricity and generally controlled by a pendulum or a balance-wheel and hairspring. Instrument panel and similar-type clocks are excluded.
(SITC, Rev.3: 88574-0, 88575-0, 88576-0, 88577-0, 88578-0, 88579-0).

Remarque générale.
Horloges, pendules et pendulettes équipées de mouvements autres que les mouvements de montres, entraînés par des poids, des ressorts ou par l'électricité et contrôlés par un pendule ou un balancier à ressort spiral.
Cette rubrique ne comprend pas les montres de tableau de bord ou similaires.
(CTCI, Rev.3: 88574-0, 88575-0, 88576-0, 88577-0, 88578-0, 88579-0).

[1] Including clocks with watch movements and instrument-panel and similar type clocks.
[2] Wall clocks.
[3] Sales.

[1] Y compris les pendulettes à mouvement de montre et montres de tableau de bord ou similaires.
[2] Pendules murales.
[3] Ventes.

Pianos
Pianos

ISIC-BASED CODE - CODE BASE CITI
3902-01

Unit : Number of units   Unité : Nombre

Country or area	1990	1991	1992	1993	1994	1995	1996	1997	1998	1999	Pays ou zone
Asia	**538849**	**546756**	**540643**	**486013**	**456669**	**435933**	**371742**	**355999**	**310639**	**301137**	**Asie**
China	36175	48958	64116	...	...	...	...	...	...	...	Chine
China, Macao, SAR[1][2]	...	...	...	2698	2395	...	1624	...	...	...	Chine, Macao PAS[1][2]
Georgia	..	...	63	57	...	20	...	0	0	0	Géorgie
Indonesia	2907	4818	6804	28135	19199	3630	...	14206	19648	...	Indonésie
Japan[3][4]	264878	231197	213312	177180	173411	167831	142365	155783	147377	134869	Japon[3][4]
Korea, Republic of	232650	259507	254109	228193	211891	212463	165562	134021	91625	95209	Corée, République de
Europe	**50708**	**118233**	**96109**	**71040**	**47110**	**43207**	**29460**	**28706**	**21506**	**25882**	**Europe**
Austria	659	...	...	...	...	...	...	...	...	...	Autriche
Belarus	..	22000	18860	12017	9279	7859	3085	3664	3360	3502	Bélarus
Estonia	..	312	149	98	90	69	150	256	262	265	Estonie
Germany	..	23211	...	17236	17291	...	...	...	13056	...	Allemagne
Germany(Fed.Rep.)	20555	..	..	..	..	..	..	..	..	..	Allemagne(Rép.féd.)
German D.R.(former)	22356	..	..	..	..	..	..	..	..	..	R.D.A. (anc.)
Latvia	..	1158	679	265	221	184	144	38	19	15	Lettonie
Poland	7138	6918	6132	4575	3748	4456	4508	3775	2885	1659	Pologne
Russian Federation	..	49707	40908	27351	11002	6833	2080	1149	1060	1824	Fédération de Russie
Slovenia	..	238	0	0	...	...	...	...	...	...	Slovénie
Ukraine	..	14030	11023	8839	4741	5369	1056	1387	126	180	Ukraine
USSR (former)	98512	..	..	..	..	..	..	..	..	..	URSS (anc.)
Total	**688069**	**664989**	**636752**	**557053**	**503779**	**479139**	**401202**	**384704**	**332145**	**327019**	**Total**

General Note.
Pianos of all types, including grand pianos and upright pianos, but excluding automatic pianos. (SITC, Rev.3: 89813-1).

Remarque générale.
Pianos de tous types, y compris les pianos à queue et les pianos droits, mais non compris les pianos dits automatiques.(CTCI, Rev.3: 89813-1).

[1] 1995 data are confidential.
[2] Beginning 1997, data are confidential.
[3] Production by establishments employing 20 or more persons.
[4] Shipments.

[1] Pour 1995, les données sont confidentielles.
[2] A partir de 1997, les données sont confidentielles
[3] Production des établissements occupant 20 personnes ou plus.
[4] Expéditions.

Musical instruments, string
Instruments de musique, à cordes

ISIC-BASED CODE - CODE BASE CITI

3902-04

Unit : Thousand units   Unité : En milliers

Country or area	1990	1991	1992	1993	1994	1995	1996	1997	1998	1999	Pays ou zone
America, South	**10**	**8**	**9**	**6**	**7**	**7**	**8**	**10**	**4**	**6**	**Amérique du Sud**
Colombia	10	...	9	6	7	7	...	10	4	...	Colombie
Asia	**2067**	**1627**	**1980**	**1805**	**1413**	**1837**	**1564**	**1717**	**1671**	**1813**	**Asie**
Indonesia	191	12	...	...	116	540	...	496	459	...	Indonésie
Japan[1]	672	597	612	440	354	323	296	275	286	247	Japon[1]
Kazakhstan	..	1	0	...	...	...	...	...	...	...	Kazakhstan
Korea, Republic of[2]	1204	1017	1066	1062	942	973	...	...	...	...	Corée, République de[2]
Europe	**297**	**1343**	**1089**	**900**	**582**	**491**	**517**	**461**	**393**	**450**	**Europe**
Belarus	..	17	16	10	7	5	6	13	18	13	Bélarus
Finland	12	11	...	...	...	...	...	...	...	...	Finlande
Germany	..	...	...	70	62	42	42	33	...	...	Allemagne
German D.R.(former)	129			..	..	..				..	R.D.A. (anc.)
Russian Federation	..	865	652	517	268	170	168	134	104	114	Fédération de Russie
Spain	154	199	201	167	191	229	262	252	226	...	Espagne
Ukraine	..	162	129	123	40	31	26	16	11	15	Ukraine
United Kingdom	...	...	...	...	2	2	...	1	1	...	Royaume-Uni
USSR (former)	1306	..	..	..	..	..	..	..	..	..	URSS (anc.)
Total	**3679**	**2978**	**3078**	**2711**	**2001**	**2334**	**2088**	**2187**	**2068**	**2269**	**Total**

General Note.
Instruments in which sound vibrations are produced by running a bow across the strings or by plucking the strings. (SITC, Rev.3: 89815-0).

Remarque générale.
Instruments dans lesquels les vibrations sonores sont produites par des cordes sous l'effet de pincements ou du frottement d'un archet. Cette rubrique ne comprend pas les pianos. (CTCI, Rev.3: 89815-0).

[1] Shipments.
[2] Including string electrical musical instruments.

[1] Expéditions.
[2] Y compris instruments de musique électriques à cordes.

Organs
Orgues

ISIC-BASED CODE - CODE BASE CITI

3902-07

Unit : Number of units
Unité : Nombre

Country or area	1990	1991	1992	1993	1994	1995	1996	1997	1998	1999	Pays ou zone
Asia	**63879**	**70493**	**74852**	**109707**	**102621**	**97389**	**106271**	**124626**	**111776**	**115793**	**Asie**
Indonesia	4131	6755	9216	43667	27265	22071	...	43056	...	...	Indonésie
Japan	...	...	...	...	50754	46710	51618	44900	39154	37293	Japon
Korea, Republic of	...	11760	15039	16825	24602	28608	...	...	...	...	Corée, République de
Europe	**813**	**1725**	**1648**	**1708**	**1239**	**851**	**665**	**485**	**312**	**285**	**Europe**
Austria [1]	...	...	...	...	...	25	43	38	...	...	Autriche [1]
Denmark [2]	53	44	38	32	18	23	24	25	24	25	Danemark [2]
Finland	18	15	22	15	...	...	...	...	...	...	Finlande
Germany	..	273	...	164	161	194	172	165	176	...	Allemagne
Germany(Fed.Rep.) [3]	198	..	..	..	..	..	..	..	..	..	Allemagne(Rép.féd.) [3]
Latvia	..	...	...	...	...	...	...	...	...	2	Lettonie
Slovenia	..	904	973	851	719	312	...	...	...	...	Slovénie
Sweden	16	15	10	5	4	5	5	28	...	...	Suède
United Kingdom	...	...	...	604	282	272	81	33	13	...	Royaume-Uni
Total	**64692**	**72218**	**76499**	**111416**	**103860**	**98240**	**106936**	**125112**	**112088**	**116078**	**Total**

General Note.

Keyboard wind instruments with or without pipes (pipe and reed organs, harmonium and similar keyboard instruments and foot-blown accordions). Orchestrions, street organs and similar pipe instruments not fitted with a keyboard are excluded. (SITC, Rev.3: 89821-0).

Remarque générale.

Instruments à vent, à clavier, munis ou non de tuyaux (orgues, harmoniums et instruments à clavier similaires, y compris les accordéons à soufflerie à pédale). Cette rubrique ne comprend pas les orchestrions, les orgues de barbarie et instruments à tuyaux similaires dépourvus de clavier. (CTCI, Rev.3: 89821-0).

[1] Beginning 1998, data are confidential.
[2] Sales.
[3] Excluding harmoniums and reed organs.

[1] A partir de 1998, les données sont confidentielles.
[2] Ventes.
[3] Non compris les harmoniums.

Musical instruments, wind
Instruments de musique, à vent

ISIC-BASED CODE - CODE BASE CITI

3902-10

Unit : Thousand units

Unité : En milliers

Country or area	1990	1991	1992	1993	1994	1995	1996	1997	1998	1999	Pays ou zone
America, South	**10**	**10**	**2**	**2**	**2**	**52**	**11**	**2**	**3**	**11**	**Amérique du Sud**
Colombia	...	...	2	2	2	52	...	2	3	...	Colombie
Asia	**314**	**349**	**317**	**320**	**363**	**245**	**344**	**292**	**372**	**313**	**Asie**
Indonesia	...	...	...	...	90	8	...	12	78	...	Indonésie
Japan[1]	267	240	247	249	259	236	276	259	273	266	Japon[1]
Kazakhstan	..	62	23	24	14	1	...	...	...	0	Kazakhstan
Europe	**2242**	**1323**	**1371**	**1156**	**1263**	**1492**	**1662**	**1335**	**1227**	**1616**	**Europe**
Germany	..	1188	...	1051	1164	1409	1531	1302	1200	...	Allemagne
Germany(Fed.Rep.)	1007	..	..	..	..	..	..	..	..	..	Allemagne(Rép.féd.)
German D.R.(former)	1158		..	..	..	..	..	..	..	..	R.D.A. (anc.)
Russian Federation	..	39	23	20	7	3	2	1	1	1	Fédération de Russie
Ukraine	..	22	13	16	26	17	7	0	0	...	Ukraine
United Kingdom	...	...	...	69	66	...	122	32	26	...	Royaume-Uni
USSR (former)	182	..	..	..	..	..	..	..	..	..	URSS (anc.)
Total	**2748**	**1683**	**1690**	**1478**	**1628**	**1789**	**2016**	**1629**	**1602**	**1939**	**Total**

General Note.
Wood and brass wind musical instruments, such as flutes, oboes, trumpets, cornets etc., excluding organs and accordions. (SITC, Rev.3: 89823-0).

Remarque générale.
Instruments de musique à vent, en bois ou en cuivre, tels que les flûtes, les hautbois, les cornets à pistons et les trompettes, etc., à l'exclusion des orgues et des accordéons. (CTCI, Rev.3: 89823-0).

[1] Shipments.

[1] Expéditions.

Dolls
Poupées

ISIC-BASED CODE - CODE BASE CITI

3909-01

Unit : Thousand units · Unité : En milliers

Country or area	1990	1991	1992	1993	1994	1995	1996	1997	1998	1999	Pays ou zone
America, North	**2040**	**1826**	**1612**	**1613**	**1630**	**1263**	**562**	**583**	**617**	**516**	**Amérique du Nord**
Mexico	...	...	...	1613	1630	1263	562	583	617	516	Mexique
America, South	**1119**	**1020**	**1259**	**665**	**500**	**728**	**722**	**713**	**469**	**227**	**Amérique du Sud**
Colombia	...	...	1259	665	500	728	...	713	469	...	Colombie
Asia	**16560**	**15929**	**48936**	**41694**	**62265**	**49416**	**48107**	**64935**	**87772**	**99677**	**Asie**
Indonesia	16560	15094	...	40951	61782	49194	...	64931	87771	...	Indonésie
Kazakhstan	..	835	896	743	483	222	67	4	1	0	Kazakhstan
Europe	**7063**	**43690**	**36873**	**31554**	**20107**	**16850**	**12021**	**12047**	**14069**	**16091**	**Europe**
Belarus	..	1411	1222	990	366	145	206	268	249	283	Bélarus
Croatia	..	...	...	...	...	...	...	...	150	...	Croatie
Denmark [1]	315	...	6161	1534	597	1436	596	517	198	27	Danemark [1]
Germany	...	...	...	...	...	1196	906	1101	887	...	Allemagne
Greece	...	...	...	299	...	166	203	90	77	...	Grèce
Hungary	...	...	...	...	...	...	...	354	1945	257	Hongrie
Latvia	..	35	...	13	234	246	218	277	596	515	Lettonie
Lithuania	..	...	960	408	104	100	14	0	2	2	Lituanie
Russian Federation	..	24125	14154	14401	6721	3574	2082	1330	1386	2701	Fédération de Russie
Spain	[2]5619	[2]6146	[2]5424	6953	8437	8474	6702	7898	8506	10954	Espagne
Ukraine	..	8057	6407	4879	1404	451	63	2	12	6	Ukraine
United Kingdom	...	...	...	...	...	60	29	60	61	...	Royaume-Uni
Total	**26781**	**62465**	**88681**	**75526**	**84502**	**68257**	**61413**	**78278**	**102927**	**116511**	**Total**

General Note.

Dolls made of rubber, artificial plastic materials, textile materials, wax, ceramic, wood, paperboard, papier mache or combinations of these materials. Toy metal soldiers and the like, as well as clay figures, are excluded. (SITC Rev.3: 89422-0)

Remarque générale.

Poupées en caoutchouc, en matières plastiques artificielles, en matières textiles, en cire, en céramique, en bois, en papier mâché, ou en combinaisons de ces matières. Cette rubrique ne comprend pas les soldats de plomb et articles similaires, ni les mannequins. (CTCI 89422-0).

[1] Sales.
[2] Excluding dolls made of rubber and artificial plastic materials.

[1] Ventes.
[2] Non compris les poupées en matière plastique ou en caoutchouc.

Fountain pens, ball-point pens, propelling pencils etc.
Porte-plumes réservoirs, stylographes, porte-mines etc.

ISIC-BASED CODE - CODE BASE CITI

3909-04

Unit : Million units   Unité : En millions

Country or area	1990	1991	1992	1993	1994	1995	1996	1997	1998	1999	Pays ou zone
Africa	**4**	**4**	**3**	**5**	**1**	**7**	**3**	**4**	**5**	**5**	**Afrique**
Ethiopia[1]	4.2	3.6	3.1	4.8	0.7	7.0	2.7	3.8	4.8	4.7	Ethiopie[1]
America, North	**305**	**365**	**428**	**415**	**426**	**500**	**843**	**837**	**801**	**786**	**Amérique du Nord**
Mexico	304.9	365.1	427.6	415.1	426.3	500.2	843.0	837.4	801.3	785.9	Mexique
America, South	**274**	**271**	**261**	**228**	**255**	**265**	**193**	**289**	**230**	**249**	**Amérique du Sud**
Colombia	...	...	71.0	49.9	84.0	99.0	...	142.4	93.1	...	Colombie
Ecuador	...	...	22.1	22.8	29.3	15.6	18.2	42.1	48.6	...	Equateur
Peru	...	...	...	...	...	149.9	84.8	103.9	87.9	81.7	Pérou
Asia	**3608**	**3838**	**3650**	**3809**	**3655**	**3850**	**3878**	**4389**	**3982**	**4150**	**Asie**
Armenia	..	0.8	0.2	0.3	0.0	0.0	0.0	0.0	0.0	0.0	Arménie
China	716.7	...	...	...	...	...	...	...	...	...	Chine
Georgia	..		12.9	...	0.1	1.2	0.3	0.0	0.0	0.0	Géorgie
Indonesia	109.8	244.9	42.6	289.8	53.5	187.2	...	227.0	27.5	...	Indonésie
Japan[2]	2503.3	2459.9	2488.0	2438.8	2489.8	2577.5	2656.3	2989.7	2718.9	2830.5	Japon[2]
Korea, Republic of[1]	278.0	365.6	343.4	324.9	379.3	362.8	348.9	448.6	509.8	...	Corée, République de[1]
Kyrgyzstan	..	46.8	45.3	34.6	13.9	3.8	6.2	6.1	6.8	2.6	Kirghizistan
Myanmar[3]	0.1	0.0	...	...	...	...	2.1	0.9	2.3	2.5	Myanmar[3]
Europe	**1481**	**2085**	**1974**	**1806**	**1825**	**1669**	**1670**	**1716**	**1825**	**1762**	**Europe**
Croatia	..	5.6	4.6	3.4	28.6	28.0	24.7	22.2	23.7	...	Croatie
Finland	3.4	3.6	3.0	3.0	5.0	4.1	5.9	...	...	...	Finlande
Germany	..	986.9	922.1	898.7	958.3	1008.2	1056.2	1141.3	1151.9	...	Allemagne
Germany(Fed.Rep.)	921.5	..	..	..	..	..	..	..	..	..	Allemagne(Rép.féd.)
Greece	21.3	25.1	25.3	...	...	...	...	...	...	...	Grèce
Hungary	29.5	11.6	11.3	10.7	14.7	11.3	27.7	26.3	21.8	20.7	Hongrie
Portugal#	...	...	0.1	...	...	...	...	...	...	...	Portugal#
Russian Federation	..	333.4	271.0	202.4	132.0	73.9	22.7	18.2	10.4	34.8	Fédération de Russie
Slovenia	..	0.7	5.3	0.2	...	...	...	...	...	...	Slovénie
Spain	302.8	339.2	301.1	248.5	291.9	253.1	269.8	234.7	328.1	277.9	Espagne
Sweden	...	...	...	...	...	...	...	7.1	8.1	7.3	Suède
Ukraine	..	149.7	196.9	185.1	122.6	36.6	20.6	14.2	9.7	8.4	Ukraine
United Kingdom	...	...	...	208.7	224.8	...	202.5	218.4	239.1	...	Royaume-Uni
Yugoslavia	..	22.4	21.1	13.8	13.1	1.1	6.0	1.5	0.0	0.0	Yougoslavie
Total	**5672**	**6563**	**6316**	**6262**	**6161**	**6291**	**6587**	**7234**	**6843**	**6951**	**Total**

General Note.
Fountain pens, stylograph pens and pencils (including ball-point pens and pencils) and other pens, pen-holders, pencil holders and similar holders, propelling pencils and sliding pencils. Mathematical drawing pens, pen nibs and nib-points, and pencil leads are excluded. (SITC, Rev.3: 89521-1).

Remarque générale.
Porte-plumes réservoirs, stylographes et porte-mines (y compris les stylos à bille) et autres porte-plumes, porte-crayons, porte-mines, etc., à l'exclusion des tire-lignes, des plumes et des mines de crayons. (CTCI, Rev.3: 89521-1).

[1] Ball-point pens only.
[2] Shipments.
[3] Government production only.

[1] Stylos à bille seulement.
[2] Expéditions.
[3] Production de l'Etat seulement.

Pencils, crayons etc.
Crayons, pastels etc.

ISIC-BASED CODE - CODE BASE CITI

3909-07

Unit : Million units   Unité : En millions

Country or area	1990	1991	1992	1993	1994	1995	1996	1997	1998	1999	Pays ou zone
America, North	**481**	**513**	**545**	**578**	**631**	**526**	**578**	**685**	**751**	**746**	**Amérique du Nord**
Mexico	...	...	...	578	631	526	578	685	751	746	Mexique
America, South	**44**	**44**	**42**	**41**	**41**	**26**	**45**	**60**	**43**	**36**	**Amérique du Sud**
Colombia	...	...	11	12	13	11	...	23	24	...	Colombie
Peru	...	...	...	...	...	15	29	37	19	11	Pérou
Asia	**3232**	**3089**	**3013**	**2227**	**2850**	**2698**	**2481**	**2168**	**1414**	**1339**	**Asie**
China	446	472	534	...	...	...	...	...	...	...	Chine
India[1]	74	90	59	59	44	30	32	...	...	...	Inde[1]
Indonesia	1501	1413	1291	689	1357	1147	...	732	30	...	Indonésie
Japan[2]	952	806	808	765	661	709	733	654	573	537	Japon[2]
Korea, Republic of[3]	235	233	188	188	203	175	...	...	...	...	Corée, République de[3]
Kyrgyzstan	..	34	28	19	9	3	4	4	4	1	Kirghizistan
Syrian Arab Republic	24	41	105	23	92	150	27	109	153	152	Rép. arabe syrienne
Europe	**673**	**693**	**664**	**504**	**469**	**382**	**313**	**398**	**325**	**458**	**Europe**
Croatia	..	27	28	45	52	49	64	126	42	...	Croatie
Germany(Fed.Rep.)	383	..	..	..	..	..	..	..	..	..	Allemagne(Rép.féd.)
Hungary	95	44	69	60	38	26	...	...	...	...	Hongrie
Russian Federation	..	322	327	268	195	121	29	56	72	175	Fédération de Russie
Spain[4]	175	198	172	108	...	...	...	...	...	...	Espagne[4]
Ukraine	..	82	48	3	1	3	3	4	4	4	Ukraine
United Kingdom	20	...	...	...	...	...	...	...	...	...	Royaume-Uni
Total	**4429**	**4339**	**4265**	**3350**	**3991**	**3632**	**3417**	**3311**	**2533**	**2578**	**Total**

General Note.
Pencil leads, slate pencils, crayons and pastels, drawing charcoals, and writing and drawing chalks. Crude chalk and medical or cosmetic pencils are excluded. (SITC, Rev.3: 89523-0).

Remarque générale.
Mines de crayons, crayons à ardoise, bâtonnets de pastel, fusains et craies pour écrire et dessiner. Cette rubrique ne comprend pas la craie brute et les crayons utilisés à des fins médicales ou cosmétiques. (CTCI, Rev.3: 89523-0).

[1] Production by large and medium scale establishments only.
[2] Shipments.
[3] Pencils only.
[4] Crayons only.

[1] Production des grandes et moyennes entreprises seulement.
[2] Expéditions.
[3] Crayons seulement.
[4] Pastels seulement.

Slide fasteners (zippers)
Fermetures à glissière

ISIC-BASED CODE - CODE BASE CITI

3909-10

Unit : Thousand metres   Unité : Milliers de mètres

Country or area	1990	1991	1992	1993	1994	1995	1996	1997	1998	1999	Pays ou zone
America, South	**18483**	**15706**	**16162**	**5969**	**20674**	**21787**	**15422**	**15452**	**14245**	**14360**	**Amérique du Sud**
Chile	6538	3761	4217	4432	4291	3872	3477	3507	2300	2415	Chili
Colombia	...	...	...	1534	16380	17912	...	...	...	...	Colombie
Ecuador	...	...	...	...	...	...	...	3	3	...	Equateur
Asia	**315655**	**306627**	**340348**	**194382**	**283225**	**279929**	**281764**	**280532**	**279299**	**278066**	**Asie**
Cyprus	*2900	*3000	2123	...	...	2374	...	...	...	...	Chypre
India [1]	616	616	615	...	...	...	...	...	...	...	Inde [1]
Indonesia	123072	98821	137702	8390	...	...	...	...	...	...	Indonésie
Korea, Republic of	189067	204190	199908	182777	188014	184943	...	...	...	...	Corée, République de
Europe	**372974**	**456210**	**486943**	**457549**	**421390**	**372644**	**348203**	**393914**	**421817**	**428484**	**Europe**
Belarus	..	...	17637	17636	11174	3923	1665	2840	4465	5946	Bélarus
Croatia	..	...	...	...	...	...	...	9	5	...	Croatie
Germany	..	98280	80271	70281	68499	69150	78585	111686	76051	...	Allemagne
Germany(Fed.Rep.)	80723			..	..	..	..	..			Allemagne(Rép.féd.)
Greece	1482	726	1159	...	...	...	...	...	...	...	Grèce
Hungary	10337	6317	4183	...	2863	2310	...	3971	5124	4264	Hongrie
Latvia	..	...	...	1714	743	821	1264	3387	2358	3006	Lettonie
Portugal	...	...	42558	28450	28450	29886	41807	20535	16497	14140	Portugal
Romania	...	...	...	1878	1681	1065	1089	964	758	729	Roumanie
Russian Federation	..	27148	55998	50667	22640	8767	4322	3056	2350	5677	Fédération de Russie
Spain	...	...	...	...	...	...	64783	100754	126723	146205	Espagne
Ukraine	..	30117	32084	35179	21778	7420	1941	2120	1733	1712	Ukraine
United Kingdom	...	...	...	136077	152816	138556	146697	143470	184631	...	Royaume-Uni
Total	**707112**	**778543**	**843453**	**657900**	**725289**	**674360**	**645390**	**689898**	**715361**	**720911**	**Total**

General Note.

Zippers of any size and for any purpose (for clothing, footwear, travel goods etc.). (SITC, Rev.3: 89985-0).

Remarque générale.

Fermetures à glissière, de toutes dimensions et pour tous usages (habillement, chaussure, bagages etc.). (CTCI, Rev.3: 89985-0).

[1] Production by large and medium scale establishments only.

[1] Production des grandes et moyennes entreprises seulement.

Electricity, total production
Electricité, production totale

ISIC-BASED CODE - CODE BASE CITI

4101-01

Unit : Million kWh   Unité : Millions de kWh

Country or area	1990	1991	1992	1993	1994	1995	1996	1997	1998	1999	Pays ou zone
Africa	**318620**	**328957**	**333432**	**344235**	**357527**	**364891**	**381472**	**400860**	**407292**	**439864**	**Afrique**
Algeria	16104	17345	18286	19415	19888	19714	*20654	21489	*23615	...	Algérie
Angola*	841	934	947	950	955	960	1028	1105	1063	...	Angola*
Benin*	5	5	5	5	6	6	6	6	6	...	Bénin*
Botswana	906	935	1157	1093	1111	1114	807	925	1000	...	Botswana
Burkina Faso	184	194	201	215	216	*242	*273	*294	*298	...	Burkina Faso
Burundi	110	136	107	111	117	*120	*120	*122	*123	...	Burundi
Cameroon*	2705	2741	2726	2731	2740	2746	2753	2758	2765	...	Cameroun*
Cape Verde*	36	36	37	37	39	39	41	41	41	...	Cap-Vert*
Central African Rep.	95	94	*96	*97	*101	*102	*104	*104	*104	...	Rép. centrafricaine
Chad	90	87	84	86	85	89	*90	*90	*91	...	Tchad
Comoros*	16	16	16	16	16	16	17	17	17	...	Comores*
Congo	508	482	428	431	431	435	438	441	*443	...	Congo
Côte d'Ivoire	2295	1819	1850	2171	2050	1761	2373	2760	*2765	...	Côte d'Ivoire
Dem. Rep. of Congo	5650	5281	6073	5545	5312	*5378	*5415	*5423	*5429	...	Rép. dém. du Congo
Djibouti*	179	180	180	182	182	184	185	187	187	...	Djibouti*
Egypt [1]	*39425	44532	*45110	48510	49500	50258	*50660	54924	*57100	...	Egypte [1]
Equatorial Guinea*	18	18	19	19	19	20	20	20	21	...	Guinée équatoriale*
Ethiopia,incl.Eritrea	1244	1176	1194	1325	1442	1500	1598	1662	*1676	...	Ethiopie,incl.Erythrée
Gabon	*1008	*1019	1035	1083	1060	1135	1213	1257	*1277	...	Gabon
Gambia	70	70	71	73	73	*74	*76	*77	*77	...	Gambie
Ghana*	5816	6123	6624	6280	6097	6138	6631	6652	6662	...	Ghana*
Guinea*	518	523	525	530	532	537	541	543	545	...	Guinée*
Guinea-Bissau	40	*41	*44	*47	49	50	51	53	*53	...	Guinée-Bissau
Kenya	3044	3227	3215	3396	3538	3747	*3745	4223	4439	...	Kenya
Liberia*	565	450	460	480	480	486	488	495	498	...	Libéria*
Libyan Arab Jamah.*	16800	16900	16950	17000	17800	18000	18300	18974	19496	...	Jamah. arabe libyenne*
Madagascar	592	586	598	*602	*660	*662	*681	*735	*785	...	Madagascar
Malawi	718	766	792	*821	*838	*859	*874	*876	*877	...	Malawi
Mali	247	256	277	299	276	312	335	391	*398	...	Mali
Mauritania	140	*143	*146	*146	*150	*152	*153	*153	*155	...	Mauritanie
Mauritius	760	833	925	988	1032	1120	1255	1278	*1283	...	Maurice
Morocco	8548	9194	9710	9895	10966	12113	12407	13207	*13440	...	Maroc
Mozambique*	485	490	490	490	806	892	964	1485	7345	...	Mozambique*
Niger*	165	230	230	231	232	232	233	233	234	...	Niger*
Nigeria	13789	14305	14834	*14505	*15531	*14483	*14991	*15338	*15716	...	Nigéria
Réunion	905	989	1091	*1130	*1206	*1298	*1386	*1471	*1566	...	Réunion
Rwanda*	171	169	176	159	162	164	164	166	166	...	Rwanda*
Sao Tome and Principe*	15	15	15	15	15	15	15	15	15	...	Sao Tomé-et-Principe*
Senegal	734	756	*897	*951	*989	*1120	*1164	1184	1252	...	Sénégal
Seychelles	101	106	110	117	126	129	133	148	159	...	Seychelles
Sierra Leone*	224	230	230	233	237	241	241	242	242	...	Sierra Leone*
Somalia*	262	265	265	268	271	272	275	276	278	...	Somalie*
St. Helena and Depend.	5	5	5	5	6	6	6	6	*6	...	St-Hélène et dépend
South Africa*	165385	168316	167956	174581	182452	187825	200266	210052	205374	...	Afrique du Sud*
Sudan*	1327	1329	1325	1328	1325	1321	1338	1340	1346	...	Soudan*
Swaziland	364	419	419	419	*419	425	*425	*425	*425	...	Swaziland
Togo*	59	89	91	91	91	93	93	94	94	...	Togo*
Tunisia	5534	5743	6181	6610	6984	7589	7837	8389	*8958	...	Tunisie
Uganda	774	*834	*895	*1018	*1057	*1097	*1170	*1258	*1273	...	Ouganda
United Rep.Tanzania	1629	1833	1852	1967	1715	*1726	*1738	*1744	*1747	...	Rép. Unie de Tanzanie
Western Sahara*	85	85	85	85	85	87	87	87	87	...	Sahara occidental*
Zambia* [2]	7771	7775	7780	7785	7785	7790	7795	7795	7603	...	Zambie* [2]
Zimbabwe [2]	9559	8832	8617	7668	8272	8017	7819	*7830	6677	...	Zimbabwe [2]
America, North	**3863690**	**3969722**	**4006169**	**4146588**	**4247813**	**4371602**	**4492792**	**4527251**	**4668615**	**4965480**	**Amérique du Nord**
Antigua and Barbuda	95	95	95	95	97	98	98	99	*99	...	Antigua-et-Barbuda
Aruba	*338	339	341	375	422	463	465	468	*470	...	Aruba
Bahamas	*950	1135	1165	1217	1278	1304	1340	1414	*1532	...	Bahamas
Barbados	468	531	541	551	577	616	650	678	*747	...	Barbade
Belize	108	125	140	157	144	148	152	167	*183	...	Belize
Bermuda	490	513	517	518	527	521	525	*530	*530	...	Bermudes
British Virgin Islands*	45	45	45	45	45	45	45	45	45	...	Iles Vierges britanniques*
Canada	482054	508474	520275	532094	555650	559981	572910	573573	*561805	...	Canada

For general note and footnotes, see end of table.   Voir la fin du tableau pour la remarque générale et les notes.

Electricity, total production (continued)
Electricité, production totale (suite)

ISIC-BASED CODE - CODE BASE CITI

4101-01

Unit : Million kWh

Unité : Millions de kWh

Country or area	1990	1991	1992	1993	1994	1995	1996	1997	1998	1999	Pays ou zone
Cayman Islands	225	234	*235	*252	*285	297	*299	*300	*302	...	Iles Caïmanes
Costa Rica	3544	3808	4144	4386	4717	4840	4894	5589	*5788	...	Costa Rica
Cuba	14678	12741	11538	11004	11964	12459	13236	14087	14768	...	Cuba
Dominica	30	*31	*31	*31	*34	*37	*37	*38	*39	...	Dominique
Dominican Republic[2]	3698	3895	5581	5874	6182	6506	6847	7335	7555	...	Rép. dominicaine[2]
El Salvador	2296	2339	2426	2833	3203	3398	3452	*3480	*3821	...	El Salvador
Greenland	220	215	216	252	*255	*257	*258	*259	*260	...	Groënland
Grenada	55	60	63	65	80	88	95	108	*110	...	Grenade
Guadeloupe	747	824	901	960	1012	1063	1128	1211	1211	...	Guadeloupe
Guatemala	2330	2493	2802	3031	3154	3413	3696	*4132	*4456	...	Guatemala
Haiti*	475	470	430	393	308	523	633	633	691	...	Haïti*
Honduras	*2287	*2319	*2313	*2486	*2672	*2838	2985	3097	*3690	...	Honduras
Jamaica	2458	2123	2199	3791	4775	5829	6038	6255	*6480	...	Jamaïque
Martinique	747	738	789	852	903	976	1019	1078	*1080	...	Martinique
Mexico[2]	122448	126807	130103	135028	145989	152548	162526	*170651	*183841	...	Mexique[2]
Montserrat*	14	15	15	16	16	17	17	18	18	...	Montserrat*
Netherlands Antilles	1209	1227	1304	1362	1415	1470	*1482	*1485	*1490	...	Antilles néerlandaises
Nicaragua	1399	1473	1578	*1682	*1688	*1796	*1919	*1907	*2153	...	Nicaragua
Panama	2771	2910	3016	3286	3475	3519	3958	4185	*4498	...	Panama
Puerto Rico*	15328	15521	16205	17434	18086	18747	19130	20005	20360	...	Porto Rico*
St. Kitts-Nevis	65	84	84	69	74	81	82	90	*92	...	St-Kitts-Nevis
St. Lucia	104	105	*107	*107	*112	*113	*115	*115	*116	...	St-Lucie
St.Pierre-Miquelon	43	45	45	43	44	42	42	43	*43	...	St-Pierre-Miquelon
St. Vincent-Grenadines	51	53	57	62	64	72	76	80	*85	...	St. Vincent-Grenadines
Trinidad and Tobago	3578	3720	3976	3912	4069	4307	4541	4844	*5191	...	Trinité-et-Tobago
Turks and Caicos Islands*	5	5	5	5	5	5	5	5	5	...	Iles Turques et Caiques*
United States[2]	3197357	3273210	3291867	3411280	3473435	3582114	3677022	3698168	*3833979	...	Etats-Unis[2]
United States Virgin Is.*	980	1000	1020	1040	1057	1071	1075	1079	1082	...	Iles Vierges américaines*
America, South	**446935**	**468476**	**482795**	**519360**	**538566**	**573263**	**601489**	**630489**	**654698**	**733875**	**Amérique du Sud**
Argentina	50907	54048	*56273	61869	65686	67085	69892	73001	*74135	...	Argentine
Bolivia	*2133	*2275	2411	2454	2843	2999	3222	3380	*3710	...	Bolivie
Brazil	222820	234366	241731	255341	260041	275601	291244	307980	321588	...	Brésil
Chile	*18372	*19961	*22362	*24004	25250	29906	32528	33292	35503	...	Chili
Colombia	36166	36661	35064	40221	43040	45246	44866	46378	*45960	...	Colombie
Ecuador	6327	6967	7165	7447	8163	8349	9225	9560	*10896	...	Equateur
Falkland Is. (Malvinas)	11	*11	*11	11	*11	*12	12	*12	15	...	Iles Falkland (Malvinas)
French Guiana	353	405	445	446	446	*450	*450	*450	*453	...	Guyane française
Guyana	312	250	233	240	567	573	693	792	830	...	Guyana
Paraguay	*27226	*29396	*27141	31454	36420	*42236	*48200	*50854	*50930	...	Paraguay
Peru	13824	15325	13418	14697	15660	17440	17280	17951	*18583	...	Pérou
Suriname	1534	1557	1573	1588	1601	1614	1621	1626	*1621	...	Suriname
Uruguay	7443	7017	8898	7977	7617	6306	6668	7147	*9570	...	Uruguay
Venezuela	*59507	*60237	*66070	71611	71221	75446	*75588	*78066	*80904	...	Venezuela
Asia	**2507405**	**2864643**	**3032129**	**3209847**	**3442074**	**3648287**	**3839109**	**4017831**	**4128857**	**4735051**	**Asie**
Afghanistan* [3]	1128	1015	703	695	687	625	565	505	485	...	Afghanistan* [3]
Armenia	..	...	9003	6294	5658	5561	6215	6022	*6190	...	Arménie
Azerbaijan	..	...	19763	19100	17583	17045	17088	16836	*17985	...	Azerbaïdjan
Bahrain	*3490	*3495	3896	4244	4550	4611	5016	*5040	*5773	...	Bahreïn
Bangladesh[1]	8057	8930	9554	9866	10600	11689	12404	12820	*13857	...	Bangladesh[1]
Bhutan	1564	*1564	1564	1684	1686	1630	1972	1838	*1801	...	Bhoutan
Brunei Darussalam	1237	1336	1447	1515	1543	1631	*1675	*1705	*1725	...	Brunéi Darussalam
Cambodia*	160	165	173	180	187	194	201	208	215	...	Cambodge*
China	621200	677550	754440	839453	928083	1007726	1081310	*1134470	*1166200	...	Chine
Hong Kong SAR	28960	31889	35076	35948	26741	27916	28440	28943	*31414	...	Hong-Kong RAS
China, Macao, SAR	790	889	992	1190	1254	1272	1372	1409	*1539	...	Chine, Macao PAS
Cyprus	1975	2077	2404	2581	2681	2473	2592	2711	*2954	...	Chypre
Georgia	..	...	11520	10124	6806	6952	7226	7172	*8069	...	Géorgie
India[4]	289439	315631	332713	356335	385557	418043	436879	464372	*494380	...	Inde[4]
Indonesia	48897	51452	54940	58888	64351	68399	78117	84096	*90027	...	Indonésie
Iran(Islamic Rep. of)[3]	59102	64126	68614	76014	82019	84969	90851	97744	*103412	...	Iran(Rép. islamique)[3]
Iraq*	29160	20810	25300	26300	28000	29000	29050	29561	30346	...	Iraq*
Israel	20897	21514	24686	26000	28316	30388	32526	35065	*37964	...	Israël

For general note and footnotes, see end of table.

Voir la fin du tableau pour la remarque générale et les notes.

Electricity, total production (continued)
Electricité, production totale (suite)

ISIC-BASED CODE - CODE BASE CITI

4101-01

Unit : Million kWh   Unité : Millions de kWh

Country or area	1990	1991	1992	1993	1994	1995	1996	1997	1998	1999	Pays ou zone
Japan	857273	888088	895266	906705	964328	989880	1009350	1037893	*1046294	...	Japon
Jordan	*3688	3723	4422	4761	5075	5616	6058	*6264	*6745	...	Jordanie
Kazakhstan	..	...	82701	77444	66397	66659	58657	52000	*49144	...	Kazakhstan
Korea,Dem.Ppl's.Rep.*	53500	53500	38000	38000	37000	36000	35000	32620	30989	...	Corée,Rép.pop.dém.de*
Korea, Republic of	118738	132228	147843	163449	184931	205102	227554	248653	240587	...	Corée, République de
Kuwait,part Ntl.Zone	18887	10880	17085	*18200	23152	24126	25925	27224	*30514	...	Koweït et prt.Zne.N.
Kyrgyzstan	..	...	11980	11273	12932	12349	13758	*12637	*11615	...	Kirghizistan
Lao People's Dem. Rep.*	870	930	910	919	1197	1044	1249	1219	1225	...	Rép. dém. pop. lao*
Lebanon	*1500	*2400	*3900	*4860	*5250	5573	*7492	*8325	*9011	...	Liban
Malaysia	25263	28335	31887	35579	40058	46656	53000	58675	*60471	...	Malaisie
Maldives	*24	28	30	40	46	57	63	*71	*82	...	Maldives
Mongolia	*3348	*3229	*2929	*2582	*2715	*2629	2614	2720	*2745	...	Mongolie
Myanmar[4]	2478	2677	2996	3385	3594	4056	4256	4550	*4139	...	Myanmar[4]
Nepal[1]	731	894	952	906	945	1000	1209	1254	*1202	...	Népal[1]
Oman	5345	5548	6237	7298	7856	8392	8979	9662	*10672	...	Oman
Pakistan[1]	37660	41042	45466	48751	50640	53545	56946	59125	*62104	...	Pakistan[1]
Philippines*	25589	25654	25870	26055	30465	33531	36663	40053	41192	...	Philippines*
Qatar	4842	4669	5183	5560	5850	*6014	*6615	*6910	*8170	...	Qatar
S.Arabia,pt.Ntrl.Zn	70115	74574	79628	87906	96880	99833	103353	107289	*112691	...	Arab.saoud,p.Zn.neut
Singapore	15618	16597	17543	18962	20676	22057	23458	26188	*28283	...	Singapour
Sri Lanka	3150	3377	3551	3979	4386	4800	4529	5145	*5683	...	Sri Lanka
Syrian Arab Republic	*11468	12350	12673	12742	15182	*15300	*17278	*18259	*19841	...	Rép. arabe syrienne
Tajikistan	..	...	16822	17741	16982	14768	13907	14005	*14422	...	Tadjikistan
Thailand	46175	52486	59698	66305	74452	83660	91467	97553	*94769	...	Thaïlande
Turkey	57544	60337	67342	73808	78322	86247	94862	103296	*111022	...	Turquie
Turkmenistan	..	...	13183	12637	10496	*9800	*10100	9498	*9416	...	Turkménistan
United Arab Emirates	17081	*17222	*18689	*21730	*23736	*24982	*26572	*28464	*31392	...	Emirats arabes unis
Uzbekistan	..	...	50911	49149	47800	47453	45418	46054	*45900	...	Ouzbékistan
Viet Nam	8722	*9300	*9691	10659	*12270	*14665	*16944	*19151	*21694	...	Viet Nam
Dem. Yemen (former)*	910	..	..	..	..	..	..	..	..	...	Yémen dém. (anc.)*
Yemen (former)*	830	..	..	..	..	..	..	..	..	...	Yémen (anc.)*
Yemen*	..	1802	1953	2051	2159	2369	2334	2557	2507	...	Yémen*
Europe	**2804960**	**4088862**	**4190651**	**4083415**	**4010163**	**4068794**	**4119767**	**4140040**	**4185246**	**4164658**	**Europe**
Albania	3197	3752	3357	3484	3903	4414	5926	5681	*5068	...	Albanie
Austria	50414	51484	51180	52675	53309	56587	54835	56854	*57437	...	Autriche
Belarus	..	..	37595	33369	31397	24918	23728	26057	*23492	...	Bélarus
Belgium	70846	71945	72259	70856	72287	74459	76447	81440	*85833	...	Belgique
Bosnia and Herzegovina	..	..	5000	*3500	1921	2203	2393	2461	*2538	...	Bosnie-Herzégovine
Bulgaria	42141	38917	35610	37997	38133	41789	*42716	42312	*41711	...	Bulgarie
Croatia	..	...	8894	9364	8280	8863	10548	9684	*10899	...	Croatie
Denmark	25857	36450	30988	34960	41456	38204	54981	48424	*46104	...	Danemark
Czechoslovakia(former)	86627	83274	..	..	..	..	..	..	..	...	Tchécoslovaquie(anc.)
Czech Republic	..	..	59293	58882	58705	60847	64261	64598	*65112	...	République tchèque
Estonia	..	..	11831	9119	9152	8693	9103	9218	*8521	...	Estonie
Finland	54379	57987	57726	61176	65642	63896	69372	69175	*70168	...	Finlande
France incl. Monaco	421203	455269	493129	472573	476780	493794	513044	509978	*504582	...	France y compris Monaco
Germany	..	539391	537135	526196	528750	537045	555325	551536	*556400	...	Allemagne
Germany(Fed.Rep.)*	452410	..	..	..	..	..	..	..	..		Allemagne(Rép.féd.)*
German D.R.(former)*	117292										R.D.A. (anc.)*
Greece	35032	35848	37449	38434	40676	41599	42123	43743	*46363	...	Grèce
Hungary	28411	29980	31689	32914	33514	34017	35091	35396	*37188	...	Hongrie
Iceland	4511	4494	4541	4780	4780	4981	5132	5586	*6281	...	Islande
Ireland	14515	15147	16016	16492	17186	17933	19219	19961	*21387	...	Irlande
Italy and San Marino	216891	222041	226319	222870	231877	242738	244424	251463	*260241	...	Italie y comp. St. Marin
Latvia	..	...	3834	3924	4440	3979	3123	4500	*5796	...	Lettonie
Lithuania	..	..	18707	14122	10021	13898	16789	14861	*17631	...	Lituanie
Luxembourg	1377	1415	1198	1072	1167	1181	1173	1158	*1159	...	Luxembourg
Malta*	1144	1279	1419	1500	1510	1512	1514	1515	1518	...	Malte*
Netherlands	71866	74252	77202	76992	79677	80832	85089	86638	*90903	...	Pays-Bas
Norway,Svlbd.J.Myn. I	121848	111009	117506	120001	113389	123136	104756	111656	*117043	...	Norvège,Svalbd,J.May
Poland	136311	134714	132750	133867	135347	139006	143173	142790	*142789	...	Pologne
Portugal	28501	29872	30081	31199	31376	33261	34520	34168	*38985	...	Portugal
Republic of Moldova	..	...	11248	10265	8228	6068	6117	5274	*4584	...	Rép. de Moldova

For general note and footnotes, see end of table.   Voir la fin du tableau pour la remarque générale et les notes.

Electricity, total production (continued)
Electricité, production totale (suite)

ISIC-BASED CODE - CODE BASE CITI

4101-01

Unit : Million kWh

Unité : Millions de kWh

Country or area	1990	1991	1992	1993	1994	1995	1996	1997	1998	1999	Pays ou zone
Romania	64307	56912	54195	55475	55136	59266	61350	57148	*53496	...	Roumanie
Russian Federation	..	...	1008450	955702	875914	860027	850381	835070	*827133	...	Fédération de Russie
Slovakia	..	...	*22520	24429	24740	26306	25278	24822	*25465	...	Slovaquie
Slovenia	..	...	12086	11692	12630	12648	12767	13166	13718	...	Slovénie
Spain	151759	155704	158505	156529	161512	167132	174520	190301	*195280	...	Espagne
Sweden	146450	147383	146450	144318	143047	147043	139386	149741	158277	...	Suède
Switzrld,Liechtenstein	55796	57802	59117	61073	66503	63080	57063	62804	*62909	...	Suisse,Liechtenstein
Ukraine			252524	229907	202922	194318	181986	178002	*172822	...	Ukraine
United Kingdom	318970	322805	320957	323070	324817	335860	347563	345867	*358714	...	Royaume-Uni
Yugoslavia	..	...	35826	33457	34528	*37176	*38093	*40312	*40651	...	Yougoslavie
T.F.Yug.Rep. Macedonia	..	...	6065	5180	5511	6085	6458	6680	*7048	...	L'ex-RY Macédoine
Yugoslavia, SFR	82905	..	..	..	..	..	..	..	..	..	Yougoslavie, RSF
USSR (former)	1764612	..	..	..	..	..	..	..	..	..	URSS (anc.)
Oceania	**192522**	**194900**	**197492**	**202934**	**207980**	**214687**	**220067**	**226025**	**238248**	**249410**	**Océanie**
American Samoa	100	108	108	122	130	*130	*130	*130	*130	...	Samoa américaines
Australia[1]	155077	156851	159761	163747	167513	173384	177672	183184	*194834	...	Australie[1]
Cook Islands*	16	16	16	16	16	16	16	16	16	...	Iles Cook*
Fiji	467	*472	*470	*480	*520	*544	*545	*545	*535	...	Fidji
French Polynesia	*291	*302	317	323	335	349	360	360	*361	...	Polynésie française
Guam*	800	800	800	800	800	825	825	825	830	...	Guam*
Kiribati*	7	7	7	7	7	7	7	7	7	...	Kiribati*
Nauru*	29	29	30	30	30	32	32	32	32	...	Nauru*
New Caledonia	1144	1166	*1170	*1170	*1280	1653	1567	1567	*1568	...	Nouvelle-Calédonie
New Zealand[4]	32266	32818	32469	33895	34999	35387	36549	36990	*37566	...	Nouvelle-Zélande[4]
Niue	3	3	3	*3	*3	*3	*3	*3	*3	...	Nioué
Pacific Islds(Trust)*	201	203	...	...	...	...	...	...	...	...	I. Pacifique (tutel.)*
Palau*	...	...	203	203	203	208	208	208	208	...	Palaos*
Papua New Guinea*	1790	1790	1790	1790	1790	1790	1790	1795	1795	...	Papouasie-Nvl-Guinée*
Samoa*	50	50	60	60	64	65	65	65	65	...	Samoa*
Solomon Islands*	30	30	30	30	30	32	32	32	32	...	Iles Salomon*
Tonga	24	25	27	*27	29	30	34	*34	34	...	Tonga
Vanuatu*	25	27	29	29	29	30	30	30	30	...	Vanuatu*
Total	**11898744**	**11915560**	**12242668**	**12506379**	**12804123**	**13241524**	**13654696**	**13942496**	**14282956**	**15288338**	**Total**

General Note.

Refers to gross production, which includes the consumption by station auxiliaries and any losses in the transformers that are considered integral parts of the station. Excluded is electricity produced from pumped storage. (SITC, Rev.3: 35100-0)

[1] Twelve months ending 30 June of year stated.
[2] Net production.
[3] Twelve months beginning 21 March of year stated.
[4] Twelve months beginning 1 April of year stated.

Remarque générale.

La production se rapporte à la production brute qui comprend la consommation des équipements auxiliaires des centrales et les pertes au niveau des transformateurs considérés comme faisant partie intégrante de ces centrales. Elle ne comprend pas l'électricité produite à partir d'une accumulation par pompage. (CTCI, Rev.3: 35100-0)

[1] Période de douze mois finissant le 30 juin de l'année indiquée.
[2] Production nette.
[3] Période de douze mois commençant le 21 mars de l'année indiquée.
[4] Période de douze mois commençant le 1er avril de l'année indiquée.

Electricity production by public utilities
Electricité, production, services publics

ISIC-BASED CODE - CODE BASE CITI

4101-02

Unit : Million kWh

Unité : Millions de kWh

Country or area	1990	1991	1992	1993	1994	1995	1996	1997	1998	1999	Pays ou zone
Africa	**305996**	**316719**	**320819**	**332459**	**345330**	**352879**	**369889**	**388930**	**395077**	**428243**	**Afrique**
Algeria	15451	16750	17677	18938	19493	19357	*20216	20983	*23065	...	Algérie
Angola*	773	866	889	900	905	910	974	1049	1009	...	Angola*
Benin*	5	5	5	5	6	6	6	6	6	...	Bénin*
Botswana	906	900	1085	1015	1011	1017	725	835	905	...	Botswana
Burkina Faso	184	194	201	215	216	*242	*273	*294	*298	...	Burkina Faso
Burundi	110	136	107	111	117	*120	*120	*122	*123	...	Burundi
Cameroon*	2705	2741	2726	2731	2740	2746	2753	2758	2765	...	Cameroun*
Cape Verde*	35	35	36	36	38	38	40	40	40	...	Cap-Vert*
Central African Rep.	95	94	*96	*97	*101	*102	*104	*104	*104	...	Rép. centrafricaine
Chad	90	87	84	86	85	89	*90	*90	*91	...	Tchad
Comoros*	16	16	16	16	16	16	17	17	17	...	Comores*
Congo	508	482	428	431	431	435	438	441	*443	...	Congo
Côte d'Ivoire	2295	1819	1850	2171	2050	1761	2373	2760	*2765	...	Côte d'Ivoire
Dem. Rep. of Congo	5461	5093	5883	5351	5115	5180	*5215	*5220	*5225	...	Rép. dém. du Congo
Djibouti*	179	180	180	182	182	184	185	187	187	...	Djibouti*
Egypt	*39125	44132	*44660	48040	49020	49758	*50150	54404	*56565	...	Egypte
Equatorial Guinea*	18	18	19	19	19	20	20	20	21	...	Guinée équatoriale*
Ethiopia,incl.Eritrea	1131	1129	1147	1278	1395	1452	1550	1614	*1628	...	Ethiopie,incl.Erythrée
Gabon	*928	*934	945	984	960	1025	1040	1082	*1100	...	Gabon
Gambia	59	59	60	61	61	*62	*64	*65	*65	...	Gambie
Ghana	5812	6119	6620	6276	6093	6134	6627	*6648	*6658	...	Ghana
Guinea*	213	216	218	220	222	225	228	229	231	...	Guinée*
Guinea-Bissau	36	*37	*40	*43	45	46	47	49	*49	...	Guinée-Bissau
Kenya	2974	3157	3145	3326	3468	3677	*3675	4153	*4369	...	Kenya
Liberia*	297	205	205	223	223	228	230	234	237	...	Libéria*
Libyan Arab Jamah.*	16800	16900	16950	17000	17800	18000	18300	18974	19496	...	Jamah. arabe libyenne*
Madagascar	480	472	484	*490	*546	*547	*563	*617	*666	...	Madagascar
Malawi	702	750	776	*805	*820	*841	*856	*858	*859	...	Malawi
Mali	244	246	262	279	250	278	295	351	*356	...	Mali
Mauritania	140	*143	*146	*146	*150	*152	*153	*153	*155	...	Mauritanie
Mauritius	570	613	679	757	822	922	1021	*1043	*1045	...	Maurice
Morocco	7320	8074	8396	8579	9453	10394	10843	11542	*11695	...	Maroc
Mozambique*	335	340	340	340	656	680	749	1269	7129	...	Mozambique*
Niger*	165	230	230	231	232	232	233	233	234	...	Niger*
Nigeria	13371	14074	14712	*14389	*15411	*14373	*14877	*15224	*15602	...	Nigéria
Réunion	879	957	959	*993	*1059	*1147	*1235	*1319	*1412	...	Réunion
Rwanda	169	167	174	157	*160	*162	*162	*164	*164	...	Rwanda
Sao Tome and Principe*	15	15	15	15	15	15	15	15	15	...	Sao Tomé-et-Principe*
Senegal	722	744	*883	*936	*974	*1104	*1148	1168	1238	...	Sénégal
Seychelles	101	106	110	117	126	129	133	148	159	...	Seychelles
Sierra Leone*	137	140	140	142	145	148	148	148	148	...	Sierra Leone*
Somalia*	262	265	265	268	271	272	275	276	278	...	Somalie*
St. Helena and Depend.	5	5	5	5	6	6	6	6	*6	...	St-Hélène et dépend
South Africa	*158565	*161496	161136	168428	176104	181927	194865	*204501	*199794	...	Afrique du Sud
Sudan*	1201	1201	1205	1207	1207	1201	1216	1218	1222	...	Soudan*
Swaziland	150	198	198	198	*198	200	*200	*200	*200	...	Swaziland
Togo	58	88	90	90	90	92	92	93	*93	...	Togo
Tunisia	4897	5096	5479	6003	6301	6909	7136	7694	*8238	...	Tunisie
Uganda	739	*796	*856	978	1017	1056	1129	1217	1232	...	Ouganda
United Rep.Tanzania	1531	1732	1750	1863	1611	*1618	*1628	*1633	*1635	...	Rép. Unie de Tanzanie
Western Sahara*	85	85	85	85	85	87	87	87	87	...	Sahara occidental*
Zambia*	¹7546	¹7550	¹7555	¹7560	¹7560	¹7565	¹7570	¹7570	7378	...	Zambie*
Zimbabwe	¹9401	¹8832	¹8617	¹7643	¹8249	¹7992	¹7794	* ¹7805	6575	...	Zimbabwe
America, North	**3592954**	**3666281**	**3654929**	**3761580**	**3833022**	**3932726**	**4044250**	**4074775**	**4183923**	**4390060**	**Amérique du Nord**
Antigua and Barbuda*	95	95	95	95	97	98	98	99	99	...	Antigua-et-Barbuda*
Aruba	*338	339	341	375	422	463	465	468	*470	...	Aruba
Bahamas	*900	1085	1115	1167	1228	1254	1290	1364	*1482	...	Bahamas
Barbados	468	527	537	548	571	613	644	672	741	...	Barbade
Belize	108	125	140	157	144	148	152	167	*183	...	Belize
Bermuda	490	513	517	518	527	521	525	*530	*530	...	Bermudes
British Virgin Islands*	45	45	45	45	45	45	45	45	45	...	Iles Vierges britanniques*
Canada	440176	466346	478520	487456	511555	513184	525149	526256	*520335	...	Canada

For general note and footnotes, see end of table.

Voir la fin du tableau pour la remarque générale et les notes.

Electricity production by public utilities (continued)
Electricité, production, services publics (suite)

ISIC-BASED CODE - CODE BASE CITI

4101-02

Unit : Million kWh | | | | | | | | | | | Unité : Millions de kWh

Country or area	1990	1991	1992	1993	1994	1995	1996	1997	1998	1999	Pays ou zone
Cayman Islands	225	234	*235	*252	*285	297	*299	*300	*302	...	Iles Caïmanes
Costa Rica	3543	3798	4122	4360	4674	4761	4652	5128	*5209	...	Costa Rica
Cuba	12912	11631	9924	9829	10779	11447	11952	12458	13060	...	Cuba
Dominica	30	*31	*31	*31	*34	*37	*37	*38	*39	...	Dominique
Dominican Republic[1]	2407	2453	3872	4075	4289	4514	4751	5090	5243	...	Rép. dominicaine[1]
El Salvador	2243	2298	2382	2783	3147	3338	3392	*3420	*3761	...	El Salvador
Greenland	165	160	161	197	*200	*202	*203	*204	*205	...	Groënland
Grenada	55	60	63	65	80	88	95	108	*110	...	Grenade
Guadeloupe	747	824	901	960	1012	1063	1128	1211	1211	...	Guadeloupe
Guatemala	2242	2395	2784	2972	3094	3346	3632	4010	*4456	...	Guatemala
Haiti*	430	437	392	364	281	495	605	605	663	...	Haïti*
Honduras	*2247	*2279	*2273	*2446	*2632	2798	2908	3053	*2211	...	Honduras
Jamaica	2008	2054	2131	1798	2398	2927	3032	3141	*3254	...	Jamaïque
Martinique	747	738	789	852	903	976	1019	1078	*1080	...	Martinique
Mexico[1]	114248	118357	121653	126568	137524	144075	151889	158401	*172223	...	Mexique[1]
Montserrat*	14	15	15	16	16	17	17	18	18	...	Montserrat*
Netherlands Antilles	789	802	854	897	947	1000	*1010	*1012	*1015	...	Antilles néerlandaises
Nicaragua	1325	1395	1528	*1635	*1645	*1727	*1834	*1807	*2052	...	Nicaragua
Panama	2660	2790	2903	3147	3361	3399	3824	4050	*4326	...	Panama
Puerto Rico*	14948	15330	16014	17243	17895	18532	18933	19814	20174	...	Porto Rico*
St. Kitts-Nevis	58	76	76	61	66	73	74	82	*84	...	St-Kitts-Nevis
St. Lucia	104	105	*107	*107	*112	*113	*115	*115	*116	...	St-Lucie
St.Pierre-Miquelon	43	45	45	43	44	42	42	43	*43	...	St-Pierre-Miquelon
St. Vincent-Grenadines	51	53	57	62	64	72	76	80	*85	...	St. Vincent-Grenadines
Trinidad and Tobago	3466	3608	3861	3817	3978	4229	4488	4787	*5131	...	Trinité-et-Tobago
Turks and Caicos Islands*	5	5	5	5	5	5	5	5	5	...	Iles Turques et Caiques*
United States[1]	2982072	3024673	2995866	3086054	3118383	3206238	3295280	3314524	*3413368	...	Etats-Unis[1]
United States Virgin Is.*	550	560	575	580	585	589	590	592	594	...	Iles Vierges américaines*
America, South	**417849**	**439961**	**451323**	**487651**	**503498**	**539195**	**563227**	**595121**	**618578**	**693038**	**Amérique du Sud**
Argentina	47007	50128	52273	57867	61207	62725	65067	68314	*68139	...	Argentine
Bolivia	*1892	*2038	*2169	2200	2622	*2772	2989	3147	*3532	...	Bolivie
Brazil	210913	221934	228711	241306	245875	260678	273300	288845	301198	...	Brésil
Chile	*16322	*17778	*20262	*21780	20426	26984	28177	30563	33244	...	Chili
Colombia	33688	*35191	31239	36626	39490	41698	42638	44113	*43946	...	Colombie
Ecuador	6327	6967	7165	7447	8163	8349	9225	9560	*10896	...	Equateur
Falkland Is. (Malvinas)	9	*9	*9	9	*9	*10	10	*10	13	...	Iles Falkland (Malvinas)
French Guiana	353	405	445	446	446	*450	*450	*450	*453	...	Guyane française
Guyana	154	120	112	114	296	338	352	395	416	...	Guyana
Paraguay	27204	29378	*27120	31416	36401	*42095	*48038	*50851	*50871	...	Paraguay
Peru	9564	11324	9849	12138	13320	14065	13578	15347	*16816	...	Pérou
Suriname	145	150	*121	*123	123	123	125	125	*127	...	Suriname
Uruguay	7358	6928	8806	7903	7551	6236	6598	7086	*9487	...	Uruguay
Venezuela	*56913	*57611	63042	68276	67569	72672	*72680	*76315	*79440	...	Venezuela
Asia	**2299847**	**2636899**	**2792975**	**2959505**	**3178795**	**3369206**	**3547991**	**3711452**	**3810299**	**4378386**	**Asie**
Afghanistan*[2]	814	735	510	505	500	442	390	340	330	...	Afghanistan*[2]
Armenia	..	...	9003	6294	5658	5561	6215	6022	*6190	...	Arménie
Azerbaijan	..	...	19673	19000	17483	16957	17005	16706	*17895	...	Azerbaïdjan
Bahrain	*3180	*3185	3885	4199	3753	3499	3854	*3683	*4507	...	Bahreïn
Bangladesh[3]	7732	8270	8894	9206	9784	10806	11474	11858	*12882	...	Bangladesh[3]
Bhutan	1557	*1560	1563	1683	1685	1630	1972	1838	*1801	...	Bhoutan
Brunei Darussalam	1172	1269	1380	1445	1471	1556	*1600	*1630	*1650	...	Brunéi Darussalam
Cambodia*	160	165	173	180	187	194	201	208	215	...	Cambodge*
China	621200	677550	754440	839453	928083	1007726	1081310	*1134470	*1166200	...	Chine
Hong Kong SAR	28960	31889	35076	35948	26741	27916	28440	28943	*31414	...	Hong-Kong RAS
China, Macao, SAR	753	854	957	1073	1159	1176	1276	1312	*1445	...	Chine, Macao PAS
Cyprus	1975	2077	2404	2581	2681	2473	2592	2711	*2954	...	Chypre
Georgia	..	...	11087	9865	6704	6903	7100	7076	*7831	...	Géorgie
India[4]	264328	287029	301362	324050	350490	379877	395889	420622	*449380	...	Inde[4]
Indonesia	34447	37102	40440	44238	49551	53449	63014	68838	*74342	...	Indonésie
Iran(Islamic Rep. of)[2]	54896	59710	63982	71335	77086	80044	85825	92310	*97862	...	Iran(Rép. islamique)[2]
Iraq*	28410	20310	24700	25600	27100	28000	28020	28491	29246	...	Iraq*
Israel	20722	20857	24019	25240	27609	29498	31352	33607	*36395	...	Israël

For general note and footnotes, see end of table.   Voir la fin du tableau pour la remarque générale et les notes.

Electricity production by public utilities (continued)
Electricité, production, services publics (suite)

ISIC-BASED CODE - CODE BASE CITI

4101-02

Unit : Million kWh   Unité : Millions de kWh

Country or area	1990	1991	1992	1993	1994	1995	1996	1997	1998	1999	Pays ou zone
Japan	757594	783111	788264	795708	849258	868028	884574	904935	*909150	...	Japon
Jordan	*3308	3341	4018	4389	4675	5215	5656	*5907	*6302	...	Jordanie
Kazakhstan	..	..	75359	70791	60511	61484	54103	47963	*45544	...	Kazakhstan
Korea,Dem.Ppl's.Rep.*	53500	53500	38000	38000	37000	36000	35000	32620	30989	...	Corée,Rép.pop.dém.de*
Korea, Republic of	107670	118619	130962	144437	164993	184661	205494	224445	215300	...	Corée, République de
Kuwait,part Ntl.Zone	18477	10780	16885	*17900	22802	23726	25475	26724	*29984	...	Koweït et prt.Zne.N.
Kyrgyzstan	..	...	11980	11273	12932	12349	13758	*12637	*11615	...	Kirghizistan
Lao People's Dem. Rep.*	870	930	910	919	1197	1044	1249	1219	1225	...	Rép. dém. pop. lao*
Lebanon	*1365	*2260	*3770	4720	*5100	5420	*6102	*7082	*7662	...	Liban
Malaysia	23549	26631	30362	34109	38543	44388	50521	*57055	*58864	...	Malaisie
Maldives	*24	28	30	40	46	57	63	*71	*82	...	Maldives
Mongolia	*3048	*2929	*2629	*2302	*2425	*2339	2329	2618	*2675	...	Mongolie
Myanmar[4]	2450	2648	2966	3355	3563	4024	4223	4516	*4105	...	Myanmar[4]
Nepal	706	869	927	881	[3]908	[3]984	[3]1193	[3]1207	* [3]1149	...	Népal
Oman	4504	4625	5113	5833	6187	6500	6802	7304	*8172	...	Oman
Pakistan	37660	41042	45466	48751	50640	53545	56946	59125	*62104	...	Pakistan
Philippines	24511	*24739	*24880	*25060	*28728	*30958	*33360	*36913	*37881	...	Philippines
Qatar	4818	4643	5153	5525	5814	*5976	*6575	*6868	*8125	...	Qatar
S.Arabia,pt.Ntrl.Zn	45266	49863	54098	61731	69941	71922	75918	81079	*86595	...	Arab.saoud,p.Zn.neut
Singapore	15618	16597	17543	18962	20676	22057	23458	26188	*28283	...	Singapour
Sri Lanka	3150	3377	3540	3979	4364	4783	4377	4910	*5569	...	Sri Lanka
Syrian Arab Republic	*10548	11249	11626	11709	14036	*14160	*16020	*16927	*18469	...	Rép. arabe syrienne
Tajikistan	..	...	16822	17741	16982	14768	13907	14005	*14422	...	Tadjikistan
Thailand	44175	50186	57098	63405	71177	80060	87467	93253	*90069	...	Thaïlande
Turkey	54182	56967	63615	69636	73702	80622	88791	95542	*100891	...	Turquie
Turkmenistan	..	...	13142	12610	10474	*9782	10080	9498	*9416	...	Turkménistan
United Arab Emirates	2226	*2312	*2420	*2689	*2890	*2915	*3050	*3223	*3813	...	Emirats arabes unis
Uzbekistan	..	...	50705	48945	47602	47274	45260	45866	*45713	...	Ouzbékistan
Viet Nam	8722	*9300	*9691	10659	*12270	*14665	*16944	*19151	*21694	...	Viet Nam
Dem. Yemen (former)*	790	..	..	..	..	..	..	..	..		Yémen dém. (anc.)*
Yemen (former)*	810	..	..	..	..	..	..	..	..		Yémen (anc.)*
Yemen*	..	1302	1453	1551	1634	1793	1767	1936	1898	...	Yémen*
Europe	**2567033**	**3801409**	**3885293**	**3776525**	**3734558**	**3790232**	**3806985**	**3807528**	**3841894**	**3812062**	**Europe**
Albania	3197	3752	3357	3484	3903	4414	5926	5681	*5068	...	Albanie
Austria	43524	44368	43784	45064	44981	47903	45872	47676	*48225	...	Autriche
Belarus	..	...	37595	33163	31203	24785	23489	25765	*23156	...	Bélarus
Belgium	68207	69274	69408	68142	69418	71571	73556	78892	*83241	...	Belgique
Bosnia and Herzegovina	..	...	5000	*3500	1921	2203	2393	2461	*2538	...	Bosnie-Herzégovine
Bulgaria	38370	35922	32956	34875	35236	38965	39896	39962	*39482	...	Bulgarie
Croatia	..	...	8391	8778	7713	8226	9933	9139	*10347	...	Croatie
Denmark	24868	36086	30430	34355	40604	37060	53428	46549	*44219	...	Danemark
Czechoslovakia(former)	76645	73926			..	..	..	..	..		Tchécoslovaquie(anc.)
Czech Republic	..	...	52350	52307	52351	54544	56972	56956	*57236	...	République tchèque
Estonia	..	...	11743	9016	9062	8594	8987	9090	*8394	...	Estonie
Finland	45693	49635	48961	51261	54871	53126	58619	57188	*56722	...	Finlande
France incl. Monaco	394360	428594	468158	446013	449701	467397	485784	481845	*474066	...	France y compris Monaco
Germany	..	459091	460930	453100	457091	462571	489077	485656	*491486	...	Allemagne
Germany(Fed.Rep.)*	386700	..	..	..	..	..	..	..	..		Allemagne(Rép.féd.)*
German D.R.(former)*	110250										R.D.A. (anc.)*
Greece	34157	34914	36520	37587	39855	40720	41221	42766	*45423	...	Grèce
Hungary	27463	29025	30711	31983	32693	33199	34207	34528	*36546	...	Hongrie
Iceland	4506	4489	4536	4773	4774	4974	5122	5577	*6272	...	Islande
Ireland	14285	14923	15764	16131	16812	17560	18849	19446	*20621	...	Irlande
Italy and San Marino	190327	192597	194212	187908	193562	202914	200983	199115	*202506	...	Italie y comp. St. Marin
Latvia	..	...	3762	3882	4408	3903	3011	4373	*5651	...	Lettonie
Lithuania	..	...	18707	14122	9987	13848	16734	14794	*17557	...	Lituanie
Luxembourg	854	833	635	501	729	863	895	977	*1079	...	Luxembourg
Malta*	1144	1279	1419	1500	1510	1512	1514	1515	1518	...	Malte*
Netherlands	59708	61753	63655	62397	67035	69075	72691	73527	*77377	...	Pays-Bas
Norway,Svlbd.J.Myn. I	108922	95623	100888	103013	101183	107846	91825	98281	*102903	...	Norvège,Svalbd,J.May
Poland	128210	126861	124599	125340	126912	130642	135039	134781	*135301	...	Pologne
Portugal	27064	28228	28276	29049	28727	30142	31281	30409	*35012	...	Portugal
Republic of Moldova	..	...	11248	10246	8218	6053	6101	5258	*4568	...	Rép. de Moldova

For general note and footnotes, see end of table.   Voir la fin du tableau pour la remarque générale et les notes.

Electricity production by public utilities (continued)
Electricité, production, services publics (suite)

ISIC-BASED CODE - CODE BASE CITI

4101-02

Unit : Million kWh   Unité : Millions de kWh

Country or area	1990	1991	1992	1993	1994	1995	1996	1997	1998	1999	Pays ou zone
Romania	61555	54703	52378	53894	53510	57936	60009	55856	*52177	...	Roumanie
Russian Federation	..	...	960442	913154	863646	852054	804121	788867	*781158	...	Fédération de Russie
Slovakia	..	..	*20100	21799	22210	23583	22746	22016	*23917	...	Slovaquie
Slovenia	..	...	11667	11319	12199	12222	12239	12687	13198	...	Slovénie
Spain	147399	151519	153587	150981	152248	156734	160007	169513	*171348	...	Espagne
Sweden	139389	140167	138769	135789	136143	139916	133406	143152	154567	...	Suède
Switzrld,Liechtenstein	51710	53457	54190	56309	60959	58839	53130	58941	*58853	...	Suisse,Liechtenstein
Ukraine	..	...	244372	222886	197459	189351	177084	173314	*167681	...	Ukraine
United Kingdom	298493	301177	300177	300513	301907	311880	326444	324143	*334978	...	Royaume-Uni
Yugoslavia	..	...	35626	33257	34328	*37029	37943	40162	*40501	...	Yougoslavie
T.F.Yug.Rep. Macedonia	..	..	5990	5134	5489	6078	6451	6670	*7002	...	L'ex-RY Macédoine
Yugoslavia, SFR	80033	..	..	..	..	..	..	..	..	..	Yougoslavie, RSF
USSR (former)	1650146	..	..	..	..	..	..	..	..	..	URSS (anc.)
Oceania	179618	181637	183855	189192	194042	200538	205398	208864	219323	230238	Océanie
American Samoa	100	108	108	122	130	*130	*130	*130	*130		Samoa américaines
Australia[3]	144080	145546	148091	151995	155744	161634	165644	170071	*180229	...	Australie[3]
Cook Islands*	16	16	16	16	16	16	16	16	16	...	Iles Cook*
Fiji	411	*412	*415	*420	*445	*469	*470	*470	*460	...	Fidji
French Polynesia	*291	*302	317	323	335	349	360	360	*361	...	Polynésie française
Guam*	800	800	800	800	800	825	825	825	830	...	Guam*
Kiribati*	7	7	7	7	7	7	7	7	7	...	Kiribati*
Nauru*	29	29	30	30	30	32	32	32	32	...	Nauru*
New Caledonia	1144	1166	*1170	*1170	*1280	1653	1567	1567	*1568	...	Nouvelle-Calédonie
New Zealand[4]	31705	32207	31844	33252	34192	34315	35235	34269	*34573	...	Nouvelle-Zélande[4]
Niue	3	3	3	*3	*3	*3	*3	*3	*3	...	Nioué
Pacific Islds(Trust)*	193	195	...	...	...	...	...	...	...	...	I. Pacifique (tutel.)*
Palau*	...	...	195	195	195	200	200	200	200	...	Palaos*
Papua New Guinea*	535	535	535	535	535	570	570	575	575	...	Papouasie-Nvl-Guinée*
Samoa*	42	45	55	55	59	60	60	60	60	...	Samoa*
Solomon Islands*	25	25	25	25	25	27	27	27	27	...	Iles Salomon*
Tonga	24	25	27	*27	29	30	34	*34	34	...	Tonga
Vanuatu*	19	21	23	23	23	24	24	24	24	...	Vanuatu*
Total	11013443	11042906	11289194	11506912	11789245	12184776	12537740	12786670	13069094	13932027	**Total**

General Note.
Public comprises the undertakings whose essential purpose is the production, transmission and distribution of electric energy. These may be private companies, co-operative organizations, local or regional authorities, nationalized undertakings or governmental organizations. (SITC, Rev.3: 35100-1).

Remarque générale.
Les producteurs publics comprennent les entreprises dont l'activité principale est la production, le transport et la distribution de l'energie électrique. Il peut s'agir de sociétés privées, de coopératives, de régies locales ou régionales et d'entreprises nationalisées ou organismes étatiques. (CTCI, Rev.3: 35100-1)

[1] Net production.
[2] Twelve months beginning 21 March of year stated.
[3] Twelve months ending 30 June of year stated.
[4] Twelve months beginning 1 April of year stated.

[1] Production nette.
[2] Période de douze mois commençant le 21 mars de l'année indiquée.
[3] Période de douze mois finissant le 30 juin de l'année indiquée.
[4] Période de douze mois commençant le 1er avril de l'année indiquée.

Gasworks gas
Gaz d'usine à gaz

ISIC-BASED CODE - CODE BASE CITI
4102-02B

Unit : Terajoules   Unité : Terajoules

Country or area	1990	1991	1992	1993	1994	1995	1996	1997	1998	1999	Pays ou zone
Africa	**27340**	**26330**	**25330**	**25094**	**25274**	**26930**	**30375**	**30312**	**31788**	**32502**	**Afrique**
Egypt*	300	300	300	350	360	370	380	380	380	...	Egypte*
Libyan Arab Jamah.	*40	*30	30	*30	*30	*30	*30	*30	*30	...	Jamah. arabe libyenne
South Africa	*27000	*26000	*25000	24714	24884	*26530	*29965	*29902	*31378	...	Afrique du Sud
America, North	**2780**	**2830**	**2830**	**2830**	**2830**	**2845**	**2900**	**2900**	**2900**	...	**Amérique du Nord**
Cuba*	2750	2800	2800	2800	2800	2800	2850	2850	2850	...	Cuba*
Panama*	30	30	30	30	30	45	50	50	50	...	Panama*
America, South	**20148**	**20888**	**20018**	**20116**	**16857**	**15623**	**15569**	**14516**	**14546**	**11183**	**Amérique du Sud**
Brazil	13826	13557	12289	11508	7835	6906	6567	5756	5991	...	Brésil
Chile	5845	6833	7235	8072	8541	8240	8491	8186	7955	...	Chili
Uruguay	477	498	494	536	481	477	511	574	*600	...	Uruguay
Asia	**228335**	**278078**	**312684**	**367205**	**394563**	**476115**	**491687**	**549417**	**554577**	**708097**	**Asie**
Hong Kong SAR	15056	16238	18207	19198	20727	21972	22989	23906	*23943	...	Hong-Kong RAS
Indonesia	6106	8589	10288	12025	15065	19807	29528	20134	*26715	...	Indonésie
Japan	160614	183261	185879	196791	182389	193517	138462	155401	*143948	...	Japon
Korea, Republic of	42553	65814	94012	134960	172162	236595	296205	345333	355141	...	Corée, République de
Philippines	210	*190	*190	*195	*198	*202	205	205	*205	...	Philippines
Singapore	2906	3187	3396	3660	3913	3978	4254	4394	*4581	...	Singapour
Sri Lanka	43	43	42	41	39	44	*44	*44	*44	...	Sri Lanka
Turkey	847	756	670	335	70	0	0	0	*0	...	Turquie
Europe	**194031**	**195334**	**142260**	**94160**	**66393**	**43933**	**44299**	**32386**	**30641**	**19792**	**Europe**
Austria	*930	574	11	43	29	*3	*0	*0	*0	...	Autriche
Croatia	..	...	822	568	386	423	436	418	*418	...	Croatie
Denmark	1780	1666	1514	1500	1405	1376	1271	1033	*924	...	Danemark
Czechoslovakia(former)	26437	24374		..	..	..	..	..	..	...	Tchécoslovaquie(anc.)
Czech Republic	..	..	22634	21108	18208	4413	8298	12045	*13499	...	République tchèque
Estonia	..	..	...	3616	4496	4968	5134	5313	*3416	...	Estonie
Finland	188	171	137	86	17	0	0	0	*0	...	Finlande
France incl. Monaco	843	1264	1494	1440	1282	1346	1498	1462	*1249	...	France y compris Monaco
Germany	..	*126600	*80000	36186	16000	*8550	7000	2300	*775	...	Allemagne
Germany(Fed.Rep.)*	16600		..	..	..	..	..	..	..		Allemagne(Rép.féd.)*
German D.R.(former)*	110000	..	..	..	..	..	..	..	..		R.D.A. (anc.)*
Greece	692	699	695	695	622	670	670	631	*635	...	Grèce
Italy and San Marino	9042	9209	9146	10287	9872	10050	9771	253	*203	...	Italie y comp. St. Marin
Poland	8034	6903	4998	3640	2588	2204	1438	689	*381	...	Pologne
Portugal	*2700	2891	2972	3045	3029	3062	3204	3163	*3419	...	Portugal
Slovenia	..	...	41	6	0	0	0	0	*0	...	Slovénie
Spain	*13199	11785	9055	7606	4816	3224	1763	1328	*1962	...	Espagne
Sweden	1608	1926	1919	2128	1757	1874	2036	1971	*2073	...	Suède
Switzrld,Liechtenstein	340	250	230	230	220	220	230	230	*200	...	Suisse,Liechtenstein
Ukraine	..	...	2076	1860	1560	*1550	*1550	*1550	...	...	Ukraine
United Kingdom	106	106	95	116	106	0	0	0	*0	...	Royaume-Uni
Yugoslavia, SFR	1532	..	..	..	..	..	..	..	..		Yougoslavie, RSF
Oceania	**8666**	**8356**	**8513**	**9849**	**9662**	**9974**	**5680**	**4865**	**4882**	**4193**	**Océanie**
Australia[1]	8561	8246	8403	9741	9554	9866	5572	4757	*4774	...	Australie[1]
New Zealand*[2]	105	110	110	...	...	...	...	...	...	...	Nouvelle-Zélande*[2]
Total	**481300**	**531816**	**511635**	**519254**	**515579**	**575420**	**590510**	**634396**	**639334**	**778716**	**Total**

General Note.
Gas produced by carbonization or total gasification with or without enrichment with petroleum products. It covers all types of gas produced to undertakings of one legal form or another whose main purpose is the production of manufactured gas. It includes gas produced by cracking of natural gas, and by reforming and simple mixing of gases. (SITC, Rev.3: 34500-2B).

Remarque générale.
Gaz obtenu par la carbonization ou par gazéfication totale, avec ou sans enrichissement au moyen de produits pétroliers. Cette rubrique comprend tous les types de gaz produits par des entreprises de quelque statut juridique que ce soit, dont l'objet principal est de produire du gaz manufacturé. Elle comprend le gaz produit par craquage du gaz naturel, ainsi que par reformage et simple mélange de differents gaz. (CTCI, Rev.3: 34500-2B).

[1] Twelve months ending 30 June of year stated.
[2] Twelve months beginning 1 April of year stated.

[1] Période de douze mois finissant le 30 juin de l'année indiquée.
[2] Période de douze mois commençant le 1er avril de l'année indiquée.

ANNEXES

ANNEXES

Annex I-A

INDEX OF COMMODITIES IN ALPHABETICAL ORDER

COMMODITY NAME	ISIC CITI	COMMODITY NAME	ISIC CITI
Abrasives, agglomerated or not (millstones, grindstones, grinding wheels etc.)	369904	Blouses, women's and girls'	322016
Abrasives, natural (pozzolan, pumice etc.)	290904	Boilers, steam-generating	381304A
Accumulators, electric, for motor vehicles	383913	Boilers, steam-generating	381304B
Acetaldehyde (ethanal)	351130	Borate minerals, crude	290222
Acetates (methyl, ethyl, butyl)	351134	Bread, ships' biscuits and other ordinary bakers' wares	311704
Acetic acid	351135	Brown-coal briquettes	354004
Acetone	351133	Building bricks, made of clay	369101A
Acetylene	351105	Building bricks, made of clay	369101B
Acrylonitrile	351143	Bulldozers	382422A
Activated carbon	351179	Buses and motor coaches, assembled from imported parts	384312
Air-conditioning machines	382925A	Buses and motor coaches, produced	384313
Alkyd resins	351310	Butter (Industrial production)	3112071
Alumina, calcined equivalent	372021	Butter (Total production)	311207
Aluminium bars, rods, angles, shapes, sections	372025	Butyl alcohol (butanol)	351122
Aluminium oxide	351161	Butylenes, butadiene	351109
Aluminium plates, sheets, strip, foil	372031	Cables	381910
Aluminium sulphate	351163	Cadmium unwrought	372052
Aluminium tubes and pipes	372034	Calcium carbide	351173
Aluminium wire	372028	Calculating machines	382504
Aluminium, unwrought (total production)	372022	Cameras, photographic	385207
Aluminium, unwrought, primary	3720221	Cans, metal	381901
Aluminium, unwrought, secondary	3720222	Carbon bisulphide	351153
Aluminium-base alloys	372023	Carbon black	352901
Amino plastics	351313	Carpets and rugs of wool, knotted	321401
Ammonia	351158	Carpets and rugs, other	321404
Andalusite, kyanite and sillimanite	2901194	Caustic soda	351159
Angles, shapes and sections (total production)	371035	Cellulosic continuous filaments	351340
Angles, shapes and sections of 80 mm or more (heavy sections)	371036	Cellulosic staple and tow	351307
		Cement	369204
Angles, shapes and sections, less than 80 mm (light sections)	371037	Central-heating apparatus, non-electric	381919
		Cereal breakfast food	311610
Aniline	351142	Chalk	290125
Antimony-bearing ores	230234M	Cheese (Industrial production)	3112101
Arsenic (Arsenic trioxide)	290225	Cheese (Total production)	311210
Asbestos	290910	Chlorine	351145
Asbestos-cement articles	369901A	Chocolate and chocolate products	311913
Aviation gasolene	353001A	Chromium-bearing ores, Cr content	230222M1
Bacon, ham and other dried, salted or smoked pig meat	311116	Cigarette paper	341128
Barytes, whether or not calcined	290219	Cigarettes	314007
Batteries and cells, primary	383910	Cigars	314004
Bauxite	230207	Clay (total production)	290119
Bed linen, articles	321204	Clocks, other, electric and non-electric	385310
Beef and veal, fresh (Industrial production)	3111011	Clocks, with watch movements	385304
Beef and veal, fresh (Total production)	311101	Coats, women's and girls'	322019
Beer	313304	Cobalt-bearing ores	230237M
Bentonite	2901191	Cocoa butter	311910
Benzene (Benzol)	351107	Cocoa powder	311907
Bicycles	384404	Coffee extracts, including instant coffee	312101
Binoculars and refracting telescopes	385201	Coke	354007
Biscuits	311707	Coke-oven gas	354013B
Bitumen (asphalt)	353034A	Combine harvester-threshers	382232
Blankets	321201	Commercial passenger and cargo planes	384507
Blockboard	331113	Compressed gas cylinders, made of metal	381907A

COMMODITY NAME	ISIC CITI	COMMODITY NAME	ISIC CITI
Compressors	382946	Ethylene	351110
Concrete blocks and bricks	369910B	Ethylene oxide	351129
Concrete blocks and bricks	369910A	Excavating machines	382425
Concrete mixers for use at construction sites	382434	Explosives	352907
Concrete pipes	369913A	Farinaceous preparations (ravioli, tortellini etc.)	311713
Concrete pipes	369913B	Ferro-chromium (including ferro-silico-chromium and	
Concrete, other products	369916A	charge chrome)	3710131
Concrete, other products	369916B	Ferro-nickel	3710132
Containers, one cubic metre and over	381916A	Ferro-silicon	3710134
Copper bars, rods, angles, shapes, sections	372010	Fertilizer distributors, animal-, hand- or tractor-operated	382263
Copper plates, sheets, strip, foil	372016	Fibreboard, compressed	341134A
Copper sulphate	351165	Fish, frozen	311401
Copper tubes and pipes	372019	Fish, salted, dried or smoked	311404
Copper wire	372013	Fish, tinned	311407
Copper, blister and other unrefined	372001	Flax, ramie and true hemp yarn	321116
Copper, primary, refined	3720041	Floor covering	321901
Copper, refined, unwrought (total production)	372004	Flour, cereal, other than wheat	311607
Copper, secondary, refined	3720042	Flour, wheat	311601
Copper-base alloys	372007	Fluorspar, excluding precious stones	290216
Copper-bearing ores	230201M	Footwear, house	324013
Cordage, rope and twine	321501	Footwear, leather, children's	324001
Cotton woven fabrics	321128A	Footwear, leather, men's	324004
Cotton woven fabrics	321128	Footwear, leather, women's	324007
Cotton woven fabrics	321128B	Footwear, other (sports, orthopedic etc.)	324010
Cotton yarn, mixed	321110	Footwear, total production, excluding rubber footwear	324000
Cotton yarn, pure	321113	Forging, stamping and die-stamping machines	382307
Cotton yarn, pure and mixed (total)	321109	Fork-lift trucks	382955
Cranes	382949	Formic acid	351137
Crude petroleum	220001A	Fountain pens, ball-point pens, propelling pencils etc.	390904
Crude steel for castings	371016	Fruit and vegetable juices, concentrated, frozen or not	311307
Crude steel, ingots	371019	Fruit and vegetable juices, unconcentrated, frozen or not	311310
Cultivators, scarifiers, weeders, hoes etc.	382202	Fruit, glace or crystalized	311901
Diamonds, gem	290919	Fruits, dried	311301
Diamonds, industrial	290901	Fruits, frozen	311313
Distilled alcoholic beverages, excluding ethyl alcohol	313101	Fruits, tinned or bottled	311316
Dolls	390901	Fuller's earth	2901192
Dresses, women's and girls'	322022	Fuses, electrical	383901
Drilling and boring machines	382301	Garden tractors	382258A
Drying machines for household use	382907	Gas-diesel oil (distillate fuel oil)	353019A
Dyestuffs, synthetic	351174	Gasworks gas	410202B
Electricity production by public utilities	410102	Generators for hydraulic turbines	383101A
Electricity, total production	410101	Generators for hydraulic turbines	383101B
Electro-mechanical hand tools	382343	Generators for steam turbines	383104B
Electronic tubes	383225	Glass bottles and other containers of common glass	362010A
Elevators, for lifting goods and persons	382952	Glass bottles and other containers of common glass	362010B
Engines, diesel	382104A	Glass fibres (including grass wool)	362005
Engines, internal combustion	382108A	Glass, cast, rolled, drawn or blown	362004A
Engines, internal combustion	382108B	Glass, drawn or blown, in rectangles, unworked	362001A
Engines, internal combustion (compression-ignition),		Glass, drawn or blown, in rectangles, unworked	362001B
for motor vehicles, diesel engines	384301A	Glass, safety, of toughened or laminated glass	362007A
Engines, internal-combustion (spark-ignition), for motor		Glycerine (Glycerol)	351125
vehicles, gasolene fueled	384304A	Gold-bearing ores	230255M
Ethanediol (ethylene glycol)	351123	Goods wagons and vans	384210A
Ethyl alcohol for all purposes	313104	Graders and levellers	382428

COMMODITY NAME	ISIC CITI	COMMODITY NAME	ISIC CITI
Gramophone records	383240	Lead, secondary, refined, soft	3720373A
Granite, porphyry, sandstone etc.	290107	Lead-base alloys	372038
Graphite, natural	290907	Lead-bearing ores	230210M
Gravel and crushed stone	290116	Light leather	323104B
Grinding and sharpening machines	382310	Lignite	210004
Gypsum, crude	290902	Limestone flux and calcareous stone	290110
Hard Coal	210001	Linen fabrics	321137B
Hard-coal briquettes	354001	Linen fabrics	321137A
Hardware, general	381107A	Linen fabrics	321137
Harrows, rotary, animal- or tractor-operated	382208	Liquefied petroleum gas from natural gas plants	3530371A
Heaters, electric space	383307	Liquefied petroleum gas from petroleum refineries	3530372A
Heavy leather	323101A	Lithopone	351178
Hides, cattle and horse, undressed (Industrial production)	3111341	Ilmenite	2302271
Hides, cattle and horse, undressed (Total production)	311134	Locksmiths' wares - locks, padlocks, keys etc.	381104B
Hoop and strip, cold-reduced	371061	Locksmiths' wares - locks, padlocks, keys etc.	381104A
Hoop and strip, hot-rolled	371064	Locomotives, diesel	384204A
Household and sanitary paper	341124	Locomotives, electric	384201A
Household ware of other ceramic materials	361004B	Looms	382410
Household ware of porcelain or china	361001A	Lorries (trucks), including articulated vehicles, assembled from imported parts	384315
Household ware of porcelain or china-	361001B	Lorries (trucks), including articulated vehicles, produced	384316
Hydraulic turbines	382116A	Lubricants	353025A
Hydrochloric acid	351146	Macaroni and noodle products, uncooked	311701
Hydrogen peroxide	351171	Machine-tools for working wood	382340
Ice-cream	311213	Machinery for making or finishing cellulosic pulp etc.	382413
Industrial refrigerators and freezers	382928	Magnesite	290122
Ingots for tubes	371022	Magnesium, unwrought (total production)	372055
Inner tubes, rubber, for bicycles and motorcycles	355102	Malt	313301
Inner tubes, rubber, for motor vehicles	355101	Manganese-bearing ores	230219M
Insecticides, fungicides, disinfectants etc.	351216	Marble, travertines etc.	290104
Insulating board	341137A	Margarine	3115011
Iron pyrites, unroasted	290213	Margarine, imitation lard and other prepared fats	311501
Iron-bearing ores	230101M	Mastics	352110
Irons, electric smoothing	383310	Mattresses	332001
Jackets, men's and boys'	322001	Meal and groats of all cereals	311604
Jams, marmalades and fruit jellies	311304	Meals, frozen prepared	311125
Jet fuels	353004A	Meat, tinned	311128
Jute fabrics	321140A	Mercury	230240M
Jute fabrics	321140B	Metal-working presses	382328
Jute fabrics	321140	Meters, electricity-supply	383119
Jute yarn	321122	Methanal (formaldehyde)	351131
Kaolin	2901193	Methanol (methyl alcohol)	351121
Kerosene	353013A	Mica in book form (sheet and splittings)	2909131
Knitted fabrics	321301	Mica waste and powder	2909132
Knitted sports shirts	321313	Milk and cream, condensed (Industrial production)	3112011
Knitted sweaters	321316	Milk and cream, condensed (Total production)	311201
Knitted undergarments	321310	Milk and cream, dried (Industrial production)	3112041
Knitting machines	382407	Milk and cream, dried (Total production)	311204
Lamps, electric	383916	Milking machines	382255
Lard (Industrial production)	3111311	Milling machines	382316
Lathes	382313	Mineral waters	313401
Lead oxides	351157	Molybdenum-bearing ores	230228M
Lead tubes and pipes	372040	Motor gasolene	353007A
Lead, primary, refined soft	3720371A	Motorcycles, scooters etc.	384401
Lead, refined, unwrought (total production)	372037		

COMMODITY NAME	ISIC CITI	COMMODITY NAME	ISIC CITI
Motors, electric, fractional horsepower	383107A	Paints, other	352107A
Motors, electric, fractional horsepower	383107B	Paints, water	352104A
Motors, electric, of one horsepower and over	383110B	Paper-cutting machines	382416
Motors, electric, of one horsepower and over	383110A	Particle board	331122
Mowers, animal-or-tractor-operated and self-propelled	382238	Passenger cars, assembled from imported parts	384307
Multinutrient fertilizers, K2O content	351213C	Passenger cars, produced	384310
Multinutrient fertilizers, N content	351213A	Pastry, cakes, and other fine bakers' wares	311710
Multinutrient fertilizers, P205 content	351213B	Peat for agricultural use	290918
Musical instruments, string	390204	Peat for fuel	290917
Musical instruments, wind	390210	Pencils, crayons etc.	390907
Mutton and lamb, fresh (Industrial production)	3111041	Perambulators and push-chairs for babies	384901
Mutton and lamb, fresh (Total production)	311104	Petroleum coke	353031
Nails, screws, nuts, bolts, rivets etc.	381913	Petroleum wax (paraffin)	353028
Naphthas	353010A	Phenol	351126
Natural gas	220010B	Phenolic and cresylic plastics	351316
Natural gasolene	220007A	Phosphate fertilizers (total production)	351203
Natural phosphates, P2O5 content	290204M	Phosphatic fertilizers, other, P2O5 content	351207
Natural phosphates, gross weight	290204	Phosphoric acid	351150
Newsprint	341119	Photographic film, sensitized, in rolls	352916
Nickel unwrought	372020	Photographic paper	352919
Nickel-bearing ores	230204M	Phthalic anhydride	351138
Niobium (Columbium) concentrates	2302291M	Pianos	390201
Nitric acid	351149	Pig Iron, foundry	371007
Nitrogenous fertilizers (total production)	351200	Pig Iron, steel- making	371010
Nitrogenous fertilizers, N content	351201	Planing, shaping and slotting machines	3823-22
Non-cellulosic continuous fibres	351337	Plastic footwear	356003
Non-cellulosic staple and tow	351304	Plates (heavy), over 4.75 mm	371040
Oil, cotton-seed, crude	311516	Plates (medium) 3 to 4.75 mm	371043
Oil, cotton-seed, refined	311519	Ploughs, animal- or tractor-operated	382218
Oil, groundnut, crude	311522	Plywood	331116
Oil, olive, crude	311528	Polyethylene	351319
Oil, soya bean, crude	311510	Polypropylene	351322
Oil, soya bean, refined	311513	Polystyrene	351325
Oils and fats of animals, unprocessed	311507	Polyvinylchloride	351328
Oils and fats of aquatic animal origin	311504	Pork, fresh (Industrial production)	3111071
Oils, other, of vegetable origin, crude	311534	Pork, fresh (Total production)	311107
Oils, other, of vegetable origin, refined	311537	Potash salts, crude	290207
Organs	390207	Potassic fertilizers (total production)	351209
Other ferro-alloys	371013	Potassic fertilizers, K2O content	351210
Other knitted outer garments	321319	Poultry, dressed, fresh (Industrial production)	3111101
Other machine-made paper and paperboard, simply finished	341131	Poultry, dressed, fresh (Total production)	311110
Other meat and edible offals, dried, salted or smoked	311119	Prepared animal feeds	312201
Other meat, fresh (Industrial production)	3111131	Printers' ink	352904
Other meat, fresh (Total production)	311113	Printing presses	382419
Other metal-cutting machine-tools	382319	Propylene	351113
Other metal-forming machine-tools	382331	Pulp of fibres other than wood	341104
Other printing and writing paper	341122	Pumps for liquids, except liquid elevators	382942
Other sea-going merchant vessels, launched	384116A	Quicklime	369201
Other sea-going merchant vessels, launched	384116B	Radio receivers	383204
Ovens, household	382901	Rail motor passenger vehicles	384207A
Overcoats, men's and boys'	322004	Rail passenger carriages	384213
Packing containers of paper or paperboard	341201	Railway track material	371067
Paints, cellulose	352101A	Raincoats, men's and boys'	322007
		Raincoats, women's and girls'	322025

Annex I-A
INDEX OF COMMODITIES IN ALPHABETICAL ORDER

COMMODITY NAME	ISIC CITI	COMMODITY NAME	ISIC CITI
Rakes, animal- or tractor-operated and self-propelled	382244	Steel castings in the rough state	371085
Raw sugar	311801	Steel forgings	371088
Razor blades	381101	Stoves, ranges, cookers	382904
Refined sugar	311804	Styrene	351103
Refrigerators for household use	382958	Sugar confectionery	311904
Regenerated cellulose	351331	Suits, men's and boys'	322010
Residual fuel oils	353022A	Suits, women's and girls'	322031
Road tractors for tractor-trailer combinations, produced	384319	Sulphur, native	290210
Rolling mills for rolling metals	382337	Sulphur, recovered as by-product	351101
Rubber footwear	355916	Sulphur, recovered from pyrites etc.	351102
Rubber, hardened (ebonite and vulcanite in blocks, plates, sheets etc.)	355910	Sulphuric acid	351147
Rubber, reclaimed	355901	Superphosphates, P2O5 content	351204
Rubber, synthetic	351301	Switches, electric	383904
Rubber, transmission, conveyor, elevator belts etc.	355913	Talc, powdered steatite and pyrophyllite	290914
Rubber, unhardened vulcanized piping and tubing	355907	Tankers, launched	384113A
Rubber, unhardened vulcanized plates, sheets etc.	355904	Tanks and vats	381301A
Salt, unrefined	290301	Tantalum and Niobium (Columbium) concentrates	230229
Sand, silica and quartz	290113	Tantalum concentrates	2302292M
Sandals and similar light footwear	324016	Tars	354016
Sanitary ceramic fittings	361007B	Telephones	383210
Sanitary ceramic fittings	361007A	Television receivers	383201
Sausages	311122	Television receivers, black and white	3832011
Sawnwood, broadleaved	331107	Television receivers, colour	3832012
Sawnwood, coniferous	331104	Threshing machines	382249
Scales, industrial	382513	Tiles, floor and wall	369107B
Scales, other than industrial	382516	Tiles, floor and wall	369107A
Scrapers	382431	Tiles, roofing, made of clay	369104A
Seeders, planters and transplanters	382226	Tiles, roofing, made of clay	369104B
Semis for tubes	371025	Tin, unwrought (total production)	372049
Sewing machines	382910	Tin, unwrought, primary	3720491
Shavers and hair clippers, electric	383304	Tin, unwrought, secondary	3720492
Sheets under 3 mm, cold-rolled, uncoated	371049	Tin-bearing ores	230216M
Sheets under 3 mm, hot-rolled	371052	Tinplate	371055
Sheets, electrical	371046	Tires for agricultural and other off-the-road vehicles	355104
Sheets, galvanized	371058	Tires for bicycles and motorcycles	355107
Shirts, men's and boys'	322034	Tires for road motor vehicles	355110
Silk fabrics	321131	Titanium oxides	351155
Silk fabrics	321131A	Tobacco, manufactured	314010
Silver-bearing ores	230246M	Tobacco, prepared leaf	314001
Skins, calf, goat and sheep, undressed (Total production)	311137	Toluene	351114
Skirts, slacks and shorts, women's and girls'	322028	Towelling	321207
Slate	290101	Tractors of 10 HP and over, other than industrial and road tractors	382261A
Slide fasteners (zippers)	390910	Trailers and semi-trailers	384322
Soap	352301	Transformers less than 5 KVA	383113A
Socks and other stockings, except women's stockings	321304	Transformers of 5 KVA and over	383116A
Soda ash	351166	Transformers of 5 KVA and over	383116B
Sodium silicates	351169	Transistors	383228
Soft drinks	313404	Trousers, men's and boys'	322013
Sound recorders	383234	Tubes, fluorescent	383919A
Sound reproducers	383237	Tubes, seamless	371076
Spiegeleisen and ferro-manganese	371004	Tubes, welded	371079
Spinning machines	382404	Tungsten-bearing ores, W content	230225M1
Steam turbines	382101B		

Annex I-A
INDEX OF COMMODITIES IN ALPHABETICAL ORDER

COMMODITY NAME	ISIC CITI	COMMODITY NAME	ISIC CITI
Typewriters	382501	Zinc, unwrought (total production)	372043
Underwear, men's and boys'	322037	Zinc, unwrought, primary	3720431
Underwear, women's and girls'	322040	Zinc, unwrought, secondary	3720432
Uranium-bearing ores	230252M		
Vacuum cleaners	383301	Zirconium ores and concentrates	230232
Vanadium-bearing ores, V content	230231M		
Vegetable tanning extracts	351175		
Vegetables, frozen	311319		
Vegetables, tinned or bottled	311322		
Veneer sheets	331110		
Vinegar	312104		
Washing machines for household use	382964		
Washing powders and detergents	352304		
Watches	385301		
Wheels, wheel centres, tires and axles	371091		
White spirit/industrial spirit	353016A		
Wine	313204		
Wire and cable, insulated	383907		
Wire rods	371028		
Wire, plain	371070		
Women's stockings	321307		
Wood pulp, dissolving grades	341107		
Wood pulp, mechanical	341101		
Wood pulp, semi-chemical	341116		
Wood pulp, sulphate and soda	341110		
Wood pulp, sulphite	341113		
Wool yarn, mixed	321104		
Wool yarn, pure	321107		
Wool yarn, pure and mixed (total)	321103		
Woollen woven fabrics	321134A		
Woollen woven fabrics	321134		
Woollen woven fabrics	321134B		
Woven fabrics of cellulosic fibres	321143B		
Woven fabrics of cellulosic fibres	321143A		
Woven fabrics of cellulosic fibres	321143		
Woven fabrics of non-cellulosic fibres	321146		
Woven fabrics of non-cellulosic fibres	321146B		
Woven fabrics of non-cellulosic fibres	321146A		
Wrapping and packaging paper and paperboard	341125		
Xylenes	351115		
Yarn of man-made staple	321119		
Yarn of other vegetable textile fibres	321125		
Zinc-base alloys	372044		
Zinc -bearing ores	230213M		
Zinc oxide	351154		
Zinc plates, sheets, strip, foil	372046		

INDICES DES PRODUITS PAR ORDRE ALPHABETIQUE

NOM DE PRODUIT	ISIC CITI	NOM DE PRODUIT	ISIC CITI
Abrasifs, agglomérés ou non (meules et pierres à moudre, à aiguiser etc.)	369904	Ascenseurs et monte-charge	382952
Abrasifs naturels (pouzzolane, pierre ponce etc.)	290904	Aspirateurs	383301
Accumulateurs pour véhicules automobiles	383913	Autocars et autobus, assemblés à partir de pièces importées	384312
Acide acétique	351135	Autocars et autobus, fabriqués	384313
Acide chlorhydrique	351146	Automobiles destinées au transport de voyageurs, assemblées à partir de pièces importées	384307
Acide formique	351137	Automobiles destinées au transport des voyageurs, fabriquées	384310
Acide nitrique	351149	Automotrices pour le transport de passagers	384207A
Acide phosphorique	351150	Autres appareils d'horlogerie, électriques et non électriques	385310
Acide sulfurique	351147	Autres balances et bascules	382516
Acier brut (lingots)	371019	Autres chaussures (pour sports, orthopédiques etc.)	324010
Acier brut pour moulages	371016	Autres engrais phosphatés, P2O5 contenu	351207
Acrylonitrile	351143	Autres ferro-alliages	371013
Acétates de méthyle, d'éthyle et de butyle	351134	Autres huiles brutes d'origine végétale	311534
Acétone	351133	Autres huiles d'origine végétale, raffinées	311537
Acétylène	351105	Autres machines-outils pour le travail des métaux	382319
Agglomérés (briquettes de houille)	354001	Autres machines-outils à former les métaux	382331
Alcool éthylique pour tous usages	313104	Autres navires marchands, mis à flot	384116A
Alcools butyliques (butanols)	351122	Autres navires marchands, mis à flot	384116B
Aldéhyde acétique (éthanal)	351130	Autres papiers d'imprimerie et d'écriture	341122
Aliments préparés pour animaux	312201	Autres papiers et cartons fabriqués à la machine simplement finis	341131
Aliments à base de céréales, pour le petit déjeûner	311610	Autres peintures	352107A
Alliages à base d'aluminium	372023	Autres produits en béton	369916A
Alliages à base de cuivre	372007	Autres produits en béton	369916B
Alliages à base de plomb	372038	Autres tapis	321404
Alliages à base de zinc	372044	Autres viandes et abats comestibles, séchés, salés ou fumés	311119
Alumine calcinée	372021	Autres viandes, non préparées (Production industrielle)	3111131
Aluminium non travaillé (production totale)	372022	Autres viandes, non préparées (Production totale)	311113
Aluminium non travaillé, neuf	3720221	Autres vêtements de dessus, en bonneterie	321319
Aluminium non travaillé, récupéré	3720222	Avions commerciaux pour le transport de passagers et de marchandises	384507
Amiante	290910	Balances et bascules industrielles	382513
Aminoplastes	351313	Barres, cornières et profilés d'aluminium	372025
Ammoniac	351158	Barres, cornières et profilés de cuivre	372010
Andalousite, cyanite et sillimanite	2901194	Barytine même calciné	290219
Anhydride phtalique	351138	Bas de dames	321307
Aniline	351142	Bas, chaussettes et socquettes	321304
Appareils d'enregistrement du son	383234	Batteuses	382249
Appareils de chauffage central, non électriques	381919	Bauxite	230207
Appareils de reproduction du son	383237	Bentonite	2901191
Appareils photographiques	385207	Benzène (Benzol)	351107
Appareils sanitaires en céramique	361007A	Bétonnières pour chantiers de construction	382434
Appareils sanitaires en céramique	361007B	Beurre (Production industrielle)	3112071
Appareils téléphoniques	383210	Beurre (Production totale)	311207
Appareils électriques pour le chauffage des locaux	383307	Beurre de cacao	311910
Ardoise	290101	Bières	313304
Argile (production totale)	290119	Biscuits	311707
Arsenic (Trioxyde d'arsenic)	290225	Bitume (brai)	353034A
Articles de ménage en autres matières céramiques	361004B	Blocs et briques en béton	369910A
Articles de ménage en porcelaine	361001A		
Articles de ménage en porcelaine	361001B		
Articles de quincaillerie, en général	381107A		
Articles de serrurerie - serrures, cadenas, clefs etc.	381104A		

NOM DE PRODUIT	ISIC CITI	NOM DE PRODUIT	ISIC CITI
Articles de serrurerie - serrures, cadenas, clefs etc.	381104B	Blouses de dames et de fillettes	322016
Boissons alcooliques distillées, à l'exclusion de l'alcool éthylique	313101	Cires de pétrole (paraffines)	353028
		Citernes et cuves	381301A
Boissons non alcooliques	313404	Clous, vis, écrous, boulons, rivets et articles similaires	381913
Bouteilles et autres récipients en verre ordinaire	362010A	Coke	354007
Bouteilles et autres récipients en verre ordinaire	362010B	Coke de pétrole	353031
Briques de construction en argile	369101A	Colorant synthétiques	351174
Briques de construction en argile	369101B	Compresseurs et ventilateurs	382946
Briquettes de lignite	354004	Compteurs d'électricité	383119
Bulldozers	382422A	Concentrés de niobium (colombium)	2302291M
Butylènes, butadiène	351109	Concentrés de tantale	2302292M
Câbles	381910	Concentrés de tantale et de niobium (colombium)	230229
Cacao en poudre	311907	Conduites en béton	369913A
Cadmium brut	372052	Conduites en béton	369913B
Cadres et autres conteneurs d'un mètre cube et plus	381916A	Confitures, marmelades et gelées de fruits	311304
Camions, y compris les véhicules articulés, assemblés à partir de pièces importées	384315	Conserves de viande	311128
		Conserves de poisson	311407
Camions, y compris les véhicules articulés, fabriqués	384316	Contreplaqués	331116
Caoutchouc durci (en blocs, plaques, feuilles etc.)	355910	Contreplaqués à âme épaisse	331113
Caoutchouc régénéré	355901	Cordes, câbles, cordages et ficelles	321501
Caoutchoucs synthétiques	351301	Cornières, profilés et poutrelles (production totale)	371035
Carbure de calcium	351173	Cornières, profilés et poutrelles de 80 mm ou plus (profilés lourds)	371036
Carburéacteurs	353004A		
Carreaux pour planchers et murs	369107A	Cornières, profilés et poutrelles de moins de 80 mm (profilés légers)	371037
Carreaux pour planchers et murs	369107B		
Castine et pierres à chaux et à ciment	290110	Costumes pour dames et fillettes	322031
Caoutchoucs synthétiques	351301	Costumes pour hommes et garçonnets	322010
Cellulose régénérée	351331	Coupe-circuits électriques	383901
Cendres sodiques	351166	Coupeuses & papier etc.	382416
Chambres à air en caoutchouc pour bicyclettes et motocyclettes	355102	Courroies transporteuses, de transmission etc., en caoutchouc	355913
Chambres à air en caoutchouc pour véhicules à moteur	355101	Couvertures	321201
Charbons activés	351179	Couvre-parquets	321901
Chariots gerbeurs	382955	Craie	290125
Charrues à traction animale ou tractées	382218	Crayons, pastels etc.	390907
Chaudières à vapeur	381304A	Crème glacée	311213
Chaudières à vapeur	381304B	Cuirs forts	323101A
Chaussures d'intérieur	324013	Cuirs légers	323104B
Chaussures de cuir pour enfants	324001	Cuivre affiné, non travaillé (production totale)	372004
Chaussures en caoutchouc	355916	Cuivre blister et autre cuivre non affiné	372001
Chaussures en cuir pour dames	324007	Cuivre, neuf, affiné	3720041
Chaussures en cuir pour hommes	324004	Cuivre, récupéré, affiné	3720042
Chaussures en matière plastique	356003	Cultivateurs, scarificateurs, extirpateurs, houes etc.	382202
Chaussures, production totale, non compris les chaussures de caoutchouc	324000	Cycles	384404
		Décapeuses (scrapers)	382431
Chaux vive	369201	Déchets et poudre de mica	2909132
Chemises d'hommes et de garçonnets	322034	Demi-produits pour tubes	371025
Chemisettes en bonneterie	321313	Diamants de joaillerie	290919
Chlore	351145	Diamants industriels	290901
Chlorure de polyvinyle	351328	Disques phonographiques	383240
Chocolat et produits à base de chocolat	311913	Distributeurs d'engrais, à traction animale, à bras ou tractés	382263
Cigares	314004	Electricité, production, services publics	410102

NOM DE PRODUIT	ISIC CITI	NOM DE PRODUIT	ISIC CITI
Cigarettes	314007	Electricité, production totale	410101
Ciments	369204	Encre d'imprimerie	352904
Engrais azotés (production totale)	351200	Fonte Spiegel et ferro-manganèse	371004
Engrais azotés, N contenu	351201	Fonte d'affinage	371010
Engrais composés, K2O contenu	351213C	Fonte de moulage	371007
Engrais composés, N contenu	351213A	Fours pour usages domestiques	382901
Engrais composés, P2O5 contenu	351213B	Fraiseuses	382316
Engrais phosphatés (production totale)	351203	Fromage (production industrielle)	3112101
Engrais potassiques (production totale)	351209	Fromage (production totale)	311210
Engrais potassiques, K2O contenu	351210	Fruits congelés	311313
Essence auto	353007A	Fruits en boîtes ou en bocaux	311316
Essence aviation	353001A	Fruits glacés ou cristallisés	311901
Etain, non travaillé (production totale)	372049	Fruits secs	311301
Etain, non travaillé, neuf	3720491	Gaz d'usine à gaz	410202B
Etain, non travaillé, récupéré	3720492	Gaz de cokerie	354013B
Ethane-diol (ethylène-glycol)	351123	Gaz de pétrole liquéfiés provenant du gaz naturel	3530371A
Ethylène	351110	Gaz de pétrole liquéfiés, des raffineries de pétrole	3530372A
Etoffes de bonneterie	321301	Gaz naturel	220010B
Explosifs	352907	Gazole/carburant diesel (mazout distillé)	353019A
Extraits et essences de café, y compris le café soluble	312101	Gazoline naturelle	220007A
Extraits tannants d'origine végétale	351175	Génératrices pour entraînement par turbines hydrauliques	383101A
Farines de céréales autres que le froment	311607	Génératrices pour entraînement par turbines hydrauliques	383101B
Farines de froment	311601	Génératrices pour entraînement par turbines à vapeur	383104B
Faucheuses, à traction animale ou tractées et automotrices	382238	Glaces ou verres de sécurité consistant en verre trempé ou feuilleté	362007A
Fer blanc	371055	Glycérine (Glycérol)	351125
Fermetures à glissière	390910	Goudrons	354016
Ferro-chrome (y compris le ferro-silicochrome et chrome de charge)	3710131	Granite, porphyre, grès etc.	290107
Ferro-nickel	3710132	Graphite naturel	290907
Ferro-silicium	3710134	Graviers et pierres concassées	290116
Fers à repasser électriques de tous types	383310	Groupes pour le conditionnement de l'air	382925A
Feuilles de tabac, traitées	314001	Grues	382949
Feuillards laminés à chaud	371064	Gypse brut	290902
Feuillards laminés à froid	371061	Herses rotatives, à traction animale ou tracté+C185es	382208
Feuilles de placage	331110	Houille	210001
Fibres continues non cellulosiques	351337	Huile d'arachides, brute	311522
Fibres de verre (y compris la laine de verre)	362005	Huile d'olives, brute	311528
Fibres discontinues et câbles non cellulosiques	351304	Huile de fèves de soya, brute	311510
Fibres et câbles cellulosiques	351307	Huile de fèves de soya, raffinée	311513
Fil d'aluminium	372028	Huile de graines de coton, brute	311516
Fil de cuivre	372013	Huile de graines de coton, raffinée	311519
Fil machine	371028	Huiles et graisses d'animaux aquatiques	311504
Fil ordinaire	371070	Huiles et graisses d'origine animale, non traitées	311507
Filaments cellulosiques continus	351340	Ilménite	2302271
Filés d'autres fibres textile végétales	321125	Imperméables pour dames et fillettes	322025
Filés de coton mélangé	321110	Imperméables pour hommes et garçonnets	322007
Filés de coton pur	321113	Insecticides, fongicides, désinfectants etc.	351216
Filés de coton pur et mélangé (production totale)	321109	Instruments de musique, à cordes	390204
Filés de fibres synthétiques et artificielles	321119	Instruments de musique, à vent	390210
Filés de jute	321122	Interrupteurs électriques	383904
Filés de laine mélangée	321104	Jumelles et longues-vues	385201
Filés de laine pure	321107	Jupes, pantalons et shorts pour dames et fillettes	322028

NOM DE PRODUIT	ISIC CITI	NOM DE PRODUIT	ISIC CITI
Filés de laine pure et mélangée (production totale)	321103	Jus concentrés de fruits et de légumes, congelés ou non	311307
Filés de lin, de ramie et de chanvre	321116	Jus non concentrés de fruits et de légumes, congelés ou non	311310
Fils et câbles électriques isolés	383907	Kaolin	2901193
Lait et crème, concentrés (production industrielle)	3112011	Minerais cuprifères	230201M
Lait et crème, concentrés (production totale)	311201	Minerais de zirconium et concentrés	230232
Lait et crème, séchés (production industrielle)	3112041	Minerais ferrifères	230101M
Lait et crème, séchés (production totale)	311204	Minerais manganifères	230219M
Lames de rasoir	381101	Minerais molybdénifères	230228M
Laminoirs à métaux	382337	Minerais nickelifères	230204M
Lampes électriques	383916	Minerais plombifères	230210M
Landaux et poussettes pour bébés	384901	Minerais stannifères	230216M
Lard entrelardé, jambon et autres viandes de porc, séchées, salées ou fumées	311116	Minerais stibifères	230234M
Légumes congelés	311319	Minerais tungstifères, W contenu	230225M1
Légumes en boîtes ou en bocaux	311322	Minerais uranifères	230252M
Lignite	210004	Minerais vanadifères, V contenu	230231M
Linge de literie	321204	Minerais zincifères	230213M
Lingots pour tubes	371022	Minéraux boratés bruts	290222
Lithopone	351178	Moissonneuses-batteuses	382232
Locomotives diesel	384204A	Montres	385301
Locomotives électriques	384201A	Moteurs diesel	382104A
Lubrifiants	353025A	Moteurs à combustion interne (à allumage par compression) pour véhicules automobiles, moteurs diesel	384301A
Machines d'excavation	382425	Moteurs à explosion pour véhicules automobiles à essence	384304A
Machines et appareils à laver, à usage domestique	382964	Moteurs à explosion, à essence	382108A
Machines pour la fabrication ou le finissage de pâte cellulosique etc.	382413	Moteurs à explosion, à essence	382108B
Machines à calculer	382504	Moteurs électriques d'un CV et plus	383110A
Machines à coudre	382910	Moteurs électriques d'un CV et plus	383110B
Machines à filer les textiles	382404	Moteurs électriques de moins d'un CV	383107A
Machines à sécher, à usage domestique	382907	Moteurs électriques de moins d'un CV	383107B
Machines à écrire	382501	Motocycles, scooters etc.	384401
Machines-outils pour le travail du bois	382340	Moulages d'acier non usinés	371085
Magnésite	290122	Naphtalène	351111
Magnésium, non travaillé (production totale)	372055	Naphtas	353010A
Malt	313301	Navires-citernes, mis à flot	384113A
Manteaux de dames et de fillettes	322019	Navires-citernes, mis à flot	384113B
Marbre, travertins etc.	290104	Nickel brut	372020
Margarine	3115011	Niveleuses-régleuses	382428
Margarine, simili-saindoux et autres graisses alimentaires préparées	311501	Noirs de carbone	352901
		Orgues	390207
Marteaux, martinets et moutons	382307	Outils et machines-outils électromécaniques, pour emploi à la main	382343
Mastics	352110	Ouvrages en amiante-ciment, cellulose-ciment et similaires	369901A
Matelas	332001	Oxide d'éthylène	351129
Matériel de voie	371067	Oxyde d'aluminium	351161
Mazout résiduel	353022A	Oxyde de zinc	351154
Mercure	230240M	Oxydes de plomb	351157
Méthanal (formaldéhyde)	351131	Oxydes de titane	351155
Méthanol (Alcool méthylique)	351121	Pain, biscuits de mer et autres produits de boulangerie ordinaire	311704
Métiers à bonneterie	382407	Panneaux de fibres, comprimés	341134A
Métiers à tisser	382410	Panneaux de particules	331122
Meuleuses et affûteuses	382310	Panneaux isolants	341137A
Mica sous forme feuilletée (en feuilles et en lamelles)	2909131		

INDICES DES PRODUITS PAR ORDRE ALPHABETIQUE

NOM DE PRODUIT	ISIC CITI	NOM DE PRODUIT	ISIC CITI
Minerais argentifères	230246M	Pantalons pour hommes et garçonnets	322013
Minerais aurifères	230255M	Papier à cigarettes	341128
Minerais chromifères, Cr contenu	230222M1	Papier journal	341119
Minerais cobaltifères	230237M	Papiers domestique et hygiénique	341124
Papiers et cartons d'empaquetage et d'emballage	341125	Pyrites de fer non grillées	290213
Papiers photographiques	352919	Raboteuses, étaux-limeurs, mortaiseuses	382322
Pâte de bois chimiques, au bisulfite	341113	Rasoirs et tondeuses, électriques	383304
Pâte de bois chimiques, au sulfate	341110	Râteaux, à traction animale ou tractés et automotrices	382244
Pâte de bois chimiques, solubles	341107	Récepteurs de radio	383204
Pâte de bois mi-chimiques	341116	Récepteurs de télévision	383201
Pâte de bois mécanique	341101	Récepteurs de télévision, en couleurs	3832012
Pâtes alimentaires	311701	Récepteurs de télévision, en noir et blanc	3832011
Pâtes de fibres autres que le bois	341104	Récipients cylindriques pour gaz comprimés, en métal	381907A
Pâtisseries, gâteaux et autres produits de boulangerie	311710	Récipients d'emballage en papier ou en carton	341201
Peaux de bovins et d'équidés, non préparées (production industrielle)	3111341	Récipients métalliques	381901
Peaux de bovins et d'équidés, non préparées (production totale)	311134	Réfrigérateurs et congélateurs industriels	382928
Peaux de veaux, de caprins et d'ovins, non préparées (production totale)	311137	Réfrigérateurs ménagers	382958
Peintures cellulosiques	352101A	Remorques et semi-remorques	384322
Peintures à l'eau	352104A	Repas préparés, congelés	311125
Pellicules photographiques sensibilisées, en rouleaux	352916	Résines alkyliques	351310
Pendulettes à mouvements de montres	385304	Robes de dames et de fillettes	322022
Perceuses	382301	Roues, centres de roues, bandages et essieux	371091
Péroxyde d'hydrogène	351171	Sables, siliceux et quartzeux	290113
Pétrole brut	220001A	Saindoux (production industrielle)	3111311
Pétrole lampant	353013A	Sandales et autres chaussures légères	324016
Phosphates naturels, P2O5 contenu	290204M	Saucissons	311122
Phosphates naturels, poids brut	290204	Savons	352301
Phénol	351126	Sciages de feuillus	331107
Phénoplastes	351316	Sciages de résineux	331104
Pianos	390201	Sel, non raffiné	290301
Piles et batteries de piles	383910	Sels de potasse bruts	290207
Pièces de forge	371088	Semoirs, planteuses et repiqueuses	382226
Plaques, feuilles etc. en caoutchouc vulcanisé non durci	355904	Semoules et gruaux de toutes céréales	311604
Plomb non travaillé, affiné (production totale)	372037	Serviettes	321207
Plomb, neuf, doux affiné	3720371A	Silicate de sodium	351169
Plomb, récupéré, doux affiné	3720373A	Soude caustique	351159
Pneumatiques et bandages pour véhicules agricoles et autres véhicules tous terrains	355104	Soufre de récupération	351102
Pneumatiques pour bicyclettes et motocyclettes	355107	Soufre en tant que sous-produit	351101
Pneumatiques pour véhicules à moteur	355110	Soufre natif	290210
Poêles, fourneaux, cuisinières	382904	Sous-vêtements de dames et de fillettes	322040
Poisson congelé	311401	Sous-vêtements pour hommes et garçonnets	322037
Poisson salé, séché ou fumé	311404	Sous-vêtements en bonneterie	321310
Polyéthylène	351319	Spath fluor, non compris les pierres precieuses	290216
Polypropylène	351322	Styrène	351103
Polystyrène	351325	Sucre brut	311801
Pompes pour liquides, non compris élévateurs à liquides	382942	Sucre raffiné	311804
Porte-plumes réservoirs, stylographes, porte-mines etc.	390904	Sucreries	311904
Poudres pour lessives et détersifs	352304	Sulfate d'aluminium	351163
		Sulfate de cuivre	351165
		Sulfure de carbone	351153
		Superphosphates, P2O5 contenu	351204
		Tabacs manufacturés	314010

NOM DE PRODUIT	ISIC CITI	NOM DE PRODUIT	ISIC CITI
Poupées	390901	Tubes et tuyaux d'aluminium	372034
Préparations à base de pâtes alimentaires	311713	Tubes et tuyaux en caoutchouc vulcanisé non durci	355907
Presses à imprimer	382419	Tubes fluorescents	383919A
Presses pour le travail des métaux	382328	Tubes sans soudure	371076
Propylène	351113	Tubes soudés	371079
Talc ou stéatite pulverisée et la pyrophyllite	290914	Tubes électroniques	383225
Tapis de laine à points noués	321401	Tuiles de couverture en argile	369104A
Terre à foulon	2901192	Tuiles de couverture en argile	369104B
Tissus de coton	321128A	Turbines hydrauliques	382116A
Tissus de coton	321128B	Turbines à vapeur	382101A
Tissus de coton	321128	Turbines à vapeur	382101B
Tissus de fibres cellulosiques	321143	Tuyaux et tubes de cuivre	372019
Tissus de fibres cellulosiques	321143A	Tuyaux et tubes de plomb	372040
Tissus de fibres cellulosiques	321143B	Verres coulés, laminés, étirés ou soufflés	362004A
Tissus de fibres non cellulosiques	321146	Verres étirés ou soufflés, de forme rectangulaire,	
Tissus de fibres non cellulosiques	321146A	non travaillés	362001A
Tissus de fibres non cellulosiques	321146B	Verres étirés ou soufflés, de forme rectangulaire,	
Tissus de jute	321140	non travaillés	362001B
Tissus de jute	321140A	Vestes pour hommes et garçonnets	322001
Tissus de jute	321140B	Viande d'ovins et de caprins, non préparée	
Tissus de laine	321134	(production industrielle)	3111041
Tissus de laine	321134A	Viande d'ovins et de caprins, non préparée	
Tissus de laine	321134B	(production totale)	311104
Tissus de lin	321137	Viande de boeuf ou de veau, non préparée	
Tissus de lin	321137A	(production industrielle)	3111011
Tissus de lin	321137B	Viande de boeuf ou de veau, non préparée	
Tissus de soie	321131	(production totale)	311101
Tissus de soie	321131A	Viande de porc, non préparée (Production industrielle)	3111071
Tôles, bandes et feuilles et papier de cuivre	372016	Viande de porc, non préparée (Production totale)	311107
Tôles, plaques, bandes et feuilles de zinc	372046	Vinaigres	312104
Tôles de moins de 3 mm, laminées à chaud	371052	Vins	313204
Tôles de moins de 3 mm, laminées à froid, sans revêtement	371049	Voitures de passagers, pour voie ferrée	384213
Tôles fortes de plus de 4,75 mm	371040	Volailles plumées et vidées, non préparées	
Tôles galvanisées	371058	(production industrielle)	3111101
Tôles magnétiques	371046	Volailles plumées et vidées, non préparées	
Tôles moyennes de 3 à 4,75 mm	371043	(production totale)	311110
Tôles, bandes et feuilles d'aluminium	372031	Vêtements de dessus pour hommes et garçonnets	322004
Toluène	351114	Wagons de marchandises et fourgons	384210A
Tourbe comme combustible	290917	White spirit/essences spéciales	353016A
Tourbe à usage agricole	290918	Xylènes	351115
Tours	382313	Zinc non travaillé, affiné (production totale)	372043
Tracteurs (autres que les tracteurs industriels et		Zinc, neuf, affiné	3720431
ceux pour train routier) de 10 CV et plus	382261A	Zinc, récupéré, affiné	3720432
Tracteurs horticoles	382258A		
Tracteurs routiers pour les ensembles tracteur-remorque,			
fabriqués	384319		
Transformateurs de 5 kva et plus	383116A		
Transformateurs de 5 kva et plus	383116B		
Transformateurs de moins de 5 kVA	383113A		
Transistors	383228		
Trayeuses	382255		
Tricots	321316		

Annex II - Annexe II

PRELIMINARY TABLE OF CORRESPONDENCE BETWEEN ISIC-BASED CODES, SITC AND HS CODES
TABLEAU PROVISOIRE DE CORRESPONDENCE ENTRE LES INDICATIFS D'APRES
LA CITI ET LES INDICATIFS DE LA CTCI ET SH

ISIC-based code, Rev. 2 Indicatif d'après la CITI Rev.2	SITC, Revised code Indicatif d'après la CTCI révisée	SITC, Rev.2 code Indicatif d'après la CTCI Rev.2	SITC, Rev. 3 code Indicatif d'après la CTCI Rev.3	Harmonized Commodity Description and Coding System (HS) Systeme Harmonise de Designation et de Codification des Marchandises (SH)
210001	32140-0	32210-0, 32220-0	32110-0, 32120-0	270111-0, 270112-0, 270119-0
210004	32160-1	32230-0	32221-0	270210-0
	33101-0A	33300-0A	33300-0A	270900-0A
220007A	33210-1A	34139-1A	34420-1A	271119-1A
220010B	34110-1B	34139-0B, 34140-0B	34310-0B, 34320-0B	271111-0B, 271121-0B
230101M	28130-1M	28150-1M, 28160-1M	28150-1M, 28160-1M	260111-1M, 260112-1M
230201M	28311-1M+	28711-1M+	28310-1M+	260300-1M+
230204M	28321-1M+	28721-1M	28410-1M+	260400-1M+
230207	28330-0	28731-0	28510-0	260600-0
230210M	28340-1M+	28740-1M+	28740-1M+	260700-1M+
230213M	28350-1M+	28750-1M+	28750-1M+	260800-1M+
230216M	28360-1M+	28760-1M+	28760-1M+	260900-1M+
230219M	28370-1M+	28770-1M+	28770-1M+	260200-1M+
2302221M	28391-1M	28791-1M	28791-1M	261000-1M
2302251M	28392-1M	28792-1M	28792-1M	261100-1M
2302271	28393-1	28793-1	28783-1	261400-1
2302272	28393-2	28793-2	28783-2	261400-2
230228M	28393-3M	28793-3M	28781-0M, 28782-0M	261300-0M
230229	28393-4	28793-4	28785-1	261590-1
2302291M	28393-41M	28793-41M	28785-11M	261590-11M
2302292M	28393-42M	28793-42M	28785-12M	261590-12M
230231M	28393-5M	28793-5M	28785-2M	261590-2M
230232	28393-6	28793-6	28784-0	261510-0
230234M	28399-1M+	28799-1M+	28799-1M	261710-0M
230237M	28399-2M+	28799-2M+	28793-0M	260500-0M
230240M	28399-3M	28799-3M	28799-2M	261790-1M
230243M	28501-1M	28901-1M	28919-1M	261690-1M
230246M	28501-2M	28901-2M	28911-1M	261610-1M
230249M	28600-1M	28600-1M	28620-0M	261220-0M
230252M	28600-2M	28600-2M	28610-0M	261210-0M
230255M	28501-3M	28901-3M	28919-2M	261690-2M
290101	27311-0	27311-0	27311-0	251400-0
290104	27312-0	27312-0	27312-0	251500-0
290107	27313-0	27313-0	27313-0	251600-0
290110	27322-0	27322-0	27322-0	252100-0
290113	27330-1	27330-1	27331-0	250510-0
290116	27340-0	27340-0	27340-0	251700-0
290119	27621-0	27821-0	27826-0, 27827-0, 27829-0	250700-0, 250800-0
2901191	27621-1	27821-1	27827-0	250810-0
2901192	27621-2	27821-2	27829-1	250820-0
2901193	27621-3	27821-3	27826-0	250700-0
2901194	27621-4	27821-4	27829-2	250850-0
2901195	27621-5	27821-5	27829-3	250830-0, 250840-0
290122	27624-0	27824-0	27824-0	251910-0
290125	27691-0	27891-0	27891-0	250900-0
290201	27110-1	27110-1	27210-1	310100-1
290204	27130-0	27130-0	27230-0	251000-0
2902041	27130-0	27130-0	27230-0	251000-0
290207	27140-0	27140-0	27240-0	310410-0
290210	27410-1	27410-1	27411-1	250310-1
290213	27420-0	27420-0	27420-0	250200-0

PRELIMINARY TABLE OF CORRESPONDENCE BETWEEN ISIC-BASED CODES, SITC AND HS CODES
TABLEAU PROVISOIRE DE CORRESPONDENCE ENTRE LES INDICATIFS D'APRES
LA CITI ET LES INDICATIFS DE LA CTCI ET SH

ISIC-based code, Rev. 2 Indicatif d'après la CITI Rev.2	SITC, Revised code Indicatif d'après la CTCI révisée	SITC, Rev.2 code Indicatif d'après la CTCI Rev.2	SITC, Rev. 3 code Indicatif d'apres la CTCI Rev.3	Harmonized Commodity Description and Coding System (HS) Systeme Harmonise de Designation et de Codification des Marchandises (SH)
290216	27654-1	27854-1	27854-0	252921-0, 252922-0
290219	27693-0	27892-0	27892-0	251100-0
290222	27697-0	27894-0	27894-0	252800-0
290225	51336-1	52229[b]-1	52222-1	280480-0
290301	27630-1	27830-1	27830-1	250100-1
290901	27510-0	27710-0	27710-0	710221-0, 719229-0
290902	27321-1	27323-0	27323-0	252010-0
290904	27523-1	27722-1	27722-1, 27729-1	251300-1
290907	27622-0	27822-0	27822-0	250400-0
290910	27640-0	27840-0	27840-0	252400-0
290913	27652-0	27852-0	27852-0	252500-0
2909131	27652-1	27852-1	27852-1	252510-0
2909132	27652-2	27852-2	27852-2	252520-0, 252530-0
290914	27695-0	27893-0	27893-0	252600-0
290917	32170-1	32240-1, 32313-1	32230-1	270300-1
290918	32170-2	32240-2	32230-2	270300-2
290919	66720-1	66721-0	66721-0	710210-0
290922	66730-1	66730-1	66731-1	710310-1
311101	01110-0	01110-0	01100-0	020100-0, 020200-0
3111011	01110-0	00111-0	01100-0	020100-0, 020200-0
311104	01120-0	01120-0	01210-0	020400-0
3111041	01120-0	01120-0	01210-0	020400-0
311107	01130-0	01130-0	01220-0	020300-0
3111071	01130-0	01130-0	01220-0	020300-0
311110	01140-1	01140-1	01231-0, 01232-0, 01234-0, 01235-0	020710-0, 020721-0, 020722-0, 020723-0, 020739-0, 020741-0, 020742-0, 020743-0
3111101	01140-1	01140-1	01231-0, 01232-0, 01234-0, 01235-0	020710-0, 020721-0, 020722-0, 020723-0, 020739-0, 020741-0, 020742-0, 020743-0
311113	01150-0+	01150-0+	01240-0, 01290-1	020500-0, 020800-1
311116	01210-0	01210-0	01610-0	021011-0, 021012-0, 021019-0
311119	01290-0	01290-0	01680-0	021020-0, 021090-0
311122	01340-0	01420-0	01720-1	160100-1
311125	01380-1	01490-1	01720-2, 01730-1, 01740-1, 01750-1, 01760-1, 01790-1	160100-2, 160220-1, 160231-1, 160239-1, 160241-1, 160242-1, 160249-1, 160250-1, 160290-1
311128	01380-2	01490-2	01730-2, 01740-2, 01750-2, 01760-2, 01790-2	160220-2, 160231-2, 160239-2, 160241-2, 160242-2, 160249-2, 160250-2, 160290-2
311131	09130-1	09130-1	41120-1	150100-1
3111311	09130-1	09130-1	41120-1	150100-1
311134	21110-0	21110-0	21110-1	410100-1
3111341	21110-0	21110-0	21110-1	410100-1
311137	21120-0, 21140-0, 21160-0	21120-0, 21140-0, 21160-0	21110-2, 21120-0, 21140-0, 21160-0	410100-2, 410210-0, 410310-0
3111371	21120-0, 21140-0, 21160-0	21120-0, 21140-0, 21160-0	21110-2, 21120-0, 21140-0, 21160-0	410100-2, 410210-0, 410310-0
311201	02210-0	02241-1, 02249-1	02223-0, 02224-0, 02232-1, 02241-1	040291-0, 040299-0, 040390-1, 040410-1
3112011	02210-0	02241-1, 02249-1	02223-0, 02224-0, 02232-1,	040291-0, 040299-0, 040390-1,

Annex II - Annexe II

PRELIMINARY TABLE OF CORRESPONDENCE BETWEEN ISIC-BASED CODES, SITC AND HS CODES
TABLEAU PROVISOIRE DE CORRESPONDENCE ENTRE LES INDICATIFS D'APRES
LA CITI ET LES INDICATIFS DE LA CTCI ET SH

ISIC-based code, Rev. 2 Indicatif d'après la CITI Rev.2	SITC, Revised code Indicatif d'après la CTCI révisée	SITC, Rev.2 code Indicatif d'après la CTCI Rev.2	SITC, Rev. 3 code Indicatif d'apres la CTCI Rev.3	Harmonized Commodity Description and Coding System (HS) Systeme Harmonise de Designation et de Codification des Marchandises (SH)
			02241-1	040410-1
311204	02220-0	02241-2, 02242-0, 02243-0, 02249-2	02221-0, 02222-0, 02232-2, 02241-2	040210-0, 040221-0, 040229-0, 040390-2, 040410-2
3112041	02220-0	02241-2, 02242-0, 02243-0, 02249-2	02221-0, 02222-0, 02232-2, 02241-2	040210-0, 040221-0, 040229-0, 040390-2, 040410-2
311207	02300-0	02300-0	02300-0	040500-0
3112071	02300-0	02300-0	02300-0	040500-0
311210	02400-1	02400-1	02410-0, 02430-0, 02491-1, 02499-0	040610-1, 040620-0, 040640-0, 040690-0
3112101	02400-1	02400-1	02410-0, 02430-0, 02491-1, 02499-0	040610-1, 040620-0, 040640-0 040690-0
311213	09909-1	09809-1	02233-1	210500-1
311301	05200-0	05730-1, 05752-1, 05760-1, 05795-1, 05796-1, 05797-1, 05799-0	05730-1, 05752-0, 05760-1 05795-1, 05796-1, 05797-1, 05799-1	080300-1, 080400-1, 080620-0, 081310-0, 081320-0, 081330-0 081340-0, 081350-1
311304	05330-0	05830-0	05810-1, 09813-0	200700-0
311307	05350-1	05850-1	05900-1	200900-1
311310	05350-2	05850-1	05900-2	200900-2
311313	05361-0, 05362-0	05861-0, 05862-0	05830-0	081100-0
311316	05390-1	05899-1	05890-1	200800-1
311319	05461-0	05461-0	05460-0, 05660-0, 05672-1, 05673-1, 05674-1	071000-0, 200200-1, 200300-1, 200400-0
311322	05552-1	05659-1, 09801-1, 09809-2	05672-2, 05673-2, 05674-2, 05675-2, 05676-1, 05677-1, 05679-1, 09812-1	200200-2, 200300-2, 200500-1
311401	03110-3	03420-0, 03440-0	03420-0, 03440-0, 03455-0	030300-0, 030420-0, 030490-0
311404	03120-0	03500-0	03500-0	030500-0
311407	03201-0	03710-0	03710-1	160400-1
311501	09140-0	09140-0	09100-0	151700-0
3115011	09140-1	09141-0	09101-0	151710-0
311504	41110-0	41110-0	41110-0	150400-0
311507	41130-0	41130-0	41120-1, 41130-1	020900-0, 150100-2, 150200-0, 150300-0, 150500-0, 150600-1
311510	42120-1	42320-1	42111-0	150710-0
311513	42120-2	42320-2	42119-0	150790-0
311516	42130-1	42330-1	42121-0	151221-0
311519	42130-2	42330-2	42129-0	151229-0
311522	42140-1	42340-1	42131-0	150810-0
311525	42140-2	42340-2	42139-0	150890-0
311528	42150-1	42350-1	42141-0, 42142-1	150910-0, 150990-1,
311531	42150-2	42350-2	42142-2	150990-2
311534	42200-1	42400-1	42151-0, 42161-0, 42171-0, 42180-1, 42211-0, 42221-0, 42231-0, 42241-0, 42250-1, 42291-1, 42299-1	151110-0, 151211-0, 151311-0, 151321-0, 151410-0, 151511-0, 151521-0, 151530-1, 151540-1, 151550-1, 151560-1, 151590-1
311537	42200-2	42400-2	42159-0, 42169-0, 42179-0, 42180-2, 42219-0, 42229-0, 42239-0, 42249-0, 42250-2, 42291-2, 42299-2	151190-0, 151219-0, 151319-0, 151329-0, 151490-0, 151519-0, 151529-0, 151530-2, 151540-2, 151550-2, 151560-2, 151590-2
311601	04601-0	04601-0	04610-0	110100-0
311604	04602-0, 04702-0	04602-0, 04702-0	04620-0, 04720-0	110300-0

Annex II - Annexe II

PRELIMINARY TABLE OF CORRESPONDENCE BETWEEN ISIC-BASED CODES, SITC AND HS CODES
TABLEAU PROVISOIRE DE CORRESPONDENCE ENTRE LES INDICATIFS D'APRES
LA CITI ET LES INDICATIFS DE LA CTCI ET SH

ISIC-based code, Rev. 2 Indicatif d'après la CITI Rev.2	SITC, Revised code Indicatif d'après la CTCI révisée	SITC, Rev.2 code Indicatif d'après la CTCI Rev.2	SITC, Rev. 3 code Indicatif d'apres la CTCI Rev.3	Harmonized Commodity Description and Coding System (HS) Systeme Harmonise de Designation et de Codification des Marchandises (SH)
311607	04701-0	04701-0	04710-0	110200-0
311610	04812-0	04812-0	04811-0	190410-0
311701	04830-0	04830-0	04830-0	190211-0, 190219-0
311704	04841-0	04841[a]-0	04849-1	190590-1
311707	04842-1	04842-1	04842-1	190530-1
311710	04842-2	04842-2	04849-2	190590-2
311713	09909-2	09809-2	09891-1	190220-1, 190240-0
311801	06110-0	06110-0	06110-0	170111-0, 170112-0
311804	06120-0	06120-0	06120-0	170191-0, 170199-0
311901	05320-0	05820-0	06210-0	200600-0
311904	06201-0	06201-0	06220-0	170400-0
311907	07220-0	07220-0	07220-0	180500-0
311910	07232-0	07232-0	07240-0	180400-0
311913	07300-0	07300-0	07300-0	180600-0
312101	07130-0	07120[a]-0	07131-0, 07132-0	210110-0, 090140-0
312104	09907-0	09807-0	09844-0	220900-0
312201	08199-0	08199-0	08195-0, 08199-0	230900-0
313101	11240-1	11240-1	11241-0, 11242-0, 11244-0, 11245-0, 11249-0	220820-0, 220830-0, 220840-0, 220850-0, 220890-0
313104	11240-2, 51224-0	11240-2, 51216-0	11243-0, 51215-0, 51216-0	220700-0, 220810-0
313201	11211-0	11211-0	05993-1	200960-0
313204	11212-0, 11213-0	11212-0, 11213-0	11210-0	220400-0, 220500-0
313301	04820-0	04820-0	04820-0	110700-0
313304	11230-0	11230-0	11230-0	220300-0
313401	11101-1	11101-1	11101-1	220110-0
313404	11102-0	11102-0	11102-0	220200-0
314001	12100-3	12120-0	12120-0	240120-0
314004	12210-0	12210-0	12210-0, 12231-1	240210-0, 240290-1
314007	12220-0	12220-0	12220-0, 12231-2	240220-0, 240290-2
314010	12230-0	12230-0	12232-0, 12239-0	240300-0
321101	26320-0	26320-0	26320-0	140420-0
321103	65121-0, 65122-0, 65125-1	65122-0, 65123-0, 65126-1	65112-0, 65113-0, 65116-1	510610-0, 510710-0, 510910-1
321104	65121-1, 65122-1, 65125-11	65122-1, 65123-1, 65126-11	65112-1, 65113-1, 65116-11	510610-1, 510710-1, 510910-11
321107	65121-2, 65122-2, 65125-12	65122-2, 65123-2, 65126-12	65112-2, 65113-2, 65116-12	510610-2, 510710-2, 510910-12
321109	65130-0	65130-1	65131-0, 65133-0	520500-0, 520710-0
321110	65130-1	65130-11	65131-1, 65133-1	520500-1, 520710-1
321113	65130-2	65130-12	65131-2, 65133-2	520500-2, 520710-2
321116	65150-1	65196-0, 65197-0, 65199[a]-0	65196-0, 65199-1	530600-0, 530820-0, 530890-1
321119	65164-1, 65165-1, 65174-1, 65175-1	65148-0, 65152-0, 65166-0, 65167-0, 65168-0, 65169-0 65174-0, 65175-0, 65176-0, 65177-0, 65182-0	65181-0, 65182-0, 65183-0, 65184-0, 65185-0, 65186-0, 65187-0	550900-0, 551000-0, 551100-0
321122	65192-1	65198-1	65197-1	530700-1
321125	65193-0	65198-2, 65199[c]-1	65197-2, 65199-2	530700-2, 530810-0, 530890-2
321128	65210-0	65210-0	65211-0, 65212-0, 65220-0	520811-0, 520812-0, 520813-0, 520819-0, 520911-0, 520912-0, 520919-0, 521011-0, 521012-0, 521019-0, 521111-0, 521112-0, 521119-0, 521211-0, 521221-0, 580211-0, 580310-0

PRELIMINARY TABLE OF CORRESPONDENCE BETWEEN ISIC-BASED CODES, SITC AND HS CODES
TABLEAU PROVISOIRE DE CORRESPONDENCE ENTRE LES INDICATIFS D'APRES
LA CITI ET LES INDICATIFS DE LA CTCI ET SH

ISIC-based code, Rev. 2 Indicatif d'après la CITI Rev.2	SITC, Revised code Indicatif d'après la CTCI révisée	SITC, Rev.2 code Indicatif d'après la CTCI Rev.2	SITC, Rev. 3 code Indicatif d'apres la CTCI Rev.3	Harmonized Commodity Description and Coding System (HS) Systeme Harmonise de Designation et de Codification des Marchandises (SH)
321128A	65210-0A	65210-0A	65211-0A, 65212-0A, 65220-0A	520811-0A, 520812-0A, 520813-0A, 520819-0A, 520911-0A, 520912-0A, 520919-0A, 521011-0A, 521012-0A, 521019-0A, 521111-0A, 521112-0A, 521119-0A, 521211-0A, 521221-0A, 580211-0A, 580310-0A
321128B	65210-0B	65210-0B	65211-0B, 65212-0B, 65220-0B	520811-0B, 520812-0B, 520813-0B, 520819-0B, 520911-0B, 520912-0B, 520919-0B, 521011-0B, 521012-0B, 521019-0B, 521111-0B, 521112-0B, 521119-0B, 521211-0B, 521221-0B, 580211-0B, 580310-0B
321131	65310-0	65410-0	65410-0	500700-0
321131A	65310-0A	65410-0A	65410-0A	500700-0A
321131B	65310-0B	65410-0B	65410-0B	500700-0B
321134	65320-1	65420-1, 65430-1	65420-1, 65430-1	511100-1, 511200-1, 580110-1
321134A	65320-1A	65420-1A, 65430-1A	65420-1A, 65430-1A	511100-1A, 511200-1A, 580110-1A
321134B	65320-1B	65420-1B, 65430-1B	65420-1B, 65430-1B	511100-1B, 511200-1B, 580110-1B
321137	65331-0	65440-0	65440-1	530911-1, 530921-1
321137A	65331-0A	65440-0A	65440-1A	530911-1A, 530921-1A
321137B	65331-0B	65440-0B	65440-1B	530911-1B, 530921-1B
321140	65340-0	65450-1	65450-1	531010-1
321140A	65340-0A	65450-1A	65450-1A	531010-1A
321140B	65340-0B	65450-1B	65450-1B	531010-1B
321143	65350-1, 65360-1	65350-1, 65360-1, 65380-1, 65390-1	65350-1, 65360-1, 65380-1, 65390-1	540800-1, 551600-1, 580131-1, 580132-1, 580133-1, 580134-1, 580135-1, 580136-1
321143A	65350-1A, 65360-1A	65350-1A, 65360-1A, 65380-1A, 65390-1A	65350-1A, 65360-1A, 65380-1A, 65390-1A	540800-1A, 551600-1A, 580131-1A, 580132-1A, 580133-1A, 580134-1A, 580135-1A, 580136-1A,
321143B	65350-1B, 65360-1B	65350-1B, 65360-1B, 65380-1B, 65390-1B	65350-1B, 65360-1B, 65380-1B, 65390-1B	540800-1B, 551600-1B, 580131-1B, 580132-1B, 580133-1B, 580134-1B, 580135-1B, 580136-1B
321146	65350-2, 65360-2	65310-1, 65320-1, 65340-1	65310-1, 65320-1, 65330-1, 65340-1, 65390-1	540700-1, 551200-1, 551300-1, 551400-1, 551500-1, 580131-1, 580132-1, 580133-1, 580134-1, 580135-1, 580136-1
321146A	65350-2A, 65360-2A	65310-1A, 65320-1A, 65340-1A	65310-1A, 65320-1A, 65330-1A, 65340-1A, 65390-1A	540700-1A, 551200-1A, 551300-1A, 551400-1A, 551500-1A, 580131-1A, 580132-1A, 580133-1A, 580134-1A, 580135-1A,

Annex II - Annexe II

PRELIMINARY TABLE OF CORRESPONDENCE BETWEEN ISIC-BASED CODES, SITC AND HS CODES
TABLEAU PROVISOIRE DE CORRESPONDENCE ENTRE LES INDICATIFS D'APRES LA CITI ET LES INDICATIFS DE LA CTCI ET SH

ISIC-based code, Rev. 2 Indicatif d'après la CITI Rev.2	SITC, Revised code Indicatif d'après la CTCI révisée	SITC, Rev.2 code Indicatif d'après la CTCI Rev.2	SITC, Rev. 3 code Indicatif d'apres la CTCI Rev.3	Harmonized Commodity Description and Coding System (HS) Systeme Harmonise de Designation et de Codification des Marchandises (SH)
				580136-1A
321146B	65350-2B, 65360-2B	65310-1B, 65320-1B, 65340-1B	65310-1B, 65320-1B, 65330-1B, 65340-1B, 65390-1B	540700-1B, 551200-1B, 551300-1B, 551400-1B, 551500-1B, 580131-1B, 580132-1B, 580133-1B, 580134-1B, 580135-1B, 580136-1B
321201	65660-0	65830-0, 77585-0	65830-0, 77585-0	630100-0
321204	65691-1	65841-0, 65842-0	65841-0, 65842-0, 65843-0	630210-0, 630221-0, 630222-0, 630229-0, 630231-0, 630232-0, 630239-0
321207	65691-2	65845-1, 65846-1,	65847-1, 65848-1	630260-0, 630291-1, 630292-1, 630293-1, 630299-1
321301	65370-0	65510-0, 65520-0	65500-0	600100-0, 600200-0
321304	84142-1	84722-1	84622-1, 84629-0	611520-1, 611591-0, 611592-0, 611593-0, 611599-0
321307	84142-2	84722-2	84622-2	611520-2
321310	84143-1	84600-1	84381-0, 84382-0, 84481-0, 84482-0, 84483-0, 84512-1, 84621-0	610711-0, 610712-0, 610719-0, 610721-0, 610722-0, 610729-0, 610811-0, 610819-0, 610821-0, 610822-0, 610829-0, 610831-0, 610832-0, 610839-0, 611100-1, 611511-0, 611512-0, 611519-0
321313	84144-1	84590-1	84370-1	610500-1
321316	84144-2	84510-1	84530-0	611000-0
321319	84144-3	84520-1, 84590-1, 84621-0, 84632-0, 84640-2	84310-0, 84320-0, 84370-2, 84410-0, 84420-0, 84470-0, 84512-0, 84524-0, 84540-0, 84562-0, 84564-0, 84590-0, 84690-0	610100-0, 610200-0, 610300-0, 610400-0, 610500-2, 610600-0, 610900-0, 611100-2, 611200-0, 611300-0, 611400-0, 611600-0, 611700-0
321401	65750-0	65921-0	65921-0	570110-0
321404	65760-0	65921-0, 65930-0, 65940-0, 65950-0, 65961-0, 65962-0	65929-0, 65930-0, 65940-0, 65950-0, 65960-0	570190-0, 570200-0, 570300-0, 570400-0, 570500-0
321501	65561-0	65751-0	65751-0	560700-0
321901	65740-0	65910-0	65911-0, 65912-0	481500-0, 590400-0
322001	84111-1	84240-0	84130-0	620331-0, 620332-0, 620333-0, 620339-0
322004	84111-2	84210-1	84110-1, 84310-1	610100-1, 620100-1
322007	84111-3, 89300-1	84210-2, 84821-1	84110-2	620100-2, 621000-1
322010	84111-4	84220-0	84120-0, 84321-0	610311-0, 610312-0, 610319-0, 620311-0, 620312-0, 620319-0, 620321-0, 620322-0, 620323-0, 620329-0
322013	84111-5	84230-0	84140-0, 84324-0	610341-0, 610342-0, 610343-0, 610349-0, 620341-0, 620342-0, 620343-0, 620349-0
322016	84112-1	84350-1	84270-0, 84470-0	610600-0, 620600-0
322019	84112-2	84310-1	84211-1, 84219-0, 84410-1	610200-1, 620200-1
322022	84112-3	84330-0	84240-0, 84424-0	610441-0, 610442-0, 610443-0, 610444-0, 610449-0, 620441-0, 620442-0, 620443-0, 620444-0, 620449-0
322025	84112-4	84310-2	84211-2	620200-2, 621000-2

PRELIMINARY TABLE OF CORRESPONDENCE BETWEEN ISIC-BASED CODES, SITC AND HS CODES
TABLEAU PROVISOIRE DE CORRESPONDENCE ENTRE LES INDICATIFS D'APRES
LA CITI ET LES INDICATIFS DE LA CTCI ET SH

ISIC-based code, Rev. 2 Indicatif d'après la CITI Rev.2	SITC, Revised code Indicatif d'après la CTCI révisée	SITC, Rev.2 code Indicatif d'après la CTCI Rev.2	SITC, Rev. 3 code Indicatif d'apres la CTCI Rev.3	Harmonized Commodity Description and Coding System (HS) Systeme Harmonise de Designation et de Codification des Marchandises (SH)
322028	84112-5	84340-0	84250-0, 84260-0, 84425-0, 84426-0	610451-0, 610452-0, 610453-0, 610459-0, 610461-0, 610462-0, 610463-0, 610469-0, 620451-0, 620452-0, 620453-0, 620459-0, 620461-0, 620462-0, 620463-0, 620469-0
322031	84112-6	84320-0	84221-0, 84421-0	610411-0, 610412-0, 610413-0, 610419-0, 620411-0, 620412-0, 620413-0, 620419-0
322034	84113-1	84410-0	84150-0, 84370-0	610500-0, 620500-0
322037	84113-2, 84143-2	84410-0, 84420-0	84160-0, 84380-0	610700-0, 620700-0
322040	84114-1, 84143-3	84430-0	84280-0, 84480-0	610800-0, 620800-0
323001	61120-0	61120-0	61120-0	411100-0
323101A	61130-1A, 61140-1A, 61190-1A	61130-1A, 61140-1A, 61150-1A, 61160-1A, 61180-1A	61130-1A, 61140-1A, 61150-1A, 61160-1A, 61170-1A, 61180-1A	410400-1A, 410500-1A, 410600-1A, 410700-1A, 410800-1A, 410900-1A
3231011A	61130-1A, 61140-1A	61130-1A, 61140-1A	61130-1A, 61140-1A	410400-1A
3231012A	61191-1A	61150-1A	61150-1A	410500-1A
3231013A	61192-1A	61161-1A	61160-1A	410600-1A
3231014A	61199-1A	61169-1A	61170-1A	410700-1A
3231015A	61193-1A, 61194-1A, 61195-1A	61180-1A	61180-1A	410800-1A, 410900-1A
323101B	61130-1B, 61140-1B, 61190-1B	61130-1B, 61140-1B, 61150-1B, 61160-1B, 61180-1B	61130-1B, 61140-1B, 61150-1B, 61160-1B, 61170-1B, 61180-1B	410400-1B, 410500-1B, 410600-1B, 410700-1B, 410800-1B, 410900-1B
3231011B	61130-1B, 61140-1B	61130-1B, 61140-1B	61130-1B, 61140-1B	410400-1B
3231012B	61191-1B	61150-1B	61150-1B	410500-1B
3231013B	61192-1B	61161-1B	61160-1B	410600-1B
3231014B	61199-1B	61169-1B	61170-1B	410700-1B
3231015B	61193-1B, 61194-1B, 61195-1B	61180-1B	61180-1B	410800-1B, 410900-1B
323104A	61130-2A, 61140-2A, 61190-2A	61130-2A, 61140-2A, 61150-2A, 61160-2A, 61180-2A	61130-2A, 61140-2A, 61150-2A, 61160-2A, 61170-2A, 61180-2A	410400-2A, 410500-2A, 410600-2A, 410700-2A, 410800-2A, 410900-2A
3231041A	61130-2A, 61140-2A	61130-2A, 61140-2A	61130-2A, 61140-2A	410400-2A
3231042A	61191-2A	61150-2A	61150-2A	410500-2A
3231043A	61192-2A	61161-2A	61160-2A	410600-2A
3231044A	61199-2A	61169-2A	61170-2A	410700-2A
3231045A	61193-2A, 61194-2A, 61195-2A	61180-2A	61180-2A	410800-2A, 410900-2A,
323104B	61130-2B, 61140-2B, 61190-2B	61130-2B, 61140-2B, 61150-2B, 61160-2B, 61180-2B	61130-2B, 61140-2B, 61150-2B, 61160-2B, 61170-2B, 61180-2B	410400-2B, 410500-2B, 410600-2B, 410700-2B, 410800-2B, 410900-2B
3231041B	61130-2B, 61140-2B	61130-2B, 61140-2B	61130-2B, 61140-2B	410400-2B
3231042B	61191-2B	61150-2B	61150-2B	410500-2B
3231043B	61192-2B	61161-2B	61160-2B	410600-2B
3231044B	61199-2B	61169-2B	61170-2B	410700-2B
3231045B	61193-2B, 61194-2B, 61195-2B	61180-2B	61180-2B	410800-2B, 410900-2B
324000	85102-0, 85103-0, 85104-0, 85105-0	85102-0, 85103-0, 85104-0, 85105-0	85115-0, 85122-0, 85124-0, 85125-0, 85140-0, 85150-0,	640300-0, 640400-0, 640500-0

PRELIMINARY TABLE OF CORRESPONDENCE BETWEEN ISIC-BASED CODES, SITC AND HS CODES
TABLEAU PROVISOIRE DE CORRESPONDENCE ENTRE LES INDICATIFS D'APRES
LA CITI ET LES INDICATIFS DE LA CTCI ET SH

ISIC-based code, Rev. 2 Indicatif d'après la CITI Rev.2	SITC, Revised code Indicatif d'après la CTCI révisée	SITC, Rev.2 code Indicatif d'après la CTCI Rev.2	SITC, Rev. 3 code Indicatif d'apres la CTCI Rev.3	Harmonized Commodity Description and Coding System (HS) Systeme Harmonise de Designation et de Codification des Marchandises (SH)
			85170-0	
324001	85102-1	85102-1	85115-1, 85140-1, 85170-1	640300-1, 640510-1
324004	85102-2	85102-2	85115-2, 85140-2, 85170-2	640300-2, 640510-2
324007	85102-3	85102-3	85115-3, 85140-3, 85170-3	640300-3, 640510-3
324010	85102-4, 85103-0, 85105-0	85102-0, 85103-0, 85105-0	85122-0, 85124-0, 85125-0, 85140-4, 85150-1, 85170-4	640411-0, 640419-1, 640420-1, 640510-4, 640520-1, 640590-1
324013	85104-1	85104-1	85140-5, 85150-2, 85170-5	640419-2, 640420-2, 640510-5 640520-2, 640590-2
324016	85104-2	85104-2	85140-6, 85150-3, 85170-6	640419-3, 640420-3, 640510-6, 640520-3, 640590-3
331101	24310-0	24810-0	24810-0	440600-0
331104	24320-0	24820-0	24820-0, 24830-0	440710-0, 440910-0
331107	24330-0	24830-0	24840-0, 24850-0	440721-0, 440722-0, 440723-0, 440791-0, 440792-0, 440799-0, 440920-0
331110	63110-0	63410-0	63410-0	440800-0
331113	63121-1	63441-0	63440-1	441200-1
331116	63121-2	63420-0	63430-0, 63440-2	441200-2
331119	63122-0	63443-0	63539-1	441800-1
331122	63142-0	63432-0	63422-0, 63423-0	441000-0
332001	82103-1	82122-1	82123-0, 82125-0	940421-0, 940429-0
332004	82103-2	82122-2	82121-0	940410-0
332005	82101-1, 82109-1	82111-1, 82192-0	82110-1, 82150-0	940100-1, 940330-0, 940340-0, 940350-0, 940360-0
341101	25120-0	25120-0	25120-0	470100-0
341104	25150-0	25192-0	25192-0	470600-0
341107	25160-0	25160-0	25130-0	470200-0
341110	25170-0	25170-0	25140-0, 25150-0	470300-0
341113	25180-0	25180-0	25160-0	470400-0
341116	25190-0	25191-0	25191-0	470500-0
341119	64110-0	64110-0	64110-0	480100-0
341122	64120-0	64121[a]-0, 64122[b]-0	64120-1, 64132-0, 64133-0, 64134-0, 64248-0	480200-1, 481011-0, 481012-0, 481021-0, 481029-0, 482351-0, 482359-0
341125	64130-0	64130-0	64140-0	480400-0
341128	64140-0	64150-1	64155-1	481390-1
341131	64150-0	64150-2	64120-2, 64151-0, 64152-0, 64154-0, 64156-0, 64157-0, 64158-0, 64159-0, 64163-0, 64164-0, 64169-0	480200-2, 480300-0, 480500-0, 480810-0, 480890-0
341134	64160-1	64161-0	63450-1	441100-1
341137	64160-2	64162-0	63450-2	441100-2
341201	64211-0	64210[a]-0	64210-0	481900-0
342000	89200-0	89200-0	89200-0	490100-0, 490200-0, 490300-0, 490400-0, 490500-0, 490600-0, 490700-0, 490800-0, 490900-0, 491000-0, 491100-0
342001	89220-0, 89299-1	89220-0, 89286-1, 89289-1	89220-0	490200-0
342002	89210-0, 89292-1, 89299-2	89210-0, 89282-1, 89289-2	89210-0	490100-0, 490300-0, 490500-0
342003	89230-0, 89240-0, 89291-0, 89292-2, 89293-0, 89294-0,	89240-0, 89281-0, 89282-2, 89283-0, 89284-0, 89285-0,	89240-0, 89280-0	482100-0, 490400-0, 490600-0, 490700-0, 490800-0, 490900-0,

Annex II - Annexe II

PRELIMINARY TABLE OF CORRESPONDENCE BETWEEN ISIC-BASED CODES, SITC AND HS CODES
TABLEAU PROVISOIRE DE CORRESPONDENCE ENTRE LES INDICATIFS D'APRES
LA CITI ET LES INDICATIFS DE LA CTCI ET SH

ISIC-based code, Rev. 2 Indicatif d'après la CITI Rev.2	SITC, Revised code Indicatif d'après la CTCI révisée	SITC, Rev.2 code Indicatif d'après la CTCI Rev.2	SITC, Rev. 3 code Indicatif d'après la CTCI Rev.3	Harmonized Commodity Description and Coding System (HS) Systeme Harmonise de Designation et de Codification des Marchandises (SH)
	89299-3, parts of 661, 666, 698, 893	89286-2, 89289-3, 89399-1, parts of 661, 666, 699		491000-0, 491100-0
351101	27410-2	27410-2	27411-2	250310-2
351102	27410-3	27410-3	27411-3	250310-3
351103	51211-0	51125-0	51125-0	290250-0
351105	51212-1	51119-1	51119-1	290129-1
351106	51212-2	51119-2	51114-1	290110-1
351107	51212-3	51122-0	51122-0	290220-0
351108	51212-4	51121-0	51121-0	290211-0
351109	51212-5	51113-0	51113-0	290123-0, 290124-0
351110	51212-6	51111-0	51111-0	290121-0
351111	51212-7	51129-1	51129-1	290290-1
351113	51212-8	51112-0	51112-0	290122-0
351114	51212-9	51123-0	51123-0	290230-0
351115	51212-10	51124-0	51124-0	290241-0, 290242-0, 290243-0, 290244-0
351116	51213-1	51139-1	51138-0	290340-0
351117	51213-2	51139-2	51136-1	290314-0
351118	51213-3	51139-3	51136-2	290312-0
351119	51213-4	51132-0	51132-0	290322-0
351120	51213-5	51133-0	51133-0	290323-0
351121	51221-0	51211-0	51211-0	290511-0
351122	51222-1	51213-0	51213-0	290513-0, 290514-0
351123	51222-2	51215-0	51221-0	290531-0
351124	51213-6	51131-0	51131-0	290321-0
351125	51226-1	51218-0	51222-0	152000-0
351126	51227-1	51234-0	51241-0	290711-0
351127	51231-1	51611-1	51616-1	290911-0
351128	51222-3	51219-1	51229-1	290532-0
351129	51232-1	51613-0	51613-0	291010-0
351130	51241-1	51621-1	51621-1	291212-0
351131	51241-2	51621-2	51621-2	291211-0
351132	51232-2	51614-0	51614-0	291020-0
351133	51243-1	51623-0	51623-0	291411-0
351134	51251-1	51372-0	51372-0	291531-0, 291532-0, 291533-0, 291534-0, 291535-0, 291539-0
351135	51251-2	51371-1	51371-1	291521-0
351137	51251-3	51379-1	51374-1	291511-0
351138	51252-1	51382-0	51382-0	291735-0
351139	51253-1	51390-1	51393-1	291822-1
351140	51252-2	51381-0	51381-0	291714-0
351141	51253-2	51390-2	51391-1	291812-0
351142	51271-1	51450-1	51454-1	292141-1
351143	51276-1	51483-0	51483-0	292610-0
351145	51321-0	52213-0	52224-0	280110-0
351146	51331-1	52221-1	52231-1	280610-0
351147	51333-0	52222-0	52232-0	280700-0
351149	51334-0	52223-1	52233-1	280800-1
351150	51335-1	52224-0	52234-2	280920-1
351151	51339-1	52229-1	52239-1	281129-1
351153	51342-1	52232-1	52242-1	281310-0

**PRELIMINARY TABLE OF CORRESPONDENCE BETWEEN ISIC-BASED CODES, SITC AND HS CODES
TABLEAU PROVISOIRE DE CORRESPONDENCE ENTRE LES INDICATIFS D'APRES
LA CITI ET LES INDICATIFS DE LA CTCI ET SH**

ISIC-based code, Rev. 2 Indicatif d'après la CITI Rev.2	SITC, Revised code Indicatif d'après la CTCI révisée	SITC, Rev.2 code Indicatif d'après la CTCI Rev.2	SITC, Rev. 3 code Indicatif d'apres la CTCI Rev.3	Harmonized Commodity Description and Coding System (HS) Systeme Harmonise de Designation et de Codification des Marchandises (SH)
351154	51351-0	52241-0	52251-0	281700-0
351155	51355-0	52246-0	52256-0	282300-0
351157	51356-0	52247-0	52257-0	282400-0
351158	51361-0	52251-0	52261-0	281400-0
351159	51362-0	52252-0, 52253-0	52262-0, 52263-0	281511-0, 281512-0
351161	51365-1	28732-0	28520-0	281820-0
351162	51365-2	52256-0	52266-0	281830-0
351163	51424-1	52319-1	52349-1	283322-0
351165	51424-2	52319-2	52349-2	283325-0
351166	51428-0	52323-0	52372-0	283620-0
351167	51431-1	52325-1	52381-1	283711-0
351168	51424-3	52318-0	52345-0	283311-0, 283319-0
351169	51433-1	52327-1	52383-1	283911-0, 283919-0
351170	51435-1	52331-1	52431-1	284130-0
351171	51492-0	52391-0	52491-0	284700-0
351173	51494-0	52393-0	52493-0	284910-0
351174	53100-0	53100-0	53110-0, 53120-0	320400-0, 320500-0
351175	53240-0	53221[a]-0	53221-1	320110-0, 320120-0, 320130-0, 320190-1
351176	51429-1	52324-1	52373-0	283630-0
351177	53310-1	53310-1	53312-0	320620-0
351178	53310-2	53310-2	53315-0	320642-0
351179	59992-0	59892[a]-0	59864-0	380210-0
351200	56110-0, 56190-1	56210-0, 56291-1, 56292-1, 56293-1, 56299-1	56210-0, 56291-1, 56293-1, 56294-1, 56295-1, 56296-1, 56299-1	310210-0, 310221-0, 310229-0, 310230-0, 310240-0, 310260-0, 310270-0, 310280-0, 310290-0, 310510-1, 310520-1, 310530-1, 310540-1, 310551-1, 310559-1, 310590-1
351201	56110-0	56210-0	56210-0	310210-0, 310221-0, 310229-0, 310230-0, 310240-0, 310260-0, 310270-0, 310280-0, 310290-0
351203	56129-0, 56190-2	56222-0, 56229-0, 56291-2, 56292-2, 56299-2	56222-0, 56229-0, 56291-2, 56292-1, 56293-2, 56294-2, 56295-2, 56296-2, 56299-2	310310-0, 310390-0, 310510-2, 310520-2, 310530-2, 310540-2, 310551-2, 310559-2, 310560-1, 310590-2
351204	56129-1	56222-0	56222-0	310310-0
351207	56129-2	56229-0	56229-0	310390-0
351209	56130-0, 56190-3	56230-0, 56291-3, 56293-3, 56299-3	56230-0, 56291-3, 56292-2, 56296-3, 56299-3	310420-0, 310430-0, 310490-0, 310510-3, 310520-3, 310560-2, 310590-3
351210	56130-0	56230-0, 56293-3, 56299-3	56230-0	310420-0, 310430-0, 310490-0
351213A	56190-1	56291-1, 56292-1, 56293-1, 56299-1	56291-1, 56293-1, 56294-1, 56295-1, 56296-1, 56299-1	310510-1, 310520-1, 310530-1, 310540-1, 310551-1, 310559-1, 310590-1
351213B	56190-2	56291-2, 56292-2, 56299-2	56291-2, 56292-1, 56293-2, 56294-2, 56295-2, 56296-2, 56299-2	310510-2, 310520-2, 310530-2, 310540-2, 310551-2, 310559-2, 310560-1, 310590-2,
351213C	56190-3	56291-3, 56293-3, 56299-3	56291-3, 56292-2, 56296-3, 56299-3	310510-3, 310520-3, 310560-2, 310590-3
351216	59920-0	59100-0	59100-0	380800-0

PRELIMINARY TABLE OF CORRESPONDENCE BETWEEN ISIC-BASED CODES, SITC AND HS CODES
TABLEAU PROVISOIRE DE CORRESPONDENCE ENTRE LES INDICATIFS D'APRES
LA CITI ET LES INDICATIFS DE LA CTCI ET SH

ISIC-based code, Rev. 2 Indicatif d'après la CITI Rev.2	SITC, Revised code Indicatif d'après la CTCI révisée	SITC, Rev.2 code Indicatif d'après la CTCI Rev.2	SITC, Rev. 3 code Indicatif d'apres la CTCI Rev.3	Harmonized Commodity Description and Coding System (HS) Systeme Harmonise dè Designation et de Codification des Marchandises (SH)
351301	23120-0	23310-0	23210-0	400200-0
351304	26620-1	26650-0, 26660-0, 26670-1	26650-0, 26660-0	550100-0, 550300-0
351307	26630-1	26711-0, 26712-0, 26713-1	26711-0, 26712-0	550200-0, 550400-0
351310	58110-1	58231-0	57432-0	390750-0
351313	58110-2	58221-0	57541-0, 57542-0, 57543-0	390910-0, 390920-0, 390930-0
351316	58110-3	58211-0	57544-0	390940-0
351319	58120-1	58310-0	57110-0	390110-0, 390120-0
351320	58120-2	58390-1	57120-0	390130-0
351322	58120-3	58321-0	57511-0	390210-0
351323	58120-4	58361-0	57520-0	390600-0
351324	58110-4	58241-0	57530-0	390800-0
351325	58120-5	58331-0	57210-0	390311-0, 390319-0
351326	58110-5	58290-1	57411-0	390710-0
351328	58120-6	58341-0	57310-0	390410-0, 390421-0, 390422-0
351329	58110-6	58231-0	57431-0	390740-0
351331	58132-0	58410-0, 58420-0, 58430-0, 58491-0, 58492-0	57550-1	391200-1
351334	58191-0	58521-0	57595-1	391390-1
351337	65160-1	65141-0, 65142-0, 65143-0, 65144-0, 65145-0, 65146-0, 65147-0, 65149-0, 65151-0	65141-0, 65150-0, 65160-0, 65188-0	540110-0, 540200-0, 540400-0, 540610-0
351340	65170-1	65171-0, 65172-0, 65173-0, 65178-0, 65181-0	65170-1	540300-1, 540600-1
352101A	53332-1A	53342-1A	53342-1A, 53343-1A	320800-1A, 321000-1A
352104A	53332-2A	53341-0A	53341-0A	320900-0A
352107A	53332-3A	53342-2A, 53343-0A, 53344-1A	53342-2A, 53343-2A, 53344-0A	320800-2A, 321000-2A, 321200-0A
352110	53335-0	53354-0	53354-0	321400-0
352200	54000-0	54000-0	54000-0	293600-0, 293700-0, 293800-0, 293900-0, 294100-0, 300100-0, 300200-0, 300300-0, 300400-0, 300500-0, 300600-0
352201	54110-0	54110-0	54110-0	293600-0
352203	54130-0	54130-0	54130-0	294100-0
352205	54140-0	54140-0	54140-0	293900-0
352207	54150-0	54150-0	54150-0	293700-0
352301	55410-0	55410-0	55410-0	340100-0
352304	55420-0	55420-0	55420-0	340200-0
352901	51327-0	52218-0	52210-1	280300-1
352904	53320-0	53320-0	53320-0	321511-0, 321519-0
352906	55430-0	55430-0	55430-0	340500-0
352907	57112-0	57212-0	59312-0	360200-0
352910	59955-0	59223-0	59224-0	350300-0
352913	86241-0	88221-0	88220-0	370100-0
352916	86242-0	88222-0	88230-0	370200-0
352919	86243-0	88223-0	88240-0	370300-0
353001A	33210-2A	33411-1	33411-1A	271000-1A
353004A	33210-3A, 33220-1A	33412-0	33412-0A	271000-2A
353007A	33210-4A	33411-2A	33411-2A	271000-3A
353010A	33210-5A, 33220-2A	33419-1A	33419-1A	271000-4A
353013A	33220-1A	33421-0A	33421-0A	271000-5A

PRELIMINARY TABLE OF CORRESPONDENCE BETWEEN ISIC-BASED CODES, SITC AND HS CODES
TABLEAU PROVISOIRE DE CORRESPONDENCE ENTRE LES INDICATIFS D'APRES
LA CITI ET LES INDICATIFS DE LA CTCI ET SH

ISIC-based code, Rev. 2 Indicatif d'après la CITI Rev.2	SITC, Revised code Indicatif d'après la CTCI révisée	SITC, Rev.2 code Indicatif d'après la CTCI Rev.2	SITC, Rev. 3 code Indicatif d'apres la CTCI Rev.3	Harmonized Commodity Description and Coding System (HS) Systeme Harmonise de Designation et de Codification des Marchandises (SH)
353016A	33220-2A	33429-1A	33429-1A	271000-6A
353019A	33230-0A	33430-0A	33430-0A	271000-7A
353022A	33240-0A	33440-0A	33440-0A	271000-8A
353025A	33250-1A	33450-1A	33450-1A	271000-9A
353028	33262-1	33512--1	33512-1	271220-0
353031	33294-0	33542-0	33542-0	271311-0, 271312-0
353034A	33295-0A	33541-1A	33541-1A	271320-0A
3530371A	34110-2A	34130-1A	34200-1A	271112-1A, 271113-1A
3530372A	34110-3A	34130-2A	34200-2A	271112-2A, 271113-2A
354001	32150-0	32311-0	32210-0	270120-0
354004	32160-2	32312-0	32222-0	270220-0
354007	32180-1	32321[b]-1, 32322-1	32500-1	270400-1
354010	32180-2	32321[b]-2, 32322-2	32500-2	270400-2
354013B	34120-1B	34150-1B	34500-1B	270500-1B
354016	52110-0	33521-0	33521-0	270600-0
355101	62910-1	62591-1	62591-1	401310-0
355102	62910-1	62591-2	62591-2	401320-0, 401390-0
355104	62910-2	62599-1	62550-0	401191-0, 401199-0
355107	62910-3	62540-0	62540-0	401140-0, 401150-0
355110	62910-4	62510-0, 62520-0	62510-0, 62520-0	401110-0, 401120-0
355901	23130-0	23321-0	23221-0	400300-0
355904	62104-0	62104-0	62132-0, 62133-0	400800-0
355907	62105-0	62105-0	62140-0	400900-0
355910	62106-1	62106-0	62991-1	401700-1
355913	62940-0	62820-0	62920-0	401000-0
355916	85101-1	85101-1	85111-1, 85113-1, 85121-1, 85123-1, 85130-1	640100-1, 640200-1
356003	85101-2	85101-2	85111-2, 85113-2, 85121-2, 85123-2, 85130-2	640100-2, 640200-2
361001A	66640-0A	66640-0A	66611-0A, 66612-0A	691100-0A
361001B	66640-0B	66640-0B	66611-0B, 66612-0B	691100-0B
361004A	66650-0A	66650-0A	66613-0A	691200-0A
361004B	66650-0B	66650-0B	66613-0B	691200-0B
361007A	81220-0A	81220-0A	81220-0A	691000-0A
361007B	81220-0B	81220-0B	81220-0B	691000-0B
362001A	66430-0A	66430-0A	66430-0A	700400-0A
362001B	66430-0B	66430-0B	66430-0B	700400-0B
362004A	66440-0A	66440-0A	66440-0A	700500-0A
362004B	66440-0B	66440-0B	66440-0B	700500-0B
362005	66494-0	66494-0	66495-0	701931-0, 701932-0, 701939-0, 791990-0
362007A	66470-0A	66470-0A	66470-0A	700700-0A
362007B	66470-0B	66470-0B	66470-0B	700700-0B
362010A	66511-0A	66511-0A	66511-0A	701090-0A
362010B	66511-0B	66511-0B	66511-0B	701090-0B
369101A	66241-0A	66241-0A	66241-1A	690410-0A
369101B	66241-0B	66241-0B	66241-1B	690410-0B
369104A	66242-0A	66242-0A	66242-1A	690510-0A
369104B	66242-0B	66242-0B	66242-1B	690510-0B
369107A	66244-0A, 66245-0A	66244-0A, 66245-0A	66244-0A, 66245-0A	690700-0A, 690800-0A
369107B	66244-0B, 66245-0B	66244-0B, 66245-0B	66244-0B, 66245-0B	690700-0B, 690800-0B

Annex II - Annexe II

PRELIMINARY TABLE OF CORRESPONDENCE BETWEEN ISIC-BASED CODES, SITC AND HS CODES
TABLEAU PROVISOIRE DE CORRESPONDENCE ENTRE LES INDICATIFS D'APRES
LA CITI ET LES INDICATIFS DE LA CTCI ET SH

ISIC-based code, Rev. 2 Indicatif d'après la CITI Rev.2	SITC, Revised code Indicatif d'après la CTCI révisée	SITC, Rev.2 code Indicatif d'après la CTCI Rev.2	SITC, Rev. 3 code Indicatif d'apres la CTCI Rev.3	Harmonized Commodity Description and Coding System (HS) Systeme Harmonise de Designation et de Codification des Marchandises (SH)
369201	66110-1	66110-1	66111-0	252210-0
369204	66120-0	66120-0	66120-0	252300-0
369901A	66183-0A	66183-0A	66183-0A	681100-0A
369901B	66183-0A	66183-0B	66183-0B	681100-0B
369904	66310-0	66310-0	66310-0	680400-0
369907	66320-0	66320-0	66320-0	680500-0
369910A	66362-1A	66332-1A	66332-1A	681011-0A
369910B	66362-1B	66332-1B	66332-1B	681011-0B
369913A	66362-2A	66332-2A	66334-1A	681020-0A
369913B	66362-2B	66332-2B	66334-1B	681020-0B
369916A	66362-3A	66332-3A	66332-2A, 66333-0A, 66334-2A	681019-0A, 681091-0A, 681099-0A
369916B	66362-3B	66332-3B	66332-2B, 66333-0B, 66334-2B	681019-0B, 681091-0B, 681099-0B
371001	56121-0	56221-0	56221-0	310320-0
371004	67110-0, 67140-0	67120-1, 67161-0	67123-2, 67140-0	720140-0, 720211-0, 720219-0
371007	67120-1	67120-2	67121-1, 67122-1, 67123-1	720110-1, 720120-1, 720130-1
371010	67120-2	67120-3	67121-2, 67122-2, 67123-2	720110-2, 720120-2, 720130-2
371013	67150-0	67162-0, 67169-0	67150-0	720221-0, 720229-0, 720230-0, 720241-0, 720249-0, 720250-0, 720260-0, 720270-0, 720280-0, 720291-0, 720292-0, 720293-0, 720299-0
3710131	67150-1	67169-1	67153-0, 67154-0	720241-0, 720249-0, 720250-0
3710132	67150-2	67169-2	67155-0	720260-0
3710133	67150-3	67169-3	67159-1	720270-0
3710134	67150-4	67169-4	67151-0	720221-0, 720229-0
371016	67230-1	67241-1, 67242-1, 67243-1, 67244-1, 67250-1	67241-1, 67247-1, 67249-1, 67260-1, 67270-1	720610-1, 720700-1, 721810-1, 722410-1
371019	67230-2	67241-2, 67242-2, 67243-2, 67244-2, 67250-2	67241-2, 67247-2, 67249-2, 67260-2, 67270-2	720610-2, 720700-2, 721810-2, 722410-2
371022	67230-3	67241-3, 67242-3, 67243-3, 67244-3	67241-3, 67247-3, 67249-3	720610-3, 721810-3, 722410-3
371025	67250-1	67250-3	67260-3, 67270-3, 67280-1	720700-3, 721890-3, 722490-1
371028	67310-0	67310-0	67610-1	721300-1, 722100-1, 722700-1
371031			67610-2, 67620-0, 67630-0, 67640-0	721300-2, 721400-0, 721500-0, 722100-2, 722210-0, 722220-0, 722230-0, 722700-0, 722810-0, 722820-0, 722830-0, 722840-0, 722850-0, 722860-0, 722880-0
371035	67340-0, 67350-0	67330-0	67680-0	721600-0, 722240-0, 722870-0, 730100-0
371036	67340-0	67332-0, 67333-1, 67334-1, 67335-1, 67337-1, 67338-1, 67339-1	67682-0, 67683-1, 67684-1, 67685-1, 67686-1, 67687-1, 67688-1	721631-0, 721632-0, 721633-0, 721640-0, 721650-1, 721660-1, 721690-1, 722240-1, 722870-1, 730100-1
371037	67350-0	67331-0, 67333-2, 67334-2, 67335-2, 67337-2, 67338-2, 67339-2	67681-0, 67683-2, 67684-2, 67685-2, 67686-2, 67687-2, 67688-2	721610-0, 721621-0, 721622-0, 721650-2, 721660-2, 721690-2, 722240-2, 722870-2, 730100-2
371040	67410-0	67410-0, 67440-0	67311-0, 67313-1, 67314-0, 67321-0, 67323-1, 67324-0,	720811-0, 720812-0, 720821-0, 720822-0, 720831-1, 720832-0,

Annex II - Annexe II

PRELIMINARY TABLE OF CORRESPONDENCE BETWEEN ISIC-BASED CODES, SITC AND HS CODES
TABLEAU PROVISOIRE DE CORRESPONDENCE ENTRE LES INDICATIFS D'APRES
LA CITI ET LES INDICATIFS DE LA CTCI ET SH

ISIC-based code, Rev. 2 Indicatif d'après la CITI Rev.2	SITC, Revised code Indicatif d'après la CTCI révisée	SITC, Rev.2 code Indicatif d'après la CTCI Rev.2	SITC, Rev. 3 code Indicatif d'apres la CTCI Rev.3	Harmonized Commodity Description and Coding System (HS) Systeme Harmonise de Designation et de Codification des Marchandises (SH)
			67316-1, 67317-1, 67326-1, 67327-1, 67339-1, 67349-1, 67351-1, 67353-1, 67531-0, 67534-0, 67537-1, 67551-0, 67556-1, 67571-1, 67572-1, 67573-1, 67574-1	720833-0, 720841-1, 720842-0, 720843-0, 720890-1, 721111-1, 721112-1, 721121-1, 721122-1, 721130-1, 721141-1, 721149-1, 721190-1, 721911-0, 721912-0, 721921-0, 721922-0, 721931-0, 721990-1, 722011-1, 722020-1, 722090-1, 722590-1, 722699-1
371043	67420-0	67450-0	67312-1, 67313-2, 67315-1, 67316-2, 67322-1, 67323-1, 67325-1, 67326-2, 67331-0, 67335-0, 67339-2, 67341-0, 67345-0, 67349-2, 67351-2, 67352-1, 67353-2, 67532-0, 67535-0, 67538-1, 67552-0, 67556-2, 67571-2, 67572-2, 67573-2, 67574-2	720813-0, 720823-0, 720831-2, 720834-0, 720841-2, 720844-0, 720890-2, 720911-0, 720921-0, 720931-0, 720941-0, 720990-1, 721111-2, 721121-2, 721130-2, 721141-2, 721149-2, 721190-2, 721913-0, 721923-0, 721932-0, 721990-2, 722012-1, 722020-2, 722090-2, 722590-2, 722699-2
371046	67430-1, 67500-1	67460-1, 67500-1	67510-0	722510-0, 722610-0
371049	67430-2	67460-2	67332-0, 67333-0, 67334-0, 67336-0, 67337-0, 67338-0, 67339-3, 67342-0, 67343-0, 67344-0, 67346-0, 67347-0, 67348-0, 67349-3, 67352-2, 67353-3, 67553-0, 67554-0, 67555-0, 67556-3, 67561-1, 67562-1, 67571-3, 67572-3, 67573-3, 67574-3	720912-0, 720913-0, 720914-0, 720922-0, 720923-0, 720924-0, 720932-0, 720933-0, 720934-0, 720942-0, 720943-0, 720944-0, 720990-2, 721130-3, 721141-3, 721149-3, 721190-3, 721933-0, 721934-0, 721935-0, 721990-3, 722020-3, 722090-3, 722550-1, 722590-3, 722692-1, 722699-3
371052	67430-3	67460-3	67312-2, 67315-2, 67319-1, 67322-2, 67325-2, 67329-1, 67351-3, 67533-0, 67536-0, 67540-1, 67571-4, 67573-4, 67574-4	720814-0, 720824-0, 720835-0, 720845-0, 720890-3, 721119-1, 721129-1, 721914-0, 721924-0, 721990-4, 722530-1, 722540-1, 722590-4, 722691-1, 722699-4
371055	67470-0, 67500-2	67470-0, 67500-2	67420-0	721011-0, 721012-0, 721210-0
371058	67480-1, 67500-3	67490-1, 67500-3	67410-0	721031-0, 721039-0, 721041-0, 721049-0, 721221-0, 721229-0, 721230-0
371061	67500-4	67500-4	67339-4, 67349-4, 67353-4, 67556-4, 67562-2, 67572-4, 67574-5	721130-4, 721141-4, 721149-4, 721190-4, 722020-4, 722090-4, 722692-2, 722699-5
371064	67500-5	67500-5	67317-2, 67319-2, 67327-2, 67329-2, 67353-5, 67537-2, 67538-2, 67543-2, 67572-5, 67574-6	721112-2, 721119-2, 721122-2, 721129-2, 721190-5, 722011-2, 722012-2, 722090-5, 722691-2, 722699-6
371067	67610-0, 67620-1	67601-0, 67602-1	67701-0, 67709-1	730210-0, 730220-0, 730240-0, 730290-0
371070	67700-0	67700-0	67800-0	721700-0, 722300-0, 722900-0
371073	67810-0	67810-0	67911-0	730300-0
371076	67820-0	67820-1	67912-0, 67913-0, 67914-0, 67915-0, 67916-0, 67917-0	730400-0
371079	67830-0	67830-0	67931-1, 67933-0, 67943-0, 67944-0	730511-0, 730512-0, 730531-0 730539-0, 730630-0, 730640-0,

PRELIMINARY TABLE OF CORRESPONDENCE BETWEEN ISIC-BASED CODES, SITC AND HS CODES
TABLEAU PROVISOIRE DE CORRESPONDENCE ENTRE LES INDICATIFS D'APRES
LA CITI ET LES INDICATIFS DE LA CTCI ET SH

ISIC-based code, Rev. 2 Indicatif d'après la CITI Rev.2	SITC, Revised code Indicatif d'après la CTCI révisée	SITC, Rev.2 code Indicatif d'après la CTCI Rev.2	SITC, Rev. 3 code Indicatif d'apres la CTCI Rev.3	Harmonized Commodity Description and Coding System (HS) Systeme Harmonise de Designation et de Codification des Marchandises (SH)
				730650-0, 730660-0
371082	67910-0	67941-0	69962-0, 69963-1	732510-0, 732591-1, 732599-1
371085	67920-0	67942-0	69963-2	732591-2, 732599-2
371088	67930-0	67930-0	69965-0	732611-0, 732619-0
371091	73170-1	79199-1	79199-1	860719-1
372001	68211-0	28712-1, 68211-0	28322-0, 68211-0	740120-0, 740200-0
372004	68212-0	68212-0	68212-0	740311-0, 740312-0, 740313-0, 740319-0
3720041	68212-1	68212-1	68212-1	740311-1, 740312-1, 740313-1, 740319-1
3720042	68212-2	68212-2	68212-2	740311-2, 740312-2, 740313-2, 740319-2
372007	68213-0	68213-0	68214-0	740321-0, 740322-0, 740323-0, 740329-0
372008	68213-0	68213-0	68213-0	740500-0
372010	68221-1	68221-1	68230-0	740700-0
372013	68221-2	68221-2	68240-0	740800-0
372016	68222-0, 68223-0	68222-0, 68223-0	68250-0, 68261-0	740900-0, 741000-0
372019	68225-1	68225-1	68271-0	741100-0
372020	68310-0	68310-0	68310-0	750200-0
372021	51365-0	28732-0, 52256-0	28520-0, 52266-0	281820-0, 281830-0
372022	68410-1	68410-1	68411-0	760110-0
3720221	68410-11	68410-11	68411-1	760110-1
3720222	68410-12	68410-12	68411-2	760110-2
372023	68410-2	68410-2	68412-1	760120-1
372024	68410-3	68410-3	68412-2	760120-2
372025	68421-1	68421-1	68421-0	760400-0
372028	68421-2	68421-2	68422-0	760500-0
372031	68422-0, 68423-0	68422-0, 68423-0	68423-0, 68424-0	760600-0, 760700-0
372034	68425-0	68425-0	68426-0	760800-0
372037	68510-1	68512-0	68512-0	780110-0
3720371A	68510-11A	68512-1A	68512-1	780110-1
3720371B	68510-12B	68512-2B	68512-2	780110-2
3720373A	68510-14A	68512-3A	68512-3	780110-3
3720373B	68510-15B	68512-4B	68512-4	780110-4
372038	68510-4	68513-1	68511-1	780191-1, 780199-1
372039	68510-5	68513-2	68511-2	780191-2, 780199-2
372040	68524-1	68524-1	68524-1	780500-1
372043	68610-1	68610-1	68611-0	790111-0, 790112-0
3720431	68610-11	68610-11	68611-1	790111-1, 790112-1
3720432	68610-12	68610-12	68611-2	790111-2, 790112-2
372044	68610-3	68610-3	68612-1	790120-1
372045	68610-4	68610-4	68612-2	790120-2
372046	68622-0	68632-0	68632-0	790500-0
372049	68710-1	68710-1	68711-0	800110-0
3720491	68710-11	68710-11	68711-1	800110-1
3720492	68710-12	68710-12	68711-2	800110-2
372052	68950-1	68999-1	68982-1	810710-1
372055	68931-0	68915-0	68915-0	810411-0, 810419-0
3720551	68931-0	68915-0	68915-1	810411-1, 810419-1
3720552	68931-0	68915-0	68915-2	810411-2, 810419-2

Annex II - Annexe II

PRELIMINARY TABLE OF CORRESPONDENCE BETWEEN ISIC-BASED CODES, SITC AND HS CODES
TABLEAU PROVISOIRE DE CORRESPONDENCE ENTRE LES INDICATIFS D'APRES
LA CITI ET LES INDICATIFS DE LA CTCI ET SH

ISIC-based code, Rev. 2 Indicatif d'après la CITI Rev.2	SITC, Revised code Indicatif d'après la CTCI révisée	SITC, Rev.2 code Indicatif d'après la CTCI Rev.2	SITC, Rev. 3 code Indicatif d'après la CTCI Rev.3	Harmonized Commodity Description and Coding System (HS) Systeme Harmonise de Designation et de Codification des Marchandises (SH)
372056	68931-0	68915-0	68915-3	810411-3, 810419-3
372057	68931-0	68915-0	68915-4	810411-4, 810419-4
381101	69603-1	69603-1	69635-0	821220-0
381102	69601-0, 69602-0, 69604-0, 69605-0, 69607-0	69604-0, 69605-0, 69607-0, 69608-0	69640-0, 69650-0, 69680-0	821100-0, 821300-0, 821400-0
381103	69606-0	69606-0	69660-0	821500-0
381104A	69811-0A	69911-0A	69911-1A	830110-0A, 830120-0A, 830130-0A, 830140-0A
381104B	69811-0B	69911-0B	69911-1B	830110-0B, 830120-0B, 830130-0B, 830140-0B
381107A	69812-0A	69913-0A	69913-0A, 69914-0A, 69915-0A, 69916-0A, 69917-0A, 69919-0A	830200-0A
381107B	69812-0B	69913-0B	69913-0B, 69914-0B, 69915-0B, 69916-0B, 69917-0B, 69919-0B	830200-0B
381201	82101-1, 82102-1	82111-1, 82121-1	82110-0, 82130-0	940100-1, 940310-0, 940320-0
381301A	69210-0A	69210-0A, 69981[a]-0A	69210-1A, 69973-1A	730900-1A, 741991-1A, 741999-1A, 761100-1A
381301B	69210-0B	69210-0B, 69981[a]-0B	69210-1B, 69973-1A	730900-1B, 741991-1B, 741999-1B, 761100-1B
381304A	71110-0A	71110-0	71110-0A	840211-0A, 840212-0A, 840219-0A, 840220-0A
381304B	71110-0B	71110-0	71110-0B	840211-0B, 840212-0B, 840219-0B, 840220-0B
381307	69110-1	69110-1	69110-0	730800-0
381308	69120-1	69120-1	69120-0	761000-0
381901	69220-1	69241-1, 69242-1	69241-0, 69242-0, 69973-2	731000-0, 741991-2, 741999-2, 761200-0
381904A	69220-2A	69241-2A, 69242-2A, 69981[a]-2A	69210-2A, 69973-3A	730900-2A, 761100-2A, 741991-3A, 741999-3A
381907A	69230-0A	69243-0A, 69244-0A	69243-0A, 69244-0A	731100-0A, 761300-0A
381907B	69230-0B	69243-0B, 69244-0B	69243-0B, 69244-0B	731100-0B, 761300-0B
381910	69310-0	69310-0	69310-0	731200-0, 741300-0, 761400-0
381913	69400-0	69400-0	69400-0	731700-0, 731800-0, 741500-0, 761610-0
381914	69331-0, 69332-0, 69341-0, 69342-0	69350-0	69350-0	731400-0, 741400-0
381916A	73163-1A	78613-0A	78630-0A	860900-0A
381916B	73163-1B	78613-0B	78630-0B	860900-0B
381919	81210-1	81210-0	81211-1, 81215-1, 81217-0	732200-1, 840310-0
382101A	71132-1A	71260[b]-1A	71210-1A	840611-1A, 840619-1A
382101B	71132-1B	71260[b]-1B	71210-1B	840611-1B, 840619-1B
382104A	71150-1A	71380-1A	71382-0A	840890-0A
382104B	71150-1B	71380-1B	71382-0B	840890-0B
382108A	71150-2A	71380-0A	71381-0A	840790-0A
382108B	71150-2B	71380-0B	71381-0B	840790-0B
382113A	71160-0A	71488-0A	71489-0A	841181-0A, 841182-0A
382113B	71160-0B	71488-0B	71489-0B	841181-0B, 841182-0B
382116A	71181-1A	71881-0A, 71889-1A	71810-1A	841000-1A
382116B	71181-1B	71881-0B, 71889-1B	71810-1B	841000-1B

PRELIMINARY TABLE OF CORRESPONDENCE BETWEEN ISIC-BASED CODES, SITC AND HS CODES
TABLEAU PROVISOIRE DE CORRESPONDENCE ENTRE LES INDICATIFS D'APRES
LA CITI ET LES INDICATIFS DE LA CTCI ET SH

ISIC-based code, Rev. 2 Indicatif d'après la CITI Rev.2	SITC, Revised code Indicatif d'après la CTCI révisée	SITC, Rev.2 code Indicatif d'après la CTCI Rev.2	SITC, Rev. 3 code Indicatif d'après la CTCI Rev.3	Harmonized Commodity Description and Coding System (HS) Systeme Harmonise de Designation et de Codification des Marchandises (SH)
382202	71210-1	72113-1	72113-1	843221-0, 843229-1
382208	71210-2	72113-2	72113-2	843229-2
382218	71210-3, 71210-4	72111-0	72111-0	843210-0
382226	71210-5	72112-1	72112-1	843230-0
382232	71220-1	72122-0	72122-0	843351-0
382238	71220-2	72121-0, 72123-1	72121-0, 72123-1	843311-0, 843319-0, 843320-0
382244	71220-3	72197-1	72123-2	843330-1, 843359-1
382249	71220-4	72123-0	72123-3	843352-0
382252	71231-0	74350-1	74351-0	842111-0
382255	71239-1	72131-0	72131-0	843410-0
382258A	71250-1A	72240-1A	72249-1A	870190-1A
382258B	71250-1B	72240-1B	72249-1B	870190-1B
382261A	71250-2A	72230-1A, 72240-2A	72230-1A, 72241-0A, 72249-2A	870110-0A, 870130-1A, 870190-2A
382261B	71250-2B	72230-1B, 72240-2B	72230-1B, 72241-0B, 72249-2B	870110-0B, 870130-1B, 870190-2B
382263	71964-1	72112-2	72112-2	843240-0
382301	71510-1	73615-0	73140-0	845910-0, 845921-0, 845929-0, 845931-0, 845939-0, 845940-0
3823011	71510-11	73615-1	73142-0, 73144-0	845921-0, 845931-0
3823012	71510-12	73615-2	73141-0, 73143-0,73145-0, 73146-0	845910-0, 845929-0, 845939-0, 845940-0
382304	71510-2	73628-1	73318-1	846299-1
3823041	71510-21	73628-11	73318-11	846299-11
3823042	71510-22	73628-12	73318-12	846299-12
382307	71510-3	73621-1	73311-1	846210-1
3823071	71510-31	73621-11	73311-11	846210-11
3823072	71510-32	73621-12	73311-12	846210-12
382310	71510-4	73619-1	73161-0, 73162-0, 73163-0, 73164-0, 73165-0, 73166-0	846011-0, 846019-0, 846021-0, 846029-0, 846031-0, 846039-0
3823101	71510-4	73619-11	73161-0, 73163-0, 73165-0	846011-0, 846021-0, 846031-0
3823102	71510-4	73619-12	73162-0, 73164-0, 73166-0	846019-0, 846029-0, 846039-0
382311	71510-9	73670-1	73121-0	845710-0
382312	71510-10	73670-2	73122-0, 73123-0	845720-0, 845730-0
3823121	71510-101	73670-21	73122-0	845720-0
3823122	71510-102	73670-22	73123-0	845730-0
382313	71510-5	73613-0	73130-0	845800-0
3823131	71510-51	73613-1	73131-0, 73135-0	845811-0, 845891-0
3823132	71510-52	73613-2	73137-0, 73139-0	845819-0, 845899-0
382316	71510-6	73614-1	73151-0, 73152-0, 73153-0, 73154-0, 73157-0	845951-0, 845959-0, 845961-0, 845969-0, 845970-0
3823161	71510-61	73614-11	73151-0, 73153-0	845951-0, 845961-0
3823162	71510-62	73614-12	73152-0, 73154-0	845959-0, 845969-0
382319	71510-7	73612-0, 73616-0, 73619-2, 73670-3	73167-0, 73169-1, 73173-0, 73175-0, 73177-0, 73179-1	846040-0, 846090-1, 846130-0, 846140-0, 846150-0, 846190-1
3823191	71510-71	73612-1, 73616-1, 73619-21, 73670-31	73167-1, 73169-11, 73173-1, 73175-1, 73177-1, 73179-11	846040-1, 846090-11, 846130-1, 846140-1, 846150-1, 846190-11
3823192	71510-72	73612-2, 73616-2, 73619-22, 73670-32	73167-2, 73169-12, 73173-2, 73175-2, 73177-2, 73179-12	846040-2, 846090-12, 846130-2, 846140-2, 846150-2, 846190-12
382322	71510-8	73617-0, 73619-3, 73670-4	73171-0, 73178-0	846110-0, 846120-0

PRELIMINARY TABLE OF CORRESPONDENCE BETWEEN ISIC-BASED CODES, SITC AND HS CODES
TABLEAU PROVISOIRE DE CORRESPONDENCE ENTRE LES INDICATIFS D'APRES
LA CITI ET LES INDICATIFS DE LA CTCI ET SH

ISIC-based code, Rev. 2 Indicatif d'après la CITI Rev.2	SITC, Revised code Indicatif d'après la CTCI révisée	SITC, Rev.2 code Indicatif d'après la CTCI Rev.2	SITC, Rev. 3 code Indicatif d'après la CTCI Rev.3	Harmonized Commodity Description and Coding System (HS) Systeme Harmonise de Designation et de Codification des Marchandises (SH)
3823221	71510-81	73617-1, 73619-31, 73670-41	73171-1, 73178-1	846110-1, 846120-1
3823222	71510-82	73617-2, 73619-32, 73670-42	73171-2, 73178-2	846110-2, 846120-2
382328	71511-1	73621-2, 73622-1, 73623-1, 73628-2, 73670-5	73311-2, 73312-1, 73313-1, 73314-1, 73315-1, 73316-1, 73317-1, 73318-2	846210-2, 846221-1, 846229-1, 846231-1, 846239-1, 846241-1, 846249-1, 846291-0, 846299-2
3823281	71511-11	73621-21, 73622-11, 73623-11, 73628-21, 73670-51	73311-21, 73312-1, 73314-1, 73316-1, 73318-21	846210-21, 846221-1, 846231-1, 846241-1, 846291-1, 846299-21
3823282	71511-12	73621-22, 73622-12, 73623-12, 73628-22, 73670-52	73311-22, 73313-1, 73315-1, 73317-1, 73318-22	846210-22, 846229-1, 846239-1, 846249-1, 846291-2, 846299-22
382331	71511-2	73622-2, 73623-2, 73670-6, 73618-0	73312-2, 73313-2, 73314-2, 73315-2, 73316-2, 73317-2, 73391-0, 73393-0, 73395-0, 73399-1	846221-2, 846229-2, 846231-2, 846239-2, 846241-2, 846249-2, 846310-0, 846320-0, 846330-0, 846390-1
3823311	71511-21	73622-21, 73623-21, 73670-61	73312-2, 73314-2, 73316-2, 73391-1, 73393-1, 73395-1, 73399-11	846221-2, 846231-2, 846241-2, 846310-1, 846320-1, 846330-1, 846390-11
3823312	71511-22	73622-22, 73623-22, 73670-62	73313-2, 73315-2, 73317-2, 73391-2, 73393-2, 73395-2, 73399-12	846229-2, 846239-2, 846249-2, 846310-2, 846320-2, 846330-2, 846390-12
382334	71511-3	73670-7	73399-2	846390-2
382337	71522-1	73721-0	73721-0	845510-0, 845521-0, 845522-0
382340	71952-0	72812-0	72812-0	846500-0
382343	72960-0	77840-0	77841-0, 77843-0, 77845-0	850810-0, 850820-0, 850880-0
382351	71980-1	72848-1	72849-1	847989-1
382401	71711-1	72441-0	72441-0	844400-0
382404	71711-2	72443-1	72443-1	844520-0
382405	71830-1	72711-0, 72722-0	72711-0, 72722-0	843780-0, 843810-0, 843820-0, 843830-0, 843840-0, 843850-0, 843860-0, 843880-0
382407	71712-1	72452-1	72452-1	844711-0, 844712-0, 844720-1
382410	71712-2	72451-0	72451-0	844600-0
382413	71811-1	72510-0	72510-0	843910-0, 843920-0, 843930-0
382416	71812-0	72520-0	72520-0	844110-0, 844120-0, 844130-0, 844140-0, 844180
382419	71829-1	72640-0	72650-0, 72661-0, 72663-0, 72665-0, 72667-0	844311-0, 844312-0, 844319-0, 844321-0, 844329-0, 844330-0, 844340-0, 844350-0
382422A	71842-1A	72341-1A	72311-0A	842911-0A, 842919-0A
382425	71842-2	72342-0, 72343-1, 72346-1	72320-0	842951-0, 842952-0, 842959-0
382428	71842-3	72341-2, 72343-2, 72346-2	72312-0	842920-0
382431	71842-4	72343-3, 72346-3	72331-0, 72346-0	842930-0, 843062-0
382434	71851-1	72833-1	72833-1	847431-0
382437	71852-1	72841-1	72841-1	847520-1
382501	71410-1	75111-0, 75112-0, 75118-1	75110-0	846900-0
3825011	71410-11	75111-1, 75118-11	75113-0	846910-0
3825012	71410-12	75111-2, 75118-12	75115-0, 75116-0	846921-0, 846929-0
3825013	71410-13	75112-1, 75118-13	75118-0, 75119-0	846931-0, 846939-0
382502	86169-1	75182-0	75130-0	900911-0, 900912-0, 900921-0, 900922-0, 900930-0

PRELIMINARY TABLE OF CORRESPONDENCE BETWEEN ISIC-BASED CODES, SITC AND HS CODES
TABLEAU PROVISOIRE DE CORRESPONDENCE ENTRE LES INDICATIFS D'APRES
LA CITI ET LES INDICATIFS DE LA CTCI ET SH

ISIC-based code, Rev. 2 Indicatif d'après la CITI Rev.2	SITC, Revised code Indicatif d'après la CTCI révisée	SITC, Rev.2 code Indicatif d'après la CTCI Rev.2	SITC, Rev. 3 code Indicatif d'apres la CTCI Rev.3	Harmonized Commodity Description and Coding System (HS) Systeme Harmonise de Designation et de Codification des Marchandises (SH)
382504	71420-1	75121-0	75121-0, 75122-0	847010-0, 847021-0, 847029-0, 847030-0
3825041	71420-11	75121-1	75121-0	847010-0
3825042	71420-12	75121-2	75122-1	847021-0
3825043	71420-13	75121-3	75122-2	847029-0
3825045	71420-14	75121-4	75122-3	847030-0
382505	71420-2	75122-0	75123-0	847040-0
382506	71420-3	75123-0	75124-0	847050-0
382507	71430-1	75210-0, 75220-0, 75230-0	75210-0, 75220-0, 75230-0 75260-0, 75270-0	847110-0, 847120-0, 847191-0 847192-0, 847193-0
3825071	71430-11	75220-1	75220-1	847120-1
3825073	71430-12	75230-0	75230-0	847191-0
3825074	71430-13	75220-2	75220-2	847120-2
3825075	71430-14	75220-3	75220-3	847120-3
3825076	71430-15	75250-1	75260-0	847192-0
3825077	71430-16	75240-0, 75250-2	75270-0	847193-0
382508	71430-2	75220-4, 75280-1	75220-4, 75290-1	847120-4, 847199-1
3825081	71430-21	75220-4	75220-4	847120-4
3825082	71430-22	75280-1	75290-1	847199-1
382510	71420-3	75280-2	75290-2	847199-2
382511	72930-1	77640-0	77640-0	854211-0, 854219-0, 854220-0, 854280-0
3825111	72930-11	77640-1	77640-1	854211-1, 854219-1, 854220-1, 854280-1
3825112	72930-12	77640-2	77640-2	854211-2, 854219-2, 854220-2, 854280-2
3825115	72930-13	77640-3	77640-3	854211-3, 854219-3, 854220-3, 854280-3
3825116	72930-14	77640-4	77640-4	854211-4, 854219-4, 854220-4, 854280-4
3825118	72930-15	77640-5	77640-5	854211-5, 854219-5, 854220-5, 854280-5
382512	72220-1	72220-0	77220-0	853400-0
382513	71963-1	74525-1	74531-1	842320-1, 842330-1, 842381-1, 842382-1, 842389-1
382516	71963-2	74525-2	74531-2, 74532-0	842310-0, 842320-2, 842330-2, 842381-2, 842382-2, 842389-2
382901	69710-1, 72505-1	69731-1, 69732-1, 69734-1, 77586-1	69731-1, 69732-1, 69734-1, 77586-I	732100-1, 741700-1, 851650-0, 851660-1
3829013	72505-11	77586-11	77586-11	851650-0
382904	69710-2, 72505-2	69731-2, 69732-2, 69734-2, 77586-2	69731-2, 69732-2, 69734-2, 77586-2	732100-2, 741700-2, 851660-2
382907	71715-1	77512-0	77512-0	845121-0
382910	71730-0	72431-0	72433-0, 72435-0	845210-0, 845221-0, 845229-0
382925A	71912-0A	74150-0A	74151-0A, 74155-0A	841510-0A, 841581-0A, 841582-0A, 841583-0A
382928	71915-0	74141-0	74143-0, 74145-0	841850-0, 841861-0, 841869-0
382931	71921-1	74288-1	74275-0	841382-0
382942	71921-2	74210-0, 74220-0, 74230-0, 74288-2	74220-0, 74230-0, 74240-0, 74250-0, 74260-0, 74271-0	841320-0, 841330-0, 841340-0, 841350-0, 841360-0, 841370-0, 841381-0
382946	71922-0	74310-0, 74330-1, 74340-1	74311-0, 74315-0, 74317-0,	841410-0, 841430-0, 841440-0,

PRELIMINARY TABLE OF CORRESPONDENCE BETWEEN ISIC-BASED CODES, SITC AND HS CODES
TABLEAU PROVISOIRE DE CORRESPONDENCE ENTRE LES INDICATIFS D'APRES
LA CITI ET LES INDICATIFS DE LA CTCI ET SH

ISIC-based code, Rev. 2 Indicatif d'après la CITI Rev.2	SITC, Revised code Indicatif d'après la CTCI révisée	SITC, Rev.2 code Indicatif d'après la CTCI Rev.2	SITC, Rev. 3 code Indicatif d'apres la CTCI Rev.3	Harmonized Commodity Description and Coding System (HS) Systeme Harmonise de Designation et de Codification des Marchandises (SH)
			74319-0, 74340-0	841451-0, 841459-0, 841460-0, 841480-0
382949	71931-1	74422-0	74430-0	842600-0
382952	71931-2	74421-0, 74424-0, 74428-1	74420-0, 74481-0, 74489-1	842511-0, 842519-0, 842520-0, 842531-0, 842539-0, 842810-0, 842860-0
382955	71932-0	74411-1	74411-0, 74412-0	842710-0, 842720-0
382958	71942-0, 72501-0	77520-0	77520-0	841810-0, 841821-0, 841822-0, 841829-0, 841830-0, 841840-0,
382961	71970-0	74910-0	74600-0	848200-0
382964	72502-0	77511-0	77511-0	845011-0, 845012-0, 845019-0
383101A	72210-1A	71622-1A	71632-1A	850161-1A, 850162-1A, 850163-1A, 850164-1A
383101B	72210-1B	71622-1B	71632-1B	850161-1B, 850162-1B, 850163-1B, 850164-1B
383104A	72210-2A	71622-2A	71632-2A	850161-2A, 850162-2A, 850163-2A, 850164-2A
383104B	72210-2B	71622-2B	71632-2B	850161-2B, 850162-2B, 850163-2B, 850164-2B
383107A	72210-3A	71610-1A, 71621-1A	71610-0A, 71620-1A 71631-1A	850110-0A, 850120-0A, 850131-1A, 850151-1A
383107B	72210-3B	71610-1B, 71621-1B	71610-0B, 71620-1B 71631-1B	850110-0B, 850120-0B, 850131-1B, 850151-1B
383110A	72210-4A	71610-2A, 71621-2A	71620-2A, 71631-2A	850131-2A, 850132-1A, 850133-1A, 850134-1A, 850140-1A, 850151-2A, 850152-1A, 850153-1A
383110B	72210-4B	71610-2B, 71621-2B	71620-2B, 71631-2B	850131-2B, 850132-1B, 850133-1B, 850134-1B, 850140-1B, 850151-2B, 850152-1B, 850153-1B
383113A	72210-5A	77110-1A	77110-1A	850431-0A, 850432-1A
383113B	72210-5B	77110-1B	77110-1B	850431-0B, 850432-1B
383116A	72210-6A	77110-2A	77110-2A	850421-0A, 850422-0A, 850423-0A, 850432-2A, 850433-0A, 850434-0A
383116B	72210-6B	77110-2B	77110-2B	850421-0B, 850422-0B, 850423-0B, 850432-2B, 850433-0B, 850434-0B
383119	72951-0	87310-1	87315-0	902830-0
383122	72992-1	73732-1	73735-0, 73736-0	851531-0, 851539-0
383125	72992-2	74131-1	74131-1, 74132-1, 74133-1	851410-1, 851420-1, 851430-1
383131	72941-1	77831-1	77831-0	851110-0, 851120-0, 851130-0, 851140-0, 851150-0, 851180-0
3831311	72941-11	77831-11	77831-1	851110-0
3831312	72941-12	77831-12	77831-2	851120-0
3831313	72941-13	77831-13	77831-3	851130-1
3831314	72941-14	77831-14	77831-4	851130-2
3831315	72941-15	77831-15	77831-5	851140-0
3831316	72941-16	77831-16	77831-6	851150-0
383201	72410-0	76100-0	76100-1	852800-1

PRELIMINARY TABLE OF CORRESPONDENCE BETWEEN ISIC-BASED CODES, SITC AND HS CODES
TABLEAU PROVISOIRE DE CORRESPONDENCE ENTRE LES INDICATIFS D'APRES
LA CITI ET LES INDICATIFS DE LA CTCI ET SH

ISIC-based code, Rev. 2 Indicatif d'après la CITI Rev.2	SITC, Revised code Indicatif d'après la CTCI révisée	SITC, Rev.2 code Indicatif d'après la CTCI Rev.2	SITC, Rev. 3 code Indicatif d'apres la CTCI Rev.3	Harmonized Commodity Description and Coding System (HS) Systeme Harmonise de Designation et de Codification des Marchandises (SH)
3832011	72410-1	76120-0	76120-1	852820-1
3832012	72410-2	76110-0	76110-1	852810-1
383202	72930-0	77610-0	77610-0	854011-0, 854012-0
383204	72420-0	76200-0	76200-0	852700-0
3832041	72420-1	76200-1	76211-0, 76221-0, 76281-0	852711-0, 852721-0, 852731-0
3832042	72420-2	76200-2	76212-0, 76222-0, 76282-0, 76289-0	852719-0, 852729-0, 852732-0, 852739-0
383210	72491-2	76410-1	76411-0	851710-0
383222	72620-0	77420-0	77420-0	902200-0
383225	72930-1	77620-1	77625-0, 77627-0	854041-0, 854042-0, 854049-0, 854081-0, 854089-0
383228	72930-2	77630-1	77632-0, 77633-0	854121-0, 854129-0
383234	89111-1	76380-1	76384-0	852000-0
383237	89111-2	76310-0, 76380-2	76330-0, 76382-0, 76383-0	851900-0
383238	Not available	76381-1	76381-0	852100-0
383240	89120-1	89830-1	89871-0	852410-0
383243	89120-2	89831-1	89840-1, 89850-1	852300-1
383245	Not available	89831-2	89840-2, 89850-2	852300-2
383301	72503-1	77571-1	77571-1	850910-0
383304	72504-0	77540-1	77541-0, 77542-0	851010-0, 851020-0
383307	72505-1	77582-0	77582-0	851621-0, 851629-0
383310	72505-2	77584-0	77584-0	851640-0
383901	72220-1	77210-1	77241-0	853510-0
383904	72220-2	77210-2	77244-0, 77255-0	853530-0, 853650-0
383907	72310-0	77310-0	77310-0	854400-0
383910	72911-0	77811-0	77811-0	850611-0, 850612-0, 850613-0, 850619-0, 850620-0
383913	72912-0	77812-0	77812-0	850710-0, 850720-0, 850730-0, 850740-0, 850780-0
383916	72920-1	77821-0	77821-0	853921-0, 853922-0, 853929-0
383919A	72920-2A	77822-0A	77822-0A	853931-0A, 853939-0A
384101A	73530-1A	79323-1A	79327-1A	890190-1A
384101B	73530-1B	79323-1B	79327-1B	890190-1B
384104A	73530-2A	79323-2A	79327-2A	890190-2A
384104B	73530-2B	79323-2B	79327-2B	890190-2B
384107A	73530-3A	79323-3A	79327-3A	890190-3A
384107B	73530-3B	79323-3B	79327-3B	890190-3B
384110A	73530-4A	79323-4A, 79324-0A, 79328-1A	79324-0A, 79327-4A 79329-1A	890190-4A, 890200-0A, 890600-1A
384110B	73530-4B	79323-4B, 79324-0B, 79328-1B	79324-0B, 79327-4B, 79329-1B	890190-4B, 890200-0B, 890600-1B
384113A	73530-5A	73530-0A	79322-0A	890120-0A
384113B	73530-5B	79322-0B	79322-0B	890120-0B
384116A	73530-6A	79321-0A, 79323-5A, 79328-2A	79326-0A, 79327-5A, 79328-0A	890110-0A, 890130-0A, 890190-5A
384116B	73530-6B	79321-0B, 79323-5B, 79328-2B	79326-0B, 79327-5B, 79328-0B	890110-0B, 890130-0B, 890190-5B
384201A	73120-1A, 73130-1A	79110-0A, 79120[B]-1A	79110-0A, 79121-0A	860100-0A, 860210-0A
384201B	73120-1B, 73130-1B	79110-0B, 79120[B]-1B	79110-0B, 79121-0B	860100-0B, 860210-0B
384204A	73130-2A	79120[b]-2A	79129-1A	860290-1A
384204B	73130-2B	79120[b]-2B	79129-1B	860290-1B

PRELIMINARY TABLE OF CORRESPONDENCE BETWEEN ISIC-BASED CODES, SITC AND HS CODES
TABLEAU PROVISOIRE DE CORRESPONDENCE ENTRE LES INDICATIFS D'APRES
LA CITI ET LES INDICATIFS DE LA CTCI ET SH

ISIC-based code, Rev. 2 Indicatif d'après la CITI Rev.2	SITC, Revised code Indicatif d'après la CTCI révisée	SITC, Rev.2 code Indicatif d'après la CTCI Rev.2	SITC, Rev. 3 code Indicatif d'apres la CTCI Rev.3	Harmonized Commodity Description and Coding System (HS) Systeme Harmonise de Designation et de Codification des Marchandises (SH)
384207A	73140-1A	79130-1A	79160-1A	860300-1A
384207B	73140-1B	79130-1B	79160-1B	860300-1B
384210A	73150-1A, 73162-1A	79140-1A, 79152-0A	79170-1A, 79182-0A	860500-1A, 860600-0A
384210B	73150-1B, 73162-1B	79140-1B, 79152-0B	79170-1B, 79182-0B	860500-1B, 860600-0B
384213	73150-2	79140-2	79170-2	860500-2
384301A	71150-4A	71320-1A	71323-0A	840820-0A
384301B	71150-4B	71320-1B	71323-0B	840820-0B
384304A	71150-5A	71320-2A	71321-0A, 71322-0A, 71381-0A	840731-0A, 840732-0A, 840733-0A, 840734-0A
384304B	71150-5B	71320-2B	71321-0B, 71322-0B, 71381-0B	840731-0B, 840732-0B, 840733-0B, 840734-0B
3843051	73260-0	78410-0	78410-0	870600-0
3843052	73281-0	78420-0	78420-0	870700-0
3843053	73289-1	78490-1	78431-1	870810-1
3843054	73289-2	78490-2	78433-1	870831-0, 870839-1
3843055	73289-3	78490-3	78434-0	870840-0
3843056	73289-4	78490-4	78435-0	870850-0
3843057	73289-5	78490-5	78436-1	870860-1
3843058	73289-6	78490-6	78439-1	870870-1
3843059	73289-7	78490-7	78439-2	870880-0
3843060	73289-8	78490-8	78439-3	870891-0
3843061	73289-9	78490-9	78439-4	870892-0
3843062	73289-10	78490-10	78439-5	870893-1
3843063	73289-11	78490-11	78439-6	870894-1
384307	73210-1	78100-1	78100-1	870300-1
384310	73210-2	78100-2	78100-2	870300-2
384312	73220-1	78310-1	78310-1	870200-1
384313	73220-2	78310-2	78310-2	870200-2
384315	73230-1	78210-1	78210-1	870400-1
384316	73230-2	78210-2	78210-2	870400-2
384319	73250-0	78320-0	78320-0	870120-0
384322	73330-1	78612-0	78620-0	871620-0, 871631-0, 871639-0
384401	73291-1	78510-1	78513-0, 78515-0, 78516-0, 78517-0, 78519-1	871120-0, 871130-0, 871140-0, 871150-0, 871190-1
384404	73311-1	78520-0	78520-0	871200-0
384501	71141-1	71311-0	71311-0	840710-0
384504	71142-0	71440-1, 71481-0	71441-0, 71481-0	841111-0, 841112-0, 841121-0, 841122-0
384507	73410-1	79210-0, 79220-0, 79230-0, 79240-0	79210-0, 79220-0, 79230-0, 79240-0	880211-0, 880212-0, 880220-0, 880230-0, 880240-0
384901	89410-0	89410-0	89410-1	871500-1
385107	86171-1	87202-1	87221-1	901831-0
385111	86181-1	87310-1	87311-0	902810-0
385112	86181-2	87310-2	87313-0	902820-0
385114	72952-1, 86182-1	87320-1, 87483-1	87321-0	902910-0
385120	72952-2, 86182-2	87320-2, 87483-2, 87489-1	87325-0	902920-0
385121	72952-3, 86191-1	87411-1, 87483-3, 87489-2	87411-0	901410-0, 901420-0, 901480-0
385130	72952-4, 86191-2	87412-1, 87483-4, 87489-3	87413-0	901510-0, 901520-0, 901530-0, 901540-0, 901580-0
385136	72952-5, 86193-1	87421-1, 87483-5, 87489-4	87422-0	901710-0, 901720-0

PRELIMINARY TABLE OF CORRESPONDENCE BETWEEN ISIC-BASED CODES, SITC AND HS CODES
TABLEAU PROVISOIRE DE CORRESPONDENCE ENTRE LES INDICATIFS D'APRES
LA CITI ET LES INDICATIFS DE LA CTCI ET SH

ISIC-based code, Rev. 2 Indicatif d'après la CITI Rev.2	SITC, Revised code Indicatif d'après la CTCI révisée	SITC, Rev.2 code Indicatif d'après la CTCI Rev.2	SITC, Rev. 3 code Indicatif d'après la CTCI Rev.3	Harmonized Commodity Description and Coding System (HS) Systeme Harmonise de Designation et de Codification des Marchandises (SH)
385137	72952-6, 86193-1	87421-2, 87483-6, 87489-5	87423-0	901730-0, 901780-0
385138	72952-7, 86197-1	87430-1, 87483-7, 87489-6	87431-0	902610-0
385140	72952-8, 86197-2	87430-2, 87483-8, 87489-7	87435-0	902620-0
385143	72952-9, 86198-1	87440-1, 87483-9, 87489-8	87441-0	902710-0
385144	72952-10, 86198-2	87440-2, 87483-10, 87489-9	87442-0	902720-0
385146	72952-11, 86198-3	87440-3, 87483-11	87443-0	902730-0
385154	72952-12, 86195-1	87453-1, 87483-12, 87489-10	87453-0	902410-0, 902480-0
385155	72952-13, 86196-1	87454-1, 87483-13, 87489-11	87455-0	902511-0, 902519-0, 902520-0 902580-0
385157	72952-14, 86197-3	87430-3, 87481-1, 87484-1	87461-0	903210-0
385159	72952-15, 86197-4	87430-4, 87481-2, 87484-2	87463-0	903220-0
385160	72952-16	87482-1	87471-0	903010-0
385163	72952-17	87483-14	87473-0	903020-0
385164	72952-18	87483-15, 87489-12	87475-0, 87478-0	903031-0, 903039-0, 903081-0 903089-0
385171	86171-2	87201-1	87211-0	901841-0
385173	86172-1	87203-1	87231-0	901910-0
385175	86172-2	87203-2	87233-0	901920-0
385201	86131-0	87101-0	87111-0, 87115-1	900510-0, 900580-1
385204	86134-0, 86133-0, 86161-1	87103-0, 87104-0, 88131-1	87131-0,87141-0,87143-0, 87145-0, 88131-0	900820-0, 901110-0, 901120-0, 901180-0, 901210-0
3852041	86133-0, 86134-0	87103-0, 87104-0	87131-0,87141-0,87143-0 87145-0	901110-0, 901120-0, 901180-0 901210-0
3852043	86161-1	88131-1	88131-0	900820-0
385207	86140-1	88111-0, 88112-0	88111-0	900610-0, 900620-0, 900630-0 900640-0, 900651-0, 900652-0, 900653-0, 900659-0
385208	86121-1	88421-1	88421-0	900311-0, 900319-0
385209	86122-0	88422-0	88423-0	900400-0
385210	86150-1	88121-1, 88122-1	88121-0	900711-0, 900719-0
3852101	86150-11	88121-11, 88122-11	88121-01	900711-01, 900719-01
385301	86411-0	88511-0	88530-0, 88540-0	910100-0, 910200-0
385304	86412-0	88512-0	88572-0, 88573-0	910300-0
385307	86421-0	88521-0	88571-0	910400-0
385310	86422-0	88522-0	88574-0, 88575-0,88576-0, 88577-0, 88578-0, 88579-0	910500-0
390201	89141-1	89811-1	89813-1	920100-1
390204	89142-0	89819-0	89815-0	920200-0
390207	89181-0	89821-0	89821-0	920300-0
390210	89183-0	89823-0	89823-0	920500-0
390901	89422-1	89422-1	89422-0	950210-0
390904	89521-0	89521-1	89521-1	960810-0, 960820-0, 960831-0, 960839-0, 960840-0, 960850-0, 960860-0, 960899-1
390907	89523-0	89523-0	89523-0	960900-0
390910	89953-0	89984-1	89985-0	960711-0, 960719-0
410101	35100-0	35100-0	35100-0	271600-0
410102	35100-1	35100-1	35100-1	271600-1
410202B	34120-2B	34150-2B	34500-2B	270500-2B

Litho in United Nations, New York   United Nations publication
51251—December 2001—2,470   Sales No. E/F.02.XVII.2
ISBN 92-1-061195-0   ST/ESA/STAT/SER.P/39
ISSN 0257-7208